THE POWER OF
FINE LITERATURE
THE MASTERY OF
LANGUAGE ARTS

PRENTICE HALL
LITERATURE

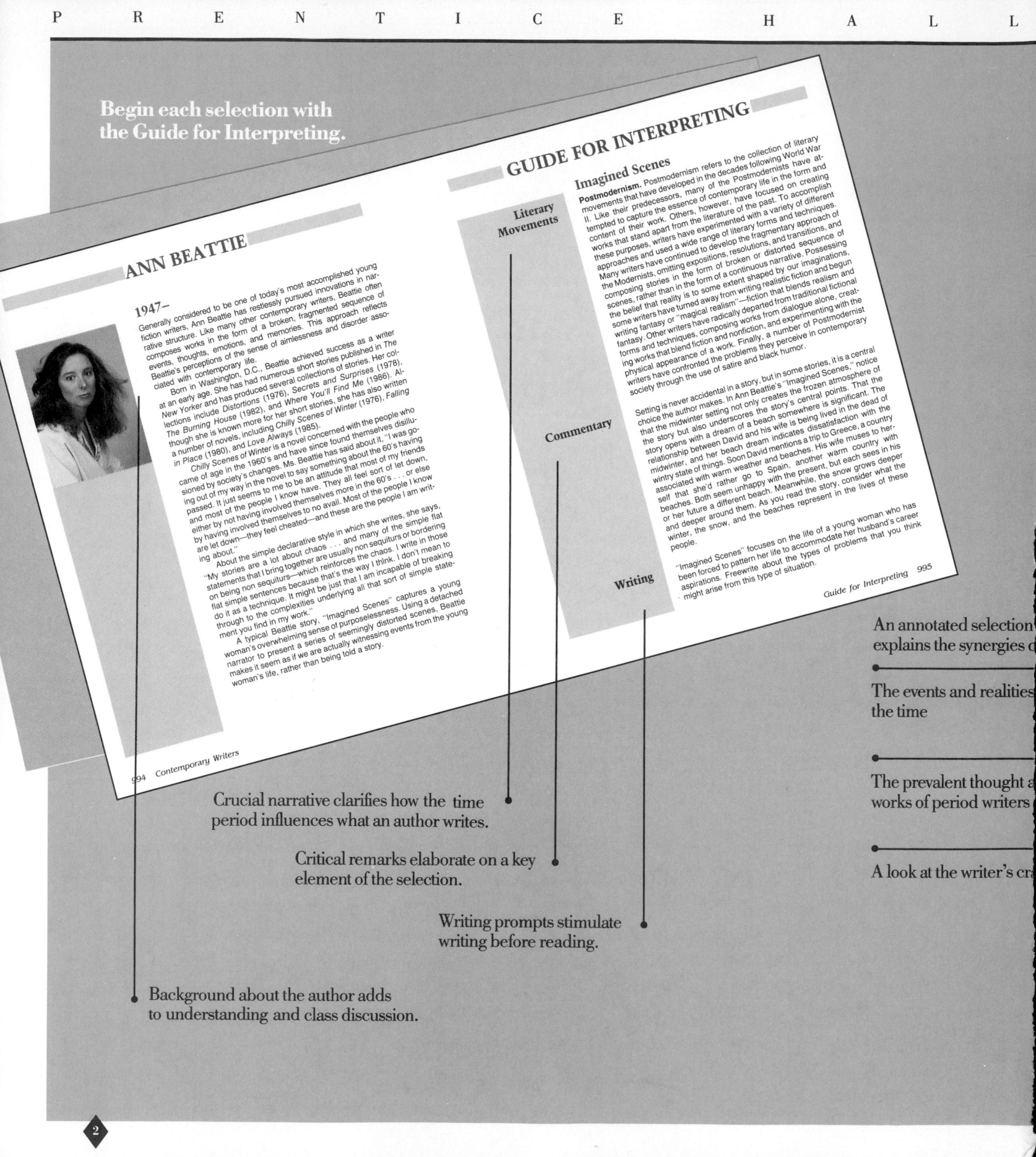

Begin each selection with
the Guide for Interpreting.

ANN BEATTIE

1947–

Generally considered to be one of today's most accomplished young fiction writers, Ann Beattie has restlessly pursued innovations in narrative structure. Like many other contemporary writers, Beattie often composes works in the form of a broken, fragmented sequence of events, thoughts, emotions, and memories. This approach reflects Beattie's perceptions of the sense of aimlessness and disorder associated with contemporary life.

Born in Washington, D.C., Beattie achieved success as a writer at an early age. She has had numerous short stories published in The New Yorker and has produced several collections of stories. Her collections include Distortions (1976), Secrets and Surprises (1978), The Burning House (1982), and Where You'll Find Me (1976), Falling in Place (1980), and Love Always (1985).

Chilly Scenes of Winter is a novel concerned with the people who came of age in the 1960's and have since found themselves disillusioned by society's changes. Ms. Beattie has said about it, "I was going out of my way in the novel to say something about the 60's having passed. It just seems to me to be an attitude that most of my friends and most of the people I know have. They all feel sort of let down, either by not having involved themselves more in the 60's . . . or else by having involved themselves to no avail. Most of the people I know are let down—they feel cheated—and these are the people I am writing about."

About the simple declarative style in which she writes, she says, "My stories are a lot about chaos . . . and many of the simple flat statements that I bring together are usually non sequiturs or bordering on being non sequiturs because that's the way I think. I don't mean to do it as a technique. It might be just that I am incapable of breaking through to the complexities underlying all that sort of simple statement you find in my work."

A typical Beattie story, "Imagined Scenes," captures a young woman's overwhelming sense of purposelessness. Using a detached narrator to present a series of seemingly distorted scenes, Beattie makes it seem as if we are actually witnessing events from the young woman's life, rather than being told a story.

994 Contemporary Writers

GUIDE FOR INTERPRETING

Imagined Scenes

Literary Movements

Postmodernism. Postmodernism refers to the collection of literary movements that have developed in the decades following World War II. Like their predecessors, many of the Postmodernists have attempted to capture the essence of contemporary life in the form and content of their work. Others, however, have focused on creating works that stand apart from the literature of the past. To accomplish these purposes, writers have experimented with a variety of different approaches and used a wide range of literary forms and techniques. Many writers have continued to develop the fragmentary approach of the Modernists, omitting expositions, resolutions, and transitions, and composing stories in the form of broken or distorted sequence of scenes, rather than in the form of a continuous narrative. Possessing the belief that reality is to some extent shaped by our imaginations, some writers have turned away from writing realistic fiction and begun writing fantasy or "magical realism"—fiction that blends realism and fantasy. Other writers have radically departed from traditional fictional forms and techniques, composing works from dialogue alone, creating works that blend fiction and nonfiction, and experimenting with the physical appearance of a work. Finally, a number of Postmodernist writers have confronted the problems they perceive in contemporary society through the use of satire and black humor.

Commentary

Setting is never accidental in a story, but in some stories, it is a central choice the author makes. In Ann Beattie's "Imagined Scenes," notice that the midwinter setting not only creates the frozen atmosphere of the story but also underscores the story's central points. That the story opens with a dream of a beach somewhere is being lived in the dead of midwinter, and her beach dream indicates dissatisfaction with the relationship between David and his wife is significant. The wintry state of things. Soon David mentions a trip to Greece, a country associated with warm weather and beaches. His wife muses to herself that she'd rather go to Spain, another warm country with beaches. Both seem unhappy with the present, but each sees in his or her future a different beach. Meanwhile, the snow grows deeper and deeper around them. As you read the story, consider what the winter, the snow, and the beaches represent in the lives of these people.

Writing

"Imagined Scenes" focuses on the life of a young woman who has been forced to pattern her life to accommodate her husband's career aspirations. Freewrite about the types of problems that you think might arise from this type of situation.

Guide for Interpreting 995

Crucial narrative clarifies how the time
period influences what an author writes.

Critical remarks elaborate on a key
element of the selection.

Writing prompts stimulate
writing before reading.

Background about the author adds
to understanding and class discussion.

An annotated selection
explains the synergies o

The events and realities
the time

The prevalent thought a
works of period writers

A look at the writer's cr

The Power of Fine Literature, The Mastery of Critical Reading.

Integrate the power of fine literature with in-depth reading to stimulate a critical response.

Begin each unit with Reading Critically.

READING CRITICALLY

The Literature of 1915–1946

Historical Context

World War I had a tremendous impact on the attitudes and outlooks of the American people. This impact is reflected in the literature of the modern age. To fully appreciate modern literature, you must understand how the nation was affected by its involvement in World War I.

Prior to World War I, the mood of American society was confident and optimistic. This mood was shattered by the horrifying realities of American involvement in World War I—a war which caused the death of hundreds of thousands of Americans and Europeans. When the war ended, many people were left with a feeling of distrust toward the ideas and values of the past. People saw the need for change, but they were unsure about the sort of changes that were needed. There was a growing sense of uncertainty, disjointedness, and disillusionment among certain members of American society.

Literary Movements

In the aftermath of World War I, a major literary movement known as Modernism developed. Abandoning many traditional forms and techniques, the Modernists sought to capture the essence of modern life in both the form and content of their work. To reflect the disjointedness of modern life, they constructed their works out of fragments, omitting the expositions, resolutions, interpretations, transitions, and summaries often used in traditional works. The Modernists also frequently expressed their views about modern life in the themes of their works, often focusing on such themes as the uncertainty, bewilderment, and apparent meaninglessness of modern life.

The Writer's Techniques

Because they believed that modern life lacked certainty, the Modernists generally suggested rather than asserted meaning in their works. The theme of a typical Modernist work is implied, not stated, forcing readers to draw their own conclusions. Often, the Modernists used symbols and allusions to suggest themes. They also generally used a limited point of view in their works, because they believed that reality is shaped by people's perceptions. Finally, the Modernists experimented with a number of new literary techniques, including shifting points of view and the stream-of-consciousness technique.

On the following pages is a selection by Sherwood Anderson, an influential modern writer. The notes in the side column show how a reader might read this selection critically.

708 The Modern Age

MODEL

Sophistication

Sherwood Anderson

It was early evening of a day in the late fall and the Winesburg County Fair had brought crowds of country people into town. The day had been clear and the night came on warm and pleasant. On the Trunion Pike, where the road after it left town stretched away between berry fields now covered with dry brown leaves, the dust from passing wagons arose in clouds. Children, curled into little balls, slept on the straw scattered on wagon beds. Their hair was full of dust and their fingers black and sticky. The dust rolled away over the fields and the departing sun set it ablaze with colors.

In the main street of Winesburg crowds filled the stores and the sidewalks. Night came on, horses whinnied, the clerks in the stores ran madly about, children became lost and cried lustily, an American town worked terribly at the task of amusing itself.

Literary Movement: The story begins without an exposition, and background information is revealed as the story progresses. This reflects the Modernist perception of life as ambiguous and fragmented.

Historical Context: The story is set just after the turn of the century.

Writer's Technique: Anderson's description of the town contrasts with the common conception that small-town life is ordered and pastoral.

WEST TISBURY FAIR
Thomas Hart Benton
Collection Mr. Arthur
Levitt, Jr., New York

Sophistication 709

3

Up to 100 Grammar in Action lessons in each ATE . . . the teachable moment for skills mastery.

7 Discussion What might postcards represent to the old man?

8 Reading Strategy Have the students invent a story that the man might tell about the postcard. Then have students discuss why the author did not include such a story, but merely alluded to one.

9 Discussion The narrator speaks very little in the scenes with the old man. What does this tell you about her character?

10 Literary Focus Have students look at the way the author establishes each scene. Many of the scenes start abruptly, in the middle of an action. What effect does this have on the reader?

11 Discussion How does this conversation add to your understanding of the relationship between David and the narrator?

7 side there is a box of tissues, a comb and brush, an alarm clock. He sits on the side of the bed, his feet not quite touching the floor, reaching into the drawer without looking. He finds what he wants: an envelope. He removes it and carefully pulls out the flap. He lets her look through the postcards. There is a bird's nest full of cherubs,[1] a picture of a lady elegantly dressed in a high, ruffled collar, curtseying beneath a flowering tree, and one that she looks at longer than the rest: a man in boots and a green jacket, carrying a rifle, is pictured walking down a path through the woods in the moonlight. Stars shine in the sky and illuminate a path in front of him. Tiny silver sparkles still adhere to the postcard. She holds it under the lamp on the night table: the lining of his jacket is silver, the edges of the rocks, a small area of the path. There is a caption: "Joseph Jefferson as Rip Van Winkle."[2] Beneath the caption is a message, ornately written: "Not yet but soon, Pa."

"Did your father write the postcard?"

8 "That's just one I found in a store long ago. I could make up a romantic story to tell you. I love to talk."

She waits, expecting the man's story. He leans back in bed, putting the envelope back in the drawer. His bedroom slippers fall to the floor, and he puts his legs under the covers.

"People get old and they can't improve things," he says, "so they lie all the time."

He waves his hand, dismissing something.

"I trust young people," he says. "I'd even tell you where my money is: in the dresser drawer, in the back of a poetry book."

The snowplow has returned, driving up the other side of the street. The lights cast patterns on the wall. He watches the shadows darken the wallpaper.

---

1. cherubs (cher′ əbz) *n.*: Representations of heavenly beings as winged children with chubby, rosy faces.
2. Rip Van Winkle: A character who sleeps for twenty years without awakening in a story by Washington Irving.

"I have real stories," he says, pointing to a photograph album on a table by the chair. "Look through and I can tell you some real stories if you want to know."

He is ready to sleep. She arranges the quilt at the bottom of the bed and starts to leave.

9 "The light doesn't bother me," he says, waving her toward the chair. "Look through my album. I'm old and cranky. I'm afraid for my pictures to leave the room."

10 It's early afternoon and no one is in the house. There are dishes on the dining-room table, records and record-album covers. There's a plate, a spoon, two bowls, three coffee cups. How many people have been here? There's no one to ask. There's some food on the counter top—things she doesn't remember buying. An apple pie. She goes into the living room and sits in a chair, looking out the window. More snow is predicted, but now the day is clear and bright, the fields shining in the sun. She goes into the kitchen again to look for the note he hasn't left. On her way to the bedroom to sleep, she looks out the window and sees David coming up the road, only a sweater and scarf on, holding a stick at his side that the dog is jumping for. On the floor by the chair the plant book is open, and several others, books he's studying for his exams. The front door is open. The dog runs into the living room, jumps on her.

"You should be asleep. You can't work at night if you're not going to sleep in the day."

"I thought I'd wait for you to come back."

"You shouldn't have waited. I could have been anywhere."

"Where would you go?"

11 He's chilled. His knuckles are bright pink, untying the scarf at his throat. He's putting another log on the fire, pushing the screen back into place.

"How's the old man?"

"He's no trouble. Last night I fixed his photograph album for him. Some of the pictures had come loose and I glued them in."

"You look like you need sleep."

Enrich your skills teaching with Grammar in Action lessons.

Grammar in Action

Indirect quotations report the substance of what a person said or thought, rather than the actual words. Unlike a **direct quotation**, an indirect quotation does not require quotation marks; it is punctuated like a simple declarative sentence. Note the following examples:

Direct quotation: "I trust young people," he says.
Indirect quotation: He says that he trusts young people.

Student Activity 1. Select three direct quotations and three indirect quotations from "Imagined Scenes." Explain why a writer would sometimes choose to report a character's words directly and, at other times, use indirect quotations.

Student Activity 2. Rewrite these indirect quotations from "Imagined Scenes" as direct quotations.
1. He told her he wouldn't be working in the fall.
2. Linus Pauling says that a sufficient intake of vitamin C will prevent colds.
3. He wants to show her his postcards.
4. The plant isn't pictured, he tells her, but it may be mentioned in the text.

998

The Power of Fine Literature, The Mastery of Grammar and Usage Skills.

Use fine literature as a springboard to teach grammar and usage skills.

"Looks like you've been working," she says, pointing to the books by the chair.

"I've had trouble concentrating. The snow was so beautiful last night. I took the dog out for long walks in the woods."

David is stroking the dog, who lies curled by the fire, panting in his sleep.

"Get some rest," he says, looking at his watch. "I met the people who moved in down the hill and told them I'd help put a sink in. He's very nice. Katherine and Larry Duane."

David kisses her on his way out. The dog wakes and wants to go with him, but at the front door he's told to stay. The dog whines when the door closes, then waits a minute longer before going back to the living room to sleep by the fireplace.

"It's awful. When you get old you expect things to be the same. Sometimes I think the cold air could clear my head. My neighbor is ten years younger than me and he jogs every day, even through snow."

"I'm leaving now," his sister says. She puts on a blue coat and a blue velvet cap that ties under the chin. Her hair is white and copper. She has small, dainty hands. She repeats that she's leaving and pats him on the shoulder, more to make sure he's listening than out of affection. "There are oranges in the bag on your bureau. Linus Pauling says that a sufficient intake of vitamin C will prevent colds."

"How would I get a cold? Every day is the same. I don't go out."

Her coat is buttoned, her hat tied securely. "That's like asking where dust comes from," she says, and disappears down the stairs.

"She's very good to come every day. I forget to thank her. I take it for granted. Fifteen years makes so much difference. She's able to do so much more, but her hands hurt her. She does embroidery so they don't go stiff."

He is looking through a book of Currier and Ives prints.[3] "I suppose I'll have to eat her oranges. There'll be more from Florida when they get back."

She looks at a picture he holds up for her to see, offers to read him science-fiction stories.

"I don't think so. My sister read them this morning. I've had enough make-believe.

3. Currier and Ives prints: Nineteenth-century lithographs depicting the manners, people, and events of the times.

PLEASURES OF WINTER
IN NEW YORK
Francis Peterson

13

12 Reading Strategy Have students predict what will happen to the characters in the rest of the story. Do the students expect there to be a change in the mood of the story?

13 Critical Thinking and Reading The old man is fond of science fiction. For what might this be a metaphor? Have students discuss the qualities of many science-fiction stories. Then have them relate science fiction to the man's postcard collection.

Humanities Note

Fine art, *Pleasures of Winter in New York*, by Francis Peterson.

Pleasures of Winter in New York is the American painter Francis Peterson's salute to urban childhood. Created in a simplified style, the artist uses bright colors to emphasize the cheer of the scene. The rural appearance of the snow-covered ground and trees is contrasted with the looming buildings visible outside the park. The activities of the children are varied and common to American youth everywhere.

You might use these questions for discussion.
1. What invitation does this scene extend to the viewer?
2. What is the response of the character in this story to a similar scene?

5. She asks him if he'll take his cane, but he wants her arm instead.
6. His sister is asking if there is any way she can come back.

Student Activity 3. Rewrite the following direct quotations from "Imagined Scenes" as indirect quotations.
1. "I don't sleep well," he tells her.
2. "I think school was canceled," she says, looking out the window.
3. "My jacket is in the hall closet," he says. "I need the air."
4. "I guess you were walking the dog in the woods," she says.
5. "We'll have to go back for my car," she says.

999

Reinforce learning with blackline masters in the Teaching Portfolio.

Guide learning with on-the-spot practice.

A writing program within a literature program.

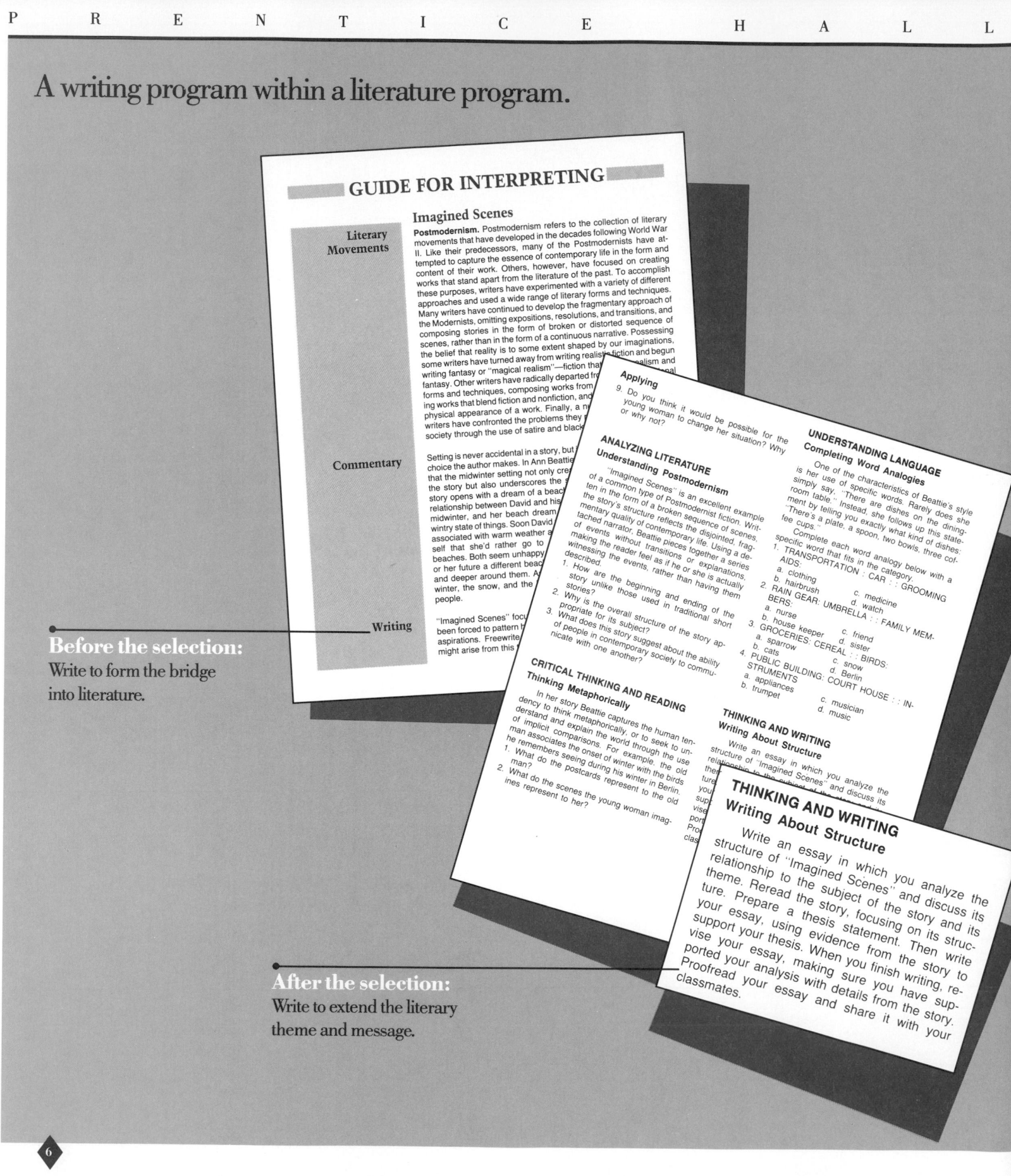

GUIDE FOR INTERPRETING

Literary Movements

Imagined Scenes

Postmodernism. Postmodernism refers to the collection of literary movements that have developed in the decades following World War II. Like their predecessors, many of the Postmodernists have attempted to capture the essence of contemporary life in the form and content of their work. Others, however, have focused on creating works that stand apart from the literature of the past. To accomplish these purposes, writers have experimented with a variety of different approaches and used a wide range of literary forms and techniques. Many writers have continued to develop the fragmentary approach of the Modernists, omitting expositions, resolutions, and transitions, and composing stories in the form of broken or distorted sequence of scenes, rather than in the form of a continuous narrative. Possessing the belief that reality is to some extent shaped by our imaginations, some writers have turned away from writing realistic fiction and begun writing fantasy or "magical realism"—fiction that [...] realism and fantasy. Other writers have radically departed fr[...] forms and techniques, composing works from [...] ing works that blend fiction and nonfiction, and [...] physical appearance of a work. Finally, a n[...] writers have confronted the problems they [...] society through the use of satire and black [...]

Commentary

Setting is never accidental in a story, but [...] choice the author makes. In Ann Beattie [...] that the midwinter setting not only cre[...] the story but also underscores the s[...] story opens with a dream of a beac[...] relationship between David and his [...] midwinter, and her beach dream [...] wintry state of things. Soon David [...] associated with warm weather a[...] self that she'd rather go to [...] beaches. Both seem unhappy [...] or her future a different beac[...] and deeper around them. A[...] winter, the snow, and the [...] people.

"Imagined Scenes" focu[...] been forced to pattern [...] aspirations. Freewrite [...] might arise from this [...]

Writing

Applying

9. Do you think it would be possible for the young woman to change her situation? Why or why not?

ANALYZING LITERATURE
Understanding Postmodernism

"Imagined Scenes" is an excellent example of a common type of Postmodernist fiction. Written in the form of a broken sequence of scenes, the story's structure reflects the disjointed, fragmentary quality of contemporary life. Using a detached narrator, Beattie pieces together a series of events without transitions or explanations, making the reader feel as if he or she is actually witnessing the events, rather than having them described.

1. How are the beginning and ending of the story unlike those used in traditional short stories?
2. Why is the overall structure of the story appropriate for its subject?
3. What does this story suggest about the ability of people in contemporary society to communicate with one another?

CRITICAL THINKING AND READING
Thinking Metaphorically

In her story Beattie captures the human tendency to think metaphorically, or to seek to understand and explain the world through the use of implicit comparisons. For example, the old man associates the onset of winter with the birds he remembers seeing during his winter in Berlin.

1. What do the postcards represent to the old man?
2. What do the scenes the young woman imagines represent to her?

UNDERSTANDING LANGUAGE
Completing Word Analogies

One of the characteristics of Beattie's style is her use of specific words. Rarely does she simply say, "There are dishes on the dining-room table." Instead, she follows up this statement by telling you exactly what kind of dishes: "There's a plate, a spoon, two bowls, three coffee cups."

Complete each word analogy below with a specific word that fits in the category.

1. TRANSPORTATION : CAR :: GROOMING AIDS:
   a. clothing   c. medicine
   b. hairbrush   d. watch
2. RAIN GEAR: UMBRELLA :: FAMILY MEMBERS:
   a. nurse   c. friend
   b. house keeper   d. sister
3. GROCERIES: CEREAL :: BIRDS:
   a. sparrow   c. snow
   b. cats   d. Berlin
4. PUBLIC BUILDING: COURT HOUSE :: INSTRUMENTS:
   a. appliances   c. musician
   b. trumpet   d. music

THINKING AND WRITING
Writing About Structure

Write an essay in which you analyze the structure of "Imagined Scenes" and discuss its relationship to the subject of the [...] ture [...] you [...] sup[...] vise [...] por[...] Pro[...] clas[...]

THINKING AND WRITING
Writing About Structure

Write an essay in which you analyze the structure of "Imagined Scenes" and discuss its relationship to the subject of the story and its theme. Reread the story, focusing on its structure. Prepare a thesis statement. Then write your essay, using evidence from the story to support your thesis. When you finish writing, revise your essay, making sure you have supported your analysis with details from the story. Proofread your essay and share it with your classmates.

Before the selection:
Write to form the bridge
into literature.

After the selection:
Write to extend the literary
theme and message.

The Power of Fine Literature,
The Mastery of Writing.

Choose from 5 writing activities for each selection.

Extend the power and breadth of your writing program with these additional activities:

- Fine Art Writing activities
- Selection Test essay questions
- Unit Test essay questions
- You the Writer Writing assignment
- You the Critic Writing assignment
- Writing Across the Curriculum activities
- Student writing models

Plus — Writing About Literature Handbook

A writing course right in the student book

Three additional writing activities in the Teaching Portfolio meet the needs of all ability levels:

- Less Challenging
- More Challenging
- The Student as Critic

Early on a snowy morning, the old man insists on going for a walk. A child bumps into him and he falls down. David, who has come to bring his wife home, helps the old man up. The old man gives her a postcard from his collection. David is angry with his wife for letting the old man go out in such slippery weather. Later, the old man's sister calls and asks the main character if she can come back. "You can come and go," the old man's sister says enviously. "You don't know what it's like to be caught."

CHECK TEST

1. To celebrate in the spring, David says they will go to _____ .
2. The old man recalls a terrible winter in the city of _____ .
3. The old man shows the nurse his collection of _____ .
4. David gives a plant to a friend who teaches _____ .
5. The old man's daughter is stuck in _____ .

COMPOSITION

Thinking and Writing
Discuss the assignment with the students. Make sure they understand the meaning of the terms *structure* and *theme.*

Prewriting: Provide classroom time for students to discuss the structure of the story. Have them consider how they might relate structure to the plot and theme. Ask them to formulate a thesis statement and to brainstorm a list of details from the story that support the thesis statement. Finally, have them discuss the requirements of their audience—their classmates.

Writing: Allow time for students to write their first draft in class.

Revising: Provide time for students to revise their writing. Direct them to make sure that they have included enough details from the story to support their thesis statement and that they have replaced any tired words with vivid ones. Have them proofread their essay and prepare a final draft. Finally, have students read each other's essays and share their impressions.

1174   Contemporary Writers

Guidelines for Evaluating Thinking and Writing
Keep the following questions in mind when evaluating students' essays.
1. Does the essay include enough details to support the argument?
2. Is the argument convincing?
3. Is the essay appropriate for its audience?
4. Are the sentences grammatically correct? Are they punctuated correctly? Are the words spelled correctly?

ALTERNATE COMPOSITION ASSIGNMENTS
Three writing assignments follow: Less Challenging, More Challenging, and The Student as Critic.

Less Challenging
Imagine that you are the old man in the story. Think abo
vacationi
write a le
thoughts
ing sure y
acter of t
letter and

More Ch
Imagine
thinking
story in
narrator
where, an
met and d
munication
Revise yo
style is co
proofread

The Stud
Beattie's
controvers

Her se
gramm
tures
boutiqu
weary
thetic

The Student as Critic

Beattie's writing style has been a source of much controversy. One critic observed:

> Her sentences are often plain, flat, their grammar exposed like the lighting fixtures in an avant-garde furniture boutique, and the effect is at first wearying. Only later does the sympathetic center of her work betray itself.

Think about the meaning of this quotation. How does it apply to "Imagined Scenes"? Then write a short composition discussing one of the following: (1) how Beattie's distinctive writing style contributes to the development of the characters and themes in the selections (2) how Beattie's story rises above the seeming simplicity of the language in which it is presented. First make a list of details from the story that support your ideas. Then organize your ideas around a good thesis statement. Write the first draft of your composition. Finally, revise your paper, checking that your ideas are clear and well-organized and that your spelling and

7

Teacher Backup
Selection background, check test, suggested readings, composition activities and evaluation guidelines, and answers to worksheets and tests.

Vocabulary Check
Reinforce or test the words taught before the selection.

Selection Test
Measure understanding of the literature through short answer questions and essay questions.

Usage and Mechanic Worksheet
Integrate grammar and editing skills with literature.

Grammar in Action Worksheet
Deepen the understanding of grammar and usage skills.

The Teaching Portfolio – Redefining the Concept of Support for all the Language Arts.

Everything you need to teach a selection is in one place.

Analyzing Literature Worksheet
Extends understanding of the literary element.

Critical Thinking and Reading Worksheet
Promotes reading and reasoning.

Language Worksheet
Beyond vocabulary to word origins, synonyms, dialects — and more.

Fine Art Transparencies

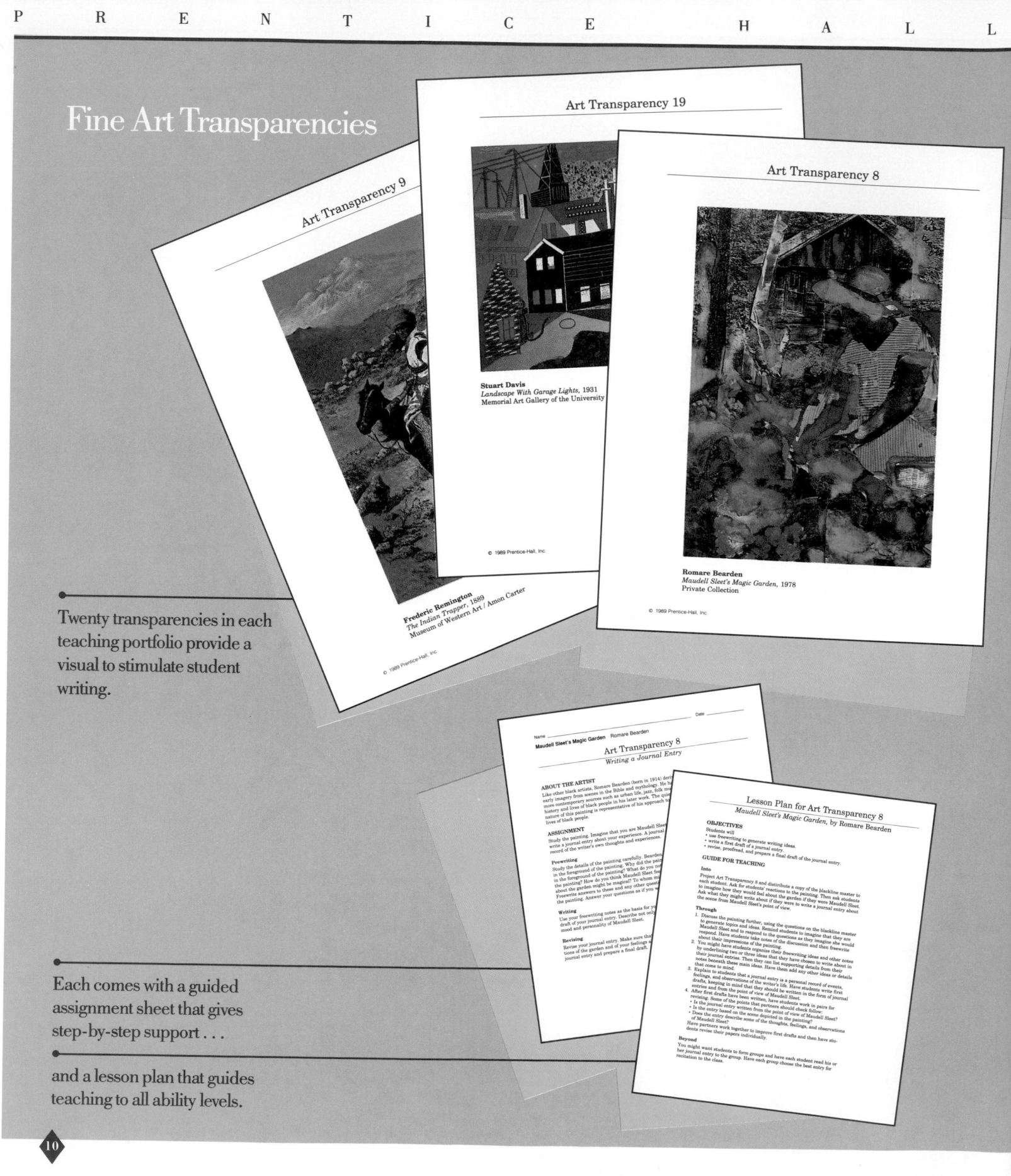

Twenty transparencies in each teaching portfolio provide a visual to stimulate student writing.

Each comes with a guided assignment sheet that gives step-by-step support . . .

and a lesson plan that guides teaching to all ability levels.

Capture the Power of Integrating Fine Literature and the Humanities.

A fine arts program and classic cinema connected with literature.

The Library of Video Classics

- Four feature length films per grade level, including the novel and the play.

- Viewing guides link the film with the literature to stimulate new ideas.

Each Viewing Guide provides:

- Previewing and After Viewing Questions — enhance critical thinking skills.

- Speaking and Listening activities — promote oral language skills through the impact of film.

- Writing activities — creative topics enhance students responsiveness.

- Ability level notes — ideas to challenge each student.

Direct students to new discoveries with the dynamic combination of literature and cinema.

Study Guides

What if your favorite novel or play is not in Prentice Hall Literature? We still provide you with teaching support. Complete teaching guides for 40 novels and plays give you fresh insights to make the classic even more interesting and relevant. Each guide contains:

- Author Background
- Synopses of Plot, Setting, Theme and More
- Chapter-by-Chapter Teaching Plans
- Writing Assignments
- Guidelines for Dealing With Provocative Themes
- Blackline Master Handouts and Test

Tailor the Literature Program to Your Own Classes.

Library of Great Works

Now, the time-honored longer works of American, British, and world cultures available with Prentice Hall Literature

- Classic, unabridged editions
- Hardbound versions insure lasting value
- A Novel Study Guide for expert teaching support to bring the work to life

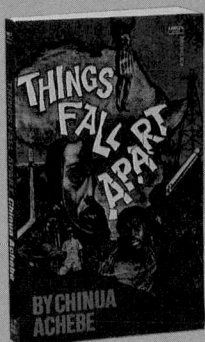

Great Works

Adventures of Huckleberry Finn	Nineteen Eighty Four
Brothers Karamazov	Our Town
Candide	Pride and Prejudice
Death of a Salesman	Red Badge of Courage
Don Quixote	Scarlet Letter
Great Gatsby	Siddartha
Hamlet	Tartuffe
Importance of Being Earnest	Things Fall Apart
Lord of the Flies	Wuthering Heights

Computer Test Bank

Customize your literature testing program with instant tests on each selection

For each selection choose from:
- Selection test
- Essay questions with evaluation guidelines
- Answer key

For each unit, choose from:
- Short answer test
- Essay tests

Powerful word processor for your made to order options.
- Write an unlimited number of new questions
- Delete questions

User friendly format for quick answers.
- Menus
- 800 customer service number

Annotated Teacher's Edition

PRENTICE HALL
LITERATURE

THE ENGLISH TRADITION

SECOND EDITION

PRENTICE HALL
Englewood Cliffs, New Jersey
Needham, Massachusetts

ISBN 0-13-688938-7

10 9 8 7 6 5 4 3 2 1

Cover and Title Page: *The Sisters*, 1900, Ralph Peacock, The Tate Gallery, London

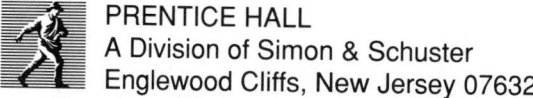

PRENTICE HALL
A Division of Simon & Schuster
Englewood Cliffs, New Jersey 07632

CONTENTS

The Prentice Hall Literature Program
OVERVIEW

THE STUDENT BOOK

The Prentice Hall Literature Program is a complete literature program, offering high-quality, appealing, traditional and contemporary literary selections, with study aids that will guide students into, through, and beyond the literature.

Organization

The selections are organized chronologically to present the literature of Great Britain in a historical context. The following list shows the units and the sections within each unit into which the selections are organized:

The Anglo-Saxon Period
The Medieval Period
The English Renaissance
The Seventeenth Century: The Schools of Donne and Jonson, The Puritan Age
The Restoration and the Eighteenth Century: The Restoration, The Age of Johnson, Pre-Romantic Poetry
The Romantic Age: Poetry, Prose
The Victorian Age: Major Victorian Poets, Other Victorian Poets, Prose
The Modern Period: Prose, Poetry, Drama
Contemporary Writers: Prose, Poetry

The number and variety of selections offer choice and flexibility in meeting curriculum requirements as well as student needs and interests.

Unique Features

Because the Prentice Hall Literature Program puts emphasis on the reading and appreciation of literature, it offers several unique features to help students become active readers.

Reading Critically Each unit begins with a feature called Reading Critically, which includes a summary of the historical context, the literary movements, and the writers' techniques of the period. This feature is followed by a Model for Reading Critically, which is annotated to demonstrate and explain to students how a good reader might apply this information to the analysis of a selection. This technique actively involves the reader in the text before reading and while reading. Such involvement and reaction are necessary if students are to learn. Students are encouraged to use this technique as they read other selections in the unit. This feature provides a method of scaffolding—giving students help and support while they acquire the skills to become successful readers of literature. To give students further practice with this process, there is an additional selection in the Teaching Portfolio which

students can annotate themselves.

Guide for Interpreting All other selections begin with a Guide for Interpreting. These pages contain useful prereading information. The Guide for Interpreting prepares students for successful reading in the following ways:
- A biography of the author provides insight into how the author came to write the selection.
- A literary focus section introduces the literary concept that is taught with the selection.
- A motivational writing activity puts students in an appropriate frame of mind.
- A primary source presents a quotation from the writer or a critic that gives and insight into the writer's work or times.
- Commentaries call out some noteworthy aspect of the work—thematic, stylistic, or meaning-oriented—and offer an insight into it.

This Guide for Interpreting provides the necessary background to enhance comprehension, motivates students to read, and gives them technical support to read successfully.

Each selection is self-contained and complete so that you can use the selections in any order.

After Reading

Features at the end of the selection are designed to foster comprehension and encourage constructive response, either personal or literary. These features encourage the growth of skills needed by students to become independent readers. These features comprise five areas:

Thinking About the Selection: These study questions are built upon three levels of comprehension: the literal, the interpretive, and the applied. The questions are grouped by three levels of increasing complexity: recalling (literal), interpreting (inference, analysis), and applying (generalization, extension, judgment). The different levels may be used as appropriate for different ability levels, or may be used to take all students through different levels of thinking.

Analyzing Literature: This section develops and reinforces the literary concept or skill introduced on the Guide for Interpreting page and applies it to the selection. It helps students to understand literary concepts and appreciate writers' techniques, thereby enabling them to respond appropriately to literature.

Critical Thinking and Reading: This section introduces students to those critical thinking and critical reading skills that are necessary for understanding literature. It gives them an opportunity to apply these skills to the literary selections.

Understanding Language: Knowledge and appreciation of language are developed in this section, which contains activities on language prompted by the selection. The activities may be geared toward helping students appreciate writers' use of language, master skills needed to increase their vocabulary, or prepare for SATs.

Thinking and Writing: This is a composition assignment arising from the selection. This assignment, which may be creative or analytical, is process-oriented, suggesting steps for prewriting, drafting, and revising.

Special Features

Several special features occur throughout this volume: **Cross Currents** present some contemporary or humanities connection to the period or content of the unit. **Great Works** introduce students to great works of literature, novels and plays that cannot be included in this anthology. This feature places the work in its historical period, indicates the significance of the work, presents a synopsis, and motivates students to read. **The Changing English Language** gives historical perspectives on the growth of the English language.

End of Unit

You the Writer, You the Critic At the end of each unit, there are six additional writing activities. Three of them, under You the Writer, are creative; three of them, under You the Critic, are analytical. Each activity is developed through the steps of the writing process.

End of Book

Three handbooks are provided at the end of *Prentice Hall Literature*: Handbook of Writing About Literature, Handbook of Critical Thinking and Reading Terms, and Handbook of Literary Terms and Techniques.

Handbook of Writing About Literature The Handbook of Writing About Literature is divided into five sections. The first section introduces the process of writing. The second requires students to analyze and interpret literature and teaches them how to write about the specific elements of literary works. The third requires students to interpret and synthesize while teaching how to write about the work as a whole. The fourth provides instruction in evaluating literary works and the fifth guides the students in the creation of their own literary works.

This Handbook may be used for direct instruction or as support for the individual writing assignments in *Prentice Hall Literature*.

Handbook of Critical Thinking and Reading Terms The Handbook of Critical Thinking and Reading Terms provides an alphabetical arrangement of the terms taught in the Critical Thinking and Reading activities at the end of selections. Each entry expands upon the original definition and provides one or more examples. This Handbook can be used to preteach terminology or to review information. It can also be used as an easy reference guide for students as they work on individual Critical Thinking and Reading assignments.

Handbook of Literary Terms and Techniques The Handbook of Literary Terms and Techniques provides an alphabetical guide to the literary terms introduced on the Guide for Interpreting page and taught in the Analyzing Literature activities at the end of selections. Each entry provides a full definition of the term or technique with one or more examples. The handbook can be used for preteaching, for review, or as a support for students as they work on individual Analyzing Literature activities.

TEACHING SUPPORT

THE ANNOTATED TEACHER'S EDITION

The annotated teacher's edition of *Prentice Hall Literature* is designed to be used both for planning and for actual in-class teaching. It offers planning aids and specific teaching suggestions for all selections. This planning and teaching material appears in the side columns next to the reduced student pages of each selection. These annotations, which correspond to the student material on that page, help you give your students positive and relevant experiences with literature by asking the right questions at the right time and by pointing out what is significant.

Preparing the Lesson: Focus

The annotations on the opening pages of the selection help you plan your presentation of the material. Each selection begins with notes that suggest ways to introduce or enhance the prereading instruction or activities presented in the students' Guide for Interpreting. These notes help you present the material or adapt it for **less advanced** or **more advanced** students. A **vocabulary** list presents, in glossary format, words from the selection that might present difficulty in reading; you may wish to preteach these words. Occasional **spelling tips** give hints for remembering the spelling of a troublesome word. A **critical evaluation** note gives a critic's point of view on the writer of the work. Objectives for each selection are keyed to the end-of-selection material. This page also includes a complete list of support material for this selection in the Teaching Portfolio and other components of the program. In the column next to the first page of the selection, you will find a **motivation/prior knowledge** suggestion and a **purpose-setting question** to prepare the students to read. Frequently, **thematic ideas** are given. These suggest other selections in this book that treat themes similar to those under discussion. You may want to use these selections together to integrate and reinforce universal concepts and themes. **ESL strategies** suggest ways to make selections accessible to ESL students. All of these annotations help you effectively prepare your lesson.

Teaching the Lesson: Presentation

You may use the notes throughout the pages of the selection to direct your discussion in class. As you and your students read the selection, you will find additional notes that enable you to customize the lesson for your class. They let you increase your students' involvement in the work and enrich their reading of it, while enabling them to deal with the particular genres. The following kinds of notes may direct your class discussions:

Master Teacher Notes These classroom tips from master teachers give an approach, a strategy, or a very special bit of information that enlivens the selection or increases appreciation.

Humanities Notes For each piece of fine art in the student book, there is a humanities note giving information on the work of art and the artist. These notes generally point out features of the piece of art that relate it to the work of literature with which it is presented. Additionally, the humanities note concludes with questions that you may use if you wish to discuss the art as part of your discussion of the selection.

Enrichment Enrichment notes provide additional information on points of interest that arise in selections. You may use this information to enrich your students' knowledge of the background of a selection and appreciation of it.

Reading Strategies Strategies to promote student comprehension of the literary text reinforce the emphasis on teaching students to read literature actively.

Clarification Words, phrases, or ideas that might be obstacles to student understanding are clarified to ensure comprehension.

Discussion Throughout the selection, you will find additional questions and points for discussion. These help you proceed through the selection with students, eliciting their understanding and appreciation of significant passages.

Literary Focus To promote understanding of the writer's techniques, literary focus annotations direct attention to those aspects of the selection that reflect the literary concept presented with it.

Critical Thinking and Reading These notes reinforce the critical thinking and reading skills developed throughout the program.

Reader's Response These notes ask a question designed to prompt the students' personal response to the selection.

Grammar in Action Grammar in Action notes integrate language arts skills. These notes demonstrate the writer's use of particular grammatical or style points. They present a direct link between grammar and writing.

Additional **commentary** and **primary source** notes add further background or insight to the selection.

There are probably more notes than you need for presenting any given selection. We emphasize the importance of selecting those annotations that are best suited to your classes and course of instruction.

Closure and Extension

Answers are provided for all questions in each feature following the selections. Where questions are open-ended, we present a suggested response or suggest points that students should note in their answers.

The annotations after the selection also include the following:

Challenge These questions take students beyond those given with the instruction.

Publishing Student Writing For many selections, additional notes suggest ways to publish the writing students have done in the Thinking and Writing feature.

Writing Across the Curriculum Where appropriate, you will see suggestions for additional assignments or suggestions for relating the Thinking and Writing assignment to students' work in another discipline.

In addition, you will find teaching suggestions for the special features in the student book—Reading Critically and You the Writer, You the Critic. You will also find annotations on the unit introductions, relating the information there to specific selections.

THE TEACHING PORTFOLIO

The Teaching Portfolio provides support for teaching and testing all of the selections and skills in *Prentice Hall Literature*.

Fine-Art Transparencies

Twenty fine-art transparencies with blackline masters are provided in the Teaching Portfolio. These can be used to introduce selections and motivate students to read, or they may be used as additional writing assignments in response to art. Each fine art transparency has a writing assignment for students and a lesson plan for teaching that assignment. Furthermore, the fine art is keyed into the selections through Master Teacher Notes in the Annotated Teacher's Edition.

Beginning of Unit

Each unit begins with a list of objectives and a skills chart listing literary elements and skills covered in the unit. The skills chart also identifies all the blackline masters in the Teaching Portfolio that correlate to each selection.

The Selections

Full teaching support is provided for each selection. This support material is organized by selection for your convenience. The support for each selection consists of the following: Teacher Backup, Grammar in Action Worksheet, Usage and Mechanics Worksheet, Vocabulary Check, Analyzing Literature Worksheet*, Critical Thinking and Reading Worksheet*, Language Worksheet* (there are always two of the starred three), and a Selection Test.

Teacher Backup Teacher Backup material is provided for each selection. This material consists of more information about the author, a critical quotation about the author, a summary of the selection, and a list of other works by the author. In addition, there is a Check Test that you can use to check if students have read the selection. Help in teaching and evaluating the writing assignment in the student text is provided as well as three alternative composition assignments for the students. One of these is less challenging than the assignment in the student text, one is more challenging, and one requires the student to write in response to literary criticism. Finally, answers to all worksheet activities and tests are provided.

Grammar in Action Worksheets The Grammar in Action Worksheet provides further instruction and practice corresponding to Grammar in Action notes in the Annotated Teacher's Edition.

Usage and Mechanics The Usage and Mechanics Worksheet provides sentences dealing with the selection that contain errors in usage and mechanics. They provide practice on such common problems as run-on sentences, sentence fragments, and subject–verb agreement as well as errors in spelling and punctuation; furthermore, the Grammar in Action skills are incorporated into these sentences wherever possible. We suggest you have your students correct these sentences orally so that they can discuss each problem.

Vocabulary Check The Vocabulary Check tests mastery of the vocabulary words listed in the Annotated Teacher's Edition on the Guide for Interpreting page before each selection. This blackline master can be used as a test or as an in-class or at-home assignment.

Worksheets The Analyzing Literature Worksheet, Critical Thinking and Reading Worksheet, and Language Worksheet support and expand upon the skills taught at the end of the selection in the student book. If no Understanding Language assignment appears in the student book, one is provided in the Teaching Portfolio.

Selections Test A Selection Test is provided for each selection. This test provides a check of comprehension as well as mastery of the skills taught at the end of the selection.

Annotated Models For each selection that is annotated as a model in the student book, a selection is provided in the Teaching Portfolio for students to annotate themselves.

End of Unit

Each unit ends with two unit tests: a short-answer test and an essay test. Guidelines are provided for evaluating student responses to the essay test questions. In addition, a list of suggested projects, a bibliography, and a list of audio-visual aids follow.

End of Portfolio

At the end of the Teaching Portfolio are models of strong and weak student writing and a guide to evaluating student writing.

STUDY GUIDES

Study Guides for major novels and plays are available with *Prentice Hall Literature*. These guides will help you teach many of the novels of your choice as part of your total literature program. Each guide contains an overview of the novel or play, chapter-by-chapter lessons, assignments leading to essays and imaginative writing, guidelines for dealing with provocative themes, a bibliography, and black-line masters of skills and a test.

COMPUTER TEST BANK

The computer test bank provides the selection test and unit tests from the Teaching Portfolio on a computer disk. The program allows you to modify the tests by deleting items from the short-answer selection tests supplied, choosing a different essay question, and writing your own test questions. You can save your test for future use.

LIBRARY OF VIDEO CLASSICS

The Library of Video Classics provides videotapes of films made of major works in this level. Each tape is accompanied by a Viewing Guide, which gives background on the film or director, a planning overview for the film, and pre-viewing and after-viewing questions and activities.

Composition Strand in Prentice Hall Literature

The following chart shows all composition activities and their location in the program. The activities are organized to take students into, through, and beyond the literature.

Feature	In the Student Materials	In the Teacher Materials	Benefit
Into the Literature			
"Writing" activity *before* each selection	"Guide for Reading" page before each selection in student text	"Guide for Reading" teaching note in margin of Annotated Teacher's Edition	Writing before reading is an ideal technique for getting students into literature
Through the Literature			
"Thinking and Writing" composition activity after each selection	End of each selection in student text	In Teaching Portfolio: teaching notes for activity labeled with writing process steps; evaluation checklist for grading writing In ATE: suggestions for publishing student writing	The writing activity that follows each selection provides an immediate opportunity to respond to the literary experience. The activity is in writing process format.
Three additional composition activities for *each* selection: Less Challenging, More Challenging, The Student as Critic		Additional activities are in the Teaching Portfolio. These can be used as assignments, or as essay questions for tests.	Three additional activities for *each* selection let you meet the needs for lower ability levels, or provide enrichment.
"Handbook of Writing About Literature," made up of two-page writing lessons	Handbook section of at least 50 pages at the end of each student text	Notes and support for using the handbook in the Teaching Portfolio	Guided lesson lead students step-by step through case studies and activities.
"Unit Test" essay questions that address several selections in a unit		Tests in Teaching Portfolio comes with evaluation checklists	Sharpen critical thinking and writing with thoughtful topics that compare and contrast thematic ideas, literary elements, and unit content.
Beyond the Literature			
"You the Writer" creative writing activity with each unit	End of each unit in student text	Guidelines for evaluating student writing are in Annotated Teacher's Edition	Students try their hand at expressive writing aided by imaginative prompts and step-by-step encouragement.
"You the Critic" literary criticism activity with each unit	End of each unit in student text	Teaching notes and guidelines for evaluating student writing in Annotated Teacher's Edition	Challenge analytical skills as your students respond to literary criticism.

Composition Strand in Prentice Hall Literature (continued)

Feature	In the Student Materials	In the Teacher Materials	Benefit
"Writing Across the Curriculum" suggestions		Suggestions in Annotated Teacher's Edition	Broaden writing opportunities to other subjects. Notes suggest assignments and interactions with other departments.
"Fine Art Writing Activity" (from full color art transparency)	Handout sheet	Twenty fine art color transparencies with accompanying blackline masters in Teaching Portfolio	Use the dynamic combination of literature and writing for a humanities-based writing activity.
"Student Writing Models"		In the Teaching Portfolio: Examples of strong and weak student compositions	Use the powerful motivator of peer learning to prompt better writing responses.

Skills Chart for Selections in Each Unit

The following chart shows the literary elements and integrated language arts skills covered with each selection. An asterisk (*) indicates that a worksheet appears in the Teaching Portfolio.

SKILLS CHART: THE ANGLO-SAXON PERIOD (449–1066)

Selection	Analyzing Literature	Critical Thinking and Reading	Understanding Language/ Speaking and Listening	Thinking and Writing	Grammar in Action
Reading Critically					
"The Seafarer," translated by Burton Raffel, p. 17	Understanding Anglo-Saxon lyric poetry*	Comparing and contrasting attitudes	Appreciating Old English*	Writing about Anglo-Saxon beliefs	
From *Beowulf,* Part 1, translated by Burton Raffel, p. 24	Understanding the Anglo-Saxon epic	Making inferences about ideals*	Using a glossary*	Writing about character traits	Recognizing appositives and appositive phrases
From *Beowulf,* Part 2, translated by Burton Raffel, p. 39	Tracing pagan and Christian elements	Identifying Old English words*	Completing word analogies*	Responding to criticism	Using action verbs*
The Wanderer, translated by Charles W. Kennedy, p. 57	Understanding exile	Appreciating a poem's structure*	Appreciating vivid adverbs*	Responding to criticism	
From *A History of the English Church and People,* Bede, p. 64	Understanding historical writing*	Making inferences about attitudes	Tracing word histories*	Writing a critical review	

SKILLS CHART: THE MEDIEVAL PERIOD (1066-1485)

Selection	Analyzing Literature	Critical Thinking and Reading	Understanding Language/ Speaking and Listening	Thinking and Writing	Grammar in Action
Reading Critically					
From *Morte d'Arthur*, Sir Thomas Malory, p. 91	Understanding legends*	Recognizing elements of fantasy*	Appreciating word origins	Writing about character	Understanding past perfect tense*
"Sir Patrick Spens," p. 104 "Get Up and Bar the Door," p. 108 "The Twa Corbies," p. 110 "Barbara Allan," p. 111	Understanding the folk ballad*	Interpreting symbols in folk ballads	Appreciating language change* Sharing folk ballads	Writing about a folk ballad	
"The Prologue," from the *Canterbury Tales*, Geoffrey Chaucer, p. 117	Understanding characterization	Making inferences about characters*	Interpreting similes*	Writing a pilgrim's tale	Using topic sentences and supporting information* Using specific words*
"The Nun's Priest's Tale," Geoffrey Chaucer, p. 141	Understanding the mock-herioc style*	Understanding courtly love*	Appreciating vivid verbs*	Writing a beast fable	Understanding debating strategies*
From "The Pardoner's Tale," Geoffrey Chaucer, p. 159	Understanding the anecdote (exemplum)*	Making inferences based on narrator's words*	Reading Middle English aloud	Writing an analysis	
From *Sir Gawain and the Green Knight*, translated by Marie Borroff, p. 170	Understanding medieval romances*	Making inferences about chivalry	Using abstract words	Evaluating the medieval romance	Understanding pronoun-antecedent agreement* Using adverbs*
From *Everyman*, p. 188	Understanding the morality play*	Interpreting names as symbols*	Performing in a play	Discussing a morality play	Understanding the evolution of the language*

SKILLS CHART: THE ENGLISH RENAISSANCE (1485–1625)

Selection	Analyzing Literature	Critical Thinking and Reading	Understanding Language/ Speaking and Listening	Thinking and Writing	Grammar in Action
Reading Critically					
"Whoso List to Hunt," Sir Thomas Wyatt, p. 219	Understanding the Petrarchan sonnet*	Interpreting figurative meaning*	Reading aloud classic British poems	Responding to criticism	
Sir Philip Sidney "Sonnet 31," p. 224 "Sonnet 39," p. 226	Understanding a sonnet sequence*		Greek and Latin word parts*	Writing a letter of response	Understanding closure*
"The Passionate Shepherd to His Love," Christopher Marlowe, p. 230	Appreciating pastoral poems	Inferring cultural attitudes*	Appreciating the multiple meanings of words*		
From *The Tragical History of the Life and Death of Dr. Faustus,* Christopher Marlowe, p. 233	Understanding historical context	Making inferences about characters*	Evaluating a dramatic reading*		Using commas*
Sir Walter Raleigh "The Nymph's Reply to the Shepherd," p. 238 "To His Son," p. 240	Identifying the speaker in a poem	Making inferences about tone* Making inferences about purpose	Understanding words based on Greek myths*	Writing an invitation in verse Writing your own reply	
Edmund Spenser From "*The Faerie Queene,*" p. 244 "Sonnet 1," p. 245 "Sonnet 26," p. 246 "Sonnet 75," p. 247	Understanding the Spenserian stanza* Understanding the Spenserian sonnet		Interpreting personification*	Comparing and contrasting sonnets	Recognizing parallelism*
"A Litany in Time of Plague," Thomas Nashe, p. 250	Understanding a litany	Generalizing from a set of assumptions*	Tracing word origins*	Writing about the concerns of a people	
William Shakespeare "Sonnet 29," p. 255 "Sonnet 73," p. 257 "Sonnet 116," p. 258 "Sonnet 130," p. 259	Understanding the Shakespearean sonnet*		Understanding prefixes and suffixes*	Comparing and contrasting sonnets	

Selection	Analyzing Literature	Critical Thinking and Reading	Understanding Language/ Speaking and Listening	Thinking and Writing	Grammar in Action
William Shakespeare "Tell Me Where is Fancy Bred?" p. 261 "It Was a Lover and His Lass," p. 262 "Fear No More the Heat o' the Sun," p. 264	Understanding Shakespeare's songs	Finding details that develop mood Selecting details that develop mood* Finding details that support purpose*		Writing about Shakespeare's songs	
William Shakespeare *Macbeth*, Act I, p. 271	Understanding blank verse*	Making inferences about characters*	Reading blank verse aloud	Comparing and contrasting characters	
Macbeth, Act II, p. 291	Understanding atmosphere*	Interpreting symbols*			Recognizing personification*
Macbeth, Act III, p. 305	Understanding irony*	Interpreting connotative meanings	Understanding figurative language*	Who is the third murderer?	
Macbeth, Act IV, p. 321	Understanding plot development*	Reading between the lines*		Writing about Macbeth's tragic flaw	Appreciating repetition*
Macbeth, Act V, p. 339	Understanding theme*		Reading Shakespearean English Understanding Shakespearean English*		Understanding tone*
From *Novum Organum*, "Idols of the Cave," Sir Francis Bacon, p. 357	Understanding aphorisms*	Reasoning	Finding Latin roots* Making words from Latin roots	Writing aphorisms	Creating unity
From the King James Bible "Psalm 23," p. 364 "The Parable of the Prodigal Son," p. 365 "I Corinthians 13," p. 367	Recognizing a psalm Understanding parables*	Analyzing the use of parallelism*			

SKILLS CHART: THE SEVENTEENTH CENTURY (1625–1660)

Selection	Analyzing Literature	Critical Thinking and Reading	Understanding Language/ Speaking and Listening	Thinking and Writing	Grammar in Action
Reading Critically					
"To the Memory of My Beloved Master, William Shakespeare," Ben Jonson, p. 391	Understanding allusions*		Tracing word origins*	Writing a letter	
The Schools of Donne and Jonson					
John Donne "Song," p. 398 Holy Sonnet 10, p. 400 Holy Sonnet 14, p. 402	Understanding paradox* Understanding metaphysical conceit*	Following an argument		Writing about a philosophical argument	
John Donne Meditation 17, p. 405	Recognizing themes*	Arguing through analogy*		Writing about the theme of a work	Using metaphors*
George Herbert "Virtue," p. 410 "Easter Wings," p. 412 "Man," p. 413	Understanding emblematic images*	Analyzing Herbert's style	Recognizing differences among synonyms*	Writing about emblematic images	
Andrew Marvell "To His Coy Mistress," p. 418 "The Picture of Little T. C. in a Prospect of Flowers," p. 420	Recognizing couplets and quatrains*		Recognizing syllables and pronunciations*	Comparing and contrasting styles	Using imagery* Using adjectives*

THE SEVENTEENTH CENTURY (1625–1660) (continued)

Selection	Analyzing Literature	Critical Thinking and Reading	Understanding Language/ Speaking and Listening	Thinking and Writing	Grammar in Action
Ben Jonson "On My First Son," p. 424 "Song: To Celia," p. 425 "Still to be Neat," p. 426	Understanding apostrophes*	Inferring the author's purpose*		Responding to criticism	
Robert Herrick "An Ode for Him (Ben Jonson)," p. 430 "To the Virgins, to Make Much of Time," p. 432	Understanding symbols*	Interpreting the difference among synonyms* Knowing differences among synonyms		Writing about thinking	
Sir John Suckling "The Constant Lover," p. 436 "Song," p. 437 Richard Lovelace "To Lucasta on Going to the Wars," p. 438 "To Althea, from Prison," p. 439	Understanding tone*	Understanding the effect of connotative meaning*		Writing about tone	Using action verbs*
The Puritan Age					
John Milton "When I Consider How My Light Is Spent," p. 444 "On His Having Arrived at the Age of Twenty-Three," p. 446	Understanding Italian sonnets*		Understanding the multiple meanings of words*	Comparing and contrasting sonnets	
John Milton, from *Paradise Lost*, p. 449	Understanding epic poetry*		Recognizing Latin roots*		Using sentences of varying lengths* Establishing tone*
From *The Pilgrim's Progress*, John Bunyan, p. 462	Recognizing allegory*	Interpreting the author's point of view*		Writing an allegory for today's world	Using conjunctive adverbs*

THE RESTORATION AND THE EIGHTEENTH CENTURY (1660–1798)

Selection	Analyzing Literature	Critical Thinking and Reading	Understanding Language/ Speaking and Listening	Thinking and Writing	Grammar in Action
Reading Critically					
"Holy Thursday," William Blake, p. 489	Understanding paradox* Using sound devices	Analyzing the effect of sound devices	Finding antonyms*	Responding to criticism	
The Restoration					
From "An Essay of Dramatic Poesy," John Dryden, p. 494	Understanding an essay	Charting an analysis Understanding analysis*	Appreciating specific words*	Writing an evaluation of an analysis	Creating coherence*
"A Song for St. Cecilia's Day," John Dryden, p. 499	Recognizing an ode*	Understanding the effect of sound	Appreciating rhythm*	Writing an ode	Creating special effects*
From The Diary, Samuel Pepys, p. 506		Finding main ideas and supporting details*	Appreciating the language of the Restoration*		Using elliptical elements*
The Age of Pope and Swift					
From A Journal of the Plague Year, Daniel Defoe, p. 514	Recognizing first-person narrative	Comparing and contrasting writers*	Distinguishing between meanings*		Understanding subordination*
From Gulliver's Travels, Jonathan Swift, p. 520	Understanding satire*	Understanding generalizations*	Using words from literature	Writing a new adventure for Gulliver	Using correlative conjunctions*
From Thoughts on Various Subjects, Jonathan Swift, p. 530	Understanding epigrams*		Completing word analogies*	Writing epigrams	

THE RESTORATION AND THE EIGHTEENTH CENTURY (1660–1798) (continued)

Selection	Analyzing Literature	Critical Thinking and Reading	Understanding Language/ Speaking and Listening	Thinking and Writing	Grammar in Action
Joseph Addison and Richard Steele "Country Manners," p. 538 "Thoughts in Westminster Abbey," p. 541	Understanding the informal essay Understanding the personal essay*	Recognizing characteristics of style* Understanding the cultural context*	Choosing the meaning that fits the context*	Writing an informal essay	Using comparison and contrast*
From *The Rape of the Lock,* Alexander Pope, p. 548	Understanding the mock epic*	Inferring the author's purpose*		Writing about tone	Using the exclamation mark*
From *An Essay on Man,* Alexander Pope, p. 561	Understanding the heroic couplet*	Generalizing	Understanding diction*	Responding to neoclassical criticism	
The Age of Johnson					
Samuel Johnson "Letter to Lord Chesterfield," p. 566 From The Preface to *A Dictionary of the English Language,* Samuel Johnson, p. 568 From *A Dictionary of the English Language,* p. 571	Analyzing diction and style*	Making inferences about tone	Word building using root words*	Comparing and contrasting styles Writing Johnsonian dictionary entries	Recognizing parallelism*
From *The Life of Samuel Johnson,* James Boswell, p. 576	Understanding biography	Recognizing subjective information Separating subjective from objective information*	Understanding how words change in meaning*	Writing from Johnson's point of view	Using commas with parenthetical expressions* Recognizing compound-complex sentences*
Pre-Romantic Poetry					
"Elegy Written in a Country Churchyard," Thomas Gray, p. 586	Understanding an elegy	Evaluating the effect of inverted sentences*	Appreciating vivid verbs*	Writing an elegy	Using participles and gerunds*
"Woman," Oliver Goldsmith, p. 593	Understanding poetic structure*		Completing word analogies*		

THE RESTORATION AND THE EIGHTEENTH CENTURY (1660–1798) (continued)

Selection	Analyzing Literature	Critical Thinking and Reading	Understanding Language/ Speaking and Listening	Thinking and Writing	Grammar in Action
Robert Burns "To a Mouse," p. 596 "To a Louse," p. 599 "Afton Water," p. 602 "John Anderson, My Jo," p. 604	Recognizing dialect*	Recognizing satire*		Comparing and contrasting two poems Writing about dialect	Appreciating dialect*
William Blake "The Lamb," p. 608 "The Tiger," p. 611 "The Human Abstract," p. 612 "Infant Sorrow," p. 613 "A Poison Tree," p. 614	Recognizing symbolism Recognizing symbols*		Appreciating Latinate words*	Writing about symbolism	

SKILLS CHART: THE ROMANTIC AGE (1798–1832)

Selection	Analyzing Literature	Critical Thinking and Reading	Understanding Language/ Speaking and Listening	Thinking and Writing	Grammar in Action
Reading Critically					
"The Solitary Reaper," William Wordsworth, p. 639	Diction	Understanding sound devices*	Appreciating vivid verbs*	Writing a poem	
Poetry					
William Wordsworth "Lines Composed a Few Miles Above Tintern Abbey," p. 644 "My Heart Leaps Up When I Behold," p. 650	Understanding Romanticism*	Comparing and contrasting experiences* Interpreting a paradox		Writing about Romanticism Writing a nature poem	Recognizing shifts in verb tense*

THE ROMANTIC AGE (1798–1832) (continued)

Selection	Analyzing Literature	Critical Thinking and Reading	Understanding Language/ Speaking and Listening	Thinking and Writing	Grammar in Action
William Wordsworth "Composed upon Westminster Bridge," p. 653 "It Is a Beauteous Evening, Calm and Free," p. 654 "London, 1802," p. 656 "The World Is Too Much With Us," p. 657	Recognizing a sonnet*		Completing word analogies*		
Samuel Taylor Coleridge "The Rime of the Ancient Mariner," p. 660	Understanding sound devices*	Analyzing the effects of sound devices	Understanding archaic words and meanings*	Responding to a statement by an author	Identifying archaic language* Recognizing similes*
Samuel Taylor Coleridge "Kubla Khan," p. 685	Understanding Romanticism*		Understanding homophones*		Using precise words*
George Gordon, Lord Byron "She Walks in Beauty," 690 "So We'll Go No More A-Roving," p. 691 "Apostrophe to the Ocean," p. 692	Understanding figurative language*		Understanding word origins*	Evaluating a poem	
George Gordon, Lord Byron from Don Juan, p. 697	Understanding the mock-epic*	Analyzing technique in relation to meaning*		Writing about the Byronic hero	
Percy Bysshe Shelley "Ozymandias," p. 702 "Ode to the West Wind," p. 704 "To a Skylark," p. 708 "To —," p. 712 "A Dirge," p. 713	Understanding poetic structure* Understanding the ode	Recognizing an author's style*		Writing an ode Comparing and contrasting views of nature	

THE ROMANTIC AGE (1798–1832) (continued)

Selection	Analyzing Literature	Critical Thinking and Reading	Understanding Language/ Speaking and Listening	Thinking and Writing	Grammar in Action
John Keats "On First Looking into Chapman's Homer," p. 716 "Bright Star, Would I Were as Steadfast as Thou Art," p. 718 "When I Have Fears That I May Cease to Be," p. 719	Understanding the sonnet*	Recognizing poetic forms*		Comparing and contrasting sonnets	
John Keats "Ode to a Nightingale," p. 721 "Ode on a Grecian Urn," p. 726 "To Autumn," p. 729	Using imagery*		Selecting music to accompany a poem Comparing rhyme schemes*	Comparing and contrasting odes	Using hyphens*
Prose					
Introduction to *Frankenstein*, Mary Wollstonecraft Shelley, p. 734	Recognizing the Gothic tradition*		Understanding Greek and Latin roots*	Writing in the Gothic tradition	Appreciating repetition*
"Dream Children: A Reverie," Charles Lamb, p. 742	Understanding the familiar essay*	Inferring tone	Using the multiple meanings of words*	Analyzing a writer's attitudes	
"Macbeth," William Hazlitt, p. 748	Understanding a critical essay*	Finding main ideas	Completing word analogies*	Evaluating literary criticism	Making direct statements*

SKILLS CHART: THE VICTORIAN AGE (1833–1901)

Selection	Analyzing Literature	Critical Thinking and Reading	Understanding Language/ Speaking and Listening	Thinking and Writing	Grammar in Action
Reading Critically					
"Ulysses," Alfred, Lord Tennyson, p. 779	Understanding dramatic monologues Understanding the speaker in poetry*	Understanding a character's motivation	Choosing the meaning that fits the context*	Writing a continuation of the poem	Studying subject-verb agreement: *There* and *Here**

THE VICTORIAN AGE (1833–1901) (continued)

Selection	Analyzing Literature	Critical Thinking and Reading	Understanding Language/ Speaking and Listening	Thinking and Writing	Grammar in Action
Major Victorian Poets					
Alfred, Lord Tennyson "The Lady of Shalott," p. 786 From *The Princess,* "Tears, Idle Tears," p. 792 "The Splendor Falls," p. 794	Recognizing meter and stanza structure Understanding meter*	Understanding an author's purpose	Fitting the context	Describing the poet's style	Appreciating details that create atmosphere*
Alfred, Lord Tennyson From *In Memoriam A. H. H.,* p. 797 "The Lotos-Eaters," p. 801 "Crossing the Bar," p. 808	Understanding an elegy Recognizing symbols	Making inferences about the subject of an elegy* Recognizing allusions Comparing attitudes	Appreciating vivid verbs* Finding antonyms	Writing about symbols	
Robert Browning "My Last Duchess," p. 812 "Home-Thoughts from Abroad," p. 817 "Love Among the Ruins," p. 818 "Prospice," p. 822	Understanding a dramatic monologue	Making inferences about the speaker* Interpreting tone Making inferences about attitudes	Understanding diction* Revealing diction	Writing a dramatic monologue Comparing and contrasting two places Comparing and contrasting two poems	Using parallelism* Appreciating contrasting rhythms*
Matthew Arnold "To Marguerite— Continued," p.826 "Self-Dependence," p. 828 "Dover Beach," p. 830	Creating imagery and mood Using figurative language Appreciating the apostrophe*		Appreciating vivid words*	Writing about imagery and mood Writing about a Victorian poet	

THE VICTORIAN AGE (1833–1901) (continued)

Selection	Analyzing Literature	Critical Thinking and Reading	Understanding Language/ Speaking and Listening	Thinking and Writing	Grammar in Action
Thomas Hardy "The Darkling Thrush," p. 834 "The Man He Killed," p. 836 "'Ah, Are You Digging on My Grave?'" p. 838	Understanding simile and metaphor* Using simile and metaphor Understanding irony*		Preparing an oral report on Wessex	Writing a response to a poem	
Gerard Manley Hopkins "God's Grandeur," p. 842 "Hurrahing in Harvest," p. 845 "Pied Beauty," p. 846 "Spring and Fall: To a Young Child," p. 847	Analyzing rhythm and rhyme*	Understanding the effects of imagery*		Writing Margaret's reply	
A. E. Housman "To an Athlete Dying Young," p. 850 "Loveliest of Trees," p. 852 "When I Was One-and-Twenty," p. 853 "With Rue My Heart Is Laden," p. 854	Finding the theme*	Understanding the multiple meanings of words*		Responding to criticism	

Selection	Analyzing Literature	Critical Thinking and Reading	Understanding Language/ Speaking and Listening	Thinking and Writing	Grammar in Action
Other Victorian Poets					
"Sonnet 43," Elizabeth Barrett Browning, p. 858 "Silent Noon," Dante Gabriel Rossetti, p. 859	Understanding a sonnet Understanding word choice in poetry*		Using prefixes and suffixes*		
"Lucifer in Starlight," George Meredith, p. 862 "A Birthday," Christina Rossetti, p. 863 "Recessional," Rudyard Kipling, p. 864 "Requiem," Robert Louis Stevenson, p. 866	Understanding imagery*		Understanding connotation and denotation*	Writing about historical content	Recognizing allusion*
Prose					
"The Signalman," Charles Dickens, p. 870	Following the plot in a ghost story Understanding plot: foreshadowing*	Separating realistic from fantastic details*	Fitting the context	Writing a ghost story	Using single quotation marks*
"The Three Strangers," Thomas Hardy, p. 882	Understanding setting and character* Understanding setting and mood	Inferring the author's attitude	Reading dialect Understanding character through dialogue*	Describing a place	Using the dash*

SKILLS CHART: THE MODERN PERIOD (1901–1945)

Selection	Analyzing Literature	Critical Thinking and Reading	Understanding Language/ Speaking and Listening	Thinking and Writing	Grammar in Action
Reading Critically					
"A Dill Pickle," Katherine Mansfield, p. 929	Understanding dialogue*	Making inferences based on dialogue	Understanding synonyms and antonyms*		
Prose					
"The Lagoon," Joseph Conrad, p. 940	Shifting point of view and theme Understanding a shifting point of view*	Making inferences about a moral code	Setting up a reader's theater Using context clues*	Responding to theme	Appreciating concrete details*
"The Schwartz-Metterklume Method," Saki (H.H. Munro), p. 952	Understanding satire*	Making inferences about tone	Understanding words with Latin roots*	Comparing and contrasting approaches	
"The Helping Hand," E. M. Forster, p. 958	Understanding direct and indirect characterization*	Making inferences about character	Understanding word origins Analyzing changes in definition*	Writing about a character	Understanding complement-subject-verb sentence patterns*
"The Lady in the Looking Glass: A Reflection," Virginia Woolf, p. 966	Recognizing stream-of-consciousness Understanding stream-of-consciousness narration*	Evaluating an author's purpose*		Using stream-of-consciousness narration	Using descriptive details*
"The Rocking Horse Winner," D.H. Lawrence, p. 974	Understanding omniscient narration	Understanding cause-and-effect relationships*	Understanding the difference between synonyms*	Telling the story	Using personification*

THE MODERN PERIOD (1901–1945) (continued)

Selection	Analyzing Literature	Critical Thinking and Reading	Understanding Language/ Speaking and Listening	Thinking and Writing	Grammar in Action
"Araby," James Joyce, p. 987	Understanding epiphany*	Analyzing Joyce's attitude	Appreciating image-making words*	Writing an extended conversation	Using semicolons*
"The Demon Lover," Elizabeth Bowen, p. 994	Considering war and the ghost story Recognizing the development of character traits*	Exploring a paradox*			Appreciating dialogue*
"Across the Bridge," Graham Greene, p. 1002	Understanding theme and point of view*	Understanding comedy and tragedy*	Learning about word completions	Analyzing the effects of point of view	Using dashes*
"Shooting an Elephant," George Orwell, p. 1012	Identifying tone*	Understanding stereotypes*	Understanding word origins	Supporting an opinion	Recognizing the active voice*
Poetry					
William Butler Yeats "When You Are Old," p. 1026 "The Lake Isle of Innisfree," p. 1027 "The Wild Swans at Coole," p. 1028 "An Irish Airman Foresees His Death," p. 1030	Understanding speaker and lyric voice*	Evaluating the use of imagery*		Writing about the use of a speaker	
William Butler Yeats "The Second Coming," p. 1033 "After Long Silence," p. 1035 "Sailing to Byzantium," p. 1036	Understanding symbols*	Understanding repetition*		Writing a poem about silence	

THE MODERN PERIOD (1901–1945) (continued)

Selection	Analyzing Literature	Critical Thinking and Reading	Understanding Language/ Speaking and Listening	Thinking and Writing	Grammar in Action
"Snake," D.H. Lawrence, p. 1039	Understanding free verse*	Making inferences about purpose	Classifying compound nouns*		Using the colon*
"Wirers," Siegfried Sassoon, p. 1046	Understanding historical context*	Understanding the multiple meanings of words*			
Rupert Brooke "The Soldier," p. 1050 "The Great Lover," p. 1051	Understanding personification* Feeling patriotism	Identifying the Georgian poets	Appreciating specific words*		
T. S. Eliot "Preludes," p. 1056 "Journey of the Magi," p. 1059	Using synecdoche* Conveying a mood*		Selecting music that evokes the poem	Writing a poem using synecdoche Analyzing Eliot's use of ambiguity	
"The Hollow Men," T. S. Eliot, p. 1063	Conveying tone*	Interpreting allusions*		Writing about tone	Omitting punctuation for effect*
Robert Graves "Interruption," p. 1070 "One Hard Look," p. 1072 "She Tells Her Love While Half Asleep," p. 1073		Recognizing traditional symbolism*	Understanding coined words*	Writing about the Modernist Movement	
W H. Auden "In Memory of W.B. Yeats," p. 1076 "Musée des Beaux Arts," W. H. Auden, p. 1078	Understanding elegy* Understanding figurative language*	Understanding the legacy of an artist		Writing about a paradox	Understanding form and tone*
Louis MacNeice "The Sunlight on the Garden," p. 1084 "Sunday Morning," p. 1086	Understanding scansion*		Appreciating concrete and abstract words*	Writing about rhyme and rhythm	

THE MODERN PERIOD (1901–1945) (continued)

Selection	Analyzing Literature	Critical Thinking and Reading	Understanding Language/ Speaking and Listening	Thinking and Writing	Grammar in Action
"What I Expected," Stephen Spender, p. 1090 "Naming of Parts," Henry Reed, p. 1092	Determining the speaker* Using satire	Comparing and contrasting speakers	Using word roots*	Comparing and contrasting two poems Writing about satire	
Dylan Thomas "The Force That Through the Green Fuse Drives the Flower," p. 1096 "Fern Hill," p. 1098 "Do Not Go Gentle into That Good Night," p. 1102	Using parallelism*	Interpreting connotative meaning*	Using words from Middle English	Writing a poem about childhood	Distinguishing that and which* Using specific words*
Drama					
George Bernard Shaw					
Preface to Pygmalion, p. 1106					Understanding persuasive writing*
Pygmalion, Act I, p. 1109	Understanding historical context	Generalizing about people Generalizing*	Understanding dialect*	Writing about historical context	
Pygmalion, Act II, p. 1121	Understanding character development*	Making inferences about characters*	Reading dialogue aloud	Comparing and contrasting characters	Appreciating dialect*

SKILLS CHART: CONTEMPORARY WRITERS (1945–PRESENT)

Selection	Analyzing Literature	Critical Thinking and Reading	Understanding Language/ Speaking and Listening	Thinking and Writing	Grammar in Action
Pygmalion, Act III, p. 1143	Using satire	Comparing and contrasting characters' attitudes*	Understanding slang*	Evaluating the effectiveness of satire	Understanding a comedy of manners*
Pygmalion, Act IV, p. 1159	Explaining crisis	Understanding cause and effect*	Understanding synonyms and antonyms* Finding synonyms and antonyms	Writing a letter of advice	
Pygmalion, Act V, p. 1169	Understanding the complete play	Summarizing a play*	Using prefixes*	Writing about the title	Using transitions* Understanding narrative writing*
Reading Critically					
"The Distant Past," William Trevor, p. 1215	Recognizing character*	Understanding a character's motivation*		Writing a dialogue	Appreciating dialect*
Prose					
"A Touch of Autumn in the Air," Sean O'Faolain, p. 1228	Understanding first-person narration*	Identifying objective and subjective information*	Learning what caricature is	Responding to a thematic subject	Using sentence fragments*
"The Truth About George," P. G. Wodehouse, p. 1238	Understanding humor*	Recognizing caricature	Using synonyms*	Writing about humor	Recognizing participial phrases*
"A Mild Attack of Locusts," Doris Lessing, p. 1252	Recognizing conflict*	Understanding the role of style*		Writing about a paradox	Using varied sentence structures*
"The Train from Rhodesia," Nadine Gordimer, p. 1260	Understanding theme	Understanding cultural attitudes*	Using concrete and abstract words*	Writing about theme	Recognizing prepositional phrases*
"The Fiddle," Alan Sillitoe, p. 1268	Understanding setting*		Understanding slang*		Recognizing the passive voice*
"A Voyage to Cythera," Margaret Drabble, p. 1276	Understanding flat and round characters*	Identifying kinds of evidence*		Writing about characterization	Using parallel structure*

CONTEMPORARY WRITERS (1945–PRESENT) (continued)

Selection	Analyzing Literature	Critical Thinking and Reading	Understanding Language/ Speaking and Listening	Thinking and Writing	Grammar in Action
Poetry					
Philip Larkin "Days," p. 1294 "The Explosion," p. 1295 "Coming," p. 1297	Understanding tone*		Understanding the multiple meanings of words*	Writing about tone	
"Taylor Street," Thom Gunn, p. 1299	Recognizing the importance of diction*		Choosing synonyms*		
Ted Hughes "Hawk Roosting," p. 1302 "The Horses," p. 1304	Using personification*		Choosing antonyms*	Using personification in a poem Comparing poems	
Stevie Smith "Not Waving but Drowning," p. 1307 "Pretty," p. 1308	Understanding voice*	Comparing and contrasting writers' attitudes*		Evaluating a poem	
Elaine Feinstein "Anniversary," p. 1311 "Out," p. 1312	Understanding style*		Word building using roots*	Writing about style	
Seamus Heaney "Follower," p. 1315 "Shore Woman," p. 1317	Understanding figurative language*	Understanding sound and meaning*		Analyzing the use of sound in a poem	
"For Doreen: A Voice in the Garden," Donald Davie, p. 1322 "Some Men Create," Molly Holden, p. 1323	Understanding imagery*		Understanding concrete language*	Writing a poem using imagery	

PRENTICE HALL
LITERATURE
THE ENGLISH TRADITION

PRENTICE HALL
LITERATURE

COPPER

BRONZE

SILVER

GOLD

PLATINUM

THE AMERICAN EXPERIENCE

THE ENGLISH TRADITION

WORLD MASTERPIECES

PRENTICE HALL
LITERATURE

THE ENGLISH TRADITION

SECOND EDITION

 PRENTICE HALL
Englewood Cliffs, New Jersey
Needham, Massachusetts

PRENTICE HALL
A Division of Simon & Schuster
Englewood Cliffs, New Jersey 07632

STAFF CREDITS FOR PRENTICE HALL LITERATURE

Editorial: Eileen Thompson, Ellen Bowler, Philip Fried, Daniel Jackson, Doug McCollum, Jane Standen, Richard Hickox, Carol Schneider, Kelly Ackley

Design: Sue Walrath, Nancy Sharkey, Leslie Osher

Photo Research: Libby Forsyth

Production: Penny Hull, Suse Cioffi, Joan McCulley, Marlys Lehmann, Lisa Meyerhoff, Cleasta Wilburn

Editorial Systems: Andrew Grey Bommarito, Ralph O'Brien

Marketing: Carol Newman, Mollie Ledwith, Tom Maksym

Manufacturing: Laura Sanderson, Denise Herckenrath

Permissions: Doris Robinson

ACKNOWLEDGMENTS

Grateful acknowledgment is made to the following for permission to reprint copyrighted material:

Edward Arnold (Publishers) Ltd.
"The Helping Hand" from *The Life to Come and Other Stories* by E.M. Forster. Copyright © 1972 The Trustees of the Late E. M. Forster.

Jonathan Cape Ltd. and the Estate of Henry Reed
"Naming of Parts" from *A Map of Verona* by Henry Reed, 1946.

Carcanet Press Ltd.
"November Sun" from *Selected Poems* by Elizabeth Daryush, 1972. Reprinted by permission of Carcanet Press Ltd.

Jonathan Clowes Ltd., London, on behalf of Doris Lessing
Excerpt from "The Small Personal Voice" from *A Small Per-*

(continued on page 1452)

vi

CONTENTS

THE SEVENTEENTH CENTURY
1625–1660

The Schools of Donne and Jonson

THE RESTORATION AND THE EIGHTEENTH CENTURY
1660–1798

THE ROMANTIC AGE
1798–1832

Poetry

Prose

CONTEMPORARY WRITERS
1945–PRESENT

xiii

BAYEUX (bà yóó′) TAPESTRY: NORMAN CAVALRY CHARGE AT THE SHIELDWALL AT THE BATTLE OF HASTINGS
The Granger Collection

Objectives

1 To learn about Britain before the arrival of the Anglo-Saxons
2 To understand the importance of the Celts' arrival in Britain
3 To learn about the Roman conquest of Britain
4 To trace the influences of the Anglo-Saxons on life in Britain
5 To examine the importance of Christianity's arrival in Britain and to trace its influence on literature
6 To study the first and second Danish invasions
7 To examine the origins and accomplishments of Anglo-Saxon poetry
8 To understand the role of prose in Anglo-Saxon writing

THE ANGLO-SAXON PERIOD
449–1066

When Angles and Saxons came hither from the east,
Sought Britain over the broad-spreading sea,
Haughty war-smiths overcame the Britons,
Valiant earls got for themselves a home.

from The Anglo-Saxon Chronicle

Focus

Historical Background Before attempting to deal with the later complexities of English literature it is necessary to treat the origins of that tradition carefully. The Anglo-Saxon Period represents the beginning of a sensitivity and wealth that continues into our own time. But its roots reach toward the centuries when magic and mayhem combined with invasions to make the islands off the western coast of Europe among the world's most mysterious places. Its dimensions must be traced by anyone interested in studying its consequences.

Motivation/Prior Knowledge Ask students to recall what they have learned about the climate and physical environment of Britain in social studies classes. Have them discuss the influence of such factors on a nation's development. Prompt them to speculate on what type of people are likely to deal well with conditions common to the British Isles.

Purpose-Setting Question What caused the migrations across Europe that were common at this time and what made people settle where they did?

ESL Teaching Strategy Pair off your ESL students with partners who are non-ESL pupils. Give them a chance to read the timelines on the following pages together quietly. Prompt the non-ESL students to provide answers to any questions that may arise. Provide guidance to those in need by circulating throughout the class while they are engaged in this activity.

Humanities Note

Fine art, *The Bayeux Tapestry: The Norman cavalry charge at the shield-wall of the Battle of Hastings.* Made about 1080, the famous Bayeux Tapestry illustrates the story of the Norman Conquest of England. It is an embroidered wool on linen tapestry, 20 inches high and 230 feet long, which now hangs in the Town Hall at Bayeux, France. This segment of the tapestry portrays the charge of Norman horsemen at the Battle of Hastings. The Saxons are on foot, while the Normans hurl their lances from horseback. That the Normans were on horseback clearly gave them an advantage. As with all of the segments of this chronicle, this battle scene is illustrated with a wonderful liveliness. The designer has integrated narrative and ornament in telling the story of William the Conqueror's invasion of England. The Bayeux Tapestry is one of the best extant examples of the art of the Middle Ages.

The passage on the previous page comes from a modern translation of *The Anglo-Saxon Chronicle,* an early record of English history. It tells of the attacks staged by warriors from Denmark and Germany on the rock-bound coast of Britain during the fifth century. Most of the fierce "war-smiths" identified themselves as Angles and Saxons, though some belonged to a smaller tribe, the Jutes. At first these pirates sailed their shallow boats across the "broad-spreading" North Sea to raid Britain's low-lying eastern coast. By A.D. 449, however, their raids had turned into a full-scale invasion.

The arrival of the Anglo-Saxons in Britain signaled the beginning of the English language. The "war-smiths" soon drove native Britons from the eastern, central, and southern portions of their island. Those areas became known as "Angles' land," or England. The closely related Germanic languages spoken by the conquering tribes developed into a new language called "Angle-ish," or English. Although that language would change a great deal over the centuries, it was the ancestor of the English we speak today. As the language took shape, so did the literature of Britain, including that of Ireland, Scotland, and Wales.

To put these early times into historical perspective, we must first examine the people whom the Angles and Saxons conquered, the settlers of Britain before 449. As you read about this period, you may want to consult the map on page 7 to locate unfamiliar geographical details.

BRITAIN BEFORE THE ANGLO-SAXONS

British historian G. M. Trevelyan has compared his country's early history to a battle scene from Shakespeare's *Macbeth* (see page 223): "Prophecy hovers around. Horns are heard blowing in the mist, and a confused uproar of savage tumult and outrage. We catch glimpses of giant figures—mostly warriors at strife. But there are ploughmen, too, it seems, breaking the primeval clod, and we hear the sound of forests crashing to the axe. Around all is the lap of waves and the cry of seamen beaching their ships."

Who were these early warriors and ploughmen? The answer is not entirely clear, for some of them arrived in Britain in the dim recesses before recorded time. Among them were Iberians from present-day Spain and Portugal, who brought late Stone Age weapons to Britain's shores. The last, and by far the most important, of the early conquerors were the Celts, a people from southern Europe who had gradually migrated west. Between 800 and 600 B.C., two groups of Celts invaded the British Isles.

Arrival of the Celts

One group, who called themselves Brythons (now spelled "Britons"), settled on the largest island, Britain. The other, known as Gaels, settled on the second largest island, known to us as Ireland.

Gaels and Britons spoke different but related languages of the Celtic family. Celtic languages had nothing in common with the Germanic ones later associated with the Angles and Saxons. 2

The Celts were farmers and hunters. They organized themselves into tightly knit clans, each with a fearsome loyalty to its chieftain. When these clans fell into argument with one another, they often looked to a class of priests known as Druids to settle their disputes. Druids presided over religious rituals including sacrifices and prayers. They also had, as their duty, the memorizing and reciting of long, heroic poems that preserved the people's myths about the past. Some of the poems may have included fables about such leaders as Old King Cole of the nursery rhyme and King Lear of Shakespeare's tragic play.

RELIGIOUS CEREMONY OF THE DRUIDS
Forrest C. Crooks
Three Lions

Humanities Note

Fine art, *Religious Ceremony of the Druids,* by Forrest C. Crooks. Forrest C. Crooks (1893–1962) was an American illustrator, who lived in New York City and was active in the 1930's.

The Druids were the priestly, learned class of the ancient Celts. The subject of this illustration is a Druid ceremony. Elements of ritual are suggested by the darkness, the fire, and the bone. Especially prominent in the foreground of the scene are an oak tree and some mistletoe, which the Celts regarded as sacred.

2 **Enrichment** Although the Celtic and the Germanic languages were very different, both belong to the Indo-European language family; that is, there are some similarities in grammar, sound structure, and vocabulary.

BRITISH EVENTS

Stonehenge

B.C.

c. 2000   Stonehenge built.

c. 500   Celts begin migrating to British Isles.

55   Julius Caesar invades Britain.

A.D.

43   Britain made a Roman province.

407   Romans withdraw from Britain.

432   St. Patrick begins missionary work in Ireland.

449   Anglo-Saxon invasion.

537   Death of the legendary hero, King Arthur.

597   St. Augustine founds Christian monastery at Canterbury, Kent.

664   Synod of Whitbyu establishes Roman Church in England.

731   **Bede** completes *A History of the English Church and People*.

c. 750   Surviving version of *Beowulf* composed.

792   Vikings attack Lindisfarne.

843   Scottish Ruler Kenneth MacAlprin unites Scots and Picts.

886   Truce with Danes establishes Saxon rule in south and Danish rule in east and north.

c. 930   Howel the Good unites kingdom of Wales.

c. 975   Saxon monks copy Old English poems into *Exeter Book*.

991   English defeated by Danes at Battle of Maldon.

1002   Brian Boru unites Kingdom of Ireland.

1034   Duncan I inherits Scottish throne.

1040   Macbeth murders Duncan I.

1042   Edward the Confessor becomes king of Saxons.

1066   Normans defeat Saxons; William the Conqueror becomes king of England.

4   *The Anglo-Saxon Period*

St. Augustine

Buddha Addressing

A Viking Sword

Danes Attacking a British Town

The Coronation of

A Roman Town After the Fall of the Empire

a Disciple

Charles Martel Battling the Moors

William the Conqueror

King Charlemagne

WORLD EVENTS

476	Western Europe: Fall of Western Roman Empire.
493	Italy: Thodoric the Great establishes Ostrogothic kingdom.
496	France: Clovis, King of Franks, converts to Christianity.
542	Eastern Europe: Plague kills half the population.
c. 550	Mexico: Toltecs defeat Mayas.
552	Japan: Buddhism introduced.
591	China: Beginning of book printing.
637	Middle East: Jerusalem conquered by Arabs.
641	Egypt: Library at Alexandria destroyed.
712	Spain: Seville conquered by Moors.
732	France: Charles Martel defeats Moors.
771	France: Charlemagne becomes king.
800	Peru: Incas build city of Machu Picchu.
c. 810	Persia: Algebra devised.
c. 821	France: Einhard writes *Life of Charlemagne*.
c. 855	Russia: Nation founded by Vikings.
861	North Atlantic: Vikings discover Iceland.
c. 900	Western Europe: Feudalism developed.
911	France: Normans establish Normandy.
982	Greenland: Eric the Red establishes first Viking colony.
c. 1000	North America: Viking explorer Leif Ericson explores Canadian coast.
1009	Middle East: Moslems destroy Holy Sepulchre in Jerusalem.
1045	Spain: Birth of El Cid, national hero who fought Moors.
1053	Italy: Normans conquer Sicily.

Introduction **5**

Clarification Point out the devastating statistics that concern the plague of 542 and tell students that the later Black Death of the fourteenth century had similarly high fatality rates wherever it struck. Explain that such rates would be extremely unlikely to occur in the modern world and ask students to list some factors that contribute significantly nowadays to the containment of contagion.

Humanities Note

Insignia of the Roman civil governor in charge of five British provinces. This illustration is from an early fifteenth-century copy of a page from the now-lost *Notitia Dignitatum Utriusque Imperii,* a fourth-century list of imperial magistrates, adorned with the symbols of their provinces. The design is roughly the shape of the island of Britain, with the symbols placed on the location of the provinces.

3 Enrichment These Roman camps, *castra,* gave their names to many English towns, in fact, all those whose names presently end in "caster," "cester," and "chester," such as Winchester and Lancaster.

4 Historical Context The Britons did not cede their country to the Germanic invaders without some struggle. The semi-legendary King Arthur organized a spirited resistance and presumably fought twelve successful battles against the Anglo-Saxons, the last of which occured at Mount Badon, sometime between the years 490 and 503. An excerpt from Sir Thomas Malory's *Morte d'Arthur* appears in the next unit, on page 91.

INSIGNIA OF THE ROMAN CIVIL GOVERNOR IN CHARGE OF THE FIVE BRITISH PROVINCES
An Early 15th-Century Copy of a Page from the Now-Lost Notitia Dignitatum Utriusque Imperii, a 4th-Century List of Imperial Magistrates, Adorned with the Symbols of their Provinces
The Granger Collection

The Roman Conquest

The next conquerors of Britain were the far more sophisticated Romans. In 55 B.C. and again the next year, the Roman general Julius Caesar made hasty invasions. Although he barely penetrated the island, he quickly declared it conquered and returned to what is now France to work on his memoirs. The true conquest of Britain occurred nearly one hundred years later during the reign of the Roman emperor Claudius. Disciplined Roman legions spread out over the island, establishing camps, which soon grew into towns.

The Romans transplanted many comforts of their urban, Mediterranean culture to the distant, rain-drenched north. In perhaps their greatest contribution, they constructed a system of well-paved roads through the woodland wilderness, highways that continued to link the island for centuries. The Romans also brought with them their skills in the art of warfare. Yet they apparently failed to teach the Britons much about self-defense.

The Roman rule of Britain lasted for more than 300 years. It ended only when northern European tribes invaded Italy and increased pressure on Rome itself. The last Roman legions departed from Britain to defend Rome in A.D. 407. By that time, some of their towns were already falling to ruin, and the Britons were easy prey for a new set of invaders.

THE ANGLO-SAXON CONQUEST

As we have seen, the next invaders were the Anglo-Saxons. Who were these ancient people? Lacking authentic first-hand accounts from the period, historians simply have to guess. Some Anglo-Saxons appear to have been deep-sea fishermen, already accustomed to marauding coasts along the Baltic Sea. Others seem to have been farmers, perhaps seeking soil richer than the sandy or marshy land at home. Ferocious as the Angles and Saxons may have been, they did not perform their piracy merely for plunder—at least not for long. They sought and won territory, apparently by rowing their shallow boats up river into the British heartland and then building camps and waging war on the Britons. Gradually the newcomers gained the upper hand over the island's settlers and took over more and more of what today is England.

Early Anglo-Saxon Life

The first Angles, Saxons, and Jutes transferred to England their highly organized tribal units. Each tribe was ruled by a king, chosen by a *witan,* or council of elders. Each community had four distinct classes. The *earls* were a hereditary class of ruling warlords who owed their position to the king. The second class, *freemen,* were allowed to own land and engage in commerce. (This class included *thanes,* early barons, who were granted their status as a reward for military service.) Lower on the social scale were *churls,* or serfs, bonded servants who worked the land in return for military protection. Lowest of all were *thralls,* or slaves, usually military prisoners or people being punished.

Invading groups set up numerous small kingdoms, and at first the various kingdoms fought frequently. As time went on, however, many of these tribal differences faded. Anglo-Saxon kingdoms traded with one another. Men married women from different tribes. Kingdoms gradually absorbed one another until seven larger ones remained. As previously mentioned, all this intermingling produced a new language. We call it Anglo-Saxon or Old English to distinguish it from our modern form.

Anglo-Saxon Beliefs

The Anglo-Saxons brought to Britain their own pagan beliefs. In the world of the sixth century, the ever-present dangers of death by accident or warfare had led these people to take a rather grim view of life. In fact, the early Anglo-Saxons believed that every human life was in the hands of fate. Their attitude was sharply different from the

5

6

5 Master Teacher Note In anticipation of the study of Shakespeare's *Macbeth,* point out to students that the early barons or *thanes* are the chief characters in this play, written in Elizabethan England but set in Anglo-Saxon Scotland.

6 Historical Context The notion of the Anglo-Saxons as a crude, insular, and barbaric people was largely belied by the discovery in 1939 of a seventh-century royal burial site at Sutton Hoo in East Anglia. Artifacts found there suggest a heroic society rich in gold and craftsmanship with evidence of far-flung trading contacts. These artifacts are on display at the British Museum.

Enrichment

Have students closely study the map on this page. Then ask them to answer the following questions:
1. What area was the most northerly on the British Isles?
2. What was the most southerly section called?
3. What is the island to the west of England called?
4. Name two of the three areas that border Mercia?
5. What seems to be the largest single territory of the map?

ANSWERS

1. Scotland
2. Wessex
3. Ireland
4. Danelaw, or Wales, or Wessex.
5. Ireland seems to be biggest.

Illumination, *Saxons, Jutes, and Angles arriving in Britain by sea.* Illumination was one of the earliest forms of book illustration. The illuminator, the "one who lightens up" a manuscript, refers to the artist who decorated the manuscripts that were produced in monasteries of the time. Many such illuminations are elaborate decorations of capital letters and marginal spaces, but others, like this one, illustrate scenes. This simple, stylized drawing represents the ships of the Anglo-Saxon invaders against whom the Britons were unable to defend themselves.

7 Literary Movement This fatalistic attitude characteristic of the Anglo-Saxons is evident both in *Beowulf* (page 24) with its frequent references to Wyrd and in "The Seafarer" (page 17).

8 Master Teacher Note To demonstrate the multi-cultural influences on our calendar, you might ask students to research the origins of the other days of the week.

9 Historical Context Columba, exiled from Ireland and remorseful because he had killed three thousand pagans in battle, settled with eleven followers on the first island from which he could no longer see his beloved native land. This island was Iona.

10 Master Teacher Note In anticipation of *Macbeth,* point out that Iona is the Columkille mentioned in the text, the burial place of Scottish kings.

SAXONS, JUTES, AND ANGLES ARRIVING IN BRITAIN BY SEA
English Manuscript Illumination
The Granger Collection

7

Christian belief in the freedom of an individual to determine his or her own path.

8

The early Anglo-Saxons worshiped ancient Germanic gods. They included Tiu, god of war and the sky; Woden, chief of the gods; and Fria, Woden's wife and goddess of the home. These gods were abandoned with the coming of Christianity. Even so, their names survive in our words *Tuesday, Wednesday,* and *Friday.*

Dispersal of the Britons

In terror of the Anglo-Saxons, the Britons retreated to the edges of their island—and beyond. Some went to Cornwall on the southwestern tip of Britain, an area that remained Celtic long after the rest of the island was Anglo-Saxon. Others fled to Britain's hilly western region, an area that become known as Wales. Still others joined the Gaels of Ireland where they formed a splinter group named Scots (from *Scotia,* the Roman word for Ireland). This group then traveled back to Britain and settled in the northern part of the island, Scotland. In all these areas, people spoke Celtic languages—Cornish, Welsh, and Irish and Scottish Gaelic—until modern times. All but Cornish are still spoken today.

THE COMING OF CHRISTIANITY

During the fourth century, the Romans had accepted Christianity and introduced it to Britain. A century later, when the Celts fled the Anglo-Saxons, they took their Christian faith with them. During this period, the faith lived on in Wales. From there it spread to Ireland, assisted by the activities of the legendary St. Patrick.

After Rome fell to barbarian tribes in A.D. 476, communications weakened between Celtic and Roman Christians. While the Roman Church was recovering from political chaos, the Celtic Christian Church continued to thrive. In 563 a group of Irish monks set sail in tiny skiffs for the west coast of Scotland. Led by a soldier and abbot named Columba, they established a Christian monastery on the island of Iona. From this headquarters, Columba and his monks moved across northern Britain in the hope of winning additional souls for the faith. In their travels, they won ready acceptance among many Scots; then among some Saxons and Angles. Their conversions led, in turn, to the establishment of other monasteries in the north.

9, 10

Resurgence of the Roman Church

Meanwhile, the Roman Church had reorganized itself and was beginning to send missionaries throughout Europe. In 597, the

Roman cleric Saint Augustine (not the early Christian Church father) arrived in southeast England and quickly converted King Ethelbert of Kent to Christianity. Augustine set up a monastery at Canterbury in Kent and began preaching his faith to other rulers in southern England. To win over a kingdom, Augustine and his followers needed only to convert the king, who would then make Christianity the religion of his realm. By the year 650, they had largely succeeded. Most of England was Christian in name, if not in fact.

The new religion had a profound effect on Anglo-Saxon civilization. It softened the ferocity of a warrior people and improved the conduct of the faithful. No longer could ruling warlords indulge themselves in the belief that they had descended from pagan gods. No longer could freemen think it permissible to treat their wives or children or slaves with cruelty. Christian clerics were now able to end old feuds by denouncing revenge and calling upon a higher law. By providing counsel to quarreling rulers, the Church promoted peace and played a major role in unifying the English people.

Christianity and Literature

The church also brought to England two elements of civilization that had been missing since the departure of the Romans: education and written literature. Christian leaders established schools at Canterbury and York and supervised the preservation of learning in the island's monasteries. Within their secluded halls, monks often worked as scribes, recording and duplicating *manuscripts,* or books written by hand. At first they worked only in Latin, the language of Church scholarship. Often several monks labored for years to complete a single manuscript. These volumes were elaborately painted and illuminated in gold and silver.

From such monastic training emerged a Northumbrian monk later considered the "father of English history." Today we know him as the Venerable Bede (673–735). Bede was a master of thorough research, tracking down information by studying earlier documents and interviewing people who had witnessed or taken part in past events. His most famous volume was *A History of the English Church and People,* a monumental work that offers the clearest account we have of early Anglo-Saxon times.

Although Christianity did indeed temper Anglo-Saxon civilization, it did not destroy the northerners' spirit. Glimpses of an earlier world lived on in the fragments of epics such as *Beowulf,* a long, narrative poem that depicted great battles between Anglo-Saxon warriors and superhuman monsters. The Anglo-Saxons remained a hardy group, fearless and loyal in their instincts even if less and less predatory in their habits. Now they were about to come face to face with a new peril from a people much like themselves— invasion by the Vikings.

AN ENGLISH MONK EXACTLY CONTEMPORARY WITH BEDE
Illumination from an early 8th-century Northumbrian Codex
The Granger Collection

Humanities Note

Illumination, *An English monk contemporary with Bede.* In the Dark Ages, classical learning and art were preserved in monasteries by monks, like the one pictured in this illumination, who copied manuscripts and illustrated them. This illumination, which is from an eighth-century Northumbrian Codex, or vellum manuscript, enables the viewer to envision Bede at work on his history.

THE FIRST DANISH INVASION

Between the eighth and twelfth centuries, a great restlessness overtook the region of northern Europe known as Scandinavia. Beset with a rising population and limited farmland, the people of Norway, the Norse, and of Denmark, the Danes, followed old traditions and took to the seas. In some of their most adventurous voyages, the Vikings (warriors) carried their piracy to the British Isles. The Norse set their sights on Northumbria, Scotland, Wales, and Ireland, whereas the Danes targeted eastern and southern England.

Viking Raids

Viking invaders sacked and plundered monasteries, destroyed manuscripts, and stole sacred religious objects. They burned entire communities and put villagers to the sword. Wherever the Vikings went, the sight of their square-sailed ships stirred specters of terror and destruction. One Anglo-Saxon prayer of the day reflected the fear that the Danish pirates inspired: "From the fury of the Northmen, O Lord, deliver us."

THE 9TH-CENTURY OSEBERG VIKING SHIP
The Granger Collection

Although the English fought back valiantly, the Danes made broad inroads. By the middle of the ninth century, most of northern, eastern, and central England had fallen to the invaders. They called their territory the Danelaw. Only the Saxon kingdom of Wessex managed to fight the Danes to a standstill.

Alfred the Great

In 871 a king ascended to the Wessex throne who would become the only ruler in England's history ever to be honored with the epithet "the Great." His name was Alfred, and he earned the title partly by resisting further Danish encroachment. Under a truce concluded in 886, England was formally divided: the Saxons acknowledged Danish rule in the east and north, but the Danes agreed to respect Saxon rule in the south. As the king of a much-expanded Wessex, Alfred the Great became a national hero.

Alfred's achievements went far beyond the field of battle, however. Not only was he instrumental in preserving the remnants of pre-Danish civilization in Britain, but he encouraged a rebirth of learning and education. To make literature and other documents more readily available, he himself translated Bede's *History* and other works from Latin into Anglo-Saxon, the everyday language of the people. In this way he fostered the growth of the English language and its literature. He also began to keep records of English history in *The Anglo-Saxon Chronicle,* today among our principal sources of information on early English life.

Danish Contributions

Gradually the Danes became more peaceful, and old animosities subsided. A once war-obsessed people settled into the workaday world of farming, beer-brewing, and moving goods to market. Even before their arrival in England, many Danes had been accustomed to the merchant's trade, however crudely it may have existed in northern Europe at the time. Now they built their Danelaw communities not only as military fortresses but as trading centers, and one result was the growth of English towns.

Like the Anglo-Saxons, the Danes spoke a Germanic language, so they were able to communicate easily with the English. In fact, many Norse words slowly crept into the English vocabulary. The word *law* is Danish, for example. Its use reflected the Danes' interest in legal procedures.

THE SECOND DANISH INVASION AND THE NORMAN CONQUEST

The peace and stability that began with Alfred's reign lasted more than a century. Immigration from Scandinavia dwindled, and

ALFRED THE GREAT ACKNOWLEDGED AS KING BY ALL MEN OF ENGLAND, 871 A.D.
Three Lions

PAGE FROM AN EARLY 12TH-CENTURY MANUSCRIPT OF THE *ANGLO-SAXON CHRONICLE* DESCRIBING THE NORMAN CONQUEST
The Granger Collection

11

Humanities Note

Alfred the Great Acknowledged as King by All Men of England, 871 A.D. This anonymous print shows Alfred becoming king of the West Saxons. He later became known as "the Great" for his achievements. He resisted the attacks of the Danes, and in the treaty of Wedmore in 878, concluded an arrangement with Guthrum, the principal Danish leader, which effectively ended the Danish raids and brought peace to the island. Education had declined because the Danes had looted the monasteries and churches; therefore, Alfred brought learned men and teachers to Wessex from other parts of Britain and Europe. Alfred died in 899.

Humanities Note

Page from an early twelfth-century manuscript of the *Anglo-Saxon Chronicle.* One of Alfred the Great's achievements was the record he kept of current events, called the *Anglo-Saxon Chronicle.* After his death, the *Chronicle* was continued until 1154. This page, describing the Norman conquest, is typical in its illuminated decorations. The decoration of this secular work indicates that works other than religious ones were also being illustrated.

11 **Enrichment** Another Danish contribution is in the place-name suffix *by,* from the Old Norse *byr* for "town." The names of approximately six hundred towns in northern England still end this way.

The Bayeux Tapestry: Edward the Confessor Speaks to Harold of Wessex. This segment of the famous Bayeux Tapestry shows Edward speaking to Harold, Earl of Wessex. When Edward died in 1066 without a direct heir to the throne, the English nobles chose Harold to succeed him. In the Norman invasion, Harold was killed and his forces defeated in the Battle of Hastings. Edward's gentle disposition and religious leanings are evident in this detail.

12 Enrichment The Normans were originally "Northmen," but their language was essentially Latin in origin rather than Germanic.

THE BAYEUX TAPESTRY: EDWARD THE CONFESSOR SPEAKS TO HAROLD OF WESSEX
The Granger Collection

the descendants of Alfred the Great were able to regain much conquered territory. Toward the close of the tenth century, however, a new series of onslaughts began as more Danes from Europe attempted to recapture and widen the Danelaw. Once they had succeeded, they forced the Saxon witan to select a succession of Danish kings.

Edward the Confessor and the Normans

Then, in 1042, the line of succession returned to a descendant of Alfred the Great. This king, Edward, had gained the title "the Confessor" because he was a deeply religious Christian. He had spent many of his early years in Normandy, a region once settled by Scandinavians and now a part of France. Norman on his mother's side, Edward had developed a close friendship with his cousin William, Normandy's ruler. Once Edward took the English throne, his association with the Normans further weakened Saxon power. His death in 1066 led directly to a Norman conquest of England and brought the end of the Anglo-Saxon period of literature, as we shall see in the next unit.

ANGLO-SAXON LITERATURE

Scholars now believe that the literature of the British Isles began with Celtic Druids. These priests assumed the function of storytellers, memorizing and reciting long, heroic poems about Celtic leaders and their deeds. In the same way, Anglo-Saxon literature began not with books, but with spoken verse and incantations. Their purpose was to pass along tribal history and values to an audience that could not read.

To be sure, some Anglo-Saxons were familiar with the written word. In the third century in northern Europe, they had devised an alphabet of letters called runes. When they came to Britain, they brought this alphabet with them and used it until the Latin alphabet we have today superseded it. Yet they employed runes chiefly for inscriptions on important buildings, on statues, and the like. Few early Anglo-Saxons could read or write.

Origins of Anglo-Saxon Poetry

The reciting of poems often occurred on ceremonial occasions such as the celebration of a military victory. A warrior's comrades would gather in his hall or castle, and the performance would begin. The performers were usually professional minstrels, known as *scops,* and their assistants, called *gleemen.* The scops and gleemen recited for hours and, in some instances, even for days.

Scholars now suppose that these recitations took place to the accompaniment of a harp. The poems followed a set formula of composition, which probably made them easier to memorize. A formal, rigid pattern of word stresses gave the lyrics a terse, sing-song effect. A mid-line pause, called a *caesura,* occurred in many lines. Another part of the pattern was *alliteration,* the repetition of sounds, especially initial consonant sounds.

Types of Anglo-Saxon Verse

Only about 30,000 lines of Anglo-Saxon verse still exist. Almost all of it is found in four works dating from about A.D. 975 to 1050. The early verse falls mainly into two categories. One is heroic poetry, which recounts the achievements of warriors involved in great battles. The other is elegiac poetry, sorrowful laments that mourn the deaths of loved ones and the loss of the past.

Copied many years after their composition, the poems have obviously undergone many changes. Later scops may have adapted them, and so may have monastic scribes. Nevertheless, pagan elements remain, particularly in the ever-present sense of an ominous fate, or *wyrd.* Consider, for example, these lines from one of the elegiac poems, "The Wanderer":

> He then, wise in soul, with weighty
> thought thinks deeply upon this dark-
> some life, this fallen fastness. . . .

The Beowulf Legend

Of the heroic poetry, the most important work is *Beowulf,* the story of a great pagan warrior renowned for his courage, strength, and dignity. *Beowulf* is an *epic,* a long heroic poem. Because it is the first such work to be composed in the English language, it is considered the national epic of England.

Like most Anglo-Saxon poets, the author of *Beowulf* is unknown. Although versions of the poem were probably recited as early as the sixth century, the text that we have today was composed in the eighth century and not written down until the eleventh. Thus, the poem includes many references to Christian ideas and Latin classics. Clearly evident in *Beowulf,* however, are the values of a warrior society, especially such values as dignity, bravery, and prowess in battle:

> And Beowulf was ready, firm with our
> Lord's
> High favor and his own bold courage and
> strength.

Emphasis on such values did not disappear in Christian times. It appeared in later Anglo-Saxon poems such as *The Battle of Maldon,* which commemorates a great military defeat of the Danes.

Poets of the Christian Era

Among the few known poets of the Christian era, two are worthy of mention—Caedmon and Cynewulf. Caedmon, who apparently

13 **Master Teacher Note** Besides these two characteristics of Anglo-Saxon poetry, you might cite other typical devices: the kenning, the four-beat line, the frequent reversal of word order. All these devices are evident in "The Seafarer," page 17, and in *Beowulf,* page 24.

14 **Historical Context** The dating of the present text has been narrowed down to the period between 680, the start of alliterative verse, and 835, the beginning of the Danish raids. After 835, such sympathetic treatment of the Danes would have been highly unlikely. The oldest extant copy, preserved in the British Museum, dates from the eleventh century.

Humanities Note

A page from the Caedmon manuscript, c. 1000. Caedmon was an English poet who lived in the late 600's. An uneducated herdsman, he entered the monastery at Whitby late in life. Bede reported in his *History* that Caedmon was commanded to sing the praises of God. He did so in what is now known as "Caedmon's Hymn." This beautifully illustrated page is from that manuscript.

15 Enrichment Caedmon, according to Bede, was a humble brother who tended the cows at Whitby Monastery and received divine inspiration for his poetry from a dream. He is generally regarded as the first English poet.

16 Historical Context Alfred's impact on English language and literature demonstrates only part of the effect this remarkable man had on ninth-century England. He dispatched diplomatic missions to fellow rulers, formulated a legal code, and established the first English "public schools."

Check Test

1. The Celtic family contained Britons and _____ .
2. The invasion of Britain in 55 B.C. was undertaken by the general named _____ .
3. Columba established a Christian monastery in 563 on the island of _____ .
4. The author of *A History of the English Church and People* was _____ .
5. The language used by the prose writers of Britain before Alfred the Great was _____ .

ANSWERS

1. Gaels
2. Julius Caesar
3. Iona
4. the Venerable Bede
5. Latin

A PAGE FROM THE CAEDMON MANUSCRIPT, c. 1000
The Granger Collection

15 lived in the seventh century, is mentioned in Bede's *History*. The poet's only authenticated verse consists of a few lines that Bede recorded, called "Caedmon's Hymn." Nevertheless, the term *Caedmonian verse* is often used to identify other early Christian poetry in English. Scholars believe that Cynewulf lived around the turn of the ninth century. He is known because he "signed" his name, spelling it out in runes, on four poems that survive today.

Anglo-Saxon Prose

Before the reign of Alfred the Great, all important prose written in the British Isles was composed in Latin. The monks who transcribed these works regarded the vernacular, the language of the common people, as a "vulgar tongue." The greatest of England's Latin scholars was the Venerable Bede, as mentioned earlier. His *History* gives an account of England from the Roman invasion to his own time.

Bede's *History* concerns itself mostly with northern England, but it is not simply the story of Northumbria or the people who settled there. The monk couples his view of the Roman Church as a universal force with a distinctly nationalistic view of a unified English people. Although Bede wrote in Latin, his *History* may nevertheless be considered the first truly English prose work. From it we derive much of what we know about early Anglo-Saxon times.

Bede's successor as the leading English scholar was Alcuin (735–804), another monk who, like Bede, won fame throughout Europe. Trained at York, Alcuin traveled widely in Europe and eventually headed the palace school of the powerful European emperor Charlemagne. By the time of his death, Alcuin had produced many major works in philosophy, religion, and Latin grammar.

Alfred the Great and His Successors

16 Historians usually credit Alfred the Great with having changed the course of British literature. The spur he gave to the English language was evident in its more widespread use among scholars after his death. Of these scholars, the foremost were Aelfric and Wulfstan, who lived in the second half of the tenth century. Aelfric, a monk of Wessex, wrote many works in the vernacular, including a series of *homilies,* or sermons, based on Bible stories. Though in prose, these sermons employ a great deal of the sort of alliteration more commonly associated with Anglo-Saxon poetry. Wulfstan, an archbishop of York, also wrote several sermons in Old English, including a famous speech on the devastation of the Danish raids.

After the Normans occupied England, they gradually transformed the English that the Anglo-Saxons spoke. Old English or Anglo-Saxon evolved into what we now call Middle English, whose literature we will explore in the next unit.

▌ENGLISH VOICES▐
Quotations by Prominent Figures of the Period

I sing of myself, a sorrowful woman.
>**Anonymous,** "A Wife's Lament," translated by Kemp Malone

This tale is true, and mine. It tells
How the sea took me, swept me back
And forth, in sorrow and fear and pain.
>**Anonymous,** "The Seafarer," translated by Burton Raffel

It is better never to begin a good work than, having begun it, to stop.
>**Bede,** *A History of the English Church and People*

Out from the marsh, from the foot of misty
Hills and bogs, bearing God's hatred,
Grendel came.

Beowulf spoke, in spite of the swollen
Livid wound, knowing he'd unwound
His string of days on earth. . . .
                              My days
Have gone by as fate willed, waiting
For its word to be spoken.
>**Anonymous,** *Beowulf,* translated by Burton Raffel

Light was first
Through the Lord's word
Named day:
Beauteous, bright creation!
>**Caedmon,** *Creation. The First Day,* translated by Benjamin
>   Thorpe

And those people should not be listened to who keep saying the voice of the people is the voice of God, since the riotousness of the crowd is always very close to madness.
>**Alcuin** in a letter to Charlemagne

Alcuin was my name; learning I loved.
>**Alcuin** in his own epitaph

Thought shall be the harder, heart the keener, courage the greater, as our might lessens.
>**Anonymous,** *The Battle of Maldon,* translated by R. K. Gordon

Master Teacher Note You might show students Art Transparency 1, *Stonehenge,* by John Constable. 1776–1837. Constable is one of Britain's supreme landscape painters. This painting was produced around 1835. The arrangement of prehistoric monoliths that still stand on Salisbury Plain may be considered an enduring symbol of early England. What purpose the stones originally served has not yet been definitely established, though reasonable speculation includes religious rites and astronomical observations. You might ask your students to describe the mood the painting evokes. Ask them to tell what the monoliths may imply about the culture of prehistoric Britain.

Reading Critically The purpose of this feature is to help students place a work of literature in its historical context, understand the literary movements of the time, and appreciate the writers' techniques used to convey the ideas of the period.

Discuss the information on this page with your students. Explain that the selection that accompanies this page, "The Seafarer," is a model for reading critically the literature of this period. It contains in the side column notes that draw attention to elements that reflect the historical context, the influence of literary movements, and the writer's techniques in the poem. Ask students to pay attention to these notes as they read the poem. Also suggest that they make their own critical comments as they read the selection.

To give students further practice with the process of reading critically, use the selection in the Teaching Portfolio, "The Wife's Lament," following the Teacher Backup, page 6 which students can annotate themselves. Encourage students to use these strategies as they read the literature in this unit.

Critical Quotation Michael Alexander, a critic and translator, insists that *The Seafarer* should not be regarded as the dialogue that it was once thought to be. "The poem," claims Alexander, "is a soliloquy: a **wraecca** that tells of the many winters [its subject has] spent at sea, and of the hardships he has borne."

READING CRITICALLY

The Literature of 449–1066

When you read literature, it is important to know its historical context. Doing so will help you to understand the writer's ideas and techniques.

Historical Context

In 449 the island of Britain was invaded by warlike Germanic peoples known as Angles and Saxons. These invaders brought with them their pagan beliefs and traditions, which appear in Anglo-Saxon poetry and legends. They also brought with them a grim, fatalistic view of the world. These Germanic invaders were followed by Roman missionaries, who converted Britain to Christianity. During this time, different kinds of literature developed, including the oral poetry of the Anglo-Saxons and written historical and religious prose. The literature of the time shows both pagan and Christian influences.

Literary Movements

Very few people were able to read during this period. Therefore, an oral tradition flourished. The Anglo-Saxons were fond of poetry, which was developed and passed on by scops, or poet-singers. Eventually, some of this oral literature was written down by monks in monasteries, who are largely responsible for having preserved oral material.

Writers' Techniques

Because most literature was oral, it was composed in such a way that it was easily memorized. Lines of poetry with regular rhythms were easier to remember than was prose. Poets used alliteration for the same reason. In addition, Anglo-Saxon poets were fond of the kenning, a compound metaphorical name for something, such as "whale's home" for the sea. The Anglo-Saxon poetry that has been preserved illustrates these techniques.

On the following pages is an Anglo-Saxon poem, "The Seafarer." The notes in the side column point out features of the poem that show the historical context or the literary techniques of the period.

16   *The Anglo-Saxon Period*

Support Material

Teaching Portfolio
Teacher Backup, p. 3
Usage and Mechanics Worksheet, p. 8
Analyzing Literature Worksheet, *Understanding Anglo-Saxon Lyric Poetry*, p. 9
Language Worksheet, *Appreciating Old English*, p. 10
Selection Test, p. 11

The Seafarer

translated by Burton Raffel

This tale is true, and mine. It tells
How the sea took me, swept me back
And forth in sorrow and fear and pain,
Showed me suffering in a hundred ships,
5   In a thousand ports, and in me. It tells
Of smashing surf when I sweated in the cold
Of an anxious watch, perched in the bow
As it dashed under cliffs. My feet were cast
In icy bands, bound with frost,
10 With frozen chains, and hardship groaned
Around my heart. Hunger tore
At my sea-weary soul. No man sheltered
On the quiet fairness of earth can feel
How wretched I was, drifting through winter
15 On an ice-cold sea, whirled in sorrow,
Alone in a world blown clear of love,
Hung with icicles. The hailstorms flew.
The only sound was the roaring sea,
The freezing waves. The song of the swan
20 Might serve for pleasure, the cry of the sea-fowl,
The death-noise of birds instead of laughter,
The mewing of gulls instead of mead.
Storms beat on the rocky cliffs and were echoed
By icy-feathered terns and the eagle's screams;
25 No kinsman could offer comfort there,
To a soul left drowning in desolation.
     And who could believe, knowing but
The passion of cities, swelled proud with wine
And no taste of misfortune, how often, how wearily,
30 I put myself back on the paths of the sea.
Night would blacken; it would snow from the north;
Frost bound the earth and hail would fall,
The coldest seeds. And how my heart
Would begin to beat, knowing once more
35 The salt waves tossing and the towering sea!
The time for journeys would come and my soul
Called me eagerly out, sent me over
The horizon, seeking foreigners' homes.

Literary Movement: Because this poem was passed on in the oral tradition, different versions of it exist.

Historical Background: The poet's subject is the sea. The sea is a common subject because the British are an island people.

Writer's Technique: Anglo-Saxon poetry frequently uses a line divided by a caesura, a pause. Alliteration joins the two parts: an important word in the first part of the line has the same initial consonant sound as an important word in the second part of the line.

Writer's Technique: "coldest seeds" is a kenning, a metaphorical name, for "hail."

The Seafarer   17

Presentation

Motivation/Prior Knowledge Read John Masefield's poem "Sea-Fever"—or another of his sea poems—and discuss the overwhelming power of the sea. Ask students if they feel that power? Are there modern occupations that might exercise this same drawing power?

Master Teacher Note Bring in pictures of Viking ships and maps of their sailing routes to introduce the subject and the period.

Thematic Idea Another selection that deals with the terrors of seafaring is "Rime of the Ancient Mariner," page 660.

Purpose-Setting Question What is the Christian message of the seafarer's story?

Enrichment Seafaring was a passion of the Anglo-Saxons' ancestors, who lived along the shores of the North Sea and from whom oral poetry like this was probably passed down.

Humanities Note

Fine art, illuminated manuscript, *The Whale*. The art of manuscript illumination underwent some changes after the Norman conquest because of the blending of the English and French cultures. The Franco-English school of illumination developed in the twelfth and thirteenth centuries. As a result, the monasteries employed more lay artists in their efforts toward higher artistic achievement.

The illumination *The Whale* is from a bestiary of that era. A bestiary is a secular collection of tales and fables about animals. In the illumination, three men in a boat are confronted by a gigantic fish. Although the whale seems content with its business of feeding, the men appear anxious and intent on navigating their craft out of the whale's reach. The sea is interpreted as an abstract shape with linear wave patterns. There is no perspective—the shapes of the boat and fish are placed flat on top of the water. The whale is fancifully depicted with an abundance of fins, hinting that the artist has never seen one first hand. It is a stylized, decorative portrayal of a fearsome marine encounter that borders on being humorous.

You might use the following questions for class discussion.

1. The seafarer speaks of his alienation and the severity of the sailing life. Does this illustration help you to visualize what he relates? Explain.

2. The poem expresses the speaker's feelings about the sea. Do the sailors in this illustration seem to share these feelings? Explain.

Enrichment Note the poet's ambivalence in lines 40–52. Some scholars think that the poem is a dialogue between an old, disillusioned sailor and a young sailor eager for adventure. Do you think the poem contains a single voice or two voices?

SHIPS WITH THREE MEN, FISH
Bodleian Library, Oxford

Historical Context: The Anglo-Saxons saw Fate as grim and overpowering.

But there isn't a man on earth so proud,
40 So born to greatness, so bold with his youth,
Grown so brave, or so graced by God,
That he feels no fear as the sails unfurl,
Wondering what Fate has willed and will do.
No harps ring in his heart, no rewards,
45 No passion for women, no worldly pleasures,
Nothing, only the ocean's heave;
But longing wraps itself around him.
Orchards blossom, the towns bloom,
Fields grow lovely as the world springs fresh,
50 And all these admonish that willing mind

Leaping to journeys, always set
In thoughts traveling on a quickening tide.
So summer's sentinel, the cuckoo, sings
In his murmuring voice, and our hearts mourn
55 As he urges. Who could understand,
In ignorant ease, what we others suffer
As the paths of exile stretch endlessly on?
      And yet my heart wanders away,
My soul roams with the sea, the whales'
60 Home, wandering to the widest corners
Of the world, returning ravenous with desire,
Flying solitary, screaming, exciting me
To the open ocean, breaking oaths
On the curve of a wave.
      Thus the joys of God
65 Are fervent with life, where life itself
Fades quickly into the earth. The wealth
Of the world neither reaches to Heaven nor remains.
No man has ever faced the dawn
Certain which of Fate's three threats
70 Would fall: illness, or age, or an enemy's
Sword, snatching the life from his soul.
The praise the living pour on the dead
Flowers from reputation: plant
An earthly life of profit reaped
75 Even from hatred and rancor, of bravery
Flung in the devil's face, and death
Can only bring you earthly praise
And a song to celebrate a place
With the angels, life eternally blessed
80 In the hosts of Heaven.
      The days are gone
When the kingdoms of earth flourished in glory;
Now there are no rulers, no emperors,
No givers of gold, as once there were,
When wonderful things were worked among them
85 And they lived in lordly magnificence.
Those powers have vanished, those pleasures are dead.
The weakest survives and the world continues,
Kept spinning by toil. All glory is tarnished.
The world's honor ages and shrinks,
90 Bent like the men who mold it. Their faces
Blanch as time advances, their beards
Wither and they mourn the memory of friends.
The sons of princes, sown in the dust.

Historical Context: Fear of Fate was balanced with a firm reliance on God.

Clarification "Givers of gold," in line 83, refers to the heroic kings of the Anglo-Saxons' ancestors, who rewarded their loyal thanes with booty.

Critical Thinking and Reading
What Christian and pagan references exist side by side in the final thirty lines of the poem? What is implied about free will in lines 117–122?

Reader's Response What would your greatest fear be if you were sailing the ocean in a small boat?

The soul stripped of its flesh knows nothing
95 Of sweetness or sour, feels no pain,
Bends neither its hand nor its brain. A brother
Opens his palms and pours down gold
On his kinsman's grave, strewing his coffin
With treasures intended for Heaven, but nothing
100 Golden shakes the wrath of God
For a soul overflowing with sin, and nothing
Hidden on earth rises to Heaven.
          We all fear God. He turns the earth,
He set it swinging firmly in space,
105 Gave life to the world and light to the sky.
Death leaps at the fools who forget their God.
He who lives humbly has angels from Heaven
To carry him courage and strength and belief.
A man must conquer pride, not kill it,
110 Be firm with his fellows, chaste for himself,
Treat all the world as the world deserves,
With love or with hate but never with harm,
Though an enemy seek to scorch him in hell,
Or set the flames of a funeral pyre
115 Under his lord. Fate is stronger
And God mightier than any man's mind.
Our thoughts should turn to where our home is,
Consider the ways of coming there,
Then strive for sure permission for us
120 To rise to that eternal joy,
That life born in the love of God
And the hope of Heaven. Praise the Holy
Grace of Him who honored us,
Eternal, unchanging creator of earth. Amen.

Literary Movement: The prayerful ending may have been added by Christian monks in recording the oral poem.

"The Seafarer" was composed by an unknown poet, probably in the eighth century. It is one of relatively few poems that survive from the oral tradition in pre-Christian Britain. Preserved by Christian copyists in monasteries, it first appeared in the *Exeter Book*, a famous collection of Anglo-Saxon poems copied around 975 and donated to Exeter Cathedral, where it remains today.

20   *The Anglo-Saxon Period*

Closure and Extension

ANSWERS TO THINKING ABOUT THE SELECTION
Recalling

1. The poet uses the image of the watch perched on the bow of a ship (lines 6–8), the image of the sea in winter, and the image of a storm beating against rocky cliffs to convey a sense of isolation.

2. Fate's three threats are illness, age, and an enemy's sword.

3. (a) "Fools who forget their God" will die;
   (b) Those who "live humbly" will be given courage and strength and faith.

Interpreting

4. The poet loves the excitement of ocean travel and visiting foreign lands, but he also recognizes the danger and loneliness seafaring entails.

THINKING ABOUT THE SELECTION

Recalling

1. What are three images the poet uses in the first stanza to convey his sense of isolation?
2. The poet names "Fate's three threats." What are they?
3. (a) What happens to "fools who forget their God"? (b) What happens to those who "live humbly"?

Interpreting

4. How might you explain the mixed feelings about the sea that the poet seems to feel?
5. Pagans in Anglo-Saxon England—that is, non-Christians—felt themselves at the mercy of forces utterly beyond their control, while Christians put their trust in salvation and heaven. In what way do lines 39 through 43 show the influence of both beliefs?
6. Explain lines 66 and 67: "The wealth / Of the world neither reaches to Heaven nor remains."
7. "The Seafarer" is a poem of contrasts. What contrast is implied in lines 80 through 102?
8. What does the poet mean by the word *home* in line 117?

Applying

9. Explain how a person can dislike something as much as the sailor dislikes life at sea and yet keep going back to it.

ANALYZING LITERATURE

Understanding Anglo-Saxon Poetry

A **lyric poem** is one that expresses intense personal emotions. "The Seafarer" mixes pagan with Christian beliefs and expresses sorrow for something lost or past. At times the poet's feelings seem to border on despair.

1. What deep personal feelings does the poet express in the first part of "The Seafarer" that show this to be a lyric poem?
2. "The Seafarer" has two distinct parts, the second of which begins at line 64. What are some of the strong emotions expressed in the second part of the poem?

CRITICAL THINKING AND READING

Comparing and Contrasting Attitudes

To **compare** two ideas or attitudes is to point out similarities. To **contrast** them is to point out differences. Most people have mixed feelings on certain subjects.

Explain what accounts for the poet's state of mind at the beginning of the poem and at the end.

UNDERSTANDING LANGUAGE

Appreciating Old English

Old English is the English language as it existed from about 500 to about 1150. Our language has changed so much since then that Anglo-Saxon poems like "The Seafarer" must be translated, just as if they came from a foreign language, if modern readers are to appreciate them. Here are lines 42 and 43 from "The Seafarer" in Old English:

þæt he a his sæfore   sorge næbbe.
to hwon hine Dryhten   gedon wille.

A few Old English words still appear in dictionaries but are seldom used any more. Find the meanings of the following words.

1. churl   4. yare
2. thane   5. yclept
3. tor

THINKING AND WRITING

Writing About Anglo-Saxon Beliefs

"The Seafarer" is not an easy poem to understand. One critic has said that almost any theory can be made to explain its meaning. What is *your* theory? What main idea do you think the poet intends to convey? In your prewriting, list the various thoughts and feelings the poet expresses in the poem. Use these notes as the basis for a thesis statement in which you summarize what you think the main idea of the poem is. In writing a first draft, support your thesis statement with evidence from the poem. When you revise, be sure you have made clear the reasons for your conclusion.

The Seafarer   21

(Answers begin on p. 20.)

this life are transient and a belief in the power of both Fate and God.

ANSWERS TO CRITICAL THINKING AND READING

At the beginning the poet is nearly in despair, and at the end he is praising God. The poet meditates on the transience of everything on earth—its hardships as well as its riches—and begins to think of another life with God.

Challenge compare and contrast the poet's references to Fate and to God.

ANSWERS TO UNDERSTANDING LANGUAGE

1. A churl is "a rude, boorish person." (In Old English, *ceorl* meant "a free man of the lowest rank.")
2. A *thane* was in Anglo-Saxon England a freeman granted land by the king in return for military service."
3. A *tor* is "a high rock or pile of rocks on the top of a hill."
4. *Yare,* when applied to a vessel, means "manageable, maneuverable."
5. *Yclept* means "known as, named, or called."

THINKING AND WRITING

For help with this assignment, students can refer to Lesson 11, "Writing About Theme," in the Handbook of Writing About Literature.

Publishing Student Writing Ask for student volunteers to read their essays aloud. Have students in the audience record at least one noteworthy feature of each essay.

Challenge How might the first half of the poem be an allegory that is explained by the second half?

---

5. Line 41 implies a belief that God bestows grace—and therefore protection, yet Line 43 indicates a belief in Fate and a lack of protection from Fate's whims
6. Worldly possessions do not extend into the next life and do not endure even in this one.
7. In these lines the poet contrasts the world of his day and the world of an earlier, heroic time.
8. The poet is referring to heaven.

Applying

9. Suggested Response: Sometimes an attachment to something outweighs any fear of its negative aspects. Here, the sailor knows the hardships and perils of life at sea, but when the time for another journey arrives, he is overpowered by his attachment to seafaring. In addition, the Anglo-Saxons were very fatalistic, and so the poet accepts dangers and isolation simply as an unavoidable part of the life to which he is accustomed.

ANSWERS TO ANALYZING LITERATURE

1. The poet expresses feelings of sorrow, loneliness, fear, excitement, and anticipation.
2. The poet expresses a deep feeling that the trappings of

Focus

More About the Work *Beowulf* is the only surviving Old English heroic epic. It deals with a pagan world, yet is informed with Christian feelings and values. Nevertheless, the poem's celebration of human endurance in a world where nothing lasts for very long implies a deeply pagan view of life.

Critical Evaluation Charles Kennedy, a translator of *Beowulf*, considers the Christian/pagan duality in the story to be extremely important. He writes: "We have seen that the primitive material of the *Beowulf* was derived from pagan folk-tale, chronicle, and legend, and slowly welded into new unities. It remained for the Old English poet to complete this process of fusion by the conversion, or transmutation, of this material from pagan to Christian. The epic emerges at last as a Christian poem. This mutation, moreover, is not merely a matter of altered phrases, or of interpolated references to the Christian faith, but is a deeply pervasive infusion of Christian spirit coloring thought and judgment, governing motive and action, a continuous and active agent in the process of transformation."

700 [?]

Composed by an unknown poet who lived more than twelve hundred years ago, *Beowulf* marks the beginning of English literature. Minstrels called scops recited this poem to audiences in England for about three hundred years before it was first written down. Only one original manuscript of the complete 3128-line poem survives, but *Beowulf* is in no danger of becoming extinct. Not only does it have lasting historical importance as a record of the Angles, Saxons, and Jutes in England, but it also tells a hair-raising tale that has electrified readers and listeners through the centuries.

Beowulf, a Geat from a region that is today southern Sweden, sets sail from his homeland to try to free Danish King Hrothgar's great banquet hall, Herot, of a monster that has been ravaging it for twelve years. This monster, Grendel, is a terrifying swampland creature of enormous size whose eyes burn "with a gruesome light." The struggle between Beowulf, a young adventurer eager for fame, and Grendel, a fierce and bloodthirsty foe, is the first of three mortal battles in the long poem. The first battle is the one described in this book. The second struggle pits Beowulf against Grendel's "water-hag" mother, and the third, fifty years later, against a dragon.

Although the action takes place in sixth century Scandinavia, the poem is unmistakably English. Recited originally in Old English, *Beowulf* is based on legends and chronicles of the various Northern Europeans who migrated to England.

Objectives

1 To understand the characteristics of the Anglo-Saxon epic
2 To make inferences about ideals when reading an epic
3 To write a story illustrating character traits

Support Material

Teaching Portfolio
Teacher Backup, p.13
Grammar in Action Worksheet, *Understanding Appositives,* p. 17
Usage and Mechanics Worksheet, p. 19
Vocabulary Check, p. 20
Critical Thinking and Reading Worksheet, *Making Inferences About Beliefs,* p. 21
Language Worksheet, *Using a Glossary,* p. 22
Selection Test, p. 23

GUIDE FOR INTERPRETING

from Beowulf

Literary Forms

Anglo-Saxon Epic Poetry. An epic is a long narrative poem, sometimes developed orally, that celebrates the deeds of a legendary or heroic figure. A few epics predate the Anglo-Saxon *Beowulf*. Well-known epics from earlier times include the Greek *Iliad* and *Odyssey* by Homer and the Roman *Aeneid* by Virgil. Typically, an epic, featuring a hero who is larger than life, concerns eternal human problems such as the struggle between good and evil. An epic is presented in a serious way, often through the use of elevated language. The hero of an epic represents widespread national, cultural, or religious values.

Beowulf is one of the oldest European epics. Its hero, Beowulf, embodies the highest ideals of his time and place: loyalty, valor, unselfishness, and a sense of justice. He represents good, while Grendel represents evil. Throughout *Beowulf* there is a prevailing yet somewhat uneasy blend of Christian ethics and pagan morality. Against a backdrop of gloom that reflects the Anglo-Saxons' stoic acceptance of fate, the story applauds the highest virtues of human nature—courage, generosity, faithfulness. Despite its blood and horror, *Beowulf* is a deeply idealistic narrative.

Anglo-Saxon epic poetry, of which *Beowulf* is the great example, has certain distinctive features. One is the two-part line. Each line is separated by a pause, known as a caesura, and there are generally two strong beats per part. Another feature is the kenning, a colorful, indirect way of naming something: The sea is a *whalepath;* a battle is *spear play;* the sun is the *candle of the skies.*

Commentary

Beowulf belongs to the present as well as the past. Perhaps the most popular contemporary works it inspired are a series of epics about the fantasy world of Middle Earth. Beginning in 1937 with *The Hobbit,* Oxford don J. R. R. Tolkein wove imaginative tales about good and evil. The enthusiastic response to his trilogy *The Lord of the Rings* (1954–1955—*The Fellowship of the Ring, The Two Towers, The Return of the King*) prompted him to continue the saga in *The Silmarillion* (1977), an account of the origins of Middle Earth. Tolkien, however, was originally far more famous for completely changing the way we read *Beowulf*. In his 1936 article "Beowulf: The Monsters and the Critics," he saw *Beowulf* as poetry rather than history, and modern *Beowulf* scholarship began.

Writing

At the time *Beowulf* was composed, the ideals of the Anglo-Saxons included loyalty, valor, unselfishness, and a sense of justice. Those are still highly regarded ideals, but they are not the only ones. List four other ideals that are important to Americans today.

Guide for Interpreting 23

Motivation/Prior Knowledge
Play a recording of "The Ballad of Davy Crockett" or another ballad as an example of how we still celebrate our heroes in song. Have students pick out Crockett's superhuman feats and keep them in mind as they read about Beowulf.

Master Teacher Note You might have students look at the picture of viking artifacts on pages 34 and 35. In addition, you might want to show pictures of other period artifacts, such as those of the Sutton Hoo archeological find in East Anglia in 1939. The British Library has Sutton Hoo slides and Anglo-Saxon postcards. For a catalog, write to British Library Publications, 46 Bloomsbury St., London WC1B3QQ, England.

In addition, the University of Toronto Media Center, 121 St. George St., Toronto, Ontario, Canada, makes available a video and a 16mm film on the Sutton Hoo archeological find.

Thematic Idea Another selection that concerns a hero going forth into danger is *Sir Gawain and the Green Knight,* page 170. You might have students compare and contrast Beowulf and Sir Gawain as heroes.

Purpose-Setting Question What are the roles of Fate and God in this epic?

1 Discussion What images does the poet use to contrast Grendel and the Danes?

2 Enrichment The king in heroic literature would build a hall for his thanes to reward them for their service to him. The name of this hall, Herot, means "hart."

from # Beowulf

translated by Burton Raffel

The selection opens during an evening of celebration at Herot, the banquet hall of the Danish king Hrothgar (hroth' gär). Outside in the darkness, however, lurks the monster Grendel, a murderous creature who poses a great danger to the people inside the banquet hall.

The Wrath of Grendel

     A powerful monster, living down
In the darkness, growled in pain, impatient
As day after day the music rang
Loud in that hall,[1] the harp's rejoicing
5 Call and the poet's clear songs, sung
Of the ancient beginnings of us all, recalling
The Almighty making the earth, shaping
These beautiful plains marked off by oceans,
Then proudly setting the sun and moon
10 To glow across the land and light it;
The corners of the earth were made lovely with trees
And leaves, made quick with life, with each
Of the nations who now move on its face. And then
As now warriors sang of their pleasure:
15 So Hrothgar's men lived happy in his hall
Till the monster stirred, that demon, that fiend,
Grendel, who haunted the moors, the wild
Marshes, and made his home in a hell
Not hell but earth. He was spawned in that slime,
20 Conceived by a pair of those monsters born
Of Cain,[2] murderous creatures banished
By God, punished forever for the crime
Of Abel's death. The Almighty drove
Those demons out, and their exile was bitter,
25 Shut away from men; they split
Into a thousand forms of evil—spirits
And fiends, goblins, monsters, giants,
A brood forever opposing the Lord's
Will, and again and again defeated.

30   Then, when darkness had dropped, Grendel
Went up to Herot, wondering what the warriors
Would do in that hall when their drinking was done.

1. hall: Herot.

2. Cain: The oldest son of Adam and Eve, who murdered his brother Abel.

3 Discussion What Christian and pagan references are used to describe Grendel? What is shown to be Grendel's motive for attacking Herot?

Fine art, *The Dragon* for *The High Kings,* 1983, by George Sharp. George Sharp is a contemporary British illustrator who began painting professionally in 1975. He studied art at the Nottingham School of Art in England. The painting to the left was done for the book *The High Kings,* by Joy Chant, published in 1983. Sharp was concerned with authenticity when creating the illustrations for this book. He spent many hours researching the myths and artifacts of ancient England. Sharp paints in a detailed illustrative style and uses transparent washes of color on a white ground. The dragon he portrays is imaginative, and it is as fearsome-looking as the dragons portrayed in historic legends.

Call your students' attention to this painting, and ask whether the artist's image of this creature agrees with their concept of Grendel. Explain.

THE DRAGON FOR "THE HIGH KINGS"
George Sharp

from *Beowulf* 25

4 Discussion What had Herot represented in the land? When it stands empty, what does this mean about the king's power?

5 Enrichment Anglo-Saxon custom dictated that a person who killed someone, even accidentally, had to pay a "man-price," or *wergild,* to the dead person's kin or risk deadly retribution. A relative who didn't exact wergild from his kin's killer was humiliated. In this darkly cynical passage, the poet notes that the only payment Grendel makes is more murder.

6 Reading Strategy Summarize the situation of the Danes.

He found them sprawled in sleep, suspecting
Nothing, their dreams undisturbed. The monster's
35 Thoughts were as quick as his greed or his claws:
He slipped through the door and there in the silence
Snatched up thirty men, smashed them
Unknowing in their beds and ran out with their bodies,
The blood dripping behind him, back
40 To his lair, delighted with his night's slaughter.
    At daybreak, with the sun's first light, they saw
How well he had worked, and in that gray morning
Broke their long feast with tears and laments
For the dead. Hrothgar, their lord, sat joyless
45 In Herot, a mighty prince mourning
The fate of his lost friends and companions,
Knowing by its tracks that some demon had torn
His followers apart. He wept, fearing
The beginning might not be the end. And that night
50 Grendel came again, so set
On murder that no crime could ever be enough,
No savage assault quench his lust
For evil. Then each warrior tried
To escape him, searched for rest in different
55 Beds, as far from Herot as they could find,
Seeing how Grendel hunted when they slept.
Distance was safety; the only survivors
Were those who fled him. Hate had triumphed.

4   So Grendel ruled, fought with the righteous,
60 One against many, and won; so Herot
Stood empty, and stayed deserted for years,
Twelve winters of grief for Hrothgar, king
Of the Danes, sorrow heaped at his door
By hell-forged hands. His misery leaped
65 The seas, was told and sung in all
Men's ears: how Grendel's hatred began,

5 How the monster relished his savage war
On the Danes, keeping the bloody feud
Alive, seeking no peace, offering
70 No truce, accepting no settlement, no price
In gold or land, and paying the living
For one crime only with another. No one
Waited for reparation from his plundering claws:
That shadow of death hunted in the darkness,
75 Stalked Hrothgar's warriors, old

6 And young, lying in waiting, hidden
In mist, invisibly following them from the edge
Of the marsh, always there, unseen.
    So mankind's enemy continued his crimes,

26   *The Anglo-Saxon Period*

80 Killing as often as he could, coming
Alone, bloodthirsty and horrible. Though he lived
In Herot, when the night hid him, he never
Dared to touch king Hrothgar's glorious
Throne, protected by God—God,
85 Whose love Grendel could not know. But Hrothgar's
Heart was bent. The best and most noble
Of his council debated remedies, sat
In secret sessions, talking of terror
And wondering what the bravest of warriors could do.
90 And sometimes they sacrificed to the old stone gods,
Made heathen vows, hoping for Hell's
Support, the Devil's guidance in driving
Their affliction off. That was their way,
And the heathen's only hope, Hell
95 Always in their hearts, knowing neither God
Nor His passing as He walks through our world, the Lord
Of Heaven and earth; their ears could not hear
His praise nor know His glory. Let them
Beware, those who are thrust into danger,
100 Clutched at by trouble, yet can carry no solace
In their hearts, cannot hope to be better! Hail
To those who will rise to God, drop off
Their dead bodies and seek our Father's peace!

The Coming of Beowulf

So the living sorrow of Healfdane's son[3]
105 Simmered, bitter and fresh, and no wisdom
Or strength could break it: that agony hung
On king and people alike, harsh
And unending, violent and cruel, and evil.
In his far-off home Beowulf, Higlac's[4]
110 Follower and the strongest of the Geats—greater
And stronger than anyone anywhere in this world—
Heard how Grendel filled nights with horror
And quickly commanded a boat fitted out,
Proclaiming that he'd go to that famous king,
115 Would sail across the sea to Hrothgar,
Now when help was needed. None
Of the wise ones regretted his going, much
As he was loved by the Geats: the omens were good,
And they urged the adventure on. So Beowulf
120 Chose the mightiest men he could find,
The bravest and best of the Geats, fourteen
In all, and led them down to their boat;
He knew the sea, would point the prow
Straight to that distant Danish shore.

3. Healfdane's (hā′ alf den′nəz) **son:** Hrothgar.

4. Higlac's (hig′ laks): Higlac was the king of the Geats (gā′ ats) and Beowulf's feudal lord and uncle.

7 **Clarification** This passage is confusing to scholars. Hrothgar and the Danes are spoken of as heathens here, even though at the beginning of the passage the scop is singing about God's creation, and later in the poem Hrothgar speaks as a Christian.

8 **Discussion** What is the Christian remedy and admonishment expressed here?

9 **Enrichment** Beowulf has chosen a heroic way of life, the goal of which is to attain glory, so he must go to fight Grendel.

10 **Discussion** Why did Beowulf's kinsmen urge him to go?

Humanities Note

Fine art, Illustration for "The High Kings," 1983, by George Sharp. This painting by George Sharp of an ancient ship was done for Joy Chant's book *The High Kings,* published in 1983. Sharp's diligent research into ancient English myth and legend is reflected in the accurately detailed rigging of the ship. Executed in transparent color washes on canvas, this painting has a misty, dreamlike quality. It is as if the scene were painted on the shore by a witness in Beowulf's time.

You may wish to ask your students the following questions.

1. Do you feel that this contemporary painting technique properly illustrates this epic? Explain.
2. What mood does this painting create?

ARTHUR GOING TO AVALON FOR "THE HIGH KINGS"
George Sharp

28   *The Anglo-Saxon Period*

125   Then they sailed, set their ship
     Out on the waves, under the cliffs.
     Ready for what came they wound through the currents,
     The seas beating at the sand, and were borne
     In the lap of their shining ship, lined
130   With gleaming armor, going safely
     In that oak-hard boat to where their hearts took them.
     The wind hurried them over the waves,
     The ship foamed through the sea like a bird
     Until, in the time they had known it would take,
135   Standing in the round-curled prow they could see
     Sparkling hills, high and green,
     Jutting up over the shore, and rejoicing
     In those rock-steep cliffs they quietly ended
     Their voyage. Jumping to the ground, the Geats
140   Pushed their boat to the sand and tied it
     In place, mail shirts and armor rattling
     As they swiftly moored their ship. And then
     They gave thanks to God for their easy crossing.
        High on a wall a Danish watcher
145   Patrolling along the cliffs saw
     The travelers crossing to the shore, their shields
     Raised and shining; he came riding down,
     Hrothgar's lieutenant, spurring his horse,
     Needing to know why they'd landed, these men
150   In armor. Shaking his heavy spear
     In their faces he spoke:
                 "Whose soldiers are you,
     You who've been carried in your deep-keeled ship
     Across the sea-road to this country of mine?
     Listen! I've stood on these cliffs longer
155   Than you know, keeping our coast free
     Of pirates, raiders sneaking ashore
     From their ships, seeking our lives and our gold.
     None have ever come more openly—
     And yet you've offered no password, no sign
160   From my prince, no permission from my people for your
        landing
     Here. Nor have I ever seen,
     Out of all the men on earth, one greater
     Than has come with you; no commoner carries
     Such weapons, unless his appearance, and his beauty,
165   Are both lies. You! Tell me your name,
     And your father's; no spies go further onto Danish
     Soil than you've come already. Strangers,
     From wherever it was you sailed, tell it,
     And tell it quickly, the quicker the better,
170   I say, for us all. Speak, say
     Exactly who you are, and from where, and why."

11

12

from *Beowulf*   29

11 Discussion What adjectives and descriptive phrases are used to describe the Geats' boat? Contrast these to the adjectives used to describe Grendel.

12 Discussion What heroic qualities does Beowulf's appearance suggest?

Their leader answered him, Beowulf unlocking
Words from deep in his breast:

"We are Geats,
Men who follow Higlac. My father
175 Was a famous soldier, known far and wide
As a leader of men. His name was Edgetho.
His life lasted many winters;
Wise men all over the earth surely
Remember him still. And we have come seeking
180 Your prince, Healfdane's son, protector
Of this people, only in friendship: instruct us,
Watchman, help us with your words! Our errand
Is a great one, our business with the glorious king
Of the Danes no secret; there's nothing dark
185 Or hidden in our coming. You know (if we've heard
The truth, and been told honestly) that your country
Is cursed with some strange, vicious creature
That hunts only at night and that no one
Has seen. It's said, watchman, that he has slaughtered
190 Your people, brought terror to the darkness. Perhaps
Hrothgar can hunt, here in my heart,
For some way to drive this devil out—
If anything will ever end the evils
Afflicting your wise and famous lord.
195 Here he can cool his burning sorrow.
Or else he may see his suffering go on
Forever, for as long as Herot towers
High on your hills."

The mounted officer
Answered him bluntly, the brave watchman:
200 "A soldier should know the difference between words
And deeds, and keep that knowledge clear
In his brain. I believe your words, I trust in
Your friendship. Go forward, weapons and armor
And all, on into Denmark. I'll guide you
205 Myself—and my men will guard your ship,
Keep it safe here on our shores,
Your fresh-tarred boat, watch it well,
Until that curving prow carries
Across the sea to Geatland a chosen
210 Warrior who bravely does battle with the creature
Haunting our people, who survives that horror
Unhurt, and goes home bearing our love."

Then they moved on. Their boat lay moored,
Tied tight to its anchor. Glittering at the top
13 215 Of their golden helmets wild boar heads gleamed,
Shining decorations, swinging as they marched,
Erect like guards, like sentinels, as though ready

Grammar in Action

Appositives are nouns or pronouns used to clarify or explain other nouns or pronouns already introduced. An **appositive phrase** is an appositive with modifiers. When you name something and then immediately rename it to give further information, you are using an appositive or an appositive phrase. If the appositive is essential to identify a noun, it is not set off by commas. If it supplies information about a noun but is not essential to the sentence's meaning, it is set off by commas. In *Beowulf,* appositives abound.

We are Geats, / *Men who follow Higlac.*

And we have come seeking / Your prince, *Healfdane's* son, protector / Of this people . . .

Have brought us stories of Herot, *the best / Of all mead-halls . . .*

In each case, the appositive phrase follows directly after the noun it explains and renames. The Geats are Higlac's men; the prince is Healfdane's son and the protector of the people; and Herot is the best of all mead-halls. None of these appositive phrases changes the original noun. Each simply adds specifics, and so each requires commas.

To fight. They marched, Beowulf and his men
And their guide, until they could see the gables
220 Of Herot, covered with hammered gold
And glowing in the sun—that most famous of all dwellings,
Towering majestic, its glittering roofs
Visible far across the land.
Their guide reined in his horse, pointing
225 To that hall, built by Hrothgar for the best
And bravest of his men; the path was plain,
They could see their way . . .

> *Beowulf and his men arrive at Herot and are about to be escorted in to see King Hrothgar.*

Beowulf arose, with his men
230 Around him, ordering a few to remain
With their weapons, leading the others quickly
Along under Herot's steep roof into Hrothgar's
Presence. Standing on that prince's own hearth,
Helmeted, the silvery metal of his mail shirt
235 Gleaming with a smith's high art, he greeted
The Danes' great lord:
                "Hail, Hrothgar!
Higlac is my cousin[5] and my king; the days
Of my youth have been filled with glory. Now Grendel's
Name has echoed in our land: sailors
240 Have brought us stories of Herot, the best
Of all mead-halls, deserted and useless when the moon
Hangs in skies the sun had lit,
Light and life fleeing together.
My people have said, the wisest, most knowing
245 And best of them, that my duty was to go to the Danes'
Great king. They have seen my strength for themselves,
Have watched me rise from the darkness of war,
Dripping with my enemies' blood. I drove
Five great giants into chains, chased
250 All of that race from the earth. I swam
In the blackness of night, hunting monsters
Out of the ocean, and killing them one
By one; death was my errand and the fate
They had earned. Now Grendel and I are called
255 Together, and I've come. Grant me, then,
Lord and protector of this noble place,
A single request! I have come so far,
Oh shelterer of warriors and your people's loved friend,
That this one favor you should not refuse me—
260 That I, alone and with the help of my men,
May purge all evil from this hall. I have heard,
Too, that the monster's scorn of men

5. cousin: Here, used as a general term for relative.

from *Beowulf* 31

14 Discussion What terms are used to describe Herot? How is Grendel's environment described elsewhere in the poem? Ask for a volunteer to give a dramatic reading of Beowulf's speech to Hrothgar.

15 Enrichment This boasting might offend some modern readers, but Beowulf is recalling his former courage as a way of making a vow of future courage.

16 Discussion Why might Beowulf want to fight Grendel alone, except for the help of his own men?

Student Activity 1. Find three more appositives or appositive phrases in *Beowulf* and point out the nouns they identify.

Student Activity 2. Identify the appositives or appositive phrases in the following sentences and punctuate them correctly.

1. My brother that tall boy is also my friend.
2. The word *anthropomorphism* is often misused.
3. Are you referring to Bob Smith the doctor or Bob Smith the car dealer?
4. My favorite relative is Luke my uncle.

17 **Discussion** What heroic quality do these lines suggest? How would you characterize Beowulf?

18 **Discussion** Why wouldn't the Danes have to sew shrouds for the Geats if Grendel triumphs?

19 **Reading Strategy** Summarize what we have learned so far about Beowulf's character.

20 **Discussion** What do we know about Grendel's physical appearance? Why do you think the author is so vague about Grendel's specific features?

17

Is so great that he needs no weapons and fears none.
Nor will I. My lord Higlac
265 Might think less of me if I let my sword
Go where my feet were afraid to, if I hid
Behind some broad linden[6] shield: my hands
Alone shall fight for me, struggle for life
Against the monster. God must decide
270 Who will be given to death's cold grip.
Grendel's plan, I think, will be
What it has been before, to invade this hall
And gorge his belly with our bodies. If he can,
If he can. And I think, if my time will have come,
275 There'll be nothing to mourn over, no corpse to prepare
For its grave: Grendel will carry our bloody
Flesh to the moors, crunch on our bones
And smear torn scraps of our skin on the walls
Of his den. No, I expect no Danes
280 Will fret about sewing our shrouds, if he wins.
And if death does take me, send the hammered
Mail of my armor to Higlac, return
The inheritance I had from Hrethel, and he
From Wayland.[7] Fate will unwind as it must!''

18

19

6. linden: A very sturdy type of wood.

7. Wayland: From Germanic folklore, an invisible blacksmith.

The Battle with Grendel

That night Beowulf and his men take the places of Hrothgar and the Danes inside Herot. While his men sleep, Beowulf lies awake, eager to meet with Grendel.

20

285   Out from the marsh, from the foot of misty
Hills and bogs, bearing God's hatred,
Grendel came, hoping to kill
Anyone he could trap on this trip to high Herot.
He moved quickly through the cloudy night,
290 Up from his swampland, sliding silently
Toward that gold-shining hall. He had visited Hrothgar's
Home before, knew the way—
But never, before nor after that night,
Found Herot defended so firmly, his reception
295 So harsh. He journeyed, forever joyless,
Straight to the door, then snapped it open,
Tore its iron fasteners with a touch
And rushed angrily over the threshold.
He strode quickly across the inlaid
300 Floor, snarling and fierce: his eyes
Gleamed in the darkness, burned with a gruesome
Light. Then he stopped, seeing the hall
Crowded with sleeping warriors, stuffed
With rows of young soldiers resting together.

305 And his heart laughed, he relished the sight,
Intended to tear the life from those bodies
By morning; the monster's mind was hot
With the thought of food and the feasting his belly
Would soon know. But fate, that night, intended
310 Grendel to gnaw the broken bones
Of his last human supper. Human
Eyes were watching his evil steps,
Waiting to see his swift hard claws.
Grendel snatched at the first Geat
315 He came to, ripped him apart, cut
His body to bits with powerful jaws,
Drank the blood from his veins and bolted
Him down, hands and feet; death
And Grendel's great teeth came together,
320 Snapping life shut. Then he stepped to another
Still body, clutched at Beowulf with his claws,
Grasped at a strong-hearted wakeful sleeper
—And was instantly seized himself, claws
Bent back as Beowulf leaned up on one arm.
325   That shepherd of evil, guardian of crime,
Knew at once that nowhere on earth
Had he met a man whose hands were harder;
His mind was flooded with fear—but nothing
Could take his talons and himself from that tight
330 Hard grip. Grendel's one thought was to run
From Beowulf, flee back to his marsh and hide there:
This was a different Herot than the hall he had emptied.
But Higlac's follower remembered his final
Boast and, standing erect, stopped
335 The monster's flight, fastened those claws
In his fists till they cracked, clutched Grendel
Closer. The infamous killer fought
For his freedom, wanting no flesh but retreat,
Desiring nothing but escape; his claws
340 Had been caught, he was trapped. That trip to Herot
Was a miserable journey for the writhing monster!
     The high hall rang, its roof boards swayed,
And Danes shook with terror. Down
The aisles the battle swept, angry
345 And wild. Herot trembled, wonderfully
Built to withstand the blows, the struggling
Great bodies beating at its beautiful walls;
Shaped and fastened with iron, inside
And out, artfully worked, the building
350 Stood firm. Its benches rattled, fell
To the floor, gold-covered boards grating
As Grendel and Beowulf battled across them.

21 **Enrichment** The poet uses fore-shadowing here. He tells us ahead of time that Grendel will die, just as the Anglo-Saxons believed that their deaths were predetermined.

22 **Reading Strategy** How will Grendel's attack on Beowulf differ from his attack on the sleeping warrior?

23 **Literary Focus** Note the profusion of kennings in this battle passage—"shepherd of evil," "guardian of crime," "the Almighty's enemy," and "hell's captive." The primary purpose of kennings in the original Anglo-Saxon was to maintain the required alliteration. The first accented syllable after the caesura had to alliterate with at least one of the accented syllables in the first half of the line.

Viking Artifacts

1. Sigurd's helmet from a pre-Viking grave in Vendel, Sweden. May have belonged to Sigurd the Volsung (d.575).
2. Viking silver coins, early ninth-century, probably struck in Hedeby, Denmark. This is an early form of coin that depended on the weight of the silver for its value. The design depicts Viking longships.
3. Prow of a restored tenth-century Viking longship, referred to as the Gokstad Ship. It was found in Norway in 1880. It is eighty feet long and built for sea and coastal maneuvers. Manned by a crew of thirty-two, it was a swift, silent raiding vessel.
4. The Oseberg Dragon, a wooden animal post head found among the furniture on the ninth-century Oseberg Ship, a royal barge used for the burial of a Norwegian queen. The post is covered with an intricate profusion of "gripping beasts," a classic Viking decorative pattern.
5. Vendel helmet, a seventh-century Swedish artifact. Composed of iron with a bronze crest and nose guard, it shows a Roman influence in the design.
6. Viking drinking horn. A cattle horn decoratively mounted with metal, it was used for drinking beer and mead. Its use required practice, as all of the liquid rushes out at once. The design prevented the horn from being put down until it was empty.

24 Master Teacher Note You might want to play a recording of *Beowulf* read in Old English at this point. Perhaps students can understand the drama of the battle scene as it was described by ancient scops. (Recording: *Beowulf,* Cadmon TC 4001)

Hrothgar's wise men had fashioned Herot
To stand forever; only fire,
355   They had planned, could shatter what such skill had put
Together, swallow in hot flames such splendor
Of ivory and iron and wood. Suddenly
The sounds changed, the Danes started
In new terror, cowering in their beds as the terrible
360   Screams of the Almighty's enemy sang
In the darkness, the horrible shrieks of pain
And defeat, the tears torn out of Grendel's
Taut throat, hell's captive caught in the arms
Of him who of all the men on earth
365   Was the strongest.
                        That mighty protector of men
Meant to hold the monster till its life
Leaped out, knowing the fiend was no use
To anyone in Denmark. All of Beowulf's
Band had jumped from their beds, ancestral
370   Swords raised and ready, determined
To protect their prince if they could. Their courage
Was great but all wasted: they could hack at Grendel

THE SO-CALLED "SIGURD'S HELMET"
Statens Historiska Museet, Stockholm
Werner Forman Archive

COINS DEPICTING VIKING LONGSHIPS
Statens Historiska Museet, Stockholm
Werner Forman Archive

THE GOKSTAD SHIP
Viking Ships Museum, Bygdøy, Oslo
Werner Forman Archive

From every side, trying to open
A path for his evil soul, but their points
375 Could not hurt him, the sharpest and hardest iron
Could not scratch at his skin, for that sin-stained demon
Had bewitched all men's weapons, laid spells
That blunted every mortal man's blade.

25

And yet his time had come, his days
380 Were over, his death near; down
To hell he would go, swept groaning and helpless
To the waiting hands of still worse fiends.

26

Now he discovered—once the afflictor
Of men, tormentor of their days—what it meant
385 To feud with Almighty God: Grendel

27

Saw that his strength was deserting him, his claws
Bound fast, Higlac's brave follower tearing at
His hands. The monster's hatred rose higher,
But his power had gone. He twisted in pain,
390 And the bleeding sinews deep in his shoulder
Snapped, muscle and bone split
And broke. The battle was over, Beowulf

28

from *Beowulf* 35

25 **Discussion** Why were Beowulf's men unable to help him kill Grendel?

26 **Enrichment** Note again the announcement of Grendel's death before it happens. After he has vividly described Grendel's murderous activities, the poet states simply—and rather anticlimatically—that Grendel will die at some future time.

27 **Discussion** Explain how the battle between Beowulf and Grendel takes on much greater significance at this point.

28 **Reading Strategy** Summarize the battle with Grendel and its outcome.

The hanging of the monster's forequarters on the wall seems to reinforce the popular notion that the Anglo-Saxons were a barbaric, insular, and in-sensitive people. However, ar-chaeological discoveries at Sutton Hoo in East Anglia in 1939 show that the seventh-century Anglo-Saxons had high artistic abilities and wide trading contacts. Also, while the epic was probably writ-ten in the mid-eighth century in England, it deals with an earlier time and place: fifth or sixth cen-tury Scandinavia.

Master Teacher Note You may want to have some of your **more advanced** pupils read John Gard-ner's novel *Grendel* or Richard Wilbur's poem "Beowulf" and compare or contrast these works with *Beowulf*.

Reader's Response What quali-ties do you think make Beowulf attractive as a hero?

Had been granted new glory: Grendel escaped,
But wounded as he was could flee to his den,
395 His miserable hole at the bottom of the marsh,
Only to die, to wait for the end
Of all his days. And after that bloody
Combat the Danes laughed with delight.
He who had come to them from across the sea,
400 Bold and strong-minded, had driven affliction
Off, purged Herot clean. He was happy,
Now, with that night's fierce work; the Danes
Had been served as he'd boasted he'd serve them; Beowulf,
A prince of the Geats, had killed Grendel,
405 Ended the grief, the sorrow, the suffering
Forced on Hrothgar's helpless people
By a bloodthirsty fiend. No Dane doubted
The victory, for the proof, hanging high
From the rafters where Beowulf had hung it, was the monster's
410 Arm, claw and shoulder and all.

THINKING ABOUT THE SELECTION

Recalling

1. (a) When does Grendel first go to Herot? (b) Explain what the warriors are doing when he arrives. (c) What does he do to them?
2. Why is Grendel afraid of touching Hrothgar's throne?
3. (a) What is Beowulf's plan for fighting Gren-del? (b) Why does he choose this plan?
4. How does Grendel die?

Interpreting

5. At the beginning of the poem, Hrothgar's warriors are happy, while Grendel is con-sumed by hatred. What causes these differ-ences in attitude?
6. How does Beowulf's remark, "Fate will unwind as it must," reflect the Anglo-Saxons' attitude toward fate?
7. What traits of Beowulf and Grendel raise the fight between them to an epic struggle be-tween two great opposing forces in the world?

Applying

8. Beowulf is thought to be a perfect hero for his times. (a) What qualities should a modern hero have? (b) In what situations might a modern hero demonstrate these heroic quali-ties? (c) Give examples of modern heroes or of heroic behavior.

ANALYZING LITERATURE

Understanding the Anglo-Saxon Epic

An **epic** is a long, narrative poem, presented in an elevated style, that celebrates episodes in a people's heroic tradition.

The Anglo-Saxon epic *Beowulf* has two dis-tinctive features. One feature is the two-part line

Closure and Extension

ANSWERS TO THINKING ABOUT THE SELECTION
Recalling

1. (a) Grendel first goes to Herot one dark evening twelve years be-fore Beowulf arrives.
   (b) King Hrothgar and his warriors are celebrating when Grendel arrives.

(c) Grendel kills thirty warriors.
2. Grendel is afraid of touching Hrothgar's throne because it is pro-tected by God.
3. (a) Beowulf's plan is to fight Grendel barehanded.
   (b) Answers may differ. Beowulf has heard that Grendel fears no weapons. Beowulf also thinks that his uncle might think less of him if he "hides behind" weapons or ˙shields. Furthermore, Beowulf has a sense that Fate has brought

him and Grendel together and that this battle will be the ulti-mate test for each of them.
4. Beowulf rips his arm off at the shoulder; Grendel escapes to his den to die.

Interpreting

5. Hrothgar's warriors are celebrating God's creation of the world; Grendel and his forebears have been exiled by God. Grendel's hate is fueled by hearing the happy war-

in which the two parts are separated by a caesura. Each part has two strong beats.

> Till the *monster stirred* / that *demon,*
> that *fiend*

The kenning is another feature in *Beowulf*. A kenning is a colorful, roundabout way of naming something.

> That *shepherd of evil, guardian of crime*

1. What are the two parts and the four strong beats in each of the following lines?

> As day after day the music rang
> Loud in that hall, the harp's rejoicing

2. In addition to the example given, find another kenning in Beowulf.
3. Explain why you do or do not find the use of kenning effective.

CRITICAL THINKING AND READING
Making Inferences About Ideals

An **inference** is a conclusion you reach from stated information in literature. The hero in an epic embodies the highest ideals of the times. The Anglo-Saxon epic *Beowulf* reflects the values of the plundering Anglo-Saxon warriors. Beowulf himself is a fighting man, eager for challenging personal encounters in a good cause.

From Beowulf's description of his previous heroic feats (lines 247–254), you can infer that his listeners respected and admired the qualities that enabled Beowulf to accomplish such deeds. In addition, you can infer that they believed that such qualities enabled Beowulf to take on the evil Grendel.

1. In what specific way does Beowulf demonstrate loyalty to his lord and king?
2. In what specific ways does he demonstrate his valor?

3. In lines 378–380, Grendel realizes that he has been beaten:

> Now he discovered—once the afflictor
> Of men, tormentor of their days—what it meant
> To feud with Almighty God.

What inference about Anglo-Saxon beliefs can you make from these lines?

UNDERSTANDING LANGUAGE
Using a Glossary

A **glossary** is a small, specialized dictionary designed to help you with unfamiliar words. Which of the following are included in the glossary entries in the back of this book?
1. pronunciation
2. part of speech
3. etymology
4. inflected forms
5. cross references
6. variant spellings

THINKING AND WRITING
Writing About Character Traits

Write a composition for your classmates in which you tell the incidents in *Beowulf* from Grendel's point of view. Begin by jotting down notes about Grendel's thoughts and feelings during his final, fatal visit to Hrothgar's hall. Then arrange these notes in a logical order to create a working outline. Next, write a draft, keeping in mind that you are giving Grendel's version of events, not your own or Beowulf's. Finally, revise your draft, improving your content and organization and correcting any errors you find in grammar or mechanics.

ANSWERS TO ANALYZING LITERATURE

1. "As *day* after *day* / the *music* rang / Loud in that *hall*, / the *harp's* re*joic*ing"
2. Answers will differ but may include "That mighty protector of men" (line 365), "mankind's enemy" (line 79), and "the Almighty's enemy" (line 360).
3. Suggested response: The kenning adds colorful language to the poem and describes characters and things in ways that enlarge our understanding of them.

ANSWERS TO CRITICAL THINKING AND READING

1. Beowulf says that he wants to fight Grendel without weapons partly to make his king proud of him. If Beowulf is killed, he wants his armor sent to Higlac.
2. When Beowulf hears of Grendel's marauding, he quickly sets out to help the Danes. Beowulf puts himself in mortal danger by waiting in Herot for Grendel, and he fights Grendel to the death.
3. The Anglo-Saxons had been Christianized and believed that God would prevail over evil.

ANSWERS TO UNDERSTANDING LANGUAGE

Glossary entries in this book include a word's pronunciation and part of speech, as well as its meaning.

THINKING AND WRITING

For help with this assignment, students can refer to Lesson 9, "Writing About Character," in the Handbook of Writing About Literature.

Publishing Student Writing Have students work in groups of four to read each other's papers and to choose the one that they think is best to read to the class.

---

riors and by knowing that he must always be "shut away" from them.
6. Beowulf feels that he and Grendel have been brought together by Fate and that he will win or lose as Fate decrees; all has been predetermined.
7. Beowulf is the greatest of the Geats and of all men; he has previously rid the earth of giants and killed sea monsters. Grendel is part of a "brood forever opposing the Lord's Will"; he is described as the embodiment of Hate, as mankind's

enemy, as the shepherd of evil, as the guardian of crime, and as the Almighty's enemy.

Applying

8. Answers may differ. (a) Students may suggest that a modern hero is self-reliant, intelligent, committed to a cause, unflinching in the face of danger, and willing to take risks —that he or she is essentially larger than life. (b) A modern hero

might demonstrate these qualities by leading a cause or struggle, by taking great risks to help others, or by taking risks to expand the frontiers of knowledge. (c) Some examples of modern heroes might be Martin Luther King, Steve Biko, John Glenn, Chuck Yeager, and Mother Teresa.

Challenge Is it easier or more difficult to be a hero today? Why?

Literary Focus Have students discuss their own experiences with films or stories inspired by "dark age" legends and folk tales. Many of them may have read Tolkien's Ring trilogy or *The Hobbit.* Others will recall reading about King Arthur and his Round Table. Much of Tolkien's work tries to recapture a purely pagan outlook, while Arthurian stories abound in Christian symbolism. You might ask students to discuss how different outlooks might affect the treatment of the same legend or tale, or even how pagan and Christian viewpoints could coexist within the same work—which was frequently the case with literature from this period.

Writing/Prior Knowledge Pair up students in your class. Before they begin freewriting, have them share ideas and tell each other about experiences in which they faced failure and then struggled to overcome it.

ESL Teaching Strategy To help with the writing assignment, pair each ESL student with a native speaker. Have the native speaker coach the ESL student on ways to create a quick list of important points that might help in writing about his or her experience.

Teaching to Ability Levels Have less advanced students make drawings of Beowulf and of Grendel's mother to show how they imagine these characters might look. Have advanced students locate Heorot Castle on a map of Denmark. (It is five miles west-southwest of the village of Roskilde.)

Vocabulary

Preteach the following vocabulary words:
massive (mas′ iv) *adj.*: Big and solid (l. 533)
loathsome (lōth′ səm) *adj.*: Disgusting (l. 555)
fetters (fet′ ərz) *n.*: Chains for the feet (l. 582)
banner (ban′ ər) *n.*: Flag (l. 791)

GUIDE FOR INTERPRETING

from **Beowulf**

Writer's Techniques

Pagan and Christian Elements. The eighth-century poet who composed *Beowulf* lived in a civilization that had become Christian only a hundred or so years before. It is not surprising, therefore, that for the characters and events of his story, he drew on pagan legends and folk tales. The magnificent monsters of *Beowulf,* for example, derive from the trolls of Scandinavian mythology, shadowy creatures who lurked around waterfalls or caves.

However, the Christian beliefs of the poets of England also penetrate the poem. For example, the poet disguises the true lineage of Grendel and his mother, giving them instead a Biblical origin:

> . . . He [Grendel] was spawned in that slime,
> Conceived by a pair of those monsters born
> Of Cain, murderous creatures banished
> By God, punished forever for the crime
> Of Abel's death . . .

In battling Grendel, Beowulf is not only a brave pagan warrior, but also a Christian hero challenging the forces of evil, the first such hero in a line that includes Sir Galahad of the Round Table and the legendary Saint George, dragon slayer and patron saint of England.

The combat with Grendel's mother, described on the following pages, also reflects the weaving together of pagan and Christian elements. The creature's underwater lair and the magic sword found by the hero are familiar from many pagan folk tales. However, in *Beowulf* God plays a role in the battle: "and Holy/God, who sent him victory, gave judgment/For truth and right . . ."

Commentary

The Christian influence on the poem is not limited to specific references to the Bible and God. As Charles W. Kennedy points out, the spirit of the newly victorious religion is evident throughout the epic: "The *Beowulf* is a tale of the pagan past in which the endurance, the loyalty, the courage, and the strength of the heroic age are tempered by union with Christian virtues. . . ." Alert readers will find this "welding of pagan heroism with Christian virtue" in the depiction of Beowulf as a young warrior and an aging king.

Writing

In his battle with Grendel's mother and later with a dragon, Beowulf faces the possibility of failure. Briefly describe a time when you had to confront the chance that you might fail. Tell how you struggled with this feeling and overcame it.

Objectives

1 To understand the characteristics of an ideal heroic warrior
2 To trace pagan and Christian elements in *Beowulf*
3 To identify Old English words
4 To respond to a critical comment about *Beowulf*

Support Material

Teaching Portfolio
Teacher Backup, pp. 25–28
Grammar in Action Worksheet, *Using Action Verbs,* p. 29
Usage and Mechanics Worksheet, p. 31
Vocabulary Check, p. 32
Critical Thinking and Reading Worksheet, *Identifying Old English Words,* p. 33

Language Worksheet, *Completing Word Analogies,* p. 34
Selection Test, pp. 35–36

Spelling Tip Write the words *fetters* and *banner* on the chalkboard. Point out to students that each has a double consonant.

from Beowulf

translated by Burton Raffel

*Hrothgar and his host celebrate Beowulf's victory over the
monster Grendel. That night, however, Grendel's mother
kidnaps and kills Hrothgar's closest friend and carries off
the claw that Beowulf tore from her child. The next day
the horrified king tells Beowulf about the two monsters
and their underwater lair.*

The Monsters' Lair

   "I've heard that my people, peasants working
In the fields, have seen a pair of such fiends
Wandering in the moors and marshes, giant
Monsters living in those desert lands.
415 And they've said to my wise men that, as well as they
    could see,
One of the devils was a female creature.
The other, they say, walked through the wilderness
Like a man—but mightier than any man.
They were frightened, and they fled, hoping to find
    help
420 In Herot. They named the huge one Grendel:
If he had a father no one knew him,
Or whether there'd been others before these two,
Hidden evil before hidden evil.
They live in secret places, windy
425 Cliffs, wolf-dens where water pours
From the rocks, then runs underground, where mist
Steams like black clouds, and the groves of trees
Growing out over their lake are all covered
With frozen spray, and wind down snakelike
430 Roots that reach as far as the water
And help keep it dark. At night that lake
Burns like a torch. No one knows its bottom,
No wisdom reaches such depths. A deer,
Hunted through the woods by packs of hounds,
435 A stag with great horns, though driven through the
    forest
From faraway places, prefers to die
On those shores, refuses to save its life
In that water. It isn't far, nor is it
A pleasant spot! When the wind stirs

Presentation

Motivation/Prior Knowledge
Tell students that they will be
reading an epic that glorifies the
great deeds of a hero. Call upon
their prior knowledge by asking
them to list words and phrases
describing heroes in other stories or poems they have read.
Then read this analysis of Beowulf's character by the critic
Alain Renoir: "Beowulf has
bridged the gap between fool-
hardiness and true courage . . .
He has learned to reflect and
listen to the voice of wisdom before making decisions; . . .
however, he has retained the will
to act, so that he has become an
embodiment of the ideal union of
wisdom and action." Ask students to discuss how this concept differs from the way they
earlier defined a hero. Suggest
they keep this discussion in mind
as they read.

Purpose-Setting Question
What kind of person is the hero of
this poem?

Thematic Idea Have students
compare Beowulf with Macbeth
(*Macbeth*, p. 271) and Satan
(*Paradise Lost*, p. 449).

1 Literary Focus Tell students that
this passage stresses the lack of
information about Grendel's ancestry and kin, but earlier in the
poem, Grendel and other monsters like him are said to have
Cain as their ancestor, the human being who committed the
first murder. Point out to students
that this is an example of the not
always consistent interweaving
of Christian and pagan elements.

2 Enrichment This passage describing a deer hunted by
hounds is one of three closely
placed echoes in *Beowulf* of the
seventh book of the *Aeneid*, a
text known to the scribes and
monks of Bede's Golden Age.

3 **Clarification** The original says that it took Beowulf almost a day to sink to the bottom of the lake. This is typical of a certain flair for exaggeration in the poem—which is also common to such American "tall tales" as those about Paul Bunyan (in which it took days for a bird to fly from one horn of the Blue Ox to the other—and longer if it was snowing).

4 **Discussion** Ask students to paraphrase the fierce and intense activity contained in this brief passage. How is this action like the frantic, swift movement in an adventure film like *Raiders of The Lost Ark* or *Indiana Jones and the Temple of Doom?*

440 And storms, waves splash toward the sky,
As dark as the air, as black as the rain
That the heavens weep. Our only help,
Again, lies with you. Grendel's mother
Is hidden in her terrible home, in a place
445 You've not seen. Seek it, if you dare! Save us,
Once more, and again twisted gold,
Heaped-up ancient treasure, will reward you
For the battle you win!''

The Battle with Grendel's Mother

Beowulf resolves to kill the "lady monster." Arriving at the lake under which she lives, Beowulf and his companions see serpents in the water and sea beasts on the rocks. The young hero kills one of the beasts with an arrow and then prepares to fight with Grendel's mother.

Then Edgetho's brave son[1] spoke:

"Remember,
450 Hrothgar, Oh knowing king, now
When my danger is near, the warm words we uttered,
And if your enemy should end my life
Then be, oh generous prince, forever
The father and protector of all whom I leave
455 Behind me, here in your hands, my belovèd
Comrades left with no leader, their leader
Dead. And the precious gifts you gave me,
My friend, send them to Higlac. May he see
In their golden brightness, the Geats' great lord
460 Gazing at your treasure, that here in Denmark
I found a noble protector, a giver
Of rings whose rewards I won and briefly
Relished. And you, Unferth,[2] let
My famous old sword stay in your hands:
465 I shall shape glory with Hrunting, or death
Will hurry me from this earth!''

As his words ended
He leaped into the lake, would not wait for anyone's
Answer; the heaving water covered him
3 Over. For hours he sank through the waves;
470 At last he saw the mud of the bottom.
And all at once the greedy she-wolf
Who'd ruled those waters for half a hundred
4 Years discovered him, saw that a creature
From above had come to explore the bottom
475 Of her wet world. She welcomed him in her claws,
Clutched at him savagely but could not harm him,

1. Edgetho's brave son: Beowolf. Elsewhere he is identified by such phrases as "the Geats' proud prince" and "the Geats' brave prince." These different designations add variety and interest to the poem.

2. Unferth: A Danish warrior who had questioned Beowolf's bravery before the battle with Grendel.

40   *The Anglo-Saxon Period*

Tried to work her fingers through the tight
Ring-woven mail on his breast, but tore
And scratched in vain. Then she carried him, armor
480 And sword and all, to her home; he struggled
To free his weapon, and failed. The fight
Brought other monsters swimming to see
Her catch, a host of sea beasts who beat at
His mail shirt, stabbing with tusks and teeth
485 As they followed along. Then he realized, suddenly,
That she'd brought him into someone's battle-hall,
And there the water's heat could not hurt him,
Nor anything in the lake attack him through
The building's high-arching roof. A brilliant
490 Light burned all around him, the lake
Itself like a fiery flame.

      Then he saw
The mighty water witch and swung his sword,
His ring-marked blade, straight at her head;
The iron sang its fierce song,
495 Sang Beowulf's strength. But her guest
Discovered that no sword could slice her evil
Skin, that Hrunting could not hurt her, was useless
Now when he needed it. They wrestled, she ripped
And tore and clawed at him, bit holes in his helmet,
500 And that too failed him; for the first time in years
Of being worn to war it would earn no glory;
It was the last time anyone would wear it. But
 Beowulf
Longed only for fame, leaped back
Into battle. He tossed his sword aside,
505 Angry; the steel-edged blade lay where
He'd dropped it. If weapons were useless he'd use
His hands, the strength in his fingers. So fame
Comes to the men who mean to win it
And care about nothing else! He raised
510 His arms and seized her by the shoulder; anger
Doubled his strength, he threw her to the floor.
She fell, Grendel's fierce mother, and the Geats'
Proud prince was ready to leap on her. But she rose
At once and repaid him with her clutching claws,
515 Wildly tearing at him. He was weary, that best
And strongest of soldiers; his feet stumbled
And in an instant she had him down, held helpless.
Squatting with her weight on his stomach, she drew
A dagger, brown with dried blood, and prepared
520 To avenge her only son. But he was stretched
On his back, and her stabbing blade was blunted
By the woven mail shirt he wore on his chest.

SLAYING OF A BULL ON THE BASE OF A CAULDRON (CELTIC ARTIFACT, 100 B.C.)
National Museum, Copenhagen
Werner Forman Archive

from *Beowulf* 41

Humanities Note

Fine art, *Slaying of a Bull on the Base of a Cauldron* (Celtic artifact, 100 B.C.). The earliest traces of the Celts, a related group of peoples, can be found in southwestern Germany and eastern France around 2000 B.C. Celtic warriors rode horses and fought with iron weapons. They spread their iron age culture over most of Europe, including Great Britain.

An identifiably Celtic style of art originated in southern Germany and eastern France during the fifth century B.C. It was characterized by fantastic, stylized plant and animal forms. Such forms were used to decorate household utensils, weapons, and body ornaments. In the first century B.C. a style characterized by asymmetrical lines came into favor.

You may want to use the following questions to discuss the art.

1. Can you identify the figures in this scene? Explain.
2. This scene appears on a utensil that was possibly used to boil food. Compare it to the scenes or designs that we use today to decorate household utensils.

6 Discussion Have students look closely at the words in this passage and list those words that they suspect have an Old English, rather than a Latin, origin. Then have them check their assumptions against the etymologies in a dictionary.

7 Discussion Ask students if it is credible that the Danes would assume that Beowulf has died, while the Geats stay on, hoping against hope. Why or why not? Point out that this detail (concerning those who leave and those who stay) appears in other Scandinavian legends of this type.

Humanities Note

Fine art, *Celtic Figure from the Side of a Bowl from a Burial Mound* (Norway, 9th century). Although this bowl was found in Norway, figures with similar large features can be found on Irish artifacts. Also, the odd square design in the center of the figure can be found on the great stone crosses still extant in Ireland. Apparently a receptacle for shield bosses (decorative knoblike forms), this Irish bowl was probably carried by a ship that was burned by pirates or raiders off the coast of Norway.

You might want to use the following questions to discuss the art.

1. Does this figure seem mysterious to you? Why or why not?
2. (a) Why do you think stone and metalwork has been our major source of information about ancient Celtic culture? (b) What kinds of art from other cultures have lasted this long?

The hammered links held; the point
Could not touch him. He'd have traveled to the bottom
  of the earth,
525 Edgetho's son, and died there, if that shining
Woven metal had not helped—and Holy
God, who sent him victory, gave judgment
For truth and right, Ruler of the Heavens,
Once Beowulf was back on his feet and fighting.

530   Then he saw, hanging on the wall, a heavy
Sword, hammered by giants, strong
And blessed with their magic, the best of all weapons
But so massive that no ordinary man could lift
Its carved and decorated length. He drew it
535 From its scabbard, broke the chain on its hilt,
And then, savage, now, angry
And desperate, lifted it high over his head
And struck with all the strength he had left,
Caught her in the neck and cut it through,
540 Broke bones and all. Her body fell
To the floor, lifeless, the sword was wet
With her blood, and Beowulf rejoiced at the sight.
  The brilliant light shone, suddenly,
As though burning in that hall, and as bright as
  Heaven's
545 Own candle, lit in the sky. He looked
At her home, then following along the wall
Went walking, his hands tight on the sword,
His heart still angry. He was hunting another
Dead monster, and took his weapon with him
550 For final revenge against Grendel's vicious
Attacks, his nighttime raids, over
And over, coming to Herot when Hrothgar's
Men slept, killing them in their beds,
Eating some on the spot, fifteen
555 Or more, and running to his loathsome moor
With another such sickening meal waiting
In his pouch. But Beowulf repaid him for those visits,
Found him lying dead in his corner,
Armless, exactly as that fierce fighter
560 Had sent him out from Herot, then struck off
His head with a single swift blow. The body
Jerked for the last time, then lay still.
  The wise old warriors who surrounded Hrothgar,
Like him staring into the monsters' lake,
565 Saw the waves surging and blood
Spurting through. They spoke about Beowulf,
All the graybeards, whispered together

CELTIC FIGURE FROM THE SIDE OF A BOWL FROM A BURIAL MOUND (NORWAY, 9TH CENTURY)
Werner Forman Archive

42   *The Anglo-Saxon Period*

Grammar in Action

Action Verbs Writers use strong action verbs—which express or describe movement, effort, or action—to make their work more vivid to the reader. By paying attention to these words and using the action verbs that are strongest, a writer can make his or her work more effective. Often, in English, this may involve a word of Old English origin rather than a word of Latin origin. Compare the following two passages. One uses bland action verbs to describe Beowulf's battle with Grendel's mother, while the other (taken from this translation) uses more vivid action verbs.

BLAND ACTION VERBS: He *removed* the sword from its scabbard, *detached* the chain on its hilt, and then *elevated* it high over his head and *impacted* it with all the strength he had left."

VIVID ACTION VERBS: "He *drew* [the sword] /From its scabbard, *broke* the chain on its hilt,/ And then . . . / . . . *lifted* it high over his head/ And struck with all the strength he had left." (lines 534–538)

And said that hope was gone, that the hero
Had lost fame and his life at once, and would never
570 Return to the living, come back as triumphant
As he had left; almost all agreed that Grendel's
Mighty mother, the she-wolf, had killed him.
The sun slid over past noon, went further
Down. The Danes gave up, left
575 The lake and went home, Hrothgar with them.
The Geats stayed, sat sadly, watching,
Imagining they saw their lord but not believing
They would ever see him again.
                           —Then the sword
Melted, blood-soaked, dripping down
580 Like water, disappearing like ice when the world's
Eternal Lord loosens invisible
Fetters and unwinds icicles and frost
As only He can, He who rules
Time and seasons, He who is truly
585 God. The monsters' hall was full of
Rich treasures, but all that Beowulf took
Was Grendel's head and the hilt of the giants'
Jeweled sword; the rest of that ring-marked
Blade had dissolved in Grendel's steaming
590 Blood, boiling even after his death.
And then the battle's only survivor
Swam up and away from those silent corpses;
The water was calm and clean, the whole
Huge lake peaceful once the demons who'd lived in it
595 Were dead.
        Then that noble protector of all seamen
Swam to land, rejoicing in the heavy
Burdens he was bringing with him. He
And all his glorious band of Geats
Thanked God that their leader had come back
    unharmed;
600 They left the lake together. The Geats
Carried Beowulf's helmet, and his mail shirt.
Behind them the water slowly thickened
As the monsters' blood came seeping up.
They walked quickly, happily, across
605 Roads all of them remembered, left
The lake and the cliffs alongside it, brave men
Staggering under the weight of Grendel's skull,
Too heavy for fewer than four of them to handle—
Two on each side of the spear jammed through it—
610 Yet proud of their ugly load and determined
That the Danes, seated in Herot, should see it.
Soon, fourteen Geats arrived

DETAIL OF A DRAGON-HEAD ON THE
MAMMEN HORSE COLLAR (VIKING
ARTIFACT, 10TH CENTURY)
National Museum, Denmark
Werner Forman Archive

from *Beowulf* 43

Student Activity 1. Find additional passages in the poem where the translator uses powerful action verbs to tell the story. Explain how these verbs contribute to the effectiveness of the passages in which they appear.

Student Activity 2. Write a brief description of an activity that requires great effort. Use powerful action verbs to communicate the struggle or excitement of the activity you are describing.

8 **Literary Focus** Have students analyze this remarkable simile and explain how, in a few lines, it is a perfect example of the pagan/Christian blend in the poem.

9 **Discussion** Ask students if they sense an air of defiance in the way the Geats carry Grendel's head back to the Danes. Could this defiance be related to the way the Danes so quickly lost hope at the lake's edge? Why or why not?

Humanities Note

Fine art, *Detail of a Dragon-Head on the Mammen Horse Collar* (Viking artifact, 10th century). This gold dragon head comes from a tenth century horse collar found at the Viking stronghold of Jutland. The Vikings were pagan, Scandanavian warriors who terrified Europe and the British Isles with their coastal raids from the 9th to the 11th centuries A.D. (the Viking Age). During this period, they were probably the best shipbuilders and sailors in the world. A typical Viking warship was powered by thirty oarsmen and carried a crew of about 90 men. It was brightly painted with striped, square sails and had rows of painted shields on both sides. (See the Ostenberg ship on page 49.)

The head reveals the Viking fascination with mythical beasts and intricate designs. Viking artisans could rival any in Europe in the making of decorative carvings like this one, or in the production of swords and armor. The secrets of their trade were handed down from father to son.

You might want to use the following questions to discuss the art.
1. How does this figure suggest the skill of Viking artisans?
2. Why do you think mythical creatures like this dragon fascinated the Vikings?

43

At the hall, bold and warlike, and with Beowulf,
Their lord and leader, they walked on the mead-hall
615 Green. Then the Geats' brave prince entered
Herot, covered with glory for the daring
Battles he had fought; he sought Hrothgar
To salute him and show Grendel's head.
He carried that terrible trophy by the hair,
620 Brought it straight to where the Danes sat,
Drinking, the queen among them. It was a weird
And wonderful sight, and the warriors stared.

The Last Battle

After being honored by Hrothgar, Beowulf and his fellow Geats return home. He is welcomed by the king, his uncle Higlac, and later becomes king himself when Higlac and his son have died. Beowulf rules Geatland for fifty years. Then a dragon menaces his kingdom. Although he is an old man, Beowulf determines to slay the beast. Before going into battle, he tells the men who have accompanied him about the history of the royal house and his exploits in its service.

And Beowulf uttered his final boast:
"I've never known fear, as a youth I fought
625 In endless battles. I am old, now,
But I will fight again, seek fame still,
If the dragon hiding in his tower dares
To face me."
Then he said farewell to his followers,
Each in his turn, for the last time:
630 "I'd use no sword, no weapon, if this beast
Could be killed without it, crushed to death
Like Grendel, gripped in my hands and torn

**GILT-BRONZE WINGED DRAGON
(SWEDISH ARTIFACT, 8TH CENTURY)**
*Statens Historiska Museet,
Stockholm*
Werner Forman Archive

Limb from limb. But his breath will be burning
Hot, poison will pour from his tongue.
635 I feel no shame, with shield and sword
And armor, against this monster: when he comes to
    me
I mean to stand, not run from his shooting
Flames, stand till fate decides
Which of us wins. My heart is firm,
640 My hands calm: I need no hot
Words. Wait for me close by, my friends.
We shall see, soon, who will survive
This bloody battle, stand when the fighting
Is done. No one else could do
645 What I mean to, here, no man but me
Could hope to defeat this monster. No one
Could try. And this dragon's treasure, his gold
And everything hidden in that tower, will be mine
Or war will sweep me to a bitter death!"
650   Then Beowulf rose, still brave, still strong,
And with his shield at his side, and a mail shirt on
    his breast,
Strode calmly, confidently, toward the tower, under
The rocky cliffs: no coward could have walked there!
And then he who'd endured dozens of desperate
655 Battles, who'd stood boldly while swords and shields
Clashed, the best of kings, saw
Huge stone arches and felt the heat
Of the dragon's breath, flooding down
Through the hidden entrance, too hot for anyone
660 To stand, a streaming current of fire
And smoke that blocked all passage. And the Geats'
Lord and leader, angry, lowered
His sword and roared out a battle cry,
A call so loud and clear that it reached through
665 The hoary rock, hung in the dragon's
Ear. The beast rose, angry,
Knowing a man had come—and then nothing
But war could have followed. Its breath came first.
A steaming cloud pouring from the stone,
670 Then the earth itself shook. Beowulf
Swung his shield into place, held it
In front of him, facing the entrance. The dragon
Coiled and uncoiled, its heart urging it
Into battle. Beowulf's ancient sword
675 Was waiting, unsheathed, his sharp and gleaming
Blade. The beast came closer; both of them
Were ready, each set on slaughter. The Geats'
Great prince stood firm, unmoving, prepared

from *Beowulf*   45

11 **Discussion** Ask students what these lines suggest about Beowulf's motivation for wanting to fight the dragon. In this last scene, when Beowulf is an old man, critics argue that he has grown in stature as a hero. Does this passage bear this argument out? Why or why not?

12 **Reading Strategy** Ask students to stop reading after this passage, summarize the dragon fight thus far, and predict how it will turn out.

13 **Discussion** Point out to students that this is the turning point of the whole poem. Ask students to say what is new here that has never been evident in Beowulf's character before. How does the writer evoke sympathy for Beowulf?

14 **Discussion** Ask students to discuss why the simplicity of this passage moves the poem beyond pathos, or mere sorrow, to something like a tragic level, in which the outcome is both mourned and accepted as part of the scheme of things. Explain what is meant when the poem says that Beowulf "stared at death." What emotions does this sentence convey?

15 **Discussion** How does the desertion of Beowulf's warriors heighten the tragic quality of the scene? If you were Wiglaf, would you be "miserable"? Explain.

Behind his high shield, waiting in his shining
680 Armor. The monster came quickly toward him,
Pouring out fire and smoke, hurrying
To its fate. Flames beat at the iron
Shield, and for a time it held, protected
Beowulf as he'd planned; then it began to melt,
685 And for the first time in his life that famous prince
Fought with fate against him, with glory
Denied him. He knew it, but he raised his sword
And struck at the dragon's scaly hide.
The ancient blade broke, bit into
690 The monster's skin, drew blood, but cracked
And failed him before it went deep enough, helped
  him
Less than he needed. The dragon leaped
With pain, thrashed and beat at him, spouting
Murderous flames, spreading them everywhere.
695 And the Geats' ring-giver did not boast of glorious
Victories in other wars: his weapon
Had failed him, deserted him, now when he needed it
Most, that excellent sword. Edgetho's
Famous son stared at death,
700 Unwilling to leave this world, to exchange it
For a dwelling in some distant place—a journey
Into darkness that all men must make, as death
Ends their few brief hours on earth.
  Quickly, the dragon came at him, encouraged
705 As Beowulf fell back; its breath flared,
And he suffered, wrapped around in swirling
Flames—a king, before, but now
A beaten warrior. None of his comrades
Came to him, helped him, his brave and noble
710 Followers; they ran for their lives, fled
Deep in a wood. And only one of them
Remained, stood there, miserable, remembering,
As a good man must, what kinship should mean.

  His name was Wiglaf, he was Wexstan's son
715 And a good soldier; his family had been Swedish,
Once. Watching Beowulf, he could see
How his king was suffering, burning. Remembering
Everything his lord and cousin had given him,
Armor and gold and the great estates
720 Wexstan's family enjoyed, Wiglaf's
Mind was made up; he raised his yellow
Shield and drew his sword—an ancient
Weapon that had once belonged to Onela's
Nephew, and that Wexstan had won, killing

Commentary: The Popularity of Beowulf in the Eighth Century

Although Beowulf was probably first written down about 1000 A.D., it had been created long before. One incident—a raid on the southern Rhine—can be definitely dated and supported by evidence outside the poem as occurring about A.D. 520. But the poem, much as we know it, was probably composed around A.D. 700 during the Northumbrian Golden Age, also called the age of the Venerable Bede. This must have occurred before Viking raids, beginning in A.D. 787, destroyed Bede's society.

Why were pagan legends like Beowulf so popular with the Christian culture of Bede's Golden Age? Possibly this was because the legends were the *Roots* of their day, telling the Northumbrians who their ancestors were.

The scholar and monk Alcuin, who was taught by Bede and who created a system of universal education for Charlemagne, wrote a famous letter home in A.D. 797, criticizing the English bishop there for allowing Christian priests, while dining, to listen to poetry about the pagan king Ingeld—one of the characters in *Beowulf*. Instead, he argued, holy scripture should be read:

725 The prince when he fled from Sweden, sought safety
With Herdred, and found death.[3] And Wiglaf's father
Had carried the dead man's armor, and his sword,
To Onela, and the king had said nothing, only
Given him armor and sword and all,
730 Everything his rebel nephew had owned
And lost when he left this life. And Wexstan
Had kept those shining gifts, held them
For years, waiting for his son to use them,
Wear them as honorably and well as once
735 His father had done; then Wexstan died
And Wiglaf was his heir, inherited treasures
And weapons and land. He'd never worn
That armor, fought with that sword, until Beowulf
Called him to his side, led him into war.
740 But his soul did not melt, his sword was strong;
The dragon discovered his courage, and his weapon,
When the rush of battle brought them together.
    And Wiglaf, his heart heavy, uttered
The kind of words his comrades deserved:
745   "I remember how we sat in the mead-hall, drinking
And boasting of how brave we'd be when Beowulf
Needed us, he who gave us these swords
And armor: all of us swore to repay him,
When the time came, kindness for kindness
750 —With our lives, if he needed them. He allowed us to
    join him,
Chose us from all his great army, thinking
Our boasting words had some weight, believing
Our promises, trusting our swords. He took us
For soldiers, for men. He meant to kill
755 This monster himself, our mighty king,
Fight this battle alone and unaided,
As in the days when his strength and daring dazzled
Men's eyes. But those days are over and gone
And now our lord must lean on younger
760 Arms. And we must go to him, while angry
Flames burn at his flesh, help
Our glorious king! By almighty God,
I'd rather burn myself than see
Flames swirling around my lord.
765 And who are we to carry home
Our shields before we've slain his enemy
And ours, to run back to our homes with Beowulf
So hard-pressed here? I swear that nothing
He ever did deserved an end
770 Like this, dying miserably and alone,
Butchered by this savage beast: we swore

3. Onela's/Nephew . . . found death: When Onela seized the throne of Sweden, his two nephews sought shelter with the king of Geatland, Herdred. Wiglaf's father, Wexstan, killed the older nephew for Onela.

GILT-SILVER BROOCH FROM GOTLAND
(PRE-VIKING SCANDINAVIA)
*Statens Historiska Museet,
Stockholm*
Werner Forman Archive

from *Beowulf* 47

"What does Ingeld have to do with Christ?" he asked. Luckily for us, the legends continued to be popular for another two hundred years, allowing Beowulf to be written down at last so that we can still enjoy it today.

48

That these swords and armor were each for us all!''
Then he ran to his king, crying encouragement
As he dove through the dragon's deadly fumes.

The Spoils

Together, Wiglaf and Beowulf kill the dragon, but the old king is mortally wounded. As a last request, Beowulf asks Wiglaf to bring him the treasure that the dragon was guarding.

775   Then Wexstan's son went in, as quickly
As he could, did as the dying Beowulf
Asked, entered the inner darkness
Of the tower, went with his mail shirt and his sword.
Flushed with victory he groped his way,
780 A brave young warrior, and suddenly saw
Piles of gleaming gold, precious
Gems, scattered on the floor, cups
And bracelets, rusty old helmets, beautifully
Made but rotting with no hands to rub
785 And polish them. They lay where the dragon left
     them;
  It had flown in the darkness, once, before fighting
18 Its final battle. (So gold can easily
  Triumph, defeat the strongest of men,
  No matter how deep it is hidden!) And he saw,
790 Hanging high above, a golden
Banner, woven by the best of weavers
And beautiful. And over everything he saw
A strange light, shining everywhere,
On walls and floor and treasure. Nothing
795 Moved, no other monsters appeared;
He took what he wanted, all the treasures
That pleased his eye, heavy plates
And golden cups and the glorious banner,
Loaded his arms with all they could hold.
800 Beowulf's dagger, his iron blade,
Had finished the fire-spitting terror
That once protected tower and treasures
Alike; the gray-bearded lord of the Geats
Had ended those flying, burning raids
805 Forever.
     Then Wiglaf went back, anxious
To return while Beowulf was alive, to bring him
19 Treasure they'd won together. He ran,
Hoping his wounded king, weak
And dying, had not left the world too soon.

SILVER PENDANT SHOWING THE HELMET OF THE VENDEL (EARLY VIKING PERIOD, 10TH CENTURY)
Statens Historiska Museet, Stockholm
Werner Forman Archive

THE OSTENBERG SHIP (VIKING ARTIFACT, C. A.D. 850)
Viking Ship Museum, Bygdoy, Oslo
Werner Forman Archive

810   Then he brought their treasure to Beowulf, and found
       His famous king bloody, gasping
       For breath. But Wiglaf sprinkled water
       Over his lord, until the words
       Deep in his breast broke through and were heard.
815   Beholding the treasure he spoke, haltingly:
         "For this, this gold, these jewels, I thank
       Our Father in Heaven, Ruler of the Earth—
       For all of this, that His grace has given me,
       Allowed me to bring to my people while breath
820   Still came to my lips. I sold my life
       For this treasure, and I sold it well. Take
       What I leave, Wiglaf, lead my people,
       Help them; my time is gone. Have
       The brave Geats build me a tomb,
825   When the funeral flames have burned me, and build
         it
       Here, at the water's edge, high
       On this spit of land, so sailors can see
       This tower, and remember my name, and call it
       Beowulf's tower, and boats in the darkness

20

from *Beowulf*   49

21

Discussion Point out to students that before the funeral, a clear prophecy in the poem suggests that the Geats as a nation will shortly perish utterly from the earth—a prediction that, historically, proved to be true. Ask students how, in the light of this fact, the funeral also enacts a mourning, not only for Beowulf, but for a whole people.

Master Teacher Note Explain to students that mythographers such as Joseph Campbell (in his book *The Hero with a Thousand Faces*) point out that heroes in myths are usually described in terms of life's peak moments. For example, young Beowulf's initiation into manhood is dramatized (the killing of Grendel and Grendel's mother), as well as his death (the dragon fight). But nothing of his fifty-year reign as king is shown in the poem.

Cooperative Learning How nations mourn and honor their fallen heroes is a subject that might interest your students. Divide your class into groups of three or four. Have each group select a president who died in office. Then have them research the way the nation mourned the president they chose.

Reader's Response Put yourself in the place of Wiglaf. How would you have reacted when Beowulf was wounded by the dragon?

Closure and Extension

ANSWERS TO THINKING ABOUT THE SELECTION

1. After making a parting speech to Hrothgar, Beowulf plunges into the water. Grendel's mother tries but fails to pierce him with her claws, then carries him to her cavern at the bottom of the lake. Beowulf's armor defends him from her and other monsters there. Just as his sword fails him, she starts bit-

830 And mist, crossing the sea, will know it.''
 Then that brave king gave the golden
Necklace from around his throat to Wiglaf,
Gave him his gold-covered helmet, and his rings,
And his mail shirt, and ordered him to use them well:
835 "You're the last of all our far-flung family.
Fate has swept our race away,
Taken warriors in their strength and led them
To the death that was waiting. And now I follow
 them.''
 The old man's mouth was silent, spoke
840 No more, had said as much as it could;
He would sleep in the fire, soon. His soul
Left his flesh, flew to glory.

The Farewell

Wiglaf denounces the soldiers who deserted Beowulf in his combat with the dragon. The Geats burn their king's body on a great funeral pyre and bitterly lament his death.

 Then the Geats built the tower, as Beowulf
Had asked, strong and tall, so sailors
845 Could find it from far and wide; working
For ten long days they made his monument,
Sealed his ashes in walls as straight
And high as wise and willing hands
Could raise them. And the riches he and Wiglaf
850 Had won from the dragon, rings, necklaces,
Ancient, hammered armor—all
The treasures they'd taken were left there, too,
Silver and jewels buried in the sandy
Ground, back in the earth, again
855 And forever hidden and useless to men.
And then twelve of the bravest Geats
Rode their horses around the tower,
Telling their sorrow, telling stories
Of their dead king and his greatness, his glory,
860 Praising him for heroic deeds, for a life
As noble as his name. So should all men
Raise up words for their lords, warm
With love, when their shield and protector leaves
His body behind, sends his soul
865 On high. And so Beowulf's followers
Rode, mourning their beloved leader,
Crying that no better king had ever
Lived, no prince so mild, no man
So open to his people, so deserving of praise.

ing holes in his helmet. Beowulf tries crushing her with his hands, but she overcomes him, and squatting on him, strikes at him with a dagger—against which his armor still holds. Then he sees an ancient giant sword hanging in the hall, seizes it, and beheads her.

2. Beowulf takes sword and shield and challenges the dragon who charges, breathing fire and smoke. Beowulf's shield begins to melt and although the sword with which he strikes draws the drag-

on's blood, it breaks in two. Then the dragon thrashes him, wraps him in fire, and mortally wounds him.

3. Answers will differ. Students may respond that the lure of the gold attracted men to this place, where the dragon killed them. The gold may symbolize avarice.

4. (a) Answers will differ. Possible answers include the description of the monster's lair, lines 425–443; the cavern under the lake, lines 485–491; the dragon's treasure,

lines 775–805; and the funeral pyre, lines 843–869. (b) In all cases, it is the concrete and specific details that make the description effective.

5. (a) The battle with Grendel is essentially similar to the one with his mother; while both creatures are monsters, they have feelings and some other human attributes as well. By contrast, the enraged dragon is wholly monstrous and animal—and nothing personal is exchanged between the adver-

THINKING ABOUT THE SELECTION
Recalling

1. Briefly summarize the battle between Beowulf and Grendel's mother.
2. Describe what occurs when Beowulf attempts to fight the dragon alone.
3. The poet writes, "So gold can easily/Triumph, defeat the strongest of men,/No matter how deep it is hidden." Explain the symbolic significance of the dragon's treasure.

Interpreting

4. Critics have praised the *Beowulf* poet's skill in describing various settings. (a) Find a passage in which the poet displays this skill. (b) Explain what makes the description so effective.
5. (a) Compare and contrast the three battles described in these excerpts. (b) How are all three battles different versions of the poem's main conflict?
6. (a) Identify the figure of speech that the poet uses in lines 576–583. (b) Explain how the figure of speech adds to the meaning of the poem.

Applying

7. Many critics claim that *Beowulf* contains themes that are relevant to modern life. Do you agree or disagree? Why?

ANALYZING LITERATURE
Tracing Pagan and Christian Elements

In *Beowulf*, we can see evidence of the Anglo-Saxon warrior culture, with its stress on heroism, and Christianity's emphasis on brotherly love and God's care for creation. For example, in the combat with the dragon, Beowulf seeks "fame" like any self-respecting warrior. As he is dying, however, he thanks "Our Father in Heaven" for the opportunity to give his people the treasure.

1. Reread the tribute to Beowulf in the last eight lines of the poem. Identify pagan and Christian influences in the qualities for which the king is praised. Give reasons for your conclusions.
2. A prominent Germanic pagan belief is that fame is the only thing that will survive a human being's death. (a) What evidence do you find in this poem of the importance placed on public esteem or reputation? (b) What value do you feel contemporary society places on fame?
3. The poem contains many references to the blind and mysterious power of *Wyrd*, or Fate, as in line 834. Do such references suggest pagan or Christian influence? Explain.

UNDERSTANDING LANGUAGE
Identifying Old English Words

Old English is the bedrock on which our language is established. Words like *sword, blood, cup,* and *flesh*—all derived from Old English and all appearing in this translation —give our language a down-to-earth, nitty-gritty quality. They contrast sharply with fancy, Latin-derived words like *perception* and *speculation*.

Scan this excerpt from *Beowulf* and find five more words that you think are Anglo-Saxon in origin. Then look up these words in a dictionary to see whether you were correct.

THINKING AND WRITING
Responding to Criticism

Burton Raffel, who made this translation, remarked that, "of all the many-sided excellences of *Beowulf*," one of the most satisfying "is the poet's insight into people." Respond to this observation, expressing your agreement or disagreement. First gather evidence. Identify instances where the poet does or does not show insight into human nature. Then write a thesis statement setting forth your point of view. Back up this statement with references to specific passages in the poem. As you revise your essay, see whether you can find other passages that support your thesis. Remember that descriptions of action can reveal character as effectively as direct statements.

from Beowulf 51

in the way the mourners raise up words of deserved praise for their lord. The Christian element can be seen in Beowulf's soul being sent on high—and in the praise he is given for being mild and open to his people.

2. (a) Many passages emphasizing the importance of fame or heroic glory include references to fame in the fight with Grendel's mother (lines 503 and 507), the gray-beards fearing Beowulf has lost fame (line 569), and Beowulf's entering the meadhall in glory (lines 616–617). (b) Possible responses include the idea that even fame itself is temporary now, as suggested by Andy Warhol's remark that soon every person would become famous for fifteen minutes.
3. The belief in the power of *Wyrd* was a powerful concept in the pre-Christian Nordic religion that underlies Beowulf. Christianity on the whole has rejected the idea of fate as having power over the individual's free will.

ANSWERS TO UNDERSTANDING LANGUAGE

Remind students that the Beowulf excerpt is a translation from the Old English, so their choices of words will not necessarily reflect these words in the original. Still, answers might well include any strong monosyllabic words such as cliffs, rocks, spray, brown, blade, and lake.

THINKING AND WRITING

Publishing Collect the responses in a looseleaf binder that is available for reading by all students.

Challenge Have students research Scandinavian (or Norse) mythology, such as the story telling how Odin, the chief god, attained wisdom and power by hanging himself on the world-tree of Yggdrasil for nine nights and days. Then have them discuss how such pagan myths might lend themselves to being translated into Christian terms.

saries. (b) All the battles involve fighting the forces of evil to end the human suffering they cause; but they are all involved, also, in the hero's quest for fame and glory by fearlessly risking his own life to benefit others.

6. (a) The figure of speech used in these lines is the simile, which is a comparison using the words "like" or "as": "like water" and "like ice" (line 580). (b) The sword melts in the creature's hot blood like ice melts in spring. After saying this,

the poet then connects the image to a Christian perspective by pointing out that both the sword's melting and the melting of ice in spring is something ordained by the "Eternal Lord" (line 581). Thus the passage anchors the powerful simile in the same Christian context that underlies the whole poem.

7. Answers will differ. Possible responses in agreement include the idea that each person is the hero of his or her own life and, like

Beowulf, must face obstacles very like Grendel and the dragon. Possible responses in disagreement include the idea that the legendary hero of long ago has no place in the modern world of the microchip; the effort now must be to increase worldwide cooperation, not to slay dragons.

ANSWERS TO ANALYZING LITERATURE

1. The pagan element can be seen

Motivation/Prior Knowledge
Tell students they will be reading about the art of translating. Ask whether they think a country's government should generously sponsor programs to have the work of its best writers translated for the benefit of other nationalities. Have them discuss the public relations advantages of such an effort and let them decide if a gesture like that would improve global understanding.

Teaching Different Ability Levels Tell your more advanced students that serious debates rage for years over the use of a single correct word in certain translations. Ask them to try to appreciate the task of a translator by deciding the single best alternate word in English for the noun "love." Have them list their synonyms in order of priority for the word. Then discuss and debate the differences of opinion that will exist.

COMPARING TRANSLATIONS

Beowulf

TRANSLATION: "A THANKLESS AND DESOLATE UNDERTAKING"

The twentieth century poet Ezra Pound once remarked that "all translation is a thankless, or at least most apt to be a thankless and desolate undertaking." Although translating *Beowulf* has proven to be an especially challenging task, an impressive number of scholars have tried their hands at it. Currently, well over half a dozen translations of *Beowulf* are in print, and a score of others are available in libraries. But judging from the problems these scholars encountered—and the criticism they received—Pound may well have had a point about the translator's task!

THE DISASTROUS FATE OF THE BEOWULF MANUSCRIPT

Most translators of *Beowulf* start with the *Beowulf* manuscript. This manuscript, however, is far from perfect. It represents the work of two tenth-century scribes copying from an older manuscript. However the text is in prose, not verse. It contains spotty punctuation and vowel markings, apparently resulting from the uncertainty of the unlearned scribes. In addition, the manuscript is damaged—a disastrous fire in 1731 scorched the manuscript, hastening its disintegration. It was sheer good fortune that Danish scholar Thorkelin made the first translation in 1787 before the manuscript crumbled further. Subsequent work showed that letters visible when Thorkelin worked have become illegible or even disappeared completely. Although steps were taken to preserve the manuscript from further harm, precious passages had already been lost forever.

THE PECULIAR PROBLEMS OF TRANSLATING BEOWULF

Aside from the dilemma of working with a damaged text, *Beowulf* presents special problems for the translator. Most notable is the metrical puzzle, for the form of Old English verse is very different from that of modern poetry. Most poetry composed after the Norman Conquest in 1066 depends on the regular pattern of stressed and unstressed syllables. Old English poetry, in contrast, is held together by four stresses and alliteration. If this dilemma is not enough to give pause to even the most determined translator, consider *Beowulf*'s content. How can a translator make the remote, unfamiliar past of a long gone civilization come alive for today's readers?

THE KENNEDY VERSUS RAFFEL TRANSLATIONS

Of all the translations now available, scholars generally agree that Charles Kennedy and Burton Raffel have produced the most useful works. That's about all they agree on, however, for each translator has his staunch defenders—and detractors.

Kennedy called his 1940 poetic translation an example of "authentic modern verse." However, he has been criticized for using such artificial expressions as "Lo! I ween" and "smote him sore." But critics

...· peꞃoð peꞃþ ðe heal ðaꞃ

V·

Sꞇꞃæꞇ paꞃ ꞅꞇan ꝼah ꞅꞇꞃꞃ ꞃꞃꞅoðe ꝣumꞙꞙ
ꞥæ ꝣæðꞡꞃe ꝣuð byꞃꞃe ꝼcan heapð
honð locen hꞃꞃꝺ men ꞅcꞃp ꞅonꝣ mꞅæꞃ
ꝥum ꝥa he coꞅele ꝼuꝺum ꞙ hyꞃa ꝣꞃy
ꞃe ꝣeꞁꞇ ꝥum ꝣanꝣan epo mon ꞅeꞇꞃon
ꞅæme þe ꞅꞃðe ꞅcylðaꞅ ꞃonðaꞅ ꞃeꝣn heapð
ꝥꞃð ꝥæꞅ ꞃeceðeꞅ ꝥeꞃl· buꝣon ꝥaꞃo benꞇe
byꞃnan hꞃꞃꝣ ðon ꝣuð ꞅæꞃo ꝣumena
ꝣaꞃaꞅ ꞅꞇoðon ꞅæ man na ꞅæꞃo ꞅamoð
æꞇ ꝣæðꞡꞃe aꞅc holꞇ uꝼan ꝣꞃæꝣ · ꞃ eꞅꞇ
ꞙ en þꞃeꞁꞇ paꞃnum ꝣe ꝥuꞃ það þaꝺꞁꞃ
pl one hæleð oꞃeꞃ meꞃꝣaꞅ æꝼꞇeꞃ hæle
þum ꝼꞃæꝣn· hꞃꞁꞃnon ꝼeꞃꞃꝣeað ꝣe ꝼaꞇ
ꞇe ꞅcylðaꞅ ꞅꞃæꝣe ꞅyꝥ can ꝺꞅꝥum helmaꞅ
heꞃe ꞅcæꞃꞃꞁ heꞁꞃ ꞙc eom hꞃoð ꝣaꞃꝩeꞅ·
aꞃ ꝺom bꞙꞇ· ne ꞅeꞁh ꞙc elꝥæðꞃꝣe þuꞅ
manꞙꝣe men moðꞙꞡlꞃcꞃan· peꞃꞙc ꝥ ꝣeꞃoꞃ
plen co nallæꞅ ꝼoꞃ ꝥꞃæꞁꞇ ꞅðum· eꞁc ꝼoꞃ huꝣe

Manuscript page from BEOWULF
The British Museum

have condemned the modern idiom Raffel used in his 1963 version as "too physical," and panned the entire work for creating "a new art rather than making available the old."

THE CASE OF THE FIRST THREE LINES

Openings set the stage for what's to follow. Which of the following two openings do you think best captures the excitement and grandeur of *Beowulf*?

Kennedy's translation

Lo! we have listened to many a lay
Of the Spear-Danes' fame, their splendor of
    old,
Their mighty princes, and martial deeds!

Raffel's translation

HEAR ME! We've heard of Danish heroes,
Ancient kings and the glory they cut
For themselves, swinging might swords!

What difference in tone do you detect between Kennedy's literal translation of the Old English "lā" into "lo" and Raffel's use of the more modern phrase "Hear me"? Is Kennedy's translation more dignified? Is Raffel's more assertive? Why might Kennedy have used the alliterative *l (lo, listened,* and *lay)* but Raffel the *h (hear, heard, heroes)* in the same first line? Why do you think Kennedy translated the original as "splendor of old" but Raffel used "glory they cut"? Notice how Raffel used *enjambment,* running the second line into the third, to set a swing to the passage, while Kennedy used a list to create a feeling of nobility and stateliness.

That two scholars can produce such different versions of only three lines shows the challenges and excitement of translation!

Enrichment Ask students to return to lines 861 through 869 of *Beowulf* on page 50. Have them read the lines again carefully and then compose paraphrases of that passage. After they have completed their "translation," have them explain why they left out some words or ideas and inserted others. Be sure to provide a chance for volunteers to read their work aloud.

CROSS CURRENTS

Beowulf and John Gardner's *Grendel*

Let's face it—against heroic Beowulf, evil Grendel just didn't stand a chance. And if Beowulf didn't kill the monster, the bad press surely would have! This situation changed recently, however, when contemporary novelist John Gardner decided to tell the monster's side of the story in his novel *Grendel*. And what a story it is! *Newsweek* called Gardner's *Grendel* "a marvelous novel, absolutely marvelous: witty, intelligent, delightful."

BEOWULF BECOMES GRENDEL?

How much of the Anglo-Saxon tale of *Beowulf* did Gardner use in his novel? Is *Grendel* simply the Beowulf legend retold from the monster's point of view? Let's start with the form of each. *Beowulf* can be divided into four parts: the episode with Grendel, the battle with Grendel's mother, the return voyage, and the dragon fight. Each part ends before the next begins, and Beowulf rules successfully for fifty years between the dragon fight and his victory over Grendel and his mother. The order of events in *Grendel* is very different, however. The novel begins with the monster attacking Hrothgar's meadhall and men, and ends right after the fight with Beowulf, as Grendel is about to die. This particular section is only about a quarter of the Anglo-Saxon poem. There is also a difference in characters. Although both Grendel's mother and the dragon appear in *Grendel*, Gardner gives each new roles.

A MONSTER WITH A NAPKIN TUCKED UNDER HIS CHIN

The main difference between the Anglo-Saxon poem and the modern "retelling,"

however, lies in the development of Grendel as a character. In *Beowulf*, the monster is static, his actions predictable. In *Grendel*, the monster is dynamic, his awareness growing as the action unfolds. Compare Grendel's attack in this excerpt from Gardner's novel to lines 285–324 of the poem (pages 32–33).

"I am swollen with excitement, bloodlust and joy and a strange fear that mingle in my chest like the twisting rage of a bone-fire," Grendel begins. "I step onto the brightly shining floor and angrily advance onto them. They're all asleep, the whole company! I can hardly believe my luck and my wild heart laughs, but I let out no sound. Swiftly, softly, I will move from bed to bed and destroy them all, swallow every man. I am blazing, half-crazy with joy. For pure, mad prank, I snatch a cloth from the nearest table and tie it around my neck to make a napkin. I delay no longer. I seize up a sleeping man, tear at him hungrily, bite through his bone-locks and suck hot, slippery blood. He goes down in huge morsels, head, chest, hips, legs, even the hands and feet. My face and arms are wet, matted. The napkin is sopping. The dark floor steams. I move on at once and I reach for another one . . . and I seize a wrist. A shock goes through me. Mistake!"

A monster tying a napkin around his neck? This is not the Grendel we've encountered in *Beowulf*! Gardner's use of the first-person point of view helps him remake Grendel from the Anglo-Saxon incarnation of blind evil, unthinking and senseless, to a conscious, rational force.

BEOWULF TAUNTS GRENDEL

Gardner plays equally sly tricks with Beowulf. In place of the noble hero of Anglo-Saxon lore we get a man who is strangely mechanical, even mad. Beowulf taunts Grendel as he kills him, demanding songs that amount to the playground surrender of ''enough.'' See how Grendel describes it in this passage:

> And now something worse. He's whispering—spilling words like showers of sleet, his mouth three inches from my ear. I will not listen. I continue whispering. As long as I whisper to myself I need not hear. His syllables lick at me, chilly fire . . . I do not listen. I am sick at heart. I have been betrayed by talk like that. ''Mama!'' I bawl . . . And still he whispers.
> Grendel, Grendel! You make the world by whispers, second by second. Are you blind to that? Whether you make it a grave or a garden of roses is not the point. Feel the wall: is it not hard? He smashes me against it, breaks open my forehead. Hard, yes! . . . Now sing of walls! Sing!
> I howl.
> Sing!
> ''I'm singing!''
> Sing words! Sing raving hymns!
> ''You're crazy! Ow!''

GRENDEL (Frontispiece from BEOWULF)
Patten Wilson
The British Library

> Sing!
> ''I sing of walls,'' I howl. ''Hooray for the hardness of walls!''

AN EXTRAORDINARY ACHIEVEMENT

What *The New York Times* called John Gardner's ''extraordinary achievement'' is far more than *Beowulf* retold from Grendel's view. It's a funny, intriguing, and ultimately touching examination of the way we look at monsters, heroes, and the world we create with both.

Focus

Literary Focus Have students discuss their own experiences with films or stories about exile or separation. Many will recall some of the basic story about the Mayflower Pilgrims, for example. Because of religious persecution, they had left England and at first settled in the Netherlands, only to uproot themselves again to settle in the New World. You might ask students to discuss how the hope of creating a better life for themselves carried the Pilgrims through what could otherwise have been overwhelming difficulties.

Writing/Prior Knowledge Pair up students in your class. Before they begin freewriting, have them share ideas and tell each other what they know of people who must leave familiar surroundings to make a new home in a strange land.

ESL Teaching Strategy To help with the writing assignment, pair each ESL student with a native speaker. Have the native speaker coach the ESL student on ways to create visual images of an immigrant or refugee.

Vocabulary

Preteach the following vocabulary words:
compassionate (kəm pash′ ən it) *adj.:* Sympathizing, pitying (l. 2)
grievous (grēv′ əs) *adj.:* Causing grief; serious (l. 7)
winsomeness (win′ səm nis) *n.:* Charm (l. 30)
rapture (rap′ chər) *n.:* Expression of joy or pleasure (l. 46)
ramparts (ram′ pärts′) *n.:* An embankment of earth; any bulwark (p. 93)
redress (ri dres′) *n.:* Compensation, as for a wrong (l. 106)

The Wanderer

Literary Elements

The Theme of Exile. Exile means separation or banishment from one's native country, region, or home. The theme of exile recurs throughout world literature—the medieval Italian poet Dante wrote his *Divine Comedy* after being banished from his beloved city of Florence—but this theme is expressed with memorable sadness and pain in Anglo-Saxon poetry.

We cannot understand what exile meant to an Anglo-Saxon warrior until we understand what he meant by home. While we identify ourselves as citizens of a certain country, an Anglo-Saxon viewed himself as the follower of a particular lord or king. The notion of loyalty toward one's country, called patriotism today, did not exist. It was the lord himself who commanded allegiance, and of course there were many lords in what is now called England. The Anglo-Saxon word for "lord," *hlaford,* came from the word *hlaf-weard,* which means "guardian of the loaf." The lord was the dispenser of bread and the source of sustenance. He was also the dispenser of the booty won in raids and skirmishes, a "gold-lord." Perhaps even more important, he guaranteed the security of his followers in a dangerous and uncertain world. In return, he expected loyalty in war. His followers would form his great shield-wall in the thick of battle.

The most important symbol of home was the mead hall (mead was an alcoholic beverage made of fermented honey and water), where the lord and his followers shared the warmth of fire, the comfort of food and drink, and the pleasures of hearing poetry recited. The pleasures of poetry were especially welcome when the *scop* praised the heroism of the listening warriors. Since we tend to identify home with individual families living in a house or an apartment, it is useful to keep in mind the image of the mead hall while reading "The Wanderer." Enlivened with a feeling of masculine fellowship, the mead hall was smoky, noisy, smelly, and crowded. It was home.

Imagine what it meant for a warrior to lose his lord and his place in the mead hall. The Anglo-Saxon exile was indeed a *wraecca,* a word meaning "wretch, stranger, unhappy man, and wanderer."

Writing

Suppose that you were forced to leave your home for an indefinite period of time. List some of the things that you would miss the most. What effect would the loss of these things eventually have on you?

56   *The Anglo-Saxon Period*

Teaching to Ability Levels Have less advanced students interview family members or neighbors about experiences of leaving their homeland for a new country. Have advanced students find out about the historical context of "The Wanderer" by researching the Scandinavian migrations that began in the fifth century.

Objectives

1 To understand the outlook of someone who has been exiled from his or her home
2 To understand exile
3 To appreciate a poem's structure
4 To respond to criticism

Support Material

Teaching Portfolio
Teacher Backup, p. 37
Usage and Mechanics Worksheet, p. 41
Vocabulary Check, p. 42
Critical Thinking and Reading Worksheet, *Understanding Structure,* p. 43
Language Worksheet, *Appreciating Vivid Adverbs,* p. 44
Selection Test, p. 45

The Wanderer

translated by Charles W. Kennedy

RECONSTRUCTED HELMET, SUTTON HOO
SHIP BURIAL (A.D. 7TH CENTURY)
The Granger Collection

Oft to the wanderer,   weary of exile,
Cometh God's pity,   compassionate love,
Though woefully toiling   on wintry seas
With churning oar   in the icy wave,
5   Homeless and helpless   he fled from fate.
Thus saith the wanderer   mindful of misery,
Grievous disasters,   and death of kin:
   "Oft when the day broke,   oft at the dawning,
Lonely and wretched   I wailed my woe.
10   No man is living,   no comrade left,
To whom I dare fully   unlock my heart.
I have learned truly   the mark of a man
Is keeping his counsel   and locking his lips,
Let him think what he will!   For, woe of heart
15   Withstandeth not fate;   a failing spirit
Earneth no help.   Men eager for honor
Bury their sorrow   deep in the breast.
   "So have I also,   often in wretchedness
Fettered[1] my feelings,   far from my kin,
20   Homeless and hapless,[2]   since days of old,
When the dark earth   covered my dear lord's face,
And I sailed away   with sorrowful heart,
Over wintry seas,   seeking a gold-lord,
If far or near   lived one to befriend me
25   With gift in the mead-hall   and comfort for grief.
   "Who bears it, knows   what a bitter companion,
Shoulder to shoulder,   sorrow can be,
When friends are no more.   His fortune is exile,
Not gifts of fine gold;   a heart that is frozen,
30   Earth's winsomeness[3] dead.   And he dreams of the hall-men,
The dealing of treasure,   the days of his youth,

---

1. Fettered (Fet' ərd): Chained, restrained.
2. hapless (hap' lis): Unlucky.
3. winsomeness (win' səm nəs): Pleasantness,
delightfulness.

Presentation

Motivation/Prior Knowledge
Tell students that they will be reading a poem about someone who today might be called a refugee or displaced person. Call upon their prior knowledge by asking them to discuss the situation of refugees they have read or heard about in the news—such as the Vietnamese boat people or Central American immigrants in the southwestern United States. Ask students to discuss how it must feel to leave a familiar world behind and seek a new life in a strange place. Suggest they keep this discussion in mind as they read.

Purpose-Setting   Question
What feelings does the wanderer express that any exile would feel?

Thematic Idea Robert Browning's "Home-Thoughts, from Abroad" expresses a longing for home similar to that expressed in "The Wanderer."

1 **Discussion** Ask students whether or not they agree with the idea expressed here, that men must bury their sorrow and not express it. To what extent is such stoic silence the mark of a warrior culture?

2 **Enrichment** Point out to students that this poem probably dates to the 700's or earlier, at a time when Scandinavia was in upheaval and many sailors fled ancestral homes there to settle finally in England. The poem, thus, might have reminded its northern English audience of the struggles their forbears met before reaching England. Ask students if they know of modern immigrants reciting poems or singing songs about their former homeland.

3 **Clarification** Tell students that these lines describe an actual ritual, usually performed annually, in which the follower (or vassal) pledged himself to his lord and was rewarded by a gift, usually made of gold.

4 **Literary Focus** Ask students to notice a persistent pattern in the poem. A happy image appears, as in a mirage of seafoam, only to be replaced by a contrasting image of the empty and desolate sea. Have students discuss how this pattern of contrasting images intensifies the theme of exile.

5 **Discussion** Point out to students that one structure in the poem is the interrupting of intensely concrete and dramatic scenes with direct advice and comment, as in this passage. Ask students if they think this passage is necessary to the poem. Why or why not? Does the wanderer in any way contradict his own advice?

Enrichment Tell students that Anglo-Saxon (or Old English) literature as a whole is the earliest, largest, and finest body of writing in all of post-Roman Europe. Just as *Beowulf* is the oldest and greatest of all early, post-classical epics, so "The Wanderer" is considered the most nearly perfect in form and feeling of all Old English lyrics. This is partly because of the intensity of its emotion and partly because it shows the fewest signs of accidental mutilation or of deliberate tamperings by later copyists.

When his lord bade welcome   to wassail[4] and feast.
But gone is that gladness,   and never again
Shall come the loved counsel   of comrade and king.

35   "Even in slumber   his sorrow assaileth,
And, dreaming he claspeth   his dear lord again,
Head on knee, hand on knee,   loyally laying,
Pledging his liege[5]   as in days long past.
Then from his slumber   he starts lonely-hearted,
40 Beholding gray stretches   of tossing sea,
Sea-birds bathing,   with wings outspread,
While hailstorms darken,   and driving snow.

Bitterer then   is the bane of his wretchedness,
The longing for loved one: his grief is renewed.
45 The forms of his kinsmen   take shape in the silence;
In rapture he greets them;   in gladness he scans
Old comrades remembered.   But they melt into air
With no word of greeting   to gladden his heart.

Then again surges   his sorrow upon him;
50 And grimly he spurs   his weary soul
Once more to the toil   of the tossing sea.
  "No wonder therefore,   in all the world,
If a shadow darkens   upon my spirit
When I reflect   on the fates of men—
55 How one by one   proud warriors vanish
From the halls that knew them,   and day by day
All this earth ages   and droops unto death.

No man may know wisdom   till many a winter
Has been his portion.   A wise man is patient,
60 Not swift to anger,   nor hasty of speech,
Neither too weak,   nor too reckless, in war,
Neither fearful nor fain,[6]   nor too wishful of wealth,
Nor too eager in vow—   ere he know the event.
A brave man must bide[7]   when he speaketh his boast
65 Until he know surely   the goal of his spirit.
  "A wise man will ponder   how dread is that doom
When all this world's wealth   shall be scattered and waste

---

4. wassail (wăs′ əl): A toast in drinking a person's health, or a celebration at which such toasts are made.
5. liege (lēj): Loyalty.
6. fain (fān): An archaic word meaning "eager"; in this context it means "too eager."
7. bide (bīd): Wait.

Commentary: Homilies in "The Wanderer"

Homiletic writing was very prevalent in the Anglo-Saxon period. A homily can be a single sermon on a Biblical text or a passage in any work that gives advice pertaining to morals and conduct. Some critics have argued that the homiletic passages in "The Wanderer"—those giving direct statements of advice, expressed in generalities—must be later additions to a poem that is otherwise remarkably terse, lyrical, intense, concrete, and dramatic. Other critics reply that the homilies are perfectly in character, even when they contradict attitudes expressed in other parts of the poem. In this view, they serve as an ironic device, showing the wanderer's belief in patience and detachment just at those moments when he is most overcome by grief.

ciuitas syrie que nunc tyrus dicit. olim
serra uocabat a pisce quodam qui illic
abundabat. quem sua lingua sar apellat
ex quo diriuatū est huius similitudinis pisciculos sardas. sardinas   qz uocari.

SERRA FLYING OVER A BOAT: ILLUMINA-
TION FROM AN ENGLISH BESTIARY
(C. 1185)
The Granger Collection

The Wanderer   59

Humanities Note

Fine art, *Serra Flying over a Boat: Illumination from an English Bestiary,* c. 1185. A medieval bestiary was a book on various animals, both real and legendary. It interpreted their habits as symbols of Christian beliefs.

An illumination is a hand-painted miniature within a text. Twelfth-century English illustrations were particularly fine. They used deep colors (influenced by those of medieval stained glass) and rhythmic, curving lines: Note, for instance, the arms of the figure on the right as he gracefully grips the boat and gestures in astonishment.

In this picture two boatmen watch a serra, a type of flying fish known today as a sawfish. Related to rays and sharks, serra are sometimes up to eighteen feet long and are able to leap high into the air. The medieval artist who depicted this serra may have exaggerated its flying ability, but bestiaries were not scientifically accurate. At any rate the painter does convey very well the wonder of the two men.

You might want to use the following questions to discuss the art.

1. How does the artist emphasize the height of the fish's leap?
2. How does this picture show the characteristic medieval mixture of realism and fantasy?
2. In medieval bestiaries various animals symbolized different aspects of Christianity. Do we use animals as symbols today? Explain.

6 Discussion Have students describe in their own words the different ways the heroes meet their deaths in this passage.

7 Discussion Have students discuss the tone of this climactic passage. How does it achieve its emotional intensity and power?

8 Discussion Point out to students that after the outcry of the previous passage, these lines return us to the present moment of the poem—a winter storm on an evening sea. Ask students how this passage completes the emotional shape of the poem.

9 Reading Strategy Have students stop and summarize the movement of the poem thus far. Then ask them whether this advice—given by the author, not the wanderer himself—is an adequate summing up of the poem. Why or why not?

Master Teacher Note Point out to students the questions beginning with the words "Where are the . . ." (lines 84–88). Tell them that this is a traditional pattern known as the *Ubi sunt* motif, after its appearance in medieval Latin lyrics, in which the two Latin words begins any variation on the question, "Where are those who lived before?" The writer may have been inspired by a Latin poem of this type, but in any case, have students discuss how the *Ubi sunt* passage in this poem heightens the sadness and poignancy of the whole poem.

Cooperative Learning How literature reflects patterns of immigration is a subject that might interest your students. Have them meet in small groups and select a modern work (such as the book *Mama's Bank Account* by Kathryn Forbes or the play or film based on it, *I Remember Mama* by John Van Druten) in which the characters are recent

As now, over all,   through the regions of earth,
Walls stand rime-covered[8]   and swept by the winds.
70 The battlements crumble,   the wine-halls decay;
Joyless and silent   the heroes are sleeping
Where the proud host fell   by the wall they defended.
Some battle launched   on their long, last journey;
One a bird bore   o'er the billowing sea;
75 One the gray wolf slew;   one a grieving earl
Sadly gave   to the grave's embrace.
The Warden of men   hath wasted this world
Till the sound of music   and revel is stilled,
And these giant-built structures   stand empty of life.
80 "He who shall muse   on these moldering ruins,
And deeply ponder   this darkling life,
Must brood on old legends   of battle and bloodshed,
And heavy the mood   that troubles his heart:
'Where now is the warrior?   Where is the war horse?
85 Bestowal of treasure,   and sharing of feast?
Alas! the bright ale-cup,   the byrny-clad[9] warrior,
The prince in his splendor   —those days are long sped
In the night of the past,   as if they never had been!'
And now remains only,   for warriors' memorial,
90 A wall wondrous high   with serpent shapes carved.
Storms of ash-spears   have smitten the earls,
Carnage of weapon,   and conquering fate.
    "Storms now batter   these ramparts of stone;
Blowing snow   and the blast of winter
95 Enfold the earth;   night-shadows fall
Darkly lowering,   from the north driving
Raging hail   in wrath upon men.
Wretchedness fills   the realm of earth,
And fate's decrees   transform the world.
100 Here wealth is fleeting,   friends are fleeting,
Man is fleeting,   maid is fleeting;
All the foundation of earth   shall fail!"
    Thus spake the sage   in solitude pondering.
Good man is he   who guardeth his faith.
105 He must never too quickly   unburden his breast
Of its sorrow, but eagerly   strive for redress;
And happy the man   who seeketh for mercy
From his heavenly Father,   our fortress and strength.

---

8. rime (rīm) -**covered:** Covered with frost.
9. byrny (bər′ nē) -**clad:** Dressed in a coat of chain-mail armor.

60   *The Anglo-Saxon Period*

immigrants. Then have each group research the biography of its writer to determine how his or her background influenced the work.

Reader's Response If you were the narrator of this poem, how might you go about recovering from the great grief that this poem expresses?

Closure and Extension
ANSWERS TO THINKING ABOUT THE SELECTION
1. (a) His lord died. (b) He is seeking a new gold-lord to befriend him.
2. Answers will differ. Possible responses include "friends," "gifts of fine gold," "Earth's winsomeness," "dealing of treasure," "youth," "wassail and feast," and "the loved counsel of comrade and king."
3. Answers will differ. Possible responses include lines 12–17 ("I have learned truly . . ."), lines 26–28 ("Who bears it . . ."), and lines 58–65 ("No man may know wisdom . . .").
4. Answers will differ. Possible responses might include images of the sea while the wanderer remembers his lord and kinsmen (lines 35–51), the descriptions of how heroes met their deaths (lines 71–76), the wall "wondrous high" (lines 89–91), or the snow storm (lines 93–97). No matter which details they choose, students

THINKING ABOUT THE SELECTION
Recalling

1. (a) What event causes the wanderer to go into exile? (b) What is the goal of his search?
2. Name three things from the past that he misses the most.
3. Identify a brief passage in which he expresses his outlook on life.

Interpreting

4. "The Wanderer" has been called an elegy, meaning a poem of mourning and lament. (a) Identify three vivid details that evoke in you a mood of mourning and lament. (b) Explain why these details are effective.
5. How does the poet's use of repetition contribute to the mood?
6. Explain the wanderer's attitude toward wisdom. Find details to support your interpretation.
7. **Tone** refers to a writer's attitude toward his subject or theme. (a) Choose two adjectives to describe the tone of this poem. (b) Give reasons for your choices.

Applying

8. What does this poem suggest about the role of women in the Anglo-Saxon world?
9. What would a modern wanderer be like? Briefly describe the causes of such a person's exile and the goal of his or her search.

ANALYZING LITERATURE
Understanding Exile

As a poem about exile, the loss of one's home, "The Wanderer" works primarily through contrast. For instance, the vivid dream-image in which the wanderer once again clasps his king, "Head on knee, hand on knee," contrasts with the waking image of the monotonous "gray stretches" of sea and the "Seabirds . . . with wings outspread." The first image conveys closeness and enfolded intimacy, while the second communicates the far-flung emptiness of exile and desolation.

1. Identify two other pairs of contrasting images in the poem and explain how they contribute to the theme of exile.
2. In addition to using contrasting images, the poet also juxtaposes his personal experience with broad generalities about human life. Would the poem be more effective or less effective if the poet's generalizations (lines 100–103) preceded his account of his exile? Why?

CRITICAL THINKING AND READING
Appreciating a Poem's Structure

Critics often seek to understand a poem by analyzing its structure, the major units of meaning into which it is divided. "The Wanderer," for example, is framed by opening (lines 1–5) and closing (lines 104–108) passages that refer to God's "pity" and "mercy." These religious invocations are clearly different from the soliloquy in the rest of the poem. The body of the poem itself, however, can also be divided into distinct parts.

1. Identify the units of meaning into which you think the poem should be divided. Indicate the lines where each begins and ends.
2. Explain why you divide the poem as you do. Consider such factors as a change in pronouns or a shift from to an individual's experience to generalities.

THINKING AND WRITING
Responding to Criticism

The scholar Michael Alexander argues that the mournful mood of "The Wanderer" is not diminished by the more comforting religious passages that appear at the beginning and end of the poem. Write an essay in which you agree or disagree with this assertion. Begin by identifying all the passages and phrases that contribute most to the poem's mood. Then write a thesis statement expressing your opinion of Alexander's critical comment. In revising your work, test your thesis by rereading the poem several times and being receptive to the mood it evokes in you.

melt into air (lines 45–51), or the list of past splendors now lost as compared to the snow storm (lines 84–98). In each case past joys are contrasted to present sorrows.
2. Answers will differ. Possible arguments for rearrangement include the idea that details following the generalization would then come as supporting examples. Possible arguments against rearrangement include the idea that the generalizations have little emotional power unless the situation of the speaker is known.

ANSWERS TO CRITICAL THINKING AND READING

1. Answers will differ. Any division into units will reflect to some extent the passages that begin with indented lines: lines 8, 18, 26, 35, 52, 66, 80, 93, and 103.
2. Answers will differ but should be supported by a close reading of the poem and should reflect an awareness of shifts in theme or approach.

THINKING AND WRITING
Writing Across the Curriculum

You may want to inform the social studies department that students are reading this selection. A social studies teacher can then help students do research on immigration patterns, both among the Scandinavians of the fifth century and among recent groups now arriving in the United States. As a writing assignment, students can compare and contrast two different waves of migration.

Challenge Tell students that some of the more philosophical passages in the poem reflect an attitude called stoicism. This attitude—of enduring both pain and pleasure without fear or longing —was as much an element of the Viking world as of the Greeks and Romans who first defined it. Have students discuss whether the wanderer in the poem is genuinely stoic or is only making an effort to control his grief.

should explain why they are effective.
5. Answers will differ. Students may respond that the repetitions in the poem emphasize the elegiac tone. In the climax of the poem (lines 84–102), where the repetitions become more frequent, the hammering quality of the verse conveys feelings of urgency, intensity, and desperation.
6. In a passage of direct statement (lines 58–65), the wanderer stresses that wisdom requires years of experience and that it

results in moderate behavior, neither rash nor fearful. In another passage (lines 12–17), the wanderer recommends the importance of suppressing sorrowful emotions.
7. (a) Possible adjectives include sorrowful, despairing, wretched, hopeless. (b) Answers should be supported by direct reference to the text of the poem.
8. Except for line 101 ("Main is fleeting, maid is fleeting"), women do not appear in the poem. The ab-

sence of references to women *might* suggest that the writer did not believe they were as important as men.
9. Answers might indicate people who became refugees in World War II or later wars, or immigrants from Korea, Japan, and Central America.

ANSWERS TO ANALYZING LITERATURE

1. Answers will differ. Possible responses include the kinsmen who

More About the Author The Venerable Bede wrote books on grammar and meter; Biblical commentary; scientific works on chronology, medicine, astronomy, and meteorology; the life stories of saints; and poems. He wrote mainly for students and other scholars. He spoke, wrote, and taught in Latin all his life, and he completed his ecclesiastical history in the last years of his life. What does this tell us about his qualifications as a historian? What does it suggest about his writing style?

Critical Evaluation According to the *Encyclopedia Britannica,* Bede's *History of the English Church and People* "leaves gaps tantalizing to the modern historian. Although overloaded with the miraculous, it is the work of a scholar anxious to access the accuracy of his sources and to record only what he regarded as trustworthy evidence. It remains as indispensable source of some of the facts and much of the feel of early Anglo-Saxon history."

BEDE

673–735

Much of what the world knows about England before A.D. 700 is based on a history written in Latin by a Benedictine monk, Bede, who is often called the father of English history. Bede was the most learned scholar of his day not only in England but in all of Western Europe. Although he wrote forty books on a variety of subjects, his reputation would be secure on the basis of a single book—his *Historia Ecclesiastica Gentis Anglorum,* or, in English, *A History of the English Church and People.*

Bede was born in Wearmouth (now the city of Sunderland) on the northeast coast of England. As a child of seven, he entered the nearby monastic school of Jarrow on the river Tyne. A diligent student, he took full advantage of the library at Jarrow, in time becoming a priest, teacher, and scholar at the monastery. He remained at Jarrow for the rest of his life.

A contemporary of the unknown author of *Beowulf,* Bede was fascinated by a broad range of ideas. His writings summarize much of the thought and learning of his time. As the earliest important English prose writer, he concentrated on the Bible but did not neglect science and history. One of his innovations was the dating of events from the birth of Christ, a system that other scholars began to follow. It was through Bede's work that the Christian chronology in use today became common throughout Europe.

Bede had a deep love for his native island and its people, which led him to write his *History of the English Church and People.* In working on his history, Bede gathered information from many kinds of documents, interviewed knowledgeable monks, and, in general, proceeded very much like a modern historian, although he accepted as fact some miracles that a modern historian would not.

In the *History,* Bede describes the conquests of the Anglo-Saxon tribes and the fortunes of the various small fiefdoms that spread across the land. His primary concern, however, was the expansion of Christianity and the growth of the Church in England. He wrote in Latin, the language of scholarship in his age. There are several surviving manuscripts, however, that have the Old English text in addition to Bede's Latin version. He became famous throughout the land as one of the most learned scholars of his age, despite the fact that he never ventured beyond Northumbria.

In the century after his death, King Alfred translated Bede's history from Latin into English. In the same century, the word *Venerable* was first applied to his name to honor his wisdom and achievements. The honor was well deserved. The Venerable Bede was largely responsible for what is sometimes called the Christian renaissance in eighth-century England.

Objectives

1 To understand the process of historical writing
2 To make inferences about attitudes in historical writing
3 To write a critical review of the excerpt from Bede's history

Support Material

Teaching Portfolio
Teacher Backup, p.47
Usage and Mechanics Worksheet, p. 51
Vocabulary Check, p. 52
Analyzing Literature Worksheet, *Understanding Historical Writing,* p. 53
Language Worksheet, *Tracing Word Histories,* p. 54
Selection Test, p. 55

GUIDE FOR INTERPRETING

from A History of the English Church and People

Writer's Techniques

Historical Writing. A history is a factual narrative or record of past events. Unless a historian has actually observed the events being described, he or she must rely on outside sources. These sources include testimony from living witnesses, accounts in letters or memoirs, records from courts, businesses, churches, armies, or other groups. Today's historian has libraries of books, newspapers, films, and other items to consult, as well as unwritten records such as buildings, artworks, and various physical remains of bygone days. An enormous amount of historical material exists.

That was not the case in Bede's time. English monastic libraries had modest collections of documents that Bede read, cross-checked, and evaluated. He made excellent use of the limited sources of his time. Bede was an innovator among historical writers, and if he sometimes accepted unlikely tales as truth, he did so far less often than did most scholars of his era.

Writing

If you were writing a history of your community, you would have to find and use a number of different sources. List at least five specific sources that might be helpful.

Primary Source

The end of a man's life is often compared to the winding up of a well-written play, where the principal persons still act in character, whatever the fate is which they undergo. JOSEPH ADDISON, *The Spectator*

Bede's own death was certainly in character, and it became the subject of historical writing in the hands of Cuthbert, a former student: "At the ninth hour, Bede said to me, 'I have a few valuables in my cask—pepper, vestments, and incense. Run quickly and bring the priests of our monastery, so that I may share among them little gifts, such as God has granted me.' And I did so with trembling. When they were all present, he addressed each and every one, urging them, imploring them they should say prayers and masses for him—which they freely promised. But they all kept weeping and sorrowing, especially because he said they must not think to see his face much longer in this world. But they rejoiced because he said, 'It is time for me, if my Maker sees fit, to be freed from the flesh and go to Him who made me out of nothing, at the time when I was nothing. I have lived a long time, and my merciful Judge has ordered my life well . . . This and much else he said for our instruction, and passed his last day happily until evening . . . upon the floor of his little cell, chanting . . . his spirit passed from the body."

Guide for Interpreting 63

Literary Focus Today, we tend to think of the monastic life as being isolating and out of the mainstream. Remind students that in Bede's day, most reading and writing was done in churches and monasteries. Therefore, Bede was in a good position to acquire a great deal of knowledge.

Writing/Prior Knowledge The historian Carlyle said, "In a certain sense, all men are historians. . . . Most men . . . speak only to narrate." Discuss this statement with students in terms of what it hints about sources. Remind students that a source is not simply a location. Any written record is a source. When they go to a library, a museum, or a historical society, the materials that they find there are their sources.

Teaching to Ability Levels You might have some of your **more advanced** students read one or more of the lives of saints which compose much of the rest of Bede's history.

Vocabulary

Preteach the following vocabulary words:
promontories (präm´ ən tôr ēz) *n*: High points of land extending into the sea (p. 64)
furlongs (fʉr´ lôŋz) *n.*: Units for measuring distance; a furlong is equal to one eighth of a mile (p. 64)
cockles (käk´ 'lz) *n.*: Edible shellfish with two heart-shaped shells (p. 64)
innumerable (i noō´ mər ə b'l) *adj.*: Too many to count (p. 64)
firth (fʉrth) *n.*: Narrow arm of the sea (p. 66)

A History of the English Church and People

Bede translated by Leo Sherley-Price

The Situation of Britain and Ireland: Their Earliest Inhabitants

Britain, formerly known as Albion, is an island in the ocean, facing between north and west, and lying at a considerable distance from the coasts of Germany, Gaul, and Spain, which together form the greater part of Europe. It extends 800 miles northwards, and is 200 in breadth, except where a number of promontories stretch farther, the coastline round which extends to 3675 miles. To the south lies Belgic Gaul,[1] from the nearest shore of which travelers can see the city known as Rutubi Portus, which the English have corrupted to Reptacestir.[2] The distance from there across the sea to Gessoriacum,[3] the nearest coast of the Morini, is 50 miles or, as some write it, 450 furlongs. On the opposite side of Britain, which lies open to the boundless ocean, lie the isles of the Orcades.[4] Britain is rich in grain and timber; it has good pasturage for cattle and draft animals,[5] and vines are cultivated in various localities. There are many land and sea birds of various species, and it is well known for its plentiful springs and rivers abounding in fish. There are salmon and eel fisheries, while seals, dolphins, and some-times whales are caught. There are also many varieties of shellfish, such as mussels, in which are often found excellent pearls of several colors: red, purple, violet, and green, but mainly white. Cockles are abundant, and a beautiful scarlet dye is extracted from them which remains unfaded by sunshine or rain; indeed, the older the cloth, the more beautiful its color. The country has both salt and hot springs, and the waters flowing from them provide hot baths, in which the people bathe separately according to age and sex. As Saint Basil says: "Water receives its heat when it flows across certain metals, and becomes hot, and even scalding." The land has rich veins of many metals, including copper, iron, lead, and silver. There is also much black jet[6] of fine quality, which sparkles in firelight. When burned, it drives away snakes, and, like amber, when it is warmed by friction, it clings to whatever is applied to it. In old times, the country had twenty-eight noble cities, and innumerable castles, all of which were guarded by walls, towers, and barred gates.

Since Britain lies far north toward the pole, the nights are short in summer, and at midnight it is hard to tell whether the evening twilight still lingers or whether dawn is approaching; for in these northern latitudes the sun does not remain long below the horizon at night. Consequently both sum-

---

1. **Belgic Gaul:** France.
2. **Reptacestir:** Richborough, part of the city of Sandwich.
3. **Gessoriacum:** Boulogne, France.
4. **Orcades:** The Orkney Isles.
5. **draft animals:** Animals used for pulling loads.

6. **jet** *n.*: A type of coal.

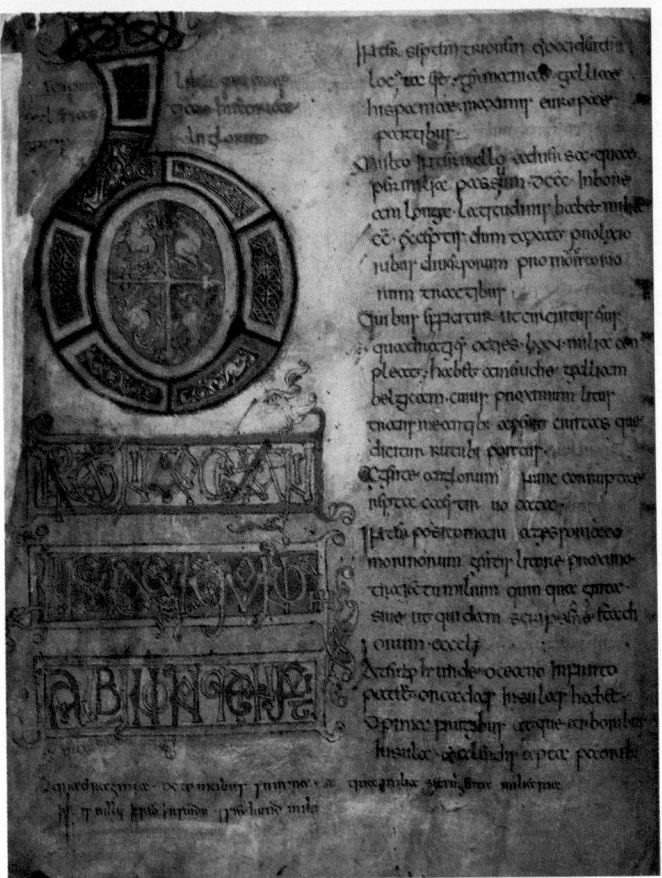

COTTON MS TIBERIUS C II FOLIO 5 VERSO
Page of Bede's History
The British Library

Humanities Note

Fine art, a page of Bede's *History*. The word *illuminator,* one who "lightens up," appeared in the language in the twelfth century. It is descriptive of the artist who decorated the written vellum manuscripts that were being produced in monasteries at the time.

This decorative page is typical of the early, painstaking work done by these artists. The enlarged decorative capital letter is embellished with the sort of geometric design that is common to all barbaric art. The colorful lozenge shapes beneath it contain decorative words. Decorated pages such as this enhanced the reader's awe and enjoyment of the manuscript. They have left us with a record of the early art of painting that has had a lasting effect on the art of succeeding generations.

You might discuss the following with your class.
1. Try to imagine the labor that this artist went through to produce this image.
2. This artist not only had to grind his own paint and ink, he also had to make his paper, brushes, pens, and even the work table that he used. Did these difficulties detract from the beauty of what he produced here?

3 mer days and winter nights are long, and when the sun withdraws southwards, the winter nights last eighteen hours. In Armenia,[7] Macedonia,[8] and Italy, and other countries of that latitude, the longest day lasts only fifteen hours and the shortest nine.

At the present time there are in Britain, in harmony with the five books of the divine law, five languages and four nations **4** —English, British, Scots, and Picts. Each of these have their own language, but all are united in their study of God's truth by the fifth, Latin, which has become a common medium through the study of the scriptures. The original inhabitants of the island were the Britons, from whom it takes its name, and who, according to tradition, crossed into Britain from Armorica,[9] and occupied the southern parts. When they had spread northwards and possessed the greater part of the islands, it is said that some Picts from Scythia[10] put to sea in a few long ships and were driven by storms around the coasts of Britain, arriving at length on the north

7. Armenia: Now part of the Soviet Union.
8. Macedonia: Now a region divided among Greece, Yugoslavia, and Bulgaria.

9. Armorica: Brittany, France.
10. Scythia (siṭh' ē ə): An ancient region in southeastern Europe.

from *A History of the English Church and People* 65

3 Clarification Bede understood the phenomenon of seasonal shifts in the earth's relation to the sun but believed that the sun, which was commonly believed to revolve around the earth, was doing the shifting.

4 Clarification "British" here refers to what we now call Welsh.

Reader's Response What parts of this section do you think Bede would change if he could revise it now?

Fine art, Illumination, *The Venerable Bede Writing His Book and Presenting It to the Bishop of Lindisfarne,* twelfth century. This illumination comes from a twelfth-century copy of Bede's *Life of St Cuthbert.*

1. Bede is an important historic figure. Does this illustration help in your appreciation of his work?
2. Are the people portrayed in this miniature that different in appearance from someone you might meet today?

5 Enrichment Most scholars think that this quotation is intended to enliven the text rather than report exact words.

6 Enrichment No one knows whether this story is true; Bede probably included it because it seemed to explain something that he did know, which was that the Pictish custom of succession was different from the one Bede knew.

7 Discussion What, then, did Bede think *Dalreudians* meant?

8 Enrichment Bede probably never went to Ireland, and he believed the geographical assumption of his day that the island extended far south of England.

9 Critical Reading and Thinking What does this passage show about Bede's attitude toward Ireland?

10 Literary Focus Love of truth is one of Bede's outstanding characteristics; when he relates a story on hearsay evidence, he carefully indicates this. Demonstrate in this and other passages.

11 Clarification This "extensive arm of the sea" is the Firth of Clyde.

MONKS
Bodleian Library, Oxford

coast of Ireland. Here they found the nation of the Scots, from whom they asked permission to settle, but their request was refused. Ireland is the largest island after Britain, and lies to the west. It is shorter than Britain to the north, but extends far beyond it to the south towards the northern coasts of Spain, although a wide sea separates them. These Pictish seafarers, as I have said, asked for a grant of land to make a settlement. The Scots replied that there was not room for them both, but said: "We can give you good advice. There is another island not far to the east, which we often see in the distance on clear days. Go and settle there if you wish; should you meet resistance, we will come to your help." So the Picts crossed

5

into Britain, and began to settle in the north of the island, since the Britons were in possession of the south. Having no women with them, these Picts asked wives of the Scots, who consented on condition that, when any dispute arose, they should choose a king from the female royal line rather than the male. This custom continues among the Picts to this day. As time went on, Britain received a third nation, that of the Scots, who migrated from Ireland under their chieftain Reuda, and by a combination of force and treaty, obtained from the Picts the settlements that they still hold. From the name of this chieftain, they are still known as Dalreudians, for in their tongue *dal* means a division.

6

7

Ireland is broader than Britain, and its mild and healthy climate is superior. Snow rarely lies longer than three days, so that there is no need to store hay in summer for winter use or to build stables for beasts. There are no reptiles, and no snake can exist there, for although often brought over from Britain, as soon as the ship nears land, they breathe its scented air and die. In fact, almost everything in this isle enjoys immunity to poison, and I have heard that folk suffering from snakebite have drunk water in which scrapings from the leaves of books from Ireland had been steeped, and that this remedy checked the spreading poison and reduced the swelling. The island abounds in milk and honey, and there is no lack of vines, fish, and birds, while deer and goats are widely hunted. It is the original home of the Scots, who, as already mentioned, later migrated and joined the Britons and Picts in Britain. There is a very extensive arm of the sea, which originally formed the boundary between the Britons and the Picts. This runs inland from the west for a great distance as far as the strongly fortified British city of Alcuith.[11] It was to the northern shores of this firth that the Scots came and established their new homeland.

8

9

10

11

11. **Alcuith** (al kü′ əth): Dumbarton, Scotland.

Closure and Extension

ANSWERS TO THINKING ABOUT THE SELECTION
Recalling

1. Germany, Gaul (France), and Spain formed the greater part of Europe.
2. (a) The four nations in Britain were the English, the British, the Scots, and the Picts;
   (b) the Latin tongue, used in the study of the Scriptures, united the four nations.
3. Deer and goats were widely hunted in Ireland.

Interpreting

4. It implies that the people in Britain dyed their cloth and that they liked bright, rich colors.

Applying

5. Britain may have consisted of many separate political entities that did not necessarily get along with one another.
6. Bede reports that almost everything in Ireland is immune to poison.

7. Bede reports both fact and legend. You might consult a source that

THINKING ABOUT THE SELECTION

Recalling

1. What countries formed the greater part of Europe at the time of Bede's history?
2. (a) In Bede's time, what were the four nations in Britain. (b) What united them?
3. What animals does Bede say were widely hunted in Ireland?

Interpreting

4. What does the explanation about scarlet dye imply about the lifestyle of the people?
5. Bede states that Britain once "had twenty-eight noble cities . . . guarded by walls, towers, and barred gates." What does this statement suggest about the political situation at the time?
6. What is one unlikely tale that Bede includes in his history?

Applying

7. If you wanted to read a reliable history of early England, you would probably choose something other than Bede's work. Why? What kind of source might you choose?

ANALYZING LITERATURE

Understanding Historical Writing

A history provides factual information about the past. This information comes from a variety of sources, including books and other printed materials, public records, and, if possible, personal letters, memoirs, and interviews. A good historian like Bede does more than just list facts, however. Bede presents his facts as part of an understandable whole.

1. Accuracy is very important in historical writing. Read the quotation from the Scots on page 66 (a) Do you think the statement is an exact quotation? (b) If not, does it cast doubt on the accuracy of Bede's history? Explain.
2. Bede sometimes relies on people's oral statements for his information. On page 66 he makes a specific reference to such a source. What is it?

CRITICAL THINKING AND READING

Making Inferences About Attitudes

Bede's history reflects his own attitudes and those of the people he is writing about. Since these attitudes tend to be revealed indirectly, you must make inferences, or draw conclusions about them. For example, Bede states that the people of England are "united in their study of God's truth." From this statement you can infer that religion played an important role in the life of the people.

1. From Bede's comments on page 66 what do you think the general attitude was in Britain toward snakes?
2. Do you think the Picts and Scots got along well with each other? Cite the evidence on which you base your inference.

UNDERSTANDING LANGUAGE

Tracing Word Histories

An **etymology** explains the origin and history of a word. It usually appears in brackets in a dictionary entry.

> **amber** n. [ME. aumbre, amber, ambergris <OFr. ambre < Ar. 'anbar, ambergris]

The present English word amber is derived from the Middle English word aumbre, which came from Old French, and originally from Arabic.

Trace the history of the following words.

1. promontory   3. migrate
2. furlong   4. cockle

THINKING AND WRITING

Writing a Critical Review

Give your opinion of this excerpt from Bede's history. First, jot down your answers to the following questions: Does the history seem accurate? Is it clearly written? What do you find to be its most striking fact? Next, write a topic sentence that states your opinion clearly. Then write a draft, using examples to support your opinion. Finally, revise your draft, making sure that its sentences are in logical order.

from *A History of the English Church and People*   67

(Answers begin on p. 66.)

2. The Picts and Scots probably did not get along. The Scots did not allow the Picts to settle in Ireland when the latter were blown ashore there. In addition, the Scots gave wives to the Picts but required the Picts to choose their rulers from the female, or Scots, lineage. Finally, the Scots eventually migrated from Ireland to the Picts's new home and displaced them "by force or treaty."

ANSWERS TO UNDERSTANDING LANGUAGE

1. *Promontory* is derived from the Medieval Latin word *promontorium,* an alteration of the Latin word *promunturium.*
2. *Furlong* is derived from the Middle English word *furlong,* which came from the Old English *furlang,* meaning "long furrow."
3. *Migrate* is derived from the inflected form *migrat-* of the Latin infinitive *migrare.*
4. *Cockle* is derived from the Middle English word *cokel,* which comes from the Old French word *coquille,* meaning "shell," which possibly came from the Vulgar Latin *conchillia,* which came from the Latin *conchylium,* which came from the Greek *konchylion,* the diminutive of *konchē,* which means "mussel."

THINKING AND WRITING

For help with this assignment, students can refer to Lesson 15, "Evaluating a Literary Work, in the Handbook of Writing About Literature.

Publishing Student Writing You might have students work in groups sharing their opinions. Perhaps each group could prepare a group opinion.

---

used not only Bede but also other surviving written records from the time, as well as archeological evidence.

ANSWERS TO ANALYZING LITERATURE

1. (a) The quotation could not be exact.
   (b) The modern reader might wonder what other quotations and "facts" have been fabricated.

Students might also mention that this could be a stylistic device.

2. Bede says that he has heard that people have been cured of snakebite by drinking water in which scrapings from the pages of Irish books have been steeped.

Challenge The British historian H.A.L. Fisher (1865–1940) once wrote "There can be . . . only one safe rule for the historian: that he

can recognize in the development of human destinies the play of the contingent and the unforeseen." Restate the quotation in your own words and explain why you think Bede would or would not have agreed with it.

ANSWERS TO CRITICAL THINKING AND READING

1. People undoubtedly hated and feared snakes.

Explain that language is at once complex and simple. Ask students if they can name gestures, like the wave of a hand or the blowing of a kiss from the fingertips, that can represent thoughts in sign language. Allow any students who know the alphabet in sign language to show the rest of the class each letter or several words they might know in sign. Then discuss the first words that youngsters use when learning to talk. Those who have siblings at two or three years of age can provide anecdotes about the successes or amusing failures of their brothers and sisters to learn to speak. Emphasize that the languages of nations, like the vocabularies of individuals, take many, many years to reach maturity.

Enrichment Before students begin to study the changing patterns of English, divide the class into several groups of three or four members each. Let the teams huddle and quietly list as many different languages as the members can think of in a two minute period of time. Congratulate those with the highest number of languages and those who listed the most languages not found on other lists.

THE CHANGING ENGLISH LANGUAGE

Old English 449–1066

"ENGLISC"

The story of English is the story of roamings and settling, invasions and war. What we call *Anglo-Saxon* or *Old English* developed through the contributions of many different peoples, including the Jutes (from Danish Jutland), the Saxons (from the region of Germany still called Lower Saxony), and scatterings of other groups. Old English began with the *Angles*, a people who originated in a section of Denmark still called *Angeln*, a word that means "an angle in the coast." The Celts called their German conquerors *Saxons* but by degrees the terms *Anglii* and *Anglia* entered their speech. Soon, people were referring to their language as *Englisc* and themselves as *Angelcynn*; literally, the relatives (*cynn* as "kin") of the Angles. By A.D. 1000 they called their country *Englisc*.

THE HUNDRED MOST COMMON WORDS

The Anglo-Saxons were farmers—when they were not at war—and they soon settled down and took over all the good farming country, chasing the Celts to the hilltops or to Wales and Ireland. Although more than half the vocabulary of modern English is borrowed, and more than half the words of Old English (some say as much as 85 percent) has vanished, the language of these Anglo-Saxon farmers became the basis of modern English. Of the hundred most common words in our speech today, every one derives from Old English; of the next hundred, eighty-three are native. Some Old English words hardly need translation—*mann* and *hus* for example—although of course we spell them differently today (man and

house). It is nearly impossible to write a modern English sentence without using a wealth of Old English vocabulary. All the words in Roosevelt's famous comforting phrase—"The only thing we have to fear is fear itself"—come from Old English. Francis Scott Key used words derived from Old English in 1814 when he saw the flag waving over Fort McHenry: "Oh say, can you see, by the dawn's early light, what so proudly we hailed at the twilight's last gleaming?" "Proud" is the only borrowing, and it's nearly a thousand years old!

RIDDLES

The Anglo-Saxons delighted in word play, riddles, and ambiguity in language. Few people could read or write, and so they had to rely on their memories. As a result, the Anglo-Saxons developed their oral tradition very fully. They liked stating their ideas in subtle, original ways, and especially admired poems that went in circles. This love of word play, which characterizes English to the present, can be seen especially in *The Exeter Book of Riddles*, a collection of Old English verse. Can you solve this one-line riddle? "On the way a miracle: water becomes bone." Ice!

THE INFLUENCE OF CHRISTIANITY

Although the English people already knew about *heofon* (heaven), *synne* (sin) and *hel* (hell), the language received a hugh boost in A.D. 597, when Christianity arrived with its enormous Latin vocabulary, more than 400 words of which survive to this day. For example, the Latin *evangelium* (good news) became the English *god-spell* which has become the modern word *gospel*. Even more importantly, words from Latin gave English speakers the ability to express abstract thoughts, including such concepts as *angel* and *discipline*. Further, Old English rejuvenated itself by giving new meaning to old words. *God, heaven,* and *hell* all assumed deeper meanings upon the arrival of Christianity.

THE VIKINGS SIMPLIFY ENGLISH

Superior numbers and literacy assured the victory of English over Danish, but the Danes left a lasting influence on English nonetheless. First, they contributed at least 900 words, such as *husbondi (house-master* or *husband)* and *syster*(sister). Second, the Danes added pronouns to English, filling a real linguistic need. Most importantly, before the arrival of the Danes, Old English conveyed meaning through word endings rather than word order. The Danes simplified language by eliminating some of the word change, called inflection, although the process would not be completed until Middle English developed.

THE SPELLING DILEMMA

Written English, however, confronted the language with a problem that still confounds us today: spelling. Almost all writing is based on symbols that stand for the sounds of the language they record. The early scribes used the Roman alphabet to record Old English. Now, the Roman alphabet did a fine job representing the sounds of Latin, for which it had been created. But Old

English included a number of decidedly un-Roman sounds, such as the sound we now write as *TH*. The scribes solved the problem by borrowing two symbols from the runic alphabet, þ and ð. Unfortunately, they used the two symbols interchangeably. This continued with other sounds, and spelling problems abounded.

So begun, English would continue to develop over the next four hundred years, becoming ever richer and more flexible.

THE ANGLO SAXON CHRONICLE
The British Library

The Changing English Language 69

YOU THE WRITER
Guidelines for Evaluating Assignment 1

1. Has the student written a narrative poem telling of the physical and mental hardships of the ocean voyage?
2. Has the student included sufficient details to describe each hardship?
3. Has the student written the narrative poem in chronological order?
4. Is the narrative poem free from grammar, usage, and mechanics errors?

Guidelines for Evaluating Assignment 2

1. Has the student presented a new view of a character or incident in Anglo-Saxon literature in a dialogue or narrative?
2. Does the paper contain sufficient detail?
3. Is the organization and structure sufficient?
4. Is the paper free from grammar, usage, and mechanics errors?

Guidelines for Evaluating Assignment 3

1. Does the article convey a clear, vivid picture of the student's day in the past?
2. Are the paragraphs fully developed and focused on a single impression or experience?
3. Does the structure and style add to the expressiveness?
4. Is the article free from grammar, usage, and mechanics errors?

YOU THE WRITER

Assignment

1. Imagine that you have been lost for many days in the north Atlantic Ocean in a small boat. At last you reach land. Write a narrative poem in which you describe the hardships, both physical and mental, that you endured. Use any verse form you feel is suitable.

Prewriting. First list several of the main sufferings you endured. Then make notes on the details of each. Think of ways to make your narrative as vivid and concrete as possible.

Writing. Write your first draft in chronological order, using description to expand on each of the basic hardships you are recounting.

Revising. When you revise, first see if you need to adjust the overall narrative structure of your poem. Then look to improve the details of each piece of description. Read your poem aloud. Can you improve its musical quality?

Assignment

2. Many notable works of literature are based on characters or incidents from earlier works. Select any character or incident from Anglo-Saxon literature and write a brief prose monologue or narrative based on the character or incident you have chosen.

Prewriting. First use your imagination to think up a new view of the character or incident. Then plan the structure and details of your monologue or narrative.

Writing. Your first draft should contain, in rough form, all the contents of your work—either your character's remarks or the details of the incident you are narrating.

Revising. When you revise, improve the organization and structure of your work. Then try to polish and perfect the details.

Assignment

3. Imagine that you have gone back in time to Anglo-Saxon England and, twenty-four hours later, have returned to the present. Write a brief magazine article whose purpose is to convey your discovery of the differences between the Anglo-Saxon world and the modern world.

Prewriting. List the details of what you saw, heard, and experienced. Then fit them into an outline that will enable you to convey a clear, vivid picture of your day in the past.

Writing. Following your outline, write fully developed paragraphs, each of which focuses on a single impression or experience. Conclude by summarizing the differences.

Revising. Can you replace one of the impressions or experiences with a better, more revealing one? Can you alter your structure or style for greater expressiveness? Revise according to these questions.

Assignment

1. Write a critical evaluation of any one of the selections from the Anglo-Saxon period. The purpose of your evaluation should be to indicate what interest the work holds for a contemporary reader.

Prewriting. Answer these questions: What is my general opinion of this work? What specifically did I admire or dislike about it? What is the basic opinion I wish to share with readers who have not yet read the work?

Writing. Write an essay in which you first state in a topic sentence your critical judgment. Then offer your reasons. Refer to details of the work to clarify and support your argument.

Revising. Revise in the light of these questions: Is my opinion fair, objective, and clearly expressed? Can I make my argument more forceful and persuasive by citing other details or aspects of the work?

Assignment

2. Some readers suppose that the earliest literature of a people tends to be crude and primitive. Write a brief essay in which you point out the literary artistry—the imaginative power, sophisticated design, or stylistic appeal—of any one of the Anglo-Saxon selections you have read.

Prewriting. First decide what you liked about the work. Then analyze it to determine the methods the writer used to make it artistically effective.

Writing. First state or describe clearly the kind of literary excellence you see in the work. Then refer to specific aspects and details of the work to embody and clarify your view.

Revising. When you revise keep in mind the question, "Have I demonstrated and illustrated the artistic excellence I see in ———?" Make changes that help you show, not just talk about, the virtues of the literary work.

Assignment

3. Write an essay with the title "Anglo-Saxon Literature: Mirror of the Times." Show how the literature you have read reflects what you have learned about Anglo-Saxon history and life.

Prewriting. Review the introduction to the Anglo-Saxon period and any other information you have gathered about it. Which work that you have read comes to mind in the course of your review? What brings this work to mind?

Writing. Write a first draft based on this last question. Tell how Anglo-Saxon history or life reveals itself in the work you have selected. Your basic approach should be a descriptive comparison of the historical background and the literary expression of it.

Revising. Concentrate on increasing the clarity and precision of your description of the link between the literature and its historical setting.

You the Critic 71

1. Does the critical evaluation begin with a topic sentence that states the student's critical judgment of a selection of Anglo-Saxon literature?
2. Is the opinion clearly stated, fair, and objective?
3. Is the argument made forceful by references to details of the work?
4. Is the essay free from grammar, usage, and mechanics errors?

Guidelines for Evaluating Assignment 2

1. Does the student explain clearly the kind of literary excellence he or she finds in the Anglo-Saxon selection?
2. Does the student refer to specific aspects and details of the work to support and clarify his or her opinion?
3. Does the student show, not just discuss, the virtues of the literary work?
4. Is the essay free from grammar, usage, and mechanics errors?

Guidelines for Evaluating Assignment 3

1. Does the essay demonstrate how Anglo-Saxon history or life is revealed in the literary work selected?
2. Has the student used a descriptive comparison of the historical background and the literary expression of it as his or her approach to the essay?
3. Is there a clear, precise description of the link between the literature and the historical setting?
4. Is the essay free from grammar, usage, and mechanics errors?

Detail of illuminated manuscript, *Pilgrims to Canterbury,* c. 1400. By 1400, illumination was a well-developed art, not limited only to religious works. This section from an English illuminated manuscript shows a group of Pilgrims on their way to Canterbury. Aspects of the time are reflected in the Pilgrims' dress and in the medieval structure in the background. Like Chaucer's pilgrims, these represent people from different walks of life, both clerical and lay.

Objectives

1 To learn about the significance of the Norman Conquest
2 To trace the rise of feudalism
3 To examine the shifts in language that expanded English vocabulary
4 To explain the dispute of Henry II with the Pope
5 To pinpoint the origins of constitutional government
6 To explain the growth of towns throughout England
7 To give an overview of the concepts of Chivalry and Romance while using the legend of King Arthur as an example of popular thinking on those subjects
8 To explain the positions of learning and literature in this age while examining the roles of poetry and drama

PILGRIMS TO CANTERBURY: DETAIL OF AN ENGLISH ILLUMINATED MANUSCRIPT. c.1400
The Granger Collection

THE MEDIEVAL PERIOD
1066–1485

A Knyght ther was, and that a worthy man
That fro the tyme that he first bigan
To riden out, he loved chivalrie,
Trouthe and honour, fredom and curteisie

Geoffrey Chaucer

73

Historical Background Just as the period of the Middle Ages throughout continental Europe saw sweeping changes and cultural diversity, so too in England did a rich complexity influence daily living. Linguistic, religious, literary, and political shifts occurred rapidly. The years between the 11th and 15th centuries witnessed a population boom followed by a diminution of people because of the rate of fatality during the Black Plague that ravished England in 1348. Civic and cultural upheaval resulted. As it does in other ages and places, literature reflected these disturbances in significant and obvious ways.

Motivation/Prior Knowledge Tell students to list ten adjectives that they associate with the Middle Ages. Ask them to place them in an order of priority. After they have read this introduction, have them consider changing the order while explaining the reasons for revising the sequence.

Purpose-Setting Question What will mark England during these years as distinctly medieval?

ESL Teaching Strategy Ask your ESL students to take notes under the headings of each section in this introduction. Have them prepare a brief outline of the contents. Be sure to provide extra credit for this task.

The Bayeux Tapestry: Duke William encourages his men at Hastings. The Bayeux Tapestry, a wool-on-linen embroidery 20 inches high and 230 feet long, records the story of the Norman Conquest of England. Its many scenes depict different aspects of the invasion of England and the Battle of Hastings. In this detail, Duke William, later to be known as William the Conqueror, is shown encouraging his men at Hastings by raising his helmet.

1 Historical Context It is very likely that Edward had, in fact, promised the throne to his cousin William in 1051 but had revoked this promise under pressure from the Godwin family, Harold and his father.

2 Master Teacher Note In order for the students to visualize the events of the Norman Conquest, you might introduce pictures of the Bayeux Tapestry, an embroidered record supervised by William's wife, Matilda.

3 Enrichment The novel *The Golden Warrior* by Hope Muntz (Scribners, 1949) presents a beautifully written and historically accurate view of the invasion from the Saxon point of view.

THE BAYEUX TAPESTRY: DUKE WILLIAM ENCOURAGES HIS MEN AT HASTINGS
The Granger Collection

The famous description on the preceding page comes from an English literary masterpiece, *The Canterbury Tales,* by Geoffrey Chaucer (1340?–1400). The passage reflects many of the ideas and attitudes held by Europeans during the fourteenth century. In these years knights lived by the code of chivalry, which stressed truth, honor, and courtesy off the battlefield and valor on it. The Roman Catholic Church had become the only force uniting most of Western Europe. Religion pervaded daily life, and to be a devout Christian —a worthy man—was important not only to knights but to all members of English society.

During these years the English language changed from its Anglo-Saxon form to one called Middle English, far more familiar to modern readers. Looking at Chaucer's words above, we can readily recognize their modern English counterparts—"knyght" is *knight,* "ther" is *there,* "fro" is *from,* "riden" is *ride,* "chivalrie" is *chivalry,* and so on. The change from Old English to Middle English took place gradually. Yet this change can be traced to one riveting event—the Norman invasion of 1066.

THE NORMAN CONQUEST

The Normans, or "north men," were descendants of Vikings who had invaded the coast of France in the ninth century. Over the years, these people had adopted many French ways. They had become devout Christians. They had accustomed themselves to speaking a dialect of the French language. They had also organized themselves according to the French political and economic system of the times—feudalism.

William, Duke of Normandy, had family ties to Edward the Confessor, the English king. When Edward died in 1066, the Saxon witan—the council of elders—chose Harold II as king. William of Normandy, meanwhile, claimed that Edward had promised him the throne. William thereupon led a few thousand Norman and French troops across the English Channel to assert his claim by force.

He met King Harold at the Battle of Hastings near a seaside village in southern England. Harold was killed, and William emerged victorious. He then headed for London, brutally crushing all resistance. At Westminster Abbey on Christmas Day, William "the Conqueror" took the throne of England as King William I.

Over the next five years, William consolidated his victory. He suppressed the Anglo-Saxon nobility and confiscated their lands. He saw to it that Normans controlled government at all levels. The Normans conducted their business in Norman French or Latin. They gradually remade England along feudal lines.

The Rise of Feudalism

Feudalism had taken root on the European continent at a time when no central government was strong enough to keep order.

Under the circumstances, nobles had to rely on their own warriors for help. The system they created was an exchange of property for personal service. The person who granted the property was the lord or overlord. The person who received it was the vassal. The vassal promised service to his lord in a ceremony called the act of homage. At the same time, the vassal usually pledged his faithfulness by taking the Christian vow of fealty.

In theory, all the land belonged to the ruler. The king kept some of it for his personal use, granted some to the church, and parceled out the rest among his powerful supporters. He gave these supporters noble titles—usually baron—and the special privileges that went with them. The parcels of land granted to the barons were known as fiefs.

As a vassal of his overlord, each baron was obliged to pay certain fees or taxes. He was also expected to supply a specified number of knights, or professional soldiers, should the king require them. In return for their services, knights usually received smaller parcels of land, called manors. The peasants who worked these manors were the lowest class in the feudal system, the serfs. Manors became the basic community of the feudal system. Most were self-sufficient, using their own craftsmen to provide nearly all their needs.

In the eleventh century, Europe had no nation-states with firm political boundaries. William and the Norman kings who followed him—William II, Henry I, and Stephen of Blois—held feudal domains in both England and France. Since they had two realms, Norman kings had far wider responsibilities than Saxon kings had faced. The situation also meant that English barons dissatisfied with their overlord could cross the English Channel and stir up trouble on the other side.

A Shifting Language

Like a great many of history's conquerors, the Normans thought themselves vastly superior to the people they had conquered. The invaders treated the Saxons and Danes as not quite human and sniffed at their language as unworthy of respect. The Normans substituted their dialect of French in the law courts as well as in the conduct of business in general. To this day, French words such as *bail* and *sergeant* remain embedded in the language of English law.

Traces of Norman discrimination against the Saxons have lingered for centuries. In his nineteenth-century novel *Ivanhoe*, Sir Walter Scott noted one aspect of Norman superiority. In the field, he wrote, a domestic animal is often referred to by its Saxon name —swine, sheep, or ox. When the same animal appears on a dinner table, however, it takes a French name—pork, mutton, or beef. In other words, the raising of farm animals was considered a Saxon activity, whereas the more elegant pursuit, dining, befitted the Normans.

A BALIFF SUPERVISING THE HARVEST (THE MONTH OF AUGUST): MANUSCRIPT ILLUMINATION, ENGLISH, EARLY 14TH CENTURY
The Granger Collection

Humanities Note

Illumination, A bailiff supervising the harvest (August). This early fourteenth-century illumination was probably from a book of days, a prayer book used by the nobility for daily prayer, with an illumination for each month. In such prayer books, a standard scene was used for each month. August, for example, would always be illustrated with a harvest scene.

This illumination shows the toil of the peasant on a manorial farm. The peasant's life was governed by the seasons, and late summer was the time for harvesting two major crops, wheat and rye.

4 Historical Context In order to obtain a record of these holdings, in 1086 William commissioned a census called the Domesday Book.

BRITISH EVENTS

1066	Saxons defeated at Hastings.
1073	Canterbury becomes England's religious center.
c. 1075	Construction on Tower of London begins.
1100	Henry I becomes king.
1110	First recorded miracle play performed at Dunstable.
c. 1130	Oxford becomes a center for learning.
c. 1136	Geoffrey of Monmouth writes *Historia Regum Britanniae*.
1151	Chess introduced to England.
1170	Thomas Becket, Archbishop of Canterbury, murdered.
1171	Henry II conquers southeastern Ireland.
1176	First Eisteddfod, Welsh festival of poetry and music.
1180	Glass windows first used in private homes.
c. 1190	Beginning of legendary era of Robin Hood.
1215	King John forced to sign Magna Carta.
1218	First Newgate Prison built in London.
1233	First coal mined at Newcastle.
1258	First commoners allowed in Parliament.
c. 1265	Roger Bacon writes *Opus Majus*.

The Murder of Thomas Becket

King John Signs the Magna Carta

Roger Bacon

Pope Gregory IX

Manuscript of

The Siege of Jerusalem During the First Crusade

Genghis Khan

The Song of Roland   Twelfth-century Chess Piece

WORLD EVENTS

1096	Europe and Middle East: First Crusade begins.
c. 1100	France: *Song of Roland* written.
c. 1120	Portugal: Alfonso VII defeats Moors.
c. 1150	Spain: First paper manufactured.
	Poem of El Cid written.
c. 1160	France: Troubadours glorify courtly love in poems and songs.
1174	Italy: Tower of Pisa built.
1189	Europe and Middle East: Third Crusade begins.
1192	Austria: Duke Leopold imprisons Richard I of England.
1194	Iceland: *Elder Edda*, a collection of Norse myths and legends, first appears.
1203	Germany: Wolfram von Eschenbach writes *Parzival*.
1214	China: Mongol leader Genghis Khan captures Peking.
1221	Italy: First known sonnet appears.
1233	Europe: Pope Gregory IX establishes Inquisition.
1241	Eastern Europe: Mongols withdraw from Poland and Hungary.
1266	Italy: Thomas Aquinas writes *Summa Theologiae*.

Introduction 77

Clarification Draw students attention to the beginnings of the Inquisition in 1233. Note that it started as a dispute over theological orthodoxy among different orders of Catholic priests (Benedictans, Dominicans, Augustinians, etc.) and did not take on interdenominational dimensions until much later.

Clarification Tell students that when the plague broke out in 1348, those who were able left the country to seek safety in areas of continental Europe where there were no reported instances of the contagion. As with other contagious infections, this probably helped to spread the disease.

BRITISH EVENTS

1272	Edward I becomes king.
c. 1281	Cambridge University founded.
1282	England conquers Wales.
c. 1285	The legendary Patrick Spens's ship wrecked off Aberdeen, Scotland.
1295	Edward I assembles Model Parliament.
1337	Beginning of Hundred Years' War with France.
1348	Black death begins sweeping through England.
1372	Bible first translated into English.
c. 1375	Surviving version of *Sir Gawain and the Green Knight* written.
1381	Peasants' Revolt.
1386	**Chaucer** begins writing *The Canterbury Tales*.
c. 1450	*The Second Shepherds' Play* first performed.
1455	Beginning of Wars of the Roses.
1460	Richard of York killed at Battle of Wakefield.
c. 1470	**Thomas Malory** writes *Morte D' Arthur*.
1476	William Caxton builds first English printing press.

François Villon

Joan of Arc

Printer's Device Used by Caxton

Black Death

Marco Polo

Johann Gutenburg Printing First Bible

Sweeps Through England

Canterbury Tales

Battle During the Hundred Years' War

WORLD EVENTS

1271	China: Marco Polo visits court of Kublai Khan.
1291	Europe and Middle East: End of Crusades.
1297	South Pacific: Moas, large flightless birds, become extinct.
1307	Italy: Dante begins writing *The Divine Comedy*.
1312	Africa: Mali Empire reaches its zenith.
1327	Mexico: Aztecs establish Mexico City.
1332	India: Bubonic plague begins.
1341	Italy: Petrarch crowned poet laureate in Rome.
1346	France: English defeat French at Crecy.
1348	Italy: Boccaccio publishes *Decameron*.
c. 1400	Italy: Beginning of Medici rule.
1416	Italy: Donatello sculpts *St. George*.
1428	France: Joan of Arc leads French in breaking Siege of Orleans.
1438	Peru: Inca Empire reaches its zenith.
c. 1450	North America: Iroquois nations unite.
1453	France: Hundred Years' War with England ends.
	Germany: First Gutenberg Bible printed.
1461	France: François Villon publishes *Grand Testament*.
1483	Portugal: John II refuses to finance Columbus.
1484	Italy: Botticelli paints *Birth of Venus*.

Introduction 79

Clarification Remind students that when Columbus was refused sponsorship by Portugal in 1483 it was not skepticism about his theories that accounted for the rejection. Other voyagers, from Ireland and the Scandanavian countries, had already established an Atlantic crossing route that brought them as far south along the coast as the location that would eventually become Boston.

5 **Historical Context** Henry II was, of course, a direct descendant of the Norman line through his mother, Maud, granddaughter of William the Conqueror.

6 **Enrichment** T. S. Eliot's play *Murder in the Cathedral* (Harcourt Brace Jovanovich, 1964) recreates this incident.

7 **Literary Movement** See the Prologue to the *Canterbury Tales* (page 117).

Reign of the Plantagenets

Although Norman influence continued for centuries, Norman rule ended in 1154 when Henry Plantagenet, Count of Anjou, came to the throne as Henry II. Henry founded the royal house of Plantagenet, otherwise known as the Angevin (from Anjou) line of English monarchs. A strongly committed ruler, Henry established a record as one of England's ablest kings. He had an avid interest in government and a keen understanding of the law.

Henry II and the Church

Henry's concern with legal matters led him into direct conflict with the Church. By the twelfth century, the Church had grown ever more powerful, obtaining the authority to put clergymen on trial in Church-run courts. Henry sought to curb some abuses connected with this privilege. When the archbishop's seat at Canterbury fell vacant, he appointed his friend Thomas Becket to the position, expecting Becket to go along with royal policy. Instead, Becket defied the king and appealed to the Pope in Rome. The Pope sided with Becket, provoking Henry to rage.

Some of Henry's knights misunderstood the royal wrath. In 1170, four of them went to Canterbury and murdered Becket in his cathedral. Henry quickly condemned the crime and tried to atone for it by making a holy journey, or pilgrimage, to Becket's tomb. Thereafter a pilgrimage to Becket's shrine at Canterbury became a common English means of showing religious devotion. The characters in Chaucer's *The Canterbury Tales,* for example, make just such a pilgrimage.

Origins of Constitutional Government

The next king, Richard I, spent most of his reign staging military expeditions overseas. His activities proved costly, and his successor, King John, inherited the debts. John tried to raise money by ordering new taxes on the barons and saved money by curtailing services such as the sending of judges to local districts to settle quarrels. The barons resisted these measures, bringing England to the edge of civil war. To avert further trouble, King John at last agreed to certain of the barons' conditions by putting his seal to the Magna Carta (Latin for "Great Charter").

In this document, the king promised not to tax land without first meeting with the barons. He also said he would choose as his officers only those "who know the law of the realm and mean to observe it well." The Magna Carta produced no radical changes in government. Yet many historians believe that the document's restrictions on royal power marked the beginning of constitutional government in England.

Constitutional government continued to develop under subsequent kings. During the reign of Henry III, the Great Council of barons who advised the king came to be called Parliament. Henry's

KING JOHN SIGNING THE MAGNA CARTA AT RUNNYMEDE, 15TH JUNE 1215: COLORED ENGRAVING, 18TH CENTURY
The Granger Collection

successor, Edward I, became the first king to summon a Parliament partly elected by "free men"—a term that included some ordinary townspeople as well as barons. By the end of the thirteenth century, then, Parliament had already been established as a cornerstone of government in the British Isles.

The Growth of Towns

It was no accident that some members of Parliament now represented townspeople. In the thirteenth century, towns were becoming increasingly important in English life. The Crusades, a series of religious wars in the twelfth and thirteenth centuries, had stimulated trade between Europe and the Middle East. As trade expanded, so did Europe's trading centers. The largest of these centers in England was London, originally built by the Romans. Four times more populous than any other English community, London had already achieved status as a city.

In London and elsewhere, townspeople organized themselves into guilds, or associations, of various sorts. The two most significant types were merchant guilds and craft guilds. Merchant guilds were formed in an effort to promote business within a town, often at the expense of other towns nearby. As these guilds became more powerful, some of them virtually took over town governments. Craft guilds, like our modern labor unions, sought to protect the interests of workers such as weavers, carpenters, and tanners. They also tried to assure the quality of the work these craftspeople produced. Such organizations operated in a world in which advancement was tightly controlled. A young person typically entered a craft as an apprentice, or beginner, and worked his way up the ladder, sometimes reaching the highest rung as master craftsman.

The growth of towns meant that wealth was no longer restricted to land ownership, which remained a privilege of the nobility.

FOUR KINGS OF ENGLAND DEPICTED ON A PAGE OF A 13TH-CENTURY MANUSCRIPT
The Granger Collection

Introduction **81**

FUNERAL OF PLAGUE VICTIM IN HOUSE OF FITZEISULF TRINITY CAPEL WINDOW, CANTERBURY CATHEDRAL, 14TH CENTURY
The Granger Collection

Unfortunately, it also meant that people lived much closer together, often under conditions that were far from sanitary. When infectious diseases came to England, they spread havoc in the towns. The worst epidemic, a great plague called the Black Death, swept the island in 1348 and 1349, killing a third of the population.

THE LATER MIDDLE AGES

By the time of the Black Death, England had already passed into the period known as the Later Middle Ages. This period lasted from the beginning of the fourteenth century to the end of the fifteenth. During these years, the house of Lancaster replaced the Plantagenets on the throne, only to be replaced in turn by the house of York. The Lancastrian kings were Henry IV, Henry V, and Henry VI, all of whom later became central figures in the historical dramas of Shakespeare.

During the Later Middle Ages, the feudal system went into a steep decline. As new towns appeared, feudal notions of land tenure seemed more and more outdated. After the Black Death swept across England, a massive labor shortage increased the value of a peasant's work. More and more land owners began paying their farmers in cash, giving these workers a greater sense of freedom. Along with freedom went frustration, as peasants began complaining about discriminatory laws and onerous taxation. Finally, in 1381, peasants in southern England staged a revolt, demanding, among other things, an end to serfdom. Although the revolt was eventually crushed, many of its causes continued, and so did the peasants' discontent.

An Attack on the Church

At about the time of the peasants' revolt, other complaints were being directed at the church. They came from an outspoken scholar, John Wycliffe (c. 1320–84), who thought that religion had traveled far from its roots. Wycliffe opposed all forms of wealth among the clergy. He showed only scorn for monks, calling them men with "red and fat cheeks and great bellies." He believed that all religious authority sprang from the Bible, not from the Church.

Wycliffe directed the translation of the Bible into English in the hope of making it more accessible to the people. He also helped to organize an order of "poor priests" known as Lollards. Eventually, the archbishop of Canterbury moved against the Lollards as heretics, people who attack Church doctrine and undermine Church authority. Yet the Lollards continued to spread Wycliffe's teachings for a number of years after the scholar's death.

Wars of the Roses

Just as the English Middle Ages had opened with a struggle for power, they closed with a similar conflict. This one began in 1453, when King Henry VI suffered the first of many bouts of madness. Parliament appointed his cousin Richard of York as temporary head of government. When Henry recovered briefly, Richard was forced from office, and Henry returned to the throne. Richard would not depart without a fight, however. The resulting civil war became known as the first War of the Roses, for it pitted the house of York, whose symbol was a white rose, against the house of Lancaster, whose symbol was a red rose.

In 1461, a Yorkist victory put Richard's son, Edward, on the throne. As Edward IV, he ruled England until his death in 1483, when his eldest son, still a boy, became Edward V. Soon afterward, Edward V and his brother died mysteriously in the Tower of London while under the supposed protection of their uncle, Richard of Gloucester. Richard, accused by many people of these "Tower murders," then proclaimed himself King Richard III.

Two years later, Henry Tudor, a distant cousin and supporter of the Lancastrian kings, led a rebellion against the unpopular King Richard and killed him. Tudor, crowned Henry VII, later married Richard's niece. By doing so, he united the houses of York and Lancaster and ended the Wars of the Roses. By the time Henry had established a new royal line, the house of Tudor, the English Middle Ages had ended.

CHIVALRY AND ROMANCE

Most societies have lived by a well-established set of ideals, and England of the Middle Ages was no exception. One set of standards by which people measured themselves during these years was the code of knightly behavior known as chivalry. The idea of chivalry first arose on the European continent at the time of the

KING HENRY VII OF ENGLAND
Panel, 1505, by Michiel Sittow
The Granger Collection

Introduction **83**

Humanities Note

Fine art, *Sir Galahad,* 1864, by Dante Gabriel Rossetti. During the medieval period, the tales of King Arthur and his knights developed. Sir Galahad, one of Arthur's knights known for his purity and nobility of spirit, is an appropriate subject for Dante Gabriel Rossetti (1828–1882). Rossetti, a Victorian artist, was the leader of a group of friends known as the Pre-Raphaelite Brotherhood, whose desire was to paint in a simple, sincere way, true to nature. Their striving to show a simpler time is reflected in Rossetti's painting of Galahad, a pure and noble knight in an idealized world.

10 Literary Movement Three great bodies of narrative developed in the Middle Ages: the matter of Britain, which concentrated mainly on the Arthurian legend; the matter of France, which centered around Charlemagne; and the matter of Rome, which celebrated classical heroes.

Crusades. Although the Crusades often involved brutality and bloodshed, they encouraged warriors to search for higher rules of conduct.

At first the code dealt mainly with loyalty and valor, both on and off the battlefield. By the thirteenth century, however, chivalry had grown considerably more complex. Every knight was supposed to pledge his service to a lady. He might also be expected to joust for his lady's favor or to rescue maidens in distress.

French poets known as troubadours popularized this tradition in songs of gallant knights. Originally these songs were written in Romance, or Roman-influenced, languages rather than Latin, and so they were called romances. At the French court, it became important for knights to treat ladies with a respect that bordered on reverence. Gradually the same ideal took root in the English court.

The Legend of King Arthur

One example illustrating the development of chivalry originated with the Celts. For centuries after their defeat by the Anglo-Saxons, the Celts had told stories of a great hero, King Arthur. Inasmuch as historians cannot say for certain whether Arthur actually lived or not, tales about him are considered legends, a blend of fiction and fact. When the Normans were battling the Anglo-Saxons, they became interested in the old Celtic legends. In about 1136, a Welsh-born scholar, Geoffrey of Monmouth (c. 1100–54), drew upon his knowledge of Celtic legends and his readings of Bede to produce a *History of the Kings of Britain.* This fanciful history, though written in Latin, quickly popularized the early Celtic king.

10 | Because of the Normans' French ties, the tales of Arthur spread not only in England but also in France. There they were influenced

SIR GALAHAD, 1864 (WATERCOLOR)
Dante Gabriel Rossetti
The Granger Collection

by other romances, often involving the French hero Charlemagne. New versions of the Arthur legend, though usually set in the past, began to depict Arthur as more modern in his practices. His Knights of the Round Table became paragons of chivalry, as adept in courtly love as they were in fighting battles. The legend also inspired *Sir Gawain and the Green Knight,* a fourteenth-century narrative poem by an anonymous author. In the poem an Arthurian knight, Sir Gawain, displays all the virtues of chivalry in his battles with the Green Knight, a supernatural figure.

Arthurian romance reached its height with *La Morte d' Arthur (The Death of Arthur),* a fifteenth-century prose work by Sir Thomas Malory (d. 1471). Translating from French sources, Malory created the most complete Middle English compilation of the various legends involving Arthur and his court. *La Morte d' Arthur* was printed in twenty-one volumes.

LEARNING AND LITERATURE

Although the Normans and French eventually had great influence on English letters, that development did not begin in 1066. To the contrary, the Norman invasion put a temporary halt to scholarship and literature in the British Isles. After the turbulence of conquest subsided, however, England experienced a "little renaissance," a small rebirth of learning, in the twelfth century. Although monasteries continued their scholastic traditions, new centers of learning emerged. Scholars flocked to the religious community at Oxford to hear lectures by noted visitors; then colleges were built to house the scholars, and the first English university was born. A second university at Cambridge followed some years later.

Probably the most famous scholar that Oxford produced in the Middle Ages was Roger Bacon (c. 1214–94), a scientist and mathematician now considered the father of English philosophy. A member of the Franciscan brotherhood, Bacon created his *Opus Majus* (Major Work), a Latin study of science, grammar, mathematics, and philosophy, at the request of the Pope. Later, however, the Church condemned Bacon as a heretic. The scholar died in obscurity, probably at Oxford, but his ideas were taken up a century later by another Franciscan, William Ockham (d. 1349). Like Bacon, Ockham attempted to use a scientific approach in exploring the universe; he, too, was accused of heresy.

While Latin remained the language of Church and university scholarship, Norman French was frequently used in government. Both languages contributed to what came to be called Middle English. Latin literature gradually gave way to literature written in the vernacular, or the language of the people. The use of the vernacular increased after 1372, when John Wycliffe began directing the English translation of the Bible. Wycliffe's work proved a major advance for literature, inasmuch as it encouraged more people to learn to read.

JOHANN GUTENBERG EXAMINING THE FIRST PROOF OF HIS PRINTED BIBLE FROM HIS PRESS AT MAINZ; AFTER THE PAINTING BY J. L. G. FERRIS
The Granger Collection

Humanities Note

Print, Johann Gutenberg examining the first proof of his printed Bible, after the painting by J. L. G. Ferris. Johannes Gutenberg, of Mainz, Germany, was the first to perfect the process of typography. The first book he printed was the Bible, now known as the Gutenberg Bible. This print from a later period shows the moment when Gutenberg sees his first proof of his Bible.

11 **Enrichment** Ockham is probably best remembered today for his law of parsimony, known as "Ockham's razor": an argument must be shaved down to its simplest terms.

A page from the Lansdowne manuscript of Chaucer's *Canterbury Tales*. This page is from an early edition of *The Canterbury Tales*. Like other manuscripts of the period, the page is illuminated with decoration in the margin and of the capital *W*.

12 Historical Context Chaucer's connection with the English court was extensive. Not only did he serve as a page in the household of Lionel, Edward III's third son, but he also married Phillipa Swynford, sister of John of Gaunt's mistress, whose offspring were later legitimatized and whose descendants became the Tudor kings.

A PAGE FROM THE LANSDOWNE MS OF GEOFFREY CHAUCER'S CANTERBURY TALES
The Granger Collection

Another important invention of the period, printing from movable type, also encouraged literacy. In 1454 a German silversmith, Johann Gutenberg, devised a printing process with individual metal letters that could be used again and again. Printing spread rapidly from Germany to other parts of Europe, and further improvements were made. In 1476 a London merchant, William Caxton (c. 1422–91) set up the first movable-type press in England. This invention meant that English literature no longer needed to be hand copied by church scribes. Now it could be produced far more quickly and made available to a much wider circle of readers.

POETRY OF THE ENGLISH MIDDLE AGES

One of Caxton's first projects was the printing of *The Canterbury Tales.* His enthusiasm for this verse showed the importance that he and others placed on poetry in general. Two key poets of the period, William Langland and Geoffrey Chaucer, lived during the later Middle Ages. Their writings reveal the changes that were taking place in the English language and in society as a whole.

William Langland

Scholars know very little about the poet they usually call William Langland. He appears to have come from western England and to have been a country boy. In his masterpiece, *Piers Plowman,* he followed a tradition of the Middle Ages by writing in the form of an allegory, a work in which most of the characters, settings, and events are arranged in a symbolical pattern. He also took a typically Anglo-Saxon delight in alliteration.

Like John Wycliffe, Langland was greatly concerned with the ways the wealthy oppress the poor. He left little doubt that his sympathies went out to those who had been treated harshly by the world. His most vivid writing concerned events he may have witnessed—tavern squabbles, for instance, or the misery of people suffering from the plague. Some scholars judge *Piers Plowman* one of the most deeply felt poems in all of English literature.

Geoffrey Chaucer

The towering figure of Middle English verse is Geoffrey Chaucer. In many estimates he ranks second only to Shakespeare as **12** England's greatest writer. Chaucer owed much of his early sophistication to his training as an attendant to King Edward III. The poet also traveled widely and familiarized himself with important Italian poets, including Dante and Petrarch.

Chaucer's major works include a number of narrative poems, such as the verse romance *Troilus and Criseyde* (1372–86) and several shorter poems. Yet his finest achievement was *The Canterbury Tales,* a series of verse stories told by different pilgrims on their way to the tomb of Thomas Becket. The pilgrims represent many walks of life—a knight, a squire, a clerk, a friar, a nun, a miller, a merchant, and so on. In Chaucer's deft hands, each storyteller emerges as a vivid personality in his or her own right. Some of the tales have religious themes; others are humorous or satiric. All in all, they provide a remarkable portrait of life in the later Middle Ages.

Lyrics and Ballads

Europeans of the Middle Ages had a fondness for a harplike instrument called the lyre. In palaces and castles, poets often strummed lyres as they recited their verse. From this custom English lyric poetry developed.

Lyric poems of this period fall into two main categories, secular and religious. The usual topics of the secular poetry are love or nature; many of them celebrate the renewal of spring or the joys of summer:

> Sumer is icumen in;
> Lhude° sing cuccu!   °Loudly

Religious lyrics might consist of a hymn praising God or a prayer of supplication. One of the most famous religious lyrics in Middle English celebrates the Virgin Mary:

> I syng of myden
>   That is makeles;°   °matchless
> Kyng of alle kynges
>   To here son che ches.   °she chose

Another includes the Latin line *Timor mortis conturbat me* ("The fear of death disturbs me") to teach the lesson that in the midst of life there is death:

> In what state that ever I be,
>   *Timor mortis conturbat me.*
>
> As I me walked in on° morning   °one
> I hard a birde both wepe and synge;
> This was the tenor of her talkynge:
>   *Timor mortis conturbat me.*

13 Another popular poetic form was the ballad, a folk song that told a story. Experts find most surviving ballads impossible to date. Those from the Scottish border probably arose long after the Middle Ages, and those from before 1485 have most likely changed a good deal over the centuries.

One surviving series of ballads concerns Robin Hood, a legendary hero who may have existed around the turn of the thirteenth century. Robin, an outlaw, lives in the woods with his band of "merrye" men, robbing from the rich and helping the poor. He and his lady friend, Maid Marian, eventually became part of traditional

ROBIN HOOD
Richard Dadd
Center for British Art,
Paul Mellon Collection

Sketch of Robin Hood by Richard Dadd. Dadd (1817–1886), a British painter, studied at the Schools of the Royal Academy. He began his career as painter of genre scenes, or scenes of ordinary life. In 1842 he illustrated the ballad "Robin Goodfellow" for Hall's *Book of British Ballads*. This sketch of his is a nineteenth-century interpretation of the legend of Robin Hood (Robin Goodfellow). The lovely woodland scene and the dramatic clothing contribute to an idealized and romanticized picture of Robin Hood.

13 Literary Movement Ballads remained a totally oral form until the eighteenth century, when Bishop Percy began collecting and recording them.

Check Test
1. _____ was a friend of Henry II's who was killed over a dispute in 1170.
2. The Latin name for The Great Charter is _____ .
3. The Black Death killed _____ percent of the population of England.
4. The shape of King Arthur's famous table was _____ .
5. The name of the author of *The Canterbury Tales* is _____ .

Answers
1. Thomas Becket
2. Magna Carta
3. 33%
4. round
5. Chaucer

May Day festivities. These folk celebrations honoring the coming of spring took place each year on the first day of May.

DRAMA OF THE MIDDLE AGES

The theater of William Shakespeare had its roots in the dramas of the Middle Ages. During early Norman times, the Church often sponsored plays as part of religious services. In time, these plays moved from the church to the churchyard and then to the marketplace. The earliest dramas were miracle plays, in England sometimes also called mystery plays. They retold stories from the Bible or dealt with some aspect of the lives of saints.

Over the years the theater gained in popularity among English townspeople. Several communities became famous for performing a particular series of plays, or cycle, which presented a Biblical history of humankind. York, the religious capital of northern England, had one of the largest cycles. Chester and Wakefield also staged multi-play productions. Clergymen usually wrote the plays, and actors performed them on wagons or fixed scaffolds. Each of the town's craft guilds would take turns producing one play.

During the turbulent years of the fifteenth century, a new kind of drama arose—the morality play. Morality plays depicted the life of an ordinary person, sometimes from birth to death. Along the way the hero meets characters who symbolize abstract qualities, such **14** as Vice or Virtue. The purpose of these allegorical dramas was to teach a moral lesson.

The most famous surviving morality play is *Everyman,* which had its origin in the Netherlands and was not adapted for English audiences until about 1500. By that time, Middle English was giving way to modern English, the form of the language we speak today. Even so, *Everyman* is usually studied as part of Middle English literature, for it is one of the most powerful examples of the kinds of morality plays performed in the later Middle Ages.

Subsequent generations of writers owe a great debt to the literature of the English Middle Ages. In Chaucer, the era produced the first major writer in English to be known and respected for his craft. With works such as *Everyman,* the period produced the foundations of the great English dramatic tradition. In addition, the romantic adventures of King Arthur and his knights became a source to which future writers would turn again and again.

Manners maketh man.
> **William of Wykeham,** Motto of two colleges at Oxford

It behooves us to place the foundations of knowledge in mathematics.
> **Roger Bacon,** *Opus Majus*

Who pulleth out this sword of this stone and anvil, is rightwise king born of all England.
> **Sir Thomas Malory,** *Morte d' Arthur*

> In a somer seson whan soft was the sonne
> Who will bell the cat?
>> **William Langland,** *Piers Plowman*

A foule may ek° a wys-man often gide.°   °also   °guide
> **Geoffrey Chaucer,** *Troilus and Criseyde*

Looke who that is moost vertuous alway,
Pryvee° and apert, and most entendeth ay   °private, secret
To do the gentil dedes that he kan;
Tak him for the grettest gentil man.
> **Geoffrey Chaucer,** "The Wife of Bath's Tale," *The Canterbury Tales*

Pacience is an heigh vertu, certeyn.
> **Geoffrey Chaucer,** "The Franklin's Tale," *The Canterbury Tales*

> When captains couragious, whom death could not daunte
> Did march to the seige of the city of Gaunt,
> They mustered their soldiers by two and by three
> And the foremost in battle was Mary Ambree.
>> **Anonymous,** "Mary Ambree"

> Come listen to me, you gallants so free,
>> All you that loves mirth for to hear,
> And I will you tell of a bold outlaw
>> That lived in Nottinghamshire.
>> **Anonymous,** "Robin Hood and Allen a Dale"

90

Reading Critically The feature on this page is designed to help students read critically the literature of the Medieval Period. The information given here helps students place a work of literature in its historical context, understand the literary movements of the time, and appreciate the writers' techniques used to convey the ideas of the period.

Discuss the information on this page with your students. Explain that the selection that accompanies this page, from *Morte D'arthur,* is a model for reading critically the literature of this period. It contains in the side column notes that draw attention to elements that reflect the historical context, the influence of literary movements, and the writer's techniques. Ask students to pay attention to these notes as they read the selection. Also suggest that they make their own critical comments as they read.

To give students further practice with the process of reading critically, use the selection in the Teaching Portfolio, "The Unquiet Grave," p. 71, following the Teacher Backup, which students can annotate themselves. Encourage students to use these strategies as they read the literature in this unit.

READING CRITICALLY

The Literature of 1066–1485

When you read literature, it is important to place it in its historical context. Doing so will help you to understand influences on the writer's ideas and techniques.

Historical Context

In 1066 the Normans conquered England by defeating the Anglo-Saxons at the Battle of Hastings. Although many Anglo-Saxon traditions and attitudes survived the invasion, the Normans dramatically changed English life by introducing a social, economic, and political system called feudalism. Under this system, land was divided among noble overlords. Controlling large, self-sufficient feudal manors, the overlords were served by knights, who provided protection, and serfs, who farmed the land and herded animals. Although it was an ideal that few of them may have actually attained, the knights tried to live according to the code of chivalry, which required them to be honorable, courteous, brave, and skillful. Toward the later part of this period, gunpower was replacing swords and the feudal order was being replaced by the aristocratic code.

Literary Movements

The concept of chivalry played an important role in shaping the literature of the Medieval Period. When chivalry was blended with such magical elements as giants, wizards, sorcerers, and dragons, the form of literature known as the romance was created. Filled with fantasy, adventure, and courtly love, romances were one of the most popular literary forms of the period. Apart from romantic literature, most of the literature of the period reflected the influence of religion. This influence is most noticeable in the two forms of drama that were popular during the period: mystery plays and morality plays.

Writers' Techniques

Although the first printing press was established toward the end of the Medieval Period, much of the literature of the period was composed orally. Folk ballads were sung or recited by common people and passed down from generation to generation. These ballads, along with most other medieval literature, were written in verse and told a story. Toward the end of the period, however, a number of writers began writing prose.

On the following pages is a selection by Thomas Malory, the first English writer to compile and arrange the numerous legends of King Arthur. The notes in the side column should help you to place the selection in its historical context.

90   *The Medieval Period*

Objectives

1 To analyze legends
2 To recognize elements of fantasy
3 To appreciate word origins
4 To write about character

Support Material

Teaching Portfolio
Teacher Backup, p. 67
Grammar in Action Worksheet, *Understanding Past Perfect Tense,* p. 72
Usage and Mechanics Worksheet, p. 74
Analyzing Literature Worksheet, *Understanding Legends,* p. 75

Critical Thinking and Reading Worksheet, *Recognizing Elements of Fantasy,* p. 76
Selection Test, p. 77
Art Transparency 2, *Morgan-le-Fay,* Frederick Sandys

from Morte d'Arthur

Sir Thomas Malory

Historical Context: Malory's Morte d'Arthur was completed around 1470. The legend of a king who adheres to the principles of chivalry is a fitting subject for this period during which feudalism was dying. The legend itself may be based on the life of a Celtic Chieftain who lived during the sixth century.

This selection begins after King Arthur has traveled to France at the insistence of his nephew, Gawain, to besiege his former friend and knight, Lancelot, for his involvement with Queen Guenevere. However, the king's attempts to punish are halfhearted, and he is soon forced to abandon them altogether when he learns that his nephew, Mordred, has seized control of England. Arthur leads his forces back to England, and Mordred attacks them upon their landing. Gawain is killed in the fighting, but before he dies, he manages to send word to Lancelot that Arthur is in need of assistance.

So upon Trinity Sunday at night King Arthur dreamed a wonderful dream, and in his dream him seemed[1] *that he saw upon a chafflet*[2] *a chair, and the chair was fast to a wheel, and thereupon sat King Arthur in the richest cloth of gold that might be made. And the King thought there was under him, far from him, an hideous deep black water, and therein was all manner of serpents, and worms, and wild beasts, foul and horrible. And suddenly the King thought that the wheel turned upside down, and he fell among the serpents, and every beast took him by a limb. And then the King cried as he lay in his bed, "Help, help!"*

And then knights, squires, and yeomen awaked the King, and then he was so amazed that he wist[3] not where he was. And then so he awaked until it was nigh day, and then he fell on slumbering again, not sleeping nor thoroughly waking. So the King seemed[4] verily that there came Sir Gawain unto him with a number of fair ladies with him. So when King Arthur saw him, he said, "Welcome, my sister's son. I weened ye had been dead. And now I see thee on-live, much am I beholden

Literary Movement: King Arthur was a common subject of medieval romances.

Literary Movement: Strange, unnatural beasts such as serpents are often depicted in medieval romances.

1. **him seemed:** It seemed to him.
2. **chafflet:** Platform.
3. **wist:** Knew.
4. **the King seemed:** It seemed to the King.

Presentation

Motivation/Prior Knowledge Students are familiar with the Arthur legend and like it very much. Allow them to share with the class what they have learned from reading or from movies about Arthur and his kingdom. You can structure this in a variety of ways from speeches to skits to debates to informal discussions.

Thematic Idea Another selection that deals with the theme of chivalry is *"Sir Gawain and the Green Knight,"* page 170.

Purpose-Setting Question The code of chivalry demands a knight be loyal to his lord, fulfill his responsibilities to his vassals, respect the Christian faith, and be an example of courtly love. How well does Arthur fulfill the chivalric ideal? Which qualities are exhibited by Sir Gawain?

Master Teacher Note Medieval man tended to believe in the truth and prophetic power of dreams. It is interesting to note that a belief in the importance of dreams was revived in the nineteenth century with the investigations of Sigmund Freud into the human psyche. The study of dreams remains an essential element in contemporary psychoanalysis. In this story, does Arthur believe his dreams?

unto Almighty Jesu. Ah, fair nephew and my sister's son, what been these ladies that hither be come with you?''

''Sir,'' said Sir Gawain, ''all these be ladies for whom I have foughten for when I was man living. And all these are those that I did battle for in righteous quarrels, and God hath given them that grace, at their great prayer, because I did battle for them for their right, that they should bring me hither unto you. Thus much hath given me leave God, for to warn you of your death. For and ye fight as tomorn[5] with Sir Mordred, as ye both have assigned, doubt ye not ye must be slain, and the most party of your people on both parties. And for the great grace and goodness that Almighty Jesu hath unto you, and for pity of you and many more other good men there shall be slain, God hath sent me to you of his special grace to give you warning that in no wise ye do battle as tomorn, but that ye take a treaty for a month from today. And proffer you largely,[6] so that tomorn ye put in a delay. For within a month shall come Sir Lancelot with all his noble knights and rescue you worshipfully and slay Sir Mordred and all that ever will hold with him.''

Then Sir Gawain and all the ladies vanished. And anon the King called upon his knights, squires, and yeomen, and charged them wightly[7] to fetch his noble lords and wise bishops unto him. And when they were come the King told them of his avision,[8] that Sir Gawain had told him and warned him that, and he fought on the morn, he should be slain. Then the King commanded Sir Lucan the Butler and his brother Sir Bedivere the Bold, with two bishops with them, and charged them in any wise to take a treaty for a month from today with Sir Mordred. ''And spare not: proffer him lands and goods as much as ye think reasonable.''

So then they departed and came to Sir Mordred where he had a grim host of an hundred thousand, and there they entreated Sir Mordred long time. And at the last Sir Mordred was agreed for to have Cornwall and Kent by King Arthur's days, and after that, all England, after the days of King Arthur.

---

5. and . . . tomorn: If you fight tomorrow.
6. proffer you largely: Make generous offers.
7. wightly: Quickly.
8. avision: Dream.

Then were they condescended[9] that King Arthur and Sir Mordred should meet betwixt both their hosts, and each of them should bring fourteen persons. And so they came with this word unto Arthur. Then said he, "I am glad that this is done," and so he went into the field.

And when King Arthur should depart, he warned all his host that, and they see any sword drawn, "Look ye come on fiercely and slay that traitor Sir Mordred, for I in no wise trust him." In like wise Sir Mordred warned his host that "And ye see any manner of sword drawn, look that ye come on fiercely, and so slay all that ever before you standeth, for in no wise I will not trust for this treaty." And in the same wise said Sir Mordred unto his host, "For I know well my father will be avenged upon me."

And so they met as their pointment[10] was and were agreed and accorded thoroughly. And wine was fetched and they drank together. Right so came an adder out of a little heathbush, and it stung a knight in the foot. And so when the knight felt him so stung, he looked down and saw the adder. And anon he drew his sword to slay the adder, and thought none other harm. And when the host on both parties saw that sword drawn, then they blew beams,[11] trumpets, and horns, and shouted grimly. And so both hosts dressed them together. And King Arthur took his horse and said, "Alas, this unhappy day!" and so rode to his party, and Sir Mordred in like wise.

And never since was there never seen a more dolefuller battle in no Christian land, for there was but rushing and riding, lunging and striking; and many a grim word was there spoken of either to other, and many a deadly stroke. But ever King Arthur rode throughout the battle[12] of Sir Mordred many times and did full nobly, as a noble king should do, and at all times he fainted never. And Sir Modred did his devoir that day and put himself in great peril.

Historical Context: Bravery and skill in battle were important aspects of chivalry.

And thus they fought all the long day, and never stinted[13] till the noble knights were laid to the cold earth. And ever

---

9. condescended: Agreed.
10. pointment: Arrangement.
11. beams: A type of trumpet.
12. battle: Battalion.
13. stinted: Stopped.

Humanities Note

Fine art, Detail of *Arthur, The Nine Heroes Tapestry*. This Gothic tapestry, woven of vegetable-dyed wool, was probably made in France about 1385. There is no record of the maker, but it may be the work of the master weaver Nicholas Bataille. The tapestry was made for Jean, Duc de Berry, the third son of John III of France.

Tapestries were often commissioned by the nobility of the fourteenth century to use as covering and decoration for the cold stone walls of their fortified castles. Their portability made them especially useful to the ruling princes who took them along to beautify transient lodgings when traveling to do battle, to collect tithes, or to oversee their lands.

The tapestry fragment, *Arthur,* from the *Nine Heroes Tapestry,* was originally part of a three-tapestry set. Each piece measured 21' × 16' and depicted a group of heroes from legend: three pagans, three Hebrews, and three Christians. Only the figure of Arthur remains on the Christian heroes tapestry; the others have been lost over time. Arthur is identified by the three crowns on his tunic and banner representing England, Scotland, and Brittany. The field of the tapestry, divided by architectural motifs, is enlivened by various small figures. Although the once brilliant colors have faded with time, they are still a pleasing hue. The extreme skill of the weaver is evident in the delicate shading of the features and clothing of the king.

In discussing this work with your class you may wish to point out that the legend of King Arthur, alive in the fourteenth century, is still with us today, due in part to the unknown artisans who wove the Gothic tapestries.

THE NINE HEROES TAPESTRIES. CHRISTIAN HEROES: ARTHUR WITH THREE CARDINALS
Probably Nicolas Bataille, Paris
The Metropolitan Museum of Art

94   *The Medieval Period*

they fought still till it was near night, and by then was there an hundred thousand laid dead upon the down. Then was King Arthur wood-wroth[14] out of measure when he saw his people so slain from him. And so he looked about him and could see no more of all his host, and good knights left no more on-live, but two knights: the t'one was Sir Lucan the Butler and the other his brother Sir Bedivere. And yet they were full sore wounded.

"Jesu, mercy," said the King, "where are all my noble knights become? Alas that ever I should see this doleful day! For now," said King Arthur, "I am come to mine end. But would to God," said he, "that I wist now where were that traitor Sir Mordred that has caused all this mischief."

Then King Arthur looked about and was ware where stood Sir Mordred leaning upon his sword among a great heap of dead men.

"Now give me my spear," said King Arthur unto Sir Lucan, "for yonder I have espied the traitor that all this woe hath wrought."

> **Writer's Technique:** King Arthur is motivated by his love for his slain knights to confront Mordred.

"Sir, let him be," said Sir Lucan, "for he is unhappy. And if ye pass this unhappy day ye shall be right well revenged upon him. And, good lord, remember ye of your night's dream, and what the spirit of Sir Gawain told you tonight, and yet God of his great goodness hath preserved you hitherto. And for God's sake, my lord, leave off by this, for, blessed be God, ye have won the field: for yet we been here three on-live, and with Sir Mordred is not one on-live. And therefore if ye leave off now, this wicked day of destiny is past."

> **Historical Context:** Sir Lucan demonstrates his loyalty to King Arthur. Loyalty to one's king or overlord was an important medieval virtue.

"Now, tide[15] me death, tide me life," said the King, "now I see him yonder alone, he shall never escape mine hands. For at a better avail shall I never have him."

"God speed you well!" said Sir Bedivere.

Then the King got his spear in both his hands and ran toward Sir Mordred, crying and saying, "Traitor, now is thy deathday come!"

And when Sir Mordred saw King Arthur he ran until him with his sword drawn in his hand, and there King Arthur smote Sir Mordred under the shield, with a thrust of his spear, throughout the body more than a fathom. And when

---

14. wood-wroth: Wild with rage.
15. tide: Befall.

from *Morte d'Arthur*   95

96

Writer's Technique: Both Mordred and Arthur exhibit their skill in battle.

Sir Mordred felt that he had his death's wound, he thrust himself with the might that he had up to the burr[16] of King Arthur's spear, and right so he smote his father King Arthur with his sword holden in both his hands, upon the side of the head, that the sword pierced the helmet and the casing of the brain. And therewith Sir Mordred dashed down stark dead to the earth.

And noble King Arthur fell in a swough to the earth, and there he swooned oftentimes, and Sir Lucan and Sir Bedivere ofttimes heaved him up. And so, weakly betwixt them, they led him to a little chapel not far from the seaside, and when the King was there, him thought him reasonably eased. Then heard they people cry in the field. "Now go thou, Sir Lucan," said the King, "and do me to wit[17] what betokens that noise in the field."

So Sir Lucan departed, for he was grievously wounded in many places. And so as he walked he saw and harkened by the moonlight how that pillagers and robbers were come into the field to pill and to rob many a full noble knight of brooches and bracelets and of many a good ring and many a rich jewel. And who that were not dead all out there they slew them for their harness and their riches. When Sir Lucan understood this work, he came to the King as soon as he might and told him all what he had heard and seen. "Therefore by my read,"[18] said Sir Lucan, "it is best that we bring you to some town."

Writer's Technique: Arthur's dream foreshadows his death.

"I would it were so," said the King, "but I may not stand, my head works so. Ah, Sir Lancelot," said King Arthur, "this day have I sore missed thee. And alas that ever I was against thee, for now have I my death, whereof Sir Gawain me warned in my dream."

Then Sir Lucan took up the King the t'one party[19] and Sir Bedivere the other party; and in the lifting up the King swooned and in the lifting Sir Lucan fell in a swoon that part of his guts fell out of his body, and therewith the noble knight's heart burst. And when the King awoke he beheld Sir Lucan how he lay foaming at the mouth and part of his guts lay at his feet.

---

16. burr: Hand guard.
17. me to wit: Let me know.
18. read: Advice.
19. party: Side.

Grammar in Action

Use the **past perfect tense** to indicate an action completed before another past action. Malory writes:

> When Sir Lucan understood this work, he came to the king as soon as he might and told him all what he *had heard* and *seen.*

What Sir Lucan heard and saw occurred before his reporting it to the king. Therefore, Malory used the past perfect form of *hear* and *see.*

The past perfect tense is also used to indicate a condition completed before another past condition.

> Bill was the captain of the baseball team. Last year, he *had been* captain of the soccer team.

Student Activity. The following paragraph is written entirely in the past tense.

Enrichment Sir Bedivere's struggle to throw Excalibur into the lake—he fails twice to fulfill Arthur's command before he successfully hurls the sword on the third try—follows a typical pattern in legends: three tries at a task, with only the last successful. Ask students to give other examples of this pattern.

"Alas," said the King, "this is to me a full heavy sight to see this noble duke so die for my sake, for he would have helped me that had more need of help than I. Alas that he would not complain him for his heart was so set to help me. Now Jesu have mercy upon his soul."

Then Sir Bedivere wept for the death of his brother.

"Now leave this mourning and weeping, gentle knight," said the King, "for all this will not avail me. For wit thou well, and I might live myself, the death of Sir Lucan would grieve me evermore. But my time passeth on fast," said the King. "Therefore," said King Arthur unto Sir Bedivere, "take thou here Excalibur my good sword and go with it to yonder water's side; and when thou comest there I charge thee throw my sword in that water and come again and tell me what thou sawest there."

"My lord," said Sir Bedivere, "your commandment shall be done, and I shall lightly[20] bring you word again."

So Sir Bedivere departed. And by the way he beheld that noble sword, that the pommel and the haft[21] was all precious stones. And then he said to himself, "If I throw this rich sword in the water, thereof shall never come good, but harm and loss." And then Sir Bedivere hid Excalibur under a tree. And so, as soon as he might, he came again unto the King and said he had been at the water and had thrown the sword into the water.

"What saw thou there?" said the King.

"Sir," he said, "I saw nothing but waves and winds."

"That is untruly said of thee," said the King. "And therefore go thou lightly again and do my commandment; as thou art to me loved and dear, spare not, but throw it in."

Then Sir Bedivere returned again and took the sword in his hand. And yet him thought sin and shame to throw away that noble sword. And so eft[22] he hid the sword and returned again and told the King that he had been at the water and done his commandment.

"What sawest thou there?" said the King.

"Sir," he said, "I saw nothing but waters wap and waves wan."[23]

Writer's Technique: Notice the dilemma here. A knight's first duty is to obey his king, but Sir Bedivere sees the value of the sword and cannot bring himself to carry out King Arthur's command.

---

20. lightly: Quickly.
21. pommel . . . haft: Hilt and hand guard.
22. eft: Again.
23. waters . . . wan: Waters lap and waves grow dark.

from *Morte d'Arthur*   97

Mary arrived at the lake at dawn. She put all her fishing tackle into the boat and rowed out to the cove. She fished for an hour without catching anything. Finally, at about seven, she caught a small bass. Then she caught a pike. By the time she rowed back to shore, she caught three more bass and two more pike.

If this paragraph began *Mary told us about her fishing trip,* the use of the past tense verb *told* would require that all the verbs that follow be changed to the past perfect tense. Rewrite the paragraph so that the verb tenses are appropriate to this new opening sentence.

"Ah, traitor unto me and untrue," said King Arthur, "now hast thou betrayed me twice. Who would have weened that thou that has been to me so loved and dear, and thou art named a noble knight, and would betray me for the riches of this sword. But now go again lightly, for thy long tarrying putteth me in great jeopardy of my life, for I have taken cold. And but if thou do now as I bid thee, if ever I may see thee I shall slay thee mine own hands, for thou wouldest for my rich sword see me dead."

Literary Movement: Magic was an important element of medieval romances.

Then Sir Bedivere departed and went to the sword and lightly took it up, and so he went to the water's side; and there he bound the girdle about the hilts, and threw the sword as far into the water as he might. And there came an arm and an hand above the water and took it and clutched it, and shook it thrice and brandished; and then vanished away the hand with the sword into the water. So Sir Bedivere came again to the King and told him what he saw.

"Alas," said the King, "help me hence, for I dread me I have tarried overlong."

Then Sir Bedivere took the King upon his back and so went with him to that water's side. And when they were at the water's side, even fast[24] by the bank floated a little barge with many fair ladies in it; and among them all was a queen; and all they had black hoods, and all they wept and shrieked when they saw King Arthur.

"Now put me into that barge," said the King; and so he did softly. And there received him three ladies with great mourning, and so they set them down. And in one of their laps King Arthur laid his head, and then the queen said, "Ah, my dear brother, why have ye tarried so long from me? Alas, this wound on your head hath caught overmuch cold." And anon they rowed fromward the land, and Sir Bedivere beheld all tho ladies go froward him.

Then Sir Bedivere cried and said, "Ah, my lord Arthur, what shall become of me, now ye go from me and leave me here alone among mine enemies?"

"Comfort thyself," said the King, "and do as well as thou mayest, for in me is no trust for to trust in. For I must into the vale of Avilion[25] to heal me of my grievous wound. And if thou hear nevermore of me, pray for my soul."

---

24. fast: Close.
25. Avilion: A legendary island.

But ever the queen and ladies wept and shrieked, that it was pity to hear. And as soon as Sir Bedivere had lost sight of the barge he wept and wailed, and so took the forest and went all that night.

And in the morning he was ware, betwixt two bare woods, of a chapel and an hermitage. Then was Sir Bedivere glad, and thither he went, and when he came into the chapel he saw where lay an hermit groveling on all fours, close thereby a tomb was new dug. When the hermit saw Sir Bedivere he knew him well, for he was but little tofore Bishop of Canterbury, that Sir Mordred put to flight.

"Sir," said Sir Bedivere, "what man is there here interred that you pray so fast for?"

"Fair son," said the hermit. "I wot not verily but by guessing. But this same night, at midnight, here came a number of ladies and brought here a dead corpse and prayed me to inter him. And here they offered an hundred tapers, and gave me a thousand gold coins."

"Alas," said Sir Bedivere, "that was my lord King Arthur, which lieth here buried in this chapel."

Then Sir Bedivere swooned, and when he awoke he prayed the hermit that he might abide with him still, there to live with fasting and prayers:

"For from hence will I never go," said Sir Bedivere, "by my will, but all the days of my life here to pray for my lord Arthur."

Writer's Technique: Sir Bedivere's request conveys his undying devotion to King Arthur.

"Sir, ye are welcome to me," said the hermit, "for I know you better than ye think that I do: for ye are Sir Bedivere the Bold, and the full noble duke Sir Lucan the Butler was your brother."

Then Sir Bedivere told the hermit all as you have heard tofore, and so he stayed with the hermit that was beforehand Bishop of Canterbury. And there Sir Bedivere put upon him poor clothes, and served the hermit full lowly in fasting and in prayers.

Thus of Arthur I find no more written in books that been authorized, neither more of the very certainty of his death heard I nor read, but thus was he led away in a ship wherein were three queens; that one was King Arthur's sister, Queen Morgan le Fay, the other was the Queen of North Galis, and the third was the Queen of the Waste Lands.

Writer's Technique: Malory's reference to the "books that been authorized" makes his account seem factual.

Now more of the death of King Arthur could I never find, but that these ladies brought him to his grave, and such one was interred there which the hermit bare witness that was

from *Morte d'Arthur* 99

Master Teacher Note Place Art Transparency 2, *Morgan-le-Fay*, by Frederick Sandys, on the overhead projector. Point out that the woman represents the artist's idea of what Morgan-le-Fay might have looked like had she been a real person. Ask your students to describe what different, and maybe even conflicting, impressions they get of her. After they have read the selection from Malory, your students might return to the painting and discuss what they think of Sandys's conception of Morgan-le-Fay.

once Bishop of Canterbury. But yet the hermit knew not in certain that he was verily the body of King Arthur; for this tale Sir Bedivere, a knight of the Table Round, made it to be written.

Yet some men say in many parts of England that King Arthur is not dead, but carried by the will of our Lord Jesu into another place; and men say that he shall come again, and he shall win the Holy Cross. Yet I will not say that it shall be so, but rather I would say: here in this world he changed his life. And many men say that there is written upon the tomb this:

> HIC IACET ARTHURUS, REX
> QUONDAM, REXQUE FUTURUS[26]

---

26. Hic . . . futurus: Here lies Arthur, who was once king and king will be again.

Sir Thomas Malory 1405[?]–1471 wrote *Morte d'Arthur* by compiling and giving order to a collection of French, English, and Latin tales about King Arthur and the Knights of the Round Table. The work was first published in 1485 by William Caxton, after Caxton had established the first printing press in England.

Although Malory seems to have stayed on the right side of the law while young, his arrest in 1451 for damaging a monastery in Lincolnshire signalled the beginning of his lifelong battles with authority. He was also brought up on charges of breaking out of jail, twice for looting the Abbey of Coombe, and for extortion—as well as various other crimes. He denied all the charges against him, but was convicted and jailed nonetheless. Malory spent most of his later years in prison, probably because he supported the Lancasters while the Yorkists ruled England during the War of the Roses. In fact, it was in prison that he wrote *Morte d' Arthur.*

Malory lived in a wild, unruly time, torn by the strife of the War of the Roses. Harassed by those in power, perhaps he defended taking the law into his own hands as a political necessity. Scholars have suggested, however, that he had a fierce temper and was not against confrontations. Malory most likely died in jail, after King Edward IV, a Yorkist, expressly barred him from two amnesties he allowed the other Lancaster supporters.

Closure and Extension

ANSWERS TO THINKING ABOUT THE SELECTION
Recalling

1. Arthur is warned not to do battle with Mordred the next day or he will die.

THINKING ABOUT THE SELECTION

Recalling

1. What warning does King Arthur receive in his dream?
2. (a) What instruction does Arthur give his men before he leaves to meet Mordred? (b) What does Mordred tell his men?
3. (a) How does Arthur slay Mordred? (b) What does Mordred do just before he dies?
4. (a) What does Sir Lucan observe when Arthur sends him back to the battlefield? (b) How does Sir Lucan die?
5. (a) What does Sir Bedivere learn on the morning after the battle? (b) What does he decide to do as a result of his discovery?

Interpreting

6. (a) How would you characterize Arthur? (b) How would you characterize Mordred?
7. What do you think are Sir Bedivere's reasons for twice failing to obey Arthur's request to throw Excalibur in the water?
8. What is ironic, or unexpected, about the way the battle begins?
9. How does the ending add to the mysterious, magical quality of the tale?

Applying

10. Why do you think the legend of King Arthur has retained its popularity for so long?

ANALYZING LITERATURE

Recognizing Legends

Legends are anonymous traditional stories popularly believed to be based on history. Generally, legends reflect the attitudes and values of the society that created them, and the heroes of legends usually possess qualities that the people of that society consider admirable. Legends also often involve evil characters who possess qualities considered undesirable.

1. What qualities does King Arthur possess that would have been considered admirable during medieval times?

2. What qualities does Mordred possess that would be considered undesirable?

CRITICAL THINKING AND READING

Recognizing Elements of Fantasy

Although legends are popularly believed to be based on history, they often involve characters with superhuman powers and contain fantastic events.

1. What incident occurs in this selection that is clearly an example of fantasy?
2. What makes the women who come for Arthur at the end of the selection seem magical and mysterious?

UNDERSTANDING LANGUAGE

Appreciating Word Origins

As a result of the Norman conquest, many French words were introduced into the English language. For example, Malory uses the word *quarrel,* which comes from the French word *querele,* meaning "complaint."

The words below are of French origin. Use your dictionary to find the French word and meaning from which each word comes.

1. vanish   3. rescue
2. preserve   4. depart

THINKING AND WRITING

Writing About Character

Write an essay in which you discuss what this excerpt reveals about King Arthur's character. Reread the selection, focusing on Arthur's comments and behavior. Also take note of how the other characters react to him. When you write your essay, use evidence from the selection to support your argument. When you finish writing, revise and proofread your essay.

from Morte d'Arthur 101

---

2. (a) If a sword is drawn, attack Mordred. (b) If a sword is drawn, attack all the men in front of them.
3. (a) Arthur kills him with the thrust of a spear. (b) Mordred hits Arthur on the side of his head with his sword.
4. (a) Lucan sees pillagers and robbers stealing from the dead and killing the wounded for their valuables. (b) He dies trying to carry Arthur.
5. (a) Bedivere learns that three mysterious women have brought a

body to the chapel for burial. (b) He decides to remain there at the chapel for the rest of his life, praying for Arthur.

Interpreting

6. (a) Arthur is a noble lord, the epitome of the chivalric king. (b) Mordred seems vindictive and insolent.
7. It seems a shame to waste such a beautiful sword. It seems almost sinful to him.

8. The battle begins by accident, when a knight tries to kill a snake that has bitten him. Neither side intentionally breaks the agreement, but neither waits for an explanation.
9. The implication that Arthur may return is a supernatural suggestion.

Applying

10. Answers will differ. Some possible answers might be that the desire

(Answers begin on p. 100.)

for perfection, the loss of love, the idea that the righteous will triumph, and the element of mystery and magic are themes of timeless popularity.

ANSWERS TO ANALYZING LITERATURE

1. Arthur's admirable qualities would be willingness to do his duty, readiness to sacrifice, loyalty to his men, honor, a respect for truth, courteousness and gentleness, bravery in battle, and courage in death.
2. Lack of loyalty to his liege, lack of honor, and greed are some of Mordred's undesirable qualities.

ANSWERS TO CRITICAL THINKING AND READING

1. The incident involving throwing Excalibur into the lake and the summoning of the women of Avalon are fantasy.
2. The women arrive just at the minute Arthur is brought to the lake shore.

ANSWERS TO UNDERSTANDING LANGUAGE

1. *Vanquish* is from *veinquis.*
2. *Preserve* is from *preserver.*
3. *Rescue* is from *rescourre.*
4. *Depart* is from *departir.*

THINKING AND WRITING

For help with this assignment, students can refer to Lesson 9, "Writing About Character," in the Handbook of Writing About Literature.

Writing Across the Curriculum
After the students have written a draft of their essays, have them consult with the psychology teacher or counselor to check the validity of their observations. Schedules and time commitments permitting, invite a counselor, a psychology teacher, or the school psychologist into class to be interviewed about Arthur's character as revealed in his comments and behavior. After the interview, have the students revise their papers, adding insights from the discussion.

More About the Ballads Since ballads were part of an oral tradition, there is no evidence that even the earliest versions we have are, in fact, the original versions. Their composition flourished during the 14th and 15th centuries, then ceased. It was not, however, until the 1765 publication of Bishop Percy's *Reliques of Ancient Popular Poetry* that they were printed and widely circulated. You might wish to point out that Percy's book was based on an old manuscript he rescued at a friend's house in Shropshire from a housemaid who was about to light the fire with it. What kinds of changes do you think might have occurred during the intervening three hundred years?

Critical Evaluation The influence of English and Scottish ballads on American folk music is considerable. Even as early as 1929, when Phillips Barry edited a text entitled *British Ballads From Maine,* efforts were being made to trace the exchanges that continue to allow the ballad to be popular. In comparing the songs he studied in Appalachia to those of northern New England, Mr. Barry pointed out the following: "We have to admit that the northern and southern texts are not only equally old but that they must have arrived about the same time from England, brought over the sea by people who knew the same version, and therefore most likely coming from the same locality. Such coincidences did not occur through the chances of later commercial intercourse, and the ballads in which they do occur are always the oldest."

English And Scottish Folk Ballads

Long before most people in Britain could read or write, they were familiar with the stories told in ballads. A **ballad** is a narrative poem, usually brief, that is meant to be sung. When the writer is unknown, the ballad is called a **folk** ballad, or sometimes a **popular** or **traditional** ballad. Such ballads as "Barbara Allan" have been recited, chanted, or sung from their earliest appearance down to the present day.

No one knows when the first folk ballads appeared in Britain, but it was probably during the twelfth century. Since the ballads were unwritten, they were passed along orally for many centuries. Most of the earliest ballads we know about probably date from the fifteenth century. Even at that time, no one paid much attention to them as literature. Not until 1765, with the publication of Bishop Thomas Percy's *Reliques of Ancient English Poetry,* did ballads come to be recognized as a fascinating part of Britain's literary heritage.

Sir Walter Scott, the author of *Ivanhoe,* was one of a number of famous writers whose interest in old ballads was sparked by Percy's *Reliques.* Scott often traveled to the Scottish-English border region to collect material on the subject. His *Minstrelsy of the Scottish Border,* published in 1803, is a pioneer work of scholarship on the background and variations of Scottish ballads.

The four ballads in this unit originated in the wild, rugged border country between England and Scotland. Their language is the Scots dialect of English. As they were passed along from person to person, place to place, and generation to generation, these ballads often acquired new words and new verses. There is no such thing as a standard version of a folk ballad, because every balladeer feels free to make alterations. Literally hundreds of versions of "Barbara Allan" have appeared in print.

Many ballads handed down to us in English have counterparts in other languages. This is because the incidents they describe are shared by much of European folklore. Both "Barbara Allan" and "The Twa Corbies" are found in other languages, for example, as is "Sir Patrick Spens," although not in its present form.

Folk ballads, with their familiar melodies, are truly songs of the people. Later writers, including Sir Walter Scott, produced literary ballads in imitation of the traditional ones. But few literary ballads have had the power of the old folk ballads to capture and hold the imagination.

Objectives

1 To analyze folk ballads
2 To understand language change

Support Material

Teaching Portfolio
Teacher Backup, p. 79
Usage and Mechanics Worksheet, p. 83
Vocabulary Check, p. 84
Analyzing Literature Worksheet, *Understanding the Folk Ballad,* p. 85
Language Worksheet, *Appreciating Language Change,* p. 86
Selection Test, p. 87

Sir Patrick Spens; Get Up and Bar the Door; The Twa Corbies; Barbara Allan

Literary Forms

Folk Ballad. It is not surprising that folk ballads appeared on the rugged English-Scottish border. Folk ballads are typically found in areas where a formal, written literature has yet to develop, or where people's lives do not permit books and reading.

A folk ballad usually presents a single dramatic episode. It is told impersonally, through action and dialogue, with very little characterization, description, or motivation. The story seems to be simple and direct, yet because it often begins in the middle, lacks transitions, and skips over incidents without explanation, it can convey an air of mystery. Ballads deal with many subjects: adventure, love, jealousy, heroism, disaster, revenge. A few folk ballads are humorous.

Most ballads have quatrains, or four-line stanzas, in which the second and fourth lines rhyme. Often, but not always, there are eight syllables in the first and third lines and six syllables in the second and fourth lines. Ballads frequently have a refrain—a regularly repeated phrase or line at the end of a stanza, or sometimes a whole separate stanza. The general effect is musical, as you would expect in poems meant to be sung.

Writing

Most popular music has a brief life span. Songs from a few years ago tend to sound dated and sentimental to listeners today. Yet folk ballads have been sung for centuries and in some places are still performed for appreciative audiences. Why? What is it that can make a song so enduring? Freewrite about the qualities that you think make a song become a long-lasting popular classic.

Primary Source

One of the most enduring modern ballads is "Taxi," Harry Chapin's haunting lament of lost love and opportunity. The story begins with the chance meeting between a down-and-out taxi driver and his seemingly successful former girl friend:

> It was raining one night in 'Frisco.
> I needed one more fare to make my night.
> A lady up ahead waved to flag me down
> She got in at the light.

"Through the too many miles and the too little smiles," the narrator remembers their dreams. By the end of the song, he realizes that neither he nor his former love are happy. What other modern ballads do you know that are meant to be sung?

Guide for Interpreting 103

Literary Focus Although ballads were once considered to be communally produced songs, modern scholars have instead focused on individual authorship. The authors, all unknown, have left few individual marks on their work. Ballads, unlike lyric poetry, generally lack reflection and sentiment. They are impersonal in tone. They almost never employ a first-person point of view. They simply present the chief incidents of a story.

Writing/Prior Knowledge Ask the students what popular songs they think will become long-lasting. Write the titles on the board. Discuss what they have in common.

Vocabulary

Preteach the following vocabulary words:
loath (lōth) *adj.:* Reluctant; unwilling (l. 29, p. 104)
fathoms (fath' əmz) *n.:* Units of measure for the depth of water; a fathom is six feet (l. 42, p. 104)
twa (twä) *n.:* Two (Scot.) (l. 13, p. 108)
gang (gaŋ)*v.:* To go or walk (Scot.) (l. 4, p. 110)
gowden (gou' d'n) *adj.:* Golden *(Scot.)* (l. 15, p. 110)
healths (helthz) *n.:* Wishes for happiness, as in drinking a series of toasts (l. 19, p. 111)

Sir Patrick Spens

This version of "Sir Patrick Spens" is in the original Middle English.

The king sits in Dumferling[1] toune,
 Drinking the blude-reid wine:
"O whar will I get guid sailor,
 To sail this schip of mine?"

5 Up and spak an eldern knicht,
 Sat at the kings richt kne:
"Sir Patrick Spens is the best sailor,
 That sails upon the se."

The king has written a braid letter,
10 And signd it wi his hand,
And sent it to Sir Patrick Spens,
 Was walking on the sand.

The first line that Sir Patrick red,
 A loud lauch lauchèd he;
15 The next line that Sir Patrick red,
 The teir blinded his ee.

"O wha is this has don this deid,
 This ill deid don to me,
To send me out this time o' the yeir,
20 To sail upon the se!

"Mak hast, mak hast, my mirry men all
 Our guid schip sails the morne:"
"O say na sae, my master deir,
 For I feir a deadlie storme.

25 "Late, late yestreen I saw the new moone,
 Wi the auld moone in hir arme,
And I feir, I feir, my deir master,
 That we will cum to harme."

O our Scots nobles wer richt laith
30 To weet their cork-heild schoone,
Bot lang owre a' the play wer playd,
 Thair hats they swam aboone.

---

1. Dumferling: A town in Scotland near Edinburgh.

MEDIEVAL BARON DINING; FROM BREVIARIUM GRIMARI, 15TH CENTURY
The Bettmann Archive

Sir Patrick Spens

This version of "Sir Patrick Spens" is in modern English.

The king sits in Dumferling town,
    Drinking the blood-red wine:
"O where will I get a good sailor,
    To sail this ship of mine?"

5 Up and spoke an ancient knight,
    Sat at the king's right knee:
"Sir Patrick Spens is the best sailor,
    That sails upon the sea."

The king has written a broad letter,
10   And signed it with his hand,
And sent it to Sir Patrick Spens,
    Was walking on the sand.

The first line that Sir Patrick read,
    A loud laugh laughed he;
15 The next line that Sir Patrick read,
    The tear blinded his eye.

"O who is this has done this deed,
    This ill deed done to me,
To send me out this time of the year,
20   To sail upon the sea!

"Make haste, make haste, my merry men all
    Our good ship sails the morn:"
"O say not so, my master dear,
    For I fear a deadly storm.

25 "Late, late yesterday evening I saw the new moon,
    With the old moon in her arm,
And I fear, I fear, my dear master,
    That we will come to harm."

O our Scots nobles were right loath
30   To wet their cork-heeled shoes,
But long before the play were played,
    Their hats they swam above.

Sir Patrick Spens 105

Presentation

Motivation/Prior Knowledge
Play a recording of a modern ballad that is familiar to students. List characteristics of ballads that students observe in the song. Ask them to notice any similarities in the ballads they are about to read.

Master Teacher Note "Sir Patrick Spens" is one of the indisputably historical ballads. The hero was a warrior–mariner of the thirteenth century, beloved by all except a small faction of enemies.

Thematic Idea Sir Patrick's unquestioning obedience can be usefully compared and contrasted with Sir Bedivere's procrastinating obedience in the selection from Malory, page 91.

Purpose-Setting Question How does this ballad conform to the standards of a ballad? We often speak of a "no-win" situation. Is Sir Patrick Spens in one?

1 **Discussion** The subject matter of ballads is traditionally tragic. Does the description of wine as "blood-red" seem to be a foreshadowing?

2 **Enrichment** In one version the king explains that he must fetch his daughter home from "Noroway."

3 **Clarification** A "broad letter" is probably an official document.

4 **Critical Thinking and Reading** Another common ballad element is repetition. In this ballad it is incremental: repetition that advances the action. In what other lines does this same incremental repetition occur?

5 **Discussion** What does Sir Patrick's question here suggest? Does he believe he has enemies at court?

O lang, lang may their ladies sit,
  Wi thair fans to their hand,
35 Or eir they se Sir Patrick Spens
  Cum sailing to the land.

O lang, lang may the ladies stand,
  Wi thair gold kems in their hair,
Waiting for thar ain deir lords,
40 For they'll se thame na mair.

Half owre, half owre to Aberdour,[1]
  It's fiftie fadom deip,
And thair lies guid Sir Patrick Spens,
  Wi the Scots lords at his feit.

---

1. **Aberdour:** A town near Edinburgh.

THINKING ABOUT THE SELECTION

Recalling

1. What problem does the king face at the beginning of the ballad?
2. From whom does the king get the idea of having Sir Patrick Spens sail for him?
3. How does Sir Patrick Spens react to the king's letter?

Interpreting

4. Why do you think the king's wine is described as "blood-red"?
5. Why does Sir Patrick Spens view the king's request as an "ill deed"?
6. In the seventh stanza, why does the sailor think the voyage is ill-fated?
7. (a) What happens to the Scots lords who dislike the idea of getting their "cork-heeled shoes" wet? (b) How do you know? (c) How is this outcome ironic?
8. In what way does Sir Patrick Spens seem to embody Medieval ideals of duty?

Applying

9. Sir Patrick Spens does his duty despite serious—and his well-founded—misgivings. What might he have done to avoid sailing? How wise would such a course of action have been?

ANALYZING LITERATURE

Understanding Folk Ballads

"Sir Patrick Spens," like most folk ballads, is short and deals with a single episode. Abrupt transitions and the absence of characterization and description force the audience to make assumptions about characters, places, and events. Dialogue moves the story along.
1. (a) How many characters are directly quoted in the poem? (b) Who are they?
2. What are some of the missing details in "Sir Patrick Spens" that, if included, would make the ballad easier to understand?

Closure and Extension

ANSWERS TO THINKING ABOUT THE SELECTION
Recalling

1. The king needs a good sailor to sail his ship.
2. An ancient knight suggests the king get Sir Patrick.
3. First Sir Patrick laughs and then he cries.

Interpreting

4. The wine is "blood-red" as a premonition of the ending.
5. It is an ill deed because the seas are treacherous that time of year.
6. The sailor notices that the moon looks strange.
7. They are drowned. (b) Line 32 states their hats swam above them. (c) More than their shoes get wet—they drown.
8. Sir Patrick obeys his king without hesitation.

Applying

9. Answers will differ but students should recognize Sir Patrick might have spoken directly with the king and tried to persuade him to change his mind. Such an attempt, however, might have been unwise, since to refuse the order could have brought disastrous results.

O long, long may their ladies sit,
    With their fans into their hand,
35 Or ever they see Sir Patrick Spens
    Come sailing to the land.

O long, long may the ladies stand,
    With their gold combs in their hair,
Waiting for their own dear lords,
40   For they'll see them no more.

Halfway over, halfway over to Aberdour,
    It's fifty fathoms deep
And there lies good Sir Patrick Spens,
    With the Scots lords at his feet.

6

6 Literary Focus The climax in these concluding stanzas is considered by ballad scholars to be superb. Do you agree? Why?

Reader's Response Which version of this poem do you favor? Why?

Challenge Write the stanzas to fill in the holes in the poem that you mentioned in Analyzing Literature?

UNDERSTANDING LANGUAGE

Recognizing Language Change

A centuries-old ballad like "Sir Patrick Spens" looks different today from how it looked when it first appeared in print. Not only is the old Scots dialect unfamiliar to most modern readers, so is much of the spelling and vocabulary of the standard English of that day.

1. What are five words in the first stanza whose spellings have changed over the years?

2. In the fifth stanza, note that the *ei* spelling has changed in two different ways. What are the two ways?

3. How is each of the following words written in modern English?
   a. knicht   d. owre
   b. lauch   e. kems
   c. schoone

Commentary

Many serious ballads reveal that love and bravery, however great, are not enough to prevent doom. In humorous ballads, in contrast, people use wit to successfully counter evil and misfortune. Sometimes humorous ballads are built around riddles as a device to outwit an opponent and defuse a dangerous situation. "The Riddle Song" illustrates this. Before you read the last stanza, see if you can guess the answer to the riddles.

1. I gave my love a cherry that has no stones,
   I gave my love a chicken that has no bones,
   I gave my love a ring that has no end.
   I gave my love a baby that's no cryen.

2. How can there be a cherry that has no stones?
   How can there be a chicken that has no bones?
   How can there be a ring that has no end?
   How can there be a baby that's no cryen?

3. A cherry when it's blooming, it has no stones,
   A chicken when it's pipping [hatching], it has no bones,
   A ring when it's rolling, it has no end,
   A baby when it's sleeping, it's no cryen.

ANSWERS TO ANALYZING LITERATURE

1. (a) There are two characters quoted. (b) They are Spens and the sailor.
2. Answers will differ. Some possible responses would be why the ancient knight suggests Sir Patrick for the journey and why the king needs to send the ship out in a dangerous season.

ANSWERS TO UNDERSTANDING LANGUAGE

1. Five words spelled differently today are *town*, *blood*, *red*, *good*, and *ship*.
2. Two ways to spell the *ei* sound are *ee* and *ea*.
3. (1) knight, (2) laugh, (3) shoes, (4) before, (5) combs

Motivation/Prior Knowledge
Discuss the following ideas with
your students. The "war" between men and women is the
subject of movies, television series, novels, and poetry. Do you
think it is real? Why or why not?

Master Teacher Note Many
works of literature deal with the
eternal question of male–female
relationships. Why is this subject
of timeless interest to writers?

Thematic Idea For a different
poetic treatment of husband-wife
relationships, see Robert Browning's "My Last Duchess," p. 812.

Purpose-Setting Question What
does this poem imply about the
war between men and women?

1 **Enrichment** In the Middle Ages
holidays were literally holy days;
consequently, seasonal references tended to be religious. *Martinmas* means *St. Martin's Mass,* or
feast day, in the same way that
Christmas means *Christ's Mass.*

2 **Enrichment** The "puddings" are
not desserts here but dishes containing suet (animal fat) boiled in a
bag. The black puddings mentioned in line 26 are probably
blood sausages.

3 **Reading Strategy** Ask the students to predict the winner of the
contest.

4 **Discussion** Why do you think the
visitors could see neither coal nor
candlelight?

Get Up and Bar the Door

1
2

It fell about the Martinmas[1] time,
    And a gay time it was then,
When our goodwife got puddings to make,
    She's boild them in the pan.

5 The wind sae cauld blew south and north.
    And blew into the floor;
Quoth our goodman to our goodwife,
    "Gae out and bar the door."

3

"My hand is in my hussyfskap,[2]
10   Goodman, as ye may see;
An it should nae be barrd this hundred year,
    It's no be barrd for me."[3]

They made a paction[4] tween them twa.
    They made it firm and sure.
15 That the first word whaeer shoud speak,
    Shoud rise and bar the door.

Then by there came two gentlemen,
    At twelve o'clock at night,
And they could neither see house nor hall,
4
20   Nor coal nor candlelight.

"Now whether is this a rich man's house,
    Or whether it is a poor?"
But neer a word wad ane o' them[5] speak,
    For barring of the door.

25 And first they[6] ate the white puddings,
    And then they ate the black:
Tho muckle[7] thought the goodwife to hersel,
    Yet neer a word she spake.

Then said the one unto the other,
30   "Here, man, take ye my knife;
Do ye tak aff the auld man's beard,
    And I'll kiss the goodwife."

1. Martinmas time:
November 11.

2. hussyfskap: Household
duties.

3. "it should . . . me": It
will not be barred in a
hundred years if it has to
be barred by me."
4. paction: Agreement.

5. them: The man and
his wife.

6. they: The strangers.

7. muckle: Much.

"But there's nae water in the house,
    And what shall we do than?"
35 "What ails ye at the pudding broo,[8]
    That boils into[9] the pan?"

⌐ 5

8. "What . . . broo:
"What's the matter with
pudding water?
    9. into: In.

O up then started our goodman,
    An angry man was he:
"Will ye kiss my wife before my een,
40   And scad[10] me wi pudding bree?"[11]

10. scad: Scald.
11. bree: Broth.

Then up and started our goodwife,
    Gied three skips on the floor:
"Goodman, you've spoken the foremost word;
    Get up and bar the door."

⌐ 6

5 **Discussion** Why does the visitor comment that there's no water in the house?

6 **Critical Thinking and Reading** Although most ballads are tragic in theme, "Get Up and Bar the Door" is an exception. It deals humorously with domestic argument. Why do you think the wife wins the argument?

Reader's Response What impression did you get from this poem's title?

THINKING ABOUT THE SELECTION
Recalling

1. Why does the goodwife refuse to bar the door when her husband first asks?
2. What agreement do the husband and wife reach about barring the door?
3. To whom does the word *one* refer in line 29?
4. What do the two strangers plan to do to (a) the goodman? (b) the goodwife?
5. (a) Who wins the battle of wills between husband and wife? (b) How?

Interpreting

6. Why does the goodman want the door barred?

7. When do the goodman and his wife first become aware of the presence of the strangers?
8. In lines 25–29, the goodwife is thinking to herself. What might she be thinking?
9. What do you think the stranger means when he suggests taking "aff the auld man's beard"?
10. What serious point does this humorous ballad make?

Applying

11. Can people be hurt by stubbornness—their own or someone else's? Explain your answer.

Get Up and Bar the Door 109

Closure and Extension

ANSWERS TO THINKING ABOUT THE SELECTION
Recalling

1. The wife is busy with her housework.
2. Whichever speaks first must bar the door.
3. It refers to one of the gentlemen.
4. (a) One plans to scald his beard to scrape it off or worse. (b) The

other will kiss the wife.
5. (a) The wife wins the contest. (b) She wins by remaining silent until her husband speaks first.

Interpreting

6. The cold wind is blowing in.
7. The couple become aware of the strangers when they enter and speak.
8. Answers will differ. A suggested response will reflect her anger about the fruits of her labor being consumed by the strangers.

9. He might be suggesting that a knife be held at the goodman's throat while the stranger kisses the wife.
10. The message is that stubbornness can have some serious consequences.

Applying

11. Answers will differ. Suggested response: Yes, stubbornness, by causing one to be unreasonable or foolish, can often hurt people.

The Twa Corbies[1]

1. Twa Corbies: Two ravens.

As I was walking all alane,
I heard twa corbies making a mane.[2]
The tane unto the tither did say,
"Whar sall we gang and dine the day?"

2. mane: Moan.

5   "In behint yon auld fail dyke,[3]
I wot[4] there lies a new-slain knight;
And naebody kens[5] that he lies there
But his hawk, his hound, and his lady fair.

3. fail dyke: Bank of earth.
4. wot: know.
5. kens: knows.

"His hound is to the hunting gane,
10   His hawk to fetch the wild-fowl hame,
His lady's ta'en anither mate,
So we may mak our dinner sweet.

"Ye'll sit on his white hause-bane,[6]
And I'll pike out his bonny blue e'en;[7]
15   Wi' ae lock o' his gowden hair
We'll theek[8] our nest when it grows bare.

6. hause-bane: Neck-bone.
7. e'en: Eyes.

8. theek: Thatch.

"Mony a one for him maks mane,
But nane sall ken whar he is gane.
O'er his white banes, when they are bare,
20   The wind sall blaw for evermair."

THINKING ABOUT THE SELECTION

Recalling

1. (a) Where is the knight lying? (b) In what condition is he?
2. Who besides the ravens knows what has happened to the knight?
3. Why is the knight's lady not interested in his fate?
4. What does one of the ravens suggest doing with the knight's golden hair?

Interpreting

5. (a) How would you describe the tone of the ballad? (b) How does the tone add to the ballad's impact?
6. What effect would be lost if the incident were described by a human speaker rather than as a conversation between two ravens?

Applying

7. Stories told from the point of view of an animal are unusual but by no means rare. What other story or stories do you recall that present the viewpoint of an animal?

Presentation

Motivation/Prior Knowledge Tell your students that the ballad is a conversation between ravens about dining on the corpse of a tollen knight. Ask what atmosphere is suggested by such a scene.

Thematic Idea Another poem about death is "In Memoriam, A. H. H.," by Tennyson, page 797.

Purpose-Setting Question What view of human life and death does the ballad present? Is it pessimistic, optimistic, or realistic? What word would you use to describe the view and mood?

Teaching to Ability Levels You might read the poem to **less advanced** students and have them follow in the text. **More advanced** students might enjoy translating it into modern English for discussion.

Master Teacher Note The word *corbie* is a chiefly Scottish term for a carrion crow or raven. Many of the folk ballads are Scottish in origin.

1 Enrichment Death by murder or accident is one of the most common themes of ballads. Treating this theme by the device of a conversation between two ravens makes "The Two Corbies" one of the more distinctive medieval ballads.

2 Literary Focus A ballad traditionally has no introduction. It begins *in medias res.* This ballad is an exception. What motive might its author have had?

3 Discussion What is your response to the device of having two ravens discuss their dining plans?

4 Critical Thinking and Reading In an English version of the poem, a "lady full of woe" discovers the body, buries him, and dies before evening. Which ending do you prefer? Why?

110

Closure and Extension

ANSWERS TO THINKING ABOUT THE SELECTION
Recalling

1. (a) The knight lies on a bank of earth. (b) He is dead.
2. Nobody knows but the knight's hawk, hound, and lady.
3. The lady has another mate already.
4. The raven wants to use it to insulate their nest.

Interpreting

5. (a) There is sadness and pathos in the poem's tone. (b) Since the poem is presented by the hungry ravens and not a sympathetic onlooker, the impact to the ballad is greater.
6. The poem would lose the objectivity that is so often a part of ballads. It would also lose its strange, haunting quality.

Applying

7. Answers will differ. *Watership Down,* by Richard Adams, is one possibility.

Thematic Idea This ballad can be usefully compared with Shakespeare's "Fear No More the Heat o' the Sun," which also adopts an unusual perspective toward death.

Barbara Allan

It was in and about the Martinmas time,[1]
    When the green leaves were a-fallin';
That Sir John Graeme in the West Country
    Fell in love with Barbara Allan.

5 He sent his man down through the town
    To the place where she was dwellin':
"O haste and come to my master dear,
    Gin[2] ye be Barbara Allan."

O slowly, slowly rase[3] she up,
10   To the place where he was lyin',
And when she drew the curtain by:
    "Young man, I think you're dyin'."

"O it's I'm sick, and very, very sick,
    And 'tis a' for Barbara Allan."
15 "O the better for me ye sal[4] never be,
    Though your heart's blood were a-spillin'.

"O dinna ye mind,[5] young man," said she,
    "When ye the cups were fillin',
That ye made the healths gae round and round,
20   And slighted Barbara Allan?"

He turned his face unto the wall,
    And death with him was dealin':
"Adieu, adieu, my dear friends all,
    And be kind of Barbara Allan."

25 And slowly, slowly rase she up,
    And slowly, slowly left him;
And sighing said she could not stay,
    Since death of life had reft[6] him.

She had not gane a mile but twa,[7]
30   When she heard the dead-bell knellin',
And every jow[8] that the dead-bell ga'ed[9]
    It cried, "Woe to Barbara Allan!"

"O mother, mother, make my bed,
    O make it soft and narrow:
35 Since my love died for me today,
    I'll die for him tomorrow."

1. Martinmas time: November 11.

2. gin: If.

3. rase: Rose.

4. sal: Shall.

5. dinna ye mind: Don't you remember.

6. reft: Deprived.

7. not . . . twa: Gone but two miles.

8. jow: Stroke.

9. ga'ed: Made.

Barbara Allan 111

Humanities Note

Fine art, *Veronica Veronese,* 1872, by Dante Gabriel Rossetti (1828 –1882). Dante Gabriel Rossetti was born in London of Italian parents. He began his training as a painter at the Royal Academy but left to apprentice with the British painter Ford Madox Brown. Rossetti, a poet as well as a painter, was a founding member of the Pre-Raphaelite Brotherhood. This was a group of young artists who admired and sought to emulate the work of the Italian painters who preceded Raphael. The Pre-Raphaelite style of painting paid close attention to natural detail and dealt with romantic, moral, and religious subjects. Although the brotherhood was short-lived, lasting only five years, their mode of painting set in motion lasting changes in British art.

The painting *Veronica Veronese* was described by Rossetti as a young woman in a "passionate reverie." The skin tones and red hair glow against the green background and lush velvet texture of her gown, giving her countenance a startling beauty. The pose is one of abstracted thought. The fluid motion of the arms, the scarf, and the branch in the birdcage all serve to draw the eye back to the haunting face. The care given to even the tiniest details, such as the chain about her neck or the tassels on her belt, are an earmark of Rossetti's technique.

You might discuss the following with your class:

1. Does the woman in the painting seem to have the same strength of character as Barbara Allen in the poem?
2. Why do you think this painting was chosen to illustrate this poem? Do you think it is an apt illustration?

VERONICA VERONESE
Dante Gabriel Rossetti
Delaware Art Museum

112   *The Medieval Period*

THINKING ABOUT THE SELECTION

Recalling

1. Why does Sir John Graeme want Barbara Allan to visit him?
2. What are Barbara Allan's first words when she sees Sir John?
3. According to Sir John, why is he "sick, and very, very sick"?
4. What reason does Barbara Allan give for acting unconcerned about his plight?
5. (a) When does Barbara Allan admit how she feels about Sir John? (b) How does she feel?

Interpreting

6. (a) At what point does the ballad make you critical of Barbara Allan? (b) When does it make you sympathize with her?
7. One critic thinks that Sir John acts "like a spineless lover who gave up the ghost without a struggle." How would you answer that criticism?

Applying

8. "Barbara Allan," like most ballads, leaves out things you might like to know. If you were adding a stanza to it (not necessarily at the end), what information would you include?

CRITICAL THINKING AND READING

Interpreting Symbols in Folk Ballads

Ballads are generally concise and direct, but sometimes their words and phrases function as symbols, thereby suggesting more than is immediately evident. A **symbol** is a word, person, or object that stands for something beyond itself. For example, the events in "Barbara Allan" (as well as in "Get Up and Bar the Door") occur "about the Martinmas time." Martinmas, a Christian festival on November 11 in honor of St. Martin, gradually came to symbolize both revelry and a warm, Indian-summer break in the autumn weather. A balladeer, by making use of a well-understood symbol like Martinmas, could add meaning to a brief story without adding an excessive number of words.

1. The literal meaning of line 18, "When ye the cups were fillin'," is that Sir John was filling people's glasses with drinks. What is the symbolic meaning?
2. When Barbara Allan asks her mother to "make my bed . . . soft and narrow," in lines 33 and 34, what kind of "bed" is probably being symbolized?

SPEAKING AND LISTENING

Sharing Folk Ballads

"Barbara Allan" is one of the most widely recorded ballads in history, sometimes under the name "Bawbie Allan," "Bonnie Barbara Allan," or a similar title. It was brought to America in the earliest days of settlement. Today there are many recorded American versions as well as many English and Scottish versions of the song. As a class project, find at least five recorded versions of "Barbara Allan" and bring them to class. Play them all, noting the differences in wording from one recording to another. Decide which version the class prefers, and why.

Then look through some poetry anthologies or collections of ballads to find a ballad you like. Read it to the class. Try to give your reading the expression and intonation it would have been given by the balladeers who first sang it.

THINKING AND WRITING

Writing About a Folk Ballad

Choose one of the four folk ballads you have read. Reread it until you are sure you understand it fully. Make notes. Write the first draft of a composition, explaining the events in the ballad and noting any details that are implied but not directly stated. Point out the literary techniques —such as rhyme, dialogue, repetition—that heighten the dramatic effect of the ballad. Go over your first draft carefully, paying close attention to what you have written. Make any changes needed. Then write the final draft.

Barbara Allan 113

More About the Author In April of 1388, when Chaucer was in his forties, he actually made a pilgrimage to Canterbury. He was not looking for material, but he was struck by the mixed company assembled at the Tabard Inn at Southwark. He remembered them ten years later when he began to write the "cavalcade of fourteenth century English life" in *The Canterbury Tales,* a work which earned him the title "the father of English poetry and perhaps the prince of it." What does the second part of this title imply about Chaucer?

Critical Evaluation In his book *An Introduction to Chaucer,* Derek Brewer made the following evaluation of the poet's work: "There is no hope of summing up in a few words, after so long a book, the greatness and diversity of Chaucer's works, and their inexhaustible interest, set as they are within the rich culture of an extraordinarily interesting as well as troubled period. The peculiar mixture of old and new, of participation with detachment, of protean sympathy with irony, of multiple points of view, all of which give variety, yet for which he seems able to preserve a basis of certainty, is surely Chaucer's outstanding artistic characteristic."

GEOFFREY CHAUCER

1343[?]–1400

In his own lifetime Geoffrey Chaucer was considered the greatest English poet, and the centuries have not dimmed his reputation. With the single exception of William Shakespeare, no English writer has surpassed Chaucer's achievements. His unfinished masterpiece, *The Canterbury Tales,* ranks as one of the world's finest works of literature. It also provides the best contemporary picture we have of fourteenth century England.

Although the exact date of Geoffrey Chaucer's birth is unknown, official records furnish many of the details of his active life as a public servant. His father was a well-to-do wine merchant in London, a man with sufficient influence to get young Geoffrey a position as a page in a household connected to that of King Edward III. As a page Chaucer's duties were humble, but the job provided him an opportunity to observe the ruling aristocracy, thus broadening his knowledge of the various classes of society. In 1359, while serving in the English army in France, he was captured and held prisoner. The king paid a £16 (sixteen pounds) ransom for his release. In 1366 Chaucer married a lady-in-waiting to the queen. His marriage to Philippa de Roet lasted until her death in 1387. Scholars believe that Chaucer and his wife had three children. Their eldest, Thomas, was apparently ambitious and advanced higher in the world than his father had. Little is known about a son, probably called Lewis, and a daughter called Elizabeth.

Throughout his life Chaucer served in key government positions. He was a controller of customs, a justice of the peace, and a one-term member of Parliament. He spent time in France and Italy on diplomatic missions, served as a supervisor of construction and repairs at Westminster Abbey and the Tower of London, and, late in life, acted as a subforester of the king's forest.

It might seem as if Chaucer would have had little time for writing, but in fact he wrote a great deal. He began producing poetry in his twenties and continued to do so for the rest of his life. Moreover, as he grew older, his literary works showed increasing depth and sophistication. In *Troilus and Criseyde,* a long poem dealing with themes from classical antiquity, he displays the dramatic flair and penetrating insight into human character that are his hallmarks. *The Canterbury Tales,* of which only 24 of the projected 124 tales were completed, shows Chaucer's absolute mastery of the storyteller's art.

Chaucer was the first person to be buried in what is now the Poet's Corner of Westminster Abbey.

THE CANTERBURY TALES

People in medieval England sometimes made pilgrimages to sacred shrines. One such shrine was the cathedral in Canterbury, a town about fifty miles southeast of London, where archbishop Thomas à Becket had been murdered in 1170. The pilgrims often traveled in groups for the sake of companionship and protection. Chaucer's masterpiece, *The Canterbury Tales,* introduces a group of "nine and twenty" pilgrims, one of whom is Chaucer himself. These pilgrims appear first at the Tabard Inn in Southwark, near London, and later on the road to Canterbury.

The Canterbury Tales is a frame story; that is, a story that includes, or frames, another story or stories. Chaucer's frame is the pilgrimage, which he originally planned as a round trip but which remained incomplete at his death. Within this frame are the 24 individual stories the pilgrims tell. Chaucer did not invent the frame-story device. The same structural scheme had been used centuries earlier in *The Thousand and One Nights;* and Boccaccio, an Italian contemporary of Chaucer, used it in the *Decameron,* published about 1350.

Chaucer's handling of his pilgrimage frame is brilliant. The stories are mostly old familiar ones, superbly retold. Perhaps even more impressive than the stories are the storytellers. Chaucer's pilgrims, all of whom are introduced briefly in his Prologue, are memorable, vividly drawn individuals whose personalities are unique but whose character traits are universal. The pilgrims interact with one another. Clashes erupt among them as one pilgrim takes offense at another's tale and proceeds to retaliate with his or her own story.

By using the vehicle of the pilgrimage, Chaucer brings together people from the three main segments of medieval society—the church, the court, and the common people. His pilgrims are drawn from the class structure of feudalism (a knight, a squire, a reeve, for example) as well as from the more open classes in the emerging cities (a merchant, an innkeeper) and the powerful, hierarchical church of the time (a nun, a friar, a pardoner). Chaucer's interest in all these people and the shrewd but affectionate pictures he draws of them make them stand out in such distinct detail that they seem real, alive, and almost modern in their foibles and concerns.

Chaucer wrote only the "Tale of Melibeus" and the "Parson's Tale" in prose. With the exception of the "Monk's Tale," he told his story in either rhymed couplets or in stanzas of seven lines. His use of iambic pentameter couplets was a forerunner of the heroic couplets perfected in the 1700's by Alexander Pope.

from *The Canterbury Tales* 115

More About *The Canterbury Tales* Another pilgrim joins the group after they leave the Tabard Inn, making a total of thirty-two persons in the company. Whether Chaucer ever had any intention of writing 124 tales is questionable. Along the road one of the Host's remarks seems to suggest that Chaucer might have halved his proposed number, but this is by no means clear. In any event, Chaucer left twenty-two finished tales, one unfinished, and another barely begun. While Chaucer made his own contribution as a writer of rhymed fiction, most of the stories did not originate with him. *The Knight's Tale* and *The Monk's Tale* are abbreviated versions of Boccaccio's stories. *The Reeve's Tale* is a version of a French fabliau. *The Man of Law's Tale* is borrowed from John Gower. Ovid and Livy are also sources for the tales. Indeed, Chaucer borrowed the framework for the Canterbury Tales itself. What is the advantage of employing a frame for a collection of narratives?

Master Teacher Note After the class has read the General Prologue, place Art Transparency 3, *The Traveling Companions,* by Augustus Leopold Egg, on the overhead projector. Conduct a class discussion on what this painting implies about how traveling changed from Chaucer's time to the nineteenth century. What other social changes come to mind when this painting is considered in relation to Chaucer's poetry?

Focus

Literary Focus Chaucer was unique among writers of his time in his ability to create the look and spirit of people and to turn characteristics into character. His dramatis personae are sharply individual, exact, and unmistakable. Through tricks of gesture, generality, accents, and complexion and by showing vices and virtues, with no ulcer or wart omitted, Chaucer carefully draws his characters. Several of the characters represent idealized people, but they all show us the values of the Medieval period. What do you discover about the ideals of the Middle Ages from reading *The Canterbury Tales?*

Writing/Prior Knowledge You might try using the directed-questioning technique here. Ask the students the questions and allow them a minute or so to freewrite the answer.

Vocabulary

Preteach the following vocabulary words:
solicitous (sə lis′ ə təs) *adj.:* Showing care or concern (l. 147)
garnished (gär′ nisht) *adj.:* Decorated; trimmed (l. 197)
preferment (pri fʉr′ mənt) *n.:* Advancement in rank (l. 301)
screeds (skrēdz) *n.:* Long, tiresome pieces of writing (l. 336)
sanguine (san′ gwin) *adj.:* Of cheerful temperament (l. 343)
avouches (ə vouch′ ez) *v.:* Asserts positively; affirms (l. 377)
whelks (hwelkz) *n.:* Pimples (l. 650)
prevarication (pri var′ ə kā′ shən) *n.:* Evasion of truth (l. 725)

The Prologue *from* The Canterbury Tales

Writer's Techniques

Characterization. Characterization refers to the personality of a fictional character as well as to the methods by which a writer creates that personality. Writers use a number of methods of characterization. Sometimes a writer makes a direct statement about a person: "Phil was hard to get to know, but those who knew him liked him." More often an author reveals character in an indirect way, through action, thoughts, and dialogue: "I should really study harder," Joan thought, laying the novel aside. "If I did, I could probably pass the test." Character can also be revealed through comments about the person by others in the story: "He's the kind of guy," said Linda, "who thinks football is the most important thing in life." A character's physical appearance and habits can help to reveal personality: "Doris wore the same threadbare dress she had worn to the party, but today she stood straighter, her shoulders squared." In defining a character, a writer will often combine these techniques to create a lifelike picture.

Writing

Jot down a few notes for a physical description of a fictional character. Choose a name for your character. Then note the following details: (1) facial features, (2) typical expression, (3) body structure, (4) typical posture, (5) clothing, (6) physical surroundings. Try to list details that not only describe the character but also help to reveal personality.

Primary Source

What was it like to live during the Middle Ages? In *The Life and Times of Chaucer,* the contemporary writer John Gardner creates a vivid picture.

> But in small things, too, we might be bothered, at least at first, by life in the Middle Ages—for instance, by Chaucer's annoying habit (or any other well-educated man's) of always reading to himself aloud, never silently, "barking on books," as one fifteenth-century playwright puts it; or, to speak of things less petty, we might be bothered by the general manners of the better class of people in the fourteenth century. They ate with their fingers, except for the occasional employment of a knife or soup spoon, and even the fingers of courtly ladies were not impeccably clean.

Objectives

1 To understand characterization
2 To make inferences about character
3 To understand similes

Support Material

Teaching Portfolio
Teacher Backup, p. 89
Grammar in Action Worksheets, *Using Topic Sentences and Supporting Information,* p. 94; *Using Specific Words,* p. 96
Usage and Mechanics Worksheet, p. 98
Vocabulary Check, p. 99

Critical Thinking and Reading Worksheet, *Making Inferences About Characters,* p. 101
Language Worksheet, *Interpreting Similes* p. 102
Selection Test, p. 103
Art Transparency 3, *The Traveling Companions,* August Leopold Egg.

The Prologue

Geoffrey Chaucer
translated by Nevill Coghill

Whan that Aprill with his shourës sootë
The droghte of March hath percëd to the rootë
And bathëd every veyne in swich licour
Of which vertu engendrëd is the flour,
5   Whan Zephirus eek with his sweetë breeth
Inspirëd hath in every holt and heeth
The tendrë croppës, and the yongë sonnë
Hath in the Ram his half cours y-ronnë,
And smalë fowelës maken melodyë
10 That slepen al the nyght with open eye,
So priketh hem Nature in hir corages,
Than longen folk to goon on pilgrymages,
And palmeres for to seken straungë strondës,
To fernë halwës kouthe in sondry londës.
15 And specially, from every shirës endë
Of Engelond, to Caunterbury they wendë,
The holy, blisful martir for to seke
That hem hath holpen whan that they were seekë.

When in April the sweet showers fall
And pierce the drought of March to the root, and all
The veins are bathed in liquor of such power
As brings about the engendering of the flower,
5   When also Zephyrus[1] with his sweet breath
Exhales an air in every grove and heath
Upon tender shoots, and the young sun
His half-course in the sign of the Ram[2] has run,
And the small fowl are making melody
10 That sleep away the night with open eye
(So nature pricks them and their heart engages)
Then people long to go on pilgrimages
And palmers[3] long to seek the stranger strands[4]
Of far-off saints, hallowed in sundry lands,
15 And specially, from every shire's end
In England, down to Canterbury they wend
To seek the holy blissful martyr,[5] quick
To give his help to them when they were sick.

1. Zephyrus (zef′ ər əs): The west wind.

2. Ram: Aries, the first sign of the zodiac. The pilgrimage began on April 11, 1387.

3. palmers: Pilgrims who wore two crossed palm leaves to show that they had visited the Holy Land.

4. strands: Shores.

5. martyr: St. Thomas à Becket, the Archbishop of Canterbury, who was murdered in the Canterbury Cathedral in 1170.

The Prologue from *The Canterbury Tales* 117

Humanities Note

Fine art, *The Tabard Inn,* 1946, by Arthur Szyk. Szyk (1894–1951), a Polish-born American artist, did much in his lifetime to revive the lost Medieval art of miniature illumination painting. His art education at the Academy of Fine Art in Krakow, Poland, and at the Beaux Arts Academy in Paris gave him the background in academic art necessary to pursue this exacting form of painting. His most famous work is a series of miniatures of the life of George Washington presented to President Franklin D. Roosevelt by the President of Poland in 1934.

The painting *The Tabard Inn,* done for *The Canterbury Tales* in 1946, was painted in miniature in the style of a medieval monk illuminating a manuscript. Despite the miniature format, this painting is rich in color and detail. The innkeeper stands proudly at the door and surveys the colorful assembly of pilgrims arriving on horseback. The expressions of the group are painted with a touch of humor that allows a glimpse into their personalities. The piety of the knight, the cunning of the friar, and the foppishness of the squire are apparent.

You may wish to ask the following questions to encourage discussion:

1. Is the humorous nature of this painting in keeping with Chaucer's attitude?
2. What does the expression and stance of the innkeeper convey?

3 Master Teacher Note Note that, after a rather formal, impersonal, high-flown opening, Chaucer descends to a simpler level: direct, informal narrative.

4 Clarification Since Southwark was a suburb at the southern end of the London Bridge, it was a logical starting point for a journey to Canterbury, about eighty miles southeast of London.

THE TABARD INN
Arthur Szyk for the Canterbury Tales
The George Macy Companies

3

      It happened in that season that one day

4   20 In Southwark[6], at The Tabard,[7] as I lay
Ready to go on pilgrimage and start
For Canterbury, most devout at heart,
At night there came into that hostelry
Some nine and twenty in a company
25 Of sundry folk happening then to fall
In fellowship, and they were pilgrims all
That towards Canterbury meant to ride.

6. Southwark (suth′ ərk): A suburb of London at the time.
7. The Tabard (ta′ bərd): An inn.

Grammar in Action

Develop paragraphs with **topic sentences** and **supporting information.** A paragraph's main idea should be stated in a topic sentence. It should be developed by supporting information —examples details, facts, reasons, and so on. Chaucer's "General Prologue" provides a number of good examples of sound paragraph development.

He had his son with him, a fine young *Squire,*
A lover and cadet, a lad of fire
With locks as curly as if they had been pressed.

The rooms and stables of the inn were wide;
They made us easy, all was of the best.
30 And shortly, when the sun had gone to rest,
By speaking to them all upon the trip
I soon was one of them in fellowship
And promised to rise early and take the way
To Canterbury, as you heard me say.
35   But nonetheless, while I have time and space,
Before my story takes a further pace,
It seems a reasonable thing to say
What their condition was, the full array
Of each of them, as it appeared to me
40 According to profession and degree,
And what apparel they were riding in;
5 And at a Knight I therefore will begin.
There was a *Knight,* a most distinguished man,
Who from the day on which he first began
6 45 To ride abroad had followed chivalry,
Truth, honor, generousness and courtesy.
He had done nobly in his sovereign's war
And ridden into battle, no man more,
As well in Christian as heathen places,
50 And ever honored for his noble graces.
    When we took Alexandria,[8] he was there.
He often sat at table in the chair
Of honor, above all nations, when in Prussia.
In Lithuania he had ridden, and Russia,
55 No Christian man so often, of his rank.
When, in Granada, Algeciras sank
Under assault, he had been there, and in
North Africa, raiding Benamarin;
In Anatolia he had been as well
60 And fought when Ayas and Attalia fell,
For all along the Mediterranean coast
He had embarked with many a noble host.
In fifteen mortal battles he had been
And jousted for our faith at Tramissene
65 Thrice in the lists, and always killed his man.
This same distinguished knight had led the van
7 Once with the Bey of Balat, doing work
For him against another heathen Turk;
He was of sovereign value in all eyes.
70 And though so much distinguished, he was wise
And in his bearing modest as a maid.
He never yet a boorish thing had said
In all his life to any, come what might;
He was a true, a perfect gentle-knight.

8. Alexandria: The site of
one of the campaigns
fought by Christians
against groups who posed
a threat to Europe during
the fourteenth century.
The place names that
follow refer to other
battlesites in these
campaigns, or crusades.

5 Enrichment Since the Knight possesses the highest social standing among the pilgrims, it is appropriate that he be the first described.

6 Enrichment When Chaucer describes the Knight as the epitome of chivalry, he is talking about an ideal from the past. By the 1380's when Chaucer began this work, feudalism and chivalry, its accompanying social code for the nobility, were all but gone.

7 Critical Thinking and Reading Although the Knight is always considered one of Chaucer's most admirable characters, indeed so admirable that he seems idealized rather than realistic, these lines suggest a somewhat less attractive side to his character. In what way do they do so?

The Prologue from *The Canterbury Tales* 119

He was some twenty years of age, I guessed.
In stature he was of a moderate length,
With wonderful agility and strength.
He'd seen some service with the cavalry
In Flanders and Artois and Picardy
And had done valiantly in little space
Of time, in hope to win his lady's grace.
He was embroidered like a meadow bright
And full of freshest flowers, red and white.

The main idea—that the knight's son is a fine young squire—is stated in the first sentence. Each subsequent sentence supports the main idea with specific descriptive details.

Student Activity 1. Choose another pilgrim's description, indicate the topic sentence, and tell how each detail supports it.

Student Activity 2. Write a paragraph in which you describe a friend or relative. State a main idea about this person in a topic sentence. Then develop your idea with apt supporting information in the sentences that follow.

8 **Discussion** What do these comments on the Knight's appearance reveal about his nature?

9 **Reading Strategy** What is the Knight's purpose in joining the pilgrimage? As you learn about the other pilgrims, watch for their motives, usually less noble than that of the knight.

10 **Critical Thinking and Reading** What seems to motivate the Squire to do well in battle? What other lines suggest his preoccupation in this same area?

11 **Discussion** How does the Squire's appearance differ from his father's? From the various references to it, what does this physical description reveal about the Squire's character?

12 **Discussion** What do we learn about the education of a well-born young man in the fourteenth century?

13 **Reading Strategy** How does Chaucer regard the Squire? Is he idealized like his father or is he more realistic, with both faults and virtues? Almost all the pilgrims will combine moral strength and weakness. Suggest that the students should be alert for this combination as they read.

14 **Critical Thinking and Reading** The description of the Yeoman concentrates primarily on his physical appearance, and there is little sense of the kind of man he is. Why do you think Chaucer has neglected any indication of his inner nature?

15 **Literary Focus** Who does the Yeoman look like? Point out that the Robin Hood resemblance is generally noted, and that the original Robin Hood was presumably a late twelfth-century figure but woodmen's garb would have changed little during the intervening years.

16 **Literary Focus** There are several references to the Yeoman's professional skill. Suggest that the students find these references. Almost all of Chaucer's pilgrims are good at what they do. He has created not only a cross-section of medieval society but a group of skilled practitioners of medieval occupations.

17 **Enrichment** The fact that he wears a St. Christopher medal does not necessarily suggest that the Yeoman is pious. St. Christopher medals were commonplace among Medieval travelers.

75 Speaking of his equipment, he possessed
Fine horses, but he was not gaily dressed.
He wore a fustian⁹ tunic stained and dark
With smudges where his armor had left mark;
Just home from service, he had joined our ranks
80 To do his pilgrimage and render thanks.
He had his son with him, a fine young *Squire*,
A lover and cadet, a lad of fire
With locks as curly as if they had been pressed.
He was some twenty years of age, I guessed.
85 In stature he was of a moderate length,
With wonderful agility and strength.
He'd seen some service with the cavalry
In Flanders and Artois and Picardy¹⁰
And had done valiantly in little space
90 Of time, in hope to win his lady's grace.
He was embroidered like a meadow bright
And full of freshest flowers, red and white.
Singing he was, or fluting all the day;
He was as fresh as is the month of May.
95 Short was his gown, the sleeves were long and wide;
He knew the way to sit a horse and ride.
He could make songs and poems and recite,
Knew how to joust and dance, to draw and write.
He loved so hotly that till dawn grew pale
100 He slept as little as a nightingale.
Courteous he was, lowly and serviceable,
And carved to serve his father at the table.
There was a *Yeoman*¹¹ with him at his side,
No other servant; so he chose to ride.
105 This Yeoman wore a coat and hood of green,
And peacock-feathered arrows, bright and keen
And neatly sheathed, hung at his belt the while
—For he could dress his gear in yeoman style,
His arrows never drooped their feathers low—
110 And in his hand he bore a mighty bow.
His head was like a nut, his face was brown.
He knew the whole of woodcraft up and down.
A saucy brace¹² was on his arm to ward
It from the bow-string, and a shield and sword
115 Hung at one side, and at the other slipped
A jaunty dirk,¹³ spear-sharp and well-equipped.
A medal of St. Christopher¹⁴ he wore
Of shining silver on his breast, and bore
A hunting-horn, well slung and burnished clean,
120 That dangled from a baldric¹⁵ of bright green.
He was a proper forester I guess.

9. fustian (fus′ chən): A coarse cloth of cotton and linen.

10. Flanders . . . Picardy: Regions in Belgium and France.

11. Yeoman (yō′ mən) *n*.: Attendant.

12. brace: Bracelet.

13. dirk *n*.: A short, straight dagger.
14. St. Christopher: The patron saint of forests and travelers.
15. baldric *n*.: A belt worn over one shoulder and across the chest to support a sword.

18 [
    There also was a *Nun*, a Prioress.[16]

19 [
    Her way of smiling very simple and coy.
    Her greatest oath was only "By St. Loy!"[17]

20 [125
    And she was known as Madam Eglantyne.
    And well she sang a service,[18] with a fine
    Intoning through her nose, as was most seemly,
    And she spoke daintily in French, extremely,
    After the school of Stratford-atte-Bowe;[19]
130 French in the Paris style she did not know.
    At meat her manners were well taught withal;
    No morsel from her lips did she let fall,
    Nor dipped her fingers in the sauce too deep;
    But she could carry a morsel up and keep
135 The smallest drop from falling on her breast.
    For courtliness she had a special zest,
    And she would wipe her upper lip so clean
    That not a trace of grease was to be seen
    Upon the cup when she had drunk; to eat,
140 She reached a hand sedately for the meat.
    She certainly was very entertaining,

21 [
    Pleasant and friendly in her ways, and straining
    To counterfeit a courtly kind of grace,
    A stately bearing fitting to her place,
145 And to seem dignified in all her dealings.

22 [
    As for her sympathies and tender feelings,
    She was so charitably solicitous
    She used to weep if she but saw a mouse
    Caught in a trap, if it were dead or bleeding.

150 And she had little dogs she would be feeding
    With roasted flesh, or milk, or fine white bread.
    And bitterly she wept if one were dead
    Or someone took a stick and made it smart;
    She was all sentiment and tender heart.
155 Her veil was gathered in a seemly way,
    Her nose was elegant, her eyes glass-gray;
    Her mouth was very small, but soft and red,

23 [
    Her forehead, certainly, was fair of spread,
    Almost a span[20] across the brows, I own;
160 She was indeed by no means undergrown.
    Her cloak, I noticed, had a graceful charm.
    She wore a coral trinket on her arm,
    A set of beads, the gaudies[21] tricked in green,
    Whence hung a golden brooch of brightest sheen
165 On which there first was graven a crowned A,
    And lower, *Amor vincit omnia.*[22]

24 [
    Another *Nun*, the chaplain at her cell,
    Was riding with her, and *three Priests* as well.

16. Prioress *n.*: In an abbey, the nun ranking just below the abbess.
17. St. Loy: St. Eligius, patron saint of goldsmiths and courtiers.
18. service: Daily prayer.

19. Stratford-atte-Bowe: A nunnery near London.

THE YEOMAN
Arthur Szyk for the Canterbury Tales
The George Macy Companies

20. span: Nine inches.

21. gaudies: Large green beads that marked certain prayers on a set of prayer beads.
22. *Amor vincit omnia* (ä môr′ wink′ it ôm′ nē ä): "Love conquers all" (Latin).

The Prologue from *The Canterbury Tales* 121

Humanities Note

Fine art, *The Yeoman*, 1946, by Arthur Szyk. In this miniature painted in 1946 for *The Canterbury Tales*, the artist shows a fully equipped medieval yeoman. He appears ready for any occurrence in the forest, from the appearance of game to an attack by highwaymen. He is portrayed as a sturdy fellow with a serious expression on his face. In painting these miniatures, Arthur Szyk, with patience and meticulous care, imitates monkish manuscript painters. Through this painstaking effort, he succeeds in capturing the charm and medieval flavor of that art.

1. How does Szyk's depiction of the yeoman compare with your image of him?
2. How closely does this depiction match Chaucer's description in lines 105–121?

18 Enrichment Chaucer introduces here the first of his various ecclesiastical pilgrims and his first woman. Of the thirty pilgrims who set out from Southwark, three are women, and of these three two are nuns.

19 Clarification An oath "by St. Loy" would have been mild and inoffensive.

20 Critical Thinking and Reading Since "Eglantyne" was the name of several clinging-vine heroines in Medieval romances, what comment does Chaucer seem to be making about the Prioress?

21 Discussion What does Chaucer's use of the verb *counterfeit* suggest?

22 Discussion Is Chaucer commending her tenderness of heart or mocking it? Although his tone in describing the Prioress is quite consistently satiric, Chaucer likes her. Why then might he use a satiric tone?

23 Clarification The Prioress would have taken a vow of poverty when she entered religious life. This vow would have precluded her owning a luxury such as little dogs. What do you think of their diet? Is it appropriate? What about the "coral trinket"? Frequently Chaucer's descriptions can be understood in two ways. Does the inscription "*Amor vincit omnia*" refer to secular or spiritual love?

24 Master Teacher Note The other nun mentioned here, her companion, is the second woman on the pilgrimage. The three priests mentioned prevent the number of pilgrims from adding up to thirty. It has been conjectured that Chaucer left this line unfinished and that someone else filled it in. It should be remembered that no manuscript for *The Canterbury Tales* exists today that Chaucer could have seen. All are copies by fifteenth-century scribes; the earliest dates back to about 1410; Chaucer died in 1400.

25 Clarification The Monk, another ecclesiastical pilgrim, held a position in his monastery somewhat like the Prioress's in her convent. Both were figures of some authority.

26 Discussion What was the Monk's attitude toward the rules of his order?

27 Master Teacher Note Here is one of the infrequent instances in the Prologue in which the narrator directly injects his own personality and opinion. It should be remembered that the ''I'' of the Prologue is not really Chaucer but an imaginary character, one who is far more naïve and impressionable than the real, urbane, tolerant, sophisticated author himself.

28 Discussion What kind of activity was expected of a Monk? What did this Monk choose to do instead?

29 Clarification To be fat in the Middle Ages was a status symbol. Only the rich had more than enough to eat; thus obesity suggested affluence.

30 Discussion Do you believe that this Monk observed the vow of poverty that he, like the Prioress, would have taken upon entering monastic life? A second vow required of the religious was a vow of obedience. How well did he fulfill these vows?

31 Enrichment Unlike monks, whose work lay within a monastery, friars were itinerant ecclesiastics whose begging supported schools, hospitals, and other church-related institutions. This Friar exemplifies the corruption to which many in these mendicant orders had sunk by Chaucer's time.

25

170   A *Monk* there was, one of the finest sort
       Who rode the country; hunting was his sport.
       A manly man, to be an Abbot able;
       Many a dainty horse he had in stable.
       His bridle, when he rode, a man might hear
175   Jingling in a whistling wind as clear,
       Aye, and as loud as does the chapel bell
       Where my lord Monk was Prior of the cell.

26

       The Rule of good St. Benet or St. Maur[23]
       As old and strict he tended to ignore;
       He let go by the things of yesterday
180   And took the modern world's more spacious way.
       He did not rate that text at a plucked hen
       Which says that hunters are not holy men
       And that a monk uncloistered is a mere
       Fish out of water, flapping on the pier,
185   That is to say a monk out of his cloister.
       That was a text he held not worth an oyster;

27

       And I agreed and said his views were sound;
       Was he to study till his head went round
       Poring over books in cloisters? Must he toil
190   As Austin[24] bade and till the very soil?
       Was he to leave the world upon the shelf?
       Let Austin have his labor to himself.

28

       This Monk was therefore a good man to horse;
       Greyhounds he had, as swift as birds, to course.
195   Hunting a hare or riding at a fence
       Was all his fun, he spared for no expense.
       I saw his sleeves were garnished at the hand
       With fine gray fur, the finest in the land,
       And on his hood, to fasten it at his chin
200   He had a wrought-gold cunningly fashioned pin;
       Into a lover's knot it seemed to pass.
       His head was bald and shone like looking-glass;
       So did his face, as if it had been greased.

29

       He was a fat and personable priest;
205   His prominent eyeballs never seemed to settle.

30

       They glittered like the flames beneath a kettle;
       Supple his boots, his horse in fine condition.
       He was a prelate fit for exhibition,
       He was not pale like a tormented soul.
210   He liked a fat swan best, and roasted whole.
       His palfrey[25] was as brown as is a berry.

31

       There was a *Friar*, a wanton[26] one and merry,
       A Limiter,[27] a very festive fellow.
       In all Four Orders[28] there was none so mellow
215   So glib with gallant phrase and well-turned speech.

122 The Medieval Period

---

23. St. Benet or St. Maur: St. Benedict, author of monastic rules, and St. Maurice, one of his followers. Benet and Maur are French versions of Benedict and Maurice.

24. Austin: English version of St. Augustine, who criticized lazy monks.

25. palfrey: Saddle horse.
26. wanton: Jolly.
27. Limiter: A friar who is given begging rights for a certain limited area.
28. Four Orders: There were four orders of friars who supported themselves by begging: Dominicans, Franciscans, Carmelites, and Augustinians.

THE MONK
Arthur Szyk for the Canterbury Tales
The George Macy Companies

Humanities Note

Fine art, *The Monk,* 1946, by Arthur Szyk. In this miniature, Szyk shows the massive and richly robed monk described in the Prologue. His wealth is apparent from his fine fur-trimmed robes, gold brooch, elaborate sword, and tooled wallet. His expression is one of haughty self-satisfaction. Szyk painted the worldly cleric with humor and wit, emphasizing the incongruity between the trappings of wealth and the man's humble vocation.

1. How does Szyk's pictorial representation of the monk compare with Chaucer's description?
2. Does this depiction look realistic or exaggerated?

The Prologue from *The Canterbury Tales* **123**

32 **Master Teacher Note** The implication here is that the Friar found husbands and dowries for women he himself had seduced. Since the third vow that religious took was the vow of chastity, his moral laxity is clear.

33 **Clarification** The Friar had received from his order a license to hear confessions without gaining permission from local priests and to give absolution for more serious sins than parish priests could. The friars were often charged with laxity in imposing penances. This Friar, in effect, allowed people to pay for having their sins forgiven.

34 **Clarification** A soft white neck was considered a mark of licentiousness.

35 **Reading Strategy** Read to discover what the Friar's attitude toward priestly duties is. What was his great talent?

32

He'd fixed up many a marriage, giving each
Of his young women what he could afford her.
He was a noble pillar to his Order.
Highly beloved and intimate was he
220 With County folk within his boundary,
And city dames of honor and possessions;
For he was qualified to hear confessions,
Or so he said, with more than priestly scope;
He had a special license from the Pope.

33

225 Sweetly he heard his penitents at shrift[29]
With pleasant absolution, for a gift.
He was an easy man in penance-giving
Where he could hope to make a decent living;
It's a sure sign whenever gifts are given
230 To a poor Order that a man's well shriven,[30]
And should he give enough he knew in verity
The penitent repented in sincerity.
For many a fellow is so hard of heart
He cannot weep, for all his inward smart.
235 Therefore instead of weeping and of prayer
One should give silver for a poor Friar's care.
He kept his tippet[31] stuffed with pins for curls,
And pocket-knives, to give to pretty girls.
And certainly his voice was gay and sturdy,
240 For he sang well and played the hurdy-gurdy.[32]
At sing-songs he was champion of the hour.

34

His neck was whiter than a lily-flower
But strong enough to butt a bruiser down.

35

He knew the taverns well in every town
245 And every innkeeper and barmaid too
Better than lepers, beggars and that crew,
For in so eminent a man as he
It was not fitting with the dignity
Of his position, dealing with a scum
250 Of wretched lepers; nothing good can come
Of dealings with the slum-and-gutter dwellers,
But only with the rich and victual-sellers.
But anywhere a profit might accrue
Courteous he was and lowly of service too.
255 Natural gifts like his were hard to match.
He was the finest beggar of his batch,
And, for his begging-district, payed a rent;
His brethren did no poaching where he went.
For though a widow mightn't have a shoe,
260 So pleasant was his holy how-d'ye-do
He got his farthing from her just the same
Before he left, and so his income came

29. **shrift:** Confession.

30. **well shriven:** Absolved of his sins.

31. **tippet:** Hood.

32. **hurdy-gurdy:** A stringed instument played by cranking a wheel.

Grammar in Action

Skilled writers use **specific words**, rather than general terms, to help their readers visualize what they are describing. For example, it is far more vivid to say that a man has "long, carrot-red, pencil-thin sideburns" than to merely note that he has "facial hair."

Chaucer makes his Canterbury pilgrims come alive by describing them with specific words. He depicts a merchant as follows:

There was a *Merchant* with a forking beard
And motley dress; high on his horse he sat,
Upon his head a Flemish beaver hat
And on his feet daintily buckled boots.

Not only does Chaucer use precise descriptions, such as *"forking* beard" and *"daintily* buckled," but the specific words he uses reveal the merchant's character. A man who would "daintily" buckle his shoes, for instance, is certainly someone who wants to impress people with his fine appearance. Just a few lines later we learn he is "in debt" but does not want anyone to know it. Here, then, is one possible reason for the care he takes with his footwear.

To more than he laid out. And how he romped,
Just like a puppy! He was ever prompt
265 To arbitrate disputes on settling days
(For a small fee) in many helpful ways,
Not then appearing as your cloistered scholar
With threadbare habit hardly worth a dollar,
But much more like a Doctor or a Pope.
270 Of double-worsted was the semi-cope[33]
Upon his shoulders, and the swelling fold
About him, like a bell about its mold
When it is casting, rounded out his dress.
He lisped a little out of wantonness
275 To make his English sweet upon his tongue.
When he had played his harp, or having sung,
His eyes would twinkle in his head as bright
As any star upon a frosty night.
This worthy's name was Hubert, it appeared.
280   There was a *Merchant* with a forking beard
And motley dress; high on his horse he sat,
Upon his head a Flemish[34] beaver hat
And on his feet daintily buckled boots.
He told of his opinions and pursuits
285 In solemn tones, and how he never lost.
The sea should be kept free at any cost
(He thought) upon the Harwich-Holland range,[35]
He was expert at currency exchange.
This estimable Merchant so had set
290 His wits to work, none knew he was in debt,
He was so stately in negotiation,
Loan, bargain and commercial obligation.
He was an excellent fellow all the same;
To tell the truth I do not know his name.
295   An *Oxford Cleric*, still a student though,
One who had taken logic long ago,
Was there; his horse was thinner than a rake,
And he was not too fat, I undertake,
But had a hollow look, a sober stare;
300 The thread upon his overcoat was bare.
He had found no preferment in the church
And he was too unworldly to make search
For secular employment. By his bed
He preferred having twenty books in red
305 And black, of Aristotle's[36] philosophy,
To having fine clothes, fiddle or psaltery.[37]
Though a philosopher, as I have told,
He had not found the stone for making gold.[38]
Whatever money from his friends he took

36 **Critical Thinking and Reading** How did his clothing reflect his character?

37 **Enrichment** The "motley" dress, made of multi-colored cloth woven in designs, suggests affluence, as do the imported beaver hat and daintily buckled boots. The Merchant is a very wealthy man.

38 **Literary Focus** "Kept free from pirates" is the implication and it reflects the Merchant's special-interest bias: the government should spare no expense in employing public funds to protect his business ventures. Does this kind of special-interest bias still exist?

39 **Discussion** Does concealment of his debts suggest that the merchant is dishonest? Does Chaucer make a moral judgment? Note that Chaucer tends to make very few explicit moral judgments. He seems extremely tolerant of human frailty.

40 **Enrichment** The term "cleric" referred to any ecclesiastical student as well as to a priest, and Oxford University in the 14th century was essentially a training ground for the religious. Chaucer's Oxford Cleric was evidently a very advanced student. Although not an ordained priest, he had undoubtedly completed most of the required course of study.

41 **Clarification** The thinness of both the Cleric and his horse as well as the threadbare condition of his coat all attest to his poverty.

42 **Clarification** It was common for men of clerical training to seek employment outside the Church. This cleric was not aggressive or materialistic enough to have found it.

33. semi-cope: Cape.

34. Flemish: From Flanders.

35. Harwich-Holland range: The North Sea between England and Holland.

36. Aristotle's (ar′ is tot′ əlz): Referring to the Greek philosopher (384–322 B.C.).

37. psaltery (sôl′ tər ē): An ancient stringed instrument.

38. stone . . . gold: At the time alchemists believed that a "philosopher's stone" existed that could turn base metals into gold.

The Prologue from *The Canterbury Tales* 125

Student Activity 1. Reread Chaucer's description of the *Oxford Cleric* and note the specific words that bring this character to life. Then choose one particular word or phrase and explain what it reveals about the cleric.

Student Activity 2. Write a brief description of someone you know, using specific words that suggest his or her personality. Include vivid adverbs, like Chaucer's *daintily,* as well as adjectives. Test the effectiveness of your description by having a classmate read it and make inferences about your subject. First be certain, however, that your classmate does not know the person you are describing.

Humanities Note

Fine art, *The Student,* 1946, by Arthur Szyk. In the miniature *The Student,* Szyk cleverly shows the student's preference for intellectual attainment over worldly matters. His drab tunic and patched knees contrast with his intent expression as he reads his book. He absently gestures with his left hand as if in conversation with himself, unaware of the picture he presents to others. Although not as decorative as the other, more richly dressed characters illustrated by Szyk, the student is detailed with care and skill.

1. Do you think Szyk's miniature captures the personality of the student as Chaucer has portrayed him?
2. Does Szyk's student remind you of any young scholar you have ever seen?

THE STUDENT
Arthur Szyk for the Canterbury Tales
The George Macy Companies

126   The Medieval Period

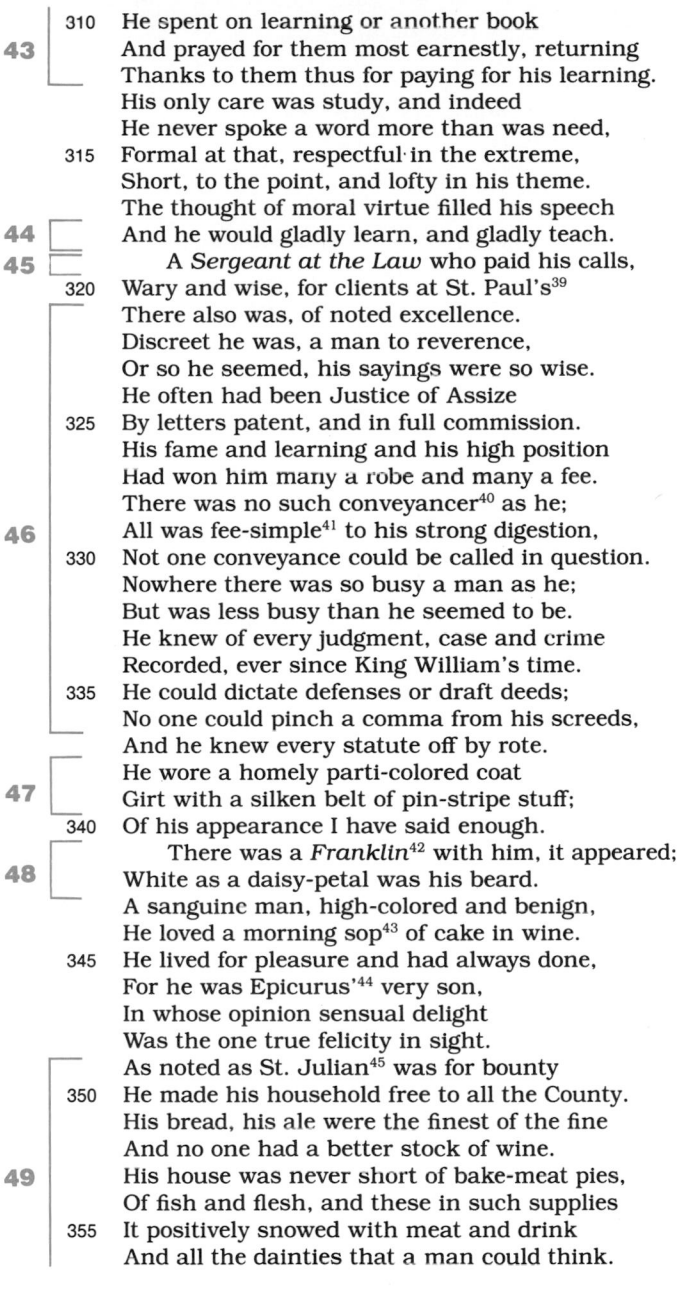

310 He spent on learning or another book
And prayed for them most earnestly, returning
Thanks to them thus for paying for his learning.
His only care was study, and indeed
He never spoke a word more than was need,
315 Formal at that, respectful·in the extreme,
Short, to the point, and lofty in his theme.
The thought of moral virtue filled his speech
And he would gladly learn, and gladly teach.

        A *Sergeant at the Law* who paid his calls,
320 Wary and wise, for clients at St. Paul's[39]
There also was, of noted excellence.
Discreet he was, a man to reverence,
Or so he seemed, his sayings were so wise.
He often had been Justice of Assize
325 By letters patent, and in full commission.
His fame and learning and his high position
Had won him many a robe and many a fee.
There was no such conveyancer[40] as he;
All was fee-simple[41] to his strong digestion,
330 Not one conveyance could be called in question.
Nowhere there was so busy a man as he;
But was less busy than he seemed to be.
He knew of every judgment, case and crime
Recorded, ever since King William's time.
335 He could dictate defenses or draft deeds;
No one could pinch a comma from his screeds,
And he knew every statute off by rote.
He wore a homely parti-colored coat
Girt with a silken belt of pin-stripe stuff;
340 Of his appearance I have said enough.

        There was a *Franklin*[42] with him, it appeared;
White as a daisy-petal was his beard.
A sanguine man, high-colored and benign,
He loved a morning sop[43] of cake in wine.
345 He lived for pleasure and had always done,
For he was Epicurus'[44] very son,
In whose opinion sensual delight
Was the one true felicity in sight.
As noted as St. Julian[45] was for bounty
350 He made his household free to all the County.
His bread, his ale were the finest of the fine
And no one had a better stock of wine.
His house was never short of bake-meat pies,
Of fish and flesh, and these in such supplies
355 It positively snowed with meat and drink
And all the dainties that a man could think.

39. St. Paul's: A London cathedral near which lawyers often met to discuss their cases.

40. conveyancer: One who draws up documents for transferring ownership of property.
41. fee-simple: Restricted ownership.

42. *Franklin:* Wealthy landowner.

43. sop: Piece.

44. Epicurus' (ep′ i kyoor′ əs): Referring to a Greek philosopher (342?–370 B.C.) who believed that happiness is the most important goal in life.
45. St. Julian: Patron saint of hospitality.

43 Discussion Do you think the Cleric took advantage of his friends by allowing them to contribute to his upkeep? Could he repay them in any way?

44 Enrichment This Oxford Cleric is considered to be one of the handful of idealized characters introduced in the Prologue. He is the model of what a student should be rather than a portrait of what a student generally is. He represents the passion for learning that was already stirring in Europe. The description ''gladly would he learn and gladly teach'' is an often-quoted encomium for the dedicated scholar.

45 Enrichment The term ''Sergeant at the Law'' referred to a member of a small, chosen group of lawyers—one who had at least sixteen years experience, was the King's legal servant, acted as judge, and was among the most eminent members of his profession. In Chaucer's day there were about twenty in this exclusive group.

46 Discussion Is the lawyer a skillful practitioner of his profession? What evidence is there of his skill?

47 Enrichment The fact that his coat was ''parti-colored'' suggests luxury. Less expensive fabric would be dyed a single color. A belt of silk would also suggest affluence, since silk would have to be imported from the Orient.

48 Clarification A franklin was a landholder of free but not noble birth. He seemed, however, to have been regarded as a gentleman with a social position equal to a knight, squire, or sergeant at law. Chaucer's Franklin is certainly a man of wealth and dignity. He corresponds to the country squire of a later period.

49 Discussion For what is the Franklin noted? What is his greatest joy in life? How admirable is this occupation?

50 **Critical Thinking and Reading**
What might Chaucer be suggesting about the Franklin's source of delicacies by abruptly ending the description with a reference to his role as Sheriff and auditor?

51 **Enrichment** In England the term *haberdasher* means "a dealer in small wares or notions." In this country it refers to a dealer in men's furnishings.

52 **Reading Strategy** Read to discover what four of the five guildsmen have in common.

53 **Master Teacher Note** Why did their wives think they should be aldermen? Is a woman's social position today determined by her husband's? Note that we learn more about the wives' characters than about the guildsmen's characters.

54 **Literary Focus** There is only one physically descriptive fact given about the Cook, and it is somewhat unappetizing. Students might theorize as to Chaucer's reason for including it.

55 **Critical Thinking and Reading**
What does Chaucer imply when he says the Skipper "rode . . . as best he could"?

According to the seasons of the year
Changes of dish were ordered to appear.
He kept fat partridges in coops, beyond,
360 Many a bream and pike were in his pond.
Woe to the cook whose sauces had no sting
Or who was unprepared in anything!
And in his hall a table stood arrayed
And ready all day long, with places laid.
365 As Justice at the Sessions[46] none stood higher;
He often had been Member for the Shire.[47]
A dagger and a little purse of silk
Hung at his girdle, white as morning milk.
As Sheriff he checked audit, every entry.
370 He was a model among landed gentry.

   A *Haberdasher*, a *Dyer*, a *Carpenter*,
A *Weaver* and a *Carpet-maker* were
Among our ranks, all in the livery
Of one impressive guild-fraternity.
375 They were so trim and fresh their gear would pass
For new. Their knives were not tricked out with brass
But wrought with purest silver, which avouches
A like display on girdles and on pouches.
Each seemed a worthy burgess,[48] fit to grace
380 A guild-hall with a seat upon the dais.
Their wisdom would have justified a plan
To make each one of them an alderman;
They had the capital and revenue,
Besides their wives declared it was their due.
385 And if they did not think so, then they ought;
To be called "*Madam*" is a glorious thought,
And so is going to church and being seen
Having your mantle carried like a queen.

   They had a *Cook* with them who stood alone
390 For boiling chicken with a marrow-bone,
Sharp flavoring-powder and a spice for savor.
He could distinguish London ale by flavor,
And he could roast and seethe and broil and fry,
Make good thick soup and bake a tasty pie.
395 But what a pity—so it seemed to me,
That he should have an ulcer on his knee.
As for blancmange,[49] he made it with the best.

   There was a *Skipper* hailing from far west;
He came from Dartmouth, so I understood.
400 He rode a farmer's horse as best he could,
In a woolen gown that reached his knee.
A dagger on a lanyard[50] falling free
Hung from his neck under his arm and down.
The summer heat had tanned his color brown,

46. Sessions: Court sessions.
47. Member . . . Shire: Parliamentary representative for the county.

48. burgess: A member of a legislative body.

49. blancmange (blə mänj'): At the time, a creamy chicken dish.

50. lanyard: A loose rope around the neck.

405 And certainly he was an excellent fellow.
Many a draught of vintage, red and yellow,
He'd drawn at Bordeaux, while the trader snored.
The nicer rules of conscience he ignored.
If, when he fought, the enemy vessel sank,
410 He sent his prisoners home; they walked the plank.
As for his skill in reckoning his tides,
Currents and many another risk besides,
Moons, harbors, pilots, he had such dispatch
That none from Hull to Carthage was his match.
415 Hardy he was, prudent in undertaking;
His beard in many a tempest had its shaking,
And he knew all the havens as they were
From Gottland to the Cape of Finisterre,
And every creek in Brittany and Spain;
420 The barge he owned was called *The Maudelayne*.

    A *Doctor* too emerged as we proceeded;
No one alive could talk as well as he did
On points of medicine and of surgery,
For, being grounded in astronomy,
425 He watched his patient's favorable star
And, by his Natural Magic, knew what are
The lucky hours and planetary degrees
For making charms and magic effigies.
The cause of every malady you'd got
430 He knew, and whether dry, cold, moist or hot;[51]
He knew their seat, their humor and condition.
He was a perfect practicing physician.
These causes being known for what they were,
He gave the man his medicine then and there.
435 All his apothecaries[52] in a tribe
Were ready with the drugs he would prescribe,
And each made money from the other's guile;
They had been friendly for a goodish while.
He was well-versed in Esculapius[53] too
440 And what Hippocrates and Rufus knew
And Dioscorides, now dead and gone,
Galen and Rhazes, Hali, Serapion,
Averroes, Avicenna, Constantine,
Scotch Bernard, John of Gaddesden, Gilbertine.[54]
445 In his own diet he observed some measure;
There were no superfluities for pleasure,
Only digestives, nutritives and such.
He did not read the Bible very much.
In blood-red garments, slashed with bluish-gray
450 And lined with taffeta,[55] he rode his way;
Yet he was rather close as to expenses
And kept the gold he won in pestilences.

The Prologue from *The Canterbury Tales* 129

51. The cause . . . hot: It was believed that the body was composed of four "humors" (cold and dry, hot and moist, hot and dry, cold and moist) and that diseases resulted from a disturbance of one of these "humors."

52. apothecaries (ə päthˈ ə ker′ ēz): Persons who prepared drugs.

53. Esculapius (es′ kyoo lā′ pē əs): In Roman mythology, the god of medicine and healing.

54. Hippocrates . . . Gilbertine: Famous physicians and medical authorities.

55. taffeta (tafˈ i tə): A fine silk fabric.

62 Enrichment Her deafness came from a blow on the ear administered by her fifth husband because she had torn several pages out of an antifeminist book he insisted on reading to her.

63 Clarification People went up to the altar to make their offerings in order of social precedence. Arguments over this precedence are stock examples in Medieval literature of the sin of pride.

64 Reading Strategy Read for the various references to her appearance. Describe the Wife of Bath. What sense do you have about her age? What evidence does Chaucer present of her affluence?

65 Master Teacher Note Medieval physiognomists believed there was a connection between character and physical features. A gap between teeth was regarded not only as a sign that a person would be lucky and would travel extensively, but also that this person was bold, false, gluttonous, and lascivious.

66 Enrichment The traditional garments or habits of those modern nuns who wear habits are simple Medieval dress. While secular styles changed, theirs did not. The cloth covering the hair, ears, and neck is the wimple that all married women wore in the Middle Ages. Nuns were considered married women, the brides of Christ.

67 Discussion Why is it no surprise to us that the Wife of Bath has an outgoing personality and is an expert on love?

68 Master Teacher Note The Parson, or parish priest, is another idealized pilgrim, one who stands in sharp contrast to those other clergy on the pilgrimage who are either worldly or corrupt. His virtues are those on which Wycliffe and other reformers laid emphasis.

69 Discussion What were his attitude toward and his actions regarding tithes? The penalty of excommunication was often imposed for their nonpayment.

Gold stimulates the heart, or so we're told.
He therefore had a special love of gold.

455   A worthy *woman* from beside *Bath*[56] city
Was with us, somewhat deaf, which was a pity.
In making cloth she showed so great a bent
She bettered those of Ypres and of Ghent.[57]
460 In all the parish not a dame dared stir
Towards the altar steps in front of her,
And if indeed they did, so wrath was she
As to be quite put out of charity.
Her kerchiefs were of finely woven ground;[58]
465 I dared have sworn they weighed a good ten pound,
The ones she wore on Sunday, on her head.
Her hose were of the finest scarlet red
And gartered tight; her shoes were soft and new.
Bold was her face, handsome, and red in hue.
470 A worthy woman all her life, what's more
She'd had five husbands, all at the church door,
Apart from other company in youth;
No need just now to speak of that, forsooth.
And she had thrice been to Jerusalem,
Seen many strange rivers and passed over them;
475 She'd been to Rome and also to Boulogne,
St. James of Compostella and Cologne,[59]
And she was skilled in wandering by the way.
She had gap-teeth, set widely, truth to say.
Easily on an ambling horse she sat
480 Well wimpled[60] up, and on her head a hat
As broad as is a buckler[61] or a shield;
She had a flowing mantle that concealed
Large hips, her heels spurred sharply under that.
In company she liked to laugh and chat
485 And knew the remedies for love's mischances,
An art in which she knew the oldest dances.

    A holy-minded man of good renown
There was, and poor, the *Parson* to a town,
Yet he was rich in holy thought and work.
490 He also was a learned man, a clerk,
Who truly knew Christ's gospel and would preach it
Devoutly to parishioners, and teach it.
Benign and wonderfully diligent,
And patient when adversity was sent
495 (For so he proved in great adversity)
He much disliked extorting tithe[62] or fee,
Nay rather he preferred beyond a doubt
Giving to poor parishioners round about
From his own goods and Easter offerings.
500 He found sufficiency in little things.

56. Bath: An English resort city.

57. Ypres (ē′ prə) **and of Ghent** (gent): Flemish cities known for wool making.

58. ground: A composite fabric.

59. Jerusalem . . . Rome . . . Boulogne . . . St. James of Compostella . . . Cologne: Famous pilgrimage sites at the time.

60. wimpled: Wearing a scarf covering the head, neck, and chin.

61. buckler: A small, round shield.

62. tithe (tīth): One tenth of a person's income, paid as a tax to support the church.

Wide was his parish, with houses far asunder,
Yet he neglected not in rain or thunder,
In sickness or in grief, to pay a call
    On the remotest, whether great or small,
505 Upon his feet, and in his hand a stave.
70 This noble example to his sheep he gave,
First following the word before he taught it,
And it was from the gospel he had caught it.
This little proverb he would add thereto
510 That if gold rust, what then will iron do?
For if a priest be foul in whom we trust
No wonder that a common man should rust;
And shame it is to see—let priests take stock—
A soiled shepherd and a snowy flock.
515 The true example that a priest should give
Is one of cleanness, how the sheep should live.
He did not set his benefice to hire[63]
71 And leave his sheep encumbered in the mire
Or run to London to earn easy bread
520 By singing masses for the wealthy dead,
Or find some Brotherhood and get enrolled.
He stayed at home and watched over his fold
So that no wolf should make the sheep miscarry.
He was a shepherd and no mercenary.
525 Holy and virtuous he was, but then
Never contemptuous of sinful men,
Never disdainful, never too proud or fine,
But was discreet in teaching and benign.
His business was to show a fair behavior
530 And draw men thus to Heaven and their Savior,
Unless indeed a man were obstinate;
And such, whether of high or low estate,
He put to sharp rebuke to say the least.
I think there never was a better priest.
535 He sought no pomp or glory in his dealings,
No scrupulosity had spiced his feelings.
Christ and His Twelve Apostles and their lore
He taught, but followed it himself before.
72   There was a *Plowman* with him there, his brother.
540 Many a load of dung one time or other
He must have carted through the morning dew.
He was an honest worker, good and true,
Living in peace and perfect charity,
And, as the gospel bade him, so did he,
73 545 Loving God best with all his heart and mind
And then his neighbor as himself, repined
At no misfortune, slacked for no content,
For steadily about his work he went

63. set . . . hire: Pay
someone else to perform
his parish duties.

The Prologue from *The Canterbury Tales* 131

74 Clarification A mare was an extremely humble steed.

75 Enrichment A miller ground wheat into flour, and he was traditionally paid with a percentage of the ground grain.

76 Enrichment Chaucer devotes considerable space to a physical description of the Miller. Medieval physiognomists would have associated his short-shouldered, stocky figure, his bushy red beard, and his warty nose with the traits of shamelessness, loquacity, belligerence, and lecherousness.

77 Reading Strategy After you read, be prepared to review the Miller's character.

78 Discussion What was the Manciple's purchasing technique?

79 Discussion How did he "outpace" or outsmart his employers? What is the narrator's attitude toward this? Why do you think he admires such skullduggery? What kind of men were the Manciple's employers? Did they deserve to be cheated?

To thrash his corn, to dig or to manure
550 Or make a ditch; and he would help the poor
For love of Christ and never take a penny
If he could help it, and, as prompt as any,
He paid his tithes in full when they were due
On what he owned, and on his earnings too.
555 He wore a tabard[64] smock and rode a mare.
     There was a *Reeve*,[65] also a *Miller*, there,
A College *Manciple*[66] from the Inns of Court,
A papal *Pardoner*[67] and, in close consort,
A Church-Court *Summoner*,[68] riding at a trot,
560 And finally myself—that was the lot.
     The *Miller* was a chap of sixteen stone,[69]
A great stout fellow big in brawn and bone.
He did well out of them, for he could go
And win the ram at any wrestling show.
565 Broad, knotty and short-shouldered, he would boast
He could heave any door off hinge and post,
Or take a run and break it with his head.
His beard, like any sow or fox, was red
And broad as well, as though it were a spade;
570 And, at its very tip, his nose displayed
A wart on which there stood a tuft of hair,
Red as the bristles in an old sow's ear.
His nostrils were as black as they were wide.
He had a sword and buckler at his side,
575 His mighty mouth was like a furnace door.
A wrangler and buffoon, he had a store
Of tavern stories, filthy in the main.
His was a master-hand at stealing grain.
He felt it with his thumb and thus he knew
580 Its quality and took three times his due—
A thumb of gold, by God, to gauge an oat!
He wore a hood of blue and a white coat.
He liked to play his bagpipes up and down
And that was how he brought us out of town.
585   The *Manciple* came from the Inner Temple;
All caterers might follow his example
In buying victuals; he was never rash
Whether he bought on credit or paid cash.
He used to watch the market most precisely
590 And go in first, and so he did quite nicely.
Now isn't it a marvel of God's grace
That an illiterate fellow can outpace
The wisdom of a heap of learned men?
His masters—he had more than thirty then—
595 All versed in the abstrusest legal knowledge,
Could have produced a dozen from their College

64. tabard: A loose jacket.

65. *Reeve*: An estate manager.

66. *Manciple*: A buyer of provisions.

67. *Pardoner*: One who dispenses papal pardons.

68. *Summoner*: One who serves summonses to church courts.

69. sixteen stone: 224 pounds. A stone equals 14 pounds.

132   The Medieval Period

Fit to be stewards in land and rents and game
To any Peer in England you could name,
And show him how to live on what he had
600 Debt-free (unless of course the Peer were mad)
Or be as frugal as he might desire,
And they were fit to help about the Shire
In any legal case there was to try;
And yet this Manciple could wipe their eye.
605   The *Reeve* was old and choleric and thin;
His beard was shaven closely to the skin,
His shorn hair came abruptly to a stop
Above his ears, and he was docked on top
Just like a priest in front; his legs were lean,
610 Like sticks they were, no calf was to be seen.
He kept his bins and garners[70] very trim;
No auditor could gain a point on him.
And he could judge by watching drought and rain
The yield he might expect from seed and grain.
615 His master's sheep, his animals and hens,
Pigs, horses, dairies, stores and cattle-pens
Were wholly trusted to his government.
And he was under contract to present
The accounts, right from his master's earliest years.
620 No one had ever caught him in arrears.
No bailiff, serf or herdsman dared to kick,
He knew their dodges, knew their every trick;
Feared like the plague he was, by those beneath.
He had a lovely dwelling on a heath,
625 Shadowed in green by trees above the sward.[71]
A better hand at bargains than his lord,
He had grown rich and had a store of treasure
Well tucked away, yet out it came to pleasure
His lord with subtle loans or gifts of goods,
630 To earn his thanks and even coats and hoods.
When young he'd learnt a useful trade and still
He was a carpenter of first-rate skill.
The stallion-cob he rode at a slow trot
Was dapple-gray and bore the name of Scot.
635 He wore an overcoat of bluish shade
And rather long; he had a rusty blade
Slung at his side. He came, as I heard tell,
From Norfolk, near a place called Baldeswell.
His coat was tucked under his belt and splayed.
640 He rode the hindmost of our cavalcade.
    There was a *Summoner* with us in the place
Who had a fire-red cherubinnish face,[72]
For he had carbuncles. His eyes were narrow,
He was as hot and lecherous as a sparrow.

70. garners *n*.: Buildings for storing grain.

71. sward *n*.: Turf.

72. fire–red . . . face: In the art of the Middle Ages, the faces of cherubs, or angels, were often painted red.

80 Master Teacher Note A reeve was generally a subordinate estate-manager. Chaucer's Reeve evidently had greater power and was more like a chief manager or steward. His choleric complexion would have denoted to physiognomists sharpness of wit, irascibility, and wantonness. Which of these traits does his description in the Prologue include?

81 Clarification His short hair indicated his servile position.

82 Discussion What specific indicators of his competency are cited? Why was he so unpopular with his inferiors?

83 Literary Focus He could please his lord by lending him some of the lord's own possessions, thus garnering thanks plus a reward. Why might he have more ready cash than his lord?

84 Literary Focus It is interesting to note that the Reeve chose his place in the cavalcade farthest away from the Miller, who led the procession. There was a traditional enmity between the two occupations. Why?

85 Enrichment His hideous skin condition was known as alopecia, a form of leprosy. Chaucer lists the most popular remedies of the day.

645 Black, scabby brows he had, and a thin beard.
Children were afraid when he appeared.
No quicksilver, lead ointments, tartar creams,
Boracic, no, nor brimstone, so it seems,
Could make a salve that had the power to bite,
650 Clean up or curve his whelks of knobby white.
Or purge the pimples sitting on his cheeks.
Garlic he loved, and onions too, and leeks,
And drinking strong wine till all was hazy.
Then he would shout and jabber as if crazy,
655 And wouldn't speak a word except in Latin
When he was drunk, such tags as he was pat in;
He only had a few, say two or three,
That he had mugged up out of some decree;
No wonder, for he heard them every day.
660 And, as you know, a man can teach a jay
To call out "Walter" better than the Pope.
But had you tried to test his wits and grope
For more, you'd have found nothing in the bag.
Then *"Questio quid juris"*[73] was his tag.
665 He was a gentle varlet and a kind one,
No better fellow if you went to find one.
He would allow—just for a quart of wine—
Any good lad to keep a concubine
A twelvemonth and dispense it altogether!
670 Yet he could pluck a finch to leave no feather:
And if he found some rascal with a maid
He would instruct him not to be afraid
In such a case of the Archdeacon's curse
(Unless the rascal's soul were in his purse)
675 For in his purse the punishment should be.
"Purse is the good Archdeacon's Hell," said he.
But well I know he lied in what he said;
A curse should put a guilty man in dread,
For curses kill, as shriving brings, salvation.
680 We should beware of excommunication.
Thus, as he pleased, the man could bring duress
On any young fellow in the diocese.
He knew their secrets, they did what he said.
He wore a garland set upon his head
685 Large as the holly-bush upon a stake
Outside an ale-house, and he had a cake,
A round one, which it was his joke to wield
As if it were intended for a shield.

86   He and a gentle *Pardoner* rode together,
690 A bird from Charing Cross of the same feather,
Just back from visiting the Court of Rome.
He loudly sang *"Come hither, love, come home!"*

73. *"Questo quid juris":* "The question is, what is the point of the law?" (Latin).

The Summoner sang deep seconds to this song,
No trumpet ever sounded half so strong.
695 This Pardoner had hair as yellow as wax,
Hanging down smoothly like a hank of flax.
In driblets fell his locks behind his head
Down to his shoulders which they overspread;
Thinly they fell, like rat-tails, one by one.
700 He wore no hood upon his head, for fun;
The hood inside his wallet had been stowed,
He aimed at riding in the latest mode;
But for a little cap his head was bare
And he had bulging eyeballs, like a hare.
705 He'd sewed a holy relic on his cap;
His wallet lay before him on his lap,
Brimful of pardons come from Rome all hot.
He had the same small voice a goat has got.
His chin no beard had harbored, nor would harbor,
710 Smoother than ever chin was left by barber.
I judge he was a gelding, or a mare.
As to his trade, from Berwick down to Ware
There was no pardoner of equal grace,
For in his trunk he had a pillowcase
715 Which he asserted was Our Lady's veil.
He said he had a gobbet[74] of the sail
Saint Peter had the time when he made bold
To walk the waves, till Jesu Christ took hold.
He had a cross of metal set with stones
720 And, in a glass, a rubble of pigs' bones.
And with these relics, any time he found
Some poor up-country parson to astound,
On one short day, in money down, he drew
More than the parson in a month or two,
725 And by his flatteries and prevarication
Made monkeys of the priest and congregation.
But still to do him justice first and last
In church he was a noble ecclesiast.
How well he read a lesson or told a story!
730 But best of all he sang an Offertory,[75]
For well he knew that when that song was sung
He'd have to preach and tune his honey-tongue
And (well he could) win silver from the crowd.
That's why he sang so merrily and loud.
735   Now I have told you shortly, in a clause,
The rank, the array, the number and the cause
Of our assembly in this company
In Southwark, at that high-class hostelry
Known as *The Tabard*, close beside *The Bell*.
740 And now the time has come for me to tell

74. gobbet: Piece.

75. Offertory: The song that accompanies the collection of the offering at a church service.

87 **Master Teacher Note** The physical description of the Pardoner would have suggested to the Medieval reader familiar with the science of physiognomy that the man was effeminate, deceptive, gluttonous, drunken, and treacherous. What physical characteristics might indicate that type of character? Do you think such characteristics are a reliable indicator of character?

88 **Discussion** How did the Pardoner take advantage of the simple country priest? Why is this chicanery particularly distasteful?

89 **Discussion** In what way is he a "noble ecclesiast"? Is this term bestowed on him naively by the pilgrim Chaucer, ironically by the poet Chaucer, or a combination of both?

90 **Reading Strategy** Review the narrator's original intentions in describing the pilgrims. Has he kept it? What aspects of life has he described in the Prologue? What classes of society does he criticize and why? What class does he favor and why?

91

How we behaved that evening; I'll begin
After we had alighted at the inn,
Then I'll report our journey, stage by stage,
All the remainder of our pilgrimage.
745 But first I beg of you, in courtesy,
Not to condemn me as unmannerly
If I speak plainly and with no concealings
And give account of all their words and dealings,
Using their very phrases as they fell.
750 For certainly, as you all know so well,
He who repeats a tale after a man
Is bound to say, as nearly as he can,
Each single word, if he remembers it,
However rudely spoken or unfit,
755 Or else the tale he tells will be untrue,
The things invented and the phrases new.
He may not flinch although it were his brother,
If he says one word he must say the other.
And Christ Himself spoke broad[76] in Holy Writ,
760 And as you know there's nothing there unfit,
And Plato[77] says, for those with power to read,
"The word should be as cousin to the deed."
Further I beg you to forgive it me
If I neglect the order and degree
765 And what is due to rank in what I've planned.
I'm short of wit as you will understand.
     Our *Host* gave us great welcome; everyone
Was given a place and supper was begun.
He served the finest victuals you could think,
770 The wine was strong and we were glad to drink.
A very striking man our Host withal,
And fit to be a marshal in a hall.
His eyes were bright, his girth a little wide;
There is no finer burgess in Cheapside.[78]
775 Bold in his speech, yet wise and full of tact,
There was no manly attribute he lacked,
What's more he was a merry-hearted man.
After our meal he jokingly began
To talk of sport, and, among other things
780 After we'd settled up our reckonings,
He said as follows: "Truly, gentlemen,
You're very welcome and I can't think when
—Upon my word I'm telling you no lie—
I've seen a gathering here that looked so spry,
785 No, not this year, as in this tavern now.
I'd think you up some fun if I knew how.
And, as it happens, a thought has just occurred
And it will cost you nothing, on my word.

76. broad: Bluntly.

77. Plato: A Greek philosopher (427?–347? B.C.).

78. Cheapside: A district in London.

Commentary

Considering that Chaucer's characters have traveled as widely as they have and experienced the ups and downs of fortune, it is interesting to trace the advances and reversals of the author himself. In a book entitled *The History of English Literature* Peter Quennell reports the following:

"Between 1370 and 1386, Chaucer undertook a variety of important diplomatic missions. Thus he made an official journey to Italy towards the end of 1372, where he visited Genoa, Pisa, Florence, and remained for over ten months; in 1377 he was despatched to Flanders and France; in 1378 he returned to France and, soon afterwards, set forth on another errand to Bernabo Visconti, Duke of Milan. His activities were well rewarded—not only with such minor privileges as the right to demand a jug of wine from the pantry of the royal butler, but with the comptrollership of the duties of wools and skins and, later, the comptrollership of the Petty Customs. In 1386 he became a knight for the shire of Kent. But that same year he suffered a temporary disgrace, lost both his comptrollerships and was obliged to borrow money. In 1389, however, he re-entered the

You're off to Canterbury—well, God speed!
790 Blessed St. Thomas answer to your need!
And I don't doubt, before the journey's done
You mean to while the time in tales and fun.
Indeed, there's little pleasure for your bones
Riding along and all as dumb as stones.
795 So let me then propose for your enjoyment,
Just as I said, a suitable employment.
And if my notion suits and you agree
And promise to submit yourselves to me
Playing your parts exactly as I say
800 Tomorrow as you ride along the way,
Then by my father's soul (and he is dead)
If you don't like it you can have my head!
Hold up your hands, and not another word."
        Well, our consent of course was not deferred,
805 It seemed not worth a serious debate;
We all agreed to it at any rate
And bade him issue what commands he would.
"My lords," he said, "now listen for your good,
And please don't treat my notion with disdain.
810 This is the point. I'll make it short and plain.
Each one of you shall help to make things slip
By telling two stories on the outward trip
To Canterbury, that's what I intend,
And, on the homeward way to journey's end
815 Another two, tales from the days of old;
And then the man whose story is best told,
That is to say who gives the fullest measure
Of good morality and general pleasure,
He shall be given a supper, paid by all,
820 Here in this tavern, in this very hall,
When we come back again from Canterbury.
And in the hope to keep you bright and merry
I'll go along with you myself and ride
All at my own expense and serve as guide.
825 I'll be the judge, and those who won't obey
Shall pay for what we spend upon the way.
Now if you all agree to what you've heard
Tell me at once without another word,
And I will make arrangements early for it."
830   Of course we all agreed, in fact we swore it
Delightedly, and made entreaty too
That he should act as he proposed to do,
Become our Governor in short, and be
Judge of our tales and general referee,
835 And set the supper at a certain price.
We promised to be ruled by his advice

civil service and received several lucrative appointments . . .
The closing years of Chaucer's existence seem to have been
calm and cheerful."

Come high, come low; unanimously thus
We set him up in judgment over us.
More wine was fetched, the business being done;
840 We drank it off and up went everyone
To bed without a moment of delay.
     Early next morning at the spring of day
Up rose our Host and roused us like a cock,
Gathering us together in a flock,
845 And off we rode at slightly faster pace
Than walking to St. Thomas' watering-place;[79]
And there our Host drew up, began to ease
His horse, and said, "Now, listen if you please,
My lords! Remember what you promised me.
850 If evensong and matins will agree[80]
Let's see who shall be first to tell a tale.
And as I hope to drink good wine and ale
I'll be your judge. The rebel who disobeys,
However much the journey costs, he pays.
855 Now draw for cut and then we can depart;
The man who draws the shortest cut shall start."

79. St. Thomas' watering-place: A brook two miles from the inn.

80. If evensong . . . agree: If what you said last night holds true this morning.

Primary Source

Seventeenth-century poet and dramatist John Dryden called Chaucer the "father of English poetry," a ranking still considered valid today. Dryden ranked Chaucer with the "same degree of veneration as the Grecians held Homer or the Romans held Virgil," and found in his work "a perpetual fountain of good sense." Writing about a hundred years later, poet and essayist Samuel Taylor Coleridge found: ". . . unceasing delight in Chaucer. His cheerfulness is especially delicious to me in my old age. How exquisitely tender he is, and yet how perfectly free from the least touch of sickly melancholy or morbid drooping. The sympathy of the poet with the subjects of his poetry is particularly remarkable in Shakespeare and Chaucer; but what Shakespeare effects by a strong act of imagination and mental changing, Chaucer does without any effort, merely by the inborn kindly joyousness of his nature. How well we seem to know Chaucer! How absolutely nothing do we know of Shakespeare!"

THINKING ABOUT THE SELECTION
Recalling

1. What does Chaucer say that people long to do when spring comes?
2. Which pilgrim is described as being (a) "modest as a maid"? (b) "all sentiment and tender heart"? (c) "a very festive fellow"?
3. Which pilgrim is described as having (a) "a special love of gold"? (b) "gap-teeth"? (c) "a store of tavern stories"?
4. How does Chaucer say he will report the events of the pilgrimage?
5. What entertainment on the journey does the host propose?

Interpreting

6. Chaucer pokes gentle fun at some of the pilgrims. What is his opinion of the Nun's singing voice and of her French?
7. Although the Friar and the Parson are both religious men, they are very different. What are some of the ways in which they differ?
8. What, if anything, does Chaucer seem to dislike about (a) the Skipper? (b) the Doctor?

Applying

9. If Chaucer were writing *The Canterbury Tales* today, what three kinds of pilgrims do you think he might consider adding to the group?

ANALYZING LITERATURE
Understanding Characterization

Chaucer sometimes makes direct statements about a character: "He was an honest worker, good and true." More often he reveals character indirectly, often through action: "She used to weep if she but saw a mouse/Caught in a trap." There is not much dialogue in the Prologue, but Chaucer frequently uses physical appearance to suggest character. Compare the appearance of the Miller ("A great stout fellow big in brawn and bone") with that of the Reeve ("old and choleric and thin"). Their looks match their personalities.

1. What nouns does Chaucer use to characterize the Squire?

2. How does Chaucer mainly characterize (a) the Doctor? (b) the Host?

CRITICAL THINKING AND READING
Making Inferences About Characters

If you are to understand fictional characters fully, you must make inferences about them. You must draw conclusions based on what the writer has told you about their actions, thoughts, words, and appearance. When Chaucer writes of the Parson, "That if gold rust, what will iron do?" you can infer that the Parson realizes he should be a model of behavior for his parishioners. What can you infer about the Pardoner from the information in lines 670–675?

UNDERSTANDING LANGUAGE
Using Similes

A **simile** is a comparison of two unlike things using *like* or *as*:

His mighty mouth was *like* a furnace door.
White *as* a daisy-petal was his beard.

The usual purpose of a simile is to give the reader an apt and striking picture of the person or object being described.

1. What three similes appear in lines 646–656 of the sketch of the Pardoner?
2. Try to find at least five other similes in the Prologue. What are they?

THINKING AND WRITING
Writing a Pilgrim's Tale

Now that you know something about each of Chaucer's pilgrims, write a tale you think one of them might tell. Choose a pilgrim and study his or her sketch carefully. When you are sure you understand the pilgrim's character, write a tale that he or she might tell. You may modernize the tale, if you wish, setting it in the present. But make sure the message of the tale fits the character of the pilgrim.

from The Canterbury Tales **139**

---

gold than his patients; he and his apothecaries worked together selling drugs at inflated prices. Also, he did not read the Bible much.

Applying

9. Answers will differ. Some possibilities are astronaut, stockbroker, professional athlete, and physical-fitness instructor.

ANSWERS TO ANALYZING LITERATURE

1. The Squire is a "lover," a "cadet," and "a lad of fire."
2. (a) Chaucer characterizes the Doctor indirectly, through action mainly. (b) Chaucer uses action, description, and several direct statements to characterize the Host.

ANSWERS TO CRITICAL THINKING AND READING

The Pardoner appears to be something of a con man.

ANSWERS TO UNDERSTANDING LANGUAGE

1. Three similes are hair "as yellow as wax," hanging "like a hank of wax," and fell "like rats-tails."
2. Answers will differ. There are many possibilities such as "as loud as does the chapel bell" (line 175), "not pale like a tormented soul" (line 209), "as brown as a berry" (line 211), "just like a puppy" (line 264), "like a bell about its mould" (line 272), "as broad as is a buckler or a shield" (line 481).

THINKING AND WRITING

For help with this assignment, students can refer to Lesson 19, "Writing a Short Story," in the Handbook of Writing About Literature.

Publishing Student Writing Ask the students to read their papers to the class. Alternatively, you might read them without revealing the writers. Ask the class to determine which pilgrim is "telling" the tale. Discuss why they thought so.

Closure and Extension

ANSWERS TO THINKING ABOUT THE SELECTION
Recalling

1. People long to go on pilgrimages.
2. The pilgrims described are (a) the Knight, (b) the Prioress, and (c) the Friar.
3. The pilgrims described are (a) the

Doctor, (b) the Wife of Bath, and (c) the Miller.
4. He will report it stage by stage —plainly, concealing nothing.
5. The host proposes that each pilgrim tell two tales going and two more on the return. The best shall receive a free dinner.

Interpreting

6. Her voice is too nasal. Her French

would be incomprehensible to a Parisian.
7. The Friar does not take his religious vows seriously; he prefers worldly pleasures and catering to the wealthy. The Parson is all that a good priest should be.
8. (a) Chaucer dislikes the Skipper because he disregards the rules of conscience—stealing wine and forcing prisoners to walk the plank. (b) The Doctor cares more about

139

Literary Focus Have students discuss their experiences with films or stories that mock people who take themselves too seriously. For example, most of them at one time or another have probably watched cartoons in which Bugs Bunny teases and eventually defeats some conceited enemy. You might want them to consider how Bugs deflates the self-importance of such characters by making them appear ridiculous.

Writing/Prior Knowledge Pair up students in your class. Before they begin freewriting, have them share ideas about trivial chores that might be made fun of in a mock-heroic way.

ESL Teaching Strategy To help with the writing assignment, pair each ESL student with a native speaker. Have the native speaker coach the ESL student on words that might be amusingly high-flown if used to describe an ordinary daily chore.

Teaching to Ability Levels Have less advanced students write brief character sketches describing the three main characters of this tale—Chanticleer, Pertelote, and Russel the Fox. Have advanced students find out something about the history of courtly love in the middle ages and see if they can apply what they have learned to Chaucer's tale.

Vocabulary

Preteach the following vocabulary words:

capital (kap′ ət 'l) n.: Wealth in money or property

timorous (tim′ ər es) adj.: Timid

derision (di rizh′ ən) n.: Contempt or ridicule

prattle (prat′ 'l) n.: Idle chatter

maxim (maks′ im) n.: A briefly expressed general truth or rule of conduct

stringent (strin′ jənt) adj.: Strict

cant (kant) n.: Insincere or meaningless talk

GUIDE FOR INTERPRETING

Writer's Techniques

The Nun's Priest's Tale

The Mock-Heroic Style. Writers use a **mock-heroic style** when they write about trivial matters in a style that would be more appropriate for great and important events. The disparity between content and style results in comic effects. For example, imagine describing a vain young man in front of his mirror as if he were participating in a solemn, religious ritual: With total devotion and concentration and hardly breathing at all, Tom carefully applied the comb to the curl that had violated the upper part of his ear . . .

In "The Nun's Priest's Tale," Chaucer uses the mock-heroic style to transform a popular animal fable into a masterpiece of comedy. He describes the barnyard interactions of animals as if he were writing an epic poem. Among the epic elements he borrows are the hero's elaborate boasts, the vivid accounts of battles, and the intervention of supernatural forces. To make his tale even more ridiculous, he includes barnyard debates about controversial issues of the day: fate versus free will and woman as the source of man's misfortune. The contrast between these lofty concerns and the animal debaters is ludicrous but appealing.

Chaucer casts a rooster and hen as his romantic leads, presenting them as if they were the lord and lady of a castle. As master of all he surveys, the rooster Chanticleer is pompous, naive, and thoroughly charming. He struts and preaches, displaying his male ego and sprinkling his conversation with learned classical allusions. Meanwhile, his hen-wife Pertelote is a comically practical heroine. She gives her lord and master advice about his health and, for all his strutting, wields emotional power over him.

The mock-heroic style works best when ridicule is tempered with affection. Chaucer certainly succeeds in this respect. His fondness for his characters, even at their most absurd, comes through in the pleasant and cheerful tone of the tale.

Writing

Think about the many little things you do every day: brushing your teeth, tying your shoe laces, opening a box of cereal. Use the mock-heroic style to describe a trivial chore or activity that is part of your daily routine. Remember to stress the contrast between style and subject matter in order to heighten the humor. After you have finished, exchange descriptions with a classmate.

Objectives

1 To understand how an egotist or vain person can be fooled by flattery
2 To understand the mock-heroic style in literature
3 To understand courtly love
4 To write a beast fable

Support Material

Teaching Portfolio
Teacher Backup, pp. 105–108
Grammar in Action Worksheet, *Understanding Debating Strategies,* p. 109
Usage and Mechanics Worksheet, p. 111
Vocabulary Check, p. 112
Analyzing Literature Worksheet, *Understanding the Mock-Heroic Style,* p. 113

Critical Thinking and Reading Worksheet, *Understanding Courtly Love,* p. 115
Language Worksheet, *Appreciating Vivid Verbs,* p. 116
Selection Test, pp. 117–118

Spelling Tip Write the words *capital* and *capitol* on the chalkboard and explain that they are perhaps more commonly confused and misspelled than any other such pair of words. Under-

The Nun's Priest's Tale

Geoffrey Chaucer

Once, long ago, there dwelt a poor old widow
In a small cottage, by a little meadow
Beside a grove and standing in a dale.
This widow-woman of whom I tell my tale
5 Since the sad day when last she was a wife
Had led a very patient, simple life.
Little she had in capital or rent,
But still, by making do with what God sent,
She kept herself and her two daughters going.
10 Three hefty sows—no more—were all her showing,
Three cows as well; there was a sheep called Molly.
  Sooty her hall, her kitchen melancholy,
And there she ate full many a slender meal;
There was no *sauce piquante*[1] to spice her veal,
15 No dainty morsel ever passed her throat,
According to her cloth she cut her coat.
Repletion[2] never left her in disquiet
And all her physic was a temperate diet,
Hard work for exercise and heart's content.
20 And rich man's gout did nothing to prevent
Her dancing, apoplexy[3] struck her not;
She drank no wine, nor white nor red had got.
Her board was mostly served with white and black,
Milk and brown bread, in which she found no lack;
25 Broiled bacon or an egg or two were common,
She was in fact a sort of dairy-woman.
  She had a yard that was enclosed about
By a stockade and a dry ditch without,
In which she kept a cock called Chanticleer.
30 In all the land for crowing he'd no peer;
His voice was jollier than the organ blowing
In church on Sundays, he was great at crowing.
Far, far more regular than any clock
Or abbey bell the crowing of this cock.
35 The equinoctial wheel and its position[4]
At each ascent he knew by intuition;
At every hour—fifteen degrees of movement—
He crowed so well there could be no improvement.

1. *sauce piquante* (pē′ kənt): French for a pleasantly sharp sauce, used for fancy and expensive meals.
2. Repletion (ri plē′ shən) *n.*: The state of having eaten too much.

3. apoplexy: An old-fashioned term for a stroke.

4. equinoctial . . . position: Chaucer and his contemporaries accounted for changes in the positions of stars and planets by imagining that the heavens circled the earth once a day, moving fifteen degrees each hour.

Presentation

Motivation/Prior Knowledge
Tell students that they will be reading a kind of fable in which thinking and talking animals are the chief characters. Call upon their prior knowledge by asking them how the animal stories they have read or watched managed to convince them momentarily that animals can really talk and think like people. Suggest they keep this discussion in mind as they read.

Purpose-Setting Question How would you describe the personality of Chanticleer in this story?

Thematic Idea Have students compare the mock-heroic style used by Chaucer with that used by Pope in "The Rape of the Lock," p. 548.

1 **Discussion** Point out to students that the first 26 lines provide the human setting within which the beast fable occurs. Ask students how true to medieval life they think this depiction of a poor dairy-farmer is. Why has Chaucer set his tale in such impoverished circumstances?

2 **Discussion** Ask students what the effect is of claiming that Chanticleer can intuitively read the position of the stars? How does this description of his crowing compare to the description of his physical appearance?

line the *o* in *capitol* and next to it write: *only a building.* Tell students that if it's *not* a building, it's always spelled with an *a.*

3 Discussion Ask students in what way the description of Pertelote would be better suited to a courtly lady. How do the adjectives describing her contribute to the comic hilarity of the passage?

4 Discussion Ask students if they think Chaucer expects his audience to believe this explanation for the ability of these animals to talk. Why or why not?

5 Discussion Ask students how they react to the courteous and elegant way the rooster and hen address each other.

His comb was redder than fine coral, tall
40 And battlemented like a castle wall,
His bill was black and shone as bright as jet,
Like azure were his legs and they were set
On azure toes with nails of lily white,
Like burnished gold his feathers, flaming bright.
45   This gentlecock was master in some measure
Of seven hens, all there to do his pleasure.
They were his sisters and his paramours,
Colored like him in all particulars;
She with the loveliest dyes upon her throat
50 Was known as gracious Lady Pertelote.
Courteous she was, discreet and debonair,
Companionable too, and took such care
In her deportment, since she was seven days old
She held the heart of Chanticleer controlled,
55 Locked up securely in her every limb;
O such happiness his love to him!
And such a joy it was to hear them sing,
As when the glorious sun began to spring,
In sweet accord *My Love is far from land*[5]
60 —For in those far off days I understand
All birds and animals could speak and sing.
    Now it befell, as dawn began to spring,
When Chanticleer and Pertelote and all
His wives were perched in this poor widow's hall
65 (Fair Pertelote was next him on the perch),
This Chanticleer began to groan and lurch
Like someone sorely troubled by a dream,
And Pertelote who heard him roar and scream
Was quite aghast and said, "O dearest heart,
70 What's ailing you? Why do you groan and start?
Fie, what a sleeper! What a noise to make!"
"Madam," he said, "I beg you not to take
Offense, but by the Lord I had a dream
So terrible just now I had to scream:
75 I still can feel my heart racing from fear.
God turn my dream to good and guard all here,
And keep my body out of durance vile![6]
I dreamt that roaming up and down a while
Within our yard I saw a kind of beast,
80 A sort of hound that tried or seemed at least
To try and seize me . . . would have killed me dead!
His color was a blend of yellow and red,
His ears and tail were tipped with sable fur
Unlike the rest; he was a russet cur.
85 Small was his snout, his eyes were glowing bright.

5. *My love is far from land:* The refrain of a popular song.

6. **durance vile:** Long imprisonment.

142   *The Medieval Period*

ENGLISH TRAVELERS SETTING FORTH
FROM THE CANTERBURY TALES
The British Library

Humanities Note

Fine Art, *English Travelers Setting Forth,* from the Canterbury Tales. This miniature painting of English travelers setting forth is from an edition of Chaucer's *Canterbury Tales.* It reveals many details of Medieval life. The pilgrims ride by a walled city with a cathedral at the center. A large manor house is at the left. The roadway is unpaved and filled with mud and the pilgrims wear hooded cloaks and heavy hats. They travel in a group for protection. In addition to the details of landscape and clothing, the artist has captured the sense of intimacy and friendship that prevailed on long pilgrimages; the figure in the center seems to be leaning towards the red-hatted man, telling a story perhaps. He is one of the characters Chaucer described, probably the monk whose "bridle jingled in the whistling wind."

By the time this picture was made, the simple decorative style of Chaucer's own day had been replaced by a more detailed and realistic technique. Note, for example, the careful attention to architecture, landscape, and clothing.

You might want to use the following questions to discuss the art.

1. What does this picture suggest about Medieval life?
2. Why do you think story-telling was one of the most popular recreations for pilgrims stopping at inns?
3. How do today's travelers entertain themselves during a journey?

6 **Discussion** Ask students if they think that women today still expect men to feel no fear in order to avoid being accused of cowardice. If not, why has this expectation changed?

7 **Discussion** Point out to students that critics have argued that Pertelote is actually more down-to-earth and practical than her husband—and that her way of viewing dreams, though unscientific, is closer to the truth than Chanticleer's point of view. Ask students if they agree with this assessment of her character. Why or why not?

It was enough to make one die of fright.
That was no doubt what made me groan and swoon."
   "For shame," she said, "you timorous poltroon![7]
Alas, what cowardice! By God above,
90 You've forfeited my heart and lost my love.
I cannot love a coward, come what may.
For certainly, whatever we may say,
All women long—and O that it might be!—
For husbands tough, dependable and free,
95 Secret, discreet, no niggard,[8] not a fool
That boasts and then will find his courage cool
At every trifling thing. By God above,
How dare you say for shame, and to your love,
That anything at all was to be feared?
100 Have you no manly heart to match your beard?
And can a dream reduce you to such terror?
Dreams are a vanity, God knows, pure error.
Dreams are engendered in the too-replete
From vapors in the belly, which compete
105 With others, too abundant, swollen tight.
   "No doubt the redness in your dream tonight
Comes from the superfluity and force
Of the red choler in your blood. Of course.
That is what puts a dreamer in the dread
110 Of crimsoned arrows, fires flaming red,
Of great red monsters making as to fight him,
And big red whelps and little ones to bite him;
Just so the black and melancholy vapors
Will set a sleeper shrieking, cutting capers
115 And swearing that black bears, black bulls as well,
Or blackest fiends are haling him to Hell.
And there are other vapors that I know
That on a sleeping man will work their woe,
But I'll pass on as lightly as I can.
120   "Take Cato[9] now, that was so wise a man,
Did he not say, 'Take no account of dreams'?
Now, sir," she said, "on flying from these beams,
For love of God do take some laxative;
Upon my soul that's the advice to give
125 For melancholy choler; let me urge
You free yourself from vapors with a purge.
And that you may have no excuse to tarry
By saying this town has no apothecary,
I shall myself instruct you and prescribe
130 Herbs that will cure all vapors of that tribe,
Herbs from our very farmyard! You will find
Their natural property is to unbind

7. poltroon (päl trōōn′) *n.*: Coward.

8. niggard: Stingy person.

9. Cato: A Roman statesman and philosopher (95–46 B.C.) with a reputation for wisdom.

And purge you well beneath and well above.
Now don't forget it, dear, for God's own love!
135 Your face is choleric and shows distension;
Be careful lest the sun in his ascension
Should catch you full of humors,[10] hot and many.
And if he does, my dear, I'll lay a penny
It means a bout of fever or a breath
140 Of tertian ague.[11] You may catch your death.
    "Worms for a day or two I'll have to give
As a digestive, then your laxative.
Centaury, fumitory, caper-spurge
And hellebore will make a splendid purge;
145 And then there's laurel or the blackthorn berry,
Ground-ivy too that makes our yard so merry;
Peck them right up, my dear, and swallow whole.
Be happy, husband, by your father's soul!
Don't be afraid of dreams. I'll say no more."
150   "Madam," he said, "I thank you for your lore,
But with regard to Cato all the same,
His wisdom has, no doubt, a certain fame,
But though he said that we should take no heed
Of dreams, by God in ancient books I read
155 Of many a man of more authority
Than ever Cato was, believe you me,
Who say the very opposite is true
And prove their theories by experience too.
Dreams have quite often been significations
160 As well of triumphs as of tribulations
That people undergo in this our life.
This needs no argument at all, dear wife,
The proof is all too manifest indeed.
    "One of the greatest authors one can read
165 Says thus: there were two comrades once who went
On pilgrimage, sincere in their intent.
And as it happened they had reached a town
Where such a throng was milling up and down
And yet so scanty the accommodation,
170 They could not find themselves a habitation,
No, not a cottage that could lodge them both.
And so they separated, very loath,
Under constraint of this necessity
And each went off to find some hostelry,
175 And lodge whatever way his luck might fall.
    "The first of them found refuge in a stall
Down in a yard with oxen and a plow.
His friend found lodging for himself somehow
Elsewhere, by accident or destiny,

8 **10. humors:** People in Chaucer's time believed that bodily fluids called humors were responsible for one's health and disposition. An excess of the fluid called yellow bile resulted in a choleric, or quick-tempered, personality. In lines 108 and 125, Chaucer seems to use the word *choler* as a synonym for the term *humor*.

11. tertian ague (tur′ shən a′ gyoo): A malarial fever.

8 **Clarification** Point out to students that the theory of humors as the cause of illness already existed centuries before Chaucer, but that the use of the word *humor* in line 137 is its first appearance in English. Another word that appears in Chaucer for the first time (in *Troilus and Criseyde*) is *tragedy*.

9 **Discussion** Ask students if they can identify what is medieval in this mock-dispute about the relative value of differing authorities. Point out that in modern times, scientists would conduct verifiable studies or experiments to settle such a dispute, rather than quoting ancient authors on the subject. How does the courteous opening to Chanticleer's reply add to the comical quality of the whole debate?

10 **Discussion** Ask students how the beginning of Chanticleer's longest anecdote is similar to the beginning of the tale as a whole. How does this setting for his anecdote create interest in finding out what happens next?

Humanities Note

Fine art, *Woman Feeding Chickens,* from an Italian manuscript (c. 1385). This painting shows a simply dressed farm woman feeding chickens in front of a chicken coop. The choice of such an earthy and unsophisticated subject for a manuscript miniature painting shows how far European taste had come toward non-religious art. Early manuscript miniatures were wholly devoted to religious themes, but by the later Middle Ages treatises on everything from farming to the art of fencing had fine illustrations. Romances, poetry, and songs were also illustrated, while scenes of warfare were—not unexpectedly—among the most common. But a humble scene such as this demonstrates the turn toward realism that began to characterize art after the Middle Ages.

The decorative picturing of hens and roosters, including one bird atop the coop, accompanies a text on farming and, no doubt, on the tasks of the farm wife.

You might use the following questions to discuss the art.
1. Is this picture realistic? Explain.
2. Does this farm scene differ from depictions of farm life today? Why or why not?

11 Reading Strategy Have students stop reading at the end of this passage and predict what the outcome of the anecdote will be.

**WOMAN FEEDING CHICKENS
FROM AN ITALIAN MANUSCRIPT (c. 1385)**
Österreichische National Bibliothek, Vienna

180 Which governs all of us and equally.
    "Now it so happened, long ere it was day,
This fellow had a dream, and as he lay
In bed it seemed he heard his comrade call,
'Help! I am lying in an ox's stall
185 And shall tonight be murdered as I lie.
Help me, dear brother, help or I shall die!
Come in all haste!' Such were the words he spoke;
The dreamer, lost in terror, then awoke.
But once awake he paid it no attention,
190 Turned over and dismissed it as invention,
It was a dream, he thought, a fantasy.
And twice he dreamt this dream successively.
    "Yet a third time his comrade came again,
Or seemed to come, and said, 'I have been slain.
195 Look, look! my wounds are bleeding wide and deep,
Rise early in the morning, break your sleep

And go to the west gate. You there shall see
A cart all loaded up with dung,' said he,
'And in that dung my body has been hidden.
200 Boldly arrest that cart as you are bidden.
It was my money that they killed me for.'
    "He told him every detail, sighing sore,
And pitiful in feature, pale of hue.
This dream, believe me, Madam, turned out true;
205 For in the dawn, as soon as it was light,
He went to where his friend had spent the night
And when he came upon the cattle-stall
He looked about him and began to call.
    "The innkeeper, appearing thereupon,
210 Quickly gave answer, 'Sir, your friend has gone.
He left the town a little after dawn.'
The man began to feel suspicious, drawn
By memories of his dream—the western gate,
The dung-cart—off he went, he would not wait,
215 Towards the western entry. There he found,
Seemingly on its way to dung some ground,
A dung-cart loaded on the very plan
Described so closely by the murdered man.
So he began to shout courageously
220 For right and vengeance on the felony,
'My friend's been killed! There's been a foul attack,
He's in that cart and gaping on his back!
Fetch the authorities, get the sheriff down
—Whosever job it is to run the town—
225 Help! My companion's murdered, sent to glory!'
    "What need I add to finish off the story?
People ran out and cast the cart to ground,
And in the middle of the dung they found
The murdered man. The corpse was fresh and new.
230   "O blessed God, that art so just and true,
Thus thou revealest murder! As we say,
'Murder will out.' We see it day by day.
Murder's a foul, abominable treason,
So loathsome to God's justice, to God's reason,
235 He will not suffer its concealment. True,
Things may lie hidden for a year or two,
But still 'Murder will out,' that's my conclusion.
    "All the town officers in great confusion
Seized on the carter and they gave him hell,
240 And then they racked the innkeeper as well,
And both confessed. And then they took the wrecks
And there and then they hanged them by their necks.
    "By this we see that dreams are to be dreaded.

12

13

12 Discussion Ask students if the end of the Chanticleer anecdote here corresponds with what they predicted earlier. If the end differs from their prediction, have them analyze how it is different. In any case, ask them to discuss the narrative strategy of Chanticleer's anecdote as a whole.

13 Discussion Ask students if they agree with Chanticleer's conclusion. Do hidden crimes always comes to light? Why or why not?

And in the self-same book I find embedded,
245 Right in the very chapter after this
(I'm not inventing, as I hope for bliss)
The story of two men who started out
To cross the sea—for merchandise no doubt—
But as the winds were contrary they waited.
250 It was a pleasant town, I should have stated,
Merrily grouped about the haven-side.
A few days later with the evening tide
The wind veered round so as to suit them best;
They were delighted and they went to rest
255 Meaning to sail next morning early. Well,
To one of them a miracle befell.
    "This man as he lay sleeping, it would seem,
Just before dawn had an astounding dream.
He thought a man was standing by his bed
260 Commanding him to wait, and thus he said:
'If you set sail tomorrow as you intend
You will be drowned. My tale is at an end.'
    "He woke and told his friend what had occurred
And begged him that the journey be deferred
265 At least a day, implored him not to start.
But his companion, lying there apart,
Began to laugh and treat him to derision.[12]
'I'm not afraid,' he said, 'of any vision,
To let it interfere with my affairs;
270 A straw for all your dreamings and your scares.
Dreams are just empty nonsense, merest japes;[13]
Why, people dream all day of owls and apes,
All sorts of trash that can't be understood,
Things that have never happened and never could.
275 But as I see you mean to stay behind
And miss the tide for wilful sloth of mind,
God knows I'm sorry for it, but good day!'
And so he took his leave and went his way.
    "And yet, before they'd covered half the trip
280 —I don't know what went wrong—there was a rip
And by some accident the ship went down,
Her bottom rent,[14] all hands aboard to drown
In sight of all the vessels at her side,
That had put out upon the self-same tide.
285 "So, my dear Pertelote, if you discern
The force of these examples, you may learn
One never should be careless about dreams,
For, undeniably, I say it seems
That many are a sign of trouble breeding.
290 "Now, take St. Kenelm's life which I've been reading:

12. derision (di rizh′ ən) *n.*: Contempt or ridicule.

13. japes: Jokes.

14. Rent: Torn.

Grammar in Action

Understanding Debating Strategies Debating strategies are those methods of argument used by either side to gain an advantage in a debate. Some strategies considered legitimate include: (1) an appeal to authority; (2) an emphasis on fact, rather than opinion; (3) a demonstration of cause and effect relationships; (4) inductive reasoning—arguing from details toward the formulation of a general principle; and (5) deductive reasoning—analyzing a principle to look closely at the details it contains. Some strategies considered questionable include: (1)

an *ad hominem* argument—attacking the debater rather than his or her ideas; (2) a class argument—attacking the group to which the debater belongs; (3) a demagogic appeal—attempting to persuade by manipulating the emotions of the audience; (4) the substitution of opinion for fact; and (5) the deliberate confusion of effect with cause.

In the argument about the meaning of dreams, Pertelote uses both *ad hominem* and class arguments against Chanticleer (lines 89–100), but then appears to argue inductively, from theory to diagnosis to prescription in the rest of her speech. She also appeals to authority (lines 120–121). But she ignores fact and provable cause/effect relationships. Chanticleer also appeals to authority but the rest of his speech uses specious

He was Kenulphus' son, the noble King
Of Mercia. Now, St. Kenelm dreamt a thing
Shortly before they murdered him one day.
He saw his murder in a dream, I say.
295 His nurse expounded it and gave her reasons
On every point and warned him against treasons
But as the saint was only seven years old
All that she said about it left him cold.
He was so holy how could visions hurt?
300   "By God, I willingly would give my shirt
To have you read his legend as I've read it;
And, Madam Pertelote, upon my credit,
Macrobius wrote of dreams and can explain us
The vision of young Scipio Africanus,[15]
305 And he affirms that dreams can give a due
Warnings of things that later on come true.
   "And then there's the Old Testament—a manual
Well worth your study; see the *Book of Daniel.*
Did Daniel think a dream was vanity?
310 Read about Joseph too and you will see
That many dreams—I do not say that all—
Give cognizance of what is to befall.
   "Look at Lord Pharaoh, king of Egypt! Look
At what befell his butler and his cook.
315 Did not their visions have a certain force?
But those who study history of course
Meet many dreams that set them wondering.
   "What about Croesus too, the Lydian king,
Who dreamt that he was sitting in a tree,
320 Meaning he would be hanged? It had to be.
   "Or take Andromache, great Hector's wife;[16]
The day on which he was to lose his life
She dreamt about, the very night before,
And realized that if Hector went to war
325 He would be lost that very day in battle.
She warned him; he dismissed it all as prattle
And sallied forth to fight, being self-willed,
And there he met Achilles and was killed.
The tale is long and somewhat overdrawn,
330 And anyhow it's very nearly dawn,
So let me say in very brief conclusion
My dream undoubtedly foretells confusion,
It bodes me ill, I say. And, furthermore,
Upon your laxatives I set no store,
335 For they are venomous. I've suffered by them
Often enough before and I defy them.
   "And now, let's talk of fun and stop all this.

15. Scipio Africanus
(sip′ ē ō af′ ri kā′ nəs):
A famous Roman general
(237–183 B.C.).

16. Andromache (an
drăm′ ə kē) **. . . wife:** She
was the wife of the
greatest warrior in Troy,
Hector, at the time of the
Trojan War.

17 Discussion Ask students what makes Chanticleer's address to Pertelote equivalent to a love-poem addressed to a courtly lady. Point out that only the word *scarlet* is ludicrously inappropriate to a woman, though quite suitable to a hen. This one word sends up the whole courtly style into utter hilarity.

18 Clarification Point out to students that a more accurate translation of the Latin saying is "Woman is man's confusion." Ask students if the irony in Chanticleer's sly deceitfulness satirizes Chanticleer—or the courtly lover.

19 Literary Focus Point out to students that having provided the setting of the story in the opening exposition and the complication in the just-concluded debate, Chaucer now moves to the climax. In doing so, he mocks the heroic style used for such transitions by describing the month and day in a typically belabored manner. Ask students what references he uses to give the transition its mock importance.

17

340
Dear Madam, as I hope for Heaven's bliss,
Of one thing God has sent me plenteous grace,
For when I see the beauty of your face,
That scarlet loveliness about your eyes,
All thought of terror and confusion dies.
For it's as certain as the Creed, I know,

18

345
Mulier est hominis confusio
(A Latin tag, dear Madam, meaning this:
'Woman is man's delight and all his bliss'),
For when at night I feel your feathery side,
Although perforce I cannot take a ride
Because, alas, our perch was made too narrow,

350
Delight and solace fill me to the marrow
And I defy all visions and all dreams!"
    And with that word he flew down from the beams,
For it was day, and down his hens flew all,
And with a chuck he gave the troupe a call

355
For he had found a seed upon the floor.
Royal he was, he was afraid no more.
He feathered Pertelote in wanton play
And trod her twenty times ere prime of day.
Grim as a lion's was his manly frown

360
As on his toes he sauntered up and down;
He scarcely deigned to set his foot to ground
And every time a seed of corn was found
He gave a chuck, and up his wives ran all.
Thus royal as a prince who strides his hall

365
Leave we this Chanticleer engaged on feeding
And pass to the adventure that was breeding.

19

    Now when the month in which the world began,
March, the first month, when God created man,
Was over, and the thirty-second day

370
Thereafter ended, on the third of May
It happened that Chanticleer in all his pride,
His seven wives attendant at his side,
Cast his eyes upward to the blazing sun,
Which in the sign of *Taurus* then had run

375
His twenty-one degrees and somewhat more,
And knew by nature and no other lore
That it was nine o'clock. With blissful voice
He crew triumphantly and said, "Rejoice,
Behold the sun! The sun is up, my seven.

380
Look, it has climbed forty degrees in heaven,
Forty degrees and one in fact, by this.
Dear Madam Pertelote, my earthly bliss,
Hark to those blissful birds and how they sing!
Look at those pretty flowers, how they spring!

385   Solace and revel fill my heart!'' He laughed.
         But in that moment Fate let fly her shaft;
      Ever the latter end of joy is woe,
      God knows that worldly joy is swift to go.
      A rhetorician[17] with a flair for style
390   Could chronicle this maxim in his file
      Of Notable Remarks with safe conviction.
      Then let the wise give ear; this is no fiction
      My story is as true, I undertake,
      As that of good Sir Lancelot du Lake[18]
395   Who held all women in such high esteem.
      Let me return full circle to my theme.
         A coal-tipped fox of sly iniquity[19]
      That had been lurking round the grove for three
      Long years, that very night burst through and passed
400   Stockade and hedge, as Providence forecast,
      Into the yard where Chanticleer the Fair
      Was wont, with all his ladies, to repair.
      Still, in a bed of cabbages, he lay
      Until about the middle of the day
405   Watching the cock and waiting for his cue,
      As all these homicides so gladly do
      That lie about in wait to murder men.
      O false assassin, lurking in thy den!
      O new Iscariot, new Ganelon!
410   And O Greek Sinon,[20] thou whose treachery won
      Troy town and brought it utterly to sorrow!
      O Chanticleer, accursed be that morrow
      That brought thee to the yard from thy high beams!
      Thou hadst been warned, and truly, by thy dreams

20

21

17. rhetorician (ret′ ə rish′ ən) *n.*: A person skilled in public speaking or writing.

18. Sir Lancelot du Lake: The most celebrated of King Arthur's knights of the Round Table.

19. iniquity (i nik′ wi tē) *n.*: Wickedness.

20. Iscariot . . . Ganelon . . . Sinon: Each of these men was famous for betrayal. Judas Iscariot betrayed Jesus Christ; Ganelon betrayed Charlemagne's greatest knight, Roland; and Sinon convinced King Priam to bring the Trojan horse, filled with Greek troops, into Troy.

THE NUN'S PRIEST
DETAIL FROM THE ELLESMERE
MANUSCRIPT
The Huntington Library, San Marino, California

The Nun's Priest's Tale   151

20 Discussion Ask students to name some of the ways this ridiculously inflated passage violates common sense. Is the maxim in lines 387–388 truly wonderful or a mere commonplace? Does Chaucer imply that the story about Lancelot is true? Or does he wickedly suggest that his fox-and-rooster tale is as much of an invention as Lancelot's story?

21 Literary Focus Explain to students that the authors of epics frequently addressed their characters in exactly this way. Is Chaucer's mockery here directed at such flowery addresses (called apostrophes) in epics themselves, or at the pomposity of using such addresses to describe a common raid by a fox on a chicken coop?

Humanities Note

Fine art, *The Nun's Priest,* detail from the Ellesmere Manuscript. Chaucer's *Canterbury Tales* appeared in numerous different editions, illustrated and illuminated by a variety of artists from his own time to the present day. Among the best known and best loved of the Chaucerian manuscripts was the Ellesmere Manuscript, from which this picture comes.

   The Ellesmere Chaucer has been dated to the early fifteenth century. Its name comes from the Ellesmere family, who owned the manuscript since the seventeenth century; today it belongs to a museum. At the beginning of each tale there is an elaborate border and the figure of the pilgrim who narrates the tale. The picture of Chaucer himself appears at the beginning of the *Tale of Melibeus.*

   The Nun's Priest is portrayed as a robust, little man on a high-stepping horse. His upraised hand suggests that he is speaking as he rides.

   You might use the following questions to discuss the art.
1. In what ways might a more contemporary artist have given a different view of this pilgrim?
2. Does the pilgrim pictured here look like the man who might have told this tale? Explain.

22 Discussion Explain to students that Chaucer was extremely interested in such philosophical questions as the conflict between God's foreknowledge and man's free will. The Nun's Priest's discussion is an accurate summation of the medieval view of this paradox. Ask students what the effect is of bringing such a lofty philosophical question to bear on the tale he is telling.

23 Enrichment Point out to students that in this era it was customary for theologians to blame women for all human woe, since Eve got Adam to eat the forbidden fruit. But possibly no male author, ancient or modern, is so remarkably free of sexism as Chaucer and generally so positive in his portrayal of women. Explain that in this passage, Chaucer's humor is based on satirizing the traditional view. The narrator, after all, is a nun's priest—that is a man assigned to hear that nun's confession. Consequently the narrator is shown as reluctant to displease anyone (namely, the nun) and blames this whole tirade on Chanticleer.

415   That this would be a perilous day for thee.
     But that which God's foreknowledge can foresee
   Must needs occur, as certain men of learning
   Have said. Ask any scholar of discerning;
   He'll say the Schools are filled with altercation
420   On this vexed matter of predestination[21]
   Long bandied by a hundred thousand men.
   How can I sift it to the bottom then?
   The Holy Doctor St. Augustine shines
   In this, and there is Bishop Bradwardine's
425   Authority, Boethius'[22] too, decreeing
   Whether the fact of God's divine foreseeing
   Constrains me to perform a certain act
   —And by "constraint" I mean the simple fact
   Of mere compulsion by necessity—
430   Or whether a free choice is granted me
   To do a given act or not to do it
   Though, ere it was accomplished, God foreknew it,
   Or whether Providence is not so stringent
   And merely makes necessity contingent.
435   But I decline discussion of the matter;
   My tale is of a cock and of the clatter
   That came of following his wife's advice
   To walk about his yard on the precise
   Morning after the dream of which I told.
440   O woman's counsel is so often cold!
   A woman's counsel brought us first to woe,
   Made Adam out of Paradise to go
   Where he had been so merry, so well at ease.
   But, for I know not whom it may displease
445   If I suggest that women are to blame,
   Pass over that; I only speak in game.
   Read the authorities to know about
   What has been said of women; you'll find out.
   These are the cock's words, and not mine, I'm giving;
450   I think no harm of any woman living.
     Merrily in her dust-bath in the sand
   Lay Pertelote. Her sisters were at hand
   Basking in sunlight. Chanticleer sang free,
   More merrily than a mermaid in the sea
455   (For *Physiologus*[23] reports the thing
   And says how well and merrily they sing).
   And so it happened as he cast his eye
   Towards the cabbage at a butterfly
   It fell upon the fox there, lying low.
460   Gone was all inclination then to crow.
   "Cok cok," he cried, giving a sudden start,

21. predestination (prē des' tə nā' shən) *n.*: The idea that God arranges beforehand everything that will happen.

22. Bishop Bradwardine's . . . Boethius' (bō ē' thē əs): Bishop Bradwardine was a well-known theologian of Chaucer's time. Boethius (A.D. 480–524) was a famous Roman philosopher.

23. *Physiologus*: A book on nature written in Latin meter.

As one who feels a terror at his heart,
For natural instinct teaches beasts to flee
The moment they perceive an enemy,
465 Though they had never met with it before.
    This Chanticleer was shaken to the core
And would have fled. The fox was quick to say
However, "Sir! Whither so fast away?
Are you afraid of me, that am your friend?
470 A fiend, or worse, I should be, to intend
You harm, or practice villainy upon you;
Dear sir, I was not even spying on you!
Truly I came to do no other thing
Than just to lie and listen to you sing.
475 You have as merry a voice as God has given
To any angel in the courts of Heaven;
To that you add a musical sense as strong
As had Boethius who was skilled in song.
My Lord your Father (God receive his soul!),
480 Your mother too—how courtly, what control!—
Have honored my poor house, to my great ease;
And you, sir, too, I should be glad to please.
For, when it comes to singing, I'll say this
(Else may these eyes of mine be barred from bliss),
485 There never was a singer I would rather
Have heard at dawn than your respected father.
All that he sang came welling from his soul
And how he put his voice under control!
The pains he took to keep his eyes tight shut
490 In concentration—then the tip-toe strut,
The slender neck stretched out, the delicate beak!
No singer could approach him in technique
Or rival him in song, still less surpass.
I've read the story in *Burnel the Ass*,[24]
495 Among some other verses, of a cock
Whose leg in youth was broken by a knock
A clergyman's son had given him, and for this
He made the father lose his benefice.
But certainly there's no comparison
500 Between the subtlety of such an one
And the discretion of your father's art
And wisdom. Oh, for charity of heart,
Can you not emulate your sire and sing?"
    This Chanticleer began to beat a wing
505 As one incapable of smelling treason,
So wholly had this flattery ravished reason.
Alas, my lords! there's many a sycophant[25]
And flatterer that fill your courts with cant

**CHAUCER RECITING TROILUS &
CRESSIDA BEFORE A COURT GATHERING
(FRONTISPIECE)**
Corpus Christi College

24. *Burnel the Ass:* A
twelfth-century poem in
which a rooster gains
revenge after being
mistreated by a priest's
son.

25. sycophant (sik' ə fənt)
n.: A person who seeks
favor by flattering
influential people.

The Nun's Priest's Tale   153

27 Literary Focus Have students analyze the elements in this passage that make it a model of the mock-heroic style.

28 Clarification Explain to students the extremely ironic nature of this passage. Chaucer is flattering the memory of a pompous writer of the past—one whom he honored and tried to imitate early in his career. By this time, however, Chaucer had thoroughly rejected the artificial and flowery methods of Vinsauf—except for use in satires, like this, of the heroic style.

Humanities Note

Fine art, *Chaucer's Canterbury Pilgrims.* This nineteenth-century version of Chaucer's pilgrims en route to Canterbury is by William Blake (1757–1827), the mystical English poet and artist. Blake chose a number of familiar themes from the Old Testament and from classics such as the *Canterbury Tales* as subject matter for his highly personal and visionary style.

Blake originally made the painting of the Canterbury pilgrims in 1809, and it was prominently featured in an exhibition of his works. Later he hoped for success with an engraving he made of the same composition, but it received little notice. The engraving (seen here) is in Blake's fluid style; it is interesting to compare this nineteenth-century version with the much earlier version of Chaucer's pilgrims seen on page 143.

You might want to use the following questions to discuss the art.

1. Why do you suppose the theme of journeys—in particular, pilgrimages—has frequently been the subject of poetry and art?
2. Compare this picture of Chaucer's pilgrims with that on page 143.

And give more pleasure with their zeal forsooth
510 Than he who speaks in soberness and truth.
Read what *Ecclesiasticus*[26] records
Of flatterers. 'Ware treachery, my lords!

27   This Chanticleer stood high upon his toes,
He stretched his neck, his eyes began to close,
515 His beak to open; with his eyes shut tight
He then began to sing with all his might.
    Sir Russel Fox then leapt to the attack,
Grabbing his gorge he flung him o'er his back
And off he bore him to the woods, the brute,
520 And for the moment there was no pursuit.
    O Destiny that may not be evaded!
Alas that Chanticleer had so paraded!
Alas that he had flown down from the beams!
O that his wife took no account of dreams!
525 And on a Friday too to risk their necks!
O Venus, goddess of the joys of sex,
Since Chanticleer thy mysteries professed
And in thy service always did his best,
And more for pleasure than to multiply
530 His kind, on thine own day is he to die?

28   O Geoffrey, thou my dear and sovereign master[27]
Who, when they brought King Richard to disaster
And shot him dead, lamented so his death,
Would that I had thy skill, thy gracious breath,
535 To chide a Friday half so well as you!
(For he was killed upon a Friday too.)
Then I could fashion you a rhapsody
For Chanticleer in dread and agony.
    Sure never such a cry or lamentation

26. *Ecclesiasticus:* Not Ecclesiastes, but a book of proverbs included with the Apocrypha in the Authorized Version of the Bible.

27. O Geoffrey . . . master: Geoffrey de Vinsauf, twelfth-century author of a book on rhetoric.

154   *The Medieval Period*

CHAUCER'S CANTERBURY PILGRIMS
William Blake
The Huntington Library, San Marino, California

Commentary: Chaucer's Political Views

Chaucer was employed as a government official by three successive kings, Edward III, Richard II, and Henry IV. Even during the conflict in which the second was replaced by the third, Chaucer himself was never threatened with the loss of his livelihood. All critics have remarked on his tolerant acceptance of people much as he found them, the good with the bad. He criticized corrupt clergy, for example, but never the church.

In *The Nun's Priest's Tale,* however, his genial, open-minded neutrality slips for a moment when he says that those pursuing the fox were more shrill than those who massacred the Flemish

540 Was made by ladies of high Trojan station,
    When Ilium fell and Pyrrhus with his sword
    Grabbed Priam by the beard, their king and lord,
    And slew him there as the *Aeneid* tells,[28]
    As what was uttered by those hens. Their yells
545 Surpassed them all in palpitating fear
    When they beheld the rape of Chanticleer.
    Dame Pertelote emitted sovereign shrieks
    That echoed up in anguish to the peaks
    Louder than those extorted from the wife
550 Of Hasdrubal,[29] when he had lost his life
    And Carthage all in flame and ashes lay.
    She was so full of torment and dismay
    That in the very flames she chose her part
    And burnt to ashes with a steadfast heart.
555 O woeful hens, louder your shrieks and higher
    Than those of Roman matrons when the fire
    Consumed their husbands, senators of Rome,
    When Nero burnt their city and their home,
    Beyond a doubt that Nero was their bale![30]
560   Now let me turn again to tell my tale;
    This blessed widow and her daughters two
    Heard all these hens in clamor and halloo
    And, rushing to the door at all this shrieking,
    They saw the fox towards the covert streaking
565 And, on his shoulder, Chanticleer stretched flat.
    "Look, look!" they cried, "O mercy, look at that!
    Ha! Ha! the fox!" and after him they ran,
    And stick in hand ran many a serving man,
    Ran Coll our dog, ran Talbot, Bran and Shaggy,
570 And with a distaff in her hand ran Maggie,
    Ran cow and calf and ran the very hogs
    In terror at the barking of the dogs;
    The men and women shouted, ran and cursed,
    They ran so hard they thought their hearts would burst,
575 They yelled like fiends in Hell, ducks left the water
    Quacking and flapping as on point of slaughter,
    Up flew the geese in terror over the trees,
    Out of the hive came forth the swarm of bees;
    So hideous was the noise—God bless us all,
580 Jack Straw and all his followers in their brawl[31]
    Were never half so shrill, for all their noise,
    When they were murdering those Flemish boys,
    As that day's hue and cry upon the fox.
    They grabbed up trumpets made of brass and box,
585 Of horn and bone, on which they blew and pooped,
    And therewithal they shouted and they whooped

28. Sure never . . . Aeneid tells: A reference to the destruction of Troy as described in the Roman poet Virgil's *Aeneid*.

29. Hasdrubal (haz′ droō bəl): A Carthaginian general.

30. bale: Evil, harm.

31. Jack Straw . . . brawl: Jack Straw was one of the leaders of the Peasants' Revolt (1381).

29 Discussion Tell students that by this point in the story, they have probably developed a sense for Chaucer's mockery that alerts them to how truly silly this passage is. Ask them to explain how Chaucer exploits the absurdities in these lines to get a laugh from the reader.

30 Discussion Ask students how the reappearance of the human characters at the climax of the story affect the tone at this point. See the Commentary below for a discussion of the reference to the Peasants' Revolt.

boys (lines 578–593). This refers to the first great popular rebellion in English history, called the Peasants' Revolt, led by Wat Tyler. Jack Straw may have been another leader—or only a contemptuous way of referring to Tyler himself.

In any case, the rebels entered London on June 13, 1381, and killed Flemish apprentices in the wool trade for taking jobs away from the English. The rebellion lasted less than a month but eyewitnesses all reported the blood-chilling cruelty of the massacre.

Probably not yet forty years old at the time, Chaucer could quite possibly have looked down on scenes of the rebellion from his rent-free quarters safely perched atop one of the gates in London's encircling wall. When he began to write *The Canterbury Tales* some six or more years later, he must still have remembered the massacre, to judge by his reference to it in this tale.

31 Enrichment Explain to students that the concept of Fortune as a goddess that ruled human affairs was extremely popular in the medieval period, despite its direct conflict with Christian doctrine. You might suggest that students listen to Carl Orff's *Carmina Burana* and follow the words of these songs to learn more about how medieval people regarded Dame Fortune.

32 Discussion Have students explain how the quick thinking here on Chanticleer's part makes him more rounded as a character and less merely an object of ridicule.

33 Discussion Point out to students that there are actually three morals at the end of the tale: the one Chanticleer draws, the one the fox draws, and the one the narrator draws. Ask them which they like best and have them explain why.

Reader's Response How would you have tried to escape from the fox if you were Chanticleer?

Master Teacher Note Chaucer's source for Sir Russel the Fox and Master Chanticleer the Cock is ultimately the French *Roman de Renart* and the German *Reinecke Fuchs.* But in England Russel first appeared as Reynard the Fox a century before Chaucer in *The Fox and the Wolf,* a comic satire expressing social unrest. In these tales Reynard represents man preying upon others out of desperation, but escaping by his cunning. Ask students if Chaucer's tale reflects any of the social unrest in the English original. Have them explain their answers and then have them keep this discussion in mind as they continue reading the tale.

Cultural Note Chaucer earned his living as a government official, particularly as a diplomat

So that it seemed the very heavens would fall.
   And now, good people, pay attention all.

31   590   See how Dame Fortune quickly changes side
And robs her enemy of hope and pride!
This cock that lay upon the fox's back
In all his dread contrived to give a quack
And said, "Sir Fox, if I were you, as God's

32   595   My witness, I would round upon these clods
And shout, 'Turn back, you saucy bumpkins all!
A very pestilence upon you fall!
Now that I have in safety reached the wood
Do what you like, the cock is mine for good;
I'll eat him there in spite of every one.'"

600   The fox replying, "Faith, it shall be done!"
Opened his mouth and spoke. The nimble bird,
Breaking away upon the uttered word,
Flew high into the tree-tops on the spot.
And when the fox perceived where he had got,

605   "Alas," he cried, "alas, my Chanticleer,
I've done you grievous wrong, indeed I fear
I must have frightened you; I grabbed too hard
When I caught hold and took you from the yard.
But, sir, I meant no harm, don't be offended,

610   Come down and I'll explain what I intended;
So help me God I'll tell the truth—on oath!
"No," said the cock, "and curses on us both,
And first on me if I were such a dunce
As let you fool me oftener than once.

615   Never again, for all your flattering lies,
You'll coax a song to make me blink my eyes;
And as for those who blink when they should look,
God blot them from his everlasting Book!"
"Nay, rather," said the fox, "his plagues be flung

33   620   On all who chatter that should hold their tongue."
   Lo, such it is not to be on your guard
Against the flatterers of the world, or yard,
And if you think my story is absurd,
A foolish trifle of a beast and bird,

625   A fable of a fox, a cock, a hen,
Take hold upon the moral, gentlemen.
   St. Paul himself, a saint of great discerning,
Says that all things are written for our learning;
So take the grain and let the chaff be still.

630   And, gracious Father, if it be thy will
As saith my Savior, make us all good men,
And bring us to his heavenly bliss.
       Amen.

who made several visits to France and Italy. Both these countries were then considered by the English to be the last word in fashionable elegance, beautiful clothes, and refined manners. Ask students to suggest how Chaucer uses the mock-heroic style to poke fun at the English admiration for continental refinement.

Cooperative Learning How Italian poetry influenced Chaucer is a subject that might interest your students. Have them meet in small groups and choose one of the three greatest Italian writers of that time, Dante, Petrarch, and Boccaccio. Dante dramatized Christian doctrine, Petrarch made courtly love popular, and Boccaccio wrote stories about all classes of society. Have each group research one of these writers to determine how he may have influenced Chaucer's writing.

THINKING ABOUT THE SELECTION
Recalling

1. Describe the living conditions of the widow who owns Chanticleer.
2. Which physical features of Chanticleer and Pertelote are presented as especially attractive?
3. What is Pertelote's advice to Chanticleer when he tells her his dream?
4. How does the fox capture Chanticleer and how does Chanticleer escape?

Interpreting

5. (a) Compare and contrast the methods of argument that Pertelote and Chanticleer use to defend their interpretations of dreams. (b) What are the fallacies in each argument?
6. The first story that Chanticleer tells has the three-part structure typical of medieval tales: an exposition describing the characters and setting, a complication or problem, and a climax. Does "The Nun's Priest's Tale" as a whole follow this pattern? Why not?
7. (a) What is the moral of this fable? (b) How seriously do you think the narrator takes this moral? Explain.
8. What does this tale suggest about its teller, the nun's priest?

Applying

9. What does this tale reveal about the concerns of people in medieval times? Do we share similar concerns today? Explain.

ANALYZING LITERATURE
Understanding the Mock-Heroic Style

Chaucer uses the **mock-heroic style** in "The Nun's Priest's Tale," portraying the domestic animals in a barnyard as if they were the heroes and heroines of a great epic. He describes Chanticleer, for example, in terms that seem more appropriate for a mighty warrior: "His comb was redder than fine coral, tall/And battlemented like a castle wall/ . . . Like burnished gold his feathers, flaming bright."

1. Epic heroes are often boastful. (a) How does the narrator portray Chanticleer's boastfulness through his words and behavior? (b) Why does this boastfulness strike a humorous note?
2. Which words and phrases in the description of Pertelote would be more suitable for a noble lady than for a hen?
3. Epics often depict the intervention of gods or goddesses in the affairs of humans. Where does Chaucer imitate this convention?

CRITICAL THINKING AND READING
Understanding Courtly Love

According to the tradition of courtly love, popular in medieval times, a knight and a noble lady could only experience love at a distance. The goal was not marriage, or even physical contact, but admiration from afar. The lady's role was to believe in the knight's heroism and to inspire him with a token of her love, like a scarf or belt. His role was to show courage and total devotion.

Does the romance between Pertelote and Chanticleer follow the rules of courtly love? Why or why not?

THINKING AND WRITING
Writing a Beast Fable

The beast epic and fable were very popular forms during the medieval period. Write your own beast fable in which you use the mock-heroic style that characterizes "The Nun's Priest's Tale." Select a situation or theme that your classmates will recognize, and decide on the moral lesson that your story will illustrate. Then choose appropriate animal characters. Before writing, briefly outline the exposition, complication, and climax of your tale. As you write, remember to describe the doings of your beasts in lofty, mock-heroic terms. Test the success of your fable by reading it aloud to a group of classmates.

The Nun's Priest's Tale 157

imaginative literature, Chanticleer proves nothing. Both deal in opinion, rather than fact.

6. Yes, the tale as a whole shows the same pattern. The characters who live in the cottage and yard are presented first, then the argument about the meaning of the dream, then the seizing of Chanticleer by the fox and Chanticleer's escape.

7. (a) The moral is "Beware of flatterers." (b) The narrator is quite serious about the moral, but seems to have a good-humored belief that our vanity will always make most of us vulnerable to flattery.

8. Answers will differ, but students may respond that the tale suggests he is learned, mild-mannered, humorous, and skeptical.

9. Answers will differ.

ANSWERS TO ANALYZING LITERATURE

1. (a) He is proud of his beautiful appearance and his crowing. He prides himself on the idea that his learning is superior to Pertelote's. He is proud of his wanton play, his manly frown and stride. (b) There are two reasons for the humor; first, roosters in chicken yards act exactly with the exaggerated pride that Chanticleer displays among his hens. But his pride in his learning is ridiculous because it is quite impossible.

2. Words and phrases more suitable for a lady include "gracious," "courteous," "discreet," "debonair," "companionable," and "care in her deportment."

3. In lines 588–590, when Chanticleer is most hopeless, Dame Fortune is invoked as if she were a goddess who could suddenly change sides and favor Chanticleer instead of the fox.

ANSWERS TO CRITICAL THINKING AND READING

Many of the elements of courtly love are present in the description of the relationship between Chanticleer and Pertelote, but these elements become ridiculous because they are applied to a cock and a hen.

THINKING AND WRITING

Publishing Have students read their fables aloud to the class.

157

Closure and Extension
ANSWERS TO THINKING ABOUT THE SELECTION

1. She is a poor dairy-farmer who lives in a small cottage with her two daughters.
2. Chanticleer's crowing is jolly and his bill, legs, toes, and feathers are brilliantly colored. All the hens are colored like him, but Pertelote has the loveliest colored throat.
3. She tells him to ignore his dream because dreams merely reflect humors and vapors caused by overeating. She advises him to eat worms and certain herbs and to stay out of the sun.
4. The fox flatters Chanticleer's singing and asks to hear a song. As Chanticleer begins to sing with closed eyes, the fox seizes him in his jaws and carries him off. Chanticleer escapes by advising the fox to turn around and taunt his pursuers. When the fox opens his mouth to do so, Chanticleer flies off into a tree.
5. (a) Both quote authorities, but Pertelote outlines the theory of humors, diagnoses Chanticleer's condition, then prescribes precise remedies for it. By contrast, Chanticleer tells long stories taken from his authorities without drawing conclusions about how to avoid what the dream "predicts." (b) Although Pertelote proceeds systematically from theory to prescription, neither offers any convincing evidence to back up either argument. By quoting anecdotes from

Literary Focus That greed is the root of all evil is exemplified by this story. What moral weaknesses besides greed do the rioters have? Suggest that your students look for them. This tale has been called the perfect short story. Does it deserve this praise? What short-story qualities does it contain? You might want to review the generally accepted short-story criteria.

Writing/Prior Knowledge Have the students freewrite about the anecdote for five minutes and then share what they have with the class.

Teaching to Ability Levels All levels would benefit from reading aloud. For **less advanced** students you might alternate reading with the students. Since Chaucer intended the tales as entertainment, encourage **more advanced** students to read with feeling and drama.

Vocabulary

Preteach the following vocabulary words:
rioters (rī′ ət ərz) *n.*: Loud, dissolute bullies (l. 1)
stile (stīl) *n.*: A step or set of steps used in climbing over a fence or wall (l. 52)
pallor (pal′ ər) *n.*: Unnatural lack of color; paleness (l. 80)
hoary (hô′ ē) *adj.*: White or gray with age (l. 85)
prating (prāt′ iŋ) *v.*: Talking much and foolishly (l. 106)
tarry (tar′ ē) *v.*: To delay, linger, be tardy (l. 195)
apothecary (ə pät/h′ ə ker′ ē) *n.*: Pharmacist or druggest (l. 196)

Spelling Tip Point out to students that the word *pallor* ends in *or,* not *er.*

The Pardoner's Tale *from* The Canterbury Tales

Writer's Techniques

Exemplum. An anecdote is a brief account of an incident or event. Although "The Pardoner's Tale" may seem rather long for an anecdote, it is a special kind of anecdote—a 238-line anecdote within a sermon, something the Pardoner would have called an *exemplum,* or example. While anecdotes are often personal or biographical, the *exemplum* in "The Pardoner's Tale" is intended to establish the truth of a moral.

The idea for "The Pardoner's Tale" did not originate with Chaucer; it goes back to antiquity. The Pardoner uses this simple but powerful anecdote as an *exemplum* to prove the maxim, *"Radix malorum est cupiditas,"* or "Greed is the root of all evil."

Writing

You have heard many sayings similar to "Greed is the root of evil." List at least five such sayings. Try to think of ones for which a good exemplum might be written.

Primary Source

In "The Pardoner's Tale," Chaucer drew from traditional stories, such as this exemplum on swearing by Thomas of Cantimpre. Preachers added detail to such exemplums to illustrate their themes more vividly. This exemplum was written before 1263.

> In the city of Louvain, within the boundaries of Brabant we saw a noble and worthy citizen who, rising to go to matins on the holy night of Good Friday, passed in front of a tavern in which dissolute young men were sitting, playing at dice and vying with one another in blasphemies and oaths. Continuing on his way, this citizen found men in the street near the tavern who were making a loud lamentation over a certain stranger who was badly wounded and bleeding. When he asked the men who had inflicted these wounds they answered: 'Those young men who are playing dice.' Entering the tavern, the citizen upbraided the young men for playing on that night and asked them sternly why they had so cruelly beaten the stranger who had been with them. Much astonished, the young men denied that anyone had come in since they had sat down, and protested that they had wounded no one either by word or blow. Going forth quickly with the citizen, they sought for the bleeding stranger but could not find him. Having now recovered their senses, each of them realized that by their terrible oaths they had again insulted the Lord Christ and by their taunts had crucified him afresh.

Objectives

1 To understand anecdote and exemplum
2 To make inferences based on the narrator's words
3 To read Middle English aloud
4 To write an analysis

Support Material

Teaching Portfolio
Teacher Backup, p. 119
Usage and Mechanics Worksheet, p. 123
Vocabulary Check, p. 124
Analyzing Literature Worksheet, *Understanding the Anecdote,* p. 125
Critical Thinking and Reading Worksheet, *Making Inferences*
Based on a Narrator's Words, p. 126
Selection Test, p. 127

from The Pardoner's Tale

Geoffrey Chaucer

translated by Nevill Coghill

During their journey to Canterbury, each of the pilgrims tells a tale. After the Knight, the Miller, the Reeve, the Nun, and the narrator have finished, the Pardoner entertains the others with a tale that supports his claim that "greed is the root of all evil."

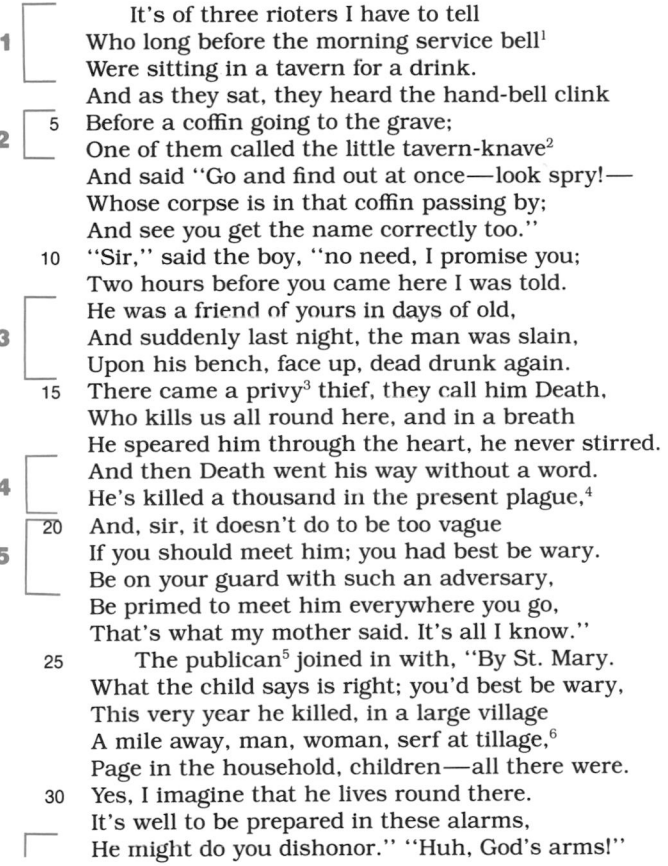

It's of three rioters I have to tell
Who long before the morning service bell[1]
Were sitting in a tavern for a drink.
And as they sat, they heard the hand-bell clink
5 Before a coffin going to the grave;
One of them called the little tavern-knave[2]
And said "Go and find out at once—look spry!—
Whose corpse is in that coffin passing by;
And see you get the name correctly too."
10 "Sir," said the boy, "no need, I promise you;
Two hours before you came here I was told.
He was a friend of yours in days of old,
And suddenly last night, the man was slain,
Upon his bench, face up, dead drunk again.
15 There came a privy[3] thief, they call him Death,
Who kills us all round here, and in a breath
He speared him through the heart, he never stirred.
And then Death went his way without a word.
He's killed a thousand in the present plague,[4]
20 And, sir, it doesn't do to be too vague
If you should meet him; you had best be wary.
Be on your guard with such an adversary,
Be primed to meet him everywhere you go,
That's what my mother said. It's all I know."
25 The publican[5] joined in with, "By St. Mary.
What the child says is right; you'd best be wary,
This very year he killed, in a large village
A mile away, man, woman, serf at tillage,[6]
Page in the household, children—all there were.
30 Yes, I imagine that he lives round there.
It's well to be prepared in these alarms,
He might do you dishonor." "Huh, God's arms!"

1. long before . . . bell:
Long before 9:00 A.M.

2. tavern-knave: Serving boy.

3. privy: Secretive.

4. plague: The Black Death, which killed over a third of the population of England in 1348 and 1349.

5. publican: Innkeeper.

6. tillage: Plowing.

from *The Pardoner's Tale* from *The Canterbury Tales*   159

Master Teacher Note This tale would be an excellent choice for a reader's theater production. Students could write their own adaptions and present them to the class.

Thematic Idea Another selection that deals with the theme of sin and false friends is "The Poison Tree" by William Blake, page 614. The excerpt from Pepy's *Diary* on page 506 is a remarkable account of a later English plague.

Presentation

Motivation/Prior Knowledge Explain that this tale takes place during a plague. The pestilence, we know now, was not one disease but two occurring simultaneously. The bubonic plague sent the victim's fever soaring and caused ugly pustules in armpit and groin but, in many cases, did not kill. The other illness was the pneumonic plague, which attacked the victim's lungs, was much more contagious, and was almost always fatal. A plague death is the impetus that begins the tale.

Purpose-Setting Question Why is it hypocritical that the Pardoner should tell a tale with the theme Greed as the root of all evil? Recalling Chaucer's description of him in the Prologue, do you find any redeeming qualities in him?

1 Literary Focus The bibulous nature of these "rioters" is quickly established. They have started drinking very early. What purpose does this fact serve in the exemplum?

2 Literary Focus What is the paradox in these lines? Another paradox is having the Pardoner preach such a moral tale. Why do you think Chaucer does this?

3 Reading Strategy How is it both prophetic and appropriate that it is their friend and fellow-rioter who has died?

4 Enrichment During sixteen months in 1348–49, the Black Plague reduced England's population from approximately four million to perhaps two million five hundred thousand.

5 Reading Strategy What advice is given to the rioters? Will they follow this good advice?

6 Discussion What vow do they swear together? Note the emphasis on their sense of brotherhood. Does this vow make sense? Or is it a result of their inebriation? Should you accept the vow literally?

7 Literary Focus Not only are these rioters drunken and profane, but they are also excessively rude and churlish. What purpose does this serve in a story conceived as an exemplum?

8 Master Teacher Note Why has the old man lived so long? For whom has he been seeking? This old man seems to be either a symbol of Death or of Old Age, Death's Messenger. Which of these interpretations seems more likely?

The rioter said, "Is he so fierce to meet?
I'll search for him, by Jesus, street by street.
35 God's blessed bones! I'll register a vow!
Here, chaps! The three of us together now,
Hold up your hands, like me, and we'll be brothers
In this affair, and each defend the others,
And we will kill this traitor Death, I say!
40 Away with him as he has made away
With all our friends. God's dignity! To-night!"
  They made their bargain, swore with appetite,
These three, to live and die for one another
As brother-born might swear to his born brother.
45 And up they started in their drunken rage
And made towards this village which the page
And publican had spoken of before.
Many and grisly were the oaths they swore,
Tearing Christ's blessed body to a shred;[7]
50 "If we can only catch him, Death is dead!"
  When they had gone not fully half a mile,
  Just as they were about to cross a stile,
They came upon a very poor old man
Who humbly greeted them and thus began,
55 "God look to you, my lords, and give you quiet!"
To which the proudest of these men of riot
Gave back the answer, "What, old fool? Give place!
Why are you all wrapped up except your face?
Why live so long? Isn't it time to die?"
60   The old, old fellow looked him in the eye
And said, "Because I never yet have found,
Though I have walked to India, searching round
Village and city on my pilgrimage,
One who would change his youth to have my age.
65 And so my age is mine and must be still
Upon me, for such time as God may will.
    "Not even Death, alas, will take my life;
So, like a wretched prisoner at strife
Within himself, I walk alone and wait
70 About the earth, which is my mother's gate,
Knock-knocking with my staff from night to noon
And crying, 'Mother, open to me soon!
Look at me, mother, won't you let me in?
See how I wither, flesh and blood and skin!
75 Alas! When will these bones be laid to rest?
Mother, I would exchange—for that were best—
The wardrobe in my chamber, standing there
So long, for yours! Aye, for a shirt of hair[8]
To wrap me in!' She has refused her grace,
80 Whence comes the pallor of my withered face.

7. Tearing . . . shred: Their oaths included expressions such as "God's arms" (line 32) and "God's blessed bones" (line 35).

8. shirt of hair: Here, a shroud.

"But it dishonored you when you began
To speak so roughly, sir, to an old man,
Unless he had injured you in word or deed.
It says in holy writ, as you may read,
85 'Thou shalt rise up before the hoary head
And honor it,' And therefore be it said
'Do no more harm to an old man than you,
Being now young, would have another do
When you are old'—if you should live till then.
90 And so may God be with you, gentlemen,
For I must go whither I have to go."

"By God," the gambler said, "you shan't do so,
You don't get off so easy, by St. John!
I heard you mention, just a moment gone,
95 A certain traitor Death who singles out
And kills the fine young fellows hereabout.
And you're his spy, by God! You wait a bit.
Say where he is or you shall pay for it,
By God and by the Holy Sacrament!
100 I say you've joined together by consent
To kill us younger folk, you thieving swine!"

"Well, sirs," he said, "if it be your design
To find out Death, turn up this crooked way
Towards that grove. I left him there today
105 Under a tree, and there you'll find him waiting.
He isn't one to hide for all your prating.
You see that oak? He won't be far to find.
And God protect you that redeemed mankind,
Aye, and amend you!" Thus that ancient man.
110 At once the three young rioters began
To run, and reached the tree, and there they found
A pile of golden florins[9] on the ground,
New-coined, eight bushels of them as they thought.
No longer was it Death those fellows sought,
115 For they were all so thrilled to see the sight,
The florins were so beautiful and bright,
That down they sat beside the precious pile.
The wickedest spoke first after a while.
"Brothers," he said, "you listen to what I say.
120 I'm pretty sharp although I joke away.
It's clear that Fortune has bestowed this treasure
To let us live in jollity and pleasure.
Light come, light go! We'll spend it as we ought.
God's precious dignity! Who would have thought
125 This morning was to be our lucky day?
"If one could only get the gold away,
Back to my house, or else to yours, perhaps—
For as you know, the gold is ours, chaps—
We'd all be at the top of fortune, hey?

9. **florins:** Coins.

from *The Pardoner's Tale* from *The Canterbury Tales*   161

9 **Reading Strategy** What do you predict that they will do now?

10 **Reading Strategy** What is the irony here?

11 Discussion Is the motive for sending one of the young men back to town alone honest and believable?

Humanities Note

Fine art, *The Pardoner,* 1946, by Arthur Szyk. The illustration uses Chaucer's description of the Pardoner in the *Prologue* to interpret his character. The stringy yellow hair, the wallet bulging with relics, and the cap upon his head are all taken from that description. The sanctimonious expression and gesture of forgiveness are from the imagination of Arthur Szyk. This miniature is finely detailed and painted in subtle glowing colors. In discussing Szyk's miniatures with your students, you may wish to mention that the costumes portrayed are close in style to those actually worn in England in Chaucer's time. Ask your students if the impression of the Pardoner that they get from this illustration is similar to or different from the impression of him they got from the Prologue.

130 But certainly it can't be done by day.
People would call us robbers—a strong gang,
So our own property would make us hang.
No, we must bring this treasure back by night
Some prudent way, and keep it out of sight.

135 And so as a solution I propose
We draw for lots and see the way it goes.
The one who draws the longest, lucky man,
Shall run to town as quickly as he can
To fetch us bread and wine—but keep things dark—

140 While two remain in hiding here to mark
Our heap of treasure. If there's no delay,
When night comes down we'll carry it away,

THE PARDONER
Arthur Szyk for the Canterbury Tales
The George Macy Companies

162   *The Medieval Period*

All three of us, wherever we have planned."
He gathered lots and hid them in his hand
145 Bidding them draw for where the luck should fall.
It fell upon the youngest of them all,
And off he ran at once towards the town.
   As soon as he had gone, the first sat down
And thus began a parley[10] with the other:
150 "You know that you can trust me as a brother;
Now let me tell you where your profit lies;
You know our friend has gone to get supplies
And here's a lot of gold that is to be
Divided equally amongst us three.
155 Nevertheless, if I could shape things thus
So that we shared it out—the two of us—
Wouldn't you take it as a friendly turn?"
   "But how!" the other said with some concern,
"Because he knows the gold's with me and you;
160 What can we tell him? What are we to do?"
   "Is it a bargain," said the first, "or no?
For I can tell you in a word or so
What's to be done to bring the thing about."
   "Trust me," the other said, "you needn't doubt
165 My word. I won't betray you, I'll be true."
   "Well," said his friend, "you see that we are two,
And two are twice as powerful as one.
Now look; when he comes back, get up in fun
To have a wrestle; then, as you attack,
170 I'll up and put my dagger through his back
While you and he are struggling, as in game;
Then draw your dagger too and do the same.
Then all this money will be ours to spend,
Divided equally of course, dear friend.
175 Then we can gratify our lusts and fill
The day with dicing at our own sweet will."
Thus these two miscreants[11] agreed to slay
The third and youngest, as you heard me say.
   The youngest, as he ran towards the town,
180 Kept turning over, rolling up and down
Within his heart the beauty of those bright
New florins, saying, "Lord, to think I might
Have all that treasure to myself alone!
Could there be anyone beneath the throne
185 Of God so happy as I then should be?"
   And so the Fiend,[12] our common enemy,
Was given power to put it in his thought
That there was always poison to be bought,
And that with poison he could kill his friends.

10. parley (pär' lē): Discussion.

11. miscreants (mis' krē onts): Villains.

12. Fiend: Satan.

12 Literary Focus Note in this passage the repeated use of words and phrases such as *trust, brother, I won't betray you,* and *I'll be true.* What is the irony here?

Challenge Does your view of the Pardoner change as a result of hearing his tale?

from *The Pardoner's Tale* from *The Canterbury Tales*   163

190 To men in such a state the Devil sends
Thoughts of this kind, and has a full permission
To lure them on to sorrow and perdition;[13]
For this young man was utterly content
To kill them both and never to repent.

195   And on he ran, he had no thought to tarry,
Came to the town, found an apothecary
And said, "Sell me some poison if you will,
I have a lot of rats I want to kill
And there's a polecat too about my yard

200 That takes my chickens and it hits me hard;
But I'll get even, as is only right,
With vermin that destroy a man by night."
    The chemist answered, "I've a preparation
Which you shall have, and by my soul's salvation

205 If any living creature eat or drink
A mouthful, ere he has the time to think,
Though he took less than makes a grain of wheat,
You'll see him fall down dying at your feet;
Yes, die he must, and in so short a while

210 You'd hardly have the time to walk a mile,
The poison is so strong, you understand."
    This cursed fellow grabbed into his hand
The box of poison and away he ran
Into a neighboring street, and found a man

215 Who lent him three large bottles. He withdrew
And deftly poured the poison into two.
He kept the third one clean, as well he might,
For his own drink, meaning to work all night
Stacking the gold and carrying it away.

220 And when this rioter, this devil's clay,
Had filled his bottles up with wine, all three,
Back to rejoin his comrades sauntered he.
    Why make a sermon of it? Why waste breath?
Exactly in the way they'd planned his death

225 They fell on him and slew him, two to one.
Then said the first of them when this was done,
"Now for a drink. Sit down and let's be merry,
For later on there'll be the corpse to bury."
And, as it happened, reaching for a sup,

230 He took a bottle full of poison up
And drank; and his companion, nothing loth,
Drank from it also, and they perished both.
    There is, in Avicenna's long relation[14]
Concerning poison and its operation,

235 Trust me, no ghastlier section to transcend
What these two wretches suffered at their end.
Thus these two murderers received their due,
So did the treacherous young poisoner too.

13. perdition: Damnation.

14. Avicenna's (aʹ və senʹ əz) **long relation:** A book on medicines written by Avicenna (980–1037), an Arab physician, which contains a chapter on poisons.

THINKING ABOUT THE SELECTION

Recalling

1. What do the three rioters pledge to do?
2. (a) What does the old man tell the rioters they will find under a tree? (b) What do they actually find there?
3. How do the two rioters decide to increase their share of the gold? Explain their plan.
4. What does the youngest rioter do when he goes to town for bread and wine?

Interpreting

5. In line 39, Death is presented as a traitor. Do you think this description appropriate? Explain you answer.
6. Do the rioters keep the pledge they made in the tavern? Why or why not?
7. Does the old man know that in directing the three rioters to the oak tree he is sending them to their deaths? Explain.

Applying

8. What person in the news today, or in the recent past, has shown character traits similar to those of the Pardoner?

ANALYZING LITERATURE

Understanding an Anecdote (Exemplum)

"The Pardoner's Tale" is an *exemplum,* a brief moral story that the Pardoner tells the pilgrims. In medieval times an *exemplum* was often included in a sermon.

1. How does the young rioter's dialogue with the chemist help to characterize both the rioter and his two companions?
2. What moral does this exemplum establish?
3. In what ways does "The Pardoner's Tale" differ from a short story?

CRITICAL THINKING AND READING

Making Inferences

In the Prologue Chaucer makes the point that he is reporting the pilgrims' tales, "using their very phrases." Therefore, although the narrator of *The Canterbury Tales* is Chaucer, the narrator of each individual tale is a particular pilgrim. You can make judgments about the Pardoner based on his own narration. Since Chaucer has already commented in the Prologue on the Pardoner's character, you have a chance to compare Chaucer's view of the Pardoner with the Pardoner's view of himself.

1. Does the topic the Pardoner chooses for his *exemplum* reflect his own interests? Explain.
2. Considering Chaucer's Prologue, how seriously do you think the Pardoner takes his moral that "Greed is the root of evil"? Explain.

SPEAKING AND LISTENING

Reading Middle English Aloud

After the Norman conquest of England in 1066, there were two languages in daily use: the French of the invaders and the Old English of the natives. As time passed, the English language began to change. By about 1150 the changes in English were notable enough for later scholars to identify the start of a new period; Middle English lasted roughly from 1150 to 1500.

Middle English is much easier to read than is Old English, but there are differences between it and the language we use today. In reading Middle English, you pronounce every syllable: *bathed* is /bath′ ed/; *soote* is /sō′ tə/. Some consonants that today are silent were sounded in Middle English: *k* in *k*nyght; *g* in *g*nawe; *l* in fo*l*k; and *gh* in drou*gh*te.

Read aloud lines 1–25 on page 159.

THINKING AND WRITING

Writing an Analysis

Write an essay analyzing "The Pardoner's Tale." An analysis is not a plot summary; it is an explanation of how the various elements in a literary work fit together. In analyzing Chaucer's tale, consider at least three of these elements: characters, plot, dialogue, moral, rhyme scheme, similes, symbolism.

die together. However, it was not the intention of the oath that they would murder each other.

7. Yes, he probably does. The old man is either Death himself or his messenger, Old Age.

Applying

8. Answers will differ. Some politicians or celebrities might be appropriate.

ANSWERS TO ANALYZING LITERATURE

1. The youngest rioter calls his companions vermin that destroy a man by night, although the apothecary assumes he is talking of rats and a polecat.
2. The moral is that greed is the root of evil.
3. It is shorter, a single episode, and the characters are completely symbolic. Moreover, it is more concerned with illustrating an idea than with re-creating experience.

ANSWERS TO CRITICAL THINKING AND READING

1. Yes, the Pardoner is a convincing preacher who wants his audience, recognizing the evil of greed, to donate money to him.
2. He takes it very seriously—as a means of satisfying his own greed.

ANSWERS TO SPEAKING AND LISTENING

You might choose to read aloud a few lines before the students attempt to read the lines. Review the material about heroic couplets to help them read effectively.

THINKING AND WRITING

Publishing Student Writing After the students have completed their compositions, have them evaluate their work in writing groups. Ask them to choose one member who seems most knowledgeable about "The Pardoner's Tale" to represent the group in a panel discussion of all seven elements of the exemplum. After the panel members have presented the elements in their papers, allow the class to ask questions.

Closure and Extension

ANSWERS TO THINKING ABOUT THE SELECTION
Recalling

1. They swear to live and die for one another
2. (a) The old man tells them they will find Death under the tree. (b) They find a pile of gold florins.
3. The two rioters decide to kill their companion by stabbing him in the back while wrestling.
4. The youngest buys poison to murder the two others.

Interpreting

5. It is appropriate inasmuch as Death betrays people, robs them of life, and hands them over to the grave.
6. Actually they do because they all

Travel Writing

Travel became important during the Middle Ages and many travelers—both fictional and real-life—kept records of their journeys. Chaucer's pilgrims set off for Canterbury, King Arthur and his knights encountered strange creatures on their quests, and the real-life Marco Polo visited the court of Kublai Khan.

Writing about travel has been important throughout the ages and across cultures. For example, traveling along the Silk Road to India in the year 648, Prince Tripitaka stopped at the oasis of Kharashahr to describe an unusual custom. "The children born of common parents," he wrote, "have their heads flattened by the pressure of a wooden board." Not all travel diaries note such remarkable customs, but then again, not all travelers encounter waters "bluish-black in color, salty and bitter in taste" in whose depths "dragons and fishes swim together; scaly monsters rise to the surface,

WORLD MAP: CATHAY AND THE EMPIRE OF THE GREAT KHAN, 1459
Mauro
Biblioteca Nazionale Marciana, Venice

and passing travelers pray to them for good fortune.''

EDUCATIONAL ACCOUNTS?

Whether the things travelers encounter on their journeys are exciting or commonplace, an astonishing number of people are moved to record their voyages in diaries. Many justify their accounts by claiming that travel is educational. E. S. Bates, for example, describes the ''educational'' sights people saw on the Continent in the 1600's:

> Torture accompanying execution was common, and branding and mutilation things that no traveller could well avoid seeing. But none seemed to want to avoid them: Evelyn [author of a famous diary] went to the Chatelet prison at Paris to look on while a prisoner underwent legal torture. The only occasions that seem to have struck them as too horrible was when the headsman bungled matters: a Dutchman at Paris saw one try sixteen times and then have to be assisted.

It appears that education, like beauty, may be in the eye of the beholder!

DIGNITY AND DECORUM

A travel diary allows one to record one's thoughts after the fact, and still maintain one's dignity. Few people were as famous for their dignity as Queen Victoria of England. Notice how she maintained her pride even as her carriage tumbled over, spilling her and Princess Alice to the ground.

A MEDIEVAL VIEW OF THE UNIVERSE
Ronald Sheridan Ancient Art and Architecture Collection

> There was an awful pause, during which Alice said: ''We are upsetting.'' In another moment— during which I had time to reflect whether we should be killed or not, and thought there were still things I had not settled and wanted to—the carriage turned over on its side, and we were all precipitated to the ground!''

According to Victoria's account, she ''precipitated'' from the carriage. No ''fall'' or ''drop'' here!

''OPEN THE HEART'S STORE''

A travel diary gives us a way to say that this is what I, not the camera, saw. This is how Clara Milburn, an ordinary Englishwoman, voiced it in her travel diary: ''There is so much background, one can't be dull, but can just open the heart's store, look round the shelves, take down the memory and live it over again. Grand!''

Cross Currents 167

Humanities Note

A Medieval View of the Universe. Medieval cartographers (mapmakers) and astronomers produced a variety of treatises on geography and the cosmic universe. They were, of course, strongly hampered by their lack of scientific knowledge. World maps included mythical beasts and imaginary half-animal, half-human creatures. It was not known that the world was round, and most people believed that the Earth was at the center of the universe.

Yet the curiosity of medieval scholars drove them to create models or pictures of the universe. In this odd illustration, a brilliant sun illuminates a flat earth and the stars seem to be painted on a shell or sphere enclosing the earth. A man who is crawling on the ground appears to have stuck his head through this sphere! Although this medieval view of the world seems humorous to us, we should remember that modern science is a comparatively recent phenomenon.

You might want to use the following questions to discuss the art.
1. What is fact and what is fantasy in this picture?
2. How does this medieval view of the world differ from our concept of it?

More About the Poem Although there are theories about the authorship of *Sir Gawain and the Green Knight,* no solid evidence exists to attribute authorship to anyone in particular. The author, called the Pearl Poet after another of his poems, was a contemporary of Chaucer's, but his work is so much more difficult to read in the original that only scholars can translate him.

Critical Evaluation The author of *A History of English Literature,* Peter Quennell, believes that the differences between Chaucer and the writer of *Sir Gawain and the Green Knight* are the result of geographic and social factors. He claims that the latter poet was "a provincial man of genius, steeped in the chivalric spirit of the Middle Ages, for whom the court of King Arthur, and the moral code it symbolized, must have seemed very much more real than the existing court at Westminster, which, unlike Chaucer, an important officer of the Crown, he may never, or very seldom, have entered."

GUIDE FOR INTERPRETING

1375[?]

Audiences in the Middle Ages enjoyed tales of adventure and fantasy, featuring heroes and rogues, magicians and monsters. One of the finest of these medieval romances, *Sir Gawain and the Green Knight,* was written by an unknown bard who lived at the time of Chaucer. "Master Anonymous," as the *Gawain* poet has been called, tells an unforgettable tale about one of the legendary knights of King Arthur's Round Table.

Although the poet is unknown, the *Gawain* manuscript (of which the British Museum owns the only copy) suggests something of its creator's background. The poet probably lived in northwestern England, judging by the poem's dialect and by its old-fashioned alliterative verse, neither of which reflects the fashion in Chaucer's London. Nevertheless, the poet is familiar with life at court and, like Chaucer, may have been connected to an aristocratic household. The poet also seems to have read widely in Latin and French as well as in English.

Sir Gawain's plot elements date back many centuries. In ancient vegetation myths, beheading is a ritual death intended to ensure the return of spring and the growth of new crops. More in line with Sir Gawain's adventure, a ninth century Irish narrative recounts a beheading contest as the supreme test of courage. Twelfth century French romances tell a similar tale, while the temptations faced by young Gawain may owe something to early French stories.

Arthurian legends, popular throughout Europe, developed orally over a long period of time. Despite this lengthy tradition, *Sir Gawain* is an original and masterful work. Not only is it excitingly told, but the poet introduces a high degree of realism into the setting. Most medieval romances take place with Camelot shimmering in the bright days of spring or summer. Not this poem. Sir Gawain's adventures occur in the bleakness of winter, with the chill desolation reinforcing the hero's trials. Nor is the hero himself without fault, as he is in so many other tales of knights and ladies. Sir Gawain is admirable but not invulnerable, which lends a psychological dimension to this medieval story. As one critic put it, the hero "gains in human credibility what he loses in ideal perfection."

Objectives

1 To understand a medieval romance
2 To make inferences about chivalric ideals
3 To understand abstract words
4 To evaluate a medieval romance

Support Material

Teaching Portfolio
Teacher Backup, p. 129
Grammar in Action Worksheets, *Understanding Pronoun/Antecedent Agreement,* p. 133; *Using Adverbs,* p. 135
Usage and Mechanics Worksheet, p. 137
Vocabulary Check, p. 138
Analyzing Literature Worksheet, *Understanding Medieval Romances,* p. 139
Critical Thinking and Reading Worksheet, *Making Inferences About Chivalric Ideals,* p. 140
Selection Test, p. 141

from Sir Gawain and the Green Knight

Literary Forms

Medieval Romance. From the twelfth to the fifteenth century, medieval romances were the popular literature of England. Based on the feudal ideal of chivalry and imbued with adventure, love, and the supernatural, medieval romances typically feature kings, knights, and damsels in distress. The earliest romances were always in verse, but later ones were sometimes in prose.

The enduring popularity of these tales of romance stems in part from their glamorous portrayal of castle life—the festivals, the feasts, the knights in armor, the courtly love. Medieval romances were for many generations the stock in trade of professional storytellers, some of whom were employed in noble households, others of whom made the rounds of modest inns and taverns. As literacy increased, the status of the minstrel declined, but the romances, preserved in written form, continue to have appeal even today.

Of all the medieval romances, the best known are those about King Arthur and his Knights of the Round Table. Arthur, who may have been a Welsh chieftain in the fifth or sixth century, is the central figure in early Arthurian romances. In later ones King Arthur's knights, such as Sir Gawain and Sir Lancelot, assume the principal roles.

Writing

In a few sentences, comment on the following statement by Charles Kingsley, nineteenth century English historian and writer: "Some say that the spirit of chivalry is past, that the spirit of romance is dead. The age of chivalry is never past, so long as there is a wrong left unredressed on earth."

Primary Source

Many authors have retold the Arthurian legend, perhaps the most spellbinding of all medieval romances. One of the most famous versions is T. H. White's *The Once and Future King*. Here, White describes some of the glories of the age:

> For there, under the window in Arthur's Gramarye, the sun's rays flamed from a hundred jewels of stained glass in monasteries and convents, or danced from the pinnacles of cathedrals and castles, which their builders had actually loved . . . Think of the glass itself, with its five grand colors stained right through. It was rougher than ours, thicker, fitted in smaller pieces . . . Picture the insides of those ancient churches . . . insides blazing with color, plastered with frescoes in which all the figures stood on tiptoe, fluttering with tapestry or with brocades from Bagdad.

Guide for Interpreting 169

Literary Focus *Sir Gawain and the Green Knight* has been called the best English example of the medieval romance, one of the most charming romances ever written anywhere, and a literary work of the highest quality, surpassed or equaled only by Chaucer's *Troilus and Criseyde*. Among the qualities for which it is admired are its picturesque language, vivid descriptions, penetrating characterizations, skillful structure, and sensitive re-creation of the drama, color, and pageantry of medieval life. Although the selection presented here is brief, it exhibits many of the cited qualities. Which qualities do you find in this excerpt?

Writing/Prior Knowledge Before you ask students to comment upon the statement, you might discuss it with them to make sure they understand chivalry and romance. You might ask them what evidence they see of these ideals today.

Vocabulary

Preteach the following vocabulary words:
assay (as ā′) *v*.: To prove or test (l. 68)
haft (haft) *n*.: A handle of a weapon or tool (l. 105)
adjure (ə joor′) *v*.: To appeal to earnestly (l. 152)
recreant (rek′ rē ənt) *adj*.: Cowardly (l. 226)
caviled (kav′ 'ld) *v*.: Raised trivial objections (l. 370)
largesse (lär jes′) *n*.: Nobility of spirit (l. 472)

Teaching to Ability Levels For **less advanced** students you might want to give an overall synopsis of the story so they can follow the plot as they read. For **more advanced** students, you might reproduce for them more of the poem; especially valuable might be Part Two.

from # Sir Gawain and the Green Knight

translated by Marie Borroff

The work begins at the start of a New Year's Eve feast at King Arthur's Court in Camelot. Before anyone has started eating, the festivities are interrupted by an immense green knight who suddenly appears at the hall door. The knight rides a green horse and is armed with a gigantic ax.

1

This horseman hurtles in, and the hall enters;
Riding to the high dais,[1] recked he no danger;
Not a greeting he gave as the guests he o'erlooked,
Nor wasted his words, but "Where is," he said,
5 "The captain of this crowd? Keenly I wish
To see that sire with sight, and to himself say my say."
      He swaggered all about
      To scan the host so gay;
      He halted, as if in doubt
10   Who in that hall held sway.

2

There were stares on all sides as the stranger spoke,
For much did they marvel what it might mean
That a horseman and a horse should have such a hue,
Grow green as the grass, and greener, it seemed.
15 Then green fused on gold more glorious by far.
All the onlookers eyed him, and edged nearer,
And awaited in wonder what he would do,
For many sights had they seen, but such a one never,
So that phantom and fairy the folk there deemed it,
20 Therefore chary[2] of answer was many a champion bold,
And stunned at his strong words stone-still they sat
In a swooning silence in the stately hall.
As all were slipped into sleep, so slackened their speech
  apace.
      Not all, I think, for dread,
25   But some of courteous grace
      Let him who was their head
      Be spokesman in that place.

Then Arthur before the high dais that entrance beholds,
And hailed him, as behooved, for he had no fear,

1. dais (dā′ is) *n.*: Platform.

2. chary (cher′ ē) *adj.*: Not giving freely.

170 *The Medieval Period*

FROM THE ROMANCE OF KING ARTHUR
AND HIS KNIGHTS OF THE ROUND TABLE
Arthur Rackham
Weathervane Books

Illustration, by Arthur Rackham. The English illustrator Arthur Rackham (1867-1936) was born in London. He studied drawing at the Lambeth School of Art there. He worked as an illustrator of magazines and bools for most of his life. Many of his original drawings are now in the collection of the Tate Gallery in London.

Arthur Rackham's style of drawing reflects his interest in prints of the German Renaissance. Although more modern in approach, his works maintain the detail and angular grace of that school. This illustration of a castle was done for a book entitled *The Romance of King Arthur*. Ever a lover of fairy-tales and scenes of fantasy, Rackham enjoyed drawing such scenes as this castle.

Consider discussing the following with your students: Does this castle convey a feeling of hospitality or does it seem forbidding? Explain.

from *Sir Gawain and the Green Knight*   171

3

Discussion Why has the Green Knight come? He states his purpose, a game, after a string of compliments and a disclaimer of warlike intent.

4 Reading Strategy Read to discover the Green Knight's attitude toward the assembled knights. Note the contempt he shows in words like "beardless" and "puny." This contemptuous tone is continued in lines 85–91.

5 Master Teacher Note Describe the game that the Green Knight proposes. Here the poet introduces the first main story element, traditionally called the "Beheading Game." This, like the other two story elements that he includes, was not his original invention. In fact, they all derive from folklore. He was, however, the first to combine them. What was the Court's immediate response to the Green Knight's proposal?

30　And said "Fellow, in faith you have found fair welcome;
　　The head of this hostelry Arthur am I;
　　Leap lightly down, and linger, I pray,
　　And the tale of your intent you shall tell us after."
　　"Nay, so help me," said the other, "He that on high sits,
35　To tarry here any time, 'twas not mine errand;
　　But as the praise of you, prince, is puffed up so high,
　　And your court and your company are counted the best,
　　Stoutest under steel-gear on steeds to ride,
　　Worthiest of their works the wide world over,
40　And peerless to prove in passages of arms,
　　And courtesy here is carried to its height,
　　And so at this season I have sought you out.
　　You may be certain by the branch that I bear in hand
　　That I pass here in peace, and would part friends,
45　For had I come to this court on combat bent,
　　I have a hauberk[3] at home, and a helm beside,
　　A shield and a sharp spear, shining bright,
　　And other weapons to wield, I ween well, to boot,
　　But as I willed no war, I wore no metal.
50　But if you be so bold as all men believe,
　　You will graciously grant the game that I ask by right."
　　　　Arthur answer gave
　　　　And said, "Sir courteous knight,
　　　　If contest here you crave,
55　　　You shall not fail to fight."

　　"Nay, to fight, in good faith, is far from my thought;
　　There are about on these benches but beardless children,
　　Were I here in full arms on a haughty[4] steed,
　　For measured against mine, their might is puny.
60　And so I call in this court for a Christmas game,
　　For 'tis Yule, and New Year, and many young bloods about;
　　If any in this house such hardihood claims,
　　Be so bold in his blood, his brain so wild,
　　As stoutly to strike one stroke for another,
65　I shall give him as my gift this gisarme[5] noble,
　　This ax, that is heavy enough, to handle as he likes,
　　And I shall bide the first blow, as bare as I sit.
　　If there be one so wilful my words to assay,
　　Let him leap hither lightly, lay hold of this weapon;
70　I quitclaim it forever, keep it as his own,
　　And I shall stand him a stroke, steady on this floor,
　　So you grant me the guerdon to give him another, sans
　　　blame.[6]
　　　　In a twelvemonth[7] and a day
　　　　He shall have of me the same;
75　　　Now be it seen straightway
　　　　Who dares take up the game."

3　172　The Medieval Period

---

3. hauberk (hô′ bərk) *n.*: Coat of armor.

4. haughty (hôt′ ē) *adj.*: Lofty.

5. gisarme (gi zärm′) *n.*: Battle-ax.

6. I . . . blame: I will stand firm while he strikes me with the ax provided that you reward me with the opportunity to do the same to him without being blamed for it.

7. twelvemonth: A year.

Grammar in Action

Make **pronouns agree** with **antecedents** in number, person, and gender. When indefinite pronouns act as antecedents, agreement rules still apply. Use plural pronouns to refer to plural indefinite pronouns (such as *all, few, many, several*) and singular pronouns to refer to singular indefinite pronouns (such as *any, each, either, one, somebody*). Notice the proper use of agreement in the following passage from *Sir Gawain and the Green Knight.*

If *any* in this house such hardihood claims,
Be so bold in *his* blood, *his* brain so wild,
As stoutly to strike one stroke for another,
I shall give *him* as my gift this gisarme noble,
This ax, that is heavy enough, to handle as *he* likes,
And I shall bide the first blow, as bare as I sit.
If there be *one* so wilful my words to assay,
Let *him* leap hither lightly, lay hold of this weapon;
I quitclaim it forever, keep it as his own . . .

Any and *one* are indefinite-pronoun antecedents in this passage. Since they are singular, all pronouns referring to them are singular as well.

If he astonished them at first, stiller were then
All that household in hall, the high and the low;
The stranger on his green steed stirred in the saddle,
80   And roisterously his red eyes he rolled all about,
Bent his bristling brows, that were bright green,
Wagged his beard as he watched who would arise.
When the court kept its counsel he coughed aloud,
And cleared his throat coolly, the clearer to speak:
85   "What, is this Arthur's house," said that horseman then,
"Whose fame is so fair in far realms and wide?
Where is now your arrogance and your awesome deeds,
Your valor and your victories and your vaunting words?
Now are the revel and renown of the Round Table
90   Overwhelmed with a word of one man's speech,
For all cower and quake, and no cut felt!"
With this he laughs so loud that the lord grieved;
The blood for sheer shame shot to his face, and pride.
       With rage his face flushed red,
95   And so did all beside.
       Then the king as bold man bred
        Toward the stranger took a stride.

And said, "Sir, now we see you will say but folly,
Which whoso has sought, it suits that he find.
100 No guest here is aghast of your great words.
Give to me your gisarme, in God's own name,
And the boon you have begged shall straight be granted."
He leaps to him lightly, lays hold of his weapon;
The green fellow on foot fiercely alights.
105 Now has Arthur his ax, and the haft grips,
And sternly stirs it about, on striking bent.
The stranger before him stood there erect,
Higher than any in the house by a head and more;
With stern look as he stood, he stroked his beard,
110 And with undaunted countenance drew down his coat,
No more moved nor dismayed for his mighty dints
Than any bold man on bench had brought him a drink of
    wine.
       Gawain by Guenevere
       Toward the king doth now incline:
115   "I beseech, before all here,
       That this melee may be mine."

"Would you grant me the grace," said Gawain to the king,
"To be gone from this bench and stand by you there,
If I without discourtesy might quit this board,
120 And if my liege lady[8] misliked it not,
I would come to your counsel before your court noble.

8. liege (lēj) **lady:**
Guenevere, the wife of the
lord, Arthur, to whom
Gawain is bound to give
service and allegiance.

from *Sir Gawain and the Green Knight*   173

6 Enrichment Sir Gawain was the son of Arthur's half-sister, the Queen of Orkney.

7 Reading Strategy Read for the characteristics of chivalry that Sir Gawain exhibits in this speech.

Student Activity. Rewrite these sentences correcting any errors in agreement.

1. Nobody ever brings their book to English class.
2. Neither of them continued their journey after that.
3. Everyone should be allowed to live their own life.
4. Few of the boys has his own car.
5. For somebody to understand the good things in life, they must experience some of the bad.

For I find it not fit, as in faith it is known,
When such a boon is begged before all these knights,
Though you be tempted thereto, to take it on yourself
125　While so bold men about upon benches sit,
That no host under heaven is hardier of will,
Nor better brothers-in-arms where battle is joined;
I am the weakest, well I know, and of wit feeblest;
And the loss of my life would be least of any;
130　That I have you for uncle is my only praise;
My body, but for your blood, is barren of worth;
And for that this folly befits not a king,
And 'tis I that have asked it, it ought to be mine,
And if my claim be not comely let all this court judge in
　　sight.''
135　　　　The court assays the claim,
　　　　And in counsel all unite
　　　　To give Gawain the game
　　　　And release the king outright.

Then the king called the knight to come to his side,
140　And he rose up readily, and reached him with speed,
Bows low to his lord, lays hold of the weapon,
And he releases it lightly, and lifts up his hand,
And gives him God's blessing, and graciously prays
That his heart and his hand may be hardy both.
145　"Keep, cousin," said the king, "what you cut with this day,
And if you rule it aright, then readily, I know,
You shall stand the stroke it will strike after."
Gawain goes to the guest with gisarme in hand,
And boldly he bides there, abashed not a whit.
150　Then hails he Sir Gawain, the horseman in green:
"Recount we our contract, ere you come further.
First I ask and adjure you, how you are called
That you tell me true, so that trust it I may."
"In good faith," said the good knight, "Gawain am I
155　Whose buffet befalls you,[9] whate'er betide after,
And at this time twelvemonth take from you another
With what weapon you will, and with no man else alive."
　　　　The other nods assent:
　　　　"Sir Gawain, as I may thrive,
160　　　　I am wondrous well content
　　　　That you this dint[10] shall drive."

"Sir Gawain," said the Green Knight, "By God, I rejoice
That your fist shall fetch this favor I seek,
And you have readily rehearsed, and in right terms,
165　Each clause of my covenant with the king your lord,

9. Whose . . . you: Whose blow you will receive.

10. dint: Blow.

Save that you shall assure me, sir, upon oath,
That you shall seek me yourself, wheresoever you deem
My lodgings may lie, and look for such wages[11]
As you have offered me here before all this host."

170   "What is the way there?" said Gawain, "Where do you
    dwell?"
I heard never of your house, by Him that made me,
Nor I know you not, knight, your name nor your court.
But tell me truly thereof, and teach me your name,
And I shall fare forth to find you, so far as I may,

175 And this I say in good certain, and swear upon oath."
"That is enough in New Year, you need say no more,"
Said the knight in the green to Gawain the noble,
"If I tell you true, when I have taken your knock,
And if you handily have hit, you shall hear straightway

180 Of my house and my home and my own name;
Then follow in my footsteps by faithful accord.
And if I spend no speech, you shall speed the better:
You can feast with your friends, nor further trace my
    tracks.[12]
        Now hold your grim tool steady

185   And show us how it hacks."
        "Gladly, sir; all ready,"
        Says Gawain; he strokes the ax.

The Green Knight upon ground girds him with care:
Bows a bit with his head, and bares his flesh:

190 His long lovely locks he laid over his crown,
Let the naked nape for the need be shown.
Gawain grips to his ax and gathers it aloft—
The left foot on the floor before him he set—
Brought it down deftly upon the bare neck,

195 That the shock of the sharp blow shivered the bones
And cut the flesh cleanly and clove it in twain,[13]
That the blade of bright steel bit into the ground.
The head was hewn off and fell to the floor;
Many found it at their feet, as forth it rolled;

200 The blood gushed from the body, bright on the green,
Yet fell not the fellow, nor faltered a whit,
But stoutly he starts forth upon stiff shanks,
And as all stood staring he stretched forth his hand,
Laid hold of his head and heaved it aloft,

205 Then goes to the green steed, grasps the bridle,
Steps into the stirrup, bestrides his mount,
And his head by the hair in his hand holds,
And as steady he sits in the stately saddle
As he had met with no mishap, nor missing were his head.

11. wages: A blow.

**12. If I tell
you . . . tracks** (lines
178–183): The Green
Knight tells Gawain that he
will let him know where he
lives after he has taken the
blow. If he is unable to
speak following the blow,
there will be no need for
Gawain to know.

13. clove it in twain: Split
it in two.

9 **Literary Focus** These lines are a
good example of the concreteness and realism of description
that contribute to *Sir Gawain and
the Green Knight*'s excellence.
Why does the result of Sir Gawain's blow to the Green Knight
evoke more terror in him and the
Court than if he had failed?

from *Sir Gawain and the Green Knight*   175

10 **Literary Focus** The picture of the disembodied head turned toward the audience and speaking is particularly vivid and gruesome. What purpose does it serve in the romance?

11 **Discussion** Why did King Arthur keep his composure and resume activities after the Green Knight left?

210   His bulk about he haled,
    That fearsome body that bled;
    There were many in the court that quailed
    Before all his say was said.

    For the head in his hand he holds right up;
215   Toward the first on the dais directs he the face,
    And it lifted up its lids, and looked with wide eyes,
    And said as much with its mouth as now you may hear:
    "Sir Gawain, forget not to go as agreed,
    And cease not to seek till me, sir, you find,
220   As you promised in the presence of these proud knights.
    To the Green Chapel come, I charge you, to take
    Such a dint as you have dealt—you have well deserved
    That your neck should have a knock on New Year's morn.
    The Knight of the Green Chapel I am well-known to many,
225   Wherefore you cannot fail to find me at last;
    Therefore come, or be counted a recreant knight."
    With a roisterous rush he flings round the reins,
    Hurtles out at the hall door, his head in his hand,
    That the flint fire flew from the flashing hooves.
230   Which way he went, not one of them knew
    Nor whence he was come in the wide world so fair.
        The king and Gawain gay
        Make a game of the Green Knight there,
        Yet all who saw it say
235   'Twas a wonder past compare.

    Though high-born Arthur at heart had wonder,
    He let no sign be seen, but said aloud
    To the comely queen, with courteous speech,
    "Dear dame, on this day dismay you no whit;
240   Such crafts are becoming at Christmastide,
    Laughing at interludes, light songs and mirth,
    Amid dancing of damsels with doughty knights.
    Nevertheless of my meat now let me partake,
    For I have met with a marvel, I may not deny."
245   He glanced at Sir Gawain, and gaily he said,
    "Now, sir, hang up your ax, that has hewn enough,"
    And over the high dais it was hung on the wall
    That men in amazement might on it look,
    And tell in true terms the tale of the wonder.
250   Then they turned toward the table, those two together,
    The good king and Gawain, and made great feast,
    With all dainties double, dishes rare,
    With all manner of meat and minstrelsy both,
    Such happiness wholly had they that day in hold.

255　　Now take care, Sir Gawain,
　　　　That your courage wax not cold
　　　　When you must turn again
　　　　To your enterprise foretold.

The following November, Sir Gawain sets out to fulfill his promise to the Green Knight. For weeks he travels alone through the cold, threatening woods of North Wales. Then, after he prays for shelter, he comes upon a wondrous castle on Christmas Eve, where he is greeted warmly by the lord of the castle and his lady. Sir Gawain inquires about the location of the Green Chapel, and the lord assures him that it is nearby and promises to provide him with a guide to lead him there on New Year's Day. Before the lord and Sir Gawain retire for the night, they agree to exchange whatever they receive during the next three days. Sir Gawain keeps his pledge for the first two days, but on the third day he does not give the lord the magic green girdle that the lady gives him because she promises that the girdle will protect him from any harm. The next day, Gawain sets out for the Green Chapel. His guide urges him not to proceed, but Gawain refuses to take this advice. He feels that it would be dishonorable not to fulfill his pledge. He is determined to accept his fate; however, he does wear the magic green girdle that the lady had given him.

12

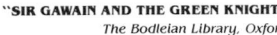

"SIR GAWAIN AND THE GREEN KNIGHT"
The Bodleian Library, Oxford

12 Master Teacher Note Another of the traditional main story elements that the poet has utilized is touched on in this summary, the "Exchange of Winnings." The third element, extremely important in the plot, is the "Temptation Story," in which the lady of the castle tries to tempt Sir Gawain.

Humanities Note

Illuminated manuscript, "Sir Gawain and the Green Knight." Medieval illuminated manuscripts were produced in monasteries by cloistered monks and by specially hired laymen. They were painted on hand-lettered vellum manuscripts to decorate and often illustrate a part of the text. Works of both a religious and secular nature were produced. Today, they provide an invaluable literary and visual historic record.

The miniature painting, *Gawain Departs Guenivere and Arthur,* is from an illuminated manuscript. The content of this manuscript is an account of the adventures of Sir Gawain. This charming painting is executed in the calligraphic, flat style that is typical of medieval art. The format, three separate scenes on a single plane, can be compared to that of today's comic strip. This lively, brightly colored account of the knight's adventures is a welcome message from the past to today's reader of ancient works.

You may wish to ask your students the following questions:

1. How does the artist show the King and Queen reacting to Gawain's departure?
2. How does this compare with the written account?

13 **Reading Strategy** Describe the Chapel Green. How does its appearance affect Sir Gawain's spirits?

14 **Discussion** What is the "barbarous din" he hears? What is the effect on the reader? On Sir Gawain?

He puts his heels to his horse, and picks up the path;
260 Goes in beside a grove where the ground is steep,
Rides down the rough slope right to the valley;
And then he looked a little about him—the landscape was
    wild,
And not a soul to be seen, nor sign of a dwelling,
But high banks on either hand hemmed it about,
265 With many a ragged rock and rough-hewn crag;
The skies seemed scored by the scowling peaks.
Then he halted his horse, and hoved there a space,
And sought on every side for a sight of the Chapel,
But no such place appeared, which puzzled him sore,
270 Yet he saw some way off what seemed like a mound,
A hillock high and broad, hard by the water,
Where the stream fell in foam down the face of the steep
And bubbled as if it boiled on its bed below.
The knight urges his horse, and heads for the knoll;
275 Leaps lightly to earth; loops well the rein
Of his steed to a stout branch, and stations him there.
He strides straight to the mound, and strolls all about,
Much wondering what it was, but no whit the wiser;
It had a hole at one end, and on either side,
280 And was covered with coarse grass in clumps all without,
And hollow all within, like some old cave,
Or a crevice of an old crag—he could not discern aright.
        "Can this be the Chapel Green?
        Alack!" said the man, "Here might
285   The devil himself be seen
        Saying matins[14] at black midnight!"

"Now by heaven," said he, "it is bleak hereabouts;
This prayer house is hideous, half covered with grass!
Well may the grim man mantled in green
290 Hold here his orisons,[15] in hell's own style!
Now I feel it is the Fiend, in my five wits,
That has tempted me to this tryst,[16] to take my life;
This is a Chapel of mischance, may the mischief take it!
As accursed a country church as I came upon ever!"
295 With his helm on his head, his lance in his hand,
He stalks toward the steep wall of that strange house.
Then he heard, on the hill, behind a hard rock,
Beyond the brook, from the bank, a most barbarous din:
Lord! it clattered in the cliff fit to cleave it in two,
300 As one upon a grindstone ground a great scythe!
Lord! it whirred like a mill-wheel whirling about!
Lord! it echoed loud and long, lamentable to hear!
Then "By heaven," said the bold knight, "That business up
    there
Is arranged for my arrival, or else I am much misled.

14. matins *n.*: Morning prayers.

15. orisons *n.*: Prayers.

16. tryst (trist) *n.*: Meeting.

Commentary

Attention has been paid to the similarities and dissimilarities between the author of *Sir Gawain and the Green Knight* and Chaucer. In commenting on the matter, critic Peter Quennell has this to say in explaining the contrasts in the two poets:

". . . whereas Chaucer's works, given a little practice and occasional reference to a glossary, are not difficult to understand, Sir Gawain, for the purposes of the ordinary reader must be translated into modern English. While Chaucer spoke the tongue that would eventually become our own, based on the culture of London, Oxford and Cambridge, the author of *Sir Gawain* was evidently a native of north-western England, from which he derived both the dialect he used and the wild landscapes that he represented."

305   Let God work! Ah me!
      All hope of help has fled!
      Forfeit my life may be
      But noise I do not dread."

Then he listened no longer, but loudly he called,
310 "Who has power in this place, high parley to hold?
For none greets Sir Gawain, or give him good day;
If any would a word with him, let him walk forth
And speak now or never, to speed his affairs."
"Abide," said one on the bank above over his head,
315 "And what I promised you once shall straightway be
   given."
Yet he stayed not his grindstone, nor stinted its noise,
But worked awhile at his whetting before he would rest,
And then he comes around a crag, from a cave in the rocks,
Hurtling out of hiding with a hateful weapon,
15 | 320 A Danish ax[17] devised for that day's deed,   **17. Danish ax:** A
With a broad blade and bright, bent in a curve,   long-bladed ax.
Filed to a fine edge—four feet it measured
By the length of the lace that was looped round the haft.
And in form as at first, the fellow all green,
325 His lordly face and his legs, his locks and his beard,
Save that firm upon two feet forward he strides,
Sets a hand on the ax-head, the haft to the earth;
When he came to the cold stream, and cared not to wade,
He vaults over on his ax, and advances amain
330 On a broad bank of snow, overbearing and brisk of mood.
        Little did the knight incline
        When face to face they stood;
        Said the other man, "Friend mine,
        It seems your word holds good!"

335 "God love you, Sir Gawain!" said the Green Knight then,
"And well met this morning, man, at my place!
And you have followed me faithfully and found me betimes,
And on the business between us we both are agreed:
Twelve months ago today you took what was yours,
340 And you at this New Year must yield me the same.
And we have met in these mountains, remote from all eyes:
There is none here to halt us or hinder our sport;
Unhasp your high helm, and have here your wages;
Make no more demur than I did myself
345 When you hacked off my head with one hard blow."
"No, by God," said Sir Gawain, "that granted me life,
I shall grudge not the guerdon,[18] grim though it prove;   **18. guerdon:** Reward.
And you may lay on as you like till the last of my part be
   paid."

from Sir Gawain and the Green Knight   179

15 Enrichment The Danish ax was named for the Vikings who used it. It was a kind of battle-ax with a very long blade, and usually without a spike on the back. The Green Knight's weapon, the gisarme, was a battle-ax complete with a spike.

16 Discussion Although a hero, Sir Gawain is humanized primarily through two actions. What are they? What is the effect of these failings on the reader? On the Green Knight? Compare this presentation of the hero with that of Beowulf. Which do you prefer and why?

17 Discussion How does the author maintain suspense in this scene? Is Sir Gawain's anger justified?

350 He proffered, with good grace,
His bare neck to the blade,
And feigned a cheerful face:
He scorned to seem afraid.

Then the grim man in green gathers his strength,
355 Heaves high the heavy ax to hit him the blow.
With all the force in his frame he fetches it aloft,
With a grimace as grim as he would grind him to bits;
Had the blow he bestowed been as big as he threatened,
A good knight and gallant had gone to his grave.

16 360 But Gawain at the great ax glanced up aside
As down it descended with death-dealing force,
And his shoulders shrank a little from the sharp iron.
Abruptly the brawny man breaks off the stroke,
And then reproved with proud words that prince among knights.
365 "You are not Gawain the glorious," the green man said,
"That never fell back on field in the face of the foe,
And now you flee for fear, and have felt no harm:
Such news of that knight I never heard yet!
I moved not a muscle when you made to strike,
370 Nor caviled at the cut in King Arthur's house;
My head fell to my feet, yet steadfast I stood,
And you, all unharmed, are wholly dismayed—
Wherefore the better man I, by all odds, must be."
Said Gawain, "Strike once more;
375 I shall neither flinch nor flee;
But if my head falls to the floor
There is no mending me!"

"But go on, man, in God's name, and get to the point!
Deliver me my destiny, and do it out of hand,
380 For I shall stand to the stroke and stir not an inch
Till your ax has hit home—on my honor I swear it!"
"Have at thee then!" said the other, and heaves it aloft,
And glares down as grimly as he had gone mad.
He made a mighty feint, but marred not his hide;
385 Withdrew the ax adroitly before it did damage.
Gawain gave no ground, nor glanced up aside,
But stood still as a stone, or else a stout stump

17 That is held in hard earth by a hundred roots.
Then merrily does he mock him, the man all in green:
390 "So now you have your nerve again, I needs must strike;
Uphold the high knighthood that Arthur bestowed,
And keep your neck-bone clear, if this cut allows!"
Then was Gawain gripped with rage, and grimly he said.

Grammar in Action

An **adverb** is a word that modifies a verb, an adjective, or another adverb. Experienced writers use adverbs to make their descriptions more detailed and precise. Note how the adverb adds color and precision to the following sentences:

WITHOUT ADVERB: She runs to her car in the parking lot.
WITH ADVERB: She runs gracefully to her car in the parking lot.
WITHOUT ADVERB: He fields the ball and throws it to first base.
WITH ADVERBS: He fields the ball smoothly and throws it effortlessly to first base.

The author of *Sir Gawain and the Green Knight* also uses adverbs effectively:

"Have at thee then!" said the other, and heaves it aloft,
And glares down as *grimly* as he had gone mad.
He made a mighty feint, but marred not his hide;
Withdrew the ax *adroitly* before it did damage.

The adverbs in this passage add a great deal of personality. They tell, respectively, *how* the green man "glares" and *the manner in which* he withdraws his ax. The adverb *adroitly*, by the way, is a very interesting word. It derives from the French word

"Why, thrash away, tyrant, I tire of your threats;
395 You make such a scene, you must frighten yourself."
Said the green fellow, "In faith, so fiercely you speak
That I shall finish this affair, nor further grace allow."
            He stands prepared to strike
            And scowls with both lip and brow;
400   No marvel if the man mislike
            Who can hope no rescue now.

He gathered up the grim ax and guided it well:
Let the barb at the blade's end brush the bare throat;
He hammered down hard, yet harmed him no whit
405 Save a scratch on one side, that severed the skin;
The end of the hooked edge entered the flesh,
And a little blood lightly leapt to the earth.
And when the man beheld his own blood bright on the
    snow,
He sprang a spear's length with feet spread wide,
410 Seized his high helm, and set it on his head,
Shoved before his shoulders the shield at his back,
Bares his trusty blade, and boldly he speaks—
Not since he was a babe born of his mother
Was he once in this world one half so blithe—
415 "Have done with your hacking—harry me no more!
I have borne, as behooved, one blow in this place;
If you make another move I shall meet it midway
And promptly, I promise you, pay back each blow with
    brand.
            One stroke acquits me here;
420   So did our covenant stand
            In Arthur's court last year—
            Wherefore, sir, hold your hand!"

He lowers the long ax and leans on it there,
Sets his arms on the head, the haft on the earth,
425 And beholds the bold knight that bides there afoot,
How he faces him fearless, fierce in full arms,
And plies him with proud words—it pleases him well.
Then once again gaily to Gawain he calls,
And in a loud voice and lusty, delivers these words:
430 "Bold fellow, on this field your anger forbear!
No man has made demands here in manner uncouth,
Nor done, save as duly determined at court.
I owed you a hit and you have it; be happy therewith!
The rest of my rights here I freely resign.
435 Had I been a bit busier, a buffet, perhaps,
I could have dealt more directly; and done you some harm.

18

from *Sir Gawain and the Green Knight*   181

18 **Discussion** When the Green Knight finally delivers the blow, what does it amount to? How does Gawain react when he sees his own blood on the snow?

droit, which means "right." Apparently, people believed that actions performed with the right hand would be done skillfully.

Student Activity 1. Find two other adverbs in the poem and explain how each makes the action more vivid.

Student Activity 2. Find a lively description in your favorite story, poem, or novel. Then identify all the adverbs that the author has used and retype the passage, eliminating every adverb. Compare and contrast the original passage with the one you have created.

Literary Focus The Green Knight discloses that his first and second feints, or pretended blows, did not touch Sir Gawain because, in their promised exchange of winnings, Sir Gawain had in fact given back to the Knight what he had won that day—in each case, a kiss from the Green Knight's wife. However, because Sir Gawain had kept the girdle that would guard him from harm and thus had not lived up to his bargain, he received the third blow, although it was only a token blow, a scratch. What is the Green Knight's assessment of Sir Gawain's overall behavior? Do you blame Sir Gawain for his act of deception? Does Sir Gawain blame himself?

First I flourished with a feint, in frolicsome mood,
And left your hide unhurt—and here I did well
By the fair terms we fixed on the first night;
440 And fully and faithfully you followed accord:
Gave over all your gains as a good man should.
A second feint, sir, I assigned for the morning
You kissed my comely wife—each kiss you restored.
For both of these there behooved but two feigned blows by
    right.
445   True men pay what they owe;
           No danger then in sight.
           You failed at the third throw,
           So take my tap, sir knight.

"For that is my belt about you, that same braided girdle,
450 My wife it was that wore it; I know well the tale,
And the count of your kisses and your conduct too,
And the wooing of my wife—it was all my scheme!
She made trial of a man most faultless by far
Of all that ever walked over the wide earth;
455 As pearls to white peas, more precious and prized,
So is Gawain, in good faith, to other gay knights.
Yet you lacked, sir, a little in loyalty there,
But the cause was not cunning, nor courtship either,
But that you loved your own life; the less, then, to blame."
460 The other stout knight in a study stood a long while,
So gripped with grim rage that his great heart shook.
All the blood of his body burned in his face
As he shrank back in shame from the man's sharp speech.
The first words that fell from the fair knight's lips:
465 "Accursed be a cowardly and covetous heart!
In you is villainy and vice, and virtue laid low!"
Then he grasps the green girdle and lets go the knot,
Hands it over in haste, and hotly he says:
"Behold there my falsehood, ill hap betide it!
470 Your cut taught me cowardice, care for my life,
And coveting came after, contrary both
To largesse and loyalty belonging to knights.
Now am I faulty and false, that fearful was ever
Of disloyalty and lies, bad luck to them both! and greed.
475   I confess, knight, in this place,
           Most dire is my misdeed;
           Let me gain back your good grace,
           And thereafter I shall take heed."

Then the other laughed aloud, and lightly he said,
480 "Such harm as I have had, I hold it quite healed.

GAWAIN RECEIVING THE GREEN GIRDLE
Woodcut by Fritz Kredel from Gardner
The Complete Works of the Gawain Poet, 1965
The University of Chicago

from *Sir Gawain and the Green Knight* **183**

Humanities Note

Fine art, *Gawain Receiving the Green Girdle,* by Fritz Kredel. Fritz Kredel (1900–1973) was a German-born American artist. He was educated in Germany at the Realgymnasium in Darmstadt and the Kunstgewerbeschule in Offenbach. Kredel worked chiefly in woodcuts, prints made from designs cut into wooden blocks. He has won many awards both in the United States and in Europe for his book illustrations.

This woodcut is done in the ancient method of a medieval woodcut. Kredel has maintained the straightforward vitality of the artists of that time. You could mention to your students that if the illustration were compared with a medieval woodcut, it would be difficult to tell, from style alone, which is contemporary.

Kredel made a point of thoroughly studying a text before he illustrated it. He felt that in illustration the artist should strive to glorify the author's work, not to overshadow it. This philosophy is a success in *Gawain.* The simple lines and sparse detail give an accurate portrayal of the characters without distracting our focus of attention from the poem.

1. Tell why you think the style and overall effect of the woodcut is or is not well suited to the poem.
2. Do you feel that highly realistic oil or watercolor paintings are usually preferable to line drawings on woodcuts such as this? Explain your answer.

20 **Discussion** Why must Sir Gawain go through this ordeal? What does the ordeal achieve for Sir Gawain? In what way is the ordeal symbolic? Note the time of year. How does this add to the symbolism?

Reader's Response Do you think that heroic acts must be dangerous and risky? Why?

You are so fully confessed, your failings made known,
And bear the plain penance of the point of my blade,
I hold you polished as a pearl, as pure and as bright
As you had lived free of fault since first you were born.

485 And I give you, sir, this girdle that is gold-hemmed
And green as my garments, that, Gawain, you may
Be mindful of this meeting when you mingle in throng
With nobles of renown—and known by this token
How it chanced at the Green Chapel, to chivalrous knights.

490 And you shall in this New Year come yet again
And we shall finish out our feast in my fair hall, with
    cheer.''

Commentary

Humorist Samuel Clemens took a lighter look at the King Arthur legend in his 1889 novel, *A Connecticut Yankee in King Arthur's Court.* A Hartford munitions maker, clunked on the head ''during a misunderstanding conducted with crowbars,'' wakes up to find himself in Camelot, England, in the year 513. ''The Boss,'' as he comes to be called, has opinions on everything. Here he discusses the proper medieval attire for following Sir Gawaine:

''I was to have an early breakfast, and start at dawn, for that was the usual way; but I had the demon's own time with my armor, and this delayed me a little. It is troublesome to get into, and there is so much detail. First you wrap a layer or two of blanket around your body, for a sort of cushion and to keep off the cold iron; then you put on your sleeves and a shirt of chain mail—these are made of small steel links woven together, and they form a fabric so flexible that if you toss your shirt onto the floor, it slumps into a pile like a peck of wet fishnet; it is very heavy and is nearly the most uncomfortablest material in the world for a nightshirt . . . then you put on your shoes—flat-boats roofed over the interleaving bands of steel . . . and you begin to feel crowded; then you hitch onto the breastplate the half-petticoat of broad overlapping bands of steel which hangs down in front but is scalloped out behind you so you can sit down, and isn't any real improvement on an inverted coalscuttle, either for looks or for wear, or to wipe your hands on; next you belt on your sword; then you put your stove-pipe joints onto your arms, your iron gauntlets onto your hands, your iron rat-trap onto your head . . . This is no time to dance. Well, a man that is packed away like that is a nut that isn't worth the cracking, there is so little of the meat, when you get down to it, by comparison to the shell.'' Imagine getting on the horse!

THINKING ABOUT THE SELECTION

Recalling

1. What kind of challenge does King Arthur at first think the Green Knight has in mind?
2. The Green Knight's challenge has two parts. (a) What is Sir Gawain to do immediately? (b) What is he to do a year later?
3. What does Sir Gawain do at the Green Chapel to cause the Green Knight to question his valor?
4. Why does the Green Knight only scratch Sir Gawain with his ax?

Interpreting

5. The Green Knight laughs at the members of the Round Table in line 92. Why?
6. When Sir Gawain sees the Green Chapel, who does he think the Green Knight may be?
7. In lines 465–477 why is Sir Gawain upset?

Applying

8. What modern occupation do you think comes closest to matching the duties and ideals of the Knights of the Round Table? Explain your answer.

ANALYZING LITERATURE

Understanding Medieval Romances

Most medieval romances
- Embody the ideals of chivalry
- Are set in a remote time or place
- Emphasize rank and social distinctions
- Convey a sense of the supernatural
- Present a hero engaged in pure adventure
- Have a loose structure, lacking in unity
- Include love as a major plot element
- Feature spontaneous, unmotivated fighting

1. Which of these characteristics does *Sir Gawain and the Green Knight* NOT display?
2. In medieval romances, a hero seldom admits failure. Does Sir Gawain follow this tradition? Explain.

CRITICAL THINKING AND READING

Making Inferences About Chivalry

Human actions and motivations reflect the ideals of the society in which people live. Today a community leader might laugh off the kind of challenge the Green Knight hurls at King Arthur. You can infer from the way Arthur and Sir Gawain react, however, that in the age of chivalry one took seriously such challenges to one's courage.

1. What ideals of medieval society can you infer from Sir Gawain's offer to accept the challenge made to Arthur?
2. What ideals can you infer from Sir Gawain's distress at the end of the poem, even after he has withstood the blow of the ax?

UNDERSTANDING LANGUAGE

Using Abstract Words

An **abstract word** expresses a quality that cannot be directly perceived through the senses. For example, although you can see a *knight* or an *ax* (concrete words), you cannot see, hear, touch, taste, or smell *chivalry, courage,* or *loyalty*. Often the best way to define an abstract word is with a specific example:

Sir Gawain set out for the Green Chapel
even though he was certain it meant death.
That is what I call *bravery*.

Write a specific example that shows the meaning of each of the following abstract words.
1. grandeur   3. perspicacity
2. temerity   4. flightiness

THINKING AND WRITING

Evaluating the Medieval Romance

One of the world's most famous novels, *Don Quixote* by Miguel de Cervantes, satirizes medieval romances like *Sir Gawain and the Green Knight*. What aspects of the medieval romance do you think Cervantes may have felt deserved satire? Jot down your answers to this question. Arrange your answers in a logical order for development in an essay. Write the essay. Make any revisions that seem necessary.

from *Sir Gawain and the Green Knight*   **185**

More About the Selection The morality play, of which *Everyman* is the finest example, emerged in English drama in the fifteenth century. Basically a dramatized sermon appealing more to the intellect than to the emotions, it strove to answer the question "How can man save his soul?" Written in the form of an allegory, the typical morality play tended to be somewhat dull and didactic. Consequently, it was often enlivened by humor, particularly in the portrayal of the evil characters. *Everyman,* however, was compelling enough to do without slapstick comedy to enthrall audiences. It has been performed by both amateur and professional actors for more than four centuries. What forms of literature or popular entertainment do we use today to teach lessons and promote values?

Critical Evaluation Contemporary attention has been given generously to *Everyman.* In a book called the *Genius of the Early English Theater* Sylvan Barnet notes that the play "has had a considerable stage history since it was revived in 1901 by William Poel, but it is best known on the stage in the German adaptation by Hugo von Hofmannsthal, *Jedermann* (1911), performed annually at Salzburg since 1920, except 1937–45, when the Nazis prohibited its production."

1475[?]

English theater began with what are called miracle plays, sometimes referred to as mystery plays. The aim of a miracle play is to dramatize an incident from the Bible. Morality plays, which came later, deal with the human struggle between virtues and vices. They feature characters that represent abstract qualities such as Beauty, Good Deeds, Knowledge, and Death. The most famous and sophisticated of the morality plays is *Everyman,* written by an unknown playwright.

The English theater originated in the medieval church. To make religious services more meaningful and impressive, the clergy began inserting bits of dialogue into the mass. These miniature dramas, much expanded, became miracle plays. The plays moved outdoors, lost their direct connection with the church, and became a popular form of entertainment. The miracle plays were performed on wagons that moved from place to place within a town or city. Each wagon stopped at designated stations, presenting the same play over and over. A viewer could sometimes see as many as fifty miracle plays by staying in one place throughout the day and watching as the procession of wagons passed by.

Morality plays such as *Everyman* grew out of these miracle plays and also out of medieval allegories, not all of them English, in which the characters are abstractions—Fear, Courtesy, Greed, Delight, and so on. *Everyman* resembles an earlier Dutch morality play, *Elckerlijk,* but since the subject matter of the two plays, the summoning of death, is so common, both may come from a single source. The theme of *Everyman* is the salvation of the soul as death approaches. When Everyman is summoned by Death, he finds that none of his friends and relatives—Fellowship, Cousin, Kindred, or Goods—will keep him company. As he makes his descent into the grave, only Good Deeds will go with him.

This play has enjoyed extraordinary success since its appearance in the fifteenth century. The allegory has been translated into many languages, has been used by later writers as the basis of their plays, and has often been performed, both as an academic revival and a commercial production, on the twentieth-century stage.

Objectives

1 To understand morality plays
2 To interpret names as symbols
3 To perform a play
4 To discuss a morality play

Support Material

Teaching Portfolio
Teacher Backup, p. 143
Grammar in Action Worksheet, *Understanding the Evolution of the Language,* p. 147
Usage and Mechanics Worksheet, p. 149
Vocabulary Check, p. 150
Analyzing Literature Worksheet, *Understanding the Morality Play,* p. 151

Language Worksheet, *Using Names As Symbols,* p. 152
Selection Test, p. 153

from Everyman

Literary Forms

Morality Play. Medieval morality plays have a singleness of purpose, to dramatize the conflict between the power of good and evil for control of one's soul. Although the plays are intended to entertain audiences, they also seek to teach strict lessons of right and wrong. Essentially religious, morality plays are allegories in which characters appear as abstract virtues and vices. By their very nature the characters are one-dimensional, lacking the complexity found in characters in more sophisticated drama. The plays were originally produced for a middle-class town audience, many of whose members could neither read nor write. For the most part the plays are anonymously written. This may seem strange to you, because *Everyman* and other moralities came into being at a time when records were kept. A main reason for the anonymity of writers is (as the morality plays teach) that worldly ambition counted for little in the Church-dominated culture of that era. Lack of credit for individual achievement was the order of the day. No one knows, for instance, who designed the magnificent Gothic cathedrals or created the stained glass and statues that adorn them. The medieval architect and sculptor, like the medieval playwright, worked primarily for the glory of God.

Commentary

Four different copies of *Everyman* survive —two whole, one damaged, one fragmentary. It is thought that all four texts were printed between 1508 and 1537. The text used most often now, known as the Britwell copy, is the one reprinted in 1904. The title page of this slender volume is printed with the well-known wood-cut of Everyman. In this picture he sports a small, round hat with a feather sticking jauntily out of the brim and a short open cape with broad lapels. He holds his hands up sadly, palms turned outward. His expression is upset as he turns toward the skeletal, eerie figure of Death, who is sternly summoning him. The background is dotted with what look like graveyard crosses; Death holds what appears to be a huge scroll, probably the list of those to be summoned next. If you were preparing an edition of *Everyman*, what cover illustration would you provide?

Writing

Assume you are writing a play to dramatize a principle such as "Honesty is the best policy" or "Haste makes waste." Write the principle. Then list at least five characters you would cast in the play. Give them abstract names like Deceit or Punctuality.

Guide for Interpreting 187

Literary Focus Review the characteristics of allegory. What will the title character represent?

Writing/Prior Knowledge Choose one of the given principles and suggest a character or two who might appear in the play. Then have students suggest other suitable characters. The class might discuss some of the actions these characters might perform that match their names.

Spelling Tip Point out to students the double *r* in *terrestrial*.

Vocabulary

Preteach the following vocabulary words:
reverence (rev′ ər əns) *n.*: Deep respect or awe (l. 2)
transitory (tran′ sə tôr′ ē) *adj.*: Temporary; fleeting (l. 6)
tempests (tem′ pistz) *n.*: Violent outbursts (l. 48)
respite (res′ pit) *n.*: Postponement; delay (l. 100)
terrestrial (tə res′ trē əl) *adj.*: Of this world; earthly (l. 155)
caitiff (kāt′ if) *n.*: An evil person (l. 171)

Motivation/Prior Knowledge
Imagine that you knew that Death was coming for you. In fact, you even had the opportunity to talk to Death. What would you say to him? What would you request of him? The title character in this play is faced with this situation.

Thematic Idea Another selection that deals with the theme of saving the soul is *Tragical History of Doctor Faustus,* by Christopher Marlowe, page 233.

Purpose-Setting Question The Messenger, whose speech serves as a prologue, opens the play with a brief summary of what it proposes to convey. What is that message?

1 **Reading Strategy** Define *transitory*. What theme is implied?

2 **Reading Strategy** Before your students read God's speech, ask them to keep the following questions in mind: How does God characterize man and the condition of the world? What has man forgotten? With what is he preoccupied? Is he improving?

from # Everyman

Here beginneth a treatise[1] how the High Father of Heaven sendeth DEATH *to summon every creature to come and give account of their lives in this world, and is in manner of a moral play.*

1. treatise: Narrative.

[*Enter* MESSENGER.]

MESSENGER. I pray, you all give your audience,
And hear this matter with reverence,
By figure[2] a moral play.
The Summoning of Everyman called it is,
5   That of our lives and ending shows
How transitory we be all day.[3]
The matter is wonder precious,
But the intent of it is more gracious
And sweet to bear away.
10   The story saith: Man, in the beginning
Look well, and take good heed to the ending,
Be you never so gay.
You think sin in the beginning full sweet,
Which in the end causeth the soul to weep,
15   When the body lieth in clay.
Here shall you see how fellowship and jollity,
Both strength, pleasure, and beauty,
Will fade from thee as flower in May.
For ye shall hear how our Heaven-King
20   Calleth Everyman to a general reckoning.
Give audience and hear what he doth say.

2. by figure: In form.

3. all day: Always.

[*Exit* MESSENGER. *Enter* GOD.]

GOD. I perceive, here in my majesty,
How that all creatures be to me unkind,[4]
Living without dread in worldly prosperity.
25   Of ghostly[5] sight the people be so blind,
Drowned in sin, they know me not for their God.
In worldly riches is all their mind:
They fear not of my righteousness the sharp rod;
My law that I showed when I for them died
30   They forget clean, and shedding of my blood red.
I hanged between two,[6] it cannot be denied:
To get them life I suffered to be dead.
I healed their feet, with thorns hurt was my head.
I could do no more than I did, truly—
35   And now I see the people do clean forsake me.

4. unkind: Thoughtless.

5. ghostly: Spiritual.

6. two: The two thieves between whom Christ was crucified.

3 They use the seven deadly sins damnable,
As pride, coveitise,[7] wrath, and gluttony
Now in the world be made commendable.
And thus they leave of angels the heavenly company.

40 Every man liveth so after his own pleasure,
And yet of their life they be nothing sure.
I see the more that I them forbear,
The worse they be from year to year:
All that liveth appaireth[8] fast.

4 45 Therefore I will, in all the haste,
Have a reckoning of every man's person.
For, and[9] I leave the people thus alone
In their life and wicked tempests,
Verily they will become much worse than beasts;

50 For now one would by envy another up eat.
Charity do they all clean forgeet.
I hoped well that every man
In my glory should make his mansion,
And thereto I had them all elect.[10]

55 But now I see, like traitors deject,[11]
They thank me not for the pleasure that I to[12] them
meant,
Nor yet for their being that I them have lent.
I proffered the people great multitude of mercy,
And few there be that asketh it heartily.[13]

60 They be so cumbered[14] with worldly riches
That needs on them I must do justice—
On every man living without fear.
Where art thou, Death, thou mighty messenger?

5 [*Enter* DEATH.]

DEATH. Almighty, God, I am here at your will,
65 Your commandment to fulfull.
6 **GOD.** Go thou to Everyman,
And show him, in my name,
A pilgrimage he must on him take,
Which he in no wise may escape;

7 70 And that he bring with him a sure reckoning
Without delay or any tarrying.
DEATH. Lord, I will in the world go run over all,[15]
And cruelly out-search both great and small.

[*Exit* GOD.]

Everyman will I beset that liveth beastly
75 Out of God's laws, and dreadeth not folly.
He that loveth riches I will strike with my dart,
His sight to blind, and from heaven to depart[16]—
Except that Almsdeeds[17] be his good friend—
In hell for to dwell, world without end.

7. coveitise: Avarice.

8. appaireth: Degenerates.

9. and: If.

10. elect: Chosen.
11. deject: Abased.
12. to: For.

13. heartily: Sincerely.
14. cumbered: Encumbered.

15. over all: Everywhere.

16. depart: Separate.
17. Almsdeeds: Deeds of mercy; good deeds.

from *Everyman* 189

3 Enrichment The Seven Deadly Sins as stated by the Church are pride, covetousness, lust, anger, gluttony, envy, and sloth.

4 Discussion In the midst of this indictment, God decides to "have a reckoning of every man's person." What does this mean?

5 Literary Focus What quality of allegory is demonstrated here?

6 Clarification Note that God here refers for the first time to Everyman as a specific person. Before this, he has used the term generally.

7 Literary Focus Again the reckoning is mentioned. Death is instructed to tell Everyman to bring it on his projected journey. What is that journey?

8 **Master Teacher Note** Point out how natural this conversation between Death and Everyman is. Everyman reacts in most predictable ways. He admits he is unready, offers a bribe, begs for a twelve-year postponement, is then willing to settle for a single day, looks for ameliorating conditions, and despairs. Is that realistic?

9 **Discussion** What is Death's rationale for refusing Everyman's bribe?

80 Lo, yonder I see Everyman walking:
Full little he thinketh on my coming;
His mind is on fleshly lusts and his treasure,
And great pain it shall cause him to endure
Before the Lord, Heaven-King.

[*Enter* EVERYMAN.]

85 Everyman, stand still! Whither art thou going
Thus gaily? Hast thou thy Maker forgeet?

EVERYMAN. Why askest thou?
Why wouldest thou weet?[18]

DEATH. Yea, sir, I will show you:
In great haste I am sent to thee
From God out of his majesty.

EVERYMAN. What! sent to me?

DEATH. Yea, certainly.
Though thou have forgot him here,
95 He thinketh on thee in the heavenly sphere,
As, ere we depart, thou shalt know.

EVERYMAN. What desireth God of me?

DEATH. That shall I show thee:
A reckoning he will needs have
100 Without any longer respite.

EVERYMAN. To give a reckoning longer leisure I crave.
This blind[19] matter troubleth my wit.

DEATH. On thee thou must take a long journay:
Therefore thy book of count[20] with thee thou bring,
105 For turn again thou cannot by no way.
And look thou be sure of thy reckoning,
For before God thou shalt answer and shew
Thy many bad deeds and good but a few—
How thou hast spent thy life and in what wise,
110 Before the Chief Lord of Paradise.
Have ado that we were in that way,[21]
For weet thou well thou shalt make none attornay.[22]

EVERYMAN. Full unready I am such reckoning to give.
I know thee not. What messenger art thou?

115 DEATH. I am Death that no man dreadeth,[23]
For every man I 'rest,[24] and no man spareth;
For it is God's commandment
That all to me should be obedient.

EVERYMAN. O Death, thou comest when I had thee least in mind.
120 In thy power it lieth me to save:
Yet of my good[25] will I give thee, if thou will be kind,
Yea, a thousand pound shalt thou have—
And defer this matter till another day.

DEATH. Everyman, it may not be, by no way.

18. **weet:** Know.

19. **blind:** Unexpected.

20. **count:** Accounts.

21. **Have ado . . . way:** Let us get started.
22. **none attornay:** None appear in your place.

23. **that no man dreadeth:** That fears no one.
24. **'rest:** Arrest.

25. **good:** Goods.

Grammar in Action

The **evolution of a language** is a complex and frequently slow process. Over the course of centuries all languages show signs of changing from their original forms to different ones that result either from native factors or from outside influences. In this sense, English as a language has altered its shape in much the same way as ancient Greek, or Hebrew, or Russian.

Specialists divide the history of such evolution with terms like Old English, Middle English, or contemporary conversational American English. Regard this example of a sentence from *Everyman* as a good sample of how a simple question was asked during the Middle Ages:

Whither art thou going
thus gaily? (1. 85)

Today we would say the same this way:

Where are you going
in such a good mood?

Another sentence, "Hast thou thy Maker forgeet," evolves from that wording into "Have you forgotten your Maker?" in today's parlance.

125   I set nought by[26] gold, silver, nor riches,
    Nor by pope, emperor, king, duke, nor princes,
    For, and I would receive gifts great,
    All the world I might get.
    But my custom is clean contrary:
130   I give thee no respite. Come hence and not tarry!
    EVERYMAN. Alas, shall I have no longer respite?
    I may say Death giveth no warning.
    To think on thee it maketh my heart sick,
    For all unready is my book of reckoning.
135   But twelve year and I might have a biding,[27]
    My counting-book I would make so clear
    That my reckoning I should not need to fear.
    Wherefore, Death, I pray thee, for God's mercy,
    Spare me till I be provided of remedy.
140   **DEATH.** Thee availeth not to cry, weep, and pray;
    But haste thee lightly[28] that thou were gone that journey,
    And prove[29] thy friends, if thou can.
    For weet thou well the tide[30] abideth no man,
    And in the world each living creature
145   For Adam's sin must die of nature.[31]
    EVERYMAN. Death, if I should this pilgrimage take
    And my reckoning surely make,
    Show me, for saint[32] charity,
    Should I not come again shortly?
150   **DEATH.** No, Everyman. And thou be once there,
    Thou mayst never more come here,
    Trust me verily.
    EVERYMAN. O gracious God in the high seat celestial,
    Have mercy on me in this most need!
155   Shall I have company from this vale terrestrial
    Of mine acquaintance that way me to lead?
    DEATH. Yea, if any be so hardy
    That would go with thee and bear thee company.
    Hie[33] thee that thou were gone to God's magnificence,
160   Thy reckoning to give before his presence.
    What, weenest[34] thou thy life is given thee,
    And thy worldly goods also?
    EVERYMAN. I had weened so, verily.
    DEATH. Nay, nay, it was but lent thee.
165   For as soon as thou art go,
    Another a while shall have it and then go therefro,
    Even as thou hast done.
    Everyman, thou art mad! Thou hast thy wits[35] five,
    And here on earth will not amend thy live![36]
170   For suddenly I do come.
    EVERYMAN. O wretched caitiff! Whither shall I flee
    That I might 'scape this endless sorrow?

26. set nought by: Care nothing for.

27. twelve year . . . biding: If I might have a twelve-year delay.

28. lightly: Quickly.
29. prove: Test.
30. tide: Time.

31. of nature: Naturally.

32. saint: Holy.

33. Hie: Hasten.

34. weenest: Suppose.

35. wits: Senses.
36. thy live: In thy life.

from *Everyman*   191

Student Activity 1. Find five other examples on these pages of short sentences that contain antiquated ways of expressing ideas. List those sentences. Then reword them to express the same thought in ways that would be correct today.

Student Activity 2. Change each of these sentences into ones using the conventions of Middle English that you have read in *Everyman.*
1. Are you going to that faraway church?
2. Where is your friend buried?
3. Why does it take so long?
4. Can you give me some help with this?
5. Would you please stop!

11
175   Now, gentle Death, spare me till tomorrow,
       That I may amend me
       With good advisement.[37]
       DEATH. Nay, thereto I will not consent,
       Nor no man will I respite,
       But to the heart suddenly I shall smite,
       Without any advisement.
180   And now out of thy sight I will me hie:
       See thou make thee ready shortly,
       For thou mayst say this is the day
       That no man living may 'scape away.
       [*Exit* DEATH.]

37. advisement: Preparation.

12
Everyman calls on Fellowship, Cousin, Kindred, and Goods (his friends, relatives, and wealth) to accompany him on his journey, but they all refuse and desert him. Everyman then summons his Good Deeds and Knowledge, and Knowledge leads him to Confession, who comforts him. Following his meeting with Confession, Everyman is assisted by Good Deeds, Knowledge, Beauty, Strength, Five-Wits (Five Senses), and Discretion (the attributes that make up an integrated person) in making up his book of accounts. Then each one, except for Good Deeds and Knowledge, leaves him as he makes final preparations for his journey to the grave.

       EVERYMAN. O Jesu, help, all hath forsaken me!
185   **GOOD DEEDS.** Nay, Everyman, I will bide with thee:
       I will not forsake thee indeed;
       Thou shalt find me a good friend at need.
       EVERYMAN. Gramercy,[38] Good Deeds! Now may I true friends
          see.
       They have forsaken me every one—
190   I loved them better than my Good Deeds alone.
       Knowledge, will ye forsake me also?
       KNOWLEDGE. Yea, Everyman, when ye to Death shall go,
       But not yet, for no manner of danger.
       EVERYMAN. Gramercy, Knowledge, with all my heart!
13 195 **KNOWLEDGE.** Nay, yet will I not from hence depart
       Till I see where ye shall become.[39]
       EVERYMAN. Methink, alas, that I must be gone
       To make my reckoning and my debts pay,
       For I see my time is nigh spent away.
200   Take example, all ye that this do hear or see,
       How they that I best loved do forsake me,
       Except my Good Deeds that bideth truly.
       GOOD DEEDS. All earthly things is but vanity.

38. Gramercy: Good thanks.

39. where ye shall become: What shall become of you.

Beauty, Strength, and Discretion do man forsake,
205 Foolish friends and kinsmen that fair spake—
All fleeth save Good Deeds, and that am I.
EVERYMAN. Have mercy on me, God most mighty,
And stand by me, thou mother and maid, holy Mary!
GOOD DEEDS. Fear not: I will speak for thee.
210 **EVERYMAN.** Here I cry God mercy!
GOOD DEEDS. Short our end, and 'minish our pain.[40]
Let us go, and never come again.
EVERYMAN. Into thy hands, Lord, my soul I commend:
Receive it, Lord, that it be not lost.
215 As thou me boughtest,[41] so me defend,
And save me from the fiend's boast,
That I may appear with that blessed host
That shall be saved at the day of doom.
In manus tuas, of mights most,
220 Forever *commendo spiritum meum.*[42]

[EVERYMAN *and* GOOD DEEDS *descend into the grave.*]

KNOWLEDGE. Now hath he suffered that we all shall endure,
The Good Deeds shall make all sure.
Now hath he made ending,
Methinketh that I hear angels sing
225 And make great joy and melody
Where Everyman's soul received shall be.
ANGEL. [*within*] Come, excellent elect spouse to Jesu![43]
Here above thou shalt go
Because of thy singular virtue.
230 Now the soul is taken the body fro,
Thy reckoning is crystal clear:
Now shalt thou into the heavenly sphere—
Unto the which all ye shall come
That liveth well before the day of doom.

[*Enter Doctor.*[44]]

235 **DOCTOR.** This memorial[45] men may have in mind:
Ye hearers, take it of worth, old and young,
And forsake Pride, for he deceiveth you in the end.
And remember Beauty, Five-Wits, Strength, and
    Discretion,
They all at the last do Everyman forsake,
240 Save his Good Deeds there doth he take—
But beware, for and they be small,
Before God he hath no help at all—
None excuse may be there for Everyman.
Alas, how shall he do than?[46]
245 For after death amends may no man make,
For then mercy and pity doth him forsake.

40. Short . . . pain: Make our death quick and diminish our pain.

41. boughtest: Redeemed.

42. *In manus . . . meum:* "Into thy hands, O greatest of powers, I commend my spirit forever." (Latin)

43. spouse to Jesu: Everyman's soul is referred to as the bride of Jesus.

44. doctor: A learned theologian.
45. memorial: Reminder.

46. than: Then.

14 Literary Focus The Doctor summarizes the message of the play in this concluding speech. Why is he chosen for that role?

from *Everyman* 193

Humanities Note

Fine Art, *The Old Man and Death,* Joseph Wright of Derby.

Joseph Wright of Derby (1734–1797) called himself "of Derby" to distinguish himself from another painter who worked at the same time, Richard Wright. Joseph Wright was a precociously talented child. He later studied portrait painting with Thomas Hudson and traveled to Italy to continue his study of art. Joseph Wright of Derby is remembered for his genre and landscape paintings.

This painting, *The Old Man and Death,* was completed about 1774. It is a commentary on man's fear of death. The choice of a subject that expressed a strong emotion shows Wright's attraction to Romanticism in art. A skillful painter, Wright was able to convey the terror of the old man and the eerie mood of the setting of the painting.

You might ask the following questions:

1. What comment is the artist making about death?
2. Explain why this painting is an appropriate illustration for *Everyman.*

If his reckoning be not clear when he doth come,
God will say, "*Ite, maledicti, in ignem eternum!*"[47]
And he that hath his account whole and sound,
250   High in heaven he shall be crowned,
Unto which place God bring us all thither,
That we may live body and soul togither.
Thereto help, the Trinity!
Amen, say ye, for saint charity.

47. Ite . . . eternum: "Depart, ye cursed, into everlasting fire." (Latin)

THE OLD MAN AND DEATH, C.1774
Joseph Wright of Derby
Wadsworth Atheneum, Hartford

THINKING ABOUT THE SELECTION

Recalling

1. On what mission does God send Death?
2. What does Everyman request when he first learns the purpose of Death's visit?
3. (a) How does Good Deeds respond to Everyman's plea for companionship? (b) How does Knowledge respond?
4. According to the Doctor, what can be done after death to make up for mistakes or oversights in life? Explain.

Interpreting

5. What is God's main complaint about the way people on earth are behaving?
6. Death repeatedly refuses to give Everyman any additional time. Why?
7. What does Death tell Everyman about the ownership of worldly goods?

Applying

8. How do you account for the fact that stage productions of *Everyman* have continued to be successful up to the present day?

ANALYZING LITERATURE

Understanding a Morality Play

The basic question in a morality play is, "What must I do to be saved?" A struggle occurs between good and evil, virtues and vices, for the possession of one's soul. The characters are persons presented as abstractions: Death, Pride, Strength, Beauty, Knowledge. *Everyman's* plot is restricted to the last part of a typical morality play—the arrival of Death.

1. Find two places in *Everyman* (not at the very beginning or end) where a line or lines directly express the play's message. Write the lines.
2. Which characters represent categories of people rather than abstract qualities?

CRITICAL THINKING AND READING

Interpreting Names as Symbols

The name of a character in literature can be used as a symbol. A **symbol** is a word, person, or object that stands for something beyond itself. For example, a star can stand for achievement. In a morality play like *Everyman,* a character is simply called Achievement, but the star symbol can be used as a character's name for the same purpose—e.g., Brenda Starr. Achievement can also be suggested by a name like Mark Winner. Choose two of the following fictional names and make them into appropriate morality play names. (Example: Mr. Bumble = Stupidity) (1) Mr. Gradgrind (2) Holly Golightly (3) Jack Armstrong (4) Lady Sneerwell (5) Tess Truehart (6) Flem Snopes (7) Daddy Warbucks.

SPEAKING AND LISTENING

Performing in a Play

When you act in a play, you must fully understand your part as the playwright intends it. You must go beyond a mere reading of lines. What is the character's personality? What is his or her motivation?

Go to the library and borrow a recording of a play for which you can also borrow the text. Choose a scene and read it a few times. Then listen to the professional actor read it. Note the stress, the pauses, the emotion. Compare the professional performance with your own.

Next, select a passage from *Everyman* and read it until you understand its meaning and purpose completely. Rehearse it until you know how you want to say every word. If possible, practice it with a tape recorder. Be prepared to read the passage in class.

THINKING AND WRITING

Discussing a Morality Play

Write an essay in which you discuss the playwright's answer in *Everyman* to the morality play question about the conduct of life. Give your opinion of the play's effectiveness. Is the play dramatic? Persuasive? Would it be better if Everyman escaped Death? Explain. When you revise, make sure you have supplied adequate support for your opinion.

from *Everyman* 195

uing success because it deals with the universal question of death and the afterlife.

ANSWERS TO ANALYZING LITERATURE

1. Choices may differ. Here are two possible answers: "For weet thou well the tide abideth no man,/ And in the world each living creature/ For Adam's sin must die of nature (lines 144–146, spoken by Death)." "All earthly things is but vanity./ . . . All fleeth save Good Deeds . . . (lines 203–206, spoken by Good Deeds)."
2. The characters are Fellowship, Cousin, and Kindred. The Doctor may be considered a representative of theologians, or religious philosophers.

ANSWERS TO CRITICAL THINKING AND READING

Answers will differ. Some possibilities are Pedantry, Amorousness, Courage or Strength, Snobbery, Loyalty or Faithfulness, Laziness, and Wealth or Greed.

SPEAKING AND LISTENING

You might consider placing students in groups and giving each group a section of the play. Have them present their portion of the play to the class in a dramatic reading or as a reader's-theater presentation.

THINKING AND WRITING

For help with this assignment, students can refer to Lesson 14, "Writing About Drama," in the Handbook of Writing About Literature.

Publishing Student Writing In writing groups have the students read one another's essays. After all essays have been read, the students should reach a consensus about the effectiveness of the play. By reading excerpts from the group's papers, students can present to the class the decision of the group and the reasons. Establish the consensus of the class.

Closure and Extension

ANSWERS TO THINKING ABOUT THE SELECTION

Recalling

1. Death is sent to bring Everyman to his reckoning.
2. He requests an extension.
3. (a) Good Deeds will follow him all the way. (b) Knowledge will follow him to the grave but no farther.
4. No man can make up for his mistakes after death. There is no mercy or pity after death. If his reckoning is sound, he goes to Heaven; if not, Hell.

Interpreting

5. God's main complaint is that people have forsaken him, forgetting his sacrifice.
6. Death refuses because time waits for no man.
7. Material things are simply lent man during his lifetime.

Applying

8. Answers will differ. One possible answer is that *Everyman* is a contin-

Middle English 1066–1485

THE NORMAN CONQUEST

In the long run, the Norman Conquest may have benefited the English language; in the short run, it was a disaster. As Normans took over the country, so they took over the language, replacing English with French. Norman clergymen ruled the English church, Norman clerks ran the English government, Norman merchants regulated English commerce—and they all spoke French. In effect, the Norman Conquest transformed England virtually overnight into a bilingual country. While most of the English still spoke English at home and among themselves, to survive many learned to understand French if not to speak it. Likewise, many of the French-speaking upper classes understood English, even if they could not speak it.

The immediate changes in English reflect the influence of the conquerors on the conquered. The English lived in a humble *cot* (cottage); the Normans, in a French *maneir* (manor or mansion) or *castel.* The English did the *werc;* the Normans relished the *leisir* and *profit.* Life for the Normans was *asie;* for the English, *hard.* In writing, Latin became the language of business. In 1154, the English monks abandoned their work on the *Anglo-Saxon Chronicle* and a great silence fell on English writing. The victory of Norman French seemed complete. Had things continued in this way, England might well have assumed the language of its conquerors.

Why did English survive? First, English was simply too well rooted to die. It was one thing for writing, controlled by a small group of educated clerks, to adopt Latin and French; it was quite another for the established daily speech of regular people to change. Second, the two cultures quickly intermarried. Thus as early as 1177, a chronicler could write that "the two nations have become so mixed that it is scarcely possible today, speaking of free men, to tell who is English, who is of Norman race." Third, around 1200 King John lost nearly all of his land in France to the French crown. In effect, this forced the Norman lords to make up their minds whether to be French or English.

ENGLISH MAKES A COMEBACK

The appearance of church sermons, prayers, and carols in English in the early part of the thirteenth century heralded the recovery of the language. English words began to sneak into Latin documents. By 1300, almost everyone in England spoke English but only a few also spoke French. A poet of the age, writing in English, was able to report that:

Lewede men cune Ffrensch non
Among an hondryd, unne pis on.

Bayeux Tapestry—Normans Attack the English

(Of French the common men know none Among a hundred, scarcely one.)

Anti-French sentiment during The Hundred Years War with France (1337–1454) greatly encouraged people to speak English rather than French. The Black Death, by causing so many deaths in monasteries and churches, gave rise to a new generation of non-French and Latin speakers who took over as abbots and prioresses.

MIDDLE ENGLISH

English had survived, but it had changed. It had become what scholars now call Middle English, a term coined in the nineteenth century to describe English from A.D. 1150 to 1500. The category is somewhat artificial, though, for much of what has come to be called Middle English is simply a written record of what had already happened to the spoken language. Therefore, while spoken English had almost certainly shed most of its inflections (word changes that indicate meaning) by 1066, it is not until the language was written down that these changes were recorded. Another important simplification in the language was the adoption of prepositions to replace the Old English word endings, a process that we know began earlier. The influence of the French also resulted in the loss of grammatical gender in the vast majority of words. Today we use gender in a few pronouns, such as *he* and *she* for male and female people, and *it* to refer to everything else. Further, words were no longer formed in the Old English style, by adding complex prefixes and suffixes. To some extent this was replaced by the use of Latin prefixes (dis-, trans-, and re-). Overall, these changes re-

sulted in a vast simplification of the language.

GEOFFREY CHAUCER

Chaucer's career illustrates the triumph of English. By deliberately writing in English, he represented the rebirth of English as a national language. His work integrates the changes English had undergone in the preceding centuries, the richness of Middle English, Latinized and Frenchified by Christianity and Conquest.

THE TRIUMPH OF ENGLISH

Seventeen years after Chaucer's death, Henry V became the first English king since Harold to use English in his official documents, including his will. In 1415, Henry crossed the Channel to fight the French. In the first letter he dictated in France he decided to write in English. This national statement indicates a turning point. English had triumphed.

The Changing English Language 197

Humanities Note

Fine art, *Beginning of prologue to* Canterbury Tales, *15th century manuscript.* This picture shows the beginning of a beautifully illuminated, or illustrated, manuscript edition of Chaucer's *Canterbury Tales.* Illuminations were done as ink outlines or full-color drawings. As miniature works of art, they were unique to the manuscript in which they appeared and in this sense different from the mass-produced book illustrations of our own time. Although only a small percentage of the population could read, illuminated manuscripts were treasured by the nobility or clergy who had commissioned them. (Today they are kept in museums.) The invention of the printing press and the wider distribution of books eventually brought to an end the art of illuminating manuscripts.

You might want to use the following questions to discuss the art.
1. What natural shapes and patterns might have inspired the decorative design around the page?
2. Are any modern books decorated in this way? Explain.

Questions Have students choose partners and let the teams compete while compiling lists of words that begin with the Latin prefixes *dis-, trans-,* and *re-.*

Answers Answers will vary but will probably include words like displease, disjointed, disappoint, translate, transfer, transform, relocate, replace, etc.

The writing assignments on page 198 have students write creatively, while those on page 199 have them think about the selections and write critically.

YOU THE WRITER
Guidelines for Evaluating Assignment 1

1. Has the student imitated a medieval ballad or narrative, emulating the style and form of the model?
2. Has the student created a "medieval" plot, characters, and setting?
3. Is the story written in a clear, interesting, well-organized manner?
4. Could the imitation almost pass for an authentic medieval ballad or narrative?
5. Is the imitation free from grammar, usage, and mechanics errors?

Guidelines for Evaluating Assignment 2

1. Does the monologue present thoughts about the life of a character from medieval literature?
2. Are there sufficient references and details in the monologue to convey the speaker's ideas and create the impression that a medieval character is speaking?
3. Has the student made the monologue sound authentic by modeling it after the selections in the unit?
4. Is the monologue well-organized and consistent in style?
5. Is the monologue free from grammar, usage, and mechanics errors?

Guidelines for Evaluating Assignment 3

1. Has the student established a viewpoint for his or her letter about an episode from medieval literature?
2. Has the student based his or her style on the selections in this unit in order to create a medieval flavor?
3. Apart from the style, is the letter a conventional personal letter?
4. Are the details vividly expressed?
5. Is the letter free from grammar, usage, and mechanics errors?

■YOU THE WRITER■

Assignment

1. Many English poets have written imitations of medieval ballads and narratives. Write your own imitation of a poem in this unit. Make your poem medieval in content as well as in form and style.

Prewriting. First think of the "medieval" plot, characters, and setting you will use in your poem. Prepare a map outlining these features. Then examine your model for the structure, verse form, and other literary aspects you will imitate.

Writing. When you write your first draft, concentrate on getting the story down on paper in a clear, interesting, well-organized way. Write in verse, but do not try to refine the poetry yet.

Revising. You may now concentrate on emulating the style and form of your model. Work on your poem until it could almost pass for an authentic medieval ballad or narrative. Read it aloud. How would it sound if it were accompanied by a musical instrument?

Assignment

2. Write a monologue in prose or verse in which one of the characters you have encountered in medieval literature presents his or her thoughts about the kind of life he or she has led or about life in general.

Prewriting. First select your character. Then decide what main idea or ideas your character will express. Then think of the references to medieval experience your character will use to illustrate and support these ideas.

Writing. Try to make your monologue sound authentically medieval by modeling it on the selections you have read in this unit. Make sure your narrator's personality shines clearly through his or her words.

Revising. Try to improve the details of the monologue so they both aptly convey the speaker's ideas and create the impression that a medieval character is speaking. Finally, make any improvements you can in the organization and style of the monologue.

Assignment

3. Imagine that you are a medieval man or woman who has witnessed any episode presented in the selections of this unit. Write a letter to a friend or relative in which you tell what you witnessed.

Prewriting. First establish your viewpoint: Where were you in relation to the characters and events? What exactly did you observe?

Writing. Try to think of yourself as a medieval person as you write your letter. Base your style of writing on the selections in this unit. Apart from the style, your letter should be a conventional personal letter.

Revising. Can you in any way express more vividly the details of what you witnessed? Can you give the letter a more medieval flavor? Revise in the light of these questions.

YOU THE CRITIC

Assignment

1. The literature of past societies provides clues to what life might have been like for the ordinary person. Write an essay in which you present your impressions of medieval life based on the selections in this unit.

    Prewriting. Ask yourself, "Judging by the literature I have read, how would I have felt living in medieval England? What would have been the troubles and the advantages of living in those days?"

    Writing. Your essay should basically answer the preceding questions. Be sure you refer to the clues you found in the selections you read.

    Revising. First check that your essay is faithful to your sense of how you would have responded to life in the Middle Ages. Then revise it for organization, style, and grammatical correctness.

Assignment

2. The literature of the past sometimes presents ideas, values, or customs that would be useful to life today. Write an essay in which you explain how one such medieval idea, value, or custom would enhance present-day life.

    Prewriting. First decide what the details of the literature you have read reveal about life and how they illustrate the quality about which you are concerned. Then list your reasons for wanting to see this quality revived or maintained today.

    Writing. Write an essay that first describes the idea, value, or custom; then illustrates it by reference to literature; and finally argues for its relevance to the present.

    Revising. Make sure the organization of your essay allows for adequate treatment of the description, illustration, and argumentation mentioned above. Check for lapses in style and usage.

Assignment

3. Choose the selection from medieval literature that you liked best, and write an essay in which you explain why you consider it superior to other selections in the unit.

    Prewriting. First choose one or two other works of medieval literature with which you can appropriately compare the selection you have chosen. Then list your reasons for preferring it to the others.

    Writing. Write an essay based on your prewriting work. Illustrate and support your reasons by apt references to the literature. Aim to make your reader see the excellence you perceive in the work of your choice.

    Revising. Concentrate on making your evaluation fair and balanced. Tone down any excessive claims for the preferred work or against the others. Finally, look for and correct any errors in grammar or lapses in style.

You the Critic   199

YOU THE CRITIC
Guidelines for Evaluating Assignment 1

1. Has the student written an essay that explains how he or she would have felt living in medieval England and identified the troubles and advantages of living at that time?
2. Does the student use examples from the literature to support his or her points about life in the Middle Ages?
3. Is the essay well-organized and consistent in style?
4. Is the essay free from grammar, usage, and mechanics errors?

Guidelines for Evaluating Assignment 2

1. Does the essay begin with a description of the medieval idea, value, or custom the student feels would be useful today?
2. Does the student illustrate his or her point by references to medieval literature?
3. Does the student effectively argue for the relevance of the value, idea, or custom to the present?
4. Is the essay well-organized and free from grammar, usage, and mechanics errors?

Guidelines for Evaluating Assignment 3

1. Does the essay explain why the chosen selection of medieval literature is superior to others?
2. Does the student illustrate and support his or her thesis by references to the literature?
3. Is the evaluation fair and balanced while showing the excellence of the student's choice?
4. Is the essay free from grammar, usage, and mechanics errors?

Humanities Note

Fine art, *Queen Elizabeth and Sir Walter Raleigh,* by Charles Edouard Boutibonne. This picture, painted two centuries after Sir Walter Raleigh's death, is a fanciful depiction of Raleigh's presentation of booty from his exploits to Queen Elizabeth I. Raleigh was, with the exception of a period of disgrace that resulted from an injudicious marriage, a long-lasting favorite of the queen. A soldier, explorer, colonizer, courtier, poet, philosopher, and historian, he exemplified the ideal Renaissance man. His fortunes fell drastically, however, when James I ascended to the throne, for the newly-crowned king feared Raleigh was part of a conspiracy against him. Condemned to death in 1603, he was executed in 1616. Cool and composed to the end, he is reported to have commented on the sharpness of the executioner's axe, saying "This is a sharp medicine, but it is a physician for all diseases."

Objectives

1 To understand the key characteristics of the Renaissance
2 To understand what England was like under the Tudors
3 To understand the conflict between James I and the Puritans
4 To appreciate the achievements of the English Renaissance

QUEEN ELIZABETH AND SIR WALTER RALEIGH
Charles Edouard Boutibonne
Three Lions

THE ENGLISH RENAISSANCE
1485–1625

This royal throne of kings, this sceptered isle,
This earth of majesty, this seat of Mars,
This other Eden, demi-paradise,
This fortress built by Nature for herself
Against infection and the hand of war,
This happy breed of men, this little world,
This precious stone set in the silver sea,
Which serves it in the office of a wall,
Or as a moat defensive to a house,
Against the envy of less happier lands,
This blessed plot, this earth, this realm, this England.

William Shakespeare

201

The ending of the Wars of the Roses and the founding of the Tudor dynasty in 1485 opened a new era in English life. Monarchs assured stability by increasing their own power and undercutting the strength of the nobles. At the same time, they dramatically changed England's religious practices. They also helped to transform England from a small, insular nation into one of the world's great powers. In this way the English people gained a new pride and sense of nationhood, clearly reflected in the patriotic lines by William Shakespeare (1564–1616) on the previous page.

THE COMING OF THE RENAISSANCE

The Renaissance was a flowering of literary, artistic, and intellectual development that began in Italy in the fourteenth century. The movement was inspired by the arts and scholarship of ancient Greece and Rome, which were rediscovered during the Crusades. Classical learning lived again as new generations of scholars and artists explored and extended the achievements of the ancients. Among the key characteristics of the Renaissance were:

- The religious devotion of the Middle Ages, with its emphasis on the afterlife, gave way to a new interest in the human being's place here on earth.
- Universities introduced a new curriculum called the humanities, which included history, geography, poetry, and modern languages.
- The invention of printing from movable type made books available to more people than ever before. A German printer, Johann Gutenberg, published a Bible in the 1450's that is believed to be the first book printed in the new manner.
- While scholars used Greek and Latin to study the ancients and students learned those languages in school, more and more writers began working in the vernacular—the local language. In England, the English language shed some of its regional differences and became increasingly standardized.

The Slow Spread of Renaissance Ideas

The Renaissance did not jump the Channel into England until the final two decades of the fifteenth century. At that time, Renaissance ideas had already been spreading across the European continent for more than a century. Because the Renaissance began in Italy, many of the leading Renaissance figures were Italian. Among them were the poet Dante Alighieri (1265–1321), author of *The Divine Comedy;* Francesco Petrarca, known as Petrarch (1304 –1374), who wrote lyric poetry in a new fourteen-line form called the sonnet; and the painter, sculptor, architect, engineer, and scientist Leonardo da Vinci (1452–1519). Because of the scope of his interests and talents, Da Vinci typifies what we call the Renaissance man—a person of broad education and interests whose curiosity knew no bounds.

MONA LISA
Leonardo Da Vinci
Three Lions

Humanities Note

Fine art, *Mona Lisa,* by Leonardo da Vinci. Born in 1452 in the town of Vinci, Leonardo was an engineer, inventor, and artist. The most famous of his portraits, *Mona Lisa* amazed the artist's contemporaries with its delicate use of light and shadow. Famous not only for the subtlety of its technique, the portrait has also fascinated viewers who are intrigued by the mysterious psychology of the sitter. Why is this smiling face so compelling? The smile not only echoes a mood but also suggests a timeless, symbolic expression. Her face embodies the quality of maternal tenderness that is Leonardo's essence of womanhood. Even the rocky landscape in the background suggests elementary generative forces. The *Mona Lisa* serves as a superb example of the artist's goal in painting: to depict the "intention of man's soul."

The Age of Exploration

The Renaissance thirst for knowledge had many practical consequences, one of which was a great burst of exploration. The Crusades had opened routes to Asia, but the merchants of the Italian city-states quickly monopolized trade over the new routes by sea and land. Seeking their own path to the riches of Asia, navigators representing Portugal and Spain began seeking an all-sea route. Aided by the development of the compass and by advances in astronomy, which freed them from the need to cling closely to the ocean's shores, these navigators ventured far and

Introduction 203

Enrichment Tell students about the events leading up to the defeat of the Spanish Armada by the English. Queen Elizabeth allowed sailors like Sir Francis Drake to carry out an undeclared war against Spanish ships, because she feared that King Philip II of Spain might invade England. When Philip II complained to Elizabeth about the activities of Drake and demanded that he be punished, Elizabeth knighted him instead. Provocations like these caused Philip to send an armada, or armed fleet, to attack England.

Tell students that the smaller, more maneuverable English ships defeated the Spanish ships in the English Channel. Then the English drove the beaten armada into the North Sea, where it was further ravaged by storms. The English later nicknamed these storms the "Protestant Wind," because they helped Protestant England overcome Catholic Spain. Some of the Spanish ships washed up on the southwestern shore of Ireland, where the sailors were slaughtered by the local populace. Recently, divers located a few of these sunken Spanish galleons off the Irish coast.

c. 1500	*Everyman* first performed.
1512	First masque performed.
1516	Thomas More publishes *Utopia*.
1520	Bowling becomes popular in London.
1534	Henry VIII issues Act of Supremacy.
	Nicholas Udall writes *Ralph Roister Doister*, first English comedy.
	Church of England established.
1535	Thomas More executed.
1541	John Knox leads Calvinist reformation in Scotland.
1547	Henry VIII dies.
1549	Book of Common Prayer issued.
1558	Elizabeth I becomes queen.
1560	Thomas Tallis publishes English cathedral music.
1563	Over 20,000 Londoners die in plague.
1576	Francis Drake returns from circumnavigating the globe.
c. 1582	**Sir Philip Sidney** writes *Astrophel and Stella*.
c. 1586	**Christopher Marlowe** writes *Tamburlaine the Great*.
1587	Mary, Queen of Scots executed.
	Christopher Marlowe completes *The Tragical History of Doctor Faustus*.
1588	English navy defeats Spanish Armada.

Sir Thomas More with His Family

Queen Elizabeth I

The Last Supper

Copernicus's Treatise of Astronomy

Columbus Sets Sail from Spain

English Navy Attacking Spanish Armada

London c. 1558

Francisco Pizarro

WORLD EVENTS

1490	Italy: Ballet introduced.
1492	Columbus lands in New World.
1495	Italy: Leonardo da Vinci paints *The Last Supper*.
1497	North America: John Cabot explores northeastern coast.
	Africa: Vasco da Gama rounds Cape of Good Hope.
1500	Italy: Michelangelo sculpts *David*.
1503	Italy: Leonardo da Vinci paints *Mona Lisa*.
1506	Italy: Construction on St. Peter's Cathedral begins.
1509	Italy: Michelangelo paints ceiling of Sistine Chapel.
1510	Japan: Ports opened to European ships.
1513	North America: Ponce de Leon explores Florida.
	Balboa sights Pacific Ocean.
1518	Africa: Algiers and Tunisia founded.
1519-1522	Magellan sails around the world.
1520	Spain: Chocolate first introduced to Europe.
1521	Mexico: Cortez conquers Aztecs.
	Italy: Pope Leo X excommunicates Martin Luther.
1530	Poland: Copernicus completes treatise on astronomy.
1532	Peru: Pizarro conquers Incas.
	France: Rabelais publishes *Gargantua and Pantagruel*, Book I.

Introduction 205

Enrichment Tell students that François Rabelais, a French doctor, writer, and classical scholar, lived during the social and religious unrest of the first half of the sixteenth century. His loosely structured book *Gargantua and Pantagruel* is one of the great works of French prose. It is a typically Renaissance mixture of seriousness and playfulness, a celebration of human freedom.

We know only a limited amount about Rabelais' life. The son of a lawyer, he was born around 1494 near the French town of Chinon in the province of Touraine and seems to have spent his late teens in a Franciscan monastery. He was greatly influenced by the effort to reform the Catholic church, and especially by the work of the Dutch humanist Erasmus of Rotterdam. Erasmus studied Greek and used it to retranslate and reinterpret the New Testament, a practice religious conservatives felt was dangerously subversive. Greek was thus a politically and religiously charged subject. For a time the conservative University of Paris banned its study, and Rabelais had his Greek books confiscated by the monastic libraries.

In 1525 Rabelais transferred to a less repressive Benedictine monastery, but in the following years he left the monastic life altogether. This decision to live life in the world was central to the values his works celebrate. He studied medicine at the University of Montpelier, earning a bachelor's degree in 1530 and a doctor's degree seven years later. His medical learning informs his book, which for all its fantasy is full of precise medical detail. In 1532 he published *Pantagruel,* the first book of his work about two good-natured giants, Gargantua and his son Pantagruel. This book announced the subjects of the following volumes: religious and social satire mixed with passages celebrating the body and others written with deep religious feeling. Through the book runs a vein of nonsense, for this first work like the rest mixes classical forms like the letter with the grotesque forms of folk-culture--tall tales, games, jokes, puns, riddles, and the rituals of holiday celebrations.

BRITISH EVENTS

Globe Theatre

1590	**Edmund Spenser** publishes *The Faerie Queene*, Part I.
1594	**Shakespeare** composes *Romeo and Juliet*.
1595	**Shakespeare's** *A Midsummer Night's Dream* first performed.
1599	Globe Theatre opens.
1600	East India Company founded.
1602	Bodeleian Library opens at Oxford.
1603	Elizabeth I dies; James I becomes king.
1605	Guy Fawkes executed for Gunpowder Plot.
	Shakespeare's *Macbeth* first performed.
1606	**Ben Jonson** publishes *Volpone*.
1609	**Shakespeare's** *Sonnets* published.
1611	King James Bible published.
1616	*Collected Works of Ben Jonson* published.
1620	**Francis Bacon** publishes *Novum Organum*.
1623	First patent laws passed.
1625	James I dies.

Galileo

Cervantes

The Pilgrims Land at Plymouth Rock

William Shakespeare

The Wedding Dance

Abkar the Great

WORLD EVENTS

1534	Spain: St. Ignatius Loyola founds Jesuit brotherhood.
1554	Italy: Cellini completes bronze statue of Perseus.
1556	India: Akbar the Great comes to power.
1565	Malta: Knights of St. John fight off Turkish invasion.
1566	Belgium: Bruegel paints *The Wedding Dance*.
1567	South America: 2,000,000 Indians die of typhoid.
	Brazil: Rio de Janeiro founded by Portuguese.
1580	France: Montaigne's *Essays* published.
1582	Italy: Pope Gregory XIII introduces new calendar.
1595	South America: Sir Walter Raleigh explores Orinoco River.
1605	Spain: Cervantes publishes Part I of *Don Quixote*.
1607	North America: British colony established at Jamestown.
1609	Italy: Galileo builds first telescope.
	North America: French colony of Quebec established.
1618	Germany: Kepler proposes laws of planetary motion.
1620	North America: Pilgrims land at Plymouth Rock.

Introduction 207

might expect. He became a member of the Parliament of Bordeaux in 1557, where he met his friend Etienne de La Boetie who was to influence his life and writing.

In 1568 he inherited his family's estate and in 1570, after years in and around the royal court, he retired from the parliament to his house to read and write. He may also have felt the need to prepare for his own death: Thirty-seven was past middle age in the Renaissance, and both his father and his friend Etienne were now dead. As it turned out, however, Montaigne lived for many years more and during his "retirement," he toured Germany, Switzerland, and Italy in 1580–1581; became mayor of Bordeaux for two terms (1583–1587); and acted as an intermediary between the Catholic French King Henry III and the Protestant leader Henry of Navarre in 1588.

In 1580 Montaigne published the first two books of his *Essays*. The word comes from a Latin verb meaning "to weigh" or "to test," and this new literary form enabled him to try out ideas, setting one belief against another and voicing his own reservations about other people's dogmatic truths. In 1575 he had a medal made with "Que sais-je" ("What do I know") on one side and a pair of scales on the other. Both sides point to the same attitude: If one cannot be certain what one knows, it is better to weigh different opinions carefully before coming to judgment.

Montaigne continued to revise and add to the *Essays* for the rest of his life. A new edition with a third book appeared in 1588. He died in 1592 and a final revision of the *Essays* was published after his death, in 1595.

Fine art, *Portrait of Erasmus,* by Hans Holbein. Holbein the Younger (1497–1543) grew up in Augsburg, a center for international commerce in southern Germany that was particularly responsive to Italy's Renaissance movements. At eighteen, he moved to Switzerland, where he became a leading artist of Basel. Most probably a gift for Thomas Moore, this portrait of Erasmus was painted soon after Holbein's move to Switzerland. A truly memorable picture of a Renaissance man, it is an intimate yet monumental photographic likeness of the great doctor of humane letters. The portrait conveys his philosophical turn of mind as well as his intellectual authority. When Holbein traveled to England to avoid the turmoil of the Protestant Reformation in Basel, Erasmus recommended him to Thomas Moore. Moore responded to Erasmus' recommendation in a letter that stated, "Your friend is a wonderful artist."

2 Master Teacher Note To review this concept of clerical abuse, you might remind students of the Pardoner from the Prologue to Chaucer's *Canterbury Tales* (page 117).

PORTRAIT OF ERASMUS
Hans Holbein
National Gallery, Parma
Scala/Art Resource

wide. Their explorations culminated in Columbus's discovery of the New World in 1492. Soon, European powers were establishing colonies in the Americas and extracting great wealth from the new lands.

England's participation in this Age of Exploration began in 1497, when the Italian-born explorer John Cabot, sailing for an English company, reached Newfoundland (an island off the east coast of what is now Canada) and perhaps also the mainland. Cabot thus laid the basis for future English claims in North America. However, English leaders would not exploit those claims until near the end of the English Renaissance.

The Protestant Reformation

Hand in hand with commercial expansion came a growing sense of nationalism, which, along with the new Renaissance spirit, led many Europeans to question the universal authority of the Roman Catholic Church. Many people had grievances against the Church. Some objected to the sale of indulgences—remissions of punishment for sins, for which people made payments that often went straight into the pockets of corrupt Church officials. Critics also objected to other forms of payment to the Church, viewing them as a form of taxation. Other people argued that Church leaders played favorites by supporting Mediterranean powers against more northerly countries. Still others—scholars who were influenced by the growth of independent thinking in the universities—questioned Church teachings and the church hierarchy.

One critical scholar was the great Dutch thinker Desiderius Erasmus (1466–1536), whose edition of the New Testament raised serious questions about standard Church interpretations of the Bible. Erasmus studied and taught in England. Through his friendship with such English writers as Thomas More (1478–1535), Erasmus focused attention on issues of morality and religion, which remained as central concerns of the English Renaissance, often overshadowing the artistic concerns that dominated the Italian Renaissance.

Although Erasmus himself remained a Roman Catholic, he helped to pave the way for a split in the Roman Church that began in 1517, when a German monk named Martin Luther (1483–1546) nailed a list of dissenting beliefs (his "ninety-five theses") to the door of a German church. Luther's protest was aimed only at reforming the Roman Catholic Church, but it ended by dividing that Church and introducing a new Christian denomination known as Protestantism. The process that Luther started has come to be called the Protestant Reformation.

Fueled by political discontent, the Protestant Reformation swept through much of Europe. It led to frequent wars between European nations whose rulers had opposing religious beliefs. Protestants and Catholics both suffered persecution, depending on where they

2

happened to live and which religion their ruler supported. Protestants themselves were divided, and in Germany the followers of Luther (called Lutherans) persecuted the followers of another Protestant reformer, John Calvin of Geneva. Calvin's ideas (called Calvinism) found a foothold in Switzerland, England, and Scotland, however, and helped bring about the establishment of the Puritan and Presbyterian sects.

ENGLAND UNDER THE TUDORS

The Tudor dynasty ruled England from 1485 to 1603. Looking back, we see this period as a time of stability and economic expansion. English wool growers were finding new markets abroad. English investors were forming trading companies to tap the riches of far-off places like India. London had grown into a metropolis of more than 180,000 people. However, those who lived in Tudor times often saw economic changes as a threat to the old familiar ways, and memories of the Wars of the Roses caused many people to fear new outbreaks of civil strife.

Henry VII and Henry VIII

The first Tudor monarch, Henry VII, inherited an England that had been depleted and exhausted by years of civil war. By the time he died in 1509, he had rebuilt the nation's treasury and established law and order. In doing so, he had restored the prestige of the monarchy and had set the stage for his successors.

Henry VII was succeeded by his handsome and athletic son,

MARTIN LUTHER FASTENING HIS 95 THESES ON THE DOOR OF ALL SAINTS CHURCH, WITTENBURG, GERMANY, ON 31 OCTOBER, 1517
19th-Century Engraving
The Granger Collection

Fine art, *Martin Luther Fastening His 95 Theses on the Door of All Saints Church, Wittenburg, Germany, on 31 October, 1517.* Outraged by Johann Tetzel's selling of indulgences, Martin Luther posted 95 theses, or questions for debate, on the door of the Wittenburg castle church, as this engraving shows. There is a certain irony in this piece of art because the Reformation initiated violent feelings against religious images, and many works of art were destroyed. Luther himself disapproved of the destruction and, condemning only their idolatrous use, stated that pictures were neither good nor bad; only people's misuse of the art made it evil.

Humanities Note

Fine art, *King Henry VIII of England,* by Hans Holbein. In 1526, Hans Holbein the Younger (1497–1543) left Basel, Switzerland for England where he hoped to receive commissions from Henry VIII. He was successful in receiving commissions from not only the king but also influential members of the court. This portrait of Henry VIII is among Holbein's most famous. The portrait shows the king, grown gross with self-indulgence. The artist painted Henry in rigid frontality conveying the authority of an absolute ruler. The immobile pose suggests an air of unapproachability while the display of precisely rendered jewels and gold embroidery creates the overwhelming sensation of Henry VIII's ruthless, commanding presence.

3 Historical Context Henry's oldest son, Arthur, who predeceased his father, had been the first husband of Catherine of Aragon. It was on the basis of this former marriage that Henry sought his annulment.

4 Enrichment Robert Bolt's play *A Man for All Seasons* (Random House, 1966) presents a beautifully written and highly sympathetic picture of More.

5 Historical Context Edward's devout Protestantism was more the product of his Seymour relatives' influence than that of his father's; doctrinally, Henry remained Catholic all his life.

6 Historical Context In order to prevent the Catholic Mary from succeeding to power upon Edward's death, his advisor Northumberland put Lady Jane Grey, Edward's first cousin, on the throne after marrying her to his son. The reign lasted nine days and ended with execution in the Tower.

KING HENRY VIII OF ENGLAND
Hans Holbein
The Granger Collection

Henry VIII. Like his father, Henry VIII was a practicing Catholic. He even wrote a book against Luther, for which a grateful Pope granted him the title "Defender of the Faith."

Henry VIII's relationship with the Pope did not last, however. Because his marriage with Catherine of Aragon had not produced a son, Henry tried to obtain an annulment from the Pope so that he could marry Anne Boleyn. When the Pope refused, Henry remarried anyway. This defiance of papal authority led to an open break with the Roman Catholic Church. Under the Act of Supremacy (1534), the king assumed full control of the Church in England and severed all ties with Rome. Henry became supreme head of the new Church of England (or Anglican Church). He seized the Catholic Church's English property and dissolved the powerful monasteries, selling some of their lands to benefit the royal treasury and granting the rest as gifts to loyal friends. **3**

Although the Protestant Reformation was not directly responsible for Henry's break with Rome, it helped to pave the way. Many people in England had resented Roman dominance, and the break helped to stir new feelings of national pride. Henry used ruthless measures to suppress opposition among monks, friars, and a few others. He even had his former friend and leading advisor, Thomas More, executed, because More had refused to renounce his faith.

Henry married six times in all. His first two marriages produced two daughters, Mary and Elizabeth. His third wife, Jane Seymour, bore a son, Edward, who was but a frail child when Henry died in 1547. **4**

Edward VI and Mary I

Henry VIII's son, Edward VI, became king at the age of nine and died at the age of fifteen. During his brief reign, a series of parliamentary acts were instituted that dramatically changed the nation's religious practices. English replaced Latin in church ritual, and the Anglican prayer book, or *Book of Common Prayer,* became required in public worship. By Edward's death in 1553, England was well on its way to becoming a Protestant nation. **5**

Roman Catholicism made a turbulent comeback, however, when Edward's half-sister, Mary, took the throne. Mary I was herself Catholic, and she restored Roman practices to the Church of England. She also restored the authority of the Pope over the English Church and insisted on marrying her Spanish cousin, Philip II, thus seeming to make England a minor appendage to the powerful Spanish state. In a time of growing national feeling, many people found these acts extremely unpatriotic. People were also disturbed by Mary's violent repression of Protestants. Ordering the execution of some 200 Protestants, she earned the nickname Bloody Mary and strengthened anti-Catholic sentiment within England. **6**

Elizabeth I

When Mary I died after a five-year reign, her half-sister, Elizabeth I, came to the throne. She would be the last of the Tudors, dying unmarried and childless, after a long and successful reign.

Strong and clever, Elizabeth was probably England's ablest monarch since William the Conqueror. She received a Renaissance education and read widely in the Greek and Latin classics. She became a great patron of the arts, gathering around her a flock of courtiers that included most of the best writers of her day. Many of the era's greatest literary works bear a dedication to the queen, and the word *Elizabethan* has come to signify the English Renaissance at its height.

Elizabeth also put an end to the religious turmoil that had existed during Mary I's reign. She reestablished the monarch's supremacy in the Church of England and restored the *Book of Common Prayer,* and she instituted a policy of religious moderation that enjoyed great popular support, although it failed to please many devout Catholics and Protestants.

Often working with England's Catholic factions were France and Spain, Europe's strongest powers at the start of Elizabeth's reign. Both nations sought to dominate England, but each was anxious that the other should not. Elizabeth and her counselors adroitly played one side against the other, dangling offers of marriage to the queen as bait. Elizabeth's clever maneuvering of French and Spanish royalty allowed England a period of peace during which commercial and maritime interests prospered.

If Elizabeth had one outstanding problem, it was her Catholic cousin Mary Stuart, queen of Scotland by birth and (as great-granddaughter of Henry VII) next in line for the throne of England. Because Catholics did not recognize Henry VIII's marriage to Elizabeth's mother, Anne Boleyn, they considered Mary Stuart the queen of England. As a prisoner in England for nineteen years, Mary became the center of numerous Catholic plots against Elizabeth. While punishing the plotters, Elizabeth let her royal cousin live. Finally, however, a court convicted Mary of plotting to murder Elizabeth, and Parliament insisted on Mary's execution. Mary went to the block in 1587, a Catholic martyr. Her famous motto, "In my end is my beginning," took on new meaning when her death led Catholic Spain to declare war on England.

Defeat of the Spanish Armada

The quarrels between Spain and England went beyond the execution of Mary. Spain rejected most English claims to territory in the Americas and resented the fact that English adventurers, known as privateers, had been attacking and plundering Spanish ships. In theory, privateers like John Hawkins and Francis Drake operated on their own, but in reality they acted on the authority of Queen Elizabeth.

QUEEN ELIZABETH I OF ENGLAND c. 1588
by or after George Gower
The Granger Collection

QUEEN ELIZABETH I KNIGHTING FRANCIS DRAKE ON BOARD THE *GOLDEN HIND* AT DEPTFORD, 4 APRIL, 1581
19th-Century Engraving
The Granger Collection

Spain's King Philip II, already infuriated by the sea pirates, considered Mary's execution the last straw. He prepared a Spanish fleet, or armada, of 130 warships and sent it to attack England. In an eight-day battle in the English Channel in 1588, English sailors outfought and outmaneuvered the Spanish fleet. The defeat of the Spanish armada marked the decline of Spain and the emergence of England as a great sea power.

STUARTS AND PURITANS

The English Renaissance continued after Elizabeth died in 1603, although a new dynasty—the Stuarts—came to the throne of England. Determined that the end of the Tudor line should not bring a dispute over the throne and a return of civil strife, Elizabeth named Scotland's King James VI as her successor. James's claim to England's throne rested on his descent from King Henry VII through his mother, Mary Stuart, Elizabeth's old antagonist. Unlike Mary, however, James was a Protestant.

THE LAUNCHING OF FIRESHIPS AGAINST THE SPANISH ARMADA
National Maritime Museum, Greenwich, England

The years of the new Stuart king (1603–25), who became England's James I, are sometimes described as the Jacobean era, from *Jacobus,* the Latin word for *James.* On the surface, the era seemed to be merely an extension of the Elizabethan age. Like his predecessor, James I was a strong supporter of the arts. He also took measures to further England's position as a world power, sponsoring the establishment of England's first successful American colony—Jamestown, Virginia.

During James's reign, however, a conflict began developing that would later erupt into war. Guided by the medieval idea of the "divine right of kings," James I often treated the Parliament with contempt. He and Parliament became involved in a power struggle, quarreling over taxes and foreign wars. James I also persecuted the Puritans, who were strongly represented in the House of Commons. Prompted by James's religious intolerance, a group of Puritans migrated to America, and established the Plymouth Colony in 1621.

ACHIEVEMENTS OF
THE ENGLISH RENAISSANCE

The Elizabethan Age produced an explosion of cultural energy. English architects designed and constructed beautiful mansions. Composers turned out new hymns to fit the Anglican service and popularized the English madrigal, a love song sung without musical accompaniment, often by several harmonizing voices. Painters and sculptors were busy, too. While the Renaissance masters generally were not English, some—like the German artist Hans Holbein the Younger (1497?–1543), court painter to Henry VIII—did move to England.

Meanwhile, the Renaissance spurred the growth of English educational institutions. Instead of depending on tutors, wealthy families began sending their sons to public schools (that is, schools outside the home—they were actually what Americans call private secondary schools). At the same time, the universities at Oxford and Cambridge were improved and expanded.

Literature in Early Tudor Times

The years from 1485 to 1558 served as a prelude to the great age of Elizabethan literature. Many major writers, such as Thomas More, continued to work in Latin. More's *Utopia* (1516) is a powerful vision of a society free of medieval superstition and prejudice. More and more writers, however, were using the vernacular—English.

7

Introduction 213

7 **Master Teacher Note** To make this colorful period even more pictorially vivid, you might show students some of Holbein's portraits, particularly those of the royal family.

Fine art, *Sir Walter Raleigh,* by Nicholas Hilliard. Elizabethan genius ran to music and literature not toward the visual arts. In general, the demand for portraits, the only art form appreciated by the Elizabethans, was filled by foreign artists visiting England. One notable exception was Nicholas Hilliard (1547–1619). A goldsmith by training, he specialized in fine jewelry and miniature portraits on parchment. These were tiny keepsakes often worn by their owners as jewelry.

This portrait of Sir Walter Raleigh is such a miniature. It is noteworthy for the amount of detail, particularly in Raleigh's collar.

8 Literary Movement See Wyatt's sonnet "Whoso List to Hunt," page 219.

9 Literary Movement See Sonnets 31 and 39 from *Astrophel and Stella,* pages 224–226.

10 Literary Movement Spenser's sonnet sequence, the *Amoretti,* is represented by Sonnets 1, 26 and 75, pages 245–247.

11 Literary Movement See Shakespeare's sonnets, pages 255–259.

SIR WALTER RALEIGH
N. Hillard
Three Lions

The poet Thomas Wyatt (1503–42), who had traveled widely on the continent, introduced the sonnet to England. Wyatt translated or adapted many of the sonnets of the Italian Renaissance poet Petrarch. A second early Tudor poet, Henry Howard, Earl of Surrey (1517–47), experimented with the sonnet form and was the first to use blank verse, the unrhymed ten-syllable lines that would later be the tool of the great Elizabethan dramatists. **8**

Elizabethan Poetry

During the lengthy reign of Elizabeth I, English literature came of age. Many of the most significant literary developments came in the area of poetry. Favoring lyric poetry, rather than the narrative poems favored by their medieval predecessors, the Elizabethan poets perfected the sonnet and began experimenting with other poetic forms.

One of the most popular literary forms during the Elizabethan age was the sonnet cycle, a series of sonnets that fit loosely together to form a story. The first of the great Elizabethan sonnet cycles was *Astrophel and Stella* by Philip Sidney (1554–86). As a member of a poetry club called Areopagus, Sidney also helped to adapt classical verse forms to fit the English language. **9**

Another major Elizabethan poet was Edmund Spenser (1552?–99). Spenser wrote intricate verse filled with rich imagery. Although Spenser wrote many fine sonnets, his most famous work, *The Faerie Queene,* is an imaginative epic, or long heroic poem, dedicated to Queen Elizabeth. Spenser wrote his epic in complex nine-line units, now called Spenserian stanzas. **10**

Christopher Marlowe (1564–93), a noted playwright, was also a gifted lyric poet. Marlowe helped popularize pastoral verse, which idealizes the rustic simplicity of rural life, in such poems as "The Passionate Shepherd to His Love."

Marlowe's poem inspired Sir Walter Raleigh (1552?–1618) to write a famous response, "The Nymph's Reply to the Shepherd." Poet, historian, courtier, soldier, and explorer, Raleigh was a typical Renaissance man whose adventurous life mirrored the restless spirit of his day.

Another brilliant lyric poet, William Shakespeare, brought the Elizabethan sonnet to new heights. In composing his sonnets, Shakespeare changed the pattern and rhyme scheme of the Petrarchan, or Italian, sonnet, employing a form now known as the English, or Shakespearean, sonnet. **11**

Elizabethan Drama

During the Elizabethan age, English drama also came into full bloom. Playwrights turned away from religious subjects and began writing more complex and sophisticated plays. Drawing upon the classical models of ancient Greece and Rome, writers reintroduced tragedies—plays in which disaster befalls a hero or heroine—and comedies—originally, plays in which a humorous situation leads to a happy resolution. Playwrights also began writing their plays in carefully crafted blank verse, using rich language, filled with vivid imagery.

Since Elizabethan dramas were almost entirely in verse, it is not surprising that many of the age's best poets were also its leading playwrights. Christopher Marlowe became the first major Elizabethan dramatist in the 1580s, writing such plays as *Tamburlaine the Great* and *The Tragical History of Doctor Faustus*. Had Marlowe lived past the age of thirty, he might well have rivaled Shakespeare as England's greatest playwright.

Shakespeare began his involvement with the theater as an actor. By 1592 he was a popular playwright, his works even having been performed at Elizabeth's court. After the Globe Theater was built in 1599, many of Shakespeare's plays were performed there. Shakespeare wrote thirty-seven plays, among them many of the greatest plays of all time. He wrote nine tragedies, including *Romeo and Juliet, Hamlet,* and *Macbeth*; several comedies, including *A Merchant of Venice* and *A Midsummer Night's Dream;* ten histories, including *Richard II, Richard III,* and *Henry V*; and a number of plays often classified as "romances" or "tragic comedies." Filled with powerful and beautiful language, his plays display his deep understanding of human nature and his compassion for all types and classes of people. Because of their eloquent language and their depth and complexity, Shakespeare's plays have retained their popularity for centuries. As the seventeenth-century writer Ben Jonson said of Shakespeare: "He was not of an age but for all time."

Elizabethan and Jacobean Prose

Prose took a back seat to poetry and drama in the English Renaissance. Scholars still preferred to write in Latin, and their English prose had a Latin flavor. Because they used long words and ornate sentences their work is often difficult to read today.

Several Elizabethan poets contributed major works of prose however. Philip Sidney's *Defence of Poesie* (about 1582) is one of the earliest works of English literary criticism. Thomas Nashe's *Unfortunate Traveler* (1594), a fictional adventure, was a forerunner of the novel. Another important work of prose, *History of the World,* was written by Walter Raleigh during his years of confinement in the Tower of London (for allegedly plotting against James I).

Perhaps the leading prose writer of the English Renaissance was Francis Bacon, a high government official under James I. "I

WILLIAM SHAKESPEARE
Artist Unknown
Three Lions

Introduction **215**

Humanities Note

Fine art, *William Shakespeare*. Over the years, Shakespeare and his plays, like Queen Elizabeth, have inspired hundreds of drawings, paintings, engravings, and other works of art. This portrait of Shakespeare by an unknown artist would have been painted during his London years, when he became well known, even outside the theater world. Queen Elizabeth admitted to being "a great admirer of the immortal Shakespeare." Shakespeare's company, The Lord Chamberlain's Men, were often summoned to Elizabeth's court at Richmond, Greenwich, or Whitehall, to participate in the festivals of the seasons. Shakespeare himself included many flattering references to the queen which were graciously accepted by her.

12 Literary Movement An excerpt from *The Tragical History of Doctor Faustus* begins on page 233.

13 Literary Movement See "To the Memory of My Beloved Master, William Shakespeare," page 391.

14 Historical Context Raleigh was eventually executed by James I, an action that increased the King's unpopularity among his subjects.

Humanities Note

Title page of the first edition of the King James Bible, London, 1611. On July 22, 1604, after considering an initial proposal from Puritan elements, James I announced that he had "appointed certain learned men, to the number four and fifty, for translating the Bible." The first edition appeared from the press of Robert Barker, the king's printer, in 1611. Barker issued many copies; some with the title page reproduced here and others with a woodcut title page he had used for the earlier Bishop's Bible (1602) which introduces the new Testament in this the first Authorized Version. After the title page comes a fulsome dedication to James, a superb preface which defends the principles of vernacular Bibles, various tables including genealogies, and a map of Canaan. Chapters were illustrated with richly engraved borders and elaborate first letters reminiscent of the illuminated manuscripts of the Middle Ages. (See page 365 for a title page reminiscent of the illuminated manuscripts of the Middle Ages. (See page 365 for a title page from the New Testament.) The King James Bible was never officially authorized; nevertheless, because of its merit, majesty of language, and music of its rhythm, it became the most generally used version and a monument to the English language.

15 **Literary Movement** See the excerpt from *Novum Organum,* page 357.

16 **Literary Movement** See the selections from the King James Bible, pages 364–367.

TITLE PAGE OF THE FIRST EDITION OF THE KING JAMES *BIBLE*
London, 1611
The Granger Collection

have taken all knowledge to be my province," Bacon wrote, and his literary output reflects his scholarship in many fields. His greatest work, the *Novum Organum* (1620), written in Latin, made major contributions to natural science and philosophy. Bacon is also known for his formal essays—short prose works focusing on single topics. His essays, including "Of Studies" and "Of Ambition," highlight the rational detachment of his clever, inquiring mind. **15**

The most monumental prose achievement of the entire English Renaissance is undoubtedly the English translation of the Bible commissioned by King James on the advice of Protestant clergymen. Fifty-four scholars labored for three years to bring this magnificent work to fruition. The King James Bible, or Authorized Version, is among the most widely quoted and influential works in the English language. **16**

The English Renaissance moved England out of its medieval past and into the modern world. No writers since have surpassed the literary achievements of Shakespeare or the majestic language of the King James Bible. These provide the standard against which all English literature has been judged right down to the present time.

Check Test

1. The Renaissance was inspired by the art and literature of ancient _____ and _____.

2. Exploration was aided by advances in astronomy and the development of the _____ .

3. The German monk Martin Luther began a religious movement that came to be called the _____ .

4. King _____ of England defied the authority of the pope.

5. Two great Elizabethan dramatists were _____ and _____ .

ANSWERS

1. Greece, Rome
2. compass
3. Protestant Reformation
4. Henry VIII
5. Christopher Marlowe, William Shakespeare

ENGLISH VOICES
Quotations by Prominent Figures of the Period

They (in Utopia) wonder much to hear that gold, which in itself is so useless a thing, should be everywhere so much esteemed.
Sir Thomas More, *Utopia*

I know I have the body of a weak and feeble woman, but I have the heart and stomach of a king, and of a king of England too.
Elizabeth I, speech to the troops on the approach of the Armada

Was this the face that launched a thousand ships,
And burnt the topless towers of Ilium?
Christopher Marlowe, *The Tragical History of Doctor Faustus*

Now is the winter of our discontent
Made glorious summer by this sun of York.
William Shakespeare, *Richard III*

The quality of mercy is not strained,
It droppeth as the gentle rain from heaven
Upon the place beneath: it is twice blessed;
It blesseth him that gives and him that takes. . . .
William Shakespeare, *The Merchant of Venice*

The fault, dear Brutus, is not in our stars,
But in ourselves, that we are underlings.
William Shakespeare, *Julius Caesar*

Something is rotten in the state of Denmark.
William Shakespeare, *Hamlet*

The world's mine oyster.
William Shakespeare, *The Merry Wives of Windsor*

Of one that loved not wisely but too well.
William Shakespeare, *Othello*

How sharper than a serpent's tooth it is
To have a thankless child!
William Shakespeare, *King Lear*

Additional Voices

They have no lawyers among them, for they consider them as a sort of people whose profession it is to disguise matters.
Sir Thomas More, *Utopia*

I am your anointed Queen. I will never be by violence constrained to do anything. I thank God I am endued with such qualities that if I were turned out of the Realm in my petticoat I were able to live in any place in Christendom.
Queen Elizabeth I

I know my life's a pain, and but a span;
I know my sense is mocked in ev'ry thing:
And to conclude, I know myself a man,
Which is a proud, and yet a wretched thing.
Sir John Davies, *Nosce Teipsum*

My nature is subdued
To what it works in, like the dyer's hand.
William Shakespeare, Sonnet 111

There was a star danced, and under that was I born.
William Shakespeare, *Much Ado About Nothing*

Men must endure
Their going hence even as their coming hither:
Ripeness is all.
William Shakespeare, *King Lear*

Reading Critically The information on this page is designed to help students read critically the literature of the English Renaissance. It is designed to help students place a literary work in its historical context, understand the literary movements of the time, and appreciate the writers' techniques used to convey the ideas of the period.

Discuss the information on this page with your students, and explain that the selection that accompanies this page, "Whoso List to Hunt," by Sir Thomas Wyatt, is a model for reading critically the literature of this period. It contains in the side column notes that draw attention to elements that reflect the historical context, the influence of literary movements, and the writer's techniques. Have students pay attention to these notes and suggest that they make their own critical comments as they read the selection.

To give students further practice with the process of reading critically, use the selection in the Teaching Portfolio, Sonnet 61, by Michael Drayton, page 173, following the Teacher Backup, which students can annotate themselves. Encourage students to use these strategies as they read the literature in this unit.

READING CRITICALLY

The Literature of 1485–1625

Historical Context

During the years from 1485 to 1625, English life changed dramatically. The feudal system disappeared, and overseas commerce transformed England into a wealthy and powerful nation. The English navy became one of the world's strongest military forces, and through exploration and colonization Britain developed into a large, rapidly expanding empire. Religious life in England also underwent a major transformation during this period. Refusing to accept the Pope's decision not to allow him to divorce his wife, King Henry VIII severed the country's connection with the Roman Catholic Church and established the Church of England, appointing himself as the church's leader.

Literary Movements

It was during this period that English literature came into full bloom. A cultural movement known as the Renaissance swept through the European continent, eventually making its way into England. Responding to this movement, Queen Elizabeth I actively supported education, science, and the arts. Her support helped to generate a tremendous amount of literary activity. Influenced by the classical works of ancient Rome and Greece, writers explored new literary forms and created some of the finest works the country has ever produced.

Writers' Techniques

The most significant developments of the period came in the areas of poetry and drama. Turning away from the long narrative poems of the Middle Ages, poets introduced a new poetic form, the lyric, into English literature. Lyrics are short, tightly structured poems in which the speaker generally focuses on conveying his or her thoughts or feelings. Most often, during this period lyrics were written in sonnet form, and they frequently dealt with the subject of love. Sonnets were often written in sequences and were generally filled with energetic, musical language. Dramas during this period were also known for their beautiful language. Written in carefully crafted verse, these dramas delve into complex characters and themes, frequently offering important insights about human nature.

On the following pages is a selection by poet Sir Thomas Wyatt. The notes in the side column should help you to place the selection in its historical context.

Objectives

1 To understand the Petrarchan sonnet
2 To interpret figurative meaning
3 To read aloud a classic poem
4 To respond to criticism

Support Material

Teaching Portfolio
Teacher Backup, p. 169
Reading Actively, Sonnet 61, p. 173
Usage and Mechanics Worksheet, p. 174
Analyzing Literature Worksheet, *Understanding the Petrarchan Sonnet*, p. 175
Critical Thinking and Reading Worksheet, *Interpreting Figurative Meaning*, p. 176
Selection Test, p. 177

VIEW OF A PARK, WITH HUNTSMEN AND DEER
Peter Tillemans
Victoria & Albert Museum Trustees

Whoso List[1] to Hunt

Sir Thomas Wyatt

Whoso list to hunt, I know where is an hind,[2]
But as for me, alas, I may no more:
The vain travail hath wearied me so sore.

> **Writer's Technique:** This poem is a Petrarchan sonnet with an *abbaabba cddcee* rhyme scheme.

---

1. Whoso list: Whoever wants.
2. hind: Doe.

I am of them that farthest cometh behind;
5 Yet may I, by no means, my wearied mind
Draw from the deer, but as she fleeth afore,
Fainting I follow. I leave off therefore,
Since in a net I seek to hold the wind.
Who list her hunt, I put him out of doubt,
10 As well as I, may spend his time in vain.
And graven with diamonds in letters plain
There is written, her fair neck round about,
"Noli me tangere,[3] for Caesar's I am,[4]
And wild for to hold, though I seem tame."

---

3. *Noli me tangere*: "Don't touch me"; words spoken by the resurrected Jesus in John 20:17.
4. Caesar's I am: At the time in which the poem was written, it was believed that Caesar attached collars inscribed with the words "Do not touch me, for I am Caesar's" to his deer to protect them from hunters.

Sir Thomas Wyatt (1503?–1542) was a diplomat and courtier in the service of King Henry VIII as well as a poet. Born in Kent, Wyatt lived an eventful and sometimes dangerous life. In 1527 while on a government mission in Italy, he became deeply interested in the works of Petrarch, the great fourteenth-century Italian poet. Already a master of traditional English lyrics, Wyatt became, under Petrarch's influence, a skillful writer of sonnets and introduced this form into England.

Wyatt was born in Kent in the castle of his father, a member of Henry's Privy Council and an executor of his will. Following in his father's footsteps, young Thomas took his place in court as a page at Princess Mary's christening. He entered Cambridge University in 1516, and married Elizabeth Brook, the daughter of Lord Cobden, in 1520.

Wyatt's poetry has been praised for its vigor and drama but is sometimes criticized for its roughness of meter. He was fortunate to have found in Petrarch an excellent form—the sonnet—which gave artistic shape to the sincerity and depth of emotion he felt when writing about love. The sonnet "Whoso List to Hunt," illustrates both the virtues of his poetry and his debt to Petrarch. It also has a special biographical interest, for it is almost certainly about his relationship with Anne Boleyn, later the wife of Henry VIII.

Sir Thomas Wyatt was the first important poet of the English Renaissance. He introduced to England a poetic form used by numerous great poets, including Shakespeare, for nearly five centuries. He ushered in the first great age of English lyric poetry. Finally, he wrote a number of poems that have a permanent place in English literature.

THINKING ABOUT THE SELECTION
Recalling

1. On the literal level, what realization has the speaker come to?
2. Tell why you think his feelings are or are not in complete harmony with this realization.
3. What are his cautionary remarks to other hunters?

Interpreting

4. (a) If this poem on the figurative level is about the poet's love for Anne Boleyn, then what does hunting a hind represent? (b) Whom does Caesar stand for?
5. What special meaning does "Noli me tangere" have?

Applying

6. Wyatt lived and wrote four and a half centuries ago. Do the feelings in "Whoso List to Hunt" seem to be outdated? Tell why you think that this poem does or does not speak to people today.

ANALYZING LITERATURE
Understanding the Petrarchan Sonnet

A sonnet is a fourteen-line poem in iambic pentameter with a fixed rhyme scheme. In the **Petrarchan sonnet** you have just read, the rhyme scheme of the octave is *abbaabba;* that of the sestet is *cddcee.*

1. To what extent is the two-part structure of the sonnet reflected in the thought content?
2. The sonnet was originally used almost exclusively for love poetry. Is there something about the sonnet form that makes it more suitable for this subject than for others? Explain your answer.

CRITICAL THINKING AND READING
Interpreting the Figurative Meaning

A poet will sometimes write a poem that has both a literal and a **figurative meaning.** "Whoso List to Hunt" is such a poem. On the literal level it is about hunting a hind. On the figurative level it is about the speaker's frustrated love for a lady. In general, you should view a poem as having a figurative meaning only when there is either internal or external evidence for such a view. Internal evidence refers to the details of a poem that clearly suggest an intended meaning beyond the literal one. External evidence refers to knowledge about the poet's life, artistic beliefs, and so on, that likewise suggests a meaning beyond the literal.

1. What external evidence do you have for interpreting Wyatt's poem as an account of his love for Anne Boleyn?
2. What internal evidence indicates that the sonnet is a love poem?

SPEAKING AND LISTENING
Reading Aloud Classic British Poems

Reading aloud older British poems may be more difficult than reading more recent poems. In older poetry you will encounter more archaic, obsolete, and unfamiliar words. The sentence structure may be more complicated and twisted. Historical references may be obscure. Such difficulties impede reading.

Practice reading "Whoso List to Hunt" aloud.

THINKING AND WRITING
Responding to Criticism

A critic of Wyatt's, J. W. Lever, remarked in his book *The Elizabethan Love Sonnet* that "Wyatt's best love poetry was really out-of-love poetry." In a brief essay, show why you think that "Whoso List to Hunt" could or could not be used as evidence to support Lever's statement.

First go over the poem carefully looking for details that help you answer the question "Is this a love poem or an out-of-love poem?" Then decide on an effective order in which to present your analyses and conclusions. When you revise, be sure you have relied on what is actually in the poem and have not read anything into it. Assume that you are writing for people who enjoy reading intelligent, well-written literary criticism.

to be presented in the octave and the speaker's thoughts and feelings about the situation to be presented in the sestet. This makes the form especially well suited to love poetry, though it can be equally effective for other subjects.

ANSWERS TO CRITICAL THINKING AND READING

1. It was rumored he was romantically involved with her. He was imprisoned with others when Anne's later infidelities were discovered.
2. The poem speaks of the pursuit of a single doe, but it makes no mention of weapons or the kill. "Her fair neck round about" hardly conjures the image of a deer; rather, it suggests interest in a woman.

SPEAKING AND LISTENING

Consider having students practice their readings in groups, where group members can give feedback and suggestions. Then have volunteers read aloud the sonnet to the class.

THINKING AND WRITING

Publishing Student Writing
After students have written their essays, you might have them take sides: those who believe that this is an "out-of-love" poem and those who do not. Have several students from each side read their essays while you list on the board the major support for each side. Perhaps you might have an informal debate about the issue to see if one side can convince the other.

Closure and Extension

ANSWERS TO THINKING ABOUT THE SELECTION
Recalling

1. The speaker realizes that he is physically unable to continue the hunt.
2. His feelings are not in harmony with this realization because his mind continues the pursuit.
3. He remarks that all is hopeless. The hind is the property of another.

Interpreting

4. (a) Hunting a hind would represent his futile pursuit of Ann Boleyn. (b) Caesar would represent Henry VIII.
5. The Latin words imply "I am already spoken for."

Applying

6. Suggested Response: The poem remains widely read because it reflects a human condition that will continue to exist.

ANSWERS TO ANALYZING LITERATURE

1. In the first part of the sonnet, the speaker addresses his situation. In the second part he gives advice to others based on what he has learned.
2. The two–part structure of the sonnet allows for a romantic situation

SIR PHILIP SIDNEY

1554–1586

Sir Philip Sidney wrote the first great sonnet sequence in English, *Astrophel and Stella.* Before Sidney, Sir Thomas Wyatt and the Earl of Surrey had written excellent sonnets, but Sidney was the first to write a series of sonnets linked by subject matter and theme. In addition, his *Defence of Poesy* marks the beginning of English literary criticism.

Sidney was born at Penshurst, the country home of his aristocratic family. After studying at Oxford and Cambridge he traveled extensively in Europe. Back in England he became a favorite at court, where his charm, intelligence, and good judgment were recognized and admired. In 1575 he made the acquaintance of Penelope Devereux, the daughter of Lord Essex. She was then thirteen. They became engaged, but the engagement was later broken off and Penelope became the wife of Lord Rich. She is the Stella of *Astrophel and Stella.*

In 1580 he fell out of favor with the court for writing a letter to Queen Elizabeth urging her not to marry the Duke of Anjou. He then retired to his sister's home, where he wrote part of *Arcadia,* a pastoral romance. Eventually he regained his status with the queen and was knighted in 1583. In 1586 during a military engagement against the Spanish Catholics in Holland, Sidney was wounded. As he lay on the ground, he refused the water offered him, insisting that it be given to another wounded soldier. Twenty-six days later Sidney died, to the great grief of his country.

As the nephew of the influential Earl of Leicester and the son of the highly respected Elizabethan statesman Sir Henry Sidney, young Philip was early groomed for success. Yet throughout his life he carried himself with modesty. Former schoolmate Fulke Greville captured Sidney's innate dignity in a line from the biography he wrote twenty-five years after his friend's death: "though I . . . knew him from a child, yet I never knew him other than a man—with such staidness of mind, lovely and familiar gravity, as carried grace and reverence above greater years."

During his life Sir Philip Sidney was widely revered as a courtier, soldier, scholar, and poet—a model gentleman of the English Renaissance. Today he is acknowledged as the first important literary critic in English. He is also recognized as the poet who inspired the sonnet sequences of later Renaissance poets and as the author of a number of eloquent sonnets that stand with the best poetry of this period.

222   *The English Renaissance*

Sonnet 31; Sonnet 39

Literary Forms

The Sonnet Sequence. A sonnet sequence is a group of sonnets linked by theme or subject. The form was brought to perfection by the fourteenth-century Italian poet Petrarch, whose *Sonnets to Laura* directly or indirectly inspired the sequences of later poets.

Again and again certain conventions appear in sonnet sequences: The lady is golden-haired, with cheeks like roses or lilies. She is proud. She cruelly rebuffs her poet-lover. The lover is unfailingly faithful. He fears her scorn and rejection but hopes for her love. Hence he describes himself as alternately freezing and burning. He is like a ship tossed by the sea. He calls upon sleep to ease his cares. Through his poetry his lady will be given eternal fame.

The widespread reliance of English Renaissance poets on such conventions makes their poetry seem somewhat artificial. In real life, love is seldom as it is depicted in poetry that makes use of Petrarchan conventions. Nevertheless, the sonnet sequences were enormously popular in their day, and the best of them are still read today.

Writing

Do love stories of today (in books, films, and TV shows) make use of widely recurring conventional ideas about men, women, and the course of love? List as many as you can recall.

Primary Source

In Sonnet 31 the speaker refers to "wit." This was one of the most important qualities of a Renaissance courtier and writer. Although the speaker here refers to intelligence rather than humor, Sonnet 31—as with much of Sidney's work—is shot through with clever, often humorous wordplays. J. C. A. Rathmell believes that Sidney's poetry "is characterized by the frequent appearance of a sly and subtle wit that is always threatening into question, albeit affectionately, the heroic and romantic values it ostensibly celebrates." Although Sidney's sonnets can be marred by over-elaboration, he continues, "what is immediately discernible, however, is his critical awareness of these elements in his work and his readiness to subject them to a good-humored scrutiny . . . an often disconcertingly dry and caustic wit are crucial components of Sidney's style, and it is their alliance with other quite contrary elements —vulnerability, sensibility, and a lingering attachment to the old high ways of romance and chivalry—that combine to make his writing so distinctive, and so winning." What examples of wit can you find in life today?

Guide for Interpreting 223

Literary Focus You might mention that the major Elizabethan poets and, to a lesser degree, John Donne were all at least indirectly indebted to earlier, Continental poets, such as Dante, Petrarch, Boccaccio, and Ronsard. The courtly, Petrarchan love literature of the Elizabethan age owes its themes, attitudes, and conventions to these earlier Italian and French authors.

Teaching to Ability Levels Make *Astrophel and Sella* available to those wishing to read more or all of it. For **less advanced** students, suggest that linking sonnets together by subject matter might be like finding a noted popular music writer linking twenty or more of his songs— that each could be sung on its own, but if all were done in sequence in concert, let's say, there would emerge a larger story form them.

Writing/Prior Knowledge Have students consider poem or story ideas that link together yet are able to stand alone.

Vocabulary

Preteach the following vocabulary work:
wan (wän) *adj.*: sickly pale (p. 224, l. 2)
languished (laŋ wisht) *v.*: made weak or sickly looking (p. 224, l. 7)
balm (bäm) *n.*: anything healing or soothing (p. 226, l. 2).

Spelling Tip Point out the silent *l* in *balm*.

Sonnet 31

Sir Philip Sidney

1 With how sad steps, O Moon, thou climb'st the skies!
    How silently, and with how wan a face!
2   What, may it be that even in heavenly place
That busy archer[1] his sharp arrows tries?
5 Sure, if that long-with-love-acquainted eyes
    Can judge of love, thou feel'st a lover's case.
3   I read it in thy looks, thy languished grace,
To me, that feel the like, thy state descries.[2]
    Then even of fellowship, O Moon, tell me
10   Is constant love deemed there but want of wit?[3]
4 Are beauties there as proud as here they be?
Do they above love to be loved, and yet
    Those lovers scorn whom that love doth possess?
    Do they call virtue there ungratefulness?

---

1. busy archer: Cupid, the Roman god of love.
2. descries: Reveals.
3. wit: Intelligence.

THINKING ABOUT THE SELECTION

Recalling

1. What four lover's complaints are expressed in the sestet?
2. Describe the appearance of the moon.

Interpreting

3. What is the connection between the appearance of the moon and the thoughts the speaker utters?

4. Paraphrase lines 3–4 and lines 5–8.
5. Judging by what is said in the sonnet, what do you infer about the speaker's relationship with his lady?

Applying

6. How would you answer the speaker's question to the moon: "O Moon, tell me/Is constant love deemed there but want of wit"? How is constancy in love viewed in the modern world? Explain your answer.

SHEPHERDS UNDER A FULL MOON
Samuel Palmer
Ashmolean Museum, Oxford

Humanities Note

Fine art, *Shepherds Under a Full Moon* by Samuel Palmer. Samuel Palmer (1805–1881), a British painter, is best known for the small, intense landscapes he painted during a seven-year period in Shoreham, Kent. A self-taught artist, Palmer was influenced by the works and person of William Blake. He belonged to a group of artists called "The Ancients," who worked with the sincerity and purity of artists in the Middle Ages. His landscapes combined direct approach and deep color with poetic vision and pantheistic joy.

Shepherds Under a Full Moon was painted during the Shoreham years, 1826–1833. Moonlit landscapes were a favorite subject of Samuel Palmer. He loved the magical transformation of shapes and forms by the cool gray light. The shepherds become ancient draped statues; the sheep become silvered forms carved from the dark, mysterious landscape. The dreamlike beauty of the scene and the mystical mood of the painting are qualities found in all the Shoreham paintings of Samuel Palmer.

You might use these questions for discussion:
1. Do the figures in the painting seem to be addressing questions to the moon as Sidney does in this sonnet?
2. How do you think the painter feels about the moon?
3. How does the painter's feelings compare with the poet's feelings about the moon?

Primary Source

London in Sidney's day held little of the beauties of nature that he described in his sonnets. Here is how Alfred H. Bill describes what the city was like when Sidney was a teenager:

"There were the aisles of the cathedral, filled with bargaining hucksters and strutting loungers. The streets were thronged with grave merchants, apprentices dodging on their errands, groups of idle serving men badged with blue and gold, whose swords and bucklers might clash at any moment in some bloody outbreak of their noble masters' rivalry at court. Gallants swaggered through the press, so extravagant in the width of their ruffs and the lengths of their swords and daggers that a law had to be passed to regulate them . . . There was the stirring of cutpurses at night. There were stage plays; and even a sensitive boy had been so toughened by the brutal sights common at the time that he could look on at a bull-baiting or a bear-baiting with as much enjoyment as one of the present day gets out of a boxing match. Criminals were strung up publicly and as nearly as might be on the scene of their wrong-doing. Dead pirates clanked on their chains in the gallows on the river-bank. With a litte luck one might see at Tyburn the ghastly business of a traitor's disembowelment alive. The heads and quarters of such, all shiny-black with the tar that preserved them from the weather, decorated the spikes above London Bridge and Temple Bar."

From this description, what picture do you get of London in Sidney's day? Would you have like to have lived there? Why or why not?

Sonnet 31 225

Closure and Extension

ANSWERS TO THINKING ABOUT THE SELECTION
Recalling

1. Constancy is treated as a form of idiocy; beauties are too proud; they scorn those who love them; and they consider their own ingratitude a virtue.

2. It climbs into the sky silently with sad steps and wan face.

Interpreting

3. The moon looks to him the way he feels, prompting his questions.
4. Lines 3-4: "Tell me, does Cupid fire his arrows even in the heavenly place where you dwell?" Lines 5-8: "If one long acquainted with love is seeing right, your appearance and manner are those of one in love."

5. He hardly suggests a joyous romance.

Applying

6. "No, constant love is not considered stupidity." In general, people value and admire constancy in love.

Motivation for Reading Ask students if they have ever felt a strange desire for sleep not because they were physically tired but because they were oppressed by cares or worries. This poem is based on the idea that sleep may offer escape from life's unhappiness.

Master Teacher Note A number of structural and content similarities exist between Sonnet 31 and Sonnet 39. Look for and discuss them, beginning with the similar first lines.

Purpose-setting Question Why does the poet seek sleep?

Purpose-setting Question What helps and comforts does Sidney attribute to sleep?

1 **Discussion** How is sleep viewed by the poet? Is this a narrow view? The phrase "poor man's wealth" is a paradox, an apparent contradiction that in fact makes sense. What does this paradox mean?

2 **Discussion** The poet continues to struggle against despair. Tribute (line 8) here means some form of payment. What good tribute might the poet offer?

3 **Discussion** Challenge your students to paraphrase the sestet. To help them, point out that the poet offers to give sleep all the things that make for a sound rest.

Reader's Response What phrase describing sleep could you add to the ones Sidney uses in lines 1–4?

Sonnet 39

Sir Philip Sidney

1
Come sleep, O sleep, the certain knot of peace,
The baiting place[1] of wit, the balm of woe,
The poor man's wealth, the prisoner's release,
The indifferent judge between the high and low;

2
5 With shield of proof[2] shield me from out the prease[3]
Of those fierce darts Despair at me doth throw:
O make in me those civil wars to cease;
I will good tribute pay, if thou do so.

3
Take thou of me smooth pillows, sweetest bed,
10 A chamber deaf to noise, and blind to light,
A rose garland, and a weary head:
And if these things, as being thine by right,
Move not thy heavy grace, thou shalt in me,
Livelier then elsewhere, Stella's image see.

---

1. **baiting place:** A place for refreshment.
2. **proof:** Proven strength.
3. **prease:** Crowd.

Commentary

"Come sleep," the speaker cries in the first line of Sonnet 39. But what exactly causes sleep? And what purpose does it serve? Scientists have made enormous strides in identifying the chemicals our brain releases to make us sleep and have described several kinds of sleep. D-sleep, for example, is so called because people awakened during these periods often report that they have been *dreaming*. S-sleep, in contrast, seems not to be marked by dreaming, although it is also a deep stage of sleep.

Despite this progress understanding the nature of sleep, no one is really sure what function sleep provides. Some scientists claim that sleep has no biological function at all—that it is simply a sort of habit! Others, however, believe that sleep does indeed play a very important role in our survival. We have more S-sleep after exercise, starvation, and other times of metabolic stress, for example. This suggests that S-sleep most likely helps rebuild the body and the brain. D-sleep appears to function in much the same way, but on a more complex level, restoring the higher-level brain functions.

The need for sleep varies tremendously. An infant sleeps 16 to 18 hours a day, at least half of which is D-sleep. A teenager, though, sleeps only 7 to 8 hours, of which 1.5 hours are spent in D-sleep. You've probably heard stories of people who do not need sleep, but such reports are unproven; everyone needs at least 4 or 5 hours of sleep a night.

Grammar in Action

The term **closure** refers to the way in which a work of art, or any piece of writing, is concluded with a feeling of finality. Writers use many different strategies to create a sense of closure. For instance, Gwendolyn Brooks ends her poem "We Real Cool," with a final statement that expresses the fate of the poem's speakers. Also contributing to the sense of closure is the abbreviated last line:

We real cool. We
Left school. We

Lurk late. We
Strike straight. We

Sing sin. We
Thin gin. We

Jazz June: We
Die soon.

In Sonnet 39 Sir Philip Sidney achieves closure with a final rhyming couplet and a reference to the person he values most highly, Stella: "And if these things, as being thine by right,/Move

THINKING ABOUT THE SELECTION

Recalling

1. What six benefits does the speaker attribute to sleep in lines 1–4?

Interpreting

2. Literally, what are the fierce darts that Despair hurls (line 6)?
3. What might the metaphor "civil wars" (line 7) signify?
4. In what sense could sleep see Stella's image in the speaker?
5. Why is the speaker addressing sleep?

Applying

6. What psychological truth about people's desire for sleep is the basis for the speaker's calling upon sleep?

ANALYZING LITERATURE

Understanding a Sonnet Sequence

The names Astrophel and Stella mean "star-lover" and "star." Since it is known that Sidney's sequence of 108 sonnets plus 11 songs is based on his love for Penelope Devereux, we know that Astrophel represents Sidney and Stella represents Penelope. The 108 sonnets do not present a love story in narrative form. Rather, they offer reflections on the course of Astrophel's love. A reader, however, can detect the story that underlies the sequence.

Since *Astrophel and Stella* makes extensive use of the love-poem conventions present in Petrarch's *Sonnets to Laura,* the sequence seems to mix the artificial and the real, convention and sincerity. In the best of Sidney's poems, the Petrarchan conventions produce an effect of courtly grace and charm, while allowing the lover's real feelings to show through.

1. Do Sidney's two sonnets seem to you primarily sincere or primarily artificial? Give reasons for your opinion.
2. Why do you suppose a poet would decide to use an elaborate set of conventional ideas and images in love poetry, rather than write of love in a realistic way?

THINKING AND WRITING

Writing a Letter of Response

If Stella had received Sonnets 31 and 39 as a gift from Sidney, how might she have responded to them? What might she have said to him in a letter acknowledging that she had received and read the sonnets? Write the letter you think Stella might have written.

First reread the material in the Guide for Reading to review the way ladies were depicted in sonnet sequences. Then decide what Stella would have said in her letter. Assume that she "got the message" Sidney's poems contain. How would she have expressed her thanks for the poems? What might she have said about what the poems imply about her and her treatment of Astrophel? When you revise, make the style of your letter as suitable as you can to the courtly, Petrarchan love depicted in Sidney's sonnets.

not thy heavy grace, thou shalt in me,/Livelier then elsewhere, Stella's image see."

Student Activity. Reread Sidney's Sonnet 31 and explain how he builds to the climax of that poem and ends it on a note of finality.

ANSWERS TO THINKING ABOUT THE SELECTION
Recalling

1. The six benefits of sleep described in lines 1-4 are the following: it assures one of peace; it restores the keen mind; it heals sorrows; it is the poor man's wealth; it allows the prisoner to wander far and wide in his dreams; and it treats all people the same.

Interpreting

2. The fierce darts of despair felt by the poet are likely the pains brought on by his feelings for Stella.
3. The "civil wars" of line 7 suggest strong internal arguments, conflicting opinions, and indecision.
4. Sleep will see Stella's image when the poet dreams of her.
5. The poet addresses sleep because he longs for all of sleep's benefits, and he longs to dream of Stella.

Applying

6. Sleep is a form of escape for people. Also, in dreams people can escape to worlds and places where their lives will not take them.

ANSWERS TO ANALYZING LITERATURE

1. Students will take sides—that the poems seem artificial and that they show strong sincerity. That they are sincere is suggested by the convincing power of language employed by Sidney in each sonnet.
2. Discuss the fact that poetry, through the use of metaphorical language, intensifies feelings and images; that the conventions used by Petrarch proved themselves to be wonderfully inspiring in Italian. In following Petrarch's lead, Sidney was using conventions of form and meaning that his English readers would expect in love poetry and would respond to favorably.

More About the Author It has also been claimed that Marlowe was actually more of what we'd call a free thinker than an atheist in an age of orthodoxy. Shakespeare was to learn much about play construction from him. Marlowe's stunning use of blank verse established it as the dramatic form to follow.

Critical Evaluation Marlowe's near-contemporary Michael Drayton (1563–1631), thinking back on the poet twenty years later, saw him as an inspired figure:

"Next Marlowe bathed in the
    Thespian springs
Had in him those brave translu-
    nary things
That the first poets had; his rap-
    tures were
All air and fire, which made his
    verses clear:
For that fine madness did he still
    retain
Which rightly should possess a
    poet's brain."

CHRISTOPHER MARLOWE

1564–1593

Though not the first English poet to write in blank verse (unrhymed iambic pentameter), Christopher Marlowe's brilliant use of it in his plays established blank verse as the preeminent meter for verse drama and ultimately for epic poetry in English. Marlowe is the author of one of the world's immortal tragedies, *Dr. Faustus*, as well as several other notable plays and poems.

Born in Canterbury, Marlowe was the son of a shoemaker. He went to Cambridge University on a scholarship usually awarded to students studying for the ministry. However, he spent much of his time writing plays and serving as a government agent. He never took holy orders. He is, indeed, reputed to have been an atheist, or at least to have held highly unorthodox religious views.

While at Cambridge Marlowe wrote *Tamburlaine,* the play that made the public aware of his dazzling abilities. It dramatizes the exploits of a fourteenth-century Scythian shepherd who conquered much of the known world. As Marlowe portrays him, Tamburlaine personifies energy and ambition and is thus a character eminently suited for the dramatist's powerful blank verse. In the remaining six years of his life, Marlowe wrote five more plays, including *Dr. Faustus* and a sequel to *Tamburlaine.* On May 30, 1593, he was killed by a dagger thrust in a tavern. His death may have been the result of a fight over the bill, or it may have been a political assassination.

Was Marlowe a spy? Hints that he may have been for a time a spy for Queen Elizabeth's secret service rest on an astonishing letter the Queen's Privy council wrote to the authorities at Cambridge in June of 1587. The letter seeks to suppress rumors that Marlowe planned to go the Rheims. "It was not in her Majesty's pleasure that anyone employed as he had been in matters touching the benefit of his country should be defamed by those who are ignorant in the affairs he went about," they wrote. Such official concern for a young divinity student suggests that Marlowe had performed an unusual service for the government.

Marlowe's fame rests primarily on his plays, especially on his "mighty line," as Ben Jonson described his dramatic blank verse. *Dr. Faustus* has been a classic of dramatic literature for four hundred years. However, Marlowe's nondramatic poetry alone would be enough to secure him a permanent place in English literature. His *Hero and Leander* is one of the finest narrative poems ever written in English, and "The Passionate Shepherd to His Love" is one of the best-known and most popular lyrics of the English Renaissance.

Objectives

1 To appreciate lyric poetry
2 To infer cultural attitudes
3 To write an invitation in verse

Support Material

Teaching Portfolio
Teacher Backup, p. 191.
Usage and Mechanics Worksheet, p. 195
Vocabulary Check, p. 196
Critical Thinking and Reading Worksheet, *Inferring Cultural Attitudes,* p. 197
Language Worksheet, *Appreciating the Multiple Meanings of Words,* p. 198

Selection Test, p. 199
Art Transparency 4, *Mrs. Richard Brinsley Sheridan,* by Thomas Gainsborough

GUIDE FOR INTERPRETING

The Passionate Shepherd to His Love

Pastoral Poetry. A lyric poem is a poem that expresses personal thoughts and feelings. As the word lyric suggests, such a poem may have some of the characteristics of a song. It is often brief and written in rhymed verse with a pronounced rhythm. Many lyric poems have, in fact, been set to music, such as the one you are about to read. Ballads, sonnets, odes, songs, and elegies are some of the more common types of lyric poetry.

"The Passionate Shepherd to His Love" is one of the most famous examples of pastoral poetry. A *pastoral poem* is a lyric that celebrates the beauty and pleasures of country life. As a tradition in English literature, pastoral poetry often makes use of a number of conventions. The speaker in a pastoral poem is frequently a shepherd. He either addresses or speaks about a shepherdess or other country maiden with whom he is in love. The world of nature is idealized. The goodness and happiness of a life in harmony with such a world are valued above all else. Pastoral poetry was especially popular during the English Renaissance, but the tradition extends from the classical era of Greece and Rome to the present.

Writing

Think of the most appealing country place you know. If you wanted to persuade a friend to visit the place, which features would you mention? List five or six and briefly describe them.

Primary Source

Perhaps because of his own experience wrestling with words, Renaissance critic, university president, and baseball commissioner A. Bartlett Giamatti had this to say about Marlowe's use of language: "Renaissance man felt he had the power to transform himself because he had the power of language. Words were units of energy. Through words man could assume forms and aspire to shapes and states otherwise beyond his reach." But "words, like men, were fallen; however, they contained, as we do, shapes of evil within them. Fallen words . . . are unstable elements; thus they are, as we are, such dangers to us. As we must always check that impulse to deformation in ourselves, so we must constantly be aware of the beast in language—Spencer calls it the Blatant Beast, whose rabid bite is vicious slander—and we must know that when we unleash a word and let it soar, we run the risk of loosing an evil force as well, one that we cannot control. We, as men using words, must stay within our limits, or what we master may master and misshape us." What power does language give you? What limits does it impose on you?

This was an era of singing. One was not educated without learning to sing and play an instrument. Lyric poems such as "The Passionate Shepherd to His Love" were often printed in songbooks before they were published elsewhere.

Writing/Prior Knowledge Have students develop lists of words and phrases that create strong and appealing country images. Have students in class select the best of them to be used by all in a paragraph or other written piece.

Vocabulary

Preteach the following vocabulary words:
dales (dālz) *n.:* Hollows, valleys (p. 230, l. 3)
madrigals (mad´ ri gəlz) *n:* Songs with parts for several voices with no musical accompaniment (p. 230, l. 8)
posies (pō´ zēz) *n.:* Bouquets (p. 231, l. 10)
swains (swānz) *n.:* Country youths (p. 231, l. 21)

Motivation for Reading Read to your students some good examples of pastoral poetry from an anthology of Elizabethan poetry.

Master Teacher Note You might point out that pastoral lyrics such as Marlowe's represent a very old tradition in Western poetry. The classical Greek and Roman poets established the tradition, which poets today have not yet abandoned.

Thematic Idea This poem should be read in conjunction with Raleigh's "Nymph's Reply to the Shepherd" (p. 238).

Purpose-Setting Question Why do you think this pastoral lyric was one of the most famous of Elizabethan songs?

1 Literary Focus This flawless lyric gained great popularity in its own day and elicited many "replies." Have students note the four-beat line, which is much quicker than a sonnet's five-beat line.

2 Discussion The idyllic setting and descriptions ignore reality. Why might a love poem present an idealized version of nature?

Humanities Note

Fine art, *The Hireling Shepherd* by William Holman Hunt. William Holman Hunt (1827–1910) was a British painter. Educated at the School of the Royal Academy in London, Hunt rebelled against the stifling academic atmosphere and became one of the original founding members of the Pre-Raphaelite Brotherhood. The Pre-Raphaelites endeavored through their painting to return art to the pure simplicity and honesty of the early Christian painters before Raphael. In his paintings, William Holman Hunt combined realistic treatment with romantic themes from literature, history, and the Bible.

1 The Passionate Shepherd to His Love

Christopher Marlowe

2
Come live with me, and be my love,
And we will all the pleasures prove[1]
That hills and valleys, dales and fields,
And all the craggy mountains yields.

5 And we will sit upon the rocks,
Seeing the shepherds feed their flocks,
By shallow rivers, to whose falls
Melodious birds sings madrigals.

THE HIRELING SHEPHERD
William Holman Hunt
The Manchester City Art Galleries

———
1. prove: Experience.

The Hireling Shepherd was painted in 1853. Hunt's approach to the traditional romantic subject matter is original in composition. Painted with carefully detailed realism, the colors of the work are bright and fresh. Hunt approached each painting with passion and sincerity. He strove to exalt the viewer and to record nature faithfully.

You may wish to ask the following questions:
1. Does the shepherd in the painting appear to be sincere? Explain.
2. Is the shepherd in the poem sincere?
3. Does the woman in this painting appear to believe the promises the shepherd is making? Explain.

And I will make thee beds of roses,
10   And a thousand fragrant posies,
A cap of flowers and a kirtle[2]
Embroidered all with leaves of myrtle;

A gown made of the finest wool,
Which from our pretty lambs we pull;
15   Fair lined slippers for the cold,
With buckles of the purest gold;

A belt of straw and ivy buds,
With coral clasps and amber studs;
And if these pleasures may thee move,
20   Come live with me, and be my love.

The shepherd swains shall dance and sing
For thy delight each May morning;
If these delights thy mind may move,
Then live with me, and be my love.

                                        3

_____
2. kirtle: Skirt.

THINKING ABOUT THE SELECTION
Recalling

1. Describe the kind of life the shepherd is offering his love.

Interpreting

2. How realistic is his representation of the kind of life he and his love will lead? Explain.

Applying

3. If a poet of today were to write a contemporary version of this poem, how might the details differ from Marlowe's?

ANALYZING LITERATURE
Appreciating Pastoral Poems

A **pastoral poem** idealizes the rustic life. Such poetry often contains an implied contrast between the good life of nature and the corrupt life of a court or city.
1. Read Marlowe's poem aloud. What qualities of it might inspire someone to set it to music?
2. Since a shepherd, not Marlowe, is the speaker, in what sense can the poem be said to express personal thoughts and feelings?
3. Would you infer from "The Passionate Shepherd to His Love" that Marlowe's Elizabethan readers valued the pastoral life because England was becoming more urbanized? Why or why not?

The Passionate Shepherd to His Love   231

3 **Discussion** Have students notice that only the month of May is mentioned, not January or February. Why?

Master Teacher Note After students have read and discussed "The Passionate Shepherd to His Love," place Gainsborough's painting of Mrs. Sheridan, Art Transparency 4, on the overhead projector. Have your class compare the mood and overall effect of the painting with the mood and effect of the poem. What are the obvious differences? Are there any similarities? What might a viewer infer about Gainsborough's feelings about his subject?

Reader's Response How do you think the woman responded to this poem?

Closure and Extension

ANSWERS TO THINKING ABOUT THE SELECTION
Recalling

1. The shepherd is offering his love a form of the good life, filled with pleasures, treasures, eternal spring, and continued happiness.

Interpreting

2. The offerings of the shepherd gen-erate a limited picture. Real life simply isn't that way. The shepherd speaks of rosebuds and May, ne-glecting the rest of the year. He speaks of sitting about while others care for the sheep.

Applying

3. A contemporary version of this poem might give less stress to wearing apparel and more to the continued peace and quiet of this pastoral setting away from the loud and hurried world we live in today.

ANSWERS TO ANALYZING LITERATURE

1. The smooth, easy flow of the words call for it to be sung, which it was.
2. It expresses the personal thoughts and feelings of an imaginary char-acter, the shepherd.
3. Life in the cities of the period left something to be desired, certainly.

This is certainly escapist verse that implies Elizabethan awareness of the possible benefits of rural living.

231

Literary Focus The Broadway musical *Damned Yankees* is a modern popular example of the many variations on this fascinating theme. Gounod's opera *Faust*, first sung in 1859, is still regularly presented around the world today.

Writing Acknowledge the challenge, if not impossibility, for most of us of creating a written record of the emotions accompanying not only imminent death but also an awareness of eternity in Hell. This aside, ask students to write about how they would spend their last hour if they were Dr. Faustus.

Vocabulary

Preteach the following vocabulary words:
firmament (fʉr′ mə mənt) *n.:* The sky, viewed poetically as a solid arch or vault (p. 233 l. 14)
nativity (nə tiv′ə tē′) *n.:* Birth, especially in regard to place and time (p. 233 l. 25)
incessant (in ses′′nt) *adj.:* never ceasing (p. 234 l. 36)
engendered (in jen′dərd) *v.:* Brought into being (p. 234 l. 48)

---

from The Tragical History of the Life and Death of Doctor Faustus

Historical Context

The Faust Legend. The Faust legend is one of the most important legends of western civilization. Numerous writers have seen it as a profound revelation of the consequences of aspiring to rise above the ordinary human condition.

The legend derives from the life and activities of an actual German scholar and magician, Johann Faust (or Faustus), who lived from about 1480 to 1540. He traveled widely, performed magic, and died under mysterious circumstances. Many Germans of the time considered him a fraud, but Martin Luther, the founder of Protestantism, believed that he had Satanic powers. Even during Faust's life he was the subject of legends. According to many of them, he had sold his soul to the devil for youth, knowledge, and magical powers.

In 1587 a crude, unreliable biography of Faust appeared. The unknown author incorporated into it many legends of other magicians. The biography concludes with Faust going to hell at the end of his life. This volume appeared in an English translation titled *The History of the Damnable Life and Deserved Death of Doctor John Faustus*. It is the immediate source of Marlowe's play, which was probably written in 1588.

Commentary

What effect did *The Tragical History of the Life and Death of Doctor Faustus* have on Elizabethan audiences? Witches and devils were very real to Elizabethans, and when Faustus signed his soul away, their blood froze. Indeed, Elizabethans often attributed to witchcraft any unexplained occurrence. Many contemporary legends sprang up about performances of *Doctor Faustus,* just as today stories will often spring up when a horror movie is made. One story concerns a performance of the play in Exeter. As Faustus summoned the devils, the actors counted one more devil than the scene called for and feared that Satan himself was in their midst. Terrified, they stopped the play, the audience ran from their seats, and the actors bolted from town early the next morning.

Writing

Create an imaginary experience you would anticipate with dread— for example, a test of some kind, a visit to a doctor or dentist, or a confrontation. What would be your thoughts and feelings as the time of the experience neared? Write a monologue that presents your thoughts as they pass through your mind. Try to write the monologue in a way that expresses your feelings without naming them.

232   *The English Renaissance*

Objectives

1 To understand the historical context of the legend
2 To make inferences about characters

Support Material

Teaching Portfolio
Teacher Backup, p. 201
Grammar in Action Worksheet, *Using Commas*, p. 204
Usage and Mechanics Worksheet, p. 206
Vocabulary Check, p. 207
Critical Thinking and Reading Worksheet, *Making Inferences About Characters*, p. 208

Speaking and Listening Worksheet, *Evaluating a Dramatic Reading*, p. 209
Selection Test, p. 210

from # The Tragical History of the Life and Death of Doctor Faustus

Christopher Marlowe

Early in the play, Dr. Faustus, the main character, contracts his soul to the devil for special powers of the mind. Now, facing death, he makes a desperate attempt to repent and save his soul.

FAUST. Ah, Faustus,
    Now hast thou but one bare hour to live
    And then thou must be damned perpetually!
    Stand still, you ever-moving spheres of heaven,
5   That time may cease and midnight never come;
    Fair Nature's eye, rise, rise again, and make
    Perpetual day; or let this hour be but
    A year, a month, a week, a natural day,
    That Faustus may repent and save his soul!
10   *O lente lente currite noctis equi.*[1]
    The stars move still,[2] time runs, the clock will strike,
    The devil will come, and Faustus must be damned.
    O, I'll leap up to my God! Who pulls me down?
    See, see, where Christ's blood streams in the firmament!
15   One drop would save my soul—half a drop! ah, my Christ!
    Rend not my heart for naming of my Christ;
    Yet will I call on him—O, spare me, Lucifer!
    Where is it now? 'Tis gone; and see where God
    Stretcheth out his arm and bends his ireful brows.
20   Mountains and hills, come, come and fall on me
    And hide me from the heavy wrath of God,
    No, no—
    Then will I headlong run into the earth:
    Earth, gape! O no, it will not harbor me.
25   You stars that reigned at my nativity,
    Whose influence hath allotted death and hell,
    Now draw up Faustus like a foggy mist

---

1. *O lente . . . equi:* "Slowly, slowly run, O horses of the night," adapted from a line in Ovid's *Amores.*
2. still: Always.

from *Tragical History of Doctor Faustus* 233

4 **Discussion** Having failed to gain some way to avoid eternal Hell, what does he ask next?

5 **Discussion** But what does he conclude?

6 **Discussion** Note that he at least partially accepts the blame for what is about to happen.

Humanities Note

Woodcut, *Faust Conjuring Up the Devil*. The earliest form of type printing in Europe was the fifteenth-century block woodcut. Designs and letters were cut into wood, inked, and pressed onto paper. This wood block print is from the title page of the 1624 edition of *Doctor Faustus*. The primitively executed design was prepared by an unknown artist for a London printer. This scene of Dr. Faustus conjuring up the devil is one of the earliest European examples of printed book illustration.

Into the entrails of yon laboring cloud
That when you vomit forth into the air,
30 My limbs may issue from your smoky mouths,
So that my soul may but ascend to heaven.

[*The watch strikes.*]

Ah, half the hour is past; 'twill all be past anon.
O God,
If thou wilt not have mercy on my soul,
35 Yet for Christ's sake whose blood hath ransomed me
Impose some end to my incessant pain:
Let Faustus live in hell a thousand years,
A hundred thousand, and at last be saved!
O, no end is limited to damnèd souls!
40 Why wert thou not a creature wanting soul?
Or why is this immortal that thou hast?
Ah, Pythagoras' *metempsychosis*[3]—were that true,
This soul should fly from me, and I be changed
Unto some brutish beast. All beasts are happy,
45 For when they die
Their souls are soon dissolved in elements,
But mine must live still to be plagued in hell.
Cursed be the parents that engendered me!
No, Faustus, curse thyself, curse Lucifer
50 That hath deprived thee of the joys of heaven.

[*The clock strikes twelve.*]

---

3. metempsychosis: The supposed passing of the soul at death into another body; from the philosophy of Pythagoras, an ancient Greek philosopher and mathematician, who lived in the sixth century B.C.

FAUST CONJURING UP THE DEVIL (WOODCUT)
Artist Unknown
The Bettmann Archive

Grammar in Action

Many individual words, phrases, and clauses need to be set off by **commas.** These include those that appear at the beginning of a sentence and nouns of direct address.

Notice the opening lines of this speech:

Ah, Faustus,
Now hast thou but one bare hour to live

And then thou must be damned perpetually!
Stand still, you ever-moving spheres of heaven, . . .

Here, the introductory word *Ah* is correctly set off by a comma. Similarly the two expressions of direct address, *Faustus* and *you ever-moving spheres of heaven,* are preceded and followed by commas, which indicate that these expressions are grammatically separate from the rest of the sentences in which they occur.

It strikes, it strikes! Now, body, turn to air
Or Lucifer will bear thee quick[4] to hell!

[*Thunder and lightning.*]

O soul, be changed to little water drops
And fall into the ocean, ne'er be found.
55 My God, my God, look not so fierce on me!

[*Enter* DEVILS.]

Adders and serpents, let me breathe awhile!
Ugly hell, gape not—come not, Lucifer—
I'll burn my books—ah, Mephistophilis!

[*Exit* DEVILS *with* FAUSTUS.]

—————————

4. quick: Alive.

THINKING ABOUT THE SELECTION

Recalling

1. What vain hopes and longings pass through Faustus's mind as midnight approaches?

Interpreting

2. Explain his exclamation "O, I'll leap up to my God! Who pulls me down? / See, see, where Christ's blood streams in the firmament!"
3. What does Faustus request of the stars in lines 25–31?
4. Paraphrase lines 40–46.
5. Analyze Marlowe's poetic technique in the excerpt. How does he convey Faustus's terror and despair?

Applying

6. Can you imagine another situation that would cause someone to feel terror and despair equal to Faustus's? Explain why you do or do not think that Faustus's terror and despair are unsurpassable.

ANALYZING LITERATURE

Understanding Historical Context

Marlowe's *Dr. Faustus* is the first great literary treatment of the Faust legend. In the centuries that have followed, a number of major writers have used the legend as the basis for literary works. The greatest of these is Goethe's poetic drama *Faust*.

The importance of the Faust legend is that it embodies what some thinkers see as an enduring impulse in Western civilization from the Renaissance to the present: the drive to go beyond ordinary bounds of knowledge and power, even at the cost of one's own soul.

1. What impression do you get of Faustus's character and personality from his speech?
2. What moral values and attitudes does the speech implicitly uphold?
3. Name one character from history who could be termed "Faustian." Explain the similarity between this character and Faust.
4. Explain why the quest for knowledge would be an appropriate theme during the English Renaissance.

from *Tragical History of Doctor Faustus*   235

Student Activity 1. Review Faustus's speech and find at least ten other examples of introductory words and expressions of direct address that are correctly set off by commas.

Student Activity 2. Write a paragraph that could serve as a brief speech in which you address directly several persons you know. Each time you address one of these persons by name, use commas to set off the name.

7 Discussion Even as the clock strikes, how does Faustus continue to react? What dramatic effect does this have?

—————————

and, saving all that, he would as soon have no soul at all to avoid his fate.

Interpreting

2. He wishes to leap up to God, but to no avail: he feels as if someone were pulling him down. The blood of Christ is believed to have been shed to save the souls of all mankind.
3. He asks that the stars draw him up into the clouds, and when they spit out the pieces his soul will have burst free to ascend to Heaven.
4. He would rather be a brutish beast whose soul is dissolved into elements than remain himself and face his fate.
5. Marlowe uses vivid and detailed imagery to depict Faustus's state of mind. He also exploits the rhythmic possibilities of blank verse to intensify the emotional level of the speech.

Applying

6. Some students might suggest that the prospect of death as a total extinction of one's being could cause one to feel as much terror and despair as Faustus feels.

ANSWERS TO ANALYZING LITERATURE

1. His speech shows Faustus to be gifted with vivid imagination, grand notions, and the ability to convey his thoughts and images with power and sensitivity.
2. It upholds the need to live within the confines of traditional morality and not to sacrifice one's soul for the more-than-human powers that evil—or the devil—can bestow.
3. Answers will vary. Encourage students to tell how the character they select went beyond the bounds of morality and ethical restraint.
4. The humanistic spirit of the Renaissance made the quest for knowledge a hallmark of Elizabethan culture. Writers would have naturally been attracted to the theme, and readers and playgoers would have responded vigorously to works that made use of it.

Closure and Extension

ANSWERS TO THINKING ABOUT THE SELECTION

Recalling

1. He asks that time cease and midnight never come, so he may repent and save his soul. He seeks but one drop of Christ's blood, when he is restrained from leaping up to Heaven; he hopes the earth will cover him; he wants to be drawn into the entrails of a cloud;

More About the Author Much of Raleigh's verse was published anonymously, the main reason for much of it's being lost. His lyrics were often written in an unconventional style, being more free in form than other verse of the period.

Critical Evaluation In evaluating Raleigh's work, Gerald Bullett wrote that "typical Elizabethan though he was, his best things, perhaps the only ones we can be quite sure are his, have an accent, a spirit, a probing melancholy wit, that seems sometimes to anticipate the mind of a later generation: a something seldom found (outside Shakespeare) in the poetry of his time."

SIR WALTER RALEIGH

1552–1618

Most people remember Sir Walter Raleigh as the courtier who supposedly covered a puddle with his cloak so that Queen Elizabeth I would not get her feet wet. Raleigh was much more than a dashing gallant, however. He is renowned as the founder of the colony of Virginia and the man who introduced tobacco to Europe. In his own time he was honored as a soldier, an explorer, and a poet. Today his actions often receive more attention than his words, but Raleigh's poems, few of which have survived, are rich and complex, reflecting the vicissitudes of his own life.

Raleigh, born into a well to-do family in Devonshire, served as a soldier for the Huguenots in France, attended Oxford briefly, and then, with others, outfitted a fleet purportedly for exploration but in fact to attack Spanish shipping. Returning to England in 1581, he gained an introduction to court and, making the most of his proud, handsome bearing and forceful personality, quickly became a favorite of Queen Elizabeth I. She showered him with honors, bestowed upon him vast estates in Ireland, and put him in charge of expeditions to colonize America, including the one that ended with the "Lost Colony" at Roanoke, Virginia.

Trouble began for Raleigh when the queen learned of his secret marriage to one of her maids of honor. His brief imprisonment at that time foreshadowed a much longer imprisonment under King James I. Accused by James of treason and convicted in an unfair trial, Raleigh spent many of the last years of his life in the Tower of London. There, surrounded by family and servants, he wrote his *History of the World,* a work intended to show God's judgment on the wicked. Released when he was past sixty, he made one final voyage to South America in search of gold. The expedition failed, and upon his return the Spanish ambassador accused him of burning a Spanish settlement. The old charge of treason was revived. Raleigh was convicted, and after calmly composing his own epitaph on October 28, 1618, he went to his execution the next day. He is reported to have run his hand along the edge of the executioner's axe and said, "Think you I fear the shadow of the axe, when I fear not the axe itself?"

Raleigh's reputation as a writer is difficult to assess because so little of his work has survived. What does survive suggests a mature poetic talent. His lyrics convey realism, humor, and largeness of spirit, with occasional flashes of bitterness that his cruel fate would seem to have warranted.

Support Material

Teaching Portfolio
Teacher Backup, p. 213
Usage and Mechanics Worksheet, p. 217
Vocabulary Check, p. 218
Critical Thinking and Reading Worksheet, *Making Inferences About Tone,* p. 220

Language Worksheet, *Understanding Words Based on Greek Myths,* p. 221
Selection Test, p. 222

GUIDE FOR INTERPRETING

The Nymph's Reply to the Shepherd; To His Son

Writer's Techniques

The Speaker. The speaker in a poem is comparable to the narrator in prose fiction. He or she is the one—not usually the poet—who presumably is delivering the lines of the poem. In Marlowe's "The Passionate Shepherd to His Love," for instance, the speaker is a love-obsessed shepherd, not the historical and very unrustic Christopher Marlowe. This distinction is important. It is easy to make the mistake of regarding the poet as the speaker when in fact poets use all sorts of speakers in their poems: kings, knights, shepherds, lovers, Greek gods, mythological heroes, and historical figures, not to mention clouds, animals, and so on. Identifying the speaker and evaluating the purpose of the speaker in a poem can help you understand poetry better.

Writing

Think of an issue or event about which you have strong feelings. It may be the lyrics of a song you dislike. It may be an aspect of school that you think could be improved. It may be a political situation that you think presents problems for your community, state, or nation. Using the cluster technique, jot down your thoughts on the issue.

Primary Source

Sir Walter Raleigh was a dynamic speaker as well as a writer. Over and over Raleigh's contemporaries commented upon the power of his eloquence and personal magnetism to move even his enemies to his side. Nowhere is this more evident than when he was fighting for his very life. His speech during his first trial, in 1603, provides an example of his remarkable appeal. An eyewitness reported that Raleigh answered his accusers with "that temper, wit, learning, courage, and judgment, that, save it went with the hazard of his life, it was the happiest day that ever he spent. In one word, never was a man so hated and so popular in so short a time." Another observer said, "Never man spoke so well in the time past, nor would in the time to come." When he first heard Raleigh speak, the man was "so led with the common hatred that he would have gone a hundred miles to see him hanged," yet he would, before they parted, "have gone a thousand to save his life."

Raleigh's persuasive eloquence characterizes his writing as well. He urges his son, for example, not to allow his passion to overcome his reason, "for that way lies misery." He ends by warning his son, "Have therefore ever more care that thou be beloved of thy wife, rather than thyself besotted [captivated] on her." Do you think Raleigh is correct in saying it is better to be loved than to love? Why or why not?

Vocabulary

Preteach the following vocabulary words:
fold (fōld) n.: A pen in which to keep sheep (p. 238, l. 5).
wanton (wän't'n) adj.: Luxuriant: said of vegetation (p. 238, l.9).
gall (gôl) n.: Something bitter or distasteful (p. 238, l. 11).
folly (fäl'ē) n.: Foolishness (p. 238, l. 16).
apace (ə pās') adv.: Swiftly: with speed (p. 240, l. 1).
asunder (ə sun'dər) adv.: Apart; in separate directions (p. 240, l. 2).
betokeneth (bi tō'k'n eth) v.: To be a sign of; to indicate (p. 240, l. 8).
frets (fretz) v.: Eats away (p. 240, l. 12).
halter (hôl'tər) n.: A rope for hanging; hangman's noose (p. 240, l. 12).

Guide for Interpreting 237

The Nymph's Reply to the Shepherd

Sir Walter Raleigh

1 *This poem was written by Raleigh as a response to the invitation presented in Christopher Marlowe's "The Passionate Shepherd to His Love."*

2 If all the world and love were young,
And truth in every shepherd's tongue,
These pretty pleasures might me move
To live with thee, and be thy love.

3 5 Time drives the flocks from field to fold,
When rivers rage and rocks grow cold,
And Philomel[1] becometh dumb,
The rest complains of cares to come.

4 The flowers do fade, and wanton fields
10 To wayward winter reckoning yields;
A honey tongue, a heart of gall,
Is fancy's spring, but sorrow's fall.

5 Thy gowns, thy shoes, thy beds of roses,
Thy cap, thy kirtle,[2] and thy posies
15 Soon break, soon wither, soon forgotten,
In folly ripe, in reason rotten.

Thy belt of straw and ivy buds,
Thy coral clasps and amber studs,
All these in me no means can move
20 To come to thee and be thy love.

6 But could youth last and love still breed,
Had joys no date[3] nor age no need,
Then these delights my mind might move,
To live with thee and be thy love.

---

1. **Philomel:** The nightingale.
2. **kirtle:** Skirt.
3. **date:** Ending.

THINKING ABOUT THE SELECTION

Recalling

1. (a) Who is the speaker in this poem? (b) Who is the person being addressed? (c) From what literary work are these two characters taken?
2. How does the speaker first suggest that the shepherd may be making unrealistic promises?

Interpreting

3. What does the speaker think about the gifts being offered her in the previous poem?
4. Under what circumstances might the speaker accept the shepherd's offer?
5. In what ways does the form of Raleigh's poem resemble that of Marlowe's?

Applying

6. If the shepherd and the nymph were to debate the question "What is love?" whose side would you take? Why?

ANALYZING LITERATURE

Identifying the Speaker in a Poem

The **speaker** in a poem is the character portrayed as delivering the lines. In "The Nymph's Reply to the Shepherd," the speaker is a nymph—the same nymph whom Marlowe's shepherd addresses in "The Passionate Shepherd to His Love" (page 230). The speaker in a poem should not be confused with the poet. In Raleigh's poem the nymph is the speaker; she is obviously not Raleigh himself. Sometimes the beliefs and attitudes of the speaker are the same as those of the poet, but not always.

1. (a) What is the speaker's attitude toward the shepherd's proposal? (b) How would you describe her emotional state?
2. Do you think Sir Walter Raleigh's own view of the shepherd's proposal is probably the same as or different from that of the nymph? Support your answer.

CRITICAL THINKING AND READING

Making Inferences About Tone

Tone is the attitude shown by a writer toward his or her subject, characters, or audience. It is often expressed as an adjective: cheerful, sarcastic, amused, lofty, sad, or any of dozens of other possibilities. The tone of "The Passionate Shepherd to His Love" might be described as optimistic. Tone is created through choice of words and details.

1. How would you describe the tone of "The Nymph's Reply to the Shepherd"?
2. What words in the poem help to convey this tone? Find at least five words.

THINKING AND WRITING

Writing an Invitation in Verse

Write a four-line or eight-line poem to invite a group of friends to a picnic in the country. Use a four-beat line and an *aabb* rhyme scheme. First think of some of the most appealing aspects of the picnic, such as the guests, the foods that will be served, and the scenic features of the picnic area. Then describe them in verse. You might conclude your invitation by repeating all or part of your opening line.

When you revise, try to make the tone of your verses lighthearted and pleasant. If you wish, idealize the pleasures of the picnic. Read the invitation aloud to check that the rhythm and rhyme sound right.

THINKING AND WRITING

Writing Your Own Reply

Using either Marlowe's (page 230) or Raleigh's poem as a model, write a poetic response of your own to one or both of the poets' views of love. Begin by making notes on what the poet says; then make a few notes on what you will say. Write your poem trying to match the form of Marlowe's or Raleigh's poem. As you revise your poem, be sure you have made your views clear. The tone of your poem can be humorous, if you wish.

"The Passionate Shepherd to His Love."
2. The first suggestion comes in the *if* clause of line 1.

Interpreting

3. She thinks the gifts are ephemeral and therefore of little value.
4. She would accept his offer if youth could last, love and joy never end, and age bring no grief.
5. Both poems are written in iambic tetrameter quatrains rhyming *aabb*.

Applying

6. Answers will vary. Idealists will probably side with the amorous shepherd, skeptics with the negativistic nymph.

ANSWERS TO ANALYZING LITERATURE

1. (a) She is skeptical toward it. (b) She seems cool and self-possessed.
2. Raleigh's conceiving the reply suggests that his view of the shepherd's proposal is probably the same as the nymph's.

ANSWERS TO CRITICAL THINKING AND READING

1. The tone is self-assured and somewhat scornful, with a hint of regret in the last stanza.
2. Some words that convey the tone are *If* (line 1), *cold* (line 6), *cares* (line 8), *gall* (line 11), and *rotten,* (line 16).

THINKING AND WRITING

For help with this assignment, students can refer to Lesson 18, "Writing a Poem," in the Handbook of Writing About Literature.

THINKING AND WRITING

For help with this assignment, students can again refer to Lesson 18, "Writing a Poem," in the Handbook of Writing About Literature.

Closure and Extension

ANSWERS TO THINKING ABOUT THE SELECTION
Recalling

1. (a) The speaker is the nymph wooed by the shepherd in Marlowe's "The Passionate Shepherd to His Love." (b) The shepherd is addressed. (c) They are taken from

Master Teacher Note With **less advanced** students, point out that the ''three things'' that the poem is about are a gallows tree, the string of a hangman's bag, and a boy sentenced to hang.

Purpose-Setting Question What do you think Raleigh's son is like?

1 **Literary Focus** This poem is written in the Shakespearean, or English, sonnet form of three quatrains and a couplet. Observe how each section expresses its own idea.

2 **Discussion** What happens when the three things that grow up apart come together?

3 **Discussion** The third quatrain describes what the three things do before they meet and after they meet. Explain.

4 **Discussion** Paraphrase the hope expressed in the closing couplet.

Reader's Response How do you think Raleigh felt about his son? Explain.

To His Son

Sir Walter Raleigh

Three things there be that prosper up apace
And flourish, whilst they grow asunder far,
But on a day, they meet all in one place,
And when they meet, they one another mar;
5 And they be these: the wood, the weed, the wag.[1]
The wood is that which makes the gallow tree;
The weed is that which strings the hangman's bag;
The wag, my pretty knave, betokeneth thee.
Mark well, dear boy, whilst these assemble not,
10 Green springs the tree, hemp grows, the wag is wild,
But when they meet, it makes the timber rot;
It frets the halter, and it chokes the child.
Then bless thee, and beware, and let us pray
We part not with thee at this meeting day.

---

1. wag *n.*: A mischievous young boy.

THINKING ABOUT THE SELECTION
Recalling

1. (a) Who is the speaker in this poem? (b) Who is the person being spoken to?
2. What happens when the wood, the weed, and the wag meet?
3. Who is the wag in the poem?
4. What is the speaker's main concern?

Interpreting

5. Given the speaker's concern, what conclusion can you draw about the behavior of the speaker's son? Explain.
6. How would you describe the poem's tone?

Applying

7. The German writer Goethe wrote, ''Behavior is the mirror in which everyone displays his own image.'' Discuss the meaning of this quotation.

CRITICAL THINKING AND READING
Making Inferences About Purpose

A poet's purpose in writing a poem involves more than just subject and theme. **Purpose** is a broad term that covers whatever the writer intends to communicate to the reader. To infer purpose, you must understand the poem's central idea and you must experience its emotional impact. When you fully understand the meaning of ''The Nymph's Reply to the Shepherd,'' for instance, you can infer that Raleigh's purpose is to refute Marlowe's idealistic and simplistic view of love and to present a more realistic view.

What do you think was Raleigh's purpose in writing this poem to his son?

240 *The English Renaissance*

Closure and Extension

ANSWERS TO THINKING ABOUT THE SELECTION
Recalling

1. (a) The speaker is a father, who may or may not be Raleigh. (b) He is addressing his potentially wayward or free-spirited son.
2. When wood, weed, and wag meet, they mar each other.
3. The wag is the son.
4. The speaker's main concern is that his son not be hanged.

Interpreting

5. We must conclude that the son has at least the potential for finding himself in serious trouble. Such a serious and strong warning would hardly be given otherwise.
6. The tone is serious and moralistic.

Applying

7. Answers will differ, though the general sense might be that how we behave reflects what we think of ourselves.

ANSWERS TO CRITICAL THINKING AND READING

Raleigh's purpose was probably to keep his son out of trouble.

PORTRAIT OF AN UNKNOWN MAN
Nicholas Hilliard

Fine art, *Portrait of an Unknown Man* by Nicholas Hilliard. Nicholas Hilliard (1547–1619) was the premier miniaturist of Elizabethan England. He was apprenticed to the Queen's jewelers and soon began producing miniatures, tiny portraits often mounted in gold and worn as jewelry. In time he was appointed limner (portraitists were called "limners") and goldsmith to Queen Elizabeth I.

This miniature portrait, also called "Young Man Among the Roses," is thought to be a portrait of Robert Devereaux, Second Earl of Essex. Approximately 5½ by 3 inches, it is not very small for a miniature. Executed on parchment glued to pasteboard, the miniature is a copy of a figure in a fresco Hilliard saw in France. With his fancy attire and handsome face, this young nobleman appears to be the perfect English court dandy.

You might use these questions for discussion:

1. Does the young man in this miniature appear to be in need of guidance and advice like that offered by Sir Walter Raleigh to his son? Explain.
2. What is it about the young man in the portrait that makes him seem unworldly and callow?

More About the Author He has been called the poet's poet because so many have learned from his artistry. He blended Platonism, Puritanism, and patriotism in the content of his work, bringing to it Heavenly love and beauty, a moral tone, and his fierce sense of pride in and devotion to what he saw as England's destiny.

Critical Evaluation The literary scholar A. Kent Hieatt wrote that "Edmund Spenser was considered in his day to be the greatest of English poets, who had glorified England and her language by his long allegorical poem *The Faerie Queene*, just as Virgil had glorified Rome and the Latin tongue by his epic poem the *Aeneid*. Spenser had a strong influence upon his immediate successors, and the sensuous features of his style, as well as his nine-line stanza-form, were later admired and imitated by such poets as Byron and Shelley in the Romantic Period of the late 18th and early 19th centuries. He is widely studied today as one of the chief begetters of the English literary Renaissance, a golden age for poetry in English, and as a master who embodied in poetic myth a view of the virtuous life in a Christian universe."

EDMUND SPENSER

1552–1599

Edmund Spenser, the "poet's poet," is one of the very greatest poets of the English Renaissance. An imaginative experimenter in verse forms, he invented the Spenserian stanza and the Spenserian sonnet, which exerted a powerful influence on the poets who followed him.

Unlike many poets of the time, Edmund Spenser was born into a working-class family. His father was a clothmaker, and Edmund attended the Merchant Taylors' School on a scholarship for a poor man's son. He went on to Cambridge University as a "sizar," a student who was required to work his way through school. During Spenser's first year at Cambridge, his earliest poems were published.

Graduating with an M.A. degree in 1576, Spenser served in a variety of positions with wealthy noblemen, including that of secretary to the Earl of Leicester, a favorite of Queen Elizabeth I. While in Leicester's service, he became friends with Sir Philip Sidney, and the two of them formed the core of a select literary group.

In 1580 Spenser took a position as secretary to the Lord Deputy of Ireland. Thereafter he spent most of his life in Ireland, acquiring Kilcolman Castle, an Irish estate, where he did much of his writing. Sir Walter Raleigh visited him at Kilcolman Castle and was so impressed by Spenser's unfinished *The Faerie Queene* that he persuaded Spenser to take the first three books to London for publication.

The Faerie Queene established Spenser's reputation as the leading poet of his day. This great work, intentionally written in an archaic style, combines two literary forms, the romance and the epic, into an allegory about "the twelve moral virtues." Dedicated to Queen Elizabeth I, *The Faerie Queene* brought Spenser a small pension but no position at court.

In 1594 Spenser married Elizabeth Boyle, whom his sonnet sequence *Amoretti* commemorates. *Amoretti*, which means "little cupids" or "little love poems," is unique in the English Renaissance for being addressed to the poet's wife.

Irish rebels destroyed Spenser's castle during an uprising, and Spenser returned to London. He died on January 13, 1599, and is buried in what is now the Poet's Corner of Westminster Abbey.

Objectives

1 To understand the Spenserian stanza
2 To understand the Spenserian sonnet
3 To understand personification
4 To compare and contrast sonnets

Support Material

Teaching Portfolio
Teacher Backup, p. 225
Grammar in Action Worksheet, *Recognizing Parallelism*, p. 230.
Usage and Mechanics Worksheet, p. 232
Vocabulary Check, p. 233
Analyzing Literature Worksheet,

Understanding the Spenserian Stanza, p. 234
Language Worksheet, *Interpreting Personification*, p. 235
Selection Test, p. 236

GUIDE FOR INTERPRETING

from The Faerie Queen; Sonnet 1; Sonnet 26; Sonnet 75

Writer's Techniques

Spenserian Poetry. Edmund Spenser had a lifelong interest in theories of poety, and he is recognized as one of the great innovators in English verse forms. Two of his innovations are especially notable.

When Spenser wrote *The Faerie Queene,* he created a new type of stanza that was named for him. A *Spenserian stanza* consists of nine lines, the first eight of which are in iambic pentamenter. The ninth line has two additional syllables and is called an *alexandrine.* The rhyme scheme of a Spenserian stanza is *ababbcbcc.*

Although most sonnets follow either the Petrarchan or the Shakespearean form, there is a third type called the Spenserian sonnet. A *Spenserian sonnet* has fourteen lines, but its rhyme scheme differs from that of other sonnets. The rhyme scheme is *abab bcbc cdcd ee.* Often there is no break in a Spenserian sonnet between the octave (first eight lines) and sestet (last six lines).

Writing

Spenser intended *The Faerie Queene,* a lengthy allegory, to consist of twelve books, but he completed only six. In each a hero representing a moral virtue was to have a series of adventures, fighting off such enemies as Envy, Pride, and Despair. Among the virtues in Spenser's plan are Holiness, Friendship, Justice, and Courtesy. All twelve books were to be unified by the presence of the legendary Prince Arthur and by Gloriana, who represents Queen Elizabeth I. Select either a virtue such as truth or honesty or a fault such as pride or envy. Freewrite about it.

Primary Source

Even in Elizabethan days poets had trouble getting paid. *The Oxford Book of Literary Anecdotes* records the following event:

Queen Elizabeth ordered that Spenser be given one hundred pounds in payment for some poems he had written in her honor. Lord Treasurer Burleigh objected to the payment, scorning Spenser's work with the comment, "What, all this for a song?" The Queen replied, "Then give him a reason" [for not being paid]. After waiting some time and receiving neither reason nor money, Spenser decided to remind the Queen of her promise. He sent her the following poem: I was promised on a time/To have reason for my rhime./From that time, unto this season,/I received nor rhime, nor reason.

The paper produced the intended effect, and the Queen, after sharply criticizing the Treasurer, immediately ordered that Spenser be paid the hundred pounds she had promised.

Guide for Interpreting 243

Literary Focus Because the alexandrine, or ninth line, of the Spenserian stanza can impede an easy flow from stanza to stanza in longer works, he often repeated the final line or continued the *c* rhyme scheme as the *a* rhyme in the next stanza.

Writing/Prior Knowledge Select one of the topics students think of and have the class discuss what allegorical figure might be used to represent it.

Vocabulary

Preteach the following vocabulary words:

ycladd (i klad′) *pp.*: Clothed, dressed (p. 244, l. 2)

curbe (kʉrb) *n.*: A chain or strap around a horse's lower jaw attached to the bit to check the horse (p. 244, l. 7)

deigne (dān) *v.*: To condescend; lower oneself (p. 245, l. 6)

moly (mō′lē) *n.*: European wild garlic (p. 246, l. 8)

coveted (kuv′it əd) *v.*: Wanted eagerly (p. 246, l. 10)

assay (a sā′) *v.*: To try, attempt (p. 247, l. 5)

eternize (i tʉr′nīz) *v.*: To make everlasting (p. 247, l. 11)

Master Teacher Note Point out that an Elizabethan reader would have responded to Spenser's verse much as a reader of today responds to late-nineteenth-century poetry. The Elizabethan would have considered Spenser's language beautiful but anti-quated.

1 **Literary Focus** Note that the spelling is somewhat archaic with the final silent e remaining on many of the words that have since lost it.

2 **Clarification** *Chide* here means "objected to." His spirited horse objected to the inhibiting bit and curb chain.

Closure and Extension

ANSWERS TO THINKING ABOUT THE SELECTION

Recalling

1. (a) The knight is wearing battered armor. (b) He carries a silver shield. (c) He is riding across a plain.

Interpreting

2. His armor bears the blows of many battles, even though he is untested in combat.
3. The knight might be described as noble.

Applying

4. Answers will vary. The type of person a student chooses is less important than the reasons he or she gives for the choice.

ANSWERS TO ANALYZING LITERATURE

The first three lines, for example, would be marked as follows:

```
U  /  U   /   U   /  U
```
1. A Gen/tle Kinght/was prick/ing
```
   /  U    /
on the plaine,
```
```
U   /  U  /  U  /   U
y  cladd/in might/ie armes/and
```

---

from The Faerie Queene

Edmund Spenser

This excerpt from Spenser's epic, The Faerie Queene, *is a description of the Redcrosse Knight, the hero of Book 1, who represents the virtue of holiness.*

1
A Gentle Knight was pricking[1] on the plaine,
Ycladd in mightie armes[2] and silver shielde,
Wherein old dints of deepe wounds did remaine,
The cruell markes of many a bloudy fielde;
5 Yet armes till that time did he never wield:[3]
2
His angry steede did chide his foming bitt,
As much disdayning to the curbe to yield:
Full jolly[4] knight he seemd, and faire did sitt,
As one for knightly giusts[5] and fierce encounters fitt.

---

1. pricking: Cantering.
2. armes: Armor.
3. Wherein . . . wield: The knight wears the armor of the Christian man, which bears the dents of every Christian's fight against evil. However, Redcrosse is wearing the armor for the first time.
4. jolly: Gallant.
5. giusts: Jousts.

THINKING ABOUT THE SELECTION
Recalling

1. (a) What is the knight wearing? (b) What is he carrying? (c) What is he doing?

Interpreting

2. What is strange about the knight's armor?
3. The knight is described as gentle and jolly (gallant). What one adjective do you think might sum up the knight's character?

Applying

4. If you were to pick a character to represent the moral virtue of truth, what kind of person would you choose?

ANALYZING LITERATURE
Understanding the Spenserian Stanza

The first eight lines of a Spenserian stanza are in iambic pentameter, or ten syllables with a pattern of alternating stressed and unstressed syllables. The ninth line, called the alexandrine, has two additional syllables.
1. Choose three lines of the stanza from *The Faerie Queene,* and mark them for stressed and unstressed syllables and for feet. Use ∪ to indicate an unstressed syllable and / to indicate a stressed syllable.
2. What is the rhyme scheme of this stanza?

```
/ ∪   /
sil/ver shielde,
```
```
∪  /  ∪  /  ∪  /    ∪
Wherein/olddints/ofdeep/wounds
```
```
/  ∪  /
did/remaine . . .
```

2. The rhyme scheme is *ababbcbcc*.

Sonnet 1

Edmund Spenser

Happy ye leaves when as those lily hands,
which hold my life in their dead doing[1] might,
Shall handle you and hold in love's soft bands,
Like captives trembling at the victor's sight,

5 And happy lines, on which with starry light,
Those lamping[2] eyes will deigne sometimes to look
And read the sorrows of my dying spright,[3]
Written with tears in heart's close[4] bleeding book.
And happy rhymes bathed in the sacred brook

10 Of Helicon[5] whence she derived is,
When ye behold that angel's blessed look,
My soul's long lacked food, my heaven's bliss.
Leaves, lines, and rhymes, seek her to please alone,
Whom if ye please, I care for other none.

1. doing: Killing.
2. lamping: Flashing.
3. spright: Spirit.
4. close: Secret.
5. sacred . . . Helicon: From Greek mythology, the Hippocrene, the fountain from which the waters of poetic inspiration flowed, located on Mt. Helicon, the sacred home of the Muses.

THINKING ABOUT THE SELECTION

Recalling

1. What three listeners does the speaker address in Sonnet 1?

Interpreting

2. Who is *she* in line 10 and *her* in line 13?
3. What is the speaker asking the listeners to do?
4. (a) To what objects does Spenser give human qualities? (b) How does Spenser tie this personification to the main idea of the sonnet?

Applying

5. What animal would you choose to personify pride? Why?

ANALYZING LITERATURE
Understanding the Spenserian Sonnet

The rhyme scheme of a Spenserian sonnet differs from that of the more familiar Petrarchan sonnet. The Spenserian rhyme Scheme is *abab bcbc cdcd ee.* Does this rhyme Scheme seem easier or harder for a poet to work with? Explain.

UNDERSTANDING LANGUAGE
Interpreting Personification

A writer who attributes human qualities to objects or animals is using **personification.** When Spenser calls the leaves in line 1 "happy," he is personifying them. Sometimes, as in allegory, personification even extends to abstract words. An idea such as beauty or honor, for example, is given human qualities.

Sonnet 1   245

1 **Discussion** What identical point is the poet making in each of these eight lines? (He states it directly in line 9.)

2 **Discussion** What further points does he make about the union of "sweet with sour"?

3 **Critical Thinking and Reading** Relate this concluding couplet to the implied love affair.

Closure and Extension

ANSWERS TO THINKING ABOUT THE SELECTION
Recalling

1. He uses "Sweet is the . . . , but . . ." in each of the first seven lines and a nearly identical pattern in line 8.
2. Spenser observes that tempering sweet with sour only makes it more desirable.

Interpreting

3. No pain, no gain.

Applying

4. Answers will vary. Some twelfth graders may mention graduation, which is sweet inasmuch as it represents the culmination of their high-school years and sour inasmuch as it represents the end of a phase of their lives.
5. Students should consult a book on Chinese philosophy.

Sonnet 26
Edmund Spenser

1
   Sweet is the rose, but grows upon a briar;
   Sweet is the juniper, but sharp his bough;
   Sweet is the eglantine,[1] but pricketh near;
   Sweet is the fir bloom, but his branches rough;
5 Sweet is the cypress, but his rynd is tough,
   Sweet is the nut, but bitter is his pill;[2]
   Sweet is the broom flower, but yet sour enough;
   And sweet is moly, but his root is ill.

2
   So every sweet with sour is tempered still,[3]
10 That maketh it be coveted the more:
   For easy things that may be got at will,
   Most sorts of men do set but little store.

3
   Why then should I account of little pain,
   That endless pleasure shall unto me gain.

---

1. eglantine: A European rose with hooked spines.
2. pill: Core.
3. still: Always.

THINKING ABOUT THE SELECTION
Recalling

1. In what ways are the lines in the octave of Sonnet 26 similar?
2. According to Spenser, what is the effect of tempering every "sweet with sour"?

Interpreting

3. How would you express in today's English what Spenser says in the closing couplet?

Applying

4. List other examples from life where the sweet is offset by the sour.
5. Find information on the Chinese principle of yin and yang.

Grammar in Action

Parallelism is the placement of equal ideas in words, phrases, or clauses of similar types. Following are examples of different types of parallelism.

   PARALLEL WORDS: John was *healthy*, *happy*, and *strong*.
   PARALLEL PHRASES: I really enjoy *shopping at small stores* and *conversing with the sales clerks*.

   PARALLEL CLAUSES: The broadcaster *whom you met last July* and *whom you saw on television yesterday* will be speaking.
   PARALLEL SENTENCES: *I visited his house, but he was away. I visited it again the next day, but he would not see me.*

Spenser uses parallel sentences in Sonnet 26 to structure the octet and emphasize that "every sweet with sour is tempered still":

   Sweet is the rose, but grows upon a briar;
   Sweet is the juniper, but sharp his bough;

Sonnet 75

Edmund Spenser

BODEGO BAY, CALIFORNIA, PACIFIC OCEAN
© Peter Arnold

> One day I wrote her name upon the strand,[1]
> But came the waves and washèd it away:
> Again I wrote it with a second hand,
> But came the tide, and made my pains his prey.
> 5 "Vain man," said she, "that dost in vain assay,
> A mortal thing so to immortalize,
> For I myself shall like to this decay,
> And eek[2] my name be wipèd out likewise."
> "Not so," quod[3] I, "let baser things devise.
> 10 To die in dust, but you shall live by fame:
> My verse your virtues rare shall eternize,
> And in the heavens write your glorious name.
> Where whenas death shall all the world subdue,
> Our love shall live, and later life renew."

---

1. strand: Beach.
2. eek: Also.
3. quod: Said.

THINKING ABOUT THE SELECTION

Recalling

1. What two events occur twice in the first quatrain of Sonnet 75?
2. (a) Who begins speaking in line 5? (b) Who begins speaking in line 9?

Interpreting

3. (a) Why does the poet believe his love's name will not be washed away by the tide? (b) Has time proven him right?

Applying

4. How do the three sonnets from Spenser's *Amoretti*—1, 26, and 75—fit the definition of a sonnet sequence?

THINKING AND WRITING

Comparing and Contrasting Sonnets

Reread Sonnet 26 and Sonnet 75 noting their similarities and differences. Write a composition in which you compare and contrast the form, tone, and meaning of the two sonnets. Begin with a chart:

	Form	Tone	Meaning
Sonnet 26			
Sonnet 75			

Use the chart as a basis for writing the first draft of your composition. Remember that to **compare** means to examine similiarities; to **contrast** means to discuss differences. When you have finished, read your first draft carefully for organization, content, grammar, mechanics, and style. Revise it as necessary.

Sweet is the eglantine, but pricketh near;
Sweet is the fir bloom, but his branches rough;
Sweet is the cypress, but his rynd is tough,
Sweet is the nut, but bitter is his pill;
Sweet is the broom flower, but yet sour enough;
And sweet is moly, but his root is ill.

Student Activity 1. Identify the type of parallelism that Spenser uses in the first four lines of Sonnet 75 and explain how it contributes to the poem.

Student Activity 2. Write a prose description of a nightmare. Use one or more types of parallelism to make your description more vivid and memorable.

More About the Author This might be a good time to note that so many of the authors of this period, like Nashe, died young. Nashe lived but 34 years.

Critical Evaluation The *Encyclopedia Brittanica* says of Nashe that he was a "pamphleteer, poet, dramatist, and author of *The unfortunate traveller, or, the life of Jack Wilton* (1594), the first picaresque novel in English."

THOMAS NASHE

1567–1601

Although Thomas Nashe is best known today for his novel *The Unfortunate Traveler,* the Elizabethans knew him better as a brash, opinionated writer of pamphlets. His personality made him stand out from his contemporaries. While they were writing lyrical poetry or plays, he was carrying on violent written arguments with the Puritans, whom he despised. In addition to his notoriety as a warring pamphleteer, he acquired a modest literary reputation as a poet, novelist, and playwright.

Nashe, the sheltered son of an English churchman, attended Cambridge as a sizar—a scholarship student who worked to defray expenses. Upon graduation he traveled briefly in France and Italy, then settled in London as a writer. He soon began turning out breezy but acidic criticisms of current literary trends and Puritan pamphleteers. At one point his running argument with Gabriel Harvey, a satirical versifier, became so heated that the government ordered both men to cease and desist.

Using material from daily life, Nashe wrote novels and roguish adventures that are filled with spirit and wit. *The Unfortunate Traveler,* published in 1594, is a remarkable work of its kind and helped to establish the adventure novel in England. As a dramatist, often in collaboration with other writers, Nashe achieved less success. One of his comedies, *The Isle of Dogs,* the text of which is now lost, so angered the authorities that Nashe was sent to Fleet prison for a time. Nashe's poetry is not as sensational as his prose, but like his prose it relies on everyday life for inspiration.

As a lyric poet Nashe is often linked with certain other sixteenth-century writers who are not widely read today. Among these excellent but less familiar poets are John Skelton, Sir Edward Dyer, Robert Southwell, and Thomas Campion. Except for the prolific Campion, most of them, like Nashe, are known for only a few poems.

Although Nashe's writing abounds with clever plays on language, he often got carried away by his own eloquence. *Pierce Penilesse his supplication to the divells* (1592), for example, is one of Nashe's most successful works. Nonetheless, it shows both the strengths and failings that characterize his writing. While the language is clever and smooth, the work lacks a consistent direction and structure. As a result the book drifts from its point. In much the same way, *The Terrors of the Night,* an attack on demonology, is frequently confusing. This resulted in an uneven quality in his work, leading one critic to label him "the first of the English prose eccentrics, an extraordinary inventor of verbal hybrids."

Objectives

1 To understand a litany
2 To learn to generalize from a set of assumptions
3 To write about the concerns of a people

Support Material

Teaching Portfolio
Teacher Backup, p. 239
Usage and Mechanics Worksheet, p. 243
Vocabulary Check, p. 244
Critical Thinking and Reading Worksheet, *Generalizing From a Set of Assumptions,* p. 245
Language Worksheet, *Tracing Word Origins,* p. 247
Selection Test, p. 248

GUIDE FOR INTERPRETING

A Litany in Time of Plague

Writer's Techniques

Litany. Strictly speaking, the word *litany* is a religious rather than a literary term. A litany is a prayer that consists of a series of alternating appeals by a minister or priest and responses by the congregation or choir. The term is sometimes applied to a poem, chant, or other recital that is echoic and repetitive.

As you read "A Litany in Time of Plague," decide which lines would be read by the minister or priest and which ones are a response by the congregation. Why is a litany particularly appropriate for a time of plague?

Commentary

Physicians could offer little help against the plague. Since many doctors thought that the plague was caused by foul air, they advised people to build bonfires to restore the atmosphere. Some suggested that "No poultry should be eaten, no waterfowl, no suckling pig . . . Cold, moist, and watery foods are generally harmful and should be avoided." People believed that the body was composed of four elements or "humors": blood (hot, moist), yellow bile (hot, dry), phlegm (cold, moist), and black bile (cold, dry). Disease resulted when the humors got unbalanced. Avoiding certain foods, they felt, would stabilize the body. Bleeding and purging were also used. Others turned to magic. Besides "magical" charms and garlic, many repeated the word "abracadabra" to ward off plague and fever.

In London's streets, children played a game to protect against plague. Holding hands, they circled clockwise as they sang a rhyme to the plague-stricken child in the middle: Ring a ring of rosies,/A pocket full of posies,/Ashes, ashes,/All fall down.

The "ring of rosies" might have been the hair garland the children wore or the rash that characterized the disease. "Posies" were the bouquets people carried to ward off the stench of death. "Ashes" might have referred to dust from which everyone came and to which they would return upon death, presumably after falling down and dying from the plague.

Writing

At the time Nashe was writing, the bubonic plague and black plague (or Black Death), two forms of the same infection, had ravaged Europe periodically. The mortality rate ran as high as 90 percent among those infected. The causes of the plague were unknown, and even the quarantining of victims had only limited effectiveness against the frightening menace. Jot down two or three threats to modern life for which a litany might be an appropriate literary form. Freewrite briefly about one of them.

Guide for Interpreting 249

Literary Focus The word litany comes from the Greek and Latin, meaning "to pray." Its use is appropriate, as the speaker faces certain death while taking a prayerful look backward and forward.

Writing/Prior Knowledge Help your students to brainstorm aloud for several possibilities.

Vocabulary

Preteach the following vocabulary words:
ope (ōp) *v.*: Open (1.25)
wantonness (wän'tˈn nis) *n.*: State of being reckless or undisciplined (1.29)
vain (vān) *adj.*: Foolish; worthless (1.33)
degree (di grē') *n.*: social class (1.36)

A Litany in Time of Plague

Thomas Nashe

Adieu, farewell earth's bliss,
This world uncertain is;
Fond[1] are life's lustful joys,
Death proves them all but toys,[2]
5 None from his darts can fly.
I am sick, I must die.
    Lord, have mercy on us!

Rich men, trust not in wealth,
Gold cannot buy you health;
10 Physic[3] himself must fade,
All things to end are made.
The plague full swift goes by;
I am sick, I must die.
    Lord, have mercy on us!

15 Beauty is but a flower
Which wrinkles will devour;
Brightness falls from the air,
Queens have died young and fair,
Dust hath closed Helen's[4] eye.
20 I am sick, I must die.
    Lord, have mercy on us!

Strength stoops unto the grave,
Worms feed on Hector[5] brave,
Swords may not fight with fate.
25 Earth still holds ope her gate;
Come! come! the bells do cry.
I am sick, I must die.
    Lord, have mercy on us!

Wit with his wantonness
30 Tasteth death's bitterness;
Hell's executioner
Hath no ears for to hear
What vain art can reply.
I am sick, I must die.
35   Lord, have mercy on us!

Haste, therefore, each degree,
To welcome destiny.
Heaven is our heritage,
Earth but a player's stage;
40 Mount we unto the sky.
I am sick, I must die.
    Lord, have mercy on us!

---

1. **fond:** Foolish.
2. **toys:** Trifles.
3. **physic:** Doctor.
4. **Helen's:** Referring to Helen of Troy, the legendary wife of the king of Sparta, whose abduction led to the start of the Trojan War.

---

5. **Hector:** A Trojan hero killed by Achilles in Homer's *Iliad*.

THINKING ABOUT THE SELECTION

Recalling

1. (a) What does the speaker believe must inevitably happen to him? (b) What line states the basis for this belief?
2. According to the speaker, what is the fate of (a) beauty? (b) strength?

Interpreting

3. After beginning a stanza with a general statement, how does the poet emphasize the truth of the statement?
4. (a) Is the speaker in despair because he must die? (b) Why or why not?
5. Do you think the speaker is suggesting that nothing on earth endures? Explain.

Applying

6. "A Litany in Time of Plague" was presented before the Archbishop of Canterbury in 1592. How does this fact indicate that the speaker in the poem—the "I"—is not Thomas Nashe himself?

ANALYZING LITERATURE

Understanding a Litany

A **litany** is a form of prayer in which appeals to God alternate with responses by the congregation. The word *litany,* when applied to a literary work, often has a meaning defined by the work itself, one that may differ from the religious meaning. In "A Litany in Time of Plague," however, there does appear to be a statement–response pattern in each stanza.

1. When this poem was presented to the Archbishop of Canterbury, it was as part of a play. What lines in each stanza do you think would be spoken in the play as a response to the "priest"?

2. What features of the poem make it appropriate for presentation as a statement–response litany?

CRITICAL THINKING AND READING

Generalizing from a Set of Assumptions

A **generalization** is a general idea, principle, or rule that you assume to be true. It is based on inductive reasoning. To make a generalization, you must look at a number of specific cases and draw conclusions from them. A *valid generalization* is one based on a sufficient amount of supporting evidence. The more evidence you have, the more reliable your generalization will be, but sometimes generalizations must be made on limited evidence or on a set of assumptions. Any assumptions you make—any guesses based on evidence—must be as sound and sensible as possible if the generalization you draw from them is to be valid.

1. What generalization can you make about the concerns of the people in London at the time Nashe wrote this poem?
2. What assumptions did you make that led you to this generalization?

THINKING AND WRITING

Writing About the Concerns of a People

What was London like in the late sixteenth century? What did people worry about? Based on your reading of "A Litany in Time of Plague" and your answers in the Critical Thinking and Reading section, write a composition explaining your answers. Use quotes from the poem to support your conclusion, and find additional evidence if you can.

Closure and Extension

ANSWERS TO THINKING ABOUT THE SELECTION

Recalling

1. (a) The speaker is anticipating death. (b) Line 5 state's the basis for this belief.
2. (a) Beauty will wither and die away. (b) Strength declines.

Interpreting

3. After each stanza's general statement, the speaker supports it with vivid examples.
4. (a) No, he is not. (b) Because the speaker looks forward to heaven after life on earth, he accepts the inevitability of death.
5. It is too strong a statement to suggest that he thinks nothing on earth endures, but he suggests that so many of the things and qualities we humans prize are as frail as life itself.

Applying

6. The speaker in the poem is dying of the plague.

ANSWERS TO ANALYZING LITERATURE

1. The refrain "I am sick, I must die./ Lord, have mercy on us!" would be the response.
2. The first five lines of each stanza are appropriate words from a member of the clergy for his parishioners, while the final two lines are clearly response lines.

ANSWERS TO CRITICAL THINKING AND READING

1. Londoners might have been concerned about how transitory and impermanent life is.
2. Answers will vary. Suggested response: Literature reflects the general concerns of a people.

WILLIAM SHAKESPEARE

1564–1616

Because of his profound understanding of the many aspects of human nature, his compassion toward all types and classes of people, and the power and beauty of his language, William Shakespeare is generally regarded as the greatest writer of English literature. More than 350 years after his death, Shakespeare's plays continue to be read widely and produced frequently throughout the world. His plays have the same powerful impact on audiences today as they did when they were first staged.

Shakespeare was born in a small country town, Stratford-on-Avon, in April (probably April 23) 1564. His father was a successful businessman who held a number of positions in the town government. Presumably educated at the Stratford grammar school, Shakespeare acquired a basic understanding of Latin, but he did not attend a university. Shakespeare married Anne Hathaway in 1582, and the couple had a daughter, Susanna, in 1583 and twins, Hamnet and Judith, in 1585. Very little is known about Shakespeare's life from the date the twins were born to his appearance in a London acting company seven years later.

By that time, however, he had already developed a reputation as an actor and had written several plays. It was not unusual for members of theater companies to do a number of different jobs, from writing to acting to designing costumes to taking care of advertising, theater arrangements, and finances. By 1594 Shakespeare was a part owner and the principal playwright of the Lord Chamberlain's Men, one of the most successful theater companies in London. In 1599 the company built the famous Globe Theater, where most of Shakespeare's plays were performed. When James I became king in 1603, following Queen Elizabeth I's death, he took control of the Lord Chamberlain's Men and renamed the company The King's Men. In about 1610 Shakespeare retired to Stratford, though he continued to write plays. Six years later, on April 23, he died and was buried in Holy Trinity Church in Stratford.

Because Shakespeare wrote his plays to be performed, not published, no one knows exactly when each of the plays was written. However, through extensive research, scholars have been able to chart several periods in Shakespeare's development as a playwright. During his early years (through most of the 1590's) Shakespeare wrote a number of comedies (including *The Comedy of Errors, Love's Labor's Lost, The Merchant of Venice,* and *A Midsummer Night's Dream*), several histories (including *Richard II, Richard III,* and *Henry IV*), and two tragedies *(Titus Andronicus and Romeo and Juliet).* Shakespeare then wrote several of his finest romantic comedies *(As You Like It, Twelfth Night,* and *Much Ado About Nothing)* just before the turn of the century. During the first decade of the seventeenth century, Shakespeare created his greatest tragedies *(Hamlet, Othello, King Lear, Macbeth, Antony and Cleopatra,* and *Coriolanus).* Finally, toward the end of his life, Shakespeare wrote several plays referred to as "romances" or "tragicomedies" *(The Winter's Tale, Cymbeline,* and *The Tempest).*

In addition to his 37 plays, Shakespeare wrote 154 sonnets and two narrative poems. He probably worked on his sonnets from 1592 through 1598, a time when sonneteering was in vogue in London. It is likely that he wrote many of them in 1592, when the London theater was closed because of a plague.

Below is a list of Shakespeare's poems and plays in roughly chronological order.

Poems

Venus and Adonis
The Rape of Lucrece
Sonnets
The Phoenix and the Turtle

Plays

The Comedy of Errors	
Love's Labor's Lost	*As You Like It*
2 Henry VI	*Twelfth Night*
3 Henry VI	*Hamlet*
1 Henry VI	*The Merry Wives of Windsor*
Richard III	*Troilus and Cressida*
Titus Andronicus	*All's Well That Ends Well*
The Taming of the Shrew	*Othello*
The Two Gentlemen of Verona	*Measure for Measure*
The Tragedy of Romeo and Juliet	*King Lear*
Richard II	*Macbeth*
A Midsummer Night's Dream	*Antony and Cleopatra*
King John	*Timon of Athens*
The Merchant of Venice	*Coriolanus*
1 Henry IV	*Pericles*
2 Henry IV	*Cymbeline*
Much Ado About Nothing	*The Winter's Tale*
Henry V	*The Tempest*
The Tragedy of Julius Caesar	*Henry VIII*

William Shakespeare 253

Literary Focus As he did throughout his career, Shakespeare took an existing form and made it his own. It has been noted that the sonnet form is so restrictive that few perfect or near perfect examples exist. Too often the final couplet fails to conclude or answer adequately within its confines. But, when it works, the sonnet soars.

Writing/Prior Knowledge As Sonnet 130 is considered a satire on Petrarchan love poetry, as an alternative assignment have students write a gentle satire on one of the other sonnets. Set guidelines and limits for their one- or two- paragraph exercise.

Vocabulary

Preteach the following vocabulary words:
haply (hap′lē) *adv.*: By chance (p. 255, l. 10)
sullen (sul′ən) *adj.*: Gloomy; dismal (p. 255, l. 12)
tempests (tem′pistz) *n.*: Violent storms (p. 258, l. 6)
dun (dun) *adj.*: Dull grayish brown (p. 259, l. 3)
belied (bi līd′) *v.*: Proved false; contradicted (p. 259, l. 14)

Writer's Techniques

Writing

Sonnet 29; Sonnet 73; Sonnet 116; Sonnet 130

Shakespearean Sonnet. During the Elizabethan period, the sonnet sequence, a group of sonnets unified by a common theme, became a popular literary form. Shakespeare's 154 sonnets, like those in other sonnet sequences, are numbered and fit loosely together to form a story. Most of the sonnets are addressed to a handsome, talented young man, urging him at first to marry and have children who can carry on his talents. The speaker also warns the young man about the destructive powers of time, age, and moral weakness. Midway through the sequence, the sonnets focus on a rival poet who has also addressed poems to the young man. Twenty-five of the later sonnets are addressed to a "dark lady," who is romantically involved with both the speaker and the young man. The focus of these later sonnets is on the grief she causes by her betrayal of the speaker.

Scholars fiercely debate the identity of the young man (Mr. W.H.), the "dark lady," and the rival poet to whom the sonnets are addressed. Leading candidates for the role of Mr. W.H. are Henry Wriothesley, third earl of Southampton, to whom Shakespeare dedicated his narrative poems, and William Herbert, third earl of Pembroke. Those favoring Southampton claim Mrs. John Davenant was the "dark lady," but the Pembroke side goes with Mary Fitton, a woman of doubtful reputation. The many nominees for the rival poet include Edmund Spenser, Christopher Marlowe, Ben Jonson, and John Donne, all Shakespeare's contemporaries—but even Chaucer, who had been dead for 200 years, has been proposed!

William Shakespeare did not invent what is now called the Shakespearean sonnet (Sir Thomas Wyatt and the Earl of Surrey did), but Shakespeare is its greatest master. A Shakespearean sonnet, fourteen lines in iambic pentameter, consists of three quatrains and a rhyming couplet. The usual rhyme scheme is *abab cdcd efef gg.* Shakespeare's sonnets ordinarily present a problem or premise in the first twelve lines and offer a solution or conclusion (sometimes a statement of the theme) in the final couplet.

Shakespeare's sonnets reflect on various aspects of life, such as personal relationships, the passing of time, and the relationship between human beings and nature. Jot down your thoughts on three aspects of life that you might consider writing about in a sonnet. Then list some of the ideas and emotions you associate with each one.

Objectives

1 To understand the Shakespearen sonnet
2 To compare and contrast sonnets

Support Material

Teaching Portfolio
Teacher Backup, p. 251
Usage and Mechanics Worksheet, p. 255
Vocabulary Check, p. 256
Analyzing Literature Worksheet, *Understanding the Shakespearean Sonnet,* p. 257

Language Worksheet, *Understanding Prefixes and Suffixes,* p. 258
Selection Test, p. 259

Sonnet 29

William Shakespeare

When in disgrace with fortune and men's eyes,
I all alone beweep my outcast state,
And trouble deaf heaven with my bootless¹ cries, ⎤ **1**
And look upon myself and curse my fate,
5 Wishing me like to one more rich in hope, ⎤
Featured like him, like him with friends possessed, **2**
Desiring this man's art, and that man's scope, ⎦
With what I most enjoy contented least. ⎤ **3**
Yet in these thoughts myself almost despising, ⎤
10 Haply I think on thee, and then my state,
Like to the lark at break of day arising
From sullen earth, sings hymns at heaven's gate; **4**
    For thy sweet love remembered such wealth brings
    That then I scorn to change my state with kings.

---

1. bootless: Futile.

THINKING ABOUT THE SELECTION

Recalling

1. With whom or what is the speaker in disfavor?
2. What are three things the speaker wishes for?
3. When the speaker thinks of the person to whom the sonnet is addressed, how does his attitude change?

Interpreting

4. How would you describe the mood (a) of the first eight lines of this sonnet? (b) of the last six lines?
5. Why is the comparison with the lark an appropriate one for the speaker to make?
6. How do the last two lines summarize the theme of the sonnet?

Applying

7. If you were to give this sonnet a title, what would it be?

ANALYZING LITERATURE

Understanding Shakespearean Sonnets

Sonnet 29 is a Shakespearean sonnet consisting of three quartains and a couplet. It has the usual rhyme scheme of such a sonnet, *abab cdcd efef gg*. In a Shakespearean sonnet, the poet typically presents a problem or premise in the first twelve lines followed by a solution or conclusion in the last two. In Sonnet 29, however, a change in direction occurs at line 9, as it does in a Petrarchan sonnet.

1. Each of the first two quatrains expresses a distinct but related thought. In your own words, what are these two thoughts?
2. What rhyming words represent (a) the *b*'s in the rhyme scheme? (b) the *e*'s? (c) the *g*'s?
3. How does the thought expressed in the last two lines of the sonnet relate to what is said in the first eight lines?
4. What is your reaction to this sonnet's theme?

Sonnet 29 255

Humanities Note

Fine art, *The Sonnet* by William Mulready. William Mulready (1786–1863) was an English painter born in Ireland. At fifteen he was supporting himself by illustrating books and by painting sets for theaters. He later attended the School of the Royal Academy in London and thereafter remained faithful to the academic training he received there.

The painting *The Sonnet* was finished in 1839. It shows Mulready's fascination with the refinement of the Dutch School of painting. This is a narrative painting, one that tells a story. The woman's expression suggests that she is moved by what she is reading. The title of the painting and the humble attitude of the man both suggest that he is the author of the sonnet.

You might use these questions for discussion:

1. What do you imagine could be the subject of the sonnet that the woman is reading?
2. How might you interpret the man's expression?

THE SONNET
William Mulready
Victoria & Albert Museum Trustees

256   *The English Renaissance*

Sonnet 73

William Shakespeare

That time of year thou mayst in me behold
When yellow leaves, or none, or few, do hang
Upon those boughs which shake against the cold,
Bare ruined choirs where late the sweet birds sang.
5   In me thou see'st the twilight of such day
As after sunset fadeth in the west,
Which by and by black night doth take away,
Death's second self that seals up all in rest.
In me thou see'st the glowing of such fire,
10 That on the ashes of his youth doth lie,
As the deathbed whereon it must expire,
Consumed with that which it was nourished by.[1]
This thou perceivest, which makes thy love more
strong,
To love that well which thou must leave ere long.

1

2

3

4

---

1. **Consumed . . . by:** Choked by the ashes of that which fueled its flame.

THINKING ABOUT THE SELECTION

Recalling

1. To what season of the year does the speaker compare himself?
2. To what time of day does the speaker compare himself?
3. What comparison does the speaker make in the third quatrain?

Interpreting

4. How does the speaker resemble the three things to which he compares himself?

5. In the "bare ruin'd choirs" of line 4, the word *choirs* refers literally to the loft where church singers perform. What does it mean as Shakespeare uses it here?
6. Explain the meaning of "Death's second self" in line 8.
7. How does the thought in the final couplet relate to the rest of the sonnet?

Applying

8. Many people regret growing old. How do you think the speaker in this sonnet feels about it? Support your answer with details from the sonnet.

Sonnet 73   257

257

Motivation for Reading What is love? Though it cannot be defined to everyone's satisfaction, Shakespeare here offers one of the most famous definitions of love in world literature.

Master Teacher Note Have students concentrate on the implications of the two metaphors in lines 5-8.

Purpose-setting Question What is Shakespeare's idea of the essence of love?

1 **Clarification** For ''marriage of true minds'' read ''true love.'' Ask students to paraphrase the opening sentence.

2 **Discussion** What does the second sentence mean? **Less advanced** students may need help in paraphrasing line 4.

3 **Discussion** In this quatrain, what metaphors does Shakespeare employ to show the constancy of true love? Explain them.

4 **Discussion** *Fool* in line 9 means ''jester'' or ''plaything.'' Why is love *not* ''Time's fool''?

Reader's Response What image would you use to describe true love?

Sonnet 116

William Shakespeare

1　Let me not to the marriage of true minds
　　Admit impediments.[1] Love is not love
2　Which alters when it alteration finds,
　　Or bends with the remover to remove.
5　O, no! It is an ever-fixèd mark
3　That looks on tempests and is never shaken;
　　It is the star to every wandering bark,[2]
　　Whose worth's unknown, although his height be taken.
　　Love's not Time's fool, though rosy lips and cheeks
4 10　Within his bending sickle's compass come;
　　Love alters not with his brief hours and weeks,
　　But bears it out even to the edge of doom.[3]
　　　　If this be error, and upon me proved,
　　　　I never writ, nor no man ever loved.

---

1. impediments: Reasons why a marriage should not be allowed to take place.
2. star . . . bark: The star that guides every wandering ship; the North Star.
3. doom: Judgment Day.

THINKING ABOUT THE SELECTION
Recalling

1. According to the speaker, what are three things that love is not?
2. To what is love compared in the second quatrain?

Interpreting

3. What are the points of similarity between true love and the North Star?
4. The speaker notes that ''Love's not Time's fool.'' (a) What does he mean? (b) How does this idea fit in with the central theme of the sonnet?
5. Ordinarily, the final couplet in a Shakespearean sonnet offers a summary or solution. This final couplet is a bit different. What point does it make about the content of the rest of the sonnet?

Applying

6. What is your opinion of the speaker's concept of true love? Explain your answer.

Closure and Extension
ANSWERS TO THINKING ABOUT THE SELECTION
Recalling

1. Love isn't true love if it can be altered when it finds changes in the other person. It isn't true love if it gives in to whoever or whatever tries to end it. It isn't true love if it is shaken by troubles.
2. It is likened to a sea-mark and to the North Star, which unlike all the other stars remains constant in the heavens.

Interpreting

3. True love and the North Star are constant and unchanging. Like the North Star, true love is a steadfast guide in one's life.
4. (a) The speaker uses the word *fool to mean ''court jester'' or ''clown''.* Time, he says, cannot make love into something laughable or contemptible. It is serious and long-lived, if not eternal. (b) This idea is one more expression of the theme that true love is unchanging and undying.
5. In the final couplet he in essence says that his argument is as indisputable as his own existence and career as a writer.

Applying

6. Answers will vary, though most should see that what he is saying is perhaps the most commonly held notion of what love is.

Sonnet 130

William Shakespeare

My mistress' eyes are nothing like the sun;
Coral is far more red than her lips' red;
If snow be white, why then her breasts are dun;
If hairs be wires, black wires grow on her head.
5   I have seen roses damasked,[1] red and white,
But no such roses see I in her cheeks;
And in some perfumes is there more delight
Than in the breath that from my mistress reeks.[2]
I love to hear her speak. Yet well I know
10   That music hath a far more pleasing sound.
I grant I never saw a goddess go;[3]
My mistress, when she walks, treads on the ground.
       And yet, by heaven, I think my love as rare
       As any she belied with false compare.

---

1. **damasked:** Variegated.
2. **reeks:** Emanates.
3. **go:** Walk.

THINKING ABOUT THE SELECTION

Recalling

1. What is less than perfect about the mistress's (a) lips? (b) cheeks? (c) breath? (d) voice?

Interpreting

2. "Sonnet 130" is often called an anti-Petrarchan sonnet. What do you think is meant by "anti-Petrarchan"?
3. There are indications even before the final couplet that the speaker loves his mistress despite her supposed imperfections. What is one such indication?

Applying

4. Would you like to have this kind of sonnet written about you, or would you prefer the more traditional kind with its idealized comparisons? Give your reasons.

THINKING AND WRITING

Comparing and Contrasting Sonnets

Choose the Shakespeare sonnet you like best. Then choose a sonnet by another writer —Wyatt, Sidney, or Spenser. Write an essay in which you compare and contrast the form, tone, and meaning of the two sonnets. Set up a chart for taking notes. Write the first draft of your essay, keeping in mind that to **compare** means to examine similarities; to **contrast** means to discuss differences.

As you write, try to incorporate direct quotations from the sonnets into your paper. When you have finished your first draft, reread it, paying special attention to the way you have punctuated direct quotations. Make any changes needed before completing your final draft. Then share it with your classmates.

Sonnet 130   259

Presentation

Motivation for Reading Exaggerated praise of one's beloved was traditional in Elizabethan poetry, including Shakespeare's. Here, however, he satirizes conventional love poetry.

Master Teacher Note A conventional Elizabethan beauty in love poetry should be bright-eyed, red-lipped, blonde-haired, and red-cheeked.

Purpose-Setting Question Is Shakespeare insulting his beloved, just having fun, or complimenting her?

Thematic Idea This poem can be read in conjunction with Sidney's and Spenser's sonnets, with which it is in marked contrast.

1 **Literary Focus** The conventional ideas of beauty expressed in Elizabethan poetry all derive ultimately from Petrarch, whose beloved Laura was, in appearance, all that Shakespeare's "dark lady" is not. The references to the sun, coral, snow, roses, perfumes, music, and a goddess are also Petrarchan stereotypes.

2 **Clarification** The last line means "as any woman falsely depicted with unjustifiable comparisons." What are the speaker's feelings about his lady's appeal?

Reader's Response Did you find this poem humorous? Why or why not?

Interpreting

2. In this context, *anti-Petrarchan* means repudiating the Petrachan ideal of feminine beauty.
3. He says that he loves to hear her speak. Further, the tone throughout is good-humored and kind, not sarcastic and cruel.

Applying

4. Answers will vary, though most will probably prefer more traditional forms of praise.

Closure and Extension

ANSWERS TO THINKING ABOUT THE SELECTION

Recalling

1. (a) They are not as red as coral. (b) Her cheeks aren't like damasked roses. (c) Perfumes offer more delight than her breath. (d) Her voice is less pleasing than music.

Literary Focus Aside from their strong entertainment value, the songs helped define the tone or mood of a scene, character or situation. Only rarely, as with the first song here, do they have a direct bearing on the plot itself.

Writing/Prior Knowledge Alternatively, have students consider a light story line all or most are familiar with from class, TV or film. Have them select areas along that story line where songs might be appropriate. More advanced students might sketch out timely lyrics.

Vocabulary

Preteach the following vocabulary words:
begot (bi gät′) v.: Brought into being (p. 261)
engendered (in jen′dərd) v.: Caused to exist (p. 261)
knell (nel) n.: Sound of a bell, especially one rung slowly, as at a funeral (p. 261)
prime (prīm) n.: Best, most mature period (p. 262)
exorciser (ek′sôr sīz′ər) n.: Sorcerer; magician (p. 264)
consummation (kän′sə mā′ hən) n.: State of fulfillment or completion (p. 264)

Tell Me Where Is Fancy Bred? It Was a Lover and His Lass; Fear No More the Heat o′ the Sun

Writer's Techniques

Shakespearean Songs. Music and song were important aspects of life during the English Renaissance. Serenades, street songs, pastoral invitations, nonsense songs, ballads—all were popular at every level of English society. Shakespeare included 124 songs in his plays. The songs serve specific purposes in the plays in which they appear; they were not added merely to capitalize on the appeal of music. Although Shakespeare's songs were sung on stage as part of the productions, none of the original printed versions of the plays includes the music. As a consequence, much of the original music has been lost. Nevertheless, the lyrics can be enjoyed as poems without music. They can also be appreciated outside the context of the plays. William Shakespeare, unparalleled playwright and poet, was also one of England's great songwriters.

Writing

Take the lyrics of a popular song and rewrite them in your own way. Your song can be as playful or as serious as you wish.

Primary Source

But supper being ended, and Musicke bookes, according to the custome being brought to the table; the mistresse of the house presented mee with a part, earnestly requesting mee to sing. But when after manie excuses, I protested unfainedly that I could not: everie one began to wonder. Yea, some whispered to others, demaunding how I was brought up . . .

Few of us today have been embarrassed by being unable to sing unfamiliar music at the dinner table! Yet young people in Shakespeare's day were expected to be able to do just that, according to Elizabethan composer Thomas Morely's account of how a young man of his acquaintance came to study music. Young men learned Latin, Greek, and French in school, but music was not taught in the classroom, for there was no need to teach music in a country where "every christening, wedding, and funeral went to the strains of flutes and trumpets and the sound of drums and singing; where May Day games and the feast of St. Nicholas resounded with music, and travelers reported everywhere the beautiful playing of violas and pandoras and that 'even in small villages the musicians wait on you for a small fee.'" At what occasions do we expect music now? How do we learn music today?

Objectives

1 To understand Shakespearian songs
2 To find details that develop mood
3 To find details that support purpose
4 To write about Shakespeare's songs

Support Material

Teaching Portfolio
Teacher Backup, p. 261
Usage and Mechanics Worksheet, p. 264
Vocabulary Check, p. 265
Critical Thinking and Reading Worksheet, *Selecting Details That Develop Mood*, p. 266

Critical Thinking and Reading Worksheet, *Finding Details That Support Purpose*, p. 267
Selection Test, p. 268

Tell Me Where Is Fancy[1] Bred

William Shakespeare

This song is sung in The Merchant of Venice *(Act III, Scene ii) while Bassanio is trying to choose between the caskets of gold, silver, and lead, knowing that only by making the correct choice will he be able to win Portia as his wife.*

Tell me where is fancy bred,
Or in the heart or in the head?
How begot, how nourishèd?
    Reply, reply.   **1**
5 It is engendered in the eyes,
With gazing fed; and fancy dies
In the cradle where it lies.   **2**
    Let us all ring fancy's knell:
I'll begin it—Ding, dong, bell.   **3**
10 Ding, dong, bell.

---

1. Fancy: Love.

THINKING ABOUT THE SELECTION

Recalling

1. What two possible sources of fancy are mentioned at the beginning of the song?
2. Where does the reply to the two questions place the origin of fancy?

Interpreting

3. The word *fancy* is central to the meaning of the poem. It means "love," to be sure, but a superficial kind of love—a love based only on outward appearances. Why is this distinction important?

4. What is it that helps fancy flourish?
5. Why do you think the speaker says that fancy dies in the cradle?
6. What does it mean to "ring fancy's knell"?

Applying

7. Bassanio must choose the correct one of three caskets if he is to win Portia. Two of the caskets are of glittering gold and silver; one is of plain lead. Bassanio chooses the lead casket. Using the words of the song as clues, why do you think he makes that choice?

Tell Me Where Is Fancy Bred? 261

261

Motivation for Reading Since this song is being sung to a couple about to be wed, students can anticipate its tone and spirit.

Master Teacher Note The refrains in this poem are common to many Elizabethan songs.

Thematic Idea Compare this song with Marlowe's "Passionate Shepherd . . ." on page 230.

Purpose-setting Question Why is springtime important to the tone, mood, and theme of this song?

1 Literary Focus In all stanzas only lines 1 and 3 change. The others constitute refrains dealing with the traditional relationships between lovers, weddings, springtime, and birdsongs.

2 Literary Focus Here Shakespeare is drawing on the classical *carpe diem* ("seize the day") theme. It is based on the assumption that since life is so brief one should seize the day of pleasure and joy while one can.

3 Discussion Students should be asked to paraphrase this line.

Reader's Response Which instruments would be suitable to accompany this song? Explain.

It Was a Lover and His Lass

William Shakespeare

This song, from As You Like It *(Act V, Scene iii), is sung by two pages to Touchstone, a clown, and Audrey, a country maid, on the day before their marriage.*

It was a lover and his lass,
    With a hey, and a ho, and a hey nonino,
That o'er the green cornfield did pass
    In the springtime, the only pretty ringtime,[1]
5 When birds do sing, hey ding a ding, ding.
Sweet lovers love the spring.

Between the acres of the rye,
    With a hey, and a ho, and a hey nonino,
These pretty country folks would lie,
10   In the springtime, the only pretty ringtime,
When birds do sing, hey ding a ding, ding.
Sweet lovers love the spring.

This carol they began that hour,
    With a hey, and a ho, and a hey nonino,
15 How that life was but a flower
    In the springtime, the only pretty ringtime,
When birds do sing, hey ding a ding, ding.
Sweet lovers love the spring.

And therefore take the present time,
20   With a hey, and a ho, and a hey nonino,
For love is crownèd with the prime
    In the springtime, the only pretty ringtime,
When birds do sing, hey ding a ding, ding.
Sweet lovers love the spring.

---

1. ringtime: Wedding season.

THE WOODCUTTER COURTING THE MILKMAID
Thomas Gainsborough
Woburn Abbey

Humanities Note

Fine art, *The Woodcutter Courting the Milkmaid*, 1775, by Thomas Gainsborough. Thomas Gainsborough (1727–1788), an English painter, was educated at the St. Martin Lane Academy in London. He embarked on his career as a painter in Ipswich and the fashionable resort of Bath, where his fame as a portraitist was established. He moved to London and became one of England's most popular portrait painters. His subjects were the wealthy and noble, whose features he idealized and beautified. He was the favorite painter of King George III and later of Queen Charlotte.

Gainsborough loved landscape painting and for his own pleasure painted what he termed "fancy pictures." These were imaginary rural landscapes with peasants, which were influenced by the French bucolic painters of his day. *The Woodcutter Courting the Milkmaid* was painted early in his career in Ipswich. The delicate pastoral scene is painted in the soft strokes of color wash that are the trademark of a Gainsborough landscape. The scene is dominated by a dying oak tree painted in sensitive detail. The figures of the milkmaid and the woodcutter are dressed more in the style of French peasants, showing the influence of the French painters Gainsborough admired. This rural scene shows Gainsborough's love for the idealized country life.

You might ask the following questions for discussion:

1. What story does this painting tell?
2. In what ways does this painting illustrate this poem?

THINKING ABOUT THE SELECTION

Recalling

1. What do lovers love?
2. To what do lovers compare life?

Interpreting

3. Why do you think springtime is called "the only pretty ringtime"?
4. What recommendation about love is made in the last stanza?

Applying

5. Love songs have always been popular. What modern love song do you think comes closest to having the same message as "It Was a Lover and His Lass"?

CRITICAL THINKING AND READING
Finding Details That Develop Mood

The **mood** of a piece of writing is the atmosphere or emotion it conveys. Mood can be created through descriptive details and word choice. For example, a dark sky, rolling thunder, and howling wind can create an eerie mood. Such words as *shivering, aghast, oppressive,* and *helplessness* can add to it.

1. How would you describe the mood in this song?
2. (a) What descriptive details help convey the mood? (b) What words help convey it?

It Was a Lover and His Lass 263

Closure and Extension

ANSWERS TO THINKING ABOUT THE SELECTION
Recalling

1. Lovers love the spring.
2. Life is compared to a flower.

Interpreting

3. Springtime is the time for love and marriage, nature's time of renewal.
4. The singer urges the hearer to take advantage of the present time, as it is joyous but all too brief.

Applying

5. Answers will vary depending on what rock and popular songs your students are currently enjoying.

ANSWERS TO CRITICAL THINKING AND READING

1. The mood is light, happy, and promising.
2. (a) Warm descriptions of spring's activities with birds singing, acres of rye (in which pretty country folk do lie), and green cornfields all suggest the mood. (b) The words *sweet lovers, green, pretty ringtime, birds . . . sing,* and *flower* are among those helping to create the mood of the song.

Fear No More the Heat o' the Sun

William Shakespeare

This song, from Cymbeline *(Act IV, Scene ii), is a lament for Imogen, the heroine, who is supposed to be dead.*

1

Fear no more the heat o' the sun,
    Nor the furious winter's rages;
Thou thy worldly task hast done,
    Home art gone, and ta'en thy wages.
5 Golden lads and girls all must,
As[1] chimney sweepers, come to dust.

2

Fear no more the frown o' the great;
    Thou art past the tyrant's stroke;
Care no more to clothe and eat;
10   To thee the reed is as the oak:
The scepter, learning, physic,[2] must
All follow this, and come to dust.

Fear no more the lightning flash,
    Nor the all-dreaded thunder stone;[3]
15 Fear not slander, censure rash;
    Thou hast finished joy and moan:
All lovers young, all lovers must
Consign to thee, and come to dust.

3

No exorciser harm thee!
20 Nor no witchcraft charm thee!
Ghost unlaid forbear thee!
Nothing ill come near thee!
Quiet consummation have;
And renownèd be thy grave!

---

1. As: Like.
2. scepter, learning, physic: Kings, scholars, doctors.
3. thunder stone: At the time it was believed that the sound of thunder was caused by falling meteorites.

THINKING ABOUT THE SELECTION

Recalling

1. What are five aspects of life that the deceased no longer has to worry about?
2. What will happen to young lovers?

Interpreting

3. In the last stanza, what do the three concerns mentioned have in common?
4. Judging by the things the deceased no longer has to fear, what status in life do you think she held?

Applying

5. If this song were to be sung today, where would a person be most likely to hear it? Explain your answer.

ANALYZING LITERATURE

Understanding Shakespeare's Songs

The songs in Shakespeare's plays are functional; that is, each serves a specific purpose. In "Fear No More the Heat o' the Sun," the purpose is to convince the audience to look upon Imogen's death as a release from the pain and sorrow of life. The details in the song all stress the idea that Imogen has no further need to fear these troubling aspects of existence.

1. What are some of the details that support the purpose of the song?
2. Suppose the lament were to take exactly the opposite approach—with the details chosen to emphasize life's vanished joys. What might some of the specific details be?

THINKING AND WRITING

Writing About Shakespeare's Songs

Write an essay about Shakespeare's songs, commenting on their themes, tone, and language. Explain how the songs do or do not match your general impression of Shakespeare's works. Begin by rereading the songs and making notes on them. Then write a thesis sentence that states the main idea you intend to develop. In writing your first draft, try to work in appropriate quotations from the songs. Reread the first draft making sure the paper is logically developed and reads smoothly. Write a final draft incorporating all changes and corrections.

Commentary

In the United States it is hard to find an inn in the thirteen original states dating back to the Revolutionary period that doesn't claim "Washington Slept Here." In England a similar situation exists in regard to Shakespeare. Although there is a lack of sure information about Shakespeare's life, traditions about the poet have become attached to places and objects. For example, tradition identifies the pew in Stratford's Guild Chapel in which Shakespeare worshipped. In 1877 the head of the grammar school proudly displayed Shakespeare's desk to visitors.

"William was a studious lad and selected that corner of the room so that he might not be disturbed by the other boys," he said, with no proof whatsoever to back up his claim. Although Shakespeare left no personal papers behind, tradition has identified and enshrined an absurd assortment of his personal effects: his pencil-case, walking stick, gloves, brooch, table, spoon, and wooden salt cellars. The owner of the Shakespeare Hotel proudly showed off Shakespeare's clock before selling it at public auction in 1880; not to be bested, the nearby Falcon Inn boasted the shovel-board at which he played.

Fear No More the Heat O' the Sun 265

ANSWERS TO THINKING ABOUT THE SELECTION
Recalling

1. Five aspects of life the deceased need not contend with are the heat of the sun, winter's rages, the frowns of the great, the lightning's flash, and the thunder's clap.
2. All young lovers will eventually die.

Interpreting

3. All are part of the supernatural and refer to harm.
4. In the play, Imogen is the daughter of the king, a fact that may not be conveyed by the words of the song, as it suggests that being clothed and eating are part of life's chores along with frowns of the great.

Applying

5. A person might hear it at an unconventional funeral service.

ANSWERS TO ANALYZING LITERATURE

1. The details include the following: the heat of the sun, the winter's rages, the displeasure of the powerful, punishments inflicted by tyrants, ordinary cares, thunder and lightning, slander, and censure. These details are what Imogen need no longer fear.
2. Answers will vary. Vanished joys might include friendship, love, family happiness, the beauties of nature, success, admiration, and so on.

THINKING AND WRITING

For help with this assignment, students can refer to Lesson 12, "Writing About a Poem," in the Handbook of Writing About Literature.

English drama came of age during the reign of Elizabeth I, developing into a sophisticated and very popular art form. While playwrights like Shakespeare were mainly responsible for the great theatrical achievements of the time, the importance of actors, audiences, and theater buildings should not be underestimated.

Before the reign of Elizabeth I, theater companies traveled about the country putting on plays wherever they could find an audience, often performing in the open courtyards of inns. Spectators watched from the ground or from the inn windows. The system persisted for years, but inns as theaters had a number of disadvantages. A permanent building solely for the production of plays was sorely needed.

England's First Playhouse

When Shakespeare was twelve years old, an actor named James Burbage built London's first theater, called The Theater, just beyond the city walls in Shoreditch. Actors—even prominent and well-to-do actors like Burbage—occupied an anomalous place in society. Despite the growing popularity of plays, actors of the time, however prosperous, were widely regarded as rogues and vagabonds. An act of Parliament in 1572 required acting companies to operate under the patronage of a respectable person or organization, and a London ordinance two years later imposed a number of licensing restrictions on theatrical groups and productions. Burbage's acting company enjoyed the patronage of the Earl of Leicester, but Burbage financed the new theater himself. His theater, once completed, proved a success, and its design set the pattern for the theaters that followed, including the famous Globe Theater in Southwark, built in 1599, where many of Shakespeare's plays were performed.

The Globe Theater

The Globe was an octagonal structure with an unroofed yard in the center where the "groundlings" stood. Groundlings were members of the audience who paid a mere penny to attend. Three tiers of seats, the galleries, rose around the perimeter of the yard and were protected by a thatched roof. Theatergoers in the galleries looked down on a rectangular wooden stage, raised a few feet off the ground, that jutted out into the yard. The groundlings were closer to the stage than were members of the gallery audience, but they had a less satisfactory view.

Permanence, however, allowed many refinements. At the back of the main stage were two doors that led to a dressing room and were used for most of the actors' entrances and exits. Built into the main stage were one or more trapdoors leading to an area below the stage. Actors playing ghosts or witches would appear and disappear through the trapdoors. Behind the main stage was a curtained recess, or inner stage, that was used (with the curtain opened) for the presentation of indoor scenes. Directly over the inner stage was an upper stage, often used as a bedroom or a balcony. Above that—at the height of the top tier of seats—was a small building known as "the heavens" where the stage crew could produce thunder and other sound effects.

Although the Globe was not a large theater, it could accommodate more than two thousand spectators, about eight hundred of whom stood in the yard. Performances were given in the afternoon, the stage being lit by daylight. Costumes were colorful and often expensive, but the sets were simple, and scenery as we think of it today was hardly used at all. The companies strove for special effects, however, such as birds and goddesses descending from the roof by means of ropes and pulleys.

Women's roles in the plays were acted by men or, more commonly, by boys. Partly because of the absence of scenery to change and the absence of a curtain across the main stage, the plays proceeded at a brisk pace. Actors spoke their lines more rapidly than they do today. A good voice and excellent diction were imperative, and Elizabethan audiences spoke of "hearing" plays rather than "seeing" them. To a theatergoer of the time, the vocabulary of Shakespeare was familiar and easily grasped. Even so, the plays had to have dramatic power to hold a popular and sometimes unruly audience. Shakespeare's plays surely had that power. They still do.

The Elizabethan Theater 267

The Tragedy of Macbeth

Macbeth is one of Shakespeare's great tragedies, a compelling and timeless drama about the success, treachery, and disintegration of a brave but flawed human being. Its diagnosis of evil is as apt today as it was when The King's Men first presented the play.

Shakespeare completed *Macbeth* in 1606, not long after the appearance of his other great tragedies—*Hamlet, Othello,* and *King Lear.* Intended as a tribute to King James I, *Macbeth* may have been first performed before the royal family at Hampton Court, a palace twelve miles from the center of London. King James, who already wore the crown of Scotland when he ascended the throne of England, would have found *Macbeth* especially intriguing. The play is set in Scotland in the eleventh century, when James's family, the Stuarts, first came to the Scottish throne. One of the strongest and most virtuous characters in the play, Banquo, is said to have been the father of the first of the Stuart kings.

Shakespeare derived the basic plot for *Macbeth* from an account of eleventh-century Scottish history in Raphael Holinshed's *Chronicles of England, Scotland, and Ireland.* In writing his play, Shakespeare altered and expanded Holinshed's history, reshaped the personalities, and invented some new characters.

The central character in *Macbeth,* as in other Elizabethan (and Greek) tragedies, is a tragic hero, a person of high rank and personal quality. Because of a fatal weakness, a tragic flaw, the hero becomes involved in a series of events that lead to his eventual downfall and destruction.

At the beginning of Shakespeare's play, the hero, Macbeth, is pictured as courageous, trustworthy, and loyal. By the end of the play, his ambition has driven him to commit a series of horrendous acts that, once begun, he is powerless to stop. While the audience is repelled by Macbeth's actions, it also pities him, understanding Macbeth's anguish and knowing how easy it is to fall prey to uncontrolled ambition or greed.

The temptations Macbeth faces are ones that have confronted people throughout time. These universal lures—along with Shakespeare's suspense-filled plot, superbly drawn characters, and masterly use of language—have contributed to the play's continuing popularity from Elizabethan days to the present.

The Whole Play

A great play like *Macbeth* weaves a variety of elements into a unified whole. No matter how impressive the individual speeches or how memorable the incidents, the play must be judged on its total effect. If the playwright has successfully blended plot, character, setting, atmosphere, diction, and imagery—and if the actors have then captured the entire rich tapestry on stage—the result is an intensely satisfying drama.

Plot

Basic to every plot is conflict, or struggle. External conflict occurs when a character struggles against another person or an outside force. In *Macbeth* there is external conflict between Macbeth and Macduff. Internal conflict is that which occurs within the mind of a character. Macbeth's agonizing over whether or not to kill Duncan is an example of internal conflict.

Character

Nothing is more important in a work of literature than the portrayal of character. *Macbeth* is a masterpiece of characterization. Macbeth, the tragic hero, is shown as being destroyed because of a tragic flaw.

Setting

Setting is the time and place in which the events in a literary work take place. The general setting of *Macbeth* is Scotland (and briefly England) in the tenth and eleventh centuries. Specific scenes are set at Inverness, on a desolate heath, in the royal palace at Forres, and so on. Because of the limited scenery in Elizabethan drama, Shakespeare often has his characters describe their surroundings.

Atmosphere

The atmosphere in *Macbeth* is one of doom and foreboding. Much of the action takes place in foul weather or in the "thick night" of darkened castles. The witches and apparitions cast a pall whenever they appear. Except for the porter's brief speech, there is little in the play resembling lightheartedness.

Diction

The term *diction* has two meanings. It can mean the pronunciation of words by an actor or other speaker. It can also mean the writer's choice of words, which in a play are delivered by the actors. A writer chooses words with care, making sure they are appropriate to the character, theme, and atmosphere of the literary work. For example, King Duncan in *Macbeth* uses language suitable for a king, while the porter speaks in a more earthy style.

Imagery

Imagery is usually visual, but it can evoke responses from any of the senses. Images, wrote one critic, like those of ". . . pouring the sweet milk of concord into hell; of the earth shaking in fever; . . . of the tale told by an idiot . . . —all keep the imagination moving 'on a wild and violent sea.' . . ."

The Shakespearean Tragedy 269

Enrichment Unlike modern audiences, Elizabethan writers and playgoers did not care if a plot was original. Many of Shakespeare's plays are based on familiar stories or readily available source material. For *Macbeth* Shakespeare took the names of his characters from Raphael Holinshed's *Chronicles,* but he was not interested in historical accuracy as he wrote. He used the events as he wanted to make a play that could be performed in two or three hours. He invented, expanded, and linked historically unconnected events in order to create this powerful tragedy.

Master Teacher Note As students read *Macbeth,* have them keep a notebook in which they jot down their thoughts and comments as they read. They might use the categories on these pages: plot, character, setting, atmosphere, diction, imagery. In addition to thoughts and comments, students might also record significant quotations from the play.

GUIDE FOR INTERPRETING

Writer's Techniques

Writing

Commentary

The Tragedy of Macbeth, Act I

Blank Verse. Like all of Shakespeare's plays, *Macbeth* is written mainly in blank verse. Blank verse is composed of unrhymed lines of iambic pentameter. Iambic pentameter has five feet, or beats, per line, and every other syllable is stressed. The following two lines are an example of blank verse from Act I of *Macbeth*.

⏑ / ⏑ / ⏑ / ⏑ / ⏑ /
Your face my thane, is as a book where men

⏑ / ⏑ / ⏑ / ⏑ / ⏑ /
May read strange manners. To beguile the time,

Blank verse, which was introduced into English literature by the Earl of Surrey, can be stately and dignified, but it can also produce an effect of smooth, natural speech more effectively than most other metrical patterns. It is one of the most flexible and versatile verse forms, a favorite not only of the poets during the English Renaissance, but of many later poets.

Because of its versatility, blank verse can be used to reproduce all kinds of speech. Listen carefully to a discussion, or think of a conversation you have recently had. Reshape this speech into dialogue written in blank verse. Try to make it sound as natural as possible.

Unlike many of Shakespeare's other plays, *Macbeth* was easy to date. Most scholars believe it was sparked by the shattering Gunpowder Plot of November 5, 1605. In writing *Macbeth* Shakespeare quickly seized on the sympathy generated by the failed conspiracy to kill James I and the Parliament. The plot originated with a group of Catholics seeking revenge against James's severe anti-Catholic laws. With the help of many, including soldier-of-fortune Guy Fawkes, the rebels planned to blow up Parliament. They rented a cellar directly beneath the House of Lords where they stored thrity-six barrels of gunpowder. Fawkes was to ignite the gunpowder on November 5 and then escape to Flanders. But one of the rebels exposed the plot and Fawkes was arrested early that day as he emerged from the cellar. After officials found fuses hidden on his person and the barrels of gunpowder, he was tortured on the rack until he confessed and revealed his associates, nearly all of whom were hanged with him on January 31, 1606. The Gunpowder Plot is celebrated in Great Britain on November 5th, when people hang effigies of Guy Fawkes.

270 *The English Renaissance*

The Tragedy of Macbeth

William Shakespeare

CHARACTERS

Duncan, King of Scotland
Malcolm } his sons
Donalbain
Macbeth
Banquo
Macduff
Lennox
Ross } noblemen of Scotland
Menteith
Angus
Caithness
Fleance, son to Banquo
Siward, Earl of Northumberland,
  general of the English forces
Young Siward, his son

Seyton, an officer attending on Macbeth
Son to Macduff
An English Doctor
A Scottish Doctor
A Porter
An Old Man
Three Murderers
Lady Macbeth
Lady Macduff
A Gentlewoman attending
  on Lady Macbeth
Hecate
Witches
Apparitions
Lords, Officers, Soldiers, Attend-
  ants, and Messengers

Setting: Scotland; England

Act I

Scene i. *An open place.*
[*Thunder and lightning. Enter* THREE WITCHES.]

FIRST WITCH. When shall we three meet again?
  In thunder, lightning, or in rain?

SECOND WITCH. When the hurlyburly's done,
  When the battle's lost and won.

5 **THIRD WITCH.** That will be ere the set of sun.

FIRST WITCH. Where the place?

SECOND WITCH.   Upon the heath.

THIRD WITCH. There to meet with Macbeth.

THE THREE WITCHES
Henry Fuseli
Courtauld Institute Galleries, London

FIRST WITCH. I come, Graymalkin.[1]

SECOND WITCH. Paddock[2] calls.

THIRD WITCH.   Anon![3]

10   **ALL.** Fair is foul, and foul is fair.
       Hover through the fog and filthy air.   [*Exit.*]

3   **Scene ii.** *A camp near Forres, a town in northeast Scotland.*
     [*Alarum within.*[1] *Enter* KING DUNCAN, MALCOLM, DONALBAIN, LENNOX,
     with ATTENDANTS, *meeting a bleeding* CAPTAIN.]

4   **KING.** What bloody man is that? He can report,
          As seemeth by his plight, of the revolt
          The newest state.

1. Graymalkin: The first witch's helper, a gray cat.
2. Paddock: The second witch's helper, a toad.
3. Anon: At once.

1. Alarum within: Trumpet call offstage.

272   *The English Renaissance*

MALCOLM.   This is the sergeant[2]
         Who like a good and hardy soldier fought
5   'Gainst my captivity. Hail, brave friend!
         Say to the king the knowledge of the broil[3]
         As thou didst leave it.

CAPTAIN.   Doubtful it stood,
         As two spent swimmers, that do cling together
         And choke their art.[4] The merciless Macdonwald—
10   Worthy to be a rebel for to that
         The multiplying villainies of nature
         Do swarm upon him—from the Western Isles[5]
         Of kerns and gallowglasses[6] is supplied;
         And fortune, on his damnèd quarrel[7] smiling,
15   Showed like a rebel's whore:[8] but all's too weak:
         For brave Macbeth—well he deserves that name—
         Disdaining fortune, with his brandished steel,
         Which smoked with bloody execution,
         Like valor's minion[9] carved out his passage
20   Till he faced the slave;
         Which nev'r shook hands, nor bade farewell to him,
         Till he unseamed him from the nave to th' chops,[10]
         And fixed his head upon our battlements.

KING. O valiant cousin! Worthy gentleman!

25 CAPTAIN. As whence the sun 'gins his reflection[11]
         Shipwracking storms and direful thunders break,
         So from that spring whence comfort seemed to come
         Discomfort swells. Mark, King of Scotland, mark:
         No sooner justice had, with valor armed,
30   Compelled these skipping kerns to trust their heels
         But the Norweyan lord,[12] surveying vantage,[13]
         With furbished arms and new supplies of men,
         Began a fresh assault.

KING.   Dismayed not this
         Our captains, Macbeth and Banquo?

CAPTAIN.   Yes;
35   As sparrows eagles, or the hare the lion.
         If I say sooth,[14] I must report they were
         As cannons overcharged with double cracks;[15]
         So they doubly redoubled strokes upon the foe.
         Except[16] they meant to bathe in reeking wounds,
40   Or memorize another Golgotha,[17]
         I cannot tell—
         But I am faint; my gashes cry for help.

2. sergeant: Officer.

3. broil: Battle.

4. choke their art: prevent each other from swimming.

5. Western Isles: The Hebrides, off Scotland.
6. Of kerns and gallowglasses: With lightly armed Irish foot soldiers and heavily armed soldiers.
7. damnèd quarrel: Accursed cause.
8. Showed . . . whore: Falsely appeared to favor Macdonwald.
9. minion: Favorite.
10. unseamed . . . chops: Split him open from the navel to the jaws.

11. 'gins his reflection: Rises.

12. Norweyan lord: King of Norway.
13. surveying vantage: Seeing an opportunity.

14. sooth: Truth.
15. cracks: Explosives.
16. except: Unless.
17. memorize . . . Golgotha (gol' gə thə): Make the place as memorable for slaughter as Golgotha, the place where Christ was crucified.

5 **Historical Focus** Holinshed suggests that Duncan's gentle nature prompted the uprising by Macdonwald.

6 **Discussion** What do we learn of Macbeth's prowess in battle?

7 **Discussion** What discomfort swells? Why?

8 Discussion What does Cawdor do? How does this battle conclude?

9 Clarification "Dollars" would have been Dutch thalers or Spanish pieces-of-eight.

Enrichment The Japanese film director Akira Kurosawa (1910–) made a movie based on *Macbeth* called *Throne of Blood* (1957). This film is set in medieval Japan rather than in Scotland, but the plot is similar to Shakespeare's and Kurosawa has his warriors encounter witches who foretell the future.

Primary Source Note

For *Macbeth*, as for many other plays, Shakespeare drew upon Raphael Holinshed's *Chronicles of England, Scotland, and Ireland* (1577). The following is Holinshed's version of the first encounter with the three witches:

KING. So well thy words become thee as thy wounds;
    They smack of honor both. Go get him surgeons.
                          [*Exit* CAPTAIN, *attended.*]

[*Enter* ROSS *and* ANGUS.]

    Who comes here?

45   MALCOLM.   The worthy Thane[18] of Ross.

LENNOX. What a haste looks through his eyes! So should he look
    That seems to[19] speak things strange.

ROSS.   God save the king!

KING. Whence cam'st thou, worthy Thane?

ROSS.   From Fife, great King;
    Where the Norweyan banners flout the sky
50   And fan our people cold.
    Norway[20] himself, with terrible numbers,
    Assisted by that most disloyal traitor
    The Thane of Cawdor, began a dismal[21] conflict;
    Till that Bellona's bridegroom, lapped in proof,[22]
55   Confronted him with self-comparisons,[23]
    Point against point, rebellious arm 'gainst arm,
    Curbing his lavish[24] spirit: and, to conclude,
    The victory fell on us.

KING.   Great happiness!

ROSS.   That now
    Sweno, the Norways' king, craves composition;[25]
60   Nor would we deign him burial of his men
    Till he disbursèd, at Saint Colme's Inch,[26]
    Ten thousand dollars to our general use.

KING. No more that Thane of Cawdor shall deceive
    Our bosom interest:[27] go pronounce his present[28] death,
65   And with his former title greet Macbeth.

ROSS. I'll see it done.

KING. What he hath lost, noble Macbeth hath won.
                                  [*Exit.*]

Scene iii. *A heath near Forres.*
[*Thunder. Enter the* THREE WITCHES.]

FIRST WITCH. Where hast thou been, sister?

SECOND WITCH. Killing swine.[1]

THIRD WITCH. Sister, where thou?

18. Thane: A Scottish title of nobility.

19. seems to: Seems about to.

20. Norway: The King of Norway.
21. dismal: Threatening.
22. Bellona's . . . proof: Macbeth is called the mate of Bellona, the goddess of war, clad in tested armor.
23. self-comparisons: Counter movements.
24. lavish: Insolent.

25. composition: Terms of peace.
26. St. Colme's Inch: Island near Edinburgh, Scotland.

27. our bosom interest: My heart's trust.
28. present: Immediate.

1. Killing swine: It was commonly believed that witches killed domestic animals.

274   *The English Renaissance*

"Shortly after happened a strange and uncouth wonder, which afterward was the cause of much trouble in the realm of Scotland, as ye shall after hear. It fortuned as Macbeth and Banquo journeyed toward Forres, where the King then lay, they went sporting by the way together without other company, save only themselves, passing through the woods and fields, when suddenly in the midst of a laund [lawn, open place] there met them three women in strange and wild apparel, resembling creatures of elder world, whom when they attentively beheld, wondering much at the sight, the first of them spake and said: 'All hail, Macbeth, Thane of Glammis!' (for he had lately entered into that dignity and office by the death of his father Sinell). The second of them said: 'Hail, Macbeth, Thane of Cawder!' But the third said: 'All hail, Macbeth, that hereafter shalt be King of Scotland!'

"Then Banquo: 'What manner of women' (saith he) 'are you, that seem so little favorable unto me, whereas to my fellow here, besides high offices, ye assign also the kingdom, appointing forth nothing for me at all?' 'Yes,' (saith the first of them) 'we promise greater benefits unto

FIRST WITCH. A sailor's wife had chestnuts in her lap,
And mounched, and mounched, and mounched.
  "Give me," quoth I.
"Aroint thee,[2] witch!" the rump-fed ronyon[3] cries.
Her husband's to Aleppo[4] gone, master o' th' Tiger:
But in a sieve[5] I'll thither sail,
And, like a rat without a tail,[6]
I'll do, I'll do, and I'll do.

SECOND WITCH. I'll give thee a wind.

FIRST WITCH. Th' art kind.

THIRD WITCH. And I another.

FIRST WITCH. I myself have all the other;
And the very ports they blow,[7]
All the quarters that they know
I' th' shipman's card.[8]
I'll drain him dry as hay:
Sleep shall neither night nor day
Hang upon his penthouse lid;[9]
He shall live a man forbid:[10]
Weary sev'nights[11] nine times nine
Shall he dwindle, peak,[12] and pine:
Though his bark cannot be lost,
Yet it shall be tempest-tossed.
Look what I have.

SECOND WITCH. Show me, show me.

FIRST WITCH. Here I have a pilot's thumb,
Wracked as homeward he did come.
                    [*Drum within.*]

THIRD WITCH. A drum, a drum!
Macbeth doth come.

ALL. The weird[13] sisters, hand in hand,
Posters[14] of the sea and land,
Thus do go about, about:
Thrice to thine, and thrice to mine,
And thrice again, to make up nine.
Peace! The charm's wound up.

[*Enter* MACBETH *and* BANQUO.]

MACBETH. So foul and fair a day I have not seen.

BANQUO. How far is 't called to Forres? What are these
So withered, and so wild in their attire,
That look not like th' inhabitants o' th' earth,
And yet are on 't? Live you, or are you aught

Line numbers: 5, 10, 15, 20, 25, 30, 35, 40

2. **Aroint thee:** Be off.
3. **rump-fed ronyon:** Fat-rumped, scabby creature.
4. **Aleppo:** A trading center in Syria.
5. **sieve:** It was commonly believed that witches often sailed in sieves.
6. **rat . . . tail:** According to popular belief, witches could assume the form of any animal, but the tail would always be missing.
7. **they blow:** To which the winds blow.
8. **card:** Compass.

9. **penthouse lid:** Eyelid.
10. **forbid:** Cursed.
11. **sev'nights:** Weeks.
12. **peak:** Waste away.

13. **weird:** Destiny-serving.
14. **Posters:** Swift travelers.

Macbeth, Act I, Scene iii 275

10 Literary Focus The power and malevolence of the witches is demonstrated by the havoc created upon the sailor-husband of this selfish woman.

11 Literary Focus Sleeplessness is a recurring theme throughout the play.

12 Clarification *Wyrd* is the Anglo-Saxon word for fate, and that is the way *weird* is used here.

13 Discussion Notice that Macbeth echoes the words of the witches from scene i. Why is it foul and fair?

thee than unto him, for he shall reign indeed, but with an unlucky end; neither shall he leave any issue behind him to succeed in his place, where contrarily thou indeed shalt not reign at all, but of thee those shall be born which shall govern the Scottish kingdom by long order of continual descent.' Herewith the foresaid women vanished immediately out of their sight. This was reputed at the first but some vain fantastical illusion by Macbeth and Banquo, insomuch that Banquo would call Macbeth, in jest, King of Scotland, and Macbeth again would call him in sport likewise the father of many kings. But afterward the common opinion was that these women were either the weird sisters, that is (as ye would say) the goddesses of destiny, or else some nymphs or fairies, imbued with the knowledge of prophecy by their necromantical science, because everything came to pass as they had spoken."

That man may question? You seem to understand me,
By each at once her choppy[15] finger laying
Upon her skinny lips. You should be women,
And yet your beards forbid me to interpret
That you are so.

MACBETH.   Speak, if you can: what are you?

FIRST WITCH. All hail, Macbeth! Hail to thee, Thane of
Glamis!

SECOND WITCH. All hail, Macbeth! Hail to thee, Thane of
Cawdor!

THIRD WITCH. All hail, Macbeth, that shalt be King
hereafter!

BANQUO. Good sir, why do you start, and seem to fear
Things that do sound so fair? I' th' name of truth,
Are you fantastical,[16] or that indeed
Which outwardly ye show? My noble partner
You greet with present grace[17] and great prediction
Of noble having[18] and of royal hope,
That he seems rapt withal:[19] to me you speak not.
If you can look into the seeds of time,
And say which grain will grow and which will not,
Speak then to me, who neither beg nor fear
Your favors nor your hate.

FIRST WITCH. Hail!

SECOND WITCH. Hail!

THIRD WITCH. Hail!

FIRST WITCH. Lesser than Macbeth, and greater.

SECOND WITCH. Not so happy,[20] yet much happier.

THIRD WITCH. Thou shalt get kings, though thou be
none.
So all hail, Macbeth and Banquo!

FIRST WITCH. Banquo and Macbeth, all hail!

MACBETH. Stay, you imperfect[21] speakers, tell me more:
By Sinel's[22] death I know I am Thane of Glamis;
But how of Cawdor? The Thane of Cawdor lives,
A prosperous gentleman; and to be King
Stands not within the prospect of belief,
No more than to be Cawdor. Say from whence
You owe[23] this strange intelligence?[24] Or why
Upon this blasted heath you stop our way
With such prophetic greeting? Speak, I charge you.
[WITCHES *vanish.*]

15. choppy: chapped.

16. fantastical: Imaginary.
17. grace: Honor.
18. having: Possession.
19. rapt withal: Entranced by it.

20. happy: Fortunate.

21. imperfect: Incomplete.
22. Sinel's (si′ nəlz): Macbeth's father's.

23. owe: Own.
24. intelligence: Information.

MACBETH AND THE WITCHES
Clarkson Stanfield
Leicestershire Museums

Fine art, *Macbeth and the Witches* by Clarkson Stanfield. William Clarkson Stanfield (1793–1867) was an English painter who began his life as a sailor. To pass time while on board ship, Stanfield drew marine views and made scenery for the sailors' play productions. Upon discharge from the navy, Stanfield took a job as a scene painter in a London theater. In subsequent years he gained an outstanding reputation for his painted scenery and worked for many theaters.

This watercolor sketch, *Macbeth and the Witches*, was done for a production of *Macbeth* at one of the theaters for which Stanfield worked. It was painted between the years 1813 and 1829. A skillful stage design, it serves to explain the popularity of Stanfield in theater circles. You may wish to ask your students this question: Does this sketch help you to visualize the impact of this scene on a theater audience?

Macbeth, Act I, Scene iii   277

16 Clarification Ross is not sure whether Cawdor aligned himself with Norway or Macdonwald. In either case he is being held for treason.

BANQUO. The earth hath bubbles as the water has,
80   And these are of them. Whither are they vanished?

MACBETH. Into the air, and what seemed corporal[25] melted
  As breath into the wind. Would they had stayed!

25. corporal: Real.

BANQUO. Were such things here as we do speak about?
  Or have we eaten on the insane root[26]
85   That takes the reason prisoner?

26. insane root: Henbane or hemlock, believed to cause insanity.

MACBETH. Your children shall be kings.

BANQUO.   You shall be King.

MACBETH. And Thane of Cawdor too. Went it not so?

BANQUO. To th' selfsame tune and words. Who's here?

[*Enter* ROSS *and* ANGUS.]

ROSS. The King hath happily received, Macbeth,
90   The news of thy success; and when he reads[27]
  Thy personal venture in the rebels' fight,
  His wonders and his praises do contend
  Which should be thine or his.[28] Silenced with that,
  In viewing o'er the rest o' th' selfsame day,
95   He finds thee in the stout Norweyan ranks,
  Nothing afeard of what thyself didst make,
  Strange images of death.[29] As thick as tale
  Came post with post,[30] and every one did bear
  Thy praises in his kingdom's great defense,
  And poured them down before him.

27. reads: Considers.
28. His wonders . . . his: His admiration contends with his desire to praise you.
29. Nothing . . . death: Killing, but not being afraid of being killed.
30. As thick . . . post: As fast as could be counted came messenger after messenger.

ANGUS.   We are sent
100
  To give thee, from our royal master, thanks;
  Only to herald thee into his sight,
  Not pay thee.

ROSS. And for an earnest[31] of a greater honor,
105   He bade me, from him, call thee Thane of Cawdor;
  In which addition,[32] hail, most worthy Thane!
  For it is thine.

31. earnest: Pledge.

32. In which addition: With this new title.

BANQUO. [*Aside*] What, can the devil speak true?

MACBETH. The Thane of Cawdor lives: why do you
  dress me
  In borrowed robes?

ANGUS.   Who was the thane lives yet,
110   But under heavy judgment bears that life
  Which he deserves to lose. Whether he was
16   combined[33]

33. combined: Allied.

With those of Norway, or did line[34] the rebel
With hidden help and vantage,[35] or that with both
He labored in his country's wrack,[36] I know not;
115   But treasons capital, confessed and proved,
Have overthrown him.

MACBETH.   [*Aside*] Glamis, and Thane of Cawdor:
The greatest is behind.[37] [*To* ROSS *and* ANGUS]
    Thanks for your pains.
[*Aside to* BANQUO] Do you not hope your children
    shall be kings,
When those that gave the Thane of Cawdor to me
Promised no less to them?

120   BANQUO. [*Aside to* MACBETH] That, trusted home,[38]
Might yet enkindle you unto[39] the crown,
Besides the Thane of Cawdor. But 'tis strange:
And oftentimes, to win us to our harm,
The instruments of darkness tell us truths,
125   Win us with honest trifles, to betray 's
In deepest consequence.
Cousins,[40] a word, I pray you.

MACBETH.   [*Aside*] Two truths are told,
As happy prologues to the swelling act
Of the imperial theme.[41]—I thank you,
    gentlemen.—
130   [*Aside*] This supernatural soliciting
Cannot be ill, cannot be good. If ill,
Why hath it given me earnest of success,
Commencing in a truth? I am Thane of Cawdor:
If good, why do I yield to that suggestion[42]
135   Whose horrid image doth unfix my hair
And make my seated[43] heart knock at my ribs,
Against the use of nature?[44] Present fears
Are less than horrible imaginings.
My thought, whose murder yet is but fantastical
140   Shakes so my single[45] state of man that function
Is smothered in surmise, and nothing is
But what is not.

BANQUO.   Look, how our partner's rapt.
MACBETH. [*Aside*] If chance will have me King, why,
    chance may crown me,
Without my stir.

BANQUO.   New honors come upon him,
Like our strange[46] garments, cleave not to their
145   mold
But with the aid of use.

34. line: support.
35. vantage: Assistance.
36. wrack: Ruin.

37. behind: Still to come.

38. home: fully.
39. enkindle you unto:
Encourage you to hope for.

40. Cousins: Often used
as a term of courtesy be-
tween fellow noblemen.

41. swelling . . . theme:
Stately idea that I will be
King.

42. suggestion: Thought
of murdering Duncan.
43. seated: Fixed.
44. Against . . . nature:
In an unnatural way.

45. single: Unaided, weak.

46. strange: New.

17 Discussion What warning does Banquo offer Macbeth?

18 Discussion With Ross's words hardly out, Macbeth is already thinking of murder. What does the thought of it do to him?

19 Literary Focus Here Macbeth expresses that what is, is not—a constantly recurring theme.

20 Discussion What decision does Macbeth seem to come to here?

Macbeth, Act I, Scene iii   279

21 **Discussion** Ask the students how they might rephrase these lines?

22 **Discussion** How did Cawdor meet his death? In doing so, how did he seem to treat his life?

23 **Discussion** Duncan's comment here is most significant to Duncan and to the play. What does he say?

24 **Literary Focus** Note the irony of Macbeth's entrance as Duncan utters these words.

21

MACBETH. [*Aside*] Come what come may,
    Time and the hour runs through the roughest day.

BANQUO. Worthy Macbeth, we stay upon your leisure.[47]

MACBETH. Give me your favor.[48] My dull brain was
    wrought
150   With things forgotten. Kind gentlemen, your pains
    Are registered where every day I turn
    The leaf to read them. Let us toward the King.
    [*Aside to* BANQUO] Think upon what hath chanced,
        and at more time,
    The interim having weighed it,[49] let us speak
    Our free hearts[50] each to other.

155 **BANQUO.** Very gladly.

MACBETH. Till then, enough. Come, friends. [*Exit.*]

Scene iv. *Forres. The palace.*
[*Flourish.*[1] *Enter* KING DUNCAN, LENNOX, MALCOLM, DONALBAIN, *and*
ATTENDANTS.]

KING. Is execution done on Cawdor? Are not
    Those in commission[2] yet returned?

MALCOLM. My liege,
    They are not yet come back. But I have spoke
    With one that saw him die, who did report
5   That very frankly he confessed his treasons,
    Implored your Highness' pardon and set forth
    A deep repentance: nothing in his life
22   Became him like the leaving it. He died
    As one that had been studied[3] in his death,
10   To throw away the dearest thing he owed[4]
    As 'twere a careless[5] trifle.

KING. There's no art
    To find the mind's construction[6] in the face:
23   He was a gentleman on whom I built
    An absolute trust.

24 [*Enter* MACBETH, BANQUO, ROSS, *and* ANGUS.]

    O worthiest cousin!
15   The sin of my ingratitude even now
    Was heavy on me: thou art so far before,
    That swiftest wing of recompense is slow
    To overtake thee. Would thou hadst less deserved,
    That the proportion both of thanks and payment
20   Might have been mine![7] Only I have left to say,
    More is thy due than more than all can pay.

47. stay upon your leisure: Await your convenience.
48. favor: Pardon.

49. The interim . . . it: When we have had time to think about it.
50. Our free hearts: Our minds freely.

1. Flourish: Trumpet fanfare.

2. in commission: Commissioned to oversee the execution.

3. studied: Rehearsed.
4. owed: Owned.
5. careless: Worthless.

6. mind's construction: A person's character.

7. Would . . . mine: If you had been less worthy, my thanks and payment could have exceeded the rewards you deserve.

Commentary: Shakespeare's Imagery

Shakespeare's imagery is a key element of his plays, commenting on and reinforcing such other elements as plot, character, atmosphere, and theme. Each of his plays, moreover, has a characteristic weave of imagery, with recognizable strands. In *Macbeth*, for instance, one strand of images concerns darkness as a cloak for evil. The murder of Duncan is so horrible a deed that Macbeth wants it to be done in darkness (I.iv.50–51): "Stars, hide your fires;/Let not light see my black and deep desires." The next two lines, even more subtly, indicate that Macbeth wants to darken or blind his own conscience: "The eye wink at the hand;/yet let that be/Which the eye fears, when it is done, to see."

These images relate to many other literary elements, hinting at the deed to come (plot), suggesting a conflict within Macbeth (character), evoking a scene of ominous darkness (atmosphere), and revealing the evil that will permeate the play (theme).

Shakespeare pursues this imagery in subsequent scenes. Lady Macbeth, on hearing that Duncan will stay at the castle,

MACBETH. The service and the loyalty I owe,
     In doing it, pays itself.[8] Your Highness' part
     Is to receive our duties: and our duties
     Are to your throne and state children and servants;
25   Which do but what they should, by doing every thing
     Safe toward[9] your love and honor.

KING.   Welcome hither.
     I have begun to plant thee, and will labor
30   To make thee full of growing. Noble Banquo,
     That hast no less deserved, nor must be known
     No less to have done so, let me enfold thee
     And hold thee to my heart.

BANQUO.   There if I grow,
     The harvest is your own.

KING.   My plenteous joys,
     Wanton[10] in fullness, seek to hide themselves
35   In drops of sorrow. Sons, kinsmen, thanes,
     And you whose places are the nearest, know,
     We will establish our estate upon
     Our eldest, Malcolm,[11] whom we name hereafter
40   The Prince of Cumberland: which honor must
     Not unaccompanied invest him only,
     But signs of nobleness, like stars, shall shine
     On all deservers. From hence to Inverness,[12]
     And bind us further to you.

MACBETH. The rest is labor, which is not used for you.[13]
45   I'll be myself the harbinger,[14] and make joyful
     The hearing of my wife with your approach;
     So, humbly take my leave.

KING.   My worthy Cawdor!

MACBETH. [*Aside*] The Prince of Cumberland! That is a
          step
     On which I must fall down, or else o'erleap,
50   For in my way it lies. Stars, hide your fires;
     Let not light see my black and deep desires:
     The eye wink at the hand;[15] yet let that be
     Which the eye fears, when it is done, to see.   [*Exit.*]

KING. True, worthy Banquo; he is full so valiant,
55   And in his commendations I am fed;
     It is a banquet to me. Let's after him,
     Whose care is gone before to bid us welcome.
     It is a peerless kinsman.   [*Flourish. Exit.*]

---

8. pays itself: Is its own reward.

9. Safe toward: With sure regard for.

10. Wanton: Unrestrained.

11. Establish . . . Malcolm: Make Malcolm the heir to my throne.

12. Inverness: Macbeth's castle.

13. The rest . . . you: Anything not done for you is laborious.
14. harbinger: An advance representative of the army or royal party who makes arrangements for a visit.

15. wink at the hand: Be blind to the hand's deed.

---

25 Literary Focus Note the irony of these lines.

26 Discussion Where does Duncan's announcement leave "chance" as a factor in Macbeth's being king?

27 Discussion What is Macbeth's state of mind by this time?

28 Literary Focus Consider the irony of this speech. How do these words relate to lines 12–14?

Master Teacher Note You might want to make sure that students know the difference between asides and soliloquies, so that they can better imagine the drama as it unfolds. Remind them that, in asides, characters secretly reveal their true thoughts to the audience in the presence of other characters. In soliloquies, characters who are alone on the stage reveal their thoughts to the audience at greater length.

Have students compare and contrast the means by which dramatists and fiction writers reveal their characters' thoughts.

Macbeth, Act I, Scene iv   281

---

echoes her husband's plea for darkness to hide the king's murder (I.v.50–54): "Come, thick night,/And pall thee in the dunnest smoke of hell,/That my keen knife see not the wound it makes." Still later, Banquo makes an apparently casual remark about the lack of starlight (II.i.4–5): "There's husbandry in heaven./Their candles are all out." To the alert reader or listener, however, this remark is far from casual, because it recalls what Macbeth and Lady Macbeth have said about darkness and murder. Though he does not realize it, Banquo is foreshadowing the death of Duncan. Imagery of darkness continues to appear at crucial points in the play; for example, II.iv.6–9 and III.ii.46–53.

Other strands of imagery develop the connection between disease and sin (IV.iii.214; V.ii.27; V.iii.43; V.iii.52), depict Macbeth as a man dressed in new or ill-fitting clothes (I.iii.108; I.iii.144; I.vii.32; II.iv.37; V.ii.15), and describe the repercussions of his deeds as loud sounds (I.vii.24; IV.iii.4; IV.iii.193).

Student Activity. Choose a type of imagery that Shakespeare uses in *Macbeth*, and identify all the passages where it occurs. Once you have compiled your list, demonstrate how the images you have chosen contribute to the atmosphere of the play, provide insight into the characters, and illuminate the theme.

29

29 Literary Focus In order to share the contents of the letter, Lady Macbeth must read it aloud. What techniques might be used in today's stage and film productions where letters remain important parts of stories?

30 Discussion What is Lady Macbeth's reaction to the prophesy? What is her concern about Macbeth in this regard? How does she describe him?

31 Literary Focus Note the words *mad* in line 31 and *dead* in line 36 used in what would otherwise be stage-business dialogue. Death and madness prevail here.

Scene v. *Inverness. Macbeth's castle.*
[Enter MACBETH'S WIFE, *alone, with a letter.*]

29

LADY MACBETH. [*Reads*] "They met me in the day of success; and I have learned by the perfect'st report they have more in them than mortal knowledge. When I burned in desire to question them further, they made themselves air, into which they van-
5   ished. Whiles I stood rapt in the wonder of it, came missives[1] from the King, who all-hailed me 'Thane of Cawdor'; by which title, before, these weird sisters saluted me, and referred me to the coming on of time, with 'Hail, King that shalt be!' This have I
10   thought good to deliver thee,[2] my dearest partner of greatness, that thou mightst not lose the dues of rejoicing, by being ignorant of what greatness is promised thee. Lay it to thy heart, and farewell."

15   Glamis thou art, and Cawdor, and shalt be
What thou art promised. Yet do I fear thy nature;
It is too full o' th' milk of human kindness
To catch the nearest[3] way. Thou wouldst be great,
Art not without ambition, but without
20   The illness[4] should attend it. What thou wouldst highly,
That wouldst thou holily; wouldst not play false,
And yet wouldst wrongly win. Thou'dst have, great Glamis,
That which cries "Thus thou must do" if thou have it;
And that which rather thou dost fear to do
25   Than wishest should be undone.[5] Hie thee hither,
That I may pour my spirits in thine ear,
And chastise with the valor of my tongue
All that impedes thee from the golden round[6]
Which fate and metaphysical aid doth seem
To have thee crowned withal.

30

[*Enter* MESSENGER.]

30   What is your tidings?
MESSENGER. The King comes here tonight.

LADY MACBETH.   Thou'rt mad to say it!
Is not thy master with him, who, were't so,
Would have informed for preparation?

31

MESSENGER. So please you, it is true. Our thane is coming.
35   One of my fellows had the speed of him,[7]
Who, almost dead for breath, had scarcely more
Than would make up his message.

1. **missives:** Messengers.

2. **deliver thee:** Report to you.

3. **nearest:** Quickest.

4. **illness:** Wickedness.

5. **that which . . . undone:** What you are afraid of doing you would not wish undone once you have done it.
6. **round:** Crown.

7. **had . . . him:** Overtook him.

282   *The English Renaissance*

LADY MACBETH. Give him tending;
He brings great news. [*Exit* MESSENGER.]
32 The raven himself is hoarse
That croaks the fatal entrance of Duncan
40 Under my battlements. Come, you spirits
That tend on mortal[8] thoughts, unsex me here,
And fill me, from the crown to the toe, top-full
Of direst cruelty! Make thick my blood,
Stop up th' access and passage to remorse[9]
33 **45** That no compunctious visitings of nature[10]
Shake my fell[11] purpose, nor keep peace between
Th' effect[12] and it! Come to my woman's breasts,
And take my milk for gall,[13] you murd'ring minis-
ters,[14]
Wherever in your sightless[15] substances
50 You wait on[16] nature's mischief! Come, thick night,
And pall[17] thee in the dunnest[18] smoke of hell,
34 That my keen knife see not the wound it makes,
Nor heaven peep through the blanket of the dark,
To cry "Hold, hold!"

[*Enter* MACBETH.]

Great Glamis! Worthy Cawdor!
Greater than both, by the all-hail hereafter!
55 Thy letters have transported me beyond
This ignorant[19] present, and I feel now
The future in the instant.[20]

MACBETH. My dearest love,
Duncan comes here tonight.

LADY MACBETH. And when goes hence?

MACBETH. Tomorrow, as he purposes.

LADY MACBETH. O, never
60 Shall sun that morrow see!
Your face, my Thane, is as a book where men
May read strange matters. To beguile the time,[21]
Look like the time; bear welcome in your eye,
Your hand, your tongue: look like th' innocent flower,
35 **65** But be the serpent under 't. He that's coming
Must be provided for: and you shall put
This night's great business into my dispatch;[22]
Which shall to all our nights and days to come
Give solely sovereign sway and masterdom.

36 **MACBETH.** We will speak further.

37 **70** **LADY MACBETH.** Only look up clear.[23]
38 To alter favor ever is to fear.[24]
Leave all the rest to me. [*Exit.*]

---

8. mortal: Deadly.
9. remorse: Compassion.
**10. compunctious . . .
nature:** Natural feelings of
pity.
11. fell: Savage.
12. effect: Fulfillment.
13. milk for gall: Kindness in exchange for bitterness.
14. ministers: Agents.
15. sightless: Invisible.
16. wait on: Assist.
17. pall: Enshroud.
18. dunnest: Darkest.

19. ignorant: Unknowing.
20. instant: Present.

21. beguile the time: Deceive the people tonight.

22. dispatch: Manage-
ment.

23. look up clear: Appear
innocent.
24. To alter . . . fear: To
show a disturbed face will
arouse suspicion.

Macbeth, Act I, Scene v 283

---

32 Clarification The raven was considered a bird of evil omen and
was thought to foretell death with
its croaking.

33 Discussion Compare the Macbeth we know so far with the Lady
Macbeth of these few lines.

34 Literary Focus Note the parallel
between Macbeth's prayer for a
shroud of darkness in scene iv,
lines 50-53, and her pleas. How
are they similar and how are they
different? What do they suggest
about the two of them?

35 Literary Focus The need for deception arises again. She fears his
face will tell all.

36 Discussion What does Macbeth's four-word answer suggest
about his feelings for the murder
his wife so ardently desires?

37 Discussion How does Lady Macbeth react to his answer?

38 Literary Focus Duncan has already declared Malcolm to be his
heir. At this point Lady Macbeth
doesn't know this. It has been
suggested that explanatory lines
may be missing here and throughout this play, which is Shakespeare's shortest.

39 Literary Focus Point out the dramatic irony here—summer, birth, delicate air are all observed by Duncan and Banquo, while the audience knows it to be a place of deception and imminent death.

40 Discussion Why is Duncan's simple, warm speech ironic?

Scene vi. *Before Macbeth's castle.*

[*Hautboys.*[1] *Torches. Enter* KING DUNCAN, MALCOLM, DONALBAIN, BANQUO, LENNOX, MACDUFF, ROSS, ANGUS, *and* ATTENDANTS.]

KING. This castle hath a pleasant seat;[2] the air
    Nimbly and sweetly recommends itself
    Unto our gentle[3] senses.

BANQUO.   This guest of summer,
5   The temple-haunting martlet,[4] does approve[5]
    By his loved mansionry[6] that the heaven's breath
    Smells wooingly here. No jutty,[7] frieze,
    Buttress, nor coign of vantage,[8] but this bird
    Hath made his pendent bed and procreant cradle.[9]
    Where they most breed and haunt,[10] I have observed
    The air is delicate.

[*Enter* LADY MACBETH.]

10 KING.   See, see, our honored hostess!
    The love that follows us sometime is our trouble,
    Which still we thank as love. Herein I teach you
    How you shall bid God 'ield us for your pains
    And thank us for your trouble.[11]

LADY MACBETH.   All our service
15   In every point twice done, and then done double,
    Were poor and single business[12] to contend
    Against those honors deep and broad wherewith
    Your Majesty loads our house: for those of old,
    And the late dignities heaped up to them,
    We rest your hermits.[13]

20 KING.   Where's the Thane of Cawdor?
    We coursed[14] him at the heels, and had a purpose
    To be his purveyor:[15] but he rides well,
    And his great love, sharp as his spur, hath holp[16] him
    To his home before us. Fair and noble hostess,
    We are your guest tonight.

25 LADY MACBETH.   Your servants ever
    Have theirs, themselves, and what is theirs, in
        compt,[17]
    To make their audit at your Highness' pleasure,
    Still[18] to return your own.

KING.   Give me your hand.
    Conduct me to mine host: we love him highly,
30   And shall continue our graces towards him.
    By your leave, hostess.   [*Exit.*]

1. **Hautboys:** Oboes announcing the arrival of royalty.
2. **seat:** Location.
3. **gentle:** Soothed.
4. **temple-haunting martlet:** The martin, a bird that usually nests in churches. In Shakespeare's time *martin* was a slang term for a person who is easily deceived.
5. **approve:** Show.
6. **mansionry:** Nests.
7. **jutty:** Projection.
8. **coign of vantage:** Advantageous corner.
9. **procreant** (prō' krē ənt) **cradle:** Nest where the young are hatched.
10. **haunt:** Visit.
11. **The love . . . trouble:** Though my visit inconveniences you, you should ask God to reward me for coming, because it was my love for you that prompted my visit.
12. **single business:** Feeble service.
13. **rest your hermits:** Remain your dependents bound to pray for you. Hermits were often paid to pray for another person's soul.
14. **coursed:** Chased.
15. **purveyor:** Advance supply officer.
16. **holp:** Helped.
17. **compt:** Trust.
18. **Still:** Always.

Scene vii. *Macbeth's castle.*
[*Hautboys. Torches. Enter a* SEWER,[1] *and diverse* SERVANTS *with dishes and service over the stage. Then enter* MACBETH.]

MACBETH. If it were done[2] when 'tis done, then 'twere well
    It were done quickly. If th' assassination
    Could trammel up the consequence, and catch,
    With his surcease, success;[3] that but this blow
5   Might be the be-all and the end-all—here,
    But here, upon this bank and shoal of time,
    We'd jump the life to come.[4] But in these cases
    We still have judgment here; that we but teach
    Bloody instructions, which, being taught, return
10   To plague th' inventor: this even-handed[5] justice
    Commends[6] th' ingredients of our poisoned chalice[7]
    To our own lips. He's here in double trust:
    First, as I am his kinsman and his subject,
    Strong both against the deed; then, as his host,
15   Who should against his murderer shut the door,
    Not bear the knife myself. Besides, this Duncan
    Hath borne his faculties[8] so meek, hath been
    So clear[9] in his great office, that his virtues
    Will plead like angels trumpet-tongued against
20   The deep damnation of his taking-off;
    And pity, like a naked newborn babe,
    Striding the blast, or heaven's cherubin[10] horsed
    Upon the sightless couriers[11] of the air,
    Shall blow the horrid deed in every eye,
25   That tears shall drown the wind. I have no spur
    To prick the sides of my intent, but only
    Vaulting ambition, which o'erleaps itself
    And falls on th' other—

[*Enter* LADY MACBETH.]

                   How now! What news?

LADY MACBETH. He has almost supped. Why have you
    left the chamber?

MACBETH. Hath he asked for me?

30 LADY MACBETH.   Know you not he has?

MACBETH. We will proceed no further in this business:
    He hath honored me of late, and I have bought[12]
    Golden opinions from all sorts of people,
    Which would be worn now in their newest gloss,
    Not cast aside so soon.

35 LADY MACBETH.   Was the hope drunk

---

1. **sewer:** Chief butler.

2. **done:** Over and done with.

3. **If . . . success:** If the assassination could be done successfully and without consequence.
4. **We'd . . . come:** I would risk life in the world to come.

5. **even-handed:** Impartial.
6. **commends:** Offers.
7. **chalice:** Cup.

8. **faculties:** Powers.
9. **clear:** Blameless.

10. **cherubin:** Angels.
11. **sightless couriers:** Unseen messengers (the wind).

12. **bought:** Acquired.

---

41 **Discussion** In Macbeth's first soliloquy, what arguments does he present against the murder and what argument or arguments in its favor? Given this argument, how, logically, should he respond?

42 **Discussion** Ask the students why is it significant that Lady Macbeth should enter at this moment?

43 **Discussion** Macbeth's words of reluctance to Lady Macbeth lack the force of his reasons in the soliloquy. Why?

Macbeth, Act I, Scene vii   285

44 Literary Focus The adage of the cat getting its feet wet foreshadows the later sleepwalking scene in which Lady Macbeth's "paws" become stained.

45 Literary Focus Manliness and masculinity as related to courage enter here. Lady Macbeth, who earlier prayed to be "un-sexed," suggests he is afraid to get his "feet wet."

46 Clarification She is challenging his manhood by, in effect saying, "When you dared to do it, then you were a real man. If you are now reluctant, you are no man."

47 Discussion While this question indicates he will go along with the plan, what does it say of Macbeth's enthusiasm for it?

48 Discussion What is Lady Macbeth's plan?

49 Discussion What does Macbeth mean by this statement?

Wherein you dressed yourself? Hath it slept since?
And wakes it now, to look so green and pale
At what it did so freely? From this time
40   Such I account thy love. Art thou afeard
To be the same in thine own act and valor
As thou art in desire? Wouldst thou have that
Which thou esteem'st the ornament of life,[13]
And live a coward in thine own esteem,
Letting "I dare not" wait upon[14] "I would,"
Like the poor cat i' th' adage? [15]

MACBETH.   Prithee, peace!
I dare do all that may become a man;
Who dares do more is none.

LADY MACBETH.   What beast was 't then
That made you break[16] this enterprise to me?
When you durst do it, then you were a man;
And to be more than what you were, you would
50   Be so much more the man. Nor time nor place
Did then adhere,[17] and yet you would make both.
They have made themselves, and that their[18] fitness now
Does unmake you. I have given suck, and know
55   How tender 'tis to love the babe that milks me:
I would, while it was smiling in my face,
Have plucked my nipple from his boneless gums,
And dashed the brains out, had I so sworn as you
Have done to this.

MACBETH.   If we should fail?

LADY MACBETH.   We fail?
60   But[19] screw your courage to the sticking-place[20]
And we'll not fail. When Duncan is asleep—
Whereto the rather shall his day's hard journey
Soundly invite him—his two chamberlains
Will I with wine and wassail[21] so convince,[22]
65   That memory, the warder of the brain,
Shall be a fume, and the receipt of reason
A limbeck only:[23] when in swinish sleep
Their drenchèd natures lies as in a death,
What cannot you and I perform upon
70   Th' unguarded Duncan, what not put upon
His spongy[24] officers, who shall bear the guilt
Of our great quell? [25]

MACBETH.   Bring forth men-children only;
For thy undaunted mettle[26] should compose
Nothing but males. Will it not be received,
75   When we have marked with blood those sleepy two

13. ornament of life: The crown.

14. wait upon: Follow.
15. poor . . . adage: From an old proverb about a cat who wants to eat fish but is afraid of getting its paws wet.

16. break: Reveal.

17. Did then adhere: Was then suitable (for the assassination).
18. that their: Their very.

19. But: Only.
20. sticking-place: The notch that holds the bow-string of a taut crossbow.

21. wassail: Carousing.
22. convince: Overpower.

23. That . . . only: That memory, the guardian of the brain, will be confused by the fumes of the drink, and the reason become like a still, distilling confused thoughts.
24. spongy: Sodden.
25. quell: Murder.

26. mettle: Spirit.

SCENE FROM MACBETH
Cattermole
By permission of The Folger Shakespeare Library

Humanities Note

Fine art, *Scene from Macbeth* by George Cattermole. George Cattermole (1800–1868), a British painter of literary and historic scenes, began his career as an architectural draftsman but became caught up in the wave of the English Romantic movement in art. He is one of the leading representatives of the painting of the past in scenes of chivalry, religion, and literary sentiment.

Scene from Macbeth is one of numerous paintings based on the plays of Shakespeare that Cattermole produced in the 1850's. The figures in the scene are described with spirit and accuracy. Cattermole had the ability to make scenes like this come alive to the viewer.

You might ask students this question: Many artists have been inspired by the works of Shakespeare. What element from *Macbeth* inspired this artist?

Commentary

Shakespeare was grateful to King James I for doubling the payment for court performances, more than doubling the number of performances, and elevating Shakespeare and his players in rank. Much of the play, then, is a tribute to the King and one of his chief interests, demonology, on which he had written a book. James's fascination with witches no doubt grew with his own brush with witchcraft. Shakespearean scholar A. L. Rowse recounts how in 1589 James suffered a stormy voyage across the North Sea on his way to Oslo to marry Anne, daughter of King Frederick of Denmark. Soon after he and his bride returned to Scotland, a number of women were arrested for witchcraft. One "witch" claimed that she and the others had gone to sea in sieves to raise a storm to wreck the ship in which James had been sailing. James conducted the first investigations of the women. One of the accused, Agnes Sampson, told him the details of a private conversation James had had with his wife on their marriage night. Soon after James began to work on his book.

Of his own chamber, and used their very daggers,
That they have done 't?

LADY MACBETH.   Who dares receive it other,[27]
As we shall make our griefs and clamor roar
Upon his death?

MACBETH.   I am settled, and bend up
80 Each corporal agent to this terrible feat.
Away, and mock the time[28] with fairest show:
False face must hide what the false heart doth know.
                                        [*Exit.*]

50

27. other: Otherwise.

28. mock the time: Mislead the world.

THINKING ABOUT THE SELECTION
Recalling

1. (a) What does the Captain tell King Duncan about Macbeth's battlefield deeds? (b) What does the King learn from Ross about the Thane of Cawdor's activities? (c) What reward for victory does Macbeth receive almost immediately from the King?
2. What do the three witches predict (a) for Macbeth? (b) for Banquo?
3. How does Macbeth react to the witches' hailing him as Thane of Cawdor?
4. (a) What happens to the Thane of Cawdor? (b) Why, despite the witches' predictions, does Macbeth have reason to doubt he will succeed Duncan as king?
5. (a) How does Lady Macbeth first learn of the witches' predictions regarding Macbeth? (b) What in Macbeth's personality does she fear may thwart his ambition?
6. (a) What action does Lady Macbeth plan to take during the King's visit? (b) How does she intend to accomplish it? (c) How does she advise Macbeth to act in King Duncan's presence?

Interpreting

7. Both the witches and Macbeth make statements about "foul" and "fair." (a) What are

two possible meanings for the witches' words? (b) What does Macbeth mean by his remark?
8. Macbeth and Banquo respond differently to the witches' predictions. (a) After becoming Thane of Cawdor, how does Macbeth react to the thought of becoming king? (b) How does Banquo view the witches' predictions?
9. In Scene vi, what is the irony in the description of the air surrounding Macbeth's castle?
10. Why is Macbeth indecisive about the idea of killing the King?
11. How does Lady Macbeth's knowledge of her husband's character help her to convince him that the murder plot should be carried out?

Applying

12. How do you think that Macbeth should have answered Lady Macbeth when, speaking of the planned murder, she said, "What beast was't then / That made you break this enterprise to me?"

ANALYZING LITERATURE
Understanding Blank Verse

Most of the lines in Shakespeare's plays are written in **blank verse,** or unrhymed iambic

---

Closure and Extension

ANSWERS TO THINKING ABOUT THE SELECTION
Recalling

1. (a) He recounts Macbeth's fearless bravery and leadership. (b)

Ross tells Duncan of Cawdor's traitorous deeds during the battles and of his defeat. (c) In the same breath that Duncan orders Cawdor's execution, he bestows the title Thane of Cawdor upon Macbeth.
2. The three witches predict (a) that Macbeth will become Thane of Cawdor and King, (b) and that Banquo shall beget kings.
3. He is startled and fearful.
4. (a) The Thane of Cawdor is executed for his misdeeds. (b) Mac-

beth, already swelled with ambition because of the predictions, sees Malcolm, Duncan's son and declared heir to the throne, as the obstacle to his becoming King.
5. (a) Lady Macbeth reads her husband's letter to her describing the encounter with the witches. (b) She shows concern that his nature, filled with the milk of human kindness, may thwart his ambition.
6. (a) Lady Macbeth plans to murder Duncan in his bed and (b) lay the

blame upon Duncan's servants, made drunk for this purpose and smeared with Duncan's blood as they sleep. (c) She warns Macbeth to hide his intents beneath a show of warm hospitality toward the happy King.

Interpreting

7. (a) The entire play turns on these reversals, here introduced in the first minutes. The great victory spells death for Duncan. Lady

pentameter. Each line has ten syllables, with the stress falling on every second syllable.

U   /   U   /U/ U   /   U   /
The King hath happily received, Macbeth,

U   /   U   /   U   /   U   /   U
The news of thy success; and when he

/
reads

Blank verse approximates the rhythm of spoken conversation. To keep the lines from becoming monotonous, Shakespeare sometimes varies the pattern of unstressed and stressed syllables or writes a shorter or longer line. Pauses at different places in the lines also help to prevent a singsong rhythm from developing.

1. *Scansion* is the analysis of verse according to its meter. Write the following lines marking stressed and unstressed syllables.

   But here, upon this bank and shoal of
   time,
   We'd jump the life to come. But in these
   cases

2. What variation does the second line show?
3. Find two successive lines in Act 1 that are in perfect iambic pentameter. Write them marking stressed and unstressed syllables.

CRITICAL THINKING AND READING
Making Inferences About Characters

When you read or see a play by Shakespeare, you must make inferences about the major characters. You have to draw your own conclusions about their personalities and motivations. Since Shakespeare's characters are complex, you should avoid hasty conclusions. For instance, Macbeth at first appears to be brave, resolute, and loyal. But later in Act I you begin to see him in a different light. Always wait until you have sufficient evidence before making inferences about an important Shakespearean character.

1. In Scene iii, from line 70 to the end, Shakespeare presents a vivid picture of Macbeth. Based on the accumulating evidence, what inferences can you draw about Macbeth's character?
2. What can you infer about Banquo from the more limited evidence in Scene iii, lines 120–126?

SPEAKING AND LISTENING
Reading Blank Verse Aloud

Since the blank-verse pattern of stressed and unstressed syllables is a natural one, you are likely to find it easier and more comfortable to read Shakespeare's plays aloud than to read rigidly rhymed verse. With blank verse you will not be tempted into the singsong trap set by rhyme. When reading blank verse, allow the meaning of the passage—and its punctuation—to guide your reading. Listening to professional actors reading Shakespeare can be highly valuable.

Choose a passage of about ten lines from Act I. Read it until you understand it fully. Then practice reading it aloud. Stop at the end of a line only when the punctuation calls for it. When you are ready, read the passage in class so that the meaning comes through clearly to your audience.

THINKING AND WRITING
Comparing and Contrasting Characters

Write a composition comparing and contrasting the character of Macbeth with that of Lady Macbeth. Find at least two passages spoken by each character that illustrate and support the points you intend to make. Include these in your first draft. When you revise, make sure the quoted passages fit logically into what you have written.

Macbeth, Act I   289

ANSWERS TO ANALYZING LITERATURE

1. Scansion:

   U   /   U/ U   /   /
   But here, upon this bank and

   /   U   /
   shoal of time,

   U   /   U   /U   /   U   /
   We'd jump the life to come. But in

   U   /   U
   these cases

2. The second line ends with an additional, unstressed syllable.
3. Answers will differ widely, of course. One possible choice is Scene vii, lines 60–61:

   U   /   U   /   U   /   U
   But screw your courage to the

   /   U   /
   sticking-place

   U   /   U   /   U   /   U   /
   And we'll not fail. When Duncan is

   U   /
   asleep—

ANSWERS TO CRITICAL THINKING AND READING

1. Macbeth appears to be instantly and dramatically fascinated with the possibilities given by the witches—this in contrast to Banquo's reaction. When he is told of the first prediction's truth, he immediately envisions murdering the king. Even though the thought unnerves him, we now share this ambitious and murderous side of Macbeth's nature.
2. While Macbeth's mind soars to grand and sordid heights, Banquo cooly wonders why these foul forces have tempted them with these predictions. Do they not have some greater evil planned, he wonders.

Challenge At this point in the play, is tragedy inevitable?

THINKING AND WRITING

Suggest that students refer to Lesson 9, "Writing About Character," in the Handbook of Writing About Literature.

Macbeth, wife of the great warrior, shows greater evil than her warrior husband, Macbeth. The promise of the crown is fulfilled but brings only pain and death. (b) Macbeth appears to be referring to the awful weather and the great victory.

8. (a) Ambition surges through Macbeth, filling his mind with the possibilities of wearing the crown. (b) Banquo wonders if the "instruments of darkness" aren't tempting them with promises only to bring harm and pain to them in the end.
9. The scene outside Macbeth's castle is deceptive—nature shows itself in its best light, disarming the king as he enters the place where the darkest deeds are being planned.
10. Macbeth's ambition struggles with his sense of decency and logic. As bad as all this is, the idea of harming your own guest makes the thought even more troublesome. Then, too, he is aware that

Malcolm must be dealt with, and that a great cry will go up at the death of this kind and good man.
11. She questions his manhood when he hesitates, and thereby spurs him on.

Applying

12. He might reply that the beast of logic holds him back. The planned action is evil, holds greater dangers than rewards, and that haste serves no purpose.

Macbeth, Act II

Writer's Techniques

Atmosphere. The atmosphere in a work of literature is its general mood or feeling. Atmosphere can often be described in one word: *fateful,* for example, or *melancholy* or *cheerful.* A writer creates atmosphere mainly through setting, word choice, and selection of specific details. Since realistic scenery was minimal and since lighting could not be controlled on the Elizabethan stage, Shakespeare often had to rely on dialogue to describe settings. His precise wording and choice of details help build the prevailing mood in each play. A great deal of the atmosphere in *Macbeth* and other Elizabethan plays depends on speech—on what the characters say. Shakespeare, like most great writers, is a master at creating atmosphere.

Writing

Choose an adjective that describes mood—*lively, dismal,* or *scary,* for example—and freewrite a passage that creates the intended atmosphere. Choose words that help to emphasize the mood. You may find it helpful to look in a thesaurus.

Primary Source

Nineteenth-century Shakespearean scholar A. C. Bradley commented on the central effect of atmosphere in *Macbeth.*

> A Shakespearean tragedy, as a rule, has a special tone or atmosphere of its own, quite as perceptible, however, difficult to describe. The effect of this atmosphere is marked with unusual strength in *Macbeth.* It is due to a variety of influences . . . so that, acting and reacting, they form a whole; and the desolation of the blasted heath, the design of the Witches, the guilt in the hero's soul, the darkness of the night, seem to emanate from one and the same source. . . . Darkness, we may even say blackness, broods over this tragedy. It is remarkable that almost all the scenes which at once recur to the memory take place either at night or in some dark spot. The vision of the dagger, the murder of Duncan, the sleepwalking of Lady Macbeth, are all night scenes. The witches dance in the thick air of a storm, or, 'black and midnight hags' receive Macbeth in a cavern. The blackness of the night is to the hero a thing of fear, even of horror; and that which he feels becomes the spirit of the play . . . The atmosphere of *Macbeth,* is not that of unrelieved blackness . . . it is really the impression of a black night broken by flashes of light and color, sometimes vivid and even glaring.

290   *The English Renaissance*

Act II

Scene i. *Inverness. Court of Macbeth's castle.*
[*Enter* BANQUO, *and* FLEANCE, *with a torch before him.*]

BANQUO. How goes the night, boy?

FLEANCE. The moon is down; I have not heard the clock.

BANQUO. And she goes down at twelve.

FLEANCE.   I take't, 'tis later, sir.

BANQUO. Hold, take my sword. There's husbandry[1] in
    heaven.
5   Their candles are all out. Take thee that[2] too.
    A heavy summons[3] lies like lead upon me,
    And yet I would not sleep. Merciful powers,
    Restrain in me the cursèd thoughts that nature
    Gives way to in repose!

[*Enter* MACBETH, *and a* SERVANT *with a torch.*]

                  Give me my sword!
10   Who's there?

MACBETH. A friend.

BANQUO. What, sir, not yet at rest? The King's a-bed:
    He hath been in unusual pleasure, and
    Sent forth great largess to your offices:[4]
15   This diamond he greets your wife withal,
    By the name of most kind hostess; and shut up[5]
    In measureless content.

MACBETH.   Being unprepared,
    Our will became the servant to defect,
    Which else should free have wrought.[6]

BANQUO.   All's well.
20   I dreamt last night of the three weird sisters:
    To you they have showed some truth.

MACBETH.   I think not of them.
    Yet, when we can entreat an hour to serve,
    We would spend it in some words upon that business,
    If you would grant the time.

BANQUO.   At your kind'st leisure.

25 **MACBETH.** If you shall cleave to my consent, when 'tis,[7]
    It shall make honor for you.

1. **husbandry:** Thrift.

2. **that:** Probably his sword belt.
3. **summons:** Weariness.

4. **largess . . . offices:** Gifts to your servants' quarters.
5. **shut up:** Retired.

6. **Being . . . wrought:** Because we did not have enough time to prepare, we were unable to entertain as lavishly as we wanted to.

7. **cleave . . . 'tis:** Join my cause when the time comes.

Macbeth, Act II, Scene i   291

5 **Discussion** How does this state-ment differ from Macbeth's re-sponse to the prophesies?

6 **Historical Focus** This play was probably written in honor of, and performed before, James I, a di-rect descendent of Banquo. Given that fact, Banquo's portrayal as a totally honorable man is under-standable, despite a less attract-ive image painted by Holinshed.

7 **Literary Focus** This famous solil-oquy is among Shakespeare's most notable. In it Macbeth's vivid imagination again surfaces in the form of a bloody dagger and other morbid imagery. In him imagina-tion is a controlling force.

BANQUO.   So[8] I lose none
In seeking to augment it, but still keep
My bosom franchised[9] and allegiance clear,
I shall be counseled.

8. **So:** Provided that.

9. **bosom franchised:** Heart free (from guilt).

MACBETH.   Good repose the while!

30 BANQUO. Thanks, sir. The like to you!
                    [*Exit* BANQUO *with* FLEANCE.]

MACBETH. Go bid thy mistress, when my drink is ready,
She strike upon the bell. Get thee to bed.
                    [*Exit* SERVANT.]

Is this a dagger which I see before me,
The handle toward my hand? Come, let me clutch
  thee.
35 I have thee not, and yet I see thee still.
Art thou not, fatal vision, sensible[10]
To feeling as to sight, or art thou but
A dagger of the mind, a false creation,
Proceeding from the heat-oppressèd brain?
40 I see thee yet, in form as palpable
As this which now I draw.
Thou marshal'st[11] me the way that I was going;
And such an instrument I was to use.
Mine eyes are made the fools o' th' other senses,
45 Or else worth all the rest. I see thee still;
And on thy blade and dudgeon[12] gouts[13] of blood,
Which was not so before. There's no such thing.
It is the bloody business which informs[14]
Thus to mine eyes. Now o'er the one half-world
50 Nature seems dead, and wicked dreams abuse[15]
The curtained sleep; witchcraft celebrates
Pale Hecate's offerings;[16] and withered murder,
Alarumed by his sentinel, the wolf,
Whose howl's his watch, thus with his stealthy pace,
With Tarquin's[17] ravishing strides, towards his de-
55   sign
Moves like a ghost. Thou sure and firm-set earth,
Hear not my steps, which way they walk, for fear
Thy very stones prate of my whereabout,
And take the present horror from the time,
60 Which now suits with it.[18] Whiles I threat, he lives:
Words to the heat of deeds too cold breath gives.
[*A bell rings.*]
I go, and it is done: the bell invites me.
Hear it not, Duncan, for it is a knell
That summons thee to heaven, or to hell.   [*Exit.*]

10. **sensible:** Able to be felt.

11. **marshal'st:** Leads.

12. **dudgeon:** Wooden hilt.
13. **gouts:** Large drops.
14. **informs:** Takes shape.
15. **abuse:** Deceive.

16. **Hecate's** (hĕk'ə tēz) **offerings:** Offerings to Hecate, the Greek goddess of witchcraft.
17. **Tarquin's:** Of Tarquin, a Roman tyrant.

18. **take . . . it:** Remove the horrible silence which suits this moment.

Grammar in Action

Personification is the attributing of human qualities to abstract ideas or nonhuman things. Good writers use it for both serious and humorous purposes; however, inexperienced writers some-times overuse it or use it unintentionally, creating humorous effects when they are not wanted.

In the following excerpt from one of Macbeth's soliloquies, Shakespeare uses personification for a serious purpose:

. . . Now o'er the one half-world

Nature seems dead, and *wicked dreams abuse*
The curtained sleep; *witchcraft celebrates*
Pale Hecate's offerings; and *withered murder,*
Alarumed by his sentinel, the wolf,
Whose howl's his watch, *thus with his stealthy pace,*
With Tarquin's ravishing strides, towards his design
Moves like a ghost. Thou sure and firm-set *earth,*
Hear not my steps, which way they walk, *for fear*
Thy very stones prate of my whereabout, . . .

As you can see, this passage is riddled with personifica-tions. Not only does Macbeth personify the abstract conceptions "Nature," "witchcraft," and "murder," but he attributes human

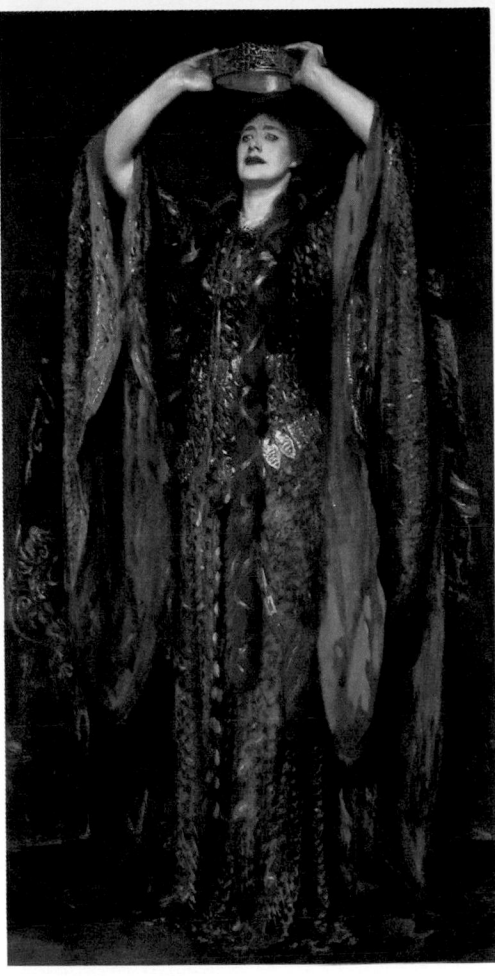

ELLEN TERRY AS LADY MACBETH
John Singer Sargent
Tate Gallery, on Loan to National Portrait Gallery, London

Scene ii. *Macbeth's castle.*
[*Enter* LADY MACBETH.]

8   **LADY MACBETH.** That which hath made them drunk hath
made me bold;
What hath quenched them hath given me fire. Hark!
Peace!

9   It was the owl that shrieked, the fatal bellman,
Which gives the stern'st good-night.[1] He is about it.

5   The doors are open, and the surfeited grooms[2]
Do mock their charge with snores. I have drugged
their possets,[3]
That death and nature do contend about them,
Whether they live or die.

1. bellman . . . good-night: It was customary for a bell to be rung at midnight outside a condemned person's cell on the night before an execution.

2. surfeited grooms: Overfed servants.

3. possets: Warm bedtime drinks.

Macbeth, Act II, Scene ii   293

Humanities Note

Fine art, *Ellen Terry as Lady Macbeth,* 1889, by John Singer Sargent. Sargent (1856–1925) was born in Italy of American parents. After training as a painter at the Paris studio of Carolus-Duran, he settled in London and was much sought after as a painter of portraits. He is considered to be the most notable portraitist of his day.

The brilliant actress Ellen Terry is one of the many famous and socially prominent people portrayed by Sargent. In executing this portrait, Sargent did not strive as much to show Lady Macbeth as to reveal the dynamic actress behind the character.

The pose in this painting is appropriately theatrical and impressive. The drapery of the costume is painted in many tones and scintillating textures that convey a richness suitable for nobility. Although the crown was not part of the original costume, Sargent used it in the painting for dramatic effect.

You might use the following questions for discussion:
1. What might the character be thinking as she holds the crown above her head?
2. Although richly dressed and regal in pose, does this woman seem suited to be a queen?
3. How does this artist's concept of Lady Macbeth compare with the other paintings of the character used to illustrate this play?

8 **Discussion** What has she done?

9 **Clarification** It was believed the sound of an owl foretold death.

qualities to "earth" and "stones." Ordinarily, such an extensive use of personification might seem a bit ridiculous. This is not an ordinary occasion, however. Macbeth, on the verge of killing Duncan, has worked himself up to a feverish pitch of guilt and anticipation. In this heightened mood, he imagines that even stones may give him away. The personifications, therefore, reveal Macbeth's state of mind at this critical point in the play.

Student Activity 1. Find other instances where Shakespeare uses personification. Explain whether the effect is humorous or serious, and tell how the personification reveals a character's personality or contributes to the mood of the scene.

Student Activity 2. Write a description in which you use exagge-rated personifications for a humorous effect. SAMPLE SENTENCE: All his appliances were out to defeat him, and every night the refrigerator whispered conspiratorially to the toaster.

10 **Literary Focus** We see here the first crack in the icy armor of Lady Macbeth. Till now she has uttered not a single word about the human factor in this awful deed.

11 **Discussion** What mood or atmosphere do these short lines create?

12 **Discussion** What is Macbeth's mood here? Is he addressing Lady Macbeth or is he not quite in contact with her after the bloody deed? What words seem to verify your answer?

13 **Historical Note** In Shakespeare's time, the hangman also tore out the vital organs of victims as part of public executions.

14 **Discussion** Of what significance is it that he is unable to say Amen? Is it significant if he is left in a spiritual void?

MACBETH.   [*Within*] Who's there? What, ho?

LADY MACBETH. Alack, I am afraid they have awaked
10   And 'tis not done! Th' attempt and not the deed
        Confounds[4] us. Hark! I laid their daggers ready;
        He could not miss 'em. Had he not resembled
        My father as he slept, I had done 't.

[*Enter* MACBETH.]

                                My husband!

MACBETH. I have done the deed. Didst thou not hear a
        noise?

LADY MACBETH. I heard the owl scream and the crickets
15   cry.
        Did not you speak?

MACBETH.   When?

LADY MACBETH.   Now.

MACBETH.   As I descended?

LADY MACBETH. Ay.

MACBETH. Hark!
        Who lies i' th' second chamber?

LADY MACBETH.   Donalbain.

20 MACBETH. This is a sorry[5] sight.

LADY MACBETH. A foolish thought, to say a sorry sight.

MACBETH. There's one did laugh in 's sleep, and one
            cried "Murder!"
        That they did wake each other. I stood and heard
            them.
        But they did say their prayers, and addressed them
        Again to sleep.

25 LADY MACBETH. There are two[6] lodged together.

MACBETH. One cried "God bless us!" and "Amen" the
            other,
        As they had seen me with these hangman's hands:
        List'ning their fear, I could not say "Amen,"
        When they did say "God bless us!"

LADY MACBETH.   Consider it not so deeply.

MACBETH. But wherefore could not I pronounce
30   "Amen"?
        I had most need of blessing, and "Amen"
        Stuck in my throat.

4. **Confounds:** Ruins.

5. **sorry:** Miserable.

6. **two:** Malcolm and Donalbain, Duncan's sons.

Commentary: Shakespeare's Diction

The English language, with its vocabulary of more than half a million words, is rich in borrowings from other tongues. These include honest and plain Anglo-Saxon words like *bread*; words from Old Norse like *billow*, which come dripping from Viking seas; French words like *amuse*, evoking the ease and sophistication of court life; and sinuous, scholarly Latinate terms like *voluminous*.

From time to time, writers or literary movements have insisted on using certain types of words rather than others. One fashion is to prefer the honest, bare-bones Anglo-Saxon, while another favors the intricacies and sophistication of Latin-derived terminology. Great writers, however, have always been alive to the full range of English diction, playing rare words against those that are more mundane.

Shakespeare is especially notable for the range and contrast of his diction. Take, for example, Macbeth's speech as he waits for Lady Macbeth to falsify the evidence at the scene of the crime (II.ii.59–62):

Will all great Neptune's ocean wash this blood
Clean from my hand? No; this my hand will rather

15 LADY MACBETH. These deeds must not be thought
After these ways; so, it will make us mad.

16
35 MACBETH. Methought I heard a voice cry "Sleep no more!
Macbeth does murder sleep"—the innocent sleep,
Sleep that knits up the raveled sleeve[7] of care,
The death of each day's life, sore labor's bath,
Balm of hurt minds, great nature's second course,[8]
Chief nourisher in life's feast—

LADY MACBETH. What do you mean?

40 MACBETH. Still it cried "Sleep no more!" to all the house:
"Glamis hath murdered sleep, and therefore Cawdor
Shall sleep no more: Macbeth shall sleep no more."

17
LADY MACBETH. Who was it that thus cried? Why, worthy
Thane,
45 You do unbend[9] your noble strength, to think
So brainsickly of things. Go get some water,
And wash this filthy witness[10] from your hand.
Why did you bring these daggers from the place?
They must lie there: go carry them, and smear
The sleepy grooms with blood.

MACBETH. I'll go no more.
50 I am afraid to think what I have done;
Look on 't again I dare not.

18
LADY MACBETH. Infirm of purpose!
Give me the daggers. The sleeping and the dead
Are but as pictures. 'Tis the eye of childhood
That fears a painted devil. If he do bleed,
55 I'll gild[11] the faces of the grooms withal,
For it must seem their guilt. [*Exit. Knock within.*]

19
MACBETH. Whence is that knocking?
How is 't with me, when every noise appalls me?
What hands are here? Ha! They pluck out mine eyes!
Will all great Neptune's ocean wash this blood
60 Clean from my hand? No; this my hand will rather
The multitudinous seas incarnadine,[12]
Making the green one red.

[*Enter* LADY MACBETH.]

LADY MACBETH. My hands are of your color, but I shame
To wear a heart so white. [*Knock.*] I hear a knocking
65 At the south entry. Retire we to our chamber.
A little water clears us of this deed:
How easy is it then! Your constancy
Hath left you unattended.[13] [*Knock.*] Hark! more
knocking.

---

7. knits . . . sleave: Straightens out the tangled threads.
8. second course: The main course; sleep.

9. unbend: Relax.

10. witness: Evidence.

11. gild: Paint.

12. incarnadine (in kär' nə din): Redden.

13. Your constancy . . . unattended: Your firmness of purpose has left you.

---

15 Literary Focus The remark is another indication of Lady Macbeth's potential vulnerability.

16 Literary Focus Macbeth acknowledges the madness of his act and predicts the destruction of anything resembling a normal life after this night. What benefits of sleep are specified here?

17 Discussion It is said Macbeth has too much imagination and Lady Macbeth too little. How do these lines and her following speeches seem to verify that opinion?

18 Literary Focus *Gild* is a grim pun here.

19 Discussion What do these lines mean both literally and figuratively?

Enrichment Although *Macbeth* is a short play, it contains some of Shakespeare's most often-quoted lines; for example, Macbeth's description of sleep (II.ii.34–42), which is probably an allusion to Sir Philip Sidney's apostrophe to sleep (See Sonnet 39, p. 226). An equally famous passage from the play is the one that begins "Tomorrow, and tomorrow, and tomorrow . . ." (V.vii.19); this speech provided William Faulkner with the title of his novel *The Sound and the Fury*. The play's well-known single lines include the following: "After life's fitful fever he sleeps well" (III.ii.23) and "All the perfumes of Arabia will not sweeten this little hand" (V.i.51–2).

The multitudinous seas incarnadine,
Making the green one red.

The words "multitudinous" and "incarnadine" are high-falutin Latin derivatives: *multitudinous* from Latin *multitudo*, meaning "many"; *incarnadine* from Latin *incarnatus*, meaning "incarnate." The size and sonority of these words seems to suggest the vastness of Macbeth's guilt: The mere spot of blood from his hand will stain the waters in all the seas!

Quickly and adeptly, however, Shakespeare contrasts these impressive but somewhat hollow terms with simple words derived from Old English: "green" and "red." This sudden shift of direction brings the sea-swollen rhetoric back to earth, as it were.

The abruptness of this change emphasizes the poignance and finality of the situation. The fact of Duncan's death and Macbeth's guilt is clinched in undeniable Anglo-Saxon.

This duality of diction also hints at a split in Macbeth's character. The Latinate rhetoric reveals him as highly imaginative, experiencing his guilt to the full, while the plain Anglo-Saxon shows him to be a straightforward soldier.

20 **Discussion** What does Macbeth wish? Why?

21 **Literary Focus** The preceding scene could hardly have been more dramatic and tension-filled for audiences. The introduction of the drunken porter here breaks the tension and carries the play forward. His references to these wrongs were surely meaningful and worthy of a laugh to the audiences of the day.

22 **Enrichment** Thomas De Quincey's essay. "On the Knocking at the Gate in *Macbeth*" provides interesting insights into this character.

23 **Clarification** He is undoubtedly holding his hand out for a tip.

24 **Literary Focus** From this point on Macduff plays a major role in the events of the drama. That he does not appear before now gives credence to those who believe sections of the play may be missing.

70 Get on your nightgown, lest occasion call us
And show us to be watchers.[14] Be not lost
So poorly in your thoughts.

MACBETH. To know my deed, 'twere best not know
myself. [*Knock.*]
Wake Duncan with thy knocking! I would thou
couldst! [*Exit.*]

14. watchers: Up late.

Scene iii. *Macbeth's castle.*
[*Enter a* PORTER.[1] *Knocking within.*]

1. porter: Doorkeeper.

PORTER. Here's a knocking indeed! If a man were porter
of hell gate, he should have old[2] turning the key.
[*Knock.*] Knock, knock, knock! Who's there, i' th'
name of Beelzebub?[3] Here's a farmer, that
5 hanged himself on th' expectation of plenty.[4] Come
in time! Have napkins enow[5] about you; here you'll
sweat for 't. [*Knock.*] Knock, knock! Who's there, in
th' other devil's name? Faith, here's an equivocator,
that could swear in both the scales against
10 either scale;[6] who committed treason enough for
God's sake, yet could not equivocate to heaven. O,
come in, equivocator. [*Knock.*] Knock, knock, knock!
Who's there? Faith, here's an English tailor come
hither for stealing out of a French hose:[7]
15 come in, tailor. Here you may roast your goose.[8]
[*Knock.*] Knock, knock; never at quiet! What are you?
But this place is too cold for hell. I'll devil-porter it no
further. I had thought to have let in some of all
professions that go the primrose way to th'
20 everlasting bonfire. [*Knock.*] Anon, anon! [*Opens an
entrance.*] I pray you, remember the porter.

2. should have old: Would have plenty of.
3. Beelzebub (bē el' zə bub): The chief devil.
4. A farmer . . . plenty: A farmer who hoarded grain, hoping that the prices would come up as a result of a bad harvest.
5. enow: Enough.
6. an equivocator . . . scale: A liar who could make two contradictory statements and swear that both were true.
7. stealing . . . hose: Stealing some cloth from the hose while making them.
8. goose: Pressing iron.

[*Enter* MACDUFF *and* LENNOX.]

MACDUFF. Was it so late, friend, ere you went to bed,
That you do lie so late?

PORTER. Faith, sir, we were carousing till the second
25 cock:[9] and drink, sir, is a great provoker of three
things.

9. second cock: 3:00 A.M.

MACDUFF. What three things does drink especially
provoke?

PORTER. Marry, sir, nose-painting, sleep, and urine.
30 Lechery, sir, it provokes and unprovokes; it provokes
the desire, but it takes away the performance: therefore much drink may be said to be an equivocator with lechery: it makes him and it mars him; it

Primary Source Note

The following is an excerpt from Thomas De Quincey's (1785–1859) famous essay "On the Knocking at the Gate in *Macbeth*":

From my boyish days I had always felt a great perplexity on one point in *Macbeth*. It was this: The knocking at the gate which succeeds to the murder of Duncan produced to my feelings an effect for which I never could account. The effect was that it reflected back upon the murderer a peculiar awfulness and a depth of solemnity; yet, however obstinately I endeavored with my understanding to comprehend this, for many years I never could see *why* it should produce such an effect.

. . . All action in any direction is best expounded, measured, and made apprehensible, by reaction. Now, apply this to the case in *Macbeth*. Here, as I have said, the retiring of the human heart and the entrance of the fiendish heart was to be expressed and made sensible. Another world has stepped in; and the murderers are taken out of the region of human things, human purposes, human desires. They are transfigured; Lady Macbeth is "unsexed"; Macbeth has forgot that he was born of woman; both are conformed to the image of devils; and the world of

35 sets him on and it takes him off; it per-
suades him and disheartens him; makes him stand
to and not stand to; in conclusion, equivocates him
in a sleep, and giving him the lie, leaves him.

MACDUFF. I believe drink gave thee the lie[10] last night.

10. **gave thee the lie:**
Laid you out.

PORTER. That it did, sir, i' the very throat on me: but I
40 requited him for his lie, and, I think, being too strong
for him, though he took up my legs some-
time, yet I make a shift to cast[11] him.

11. **cast:** Vomit.

MACDUFF. Is thy master stirring?

[Enter MACBETH.*]*

Our knocking has awaked him; here he comes.

LENNOX. Good morrow, noble sir.

45 **MACBETH.**   Good morrow, both.

MACDUFF. Is the king stirring, worthy Thane?

25 **MACBETH.**   Not yet.

MACDUFF. He did command me to call timely[12] on him:
I have almost slipped the hour.

12. **timely:** Early.

MACBETH.   I'll bring you to him.

MACDUFF. I know this is a joyful trouble to you;
50 But yet 'tis one.

MACBETH. The labor we delight in physics pain.[13]
This is the door.

13. **labor . . . pain:** Labor
that we enjoy cures discomfort.

MACBETH.   I'll make so bold to call,
For 'tis my limited service.[14]   *[Exit* MACDUFF.*]*

14. **limited service:** Assigned duty.

LENNOX. Goes the king hence today?

MACBETH.   He does: he did appoint so.

55 **LENNOX.** The night has been unruly. Where we lay,
Our chimneys were blown down, and, as they say,
Lamentings heard i' th' air, strange screams of
death,
And prophesying with accents terrible
Of dire combustion[15] and confused events
60 New hatched to th' woeful time: the obscure bird[16]
Clamored the livelong night. Some say, the earth
Was feverous and did shake.

26

15. **combustion:** Confusion.
16. **obscure bird:** Bird of
darkness, the owl.

27 **MACBETH.**   'Twas a rough night.

LENNOX. My young remembrance cannot parallel
A fellow to it.

Macbeth, Act II, Scene iii   297

25 Literary Focus Note the dramatic
irony here.

26 Literary Focus The horror of the
night before was matched by an
unnatural series of storms and
howlings, all seeming to prophesy
some terrible event. Shakespeare
again intensifies dramatic events
with corresponding natural phenomena. Further, the murder of an
anointed king would be viewed by
Elizabethans as a most heinous
crime against nature itself.

27 Literary Focus Note the understatement.

Enrichment The Elizabethans
believed that the universe extended in a great chain of being
from God down to the lowliest
creature. Every item in this chain
had its proper place, reflecting a
universal order. Harmony in
heaven mirrored harmony in the
natural world, the political state,
and the family. When this order
was disrupted, the whole structure of the universe was at risk.
Elizabethan spectators were
probably not surprised, therefore, when the killing of Duncan
led to disturbances in nature. As
Shakespeare wrote in *Troilus and
Cressida* (I.iii. 109–110): "Take
but degree [established rank]
away, untune that string,/And,
hark, what discord follows! . . ."

devils is suddenly revealed. But how shall this be conveyed and made palpable? In order that a new world may
step in, this world must for a time disappear. The murderers and the murder must be insulated—cut off by an
immeasurable gulf from the ordinary tide and succession
of human affairs—locked up and sequestered in some
deep recess; we must be made sensible that the world of
ordinary life is suddenly arrested, laid asleep, tranced,
racked into a dread armistice; time must be annihilated,
relation to things without abolished; and all must pass
self-withdrawn into a deep syncope and suspension of
earthly passion. Hence it is that, when the deed is done,
when the work of darkness is perfect, then the world of
darkness passes away like a pageantry in the clouds: the
knocking at the gate is heard, and it makes known audibly
that the reaction has commenced; the human has made its
reflux upon the fiendish; the pulses of life are beginning to
beat again; and the re-establishment of the goings-on of
the world in which we live first makes us profoundly
sensible of the awful parenthesis that had suspended
them.

LADY MACBETH SEIZING THE DAGGERS
Henry Fuseli
The Tate Gallery, London

[*Enter* MACDUFF.]

65   **MACDUFF.** O horror, horror, horror! Tongue nor heart
     Cannot conceive nor name thee.

   MACBETH AND LENNOX.   What's the matter?

   MACDUFF. Confusion[17] now hath made his masterpiece.
     Most sacrilegious murder hath broke ope
     The Lord's anointed temple,[18] and stole thence
     The life o' th' building.

70   **MACBETH.**   What is 't you say? The life?

   LENNOX. Mean you his Majesty?

     MACDUFF. Approach the chamber, and destroy
     your sight

17. Confusion: Destruction.

18. The Lord's anointed temple: The King's body.

298   *The English Renaissance*

With a new Gorgon:[19] do not bid me speak;
See, and then speak yourselves. Awake, awake!

[*Exit* MACBETH *and* LENNOX.]

75 Ring the alarum bell. Murder and Treason!
Banquo and Donalbain! Malcolm! Awake!
Shake off this downy sleep, death's counterfeit,
And look on death itself! Up, up, and see
The great doom's image![20] Malcolm! Banquo!
80 As from your graves rise up, and walk like sprites,[21]
To countenance[22] this horror. Ring the bell.

[*Bell rings. Enter* LADY MACBETH.]

LADY MACBETH. What's the business,
That such a hideous trumpet calls to parley[23]
The sleepers of the house? Speak, speak!

MACDUFF.   O gentle lady,
85 'Tis not for you to hear what I can speak:
The repetition, in a woman's ear,
Would murder as it fell.

[*Enter* BANQUO.]

                                    O Banquo, Banquo!
Our royal master's murdered.

LADY MACBETH.   Woe, alas!
What, in our house?

BANQUO.   Too cruel anywhere.
90 Dear Duff, I prithee, contradict thyself,
And say it is not so.

[*Enter* MACBETH, LENNOX, *and* ROSS.]

MACBETH. Had I but died an hour before this
      chance,
I had lived a blessèd time; for from this instant
There's nothing serious in mortality:[24]
95 All is but toys.[25] Renown and grace is dead,
The wine of life is drawn, and the mere lees[26]
Is left this vault[27] to brag of.

[*Enter* MALCOLM *and* DONALBAIN.]

DONALBAIN. What is amiss?

MACBETH.   You are, and do not know 't.
The spring, the head, the fountain of your blood
100 Is stopped; the very source of it is stopped.

MACDUFF. Your royal father's murdered.

MALCOLM.   O, by whom?

19. Gorgon: Medusa, a mythological monster whose appearance was so ghastly that those who looked at it turned to stone.

20. great doom's image: Likeness of Judgment Day.
21. sprites: Spirits.
22. countenance: Be in keeping with.

23. parley: A war conference.

24. serious in mortality: Worthwhile in mortal life.
25. toys: Trifles.
26. lees: Dregs.
27. vault: World.

28 **Discussion** Why are these lines to Lady Macbeth so ironic?

29 **Discussion** Is this comment from Lady Macbeth believable? Is it helpful in establishing her innocence? Note Banquo's sharp reply.

30 **Discussion** What is the irony about this passionate speech? How does it reflect his words of the night before?

Macbeth, Act II, Scene iii   299

31 **Discussion** What do we see happening to Macbeth and the direction of his actions following the murder of Duncan? What more can we expect?

32 **Discussion** Discuss the visible reactions of Macbeth and Lady Macbeth the morning after the murder. What do these reactions imply about each of them at this point?

33 **Discussion** What reason does Macbeth give for killing the grooms? What is the real reason?

34 **Discussion** What does he mean?

35 **Literary Focus** Lady Macbeth faints. Scholars argue about the legitimacy of this action. Is she fainting or is she pretending to faint? Which seems more likely? Why?

LENNOX. Those of his chamber, as it seemed, had
    done 't:
Their hands and faces were all badged[28] with blood;
So were their daggers, which unwiped we found
105   Upon their pillows. They stared, and were distracted.
No man's life was to be trusted with them.

MACBETH. O, yet I do repent me of my fury,
    That I did kill them.

MACDUFF.   Wherefore did you so?

MACBETH. Who can be wise, amazed, temp'rate and
    furious,
110   Loyal and neutral, in a moment? No man.
The expedition[29] of my violent love
Outrun the pauser, reason. Here lay Duncan,
His silver skin laced with his golden blood,
And his gashed stabs looked like a breach in nature
115   For ruin's wasteful entrance: there, the murderers,
Steeped in the colors of their trade, their daggers
Unmannerly breeched with gore.[30] Who could
    refrain,
That had a heart to love, and in that heart
Courage to make 's love known?

LADY MACBETH.   Help me hence, ho!

MACDUFF. Look to the lady.

MALCOLM. [*Aside to* DONALBAIN] Why do we hold our
120   tongues,
That most may claim this argument for ours?[31]

DONALBAIN. [*Aside to Malcolm*] What should be spoken
    here,
Where our fate, hid in an auger-hole,[32]
May rush, and seize us? Let's away:
Our tears are not yet brewed.

125   **MALCOLM.** [*Aside to* DONALBAIN] Nor our strong sorrow
Upon the foot of motion.[33]

BANQUO.   Look to the lady.
                [LADY MACBETH *is carried out.*]
And when we have our naked frailties hid,[34]
That suffer in exposure, let us meet
And question[35] this most bloody piece of work,
130   To know it further. Fears and scruples[36] shake us.
In the great hand of God I stand, and thence
Against the undivulged pretense[37] I fight
Of treasonous malice.

MACDUFF.   And so do I.

28. badged: Marked.

29. expedition: Haste.

30. breeched with gore: Covered with blood.

31. That most . . . ours: Who are the most concerned with this topic.

32. auger-hole: Tiny hole, an unsuspected place because of its size.

33. Our tears . . . motion: We have not yet had time for tears nor to turn our sorrow into action.
34. when . . . hid: When we have put on our clothes.
35. question: Investigate.
36. scruples: Doubts.

37. undivulged pretense: Hidden purpose.

300   *The English Renaissance*

ALL.   So all.
MACBETH. Let's briefly[38] put on manly readiness,
And meet i' th' hall together.

135   **ALL.**   Well contented.
                    [*Exit all but* MALCOLM *and* DONALBAIN.]

MALCOLM. What will you do? Let's not consort with
        them.
To show an unfelt sorrow is an office[39]
Which the false man does easy. I'll to England.

DONALBAIN. To Ireland, I; our separated fortune
140   Shall keep us both the safer. Where we are
There's daggers in men's smiles; the near in blood,
The nearer bloody.[40]

MALCOLM.   This murderous shaft that's shot
Hath not yet lighted,[41] and our safest way
Is to avoid the aim. Therefore to horse;
145   And let us not be dainty of leave-taking,
But shift away. There's warrant[42] in that theft
Which steals itself[43] when there's no mercy left.
                                                    [*Exit.*]

Scene iv. *Outside Macbeth's castle.*
[*Enter* ROSS *with an* OLD MAN.]

OLD MAN. Threescore and ten I can remember well:
Within the volume of which time I have seen
Hours dreadful and things strange, but this sore[1]
        night
Hath trifled former knowings.

ROSS.   Ha, good father,
5   Thou seest the heavens, as troubled with man's act,
Threatens his bloody stage. By th' clock 'tis day,
And yet dark night strangles the traveling lamp:[2]
Is 't night's predominance, or the day's shame,
That darkness does the face of earth entomb,
When living light should kiss it?

10   **OLD MAN.**   'Tis unnatural,
Even like the deed that's done. On Tuesday last
A falcon, tow'ring in her pride of place,[3]
Was by a mousing owl hawked at and killed.

ROSS. And Duncan's horses—a thing most strange
        and certain—
15   Beauteous and swift, the minions of their race,
Turned wild in nature, broke their stalls, flung out,
Contending 'gainst obedience, as they would make
War with mankind.

---

38. briefly: Quickly.

39. office: Function.

**40. the near . . .
bloody:** The closer we are
in blood relationship to
Duncan, the greater our
chance of being murdered.
41. lighted: Reached its
target.
42. warrant: Justification
43. that theft . . . itself:
stealing away.

1. sore: Grievous.

2. traveling lamp: The
sun.

3. tow'ring . . . place:
Soaring at its summit.

---

36 Discussion Why do Malcolm and Donalbain decide to flee?

37 Literary Focus The first half of this brief scene recapitulates nature's upheaval mentioned previously. In past ages, it was widely believed that chaos in the social and political orders of life was reflected in the natural and cosmic orders.

38 Literary Focus Day is night. Again the reference to disorder and unnatural events.

39 Literary Focus The old man refers here to the rumor that Duncan's sons were responsible for his death.

40 Literary Focus Have your students take note that it is a female hawk that was pulled from its high place by an owl. What might this suggest?

Macbeth, Act II, Scene iv   301

Literary Focus The latter part of this short scene establishes that Duncan's sons, having fled, are the prime suspects, and that Macbeth is already named to succeed Duncan.

Reader's Response What do you think Macbeth and Lady Macbeth look like?

OLD MAN. 'Tis said they eat[4] each other.

ROSS. They did so, to th' amazement of mine eyes,
That looked upon 't.

[*Enter* MACDUFF.]

20 Here comes the good Macduff.
How goes the world, sir, now?

MACDUFF. Why, see you not?

ROSS. Is 't known who did this more than bloody deed?

MACDUFF. Those that Macbeth hath slain.

ROSS. Alas, the day!
What good could they pretend?[5]

MACDUFF. They were suborned:[6]
25 Malcolm and Donalbain, the king's two sons,
Are stol'n away and fled, which puts upon them
Suspicion of the deed.

ROSS. 'Gainst nature still.
Thriftless ambition, that will ravin up[7]
Thine own life's means! Then 'tis most like
30 The sovereignty will fall upon Macbeth.

MACDUFF. He is already named, and gone to Scone[8]
To be invested.

ROSS. Where is Duncan's body?

MACDUFF. Carried to Colmekill,
The sacred storehouse of his predecessors
And guardian of their bones.

35 ROSS. Will you to Scone?

MACDUFF. No, cousin, I'll to Fife.[9]

ROSS. Well, I will thither.

MACDUFF. Well, may you see things well done there.
Adieu,
Lest our old robes sit easier than our new!

ROSS. Farewell, father.

40 OLD MAN. God's benison[10] go with you, and with those
That would make good of bad, and friends of foes!
[*Exit.*]

4. eat: Ate.

5. pretend: Hope for.

6. suborned: Bribed.

7. ravin up: Devour greedily.

8. Scone (skōōn): Where Scottish kings were crowned.

9. Fife: Where Macduff's castle is located.

10. benison: Blessing.

Closure and Extension

ANSWERS TO THINKING ABOUT THE SELECTION
Recalling

1. (a) Macbeth sees a dagger, which becomes covered with blood. (b)

When the bell rings at the end of scene i, Macbeth leaves to kill Duncan.

2. (a) Lady Macbeth would have killed him herself, except that he resembled her father as he lay asleep. (b) Macbeth still holds the daggers after the murder. (c) Lady Macbeth is concerned about Macbeth's reaction to the killing, part of which is his maintaining the bloody knives. She fears his reaction may spoil their plan. (d) She takes the knives and the re-

sponsibility for the details after the murder.

3. (a) The porter imagines he stands at the gates of hell observing the entrants, whom he describes as they pass. (b) Macbeth now wishes the knocking could awaken Duncan. (c) Macduff and Lennox knock, as they were obliged to awaken the King.

4. (a) Macduff enters the King's chamber to find him slaughtered. (b) Macbeth rushes in and kills the blood-smeared grooms. (c) Mal-

colm and Donalbain flee for fear that their lives are in jeopardy, too, as they realize there is a killer among them.

5. (a) The assumption is made that the grooms killed the King, at the orders of Malcolm and Donalbain. That would explain why they fled as they did.

Interpreting

6. Simply, he will sleep no more, because the thoughts of his horri-

THINKING ABOUT THE SELECTION

Recalling

1. (a) What is it that Macbeth thinks he sees in his "fatal vision"? (b) When the bell rings at the end of Scene i, what does Macbeth do?
2. (a) Why, according to Lady Macbeth, did she not kill the King herself? (b) What does Macbeth do with the daggers after the murder? (c) Why does this bother Lady Macbeth? (d) What action does she take?
3. (a) What does the drunken porter imagine he is doing in response to the knocking at the door? (b) What does Macbeth wish the knocking could do? (c) Who is doing the knocking? Why?
4. (a) Who first learns that a murder has taken place? (b) What action does Macbeth take against the grooms? (c) Why do Malcolm and Donalbain leave Macbeth's castle?
5. (a) Who does Macduff say has killed King Duncan? Why do Malcolm and Donalbain fall under suspicion, according to Macduff?

Interpreting

6. What does Macbeth mean by saying he has "murdered sleep"?
7. What is ironic about Lady Macbeth's remark "A little water clears us of this deed"?
8. (a) Why do you think critics consider the porter's speech to be comic relief? (b) How do the porter's comments on the people arriving at "hell gate" mirror Macbeth's dilemma?
9. What do you think causes Lady Macbeth to faint?
10. (a) Why does Ross have doubts about accepting the grooms as the murderers? (b) Why is Macduff concerned that "our old robes" may fit "easier than our new"?

Applying

11. In his soliloquy in Scene i, Macbeth speaks of "vaulting ambition." (a) How can vaulting ambition bring with it great success? (b) How can it bring with it destruction?

ANALYZING LITERATURE

Understanding Atmosphere

Atmosphere is the general mood or feeling in a literary work. In *Macbeth* the murder of the King occurs on an unusually dark, moonless night. The blackness of the night, which is conveyed through dialogue, matches the blackness of the deed. The grim, foreboding atmosphere reinforces the emotional states of the characters.

1. What is eerie about Macbeth's soliloquy in Scene i?
2. Reread Lennox's description of the night, Scene iii, lines 43–50. How does this description add to the atmosphere of the scene?
3. (a) How do the strange natural occurrences mentioned in Scene iv affect the atmosphere? (b) How do they relate to the night's events at Inverness Castle?

CRITICAL THINKING AND READING

Interpreting Symbols

A **symbol** is a word, person, object, or action that stands for something beyond itself. A flag, for example, is more than a piece of cloth; it stands for a country, its people, its ideals. Similarly, the ringing of the bell in Scene i is more than just a sound. It symbolizes an imminent death, much like the bell announcing an execution at London's Newgate prison or the small handbell that was rung outside a condemned person's cell at midnight to urge repentance.

1. In Scene ii, Lady Macbeth compares an owl's shriek to the "fatal bellman." How does this comparison extend the symbol of the bell?
2. Blood and water function as symbols in Scene ii, lines 44–68. (a) What does each symbolize? (b) What indication is there that Macbeth is less impressed by this symbolism than his wife is?
3. It has been suggested that the Old Man in Scene iv is a symbol for the people of Scotland. What is there about the Old Man that makes this suggestion plausible?

gained. (b) "Vaulting ambition" entails risks, including the possibility of failure and death.

ANSWERS TO ANALYZING LITERATURE

1. The eerie vividness of Macbeth's imaginings is intensified by the fact that an audience would not see the bloody dagger—it would see a man thoroughly at the mercy of his own morbid mental processes.
2. The description tells of an unruly night, filled with the sounds of lamentings and strange screams of death and prophesying. Confusion reigns. "Some say, the earth did . . . shake." It is such a night within the castle, as well.
3. (a) Day is night. The world is turned upside down, or so it seems. (b) All of the unnatural natural events reflect the murder of the King. So heinous an act is the killing of a monarch that the forces of the world are being wrenched by it.

ANSWERS TO CRITICAL THINKING AND READING

1. With this comparison, the owl's screeches become like the bell—fatal signals.
2. (a) Blood symbolizes murder and the stain of guilt; water symbolizes the removal of guilt. (b) Macbeth argues that the stain of blood is so great that his hands will turn the ocean red.
3. He certainly can be a symbol for all good people. He abhors the terrible deed of the night before; he has witnessed good and bad in this land for many years; and he wishes success for Ross and MacDuff, who refer to him as father.

Macbeth, Act II 303

---

ble deed will never leave him or allow him any peace.
7. Unlike her husband, she believes, or would like to believe, that a bit of scrubbing will wash away this deed as it does the blood. Later in the play during her sleepwalking scene, she will utter "out damned spot" as the stains of this deed persist.
8. (a) There isn't much doubt of its being comic relief—critics have differed about its appropriateness here. It is generally agreed Shake-

speare injected the drunken porter as an effective way to alter the mood from the horror and power of the preceding scene. (b) The imagined characters entering hell are all liars and cheats who thought they could get away with their misdeeds. In the end, each must pay.
9. Critics argue about her fainting. Some think she does, and others think she pretends in order to demonstrate her shock over Duncan's death. Shakespeare doesn't

tell us. If she really faints, it could be a first sign of the instability that destroys her. Have students discuss the possibilities.
10. (a) Ross wonders what the grooms had to gain by killing the King. (b) Macduff suggests that unless they do things well and carefully from here on, they could end up dead, also.

Applying

11. (a) Nothing ventured, nothing

Literary Focus Point out to the students that authors of stories or plays about historical figures or events often use dramatic irony because they can presuppose readers' or viewers' knowledge of the events. A story about a couple meeting and falling in love aboard the *Titanic* might be an obvious and overworked example. Have students give examples of their own.

Writing/Prior Knowledge Have less-advanced students sketch out ironic situations.

Vocabulary

Preteach the following vocabulary words:

indissoluble (in′ di säl′ yσο b'l) *adj.*: Not able to be dissolved or undone (Sc.i, l. 17)

dauntless (dônt′ lis) *adj.*: Fearless (Sc. i, l. 52)

jocund (jäk′ənd) *adj.*: Cheerful; jovial (Sc. ii, l. 40)

infirmity (in fʉr′ mə tē) *n.*: Physical or mental defect; illness (Sc. iv, l. 87)

malevolence (mə lev′ ə ləns) *n.*: Ill will; spitefulness (Sc. vi, l. 28)

GUIDE FOR INTERPRETING

Macbeth, Act III

Writer's Techniques

Irony. In general, irony is a contrast between what is said and what is meant or between what is expected and what occurs. There are three kinds of irony in literature, all of which occur in *Macbeth*.

Dramatic irony exists when the words or acts of a character in a play carry a meaning the character does not understand but the audience does. An example of dramatic irony occurs in *Macbeth* at the beginning of Act I, Scene vi, when Banquo and Duncan discuss the pleasant and delicate air as they arrive at Inverness. The audience knows, but Banquo and Duncan do not, that a murderous plot is being hatched behind the castle walls.

Situational irony occurs when the expected results of an action or situation differ from the actual results.

Verbal irony exists when a speaker says one thing and means the opposite. In a famous speech in Shakespeare's *Julius Caesar*, for example, when Mark Antony says of the assassins of Caesar, "So are they all, all honorable men," he means exactly the opposite of what he says. To him, the assassins are *not* honorable men. Antony's words are therefore verbal irony.

Commentary

The Elizabethans believed that ghosts of dead people could return to earth. Spirits could appear to whomever they wanted, whenever they wanted, so that one person in a crowd might see a ghost while the others did not. Ghosts were especially likely to return when their originals were troubled. In Shakespeare's plays, ghosts often return to haunt a murderer. Although clergymen preached that the belief in ghosts was wicked and sinful, people remained convinced that ghosts were real, and well-stocked Elizabethan households boasted a stockpile of charms to ward off ghosts.

Perhaps William Shakespeare had his country folks' belief in ghosts in mind when he chose this epitaph for his own grave:

> Good friend, for Jesus' sake forbare
> To dig the dust encloséd here.
> Blest be the man that spares these stones,
> And curst be he that moves my bones.

Writing

At this point in *Macbeth*, you know a great deal about the major characters—more, in fact, than they know about themselves. Based on your knowledge, make notes on what you think will happen to the following characters by the end of the play: Macbeth, Lady Macbeth, Banquo, Macduff.

Objectives

1 To understand irony
2 To interpret connotative meanings
3 To write a speculative essay

Support Material

Teaching Portfolio
Teaching Backup, p. 295
Usage and Mechanics Worksheet, p. 298
Vocabulary Check, p. 299
Analyzing Literature Worksheet, *Understanding Irony*, p. 300
Language Worksheet, *Understanding Figurative Language*, p. 301
Selection Test, p. 302

Act III

Scene i. *Forres. The palace.*
[*Enter* BANQUO.]

BANQUO. Thou hast it now: King, Cawdor, Glamis, all,
As the weird women promised, and I fear
Thou play'dst most foully for 't. Yet it was said
It should not stand[1] in thy posterity,
5   But that myself should be the root and father
Of many kings. If there come truth from them—
As upon thee, Macbeth, their speeches shine—
Why, by the verities on thee made good,
May they not be my oracles as well
10 And set me up in hope? But hush, no more!

[*Sennet[2] sounded. Enter* MACBETH *as King,* LADY MACBETH,
LENNOX, ROSS, LORDS, *and* ATTENDANTS.]

MACBETH. Here's our chief guest.

LADY MACBETH.   If he had been forgotten,
It had been as a gap in our great feast,
And all-thing[3] unbecoming.

MACBETH. Tonight we hold a solemn[4] supper, sir,
And I'll request your presence.

15 **BANQUO.**   Let your Highness
Command upon me, to the which my duties
Are with a most indissoluble tie
For ever knit.

MACBETH. Ride you this afternoon?

BANQUO.   Ay, my good lord.

20 **MACBETH.** We should have else desired your good advice
(Which still hath been both grave and prosperous[5])
In this day's council; but we'll take tomorrow.
Is 't far you ride?

BANQUO. As far, my lord, as will fill up the time
25 'Twixt this and supper. Go not my horse the better,[6]
I must become a borrower of the night
For a dark hour or twain.

MACBETH.   Fail not our feast.

BANQUO. My lord, I will not.

MACBETH. We hear our bloody cousins are bestowed
30 In England and in Ireland, not confessing
Their cruel parricide, filling their hearers
With strange invention.[7] But of that tomorrow,

1. **stand:** Continue.

2. **Sennet:** Trumpet call.

3. **all-thing:** Altogether.

4. **solemn:** Ceremonious.

5. **grave and prosperous:**
Weighty and profitable.

6. **Go not . . . better:** Unless my horse goes faster than I expect.

7. **invention:** Lies.

Macbeth, Act III, Scene i   305

4 **Discussion** How does all that follows hinge upon the meaning of this line? What does it imply about Macbeth's character?

4 **Discussion** How does all that follows hinge upon the meaning of this line? What does it imply about Macbeth's character?

5 **Discussion** The soliloquy is divided into two parts, with Macbeth's reasons for fearing Banquo in the first part and, in the second, Macbeth's resentment of Banquo's prophecy. What is the chief reason he feels Banquo is a threat to him? What is the source of the resentment about the prophecy? Does it seem likely that Banquo might try to wrench the throne from him, or is this more of Macbeth's fevered imagination?

6 **Discussion** What does this challenge indicate about Macbeth's state of mind at this point?

When therewithal we shall have cause of state
Craving us jointly.[8] Hie you to horse. Adieu,
35 Till you return at night. Goes Fleance with you?

BANQUO. Ay, my good lord: our time does call upon 's.

MACBETH. I wish your horses swift and sure of foot,
And so I do commend you to their backs.
Farewell.   [*Exit* BANQUO.]
40 Let every man be master of his time
Till seven at night. To make society
The sweeter welcome, we will keep ourself
Till suppertime alone. While[9] then, God be with you!

[*Exit* LORDS *and all but* MACBETH *and a* SERVANT.]

Sirrah,[10] a word with you: attend those men
45 Our pleasure?

ATTENDANT. They are, my lord, without the palace gate.

MACBETH. Bring them before us.   [*Exit* SERVANT.]

4   To be thus[11] is nothing, but[12] to be safely thus—
Our fears in Banquo stick deep,
50 And in his royalty of nature reigns that
Which would be feared. 'Tis much he dares;
And, to[13] that dauntless temper of his mind,
He hath a wisdom that doth guide his valor
To act in safety. There is none but he
55 Whose being I do fear: and under him
My genius is rebuked,[14] as it is said
Mark Antony's was by Caesar. He chid[15] the sisters,
When first they put the name of King upon me,
And bade them speak to him; then prophetlike
5 60 They hailed him father to a line of kings.
Upon my head they placed a fruitless crown
And put a barren scepter in my gripe,[16]
Thence to be wrenched with an unlineal hand,
No son of mine succeeding. If 't be so,
65 For Banquo's issue have I filed[17] my mind;
For them the gracious Duncan have I murdered;
Put rancors in the vessel of my peace
Only for them, and mine eternal jewel[18]
Given to the common enemy of man,[19]
70 To make them kings, the seeds of Banquo kings!
Rather than so, come, fate, into the list,
6   And champion me to th' utterance![20] Who's there?

[*Enter* SERVANT *and* TWO MURDERERS.]

Now go to the door, and stay there till we call.
                    [*Exit* SERVANT.]
Was it not yesterday we spoke together?

8. cause . . . jointly: Matters of state demanding our joint attention.

9. While: Until.

10. Sirrah: A common address to an inferior.

11. thus: King.
12. but: Unless.

13. to: Added to.

14. genius is rebuked: Guardian spirit is cowed.
15. chid: Scolded.

16. gripe: Grip.

17. filed: Defiled.

18. eternal jewel: Soul.
19. common . . . man: The Devil.

20. champion me to th' utterance: Fight against me to the death.

Primary Source Note

Laurence Olivier played Macbeth in 1937 and 1955. In his book *On Acting,* he discusses the differences between these two productions and the changes in his conception of the role:

> The director of my 1937 *Macbeth* was Michel St.-Denis, a star director full of wit and imagination, though on this particular production neither seemed to be on our side. When I told Ralph Richardson I was going down to the Vic, he asked, "What are you going to play?" and when I said,

"Macbeth," he said, "You'll break your neck, my dear boy. You don't want to play Macbeth at your age; be very, very careful." It was what you might call a stylized production. Everything in godlike proportions. The makeups were masklike. I had a huge false face on, a nose that went down, a stuck-on chin and a putty forehead with vast eyebrows. The idea was to make something real through a highly poetic and unreal approach. I put myself entirely in St.-Denis' hands, but felt I was not good in such a theatrical production. I "made up" to play Macbeth, instead of letting Macbeth play through me. I had everything outwardly and not enough inwardly. I think, in that production Macbeth was nearer my sleeve than my heart.

MURDERERS. It was, so please your Highness.

75 **MACBETH.**   Well then, now
Have you considered of my speeches? Know
That it was he in the times past, which held you
So under fortune,[21] which you thought had been
Our innocent self: this I made good to you
80 In our last conference; passed in probation[22] with
     you,
How you were born in hand,[23] how crossed, the
     instruments,
Who wrought with them, and all things else that
     might
To half a soul[24] and to a notion[25] crazed
Say "Thus did Banquo."

FIRST MURDERER.   You made it known to us.

85 **MACBETH.** I did so; and went further, which is now
Our point of second meeting. Do you find
Your patience so predominant in your nature,
That you can let this go? Are you so gospeled,[26]
To pray for this good man and for his issue,
90 Whose heavy hand hath bowed you to the grave
And beggared yours for ever?

FIRST MURDERER.   We are men, my liege.

MACBETH. Ay, in the catalogue ye go for[27] men;
As hounds and greyhounds, mongrels, spaniels,
     curs,
Shoughs, water-rugs[28] and demi-wolves, are clept[29]
95 All by the name of dogs: the valued file[30]
Distinguishes the swift, the slow, the subtle,
The housekeeper, the hunter, every one
According to the gift which bounteous nature
Hath in him closed,[31] whereby he does receive
100 Particular addition,[32] from the bill
That writes them all alike: and so of men.
Now if you have a station in the file,[33]
Not i' th' worst rank of manhood, say 't,
And I will put that business in your bosoms
105 Whose execution takes your enemy off,
Grapples you to the heart and love of us,
Who wear our health but sickly in his life,[34]
Which in his death were perfect.

SECOND MURDERER.   I am one, my liege,
Whom the vile blows and buffets of the world
110 Hath so incensed that I am reckless what
I do to spite the world.

Macbeth, Act III, Scene i 307

---

21. held . . . fortune: Kept you from good fortune.
22. passed in probation: Reviewed the proofs.
23. born in hand: Deceived.

24. half a soul: A halfwit.
25. notion: Mind.

26. gospeled: Ready to forgive.

27. go for: Pass as.
28. Shoughs (shuks), **water-rugs:** Shaggy dogs, long-haired dogs.
29. clept: Called.
30. valued file: Classification by valuable traits.

31. closed: Enclosed.
32. addition: Distinction (to set it apart from other dogs).
33. file: Ranks.

34. wear . . . life: Are sick as long as he lives.

---

7 Discussion Note that there is little subtlety here in labeling these two as murderers. This is a second meeting. What has Macbeth suggested about Banquo to stimulate their anger?

8 Literary Focus Note that Macbeth, in attacking their manhood, uses the same argument as did Lady Macbeth against him.

9 Discussion How does the Second Murderer assess his rank among men and how does he react?

Though I have relied a great deal on makeup and appearances over the years, I still maintain that the real look should come from inside. Of course, I was to play it again some years later, at Stratford in 1955, directed by Glen Byam Shaw, with a considerable degree of success. My voice was infinitely stronger and more powerful, and the extra chunk of life experience I had had since I'd first played the part really counted. The first time, I had played age through pure imagination; now I could bring knowledge to bear. I was also happy with the makeup and the costumes. I found that it was genuinely possible to make every second of Macbeth human despite all that murdering of children. By luck that second time I found a complete experience which belonged to the part and was able to get the right mixture of style and down-to-earth bone reality. I found the right cocktail, the right mixture, the right ingredients in the right proportion.

10 Discussion Paraphrase this statement. Does it sound sincere?

11 Discussion What reason does Macbeth give for not being able to openly use his power as king to punish Banquo?

12 Discussion Notice that Macbeth mentions Fleance almost as an afterthought. How important to Macbeth is Fleance's death? Why?

10

FIRST MURDERER. And I another
So weary with disasters, tugged with fortune,
That I would set[35] my life on any chance,
To mend it or be rid on 't.

MACBETH. Both of you
Know Banquo was your enemy.

115 **BOTH MURDERERS.** True, my lord.

MACBETH. So is he mine, and in such bloody distance[36]
That every minute of his being thrusts
Against my near'st of life:[37] and though I could
With barefaced power sweep him from my sight
120 And bid my will avouch[38] it, yet I must not,

11

For certain friends that are both his and mine,
Whose loves I may not drop, but wail his fall[39]
Who I myself struck down: and thence it is
That I to your assistance do make love,
125 Masking the business from the common eye
For sundry weighty reasons.

SECOND MURDERER. We shall, my lord,
Perform what you command us.

FIRST MURDERER. Though our lives—

MACBETH. Your spirits shine through you. Within this
hour at most
I will advise you where to plant yourselves,
130 Acquaint you with the perfect spy o' th' time,
The moment on 't;[40] for 't must be done tonight,
And something[41] from the palace; always thought[42]
That I require a clearness:[43] and with him—

12

To leave no rubs[44] nor botches in the work—
135 Fleance his son, that keeps him company,
Whose absence is no less material to me
Than is his father's, must embrace the fate
Of that dark hour. Resolve yourselves apart:[45]
I'll come to you anon.

MURDERERS. We are resolved, my lord.

140 **MACBETH.** I'll call upon you straight.[46] Abide within.
It is concluded: Banquo, thy soul's flight,
If it find heaven, must find it out tonight. [*Exit.*]

Scene ii. *The palace.*
[*Enter* MACBETH'S LADY *and a* SERVANT.]

LADY MACBETH. Is Banquo gone from court?

SERVANT. Ay, madam, but returns again tonight.

35. set: Risk.

36. distance: Disagreement.

37. near'st of life: Most vital parts.

38. avouch: Justify.

39. wail his fall: (I must) bewail his death.

40. the perfect . . . on 't: The exact information of the exact time.
41. something: Some distance.
42. thought: Remembered.
43. clearness: Freedom from suspicion.
44. rubs: Flaws.
45. Resolve yourselves apart: Make your own decision.

46. straight: Immediately.

LADY MACBETH. Say to the King, I would attend his
    leisure
For a few words.

SERVANT.   Madam, I will.   *[Exit.]*

LADY MACBETH.   Nought's had, all's spent,
5   Where our desire is got without content:
'Tis safer to be that which we destroy
Than by destruction dwell in doubtful joy.

[Enter MACBETH.*]*

How now, my lord! Why do you keep alone,
Of sorriest fancies your companions making,
10   Using those thoughts which should indeed have died
With them they think on? Things without all remedy
Should be without regard: what's done is done.

MACBETH. We have scotched[1] the snake, not killed it:
She'll close[2] and be herself, whilst our poor malice
15   Remains in danger of her former tooth.[3]
But let the frame of things disjoint,[4] both the worlds[5]
    suffer,
Ere we will eat our meal in fear, and sleep
In the affliction of these terrible dreams
That shake us nightly: better be with the dead,
20   Whom we, to gain our peace, have sent to peace,
Than on the torture of the mind to lie
In restless ecstasy.[6] Duncan is in his grave;
After life's fitful fever he sleeps well.
Treason has done his worst: nor steel, nor poison,
25   Malice domestic, foreign levy,[7] nothing,
Can touch him further.

LADY MACBETH.   Come on.
Gentle my lord, sleek o'er your rugged looks;
Be bright and jovial among your guests tonight.

MACBETH. So shall I, love; and so, I pray, be you:
30   Let your remembrance apply to Banquo;
Present him eminence,[8] both with eye and tongue:
Unsafe the while, that we must lave[9]
Our honors in these flattering streams
And make our faces vizards[10] to our hearts,
Disguising what they are.

35 **LADY MACBETH.**   You must leave this.

MACBETH. O, full of scorpions is my mind, dear wife!
Thou know'st that Banquo, and his Fleance, lives.

LADY MACBETH. But in them nature's copy's not eterne.[11]

Macbeth, Act III, Scene ii   309

---

1. **scotched:** Wounded.
2. **close:** Heal.
3. **in . . . tooth:** In as much danger as before.
4. **frame of things disjoint:** Universe collapse.
5. **both the worlds:** Heaven and earth.

6. **ecstasy:** Frenzy.

7. **Malice . . . levy:** Civil and foreign war.

8. **Present him eminence:** Honor him.
9. **Unsafe . . . lave:** We are unsafe as long as we have to wash.
10. **vizards** (viz′ ərdz): Masks.

11. **nature's . . . eterne:** Nature's lease is not eternal.

---

13 **Discussion** Paraphrase the first line of this telling statement. When she says "we destroy," what does she mean? What did they destroy?

14 **Literary Focus** It was indicated earlier that Lady Macbeth has no imagination; we are seeing the results of the lack here. What would seem glaringly obvious to most people she is only now coming to realize—too late.

15 **Literary Focus** Note how she tries to cover her own depression in trying to elevate her husband's spirits, advising him to do what she herself, in private, cannot.

16 **Discussion** What is Macbeth suggesting might be better than the terrible dreams that torment him nightly? Who is "sleeping" more soundly than he?

17 **Discussion** In assuring Lady Macbeth that he will strike the proper mood at the party, what do we learn about Macbeth and his relationship with his wife at this point through these few lines?

BANQUO AT THE GATE, WOOD ENGRAVING AFTER SIR JOHN GILBERT
The Granger Collection

18

MACBETH. There's comfort yet; they are assailable.
40   Then be thou jocund. Ere the bat hath flown
    His cloistered flight, ere to black Hecate's summons
    The shard-borne[12] beetle with his drowsy hums
    Hath rung night's yawning peal, there shall be done
    A deed of dreadful note.

LADY MACBETH.   What's to be done?

45 **MACBETH.** Be innocent of the knowledge, dearest
       chuck,[13]
    Till thou applaud the deed. Come, seeling[14] night,
    Scarf up[15] the tender eye of pitiful day,
    And with thy bloody and invisible hand
    Cancel and tear to pieces that great bond[16]
50   Which keeps me pale! Light thickens, and the crow
    Makes wing to th' rooky[17] wood.
    Good things of day begin to droop and drowse,
    Whiles night's black agents to their preys do rouse.
    Thou marvel'st at my words: but hold thee still;
55   Things bad begun make strong themselves by ill:
    So, prithee, go with me.   [*Exit.*]

19

12. shard-borne: Borne on scaly wings.

13. chuck: A term of endearment.
14. seeling: Eye-closing. Falconers sometimes sewed a hawk's eyes closed in order to train it.
15. Scarf up: Blindfold.
16. great bond: Between Banquo and fate.
17. rooky: Full of rooks, or crows.

Scene iii. *Near the palace.*

[*Enter* THREE MURDERERS.]

FIRST MURDERER. But who did bid thee join with us?

THIRD MURDERER.   Macbeth.

SECOND MURDERER. He needs not our mistrust; since he
    delivers
Our offices[1] and what we have to do
To the direction just.[2]

FIRST MURDERER.   Then stand with us.
5   The west yet glimmers with some streaks of day.
Now spurs the lated traveler apace
To gain the timely inn, and near approaches
The subject of our watch.

THIRD MURDERER.   Hark! I hear horses.

BANQUO. [*Within*] Give us a light there, ho!

SECOND MURDERER.   Then 'tis he. The rest
10   That are within the note of expectation[3]
Already are i' th' court.

FIRST MURDERER.   His horses go about.[4]

THIRD MURDERER. Almost a mile: but he does usually—
So all men do—from hence to th' palace gate
Make it their walk.

[*Enter* BANQUO *and* FLEANCE, *with a torch.*]

SECOND MURDERER. A light, a light!

THIRD MURDERER.   'Tis he.

15   **FIRST MURDERER.**   Stand to 't.

BANQUO. It will be rain tonight.

FIRST MURDERER.   Let it come down.

[*They set upon* BANQUO.]

BANQUO. O, treachery! Fly, good Fleance, fly, fly, fly!
                    [*Exit* FLEANCE.]

             Thou mayst revenge. O slave! [*Dies.*]

THIRD MURDERER. Who did strike out the light?

FIRST MURDERER.   Was't not the way?[5]

20   **THIRD MURDERER.** There's but one down; the son is fled.

SECOND MURDERER. We have lost best half of our affair.

FIRST MURDERER. Well, let's away and say how much is
    done.   [*Exit.*]

Macbeth, Act III, Scene iii   311

1. offices: Duties.
2. direction just: Exact detail.

3. within . . . expectations: On the list of expected guests.
4. His . . . about: His horses have been taken to the stable.

5. way: Thing to do.

24 **Literary Focus** Macbeth's conversation with the Murderer would take place at the side of the stage, presumably out of sight and out of earshot of the guests.

25 **Literary Focus** It has also been argued that this is the climax, when Macbeth learns of the escape of Fleance.

26 **Discussion** Was he in fact as whole as marble and as well as these lines imply? Why or why not?

27 **Clarification** *Worm* held a broader meaning in Shakespeare's time, often referring to a snake.

Scene iv. *The palace.*
[*Banquet prepared. Enter* MACBETH, LADY MACBETH, ROSS, LENNOX, LORDS, *and* ATTENDANTS.]

MACBETH. You know your own degrees;[1] sit down:
    At first and last, the hearty welcome.

LORDS. Thanks to your Majesty.

MACBETH. Ourself will mingle with society[2]
5   And play the humble host.
    Our hostess keeps her state,[3] but in best time
    We will require[4] her welcome.

LADY MACBETH. Pronounce it for me, sir, to all our friends,
    For my heart speaks they are welcome.

[*Enter* FIRST MURDERER.]

MACBETH. See, they encounter thee with their hearts' thanks.
10   Both sides are even: here I'll sit i' th' midst:
    Be large in mirth; anon we'll drink a measure[5]
    The table round. [*Goes to* MURDERER] There's blood upon thy face.

MURDERER. 'Tis Banquo's then.

15 MACBETH. 'Tis better thee without than he within.[6]
    Is he dispatched?

MURDERER. My lord, his throat is cut; that I did for him.

MACBETH. Thou art the best o' th' cutthroats.
    Yet he's good that did the like for Fleance;
20   If thou didst it, thou art the nonpareil.[7]

MURDERER. Most royal sir, Fleance is 'scaped.

MACBETH. [*Aside*] Then comes my fit again: I had else been perfect,
    Whole as the marble, founded as the rock,
    As broad and general as the casing[8] air:
25   But now I am cabined, cribbed, confined, bound in
    To saucy[9] doubts and fears.—But Banquo's safe?

MURDERER. Ay, my good lord: safe in a ditch he bides,
    With twenty trenchèd[10] gashes on his head,
    The least a death to nature.[11]

MACBETH.   Thanks for that.
    [*Aside*] There the grown serpent lies; the worm
30   that's fled

1. **degrees:** Ranks. At state banquets guests were seated according to rank.

2. **society:** The company.

3. **keeps her state:** Remains seated on her throne.
4. **require:** Request.

5. **measure:** Toast.

6. **thee . . . within:** You outside than he inside.

7. **nonpareil:** Without equal.

8. **as . . . casing:** As unrestrained as the surrounding.
9. **saucy:** Insolent.

10. **trenchèd:** Trenchlike.
11. **nature:** Natural life.

312   The English Renaissance

Commentary:
Ghosts and Witches at the Globe

The arrival of Banquo's ghost at the banquet might prompt curiosity about how Elizabethan theater companies managed the entrances and exits of supernatural beings. You may recall that the outer stage of the Globe Playhouse thrust forward into the ground-floor audience. Actors standing at the edge of this stage could therefore play to a surrounding crowd. Behind the outer stage, was a smaller area called the rear stage, open to the audience but enclosed by a rigid wall in the back and cloth hangings on the sides.

The trap-door (trap) in the floor of the rear stage was the means by which Banquo's ghost made an entrance. Since this trap operated silently, there was no need for accompanying music to disguise the creaking of ropes. It also had the advantage of not being completely visible to the audience. This trap was therefore ideal for the stealthy, unannounced appearance of a spirit. In addition to accommodating the apparition of Banquo, it served as the entrance for Caesar's ghost in *Julius Caesar,* IV.iii, and for the ghosts of the family of Posthumus in *Cymbeline,* V.iv.

Hath nature that in time will venom breed,
No teeth for th' present. Get thee gone. Tomorrow
We'll hear ourselves[12] again.   [*Exit* MURDERER.]

LADY MACBETH.   My royal lord,
You do not give the cheer.[13] The feast is sold
35 That is not often vouched, while 'tis a-making,
'Tis given with welcome.[14] To feed were best at home;
From thence, the sauce to meat is ceremony;[15]
Meeting were bare without it.

[*Enter the* GHOST OF BANQUO, *and sits in* MACBETH'*s place.*]

MACBETH.   Sweet remembrancer!
Now good digestion wait on appetite,
And health on both!

40 **LENNOX.**   May 't please your Highness sit.

MACBETH. Here had we now our country's honor roofed,[16]
Were the graced person of our Banquo present—
Who may I rather challenge for unkindness
Than pity for mischance![17]

ROSS.   His absence, sir,
Lays blame upon his promise. Please 't your
45   Highness
To grace us with your royal company?

MACBETH. The table's full.

LENNOX.   Here is a place reserved, sir.

MACBETH. Where?

LENNOX. Here, my good lord. What is 't that moves your
    Highness?

MACBETH. Which of you have done this?

50 **LORDS.**   What, my good lord?

MACBETH. Thou canst not say I did it. Never shake
    Thy gory locks at me.

ROSS. Gentlemen, rise, his Highness is not well.

LADY MACBETH. Sit, worthy friends. My lord is often thus,
55   And hath been from his youth. Pray you, keep seat.
The fit is momentary; upon a thought[18]
He will again be well. If much you note him,
You shall offend him and extend his passion.[19]
Feed, and regard him not.—Are you a man?

60 **MACBETH.** Ay, and a bold one, that dare look on that
    Which might appall the devil.

12. hear ourselves: Talk it over.

13. give the cheer: Make the guests feel welcome.
14. The feast . . . welcome: The feast at which the host fails to make the guests feel welcome while the food is being prepared is no more than a bought dinner.
15. From . . . ceremony: Ceremony adds a pleasant flavor to the food.

16. our . . . roofed: The most honorable men in the country under one roof.

17. Who . . . mischance: Whom I hope I may reproach for being absent due to discourtesy rather than pity because he has had an accident.

18. upon a thought: In a moment.
19. passion: Suffering.

28 Literary Focus The stage direction for the entrance of the ghost suggests a ghostlike figure appearing on the Elizabethan stage. In modern productions, the seat usually remains empty, the ghost being a figment of Macbeth's imagination. In contrast, the ghost of Hamlet's father appears nightly on the battlements, where he is seen by the guards as well as by Hamlet himself.

Enrichment In 1989, the remains of the Rose Theater were excavated in London. Shakespeare began his writing career at this playhouse. He created *Titus Andronicus* and *Henry VI, Parts I, II, and III* for the troupe that played at the Rose, before he became associated with the Globe Theater. A surprise result of the excavation is the discovery that the Rose could only accommodate a small audience of several hundred.

Macbeth, Act III, Scene iv 313

As for the first appearance of the three Witches, they rose through a trap in the floor of the outer stage. This trap, with a platform raised by rope and pulley, was frequently required to lift such prodigious items as "a King . . . riding upon a Lyon or dragon" or "a Tree of gold laden with Diadems & Crownes of gold." The witches, being supernatural creatures, probably appeared with a racket of thunder and lightning, trumpeting, and falling chains. Not only did this commotion convey a proper feeling of terror, but it disguised the less bloodcurdling noise of the trap's straining ropes.

It is widely agreed that the character Hecate, leader of the witches, was inserted into the play by the dramatist Middleton. Despite this irregular entrance into the proceedings, she had a sufficiently spectacular exit. At the end of III.v, she was hoisted up from the stage on a chair by a rope-and-pulley mechanism on the superstructure of the theater. Folds of light cloth disguised the ropes and gave the appearance of "a foggy cloud."

29 **Literary Focus** These lines would not be overheard by the guests.

30 **Literary Focus** His efforts to make her see the ghost are futile, as it is visible only in his mind.

31 **Literary Focus** Note that she again questions his manhood in order to snap him out of his distraction.

32 **Discussion** What happens that makes the ghost reappear for Macbeth?

LADY MACBETH.   O proper stuff!
This is the very painting of your fear.
This is the air-drawn dagger which, you said,
Led you to Duncan. O, these flaws[20] and starts,
Impostors to true fear, would well become
A woman's story at a winter's fire,
Authorized[21] by her grandam. Shame itself!
Why do you make such faces? When all's done,
You look but on a stool.

MACBETH.   Prithee, see there!
Behold! Look! Lo! How say you?
Why, what care I? If thou canst nod, speak too.
If charnel houses[22] and our graves must send
Those that we bury back, our monuments
Shall be the maws of kites.[23]   [*Exit* GHOST.]

LADY MACBETH.   What, quite unmanned in folly?

MACBETH. If I stand here, I saw him.

LADY MACBETH.   Fie, for shame!

MACBETH. Blood hath been shed ere now, i' th' olden time,
Ere humane statute purged the gentle weal;[24]
Ay, and since too, murders have been performed
Too terrible for the ear. The times has been
That, when the brains were out, the man would die,
And there an end; but now they rise again,
With twenty mortal murders on their crowns,[25]
And push us from our stools. This is more strange
Than such a murder is.

LADY MACBETH.   My worthy lord,
Your noble friends do lack you.

MACBETH.   I do forget.
Do not muse at me, my most worthy friends;
I have a strange infirmity, which is nothing
To those that know me. Come, love and health to all!
Then I'll sit down. Give me some wine, fill full.

[*Enter* GHOST.]

I drink to th' general joy o' th' whole table,
And to our dear friend Banquo, whom we miss;
Would he were here! To all and him we thirst,[26]
And all to all.

LORDS.   Our duties, and the pledge.

65

70

75

80

85

90

20. flaws: Gusts of wind; outbursts of emotion.

21. Authorized: Vouched for.

22. charnel houses: Vaults containing human bones dug up in making new graves.

23. our . . . kites: Our tombs shall be the bellies of birds of prey.

24. Ere . . . weal: Before humane laws civilized the state and made it gentle.

25. mortal . . . crowns: Deadly wounds on their heads.

26. thirst: Drink.

MACBETH. Avaunt![27] and quit my sight! Let the earth
    hide thee!
95   Thy bones are marrowless, thy blood is cold;
    Thou hast no speculation[28] in those eyes
    Which thou dost glare with.

LADY MACBETH.   Think of this, good peers,
    But as a thing of custom, 'tis no other.
    Only it spoils the pleasure of the time.

100 **MACBETH.** What man dare, I dare.
    Approach thou like the rugged Russian bear,
    The armed rhinoceros, or th' Hyrcan[29] tiger;
    Take any shape but that,[30] and my firm nerves
    Shall never tremble. Or be alive again,
105   And dare me to the desert[31] with thy sword.
    If trembling I inhabit[32] then, protest me
    The baby of a girl. Hence, horrible shadow!
    Unreal mock'ry, hence!   [*Exit* GHOST.]
                Why, so: being gone,
    I am a man again. Pray you, sit still.

LADY MACBETH. You have displaced the mirth, broke the
110   good meeting,
    With most admired[33] disorder.

MACBETH.   Can such things be,
    And overcome us[34] like a summer's cloud,
    Without our special wonder? You make me strange
    Even to the disposition that I owe,[35]
115   When now I think you can behold such sights,
    And keep the natural ruby of your cheeks,
    When mine is blanched with fear.

ROSS.   What sights, my lord?

LADY MACBETH. I pray you, speak not: He grows worse
    and worse;
    Question enrages him: at once, good night.
120   Stand not upon the order of your going,[36]
    But go at once.

LENNOX.   Good night; and better health
    Attend his Majesty!

LADY MACBETH.   A kind good night to all!
                [*Exit* LORDS.]

MACBETH. It will have blood, they say: blood will have
    blood.
    Stones have been known to move and trees to
    speak;

27. Avaunt: Be gone!

28. speculation: sight.

29. Hyrcan (hər' kən):
From Hyrcania, a province
of the ancient Persian and
Macedonian empires south
of the Caspian Sea.
30. that: Banquo's shape.
31. desert: A place where
neither of us could escape.
32. inhabit: Remain indoors.

33. admired: Amazing.

34. overcome us: Come
over us.

35. disposition . . . owe:
My own nature.

36. Stand . . . going: Do
not wait to depart in order
of rank.

33 Discussion Might this be a kind
of response to Lady Macbeth's
suggestion that he is "unmanned"?

Macbeth, Act III, Scene iv   315

34 **Clarification** What time is it? (Almost morning.)

35 **Literary Focus** Macbeth has established a kind of police state with paid informers in the houses of important people.

36 **Clarification** "For mine own good . . . way" means "My own interests and needs take precedence over all else." Is this a proper attitude for a king?

37 **Discussion** He then indicates that at this point retreating would be as difficult as going ahead with more bloodletting. Is that true? Would it even be possible to retreat at this point?

38 **Discussion** How does he rationalize the appearance of the ghost?

39 **Literary Focus** This scene is almost unanimously regarded as spurious and is generally considered not to have been written by Shakespeare. Because Elizabethan audiences so thoroughly enjoyed the witches, it is thought that Thomas Middleton wrote and interjected this scene, which contributes nothing to the action of the play. In 1612 Middleton wrote a play entitled *The Witch.*

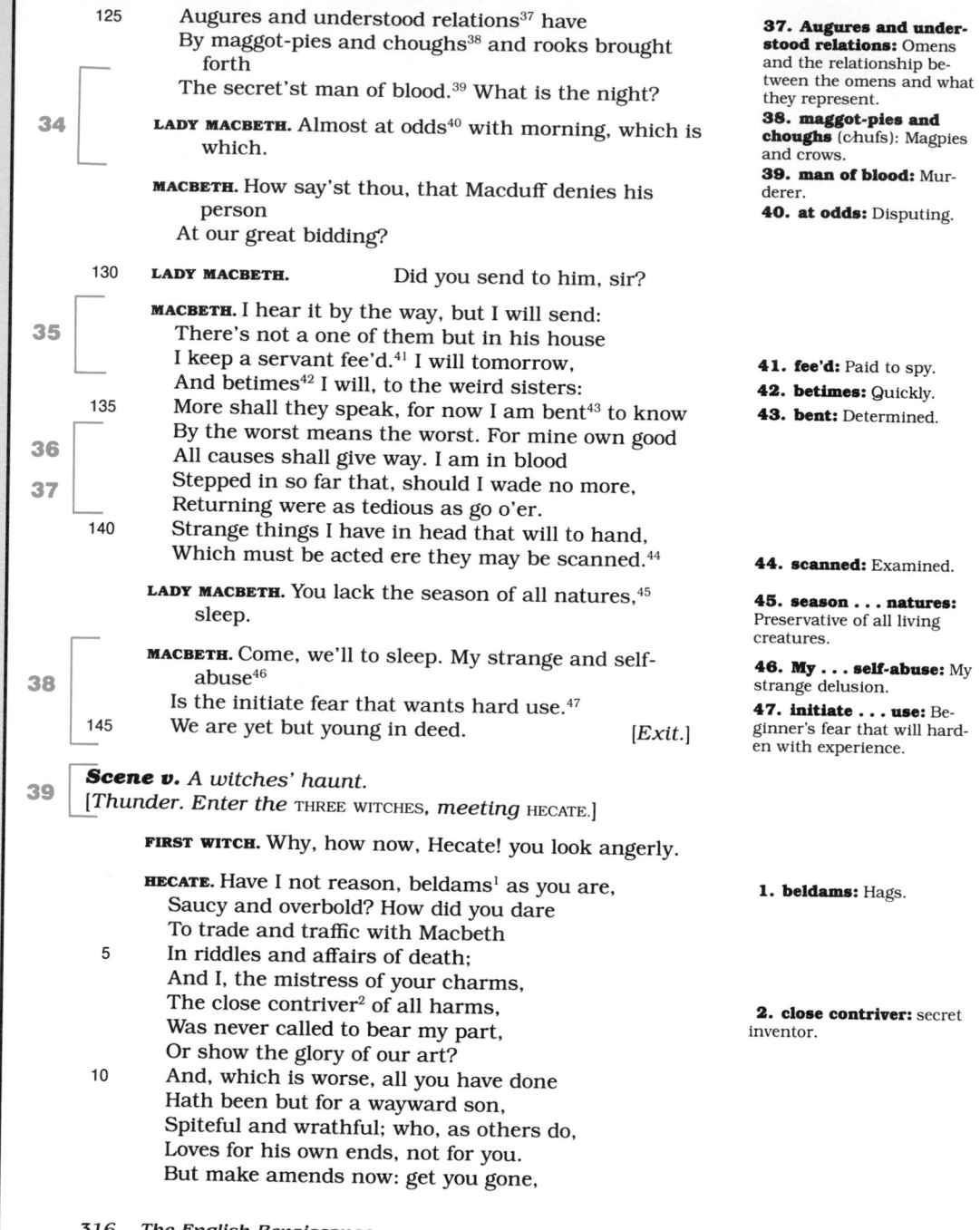

125 Augures and understood relations[37] have
By maggot-pies and choughs[38] and rooks brought forth
The secret'st man of blood.[39] What is the night?

34 **LADY MACBETH.** Almost at odds[40] with morning, which is which.

MACBETH. How say'st thou, that Macduff denies his person
At our great bidding?

130 **LADY MACBETH.**   Did you send to him, sir?

35 **MACBETH.** I hear it by the way, but I will send:
There's not a one of them but in his house
I keep a servant fee'd.[41] I will, to-morrow,
And betimes[42] I will, to the weird sisters:
135 More shall they speak, for now I am bent[43] to know
By the worst means the worst. For mine own good
36 All causes shall give way. I am in blood
Stepped in so far that, should I wade no more,
37 Returning were as tedious as go o'er.
140 Strange things I have in head that will to hand,
Which must be acted ere they may be scanned.[44]

LADY MACBETH. You lack the season of all natures,[45] sleep.

38 **MACBETH.** Come, we'll to sleep. My strange and self-abuse[46]
Is the initiate fear that wants hard use.[47]
145 We are yet but young in deed.   [*Exit.*]

39 **Scene v.** *A witches' haunt.*
[*Thunder. Enter the* THREE WITCHES, *meeting* HECATE.]

FIRST WITCH. Why, how now, Hecate! you look angerly.

HECATE. Have I not reason, beldams[1] as you are,
Saucy and overbold? How did you dare
To trade and traffic with Macbeth
5 In riddles and affairs of death;
And I, the mistress of your charms,
The close contriver[2] of all harms,
Was never called to bear my part,
Or show the glory of our art?
10 And, which is worse, all you have done
Hath been but for a wayward son,
Spiteful and wrathful; who, as others do,
Loves for his own ends, not for you.
But make amends now: get you gone,

37. **Augures and understood relations:** Omens and the relationship between the omens and what they represent.
38. **maggot-pies and choughs** (chufs): Magpies and crows.
39. **man of blood:** Murderer.
40. **at odds:** Disputing.

41. **fee'd:** Paid to spy.
42. **betimes:** Quickly.
43. **bent:** Determined.

44. **scanned:** Examined.

45. **season . . . natures:** Preservative of all living creatures.
46. **My . . . self-abuse:** My strange delusion.
47. **initiate . . . use:** Beginner's fear that will harden with experience.

1. **beldams:** Hags.

2. **close contriver:** secret inventor.

316   *The English Renaissance*

15 And at the pit of Acheron[3]
Meet me i' th' morning: thither he
Will come to know his destiny.
Your vessels and your spells provide,
Your charms and everything beside.
20 I am for th' air; this night I'll spend
Unto a dismal and a fatal end:
Great business must be wrought ere noon.
Upon the corner of the moon
There hangs a vap'rous drop profound;
25 I'll catch it ere it come to ground:
And that distilled by magic sleights[4]
Shall raise such artificial sprites[5]
As by the strength of their illusion
Shall draw him on to his confusion.[6]
30 He shall spurn fate, scorn death, and bear
His hopes 'bove wisdom, grace, and fear:
And you all know security[7]
Is mortals' chiefest enemy.

[*Music and a song.*]

Hark! I am called; my little spirit, see,
35 Sits in a foggy cloud and stays for me.   [*Exit.*]

[*Sing within,* "Come away, come away," *etc.*]

FIRST WITCH. Come, let's make haste; she'll soon be back
again.   [*Exit.*]

40 *Scene vi.* *The palace.*
[*Enter* LENNOX *and another* LORD.]

41

LENNOX. My former speeches have but hit[1] your
thoughts,
Which can interpret farther.[2] Only I say
Things have been strangely borne.[3] The gracious
Duncan
Was pitied of Macbeth: marry, he was dead.
5 And the right-valiant Banquo walked too late;
Whom, you may say, if 't please you, Fleance killed,
For Fleance fled. Men must not walk too late.
Who cannot want the thought,[4] how monstrous
It was for Malcolm and for Donalbain
10 To kill their gracious father? Damnèd fact![5]
How it did grieve Macbeth! Did he not straight,
In pious rage, the two delinquents tear,
That were the slaves of drink and thralls[6] of sleep?
Was not that nobly done? Ay, and wisely too;
15 For 'twould have angered any heart alive
To hear the men deny 't. So that I say

3. Acheron (ak′ ə ron′):
Hell; in Greek mythology
the river of Hades.

4. sleights: Devices.
5. artificial sprites: Spirits created by magic.
6. confusion: Ruin.

7. security: Overconfi-
dence.

1. hit: Coincided.

2. Which . . . farther:
From which you can draw
your own conclusions.
3. borne: Managed.

4. cannot . . . thought:
Can fail to think.
5. fact: Deed.

6. thralls: slaves.

40 Literary Focus This scene is totally expository, allowing the audience insight into what is happening in Scotland under Macbeth's
rule. Some scholars suggest the
scene should follow rather than
precede Act IV, scene i. Seek
student's thoughts as you read
on.

41 Discussion Do we detect sarcasm here? What is Lennox really
saying?

Macbeth, Act III, Scene vi   317

Side notes (left margin)

42 Discussion What does this line tell us of their feelings?

43 Discussion Where has Macduff gone? Why?

44 Discussion How is Macbeth reacting to all this?

45 Clarification Read as "You'll be sorry."

Reader's Response Is there a kind of grim humor in the scene where Banquo's ghost appears? Explain.

Main text

He has borne all things well: and I do think
That, had he Duncan's sons under his key—
As, an 't[7] please heaven, he shall not—they should find
20 What 'twere to kill a father. So should Fleance.
But, peace! for from broad[8] words, and 'cause he failed

42 His presence at the tyrant's feast, I hear,
Macduff lives in disgrace. Sir, can you tell
Where he bestows himself?

LORD.   The son of Duncan,
25 From whom this tyrant holds the due of birth,[9]
Lives in the English court, and is received
Of the most pious Edward[10] with such grace
That the malevolence of fortune nothing
Takes from his high respect.[11] Thither Macduff
30 Is gone to pray the holy King, upon his aid[12]
To wake Northumberland and warlike Siward;[13]
That by the help of these, with Him above
To ratify the work, we may again
Give to our tables meat, sleep to our nights,
35 Free from our feasts and banquets bloody knives,
Do faithful homage and receive free honors:[14]

44 All which we pine for now. And this report
Hath so exasperate the King that he
Prepares for some attempt of war.

LENNOX.   Sent he to Macduff?

40 **LORD.** He did: and with an absolute "Sir, not I,"
The cloudy[15] messenger turns me his back,
And hums, as who should say "You'll rue the time

45 That clogs[16] me with this answer."

LENNOX.   And that well might
Advise him to a caution, t' hold what distance
45 His wisdom can provide. Some holy angel
Fly to the court of England and unfold
His message ere he come, that a swift blessing
May soon return to this our suffering country
Under a hand accursed!

LORD.   I'll send my prayers with him.
                              [*Exit.*]

Right margin notes

7. an 't: If it.

8. broad: Unguarded.

9. due of birth: Birthright, claim to the throne.
10. Edward: Edward the Confessor, King of England 1042–1066.
11. with . . . respect: Does not diminish the high respect he is given.
12. upon his aid: To aid Malcolm.
13. To . . . Siward: To call to arms the commander of the English forces, the Earl of Northumberland, and his son Siward.
14. free honors: Honors given to free men.

15. cloudy: Disturbed.

16. clogs: Burdens.

Closure and Extension

ANSWERS TO THINKING ABOUT THE SELECTION
Recalling

1. (a) Because the prophecies have come true for Macbeth, he wonders if they will indeed come true for him as well, making him the father of a line of kings. (b) Macbeth is now concerned that the blood he has spilled will serve the heirs of Banquo, as Macbeth is childless.
2. (a) The murderers are instructed by Macbeth to kill Banquo and his son, Fleance. (b) The death of Fleance is important to Macbeth's plans and wishes in order to halt the possible succession to the throne of Banquo's heirs.
3. The plans partially fail as Fleance escapes.
4. (a) In scene iv, Macbeth is tormented by the vision of the dead Banquo sitting in his place at the banquet table. (b) Lady Macbeth explains to the guests that Macbeth suffers from a childhood affliction that occasionally overtakes him.
5. (a) Macbeth seeks out the witches again to learn where all this killing is going to lead—to learn the worst, as he says. (b) Lady Macbeth urges him to get some sleep, which he has sorely lacked and by which he may regain his wits.
6. (a) Macduff lives in disgrace for failing to attend Macbeth's banquet. (b) Macduff has gone off to England to seek the aid of the king, Northumberland, and his son, Siward, in an effort to dethrone Macbeth and free Scotland from his tyranny.

Interpreting

7. The moral decline of Macbeth is evident. Prior to Duncan's murder, he was driven by raw ambition, which would have been checked

THINKING ABOUT THE SELECTION
Recalling

1. (a) In Scene i, what are Banquo's thoughts about the witches' prophecies? (b) What are Macbeth's thoughts about the prophecies?
2. (a) What two people are the murderers told to kill? (b) Why is it necessary to kill both?
3. What goes wrong with the murderers' plans?
4. (a) In Scene iv, why does Macbeth not sit down at the banquet table? (b) How does Lady Macbeth explain his behavior?
5. (a) Why does Macbeth want to see the witches again? (b) What does Lady Macbeth think Macbeth needs most?
6. (a) In Scene vi, what reason does Lennox give for Macduff's being in disgrace? (b) What is Macduff trying to accomplish in England?

Interpreting

7. Macbeth's soliloquy in Scene i shows that his attitude toward those who stand in his way has changed. Recall the soliloquy prior to Duncan's murder. What change or changes have occurred?
8. How does Macbeth's technique of persuading the murderers resemble Lady Macbeth's earlier method of persuading Macbeth?
9. How has the relationship between Macbeth and Lady Macbeth changed?
10. Events at the banquet show that Macbeth can no longer pretend to be innocent. What evidence is there that he will continue to kill those who threaten him?

Applying

11. By the end of Act III, Macbeth is in desperate trouble. What advice would you give him concerning his best course of action?

ANALYZING LITERATURE
Understanding Irony

In *verbal irony* there is a contrast between what is said and what is meant. An example of verbal irony occurs in Act III, Scene i, when Macbeth says to Banquo, "Here's our chief guest," knowing that Banquo will be murdered on his orders before the great feast begins.

1. What three additional examples of verbal irony can you find in the conversation in Scene i between Macbeth and Banquo?
2. In Scene vi Lennox appears to accept Macbeth's version of the various murders. (a) How can you tell from what Lennox says that he does not really believe in Macbeth's innocence? (b) What are three examples of verbal irony in Lennox's opening speech?

CRITICAL THINKING AND READING
Interpreting Connotative Meanings

The **connotation** of a word is what is suggested by the word in addition to its literal meaning, or denotation. For instance, the denotation of the word *home* is "the place where one lives." The associations of *home* give the word its *connotative meanings:* "warmth, love, peace." Shakespeare, like all good writers, chooses words for their connotative meanings.

1. When the ghost of Banquo exits (Scene iv, line 108), Macbeth says, "I am a man again." What are the connotative meanings of *man*?
2. When Macbeth is talking to the murderers (Scene i, lines 90–91), he says, "Whose heavy hand hath bowed you to the grave / And *beggared* yours forever?" What are the connotative meanings of *beggared*?

THINKING AND WRITING
Who Is the Third Murderer?

Shakespeare never reveals the identity of the third murderer. Who do you think the third murderer might be? Write an essay supporting your theory of his or her identity. Reread Scene iii carefully. Then build a logical case using facts and lines from the play to support your theory. Use the process of elimination to exonerate some of the major characters. Remember, though, that the third murderer may have been sent by someone—even the witches—for a specific purpose (perhaps the killing of Banquo or the escape of Fleance). In revising your paper, make sure you have left no logical holes in your argument. Proofread and prepare a final draft.

Macbeth, Act III **319**

---

by his natural decency, had it not been for Lady Macbeth. Now he coldly plans the deaths of Banquo and Fleance because of the witches' predictions and because he is childless. In this soliloquy we find no evidence of decency or compassion.

8. Macbeth implies that they are less than men if they choose to stand by and let the wrongs of Banquo —most likely fabricated by Macbeth—go unpunished. Lady Macbeth's implications were similar when her husband seriously questioned the wisdom of their awful plan.

9. Macbeth has drawn into himself. Lady Macbeth is not apprised of, much less consulted about, his plans for Banquo and Fleance. His letter to her early in the play suggests much communication and sharing before all this.

10. He says that he is so deep in blood now that there is no turning back, implying that future sacrific-

es will be made to protect their bloody gains.

Applying

11. Answers will vary. However, given Macbeth's character and situation it seems likely that the only advice he would heed would be to continue along his murderous—and tragic—course. Advice grounded in traditional morality would, no doubt, be of no avail with Macbeth.

(Answers begin on p. 318.)

ANSWERS TO ANALYZING LITERATURE

1. In lines 13–14 Macbeth again requests Banquo's presence, not knowing that his ghost will indeed attend. In line 22 Macbeth says that he will seek Banquo's good advice tomorrow, knowing there will be no tomorrow for Banquo. In line 28, Banquo assures Macbeth he will not fail to attend the banquet. In fact, his ghost attends.
2. (a) His equivocations and exaggerations lead one to question immediately his true meaning, for example in line 7. The language seems purposely bloated and overdone, suggesting that he means the opposite of what he says. Finally, he refers to Macbeth as the tyrant, leaving no doubt of his true meaning. (b) Lennox says that Macbeth pitied the murdered Duncan, that it was monstrous of Malcolm and Donalbain to murder their gracious father, and that Macbeth's killing of the servants was understandable under the circumstances.

ANSWERS TO CRITICAL THINKING AND READING

1. When Macbeth says he is a "man" again, he is saying he is strong, fearless, composed, clear-headed, of good humor, and clever.
2. He is saying Banquo has put these two in a state where they will become beggars, a level of human life frightening and disturbing to everyone, as it saps people of their dignity.

THINKING AND WRITING

Publishing Student Writing Students might enjoy hearing one another's essays. Ask for volunteers to share their essays with the class.

Literary Focus By now most students know about plot. For those who do not, explain that plot is what you tell someone when you explain the story line of a TV show or movie. Draw a line on the board moving form left to right that swings upward then downward. At the point where the line turns downward is the climax. You might want to mark points along the line that correspond with actions of the play so far.

Writing/Prior Knowledge Have students discuss why, in a work of literary merit, the characters drive the plot, and not the other way around. To be sure students understand this important concept, ask them to explain how the character of Lady Macbeth dictates the shape of a segment of the plot of the play. What if Macbeth had married the woman who became Lady Macduff? How would she have reacted to his letter in the beginning of Act II?

Vocabulary

Preteach the following vocabulary words:
pernicious (pər nish′ əs) *adj.*: Evil; wicked (Sc. i, l. 133)
judicious (jσσ dish′ əs) *adj.*: Showing good judgment (Sc. ii, l. 16)
sundry (sun′ drē) *adj.*: Various; miscellaneous (Sc. iii, l. 48)
intemperance (in tem′ pər əns) *n.*: Lack of restraint (Sc. iii, l. 66)
avarice (av′ ər is) *n.*: Greed (Sc. iii, l. 78)
credulous (krej′ σσ ləs) *adj.*: Tending to believe too readily (Sc. iii, l. 120)

GUIDE FOR INTERPRETING

Writer's Techniques

Writing

Commentary

Macbeth, Act IV

Plot Development. The plot of a literary work is the sequence of related events that create and then resolve a conflict. Conflict is the struggle, or interplay of forces, that takes place within the story. The main character may be in conflict with another person, with a value system, with fate, or with nature. Certain background information is necessary for an understanding of the action. This information is called **exposition,** and it usually appears early in the story. The plot movement at the beginning is one of *rising action* toward a climax. The *climax,* or *crisis,* is the peak of tension, a dramatic turning point. In a tragedy like *Macbeth,* the climax often occurs near the middle of the play. Then comes a period of *falling action,* which, in tragedy, shows the downfall of the tragic hero. The falling action leads finally to the *resolution,* or *denouement,* the point at which the conflict ends and the outcome is made clear.

Plot is closely intertwined with character. Indeed, in a work of literary merit, you will find that character largely drives the plot, not the other way around. Make some notes analyzing that character of Macbeth. List his virtues as well as his faults, for the complexity of Macbeth's character lies at the heart of his difficulties.

Although Shakespeare began with Holinshed's account of two different murders, he transformed these historical tales into an entirely original plot. The first influence was the story of Duncan's assassination (c. 1040) by Macbeth and several rebels—including the treacherous Banquo, a detail Shakespeare obviously changed. He combined this with the earlier murder of another Scottish monarch, King Duff. As in *Macbeth,* the King was murdered on orders of his host while at his home; unlike the murder of Duncan in *Macbeth,* the King was killed by servants. The Bard also added parts of Holinshed's tale of King Kenneth. To Lady Macbeth went the King's inability to sleep and terrifying guilt at being part of a murder, but the playwright rejected the murder itself (of a nephew) and the haunting by a mysterious voice promising divine punishment. He also compressed the events of Macbeth's seventeen year reign into as many weeks. Finally, two of the greatest scenes in *Macbeth* are both original to Shakespeare. Both have to do with guilt: the banquet scene (III, iii) and the sleepwalking scene (V,i). Many critics feel that Shakespeare's most brilliant invention in the play is the banquet scene, which draws together the plot by dramatizing many of the ideas previously implied.

Objectives

1 To understand plot development
2 To read between the lines
3 To understand the idea of the tragic flaw

Support Material

Teaching Portfolio:
Teacher Backup, p. 305
Grammar in Action Worksheet, *Appreciating Repetition,* p. 309
Usage and Mechanics Worksheet, p. 311
Vocabulary Check, p. 312
Analyzing Literature Worksheet, *Understanding Plot Development,* p. 313

Critical Thinking and Reading Worksheet, *Reading Between the Lines,* p. 314
Selection Test, p. 315

Act IV

Scene i. *A witches' haunt.*

[*Thunder. Enter the* THREE WITCHES.]

1, 2

FIRST WITCH. Thrice the brinded[1] cat hath mewed.

SECOND WITCH. Thrice and once the hedge-pig[2] whined.

THIRD WITCH. Harpier[3] cries. 'Tis time, 'tis time.

FIRST WITCH. Round about the caldron go:
5   In the poisoned entrails throw.
    Toad, that under cold stone
    Days and nights has thirty-one
    Swelt'red venom sleeping got,[4]
    Boil thou first i' th' charmèd pot.

10 **ALL.** Double, double, toil and trouble;
    Fire burn and caldron bubble.

SECOND WITCH. Fillet of a fenny snake,
    In the caldron boil and bake;
    Eye of newt and toe of frog,
15   Wool of bat and tongue of dog,
    Adder's fork[5] and blindworm's[6] sting,
    Lizard's leg and howlet's[7] wing,
    For a charm of pow'rful trouble,
    Like a hell-broth boil and bubble.

3

20 **ALL.** Double, double, toil and trouble;
    Fire burn and caldron bubble.

THIRD WITCH. Scale of dragon, tooth of wolf,
    Witch's mummy, maw and gulf[8]
    Of the ravined[9] salt-sea shark,
25   Root of hemlock digged i' th' dark,
    Liver of blaspheming Jew,
    Gall of goat, and slips of yew
    Slivered in the moon's eclipse,
    Nose of Turk and Tartar's lips,[10]
30   Finger of birth-strangled babe
    Ditch-delivered by a drab,
    Make the gruel thick and slab:[11]
    Add thereto a tiger's chaudron,[12]
    For th' ingredience of our caldron.

35 **ALL.** Double, double, toil and trouble;
    Fire burn and caldron bubble.

SECOND WITCH. Cool it with a baboon's blood,
    Then the charm is firm and good.

[*Enter* HECATE *and the other* THREE WITCHES.]

---

1. **brinded:** Striped.

2. **hedge-pig:** Hedgehog.

3. **Harpier:** One of the spirits attending the witches.

4. **Swelt'red . . . got:** Venom sweated out while sleeping.

5. **fork:** Forked tongue.
6. **blindworm's:** Small, limbless lizard's.
7. **howlet's:** A small owl's.

8. **maw and gulf:** Stomach and gullet.
9. **ravined:** Ravenous.

10. **blaspheming Jew . . . Tartar's lips:** For many in Shakespeare's audience, the words ''Jew,'' ''Turk,'' and ''Tartar'' evoked stereotypical enemies of Christianity.
11. **slab:** sticky.
12. **chaudron** (shô′ drən): Entrails.

Macbeth, Act IV, Scene i   321

---

4 Literary Focus The entrance of Hecate and her companions here has little to do with the action of the play, and is considered in the same light as the previous witch scene. Compare these passages with the witch scenes of Act I.

5 Literary Focus Note the irony in the witches' evaluation of Macbeth.

6 Discussion What does this greeting imply about Macbeth?

7 Discussion Macbeth demands an answer to his questions, no matter what the consequences. What possible consequences does he conjure up? What does this speech tell us about his kingly qualities? What should a leader's first consideration be?

HECATE. O, well done! I commend your pains;
40 And every one shall share i' th' gains:
And now about the caldron sing,
Like elves and fairies in a ring,
Enchanting all that you put in.

[*Music and a song: "Black Spirits," etc. Exit* HECATE *and the other* THREE WITCHES.]

SECOND WITCH. By the pricking of my thumbs,
45 Something wicked this way comes:
Open, locks,
Whoever knocks!

[*Enter* MACBETH.]

MACBETH. How now, you secret, black, and midnight hags!
What is 't you do?

ALL. A deed without a name.

MACBETH. I conjure you, by that which you profess,
50 Howe'er you come to know it, answer me:
Though you untie the winds and let them fight
Against the churches; though the yesty[13] waves
Confound[14] and swallow navigation up;
55 Though bladed corn be lodged[15] and trees blown down;
Though castles topple on their warders' heads;
Though palaces and pyramids do slope[16]
Their heads to their foundations; though the treasure
Of nature's germens[17] tumble all together,
60 Even till destruction sicken, answer me
To what I ask you.

FIRST WITCH. Speak.

SECOND WITCH. Demand.

THIRD WITCH. We'll answer.

FIRST WITCH. Say, if th' hadst rather hear it from our mouths,
Or from our masters?

MACBETH. Call' em, let me see 'em.

FIRST WITCH. Pour in sow's blood, that hath eaten
65 Her nine farrow;[18] grease that's sweaten
From the murderer's gibbet[19] throw
Into the flame.

ALL. Come, high or low,

13. **yesty:** Foamy.
14. **Confound:** Destroy.
15. **lodged:** Beaten down.

16. **slope:** Bend.

17. **nature's germens:** Seeds of all life.

18. **farrow:** Young pigs.
19. **gibbet** (jib' it): Gallows.

Grammar in Action

The **repetition** of words, phrases, and clauses may seem like a simple device, but poets have used it to create both musical and dramatic effects. Gerard Manley Hopkins uses repetition in the beginning of his sonnet "God's Grandeur":

The world is charged with the grandeur of God.
It will flame out, like shining from shook foil;
It gathers to a greatness, like the ooze of oil
Crushed. Why do men then now not reck his rod?

Generations *have trod, have trod, have trod;*
And all is seared with trade; bleared, smeared with toil

In the fifth line, the repeated words imitate the passing of generation after generation.

Repetition is an important device in *Macbeth* as well. In his speech conjuring the witches (IV.i.48–59), Macbeth's repetitions indicate that he is determined to have an answer no matter how much destruction he causes. These repetitions therefore suggest the desperation that Macbeth feels at this point in the play: "Though you untie the winds and let them fight/Against the churches; though the yesty waves/Confound and swallow navigation up;/Though bladed corn be lodged . . ."

Thyself and office²⁰ deftly show!

[*Thunder.* FIRST APPARITION: *an Armed Head.*²¹]

MACBETH. Tell me, thou unknown power—

FIRST WITCH.   He knows thy thought:
70   Hear his speech, but say thou nought.

FIRST APPARITION. Macbeth! Macbeth! Macbeth! Beware
     Macduff!
     Beware the Thane of Fife. Dismiss me: enough.
                                   [*He descends.*]

MACBETH. Whate'er thou art, for thy good caution
     thanks:
     Thou hast harped²² my fear aright. But one word
     more—

FIRST WITCH. He will not be commanded. Here's
75   another,
     More potent than the first.

[*Thunder.* SECOND APPARITION: *a Bloody Child.*²³]

SECOND APPARITION. Macbeth! Macbeth! Macbeth!

MACBETH. Had I three ears, I'd hear thee.

SECOND APPARITION. Be bloody, bold, and resolute! Laugh
     to scorn
80   The pow'r of man, for none of woman born
     Shall harm Macbeth.   [*Descends.*]

MACBETH. Then live, Macduff: what need I fear of thee?
     But yet I'll make assurance double sure,
     And take a bond of fate.²⁴ Thou shalt not live;
85   That I may tell pale-hearted fear it lies,
     And sleep in spite of thunder.

[*Thunder.* THIRD APPARITION: *a Child Crowned, with a
tree in his hand.*²⁵]

                              What is this,
     That rises like the issue of a king,
     And wears upon his baby-brow the round
     And top of sovereignty? ²⁶

ALL.   Listen, but speak not to 't.

90   THIRD APPARITION. Be lion-mettled, proud, and take no
     care
     Who chafes, who frets, or where conspirers are:
     Macbeth shall never vanquished be until
     Great Birnam Wood to high Dunsinane Hill
     Shall come against him.   [*Descends.*]

Macbeth, Act IV, Scene i   323

---

20. **office:** Function.

21. **an Armed Head:** A symbol of Macduff.

22. **harped:** Hit upon.

23. **a Bloody Child:** A symbol of Macduff at birth.

24. **take . . . fate:** Get a guarantee from fate (by killing Macduff).

25. **a Child . . . hand:** A symbol of Malcolm.

26. **top of sovereignty:** Crown.

---

8 Discussion What is the first of the three messages?

9 Discussion What does the second apparition predict?

10 Discussion How does Macbeth react? Why doesn't he pause to consider if the prediction might have some hidden meaning? What precaution will he take?

11 Discussion What is the third prophecy?

Student Activity 1. Find an example of repetition on page 323. Then explain how this repetition contributes to the mood of the scene.

Student Activity 2. Write a dramatic speech for the ghost of Banquo. Use repeated words or phrases to emphasize a point, reveal Banquo's state of mind, or evoke a mood.

12 **Discussion** Why is Macbeth pleased with this prophecy's content, and what does he conclude?

13 **Clarification** Hautboys are wooden pipe-like instruments.

14 **Discussion** What does Macbeth learn from the appearance of the kings and Banquo? What should he learn about the prophecies, but apparently does not?

Enrichment James I was a Stuart king, part of a royal family whose traditions extended back to medieval Scotland. Since Banquo was supposedly an ancestor of the Stuarts, Shakespeare was paying James a compliment in having the Witches prophecy the success of Banquo's descendants.

MACBETH.   That will never be.
95 Who can impress[27] the forest, bid the tree
Unfix his earth-bound root? Sweet bodements,[28] good!
Rebellious dead, rise never, till the Wood
Of Birnam rise, and our high-placed Macbeth
100 Shall live the lease of nature,[29] pay his breath
To time and mortal custom.[30] Yet my heart
Throbs to know one thing. Tell me, if your art
Can tell so much: shall Banquo's issue ever
Reign in this kingdom?

ALL.   Seek to know no more.

MACBETH. I will be satisfied. Deny me this,
105 And an eternal curse fall on you! Let me know.
Why sinks that caldron? And what noise is this?

[*Hautboys.*]

FIRST WITCH. Show!

SECOND WITCH. Show!

THIRD WITCH. Show!

110 **ALL.** Show his eyes, and grieve his heart;
Come like shadows, so depart!

[*A show of eight* KINGS *and* BANQUO, *last* KING *with a glass*[31] *in his hand.*]

MACBETH. Thou art too like the spirit of Banquo. Down!
Thy crown does sear mine eyelids. And thy hair,
Thou other gold-bound brow, is like the first.
115 A third is like the former. Filthy hags!
Why do you show me this? A fourth! Start, eyes!
What, will the line stretch out to th' crack of doom?
Another yet! A seventh! I'll see no more.
And yet the eighth appears, who bears a glass
120 Which shows me many more; and some I see
That twofold balls and treble scepters[32] carry:
Horrible sight! Now I see 'tis true;
For the blood-boltered[33] Banquo smiles upon me,
And points at them for his.[34] What, is this so?

125 **FIRST WITCH.** Ay, sir, all this is so. But why
Stands Macbeth thus amazedly?
Come, sisters, cheer we up his sprites,
And show the best of our delights:
I'll charm the air to give a sound,
130 While you perform your antic round,[35]
That this great king may kindly say
Our duties did his welcome pay.

27. **impress:** Force into service.
28. **bodements:** Prophecies.

29. **lease of nature:** Natural lifespan.
30. **mortal custom:** Natural death.

31. **glass:** Mirror.

32. **twofold . . . scepters:** Coronation emblems and insignia of the kingdoms of England, Scotland, and Ireland, united in 1603 when James VI of Scotland became James I of England.
33. **blood-boltered:** With his hair matted with blood.
34. **his:** His descendants.
35. **antic round:** Grotesque circular dance.

Commentary:
King James I and Witchcraft

Macbeth was probably performed for King James I and his brother-in-law in the summer of 1606. If so, the king would have found much to interest him in the play. The subject was Scottish, as was the king himself, and the action turned on the prophecies of witches. King James I was an authority on witchcraft, having taken part in a lively controversy about this subject.

While some Elizabethans believed in witches, others were skeptical. Among the skeptics was Reginald Scot, who wrote *Discovery of Witchcraft* (1584) to demonstrate "that the compacts and contracts of witches with all Devils and all Infernal Spirits or Familiars are but erroneous novelties and imaginary conceptions." Scot stated unequivocally that magical spells could not make people fall sick or die: "Witchcraft and enchantment is the cloak of ignorance: whereas indeed evil humors, and not strange words, witches, or spirits are the causes of such diseases." The "evil humors" to which he refers were bodily fluids that Elizabethans believed to be the cause of health or illness.

The king, when he was still King James VI of Scotland, objected to Scot's "damnable opinions" about witches and wrote

Humanities Note

Fine art, *Macbeth and the Witches,* engraved by Robert Thew. Robert Thew (1758–1802), a British engraver, had little formal training as an artist. He was, however, a man of great natural ability and motivation. He taught himself the art of engraving and attained excellence in it. He used this art to create shop bills and business cards until a stroke of good fortune won him an introduction to the eminent publisher and engraver John Boydell (1719-1804). Boydell enlisted Thew's services on a large project involving the engraving of twenty-two paintings on Shakespearean subjects by England's leading artists for a subscription series of prints.

The engraving *Macbeth and the Witches,* published in 1802, was done after a painting by Sir Johsua Reynolds (1723–1792), who was one of England's most respected portrait painters. Boydell's employment of Robert Thew was considered an endorscment of the engraver's considerable talents and thereby established his fame.

You might use the following questions in your discussion:
1. How does this artist's conception of the witches differ from the common stereotype of a witch?
2. What about this engraving makes it seem like a painting?

[*Music.* THE WITCHES *dance, and vanish.*]

MACBETH. Where are they? Gone? Let this pernicious
  hour
  Stand aye accursèd in the calendar!
  Come in, without there!

[*Enter* LENNOX.]

135 **LENNOX.**   What's your Grace's will?

MACBETH. Saw you the weird sisters?

LENNOX.   No, my lord.

MACBETH. Came they not by you?

LENNOX.   No indeed, my lord.

MACBETH. Infected be the air whereon they ride,
  And damned all those that trust them! I did hear
140 The galloping of horse. Who was 't came by?

Macbeth, Act IV, Scene i   325

a book entitled *Daemonology* (1597) to state his case. King James's strong opinions on this matter came from personal experience. A group of Scottish witches had been accused of plotting against his life. One of the suspects, Agnes Sampson, made such wild statements that James was convinced the whole affair was absurd. At that point, Agnes Sampson spoke to the king in private and "declared unto him the very words which passed between the King's Majesty and his Queen at Upslo in Norway the first night of their marriage; whereat the King wondered greatly and swore by the living God that he believed that all the devils in Hell could not have discovered the same." Sampson's clairvoyance or lucky guess made the king a firm believer in the power of witchcraft.

The sensational news from this trial was fully covered in England, and it is tempting to imagine Shakespeare reading this account and storing it up for future use. The critic G.B. Harrison, in fact, points out that "the witches in *Macbeth* behave in much the same way as the witches in this case."

At any rate, we can certainly imagine the king viewing the witch scenes in *Macbeth* with complete credulity.

15 **Discussion** What does this decision tell us about Macbeth's continuing moral decline? In what way are these murders worse than those he has already committed?

16 **Discussion** To whom is Lady Macduff referring?

17 **Discussion** What argument does she make against his flight?

LENNOX. 'Tis two or three, my lord, that bring you word
    Macduff is fled to England.

MACBETH.   Fled to England?

LENNOX. Ay, my good lord.

MACBETH. [*Aside*] Time, thou anticipat'st[36] my dread
    exploits.
145 The flighty purpose never is o'ertook
    Unless the deed go with it.[37] From this moment
    The very firstlings of my heart[38] shall be
    The firstlings of my hand. And even now,
    To crown my thoughts with acts, be it thought and
    done:
150 The castle of Macduff I will surprise;
    Seize upon Fife; give to th' edge o' th' sword
    His wife, his babes, and all unfortunate souls
    That trace[39] him in his line. No boasting like a fool;
    This deed I'll do before this purpose cool:
155 But no more sights!—Where are these gentlemen?
    Come, bring me where they are.   [*Exit.*]

Scene ii. *Macduff's castle.*
[*Enter* MACDUFF'S WIFE, *her* SON, *and* ROSS.]

LADY MACDUFF. What had he done, to make him fly the
    land?

ROSS. You must have patience, madam.

LADY MACDUFF.   He had none:
    His flight was madness. When our actions do not,
    Our fears do make us traitors.

ROSS.   You know not
5 Whether it was his wisdom or his fear.

LADY MACDUFF. Wisdom! To leave his wife, to leave his
    babes,
    His mansion and his titles,[1] in a place
    From whence himself does fly? He loves us not;
    He wants the natural touch:[2] for the poor wren,
10 The most diminutive of birds, will fight,
    Her young ones in her nest, against the owl.
    All is the fear and nothing is the love;
    As little is the wisdom, where the flight
    So runs against all reason.

ROSS.   My dearest coz,[3]
15 I pray you, school[4] yourself. But, for your husband,
    He is noble, wise, judicious, and best knows

36. anticipat'st: Foretold.

37. The flighty . . . it: The fleeting plan is never fulfilled unless it is carried out at once.

38. firstlings . . . heart: First thoughts, impulses.

39. trace: Succeed.

1. titles: possessions.

2. wants . . . touch: Lacks natural affection.

3. coz: Cousin.
4. school: Control.

Commentary:
Fate Versus Free Will in *Macbeth*

Scholars have long debated whether Macbeth's tragedy results from the inexorable pressures of fate or from his own free choice of evil. This debate tends to focus on the role of the Witches. The great Shakespearean scholar George Lyman Kittredge argued that these weird sisters were not just run-of-the-mill crones but arbiters of human destiny. He identified them with the Norns, Scandanavian goddesses of fate:

> The Norns were goddesses who shaped beforehand the life of every man. Sometimes they came in the night and stood by the cradle of the new-born child, uttering their decrees. . . . Sometimes they were met in wild places and at unexpected moments. . . . They were great powers of destiny. . . . they not only foresaw the future, but decreed it.

If the Witches do in fact determine Macbeth's fate, then he has no power of choice and is lost from the instant he sets eyes upon them. In this view, he is a merely a plaything of fate.

The fits o' th' season.[5] I dare not speak much further:
But cruel are the times, when we are traitors
And do not know ourselves;[6] when we hold rumor
20 From what we fear,[7] yet know not what we fear,
But float upon a wild and violent sea
Each way and move. I take my leave of you.
Shall not be long but I'll be here again.
Things at the worst will cease, or else climb upward
25 To what they were before. My pretty cousin,
Blessing upon you!

LADY MACDUFF. Fathered he is, and yet he's fatherless.

ROSS. I am so much a fool, should I stay longer,
It would be my disgrace and your discomfort.[8]
I take my leave at once.   [*Exit* ROSS.]

30 **LADY MACDUFF.**   Sirrah, your father's dead;
And what will you do now? How will you live?

SON. As birds do, mother.

LADY MACDUFF.   What, with worms and flies?

SON. With what I get, I mean; and so do they.

LADY MACDUFF. Poor bird! thou'dst never fear the net nor
lime,[9]
35 The pitfall nor the gin.[10]

SON. Why should I, mother? Poor birds they are not set
for.
My father is not dead, for all your saying.

LADY MACDUFF. Yes, he is dead: how wilt thou do for a
father?

SON. Nay, how will you do for a husband?

40 **LADY MACDUFF.** Why, I can buy me twenty at any market.

SON. Then you'll buy 'em to sell[11] again.

LADY MACDUFF. Thou speak'st with all thy wit, and yet
i' faith,
With wit enough for thee.[12]

SON. Was my father a traitor, mother?

45 **LADY MACDUFF.** Ay, that he was.

SON. What is a traitor?

LADY MACDUFF. Why, one that swears and lies.[13]

SON. And be all traitors that do so?

5. fits o' th' season: Disorders of the time.

6. when . . . ourselves: When we are treated as traitors but do not know of any treason.

7. when . . . fear: Believe rumors based on our fears.

8. It . . . discomfort: I would disgrace myself and embarrass you by weeping.

9. lime: Birdlime, a sticky substance smeared on branches to catch birds.
10. gin: Trap.

11. sell: Betray.

12. for thee: For a child.

13. swears and lies: Takes an oath and breaks it.

18 **Discussion** What is the temper of the country and its people?

19 **Discussion** Explain this paradoxical line.

20 **Literary Focus** This exchange between Lady Macduff and her son is one of the few tender and witty passages in the play. Little Macduff is a precocious child who is doted on by his mother. Our knowledge of Macbeth's intentions makes the scene doubly poignant. Why might Shakespeare have included this scene?

Macbeth, Act IV, Scene ii   327

Irving Ribner, among others argued against this position. He felt that Shakespeare was writing from a Christian rather than a pagan perspective. While Christians acknowledge the reality of evil, in the person of the devil, they believe that God gave humans the power to choose evil or good. Though he is presented with a temptation to do wrong, Macbeth chooses his own course. An argument for Macbeth's free will is that Banquo, subject to the same or a similar temptation, remains virtuous.

Still another response to this controversy is that Shakespeare deliberately keeps the issue ambiguous, as it is in life. If Macbeth were simply a toy of fate, then his stature would diminish. He would be pitiful and little more. On the other hand, if we felt that the choice of evil were entirely his, we might condemn him but feel little pity for his fate. Shakespeare maximizes our response by showing Macbeth as a free agent, with Banquo as his foil, but also using the weird sisters to suggest that evil was somehow lying in wait for the Thane of Glamis.

You might want to ask groups of students to gather evidence from the play for each of these three perspectives. After the groups present their findings to the class, lead students in a discussion of this controversy.

Fine art: Drawing of Lady Macduff by Sir John Gilbert. Sir John Gilbert (1817–1897) did this drawing of Lady Macduff and the murderers for Mackey's *Shakespeare,* an illustrated book in a series that won him great popularity as an illustrator. The ease with which the figures are drawn and the scene composed shows the superior sketching ability that Gilbert achieved through continuous practice. This drawing is dramatic, narrative, and spirited. It appeals even to today's viewer.

You might use the following questions for discussion:
1. A narrative drawing is one that tells a story. What story does this drawing tell?
2. How does the artist portray the fear and tension of this scene?

21 Discussion Of what significance is this discussion of traitors beyond showing us how clever and bright the young Macduff is?

WOOD ENGRAVING AFTER SIR JOHN GILBERT
The Granger Collection

LADY MACDUFF. Every one that does so is a traitor, and must be hanged.

21 | 50 **SON.** And must they all be hanged that swear and lie?

LADY MACDUFF. Every one.

SON. Who must hang them?

328   *The English Renaissance*

LADY MACDUFF. Why, the honest men.

SON. Then the liars and swearers are fools; for there are
55   liars and swearers enow[14] to beat the honest men
and hang up them.

LADY MACDUFF. Now, God help thee, poor monkey! But
how wilt thou do for a father?

SON. If he were dead, you'd weep for him. If you would
60   not, it were a good sign that I should quickly have a
new father.

LADY MACDUFF. Poor prattler, how thou talk'st!

[Enter a MESSENGER.*]*

MESSENGER. Bless you, fair dame! I am not to you known,
Though in your state of honor I am perfect.[15]
65   I doubt[16] some danger does approach you nearly:
If you will take a homely[17] man's advice,
Be not found here; hence, with your little ones.
To fright you thus, methinks I am too savage;
To do worse to you were fell[18] cruelty,
70   Which is too nigh your person. Heaven preserve you!
I dare abide no longer.   *[Exit* MESSENGER.*]*

LADY MACDUFF.   Whither should I fly?
I have done no harm. But I remember now
I am in this earthly world, where to do harm
Is often laudable, to do good sometime
75   Accounted dangerous folly. Why then, alas,
Do I put up that womanly defense,
To say I have done no harm?—What are these faces?

[Enter MURDERERS.*]*

MURDERER. Where is your husband?

LADY MACDUFF. I hope, in no place so unsanctified
Where such as thou mayst find him.

80 **MURDERER.**   He's a traitor.

SON. Thou li'st, thou shag-eared[19] villain!

MURDERER.   What, you egg!

            [Stabbing him.]

    Young fry[20] of treachery!

SON.   He has killed me, mother:
    Run away, I pray you! *[Dies.]*

            [Exit LADY MACDUFF *crying "Murder!"*
                followed by MURDERERS.*]*

14. enow: Enough.

15. in . . . perfect: I am
fully informed of your honorable rank.
16. doubt: Fear.
17. homely: Simple.

18. fell: Fierce.

19. shag-eared: Hairy-
eared.

20. fry: Offspring.

22 Discussion What can we judge of
Lady Macduff's character from
this and earlier comments? Compare her to Lady Macbeth.

22

Macbeth, Act IV, Scene ii   329

23 Historical Focus The English court to which Malcolm earlier fled, and the scene of this meeting with Macduff, is the court of Edward the Confessor. The action of this play would have concluded in the year 1054, when Malcolm III, called Malcolm Canmore, ascended the Scottish throne. His daughter Matilda married Henry I of England.

24 Discussion What does his initial suggestion to Macduff suggest about Malcolm's character? Is this judgment compatible with his behavior earlier in the play?

25 Discussion Compare the tone of Macduff's response. Why is it appropriate to what we know about Macduff?

26 Discussion What concern does Malcolm voice?

27 Discussion Why is Macduff's simple answer not convincing to Malcolm?

28 Literary Focus The theme of appearances and realities is continued here. In this case how is Malcolm dealing with them?

29 Discussion Why does the fact that Macduff left his family unprotected in Scotland give Malcolm doubts?

---

23   *Scene iii. England. Before the King's palace.*
[*Enter* MALCOLM *and* MACDUFF.]

24

MALCOLM. Let us seek out some desolate shade, and there
    Weep our sad bosoms empty.

25   5

MACDUFF.   Let us rather
    Hold fast the mortal[1] sword, and like good men
    Bestride our down-fall'n birthdom.[2] Each new morn
    New widows howl, new orphans cry, new sorrows
    Strike heaven on the face, that it resounds
    As if it felt with Scotland and yelled out
    Like syllable of dolor. [3]

26   10

MALCOLM.   What I believe, I'll wail;
    What know, believe; and what I can redress,
    As I shall find the time to friend,[4] I will.
    What you have spoke, it may be so perchance.
    This tyrant, whose sole[5] name blisters our tongues,
    Was once thought honest:[6] you have loved him well;
    He hath not touched you yet. I am young; but something
    You may deserve of him through me;[7] and wisdom[8]
    To offer up a weak, poor, innocent lamb
    T' appease an angry god.

15

MACDUFF. I am not treacherous.

27
28   20

MALCOLM.   But Macbeth is.
    A good and virtuous nature may recoil
    In an imperial charge.[9] But I shall crave your pardon;
    That which you are, my thoughts cannot transpose:[10]
    Angels are bright still, though the brightest[11] fell:
    Though all things foul would wear[12] the brows of grace,
    Yet grace must still look so. [13]

MACDUFF.   I have lost my hopes.

29   25

MALCOLM. Perchance even there where I did find my doubts.
    Why in that rawness[14] left you wife and child,
    Those precious motives, those strong knots of love,
    Without leave-taking? I pray you,
    Let not my jealousies[15] be your dishonors.

30   But mine own safeties.[16] You may be rightly just
    Whatever I shall think.

MACDUFF.   Bleed, bleed, poor country:
    Great tyranny, lay thou thy basis sure,

1. mortal: Deadly.

2. Bestride . . . birthdom: Protectively stand over our native land.

3. Like . . . dolor: A similar cry of anguish.

4. to friend: Be friendly.

5. sole: Very.
6. honest: Good.

7. deserve . . . me: Earn by betraying me to Macbeth.
8. wisdom: It is wise.

9. recoil . . . charge: Give way to a royal command.
10. transpose: Transform.
11. the brightest: Lucifer.
12. would wear: Desire to wear.
13. so: Like itself.

14. rawness: Unprotected state or condition.

15. jealousies: Suspicions.
16. safeties: Protections.

330   *The English Renaissance*

For goodness dare not check thee: wear thou thy
　　wrongs:
The title is affeered.[17] Fare thee well, lord:
35　I would not be the villain that thou think'st
For the whole space that's in the tyrant's grasp
And the rich East to boot.

MALCOLM.　　　　　　　　Be not offended:
I speak not as in absolute fear of you.
I think our country sinks beneath the yoke;
40　It weeps, it bleeds, and each new day a gash
Is added to her wounds. I think withal
There would be hands uplifted in my right;[18]
And here from gracious England[19] have I offer
Of goodly thousands: but, for all this,
45　When I shall tread upon the tyrant's head,
Or wear it on my sword, yet my poor country
Shall have more vices than it had before,
More suffer, and more sundry ways than ever,
By him that shall succeed.

MACDUFF.　　　　　　　　What should he be?

50　MALCOLM. It is myself I mean, in whom I know
All the particulars of vice so grafted[20]
That, when they shall be opened,[21] black Macbeth
Will seem as pure as snow, and the poor state
Esteem him as a lamb, being compared
With my confineless harms. [22]

55　MACDUFF.　　　　　　　　Not in the legions
Of horrid hell can come a devil more damned
In evils to top Macbeth.

MALCOLM.　　　　　　　　I grant him bloody,
Luxurious,[23] avaricious, false, deceitful,
Sudden,[24] malicious, smacking of every sin
60　That has a name: but there's no bottom, none,
In my voluptuousness: your wives, your daughters,
Your matrons and your maids, could not fill up
The cistern of my lust, and my desire
All continent impediments[25] would o'erbear,
65　That did oppose my will. Better Macbeth
Than such an one to reign.

MACDUFF.　　　　　　　　Boundless intemperance
In nature[26] is a tyranny; it hath been
Th' untimely emptying of the happy throne,
And fall of many kings. But fear not yet
70　To take upon you what is yours: you may
Convey[27] your pleasures in a spacious plenty,

17. **affeered:** Legally confirmed.

18. **in my right:** On behalf of my claim.
19. **England:** The King of England.

20. **grafted:** Implanted.
21. **opened:** In bloom.

22. **confineless harms:** Unbounded evils.

23. **luxurious:** Lecherous.
24. **Sudden:** Violent.

25. **continent impediments:** Restraints.

26. **nature:** Man's nature.

27. **Convey:** Secretly manage.

Macbeth, Act IV, Scene iii　331

30 Discussion Malcolm suggests that he is worse than Macbeth. What three specific evils does he accuse himself of in the lines that follow? Do these self-accusations seem believable?

31 Discussion How does Macduff address the first of Malcolm's claims to evil?

32 **Discussion** How does he compare the second failing with Malcolm's first? How does he suggest it be overcome?

33 **Discussion** What does Malcolm say he has none of?

34 **Clarification** For *concord,* read "harmony."

35 **Discussion** What is Macduff's reaction to Malcolm's third failing?

And yet seem cold, the time you may so hoodwink.
We have willing dames enough. There cannot be
That vulture in you, to devour so many
75   As will to greatness dedicate themselves,
Finding it so inclined.

MALCOLM.   With this there grows
In my most ill-composed affection[28] such
A stanchless[29] avarice that, were I King,
I should cut off the nobles for their lands,
80   Desire his jewels and this other's house:
And my more-having would be as a sauce
To make me hunger more, that I should forge
Quarrels unjust against the good and loyal,
Destroying them for wealth.

MACDUFF.   This avarice
85   Sticks deeper, grows with more pernicious root
Than summer-seeming[30] lust, and it hath been
The sword of[31] our slain kings. Yet do not fear.
Scotland hath foisons[32] to fill up your will
Of your mere own.[33] All these are portable,[34]
90   With other graces weighed.

MALCOLM. But I have none: the king-becoming graces,
As justice, verity, temp'rance, stableness,
Bounty, perseverance, mercy, lowliness,
Devotion, patience, courage, fortitude,
95   I have no relish of them, but abound
In the division of each several crime,[35]
Acting it many ways. Nay, had I pow'r, I should
Pour the sweet milk of concord into hell,
Uproar the universal peace, confound[36]
All unity on earth.

100   MACDUFF.   O Scotland, Scotland!

MALCOLM. If such a one be fit to govern, speak:
I am as I have spoken.

MACDUFF.   Fit to govern!
No, not to live. O nation miserable!
With an untitled[37] tyrant bloody-sceptered,
105   When shalt thou see thy wholesome days again,
Since that the truest issue of thy throne[38]
By his own interdiction[39] stands accursed,
And does blaspheme his breed?[40] Thy royal father
Was a most sainted king: the queen that bore thee,
110   Oft'ner upon her knees than on her feet,
Died[41] every day she lived. Fare thee well!
These evils thou repeat'st upon thyself

28. affection: Character.
29. stanchless: Never-ending.

30. summer-seeming: Summerlike.
31. of: That killed.
32. foisons (foi′ zənz): Plenty.
33. mere own: Own property.
34. portable: Bearable.

35. division . . . crime: Variations of each kind of crime.

36. confound: Destroy.

37. untitled: Having no right to the throne.
38. truest . . . throne: Child of the true king.
39. interdiction: Exclusion.
40. blaspheme his breed: Slander his ancestry.
41. Died: Prepared for heaven.

Hath banished me from Scotland. O my breast,
Thy hope ends here!

MALCOLM.   Macduff, this noble passion,
115   Child of integrity, hath from my soul
Wiped the black scruples, reconciled my thoughts
To thy good truth and honor. Devilish Macbeth
By many of these trains[42] hath sought to win me
Into his power; and modest wisdom[43] plucks me
120   From over-credulous haste: but God above
Deal between thee and me! For even now
I put myself to thy direction, and
Unspeak mine own detraction,[44] here abjure
The taints and blames I laid upon myself,
125   For[45] strangers to my nature. I am yet
Unknown to woman, never was forsworn,
Scarcely have coveted what was mine own,
At no time broke my faith, would not betray
The devil to his fellow, and delight
130   No less in truth than life. My first false speaking
Was this upon myself. What I am truly,
Is thine and my poor country's to command:
Whither indeed, before thy here-approach,
Old Siward, with ten thousand warlike men,
135   Already at a point,[46] was setting forth.
Now we'll together, and the chance of goodness
Be like our warranted quarrel![47] Why are you silent?

MACDUFF. Such welcome and unwelcome things at once
'Tis hard to reconcile.

[Enter a DOCTOR.]

MALCOLM. Well, more anon. Comes the King forth, I pray
140   you?

DOCTOR. Ay, sir. There are a crew of wretched souls
That stay[48] his cure: their malady convinces
The great assay of art;[49] but at his touch,
Such sanctity hath heaven given his hand,
They presently amend.[50]

MALCOLM.   I thank you, doctor.
145   [Exit DOCTOR.]

MACDUFF. What's the disease he means?

MALCOLM.   'Tis called the evil:[51]
A most miraculous work in this good King,
Which often since my here-remain in England
I have seen him do. How he solicits heaven,
150   Himself best knows: but strangely-visited people,

42. **trains:** Enticements.
43. **modest wisdom:** Prudence.

44. **detraction:** Slander.

45. **For:** As.

46. **at a point:** Prepared.

47. **the chance . . . quarrel:** May our chance of success equal the justice of our cause.

48. **stay:** Wait for.
49. **convinces . . . art:** Defies the efforts of medical science.
50. **presently amend:** Immediately recover.

51. **evil:** Scrofula (skrof′ yə lə), a skin disease called "the king's evil" because it was believed that it could be cured by the king's touch.

36 Literary Focus Here Malcolm explains that he was testing Macduff. He goes on to give him some good news. What is it?

37 Historical Focus This brief scene with the doctor is a digression, presumably written to compliment James I. Edward the Confessor supposedly had the power to cure the disease scrofula with his saintly touch. This power and the kings' use of it to cure their subjects appeared to come to an end with James I, who was reluctant to continue the practice until persuaded by his ministers. These lines praise his decision.

Macbeth, Act IV, Scene iii   333

All swoll'n and ulcerous, pitiful to the eye,
The mere[52] despair of surgery, he cures,
Hanging a golden stamp[53] about their necks,
Put on with holy prayers: and 'tis spoken,
155 To the succeeding royalty he leaves
The healing benediction. With this strange virtue
He hath a heavenly gift of prophecy,
And sundry blessings hang about his throne
That speak him full of grace.

52. mere: Utter.
53. stamp: Coin.

[*Enter* ROSS.]

MACDUFF.   See, who comes here?

160 **MALCOLM.** My countryman; but yet I know him not.

MACDUFF. My ever gentle[54] cousin, welcome hither.

54. gentle: Noble.

MALCOLM. I know him now: good God, betimes[55] remove
The means that makes us strangers!

55. betimes: Quickly.

ROSS.   Sir, amen.

MACDUFF. Stands Scotland where it did?

ROSS.   Alas, poor country!
165 Almost afraid to know itself! It cannot
Be called our mother but our grave, where nothing[56]
But who knows nothing is once seen to smile;
Where sighs and groans, and shrieks that rent the
    air,
Are made, not marked, where violent sorrow seems
170 A modern ecstasy.[57] The dead man's knell
Is there scarce asked for who,[58] and good men's lives
Expire before the flowers in their caps,
Dying or ere they sicken.

56. nothing: No one.

57. modern ecstasy: Ordinary emotion.
58. The dead . . . who: People can no longer keep track of Macbeth's victims.

MACDUFF.   O, relation
Too nice,[59] and yet too true!

59. nice: Exact.

MALCOLM.   What's the newest grief?

175 **ROSS.** That of an hour's age doth hiss the speaker;[60]
Each minute teems[61] a new one.

60. That . . . speaker: The report of the grief of an hour ago is hissed as stale news.
61. teems: Gives birth to.

MACDUFF.   How does my wife?

ROSS. Why, well.

MACDUFF.   And all my children?

ROSS.   Well too.

MACDUFF. The tyrant has not battered at their peace?

38 **ROSS.** No; they were well at peace when I did leave 'em.

MACDUFF. Be not a niggard of your speech: how goes 't?

180

ROSS. When I came hither to transport the tidings,
Which I have heavily borne, there ran a rumor
Of many worthy fellows that were out;[62]
Which was to my belief witnessed[63] the rather,
For that I saw the tyrant's power[64] afoot.

185

Now is the time of help. Your eye in Scotland
Would create soldiers, make our women fight,
To doff[65] their dire distresses.

MALCOLM.   Be 't their comfort
We are coming thither. Gracious England hath
Lent us good Siward and ten thousand men;

190

An older and a better soldier none
That Christendom gives out.

ROSS.   Would I could answer
This comfort with the like! But I have words
That would be howled out in the desert air,
Where hearing should not latch[66] them.

195

MACDUFF.   What concern they?
The general cause or is it a fee-grief[67]
Due to some single breast?

ROSS.   No mind that's honest
But in it shares some woe, though the main part
Pertains to you alone.

MACDUFF.   If it be mine,

200

Keep it not from me, quickly let me have it.

ROSS. Let not your ears despise my tongue for ever,
Which shall possess them with the heaviest sound
That ever yet they heard.

MACDUFF.   Humh! I guess at it.

ROSS. Your castle is surprised; your wife and babes

205

Savagely slaughtered. To relate the manner,
Were, on the quarry[68] of these murdered deer,
To add the death of you.

MALCOLM.   Merciful heaven!
What, man! Ne'er pull your hat upon your brows;
Give sorrow words. The grief that does not speak

210

Whispers the o'er-fraught[69] heart and bids it break.

MACDUFF. My children too?

ROSS.   Wife, children, servants, all
That could be found.

39

---

62. out: In rebellion.
63. witnessed: Confirmed.
64. power: Army.

65. doff: Put off.

66. latch: Catch.

67. fee-grief: Personal grief.

68. quarry: Heap of game slain in a hunt.

69. o'er-fraught: Overburdened.

39 Literary Focus Ross turns to Malcolm to tell him that his presence in Scotland would support an uprising against Macbeth, who is by now nothing short of a tyrant. Only after Malcolm's response does he painfully and haltingly return to the terrible news about Macduff's family.

Macbeth, Act IV, Scene iii **335**

336

40 Literary Focus Macduff's struggle to absorb this terrible news adds emotional power and realism to this scene.

41 Discussion What does Macduff mean by this line?

42 Discussion Whom does Macduff blame? Why?

43 Literary Focus Explain this metaphor.

44 Literary Focus The imagery of night and day returns again. The evil associated with this play has occurred mostly at night. It is fitting and conscious that this last line of Act IV acknowledges that day will follow even the longest of nights. Even as we struggle with these most mindless of murders, one senses that the struggle will soon be over.

Reader's Response If you wanted to modernize the witches in *Macbeth*, how would you have them dress and speak?

40

MACDUFF.   And I must be from thence!
My wife killed too?

ROSS.   I have said.

MALCOLM.   Be comforted.
215   Let's make us med'cines of our great revenge,
To cure this deadly grief.

41 MACDUFF. He has no children. All my pretty ones?
Did you say all? O hell-kite![70] All?
What, all my pretty chickens and their dam
At one fell swoop?

MALCOLM. Dispute it[71] like a man.

220 MACDUFF.   I shall do so;
But I must also feel it as a man.
I cannot but remember such things were,
That were most precious to me. Did heaven look on,
And would not take their part? Sinful Macduff,
42 225   They were all struck for thee! Naught[72] that I am,
Not for their own demerits but for mine
Fell slaughter on their souls. Heaven rest them now!

43 MALCOLM. Be this the whetstone of your sword. Let grief
Convert to anger; blunt not the heart, enrage it.

230 MACDUFF. O, I could play the woman with mine eyes,
And braggart with my tongue! But, gentle heavens,
Cut short all intermission; front to front[73]
Bring thou this fiend of Scotland and myself;
Within my sword's length set him. If he 'scape,
Heaven forgive him too!

MALCOLM.   This time goes manly.
Come, go we to the King. Our power is ready;
Our lack is nothing but our leave.[74] Macbeth
Is ripe for shaking, and the pow'rs above
Put on their instruments.[75] Receive what cheer you
may.
44 240   The night is long that never finds the day.   [*Exit.*]

---

70. hell-kite: Hellish bird of prey.

71. Dispute it: Counter your grief.

72. Naught: Wicked.

73. front to front: Face to face.

74. Our . . . leave: We need only to take our leave.
75. Put . . . instruments: Urge us onward as their agents.

Closure and Extension

ANSWERS TO THINKING ABOUT THE SELECTION
Recalling

1. (a) The first apparition tells Macbeth to beware of Macduff. (b) The second apparition says that none of woman born shall harm Macbeth, who naturally assumes Macduff is of woman born. (c) The third apparition tells Macbeth that he'll not be vanquished till Burnam Wood comes to his castle, Dunsinane.
2. Macbeth seeks to know if Banquo's descendants will rule Scotland. The witches do not tell him, but (b) they do generate images of future kings and the dead Banquo to prove that his offspring become kings.
3. (a) Lennox tells Macbeth that Macduff has fled to England. (b) He decides to slay Macduff's wife, children, and others at the unprotected castle.
4. (a) Malcolm is testing Macduff's loyalty to Scotland and his abhorrence of Macbeth and his plots when he claims to be worse than Macbeth. (b) Upon hearing of Malcolm's proclaimed failings, Macduff says he cannot support him in his quest to rule his beloved Scotland. With this Malcolm admits his ruse.

THINKING ABOUT THE SELECTION

Recalling

1. (a) What does the first apparition tell Macbeth? (b) How does the prophecy of the second apparition seem to contradict that of the first? (c) What does the third apparition promise?
2. (a) What question do the witches refuse to answer? (b) What vision do they parade before Macbeth?
3. (a) Where does Lennox say Macduff has gone? (b) On learning of Macduff's absence, what does Macbeth decide to do to Macduff's family?
4. (a) In his conversation with Macduff, why does Malcolm pretend to have all of Macbeth's vices and more? (b) What convinces Malcolm that Macduff is trustworthy?
5. (a) What good news about "gracious England" does Ross bring Malcolm? (b) What bad news does Ross bring Macduff?

Interpreting

6. Why does Macbeth readily accept the predictions made by the second and third apparitions?
7. (a) In the witches' procession of kings, why do some kings carry double and triple scepters? (b) Why does Banquo carry a mirror?
8. (a) What is Macbeth's reason for killing Macduff's wife and child? (b) How do these murders differ from the previous ones?
9. How would you describe Macbeth's character at this point in the play?
10. How is Malcolm's character revealed in the dialogue with Macduff in Scene iii?
11. Based on Macduff's reaction to the murder of his wife and son, how would you describe Macduff's character?

Applying

12. In staging *Macbeth,* some producers eliminate Scene ii, the murder of Lady Macduff and her son. (a) What reasons do you think they give for doing so? (b) What is your reaction to that kind of cut?

ANALYZING LITERATURE

Understanding Plot Development

Plot is a series of related incidents progressing through a period of *rising action* to a *climax.*
1. How do the apparitions' prophecies in Scene i prepare the audience for the plot developments to follow?
2. By the end of Act IV, the character of each major living participant—Macbeth, Lady Macbeth, Malcolm, Macduff, even Ross—has been made clear. How has this portrayal of character laid the groundwork for later events?

CRITICAL THINKING AND READING

Reading Between the Lines

In a play as carefully crafted as *Macbeth,* there are very few insignificant lines. For instance, in Act IV when one of the witches says, "'Tis time, 'tis time," the reader should think, "Time for what? Time for the witches to exact their price from Macbeth?"

Even today, critics have differing opinions about the character of Ross, a man who can be evaluated only by reading between the lines. What is your opinion of Ross's character—is he a toadying politician, a loyal Scot, or something else? Defend your assessment.

THINKING AND WRITING

Writing About Macbeth's Tragic Flaw

Macbeth is a tragic hero, a person of high rank who is brought to eventual ruin by a flaw in his character. Macbeth's tragic flaw is his ambition, which leads him into a series of bloody and increasingly indefensible acts. Write a composition in which you relate Macbeth's character to the plot development of the play. First make some notes on how Macbeth's personality and motivations get him into trouble and prevent him from getting out. Then write a first draft. When you revise, make sure each of your major points ties Macbeth's character to a plot element.

Macbeth, Act IV 337

---

10. While Malcolm claims a great list of character flaws, his speeches hardly confirm his claims. He seems a good and caring man. Then upon learning of the murders of Macduff's family, he demonstrates his strength of character and good sense.
11. *Admirable* seems an appropriate word to describe Macduff's character as it is shown when he struggles with the knowledge of the loss of his family. He behaves nobly under the crushing reality.

Applying

12. (a) One good reason would be that the slaughter is melodramatic and pitiful, not tragic. (b) Answers will vary.

ANSWERS TO ANALYZING LITERATURE

1. Macbeth is warned to beware of Macduff. Knowing his deteriorating state of mind, we can assume he will try to act against Macduff or his family. He seems to read the other predictions as an assurance that he will live out his life uncontested. Given this, he now feels he can do whatever he likes, which he seems to be doing. This behavior is leading to an uprising.
2. If character development dictates plot, as it should, a confrontation between good and evil is imminent. Malcolm and Macduff have rallied their forces. Macbeth has armed himself with prophecies that he reads as making him immune to being overcome. Lady Macbeth will likely continue her passage away from center stage as her actions continue to destroy her from within.

ANSWERS TO CRITICAL THINKING AND READING

As critics differ in their opinions, so will you find varying answers from student readers. His loyalties remain ambiguous, it seems, until he is sure about where the power will lie. A character such as he opens possibilities for lively discussion.

---

5. (a) Ross tells Malcolm that England has provided ten thousand soldiers to fight against Macbeth. (b) Then he sadly tells Macduff about the murder of his family and household.

Interpreting

6. Macbeth knows that the predictions made earlier came true; therefore he assumes these predictions are accurate, too. Rather than wonder if they are in some riddle form, however, he quickly assumes he is safe till he dies of old age.
7. (a) The double and triple scepters are the insignia of the Kingdoms of England, Scotland, and Ireland, united in 1603 when James VI of Scotland, Banquo's heir, became James I of England. (b) The eighth king carries a mirror to show images of more kings—including perhaps King James—beyond him in whom Banquo's blood will flow.
8. (a) They pose little or no threat to Macbeth, but as the castle is unprotected, and he was warned to beware Macduff, he feels he should act quickly against his enemy's family. (b) There is no sensible reason for these murders. As twisted as the logic was for the other killings, we can understand why they happened.
9. Macbeth is mentally unstable at this point. He has become a despot.

Literary Focus
You might have students practice identifying the themes of applicable stories recently studied, as theme identification can be elusive. While it is usually more complex, a theme can be likened to the moral of a fable.

Writing/Prior Knowledge
Alternatively, identify a worthy story, possibly a recent popular film, known to everyone in the class. Have the students identify its theme and give some explanation to support their answers.

Motivation for Reading
Everything is in place for the conclusion of the play. Have the students recall that Macbeth pins his hopes for a lengthy reign as king upon ambiguous prophecies.

Master Teacher Note
As you discuss Act V, point out how earlier incidents, events, foreshadowings, and images are culminated here.

Purpose-Setting Question
What is your final judgment on Macbeth and the outcome of his deeds?

Vocabulary
Preteach the following vocabulary words:
perturbation (pʉr′ tər bā′ shən) *n.*: Disorder (Sc. ik l.9)
pristine (pris′tēn) *adj.*: Pure; untouched; unspoiled (Sc. iv, l.53)
clamorous (klam′ər əs) *adj.*: Noisy (Sc. vi, l.10)
harbingers (här′bin jərz) *n.*: Forerunners (Sc. vi, l.10)

Writer's Techniques

Writing

Primary Source

Macbeth, Act V

Theme. The theme of a literary work is its central idea, an idea that can usually be expressed as a general statement about life. Every element in a work of literature—plot, character, setting, and so on—contributes to the theme. In many works of literature, including *Macbeth,* the theme pertains not only to the lives of the characters on stage but also, and more importantly, to the lives of the members of the audience. Sometimes it is possible to state a theme in one sentence, although complex literary works may require a lengthier explanation. A theme may be directly stated, but more commonly it is implied.

Jot down a few lines from Act V of *Macbeth* (and perhaps from earlier acts) that seem to imply the theme of the play. While the theme is not directly stated, the dialogue gives many indications that you will find helpful. Remember that the theme cannot be expressed in a single word or phrase. It requires at least a complete sentence and often more.

The theme of *Macbeth* is reinforced by the imagery of blood that permeates the play. Critic Mark Von Doren claimed,

> Never in a play has there been so much of this substance, and never has it been so sickening . . . The second scene opens with a messenger running in to Duncan red with wounds. And blood darkens every scene thereafter. It is not bright red, nor does it run freely and wash away . . . It is so real that we see, feel, and smell it on everything. And it sticks. "This is a sorry sight," says Macbeth as he comes from Duncan's murder, staring at his hands. He had not thought there would be so much blood on them, or that it would stay like that. Lady Macbeth is for washing the "filthy witness" off, but Macbeth knows that all great Neptune's oceans will not make him clean; rather his hand, plunged into the green, will make it all one red. The blood of the play is everywhere physical in its looks and gross in its quantity.

> That the blood imagery deeply impressed Shakespeare's contemporaries is shown in a reference to it the very next year in *The Knight of the Burning Pestle:*

> When thou art at thy table with thy friends,
> Merry in heart, and filled with swelling wine,
> I'll come in midst of all thy pride and mirth,
> Invisible to all men but thyself . . .

338 *The English Renaissance*

Objectives
1 To understand the theme
2 To read Shakespearean English

Support Material

Teaching Portfolio
Teacher Backup, p. 317
Grammar in Action Worksheet, *Understanding Tone,* p. 320
Usage and Mechanics Worksheet, p. 322
Vocabulary Check, p. 323
Analyzing Literature Worksheet, *Understanding Theme,* p. 324
Language Worksheet, *Understanding Shakespearean English,* p. 325
Selection Test, p. 326

Act V

1 **Scene i.** *Dunsinane. In the castle.*
[*Enter a* DOCTOR OF PHYSIC *and a* WAITING-GENTLEWOMAN.]

2,3

DOCTOR. I have two nights watched with you, but can
perceive no truth in your report. When was it she last
walked?

5   **GENTLEWOMAN.** Since his Majesty went into the field.[1] I
have seen her rise from her bed, throw her nightgown
upon her, unlock her closet,[2] take forth paper, fold it,
write upon 't, read it, afterwards seal it, and again
return to bed; yet all this while in a most fast sleep.

10   **DOCTOR.** A great perturbation in nature, to receive at
once the benefit of sleep and do the effects of watching![3] In this slumb'ry agitation, besides her walking
and other actual performances, what, at any time,
have you heard her say?

GENTLEWOMAN. That, sir, which I will not report after
15   her.

DOCTOR. You may to me, and 'tis most meet[4] you should.

4   **GENTLEWOMAN.** Neither to you nor anyone, having no
witness to confirm my speech.

[*Enter* LADY MACBETH, *with a taper.*]

Lo you, here she comes! This is her very guise,[5]
20   and, upon my life, fast asleep! Observe her; stand
close.[6]

DOCTOR. How came she by that light?

5   **GENTLEWOMAN.** Why, it stood by her. She has light by her
continually. 'Tis her command.

25   **DOCTOR.** You see, her eyes are open.

GENTLEWOMAN. Ay, but their sense[7] are shut.

DOCTOR. What is it she does now? Look, how she rubs
her hands.

6   **GENTLEWOMAN.** It is an accustomed action with her, to
30   seem thus washing her hands: I have known her
continue in this a quarter of an hour.

LADY MACBETH. Yet here's a spot.

DOCTOR. Hark! She speaks. I will set down what comes
from her, to satisfy[8] my remembrance the more
35   strongly.

---

1. field: Battlefield.

2. closet: Chest.

3. effects of watching:
Deeds of one awake.

4. meet: Suitable.

5. guise: Custom.

6. close: Hidden.

7. sense: Powers of sight.

8. satisfy: Support.

Macbeth, Act V, Scene i   339

1 Literary Focus Notice that this scene takes place at Dunsinane, the castle cited in the prophecy, and that nearby is Birnam Wood. Does Macbeth seem to be tempting fate to fortify himself here? Why might he have little concern about this detail?

2 Literary Focus Notice that this scene is written almost entirely in prose. Blank verse was not used for the language of servants and other working folk.

3 Discussion Why are these two characters here?

4 Literary Focus Point out how with only a few lines of dialogue even a minor character can be developed. What does this answer tell us about the gentle-woman?

5 Discussion Why is it ironic that Lady Macbeth is now afraid of the dark?

6 Literary Focus The same Lady Macbeth who in Act II, scene ii, said, "A little water clears us of this deed," now cannot clean the blood from her hands.

Fine art, *Mrs. Siddons as Lady Macbeth,* 1812, by George Henry Harlow. George Harlow (1787–1819), was British, a painter of historical scenes and landscapes as well as a clever and apt portraitist. He studied painting and drawing with several leading British painters. His knack for capturing an individual's personality on canvas led to many portrait commissions from famous people, including artists Benjamin West and Henry Fuseli and the actress Sarah Siddons.

Mrs. Siddons as Lady Macbeth was commissioned to commemorate the farewell performance of the actress in the play *Macbeth.* In this portrait, Sarah Siddons has a glowing, ethereal quality that seems almost supernatural. Her features are delineated with beauty and grace. It is an appropriate tribute to the leading tragic actress of the day.

In discussing this portrait with your class, you may wish to compare this artist's rendition of the character with those of the other two artists, Fuseli and Sargent, who painted Lady Macbeth. You might use the following questions for discussion:

1. Which portrait is most in keeping with your concept of Lady Macbeth?

2. Which portrait is the least effective illustration for the play? Why?

3. Do you feel that the use of portraits of legendary actresses to illustrate this play has enriched your study of it?

MRS. SIDDONS AS LADY MACBETH
G. H. Harlow
Garrick Club
E. T. Archive

LADY MACBETH. Out, damned spot! Out, I say! One: two: why, then 'tis time to do 't. Hell is murky. Fie, my lord, fie! A soldier, and afeard? What need we fear who knows it, when none can call our pow'r to
40   accompt?[9] Yet who would have thought the old man to have had so much blood in him?

9. to accompt: Into account.

DOCTOR. Do you mark that?

340   *The English Renaissance*

Commentary: Sarah Siddons and Ellen Terry as Lady Macbeth

Sarah Siddons (1755–1831) was a great English actress known for her portrayal of Lady Macbeth. She played this part a number of times over a span of twenty-seven years, and it was in this role that she gave the farewell performance of her acting career (1812). Her charisma is suggested by the dramatic picture of her on the student page above. The picture cannot convey, however, the richness and warmth of her voice.

Siddons portrayed Lady Macbeth as a strong, manlike woman, chilling in her ruthlessness. Her private notes, however, reveal that she saw a side to Lady Macbeth that she was unwilling or unable to communicate in performance. She wrote, for instance, that Lady Macbeth is "fair, feminine, nay, perhaps, even fragile" and "captivating in feminine loveliness."

Years later, the equally famous actress Ellen Terry (see her picture on page 245 of the student text) (1848–1928) would try to express this "feminine" quality of Lady Macbeth in her interpretation of the role. Terry wrote the following note to herself about the

LADY MACBETH. The Thane of Fife had a wife. Where is
    she now? What, will these hands ne'er be clean? No
45   more o' that, my lord, no more o' that! You mar all
    with this starting.

DOCTOR. Go to, go to! You have known what you should
    not.

GENTLEWOMAN. She has spoke what she should not, I am
50   sure of that. Heaven knows what she has known.

LADY MACBETH. Here's the smell of the blood still. All the
    perfumes of Arabia will not sweeten this little hand.
    Oh, oh, oh!

DOCTOR. What a sigh is there! The heart is sorely
55   charged.[10]

GENTLEWOMAN. I would not have such a heart in my
    bosom for the dignity[11] of the whole body.

DOCTOR. Well, well, well—

GENTLEWOMAN. Pray God it be, sir.

60 **DOCTOR.** This disease is beyond my practice. Yet I have
    known those which have walked in their sleep who
    have died holily in their beds.

LADY MACBETH. Wash your hands; put on your night-
    gown; look not so pale! I tell you yet again, Banquo's
65   buried. He cannot come out on 's[12] grave.

DOCTOR. Even so?

LADY MACBETH. To bed, to bed! There's knocking at the
    gate. Come, come, come, come, give me your hand!
70   What's done cannot be undone. To bed, to bed, to
    bed!   [*Exit* LADY MACBETH.]

DOCTOR. Will she go now to bed?

GENTLEWOMAN. Directly.

DOCTOR. Foul whisp'rings are abroad. Unnatural deeds
    Do breed unnatural troubles. Infected minds
    To their deaf pillows will discharge their secrets.
75   More needs she the divine than the physician.
    God, God forgive us all! Look after her;
    Remove from her the means of all annoyance,[13]
    And still keep eyes upon her. So good night.
    My mind she has mated[14] and amazed my sight:
80   I think, but dare not speak.

GENTLEWOMAN.   Good night, good doctor.
                         [*Exit.*]

Macbeth, Act V, Scene i   341

10. **charged:** Burdened.

11. **dignity:** Worth.

12. **on 's:** Of his.

13. **annoyance:** Injury.

14. **mated:** Baffled.

7 Discussion Pick out the specific events that Lady Macbeth's fragementary speech recalls through line 69.

8 Discussion Is there some wisdom in the doctor's conclusion that she has more need of spiritual help than medical or physical help? What signs existed that pointed toward a mental collapse?

9 Discussion What does the doctor mean when he tells the gentlewoman to remove the means of all annoyance? What does he anticipate?

Enrichment The appearance of a doctor at this point in the play may arouse students' curiosity about the prevalence of disease and the practice of medicine in Elizabethan England. You might want to tell them that the lack of sewers in big cities like London contributed to the spread of disease. During Shakespeare's life, there were two great epidemics of bubonic plague. In 1592 and 1593, about 20,000 people died from the plague and in 1603, about 30,000 perished.

Childbirth was often supervised by women who had no special training in midwifery. The rate of birth was extremely high, but so was infant mortality.

Only the rich could afford physicians who had studied at the great medical centers of Europe—Padua, Bologna, or Montpelier. The poor had to do without medical help or rely on unscrupulous fakes.

---

part: "Be damn'd *charming*." She also wrote as a stage instruction to herself: "Play with his [Macbeth's] hands and *charm* him."

In a letter to the critic Clement Scott, Terry attempted to explain her conception of the character. The informal and unorthodox punctuation makes it seem as if she is thinking out loud, groping for her conclusions:

. . . —Mind you though Mr. Clement, although certainly I know I cannot do what I *want* to do in this part, I don't even *want* to be 'a fiend'—& *won't* believe for a moment [moment is crossed out] *can't* believe for a moment that she *did* "conceive" that murder—that *one* murder of which she is accused—Most women break the law during their lives, few women realize the consequences of *that they do to*

day . . ."

In still another letter, to the critic William Winter, she was even clearer about wanting to break away from the traditional Siddons portrayal of Lady Macbeth as a monster:

Everyone seems to think Mrs. McB is a *Monstrousness* & I can only see that she's a *woman*—a mistaken woman—& *weak* —not a Dove—of course not—*but first of all* **a wife**—I don't think she's *at all clever* ("Lead Macbeth" *indeed!* —she's not even clever enough to *sleep!*)

10 Literary Focus In this largely expository scene, the thanes who enter are obviously the Scottish rebels referred to in Act IV, scene iii.

11 Discussion What is about to happen at Birnam Wood? Why is this significant?

12 Literary Focus Take note of the simile.

Scene ii. *The country near Dunsinane.*
[*Drum and colors. Enter* MENTEITH, CAITHNESS, ANGUS, LENNOX, SOLIDERS.]

MENTEITH. The English pow'r[1] is near, led on by Malcolm,
His uncle Siward and the good Macduff.
Revenges burn in them; for their dear causes
Would to the bleeding and the grim alarm
Excite the mortified man.[2]

5 ANGUS.   Near Birnam Wood
Shall we well meet them; that way are they coming.

CAITHNESS. Who knows if Donalbain be with his brother?

LENNOX. For certain, sir, he is not. I have a file[3]
Of all the gentry: there is Siward's son,
10 And many unrough[4] youths that even now
Protest[5] their first of manhood.

MENTEITH.   What does the tyrant?

CAITHNESS. Great Dunsinane he strongly fortifies.
Some say he's mad; others, that lesser hate him,
Do call it valiant fury: but, for certain,
15 He cannot buckle his distempered cause
Within the belt of rule.[6]

ANGUS.   Now does he feel
His secret murders sticking on his hands;
Now minutely revolts upbraid his faith-breach.[7]
Those he commands move only in command,
20 Nothing in love. Now does he feel his title
Hang loose about him, like a giant's robe
Upon a dwarfish thief.

MENTEITH.   Who then shall blame
His pestered[8] senses to recoil and start,
When all that is within him does condemn
Itself for being there?

25 CAITHNESS.   Well, march we on,
To give obedience where 'tis truly owed.
Meet we the med'cine of the sickly weal,[9]
And with him pour we, in our country's purge,
Each drop of us.[10]

LENNOX.   Or so much as it needs
30 To dew the sovereign flower and drown the weeds.[11]
Make we our march towards Birnam.
                              [*Exit, marching.*]

1. **pow'r:** Army.

2. **Would . . . man:** Would incite a dead man to join the bloody and grim call to arms.

3. **file:** List.

4. **unrough:** Beardless.
5. **Protest:** Assert.

6. **rule:** Self-control.

7. **minutely . . . faith-breach:** Every minute revolts rebuke his disloyalty.

8. **pestered:** Tormented.

9. **med'cine . . . weal:** Malcolm and his supporters are "the med'cine" that will heal "the sickly" commonwealth.
10. **Each . . . us:** Every last drop of our blood.

11. **dew . . . weeds:** Water the royal flower (Malcolm) and drown the weeds (Macbeth).

342   *The English Renaissance*

Scene iii. *Dunsinane. In the castle.*

[*Enter* MACBETH, DOCTOR, *and* ATTENDANTS.]

MACBETH. Bring me no more reports; let them fly all![1]
   Till Birnam Wood remove to Dunsinane
   I cannot taint[2] with fear. What's the boy Malcolm?
   Was he not born of woman? The spirits that know
5   All mortal consequences[3] have pronounced me thus:
   "Fear not, Macbeth; no man that's born of woman
   Shall e'er have power upon thee." Then fly, false thanes,
   And mingle with the English epicures.[4]
   The mind I sway[5] by and the heart I bear
10   Shall never sag with doubt nor shake with fear.

[*Enter* SERVANT.]

   The devil damn thee black, thou cream-faced loon.[6]
   Where got'st thou that goose look?

SERVANT. There is ten thousand—

MACBETH.   Geese, villain?

SERVANT.   Soldiers, sir.

MACBETH. Go prick thy face and over-red thy fear.
15   Thou lily-livered boy. What soldiers, patch?[7]
   Death of thy soul! Those linen[8] cheeks of thine
   Are counselors to fear. What soldiers, whey-face?

SERVANT. The English force, so please you.

MACBETH. Take thy face hence.   [*Exit* SERVANT.]
              Seyton!—I am sick at heart.
20   When I behold—Seyton, I say!—This push[9]
   Will cheer me ever, or disseat[10] me now.
   I have lived long enough. My way of life
   Is fall'n into the sear,[11] the yellow leaf,
   And that which should accompany old age,
25   As honor, love, obedience, troops of friends,
   I must not look to have; but, in their stead,
   Curses not loud but deep, mouth-honor, breath,
   Which the poor heart would fain deny, and dare not.
   Seyton!

[*Enter* SEYTON.]

SEYTON. What's your gracious pleasure?

30 MACBETH.   What news more?

SEYTON. All is confirmed, my lord, which was reported.

Footnotes

1. **let . . . all:** Let them all desert me!

2. **taint:** Become infected

3. **mortal consequences:** Future human events.

4. **epicures:** Gluttons.

5. **sway:** Move.

6. **loon:** Fool.

7. **patch:** Fool.
8. **linen:** Pale as linen.

9. **push:** Effort.
10. **disseat:** Unthrone.

11. **the sear:** A withered state.

Margin notes

13 **Discussion** Macbeth sums up the situation in these lines. What is happening as he prepares for battle? Why does he claim no fear? Do you think he is sincere?

14 **Clarification** The loon is a large diving, fish-eating northern waterfowl whose weird laughing cry has an almost insane human quality about it.

15 **Literary Focus** Notice the array of insulting epithets about the servant's pallor. How do you account for this extravagantly offensive behavior?

16 **Discussion** Paraphrase lines 16–17.

17 **Clarification** Seyton, his attendant, is off stage. Macbeth raises his voice to summon him; otherwise, this brief soliloquy is spoken quietly.

18 **Literary Focus** Point out Macbeth's subdued behavior now that he is alone. Does this speech elicit our sympathy? Shakespeare wants to remind us that this is a tragedy, and that the audience is witnessing the fall of a once great man.

19 **Clarification** For *mouth-honor* (line 27), read "lip service."

20 **Discussion** What does it indicate about Macbeth's state of mind that he will don his armor before it is needed? Remember, eleventh-century armor was quite heavy, cumbersome, and tiring to wear.

21 **Discussion** When Macbeth asks the doctor if he can "minister to a mind diseased" and otherwise attend to what might seem to be Lady Macbeth's problems, does he hope some cure might exist for him, too?

22 **Literary Focus** Point out the hysterical quality of this speech as Macbeth speaks with the doctor while showing impatience with Seyton about his armor.

23 **Literary Focus** One must sympathize with the doctor, whose house call embroils him in a deadly confrontation.

24 **Literary Focus** Note that the rebels have joined with the British forces.

20

MACBETH. I'll fight, till from my bones my flesh be hacked.
Give me my armor.

SEYTON.   'Tis not needed yet.

MACBETH. I'll put it on.
35 Send out moe[12] horses, skirr[13] the country round.
Hang those that talk of fear. Give me mine armor.
How does your patient, doctor?

DOCTOR.   Not so sick, my lord,
As she is troubled with thick-coming fancies
That keep her from her rest.

21

MACBETH.   Cure her of that.
40 Canst thou not minister to a mind diseased,
Pluck from the memory a rooted sorrow,
Raze out[14] the written troubles of the brain,
And with some sweet oblivious antidote
Cleanse the stuffed bosom of that perilous stuff
Which weighs upon the heart?

45 DOCTOR.   Therein the patient
Must minister to himself.

22

MACBETH. Throw physic[15] to the dogs, I'll none of it.
Come, put mine armor on. Give me my staff.
Seyton, send out.—Doctor, the thanes fly from me.—
50 Come, sir, dispatch. If thou couldst, doctor, cast
The water[16] of my land, find her disease
And purge it to a sound and pristine health,
I would applaud thee to the very echo,
That should applaud again.—Pull 't off,[17] I say.—
55 What rhubarb, senna, or what purgative drug,
Would scour these English hence? Hear'st thou of them?

DOCTOR. Ay, my good lord; your royal preparation
Makes us hear something.

MACBETH.   Bring it[18] after me.
I will not be afraid of death and bane[19]
60 Till Birnam Forest come to Dunsinane.

23

DOCTOR. [Aside] Were I from Dunsinane away and clear,
Profit again should hardly draw me here.   [Exit.]

24

Scene iv. *Country near Birnam Wood.*
[*Drum and colors. Enter* MALCOLM, SIWARD, MACDUFF, SIWARD's SON, MENTEITH, CAITHNESS, ANGUS, *and* SOLDIERS, *marching.*]

12. moe: More.
13. skirr: Scour.

14. Raze out: Erase.

15. physic: Medicine.

16. cast the water: Diagnose the illness.

17. Pull 't off: Pull off a piece of armor which has been put on incorrectly in Macbeth's haste.

18. it: His armor.
19. bane: Destruction.

MALCOLM. Cousins, I hope the days are near at hand
That chambers will be safe.[1]

MENTEITH.   We doubt it nothing.

SIWARD. What wood is this before us?

MENTEITH.   The Wood of Birnam.

MALCOLM. Let every soldier hew him down a bough
And bear 't before him. Thereby shall we shadow[2]
The numbers of our host, and make discovery[3]
Err in report of us.

SOLDIERS.   It shall be done.

SIWARD. We learn no other but the confident tyrant
Keeps still in Dunsinane, and will endure
Our setting down before 't.[4]

MALCOLM.   'Tis his main hope,
For where there is advantage to be given
Both more and less[5] have given him the revolt,
And none serve with him but constrainèd things
Whose hearts are absent too.

MACDUFF.   Let our just censures
Attend the true event,[6] and put we on
Industrious soldiership.

SIWARD.   The time approaches,
That will with due decision make us know
What we shall say we have and what we owe.[7]
Thoughts speculative their unsure hopes relate,
But certain issue strokes must arbitrate:[8]
Towards which advance the war.[9] [*Exit, marching.*]

Scene v. *Dunsinane. Within the castle.*
[*Enter* MACBETH, SEYTON, *and* SOLDIERS, *with drum and colors.*]

MACBETH. Hang out our banners on the outward walls.
The cry is still "They come!" Our castle's strength
Will laugh a siege to scorn. Here let them lie
Till famine and the ague[1] eat them up.
Were they not forced[2] with those that should be ours,
We might have met them dareful,[3] beard to beard,
And beat them backward home.
    [*A cry within of women.*]
                            What is that noise?

SEYTON. It is the cry of women, my good lord.   [*Exit.*]

Line numbers: 5, 10, 15, 20 (first column); 5 (Scene v)

Section markers: 25, 26, 27

1. That . . . safe: That people will be safe in their own homes.

2. shadow: Conceal.
3. discovery: Those who see us.

4. setting down before 't: Laying siege to it.

5. more and less: People of high and low rank.

6. our . . . event: True judgment await the actual outcome.

7. owe: Own.

8. strokes . . . arbitrate: Fighting must decide.
9. war: Army.

1. ague: Fever.
2. forced: Reinforced.
3. dareful: Boldly.

25 **Discussion** How does this order recall the prophecy made to Macbeth?

26 **Discussion** Why doesn't Macbeth meet these opposing forces in battle, rather than let them lay siege to the castle?

27 **Discussion** What is Macbeth's claim as the siege begins? Is this realistic or more bravado?

Macbeth, Act V, Scene v   345

28 Discussion When in the play was this true?

29 Discussion How do you interpret the first line of this speech? Is he being totally callous or is he suggesting that her death at any other time would allow him time for sympathy?

30 Literary Focus Here is Macbeth's most notable speech in the play, a powerful expression of life's futility as he is being crushed from all sides. Is Macbeth's story "a tale . . . full of sound and fury/ Signifying nothing"?

31 Discussion Macbeth is now told of Birnam Wood's moving toward Dunsinane. How does he react? Why?

32 Clarification *Equivocation* means "the ambiguous language of the prophecy."

28

MACBETH. I have almost forgot the taste of fears:
10   The time has been, my senses would have cooled
  To hear a night-shriek, and my fell[4] of hair
  Would at a dismal treatise[5] rouse and stir
  As life were in 't. I have supped full with horrors.
  Direness, familiar to my slaughterous thoughts,
  Cannot once start[6] me.

4. fell: Scalp.
5. treatise: Story.

6. start: Startle.

[*Enter* SEYTON.]

15   Wherefore was that cry?

SEYTON. The Queen, my lord, is dead.

29

MACBETH. She should[7] have died hereafter;
  There would have been a time for such a word.[8]

7. should: Inevitably would.
8. word: Message.

30

  Tomorrow, and tomorrow, and tomorrow
20   Creeps in this petty pace from day to day,
  To the last syllable of recorded time;
  And all our yesterdays have lighted fools
  The way to dusty death. Out, out, brief candle!
  Life's but a walking shadow, a poor player
25   That struts and frets his hour upon the stage
  And then is heard no more. It is a tale
  Told by an idiot, full of sound and fury
  Signifying nothing.

[*Enter a* MESSENGER.]

  Thou com'st to use thy tongue; thy story quickly!

30 **MESSENGER.** Gracious my lord,
  I should report that which I say I saw,
  But know not how to do 't.

MACBETH.   Well, say, sir.

MESSENGER. As I did stand my watch upon the hill,
  I looked toward Birnam, and anon, methought,
  The wood began to move.

35 **MACBETH.**   Liar and slave!

31

MESSENGER. Let me endure your wrath, if 't be not so.
  Within this three mile may you see it coming;
  I say a moving grove.

MACBETH.   If thou speak'st false,
  Upon the next tree shalt thou hang alive,
40   Till famine cling[9] thee. If thy speech be sooth,[10]
  I care not if thou dost for me as much.
  I pull in resolution, and begin

9. cling: Wither.
10. sooth: Truth.

32

  To doubt th' equivocation of the fiend
  That lies like truth: "Fear not, till Birnam Wood

Grammar in Action

Make the **tone** of your writing appropriate to your feelings about your subject. Notice how the tone of Macbeth's speech below matches his world-weariness and despair with life.

Tomorrow, and tomorrow, and tomorrow
Creeps in this petty pace from day to day,
To the last syllable of recorded time;
And all our yesterdays have lighted fools
The way to dusty death. Out, out, brief candle!
Life's but a walking shadow, a poor player
That struts and frets his hour upon the stage
And then is heard no more. It is a tale
Told by an idiot, full of sound and fury
Signifying nothing.

45   Do come to Dunsinane!" And now a wood
    Comes toward Dunsinane. Arm, arm, and out!
    If this which he avouches[11] does appear,
    There is nor flying hence nor tarrying here.
    I 'gin to be aweary of the sun,
50   And wish th' estate o' th' world were now undone.
    Ring the alarum bell! Blow wind, come wrack!
    At least we'll die with harness[12] on our back. [*Exit.*]

11. avouches: Asserts.

12. harness: Armor.

Scene vi. *Dunsinane. Before the castle.*
[*Drum and colors. Enter* MALCOLM, SIWARD, MACDUFF, *and their army, with boughs.*]

MALCOLM. Now near enough. Your leavy[1] screens throw
    down,
    And show like those you are. You, worthy uncle,
    Shall, with my cousin, your right noble son,
    Lead our first battle.[2] Worthy Macduff and we
5   Shall take upon 's what else remains to do,
    According to our order.[3]

1. leavy: Leafy.

2. battle: Battalion.

3. order: Plan.

SIWARD.   Fare you well.
    Do we but find the tyrant's power[4] tonight,
    Let us be beaten, if we cannot fight.

4. power: Forces.

MACDUFF. Make all our trumpets speak; give them all
    breath,
10   Those clamorous harbingers of blood and death.
                          [*Exit. Alarums continued.*]

Scene vii. *Another part of the field.*
[*Enter* MACBETH.]

MACBETH. They have tied me to a stake; I cannot fly,
    But bearlike I must fight the course.[1] What's he
    That was not born of woman? Such a one
    Am I to fear, or none.

1. bearlike . . . course: Like a bear chained to a stake being attacked by dogs, I must fight until the end.

[*Enter* YOUNG SIWARD.]

YOUNG SIWARD. What is thy name?

5 **MACBETH.**   Thou'lt be afraid to hear it.

YOUNG SIWARD. No; though thou call'st thyself a hotter
    name
    Than any is in hell.

MACBETH.   My name's Macbeth.

YOUNG SIWARD. The devil himself could not pronounce a
    title
    More hateful to mine ear.

MACBETH.   No, nor more fearful.

Macbeth, Act V, Scene vii   347

33 Literary Focus He wearies of life. Further, we witness one more reference to the day–night theme.

34 Literary Focus The action in these final three scenes is continuous, focusing in turn on different groups of soldiers and different parts of the battlefield.

35 Discussion What are Macbeth's chances at this point? What does he see as his only hope?

Having just learned of his wife's death, Macbeth is at this moment almost anticipating his own. Notice how a somber tone is created by apt words and phrases: *creeps, fools, dusty death, walking shadow, nothing.* The rhythm of his words—especially of the first line—also contributes to the tone. Life to him is meaningless and monotonous, "to the last syllable of recorded time." Shakespeare's lines hang as heavily as Macbeth's heart, and it is this heavy slowness of the lines coupled with the meaning of the words that gives this speech its power.

Student Activity 1. Read Macbeth's reply to the news that Birnam Wood "began to move," pages 346–347, lines 39–52. How does the tone differ from that of the "tomorrow and tomorrow" speech? Why is the difference appropriate?

Student Activity 2. Rewrite the Birnam Wood speech in prose. Change the ideas and phrasing so that the tone resembles that of the "tomorrow and tomorrow" speech.

36 **Discussion** Is it surprising that Macbeth so easily destroys Siward? What force is driving him? Notice how he and Macduff narrowly miss a confrontation.

37 **Clarification** *Kerns* were "hired Irish foot soldiers."

38 **Discussion** What is the outcome by the end of this scene? How have Macbeth's soldiers been fighting?

39 **Discussion** What decision does Macbeth make about how he will accept the loss of the battle and the kingdom?

40 **Discussion** Why has Macbeth avoided Macduff during the battle? Does it suggest he has some feelings about what he did?

36

10 **YOUNG SIWARD.** Thou liest, abhorrèd tyrant; with my sword
I'll prove the lie thou speak'st.
[*Fight, and* YOUNG SIWARD *slain.*]

MACBETH. Thou wast born of woman.
But swords I smile at, weapons laugh to scorn,
Brandished by man that's of a woman born. [*Exit.*]

[*Alarums. Enter* MACDUFF.]

37

MACDUFF. That way the noise is. Tyrant, show thy face!
15 If thou be'st slain and with no stroke of mine,
My wife and children's ghosts will haunt me still.
I cannot strike at wretched kerns, whose arms
Are hired to bear their staves.[2] Either thou, Macbeth,
Or else my sword, with an unbattered edge,
20 I sheathe again undeeded.[3] There thou shouldst be;
By this great clatter, one of greatest note
Seems bruited.[4] Let me find him, Fortune!
And more I beg not. [*Exit. Alarums.*]

2. staves: Spears.

3. undeeded: Unused.

4. bruited: Reported.

[*Enter* MALCOLM *and* SIWARD.]

38

SIWARD. This way, my lord. The castle's gently rend'red:[5]
25 The tyrant's people on both sides do fight;
The noble thanes do bravely in the war;
The day almost itself professes yours,
And little is to do.

5. gently rend'red: Easily surrendered.

MALCOLM. We have met with foes
That strike beside us.[6]

SIWARD. Enter, sir, the castle.
[*Exit. Alarum.*]

6. strike . . . us: Deliberately miss us.

Scene viii. *Another part of the field.*
[*Enter* MACBETH.]

39

MACBETH. Why should I play the Roman fool, and die
On mine own sword?[1] Whiles I see lives,[2] the gashes
Do better upon them.

1. play . . . sword: Die like Brutus or Cassius, who killed themselves with their own swords in the moment of defeat.
2. Whiles . . . lives: So long as I see living men.

[*Enter* MACDUFF.]

MACDUFF. Turn, hell-hound, turn!

40

MACBETH. Of all men else I have avoided thee.
5 But get thee back! My soul is too much charged
With blood of thine already.

MACDUFF. I have no words:
My voice is in my sword, thou bloodier villain
Than terms can give thee out![3]
[*Fight. Alarum.*]

3. terms . . . out: Words can describe you.

348 *The English Renaissance*

Commentary: Sword-play on the Elizabethan Stage

Macbeth ends with a flurry of sword-play. In furious succession, the villainous king stabs Young Siward and then is outdueled by the virtuous Macduff. As seasoned viewers of Hollywood stunt men, we may wonder just how realistically these battle scenes were staged for an Elizabethan audience.

Actually, Londoners of Shakespeare's time were connoisseurs of the art of fencing. They would have been just as disappointed to see a half-hearted duel as a modern movie audience would be to see a car-chase at 20 miles per hour. Consequently, Elizabethan actors had to study hard to be reasonably good fencers. They had to learn how to thrust with rapiers and parry with daggers, coming perilously close to their opponents without actually injuring them. The challenge of such a dangerous exercise is probably not so different from that of a demonstration karate match.

Some Elizabethan actors became so skillful at fencing that they won awards for it. Richard Tarleton, for example, a theater

MACBETH.   Thou losest labor:
As easy mayst thou the intrenchant[4] air
With thy keen sword impress[5] as make me bleed:
Let fall thy blade on vulnerable crests;
I bear a charmèd life, which must not yield
To one of woman born.

MACDUFF.   Despair thy charm,
And let the angel[6] whom thou still hast served
Tell thee, Macduff was from his mother's womb
Untimely ripped.[7]

MACBETH. Accursèd be that tongue that tells me so,
For it hath cowed my better part of man![8]
And be these juggling fiends no more believed,
That palter[9] with us in a double sense;
That keep the word of promise to our ear,
And break it to our hope. I'll not fight with thee.

MACDUFF. Then yield thee, coward,
And live to be the show and gaze o' th' time:[10]
We'll have thee, as our rarer monsters[11] are,
Painted upon a pole,[12] and underwrit,
"Here may you see the tyrant."

MACBETH.   I will not yield,
To kiss the ground before young Malcolm's feet,
And to be baited with the rabble's curse.
Though Birnam Wood be come to Dunsinane,
And thou opposed, being of no woman born,
Yet I will try the last. Before my body
I throw my warlike shield. Lay on, Macduff;
And damned be him that first cries "Hold, enough!"

[*Exit, fighting. Alarums.*]

[*Re-enter fighting, and* MACBETH *slain. Exit* MACDUFF, *with*
MACBETH. *Retreat and flourish.*[13] *Enter, with drum and*
colors, MALCOLM, SIWARD, ROSS, THANES, *and* SOLDIERS.]

MALCOLM. I would the friends we miss were safe arrived.

SIWARD. Some must go off;[14] and yet, by these I see,
So great a day as this is cheaply bought.

MALCOLM. Macduff is missing, and your noble son.

ROSS. Your son, my lord, has paid a soldier's debt:
He only lived but till he was a man;
The which no sooner had his prowess confirmed
In the unshrinking station[15] where he fought,
But like a man he died.

SIWARD.   Then he is dead?

4. intrenchant: Incapable of being cut.
5. impress: Make a dent in.

6. angel: Fallen angel, fiend.
7. his . . . ripped: Macduff's mother died before giving birth to him.
8. better . . . man: Courage.
9. palter: Juggle.

10. gaze o' th' time: Spectacle of the age.
11. monsters: Freaks.
12. Painted . . . pole: Pictured on a banner stuck on a pole by a showman's booth.

13. Retreat and flourish: Trumpet call to withdraw and fanfare.

14. go off: Die.

15. unshrinking station: Place where he stood firmly.

Macbeth, Act V, Scene viii   349

41 **Discussion** What does Macbeth tell Macduff about a confrontation between them? How does Macduff crush Macbeth's final hope?

42 **Discussion** What is he saying about the witches here?

43 **Discussion** If Macbeth gives himself up, what does Macduff suggest they will do with him?

44 **Literary Focus** In his final lines, Macbeth at least redeems himself as a brave and determined warrior.

45 **Discussion** Paraphrase these lines.

Enrichment In a repertory company, actors often have the opportunity to play more than one role in a drama on successive nights. A particularly strong actor, however, can dominate a play even when he plays a comparatively minor role. Some years ago, James Earl Jones traveled around New York City doing *Macbeth* with Joseph Papp's Shakespeare company. One evening, theatergoers would hear Jones's rich, deep voice reciting, "Tomorrow, and tomorrow . . ." The next evening, however, they would hear that same voice declaring, in the role of Macduff, "Then yield thee, coward . . ." Jones had such a dominating stage presence that, on alternate nights, it seemed that the play should be retitled *Macduff*!

star of the 1580's, was made Master of Fence. As the highest degree offered by fencing schools, this designation was something like today's black belt in karate.

Elizabethan audiences, however, wanted blood as well as skill. After all, they were used to seeing such entertainments as bullbaiting or bearbaiting. In the latter "sport," a bear fought against dogs or a blind bear was whipped until it began to bleed. (This was a cruel and savage practice, but we might reflect that another culture could view our numerous traffic fatalities as a form of savagery.) Macbeth even compares himself to a baited bear in this final combat (V.vii.1–2): "They have tied me to a stake; I cannot fly,/But bearlike I must fight the course . . ."

Paradoxically, theater companies often relied on such meek animals as sheep for spectacular, bloody effects. An actor, for example, might hide on his person a bladder of sheep's blood—ox blood was tried but found to be too viscous—that could spurt out the instant he was "stabbed." If a scene called for an actor to be disembowelled, sheep's viscera could be added to the blood. It is worth noting, by the way, that these theatrical illusions did not rely on tricky lighting. They were created in plain daylight.

The chances are that Elizabethan theater-goers watched Macbeth die after a dazzling exhibit of sword-play and a copious spilling of blood.

46 **Clarification** Wounds in the back would suggest a cowardly death during flight. His wounds in front tell the story that he died bravely.

47 **Discussion** How does the old soldier, Siward, react to his son's death? Is he being heartless, or is there another explanation?

48 **Literary Focus** The "newer comfort" is Macbeth's head, a compelling reason for the actual killing to take place off stage.

49 **Literary Focus** The final upbeat speech that closes the play is typical of Shakespeare's tragedies. It is intended to resolve any questions that may remain. Lines 70–71 confirm that Lady Macbeth took her own life. Was there an indication of this given earlier?

Reader's Response How would you stage the approach of Birnham Wood to Dunsinane? Explain.

ROSS. Ay, and brought off the field. Your cause of sorrow
45   Must not be measured by his worth, for then
    It hath no end.

46

SIWARD.   Had he his hurts before?

ROSS. Ay, on the front.

SIWARD.   Why then, God's soldier be he!
    Had I as many sons as I have hairs,
    I would not wish them to a fairer death:
    And so his knell is knolled.

50 MALCOLM.   He's worth more sorrow,
    And that I'll spend for him.

SIWARD.   He's worth no more:
    They say he parted well and paid his score:
47   And so God be with him! Here comes newer comfort.
48

[*Enter* MACDUFF, *with* MACBETH'S *head.*]

MACDUFF. Hail, King! for so thou art: behold, where stands
55   Th' usurper's cursèd head. The time is free.[16]
    I see thee compassed with thy kingdom's pearl,[17]
    That speak my salutation in their minds,
    Whose voices I desire aloud with mine:
    Hail, King of Scotland!

ALL.   Hail, King of Scotland!

[*Flourish.*]

60 MALCOLM. We shall not spend a large expense of time
    Before we reckon with your several loves,[18]
    And make us even with you.[19] My thanes and kinsmen,
    Henceforth be earls, the first that ever Scotland
    In such an honor named. What's more to do,
65   Which would be planted newly with the time[20]—
49   As calling home our exiled friends abroad
    That fled the snares of watchful tyranny,
    Producing forth the cruel ministers
    Of this dead butcher and his fiendlike queen,
70   Who, as 'tis thought, by self and violent hands
    Took off her life—this, and what needful else
    That calls upon us, by the grace of Grace
    We will perform in measure, time, and place:[21]
    So thanks to all at once and to each one,
    Whom we invite to see us crowned at Scone.

                  [*Flourish. Exit all.*]

16. The . . . free: Our country is liberated.
17. compassed . . . pearl: Surrounded by the noblest people in the kingdom.

18. reckon . . . loves: Reward each of you for your devotion.
19. make . . . you: Pay what we owe you.

20. What's . . . time: What remains to be done at the beginning of this new age.

21. in measure . . . place: Fittingly at the appropriate time and place.

Closure and Extension

ANSWERS TO THINKING ABOUT THE SELECTION
Recalling

1. (a) The gentlewoman has observed Lady Macbeth walking in her sleep on several occasions prior to seeking the doctor's help. (b) She will not tell him the troubling words she has overheard.

2. (a) She refers to the murders of Duncan, Banquo, and Macduff's family. (b) She comes back again and again to the murder of Duncan, the only one she participated in and because of which all the others followed.

3. (a) The four Scottish lords are crossing over to the other side to assist in the overthrow of Macbeth. (b) They will meet the English forces by Birnam Wood.

4. (a) He tells Macbeth that Lady

THINKING ABOUT THE SELECTION
Recalling

1. (a) Why are the doctor and the gentlewoman watching Lady Macbeth? (b) What does the gentlewoman refuse to tell the doctor?
2. (a) While Lady Macbeth is sleepwalking, to to what three prior events does she refer? (b) To which event does she keep coming back?
3. (a) In Scene ii what are the four Scottish lords preparing to do? (b) Where will they meet the English forces?
4. (a) What news does Seyton bring Macbeth in Scene v? (b) What in the messenger's report makes Macbeth fear that the apparitions' second prophecy is coming true?
5. (a) In Scene viii why does Macbeth tell Macduff he does not wish to fight him? (b) What does Macduff tell Macbeth concerning the apparitions' third prophecy?
6. (a) Whom does Macbeth kill in the encounter with the English forces? (b) Whom does Macduff kill? (c) At the end of the play, who is to be crowned King of Scotland?

Interpreting

7. Why do you think it is an "accustomed action" for Lady Macbeth to wash her hands while sleepwalking?
8. (a) Why does Macbeth remain confident of surviving the battle with Malcolm's army despite his own troops' desertion? (b) Judging by the way Macbeth behaves in Scene iii, describe his state of mind.
9. What changes in his personality is Macbeth describing in Scene v, lines 9–14?
10. Why does Macbeth say, "She should have died hereafter," upon learning of the death of Lady Macbeth?
11. Macbeth, mad and murderous though he is, shows certain admirable traits to the very end. What are some of his better traits?

Applying

12. If Macbeth had defeated Malcolm's forces and remained King of Scotland, what actions do you think he would have taken in regard to (a) Malcolm? (b) the rebellious Scottish lords? (c) the witches?

ANALYZING LITERATURE
Understanding Theme

Theme is the central or dominating idea in a literary work. In a tragedy the theme is based on the actions of a tragic hero—a basically moral person, often of noble stature, whose downfall usually results from a bad choice. The bad choice stems from a tragic flaw in the hero's character.

1. What is the tragic flaw in Macbeth's character? Support your answer.
2. What is the theme of *Macbeth?* State the theme. Your statement should be in the form of a universal truth, not restricted to Macbeth's tragic flaw and its consequences.
3. What events in Act V show Macbeth's downfall to be complete and irreversible?

UNDERSTANDING LANGUAGE
Reading Shakespearean English

The language of Shakespeare is Early Modern English, the direct ancestor of our own Modern English. Around the year 1500, Middle English, the language of Chaucer, began to undergo a number of gradual, systematic changes. One was the elimination of the vowel sound at the end of many words. The word *name,* for example, had two syllables in Middle English but only one by Shakespeare's time. Other changes occurred. The so-called "Great Vowel Shift" resulted in many changes in pronunciation: *he* in Middle English had sounded like *hey, mouse* like *moose,* and *moon* like *moan.* The renewed interest in Greek and Latin added many words of classical origin to the language. Certain consonants, such as the *l* in *would* and *could,* were still pronounced in Shakespeare's day. The pronouns *thou* and *thee* were in common use, as were the verbs *hath* and *doth* and the expressions *anon, prithee,* and *fie.*

1. In Scene iii, lines 35–37, find and list three examples of how Shakespearean English differs from today's.
2. In Scene v, lines 38–41, find and list three more examples of these differences.

Macbeth, Act V   351

(Answers begin on p. 350.)

in more than one way. It suggests that he would wish it to have happened at another time, when he could properly mourn, or possibly he's saying she would have died soon, anyway, so what difference does her death make?

11. Macbeth chooses to die doing battle, like a soldier, even though all is lost. He will not kill himself, nor will he simply give himself up. In this he shows his bravery and courage.

Applying

12. Answers will vary. (a) He almost certainly would have slain Malcolm. (b) He might have punished them or attempted to win back their loyalty. (c) He might have forgotten about them or occasionally consulted them.

ANSWERS TO ANALYZING LITERATURE

1. Answers will differ. Ruthless ambition might be considered the flaw, since this drives Macbeth to commit the crime that ultimately eventuates in his death.
2. The theme of Macbeth might be stated thus: Succumbing to a lust for power at any cost will inevitably lead to turmoil and destruction.
3. In Act V we learn that the unlikely prophecies of moving forests and a man not of woman born come true. We see an army laying siege to Macbeth's castle as his own forces abandon him and those who remain show no will to resist. Further, Macbeth shows no remorse or repentence.

ANSWERS TO UNDERSTANDING LANGUAGE

1. The words *moe* for *more, skirr* for *scour,* and *mine* for *my* are clear examples of the differences.
2. The use of *thou* for *you, speak'st* for *speak* and *shalt* for *shall* are three more examples.

Macbeth is dead. (b) The messenger tells Macbeth that Birnam Wood seems to be moving toward the castle.

5. (a) He does not wish to fight Macduff, he says, because enough of Macduff's family's blood has already been spilled. (b) Macduff startles Macbeth with the news that he was taken from his mother's womb—he was, therefore, not born, in the strict sense of the word.

6. (a) Macbeth kills the young Siward in battle. (b) Macduff in turn kills Macbeth. (c) Malcolm is to be crowned king of Scotland.

Interpreting

7. Lady Macbeth is haunted by the terrible deed she helped commit contrary to her initial belief that "a little water" would wash away the blood. The blood is the guilt that she obsessively tries to wash away.

8. (a) Macbeth believes he is shielded by the substance of the prophecies. (b) Macbeth is struggling with his emotions here. He is almost unstrung, judging by his words and actions.

9. Here we see Macbeth's emotions taking a swing all the way back. He seems now unable to respond at all to the terrible sounds he hears.

10. (a) This line could be interpreted

HAMLET
by William Shakespeare

DELACROIX AS HAMLET
Delacroix
le Louvre, Paris

"What a Sensational Story!"

"*Hamlet* is the most wonderful play ever written," claims critic A. C. Bradley. "What a sensational story! Why, there are some eight violent deaths, not to speak of a ghost, a mad woman, and a fight in a grave!" Whether we agree with Bradley's assessment or not, no one can deny that *Hamlet* is certainly among the most enthralling plays in the world. From the very first scene, we are plunged into a dark world of mystery and excitement.

"Something Is Rotten in the State of Denmark"

The play opens at midnight on the battlements of Elsinore Castle. The soldiers on duty are tired and edgy, for unnerving things have been happening lately. Moments later, the uneasy quiet is shattered by the appearance of a ghost, the very image of the former King of Denmark, down to his majestic presence and full armor. The guards and Horatio, Hamlet's friend, beg the ghost to tell them why it has been haunting the battlements, but it refuses to answer, and vanishes. The men decide to tell Hamlet, the dead king's son, what they have seen that night. If things weren't bad enough, we

OPHELIA
Sir John Everett illais
The Tate Gallery, London

Humanities Note

Fine art, *Ophelia*, by John Everett Millais. Millais (1829–1896) was a highly regarded nineteenth-century English artist. For a brief period, he was a member of the Pre-Raphaelite Brotherhood, a group dedicated to revitalizing craftsmanship, design, and decorative naturalism in an increasingly machine-dominated society. Throughout his career, he was known for his detailed, realistic paintings and illustrations. Because of his attention to detail, his works were often used to illustrate the work of major British writers.

In this painting Millais depicts Ophelia's death scene. This scene is not acted out on the stage, but it is described in vivid detail by one of the characters.

You might want to use the following questions to discuss the art.

1. What impression of Ophelia does this painting convey? Explain.
2. If you had to choose a piece of music to accompany this picture, what would you select?

learn that Norway is poised to attack Denmark, as young Fortinbras is intent on getting revenge on Denmark for his father's death in battle. There is profound trouble afoot in Denmark.

"Frailty, Thy Name Is Woman!"

Yet in the next scene it appears that matters are well in hand—at least on the surface. Claudius, charming and smooth, has assumed the throne after his brother's death, and married his wife, to boot. The only thing disturbing about this picture of domestic and political bliss is the presence of Prince Hamlet. In contrast to the colorful clothing of the royal couple and the courtiers, Hamlet is dressed entirely in the "inky cloak" of deep black mourning and stands well apart from the jovial mood of the others. "O! that this too too solid flesh would melt,/ Thaw and resolve itself into a dew," he exclaims in his first soliloquy, pouring out his bitterness at his uncle's falsity. His anger is directed especially at his mother's hasty remarriage to her former brother-in-law—less than two months after the death of her tender and loving husband.

Hamlet bravely sets out to the battlements at midnight to confront the ghost and learn what it is, if he can. But Shakespeare keeps us in suspense as he introduces us to Claudius's chief advisor, Polonius, and Polonius's two children, Laertes and Ophelia. We learn that Hamlet has declared his love to Ophelia, but Polonius doubts the sincerity of his words and has forbidden

Great Works   353

Humanities Note

Fine art, *Hamlet and Horatio*, by Eugène Delacroix. This picture is based on the famous gravedigger scene in Act V of *Hamlet*. Prince Hamlet, who has recently escaped from Claudius' spies, is with his good friend Horatio in a graveyard. The gravedigger is handing him the skull of Yorick, the former court jester. Hamlet is about to say, "Alas, poor Yorick! I knew him, Horatio: a fellow of infinite jest, of most excellent fancy: he hath borne me on his back a thousand times; and now, how abhorred in my imagination it is! My gorge rises at it. Here hung those lips that I have kissed I know not how oft. Where be your gibes now? your gambols? your songs? your flashes of merriment, that were wont to set the table on a roar. . . ."

You might want to use the following questions to discuss the art.

1. Which details in the picture add to its dramatic impact?
2. What mood does the picture create? Explain.

HAMLET AND HORATIO
Delacroix
le Louvre, Paris

Ophelia to have anything more to do with Hamlet.

But it is to the eerie night air that our attention turns. What will happen when Hamlet confronts the ghost?

Murder Most Foul!

As the men talk of Claudius's lavish parties, the ghost suddenly appears. It beckons Hamlet to follow him. Is the ghost sent to bring Hamlet crashing down the battlements to his doom? His friends try to hold him back, but Hamlet insists on following the ghost to a secluded spot. There, the ghost tells him that it is indeed his father's spirit, poisoned by his brother Claudius. He entreats Hamlet to "revenge his foul and most unnatural murder." Hamlet swears to do so. But how? He vows to "put on an antic disposition"—to feign madness—to better accomplish his mission. Can we trust him? Is this an act, or reality?

"Though This Be Madness, Yet There Is Method in 't"

Ophelia, at least, is convinced of his madness when he appears soon after in her room and acts most strangely. Polonius, too, is persuaded, but Claudius is not as certain, and sets spies on his stepson. Hamlet makes a mockery of the clumsy spies, his former friends Rosencrantz and Guildenstern, and has a great deal of fun tweaking Polonius as well. But his melancholy hangs on him as his black cloak, as he must find a way to verify the ghost's claim and achieve his revenge. "O! what a rogue and peasant slave am I," he exclaims, vowing to take action at once.

"The Play's the Thing, Wherein I'll Catch the Conscience of the King"

Just then the troop of traveling players arrive on its annual visit. To verify Claudius's guilt, Hamlet decides to insert a reenactment of the murder in one of the plays. But his sadness has grown so deep that he cannot help but reproach himself. In his most famous soliloquy, Hamlet cries:

> To be, or not to be: that is the question:
> Whether 'tis nobler in the mind to suffer
> The slings and arrows of outrageous fortune,
> Or to take arms against a sea of troubles,
> And by opposing, end them.

Claudius's violent reaction leaves no doubt of his guilt, and his later confession seals his fate. Mistaking Polonius for Claudius, Hamlet kills him, sending Ophelia into madness. Claudius arranges to have Hamlet killed, but he escapes and returns to Denmark's shores. He achieves his revenge brilliantly, but at a terrible price.

Shakespeare Today

Why then do we continue to read Shakespeare 400 years after his death? According to writer Pablo Neruda, it is because we so clearly see ourselves—our hopes, uncertainties, terrors—so clearly through his works.

One reason more, then, to love William Shakespeare, the greatest of all human beings. There will always be time and space to explore in Shakespeare, to lose ourselves, or begin the long journey around his statue, like the Lilliputians around Gulliver. And though we may go a long way without reaching the end, we always return with hands filled with fragrance and blood, with flowers and sorrows, with mortal treasures.

At this solemn moment, it is my pleasure to open the door of tributes, raising the curtain so the dazzling, pensive figure of the Bard may appear. And across four centuries I would say to him: "Greetings, Prince of Light! Good health, sir itinerant actor! We are the heirs to your great dreams; we dream them still. Your words do honor to the entire world."

And, more quietly, I would whisper into his ear: "My friend, I thank you."

THE PLAY SCENE IN HAMLET
Daniel Maclise
The Tate Gallery, London

Fine art, *The Play Scene in Hamlet*, by Daniel Maclise. Daniel Maclise (1811–1870) was a British painter famous for his portraits. For instance, he did a portrait of his friend Charles Dickens that now hangs in the National Gallery, London. Maclise also painted dramatic historical scenes such as *The Death of Nelson*. Horatio Nelson was the British admiral who won a victory over the French navy off Cape Trafalgar (1805), but died in the course of the battle.

The play within the play in *Hamlet* occurs in Act III, scene ii.

You might want to use the following questions to discuss the art.

1. Identify the "audience" in this scene.
2. Why do you think the artist chose to depict this particular scene?

from Novum Organum:
Idols of the Cave

Sir Francis Bacon (1561–1626) was born in London, the son of Sir Nicholas Bacon, Lord Keeper of the Great Seal. Although he made no discoveries in natural science and proposed no new scheme of philosophy, he gave to the seventeenth century something that it lacked, a "science of science" and a "philosophy of philosophy." Bacon's *Essays,* fifty-eight in all, appeared between 1597 and 1625. Full of practical wisdom and noted for their style, they reflect the experiences of Bacon's own life.

An account of Sir Francis Bacon's last days survives in a report by his friend, John Aubrey. According to Aubrey, Bacon was riding in a coach through the snow on the way to Highgate. With him was Dr. Witherborne, the King's physician. Looking at the snow, Bacon got the idea that meat might be preserved in cold, as it was in salt. Bacon and the doctor decided to try the experiment at once. They stopped the coach in front of a poor woman's home in Highgate, bought a hen from her and had her kill it and removed its innards. The two men then stood in the frigid air and stuffed the dead fowl with snow. Sir Francis got so chilled that he immediately fell deathly ill. Unable to complete the journey home, he went to a friend's house at Highgate. The only bed available was very damp, for it had not been used for about a year. Although Bacon's host warmed the bed with a pan, the bed was still so damp that the scientist's symptoms worsened. He died two or three days later. Imagine his amazement at the frozen food cases in our supermarkets today!

Writer's Techniques

Aphorism. An aphorism is a short statement that expresses a wise or clever observation about life. The term comes from Hippocrates's *Aphorisms,* a collection of tersely worded medical principles written by the early Greek physician. Hippocrates's opening sentence is a famous example of an aphorism: "Life is short, art is long, opportunity fleeting, experimenting dangerous, reasoning difficult."

As you read Bacon's "Idols of the Cave" from *Novum Organum,* look for the aphorisms. What insights about life do they provide?

Writing

Write the following headings across the top of a piece of paper: *Being a teenager, Being a student, Being a friend, Being a son* or *daughter.* Under each heading write two or more observations you have made or facts you have learned from your experience.

from Novum Organum[1]
Idols[2] of the Cave
Sir Francis Bacon

53

The *Idols of the Cave* take their rise in the peculiar constitution, mental or bodily, of each individual; and also in education, habit and accident. Of this kind there is a great number and variety; but I will instance those the pointing out of which contains the most important caution, and which have most effect in disturbing the clearness of the understanding.

54

Men become attached to certain particular sciences[3] and speculations, either because they fancy themselves the authors and inventors thereof, or because they have bestowed the greatest pains upon them and become most habituated to them. But men of this kind, if they betake themselves to philosophy and contemplations of a general character, distort and color them in obedience to their former fancies; a thing especially to be noticed in Aristotle,[4] who made his natural philosophy a mere bondservant to his logic, thereby rendering it contentious and well nigh useless. The race of chemists[5]

again out of a few experiments of the furnace have built up a fantastic philosophy, framed with reference to a few things; and Gilbert[6] also, after he had employed himself most laboriously in the study and observation of the loadstone,[7] proceeded at once to construct an entire system in accordance with his favorite subject.

55

There is one principal and, as it were, radical distinction between different minds, in respect of philosophy and the sciences, which is this: that some minds are stronger and apter to mark the differences of things, others to mark their resemblances. The steady and acute mind can fix its contemplations and dwell and fasten on the subtlest distinctions: the lofty and discursive mind recognizes and puts together the finest and most general resemblances. Both kinds however easily err in excess, by catching the one at gradations, the other in shadows.

56

There are found some minds given to an extreme admiration of antiquity, others to an extreme love and appetite for novelty; but few so duly tempered that they can hold the mean, neither carping at what has been well

---

1. **Novum Organum:** The New Instrument of Learning.
2. **Idols:** Misleading images of truth.
3. **sciences:** Ideas.
4. **Aristotle:** Ancient Greek philosopher (384–322 B.C.).
5. **chemists:** Alchemists; people who practiced alchemy, an early form of chemistry, involving the study of philosophical and magical associations.

6. **Gilbert:** William Gilbert (1540?–1603), an English physician, known for his studies of magnetic force.
7. **loadstone** *n*: A strongly magnetic variety of the mineral magnetite.

Presentation

Motivation for Reading Bacon draws attention to four obstacles to clear thinking. Have students seek them out and identify each.

Master Teacher Note Introduce several more contemporary aphorisms and their creators—Mark Twain, Yogi Berra, and Will Rogers, among others, might be good choices.

Purpose-Setting Question What four obstacles to clear thinking does Bacon discuss in this work?

1 **Clarification** Many students are familiar with the definition of *idol* as a "god" or "false god." The less-used definition applies here —*idol* as "a false or misleading idea or fallacy."

2 **Discussion** Bacon suggests that many fallacies of the mind exist and for many reasons. Which of them will he discuss here?

3 **Discussion** Why do men become particularly attached to certain views or viewpoints? What happens when these men turn their attentions to other, more general fields of thought?

4 **Discussion** What does Bacon see as the main distinction between the scientific and the philosophic mind? How is each inclined to go too far?

5 **Discussion** What two extreme attitudes does Bacon criticize? What is the ideal, instead? Where does he feel truth can be found?

Grammar in Action

Strive for **unity** in a paragraph. All ideas expressed within a paragraph must relate to each other as well as to the main idea. Supporting information should develop the idea introduced in the topic sentence while maintaining a consistent tone. Notice how Sir Francis Bacon achieves paragraph unity in 55.

The paragraph states in its topic sentence that one "radical distinction" differentiates philosophical and scientific minds. It then clearly states the nature of that distinction. The next sentence elaborates on it by giving a specific example of how each kind of mind operates. The paragraph concludes with a sentence connecting the two through a similar fault, their tendency to "easily err in excess."

Student Activity 1. Choose another paragraph from the selection and describe how it is unified.

Student Activity 2. Write a unified paragraph about some truth you have discovered. Be sure you keep to one topic and develop it with relevant sentences.

6 Discussion What problems arise in the study of nature and bodies? What does Bacon see as the ideal way to study them?

7 Discussion What, then, are the four reasons for the growth of the Idols of the Cave? Note that this section summarizes the previous four. What should every student of nature take as his general rule?

Reader's Response What prejudices and distortions prevent the discovery of truth in our time?

laid down by the ancients, nor despising what is well introduced by the moderns. This however turns to the great inquiry of the sciences and philosophy; since these affectations of antiquity and novelty are the humors of partisans rather than judgments; and truth is to be sought for not in the felicity of any age, which is an unstable thing, but in the light of nature and experience, which is eternal. These factions therefore must be abjured, and care must be taken that the intellect be not hurried by them into assent.

57

Contemplations of nature and of bodies in their simple form break up and distract the understanding, while contemplations of nature and bodies in their composition and configuration overpower and dissolve the understanding:[8] a distinction well seen in the school of Leucippus and Democritus[9] as compared with the other philosophies. For

8. **contemplations . . . understanding:** Neither reducing nature to the most basic principles nor trying to observe all of nature's particulars can produce a true understanding of it.
9. **Leucippus and Democritus:** Ancient Greek philosophers.

that school is so busied with the particles that it hardly attends to the structure; while the others are so lost in admiration of the structure that they do not penetrate to the simplicity of nature. These kinds of contemplation should therefore be alternated and taken by turns; that so the understanding may be rendered at once penetrating and comprehensive, and the inconveniences above mentioned with the idols which proceed from them, may be avoided.

58

Let such then be our provision and contemplative prudence for keeping off and dislodging the *Idols of the Cave,* which grow for the most part either out of the predominance of a favorite subject, or out of an excessive tendency to compare or to distinguish, or out of partiality for particular ages, or out of the largeness or minuteness of the objects contemplated. And generally let every student of nature take this as a rule —that whatever his mind seizes and dwells upon with peculiar satisfaction is to be held in suspicion, and that so much the more care is to be taken in dealing with such questions to keep the understanding even and clear.

THINKING ABOUT THE SELECTION
Recalling

1. In 53 what four sources of the "Idols of the Cave" does Bacon identify?
2. What two reasons are mentioned in 54 for people becoming attached to certain ideas?
3. What is the main distinction noted in 55 between different minds?
4. According to Bacon in 57, what is the main fault with the philosophy of Leucippus and Democritus?

Interpreting

5. In your own words, what does Bacon think is wrong with Aristotle's philosophy?

6. (a) If Bacon were to put himself into one of the two categories in 55, which one would it be? (b) Why?
7. In both 55 and 56, Bacon warns against going to extremes. How does he suggest doing it?
8. What purpose does the advice in 58 serve?

Applying

9. (a) In your own words, what is the rule Bacon recommends in 58 for a "student of nature"? (b) What is your opinion of the rule? (c) What, if any, instances can you think of in your personal experience where it might apply?

358 *The English Renaissance*

358

Closure and Extension

ANSWERS TO THINKING ABOUT THE SELECTION
Recalling

1. Bacon identifies the mental or bodily constitution of an individual, along with education, habit, and accident as four sources of the

ANALYZING LITERATURE
Understanding Aphorism

An **aphorism** is a concise statement expressing a wise or clever observation about life. In a very few words it summarizes a great deal of information or experience. Explaining the meaning of an aphorism requires many more words than those in the aphorism. Sometimes an example helps to make the meaning of an aphorism clear. In your own words, give the meaning of each of the following aphorisms from the works of Sir Francis Bacon.

1. "Revenge is a kind of wild justice, which the more man's nature seems to run to, the more ought law to weed it out."
2. "Virtue is like a rich stone—best plain set."
3. "There is no excellent beauty that hath not some strangeness in the proportion."
4. "Prosperity is not without many fears and distastes; and adversity is not without comforts and hopes."

CRITICAL THINKING AND READING
Reasoning

Before Bacon's time, science was based on *deductive reasoning*—the process of applying an already accepted general principle to specific facts. Bacon considered that method to be backwards. He argued that true science requires *inductive reasoning*—the process of examining specific facts in order to derive a general principle. From "some good quantity of observation" Bacon created his aphorisms in *Novum Organum*. Bacon's aphorisms therefore demonstrate in style as well as content the method of inductive reasoning.

When inductive reasoning is carried out logically, it results in a *valid generalization*—a statement, supported by evidence, that holds true in a large number of cases. If you make a generalization on the basis of only a few examples, without taking exceptions or qualifying facts into account, you produce a *hasty generalization*. A hasty generalization may be valid but only by accident, since the process of reaching it is flawed.

Read the following examples and decide which are valid generalizations and which are hasty generalizations.

1. I did worse on today's calculus test than I did on the three previous ones. I'm going to get a bad grade in calculus.
2. In the ninth inning I struck out with the bases loaded. I'll never be a good baseball player.
3. I helped my aunt run her day-care center for six toddlers this summer. I worked every day for two months. It takes skill and patience to care for young children.
4. It rained on my birthday for the last two years. It's almost sure to rain on it this year, too.

UNDERSTANDING LANGUAGE
Words from Latin Roots

Many words in the English language came from Latin. Sometimes the entire word was borrowed—*senator,* for example—but more often the Latin base, or root, was used in combination with something else to create a new word.

Use each of the following Latin roots to make at least two English words. If necessary, use a dictionary. You may have to change the spelling of the Latin root when you write the English word. For example, the Latin root *aer* (air) gives us *airplane* and *airmail.*

1. *omni* (all)
2. *viv* (live)
3. *flex* (bend)
4. *avis* (bird)
5. *sect* (cut)
6. *fid* (faith)
7. *rupt* (break)
8. *aqua* (water)
9. *grat* (thank)
10. *locut* (speak)

THINKING AND WRITING
Writing Aphorisms

Choose three of the observations that you made for the Writing assignment. Rewrite each observation in the form of an aphorism. Be sure that your aphorism, like those of Sir Francis Bacon, is a valid generalization. This requires that your observation be based on sufficient evidence to make the resulting aphorism express a general truth, one that cannot be easily disproved.

Idols of the Cave 359

(Answers begin on p. 358.)

is to be suspicious of whatever notion one's mind finds special. (b) Answers will vary, though at least some students should argue for its usefulness. (c) Answers again will vary, though some should mention the applicability of the rule to interpersonal relationships.

ANSWERS TO ANALYZING LITERATURE

1. Legal punishments for revenge should increase in intensity and severity in direct proportion to its occurrence.
2. Virtue needs little beyond its own richness and luster to make its value known.
3. The most prized kind of beauty has at least a touch of strangeness to it.
4. The rich fear losing their wealth; the poor can hope to attain riches.

ANSWERS TO CRITICAL THINKING AND READING

1. This is an invalid generalization, as the one poor test grade may be offset by a superior grade on the next test.
2. This is a hasty generalization. Striking out once is no indication of a batter's ability.
3. This is a valid generalization, arrived at through solid experience.
4. This is a hasty generalization, of course.

ANSWERS TO UNDERSTANDING LANGUAGE

1. omniscient, omnipresent
2. revive, vivacious
3. flexible, reflexes
4. aviary, aviation
5. intersect, section
6. fidelity, confidence
7. interrupt, rupture
8. aquatic, aquarium
9. gratitude, grateful, ingrate
10. elocution, eloquent

THINKING AND WRITING

Publishing Student Writing The best efforts of your students can be printed in enlarged form and displayed on a bulletin board.

Idols of the Cave.

2. Two reasons people become attached to certain ideas are that they consider themselves the authors or inventors of them, or that they've spent great time and trouble with them, making them their own.
3. Some minds are able to note differences in things, while others note similarities or resemblances in things.
4. The school of Leucippus and Democritus was so concerned with the particles of things that it overlooked the structure of things.

Interpreting

5. Suggested Response: Bacon felt Aristotle's philosophy was made a bondservant to his logic; that is, his logic kept his philosophy within very tight limits.
6. (a) Suggested Response: Bacon considered his mind to be lofty and discursive. It is possible he considered himself of both minds, however. (b) He dealt with resemblances.
7. He suggests that the intellect not allow itself to be hurried into extreme decisions.
8. The advice in 58 summarizes the four points he made earlier. It also leads to a generalization that students of nature should beware of thoughts or ideas the mind is content or satisfied with.

Applying

9. (a) Suggested Response: The rule

Ask students what they think is meant by the term "world view." Lead them to see that it means the beliefs about the world held by people of a particular period. Have students describe some of the elements of our contemporary world view. What, for instance, do scientists believe about the origin and nature of the universe? Then tell students that they will be reading about the world view of the Elizabethans.

Humanities Note

Fine art, *The Primum Mobile* from *The Cosmographical Glass*, 1559, from William Cuningham. This picture shows Atlas holding the world on his shoulders, a scene from Greek mythology. In this case, however, the globe represents the Elizabethan view of the world. Notice the earth in the center of the globe. Surrounding the earth are the spheres of the various planets. The outermost circle is the primum mobile (Latin for "first mover"), the sphere that moves all the others.

You might want to use the following questions with the art.
1. Find the Earth, the various planets, and the primum mobile in this illustration.
2. How does our view of the universe differ from this one?

CROSS CURRENTS

The Elizabethan World View

ORDER IN THE LAND!

The Elizabethans viewed the world as an ordered, rational place. Each person occupied a specific rung on the social ladder. With each rank came understood responsibilities to those above and below in the chain. Everyone understood and accepted this hierarchy, and it was constantly reinforced in daily life. On Sunday, during compulsory services at the Established Church of England, for example, ministers explained that "Every degree of people . . . hath appointed to them, their duty and order. Some are in high degree, some are in low, some kings and princes, some inferiors and subjects. Almighty God hath created and appointed all things . . . in a most excellent and perfect order."

The social ranking of people extended to everything in the universe, as each element, creature, and spiritual being occupied a fixed place in the universe.

THE PRIMUM MOBILE from THE COSMOGRAPHICAL GLASS, 1559
from William Cuningham
The Huntington Library, San Marino, California

HEAVENLY BODIES

This divinely directed order began with the heavens themselves. To the Elizabethans, the entire universe was enclosed by a sphere called the *primum mobile*. Beneath it lay the fixed stars. Next came the planets, whose motion was directed by the primum mobile. While opinion differed on exactly how many planets made up the universe—was it nine? ten? eleven?—no one with any sense doubted that these spheres circled around a fixed earth. Copernicus had a wild idea that the sun, not the earth, was the center of the universe. He even went so far as to claim that the earth was actually in motion, not fixed in place!

The angels too obeyed a strict hierarchy. The three different classes ranged from the highest, the Seraphs, to the lowest, the angels. Shakespeare commented on this order in *Troilus and Cressida* when Ulysses remarked that "the heavens themselves, the planets, and this center Observe degree, priority, and place."

THE GREAT CHAIN OF BEING

Heaven and its inhabitants were linked to the rest of the universe through a belief called The Great Chain of Being. It stretched from the humblest thing in the universe all the way up to God, and the order of each world was reflected in all others. England's rulers, for example, were arranged in order, which corresponded to the order of the rest of creation. The Sovereign was analogous to fire, the chief element; the sun, the chief planet; and the eagle, the chief bird, for instance.

Naturally, humans were expected to exceed the other worlds because of their superior intellect. A woman in *A Comedy of Errors* points this out while lecturing to her sister:

> The beasts, the fishes, and the
> winged fowl,
> Are their males' subjects and at
> their controls.
> Man, more divine, the master of all
> these,
> Lord of the wide world and wilde
> watery seas,
> Endued with intellectual sense and
> souls,
> Of more preeminence than fish and
> fowls,
> Are masters to their females, and
> their lords;
> Then let your will attend on their
> accords.

Although her sister resents being told she ought to be submissive to men, the Elizabethans saw the dominance of the man within the family as a model for the broader world order.

FATHER KNOWS BEST

As the king ruled over the kingdom, so the man of the family ruled over his wife and children. He had absolute right to dispose of his daughters in marriage, for example. Old Capulet would be considered an extremely considerate father to the Elizabethans, for when the question of Juliet's marriage to Paris is first discussed, he is willing to let her refuse. It is not until she defies him that he gives commands. Children were brought up to fear and respect their parents. They called their father "Sir" and stood in his presence. The power and authority of the father was recognized as part of the social order.

DRESS FOR SUCCESS

This rigid hierachy was even seen in the clothing laws, which decreed who was allowed to wear what. Clothing Acts were passed to halt the "intolerable abuse and unmeasurable disorder" caused by the poorer people dressing as their betters. No one under the rank of knight, for example, could wear velvet cloaks or silk stockings; only countesses and higher appeared in purple silk; gold and silver cloth were allowed only for nobles. But most people ignored the laws, much to the dismay of the lawmakers.

THE LINKS WEAKEN

The explosion of education and exploration caused people to cling even more tenaciously to the comfort of hierarchy. But combined with the avalanche of inventions and discoveries, the neat order of the world increasingly came under fire.

Cross Currents 361

More About the Author Although the scholars who worked on the King James Version knew Latin and Greek, they were told to use earlier English versions of the bible as the basis for their work. Five important versions of the Bible had been published in English from 1535 to 1568. This renewed interest in the Bible was inspired by Henry VIII's dramatic and decisive break with the Roman Church (1534).

Critical Evaluation Robert Mc-Crum, William Cran, and Robert MacNeil wrote that "The King James Bible was published in the year Shakespeare began work on his last play, *The Tempest*. Both the play and the Bible are masterpieces of English, but there is one crucial difference between them. Whereas Shakespeare ransacked the lexicon, the King James Bible employs a bare 8000 words—God's teaching in homely English for everyman."

THE KING JAMES BIBLE

1611

King James I, son of Mary Queen of Scots, ascended the English throne upon the death of Queen Elizabeth I. One of the first demands the new king faced was that of the Puritans for a uniform English version of the Bible. At the Hampton Court Conference in 1604, James accepted their demand. He commissioned fifty-four English scholars and clergymen to compare all extant texts of the Bible and to produce a definitive English edition. They succeeded perhaps beyond their expectations. The King James Version of the Holy Bible, published in 1611, has been called "the only classic ever created by a committee." From its earliest appearance until the present day it has been regarded as one of the great works of English literature.

The Bible, a collection of books developed over a period of more than twelve hundred years, consists of two main parts, the Old Testament and the New Testament. The Old Testament was originally written in Hebrew, the New Testament in Greek. In A.D. 382, St. Jerome translated the Bible into Latin, and his translation, called the Vulgate Version, remained the standard Bible in the West for centuries. An English reformer, John Wyclif, along with his followers, produced the first English translation from Latin in the late 1300's.

It was the Reformation in the 1500's, however—and the growing use of Gutenberg's movable type—that increased the demand for a Bible in the vernacular, or common language of the people. William Tyndale, a Protestant chaplain and tutor, decided to prepare a new English translation from Hebrew and Greek. Faced with clerical opposition at home, he went to Germany, where he translated and printed the New Testament in English. Arrested for heresy while at work on the Old Testament, Tyndale was executed near Brussels, Belgium, in 1536. The importance of Tyndale's New Testament is that the King James committee, impressed by its diction and rhythm, followed it more closely than any other translation in working on their 1611 masterpiece.

Other Bibles preceded the King James Version. None had the immense impact of the King James or Authorized Version, which in fact was never officially "authorized." It won its acceptance through use. Generations of people in Great Britain and the United States grew up reading its text and adding its wisdom to the common store of knowledge. Hundreds of expressions—"swords into plowshares," "fat of the land," "out of the mouths of babes"—are familiar to nearly every English-speaking person, while the magnificent rhythms of the Bible have influenced English prose and poetry throughout its history.

Objective
To recognize a psalm

Support Material

Teaching Portfolio
Teacher Backup, p. 343
Usage and Mechanics Worksheet, p. 347
Vocabulary Check, p. 348
Analyzing Literature Worksheet, *Understanding Parables*, p. 349

Critical Thinking and Reading Worksheet, *Analyzing the Use of Parallelism*, p. 350
Selection Test, p. 351

GUIDE FOR INTERPRETING

Psalm 23; The Parable of the Prodigal Son; I Corinthians 13

Literary Forms

Psalm and Parable. The Bible, particularly the Old Testament, contains a wide variety of literary forms in both prose and poetry. Many of them are already familiar to you, but two may not be. A psalm is a song or lyric poem in praise of God. Psalms were originally meant to be sung to the accompaniment of a stringed instrument. Today the word *psalm* generally refers to one of the 150 poetic pieces in the Old Testament Book of Psalms. Although the Hebrew authors of the psalms are mostly unknown, King David is often credited with having composed a few of them. The subject matter of the psalms varies widely. Some are hymns for public worship; others tell of historical events; still others portray everyday life in the Holy Land.

A parable is a short, simple story, usually about a common kind of occurrence, from which a moral or religious lesson can be drawn. Some parables, such as that of the unproductive vineyard, appear in the Old Testament. In the New Testament, Jesus often answers a question by telling a brief story based on an experience familiar to his listeners. Among the best known New Testament parables are those of the good Samaritan, the mustard seed, and the prodigal son.

Commentary

The *King James Bible* was published the same year that Shakespeare began his last play, *The Tempest*. While both works are masterpieces of the English language, there is one significant difference between them—words. Shakespeare nearly turned the language on its ear in his search for words. This is evident in the stunning array of different words he used in *The Tempest* (as well as his other works). The authors of the *King James Bible,* in contrast, used but 8,000 different words to convey their message. Noting this contrast moved one critic to remark that "from that day to this, the Shakespearean cornucopia and the biblical iron rations represent, as it were, the North and South poles of the language, reference points for writers and speakers throughout the world, from the Shakespearean splendor of a Joyce or Dickens to the biblical rigor of a Bunyan or Hemingway."

Writing

Think of an incident that would make a good parable. It should be an everyday occurrence whose outcome conveys a moral lesson. Jot down some notes about what happened. Indicate why you think the incident you have chosen fits the requirements for a parable.

Literary Focus Among the literary devices used most effectively in the King James Bible is parallelism, the repetition of phrases that are similar in structure. Another is imagery.

Writing/Prior Knowledge You might suggest, as an alternative, that when your students have read the Parable of the Prodigal Son they write an essay about the father and his two sons aimed at bringing some insight to the parable. They might, for example, concentrate on the universal implications of the story.

Motivation for Reading Ask students to enjoy the poetic rhythms and imagery of this best known of the psalms before seeking to analyze its meanings.

Master Teacher Note Discuss with your class why this poem is a traditional element in burial services for both Christians and Jews.

Purpose-Setting Question How does the psalm carry the Lord-as-shepherd image through from beginning to end?

1 Discussion How do these lines enhance the shepherd idea? How do they go beyond it?

2 Discussion How is the speaker supported and comforted by this guidance?

3 Discussion What future benefits does the speaker anticipate?

Reader's Response Why do you think many people recite this psalm in times of great distress and danger?

Psalm 23

1 The Lord is my shepherd; I shall not want.
He maketh me to lie down in green pastures: he leadeth me beside the still waters.
He restoreth my soul: he leadeth me in the paths of righteousness for his name's sake.

2 Yea, though I walk through the valley of the shadow of death, I will fear no evil: for thou art with me; thy rod and thy staff they comfort me.

5 Thou preparest a table before me in the presence of mine enemies; thou anointest my head with oil; my cup runneth over.

3 Surely goodness and mercy shall follow me all the days of my life: and I will dwell in the house of the Lord forever.

THINKING ABOUT THE SELECTION
Recalling

1. In the first part of the psalm, what images carry out the idea of the Lord as a shepherd?
2. At what point does the psalmist change from speaking of the Lord as a shepherd to viewing Him as a host preparing a feast?

Interpreting

3. Why would the Lord's (shepherd's) rod and staff comfort the psalmist (sheep)?
4. Why is it significant that the table is prepared "in the presence of mine enemies"?

Applying

5. Two years before the King James Bible appeared, the Douay Version, an English translation from Latin, was published in France. Following are the last three lines of Psalm 23 in the Douay Bible. What stylistic features of the King James Version distinguish it from the Douay Version?

Thou hast fatted my head with oil,
  and my chalice inebriating how
    goodly is it!
And thy mercy shall follow me
  all the days of my life
And that I may dwell in the house
  of the Lord in longitude of days.

ANALYZING LITERATURE
Recognizing a Psalm

A **psalm** is a sacred song or lyric poem. The psalms in the Book of Psalms, originally in Hebrew, were meant to be sung to the accompaniment of a stringed instrument. Since none of the Biblical translations really advanced that purpose, the paraphrasing of psalms into metrical verse began during the Reformation. This rephrasing, which permitted the psalms to be sung by congregations, emphasized the lyrical nature of the original compositions.

What qualities of Psalm 23 make it especially lyrical?

Closure and Extension

ANSWERS TO THINKING ABOUT THE SELECTION
Recalling

1. The Lord provides for the speaker; he guides him to places where there is plenty; he restores his inner well-being; he helps him lead a righteous life: and he protects him from the fears of death and evil.

2. The change occurs with the line that begins "Thou preparest a table . . . ," the speaker refers to the Lord as a host.

Interpreting

3. The rod and staff, or the lord's power, will be used to protect the psalmist.
4. A point is made that all, even the psalmist's enemies, are aware of the protection and sustenance offered by the lord.

Applying

5. The King James Version is simpler. It avoids such Latinate phrases as "chalice inebriating" and "longitude of days."

ANSWERS TO ANALYZING LITERATURE

Suggested Response: Its rhythm and phrasing make it lyrical.

Luke 15:11–32

The Parable of the Prodigal Son

A certain man had two sons. And the younger of them said to his father, "Father, give me the portion of goods that falleth to me." And he divided unto them his living.

And not many days after the younger son gathered all together, and took his journey into a far country, and there wasted his substance with riotous living. And when he had spent all, there arose a mighty famine in that land; and he began to be in want. And he went and joined himself to a citizen of that country; and he sent him into his fields to feed swine. And he would fain[1] have filled his belly with the husks that the swine did eat and no man gave unto him.

And when he came to himself, he said, "How many hired servants of my father's have bread enough and to spare, and I perish with hunger! I will arise and go to my father, and will say unto him, "Father, I have sinned against heaven, and before thee, and am no more worthy to be called thy son. Make me as one of thy hired servants."

And he arose, and came to his father. But when he was yet a great way off, his father saw him, and had compassion and ran, and fell on his neck, and kissed him. And the son said unto him, "Father, I have sinned against heaven, and in thy sight, and am no more worthy to be called thy son."

---

1. fain *adv.*: Gladly.

KING JAMES BIBLE, 1611
Title page of the New Testament
The Folger Shakespeare Library

Motivation for Reading Have students discuss why a well-told parable can teach a lesson more effectively than an argumentative or expository form of expression.

Master Teacher Note Explain that parables—didactic stories—are a universal means of teaching in comparatively unsophisticated or unschooled societies. Since Christ's hearers were often simple country people, it was inevitable that he should use parables to teach them.

Purpose-setting Question Have students keep in mind as they read that a moral or spiritual lesson is being taught. What is it? Is the older son justified in his unhappiness? What point is expressed in the last three paragraphs?

1 Clarification Be sure students understand the roles of elder and younger sons in a landholding family: that the elder son will take over the land and titles—a condition that remains in many situations even today.

2 Discussion Why do you suppose he does not return to the home of his family?

3 Discussion Under what conditions does he at last allow himself to return?

Humanities Note

King James Bible, 1611, title page of the New Testament. This frontispiece appeared in the first edition of the English Bible of 1611, known as the King James Version. The art for the title page was executed by an unknown artist in the employ of Robert Barker (d.1645). Robert Barker held the office of King's printer, which entitled him to a royally granted monopoly on the printing of English bibles, prayer books, statutes, and proclamations. This handsome page with the classically depicted biblical figures appeared in both of the editions issued in 1611. These books were the most noteworthy issue of the Barker family.

You may wish to ask your students what the style of the drawing indicates about the content of the book.

4 **Clarification** To kill and feast upon the fatted calf bestows great honor upon an event or people for whom it is done. Even the killing of a baby goat, a kid, as mentioned below, was done for some festive occasion.

5 **Discussion** Why does the father say that his son "was dead"?

Reader's Response Do you think the Father's response at the end of the parable calmed the elder son? Why or why not?

But the father said to his servants, "Bring forth the best robe, and put it on him; and put a ring on his hand, and shoes on his feet; and bring hither the fatted calf, and kill it; and let us eat, and be merry: for this my son was dead, and is alive again; he was lost, and is found." And they began to be merry.

Now his elder son was in the field; and as he came and drew nigh to the house, he heard music and dancing. And he called one of the servants, and asked what these things meant. And he said unto him, "Thy brother is come; and thy father hath killed the fatted calf, because he hath received him safe and sound."

And he was angry, and would not go in:

therefore came his father out, and entreated him. And he answering said to his father, "Lo, these many years do I serve thee, neither transgressed I at any time thy commandment; and yet thou never gavest me a kid, that I might make merry with my friends; but as soon as this thy son was come, which hath devoured thy living, thou hast killed for him the fatted calf."

And he said unto him, "Son, thou art ever with me, and all that I have is thine. It was meet[2] that we should make merry, and be glad: for this thy brother was dead, and is alive slain; and was lost, and is found."

---

2. meet *adj.*: Fitting.

THINKING ABOUT THE SELECTION
Recalling

1. What happens to the younger son's money?
2. (a) Why does the younger son decide to return home? (b) What does he intend to say to his father?
3. How does the father react to the return of his younger son?
4. (a) Why is the older son angry? (b) How does his father answer the complaint?

Interpreting

5. From the limited evidence given in the parable, how repentant do you think the younger son is?

6. Why is the father happy rather than unhappy at the sight of his younger son?
7. To what extent do you think the older son is justified in being angry at the treatment given his brother?

Applying

8. A parable is meant to teach a moral or spiritual lesson. What lesson do you draw from this one?
9. Sometimes this parable is called "The Parable of the *Lost* Son." How might that title affect your reaction to it?

Closure and Extension

ANSWERS TO THINKING ABOUT THE SELECTION
Recalling

1. He spends it foolishly in extravagant ways.
2. (a) He is forced to take menial work to barely survive, and decides he can work as a hired servant at home and avoid starvation. (b) He intends to admit he has sinned against heaven, beg his father's forgiveness for squandering his money, and seek to work as a servant.
3. His father, elated with his son's return, orders a feast in his honor.
4. (a) The older son is angry that his brother is honored despite his failings, while he receives little recognition for his own hard work and clean living. (b) He tells his older son that everything of the father's is his, and that they should be glad that the younger brother, whom they considered literally or figuratively dead, has returned.

Interpreting

5. The evidence is very limited, indeed. He has at least tasted hard times and suffering.
6. The father had given his son up for dead, or at least had feared he would never see him again.
7. There is an implication that the older son is as hard working and obedient as the younger son was unwise and extravagant, and perhaps the feelings expressed have been long held by the obedient

brother. A suggestion of "he always liked you better" seems possible.

Applying

8. Suggested Response: One lesson might be that it is never too late to repent and reform oneself.
9. The word *lost* would emphasize the loss of the son to his family. The word *prodigal* on the other hand, emphasizes the son's moral failings.

I Corinthians 13

1   Though I speak with the tongues of men and of angels, and have not charity, I am become as sounding brass, or a tinkling cymbal. And though I have the gift of prophecy, and understand all mysteries, and all knowledge; and though I have all faith, so that I could remove mountains, and have not charity, I am nothing. And though I bestow all my goods to feed the poor, and though I give my body to be burned, and have not charity, it profiteth me nothing. Charity suffereth long, and is kind; charity envieth not; charity vaunteth not itself, is not puffed up, doth not behave itself unseemly, seeketh not her own, is not easily provoked, thinketh no

2 evil; rejoiceth not in iniquity, but rejoiceth in the truth; beareth all things, believeth all things, hopeth all things, endureth all things. Charity never faileth: but whether there be prophecies, they shall fail; whether there be tongues, they shall cease; whether there be knowledge, it shall vanish away. For we know in part, and we prophesy in part. But when that which is perfect is come,

3 then that which is in part shall be done away. When I was a child, I spake as a child, I understood as a child, I thought as a child: but when I became a man, I put away childish things. For now we see through a glass darkly; but then face to face: now I know in part; but then shall I know even as also I am known. And now abideth faith, hope, charity, these three; but the greatest of these is charity.

THINKING ABOUT THE SELECTION

Recalling

1. In each of the first three sentences, the apostle Paul mentions some impressive personal achievements. (a) What are they? (b) In each case, if he lacks charity, what is the result?
2. The sentence beginning "Charity suffereth long" describes the nature of charity. (a) What does charity do? (b) What does it not do?
3. This passage is a letter to the Corinthians. In it Paul advises them to prepare for the coming perfect times with God. What analogy does he use to make his point clear?

Interpreting

4. Knowing what Paul means by *charity* is vital to an understanding of the passage. He does *not* mean "human kindness" or "doing good." What does the word *charity* mean, as Paul uses it? Context clues can help, but you may also need to consult a dictionary.
5. (a) Given this definition of *charity,* how do faith and hope relate to charity? (b) Why is charity "the greatest of these"?
6. (a) Find two uses of parallelism. (b) Does the use of parallelism make the writing more or less effective? Explain.

Applying

7. The apostle Paul is giving advice to the Corinthians on how to live a spiritual life. How, if at all, do you think it would be possible to know whether a person is following Paul's advice concerning charity?

I Corinthians 13   367

Motivation/Prior Knowledge
Have students think of words that came to English from another language. Verify their examples by looking them up in a dictionary. Then tell them that during the English Renaissance, English gained words from French, Dutch, Spanish, Latin, and other languages.

Enrichment Tell students that for 150 years after the Norman invasion, French was an essential language for the English upper class. In the thirteenth century, however, English came into greater use among the nobility. Noting this shift, Albert C. Baugh and Thomas Cable asserted, "There is evidence that by the close of the century some children of the nobility spoke English as their mother tongue and had to be taught French through the medium of manuals equipped with English glosses."

THE CHANGING ENGLISH LANGUAGE

Shakespearean English 1485–1625

A BLOODLESS INVASION

After the Normans invaded England in 1066, there were no more major assaults by foreign armies, but there did come another invasion of a kind—the onslaught of European culture.

Throughout the reign of the Tudors, England quarreled with her neighbors on the continent. Henry VIII severed allegiance with Rome. His daughter Elizabeth constantly sparred with the superpowers of the day, France and Spain. Through these skirmishes came the increasing interchange of words. Sailors returning from France brought cargo in the holds and *bigot* and *detail* on their lips. From Italy came *cupola* and *stucco;* the Dutch countries contributed *smuggle* and *reef.* Spenser's poetry even contains slang from the sailors who defeated the Armada!

WHAT SHALL WE CALL IT?

When they weren't off negotiating, exploring, or trading, the English were inventing and discovering wondrous new things, which all had to be named. From physics came *paradox* and *chronology;* from biology, *skeleton.* Through Versalius's work with anatomy we learned how *strenuous* activity could be. Soon, people needed an *encyclopedia* to learn about *gravity!*

LATIN AND GREEK ENTER THE MIX

The renewed focus on scholarship also helped the English language to grow. This interest in learning sparked a new class of scholars concerned with the refinement of writing style. Such writers as Thomas More and Francis Bacon rebelled against what they saw as the awkwardness of English. Bacon, for example, preferred to write in Latin, which was still the language of scholarship. English, he sneered, will "play the bankrupts with books." When forced to write in English, these men decorated their sentences with Latinate words they had gleaned from classical texts. From Latin they took *agile, capsule, habitual,* for instance; from Greek, *catastrophe, lexicon,* and *thermometer.*

A RETURN TO BASICS?

Not everyone was enthusiastic about the deluge of new words pouring into the language. Elizabeth's subjects felt as proud of their native tongue as they did of their land —and took both very seriously. Thomas Chaloner is often cited for his attack on writers who "serche . . . out of some rotten Pamphlet foure or fyve disused woords of antiquitee, therewith to darken the sence unto the reader." But others endorsed the importation of foreign terms: "Seeing that we borrow (and not shamefully) from the Dutch, the Breton, the Roman, the Dane, and French, Italian, and Spaniard, how can our stock be other than exceeding plentiful?" The battle between these two camps spilled over onto the stage. One of Ben Jonson's plays shows a poet cleansed of such borrowed Latin words as *retrograde* and *inflate.* Despite such protests, this mix of domestic and foreign words resulted in a language that one critic has called "of unsurpassed richness and beauty, which, however, defies all the rules."

AND NOW TO THOSE RULES . . .

This rich outpouring of foreign words into English did have its drawbacks, however. Chief among them, the matter of consistent rules for the different parts of speech. During the Renaissance, almost any English word could be used as almost every part of speech. Adverbs could become verbs, for example, and nouns could become adjectives; nouns and adjectives could even take the place of verbs and adverbs. In Elizabethan English you could *happy* your friend, *malice* or *foot* your enemy, or *fall* an axe on his neck. Words could be spelled any number of different ways—even within the same sentence! Nouns didn't have to match their verbs. The order of words in a sentence was up for grabs as well: Objects could come before verbs and adjectives could come after nouns, for example. Despite the linguistic model of Latin, the order of the day was disorder. In general, people felt that it was more important for language to be strong and interesting than logical.

IT LOOKS FAMILIAR . . .

Since the language of the Renaissance was shaped to appeal to listeners, why does it seem hard to understand today? It is simply that language changes. As it grew during the Renaissance, so it has developed through the centuries, and many words used in the past have long been discarded, replaced by terms that describe our life now. Someone from the Renaissance who arrived in America today would be baffled by "television" and "computer," as we are by their "chopine" (a high-heeled shoe) and "kecksey" (a wild plant). Even more perilous are the words that look familiar—those we think we know but that mean something entirely different today. For example, when someone in a Shakespearean play remarks, "I love not the *humor* of it," he is talking about the general tone of a situation, not its amusing aspects.

But it is only through such change that language remains fascinating—even challenging—and always alive.

Letter from Patent from Elizabeth I to Francis Drake

Elizabeth. To establish his claim, he erected a post bearing a brass plate with the queen's name, the date of his landing (1579), and a declaration that the land belonged to the queen. He also affixed on the plate a silver sixpence with the queen's likeness.

Unable to find Frobisher's passage in the "most vile and stinking fogs," Drake finally sailed west across the Pacific, completing his circumnavigation of the globe and arriving back in England in 1580. When he docked at Plymouth, Queen Elizabeth was so delighted with his exploits that she knighted him. This picture shows the patent that she gave him. A patent is a document giving the recipient the right or rights to an office, land, or a franchise.

You might want to use the following questions to discuss this document.

1. Queen Elizabeth permitted Drake to raid Spanish ships, even though England and Spain were not at war. What does Elizabeth's action suggest about the relationship between England and Spain?
2. Do you think there is any relationship between the vitality of Elizabethan literature and exploits like Drake's? If so, what connection might there be?

Humanities Note

Letter from Patent from Elizabeth I to Francis Drake. Sir Francis Drake (1540–1596), a fearless sea raider, was the first Englishman to sail around the world. He had heard about a passage to the Indies from the explorer Martin Frobisher (1535?–1594), who thought he had discovered a route across America by sea. Drake conceived of a bold plan to sail around South America to the Pacific, meanwhile raiding Spanish ships carrying treasure from the New World, and to return via Frobisher's new route.

In 1577 Drake left England and sailed into the Pacific through the Straits of Magellan, a seaway that separates South America from Tierra del Fuego. (Magellan was a Portuguese navigator in the service of Spain; members of his crew had completed a trip around the world in 1522.) He also plundered Spanish treasure ships, capturing the equivalent of five million dollars worth of gold. Drake then sailed up the coast of California, searching for Frobisher's passage through America. He went ashore, calling the land New Albion (an old poetic name for England) and claiming it for Queen

The writing assignments on page 370 have students write creatively, while those on page 371 have them think about the selections and write critically.

YOU THE WRITER
Guidelines for Evaluating Assignment 1

1. Has the student written a sonnet that is modeled on one from this unit?
2. Has the student devoted the octave to one main idea and used the sestet to comment upon it?
3. Does the sonnet have fourteen five-beat lines and a rhyme scheme like that of the model?
4. Is the sonnet free from grammar, usage, and mechanics errors?

Guidelines for Evaluating Assignment 2

1. Has the student written a scene showing two individuals in conflict, which is modeled on the dialogue of Marlowe or Shakespeare?
2. Does the scene reveal the nature of the conflict and aspects of their personalities?
3. Does the scene begin slowly and gradually build the conflict?
4. Is the scene free from grammar, usage, and mechanics errors?

Guidelines for Evaluating Assignment 3

1. Has the student written ten personifications modeled on figurative speech found in Elizabethan poetry?
2. Is each of the personifications expressed in a complete sentence?
3. Are the personifications appropriate and clear?
4. Is each of the personification free from grammar, usage, and mechanics errors?

YOU THE WRITER

Assignment

1. Write a sonnet modeled on any one contained in this unit. Your poem should have fourteen five-beat lines and the same rhyme scheme as your model.

Prewriting. Before you write, make a list of subjects that interest you—places, sports, hobbies, people you know, and so on. Then, from this list, choose the topic that appeals to you most and freewrite about it.

Writing. Write the first draft of your sonnet. You might devote the octave to one main idea and use the sestet to comment on it.

Revising. When you revise, check to see that your sonnet has fourteen five-beat lines and a rhyme scheme like that of one of the sonnets you have read.

Assignment

2. Write a scene modeled on the dramatic literature of this period, showing two individuals in conflict. As the characters talk, have them reveal the nature of the conflict between them and aspects of their personalities.

Prewriting. Before you write, make notes on the conflict between the characters. What is it about? How will it develop? How will it conclude?

Writing. Start the scene off slowly and gradually build the conflict. Although you need not use blank verse, try to emulate the style of the speeches in Marlowe or Shakespeare.

Revising. See if you can improve the way you developed and concluded the conflict. Then read the dialogue aloud. Can you improve the style of the speeches? Have you followed the conventions of drama in writing your scene?

Assignment

3. One of the most effective types of figurative language is personification. When a poet uses personification, he or she speaks about a nonhuman thing as if it were a person, maybe by saying something like "The sun is smiling." Write ten examples of personification modeled on the use of this figure of speech in Elizabethan poetry that you have read.

Prewriting. Before you write, look around you at the objects in your room, on the street outside your window, in your back yard. Let your imagination picture some of the objects you see doing things that human beings might do—singing, dancing, smiling, and so on.

Writing. Now, using the ideas you obtained by letting your imagination work, write your ten examples of personification.

Revising. When you revise, be sure that each of your examples is expressed in a complete sentence and that the personification is appropriate and clear.

370   *The English Renaissance*

YOU THE CRITIC

Assignment

1. Choose a character from a play in this unit and write an essay discussing the changes he or she undergoes. Tell (1) what the character was like at first, (2) what caused him or her to change, and (3) what he or she was like after the change.

Prewriting. Scan the play of your choice for a character who undergoes a change. When you have found this character, divide a sheet of paper into three columns and make notes on the three focal points mentioned above.

Writing. In your opening paragraph, state your main idea about the change the character undergoes. In the paragraphs that follow, discuss each of the focal points. In your concluding paragraph, restate your main idea in an interesting way.

Revising. When you revise, see if you can improve the organization and style of your essay.

Assignment

2. The theme of a poem is the central idea or insight the poem presents. Choose two poems from this section and write an essay stating the theme of each. In addition, identify the images, lines, and figures of speech that helped the author of each poem to express the theme.

Prewriting. Reread two of the poems you liked best. As you read each poem, ask yourself this question: What is the main idea this poem is expressing? The answer to this question is the theme. Now ask yourself how the poet developed and expressed the theme by using images, figures of speech, and other poetic devices.

Writing. Discuss each poem separately. For each poem state the theme and identify the specific devices that the poet used to develop it.

Revising. When revising, check that your remarks are clear and well supported by apt references to the literature.

Assignment

3. Write an essay about a sonnet from this section, discussing the following: (1) the subject of the sonnet, (2) the poet's attitude toward this subject, and (3) the passages in the poem where this attitude is revealed most clearly.

Prewriting. Reread the poem and try to grasp the author's tone of voice, for this tone reveals the poet's attitude. Where do you hear this tone most clearly—in what lines, words, images?

Writing. In your opening paragraph, identify the subject of the poem and the author's attitude toward it. Then in the body paragraphs, discuss in detail the specific lines in the poem where this attitude is revealed most clearly.

Revising. Revise to improve the clarity and organization of your essay. Then correct any errors in grammar and style that you find.

You the Critic **371**

YOU THE CRITIC
Guidelines for Evaluating Assignment 1

1. Does the student begin the essay by stating his or her thesis about the change the character undergoes?
2. Does the body of the essay discuss what the character was like at first, what caused him or her to change, and what he or she was like after the change?
3. Does the concluding paragraph restate the main idea in an interesting way?
4. Is the essay well-organized and free from grammar, usage, and mechanics errors?

Guidelines for Evaluating Assignment 2

1. Does the student discuss separately the theme of two poems from the Elizabethan period?
2. Has the student explained how images, lines, and figures of speech have contributed to the development of the theme?
3. Has the student supported his or her ideas with sufficient references to the literature?
4. Is the essay free from grammar, usage, and mechanics errors?

Guidelines for Evaluating Assignment 3

1. Has the student identified the subject of the poem and the author's attitude toward it in the opening paragraph?
2. Does the body of the essay discuss with clarity and in detail the specific lines in the poem where this attitude is clearly revealed?
3. Is there a satisfactory concluding paragraph?
4. Is the essay well-organized and free from grammar, usage, and mechanics errors?

Humanities Note

Fine art, *The Thames at Westminster Stairs*, by Claude de Jongh. Little is known about the life of the Dutch painter Claude de Jongh (c. 1600–1663). He worked in Utrecht during the 1620's and 1630's and later traveled to London. It was there that he painted scenes of the Thames River and London Bridge.

The Thames at Westminster Stairs is one of his views of the London Bridge and the Thames during the seventeenth century. In this view the thickly developed bank of the Thames is in sharp contrast with the openness in the distance.

THE THAMES AT WESTMINSTER STAIRS
Claude de Jongh, c. 1631 or 1637
Yale Center for British Art, Paul Mellon Collection

Objectives

1 To understand the roots of civil conflict in seventeenth-century England
2 To appreciate the literature of a turbulent age
3 To understand the schools of Jonson and Donne
4 To appreciate the Puritan writers of the seventeenth-century

THE SEVENTEENTH CENTURY
1625–1660

During the time men live without a common power to keep them all in awe, they are in that condition which is called war, and such a war as is of every man against every man. . . . In such condition there is no place for industry, because the fruit thereof is uncertain, and consequently no culture of the earth; no navigation, nor use of the commodities that may be imported by sea; no commodious building; . . . no arts; no letters; no society; and, which is worst of all, continual fear, and danger of violent death; and the life of man, solitary, poor, nasty, brutish, and short.

Thomas Hobbes

1

Focus

Historical Background Explain to students that the seventeenth-century witnessed a civil war in England between the Cavaliers, who supported the king, and the Roundheads, Puritan dissenters who backed Parliament against the king. Despite the turbulence of this period, however, poets like Ben Jonson and John Donne produced work of the highest quality.

Writing to Learn Have students write down what they know about the civil conflict in England and such figures as Oliver Cromwell and Charles I. Ask them to re-read this assignment after they have finished the introduction. Encourage them to evaluate the accuracy of the statements they made.

ESL Teaching Strategy Have ESL students report to the class on civil conflicts that occurred in their own society. Also, ask ESL students to make a simple chart summarizing the difference between the Cavaliers and Round-heads. Have them work with a non-ESL student to make sure their chart is accurate.

1 **Enrichment** This passage from Hobbes is derived from his famous political treatise, *Leviathan.*

Motivation/Prior Knowledge
Have students tell what they know about the American Civil War. Then explain to them that the English Civil War, which they will read about in the following pages, was also a bloody conflict.

Enrichment Tell students that while Queen Elizabeth had generally kept on good terms with Parliament, her successor James I had disputes with Parliament about religion, money, and foreign policy.

Among members of Parliament were wealthy merchants who were Puritans. Like most Puritans they wanted the Anglican Church, the official Protestant church of England, to eliminate Catholic rituals and ceremonies. They also wanted religious congregations to be able to administer their own affairs, without interference from higher church officials. James I had no sympathy for these goals. He did, however, frequently ask Parliament for money. His court expenses were high and England still had to pay off the debts it incurred during its war with Spain. Parliament would refuse the king's requests for money, insisting that he enact the religious reforms it wanted. To this demand James would answer that, as king, he had the "divine right" to do as he pleased.

Members of Parliament also protested against the king's conduct of foreign policy. They thought he should not have made peace with Catholic Spain and they were doubly offended when he tried to marry his son to a Spanish princess.

In the passage above, Thomas Hobbes pictures the terrible condition of people who lived before there were kings to bring order to society. Without rulers to keep people "in awe," Hobbes insisted, society would dissolve in chaos, and life would be "poor, nasty, brutish, and short." Hobbes claimed he was writing about a "state of nature" that existed before the dawn of history. But, in 1651, he had good reason to worry about the breakdown of society. The English had shocked the world by beheading their king in 1649 and abolishing the monarchy. Perhaps England had not quite reverted to the state of nature Hobbes imagined. But Hobbes, like many conservatives, believed that the violence would continue until the English again had "a common power to keep them all in awe."

It is difficult to believe that civil war followed so closely on the Golden Age of Elizabeth, with its triumphant defeat of the Spanish Armada and its brilliant literary achievements. Looking back, we see the English Renaissance as a time of unsurpassed accomplishments, but to people at the time, the age was one of frightening doubts as well as great expectations.

In science, philosophy, religion, and politics, long-held beliefs and ideas were discredited. The Ptolemaic world view—according to which Earth is the center of a finite universe—was giving way to the Copernican theory of an infinite universe in which the Earth is merely one planet in one of countless solar systems, and not even at the center of its own solar system. William Gilbert's studies of magnetism and William Harvey's discovery of the circulation of the blood opened new realms to the human imagination as well as to the human understanding. Sir Francis Bacon's writings popularized a reliance on observation and experimentation, as opposed to ancient authority, in scientific and intellectual pursuits. And, later in the century, Sir Isaac Newton created the classical physics that remained unchallenged until our own century. The triumph of the modern scientific spirit in the seventeenth century is symbolized by the establishment of the Royal Society in 1662.

Moreover, religious and political grievances, masked by the brilliance of Elizabeth I, began to emerge in the reign of the first Stuart king, James I. During the reign of Charles I, they led to a full-scale civil war. The Civil War unleashed new forces in English society, challenging the most basic ideas of order, even the monarchy itself. It swept away the rigid structure of the old society, in which the court was the center of political power and literary activity. In its place grew a new, competitive society, with a looser social structure and greater freedom in religion and politics.

THE ROOTS OF CIVIL CONFLICT

The roots of the religious and political conflicts that underlay the Civil War stretched back many years. Under Elizabeth the Anglican

Church held to a middle course between Catholicism and Calvinism. Puritans still worshiped and held positions in the Anglican Church, even though they disagreed with some of the Church's practices. That situation started to change after James I became king in 1603. James made no secret of his hostility toward Calvinism. He used his power as head of the Anglican Church to dismiss Puritan clergymen.

Charles I

In 1625, Charles I inherited all the religious problems his father had faced—and made them worse. He was married to the daughter of the king of France, a Catholic. That fact alone alarmed the people of England, most of whom were firmly Protestant.

Like his father, Charles had little love for Puritans. The king wholeheartedly supported Archbishop Laud, the reactionary leader of the anti-Puritans. Laud insisted that clergymen "conform," or observe all the church ceremonies, including those the Puritans disliked. In this way, Laud pulled the Anglican Church back toward Catholicism. Laud retreated so far from Protestantism, in fact, that the Pope offered to make him a Catholic bishop. Laud refused, but many Protestants still saw him as a Catholic in all but name.

Money Troubles

Charles I was like his father in another way. He was determined, in the words of Charles Dickens, "to be a high and mighty king not to be called to account by anybody." This attitude put Charles on a collision course with Parliament, and the crash came quickly over a basic question: money.

Charles had instigated wars against Spain and France and needed money to fight both enemies. Under English law, the money had to be granted to him by Parliament. But Parliament supported neither venture, and the king had to turn elsewhere. From his wealthy subjects Charles extorted loans by threatening them with prison. Charles lost popularity with commoners by pressing the poor into service as soldiers and sailors.

The king's abuse of his power angered many subjects. When Parliament met in 1628, its members boldly stood up to the king by passing the Petition of Right. This document spelled out the basic rights of Englishmen—at the time women had no political rights. Charles unhappily accepted the Petition of Right in order to get approval for new revenues. He soon showed that he had no intention of abiding by it. When leaders of Parliament protested, Charles had them arrested and then dissolved Parliament. For the next eleven years, Charles ruled without so much as calling Parliament into session.

Enrichment Tell students that some scholars have argued that Charles I brought about his own downfall. He simply did not understand the political and religious issues that were dividing his kingdom. Moreover, he received bad advice from men like George Villiers, duke of Buckingham.

Enrichment Inform students that the Petition of Right (1628) set forth basic civil liberties that the king could not violate: Taxes could not be levied without the approval of Parliament, subjects could not be imprisoned without cause, soldiers could not be quartered in citizens' houses, and martial law could not be declared during peacetime. As one might suspect, each of these demands was a response to specific abuses.

BRITISH EVENTS

1625   Full-bottomed wigs come into fashion.

1627   **Sir Francis Bacon** publishes *The New Atlantis*.

1628   William Harvey explains blood circulation.

1633   **John Donne's** *Poems* published.

        George Herbert's *The Temple* published.

1634   Covent Garden Market opens.

1635   Public mail service established.

1637   Charles I summons Long Parliament.

        John Milton publishes *Lycidas*.

1640   **John Donne's** *Devotions upon Emergent Occasions* published.

1642   English Civil War begins.

        Puritans close theaters.

1644   **John Milton** writes *Areopagitica*.

1645   **John Milton** publishes *Poems*.

1646   **John Suckling** publishes *Fragmenta Aurea*.

1647   First newspaper ad appears.

1648   George Fox founds Society of Friends (Quakers).

        Robert Herrick publishes *Hesperides*.

1649   Charles I beheaded.

        Richard Lovelace publishes *Lucasta*.

1651   Thomas Hobbes publishes *Leviathan*.

1653   Oliver Cromwell becomes Lord Protector.

1658   Oliver Cromwell dies.

1659   Puritan government collapses.

1660   Monarchy restored.

        Theaters reopened.

Sir Francis Bacon

Execution of Charles I

The Night Watch

John Milton

Covent Garden Market

New Amsterdam

Molière

King Louis XIV

Andrew Marvell

WORLD EVENTS

1626	North America: Dutch found New Amsterdam.
1630	France: Beginning of public advertising.
	North America: William Bradford begins writing *Of Plymouth Plantation*.
	Boston founded by John Winthrop.
1636	North America: Rhode Island founded by Roger Williams.
	Harvard University founded.
	France: Corneille publishes *Le Cid*.
1637	Japan: All Europeans expelled.
1639	India: English settlement established at Madras.
1640	North America: *Bay Psalm Book* published in Massachusetts.
	Italy: First European cafe opens in Venice.
	Holland: Rembrandt paints *Self-Portrait*.
1642	Holland: Rembrandt paints *Night Watch*.
	North America: Education becomes compulsory in Massachusetts.
1643	France: Molière founds Comédie Française.
1644	France: Descartes publishes *Principia Philosophicae*.
	China: Ming Dynasty ends.
1647	North America: Massachusetts establishes free public schools.
1651	North America: William Bradford finishes *Of Plymouth Plantation*.
1654	France: Louis XIV becomes king.
1657	France: First stockings manufactured.
1659	France: Molière publishes *The Flying Doctor*.
1660	South Africa: First Dutch settlers arrive.

Introduction 377

Humanities Note

Fine art, *Portrait of Charles I,* c. 1635, by Anthony van Dyck. Anthony van Dyck (1599–1641) was an important Baroque artist, who attained international stature. He was court painter in England to Charles I from 1632 to 1644. He is best known for the portraits he painted during this time. The flourishing aristocratic society of this period was charmed by this handsome painter, friend of Charles I.

Van Dyck created a new aristocratic portrait tradition that continued into the late eighteenth century. He had the ability to capture a vivid likeness but with an elegant style. This portrait of Charles I hunting shows the king at ease in a less rigid pose than a formal state portrait, but hardly less grand. The fluid backdrop with landscape, horse, and two grooms contrasts with the elegance of the king's pose.

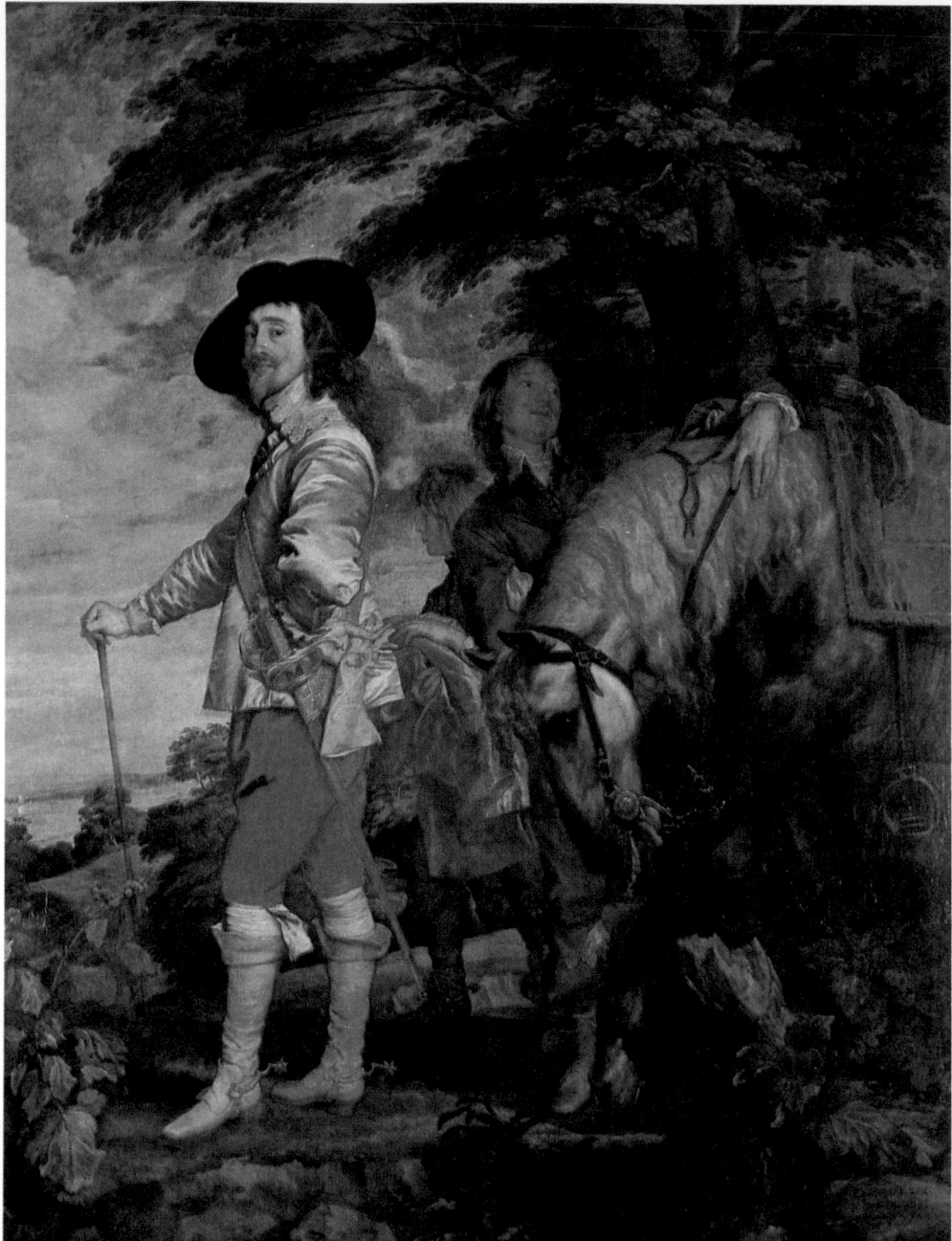

PORTRAIT OF CHARLES I
Anthony van Dyck
The Louvre, Paris

Conflict with the Puritans

Many English subjects were disgusted with Charles, but none more so than the Puritans. The king's ally, Archbishop Laud, had stepped up his persecution of these Calvinist "dissenters." In brutal public ceremonies, Puritan leaders had their noses slit, their cheeks branded, and their ears cropped off. The Puritans often displayed such faith and resolve during these mutilations that they won the hearts of onlookers. "The more I am beaten down, the more I am lifted up!" exclaimed one Puritan as a torturer finished his work.

It was no accident that Laud and the "High Church" Anglicans supported the king, while most Puritans opposed him. The Puritan religious outlook had implications for politics. Radical Puritans wanted to do away with bishops and the whole hierarchy of the Anglican Church. They believed that each congregation, or group of worshipers, had the right to choose its own minister. As you can see, this belief resembled democracy in politics.

Most Puritans were dead set against the idea of a king's "divine right" to rule, on which Charles I insisted. One Puritan put the matter plainly: "A King is a thing men have made for their own sakes." It was only a short step further to the idea that men could *un*make a king. James I had understood this danger and summed it up in the curt phrase, "No bishop, no king."

The Long Parliament

The policies of Charles and Archbishop Laud were unpopular enough in England. But when the king and archbishop tried to force conformity on Scottish Calvinists, the Scots rose up in defiance. In 1639, King Charles had to lead an army north to put down the rebellion. With the war stalemated, Charles returned to London, once again desperate for funds.

Parliament, however, was in no mood to grant the king's request without guarantees in return. Among other things, Parliament demanded the trial of Laud and Thomas Wentworth, the hated leader of the king's army. Both were tried and later executed. The legislators also insisted on reforms to limit the power of the king. As the session went on in the stormy atmosphere of London, one demand led to another. At last, in 1642, Parliament condemned Charles as a tyrant.

Charles struck back by sending armed men into Parliament to seize the opposition leaders. The leaders escaped, and Parliament began raising its own army. Charles fled north, rallying loyalists to his side. For the next eleven years, the "Long Parliament" ruled England. The Civil War had begun.

The Civil War

When war came, the people of England were forced to choose sides. The king's supporters were called Cavaliers, since many of

2 Historical Context According to Divine Right belief, power comes *down* from God to the king; according to Puritan belief, power rises *up* from the people to the king.

THE EXECUTION OF KING CHARLES I OF ENGLAND AT WHITEHALL, LONDON, JANUARY 30, 1649
Colored woodcut from Contemporary Ballad-Sheet
The Granger Collection

these aristocrats were skilled horsemen, or cavalry. They generally lived in the countryside. Parliament drew its followers from London and the towns, where Puritanism ran strong. Because these austere Calvinists cut their hair short, they were known as Roundheads.

The same grit Puritans had shown under the torturer's hand made them fierce enemies. The dour Puritan leader Oliver Cromwell took charge of Parliament's forces. He drilled them into an unparalleled fighting machine called the New Model Army. At the Battle of Marston Moor, the New Model Army showed the power of its training. The next year, in 1645, Cromwell's troops defeated a Cavalier army and captured Charles I.

Meanwhile, a battle of another kind was going on in Parliament. There, members of the different Protestant factions were struggling for power. Gradually, the most radical Puritans won out. In 1648, they shut the doors on moderate members. Then the radicals brought Charles I to trial. With no moderates to oppose them, the radical Puritans found the king guilty of treason. Charles I was beheaded on January 1, 1649. Parliament, or the few members who remained, declared that the monarchy was over and that England was a republic.

From Commonwealth to Protectorate

The monarchy was gone, but what would replace it? Oliver Cromwell became leader of the new English Commonwealth, as the new government was called. Cromwell, ruling with the radicals left in Parliament, faced the hopeless task of uniting a nation divided not into two but numerous factions. Many subjects had turned against Parliament after the execution of Charles I. A popular poem of the time lamented:

> On Tuesday last his Grace,
> Cheerfully, cheerfully,
> Went to his dying place,
> to end all strife,
> Where many a weeping eye,
> With groans unto the skie,
> To see his Majesty,
> There end his life.

Discontent among the English people was fueled by the severe policies of the Puritans. They outlawed gambling, horse racing, newspapers, fancy clothes, public dancing, and theater. Cromwell faced perils from outside England, too. In Scotland, rebels rallied to Charles II, son of the executed king. In Ireland, Catholics had risen against Protestant landowners. Cromwell himself led the force that savagely repressed that rebellion. In addition, England was at war against Spain and Holland.

These disorders forced Cromwell to give up even the pretense of republican government. In 1653, he dissolved Parliament and named himself Lord Protector. He ruled as a virtual dictator until his death in 1658, when his son became Lord Protector. By then the English people were thoroughly sick of the endless taxations, violence, and disorder. Parliament reconvened and asked Charles II to become king. In 1660, the monarchy was restored. Though Cromwell inspired as much fear and hatred as love and reverence, he always remained true to his own high moral purposes. The measures he resorted to as ruler of England were stern and painful, yet they were probably necessary to achieve order in such a troubled, disorderly period of English history.

LITERATURE OF A TURBULENT AGE

The reign of Charles I and the Interregnum, or period between reigns, that followed were a time of intense religious and political conflict. Under Charles I, the court remained the center of literary life. Poets upheld the traditional courtly values of loyalty to crown and church and the strict code of honor. Not surprisingly, the poets often fought on the side of the king.

The literature of the turbulent years from 1625 to 1660 in part continues the styles of the Renaissance and in part reflects changing conditions. Although Ben Jonson and others wrote plays that were more popular than Shakespeare's, the period is not remembered for its drama. Rather, it is an age that produced some of the best-loved poems in English—Jonson's crystalline lyrics and digni-

5

Fine art, *Oliver Cromwell,* by Sir Peter Lely. Peter Lely was a Flemish school portrait painter. Upon arriving in England, he studied the paintings of Van Dyck (who had just died), and his earlier portraits often approach the great master's style. During the Civil War, Lely received portrait commissions from members of both political parties.

Oliver Cromwell (1599 –1658), the powerful military leader, foe of Charles I, and "Lord Protector" of Britain, headed a virtual dictatorship under a constitution drafted by officers of the army. Lely painted this portrait showing Cromwell in military garb, but not with the sternness and implacability often associated with him. During the period known as the Restoration, Charles II knighted Lely and appointed him court painter.

OLIVER CROMWELL
Sir Peter Lely (Peter Van Der Faes)
Firenze, Galleria Palatina
Art Resource

fied longer poems modeled after classical precedents; John Donne's brilliant, intellectually ingenious amorous and religious verses; and Andrew Marvell's lyrics combining the classical polish of Jonson and the intellectual brilliance of Donne. Appropriate to a society cleft by civil war, the literature of the age had another side. The Puritan writers John Milton and John Bunyan produced deeply religious works very much different in style and substance from those of Jonson, Donne, and their followers.

Jonson's Life

The most influential writer of the early 1600s was Ben Jonson. Jonson's life is a mirror of the tensions of his time. Jonson rose from humble origins—his stepfather was a bricklayer. The family lived near Westminster Abbey, however, and Jonson was lucky enough to attend its school. There he read the Greek and Latin authors that shaped so much of his own later writing. Although he hoped to attend college, the young Jonson found himself laying bricks. But he refused to give up his ambitions. One friend described him as having "a trowel in his hand . . . and a book in his pocket."

Jonson set down his trowel to become a soldier, and later turned up as an actor in London. One of his earliest works, a satirical play, was condemned as slanderous and landed Jonson in jail. A later play was well received, but Jonson had little chance to bask in the praise. He argued with an actor, killed him in a duel, and was once again imprisoned. There Jonson converted to Catholicism, though he later returned to the Anglican church—another sign of the changeable times he lived in.

Ultimately, Jonson became a great favorite of James I and was friendly with many noblemen and with other writers—including Shakespeare, who acted in one of Jonson's earliest plays and is the subject of one of his finest poems. By the 1620s Jonson was the best-known poet in a city of poets. As one admirer said, Jonson was the "fairest light in no darke time."

THE SCHOOLS OF JONSON AND DONNE

Jonson's Work

6   In Jonson's life we can see the turmoil of his age—violence, persecution, religious conflict. But in his writing Jonson strove for the perfection and harmony he found in his beloved classical authors, turning away from the ornate style of Elizabethan times. Although Jonson was steeped in, and greatly influenced by, the classics, he was not an imitator. He created his own voice, which people of the time recognized as distinctively modern and strong.

7   Jonson took seriously the role of poet. He believed, in fact, that no other profession could compare to it. Poets, he wrote, encourage "young men to all good disciplines, inflame grown men to all great virtues, [and] keep old men in their best and supreme state." A person could not be "the good poet without first being a good man," he asserted. Jonson lived up to this moral duty in several ways: by giving good advice in some poems; by honoring worthy men and women in others; and, in his plays, by satirizing corruption and immorality.

The School of Donne

The other great poet of the early 1600's was John Donne (1572?–1631). Whereas Jonson did all he could to raise the prestige of poets, and personally oversaw the printing of his poems, Donne

BEN JONSON
The Granger Collection

Humanities Note

Fine art, *Ben Jonson.* Portraiture was the most common and respected form of art in the seventeenth century. The sober, restrained style of this portrait of Ben Jonson reflects the artistic trends following the Reformation and the strength of Protestant, and particularly Puritan, beliefs in the country.

6 **Literary Movement** This classical clarity is evident in the lyrics "On My First Son," page 424; "Song to Celia," page 425; and "Still to Be Neat," page 426.

7 **Enrichment** Jonson's plays *Volpone* and *The Alchemist,* for example, both satirize avarice.

never tried to make writing a career. His poems, in fact, were not published until two years after his death. But manuscripts of his work circulated at court, and his witty, cerebral poems created a widely admired style in English literature: metaphysical poetry.

Donne's life, like Jonson's, reflected his turbulent age. Donne was raised a Roman Catholic. After studying at Oxford, he traveled abroad, fighting against the Spanish in the 1590's. As a young man, Donne took an active part in the life of the court and composed many fine love poems. (According to Ben Jonson, Donne wrote "all his best pieces ere he was twenty-five.") Later, Donne turned to the Protestant faith. In 1615, he was ordained as an Anglican minister. His sermons in St. Paul's Cathedral, which often lasted for hours, held hundreds of listeners at rapt attention. They are among the finest prose works of the century. After the death of his wife, Donne withdrew from society. In contrast to the fervent love poems of his youth, Donne's later poetry expresses intense religious feeling, often penitential in character. Given Donne's evolution from courtier to minister, it is not surprising that his poetry often embodies the conflict between the spirit and the world.

More than any other poet, Donne is associated with the metaphysical school of poetry. Metaphysical poetry is characterized by an unusual degree of intellectualism. Even in his love poems, Donne will base his images and figures of speech on material drawn from law, medieval theology and philosophy, natural science, metalurgy, medicine, astronomy, old legends, and other sources that more conventional poets seldom make use of. Moreover, Donne's poems are frequently structured like ingenious, subtle arguments involving complicated—and often witty—reasoning. Finally, they often employ a type of metaphor termed a *conceit*. A conceit is a comparison in which the subject is likened to something that would never normally be associated with it. In Donne's most famous conceit, for example, he likens his and his beloved's souls to the legs of a geometrician's compass:

> If they be two, they are two so
>   As stiff twin compasses are two;
> Thy soul, the fixed foot, makes no show
>   To move, but doth if the other do.
>
> And though it in the center sit,
>   Yet, when the other far doth roam,
> It leans and hearkens after it,
>   And grows erect as that comes home.

The Sons of Ben

Jonson and Donne were the dominant poets of their age. Later poets of the seventeenth century are usually classified as being

JOHN DONNE
The Granger Collection

disciples of either Jonson or Donne. Like all such categorizations, these are only partly correct. The "Sons of Ben" were influenced by Donne's work, and the "School of Donne" read and admired Ben Jonson. The basic distinction is useful nonetheless.

Among the best-known sons of Ben were Robert Herrick, Sir John Suckling, and Richard Lovelace. These Sons of Ben are also called Cavalier poets, since they are identified with the king's cause. Robert Herrick (1591–1674) was probably closest to Jonson in style and temperament. Although he lived through the Civil War and Interregnum, Herrick's poetry gives little evidence of these worldly disturbances. He concentrated instead on things that could not be touched by war: "I sing of Brooks, of Blossomes, Birds, and Bow-

11

Introduction 385

12 **Literary Movement** Both "The Constant Lover," page 436, and "Song," page 437, echo an attitude prevalent among the Cavalier poets: cynicism about love.

13 **Master Teacher Note** To dramatize the diametrically different attitudes toward love of the Elizabethans and the Cavaliers, you might ask students to compare "The Constant Lover," page 436, with Shakespeare's Sonnet 116, page 258.

14 **Literary Movement** See "To Lucasta, on Going to the Wars," page 438, and "To Althea, from Prison," page 439, both of which voice these views.

15 **Literary Movement** Herbert's "Man," page 413, contains a number of conceits, as do "Virtue," page 410, and "Easter Wings," page 412, to a lesser degree.

16 **Enrichment** T.S. Eliot showed his great admiration for "To His Coy Mistress," page 418, by quoting and paraphrasing passages from it in both "The Love Song of J. Alfred Prufrock" and "The Waste Land." Marvell's poem is another example of the *carpe diem* tradition.

ers; /Of April, May, of June and July-Flowers." Herrick, who became an Anglican minister, also wrote graceful religious poems.

Sir John Suckling (1609–1642), an admirer of Jonson's style but not of his moral severity, was also influenced by Donne's early love poems. Suckling, the perfect courtier, was everything the Puritans despised. A gambler, cardsharp, and pleasure seeker, he is remembered today for his love poems. In 1639, Suckling marched north with Charles I to put down the Scottish rebellion. He fled England two years later after becoming involved in a political intrigue and died in France at a young age.

Richard Lovelace (1618–1656?) was, like Suckling, a luminary of Charles I's court. A strikingly handsome man, Lovelace wrote about themes near the heart of the Cavaliers: honor, bravery, true love, and stoical resolve. Lovelace also fought for the king's cause and went to prison for it. It was there that he wrote many of his finest poems.

The School of Donne

The most notable followers of John Donne were George Herbert (1593–1633) and Andrew Marvell (1621–1678). Herbert's mother was a friend of Donne's, and in many ways the life of Herbert parallels Donne's. He keenly felt the tension between religious and worldly drives. At first intending to enter the church, Herbert was tempted for a time to enjoy the sparkling life at the court of James I. Later Herbert became an Anglican deacon and gave himself to the care of his parish. Like Donne, Herbert excelled at the conceit and the other stylistic features of metaphysical poetry. However, Herbert's best poems are almost all religious lyrics. When read together, in his volume *The Temple*, they reveal a greater range of religious feelings than are found in Donne's religious verse.

Andrew Marvell was born later than the other metaphysical and Cavalier poets and is in many ways a figure of transition. Marvell was still a young man when the Civil War began and had little connection with the court. In fact, for three years Marvell tutored the daughter of a Puritan leader. Later Marvell became the assistant of John Milton, the greatest of the Puritan poets. When the monarchy was restored in 1660, Marvell used his influence at court to prevent Milton's execution for treason.

Marvell's best lyrics blend the metaphysical brilliance of Donne and Herbert and the classical finish of Jonson and Herrick. They offer observations on nature, love, and God that, at first, seem urbane and conventional but, on closer inspection, prove profound and problematical. His best-known poem, "To His Coy Mistress," is one of the very best lyrics in English literature.

GEORGE HERBERT
The Granger Collection

THE PURITAN WRITERS

So far we have been looking at poets connected with the court of the Stuarts. But perhaps the greatest poet of the seventeenth century was a Puritan, not a Cavalier: John Milton. The Puritan movement also produced the best-selling prose writer of the century, John Bunyan. Only the Bible sold more copies than Bunyan's religious narrative *The Pilgrim's Progress*.

John Milton

In John Milton (1608–1674) the streams of the Renaissance and the Reformation flow together. Like Ben Jonson, he was a learned disciple of the Greek and Latin authors. But unlike Elizabethan humanists and the Cavalier poets, Milton was a profound Calvinist who studied the Old Testament in Hebrew.

17 Literary Movement See Milton's sonnet "When I Consider How My Light Is Spent," page 444.

18 Enrichment When Bunyan went to prison for refusing to refrain from preaching Puritan doctrine, he took two books with him: Foxe's *Book of Martyrs* and the Bible. They provided his inspiration for *The Pilgrim's Progress.*

19 Literary Movement An excerpt from *The Pilgrim's Progress* begins on page 462.

Check Test

1. The English subjects most angry at Charles I were the _____ .

2. After King Charles I was killed, _____ became the leader of the new English Commonwealth.

3. The two greatest poets of the early 1600's were _____ and _____ .

4. John Milton was strongly influenced by the intellectual currents of the Renaissance and the religious movement known as the _____ .

5. John Bunyan's allegory, entitled _____ , tells about a man who flees sin to lead a holy life.

ANSWERS

1. Puritans
2. Oliver Cromwell
3. Ben Jonson and John Donne
4. Reformation
5. *The Pilgrim's Progress*

Milton was born in London to a prosperous middle-class family. He got a good basic education, studied at Cambridge, and spent six years after college reading and studying on his own. In the 1640's, Milton was working as a private tutor in London. As the battle between Charles I and Parliament grew hotter, Milton began writing political pamphlets for the Roundhead cause. His part in the "pamphlet wars" produced *Areopagitica,* a ringing call for freedom of the press.

Milton supported the Commonwealth and Protectorate and even defended the execution of Charles I. As Cromwell's rule turned to a dictatorship, however, Milton lost hope in the possibility of forming a just society on earth. Milton, who went completely blind by 1652, set about composing an epic that would offer a poetic explanation as to why God allows suffering and unhappiness in this world.

Paradise Lost, published in 1667, reflects Milton's humanistic love of poetry and his Puritan devotion to God. In Book I of *Paradise Lost,* Milton voices his poetic ambition: to create "things unattempted yet in Prose or Rhyme." A few lines later he asserts his religious aim: to "justify the ways of God to men." The poem is both a heroic epic that recounts the expulsion of Adam and Eve from Eden and a vindication of God's wisdom.

John Bunyan

After decades of political activity, Milton concluded that the best humans could hope for was to lead their individual lives blamelessly. That was the premise that John Bunyan began with. Unlike Milton, Bunyan had little education beyond reading the Bible, but what his reading and studies lacked in variety they made up for in profundity. A tinker by trade, Bunyan wandered from town to town in rural England, preaching wherever people would listen. After the restoration of Charles II, Bunyan was imprisoned, and it was there he wrote *The Pilgrim's Progress.*

The simplicity of the work in form and style was no small factor in its success. The allegory tells the story of a man who flees sin to lead a holy life. In his "apology" for the work Bunyan tells his readers:

This book will make a traveller of thee,
If by its counsel thou wilt ruled be;
It will direct thee to the Holy Land,
If thou wilt its directions understand.

Bunyan and Milton produced the greatest literary works of the Puritan revolution. The Commonwealth had failed, but left behind a new culture that was neither courtly nor Puritan. The next age would belong to professional writers, journalists, and playwrights, not to courtly poets or Puritan proselytizers. The revolution that had begun in the mid-seventeenth century would continue in the eighteenth.

ENGLISH VOICES
Quotations by Prominent Figures of the Period

No man is an Island, entire of itself; . . . any man's death diminishes me, because I am involved in Mankind; and therefore never send to know for whom the bell tolls; it tolls for thee.
> **John Donne,** "Meditation XVII"

Art hath an enemy called Ignorance.
> **Ben Jonson,** "Every Man Out of His Humor"

Drink to me only with thine eyes
And I will pledge with mine.
> **Ben Jonson,** "To Celia"

Gather ye rosebuds while ye may,
Old Time is still a-flying.
> **Robert Herrick,** "To the Virgins, to Make Much of Time"

They also serve who only stand and wait.
> **John Milton,** "Sonnet: On His Blindness"

But at my back I always hear
Time's winged chariot hurrying near.
> **Andrew Marvell,** "To His Coy Mistress"

I have laid aside business, and gone a-fishing.
> **Izaak Walton,** *The Compleat Angler*

Stone walls do not a prison make,
Nor iron bars a cage.
> **Richard Lovelace,** "To Althea, from Prison"

Additional Voices

Twice or thrice had I loved thee,
Before I knew thy face or name;
So in a voice, so in a shapeless flame,
Angels affect us oft, and worshipped be.
> **John Donne,** "Air and Angels"

At the round earth's imagined corners, blow
Your trumpets, angels; and arise, arise
From death, you numberless infinities
Of souls, and to your scattered bodies go.
> **John Donne,** "Holy Sonnet 7"

Love bade me welcome: yet my soul drew back,
Guilty of dust and sin.
But quick-eyed Love, observing me grow slack
From my first entrance in,
Drew nearer to me, sweetly questioning
If I lacked anything.
> **George Herbert,** "Love (III)"

I saw eternity the other night
Like a great ring of pure and endless light,
All calm as it was bright;
And round beneath it, Time, in hours, days, years,
Driven by the spheres,
Like a vast shadow moved, in which the world
And all her train were hurled.
> **Henry Vaughan,** "The World"

What wondrous life is this I lead!
Ripe apples drop about my head;
The luscious clusters of the vine
Upon my mouth do crush their wine;
The nectarine and curious peach
Into my hands themselves do reach;
Stumbling on melons, as I pass,
Insnared with flowers, I fall on grass.
> **Andrew Marvell,** "The Garden"

Reading Critically The purpose of this page is to guide students in the critical reading of seventeenth century English literature. The information offered here will allow students to place a work of literature in its historical context, identify literary movements of the time, and appreciate the techniques used by writers of the period.

As you discuss the information on the page with the class, explain that the poem "To the Memory of My Beloved Master, William Shakespeare" by Ben Jonson beginning on page 391, is a model for reading critically. The side columns contain notes that draw students' attention to elements that reflect the historical context, the influence of the literary movements, and the writer's techniques.

To give students further practice with the process of reading critically, use the selection in the Teaching Portfolio, "Bermudas," by Andrew Marvell, on page 377 which students can annotate themselves. Encourage students to use these strategies as they read the literature in this unit.

Teaching to Ability Levels For less advanced students, you might review any difficult vocabulary words with the class before reading. Also, summarize the poem for the class before they read. More advanced students might appreciate reading the poem aloud.

READING CRITICALLY

The Literature of 1625–1660

When you read literature, it is important to place it in its historical context. Doing so will help you to understand influences on the writer's ideas and techniques.

Historical Context

During the years from 1625 to 1660, England suffered from tremendous political and religious unrest. Shortly after Charles I inherited the throne in 1625, he became involved in a power struggle with the Parliament, whose members strongly objected to his efforts to limit Parliamentary authority. Charles I's continuing suppression of Puritans also aroused a great deal of anger among certain members of the Parliament, many of whom were Puritans. This controversy resulted in a civil war that began in 1642 and brought about the temporary downfall of the monarchy in 1649. Oliver Cromwell, a Puritan member of Parliament, ruled the nation for nine years before dying in 1658 and leaving the country in the hands of his son, Richard. Richard proved to be an ineffective ruler, however, and in 1660 the monarchy was restored.

Literary Movements

The writers from this period can be divided essentially into two groups: the metaphysical poets and the Sons of Ben. A group consisting of John Donne and several of his followers, the metaphysical poets are known for their intellectual verse filled with complex, elaborate, and striking comparisons. In contrast, the Sons of Ben, led by the influential poet Ben Jonson, are known for their precise, witty, and elegant poetry. However, John Milton, probably the most significant writer of the period, did not fit into either of these categories. Drawing upon a variety of literary traditions, Milton produced a range of different types of works.

Writers' Techniques

Among the metaphysical poets, the conceit, an especially striking type of metaphor, was a popular literary device. Influenced by the works of the ancient Greeks and Romans, the Sons of Ben relied on classical poetic forms and often used allusions in their works. Milton, on the other hand, made extensive use of both metaphors and allusions.

On the following pages is a poem by Ben Jonson. The notes in the side column should help you to place the poem in its historical context.

Objectives

1 To analyze allusions
2 To analyze the effect of allusions
3 To write an informal letter offering an opinion

Support Material

Teaching Portfolio
Teacher Backup, p. 373
Reading Critically, "Bermudas," p. 377
Usage and Mechanics Worksheet, p. 378
Analyzing Literature Worksheet, *Understanding Allusions*, p. 380

Language Worksheet, *Tracing Word Origins*, p. 381
Selection Test, p. 382

To the Memory of My Beloved Master, William Shakespeare

Ben Jonson

To draw no envy, Shakespeare, on thy name,
Am I thus ample[1] to thy book and fame:
While I confess thy writings to be such
As neither man nor Muse can praise too much.
5 'Tis true, and all men's suffrage.[2] But these ways
Were not the paths I meant unto thy praise:
For silliest[3] ignorance on these may light,
Which, when it sounds at best, but echoes right;
Or blind affection,[4] which doth ne'er advance
10 The truth, but gropes, and urgeth all by chance;
Or crafty malice, might pretend this praise,
And think to ruin, where it seemed to raise . . .
But thou art proof against them, and indeed
Above the ill fortune of them, or the need.
15 I, therefore will begin. Soul of the age!
The applause! delight! the wonder of our stage!
My Shakespeare, rise; I will not lodge thee by
Chaucer, or Spenser, or bid Beaumont[5] lie
A little further, to make thee a room:
20 Thou art a monument, without a tomb,
And art alive still, while thy book doth live,
And we have wits to read, and praise to give.

Historical Context: This poem first appeared in the opening pages of the first edition of Shakespeare's collected plays, published in 1623.

Literary Movement: Jonson stresses a rational, intellectual examination of Shakespeare's achievements.

Writer's Technique: Jonson uses apostrophe, directly addressing Shakespeare in the poem.

Literary Movement: Jonson uses the type of strong and elegant yet simple and precise language that characterized the poetry of the Sons of Ben.

---

1. ample: Liberal.
2. suffrage: Agreement.
3. silliest: Simplest.
4. blind affection: Prejudice.
5. Beaumont: Francis Beaumont (1584–1616), a playwright who was one of Shakespeare's contemporaries. Chaucer, Spenser, and Beaumont were buried in Westminster Abbey; Shakespeare was buried in Stratford. Jonson believes that it is proper for Shakespeare to be buried apart from these other important writers.

Presentation

Motivation for Reading Imagine that you were given the assignment of writing an introduction to a collection of Shakespeare's plays. What would you say about them? In what literary form would you choose to write? Ben Jonson, a follower of Shakespeare, was in that position. He wrote a poem.

Purpose-Setting Question Jonson was not only a poet but also a playwright. This introduction seems particularly generous because Shakespeare's plays were competing with and receiving more acclaim than Jonson's. What does this praise of Shakespeare indicate about Jonson's character?

Enrichment A close intimacy sprang up between Shakespeare and Jonson. Together they drew a great circle of friends around them. The company often met at the Mermaid Tavern, which boasted about entertaining "the tribe of Ben."

Clarification In line 19, Jonson is referring to the south transept of Westminster Abbey, the Poets' Corner. Many of England's greatest poets are buried there; among them Geoffrey Chaucer, Edmund Spenser, John Dryden, Thomas Gray, Alfred Tennyson, and Robert Browning. Nearby lie the men of letters.

Fine art, *Shakespeare and Ben Jonson at Chess*, 1603, attributed to Karel von Mander. Von Mander (1548-1606) was a well-known Dutch painter of portraits and historical subjects. Although Shakespeare and Ben Jonson could have been models for this painting, it is doubtful that they posed for it. The painting is more likely the artist's conception of the scene. The simple composition in pleasant, earthy tones is accented in white. The light source from above highlights the men's features and the game. This portrait of William Shakespeare (left) and Ben Jonson (right) companionably holding a chessboard at their knees gives a unique glimpse into the friendship they shared.

You might ask students these questions:
1. What might have prompted the artist to paint this scene?
2. What does this scene suggest about the relationship between Shakespeare and Ben Jonson?
3. What seems to be the attitude of the painter toward the two writers?

SHAKESPEARE AND BEN JONSON AT CHESS
Karel van Mander

Writer's Technique:
Jonson uses regular rhyme and rhythm throughout the poem.

That I not mix thee so, my brain excuses,
I mean with great, but disproportioned[6] Muses;
25 For, if I thought my judgment were of years,
I should commit thee surely with thy peers,
And tell, how far thou didst our Lyly outshine,
Or sporting Kyd, or Marlowe's[7] mighty line.

Writer's Technique:
Jonson alludes to classical Greek and Roman tragic playwrights.

And though thou hadst small[8] Latin, and less Greek,
30 From thence to honor thee, I would not seek
For names; but call forth thund'ring Aeschylus,
Euripides, and Sophocles to us,
Paccuvius, Accius,[9] him of Cordova dead,[10]
To life again, to hear thy buskin[11] tread,
35 And shake a stage: Or, when thy socks[12] were on,

---

6. disproportioned: Not comparable.
7. Lyly . . . Kyd . . . Marlowe: Elizabethan playwrights who influenced Shakespeare.
8. small: A limited knowledge of.
9. Aeschylus (es′ kɔ ləs), **Euripides** (yoo rip′ ə dēz′) **. . . Sophocles** (sof′ ə klēz′) **. . . Paccuvius** (pə kōo′ vē əs), **Accius** (ak′ ē əs): Classical Greek and Roman tragic playwrights.
10. him . . . dead: Classical Roman playwright, Seneca, born in Cordova, Spain.
11. buskin: Symbolizes tragedy. Tragic actors wore shoes with thick ''buckskin'' soles.
12. socks: Symbolize comedy. Comic actors wore thin-soled shoes called ''socks.''

Leave thee alone, for the comparison
Of all, that insolent Greece, or haughty Rome
Sent forth, or since did from their ashes come.
Triumph, my Britain, thou hast one to show,
40 To whom all scenes[13] of Europe homage owe.
He was not of an age, but for all time!
And all the Muses still were in their prime,
When like Apollo[14] he came forth to warm
Our ears, or like a Mercury[15] to charm!
45 Nature herself was proud of his designs,
And joyed to wear the dressing of his lines!
Which were so richly spun, and woven so fit,[16]
As, since, she will vouchsafe no other wit.
The merry Greek, tart Aristophanes,
50 Neat Terence, witty Plautus,[17] now not please,
But antiquated, and deserted lie
As they were not of Nature's family.
Yet must I not give Nature all; thy art,
My gentle Shakespeare, must enjoy a part.
55 For though the poet's matter nature be,
His art doth give the fashion.[18] And, that he
Who casts[19] to write a living line, must sweat,
(Such as thine are) and strike the second heat
Upon the Muse's anvil; turn the same,
60 (And himself with it) that he thinks to frame,
Or for the laurel[20] he may gain a scorn;
For a good poet's made, as well as born.
And such wert thou. Look how the father's face
Lives in his issue, even so, the race
65 Of Shakespeare's mind, and manners brightly shines
In his well torned, and true filèd[21] lines;
In each of which, he seems to shake a lance,[22]
As brandished at the eyes of ignorance.

Writer's Technique:
Jonson alludes to figures from Greek and Roman mythology.

Writer's Technique:
Jonson alludes to classical Greek and Roman comic dramatists. Jonson's frequent use of allusions to classical Greece and Rome reflects the influence of classical writing and ideas on his work.

Writer's Technique:
Jonson uses the work of a blacksmith as a metaphor for the tasks of a poet.

Literary Movement:
Jonson stresses the importance of education and hard work in shaping a poet's talent.

---

13. **scenes:** Stages.
14. **Apollo:** In Greek and Roman mythology, the god of light, music, and poetry.
15. **Mercury:** In Roman mythology, the messenger of the gods and the god of cleverness.
16. **fit:** Appropriately.
17. **Aristophanes** (ar′ is tof′ ə nēz′) **. . . Terence** (ter′ əns) **. . . Plautus** (plô′ təs): Classical Greek and Roman comic playwrights.
18. **fashion:** Form.
19. **casts:** Undertakes.
20. **laurel:** Fame.
21. **true filèd:** Accurately polished.
22. **shake a lance:** A pun on Shakespeare's name.

To the Memory of My Beloved Master, William Shakespeare 393

Enrichment Elaborately turned, polite compliments characterize certain kinds of poetry in the seventeenth century. Wit was more prevalent in serious poetry than it is today. Lines 64-66 contain an example of a witty compliment.

Master Teacher Note It is fairly well established that Shakespeare acted in Jonson's play *Every Man in His Humor.* Some have suggested that Shakespeare's portrait in the 1623 folio shows him in the part of Old Knowell.

For Further Study Biographical information on Jonson appears on page 422, and other poems by him are on pages 424-426.

Closure and Extension

ANSWERS TO THINKING ABOUT THE SELECTION
Recalling

1. The wrong reasons for praising Shakespeare are simple ignorance which will make the praise sound empty, affectionate prejudice which will disregard the truth, or malice which would attempt to ruin while pretending to flatter.
2. Since Shakespeare's death, the stage has mourned and despaired.

Interpreting

3. Jonson suggests that Shakespeare's genius is universal; his works will have meaning throughout time.
4. Jonson is comparing the effort of writing to a blacksmith's forging iron. Like a blacksmith, a writer must work and rework a line until it is right.
5. (a) The poem reveals Jonson's great admiration and respect for Shakespeare. (b) To Jonson, writing is difficult. Although one may have a talent, it must be shaped and disciplined by hard work and "sweat."
6. (a) By understanding the greatness of the playwrights or the characteristics of the gods in the allusions, the reader can recognize how great Jonson feels Shakespeare actually is.
7. Jonson's allusions imply his thorough knowledge of classical literature and his belief that this literature represents the standard by which later writers may be judged.

Applying

8. Answers will differ. Suggested Response: A writer can be immortalized because his or her ideas live on in the works. Future generations will have the opportunity to explore a writer's opinions and thoughts, thus keeping alive aspects of the writer.

Sweet swan of Avon![23] what a sight it were
70 To see thee in our waters yet appear,
And make those flights upon the banks of Thames
That so did take Eliza and our James![24]
But stay, I see thee in the hemisphere
Advanced, and made a constellation there!
75 Shine forth, thou star of poets, and with rage[25]
Or influence, chide, or cheer the drooping stage,
Which, since thy flight from hence, hath mourned like night,
And despairs day, but for thy volume's light.

Historical Context: Jonson refers to Queen Elizabeth I and King James I, who encouraged and supported Shakespeare and other writers.

---

23. Avon: The river on which Shakespeare's home town, Stratford, is located.
24. Eliza . . . James: Queen Elizabeth I and King James I.
25. rage: Poetic inspiration.

THINKING ABOUT THE SELECTION
Recalling

1. According to lines 1–12, what are the wrong reasons for praising Shakespeare?
2. According to the final two lines, how has the stage reacted since Shakespeare's death?

Interpreting

3. What does Jonson mean when he comments that Shakespeare was "not of an age, but for all time"?
4. What is the meaning of the metaphor in lines 57–59?
5. (a) What does this poem reveal about Jonson's attitude toward Shakespeare? (b) What does it reveal about his attitudes concerning the art of writing?
6. (a) How does your awareness of the meaning of the allusions contribute to your overall understanding of Jonson's poem? (b) How does Jonson's use of allusions help to give you a sense of Shakespeare's place in literary history?

7. How do Jonson's allusions reflect his interest in classical Greek and Roman literature?

Applying

8. In this poem, Jonson expresses the idea that a writer can be immortalized through his or her work. Explain whether you agree with this suggestion.

THINKING AND WRITING
Writing a Letter

Write a letter to Ben Jonson in which you tell him whether you agree with the attitudes he expresses concerning Shakespeare and the art of writing. Reread the poem, focusing on Jonson's attitudes. Brainstorm about your own attitudes on these subjects. Then express your opinions in a personal letter. Use an informal, conversational writing style, but be sure to support your opinions. When you revise, make sure you have not included any unnecessary information. Proofread your letter and prepare a final draft.

394   *The Seventeenth Century*

THINKING AND WRITING

Publishing Student Writing
Read a few letters to the class. Ask the class to respond to the criticism. Determine the class's consensus on Jonson's opinion about Shakespeare and about writing.

The Schools of Donne and Jonson

GREENWICH PALACE FROM THE NORTHEAST WITH A MAN-OF-WAR AT ANCHOR (detail) *c.* 1630
National Maritime Museum

Humanities Note

Fine art, *Greenwich Palace from the Northeast with a Man-of-War at Anchor,* c. 1630. The influence of the Dutch landscape painters is evident in dark and somber coloring of this painting by an unknown artist. The peaceful mood reflects the pride and security the English navy provided for the nation during this time. The navy was among the strongest in the world. It enabled the English to expand its territories abroad. The prominent position of the flag reflects the pride and patriotism associated with the navy, despite the political and religious turmoil in the country.

More About the Author Although a great church man, John Donne was known in his youth for his love poems, which were circulated in manuscript but were not published until years later. Donne's love poetry is more intimate and personal than that of his predecessors. This song is a farewell, or valedictory, poem, written on the occasion of an impending departure from his wife. Ask students to consider the feelings husband and wife might have as they anticipate the separation. What might be their concerns?

Critical Evaluation Reflecting on the influence of Donne's poetry, the scholar Douglas Bush remarked that "The revival of Donne and other 'metaphysical' poets has of course, been a main movement of our time; quickening in the 1890's and proceeding slowly, it came to a rather sudden peak in the third decade of this century, the period after the First World War. It not only brought a relatively neglected body of writing into active life but strongly affected modern poetry and criticism and indeed altered the whole contour map of English poetry of the last three centuries and a half. Metaphysical poetry, or simply Donne, became for a time the virtual criterion of all good poetry."

JOHN DONNE

1572(?)–1631

John Donne's reputation has changed over time. He was very popular during his own lifetime, but his writings went out of favor soon after his death. At the beginning of the twentieth century, however, interest in his works revived. Now Donne occupies a major position in literature. Modern critics place him with William Shakespeare and John Milton at the very pinnacle of English poetry.

Donne was raised by his widowed mother, who was a devout Catholic and a member of the family of St. Thomas More. At the time, being Catholic was difficult, for Roman Catholics were severely discriminated against in Queen Elizabeth's England. Indeed, Donne later recanted his Catholicism and joined the Anglican Church. Scholars are divided as to his motives. They wonder whether he experienced a genuine conversion or made a shrewd move to try to gain advancement in courtly society.

Donne's life is generally described as falling into two parts. The first is often thought of as the "wild youth of Jack Donne, ambitious man about town." Bright, clever, and charming, Donne was welcomed into the most exclusive courtly circles and served as private secretary to one of the Queen's highest-ranking officials. He was so charming that he wooed and won the hand in marriage of Anne More, his employer's niece.

As with his religious conversion, some scholars have questioned Donne's motives. Cynics thought that through this marriage Donne had made a shrewd move to advance his career. However, the marriage did not work out that way. Because of the opposition of Anne's father, Donne's marriage ruined his chances for advancement. As a consequence, the devoted couple and their many children experienced seventeen years of poverty, illness, and despair. During these years Donne eked out a living as a writer of religious tracts and as the temporary secretary of several aristocrats. He also became during this difficult period one of the most widely read and influential poets of the age.

Later Donne was ordained and made dean of St. Paul's Cathedral in London. He now entered the second part of his life, which has been described as the "sacred calling of Dr. John Donne, Dean of St. Paul's." From this time until his death, Donne was the most popular preacher in England; his meditations and sermons were published during his life and went through several editions.

We should not, however, emphasize too much the differences between the younger and older Donne. All of his writings, whether on love or faith, were written with the same intensity and wit.

Objectives

1　To understand paradox
2　To understand metaphysical conceits
3　To follow an argument
4　To write about a philosophical argument

Support Material

Teaching Portfolio
Teacher Backup, p. 385
Usage and Mechanics Worksheet, p. 389
Vocabulary Check, p. 390
Analyzing Literature Worksheet, *Understanding Paradox,* p. 391
Analyzing Literature, *Understanding Metaphysical Conceit,* p. 392
Selection Test, p. 393

GUIDE FOR INTERPRETING

Writer's Techniques

Song, Holy Sonnet 10, Holy Sonnet 14

Donne was a leading writer of what has come to be called *metaphysical poetry* because of its concern with philosophical and religious issues. This kind of poetry is characterized by the extensive use of paradoxes and conceits.

Paradox. In literature, a paradox is an apparent self-contradiction that reveals a kind of truth. One of the most famous literary paradoxes is present in Donne's "Holy Sonnet 14": "Take me to You, imprison me, for I, / Except You enthral me, never shall be free." Finding "freedom" in prison or in slavery would seem to many people a contradiction. But here, "prison" and "enthral" (enslave) are metaphors for submissive devotion to God, which to the deeply religious person represents true freedom.

Metaphysical Conceit. A conceit is an extended, fanciful metaphor that makes a surprising or unexpected comparison. In the sixteenth century, the Elizabethans fell in love with long, elaborate conceits, as in Sir Philip Sidney's comparison of the moon with a languishing lover in "Sonnet 31." The metaphysical poets, such as John Donne and Andrew Marvell, wrote ingenious, often shocking conceits in which very dissimilar objects are compared.

Commentary

Sir George Moore was so furious that his seventeen-year-old daughter Anne married John Donne against his wishes that he not only threw her and his son-in-law out of his home, but also convinced Lord Chancellor Egerton to fire Donne from his position as Secretary to the Great Seal and arranged to have the young poet imprisoned. Donne and his wife found sanctuary in a house in Pyrford, but near Anne's father, who lived in Surrey. Legend has it that one of the first actions Donne took upon his arrival in Pyrford was to write the following lines on a pane of glass in his new home:

> John Donne
>
> An Donne
>
> Undone.

Was Donne really "undone"? According to what he says in "Song," what did he lose—and what did he win?

Writing

Write a short composition in which you use metaphors to explain yourself. Try to convince someone of an unusual experience you have had. Find objects, ideas, or common experiences that you can compare with your own experience and explain the connections.

Vocabulary

Preteach the following vocabulary words:

divining (də vīn′ iŋ) *adj.:* Guessing; intuitive (p. 399, l. 33)

forethink (fôr think′) *v.:* Foretell; predict (p. 399, l. 34)

usurped (yo͞o sʉrp′d′) *adj.:* Wrongfully seized (p. 402, l. 5)

chaste (chãst) *adj.:* Pure; untainted; unblemished (p. 402, l. 14)

ravish (rav′ ish) *v.:* Violate; (p. 402, l. 14).

Song

John Donne

1

Sweetest love, I do not go,
    For weariness of thee,
Nor in hope the world can show
    A fitter love for me;
5   But since that I
Must die at last, 'tis best
To use[1] myself in jest,

2

    Thus by feigned[2] deaths to die.

3

Yesternight the sun went hence,
10   And yet is here today;
He hath no desire nor sense,
    Nor half so short a way;
      Then fear not me,
But believe that I shall make
15 Speedier journeys, since I take
    More wings and spurs than he.

4

O how feeble is man's power,
    That if good fortune fall,
Cannot add another hour,
20   Nor a lost hour recall!
      But come bad chance,
And we join to it our strength,
And we teach it art and length,
    Itself o'er us to advance.

5

25 When thou sigh'st, thou sigh'st not wind,
    But sigh'st my soul away;
When thou weep'st, unkindly kind,
    My life's blood doth decay.
      It cannot be
30 That thou lovest me as thou say'st,
If in thine my life thou waste,
    That art the best of me.

---

1. use: Condition.
2. feigned: Imagined.

              Let not thy divining heart
                  Forethink me any ill,
      35 Destiny may take thy part,
                  And may thy fears fulfill;
                  But think that we
              Are but turned aside to sleep.   6
              They who one another keep
      40   Alive, ne'r parted be.

THINKING ABOUT THE SELECTION
Recalling

1. What are the speaker's reasons for leaving his beloved?
2. What does the speaker say happens when "bad chance" comes (ll. 21–24)?
3. How do the beloved's sighs and tears affect the speaker?
4. How does the speaker suggest that his beloved think of their parting?

Interpreting

5. To what is the sun in stanza 2 compared?
6. Of what is the speaker trying to convince his beloved? How would you outline the speaker's argument?
7. What is the tone of the poem? Is it angry, beseeching, reassuring, uncertain, mocking?

Applying

8. The speaker in this poem resorts to exaggeration as an instrument of persuasion. Do you think that exaggerating in order to win is a valid persuasive technique? Explain your answer.

9. Although this is a love poem, it is cast in the form of an argument. Why is that appropriate?

ANALYZING LITERATURE
Understanding Paradox

A paradox is an apparent self-contradiction that reveals a truth. A very well-known one is the statement of Jesus in Matthew 16:25, "For whosoever will save his life shall lose it." A related paradox can be found in Donne's Holy Sonnet 10: ". . . poor death, nor yet canst thou kill me." In this example, the speaker says death cannot kill him because as a devout Christian he will have eternal life. Our very puzzlement adds zest to our understanding once we have figured out the meaning of the paradox, which is why religious leaders and writers so often employ them.

Donne's "Song" contains a couple of paradoxes. Explain why the following quote is a paradox, what it means, and how it works in the poem: "When thou weep'st, unkindly kind" (line 27).

Song 399

6 **Discussion** What does Donne's wife fear? What is Donne's attitude toward this fear?

Reader's Response How would you comfort a loved one you were leaving to go on a long trip?

as in this poem, exaggeration can sometimes make arguments more vivid and compelling.

9. The speaker's purpose is to persuade his beloved not to grieve over their separation.

ANSWERS TO ANALYZING LITERATURE

The speaker's wife is "kind" because she mourns his departure. But the speaker sees this grieving as actually unkind because her grieving "wastes" and weakens him. "Unkindly kind" is an oxymorom, a figure of speech that is a short, self-contradictory phrase, an abbreviated paradox.

Challenge "Song" comes full circle by returning at the end to the theme of death. Why is this structure appropriate to the theme of departure in the poem?

Speaking and Listening Although Donne is often accused of being irregular and harsh in his versification, here he has used regular, melodious meter and smooth diction. Have volunteers rehearse and then read the poem aloud. Discuss why the rhythm, structure, and diction should make the title "Song" appropriate.

Closure and Extension

ANSWERS TO THINKING ABOUT THE SELECTION
Recalling

1. He says that his departure is a preparation for his ultimate departure in death.
2. By our actions, we make misfortune worse.
3. They weaken him.
4. He asks her to think that as long as two people remember each other, they are not really parted but rather separated, as in sleep.

Interpreting

5. As the sun disappears and returns predictably each day, so too will the speaker return.
6. He asks her not to grieve over their separation by offering the following arguments: that his departure will be a rehearsal for his death; that like the sun, he will inevitably return; that his beloved's grieving weakens him; and that she should think of them as merely turned aside in sleep.
7. The tone is tender and reassuring.

Applying

8. Answers will differ. Suggested response: Although it is often tempting to exaggerate the facts of an argument, exaggeration can undermine credibility. On the other hand,

399

Presentation

Motivation for Reading Point out that John Gunther used the opening words of this sonnet as the title for his book *Death Be Not Proud* about the death of his son. Why should Gunther, like many others, have looked to this poem as a source of comfort?

Master Teacher Note Point out that, like "Song" and many of his other poems, Donne develops this sonnet through a series of discrete arguments, each developed in a separate quatrain.

Thematic Idea Other selections on death that might be compared to this sonnet are Browning's "Prospice," page 822, and Thomas's "Do Not Go Gentle into That Good Night," page 1102.

Purpose-Setting Question Why does Donne begin the poem with a challenge? How do the first four words set the tone for the rest of the poem?

1 Enrichment This sonnet begins with an apostrophe, the figure of speech in which an absent person or a personified object or quality is addressed directly.

2 Discussion How does stating that Death must be pleasurable deflate its power?

3 Literary Focus An even more vigorous attack is launched here. In what way is Death the slave of fate? of chance? of kings? of desperate men?

4 Discussion In what way does the couplet represent the climax of the poem? What is the tone of the poem? Is it somber and funereal? Or is it instead contemptuous and superior? Is the tone of the poem what you would expect in a poem on death?

Holy Sonnet 10

John Donne

1   Death be not proud, though some have called thee
Mighty and dreadful, for thou art not so;
For those whom thou think'st thou dost overthrow,
Die not, poor death, nor yet canst thou kill me.
5   From rest and sleep, which but thy pictures[1] be,
2   Much pleasure; then from thee much more must flow,
And soonest our best men with thee do go,
Rest of their bones, and soul's delivery[2]
3   Thou art slave to fate, chance, kings, and desperate men,
10   And dost with poison, war, and sickness dwell,
And poppy,[3] or charms can make us sleep as well
And better than thy stroke; why swell'st[4] thou then?
4   One short sleep past, we wake eternally,
And death shall be no more; Death, thou shalt die.

---

1. pictures: Images.
2. And . . . delivery: Our best men go with you to rest their bones and find freedom for their souls.
3. poppy: Opium.
4. swell'st: Swell with pride.

THINKING ABOUT THE SELECTION
Recalling

1. In the first four lines, why does the speaker say that death should not be proud?
2. Why does the speaker say in lines 5–8 that death is pleasant? What within these lines indicates that death is a source of pleasure?
3. How does the speaker characterize death in lines 9–12?
4. Why does the speaker say that death shall be no more?

Interpreting

5. (a) What does the speaker mean when he says in lines 3–4: "For those whom thou think'st thou dost overthrow, / Die not, poor death, nor yet canst thou kill me"? (b) In what way is this meaning reinforced by the last two lines?
6. (a) What does the paradox "Death, thou shalt die" mean? What makes it paradoxical? (b) In what way does the final paradox serve as the conclusion to the argument of the poem?

Applying

7. In the poem, the speaker gives human characteristics to death. This is called *personification*. Death has often been personified in art and literature, sometimes as the grim reaper carrying a scythe, at other times as an angel with black wings and a net, and at still other

Reader's Response Did you find this poem comforting? Why or why not?

Closure and Extension

ANSWERS TO THINKING ABOUT THE SELECTION
Recalling

1. In reality Death has no power.
2. Rest and sleep are pleasant, and since death resembles a deep sleep, it must be even more pleasant. Death rests the body and delivers the soul to heaven.
3. Death is paired with ugly and sor-

SIR THOMAS ASTON AT THE DEATHBED OF HIS WIFE
John Souch
Manchester City Art Galleries

Humanities Note

Fine art, *Sir Thomas Aston at the Deathbed of His Wife,* by John Souch. Souch was a British portrait painter who was active from 1617 to 1636. He gained his training as a painter during an apprenticeship under a painter of heraldry, (coats of arms), named Randle Holme.

Of the few portraits of Souch that survive, *Sir Thomas Aston at the Deathbed of His Wife,* is the most important. Painted in 1635, this group portrait of the high sheriff of Cheshire, Thomas Aston, and one of his children at the deathbed of his first wife, Magdalene, is interesting for Souch's use of the medieval device of portraying Lady Aston simultaneously as dead, on her deathbed, and alive, on the bottom right of the painting. The artificial pose of the figures is relieved by the concentration of skill used to paint the heads. The mood and personality of each person is captured by the artist's depiction of their countenance. The work is painted in high-gloss colors that give the jewel-like appearance of an enamelled miniature. This work was most likely commissioned as a memorial to the first Lady Aston.

You might use the following questions for discussion:
1. In what ways does this painting reflect the ideas of the sonnet?
2. What do you think the artist meant to convey by the dual portrait of Lady Aston?

times as a fierce horseman whose head is often a skull. Think of other ways you may have seen death personified in literature or art. Discuss with your classmates what each of these images implies about our attitudes toward death. How does Donne's poem address these attitudes?

ANALYZING LITERATURE
Understanding Metaphysical Conceit

The term *conceit* comes from the Italian word *concetto,* meaning "conception." Meta-physical poets often worked out complex, far-fetched conceits, and Donne's are among the best of them. Sometimes a metaphysical conceit is an elaborate image; sometimes it can be just a line or two. What is essential to all metaphysical conceits, however, is the startling conjunction of dissimilar concepts, ideas, images, or objects. The underlying conceit of Holy Sonnet 10 is the likening of death to a proud but ultimately ineffectual tyrant.
1. What are the images in the poem that illustrate the conceit?
2. How do they relate with each other to form a single image of a powerless Death?

did things.
4. We will awaken to be with God.

Interpreting

5. (a) Those whom Death thinks it has taken are really not dead. (b) The last two lines explain how this paradox can be so: the dead will awaken to eternal life.
6. (a) Death will be powerless and meaningless. The statement is paradoxical because only Death has the power to kill and thus will be killing itself. (b) The final paradox is the logical culmination of the argument promised on the Christian belief in life after death.

Applying

7. Suggested Response: Each of these images shows death as frightening and powerful. Donne shows death as pleasant (a deep sleep), powerless, and even pitiable.

ANSWERS TO ANALYZING LITERATURE

1. Death is merely a form of sleep and not even as good a form as can be gained with medication or hypnosis. Death is a "slave" since it can be summoned by anyone. Death keeps company with such unsavory elements as poison and sickness. Most important, it is only a temporary condition before entering eternal life.
2. Each image belittles death.

Challenge What does Donne gain by addressing Death directly, rather than describing it in the third person?

Presentation

Motivation for Reading Discuss with students situations where they have wanted to do, or to stop doing, something, but have been unable to do it.

Master Teacher Note Ask students what kinds and degrees of emotion they can find in the sonnet—for example, anger, guilt, and desperation. What words and passages do they find most intensely emotional? Why?

Thematic Idea Other selections that deal with man's attempt to reach God are *Everyman,* page 188, and *The Pilgrim's Progress,* page 462.

Purpose-Setting Question What is the effect of Donne's unusual reliance on action verbs in the sonnet?

1 Discussion What image is Donne suggesting with words like "batter," "shine," "bend your force," "break," "blow," and "burn"? Note that Donne sees God as a tinker, smithy, or mender of pottery and himself as a broken vessel in need of repair. Point out that there are fourteen verbs in this quatrain. What cumulative tone emerges from them? Note that the verbs are clumped in threes to further develop the triune quality of God. What is the effect of alliteration in the quatrain?

2 Discussion What image does this quatrain evoke with words like "usurped town," "viceroy," and "captived"? What tone do these words suggest? What is the soul trying to do? How is its attempt being frustrated?

3 Discussion A third image emerges here with words like "love," "betrothed," "divorce," and "knot." What is it?

4 Literary Focus This line contains the central paradox of the poem.

Holy Sonnet 14

John Donne

1   Batter my heart, three-personed God;[1] for You
  As yet but knock, breathe, shine, and seek to mend;
  That I may rise, and stand, o'erthrow me, and bend
  Your force, to break, blow, burn and make me new.

2 5 I, like an usurped town, to another due,
    Labor to admit You, but O, to no end,
  Reason Your viceroy[2] in me, me should defend,
  But is captived, and proves weak or untrue.

3   Yet dearly I love You, and would be loved fain,
 10 But am betrothed unto Your enemy.
  Divorce me, untie, or break that knot again;

4   Take me to You, imprison me, for I,
  Except You enthral[3] me, never shall be free,

5   Nor ever chaste, except You ravish me.

---

1. three-personed God: The Trinity:
the Father, the Son, and the Holy Ghost.
2. viceroy: Deputy.
3. enthral: Enslave.

Primary Source

The great critic and writer Samuel Johnson was the first to identify—and indict—the metaphysical poets. His discussion appeared in 1779 in his *Lives of the English Poets.* He explains:

"About the beginning of the seventeenth century appeared a race of writers that may be termed the metaphysical poets . . . (They) were men of learning, and to show their learning was their whole endeavor; but, unluckily resolving to show it in rhyme, instead of writing poetry, they only wrote verses, and, very often, such verses as stood the trial of the finger better than of the ear; for the modulation was so imperfect that they were only found to be verses by counting the syllables.

"Their thoughts are often new, but seldom natural; they are not obvious, but neither are they just; and the reader, far from wondering that he missed them, wonders more frequently by what perverseness of industry they were ever found. . . .

"The most heterogeneous ideas are yoked by violence together; nature and art are ransacked for illustrations, comparisons, and allusions; their learning instructs, and their subtilty surprises; but the reader commonly thinks his improvement dearly bought, and, though he sometimes admires, is seldom pleased . . .

"From this account of their compositions it will be readily inferred that they were not successful in representing or moving the affections . . . Their wish was only to say what they hoped had never been said before."

In what way can imprisonment lead to freedom?

5 Literary Focus The image of Christ as a bridegroom is traditional. Nevertheless, Donne's treatment of the image is quite startling. Why? How does it represent a culmination of the imagery elsewhere in the poem?

Reader's Response Do you think that Donne addresses God in an unusual way? Explain.

THINKING ABOUT THE SELECTION

Recalling

1. In the first four lines what does the speaker ask God to do?
2. (a) To what does the speaker compare himself in line 5? (b) Of what does the speaker complain in lines 6–8? (c) How is reason characterized in lines 7 and 8?
3. (a) How does the speaker describe his condition in lines 9 and 10? (b) What does the speaker ask God to do in lines 11–12? (c) What reason does he give for his request in lines 13–14?

Interpreting

4. In line 2 why does the speaker complain of God's gentleness? Why does the speaker want God to treat him violently?
5. What are the paradoxes in lines 3, 13, and 14? What do they mean? How do they affect you, the reader?
6. Who is the "enemy" to whom the speaker is "betrothed"?
7. What is the tone in this poem? Is it belligerent, argumentative, pleading, arrogant, or contemptuous?

Applying

8. In the poem the speaker wants to be overwhelmed with emotion. There are many instances when a person might want to experience a deep emotion. What are some of these instances?

CRITICAL THINKING AND READING

Following an Argument

Metaphysical poets were said to combine "passion with reason." Reason is the chief tool of philosophy, and arguments are the chief tools of reason. A philosophical argument—which is much different from the shouting match we usually think of—is a logical or reasonable demonstration of how certain facts or ideas can or must lead to a conclusion. When you say, "I believe such and such because of this, that, and the other," you are offering an *argument* for your beliefs.

But of course, few if any literary works display their "arguments" as nakedly as we have just done. For example, if we think of Holy Sonnet 14 as an argument—rather than as a prayer or an appeal, which is another way to view the poem—then we might ask why the speaker is saying, in effect, "God, please beat down my resistance so that I can worship you." After reflection, we might come up with the proposition: "Suffering overwhelms doubt and leads to the love of God."

Reread Holy Sonnet 14 and support the proposition with the images and metaphors of the poem. First state the proposition or thesis, then give evidence supporting the proposition. Finally restate the proposition as a conclusion in such a way as to indicate it follows from the evidence.

THINKING AND WRITING

Writing a Philosophical Argument

Take your argument—thesis or proposition, supporting evidence, and conclusion—for Donne's poem and discuss it in a 500-word composition. Make sure you express your opinion of Donne's argument. Include in your discussion evidence supporting your opinion.

Take off from Donne's poem and write your own philosophical argument. For example, Holy Sonnet 14 might suggest questions about the difficulty of making a commitment or of feeling an attachment to a transcendent or abstract idea. Freewrite, exploring your answer to this question. After you have arrived at an answer to your question, take that as your thesis or proposition. Develop supporting evidence; take into account opposing views, if there are any; answer them; and present your conclusion. When you revise, keep in mind that when writing an argumentative essay, you have to persuade your readers that your views are correct. Are your supporting details arranged so that they will have a powerful effect? Have you provided enough support? Proofread your essay and prepare a final draft.

free if God imprisons him; he can only be chaste if he is taken passionately by God. In each case he is begging God to take control of him so that he can be faithful.
6. He is "betrothed" to the devil.
7. The tone is passionately pleading and argumentative.

Applying

8. We might wish that we could return greater love to someone who loves us. We might wish that we could more fully appreciate the objects and interests that are important to the people close to us. We might wish that we could feel deeper religious faith.

ANSWER TO CRITICAL THINKING AND READING

Proposition: Suffering overwhelms doubt and leads to the love of God.

Evidence: (images of suffering) Speaker asks that God use Force to overcome doubt—"batter my heart," "bend/Your force, to break, blow, burn and make me new," "am betrothed to Your enemy," "imprison me," and "except You ravish me."

Conclusion: The speaker desires that doubt and temptation be forcibly removed so that the speaker is free to love God.

Challenge Rewrite the poem using different verbs, for example, "strike" or "hit" instead of "Batter," or "attached" instead of "betrothed," and so forth. How would the effect of the poem change?

THINKING AND WRITING

For help with this assignment, students can refer to Lesson 21, "Writing a Personal Essay," in the Handbook of Writing About Literature.

Publishing Student Writing You might read aloud several of the better arguments and use them as models for other students in revising their arguments.

Closure and Extension

ANSWERS TO THINKING ABOUT THE SELECTION

Recalling

1. He wants God to force him to have faith and thus make him new.
2. (a) He compares himself to a town that has been seized by force. (b) He complains that his reason, which should convince him to be faithful, is ineffective. (c) Reason is personified as the imprisoned deputy of God.
3. (a) He would gladly love God but is betrothed to the devil. (b) He wants God to take him by force from the devil. (c) He thinks that unless he is completely possessed by God he cannot be free of evil.

Interpreting

4. God's attempts are too weak to help the speaker attain salvation. He thinks that he can only be faithful if God forces him to have faith.
5. The speaker can only rise if God knocks him down; he can only be

GUIDE FOR INTERPRETING

Writer's Techniques

Meditation 17

Theme. The central or main idea of a literary work is its *theme*. In some works, the theme is stated directly. At the beginning of Sir Francis Bacon's "Idols of the Cave," for example, he says that prejudices derived from "education, habit, and accident" may interfere with the ability to understand things clearly. More often, though, the theme of a literary work is presented indirectly. An example of this can be found in John Donne's "Song." We can say the theme of the poem is something like: "Separation may seem like death, but it is really more like sleep, and lovers would suffer less if they viewed their separation this way."

Many works of literature have more than one theme. When they do, there is usually one dominant or controlling idea and several secondary or subordinate ones. For example, the major theme of *Macbeth* is the effects of ruthless ambition. This is not, however, the only theme in the play. To it can be added as secondary themes: cruelty by rulers causes rebellion; illegitimate power will be overthrown; and evil deeds bring their own punishment.

No matter the kind of writing, themes arise from the elements of the work. In a poem, for example, metaphor, image, and choice of words frequently develop the theme; in a play or novel, plot, character, and dialogue usually illustrate the theme; and in an essay, subordinate ideas and the ways in which language is used.

Commentary

In 1940, Ernest Hemingway sparked a run on copies of "Meditation 17" when he used a phrase from it for the title of his bestselling novel, *For Whom the Bell Tolls*. To underscore the parallel between the theme of Donne's meditation and that of his book, Hemingway also quoted a portion of the meditation on the book's inside front cover. Hemingway used the theme of Donne's "Meditation 17" as a call for personal involvement in the Spanish Civil War, the subject of his novel, and by extension, World War II.

Publishers rushed to reissue "Meditation 17." The Oxford Press, for example, reported that all its editions of Donne's poetry sold out, while "fifteen hundred sheets [of 'Meditation 17'] ordered by Random House were bombed out of existence."

What do you think there was in Donne's theme in "Meditation 17" that captured the mood of the war years?

Writing

Jot down ideas as they come to you while reading Donne's meditation. Then assign numbers to your jottings according to their importance to you. Number one will be your main theme.

Meditation 17

John Donne

Nunc lento sonitu dicunt, Morieris.

(Now, this bell tolling softly for another, says to me, Thou must die.)

Perchance he for whom this bell tolls may be so ill as that he knows not it tolls for him; and perchance I may think myself so much better than I am as that they who are about me and see my state may have caused it to toll for me, and I know not that. The church is catholic, universal, so are all her actions; all that she does belongs to all. When she baptizes a child, that action concerns me; for that child is thereby connected to that head which is my head too, and ingrafted into that body[1] whereof I am a member. And when she buries a man, that action concerns me: all mankind is of one author and is one volume; when one man dies, one chapter is not torn out of the book, but translated[2] into a better language; and every chapter must be so translated. God employs several translators; some pieces are translated by age, some by sickness, some by war, some by justice; but God's hand is in every translation, and his hand shall bind up all our scattered leaves again for that library where every book shall lie open to one another. As therefore the bell that rings to a sermon calls not upon the preacher only, but upon the congregation to come, so this bell calls us all; but how much more me, who am brought so near the door by this

1. **body:** The Church
2. **translated:** Carried across on a spiritual level from one sphere to another.

sickness. There was a contention as far as a suit[3] (in which both piety and dignity, religion and estimation,[4] were mingled) which of the religious orders should ring to prayers first in the morning; and it was determined that they should ring first that rose earliest. If we understand aright the dignity of this bell that tolls for our evening prayer, we would be glad to make it ours by rising early, in that application, that it might be ours as well as his whose indeed it is. The bell doth

3. **suit:** Lawsuit.
4. **estimation:** Self-esteem.

Presentation

Motivation for Reading Everyone at some time has contemplated his or her own death. In Holy Sonnet 10 Donne confronts the idea in a self-assured apostrophe to Death. How is his attitude toward death different now?

Master Teacher Note From what students know of Donne's poetry, ask them what they expect to find in the meditation. Answers should include a series of metaphysical conceits, paradox, and a series of arguments.

Thematic Idea Another selection in which someone contemplates his own death is Keat's "When I Have Fears that I May Cease to Be," page 719.

Purpose-Setting Question How does Donne maintain the bell motif throughout the meditation?

1 **Enrichment** The tradition of tolling the church bell to indicate a death is an old one. Students might find out where this custom originated.

2 **Literary Focus** Recall that a conceit is an extended metaphor comparing two basically dissimilar things. In this meditation, Donne uses several conceits. The first sees people as chapters in a book. What is the second? The third?

Grammar in Action

Metaphors connect dissimilar things. The implied comparison of a metaphor is striking because it declares that one thing is the other. When a metaphor is drawn to some length, it may also be called an analogy. Notice Donne's use of extended metaphor.

No man is an island, entire of itself; every man is a piece of the continent, a part of the main. If a clod be washed away by the sea, Europe is the less, as well as if a promontory were, as well as if a manor of thy friend's or of thine own were.

Donne's metaphor dramatically suggests that all people are connected, just as all clods of dirt form the continent. He further states that subtracting one clod makes Europe smaller, and implies that mankind is smaller if one person dies. He goes on to suggest that losing a clod of dirt (one small person, perhaps) is the same as losing a large finger of land (a mass of people), or a friend's house (your friend), or even your own house (or your own life). His point is emotionally appealing because he uses metaphor. To have ex-
(continued)

Enrichment The passage beginning "No man is an island" contains some of the most quoted prose in English literature. Ernest Hemingway, for example, borrowed from it his title *For Whom the Bell Tolls.*

4 **Discussion** What does Donne mean when he says that "affliction is a treasure"? Note that a similar idea appears in "Song," lines 21-24. Do you agree? Explain his parallel between tribulation and money.

Reader's Response Is it true that "No man is an island"? Why or why not?

---

toll for him that thinks it doth; and though it intermit again, yet from that minute that that occasion wrought upon him, he is united to God. Who casts not up his eye to the sun when it rises? but who takes off his eye from a comet when that breaks out? Who bends not his ear to any bell which upon any occasion rings? but who can remove it from that bell which is passing a piece of himself out of this world? No man is an island, entire of itself; every man is a piece of the continent, a part of the main.[5] If a clod be washed away by the sea, Europe is the less, as well as if a promontory were, as well as if a manor of thy friend's or of thine own were. Any man's death diminishes me because I am involved in mankind, and therefore never send to know for whom the bell tolls; it tolls for thee. Neither can we call this a begging of misery or a borrowing of misery, as though we were not miserable enough of

3

---

5. main: Mainland.

ourselves but must fetch in more from the next house, in taking upon us the misery of our neighbors. Truly it were an excusable covetousness if we did; for affliction is a treasure, and scarce any man hath enough of it. No man hath affliction enough that is not matured and ripened by it, and made fit for God by that affliction. If a man carry treasure in bullion, or in a wedge of gold, and have none coined into current money, his treasure will not defray him as he travels. Tribulation is treasure in the nature of it, but it is not current money in the use of it, except we get nearer and nearer our home, heaven, by it. Another man may be sick too, and sick to death, and this affliction may lie in his bowels as gold in a mine and be of no use to him; but this bell that tells me of his affliction digs out and applies that gold to me, if by this consideration of another's danger, I take mine own into contemplation and so secure myself by making my recourse to my God, who is our only security.

4

Primary Source

Poet and critic T. S. Eliot ignited a literary bonfire in 1921 when he set about establishing Donne as the speaker for the twentieth-century mood. Eliot believed that:

"In the seventeenth century a dissociation of sensibility set in, from which we have never recovered; and this dissociation . . . was aggravated by the influence of the two most powerful poets of the century, Milton and Dryden.

"Each of these men performed certain poetic functions so magnificently well that the magnitude of the effect concealed the absence of others. The language went on and in some respects improved; the best verse of Collins, Gray, Johnson, and even Goldsmith satisfies some of our fastidious demands better than that of Donne or Marvell or

King. But while the language became more refined, the feeling became more crude. The feeling, the sensibility, expressed in the 'Country Churchyard' is cruder than that in 'Coy Mistress' . . .

"We can only say that it appears likely that poetry in our civilization, as it exists at present, must be *difficult.* Our civilization comprehends great variety and complexity, and this variety and complexity, playing upon a refined sensibility, must produce more . . . complex results. The poet must become more and more comprehensive, more allusive, more indirect, in order to force, to dislocate if necessary, language into his meaning."

His remarks set the standard for a generation of students: Donne soared; Milton and Dryden plummeted.

---

406   *The Seventeenth Century*

---

pressed it directly would have been preachy and therefore less effective.

Student Activity 1. Find another metaphor in "Meditation 17." What does the metaphor mean to say? Why is the idea more effective in metaphor than it would be in literal language?

Student Activity 2. Write a sentence of your own containing a metaphor.

THINKING ABOUT THE SELECTION

Recalling

1. In "Meditation 17," what are the circumstances that cause church bells to toll?
2. Why does Donne say the tolling bell applies to him as well as to others?
3. At the conclusion, why does Donne say that contemplation of the tolling bell brings one close to God?

Interpreting

4. To what do the metaphors "chapter," "book," "language," and "translated" refer?
5. What is meant by "No man is an island entire of itself; every man is a piece of the continent"?

Applying

6. At the beginning of the Second World War, Donne's phrase "No man is an island" became widely used as a slogan by those fighting Nazi Germany. It served to explain why Great Britain went to war in defense of Poland and France, and why the United States helped Britain in its most difficult times. Given this historical context, how did the meaning of the phrase match the meaning intended by Donne?
7. What is Donne's attitude toward death in "Meditation 17"? How does it compare with his view of death in Holy Sonnet 10?

ANALYZING LITERATURE

Recognizing Themes

Themes are the central ideas of literary works. Some works have several themes in the same piece, one dominant and others subordinate. The subordinate ideas usually play a supporting role by backing up or reinforcing the main idea.

1. In the following list of ideas from "Meditation 17," which one is central and which are secondary?
   a. Death comes to everyone.
   b. There is life after death.
   c. All humans share the same experiences.
   d. Contemplation of another's death and suffering can prepare one for life after death.
   e. By empathizing with another's suffering, we recognize our common humanity.
   f. No individual exists alone.
2. Explain how the secondary ideas support the main one, and show how Donne's theme controls the other ideas.

CRITICAL THINKING AND READING

Arguing Through Analogy

An **analogy** is a comparison pointing up the resemblance between two or more things, ideas, or people. For example, one might draw an analogy between a teacher, who takes students through the difficulties of a subject, and a guide who takes travelers over some difficult or dangerous terrain.

Analogies are often used to explain complicated ideas or argue difficult points. As a rule, an analogy compares an unusual or abstract concept to something familiar or concrete. A frequent analogy, for example, is the comparison of the effect of a person's attractiveness to the action of a magnet on metal, as when we talk of an individual's "magnetism."

To "prove" that there is an afterlife and that death is not final, Donne draws an analogy. What is that analogy? How does this analogy contribute to the overall argument of "Meditation 17"?

THINKING AND WRITING

Writing About the Theme of a Work

Take the idea that you chose in Analyzing Literature as central to "Meditation 17" and discuss how Donne developed it. Show how he hammered away at certain ideas through repetition. Also show how one idea supported another in an almost pyramidal fashion, with Donne's major theme at the apex.

moved from the book but "translated" or transferred to a "better language," in other words, to be with God.
5. No one is isolated but is connected to everyone else.

Applying

6. It matched Donne's intended meaning: that we are all involved with one another.
7. Donne sees the death of others as a useful reminder that we are not isolated and that we should make ourselves closer to God. In Holy Sonnet 10, he sees death as haughty and ultimately powerless.

ANSWERS TO ANALYZING LITERATURE

1. Though all of these ideas are present in "Meditation 17," the idea that contemplating another's death and suffering can bring us closer to God is perhaps central.
2. The other ideas are implied in the central one. Donne's language —as in the "No man is an island" passage—relates these other ideas to the central idea and, thereby, to his main purpose: to encourage believing Christians to contemplate death and turn to God as their "only security."

The central theme of "Meditation 17" is that by empathizing with another's suffering, we recognize our common humanity. The other themes listed are secondary.

ANSWERS TO CRITICAL THINKING AND READING

Donne compares dying with being "translated" from one language to another. When one chapter of the volume to which we all belong is torn out, the loss affects us all and reminds us of our closeness to God.

Challenge Which is Donne's most effective metaphor? Why?

THINKING AND WRITING

For help with this assignment, students can refer to Lesson 11, "Writing About Theme," in the Handbook of Writing About Literature.

Closure and Extension

ANSWERS TO THINKING ABOUT THE SELECTION

Recalling

1. The bell tolls to signal a death.
2. The death of one person affects everyone.
3. The tolling bell reminds one of one's own death and the necessity of assuring one's salvation.

Interpreting

4. Donne compares humankind to a book and individual people to the chapters. When a person dies, however, the chapter is not re-

More About the Author According to his biographer, Izaak Walton, on the night of his installation as a country pastor, George Herbert told a friend, ''I now look back upon my aspiring thoughts and think myself more happy than if I had attained what then I so ambitiously thirsted for.'' What different kinds of satisfactions might one find upon moving from an active life in the city to life in a rural village? What might be one's interests and priorities?

Critical Evaluation Douglas Bush wrote that ''Herbert does not electrify the nerves so often or so startlingly as Donne, but, instead of Donne's fevered preoccupation with death and judgment, he has a far more truly religious preoccupation with everyday fulfillment of the divine will here and now; the quiet Herbert is also a more subtle artist than the explosive Donne. If the modern reader sees inner tension as a prime essential of metaphysical poetry, no writer has more than the man whose manuscript was 'a picture of the many spiritual conflicts that have past betwixt God and my Soul. . . .''

GEORGE HERBERT

1593–1633

Herbert was born to a wealthy and influential aristocratic family. Instead of becoming a high-ranking official at the English court, however, he became a country parson at one of the smallest rural churches in England. There he served the poor and wrote the poems that gained him fame.

Like many wealthy young men, George Herbert first looked toward worldly success. He served as spokesman for Cambridge University, usually a steppingstone to high public office, and became a favorite of King James I. It was during this period of great promise that Herbert also served for two years as a Member of Parliament. With the deaths of his mother and several patrons, he withdrew from London. In 1630 he accepted a parish assignment in a remote part of England. For the remaining three years of his life he devoted himself to his church: He restored the church buildings at his own expense, tended to his parishioners, performed music for his congregation, and composed his devotional poems.

In many ways, Herbert's poetry shows the influence of John Donne. This is understandable, since Donne was older and a good family friend. Herbert's temperament, however, was very different from that of his doubt-ridden, anxious mentor. The poetry Herbert wrote is graceful, pious verse intended to instill devotion by giving pleasure. As he himself put it: ''A verse may find him who a sermon flies, / And turn delight into a sacrifice.''

Herbert organized his poems in a particular sequence and called his collection *The Temple.* Just before his death, he sent the manuscript of *The Temple* to a profoundly religious friend named Nicholas Ferrar with a special request. If Ferrar found the poems worthy, then he should have them published; if not, they should be burned. Fortunately, Ferrar found the poems worthy. *The Temple,* as it turned out, was enormously popular throughout the seventeenth century.

Herbert had carefully given his collection of 160 very different poems a unifying concept. Taken together, all the poems represent the experience of attending church. *The Temple* opens with the rather long poem ''The Church Porch'' and then, in a wide variety of verse forms, represents parts of a church building, religious services, sacred objects, and private devotions. We can glimpse the large assortment of forms and themes present in Herbert's collection of poems by examining the three reprinted in this volume.

Objectives

1 To understand Herbert's use of emblems and symbols
2 To analyze Herbert's style
3 To write about emblematic images

Support Material

Teaching Portfolio
Teacher Backup, p. 407
Usage and Mechanics Worksheet, p. 411
Vocabulary Check, p. 412
Analyzing Literature Worksheet, *Understanding Emblematic Images,* p. 414

Language Worksheet, *Recognizing Differences Among Synonyms,* p. 415
Selection Test, p. 416

Virtue, Easter Wings, Man

Emblematic Images. Emblems were usually pictures accompanied by mottoes or labels and poems connecting or explaining the pictures and the mottoes. In some instances the poem itself was shaped so as to serve as picture, motto, and explanation. George Herbert's "Easter Wings" is such a poem. Verses of this type are called *emblematic images* or *emblem poems*.

Emblem poems were written so that visual image and verbal image could reinforce one another. "Easter Wings," for example, is concerned with the resurrection of the spirit, and angelic wings may well help the troubled soul to rise and take flight. When this poem was first published, it was printed on its side. In this way, the poem *looked* as if an angel or bird were flying, wings spread apart.

Shaped poems, such as "Easter Wings," have been produced intermittently since ancient times. An ancient Roman, writing about a sea fight, had the lines of his poems written so that they made pictures of ships at battle. Shaped poems were not produced after the classical period until their revival at the beginning of the Renaissance. Then they became popular. One Renaissance poet wrote a drinking song shaped like a bottle. Other poets wrote their verses so as to make shapes of crosses, altars, hearts, tears, and so forth. Shaped poems are still being written today, and they often still serve a kind of emblematic purpose.

Write the name of a picture that appeals to you. For example, you might choose the painting, *Mona Lisa,* by Leonardo da Vinci, or the photograph of the Beatles dressed as *Sergeant Pepper's Lonely Hearts Club Band.* Use the name as the motto and write a short comment for motto and picture.

What kind of preacher was Herbert? Were his sermons full of the clever word plays that characterize his verse? One source tells us that Herbert delivered his first sermon "after a most florid manner, both with great learning and eloquence," but promised that "since Almighty God does not intend to lead men to heaven by hard questions, he would not therefore fill their heads with unnecessary notions; but that for their sakes, his language and his expressions should be more plain and practical in his future sermons . . . He often tells them, that sermons are dangerous things, that none goes out of church as he came in, but either better or worse; that none is careless before his Judge, and that the word of God shall judge us. By these and other means the parson procures attention; but the character of his sermon is holiness; he is not witty, or learned, or eloquent, but holy."

Guide for Interpreting 409

Literary Focus Herbert viewed the poet's task as uncovering God's hidden meanings. As God created emblems, or meaningful pictures, for man to discover, the writer created poetry that reflected these symbols. Poetry thus represented for Herbert the highest form of praise for God.

Writing/Prior Knowledge Have less advanced students write a brief essay explaining how their motto is appropriate to the picture they chose.

Vocabulary

Preteach the following vocabulary words:

compacted (kəm pakt′d) *v.:* Put together (p. 410)

virtuous (vʉr′cho͞o wəs) *adj.:* Pure, righteous (p. 410)

harmoniously (här mō′ nē əs le) *adv.:* In a manner that is in accordance (p. 412)

affliction (ə flik′shən) *n.:* Suffering (p. 412)

habitation (hab′ə tā′shən) *n.:* Home; dwelling (p. 413)

symmetry (sim′ə trē) *n.:* Balance of form (p. 413)

amity (am′ə tē) *n.:* Peaceful relationships (p. 413)

Motivation for Reading Have students imagine and then describe feeling a sense of intimacy and cooperation with God. How would they express this intimacy? What objects might they choose as symbols to help them describe their feeling?

Master Teacher Note Although Herbert was known for his saintliness and deep devotion to the church, his poetry is neither sentimental nor pompous. Instead, it is unusual and inventive. Herbert delighted in odd forms and patterns. Discuss examples of this combination of piety and playfulness in his poetry—for example the refrain in "Virtue," the shape of "Easter Wings," and the image of the canopied bed in "Man," lines 31-32.

Thematic Idea Another devotional poet who may be compared with Herbert is Gerard Manley Hopkins, pages 840–847.

Purpose-Setting Question What is the theme of each poem?

1 **Enrichment** In the Prologue to *Canterbury Tales*, Chaucer uses the word *vertu* to mean "power" or "strength." What meanings does *Virtue* have in Herbert's poem?

2. **Discussion** How is the day "the bridal of the earth and sky"?

3 **Discussion** Why does Herbert make the last line of each stanza shorter than the rest?

4 **Discussion** Why does the beauty of the rose bring tears to the gazer's eyes? Why is the gazer "rash"?

5 **Discussion** How does the spring represent the culmination of the images of the previous stanzas? To what senses does this stanza appeal?

410

Virtue

George Herbert

Sweet day, so cool, so calm, so bright,
The bridal of the earth and sky;
The dew shall weep thy fall tonight;
    For thou must die.

5 Sweet rose, whose hue angry and brave[1]
Bids the rash gazer wipe his eye:
Thy root is ever in its grave,
    And thou must die.

Sweet spring, full of sweet days and roses,
10 A box where sweets[2] compacted lie;
My music shows ye have your closes,[3]
    And all must die.

Only a sweet and virtuous soul,
Like seasoned timber, never gives;
15 But though the whole world turn to coal,[4]
    Then chiefly lives.

---

1. angry and brave: Red (the hue of anger) and splendid.
2. sweets: Perfumes.
3. closes: The concluding sounds.
4. turn to cinder: Be reduced to cinder and ash by the fires of the Last Judgment (see II Peter 3:10).

THINKING ABOUT THE SELECTION
Recalling

1. In the first three stanzas of "Virtue," what happens to "sweet day," "sweet rose," and "sweet spring"?
2. In the last stanza, what happens to the "sweet and virtuous soul"?

Interpreting

3. (a) What do the last lines of each of the four stanzas say? (b) How is the last line in the fourth stanza different from the other three? (c) When combined, what additional meaning do they gain?
4. How is the thought that all of nature dies but the soul lives eternally shown in this poem?
5. If death means a permanent end to existence, in what sense can one say that *days, roses,* and *spring* actually die?
6. Mark the rhyme scheme of the poem. What rhyming sound is most often repeated? What rhyming sound replaces this in the last stanza? In what way does the rhyme emphasize the theme or main point of the poem?

6 **Discussion** What other adjective is added to "sweet" in this stanza? Why is the soul like "seasoned timber"? Help students see the difference in durability between green and seasoned wood.

Reader's Response What is your idea of virtue?

Closure and Extension

ANSWERS TO THINKING ABOUT THE SELECTION
Recalling

1. They all must die.
2. It lives eternally.

Interpreting

3. (a) Taken together, they state that everything dies except the soul. (b)

THE MILKMAID
Myles Birket Foster

Humanities Note

Fine art, *The Milkmaid* by Myles Birket Foster. Miles Birket Foster (1825–1899), a British watercolorist, showed a precocious talent for drawing and was encouraged by his family. At the age of sixteen, he was apprenticed to a wood engraver for five years. He subsequently worked as a book illustrator and painter. His reputation was established in a bizarre way. When his father died, the death was mistaken for his, and art critics wrote flowery eulogies praising his talent and mourning the great loss to the world of art. When this confusion was cleared up, he was famous and remained so.

Foster loved to paint dainty, rustic scenes of rural England. He is best known for watercolors of gentle subjects painted with charm, grace, and fresh color. *The Milkmaid* is one of these paintings. It shows Foster's leaning toward the Pre-Raphaelite style in his careful attention to detail and the romantic mood of the subject. The stippled application of paint, uniquely his, creates a dreamy effect.

You may wish to use the following questions for discussion:

1. What is the difference between what the poet Herbert and the painter Foster see in the glory of spring?
2. Why is this painting a suitable illustration for this contemplative poem?

Applying

7. Basically, this poem says that the virtuous soul need not fear death. What other poem in this book imparts a similar message?

ANALYZING LITERATURE

Understanding Emblematic Images

Although emblematic images are usually associated with pictures and shaped verse, it is sometimes possible to see a kind of emblematic impulse in more traditionally formed poems. To see the emblematic image in a poem such as "Virtue," for example, we need to probe the meaning of the word *emblem*. The word comes into English from the Latin meaning "inlaid," as in mosaic pictures, which are made of little pieces of stone put together according to a pattern that forms an image. From this use it came to mean "symbol," one thing standing for another.

In early Renaissance emblems, poems were written to comment on or explain pictorial symbols. After a while, poems and pictures became separated and the reader of an emblematic poem had to imagine the symbolic picture to which it related.

Explain the symbolism of "sweet day," "sweet rose," and "sweet spring." Then explain what "seasoned timber" might represent and how it relates to the sweet day, rose, and spring symbols. Describe the pictorial image you think this poem might fit.

Virtue 411

The first three stanzas culminate in the words "must die"; the fourth, with the word "lives." (c) They gain the meaning that a virtuous soul triumphs over death.

4. The poem presents three examples of things that die, followed by an example of something that does not.
5. They cease to be.
6. The rhyme scheme is *abab, cbcb, dbdb, efef*. The long *i* sound is repeated in the first three stanzas. The *ives* sound replaces it in stanza four. The main rhyme is based on the word "die." The idea of the living soul is associated with a different rhyme.

Applying

7. Donne's Holy Sonnet 10 has a similar theme.

ANSWERS TO ANALYZING LITERATURE

"Sweet day," "Sweet rose," and "Sweet spring" are three symbols of the beauty and mortality of merely natural life. "Seasoned timber" symbolizes something natural that has been prepared to survive death. Seasoned timber, therefore, contrasts with the three preceding symbols. The pictorial image implied is that of sound, lasting wood in a natural setting where all other things are drooping or already dead.

412

Easter Wings

George Herbert

Lord, who createdst man in wealth and store,[1]
   Though foolishly he lost the same,
      Decaying more and more,
         Till he became
           Most poor:
         With thee
      O let me rise
   As larks, harmoniously,
 And sing this day thy victories:
Then shall the fall further the flight in me.

My tender age in sorrow did begin.
   And still with sickness and shame
      Thou didst so punish sin,
         That I became
           Most thin.
         With thee
      Let me combine
   And feel this day thy victory:
 For, if I imp[2] my wing on thine,
Affliction shall advance the flight in me.

Line numbers: 5, 10, 15

---

1. store: Abundance.
2. imp: Graft.

THINKING ABOUT THE SELECTION
Recalling

1. At the end of the poem, why does the speaker say he wants to "combine" with God? In what way does this echo lines 6–10?

Interpreting

2. (a) In line 11, what does the speaker mean when he says: "My tender age in sorrow did begin"? Why should he have begun in sorrow? (b) How does this line echo lines 1–5?

3. In what way is line 10 a paradox?
4. How are the title and shape of the poem appropriate to its meaning or theme?

Applying

5. George Herbert was sickly as a child and remained in frail health throughout his rather short life. He also moved from the pomp of the royal court to the poverty of a rural church. In what way are these personal experiences reflected in "Easter Wings"?

Sidebar notes

1 Discussion What is the significance of the title? Point out that for Christians, Easter is the day of resurrection, the time of Christ's rising from the dead. The poet wishes to rise above sin and spiritual poverty. Note the references to flight in the poem.

2 Literary Focus Notice how the physical shape of the poem reflects its content. For example, line 1 deals with the abundance with which man was created; in line 2, some of that abundance has been lost; and in line 3, there is further decay, which reaches its maximum in line 5, with "Most poor." Then, after line 6, "With thee," spiritual growth begins. The same progression of ideas occurs in the second stanza. See if students can trace the debilitating effects of sorrow, sickness, shame, and sin, with the same mid-stanza reversal in stanza 2.

3 Discussion To what "victory" does the speaker refer?

4 Enrichment In the Bible, Malachi says, "Son of man shall rise with feeling in his wings." Isaiah says, "through affliction we shall rise on wings." Have students compare these images with the last two lines of this poem and with the similar statement at the end of Donne's "Meditation 17" that adversity helps us better appreciate God's gifts.

Reader's Response How can a sense of loss lead to positive feelings?

Closure and Extension

ANSWERS TO THINKING ABOUT THE SELECTION
Recalling

1. He thinks that if he can "combine" with God, he can imitate Christ's suffering and thereby rise to God. In both passages, he wants to praise Christ's "victory" of rising from the dead.

Interpreting

2. (a) He had been ill and frail since an early age. (b) Lines 1-5 state that humankind in general has been afflicted with pain; lines 11-15 say how the speaker himself was afflicted with pain.
3. The speaker states that the Fall will make him rise closer to God.
4. The wing-like shape of the poem is an emblem for its title. At Easter, the spirit is reborn and able to fly to God.

Applying

5. Herbert refers directly to his personal "sickness and shame," and also implies his religiosity and prayerful spirituality.

Man

George Herbert

1

       My God, I heard this day,
That none doth build a stately habitation,
      But he that means to dwell therein.
      What house more stately hath there been,
5 Or can be, than is man? to whose creation
      All things are in decay.[1]

       For Man is every thing,
And more: He is a tree, yet bears more fruit;
      A beast, yet is, or should be more:[2]
10   Reason and speech we only bring.[3]
Parrots may thank us, if they are not mute,
      They go upon the score.[4]

2

       Man is all symmetry,
Full of proportions, one limb to another,
15   And all to all the world besides:
      Each part may call the furthest, brother:
For head with foot hath private amity,
      And both with moons and tides.

       Nothing hath got so far,
20 But man hath caught and kept it, as his prey.
      His eyes dismount the highest star:

3

      He is in little all the sphere.
Herbs gladly cure our flesh; because that they
      Find their acquaintance there.

25   For us the winds do blow,
The earth doth rest, heaven move, and fountains flow.
      Nothing we see, but means our good,
      As our delight, or as our treasure:
The whole is, either our cupboard of food,
30   Or cabinet of pleasure.

---

1. **to . . . decay:** In comparison to created man, all other things are in decay.
2. **For . . . more:** Man has an animal, vegetable, and spiritual nature.
3. **Reason . . . bring:** Man alone is capable of speaking and using reason.
4. **Parrots . . . score:** Parrots may also seem to be able to speak, but only because man has taught them how.

1 **Enrichment** Here Herbert expresses the theory of the nature of man common to the Renaissance: in a hierarchy man is at the top of creation next to God.

2 **Enrichment** Note that man's "symmetry" is not only internal so that the parts of his body operate in unity with each other, but also external so that he operates in unity with all the world, including the moon and tides.

3 **Discussion** How is man "in little all the sphere"?

4 **Discussion** What is the image created in lines 31-32?

5 **Discussion** Who are the innumerable servants who wait on man? What is the other world that attends man?

Reader's Response Do you think Herbert would have the same opinions about humankind if he were alive today? Explain.

The stars have us to bed;
Night draws the curtain, which the sun withdraws;
Music and light attend our head.
All things unto our flesh are kind
35 In their descent and being; to our mind
In their ascent and cause.

Each thing is full of duty:
Waters united are our navigation;
Distinguished, our habitation;
40 Below, our drink; above, our meat;
Both are our cleanliness. Hath one such beauty?
Than how are all things neat?[5]

More servants wait on man,
Than he'll take notice of: in every path
45 He treads down that which doth befriend him,
When sickness makes him pale and wan.[6]
Oh mighty love! Man is one world, and hath
Another to attend him.

Since then, my God, thou hast
50 So brave a palace built; O dwell in it,
That it may dwell with thee at last!
Till then, afford us so much wit;
That, as the world serves us, we may serve thee,
And both thy servants be.

---

5. Each . . . neat: Each element serves man in a number of ways. Water is used as an example. Oceans are used for navigation; dividing waters created the earth that man inhabits (Genesis 1:6-7); water provides man with food and drink; and water allows man to cleanse himself. If one element can serve man so well, how beautiful is the sum of the elements.
6. He . . . won: Man treads down the herb that can cure him when he is sick.

THINKING ABOUT THE SELECTION
Recalling

1. In the first stanza of "Man," what question does the speaker ask?
2. How is man described in lines 7–24?
3. In lines 25–42, what does the speaker say is the relation of nature to man?
4. As shown in the next-to-last stanza, how does man behave toward nature?
5. In the final stanza, what are the two requests the speaker makes?

Interpreting

6. To what specific categories do the items mentioned in lines 7–10 belong? In broad general terms, how is man characterized in these lines?
7. To what does the "brave palace" of line 50 refer? In what way does this metaphor recall lines 4 and 5? How does this echoing serve to conclude or "close" the poem?

Applying

8. In a certain sense, this poem can be read as a criticism of human disregard for the rich bounties of nature. If modern environmentalists were to make the same criticism, as they often do, what would they say? To whom would they address their pleas? How would they present their position or viewpoint?

CRITICAL THINKING AND READING
Analyzing Herbert's Style

The word *style* refers to the characteristic way in which an individual does something, such as dressing, swimming, painting a picture, or writing a poem. In literature, style refers specifically to the way an individual uses language.

When we analyze a literary style, we examine a writer's characteristic choice of words, use of figures of speech, arrangement of sentences, organization of paragraphs, and, in poetry, treatment of rhythm and rhyme. Sometimes we also look at an author's use of certain literary devices —such as paradox, imagery, or symbolism —and his or her seeming preference for certain subjects or themes. John Donne, for example, seems to prefer themes that reflect anxiety, uncertainty, or suffering. He often uses exaggerated language when treating these difficult matters, thereby creating discomfort and heightening the emotional response to his writing. Donne's style could thus be described as highly provocative.

George Herbert stands in marked contrast to Donne. The poems Herbert wrote tend to make the reader feel comfortable, perhaps even soothed, as if listening to the gentle murmur of continuous prayer. Herbert's diction, or vocabulary, is essentially quiet, never clangorous as is Donne's on many occasions. Even when dealing with so potentially traumatic a subject as the Fall of Man, or his own approaching death, Herbert's words are mild, almost as if spoken in a whisper.

Reread "Easter Wings" and look closely at the way Herbert uses language. For example, notice the way he uses rhyme (in Herbert's day, "poor" rhymed with "more" and "store"); notice also that in the second half of each stanza, the only perfect rhyme for "thee" is "me," and "thee" of course refers to God. Describe Herbert's style in this poem and show how it complements his main idea. In addition to his use of rhyme, take into account his choice of words, his changes in line lengths, and his treatment of metaphors and similes.

THINKING AND WRITING
Writing About Emblematic Images

Properly speaking, an emblem consisted of a picture, a motto, and a poem. Over time, however, picture and poem came to be separated. As a result, many poems were written as if they contained their own picture, as in "Easter Wings," for example, or as if they were written to explain or comment on a picture in the poet's mind, as might be said of "Virtue" or of "Man."

Reread "Man" and describe the picture that might have been in Herbert's mind or that could accompany the poem today. Explain your description by referring to the details of the poem. When you revise, make sure you have included

kingdom, the beast the animal kingdom, reason and speech the realm of human beings. Man is connected to all other living creatures but superior to them.

7. The "palace" is the human person. Herbert begins the poem with the metaphor of a fine house to represent the human person. The poem comes full circle with its return to the opening metaphor.

Applying

8. Herbert believes that nature exists for man's use and should be respected as such. Modern environmentalists stress that the earth is an ecosystem with all forms of life existing interdependently. They address their pleas to people who think that nature exists only for their use and would exploit it. They usually express their views in speeches, and in newspaper and magazine articles, although occasionally in poetry.

ANSWERS TO CRITICAL THINKING AND READING

Students might point out, among other things, that Herbert's elaborate rhymes and complex but regularly recurring metrical patterns are especially appropriate in a poem that celebrates man's special place in a complex but orderly and purposeful universe maintained by God. The scientific and cosmological references, along with the generally intellectual manner of the poem, are in harmony with the poem's rational theology: Herbert's view of man in relation to the universe and God is rooted in centuries of orthodox Christian theology and thought.

THINKING AND WRITING
Publishing Student Writing Have students share their emblematic images by reading them aloud.

Closure and Extension

ANSWERS TO THINKING ABOUT THE SELECTION
Recalling

1. Why would anyone build a grand home unless he planned to live there?
2. Man is better than trees or beasts; his body is in perfect harmony; and he is in perfect command of nature.
3. Everything in nature exists for man's nourishment or pleasure.
4. Man is arrogant and wasteful of nature, which he dominates.
5. The speaker wants God to dwell with him so that he may eventually dwell with God; in the meantime, he asks for the intelligence and perception to serve God while he is on earth.

Interpreting

6. The tree represents the vegetable

More About the Author Andrew Marvell was an intensely private man whose lyric poetry remained almost unknown in his own time. After his death, he was chiefly remembered as a member of Parliament and as a political writer. It was only in the late nineteenth century that Marvell was rediscovered as a poet. What are some reasons that a writer's work would be neglected and then rediscovered?

Critical Evaluation The literary scholar Robert M. Adams said that the reputation of Marlowe's poems "has never stood higher than in our own time. For it is now clear that Marvell's is the most major minor verse in English. Playful, casual, and witty in tone, always light on its metrical feet and exact in its diction, it displays depth and intellectual hardness in unexpected places; its texture is extraordinarily rich."

ANDREW MARVELL

1621–1678

Although seemingly easy and relaxed in style, Andrew Marvell was actually tough in poetry and politics. Beneath his graceful lyrics lie somber ideas and rigorous structures. Alongside his ready adaptability resided a firm attachment to his friends and beliefs.

Marvell was the son of a Puritan minister who was appointed to a church in Hull, a small town on the Humber River in northern England. There young Andrew remained until he entered Cambridge University at the age of twelve. While at Cambridge, he wrote several poems in Greek and Latin that were published by the university in a volume dedicated to King Charles I. After his father's death, Marvell traveled in Europe, where he learned to speak several modern European languages.

During his stay in Europe, the English Parliament, dominated by Puritans, rebelled against the king. On first returning to England, Marvell established friendships with royalist supporters of Charles I. At this time he wrote several verses commemorating these friends, among whom was the poet Richard Lovelace. Somewhat later, he was hired by Lord Fairfax, the commanding general of the anti-royalist Parliamentary army, to teach his daughter foreign languages. Marvell held this position for about two years, at which time he may have written most of the poems for which he is now famous.

Several years after ceasing to teach Fairfax's daughter, Marvell became tutor to the ward of Oliver Cromwell, leader of the Puritan rebellion and ruler of England. Shortly afterward, Marvell served as unofficial court poet to Cromwell himself. Obviously capable, Marvell gained the attention and sponsorship of the great English poet John Milton, who was at the time Latin Secretary to Cromwell's Council of State. Several years later, Marvell became Milton's assistant. Throughout this period, Marvell wrote several political and commemorative poems.

In 1659, after Cromwell's death and shortly before the monarchy was restored, Marvell was elected the Member of Parliament from Hull. He was regularly returned to Parliament until his death, almost twenty years later. It is believed that while a member, he was mainly responsible for saving Milton from a long imprisonment and possible death sentence.

Marvell showed an extraordinary ability to adjust to the realities of his time. He also displayed, however, an equal firmness of principle. After the Restoration of Charles II, Marvell wrote political satires and prose pamphlets attacking the abuses of monarchy and defending democratic concepts.

Objectives

1 To recognize couplets and hidden quatrains in the poems
2 To analyze tone
3 To compare and contrast authors' styles

Support Material

Teaching Portfolio
Teacher Backup, p. 419
Grammar in Action Worksheets, *Using Imagery,* p. 423; *Using Adjectives,* p. 425
Usage and Mechanics Worksheet, p. 427
Vocabulary Check, p. 428
Analyzing Literature Worksheet, *Recognizing Couplets and Quatrains,* p. 429

Language Worksheet, *Recognizing Syllables and Pronouncations,* p. 431)
Selection Test, p. 432

GUIDE FOR INTERPRETING

To His Coy Mistress, The Picture of Little T. C. in a Prospect of Flowers

Writer's Techniques

Couplets and Quatrains. Two of the most common structural elements in poetry are couplets and quatrains. Two lines rhyming together are called a *couplet,* and four lines rhyming in various ways are called a *quatrain.* Here is an example of a couplet and a quatrain. The verses are by Andrew Marvell, who used these forms in an early poem that he wrote as a debate between the Soul and Pleasure.

Quatrain:	PLEASURE	
	Wilt thou all the glory crave	a
	That war or peace commend?	b
	Half the world shall be thy slave,	a
	The other half they friend.	b
Couplet:	SOUL	
	What friends, if to my self untrue!	c
	What slaves, unless I captive you!	c

Although both the couplet and the quatrain are often used as complete stanzas by themselves, they are also frequently used as parts of longer stanzas.

Writing

Write two lines that rhyme, then write several more two-line rhymes. If four of these rhyming lines seem related, perhaps because they deal with the same subject or central idea, join them together. Now write four new lines in which the rhymes alternate. You might then have one quatrain rhyming *a b a b* and another rhyming *a a b b.*

Primary Source

Charles II decided to show his respect for Marvell's wit and intelligence as well as buy his allegiance. He sent a messenger who told Marvell that the king would grant him a favor. When Marvell refused, the messenger offered a thousand gold pieces. With a smile Marvell replied, "Surely, my good Lord, you do not mean to treat me ludicrously by these munificent offers, which seem to interpret a poverty on my part. Pray, my Lord Treasurer, do these apartments wear in the least the air and mark of need? And as for my living, that is plentiful and good, which you shall have from the mouth of the servant. —Pray, what had I to dinner yesterday? —'A shoulder of mutton, sir.'" The messenger left with a smile, and Marvell went to ask his bookseller for a loan.

How do you see Marvell's independent streak in these poems?

Guide for Interpreting 417

Literary Focus In the English sonnet, the concluding couplet provides a sense of closure, often summarizing the material that has preceded it. Couplets also lend themselves to aphorism—short, witty sayings that express a general truth. A couplet such as Marvell's "The grave's a fine and private place,/ But none I think do there embrace" displays the pithy wit of an aphorism.

Writing/Prior Knowledge Have more advanced students choose one of the quatrains they wrote for their freewriting assignment. Have them complete a poem of several stanzas that continues the same rhyme scheme.

Vocabulary

Preteach the following vocabulary words:

coy (koi) *adj.:* Reluctant to make a commitment; it is important to recognize that the modern sense of "pretending to be shy" is absent from the poem (p. 418, title)

hew (hyoo) *n.:* Color; hue (p. 418, l. 33)

nymph (nimf) *n.:* In classical mythology, a minor nature goddess usually shown as a lovely young girl (p. 420, l. 2)

compound (käm' pound) *v.:* Join; combine (p. 420, l. 17)

parley (pär'lē) *v.:* Talk; converse (p. 420, l. 17)

prime (prīm) *n.:* Best stage or time (p. 421, l. 37)

Grammar in Action

Vigorous writing appeals to the senses through strong **imagery.** Note the vivid images that build Andrew Marvell's argument in lines 21–32.

Marvell uses images of time and the grave to persuade his lady to succumb to his advances. "Time's winged chariot hurrying near" suggests urgency. The next image directs the lady's vision to what lies ahead, "Deserts of vast eternity," implying the endless desolation of death. Marvell then shifts his imagery to within her grave, where his "echoing songs" will not be heard and "worms shall try that long-preserved virginity." At last, all is reduced to dust and ashes. Marvell's imagery, by appealing to the lady's senses, may move her more than would a mere argument appealing to her mind.

Student Activity 1. Read the final section of the poem, ll 33–46. What vivid images do you find there? How do they enhance the meaning of the poem?

Student Activity 2. Write a letter in which you urge an imaginary acquaintance to mend some serious flaw in his or her character. Use concrete, vivid images to express your main idea.

Motivation for Reading Both "To His Coy Mistress" and "Little T.C." focus on the value of youth. How do we regard youth in our culture? Why? How is this similar or different from the way Marvell presents youth?

Master Teacher Note Explain the Ovidian tradition of *carpe diem*, or "seize the day," which urges taking advantage of the pleasures of the moment. Discuss whether this philosophy is a sound one.

Thematic Idea Other poems on the theme of *carpe diem* are Raleigh's "The Nymph's Reply to the Shepherd" on page 238 and Herrick's "To the Virgins, to Make Much of Time," page 432. Marvell can also be compared with Wordsworth, whom he anticipates in his appreciation of the open air and countryside.

Purpose-Setting Question Which words signal shifts in focus or time frame? (*But* and *Now* in "To His Coy Mistress"; *Meantime* in "Little T.C.")

1 **Discussion** Why does the speaker call his love "vegetable"?

2 **Enrichment** Praise of the lover's body was a poetic convention called a "blazon." Here it is satirized by Marvell. Students might compare this passage to Shakespeare's Sonnet 130.

3 **Literary Focus** Point out the use of personification in these lines. "Time's winged chariot" is a classical image, many of which appear in Marvell's poetry.

4 **Discussion** How do these lines express the theme of *carpe diem*?

To His Coy Mistress

Andrew Marvell

Had we but world enough, and time,
This coyness lady were no crime.
We would sit down, and think which way
To walk, and pass our long love's day.
5   Thou by the Indian Ganges' side
Should'st rubies find; I by the tide
Of Humber[1] would complain. I would
Love you ten years before the Flood,
And you should if you please refuse
10   Till the conversion of the Jews.[2]
My vegetable love should grow
Vaster than empires, and more slow;
An hundred years should go to praise
Thine eyes, and on thy forehead gaze;
15   Two hundred to adore each breast,
But thirty thousand to the rest;
An age at least to every part,
And the last age should show your heart.
For, lady, you deserve this state,[3]
20   Nor would I love at lower rate.
      But at my back I always hear
Time's winged chariot hurrying near:
And yonder all before us lie
Deserts of vast eternity.
25   Thy beauty shall no more be found,
Nor, in thy marble vault, shall sound
My echoing songs; then worms shall try
That long-preserved virginity,
And your quaint honor turn to dust,
30   And into ashes all my lust:
The grave's a fine and private place,
But none I think do there embrace.
      Now therefore, while the youthful hew
Sits on thy skin like morning dew,
35   And while thy willing soul transpires[4]
At every pore with instant fires,

---

1. **Humber:** River flowing through Hull, Marvell's home town.
2. **conversion of the Jews:** According to Christian tradition, the Jews were to be converted immediately before the Last Judgment.
3. **state:** Dignity.
4. **transpires:** Breathes out.

Now let us sport us while we may,
And now, like amorous birds of prey,
Rather at once our time devour
40 Than languish in his slow-chapped[5] power.
Let us roll all our strength, and all
Our sweetness, up into one ball,
And tear our pleasures with rough strife
Thorough[6] the iron gates of life:
45 Thus, though we cannot make our sun
Stand still, yet we will make him run.

5. **slow-chapped:** Slow-jawed.
6. **thorough:** Through.

THINKING ABOUT THE SELECTION
Recalling

1. According to line 1 of "To His Coy Mistress," under what conditions would the lady's coyness not be a crime?
2. In lines 3–7, what would the lady and the speaker each do, separately and together?
3. Starting at the end of line 7 and continuing to line 20, how does the speaker express his love?
4. In lines 21–24, what does the speaker hear at his back, and what lies before him and the lady?
5. In what place does the action described in lines 25–32 occur?
6. In lines 33–40, why does the speaker urge the lady to act "now"?
7. In conclusion (lines 41–46), what does the speaker say that he and the lady should do?

Interpreting

8. If you had to state the speaker's objections to the lady's resistance in one sentence, what would that sentence be?
9. Since time is central to the poem, how is it expressed? Point to the word pictures or images and to the comparisons or metaphors that stand for and represent time.

Applying

10. The lines "But at my back I always hear / Time's winged chariot hurrying near" have a great deal of meaning. What is the modern experience that these lines express?

ANALYZING LITERATURE
Recognizing Couplets and Quatrains

Couplets are two lines that rhyme and quatrains are four lines that rhyme in various ways. One of the ways to make a quatrain is to join two couplets that deal with one idea, word picture, or comparison. This is sometimes done in long poems, although the quatrain may thus be "hidden."

There are indeed several hidden quatrains in this poem made up entirely of couplets. For example, look at lines 21–24.

These four lines make a single unit, a quatrain. The preceding lines all deal with praising the beauty of the lady; the following lines describe what happens to the body after death. By contrast, the quatrain deals directly with the experience of time.

Find at least one other hidden quatrain. Explain how Marvell's ideas, word pictures, and comparisons move through his couplets.

To His Coy Mistress 419

---

5 Clarification For "we will make him run" read "we'll give him a run for his money!"

Reader's Response How do you think the lady Marvell was addressing responded to his poem?

as having "slow-chapped power"; and the sun.

Applying

10. These lives express the feeling that death and extinction are imminent.

ANSWERS TO ANALYZING LITERATURE

Hidden quatrains include lines 13–17, 33–36, 37–40, and 41–44. Within each of the three verse paragraphs, the images and ideas are linked by association—they simply fit together to express ideas. However, the three verse paragraphs taken together have a logical structure that may be summarized thus: If we had all of time and space at our command, your coyness would be acceptable (Paragraph 1). However, we don't (Paragraph 2). Therefore, let us enjoy life and love while we can (Paragraph 3).

Closure and Extension

ANSWERS TO THINKING ABOUT THE SELECTION
Recalling

1. If the lovers had all space and time in which to live and love, then her coyness would not matter.
2. Together they would sit and think about which way to walk; on opposite sides of the world, she would find rubies and he would lament.
3. He expresses his love in terms of how much time he would use to praise her.
4. He hears Time at his back, reminding him of his death ahead.
5. These lines describe what it's like in a grave.
6. He wants her to act now while she is still young, beautiful, and full of vitality.
7. He wants them to seize all the pleasure they can, while they can.

Interpreting

8. She keeps wasting time rather than taking advantage of her youth.
9. Marvell uses the following images: the lovers thinking about which way to walk; references to the flood and "the conversion of the Jews"; description of love as "vegetable"; the hyperbolic description of the lady; "Time's winged chariot"; time personified

419

The Picture of Little T. C. in a Prospect¹ of Flowers

Andrew Marvell

1

See with what simplicity
This nymph begins her golden days!
In the green grass she loves to lie,
And there with her fair aspect tames
5 The wilder flowers and gives them names,
But only with the roses plays,
     And them does tell
What color best becomes them, and what smell.
Who can foretell for what high cause
10 This darling of the gods was born!
Yet this is she whose chaster laws
The wanton love shall one day fear,
And, under her command severe
See his bow broke and ensigns² torn.
15   Happy who can
Appease this virtuous enemy of man!
O then let me in time compound
And parley with those conquering eyes
Ere they have tried their force to wound,
20 Ere, with their glancing wheels, they drive
In triumph over hearts that strive,
And them that yield but more despise:
     Let me be laid,
Where I may see thy glories from some shade.
25 Meantime, whilst every verdant³ thing
Itself does at thy beauty charm,
Reform the errors of the spring;
Make that the tulips may have share
Of sweetness, seeing they are fair;
30 And roses of their thorns disarm:
     But most procure

---

1. prospect: Landscape.
2. ensigns: Flags.
3. verdant *adj.*: Green.

1 **Clarification** T.C. was possibly Theophilia Cornewall, a young girl who may have been seven or eight when Marvell wrote the poem. The name "Theophilia" can be translated from the Greek as "God's beloved," in which connection see line 10, "This darling of the gods."

2 **Enrichment** The adjective "golden" indicates the era that Marvell is describing—a golden age of perfection.

3 **Enrichment** Before the Fall, Eve also named the flowers.

4 **Discussion** What does T.C.'s life seem to represent?

5 **Enrichment** Cupid, personified as "The wanton love," was often shown carrying a bow and arrows as his insignia.

6 **Discussion** Note the development of the word *enemy* into a military conceit. What weapon does T.C. use in this war? Note the double meaning of "glancing wheels" in line 20.

7 **Discussion** Why would she more despise those that yield?

8 Why does the poet wish to watch from the shade?

9 **Discussion** How does the mood change at the end of the poem?

Grammar in Action

An **adjective** is a word that modifies a noun. When writers use too many adjectives, their writing can seem as overstuffed as a bulky seat cushion—and just as uncomfortable! However, a telling adjective, inserted at just the right point, can lend force and color to a description. Note the following examples.

OVERUSE OF ADJECTIVES: The *lanky young* boy ran to the *old-fashioned, decrepit, brown-and-white* house with the *crumbling, hickory* stoop and looked up at the *wide, imposing* facade.

USE OF TWO TELLING ADJECTIVES: Any man doing *dusty* business on the *cheap* side of town could answer your question.

In "The Picture of Little T. C. in a Prospect of Flowers," Andrew Marvell uses adjectives with care and precision:

    And, under her command *severe*,
    See his bow broke and ensigns torn.

The adjective *severe* is especially effective because it conjures

That violets may a longer age endure.
But O, young beauty of the woods,
Whom nature courts with fruits and flowers,
35 Gather the flowers, but spare the buds,
Lest Flora[4] angry at thy crime
9   To kill her infants in their prime,
Do quickly make th' example yours;
        And ere we see,
40 Nip in the blossom all our hopes and thee.

---

4. Flora: The Roman goddess of flowers.

THINKING ABOUT THE SELECTION
Recalling

1. What is the nymph doing in stanza 1?
2. In stanza 2, what will Love fear?
3. Why does the speaker, in stanza 3, want to converse with "those conquering eyes"?
4. To whom are stanzas 4 and 5 addressed?
5. What is asked for in the fourth stanza?
6. Of what is the "young beauty" warned in the last stanza?

Interpreting

7. Nymphs are pretty young nature goddesses from classical mythology. They were often depicted in art and literature as rejecting ardent lovers, many of whom were gods. What details in the poem identify little T.C. with a wood nymph?
8. The speaker at first addresses someone outside the poem, then suddenly shifts and addresses directly little T.C. Where in the poem does this shift occur? What word signals the shift?

Applying

9. Each stanza of this poem ends in a couplet, two lines that rhyme together. What other poems that you have read in this volume end their stanzas with couplets?
10. In a sense, "The Picture of Little T. C. in a Prospect of Flowers" can be thought of as an emblem poem such as George Herbert might have written. Emblems were pictures with mottoes and poems. What sort of picture do you think would be appropriate for this poem by Marvell?

THINKING AND WRITING
Comparing and Contrasting Styles

A literary style is a distinctive use of language. Individual writers have their own style, true enough, but sometimes groups of writers also share a common style. The metaphysical poets were such a group. Among the stylistic traits shared by these poets were a fondness for conceits (extended, farfetched comparisons), paradoxes (apparent contradictions), arguments (efforts at persuasion), and obscure bits of knowledge. Choose two metaphysical writers. List the characteristics of their style. Write an essay comparing and contrasting their styles. When you revise make sure you have included details from their poems to support your ideas.

The Picture of Little T. C. in a Prospect of Flowers 421

ANSWERS TO THINKING ABOUT THE SELECTION
Recalling

1. She is lying on the grass in a flower garden.
2. Love will fear her rejection.
3. He wants to flirt with her before she becomes wise to her womanly powers.
4. They are addressed to the girl.
5. He asks that she make the flowers more perfect.
6. She is warned not to antagonize the goddess of flowers.

Interpreting

7. She is associated throughout with nature; in addition, the speaker fears that she will one day spurn love.
8. The shift occurs at the beginning of the fourth stanza with the word *thy*.

Applying

9. English sonnets such as Shakespeare's, Spenser's sonnets, and Raleigh's "To His Son" end their final stanza with a couplet.
10. Little T.C. might be shown lying on the grass, fingering the abundance of flowers surrounding her. The background would be lush and highly decorated. Cupid might be waiting in the background on one side; Flora might be jealously watching on the other.

THINKING AND WRITING

For help with this assignment, students can refer to Lesson 12, "Writing About a Poem," in the Handbook of Writing About Literature.

Publishing Student Writing You might read aloud the better papers to stimulate further discussion of Donne's themes.

Challenge In both "To His Coy Mistress" and "Little T.C.," Marvell creates perfect worlds that are belied by reality. Describe these perfect worlds. Why can't they be attained?

---

up the image of a virtuous, even chilly young woman. At the same time, this adjective reveals the poet's partly humorous tone, because the words *command severe* are more suitable to describe a military leader than a pretty girl.

Student Activity 1. Identify two other passages in which Marvell uses telling adjectives and explain why the adjectives are so effective.

Student Activity 2. Write a description and deliberately use too many adjectives. Make your overuse of adjectives as humorous as possible. When you have finished, exchange descriptions with a classmate and enjoy his or her overstuffed prose.

Reader's Response If you were writing a poem to a younger friend or relative, what would you say?

More About the Author Ben Jonson was vain, pugnacious, and given to excessive drinking, as well as enormously charismatic and revered as a writer. In the Preface to his play *Volpone,* he wrote of "the impossibility of any man's being a good poet without first being a good man." What do you think Jonson meant by this statement? Do you agree with it?

Critical Evaluation Douglas Bush made the following evaluation of Jonson's work: "Reacting against Elizabethan vagaries of matter, form, and style, Jonson demanded, and unceasingly strove for, the ageless classical virtues of clarity, unity, symmetry, and proportion; in short, the control of the rational intelligence. His poems are wholes, not erratic displays of verbal fireworks, and false taste always pronounces such writing 'barren, dull, leane.' The curt phrase, 'Shaksperr wanted Arte,' which only bardolaters have resented, is probably nearer Ben's considered judgement than the lapidary generosity of his noble tribute in verse."

BEN JONSON

1572–1637

From bricklayer to literary dictator, Ben Jonson's life story is the perfect tale of rags to riches. Not only does his life suggest myth, his physique does too. He was a large man with boundless energy and enormous courage. Friend of Shakespeare and Donne, Jonson was their chief rival in drama and lyric. In addition, Jonson was a classical scholar, an astute critic, a superb prose stylist, a skillful translator, and the chief arbiter of taste for an entire generation of writers.

Adopted when an infant by a bricklayer, Jonson worked for his stepfather a number of years while attending the equivalent of high school under one of the leading teachers of the age. Too poor to pursue his education further, Jonson enlisted in the army and fought in the wars for Dutch independence from Spain. At one point as a soldier, he fought in single combat the champion of the enemy before the massed armies of Holland and Spain. Jonson won.

On returning to England, Jonson went on the stage as an actor. His early years in the theater were stormy ones: He was jailed one time for taking part in a "seditious and slanderous" play; another time he was almost hanged for killing a fellow actor in a duel; and still later he was suspected of having a part in a plot on the life of King James I. Despite the turbulence of his life, however, Jonson learned his stagecraft well and became a major dramatist in his own right. His first play had William Shakespeare in a major role, and his later plays were performed by the chief acting companies of the day, including Shakespeare's.

Jonson was so successful he was granted a handsome pension by King James I and treated as if he were poet laureate of England. Over many years he had written masques, elaborate entertainments, for the royal court, where he was a favorite writer. During these years he was enormously influential, functioning as virtual dictator over the literary efforts of the day.

A number of the brightest and best of the young courtly writers flocked about Jonson and called themselves the "Sons" or "Tribe of Ben." Among the outstanding Sons of Ben can be counted Robert Herrick and John Suckling. Although not himself one of the "Sons," Richard Lovelace was also much influenced by Jonson. Indeed, Jonson's direct influence extended beyond these poets to the end of the seventeenth century and into the eighteenth. It is still felt today. What Jonson said of Shakespeare can be said of him as well: "He was not of an age, but for all time."

Objectives

1 To understand apostrophe
2 To infer the author's purpose
3 To write a letter defending the lady in "Still to Be Neat"

Support Material

Teaching Portfolio
Teacher Backup, p. 435
Usage and Mechanics Worksheet, p. 439
Vocabulary Check, p. 440
Analyzing Literature Worksheet, *Understanding Apostrophe,* p. 441

Critical Thinking and Reading Worksheet, *Inferring the Author's Purpose,* p. 442
Selection Test, p. 443
Art Transparency 6, *Abelard Soliciting the Hand of Heloise,* by Angelica Kauffman

GUIDE FOR INTERPRETING

On My First Son, Song: To Celia, Still to Be Neat

Writer's Techniques

Apostrophe. An apostrophe is a figure of speech in which an abstract idea or quality, a place or inanimate thing, or a dead or absent person is addressed as if present and able to hear and understand what is said. Ben Jonson used an apostrophe when he directly addressed William Shakespeare, who had been dead for several years, in his poem "To the Memory of My Beloved Master, William Shakespeare."

Apostrophes have been used since very early times by the ancient Greeks and Romans. Here is the opening line to Homer's *Odyssey:*

> Tell me, Muse, of the man of many ways. . . .

Although it is rare to find a modern poet apostrophizing, it does sometimes occur. Dylan Thomas apostrophized part of his anatomy in his poem "All All and All the Dry World's Lever."

> Know, O my bone, the jointed lever.

For the most part, though, use of the apostrophe today sounds old-fashioned, which brings to mind an ancient Roman apostrophe.

> O time! O custom!

Writing

Often people have unfinished conversations with others, conversations that they complete many times over in the privacy of their homes. Complete an unfinished conversation.

Primary Source

Few comments have been as controversial as Jonson's remarks about Shakespeare: "I remember, the players have often mentioned it as an honor to Shakespeare, that in his writing . . . he never blotted out a line. My answer hath been, would he had blotted a thousand. Which they thought was a malevolent speech . . . And to justify mine own candor (for I loved the man, and do honor his memory, on this side of idolatry, as much as any). He was (indeed) honest, and of an open, and free nature: he had an excellent fancy; brave notions, and gentle expressions . . . But he redeemed his vices, with his virtues. There was ever more in him to be praised, than to be pardoned." How do you think Jonson really felt about Shakespeare? As you read, look for the feelings Jonson expresses about the person in each poem.

Guide for Interpreting 423

424

On My First Son

Ben Jonson

Farewell, thou child of my right hand,[1] and joy;
   My sin was too much hope of thee, loved boy,
Seven years thou wert lent to me, and I thee pay,
   Exacted by thy fate, on the just[2] day.
5 O, could I lose all father,[3] now. For why
   Will man lament the state he should envy?
To have so soon scaped world's, and flesh's rage,
   And, if no other misery, yet age?
Rest in soft peace, and, asked, say here doth lie
10 Ben Jonson his best piece of poetry.
For whose sake, henceforth, all his vows be such,
   As what he loves may never like too much.

---

1. child . . . hand: The literal translation of the Hebrew name Benjamin. Jonson's son was born in 1596 and died in 1603.
2. just: Exact.
3. lose . . . father: Give up all thoughts of being a father.

THINKING ABOUT THE SELECTION
Recalling

1. What is the epitaph Jonson has composed for his son in lines 9–12? What vow does Jonson make as part of the epitaph?

Interpreting

2. How would you rephrase the "sin" Jonson attributes to himself in line 2? What details in the poem support this reading?
3. Why does Jonson say in line 6 that his son's death is enviable?

Applying

4. Compare Jonson's poem on his son's death with Donne's meditation and sonnet. Does Jonson express as much anguish or suffering as Donne?

ANALYZING LITERATURE
Understanding Apostrophes

The apostrophe is a literary convention that allows an author to bring vividly to the mind of a reader the subject of the apostrophe. It endows that subject with a degree of life it might not otherwise have and thereby makes it easier for the reader to share the writer's emotion.

1. To whom is this poem addressed?
2. What question does Jonson ask in lines 5–8?
3. Explain how the device of the apostrophe allows him to clearly express his emotions.

Song: To Celia

Ben Jonson

Drink to me only with thine eyes,
And I will pledge with mine;
Or leave a kiss but in the cup,
And I'll not look for wine.
5   The thirst that from the soul doth rise,
Doth ask a drink divine:
But might I of Jove's[1] nectar sup,
I would not change for thine.

I sent thee late[2] a rosy wreath,
10   Not so much honoring thee,
As giving it a hope, that there
It could not withered be.
But thou thereon did'st only breathe,
And sent'st it back to me;
15   Since when it grows and smells, I swear,
Not of itself, but thee.

———————

1. Jove's: Jupiter's. In Roman mythology, Jupiter
is the ruler of the gods.
2. late: Recently.

THINKING ABOUT THE SELECTION
Recalling

1. What does the speaker ask for in the first four lines of "Song: To Celia"?
2. In the next four lines, what does the speaker say the soul requires and what substitutes does it desire?
3. (a) Why, according to lines 11–12, did the speaker send the "rosy wreath" to Celia? (b) In lines 14–16, what does the speaker say happened to the wreathe?

Interpreting

4. The speaker says a number of times that he prefers expressions of love to drink, whether wine or nectar. (a) What does love give him that drink cannot? (b) In which lines does he say this?

Applying

5. Many of Jonson's songs were updated versions of classical Latin and Greek poems. If you were asked to update "Song: To Celia," how would you do so?
6. In your opinion, why has this song been so popular down through the centuries?

Song: To Celia   425

Reader's Response What instruments would you use in setting this poem to music? Explain.

Master Teacher Note You might wish to compare the affection expressed in "To Celia" with that depicted in *Abelard Soliciting the Hand of Heloise,* by Angelica Kauffmann. You may wish to explain that Pierre Abelard was a notable twelfth-century thinker and teacher and that Heloise was at first his student and later his wife. The story of their love is one of the most famous in history. Ask your students to tell what feelings the scene implies. Are the feelings in "To Celia" similar or different?

Enrichment Jonson developed this song from some prose pieces written by Philostratus, a Greek letter writer of the third century. Set to music, it has been a familiar and popular song for almost four hundred years. Jonson's lyrics owe a great deal to Roman and Greek lyrics with their sense of proportion, structural beauty, lucidity and conciseness of style, and freedom from extravagance.

Closure and Extension

ANSWERS TO THINKING ABOUT THE SELECTION
Recalling

1. He asks that Celia toast him with her eyes and send him a kiss.
2. The soul asks for divine love; but even if the speaker could have the food of the gods, he would prefer Celia's love.
3. (a) He says that the wreath would not wither if it were in Celia's presence. (b) Celia sent it back to the speaker, but it acquired Celia's scent.

Interpreting

4. (a) Love gives him greater delight. (b) He implies this in lines 7–8.

Applying

5. Answers will differ but students might make the following points: one might modernize the language and change the reference to Jove, and one might also change the extravagant conceit about the wreath and possibly focus on the modern uneasiness with the idea of perfect love or on the dynamics between the man and woman.
6. The song is charming, rhythmic, and accessible. It deals with the always interesting topics of flirting, wine, and devoted love.

426

Still to Be Neat

Ben Jonson

> Still to be neat, still to be dressed,
> As, you were going to a feast;
> Still to be powdered, still perfumed:
> Lady, it is to be presumed,
> 5 Though arts hid causes are not found,
> All is not sweet, all is not sound.
>
> Give me a look, give me a face,
> That makes simplicity a grace;
> Robes loosely flowing, hair as free:
> 10 Such sweet neglect more taketh me,
> Then all th'adulteries of art.
> They strike mine eyes, but not my heart.

THINKING ABOUT THE SELECTION

Recalling

1. To whom is the first stanza of "Still to Be Neat" addressed?
2. In stanza 1, what is the speaker saying about the Lady's appearance?
3. What does the speaker ask for in the second stanza?

Interpreting

4. The speaker's tone in the first stanza is one of complaint and criticism. What words convey this tone?

5. Where does the speaker say that art raises questions about the good and the true?
6. Essentially, the poem says that art is false, and that naturalness is both more truthful and more appealing. What statements in the poem support this theme or main idea?

Applying

7. A modern writer once said, "Nature imitates art." What does this statement reveal about modern attitudes toward art and nature, and how does it contrast with the attitude expressed by Jonson?

MARRIAGE À LA MODE IV:
THE COUNTESS'S MORNING LEVÉE
William Hogarth
National Gallery, London

THINKING AND WRITING

Responding to Criticism

Imagine that you are either the Lady or the Lady's friend and are called upon to respond to the speaker's criticism. Write a letter to the speaker defending the Lady, the virtue of neatness, and the truthfulness of art. Remember, you do not want to offend the speaker; if possible, you would like to persuade him that he is mistaken. It would be a nice touch if you could write your letter as a poem, but prose will do as well.

More About the Author While a young man living in London, Robert Herrick was a "Son of Ben," one of the followers of Ben Jonson. Many people feel that Herrick surpassed his master in charm, craftsmanship, and spontaneity. What might be some of the advantages and disadvantages for a young artist of having an older mentor, or more experienced advisor?

Critical Evaluation Robert M. Adams asserted that "Jonson taught Herrick the art of the polished trifle, the light touch, and the quiet mood. For both of them life was a sacrament—and Herrick brought to that sometimes portentous view of things a modesty and sense of proportion that are uniquely his own."

ROBERT HERRICK

1591–1674

Called the greatest songwriter of the English language, Herrick's verses please the ear more than the mind. Although he lived through one of the most controversial periods of English history, little of this is reflected in his poetry. His poems are light, whimsical, highly polished, and extremely artificial. They are also a joy to read and hear.

Born to a wealthy goldsmith in London who died when Robert was young, Herrick was apprenticed to his even wealthier uncle, who was also a goldsmith. Although there are no records of his early education, Herrick went up to Cambridge when he was 22 and graduated when he was 29 with a master's degree. Shortly afterward he was ordained a minister and served as a chaplain with English troops fighting in France. On his return from France he was assigned a rural parish in southwestern England. At first unhappy at his "internal exile," Herrick soon adjusted to the lovely countryside and easy life of a country parson. There he wrote his charming verse that celebrated equally the passage of time, the beauty of nature, the joys of love, the pleasures of paganism, and the modesty of Christian devotion.

Although not politically active, Herrick was evicted from his parish by triumphant Puritans after the final defeat of Charles I. Returning to his native and much-loved London, Herrick published his poems in a single, thick little volume with two titles: *Hesperides* and *Noble Numbers. Hesperides,* which is the classical Greek name for a mythological garden at the western edge of the world, contained Herrick's secular poems, for which he is best known today. *Noble Numbers* contained his religious verse. Published at a politically turbulent time in London, Herrick's light and graceful poems were ignored by his contemporaries. Interest in them was revived in the nineteenth century, and they are highly regarded today.

With the Restoration in 1660, Herrick went back to his parish in the west country and remained there until his death. When he was young, he had been one of the most ardent disciples of Ben Jonson. From the older poet, Herrick had learned the virtues of a light touch, of a polished surface, and of a restrained manner. He carried his lessons well into his exile, where he sang "of brooks, of blossoms, birds, and bowers: / Of April, May, of June, and July flowers."

Objectives
1 To understand symbols
2 To make inferences about the *carpe diem* tradition
3 To write a reply in verse to "To the Virgins . . ."
4 To write about the thinking process

Support Material

Teaching Portfolio
Teacher Backup, p. 445
Usage and Mechanics Worksheet, p. 449
Vocabulary Check, p. 450
Analyzing Literature Worksheet, *Understanding Symbols,* p. 452

Critical Thinking and Reading Worksheet, *Interpreting the Difference Among Synonyms,* p. 453
Selection Test, p. 455

GUIDE FOR INTERPRETING

An Ode for Him,
To the Virgins, to Make Much of Time

Writer's Techniques

Symbols. A symbol stands for something other than itself while at the same time making us aware of itself. For example, although we realize that the American flag is a piece of cloth, we also recognize that it stands for the United States, its system of government, and the kinds of freedom that are enjoyed here. Writers often use symbols because they are such economical ways of expressing complex ideas. For example, the rose is used frequently to express the idea of the swift passage of time and the short duration of beauty and freshness. Feasts or meals often symbolize sharing, affection, community, and close companionship. The rose and the feast are central symbols in the following two poems by Herrick.

Commentary

In "To the Virgins, to Make Much of Time," Herrick advises young women to marry while they can. How does Herrick's advice relate to the reality of marriage-making in the seventeenth century?

Marriages were essentially economic, not romantic, affairs. In most cases, the parents made all the arrangements. A daughter would almost always agree to marry the man that her parents had selected, for she was usually still a teenager and had been brought up to expect her parents to select her husband. Often, as with the very wealthy, the negotiations for marriage began when the prospective brides were still infants. Sometimes, however, girls flatly refused to accept their parents' choices.

Fourteen-year-old Mary Boyle, the daughter of the Earl of Cork, for example, stood her ground against the match her parents had arranged. In turning down James Hamilton, she wrote, "My aversion for him was extraordinary. I could never be brought by fair means or foul to it." Dorothy Osborn was equally determined to marry for love rather than for social and economic advantage. Although the family estates were ruined by the Civil War, her father's health was declining, and her mother was dead, she steadily refused the stream of prospective husbands that her brother provided. "I am certain," she wrote, "I could not love the most perfect person in the world unless I did first believe he had a passion for me."

In light of the realities of the seventeenth-century marriage mart, why do you think Herrick advises women to marry young?

Writing

Write the name of an object, such as a flag, a flower, a football, a catcher's mitt, a sewing needle, or a rolling pin. First describe the object as it actually exists: the way it looks, what it is used for. Then write down all the associations you have with the object.

Guide for Interpreting   429

Literary Focus Have students work in pairs or small groups to brainstorm for a list of symbolic items. Have them share their lists with the class.

Vocabulary

Preteach the following vocabulary words:

ode (ōd) *n.*: A poem of varying line lengths and usually several stanzas, often addressed to someone; in classical literature, a poem to be sung, usually in praise of someone (p. 430, title)

lyric (lir′ ik) *n.*: A poem, one of the major categories of poetry; in classical literature, a song accompanied by a lyre (p. 430, l. 4)

clusters (klus′ tərz) *n.*: Groups, gatherings; bunches, as of grapes for wine (p. 430, l. 7)

frolic (fräl′ ik) *adj.*: Merry (p. 430, l.10)

wit (wit) *n.*: Intelligence, wisdom (p. 430, l.14)

overplus (ō′ vər plus′) *n.*: Surplus, abundance; enough left over for others (p. 430, l.14)

talent (tal′ ənt) *n.*: A Biblical unit of money; native ability (p. 430, l.17)

succeed (sək sēd′) *v.*: Follow; come after (p. 432, l.12)

former (fôr′ mər) *adj.*: Earlier; coming before (p. 432, l.12)

coy (koi) *adj.*: Unwilling to make a commitment, *not* the modern sense of "pretending to be shy" (p. 432, l.13)

prime (prīm) *n.*: Youth (p. 432, l.15)

tarry (tar′ ē) *v.*: Linger, abide; continue in the same condition (p. 432, l.16)

An Ode for Him (Ben Jonson)

Robert Herrick

Ah Ben!
Say how, or when
Shall we thy guests
Meet at those lyric feasts,
5   Made at the Sun,
The Dog, the Triple Tun?[1]
Where we such clusters had,
As made us nobly wild, not mad;
And yet each verse of thine
10 Outdid the meat, outdid the frolic wine.

My Ben
Or[2] come again:
Or send to us,
Thy wits great overplus;
15   But teach us yet
Wisely to husband[3] it;
Lest we that talent spend:
And having once brought to an end
That precious stock; the store
20 Of such a wit the world should have no more.

---

1. Sun . . . Dog . . . Triple Tun: The names of taverns where "The Tribe of Ben" (see p. 444) would gather.
2. or: Either.
3. husband: Conserve.

---

1 **Discussion** The term *ode* implies a poem that is serious, formal, and dignified, usually written to commemorate a person or event. Odes often have an elaborate stanzaic pattern. Does Herrick's poem fit this definition?

2 **Discussion** What is meant by "lyric feasts"?

3 **Discussion** What is meant by "nobly wild"?

4 **Discussion** "Stock" is a metaphor for what commodity referred to in the poem? How is that image developed throughout?

Reader's Response How would you praise the wittiest person you know?

THINKING ABOUT THE SELECTION
Recalling

1. What question is asked in the first six lines?
2. In lines 7–10, what does the speaker say took place at Ben Jonson's favorite taverns?
3. (a) In lines 11–16, what does the speaker ask of Ben? (b) In lines 17–20, what risks does the speaker describe if Ben does not respond?

Interpreting

4. In what way were the speaker and others Ben Jonson's guests?
5. The tone of this poem is melancholy. What words, phrases, and thoughts contribute to setting this melancholy tone?

Applying

6. "An Ode for Him" is a poem praising Ben Jonson. Today, there are many occasions when we speak words of praise. What are those occasions and how would you express yourself on such occasions?

CRITICAL THINKING AND READING
Knowing Differences Among Synonyms

A **synonym** is a word that has the same or similar meaning as another word, as, for example, *error* and *mistake*. Sometimes, several words are synonyms, such as *error, mistake, slip-up,* and *blunder.* They all mean "incorrectness" or "inaccuracy," but there are slight differences among them. *Error* often implies that the incorrectness is the result of *stubborness,* as when we say, "That was an error in judgment." In contrast, *mistake* is much less harsh in implication. It does not, for example, suggest *willfulness,* as does *error.* The word *mistake* also often suggests that the incorrectness or inaccuracy is minor, as when we say, "Oh well, he just made a mistake." We would never use the word *error* in that sentence.

We might, though, use the word *slip-up* if we felt the mistake was a result of carelessness. *Slip-up* is even less formal than *mistake* and would not be used in a report to the top boss of a corporation, for instance. On the other hand, *blunder,* which is far more formal than *slip-up* and *mistake,* is much farther from *error* in its associated meanings than the other two. The senses of *stupidity, clumsiness,* and *sloppiness* are part of the meaning of *blunder.*

If we were to arrange our three words according to how close they are to the word *error,* we would put them in the following order: *error,* (1) mistake, (2) slip-up, and (3) blunder. Do the same with the following synonyms taken from "An Ode for Him." Look each word up in the dictionary, number them according to how close they are to the main word, and explain how they differ from one another.

1. *feast:* meal, banquet, religious celebration
2. *wild:* uncivilized, uncontrolled, impassioned
3. *teach:* guide, train, instruct

THINKING AND WRITING
Writing About Thinking

Imagine that you are writing a letter to a friend explaining how you arranged the synonyms. In your letter, answer the following questions. What was the basis for the order in which you placed the synonyms? Did you first look in the dictionary to find out what the words mean? How did you know the dictionary definition was correct? Did you try to make up sentences to fit the definitions? Did you try out the definitions and sentences on people you know? What was their reaction? Did you check out the order of the synonyms with these people? How did they react to that? Did they confirm your judgment? If not, what did you do? At the end of your letter, ask your friend what he thinks the order of the synonyms should be and why. Revise your letter and prepare a final draft.

An Ode for Him 431

431

Motivation for Reading Ask students to imagine that they are song-writers. What would they say in a song urging young women to take advantage of their youth and energy before they get old?

Master Teacher Note Ask students how many have heard the line "Gather ye rosebuds while ye may." Ask them to explain this line. Why is it so famous?

Thematic Idea Other poems on the theme of *carpe diem* are "The Nymph's Reply to the Shepherd" on page 238 and "To His Coy Mistress" on page 418.

Discussion Describe the rhyme scheme and rhythm of the poem. How do they contribute to the poem's overall effect?

Reader's Response How would you express the idea of this poem in a modern, but memorable, way?

To the Virgins, to Make Much of Time

Robert Herrick

Gather ye rosebuds while ye may,
    Old time is still a-flying;
And this same flower that smiles today
    Tomorrow will be dying.

5   The glorious lamp of heaven, the sun,
    The higher he's a-getting,
The sooner will his race be run,
    And nearer he's to setting.

That age is best which is the first,
10   When youth and blood are warmer;
But being spent, the worse, and worst
    Times still succeed the former.

Then be not coy, but use your time,
    And, while ye may, go marry;
15 For, having lost but once your prime,
    You may forever tarry.[1]

---

1. tarry (tar′ē) *v.*: Delay.

THINKING ABOUT THE SELECTION
Recalling

1. In stanza 1, why does the speaker advise the girls to gather the rosebuds while they may?
2. In the second stanza, what happens to the sun as it gets higher in the sky?
3. According to the third stanza, what is the best age and what happens when it is passed?
4. In stanza 4, why does the speaker suggest that the young girls stop delaying and marry?

Interpreting

5. The central theme or idea of this poem is the swift passage of time. What images express this theme?

Applying

6. This poem is in one sense advice to young women to marry while still young. In what way does it also express the "carpe diem" or "seize the day" tradition? Why do you think

Closure and Extension

ANSWERS TO THINKING ABOUT THE SELECTION
Recalling

1. The rosebuds—the joys of youth—last a very short time.
2. It gets closer to setting.
3. The best age is youth and after that things get worse and worse.
4. If they don't marry now, maybe they never will.

Interpreting

5. Images that express the passage of time are the rosebuds, the sun, and the different stages of life.

Applying

6. Throughout, the poem expresses the idea that time flies and pleasures must be seized while they are available. This is the essence of the "carpe diem" theme. One special reason for the popularity of the tradition is that it is a staple of Classical poetry, which most English poets of this time knew well and admired.

ANSWERS TO ANALYZING LITERATURE

1. Symbols of time include rosebuds, flowers that smile today and die tomorrow, and the course of the sun.
2. These symbols work together to create a vivid impression of the

THREE LADIES ADORNING A TERM OF HYMEN
Sir Joshua Reynolds
The Tate Gallery, London

Humanities Note

Fine art, *Three Ladies Adorning a Term of Hymen,* 1773, by Sir Joshua Reynolds. An English painter, Sir Joshua Reynolds (1723–1792) began his artistic education as an apprentice to the artist Thomas Hudson. His education continued as he traveled to Italy where he studied the works of the masters, particularly Rubens and Michelangelo. After his return to England, he became famous for his portraits of the British upper class done with classical themes and backgrounds of ancient landscapes and architecture. He was instrumental in the formation of the Royal Academy and became its first president.

The painting *Three Ladies Adorning a Term of Hymen* was posed for by three daughters of a London gentleman. It was painted more as a "conversation piece" than as a portrait. The three young women, in classical drapery, are shown holding a garland of flowers before a term (stone figure used by ancient Romans to mark boundries) of the god of marriage. The classical theme is further carried out in the details of the amphora and shield to the right. The pose is artificial and theatrical in a good-natured way. When viewing this painting with your students, you might mention that although the painting was produced more than a century after the poem was written, the sentiments expressed in both are the same.

Master Teacher Note After reading Herrick's "To the Virgins, to Make Much of Time," place *Young Girl and Death,* by Marianne Stokes, on the overhead projector. Ask your students to summarize the "message" of Herrick's poem. Then ask them to suggest what underlying similarity of idea is present in Stokes's strange painting. If necessary, you might prompt discussion by pointing out that even for young girls life does not last forever.

this tradition was so popular during the seventeenth century?

ANALYZING LITERATURE
Understanding Symbols

Symbols are at the same time themselves and stand for something else. The poets of the sixteenth and seventeenth centuries loved playing with the conventions of their art. One of the most popular conventions of the period was the combination of a swiftly passing time and an urgent need to love. Robert Herrick was one of the most successful players of this conventional game.

1. Point to all the symbols of time in "To the Virgins, to Make Much of Time."
2. How do these symbols work together to suggest "blossoming youth" and "decaying age"?

To the Virgins, to Make Much of Time 433

transience of all young, lovely growing things.

THINKING AND WRITING
Publishing Student Writing Possible arguments that might be included in a response to Herrick are: love can be enjoyed at any time in life; mature love is deeper than youthful love; and youthful love is often merely infatuation. You might consider having students' share their responses in a class magazine.

Critical Evaluation Robert M. Adams noted that Suckling exemplified a quality that Baldassare Castiglione had written about "in his dialogue *The Courtier* (1528)': "a certain fine carelessness as the natural quality of a great gentleman. It meant that no matter how hard one had worked on some accomplishment—a poem, a costume, swordsmanship—one should treat it always as if it were a natural, easy, spontaneous action. Sir John Suckling above all the other 'Cavalier' poets who gallantly supported the lost cause of Charles Stuart, cultivated this special quality of instinctive, careless poise."

Douglas Bush wrote that "As soldier, courtier, lover, poet, scholar, musician, and connoisseur of painting, the 'extraordinary handsome' Lovelace exemplified the tradition of Sidney and Castiglione. His poems display the extreme unevenness of a gentleman amateur, and fame has rightly fixed upon the few lyrics in which he struck a simple, sincere, and perfect attitude; in these, with pure and exalted idealism, he enshrined the cavalier trinity, beauty, love, and loyal honor."

BIOGRAPHIES

Sir John Suckling (1609–1642)
Richard Lovelace (1618–1657)

The works of Suckling and Lovelace have been linked together as the prime examples of the courtly lyrics known as *Cavalier poetry*. Both poets wrote a light and easy kind of verse associated with the court of Charles I. Both affected a tone of gentlemanly nonchalance in their poems; both were courtiers under Charles.

Suckling came from an extremely wealthy family and used up his inheritance in extravagant living. At one point he hired one hundred fighting men, dressed them up in fancy uniforms, went off to fight for the king in Scotland, and was roundly beaten by the sullen, unfashionably dressed Scots. When he was not engaged in futile fights, he wasted his wealth in gambling. However, he was also a serious patron of many excellent poets, wrote four plays that were spectacularly staged and published at his own exorbitant cost, and composed the delicate lyrics that have gained him fame for over 300 years. As Parliament rebelled against King Charles and gained control of the government, Suckling joined in a conspiracy to free a Royalist leader from the Tower of London. The plot was exposed and Suckling fled to France. There he died impoverished and in despair.

Also from an extremely wealthy family, Lovelace was the pretty boy of Cavalier poetry. He was so handsome that the king and queen ordered that he be granted a master's degree before he completed his studies at Oxford. He was, however, also talented. While at Oxford he wrote a play, painted some fine pictures, and performed credibly on several musical instruments. Perhaps because he was so attractive, Lovelace was chosen by the Royalists to present to Parliament a demand for the restoration of the king's right to absolute authority. Lovelace was immediately arrested. It was while imprisoned that he wrote "To Althea" as a justification for siding with the king even though it meant being confined in jail. After his release from prison, he rejoined Charles's forces in the civil war and spent most of his fortune to help equip the king's army. Upon Charles's defeat in 1645, Lovelace went to France and fought against Holland. Returning to England some while later, he was once again imprisoned by the Puritans. It was during this second imprisonment that he prepared for publication the volume of poems that included "To Lucasta." Although no one knows for certain, it is believed that he died in poverty.

Objectives

1 To write about tone
2 To understand the effect of connotative meaning
3 To compare and contrast the poetry of Suckling and Lovelace

Support Material

Teaching Portfolio
Teacher Backup, p. 457
Grammar in Action Worksheet, *Using Action Verbs,* p. 462
Usage and Mechanics Worksheet, p. 464
Vocabulary Check, p. 465
Analyzing Literature Worksheet, *Understanding Tone,* p. 467

Critical Thinking and Reading Worksheet, *Understanding the Effect of Connotative Meaning,* p. 468
Selection Test, p. 469

GUIDE FOR INTERPRETING

The Constant Lover; Song; To Lucasta, on Going to the Wars; To Althea, from Prison

Writer's Techniques

Tone. In literature, *tone* refers to the attitude expressed by an author toward his or her subject or audience. A writer's attitude is conveyed through language, characterization, setting, point of view, and details of appearance, voice, location, and the like. Whether in prose or poetry, recognizing the writer's tone is essential to an understanding of the work. Without this recognition, we cannot tell if an author is serious or playful, mocking or admiring, angry or joking, laughing or crying. Very often the tone of a piece of writing can shift from one quality to another.

Writing

Describe the way you feel about something. Your subject can be either serious or trivial. The important thing about your writing is that you reveal how you feel through the words and details you choose. Do not say directly how you feel; do not say, "I am angry," "I am amused," "I am proud," or "I am sorry."

Primary Source

A man investigating prison conditions in the seventeenth century wrote, "Lord Bless me! What a Sight is here! I do not think there had been so much cruelty in the Hearts of Englishmen, to use Englishmen in this manner." What he saw was appalling indeed.

Prisoners were herded together, without privacy or comfort. They slept on piles of straw, usually directly on the cold ground. Since there was no indoor plumbing, bathing was virtually impossible. A few prisons had fireplaces and jailers might provide coals for a fee, but more than a century later the majority of English prisons still did not have heating or baths. Prisoners were given only a quarter of a loaf of bread daily, supplemented by what their family and friends could supply. Scores perished from jail fever. For this, prisoners paid five pounds a year!

Because jailers had to pay a tax on windows, fresh air was scarcer than water and heat. One eyewitness wrote, "The most pernicious infection next to the plague is the smell of a jail, whereof we have had, in our time, experience once or twice." One visitor protected himself by "smelling to vinegar, while I was in those places, and changing my apparel afterwards."

How does the tone of "To Althea, from Prison" reflect prison life in the seventeenth century?

Guide for Reading 435

Literary Focus One tone of voice that will be familiar to students is sarcasm. Ask volunteers to repeat the words *Nice catch* seriously and then sarcastically.

Writing/Prior Knowledge Have students read aloud the descriptions they wrote for their freewriting assignment. Have members of the class guess the tone each description is trying to convey.

Vocabulary

Preteach the following vocabulary words:

constant (kän′ stənt) *adj.*: Faithful; unchanging; unceasing (p. 436, title)

molt (mōlt) *v.*: Cast off; shed, as skin or feathers (p. 436, l.5)

wan (wän) *adj.*: [Archaic] Gloomy, not the modern sense of sickly pale (p. 437, l.1)

fond (fänd) *adj.*: [Archaic] Foolish, not the modern sense of having affection for someone or something (p. 437, l.1)

nunnery (nun′ ər ē) *n.*: Convent, a dwelling place for nuns (p. 438, l.2)

inconstancy (in kän′ stən sē) *n.*: Fickleness; changeableness (p. 438, l.9)

grates (grāts) *n.*: A frame of metal bars used as a partition (p. 439, l.4)

fettered (fet′ ər'd) *adj.*: Chained; confined (p. 439, l.6)

hermitage (hʉr′ mit ij) *n.*: A retreat suitable for meditation; originally, a hermit's dwelling (p. 440, l.28)

436

The Constant Lover

Sir John Suckling

1
Out upon it! I have loved
        Three whole days together;
And am like to love three more,
2
        If it prove fair weather.

5   Time shall molt away his wings,
        Ere he shall discover
In the whole wide world again
        Such a constant lover.

But the spite on 't is, no praise
10   Is due at all to me:
3
Love with me had made no stays,
        Had it any been but she.

Had it any been but she,
        And that very face,
15 There had been at least ere this
        A dozen dozen in her place.

THE INTERRUPTED SLEEP
François Boucher
The Metropolitan Museum of Art

THINKING ABOUT THE SELECTION

Recalling

1. In the first stanza of "The Constant Lover," how long has the speaker loved?
2. According to lines 3 and 4, what conditions are necessary for the speaker to continue to love?
3. In the second stanza, how long will it be before Time will find a lover as faithful as the speaker?
4. According to stanza 3, why is praise not due the speaker?
5. In the last stanza, what reason does the speaker give for not leaving his lady for another "dozen dozen" women?

Interpreting

6. The poem is an elaborate compliment to a lady. What are the elements that contribute to this compliment?
7. When an inanimate object or an abstract idea, such as Time or Death, is given human characteristics, it is called *personification*. What is personified in stanza 2 and how does it work in the poem?
8. (a) What attitude toward love and the woman are evident? (b) In what way is the word *constant* in the title ironic?

Applying

9. What qualities do you think characterize a *constant* lover?

Song

Sir John Suckling

1

FAIR IS MY LOVE
Edwin A. Abbey
The Harris Museum and Art Gallery, Preston

Why so pale and wan, fond lover?
　　Prithee, why so pale?
Will, when looking well can't move her,
　　Looking ill prevail?
5　　　Prithee, why so pale?

Why so dull and mute, young sinner?
　　Prithee, why so mute?
Will, when speaking well can't win her,
　　Saying nothing do't?
10　　Prithee, why so mute?

Quit, quit, for shame; this will not move,
　　This cannot take her.
If of herself she will not love,
　　Nothing can make her:
15　　The devil take her!

2
3

THINKING ABOUT THE SELECTION

Recalling

1. In the first stanza of "Song," how does the lover look?
2. What is the question the speaker asks in the second stanza?
3. What advice to the lover does the speaker give in the third stanza?

Interpreting

4. The third stanza is different from the two preceding ones. In what way is it different?
5. What has caused the "fond" lover to look and behave in the way described by the speaker?
6. What do you think is the lover's emotional state? Explain your answer.

Applying

7. This poem is in a sense an early example of advice to the lovelorn. If a good friend broke up with a loved one, what sort of advice would you give? What would you say and how would you say it?

THINKING AND WRITING

Writing About Tone

Write an essay in which you discuss the tone of Suckling's "Song." Imagine that you will deliver this paper to a scholarly audience. For this audience you will want to discuss the use of irony and wit as instruments for expressing the poet's attitude toward his subject.

1 **Discussion** In what ways is the poem a song?

2 **Enrichment** In the tradition of Petrarch, the Italian sonneteer, the lover became pale and silently wasted away for want of his beloved.

3 **Discussion** What is the speaker's attitude toward love?

Humanities Note

Fine art, *Fair is My Love,* by Edwin Austin Abbey. Abbey (1852-1911) was an expatriate American painter, muralist, and illustrator who lived in England. An apt and clever draftsman in pen and ink, Abbey had a definite attraction for scenes from the British middle ages. The painting *Fair is My Love* was done after 1890 during a period when Edwin Abbey turned to the medium of oil paint. A sweet and charming scene, set in a castle garden, it is historically correct in every detail.

　　You might use these questions for discussion:
1. How would you describe this painting?
2. In what ways does the painting illustrate Suckling's poem?

Reader's Response Do you share this speaker's attitude toward love? Why or why not?

Applying

9. Answers will vary, although all students should include faithfulness, or a similar quality.

ANSWERS TO THINKING ABOUT THE SELECTION
Recalling

1. The lover looks ill.
2. Why is the lover so silent?
3. His advise is to forget about the girl.

Interpreting

4. The third stanza consists of commands rather than questions.
5. He is unhappy that he cannot win his lady.
6. The lover is depressed.

Applying

7. Answers will differ, but common advice might be to find another lover.

Humanities Note

Fine art, *Going to the Battle,* 1858, by Sir Edward Coley Burne-Jones. Burne-Jones (1833–1898), a British painter, abandoned studies in theology to become a painter. After a brief apprenticeship with Dante Gabriel Rossetti, a founding member of the Pre-Raphaelite brotherhood, he began his lifetime work as a painter. His work exemplifies the Pre-Raphaelite style in its use of subjects from medieval times, allegory and myth, careful attention to detail, and purity of color and form.

Going to the Battle is a pen and ink study of a medieval theme. The graceful maidenly figures are formalized in the manner of a carved frieze. The draped folds and rich patterns of their clothing add to the enchantment of the scene.

Consider using these questions for discussion:

1. What seems to be the attitude of the knight in this drawing?
2. What aspects of the poem are reflected in this drawing?

GOING TO THE BATTLE
Edward Burne-Jones
Fitzwilliam Museum, Cambridge

To Lucasta, on Going to the Wars

Richard Lovelace

1 Tell me not, Sweet, I am unkind,
        That from the nunnery
   Of thy chaste breast, and quiet mind,
        To war and arms I fly.

2 5 True, a new mistress now I chase,
        The first foe in the field;
   And with a stronger faith embrace
        A sword, a horse, a shield.

   Yet this inconstancy is such,
   10   As you too shall adore;
   I could not love thee, Dear, so much,
3   Loved I not honor more.

THINKING ABOUT THE SELECTION

Recalling

1. In the first stanza of "To Lucasta, on Going to the Wars," from whom is the speaker going and toward what is he "flying"?
2. In the second stanza, whom does the speaker chase and what will he embrace?
3. According to the last stanza, why will the abandoned lady "adore" the speaker's "inconstancy"?

Interpreting

4. What is the "new mistress" the speaker refers to in the second stanza?
5. What do you believe is the "stronger faith" mentioned by the speaker in line 7?
6. What does the speaker mean when he says in lines 11–12, "I could not love thee, Dear, so much / Loved I not honor more"?
7. This poem is an argument made by the speaker to his lady-love in an effort to convince her to accept his leaving her for war. What details in the poem support this interpretation?

Applying

8. If you were to leave a loved one to go off to fight, what would you say to convince that person to accept your departure?
9. In "Song" (pages 420–421), John Donne also wrote an argument trying to persuade his beloved to accept his leaving her. Compare the poems by Donne and Lovelace. How do they differ? In what one respect are they similar?

438   *The Seventeenth Century*

To Althea, from Prison

Richard Lovelace

When love with unconfined wings
    Hovers within my gates,
And my divine Althea brings
    To whisper at the grates;
5 When I lie tangled in her hair
    And fettered to her eye,
The gods[1] that wanton[2] in the air
    Know no such liberty.

    When flowing cups run swiftly round,
10   With no allaying Thames,[3]
Our careless heads with roses bound,
    Our hearts with loyal flames;
When thirsty grief in wine we steep,
    When healths[4] and drafts[5] go free,
15 Fishes that tipple in the deep,
    Know no such liberty.

When, like committed linnets,[6] I
    With shriller throat shall sing
The sweetness, mercy, majesty,
20   And glories of my King;
When I shall voice aloud how good
    He is, how great should be,
      Enlarged[7] winds that curl the flood,
      Know no such liberty.

---

1. gods: The word *gods* is replaced by *birds* in some versions of this poem.
2. wanton: Play.
3. cups . . . Thames (temz): Wine that has not been diluted by water (from the river Thames).
4. healths: Toasts.
5. drafts: Drinks.
6. committed linnets: Caged finches.
7. enlarged: Released.

1 **Literary Focus** In this stanza Lovelace makes use of the literary device of paradox. What is the paradox? What are the paradoxes in the following stanzas?

2 **Discussion** Why are fish appropriate symbols of liberty here?

3 **Discussion** Why are winds an appropriate symbol here?

4 **Discussion** Why are the angels an appropriate symbol here?

Reader's Response What is a modern example that proves "Stone walls do not a prison make"?

Closure and Extension

ANSWERS TO THINKING ABOUT THE SELECTION
Recalling

1. (a) The god is hovering within the prison gates. (b) She is whispering outside the bars of his cell.
2. (a) Being with Althea gives him the greatest freedom. (b) Celebrating with friends gives him the greatest freedom.
3. Praising King Charles gives him the greatest liberty.
4. (a) He needs freedom for his mind, heart, and soul. (b) Gods, fish, winds, and angels will experience no greater freedom than he. (c) He compares his freedom to that of an angel.

Interpreting

5. (a) He moves from love of a woman, to celebrating with his friends, to love for the king, or from personal to public pleasures. (b) Freedom doesn't depend on where you are but on whether the heart and mind are free.
6. (a) The poem is about what constitutes true freedom. (b) Each stanza focuses on one expression of liberty: love, friendship, and love of one's country.
7. Answers will differ, but students might note that the title and the fact that the speaker returns to the idea of love at the end argue that it is a love poem. The fact that the speaker is not complaining while in prison suggests that the poem is an expression of devotion for the king.

Applying

8. Answers will differ but students might point out that the sentiment is reassuring and pithily expressed.

---

25   Stone walls do not a prison make,
        Nor iron bars a cage;
     Minds innocent and quiet take
        That for an hermitage;
     If I have freedom in my love,
30   And in my soul am free,
     Angels alone that soar above,
        Enjoy such liberty.

4 [

THINKING ABOUT THE SELECTION
Recalling

1. (a) According to lines 1–4, where is the god Love hovering? (b) Where is the "divine Althea" whispering?
2. (a) In lines 5–8, what does the speaker say gives him the greatest freedom? (b) What conditions does the speaker describe in the second stanza as yielding the greatest freedom?
3. In the third stanza, when will the speaker know the greatest "liberty"?
4. (a) What, in the last stanza, does the speaker say is required to enable him to enjoy the maximum freedom? (b) What or who does the speaker say in the first three stanzas will experience no greater freedom than he? (c) To what does the speaker compare his freedom in the last stanza?

Interpreting

5. (a) The conditions for the speaker's freedom form a progressive movement in the first three stanzas. What is that movement? (b) Summarize the speaker's conception of freedom.
6. In seventeenth-century England, part of the conflict between King Charles I and his rebellious Parliament was over freedom. Charles wanted to rule by "divine right," which meant basically that he could do as he wished. Parliament wished to take that right away from him. To Charles, this meant a loss of freedom. The Puritans in Parliament, on the other hand, felt that Charles had tried to take away their freedom of religion. From their point of view, it was either his freedom or their freedom that was at stake.
   (a) In what way does Lovelace's poem, "To Althea," reflect this issue? (b) Why does each stanza turn on the idea of "liberty"?
7. Some critics have called "To Althea" a love poem; others have said it was an expression of devotion to King Charles. Which interpretation do you believe is right and why?

Applying

8. The first two lines of the fourth stanza of "To Althea" are very famous. They have been repeated down through the ages, often by people who did not know their source. Aside from their poignancy, why, in your opinion, have these lines been so very popular?

Grammar in Action

Use precise **action verbs** to make writing lively. Vague or weak verbs leech vigor from writing. Notice how Richard Lovelace uses precise action verbs.

    When love with unconfined wings
        Hovers within my gates . . .

    When I lie *tangled* in her hair
        And *fettered* to her eye . . .

The Puritan Age

THE FARRIER'S SHOP, *c. 1620–1687*
Gael Barend
Guildhall Art Gallery, London

Humanities Note

Fine art, *The Farrier's Shop,* Gael Barend (c. 1600–1663). During the latter part of the seventeeth century, other forms of painting besides portraiture emerged, perhaps influenced by the art of Holland and France. At the same time, interest was growing in genre scenes, scenes of everyday life in the country, like the scene in *The Farrier's Shop.* A farrier is one who shoes horses or one who treats them medically. This scene centers on the farrier about his business, a common scene in village life of the seventeenth century.

Lovelace's vivid verbs give life to his sentences. Compare the following weaker sentences with Lovelace's:

When love with unconfined wings stays within my gates . . .

When I lie caught in her hair and joined to her eye . . .

Student Activity 1. Replace the verbs in the following sentences with stronger, more precise ones.

1. The rival squad made a disturbance in the gym.
2. Patsy danced wildly across the floor.
3. The batter laughed at the pitcher's wild pitch.
4. The family lived from day to day trying to make ends meet.

Student Activity 2. Write two sentences using precise, strong, action verbs.

More About the Author John Milton was known in his time as a fiery revolutionary and writer of political tracts as well as a poet. Toward the end of his life, poor and blind, with his cause lost, he retired to his writing, hoping to "leave something to aftertimes as they should not willingly let die." What does this quotation reveal about Milton's view of himself as a poet?

Critical Evaluation Douglas Bush asserted that "John Milton stands next to Shakespeare among English poets; his writings and his influence are a very important part of the history of English literature, culture, and libertarian thought. He is best known for his long epic poem Paradise Lost, in which his 'grand style' is used with superb power; its characterization of Satan is one of the supreme achievements of world literature."

JOHN MILTON

1608–1674

Ranked with William Shakespeare and Geoffrey Chaucer as one of the greatest poets of the English language, John Milton actually produced comparatively few poems. The major part of his life he spent either studying literature or writing political tracts. Yet *Paradise Lost* by itself would have been enough to earn him a place among the immortals of English literature.

Born in London to a middle-class family, Milton grew up in a highly cultured environment. His father was a composer and musician of considerable ability as well as a professional scribe or notary. Milton's father was also deeply religious and devoted to the Protestant cause. Educated first at home by tutors, Milton started his formal education in the equivalent of high school when he was about thirteen. While a student at this school he mastered Greek, Latin, and Hebrew as well as several modern European languages. Then he went on to college.

It was while at Cambridge University that Milton decided to prepare himself for a career as a great poet ("God's poet," was how he described it). From this point onward until the English Civil War broke out, Milton devoted himself to a life of study. After earning his degrees from Cambridge, he withdrew to his father's house at Horton for five years, where he is reputed to have read everything that was written in the ancient and modern languages that he knew. It was during this long period of study that Milton wrote "L'Allegro," "Il Penseroso," and "Lycidas," which by themselves would have earned him a lasting position as a major poet. Following his stay at Horton, he went on the Grand European Tour for two years.

While Milton was in Europe, Parliament rebelled against King Charles I; learning of the revolt, Milton cut short his trip and rushed back to England. There, he immediately took up the cudgels in defense of the Parliamentary and Puritan cause. It was in this role that he took part in the pamphlet war of the time and became a leading exponent of republican principles. As a result of his brilliant writings, Oliver Cromwell made Milton Latin Secretary of the Commonwealth. It was in this job that he went blind. Upon restoration of the monarchy, he was at first imprisoned and then released. Andrew Marvell, his former assistant and now Member of Parliament, may have argued in his behalf.

After Milton's release and the loss of most of his property, he withdrew into his blindness and poverty to write *Paradise Lost,* the greatest epic of the English language.

Objectives

1 To recognize the Italian sonnet
2 To understand multiple meaning of words
3 To explain an allusion in poetry and use an allusion in writing
4 To compare and contrast the English and the Italian sonnet

Support Material

Teaching Portfolio
Teacher Backup, p. 471
Usage and Mechanics Worksheet, p. 475
Vocabulary Check, p. 476
Analyzing Literature Worksheet, *Understanding Italian Sonnets,* p. 478

Language Worksheet, *Understanding the Multiple Meanings of Words,* p. 479
Selection Test, p. 480

GUIDE FOR INTERPRETING

When I Consider How My Light Is Spent; On His Having Arrived at the Age of Twenty-Three

Writer's Techniques

The Italian Sonnet. The sonnet is one of the major forms of English poetry, but it was invented by the Italians in the thirteenth century. It was imported into England by Wyatt and Surrey in the middle of the sixteenth century. The Italian sonnet is a fourteen-line lyric poem. It is usually divided into two segments, an octave of eight lines and a sestet of six lines. According to the sonnet convention, the octave is supposed to present a situation or problem and the sestet is supposed to offer an answer or response. The rhyme scheme also follows a fairly strict pattern. The octave rhymes *abbaabba* and the sestet usually varies, although within a fairly narrow range. In English, sonnets, whether Italian or not, are written in ten-syllable lines, five beats to the line with a stress pattern that goes like this:

$$\breve{U} / \breve{U} / \breve{U} \quad / \quad \breve{U} / \breve{U} /$$
open unto the fields and to the sky.

Commentary

In "On His Having Arrived at the Age of Twenty-Three," Milton assesses his life. People completing their education today sometimes assess their lives as they prepare to embark on a career. Some people even feel that they should have acccomplished more. Imagine how they would feel hearing the stories of child prodigies who have already achieved a lifetime of accomplishments before reaching their teens!

Wolfgang Amadeus Mozart (1756–1791), for example, began music lessons at age four, and by five was composing minuets. A year later his ability to sight read music caused a sensation throughout Europe. He wrote his first symphony at eight; at twelve, he wrote two operas and a mass. His achievements grew as he matured, and today he is considered a musical genius.

John Stuart Mill (1806–1873) was fluent in Greek at three, Latin at eight—not to mention history and mathematics. By twelve he had read the classics in the original. He became an important theorist and writer in politics, economics, and philosopy who dedicatd himself to justice and the public good.

According to the poem, how does Milton believe he will accomplish his goals?

Writing

Jot down some ideas on reaching whatever age you might now be—16, 17, 18. Try to include some ideas reflecting your view of your accomplishments to date and what you expect from the future.

Guide for Interpreting   443

Literary Focus Almost every major poet, even into the twentieth century, has tried his or her hand at writing sonnets. What do you think writers and readers find so appealing about the sonnet? Why should it be such a popular form?

Writing/Prior Knowledge Have **less advanced** students write about their accomplishments in prose.

Vocabulary

Preteach the following vocabulary words:

spent (spent) *adj.*: Used up; gone (p. 444, l.1)

bent (bent) *adj.*: Determined; resolved (p. 444, l.4)

chide (chīd) *v.*: Scold; rebuke (p. 444, l.6)

exact (ig zakt') *v.*: Demand; compel (p. 444, l.7)

yoke (yōk) *n.*: A wooden contrivance joining the heads of two draft animals, such as oxen, to make them capable of pulling heavier loads (p. 444, l.11)

subtle (sut' 'l) *adj.*: Cunning; ingenious (p. 446, l.1)

semblance (sem' bləns) *n.*: Appearance; image (p. 446, l.5)

measure (mezh' ər) *n.*: Quantity, dimensions, size (p. 446, l.10)

even (ē' vən) *adj.*: Parallel; on the same level with; conforming to (p. 446, l.10)

grace (grās) *n.*: God's favor or approval (p. 446, l.13)

When I Consider How My Light Is Spent

John Milton

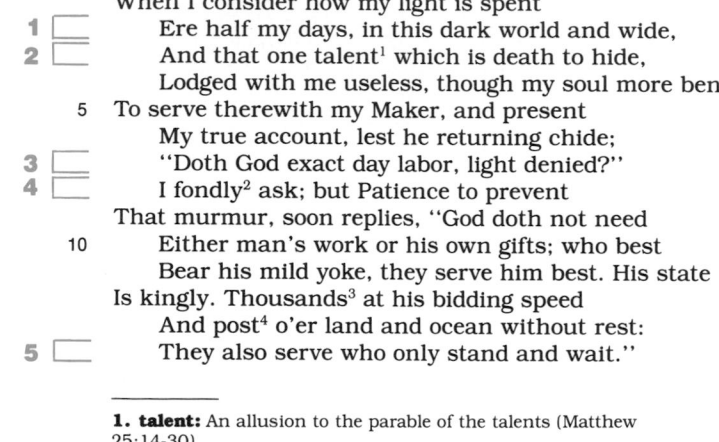

When I consider how my light is spent
    Ere half my days, in this dark world and wide,
    And that one talent[1] which is death to hide,
    Lodged with me useless, though my soul more bent
5 To serve therewith my Maker, and present
    My true account, lest he returning chide;
    "Doth God exact day labor, light denied?"
    I fondly[2] ask; but Patience to prevent
That murmur, soon replies, "God doth not need
10   Either man's work or his own gifts; who best
    Bear his mild yoke, they serve him best. His state
Is kingly. Thousands[3] at his bidding speed
    And post[4] o'er land and ocean without rest:
    They also serve who only stand and wait."

---

1. talent: An allusion to the parable of the talents (Matthew 25:14-30).
2. fondly: Foolishly.
3. thousands: Thousands of angels.
4. post: Travel.

THINKING ABOUT THE SELECTION

Recalling

1. According to lines 1–2, at what point in the speaker's life does his eyesight fail?
2. What three qualities does the second speaker attribute to God?

Interpreting

3. The first speaker in this poem expresses a sense of failure. What is the nature of that failure?

4. Why, in your opinion, might Milton have felt that his blindness made his talent useless?
5. Explain the last line of the poem: "They also serve who only stand and wait."
6. This sonnet, unlike most other sonnets, is like the dialogue in a play. How does this unusual formal arrangement affect your understanding of the poem?

Applying

7. Do you feel it is necessary for people to use their talents? Explain your answer.

444   *The Seventeenth Century*

ANALYZING LITERATURE
Understanding Italian Sonnets

The rhyme scheme of Milton's sonnet on his blindness is *abbaabba cdecde,* which is common to the Italian sonnet. To emphasize their rhyme scheme, most sonneteers end-stop their lines. When a natural pause occurs at the end of a line, the line is called *end-stopped.* An example of end stopping is the third line of Milton's "When I Consider . . . " This can be contrasted with the next line, the normal reading of which carries one over to the following or fifth line. This kind of carry-over is called *enjambment* or a *run-on line.* Run-on lines tend to obscure end rhymes and thereby make the rhyme scheme more subtle than it might otherwise be. There are a number of run-on lines in Milton's poem.

Another characteristic of the sonnet is the change that takes place between the first eight lines, or octave, and the followig six lines, or sestet. Most often the change is very subtle in the Italian sonnet. In Milton's "When I Consider . . ." it is very obvious.

1. Which rhyme sounds are end-stopped and which run-on in the octave?
2. How many end-stopped lines are there in the sestet?

3. Did you read the run-on lines as if you were reading prose? Explain your answer.
4. Which seemed more natural to you, the end-stopped lines or the run-on ones? Which more artifical?
5. What shift in tone did you experience between the octave and sestet when reading aloud? How do you account for this shift?

UNDERSTANDING LANGUAGE
Understanding Multiple Meanings

Most words have more than one meaning. Picking the word *friend* at random, one dictionary indicates five different meanings; another indicates seven.

Poets often use words in such a way as to exploit several meanings of a word at the same time. In this way they enrich an image or a poem.

1. What are the two meanings of the word *talent*?
2. Which is the primary one in the poem?
3. How does the secondary one reinforce the meaning of the primary sense of *talent*?
4. In Milton's mind, what was his chief, perhaps only, talent? What had he spent most of his early life preparing for?
5. What kind of "death" might Milton have experienced if he "hid" or did not use his talent?

ANSWERS TO ANALYZING LITERATURE

1. End-stopped lines: 2, 3, 6, 7
   Run-on lines: 1, 4, 5, 8
2. There are only two end-stopped lines in the sestet, lines 13 and 14.
3. The lines still have the rhythm of poetry and read as such.
4. The run-on lines seem more natural because they follow natural speech patterns; the end-stopped lines seem more artificial.
5. The tone changes from anxiety to assurance. The shift occurs because the speakers change.

ANSWERS TO UNDERSTANDING LANGUAGE

1. *Talent* is a natural ability and is also an ancient coin.
2. The primary meaning is "ability."
3. The secondary meaning emphasizes the worth of his talent by comparing it to a valuable coin.
4. His chief talent is as a writer. He had spent most of his early life preparing to be a writer.
5. He would have experienced a spiritual death.

Primary Source

Milton's essay, "The Second Defense of the English People," written in 1654, offers an intriguing glimpse into his life. In the following excerpt, he discusses his childhood and describes what he sees as the cause for his later blindness:

"I will now mention who and whence I am. I was born at London, of an honest family; my father was distinguished by the undeviating integrity of his life; my mother, by the esteem in which she was held, and the alms which she bestowed. My father destined me from a child to the pursuits of literature; and my appetite for knowledge was so voracious, that, from twelve years of age, I hardly ever left my studies, or went to bed before midnight. This primarily led to my loss of sight. My eyes were naturally weak, and I was subject to frequent head-aches; which, however, could not chill the ardor of my curiosity, or retard the progress of my improvement."

On His Having Arrived at the Age of Twenty-Three

John Milton

How soon hath Time, the subtle thief of youth,
    Stolen on his wing my three and twentieth year!
    My hasting days fly on with full career,[1]
    But my late spring no bud or blossom showeth.
Perhaps my semblance might deceive[2] the truth,
    That I to manhood am arrived so near,
    And inward ripeness doth much less appear,
    That some more timely-happy spirits[3] endueth.[4]
Yet be it less or more, or soon or slow,
    It shall be still[5] in strictest measure even,
    To that same lot,[6] however mean or high,
Toward which Time leads me, and the will of Heaven;
    All is, if I have grace to use it so,
    As ever in my great Taskmaster's eye.

---

1. career: Speed.
2. deceive: Prove false.
3. timely-happy spirits: Other people who seem to be more accomplished poets at the age of twenty-three.
4. endueth: Endoweth.
5. still: Always.
6. lot: Fate.

THINKING ABOUT THE SELECTION
Recalling

1. According to the first line, who or what is the "subtle thief of youth"?
2. According to the second line, what was stolen?
3. What, according to line 3, flies on swiftly?
4. In line 4, what is not shown?
5. In lines 5–6, what is the speaker's image that "might deceive the truth"?
6. According to lines 7–8, what does not appear that others seem to have?
7. According to lines 8–12, to what will the speaker's accomplishments eventually conform?
8. What, according to lines 13–14, is forever in the "great Taskmaster's eye"?

Interpreting

9. A metaphor is a comparison of two unlike things. In line 4, Milton uses two metaphors: one for the advanced stage of his youth, the other to represent the early or full development of his poetic ability. Which words are the metaphors?
10. Compare and contrast the concerns of the first four and second four lines of the poem.
11. Overall, what concerns the speaker in the first eight lines?
12. How do the last six lines answer the concern expressed in the first eight lines?

Applying

13. One reason Milton may have felt he hadn't achieved much is that he hadn't yet decided on a career. He had first thought of entering the church and becoming a minister, but by the time he was twenty-three had decided against it. How many people do you know who have made career decisions by the time they were twenty-three? Why do you think it is so difficult to do this?

THINKING AND WRITING
Comparing and Contrasting Sonnets

Write an essay comparing and contrasting the Italian and English sonnets. Imagine you are writing this explanation for your school newspaper.

The English sonnet, which is also commonly known as the Shakespearean sonnet, is markedly different from the Italian form. The sonnet was first developed by the Italians as a fourteen-line love poem with a strict rhyme scheme and structure. The structure is divided into an eight-line octave and a six-line sestet.

The English sonnet, which derives from the Italian, has an entirely different structure and rhyme scheme. In this instance, the sonnet is divided into three four-line quatrains and a concluding two-line couplet. Each of these units has a different set of rhymes and a slightly different thought or image.

Use Shakespeare's "Sonnet 73" (page 257) and Milton's "On His Having Arrived at the Age of Twenty-Three" as your models. Analyze the ryhme scheme for both poems and explain the shifts in thought and image for both poems. Also describe the subjects of both poems. In what way are the subjects similar? How are they different? When you revise, make sure you have arranged your information in logical order. Proofread your essay and prepare a final draft.

Applying

13. Answers will differ. Students might mention that many who make career decisions early in life change their careers in the future.

THINKING AND WRITING

For help with this assignment, students can refer to Lesson 16, "Writing a Comparative Evaluation," in the Hankbook of Writing About Literature.

Publishing Student Writing
After reading the essays, you may want to read several of the best to your class as models of thoughtful, well-organized comparisons.

Closure and Extension

ANSWERS TO THINKING ABOUT THE SELECTION
Recalling

1. Time is the "subtle thief of youth."
2. His twenty-third year was stolen.
3. His life flies on swiftly.
4. No buds or blossoms are shown.
5. His appearance, or "semblance," might "deceive the truth."
6. An "inward ripeness" does not seem to appear.
7. They will eventually conform to what he should accomplish according to his age and God's will.
8. God's eye envisions Milton's destiny as a poet.

Interpreting

9. The bud represents youth, the blossom his poetic development.
10. In the first stanza, he is concerned that so much time has passed and that he has accomplished so little. In the second stanza, he is concerned that his outward appearance does not reflect his inward maturity. Both stanzas use horticultural metaphors, such as bud, blossom, and ripeness.
11. He is concerned about his lack of accomplishments.
12. These lines express the speaker's acceptance of God's will as the chief determinant of his life.

GUIDE FOR INTERPRETING

from Paradise Lost

Epic Poetry. An epic is a long narrative poem written in an elevated style. It tells the story of a major cultural hero and reflects the values of the society in which it was produced. The early English epic *Beowulf* exhibits the values of the Anglo-Saxon warriors for whom it was composed. John Milton's epic *Paradise Lost* expresses the values of Christian England in the late seventeenth century. It also expresses, however, ideas that are so universal that the poem has become *the* epic of the English-speaking world.

Milton based his poem on the Biblical story of Adam and Eve and his style on the classical epics of ancient Greece and Rome. Like the *Aeneid,* the epic of classical Rome, Milton divided *Paradise Lost* into twelve books. He wrote the poem in blank verse, which no one writing in English had done before except in plays. Milton chose blank verse, which uses an unrhymed iambic pentameter line, because the great epics of ancient Greece and Rome did not rhyme.

Paradise Lost had to be licensed by the Archbishop of Canterbury before it could be published. As was the practice, the Archbishop passed the manuscript to a deputy. In this case the deputy was a chaplain named Tomkyns who had written pamphlets against the dissenters. Fortunately, Tomkyns did not wish to direct attention to himself and so chose to ignore anti-monarchy passages in the manuscript that might even have gotten Milton hanged. Tomkyns might also have thought that *Paradise Lost* was religious verse that would never be read at court, and therefore its contents were not important. He passed it on.

After his manuscript was licensed by the Archbishop, Milton found a publisher for it in Aldersgate, which had not been destroyed in the recent Great Fire. The contract, still preserved in the national museum, records that the agreement was drawn up between the author "John Milton, gent. of the one parte, and Samuel Symons, printer, of the other parte." For his work Milton received five pounds down and was to receive a second five pounds each for the sale of the first, second, and third editions, respectively.

Milton earned only five more pounds for the sale of the first edition. All told, he received ten pounds for his masterpiece. Do you think the market has changed today for serious literature?

Jot down all the information you remember of the Biblical story of the fall of Adam and Eve.

448   *The Seventeenth Century*

from Paradise Lost

John Milton

Of man's first disobedience, and the fruit
Of that forbidden tree, whose mortal[1] taste
Brought death into the world, and all our woe,
With loss of Eden, till one greater Man[2]
5 Restore us, and regain the blissful seat,
Sing Heavenly Muse,[3] that on the secret top
Of Oreb, or Sinai,[4] didst inspire
That shepherd, who first taught the chosen seed,
In the beginning how the Heavens and Earth
10 Rose out of Chaos: or if Sion hill[5]
Delight thee more, and Siloa's brook[6] that flowed
Fast[7] by the oracle of God, I thence
Invoke thy aid to my adventurous song,
That with no middle flight intends to soar
15 Above the Aonian mount,[8] while it pursues
Things unattempted yet in prose or rhyme.
And chiefly thou O Spirit,[9] that dost prefer
Before all temples the upright heart and pure,
Instruct me, for thou know'st; thou from the first
20 Wast present, and with mighty wings outspread
Dovelike sat'st brooding on the vast abyss
And mad'st it pregnant: what in me is dark
Illumine, what is low raise and support;
That to the height of this great argument[10]

---

1. mortal: Deadly.
2. one . . . Man: Christ.
3. Heavenly Muse: Urania, the muse of astronomy and sacred poetry in Greek mythology. Here, Milton associates Urania with the holy spirit that inspired Moses ("That shepherd,") to receive and interpret the word of God for the Jews ("the chosen seed"). To convey the message of God to his people, Moses wrote the first five books of the Bible, including Genesis. Genesis is the book on which *Paradise Lost* is based.
4. Oreb (ôr′ ĕb) **. . . Sinai** (sī′ nī′): Alternate names for the mountain where God communicated the laws to Moses.
5. Sion (sī′ ən) **hill:** The hill near Jerusalem on which the temple ("the oracle of God,") stood.
6. Siloa's (sī lō′ əz) **brook:** A stream near Sion hill.
7. fast: Close.
8. Aonian (ā ō′ nē ən) **Mount:** Mount Helicon in Greek mythology, home of the Muses. Milton is drawing a comparison between the epic he is now presenting and the epics written by the classical Greek poets, Homer and Virgil.
9. Spirit: The Holy Spirit, the voice that provided inspiration for the Hebrew prophets.
10. argument: Theme.

from *Paradise Lost*   449

Presentation

Motivation for Reading Ask students to describe their own images of Satan and Hell.

Master Teacher Note Read aloud the Biblical description of the Fall (Genesis 2 and 3).

Thematic Idea Another selection that deals with the theme of evil is Shakespeare's *Macbeth,* p. 271.

Purpose-Setting Question In what ways does Milton portray Satan as a fully realized character?

1 Discussion What are the "Things unattempted yet in prose or rhyme"?

2 Discussion Ask students what they think Milton might mean in this line.

3 Reading Strategy The epic, like its Classical predecessors, begins *in medias res,* in the middle of things. Ask students to discuss what action has preceded this section.

25 I may assert Eternal Providence,
And justify the ways of God to men.
　　Say first, for Heaven hides nothing from thy view
Nor the deep tract of Hell, say first what cause
Moved our grand[11] parents in that happy state,
30 Favored of Heaven so highly, to fall off
From their Creator, and transgress his will
For[12] one restraint,[13] lords of the world besides?[14]
Who first seduced them to that foul revolt?
The infernal Serpent; he it was, whose guile
35 Stirred up with envy and revenge, deceived
The mother of mankind, what time his pride
Had cast him out from Heaven, with all his host
Of rebel angels, by whose aid aspiring
To set himself in glory above his peers,
40 He trusted to have equaled the Most High,
If he opposed; and with ambitious aim
Against the throne and monarchy of God
Raised impious war in Heaven and battle proud
With vain attempt. Him the Almighty Power
45 Hurled headlong flaming from the ethereal sky
With hideous ruin and combustion down
To bottomless perdition, there to dwell
In adamantine[15] chains and penal fire,
Who durst defy the Omnipotent to arms.
50 Nine times the space that measures day and night
To mortal men, he with his horrid crew
Lay vanquished, rolling in the fiery gulf,
Confounded though immortal. But his doom
Reserved him to more wrath; for now the thought
55 Both of lost happiness and lasting pain
Torments him; round he throws his baleful eyes
That witnessed[16] huge affliction and dismay,
Mixed with obdurate pride and steadfast hate.
At once as far as angels' ken,[17] he views
60 The dismal situation waste and wild:
A dungeon horrible, on all sides round,
As one great furnace flamed, yet from those flames
No light, but rather darkness visible
Served only to discover sights of woe,
65 Regions of sorrow, doleful shades, where peace

11. **grand:** First in importance and in time.
12. **for:** Because of.
13. **one restraint:** That Adam and Eve should not eat of the fruit of the tree of knowledge.
14. **besides:** In every other respect.
15. **adamantine** (ad' ə man' tēn) *adj*: Unbreakable.
16. **witnessed:** Gave evidence of.
17. **ken:** Can see.

Grammar in Action

Skillful writers sometimes use **sentences of varying lengths** to create dramatic effects. Milton is known for his long sentences and complex syntax; however, he sometimes follows such sentences with a short, dramatic exclamation or question. Milton uses this pattern, for example, in a passage where Satan describes his rebellion against God:

" 'Yet not for those,
Nor what the potent Victor in his rage
Can else inflict, do I repent or change,
Though changed in outward luster, that fixed mind
And high disdain, from sense of injured merit,
That with the Mightiest raised me to contend,

And rest can never dwell, hope never comes
That comes to all; but torture without end
Still urges,[18] and a fiery deluge, fed
With ever-burning sulfur unconsumed:
70 Such place eternal justice had prepared
For these rebellious, here their prison ordained
In utter darkness, and their portion set
As far removed from God and light of Heaven
As from the center thrice to the utmost pole.[19]
75 O how unlike the place from whence they fell!
There the companions of his fall, o'erwhelmed
With floods and whirlwinds of tempestuous fire,
He soon discerns, and weltering by his side
One next himself in power, and next in crime,
80 Long after known in Palestine, and named
Beelzebub.[20] To whom the archenemy,
And thence in Heaven called Satan, with bold words
Breaking the horrid silence thus began:
   "If thou beest he; but O how fallen! how changed
85 From him, who in the happy realms of light
Clothed with transcendent brightness didst outshine
Myriads though bright: if he whom mutual league,
United thoughts and counsels, equal hope
And hazard in the glorious enterprise,
90 Joined with me once, now misery hath joined
In equal ruin: into what pit thou seest
From what height fallen, so much the stronger proved
He with his thunder:[21] and till then who knew
The force of those dire arms? Yet not for those,
95 Nor what the potent Victor in his rage
Can else inflict, do I repent or change,
Though changed in outward luster, that fixed mind
And high disdain, from sense of injured merit,
That with the Mightiest raised me to contend,
100 And to the fierce contention brought along
Innumerable force of spirts armed
That durst dislike his reign, and me preferring,
His utmost power with adverse power opposed
In dubious battle on the plains of Heaven,
105 And shook his throne. What though the field be lost?
All is not lost; the unconquerable will,

---

18. urges: Afflicts.
19. center . . . pole: Three times the distance from the center of the universe (earth) to the outermost sphere of the universe.
20. Beelzebub (bē el′ zə bub′): Traditionally, the chief devil, or Satan. In this poem, Satan's chief lieutenant among the fallen angels.
21. He . . . thunder: God.

from *Paradise Lost* 451

And to the fierce contention brought along
Innumerable force of spirits armed
That durst dislike his reign, and me preferring,
His utmost power with adverse power opposed
In dubious battle on the plains of Heaven,
And shook his throne. What though the field be lost?' "

Coming after the complicated, long sentence, the brief question dramatically sums up Satan's defiance.

Student Activity 1. Identify another passage in which a long sentence is followed by a short one. Then explain the effect of the contrast.

Student Activity 2. Write a description of Satan in which you use sentences of varying lengths to create a dramatic effect.

4 Discussion In line 106, Satan states that all is not lost. What do they still have?

5 Discussion Contrast Beelzebub's attitude toward his banishment with Satan's.

4

And study[22] of revenge, immortal hate,
And courage never to submit or yield:
And what is else not to be overcome?
110 That glory never shall his wrath or might
Extort from me. To bow and sue for grace
With suppliant knee, and deify his power
Who from the terror of this arm so late
Doubted[23] his empire, that were low indeed,
115 That were an ignominy and shame beneath
This downfall; since by fate the strength of gods
And this empyreal substance[24] cannot fail,
Since through experience of this great event,
In arms not worse, in foresight much advanced,
120 We may with more successful hope resolve
To wage by force or guile eternal war
Irreconcilable, to our grand Foe,
Who now triumphs, and in the excess of joy
Sole reigning holds the tyranny of Heaven."
125   So spake the apostate angel, though in pain,
Vaunting aloud, but racked with deep despair;
And him thus answered soon his bold compeer.[25]
    "O prince, O chief of many throned Powers,
That led the embattled Seraphim[26] to war

5

130 Under thy conduct, and in dreadful deeds
Fearless, endangered Heaven's perpetual King,
And put to proof his high supremacy,
Whether upheld by strength, or chance, or fate!
Too well I see and rue the dire event[27]
135 That with sad overthrow and foul defeat
Hath lost us Heaven, and all this mighty host
In horrible destruction laid thus low,
As far as gods and heavenly essences
Can perish: for the mind and spirit remains
140 Invincible, and vigor soon returns,
Though all our glory extinct, and happy state
Here swallowed up in endless misery.
But what if he our conqueror (whom I now
Of force[28] believe almighty, since no less
145 Than such could have o'erpowered such force as ours)
Have left us this our spirit and strength entire
Strongly to suffer and support our pains,

---

22. study: Pursuit.
23. doubted: Feared for.
24. empyreal (em pir' ē əl) **substance:** The indestructible substance of which Heaven, or the empyrean, is composed.
25. compeer: Comrade, equal.
26. Seraphim (sĕr' ə fim): The highest order of angels.
27. event: Outcome.
28. of force: Necessarily.

Primary Source Note

Douglas Bush made the following comments about Milton's style:

"More or less hostile critics, old and new, have charged him with un-English diction and syntax, a charge which is not strengthened by irrelevant comparisons with Donne, with Shakespeare's dramatic speech, and with Dante's

totally different kind of epic. Milton's poetic and critical heritage and his own purpose prescribed a long poem, and in such a long poem the reader must be made to feel the continuity, 'the enormous onward pressure of the great stream' on which he is embarked. In short, epic style must be stylized, and Milton's style is surely no more remote

That we may so suffice[29] his vengeful ire,
Or do him mightier service as his thralls
150 By right of war, whate'er his business be
Here in the heart of Hell to work in fire,
Or do his errands in the gloomy deep?
What can it then avail though yet we feel
Strength undiminished, or eternal being
155 To undergo eternal punishment?''
Whereto with speedy words the Archfiend replied:
    ''Fallen cherub, to be weak is miserable,
Doing or suffering:[30] but of this be sure,
To do aught[31] good never will be our task,
160 But ever to do ill our sole delight,
As being the contrary to his high will
Whom we resist. If then his providence
Out of our evil seek to bring forth good,
Our labor must be to pervert that end,
165 And out of good still[32] to find means of evil;
Which oft times may succeed, so as perhaps
Shall grieve him, if I fail not,[33] and disturb
His inmost counsels from their destined aim.
But see the angry Victor[34] hath recalled
170 His ministers of vengeance and pursuit
Back to the gates of Heaven: the sulfurous hail
Shot after us in storm, o'erblown hath laid
The fiery surge, that from the precipice
Of Heaven received us falling, and the thunder,
175 Winged with red lightning and impetuous rage,
Perhaps hath spent his shafts, and ceases now
To bellow through the vast and boundless deep.
Let us not slip[35] the occasion, whether scorn,
Or satiate[36] fury yield it from our Foe.
180 Seest thou yon dreary plain, forlorn and wild,
The seat of desolation, void of light,
Save what the glimmering of these livid flames
Casts pale and dreadful? Thither let us tend
From off the tossing of these fiery waves,
185 There rest, if any rest can harbor there,
And reassembling our afflicted powers,[37]
Consult how we may henceforth most offend

---

29. suffice: Satisfy.
30. doing or suffering: Whether one is active or passive.
31. aught: Anything.
32. still: Always.
33. if . . . not: Unless I am mistaken.
34. angry Victor: God.
35. slip: Fail to take advantage of.
36. satiate: Satisfied.
37. afflicted powers: Overthrown armies.

from popular English than Virgil's is from popular Latin or Homer's from popular Greek. Like the ancients, Milton wore his singing robes; a ritualistic elevation of style and movement was essential to a heroic and religious theme of cosmic dimensions. Classical theory and practice had been restated for the Renaissance by such a poet-critic as Tasso, and his precepts for the attaining of epic elevation are illustrated in *Paradise Lost*. One essential function of stylized elevation is the preserving of aesthetic distance, in the depiction of hell, heaven, chaos, and most of all Eden; presented realistically, Adam and Eve would be a pair of suburban nudists.''

Fine art, Engraving, *Paradise Lost,* by Jacob Tonson (1656–1736), a London printer. This engraving was produced as an illustration for *Paradise Lost*. It is from a lavish folio published in 1688. This engraving reflects the baroque style in art (elaborate decoration characterized by overuse of the curve) that was in full flower in England at the time. Grotesque and nightmarish, this engraving is an appropriate visualization of the subject it illustrates.

Listed below are questions for class discussion of this illustration:

1. Do you think this artist's concept of Satan agrees with Milton's characterization of him? Explain.
2. Is this illustration an accurate visualization of Milton's text? Explain.

Our Enemy, our own loss how repair,
How overcome this dire calamity,
190 What reinforcement we may gain from hope,
If not what resolution from despair."
        Thus Satan talking to his nearest mate,
With head uplift above the wave, and eyes
That sparkling blazed; his other parts besides,
195 Prone on the flood, extended long and large,

PARADISE LOST, 1688
From the British Library

Grammar in Action

Language choice creates tone. **Tone** is the pervading mood of a piece of writing or a passage within it. One factor that contributes to tone is the writer's word choice. Notice how John Milton's choices contribute to the grand, elevated tone of *Paradise Lost*.

Forthwith upright he rears from off the pool
His mighty stature; on each hand the flames
Driven backward, slope their pointing spires, and rolled
In billows leave in the midst a horrid vale.
Then with expanded wings he steers his flight
Aloft, incumbent on the dusky air
That felt unusual weight, till on dry land
He lights . . .

Lay floating many a rood,[38] in bulk as huge
As whom the fables name of monstrous size,
Titanian, or Earthborn, that warred on Jove,
Briareos or Typhon,[39] whom the den

6

200   By ancient Tarsus[40] held, or that sea beast
Leviathan,[41] which God of all his works
Created hugest that swim the ocean stream:
Him haply slumbering on the Norway foam
The pilot of some small night-foundered skiff,

205   Deeming some island, oft, as seamen tell,
With fixed anchor in his scaly rind
Moors by his side under the lee, while night
Invests[42] the sea, and wished morn delays:
So stretched out huge in length the Archfiend lay

7

210   Chained on the burning lake, nor ever thence
Had risen or heaved his head, but that the will
And high permission of all-ruling Heaven
Left him at large to his own dark designs,
That with reiterated crimes he might

215   Heap on himself damnation, while he sought
Evil to others, and enraged might see
How all his malice served but to bring forth
Infinite goodness, grace and mercy shown
On man by him seduced, but on himself

220   Treble confusion, wrath and vengeance poured.
Forthwith upright he rears from off the pool
His mighty stature; on each hand the flames
Driven backward, slope their pointing spires, and rolled
In billows leave in the midst a horrid vale.

225   Then with expanded wings he steers his flight
Aloft, incumbent[43] on the dusky air
That felt unusual weight, till on dry land
He lights, if it were land that ever burned
With solid, as the lake with liquid fire;

230   And such appeared in hue, as when the force
Of subterranean wind transports a hill
Torn from Pelorus, or the shattered side

---

38. rood: An old unit of measure, equal to seven or eight yards.
39. Titanian (tī tā′ nē ən) **. . . Earthborn . . . Briareos** (brī är′ ē əs) **. . . Typhon** (tī′ fən): In classical mythology, both the Titans, led by Briareos, who had a hundred hands, and the Giants (Earthborn), led by Typhon, a hundred-headed serpent monster, fought with Jove. As punishment for their rebellion, both Briareos and Typhon were thrown into the underworld.
40. Tarsus (tär′ səs): The capital of Cilicia (sə lish′ ə). Typhon is said to have lived in Cilicia near Tarsus.
41. Leviathan (lə vī′ ə thən): A great sea monster.
42. invests: Covers.
43. incumbent: Lying.

from *Paradise Lost*   455

6 **Discussion** How will Satan's plan for destruction be thwarted by Heaven?

7 **Discussion** How do Satan and his mate escape the flames? Note the epic simile here.

There is nothing light or subtle about this tone, nor is there anything light or subtle about Satan as he rises from the fiery lake and alights on the burning ground. He is a fallen angel, grown heavy and dark, and his bulk is weighty, "incumbent on the dusky air/That felt unusual weight." Milton chooses verbs that add weight and resonance to the tone. Satan "rears" and "steers," he does not *rise* or *guide*, which are lighter verbs. Milton's adjectives also increase the tone's thickness: "horrid vale," "expanded wings," "incumbent flight," and "dusky air." How different the tone would be if Milton had chosen *appalling, outstretched, burdensome,* and *dim.*

Student Activity. Locate the sentence on page 450, line 44, that begins with "Him the Almighty Power . . ." Look up any words you do not know in a dictionary. Then find a word to describe the tone of the sentence. Now substitute synonyms for the verbs and adjectives. What happens to the tone?

8 Discussion Help students to paraphrase this elaborate comparison. Point out that the main clause is "such resting found the sole/Of unblessed feet.

9 Discussion Explain Satan's philosophy in these lines.

10 Discussion Ask students if they are surprised at Satan's decision to exclude the others from his Kingdom. Why or why not?

Reader's Response Is there anything admirable about Satan? Explain.

Of thundering Etna,[44] whose combustible
And fueled entrails thence conceiving fire,
235 Sublimed[45] with mineral fury, aid the winds,
And leave a singed bottom all involved[46]
With stench and smoke: such resting found the sole
Of unblessed feet. Him followed his next mate,
Both glorying to have scaped the Stygian[47] flood
240 As gods, and by their own recovered strength,
Not by the sufferance[48] of supernal[49] power.
      "Is this the region, this the soil, the clime,"
Said then the lost Archangel, "this the seat
That we must change[50] for Heaven, this mournful gloom
245 For that celestial light? Be it so, since he
Who now is sovereign can dispose and bid
What shall be right: farthest from him is best,
Whom reason hath equaled, force hath made supreme
Above his equals. Farewell happy fields,
250 Where joy forever dwells. Hail horrors! Hail
Infernal world! and thou, profoundest Hell
Receive thy new possessor, one who brings
A mind not to be changed by place or time.
The mind is its own place, and in itself
255 Can make a Heaven of Hell, a Hell of Heaven.
What matter where, if I be still the same,
And what I should be, all but less than he
Whom thunder hath made greater? Here at least
We shall be free; the Almighty hath not built
260 Here for his envy, will not drive us hence:
Here we may reign secure, and in my choice
To reign is worth ambition though in Hell:
Better to reign in Hell than serve in Heaven.
But wherefore[51] let we then our faithful friends,
265 The associates and copartners of our loss
Lie thus astonished[52] on the oblivious[53] pool,
And call them not to share with us their part
In this unhappy mansion, or once more
With rallied arms to try what may be yet
270 Regained in Heaven, or what more lost in Hell?"

---

44. **Pelorus** (pə lôr′ əs) **. . . Etna:** Volcanic mountains in Sicily.
45. **sublimed:** Vaporized.
46. **involved:** Enveloped.
47. **Stygian** (stij′ ē ən): Of the river Styx, which, in Greek mythology, encircled Hades, the home of the dead.
48. **sufferance:** Permission.
49. **supernal:** Heavenly.
50. **change:** Exchange.
51. **wherefore:** Why.
52. **astonished:** Stunned.
53. **oblivious:** Causing forgetfulness.

Recalling

1. The first five lines of *Paradise Lost* allude to the Biblical story of Adam and Eve and their expulsion from Paradise. What are the five elements of the story that Milton chooses to emphasize?

2. Lines 6–26 are the invocation to the muse. Which lines state the help that Milton is seeking?

3. In lines 29–36, Milton fills out a bit of the story of Adam and Eve. What new element does he introduce here?

4. (a) Lines 34–53 tell of another, earlier fall from grace. Who fell that earlier time? (b) What caused that earlier fall?

5. Lines 59–74 describe Hell. What are its main features?

6. (a) In lines 84–155 Satan addresses Beelzebub and speaks of eternal rebellion and war against God. What are his motives for continuing the war? (b) Explain Beelzebub's advice.

7. From lines 193 to 209, Milton describes the size of Satan. To what creatures is Satan compared?

Interpreting

8. Throughout his invocation, from the first line to the twenty-sixth, Milton mixes references to the Hebrew Bible and classical mythology. What effect is created by Milton's combination of Hebrew and Greek-Roman elements?

9. In what ways are the Fall of Adam and Eve paralleled by the Fall of Satan and his cohorts? Point out the parallels in the poem.

10. Between lines 200 and 208 Milton uses an epic simile in which he compares Satan to the sea beast Leviathan. How does Milton convey the huge size of Leviathan, the point of the comparison?

11. From lines 242 until the end of this excerpt at line 270, Satan expresses simultaneously his despair at losing heaven and his resolve to glory in his lost condition. What words, phrases, and lines show Satan's feelings?

12. How would you describe Satan's character? Is he petty, mean, grand, self-pitying, heroic, stubborn, weak, or rebellious? You may combine several of these characterizations, but support your choices with references to the poem.

Applying

13. The eighteenth-century poet William Blake said "Milton was of the Devil's party." What do you think this statement means? Explain why you agree or disagree with this statement. Find evidence from the poem to support your answer.

ANALYZING LITERATURE

Understanding Epic Poetry

Epic poems express the values of their cultures through stories of heroes and villains in conflict. As in any other kind of story, the conflict is central and can be of many different kinds. Some conflicts are between characters, some are between a character and the environment, and some are within a character's mind.

The conflict in *Paradise Lost* is essentially between Satan and God, and the arena in which the struggle takes place is in the heart and mind first of Eve and then of Adam. The most illuminating insights into the struggle, however, come from the mind of Satan, which is always conscious of the beauty of goodness as it plans evil.

1. What causes Satan the greatest mental anguish?
2. How does he view Heaven? Contrast this to his view of Hell.
3. Interpret his statement: "The mind is its own place, and in itself / Can make a Heaven of Hell, a Hell of Heaven."

from *Paradise Lost* 457

Closure and Extension

ANSWERS TO THINKING ABOUT THE SELECTION
Recalling

1. Milton emphasizes Adam and Eve's disobedience, their eating of the apple, the death and evil that their disobedience caused, the loss of Eden, and the salvation of man through Christ.
2. Lines 22-26 state the help.
3. Milton writes that Satan deceived Eve out of revenge on God for casting him out of heaven.
4. (a) Satan himself fell earlier. (b) Satan fell because he challenged God's sovereign rule.
5. Hell is dark, eternally burning, and filled with tortured souls who have no hope of relief.
6. (a) Satan wants to continue the war because God has humiliated him and because the experience of the last rebellion has made them stronger and wiser. (b) Beelzebub's advice is to accept the fact that God is almighty and therefore cannot be overthrown by the powers of hell.
7. Satan is compared to the Titans and to the Leviathan.

Interpreting

8. The references place the poem on a grand scale because the poem seems to encompass all Western cultures.
9. Adam and Eve, like Satan, question God's sovereignty. God punished Satan by exiling him from heaven and punished Adam and Eve by exiling them from Eden. Both had been God's favorites.
10. Milton conveys his size by telling how the pilot of a small boat might mistake him for an island.
11. Students may select different lines, but a good choice might be lines 249-251 or line 263.
12. Satan is certainly rebellious and stubborn—Beelzebub speaks of Satan's "fixed mind," line 97—but he is also courageous in refusing to be conquered.

Applying

13. Blake felt that Milton—at least subconciously—admired Satan's energy, heroic qualities, and rebelliousness against a God who is depicted as rational and authoritarian.

ANSWERS TO ANALYZING LITERATURE

1. Satan's greatest mental anguish is caused by his humiliation at having been cast out of heaven.
2. Satan views Heaven as the place of all goodness. He views Hell as the place of all evil.
3. The statement suggests that Heaven and Hell, or good and evil, are merely states of mind.

Ask students to describe the most beautiful place they can imagine. Tell them that it does not have to be a place they have actually seen. Encourage them to be as vivid and detailed as possible in their descriptions. Then tell them that they will be reading about different versions of paradise—in other words, the loveliest place that can be imagined.

Enrichment You might want to read aloud to students the description of the Garden of Eden in Genesis 2:

"8 And the Lord God planted a garden eastward in Eden; and there he put the man whom he had formed.

9 And out of the ground made the Lord God to grow every tree that is pleasant to the sight, and good for food; the tree of life also in the midst of the garden, and the tree of knowledge of good and evil.

10 And a river went out of Eden to water the garden; and from thence it was parted, and became into four heads.

11 The name of the first is Pison: that is it which compasseth the whole land of Havilah, where there is gold;

12 And the gold of that land is good: there is bdellium and the onyx stone.

13 And the name of the second river is Gihon: the same is it that compasseth the whole land of Ethiopia.

14 And the name of the third river is Hiddekel: that is it which goeth toward the east of Assyria. And the fourth river is Euphrates."

CROSS CURRENTS

Views of Paradise

You're plodding through the gray slush, an icy wind tearing at your eyes. Your cheeks are flushed crimson, your fingers nearly frozen. Suddenly a car veers too close to the curb, an angry face glares out, and a blast of icy slush dives into your shoes. In desperation, your thoughts drift to a lush green garden overflowing with sweet fruit. Peace and freedom reign, as people live in harmony and freedom with each other and their animal companions. The birds sing lyrically, the flowers sway softly, and a fresh breeze wafts gently over all. Paradise!

The word *paradise* came from the Old Persian word *pairidaeza,* which meant a "walled enclosure, pleasure park, garden." Curiously, the description of paradise differs little among various cultures. Cross-culturally and throughout the ages, it is seen as a beautiful garden free from violence or pain.

CUNIFORM TABLETS

An early account of paradise appears on tablets produced by the Sumer tribe in southern Mesopotamia around the year 5000 B.C. The inscription opens with praise for the plain of Babylon, called "Edinn." In this innocent, clean, and sun-filled land, gods are forever young, healthy, and amiable. The only thing lacking is water, but this is soon brought by the sun god Utu at the command of the water god Enki. Water completes paradise by creating a lush garden bursting with fruit.

THE GARDEN OF EDEN

In *Paradise Lost,* Milton gives the traditional description of the Garden of Eden. Again we have a garden: this time, an en-

closed area on the top level of a steep hill whose sides are covered with rows of shrubs. The entire scene is illuminated by the glorious light of the sun. The image suggests the power of humanity as well as the beauty and security of paradise.

Milton's account owes much to the traditional seventeenth-century European gardens. These were private estates and parks, carefully and cleverly planted in geometrical patterns, and stocked for their wealthy owners. These lavish formal gardens were an idealized setting for thought and learning.

THE GOLDEN APPLES OF THE SUN

In Greek mythology, paradise is the garden of the Hesperides, the home of the daughters of Atlas, the evening star. Assisted by a dragon, the inhabitants guard the tree that gives the golden apples. The tree, with branches and leaves of gold, had been a wedding gift to the goddess Hera from Gaea, Mother Earth. The apples were so closely guarded that theft was thought impossible; in fact, one of the hero Hercules' twelve labors was to bring back the golden apples of the Hesperides.

AFRICAN, BUDDHIST, AND HINDU TALES OF PARADISE

Although every culture has a different word for "paradise," the tales are curiously alike. In African tales, for example, paradise is a beautiful garden with ample food and leisure. There is no death or disease. Humans live in harmony with animals, able to understand their language. But something happened that ended paradise, making life what it is today.

THE GARDEN OF EDEN
Estratus S. Field

To the Buddhists, India will become paradise when the next Buddha, called "Maitreya," appears. Evil will vanish and people will be strong and healthy. The earth will effortlessly yield an abundance of rice. Calm, broad rivers will nourish a wonderful variety of fruits and flowers.

Perhaps the most striking example of paradise is the Hindu belief in the world ages, called "yugas." There are four world ages in each cycle, all related to the ages of the life of the god Brahma. The "krtayuga" is the golden age, equivalent to paradise, where equality, prosperity, and fulfillment rein. This is followed by three ages of increasing decay, climaxing in the dark age, when people and the world are at their worst. By some Buddhist accounts, we are now unfortunately in the dark age, slated to last 432,000 human years.

PARADISE ON EARTH?

People have long searched the four corners of the globe for paradise. The Guarani Indians of South America provide perhaps the best recorded instance of an actual quest. They believe that paradise really exists on earth, but that it is cleverly concealed. For more than four hundred years, the tribe has conducted numerous voyages to find what they call the "land without evil."

Christopher Columbus claimed that the freshwater tides he found in the Gulf of Paria between Trinidad and the coast of South America originated in the four rivers that flow out of Eden. He took as proof the area's sweet climate, fragrant flowers, and lush vegetation. But paradise has also been "discovered" in less logical places, such as the North Pole!

Cross Currents 459

Questions

1. Why do you think there are descriptions of paradise in many different cultures?
2. What do these various descriptions have in common?
3. How is the quest of the Guarani Indians symbolic of a universal quest of many different peoples?
4. Now that the Earth has been completely explored, do you think that people will imagine a paradise in outer space? Explain.
5. In what way does paradise exist within us rather than outside us?

Activities

1. Have students research and report on myths and legends about paradise in different cultures.
2. Ask students to work in small groups to create their own versions of paradise. Then each group can present its description of paradise to the class.
3. Have students research and report on seventeenth-century European gardens. Encourage them to bring in pictures of these gardens, if possible.

459

JOHN BUNYAN

1628–1688

Perhaps the most widely read book by any English author, *The Pilgrim's Progress* was written by an ill-educated traveling tinker or mender of pots, pans, and other household utensils. John Bunyan's father had been a tinker before him and had trained him in his craft. As a child John received some education at the local grammar school. After marriage, Bunyan educated himself by reading two religious tracts that his wife brought as a dowry and the Bible. On the basis of this background he wrote a great many religious books and tracts, culminating in the most popular, *The Pilgrim's Progress*.

Born and raised near Bedford in central England, he left there at sixteen to join the Parliamentary army and did not return until a number of years later. At twenty-one he married and at twenty-five he started to preach after several years of an intense spiritual struggle in the dark night of the soul. Bunyan had joined a nonconformist sect and was an unlicensed preacher to its congregation at Bedford. Upon the restoration of the Stuart monarchy, Bunyan, as well as many other nonconformist preachers, was arrested. Refusing to renounce his faith, he remained imprisoned for twelve years, during which time he wrote a fairly large number of religious works. Upon his release as a result of a general amnesty, Bunyan returned to Bedford as a licensed preacher. Except for a short period during which he was imprisoned again, Bunyan remained in Bedford for the rest of his life. There he preached to his congregation and an increasing audience in the barn that served as his church and continued to work at his trade as a tinker. During his second imprisonment, Bunyan wrote the first part of *The Pilgrim's Progress*. Several years later he wrote the second part of this work and a number of other fairly successful books. Altogether Bunyan wrote and published nearly sixty works, yet at his death he was almost as poor as when he was born.

From the seventeenth century through the nineteenth, *The Pilgrim's Progress* was the most successful Christian text written by an Englishman. It was translated into well over 100 languages. Once you have read it, you can understand why the book was so popular. Bunyan was a superb storyteller. He wrote with humor; drew vivid, easily understandable characters; provided suspense and action; and sent a clear, unambiguous message. Moreover, his language, though simple and colloquial, is charged with echoes of the Bible. In essence, Bunyan's tale reflected the main cultural values of his audience.

GUIDE FOR INTERPRETING

from *The Pilgrim's Progress*

Writer's Techniques

Allegory. When the plot, characters, and setting of a story clearly represent abstract ideas, the narrative is called an *allegory*. An allegory can be prose or poetry. It operates on at least two levels: an on-the-surface level and a beneath-the-surface level.

The interest in allegory goes back very far in human history. In fact, the word itself comes from ancient Greece. However, allegory as a way of creating literature hit its stride in the Middle Ages. There are several kinds of allegories. *The Faerie Queene,* for example, is primarily a social allegory, although it has religious, moral, and political elements as well. *Everyman,* on the other hand, is almost entirely a moral allegory, and *The Pilgrim's Progress* is almost entirely a religious one.

The purpose of all allegory is to teach entertainingly. As Bunyan put it in his preface to *The Pilgrim's Progress:*

> [Fish] must be groped for, and tickled too,
> Or they will not be catch'd, whate'er you do.

To make their instruction clear, writers of allegories draw simple, one-dimensional characters and settings, which are then assigned the names of their governing traits. For example, *The Pilgrim's Progress* is an allegory of Christian redemption and salvation. The hero's name is Christian. He leaves the City of Destruction (this world) and goes toward the Celestial City (the place of salvation or heaven). Some of the characters on his journey are Obstinate, Faithful, and Mr. Worldly Wiseman.

Writing

Jot down the names of several traits, such as Happy, Dour, Mr. Cynic, or Miss Know-it-All. Then write little scenes in which characters bearing these names display the traits.

Primary Source

"Vanity Fair" is an allegorical version of a country fair. Fairs were common in Bunyan's day. A disgruntled seventeenth-century shopper, annoyed at the price and quality offered, reports that "There are (as I take it) few great towns in England that have not their weekly markets . . . where all manner of provisions for household is to be bought and sold, for ease and benefit of the country round about . . . And, as these have been in times past erected for the benefit of the realm, so are they in many places too, too much abused: for the relief and ease of the buyer is not so much intended in them as the benefit of the seller . . . For, in most of these markets, neither . . . bread nor . . . sweetness of grain are any whit looked unto, but each one suffered to sell or set up what and how himself listeth."

Guide for Interpreting 461

Writing/Prior Knowledge Divide **more advanced** students into small groups. Have them write brief scenes in which the characters from their freewriting assignments meet and share an adventure.

Vocabulary

Preteach the following vocabulary words:

vanity (van′ ə tē) *n.*: A trifle, knickknack, or other insignificant thing (p. 462, subtitle)

knaves (nāvz) *n.*: Scoundrels; cheaters (p. 462)

reverence (rev′ ər əns) *n.*: Great respect (p. 464)

raiment (rā′ mənt) *n.*: Clothing (p. 464)

traffic (traf′ ik) *n.*: Business (p. 464)

carriages (kar′ ij iz) *n.*: Ways of bearing oneself; deportment (p. 464)

from The Pilgrim's Progress

John Bunyan

Vanity Fair

This is probably the best-known episode of The Pilgrim's Progress. *The book's hero, Christian, and his companion, Faithful, pass through the town of Vanity during the season of the local fair. Local fairs were an important British tradition, giving people the opportunity to buy wares sold by merchants from all over Europe. At the same time, these fairs involved a good deal of eating and drinking and offered a wide variety of entertainment. In this selection, Bunyan uses the fair to demonstrate how worldly attractions can corrupt religious life.*

Then I saw in my dream, that when they were got out of the wilderness, they presently saw a town before them, and the name of that town is Vanity; and at the town there is a fair kept, called Vanity Fair. It is kept all the year long. It beareth the name of Vanity Fair, because the town where it is kept, is lighter than vanity, and also, because all that is there sold, or that cometh thither, is vanity; as is the saying of the wise, ''All that cometh is vanity'' (Ecclesiastes 1:2, 14; 2:11, 7; 11:8; Isaiah 11:17).

This fair is no new-erected business, but a thing of ancient standing. I will show you the original of it.

Almost five thousand years ago, there were pilgrims walking to the Celestial City,[1] as these two honest persons are; and Beelzebub,[2] Apollyon,[3] and Legion,[4] with their companions, perceiving by the path that the pilgrims made, that their way to the city lay through this town of Vanity, they contrived here to set up a fair; a fair wherein should be sold all sorts of vanity, and that it should last all the year long. Therefore at this fair are all such merchandise sold as houses, lands, trades, places, honors, preferments,[5] titles, countries, kingdoms, lusts, pleasures, and delights of all sorts, as harlots, wives, husbands, children, masters, servants, lives, blood, bodies, souls, silver, gold, pearls, precious stones, and what not.

And moreover, at this fair there is at all times to be seen jugglings, cheats, games, plays, fools, apes, knaves, and rogues, and that of every kind.

Here are to be seen, too, and that for nothing, thefts, murders, adulteries, false swearers, and that of a blood-red color.

And as, in other fairs of less moment, there are the several rows and streets under

---

1. Celestial City: The source of salvation.
2. Beelzebub (bē el' zə bub): Prince of the devils (Matthew 12:24).
3. Apollyon (a pol' yən): The angel of the bottomless pit (Revelation 9:11).
4. Legion: The unclean spirit (Mark 5:9).

5. preferments: Appointments and promotions to political or ecclesiastical positions.

their proper names, where such and such wares are vended; so here likewise you have the proper places, rows, streets (namely, countries and kingdoms), where the wares of this fair are soonest to be found. Here is the Britain Row, the French Row, the Italian Row, the Spanish Row, the German Row, where several sorts of vanities are to be sold. But as in other fairs some one commodity is as the chief of all the fair, so the ware of Rome and her merchandise is greatly promoted in this fair; only our English nation, with some others, have taken a dislike thereat.

Now, as I said, the way to the Celestial City lies just through this town where this lusty[6] fair is kept; and he that would go to the city, and yet not go through this town, "must needs go out of the world" (I Corinthians 5:10). The Prince of princes himself, when here, went through this town to his own country, and that upon a fair day too;[7] yea, and, as I think, it was Beelzebub, the

---

6. lusty: Merry.
7. The Prince . . . too: Refers to the temptation of Christ in the wilderness (Matthew 4:1–11).

PILGRIM'S PROGRESS
Angels/Pilgrim/Knight Figures
John Bunyan
The British Library

2 **Clarification** The "ware of Rome" is the Roman Catholic Church, which England had broken away from.

Humanities Note

Illustration for *The Pilgrim's Progress.* This illustration was made for the first edition of the second part of *The Pilgrim's Progress,* published in 1682. The identity of the artist is unknown. It is a woodcut engraving, a printing process by which prints are made from designs cut into wooden blocks that are inked and pressed onto paper, thereby transferring the design. The subject is a depiction of an episode from Bunyan's text involving the character Christian on his pilgrimage.

You may wish to use the following questions for discussion:

1. This art deals with a religious subject, as does the art used to illustrate the King James Version of the Bible, (page 389). How do the styles of the two examples of art compare?
2. Do you feel that the difference in styles is a reflection of the difference in religious outlook of the two eras in English history? Explain.

Grammar in Action

Conjunctive adverbs act as transitions between complete ideas and indicate the logical connections between them. Common conjunctive adverbs include *accordingly, again, besides, consequently, finally, furthermore, however, moreover, nevertheless, then, therefore,* and *thus.* Notice how the conjunctive adverb *therefore* shows the logical connection between the last two sentences of the excerpt.

But they that were appointed to examine them did not believe them to be any other than bedlams and mad, or else such as came to put all things into a confusion in the fair. *Therefore* they took them and beat them, and besmeared them with dirt, and then put them into the cage, that they might be made a spectacle to all the men of the fair.

Omit the conjunctive adverb and the relationship between the ideas is obscured. *(continued)*

3 Discussion How do you think the pilgrims were dressed?

4 Discussion What is the significance of the pilgrims' degradation? How does it recall Christ's humiliation by the Romans?

Reader's Response What did you find most vivid and appealing about this episode?

chief lord of this fair, that invited him to buy of his vanities; yea, would have made him lord of the fair, would he but have done him reverence as he went through the town. Yea, because he was such a person of honor, Beelzebub had him from street to street, and showed him all the kingdoms of the world in a little time, that he might, if possible, allure that Blessed One to cheapen[8] and buy some of his vanities; but he had no mind to the merchandise, and, therefore, left the town without laying out so much as one farthing upon these vanities. This fair, therefore, is an ancient thing of long standing, and a very great fair.

Now these pilgrims, as I said, must needs go through this fair. Well, so they did; but, behold, even as they entered into the fair, all the people in the fair were moved, and the town itself, as it were, in a hubbub about them, and that for several reasons: for

First, the pilgrims were clothed with such kind of raiment[9] as was diverse from the raiment of any that traded in that fair. The people, therefore, of the fair made a great gazing upon them: some said they were fools, some they were bedlams[10] and some they were outlandish men[11] (I Corinthians 2:7,8).

Secondly, and as they wondered at their apparel, so they did likewise at their speech; for few could understand what they said. They naturally spoke the language of Canaan,[12] but they that kept the fair were the men of this world; so that, from one end of the fair to the other, they seemed barbarians each to the other (Job 12:4; I Corinthians 4:9).

Thirdly, but that which did not a little amuse the merchandisers was that these pilgrims set very light by their wares; they

cared not so much as to look upon them; and if they called upon them to buy, they would put their fingers in their ears, and cry, "Turn away mine eyes from beholding vanity," and look upwards, signifying that their trade and traffic was in heaven (Psalms 129:37; Philippians 3:19, 20).

One chanced mockingly, beholding the carriages of the men, to say unto them, "What will ye buy?" But they, looking gravely upon him, said, "We buy the truth" (Proverbs 23:23). At that there was an occasion taken to despise the men the more; some mocking, some taunting, some speaking reproachfully, and some calling upon others to smite them. At last things came to a hubbub and great stir in the fair, insomuch that all order was confounded. Now was word presently brought to the great one of the fair, who quickly came down, and deputed some of his most trusty friends to take these men into examination, about whom the fair was almost overturned. So the men were brought to examination; and they that sat upon[13] them, asked them whence they came, whither they went, and what they did there, in such an unusual garb? The men told them that they were pilgrims and strangers in the world, and that they were going to their own country, which was the Heavenly Jerusalem (Hebrews 11:13–16); and that they had given no occasion to the men of the town, nor yet to the merchandisers, thus to abuse them, and to let[14] them in their journey, except it was for that, when one asked them what they would buy, they said they would buy the truth. But they that were appointed to examine them did not believe them to be any other than bedlams and mad, or else such as came to put all things into a confusion in the fair. Therefore they took them and beat them, and besmeared them with dirt, and then put them into the cage, that they might be made a spectacle to all the men of the fair.

---

8. cheapen: Ask the price of.
9. raiment: Clothing.
10. bedlams: Lunatics from Bethlehem Hospital, the insane asylum in London.
11. outlandish men: Foreigners.
12. Canaan: The Promised Land. The "language of Canaan" is the language of the Bible.

13. sat upon: Interrogated and tried them.
14. let: Hinder.

Student Activity 1. Find another conjunctive adverb in *The Pilgrim's Progress.* Explain the logical connection it establishes.

Student Activity 2. Supply conjunctive adverbs to join the following complete ideas.

1. I don't like dancing. I do it once in a while.
2. I fell from a ladder once. I am afraid of heights.
3. We've never been to Hawaii. It's time for a trip.
4. Joe can't attend the meeting. He thinks you should go.

THINKING ABOUT THE SELECTION
Recalling

1. In *The Pilgrim's Progress*, on what path or route is the town of Vanity located?
2. When in time was the fair established at Vanity?
3. Who were the ones that first set up the fair?
4. What can be seen at the fair?
5. Which individuals *must* go through the town and hence through the fair as well?
6. What were the three reasons the two pilgrims caused such a stir at the fair?
7. What did the pilgrims say that led to their being examined by "the great one's trusty friends"?

Interpreting

8. Why do the travelers have to pass through the fair to reach their destination?
9. What does the fair represent?
10. Why were the pilgrims so uppity toward the inhabitants of the fair?

Applying

11. "Vanity Fair," as well as the whole of *The Pilgrim's Progress*, represents a level and type of writing that is no longer common. If you were to write something like "Vanity Fair" today, how would you go about it?

ANALYZING LITERATURE
Recognizing Allegory

Everything in an **allegory** is geared toward delivering a message. The plot, characters, dialogue, and setting all contribute to the same end—to make the author's ideas immediately understandable.

1. How does the allusion to the temptation of Jesus in the wilderness relate to the purpose of the fair at Vanity?
2. Why is the town and its fair astride the path the true Christian must follow?
3. Why is the fair run by Beelzebub?
4. In relation to Christian virtue, what does the fair represent?

CRITICAL THINKING AND READING
Interpreting the Author's Point of View

Point of view refers to the way a story is told. Stories are told by *someone* and that someone or narrator is represented by a grammatical form or person. The first-person narrator is the character in the story who says "I," like the dreamer in *The Pilgrim's Progress*. The third-person narrator is the one who says "he," "she," or "it." In *The Pilgrim's Progress* the dreamer is also a third-person narrator.

In this excerpt from the "Vanity Fair" episode, there is a first-person and third-person narrator.

1. Point out where each occurs and what the function of the narrator is in any one circumstance.
2. Describe which kind of third-person narrator is being used.
3. Discuss the effect that using two kinds of narrators has on Bunyan's story.
4. In what way might this device suit Bunyan's purpose and allow him the freedom to express his own point of view?

THINKING AND WRITING
Writing an Allegory for Today's World

Allegories generally use one-dimensional characters and situations to present clear ideas about religious, moral, political, or social issues. Write an allegory about the modern world for your fellow students. Remember, allegories are stories, and all stories have conflict. In allegories, this conflict is between characters representing abstract ideas. You should have one central character that the reader can identify with. Do not forget to choose a particular point of view when writing your narrative. You may wish to use a first-person or third-person narrator, or you may wish to alternate between the two, as Bunyan did.

temptation before they can reach salvation.
9. The fair represents worldly corruption.
10. The pilgrims felt superior because they were on the road to salvation and the others were not.

Applying

11. Answers will differ, but students would probably approach such a task using more rounded characters and realistic situations.

ANSWERS TO ANALYZING LITERATURE

1. The fair represents worldly temptations such as the devil offered Jesus.
2. Like Christ, the Christian must be tested in order to prove his true resolve.
3. Beelzebub is the most appropriate figure to preside over a collection of temptations because he represents the greatest evil.
4. The fair represents everything that might corrupt Christian virtue.

ANSWERS TO CRITICAL THINKING AND READING

The excerpt begins with a first-person narrator, then shifts to a story told by a third-person narrator. The first-person narrator provides a link to the rest of the book by tying the adventures together and helps the allegory seem more personal. The third-person narrator gives Bunyan the scope to tell a story outside the experience of his central character.

THINKING AND WRITING

For help with this assignment, students can refer to Lesson 19, "Writing a Short Story," in the Handbook of Writing About Literature.

Challenge Both Milton and Bunyan were writers with strong religious beliefs that were reflected in their works. Compare the place of faith in their works, their purpose in writing, their use of the Bible, and their views of God and the devil.

Closure and Extension

ANSWERS TO THINKING ABOUT THE SELECTION
Recalling

1. Vanity is on the road to the Celestial City.
2. The fair was set up "almost five thousand years ago."
3. The devils Beelzebub, Apollyon, and Legion set up the fair.
4. Everything corrupt and with the potential to corrupt can be seen at the fair.
5. Everyone must go through the fair.
6. The pilgrims created a stir because of their clothes, their speech, and their lack of interest in the wares.
7. The pilgrims said, "We buy the truth."

Interpreting

8. They have to face and conquer

THE CHANGING ENGLISH LANGUAGE

Presentation

Motivation/Prior Knowledge
Ask students what they know about the first settlers to come to the New World. Have them discuss the Puritans and the settlements in Jamestown, Virginia, and Plymouth, Massachusetts. Then tell students that they will learn how the settlement of the New World affected the English language.

Enrichment Tell students that the islands of Chesapeake Bay, off the coasts of Maryland and Virginia, are a perfect laboratory for the study of the English language. The language has changed very little on these islands since the first settlers came. It therefore contains many echoes of the West Country English dialect of the seventeenth century. For example, the word *sink* is pronounced *zink* and the word *ball* is pronounced so it sounds like *bull*.

Humanities Note

Fine art, *Captain John Smith,* Captain John Smith, (1580–1631) seen here in an engraving from the frontispiece of his own account of his travels, was a remarkable Elizabethan. His voyages to the New World were only part of his extraordinary life, which he chronicled in several volumes, including *The True Travels, Adventures, and Observations of Captain John Smith.* For some three hundred years after its publication, its facts were generally accepted as true, but in the mid-nineteenth century skeptics decided that Smith was more a fantasist than a true historian. Recent research has shown, however, that most of what Smith said about his Virginia experiences was indeed true, and his maps and descriptions are now accepted as first-hand evidence of the early exploration and settlement on the Virginia coast.

466

New Worlds, New Words

The Renaissance had sparked the rebirth of spoken and written English. The language continued to grow and spread during the reign of James I. As the seventeenth century opened, English was poised on the edge of worldwide recognition.

The story of English in the seventeenth century is largely the story of the New World. Sparked by a combination of optimism,

CAPTAIN JOHN SMITH
The Granger Collection

faith, and self-interest, thousands of people undertook the brutal voyage to America. Captain John Smith established the first permanent British colony in Jamestown, Virginia, in 1607; the Puritans anchored the Mayflower at Plymouth Bay in December, 1620. With these voyages, the English language was planted—and took root—in an entirely new land.

Initially, the majority of people who braved the terrors of the unknown were Puritans from a section of England called East Anglia, the Puritan stronghold. Cromwell himself was from East Anglia and had trained his New Model Army there. Throughout the period, Puritans from East Anglia would continue to pour into the New World, seeking to establish a stronghold of their faith and better their lot in life. As they brought their dreams across the ocean, so they brought their language.

SEVENTEENTH-CENTURY ENGLISH LINGERS TODAY

This mass immigration to the New World had an exciting effect on the English language. Thomas Jefferson commented on the results of this movement nearly two hundred years after the first settlers established their fragile beachheads on the shores of the New World. "New circumstances," he said, "call for new words, new phrases, and the transfer of old words to new objects."

Even today, visitors from England can hear distinctive traces of seventeenth-century British speech in American English. To the ears of the British, these words

In this engraving, which appears in slightly different versions in each edition of his writings, he is a strong-looking, wily Elizabethan general, described in the frame as "Admirall of New England". His doublet, high collar, sword hilt, and rounded beard place him properly in the Elizabethan age; this drawing is dated about 1616.

You might use the following questions to discuss the art:

1. How do you suppose clothing such as he wears here would have suited the climate and lifestyle of the first settlers in Virginia?
2. Why do you suppose that an adventurer like Captain Smith found the exploration of the New World an inviting prospect?

are clearly archaic. For example, today in American English we use "gotten" in place of "got," a term commonplace in England until the late eighteenth century. American speakers still use the term "mad" to mean "angry," another remnant of seventeenth-century English. In England today, "sick" means "nausea," not illness in general, as is the case in modern America, where we have retained the older definition. "Platter," meaning "dish," is a commonplace term in America; it is largely unknown in contemporary England. Another frequently used American term carried over on those first ships is "I guess"; scholars have identified it as dating back as far as Chaucer's age. The English use "autumn" to refer to the season before winter; we interchange it with the seventeenth-century word "fall."

YOU SAY POTATO . . .

And how did all this sound? Despite the growing discontent with monarchy in the beginning of the seventeenth century, the speech of the court still set the standard for "proper" spoken and written English throughout the land. The sound of this "standard English" was different enough from the speech of the villages to be discernible, however. A country visitor to the court was easily able to identify what he called a "true kynde of pronunciation," one of the first references to what was to become standard English. As we can tell from this remark, those who spoke in courtly tones thought themselves vastly superior to those who used country dialect. Another contemporary noted this elitist attitude when he wrote:

> There be gentlemen and other that speake, but specially write, as good Southerne as we of Middlesex or Surrey do, but not the common people or every shire, of whome the gentlemen, and also their learned clarkes, do for the most part condescend.

Since Johnson had yet to write his dictionary, people tended to spell words as they sounded, which offers us clues as to their pronunciation. From the above quotation, for example, we can see that "clerkes" was pronounced "clarkes" because of the way it was spelled. Many of the rhymes found in poetry of the age—such as "tea" with "tay," and "sea" with "say"—also offer hints. From these clues and others, scholars believe that seventeenth-century standard English most likely sounded like a combination of the Irish and West Country speech of today.

CALLS FOR LANGUAGE REFORM

Carried across the vast ocean by eager pilgrims, English took firm root in the fertile linguistic soil of the new land. But back home in England, many people were beginning to feel that language matters had gotten out of hand. English, perhaps like the bulk of English society itself, was willful and coarse. In the decades to come, writers and scholars would be increasingly concerned with reining in the unruly mother tongue.

Questions

1. From which region of England did most of the early settlers come?
2. Why is it important from the perspective of linguistic history that most of these settlers came from the same region?
3. Why do you think the discovery and settlement of the New World had such a great influence on the English language?
4. (a) Which English institution set the standard for language in the seventeenth century? (b) Why do you think this institution exerted such a strong influence?
5. How can a poet's rhymes provide clues to the way in which English words were pronounced in the seventeenth century?

Activities

1. Show students appropriate portions of the PBS television series *The Story of English*. Have the class discuss the program after they view it.
2. Ask students to read and report on relevant chapters from the book *The Story of English*, which serves as a companion to the PBS series.

■ YOU THE WRITER ■

Assignment

1. Several poems in this unit are addressed to a person. Select one of these poems and turn it into a personal letter such as the poet might have conceivably written.
    Prewriting. Write a line-by-line paraphrase of the poem. Then decide how this material should be developed in prose.
    Writing. When you write the letter, use modern English, but try to capture the personality and tone of your seventeenth-century author.
    Revising. Think of the purpose or main point of your letter. What changes can you make to improve the letter's effectiveness? See if you can add to its seventeenth-century style and tone.

Assignment

2. Many of the authors in this unit led adventurous lives. Write a brief short story in which the main character is an author from this unit.
    Prewriting. Review the author's biography and his works. Jot down notes about this author. List details that make him come alive. Then use your imagination. In what scene or situation can you picture him? What other characters are present? How does the scene or situation conclude? Make a map outlining the events in your short story.
    Writing. Write the first draft of your short story. Aim to give the reader a glimpse of the author's personality and style. Your narrative should have a beginning, middle, and end. Arrange events in chronological order.
    Revising. Make whatever changes will enhance the seventeenth-century character of your narrative. Does the dialogue sound appropriate to the time and place? Then see if you can improve the narrative flow and style.

Assignment

3. Several poems in this unit are about specific people. Write a poem about a person you know, modeling your verses on one of the seventeenth-century poems.
    Prewriting. Think of the person your poem will be about and jot down whatever comes to mind about him or her. Then select thoughts and images that can be linked in a poem structured like your seventeenth-century model.
    Writing. You might first write a prose passage that contains all the ideas you wish to express. Then turn the passage into verse, following the rhythm, rhyme scheme, and stanza pattern of your model.
    Revising. Rewrite your verses until they can stand alone as a satisfactory imitation of seventeenth-century poetry. Read it aloud. Listen to the way it sounds.

YOU THE CRITIC

Assignment

1. Jacobean poetry is distinguished by the presence of striking, highly imaginative figures of speech. Write an essay in which you develop this point by citing and analyzing such figures in the work of three Jacobean poets.

 Prewriting. Review the poems you have read and scan them for figures of speech. Analyze the figures to determine what makes them effective vehicles of meaning.

 Writing. Write the first draft of your essay. Discuss the figures of speech in a systematic way to prove and illustrate the idea that striking and imaginative figures of speech are a distinctive characteristic of seventeenth-century poetry.

 Revising. First check that your separate analyses all relate to and support your main point. Then look for and correct lapses in grammar and style.

Assignment

2. Write an essay in which you compare one humorous and one serious love poem from this unit. Show how each presents a distinctive attitude toward love or the poet's beloved.

 Prewriting. Once you have chosen the poems you plan to write about, find the lines, words, ideas, and images that create the humorous or serious tone of each poem.

 Writing. Begin with a topic sentence that sums up the different attitude toward love seen in each poem. Then write about each poem separately, supporting your thesis sentence with the evidence you gathered in your prewriting work.

 Revising. First check that you have compared the poems in a way that shows clearly the different feelings and attitudes they express. Then look for and correct errors in grammar and style.

Assignment

3. How does seventeenth-century English literature in general differ from the literature of earlier periods? Write an essay in which you answer this question.

 Prewriting. First think of one or two differences in subject matter between seventeenth-century and earlier English literature. Then think of one or two differences in style or artistic technique. What specific works or parts of works would you cite to support your views?

 Writing. You might first discuss the differences in subject matter and then the differences in style or technique. Be sure to refer to specific works or passages to support your ideas.

 Revising. Pay particular attention to improving the organization of your essay so that the characteristics you are concerned with emerge clearly and vividly.

You the Critic   469

YOU THE CRITIC
Guidelines for Evaluating Assignment 1

1. Does the essay develop the ideas that Jacobean poetry is distinguished by the presence of striking, highly imaginative figures of speech?
2. Is the thesis supported by examples from the literature?
3. Are the points developed systematically?
4. Is the essay free from grammar, usage, and mechanics errors?

Guidelines for Evaluating Assignment 2

1. Does the essay begin with a statement that sums up the different attitudes toward love seen in two seventeenth-century poems?
2. Does the student write about each poem separately while supporting the thesis with evidence from the poems?
3. Has the student offered lines, words, ideas, and images to show clearly the humorous and serious tones of the poems?
4. Is the essay free from grammar, usage, and mechanics errors?

Guidelines for Evaluating Assignment 3

1. Does the essay demonstrate the difference between seventeenth-century English literature and earlier works?
2. Does the student base the comparison on differences in subject matter, style, and technique?
3. Does the student refer to specific works and passages to clarify and illustrate his or her ideas?
4. Is the essay free from grammar, usage, and mechanics errors?

Humanities Note

Fine art, *Morville Hall, Shropshire,* by John Inigo Richards. Richards (c. 1720–1810) was a theatrical scene painter and landscapist.

Throughout the eighteenth century, a "rediscovery," of England was taking place. This interest in the country was manifested in a profusion of illustrated town histories, finely engraved maps, and pictorial records of travel in various regions. The countryside was changing: Open land was disappearing; farm land was being developed, land values were growing, and common land was being enclosed. There was a desire to record the disappearing way of life.

John Inigo Richards wavered between an imitative classical landscape and the reality of the English countryside. In this painting of a Shropshire scene, he has created a fine open vista, no doubt influenced by his experience with theatrical scene painting.

MORVILLE HALL, SHROPSHIRE
John Inigo Richards
Roy Miles Fine Paintings, London

Objectives

1 To provide an overview of the Restoration and the Eighteenth Century in England
2 To trace the growth of democracy during the restoration of the monarchy
3 To understand the significance of William and Mary's "Glorious Revolution"
4 To examine the role of the cabinet and prime minister in British affairs
5 To trace the change of Britain's economy from an agricultural to an industrial system
6 To evaluate the ideals of the Enlightenment

as they were presented by neoclassical English writers
7 To define the borders of the literary world with the ages of Dryden, Swift and Pope, and Johnson
8 To investigate the eclipse of the Enlightenment

THE RESTORATION AND THE EIGHTEENTH CENTURY

1660–1798

All Nature is but art, unknown to thee,
All chance, direction which thou canst not see;
All discord, harmony not understood;
All partial evil, universal good.

Alexander Pope

471

2 **Literary Movement** See the excerpt from Daniel Defoe's *Journal of the Plague Year,* page 514, a vivid re-creation of the Black Death's emergence in England in 1665. Defoe's *Journal* reads like an eyewitness account although Defoe was only five years old when the plague occurred.

ESL Teaching Strategy Have your ESL students pair off with non-ESL partners. Let them scan the events and dates on pages 474 and 475 together. Allow time for the partners to share questions and answers quietly about the events listed in the columns.

In 1660, England stood at the threshold of a new age. The religious conflicts that had brought on the Civil War had been settled, and a king once again sat on the throne. The people of England could look forward to a period of stability, order, and progress.

This happy prospect was reinforced by the ideas of a scientific revolution then sweeping Europe. From their close observation of nature, Isaac Newton and other scientists concluded that harmony and order underlay all the events in the world. They also believed that human beings were capable of discovering and understanding that order.

The Scientific Revolution ushered in a new era called the Age of Reason, or the Enlightenment. During the Enlightenment, confidence in human reason spread beyond the realm of science. In the verses quoted on page 471, for example, Alexander Pope asserted that everything in nature has a design and purpose. Disharmony is an illusion—no more than "harmony not understood." Like scientists, Pope believed, poets must struggle to see beneath the superficial chaos and grasp the underlying harmony of the world.

The Enlightenment thus put great emphasis on order, harmony, and stability. At the same time, however, it was an age that believed in progress, and progress meant change. Great changes indeed overtook England between 1660 and the late 1700's. As Parliament restricted the power of the monarch, England improved what was already an admirably democratic political system in Europe. Even more profound changes took place in the economic sphere. English merchants were accumulating great wealth, in part because of their trade with England's colonial empire. In the late 1700's they began to invest in the first factories of the Industrial Revolution. By 1800, Britain had surpassed its ancient rival, France, as the foremost military and economic power in Europe.

From 1660 to the late 1700's, British literature continued to exhibit order and harmony in spite of, or perhaps because of, the rapid transformation of British society. Before discussing the literature of the period, however, it will be helpful to look in more detail at the political, social, and economic developments that took place in England from 1660 to the end of the 1700's.

THE GROWTH OF ENGLISH DEMOCRACY

The Restoration of Monarchy

Soon after Oliver Cromwell's death, in 1658, Parliament offered the crown to the exiled son of Charles I. In 1660, he became Charles II. Most English people fervently hoped that the restoration of the House of Stuart would end the fighting between Puritans and Anglicans and between Parliament and the Crown.

The omens in the first years of Charles II's reign were not good.
2 In 1665, a plague swept the city of London, killing 70,000 people. A

year later, the Great Fire destroyed over half the city's houses. Yet these calamities were quickly overcome. London was rebuilt on a grander scale under the direction of the brilliant architect Christopher Wren (1632–1723). Profits from the global trade carried on by British merchants furthered London's growth.

Charles II had lived in Paris during Cromwell's Protectorship. In sharp contrast to the drab Puritan leaders, Charles II enjoyed elegance. His court copied the plush clothing, rich jewelry, and elaborate wigs of Paris. An avid patron of the arts, Charles also invited Italian composers and Dutch painters to live and work in London. In 1662 he advanced the scientific spirit of the age by chartering the Royal Society, devoted to the study of natural science.

Although some critics said Charles cared more about pleasure than power, he was a shrewd ruler. He kept his Catholic convictions to himself even while accepting money from the Catholic king of France. The problem of having a Catholic king rule a Protestant nation could not, however, be kept in check forever. After Charles II died, James, son of Charles I, became king. James II was a stubborn ruler and a devout Catholic. Trouble loomed when James appointed Catholics to high offices and dismissed Parliament for failing to obey his wishes.

A Glorious Revolution

The crisis came in 1688, when James II's wife gave birth to a son. To the people of England, this meant that another Catholic king would someday sit on the throne. Parliament reacted quickly. Several leaders invited Mary, the Protestant daughter of James II, to rule England jointly with her husband, William of Orange. William was a prince of Holland and a champion of Protestantism in Europe. | 3

When William and Mary arrived in England, they were prepared to fight for the throne if necessary. But James, recalling the fate of his father, escaped to France. The people of England hailed the event as a "Glorious Revolution," since not a drop of blood had been shed. The next year, William and Mary agreed to respect a Bill of Rights passed by Parliament. Among other things, it guaranteed Parliament the right to approve all taxes and said that a king could not suspend the law. With the Bill of Rights, England attained a limited, or constitutional, monarchy. Although it was far from being a democracy in the modern sense, England was among the most democratic nations of Europe. | 4

Political Parties Emerge

After William of Orange followed his wife Mary to the grave in 1702, Mary's sister Anne, a Protestant, became queen. Under Queen Anne, England grew stronger and more united. One important act of her reign was the joining of the realms of England and Scotland. The Act of Union, passed in 1707, created the nation of Great Britain, with a central government in London.

Introduction 473

3 **Historical Context** James's two daughters, offspring of his first marriage, were safely Protestant. It was his second marriage to the Catholic Mary of Modena that produced the Catholic son who so threatened Parliament.

4 **Historical Context** William and Mary were joint monarchs. They were first cousins, both grandchildren of Charles I (William through Charles's daughter Mary), both with royal Stuart blood in their veins. Thus when Mary died, William retained the throne.

BRITISH EVENTS

1660   **Samuel Pepys** begins *Diary*.

1662   Royal Society chartered.

1663   Drury Lane Theater opens.

1666   Great Fire of London.

       First cheddar cheese produced.

1667   **John Milton's** *Paradise Lost* published.

1668   **John Dryden** publishes *An Essay of Dramatic Poesy*.

1685   James II becomes king.

1687   Isaac Newton publishes *Philosophiae Naturalis Principia Mathematica*.

1688   Glorious Revolution.

1689   Bill of Rights becomes law.

1690   John Locke publishes *Essay Concerning Human Understanding*.

1700   William Congreve publishes *The Way of the World*.

1701   Act of Settlement.

1702   England enters War of the Spanish Succession.

       First daily newspaper begins publication.

1707   Great Britain created by Act of Union.

1709   First Copyright Act.

       First literary magazine, *The Tatler*, begins publication.

1712   **Alexander Pope** publishes *The Rape of the Lock*.

1714   George I becomes king.

1719   First organized cricket match takes place.

       Daniel Defoe publishes *Robinson Crusoe*.

Palace at Versailles

The Syndics

Samuel Pepys

John Locke

The Great Fire of London

La Salle Visits Indian Village

AMACAO.

Major Port for Trade with China

Johann Sebastian Bach

WORLD EVENTS

1661	Holland: Rembrandt paints *The Syndics*.
1662	France: Louis XIV begins palace at Versailles.
1664	North America: Britain seizes New Netherlands.
1665	Holland: Vermeer paints *The Artist's Studio*.
1666	Italy: Stradivari labels first violin.
1669	France: Molière's *Tartuffe* first performed.
1677	France: Racine's *Phèdre* first performed.
1678	North America: La Salle explores Great Lakes.
1680	Dodo becomes extinct.
1685	China: All ports opened to foreign trade.
1690	India: Calcutta founded by British.
1700	Japan: Kabuki Theater developed.
1703	Russia: Peter the Great begins building St. Petersburg.
1714	Holland: Fahrenheit constructs mercury thermometer.
1715	France: Louis XV succeeds to throne.
1721	Germany: Bach composes *Brandenburg Concertos*.
1727	Brazil: First coffee planted.
1728	Pacific: Behring explores Alaskan waters.
1735	Russia: Ballet school opens in St. Petersburg.
1740	Prussia: Frederick the Great succeeds to throne.
1748	France: Montesquieu publishes *The Spirit of the Law*.
1749	Portugal: Sign language invented.

Introduction 475

Enrichment Tell students that the effort in Portugal to formalize the system of sign language was designed in part to assist in the teaching of deaf students. Point out that Europeans were impressed at that same time by the ability of the American Indian tribes to communicate well with each other, despite linguistic differences, in a system that combined common words and signs. That native American method of sign language, known to the majority of the tribes on the North American Plains, provided a common if limited means of communication among many groups including the Blackfoot, Cree, Cheyenne, and Apache.

Enrichment Mention that Gray's "Elegy in a Country Churchyard," published in 1750, might have been more than five years in the making despite its relative brevity. One of his friends, William Mason, received a version as early as 1742; others who corresponded with the poet say that he did not begin the work until 1745 or 1746. In any event, Gray was extremely reluctant to have the piece published and was, in effect, forced into admitting that he wrote the work after being told that an editor intended to print the poem even though it was not submitted for publication by Gray himself.

BRITISH EVENTS

1726   **Jonathan Swift** publishes *Gulliver's Travels*.

1735   William Hogarth paints *The Rake's Progress*.

1745   Last Jacobite rebellion in Scotland.

1749   Henry Fielding publishes *Tom Jones*.

1750   **Thomas Gray** publishes "Elegy in a Country Churchyard".

1755   **Samuel Johnson** publishes *Dictionary of the English Language*.

1756   Britain enters Seven Years' War.

1766   **Oliver Goldsmith** publishes *The Vicar of Wakefield*.

1775   Actress Sarah Siddons debuts at Drury Lane Theater.

1786   **Robert Burns** publishes *Poems Chiefly in Scottish Dialect*.

1789   **William Blake** publishes *Songs of Innocence*.

1791   **James Boswell** publishes *The Life of Samuel Johnson*.

1793   England goes to war with France.

1798   Admiral Nelson defeats French at Aboukir Bay.

Illustration from *Gulliver's Travels*

The American Revolution Begins

Robert Burns   Johnson and Boswell

Captain Cook Explores the South Pacific

The Storming of the Bastille

Benjamin Franklin   Mozart

The Boston Tea Party

WORLD EVENTS

1752	North America: Benjamin Franklin invents lightning rod.
1759	Canada: British troops capture Québec.
1765	North America: Stamp Act imposed.
1769	Pacific: Captain Cook explores New Zealand and Australia (to 1770).
1772	France: Diderot publishes *Encyclopédie*.
1773	Austria: Waltz introduced.
	North America: Boston Tea Party.
1774	France: Louis XVI succeeds to throne.
	Germany: Goethe publishes *The Sorrows of Young Werther*.
1775	United States: Revolution begins.
1776	United States: Thomas Jefferson writes Declaration of Independence.
1780	Peru: Rebellion against Spanish rule.
1781	France: Rousseau's *Confessions* published.
	Germany: Kant publishes *Critique of Pure Reason*.
1784	France: First school for the blind established.
1786	Austria: Mozart's *Marriage of Figaro* first performed.
1789	France: Revolution begins with storming of Bastille.
1791	Austria: Haydn composes *Surprise Symphony*.
1793	France: Reign of Terror begins.
1795	Africa: Mungo Park explores Niger River.

Introduction 477

Enrichment Give students an opportunity to compare the events happening around the world with those mentioned in the previous timelines on events in Britain. Prompt them to consider how interrelated occurrences can be. Ask them to estimate whether Cook's exploration of the South Pacific in 1769 would have been more apparently newsworthy to England's citizens than the Boston Tea Party of 1773.

Humanities Note

Fine art, *Queen Anne and the Knights of the Garter,* by Peter Angelis. The Flemish painter Peter Angelis (1685–1734) was born in Dunkirk (his original name, Pierre Angillis, has become Anglicized among English-speaking writers). After traveling in Flanders, he lived in England between about 1719 and 1727. Angelis is admired for his carefully executed pastoral scenes and pleasingly decorative genre paintings, showing ordinary people in simple, domestic settings. Angelis also painted more formal scenes, such as this court scene of Queene Anne in a ceremonial role, installing the Knights of the Garter in 1713.

5 Historical Context Although Ann had many children, they all predeceased her. Thus her successor was George of Hanover, a great-grandson of James I through his daughter Elizabeth.

During Anne's reign, there was another important political development. Once again, France and Britain were at war. The war helped to crystallize two political factions in Parliament, the Tories and the Whigs. The Tories included aristocrats and lesser landowners. As a group, they were conservatives who were against the changes taking place in Britain. Most Tories opposed the war with France as a waste of tax money. Whigs, on the other hand, supported the war. Many Whigs came from Britain's growing class of merchants, who made handsome profits supplying war goods. They also wanted Britain to crush France once and for all and become the undisputed trade leader of Europe. The split between Tories and Whigs would remain a basic fact of British politics for many decades.

Favoring the Tories, Queen Anne signed a treaty to end the war in 1713, the same year she fell ill. Earlier, Parliament had passed a law stipulating that only a Protestant could inherit the throne. When **5** Anne died in 1714, the throne passed to a little-known relative of James I who ruled a small principality in Hanover, Germany.

QUEEN ANNE AND THE KNIGHTS OF THE GARTER, 1713
Peter Angelis
The Granger Collection

A Cabinet and Prime Minister

The new king, George I, spoke no English and had little interest in the affairs of Britain. He seemed an unlikely figure to advance democracy in Britain, but in fact he did. George I relied on ministers, chosen from Parliament, to run the country. This group of ministers was called the cabinet, and the chief among them came to be known as the prime minister. Robert Walpole, a brilliant and energetic Whig was the first man to unify the cabinet government in the person of the prime minister. Thus began the cabinet system still used in Britain today. Through the cabinet, Parliament gained a greater voice in the nation's policies.

In 1760, another Hanoverian king came to the British throne. Born in Britain, George III thought of himself as an Englishman, not a German. He was a strong-willed man who took his mother seriously when she said, "George, be a king." Using his wealth and influence, the king packed Parliament with men loyal to him. He then set about pursuing his own policies. His strong-headed handling of the American colonies helped bring about the American Revolution.

The king's disastrous policies toward America angered Parliament. In 1782, a fiery twenty-four-year-old became prime minister. William Pitt, the youthful Tory leader, had great plans for reform of the British government. Before he had a chance to put them into effect, however, France erupted in revolution. Soon thereafter, Britain and France were at war again, putting off any chance of reform.

THE TRANSFORMATION OF BRITAIN'S ECONOMY

An Agricultural Revolution

After the Restoration, Britain's system of government became gradually more democratic. Gradual changes also occurred in the economic life of the nation.

In 1660, the vast majority of the British people were farmers. Most either rented their fields from a landlord or cultivated a patch of common land. By the late 1600's, however, new economic forces were changing life in the countryside. New farm tools made it possible for farmers to plant and harvest a much bigger crop. As a result, landlords began to fence in the land they had once rented out, hiring laborers to work the land for them.

Bigger, more efficient estates replaced the small holdings of earlier times. By the mid-1700's, British farms were producing much more food. With more food available, the population of the small island surged upward. Since fewer farmhands were needed, many people left the countryside. In the growing towns, they became the factory hands who ran the machines of the early Industrial Revolution.

KING GEORGE III OF ENGLAND, c. 1760
Allan Ramsay
The Granger Collection

Humanities Note

Fine art, *George III of England,* c. 1760, by Allan Ramsay. Scottish-born Allan Ramsay (1713–1784) studied painting in Italy. In the 1730's he settled in London, where he became a well-known portrait painter. Ramsay cultivated a style of depicting some of his subjects in the costume or the pose of a famous ancient person or statue, such as that of Apollo. His works done in a simpler manner are less formal and, at least to modern tastes, more appealing.

Through Ramsay's patron, the Prince of Wales's tutor, the artist received commissions to paint a portrait of the Prince (1757) and, about 1760, when the young monarch ascended to the throne, of King George III. In 1761 Ramsay was appointed painter-in-ordinary to the king.

6 **Enrichment** These "Enclosure Acts," driving people off the land, provide the background for Oliver Goldsmith's famous poem, "The Deserted Village." Goldsmith himself, whose poem "Woman" appears on page 593, has the unique distinction of having created a literary masterpiece in three separate fields: poetry, the drama with *She Stoops to Conquer,* and the novel with *The Vicar of Wakefield.*

The Industrial Age Dawns

The Industrial Revolution began in Britain. A series of British inventions after 1750 made the spinning and weaving of cloth much more efficient. At the same time, the steam engine was perfected and adapted to run a power loom. These machines were brought together in factories, which were soon producing vast quantities of cotton cloth. Merchants sold the goods all over the world, adding more gold to the nation's coffers.

Although the Industrial Revolution happened first in England, the nation did not become predominantly industrial until the 1800's. As late as the 1790's, a majority of British people still earned their living as farmers. Yet the economic changes of the 1700's had major significance. They profoundly affected ways of thinking about the world.

NEW IDEAS FOR A NEW AGE

The Enlightenment

In a sense, the Industrial Revolution began when British inventors found practical ways to apply the ideas of the Scientific Revolution. The Scientific Revolution led to other developments as well. Works by Enlightenment thinkers in many other fields can all be considered its offspring.

In 1687, Sir Isaac Newton published his monumental study of gravity and the movement of the planets. Popular awareness of Newton's achievement is reflected in this couplet from a poem by Alexander Pope:

> Nature and Nature's laws lay hid in night:
> God said, Let Newton be! and all was light.

Each breakthrough in astronomy, physics, and chemistry seemed to affirm the hope that human beings would someday perfect their knowledge of the world. Thinkers in other fields tried to make their studies as orderly and rational as the studies of a scientist. In *The Wealth of Nations,* for example, Adam Smith suggested that economic life is ruled by laws as discoverable as scientific laws.

One of the greatest figures of the Enlightenment was John Locke, a British philosopher and political theorist. After the Glorious Revolution, Locke brought the rationalism of the age to his study of government. Kings, said Locke, did not have a "divine right" to hold power. Rather, a monarch's authority came from the consent of the people. If the monarch abuses his subjects, they "are thereupon absolved from any further obedience." Locke's enlightened ideas about government helped shape the arguments of the American colonists during their disputes with George III.

The scientific advances of the Enlightenment established the

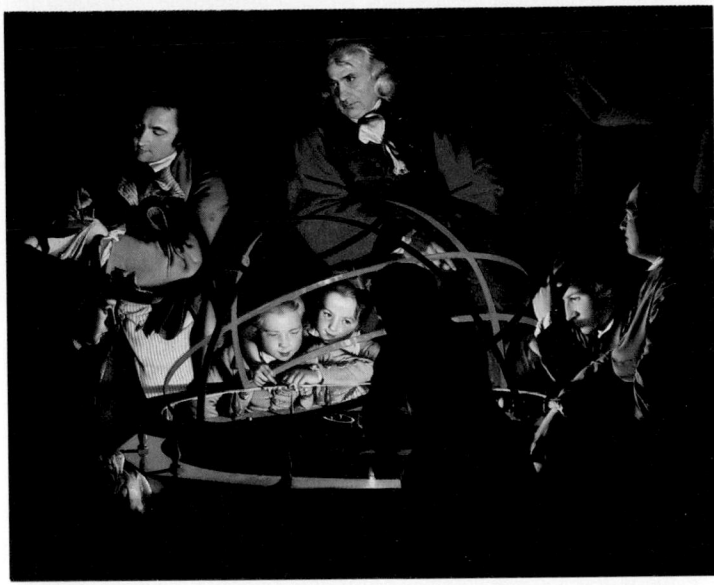

A PHILOSOPHER LECTURING ON
THE ORRERY
Joseph Wright of Derby
Derby Art Gallery

Humanities Note

Fine art, *A Philosopher Lecturing on the Orrery*, by Joseph Wright of Derby. Joseph Wright of Derby (1734–1797) studied in London with the master painter Joshua Reynolds. He first became a portrait painter but later devoted himself to landscape and genre painting. He made many sketches of flame effects and has been called a painter of light.

His interest in the effects of light are obvious in this painting. The focus of the picture is the orrery, a mechanical apparatus for illustrating, with balls of various sizes, the movements and phases of the planets in the solar system. It was named after Charles Boyle, Earl of Orrery, for whom one was made.

basis for the new technology of the Industrial Revolution. But beyond that, a new confidence in human ability encouraged inventors to experiment with new devices, and capitalists to risk their money on untested ideas. Hence, the Industrial Revolution both grew out of and reinforced the new scientific spirit.

The Neoclassical Ideal

Everywhere they looked, the Enlightenment thinkers discerned what they took to be evidence of the world's harmony and order. When Alexander Pope and others sought kindred spirits in the past, they often found them among the writers of ancient Greece and Rome. In the works of Homer, Virgil, Horace, and other classical authors, Enlightenment thinkers and artists discovered harmony, restraint, and clarity—the very qualities they admired most.

English writers of the Enlightenment are often called *neoclassical* because they emulated classical styles. The features of neoclassicism are easy to identify. One feature is the frequent use of classical allusions—that is, references to the myths, gods, and heroes of ancient times. Another is an inclination to generalize about the world rather than to describe it from a particular individual's point of view. John Dryden, Alexander Pope, and Samuel Johnson often put their generalizations about the world in the form of *aphorisms*—short, quotable sentences, such as "The proper study of mankind is man." (See the quotations on page 487.)

7 **Literary Movement** See Samuel Johnson's "Letter to Lord Chesterfield," page 566, as a comment on and a repudiation of patrons. This letter was said to have broken the patronage system; subsequent writers looked more to public support than to private encouragement.

8 **Master Teacher Note** To help students gain a better understanding of the position of poet laureate, you might ask them to research all the poets laureate up to the present. You might also ask them to research America's recent recognition of poets with the establishment of a laureateship here.

One other feature of neoclassicism makes the work of Pope and others lively and amusing: a fondness for satire, the literary ridicule of the vices, follies, and stupidities of society. Such classical poets as Horace, Juvenal, and Martial provided the English poets of the eighteenth century with superb models of the genre.

Most of the satires of the time were mild and inoffensive, usually written in a formal, neoclassical style. Pope, for example, wrote a long poem, *The Dunciad,* in a high-flown, heroic style—but the poem is a satirical celebration of stupidity. Other satirists, such as Jonathan Swift, were less polite. His *Gulliver's Travels* includes savage attacks on lawyers, princes, and mankind in general. In *A Modest Proposal,* Swift suggests a way "for preventing the children of poor people in Ireland from being a burden to their parents or country." Swift's ironic solution—to eat them—is the modest proposal at the heart of a bitter satire directed against the English absentee landlords who were destroying Ireland.

The Literary World Expands

As Britain grew wealthier, more men and women could afford an education. The number of people who could read grew, as did the number who could spend money on books. This change had several results. Daily newspapers began to appear. The first real magazine, the *Gentleman's Magazine,* began publication in 1731. The first private lending libraries, which charged their members a fee, also opened in the early 1700's.

In London, coffeehouses and clubs became popular places for middle-class men to stop in, read the newspapers, and chat about politics. Expanding literacy presented writers with a real opportunity. No longer did they have to rely on a few wealthy patrons for their livelihood. For the first time, writers could at least survive on the money they made from their books and articles. The modern world of publishers, copyright laws, and royalties began to take shape in London during the 1700's.

THREE LITERARY AGES

The literature of the Restoration and eighteenth century may be thought of as comprising three broad divisions, or "ages": the Age of Dryden, the Age of Pope and Swift, and the Age of Johnson.

The Age of Dryden

The Age of Dryden in literature extends from the year of the restoration of Charles II, 1660, to 1700, the year of Dryden's death. In history, this forty-year period is called the Restoration. Dryden, whose works included poems, plays, and essays, dominated the period. He was named poet laureate, England's official poet, by Charles II.

Among Dryden's most famous works are his satirical poems,

THE RAKE'S PROGRESS: NO. 5, THE MARRIAGE
William Hogarth
The Granger Collection

especially *MacFlecknoe,* written in 1682. These satires included unflattering portraits of real people of his time. Although the poems employ lofty, heroic language, they actually ridicule their "heroes." For this reason they are often called mock heroic poems, or mock epics. Dryden also created several celebratory poems for royal and other public events. These poems, in true Enlightenment spirit, hail the achievements of humanity. A famous example is "A Song for St. Cecilia's Day," an ode in honor of music.

9

The Restoration was also noted for its drama, especially comedies. When he became king, Charles II reopened the London theaters, which the disapproving Puritans had closed. The Restoration theaters, fancier and more costly than those of Shakespeare's time, did a thriving business. Dryden himself wrote the best tragedy of the period. Entitled *All for Love,* it recounts the ill-fated romance of Antony and Cleopatra.

10

Introduction 483

11

11 Literary Movement See the excerpt from Dryden's "An Essay on Dramatic Poesy," page 494, written in the precise and graceful style that earned him the title, "father of modern English prose." It was in these critical essays that Dryden established Chaucer's and Shakespeare's modern reputations.

12 Literary Movement The excerpt from Pepys's diary, page 506, not only records in accurate detail the major events of London life in the 1660's but also contains many interesting personal observations. Pepys was extremely frank—indeed, his diary was written in a code that was not deciphered until almost one hundred years after his death.

13 Literary Movement See the excerpt from Pope's *The Rape of the Lock,* page 548, which not only satirizes the folly of man but also mocks the elaborate and stylized conventions of the epic form.

14 Enrichment Samuel Richardson's *Pamela,* published more than twenty years later, is often considered the first modern English novel.

11
12
Prose writing also flourished in the Restoration. Dryden wrote a series of essays about drama that laid the foundation for British literary criticism. These, along with his translations of Plutarch and other prose compositions, represent what many literary historians consider the first modern prose. They are clear, plain, direct, colloquial in tone, and—for people of today—easy to read. Probably the most fascinating prose work of the period, however, was the diary kept by Samuel Pepys (1633–1703). Pepys kept his journal for nine years, beginning in 1660. With remarkable frankness he recorded the daily events in London during those turbulent years, including the deadly plague of 1665 and the Great Fire.

The Age of Pope and Swift

During the reign of Queen Anne in the early 1700's, one of the most admired writers in London was Alexander Pope. Pope's poetry is a shining example of neoclassical style, exhibiting wit, elegance, and moderation. All these qualities show forth in his most famous work, *The Rape of the Lock,* a mock-heroic poem that satirizes the absurdities of a war between the sexes.

13

Pope also had enormous influence as a literary critic. His principles found eloquent expression in *An Essay on Criticism,* a long verse essay in heroic couplets. Many well-known aphorisms can be traced to that work, including the following couplet:

> True wit is Nature to advantage dress'd;
> What oft was thought, but ne'er so well express'd.

Pope, a Tory, was a special favorite of Queen Anne. When George I came to power in 1714, the Tories fell out of favor, and Pope retired to his country house. There he wrote *An Essay on Man,* a long poem that asserts the essential order and goodness of the universe and the rightness of humanity's place in it.

Another Tory writer of the time was Jonathan Swift (1667–1745). Swift, a close friend of Pope's, wrote mild satires while Queen Anne reigned. After her death and the fall of the Tories, Swift grew increasingly bitter. The behavior of the rising merchants, whom he viewed as shameless money grubbers, enraged Swift. *Gulliver's Travels* and *A Modest Proposal* date from this later period. Swift stood apart from many of his contemporaries by his antagonism to the idea that human nature is essentially good. In his great satires he presents the older view that human nature is deeply flawed, and that improvement must begin with a recognition of our intellectual and moral limitations.

14
One book that enjoyed a huge success at the time told about a shipwrecked British sailor struggling to survive on a deserted island. The work, *Robinson Crusoe,* has been called the first novel in English. It was such a success that its author, Daniel Defoe, immediately set to work on other novels. Defoe's experiments with

the novel opened up a new form of fiction that, in the 1800's, would become the favorite reading matter of the middle classes.

England's first literary periodicals, *The Tatler* and *The Spectator,* also appeared in the early 1700's. Written by Joseph Addison (1672–1719) and Richard Steele (1672–1729), these one-page papers included crisply written reflective essays and news. The essays quickly became models for other prose writers.

The Age of Johnson

Alexander Pope died in 1744, and Jonathan Swift the following year. The dominant literary figure of the next generation was Samuel Johnson. Like many young writers after him, Johnson honed his writing style by working as a journalist. He later published his own magazine, *The Rambler*. Johnson also wrote poetry, literary criticism, and a novel. His most important work, however, was the *Dictionary of the English Language,* published in 1755. It was the first dictionary that could be considered a standard and authoritative reference work on English.

Samuel Johnson dominated his age not only by his writings but also by his conversation and acquaintanceships. A brilliant and inexhaustible talker, he was friendly with most of the writers, painters, and actors of his time. His wise advice helped nurture the careers of many younger talents.

One reason we know so much about Samuel Johnson is that one of those younger talents, James Boswell (1740–1795), wrote his biography. Boswell followed his friend and mentor from club to coffeehouse to dinner party, faithfully recording Johnson's comments and witticisms. The result, Boswell's *Life of Samuel Johnson,* was the first modern biography written in English. It gives a vivid portrait not only of Johnson but of life in London in the 1700's.

The Age of Johnson saw other literary accomplishments. On the stage, the Restoration tradition of satire was carried on by Oliver Goldsmith and other comic playwrights. Among the many important works of prose, Edward Gibbon's history of Rome stands out. And novelists, working in the tradition begun by Defoe, produced a spate of popular books. Among the best were Samuel Richardson's *Pamela* and *Clarissa*, Fanny Burney's *Evelina,* Henry Fielding's *Tom Jones* and *Joseph Andrews*, and Lawrence Sterne's *Tristram Shandy.*

THE ECLIPSE OF THE ENLIGHTENMENT

By 1750 Britain was launched on a course of rapid industrialization. In the new industrial towns, mills and factories belched smoke into the country air. Inside the factories, men, women, and children toiled at machines for twelve and fourteen hours a day. Every year

15 Literary Movement See the examples of Addison and Steele's essays, pages 538 and 541; these famous literary partners are given credit for creating the familiar essay. Steele was considered the more original thinker, Addison the more polished writer.

16 Literary Movement See the excerpts from Johnson's Preface, page 568, and from his dictionary proper, page 571. His dictionary is extremely idiosyncratic and often strongly colored by the author's own biases.

17 Literary Movement See the excerpts from Boswell's *Life of Samuel Johnson,* page 576, a work to which he dedicated thirty years. It was Dryden who first defined the word *biography* as "the history of particular men's lives."

Fine art, *Sir Isaac Newton,* c. 1726, by John Vanderbank. Vanderbank (c. 1694–1730) painted during the first part of the eighteenth century. This portrait of Sir Isaac Newton is considered one of his best works. Newton is shown in a studious pose with an open book in front of him, an appropriately symbolic scene for the Age of Reason.

18 Literary Movement Although Gray's "Elegy Written in a Country Churchyard," page 586, exhibits some of the emotion and language of the revolt against neo-classicism, Gray is very much a transitional figure who retains formal and impersonal eighteenth-century diction. He is more revolutionary and "romantic" in his content: sympathy for the common person.

19 Literary Movement Blake's lyrics, on pages 608–614, taken from his *Songs of Innocence* and his *Songs of Experience,* reveal his preoccupation with "contraries": the contrasts between the innocence of childhood and the wisdom of experience as well as the necessity for both.

Check Test

1. The Plague of 1665 killed _____ people in the city of London.
2. The "Glorious Revolution" allowed _____ to assume control of the English throne.
3. _____ was the king of England when the American colonies revolted.
4. Jonathan Swift's allegory, _____, was a savage attack on lawyers, princes, and mankind in general.
5. *Robinson Crusoe,* the first English novel, was written by _____.

SIR ISAAC NEWTON, c. 1726
Attributed to John Vanderbank
The Granger Collection

more poor people crowded into the towns and cities, unable to find regular work and barely able to survive.

As a result of these changes, writers and intellectuals began to lose faith in the ability of human reason to solve every problem. The thinkers in the Age of Reason looked to science to make life better for humanity. Yet by the late 1700's, "progress" seemed to be bringing misery to millions.

As they began to doubt the basic assumptions of the Enlightenment, writers turned away from the standards of neoclassicism. Instead of using the impersonal, high-flown style of the early 1700's, some wrote in the common language of everyday life. Departing from the spirit of rationalism, they charged their poems with powerful emotions. Thomas Gray's *Elegy Written in a Country Churchyard,* completed in 1750, exemplifies the transition from the formal, classical poetic styles of the early eighteenth century to the more emotional manner of the Romantic era. **18**

William Blake broke even more sharply with the ideas and attitudes of Pope and the neoclassicists. In simple language, he conveyed mystical ideas and biting attacks on what England was becoming. In one poem he derided those who held to a complacent faith in human rationality, while ignoring the spiritual side of human existence: **19**

> You don't believe—I won't attempt to make ye;
> You are asleep—I won't attempt to wake ye.
> Sleep on! Sleep on! while in your pleasant dreams
> Of Reason you may drink of Life's clear streams.
> Reason and Newton, they are quite two things;
> For so the swallow and the sparrow sings.

The Age of Reason, with its unbounded faith in human intelligence, was coming to an end. New voices were being raised, and they no longer spoke in the clipped and polished language of rationalist neoclassicism. They would make the 1800's a new literary age.

ANSWERS

1. 70,000
2. William and Mary
3. George III
4. *Gulliver's Travels*
5. Daniel Defoe

ENGLISH VOICES
Quotations by Prominent Figures of the Period

Errors, like straws, upon the surface flow;
He who would search for pearls must dive below.
> **John Dryden,** *All for Love*

Titles are shadow, crowns are empty things,
The good of subjects is the end of kings.
> **Daniel Defoe,** *The True-Born Englishman*

Satire is a sort of glass, wherein beholders do generally discover everybody's face but their own.
> **Jonathan Swift,** "The Battle of the Books"

Proper words in proper places, make the true definition of a style.
> **Jonathan Swift,** "Letter to a Young Clergyman"

Sweet are the slumbers of the virtuous man.
> **Joseph Addison,** *Cato*

Reading is to the mind what exercise is to the body.
> **Richard Steele,** *The Tatler*

The noblest motive is the public good.
> **Richard Steele,** *The Spectator*

To err is human, to forgive divine.
> **Alexander Pope,** *An Essay on Criticism*

Fools rush in where angels fear to tread.
> **Alexander Pope,** *An Essay on Criticism*

When a man is tired of London, he is tired of life.
> **Samuel Johnson,** Quoted by James Boswell in *The Life of Samuel Johnson*

The paths of glory lead but to the grave.
> **Thomas Gray,** "Elegy Written in a Country Churchyard"

The best laid plans o' mice and men
Gang aft a-gley.
> **Robert Burns,** "To a Mouse."

Additional Voices

There is a pleasure sure in being mad which none but madmen know.
> **John Dryden,** *The Spanish Friar*

I pray God to keep me from being proud.
> **Samuel Pepys,** *Diary*

There is nothing in this world constant, but inconstancy.
> **Jonathan Swift,** *Journal*

Satire's my weapon, but I'm too discreet
To run amuck, and tilt at all I meet.
> **Alexander Pope,** *Imitation of Horace*

Reading Critically The purpose of this page is to guide students in the critical reading of literature written between 1660–1798. The information here will enable students to place a work of literature in its historical context, identify the literary movements of the time, and appreciate the techniques used by writers to convey the ideas of the period.

As you discuss this information with your class, explain that the poem "Holy Thursday" by William Blake beginning on the facing page is a model for reading critically. The side columns contain notes that draw students' attention to elements that reflect the historical context, the influence of the literary movements, and the writer's techniques.

To give students further practice with the process of reading critically, use the excerpt from Pepys's *Diary* (Coronation of Charles II) in the **Teaching Portfolio,** page 530, which students can annotate themselves. Encourage students to use these strategies as they read the literature in this unit.

Teaching to Ability Levels For **less advanced** students, you might discuss the meaning of the title before reading the poem. (See clarification note on page 489). **More advanced** students might wish to interpret the title's significance before reading the poem.

The Literature of 1660–1798

When you read literature, it is important to place it in its historical context. Doing so will help you to see how it was shaped by the dominant attitudes of the period and to appreciate the techniques the writer used to convey these attitudes.

Historical Context

During the years from 1660 to 1798, English life was dominated by a desire for social and political stability. The nation had been severely shaken by the events of the civil war and the Puritan dictatorship and sought to reestablish a sense of order and security. Although the monarchy had been restored, the Parliament developed into the nation's supreme ruling force. Despite this shift in power, the English people generally remained complacent. The nation prospered financially and its citizens tended to be patriotic and optimistic. This sense of optimism resulted in part from scientific and philosophical advances that helped create a belief that everything in the universe could be explained.

Literary Movements

The literature written between 1660 and 1798 generally reflects the faith in reason and the desire for stability that characterized English life at the time. Strongly influenced by the works of classical Greek and Roman writers, writers generally displayed their intelligence, education, and sense of discipline in their works. Their works also conveyed their faith in English traditions and captured the elegance of English aristocratic life at the time. Toward the end of the eighteenth century, however, some poets, who are often referred to as Preromantics, began to react against the emphasis on reason and the intellect.

Writer's Techniques

During this period English prose flourished. Writers wrote formal essays on a variety of subjects, presenting logical, scientific arguments. The literary letter became a popular form; the first modern biography was written; and literary criticism and fiction flourished. In poetry, writers generally turned away from the lyric and wrote formally structured poems, often filled with classical allusions. Writers often displayed their wit by satirizing the society of their day in both poems and essays. The Preromantic poets, however, disregarded the tastes of the time and reestablished the lyric.

On the following page is a poem by William Blake, a Preromantic poet. The notes in the side column should help you to place the selection in its historical context.

Objectives

1 To analyze sound devices
2 To analyze the effect of sound devices
3 To respond to criticism

Support Material

Teaching Portfolio
Teacher Backup, p. 527
Reading Critically, *The Diary,* p. 530
Usage and Mechanics Worksheet, p. 532
Analyzing Literature Worksheet, *Understanding Paradox,* p. 533
Language Worksheet, *Finding Antonyms,* p. 534
Selection Test, p. 535

Holy Thursday

William Blake

Is this a holy thing to see,
In a rich and fruitful land,
Babes reduced to misery,
Fed with cold and usurious[1] hand?

5 Is that trembling cry a song?
Can it be a song of joy?
And so many children poor?
It is a land of poverty!

And their sun does never shine,
10 And their fields are bleak and bare,
And their ways are filled with thorns;
It is eternal winter there.

For where-e'er the sun does shine,
And where-e'er the rain does fall,
15 Babe can never hunger there,
Nor poverty the mind appall.

---

1. usurious (yōō zho͞or′ ē əs) *adj.*: Lending money at a high rate of interest.

Historical Context: Although England was a wealthy and prosperous nation during the eighteenth century, the poor were generally neglected.

Literary Movement: Unlike most writers of the time, the Preromantic poets often wrote about lower-class people.

Writer's Technique: This poem is a lyric in which the speaker expresses his thoughts and feelings concerning the poor.

Literary Movement: Blake appeals to both the reader's emotions and sense of reason.

Holy Thursday 489

Clarification The title refers to Ascension Day, the Fortieth day after Easter, when children from London's charity schools were marched to St. Paul's to sing before their patrons.

Presentation

Motivation/Prior Knowledge Ask the students to discuss injustices that they see in today's society. Problems of homelessness, and poverty are examples. Explain that such problems are not unique to our society and era but were also common during the Pre-Romantic period during which William Blake wrote. A courageous man both physically and mentally, Blake wrote "Holy Thursday" attacking a serious social problem of his day, which is still a familiar one today.

Master Teacher Note An engraver by profession, Blake, with the help of his wife, published his poetry in a unique way. Instead of using a printing press, his poems were drawn on metal plates with varnish and designs sketched into the margins. The metal plates were plunged into acid baths, which ate away the unvarnished portions. The letters and illustrations stood out like engravings. Blake and his wife then painstakingly colored them, sometimes with gold leaf. The process is remarkable because, in order to appear correct to the reader, the letters had to be written backward. Most of Blake's books were prepared in this manner.

For examples of this work, see pages 609, 610, and 614.

Purpose-Setting Question Blake uses sound devices to reinforce his outrage about the inhumane conditions suffered by the children of the poor. How effective is his use of sound devices in emphasizing his theme?

For Further Study Biographical information on Blake appears on page 606, and other poems by him are on pages 608–614.

1. Blake characterizes England as a rich and fruitful land in the first stanza. (b) In the second stanza he brands the country a land of poverty.
2. The poor never see the sun shine, they own bleak and bare fields, and have thorns filling their paths. They live in an eternal winter.
3. Where the sun shines and the rain falls, babies can never be hungry, and poverty will never horrify.

Interpreting

4. Suggested response: Because Holy Thursday is a happy day, the title is ironic. Blake uses the title to point out the contrast between the way things are and the way they should be.
5. (a) A suggested response: Lines 13 and 14 are parallel. (b) The parallel structure of these lines recalls the parallel structure of the lines 9, 10, and 11. This underscores the contrast between the poverty and the ideal.
6. (a) In "Holy Thursday" Blake is decrying miserable conditions forced upon the urban poor, especially the children, during the Industrial Revolution. (b) By writing the poem, he hoped to bring attention to the problem, thereby creating an impetus to rectify the miserable situation.

Applying

7. Answers will differ. Suggested response: Yes, this poem might be applied to the contemporary United States. There are many homeless people—many of them children. The poor are often malnourished and hungry, while many more affluent people live in comfort.

Challenge Write a protest poem about a problem you see in American society.

THINKING ABOUT THE SELECTION
Recalling

1. (a) How does Blake characterize England in the first stanza? (b) How does he characterize the country in the second stanza?
2. What observations about the poor does Blake make in the third stanza?
3. According to the final stanza, what can never happen "where-e'er the sun does shine" and "the rain does fall"?

Interpreting

4. Holy Thursday is another name for Ascension Day, the day on which Jesus' ascension into heaven is celebrated. Why do you think Blake used this name as the title of his poem?
5. (a) Find one example of Blake's use of parallelism—the repetition of phrases, clauses, or sentences that are similar in meaning or structure? (b) How does his use of parallelism reinforce the meaning of the poem?
6. (a) What is the theme, or main point, of the poem? (b) What was Blake's purpose in writing the poem?

Applying

7. Do you think this poem could be applied to contemporary American society? Why or why not?

ANALYZING LITERATURE
Using Sound Devices

Alliteration, consonance, and assonance are three sound devices used in poetry. **Alliteration** is the repetition of consonant sounds at the beginnings of words or accented syllables. For example, the *th* sound is repeated in line 1 of "Holy Thursday": "Is *th*is a holy *th*ing to see." **Consonance** is the repetition of consonant sounds at the ends of words or accented syllables. Notice the repetition of the *d* sound in line 4 of Blake's poem: "Fe*d* with col*d* an*d* usurious han*d*." **Assonance** is the repetition of vowel sounds. For example, the short *i* sound is repeated in "*i*s," "th*i*s," "*i*n," and "r*i*ch" in the first two lines of "Holy Thursday."

1. Find another example of alliteration in "Holy Thursday."
2. Find another example of consonance.
3. Find another example of assonance.

CRITICAL THINKING AND READING
Analyzing the Effect of Sound Devices

Sound devices cause poetry to have a musical quality. The repetition of sounds also adds emphasis to certain words and reinforces the meaning of a poem.

1. Find two cases in which Blake's use of a sound device adds emphasis to important words.
2. How does the emphasis of these words reinforce the meaning of the poem?

THINKING AND WRITING
Responding to Criticism

A critic has stated that Blake had "the ability to establish direct contact with readers, however remote in time or space." Write an essay in which you discuss this comment in relation to "Holy Thursday." Consider the meaning of the critic's comment. Reread the poem with the critic's statement in mind. Prepare a thesis statement. Then write your essay, using evidence from the poem to support your thesis. When you revise, make sure you have not included any unnecessary information.

1. Another example of alliteration is "And their *s*un does never *s*hine . . ."
2. Another example of consonance is "Babe can never hunger there . . . "
3. Another example of assonance is "And their fields are bleak and bare . . . "

1. The "b" sounds in line 10 and the long "e" sounds in the same line add emphasis to the words.
2. These sounds are harsh sounds, sounds of crying and sadness. They reinforce the misery being presented in the poem.

Publishing Student Writing Using writing groups, have students choose one essay that their group likes the best from essays written by another group. Have a member of the group read the essay to the class. After all choices have been read, discuss the points made. Determine whether the class agrees with the critic's statement.

The Restoration

THE ELECTION—THE POLLING
William Hogarth
Sir John Soane's Museum, London

Humanities Note

Fine art, *The Election—the Polling.* 1755, by William Hogarth. Hogarth (1697–1764) was first apprenticed to a silver plate engraver but later studied painting, learning the decorative style of James Thornhill. He emerged as a painter of portraits and conversation pieces but later turned to paintings of moral subjects. His most famous works were those in which he painted a dramatic series of scenes with a moral point.

The Election—the Polling is one painting in the last series that Hogarth painted. It is possible that Hogarth was inspired by the lively scenes that marked the election of 1754.

back on the last half of the seventeenth century in England, which had seen political upheaval and civil strife, followed by the folly and indulgence of the Restoration, John Dryden wrote: "Thy wars brought nothing about/Thy lovers were all untrue./'Tis well an old age is out,/And time to begin a new." Dryden's answer to the excesses of the earlier seventeenth century was to praise the virtues of order, balance, and harmony, words which appear often in his writing. As the most influential poet of his time, he, more than any other single person, brought about a change in intellectual attitudes that led to a new age in literature. Do you think it is possible for a single individual today to have such a pronounced effect on the attitudes of this country? If so, support your answer with examples. If not, explain your answer.

Critical Evaluation T.S. Eliot, a poet who also praised order, balance, and harmony as Dryden did, might be considered as a good example of an influential thinker who shaped the thinking of his generation in the mid-twentieth century. Eliot has this to say about his seventeenth century counterpart: ". . . where Dryden fails to satisfy, the nineteenth century does not satisfy us either; and where that century has condemned him, it is itself condemned. In the next revolution of taste it is possible that poets may turn to the study of Dryden. He remains one of those who have set standards for English verse which it is desperate to ignore."

JOHN DRYDEN

1631–1700

John Dryden dominated the literary scene in the last quarter of the seventeenth century. The most accomplished poet of the period, he also ranks high in English letters as a dramatist, essayist, satirist, and critic. His versatility and professionalism helped to establish writing as a legitimate career in England. The poet T. S. Eliot has maintained that Dryden "is the ancestor of nearly all that is best in the poetry of the eighteenth century," while the poet Matthew Arnold observed, "Here at last we have the true English prose, a prose such as we would all gladly use if only we knew how."

Born at the vicarage of Aldwinkle All Saints, Northamptonshire, where his father was a country gentleman, young Dryden studied at Westminster School. He graduated from Trinity College, Cambridge, in 1654, and five years later published his first important poem, *Heroic Stanzas.* The poem commemorates the death of Oliver Cromwell, under whose protectorate Dryden seems to have held a minor political post. A year later, in *Astraea Redux,* he did a political about-face and hailed the return to the throne of King Charles II. While in his fifties, Dryden, who had once been a Puritan and then an Anglican, became a convert to Roman Catholicism.

Dryden first came to prominence as a playwright, producing blank-verse tragedies and comedies. He was appointed poet laureate in 1668, a position that was supposed to pay an annual salary of two hundred pounds, but because of problems in the Royal Treasury, he received only half. His best play, *All for Love* (1677), is a rewriting of Shakespeare's *Antony and Cleopatra* in a clear, simple style. He displays his full power in *Absalom and Achitophel,* a political poem published in 1681. This poem was followed a year later by the equally impressive *The Medall,* also on politics.

After the Revolution of 1688 in England, which brought the Protestants William and Mary to the throne, Dryden lost his laureateship. He was replaced by Thomas Shadwell, whom Dryden had satirized a few years earlier in the poem *MacFlecknoe.* To compensate for his lost income, Dryden increased his literary output, translating classical writers and writing prologues and miscellaneous pieces. The last of these efforts, his *Fables, Ancient and Modern*—translations from Chaucer, Boccaccio, and Ovid —appeared the year he died.

As a writer, Dryden was uniquely a man of his era. He expressed himself on virtually every important issue of the day. His friend William Congreve, a fellow playwright, pays tribute to Dryden's talents, saying that "no man hath written in our language so much . . . and in so various manners so well. . . ."

Objectives

1 To understand formal and informal essays
2 To chart an analysis of an essay
3 To write an evaluation of an analysis

Support Material

Teaching Portfolio
Teacher Backup, p. 537
Grammar in Action Worksheet, *Coherence,* p. 541
Usage and Mechanics Worksheet, p. 543
Vocabulary Check, p. 544
Critical Thinking and Reading Worksheet, *Understanding Analysis,* p. 545

Language Worksheet, *Appreciating Specific Words,* p. 546
Selection Test, p. 547

GUIDE FOR INTERPRETING

from An Essay of Dramatic Poesy

Literary Forms

Essay. An essay is a prose composition that expresses the writer's viewpoint on a limited topic. Essays vary in length from several paragraphs to the equivalent of an entire book. Modern essays are generally short, but in the eighteenth century, when the essay flourished as a popular literary form, essays were considerably longer. Dryden's complete essay on dramatic poesy—about thirty-five printed pages—is of average length for the time. Essays can be classified as formal or informal. A *formal essay* is one that deals with a serious subject in a carefully organized and often lofty way. An *informal essay,* or *personal essay,* is lighter and less structured than a formal essay. It may be humorous, and—even though classified as nonfiction—it may stretch the truth considerably or abandon it entirely. An informal essay is generally written in a conversational tone, reflecting the personality of the author and displaying distinctly personal touches.

Commentary

Writing style, as with style in fashion, changes throughout the years. Dryden's style of writing, however, has become "classic"—the standard by which we measure all other writing—because it is clear, direct, and elegant. To Samuel Johnson, for example, Dryden does not appear "to have any other art than that of expressing with clearness what he thinks with vigor. His style could not easily be imitated, either seriously or ludicrously; for, being always equable and always varied, it has no prominent or discriminative characters." What are the qualities of Dryden's style?

His sentences are basically subject-verb-object, with just enough variety to avoid monotony. While his sentences are usually longer than was fashionable in the seventeenth century, they are still not overly long, when judged by earlier standards. Clear and concise, they have a conversational tone and avoid excessive figurative language. What other elements of style can you find in the following essay that contribute to Dryden's concise, clear, and dignified writing?

Writing

When you read a work of fiction, what do you look for? An exciting plot? Well-developed, believable characters? Insights into human nature? List at least five characteristics that you think a work of fiction should have. Then make a second list in which you include the characteristics that detract from a work of fiction—for example, dull characters or an unbelievable plot.

Literary Focus Have students bring in examples of articles from newspapers and magazines that fit the definitions of formal and informal essays. Under each type, make a list of the essay subjects brought in. Discuss whether some subjects are better treated in a formal or informal manner.

Writing/Prior Knowledge Have students think of a work of fiction they read recently. Have **less advanced** students write a few sentences explaining whether or not the work exhibits one of the positive characteristics they listed. Challenge **more advanced** students to write a brief essay on two characteristics, using examples to support their points.

Vocabulary

Preteach the following vocabulary words:
insipid (in sip′ id) *adj.*: Not exciting or interesting; dull; lifeless (p. 494)
dotages (dōt′ ij əz) *n.*: Second childhoods; states of senility (p. 494)
judicious (jo͞o dish′ es) *adj.*: Having or showing good judgment (p. 494)
laboriously (lə bôr′ē əs lē) *adv.*: In a manner involving much hard work (p. 496).

from An Essay of Dramatic Poesy

John Dryden

Shakespeare and Ben Jonson Compared

To begin, then, with Shakespeare. He was the man who of all modern, and perhaps ancient poets, had the largest and most comprehensive soul. All the images of nature were still present to him, and he drew them, not laboriously, but luckily; when he describes anything, you more than see it, you feel it too. Those who accuse him to have wanted[1] learning, give him the greater commendation: he was naturally learned; he needed not the spectacles of books to read nature; he looked inwards, and found her there. I cannot say he is everywhere alike; were he so, I should do him injury to compare him with the greatest of mankind. He is many times flat, insipid; his comic wit degenerating into clenches,[2] his serious swelling into bombast. But he is always great, when some great occasion is presented to him; no man can say he ever had a fit subject for his wit, and did not then raise himself as high above the rest of poets,

Quantum lenta solent inter viburna cupressi[3]

The consideration of this made Mr. Hales of Eton say that there was no subject of which any poet ever writ, but he would produce it much better done in Shakespeare; and however others are now generally preferred before him, yet the age wherein he lived, which had contemporaries with him Fletcher[4] and Jonson, never equaled them to him in their esteem: and in the last king's court, when Ben's reputation was at highest, Sir John Suckling, and with him the greater part of the courtiers, set our Shakespeare far above him. . . .

As for Jonson, to whose character I am now arrived, if we look upon him while he was himself (for his last plays were but his dotages), I think him the most learned and judicious writer which any theater ever had. He was a most severe judge of himself, as well as others. One cannot say he wanted wit, but rather that he was frugal of it. In his works you find little to retrench[5] or alter. Wit, and language, and humor also in some measure, we had before him; but something of art was wanting to the drama till he came.

---

1. wanted: Lacked.
2. clenches: Puns.
3. *Quantum . . . cupressi*: As do cypresses among the bending shrubs. From Virgil's *Eclogues* 1:25.

4. Fletcher: John Fletcher (1579–1625), an Elizabethan playwright.
5. retrench: Delete.

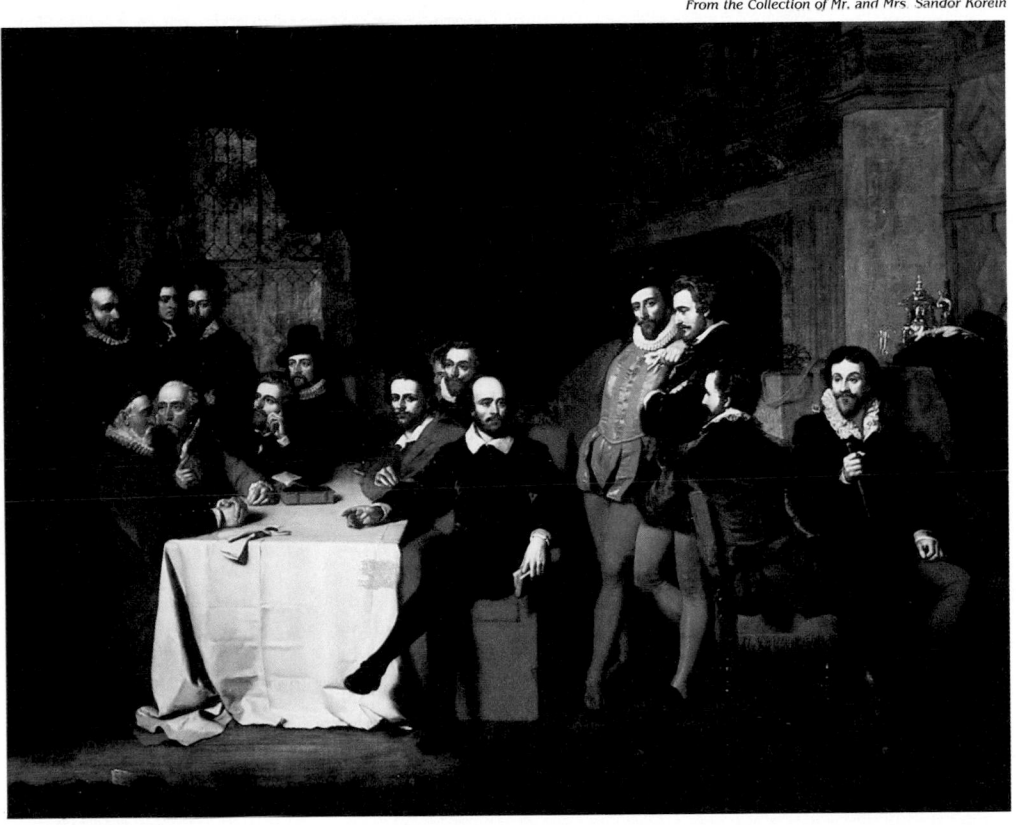

Humanities Note

Fine art, *Shakespeare and His Contemporaries* by John Faed. John Faed (1820–1902) was a Scottish painter and miniaturist. Born into an artistically talented family, he is considered a self-taught artist. At the age of eleven, he was successfully painting miniature portraits. He continued doing so for forty years before switching to larger-format canvases. In these larger works, he preferred subjects from Shakespeare, the Bible, and Scottish history.

The painting *Shakespeare and his Contemporaries (at the Mermaid Tavern),* was painted after 1862. John Faed's detailed style of portraiture reflects his experience as a miniaturist. Although his paintings are carefully finished, they lack interesting color and atmosphere. Narrative, historic subjects like this were favored in Victorian England. This painting inspired an engraving by John Faed's brother, James, which was widely circulated as a popular print.

You may wish to discuss the following with your class:

1. What does this painting show about Shakespeare's character?
2. What does it reveal about Elizabethan life?
3. The painter Faed and the writer Dryden are artists from different eras. Despite this, what do you think their works have in common?

from *An Essay of Dramatic Poesy* 495

Grammar in Action

Ideas should be presented in logical order with smooth connections between them. This is the principle of **coherence.** Coherent paragraphs follow a clear pattern of arrangement. Notice how John Dryden shapes the following passage.

As for Jonson, to whose character I am now arrived, if we look upon him while he was himself (for his last plays were but his dotages), I think him the most learned and judicious writer which any theater ever had. He was a most severe judge of himself, as well as others. One cannot say he wanted wit, but rather that he was frugal of it. In his works you find little to retrench or alter. Wit, and language, and humor also in some measure, we had before him; but something of art was wanting to the drama till he came.

Dryden introduces his subject, Jonson, and his thesis about him, that he was the "most learned and judicious writer which any theater ever had," in a clear topic sentence. He supports the thesis with the detail that Jonson was "a most severe judge of himself, as

12 **Discussion** Restate this sentence in your own words.

13 **Discussion** Explain what Dryden means by idiom.

14 **Clarification** Homer was a Greek epic poet traditionally believed to have been the author of the *Iliad* and the *Odyssey*. Virgil was a Roman poet, author of the epic poem the *Aeneid*. To Dryden, both were to be admired for the order, balance, and harmony of their writings.

15 **Discussion** What value judgments are implied in the words *admire* and *love*?

Reader's Response Choose your own favorite writer or singer and explain why you enjoy that person's work.

12 He managed his strength to more advantage than any who preceded him. You seldom find him making love in any of his scenes or endeavoring to move the passions; his genius was too sullen and saturnine[6] to do it gracefully, especially when he knew he came after those who had performed both to such a height. Humor was his proper sphere: and in that he delighted most to represent mechanic people.[7] He was deeply conversant in the ancients, both Greek and Latin, and he borrowed boldly from them: there is scarce a poet or historian among the Roman authors of those times whom he has not translated in *Sejanus* and *Catiline*.[8] But he has done his robberies so openly, that one may see he fears not to be taxed by any law. He invades authors like a monarch; and what would be theft in other poets is only victory in him. With the spoils of these writers he so represents old Rome to us, in its rites, ceremonies, and customs, that if one of their poets had written either of his tragedies, we had seen less of it than in him. If there was any fault in his language, 'twas that he weaved it too closely and laboriously, in his serious plays; perhaps, too, he did a little too much Romanize our tongue, leaving the words which he translated almost as much Latin as he found them, wherein, though he learnedly followed the idiom of their language, he did not enough comply with the idiom of ours. If I would compare him with Shakespeare, I must acknowledge him the more correct poet, but Shakespeare the greater wit. Shakespeare was the Homer, or father of our dramatic poets; Jonson was the Virgil, the pattern of elaborate writing; I admire him, but I love Shakespeare. . . .

13

14

15

---

6. **saturnine:** Heavy.
7. **mechanic people:** Artisans.
8. ***Sejanus* and *Catiline*:** Two of Jonson's plays.

THINKING ABOUT THE SELECTION
Recalling

1. How does Dryden respond to the criticism that Shakespeare lacked learning?
2. What was the opinion of Shakespeare held by Mr. Hales of Eton?
3. According to Dryden, what was missing from English drama before Ben Jonson started writing?
4. Far from accusing Jonson of theft, what does Dryden say about his borrowing from classical writers?

Interpreting

5. In your own words, what does Dryden mean by saying that Shakespeare "had the largest and most comprehensive soul"?

6. Dryden uses a Latin quotation from Virgil to describe Shakespeare's achievement. How does this quotation relate to the comment that immediately precedes it?
7. In what sense does Dryden mean that Shakespeare was not a "correct poet"?

Applying

8. Assume that the virtues of Shakespeare and Jonson represent the qualities Dryden admired in all writers. (a) What qualities would Dryden's perfect writer have? (b) What writer, in your opinion, comes closest to having those qualities? Explain the reasons for your choice.

well as others," while linking "judge" with "judicious" to increase logical flow. Next, Dryden adds two new details to support his thesis—that Jonson was "frugal" of "wit" and that his language left "little to retrench or alter." Both details show frugality and discerning judgment, and so they relate to each other as well as to the paragraph's chain of logic. Dryden progresses to his final, dramatic statement about Jonson over the bridge of "wit" and "language." "Wit, and language, and humor . . . we had before him; but something of art was wanting to the drama till he came." Thus the passage links logically one piece to another.

Student Activity. Write a paragraph in which you link your ideas logically sentence by sentence.

ANALYZING LITERATURE

Understanding an Essay

An **essay** is a prose composition, usually short, that deals with one topic. Typically, the writer of an essay states his or her personal views on the topic. A formal essay is serious and dignified. An informal essay is lighter and more conversational. Dryden's "Essay of Dramatic Poesy," written more than three hundred years ago, may not seem like an informal essay, but it is. It is written in the form of a conversation among four friends as they are boating on the Thames. One of them, named Neander, represents Dryden. He is the person speaking in the excerpt included in this book.

1. Two signs of informality in writing are (a) the occasional use of sentence fragments and (b) the occasional use of a conjunction to start a sentence. Find an example of each of these in the excerpt from Dryden's essay.
2. Compare Dryden's essay with Bacon's "Idols of the Cave" (pages 357–358). What are three noticeable differences in prose style between the two essays. (In examining prose style, look at sentence structure, sentence length, rhetorical devices, word choice, and so on.)

CRITICAL THINKING AND READING

Charting an Analysis

Dryden's "An Essay of Dramatic Poesy" is an analysis of the literary merits of William Shakespeare and Ben Jonson. The essay contains a number of specific statements praising, criticizing, or comparing the two writers. On a sheet of paper, list as many properties of a writer as you can find in Dryden's essay. These properties can be good or bad. Beside each property on your list, state in a phrase or short sentence how

Dryden rates each writer in regard to it. For example, you might list "Education" as a property. Your entry for Shakespeare might then read, "Lacked formal education but was thoroughly self-educated."

Property	Shakespeare	Jonson
1. Education	Lacked formal education but was thoroughly self-educated	

If nothing is said about one of the two writers in regard to a particular property, write, "No comment." Complete your chart with a statement summarizing Dryden's overall opinion of Shakespeare and Jonson as writers.

THINKING AND WRITING

Writing an Evaluation of an Analysis

Review the chart you prepared on Shakespeare and Jonson. Also review the lists you made before reading. Use these materials as the basis for an essay in which you evaluate Dryden's analysis of the literary merits of Shakespeare and Jonson. Take into account your own opinion of Shakespeare and Jonson as well. Is Dryden fair to Shakespeare? Does Dryden overrate Jonson? These and other questions should occur to you as you write the first draft. When you are ready to revise, reread the Dryden excerpt to be sure you are interpreting his opinions accurately. Be sure you have supported your own opinions well. Make any needed changes. Then write your final draft.

Closure and Extension

Literary Focus Make sure that students grasp the essential idea of an ode: a poem on a dignified subject in a formal and elevated style. You might also mention that Dryden's ode was set to music by Handel.

Writing/Prior Knowledge Lead the class in brainstorming for suitable subjects.

Vocabulary

Preteach the following vocabulary word:
sequacious (si kwā′ shəs) *adj.: Archaic.* Tending to follow dutifully; in service of (p. 501, l. 50)

A Song for St. Cecilia's Day

Literary Forms

Ode. An ode is a lyric poem, usually rhymed, that addresses and praises a person, an object, or a quality. Most odes are dignified or exalted in subject matter and style. The word *ode* comes from a Greek word meaning "song." The earliest odes, dating back to ancient Greece, were elaborate chants with themes and responses sung by a divided choir. Pindar, a Greek poet of the fifth century B.C., refined the form, becoming one of its great masters. The form he devised has been considerably changed over the centuries. Although Dryden patterned his odes loosely on classical models, later writers varied the form in many ways. Once recognizable by its shape, the ode today is more a matter of tone and intention than of structure.

Commentary

In his day it was common knowledge among literary circles that Dryden was a solemn, dignified person who was not much given to making amusing remarks. He admitted this himself on numerous occasions. One of his witty rejoinders, however, has been passed down.

According to many reports, he and his wife, Lady Elizabeth, do not seem to have been on very friendly terms with each other. If we trust the gossip of his day, the relationship got off to a rocky start when Dryden had been forced into marriage with the woman by one of her brothers. Regardless of the reason, the union was less than cordial.

One day, so the story goes, Lady Elizabeth began to feel more than usually neglected by her husband, who spent a great deal of time alone with his books and papers. Marching into the study, she burst out, "Lord, Mr. Dryden, how can you always be pouring over those musty books? I wish I were a book, and then I should have more of your company." Dryden was ready with a quick answer. "Pray, my dear," he replied, "if you do become a book let it be an almanack, for then I shall change you every year."

What contrast do you see between "A Song for St. Cecilia's Day" and Dryden's domestic situation?

Writing

Jot down some thoughts on a person, thing, or event you think deserves to be honored. Then freewrite a short tribute, either in a paragraph or in a few lines of poetry, in which you make clear the qualities of the person, thing, or event that you believe justify the tribute.

Objectives

1 To understand the ode as a literary form
2 To understand the effect of sound in poetry
3 To write an ode

Support Material

Teaching Portfolio
Teacher Backup, p. 549
Grammar in Action Worksheet, *Special Effects,* p. 552
Usage and Mechanics Worksheet, p. 554
Analyzing Literature Worksheet, *Recognizing the Ode,* p. 555
Language Worksheet, *Appreciating Rhythm,* p. 556
Selection Test, p. 557

A Song for St. Cecilia's Day[1]

John Dryden

1

From harmony, from heavenly harmony
    This universal frame[2] began;
    When Nature underneath a heap
    Of jarring atoms[3] lay,
5   And could not heave her head,
The tuneful voice was heard from high,
    "Arise, ye more than dead."

Then cold and hot and moist and dry[4]
    In order to their stations leap,
10   And Music's power obey.
From harmony, from heavenly harmony
    This universal frame began:
    From harmony to harmony
Through all the compass of the notes it ran,
15 The diapason[5] closing full in Man.

2

What passion cannot Music raise and quell?
    When Jubal[6] struck the chorded shell,
    His listening brethren stood around,
    And, wondering, on their faces fell
20   To worship that celestial sound.

---

1. "A Song for St. Cecilia's Day" was composed for the Festival of St. Cecilia on November 22, 1687. According to legend, St. Cecilia was an early Christian martyr, who became the patron saint of music.
2. universal frame: The structure of the universe.
3. jarring atoms: The chaos that preceded the creation of the universe.
4. cold . . . dry: Earth, fire, water, and air, the four elements out of which everything was composed, according to the ancient Greeks.
5. diapason (dī′ ə pā′ zən): The entire range of tones on a musical scale. Dryden is also making reference to the Chain of Being, the ordered creation from inanimate nature up to man.
6. Jubal: In Genesis 4:21, Jubal is said to be the inventor of the lyre and the pipe.

Presentation

Motivation/Prior Knowledge
Play for students some dramatically different types of music that evoke different moods. Then discuss how music can affect our emotions.

Master Teacher Note Dryden's ode dramatizes the ancient conception of the universe as a harmony created by God of the warring elements of chaos. The spheres that encased the planets and stars were believed to create a divine music inaudible to humans.

Purpose-Setting Question How does the poet use sound to enhance the poem's meaning?

1 **Discussion** What figure of speech is used in these lines?

2 **Discussion** What does man represent?

3 **Clarification** Dryden centers his poem on this line.

Fine art, *The Music of a Bygone Age,* by John Melhuish Strudwick. Strudwick (1849–1937) was a British painter of the Pre-Raphaelite school (painters who emulated the works of primitive Christian painters before Raphael, the Italian Renaissance master). He left the School of the Royal Academy to assist at the studios of eminent Pre-Raphaelite artists, Spencer-Stanhope and Burne-Jones. The works of these men and Strudwick's admiration for Italian art greatly influenced his style.

The Music of a Bygone Age was painted in 1890. The influence of his teachers is apparent in the poetic subject matter, the classically draped clothing, and the resemblance of the figures to angels from Italian religious paintings. The almost startling detail and the clear glowing colors of this painting are trademarks of the Pre-Raphaelite style.

You might use the following questions for discussion:

1. Which instruments appear in both the painting and the poem?
2. Is the angelic appearance of the figures in this painting similar to any aspect of this poem? Explain.
3. What sort of music would you expect to hear from the musicians in this painting?

THE MUSIC OF A BYGONE AGE
John Melhuish Strudwick
Art Resource

Grammar in Action

Rhythm is one of the **special effects** that writers use to emphasize their themes and capture readers' attention. This device is used by poets and prose writers alike. The following sentence, from Doris Lessing's "A Mild Attack of Locusts" (page 1252), is an example of effective rhythms in prose.

RHYTHMS IN PROSE: From down on the lands came *the beating and banging and clanging* of a hundred gasoline cans and bits of metal.

The use of three gerunds, *beating, banging,* and *clanging,* joined by two conjunctions, emphasizes the insistent rhythm of the noise being described.

Prose writers can often learn a great deal from poets about the effects of rhythm. In "A Song for St. Cecilia's Day," Dryden imitates in language the rhythms of musical instruments. Here, for example, is his description of a drum:

Less than a god they thought there could not dwell
　　　Within the hollow of that shell
　　　That spoke so sweetly, and so well.
What passion cannot Music raise and quell?

3

25　　　The trumpet's loud clangor
　　　　Excites us to arms
　　　With shrill notes of anger
　　　　And mortal alarms.
　　　The double double double beat
30　　　Of the thundering drum
　　　Cries, "Hark! the foes come:
Charge, charge, 'tis too late to retreat."

4

　　　The soft complaining flute
　　　In dying notes discovers[7]
35　　　The woes of hopeless lovers,
Whose dirge is whispered by the warbling lute.

5

　　　Sharp violins proclaim
　　　Their jealous pangs and desperation.
　　　Fury, frantic indignation,
40　　　Depth of pains and height of passion,
　　　　For the fair, disdainful dame.

6

　　　But Oh! What art can teach,
　　　What human voice can reach
　　　　The sacred organ's praise?
45　　　　Notes inspiring holy love,
　　　Notes that wing their heavenly ways
　　　　To mend the choirs above.

7

　　　Orpheus[8] could lead the savage race,
　　　And trees unrooted left their place,
50　　　　Sequacious of the lyre:
　　　But bright Cecilia raised the wonder higher:

---

7. discovers: Reveals.
8. Orpheus (ôr′ fē əs): In Greek mythology, a poet and musician whose magic musical powers enabled him to charm rocks, trees, and wild beasts by playing his lyre.

A Song for St. Cecilia's Day　501

---

4 Discussion What passion is referred to in this stanza? Are the instruments referred to appropriate symbols for this passion?

5 Discussion How does this stanza contrast in mood with the previous stanza?

6 Discussion Is the violin an appropriate instrument to represent the "Depth of pains and height of passion"? Why or why not?

7 Discussion With what passion does Dryden associate the organ?

8 Reading Strategy Stanzas three through six describe the four passions that music can "raise and quell." What are they?

The double double double beat
Of the thundering drum
Cries, "Hark! the foes come:
Charge, charge, 'tis too late to retreat."
The word *double,* repeated three times, mimics the insistent repetition of the drums themselves, and the repetition of the word *charge* emphasizes the urgency that the drums inspire.

Student Activity 1. Find another instance where Dryden uses rhythm effectively and explain his success. Remember that there are many rhythmic devices other than simple repetition. You might want to focus, for example, on the pattern of stresses in several lines or on the varying lengths of lines.

Student Activity 2. Write a prose description of some type of work. Use sentence rhythms to emphasize the rhythmic patterns of the labor you are describing.

9 Discussion Explain the paradox in this line?

Reader's Response What kind of music would you use to accompany a reading of this poem?

When to her organ vocal breath was given,
An angel heard, and straight appeared
    Mistaking earth for heaven.

GRAND CHORUS

55   *As from the power of sacred lays*[9]
      The spheres began to move.[10]
    And sung the great Creator's praise
      To all the blessed above;
    So when the last and dreadful hour
60   *This crumbling pageant*[11] *shall devour,*
    The trumpet shall be heard on high,[12]
    The dead shall live, the living die,
    And Music shall untune the sky.

---

9. lays: Songs.
10. spheres . . . move: According to legend, the celestial bodies (spheres) were put into motion by angelic song. The motion of the spheres was believed to produce harmonious music, a hymn of "praise" for the "Creator," sung by the created.
11. pageant: The universe.
12. trumpet . . . high: From I Corinthians 15:52, the last trumpet that will announce the Last Judgment, or the end of the universe.

Primary Source

For people in the eighteenth century, music was a social as well as an intellectual pastime. In the summer concerts were offered in public gardens, where people strolling among the "regular rows of young trees" feasted on fruit tarts, almond cheesecakes, and fine Epping butter. Sometimes there were fireworks as well, brilliant displays "splendid beyond conception." The following contemporary advertisement promised exotically named fireworks as well as music:

"Marybone Gardens.—This day, June 2, will be performed a Concert of Vocal and Instrumental Music. In the course of which will be sung for the first time this season an Entertainment of Music called 'The MAGNET.' The Vocal Parts by Mr. Reinhold, Miss Wilde, and Miss Wewitzer. The celebrated Mons. Ladell, Musician to the King of Portugal, will perform a Concert on the German Flute. Admittance Two Shillings and Sixpence. The Doors will be opened at Five o'clock. The Concert will begin at Half Past Six o'clock . . . To-morrow Sig. Torre's Second Exhibition; when he will repeat the Forge of Vulcan, as it was performed at the Marriage of his Royal Highness the Count d'Artois.

"Marybone Gardens will open To-morrow Evening immediately after Five o'clock for Company to walk in. Tea, Coffee, and other Refreshments may be had at the Bar. To prevent Improper company each Person to pay sixpence at the Door."

THINKING ABOUT THE SELECTION

Recalling

1. According to the first stanza, what was the condition of Nature when the universe took shape?
2. In addition to the corded shell, what musical instruments are mentioned in the poem?
3. What does Dryden claim an angel did upon hearing Cecilia play the organ?
4. What instrument will announce Judgment Day?

Interpreting

5. The word *harmony* dominates the first stanza. What meaning, or meanings, does it have as Dryden uses it?
6. (a) What musical instrument does Dryden suggest is the most heavenly? (b) In view of the day the poem celebrates, why is this praise especially appropriate?
7. Why will music "untune the sky" in "the last and dreadful hour"?

Applying

8. Dryden is often called an "occasional" poet, because he wrote in response to major news events, literary developments, and, as in this poem, to celebrate special days. Occasional poetry is no longer popular. What do people do today to commemorate special events and heroes?

ANALYZING LITERATURE

Recognizing an Ode

An **ode** is a lyrical poem that pays homage to a person, thing, or quality. The earliest odes are from classical times, such as those of the Greek poet Pindar (522?–443 B.C.) and the Latin poet Horace (65–8 B.C.). The Greek ode, which is the ancestor of the odes written by Dryden, is composed of three-part stanzas called *triads*. Each triad is made up of a *strophe* (sung by one half the singers in a choir), an *antistrophe* (sung by the other half), and an *epode* (sung by the entire choir). Dryden and other poets of the seventeenth century use a much looser prosodic system than Pindar's, as do later writers.

1. In "A Song for St. Cecilia's Day," how many lines are (a) in each numbered stanza? (b) in the Grand Chorus?
2. (a) Which stanzas have regular patterns of rhyme? (b) What are these patterns? (Use *a, b, c,* and so on, to show patterns.)
3. Why do you think Dryden uses such an irregular stanza and rhyme scheme for his poem?

CRITICAL THINKING AND READING

Understanding the Effect of Sound

Dryden's words carry meaning not only in a lexical, or dictionary, sense but also through their sound. For example, in the third stanza, the word *shrill* echoes—that is, imitates the sound of—the insistent cry of the trumpet. The word *double,* while not in itself echoic of a drum, becomes so when repeated like a drumbeat—"double, double, double."

1. What word in the third stanza besides *double* has a sound that echoes the pounding of the drum?
2. What words in the fourth stanza have sounds that echo the melodic flute and lute?
3. What sounds in the fifth stanza echo the piercing tone of the violin?

THINKING AND WRITING

Writing an Ode

Choose one of the following topics and write an ode concerning it. You may decide on the number of stanzas and the length of lines, but try to follow at least two of the rhyme patterns used by Dryden in "A Song for St. Cecilia's Day." Also, use as many echoic, or sound-imitative, devices as you can. Read your ode aloud to judge its effect. After revising, proofread it and prepare a final draft.

1. The United States
2. A season of the year
3. A brother or sister
4. Honesty

---

roes people stay home from work and enjoy themselves. A feast or parade is often involved.

ANSWERS TO ANALYZING LITERATURE

1. (a) There are, respectively, fifteen, nine, eight, four, five, six, and seven lines in each numbered stanza. (b) There are nine lines in the Grand Chorus.
2. (a) There are no regular patterns of rhyme; each stanza has a different pattern. (b) 1a, b, c, d, e, f, e, f, c, d, a, b, a, b, b; 2a, a, b, a, b, a, a, a, a; 3a, b, a, c, d, e, e, d; 4a, b, b, a; 5a, b, b, b, a; 6a, a, b, c, b, c; 7a, a, b, b, c, d, c; chorus a, b, a, c, d, d, c, e, e
3. Answers will differ. A possible answer is: The first stanza is highly irregular to show the emergence of harmony out of chaos. The second stanza consists mostly of couplets to suggest the sweet harmony described. The other stanzas are irregular to suggest the different instruments being described. In the Grand Chorus, a highly irregular pattern is again used as chaos returns.

ANSWERS TO CRITICAL THINKING AND READING

1. The word *thundering* echoes the drum's pounding.
2. The words *soft, woes, whispered,* and *warbling* have sounds that echo the flute and lute.
3. The words *proclaim, pangs, desperation, indignation, pains,* and *passion* echo the tone of the violin.

Challenge What figure of speech uses words with sounds that imitate or suggest their meanings?

ANSWERS TO THINKING AND WRITING

For help with this assignment, students can refer to Lesson 18, "Writing a Poem," in the Handbook of Writing About Literature.

Publishing Student Writing Suggest that students submit their odes to the school literary magazine for publication. Alternatively, you might prepare a class magazine with students' odes.

Closure and Extension

ANSWERS TO THINKING ABOUT THE SELECTION

Recalling

1. Nature was buried under a heap of jarring atoms.
2. The musical instruments mentioned are the trumpet, drum, flute, lute, violin, organ, and lyre.
3. Hearing the sound, an angel appeared, thinking earth was heaven.
4. The trumpet will announce it.

Interpreting

5. The word *harmony* refers to musical sweetness and also to order and symmetry.

6. (a) Dryden thinks the organ is the most heavenly instrument. (b) Since St. Cecilia is regarded as the inventor of the organ, his praise is especially appropriate.
7. When the universe ends, on the biblical Judgment Day, there will no longer be harmony.

Applying

8. To commemorate events and he-

More About the Author In addition to being a man of action, Samuel Pepys was quite a scholar. He had a good working knowledge of several languages —Latin, Greek, French, Spanish, and some Italian—and he sometimes put these languages to use in his diary. He and Mrs. Pepys frequently spoke French, and Pepys liked to read books in Latin, especially the scientific and philosophical works of his favorite writer, Sir Francis Bacon. What does Pepys's classical education and proficiency in languages tell you about the education of the day? Do you think he was atypical of other men of his station in life?

Critical Quotation Pepys's motto was *Mens cujusque is est quisque,* a Latin quotation from Cicero that can be translated as "what a man's mind is, that is what he is." In commenting on the expression, biographer Richard Ollard has this to say: "For Pepys, the *mens,* the mind, the intellect, reason, was the quality that set a man above the beasts that perish and thus, implicit in the phrase if not in logic, his passport to immortality. It was the surest mark of the Divine hand, the thread to follow through the labyrinth in which generations of theologians had imprisoned their victims."

SAMUEL PEPYS

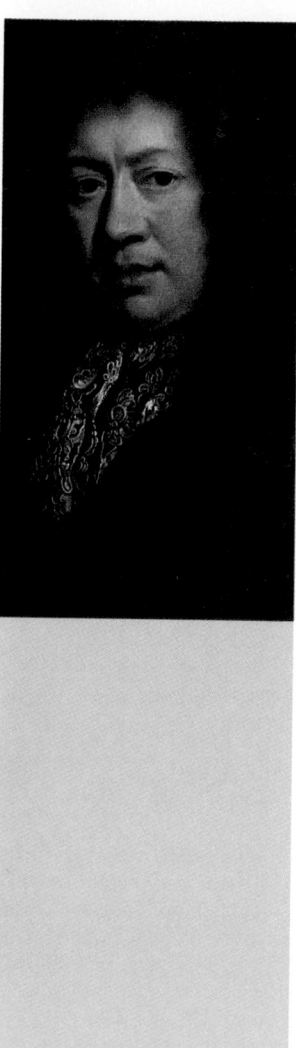

1633–1703

Samuel Pepys (pēps) is an unusual figure in English literature, not so much because his fame rests on a single work but rather the one work, his *Diary,* was never intended for publication. This *Diary,* which Pepys kept in shorthand and in his own private code, was not deciphered until the nineteenth century.

The man who painted this vivid portrait of his times was a "very worthy, industrious, and curious person," according to his friend John Evelyn. Born in London, the son of a tailor, Pepys studied at St. Paul's School and Magdalene (mag′ də lēn) College, Cambridge. Upon graduation in 1653, he became secretary to his influential cousin, Edward Montagu, later the Earl of Sandwich. Two years later he married Elizabeth St. Michel, a girl of fifteen. The *Diary* contains many details of their strife-ridden union, which survived Pepys countless infidelities and lasted until her early death in 1669.

Pepys began his career as a naval man—as well as his famous *Diary*—in 1660, when he was appointed clerk of the King's ships and clerk of the privy seal. His advancement, as the *Diary* notes, was rapid, and with each new position, Pepys grew richer. Yet his life was not without its tragedies. In the same year his wife died, Pepys's failing eyesight caused him to stop keeping the *Diary.* In 1679 he was imprisoned briefly in the Tower of London, accused of popery and treason, and in 1690 he once again spent some time in prison on charges of intrigue.

The *Diary,* originally in six manuscript volumes, remained in cipher until 1819 when a student at Magdalene College, Cambridge, began transcribing it. Published in 1825, the *Diary* proved a fascinating mix of candid private revelations and keenly observed public scenes. The 1660's, during which the diary was kept, saw Pepys' personal rise in the world from obscure clerk to highly regarded public servant. It also saw—and through Pepys's eyes modern readers can see—the coronation of King Charles II, the devastating London plague of 1665, and the Great Fire of 1666.

In the centuries since his death, some readers have dismissed Pepys as a shallow figure and his observations as mere gossip. But the Samuel Pepys who emerges from between the lines of the *Diary* is more than just a government careerist with a roving eye. He is a man of intelligence and great diplomacy, much admired by the people of his time, and evidently deserving of that admiration. He is also a diarist of exceptional honesty and perception. Readers of today who wish to know about life in seventeenth-century London are greatly in his debt.

Support Material

Teaching Portfolio
Teacher Backup, p. 559
Grammar in Action Worksheet, *Ellipitical Elements,* p. 563
Usage and Mechanics Worksheet, p. 565
Vocabulary Check, p. 566

Critical Thinking and Reading Worksheet, *Finding Main Ideas and Supporting Details,* p. 567
Language Worksheet, *Appreciating the Language of the Restoration,* p. 569
Selection Test, p. 571

GUIDE FOR INTERPRETING

from **The Diary**

Literary Forms

Diary. A diary is a personal day-by-day record of events, experiences, and observations. Perhaps you think of a diary as simply a collection of notes about the small details in one's life, such as what the diarist had for breakfast. Many diaries fit that definition but not all. The diaries that become literature are usually those that provide insights into important historical events or periods. *The Diary of Anne Frank,* for instance, gives readers a poignant glimpse of a young Jewish girl's ultimately futile attempt to escape Nazi persecution by hiding with her family in Nazi-occupied Netherlands in World War II. The events have an importance beyond Anne Frank's individual fate. Moreover, as with most diaries that are regarded as literature, it is exceptionally well written.

Commentary

Pepy's diary gives us first-hand information about life in London. As we know from Pepys's account, there was considerable danger from fire in the town and countryside. Once started, fires spread with terrible speed. Water could be obtained only by great difficulty through pumps and conduits. Homes in town were supplied through a huge water wheel at London Bridge, but people in the country had to rely on well water or store rainwater in huge lead casks. By the beginning of the eighteenth century, with memories of the Great Fire still fresh, stronger measures were being taken against the threat of fire.

In 1708, for example, an Act was passed "for the better preventing of mischiefs that may happen by fire." Some shops carried rope ladders and other devices to help people escape from burning buildings. Most noteworthy, perhaps, was the establishment of the first insurance companies. These included the symbolically named "Phoenix," "The Friendly Society," and "The Amicable Contributors." The firms all had offices in London coffeehouses, centers for the exchange of news and views, and meeting places for businessmen, wits, and idlers. The fire insurance companies could be easily identified by their own specially uniformed firemen.

What evidence do you have from Pepys's account that adequate measures were not yet in place to combat the fires?

Writing

Make some notes about an especially memorable event you have experienced. These notes can be in the form of a diary entry; that is, they do not have to be written in grammatically complete sentences or arranged in an orderly sequence.

Guide for Interpreting   505

Literary Focus Ask students how many of them keep or have kept a diary. Discuss whether they would like others to read their diaries.

Writing/Prior Knowledge Suggest that **more advanced** students write a poem about the event and compare the effect of the two literary forms.

Vocabulary

Preteach the following vocabulary words:
apprehensions (ap rə hen′ shənz) *n.:* Fears, concerns (p. 506)
abated (ə bāt′id) *v.:* Lessened (p. 506)
lamentable (lam′ ən tə b′l) *adj.:* Distressing (p. 506)
discoursing (dis kôrs′ ′iŋ) *v.:* Talking about; discussing (p. 510)

Motivation/Prior Knowledge
Ask students to imagine what it would be like to be involved in a huge disaster, such as a fire or an epidemic. Assuming they were not yet personally involved, what would their first reaction be: to try to get away or to help those in need?

Master Teacher Note Pepys's travel experiences, intellectual interests, and governmental activities make his diary an important historical document. His candid revelations of private personal experience make the diary a fascinating human document of great psychological interest.

Purpose-Setting Question As you read, decide whether Pepys wrote his diary for personal information or if he had in mind a larger audience at some time.

Thematic Idea Read and discuss Thomas Nashe's "A Litany in Time of Plague," on page 250, in conjunction with the excerpts from Pepys' work.

1 **Discussion** What can you infer about Pepys's position in the community?

2 **Discussion** Why were public funerals not allowed during the plague?

3 **Discussion** What does this tell you about Pepys's personality?

4 **Discussion** What was Pepys's job at this time?

5 **Discussion** Why is Pepys both elated and disturbed by news about the plague?

6 **Critical Thinking and Reading** List five specific examples that Pepys uses to back up his growing fear of the plague.

from The Diary

Samuel Pepys

The Plague

Sept. 3, 1665. (Lord's Day.) Church being done, my Lord Bruncker, Sir J. Minnes, and I up to the vestry[1] at the desire of the Justices of the Peace, Sir Theo. Biddulph and Sir W. Boreman and Alderman Hooker, in order to the doing something for the keeping of the plague from growing; but Lord! to consider the madness of the people of the town, who will (because they are forbid) come in crowds along with the dead corps[2] to see them buried; but we agreed on some orders for the prevention thereof.[3] Among other stories, one was very passionate, methought, of a complaint brought against a man in the town for taking a child from London from an infected house. Alderman Hooker told us it was the child of a very able citizen in Gracious Street, a saddler,[4] who had buried all the rest of his children of the plague, and himself and wife now being shut up and in despair of escaping, did desire only to save the life of this little child; and so prevailed to have it received stark-naked into the arms of a friend, who brought it (having put it into new fresh clothes) to Greenwich; where upon hearing the story, we did agree it should be permitted to be received and kept in the town. Thence with my Lord Bruncker to Captain Cocke's, where we mighty merry and supped, and very late I by water to Woolwich, in great apprehensions of an ague. . . .

Sept. 14, 1665. When I come home I spent some thoughts upon the occurrences of this day, giving matter for as much content on one hand and melancholy on another, as any day in all my life. For the first; the finding of my money and plate,[5] and all safe at London, and speeding in my business of money this day. The hearing of this good news to such excess, after so great a despair of my Lord's doing anything this year; adding to that, the decrease of 500 and more, which is the first decrease we have yet had in the sickness since it begun: and great hopes that the next week it will be greater. Then, on the other side, my finding that though the bill[6] in general is abated, yet the city within the walls is increased, and likely to continue so, and is close to our house there. My meeting dead corpses of the plague, carried to be buried close to me at noonday through the city in Fanchurch Street. To see a person sick of the sores, carried close by me by Grace church in a

---
1. **vestry** (ves′ trē) *n.*: A church meeting room.
2. **corps:** corpses.
3. **but we . . . thereof:** Funeral processions were forbidden in London during the plague. However, the law was often ignored.
4. **saddler** *n.*: A person who makes, sells, and repairs saddles.

---
5. **plate:** Valuable serving dishes and flatware.
6. **bill:** Weekly list of burials.

hackney coach.[7] My finding the Angell Tavern at the lower end of Tower Hill, shut up, and more than that, the alehouse at the Tower Stairs, and more than that, the person was then dying of the plague when I was last there, a little while ago, at night, to write a short letter there, and I overheard the mistress of the house sadly saying to her husband somebody was very ill, but did not think it was of the plague. To hear that poor Payne, my waiter, hath buried a child, and is dying himself. To hear that a laborer I sent but the other day to Dagenhams, to know how they did there, is dead of the plague; and that one of my own watermen, that carried me daily, fell sick as soon as he had landed me on Friday morning last, when I had been all night upon the water (and I believe he did get his infection that day at Brainford), and is now dead of the plague. To hear that Captain Lambert and Cuttle are killed in the taking these ships; and that Mr. Sidney Montague is sick of a desperate fever at my Lady Carteret's, at Scott's Hall. To hear that Mr. Lewes hath another daughter sick. And, lastly, that both my servants, W. Hewer and Tom Edwards, have lost their fathers, both in St. Sepulcher's parish, of the plague this week, do put me into great apprehensions of melancholy, and with good reason. But I put off the thoughts of sadness as much as I can, and the rather to keep my wife in good heart and family also. After supper (having eat nothing all this day) upon a fine tench[8] of Mr. Shelden's taking, we to bed.

The Fire of London

Sept. 2, 1666. (Lord's day.) Some of our maids sitting up late last night to get things ready against our feast today, Jane called us up about three in the morning, to tell us of a great fire they saw in the city. So I rose and slipped on my night-gown, and went to her window, and thought it to be on the back side of Mark Lane at the farthest; but, being unused to such fires as followed, I thought it far enough off; and so went to bed again and to sleep. About seven rose again to dress myself, and there looked out at the window, and saw the fire not so much as it was and farther off. So to my closet to set things to rights after yesterday's cleaning. By and by Jane comes and tells me that she hears that above 300 houses have been burned down tonight by the fire we saw, and that it is now burning down all Fish Street, by London Bridge. So I made myself ready presently, and walked to the Tower,[9] and there got up upon one of the high places, Sir J. Robinson's little son going up with me; and there I did see the houses at that end of the bridge all on fire, and an infinite great fire on this and the other side the end of the bridge; which, among other people, did trouble me for poor little Michell and our Sarah on the bridge. So down, with my heart full of trouble, to the Lieutenant of the Tower, who tells me that it begun this morning in the King's baker's house in Pudding Lane, and that it hath burned St. Magnus's Church and most part of Fish Street already. So I down to the waterside, and there got a boat and through bridge, and there saw a lamentable fire. Poor Michell's house, as far as the Old Swan, already burned that way, and the fire running farther, that in a very little time it got as far as the steel yard, while I was there. Everybody endeavoring to remove their goods, and flinging into the river or bringing them into lighters that lay off; poor people staying in their houses as long as till the very fire touched them, and then running into boats, or clambering from one pair of stairs by the waterside to another. And among other things, the poor pigeons, I perceive, were loth to leave their houses, but hovered about the windows and balconies

7. **hackney coach:** A carriage for hire.
8. **tench** *n*.: A type of fish.

9. **Tower:** The Tower of London.

7 **Discussion** What does Pepys achieve by briefly listing those who have died rather than developing a single story?

8 **Discussion** Give examples that illustrate that Pepys is a man of action.

9 **Discussion** What does the fact that Pepys noticed the plight of the pigeons tell you about the man?

Fine art, *The Great Fire of London, 1666.* This painting of *The Great Fire of London,* by an unknown artist hangs in the Museum of London, England. Even today this spectacle of an uncontrolled inferno is terrifying to behold. Paintings such as this and accounts such as the diary of Samuel Pepys give an idea of the effect of this disaster upon the inhabitants of the seventeenth-century city.

You may wish to ask the following questions:

1. What line from Pepys's account of the fire would be an appropriate caption for this painting?
2. Do you think the artist of this painting was an eyewitness to this fire? Explain.

THE GREAT FIRE OF LONDON, 1666
The Museum of London

till they were, some of them burned, their wings, and fell down. Having stayed, and in an hour's time seen the fire rage every way, and nobody, to my sight, endeavoring to quench it, but to remove their goods, and leave all to the fire, and having seen it get as far as the steel yard, and the wind mighty high and driving it into the city; and everything, after so long a drought, proving combustible, even the very stones of churches, and among other things the poor steeple by which pretty Mrs.— lives, and whereof my old schoolfellow Elborough is parson, taken fire in the very top, and there burned till it fell down. I to Whitehall (with a gentleman with me who desired to go off from the Tower, to see the fire, in my boat), and there up to the King's closet in the chapel, where people come about me, and I did give them an account dismayed them all, and word was carried in to the King. So I was called for, and did tell the King and Duke of York what I saw, and that unless his Majesty did command houses to be pulled down nothing could stop the fire. They seemed much troubled, and the King commanded me to go to my Lord Mayor from him, and command him to spare no houses, but to pull down before the fire every way. The Duke of York bid me tell him that if he would have any more soldiers he shall; and so did my Lord Arlington afterwards, as a great secret. Here meeting with Captain Cocke, I in his coach, which he lent me, and Creed with me to Paul's,[10] and there walked along Watling Street, as well as I could, every creature coming away loaden with goods to save, and here and there sick people carried away in beds. Extraordinary good goods carried in carts and on backs. At last met my Lord Mayor in Canning Street, like a man spent,

---

10. Paul's: St. Paul's Cathedral.

Grammar in Action

Elliptical elements are phrases or clauses with omitted words that a reader's mind will supply correctly. Omitting understood words will tighten text and minimize needless repetition of simple elements, but use caution when doing so. Remember, omissions should clarify not obscure meaning. Notice how Samuel Pepys omits words that will be understood in the following italicized elliptical constructions.

By this time it was about twelve o'clock; *and so home.*

Their order was only to pull down houses apace, *and so below bridge at the waterside;* but little was or could be done, the fire coming upon them so fast.

Pepys's diary was written for himself, not the public, so he uses elliptical elements more frequently than writers usually do. In the first example, he omits *I went,* yet the statement is still clear. The second example is more complex: and [*to do*] so below [*the*] bridge requires more mental agility on the part of the reader. This example has a second ellipsis—"the fire [*was*] coming"—but it is clearer than the first. Most writers prefer to leave out only repeated elements and relative pronouns.

with a handkerchief about his neck. To the King's message he cried, like a fainting woman, "Lord! what can I do? I am spent: people will not obey me. I have been pulling down houses; but the fire overtakes us faster than we can do it." That he needed no more soldiers; and that, for himself, he must go and refresh himself, having been up all night. So he left me, and I him, and walked home, seeing people all almost distracted, and no manner of means used to quench the fire. The houses, too, so very thick there-abouts, and full of matter for burning, as pitch and tar, in Thames Street; and ware-houses of oil, and wines, and brandy, and other things. Here I saw Mr. Isaake Houblon, the handsome man, prettily dressed and dirty, at his door at Dowgate, receiving some of his brothers' things, whose houses were on fire; and, as he says, have been removed twice already; and he doubts (as it soon proved) that they must be in a little time removed from his house also, which was a sad consideration. And to see the churches all filling with goods by people who them-selves should have been quietly there at this time. By this time it was about twelve o'clock; and so home. Soon as dined, and walked through the city, the streets full of nothing but people and horses and carts loaden with goods, ready to run over one another, and removing goods from one burned house to another. They now remov-ing out of Canning Street (which received goods in the morning) into Lumbard Street, and farther; and among others I now saw my little goldsmith, Stokes, receiving some friend's goods, whose house itself was burned the day after. I to Paul's Wharf, where I had appointed a boat to attend me, and took in Mr. Carcasse and his brother, whom I met in the street, and carried them below and above bridge to and again to see the fire, which was now got farther, both below and above, and no likelihood of stop-ping it. Met with the King and Duke of York in their barge, and with them to Queen-hithe, and there called Sir Richard Browne

to them. Their order was only to pull down houses apace, and so below bridge at the waterside; but little was or could be done, the fire coming upon them so fast. Good hopes there was of stopping it at the Three Cranes above, and at Buttolph's Wharf below bridge, if care be used; but the wind carries it into the city, so as we know not by the waterside what it do there. River full of lighters and boats taking in goods, and good goods swimming in the water, and only I observed that hardly one lighter or boat in three that had the goods of a house in, but there was a pair of virginals[11] in it. Having seen as much as I could now, I away to Whitehall by appointment, and there walked to St. James's Park, and there met my wife and Creed and Wood and his wife, and walked to my boat; and there upon the water again, and to the fire up and down, it still increasing, and the wind great. So near the fire as we could for smoke; and all over the Thames, with one's face in the wind, you were almost burned with a shower of firedrops. This is very true; so as houses were burned by these drops and flakes of fire, three or four, nay, five or six houses, one from another. When we could endure no more upon the water, we to a little alehouse on the Bankside, over against the Three Cranes, and there stayed till it was dark almost, and saw the fire grow; and, as it grew darker, appeared more and more, and in corners and upon steeples, and between churches and houses, as far as we could see up the hill of the city, in a most horrid malicious bloody flame, not like the fine flame of an ordinary fire. Barbary and her husband away before us. We stayed till, it being darkish, we saw the fire as only one entire arch of fire from this to the other side the bridge, and in a bow up the hill for an arch of above a mile long: it made me weep to see it. The churches, houses, and all on fire and flaming at once; and a horrid noise the flames made, and the cracking of houses

---

11. virginals *n.*: Small, legless harpsichords.

10 Enrichment Look at pictures of London in 1666. Notice the close-ness of the buildings and the wooden structures.

11 Discussion What seems to be the primary activity during the fire?

12 Discussion Why do they find it difficult to remain on the river?

13 Literary Focus How does Pepys's description differ from, say, a newspaper account of the fire?

Student Activity 1. Find another sentence in which Pepys successfully uses an elliptical element.

Student Activity 2. Supply the omitted element in each of the following sentences:

1. I fixed the tire, but then ran out of gas. More trouble.
2. "Would you like a sandwich?" she asked. "Please," I replied.
3. My boss is as nice as John's.
4. We knew you would help when asked.

14 **Discussion** Why would Pepys's iron chests be safe in his cellar?

Reader's Response How would you respond to a fire like the one described here?

at their ruin. So home with a sad heart, and there find everybody discoursing and lamenting the fire; and poor Tom Hater come with some of his few goods saved out of his house, which is burned upon Fish Street Hill. I invited him to lie at my house, and did receive his goods, but was deceived in his lying there, the news coming every moment of the growth of the fire; so as we were forced to begin to pack up our own goods, and prepare for their removal; and did by moonshine (it being brave dry, and moonshine, and warm weather) carry much of my goods into the garden, and Mr. Hater and I did remove my money and iron chests into my cellar, as thinking that the safest place. And got my bags of gold into my office, ready to carry away, and my chief papers of accounts also there, and my tallies into a box by themselves. So great was our fear, as Sir W. Batten hath carts come out of the country to fetch away his goods this night. We did put Mr. Hater, poor man, to bed a little; but he got but very little rest, so much noise being in my house, taking down of goods.

3rd. About four o'clock in the morning, my Lady Batten sent me a cart to carry away all my money, and plate, and best things, to Sir W. Rider's at Bednall Green. Which I did, riding myself in my nightgown in the cart; and, Lord! to see how the streets and the highways are crowded with people running and riding, and getting of carts at any rate to fetch away things. I find Sir W. Rider tired with being called up all night, and receiving things from several friends. His house full of goods, and much of Sir W. Batten's and Sir W. Pen's. I am eased at my heart to have my treasure so well secured. Then home, with much ado to find a way, nor any sleep all this night to me nor my poor wife.

THINKING ABOUT THE SELECTION
Recalling

1. In his entry for September 3, 1665, Pepys tells a story of a saddler's family. What is the story of the last living child?
2. In his entry for September 14, 1665, Pepys gives two reasons for feeling content. One is that his valuables are safe. What is the other?
3. (a) When does Pepys first learn of the great fire? (b) When Pepys looks out his window at seven in the morning on September 2, 1666, what does he observe about the fire?
4. (a) What does Pepys recommend to the King and the Duke of York? (b) What is the reply?
5. Summarize Pepys's actions on September 3, 1666.

Interpreting

6. In the entry for September 14, 1665, Pepys states that he has despaired "of my Lord's doing anything this year." (a) What does he mean by the statement? (b) What does it show about Pepys's beliefs?
7. On September 2, 1666, Pepys sees "the churches all filling with goods by people who themselves should have been quietly there at this time." (a) Why do you think people are storing goods in churches? (b) Why do you think they themselves should have been there at the time?
8. From the evidence of these diary entries, how would you describe Pepys's character and personality?

Applying

9. (a) In Pepys's London, which do you think was the greater disaster—the plague or the great fire? Explain. (b) What disasters in modern times, if any, compare with the London plague of 1665 and the great fire of 1666?

The Age of Pope and Swift

CONVERSATION IN A PARK
Thomas Gainsborough
The Louvre, Paris

Humanities Note

Fine art, *Conversation in a Park,* by Thomas Gainsborough. Gainsborough (1727–1788) was an English painter of portraits, landscapes, and genre subjects. He studied in London and was influenced by the Dutch naturalistic manner and the French rococo style. He became a member of the Royal Academy in 1768. By 1780 Gainsborough was receiving portrait commissions from the Royal family. Although he became the favorite portraitist of British high society, Gainsborough often said that his heart was in landscapes not portraits.

This painting, *Conversation in a Park,* combines portraiture with landscape. It has also been called *Lady and Gentleman in Landscape* and *Thomas Sandby and Wife,* but it may well be the painter and his wife. In the background is an English landscape garden. These gardens were carefully planned to appear natural and picturesque. Little temples and artificial ruins were used to show the superiority of the ancients.

This portrait was painted during Gainsborough's Suffolk period. He presumably settled in Suffolk about 1748, where he painted many portraits of unidentified sitters.

DANIEL DEFOE

1660–1731

Although Daniel Defoe produced an impressive number of pamphlets, essays, and poems throughout his life, he was nearly sixty years old before he began writing the novels that established him as a writer of genius. Defoe's *Robinson Crusoe,* a book that recounts the mostly imaginary adventures of a real person, marked the beginning of the modern English novel. Defoe's realistic, almost documentary narrative of a man marooned on a desert island was something new in English literature. It established a genre.

Defoe's life was an odd mixture of business, politics, religion, and journalism. Born to a middle-class family named Foe (he added the "De" later), Defoe attended a school run by the Dissenters, a loosely knit group that refused to accept the principles set down by the Church of England. He considered entering the Presbyterian ministry but instead turned his attention to commerce. He invested heavily and not always well in a variety of ventures—a ship, diving bells, wines, civet cats. The scope of his activities is shown by the size of his debt. When he declared bankruptcy in 1692, he owed his creditors 17,000 pounds.

At that point, he turned to writing (and to patrons for his writing) to try to improve his fortunes. His pen, however, also got him into trouble. After enjoying brief success with *The True-Born Englishman* (1701), a defense of King William III against his detractors, he wrote an ill-advised satire, *The Shortest Way with the Dissenters* (1702), that landed him in jail and in the pillory. Published anonymously, this pamphlet condemned the very religious group Defoe favored. Its irony amused neither the Dissenters nor members of the Church of England, but Defoe had enough popularity to attract cheering supporters rather than rock throwers at his pillory appearance.

Late in life Defoe turned to writing books that purported to be memoirs, among them *Robinson Crusoe* (1719) and *Moll Flanders* (1722). As published, these books were not novels in the strict sense, since they were sold as nonfiction. Although Defoe has been accused "of forging a story, and imposing it on the world for truth," these books are generally regarded as novels today—and as outstanding novels at that.

Defoe's journalistic talents served him well in writing *A Journal of the Plague Year* (1722). He studied official documents, interviewed survivors of the plague, and may have drawn upon his own memories as a young child. The vivid historical re-creation of the plague is a triumph of Defoe's energetic, detailed style in a genre that set English fiction upon a new path.

GUIDE FOR INTERPRETING

from A Journal of the Plague Year

First-person Narrative. Fiction is written from one of two main points of view—first person or third person. The narrator's perspective can vary somewhat in each of them. A third-person narrator, for example, can be *omniscient* (all-knowing) or *limited* (restricted to the mind of one character). A first-person narrator ("I") can be a *participant* (directly involved in the action) or an *observer* (reporting on the actions of another, as Watson reports on Sherlock Holmes). From a writer's standpoint, first-person narration imposes severe limitations. The narrator must be physically present at all times and involved in most of the important action. Everything must be observed through the eyes and mind of that narrator; there can be no omniscience, no multiple viewpoints. If the first-person narrator is a participant, the story will sound very much like a personal memoir or an autobiography. If the writing is highly realistic and plausible, you may think (unless told otherwise) that you are reading nonfiction. In *A Journal of the Plague Year,* that is exactly what Defoe had in mind.

Writing

Choose an imaginary setting for a description, such as a new planet inhabited by an unfamiliar species or your own community at a time in the distant past or future. Using that setting, list some of the specific details you would include in a first-person narrative.

Primary Source

Plague struck with terrifying frequency, but it was only one of a series of epidemics that ravaged England in the seventeenth century. More frequent were outbreaks of smallpox, dysentery, and measles. Herbal and folk remedies were passed down through the generations. Every area had its treatments, and both men and women took an active interest in doctoring.

To relieve measles, for example, people advised that a live sheep be laid on the bed of the afflicted one, "because these creatures are easily infected and draw the venom to themselves, by which means some ease may happen to the sick person." To treat plague, you were advised:

> "Take halfe a handfull of Rew, likewise of Mandragories, Featherfew, Sorrell Burnet, and a quantity of the Crops and rootes of Dragons, and wash them clean, and seeth them with a soft fire in running water for a potle to a quart, and then straine them together through a cleane cloth, and if it be bitter, put thereto a quantity of sugar-candy, and if this medicine be used before the Purples do arise, yee shall be whole by God's grace."

Guide for Interpreting 513

Literary Focus Review with students the view of the plague depicted in Samuel Pepys's *Diary.* Discuss whether the limitations of a first-person participant narrator overshadowed the benefits of reading about the plague through Pepys's eyes. Have students give examples to support their opinions.

Writing/Prior Knowledge Remind students to use sensory words to provide a clearer image of their imaginary setting.

Spelling Tip Point out the double *p* and double *s* in *oppressed.*

Vocabulary

Preteach the following vocabulary words:
distemper (dis tem′ pər) *n.:* An infectious disease, in this case the plague (p. 515)
oppressed (ə prest′) *v.:* Burdened (p. 516)
importuning (im′ pôr tōōn′iŋ) *v.:* Begging; urging (p. 516)
promiscuously (prə mis′ kyσo əs lē) *adv.:* Without care or thought (p. 516)
prodigious (prə dij′ ′s) *adj.:* Enormous; huge (p. 517)

from A Journal of the Plague Year

Daniel Defoe

The face of London was now indeed strangely altered, I mean the whole mass of buildings, city, liberties, suburbs, Westminster, Southwark, and altogether; for as to the particular part called the city, or within the walls, that was not yet much infected.

THE DEAD CART
The British Library

But in the whole the face of things, I say, was much altered; sorrow and sadness sat upon every face; and though some parts were not yet overwhelmed, yet all looked deeply concerned; and as we saw it apparently coming on, so everyone looked on himself and his family as in the utmost danger. Were it possible to represent those times exactly to those that did not see them, and give the reader due ideas of the horror that everywhere presented itself, it must make just impressions upon their minds and fill them with surprise. London might well be said to be all in tears; the mourners did not go about the streets indeed, for nobody put on black or made a formal dress of mourning for their nearest friends; but the voice of mourning was truly heard in the streets. The shrieks of women and children at the windows and doors of their houses, where their dearest relations were perhaps dying, or just dead, were so frequent to be heard as we passed the streets, that it was enough to pierce the stoutest heart in the world to hear them. Tears and lamentations were seen almost in every house, especially in the first part of the visitation; for toward the latter end men's hearts were hardened, and death was so always before their eyes, that they did not so much concern themselves for the loss of their friends, expecting that themselves should be summoned the next hour. . . .

I went all the first part of the time freely

about the streets, though not so freely as to run myself into apparent danger, except when they dug the great pit in the churchyard of our parish of Aldgate. A terrible pit it was, and I could not resist my curiosity to go and see it. As near as I may judge, it was about forty feet in length, and about fifteen or sixteen feet broad, and, at the time I first looked at it, about nine feet deep; but it was said they dug it near twenty feet deep afterwards in one part of it, till they could go no deeper for the water; for they had, it seems, dug several large pits before this. For though the plague was long a-coming to our parish, yet, when it did come, there was no parish in or about London where it raged with such violence as in the two parishes of Aldgate and Whitechapel.

I say they had dug several pits in another ground, when the distemper began to spread in our parish, and especially when the dead carts began to go about, which was not, in our parish, till the beginning of August. Into these pits they had put perhaps fifty or sixty bodies each; then they made larger holes, wherein they buried all that the cart brought in a week, which, by the middle to the end of August, came to from 200 to 400 a week; and they could not well dig them larger, because of the order of the magistrates confining them to leave no bodies within six feet of the surface; and the water coming on at about seventeen or eighteen feet, they could not well, I say, put more in one pit. But now, at the beginning of September, the plague raging in a dreadful manner, and the number of burials in our parish increasing to more than was ever buried in any parish about London of no larger extent, they ordered this dreadful gulf to be dug, for such it was rather than a pit.

They had supposed this pit would have supplied them for a month or more when they dug it, and some blamed the churchwardens for suffering[1] such a frightful thing,

telling them they were making preparations to bury the whole parish, and the like; but time made it appear the churchwardens knew the condition of the parish better than they did, for the pit being finished the 4th of September, I think, they began to bury in it the 6th, and by the 20th, which was just two weeks, they had thrown into it 1114 bodies, when they were obliged to fill it up, the bodies being then come to lie within six feet of the surface. I doubt not but there may be some ancient persons alive in the parish who can justify the fact of this, and are able to show even in what place of the churchyard the pit lay better than I can. The mark of it also was many years to be seen in the churchyard on the surface, lying in length parallel with the passage which goes by the west wall of the churchyard out of Houndsditch, and turns east again into Whitechapel, coming out near the Three Nuns' Inn.

It was about the 10th of September that my curiosity led, or rather drove, me to go and see this pit again, when there had been near 400 people buried in it; and I was not content to see it in the daytime, as I had done before, for then there would have been nothing to have been seen but the loose earth; for all the bodies that were thrown in were immediately covered with earth by those they called the buriers, which at other times were called bearers; but I resolved to go in the night and see some of them thrown in.

There was a strict order to prevent people coming to those pits, and that was only to prevent infection. But after some time that order was more necessary, for people that were infected and near their end, and delirious also, would run to those pits, wrapped in blankets or rugs, and throw themselves in, and, as they said, bury themselves. I cannot say that the officers suffered any willingly to lie there; but I have heard that in a great pit in Finsbury, in the parish of Cripplegate, it lying open then to the fields, for it was not then walled about,

---

1. **suffering:** Allowing.

from *A Journal of the Plague Year*   515

6 **Discussion** Do you think it was strange that the narrator wanted to see the pit? Explain.

7 **Literary Focus** How does the use of proper names add to the realism of the narrative?

8 **Literary Focus** What is the effect of citing dates and numbers of bodies?

9 **Literary Focus** What purpose does this seemingly useless detail serve?

10 **Literary Focus** What is the effect of the narrator's correcting himself?

11 **Discussion** Why were buriers sometimes called "bearers"?

Grammar in Action

Subordination connects unequal but related information. It distinguishes main ideas from less important (subordinate) ideas in clauses or phrases. Notice Daniel Defoe's subordination in this passage from page 516:

I got admittance into the churchyard by being acquainted with the sexton who attended, who, though he did not refuse me at all, yet earnestly persuaded me not to go, telling me very seriously, for he was a good, religious, and sensible man, that it was indeed their business and duty to venture, and to run all hazards, and that in it they might hope to be preserved; but that I had no apparent call to it but my own curiosity, which, he said, he believed I would not pretend was sufficient to justify my running that hazard.

Defoe's main idea is that he was admitted into the churchyard. Compare the following:

12 Discussion Why does the narrator feel that "no tongue can express" the dreadful condition?

13 Discussion What "uses" do you think the narrator might find for what he was about to see?

14 Discussion Why would the pit be a "sermon"?

15 Discussion What do you think the sexton meant by "voice" and "speaking sight"?

16 Discussion What happens to strengthen the narrator's resolve to see the pit?

17 Discussion What is the effect of including the story of the desperate mourner?

Master Teacher Note Toward the end of the *Journal* the narrator comments on the susceptibility of the city to plague. "The Plague like a great Fire, if a few Houses only are contiguous where it happens, can only burn a few Houses; or if it begins in a single, or as we call it a lone House, can only burn that lone House where it begins: but if it begins in a close built Town, or city, and gets a Head, there its fury encreases, it rages over the whole Place, and consumes all it can reach." How does this comment apply to what you know about the devastating London fire described in Samuel Pepys's *Diary*?

[some] came and threw themselves in, and expired there, before they threw any earth upon them; and that when they came to bury others, and found them there, they were quite dead, though not cold.

This may serve a little to describe the dreadful condition of that day, though it is impossible to say anything that is able to give a true idea of it to those who did not see it, other than this, that it was indeed very, very, very dreadful, and such as no tongue can express.

I got admittance into the churchyard by being acquainted with the sexton who attended, who, though he did not refuse me at all, yet earnestly persuaded me not to go, telling me very seriously, for he was a good, religious, and sensible man, that it was indeed their business and duty to venture, and to run all hazards, and that in it they might hope to be preserved; but that I had no apparent call to it but my own curiosity, which, he said, he believed I would not pretend was sufficient to justify my running that hazard. I told him I had been pressed in my mind to go, and that perhaps it might be an instructing sight, that might not be without its uses. "Nay," says the good man, "if you will venture upon that score, name of God go in; for, depend upon it, 't will be a sermon to you, it may be, the best that ever you heard in your life. 'T is a speaking sight," says he, "and has a voice with it, and a loud one, to call us all to repentance"; and with that he opened the door and said, "Go, if you will."

His discourse had shocked my resolution a little, and I stood wavering for a good while, but just at that interval I saw two links[2] come over from the end of the Minories, and heard the bellman, and then appeared a dead cart, as they called it, coming over the streets; so I could no longer resist my desire of seeing it, and went in. There was nobody, as I could perceive at first, in the church-yard, or going into it, but the buriers and the fellow that drove the cart, or rather led the horse and cart; but when they came up to the pit they saw a man go to and again,[3] muffled up in a brown cloak, and making motions with his hands under his cloak, as if he was in a great agony, and the buriers immediately gathered about him, supposing he was one of those poor delirious or desperate creatures that used to pretend, as I have said, to bury themselves. He said nothing as he walked about, but two or three times groaned very deeply and loud, and sighed as he would break his heart.

When the buriers came up to him they soon found he was neither a person infected and desperate, as I have observed above, or a person distempered in mind, but one oppressed with a dreadful weight of grief indeed, having his wife and several of his children all in the cart that was just come in with him, and he followed in an agony and excess of sorrow. He mourned heartily, as it was easy to see, but with a kind of masculine grief that could not give itself vent by tears; and calmly defying the buriers to let him alone, said he would only see the bodies thrown in and go away, so they left importuning him. But no sooner was the cart turned round and the bodies shot into the pit promiscuously, which was a surprise to him, for he at least expected they would have been decently laid in, though indeed he was afterwards convinced that was impracticable; I say, no sooner did he see the sight but he cried out aloud, unable to contain himself. I could not hear what he said, but he went backward two or three steps and fell down in a swoon. The buriers ran to him and took him up, and in a little while he came to himself, and they led him away to the Pie Tavern over against the end of Houndsditch, where, it seems, the man was known, and where they took care of him. He looked into the pit again as he went away,

---

2. links: Torches.

3. to and again: To and fro.

I got admittance into the churchyard by being acquainted with the sexton. He attended it. He did not refuse me at all. He was a good, religious, and sensible man. He earnestly persuaded me not to go. . . .

Such writing puts all the ideas on the same level of importance. It fails to indicate that one idea is more important than the others.

Student Activity. Rewrite Defoe's passage in contemporary English, but use subordination to indicate the relative importance of the ideas.

but the buriers had covered the bodies so immediately with throwing in earth, that though there was light enough, for there were lanterns, and candles in them, placed all night round the sides of the pit, upon heaps of earth, seven or eight, or perhaps more, yet nothing could be seen.

This was a mournful scene indeed, and affected me almost as much as the rest; but the other was awful and full of terror. The cart had in it sixteen or seventeen bodies; some were wrapped up in linen sheets, some in rags, some little other than naked, or so loose that what covering they had fell from them in the shooting out of the cart, and they fell quite naked among the rest; but the matter was not much to them, or the indecency much to anyone else, seeing they were all dead, and were to be huddled together into the common grave of mankind, as we may call it, for here was no difference made, but poor and rich went together; there was no other way of burials, neither was it possible there should, for coffins were not to be had for the prodigious numbers that fell in such a calamity as this.

18

THINKING ABOUT THE SELECTION
Recalling

1. (a) Describe the great pit in the churchyard of Aldgate parish. (b) What was the purpose of the pit?
2. (a) What limited the depth to which the pit could be dug? (b) What restriction did an order of the magistrates put on the use of the pit?
3. How many bodies does the narrator say were buried in the great pit between September 6 and September 20?
4. (a) What prompts the narrator to visit the pit? (b) Why does he go at night?
5. (a) What kind of person did the buriers at first suppose the man in the brown cloak to be? (b) Summarize the incident concerning the man in the brown cloak.

Interpreting

6. Why do you think the narrator describes the great pit in such a specific and detailed way?
7. Judging by the tone of this excerpt and the narrator's reason for visiting the pit, what kind of person do you think the narrator is?
8. Why does the sexton at the churchyard say that visiting the pit will "be a sermon to you . . . a voice . . . to call us all to repentence"?

9. What causes the "masculine grief" of the man in the brown cloak to turn suddenly to anguish?

Applying

10. Many writers have written fictional accounts of great disasters or have used disasters as backgrounds for their fiction. Why do you think disasters have this fictional appeal?

ANALYZING LITERATURE
Recognizing First-person Narrative

A **first-person narrative** is one told by an "I" narrator—a person present at the events being described. A first-person narrator can be either a participant or an observer in the main action. Defoe's *A Journal of the Plague Year* claims to be a first-person narrative of a London resident, one "H. F.," written during the great plague of 1665. In reality, it is a fictional reconstruction written by Defoe more than fifty years later.

1. Why do you think Defoe chose a first-person narrator, an "eyewitness," to present this account of the plague year?
2. Defoe has been called the father of modern journalism. (a) If "H. F.'s" first-person account of the plague were true, what features would qualify it as good journalism? (b) What features would you not find in the usual modern news story?

from *A Journal of the Plague Year*   517

More About the Author In a letter to his friend Alexander Pope, written in 1725, Jonathan Swift declared that "the chief end I propose to myself in all my labors is to vex the world rather than divert it." In spite of this dour credo, *Gulliver's Travels*, when it came out, was "the conversation of the whole town [London] . . . the whole impression [edition] sold in a week . . ." After you read the excerpts here, think about whether his readers might have missed the bitter satire of his book, and simply mistook it for amusing fiction, or that, however vexing Swift hoped to be, people find satire entertaining? In other words with what motive do people read satire? Do they hope to better themselves? Or do they hope simply to find themselves shaking their heads in wry agreement with the author? Can you think of any present day works, written or visual, that seem to be created with the intention of "vexing the world"? And does the public generally find this type of work vexing, or entertaining?

Critical Evaluation Because of the popularity of his writings there is a temptation to overlook an important part of Swift's personality. It is with this in mind that A.L. Rowse notes the following: "One side of Swift's mind is hardly at all noticed—the scholarly side. He was extraordinarily widely read, and one must place the emphasis on the width of his intellectual interests. We know that at Moor Park he laid in a stock of reading sufficient to last a lifetime."

JONATHAN SWIFT

1667–1745

The life of Jonathan Swift is a tale of thwarted ambition coupled with brilliant literary achievement. In the Church of England and in British politics, he sometimes seemed on the verge of great success, only to have an unkind fate baffle his expectations. In literature, on the other hand, he achieved an almost unparalleled triumph with *Gulliver's Travels,* a book that can be read—and has been read since its publication—as a children's story, a fantasy, a parody of travel books, and a sophisticated satire on English politics.

Jonathan Swift was born in Dublin, Ireland, to English parents. His father died before he was born, and young Jonathan, through the assistance of relatives, attended Kilkenny Grammar School and Trinity College, Dublin. Later he joined the household of Sir William Temple, a retired diplomat, who lived at Moor Park, Surrey, England. Swift read, studied, and wrote for the next few years. Receiving none of the hoped-for political support from Sir William, he decided on a career in the church.

After Temple's death in 1699, Swift was given a small parish near London. The satirical writing he had done while in the Temple household was somewhat out of character for a clergyman, but its brilliance was widely acknowledged when it appeared as two separate books in 1704. Published anonymously, *A Tale of a Tub* satirizes excesses in religion and learning, while *The Battle of the Books* describes a comic encounter between ancient and modern literature.

Although *A Tale of a Tub* dashed his hopes for advancement to the rank of bishop in the Church of England, Swift remained a defender of the Anglican faith. In 1710, he changed his political allegiance from the conservative Whig party to the Tory party favored by Queen Anne. He benefited immediately from this switch. As the leading party writer for the government, he wrote many pamphlets and wielded considerable political influence. The glory was short-lived, however. Anne died in 1714; the Whigs regained power; and Swift, embittered, returned to Ireland as dean of St. Patrick's Cathedral, a position he held for more than thirty years.

Back in Ireland, he continued to write satires, including *Drapier Letters* (1724) and *A Modest Proposal* (1729), which championed the Irish cause. With the publication of *Gulliver's Travels* (1726), he reached the height of his literary power. In his later years, he suffered what was probably Ménière's disease, marked by a serious loss of memory and balance. His death in 1745 deprived the world of one of its great writers—a generous and learned man who despised the fanaticism, selfishness, and pride of people in general but admired individual human beings.

Objectives

1 To familiarize the student with satirical writing and its usual targets
2 To understand generalizations
3 To acquaint the student with words derived from literature

Support Material

Teaching Portfolio
Teacher Backup, p. 587
Grammar in Action Worksheet, *Correlative Conjunctions,* p. 592
Usage and Mechanics Worksheet, p. 594
Vocabulary Check, p. 595
Analyzing Literature Worksheet, *Understanding Satire,* p. 597

Critical Thinking and Reading Worksheet, *Understanding Generalizations,* p. 599
Selection Test, p. 600
Art Transparency 7, *St. Michael's Mount, Cornwall,* Arthur Joseph Meadows

GUIDE FOR INTERPRETING

from Gulliver's Travels

Satire. Satire is writing that uses wit and humor to ridicule vices, follies, stupidities, and abuses. Irony is often an element in satire, as is sarcasm. Satire can take the form of prose, poetry, or drama. Satirists, by directing their barbs toward those they view as offenders, hope to improve the situation—to reform individuals, groups, or humanity as a whole. Satire may be gentle and amusing, or it may be cruel and even vicious. Whatever its tone, satire is usually subtle enough to require the reader to make at least a small mental leap to connect it with its target.

Think about current social or political problems or situations that might be suitable subjects for satire. Try to suggest at least two. Jot these ideas down. After each subject, give one aspect of it that is particularly open to ridicule.

The allure of distant lands is timeless. In Swift's day, as in our own, writers offered advice to would-be travelers. Perhaps these "Hints for Travellers," from the late seventeenth century, would have helped Gulliver in his voyages!

> In such a one going to travel; there is required–
> First. A competent age. That he be above eighteen or twenty years old: although the years of fourteen or fifteen are more proper for learning the true accent of any language . . .
> Secondly. That he hath the Latin tongue.
> Thirdly. That he be skillful in architecture: able so well to limn or paint, as to take in paper the situation of a castle or a city, or a platform [plan] of a fortification.
> Fourthly. That he be well grounded in the true religion: lest he be seduced and perverted.
> Fifthly. He should be first well acquainted with his own country, before he go abroad; as to the places and government.
> Sixthly. It were of use to inform himself, before he undertakes his voyage, by the best . . . map of . . . the country he goes to; both in itself, and relatively to the universe.
> Men that travel must be very cautious both of speech and demeanor. The Italian proverb saith, "For a man to travel safely through the world; it behoveth him to have a falcon's eye, an ass's ears, a monkey's face, a merchant's words, a camel's back, a hog's mouth, and a deer's feet.

Guide for Interpreting 519

Writing/Prior Knowledge Another source for situations to satirize might come from political cartoons. Suggest that your students collect several that please them, then let them consider if they could translate visual indignation into a written satire.

Spelling Tip Point out the two words containing the letters -*ious*: *perfidiousness*, *odious*.

Vocabulary

Preteach the following vocabulary words:
conjecture (kən jek′ chər) *v.:* To guess (p. 520)
fomented (fō ment′ id) *v.:* Stirred up; incited (p. 521)
expostulate (ik späs′ chə lāt) *v.:* To reason earnestly with (p. 521)
schism (siz′ 'm) *n.:* A division into groups or factions (p. 521)
expedient (ik spē′dē ənt) *n.:* A device used in an emergency (p. 522)
encomiums (en kō′ mē əmz) *n.:* Formal expressions of praise or tribute (p. 523)
habituate (hə bich′ ͞oo wāt′) *v.:* To make used to (p. 524)
perfidiousness (pər fid′ ē əs nis) *n.:* Betrayal of trust (p. 525)
panegyric (pan′ ə jir′ ik) *n.:* A speech giving praise (p. 525)
odious (ō′dē əs) *adj.:* Hateful; disgusting (p. 525)

Literary Focus Satire walks a shaky tightrope between cynicism and idealism. In tone it is often ironic, sarcastic, or even despairing. Our impression of the writer may be the rather off-putting one of a bitterly disgusted person. But at its best satire does more than ridicule, it hopes to change a situation. Behind the anger we may catch glimpses of a wistfulness for the world that should be.

from Gulliver's Travels

Jonathan Swift

In Gulliver's Travels, *Swift exposes the corruption and defects in England's political, social, and economic institutions. The work centers on the four imaginary voyages of Lemuel Gulliver, the narrator, a well-educated but unimaginative ship's surgeon. Each of these voyages takes Gulliver to a different remarkable and bizarre world. During his stays in these imaginary lands, Gulliver is led toward realizations about the flawed nature of the society from which he had come, and he returns to England filled with disillusionment.*

from A Voyage to Lilliput

After being shipwrecked, Gulliver swims to shore and drifts off to sleep. When he awakens, he finds that he has been tied down by the Lilliputians (lil' ə pyoo' shənz), a race of people who are only six inches tall. Though he is held captive and his sword and pistols are taken from him, Gulliver gradually begins to win the Lilliputians' favor because of his mild disposition, and he is eventually granted his freedom. Through Gulliver's exposure to Lilliputian politics and court life, the reader becomes increasingly aware of the remarkable similarities between the English and Lilliputian affairs of state. The following excerpt begins during a discussion between the Lilliputian Principal Secretary of Private Affairs and Gulliver concerning the affairs of the Lilliputian empire.

We are threatened with an invasion from the island of Blefuscu,[1] which is the other great empire of the universe, almost as large and powerful as this of his Majesty. For as to what we have heard you affirm, that there are other kingdoms and states in the world, inhabited by human creatures as large as yourself, our philosophers are in much doubt, and would rather conjecture that you dropped from the moon, or one of the stars; because it is certain, that an hundred mortals of your bulk would, in a short time, destroy all the fruits and cattle of his Majesty's dominions. Besides, our histories of six thousand moons make no mention of any other regions, than the two great empires of Lilliput and Blefuscu. Which two mighty powers have, as I was going to tell you, been engaged in a most obstinate war for six and thirty moons past. It began upon the following occasion. It is allowed on all hands, that the primitive way of breaking eggs before we eat them, was upon the larger end; but his present Majesty's grandfather, while he was a boy, going to eat an egg, and breaking it according to the ancient practice, happened to cut one of his fingers. Whereupon the Emperor, his father, published an edict,

---

1. Blefuscu: Represents France.

commanding all his subjects, upon great penalties, to break the smaller end of their eggs. The people so highly resented this law that our histories tell us there have been six rebellions raised on that account; wherein one emperor lost his life, and another his crown.[2] These civil commotions were constantly fomented by the monarchs of Blefuscu; and when they were quelled, the exiles always fled for refuge to that empire. It is computed that eleven thousand persons have, at several times, suffered death rather than submit to break their eggs at the smaller end. Many hundred large volumes have been published upon this controversy; but the books of the Big-Endians have been long forbidden, and the whole party rendered incapable by law of holding employments.[3] During the course of these troubles, the emperors of Blefuscu did frequently expostulate by their ambassadors, accusing us of making a schism in religion, by offending against a fundamental doctrine of our great prophet Lustrog, in the fifty-fourth chapter of the *Brundecral* (which is their Alcoran[4]). This, however, is thought to be a mere strain upon the text, for the words are these: That all true believers shall break their eggs at the convenient end; and which is the convenient end, seems, in my humble opinion, to be left to every man's conscience, or at least in the power of the chief magistrate[5] to determine. Now the Big-Endian exiles have found so much credit in the Emperor of Blefuscu's court, and so much private assistance and encouragement from their party here at home, that a bloody war hath been carried on between the two empires for

six and thirty moons with various success; during which time we have lost forty capital ships, and a much greater number of smaller vessels, together with thirty thousand of our best seamen and soldiers; and the damage received by the enemy is reckoned to be somewhat greater than ours. However, they have now equipped a numerous fleet, and are just preparing to make a descent upon us; and his Imperial Majesty, placing great confidence in your valor and strength, hath commanded me to lay this account of his affairs before you.

I desired the Secretary to present my humble duty to the Emperor, and to let him know, that I thought it would not become me, who was a foreigner, to interfere with parties; but I was ready, with the hazard of my life, to defend his person and state against all invaders.

The empire of Blesfuscu is an island situated to the north-northeast side of Lilliput, from whence it is parted only by a channel of eight hundred yards wide. I had not yet seen it, and upon this notice of an intended invasion, I avoided appearing on that side of the coast, for fear of being discovered by some of the enemy's ships, who had received no intelligence of me, all intercourse between the two empires having been strictly forbidden during the war, upon pain of death, and an embargo laid by our Emperor upon all vessels whatsoever. I communicated to his Majesty a project I had formed of seizing the enemy's whole fleet; which, as our scouts assured us, lay at anchor in the harbor ready to sail with the first fair wind. I consulted the most experienced seamen upon the depth of the channel, which they had often plumbed, who told me, that in the middle at high water it was seventy *glumgluffs* deep (which is about six feet of European measure), and the rest of it fifty *glumgluffs* at most. I walked to the northeast coast over against Blefuscu, where, lying down behind a hillock, I took out my small pocket perspective-glass, and

---

2. It is allowed . . . crown: Here, Swift satirizes the dispute in England between the Catholics (Big-Endians) and Protestants (Little-Endians). King Henry VIII who "broke" with the Catholic church, King Charles I who "lost his life," and King James who lost his "crown" are each referred to in the passage.

3. the whole party . . . employments: The Test Act (1673) prevented Catholics from holding office.

4. Alcoran: Koran, the sacred book of the Moslems.
5. chief magistrate: Ruler.

from *Gulliver's Travels* 521

3 Discussion Note that clergyman Swift does not equate the Lilliputians's sacred book with the Bible. This puts him two steps removed from the true object of his satire. Does that insulation perhaps make him feel safer?

4 Literary Focus Have a student explain the irony of this sentence. Swift also seems to be saying that there may not be so much difference between religions as some men think, and also, that at least some matters of religion might be best left to each man's conscience. Would that have been a daring opinion for a clergyman to hold in that day and age?

5 Enrichment France lies east-southeast of England. Separating the two countries is the English Channel, twenty-one miles wide at its narrowest point.

6 Discussion What is the effect of including words such as *glumgluffs* that are unique to the Lilliputian vocabulary?

viewed the enemy's fleet at anchor, consisting of about fifty men of war, and a great number of transports. I then came back to my house and gave order (for which I had a warrant) for a great quantity of the strongest cable and bars of iron. The cable was about as thick as packthread, and the bars of the length and size of a knitting-needle. I trebled the cable to make it stronger, and for the same reason I twisted three of the iron bars together, bending the extremities into a hook. Having thus fixed fifty hooks to as many cables, I went back to the northeast coast and, putting off my coat, shoes, and stockings, walked into the sea in my leathern jerkin, about half an hour before high water. I waded with what haste I could, and swam in the middle about thirty yards until I felt ground; I arrived at the fleet in less than half an hour. The enemy was so frightened when they saw me, that they leaped out of their ships, and swam to shore, where there could not be fewer than thirty thousand souls. I then took my tackling, and, fastening a hook to the hole at the prow of each, I tied all the cords together at the end. While I was thus employed, the enemy discharged several thousand arrows, many of which struck in my hands and face and, besides the excessive smart, gave me much disturbance in my work. My greatest apprehension was for my eyes, which I should have infallibly lost, if I had not suddenly thought of an expedient. I kept among other little necessaries a pair of spectacles in a private pocket, which, as I observed before, had escaped the Emperor's searchers. These I took out and fastened as strongly as I could upon my nose and thus armed went on boldly with my work in spite of the enemy's arrows, many of which struck against the glasses of my spectacles, but without any other effect further than a little to discompose them. I had now fastened all the hooks

Illustration for Gulliver's Travels, *by Willy Pogany*
The Donnell Library Children's Room, New York Public Library

and, taking the knot in my hand, began to pull; but not a ship would stir, for they were all too fast held by their anchors, so that the boldest part of my enterprise remained. I therefore let go the cord, and, leaving the hooks fixed to the ships, I resolutely cut with my knife the cables that fastened the anchors, receiving above two hundred shots in my face and hands; then I took up the knotted end of the cables to which my hooks were tied and, with great ease, drew fifty of the enemy's largest men-of-war after me.

The Blefuscudians, who had not the least imagination of what I intended, were at first confounded with astonishment. They had seen me cut the cables and thought my design was only to let the ships run adrift or fall foul on each other; but when they perceived the whole fleet, moving in order, and saw me pulling at the end, they set up such a scream of grief and despair that it is almost impossible to describe or conceive. When I had got out of danger, I stopped a while to pick out the arrows that stuck in my hands and face, and rubbed on some of the same ointment that was given me at my first arrival, as I have formerly mentioned. I then took off my spectacles, and, waiting about an hour until the tide was a little fallen, I waded through the middle with my cargo and arrived safe at the royal port of Lilliput.

The Emperor and his whole court stood on the shore expecting the issue of this great adventure. They saw the ships move forward in a large half-moon but could not discern me, who was up to my breast in water. When I advanced to the middle of the channel, they were yet more in pain, because I was under water to my neck. The Emperor concluded me to be drowned, and that the enemy's fleet was approaching in a hostile manner; but he was soon eased of his fears; for, the channel growing shallower every step I made, I came in a short time within hearing, and holding up the end of the cable by which the fleet was fastened, I cried in a loud voice, Long live the most puissant[6] Emperor of Lilliput! This great prince received me at my landing with all possible encomiums and created me a *Nardac* upon the spot, which is the highest title of honor among them.

His Majesty desired I would take some other opportunity of bringing all the rest of his enemy's ships into his ports. And so unmeasurable is the ambition of princes, that he seemed to think of nothing less than reducing the whole empire of Blefuscu into a province and governing it by a viceroy; of destroying the Big-Endian exiles and compelling that people to break the smaller end of their eggs, by which he would remain sole monarch of the whole world. But I endeavored to divert him from this design by many arguments drawn from the topics of policy as well as justice, and I plainly protested that I would never be an instrument of bringing a free and brave people into slavery. And when the matter was debated in council, the wisest part of the ministry were of my opinion.

This open bold declaration of mine was so opposite to the schemes and politics of his Imperial Majesty that he could never forgive me; he mentioned it in a very artful manner at council, where I was told that some of the wisest appeared, at least, by their silence, to be of my opinion; but others, who were my secret enemies, could not forbear some expressions, which by a sidewind reflected on me. And from this time began an intrigue between his Majesty and a junta of ministers maliciously bent against me, which broke out in less than two months and had like to have ended in my utter destruction. Of so little weight are the greatest services to princes when put into the balance with a refusal to gratify their passions.

from **A Voyage to Brobdingnag**

Gulliver's second voyage leads him to

---

6. puissant (pyōō′ i sənt): Powerful.

8 Discussion Why does Gulliver acquire many enemies after this feat?

9 Clarification A *junta* is a Spanish word meaning "an assembly or council, or a group of political intriguers." This is one of the earliest known uses of the word in the English language.

10 Master Teacher Note To introduce "A Voyage to Brobdingnag," locate reproductions of three works by Goya—a painting and an etching each entitled *The Giant*, and an etching from the Caprichos, no. 43, *The Sleep Of Reason Produces Monsters*. The first two works relate directly to this selection. In the notes that come with the third, the artist sets down a credo with which Swift would surely have agreed. "A universal language. The artist dreaming. His sole intention is to banish harmful errors and perpetuate with this work of Caprichos the solid testimony of truth."

Brobdingnag (brob′ ding nag′), an island located near Alaska that is inhabited by giants twelve times as tall as Gulliver. After being sold to the Queen of Brobdingnag, Gulliver describes the English social and political institutions to the king, who reacts to his description with contempt and disgust.

It is the custom that every Wednesday (which, as I have before observed, was their Sabbath), the King and Queen, with the royal issue of both sexes, dine together in the apartment of his Majesty, to whom I was now become a favorite; and at these times my little chair and table were placed at his left hand before one of the saltcellars. This prince took a pleasure in conversing with me, inquiring into the manners, religion, laws, government, and learning of Europe, wherein I gave him the best account I was able. His apprehension was so clear, and his judgment so exact, that he made very wise reflections and observations upon all I said. But I confess, that after I had been a little too copious in talking of my own beloved country, of our trade, and wars by sea and land, of our schisms in religion, and parties in the state, the prejudices of his education prevailed so far, that he could not forbear taking me up in his right hand, and stroking me gently with the other, after an hearty fit of laughing, asked me whether I were a Whig or a Tory.[7] Then turning to his first minister, who waited behind him with a white staff, near as tall as the mainmast of the *Royal Sovereign*,[8] he observed how contemptible a thing was human grandeur, which could be mimicked by such diminutive insects as I. And yet, said he, I dare engage, those creatures have their titles and distinctions of honor, they contrive little nests and burrows, that they call houses and cities; they make a figure in dress and equipage;[9] they love, they fight, they dispute, they cheat, they betray. And thus he continued on, while my color came and went several times, with indignation to hear our noble country, the mistress of arts and arms, the scourge of France, the arbitress of Europe, the seat of virtue, piety, honor and truth, the pride and envy of the world, so contemptuously treated. . . .

He laughed at my odd kind of arithmetic (as he was pleased to call it) in reckoning the numbers of our people by a computation drawn from the several sects among us in religion and politics. He said he knew no reason why those who entertain opinions prejudicial to the public should be obliged to change or should not be obliged to conceal them. And, as it was tyranny in any government to require the first, so it was weakness not to enforce the second; for, a man may be allowed to keep poisons in his closets, but not to vend them about as cordials.

He observed, that among the diversions of our nobility and gentry[10] I had mentioned gaming.[11] He desired to know at what age this entertainment was usually taken up, and when it was laid down. How much of their time it employed; whether it ever went so high as to affect their fortunes. Whether mean vicious people by their dexterity in that art might not arrive at great riches, and sometimes keep our very nobles in dependence, as well as habituate them to vile companions, wholly take them from the improvment of their minds, and force them, by the losses they received, to learn and practice that infamous dexterity upon others.

He was perfectly astonished with the historical account I gave him of our affairs during the last century, protesting it was only an heap of conspiracies, rebellions, murders, massacres, revolutions, banishments, the very worst effects that avarice,

---

7. Whig . . . Tory: British political parties.
8. *Royal Sovereign:* One of the largest ships in the British Navy.
9. equipage (ek′ wə pij): Horses and carriages.

10. gentry: The class of landowning people ranking just below the nobility.
11. gaming: Gambling.

Grammar in Action

Use **correlative conjunctions** to join elements of equal grammatical weight. Conjunctions such as *as . . . so, both . . . and, either . . . or, neither . . . nor, not only . . . but also,* and *whether . . . or* work as coordinating conjunctions do, but they add balance and often suggest something about the relationship between the two coordinated items. Jonathan Swift uses correlative conjunctions to advantage.

. . . after an hearty fit of laughing, [he] asked me *whether* I were a whig *or* a Tory.

. . . but this prince happened to be so curious and inquisitive upon every particular that it could not consist *either* with gratitude *or* good manners to refuse giving him what satisfaction I was able.

faction, hypocrisy, perfidiousness, cruelty, rage, madness, hatred, envy, lust, malice, and ambition could produce.

His Majesty in another audience was at the pains to recapitulate the sum of all I had spoken; compared the questions he made with the answers I had given; then taking me into his hands, and stroking me gently, delivered himself in these words, which I shall never forget, nor the manner he spoke them in. "My little friend Grildrig, you have made a most admirable panegyric upon your country. You have clearly proved that ignorance, idleness, and vice are the proper ingredients for qualifying a legislator. That laws are best explained, interpreted, and applied by those whose interest and abilities lie in perverting, confounding, and eluding them. I observe among you some lines of an institution, which in its original might have been tolerable, but these half erased, and the rest wholly blurred and blotted by corruptions. It doth not appear from all you have said how any one perfection is required toward the procurement of any one station among you, much less that men are ennobled on account of their virtue, that priests are advanced for their piety or learning, soldiers for their conduct or valor, judges for their integrity, senators for the love of their country, or counselors for their wisdom. As for yourself, continued the King, who have spent the greatest part of your life in traveling, I am well disposed to hope you may hitherto have escaped many vices of your country. But, by what I have gathered from your own relation, and the answers I have with much pains wringed and extorted from you, I cannot but conclude the bulk of your natives to be the most pernicious race of little odious vermin that nature ever suffered to crawl upon the surface of the earth."

16 | Nothing but an extreme love of truth could have hindered me from concealing this part of my story. It was in vain to discover my resentments, which were always turned into ridicule; and I was forced to rest with patience while my noble and most beloved country was so injuriously treated. I am heartily sorry as any of my readers can possibly be that such an occasion was given, but this prince happened to be so curious and inquisitive upon every particular that it could not consist either with gratitude or good manners to refuse giving him what satisfaction I was able. Yet thus much I may be allowed to say in my own vindication that I artfully eluded many of his questions and gave to every point a more favorable turn by many degrees than the strictness of truth would allow. For I have always borne that laudable partiality to my own country, which Dionysius Halicarnassensis[12] with so much justice recommends to an historian. I would hide the frailties and deformities of my political mother and place her virtues and beauties in the most advantageous light. This was my sincere endeavor in those many discourses I had with that mighty monarch, although it unfortunately failed of success.

17

But great allowances should be given to a king who lives wholly secluded from the rest of the world, and must therefore be altogether unacquainted with the manners and customs that most prevail in other nations: the want of which knowledge will ever produce many prejudices, and a certain narrowness of thinking, from which we and the politer countries of Europe are wholly exempted. And it would be hard indeed, if so remote a prince's notions of virtue and vice were to be offered as a standard for all mankind.

18

To confirm what I have now said, and further to show the miserable effects of a confined education, I shall here insert a passage which will hardly obtain belief. In hopes to ingratiate myself farther into his Majesty's favor, I told him of an invention discovered between three and four hundred

---

12. **Dionysius** (dī′ ə nish′ əs) **Halicarnassensis** (hal′ ə kär na sen′ sis): A Greek writer who lived in Rome and attempted to persuade the Greeks to submit to their Roman conquerors.

from *Gulliver's Travels*   525

---

16 Discussion The phrase "an extreme love of truth" has a double meaning. On the ironical level, Gulliver protests too much that only his love for the truth lets him pass on the King's painfully frank opinions. On another level entirely, it is Swift's indignant love of truth that inspires him to write of his country's iniquities.

17 Literary Focus Why is it necessary for Gulliver to insist on his loyalty to his country?

18 Critical Thinking and Reading Discuss the scathing irony of this paragraph.

And, *as* it was tyranny in any government to require the first, *so* it was weakness not to enforce the second; . . .

The first two examples emphasize choice between two items. Sense remains clear and simple because the correlative conjunctions eliminate all other possibilities. The third example emphasizes an equivalence between the two clauses the conjunctions link.

Student Activity. Use each of the following paired elements in a sentence. Use correlative conjunctions to join the elements.

1. early in the morning / late at night
2. my great talent / my lack of discipline
3. taller / thinner
4. mountain bike trip / ski weekend

19 Discussion What is Gulliver offering to make for the King?

20 Enrichment Gunpowder *is* a very simple compound, consisting of sulfur, saltpeter, and charcoal.

Reader's Response How would you feel if you became a giant among small people?

Humanities Note

Fine Art: Illustration for *Gulliver's Travels* by Willy Pogany. Willy Pogany was much admired as an illustrator. His drawings for *Gulliver's Travels* were produced during a prolific period (1940–1951) in his career, in which he illustrated more than 150 books. This pen–and–ink drawing is a visualization of Gulliver explaining the use of gunpowder to the King of Brobdingnag. The humor of the situation is emphasized by the horrified expression on the face of the King. In these illustrations Pogany made every effort to present simple, pleasing drawings that a child would find appealing.

Consider asking the following question: Swift employed humor to make his point in *Gulliver's Travels*. How does the artist use this same device in his drawing?

Master Teacher Note Bring in copies of *Mad* Magazine and *National Lampoon*, and also satirical comic strips such as *Doonesbury* or *Bloom County*. Also bring in some satirical columns by Art Buchwald or Russell Baker. Allow your students to work in groups and ask them to identify the topics being satirized by the artists and writers, then to share their findings with the class. Ask them also to decide on the tone of each satirical piece. Is it a bitter satire? a funny or gentle one? You might let the class vote on which satire they think is most effective in getting its point across.

years ago, to make a certain powder, into an heap of which the smallest spark of fire falling, would kindle the whole in a moment, although it were as big as a mountain, and make it all fly up in the air together, with a noise and agitation greater than thunder. That a proper quantity of this powder rammed into an hollow tube of brass or iron, according to its bigness, would drive a ball of iron or lead with such violence and speed as nothing was able to sustain its force. That the largest balls, thus discharged, would not only destroy whole ranks of an army at once, but batter the strongest walls to the ground, sink down ships, with a thousand men in each, to the bottom of the sea; and when linked together by a chain, would cut through masts and rigging, divide hundreds of bodies in the middle, and lay all waste before them. That we often put this powder into large hollow balls of iron, and discharged them by an engine into some city we were besieging, which would rip up the pavement, tear the houses to pieces, burst and throw splinters on every side, dashing out the brains of all who came near. That I knew the ingredients very well, which were cheap, and common; I understood the manner of compounding them, and could direct his workmen how to make those tubes of a size proportionable to all other things in his Majesty's kingdom, and the largest need not be above two hundred foot long; twenty or thirty of which tubes, charged with the proper quantity of powder and balls, would batter down the walls of the strongest town

Illustration for Gulliver's Travels, *by Willy Pogany*
The Donnell Library Children's Room, New York Public Library

in his dominions in a few hours, or destroy the whole metropolis, if ever it should pretend to dispute his absolute commands. This I humbly offered to his Majesty as a small tribute of acknowledgment in return of so many marks that I had received of his royal favor and protection.

The King was struck with horror at the description I had given of those terrible engines and the proposal I had made. He was amazed how so impotent and groveling an insect as I (these were his expressions) could entertain such inhuman ideas, and in so familiar a manner as to appear wholly unmoved at all the scenes of blood and desolation which I had painted as the common effects of those destructive machines; whereof he said some evil genius, enemy to mankind, must have been the first contriver. As for himself, he protested that although few things delighted him so much as new discoveries in art or in nature, yet he would rather lose half his kingdom than be privy to such a secret, which he commanded me, as I valued my life, never to mention any more.

THINKING ABOUT THE SELECTION
Recalling

1. (a) Describe the conflict between Lilliput and Blefuscu over the breaking of eggs. (b) How many people have died as a result?
2. (a) How does Gulliver capture the Blefuscudian fleet? (b) What problem do the enemy arrows cause him? (c) How does he solve the problem?
3. (a) What are some of the words the king of Brobdingnag uses to describe English history over the preceding hundred years? (b) How does he describe the English people?
4. (a) What invention does Gulliver describe to the King of Brobdingnag? (b) What is the King's reaction to the invention?

Interpreting

5. In the dispute between English Catholics and Protestants, what does Swift's attitude seem to be? Explain.
6. Why does Gulliver lose favor with the Lilliputian King in spite of having captured the Blefuscudian fleet?

7. If the views of the King of Brobdingnag represent Swift's own views, what is Swift's general opinion of recent English history and politics?
8. (a) Why do you think Gulliver supposes that his gunpowder proposal to the King of Brobdingnag will be regarded favorably? (b) How is it regarded? (c) Why?

Applying

9. Why do you think Swift makes one of the races Gulliver visits tiny in comparison with him and the other race gigantic?

ANALYZING LITERATURE
Understanding Satire

Satire is writing that uses wit and humor to expose and ridicule human vice and folly. Instead of praising the ideal, the satirist focuses on what is false, despicable, or foolish. Since people perceive things differently, not everyone will agree on what deserves to be satirized. Yet effective satire is so ingenious in its presentation and, at the same time, so clear in its purpose that most readers will appreciate the writing and grasp the point, regardless of their personal

from *Gulliver's Travels*   527

---

massacres . . . the very worst effects that avarice . . . cruelty [and] malice could produce." (b) He describes the English as "the most pernicious race of little odious vermin that nature ever suffered to crawl upon the surface of the earth."
4. (a) Gulliver describes gunpowder to the King. (b) The King is horrified, and bids Gulliver never mention it again, if he values his life.

Interpreting

5. Swift seems to think that the dispute is as silly as the dispute over the proper way to break an egg. He seems to suggest that the matter might at best be left to each man's conscience, or failing that, to his own monarch's decision.
6. He refuses to help him enslave the Blefuscudians.
7. Swift's general opinion of recent English history seems to be that it has been foolish, bloody, and barbaric.
8. (a) Gulliver supposes that the King will be interested in his gunpowder proposal because, in Gulliver's experience, monarchs delight in owning and using lethal weapons. (b) In fact, the King regards his proposal with horror. (c) He values gains in science or art, rather than technological advances in "destructive machinery."

Applying

9. Swift may have several reasons for making one of his races tiny, and the other gigantic. First, this gives us variety and symmetry, both distinguishing and yet uniting these two stories. Second, it is interesting that, each time, the criticized race is the smaller one. "To act small" is a phrase of contempt. Third, does Swift perhaps wish to avoid directly condemning the Protestant–Catholic disputes? Notice that the religious idiocies are assigned to the Lilliputians. The other vices and actions are laid directly at the door of the English, by the King of Brobdingnag.

Closure and Extension

ANSWERS TO THINKING ABOUT THE SELECTION
Recalling

1. (a) The Emperor of the Lilliputians ordered his subjects to break the small end of their eggs. The Blefuscudians have supported the Lilliputian rebels who wished to continue breaking their eggs at the large end. (b) Some forty-one thousand Lilliputians have died as a result of this edict.
2. (a) Gulliver captures the fleet by cutting their anchor cables, then towing them away. (b) The arrows smart, and they threaten his eyes. (c) He puts on a pair of spectacles.
3. (a) He calls it a "heap of conspiracies, rebellions, murders [and]

ANSWERS TO ANALYZING LITERATURE

1. Swift is satirizing domestic and international schisms in religion, and people's belligerence and cruelty to people in general.
2. It varies from warily ironic Lilliput to savagely ironic in Brobdingnag.
3. (a) In "A Voyage to Lilliput," the Principal Secretary of Private Affairs notes that the philosophers of Lilliput doubt that Gulliver comes from somewhere on earth, since their histories make no mention of any countries besides Lilliput and Blefuscu. The irony here is directed against closed minds, to which if a thing is not known, it is judged not to exist at all. (b) When Gulliver maintains, in his accounts to the King of Brobdingnag, that he "gave every point a more favorable turn . . . than the strictness of truth would allow," he is being ironic, for his gloss of the truth is enough to horrify that ruler. (c) In the following paragraph, Swift refers to the King's "narrowness of thinking, from which we and the politer countries of Europe are wholly exempted."

ANSWERS TO CRITICAL THINKING AND READING

1. The King observes "how contemptible a thing was human grandeur, which could be mimicked by such diminutive insects as [Gulliver]."
2. The King makes the following generalizations about (a) legislators —"that ignorance, idleness and vice are the proper" qualifications to become one. (b) priests—are not "advanced for their piety or learning" (c) soldiers—are not promoted "for their conduct or their valor" (d) judges—are not hired "for their integrity" nor are (e) senators—chosen "for the love of their country."
3. He concludes that the bulk of the human race is "an odious vermin."

ANSWERS TO UNDERSTANDING LANGUAGE

1. Yahoo: Any of a race of brutish, degraded creatures; degraded, vicious humans
2. Lilliputian: Tiny, or narrow minded and petty

views. Satire can be light and good-humored, or it can be bitter and unsparing. An important ingredient of much satire is irony—that is, a contrast between what is said and what is meant. For example, when Gulliver says that his "color came and went several times, with indignation to hear our noble country . . . the seat of virtue, piety, honor . . . the pride and envy of the world, so contemptuously treated," you can be quite sure that Swift is being ironic.

1. What is Swift satirizing in *Gulliver's Travels*?
2. From the excerpts you have read, how would you describe the tone of Swift's prose?
3. Point out at least three examples of irony in the excerpts from *Gulliver's Travels*.

CRITICAL THINKING AND READING
Understanding Generalizations

A **generalization** is a conclusion based on the accumulation of evidence. This evidence may come in the form of facts, statistics, incidents, and so on. In the excerpt from "A Voyage to Lilliput," Gulliver uses a single striking example as the basis for this generalization: "Of so little weight are the greatest services to princes when put into the balance with a refusal to gratify their passions." In "A Voyage to Brobdingnag," the King makes a number of generalizations about the English and other Europeans based on what Gulliver tells him.

1. What generalization does the King make to his first minister after Gulliver, sitting at a little table and chair . . . before one of the salt cellars," has told him about European manners, religion, laws, government, and learning? Is the generalization valid, or sound in light of the information the king has? Explain your answer.
2. After listening to Gulliver's historical account of "our affairs during the last century," what generalization does the King make about each of the following groups?
   a. legislators
   b. priests
   c. soldiers

d. judges
e. senators
3. What broader generalization does the King make about *all* the groups listed above?

UNDERSTANDING LANGUAGE
Using Words from Literature

Sometimes the names invented by writers become so closely associated with certain character traits or behaviors that they enter the language as standard English words. The word *lilliputian*, for example, can be found in most dictionaries. Several other words from *Gulliver's Travels* have joined the mainstream of modern English. Look up each of the following words in a standard dictionary. On a sheet of paper, write (a) each word you find and (b) its definition(s). Indicate capitalization where needed.
1. yahoo 2. lilliputian 3. brobdingnagian

THINKING AND WRITING
Writing a New Adventure for Gulliver

In addition to his trips to Lilliput and Brobdingnag, Lemuel Gulliver journeys to a place called Laputa and to the land of the Houyhnhnms. In Laputa, Swift's satire is directed against learned fools, impractical professors who, among other silly enterprises, are trying to extract sunshine from cucumbers. In the land of the Houyhnhnms, he encounters a race of noble, intelligent horses that are served by vile, human-like Yahoos. Create a fifth land for Gulliver to visit. Remember the types of creatures he has already encountered and the things he has learned along the way. In a narrative passage of a page or two, write your version of a new voyage by Gulliver. Give the land a name. Give its inhabitants names and characteristics. Include the truths about humans that Gulliver hears uttered by his hosts in this strange land. When you revise, make sure you have told your tale in chronological order.

3. Brobdingnagian: Of gigantic proportions

THINKING AND WRITING

Publishing Student Writing Give your students the opportunity to read aloud and listen to one another's stories.

GUIDE FOR INTERPRETING

from Thoughts on Various Subjects

Writer's Techniques

Epigram. The word *epigram* has two meanings. An epigram can be a short poem with a witty or satirical point, or it can be a brief, clever statement that often pairs opposite thoughts. This pairing of opposite thoughts is called *antithesis*. In an epigram terseness is vital—the writer must state the point as concisely as possible.

As you read the excerpts from Swift's "Thoughts on Various Subjects," note the humor in the epigrams. Also look for examples of antithesis.

Commentary

Swift did not confine his sense of humor only to witty epigrams and satires; it spilled over into his daily life as well. One example of his keen wit concerns a joke he played on Lady Berkeley.

While visiting London, Swift stayed with the Berkeley family, acting as their chaplain. At Lady Berkeley's request Swift read Boyle's *Meditations* to her, which he found unbearably dull. He decided to end the readings. Sneaking into the room, he inserted his own "Meditation on a Broom-stick," and replaced the book.

When Lady Berkeley next asked him to read one of the meditations, he opened to the page he had inserted, and calmly read the title. Astonished, she exclaimed, "A Meditation on a Broom-stick! Bless me, what a strange subject! But there is no knowing what useful lessons of instruction this wonderful man may draw from things apparently the most trivial. Pray let us hear what he says upon it." Swift solemnly read the silly piece. Lady Berkeley was convinced that she was indeed hearing a serious meditation.

As the room filled with others, Swift left. Lady Berkeley praised Boyle, saying, "The Doctor has been just reading one to me which surprised me more than all the rest . . . the excellent 'Meditation on a Broom-stick.' When everyone protested that they had never heard of it, she urged them to look for themselves.

When they found the meditation written in Swift's handwriting, everyone burst out laughing. History has recorded that Lady Berkeley was a good sport. Laughing along with the rest, she said, "What a vile trick has the rogue played on me. But it is his way, he never baulks [restrains] his humor in anything." The affair ended with general good feelings—and Swift never had to read Boyle's *Meditations* again.

Writing

Think of a well-known short story or choose one of the stories in this book. Consider the theme of the story. Then write a one-sentence summary of the theme. Make it as concise and epigrammatic as possible.

Guide for Interpreting 529

Teaching to Ability Levels Your less advanced students may have problems with the concept of antithesis. Suggest that they first look for the word *but* in any of the epigrams, and then try to spot two words or ideas within that epigram that seem to have opposite meanings; for example, fat and thin. Ask your **more advanced** students to explain the phrase "We're from the government, and we're here to help you." Why do most adults find this amusing? Is this statement antithetical?

Writing/Prior Knowledge You might suggest that your students approach this exercise as if they were whittling a block of wood. Ask them to first "rough in" the theme in three or four declarative sentences. Then see if they can introduce an antithesis into their short paragraph. Is there a "but" within their rough theme? Then ask them to reduce their theme to one declarative sentence. At that point, after they have dealt with the content of their epigram, they should be ready to shape it into its final, epigrammatic form and to polish it. For your **less advanced** students, a good source for their themes might be *Aesop's Fables,* since each of those is constructed rather tightly around a particular lesson. A second source for clearcut themes might be Kipling's *Just So* stories.

Vocabulary

Preteach the following vocabulary words:
solicit (sə lis′ it) v.: Ask for; plead for (p. 530)
inconsistencies (in′ kən sis′ tən sēz) n.: contradictions (p. 530)
fluency (floo′ ən sē) n.: Easy flow; smoothness (p. 530)
diversion (də vər′ zhən) n.: Pastimes; amusements (p. 531)

Objective

1 To write epigrams

Support Material

Teaching Portfolio
Teacher Backup, p. 603
Usage and Mechanics Worksheet, p. 606
Analyzing Literature Worksheet, *Understanding Epigrams,* p. 607
Language Worksheet, *Completing Word Analogies,* p. 608
Selection Test, p. 609

Literary Focus Point out to students that they know quite a few epigrams already. Folk sayings and mothers' admonitions are often epigrammatic. Consider "Pretty is as pretty does"; "All that glitters is not gold"; and "His eyes were bigger than his stomach." See if the class can contribute other examples.

Motivation/Prior Knowledge
An idea can be one of the most enduring artifacts in the world. Thoughts that endure have two characteristics. They are short, and they offer a truth that holds good through the centuries. If the thought is a funny one, it is that much more memorable. Let the students imagine that they want to do one of three things: They want to pass on a piece of wisdom to a beloved grandchild. They want to write an epitaph for a friend's grave. They want to insult an enemy in a way that no one will ever forget. And for each of these, they want their words, to be remembered. Have them devise a sentence of twenty words or fewer that accomplishes their purpose.

Master Teacher Note Because he was learned in the classics, Swift was inclined toward the classical ideal of giving terse, pointed expression to his thoughts. The epigrammatic tradition in English poetry and prose issues from the great writers of ancient Greece and Rome.

Purpose-Setting Question Which of the following "Thoughts" apply to what you have observed of life?

1 Discussion How might this epigram be applied to the religious differences and wars in the Middle East and in Ireland? Can the class think of other disputes that this saying brings to mind?

2 Discussion Do you think this is true? Could you give an example from your own experience?

3 Reading Strategy Ask one of your students to rephrase this epigram in his or her own words.

4 Discussion What do your students think about this? Have they noticed any great changes in their

from Thoughts on Various Subjects

Jonathan Swift

Thoughts on Various Subjects developed out of an agreement between Alexander Pope and Swift to record their passing thoughts. The following are some of Swift's ideas and impressions, which were included in his commonplace book, or book of collected passages.

1 We have just enough religion to make us hate, but not enough to make us love one another.

2 When we desire or solicit anything, our minds run wholly on the good side or circumstances of it; when 'tis obtained, our minds run wholly on the bad ones.

When a true genius appears in the world, you may know him by this sign: that the dunces are all in confederacy against him.

3 It is in disputes as in armies where the weaker side sets up false lights and makes a great noise to make the enemy believe them more numerous and strong than they really are.

I have known some men possessed of good qualities which were very serviceable to others but useless to themselves, like a sundial on the front of a house, to inform the neighbors and passengers but not the owner within.

4 If a man would register all his opinions upon love, politics, religion, learning, etc. beginning from his youth, and so go on to old age, what a bundle of inconsistencies and contradictions would appear at last.

5 Ambition often puts men upon doing the meanest offices; so climbing is performed in the same posture with creeping.

Ill company is like a dog who dirts those most whom he loves best.

No wise man ever wished to be younger.

The common fluency of speech in many men and most women is owing to a scarcity of matter and scarcity of words; for whoever is a master of language and hath a mind full of ideas, will be apt, in speaking, to hesitate upon the choice of both; whereas common speakers have only one set of ideas and one set of words to clothe them in, and these are always ready at the mouth: So people come faster out of a church when it is almost empty than when a crowd is at the door.

own thoughts yet? Have their opinions changed as to what would make them happy? As to what they'd like to be when they grow up? As to where they might like to go to college?

5 Literary Focus Could this epigram be applied to Macbeth? Explain.

Closure and Extension

ANSWERS TO THINKING ABOUT THE SELECTION
Recalling

1. Swift compares armies to disputes. In this usage, those engaged in arguement might be either individuals or groups.
2. Swift says that no wise man ever wished to be younger.
3. He says that most forms of play resemble fighting.

Dignity, high station, or great riches are in some sort necessary to old men in order to keep the younger at a distance who are otherwise too apt to insult them upon the score of their age.

6

Every man desires to live long, but no man would be old.

7

Most sorts of diversion in men, children, and other animals are an imitation of fighting.

8

Very few men, properly speaking, live at present but are providing to live another time.

9

THINKING ABOUT THE SELECTION

Recalling

1. To what does Swift compare armies that attempt to confuse the enemy by means of false lights and great noise?
2. According to Swift, what does a wise man never wish?
3. What does Swift say that most forms of play resemble?

Interpreting

4. The American writer Ralph Waldo Emerson observed, "A foolish consistency is the hobgoblin of little minds." Of which Swift epigram does Emerson's thought remind you?
5. In your own words, what is Swift's view of the difference between the speaking habits of a master of language and a common speaker?

Applying

6. Using a standard book of quotations arranged by subject matter, find other epigrams on three of the subjects dealt with by Swift.

THINKING AND WRITING

Writing Epigrams

In an epigram, as in lyric poetry, every word counts. The aim is to express an original thought in a brief, witty, memorable way. Review the epigrams from Swift's *Thoughts on Various Subjects,* paying close attention to how Swift uses wit and antithesis. Then write three epigrams of your own. Take your time in planning and writing the epigrams. Revise carefully. Although a good epigram looks simple, it requires considerable thought and imagination.

from *Thoughts on Various Subjects*   531

ROBINSON CRUSOE
by Daniel Defoe

Illustration from ROBINSON CRUSOE
N. C. Wyeth
The Granger Collection

Around 1742, so the story goes, a certain village in England was without a place of worship—the closest parish church being more than five miles away. Although the village also lacked a Bible, the inhabitants did have a Testament and a Common Prayer-book, bound together, that they shared. This valuable possession belonged to the innkeeper, who kept it safely tucked away on a kitchen shelf with her other prize, a copy of *Robinson Crusoe.*

Surprised by a sudden, fierce thunderstorm one summer's afternoon, a group of villagers made a wild dash for the inn's kitchen, the closest shelter. The terrified people decided prayers were in order and called for Jack, the innkeeper's helper, who had the rare good fortune to know how to read. Dropping to their knees in the large dining room, the villagers sent Jack back into the kitchen to get the one-volume Testament and Prayer-book, which was, you will recall, kept next to *Robinson Crusoe.* What with all the screaming and moaning, Jack took down the wrong book.

Rushing back into the dining room, he fell to his knees and began reading as quickly as he could. In his own fright, he mispronounced many words, and thus continued reading for quite some time until the villagers began to realize that they were not listening to prayers at all. Finally, when he

Illustration from ROBINSON CRUSOE
N. C. Wyeth
The Granger Collection

read the name of Robinson Crusoe's servant, Friday, the innkeeper cried out, "Why, Jock! thee hast got the wrong book! sure thee'st reading prayers out of *Robinson Crusoe!*" The lad, taking this comment as an insult, stubbornly continued to read, declaring that "*Robinson Crusoe* would as soon stop the thunder as the prayer-book."

The Masterpiece of the Age

Whether *Robinson Crusoe* did indeed have the power to stop the thunder has not been recorded, but the astonishing popularity of Defoe's book can easily be verified. Upon its publication in 1719, *Robinson Crusoe* was hailed as the masterpiece of the century. No less a critic than Samuel Johnson asserted that Defoe's fictional story of a sailor shipwrecked on a desert isle was sufficient alone to establish Defoe's reputation. "How few books are there of which one ever can possibly arrive at the last page!" he exclaimed. "Was there ever yet anything written by a mere man that was wished longer by its readers, excepting *Don Quixote, Robinson Crusoe,* and the *Pilgrim's*

Great Works 533

Illustration from ROBINSON CRUSOE
N. C. Wyeth
The Granger Collection

"The Wonders of this Man's Life"

Robinson Crusoe claims to be the autobiography of a young man who throws all warning aside to lead a life of adventure on the high seas. In the short opening, Crusoe tells about his life before he is shipwrecked on a distant island. The rest of the book is his firsthand journal of his experiences on the island.

Eight years after defying his parents by going to sea, Crusoe's ship runs aground during a fierce storm somewhere in the West Indies. His crew lost, only he makes it to shore, barely alive. For the next eleven days he ransacks the ship for supplies, until it is swallowed up by another storm. Practical, independent, and resourceful, he sets about building shelter, finding food, and keeping a record of his new life. Despite serious illness and extreme loneliness, Crusoe's faith and common sense see him through. By his eleventh year on the island, our hero has everything he could need—food, utensils, even pets—except human companionship. This too is solved; his twenty five years of solitude come to a dramatic end with the arrival of a man he calls "Friday" (to commemorate the day they met), a native destined to become his servant and friend. Will Crusoe and Friday survive? Will they be rescued?

Progress?" An 1810 critic was equally lavish in his praise, writing: "Perhaps there exists no work, either of instruction or entertainment, in the English language, which has been more generally read, and more universally admired, than the *Life and Adventures of Robinson Crusoe. . . .* Society is forever indebted to the memory of Defoe for his production of a work, in which the ways of Providence are simply and pleasingly vindicated, and a lasting and useful moral is conveyed through the channel of an interesting and delightful story."

Alexander Selkirk

Eighteenth-century readers relished travel, escape, and adventure books, as we do today. Defoe had copies of all the popular books of the day, including the one on which he based *Robinson Crusoe:* Captain Roger's *Cruising Voyage Around the World.* This is the true story of Alexander Selkirk, the Scottish sailor marooned on a Pacific island for four years. Most of Defoe's readers assumed that *The Life and Strange Surprising Adventures of Robinson Crusoe, of*

York, Mariner was also a true account. Defoe kept mum on the issue, for it boosted sales.

Storytelling at Its Best

But ultimately the appeal of the novel lies with Defoe's skill in making the impossible seem possible. At his hands, wild storms, pirate attacks, shipwrecks, cannibalism, and the attack of five hundred savage wolves all seem realistic. As a storyteller Defoe has few rivals; as an adventure tale *Robinson Crusoe* enthralls us today as it did in 1719.

Illustration from ROBINSON CRUSOE
N. C. Wyeth
The Granger Collection

Enrichment Have students discuss possible answers to each of these inquiries:

1. How afraid would you be if you were shipwrecked alone on an island?
2. What would have to be done immediately on an island like that in order to survive?
3. If there were limited supplies and you could only take three tools with you, which would you choose? Why?
4. What medicines would you want to have along?
5. What would you miss most about civilization while living on an isolated island? Why?

BIOGRAPHIES

Joseph Addison (1672–1719)
Sir Richard Steele (1672–1729)

Although great writing seldom results from a team effort, the collaboration of Joseph Addison and Richard Steele is an exception to the general rule. Addison and Steele's work on two precedent-setting periodicals, *The Tatler* and *The Spectator,* has earned both authors a permanent place in literary history.

The two men, born a few weeks apart, were opposites in many ways. Joseph Addison, dignified, shy, and rather cold, enjoyed a reputation as a Latin scholar. Richard Steele, energetic, witty, and outgoing, was a man-about-town. Nevertheless, for most of their lives they were close friends, temperamentally different but sharing similar aims and values. Addison, born in a village in Wiltshire, England, and Steele, born in Dublin, Ireland, met as classmates at the Charterhouse School in London. They then went on to Oxford, where Addison graduated but Steele did not.

Instead, Steele took a commission in the army and immersed himself in the London literary scene. Steele had a tendency to live beyond his means, and in 1709, to earn some extra money, he started *The Tatler,* a periodical dealing with "gallantry, pleasure and entertainment." *The Tatler* proved highly popular in London coffeehouses, appearing three times a week from April 1709 to January 1711.

Since his undergraduate days, Addison had pursued a different path from that of Steele. An outstanding student, he became a Fellow of Magdalen College, Oxford, and was invited by John Dryden to do translations of Virgil. After four years of European study and travel, he produced a hugely successful epic poem, "The Campaign," celebrating the Duke of Marlborough's victory at the Battle of Blenheim. In 1706 Addison was named undersecretary of state, and two years later was elected to the House of Commons, where he remained until his death.

In 1709, while serving briefly as secretary to the Lord Lieutenant of Ireland, he began reading the newly published *Tatler.* Despite Steele's pen name, "Isaac Bickerstaff," Addison recognized the writing as that of his old friend, and he began to submit contributions, notes, and suggestions. *The Tatler,* mostly the work of Steele, was succeeded by *The Spectator,* issued daily except Sunday from March 1711 to December 1712, and revived briefly in 1714. *The Spectator* was mostly the work of Addison, although Steele contributed regularly.

GUIDE FOR INTERPRETING

Country Manners;
Thoughts in Westminster Abbey

Literary Forms

Informal Essay. An *informal essay*, like a formal essay, presents the observations and opinions of its author, but it does so in a more relaxed and conversational manner. The informal essay is sometimes called a *familiar essay*, a *personal essay*, or, when printed in a magazine or newspaper, a *periodical essay*. The eighteenth century was a time in which the formal essay flourished. The formal essay was first used in England by Sir Francis Bacon. The informal essay, introduced by the sixteenth-century French writer Michel de Montaigne, had a great influence on English writers through the vigorous translation of John Florio. An informal essay, less structured than a formal essay, is written in a personal, often anecdotal, sometimes humorous way.

The informal essays of Addison and Steele were published regularly in *The Tatler* and *The Spectator*. These two publications are notable for their wide-ranging, nonpolitical content and their graceful tone and style. Steele was the more imaginative writer, Addison the better craftsman. Both set a high standard for later periodical essayists and journalists.

Commentary

How were the periodicals of Addison and Steele different from the newspapers of the day? The newspapers recorded events; *The Spectator* and *The Tatler* transformed journalism into literature.

Influential men employed writers to provide them with news of the Court in their absence. By the beginning of the seventeenth century, this expanded into the news-book, sixteen pages of foreign news, much of it scurrilous, including torrents of abuse and outright lies. This led to years of suppression, but the pamphlets flourished, and by the middle of the century the newspaper was firmly entrenched. Advertisements appeared in 1655. These ads seem meek by today's standards; coffee, for instance, was promoted as "a simple Innocent thing incomparable good for those that are troubled with melancholy." By 1715 the newspaper was established, and the press was a power recognized by every political party.

Writing

Think of a topic on which opinion varies. It should be a topic about which you have strong opinions of your own. Jot down notes about this topic. These notes should include not only support for your own viewpoint but also evidence that helps to refute the opposing viewpoint. Save these notes for later use.

Guide for Interpreting 537

Writing/Prior Knowledge Ask your students to tell what topics they have thought of. Select a few for class discussion. Then invite the class to offer *pro* and *con* opinions.

Spelling Tip Write the following pairs of words on the board:
superfluity-superfluities
precedency-precedencies
repository-repositories
Point out to students that to form the plural of a word ending with a consonant and *y*, we change the *y* to *i* and add *es*.

Literary Focus In the *Spectator* Addison wrote about the disadvantages of the brief informal essay. "We must immediately fall into our Subject, and treat every part of it in a lively Manner, or our Papers are thrown by as dull and insipid: Our Matter must lie close together, and either be wholly new in itself, or in the Turn it receives from our Expressions. . . . it is often expected that every Sheet should be a kind of Treatise, and make out in thought what it wants in Bulk; that a Point of Humour should be worked up in all its Parts; and a subject touched upon in its most essential articles, without the Repetitions, Tautologies, and Enlargements that are indulged to longer Labours. An Essay Writer must . . . give the Virtue of a full draught in a few Drops." Discuss whether you agree with Addison's points.

Vocabulary

Preteach the following vocabulary words:

deferences (def′ ər ən sez) n.: Courtesies (p. 538)

complaisance (kəm plā′ z'ns) n.: Desire to be agreeable (p. 538)

modish (mōd′ish) adj.: Fashionable (p. 538)

superfluities (sōō′ pər flōō′ ə tēz) n.: Excesses (p. 538)

precedency (pres′ ə dən sē) n.: Priority because of rank (p. 538)

rostral (räs′trəl) adj.: Having a beaklike projection, or rostrum, as at the prow of a ship (p. 543)

repository (ri päz′ ə tôr′ ē) n.: A center for accumulation and storage (p. 543)

timorous (tim′ ər əs) adj.: Fearful; timid (p. 543)

inordinate (in ôr′d'n it) adj.: Beyond reasonable limits (p. 543)

Country Manners

Joseph Addison

The Spectator, July 17, 1711

The first and most obvious reflections which arise in a man who changes the city for the country are upon the different manners of the people whom he meets with in those two different scenes of life. By manners I do not mean morals, but behavior and good breeding as they show themselves in the town and in the country.

And here, in the first place, I must observe a very great revolution that has happened in this article of good breeding. Several obliging deferences, condescensions, and submissions, with many outward forms and ceremonies that accompany them, were first of all brought up among the politer part of mankind, who lived in courts and cities and distinguished themselves from the rustic part of the species (who on all occasions acted bluntly and naturally) by such a mutual complaisance and intercourse of civilities. These forms of conversation by degrees multiplied and grew troublesome; the modish world found too great a constraint in them, and have therefore thrown most of them aside. Conversation was so encumbered with show and ceremony that it stood in need of a reformation to retrench its superfluities and restore its natural good sense and beauty. At present, therefore, an unconstrained carriage and a certain openness of behavior are the height of good breeding. The fashionable world is grown free and easy; our manners sit more loose upon us; nothing is so modish as an agreeable negligence. In a word, good breeding shows itself most where to an ordinary eye it appears the least.

If after this we look on the people of mode in the country, we find in them the manners of the last age. They have no sooner fetched themselves up to the fashion of a polite world, but the town has dropped them, and are nearer to the first stage of nature than to those refinements which formerly reigned in the court and still prevail in the country. One may now know a man that never conversed in the world by his excess of good breeding. A polite country squire[1] shall make you as many bows in half an hour as would serve a courtier[2] for a week. There is infinitely more to do about place and precedency in a meeting of justices' wives than in an assembly of duchesses.

This rural politeness is very troublesome to a man of my temper who generally takes the chair that is next me and walks first or last, in the front or in the rear, as chance directs. I have known my friend Sir Roger's dinner almost cold before the company could adjust the ceremonial and be prevailed upon to sit down; and have heartily pitied my old friend when I have seen him forced to pick and cull his guests, as they sat at the several parts of his table, that he might drink their healths according to their respective ranks and qualities. Honest Will Wimble, who I should have thought had

---

1. squire n.: A country gentleman or landed proprietor.
2. courtier (kôr′ tē ər) n.: An attendant at a royal court.

Grammar in Action

Comparison and contrast is one of the most effective methods writers use to achieve clear, forceful expression. Notice the second and third paragraphs of "Country Manners." First the essay contrasts city people of "good breeding" in the past and such people in the present. Then, in the third paragraph, city manners are contrasted with country manners.

been altogether uninfected with ceremony, gives me abundance of trouble in this particular. Though he has been fishing all the morning, he will not help himself at dinner till I am served. When we are going out of the hall, he runs behind me; and last night, as we were walking in the fields, stopped short at a stile till I came up to it and, upon my making signs to him to get over, told me, with a serious smile, that sure I believed they had no manners in the country.

There has happened another revolution in the point of good breeding which relates to the conversation among men of mode and which I cannot but look upon as very extraordinary. It was certainly one of the first distinctions of a well-bred man to express everything that had the most remote appearance of being obscene in modest terms and distant phrases; whilst the clown, who had no such delicacy of conception and expression, clothed his ideas in those plain homely terms that are the most obvious and natural. This kind of good manners was perhaps carried to an excess so as to make conversation too stiff, formal, and precise; for which reason (as hypocrisy in one age is generally succeeded by atheism in another) conversation is in a great measure relapsed into the first extreme; so that at present several of our men of the town, and particularly those who have been polished in France, make use of the most coarse, uncivilized words in our language and utter themselves often in such a manner as a clown would blush to hear.

This infamous piece of good breeding, which reigns among the coxcombs[3] of the town, has not yet made its way into the country; and as it is impossible for such an irrational way of conversation to last long among a people that makes any profession of religion or show of modesty, if the country gentlemen get into it, they will certainly be left in the lurch. Their good breeding will come too late to them, and they will be thought a parcel of lewd clowns, while they fancy themselves talking together like men of wit and pleasure.

As the two points of good breeding, which I have hitherto insisted upon, regard behavior and conversation, there is a third which turns upon dress. In this too the country are very much behindhand. The rural beaus are not yet got out of the fashion that took place at the time of the Revolution[4] but ride about the country in red coats and laced hats; while the women in many parts are still trying to outvie one another in the height of their headdresses.

But a friend of mine, who is now upon the western circuit, having promised to give me an account of the several modes and fashions that prevail in the different parts of the nation through which he passes, I shall defer the enlarging upon this last topic till I have received a letter from him, which I expect every post.

---

3. coxcombs *n.*: Silly, vain men; dandies.
4. the Revolution: The "Glorious Revolution" of 1688, during which James II was expelled from the throne.

5 Clarification As it is used here, the word *clown* means an "uncouth person," or a "yokel." To what group is the clown's language comparable?

6 Discussion What does the author think about this latest example of good breeding? What is ironic about such an expression of "good breeding"?

Reading Strategy Summarize the three points of good breeding the essay discusses.

Reader's Response How does your behavior change when you travel to cities or to suburbs?

Country Manners   539

If after this we look on the people of mode in the country, we find in them the manners of the last age. They have no sooner fetched themselves up to the fashion of a polite world, but the town has dropped them.

Our view of the manners of country people is all the more sharp and clear because of the contrast with the manners of city people.

Student Activity 1. "Country Manners" contains other examples of comparison and contrast. Point out at least two of them and show how they contribute to the main point of the essay.

Student Activity 2. Write a two-paragraph essay in which you compare and contrast two well-known people, such as actors, professional athletes, or people in public life. Devote the first paragraph to one of the people, the second paragraph to the other.

Closure and Extension

ANSWERS TO THINKING ABOUT THE SELECTION
Recalling

1. (a) Members of polite society introduced mannerisms into conversation that distinguished them from rustics. (b) The revolution occurred in the courts and cities. (c) Modish society rejected the forms of conversation as too complicated and troublesome.
2. Country gentlemen kept the conversational mannerisms after they were rejected by city folk.
3. (a) Sir Roger lets his dinner grow cold while he follows outmoded ceremonies of politeness. (b) Will Wimble's excessive deference.
4. (a) The second revolution involved abandoning polite words in favor of obscene ones. (b) It occurred first in France and was brought to London. (c) The words were obscene and uttered in a crude manner.
5. (a) The country has ignored it. (b) Country gentlemen may someday react to a change in dress.

Interpreting

6. New ideas usually begin in centers of intellectual activity; in the country, people are more concerned with simple pleasures.
7. Styles have changed; the excesses of good breeding are now perceived for exactly what they are—ridiculous conventions that stand in the way of common sense.
8. (a) The writer considers himself a member of the "politer part of mankind." (b) He is unaware of what is in vogue in different parts of the nation.

Applying

9. Answers will differ. A possible answer is that modern transportation and communication have minimized the differences between country and city manners.
10. Though Addison and Steele would have understood Whitman's remark, their natural politeness and decorum would have inclined them to reject his tolerance of bad manners.

540

THINKING ABOUT THE SELECTION
Recalling

1. (a) What happened in the first "great revolution . . . of good breeding"? (b) Where did the revolution occur? (c) What brought about the change?
2. How did "country gentlemen" react to the change in city manners?
3. What annoys the writer about the behavior of (a) Sir Roger? (b) Honest Will Wimble?
4. (a) What did the second revolution in good breeding involve? (b) Where did it occur? (c) Why might its effects make "a clown . . . blush"?
5. (a) How has the country reacted to the revolution in conversation? (b) In what other area of good breeding may country gentlemen someday react?

Interpreting

6. Why do you think the country lags behind the city in manners?
7. Why would a city dweller who had once expected an "excess of good breeding" now be annoyed by it?
8. (a) To which group mentioned in the essay does the writer belong? (b) Why must he await a letter before he can comment on the fashion prevailing in the country?

Applying

9. In the United States today, what are the differences, if any, between country manners and city manners? Explain.
10. In nineteenth-century America, Walt Whitman wrote, "To the real artist in humanity, what are called bad manners are often the most picturesque and significant of all."

How do you think Addison and Steele would have reacted to Whitman's comment? Explain your answer.

ANALYZING LITERATURE
Understanding Informal Essay

As its name implies, an informal essay expresses the observations and opinions of its author in a personal, conversational way. The informal essay is less rigid than the formal essay. The views stated can be highly individual, even outrageous. Although Addison and Steele are seldom outrageous, they do express unequivocal, thought-provoking opinions.

1. For each of the three "points of good breeding" in "Country Manners," find one statement that you consider highly opinionated.
2. A personal essay shows clear signs of having been written by the specific individual whose opinions it expresses. What are three such signs in "Country Manners"?

THINKING AND WRITING
Writing an Informal Essay

Use the topic that you chose for Writing, page 537, or else select a new topic on which opinions vary. Possible general topic areas include politics, sports, arts, and leisure. If you are using the topic you chose earlier, you have existing notes for it. If not, begin by stating your opinion clearly in one sentence. Then jot down notes before you start to write. When writing the first draft of your informal essay, use a personal, conversational style. In revising the first draft, pay close attention to tone. A good conversational style is friendly and down-to-earth but not overly clever.

ANSWERS TO ANALYZING LITERATURE

1. Three highly opinionated statements are (1) ". . . good breeding shows itself most where to an ordinary eye it appears the least." (2) ". . . as it is impossible for such an irrational way of conversation to last long among a people that makes any profession of religion or show of modesty, if the country gentlemen get into it, they will certainly be left in the lurch." (3) "The rural beaus are not yet got out of the fashion that took place at the time of the Revolution . . ."
2. Three signs are (1) "I have known my friend Sir Roger's dinner almost cold . . ." (2) Honest Will Wimble . . . gives me abundance of trouble in this particular." (3) ". . . I shall defer the enlarging upon this last topic until I have received a letter from him, which I expect every post."

THINKING AND WRITING

Publishing Student Writing Have students submit their essays to the school newspaper or literary magazine.

Thoughts in Westminster Abbey[1]

Joseph Addison

The Spectator, March 30, 1711

When I am in a serious humor, I very often walk by myself in Westminster Abbey; where the gloominess of the place, and the use to which it is applied, with the solemnity of the building, and the condition of the people who lie in it, are apt to fill the mind with a kind of melancholy, or rather thoughtfulness, that is not disagreeable. I yesterday passed a whole afternoon in the churchyard, the cloisters, and the church, amusing myself with the tombstones and inscriptions that I met with in those several regions of the dead. Most of them recorded nothing else of the buried person, but that he was born upon one day, and died upon another: the whole history of his life being comprehended in those two circumstances, that are common to all mankind. I could not but look upon these registers of existence, whether of brass or marble, as a kind of satire upon the departed persons; who had left no other memorial of them, but that they were born and that they died. They put me in mind of several persons mentioned in the battles of heroic poems, who have sounding names given them, for no other reason but that they may be killed, and are celebrated for nothing but being knocked on the head.

Upon my going into the church, I entertained myself with the digging of a grave; and saw in every shovelful of it that was thrown up, the fragment of a bone or skull intermixed with a kind of fresh moldering earth that some time or other had a place in the composition of a human body. Upon this I began to consider with myself what innumerable multitudes of people lay confused together under the pavement of that ancient cathedral; how men and women, friends and enemies, priests and soldiers, monks and prebendaries,[2] were crumbled amongst one another, and blended together in the same common mass; how beauty, strength, and youth, with old age, weakness, and deformity, lay undistinguished in the same promiscuous heap of matter.

After having thus surveyed this great magazine of mortality, as it were, in the lump; I examined it more particularly by the accounts which I found on several of the monuments which are raised in every quarter of that ancient fabric. Some of them were covered with such extravagant epitaphs that, if it were possible for the dead person to be acquainted with them, he would blush at the praises which his friends have bestowed upon him. There are others so excessively modest, that they deliver the character of the person departed in Greek or

---

1. **Westminster Abbey:** A famous church in Westminster, England, where English monarchs are crowned, and where English monarchs and many famous writers and statesmen are buried.

2. **prebendaries** (preb′ ən der′ ēz) *n.*: In the Church of England, honorary clergymen.

6 Discussion What does this mean in light of what you have learned about Poets' Corner?

7 Discussion How would a foreigner draw conclusions about a nation's ignorance or politeness from its tombstones?

8 Discussion According to the author, what is incongruous about this picture?

Humanities Note

Fine art, *St. Edmunds Chapel in Westminster Abbey,* John Fulleylove. The British artist John Fulleylove (1845–1908) specialized in painting and drawing landscapes, gardens, buildings, and interiors. He traveled through England, France, and Italy in search of subjects. His works were exhibited for sale at various galleries and societies in England.

In 1904 a group of excellent pencil sketches were exhibited at the Gouper Gallery in London. Among them was this view of the St. Edmunds Chapel in Westminster Abbey. Always noteworthy as a fine architectural draftsman, Fullylove shows his skill in this drawing. Every detail of the carvings, arches, and tombs is confidently and solidly drawn with perfect perspective. This drawing was reproduced in color in 1907 as an illustration in a guidebook. The accuracy and detail of Fullylove's works made them particularly desirable as illustrations.

You might ask the following questions:

1. What information about Westminster Abbey does this drawing give?
2. How is a drawing like this similar to and different from a photograph? Which do you think is more effective? Why?

Hebrew, and by that means are not understood once in a twelvemonth. In the poetical quarter, I found there were poets who had no monuments, and monuments which had no poets. I observed, indeed, that the present war[3] had filled the church with many of these uninhabited monuments, which had been erected to the memory of persons whose bodies were perhaps buried in the plains of Blenheim,[4] or in the bosom of the ocean.

I could not but be very much delighted with several modern epitaphs, which are written with great elegance of expression and justness of thought, and therefore do honor to the living as well as to the dead. As a foreigner is very apt to conceive an idea of the ignorance or politeness of a nation, from the turn of their public monuments and inscriptions, they should be submitted to the perusal of men of learning and genius, before they are put in execution. Sir Cloudesly Shovel's[5] monument has very often given me great offense: instead of the brave rough English admiral, which was the distinguishing character of that plain gallant man, he is represented on his tomb by the figure of a beau, dressed in a long periwig,[6] and reposing himself upon velvet cushions under a canopy of state. The inscription is answerable to the monument; for instead of celebrating the many remarkable actions he had performed in the service of his country, it acquaints us only with the manner of his death, in which it was impossible for him to reap any honor. The Dutch,

---

3. the present war: The War of the Spanish Succession, in which England and several other European nations fought against an alliance led by the French and Spanish.
4. Blenheim (blen′ əm): Village in western Bavaria that was the site of an important battle (1704) during the War of the Spanish Succession.

5. Sir Cloudesly Shovel (1650–1707): English admiral and commander of the British fleet.
6. periwig (per′ ə wig′) n.: A type of wig often worn by men during the seventeenth and eighteenth centuries.

ST. EDMUND'S CHAPEL, WESTMINSTER ABBEY
John Fulleylove

whom we are apt to despise for want of genius, show an infinitely greater taste of antiquity and politeness in their buildings and works of this nature, than what we meet with in those of our own country. The monuments of their admirals, which have been erected at the public expense, represent them like themselves; and are adorned with rostral crowns and naval ornaments, with beautiful festoons of seaweed, shells, and coral.

But to return to our subject. I have left the repository of our English kings for the contemplation of another day, when I shall find my mind disposed for so serious an amusement. I know that entertainments of this nature are apt to raise dark and dismal thoughts in timorous minds and gloomy imaginations; but for my own part, though I am always serious, I do not know what it is to be melancholy; and can therefore take a view of nature in her deep and solemn scenes, with the same pleasure as in her most gay and delightful ones. By this means I can improve myself with those objects which others consider with terror. When I look upon the tombs of the great, every emotion of envy dies in me; when I read the epitaphs of the beautiful, every inordinate desire goes out; when I meet with the grief of parents upon a tombstone, my heart melts with compassion; when I see the tomb of the parents themselves, I consider the vanity of grieving for those whom we must quickly follow: when I see kings lying by those who deposed them, when I consider rival wits placed side by side, or the holy men that divided the world with their contests and disputes, I reflect with sorrow and astonishment on the little competitions, factions, and debates of mankind. When I read the several dates of the tombs, of some that died yesterday, and some six hundred years ago, I consider that great day when we shall all of us be contemporaries, and make our appearance together.

THINKING ABOUT THE SELECTION

Recalling

1. (a) At what times does the author say he visits Westminster Abbey? (b) Why does he go then?
2. (a) Who was Sir Cloudsley Shovel? (b) What kind of man was he? (b) Why does the author object to Shovel's monument?
3. On what does the author reflect with "sorrow and astonishment"?

Interpreting

4. What two kinds of epitaphs seem to offend the author most?

5. The author states that some modern epitaphs "do honor to the living as well as to the dead." (a) What does he mean? (b) Why does he think proposed monuments and epitaphs should be reviewed by "men of learning and genius"?
6. What does the author mean by "that great day when we shall all of us be contemporaries"?

Applying

7. At the end of the essay the author lists a number of ironies he sees in Westminster Abbey. (a) Which of them seems the most poignant to you? (b) What ironies can you think of that might be added to the list?

Thoughts in Westminster Abbey   543

9 **Discussion** What irony is implied here?

10 **Literary Focus** What is the effect of the sentence fragment?

11 **Discussion** What is the difference between being serious and melancholy?

12 **Discussion** Why might objects that fill others with terror affect the author in a different way?

13 **Literary Focus** You might wish to read the latter part of this paragraph aloud. The prose style here blends richness and depth of feeling with neoclassical balance and elegance. Ask your students what the "great day" is that the author alludes to.

2. (a) Sir Cloudsley Shovel was an English admiral. (b) He was a brave, plain, and gallant man who had served his country well. (c) The picture on the monument bears no resemblance to the man and the inscription honors his death rather than his life.
3. He reflects with "sorrow and astonishment" on the competitions, factions, and debates of mankind.

Interpreting

4. The author is annoyed by overly extravagant or excessively modest epitaphs.
5. (a) Good epitaphs honor the person who has died and do not offend those who read them. (b) Men of learning and genius would presumably make sure that poorly written epitaphs did not appear on tombstones.
6. He means Judgment Day, when the dead shall arise from their graves.

Applying

7. Answers will differ. Possible answers are: (a) The most poignant concerns meeting with the grief of parents upon a tombstone. (b) Other ironies include beggars' lying next to the wealthy, murderers next to those murdered, and the religious next to atheists.

Closure and Extension

ANSWERS TO THINKING ABOUT THE SELECTION
Recalling

1. (a) The author goes to Westminster Abbey when he is feeling serious. (b) He goes then because the place fills his mind with an agreeable thoughtfulness.

543

CROSS CURRENTS

Literary Magazines Today

Editor Reginald Gibbons recently observed in the *Chicago Tribune*, "It's no accident that almost every writer of our century who is now regarded as the author of great and enduring work was first published in the little literary magazines, some of which, like T. S. Eliot's famous *Criterion*, had as few as 700 subscribers."

Many literary magazines from the early part of the twentieth century have passed into legend, but not before leaving an indelible mark on literature and culture. *The Masses, The Pagan, The Dial,* and *The Fugitive* published the early works of T. S. Eliot, Ezra Pound, Wallace Stevens, as well as many other landmark writers. The mass-market magazines, in contrast, published the long-forgotten verse of such authors as Anne Bunner and Fannie Stearns Davis. But before we can consider the affect of today's literary magazines, we have to be sure we know how to recognize one!

WHAT IS A LITERARY MAGAZINE?

The Coordinating Council of Literary Magazines includes among its members 380 literary magazines. They define a literary magazine as "a noncommercial magazine in which fiction, poetry, or literary essay comprises at least 50% of the editorial material." Yet many of these journals are indeed published for a profit. *Granta,* for instance, is published by Penguin Books. This notable magazine, begun by students at Cambridge University in 1888, has showcased the work of A. A. Milne (of Winnie the Pooh fame), E. M. Forster, Sylvia Plath, Graham Greene, and Saul Bellow, to mention just a few. In a

similar fashion, the publishing house of W. W. Norton supports the literary magazine *Antaeus,* and Vintage Books publishes *The Quarterly.*

According to this definition, mass-market literary magazines are an entirely different kettle of literature. Yet *The New Yorker, Atlantic, Harper's, The New York Review of Books, The Times Literary Supplement,* and *Partisan Review* devote the majority of their editorial space to publishing some of today's most important fiction, poetry, and literary essays. Twenty-five percent of the 155 short stories published in single volumes in 1987 were first published in *The New Yorker; The Atlantic* came in a laudable second. Virtually all the stories published in these magazines, however, were by already-famous writers.

But whether they are published for profit or not, literary magazines offer an astonishing diversity of style and content. At one end of the spectrum are the long-established publications such as *The Paris Review.* Founded as a journal where undiscovered writers could gain public notice, *The Paris Review* has enjoyed the same fate as many of its original contributors: It's gone mainstream. Now they publish the work of such well-known writers as Nadine Gordimer and John Irving. At the other end of the scale are such "hip lit" publications as *Bomb* and *Between C & D.* The latter, for example, has rejected the understated in favor of shock: The entire print run of 600 copies, printed directly from a home computer, is distributed with sprocket holes still attached and the pages connected in a single, long accordion of folded pages. The content is as offbeat as the style.

Cooperative Learning Students who intend to contact the sources listed on page 544 should choose partners prior to calling or writing. They ought to begin coordinating their efforts by listing questions they want answered and then placing the same in an order of priority. This is particularly useful if they intend to contact the groups by telephone.

HOW ARE LITERARY MAGAZINES DISTRIBUTED?

How do people hear about literary magazines? Many are distributed through universities and colleges; others are publicized through word of mouth. A surprising number of literary magazines are distributed through bookstores. These include the more famous titles—*Antioch Review*, *VLS (Voice Literary Supplement)*, *Yale Literary Magazine*, *Hudson Review*, *TriQuarterly*, *American Poetry Review*, *Hornbook*, *Paris Review*, *American Book Review*, *American Poetry Review*, and *October*—as well as the often colorfully named newer productions —*Coyote's Journal*, *Callaloo*, *Southpaw*, *Sulphur*, *Zyzzyva*, *Alcatraz*, *Imagine*, and *AMC (Another Chicago Magazine)*.

Often, bookstores alert their customers to new literary magazines through poetry readings, book signings, and fancy receptions. Although literary magazines often sell only a handful of copies, they are surprisingly profitable to bookstore owners. Richard Bray, owner of Guild Books in Chicago, remarked, "We don't lose money on them. It's profitable from the standpoint that people who buy and browse these magazines are probably, more than any other category, book buyers. Just as magazines in general are a draw to help sell books, I'd say literary magazines are—and more so."

THE IMPORTANCE OF LITERARY MAGAZINES

Although the number of people reading literary magazines is limited, these publications nonetheless play a very significant role in the literary scene. They give famous writers a chance to take a chance and try a new writing style or topic, but, even more important, they allow readers to see new and unusual literary experiments by writers who are still developing a career. You might be the one to discover the next "classic" writer!

ALEXANDER POPE

1688–1744

From the age of eight or nine, Alexander Pope knew that he wanted to become not just a poet but a great poet. Before he was twenty-one, his *Essay on Criticism* had brought him to the attention of the leading literary figures of England. His satiric *The Rape of the Lock,* probably the best mock-epic poem in English, followed when he was twenty-four. Despite a crippling childhood disease and persistent ill health, Pope triumphantly achieved his boyhood ambition. A brilliant satirist in verse, he gave his name (the Age of Pope and Swift) to the literary era in which he lived and wrote.

Born into the Roman Catholic family of a London linen merchant, Pope had to struggle for position. After the expulsion of King James II, English Catholics could not legally vote, hold office, attend a university, or live within ten miles of London. To comply with the rule of residency, his family moved to Binfield, near Windsor Forest, a rural setting where Pope spent his formative years writing poetry, studying the classics, and becoming broadly self-educated. Pope's physical problems were as severe as his religious ones. Deformed by tuberculosis of the spine, Pope stood only about four and a half feet tall—"the little Alexander whom the women laugh at," he said—and he suffered from nervousness and excruciating headaches throughout his life. In 1718 Pope moved to a five-acre estate at Twickenham (twit′ nam), a village on the Thames, where he lived until his death.

Although Pope, "the Wasp of Twickenham," is more often remembered for his quarrels than for his cordiality, he became friends, and remained so for life, with members of a Tory group that included Jonathan Swift, John Gay, and Lord Bolingbroke. Pope instigated the formation of the Scriblerus Club, the purpose of which was to ridicule what its members regarded as "false tastes in learning." The satiric emphasis of the club probably gave some impetus to the writing of Swift's *Gulliver's Travels,* Gay's *Beggar's Opera,* and Pope's *The Dunciad*—a "burlesque heroick" attack on Pope's literary enemies (most of whom are now forgotten).

In the 1730's Pope's writing turned increasingly philosophical. He embarked on a massive work concerning morality and government, but completed only *An Essay on Man* and *Moral Essays.* Nevertheless, the entire body of his work is sufficient for critics today to accord him exceptionally high praise. The twentieth-century poet Edith Sitwell calls Pope "perhaps the most flawless artist our race has yet produced."

GUIDE FOR INTERPRETING

from The Rape of the Lock

Literary Forms

Mock Epic. A mock epic is a long, humorous narrative poem that treats a trivial subject in the grand, elevated style of a true epic such as the *Odyssey* or *Paradise Lost*. Sometimes called a *mock-heroic* poem, this literary form reached the height of its popularity in the eighteenth century. The *conventions,* or standard elements, of an epic require both the characters and the action to be of heroic proportions. The theme of a true epic concerns fundamental human problems. In a classical epic, gods and goddesses oversee and sometimes intervene in human affairs. When these conventions of an epic are satirically applied to a subject of little consequence, the result can be highly amusing.

Writing

Freewrite about an incident you have heard or read about that you think has been magnified beyond its importance. In your writing, carry the incident to an illogical extreme, as the writer of a mock epic would do.

Primary Source

Concerned that the publication of his poem could cause greater hard feelings, Pope wrote a dedication to Arabella Fermor, the model for Belinda, intended to coax her into a good mood. After you read the following excerpt, decide whether Pope succeeded.

> Madam,
> It will be in vain to deny that I have some Regard for this Piece, since I Dedicate it to You. Yet . . . it was intended only to divert a few young ladies, who have good Sense and good Humor enough, to laugh not only at their Sex's little unguarded Follies, but at their own. But as it was communicated with the Air of A Secret, it soon found its Way into the World. . . .
> As to the following Cantos, all the Passages in them are as Fabulous, as the Vision at the Beginning, or the Transformation at the end; (except the Loss of your Hair, which I always mention with Reverence). The Human Persons are as Fictitious as the Airy ones; and the Character of Belinda, as it is now manag'd, resembles you in nothing but in Beauty.
> If this Poem had as many Graces as there are in Your Person, or in Your Mind, yet I could never hope it would pass thro' the World half so Uncensured as You hace done. But let its Fortune be what it will, mine is happy enough, to have given you this Occasion of assuring You that I am, with the truest Esteem . . . A. Pope

Guide for Interpreting 547

Master Teacher Note Pope first published the poem in 1712 in two cantos. Two years later he expanded the work to five cantos. This later version included the supernatural elements. These were taken from Rosicrucian mythology, in which the four elements —earth, air, fire, and water—were inhabited by sylphs and gnomes. Even though invisible, they were active in human affairs—sylphs as guardian spirits and gnomes as mischief makers. In this poem Ariel is the chief sylph and Belinda's guardian.

Reading Strategy Most poetry —and certainly the mock epic —benefits from being read aloud. Pick two accomplished readers to take the parts of Belinda and the Baron in Canto V. Choose a third student to act as the narrator. Have this canto read aloud by the three students, interpreting the lines as they might be delivered on stage.

Purpose-Setting Question What elements of an epic do you find in these excerpts?

1 Literary Focus Note the use of zeugma (zōog′me), a figure of speech Pope was fond of employing. This is a device in which a word—in this case, *fall*—modifies or governs two or more words, although it makes sense with only one. The word *take,* in line 8, is another example of the figure. Ask students to be alert for this rhetorical device in the poem.

from **The Rape of the Lock**

Alexander Pope

The Rape of the Lock, a mock epic, or a humorous poem written in the style of and recalling situations from the famous epic poems of Homer, Virgil, and Milton, is based on an actual incident. When Lord Petre, a wealthy baron, cut a lock of hair from the head of the beautiful Arabella Fermor, a great quarrel developed between the lady's family and the family of Lord Petre. Following the incident, Pope's friend John Caryll suggested that Pope write a poem mocking the trivial incident to point out the absurdity of the families' reactions. In writing The Rape of the Lock, *however, Pope went far beyond the ridiculous incident that inspired it. The poem, filled with allusions to the great literary works of the past, is a poignant appraisal of the social manners and human behavior of the time.*

The first of the poem's five cantos opens with a formal statement of theme and an invocation to the Muse for poetic inspiration. Then Belinda, the poem's heroine, receives a warning from the sylph Ariel that a dreadful event will take place in her immediate future. In Canto II, during a boat ride on the Thames, an adventurous baron admires Belinda's hair and is determined to cut two bright locks from her head and keep them as a prize. Aware of the baron's desires, Ariel urges the spirits to protect Belinda.

Canto III

Close by those meads, forever crowned with flowers,
Where Thames with pride surveys his rising towers,
There stands a structure of majestic frame,[1]
Which from the neighboring Hampton takes its name.
5 Here Britain's statesmen oft the fall foredoom
Of foreign tyrants, and of nymphs at home;
Here thou, great Anna![2] whom three realms obey,

---

1. structure . . . frame: Hampton Court, a royal palace near London.
2. Anna: Queen Anne, who ruled England, Ireland, and Scotland from 1702 through 1714.

Commentary: The Mock Epic

Alexander Pope described writing a mock epic as "using a vast force to lift a feather." In his famous mock epic, *The Rape of the Lock,* Pope blows up a trivial event to epic proportions by drawing parallels between it and events in such classical works as the *Iliad,* the *Odyssey,* and the *Aeneid.* For example, the abduction of Helen in these works becomes the rape of a lock of hair. As do these classical epics, *The Rape of the Lock* begins with an invocation and a description of a hero arming for battle. In this case, however, the "hero" is the nubile belle Belinda, the "arming" is the application of her cosmetics in "the sacred rite of

THE BARGE, 1895–96
Aubrey Beardsley

10 To taste awhile the pleasures of a court;
In various talk th' instructive hours they passed,
Who gave the ball, or paid the visit last;
One speaks the glory of the British Queen,
And one describes a charming Indian screen;
15 A third interprets motions, looks, and eyes;
At every word a reputation dies.

2

from *The Rape of the Lock*   549

Humanities Note

Fine art, *The Barge* by Aubrey Beardsley. The British illustrator Aubrey Beardsley (1872–1898) achieved in his six productive years a strange and wonderful style that would have taken many artists a lifetime. His only formal art training was one year of lessons at the Westminster School of Art in London. His lifelong illness, tuberculosis, did not leave him the strength to explore oil painting or any form of artistic expression other than the pen-and-ink drawing for which he is remembered. He received his first illustration commission by chance through a bookseller he frequented. This commission led to many others and to fame as an illustrator. His career ended abruptly with his death at the age of twenty-six.

The illustrations for Alexander Pope's "The Rape of the Lock" were done for an 1896 edition of that work. *The Barge* is one of the nine pen-and-ink drawings Beardsley produced. In executing this drawing, he introduced a technique of using dots to give texture and variety to his usually severe lines. Embellished decoratively, this drawing still demonstrates Beardsley's elegance of form and his grasp of the formal rules of good composition.

You might use this question for discussion: Has the artist approached this drawing of Belinda with sincerity or satire? Explain.

2 Discussion What kind of world does Belinda live in? How "instructive" are the subjects Belinda and her friends talk about?

Pride"; and the "battle" is a game of cards. Pope even parodies Aeneas' portentous epic journey to the underworld, called here "the gloomy cave of Spleen," and Aeneas' journey up the Tiber becomes Belinda's up the Thames.

In addition, Pope makes frequent references to that great English epic, Milton's *Paradise Lost*. For example, the sylph cut in half while defending Belinda's sacred lock but magically united again recalls Milton's doughty and likewise invulnerable angels. Also, Pope's great battle between the beaus and the belles parodies Milton's battle between the angels and devils.

The play on epic conventions is obvious, but what is its intent? Our first impulse may be to answer that Pope is mocking and deflating the values of Augustan high society. This is certainly true, as far as it goes. The perspective from Homer's or Milton's view indicates that the cause celebre of the rape of the lock is a tempest in a teapot, or more appropriately, a coffee pot. Such an answer, however, ignores the complexities of tone in *The Rape of the Lock*. Perhaps the poem shows, as some critics maintain, that Pope is "as much charmed by his subject as he was critical of it" and he sensed that "the loss of the lock of hair touches a girl deeply."

Pope, then, gets to have his cake and eat it too, simultaneously satirizing Augustan manners and expressing delight in them. No wonder the poem was and is so popular!

3 **Discussion** What elements of a card game are appropriate for imitating a battle?

4 **Clarification** Belinda leads with the ace of spaces. Nine tricks make up the game. To win, one person must take at least five.

5 **Clarification** She plays the two of spades.

Snuff, or the fan,[3] supply each pause of chat,
With singing, laughing, ogling, and all that.
    Meanwhile, declining from the noon of day,
20 The sun obliquely shoots his burning ray;
The hungry judges soon the sentence sign,
And wretches hang that jurymen may dine;
The merchant from th' Exchange[4] returns in peace,
And the long labors of the toilet[5] cease.
25 Belinda now, whom thirst of fame invites,
Burns to encounter two adventurous knights,
At omber[6] singly to decide their doom;
And swells her breast with conquests yet to come.
Straight the three bands prepare in arms to join,
30 Each band the number of the sacred nine.[7]
Soon as she spreads her hand, th' aerial guard
Descend, and sit on each important card:
First Ariel perched upon a Matadore,[8]
Then each, according to the rank they bore;
35 For sylphs, yet mindful of their ancient race,
Are, as when women, wondrous fond of place.
    Behold, four kings in majesty revered,
With hoary whiskers and a forky beard;
And four fair queens whose hands sustain a flower,
40 Th' expressive emblem of their softer power;
Four knaves in garbs succinct,[9] a trusty band,
Caps on their heads, and halberts[10] in their hand;
And particolored troops, a shining train,
Draw forth to combat on the velvet plain.
45   The skilful nymph reviews her force with care:
Let spades be trumps! she said, and trumps they were.
    Now move to war her sable Matadores,
In show like leaders of the swarthy Moors.
Spadillio[11] first, unconquerable Lord!
50 Led off two captive trumps, and swept the board.
As many more Manillio[12] forced to yield,
And marched a victor from the verdant field.[13]

---

3. snuff . . . fan: At the time, gentlemen commonly took snuff, and ladies usually carried a fan.
4. Exchange: The London financial center where merchants, bankers, and brokers conducted business.
5. toilet: Dressing tables.
6. omber: A popular card game.
7. sacred nine: A reference to the nine Muses of Greek mythology.
8. Matadore: A powerful card that could take a trick.
9. succinct (sək siŋkt′): Belted.
10. halberts: Long-handled weapons.
11. Spadillio: The ace of spades.
12. Manillio: The two of spades.
13. verdant field: The card table, covered with a green cloth.

Primary Source

Periodicals like the *Spectator,* the *Tatler,* and the *Guardian* were extremely important in building a readership for Pope's work. They encouraged the middle classes, women especially, to read literature and tutored them in its appreciation. One reason why such periodicals are fascinating for us today is that they also reflect the world that Pope depicted in *The Rape of the Lock.*

What was upper-class society like in Pope's day? Could anyone be as foppish as the Baron in *The Rape of the Lock*? Here is an excerpt from the *Tatler* (December 29, 1709) listing the personal effects of a deceased gentleman, a beau not very different from the Baron in Pope's mock epic:

"A very rich Tweezer-Case, containing Twelve Instruments for the Use of each Hour in the Day.

    Four Pounds of scented Snuff, with Three gilt Snuff-Boxes; one of them with an invisible Hinge, and a Looking-glass in the Lid.

    Two more of Ivory with the Portraitures on their Lids of Two Ladies of the Town . . .

    A Sword with a Steel Diamond Hilt . . .

Him Basto[14] followed, but his fate more hard
Gained but one trump and one plebeian card.
55 With his broad saber next, a chief in years,
The hoary majesty of spades appears,
Puts forth one manly leg, to sight revealed,
The rest, his many-colored robe concealed.
The rebel knave, who dares his prince engage,
60 Proves the just victim of his royal rage.
Even mighty Pam,[15] that kings and queens o'erthrew
And mowed down armies in the fights of loo,
Sad chance of war! now destitute of aid,
Falls undistinguished by the victor spade!
65   Thus far both armies to Belinda yield;
Now to the baron fate inclines the field.
His warlike Amazon her host invades,
Th' imperial consort of the crown of spades.
The club's black tyrant first her victim died,
70 Spite of his haughty mien, and barbarous pride.
What boots[16] the regal circle on his head,
His giant limbs, in state unwieldy spread;
That long behind he trails his pompous robe,
And, of all monarchs, only grasps the globe?
75   The baron now his diamonds pours apace;
Th' embroidered king who shows but half his face,
And his refulgent queen, with powers combined
Of broken troops an easy conquest find.
Clubs, diamonds, hearts, in wild disorder seen,
80 With throngs promiscuous strew the level green.
Thus when dispersed a routed army runs,
Of Asia's troops, and Afric's sable sons,
With like confusion different nations fly,
Of various habit, and of various dye,
85 The pierced battalions disunited fall,
In heaps on heaps; one fate o'erwhelms them all.
    The knave of diamonds tries his wily arts,
And wins (oh shameful chance!) the queen of hearts.
At this, the blood the virgin's cheek forsook,
90 A livid paleness spreads o'er all her look;
She sees, and trembles at th' approaching ill,
Just in the jaws of ruin, and codille.[17]
And now (as oft in some distempered state)
On one nice trick depends the general fate.

14. Basto: The ace of clubs.
15. Pam: The knave of clubs, the highest card in the game called "100."
16. what boots: Of what benefit is.
17. codille: A term meaning the defeat of a hand of cards.

6 Clarification She plays the ace of clubs, the third highest card.

7 Clarification She plays the king of spades and wins her fourth trick. But this uses up the last of her trump cards.

8 Clarification She plays the king of clubs, which the Baron trumps with his queen of spades.

9 Clarification The Baron plays his high diamonds, for Belinda is out of trump cards.

10 Clarification He takes a trick with the queen of diamonds

11 Clarification His jack of diamonds takes her queen of hearts, since she cannot follow suit.

Six clean Packs of Cards, a Quart of Orange-Flower-
Water, a Pair of *French* Scissors, a Tooth-pick Case, and an
Eyebrow Brush.
Ask students to discuss the picture they form of this man after
reading the list of his personal effects.

12 Clarification The Baron plays his ace of hearts. Since hearts are not trumps, though, this card is worth less than the face cards of the heart suit. Belinda wins.

Humanities Note

Fine art, *The Rape of the Lock* by Aubrey Beardsley. The drawing entitled *The Rape of the Lock* is one of the nine produced by Aubrey Beardsley for an 1896 edition of Alexander Pope's comic poem of the same name. The satiric nature of the poem appealed to Beardsley's sense of the burlesque. He depicts the incident of the cutting of the hair with a mocking humor comparable to Pope's. The rococo extravagance of the drawing room and attire of the figures also matches the satiric exaggeration of the situation by Pope. The artist's appreciation of the poet's wit and humor adds an extra element to these drawings.

You may wish to discuss the following with your class: In his poem Pope glorifies a trivial incident. Would you say that the artist does the same in his drawing? Explain.

An ace of hearts steps forth; the king unseen
Lurked in her hand, and mourned his captive queen.
He springs to vengeance with an eager pace,
And falls like thunder on the prostrate ace.
The nymph exulting fills with shouts the sky;
100 The walls, the woods, and long canals reply.
    Oh thoughtless mortals! ever blind to fate,
Too soon dejected, and too soon elate.
Sudden, these honors shall be snatched away,
And cursed forever this victorious day.

THE RAPE OF THE LOCK, 1895–96
Aubrey Beardsley

552   The Restoration and the Eighteenth Century

Grammar in Action

An **exclamation mark** calls attention to an exclamatory sentence, an imperative sentence, or an interjection. When writers use exclamation marks to emphasize the drama of a statement, they usually do so sparingly. Overuse of this endmark can tire or annoy a reader, as in the following example.

OVERUSE OF THE EXCLAMATION MARK: Imagine her shock and horror! When she opened the door to her apartment, all her jellybeans were on the floor! And the dog was shamelessly devouring them!

Reading such a series of exclamatory statements is like being hit over the head repeatedly with a rubber mallet. Instead of being powerfully dramatic, the description just seems silly.

In "The Rape of the Lock," however, Pope deliberately overuses the exclamation mark in order to achieve a comic effect. When the Baron is thinking of cutting Belinda's lock, Pope uses three exclamation marks in rapid succession:

Ah cease, rash youth! desist ere 'tis too late,/Fear the just gods, and think of Scylla's fate!/Changed to a bird, and sent to flit in air,/She dearly pays for Nisus' injured hair!

105   Fo lo! the board with cups and spoons is crowned,
The berries crackle, and the mill turns round;[18]
On shining altars of Japan[19] they raise
The silver lamp; the fiery spirits blaze;
From silver spouts the grateful liquors glide,
110 While China's earth[20] receives the smoking tide.
At once they gratify their scent and taste,
And frequent cups prolong the rich repast.
Straight hover round the fair her airy band;
Some, as she sipped, the fuming liquor fanned,
115 Some o'er her lap their careful plumes displayed,
Trembling, and conscious of the rich brocade.
Coffee (which makes the politician wise,
And see through all things with his half-shut eyes)
Sent up in vapors to the baron's brain
120 New stratagems, the radiant lock to gain.
Ah cease, rash youth! desist ere 'tis too late,
Fear the just gods, and think of Scylla's fate![21]
Changed to a bird, and sent to flit in air,
She dearly pays for Nisus' injured hair!
125   But when to mischief mortals bend their will,
How soon they find fit instruments of ill!
Just then, Clarissa drew with tempting grace   ☐ **13**
A two-edged weapon from her shining case:
So ladies in romance assist their knight,
130 Present the spear, and arm him for the fight.
He takes the gift with reverence, and extends
The little engine[22] on his fingers' ends;
This just behind Belinda's neck he spread,
As o'er the fragrant steams she bends her head.
135 Swift to the lock a thousand sprites repair,
A thousand wings, by turns, blow back the hair;
And thrice they twitched the diamond in her ear;
Thrice she looked back, and thrice the foe drew near.
Just in that instant, anxious Ariel sought
140 The close recesses of the virgin's thought;
As on the nosegay in her breast reclined,   **14**
He watched th' ideas rising in her mind,
Sudden he viewed, in spite of all her art,
An earthly lover lurking at her heart.[23]

---

18. the berries . . . round: The coffee beans are ground in a hand mill at the table.
19. altars of Japan: Small imported lacquer tables.
20. China's earth: Earthenware cups imported from China.
21. Scylla's (sĭl′ əz) **fate:** Scylla, the daughter of King Nisus, was turned into a sea bird because she cut off the lock of her father's hair on which his safety depended and sent it to his enemy.
22. engine: Instrument.
23. earthly lover . . . heart: If in her heart Belinda wants the baron to succeed, they cannot protect her.

from *The Rape of the Lock*   553

13 Clarification Clarissa is an unidentified friend of Belinda. What purpose does Clarissa have?

14 Clarification Note that Ariel loses his power, for Belinda's thoughts are now possessed by an earthly lover.

This outburst is clearly a case of exclamatory overkill (the potential deed is not equivalent to murder, as in the case of Scylla) and Pope indulges in it with a wink at the audience.

Student Activity 1. Find other instances in the poem where Pope deliberately misuses the exclamation mark for comic purposes. Explain how this misuse is in harmony with the mock–heroic genre.

Student Activity 2. Write a dramatic account of a trivial event, deliberately misusing the exclamation mark for comic purposes.

15 **Literary Focus** Note the use of zeugma.

16 **Discussion** What is the victor's "glorious prize"?

145   Amazed, confused, he found his power expired,
    Resigned to fate, and with a sigh retired.
       The peer now spreads the glittering forfex[24] wide,
    T' enclose the lock; now joins it, to divide.
    Even then, before the fatal engine closed,
150   A wretched sylph too fondly interposed;
    Fate urged the shears, and cut the sylph in twain,
    (But airy substance soon unites again).
    The meeting points the sacred hair dissever
    From the fair head, forever, and forever!
155   Then flashed the living lightning from her eyes,
    And screams of horror rend th' affrighted skies.
    Not louder shrieks to pitying heaven are cast,
    When husbands, or when lap dogs breathe their last;
    Or when rich China vessels fallen from high,
160   In glittering dust, and painted fragments lie!
       "Let wreaths of triumph now my temples twine,"
    The victor cried, "the glorious prize is mine!"
    While fish in streams, or birds delight in air,
    Or in a coach and six the British Fair,
165   As long as *Atalantis*[25] shall be read,
    Or the small pillow grace a lady's bed,
    While visits shall be paid on solemn days,
    When numerous wax lights in bright order blaze,
    While nymphs take treats, or assignations give,
170   So long my honor, name, and praise shall live!
    What time would spare, from steel receives its date,[26]
    And monuments, like men, submit to fate!
    Steel could the labor of the gods destroy,
    And strike to dust th' imperial towers of Troy;
175   Steel could the works of mortal pride confound,
    And hew triumphal arches to the ground.
    What wonder then, fair nymph! thy hairs should feel,
    The conquering force of unresisted steel?

from Canto V

    In Canto IV, *after Umbriel, "a dusky, melancholy sprite," empties a bag filled with "the force of female lungs, sighs, sobs, and passions, and the war of tongues" onto Belinda's head, the lady erupts over the loss of her lock. Then she "bids her beau," Sir Plume, to "demand the precious hairs," but Plume is unable to persuade the baron to return the hair.*

---

24. forfex: Scissors.
25. *Atalantis*: A popular book of scandalous gossip.
26. receives its date: Is destroyed.

Commentary: True Wit

In *An Essay on Criticism* (1711), Pope discussed the role of wit in literature and memorably defined "True Wit" as "Nature to advantage dress'd/What oft was thought but ne'er so well express'd." This impressive poetic essay, written by a young man of twenty–two, appeared at a crucial time in literary history. Earlier, the term *wit* had been associated with poetic inspiration and the highly imaginative conceits of metaphysical poets like Donne. More recently, however, Dryden had defined wit as "a propriety of thoughts and words," stressing decorum over scintillation. Just as significant was Locke's influential discrimination between "false wit," responsible for the deceptions of expressive language, and a more appropriate kind of wit, which performed the functions of analysis and judgment. Wit was also viewed suspiciously by the Protestant middle–class, who associated it with the immorality of the Restoration period.

    At the other extreme, the Restoration dramatist Wycherley, launching a new career as a lyric poet, argued that "To sacrifice . . . flashes of wit to an ordered design . . . is to sacrifice poetry itself . . ." Pope could not agree with this radical opinion and

In the beginning of Canto V, *Clarissa, a level-headed nymph, tries to bring an end to the commotion, but rather than being greeted with applause, her speech is followed by a battle cry.*

"To arms, to arms!" the fierce virago[27] cries,
And swift as lightning to the combat flies.
All side in parties, and begin th' attack;
Fans clap, silks rustle, and tough whalebones crack;
5 Heroes' and heroines' shouts confusedly rise,
And bass and treble voices strike the skies.
No common weapons in their hands are found,
Like gods they fight, nor dread a mortal wound.
    So when bold Homer makes the gods engage,
10 And heavenly breasts with human passions rage;
'Gainst Pallas, Mars, Latona, Hermes[28] arms;
And all Olympus[29] rings with loud alarms:
Jove's[30] thunder roars, heaven trembles all around,
Blue Neptune[31] storms, the bellowing deeps resound;
15 Earth shakes her nodding towers, the ground gives way,
And the pale ghosts start at the flash of day!
    Triumphant Umbriel on a sconce's height[32]
Clapped his glad wings, and sat to view the fight;
Propped on their bodkin spears,[33] the sprites survey
20 The growing combat, or assist the fray.
    While through the press enraged Thalestris[34] flies,
And scatters death around from both her eyes,
A beau and witling[35] perished in the throng,
One died in metaphor, and one in song.
25 "O cruel nymph! a living death I bear,"
Cried Dapperwit, and sunk beside his chair.
A mournful glance Sir Fopling[36] upwards cast,
"Those eyes are made so killing"—was his last.

17

---

27. virago (və rā′ gō): Scolding woman.
28. Pallas . . . Hermes: Gods who directed the Trojan War. Pallas and Hermes supported the Greeks, while Mars and Latona sided with the Trojans.
29. Olympus: The mountain which was supposed to be the home of the gods.
30. Jove's: Referring to Jupiter, the ruler of the Gods in Roman mythology; identified with Zeus in Greek mythology.
31. Neptune: The Roman god of the sea; identified with Poseidon in Greek mythology.
32. sconce's height: A candleholder attached to the wall.
33. bodkin spears: Large needles.
34. Thalestris (thə lĕs′ tris): An Amazon (a race of female warriors supposed to have lived in Scythia) who played a role in the medieval tales of Alexander the Great.
35. witling: A person who fancies himself or herself a wit.
36. Dapperwit, Sir Fopling: Names of amusing characters in comedies of the time.

from *The Rape of the Lock*   555

---

dared to tell the older poet so in correspondence. The young poet, however, was faced with the problem of reaffirming the importance of wit in an increasingly sober and scientific age, while avoiding the "wild heap of wit" that Wycherley advocated.

"True Wit," for Pope, related more to the balance of the whole work than to the sputtering fireworks in particular lines or images. At the same time, wit was not merely decorous or proper. It was a vital faculty that derived from the creative power of "Nature" itself. By "Nature" Pope understood not just the natural world or even human nature but a godlike entity that actively promoted universality. Dressing "Nature to Advantage" meant finding universal values. Similarly, "What oft was thought . . ." referred not to platitudes but to widely applicable truths.

Pope believed that the works of ancient authors like Homer were superlative embodiments of "True Wit." These works had stood the test of time because they spoke to all of humanity. As Pope wrote, "To copy nature is to copy them." That he did not mean slavish imitation, however, is evident from his own writing. He had immersed himself in the ancients and yet had produced, in his biographer Maynard Mack's words, "a fully contemporary 'conversational' idiom, pithy, pointed, witty, and smart. . . ."

Thus on Maeander's[37] flowery margin lies
30 Th' expiring swan, and as he sings he dies.
    When bold Sir Plume had drawn Clarissa down,
Chloe[38] stepped in, and killed him with a frown;
She smiled to see the doughty hero slain,
But, at her smile, the beau revived again.
35   Now Jove suspends his golden scales in air,
Weighs the men's wits against the lady's hair;
The doubtful beam long nods from side to side;
At length the wits mount up, the hairs subside.
    See, fierce Belinda on the baron flies,
40 With more than usual lightning in her eyes;
Nor feared the chief th' unequal fight to try,
Who sought no more than on his foe to die.
But this bold lord with manly strength endued,
She with one finger and a thumb subdued:
45 Just where the breath of life his nostrils drew,
A charge of snuff the wily virgin threw;
The gnomes direct, to every atom just,
The pungent grains of titillating dust.
Sudden with starting tears each eye o'erflows,
50 And the high dome re-echoes to his nose.
    "Now meet thy fate," incensed Belinda cried,
And drew a deadly bodkin[39] from her side . . .
    "Boast not my fall," he cried, "insulting foe!
Thou by some other shalt be laid as low.
55 Nor think, to die dejects my lofty mind;
All that I dread is leaving you behind!
Rather than so, ah let me still survive,
And burn in Cupid's flames—but burn alive."
    "Restore the lock!" she cries; and all around
60 "Restore the lock!" the vaulted roofs rebound.
Not fierce Othello in so loud a strain
Roared for the handkerchief that caused his pain.[40]
But see how oft ambitious aims are crossed,
And chiefs contend till all the prize is lost!
65 The lock, obtained with guilt, and kept with pain,
In every place is sought, but sought in vain.
With such a prize no mortal must be blessed,
So Heaven decrees! with Heaven who can contest?

---

37. Maeander's: Referring to a river in Asia.
38. Chloe (klō′ ē): The heroine of the ancient Greek pastoral romance, *Daphnis and Chloe*.
39. bodkin: An ornamental pin shaped like a dagger.
40. not . . . pain: In Shakespeare's *Othello*, the hero is convinced that his wife is being unfaithful to him when she cannot find the handkerchief that he had given her. Actually, the handkerchief had been taken by the villain, Iago, who uses it as part of his evil plot.

THE BATTLE OF THE BEAUX AND BELLES
Aubrey Beardsley

Fine art, *The Battle of the Beaux and the Belles* by Aubrey Beardsley. This drawing is one of the nine pen-and-ink drawings by Beardsley for the 1896 edition of Alexander Pope's "The Rape of the Lock." This rococo scene is executed with the skill and mocking wit for which Beardsley is noted. The abundance of ruffles and flounces and the extravagance of embroidery and pattern serve to emphasize the silliness of the situation depicted. Beardsley's satiric style appropriately illustrates this social parody by Pope.

You may wish to ask this question: Do you feel that the elaborate decorative style of the drawing is similar to the language of the poem? Explain.

from *The Rape of the Lock*   557

19 **Discussion** What happens, finally, to the lock of Belinda's hair? In light of the poem, is this an appropriate resolution? Why, or why not?

Reader's Response Describe a great dispute you saw resulting from a disagreement over some minor matter.

Some thought it mounted to the lunar sphere,
70   Since all things lost on earth are treasured there.
There heroes' wits are kept in ponderous vases,
And beaux' in snuffboxes and tweezer cases.
There broken vows and deathbed alms are found,
And lovers' hearts with ends of riband bound . . .
75   But trust the Muse—she saw it upward rise,
Though marked by none but quick, poetic eyes . . .
A sudden star, it shot through liquid[41] air
And drew behind a radiant trail of hair . . .[42]
       Then cease, bright Nymph! to mourn thy ravished hair,
80   Which adds new glory to the shining sphere!
Not all the tresses that fair head can boast,
Shall draw such envy as the lock you lost.
For, after all the murders of your eye,[43]
When, after millions slain, yourself shall die;
85   When those fair suns shall set, as set they must,
And all those tresses shall be laid in dust,
This lock, the Muse shall consecrate to fame,
And midst the stars inscribe Belinda's name.

---

41. liquid: Clear.
42. trail of hair: The word "comet" comes from a Greek word meaning "long-haired."
43. murders . . . eye: Lovers struck down by her glances.

THINKING ABOUT THE SELECTION
Recalling

1. (a) In what activity is Belinda engaged during the first half of Canto III? (b) What is the outcome?
2. (a) What is the group doing when the "berries crackle, and the mill turns round"?
3. (a) What is the "two-edged weapon" that Clarissa gives the baron? (b) How many times does the baron fail to get the lock of hair? (c) How does Belinda respond when he does get it? (d) How does the baron react?
4. (a) In Canto V, what noises accompany the attack that follows Belinda's cry of "To arms, to arms!"? (b) With what weapon does Belinda threaten the baron's life? (c) What does she demand that he do?
5. (a) Who has possession of the lock at the end of Canto V? (b) What do some people think has happened to it?

Interpreting

6. Why do you think Pope precedes the trivial episodes in Canto III with such a grisly image as "wretches hang that jurymen may dine"?
7. What similarity is there between Pope's description of the omber game and his description of the events following the theft of the lock?

8. Lines 79–88 in Canto V are "elegant spoofing," according to one critic. Yet in a sense Pope made the poem's extravagant claim come true. How did he do it?

Applying

9. Pope based *The Rape of the Lock* on an actual incident. What incident in the news today might provide the basis for a similar mock epic? (Your freewriting on page 547 may supply an answer to this question.)

ANALYZING LITERATURE
Understanding Mock Epic

A **mock epic** is a humorous narrative poem done in the manner of a true epic. It may resemble classical epics such as the *Odyssey* or the *Iliad*. It may contain elements of English epics such as *Beowulf* or *Paradise Lost*. Or, as in *The Rape of the Lock,* a mock epic may show traces of both types. In either case it will have characters who perform what appear to be heroic deeds. It may also contain references from mythology and include impossible or supernatural events.

1. (a) What are three trivial incidents in *The Rape of the Lock* that Pope presents in a heroic manner? (b) What are three characteristics of the heroic manner that the poem exhibits?
2. What are some of the mythical creatures, including deities and muses, mentioned in the poem? Try to find at least seven.

CRITICAL THINKING AND READING
Inferring the Author's Purpose

Up to a point, you know the author's purpose in writing *The Rape of the Lock*. Pope is mocking the overwrought reaction of two noble families to a hair-cutting prank. In his own words, Pope is "using a vast force to lift a feather." But that is not his only intent. The author has a more serious purpose than just memorializing a silly incident. To understand what it is, you have to read between the lines—to infer—what Pope believes about human behavior and social manners. The

following lines from the poem give clues to the author's purpose. First interpret the lines in your own words. Then write a general statement expressing what you believe to be Pope's purpose in writing the poem.

1. "Oh thoughtless mortals! ever blind to fate,/ Too soon dejected, and too soon elate." (Canto III, lines 101–102)
2. "But when to mischief mortals bend their will,/How soon they find fit instruments of ill!" (Canto III, lines 125–126)
3. "But see how oft ambitious aims are crossed,/ And chiefs contend till all the prize is lost!" (Canto V, lines 63–64)

THINKING AND WRITING
Writing About Tone

Tone is sometimes easier to recognize than to describe. You can easily see that the tone of *The Rape of the Lock* is high-flown and heroic. But what are the features of Pope's language that lend the poem its distinctive tone? Ask yourself these questions. You will find it helpful to take notes in answering them.

1. How do the words in the poem differ from the words you use in ordinary speaking and writing? (Consider figurative as well as literal meanings of words.)
2. How does the arrangement of words in sentences differ from that in most sentences in everyday English? (Pay attention to inverted elements, modifier placement, parallelism, and so on.)
3. More broadly, what is the total effect of Pope's language? (Look at his overstatement, allusions, choice of details—indeed, anything that makes the poem high-flown and mock heroic.)

Use your answers to these questions to write a composition on the tone of *The Rape of the Lock*. Begin by stating what you believe the tone of the poem to be. Support that statement by citing examples from the poem. Use quotations. Revise, checking especially your organization and coherence.

Closure and Extension

ANSWERS TO THINKING ABOUT THE SELECTION
Recalling

1. (a) Belinda is engaged in a social "hour," which includes a card game. (b) Belinda beats the Baron at omber, the card game.
2. They are reflecting on the outcome of the card game.

3. (a) Clarissa gives the Baron a pair of scissors. (b) The Baron fails three times. (c) She screams with horror. (d) The Baron cries out in glee.
4. (a) The shouts of people, the rustling of their clothes, and handclaps are likened to thunder, roaring gods, and the ringing of loud alarms. (b) Belinda threatens the Baron with a hairpin. (c) She demands that he return the lock of hair.

5. (a) In the end the lock flies heavenward. (b) It changes into a star in the heavens, bearing Belinda's name.

Interpreting

6. Answers will differ but should include the idea that such biting satire is quite typical of Pope.
7. Answers will differ but should include the idea that both are elevated to the dignity of a true epic by the use of innumerable allusions.

8. Answers will differ but should include the notion that Pope, by immortalizing Belinda in this poem, made good on his extravagent claim.

Applying

9. Answers will differ. Some students may find an incident involving celebrities.

ANSWERS TO ANALYZING LITERATURE

1. (a) Pope presents in a heroic manner the card game, the theft of the lock, and the battle scene following it. (b) The poem includes a heroine, a battle scene, and the intervention of gods and goddesses (sylphs and gnomes) in human affairs.
2. Among the creatures listed are Scylla, Pallas, Hermes, Olympus, Jove, Neptune, Muses, and Cupid.

ANSWERS TO CRITICAL THINKING AND READING

1. Most people do not consider the long-term ramifications of an action, so they either celebrate, or mourn, its hoped-for ends before the results are really known.
2. People are usually quite ingenious in devising ways to get what they want and in rationalizing the means they use to gain the desired end.
3. Selfish ambition keeps people from compromising, preferring instead to see that no one wins if they themselves do not.
   Students will express differently Pope's purpose, but they all should see that it is primarily moral and aims to uphold conventional norms of conduct and behavior.

Challenge Have students compare the satiric style of Swift and of Addison and Steele with that of Pope. Which is the most biting? Which the cleverest? Which has the most telling impact?

THINKING AND WRITING

Publishing Student Writing You may want to have several students volunteer to read aloud their compositions.

A little learning is a dangerous
thing;
Drink deep, or taste not the
Pierian spring . . .

Honor and shame from no condition rise;
Act well your part; there all
the honor lies.

'Tis education forms the common
mind:
Just as the twig is bent, the
tree's inclined.

Hope springs eternal in the
human breast:
Man never is, but always to be
blest.

Writing/Prior Knowledge You might provide your students with some brief, witty quotations from Bartlett's or some other collection of quotations. They can then versify them.

Spelling Tip Point out the silent letters *th* in *isthmus*.

Vocabulary

Preteach the following vocabulary words:
isthmus (is′məs) n.: A narrow strip of land, with water on each side, con-necting two larger land masses (l. 3)
stoic (stō′ik) n.: A person indifferent to pleasure or pain (l. 6)
disabused (dis′ə byo͞ozd′) adj.: Freed from false ideas (l. 14)

GUIDE FOR INTERPRETING

Writer's Techniques	*from* **An Essay on Man**

Heroic Couplet. A heroic couplet is a rhyming pair of lines in iambic pentameter. Since it requires the clear thought and precise wording admired by classically inspired writers, it was a favorite verse form among Restoration and eighteenth-century poets. Dryden, Swift, and Pope are among the best-known users of the form. The heroic couplet, concise and quotable, is often used in satire. The following lines from Pope's *The Rape of the Lock* are a heroic couplet.

U / U / U / U / U /
He springs to vengeance with an eager pace,

U / U / U / U / U /
And falls like thunder on the prostrate ace.

Writing

Many of Pope's heroic couplets are closed couplets—that is, their two lines represent a complete thought.

True wit is Nature to advantage dress'd,
What oft was thought, but ne'er so well expressed.

That couplet, a complete thought, is from Pope's *Essay on Criticism*. Create a closed couplet; it will consist of two rhyming lines with ten syllables each, the stress falling on every second syllable. As a closed couplet, it will make a complete, understand-able statement, ideally in an effective and memorable way.

Primary Source

The form of the heroic couplet makes it an easy form to mock and makes Pope, because of his tendency to quarrel with others, an easy target as well. The following is an excerpt of a parody of Pope's style from *A Pipe of Tobacco* (1736) by Isaac Hawkins Browne.

The parody is agreeable and skillful, and though it lacks any bite, was very much admired in its own day, as was its author. Although sensitive about his work, Pope spoke highly of Browne and his parody, remarking: "Browne is an excellent copyist, and those who talk ill of him are very much in the wrong."

. . . Nor less, the critic owns thy genial aid,
While supperless he plies the piddling trade.
What tho' to love and soft delights a foe,
By ladies hated, hated by the beau,
Yet social freedom, long to courts unknown,
Fair health, fair truth, and virtue are thy own.
Come to thy poet, come with healing wings,
And let me taste thee unexcis'd by kings.

Objectives

1 To introduce the heroic couplet as a literary form
2 To generalize about emotion and intellect
3 To respond to neoclassical criticism

Support Material

Teaching Portfolio
Teacher Backup, p. 649
Usage and Mechanics Work-sheet, p. 652
Vocabulary Check, p. 653
Analyzing Literature Worksheet, *Understanding the Heroic Cou-plet,* p. 654
Language Worksheet, *Under-standing Diction,* p. 656
Selection Test, p. 658

from An Essay on Man

Alexander Pope

An Essay on Man is an examination of human nature, society, and morals. In describing the work, Pope comments that it is "a general map of man, marking out . . . the greater parts, their extent, their limits, and their connection." The following excerpt is from the second epistle, in which Pope attempts to show how it is possible for man to achieve a psychological harmony through self-understanding and self-love.

Know then thyself, presume not God to scan;
The proper study of mankind is man.
Placed on this isthmus of a middle state,
A being darkly wise, and rudely great:
5   With too much knowledge for the skeptic side,
With too much weakness for the stoic's pride,
He hangs between; in doubt to act, or rest;
In doubt to deem himself a god, or beast;
In doubt his mind or body to prefer;
10   Born but to die, and reasoning but to err;
Alike in ignorance, his reason such,
Whether he thinks too little, or too much:
Chaos of thought and passion, all confused;
Still by himself abused, or disabused;
15   Created half to rise, and half to fall;
Great lord of all things, yet a prey to all;
Sole judge of truth, in endless error hurled:
The glory, jest, and riddle of the world!

from *An Essay on Man*   561

Master Teacher Note Pope's *Essay on Man* was never completed. It's purpose was, in his own words, "to vindicate the ways of God to man." The *Essay,* or the part of it that was completed, is made up of four Epistles. The first deals with the order and goodness of the world and the right of man to be a part of it. The third deals with man in the society he created; and the fourth deals with happiness.

Presentation

Motivation/Prior Knowledge Challenge your students to find any statement here that is not a wise and memorable description of the human condition.

Purpose-Setting   Question Pope's poetry is noted for its compression of language—for the clarity, glitter, beauty, and exactness of his phrasing. Which couplets do you find remarkable for these qualities? Which might you wish to memorize?

1 Discussion How does the poet show that man's condition is a middle state?

2 Discussion What purpose does the repetition of *doubt* serve in reinforcing the poet's point of view?

3 Discussion What is Pope's view of our mental powers? In general, how would you sum up Pope's description of man in these lines? Do you agree or disagree with his view?

4 Discussion Reread the closing line. Give an example of present-day man as the glory of the world, as the jest of the world, and as the riddle of the world. What actions might portray man in each of these phrases?

Reader's Response What else, besides man, do you think the proper study of mankind might include?

Challenge It has been said that Pope has been kept alive as a poet more because of his way with words than by his philosophy. Do these lines suggest that he was a shallow-thinker?

Closure and Extension

1. The proper study of mankind, says Pope, is man.
2. (a) Too much knowledge keeps man from becoming a skeptic. (b) Too much weakness keeps man from becoming a stoic.
3. The word *doubt* suggests a world of chaos and error.

Interpreting

4. (a) At one end of the isthmus is the skeptic (or beast); (b) on the other is the stoic (or god).
5. The line suggests that man has trouble deciding whether to be ruled by his mind or by his passions.
6. Answers will differ but may include the idea that a person should always be as self-critical as possible, knowing that great care must be exercised to avoid errors of judgment.

Applying

7. Answers will differ. However, encourage your students to support their opinions with reasons and, if possible, references to works of didactic literature.

ANSWERS TO ANALYZING LITERATURE

1. The words *thyself* and *presume* (line 1), *mankind* (line 2), *between* (line 7), *himself* (line 8), and *alike* (line 11) function as iambs.
2. (a) In lines 7–8 the words *rest* and *beast* are examples of near rhyme, in which there are changes within the vowel sounds of words meant to rhyme. (b) In the "Rape of the Lock" lines 5–6, 7–8, 27–28, 29–30, 45–46, 49–50, and 111–112 in Canto III are near rhymes. In Canto V lines 7–8, 69–70, 79–80, and 81–82 are examples. Near rhyme is a perfectly acceptable technique in poetry.

ANSWERS TO CRITICAL THINKING AND READING

1. Answers will differ but should in-

THINKING ABOUT THE SELECTION
Recalling

1. What does Pope say should be the object of man's study?
2. According to Pope, what prevents man from being (a) a skeptic? (b) a stoic?
3. What word, repeated three times, suggests the world of chaos and error in which human beings exist?

Interpreting

4. Pope writes that man stands on an "isthmus of a middle state." He describes the middle state in detail. In a single word, what is (a) at one end of the isthmus? (b) at the other end?
5. What do you think Pope means by the line, "In doubt his mind or body to prefer"?
6. "Know then thyself," writes Pope. How can a person "in mindless error hurled" achieve that goal?

Applying

7. Most writers today reject the idea of literature presenting an obvious moral. Pope believed just the opposite. He felt that poetry has a didactic, or instructional, role to play. What do you think?

ANALYZING LITERATURE
Understanding a Heroic Couplet

A heroic couplet is a pair of rhymed lines in iambic pentameter. An *iamb* is a metrical foot consisting of one short syllable followed by one long syllable or one unstressed syllable followed by one stressed syllable. The word *apply* (ə plī′), for instance, could function as an iamb:

$$\overset{\cup}{\text{ap}}\overset{/}{\text{ply}}$$

apply

1. Find one word that functions as an iamb in each of the following lines: 1, 2, 7, 8, 11.
2. Since it is a heroic couplet, lines 7–8 should rhyme, but they seem not to. (a) What explanation can you suggest for this apparent mistake? (Hint: Look up in a dictionary the

pronunciation of the adjective *bestial.*) (b) Find five similarly nonrhyming pairs of words in *The Rape of the Lock*. How can you explain them?

CRITICAL THINKING AND READING
Generalizing

To some extent—except for stable religious convictions—each era sets its own moral and intellectual standards. What is viewed as acceptable in one century may seem outrageous in another. For example, the word *leg* (referring to that part of the human anatomy) was considered so scandalous by Victorians that even chairs and tables were said to have *limbs*. Today the word *leg* seems innocuous.

1. If Pope's observations represent the thought of his day, how did people in the eighteenth century view the relationship between the intellect and the emotions?
2. What differences, if any, do you see in that relationship today?

THINKING AND WRITING
Responding to Neoclassical Criticism

In the preface to his poem "Religio Laici," John Dryden offers his critical opinion of how poetry should be written:

> The expressions of a poem designed purely for instruction ought to be plain and natural, and yet majestic; for the poet is . . . a kind of lawgiver, and those three qualities which I have named are proper to the legislative style.

In an essay of no more than one page, state (1) whether you agree with Dryden as to how a poem "purely for instruction" should be written, and (2) whether you think *An Essay on Man* (based on the excerpt you have read) has the three elements named. Draw freely from the poem to support your opinion. When you revise, make sure you have provided adequate support for your opinion.

clude the idea that in Pope's time people believed in a rational order of things and in their willingness to subordinate their emotions to the intellect.
2. Answers will differ but will likely include the idea that today people are more trusting in the free expression of emotion.

THINKING AND WRITING

Publishing Student Writing Students with differing opinions might read their essays to the class. Classmates could then evaluate their essays.

The Age of Johnson

Oliver Goldsmith, James Boswell,
And Samuel Johnson At The
Mitre Tavern
Nineteenth-century colored engraving
The Granger Collection

Engraving, *Oliver Goldsmith, James Boswell, and Samuel Johnson at the Mitre Tavern.* This engraving presents three men of the period who frequently spent time in conversation. Johnson is on the right in this picture, the admiring Boswell in the back, and Oliver Goldsmith, the playwright and poet, is on the left.

More About the Author Samuel
Johnson's "theme of themes," as
it has been called, is expressed in
the title of his poem "The Vanity of
Human Wishes." By this Johnson
means the hunger of imagination
which preys upon life to make us
see things as we wish they were
rather than as they are—a representative eighteenth-century
viewpoint. What relevance does
Johnson's view hold for the present day?

Critical Evaluation It is difficult
to summarize the concepts that
informed Johnson's efforts on the
dictionary he produced. But in
an effort to do so, co-authors
James Sledd and Gwin Kolb
have written the following on his
theories of language: ". . . They
are theories which many writers
had expressed before him.
Words, he says, are the signs of
ideas, names imposed by man,
not by God, and hence arbitrary
and governed by custom. On the
other hand, some usages remain
barbarous and improper, whatever custom may be and whoever may be cited as authority for
them, and here etymology may
rightly be invoked to determine
propriety; for, although every language as a whole is arbitrary, its
native structure should not be
weakened or distorted by unwise
innovation."

SAMUEL JOHNSON

1709–1784

Many readers know Samuel Johnson only through the biography
written by his contemporary and ardent admirer, James Boswell.
That is unfortunate, because the Samuel Johnson who is revealed
through his own writings is a man with much to say on a variety of
subjects—a man who, despite the excellence of Boswell's portrait,
is best read firsthand. During his own lifetime, Johnson was widely
recognized as the most influential literary figure of his day as well as
a brilliant and witty conversationalist. Indeed, the second half of the
eighteenth century is often called the Age of Johnson.

Johnson's success was hard-won. The son of a bookseller in
Lichfield, a small town north of Birmingham, he grew up in poverty.
He described himself as a "poor diseased infant." A series of
childhood illnesses left him physically weak and facially disfigured.
A brilliant child who read *Hamlet* at the age of eight, Johnson feared
that insanity would deprive him of his single advantage, his intellect.
He entered Pembroke College, Oxford, in 1728, but was forced to
leave after fourteen months because of a lack of funds. For six years
thereafter, until deciding to pursue a literary career in earnest, he
was a Lichfield bookseller and schoolmaster, reading widely and
occasionally working on translations. At the age of twenty-six he
married a widow much older than he, to whom he remained devoted
until her death.

In 1737 he moved to London. Despite critical praise for his early
writing, he failed to gain a large audience. It was Johnson's
Dictionary of the English Language, published in 1755, that earned
him a permanent place in English letters. For the next two years, he
wrote *The Idler,* a series of articles for a weekly newspaper, in
addition to completing one of his best-loved works, *Rasselas,* a
moral romance.

Johnson was awarded an annual pension of three hundred
pounds in 1762, which made him something of a man of leisure. The
next year he and twenty-three-year-old James Boswell met for the
first time in the back parlor of Tom Davis's bookshop. It was a fateful
meeting, one that led, after many further meetings, to Boswell's *Life
of Johnson,* a book generally regarded as the finest biography in
English.

In 1765 Johnson published an acclaimed edition of Shakespeare. His last important work, *The Lives of the Poets,* appeared in
ten volumes between 1779 and 1781. It is a group of fifty-two critical
biographies that cover about two hundred years of English literary
history. Late in life Johnson received honorary degrees from Oxford
and from Trinity College, Dublin—thus the "Dr." that often precedes
his name. He is buried in Westminster Abbey.

Objectives

1 To understand diction
 and style in prose
 writings
2 To compare and contrast
 writing styles
3 To make inferences
 about tone
4 To write dictionary
 entries

Support Material

Teaching Portfolio
Teacher Backup, p. 661
Grammar in Action Worksheet,
 Parallelism, p. 666
Usage and Mechanics Work-
 sheet, p. 668
Vocabulary Check, p. 669
Analyzing Literature Worksheet,
 Analyzing Diction and Style,
 p. 671

Language Worksheet, *Word
 Building Using Root Words,*
 p. 673
Selection Test, p. 674

GUIDE FOR INTERPRETING

Letter to Lord Chesterfield; *from* The Preface to A Dictionary of the English Language; *from* A Dictionary of the English Language

Writer's Techniques

Diction and Style. In written communication, *diction* means word choice. A careful writer chooses words that are clear, correct, and effective. The words that are chosen are at the same time combined in phrases, sentences, and paragraphs. The distinctive way in which words are combined is called *style*. Diction and style change over the years, just as fashion changes. Writing tends to be more casual today than it was two hundred years ago, although formal situations still require formal diction and style. The intended audience for a piece of writing helps to determine appropriate diction and style.

Commentary

According to contemporary reports, Johnson was enthralled by words, especially their histories. No doubt this led to his keen interest in diction and style. The following story sheds light on the process of compiling a dictionary—as well as on Samuel Johnson's character.

The story has it that an anonymous source once sent Johnson a letter containing his derivation of "curmudgeon," an ill-tempered person. The unknown donor claimed that the word came from the French *coeur méchant;* literally, "heart wicked," or wicked heart. This wild guess so pleased Johnson that he used it in his *Dictionary,* giving due credit to the "unknown correspondent."

The matter came up again twenty years later, when Dr. John Ash, compiling his own dictionary, came across the entry in Johnson's *Dictionary*. He, too, found it interesting and decided to use it. Unlike Johnson, however, Ash wanted to claim full credit for discovering the word's history, so he wrote that "curmudgeon" was created from *coeur,* meaning "unknown," and *mechant,* meaning "correspondent." Do you think it is necessary to give credit for a word's history? Can anyone "own" a word?

Writing

In your local newspaper, find a letter to the editor with which you disagree. Jot down your points of disagreement. Then write the opening paragraph of a response. Try to match your diction and style to that of the published letter you have chosen.

Guide for Interpreting 565

Literary Focus Review diction and style as they are reflected in the works of Swift, page 520, whose own style is noted for its simplicity. As an example of present-day formal writing, a governmental proclamation will prove useful. Point out that Johnson's usual diction and style are formal—too formal for the taste of most readers today. Although no one now is likely to imitate Johnson's prose, exposure to his craftsmanship can be beneficial to those trying to write with dignity and elegance.

Writing/Prior Knowledge Have students compare the diction and style of several letters to the editor. Choose from serious, angry, bewildered, and humorous letters.

Letter to Lord Chesterfield

Samuel Johnson

Shortly after the completion of the Dictionary, *Lord Chesterfield published two articles praising it. He had earlier ignored Johnson's appeals for financial assistance for the writing of the* Dictionary.

To the Right Honorable
the Earl of Chesterfield

February 7, 1755

My Lord:

I have been lately informed by the proprietor of the *World*[1] that two papers in which my *Dictionary* is recommended to the public were written by your Lordship. To be so distinguished is an honor which, being very little accustomed to favors from the great, I know not well how to receive, or in what terms to acknowledge.

When upon some slight encouragement I first visited your Lordship, I was overpowered like the rest of mankind by the enchantment of your address,[2] and could not forbear to wish that I might boast myself *"Le vainqueur du vainqueur de la terre"*;[3] that I might obtain that regard for which I saw the world contending, but I found my attendance so little encouraged that neither pride nor modesty would suffer me to continue it. When I had once addressed your Lordship in public, I had exhausted all the art of pleasing which a retired and uncourtly scholar can possess. I had done all that I could; and no man is well pleased to have his all neglected, be it ever so little.

Seven years, my Lord, have now passed since I waited in your outward rooms or was repulsed from your door, during which time I have been pushing on my work through difficulties of which it is useless to complain and have brought it at last to the verge of publication without one act of assistance, one word of encouragement, or one smile of favor. Such treatment I did not expect, for I never had a patron before.

The shepherd in Virgil grew at last acquainted with love, and found him a native of the rocks.[4] "Is not a patron, my Lord, one who looks with unconcern on a man struggling for life in the water and when he has reached ground encumbers him with help. The notice which you have been pleased to take of my labors, had it been early, had been kind; but it has been delayed till I am indifferent and cannot enjoy it, till I am solitary and cannot impart it, till I am known and do not want[5] it.

---

1. the *World*: A newspaper in which Lord Chesterfield had praised Johnson's *Dictionary*.
2. address: Conversation.
3. *Le vainqueur du vainqueur de la terre* (lə van kər′ dyōo van kər′ də lä ter′): French for "the conqueror of the conqueror of the earth."

4. The shepherd . . . rocks: In Virgil's *Eclogue*, a shepherd complains that love must have been born among jagged rocks.
5. want: Need.

3   I hope it is no very cynical asperity not to confess obligation where no benefit has been received, or to be unwilling that the public should consider me as owing that to a patron which Providence has enabled me to do for myself.

    Having carried on my work thus far with so little obligation to any favorer of learning,

I shall not be disappointed though I should conclude it, if less possible, with less; for I have been long wakened from that dream of hope, in which I once boasted myself with so much exultation, my Lord,

Your Lordship's most humble,
most obedient servant,
Samuel Johnson

4

THINKING ABOUT THE SELECTION
Recalling

1. (a) How did Johnson learn of Lord Chesterfield's articles in the *World*? (b) Why does he feel the need to respond?
2. How much time has passed since Johnson first tried to get financial assistance from Lord Chesterfield for work on the *Dictionary*?
3. What does Johnson say will not cause him any disappointment at this point?

Interpreting

4. How does the definition of a patron in the fourth paragraph apply to Johnson's experience with Lord Chesterfield?
5. From Johnson's remarks in the next to last paragraph, what misinformation do you think Chesterfield may have conveyed in his *World* articles concerning his relationship with Johnson?

Applying

6. Suppose Lord Chesterfield had assisted Johnson throughout the development of his dictionary. How do you think Johnson would

then have responded to the articles in the *World*?

ANALYZING LITERATURE
Diction and Style

    Diction in writing is word choice. **Style** is the overall effect of a writer's choice and arrangement of words. In fact, Lord Chesterfield once called style "the dress of thought." Diction and style are influenced by purpose, audience, and the period in which the writing is done. In his "Letter to Lord Chesterfield," Samuel Johnson intends his diction and style to deliver an unmistakable message.

1. (a) What is the purpose of the letter? (b) What is its audience? (c) How does Johnson feel about the audience?
2. What are ten words that you consider to be especially well chosen for the point Johnson wants to make and the way in which he wants to make it?
3. What are three stylistic devices that Johnson uses effectively? Give one example of each from the letter. (Among the possibilities, consider parallelism, understatement, overstatement, and quotation.)

Letter to Lord Chesterfield   567

3 **Discussion** Restate this one-sentence paragraph in your own words.

4 **Discussion** What is the tone of the closing?

Reader's Response How would you feel about someone who refused to help you after you asked for assistance?

---

one to think he was obligated to Chesterfield for the latter's help, which never was forthcoming.
2. Seven years have passed.
3. At this point Johnson will not be disappointed that he has had no encouragement, no financial help.

Interpreting

4. Johnson was rejected by Lord Chesterfield; the definition is quite personal.
5. The earl may have suggested he had encouraged and abetted Johnson all along.

Applying

6. Answers will differ but should include the idea that Johnson would no doubt have responded with a finely phrased expression of humble gratitude.

ANSWERS TO ANALYZING LITERATURE

1. (a) The purpose of the letter is to express his disapproval at Chesterfield's misleading praise for his work. (b) His audience is Lord Chesterfield himself, then anyone else who had the good fortune to read the letter. (c) Johnson is not pleased with Chesterfield's actions.
2. Answers will differ. Possibilities are *overpowered, neglected, repulsed, patron, struggling, encumbers, labors, delayed, indifferent, obligation.*
3. Answers will differ. Possibilities are overstatement as in sentence 1 of paragraph 2, parallelism as at the end of sentence 1 of paragraph 3, and the allusion to Virgil's shepherd in sentence 1 of paragraph 4.

ANSWERS TO THINKING ABOUT THE SELECTION
Recalling

1. (a) The owner of the *World* told Johnson. (b) He does not wish any-

Motivation/Prior Knowledge
Can you imagine having to write, read, and speak English without having a dictionary for a reference tool? How would you find the meanings of unfamiliar words? How would you know the correct spelling, or pronunciation?

Master Teacher Note Johnson's efforts to compile his dictionary were truly heroic. Today such work would be carried out by numerous committees overseeing staffs of specialists, and with the aid of computers. Suggest that your students read Johnson's "Preface" with the aim of discerning some of the difficulties he had to overcome.

Purpose-Setting Question While a writer's style may remain constant, the tone often changes from selection to selection, depending on its audience and its purpose. How does the tone of the "Preface" differ from that of the letter to Lord Chesterfield?

1 **Discussion** Do you agree with this point of view?

2 **Discussion** Explain how this passage could be considered hyperbole. What other examples do you find in the "Preface"?

3 **Enrichment** Like the French and Italian academies, which had produced dictionaries, Johnson at first wanted to "fix" the language; he looked upon change with suspicion; he felt change was likely to corrupt the language.

4 **Discussion** Do you agree? Besides writers, what other groups of people might be included in the term *authors*? Explain your choices.

from # The Preface to A Dictionary of the English Language

Samuel Johnson

1   It is the fate of those who toil at the lower employments of life, to be rather driven by the fear of evil, than attracted by the prospect of good; to be exposed to censure, without hope of praise; to be disgraced by miscarriage, or punished for neglect, where success would have been without applause, and diligence without reward.

2   Among these unhappy mortals is the writer of dictionaries; whom mankind have considered, not as the pupil, but the slave of science, the pioneer of literature, doomed only to remove rubbish and clear obstructions from the paths through which learning and genius press forward to conquest and glory, without bestowing a smile on the humble drudge that facilitates their progress. Every other author may aspire to praise; the lexicographer can only hope to escape reproach, and even this negative recompense has been yet granted to very few.

    I have, notwithstanding this discouragement, attempted a dictionary of the English language, which, while it was employed in the cultivation of every species of literature, has itself been hitherto neglected; suffered to spread under the direction of chance, into wild exuberance; resigned to the tyranny of time and fashion: and exposed to the corruptions of ignorance and caprices of innovation.

3   When I took the first survey of my undertaking, I found our speech copious without order and energetic without rule: wherever I turned my view, there was perplexity to be disentangled and confusion to be regulated; choice was to be made out of boundless variety, without any established principle of selection; adulterations were to be detected, without a settled test of purity; and modes of expression to be rejected or received, without the suffrages of any writers of classical reputation or acknowledged authority.

    Having therefore no assistance but from general grammar, I applied myself to the perusal of our writers; and noting whatever might be of use to ascertain or illustrate any word or phrase, accumulated in time the materials of a dictionary, which, by degrees, I reduced to method, establishing to myself, in the progress of the work, such rules as experience and analogy suggested to me; experience, which practice and observation were continually increasing; and analogy, which, though in some other words obscure, was evident in others . . .

    In hope of giving longevity to that which its own nature forbids to be immortal, I have devoted this book, the labor of years, to the honor of my country, that we may no longer yield the palm of philology, without a contest to the nations of the continent. The chief glory of every people arises from its 4 authors. Whether I shall add anything by my own writings to the reputation of English literature, must be left to time. Much of my life has been lost under the pressures of disease; much has been trifled away; and

Grammar in Action

One of the cardinal rules of clear, effective writing is to present equal ideas in words, phrases, and clauses of similar grammatical structures. This stylistic device is called **parallelism.** Samuel Johnson was a master of it.

> When I took the first survey of my undertaking, I found our speech copious without order and energetic without rule: wherever I turned my view, there was perplexity to be disentagled and confusion to be regulated.

much has always been spent in provision for the day that was passing over me; but I shall not think my employment useless or ignoble, if by my assistance foreign nations and distant ages gain access to the propagators of knowledge, and understand the teachers of truth; if my labors afford light to the repositories of science, and add celebrity to Bacon, to Hooker, to Milton, and to Boyle.[1]

When I am animated by this wish, I look with pleasure on my book, however defective, and deliver it to the world with the spirit of a man that has endeavored well. That it will immediately become popular, I have not promised to myself. A few wild blunders, and risible absurdities, from which no work of such multiplicity was ever free, may for a time furnish folly with laughter, and harden ignorance into contempt; but useful diligence will at last prevail, and there never can be wanting some who distinguish desert; who will consider that no dictionary of a living tongue ever can be perfect, since, while it is hastening to publication, some words are budding, and some falling away; that a whole life cannot be spent upon syntax and etymology, and that even a whole life would not be sufficient; that he, whose design includes whatever language can express, must often speak of what he does not understand; that a writer will sometimes be hurried by eagerness to the end, and sometimes faint with weariness under a task which Scaliger[2] compares to the labors of the anvil and the mine; that what is obvious is not always known, and what is known is not always present; that sudden fits of inadvertency will surprise vigilance, slight avocations[3] will seduce attention, and casual eclipses of the mind will darken learning; and that the writer shall

often in vain trace his memory at the moment of need, for that which yesterday he knew with intuitive readiness, and which will come uncalled into his thoughts tomorrow.

In this work, when it shall be found that much is omitted, let it not be forgotten that much likewise is performed; and though no book was ever spared out of tenderness to the author, and the world is little solicitous to know whence proceed the faults of that which it condemns; yet it may gratify curiosity to inform it, that the *English Dictionary* was written with little assistance of the learned, and without any patronage of the great; not in the soft obscurities of retirement, or under the shelter of academic bowers, but amidst inconvenience and distraction, in sickness and in sorrow. It may repress the triumph of malignant criticism to observe that if our language is not here fully displayed, I have only failed in an attempt which no human powers have hitherto completed. If the lexicons of ancient tongues, now immutably fixed and comprised in a few volumes, be yet, after the toil of successive ages, inadequate and delusive; if the aggregated knowledge and cooperating diligence of the Italian academicians did not secure them from the censure of Beni;[4] if the embodied critics of France, when fifty years had been spent upon their work, were obliged to change its economy[5] and give their second edition another form, I may surely be contented without the praise of perfection, which, if I could obtain, in this gloom of solitude, what would it avail me? I have protracted my work till most of those whom I wished to please have sunk into the grave,[6] and success and miscarriage are empty sounds: I therefore dismiss it with frigid tranquility, having little to fear or hope from censure or from praise.

---

1. **Bacon . . . Boyle:** Writers quoted by Johnson in the *Dictionary*.
2. **Scaliger:** Joseph Justus Scaliger (1540–1609), a scholar who suggested that criminals should be condemned to writing dictionaries.
3. **avocation:** Something that calls one away or distracts one from something.

4. **Beni:** Paolo Beni severely criticized the first Italian dictionary.
5. **economy:** Organization.
6. **sunk . . . grave:** Johnson's wife had died three years earlier.

from The Preface to A Dictionary of the English Language   569

5 Enrichment Here, Johnson admits that language cannot be "fixed"; rather it is a living thing, constantly changing.

6 Discussion Under what conditions did Johnson write the *Dictionary?*

Enrichment Boswell had this to say about Johnson's monumental project: "The world contemplated with wonder [a work] achieved by one man, while other countries had thought such undertakings fit only for whole academies." To produce his *Dictionary*, Johnson labored alone for seven years. By way of comparison, to complete the authoritative *Dictionary* of the French Academy required the labors of forty scholars for forty years.

Notice how "copious without order" is paralleled in grammatical form by "energetic without rule," and "perplexity to be disentangled" by "confusion to be regulated." Such parallelism makes writing readable.

Student Activity 1. Find at least six more examples of grammatical parallelism in Johnson's Preface.

Student Activity 2. Rewrite the following paragraph using parallelism to improve clarity and readability.

I invited John, who brought his albums. I also invited Joan. She brought lemonade. Phil and Bob were also invited, and they came, Phil bringing a box of sandwiches. Bob brought snacks. I also invited my brother, and he brought a couple of his funny friends.

Closure and Extension

ANSWERS TO THINKING ABOUT THE SELECTION
Recalling

1. (a) Writers of dictionaries are among those "who toil at the lower employments of life." (b) The lexicographer's "negative recompense" is "to escape reproach."
2. (a) Among other things, Johnson found English to be lacking in order and in rules. (b) General grammar was his only assistance.
3. Johnson devoted his *Dictionary* to the honor of England.
4. Any living tongue is constantly changing—adding words, dropping words, changing meanings, and so on.

Interpreting

5. (a) Johnson wrote the *Dictionary* to help codify English—that is, put some order into the language. (b) Students' answers will differ, but it can be inferred that previous dictionary-making was not effective.
6. Johnson collected words by reading the principal writers of his and earlier times.
7. Students' answers will differ, but it is quite likely that Johnson was both hopeful and pessimistic about his work. The final words of the "Preface" have a mock-serious tone about them.

Applying

8. Johnson would likely have a low opinion of today's dictionary writers, many of whom look upon themselves as reporters of the language and its usage rather than arbiters of good taste and correctness in language.
9. Computers have simplified the organization of information, the storage of information, and the changing or updating of information.

THINKING AND WRITING

Publishing Student Writing Students comparing or contrasting styles of the same authors might be interested in reading each other's essays.

570

THINKING ABOUT THE SELECTION
Recalling

1. (a) Among what class of workers does Johnson place writers of dictionaries? (b) What is the lexicographer's "negative recompense"?
2. (a) When Johnson "took the first survey," what did he find English speech to be lacking? (b) What gave him his only assistance?
3. To whom or what does Johnson say he has "devoted this book"?
4. Why, according to "The Preface," can "no dictionary of a living tongue ever be perfect"?

Interpreting

5. (a) What is Johnson's reason for having undertaken the task of writing a dictionary of English? (b) What can you conclude about prior dictionary-making in England?
6. How did Johnson collect the words for his dictionary?
7. Johnson seems to have mixed feelings about his efforts. (a) Do you think he is hopeful or pessimistic (or perhaps both) about the fate of his dictionary? Explain. (b) How have his efforts held up against the test of time?

Applying

8. What opinion do you think Johnson would have of today's unabridged English dictionaries?

9. How have computers changed the role of dictionary makers?

THINKING AND WRITING
Comparing and Contrasting Styles

A **writer's style** is the distinctive way that he or she uses language. No two writers have exactly the same style, although you may notice obvious similarities, especially among writers of the same era. Think about other writers' works that you have read so far in this book. Which writer has a style the most like—or, if you prefer, the least like—that of Samuel Johnson? To answer the question, you will need to consider diction, sentence structure, tone, and point of view. Style is a complex matter; parallels can be difficult. Once you have made your choice, write a short essay in which you compare and contrast the style of Johnson with that of the other writer you have chosen. Take notes before you start to do your first draft. Be specific as to the similarities and differences between the two styles you are comparing. When you revise for your final draft, go back to make sure that your observations about style are accurate and that your quoted excerpts are correct.

from # A Dictionary of the English Language

Samuel Johnson

athle′tick. Strong of body; vigorous; lusty; robust.

> Science distinguishes a man of honor from one of those _athletick_ brutes, whom underservedly we call heroes. Dryden.

bang. A blow; a thump; a stroke: a low word.

> I am a bachelor. That's to say, they are fools that marry; you'll bear me a _bang_ for that. Shakespeare, _Julius Caesar._

to ba′rbecue. A term used in the West Indies for dressing a hog whole; which, being split to the backbone, is laid flat upon a large gridiron, raised about two foot above a charcoal fire, with which it is surrounded.

> Oldfield, with more than harpy throat endu'd,
>
> Cries, send me, gods, a whole hog _barbecu'd._ Pope.

bu′ffleheaded. A man with a large head, like a buffalo; dull; stupid; foolish.

cream. The unctuous or oily part of milk, which, when it is cold, floats on the top, and is changed by the agitation of the churn into butter; the flower of milk.

electri′city. A property in some bodies, whereby, when rubbed so as to grow warm, they draw little bits of paper, or such like substances, to them. Quincy.

> Such was the account given a few years ago of electricity; but the industry of the present age, first excited by the experiments of Gray, has discovered in electricity a multitude of philosophical wonders. Bodies electrified by a sphere of glass, turned nimbly round, not only emit flame, but may be fitted with such a quantity of the electrical vapor as, if discharged at once upon a human body, would endanger life. The force of this vapor has hitherto appeared instantaneous, persons at both ends of a long chain seeming to be struck at once. The philosophers are now endeavoring to intercept the strokes of lightning.

to fu′rnace. To throw out as sparks from a furnace. A bad word.

> He _furnaces_
>
> The thick sighs from him. Shakespeare's _Cymbeline._

gang. A number herding together; a troop; a company; a tribe; a herd. It is seldom used but in contempt or abhorrence.

ha′tchet-face. An ugly face; such, I suppose, as might be hewn out of a block by a hatchet.

Motivation/Prior Knowledge Ask students why dictionaries are important.

Purpose-Setting Question Johnson's is a highly personal dictionary, quite unlike modern works. As such, you can expect the tone of his entries to be affected by his attitude toward the words. Try to describe the tone of each entry as you read it.

1 Enrichment Note that unlike modern dictionaries, Johnson's offers no help in pronouncing words, beyond the inclusion of accents.

2 Discussion What is the meaning of this word today?

3 Discussion Having read the letter to Lord Chesterfield, is this the definition you would have expected? Why, or why not?

4 Discussion What is the present-day spelling of this word?

5 Enrichment Note that Johnson identifies verbs by the use of the word *to*.

Reader's Response What do you think would be the hardest part of compiling a dictionary?

An ape his own dear image will embrace;
An ugly beau adores a *hatchet-face*. Dryden.

lifegua'rd. The guard of a king's person.

mo'dern. In Shakespeare, vulgar; mean; common.
We have our philosophical persons to make *modern* and familiar things supernatural and causeless. Shakespeare.

pa'tron. One who countenances, supports or protects. Commonly a wretch who supports with insolence, and is paid with flattery.

pi'ckle. Condition; state. A word of contempt and ridicule.
How cam'st though in this *pickle?* Shakespeare.

plu'mper. Something worn in the mouth to swell out the cheeks.
She dex'trously her *plumpers* draws,
That serve to fill her hollow jaws. Swift's *Miscellanies*.

shill-I-shall-I. A corrupt reduplication of *shall I?* The question of a man hesitating. To stand *shill-I-shall-I*, is to continue hesitating and procrastinating.
I am somewhat dainty in making a resolution, because when I make it, I keep it; I don't stand *shill-I-shall-I* then; if I say't, I'll do't. Congreve's *Way of the World*.

to sneeze. To emit wind audibly by the nose.

wi'llow. A tree worn by forlorn lovers.

to wipe. To cheat; to defraud.
The next bordering lords commonly encroach one upon another, as one is stronger, or lie still in wait to *wipe* them out of their lands. Spenser, *On Ireland*.

you'ngster, you'nker. A young person. In contempt.

youth. The part of life succeeding to childhood and adolescence; the time from fourteen to twenty-eight.

THINKING ABOUT THE SELECTION

Recalling

1. What is Johnson's definition of (a) *lifeguard* and (b) *modern*?
2. According to Johnson, what is (a) a "tree worn by forlorn lovers"? (b) a person "from fourteen to twenty-eight"?

Interpreting

3. How does Johnson indicate that a word is a verb?
4. Why do you think the word *electricity* receives such a long definition?
5. Given what you know of Johnson's life, how do you account for his comment about *patron:* "a wretch who supports with insolence, and is paid with flattery"?
6. (a) In a modern dictionary, how is the entry for *shill-I-shall-I* spelled? (b) What inferences do you make about Johnson based on his definition?

Applying

7. Dictionaries are generally scientific, objective works. Johnson's dictionary, however, is filled with opinions and value judgments. What are three conspicuous examples of the kind of wording that would not appear in a modern dictionary?

CRITICAL THINKING AND READING

Making Inferences About Tone

Tone, the manner in which a writer communicates, shows the writer's attitude toward his or her subject. It often displays traces of the writer's personality or set of values. When tone seems to be completely straightforward, as in a newspaper report, a reader will tend to accept the writer's message at face value. If tone appears to be ironic or sarcastic, as in a satirical essay, a reader will be on guard for less obvious meanings. Tone can usually be described by one or two adjectives. Review Johnson's definitions of the following words. Then, in a brief paragraph, tell what you can infer from them about Johnson's tone.

1. bang
2. cream
3. to furnace
4. hatchet-face
5. youngster

THINKING AND WRITING

Writing Johnsonian Dictionary Entries

Take a look once again at the entries from Johnson's *Dictionary*. Pay close attention to exactly how they are written. Then search through a standard modern dictionary of the English language and find at least five words that might be imaginatively redefined through Johnson's eyes. Finally, write Johnsonian definitions for these words. Follow his style in every way possible, including accenting, diction, and outspokenness.

ANSWERS TO THINKING ABOUT THE SELECTION
Recalling

1. (a) According to Johnson, a *lifeguard* is the guard of a king's person. (b) The word *modern* means "vulgar," "mean," or "common."
2. (a) According to Johnson, "a tree worn by forlorn lovers" is a willow; (b) a person "from fourteen to twenty-eight" is a youth.

Interpreting

3. Johnson indicates verbs by using the word *to*.
4. The entry for *electricity* is quite long, perhaps in order to explain it in detail, thinking that most people would be completely unfamiliar with the term.
5. Johnson's definition of *patron* is in keeping with his experiences with Lord Chesterfield.
6. (a) The word is spelled *shilly-shally*. (b) Johnson may either have had difficulty making decisions, or he may have felt contempt for indecisive people.

Applying

7. Students' answers will differ, but should include the entries for words like *electricity, gang,* and *youngster.*

ANSWERS TO CRITICAL THINKING AND READING

1. The tone of *bang* is pejorative.
2. The tone of *cream* is matter-of-fact.
3. The tone of *to furnace* is pedantic.
4. The tone of *hatchet-face* is matter-of-fact.
5. The tone of *youngster* is matter-of-fact.

Challenge Have students compile a dictionary of present-day slang they commonly use. Their definitions should be as subjective as those Johnson used.

THINKING AND WRITING

Publishing Student Writing Students' definitions could be collected in a dictionary.

More About the Author It is iron-ic that a man who had such an inferiority complex should write what is regarded as the finest biography ever. It is doubly ironic that thanks to the discovery of James Boswell's personal papers in the 1920's, more is known today about Boswell himself than about the great man he so ad-mired. Give an example of irony in your own life or the life of some-one you know.

Critical Evaluation In addition to the praise bestowed on Bos-well's biography there has also been a cautionary note sounded about it by those who think its influence creates problems. Here is the way literary historian Edmund Wilson expressed his concern on the topic: "It is a pity that Boswell's *Life of Johnson* should have so largely supplant-ed for the general reader the writings of Johnson himself. If we know nothing but Boswell and Macaulay's essay, which is read in so many schools, we are likely to have a picture of a great ec-centric who was even a bit of a clown. Boswell, in spite of his great respect and of the filial role he assumed, could not help mak-ing Johnson a character in an eighteenth century comedy of manners . . . That Johnson him-self was really one of the best English writers of his time, that he deserved his great reputation, is a fact that we are likely to lose sight of."

JAMES BOSWELL

(1740–1795)

Not until the twentieth century did James Boswell rise from the fringes of literary history to take his place as perhaps the greatest biographer in English literature. Best known for his biography of Samuel Johnson, Boswell wrote with vigor, training his eye now on the picturesque, now on the grotesque.

Born into an aristocratic family in Edinburgh, Scotland, Boswell was educated at the University of Glasgow, the University of Edinburgh, and the University of Utrecht. Although he received his degree in law and was admitted to the bar in both Scotland and England, Boswell's true passion was literature. His father, a promi-nent judge, was angered by what he saw as his son's "shallow" values. The extremely sensitive young Boswell interpreted this dissatisfaction as rejection, which led in turn to feelings of inferiority. In an effort to overcome his low self-esteem and at the same time find a suitable father figure, Boswell became a celebrity chaser, seeking out the acquaintanceship of the great men and women of his day. To his credit, many of them became his lifelong friends.

Among these was the writer Samuel Johnson, whom Boswell met while visiting London in 1763. After his acceptance into the prestigious Literary Club, Boswell devoted thirty years to compiling detailed records of Johnson's activities and conversations. From these assorted bits and pieces he distilled his famous work, *The Life of Samuel Johnson,* a precise yet wonderfully intimate portrait of the colorful poet. "The great art of biography," Boswell wrote, "is to keep the person whose life we are giving always in the reader's view." This he does by depicting Johnson variously as "a rhinocer-os, in a kind of good humoured growl," and as "blowing out his breath like a whale" following an argument.

In addition to his portrait of Johnson, Boswell wrote numerous personal journals. *An Account of Corsica* (1768) is a sympathetic report of his meeting with the Corsican patriot Paoli and of Corsica's struggle for independence. His *Journal of a Tour in the Hebrides* (1785), published after Johnson's death, tells of the trip he made with the sage to Scotland.

During his lifetime Boswell's popularity was stifled by the biting criticism leveled at his work by the poet Thomas Gray, who caustically noted that "any fool may write a valuable book by chance, if he will only tell what he heard and saw. . . ." It is only since the 1920's, in fact, when a batch of Boswell's private papers were discovered in Malahide Castle, that the reading public has had any real awareness of this often rowdy, often vain young gentleman who gave the world its closest look at Samuel Johnson.

GUIDE FOR INTERPRETING

from The Life of Samuel Johnson

Literary Forms

Biography. A biography is an account of a person's life, usually written, though sometimes communicated orally, by another person. Effective biography will represent the subject's life accurately and thoroughly. A good biography, in other words, paints a complete portrait, giving as much space to the subject's flaws and limitations as to his or her most admirable traits. An important milestone in the writing of biography was James Boswell's *The Life of Samuel Johnson.* In his work Boswell displayed an impressive grasp of Johnson's character by presenting countless particular details rather than a distant and generalized view of the man. The art of the biography has continued into the present century with such monumental works as Carl Sandburg's massive work on the life of Abraham Lincoln, which spans several volumes.

Commentary

Boswell claimed that his biography of Johnson would be the most complete life of a person ever penned, but in a curious way he was proven wrong: The one he wrote about himself is far more complete. When his eighteen volumes of journals were published after his death, he became, according to critic J. W. Krutch, "perhaps the best self-documented man in all history."

Boswell began jotting down occasional notes in 1758. By 1762 he was writing in his journal regularly, a practice he continued until about thirteen months before he died. He published only a few excerpts from his journals during his life. As he did not intend the bulk of the material for public eyes, the *Journals* are free and open expressions of his feelings and clearly reveal his decision to write the truth about himself.

Since he had no intention of publishing his journals, why did he spend so much time on them? As he wrote, "Know thyself, for surely this knowledge is of all the most important." And what better way for a person to gain self-awareness than by "attending to the feelings of his heart and to his external actions. . . . I have therefore determined to keep a daily journal in which I shall set down my various conduct, which will be not only useful but very agreeable."

What do Boswell's accounts of Johnson reveal about himself?

Writing

Imagine that you were able to interview a person whom you greatly admire. The person in question may be an athlete, film star, author, or the like. Prepare a list of questions that you think would reveal the individual behind the public mask.

Guide for Interpreting 575

Literary Focus Discuss the term *biography* and ask students what biographies they have read. Ask them whether the biography gave an intimate picture of the individual or whether it presented a distant and generalized view. Which is preferable in a biography and why?

Spelling Tip Point out the *ch* spelling of the sound /k/ in *chimerical.* Have students list other words in which /k/ is spelled by *ch*; for example, *chemical, chaos, character.*

Writing/Prior Knowledge Boswell stated that his aim in writing a biography of Johnson was "to write, not his panegyrick, which must be all praise, but his Life; which, great and good as he was, must not be supposed to be entirely perfect . . . in every picture there should be shade as well as light." Discuss whether reporters have an obligation to present both "shade" and "light" when they write about a public person. Where does a celebrity's private life end and his or her public life begin? What kinds of questions, if any, should an interviewer avoid?

Vocabulary

Preteach the following vocabulary words:

abasement (ə bās′ mənt) *n.*: Condition of being put down or humbled (p. 576)

animadversion (an′ə mad vʉr′ zhən) *n.*: Unfavorable comment (p. 578)

chimerical (ki mir′i k'l) *adj.*: Imaginary; unreal (p. 578)

credulity (krə doo′ lə tē) *n.*: Tendency to believe too readily (p. 579)

malignity (mə lig′nə tē) *n.*: Strong desire to harm others (p. 580)

impetuous (im pech′ oo wəs) *adj.*: Acting rashly (p. 580)

petulance (pech′′ oo ləns) *n.*: Insolent behavior (p. 580)

tincture (tiŋk′ chər) *n.*: Tint (p. 581)

pernicious (pər nish′əs) *adj.*: Causing serious injury; deadly (p. 581)

inculcated (in kul′kāt id) *v.*: Impressed upon the mind by frequent repetition (p. 581)

from The Life of Samuel Johnson

James Boswell

Boswell Meets Johnson
1763

1 This is to me a memorable year; for in it I had the happiness to obtain the acquaintance of that extraordinary man whose memoirs I am now writing; an acquaintance which I shall ever esteem as one of the most fortunate circumstances in my life. Though then but two-and-twenty, I had for several years read his works with delight and instruction, and had the highest reverence for their author, which had grown up in my fancy into a kind of mysterious veneration, by figuring to myself a state of solemn elevated abstraction, in which I supposed him to live in the immense metropolis of London. . . .

Mr. Thomas Davies[1] the actor, who then kept a bookseller's shop in Russel Street, Covent Garden, told me that Johnson was very much his friend, and came frequently to his house, where he more than once invited me to meet him; but by some unlucky accident or other he was prevented from coming to us.

2,3 At last, on Monday the 16th day of May, when I was sitting in Mr. Davies's back parlor, after having drunk tea with him and Mrs. Davies, Johnson unexpectedly came into the shop; and Mr. Davies having perceived him through the glass door in the room in which we were sitting, advancing towards us—he announced his aweful[2] approach to me, somewhat in the manner of an actor in the part of Horatio, when he addresses Hamlet on the appearance of his father's ghost, "Look, my Lord, it comes,"[3] I found that I had a very perfect idea of Johnson's figure, from the portrait of him painted by Sir Joshua Reynolds[4] soon after he had published his *Dictionary*, in the attitude of sitting in his easy chair in deep meditation, which was the first picture his friend did for him, which Sir Joshua very kindly presented to me, and from which an engraving has been made for this work. Mr. Davies mentioned my name, and respectfully introduced me to him. I was much agitated; and recollecting his prejudice against the Scotch, of which I had heard much, I said to Davies, "Don't tell where I come from." "From Scotland," cried Davies roguishly. "Mr. Johnson," said I, "I do indeed come from Scotland, but I cannot help it." I am willing to flatter myself that I meant this as light pleasantry to sooth and conciliate him, and not as an humiliating abasement at the expense of my country. But however that might be, this speech was somewhat

---

1. Thomas Davies: An English bookseller and unsuccessful actor (1712–1785).

2. aweful: Awe-inspiring.
3. Horatio " . . . it comes": From Shakespeare's *Hamlet* (Act I, Scene iv).
4. Sir Joshua Reynolds: A celebrated portrait painter at the time (1723–1792).

JOHNSON AND BOSWELL
© The Trustees of the British Museum

from *The Life of Samuel Johnson* 577

Humanities Note

Engraving, *Johnson and Boswell*. This engraving of the ghost of Samuel Johnson haunting his biographer, Boswell, appeared in the 1803 edition of the play *The Way of the World* by William Congreve. The artist, whose identity is unknown, was in the employ of the publisher, C. Bestland of West End, Hempstead, England. William Congreve (1670–1729) was known to Boswell and Johnson, who admired him greatly.

You may wish to use the following questions for discussion.

1. Boswell admits in his biography that he himself was a silly fop next to the stern and stately Johnson. Does this comparison come across in the illustration? Explain.

2. What facts did Boswell reveal about Johnson that may have made him return to "haunt" his biographer, as shown in this illustration?

4 Discussion What does Johnson mean by this statement?

5 Discussion How, according to Johnson, does Providence preserve equality among mankind?

6 Literary Focus What does this statement tell you about Johnson's view of the monarchy? of punishment for sedition?

unlucky; for with that quickness of wit for which he was so remarkable, he seized the expression "come from Scotland," which I used in the sense of being of that country; and, as if I had said that I had come away from it, or left, retorted, "That, Sir, I find, is what a very great many of your countrymen cannot help." This stroke stunned me a good deal; and when we had sat down, I felt myself not a little embarrassed, and apprehensive of what might come next. He then addressed himself to Davies: "What do you think of Garrick?[5] He has refused me an order for the play for Miss Williams, because he knows the house will be full, and that an order would be worth three shillings." Eager to take any opening to get into conversation with him, I ventured to say, "O, Sir, I cannot think Mr. Garrick would grudge such a trifle to you." "Sir," said he, with a stern look, "I have known David Garrick longer than you have done: and I know no right you have to talk to me on the subject." Perhaps I deserved this check; for it was rather presumptuous in me, an entire stranger, to express any doubt of the justice of his animadversion upon his old acquaintance and pupil. I now felt myself much mortified, and began to think that the hope which I had long indulged of obtaining his acquaintance was blasted. And, in truth, had not my ardor been uncommonly strong, and my resolution uncommonly persevering, so rough a reception might have deterred me forever from making any further attempts. Fortunately, however, I remained upon the field not wholly discomfited; and was soon rewarded by hearing some of his conversation, of which I preserved the following short minute,[6] without marking the questions and observations by which it was produced.

"People," he remarked, "may be taken in once, who imagine that an author is

greater in private life than other men. Uncommon parts require uncommon opportunities for their exertion."

"In barbarous society, superiority of parts is of real consequence. Great strength or great wisdom is of much value to an individual. But in more polished times there are people to do everything for money; and then there are a number of other superiorities, such as those of birth and fortune, and rank, that dissipate men's attention, and leave no extraordinary share of respect for personal and intellectual superiority. This is wisely ordered by Providence, to preserve some equality among mankind."

"Sir, this book (*The Elements of Criticism*,[7] which he had taken up) is a pretty essay, and deserves to be held in some estimation, though much of it is chimerical."

Speaking of one[8] who with more than ordinary boldness attacked public measures and the royal family, he said, "I think he is safe from the law, but he is an abusive scoundrel; and instead of applying to my Lord Chief Justice to punish him, I would send half a dozen footmen and have him well ducked."[9]

"The notion of liberty amuses the people of England, and helps to keep off the *taedium vitae*.[10] When a butcher tells you that his heart bleeds for his country, he has, in fact, no uneasy feeling."

"Sheridan[11] will not succeed at Bath with his oratory. Ridicule has gone down before him, and, I doubt,[12] Derrick[13] is his enemy."

---

5. Garrick: David Garrick (1717–1779), a famous actor who had been educated by Johnson. Garrick was also one of the managing partners of the Drury Lane Theater in London.
6. minute: Note.

7. Elements of Criticism: One of the works of Scottish philosophical writer Henry Home (1696–1782).
8. one: John Wilkes (1727–1797), an English political agitator.
9. ducked: Tied to a chair at the end of a plank and plunged into water.
10. taedium vitae (tī′dē əm vē′ tī): Boredom.
11. Sheridan: Thomas Sheridan (1719–1788), an Irish actor and author. At the time, Sheridan was reading lectures at the Oratory at Bath.
12. doubt: Fear.
13. Derrick: The Master of Ceremonies of the Oratory at Bath.

Grammar in Action

Use commas to enclose all **parenthetical expressions** that interrupt the flow of a sentence. Notice how James Boswell encloses his many parenthetical expressions between commas.

The character of Samuel Johnson has, *I trust,* been so developed in the course of this work . . .

Man is, *in general,* made up of contradictory qualities . . .

I had, *for a part of the evening,* been left alone with him . . .

Using commas to set off parenthetical expressions within sentences maintains clarity. It does so by indicating that such expressions are of secondary importance to the sense the writer wishes to communicate.

"Derrick may do very well, as long as he can outrun his character; but the moment his character gets up with him, it is all over."

It is, however, but just to record, that some years afterwards, when I reminded him of this sarcasm, he said, "Well, but Derrick has now got a character that he need not run away from."

I was highly pleased with the extraordinary vigor of his conversation, and regretted that I was drawn away from it by an engagement at another place. I had, for a part of the evening, been left alone with him, and had ventured to make an observation now and then, which he received very civilly; so that I was satisfied that though there was a roughness in his manner, there was no ill nature in his disposition. Davies followed me to the door, and when I complained to him a little of the hard blows which the great man had given me he kindly took upon him to console me by saying, "Don't be uneasy. I can see he likes you very well."

Johnson's Character

The character of Samuel Johnson has, I trust, been so developed in the course of this work, that they who have honored it with a perusal, may be considered as well acquainted with him. As, however, it may be expected that I should collect into one view the capital and distinguishing features of this extraordinary man, I shall endeavor to acquit myself of that part of my biographical undertaking, however difficult it may be to do that which many of my readers will do better for themselves.

His figure was large and well formed, and his countenance of the cast of an ancient statue; yet his appearance was rendered strange and somewhat uncouth by convulsive cramps, by the scars of that distemper[14] which it was once imagined the royal touch could cure,[15] and by a slovenly mode of dress. He had the use only of one eye; yet so much does mind govern and even supply the deficiency of organs, that his visual perceptions, as far as they extended, were uncommonly quick and accurate. So morbid was his temperament, that he never knew the natural joy of a free and vigorous use of his limbs: when he walked, it was like the struggling gait of one in fetters; when he rode, he had no command or direction of his horse, but was carried as if in a balloon. That with his constitution and habits of life he should have lived seventy-five years, is a proof that an inherent *vivida vis*[16] is a powerful preservative of the human frame.

Man is, in general, made up of contradictory qualities; and these will ever show themselves in strange succession, where a consistency in appearance at least, if not in reality, has not been attained by long habits of philosophical discipline. In proportion to the native vigor of the mind, the contradictory qualities will be the more prominent, and more difficult to be adjusted; and, therefore, we are not to wonder that Johnson exhibited an eminent example of this remark which I have made upon human nature. At different times, he seemed a different man, in some respects; not, however, in any great or essential article, upon which he had fully employed his mind, and settled certain principles of duty, but only in his manners and in the display of argument and fancy in his talk. He was prone to superstition, but not to credulity. Though his imagination might incline him to a belief of the marvelous and the mysterious, his vigorous reason examined the evidence with jealousy.[17] He was a sincere and zealous Christian, of high Church of England and monarchical princi-

14. **distemper** *n.*: Scrofula, a type of tuberculosis that causes swelling and scarring of the neck.

15. **royal touch . . . cure:** It was at one time believed that the touch of an English monarch had the power to heal. As a child Johnson was taken to Queene Anne to receive her touch in the hope that it would cure him.
16. *vivida vis:* Lively force.
17. **jealousy:** Suspicion.

from *The Life of Samuel Johnson*   579

7 **Literary Focus** What does this statement show about Johnson's flexibility?

8 **Discussion** How is Boswell's sense of inferiority revealed here?

9 **Discussion** Do you think this is false modesty?

10 **Discussion** What one characteristic of Johnson's always remained the same?

Student Activity 1. Insert commas before and after the parenthetical expressions in the following sentences.

1. Next time you're in the area unless you're pressed for time be sure to look me up.
2. My little sister much to her surprise was the hit of the show.
3. We talked on the phone to the alarm of my parents for two hours.
4. Never buy a used car she warned me from a person you don't know.

Student Activity 2. Write three sentences each of which includes a parenthetical expression. Punctuate the expression correctly.

11 **Critical Thinking and Reading**
How does Boswell excuse Johnson's many prejudices?

12 **Critical Thinking and Reading**
How does Boswell excuse Johnson's "hasty and satirical sallies even against his best friends"?

13 **Discussion** Considering Pope, Swift, and other writers of the time, why do you think satirists were in such vogue during the "Age of Enlightenment"?

14 **Critical Thinking and Reading**
How does the manner in which Boswell presents Johnson's weaknesses help to lessen their seriousness?

ples, which he would not tamely suffer to be questioned; and had, perhaps, at an early period, narrowed his mind somewhat too much, both as to religion and politics. His being impressed with the danger of extreme latitude in either, though he was of a very independent spirit, occasioned his appearing somewhat unfavorable to the prevalence of that noble freedom of sentiment which is the best possession of man. Nor can it be denied, that he had many prejudices; which, however, frequently suggested many of his pointed sayings that rather show a playfulness of fancy than any settled malignity. He was steady and inflexible in maintaining the obligations of religion and morality; both from a regard for the order of society, and from a veneration for the Great Source of all order; correct, nay, stern in his taste; hard to please, and easily offended; impetuous and irritable in his temper, but of a most humane and benevolent heart, which showed itself not only in a most liberal charity, as far as his circumstances would allow, but in a thousand instances of active benevolence. He was afflicted with a bodily disease, which made him often restless and fretful; and with a constitutional melancholy, the clouds of which darkened the brightness of his fancy, and gave a gloomy cast to his whole course of thinking: we, therefore, ought not to wonder at his sallies of impatience and passion at any time; especially when provoked by obtrusive ignorance, or presuming petulance; and allowance must be made for his uttering hasty and satirical sallies even against his best friends. And, surely, when it is considered, that, "amidst sickness and sorrow," he exerted his faculties in so many works for the benefit of mankind, and particularly that he achieved the great and admirable Dictionary of our language, we must be astonished at his resolution. The solemn text, "of him to whom much is given, much will be required," seems to have been ever present to his mind, in a rigorous sense, and to have made him dissatisfied with his labors and

acts of goodness, however comparatively great; so that the unavoidable consciousness of his superiority was, in that respect, a cause of disquiet. He suffered so much from this, and from the gloom which perpetually haunted him and made solitude frightful, that it may be said of him, "If in this life only he had hope, he was of all men most miserable."[18] He loved praise, when it was brought to him; but was too proud to seek for it. He was somewhat susceptible of flattery. As he was general and unconfined in his studies, he cannot be considered as master of any one particular science; but he had accumulated a vast and various collection of learning and knowledge, which was so arranged in his mind, as to be ever in readiness to be brought forth. But his superiority over other learned men consisted chiefly in what may be called the art of thinking, the art of using his mind; a certain continual power of seizing the useful substance of all that he knew and exhibiting it in a clear and forcible manner; so that knowledge, which we often see to be no better than lumber[19] in men of dull understanding, was, in him, true, evident, and actual wisdom. His moral precepts are practical; for they are drawn from an intimate acquaintance with human nature. His maxims carry conviction; for they are founded on the basis of common sense, and a very attentive and minute survey of real life. His mind was so full of imagery, that he might have been perpetually a poet; yet it is remarkable, that, however rich his prose is in this respect, his poetical pieces, in general, have not much of that splendor, but are rather distinguished by strong sentiment and acute observation, conveyed in harmonious and energetic verse, particularly in heroic couplets. Though usually grave, and even aweful, in his deportment, he possessed uncommon and peculiar powers of wit and humor; he frequently indulged himself in colloquial pleasantry; and the hearti-

---

18. **"If . . . miserable":** From I Corinthians 15:19.
19. **lumber:** Rubbish.

Grammar In Action

Compound-Complex sentences indicate a mature style of writing. A compound-complex sentence consists of two or more independent clauses and one or more subordinate clauses.

Reread these sentences from *The Life of Samuel Johnson:*

Though usually grave, and even aweful, in his deportment, he possessed uncommon and peculiar powers of wit and humor; he frequently indulged himself in colloquial pleasantry; and the heartiest merriment was often enjoyed in his company.

Exulting in his intellectual strength and dexterity, he could, when he pleased, be the greatest sophist that ever contended in the lists of declamation; and, from a spirit of contradiction and a delight in showing his powers, he would often maintain the wrong side with equal warmth and ingenuity.

Each of these sentences is compound: each has two independent clauses separated by a semicolon. Notice that there is a complete sentence on each side of the semicolon. With the deletion of the word *and* as well as the dropping of the est merriment was often enjoyed in his company; with this great advantage, that as it was entirely free from any poisonous tincture of vice or impiety, it was salutary to those who shared in it. He had accustomed himself to such accuracy in his common conversation, that he at all times expressed his thoughts with great force, and an elegant choice of language, the effect of which was aided by his having a loud voice, and a slow deliberate utterance. In him were united a most logical head with a most fertile imagination, which gave him an extraordinary advantage in arguing: for he could reason close or wide, as he saw best for the moment. Exulting in his intellectual strength and dexterity, he could, when he pleased, be the greatest sophist[20] that ever contended in the lists of declamation; and, from a spirit of contradiction and a delight in showing his powers, he would often maintain the wrong side with equal warmth and ingenuity; so that, when there was an audience, his real opinions could seldom be gathered from his talk; though when he was in company with a single friend, he would discuss a subject with genuine fairness: but he was too conscientious to make error permanent and pernicious, by deliberately writing it; and, in all his numerous works, he earnestly inculcated what appeared to him to be the truth; his piety being constant, and the ruling principle of all his conduct.

Such was Samuel Johnson, a man **15** whose talents, acquirements, and virtues, were so extraordinary, that the more his character is considered the more he will be regarded by the present age, and by posterity, with admiration and reverence.

---

20. sophist (säf′ ist) *n.*: One who makes misleading arguments.

from *The Life of Samuel Johnson*   581

---

15 Reading Strategy Summarize the contradictory qualities Boswell found fascinating in Johnson.

Reader's Response Whose biography would you enjoy writing and how would you research the matter?

---

semicolon and the addition of a capital letter, two separate sentences could be created.

Each of these sentences is also complex: each contains at least one subordinate clause beginning with a subordinating conjunction *(though, when).*

Student Activity 1. Copy out these example sentences. Underline the independent clauses and put parentheses around the subordinate clauses.

Student Activity 2. Write three compound-complex sentences of your own.

Closure and Extension

ANSWERS TO THINKING ABOUT THE SELECTION
Recalling

1. His body cramped convulsively; he was scared; his clothes were slovenly; one eye was useless; and he walked with a struggling gait.
2. (a) He was superstitious but not gullible. (b) He was a zealous Christian. (c) He loved praise. (d) He was somewhat susceptible to flattery.

Interpreting

3. (a) The art of using his mind and his powers of wit and humor explain his sarcastic remark. (b) He was charitable and actively benevolent. (c) He was impatient when provoked by ignorance.
4. Answers will differ. A possible answer is: Boswell's inferiority complex, which led him to become a celebrity chaser, probably led him to exaggerate Johnson's brilliance and wit, although the man undoubtedly had a good measure of both.

Applying

5. Answers will differ. Possible answers are: (a) "Man is, in general, made up of contradictory qualities . . ."; "At different times, he seemed a different man . . ."; ". . . he had many prejudices . . ."; and "He was somewhat susceptible of flattery." (b) No, because they help to form a complete picture of the man.
6. Answers will differ. Possible answers are: (a) Most celebrities seem to enjoy attention and to assume they are welcome to "drop in" on friends and acquaintances. They also assume that whatever they have to say is important. (b) One difference between Johnson and celebrities today is that today's celebrities would not generally appear in public in "a slovenly mode of dress."

ANSWERS TO ANALYZING LITERATURE

Answers will differ.
1. Boswell was so impressed by Johnson even before he met him and so anxious to impress him when he

THINKING ABOUT THE SELECTION
Recalling

1. What aspects of Johnson's appearance prompt Boswell to describe him as "strange and somewhat uncouth"?
2. (a) What, according to the selection, was Johnson's position on superstition? (b) On religion? (c) On praise? (d) On flattery?

Interpreting

3. (a) What details of Johnson's personality described in this excerpt explain his sarcastic remark about Scotland in "Boswell Meets Johnson"? (b) His desire to obtain a free theater ticket for a friend? (c) His harsh reply to Boswell's comment on Garrick?
4. What do you learn about Boswell himself from this passage? Support your comments with evidence.

Applying

5. (a) Which of the observations presented in this excerpt do you think apply more or less to most people? (b) Do you think the inclusion of these details detracts from the integrity of Boswell's biography? Explain your answer.
6. (a) What similarities do you detect between the lifestyles and habits of celebrities of the eighteenth century and those of our own age? (b) What differences do you detect?

ANALYZING LITERATURE
Understanding Biography

A **biography** is a history of a person told or written by others. A good biography meets several criteria. It presents (1) the subject in an impartial light; (2) a complete and unified picture of the subject; (3) the subject against the backdrop of the times in which he or she lived. Based on the excerpt from Boswell's *The Life of Samuel Johnson,* state how well you think the work meets these criteria. In making your assessment, consider the following questions.

1. Can Boswell's statement that he "was much agitated" upon meeting Johnson be taken as an admission that he was not in a frame of mind to report facts impartially? Why?
2. On page 578, Boswell notes that he preserved Johnson's observations "without marking the questions and observations" that led up to them. Does this suggest a lack of completeness? Why?

CRITICAL THINKING AND READING
Recognizing Subjective Information

Subjective information is information colored by a person's own attitudes and feelings. *Objective* information is information that preserves some widely held truth. The statement "I like to eat chicken" is a piece of subjective information. The statement "Chicken is a source of protein" is a piece of objective information. Biography, if it is interesting, will usually contain a mixture of subjective and objective statements.

Bearing in mind what you read about Boswell in the biographical sketch of him on page 574, which of the details presented in this excerpt do you suspect of being the most subjective? Explain your answer.

THINKING AND WRITING
Writing from Johnson's Point of View

Write an account of the meeting described in this excerpt from Samuel Johnson's point of view. Before beginning, review Boswell's quotations of Johnson in order to help you form an impression of the older man's prose style and general attitude toward life. Feel free to add original details that may have escaped Boswell's attention.

did that he probably could not have been impartial.
2. The statements provide a good picture of Johnson even without the questions and observations that led up to them.

ANSWERS TO CRITICAL THINKING AND READING

Answers will differ. Students should provide support for their choices.

THINKING AND WRITING

For help with this assignment, students can use Lesson 10, "Writing About Point of View," in the Handbook of Writing About Literature.

Pre-Romantic Poetry

HAYMAKERS, 1785
George Stubbs
The Granger Collection

More About the Author Thomas Gray remains one of the best known and respected of all English poets, yet his reputation rests entirely on the basis of three major poems and three or four short lyrics. Ask students to discuss the relative value of quality versus quantity in determining ranking in any field. Should a person who has contributed only, say, two or three admittedly brilliant poems—or songs, or books, etc.—be ranked with artists who have contributed much more —even if the works of the more productive artists are not all first rate?

Critical Evaluation Joseph Wood Krutch, noted literary historian and critic, has selected and edited the correspondence of Thomas Gray. In explaining his understanding of why Gray seems to have written so limited an amount of poetry, Krutch has this to say about his subject's habits: "Gray was a reluctant poet as he was a reluctant everything else. Whether one calls it timidity, pride, disdain, or even the desire for perfection, something made him hesitate to write, hesitate to show what he had written and hesitate above all to publish." In the introduction to his collection of Gray's letters, Krutch examines various theories for the poet's hesitancy. He dismisses those, like Roger Martin, who argue that Gray's habits were the result of physical and psychological disorders over which the artist had no control.

THOMAS GRAY

(1716–1771)

Although Thomas Gray produced precious little poetry during his lifetime, his scant output was more a result of his perfectionism than it was of any lack of ideas. Gray was a scholar, with interests ranging from literature to art to science and beyond. Had he lived in an era more compatible with the romantic yearnings of his soul, he might, as the poet Matthew Arnold suggested, have been capable of far greater things.

Gray was born in the Cornhill section of London. Gray himself suffered from convulsions, a condition that forced his mother on at least one occasion to open a vein in his head to relieve pressure on his brain. He was educated at Eton and Cambridge and, after completing his studies, traveled through Europe with his friend Horace Walpole.

At the end of three years, Gray returned to England and lived for a time with his mother and sister in the village of Stoke Poges. It was in this sleepy hamlet during the summer of 1742 that he wrote his first important poems—"On the Spring," "On a Distant Prospect of Eton College," and "Hymn to Adversity." It was also around this time that Gray penned his most famous poetic work, "Elegy Written in a Country Churchyard." A copy of the elegy that he sent to Walpole accidentally fell into the hands of a dishonest editor. Ultimately it was retrieved, though only after a great struggle, which adds a touch of irony to Gray's having refused to accept payment for the poem when at last it was published.

After reaching the age of thirty, Gray lived an increasingly quiet country life, becoming something of a hermit. A confirmed bachelor, he busied himself with books and experimented with new poetic forms, while conducting private studies in classical literature at Cambridge. His work of this period, which includes the odes "The Bard" (1757) and "The Descent of Odin" (1761), reflects his love of Celtic and Norse mythology and his interest in history and language. In 1771 while planning a visit to a friend in Switzerland, the poet suffered a violent attack of gout and died on July 30. Seven years after his death, a monument honoring him was erected in Westminster Abbey.

Although Gray was a less than energetic poet, the small body of works that he left behind is notable for its juxtaposing of established forms and novel sentiments. His "Elegy Written in a Country Churchyard," in particular, skillfully combines the neoclassical style of his own century with the Romantic ideals of the next one.

Objectives

1 To understand the elegy as a literary form
2 To evaluate the effect of inverted sentences in verse
3 To appreciate vivid verbs in verse
4 To write an elegy

Support Material

Teaching Portfolio
Teacher Backup, p. 695
Grammar in Action Worksheet, *Participles and Gerunds,* p. 700
Usage and Mechanics Worksheet, p. 702
Vocabulary Check, p. 703

Critical Thinking and Reading Worksheet, *Evaluating The Effect of Inverted Sentences,* p. 704
Language Worksheet, *Appreciating Vivid Verbs,* p. 705
Selection Test, p. 706

GUIDE FOR INTERPRETING

Elegy Written in a Country Churchyard

Literary Forms

Elegy. An elegy is a lyric poem or musical composition that laments a death. The form, which dates back to ancient Greece and Rome, flourished during the European Renaissance that spanned the fourteenth through the sixteenth centuries. Although an elegy usually mourns the death of an individual, it may also address the ravages of time or may function as a meditation on the nature of loss. The elegy, while conforming to no rigid structural guidelines, often opens with an expression of grief and moves gradually toward a philosophical acceptance of the loss. Thomas Gray's "Elegy Written in a Country Churchyard," inspired by the death of the poet's close friend Richard West, marks one of three highpoints of the elegiac form in English literature, the other being Milton's "Lycidas" and Tennyson's *In Memoriam.*

Writing

Gray's elegy ends with an epitaph, a poetic inscription intended to appear on a gravestone. Often an epitaph mentions a property or trait of the deceased for which he or she might best be remembered. Write an epitaph for yourself or for a friend. Focus, using as few words as possible, on the individual's most memorable quality.

Primary Source

Whether Gray wrote his own epitaph has not been recorded, but several other writers of the time did leave behind the poems they wanted inscribed on their gravestones. Alexander Pope, for example, left the following lines for his gravestone:

> Under this marble, or under the sill,
> Or under this turf, or e'en what they will;
> Whatever an heir, or a friend in his stead,
> Or any good creature shall lay o'er my head;
> Lies he who ne'er car'd, and still cares not a pin,
> What they said, or may say of the mortal within.
> But who living and dying, serene still and free,
> Trusts in God, that as well as he was, he shall be.

Several years later, Coleridge penned this epitaph for himself:

> Here sleeps at length poor Col., and without screaming;
> Who died as he lived, a-dreaming:
> Shot dead, while sleeping, by the gout within—
> All alone and unknown, at Edinbro' in an inn.

As you read, look for the differences between the epitaph that ends Gray's elegy and the ones Pope and Coleridge wrote for themselves.

Guide for Interpreting 585

Literary Focus Stress the fact that the elegy is a meditative poem lamenting the death of a particular person. Gray's elegy, however, laments not the death of a specific person, but dwells on death as the ultimate fate of all people, rich and poor alike.

Writing/Prior Knowledge You might lead your students in writing a group epitaph in the form of a quatrain rhyming *abab.* Begin with the formula phrase *Here lies . . .*

Vocabulary

Preteach the following vocabulary words:
knell (nel) *n.:* Sound of a bell rung slowly (p. 586, l. 1)
jocund (jäk'ənd) *adj.:* Cheerful (p. 589, l. 27)
pregnant (preg'nənt) *adj.:* Full of ideas; inventive (p. 589, l.46)
penury (pen'yə rē) *n.:* Poverty (p. 589, l.51)
inglorious (in glôr'ē əs) *adj.:* Little-known (p. 589, l. 59)
circumscribed (sʉr' kəm skrīb'd) *v.:* Limited; confined (p. 589, l. 65)
ingenuous (in jen'yoo wəs) *adj.:* Naive; simple (p. 590, l.69)
tenor (ten'ər) *n.:* General tendency or course (p. 591, l. 76)

Spelling Tip Point out the silent *k* in *knell.*

Presentation

Motivation/Prior Knowledge
Suggest that your students look for the democratic spirit that pervades this poem. What seems to be Gray's attitude toward the ordinary, humble man and woman.

Master Teacher Note Gray is a transitional figure, a bridge between the eighteenth-century classical ideals and the Romantic movement of the nineteenth century. As his "Elegy . . ." reveals, Gray reflects the former in his respect for established literary forms and in his knowledge of Greek and Roman culture. At the same time elements of Romanticism are revealed—in the subject matter and in the dignified tone of the poem.

Purpose-Setting Question
Whom does the poet lament in this elegy?

Thematic Idea Compare Gray's poem with the excerpt from John Donne's "Meditation 17," on page 405. How are they similar in content; how are they different? A similar comparison may be made with "Thoughts in Westminster Abbey," page 541.

1 Literary Focus Note that the poem is written in iambic-pentameter quatrains, with an alternating rhyme scheme, *abab.* This is a typical eighteenth-century elegiac form.

2 Reading Strategy Have students sum up the content of the opening three stanzas. Note how they establish the setting and mood of the poem. What time of day is it? Where is the speaker? How do you know it is set in the country? What is the mood of these stanzas?

3 Literary Focus In line 13 the speaker shifts attention to the graveyard and its inhabitants. This stanza and the next nineteen offer

Elegy Written in a Country Churchyard

Thomas Gray

1

The curfew tolls the knell of parting day,
    The lowing herd winds slowly o'er the lea,[1]
The plowman homeward plods his weary way,
    And leaves the world to darkness and to me.

5 Now fades the glimmering landscape on the sight,
    And all the air a solemn stillness holds,
Save where the beetle wheels his droning flight,
    And drowsy tinklings lull the distant folds;

2 10 Save that from yonder ivy-mantled tower,
    The moping owl does to the moon complain
Of such as, wandering near her secret bower,
    Molest her ancient solitary reign.

3 Beneath those rugged elms, that yew tree's shade,
    Where heaves the turf in many a moldering heap,
15 Each in his narrow cell forever laid,
    The rude[2] forefathers of the hamlet sleep.

4, 5 The breezy call of incense-breathing morn,
    The swallow twittering from the straw-built shed,
The cock's shrill clarion, or the echoing horn,[3]
20   No more shall rouse them from their lowly bed.

6, 7 For them no more the blazing hearth shall burn,
    Or busy housewife ply her evening care;
No children run to lisp their sire's return,
    Or climb his knees the envied kiss to share.

---

1. lea: Meadow.
2. rude: Uneducated.
3. horn: The hunter's horn.

some general reflections prompted by the setting.

4 Clarification A clarion is a trumpet-like sound.

5 Discussion Note the morning sounds described in lines 17–20. How are they different from the evening sounds in the first three stanzas?

6 Discussion Lines 21–28 illustrate activities in the daily lives of these simple people. What kinds of activities are mentioned? How did they feel about their work? Does the speaker sympathize with or mock their lives?

7 Literary Focus Gray's sympathy with common people and his sense that working close to nature is both joyful and ennobling are Romantic attitudes.

8 **Literary Focus** In lines 29–44 the speaker shifts to talk about the inevitability of death—even for the mighty. Note the formal style.

9 **Literary Focus** Line 36 is one of the many lines often quoted from this poem. Note the use of personification in this line.

25 Oft did the harvest to their sickle yield,
        Their furrow oft the stubborn glebe[4] has broke;
    How jocund did they drive their team afield!
        How bowed the woods beneath their sturdy stroke!

    Let not Ambition mock their useful toil,
30   Their homely joys, and destiny obscure;
    Nor Grandeur hear with a disdainful smile
        The short and simple annals of the poor.

    The boast of heraldry,[5] the pomp of power,
        And all that beauty, all that wealth e'er gave,
35 Awaits alike the inevitable hour.
        The paths of glory lead but to the grave.

---

4. glebe: Soil.
5. heraldry: Noble descent.

Elegy Written in a Country Churchyard   587

10 Clarification "Hands, that the rod of empire might have swayed" means "mighty ruler." "Or waked to ecstasy the living lyre" is a way of saying "poet."

11 Discussion What kept these dead from realizing their potential? Point out that the word *rage* means "ardor or enthusiasm." The phrase *genial current* means "natural potentialities."

12 Literary Focus Lines 53–56 are often quoted. In your own words summarize the meaning. How apt are the lines, considering the theme of the poem?

13 Clarification Lines 61–72 might be summarized as "Their lot in life prevented them from becoming great statesmen and benefactors, but it also prevented them from becoming tyrants." Explain that the phrase *ingenuous shame* might mean "the shame a good person feels when he or she doesn't live up to ideals."

Nor you, ye proud, impute to these the fault,
    If memory o'er their tomb no trophies[6] raise,
Where through the long-drawn aisle and fretted vault[7]
40   The pealing anthem swells the note of praise.

Can storied urn,[8] or animated[9] bust,
    Back to its mansion call the fleeting breath?
Can honor's voice provoke[10] the silent dust,
    Or Flattery soothe the dull cold ear of Death?

45 Perhaps in this neglected spot is laid
    Some heart once pregnant with celestial fire;
Hands, that the rod of empire might have swayed,
    Or waked to ecstasy the living lyre.

But Knowledge to their eyes her ample page
50   Rich with the spoils of time did ne'er unroll;
Chill Penury repressed their noble rage,
    And froze the genial current of the soul.

Full many a gem of purest ray serene
    The dark unfathomed caves of ocean bear:
55 Full many a flower is born to blush unseen,
    And waste its sweetness on the desert air.

Some village Hampden,[11] that, with dauntless breast,
    The little tyrant of his fields withstood,
Some mute inglorious Milton[12] here may rest,
60   Some Cromwell[13] guiltless of his country's blood.

The applause of listening senates to command,
    The threats of pain and ruin to despise,
To scatter plenty o'er a smiling land,
    And read their history in a nation's eyes,

65 Their lot forbade: nor circumscribed alone
    Their growing virtues, but their crimes confined
Forbade to wade through slaughter to a throne,
    And shut the gates of mercy on mankind,

6. trophies: Symbolic figures or pictures depicting the achievements of the dead man.
7. fretted vault: A church ceiling decorated with intersecting lines.
8. storied urn: A funeral urn with an epitaph inscribed on it.
9. animated: Lifelike.
10. provoke: Call forth.
11. Hampden: John Hampden (1594–1643), an English statesman who defied King Charles I by resisting the king's efforts to revive the obsolete tax of ship-money without the authority of Parliament.
12. Milton: English poet, John Milton (1608–1674).
13. Cromwell: Oliver Cromwell (1599–1658), English revolutionary leader and Lord Protector of the Commonwealth from 1653 to 1658.

Grammar in Action

Participles and **gerunds** should not be confused. Both are verb forms and can end in *-ing,* but participles act as adjectives in sentences while gerunds act as nouns. Notice how Thomas Gray uses participles and gerunds in his poem.

The curfew tolls the knell of *parting* day,
    The *lowing* herd winds slowly o'er the lea,
The plowman homeward plods his weary way,
    And leaves the world to darkness and to me.

Now fades the *glimmering* landscape on the sight,
    And all the air a solemn stillness holds,
Save where the beetle wheels his *droning* flight,
    And drowsy *tinklings* lull the distant folds;

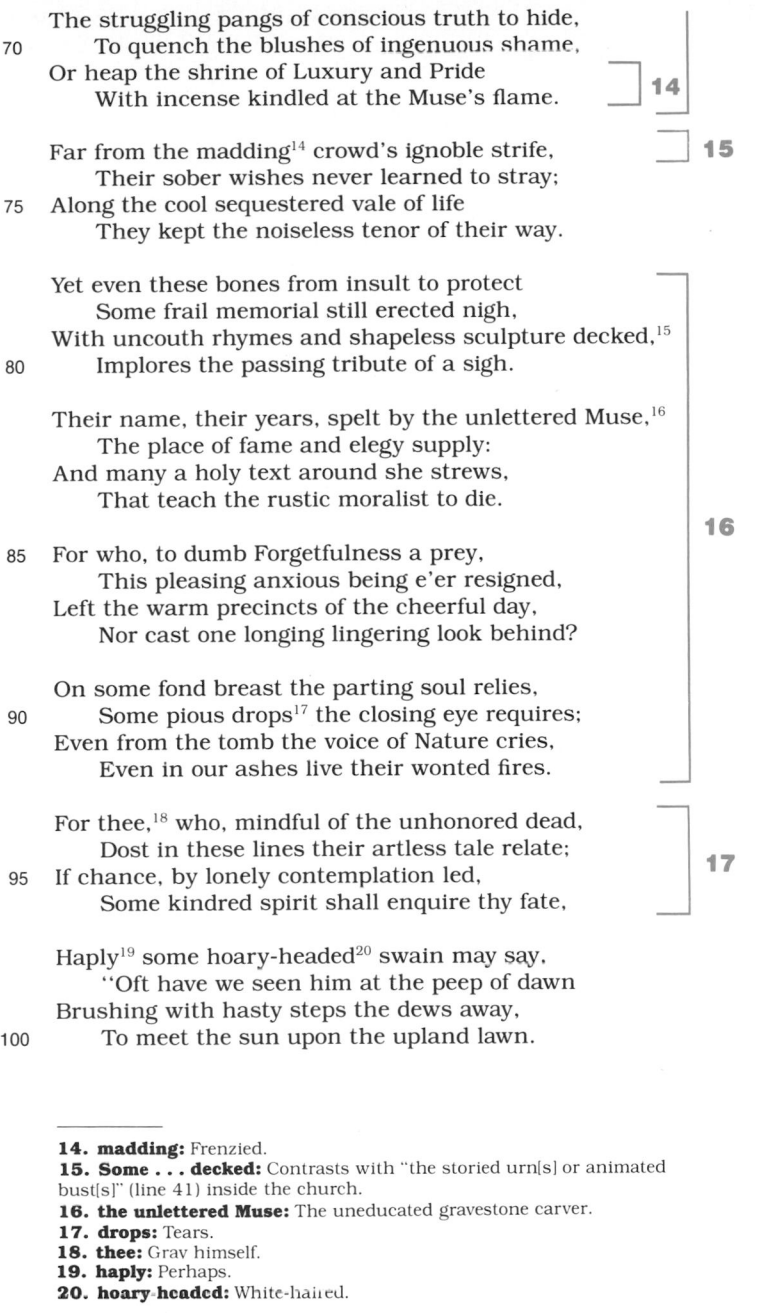

The struggling pangs of conscious truth to hide,
70   To quench the blushes of ingenuous shame,
Or heap the shrine of Luxury and Pride
    With incense kindled at the Muse's flame. **14**

Far from the madding[14] crowd's ignoble strife, **15**
    Their sober wishes never learned to stray;
75 Along the cool sequestered vale of life
    They kept the noiseless tenor of their way.

Yet even these bones from insult to protect
    Some frail memorial still erected nigh,
With uncouth rhymes and shapeless sculpture decked,[15]
80   Implores the passing tribute of a sigh.

Their name, their years, spelt by the unlettered Muse,[16]
    The place of fame and elegy supply:
And many a holy text around she strews,
    That teach the rustic moralist to die. **16**

85 For who, to dumb Forgetfulness a prey,
    This pleasing anxious being e'er resigned,
Left the warm precincts of the cheerful day,
    Nor cast one longing lingering look behind?

On some fond breast the parting soul relies,
90   Some pious drops[17] the closing eye requires;
Even from the tomb the voice of Nature cries,
    Even in our ashes live their wonted fires.

For thee,[18] who, mindful of the unhonored dead,
    Dost in these lines their artless tale relate; **17**
95 If chance, by lonely contemplation led,
    Some kindred spirit shall enquire thy fate,

Haply[19] some hoary-headed[20] swain may say,
    "Oft have we seen him at the peep of dawn
Brushing with hasty steps the dews away,
100   To meet the sun upon the upland lawn.

---

14. **madding:** Frenzied.
15. **Some . . . decked:** Contrasts with "the storied urn[s] or animated bust[s]" (line 41) inside the church.
16. **the unlettered Muse:** The uneducated gravestone carver.
17. **drops:** Tears.
18. **thee:** Gray himself.
19. **haply:** Perhaps.
20. **hoary-headed:** White-haired.

Elegy Written in a Country Churchyard 589

14 **Clarification** Lines 71–72 are an allusion to people who write poetry that extols the vices of powerful people.

15 **Literary Focus** Thomas Hardy chose "Far from the madding crowd" as the title of one of his novels.

16 **Literary Focus** In lines 77–92 the speaker shifts focus to the desire of humble people for some kind of immortality in the minds of the living. Lines 85–92 offer a reason why these people need a memorial of some kind. What is that reason? Explain that the phrase *this pleasing anxious being* means "the living human body."

17 **Clarification** The *thee* is the *me* of line 4. The speaker is addressing himself, imagining the death of the kind of person he is. *If chance* means "if it happens that."

Gray uses many *-ing* verb forms in the poem. Most are participles modifying nouns, as in "parting day", "lowing herd", "glimmering landscape", and "droning flight." Occasionally, however, he uses a gerund, such as "tinklings," which functions here as the subject of the clause "drowsy tinklings lull the distant folds." It is important to remember that *-ing* endings can also be found on verbs acting as verbs. The only way to correctly identify an *-ing* word as a participle or gerund is to examine its use in the sentence.

Student Activity 1. Read lines 17 through 20 in the poem and tell whether each *-ing* word is a participle, a gerund, or a verb.

Student Activity 2. Identify the participles and gerunds in the following sentences and explain how each functions.

1. Mowing the lawn is not my idea of a rollicking good time.
2. My poor aching back hates mowing more than anything.
3. I think hiring a gardner is an exciting idea!

19 **Literary Focus** This imaginary
epitaph is written for a person
very much like Gray himself, although it does not appear on the
poet's own gravestone. Even after
the "Elegy . . ." was published
and brought him fame, Gray remained both indifferent to and
suspicious of it. Explain how the
epitaph is a logical summation of
the poem.

Reader's Response What do
you think about when you see
graveyards?

Challenge Explain why passages
like lines 3, 8, and 88 have been
acclaimed for their blend of sound
and sense. What other memorable passages did you find? Explain your choices.

"There at the foot of yonder nodding beech,
  That wreathes its old fantastic roots so high,
His listless length at noontide would he stretch,
  And pore upon the brook that babbles by.

105 "Hard by yon wood, now smiling as in scorn,
  Muttering his wayward fancies he would rove;
Now drooping, woeful wan, like one forlorn,
  Or crazed with care, or crossed in hopeless love.

18 110 "One morn I missed him on the customed hill,
  Along the heath, and near his favorite tree;
Another came; nor yet beside the rill,[21]
  Nor up the lawn, nor at the wood was he;

"The next, with dirges due in sad array
  Slow through the churchway path we saw him borne.
115 Approach and read (for thou canst read) the lay
  Graved on the stone beneath yon aged thorn."[22]

The Epitaph

*Here rests his head upon the lap of Earth
  A youth, to Fortune and to Fame unknown.
Fair Science[23] frowned not on his humble birth,
120 And melancholy marked him for her own.*

19
*Large was his bounty, and his soul sincere,
  Heaven did a recompense as largely send:
He gave to misery (all he had) a tear,
  He gained from Heaven ('twas all he wished) a friend.*

125 *No farther seek his merits to disclose,
  Or draw his frailties from their dread abode
(There they alike in trembling hope repose),
  The bosom of his Father and his God.*

---

21. **rill:** Brook.
22. **thorn:** Hawthorn tree.
23. **Science:** Learning.

THINKING ABOUT THE SELECTION

Recalling

1. The first four stanzas establish the setting of the poem. (a) Where is the speaker? (b) What time of day is it?
2. According to lines 21–25, what pleasure will these "rude forefathers" no longer partake of?
3. What sorts of lives does the speaker speculate, in lines 57–60, that these people might have led under other circumstances?
4. To whom is "The Epitaph" in the last three stanzas dedicated?

Interpreting

5. (a) What do you think is meant by "the inevitable hour" in line 35? (b) By "its mansion" in line 42?
6. (a) How would you summarize the sentiment expressed in lines 53–56? (b) In lines 77–92?

Applying

7. (a) Tell who or what the poet is elegizing. (b) State whether you share his sense of loss, giving reasons for your answer.

ANALYZING LITERATURE

Understanding an Elegy

An **elegy** is a lyric poem that expresses mourning. Usually the object of this mourning is the death of an individual, though an elegy can also grieve the toll that time's passage takes on youth or beauty. Typically the elegy begins solemnly, with the poet's expression of sadness over his or her loss, and ends with an insight that enables the poet to cope with this loss.

1. (a) Whom does the poet grieve in "Elegy Written in a Country Churchyard"? (b) What do these people seem to represent to the poet? (c) What words express the poet's sadness?
2. (a) Does the poet come to accept his loss by the end of the poem? Explain your answer. (b) What insight helps him to reach this acceptance? (c) What ideas or thoughts bridge his grief and his acceptance?

CRITICAL THINKING AND READING

Evaluating Inverted Sentences

In English the most common sentence structure is subject-verb-object. That is, the "doer" of the action is usually named first, the word specifying the action appears second, and the recipient of the action comes last. In poetry the parts of the sentence are sometimes **inverted,** or reversed, to emphasize a particular idea. In line 90, for example, the poet places the object *some pious drops* before both the subject and verb of the sentence, to focus the reader's attention on the idea of tears. Locate the following lines, and identify the order of the sentence parts. Then tell what idea is being stressed.

1. Line 5
2. Lines 13–16
3. Lines 49–50
4. Lines 81–82

UNDERSTANDING LANGUAGE

Appreciating Vivid Verbs

The words a poet uses can help convey the poem's mood and can influence the feelings the poem arouses in the reader. In the opening stanzas of Gray's "Elegy," the mood is one of quiet solemnity. To carry this feeling across to the reader, the poet chooses **vivid,** or highly descriptive, verbs. Notice, for instance, Gray's use of the verb *plod* in line 3, to suggest slow and weary movement. Imagine how bland the line would have seemed if the poet had instead chosen the verb *goes.*

Find five vivid verbs in this elegy and explain the effect of each.

THINKING AND WRITING

Writing an Elegy

Using the epitaph you created for the Writing activity on page 585 as a starting point, write an elegy. Imitate as many of the features of Gray's "Elegy" as you can, including inverted sentence structure and vivid verbs. Remember to begin your elegy with an expression of your grief and to end it with a statement of acceptance.

(Answers begin on p. 590)

ANSWERS TO CRITICAL THINKING AND READING

1. Line 5 is verb-subject. Here the poet stresses the word *fades.*
2. Lines 13–16 begin with a series of subordinate clauses, and end with a subject-verb arrangement. The poet uses the subordinate clauses to build the reader's emotions, climaxing with the final, main clause.
3. Lines 49–50 offer a similar arrangement. Subordinate matter precedes the subject; more intervening subordinate matter follows the subject; and the lines end with the verb.
4. Lines 81–82 offer a subordinate clause, with its modifiers, followed by the subject and verb; again the poet reverses the normal word order to build emotional suspense.

ANSWERS TO UNDERSTANDING LANGUAGE

Answers will differ. Possibilities include

1. In line 8 the verb *lull* helps build a mood of somnolence.
2. In line 14 the verb *heaves* helps build a mood of energetic motion.
3. In line 23 the verb *lisp* helps build a mood of playful innocence and love.
4. In line 28 the verb *bowed* helps build a mood of aquiescence.
5. In line 40 the verb *swells* helps build a mood of pride.

Challenge Ask students to consider whether it is better to lead a quiet, obscure life, or one in which the person is famous. Once they have marshalled their ideas pro and con, have them write a paper of four or five paragraphs defending their choice.

THINKING AND WRITING

Publishing Student Writing Invite students to read their elegies in class.

---

3. These people, under other circumstances, might have been great leaders—in literature and in politics, for example.
4. "The epitaph" is dedicated to all the humble, unknown people buried in the churchyard.

Interpreting

5. (a) The "inevitable hour" is the moment of death. (b) "Its mansion" is life itself.

6. (a) Answers will differ but should include the idea that many wonderful things in nature go unnoticed. (b) Answers will differ but should include the idea that the humble people long for some kind of immortality in the minds of the living.

Applying

7. (a) The poet is elegizing the death of all people, the mighty and the common. (b) Answers will differ.

ANSWERS TO ANALYZING LITERATURE

1. (a) The poet grieves for the common people, whose lives go unnoticed. (b) They seem to represent the Romantic attitude that working close to nature is both joyful and ennobling. (c) Answers to the last question in this item will differ.
2. (a) and (b) The poet accepts his loss, believing that these dead repose in heaven with God. (c) Answers to the last question in this item will differ.

More About the Author The poem "Woman" is from Oliver Goldsmith's novel *The Vicar of Wakefield*. In 1762, Dr. Samuel Johnson, a good friend of Goldsmith, learned that Goldsmith had been arrested for not paying his rent. When Johnson arrived at the scene, Goldsmith admitted that his only asset was the unpublished manuscript of the novel. Johnson was able to sell the manuscript to a publisher for enough money to keep Goldsmith out of jail. On another occasion Goldsmith gambled away most of his passage money for a planned trip to America and gave the rest to a poor woman with eight children. What do these anecdotes tell you about Goldsmith's personality and in particular, his ability to handle money?

Literary Focus How do the theme and open pattern of the poem "Woman" show Goldsmith's transition from a neoclassicist—a believer in the orderly rationality of ancient Greece and Rome—to a Romantic poet?

Writing/Prior Knowledge For inspiration students may read several advice columns.

Vocabulary

Preteach the following vocabulary words:
folly (fäl′ē) *n.*: Foolish action or belief (l. 1)
melancholy (mel′ən käl′ē) *n.*: Sadness; lowness of spirit (l. 3)

GUIDE FOR INTERPRETING

Woman

Oliver Goldsmith (1728–1774) was generally regarded as an essayist of the highest standing. Much of what is known of the first half of Goldsmith's life is known through his own accounts. In 1766, four years after the publication of an important collection of essays titled *The Citizen of the World,* he produced his only novel, *The Vicar of Wakefield*. Later, Goldsmith turned to poetry and enjoyed both critical and financial success

Goldsmith's early years gave no indication of his future success. As a child, he was badly scarred by smallpox and was ill-suited for sports. He was an unmotivated student whom others judged lazy and thick. Nonetheless, his clergyman father enrolled him in Trinity College, Dublin, as a scholarship student. Although he received his degree in 1749, he still had no clear idea of what path he wished to pursue. A relative paid his way to medical college in Scotland, but he found the study not to his liking and instead roamed through Europe for several years. After somehow procuring a medical degree, he returned to England when he was twenty-eight years old but was unable to make a living as a doctor. He ended up trying his hand at writing. He had found his niche.

His writings are remarkable for their quality and variety, including such brilliant comedies as the play *She Stoops to Conquer* and the elegant poem "The Deserted Village."

Writer's Technique

Poetic Structure. Poetic structure is the pattern or formal design of a poem. Several factors determine a poem's structure: number of stressed syllables per line, line length, and rhyme scheme. Also grouped under the heading of structure are such considerations as the size and shape of the stanzas and the relationship among ideas, images, and sound devices used by the poet. Generally poems are categorized, in terms of their structure, as either closed-pattern or open-pattern. Closed-pattern poems are those that exhibit some or all of the properties of a well-defined traditional poetic form; sonnets and ballads are two examples of closed-pattern poems. Open-pattern poems exhibit no such properties. Oliver Goldsmith's "Woman" is an example of an open-pattern poem.

Writing

Imagine that you write an advice column for a local newspaper. You have received a letter from a young man or woman who is heartbroken. Write a response in the form of a poem offering original suggestions that will help the person get through this difficult period.

Teaching to Ability Levels Review with **less advanced** students the poetic structure of such closed-pattern forms as a sonnet and a ballad. A sonnet has fourteen iambic pentameter lines rhyming according to one of two general schemes. A ballad has four lines of poetry with a rhyme scheme *abcb*. You may also want to review meter.

Objectives

To understand poetic structure

Support Material

Teaching Portfolio
Teacher Backup, p. 709
Usage and Mechanics Worksheet, p. 712
Vocabulary Check, p. 713
Analyzing Literature Worksheet, *Understanding Poetic Structure,* p. 714
Language Worksheet, *Completing Word Analogies,* p. 715
Selection Test, p. 716

Woman

Oliver Goldsmith

When lovely woman stoops to folly,
    And finds too late that men betray,   **1**
What charm can soothe her melancholy?
    What art can wash her tears away?

5 The only art her guilt to cover,
    To hide her shame from every eye,   **2**
To give repentance to her lover,
    And wring his bosom is—to die.

THINKING ABOUT THE SELECTION

Recalling

1. What has made the woman in the poem melancholy?
2. (a) What question does the speaker ask? (b) What answer does he give?

Interpreting

3. Judging from its usage in lines 4 and 5, what do you think is meant by the term "art"?
4. Do you think the poet is being serious in his solution for melancholy of the sort described in the poem? Explain why you feel as you do?

Applying

5. What does the poet's addressing this poem exclusively to women suggest about the values of his era?

ANALYZING LITERATURE

Understanding Poetic Structure

    Poetic structure is the shape or general pattern of a poem. The elements that determine a poem's structure include the number of beats per line, line length, rhyme scheme, and stanza size. Depending on their structure, poems fall into either the closed-pattern or open-pattern category. Closed-pattern poems are those that follow a well-defined set of structural rules. The sonnet, which is required among other things to have exactly fourteen lines, is an example of a closed-pattern poetic form. Open-pattern poems, by contrast, are free of such rigid constraints. The structure a poet chooses for a particular poem is often a function of the poem's content and theme.

1. (a) What aspects of the content and theme in "Woman" do you think led the poet to choose an open pattern for the poem? (b) Why do you think he wrote his poem in a total of two four-line stanzas?
2. What effect is created by the short, almost abrupt, lines?
3. What other factors can you think of that may have led to the poet's use of rhyming lines and a regular number of stressed syllables? Support your answer.

Woman   593

More about the Author Although Robert Burns liked to portray himself as an artist whose work came naturally from his emotions, he was actually quite well educated by the time he started to write. Similarly, although his public image was that of a simple Scottish farmer (he was called the "Peasant Poet"), his work won him acceptance into Edinburgh high society, and he spent a great deal of time in that city enjoying his literary and social success. But at the height of his popularity Burns decided to leave Edinburgh and return to farming. He said, "I see the time not distant far when the popular tide shall recede with silent celerity and leave me a barren waste of sand." What did Burns mean by these words? Can you think of any modern-day examples of personalities for whom "the popular tide receded"?

Critical Evaluation Those who find the dialect used by Burns confusing might do well to keep the following in mind. It is an insightful summation of the poet's approach written by Robert Fitzhugh, one of Burns' biographers.

"He developed a highly individualized style and idiom. He devised a mixture of general English and of Scots spoken in no particular area and by no particular group, to create the informal and conversational manner he wanted. He shifts back and forth from English to Scots as it suits his purpose, his rhythm, his rhyming need, his poetic mood. He tries to be simple, clear, and exciting. He speaks naturally, and to the heart."

ROBERT BURNS

1759–1796

No other name is more synonymous with the title "The voice of Scotland" than that of the poet Robert Burns. A farmer and a farmer's son, Burns was born at Alloway, in Ayrshire, and spent his early years in the two-room clay cottage his father had built. Although poverty prevented Burns from receiving a formal education, with his father's encouragement he read widely, studying the Bible, Shakespeare, and Alexander Pope on his own. His mother, though herself illiterate, instilled in him a love of Scottish folk songs, legends, and proverbs.

In 1786 Burns published his first collection of poems at a small local press. Although the collection, which included "To a Mouse," was successful, Burns only first came to the attention of the public at large the following year when a fuller collection, *Poems: Chiefly in Scottish,* was published at Edinburgh. He was invited to the Scottish capital, where he was swept into the social scene, if only as something of a rustic curiosity. He left Edinburgh in 1788, to explore the English border region and the Highlands.

Later that year he married Jean Armour, his sweetheart of many years, and returned to the farm to work the land. The soil proved unproductive, however, and so to supplement his income he took a position with the Excise Service—Scotland's department of taxation. All the while he continued to refine his poetic style, turning out some of his finest verses. At the outbreak of the French Revolution, he became an outspoken supporter of the republican cause, a move that threatened his job and alienated many of his friends. His spirits low and his health taxed by a weak heart he had had since childhood, Burns contracted a fever from which he never recovered. Thousands of people from all social levels followed his coffin to the grave, and he was acclaimed the national poet of Scotland.

Burns's numerous adventures produced many lyrics that figure among the most natural and spontaneous the English language has produced. His poems, written for the most part in dialect, are characterized by innocence, honesty, and simplicity. First and last a people's poet, Burns crafted poetic "melodies" that speak to "the sons and daughters of labor and poverty"—and for them. Though some of the poet's work had its origins in folk tunes, "it is not," as James Douglas wrote, "easy to tell where the vernacular ends and the personal magic begins."

Objectives

1 To understand Robert Burns's use of dialect
2 To recognize satire as a form of humor
3 To compare and contrast two poems in writing
4 To write about dialect

Support Material

Teaching Portfolio
Teacher Backup, p. 719
Grammar in Action Worksheet, *Appreciating Dialect,* p. 724
Usage and Mechanics Worksheet, p. 726
Vocabulary Check, p. 727
Analyzing Literature Worksheet, *Recognizing Dialect,* p. 729

Critical Thinking and Reading Worksheet, *Recognizing Satire,* p. 730
Selection Test, p. 732

GUIDE FOR INTERPRETING

To a Mouse; To a Louse; Afton Water; John Anderson, My Jo

Writer's Technique

Dialect. Dialect is the language, and particularly the speech habits, of a particular social class, region, or group. A dialect may vary from the standard form of a language in grammar, in pronunciation, and in the use of certain expressions. In literature it can serve to establish character, tone, and setting. The use of dialect by a writer or poet can also add to the immediacy and familiarity of a piece of literature.

In the eighteenth century, the belief was widespread among writers that only formal diction was acceptable in poetry. Rules were thus developed concerning the subjects and styles that were thought to be appropriate for poetry. Common life and colloquial language were almost always excluded from the poet's domain. Robert Burns rebelled against these rules, both with his use of Scottish dialect and his celebration of the rural and working life. Like so many poets of the age that ushered in the Romanticism of the next generation, Burns strived to capture in words the language and experiences of the human heart.

Writing

Write an account titled A Day in the Life of a _____, filling in the blank with one of the following: dog, cat, bird, squirrel, goldfish, or gerbil. Try to get inside the mind of the subject of your narrative, imagining the triumphs, defeats, fears, and hopes your creature experiences on a typical day.

Primary Source

As with many writers, Burns kept a Commonplace Book, a place to record scraps of lyrics, topics for poetry, and various thoughts and ideas on numerous different topics. A number of his entries reveal that he had long considered using dialect and adapting legendary Scotch songs in his poetry. In one entry, he remarked:

> There is a degree of wild irregularity in many of the compositions & Fragments which are daily sung to them by my compeers, the common people—a certain happy arrangement of old Scotch syllables, & yet, very frequently, nothing, not even like rhyme, or sameness of jingle at the ends of the lines. —This has made me sometimes imagine that perhaps, it might be possible for a Scotch Poet, with a nice, judicious ear, to set compositions to many of our favorite airs, particularly the class of them mentioned above, independent of rhyme altogether.—

Literary Focus Ask students to consider what aspects of Robert Burns's life and work made him stand out from poets and prose writers who preceded him.

Writing/Prior Knowledge Ask students about movies or television shows they have seen or stories they have read which are told from an animal's point of view. Discuss whether the author was successful in getting "inside the mind" of the animal. If the author was successful, suggest that they use similar techniques in writing their own accounts.

Vocabulary

Preteach the following vocabulary words:

keen (kēn) *adj.*: Having a sharp edge or point (p. 597, l. 24)

drear (drir) *adj.*: Dreary; melancholy (p. 598, l. 46)

impudence (im' pyoo dəns) *n.*: Quality of being rash or contrary (p. 599, l. 2)

kindred (kin'drid) *n.*: Relatives; relations (p. 599, l. 15)

rills (rilz) *n.*: Little brooks (p. 602, l. 10)

wanton (wän't'n) *adj.*: Frisky; playful (p. 603, l. 19)

stems (stemz) *v.*: Stops; dams up (p. 603, l. 20)

lays (lāz) *n.*: Short poems to be sung (p. 603, l. 22)

Motivation/Prior Knowledge
To help familiarize students with the Scottish dialect and to make it easier for them to understand, play a recording of the poem or read it aloud.

Master Teacher Note One of Burns's many Romantic qualities is his original metrical form. Breaking away from the heroic couplet in both this poem and "To a Louse," he employs a six line stanza with lines 1, 2, 3, and 5 all rhyming and written in iambic tetrameter; lines 4 and 6, written in iambic dimeter, provide a second rhyme sound.

Purpose-Setting Question How does Burns's use of dialect add to the poem's appeal?

1 **Discussion** What does Burns's sympathy for the mouse's situation tell you about the man himself?

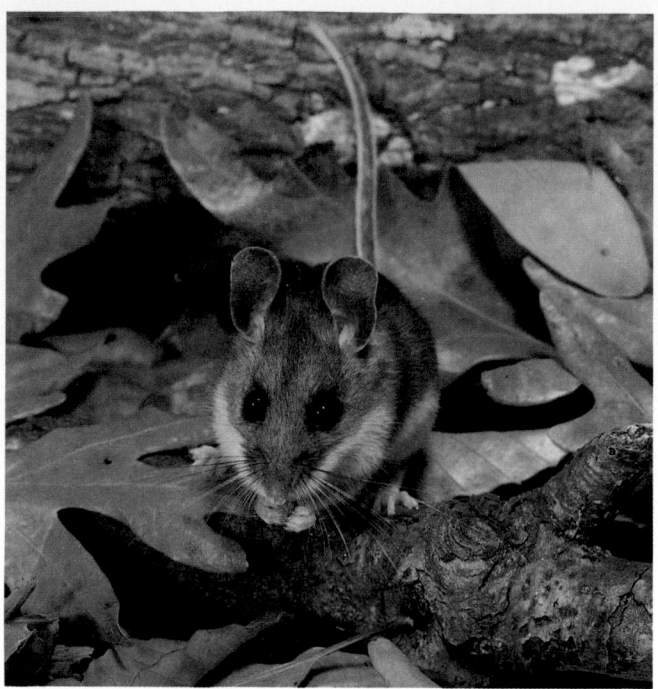

To a Mouse

On Turning Her up in Her Nest with the Plow, November, 1785

Robert Burns

1
    Wee, sleekit,[1] cow'rin', tim'rous beastie,
    O, what a panic's in thy breastie!
    Thou need na start awa sae hasty,
        Wi' bickering brattle![2]
5 I wad be laith[3] to rin an' chase thee
        Wi' murd'ring pattle![4]

---

1. sleekit: Sleek.
2. Wi' . . . brattle: In sudden flight.
3. wad be laith: Would be loath.
4. pattle: Paddle for cleaning a plow.

Grammar In Action

Dialect is the form of language peculiar to a particular region or social group. By using dialect, writers can capture the flavor of a particular area.

Dialect may contain special vocabulary words or may violate standard rules of grammar or spelling. For example, look at the following dialect from "To a Mouse."

O, what a panic's in thy breastie!

Thou need na start awa sae hasty
I wad be laith to rin an' chase thee
An' lea'e us nought but grief an' pain

Student Activity 1. Rewrite each of the examples above following the rules of standard grammar. Which sentences seem more appropriate for this selection—the ones you have written or the original ones? Why?

Student Activity 2. Pick a particular area of the country. Using dialect, write a conversation between two people from this region. Be sure to include variations of correct spelling that will enable readers to "hear" the way your speakers pronounce words.

I'm truly sorry man's dominion
Has broken Nature's social union,
An' justifies that ill opinion,
      Which makes thee startle,
10 At me, thy poor, earth-born companion,
      An' fellow-mortal!

I doubt na, whyles,[5] but thou may thieve;
What then? poor beastie, thou maun[6] live!
15 A daimen icker in a thrave[7]
      'S a sma' request:
I'll get a blessin' wi' the lave,[8]
      And never miss't!

Thy wee bit housie, too, in ruin!
20 Its silly wa's[9] the win's are strewin'!
An' naething, now, to big[10] a new ane,
      O' foggage[11] green!
An' bleak December's winds ensuin',
      Baith snell[12] an keen!

25 Thou saw the fields laid bare and waste,
An' weary winter comin' fast,
An' cozie here, beneath the blast,
      Thou thought to dwell,
Till crash! the cruel coulter[13] past
30   Out through thy cell.

That wee bit heap o' leaves an' stibble,
Has cost thee mony a weary nibble!
Now thou's turned out, for a' thy trouble,
      But[14] house or hald,[15]
35 To thole[16] the winter's sleety dribble,
      An' cranreuch[17] cauld!

---

5. whyles: At times.
6. maun: Must.
7. A . . . thrave: An occasional ear of grain in a bundle.
8. lave: Rest.
9. silly wa's: Feeble walls.
10. big: Build.
11. foggage: Rough grass.
12. snell: Sharp.
13. coulter: Plow blade.
14. But: Without.
15. hald: Property.
16. thole: Withstand.
17. cranreuch (krɔn' rəkh): Frost.

To a Mouse   597

2 **Discussion** What is the speaker apologizing for?

3 **Discussion** Why is the destruction of the mouse's house so serious?

4 **Literary Focus** Here Burns seems to be viewing the situation from the mouse's point of view.

Literary Focus At this point the poet changes focus. From a specific account of a small, poignant incident Burns moves to a general statement that relates to the human experience. John Steinbeck borrowed from this stanza the title *Of Mice and Men* for his novel that treats of plans gone fatally awry.

Reader's Response Describe a time when you responded with wonder to the sudden appearance of an animal.

Closure and Extension

ANSWERS TO THINKING ABOUT THE SELECTION

Recalling

1. (a) The poem takes place on Burns's farm in Scotland in November.
2. The speaker apologizes to the mouse for frightening it.
3. The speaker has plowed under the moss the mouse needs to build a home.
4. The mouse's problem is one it must deal with now. The speaker has both past misfortunes and future problems to worry about.

Interpreting

5. The "social union" refers to the balance among natural things.
6. The sentiment suggests that the speaker believes that the end justifies the means.
7. (a) "The best laid schemes o' mice an' men Gang aft a-gley" carries the poem's theme. (b) You cannot always count on things working out the way you expect them to.

Applying

8. Answers will differ but students should support their positions.

ANSWERS TO ANALYZING LITERATURE

1. (a) The dialect suggests that the speaker is uneducated and low in social standing. (b) Both the speaker and the mouse are poor, lowly

---

But, Mousie, thou art no thy lane,[18]
In proving foresight may be vain:
The best laid schemes o' mice an' men
    Gang aft a-gley,[19]
40 An' lea'e us nought but grief an' pain,
    For promised joy.

Still thou art blest, compared wi' me!
The present only toucheth thee:
45 But, och! I backward cast my e'e
    On prospects drear!
An' forward, though I canna see,
    I guess an' fear!

5

---

18. **no thy lane:** Not alone.
19. **Gang aft a-gley:** Go often awry.

THINKING ABOUT THE SELECTION

Recalling

1. What is the setting of the poem?
2. For what reason does the speaker apologize to the mouse?
3. Why is the mouse unable to build a new home?
4. Why does the speaker say that, compared with him, the mouse is blessed?

Interpreting

5. To what "social union" do you think the speaker is referring in line 7?
6. What does the sentiment in lines 13–14 suggest about the speaker's own moral code?
7. (a) What famous line in the poem carries the poem's theme? (b) How might you state this theme in your own words?

Applying

8. What value do you place on foresight? Explain your answer.

ANALYZING LITERATURE

Recognizing Dialect

Dialect is a collection of speech habits and patterns belonging to a specific group, class, or region. Often, a dialect will possess its own unique grammar, pronunciation, and vocabulary. One of the first poets to write using the Scottish dialect of English, Robert Burns placed himself in direct opposition to the poetic standards of the eighteenth century.

1. (a) What does the use of dialect in this poem suggest about the speaker's social station? (b) How does it help carry across the poem's theme?
2. Like the standard language, dialects of a language follow rules. Find at least two examples in the poem of each of the following pronunciation rules for Scottish English. (a) Final consonants are dropped. (b) The letter *o* is replaced by either *ae* or *a*.
3. How would the effect of this poem have been different if it had been written in standard English?

---

creatures subject to life's twists and turns.
2. (a) Answer will differ but may include the following. Final consonants are dropped in *cowrin'* (cowering) and *sma'* (small), and *wi'* (with). (b) The letter *o* is replaced by *a* in *hald* (holding), *lane* (alone), and *canna* (cannot).
3. The poem would lack the intimacy it now possesses, the flavor of the place and the speaker.

To a Louse

On Seeing One on a
Lady's Bonnet at Church

Robert Burns

Ha! whare ye gaun, ye crowlin' ferlie![1]
Your impudence protects you sairly:[2]
I canna say but ye strunt[3] rarely,
    Owre gauze and lace;
5 Though faith! I fear ye dine but sparely
    On sic a place.

Ye ugly, creepin', blastit wonner,[4]
Detested, shunned by saunt an' sinner,
How dare ye set your fit[5] upon her,
10   Sae fine a lady?
Gae somewhere else, and seek your dinner
    On some poor body.

Swith![6] in some beggar's haffet[7] squattle;[8]
There ye may creep, and sprawl, and sprattle[9]
15 Wi' ither kindred, jumping cattle,
    In shoals and nations:
Whare horn nor bane[10] ne'er dare unsettle
    Your thick plantations.

Now haud[11] ye there, ye're out o' sight,
20 Below the fatt'rels,[12] snug an' tight;
Na, faith ye yet![13] ye'll no be right
    Till ye've got on it,
The vera tapmost, tow'ring height
    O' Miss's bonnet.

---

1. **crowlin' ferlie:** Crawling wonder.
2. **sairly:** Sorely.
3. **strunt:** Strut.
4. **blastit wonner:** Blasted wonder.
5. **fit:** Foot.
6. **swith:** Swift.
7. **haffet:** Locks.
8. **squattle:** Sprawl.
9. **sprattle:** struggle.
10. **horn nor bane:** Comb nor poison.
11. **haud:** Hold.
12. **fatt'rels:** Ribbon ends.
13. **Na faith ye yet!:** Confound you!

Presentation

Motivation/Prior Knowledge
Ask students how they might react if they saw a louse on a lady's hat in a church.

Literary Focus Although this poem shares many of the Romantic characteristics of "To a Mouse," its satiric tone puts it at least partly in the neo-classical tradition.

Master Teacher Note Have students look up the word *lousy* in a good dictionary and note the various meanings of the word ("infested with lice"; "mean"; "painful"; "inferior"; "abundantly supplied"). How do the meanings of the word, which derives from the word *louse*, reflect the message of this poem?

Purpose-Setting Questions
How does this poem illustrate Burns's sense of humor? How do the number of stanzas and the rhyme scheme in this poem compare with "To a Mouse"?

1 Clarification Explain that in Burns's time lice—small, wingless creatures that suck the blood of animals and humans—were quite common. Today, better standards of hygiene have helped to keep the insects under control.

2 Discussion What is the speaker's attitude toward the louse?

3 Literary Focus These lines reflect Burns's satiric tone. Is he saying that the louse should be on a poor person or that it is a common expectation that lice will be on poor people? This idea is repeated in lines 31–36.

4 Discussion Burns pursues this idea with great originality here, suggesting several reasons why the louse would be happier on a poor person's head. What are those reasons?

5 **Literary Focus** Point out that this stanza echoes the second stanza.

6 **Literary Focus** This stanza marks a change in the poem. Instead of speaking to the louse, the speaker addresses Jenny.

7 **Discussion** As in "To a Mouse," Burns moves from the specific to the general. Is he generalizing the folly of the louse or humans or both? Explain.

Reader's Response What other creatures would you regard as unlikely subjects for poetic reflection?

25   My sooth! right bauld ye set your nose out,
        As plump and gray as onie grozet;[14]
        O for some rank, mercurial rozet,[15]
            Or fell,[16] red smeddum,[17]
        I'd gie you sic a hearty dose o't,
30   Wad dress your droddum![18]

5   I wad na been surprised to spy
        You on an auld wife's flannen toy;[19]
        Or aiblins some bit duddie boy,[20]
            On's wyliecoat;[21]
35   But Miss's fine Lunardi![22] fie,
            How daur ye do't?

6   O, Jenny, dinna toss your head,
        An' set your beauties a' abroad![23]
        Ye little ken what cursèd speed
40   The blastie's[24] makin'!
        Thae[25] winks and finger-ends, I dread,
            Are notice takin'!

7   45 O wad some Pow'r the giftie gie us
        To see oursels as ithers see us!
        It wad frae monie a blunder free us
            And foolish notion:
        What airs in dress an' gait wad lea'e us,
            And ev'n devotion!

---

14. onie grozet (grŏz' it): Any gooseberry.
15. rozet (rŏz' it): Rosin.
16. fell: Sharp.
17. smeddum: Powder.
18. Wad . . . droddum: Would put an end to you.
19. flannen toy: Flannel cap.
20. Or . . . boy: Or perhaps on some little ragged boy.
21. wyliecoat (wī' lē kōt'): Undershirt.
22. Lunardi: A balloon-shaped bonnet, named for Vincenzo Lunardi, a balloonist of the late 1700's.
23. abread: Abroad.
24. blastie's: Creature's.
25. Thae: Those.

THINKING ABOUT THE SELECTION

Recalling

1. (a) What is the louse doing? (b) What does the speaker command it to do instead?
2. What does the speaker say he would like to do in lines 27–30?
3. (a) Whom does the speaker address in the seventh stanza? (b) What does he warn her against?

Interpreting

4. (a) What conclusions can you draw about Jenny's character? (b) What evidence supports these assumptions?
5. What is the poet's tone—that is, his attitude toward his subject?
6. Like "To a Mouse," this poem contains a famous line that suggests the poem's theme. (a) What is that line? (b) What is the poem's theme?

Applying

7. William Hazlitt wrote, "Life is the art of being well deceived." How do you think Burns would respond to this statement? Explain your answer.

CRITICAL THINKING AND READING

Recognizing Satire

Satire is writing that uses humor and wit to expose folly and flaws of humans or institutions. Popular since ancient Greek and Roman times, satire has long been an effective tool of both writers and reformers. In order to recognize the target of the poet's satire, reread the brief biography of Robert Burns on page 594. Based on information you find there and on the poem itself, answer the following questions about "To a Louse."

1. (a) What do you imagine to be the social class of the speaker? Why? (b) Of Jenny? Why?
2. (a) What is the louse's "crime"? What does the speaker have in common with those to whom he seems to feel the louse belongs? (b) What is ironic about this?

THINKING AND WRITING

Comparing and Contrasting Two Poems

"To a Mouse" and "To a Louse" are often considered to be companion poems. Indeed, both poems address creatures of nature, and both are written in the Scottish dialect. Apart from these obvious similarities, consider other traits the poems share in common, as well as features that set the two apart. Consider in particular the theme of the poems and the attitude of the poet toward society. Discuss your findings with your classmates. Then write an essay comparing and contrasting the two poems. When you revise, make sure you have presented both similarities and differences. Proofread your essay and prepare a final draft.

Challenge Do you agree or disagree with Burns's message in the poem?

ANSWERS TO THINKING ABOUT THE SELECTION

Recalling

1. (a) The louse is crawling on a lady's hat while she is sitting in church. (b) The speaker commands the louse to find its dinner on the head of some beggar.
2. He would like to kill it by giving it a dose of deadly red powder.
3. (a) The speaker addresses Jenny, the woman wearing the bonnet. (b) He warns her against shaking her head.

Interpreting

4. (a) In the speaker's opinion, Jenny is vain. There is the suggestion that she comes to church to be seen, rather than to worship. (b) In the last stanza Burns suggests that people could save themselves from many a blunder if they could see themselves as others see them. He specifically refers to "airs in dress an' gait."
5. The poet's tone is one of quiet anger and gentle ridicule.
6. (a) The line that suggests the poem's theme is "O wad some Pow'r the giftie gie us/To see oursels as ithers see us!" (b) The theme is that people who put on airs are seen as foolish by others.

Applying

7. Answers will vary, but this poem suggests that Burns might reply, "Yes, unfortunately, that is what life is for many."

ANSWERS TO CRITICAL THINKING AND READING

1. The dialect suggests that the speaker is from a low social class. Jenny is probably an upper-class woman, since the speaker calls her a fine lady.
2. The louse's crime is that it chose a fine bonnet to crawl on rather than some "poor body." Like those he feels the louse belongs on, the speaker is poor. The irony is that the louse chose the body of someone with social standing, rather than the kind of body it would be expected to be on.

Afton¹ Water

Robert Burns

1
Flow gently, sweet Afton, among thy green braes,²
Flow gently, I'll sing thee a song in thy praise;
My Mary's asleep by thy murmuring stream,
Flow gently, sweet Afton, disturb not her dream.

2
5 Thou stock-dove whose echo resounds through the glen,
Ye wild whistling blackbirds in yon thorny den,
Thou green-crested lapwing, thy screaming forbear,
I charge you, disturb not my slumbering fair.

How lofty, sweet Afton, thy neighboring hills,
10 Far marked with the courses of clear, winding rills;
There daily I wander as noon rises high,
My flocks and my Mary's sweet cot³ in my eye.

---

1. Afton: The Afton is a river in Ayrshire, a former county in Southwestern Scotland.
2. braes (brāz): Slopes.
3. cot: Cottage.

THE RIVER DEE NEAR EATON HALL
Richard Wilson
The Barber Institute of Fine Arts
The University of Birmingham

How pleasant thy banks and green valleys below,
Where wild in the woodlands the primroses blow;
15 There oft as mild evening weeps over the lea,[4]
The sweet-scented birk[5] shades my Mary and me.

Thy crystal stream, Afton, how lovely it glides,
And winds by the cot where my Mary resides;
How wanton thy waters her snowy feet lave,
20 As gathering sweet flowerets she stems thy clear wave.

Flow gently, sweet Afton, among thy green braes,
Flow gently, sweet river, the theme of my lays;
My Mary's asleep by thy murmuring stream,
Flow gently, sweet Afton, disturb not her dream.

3

---

4. lea: Meadow.
5. birk: Birch.

THINKING ABOUT THE SELECTION
Recalling

1. (a) Why does the speaker ask the Afton to "flow gently"? (b) What other three things does he command to be silent?
2. What is the speaker's occupation?

Interpreting

3. (a) What is the poem's mood—the feeling it conveys to the reader? (b) What words and phrases help achieve this mood?
4. (a) What assumptions can you make about Mary based on the poem? (b) About the speaker's feelings toward her?
5. Do you think the author, in composing these lines, had any purpose in mind other than to entertain? Explain your answer.

Applying

6. What songs or lullabies are you familiar with that carry the same message as this poem?

Afton Water 603

John Anderson, My Jo[1]

Robert Burns

John Anderson, my jo, John,
    When we were first acquent,
Your locks were like the raven,
    Your bonnie[2] brow was brent;[3]
5 But now your brow is beld,[4] John,
    Your locks are like the snow;
But blessings on your frosty pow,[5]
    John Anderson, my jo.

John Anderson, my jo, John,
10   We clamb[6] the hill thegither;
And monie[7] a canty[8] day, John,
    We've had wi' ane anither:
Now we maun[9] totter down, John,
    And hand in hand we'll go,
15 And sleep thegither at the foot,
    John Anderson, my Jo.

---

1. jo: Joy.
2. bonnie: Pretty.
3. brent: Unwrinkled.
4. beld: Bald.
5. pow: Head.
6. clamb: Climbed.
7. monie: Many.
8. canty: Cheerful.
9. maun: Must.

THINKING ABOUT THE SELECTION

Recalling

1. (a) How does the speaker say John Anderson looked when she and he first met? (b) How does he look now?
2. What does the speaker say she and John Anderson will do now?

Interpreting

3. What do you suppose to be the relationship between the speaker and John Anderson? Explain your assumption.
4. (a) How would you paraphrase what the speaker is saying in the first four lines of the second stanza? (b) In the last four lines?

Applying

5. It has been noted that "John Anderson, My Jo" reveals Robert Burns's great talent for writing romantic poetry. Explain why you agree or disagree with this observation.

THINKING AND WRITING

Writing About Dialect

Three of the four poems you have read by Robert Burns are written in dialect. In an essay, explain how you believe the impact of these poems would have been altered had the poet chosen to write them instead in standard English. Before writing consider the following questions. What factors do you think influenced Burns's decision to use dialect? What qualities of tone are communicated through the use of dialect? Of theme? What aspects of the message in "Afton Waters" may have prompted the poet to write in standard English?

ANSWERS TO THINKING ABOUT THE SELECTION
Recalling

1. (a) When she first met him he had dark hair and a smooth, unwrinkled brow. (b) Now John is balding, with white hair.
2. They will grow old together.

Interpreting

3. The speaker and John Anderson are husband and wife.
4. (a) When we were young we spent many happy days together. (b) Now that we are old we will enjoy each other until we die.

Applying

5. Answers will differ. Suggested response: Love is a constant theme in Romantic poetry. While most Romantic poets extoll the virtues of young love or unrequited love, Burns extolls a happy love that has reached old age. The poem is direct, natural, and passionate—all indicative of his great talent.

THINKING AND WRITING

Publishing Student Writing You might have students meet in small groups and choose one essay from the group to be read aloud to the class.

More About the Author William Blake's belief in a union of opposites is reflected in his famous "Doctrine of Contraries": "Without Contraries," he wrote, "is no progression. Attraction and repulsion, reason and energy, love and hate, are necessary to human existence." Do you agree with this view? Explain.

Critical Evaluation In an article explaining the connections between poetry and design in Blake's work, the critic Northrop Frye makes a point of emphasizing how unusual his subject's combined talent was. He writes: "The ability to paint and the ability to write have often belonged to the same person; but it is rare to find them equally developed. Most people so gifted have been either writers who have made a hobby of painting . . . or painters who have made a hobby of writing . . . One usually predominates . . . Besides being a poet and painter, Blake was a professional engraver and a tireless and versatile experimenter in a great variety of media. He was an artisan or craftsman who was an expert in an important minor art as well as two major ones."

WILLIAM BLAKE

1757–1827

When William Blake was four years old, he screamed because he saw God at his window. At age eight, while walking in the fields, he saw a tree filled with angels. To outside observers, Blake's "spells" might have seemed a cause for grave concern. In the home of his parents—themselves followers of the mystical teachings of Emanuel Swedenborg—the boy's "gift of vision" was something to be revered and nurtured. At least partly as a result of the family's way of life, the century and the world received a painter and a poet whose contributions are as rare as they are brilliant.

Blake was born in London, where his father ran a hosiery shop. He was never sent to school but instead, after expressing a desire to become a painter, was apprenticed to an engraver. Ultimately self-taught, he found his way into art and literature.

Between the ages of twelve and twenty, Blake wrote a series of poems, *Poetical Sketches,* that followed the tradition of English lyric poetry, while bringing a new innocence to his subject matter. When he was thirty-two, he published his *Songs of Innocence,* which he had composed when he was younger, and which explored his favorite subject—the destiny of the human spirit. Instead of printing the collection, he developed a unique process whereby the words and illustrations were etched on metal plates with varnish, then painted in by hand. Because the process was time-consuming, few books could be produced, and so to support himself, Blake hired himself out to other authors as an illustrator and sold what he could of his own works for one pound apiece. He also continued to write and in 1794 brought out a companion to *Songs of Innocence* titled *Songs of Experience.*

In *Songs of Innocence* Blake had suggested that by recapturing the imagination and wonderment of childhood, we could achieve the goal of self-awareness. The poems thus present views of the world as filtered through the eyes and mind of a child. In *Songs of Experience* he now insisted that a return to innocence was not, at least by itself, sufficient for us to attain an awareness of our true identity—that we must also recognize and attempt to understand the evils around us. Thus Blake's credo was that there must be a union of opposites, a fusion of innocence and experience.

Unrecognized by his peers and living only slightly above poverty level, Blake spent his seventy years in constant creative activity. Only later, many years after his death, was the system behind his work understood. His poetry operates on two levels, one of them symbolic, the other literal. Both of them address a single purpose—the renewal of the human spirit.

Objectives
1 To recognize symbolism
2 To write about William Blake's symbolism as illustrated in his poetry

Support Material

Teaching Portfolio
Teacher Backup, p. 735
Usage and Mechanics Worksheet, p. 739
Vocabulary Check, p. 740
Analyzing Literature Worksheet, *Recognizing Symbols,* p. 741
Language Worksheet, *Appreciating Latinate Words,* p. 742
Selection Test, p. 743

GUIDE FOR INTERPRETING

The Lamb; The Tiger; The Human Abstract; Infant Sorrow; A Poison Tree

Writer's Technique

Symbolism. Symbolism is the use of a person, an object, a place, or an idea to represent itself and something beyond itself at the same time. Two well-known examples of symbolism are the use of the Stars and Stripes to represent the United States and the use of a skull and crossbones to represent something poisonous. While symbolism occurs in all types of literature, poetry, by virtue of its purity as an art form, is an especially natural vehicle for the presentation of ideas in symbolic form. Symbolism also permits the poet to introduce in relatively little space concepts and ideas that would ordinarily require more extensive treatment. In "The Tiger," William Blake uses the jungle cat as a symbol for the savage and untamed forces in the world that prompt human beings to perform evil actions.

Writing

Imagine that suddenly you are four or five years old again. Look around you, at the people and objects in your presence, and describe what you see. Use words that you believe would be appropriate to a small child, and remember that much which you take for granted would seem new and wonderful to a younger you.

Primary Source

To realize Blake's importance in the history of engraving, it is important to know that since the masterpieces of Albrecht Dürer, the sixteenth-century German engraver/printer, engraving on metal had been abandoned. It was replaced by the easier method of etching, which did not involve as much labor and training.

Much attention has been focused on Blake's mastery of this difficult art form. The following excerpt is from the famous description of Blake's process of engraving and the explanation of its discovery that appeared the year after he died:

> Blake, after deeply perplexing himself as to the mode of accomplishing the publication of his illustrated songs, without their being subject to the expense of letter-press, his brother Robert stood before him in one of his visionary imaginations, and so decidedly directed him in the way in which he thought he ought to proceed, that he immediately followed his advice, by writing his poetry, and drawing his marginal subjects of embellishments in outline upon the copper-plate with an impervious liquid, and then eating the plain parts or lights away with aqua fortis considerably below them, so that the outlines were left as a stereotype.

Guide for Interpreting 607

Literary Focus Distinguish between a sign and a symbol. Point out that a sign—such as a traffic light or stop sign—has a single, distinct meaning. A symbol, however, may have an indefinable meaning, a number of different meanings, or a meaning that can vary from one interpreter to another.

Writing/Prior Knowledge In writing about innocence, Blake was describing a mystical state, rather than childhood, but he identifies the two so closely that his poems seem to be spoken by the very children themselves. He does not look at children; he actually enters their minds and speaks through their mouths.

Vocabulary

Preteach the following vocabulary words:

vales (vālz) *n.*: Valleys (p. 608, l. 8)
symmetry (sim'ə trē) *n.*: Beauty resulting from balance of form (p. 611, l. 4)
aspire (ə spīr') *v.*: Rise high (p. 611, l. 7)
sinews (sin'yōōz) *n.*: Muscular power; force (p. 611, l. 10)
abstract (ab'strakt) *n.*: Brief summary stating main points (p. 612, title)
swaddling (swäd'liŋ) *adj.*: Long, narrow bands of cloth wrapped around newborn babies (p. 613, l. 6)

Spelling Tip Point out the double *m* in *symmetry*.

Motivation/Prior Knowledge
Ask students if important ideas can be expressed in simple words. Have students give examples.

Master Teacher Note You may want to consider teaching the "The Lamb" and "The Tiger" together, as they suggest such totally different attributes of the same God. Taken together the two poems exemplify Blake's belief in contrasts.

Purpose-Setting Question What symbols does Blake use in the poem? What do they stand for?

1 Discussion Note that the words in the poem are mostly monosyllabic and extremely simple, as is the rhyme scheme. Why do you think Blake uses such simple diction?

2 Discussion What is the rhyme scheme? How does it enhance the meaning of the poem?

3 Clarification Jesus was described as "the Lamb" by John the Baptist in the Bible, in John 1:20 and Revelations 5:18. In what special sense was Christ the Lamb of God?

4 Discussion Who is the speaker in the poem?

Reader's Response What creatures in addition to the lamb might prompt a person to reflect on the wonders of existence?

The Lamb

William Blake

Little Lamb, who made thee?
  Dost thou know who made thee?
Gave thee life, and bid thee feed,
By the stream and o'er the mead;
5 Gave thee clothing of delight,
Softest clothing, woolly, bright;
Gave thee such a tender voice,
Making all the vales rejoice!
  Little Lamb, who made thee?
10 Dost thou know who made thee?

  Little Lamb, I'll tell thee,
  Little Lamb, I'll tell thee.
He is called by thy name,
For He calls Himself a Lamb.
15 He is meek, and He is mild;
He became a little child.
I a child, and thou a lamb,
We are callèd by His name.
  Little Lamb, God bless thee!
20 Little Lamb, God bless thee!

THINKING ABOUT THE SELECTION
Recalling

1. (a) What questions does the speaker ask in the first stanza? (b) What answer does he give in the second?
2. How does the speaker identify himself in the second stanza?

Interpreting

3. Blake uses repetition to create a mood, or overall feeling, in this poem. (a) What types of words does he repeat? (b) What feeling is created?
4. (a) How would you characterize the creator imagined in this poem? (b) Find at least three words that support your opinion.

Applying

5. Assume that you were asked to illustrate this poem. (a) What kinds of images would you use to represent the words? (b) What style of drawing might you use?

ANALYZING LITERATURE
Recognizing Symbolism

A **symbol** is a thing, idea, person, or place that has a meaning in and of itself but also stands for more. An old, bent man with a scythe symbolizes the end of the year. In poetry, symbolism—the systematic use of symbols—adds particular clarity to a poet's point. In "The Lamb," Blake offers two separate but related symbolic representations for the animal named in the title.

1. What two things does the lamb symbolize? What properties of the lamb suggest its use as a symbol? What is the origin of the symbolic interpretation of the lamb in the second stanza?
2. Restate "The Lamb" in purely literal language. What is the poet's message? How is that message altered, if at all, by restating the poem in literal terms?

ANSWERS TO THINKING ABOUT THE SELECTION
Recalling

1. (a) The speaker asks the Lamb who its maker was, who fed and clothed it, and who gave it its voice. (b) God made the Lamb.
2. The speaker identifies himself as a child and a Christian.

Interpreting

3. (a) The words *Little Lamb, thee, He,* and *God* are repeated. (b) The feeling is that all the creatures in the world are one with God, the creator. The repetition also suggest a child's limited vocabulary.
4. Answers will differ. Possible answers are: (a) The creator is gentle and compassionate. (b) The creator provided the Lamb with soft, bright clothing and a tender voice—signs of compassion. The speaker calls the creator "meek" and "mild."

Applying

5. Answers will differ. Possible answers are: (a) An image of a child playing with a lamb in the country would be an appropriate image. (b) The style should be soft, perhaps painted in watercolors or drawn in pastels.

Little Lamb who made thee?
Dost thou know who made thee?
Gave thee life & bid thee feed.
By the stream & o'er the mead;
Gave thee clothing of delight,
Softest clothing wooly bright;
Gave thee such a tender voice,
Making all the vales rejoice:
  Little Lamb who made thee?
  Dost thou know who made thee?

Little Lamb I'll tell thee,
Little Lamb I'll tell thee:
He is called by thy name,
For he calls himself a Lamb:
He is meek & he is mild,
He became a little child:
I a child & thou a lamb.
We are called by his name.
  Little Lamb God bless thee.
  Little Lamb God bless thee.

From a manuscript of "The Lamb," by William Blake
Lessing J. Rosenwald Collection, Library of Congress,
Washington, D. C.

The Lamb 609

Fine Art, *The Tiger,* 1794, by William Blake. The engraving "The Tiger," lightly printed in brown ink and hand-colored with watercolor, was done by Blake himself. Note how the trees in the print repeat the straight symmetry of the tiger's stripes. The simplicity of the drawing complements the simple language of the poem. You might ask the students whether the drawing as well as the poem is meant to convey a more complex meaning.

From a manuscript of "The Tiger," by William Blake
The Metropolitan Museum of Art

610   *The Restoration and the Eighteenth Century*

Enrichment It has been suggested that Blake's choice of the tiger symbol may have been a reflection of the times. The tiger seemed to be an image that often came to English minds in a effort to describe the French Revolution, which coincided with Blake's work on his *Songs of Innocence. The London Times* of January 7, 1792, tells us that the French people are now "loose from all restraints, and in many instances, more vicious than wolves and tigers." Another comment stated that the "mob were barbarous beyond the tiger's cruelty." Years later Wordsworth looked back on the Paris of 1792 as "a place of fear . . . Defenceless as a wood where tigers roam."

The Tiger

William Blake

1
Tiger! Tiger! burning bright
In the forests of the night,
What immortal hand or eye
Could frame thy fearful symmetry?

2
5   In what distant deeps or skies
Burnt the fire of tnine eyes?
On what wings dare he aspire?
What the hand dare seize the fire?

3
10 And what shoulder, and what art,
Could twist the sinews of thy heart?
And when thy heart began to beat,
What dread hand? and what dread feet?

4
What the hammer? what the chain?
In what furnace was thy brain?
15 What the anvil? what dread grasp
Dare its deadly terrors clasp?

5
When the stars threw down their spears,
And watered heaven with their tears,
6
Did he smile his work to see?
20 Did he who made the Lamb make thee?

7
Tiger! Tiger! burning bright
In the forests of the night,
What immortal hand or eye
Dare frame thy fearful symmetry?

THINKING ABOUT THE SELECTION

Recalling

1. (a) What question is raised in the first stanza? (b) In the second stanza? (c) In the fifth stanza?

Interpreting

2. (a) What properties of the tiger are suggested by the images mentioned in the fourth stanza? (b) What emotional impact is created by those images?

3. (a) What do you suppose to be the answer to the central question of the poem? (b) Is it the same answer as that given in "The Lamb"? Explain.

Applying

4. "The Lamb" was included in *Songs of Innocence,* "The Tiger" in *Songs of Experience.* What does the use of the tiger as a symbol of the world of experience suggest about Blake's view of that world?

Motivation/Prior Knowledge
Read the Biblical version of the creation, which describes Adam and Eve's fall from grace as a result of eating fruit from the tree of knowledge. Discuss what happened after they ate the fruit. Tell students to keep the symbolism of the Biblical account in mind as they read "The Human Abstract."

Master Teacher Note This poem is from *Songs of Experience*. Its complement in *Songs of Innocence* is "The Divine Image," which celebrates mercy, pity, peace, and love. "The Human Abstract" shows their antitheses: exploitation, cruelty, conflict, and hypocritical humility.

Purpose-setting Question Does this poem seem to belong in *Songs of Innocence* or *Songs of Experience*? Support your choice by referring to specific statements in the poem.

1 **Discussion** Do you think Blake is being sarcastic here? Why or why not?

2 **Discussion** Who do you think Blake means by "we"?

3 **Discussion** Give a modern political example of how selfish love can affect peace.

4 **Discussion** What figure of speech is employed here?

5 **Discussion** Why would the raven choose the tree's thickest shade to make its nest?

6 **Literary Focus** What does Nature symbolize?

The Human Abstract

William Blake

1 Pity would be no more,
If we did not make somebody Poor;
2 And Mercy no more could be,
If all were as happy as we;

3 5 And mutual fear brings peace,
Till the selfish loves increase;
Then Cruelty knits a snare,
And spreads his baits with care.

4 He sits down with holy fears,
10 And waters the ground with tears;
Then Humility takes its root
Underneath his foot.

Soon spreads the dismal shade
Of Mystery over his head;
15 And the Caterpillar and Fly
Feed on the Mystery.

And it bears the fruit of Deceit,
Ruddy and sweet to eat;
And the Raven his nest has made
20 In its thickest shade. 5

The Gods of the earth and sea,
Sought through Nature to find this Tree, 6
But their search was all in vain:
There grows one in the Human Brain.

THINKING ABOUT THE SELECTION
Recalling

1. (a) What, according to the first stanza, would happen if no one in the world were poor? (b) If everyone were happy?
2. A tree is described in the third and following stanzas? Where is this tree said to grow?

Interpreting

3. In the fifth stanza Blake writes of "the fruit of Deceit." (a) What do you think this phrase is intended to symbolize? (b) What other symbols are present in the poem? (c) How do they expand the poem's meaning?

Applying

4. (a) What does the title suggest about the poet's outlook? (b) Do you agree with the view he presents here? Explain your answer.

Closure and Extension

ANSWERS TO THINKING ABOUT THE SELECTION
Recalling

1. (a) If no one were poor, there would be no pity. (b) If everyone were happy, there would be no mercy.
2. The tree of Humility grows under the feet of Cruelty.

Interpreting

3. (a) The fruit of Deceit suggests the apple that caused Eve to lie to Adam and resulted in her fall from grace. (b) The Tree of Mystery symbolizes the tree of knowledge, or experience; the seed of the fatal tree is man's cruelty, its root is false humility, and its fruit is deceit. The caterpillar and the fly symbolize the evil in life that feeds on man's weaknesses, and the raven is a symbol for death. (c) The symbols point out the dangers of experience; it can bring about people's downfall.

Applying

4. (a) Blake calls this image of a tree which is life-destroying a "Human Abstract" because it is false and unnatural, existing only in the human mind—unlike nature, the impulse of life, which is concrete and real. (b) Answers will differ.

Infant Sorrow

William Blake

My mother groaned, my father wept,   **1**
Into the dangerous world I leapt;
Helpless, naked, piping loud,
Like a fiend hid in a cloud.   **2**

5   Struggling in my father's hands,
Striving against my swaddling bands,
Bound and weary, I thought best   **3**
To sulk upon my mother's breast.

THINKING ABOUT THE SELECTION

Recalling

1. (a) How does the speaker describe each of his parents in the opening stanza? (b) The world?
2. What event has just occurred?

Interpreting

3. How would you describe this poem's tone —the feelings it awakens in the reader? What words contribute to these feelings?
4. (a) In what sense do you think the speaker is "bound," as he describes himself in line 7? (b) Where do you suppose he would prefer to be?

Applying

5. In which of the two volumes, *Songs of Innocence* or *Songs of Experience,* do you think this poem was included? Explain your assumption.

Motivation/Prior Knowledge
Have students discuss the last time they felt anger. How did they deal with it? Discuss whether it is better to express anger or to repress it.

Purpose-setting Question How does the tree here resemble the tree in "The Human Abstract"?

Master Teacher Note This poem may be interpreted as a symbolic depiction of the psychology of unresolved enmity. When anger and animosity are cultivated, like a tree, they can kill.

1 Discussion What is the meter of the stanza?

2 Literary Focus What do you think the apple symbolizes?

3 Literary Focus What does the garden symbolize?

4 Literary Focus What does this image symbolize? How does Blake use mixed meters in this concluding stanza to build and then relieve tension?

Humanities Note

Fine art, Illustration from a manuscript of "A Poison Tree" by William Blake. William Blake was a painter as well as a poet of mystic vision. His apprenticeship to an engraver gave him the background necessary to produce the bound volumes of his poems. In these books, Blake composed both the text and illustrations, which were printed simultaneously on a single page that he later hand-tinted with watercolor. These beautiful, lyrical books, laboriously produced in a small number, are considered to be Blake's finest effort.

The page "A Poison Tree" is from one of Blake's handmade books entitled *Songs of Experience,* published in 1794. The illustrations and poems for this work

A Poison Tree

William Blake

1
I was angry with my friend:
I told my wrath, my wrath did end.
I was angry with my foe:
I told it not, my wrath did grow.

5 And I watered it in fears,
Night and morning with my tears;
And I sunnèd it with smiles,
And with soft deceitful wiles.

And it grew both day and night,
2 10 Till it bore an apple bright.
And my foe beheld it shine,
And he knew that it was mine,

3 And into my garden stole
When the night had veiled the pole;[1]
15 In the morning glad I see
4 My foe outstretched beneath the tree.

——————
1. pole: Sky.

From a manuscript of "A Poison Tree," by William Blake
Lessing J. Rosenwald Collection, Library of Congress, Washington, D. C.

are of a darker nature than those done for *Songs of Innocence.* The tortured, evil-looking tree symbolizes the growth of the nurtured anger mentioned in the poem. The written poem becomes an integral part of the visual design of this page.

You may wish to discuss the following:
1. Does this drawing accurately depict the anguish of the speaker in the poem? Explain your answer.
2. What is it about this drawing that gives it an ominous mood?
3. How does the mood of this page compare to the page done for "The Lamb" shown on page 608.

THINKING ABOUT THE SELECTION

Recalling

1. (a) What does the speaker say occurred when he revealed his anger? (b) When he did not?
2. What "grows" out of the speaker's anger?

Interpreting

3. What sort of person do you find the speaker of this poem to be? What evidence can you find in support of your view?
4. (a) What symbols are used in the poem? (b) How effective do you find them to be?

Applying

5. In what other famous piece of literature does an apple appear as a symbol? What relationship can you detect between its symbolic value there and here?
6. (a) Which of the four other poems by Blake printed here is this one most reminiscent of in theme, structure, and symbolism? (b) Which of the two poems do you think states its message most clearly? Give your reasons.

THINKING AND WRITING

Writing About Symbolism

Blake wrote to communicate his deeply mystical belief that coming of age forces a child to leave "Eden and struggle with a world that has lost its Paradise." For Blake, the uniting of innocence and experience carries with it an awareness of the inseparability of good and evil. His poems make extensive use of symbolism to convey that notion. List the symbols used by Blake in the six poems to represent these opposing forces of good and evil. Then in an essay discuss how these symbols clarify and add dimension to the notion underlying the poems. When you revise, make sure you have included adequate examples. Proofread your essay and prepare a final draft.

Primary Source

Why do people come to respect each other? It is intriguing to speculate on the interactions of great contemporaries and to wonder why this one or that one could not plainly see the merits of the other—which seem so clear to us from a distance of two centuries! An article that appeared in *The Examiner* in 1809, for example, discribed Blake as "an unfortunate lunatic whose personal inoffensiveness secures him from confinement." His now-famous *Descriptive Catalogue* was blasted as "the wild effusions of a distempered brain." At least one well-regarded peer did recognize Blake's talent, however.

In a letter dated May 24, writer Charles Lamb described Blake as "a most extraordinary man. . . . [His] wild designs accompany a splendid folio edition of the Night Thoughts. . . . He paints in water colors marvelous strange pictures, visions of his brain, which he asserts that he has seen. They have great merit. He has *seen* the Old Welsh bards on Snowdon . . . and has painted them from memory (I have seen his paintings). . . . His Pictures—one in particular, the Canterbury Pilgrims (far above Stothard's)—have great merit, but hard, dry, yet with grace. He has written a Catalogue of them, with a most spirited criticism on Chaucer, but mystical and full of Vision. . . . There is one [song] to a tiger, which I have heard recited . . . which is glorious, but alas! I have not the book; for the man is flown, whither I know not. . . . But I must look on his as one of the most extraordinary persons of the age."

ANSWERS TO THINKING ABOUT THE SELECTION

Recalling

1. (a) When he revealed his anger to a friend, the wrath ended. (b) When he did not reveal his anger to a foe, it grew.
2. A tree of wrath grew out of the speaker's anger.

Interpreting

3. The speaker is a person who refuses to resolve his enmity with a foe. The second stanza offers evidence of the speaker's active cultivation of wrath.
4. (a) The chief symbols are the tree and the apple. The tree is a symbol of nurtured, cultivated enmity. The apple is a symbol of the fruit, or consequence, of hatred—death.

Applying

5. The apple is a symbol in the story from Genesis about man's fall from grace. God banished Adam and Eve from the Garden of Eden after they had eaten of the apple. Here the foe is banished from the garden by death.
6. (a) This poem is most reminiscent of "The Human Abstract" in theme, structure, and symbolism. (b) "A Poison Tree" states its message more clearly because the symbols are more universal. In "The Human Abstract" many of the symbols refer to Blake's private philosophy and their interpretation is more uncertain.

THINKING AND WRITING

Publishing Student Writing Student essays could be collected in a booklet and displayed in the classroom.

Presentation

Motivation/Prior Knowledge
Tell students that confusion in a language's history sometimes results from people using words to mean things other than what they usually mean. Remind students that there are words, even simple ones like "cool," "bad," "heavy," or "hot" that have several, sometimes contradictory meanings. Have the class discuss the consequences of such use or misuse of language. Ask if there are humorous dimensions to such irregular use of vocabulary.

Enrichment Allow each student to choose a partner and provide dictionaries for each of the couples in your class. Set a brief time limit and ask the groups to search for Latin roots that have multiple English derivatives. Have them list the root word and the words derived from it.

The Restoration and the Eighteenth Century 1660–1798

A CALL FOR ORDER

The spirit of adventure, independence, and individualism that had characterized the sixteenth and early seventeenth centuries gave way in the eighteenth century to a desire for order, regularity, and certainty in all aspects of life. "How barbarously we yet write and speak," exclaimed John Dryden, uttering a commonly held view. Different versions of English were still used in different regions, including, for example, the Scots dialect Robert Burns immortalized. As with society itself, English had simply gotten out of hand! From 1660 to the end of the eighteenth century, one of the most important concerns facing the literary establishment was the reform of English.

LATIN PROVIDES A MODEL

Many looked back to Latin, the language of mathematics and theology, for a model of regular grammar, spelling, and style. Dryden, for example, confessed that at times he had to translate an idea into Latin in order to decide on the correct way to express it in English! It seemed to some that English, in its current wild state, could not last. Latin, on the other hand, had prevailed because it had a definite set of rules.

"A PROPOSAL FOR CORRECTING, IMPROVING, AND ASCERTAINING THE ENGLISH TONGUE"

Jonathan Swift was a particularly strong voice in the call for language reform. For example, he objected to words being shortened. While many of these words—such as *rep* for "reputation" and *incog* for "incognito"—have passed out of use, we have retained *mob* for "mobile," as well as inventing scores of new ones, such as *taxi, bus,* and *phone.* He equally detested the shortening of verbs, calling such words as *rebuk'd* and *disturb'd* "the disgrace of our language." He also proposed an end to slang terms, condemning "all the modern terms of art, *sham, banter, mob, bubble, bully, cutting, shuffling,* and *palming.*"

His 1712 call for the establishment of an English Academy—"A Proposal for Correcting, Improving, and Ascertaining the English Tongue"—was echoed in many quarters. Some gathered support from Italian and French models of language improvement. The Italians, for example, had specifically commissioned an Academy to order their language. In France Cardinal Richelieu had founded the Académie Française to purify French. Their task was "to labor with all possible care and diligence to give definite rules to our language, and to render it pure, eloquent and capable of treating the arts and sciences."

Nonetheless, the idea of an English Academy never gathered enough support to become a reality. Writer Daniel Defoe, for example, lent his voice to those opposing the idea, for he felt that if an official Academy was established to dictate correct grammar, "it would be as criminal to coin words as money."

THE QUESTION OF GRAMMAR AND SPELLING

But more and more educated people seriously examined English. They began with grammar, but to their dismay, they discovered that English had no grammar. Latin had rules; English had none. Even the notion that there should be a right way of spelling was foreign to many letter writers and printers, as the uneven spelling of their books and papers shows. Swift had this to say about the turmoil of English spelling:

> Another Cause . . . which hath contributed not a little to the maiming of our Language, is a foolish Opinion, advanced of late Years, that we ought to spell exactly as we speak; which besides the obvious Inconvenience of utterly destroying our Etymology, would be a thing we should never see an End of. Not only the several Towns and Countries of England have a different way of Pronouncing, but even here in London, they clip their Words after one Manner about the Court, another in the City, and a third in the Suburbs. . . .

The practice of spelling as you spoke had produced such monstrosities as "sartinly" (certainly), "gine" (join), and "byled" (boiled). Things had gotten even more confusing when writers had changed words based on mistaken derivations, so that *iland* became "island," *sissors,* "scissors." The time had come for a standardized source book.

SAMUEL JOHNSON'S *DICTIONARY*

While there had been other dictionaries, none approached the scope of Johnson's *Dictionary.* Johnson and his six assistants worked nine years, filling eighty large notebooks with the practical definitions of more than 40,000 words. His resulting two-volume work is a landmark that stood unrivalled for more than a century. In Boswell's words the *Dictionary* "conferred stability on the language of his country."

As the century drew to a close, English became increasingly refined and standardized as the language of power and learning.

Allegory of the Royal Society by Hollar
The Mansell Collection

The Changing English Language   617

Humanities Note

Fine art, *Allegory of the Royal Society,* by Vaclav Hollar. The Royal Society, a scientific organization incorporated in 1662, was founded to promote research in the physical sciences and to recognize achievements in related fields. Its classical associations are highlighted here in the work of Hollar (1607–1677), a Bohemian etcher who settled in England after completing his studies on the continent and who worked regularly for Charles I. Hollar produced more than 2,500 plates of great variety, including portraits, animal studies, and works on still life, religious, and architectural subjects.

You may wish to use the following questions to discuss the art:

1. What is the most engaging aspect of this illustration?
2. How do you imagine the artist wants you to feel about the members of the Royal Society?
3. What can you tell about the Royal Society from the way this room is furnished and the members are dressed?

The writing assignments on page 618 have students write creatively, while those on page 619 have them think about the selections and write critically.

YOU THE WRITER
Guidelines for Evaluating Assignment 1

1. Has the student written additional stanzas for an eighteenth-century poem that are consistent with the original in content?
2. Has the student followed the model's meter and rhyme?
3. Is the style of the student's lines appropriate?
4. Are the new stanzas free from grammar, usage, and mechanics errors?

Guidelines for Evaluating Assignment 2

1. Has the student written a narrative or essay modeled on one of the selections of eighteenth-century literature that has content reflecting the ideas and beliefs of the period?
2. Has the student written the essay with the values and outlook of an author in mind?
3. Has the student chosen an appropriate style that is consistent with the author's?
4. Is the essay free from grammar, usage, and mechanics errors?

Guidelines for Evaluating Assignment 3

1. Does the letter express thoughts about a major event or concern of the eighteenth century?
2. Does the letter maintain an eighteenth-century outlook, character, and flavor?
3. Has the student written the letter in a clear, well-organized way?
4. Is the letter free from grammar, usage, and mechanics errors?

YOU THE WRITER

Assignment

1. Select a poem from this unit and write a stanza or two that could be added onto the end as a continuation of the original. Your additional lines should follow the verse form and style of the original.

Prewriting. Freewrite, exploring the meaning of the original poem. Decide what you might say that would be in harmony with the content of the original. Then study the meter and rhyme of this poem.

Writing. Write your lines in verse, trying to keep to the meter and rhyme of the original. Your first concern, however, should be with the content.

Revising. Refine your verse. Have you followed your model's meter and rhyme? Is the style of your lines appropriate? Finally, check over the content. Does it seem in keeping with that of the original?

Assignment

2. Write a prose narrative or essay modeled on one of the selections in this unit. The content should reflect the ideas and beliefs of the period. The style should closely follow that of your model.

Prewriting. Reread the selection you have chosen. Decide what subject matter, ideas, and viewpoint would make your narrative or essay a close imitation of the original.

Writing. When you write your first draft, try to keep within the mind and outlook of the author whose work you are following. As well as you can, follow his style.

Revising. First check that the content of your writing is in keeping with the era of the original. Then check that the style is also appropriate. Finally, look for and correct any lapses in grammar and style.

Assignment

3. Imagine you are a young lady or gentleman of the eighteenth century. Write a letter to a friend in which you express your thoughts on any major event or concern of the day.

Prewriting. Review the introduction to this unit and any other information you have gathered about the era. Select your subject from this material. Then outline what you will say to your friend. Remember that you are an eighteenth-century person and your comments should reflect the standards and concerns of this time.

Writing. When you write your letter, concentrate on expressing your thoughts in a clear, well-organized way. Try, however, to maintain an eighteenth-century outlook.

Revising. See if you can enhance the eighteenth-century character and flavor of your letter. Although your letter is to a friend, it should have a somewhat formal tone. Make sure your language is appropriate. Then correct any errors in grammar that you notice.

618   *The Restoration and the Eighteenth Century*

YOU THE CRITIC

Assignment

1. The era called Restoration and the Eighteenth century makes up one of the great periods of English prose. Write a descriptive essay in which you compare and contrast the prose of the period with the prose you find in magazines and newspapers of today.

Prewriting. First decide what you find especially admirable in one or two of the selections you have read. What adjectives would you use to describe this quality? What passages would you cite to illustrate it? How is the prose of today different?

Writing. Write an essay based on your prewriting work. Strive to be clear and precise in your descriptions.

Revising. Ask yourself, "Am I conveying clearly the qualities I see in the prose? Am I using comparison and contrast effectively to differentiate eighteenth-century prose from the prose of today?"

Assignment

2. A line from Alexander Pope, "What oft was thought, but ne'er so well expressed," could be applied to some of the best literature of this period. Choose at least two works from this unit and show how they express traditional ideas both elegantly and memorably.

Prewriting. Review selections you have read and find statements or passages that could stand alone as memorable quotations. Jot down notes about the meaning of each passage. Then decide in what order you will quote and comment on them.

Writing. First write a topic sentence that sums up your general opinion of the style and content of the lines and passages you are concerned with. Then present your quotations with comments on their literary effectiveness.

Revising. Look for and correct any lapses in the style and organization of your essay or in grammar.

Assignment

3. Literature reflects the times in which it is created. Write an essay showing how the literature you have read in this unit reflects the historical developments and trends of the period.

Prewriting. Review the introduction to the unit and any other related knowledge you may have. Which of the selections you have read comes to mind during your review? How do they reflect their times? Freewrite, exploring your answers.

Writing. Write an essay based on your prewriting work. You might first mention a historical development or trend and then describe how it is reflected in one of the works you have read.

Revising. Check that your essay is well organized and unified by a topic sentence, and that your explanations are clear and well developed. Finally, correct any errors in grammar or style.

You the Critic **619**

YOU THE CRITIC
Guidelines for Evaluating Assignment 1

1. Has the student used comparison and contrast to write a descriptive essay about eighteenth-century prose and prose found in magazines and newspapers today?
2. Has the student described what is admirable about eighteenth-century prose?
3. Has the student provided clear and precise evidence to support the main idea?
4. Is the essay free from grammar, usage, and mechanics errors?

Guidelines for Evaluating Assignment 2

1. Does the student begin the essay with a statement that sums up his or her general opinion of the style and content of the lines and passages chosen?
2. Does the student present the quotations chosen from eighteenth-century literature and comment on their literary effectiveness?
3. Does the student prove that eighteenth-century authors expressed traditional ideas elegantly and memorably?
4. Is the essay free from grammar, usage, and mechanics errors?

Guidelines for Evaluating Assignment 3

1. Has the student begun the essay by describing an historical development or trend of the eighteenth century?
2. Does the student describe how the development or trend is reflected in one of the works of the period?
3. Has the student used sufficient evidence from the work to support his or her main idea?
4. Is the essay free from grammar, usage, and mechanics errors?

Humanities Note

Fine art, *View in Hampshire,* by Patrick Nasmyth. Patrick Nasmyth (1787–1831) was born in Edinburgh, Scotland, one of eleven children of the landscape painter Alexander Nasmyth. In 1807 Patrick moved to London. He overcame the handicap of an injury to his right hand by learning to use his left hand with as much skill as if he had been left-handed.

View in Hampshire, like many of Nasmyth's oils, is in the style of Dutch landscape painters, whose works are marked by somber colors, emphasis on light and shadow, careful attention to detail, and, generally, a sense of quiet calmness. *View in Hampshire,* showing a rural scene in a locality southwest of London, is characterized in particular by its simplicity and gentleness. The most significant figure against the rustic background is the grazing horse. It is the sort of pastoral scene that has come to be associated with the Romantics.

Objectives

1 To learn about the American and French Revolutions and the reactions to them
2 To learn about the Reign of Terror in France
3 To learn about the problems in society during the Romantic Age
4 To learn about the beginnings of Romanticism
5 To learn about the Romantic Age in British poetry
6 To learn about the Romantic Age in British prose

VIEW IN HAMPSHIRE
Patrick Nasmyth

THE ROMANTIC AGE
1798–1832

One impulse from a vernal wood
   May teach you more of man,
Of moral evil and of good,
   Than all the sages can.

Sweet is the lore which Nature brings;
   Our meddling intellect
Misshapes the beauteous forms of things—
   We murder to dissect.

Enough of Science and of Art;
   Close up those barren leaves;
Come forth, and bring with you a heart
   That watches and receives.

from "The Tables Turned"
William Wordsworth

621

Fine art, *Capture of the Bastille, 14 July, 1789,* by Claude Cholat. The Bastille was originally built, in the 1370's, as a fortified gate to protect the French against British attack. Over the centuries the fortification was added to, until it had eight towers 100 feet high, surrounded by an 80-foot moat. In the seventeenth century, under Cardinal Richelieu, chief minister to King Louis XIII, political prisoners were sent to the Bastille for the first time; even banned books were kept within its walls.

At the time of the storming of the Bastille, only seven prisoners were being held. The original intention of the crowd was to ask that arms kept in the Bastille be distributed. Angered at the arrogant response of the prison head, however, they forced their way in. Two days later the legislative assembly in Paris decided that the Bastille must be torn down—a procedure that took several years. In any event, the structure, in Paris, had become the symbol of the tyranny of the French monarchy and aristocracy.

Presentation

Motivation/Prior Knowledge Have students discuss what they know about the French and American Revolutions, especially the effect of the conflicts on Britain. If students participated in the Writing to Learn exercise outlined on p. 621, they might share their notes with the class.

Purpose-Setting Question How did the political and social events during the years 1798–1832 influence the writers and artists of the Romantic Age?

1 **Enrichment** The young poet Shelley shared much of the radical William Godwin's revolutionary ardor and eventually became his son-in-law, marrying Mary Godwin after the suicide of his young wife.

CAPTURE OF THE BASTILLE, JULY 14, 1789
Claude Cholat
The Granger Collection

The preceding stanzas from "The Tables Turned," written in 1798, capture some of the main sentiments of a new age in British literature, an age in which writers "turned the tables" on eighteenth century thinking, insisting that the world be viewed through the heart, not the mind. During this period, which was named the Romantic Age by historians during the late 1800's, nearly all the attitudes and tendencies of eighteenth-century classicism and rationalism were redefined or changed dramatically. To understand how these changes occurred, it is necessary to examine not only the impact of events in Britain, but also the effects of the social and political upheaval that began taking place in other parts of the world.

REVOLUTION AND REACTION

Toward the end of the eighteenth century, two revolutions occurred outside England that indirectly threatened the stability of the British political and social systems. During the 1770's the American colonies revolted against British rule, eventually winning their independence and forming a government based on the principles of freedom and equality. While the American Revolution divided British public opinion and aroused some awareness of the need for reform, its impact on British society was not nearly as great as that of the French Revolution, which demonstrated that it was possible for a long-standing government to be successfully challenged on its own soil.

The French Revolution began on July 14, 1789, when a group of French citizens stormed the Bastille, a Paris prison for political prisoners. In the weeks that followed, the revolutionaries placed limits on the powers of King Louis XVI, established a new government, and approved a document called the Declaration of the Rights of Man, affirming the principles of "liberty, equality, and fraternity." France became a constitutional monarchy.

Opposing Views

From the start, the revolution evoked strong reactions from both liberals and conservatives throughout the rest of Europe. In England the ruling class felt threatened by the implications of the events in France, while most intellectuals, including several of the most important and influential writers of the Romantic Age, enthusiastically supported the revolution and the democratic ideals on which it was grounded. One ardent supporter of the revolution was Charles James Fox, leader of the Whig party, who declared, "How much the greatest event it is that ever happened in the world! and how much the best!" Poet William Wordsworth also spoke out in support of the revolution, and philosopher and novelist William Godwin (1756–1836) reacted to the revolution by writing *An Enquiry Concerning Social Justice* (1793), in which he predicted that British society would evolve peacefully into a nation characterized by freedom and equality. In contrast, Whig political thinker Edmund Burke (1729–1797), who had sympathized with the American Revolution, condemned the events in France. In *Reflections on the Revolution in France* (1790), he argued that the French, unlike the Americans, were attacking the very fabric of their society with complete disregard for their roots and ancestry. Burke warned that the revolution was bound to grow violent and mourned that "the age of chivalry is gone . . . and the glory of Europe is extinguished forever."

THE REIGN OF TERROR

Burke's views did not win wide acceptance in Britain until his dire predictions began coming true. As royalists, moderates, and radicals jockeyed for power, the French Revolution became more and more chaotic. In 1792, France declared war on Austria, touching off an invasion by Austrian and Prussian troops, whose leader proclaimed the intention of restoring the French king to full authority. Fuming with patriotic indignation, a radical group called the Jacobins gained control of the French legislative assembly, abolished the monarchy, and declared the nation a republic. Mobs attacked and killed many prisoners—including former aristocrats and priests—and soon French refugees began pouring into England with tales of these bloody "September massacres." Within weeks the revolutionaries had tried and convicted Louis XVI on a charge of treason. When Louis XVI went to the guillotine early in 1793, a revolutionary leader, Georges Danton, exclaimed: "The kings of Europe would challenge us. We throw them the head of a king!"

Following the execution, revolutionary violence reached its peak, as the Jacobins, under the leadership of Maximilien Robespierre, began what is called the Reign of Terror. Before the terror ended in the summer of 1794, revolutionary authorities had imprisoned thousands of royalists, moderates, and even radicals, sending some 4000 of them—including Danton and finally Robespierre himself—to the guillotine.

British Reaction

The September massacres and the Reign of Terror were so shocking that even Britons who had sympathized with the French Revolution now turned against it. Conservative Britons, already hostile to the Revolution, demanded a crackdown on reformers within Britain, whom they denounced as dangerous Jacobins. Adding to British alarm was the success of France's new "citizen army," which expelled the Austrian and Prussian invaders and then set out to "liberate" other European nations from despotic rule. British leaders did not want France or any other nation to win dominance on the European continent. In 1793, France took the initiative by declaring war on Britain. Thus began a series of wars

2 Master Teacher Note For a vivid recreation of the Reign of Terror, you might suggest that students read Charles Dickens's *A Tale of Two Cities,* Dickens's only historical novel.

Enrichment Considered one of the greatest naval battles in history, the Battle of Trafalger took place on October 21, 1805, off Cape Trafalger on the southwest coast of Spain. The British fleet, under Horatio Nelson, defeated a superior number of French and Spanish vessels under Pierre de Villeneuve.

Nelson's strategy was to divide his fleet into two sections and cut through the enemy battle line. This maneuver surprised the French fleet, who lost over half of their ships through capture or destruction. Although the British did not lose a single ship, they did lose their leader. Admiral Nelson was killed by a bullet fired from an enemy ship.

The victory of the British fleet insured Britain's control of the sea during the Napoleonic wars and forced Napoleon to abandon plans to invade England. Trafalgar Square in London is named in honor of Nelson and this great British naval victory.

BRITISH EVENTS

1798	**William Wordsworth** and **Samuel Taylor Coleridge** publish *Lyrical Ballads*.
	Wolfe Tone Rebellion in Ireland.
1801	Act of Union creates United Kingdom of Great Britain and Ireland.
	Union Jack becomes official flag.
1802	J.M.W. Turner's *Calais Pier* exhibited in London.
1803	Henry Shrapnel invents exploding shell.
1805	Battle of Trafalgar.
1807	Thomas Moore writes *Irish Melodies*.
1811	King George III declared permanently insane.
1812	**Byron** publishes *Childe Harold's Pilgrimage*.
1813	Waltz becomes acceptable in London ballrooms.
	Jane Austen publishes *Pride and Prejudice*.
1814	George Stephenson constructs first successful steam locomotive.
	Walter Scott publishes *Waverley*.
1815	John MacAdam constructs roads of crushed stone.
1817	**William Hazlitt** writes *Characters of Shakespeare's Plays*.
1818	Thomas Bowdler publishes censored edition of Shakespeare's plays.
	Mary Wollstonecraft Shelley publishes *Frankenstein, or the Modern Prometheus*.

624   *The Romantic Age*

William Wordsworth

George Stephenson's

Jane Austen

Union Jack

Rosetta Stone

Sir Walter Scott and Robert Burns

Locomotive

Napoleon

Beethoven

Robert Fulton's Steamboat

WORLD EVENTS

1799	France: Napoleon becomes head of revolutionary government.
	Egypt: Rosetta Stone, key to deciphering hieroglyphics, discovered.
1800	Italy: Volta builds first electric battery.
	Spain: Goya paints *The Two Majas*.
1802	Haiti: Toussaint L'Ouverture leads rebellion against French rule.
1803	United States: Louisiana Territory purchased from France.
	Germany: French occupy Hanover.
1804	Germany: Beethoven composes *Symphony No. 3*.
	France: Napoleon crowns himself emperor.
1805	Eastern Europe: Napoleon defeats allies at Austerlitz.
1807	United States: Fulton's steamboat navigates Hudson River.
1808	Italy: Excavation of Pompeii begins.
	Germany: Goethe publishes *Faust*, Part I.
1809	United States: Washington Irving writes "Rip Van Winkle."
1810	South America: Simón Bolívar leads rebellions against Spanish rule.
1812	Russia: Napoleon loses hundreds of thousands of troops in retreat from Moscow.
	Spain: Wellington drives French from Madrid.
	United States: War with Britain declared.
1813	Germany: Allies defeat Napoleon at Leipzig.
	Mexico: Independence declared.

Introduction 625

Enrichment In the spring of 1812, Napolean unleashed the Grand Army on Russia and sent 453,000 French troops marching toward Moscow. The invasion did not surprise the Russians, as tensions had been mounting between the two countries for several years. As a result, the Russians had devised a strategy that would ultimately enable them to turn back Napolean's forces.

Instead of engaging the French forces in direct clashes, the Russian army simply retreated as Napoleon's army advanced. This strategy avoided the possibility of an early defeat and lured the French farther and farther from their source of supplies. When the French reached Moscow in September of 1812, they expected to find food and shelter. Instead they found a burning city devoid of people or food. Realizing the folly of continuing forward, Napoleon ordered his troops to retreat.

The ensuing retreat was a disaster for the French. They were constantly harassed by Russian snipers and were forced to contend with the sudden onset of the Russian winter. Without adequate food or supplies, countless soldiers died of exposure and starvation. In the end, two-thirds of the Grand Army had perished. The unsuccessful invasion of Russia and the disastrous retreat that followed signaled the beginning of the end for Napoleon and his empire.

Enrichment Buckingham Palace was built in 1703 by the Duke of Buckingham. In 1761, King George III purchased the residence. It was then remodeled by John Nash (1752–1835), an English architect especially noted for his skills in town planning. Buckingham Palace became the residence of British sovereigns in 1837.

Further additions have been made to the palace, including an eastern facade in 1847 and a great ballroom in 1856. In 1913 Sir Aston Webb designed a new front. The palace has nearly 600 rooms and a collection of paintings, including many royal portraits.

BRITISH EVENTS

1819   Peterloo Massacre in Manchester.

        Percy Bysshe Shelley publishes "Ode to the West Wind".

1820   King George III dies.

        John Keats publishes "Ode on a Grecian Urn".

1821   *Manchester Guardian* begins publication.

        John Constable paints *The Grove*

1823   **Charles Lamb** publishes *Essays of Elia*.

1824   First labor unions permitted.

1825   Horse-drawn buses begin operating in London.

        John Nash completes rebuilding of Buckingham Palace.

1827   System for purifying London water installed.

1829   Catholic Emancipation Act passed.

        Robert Peel establishes Metropolitan Police in London.

1830   Liverpool-Manchester railway opens.

1831   Michael Faraday demonstrates electromagnetic induction.

1832   First Reform Act extends voting rights.

John Keats

The Grove

London in the 1820's

Charles Lamb

Liverpool-Manchester

The Peterloo Massacre

THE
LAST OF THE MOHICANS.

BY
JAMES FENIMORE COOPER.

NEW YORK:
D. APPLETON AND COMPANY, PUBLISHERS.

The Last of the Mohicans

Savannah, the First Steamer to Cross the Atlantic

Railway

Edgar Allan Poe

WORLD EVENTS

1814   France: Napoleon abdicates and is exiled to Elba.

1815   France: Napoleon returns for "Hundred Days."

      Belgium: Napoleon defeated at Waterloo.

      France: Napoleon exiled to St. Helena.

1816   Italy: Rossini composes *The Barber of Seville*.

1817   United States: William Cullen Bryant publishes "Thanatopsis."

      Germany: Hegel publishes *Encyclopedia of the Philosophical Sciences*.

1818   First steamship crosses Atlantic.

1821   Greece: War with Turkey begins.

      Germany: Heinrich Heine publishes *Poems*.

1822   Austria: Schubert begins *Symphony No. 8* ("Unfinished Symphony").

      Russia: Aleksandr Pushkin publishes *Eugene Onegin*.

1823   United States: Monroe Doctrine closes Americas to further European colonization.

1825   Russia: Bolshoi Ballet established.

1826   Germany: Mendelssohn composes *Overture to A Midsummer Night's Dream*.

      United States: James Fenimore Cooper publishes *The Last of the Mohicans*.

1827   France: Alexandre Dumas publishes *The Three Musketeers*.

1830   France: Stendhal publishes *The Red and the Black*.

1831   United States: Edgar Allan Poe publishes *Poems*.

      France: Victor Hugo publishes *The Hunchback of Notre Dame*.

Introduction   627

Enrichment In addition to writing beautiful love poems, German poet Heinrich Heine (1797–1856) wrote many satirical and political works that outraged the German government. As a result of his outspoken political beliefs, Heine was a controversial figure in his homeland and in other countries.

Heine achieved literary success with the publication of his first book of poetry in 1821. In 1827 he published *Book of Songs,* considered by many to be his finest work. His poetry was influenced by the Romantic Movement and inspired by a deep attachment to his uncle's daughter.

Following his initial success as a poet, Heine moved to Paris in 1831 where he wrote a series of works critical to the German government. These works were inspired by Romantic ideals and the continuing experiment with limited democracy in France. His political beliefs eventually overshadowed his popularity in Germany as a poet. He was not allowed to return to Germany and all of his books were banned.

Heine remained a controversial figure after his death. When the Nazis assumed power in the 1930's many of his works were suppressed. He was controversial in other countries because his political beliefs were similar to Marxism. Despite the controversy over his politics, however, Heine is still regarded as one of the finest writers of the eighteenth century.

Fine art, *The Battle of Trafalgar,* c. 1823, by J. M. W. Turner. John Mallord William Turner had a precocious talent and exhibited his first painting at the Royal Academy when he was fifteen. He became very successful, frequently exhibiting paintings there. In 1823, Turner was commissioned to paint a vast representation of the Battle of Trafalgar. This piece now hangs in the National Maritime Museum in Greenwich, England. In this work Turner projected all his patriotism and his love of the sea. However, he was unable to meet the criticisms of the seaman who wanted complete historical accuracy. Like most of Turner's work, this one is large in scope, showing a dramatic sea and sky. In true Romantic fashion, the natural elements are emphasized over the human ones.

that would drag on for twenty-two years, creating fear and rigidity within Britain and effectively squelching during that time all hope of reform within British society.

The Tory government led by William Pitt (the Younger) began the reaction by outlawing all talk of parliamentary reform outside the halls of Parliament, banning public meetings, and suspending certain basic rights. Later, Pitt's government crushed a rebellion in Ireland. Liberal-minded Britons had no political outlet for their hopes and dreams. Many turned to literature and art as a way to find in the pristine world of romanticized nature the source of beauty and truth.

The Napoleonic Wars

Britain's battles against France took a new turn after 1799, when a military leader named Napoleon Bonaparte came to power in Paris. Napoleon had grandiose plans for French military expansion, and he was an able leader. After a brief break in French-British hostilities in 1802–03, war resumed in earnest. Napoleon, who had declared himself emperor of France, planned an invasion of Britain, but had to abandon the plan after a British fleet under Lord Nelson defeated the French fleet at the Battle of Trafalgar, off Spain, in 1805. Napoleon's armies fought well against Britain's European allies, however, and by 1807 they controlled almost all of Europe as far east as the borders of Russia. Britain ruled the ocean, but Napoleon ruled Europe.

In 1812 Napoleon finally overextended himself by invading Russia. There his armies suffered a series of bloody defeats. At the same time, Napoleon was experiencing reverses in the west. His forces were defeated in the Peninsular War (1808–13) in Portugal

THE BATTLE OF TRAFALGAR
J. M. W. Turner
The Granger Collection

628   *The Romantic Age*

and Spain and, in 1814, British and allied armies closed in on him and forced him to abandon his crown. Napoleon was not finished, however. Exiled to the Mediterranean island of Elba, he plotted a return, and in 1815 he managed to escape to France, assemble an army, and resume rule for a period known as the Hundred Days. Napoleon's attempt to regain his former glory ended on the battlefield at Waterloo, Belgium, in 1815, when the Duke of Wellington, British hero of the Peninsular War, led an allied army to a decisive victory.

All over Britain, people celebrated the end of the Napoleonic Wars with bonfires and other festivities. Royalists hailed the restoration of monarchical authority throughout Europe, while radicals mourned the failure of the revolutionary ideals of liberty and equality.

COPING WITH SOCIETY'S PROBLEMS

Throughout the long wars with France, Britain's government kept a tight lid on domestic dissent. It ignored the problems caused by the Industrial Revolution—including the overcrowding of factory towns, the unpleasant and unsafe working conditions in the factories, and the long working hours, and low pay experienced by the workers—and the problems only got worse.

Rumblings Among the People

Britain's government claimed to be following a hands-off policy, but in fact it sided openly with employers against workers even helping to crush the workers' attempts to form unions. Meanwhile, the working class grew steadily larger and more restless. In the factory towns of northern England, workers protested the loss of jobs to new machinery in the violent Luddite Riots (1811–13). In Manchester, mounted soldiers charged a peaceful mass meeting of cotton workers and killed several of them in what came to be known as the Peterloo Massacre (1819). To many, it seemed that British society was splitting into two angry camps—the working classes, who demanded reform, and the ruling classes, who resisted fiercely.

Beginnings of Reform

During this time, Britain had a series of weak and ineffective royal heads. George III, long subject to bouts of insanity, went irretrievably mad in 1811. His eldest son, the scandal-plagued and unpopular George, Prince of Wales, ruled as Regent from 1811 to 1820—a period known as the Regency. Then the old king died and the Regent became George IV. When he died in 1830, his brother took over as William IV—an old and weak but amiable king, who ruled until 1837.

The weakness of these kings helped to enhance the power of the prime ministers—in theory named by the king, but in practice

NAPOLEON (THE CAMPAIGN IN FRANCE, 1814)
J. L. E. Meissonier
The Granger Collection

KING WILLIAM IV OF ENGLAND
Sir Martin Archer Shee
The Granger Collection

Introduction 629

3 Historical Context The Victorian novelist William Thackeray characterized him as "the last and worst of all the Georges" because of his extravagance and his treatment of his consort. The poet Leigh Hunt was sentenced to a two-year prison term for calling him a "fat Adonis."

Humanities Note

Fine art, *Napoleon (The Campaign in France, 1814),* 1864, by J. L. E. Meissonier. Jean Louis Ernest Meissonier (1815–1891) accompanied Napoleon III, Napoleon Bonaparte's nephew, to Italy in the 1850's. Meissonier did a series of paintings of Napoleon I. This detail of *The Campaign in France, 1814* shows the French general in a typical pose, leading his troops on a light-colored horse. The invasion of France by Britain and Spain in 1814 led to the downfall of the emperor, and thus the painting depicts a great leader whose defeat is imminent.

Humanities Note

Fine art, *King William IV of England* by Sir Martin Archer Shee. When he was nineteen Martin Archer Shee (1769–1850), who had studied art in his native Dublin, went to London, at the urging of the famous American portrait painter Gilbert Stuart. Through influential connections, Shee entered the Royal Academy, in 1790, and later became a successful portrait painter whose subjects included members of the royal family.

Shee's full-length portrait of the King William IV is a typical formal pose of a monarch. It was painted by a man whose conservative views on art were expressed in two poems Shee wrote: "Rhymes on Art, or the Remonstrance of a Painter" (1805) and "Elements of Art" (1809). Shee's interest in both painting and literature led his friend the poet Lord Byron, perhaps satirically, to write: "And here let Shee and genius find a place,/Whose pen and pencil yield an equal grace. . . ."

Fine art, Sketch for *Hadleigh Castle,* c. 1828–9, by John Constable. All of the paintings of John Constable (1776–1837) show familiar and realistic scenes of the English countryside. Constable wanted to paint what he saw with his own eyes, for he believed that landscape painting must be based on observable facts. He went out into the countryside to make sketches from nature and painted final versions in his studio. This working sketch for *Hadleigh Castle* is an example of his work in progress. This detail shows a literal rendering, with freshness in color resulting from working in natural light outdoors.

4 Enrichment Wordsworth in particular among the older Romantic poets supported the French Revolution, although both Coleridge and Southey were ardent revolutionaries in their youth.

5 Literary Movement Wordsworth's "London, 1802," page 656, expresses his reaction to the disappointing outcome of the French Revolution and the growing reactionary spirit in England.

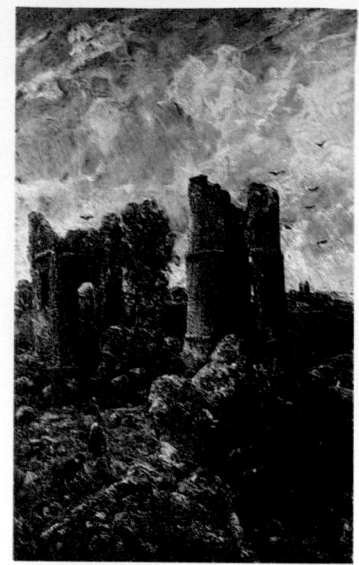

SKETCH FOR HADLEIGH CASTLE, c. 1828–9
John Constable
The Granger Collection

chosen by the strongest party in Parliament. The Tory leaders who held power during and immediately after the Napoleonic Wars rejected all suggestions of reform. A new generation of Tories emerged in the 1820's, however, and a trickle of reforms began. However, a law was passed in 1824 permitting Britain's first labor unions to organize; and in 1829 the Catholic Emancipation Act restored economic and religious freedoms to Roman Catholics.

The trickle grew into a stream of reforms following a Whig victory in the election of 1830. The Reform Law of 1832 brought sweeping changes to British political life. By extending voting rights to the small but important middle class (males only), this law threatened the traditional dominance of land-owning aristocrats in Parliament. Moreover, in 1833 Parliament passed the first law governing factory safety. That same year, it also abolished slavery.

THE BEGINNINGS OF ROMANTICISM

Writers of the Romantic Age reacted strongly to the events of their time. They felt stirrings of excitement or repulsion as they contemplated the French Revolution. They saw the dramatic changes being wrought by the Industrial Revolution and longed for the simplicity and purity of the past. They sensed the rumblings of discontent and desperation that could not be silenced, even by the repressive measures of the war years. Those who had applauded the French Revolution, envisioning a new age of democracy and equality in Britain, were left in a state of bitter disappointment. They turned their attention to literary endeavors, creating a Romantic style that offered a new perspective on the world—a perspective that focused on nature and "the common people."

4

5

New Literary Concerns

Just as the French revolutionaries had at first discarded the customs and procedures that had traditionally governed French society, the Romantic writers abandoned many of the dominant attitudes and principles of eighteenth-century literature. New literary concerns emerged, many of which had been shaped either by the French revolutionary spirit or by the effects of the Industrial Revolution. The Romantic writers' interest in the trials and dreams of common people and their desire for radical change developed out of the democratic idealism that characterized the early part of the French Revolution, while their deep attachment to nature was a response to the consequences of industrialization. These and other characteristics of Romantic literature represent a distinct departure from the concerns associated with eighteenth-century classicism and rationalism. Because of this dichotomy, the prevailing ideas and attitudes of Romanticism are most easily grasped when viewed in contrast to those of the eighteenth century. The following chart identifies some of the contrasting tendencies.

	CLASSICISM AND RATIONALISM	ROMANTICISM
SOURCES OF INSPIRATION	scientific observation of the outer world; logic	examination of inner feelings, emotions; imagination
	classical Greek and Roman literature	the literature of the Middle Ages
ATTITUDES AND INTERESTS	pragmatic	idealistic
	interested in science, technology	interested in the mysterious and supernatural
	concerned with general, universal experiences	concerned with the particular
	believed in following standards and traditions	sought to develop new forms of expression
	felt optimistic about the present	romanticized the past
	emphasized moderation and self-restraint	tended toward excess and spontaneity
	appreciated elegance, refinement	appreciated folk traditions
SOCIAL CONCERNS	valued stability and harmony	desired radical change
	favored a social hierarchy	favored democracy
	interested in maintaining the aristocracy	concerned with common people
	concerned with society as a whole	concerned with the individual
	believed that nature should be controlled by humans	felt that nature should be untamed

It is customary to set the beginning of Britain's Romantic Age in 1798, the year in which William Wordsworth and Samuel Taylor Coleridge published the *Lyrical Ballads,* establishing the Romantic principles that would dominate British literature for several decades. However, the ideas of Romanticism arose on continental Europe well before the turn of the century. Even in Britain a handful of poets—most notably Thomas Gray, Robert Burns, and William Blake—had displayed some of the characteristics of Romantic thinking before *Lyrical Ballads* was published.

Jean-Jacques Rousseau

Though he died before the start of the Romantic Age, Swiss-born writer Jean-Jacques Rousseau (1712–1778), a leading philosopher of eighteenth-century France, planted one of the seeds from

RAIN, STEAM, AND SPEED—THE GREAT WESTERN RAILWAY 1844
J. M. W. Turner
The Granger Collection

Introduction 631

PORTRAIT OF GOETHE
Joseph Karl Stieler
Three Lions

which Romanticism grew. Rousseau saw society as a force of evil that infringed on personal liberty and human happiness. "Man is born free," he wrote, "and everywhere he is in chains." He reasoned that humanity should revert to its natural state, abandoning its stifling social institutions and outworn philosophies and listening instead to nature, instinct, and intuition.

6

Rousseau prepared the way for political revolution. The Americans who declared their independence in 1776 quoted Rousseau often, and the French revolutionaries of 1789 quoted him even more frequently. Rousseau also prepared the way for a new artistic movement, Romanticism. During the latter part of the eighteenth century, in the German-speaking areas of Europe, which were not yet a unified nation and often suffered from the repressive policies of powerful Prussia and Austria, a group of nationalistically minded writers began incorporating Rousseau's ideas into major works of poetry, drama, and fiction.

7

Johann Wolfgang von Goethe

The most influential of this group was Johann Wolfgang von Goethe (1749–1832). In search of inspiration, Goethe turned to the German literature of the Middle Ages, early vernacular works filled with myth and superstition, adventure and passion, not unlike the Anglo-Saxon *Beowulf.* In these works Goethe found not only a source of pride for a new generation of German writers but also a primitive simplicity much in keeping with Rousseau's ideas and values. A fascination with medieval times—the same Middle Ages that "enlightened" thinkers had despised—soon became characteristic of the emerging artistic movement. In fact, the movement would later be named the Romantic Age because of its interest in medieval *romances*—imaginary tales of adventure written in one of the Roman dialects, the early forms of languages derived from Latin.

THE ROMANTIC AGE IN BRITISH POETRY

Romanticism was a movement that affected not only literature but all the arts. In music, it produced such brilliant European composers as Germany's Ludwig van Beethoven (1770–1827) and Austria's Franz Schubert (1797–1828), but no one of comparable stature in Britain. In painting, it influenced the intensely personal and warmly spontaneous rural landscapes of Britain's John Constable (1776–1837) and J. M. W. Turner (1775–1851). However, it is for literature, and especially for poetry, that Britain's Romantic Age is most famous.

8

Wordsworth and Coleridge: A Break with the Past

When William Wordsworth (1770–1850) asked his friend Samuel Taylor Coleridge (1772–1834) to collaborate with him in the publication of *Lyrical Ballads,* he was well aware that their collection

CALAIS PIER: AN ENGLISH PACKET ARRIVING
J. M. W. Turner
The Granger Collection

Humanities Note

Fine art, *Calais Pier, with French Poissards preparing for sea: an English packet arriving,* 1803, by J. M. W. Turner. Turner's vision of the world was a fantastic one, bathed in dramatic light filled with dazzling pageantries. In many of his pictures, like *Calais Pier,* he crowded in every effect that would make them more dazzling and striking. He shows the power of nature, which is not always kind to humans. Here Turner presents dazzling light in stark contrast with the dark shadows of the storm clouds. The viewer can feel the rush of the wind and the impact of the waves, against which the humans struggle.

of poetry would make a distinct break with the past. To underscore that break, Wordsworth included in the second (1800) and third (1802) editions of *Lyrical Ballads* a preface explaining the new poetic principles he and Coleridge had employed. That preface defined poetry as "the spontaneous overflow of powerful feelings" and explained that poetry "takes its origin from emotion recollected in tranquillity." An emphasis on the emotions, then, was central to the new Romantic poetry the two men were creating.

Equally important was subject matter. According to the preface, poetry should deal with "incidents and situations from common life" over which the poet throws "a certain coloring of imagination, whereby ordinary things should be presented . . . in an unusual way." Wordsworth's poems gave "the charm of novelty to things of every day," as Coleridge later said. Coleridge, on the other hand, provided the "coloring of imagination," creating imaginative settings and mysterious sequences of events.

Finally, Wordsworth's preface spoke about incorporating human passions with "the beautiful and permanent forms of nature." An emphasis on nature would become another important characteristic of British Romantic verse, and Wordsworth would frequently be described as a "nature poet."

The Romantic view of nature was quite different from that of most eighteenth-century literature. Nature was not a force to be tamed and analyzed scientifically; rather, it was a wild, free force that could inspire poets to instinctive spiritual understanding. In "The Tables Turned," Wordsworth advised readers to

> Come forth into the light of things,
> Let Nature be your Teacher.

SAMUEL TAYLOR COLERIDGE
Peter Vandyke
The Granger Collection

Humanities Note

Fine art, *Samuel Taylor Coleridge,* 1795, by Peter Vandyke. A native of the Netherlands, Peter Vandyke (b. 1729; death date uncertain) was asked to come to England by Sir Joshua Reynolds, the widely acclaimed British portrait painter. In England Vandyke assisted Reynolds, and he also painted portraits of his own; he exhibited some of them in London in the 1760's.

It was at the invitation of a publisher that Vandyke painted his portrait of Samuel Taylor Coleridge, which now hangs in London's National Portrait Gallery. The portrait of Coleridge is formal —perhaps in something of the "grand style" favored by Reynolds—and yet it displays warmth and humanity, especially in the expressiveness of the subject's eyes.

Introduction 633

9 **Literary Movement** Coleridge's "The Rime of the Ancient Mariner," page 660, is considered to be his one complete and perfectly executed masterpiece. Coleridge planned many works, but his temperament prevented their completion; his fragment "Kubla Khan," page 685, a rich and evocative dream picture, gives evidence of the abortive nature of much of his inspiration.

10 **Literary Movement** Wordsworth's "Lines Composed a Few Miles Above Tintern Abbey," page 644, and "My Heart Leaps Up When I Behold," page 650, give a personal history of his own commitment to Nature. Both these poems are prefatory to his great "Ode: Intimations of Immortality from Recollections of Early Childhood."

11 **Literary Movement** In Wordsworth's "The World is Too Much with Us," page 657, the poet truly sees untamed Nature as an elemental spiritual force.

12 Enrichment Wordsworth became so extremely conservative, even reactionary, in his old age that his ideas came to be denounced by younger writers. The Victorian poet Robert Browning, for example, in his poem "The Lost Leader," mourned Wordsworth's decline from liberalism.

13 Enrichment Although Byron was an outstandingly attractive man, he did have one physical flaw: a clubfoot.

14 Enrichment Byron's "English Bards and Scotch Reviewers" treats all three "first generation Romantics" with contempt; he calls Wordsworth idiotic, Coleridge turgid, and Southey long-winded.

15 Literary Movement Both Emily Brontë's *Wuthering Heights* and Charlotte Brontë's *Jane Eyre* (information on *Wuthering Heights* can be found in the Great Works feature, page 898) contain Byronic heroes in the characters of Heathcliff and Rochester.

16 Literary Movement See the excerpt from Byron's *Don Juan*, page 697, for a work whose satirical tone is definitely anti-Romantic.

17 Enrichment Although Shelley was a political radical, his self-imposed exile was based more on his personal than his political unpopularity. The English public was unforgiving of his abandonment of his wife, her subsequent suicide, and his immediate remarriage to a woman who had already borne him two children.

Use your judgment in deciding whether to share this sort of sensitive material with your students.

In idealizing unspoiled nature, Wordsworth and the other Romantics were not merely abandoning the philosophies of classicism and rationalism; they were condemning the Industrial Revolution and its encroachment on the English countryside.

Lyrical Ballads met a cool reception at first, but with time it came to be regarded as the cornerstone of Britain's Romantic Age. Also with time, Wordsworth and Coleridge became respected members of Britain's literary establishment. Their literary ideas began to seem less radical than they once had, and their political thinking—deeply marked by events in France—grew more conservative.

The Second Generation of Romantic Poets

Wordsworth and Coleridge blazed the way for a new generation of British Romantic poets—the so-called "second generation" of poets, which included Byron, Shelley, and Keats. Coming of age during the Napoleonic era and the Regency, these younger poets rebelled even more strongly than Wordsworth and Coleridge against the British conservatism of the time. All three died abroad after tragically short lives, and their viewpoints were those of disillusioned outsiders.

George Gordon, Lord Byron (1788–1824), did not begin life as an outsider. On the contrary, he was part of the British aristocracy—a member of the House of Lords, an intimate of high-born men and women. Although critics responded unfavorably to his early poetry, Byron persisted and finally achieved success when he published *Childe Harold's Pilgrimage* (1812). Handsome, egotistical, and aloof, Byron became the darling of elegant society—but not for long. Shocked by Byron's radical politics and scandalous love affairs, London hostesses began to shun him, and Byron left Britain in 1816, never to return. He died of a fever while fighting with Greek revolutionaries in their struggle to win independence from Turkey.

Because they had abandoned their democratic ideals, Byron wrote scornfully about Wordsworth and Coleridge. However much of his work reflects their Romantic style. His long narrative poems often feature brooding, passionate, rebellious figures. Such "Byronic" heroes and heroines became a common feature of the literature of the Romantic Age. On the other hand, some of Byron's work —such as his poem *Don Juan* (1819–24)—owes more to eighteenth-century mock epics than it does to Wordsworth and Coleridge.

Byron's friend Percy Bysshe Shelley (1792–1822) was also well-born and politically radical—more consistently radical, in fact, than Byron. In poems such as "Song to the Men of England" (1819), Shelley urged England's lower classes to rebel.

Like Byron, Shelley was shunned for his radical ideas; he left Britain for good in 1818. Unlike Byron, however, Shelley did not attain fame in his own lifetime. Yet he is now remembered for the fervor he brought to lyric poetry in such intensely personal and emotional verses as "To a Skylark" (1821).

John Keats (1795–1821), the third great figure in the second generation of Romantic poets, was also a master of lyrical poetry. Unlike Byron and Shelley, Keats was born outside elegant society, the son of a London stable keeper. Keats trained to be a doctor, then abandoned his medical career to pursue his passion for poetry. He produced many of his greatest poems in a burst of creativity during the first nine months of 1819—works like *The Fall of Hyperion* and "Ode on a Grecian Urn." Unfortunately, however, Keats was already struggling against tuberculosis. Hoping to recuperate in a warmer climate he traveled to Italy, where he died at the age of twenty-five. By his own request, his epitaph reads: "Here lies one whose name was writ in water."

THE ROMANTIC AGE IN BRITISH PROSE

Poetry was the dominant literary form during the Romantic Age, but not the only one. Many significant prose works also appeared, mainly in the form of essays and novels. This was a dry period for drama; only two theaters were licensed to produce plays, and they tended to feature popular spectacles rather than serious plays. However, Shelley and other poets did write closet dramas, verse works intended to be read rather than produced on the stage.

The Romantic Essayists

British readers of the Romantic Age could find brilliant literary criticism and topical essays in a variety of new periodicals. The earliest of these periodicals reflected the conservative and neoclassical ideals of an earlier age; they roundly condemned the Romantic poets and their work. In time, however, periodicals that were more sympathetic to the Romantics came into being. One such publication, *The London Magazine*, although it appeared only from 1820 to 1829, attracted major contributions from the three greatest essayists of the era: Charles Lamb (1775–1834), William Hazlitt (1778–1830), and Thomas De Quincey (1785–1859). Lamb, in particular, transformed the informal essay of the eighteenth century into a more personal, more introspective Romantic composition.

The Romantic Novelists

Unlike the Romantic poets, the novelists of the Romantic Age did not make a sharp break with the past. In fact, the three main types of Romantic novels—the Gothic novel, the novel of manners, and the historical romance—all represented elaborations on earlier forms.

The Gothic novel first appeared in the middle of the eighteenth

JOHN KEATS
Joseph Severn
The Granger Collection

18 **Literary Movement** See Shelley's "To a Skylark," page 708, and his "Ode to the West Wind," page 704, for examples of his consummate poetic skill and great lyric beauty.

Humanities Note

Fine art, *John Keats,* 1818, by Joseph Severn. In 1820, when Keats was suffering from tuberculosis, his publisher arranged for the poet to go to Rome, to a warmer climate. Joseph Severn (1793–1879), a painter who had been a close friend of Keats for several years, accompanied the poet to Italy and took care of him until Keats died.

The portrait of Keats depicts the poet in a subdued, pensive mood—perhaps not what one would imagine of the poet who produced such intensely creative works within such a short period of time. Another portrait Severn made of Keats, a charcoal drawing, has a more expressive look. Probably done more rapidly than the painting, the drawing captures the poet in a more spontaneous pose.

19 **Literary Movement** See "Ode on a Grecian Urn," page 726, for the famous statement that epitomizes Keats's passionate commitment to beauty.

20 **Enrichment** Most of the Romantic writers were strongly criticized when their poetry first appeared. The *Edinburgh Review* was particularly harsh; its negative tone inspired Byron's retort, "English Bards and Scotch Reviewers." The critics' savaging, in the *Quarterly Review,* has popularly but erroneously been considered a contributory cause for Keats's early death at the age of twenty-six.

21 **Literary Movement** Charles Lamb's essay, "Dream Children," page 742, reveals both his gentle nature and the disappointments of a life that precluded domestic happiness: Because his sister Mary had killed their mother in a fit of insanity, Lamb was afraid to marry and have children.

Humanities Note

Fine art, *Sir Walter Scott/ Abbotsford Family,* by Sir David Wilkie. Some of the earlier works of David Wilkie (1785–1841), such as *The Blind Fiddler* (1807), are in the tradition of seventeenth-century Dutch genre painting —they depict, with great technical skill, the everyday lives of ordinary people. Wilkie's unsentimental, unpretentious scenes of village life, painted on a small scale, were quite popular and influential in his day. Wilkie helped establish a style of painting that suggested a ''story,'' possibly with an implied moral.

Wilkie, who had left his native Scotland in 1805 to go to London, returned to the north for a visit in 1817. He stayed, at that time, with Sir Walter Scott. Some six years earlier Scott had purchased land in Roxburghshire, Scotland, and, between 1817 and 1824, had his house, called Abbotsford, built for him. In Wilkie's painting, Scott is shown with people from the village. The writer, who limped as a result of childhood polio, holds a cane. The work is a tribute both to a famous literary man and to the simple people among whom he lived.

22 Literary Movement See the introduction to Mary Shelley's *Frankenstein,* page 734, a story she reportedly devised when the Shelleys and Byron were whiling away a rainy evening together in Italy during their exiles.

23 Literary Movement See the excerpt from Jane Austen's *Pride and Prejudice,* page 752, unarguably the finest novel of the Romantic period, a masterpiece of insightful character development and gentle satire.

**SIR WALTER SCOTT/ABBOTSFORD FAMILY,
1804**
Sir David Wilkie
The Granger Collection

century. It featured a number of standard ingredients, including brave heroes and heroines, threatening scoundrels, vast eerie castles, and ghosts. The Romantic fascination with mystery and the supernatural made such novels quite popular during the Romantic Age. One of the most successful was *Frankenstein, or the Modern Prometheus* (1818), written by Shelley's wife, Mary Wollstonecraft Shelley (1797–1851).

22

The Romantic novel of manners carried on in the tradition of earlier writers by turning a satirical eye on British customs. The most highly regarded writer of novels of manners was Jane Austen (1775–1817) whose works include *Sense and Sensibility* (1811) and *Pride and Prejudice* (1813). Her incisive portrayals of character are more reflective of the classical sensibility of the eighteenth century than the Romantic notions of the new age.

23

Historical romances—imaginative works of fiction built around a real person or historical event—had appeared long before the Romantic Age, but they attained their peak of popularity in the work of Sir Walter Scott (1771–1832). Passionately devoted to his native Scotland, Scott wrote about the days of knights and chivalry. Although he expressed a Scottish nationalism not unlike the nationalism of Germany's Romantic writers, Scott remained popular with England's ruling class, who apparently did not view his tales of a bygone age as a threat to the status quo.

The close of Britain's Romantic Age is usually set in 1832, the year of the passage of the First Reform Bill. However, the ideas of Romanticism remained a strong influence on many writers from following generations. In fact, even today we can detect elements of Romanticism in many major works of contemporary fiction and poetry as well as in TV dramas, movies, and popular songs.

636   *The Romantic Age*

Check Test

1. In 1789, the French Revolution was touched off by the storming of the _____.
2. The events in France became especially alarming to Britain with the period of violence known as the Reign of _____.
3. The French army had great success after _____ took power.
4. The beginning of the Romantic Age is marked by the publication of a book of verses by Samuel Coleridge and _____.
5. One of the most popular novels from the Romantic Age is Mary Shelley's _____.

Answers to the Check Test

1. Bastille
2. Terror
3. William Wordsworth
4. *Frankenstein, or the Modern Prometheus*

ENGLISH VOICES
Quotations by Prominent Figures of the Period

Bliss was it on that dawn to be alive . . .
France standing on the top of golden hours
And human nature seemed born again.
> **William Wordsworth,** *The Prelude*

But yet I know, where'er I go.
That there hath past away a glory from the earth . . .
nothing can bring back the hour
Of splendor in the grass, of glory in the flower.
> **William Wordsworth,** "Ode: Intimations of Immortality from Recollections of Early Childhood"

Poetry is not the proper antithesis to prose, but to science.
> **Samuel Taylor Coleridge,** *Definitions of Poetry*

One half the world cannot understand the pleasures of the other.
> **Jane Austen,** *Emma*

It is a truth universally acknowledged that a man in possession of a good fortune must be in want of a wife.
> **Jane Austen,** *Pride and Prejudice*

Clear writers, like fountains, do not seem so deep as they are.
> **Charles Lamb,** *Imaginary Conversation*

I love not man the less, but Nature more.
> **George Gordon, Lord Byron,** *Childe Harold's Pilgrimage*

If Winter comes, can Spring be far behind?
> **Percy Bysshe Shelley,** "Ode to the West Wind"

The poetry of earth is never dead.
> **John Keats,** "Sonnet: On the Grasshopper and the Cricket"

"Beauty is truth, truth beauty"—that is all
Ye know on earth, and all ye need to know.
> **John Keats,** "Ode on a Grecian Urn"

Additional Voices

Until you understand a writer's ignorance, presume yourself ignorant of his understanding.
> **Samuel Taylor Coleridge,** *Biographia Literaria*

All love is sweet,
Given or returned. Common as light is love,
And its familiar voice wearies not ever. . . .
> **Percy Bysshe Shelley,** *Prometheus Unbound*

I beheld the wretch—the miserable monster whom I had created.
> **Mary Wollstonecraft Shelley,** *Frankenstein*

The human species, according to the best theory I can form of it, is composed of two distinct races, the men who borrow, and the men who lend.
> **Charles Lamb,** *The Two Races of Men*

There is not a more mean, stupid, dastardly, pitiful, selfish, spiteful, envious, ungrateful animal than the Public. It is the greatest of cowards, for it is afraid of itself.
> **William Hazlitt,** *On Living to One's Self*

The love of liberty is the love of others; the love of power is the love of ourselves.
> **William Hazlitt,** *Political Essays. The Times Newspaper*

Reading Critically The purpose of this page is to guide students in the critical reading of literature of the Romantic Age. The information offered here will allow students to place a work of literature in its historical context, identify literary movements of the time, and appreciate the techniques used by writers of the period.

As you discuss the information on the page with the class, explain that the poem "The Solitary Reaper" by William Wordsworth beginning on page 649, is a model for reading critically. The side columns contain notes that draw students' attention to elements that reflect the historical context, the influence of the literary movements, and the writer's techniques.

To give students further practice with the process of reading critically, use the selection in the **Teaching Portfolio,** "I Am" by John Clare, page 768, following the Teacher Backup, which students can annotate themselves. Encourage students to use these strategies as they read the literature in this unit.

Teaching to Ability Levels For **less advanced** students, discuss any difficult vocabulary words before reading. You might wish to have them read the poem aloud after they have read it silently.

READING CRITICALLY

The Literature of 1798–1832

When you read literature, it is important to place it in its historical context. Doing so will help you to see how it reflects the dominant ideas of its time and appreciate the techniques the writer used in conveying these ideas.

Historical Context

During the years from 1798 to 1832, English life was dramatically influenced by the aftereffects of the French Revolution and the realities of industrialization. While many English intellectuals supported the democratic ideals upon which the French Revolution was grounded, the English ruling class took measures to ensure that a similar revolution could not occur in England. At the same time, the industrial revolution was having a profound social and economic impact on the nation. English cities grew rapidly and became the nation's economic centers. Factory workers labored long hours for extremely low wages, and young children often had to work to help support their families. It became increasingly clear that new governmental policies were needed to accommodate these changes. Yet few political changes occurred until 1832, when the First Reform Bill was passed.

Literary Movements

Toward the end of the eighteenth century, an artistic movement known as Romanticism developed as a reaction against the dominant ideas and standards of Rationalism. Unlike the Rationalists, who stressed logic and reason, the Romantics emphasized emotions and the imagination. The Romantics also possessed a strong belief in democracy, an interest in mystery and the supernatural, a belief in excess and spontaneity, a concern for common people, and a love of nature.

Writers' Techniques

The Romantic period was an age in which poetry flourished. Using the language of common people, the Romantics wrote lyric poems that generally focused on ordinary situations and ordinary people. Although poetry was the major form of literary expression during the period, a number of significant novels and essays were also produced. Like Romantic poetry, these works reflect the dominant ideas and attitudes of the age.

On the following pages is a poem by William Wordsworth, a major Romantic poet. The annotations in the side column should help you to place the selection in its historical context.

Objectives

1 To analyze diction
2 To appreciate sound devices
3 To write a poem

Support Material

Teaching Portfolio
Teacher Backup, p. 765
Reading Critically, *"I Am"* by John Clare, p. 768
Usage and Mechanics Worksheet, p. 769
Critical Thinking and Reading Worksheet, *Understanding Sound Devices,* p. 770

Language Worksheet, *Appreciating Vivid Verbs,* p. 771
Selection Test, p. 772

MODEL

The Solitary Reaper

William Wordsworth

This poem was inspired by a passage from Thomas Willkinson's Tour of Scotland (1824): "Passed a female who was reaping alone; she sung in Erse (Scottish Gaelic) as she bended over her sickle; the sweetest human voice I ever heard: her strains were tenderly melancholy, and felt delicious long after they were heard no more."

Behold her, single in the field,
Yon solitary Highland lass!
Reaping and singing by herself;
Stop here, or gently pass!
5   Alone she cuts and binds the grain,
And sings a melancholy strain;
O listen! for the vale profound
Is overflowing with the sound.

No nightingale did ever chaunt
10   More welcome notes to weary bands
Of travelers in some shady haunt,
Among Arabian sands;
A voice so thrilling ne'er was heard
In springtime from the cuckoo-bird,
15   Breaking the silence of the seas
Among the farthest Hebrides.

Will no one tell me what she sings?—
Perhaps the plaintive numbers flow
For old, unhappy, far-off things,
20   And battles long ago;
Or is it some more humble lay,
Familiar matter of today?
Some natural sorrow, loss, or pain,
That has been, and may be again?

25   Whate'er the theme, the maiden sang
As if her song could have no ending;

Literary Movement: Wordsworth uses his imagination to transform a passage from Wilkinson's book into a poem. The poem's subject reflects the Romantic interest in common people and rural life.

Literary Movement: Wordsworth's references to the songs of birds reflect the Romantic love of nature.

Writer's Technique: The poem is a lyric written in octaves, or eight-line stanzas, using an *ababccdd* rhyme scheme.

Writer's Technique: The poem is written in common, everyday language.

The Solitary Reaper   639

Presentation

Motivation/Prior Knowledge
Have the students discuss times in their lives when a commonplace event, and everyday place, or an ordinary person took on special significance. Share one of your special times with the class. Explain that Wordsworth used one of those experiences a friend had written about as a springboard for this poem.

Purpose-setting Question
When Wordsworth wrote this poem, he was experimenting with "how far the language of conversation is adapted for the purposes of poetic pleasure." How does the diction or word choice contribute to the success of this poem?

Master Teacher Note Wordsworth stated that his purpose in writing poetry was to give "the charm of novelty to things of every day . . . by awakening the mind's attention and directing it to the loveliness and wonders of the world before us." Discuss whether students think that this is possible. From this statement and from the title, have the class predict what the poem might include before they read.

Clarification The Hebrides is a group of about 500 islands in the Atlantic Ocean off the west coast of Scotland. Fewer than one hundred of the Hebrides are populated, with most of the inhabitants living on four of the islands. Only one of these islands, Skye, is a part of the farthest Hebrides, or Outer Herbrides. (Refer students to the map on p. 1328.)

Master Teacher Note In his lyrics Wordsworth freely used conversational language in contrast to traditional poetic speech. This conversation-like diction tightened Wordsworth's lyrics, and, combined with Wordsworth's kinship with nature, helped create poems with a frank and noble simplicity.

For Further Study Biographical information on Wordsworth appears on page 642, and other poems by him are on pages 644–657.

Literary Movement: The speaker examines his inner feelings and explores the emotional impact of the experience.

I saw her singing at her work,
And o'er the sickle bending;
I listened, motionless and still;
30   And, as I mounted up the hill,
The music in my heart I bore,
Long after it was heard no more.

THINKING ABOUT THE SELECTION

Recalling

1. What is the "solitary Highland lass" doing when the speaker sees her?
2. To what does the speaker compare the woman's singing in the second stanza?
3. What possible subjects of the woman's song does the speaker imagine?
4. What does the speaker bear in his heart as he continues his walk?

Interpreting

5. What do the comparisons in the second stanza suggest about the woman's song?
6. What does the final stanza reveal about the impact of the experience on the speaker?

Applying

7. In what ways does the type of life portrayed in the poem contrast with the type of life you would imagine the nineteenth-century factory workers must have lead?

ANALYZING LITERATURE

Appreciating a Writer's Diction

Diction refers to a writer's choice of words. A writer uses language appropriate for the subject and characters.
1. In this poem Wordsworth uses simple, direct language. Why is this type of language appropriate?

2. Why would the poem be less effective if it were written using elegant, ornate language?

CRITICAL THINKING AND READING

Understanding Sound Devices

In "The Solitary Reaper," Wordsworth uses a number of sound devices to give the poem a musical quality. For example, he uses alliteration—the repetition of consonant sounds at the beginnings of words—in line 9, repeating the *n* sound: "*No nightingale* did ever chant." Wordsworth also uses assonance, or the repetition of similar vowel sounds. Notice the repetition of the *i* sound in line 1: "Behold her, s*i*ngle *i*n the field."
1. Find two more examples of alliteration.
2. Find two more examples of assonance.
3. How does the poem's musical quality reflect its meaning?

THINKING AND WRITING

Writing a Poem

Write a poem in which the Highland lass describes the experience that Wordsworth's speaker observes. Use your imagination to develop her character. When writing your poem, make sure it conveys the character you have developed. In your poem, reveal the subject of her song and present her impressions of the speaker of Wordsworth's poem. When you revise, make sure you have used concrete images, or word pictures.

640   The Romantic Age

Closure and Extension

ANSWERS TO THINKING ABOUT THE SELECTION
Recalling

1. The Lass is singing and reaping wheat.
2. Wordsworth compares the woman's singing to the songs of a nightingale and a cuckoo-bird.
3. The speaker feels she might be singing an old, sad ballad about battles or a less noble song about the sorrows human beings feel.
4. The speaker bore the music of her song in his heart.

Interpreting

5. The comparisons suggest that her singing is a part of nature, and they imply that the song is very welcome and beautiful.
6. The woman's song had a tremendous impact on the speaker because he would remember the experience forever.

Applying

7. Answers will differ. Suggested Response: The factory workers of the period worked under horrible conditions, laboring many grueling hours in factories with no health or safety regulations. They had little time to enjoy the outdoors and certainly

640

had little opportunity to work in a natural environment.

ANSWERS TO ANALYZING LITERATURE

1. Wordsworth's simple language is appropriate because he is writing about commonplace subjects and events.
2. Since the poem was written to show the charm of everyday things, elegant language would conflict

with the ordinariness of the setting.

ANSWERS TO CRITICAL THINKING AND READING

1. Two possibilities are "Breaking the silence of the seas" and "Perhaps the plaintive numbers flow."
2. One possibility is " . . . bands of travelers . . . "; another is " . . . heard no more."
3. Since the poem is about a woman's beautiful singing, the musical quality mirrors the subject of the poem.

THINKING AND WRITING

For help with this assignment, students can refer to Lesson 18, "Writing a Poem," in the Handbook of Writing About Literature.

Publishing Student Writing Have the students make posters of their poems by illustrating their poems with original art, photographs, or pictures from magazines. Display the posters.

Poetry

SALISBURY CATHEDRAL
John Constable
Musea de Arte, Sao Paulo,
Art Resource

Humanities Note

Fine art, *Salisbury Cathedral,* by John Constable. Constable (1776–1837) is one of Britain's supreme landscape painters. He studied art in London as a young man and exhibited his first landscape in 1803. Constable preferred to go out into the countryside to make sketches and then return to his studio to make final versions. Sketching live outside enabled him to capture individuality in movement, light, and atmosphere, which were the elements that interested him. *Salisbury Cathedral* emphasizes the cathedral by bathing it in light, while the foreground, in shadow, presents a dramatic frame.

WILLIAM WORDSWORTH

1770–1850

William Wordsworth is among the small group of writers and poets who truly deserve the title "pioneer." His name is almost synonymous with the movement known as *Romanticism*. Wordsworth demonstrated that poetry was a free—a *living*—form of artistic expression, a view that contrasted sharply with that held by the generation writing before him. Whereas the Neoclassicists, as these earlier poets were called, insisted that poetry address a narrow range of topics and be rigidly structured, Wordsworth's poems were written for the common people—and in a common language.

Born in the beautiful Lake District of England, Wordsworth loved to roam the hills and sit and meditate by the streams. He was well-suited to country living and in later years found nature to be the source of his poetic inspiration and internal peace. Though his parents died when he was young—his mother when he was eight, his father when he was thirteen—Wordsworth's education was seen to, and in 1787 he entered Cambridge. After graduation he traveled through Europe, spending considerable time in France. Here he became caught up in the popular side of the French Revolution, with its emphasis on the rights of the individual. He also found time to fall in love with a young woman named Annette Vallon.

Wordsworth's involvement in the Revolution and his affair with Annette ended abruptly, however, when England declared war on France in 1793 and he was forced to return to his homeland. A year later, the Revolution was halted altogether with the execution of its leader, Robespierre. Wordsworth, seeing his ideals dashed, lapsed into a deep depression. Two people who came to his spiritual rescue were his sister Dorothy and his good friend Samuel Taylor Coleridge.

With Coleridge, Wordsworth composed *Lyrical Ballads* (1798), a collection of poems that reflected his "revolutionary" approach to poetry. In the preface to the collection, Wordsworth put forth his view that poetry should deal with common people and ordinary experiences—that its style and form should reflect "a spontaneous overflow of emotion." Though the book was not received favorably at first, it eventually gained recognition as a major poetic work and is seen today as one of the most influential works on poetic theory ever written in the English language.

642   *The Romantic Age*

GUIDE FOR INTERPRETING

Lines Composed a Few Miles Above Tintern Abbey; My Heart Leaps Up When I Behold

Writer's Technique

Romanticism. Romanticism was a literary movement in Europe in the late eighteenth century. It grew out of a negative reaction to the rigid, formal guidelines and forced subject matter that typified the poetry and art of the previous age. Whereas rationalism and a reliance on scientific doctrine were highly valued by the earlier Neoclassicists, Romanticists believed in the virtues of the imagination and fantasy. The Romantic writer was not only permitted, but encouraged, to give vent to his or her emotions—to write spontaneously, from the heart. Love of nature and an idealization of rural life were naturals for the Romantic poet. Many of these aspects of the Romantic credo figure in the poems of William Wordsworth. Subjectivity in particular is clearly visible in his "Lines Composed a Few Miles Above Tintern Abbey."

Writing

Think about a place you have been that made a vivid impression on you. You might choose a place you visited on vacation or one where you lived. Close your eyes and try to visualize this locale, concentrating on details. Then, freewrite, describing everything you "see."

Primary Source

To offset the cost of a hike to the Valley of Stones, Wordsworth and Coleridge planned to collaborate on a ballad for publication in *The New Monthly Magazine.* They began to compose "The Ancient Mariner" as they walked but soon realized that their styles were too different. Instead, they decided to collaborate on a book of poems. Twenty years later, in 1817, Coleridge described the division of labor:

> The thought suggested itself (to which of us I do not recollect) that a series of poems might be composed of two sorts. In the one, the incidents and agents were to be, in part at least, supernatural. . . . For the second class, subjects were to be chosen from ordinary life; the characters and incidents were to be such as will be found in every village and vicinity. . . .

Guide for Interpreting 643

Motivation/Prior Knowledge
Have students think of a place they knew and loved as a child. What was it about the place that fascinated them then? Now, have them suppose that after several years they are to return to the place. Will they expect the place to be the same? Will they expect their feelings about it to be the same? Do they think they can—or would want to—recapture their original feelings about the place?

Purpose-Setting Question What evidences of Wordsworth's suggestion that one should "Let Nature be your teacher" do you find in the poem?

1 **Discussion** What sort of scene is described in these lines? Is anything missing from the scene? If so, what?

2 **Clarification** Copses (line 14) are thickets of small trees.

3 **Reading Strategy** The poem artfully develops by introducing new ideas at key junctures. These occur at lines 22, 49, 57-8, and 111. Have students summarize the main idea in a section before they move on to the next.

4 **Discussion** Why is the simile of the blind man's eye so effective?

5 **Discussion** In lines 26-41, the poet tells how scenes of the Abbey have influenced him over the past five years. How have they done so? Where has he spent those years?

Lines Composed a Few Miles Above Tintern Abbey

William Wordsworth

This poem was written in 1798 during Wordsworth's second visit to the valley of the River Wye and the ruins of Tintern Abbey, once a great medieval church, in Wales. Having passed through the region alone five years earlier, Wordsworth brought his sister with him to share the experience this time. Of this experience and the poem it inspired, Wordworth wrote, "No poem of mine was composed under circumstances more pleasant for one to remember than this."

Five years have past; five summers, with the length
Of five long winters! and again I hear
These waters, rolling from their mountain springs
With a soft inland murmur. Once again
5 Do I behold these steep and lofty cliffs,
That on a wild secluded scene impress
Thoughts of more deep seclusion; and connect
The landscape with the quiet of the sky.
The day is come when I again repose
10 Here, under this dark sycamore, and view
These plots of cottage ground, these orchard tufts,
Which at this season, with their unripe fruits,
Are clad in one green hue, and lose themselves
'Mid groves and copses. Once again I see
15 These hedgerows, hardly hedgerows, little lines
Of sportive wood run wild: these pastoral farms,
Green to the very door; and wreaths of smoke
Sent up, in silence, from among the trees!
With some uncertain notice, as might seem
20 Of vagrant dwellers in the houseless woods,
Or of some hermit's cave, where by his fire
The hermit sits alone.

                  These beauteous forms,
Through a long absence, have not been to me
As is a landscape to a blind man's eye:
25 But oft, in lonely rooms, and 'mid the din
Of towns and cities, I have owed to them

Primary Source

In the Preface to the second edition of *Lyrical Ballads,* Wordsworth wrote the following about his objectives as a poet:

> The principal object, then, proposed in these Poems, was to choose incidents and situations from common life, and to relate or describe them throughout, as far as was possible, in a selection of language really used by men, and, at the same time, to throw over them a certain colouring of imagination, whereby ordinary things should be presented to the mind in an unusual aspect; and further, and above all, to make these incidents and situations interesting by tracing in them, truly though not ostentatiously, the primary laws of our nature: chiefly, as far as regards the manner in which we associate ideas in a state of excitement. Humble and rustic life was generally chosen, because in that condition the essential passions of the heart find a better soil in which they can attain their maturity, are less under restraint, and speak a plainer and more emphatic language; because in that condition of life our elementary feelings co-exist in a state of greater simplicity, and, consequently, may be more accurately contemplated, and more forcibly communicated; because

TINTERN ABBEY
J. M. W. Turner
British Museum

Lines Composed a Few Miles Above Tintern Abbey 645

Humanities Note

Fine art, *Tintern Abbey* by J. M. W. Turner. Joseph Mallord William Turner (1775-1851) was a premier British landscape painter. A precocious talent, Turner exhibited his first paintings at the age of fifteen. He subsequently studied at the Schools of the Royal Academy and took lessons from an architectural draftsman. Upon completion of his education, he toured England on foot and made watercolors of regional scenes, which he sold to an appreciative public. He later developed his unique, almost abstract approach to painting the light and atmosphere of a landscape, for which he became notable.

The watercolor *Tintern Abbey* was painted early in his career on one of his sketching tours. The skilled depiction of the architectural elements of this painting reflect his training with the draftsman. Romantic, pretty, and decorative, it appealed to the picture-buying public of his day.

Consider using these questions for class discussion:
1. What feature, do you think, inspired Turner to paint this ruin?
2. What adjectives would you use to describe the style?

the manners of rural life germinate from those elementary feelings, and, from the necessary character of rural occupations, are more easily comprehended, and are more durable; and, lastly, because in that condition the passions of men are incorporated with the beautiful and permanent forms of nature. The language, too, of these men has been adopted (purified indeed from what appear to be its real defects, from all lasting and rational causes of dislike or disgust), because such men hourly communicate with the best objects from which the best part of language is originally derived; and because, from their rank in society and the sameness and narrow circle of their intercourse, being less under the influence of social vanity, they convey their feelings and notions in simple and unelaborated expressions. Accordingly, such a language, arising out of repeated experience and regular feelings, is a more permanent, and far more philosophical language, than that which is frequently substituted for it by Poets, who think that they are conferring honour upon themselves and their art in proportion as they separate themselves from the sympathies of men, and indulge in arbitrary and capricious habits of expression, in order to furnish food for fickle tastes and fickle appetites of their own creation.

In hours of weariness, sensations sweet,
Felt in the blood, and felt along the heart;
And passing even into my purer mind,
30 With tranquil restoration—feelings too
Of unremembered pleasure: such, perhaps,
As have no slight or trivial influence
On that best portion of a good man's life.
His little, nameless, unremembered, acts
35 Of kindness and of love. Nor less, I trust,
To them I may have owed another gift,
Of aspect more sublime; that blessed mood,
In which the burthen[1] of the mystery,
In which the heavy and the weary weight
40 Of all this unintelligible world,
Is lightened—that serene and blessed mood,
In which the affections gently lead us on—
Until, the breath of this corporeal frame[2]
And even the motion of our human blood
45 Almost suspended, we are laid asleep
In body, and become a living soul;
While with an eye made quiet by the power
Of harmony, and the deep power of joy,
We see into the life of things.

                              If this
50 Be but a vain belief, yet, oh! how oft—
In darkness and amid the many shapes
Of joyless daylight; when the fretful stir
Unprofitable, and the fever of the world,
Have hung upon the beatings of my heart—
55 How oft, in spirit, have I turned to thee,
O sylvan[3] Wye! thou wanderer through the woods,
How often has my spirit turned to thee!

        And now, with gleams of half-extinguished thought,
With many recognitions dim and faint,
60 And somewhat of a sad perplexity,
The picture of the mind revives again;
While here I stand, not only with the sense
Of present pleasure, but with pleasing thoughts
That in this moment there is life and food
65 For future years. And so I dare to hope,
Though changed, no doubt, from what I was when first
I came among these hills; when like a roe[4]

---

1. **burthen:** Burden.
2. **corporeal** (kôr pôr′ ē əl) **frame:** Body.
3. **sylvan** (sil′ vən): Wooded.
4. **roe:** A type of deer.

Grammar in Action

A good writer never shifts **verb tenses** unnecessarily. If a poem, story, or essay is written in the past tense, for example, and we encounter another tense form, that tense shift is a signal that the writer is moving the account into a different time frame. In "Lines Composed a Few Miles Above Tintern Abbey," Wordsworth skillfully interweaves memories of his youth with thoughts of the present and his hopes for the future. He does so by correctly shifting verb tenses to indicate shifts in thought from past to present and from present to future. Notice how the shift in verb tense in the following lines indicates a shift in the time frame of the speaker's thoughts:

While here I stand, not only with the sense
Of present pleasure, but with pleasing thoughts
That in this moment there is life and food
For future years. And so I dare to hope,
Though changed, no doubt from what I was when first
I came among these hill; when like a roe
I bounded o'er the mountains, by the sides
Of the deep rivers, and the lonely streams,
Wherever nature led:

The verbs in the first four lines are in the present tense, while in the final five lines the verbs shift to the past tense.

I bounded o'er the mountains, by the sides
Of the deep rivers, and the lonely streams,
70 Wherever nature led: more like a man
Flying from something that he dreads, than one
Who sought the thing he loved. For nature then
(The coarser pleasures of my boyish days,
And their glad animal movements all gone by)
75 To me was all in all—I cannot paint
What then I was. The sounding cataract ⌐ 6
Haunted me like a passion; the tall rock,
The mountain, and the deep and gloomy wood,
Their colors and their forms, were then to me
80 An appetite; a feeling and a love,
That had no need of a remoter charm,
By thought supplied, nor any interest
Unborrowed from the eye. That time is past,
And all its aching joys are now no more,
85 And all its dizzy raptures. Not for this
Faint⁵ I, nor mourn nor murmur; other gifts
Have followed; for such loss, I would believe,
Abundant recompense. For I have learned
To look on nature, not as in the hour
90 Of thoughtless youth; but hearing oftentimes
The still, sad music of humanity,
Nor harsh nor grating, though of ample power
To chasten and subdue. And I have felt
A presence that disturbs me with the joy
95 Of elevated thoughts; a sense sublime
Of something far more deeply interfused, ⌐ 7
Whose dwelling is the light of setting suns,
And the round ocean and the living air,
And the blue sky, and in the mind of man;
100 A motion and a spirit, that impels
All thinking things, all objects of all thought,
And rolls through all things. Therefore am I still
A lover of the meadows and the woods
And mountains; and of all that we behold
105 From this green earth; of all the mighty world
Of eye, and ear—both what they half create,
And what perceive; well pleased to recognize ⌐ 8
In nature and the language of the sense,
The anchor of my purest thoughts, the nurse,
110 The guide, the guardian of my heart, and soul ⌐ 9
Of all my moral being.

                    Nor perchance.
If I were not thus taught, should I the more

_____
5. faint: Lose heart.

6 **Clarification** A cataract is a waterfall.

7 **Discussion** What is the "something" the poet refers to?

8 **Clarification** The word *sense* means "senses."

9 **Discussion** Ask students to tell in their own words what the poet recognizes in nature? Help less advanced students to paraphrase these metaphors.

Student Activity 1. Find another passage from the poem in which the speaker shifts verb tenses. Identify the change in verb tense, and explain what this indicates about the speaker's thoughts.

Student Activity 2. Imagine that you are standing in a place that you have visited in the past and hope to visit in the future. Write a short description of your thoughts about how you have changed since you last visited this place, and how you hope to change in the future. Use shifts in verb tense to correctly show your shifts in thought.

Master Teacher Note This work is written in blank verse—lines of unrhymed iambic pentameter, five metrical feet to each line. It is a verse form often used with serious, even stately, works. Students might compare Wordsworth's use of blank verse with that of Shakespeare in *Macbeth*, page 271.

Reader's Response What are your own feelings and attitudes toward nature?

Suffer[6] my genial spirits[7] to decay;
For thou art with me here upon the banks
115 Of this fair river; thou my dearest Friend,[8]
My dear, dear Friend, and in thy voice I catch
The language of my former heart, and read
My former pleasures in the shoooting lights
Of thy wild eyes. Oh! yet a little while
120 May I behold in thee what I was once,
My dear, dear Sister! and this prayer I make,
Knowing that Nature never did betray
The heart that loved her; 'tis her privilege,
Through all the years of this our life, to lead
125 From joy to joy; for she can so inform
The mind that is within us, so impress
With quietness and beauty, and so feed
With lofty thoughts, that neither evil tongues,
Rash judgments, nor the sneers of selfish men,
130 Nor greetings where no kindness is, nor all
The dreary intercourse of daily life,
Shall e'er prevail against us, or disturb
Our cheerful faith, that all which we behold
Is full of blessings. Therefore let the moon
135 Shine on thee in thy solitary walk;
And let the misty mountain winds be free
To blow against thee: and, in after years,
When these wild ecstasies shall be matured
Into a sober pleasure; when thy mind
140 Shall be a mansion for all lovely forms,
Thy memory be as a dwelling place
For all sweet sounds and harmonies; oh! then,
If solitude, or fear, or pain, or grief,
Should be thy portion, with what healing thoughts
145 Of tender joy wilt thou remember me,
And these my exhortations! Nor, perchance—
If I should be where I no more can hear
Thy voice, nor catch from thy wild eyes these gleams
Of past existence—wilt thou then forget
150 That on the banks of this delightful stream
We stood together; and that I, so long
A worshipper of Nature, hither came
Unwearied in that service: rather say
With warmer love—oh! with far deeper zeal
155 Of holier love. Nor wilt thou then forget,
That after many wanderings, many years

---

6. suffer: Allow.
7. genial spirits: Creative powers.
8. Friend: His sister Dorothy.

Of absence, these steep woods and lofty cliffs,
And this green pastoral landscape, were to me
More dear, both for themselves and for thy sake!

THINKING ABOUT THE SELECTION
Recalling

1. In "Lines Composed a Few Miles Above Tintern Abbey," how have the poet's memories of his first visit to the Wye valley altered him?
2. (a) Apart from his pleasure at the moment, what does the poet hope to gain from his second visit to the valley? (b) What does he hope his sister will gain?

Interpreting

3. (a) At what time of year does the poet make his second visit to the area near Tintern Abbey? (b) Find evidence in the poem that supports your answer.
4. In line 35 of the poem, the poet mentions "another gift" which his contact with this rural scene has bestowed upon him. Briefly describe this gift.
5. To what is the poet referring in line 109 as the "anchor of my purest thoughts?"

Applying

6. Do you think it was Wordsworth's wish that everyone attempt to share his experience with and attitudes toward nature? Do you think he believed everyone was capable? Explain.

ANALYZING LITERATURE
Understanding Romanticism

Romanticism stressed the importance of emotion and imagination as tools of the artist. To Wordsworth, one of the movement's foremost practitioners, Romanticism also meant a return to nature and an escape from the contamination of modern civilization. Wordsworth urged the poet to explore his or her innermost feelings—to become attuned to the stirrings of the soul. For this reason, much of Romantic art and poetry has a spiritual, at times almost mystical, quality about it.

Look again at "Lines Composed a Few Miles Above Tintern Abbey," and as you read be on the lookout for the words *soul, heart,* and *spirit.* Paraphrase (state in your own words) each of the poet's thoughts that contains one or more of these words. Explain how each thought relates to the ideals of the Romantic movement.

CRITICAL THINKING AND READING
Comparing and Contrasting Experiences

A careful reading of "Tintern Abbey" reveals that even as a young man Wordsworth was a sensitive and perceptive person. And yet the poem details certain differences between his first and second trips to the Wye valley. Skim the poem for details and then describe:
1. the differences in the poet's behavior.
2. the differences and similarities in his thoughts and attitudes.

THINKING AND WRITING
Writing About Romanticism

The twentieth-century American writer Thomas Wolfe defined the true Romantic feeling as "not the desire to escape life, but to prevent life from escaping you." Freewrite, exploring the meaning of this quotation. Then write an essay explaining how "Tintern Abbey" typifies the true Romantic feeling as defined by Wolfe. When you revise make sure you have supported your opinion with details from the poem.

Lines Composed a Few Miles Above Tintern Abbey   649

Interpreting

3. (a) The time of year is summer. (b) We learn this from lines 10-14.
4. The gift is the ability nature has to ease our burdened minds.
5. He refers to nature and the language of the senses.

Applying

6. Suggested Response: By implication rather than direct statement, the poet not only wishes that everyone would try to share his experiences and attitudes towards nature, he also believes everyone is capable of doing so. The many suggestions to likenesses between man and nature bear this out.

ANSWERS TO ANALYZING LITERATURE

Responses will differ; however, responses should come from lines 28, 54-57, 110, 117, and 123.

ANSWERS TO CRITICAL THINKING AND READING

1. The poet experienced nature as a youth with the boundless energy of the young; he never stopped to contemplate what nature means; rather, full of "aching joys" and "dizzy raptures," he merely enjoyed nature for its own sake. As a mature adult, the poet casts off that boundless energy to replace it with a serious contemplative attitude.
2. As a boy the poet experienced nature as an object of pure sensual pleasure. As a mature person he observes it as the heart and soul of all his moral being. The similarity is that his abiding love for nature has not altered; only the way in which he expresses that love has changed.

THINKING AND WRITING

Publishing Student Writing Post the papers written as a result of the Thinking and Writing activity on a bulletin board for several days. Have students vote for the papers that they think are best. Present these to the school newspaper for possible publication.

Closure and Extension

ANSWERS TO THINKING ABOUT THE SELECTION
Recalling

1. He has changed from a youth charged with the wild ecstacy of his love for nature into a mature person who cherishes the solace nature now affords him.
2. (a) He hopes to reinforce his sense of the solace nature provides in such a way that it will carry through his entire life. (b) He hopes that his sister will experience the same feelings for nature that he now has.

My Heart Leaps Up When I Behold

William Wordsworth

My heart leaps up when I behold
    A rainbow in the sky:
So was it when my life began;
So is it now I am a man;
So be it when I shall grow old,
    Or let me die!
The child is father of the Man;
And I could wish my days to be
Bound each to each by natural piety.[1]

———

1. natural piety: Devotion to nature.

1 ⌐

LANDSCAPE WITH RAINBOW
Joseph Wright of Derby
Derby Art Gallery

THINKING ABOUT THE SELECTION

Recalling

1. What is the poet's hope in the poem "My Heart Leaps Up"?

Interpreting

2. What general statement might the poet have used in place of the first two lines?
3. What do you think the poet means when he speaks of "natural piety"?

Applying

4. (a) What interest of yours would you like to share with other people? (b) How best might you communicate this to them?

CRITICAL THINKING AND READING

Interpreting a Paradox

A **paradox** is a statement that makes sense in spite of an apparent contradiction. "Youth is wasted on the young," for example, is paradoxical. However, it makes perfect sense when we consider that hindsight, or the experience of age, can help us better appreciate the value of what we have when we are young.

1. The statement, "The child is Father of the Man" is one of the most famous paradoxes in literature. Explain how this seeming contradiction can be true.
2. Explain what belief of the Romantic movement this paradox illustrates.

THINKING AND WRITING

Writing a Nature Poem

Write a short poem about the joy you find in some aspect of nature. The poem need not rhyme but should contain ample description of the source of your pleasure, as well as an account of precisely how this aspect of nature makes you feel.

When you revise, make sure you have used sensory details to make your description of nature vivid. Have you chosen words that carry the appropriate connotations?

Primary Source

In his memoirs, Christopher Wordsworth, William's youngest brother, describes the countryside that inspired his brother's lyrical verse. What elements in the following scene do you think would make your heart "leap up"?

"The weather being fine, Wordsworth agreed to go with us into Easedale . . . he trudging before, with his green gauze shade over his eyes, and in his plaid jacket and waistcoat. First, he turned aside at a little farmhouse, and took us into a swelling field, to look down on the tumbling stream which bounded it, and which we saw precipitated at a distance, in a broad white sheet, from the mountain. . . . Oh, what a scene! The day one of the softest and brightest in autumn; the lights various; the mountains in the richest coloring, fern covering them with reddish gold in great part; here and there, trees in every variety of autumn foliage; and the rock itself of a kind of lilac tint; the outlines of the mountains very fine; the Tarn, which might almost be called a lake for size and abundance of water, with no culture, trees, or habitation around it, here and there a great rock stretching into it like a promontory, and high mountains surrounding it on three sides, on two of them almost precipitate; on the fourth side, it is more open, and on this the stream, crossed by four great steppingstones, runs out of it, and descends into Grasmere vale and lake."

Closure and Extension

ANSWERS TO THINKING ABOUT THE SELECTION
Recalling

1. His hope is that his emotional love of nature will remain with him all his life.

Interpreting

2. Answers will differ. Suggested response: The poet might have used an expression such as "Events of nature excite me."
3. The poet probably means innate goodness as well as the goodness one acquires from maintaining a close relationship with nature.

Applying

4. (a) Answers will differ. (b) Answers will differ, though students might well mention written and oral communication.

ANSWERS TO CRITICAL THINKING AND READING

1. Suggested Response: What one is as a child generates what one is as an adult.
2. Suggested Response: This paradox illustrates the belief in the natural goodness of things and in the natural goodness in a child that might be lost in an adult.

THINKING AND WRITING

For help with this assignment, students can refer to Lesson 18, "Writing a Poem," in the Handbook of Writing About Literature.

Publishing Student Writing Encourage students to volunteer to read their poems aloud. You might have the class select the best to submit to your school's literary magazine.

Challenge Think back on your own life. What beliefs that you hold now were formed in those early years? Organize your thoughts into an essay of three or four paragraphs.

Vocabulary

Preteach the following vocabulary words:

steep (stēp) *v.*: Become saturated with (p. 653)

stagnant (stag'nənt) *adj.*: Standing still, as water (p. 656)

sordid (sor'did) *adj.*: Unclean, dirty (p. 657)

boon (bo͞on) *n.*: Something good or pleasant that is given, like a blessing (p. 657)

GUIDE FOR INTERPRETING

Composed Upon Westminster Bridge, September 3, 1802; It Is a Beauteous Evening, Calm and Free; London, 1802; The World Is Too Much with Us

Literary Forms

The Sonnet. A sonnet is a fourteen-line poem in which each line contains five strong beats and five weak beats. While most sonnets follow one of two general rhyme schemes—the Shakespearean (or English) and the Petrarchan (or Italian)—many poets adapt the rhyme to fit their own needs. The sonnet occupies a particular place of distinction among the poems of Wordsworth. Though a champion of freedom and spontaneity in poetry, Wordsworth nevertheless recognized the importance of order and discipline. The sonnet, as a relatively short and decisive poetic statement, was the logical vehicle for treating such subjects as the human condition and the importance of nature to the human spirit. "Scarcely one of my poems," Wordsworth wrote, "does not aim to direct attention to some moral sentiment." His purpose, as he saw it, was "to console the afflicted" and "to add sunshine to daylight by making the happy happier." These and related other goals could best be served, he felt, through the sonnet.

Writing

Think of a topic that holds importance for you. The topic could range from such social issues as finding shelter for the homeless of our country to such personal ones as the love between a pet and a person. Write down specific details of your topic that might be covered in a poem.

Primary Source

The journal that Wordsworth's younger sister Dorothy kept from 1895, when she was twenty-four, until her death five years after her brother's, provides an invaluable clue to the life of a great poet. Wordsworth and his sister enjoyed a close relationship; in his own journals, the poet wrote that Dorothy "preserved me still a Poet" through times of personal crisis. In her journal for September 3, 1802, Dorothy records the following entry:

> It was a beautiful morning. The city, St. Paul's, with the river and a multitude of little boats, made a most beautiful sight as we crossed Westminster Bridge. The houses were not overhung by their cloud of smoke, and they were spread out endlessly, yet the sun shone so brightly, with such a fierce light, that there was even something like the purity of one of nature's own grand spectacles.

652 *The Romantic Age*

Objective

To recognize a sonnet

Support Material

Teaching Portfolio
Teacher Backup, p. 789
Usage and Mechanics Worksheet, p. 792
Vocabulary Check, p. 793
Analyzing Literature Worksheet, *Recognizing a Sonnet,* p. 794
Language Worksheet, *Completing Word Analogies,* p. 795
Selection Test, p. 796

Composed Upon Westminster Bridge

September 3, 1802

William Wordsworth

Earth has not anything to show more fair:
Dull would he be of soul who could pass by
A sight so touching in its majesty;
This City now doth, like a garment, wear   **1**
5   The beauty of the morning; silent, bare,
Ships, towers, domes, theaters, and temples, lie
Open unto the fields, and to the sky;
All bright and glittering in the smokeless air, **2**
Never did sun more beautifully steep
10 In his first splendor, valley, rock, or hill;
Ne'er saw I, never felt, a calm so deep!
The river glideth at his own sweet will:
Dear God! the very houses seem asleep:
And all that mighty heart is lying still!

THINKING ABOUT THE SELECTION

Recalling

1. At what time of day is the poem "Composed Upon Westminster Bridge" set?
2. What sights does the poet see around him?

Interpreting

3. In lines 9–10, the poet sums up his reaction to his own description of the first eight lines. State this reaction in your own words.
4. Paraphrase the last four lines of this poem.

Applying

5. In what way is this poem contrary to some of the ideas expressed by Wordsworth in "My Heart Leaps Up"? How can you account for these differences? With which attitude are you more in sympathy? Explain your answer.

Composed Upon Westminster Bridge, September 3, 1802   653

1 **Discussion** List the words in the first five lines that describe the evening's mood.

2 **Clarification** *Being* here refers to the sea.

3 **Clarification** The "Dear Child" is Wordsworth's daughter Caroline.

4 **Clarification** The "inner shrine" is the inner recess of the Jerusalem Temple, which is entered only on the Day of Atonement.

5 **Literary Focus** As a sonnet with an octave-sestet structure, this poem raises a question or an issue in the first eight lines and addresses it in the closing six. Explain what the issue is and how it is resolved.

Reader's Response What feelings or emotions does this poem convey?

It Is a Beauteous Evening, Calm and Free

William Wordsworth

It is a beauteous evening, calm and free,
The holy time is quiet as a Nun
Breathless with adoration; the broad sun
Is sinking down in its tranquility;
5   The gentleness of heaven broods o'er the Sea:
Listen! the mighty Being is awake,
And doth with his eternal motion make
A sound like thunder—everlastingly.
Dear Child! dear Girl! that walkest with me here,
10   If thou appear untouched by solemn thought,
Thy nature is not therefore less divine:
Thou liest in Abraham's bosom[1] all the year;
And worship'st at the Temple's inner shrine,
God being with thee when we know it not.

_____
1. **Abraham's bosom:** Heaven (Luke 16:22).

THINKING ABOUT THE SELECTION

Recalling

1. Describe the setting of "It Is a Beauteous Evening."
2. Who is the poet's companion?

Interpreting

3. What is meant by "eternal motion" and "thunder"?

4. How does the poet's response to the scene differ from that of the child?
5. (a) How would you summarize the poet's advice to the child? (b) to the reader?

Applying

6. What differences in the last six lines of the poem might you expect if they were addressed to another adult? Explain.

CORNFIELD BY MOONLIGHT
Samuel Palmer
British Museum

ANALYZING LITERATURE
Recognizing a Sonnet

A **sonnet** is a poem with fourteen lines, each with five strong and five weak beats. Sonnets are generally divided into two main types, Shakespearean or Petrarchan, on the basis of rhyme scheme and stanza division. The Shakespearean sonnet is divided into three *quatrains* (or stanzas of four lines) and a closing *couplet* (pair of lines). Its rhyme scheme is most often *abab cdcd efef gg.* The Petrarchan sonnet, by con-trast, is composed of a group of eight lines (called an *octet*), followed by a group of six (the *sestet*). The rhyme scheme is usually *abbaabba cdecde,* though variations exist in the sestet.

1. Which kind of sonnet is "It Is a Beauteous Evening, Calm and Free"?
2. What is its rhyme scheme?
3. (a) What is the subject matter of the first eight lines? (b) What is the subject matter of the last six lines? (c) Explain how both parts comple-ment each other.

Humanities Note

Fine art, *Cornfield by Moonlight,* 1830, by Samuel Palmer. Samuel Palmer (1805–1881), an English Romantic painter, was a preco-cious artist, exhibiting paintings at the Royal Academy when he was fourteen. His works—visionary, idealized landscapes and pastorals—were influenced by the English mystic poet and paint-er William Blake. Palmer became a member of "the Ancients," a group of artists who sought to return art to the state of purity it attained in the Middle Ages. This group settled in Shoreham, Kent. There Palmer painted what are considered to be his finest works. *Cornfield by Moonlight* exempli-fies the work achieved by Palmer at Shoreham.

Inspired by the beautiful summer evening, Palmer translat-ed his mystical feelings into a painted scene, executed in water-color and gouache, which is opaque watercolor. Lit by the moon and a magical evening star, the harvested sheaves of wheat seem to symbolize all that is boun-tiful and good in the world. The figure, gilded with moonlight, seems to be in total harmony with the landscape.

You might point out to the students that Samuel Palmer re-vered nature, and ask them why this reverence makes this painting a suitable illustration for Words-worth's poem.

ANSWERS TO ANALYZING LITERATURE

1. "It Is a Beauteous Evening, Calm and Free" is a Petrarchan sonnet.
2. Its rhyme scheme is abbaacca, *defdfe.*
3. (a) The subject of the octet is the lovely, moving evening. (b) The subject of the sestet is the speak-er's awareness of the divine nature of the child with him. (c) The speak-er sees the divine presence as manifested in the evening reflected in the child.

Closure and Extension

ANSWERS TO THINKING ABOUT THE SELECTION
Recalling

1. The poem is set by the ocean on a calm, quiet evening.
2. The poet's companion is a little child, a girl.

Interpreting

3. The "eternal motion" is the move-ment of the sea; the "thunder" is the roar of the surf.
4. The poet is moved to solemn thoughts about nature and life; the child, so young, is unaware of such things.
5. (a) Answers will differ, but they should include the ideas that al-though the child is unaware of the majesty of the scene she is no less divine a creature, and that (b) all creatures, young and old, are pos-sessed of an innate goodness.

Applying

6. Answers may differ, but they should include the idea that in talk-ing to another adult rather than a child, the poet would likely have stressed the adult's knowledge of God's presence in nature.

London, 1802

William Wordsworth

Milton! thou shouldst be living in this hour:
England hath need of thee: she is a fen[1]
Of stagnant waters: altar, sword, and pen,
Fireside, the heroic wealth of hall and bower,
5 Have forfeited their ancient English dower
Of inward happiness. We are selfish men;
Oh! raise us up, return to us again;
And give us manners, virtue, freedom, power.
Thy soul was like a Star, and dwelt apart,
10 Thou hadst a voice whose sound was like the sea:
Pure as the naked heavens, majestic, free,
So didst thou travel on life's common way,
In cheerful godliness; and yet thy heart
The lowliest duties on herself did lay.

---

1. fen: Bog.

THINKING ABOUT THE SELECTION

Recalling

1. (a) What other poet does Wordsworth address in "London, 1802"? (b) What does he ask that poet to do?

Interpreting

2. According to the poet, in what way is England like a "fen/Of stagnant waters"?

3. Which classes do you think are represented by the terms "altar," "sword," "pen," and "fireside"?

Applying

4. (a) In what ways does the poet's image of London differ with that expressed in "Composed Upon Westminster Bridge," written in the same year? (b) How might Wordsworth explain these differences?

The World Is Too Much with Us

William Wordsworth

The world is too much with us; late and soon,
Getting and spending, we lay waste our powers:
Little we see in Nature that is ours;
We have given our hearts away, a sordid boon![1]
5   This sea that bares her bosom to the moon;
The winds that will be howling at all hours,
And are upgathered now like sleeping flowers;
For this, for everything, we are out of tune;
It moves us not.—Great God! I'd rather be
10 A Pagan suckled in a creed outworn;[2]
So might I, standing on this pleasant lea,[2]
Have glimpses that would make me less forlorn;
Have sight of Proteus[3] rising from the sea;
Or hear old Triton[4] blow his wreathèd horn.

---

1. boon: Favor.
2. lea: Meadow.
3. Proteus (prō′ tyōōs): In Greek mythology, a sea god who could change his appearance at will.
4. Triton: In Greek mythology, a sea god with the head and upper body of a man and the tail of a fish.

THINKING ABOUT THE SELECTION

Recalling

1. In "The World Is Too Much with Us," what does the poet say "we" have given away?

Interpreting

2. Explain what the poet means by the words *world* and *Nature.*
3. (a) Why would the poet rather be "A Pagan suckled in a creed outworn"? (b) How would even a "creed outworn" be preferable to the materialistic faith Wordsworth observed?

Applying

4. In 1955 in the United States, Erich Fromm wrote, "We live in a world of things, and our only connection with them is that we know how to manipulate or to consume them." How do you think Wordsworth would respond to this contemporary viewpoint?

SAMUEL TAYLOR COLERIDGE

1772–1834

Samuel Taylor Coleridge is the classic case of the gifted writer whose genius was hampered by lifelong problems, among them self-doubt and poor health. Coleridge was born in Ottery St. Mary on the Devon coast of England, the last of fourteen children, only four of whom survived. Spoiled by his father, Coleridge withdrew into a world of books and fantasy. At age nine, after his father died, Coleridge was sent to school in London. There the boy excelled and began developing an ability to speak on such matters as philosophy in a way that left his fellow students spellbound.

In 1791 Coleridge entered Cambridge University on a scholarship, but left before he graduated. He discussed plans with several other thinkers of the age to start up a colony in America whose members would live on a high intellectual plane. It was agreed that each member would have a wife. Though the plans for the community fell through, Coleridge's marriage plans did not, and in 1795 he married Sara Fricker.

With his wife, Coleridge moved in 1797 to Somerset, where he developed a close friendship with William Wordsworth, an important poet of the period. In 1798 the two turned out *Lyrical Ballads*, a joint collection of their work. The four poems that make up Coleridge's contribution to the volume deal with matters of the spiritual world and include his masterpiece, ''The Rime of the Ancient Mariner.'' Though at first public response to this collection of poems was lukewarm, the book slowly gained critical attention, ultimately causing a revolution in poetic style and thought and firmly establishing the movement known as Romanticism.

As Coleridge's fame grew, his marriage, his health, and his friendship with Wordsworth all gradually failed. He suffered increasingly from asthma and rheumatism, and he began to rely heavily on painkillers, which dulled his creative powers. Still, Coleridge managed to turn out a good deal of work in the years left him, and in a variety of areas. He worked variously as a journalist, as a lecturer on Shakespeare and Milton, as an essayist, and as a playwright, earning a tidy sum of money in 1812 with his tragedy *Remorse*. And all the time, despite his personal hardships, Coleridge continued to make himself available to visitors, which ultimately proved to have a great impact on the young crop of Romanticists writing at that time.

Perhaps Coleridge's greatest legacy was the insight he affords his reader on the role of imagination in literature. His belief that literature is a magical blend of thought and emotion is at the very heart of his greatest works, in which the unreal is often made to seem real.

GUIDE FOR INTERPRETING

The Rime of the Ancient Mariner

Writer's Technique

Sound Devices. The relationship between poetry and music has often been noted. Just as music achieves its effect through rhythms and harmonies, so poetry achieves its effect through sound devices, or techniques that enhance the meter and rhyme of a poem.

Chief among the sound devices available to the poet is *alliteration,* the repetition of a given consonant sound at the beginning of words or accented syllables that occur close together. Notice, for example, the repeated *f* sound in these lines from "The Rime of the Ancient Mariner": "The *f*air breeze blew, the white *f*oam *f*lew,/ The *f*urrow *f*ollowed *f*ree. . . ."

Consonance, a device related to alliteration, is the repetition of a given consonant sound at the end of words or accented syllables appearing close by. Consider another line from Coleridge, this one capitalizing on the *v* sound: "When the i*v*y tod is hea*v*y with snow . . ."

In the sound device known as *assonance,* it is a vowel sound that is repeated in nearby words or syllables. In the following passage, the long *a* sound is so treated: "The western w*a*ve was all *a*flame./ The d*a*y was well-nigh done!"

Internal rhyme, a fourth sound device, features rhyming words within the space of a single line. As an example, note the following line: "With heavy *thump,* a lifeless *lump* . . ."

Commentary

Coleridge once opened an essay by asking his readers to "sit down to a book . . . as a well-behaved visitor does to a banquet." But he knew that good readers need more than manners. To make his point, he discussed what he saw as the four kinds of readers:

1. Sponges, who absorb all they read and return it nearly in the same state, only a little dirtied.
2. Sand glasses, who retain nothing and are content to get through a book for the sake of getting through the time.
3. Strain-bags, who retain merely the dregs of what they read.
4. Mogul diamonds, equally rare and valuable, who profit from what they read and enable others to profit by it also.

What type of reader are you?

Writing

Imagine a contest: A friend has dreamed of a skeleton ship manned by spectral figures. You and a group of friends decide to flesh out the dream. The best narrative will win the contest. Write your tale of this skeleton ship.

Guide for Interpreting 659

Literary Focus Sound goes hand in hand with sense in this poem. Provide students with examples of poetic sound devices such as alliteration, onomatopoeia, consonance, assonance, and rhyme.

Writing/Prior Knowledge Have students discuss Coleridge's belief that poetry involves a "willing suspension of disbelief for the moment." Once the discussion has run its course, students should sum up in their own words, in writing, what the statement means to them.

Vocabulary

Preteach the following vocabulary words:
averred (ə vʉrd′) *v*.: Stated to be true (p. 664)
sojourn (sō jʉrn) *v*.: Stay for a while (p. 671)
expiated (ēk′ spē āt′ əd) *v*.: Forgiven; absolved (p. 677)
reverence (rēv′ ər əns) *n*.: Respect (p. 682)

Spelling Tip Have students note that the *r* is doubled when the past tense ending is added to *aver*.

Motivation/Prior Knowledge
Coleridge based this poem on a deep human experience—the sense of isolation and guilt. Ask students if they recall any characters from fiction they have read whose story is based on the same human experience. Did the character overcome those feelings? If so, how?

Master Teacher Note Charles Lamb, in a letter to Wordsworth, had this to say about the poem: "For me, I was never so affected with any human Tale. After first reading it, I was totally possessed with it for many days—I dislike all the miraculous part of it, but the feelings of the man under the operation of such scenery dragged me along like Tom Piper's magic whistle."

Purpose-Setting Question How important are literary devices that emphasize sound to establishing the mood and sense of a poem?

1 **Enrichment** This poem was the opening selection in Wordsworth's and Coleridge's famous *Lyrical Ballads* (1798). Later, Wordsworth expressed doubt about placing the poem first, thinking it would put readers off with its mystical and supernatural feeling. Wordsworth's own "Tintern Abbey," page 644, was the final poem in the collection.

2 **Reading Strategy** Since the poem is a narrative it has all the elements of fiction—characters, setting, plot, conflict, point of view, and theme. Students should be aware of this as they read.

3 **Enrichment** Sometime between 1798 and 1817, when the poem reappeared, Coleridge added the marginal notes.

4 **Clarification** The "glittering eye" suggests that the Mariner is a hypnotist.

The Rime of the Ancient Mariner

Samuel Taylor Coleridge

The Rime of the Ancient Mariner, *based on a dream of Coleridge's friend, John Cruikshank, was originally planned as a collaboration between Coleridge and Wordsworth. Eventually Wordsworth dropped out of the project, but not before making a number of valuable suggestions, including the shooting of the albatross and the navigation of the ship by the dead men. Several years after the poem was first published in* Lyrical Ballads *(1798), Coleridge added the prose explanations in the margins to aid the reader in understanding the poem's meaning.*

Argument

How a Ship having passed the Line[1] was driven by storms to the cold Country towards the South Pole: and how from thence she made her course to the tropical Latitude of the Great Pacific Ocean; and of the strange things that befell: and in what manner the Ancyent Marinere came back to his own Country.

Part I

An ancient Mariner meeteth three Gallants bidden to a wedding feast and detaineth one.

It is an ancient Mariner,
And he stoppeth one of three.
"By thy long gray beard and glittering eye,
Now wherefore stopp'st thou me?

"The Bridegroom's doors are opened wide,   5
And I am next of kin;
The guests are met, the feast is set:
May'st hear the merry din."

---

1. Line: Equator.

Discussion The account of the Wedding Guest's reactions in Part I serves as a frame for the Mariner's tale. Why do you think the poet has chosen a wedding, normally a happy occasion, against which to relate the tale?

Reading Strategy Students will need to identify speakers at points where characters other than the Mariner are speaking. Stress this at the opening of the tale. See also lines 80, 224, 345, 400, 410, and 527.

The Wedding Guest is spellbound by the eye of the old seafaring man and constrained to hear his tale.

He holds him with his skinny hand,
"There was a ship," quoth he.   10
"Hold off! unhand me, graybeard loon!"
Eftsoons[2] his hand dropped he.

He holds him with his glittering eye—
The Wedding Guest stood still,
And listens like a three years' child: 15
The Mariner hath his will.

The Wedding Guest sat on a stone:
He cannot choose but hear;
And thus spake on that ancient man,
The bright-eyed Mariner.   20

The Mariner tells how the ship sailed southward with a good wind and fair weather till it reached the Line.

"The ship was cheered, the harbor cleared,
Merrily did we drop
Below the kirk,[3] below the hill,
Below the lighthouse top.

"The Sun came up upon the left,   25
Out of the sea came he!
And he shone bright, and on the right
Went down into the sea.

"Higher and higher every day,
Till over the mast at noon[4]—"   30
The Wedding Guest here beat his breast,
For he heard the loud bassoon.

The Wedding Guest heareth the bridal music; but the Mariner continueth his tale.

The bride hath paced into the hall.
Red as a rose is she;
Nodding their heads before her goes   35
The merry minstrelsy.

The Wedding Guest he beat his breast,
Yet he cannot choose but hear;
And thus spake on that ancient man
The bright-eyed Mariner.   40

The ship driven by a storm toward the South Pole.

"And now the Storm blast came, and he
Was tyrannous and strong:
He struck with his o'ertaking wings,
And chased us south along.

---

2. eftsoons: Immediately.
3. kirk: Church.
4. over . . . noon: The ship has reached the equator.

The Rime of the Ancient Mariner   661

6 **Literary Focus** Another sound device prominent in the poem is onomatopoeia. Line 61 offers a fine example of this device. Be sure students are aware of the importance of onomatopoeia in the poem.

7 **Enrichment** It was Wordsworth, not Coleridge, who thought of the albatross.

"With sloping masts and dipping prow,   45
As who pursued with yell and blow
Still treads the shadow of his foe,
And forward bends his head,
The ship drove fast, loud roared the blast,
And southward aye[5] we fled.   50

"And now there came both mist and snow.
And it grew wondrous cold;
And ice, mast-high, came floating by,
As green as emerald.

The land of ice, and of fearful sounds, where no living thing was to be seen.

"And through the drifts the snowy clifts[6]   55
Did send a dismal sheen;
Nor shapes of men nor beasts we ken[7]—
The ice was all between.

"The ice was here, the ice was there,
The ice was all around;   60
6 It cracked and growled, and roared and howled,
Like noises in a swound![8]

Till a great sea bird, called the Albatross, came through the snow-fog, and was received with great joy and hospitality.

7 "At length did cross an Albatross,
Thorough[9] the fog it came;
As if it had been a Christian soul,   65
We hailed it in God's name.

"It ate the food it ne'er had eat,[10]
And round and round it flew.
The ice did split with a thunder-fit;
The helmsman steered us through!   70

And lo! the Albatross proveth a bird of good omen, and followeth the ship as it returned northward through fog and floating ice.

"And a good south wind sprung up behind;
The Albatross did follow,
And every day, for food or play,
Came to the mariner's hollo!

"In mist or cloud, on mast or shroud,[11]   75
It perched for vespers[12] nine;
Whiles all the night, through fog-smoke white,
Glimmered the white Moonshine."

---

5. aye: Ever.
6. cliffs: Icebergs.
7. ken: knew.
8. swound: swoon.
9. thorough: Through.
10. eat (et): Old form of *eaten*.
11. shroud *n.*: Ropes stretching from the ship's side to the masthead.
12. vespers: Evenings.

662   *The Romantic Age*

Grammar in Action

Throughout "The Rime of the Ancient Mariner," Coleridge makes extensive use of **archaic words,** words that are no longer used in everyday speech and writing. The archaic words make the poem seem as if it were written long ago. For example, the word *aye* in line 50, meaning "ever," and the word *ken* in line 57, meaning "knew," are from Middle English. *Thorough* and *eat* are old forms of "through" and "eaten." You can figure out the meanings of many of these words from their context or from footnotes. Also, many dictionaries have entries for archaic words.

Student Activity 1. For each of the following lines from the poem, identify the archaic words and explain their meaning. If possible, look up the origin of the words.
1. "Nor dim nor red, like God's own head, The glorious Sun uprist;"
2. "With throats unslaked, with black lips bakes, Agape they heard me call: Gramercy! they for joy did grin,"
3. "See! see! (I cried) she tacks no more! Hither to work us weal;"
4. "I looked to heaven, and tried to pray; But or ever a prayer had gushed,"
5. "Sometimes all little birds that are, How they seemed to fill the sea and air With their sweet jargoning!"

ENGRAVING BY GUSTAVE DORÉ FOR THE RIME OF THE ANCIENT MARINE
by Samuel Taylor Coleridge

Humanities Note

Fine art, illustration, 1875, by Gustave Doré. The French illustrator Gustave Doré (1832–1883) began his career as a cartoonist and caricaturist in Paris. His fame spread, and he was soon established as one of the best illustrators in Paris. Doré was self-taught; he refined his technique through independent study of engravings at the National Library in Paris.

Inspired by "The Rime of the Ancient Mariner," Doré published a set of illustrations for the poem in 1875. Doré's obsession with this poem led to some of his most eerie and disturbing images. Although this illustrated volume of Coleridge's poem was not a commercial success, it is considered to be an artistic triumph for Gustave Doré.

This engraving was intended to illustrate the first two lines of the poem. The surprise of the wedding guest and the desperation of the Mariner are both skillfully portrayed by Doré. His mastery of figure drawing and composition are evident in this drawing.

You might discuss the following with your students.
1. What can you say about the eye of the Mariner in this engraving?
2. How does the artist accurately portray the reluctant demeanor of the wedding guest?

Student Activity 2. Find five other archaic words in the poem. For each, rewrite the line or lines that contain the word, substituting modern English for the archaic words. Then explain how the effect of the line is changed when the modern English is used.

8 **Discussion** What significant event happens at the end of Part I?

9 **Reading Strategy** Have students summarize the events of Part I.

10 **Literary Focus** Note the use of alliteration and internal rhyme in these lines.

11 **Discussion** What is the immediate consequence of the Mariner's actions? What soon follows? How does the crew feel about the Mariner?

The ancient Mariner inhospitably killeth the pious bird of good omen.

"God save thee, ancient Mariner!
From the fiends, that plague thee thus!—
Why look'st thou so?"[13] "With my crossbow
I shot the Albatross."   80

8 ⌐

9 ⌐

Part II

"The Sun now rose upon the right:[14]
Out of the sea came he,
Still hid in mist, and on the left   85
Went down into the sea.

"And the good south wind still blew behind,
But no sweet bird did follow.
Nor any day for food or play
Came to the mariners' hollo!   90

His shipmates cry out against the ancient Mariner for killing the bird of good luck.

10 ⌐ "And I had done a hellish thing,
And it would work 'em woe:
For all averred, I had killed the bird
That made the breeze to blow.
Ah wretch! said they, the bird to slay,   95
That made the breeze to blow!

But when the fog cleared off, they justify the same, and thus make themselves accomplices in the crime.

11 ⌐ "Nor dim nor red, like God's own head,
The glorious Sun uprist;[15]
Then all averred, I had killed the bird
That brought the fog and mist.   100
'Twas right, said they, such birds to slay,
That bring the fog and mist.

The fair breeze continues; the ship enters the Pacific Ocean, and sails northward, even till it reaches the Line.

"The fair breeze blew, the white foam flew,
The furrow[16] followed free;
We were the first that ever burst   105
Into that silent sea.

The ship hath been suddenly becalmed.

"Down dropped the breeze, the sails dropped
       down,
'Twas sad as sad could be;
And we did speak only to break
The silence of the sea!   110

---

13. God . . . so: Spoken by the Wedding Guest.
14. The Sun . . . right: The ship is now headed north.
15. uprist: Arose.
16. furrow: Ship's wake.

ENGRAVING BY GUSTAVE DORÉ FOR THE RIME OF THE ANCIENT MARINER
by Samuel Taylor Coleridge

Humanities Note

Fine art, illustration, 1875, by Gustave Doré. Doré's engraving of the shooting of the albatross is created with skill and imagination. Ask the students why the artist might have chosen to illustrate the moment before the arrow struck the bird.

Fine art, illustration, 1875, by Gustave Doré. Doré's engraving of the ship tossing on a heavy sea evokes the sense of hopelessness that a person at the mercy of the sea must feel.

You might ask the following questions.

1. What details convey the peril of the ship in this engraving?
2. What mood does this illustration evoke?

ENGRAVING BY GUSTAVE DORÉ FOR THE RIME OF THE ANCIENT MARINER
by Samuel Taylor Coleridge

666   The Romantic Age

Primary Source

In the following excerpt from *Biographia Literaria,* Coleridge outlines the thinking that led to his writing "The Rime of the Ancient Mariner" for inclusion in *Lyrical Ballads:*

During the first year that Mr. Wordsworth and I were neighbors, our conversations turned frequently on the two cardinal points of poetry, the power of exciting the sympathy of the reader by a faithful adherence to the truth of nature, and the power of giving the interest of novelty by modifying colors of the imagination. The sudden charm, which accidents of light and shade, which moonlight or sun-set diffused over a known and familiar landscape, appeared to represent the practicability of combining both. These are the poetry of nature. The thought suggested itself (to which of us I do not recollect) that a series of poems might be composed of two sorts. In the one, the incidents and agents were to be in part at least, supernatural . . . For the second class, subjects were to be chosen from ordinary life . . .

In this idea originated the plan of the "Lyrical Ballads"; in which it was agreed, that my endevours should be directed to persons and characters supernatural, or at

"All in a hot and copper sky,
The bloody Sun, at noon,
Right up above the mast did stand,
No bigger than the Moon.

"Day after day, day after day,   115
We stuck, nor breath nor motion;
As idle as a painted ship
Upon a painted ocean.

And the Albatross begins
to be avenged.

"Water, water, everywhere,
And all the boards did shrink;   120
Water, water, everywhere,
Nor any drop to drink.

"The very deep did rot: O Christ!
That ever this should be!
Yea, slimy things did crawl with legs   125
Upon the slimy sea.

"About, about, in reel and rout[17]
The death fires[18] danced at night;
The water, like a witch's oils,
Burned green, and blue and white.   130

A Spirit had followed
them; one of the invisible
inhabitants of this planet,
neither departed souls
nor angels. They are very
numerous, and there is
no climate or element
without one or more.

"And some in dreams assurèd were
Of the Spirit that plagued us so;
Nine fathom deep he had followed us
From the land of mist and snow.

"And every tongue, through utter drought,   135
Was withered at the root;
We could not speak, no more than if
We had been choked with soot.

The shipmates, in their
sore distress, would fain
throw the whole guilt on
the ancient Mariner: in
sign whereof they hang
the dead sea bird round
his neck.

"Ah! well a-day! what evil looks
Had I from old and young!   140
Instead of the cross, the Albatross
About my neck was hung.

---

17. rout: Disorderly crowd.
18. death fires: St. Elmo's fire, a visible electrical discharge from a
ship's mast, believed by sailors to be an omen of disaster.

The Rime of the Ancient Mariner 667

least romantic; yet so as to transfer from our inward nature
a human interest and a semblance of truth sufficient to
procure for these shadows of imagination that willing
suspension of disbelief for the moment, which constitutes
poetic faith. Mr. Wordsworth, on the other hand, was to
propose to himself as his object, to give the charm of
novelty to things of every day, and to excite a feeling
analogous to the supernatural, by awakening the mind's
attention from the lethargy of custom, and directing it to the
loveliness and the wonders of the world before us . . .

Part III

"There passed a weary time. Each throat
Was parched, and glazed each eye.
A weary time! a weary time!   145
How glazed each weary eye,
When looking westward, I beheld
A somethling in the sky.

The ancient Mariner be-
holdeth a sign in the ele-
ment afar off.

"At first it seemed a little speck,
And then it seemed a mist;   150
It moved and moved, and took at last
A certain shape, I wist.[19]

"A speck, a mist, a shape, I wist!
And still it neared and neared:
As if it dodged a water sprite,   155
It plunged and tacked and veered.

At its nearer approach, it
seemeth him to be a ship;
and at a dear ransom he
freeth his speech from the
bonds of thirst.

"With throats unslaked, with black lips baked,
We could nor laugh nor wail;
Through utter drought all dumb we stood!
I bit my arm, I sucked the blood,   160
And cried, A sail! a sail!

"With throats unslaked, with black lips
    baked,
Agape they heard me call:

A flash of joy;

Gramercy![20] they for joy did grin,
And all at once their breath drew in,   165
As they were drinking all.

And horror follows. For
can it be a ship that
comes onward without
wind or tide?

"See! see! (I cried) she tacks no more!
Hither to work us weal;[21]
Without a breeze, without a tide,
She steadies with upright keel!   170

"The western wave was all aflame.
The day was well nigh done!
Almost upon the western wave
Rested the broad bright Sun;
When that strange shape drove suddenly   175
Betwixt us and the Sun.

---

19. wist: Knew.
20. Gramercy (grə mur' sē): Great thanks.
21. work us weal: Assist us.

It seemeth him but the skeleton of a ship.

"And straight the Sun was flecked with bars,
(Heaven's Mother send us grace!)
As if through a dungeon grate he peered
With broad and burning face.   180

And its ribs are seen as bars on the face of the setting Sun. The Specter Woman and her Death-mate, and no other on board the skeleton ship.

"Alas! (thought I, and my heart beat loud)
How fast she nears and nears!
Are those *her* sails that glance in the Sun,
Like restless gossameres?[22]

"Are those *her* ribs through which the
    Sun   185
Did peer, as through a grate?
And is that Woman all her crew?
Is that a Death? and are there two?
Is Death that woman's mate?

Like vessel, like crew!

Death and Life-in-Death have diced for the ship's crew, and she (the latter) winneth the ancient Mariner.

"*Her* lips, were red, *her* looks were free,   190
Her locks were yellow as gold;
Her skin was as white as leprosy,
The Nightmare Life-in-Death was she,   ⬜ **14**
Who thicks man's blood with cold.

"The naked hulk alongside came,   195
And the twain were casting dice;
'The game is done! I've won! I've won!'   ⬜ **15**
Quoth she, and whistles thrice.

No twilight within the courts of the Sun.

"The Sun's rim dips; the stars rush out:
At one stride comes the dark;   200
With far-heard whisper, o'er the sea,
Off shot the specter bark.

At the rising of the Moon,

"We listened and looked sideways up!
Fear at my heart, as at a cup,
My lifeblood seemed to sip!   205
The stars were dim, and thick the night,
The steersman's face by his lamp gleamed
    white;
From the sails the dew did drip—
Till clomb[23] above the eastern bar
The hornèd[24] Moon, with one bright star   210
Within the nether tip.

---

22. gossameres: Floating cobwebs.
23. clomb: Climbed.
24. hornèd: Crescent.

14 Discussion What do you make of the term "Life-in-Death" for the specter who gambled and won the souls of the crew? How apt is the name?

15 Clarification She won the lives of the crew, except for the Mariner, who will live on to suffer.

Reading Strategy Have students summarize the events in Part III.

Literary Focus Note the alliteration and assonance in lines 232-235, which give this stanza a haunting, mournful sound.

Literary Focus Note the simile in line 247. Ask students to tell what is implied by it?

One after another.

"One after one, by the star-dogged Moon,[25]
Too quick for groan or sigh,
Each turned his face with a ghastly pang,
And cursed me with his eye.   215

His shipmates drop down dead.

"Four times fifty living men,
(And I heard nor sigh nor groan)
With heavy thump, a lifeless lump,
They dropped down one by one.

But Life-in-Death begins her work on the ancient Mariner.

"The souls did from their bodies fly—   220
They fled to bliss or woe!
And every soul, it passed me by,
Like the whizz of my crossbow!"

16

Part IV

The Wedding Guest feareth that a Spirit is talking to him;

"I fear thee, ancient Mariner!
I fear thy skinny hand!   225
And thou art long, and lank, and brown,
As is the ribbed sea sand.

"I fear thee and thy glittering eye,
And thy skinny hand, so brown."

But the ancient Mariner assureth him of his bodily life, and proceedeth to relate his horrible penance.

"Fear not, fear not, thou Wedding Guest!   230
This body dropped not down.

17

"Alone, alone, all, all alone,
Alone on a wide wide sea!
And never a saint took pity on
My soul in agony.   235

He despiseth the creatures of the calm.

"The many men, so beautiful!
And they all dead did lie:
And a thousand thousand slimy things
Lived on; and so did I.

And envieth that they should live, and so many lie dead.

"I looked upon the rotting sea,   240
And drew my eyes away;
I looked upon the rotting deck,
And there the dead men lay.

"I looked to heaven, and tried to pray;
But or[26] ever a prayer had gushed,   245
A wicked whisper came, and made

18 My heart as dry as dust.

---

25. star-dogged Moon: An omen of impending evil to sailors.
26. or: Before.

670   *The Romantic Age*

Primary Source

In his introduction to *Twentieth Century Interpretations of The Rime of the Ancient Mariner,* James D. Boulger discusses the imaginative, other-worldly qualities of the Mariner's voyage:

In the world of Imagination in which the voyage takes place four aspects are noticeable, as evidence that the world of the poem is quite different from the land world—

1. the "Dream" quality of the voyage and all its events, with the participation of reality, living and nonliving in one organic whole, and the unending series of shifts between subjects and objects, sights and sounds, in the phenomena of the perceived world;
2. a special kind of logic, or "non-logic" if you will, in the main events and symbols of the poem;
3. a machinery of "spirits" of various orders not found in the ordinary world;
4. a special definition of appearance and reality, substance and surface, developed in the descriptions of objects, especially the sea, during the voyage.

Taken together, this special world contributes to define the nature of the major parable (Fall, redemption, scepticism, spiritual will, and Faith) not by mere fiat and statement, but

19 **Discussion** How might the Mariner's change in attitude lead to his salvation?

20 **Discussion** What might be the significance of line 285 as a step in the Mariner's salvation?

"I closed my lids, and kept them close,
And the balls like pulses beat;
For the sky and the sea and the sea and the
   sky   250
Lay like a load on my weary eye,
And the dead were at my feet.

But the curse liveth for
him in the eye of the
dead men.

"The cold sweat melted from their limbs,
Nor rot nor reek did they;
The look with which they looked on me   255
Had never passed away.

"An orphan's curse would drag to hell
A spirit from on high;
But oh! more horrible than that
Is the curse in a dead man's eye!   260
Seven days, seven nights, I saw that curse,
And yet I could not die.

In his loneliness and fix-
edness he yearneth to-
wards the journeying
Moon, and the stars that
still sojourn, yet still
move onward; and every-
where the blue sky be-
longs to them, and is
their appointed rest, and
their native country and
their own natural homes,
which they enter unan-
nounced, as lords that
are certainly expected
and yet there is a silent
joy at their arrival.
By the light of the Moon
he beholdeth God's crea-
tures of the great calm.

"The moving Moon went up the sky,
And nowhere did abide:
Softly she was going up,   265
And a star or two beside—

"Her beams bemocked the sultry main,[27]
Like April hoarfrost spread;
But where the ship's huge shadow lay,
The charmèd water burned alway   270
A still and awful red.

"Beyond the shadow of the ship,
I watched the water snakes:
They moved in tracks of shining white,
And when they reared, the elfish light   275
Fell off in hoary flakes.

"Within the shadow of the ship
I watched their rich attire:
Blue, glossy green, and velvet black,
They coiled and swam; and every track   280   **19**
Was a flash of golden fire.

Their beauty and their
happiness.

"O happy living things! no tongue
Their beauty might declare:
A spring of love gushed from my heart,
And I blessed them unaware;   285   **20**
Sure my kind saint took pity on me,

He blesseth them in his
heart.

And I blessed them unaware.

---

27. main: Open sea.

The Rime of the Ancient Mariner   671

as the total poetic logic of the poem.

The world of primary Imagination is conveyed in immediate and existential ways, not in abstract definition of terms. The notable means are appeals to the state of dreams, which we all recognize as different from the ordinary waking world, and appeals to unusual combinations of sounds and sights acceptable in the world of the poem but certainly "confusing" if considered under normal circumstances. As the voyage begins, the Sun and Storm-Blast are both personified as HE, typical of the dream-state that animates all things, living and nonliving, good and malevolent. The strange noises of the ice, "It cracked and growled, and roared and howled" (61) are compared directly to the dream-state of sensation, "Like noises in a swound!" (62) The dream-state is appealed to directly many times to explain the mysterious actions of the poem . . .

The spell begins to break.

21
"The selfsame moment I could pray;
And from my neck so free
The Albatross fell off, and sank   290
Like lead into the sea.

Part V

22
"Oh sleep! it is a gentle thing,
Beloved from pole to pole!
To Mary Queen the praise be given!
She sent the gentle sleep from Heaven,   295
That slid into my soul.

By grace of the holy Mother, the ancient Mariner is refreshed with rain.

"The silly[28] buckets on the deck,
That had so long remained,
I dreamed that they were filled with dew;
And when I awoke, it rained.   300

"My lips were wet, my throat was cold,
My garments all were dank;
Sure I had drunken in my dreams,
And still my body drank.

"I moved, and could not feel my limbs: 305
I was so light—almost
I thought that I had died in sleep,
And was a blessèd ghost.

He heareth sounds and seeth strange sights and commotions in the sky and the element.

"And soon I heard a roaring wind:
It did not come anear;   310
But with its sound it shook the sails,
That were so thin and sere.[29]

"The upper air burst into life!
And a hundred fire flags sheen,[30]
To and fro they were hurried about!   315
And to and fro, and in and out,
The wan stars danced between.

"And the coming wind did roar more loud,
And the sails did sigh like sedge;[31]
And the rain poured down from one black
   cloud;   320
The Moon was at its edge.

---

28. silly: Empty.
29. sere: Dried up.
30. fire flags sheen: The aurora australis, or southern lights, shone.
31. sedge *n.*: A rushlike plant that grows in wet soil.

ENGRAVING BY GUSTAVE DORÉ FOR THE RIME OF THE ANCIENT MARINER
by Samuel Taylor Coleridge

Humanities Note

Fine art, illustration, 1875, by Gustave Doré. Doré's engraving of the haunted, ice-bound ship is an unforgettable, eerie vision. Trapped in a frozen sea, the cursed ship glitters with ice. It seems to be lit from within by an evil light.

You might ask the following questions.

1. The poet uses words to create and describe situations. How does this artist visually describe the situation?
2. If you had seen this illustration before reading the poem, what mood would it evoke?

"The thick black cloud was cleft, and still
The Moon was at its side:
Like waters shot from some high crag,
The lightning fell with never a jag,   325
A river steep and wide.

The bodies of the ship's crew are inspired[32] and the ship moves on;

"The loud wind never reached the ship,
Yet now the ship moved on!
Beneath the lightning and the Moon
The dead men gave a groan.   330

"They groaned, they stirred, they all uprose,
Nor spake, nor moved their eyes;
It had been strange, even in a dream,
To have seen those dead men rise.

"The helmsman steered, the ship moved
    on: 335
Yet never a breeze up-blew;
The mariners all 'gan work the ropes,
Where they were wont[33] to do;
They raised their limbs like lifeless tools—
We were a ghastly crew.   340

"The body of my brother's son
Stood by me, knee to knee:
The body and I pulled at one rope,
But he said nought to me.

But not by the souls of the men, nor by demons of earth or middle air, but by a blessed troop of angelic spirits, sent down by the invocation of the guardian saint.

"I fear thee, ancient Mariner!"   345
"Be calm, thou Wedding Guest!
'Twas not those souls that fled in pain,
Which to their corses[34] came again,
But a troop of spirits blessed:

"For when it dawned—they dropped their
    arms,   350
And clustered round the mast;
Sweet sounds rose slowly through their
    mouths,
And from their bodies passed.

---

32. inspired: Inspirited.
33. wont: Accustomed.
34. corses: Corpses.

Primary Source

In the headnote to the poem "We Are Seven," William Wordsworth wrote about the origins of "The Rime of the Ancient Mariner":

"In reference to this poem I will here mention one of the most remarkable facts in my own poetic history and that of Mr. Coleridge. In the spring of the year 1798, he, my sister, and myself, started from Alfoxden, pretty late in the afternoon, with a view to visit Lenton and the valley of Stones near it; and as our united funds were very small, we agreed to defray the expense of the tour by writing a poem, to be sent to the new *Monthly Magazine* . . . .Accordingly we set off and proceeded along the Quantock Hills towards Watchet, and in the course of this walk was planned the poem of *The Ancient Mariner,* founded on a dream, as Mr. Coleridge said, of his friend, Mr. Cruikshank. Much the greatest part of the story was Mr. Coleridge's invention; but certain parts I myself suggested:—for example, some crime was to be committed which should bring upon the old navigator, as Coleridge afterwards delighted to call him, the spectral persecution, as a consequence of that crime, and his own wanderings. I had been reading in

"Around, around, flew each sweet sound,
Then darted to the Sun;   355
Slowly the sounds came back again,
Now mixed, now one by one.

"Sometimes a-dropping from the sky
I heard the skylark sing;
Sometimes all little birds that are,   360
How they seemed to fill the sea and air
With their sweet jargoning!³⁵

"And now 'twas like all instruments,
Now like a lonely flute;
And now it is an angel's song,   365
That makes the heavens be mute.

"It ceased; yet still the sails made on
A pleasant noise till noon,
A noise like of a hidden brook
In the leafy month of June,   370
That to the sleeping woods all night
Singeth a quiet tune.

"Till noon we quietly sailed on,
Yet never a breeze did breathe;
Slowly and smoothly went the ship,   375
Moved onward from beneath.

The lonesome Spirit from the South Pole carries on the ship as far as the Line, in obedience to the angelic troop, but still requireth vengeance.

"Under the keel nine fathom deep,   □ 23
From the land of mist and snow,
The spirit slid; and it was he
That made the ship to go.   380
The sails at noon left off their tune,
And the ship stood still also.

"The Sun, right up above the mast,
Had fixed her to the ocean:
But in a minute she 'gan stir,   385
With a short uneasy motion—
Backwards and forwards half her length
With a short uneasy motion.

"Then like a pawing horse let go,
She made a sudden bound: 390
It flung the blood into my head,
And I fell down in a swound.   □ 24

---
35. **jargoning:** Singing.

23 Clarification A fathom is equal to six feet; therefore, water which is "nine fathom deep" is water that is fifty-four feet deep.

24 Clarification A swound is a swoon or faint.

Shelvock's *Voyages* a day or two before that while doubling Cape Horn they frequently saw albatrosses in that latitude, the largest sort of sea-fowl, some extending their wings twelve or fifteen feet. "Suppose," said I, "you represent him as having killed one of these birds on entering the South Sea, and that the tutelary Spirits of those regions take upon them to avenge the crime." The incident was thought fit for the purpose and adopted accordingly. I also suggested the navigation of the ship by the dead men, but do not recollect that I had anything more to do with the scheme of the poem. . . . We began the composition together on that, to me, memorable evening. I furnished two or three lines at the beginning of the poem, in particular:—
    'And listened like a three years' child;
    The Mariner had his will.'
. . . As we endeavored to proceed conjointly . . . our respective manners proved so widely different that it would have been quite presumptuous in me to do anything but separate from an undertaking upon which I could only have been a clog."

25 Discussion What fate remains in store for the Mariner?

26 Reading Strategy Have students summarize the events in Part V.

The Polar Spirit's fellow demons, the invisible inhabitants of the element, take part in his wrong; and two of them relate, one to the other, that penance long and heavy for the ancient Mariner hath been accorded to the Polar Spirit, who returneth southward.

"How long in that same fit I lay,
I have not to declare;
But ere my living life returned,   395
I heard and in my soul discerned
Two voices in the air.

" 'Is it he?' quoth one, 'Is this the man?
By him who died on cross,
With his cruel bow he laid full low   400
The harmless Albatross.

" 'The spirit who bideth by himself
In the land of mist and snow,
He loved the bird that loved the man
Who shot him with his bow.'   405

"The other was a softer voice,
As soft as honeydew:
25 Quoth he, 'The man hath penance done,
And penance more will do.'

26

Part VI

FIRST VOICE

" 'But tell me, tell me! speak again,   410
Thy soft response renewing—
What makes that ship drive on so fast?
What is the ocean doing?'

SECOND VOICE

" 'Still as a slave before his lord,
The ocean hath no blast;   415
His great bright eye most silently
Up to the Moon is cast—

"If he may know which way to go;
For she guides him smooth or grim.
See, brother, see! how graciously   420
She looketh down on him.'

FIRST VOICE

The Mariner hath been cast into a trance; for the angelic power causeth the vessel to drive northward faster than human life could endure.

" 'But why drives on that ship so fast,
Without or wave or wind?'

Grammar in Action

Similes are explicit comparisons between two dissimilar things indicated by the words like or as. Writers use similes to enliven their descriptions and to enable readers to visualize connections that their senses may not be able to perceive. Thus similes make descriptions striking and memorable. Note the similes in the following passages from "The Rime of the Ancient Mariner":

"The other was a softer voice,
As soft as honeydew:"

"*Still as a slave before his lord,*
The ocean hath no blast;"

"But soon there breathed a wind on me, . . ."
"It raised my hair, it fanned my cheek
Like a meadow-gale of spring—"

Student Activity 1. Identify the similes in each of the following passages from "The Rime of the Ancient Mariner." Then explain the impression conveyed by each simile.

1. He holds him with his glittering eye—The Wedding Guest stood still, And listens like a three years' child: The Mariner hath his will.

2. "Day after day, day after day, We stuck, nor breath nor motion; As idle as a painted ship Upon a painted ocean."

27 Literary Focus Note the simile in lines 456-7. Why is the reference to a meadow especially significant?

" 'The air is cut away before,
And closes from behind.   425

"Fly, brother, fly! more high, more high!
Or we shall be belated;
For slow and slow that ship will go,
When the Mariner's trance is abated.'

The super-natural motion is retarded; the Mariner awakes, and his penance begins anew.

"I woke, and we were sailing on   430
As in a gentle weather;
'Twas night, calm night, the moon was high;
The dead men stood together.

"All stood together on the deck,
For a charnel dungeon[36] litter;   435
All fixed on me their stony eyes,
That in the Moon did glitter.

"The pang, the curse, with which they died,
Had never passed away;
I could not draw my eyes from theirs,   440
Nor turn them up to pray.

The curse is finally expiated.

"And now this spell was snapped; once more
I viewed the ocean green,
And looked far forth, yet little saw
Of what had else been seen—   445

"Like one, that on a lonesome road
Doth walk in fear and dread,
And having once turned round walks on,
And turns no more his head;
Because he knows, a frightful fiend   450
Doth close behind him tread.

"But soon there breathed a wind on me,
Nor sound nor motion made:
Its path was not upon the sea,
In ripple or in shade.   455

"It raised my hair, it fanned my cheek   ⌐ **27**
Like a meadow-gale of spring—
It mingled strangely with my fears,
Yet it felt like a welcoming.

---

36. charnel dungeon: Vault where corpses or bones are deposited.

The Rime of the Ancient Mariner   677

---

3. "A speck, a mist, a shape, I wist! And still it neared and neared: As if it dodged a water sprite, It plunged and tacked and veered."
4. "The souls did from their bodies fly—They fled to bliss or woe! And every soul, it passed me by, Like the whizz of my crossbow!"
5. "The selfsame moment I could pray; And from my neck so free The Albatross fell off, and sank Like lead into the sea."

Student Activity 2. Write either a descriptive paragraph containing at least five similes or five separate sentences that each contain one simile.

28 Discussion Explain how the Mariner's ship returns home. Is it a normal sailing, or one with miraculous overtones?

29 Literary Focus Note the simile in line 472. Is it effective, or is it trite and unimaginative?

28
"Swiftly, swiftly flew the ship,   460
Yet she sailed softly too:
Sweetly, sweetly blew the breeze—
On me alone it blew.

And the ancient Mariner beholdeth his native country.

"Oh! dream of joy! is this indeed
The lighthouse top I see?   465
Is this the hill? is this the kirk?
Is this mine own countree?

"We drifted o'er the harbor bar,
And I with sobs did pray—
O let me be awake, my God!   470
Or let me sleep alway.

29
"The harbor bay was clear as glass,
So smoothly it was strewn![37]
And on the bay the moonlight lay,
And the shadow of the Moon.   475

"The rock shone bright, the kirk no less,
That stands above the rock;
The moonlight steeped in silentness
The steady weathercock.

"And the bay was white with silent light,   480
Till rising from the same,
Full many shapes, that shadows were,
In crimson colors came.

The angelic spirits leave the dead bodies,

"A little distance from the prow
Those crimson shadows were;   485
I turned my eyes upon the deck—
Oh, Christ! what saw I there!

And appear in their own forms of light.

"Each corse lay flat, lifeless and flat,
And, by the holy rood![38]
A man all light, a seraph[39] man,   490
On every corse there stood.

"This seraph band, each waved his hand:
It was a heavenly sight!
They stood as signals to the land,
Each one a lovely light;   495

---

37. strewn: spread.
38. rood: Cross.
39. seraph: Angel.

678   *The Romantic Age*

678

"This seraph band, each waved his hand,
No voice did they impart—
No voice; but oh! the silence sank
Like music on my heart.

"But soon I heard the dash of oars,   500
I heard the Pilot's cheer;
My head was turned perforce away
And I saw a boat appear.

"The Pilot and the Pilot's boy,
I heard them coming fast: 505
Dear Lord in Heaven! it was a joy
The dead men could not blast.

"I saw a third—I heard his voice:
It is the Hermit good!
He singeth loud his godly hymns   510
That he makes in the wood.
He'll shrieve[40] my soul, he'll wash away
The Albatross's blood.

Part VII

The Hermit of the Wood.

"This Hermit good lives in that wood
Which slopes down to the sea.   515
How loudly his sweet voice he rears!
He loves to talk with mariners
That come from a far countree.

"He kneels at morn, and noon, and eve—
He hath a cushion plump: 520
It is the moss that wholly hides
The rotted old oak-stump.

"The skiff boat neared; I heard them talk.
'Why, this is strange, I trow![41]
Where are those lights so many and fair,   525
That signal made but now?'

*Approacheth the ship
with wonder.*

" 'Strange, by my faith!' the Hermit said—
'And they answered not our cheer!
The planks looked warped! and see those
   sails,
How thin they are and sere!   530
I never saw aught like to them,
Unless perchance it were

---

40. shrieve (shrēv): Absolve from sin.
41. trow: Believe.

30 Discussion In the final stanza of Part VI the Mariner's words imply a fervent wish. What is that wish?

31 Reading Strategy Have students summarize the events of Part VI.

" 'Brown skeletons of leaves that lag
My forest brook along;
When the ivy tod[42] is heavy with snow,   535
And the owlet whoops to the wolf below,
That eats the she-wolf's young.'

" 'Dear Lord! it hath a fiendish look'
(The Pilot made reply)
'I am a-feared'—'Push on, push on!'   540
Said the Hermit cheerily.

"The boat came closer to the ship,
But I nor spake nor stirred;
The boat came close beneath the ship,
And straight[43] a sound was heard.   545

The ship suddenly sinketh.

"Under the water it rumbled on,
Still louder and more dread;
It reached the ship, it split the bay;
The ship went down like lead.

The ancient Mariner is saved in the Pilot's boat.

"Stunned by that loud and dreadful sound,   550
Which sky and ocean smote,
Like one that hath been seven days drowned
My body lay afloat;
But swift as dreams, myself I found
Within the Pilot's boat.   555

"Upon the whirl, where sank the ship,
The boat spun round and round;
And all was still, save that the hill
Was telling of the sound.

"I moved my lips—the Pilot shrieked   560
And fell down in a fit;
The holy Hermit raised his eyes,
And prayed where he did sit.

"I took the oars; the Pilot's boy,
Who now doth crazy go,   565
Laughed loud and long, and all the while
His eyes went to and fro.
'Ha! ha!' quoth he, 'full plain I see,
The Devil knows how to row.'

----

42. tod: Bush.
43. straight: Immediately.

"And now, all in my own countree,   570
I stood on the firm land!
The Hermit stepped forth from the boat,
And scarcely he could stand.

"'O shrieve me, shrieve me, holy man!'
The Hermit crossed his brow.[44]   575
'Say, quick,' quoth he, 'I bid thee say—
What manner of man art thou?'

"Forthwith this frame of mine was wrenched
With a woful agony,
Which forced me to begin my tale;   580
And then it left me free.

"Since then, at an uncertain hour,
That agony returns;
And till my ghastly tale is told,
This heart within me burns.   585

"I pass, like night, from land to land;
I have strange power of speech;
That moment that his face I see,
I know the man that must hear me:
To him my tale I teach.   590

"What loud uproar bursts from that door!
The wedding guests are there;
But in the garden bower the bride
And bridemaids singing are;
And hark the little vesper bell,   595
Which biddeth me to prayer!

"O Wedding Guest! this soul hath been
Alone on a wide wide sea:
So lonely 'twas, that God himself
Scarce seemed there to be.   600

"O sweeter than the marriage feast,
'Tis sweeter far to me,   **32**
To walk together to the kirk
With a goodly company!—

---

44. crossed his brow: Made the sign of the cross on his forehead.

The Rime of the Ancient Mariner   681

32 Discussion In these lines the Mariner admits that the company of living people is the sweetest blessing he can seek. Why does he feel this way?

33 **Discussion** These lines reveal the theme, or moral, of the tale. Restate that theme in your own words. What other lines in the poem can you find that relate to the moral?

34 **Reading Strategy** Have students summarize the events in Part VII.

Challenge How does the blend of Christian and pagan imagery extend the poet's intention to write a poem that deals with the supernatural? The imagery in the poem, while often eerie, is always quite vivid. What images stand out as most forceful?

Thematic Idea Turn back to the ballad "Sir Patrick Spens," page 104. What similarities do you see in form and style between that ballad and this one? What are the chief differences, aside from length?

Reader's Response Did you enjoy the poem more for the symbolic and thematic ideas it conveyed or for its narrative qualities? Explain.

"To walk together to the kirk,   605
And all together pray,
While each to his great Father bends,
Old men, and babes, and loving friends
And youths and maidens gay!

And to teach, by his own example, love and reverence to all things that God made and loveth.

"Farewell, farewell! but this I tell   610
To thee, thou Wedding Guest!
He prayeth well, who loveth well
Both man and bird and beast.

33

"He prayeth best, who loveth best
All things both great and small;   615
For the dear God who loveth us,
He made and loveth all."

The Mariner, whose eye is bright,
Whose beard with age is hoar,
Is gone; and now the Wedding Guest   620
Turned from the bridegroom's door.

34

He went like one that hath been stunned
And is of sense forlorn;
A sadder and a wiser man,
He rose the morrow morn.   625

THINKING ABOUT THE SELECTION

Recalling

1. (a) What happens to the ship as a result of the storm? (b) What change occurs when the Albatross appears?
2. (a) What "hellish thing" does the Mariner do? (b) How do the other sailors at first react to this deed? (c) What changes their minds?
3. (a) Who is the crew of the strange ship that appears in Part III? (b) What happens to the Mariner's shipmates soon after the appearance of this ship?
4. (a) What changes take place in the Mariner in Part IV? (b) What burden is he freed of as a result of these changes?

5. (a) According to the margin notes in Part V, what force causes the ship to move? (b) Who serves as the crew of the ship on this leg of its journey? (c) What force takes control of the ship at the equator?
6. What does the Mariner hope the Hermit will do for him?
7. What is the Mariner's lifelong penance?

Interpreting

8. What do you think the Albatross symbolizes, or stands for? Find evidence to support your answer.
9. In what ways might the journey of the Mariner be seen as spiritual as well as actual?
10. Some of the events Coleridge describes are

682   *The Romantic Age*

Closure and Extension

ANSWERS TO THINKING ABOUT THE SELECTION
Recalling

1. (a) The storm drove the ship south into an ice field. (b) The ice split, a good south wind blew up, and the ship headed back north.

2. (a) The Mariner shoots the Albatross with a crossbow. (b) At first the other sailors think the Mariner has done a good thing. (c) They change their minds when the ship is becalmed.
3. (a) The Specter Woman and her Death-mate are the crew. (b) One after another, the Mariner's shipmates drop dead.
4. (a) The Mariner's initial feelings of dismay, envy, and anger change

to those of love when he finds he can pray. (b) The Mariner having learned to pray, the Albatross falls off him.
5. (a) The Polar Spirit from the South carries the ship on its way. (b) A troop of angelic spirits make up the crew. (c) Fellow demons of the Polar Spirit take over the ship once it reaches the equator.
6. The Mariner hopes the hermit will absolve him of his sin.
7. His penance is to wander the

real and some are supernatural. Why do you think he includes both kinds in this poem?

Applying

11. Reread lines 614–617. How might this advice be useful for today's world?
12. What do we mean when we say that some past action stays with a person "like an albatross around his or her neck"?

ANALYZING LITERATURE
Understanding Sound Devices

Alliteration, consonance, assonance, and internal rhyme are four sound devices used to enhance the meaning and create the mood of a poem. **Alliteration** is the repetition of a first consonant sound in words or accented syllables ("the owlet *whoops* to the *wolf*"). **Consonance** is the repetition of a final consonant sound in words or accented syllables ("thy ski*nn*y ha*nd*, so brow*n*"). **Assonance** is the repetition of a vowel sound ("the Sun's r*i*m d*i*ps"). **Internal rhyme** is a rhyme within a line ("on the b*ay* the moonlight l*ay*").

Identify the sound device or devices in each of the following lines from "The Rime of the Ancient Mariner."

1. lines 7–8   4. lines 236–237
2. lines 31–32   5. lines 452–453
3. lines 121–122   6. lines 478–479

CRITICAL THINKING AND READING
Analyzing the Effects of Sound Devices

Sound devices in poetry please the ear and also reinforce meaning and create moods. In lines 41–44, for example, the repetition of the *s* sound, through both alliteration and consonance, enables us almost to hear the hissing of the sea foam as the ship is tossed about.

1. Reread lines 331–340. Identify the sound devices used and explain how they add to the eerie mood of the scene.
2. Reread lines 472–483. State the feeling you think Coleridge was trying to establish in his reader. Tell whether, in your opinion, his use of sound devices helps, and give your reasons.

UNDERSTANDING LANGUAGE
Using Archaic Words and Meanings

To give his poem the feeling of something written long ago, Coleridge used archaic, or outdated, language in "The Rime of the Ancient Mariner." Old verb forms such as *stoppeth* (line 2), Middle English words such as *eftsoons* (line 12), and earlier meanings of familiar words, such as *silly* to mean "empty" (line 297) all sounded as odd to Coleridge's original audience as they do to us today.

Find at least one other example each of old verb forms, Middle English words, and former word meanings in the poem. State whether you feel they help achieve the feeling Coleridge was striving after.

THINKING AND WRITING
Responding to a Statement

Coleridge wrote that successful poetry is poetry that will arouse "the sympathy of the reader by a faithful adherence to the truth of nature" while, at the same time, "giving the interest of novelty by the modifying colors of imagination." In an essay, argue whether or not you feel Coleridge met these standards in "The Rime of the Ancient Mariner." Begin by defining *sympathy* and *interest* as you believe he has used the words here. Support your claims by quoting passages from the poem. When you revise make sure you have included details from the poem to support your judgment. Proofread your essay and prepare a final draft.

The Rime of the Ancient Mariner 683

2. Lines 31-32 contain internal rhyme, alliteration, assonance, and consonance.
3. Lines 121-122 contain alliteration and assonance.
4. Lines 236-237 contain alliteration, assonance, and consonance.
5. Lines 452-453 contain alliteration, assonance, and consonance.
6. Lines 478-479 contain alliteration.

ANSWERS TO CRITICAL THINKING AND READING

1. In lines 331-340 the use of alliteration and assonance—especially the long *o* sound in the latter—reinforces the eeriness of the scene.
2. In lines 472-483 the poet succeeds in evoking a ghostly feeling through the use of sound devices, especially alliteration and assonance. Students' reasons should refer to the effects of specific sound devices.

ANSWERS TO UNDERSTANDING LANGUAGE

Examples of archaic words abound in the poem; they include *hath, spake, ken, o'ertaking, swound, look'st, uprist, reel* and *rout, wist, gramercy, nigh, twain, quoth, clomb, anear, corses, singeth, bideth, looketh,* and *shrieve,* all of which add to the supernatural, otherworldly effect that permeates the tale.

Writing Across the Curriculum
Today many people are concerned with preserving the delicate ecological balance that allows all life to co-exist. How does the Mariner's philosophy support the concerns of scientists? Of ordinary citizens? Consider working with the science department on this question. Science teachers might contribute current information on ecological concerns.

Challenge Compare and contrast the Mariner's philosophy with the Renaissance concept of the "Great Chain of Being."

earth telling his tale and teaching love and reverence for all things.

Interpreting

8. Suggested Response: The Albatross symbolizes nature as an evocation or test of human moral responses.
9. The Mariner's journey can also be thought of as an allegory of one's passage through life—from innocence through sin to grace and penitence. Sin makes an outcast

of the person; Grace and penitence readmit the person back into society.
10. Answers will differ. Suggested Response: Including the real and the supernatural results in a poem whose images are more vivid and lasting, as well as more credible.

Applying

11. Answers may differ but should include the idea that the moral of the poem is to love all things, both

great and small. Certainly applying this moral to the world today would lessen tensions between people and nations.
12. "Having an albatrass around one's neck" means that a person is unable to escape the effects of the past action.

ANSWERS TO ANALYZING LITERATURE

1. Lines 7-8 contain internal rhyme and consonance.

Literary Focus Point out that although Romanticism is most often thought of as an attempt to return to nature, a concern with the exotic, the strange, the far-away is a powerful strain in all forms of Romantic art. "Kubla Khan" is one of the greatest expressions of this form of Romanticism.

Writing/Prior Knowledge Have students discuss the term *exotic* in an attempt to define it and to give examples. They can then complete the writing activity.

Enrichment Go over the words before reading the poem. Consider adding these words to the list: *damsel* (young girl, maiden); *decree* (official decision, law); *tumult* (violent disturbance, confusion, or excitement).

Vocabulary

Preteach the following vocabulary words:
sinuous (sin′ yo͞o əs) *adj.*: Winding, twisting (p. 685)
tumult (to͞o′mult) *n.*: Noisy confusion (p. 686)
prophesying (prŏf′ ə sī′ iŋ) *v.*: Predicting (p. 686)

Kubla Khan

Literary Movements

Romanticism. Romanticism was a literary and artistic movement that began in Europe toward the end of the eighteenth century. A rebellion against the cold rationalism and strict adherence to form that typified the earlier Neoclassical movement, Romanticism stressed imagination and subjectivity as key literary virtues. The Romantic writer was free to express his or her personal views in a spontaneous and nonlogical fashion. The goal of the Romantics thus was to bring people to an awareness of their "oneness" with all other living things. It was in the spirit of this movement and its goal that Coleridge gave his poem "Kubla Khan" the subtitle "A Vision in a Dream." The word *vision* here reminds us that the Romantics were fond of mysticism and fantasy—the stuff of visions. The word *dream* calls to mind a freedom from the rules and logical order of the day-to-day world—traits that were at the very heart of Romanticism.

Writing

Recall as best you can a dream you had in which you made a trip to a strange place. Write a vivid description. Use as many details of sight, sound, touch, taste, and smell as you are able.

Primary Source

From his memories of childhood, it is apparent that Romanticism exerted a tug at Coleridge's nature from the very start. He was especially taken with mystery and fantasy:

> My father's sister kept an *every-thing* shop at Crediton," he recalled, "and there I read through all the gilt-covered little books that could be had at that time, and likewise all the uncovered tales of *Tom Hickathrift, Jack the Giant-Killer,* etc. and . . . I used to lie by the wall, and mope—and my spirits used to come upon me suddenly, and in a flood—and then I was accustomed to run up and down the church-yard, and act over all I had been reading on the docks, the nettles, and the rank-grass. At six years old . . . I found the Arabian Nights entertainments—one tale of which . . . made so deep an impression on me (I had read it in the evening while my mother was mending stockings) that I was haunted by specters whenever I was in the dark—and I distinctly remember the anxious and fearful eagerness with which I used to watch the window in which the books lay—and whenever the sun lay upon them, I would seize it, carry it by the wall, and bask, and read. My father found out the effect which these books had produced—and burnt them. So I became a dreamer. . . .

684   *The Romantic Age*

Objective
1 To understand the beliefs of Romanticism

Support Material

Teaching Portfolio
Teacher Backup, p. 813
Grammar in Action Worksheet, *Using Precise Words,* p. 816
Usage and Mechanics Worksheet, p. 818
Vocabulary Check, p. 819
Analyzing Literature Worksheet, *Understanding Romanticism,* p. 820

Language Worksheet, *Understanding Homophones,* p. 821
Selection Test, p. 822

Kubla Khan

Samuel Taylor Coleridge

This poem was inspired by a passage about Kubla Khan (kōō' ble kän'), the founder of the Mongol dynasty in China in the thirteenth century, in Samuel Purchas's Purchas His Pilgrimage *(1613): "Here the Khan Kubla commanded a palace to be built, and a stately garden thereunto. And thus ten miles of fertile ground were inclosed with a wall." Coleridge claims to have fallen asleep while reading this passage due to the effects of medication he was taking for an illness at the time (1797). Three hours later, he awoke from a dream, finding his mind was filled with two to three hundred lines of poetry, which were an elaboration of the description he had read immediately before drifting off to sleep. Coleridge immediately began to write down the lines that filled his head, but when he was interrupted by a visitor, he forgot the lines that he had not yet transcribed. As a result, he was unable to complete the poem.*

In Xanadu[1] did Kubla Khan
A stately pleasure dome decree:
Where Alph,[2] the sacred river, ran
Through caverns measureless to man
5   Down to a sunless sea.
So twice five miles of fertile ground
With walls and towers were girdled round;
And there were gardens bright with sinuous rills,[3]
Where blossomed many an incense-bearing tree;
10 And here were forests ancient as the hills,
Enfolding sunny spots of greenery.

But oh! that deep romantic chasm which slanted
Down the green hill athwart[4] a cedarn cover![5]
A savage place! as holy and enchanted
15 As e'er beneath a waning moon was haunted
By woman wailing for her demon lover!
And from this chasm, with ceaseless turmoil seething,
As if this earth in fast thick pants were breathing.

1. Xanadu (zan' ə dōō): An indefinite area in China.
2. Alph: Probably derived from the Greek river Alpheus, the waters of which, it was believed in Greek mythology, joined with a stream to form a fountain in Sicily.
3. rills: Brooks.
4. athwart: Across.
5. cedarn cover: Covering of cedar trees.

Kubla Khan 685

Grammar in Action

Precise words bring writing alive. Vivid, specific nouns, verbs, adjectives, and adverbs create graphic pictures and add greatly to emotional tone. Samuel Taylor Coleridge demonstrates superb use of such words in the opening lines of "Kubla Khan."

In Xanadu did Kubla Khan
A *stately* pleasure dome decree:
Where Alph, the *sacred* river, ran
Through caverns *measureless* to man
     Down to a *sunless* sea. . . .
And there were gardens *bright* with *sinuous rills*
Where *blossomed* many an *incense-bearing* tree . . .

(*continued*)

Presentation

Motivation/Prior Knowledge
Ask students to imagine they have just awakened from a vivid dream of some exotic place. Would they try to hold onto the images the dream evoked? Why or why not?

Master Teacher Note Scholars have discovered that passages in the poem derive from about eight travel writers besides Purchas, as well as landscapes that Coleridge himself had seen.

Purpose-Setting Question What evidence of passion, mysticism, and fantasy do you find in "Kubla Khan"?

1 Enrichment Coleridge said that Lord Byron convinced him to publish "Kubla Khan," which he did, "rather as a psychological curiosity, than on the ground of any supposed *poetic* merits."

2 Literary Focus The indefinite Oriental setting exemplifies Romantic fascination with the exotic, strange, and faraway. However, the "measureless" caverns, the gardens, and the ancient forests recall the more conventional Romantic interest in nature. You might read these lines aloud and ask your students to describe the mood and atmosphere they create.

3 Discussion With more advanced, or more mature, students, you may wish to point out the mixture of savagery, holiness, enchantment, passion, and demonolatry in these lines. Imagery and connotation combine to make these verses especially memorable. Ask what feelings this place seems to stir in the poet.

5 **Discussion** What new emotion is introduced in lines 29–30? Point out that in lines 31–36 the delicacy of the "pleasure dome" is suggested and therefore its vulnerability to war.

6 **Literary Focus** Point out that the abrupt transition to the damsel is typical of the free-flowing nature of a dream. Coleridge's use of a non-logical structure in "Kubla Khan" is characteristically Romantic. Classical and neoclassical poets, conversely, tend to rely on a logical structure in their poems.

7 **Discussion** Point out that the poem becomes personal at the end. Ask students to summarize the poet's vision of himself here. In what sense would he "build that dome in air"? You may need to explain that line 51 describes a magical ritual intended to protect the inspired, frenzied poet from intrusion. The image of the poet as a divinely inspired madman is common in some of the more extreme forms of Romanticism.

Reader's Response Why do you think that dreams can be so richly imaginative and fascinating?

A mighty fountain momently was forced;
20   Amid whose swift half-intermitted burst
Huge fragments vaulted like rebounding hail,
Or chaffy grain beneath the thresher's flail;
And 'mid these dancing rocks at once and ever
It flung up momently the sacred river.
25   Five miles meandering with a mazy motion
Through wood and dale the sacred river ran,
Then reached the caverns measureless to man,
And sank in tumult to a lifeless ocean:
And 'mid this tumult Kubla heard from far
30   Ancestral voices prophesying war!
    The shadow of the dome of pleasure
    Floated midway on the waves;
    Where was heard the mingled measure
    From the fountain and the caves.
35   It was a miracle of rare device.[6]
A sunny pleasure dome with caves of ice!

    A damsel with a dulcimer[7]
    In a vision once I saw:
    It was an Abyssinian[8] maid,
40   And on her dulcimer she played.
    Singing of Mount Abora.[9]
    Could I revive within me
    Her symphony and song,
    To such a deep delight 'twould win me,
45   That with music loud and long,
I would build that dome in air,
That sunny dome! those caves of ice!
And all who heard should see them there,
And all should cry, Beware! Beware!
50   His flashing eyes, his floating hair!
Weave a circle round him thrice,
And close your eyes with holy dread,
For he on honeydew hath fed,
And drunk the milk of Paradise.

---

6. device: Design.
7. dulcimer: (dul' sə mər) *n.*: A musical instrument with metal strings which produce sounds when struck by two small hammers.
8. Abyssinian (ab ə sin' ē ən): Ethiopian.
9. Mount Abora: Probably Mount Amara in Abyssinia.

Notice how the italicized words in the following couplet express the tumult of the river.

    And from this chasm, with *ceaseless turmoil seething*,
    As if this earth in *fast thick pants* were *breathing* . . .

Student Activity. Write a brief description of an extraordinary phenomenon of nature. Concentrate on selecting words that are especially vivid and precise.

Closure and Extension

ANSWERS TO THINKING ABOUT THE SELECTION
Recalling

1. The pleasure dome was "twice five miles" in size.
2. "A mighty fountain" was forced up.

KUBLAI KHAN
Chinese Silk Album Leaf, Yuan Dynasty
The Granger Collection

Humanities Note

Fine art, *Kublai Khan,* Chinese silk album leaf, Yuan Dynasty. Chinese painting differs from European painting in several ways: the subject matter is always related to Chinese spirituality; the purpose of the painting is to evoke a mood or emotional response in a sensitive viewer; and the surface is usually fabric, most often silk.

This painting on silk of Kubla Khan is spare and stylized, yet it captures a formal authority in the bearing of Kubla Khan.

You may wish to ask the following question: How does the artist's conception of the great Kubla Khan compare with Coleridge's?

(Answers begin on p. 686.)

THINKING ABOUT THE SELECTION

Recalling

1. What was the size of the palatial estate that Kubla Khan ordered built?
2. What, according to the second stanza, was forced up through "that deep romantic chasm"?
3. What did Kubla Khan hear in the noise made by the river emptying into the ocean?
4. (a) According to the last stanza, what did the speaker once see in a vision? (b) What part of that vision does the speaker wish he could revive?

Interpreting

5. Using your own words, what does the speaker say would happen to him and "all who heard" if he were able to revive his vision?

6. What statement do you think Coleridge is making here about the power of imagination?
7. (a) Find one example each of Coleridge's use of alliteration and assonance. (b) Explain how each example enhances the meaning or mood of the words.
8. (a) Do you feel that Coleridge's imagination and "music" combine to make his vision seem real for the reader? (b) Support your answer with quotations from the poem.

Applying

9. Do you think people should be governed more by their emotions or their reason? Do you think there should be a balance between the two? Explain your answer.

Kubla Khan 687

---

erns, the "deep romantic chasm," the sacred river, and the maid with the dulcimer would be appropriate choices.

Applying

9. Answers will differ. In their answers students should cite the advantages and disadvantages of being governed by emotion and reason.

Challenge More than one critic has noted that "Kubla Khan" oscillates between giving and taking away, between what the critic Elisabeth Schneider, for example, describes as "bright affirmation and sunless negation." Defend or attack this interpretation, citing specific passages from the poem to support your view.

---

3. Kubla heard "Ancestral voices prophesying war!"
4. (a) The speaker once saw a "damsel with a dulcimer." (b) The speaker wishes he could revive "Her symphony and song." (c) The vision would win him over to build the sunny pleasure dome.

Interpreting

5. He would re-create in his imagination Kubla Khan's pleasure dome

and the cover of ice. Those who heard him would look upon him as an inspired madman and seal him off from ordinary people.

6. Answers will differ but should mention that imagination has the power to create a vision that amounts to a kind of reality. Coleridge is also suggesting that the imagination is a form of divinely inspired lunacy.

7. (a) Line 4 contains alliteration; line 6 contains assonance. (b) Alliteration

in line 4 draws the reader's attention to the key words *measureless* and *man*. In line 6 the long *i* sound "lifts" the tone of the poem from the depths—of sound as well as sense—of the preceding lines.

8. (a) Answers will differ but should affirm that imagination and music do indeed combine to make the vision seem real. (b) Students' supporting quotations will differ. However, the descriptions of the cav-

More About the Author Lord Byron was once as celebrated for his lifestyle as for the remarkable quality of his works. Indeed, he gave rise to the term *Byronic hero*—a kind of hero as outcast, a person in whom, as Byron himself once suggested, there is much to admire and much to hate. Ask students to discuss any public figures they think might qualify as Byronic heroes.

Critical Evaluation According to literary scholar Kenneth Hopkins, "The reader coming newly to Byron is embarrassed by the richness of available comment, and the diversity of views upon him. Perhaps no English poet has been written about so copiously, and so diversely, except (as always) Shakespeare. Biographical accounts of him began to appear before his death, and multiplied after it; and with justice, for his life is perennially interesting to read about, and remains of great interest even after the outline becomes familiar; he was far more alive, perverse, human, likeable, infuriating, understandable, baffling, complex and diverse than his contemporaries —more so even than Shelley, the next most appealing as a subject for a biography. . . . (A)s a person to *read about* and to read about at any moment of his brief and crowded life, Byron stands supreme and alone among the literary figures of his time. This has tended, often enough, to divert the reader from his works, and at any time this past hundred years there have always been more people who could recite the outline details of Byron's life than tell the story of *Don Juan*. But *Don Juan* might well be called the most thoroughly *readable* work in the whole of English literature."

GEORGE GORDON, LORD BYRON

1788–1824

In his life as well as in his work, George Gordon, Lord Byron, typified the Romanticist's zest for life. As much a public figure as a literary genius, Byron lived life "in the fast lane"—a point that was looked on with disapproval by his contemporaries.

Whether distasteful behavior is purely a matter of example is open to debate. Nevertheless, it is significant to note that Byron was born in London to a father whose good looks—which his son inherited—made him irresistible to women. The father, John Byron, died when his son was three. When the young Byron was ten, the death of a great-uncle brought him the title of Baron, along with an estate at Newstead. Here the boy and his mother went to live until, at seventeen, Byron left home to attend Trinity College at Cambridge. At college, Byron made many friends, played many sports, and spent much money. He also published his first book of poems, *Hours of Idleness* (1807), which received harsh criticism from the *Edinburgh Review*. He was hurt but not crushed by this attack on his work, and two years later he came out with *English Bards and Scotch Reviewers,* a poem poking fun at the magazine.

That same year, Byron journeyed to the Near East, and spent the next two years traveling. When he returned home, he brought with him two sections of a book-length poem titled *Childe Harold,* which depicted a young hero not unlike himself—moody, reckless, sensitive, and adventuresome. The work was received with great enthusiasm, and Byron became a very popular figure in important English circles. So great was his popularity, in fact, that his next published work, *The Corsair,* sold 10,000 copies in one day.

During this period Byron saw a great many women. In 1815 he married Ann Isabella Milbanke, with whom he had a daughter. The couple seemed mismatched from the start and, after about a year, separated. Hurt by nasty gossip, Byron left England, never to return. It was in Italy that he began work on his most ambitious opus, *Don Juan* (pronounced "JOO-en"), a mock epic of the Romantic hero.

It was also at this point that tragedy struck, and then struck again—first with the death of his daughter, later with that of his friend, the poet Shelley. In 1823 Byron joined a group of revolutionaries seeking to free Greece from Turkish rule. Before the revolt got underway, however, Byron died of rheumatic fever, at the age of thirty-six.

Although Byron openly spurned the works of other Romantics, including Wordsworth and Coleridge, his independence was a hallmark of the Romantic movement.

688   *The Romantic Age*

GUIDE FOR INTERPRETING

She Walks in Beauty;
So We'll Go No More A-Roving;
Apostrophe to the Ocean

Writer's Technique

Figurative Language. Figurative language is the name given to a class of literary conventions that purposely distort language to make ideas more interesting and memorable. As opposed to literal language, or language "by the rules," figurative language is not to be taken at face value. When a poet writes, for instance, of trees "standing by the side of the road like sentinels," he or she is attempting to get the reader to picture trees that are very upright, much like soldiers.

Writing

Develop a list of about twenty adjectives and descriptive phrases, such as *blue, filled with holes, slippery,* and so on. Randomly choose three entries from your list, and write them at the top of a sheet of paper. Then try to think of two objects that share each of the three traits. Write a sentence that compares one of the objects to the other. Try this with at least four pairs of objects.

Primary Source

Lady Caroline Lamb, wildly in love with Byron, confided in her diary that he was "Mad, bad, and dangerous to know." Whether we completely believe the lovesick, we cannot deny that Byron had an astonishing affect on those he met. Critic Gilbert Highet has an intriguing theory to explain Byron's remarkable personality.

Highet claims that Byron was "not naturally a slender, elegant, athletic, grave young man at all. Naturally, he was a plump, pleasant, pot-bellied person, and he spent tremendous, almost unremitting efforts on keeping down his natural fat. He was about five feet eight. When he was nineteen years old, he weighed 202 pounds. . . . He resolved to get it off, and keep it off. He did so by painful exercises and the most Spartan regime of dieting, which may well have wrecked his liver. He took exercise wearing seven waistcoats and a heavy topcoat; then he took hot baths; he ate hardly anything. By the time he was twenty, he had got down to 147 pounds. . . . He was starving.

"He was a thin man, and inside him was a fat man roaring to be set free. . . . Byron had several vultures with their beaks buried deep into his vitals; but the one which he felt most constantly, if not most painfully, was that haggard-eyed, sharp-clawed, tireless monster, a starvation diet."

Literary Focus With less advanced students, explain that literal language means what it says, whereas figurative language says one thin but means much more. Presenting several metaphors to illustrate how figurative language works should prove helpful.

Writing/Prior Knowledge Give the class an example to help them get started: for a snowy evening write, "An infinity of down blanketed the sleeping earth." Have a few students volunteer their figurative descriptions.

Vocabulary

Preteach the following vocabulary words:

gaudy (gôd′ ē) *adj.*: Showy in a tasteless way (p. 690)

impaired (im per′d) *v.*: Diminished (p. 690)

tress (tres) *n.*: Lock of human hair (p. 690)

eloquent (el′ ə kwənt) *adj.*: Very expressive (p. 690)

armaments (är′ mə ments) *n.*: Arms, weapons (p. 693)

arbiter (är′ bə tər) *n.*: Judge, umpire (p. 693)

torrid (tôr′ id) *adj.*: Hot, scorching (p. 694)

Motivation/Prior Knowledge
Inform the class that this is one of
the most famous descriptions of
womanly beauty in English poetry. Challenge them to describe
in prose Lady Horton's beauty.

Master Teacher Note The poem
was published in Byron's *Hebrew
Melodics,* which was written to be
set to adaptations of traditional
Jewish tunes.

Purpose-Setting Question: What
figures of speech and images
does Byron use to express his
sense of the lady's beauty?

Thematic Idea Compare and
contrast this poem with Shakespeare's Sonnet 130, page 259.

Reader's Response Why do you
think that the theme of beauty is
so well suited to poetry?

1 Enrichment Byron wrote this lyric
for Lady Horton as soon as he had
returned to his room following a
dance at which he saw her.

2 Discussion The opening simile is
justly famous. How apt is it? How
is Lady Horton like the night?

3 Discussion Does Byron's picture
emphasize the physical or the
spiritual aspect of the lady?

Challenge Compare the rhythm,
the meter, and the rhyme
scheme in this poem to those in
the heroic couplets of Pope's
"Rape of the Lock," page 548.

She Walks in Beauty

George Gordon, Lord Byron

*This poem, written to be set to music, was inspired by
Byron's first meeting with Lady Wilmot Horton, his cousin
by marriage, who wore a black mourning gown with
spangles.*

She walks in beauty, like the night
    Of cloudless climes and starry skies;
And all that's best of dark and bright
    Meet in her aspect and her eyes:
5 Thus mellowed to that tender light
    Which heaven to gaudy day denies.

One shade the more, one ray the less,
    Had half impaired the nameless grace
Which waves in every raven tress,
10   Or softly lightens o'er her face;
Where thoughts serenely sweet express
    How pure, how dear their dwelling place.

And on that cheek, and o'er that brow,
    So soft, so calm, yet eloquent,
15 The smiles that win, the tints that glow,
    But tell of days in goodness spent,
A mind at peace with all below,
    A heart whose love is innocent!

THINKING ABOUT THE SELECTION
Recalling

1. In "She Walks in Beauty," to what does the
speaker of the poem compare the lady's
beauty?
2. What color is the lady's hair?

Interpreting

3. What do you think is the meaning of "that
tender light" in line 5?
4. What does the speaker believe the woman's
appearance reveals about her character?

Applying

5. (a) Why was nature a logical choice for Byron
as something with which to compare a lady's
beauty? (b) Why would it be a logical choice
for any comparison by Byron?

**ANSWERS TO THINKING
ABOUT THE SELECTION**
Recalling

1. The speaker compares the lady's
beauty to a starry night.
2. Her hair is black.

Interpreting

3. "Tender light" refers to the lady's
fair complexion.
4. Her appearance suggests a character imbued with peace and innocent love.

Applying

5. Suggested Responses: (a) Putting
aside Byron's place among Romantic poets, nature was a logical
choice for Byron's comparison because nature offers various images
of beauty. (b) It would be logical
because Byron, living in the great
age of nature poetry, would naturally have been predisposed to look to
nature for figurative comparisons.

So We'll Go No More A-Roving

George Gordon, Lord Byron

This poem was included in a letter to Thomas Moore, written from Venice on February 28, 1817. Carnival season had just passed and Byron, at the age of twenty-nine, found himself in a prolonged period of reflection. The poem is based on the refrain of the Scottish song, "The Jolly Beggar."

So we'll go no more a-roving
   So late into the night,
Though the heart be still as loving,
   And the moon be still as bright.

5 For the sword outwears its sheath,
   And the soul wears out the breast,
And the heart must pause to breathe,
   And Love itself have rest.

Though the night was made for loving,
10   And the day returns too soon,
Yet we'll go no more a-roving
   By the light of the moon.

THINKING ABOUT THE SELECTION

Recalling

1. What does the speaker say that "Love itself" must have?

Interpreting

2. (a) What do you think is meant by the line "And the soul wears out the breast"? (b) Why must the heart "pause to breathe"?

3. (a) Why will the speaker "go no more a-roving"? (b) How might you summarize in one sentence the speaker's message?

Applying

4. Which properties of the Romantic spirit are evident in this poem?

So We'll Go No More A-Roving   691

from Childe Harold's Pilgrimage

Apostrophe to the Ocean

George Gordon, Lord Byron

There is a pleasure in the pathless woods,
There is a rapture on the lonely shore,
There is society, where none intrudes,
By the deep sea, and music in its roar;
5 I love not man the less, but nature more,
From these our interviews, in which I steal
From all I may be, or have been before,
To mingle with the universe, and feel
What I can ne'er express, yet cannot all conceal.

10 Roll on, thou deep and dark blue ocean—roll!
Ten thousand fleets sweep over thee in vain;
Man marks the earth with ruin—his control
Stops with the shore; upon the watery plain
The wrecks are all thy deed, nor doth remain
15 A shadow of man's ravage, save[1] his own,
When, for a moment, like a drop of rain,
He sinks into thy depths with bubbling groan,
Without a grave, unknelled, uncoffined, and unknown.

His steps are not upon thy paths—thy fields
20 Are not a spoil for him—thou dost arise
And shake him from thee; the vile strength he wields
For earth's destruction thou dost all despise,
Spurning him from thy bosom to the skies,
And send'st him, shivering in thy playful spray
25 And howling, to his gods, where haply[2] lies
His petty hope in some near port or bay,
And dashest him again to earth—there let him lay.[3]

---

1. save: Except.
2. haply: Perhaps.
3. lay: A note on Byron's proof suggests that he intentionally made this grammatical error for the sake of the rhyme.

SHIPWRECK
J.C.C. Dahl
Munich Neue Pinakothek/Kavaler

The armaments which thunderstrike the walls
Of rock-built cities, bidding nations quake,
30   And monarchs tremble in their capitals,
The oak leviathans,[4] whose huge ribs make
Their clay creator[5] the vain title take
Of lord of thee, and arbiter of war—
These are thy toys, and, as the snowy flake,
35   They melt into thy yeast of waves, which mar
Alike the Armada's[6] pride or spoils of Trafalgar.[7]   ⌐ **6**

Thy shores are empires, changed in all save thee—
Assyria, Greece, Rome, Carthage, what are they?
Thy waters washed them power while they were free,
40   And many a tyrant since; their shores obey

---

4. leviathans (lə vī′ ə thənz): Monstrous sea creatures, described in the Old Testament. Here the word means giant ships.
5. clay creator: Human beings.
6. Armada's: Refers to the Spanish Armada, defeated by the English in 1588.
7. Trafalgar: The battle in 1805 during which the French and Spanish fleets were defeated by the British fleet led by Lord Nelson.

Apostrophe to the Ocean 693

8 **Discussion** Throughout the poem, the speaker creates an image of the ocean as all powerful and relentless. Yet in the last stanza he expresses great love and delight in the ocean. Why is this not surprising?

Master Teacher Note After reading Byron's "Apostrophe to the Ocean," you might wish to place Art Transparency 8, Henry Moore's *Arran*, on your overhead projector. Arran is an island in the Firth of Clyde, in southwest Scotland. Ask your students to examine how Moore has depicted the water. What impression was he trying to convey? How well has he succeeded? Compare this painting with Byron's poem. What do you think Byron's intention was? How does it compare with Moore's?

Reader's Response What thoughts and feelings do you associate with the ocean?

The stranger, slave, or savage; their decay
Has dried up realms to deserts—not so thou,
Unchangeable, save to thy wild waves' play.
Time writes no wrinkle on thine azure brow;

7 | 45 Such as creation's dawn beheld, thou rollest now.

Thou glorious mirror, where the Almighty's form
Glasses[8] itself in tempests; in all time,
Calm or convulsed—in breeze, or gale, or storm,
Icing the pole, or in the torrid clime

50 Dark-heaving—boundless, endless, and sublime;
The image of eternity, the throne
Of the Invisible; even from out thy slime
The monsters of the deep are made; each zone
Obeys thee; thou goest forth, dread, fathomless, alone.

8 | 55 And I have loved thee, ocean! and my joy
Of youthful sports was on thy breast to be
Borne, like thy bubbles, onward; from a boy
I wantoned with thy breakers—they to me
Were a delight; and if the freshening sea

60 Made them a terror—'twas a pleasing fear,
For I was as it were a child of thee,
And trusted to thy billows far and near,
And laid my hand upon thy mane—as I do here.

---

8. glasses: Mirrors.

Primary Source

How do poets evaluate their own works? How did Byron feel about his much-celebrated "Childe Harold's Pilgrimage"? In a letter to his printer, Byron offered his opinion.

Dear Sir,
I enclose a sheet for correction, if you ever get to another edition. You will observe the blunder in printing makes it appear as if the Château was over St. Gingo, instead of being on the opposite shore of the Lake, over Clarens. So, separate the paragraphs, otherwise my topography will be seen as inaccurate as your typography on this occasion.
The other day I wrote to convey my proposition with regard to the 4th and concluding canto [of "Childe Harold's Pilgrimage"]. I have gone over and extended it to one hundred and fifty stanzas. . . . I look upon Childe Harold as my best; and as I begun, I think of concluding with it. But I make no resolutions on that head, as I broke my former intention with regard to "The Corsair." However, I fear that I shall never do better; and yet, not being thirty years of age, for some moons to come, one ought to be progressive as far as Intellect goes for many a good year. But I have had a devilish deal of wear and tear of mind and body in my time, besides having published too often and much already.

694   The Romantic Age

THINKING ABOUT THE SELECTION

Recalling

1. How does the speaker of the poem say the ocean makes him feel?
2. How does he say the ocean treats such things as warships and sea monsters?
3. What childhood memories of the ocean does the speaker have?

Interpreting

4. In line 10, the speaker describes the movement of ships over the ocean as "in vain." What might he mean by this?
5. What property of the ocean does the speaker admire in the fifth stanza?
6. What double meaning might the speaker have intended in his reference to the ocean as a glorious mirror in line 46?

Applying

7. Do you believe it is still true today that humans control of the planet "stops with the shore," as Byron puts it in "Apostrophe to the Ocean"? Explain.

ANALYZING LITERATURE

Understanding Figurative Language

Figurative language is language that links, in one way or another, things or ideas that are generally unrelated. Also known as figures of speech, figurative language is actually a category heading for a number of literary devices. Simile, among the best known of these, is a comparison using a word such as *like* or *as*. The line "the sheen of their spears was like stars on the sea" contains a simile.

Metaphor, often thought of as a companion to the simile, compares two objects without making use of a linking word. The line "The moon was a ghostly galleon tossed upon cloudy seas" contains a metaphor.

A third device, personification, gives human characteristics to nonhuman subjects. The line "The moon peeked out from behind a cloud" contains an example of personification.

Identify the type of figurative language in each quotation, and express in your own words what it adds to the poem.

1. "She walks in beauty, like the night . . ." (p. 690)
2. ". . . the heart must pause to breathe . . ." (p. 691)
3. ". . . like a drop of rain,/He sinks into thy depths . . ." (p. 692)
4. "These are thy toys, and, as the snowy flake,/They melt into the yeast of waves . . ." (p. 693)
5. "Thou glorious mirror, where the Almighty's form/Glasses itself . . ." (p. 694)

THINKING AND WRITING

Evaluating a Poem

When you read a review of a film or book in a newspaper, you are reading an evaluation. Write an evaluation of one of the three poems by Byron. First jot down ideas about this poem. Then write your first draft. Mention such things as language, style, and subject matter, and conclude with your personal reactions to the piece, giving conclusive reasons for why you feel as you do. When you revise make sure that your arguments are sound. Proofread your essay and prepare a final draft.

Writing Across the Curriculum

Ask students to find passages from a science book describing the ocean, or one phase of it, such as storms or tides. Science teachers might suggest sources. Have students contrast the scientific approach to describing the ocean to the poet's.

ANSWERS TO THINKING ABOUT THE SELECTION
Recalling

1. The ocean fills the speaker with emotion to the point that he cannot express himself.
2. The ocean treats warships and sea monsters with disdain.
3. He remembers the ocean as a wonderful, if at times terror-filled, place to swim and play.

Interpreting

4. No matter how important the fleets of warships are to men, they cannot challenge the ocean nor can they damage it.
5. The speaker admires the ocean's being unchangeable.
6. The poet may be using the term *mirror* in the sense of "reflecting" and also in the sense of a reflection of life as a whole.

Applying

7. Answers will differ but should include ideas about recent, and not so recent, attempts to control the sea, as in Holland, through the use of elaborate dykes, as in dredging harbor inlets, and as in experiments with "farming" the sea for minerals.

ANSWERS TO ANALYZING LITERATURE

1. This image is a simile.
2. This image personifies the heart.
3. This image is a simile.
4. The images here are metaphors and a simile.
5. The image is a metaphor.

Answers about the effect of each type of figurative language will differ but should include the idea that figurative language makes any work more interesting and vivid, as well as easier to understand.

Thinking and Writing

For help with this assignment, students can refer to Lesson 15, "Evaluating a Literary Work," in the Handbook of Writing About Literature.

Focus

Literary Focus *Don Juan* (pronounced Jōō ən) was begun in July of 1818, and Byron worked on it almost until his death, in 1824. He had read the Italian seriocomic versions of medieval chivalric romances, and from them learned how to manage the ottava-rima stanza, with its *abababcc* rhyme scheme. He also learned how effective an alternation of sublimity and ridiculousness could be in a mock epic.

Writing Pick one of these activities, and ask students to suggest pompous and inflated descriptions that might apply to it. For example, walking a dog could be described as "perambulating with my pooch."

Vocabulary

Preteach the following vocabulary words:
retort (ri tôrt′) *n.*: Come back with a smart answer or wisecrack (p. 697)
credulous (krej′ oͦ ləs) *adj.*: Willing to believe (p. 698)
copious (kō′ pē əs) *adj.*: Abundant, plentiful (p. 698)
avarice (av′ ər is) *n.*: Greed (p. 698)

from Don Juan

Literary Forms

Mock Epic. A mock epic is a long poem that mocks, or pokes fun at, a trivial subject by treating it in the grand style of epic poetry. The epic poem, which found its loftiest expression in such timeless works as the *Iliad*, the *Odyssey*, and *Paradise Lost*, was defined not only by its style but also by certain regular features. The poem usually began, for example, with an *invocation*, or request for inspiration and guidance from a muse or deity, and it was usually divided into long sections called *cantos* or books. In addition, the epic generally contained lengthy and carefully worded speeches by heroes and included descriptions of battles fought by noble warriors. In a mock epic, this combination of ingredients—a lofty style and a base subject—leads to humorous results. When, for example, the romantic adventures of a beautiful young man are narrated in a grand fashion, as is the case in *Don Juan*, the end product is hilarious.

Writing

Think of an activity that is especially trival or commonplace, such as walking a dog or going to the supermarket for groceries. Now think of several adjectives that might be used—or *misused*—to describe this activity in a heroic manner. Finally, write a "mini-mock epic" that paints a lofty picture of this routine task.

Commentary

Despite a great enthusiasm for reading, public taste became increasing conservative during the Romantic Age. Groups such as the Society for the Suppression of Vice were remarkably effective in controlling public taste. The fear of prosecution made many booksellers unwilling to print works that were either risqué or immoral. Byron's publisher, for example, was reluctant to print the first two cantos of *Don Juan* because he feared he might be prosecuted. When *Don Juan* did appear, although the vice society took no action against it, many reviewers denounced it as indecent and immoral. The *Eclectic Review*, for example, warned that Byron wrote poetry "such as no brother could read aloud to his sister, no husband to his wife—poetry in which the deliberate purpose of the author is to corrupt by inflaming the mind." One woman was horrified when a clergyman told her he had bought an edition of Byron's poems, though he "boasted that he had burned *Don Juan*."

What do you see in this excerpt from *Don Juan* that might inflame readers in Byron's day?

Objective

1 To write about the Byronic hero

Support Material

Teaching Portfolio
Teacher Backup, p. 835
Usage and Mechanics Worksheet, p. 838
Vocabulary Check, p. 839
Analyzing Literature Worksheet, *Understanding the Mock-Epic*, p. 840

Critical Thinking and Reading Worksheet, *Analyzing Technique in Relation to Meaning*, p. 841
Selection Test, p. 842

from Don Juan

George Gordon, Lord Byron

Though it is unfinished, Don Juan *is generally regarded as Byron's finest work. The long poem, a mock epic that was described by Shelley as being "something wholly new and relative to the age," satirizes the political and social problems of Byron's time.*

Traditionally the character of Don Juan, the poem's hero, had been portrayed as being a wicked and immoral man driven solely by his obsession with beautiful women. In Byron's work Don Juan is depicted as an innocent young man whose physical beauty, charm, and spirit prove to be extremely alluring for ladies, leading him into many difficult situations.

Many people feel that what makes Don Juan *such a great poem is the lapses in the story, during which the speaker drifts away from the subject. During these lapses the speaker comments on the issues of the time and on life in general. In this excerpt the speaker abandons his hero to reflect on old age and death.*

But now at thirty years my hair is gray
    (I wonder what it will be like at forty?
I thought of a peruke¹ the other day)—
    My heart is not much greener; and, in short, I
5 Have squandered my whole summer while 'twas May,
    And feel no more the spirit to retort; I
Have spent my life, both interest and principal,
And deem not, what I deemed, my soul invincible.

No more—no more—Oh! never more on me
10   The freshness of the heart can fall like dew,
Which out of all the lovely things we see
    Extracts emotions beautiful and new,
Hived in our bosoms like the bag o' the bee:
    Think'st thou the honey with those objects grew?
15 Alas! 'twas not in them, but in thy power
To double even the sweetness of a flower.

No more—no more—Oh! never more, my heart,
    Canst thou be my sole world, my universe!

---

1. peruke (pə rook′): Wig.

Presentation

Motivation/Prior Knowledge Ask your students to tell how it might feel to think that the best of life is already in the past and the future promises very little that seems to matter.

Master Teacher Note Consider introducing the poem by reading Herrick's "To the Virgins . . .," on page 432, to awaken students to the notion of youth as something that quickly passes.

Purpose-Setting Question What evidence do you see that Byron is poking fun at his subject?

1 **Enrichment** *Don Juan* is written in ottava rima, an Italian stanza form of eight iambic pentameter lines with a rhyme scheme of *abababcc*.

2 **Discussion** Explain the aptness of the word *greener* in line 4. What does the color green often symbolize? As a symbol of a stage of life, what would its opposite color be?

3 **Literary Focus** Note the simile in line 13. What is being compared to what?

4 Enrichment Stanzas three and four represent Byron's version of Wordsworth's famous "Ode: Intimations of Immortality. . . ." In lines 22–23 what does the poet tell us has replaced frivolous emotions?

5 Discussion How did the poet manage to lose his ambition?

6 Discussion According to the poet, what is the end of fame? Do you agree with his view?

7 Thematic Idea Compare the allusion to Cheops with Shelley's poem "Ozymandias," on page 702.

Once all in all, but now a thing apart,
20   Thou canst not be my blessing or my curse:
The illusion's gone forever, and thou art
       Insensible, I trust, but none the worse,
And in thy stead I've got a deal of judgment,
Though heaven knows how it ever found a lodgment.

25   My days of love are over; me no more
       The charms of maid, wife, and still less of widow
Can make the fool of which they made before—
       In short, I must not lead the life I did do;
The credulous hope of mutual minds is o'er,
30   The copious use of claret is forbid too,
So for a good old-gentlemanly vice,
I think I must take up with avarice.

Ambition was my idol, which was broken
       Before the shrines of Sorrow and of Pleasure;
35   And the two last have left me many a token
       O'er which reflection may be made at leisure:
Now, like Friar Bacon's brazen head, I've spoken,
       "Time is, Time was, Time's past,"[2] a chymic[3] treasure
Is glittering youth, which I have spent betimes—
40   My heart in passion, and my head on rhymes.

What is the end of fame? 'tis but to fill
       A certain portion of uncertain paper:
Some liken it to climbing up a hill,
       Whose summit, like all hills, is lost in vapor;
45   For this men write, speak, preach, and heroes kill,
       And bards burn what they call their "midnight taper,"
To have, when the original is dust,
A name, a wretched picture, and worse bust.

What are the hopes of man? Old Egypt's King
50   Cheops erected the first pyramid
And largest, thinking it was just the thing
       To keep his memory whole, and mummy hid:
But somebody or other rummaging
       Burglariously broke his coffin's lid:
55   Let not a monument give you or me hopes,
Since not a pinch of dust remains of Cheops.

---

2. Friar Bacon . . . Time's past": In Robert Greene's comedy *Friar Bacon and Friar Burgandy* (1594), these words are spoken by a bronze bust, made by Friar Bacon.
3. chymic (kim' ik): Alchemic; counterfeit.

Primary Source

Literary scholar Helen Gardner concluded her essay, "Don Juan," with the following thoughts about Byron's relevance to readers today:

> Although Byron's vision of man and the world is not very flattering to our self-esteem, or very comforting to our hopes, it is not discouraging. Man may not be a very noble animal, but he has his moments of glory, and life provides pleasures and satisfactions of many kinds. Although most men are fools, by no means all are knaves. The human race has even produced a few heroes, and common men are capable of loyalty and kindness. "Chequered as is seen our human lot," it is still better to be alive than dead, better to be young than old, better to be generous than cautious, and better to be compassionate than censorious. For all its bursts of cynicism, savagery, and melancholy, there is a fundamental good humor in *Don Juan* which becomes the dominant tone when Byron finally gets his hero to England. Byron should be congenial reading today. There are many and obvious affinities between his age and ours, both exhausted by a great revolution and its aftermath of war;

But I, being fond of true philosophy,
  Say very often to myself, "Alas!
All things that have been born were born to die,
60 And flesh (which Death mows down to hay) is grass;
You've passed your youth not so unpleasantly,
  And if you had it o'er again—'twould pass—
So thank your stars that matters are no worse,
And read your Bible, sir, and mind your purse."

65 But for the present, gentle reader! and
  Still gentler purchaser! the bard—that's I—
Must, with permission, shake you by the hand,
  And so your humble servant, and good-bye!
We meet again, if we should understand
70 Each other; and if not, I shall not try
Your patience further than by this short sample—
'Twere well if others followed my example.

"Go, little book, from this my solitude!
  I cast thee on the waters—go thy ways!
75 And if, as I believe, thy vein be good,
  The world will find thee after many days."[4]
When Southey's read, and Wordsworth understood,
  I can't help putting in my claim to praise—
The four first rhymes are Southey's, every line:
80 For God's sake, reader! take them not for mine!

---

4. "Go . . . days": The lines are from the last stanza of Robert
Southey's (1774–1843) *Epilogue to the Lay of the Laureate.*

THINKING ABOUT THE SELECTION
Recalling

1. What causes the speaker to think of a peruke, or wig?
2. (a) What, according to lines 17 and 18 does the speaker say has been his "sole world" and "universe" up until now? (b) According to the fourth stanza, with what "old-gentlemanly vice" will he replace it?

Interpreting

3. In the fifth stanza, the speaker notes that "glittering youth" is a "chymic," or counterfeit, "treasure." In what way do you think he means this?
In what way do you think he means this?

4. Summarize in your own words the point the speaker is making in his mention of Cheops.

Applying

5. What do you think is meant by the remark "flesh . . . is grass" in line 60?

THINKING AND WRITING
Writing About the Byronic Hero

Byron saw himself as melancholy, sensitive, rebellious, fearless, moody, and adventurous. These traits, characterize the "Byronic hero." Choose a fictional character that comes close to fitting this description. In an essay, explain in what ways this character is, and is not, a Byronic hero. When you revise be sure you have supported your main idea.

from *Don Juan* 699

and no writer has been more heartily and consistently "against the Establishment." But although Byron can be bitter and astringent he is not sour. His skepticism and irreverence are echoed today; but not his high spirits, and his zest for life. It is rather doubtful if we rise from reading *Don Juan* as wiser men. Wisdom of the highest kind Byron did not attain to, and this prevents him from ranking with the greatest poets. But if we are not wiser we are certainly not sadder from reading *Don Juan,* and there is something for us to learn from the courage and buoyancy with which Byron came to terms with a world as shabby and confused as ours.

8 Discussion Describe the tone in this stanza.

Reader's Response Why do you think that many young people feel, as the speaker felt, "my soul invincible"?(1.8)

Closure and Extension

ANSWERS TO THINKING ABOUT THE SELECTION
Recalling

1. Growing older makes the speaker think of growing bald, and so the need for a wig.
2. (a) His heart—his passion—has been his whole world—his universe. (b) He will take up avarice.

Interpreting

3. Answers will differ but might include the idea that youth is full of dreams and misdirected ambitions or that it quickly passes.
4. Answers will differ but should include the idea that nothing man builds does or hopes for remains long after he has died.

Applying

5. Flesh, like grass, will be cut down in death.

Thinking and Writing

For help with this assignment, students can refer to Lesson 9, "Writing About Character," in the Handbook of Writing About Literature.

700

PERCY BYSSHE SHELLEY

1792–1822

When he died in a boating accident at age thirty, Percy Bysshe Shelley was eulogized by his friend Byron as "without exception the best and least selfish man I ever knew." This seems strange praise indeed, considering it was directed at a man whose disenchantment with the world was at least as great as his appreciation of its beauties. At once modest and intense, Shelley was a poet of rare gift. He was also a self-appointed reformer who believed that humankind was capable of attaining a more perfect society.

Shelley was born in Sussex and raised on a fine country estate where he spent a quiet childhood. He was sent to excellent schools—first Eton, a prestigious boarding school, and later Oxford —but was never able to settle into the routine of a student. Instead he preferred to wander over the countryside or perform private scientific experiments. At Oxford Shelley became friends with a young man named Thomas Jefferson Hogg, whose political views were as strong as his own. The friendship further fueled Shelley's rebellious nature, and when with Hogg's support he wrote a pamphlet titled *The Necessity of Atheism;* both were expelled.

The incident led to trouble between Shelley and his father, and instead of going home Shelley headed for London. There he met sixteen-year-old Harriet Westbrook, who played on his sympathy for the underdog by describing her miserable situation at home and at school. The two married and went to Ireland, where Shelley tried unsuccessfully to "deliver the Irish people from tyranny."

In 1813 he completed his first important poem, "Queen Mab," a philosophical work that explored some of the ideas he had read about in Godwin's *Political Justice.* The view that Shelley put forth—that government and institutions should be reshaped to better conform to the will of the people—was evident in much of his poetry, even in his nature poems.

Shelley's marriage, meanwhile, was in trouble. Harriet felt she could not keep up with her husband, whose political ideals, in any case, she had come to question. Shelley was unhappy too, and after divorcing Harriet in 1814 he married Mary Wollstonecraft Godwin.

Shelley spent the last four years of his life in Italy, where he became close friends with Byron. Here Shelley wrote some of his best poetry, including "Ode to the West Wind" and *Prometheus Unbound,* the second of these a long poem predicting that someday humanity would be free of tyranny.

Shelley has been called the perfect poet of the Romantic era. One need only consider his emotional response to life and his belief in personal freedom to appreciate how fitting that title is.

Ozymandias; Ode to the West Wind; To a Skylark; To—; A Dirge

Literary Forms

The Ode. Poetic structure is the framework or blueprint on which a poem is built. The structure takes into account the number of stanzas, the rhyme scheme, and the rhythmic patterns to be used.

An *ode* is a lyrical poem that pays homage to a person, a quality, or a thing. The first odes were written in Classical times by the Greek poet Pindar (552?–443? B.C.) and the Latin poet Horace (65–8 B.C.) The Pindaric ode, which is the more often imitated of the two types, consists mainly of three-line stanzas called *triads*. Shelley's "Ode to the West Wind" is a Pindaric ode.

Writing

Think of several individuals, objects, and qualities which you hold in high regard. To get yourself started, you might think of people who do important work in your community, and who have such character traits as honesty and reliability. Write each at the top of a sheet of paper and under it jot down some of your thoughts.

Commentary

The following story is told about Shelley's death. Notice how it illuminates the men. On July 8, 1822, Shelley and Edward Williams boarded their small boat to return to their summer home on the Gulf of Spezia, but their friend E. J. Trelawny was denied port clearance. As he stood sullenly on the dock watching his friends sail off, a sailor pointed to the water and said, "Look at the smoke on the water; the devil is brewing mischief." Oppressed by the heat, Trelawny dozed off. When he awoke around dinner time, a fierce storm had blown in. Although Trelawny anxiously scanned every dot on the horizon, he could see no sign of Shelley's small boat. Three days passed in terrible anxiety as he spoke with the crews of all returning boats.

On the morning of the third day, Trelawny rode to Pisa where he summoned Byron and dispatched a number of searchers. A water-keg and some bottles from Shelley's boat had washed up on the sand. Over a week later the two bodies were found on the shore. Although the bodies were badly mutilated, Trelawny recognized his friend by the volume of Sophocles in one pocket and a copy of Keats's poems in the other. In a similar fashion he identified Williams's body. Shortly thereafter he arranged to have both bodies cremated. Despite the fierce blaze, the poet's heart did not burn. Trelawny snatched it out of the fire, badly burning his hand. He gave the relic to Mary Shelley. He took the remains to a Protestant cemetery near Rome, where they were buried. When he died in 1881, his ashes were buried in a tomb beside that of his friend.

Guide for Interpreting 701

Writing/Prior Knowledge Have students bring to class articles about people who have made admirable achievements. Make a list of those people on the chalkboard, and have students who brought in the articles write their achievements under the names on the board. Students may then proceed to make their own lists.

Enrichment Give students ten minutes to study the vocabulary words as you write the words on the chalkboard. Give a quiz in which you supply the definition and students choose the word being defined from among the words on the board. Your **less advanced** students may need help with these additional words: *colossal* (page 702), *azure* (page 704), and *unpremeditated* (page 708).

Literary Focus Originally, an ode was a poem meant to be sung. However, in English poetry an ode is a lyric poem with two primary characteristics: a dignified theme and a formal, elevated style.

Vocabulary

Preteach the following vocabulary words:

visage (viz′ij) *n.*: A person's face or facial expression (p. 702, l.4)

pestilence (pes′t'l əns) *n.*: Highly contagious disease, such as plague (p. 704, l.5)

verge (vʉrj) *n.*: Edge, rim (p. 705, l.21)

sepulcher (sep′'l kər) *n.*: Tomb (p. 705, l.25)

cleave (klēv) *v.*: Split apart, especially in two (p. 706, l.38)

despoil (di spoil′) *v.*: Take away one's possessions (p. 706, l.42)

tumult (too′ mult) *n.*: Commotion, disturbance (p. 706, l.59)

impetuous (im pech′ oo wəs) *adj.*: Tending to act impulsively, without thinking (p. 707, l.62)

blithe (blīth) *adj.*: Cheerful (p. 708, l.1)

profuse (prə fyoos′) *adj.*: Abundant, pouring out (p.708, l.5)

vaunt (vônt) *v.*: Speak boastfully (p. 710, l.69)

languor (laŋ′ gər) *n.*: Weakness, fatigue (p. 710, l.77)

satiety (sə tī′ ə tē) *n.*: State of being filled to excess (p. 710, l.80)

dirge (dʉrj) *n.*: Song of mourning (p. 713, title)

Motivation/Prior Knowledge
Ask students to review the term *irony,* a contrast between an expected outcome and the actual outcome or between appearance and reality. Then ask if they think the term applies to Shelley's life. For example, Shelley died unexpectedly at a very young age, before his work received recognition. Ask if they can think of any examples of irony in their own lives. Tell them that irony is an important device in the poem "Ozymandias."

Master Teacher Note In conjunction with this poem you may want to teach the poem "Ozymandias Revisited," a parody by Morris Bishop.

Purpose-Setting Question What generalization about grand human achievements might a reader draw from this poem?

1 **Enrichment** Ozymandias was a pharoah who ruled Egypt during the thirteenth century B.C. He was known for his extensive building programs and as the pharoah who oppressed the Israelites. He was responsible for the largest statue in Egypt, on which were carved the words: "I am Ozymandias, king of kings; if anyone wishes to know what I am and where I lie, let him surpass me in some of my exploits."

Speaking and Listening Remind students that poetry is meant to be read aloud. Choose a volunteer to read "Ozymandias" aloud to the class.

Ozymandias[1]

Percy Bysshe Shelley

I met a traveler from an antique land
Who said: Two vast and trunkless legs of stone
Stand in the desert. Near them, on the sand,
Half sunk, a shattered visage lies, whose frown,
5   And wrinkled lip, and sneer of cold command,
Tell that its sculptor well those passions read
Which yet survive, stamped on these lifeless things,
The hand that mocked them and the heart that fed:
And on the pedestal these words appear:
10   "My name is Ozymandias, king of kings:
Look on my works, ye Mighty, and despair!"
Nothing beside remains. Round the decay
Of that colossal wreck, boundless and bare,
The lone and level sands stretch far away.

---

1. Ozymandias (ŏz ĭ măn′ dē əs): The Greek name for Ramses. Ramses II, the king referred to in the poem, was a pharoah who ruled Egypt during the thirteenth century B.C. and built many great palaces and statues. One statue was inscribed with the words: "I am Ozymandias, king of kings, if anyone wishes to know what I am and where I lie, let him surpass me in some of my exploits."

THINKING ABOUT THE SELECTION
Recalling

1. (a) Whom has the speaker met? (b) What sight does this person describe?

Interpreting

2. What sort of person is suggested by the visage that is described?
3. Think of the words on the pedestal. (a) Why is it ironic that the statue has crumbled? (b) Why is it ironic that it is surrounded by desert?
4. What is the theme of this poem?

Applying

5. (a) What is your definition of power? (b) What is your definition of pride? (c) In what way do the two complement each other?

ANALYZING LITERATURE
Understanding Poetic Structure

The poetic structure of a poem is the plan on which it is built. Poetic structure includes such elements as rhyme, rhythm, and number of stanzas. Analyze the poetic structure of "Ozymandias." State whether or not you feel this structure enhances the poem's message. When you revise make sure you have provided adequate support for your main idea.

Closure and Extension

ANSWERS TO THINKING ABOUT THE SELECTION
Recalling

1. (a) The speaker met a traveler from an antique (ancient) land. (b) In the desert are the crumbling remains of a statue of the Egyptian pharaoh Ozymandias.

Interpreting

2. The person suggested is cold, cruel, and conceited.
3. (a) It is ironic that the statue of a ruler who claimed great works is now surrounded by emptiness. (b) This is another irony; the crumbling statue mocks the pride of the once great ruler.
4. Answers will differ. Suggestions include "How the mighty have fallen," Don't get too big for your britches," and "A man's pride shall bring him low."

THE COLOSSI OF MEMNON

Humanities Note

The Colossi of Memnon at Thebes, Egypt. Thebes, on the west bank of the Nile River, served as a capital for many Egyptian kings during a period of power and prosperity. During this period, royal tombs reached unequaled material splendor, and figures such as the colossus (huge statue) pictured in this photograph represented the power and divine kingship of Pharaohs.

   Consider using these questions for discussion:
1. What characteristics of this statue indicate power and authority?
2. How might a statue such as this have inspired Shelley to wriite "Ozymandias?"

Applying

5. Answers will differ. Suggested responses: (a) Power is authority. (b) Pride is a sense of one's self respect. (c) Power and pride in proper proportions can balance each other.

ANSWERS TO ANALYZING LITERATURE

"Ozymandias" is a sonnet. Its fourteen lines, written in iambic pentameter, are divided into two parts in which the first eight lines, the octave, describe the statue of Ozymandias, and the last six lines, the sestet, bring out the irony implicit in the wreckage. It was appropriate for Shelley to choose this traditional structure, since it helps to emphasize his message—the first part of the poem strikes the reader with the image of the ruined statue, while the second part reinforces the irony of the statue's condition.

The sonnet format presents a challenge to a poet. Shelley more than met the challenge by incorporating an unconventional—and difficult—rhyme scheme. Perhaps he wanted to show that he could in fact surpass Ozymandias in his exploits by creating a great work of art that, unlike the statue, would last forever.

Challenge Tell why you think that this poem should or should not be considered a Romantic poem.

Ode to the West Wind

Percy Bysshe Shelley

Shelley composed this poem in the woods near Florence, Italy. He described the day of its composition as one "when that tempestuous wind, whose temperature is at once mild and animating, was collecting the vapors which pour down the autumnal rains."

I

O wild West Wind, thou breath of Autumn's being,
Thou, from whose unseen presence the leaves dead
Are driven, like ghosts from an enchanter fleeing,

Yellow, and black, and pale, and hectic red,
5   Pestilence-stricken multitudes: O thou,
Who chariotest to their dark and wintry bed

The wingèd seeds, where they lie cold and low,
Each like a corpse within its grave, until
Thine azure sister of the Spring[1] shall blow

10   Her clarion[2] o'er the dreaming earth, and fill
(Driving sweet buds like flocks to feed in air)
With loving hues and odors plain and hill:

Wild Spirit, which art moving everywhere;
Destroyer and preserver; hear, oh, hear!

II

15   Thou on whose stream, 'mid the steep sky's commotion,
Loose clouds like earth's decaying leaves are shed,
Shook from the tangled boughs of Heaven and Ocean,

Angels[3] of rain and lightning: there are spread
On the blue surface of thine aery surge,
20   Like the bright hair uplifted from the head

---

1. sister of Spring: The south wind.
2. clarion: *n.*: A trumpet producing clear, sharp, shrill tones.
3. angels: Messengers.

Of some fierce Maenad,[4] even from the dim verge
Of the horizon to the zenith's height,
The locks of the approaching storm. Thou dirge

Of the dying year, to which this closing night
25   Will be the dome of a vast sepulcher,
Vaulted with all thy congregated might

Of vapors, from whose solid atmosphere
Black rain, and fire, and hail will burst: oh, hear!

III

Thou who didst waken from his summer dreams
30   The blue Mediterranean, where he lay,
Lulled by the coil of his crystalline streams,

---

4. Maenad (mē′ nad): A priestess of Bacchus, the Greek and Roman
god of wine and revelry.

Humanities Note

Fine art, *Cirrus Cloud Study*, 1882, by John Constable. England's John Constable (1776–1937) is one of that country's most notable landscape painters. His paintings differed from those of his contemporaries in their fresh, vibrant use of color and in their close observance of nature. A lover of the outdoors, Constable was ever conscious of the effects of light, weather, and season upon the landscape.

Cirrus Cloud Study was painted in 1822. He felt that as the sky was a large and important part of a landscape painting, it was very important to paint it realistically and effectively. Studies such as this caught the effects of light, cloud, wind, and sky with consummate mastery.

You might ask the following questions:
1. The wind is an invisible force; we can only see its effect. How has the artist allowed us to "see" the wind in this painting?
2. What do you think are the artist's feelings about the wind?

2 **Discussion** How do the last two sections differ from the first three? What function do they serve?

3 **Discussion** Does the poem end on an optimistic or a pessimistic note? Explain.

Master Teacher Note After students have read and discussed "Ode to the West Wind," you might display Art Transparency 5, *The Storm, Antigonus Pursued by the Bear,* by Joseph Wright, on the overhead projector. Lead the class in a discussion of how the painting emphasizes some of the Romantic concerns. For example, the painting portrays nature as an untamable and inspiring force. What details from the painting contribute to this effect? What other Romantic concerns are conveyed in the painting?

Beside a pumice⁵ aisle in Baiae's bay,⁶
And saw in sleep old palaces and towers
Quivering within the wave's intenser day,

35 All overgrown with azure moss and flowers
So sweet, the sense faints picturing them! Thou
For whose path the Atlantic's level powers

Cleave themselves into chasms, while far below
The sea-blooms and the oozy woods which wear
40 The sapless foliage of the ocean, know

Thy voice, and suddenly grow gray with fear,
And tremble and despoil themselves: oh, hear!

IV

If I were a dead leaf thou mightest bear;
If I were a swift cloud to fly with thee;
45 A wave to pant beneath thy power, and share

The impulse of thy strength, only less free
Than thou, O uncontrollable! If even
I were as in my boyhood, and could be

The comrade of thy wanderings over Heaven,
50 As then, when to outstrip thy skyey speed
Scarce seemed a vision; I would ne'er have striven

As thus with thee in prayer in my sore need.
Oh, lift me as a wave, a leaf, a cloud!
I fall upon the thorns of life! I bleed!

55 A heavy weight of hours has chained and bowed
One too like thee: tameless, and swift, and proud.

V

Make me thy lyre,⁷ even as the forest is:
What if my leaves are falling like its own!
The tumult of thy mighty harmonies

---

5. pumice (pum′ is) *n.*: Volcanic rock.
6. Baiae's (bā′ yēz) **bay:** An ancient Roman resort near Naples.
7. lyre: Aeolian (ē o′ lē ən) lute, or wind harp, a stringed instrument which produces musical sounds when the wind passes over it.

60   Will take from both a deep, autumnal tone,
     Sweet though in sadness. Be thou, Spirit fierce,
     My spirit! Be thou me, impetuous one!

     Drive my dead thought over the universe
     Like withered leaves to quicken a new birth!
65   And, by the incantation of this verse,

     Scatter, as from an extinguished hearth
     Ashes and sparks, my words among mankind!
     Be through my lips to unawakened earth

     The trumpet of a prophecy! O Wind,
70   If Winter comes, can Spring be far behind?

THINKING ABOUT THE SELECTION
Recalling

1. According to the poem, with what season is the west wind associated?
2. (a) What does the wind do to dead leaves? (b) What does it do to the ocean?
3. What does the speaker ask of the wind in section V of the poem?

Interpreting

4. In what sense is the wind a "destroyer and preserver"?
5. (a) How, according to section IV, has the speaker changed? (b) What caused this change?
6. Whose "new birth" (line 65) do you think the speaker wishes to bring about?
7. (a) Interpret the last line of this poem. (b) How does this famous last line tie the poem together?

Applying

8. In what way is the message in this poem related to Shelley's lifelong mission?

ANALYZING LITERATURE
Understanding the Ode

An ode is a poem that honors an individual, a thing, or a trait. The form dates back to classical times, when it was written to be sung at a festival or as part of a play. Many features of the classical ode are to be found in "Ode to the West Wind." Find evidence in Shelley's poem of each of the following properties.
1. Direct form of address to the individual, trait, or thing being honored
2. An almost fearful reverence for the thing or person being honored
3. Dignified and lofty language and examples

Ode to the West Wind   707

6. The speaker is seeking a new age of freedom for all people.
7. Suggested Response: (a) The west wind brings winter, or death, but after winter spring brings new life. (b) It sums up metaphorically the poem's theme of hope for a new beginning.

Applying

8. Suggested Response: Shelley was against any kind of tyranny; he believed strongly in personal freedom for all people. In this poem Shelley proclaims his faith that there can be a society free from oppression and unjust authority.

Challenge In his essay "A Defense of Poetry," Shelley wrote that "poets are the unacknowledged legislators of the world." How does "Ode to the West Wind" help to explain what Shelley meant?

ANSWERS TO ANALYZING LITERATURE

1. Answers will differ. Suggested Response: Shelley addresses the wind directly in the opening line of the poem: "O wild West Wind. . . ."
2. Answers will differ. Suggested Response: Shelley calls the wind "O uncontrollable!"
3. Suggested Response: Shelley compares "the locks" of an approaching storm carried on the wind to the "bright hair uplifted from the head/Of some fierce Maenad."

Closure and Extension

ANSWERS TO THINKING ABOUT THE SELECTION
Recalling

1. The west wind is associated with autumn.
2. (a) The wind drives the dead leaves. (b) It forms waves on the ocean.

3. The speaker asks the wind to scatter his thoughts and words among mankind.

Interpreting

4. The west wind brings winter, which destroys plant life. But it also preserves seeds which come to life in the spring.
5. (a) In section IV the speaker loses some of his awe of the wind and wishes to share its power and freedom. (b) The speaker has experienced the thorns, or pains, of life.

Motivation/Prior Knowledge
Discuss with students what freedom means to them. Ask students to come up with their own symbol for freedom.

Purpose-Setting Question As you read the poem, compare its form with that of "Ode to the West Wind." Consider how the form enhances the poem's message.

Thematic Idea: Compare and contrast the "Ode to the West Wind" (page 704) and "To a Skylark" for what they imply about the individual in relation to society.

1 **Discussion** Why does the speaker say the skylark is not a bird? As you read on, look for an answer to this question.

To a Skylark

Percy Bysshe Shelley

1
    Hail to thee, blithe spirit!
      Bird thou never wert,
    That from heaven, or near it,
      Pourest thy full heart
5 In profuse strains of unpremeditated art.

    Higher still and higher,
      From the earth thou springest
    Like a cloud of fire;
      The blue deep thou wingest,
10 And singing still dost soar, and soaring ever singest.

    In the golden lightning
      Of the sunken sun,
    O'er which clouds are brightening,
      Thou dost float and run;
15 Like an unbodied joy whose race is just begun.

    The pale purple even[1]
      Melts around thy flight;
    Like a star of heaven,
      In the broad daylight
20 Thou art unseen, but yet I hear thy shrill delight,

    Keen as are the arrows
      Of that silver sphere,[2]
    Whose intense lamp narrows
      In the white dawn clear,
25 Until we hardly see—we feel that it is there.

    All the earth and air
      With thy voice is loud,
    As, when night is bare,
      From one lonely cloud
30 The moon rains out her beams, and Heaven is overflowed.

---

1. even: Evening.
2. silver sphere: The morning star.

Primary Source

In his *Recollections of the Last Days of Shelly and Byron* (1858) Edward John Trelawny wrote about the two poets when they were in Italy. The following is his description of Shelley:

> Shelley came of a long-lived race, and, barring accidents, there was no reason why he should not have emulated his forefathers in attaining a ripe age. . . . He was tall, slim, and bent from eternally poring over his books; this habit had contracted his chest. His limbs were well proportioned, strong and bony—his head was very small—and his features were expressive of great sensibility, and decidedly feminine. There was nothing about him outwardly to attract notice, except his extraordinarily juvenile appearance. At twenty-nine, he still retained on his tanned and freckled cheeks, the fresh look of a boy—although his long wild locks were coming into blossom, as a polite hairdresser once said to me, whilst cutting mine.
>
> It was not until he spoke that you could discern anything uncommon in him—but the first sentence he uttered, when excited by his subject, riveted your attention. The light from his very soul streamed from his eyes, and every mental emotion of which the human mind is suscepti-

CLOUD STUDY, 1821
John Constable
Yale Center for British Art

What thou art we know not;
　　What is most like thee?
From rainbow clouds there flow not
　　Drops so bright to see,
35　As from thy presence showers a rain of melody.

Like a poet hidden
　　In the light of thought,
Singing hymns unbidden,
　　Till the world is wrought
40　To sympathy with hopes and fears it heeded not:

Like a highborn maiden
　　In a palace tower,
Soothing her love-laden
　　Soul in secret hour
45　With music sweet as love, which overflows her bower:

Like a glowworm golden
　　In a dell of dew,
Scattering unbeholden
　　Its aerial hue
50　Among the flowers and grass, which screen it from the
　　view!

2

To a Skylark 709

Humanities Note

Fine art, *Cloud Study*, 1821, by John Constable. John Constable (1776–1837) is one of Britain's most noteworthy landscape painters. Educated at the Royal Academy, Constable disagreed with some of the artificial academic techniques of painting and sought to paint landscapes with truth and originality. His works were painted outdoors instead of in a studio, and he used bright colors that were closer to nature. He painted the landscape in all lights and seasons, paying close attention to changes brought about by weather conditions.

Cloud Study, a study of stratocumulus cloud formations, was painted in 1821. It is one of a group of small oil sketches that Constable did in order to study the effects of weather, time of day, and time of year on the sky. He carefully noted the weather conditions, time, and date on each study. This intense preparation, which resulted in the painting of this lovely patch of sky, is one of the many reasons John Constable was able to paint such successful landscapes.

You may wish to ask the following questions.
1. Which lines from Shelley's poem do you feel this painting illustrates best?
2. How does the poet's appreciation of nature differ from the painter's?

2 Discussion What is the central element of each simile in these stanzas?

ble, was expressed in his pliant and ever-changing features. He left the conviction on the minds of his audience, that however great he was as a Poet, he was greater as an orator. There was another and most rare peculiarity in Shelley,—his intellectual faculties completely mastered his material nature, and hence he unhesitatingly acted up to his own theories, if they only demanded sacrifices on his part,—it was where they implicated others that he forbore. Mrs. Shelley has observed, "Many have suggested and advocated far greater innovations in our political and social system than Shelley; but he alone practised those he approved of as just."

Like a rose embowered
　　In its own green leaves,
By warm winds deflowered,[3]
　　Till the scent it gives
55　Makes faint with too much sweet those heavy-wingèd
　　　thieves.[4]

Sound of vernal showers
　　On the twinkling grass,
Rain-awakened flowers,
　　All that ever was
60　Joyous, and clear, and fresh, thy music doth surpass:

Teach us, sprite or bird,
　　What sweet thoughts are thine:
I have never heard
　　Praise of love or wine
65　That panted forth a flood of rapture so divine.

Chorus Hymeneal,[5]
　　Or triumphal chant,
Matched with thine would be all
　　But an empty vaunt,
70　A thing wherein we feel there is some hidden want.

What objects are the fountains[6]
　　Of thy happy strain?
What fields, or waves, or mountains?
　　What shapes of sky or plain?
75　What love of thine own kind? what ignorance of pain?

With thy clear keen joyance
　　Languor cannot be;
Shadow of annoyance
　　Never came near thee:
80　Thou lovest—but ne'er knew love's sad satiety.

Waking or asleep,
　　Thou of death must deem[7]
Things more true and deep
　　Than we mortals dream,
85　Or how could thy notes flow in such a crystal stream?

---

3. deflowered: Fully open.
4. thieves: The "warm winds."
5. Chorus Hymeneal (hī′ mə nē′ əl): Marriage song, named after
Hymen, the Greek god of marriage.
6. fountains: Sources, inspiration.
7. deem: Know.

We look before and after,
   And pine for what is not;
Our sincerest laughter
   With some pain is fraught;
90 Our sweetest songs are those that tell of saddest thought.

Yet if[8] we could scorn
   Hate, and pride, and fear;
If we were things born
   Not to shed a tear,
95 I know not how thy joy we ever should come near.

Better than all measures
   Of delightful sound,
Better than all treasures
   That in books are found,
100 Thy skill to poet were,[9] thou scorner of the ground!

Teach me half the gladness
   That thy brain must know,
Such harmonious madness
   From my lips would flow,
105 The world should listen then, as I am listening now.

3

---

8. **if:** Even if.
9. **were:** Would be.

THINKING ABOUT THE SELECTION
Recalling

1. At what time of day does the "blithe spirit" fly?
2. (a) To what four things does the speaker compare the bird in lines 36–55? (b) In what ways does he say the bird is like these things?

Interpreting

3. Why does the poet say of the bird, "Bird thou never wert"?
4. What do you suppose the speaker means in line 80 by "love's sad satiety"?
5. (a) How is the poet's song different from the

bird's song? (b) Why can the bird's song "flow in such a crystal stream"?
6. (a) What does the speaker ask the skylark to teach him? (b) What effect does he think this would have on the world? (c) Why does he feel this way?

Applying

7. The twentieth-century poet W. H. Auden wrote, "A verbal art like poetry is reflective; it stops to think. Music is immediate; it goes on to become." Discuss the meaning of this quotation.

To a Skylark   711

Discussion Even if the conditions suggested in this stanza were met, why couldn't man hope to experience the joy of the skylark?

Reader's Response Do you agree with Shelley that "Our sincerest laughter With some pain is fraught; Our sweetest songs are those that tell of saddest thought."? Why or why not?

Closure and Extension

ANSWERS TO THINKING ABOUT THE SELECTION
Recalling

1. The "blithe spirit" flies at sundown.
2. (a) The speaker compares the bird to a poet, a high-born maiden, a glowworm, and a rose. (b) Like these things, the bird is artless; it performs for itself alone.

Interpreting

3. The bird's song is full of joy; it has not experienced the pains of life that mortals must endure.
4. Loving too much can bring sadness.
5. (a) The bird's song is for itself alone while the poet's song is intended to be delivered to an audience. (b) The bird's song flows "in such a crystal stream" because its source is pure.

6. (a) The speaker asks the bird to teach him how to enjoy life. (b) The world would learn how to live in harmony. (c) The bird's song is so full of gladness that he is sure the world would listen, just as he has.

Applying

7. Answers will differ. Students might suggest that the appreciation of poetry takes time, while the melodies of music provide immediate gratification.

711

Motivation/Prior Knowledge
Discuss why memories are so important to us.

Purpose-Setting Question How do the simple rhyme scheme and short lines add to the poem's effectiveness?

1 Discussion What three images are mentioned in the first six lines of the poem?

2 Discussion How is the fourth image like the first three?

Reader's Response Do you think that this is an appropriate and effective description of the thoughts of love? Why or why not?

Closure and Extension

ANSWERS TO THINKING ABOUT THE SELECTION
Recalling

1. Thoughts of his love will remain in his memory.

Interpreting

2. Music, odors, and roses all have lingering qualities that live on in memory.
3. Love never dies.

Applying

4. Answers will differ. Suggested Response: Like the music, odors, and roses in the poem, poetry with its sensory language and rhythmic sound, has qualities that linger in memory. Some of these qualities are lost in prose.

ANSWERS TO CRITICAL THINKING AND READING

Answers will differ depending on the poem chosen, but students should mention the rhythmic pattern of the sentences, arrangement of words, and sentence and line length. All points should be supported with examples from Shelley's poems.

To———

Percy Bysshe Shelley

1
Music, when soft voices die,
Vibrates in the memory—
Odors, when sweet violets sicken,
Live within the sense they quicken.

5 Rose leaves, when the rose is dead,
Are heaped for the belovèd's bed;
2 And so thy thoughts,[1] when thou art gone,
Love itself shall slumber on.

---

1. thy thoughts: Thoughts of thee.

THINKING ABOUT THE SELECTION
Recalling

1. What does the speaker of the poem say will happen to "thy thoughts, when thou art gone"?

Interpreting

2. Explain how music, odors, and roses will live on.
3. What idea about love is the speaker communicating?

Applying

4. How differently would this idea come across if it were presented in simple prose rather than as a poem? Explain.

CRITICAL THINKING AND READING
Recognizing an Author's Style

Style is the way an author chooses and arranges words to express ideas. Just as no two

personalities are identical, no two writing styles are identical. Sentence length, variation in sentence patterns, and word usage are among the features that define a writer's style. Carefully reread "To———" and any other poem of your choice by Shelley, noting stylistic similarities in the areas mentioned above. Briefly describe this style, and tell whether or not you like it, and why. When you revise make sure you have included details from the poems to support your thesis.

THINKING AND WRITING
Writing an Ode

Select one of the objects about which you jotted down some thoughts before you read these poems by Shelley. Examine the observations you made regarding that person, thing, or trait, and decide whether you want to change, add, or remove any of these observations. Then write an ode to that person, quality, or thing. When you revise make sure you have created a vivid description.

712   The Romantic Age

THINKING AND WRITING

For help with this assignment, students can refer to Lesson 18, "Writing a Poem," in the Handbook of Writing About Literature.

A Dirge

Percy Bysshe Shelley

Rough wind, that moanest loud
    Grief too sad for song;
Wild wind, when sullen cloud
    Knells all the night long;
5   Sad storm, whose tears are vain,
Bare woods, whose branches strain,
Deep caves and dreary main,—
    Wail, for the world's wrong!

THINKING ABOUT THE SELECTION
Recalling

1. What does the speaker of the poem ask the wind, a storm, and bare branches to do?

Interpreting

2. What do you think the speaker means by "the world's wrong"?

3. What effect is created by calling upon the natural elements to bemoan the world's wrong? How does this device help portray the poet's sense of moral indignation?

Applying

4. If Shelley were living in the contemporary world, what aspects of life might he bemoan?

THINKING AND WRITING
Comparing and Contrasting Nature Views

Select a poem by one of the other Romantic poets you have read so far, and compare that poet's view of nature with Shelley's. Start by jotting down notes about each poem. Use quotes from each of the poems to illustrate similarities and differences. When you revise make sure you have presented your information in a logical order.

A Dirge 713

Presentation

Literary Focus Ask students to list the verbs and adjectives in the poem which determine the poem's mood.

Master Teacher Note This poem, like "Ode to the West Wind" and "To a Skylark" is in the form of an apostrophe to several different natural phenomena.

Purpose-Setting Question What two figures of speech are primary in the poem?

1 Clarification The word *dirge* means "a mournful song, often accompanying a funeral." It can also refer to something, such as a poem, that has the qualities of a dirge.

2 Discussion After reading the poem aloud, ask your students to tell how the sound of the poem, especially the rhymes, matches the description of the natural forces. Why does the poet ask nature to wail?

Closure and Extension

ANSWERS TO THINKING ABOUT THE SELECTION
Recalling

1. The speaker asks them to wail.

Interpreting

2. The speaker sees the world as full of hypocrisy and injustice.
3. The poet sees the natural elements as superior to conditions developed by humans. Therefore, it is appropriate that the natural world take the human world to task for its wrongs.

Applying

4. Answers will differ. Students might mention excessive materialism, war, and the threat of nuclear destruction.

Challenge In this poem Shelley illustrates his belief that nature has compassion for man, or at least can be responsive to his situation. Do you think man has compassion for nature? Why or why not?

JOHN KEATS

1795–1821

Despite his early death and the fact that the most important of his works were composed in the space of two years, John Keats remains one of the major influences on English poetry. Known as a pure artist, Keats saw the appreciation of beauty as an end in itself and made the pursuit of beauty the goal of his poetry. As Keats himself so eloquently put it, "Beauty is truth, truth beauty."

Born in London of working-class parents, Keats was unusually handsome and active as a child. He developed a reputation for fighting, not so much out of rowdiness as from a readiness to take sides in a worthy cause. It was not until he became a close friend of his schoolmaster's son, Charles Cowden Clarke, that Keats developed an interest in poetry and became an avid reader.

In 1815 Keats began the study of medicine at a London hospital. By this time he had already begun writing poetry, and though his studies earned him a pharmacist's license, he ultimately abandoned medicine for a career as a poet. His first major effort, *Endymion,* published in the spring of 1818, was severely attacked by the journals of the day. Part of the reason for the harsh criticism was Keats's association with Leigh Hunt, a radical poet, but much of it had to do with the verse itself. Far from being crushed by the assault, Keats began the second of his long poems, *Hyperion,* which was never completed.

The end of the year found Keats mourning the loss of his brother Tom to tuberculosis. It also found the poet deliriously happy over his engagement to Fanny Brawne, a lively 18-year-old who was a light in Keats's life. The following year, 1819, was when Keats turned out his finest work, including "The Eve of St. Agnes," "The Eve of St. Mark," and his famous odes. This might have been only the beginning, but Keats's health took a turn for the worse. He moved to Italy, which promised a warmer climate, but to no avail. After a long battle with tuberculosis, the disease that had claimed his brother, he died at 25.

Though Keats and Shelley knew each other, their visions of what the poet should be could not have been more different. Keats did not share Shelley's rebellious spirit, not did he feel that poetry was the proper vehicle for political statements. Rather Keats sought to refine his idea of beauty, and in so doing, refined ours. His extraordinary sensitivity enabled him to see beauty in the most ordinary of circumstances, while his mastery of verse enabled him to unveil that beauty to the world.

GUIDE FOR INTERPRETING

On First Looking into Chapman's Homer; Bright Star! Would I Were Steadfast as Thou Art; When I Have Fears That I May Cease to Be

Literary Forms

The Sonnet. The sonnet is a poem of fourteen lines arranged according to a specific rhyme scheme, with five strong beats and five weak beats per line. In each of the two basic types of sonnet, Petrarchan and Shakespearean, a portion of the poem is used to present a problem or ask a question, and another portion to resolve it. Despite the demands of its form, the successful sonnet is one that flows smoothly, creates powerful impressions, and delivers an important message without sounding forced. These features are hallmarks of the sonnets written by Keats.

Writing

Think about a book you have read or a film or work of art you have seen that in some way has changed your life. Consider what particular features of the work led to this change. Then freewrite, comparing this experience to other moving experiences people have.

Primary Source

We now know that ill health, aggravated by severe financial and family problems, is the true cause of Keats's premature death. However, for many years his early death was blamed on the effects of two vicious articles in leading literary journals of his day.

Both attacks were anonymous. One article assaulted Keats as a member of fellow-author Leigh Hunt's radical literary circle in London. The other piece ripped into his poem "Endymion." Although Keats himself had the common sense to see that the attacks were brought about by political and social snobbery, many of his contemporaries supported the myth of the cause of his death. One in particular was Lord Byron, who penned the following epitaph:

> John Keats, who was really killed off by one critique
>> Just as he really promised something great,
> If not intelligible, without Greek
>> Contrived to talk about the gods of late
> Much as they might have been supposed to speak.
>> Poor fellow! His was an untoward fate;
>>> 'Tis strange the mind, that very fiery particle,
>>> Should let itself be snuffed out by an article.

Literary Focus Preview the technical aspects of each kind of sonnet with students.

Writing/Prior Knowledge Lead a discussion in which students contribute experiences with media or art that have influenced them. Then have them do the writing activity.

Vocabulary

Preteach the following vocabulary words:

expanse (ik spans') *n.*: Wide, continuous stretch, as of land (p. 716, l.5)

ken (ken) *n.*: Range of sight or knowledge (p. 716, l.10)

surmise (sər mīz') *v.*: Guess, assume (p. 716, l.13)

ablution (ab lōō' shən) *n.*: Washing or cleansing of the body (p. 718, l.6)

gleaned (glēnd) *v.*: Picked from, as crops—in this case thoughts (p. 719, l.2)

teeming (tēm' iŋ) *adj.*: Filled to overflowing (p. 719, l.2)

Motivation/Prior Knowledge
Have students recall a time when
they were awed by some discovery, perhaps quite by accident.
What were their impressions?

Master Teacher Note Students
should hear this poem read aloud
to get the full impact of the masterly blend of rhythm and meaning. Read the poem aloud yourself, or play a recording of it.

Purpose-Setting Question How
apt is the sonnet form for the
meaning the poet wishes to convey?

Literary Focus Note Keats's use
of diction. Point out the archaic
words in the octave—*goodly,
bards, fealty, demesne*—which
suggest the dignified antiquity of
classical poetry and Homer. Compare this archaic diction to the
simple language in the sestet
which suggests the excitement of
the discoveries of a planet and the
Pacific.

1 **Discussion** Are the travels Keats
talks about in the octave real or
imaginary? What are the "realms
of gold" in line 1? What does
Homer's demesne contain?

2 **Discussion** What two similes
does Keats use to compare the
sense of excitement at reading
Chapman for the first time? How
apt are these similes? Does the
fact that Balboa, not Cortez, discovered the Pacific weaken the
poem? Why or why not?

Reader's Response Have you
ever had an experience similar to
that described in this poem? Explain.

On First Looking into Chapman's Homer

John Keats

*When Keats was twenty-one, his former teacher,
Charles Cowden Clarke, introduced him to a translation of
Homer by Elizabethan poet George Chapman. The two men
spent the evening reading this book, and early the next
morning Keats presented this sonnet to Clarke.*

Much have I traveled in the realms of gold,
   And many goodly states and kingdoms seen;
   Round many western islands have I been
Which bards in fealty to Apollo[1] hold.
5 Oft of one wide expanse had I been told
   That deep-browed Homer ruled as his demesne;[2]
   Yet did I never breathe its pure serene[3]
Till I heard Chapman speak out loud and bold:
Then felt I like some watcher of the skies
10   When a new planet swims into his ken;
Or like stout Cortez[4] when with eagle eyes
   He stared at the Pacific—and all his men
Looked at each other with a wild surmise—
   Silent, upon a peak in Darien.[5]

---

1. Apollo: In Greek and Roman mythology, the god of music, poetry,
and medicine.
2. demesne (di mān'): Realm.
3. serene: Clear air.
4. Cortez: Here, Keats was mistaken. The Pacific was discovered in
1513 by Balboa, not Cortez.
5. Darien (der' ē ən): The Isthmus of Panama.

716   *The Romantic Age*

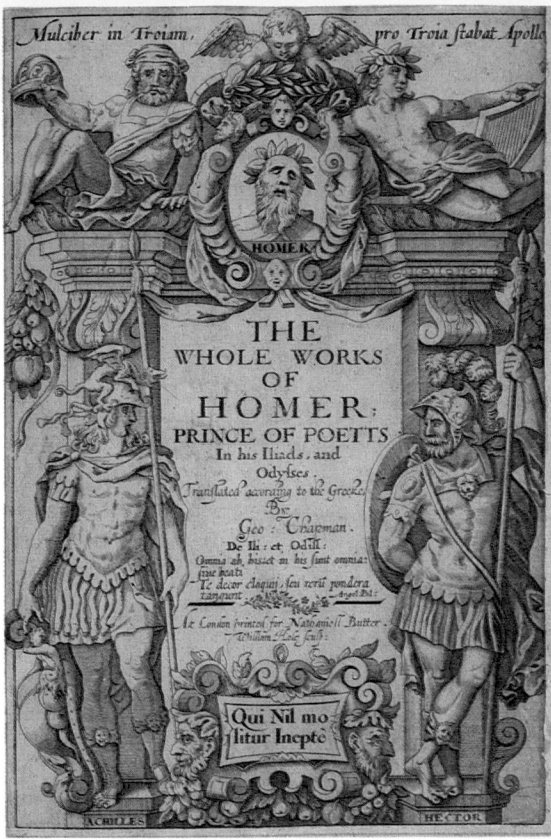

FRONTISPIECE, HOMER'S ILIAD AND ODYSSEY, 1612
William Hole
The British Library

Fine art, Engraving, Frontispiece by William Hole. The frontispiece to the 1612 edition of George Chapman's *The Whole Works of Homer, Prince of Poetts* (sic) was designed and engraved by William Hole (or Holle, fl. 1600–1630). William Hole, one of the earliest English engravers, is noteworthy for his engravings of sheet music, authors' portraits, and title pages for volumes of works by Gibbons, Coryat, and Chapman, among others.

The architectural frame surrounding the title reflects the classic style of the famous architect of the day, Inigo Jones. The two columns are protected by Hector and Achilles, figures from Greek mythology. A portrait medallion of Homer wreathed in laurel, the leaves used by the ancients to crown heros and honored ones, surmounts the whole. This engraving is a flowery presentation that shows the beginnings of the baroque style.

You may wish to discuss the following with your students:

1. From the design of this engraving what would you predict about the content of the book?
2. Keats felt Homer to come alive for him after reading this translation by George Chapman. Do you feel that the artist of this engraving also felt that way about the work of Chapman? Explain.

THINKING ABOUT THE SELECTION

Recalling

1. What does the speaker of the poem claim he missed before reading Chapman?

Interpreting

2. (a) What transportation did the speaker use in his "travels"? (b) To what does he compare his new-found wonderment?
3. Dante Gabriel Rossetti, a poet of the nineteenth century, wrote that "A Sonnet is a coin: its face reveals/The soul—it converse, to what Power tis due." (a) How would you describe Keats's "soul," as it is revealed in "On First Looking into Chapman's Homer"? (b) What is the "power" to which that soul owes its due?

Applying

4. Do you think books can change people's lives? Explain your answer.

Closure and Extension

ANSWERS TO THINKING ABOUT THE SELECTION

Recalling

1. The speaker missed the true import, as well as the beauty and majesty, of Homer's works.

Interpreting

2. (a) The speaker has traveled figuratively—through books. (b) He compares his new-found wonderment to that of an astronomer discovering a star and an explorer discovering the Pacific.
3. Suggested Responses: (a) Keats's soul is open to new ideas and impressions and is capable of awestruck appreciation. (b) That "power" might be ideas found in books.

Applying

4. Answers will differ but should include the idea that one should always be open to new ideas and new interpretations, and these can be found in books.

Bright Star, Would I Were Steadfast as Thou Art

John Keats

1   Bright star, would I were steadfast as thou art—
     Not in lone splendor hung aloft the night
  And watching, with eternal lids apart,
     Like nature's patient, sleepless Eremite,[1]
5 The moving waters at their priestlike task
     Of pure ablution round earth's human shores,
2 Or gazing on the new soft-fallen mask
     Of snow upon the mountains and the moors—
  No—yet still steadfast, still unchangeable,
10   Pillowed upon my fair love's ripening breast,
3 To feel forever its soft fall and swell,
     Awake forever in a sweet unrest,
  Still, still to hear her tender-taken breath,
  And so live ever—or else swoon to death.

---

1. Eremite (ĕr′ ə mīt′): Hermit.

THINKING ABOUT THE SELECTION

Recalling

1. What two things does the speaker say the star watches from its position in the sky?

Interpreting

2. (a) In what ways does the speaker wish to be like the star? (b) In what ways does he wish to be different?
3. What do do think is meant by "sweet unrest" in line 12?
4. In a Petrarchan, or Italian, sonnet, the first eight lines pose a question or problem, while the last six lines offer a solution or comment on or extend the issue. (a) What question or problem is presented in the octave, or first eight lines? (b) What response is given in the sestet, or next six lines? (c) What word signals this response?

Applying

5. Based on this poem, describe Keats's attitudes toward nature and emotion. Explain how these attitudes are typical of the Romantic movement.

When I Have Fears
That I May Cease to Be

John Keats

1

When I have fears that I may cease to be
    Before my pen has gleaned my teeming brain,
Before high-piled books, in charactery,[1]
    Hold like rich garners[2] the full ripened grain;

2

5 When I behold, upon the night's starred face,
    Huge cloudy symbols of a high romance,
And think that I may never live to trace
    Their shadows, with the magic hand of chance;[3]

3

And when I feel, fair creature of an hour,
10   That I shall never look upon thee more,
Never have relish in the fairy power
    Of unreflecting love—then on the shore

4

Of the wide world I stand alone, and think
Till love and fame to nothingness do sink.

---

1. charactery: Written or printed letters of the alphabet.
2. garners: Storehouses for grain.
3. chance: Inspiration.

JOHN KEATS, 1821
Joseph Severn
By Courtesy of the National Portrait Gallery, London

THINKING ABOUT THE SELECTION

Recalling

1. (a) What does the speaker say he fears missing in lines 1–8? (b) In lines 9–12?

Interpreting

2. What do you think is meant by "cloudy symbols of a high romance" in line 6?
3. Whom is the speaker addressing in line 10?
4. How does the speaker resolve his fears?

Applying

5. What does this poem suggest about Keats's views on death? Do you feel these views would be held by the other Romantic poets you have read? Why or why not?

THINKING AND WRITING

Comparing and Contrasting Sonnets

Choose one of the sonnets by William Wordsworth (pages 653–657). On a sheet of paper take notes on how this sonnet is similar to and different from the sonnets of Keats in form, subject matter, word usage, and theme. In an essay of one page or more write about your findings. When you revise make sure you have included details from the poems as support.

Closure and Extension

ANSWERS TO THINKING ABOUT THE SELECTION
Recalling

1. (a) The poet fears not having the time to write all that is in his mind and not being able to write everything his imagination can conceive. (b) The poet fears he will never experience reciprocal love.

Interpreting

2. By "cloudy symbols of high romance" the poet may mean his imagination or images and thoughts that inspire him.
3. "Thee" refers to someone he loves or might come to love.
4. The poet realizes that in the larger sense personal love and fame are of little account.

Applying

5. Answers will differ, but based on the meaning and contents of this sonnet, it appears that Keats is not concerned with the idea of an afterlife. This would seem somewhat out of character with the other Romantics, all of whom embraced personal beliefs of eternity and afterlife. Throughout his poetry, however, Keats's views of eternity seem clouded with moods of doubt and mystery.

Literary Focus After discussing imagery review the ode form before beginning a study of the poem. See Shelley's "Ode to the West Wind" on page 704. While Shelley's ode is in the Pindaric mode, Keats devised his own stanza form. This ode is written in ten-line stanzas of essentially iambic pentameter, except that the eighth line in each stanza is iambic trimeter. Keats's rhyme scheme is *ababcdecde*. Point out the heavy use of allusion in the ode. Note that authors who use allusions assume a certain kowledge on the part of their readers.

Writing Have students tell what images they thought of to describe the various features.

Vocabulary

Preteach the following vocabulary words:

opiate (ō′ pe it) *n*.: Something that brings on relaxation or sleep (p. 721, l.3)

vintage (vin′tij) *n*.: Wine or nectar of high quality (p. 721, l.11)

requiem (rek′ wē əm) *n*.: Musical composition or service honoring the dead (p. 724, l.60)

unravished (un rav′ ishd) *adj*.: Undisturbed, unspoiled (p. 726, l.1)

cloyed (kloɪd) *adj*.: Made sick by an overdose (p. 727, l.29)

Writer's Technique

Commentary

Writing

Ode to a Nightingale; Ode on a Grecian Urn; To Autumn

Imagery. Imagery is language that helps a reader form a mental picture of an object or idea by appealing to one or more of the five senses. Taken by itself the word *bread,* for example, is nothing more than just that—a word. When, however, the word is part of the image "warm loaf of freshly baked bread," our sense of sight and especially our sense of smell are both called into play. In his odes Keats used imagery with a degree of skill that few poets before or since have achieved.

We all have different methods of writing, depending on our audience, topic, and purpose as well as our personalities and moods. Sometimes we need a great deal of time to gather and arrange our thoughts; other times we can write with feverish haste, inspired perhaps by a vivid image or idea.

It's not easy to describe the writing process. At times, too, we may want to recount our creative experiences somewhat differently from how they actually occurred. Perhaps we want to make the story more impressive, or try to conform to prevailing ideas of creativity.

After Charles Brown found the scraps of paper containing Keats's ode to the nightingale, he continued his search for more of Keats's work. With his friend's help, Brown found other short poems, which otherwise might have vanished. "From that day on he gave me permission to copy any verses he might write," Brown recounts. "He cared so little for them himself when once, as it appeared to me, his imagination was released from their influence, that it required a friend at hand to preserve them."

We have no reason to doubt Brown's account, yet perhaps his version is colored by the Romantic notion of creativity. What do you see in Brown's account and Keats's poetry that supports the Romantic idea that poetry is "the spontaneous overflow of powerful feelings"? What other Romantic ideas do you find here?

Picture a setting in nature with which you are very familiar—a park, a wooded area, or the like. On a sheet of paper jot down as many physical features of the scene as you can. You might, for instance, mention trees, grass, rocks, and sky. Lastly, think up an image for each feature you mentioned that would enable a reader to develop a strong mental picture.

720   *The Romantic Age*

Objectives

1 To find equivalent imagery
2 To select music to accompany a poem
3 To compare and contrast odes

Support Material

Teaching Portfolio
Teacher Backup, p. 865
Grammar in Action Worksheet, *Using Hyphens,* p. 868
Usage and Mechanics Worksheet, p. 870
Vocabulary Check, p. 871
Analyzing Literature Worksheet, *Using Imagery,* p. 872

Critical Thinking and Reading Worksheet, *Comparing Rhyme Schemes,* p. 873
Selection Test, p. 875

Ode to a Nightingale

John Keats

*Keats composed the following ode in 1819, while living
in Hampstead with his friend Charles Brown. Brown wrote
the following description about how the ode was composed:
"In the spring of 1819 a nightingale had built her nest near
my house. Keats felt a tranquil and continued joy in her
song; and one morning he took his chair from the breakfast
table to the grass plot under the plum tree, where he sat for
two or three hours. When he came into the house, I perceived he had some scraps of paper in his hand, and these
he was quietly thrusting behind the books. On inquiry, I
found those scraps, four or five in number, contained his
poetic feeling on the song of our nightingale."*

I

My heart aches, and a drowsy numbness pains
    My sense, as though of hemlock[1] I had drunk,
Or emptied some dull opiate to the drains
    One minute past, and Lethe-wards[2] had sunk:
5 'Tis not through envy of thy happy lot,
    But being too happy in thine happiness,—
      That thou, light-winged Dryad[3] of the trees,
        In some melodious plot
Of beechen green, and shadows numberless,
10   Singest of summer in full-throated ease.

II

O, for a draft[4] of vintage! that hath been
    Cooled a long age in the deep-delved earth,
Tasting of Flora[5] and the country green,
    Dance, and Provençal[6] song, and sunburnt mirth!

---

1. hemlock: A poisonous herb.
2. Lethe-wards: Toward Lethe, the river of forgetfulness in Hades,
the underworld, in classical mythology.
3. Dryad (drī′ əd): In classical mythology, a wood nymph.
4. draft: Drink.
5. Flora: In classical mythology, the goddess of flowers, or the flowers
themselves.
6. Provençal (prō′ vən säl′): Pertaining to Provence, a region in
southern France, renowned in the late Middle Ages for its
troubadours, who composed and sang love songs.

Ode to a Nightingale 721

Master Teacher Note This poem
is an example of what Keats
termed "negative capability"
—one of the most famous and
elusive phrases ever uttered by a
great poet. Part of its meaning
may be stated thus: the capability
of a poet to negate himself or
herself and enter fully into his or
her subject so as to represent it
with an especially rich and vibrant
objectivity.

Purpose-Setting Question What
thoughts and feelings in the poet
does the nightingale evoke?

1 **Discussion** As the poem opens,
what is the poet's state of mind?

2 **Clarification** The word *thy* refers
to the nightingale.

3 **Discussion** In stanza two the
poet says he longs to leave the
world behind to join the nightingale. By what means would he
accomplish this?

4 **Discussion** What senses does
Keats appeal to in stanza two?

Humanities Note

Fine art, *Small Bird on a Flowering Plum Branch*, attributed to Ma Lin. Ma Lin was a landscape painter of the Sung Dynasty (12th–13th centuries). The bird and flower were a favored Sung motif.

This delicate Chinese painting on silk shows a bird perched on a branch. The serenity of the scene suggests the freedom from earthly concerns for which Keats longs in his "Ode to a Nightingale."

As students read the poem and look at the art, you might use these questions for discussion.
1. How has the artist suggested peacefulness and serenity in this painting?
2. What "among the leaves hast [the bird] never known"?
3. What elements of Beauty would Keats admire in this painting?

SMALL BIRD ON A FLOWERING PLUM BRANCH
Attributed to Ma Lin
The Gotoh Museum

15   O for a beaker full of the warm South,
      Full of the true, the blushful Hippocrene,[7]
        With beaded bubbles winking at the brim,
          And purple-stained mouth;
      That I might drink, and leave the world unseen,
20   And with thee fade away into the forest dim:

---

7. Hippocrene (hĭp′ ə krēn′): In classical mythology, the fountain of the Muses on Mt. Helicon. From this fountain flowed the waters of inspiration.

Primary Source

Literary scholar Douglas Bush wrote the following about Keats's greatness as a poet:

Keats is probably the only romantic poet, apart from Blake, whose present rank is conspicuously higher than it was in the nineteenth century, and the rank given him by critics and poets of that period was not low. What is there in Keats that has enabled him to emerge from modern scrutiny a larger figure than ever before? In the first place, he carries relatively little excess baggage in the way of mediocre writing or "dated" ideas from which, in various ways and degrees, Wordsworth, Coleridge, Byron and Shelley must be cut loose. Keats speaks to us directly, almost as one of ourselves; we do not need to approach him through elaborate reconstructions of dead philosophies or dead poetical fashions. The romantic elements in him remained, so to speak, central, sane, normal—in everything but their intensity—and did not run into transcendental or pseudo-romantic or propagandist excesses. It is one of Keats's essential links with some poetic leaders of our own age that he, alone among the romantic poets, consciously strove to

III

Fade far away, dissolve, and quite forget
    What thou among the leaves hast never known,
The weariness, the fever, and the fret
    Here, where men sit and hear each other groan;
25 Where palsy shakes a few, sad, last gray hairs,
    Where youth grows pale, and specter-thin, and dies;[8]
      Where but to think is to be full of sorrow
        And leaden-eyed despairs,
    Where Beauty cannot keep her lustrous eyes,
30   Or new Love pine at them beyond tomorrow.

5

IV

Away! away! for I will fly to thee,
    Not charioted by Bacchus[9] and his pards,
But on the viewless[10] wings of Poesy,[11]
    Though the dull brain perplexes and retards:
35 Already with thee! tender is the night,
    And haply[12] the Queen-Moon is on her throne,
      Clustered around by all her starry Fays;[13]
        But here there is no light,
    Save what from heaven is with the breezes blown
40   Through verdurous[14] glooms and winding mossy
      ways.

6, 7

V

I cannot see what flowers are at my feet,
    Nor what soft incense hangs upon the boughs,
But, in embalmed[15] darkness, guess each sweet
    Wherewith the seasonable month endows
45 The grass, the thicket, and the fruit-tree wild;
    White hawthorn, and the pastoral eglantine;[16]
      Fast fading violets covered up in leaves;
        And mid-May's eldest child,
    The coming musk-rose, full of dewy wine,
50   The murmurous haunt of flies on summer eves.

8

---

8. youth . . . dies: Keats is referring to his brother, Tom, who had died from tuberculosis the previous winter.
9. Bacchus (băk′ əs): In classical mythology, the god of wine, who was often represented in a chariot drawn by leopards ("pards").
10. viewless: Invisible.
11. Poesy: Poetic fancy.
12. haply: Perhaps.
13. Fays: Fairies.
14. verdurous: Green-foliaged.
15. embalmed: Perfumed.
16. eglantine (eg′ lən tin′): Sweetbrier or honeysuckle.

Ode to a Nightingale   723

---

5 Discussion In stanza three the poet says he would like to fade into the forest trees with the nightingale. What advantage does he see in this?

6 Discussion In stanza four the poet chooses his vehicle of escape. What is it?

7 Enrichment The phrase "tender is the night" (line 35) was borrowed by F. Scott Fitzgerald as the title of one of his novels.

8 Enrichment Stanza five is justly acclaimed as a beautifully lyrical evocation of the scents and sounds of an early summer woodland evening. Point out how much of the stanza consists of rich, sensuous imagery. The word *sweet* (line 43) means "sweet smells."

---

escape from self-expression into Shakespearean impersonality.

Moreover, there is nowadays a much more general understanding of the solid strength of Keats's mind and character, of his philosophic attitude toward life and art, of his astonishing self-knowledge and capacity for growth, of his unceasing struggle to achieve poetic integrity. In all these respects, and especially in the last, he is linked with the serious poets of the present. Certain fundamental questions are always tormenting him; he can neither put them aside nor finally answer them. Has the artist a right to exist at all in the midst of chaos and wrong and suffering? If his existence is justified, can he allow his imagination to be self-centered, in the large sense "lyrical," or should it be dramatic and rooted in the heart of man and human life? Is truth, the truth which is the soul of poetry, to be won by sensuous intuition or by study and conscious thought? From first to last Keats's important poems are related to, or grow directly out of, these inner conflicts, conflicts which are all the more acute because his poetic ambitions are so often at odds with his poetic gifts.

9 **Discussion** If, as the poet says in stanza six, he should die, what would happen to the nightingale's song?

10 **Discussion** Stanza seven develops one of Keats's basic beliefs—the permanence and changelessness of beauty. In what sense was the nightingale "not born for death"? How does he use the nightingale's song to express this idea?

11 **Discussion** In stanza eight the poet is brought back to reality from his reverie. What meaning do lines 73–74 hold? Note that *fancy* (line 73) means "imagination."

Reader's Response Do you agree with Keats that beauty is permanent and changeless? Why or why not?

VI

Darkling[17] I listen; and, for many a time
    I have been half in love with easeful Death,
Called him soft names in many a mused[18] rhyme,
    To take into the air my quiet breath;
55 Now more than ever seems it rich to die,
    To cease upon the midnight with no pain,
      While thou art pouring forth thy soul abroad
        In such an ecstasy!
    Still wouldst thou sing, and I have ears in vain—
60   To thy high requiem become a sod.

VII

Thou wast not born for death, immortal Bird!
    No hungry generations tread thee down;
The voice I hear this passing night was heard
    In ancient days by emperor and clown:
65 Perhaps the selfsame song that found a path
    Through the sad heart of Ruth,[19] when, sick for home,
    She stood in tears amid the alien corn;
      The same that ofttimes hath
Charmed magic casements, opening on the foam
70   Of perilous seas, in fairylands forlorn.

VIII

Forlorn! the very word is like a bell
    To toll me back from thee to my sole self!
Adieu! the fancy cannot cheat so well
    As she is famed[20] to do, deceiving elf.
75 Adieu! adieu! thy plaintive anthem[21] fades
    Past the near meadows, over the still stream,
      Up the hillside; and now 'tis buried deep
        In the next valley-glades:
    Was it a vision, or a waking dream?
80   Fled is that music:—Do I wake or sleep?

---

17. darkling: In the dark.
18. mused: Meditated.
19. Ruth: In the Bible (Ruth 2:1–23), a widow who left her home and went to Judah to work in the corn (wheat) fields.
20. famed: Reported.
21. anthem: Hymn.

Recalling

1. What is the speaker's mood in stanza I?
2. (a) What wish does the speaker express at the end of stanza II and at the beginning of stanza III? (b) According to stanza IV, how will he accomplish this wish?
3. What effect does the word "forlorn" have on the speaker in stanza VIII?

Interpreting

4. (a) What is the "draught of vintage" the speaker craves in stanza II? (b) What would it help him to escape?
5. (a) What differences between the speaker's world and the bird's are described in stanza IV? (b) What is meant in line 38 by "here there is no light"?
6. (a) What does the speaker find tempting in stanza VI? (b) What changes his mind in stanza VII?

Applying

7. The poem ends with a question. What is its relevance, both to the poem and to the spirit of the Romantic movement?

8. The twentieth-century American novelist F. Scott Fitzgerald took the title of one of his novels from line 35: "Already with thee! Tender is the night." (a) In what way can the night be tender? (b) Why are the words "tender is the night" especially appropriate for one who has been "half in love with easeful Death"?

ANALYZING LITERATURE

Using Imagery

Imagery is language that appeals to the senses and, by so doing, creates a vivid picture in the reader's mind. The phrase "blustery, wind-swept day" provides the reader with a strong impression that the simple phrase "cold day" does not. Such is the impact of imagery. Find an everyday equivalent for each of the following images from "Ode to a Nightingale." Then state which of Keats's words are central to his image.
1. "With beaded bubbles winking at the brim,/ And purple-stained mouth;" (lines 17–18)
2. "Where palsy shakes a few, sad, last gray hairs,/Where youth grows pale, and specter-thin, and dies;" (lines 25–26)
3. The coming musk-rose, full of dewy wine,/The murmurous haunt of flies on summer eves." (lines 49–50)

Ode to a Nightingale 725

world and fade into the forest with the nightingale.
3. The word *forlorn* brings the poet out of his reverie.

Interpreting

4. (a) The poet craves a draft of wine. (b) The wine, he thinks, will help him leave the real world.
5. (a) The real world is one in which the brain is perplexed and dulled; the nightingale's world is one of permanence, through his song. (b) The line suggests the real world lacks the joy, as well as brightness, of nature's world, as exemplified by the nightingale.
6. (a) The poet finds the idea of death tempting. (b) The nightingale's song evokes the idea of immortality.

Applying

7. Suggested Response: The question means "Was my reverie of the nightingale a dream—a form of sleep—or is my return to ordinary thoughts and feelings a kind of sleep?" For both the poem and the entire Romantic movement, the poet's vision is a kind of awakening to intenser life; a return to ordinary living is, by comparison, a sleep.
8. Suggested Responses: (a) The darkness of the night can often soothe one's emotions or blot out painful realities. (b) The resemblance of night to death makes it appealing to the speaker; hence the words are appropriate to his feelings about the night.

ANSWERS TO ANALYZING LITERATURE

1. The image in lines 17–18 refers to a glass of wine.
2. The image in lines 25–26 refers to the process of aging and death.
3. The image in lines 49–50 refers to rosebuds about to burst, with insects hovering about them.
   In all of the images, the nouns and adjectives—and to a lesser extent the verbs—are of central expressive importance. The other words are little more than connectives.

Challenge Trace each of the mythological allusions in a handbook such as Bullfinch's. Then explain the aptness of each allusion.

Closure and Extension

ANSWERS TO THINKING ABOUT THE SELECTION
Recalling

1. The poet's mood can be described as one of sadness, even depression.
2. (a) The poet wishes to leave the world behind and join the nightingale. (b) He wishes to leave the

Ode on a Grecian Urn

John Keats

I

Thou still unravished bride of quietness,
    Thou foster child of silence and slow time,
Sylvan[1] historian, who canst thus express
    A flowery tale more sweetly than our rhyme:
5   What leaf-fringed legend haunts about thy shape
        Of deities or mortals, or of both,
          In Tempe[2] or the dales of Arcady?[3]
      What men or gods are these? What maidens loath?[4]
What mad pursuit? What struggle to escape?
10   What pipes and timbrels?[5] What wild ecstasy?

II

Heard melodies are sweet, but those unheard
    Are sweeter; therefore, ye soft pipes, play on;
Not to the sensual[6] ear, but, more endeared,
    Pipe to the spirit ditties of no tone:
15 Fair youth, beneath the trees, thou canst not leave
      Thy song, nor ever can those trees be bare;
        Bold Lover, never, never canst thou kiss,
Though winning near the goal—yet, do not grieve;
      She cannot fade, though thou hast not thy bliss,
20   Forever wilt thou love, and she be fair!

III

Ah, happy, happy boughs! that cannot shed
    Your leaves, nor ever bid the Spring adieu;
And, happy melodist, unwearied,
    Forever piping songs forever new;

---

1. sylvan: Rustic, representing the woods or forest.
2. Tempe (tem′ pē): A beautiful valley in Greece that has become a symbol of supreme rural beauty.
3. Arcady (är′ kə dē): A region in Greece that has come to represent supreme pastoral contentment.
4. loath: Unwilling.
5. timbrels: Tambourines.
6. sensual: Involving the physical sense of hearing.

25 More happy love! more happy, happy love!
        Forever warm and still to be enjoyed,
            Forever panting, and forever young;
    All breathing human passion far above,
        That leaves a heart high-sorrowful and cloyed,
30   A burning forehead, and a parching tongue.

                        IV
    Who are these coming to the sacrifice?
        To what green altar, O mysterious priest,
    Lead'st thou that heifer lowing at the skies,
        And all her silken flanks with garlands dressed?
35 What little town by river or seashore,
        Or mountain-built with peaceful citadel,
            Is emptied of this folk, this pious morn?
    And, little town, thy streets forevermore
        Will silent be; and not a soul to tell
40   Why thou art desolate, can e'er return.

COLUMN KRATER (CALLED THE "ORCHARD VASE"),
SIDE A: WOMEN GATHERING APPLES
The Metropolitan Museum of Art

Ode on a Grecian Urn   727

Humanities Note

The Column Krater (Orchard Vase): Women Gathering Apples. Artifacts from the early Greek period include many painted vessels, called vases or urns. In spite of their utilitarian function, these vases were in many cases works of art. The highly individual drawings on them show scenes from mythology, legend, and everyday life. This vase, in the red-figured style, shows a common scene. The women are in profile with well-proportioned and realistic features.

As students look at this typical Greek vase, you might ask these questions.
1. What common activity is happening in this painting?
2. To what aspects of an urn like this might Keats be referring in his ode?
3. What rhetorical questions might Keats have posed about this particular vase?

5 Discussion In the last stanza Keats steps back to summarize his contemplations. What message does the urn have? Consider the antecedent of *that* to be all of lines 46–49. Then the message might be that the beauty of the urn shall comfort future generations with its linking of truth and beauty.

Enrichment Keats wrote in a letter that what the imagination seizes as beauty must be truth. Critic Harold Bloom extends this statement to speculate that "the urn's beauty is truth because age cannot waste it; our woes cannot consume it. The urn's truth, its existence out of time, is beauty because such freedom is beautiful to us. The condition of man, for Keats, is such that all we shall ever know we know on earth, and the sum of our knowledge is the identity of beauty and truth, when beauty is defined as what gives joy forever, and truth is what seizes upon us as beauty."

Reader's Response What do the final two lines of the poem mean to you?

Closure and Extension

ANSWERS TO THINKING ABOUT THE SELECTION
Recalling

1. (a) In stanza two the speaker addresses the "fair youth" who is pursuing his love. (b) In stanza three the poet addresses the trees and a musician.
2. The ritual is the sacrifice of an animal to the gods.

Interpreting

3. (a) It is a sylvan historian because the forest painted on it witnesses the events depicted. (b) It tells its tale through pictures whose beauty the poet feels he cannot emulate.

728

V

O Attic[7] shape! Fair attitude! with brede[8]
　　Of marble men and maidens overwrought,[9]
With forest branches and the trodden weed;
　　Thou, silent form, dost tease us out of thought
45　As doth eternity: Cold[10] Pastoral!
　　When old age shall this generation waste,
　　　Thou shalt remain, in midst of other woe
Than ours, a friend to man, to whom thou say'st,
　　"Beauty is truth, truth beauty,"—that is all
50　　Ye know on earth, and all ye need to know.

---

7. Attic: Attica was the region of Greece in which Athens was located; a region characterized by grace and simplicity.
8. brede: An interwoven pattern.
9. overwrought: All over.
10. cold: Unchanging.

THINKING ABOUT THE SELECTION
Recalling

1. As the speaker studies the scene on a Grecian urn, it takes hold of his imagination. (a) Whom does the speaker address in stanza II of the poem? (b) Whom does he address in stanza III?
2. What ritual is described in the first four lines of stanza IV?

Interpreting

3. (a) In what way is the urn a "Sylvan historian"? (b) How can it tell its "flowery tale more sweetly than our rhyme"?
4. (a) Interpret lines 11–12: "Heard melodies are sweet, but those unheard/Are sweeter . . ." (b) What do these lines indicate about the power of the imagination?

5. (a) Why might the lover in stanza II grieve? (b) Why does the speaker advise him not to grieve?
6. (a) What is the "Cold Pastoral" mentioned in line 45? (b) With what does the speaker contrast it?

Applying

7. (a) Explain the meaning of the last two lines of the poem. (b) In what ways might this finish have been appropriate to "Ode to a Nightingale"?
8. In *Endymion*, John Keats wrote, "A thing of beauty is a joy forever;/Its loveliness increases; it will never/Pass into nothingness." Compare and contrast the idea of beauty expressed in these lines with that expressed in lines 49–50 of "Ode on a Grecian Urn".

---

4. (a) "Unheard melodies" are those of the imagination. (b) The power of the imagination is very strong. Things that do not exist in the senses can exist in the imagination.
5. (a) The lover might grieve because he never catches his love. (b) The lover should not grieve because his love will always be strong and the maiden always fair and young.
6. (a) The "Cold Pastoral" is the scene frozen in time by art. (b) It is contrasted with real life.

Applying

7. (a) Answers will differ but should suggest that truth and beauty are linked. (b) Answers will differ but should suggest that in "Ode to a Nightingale" the beauty associated with nature constitutes truth for the poet.
8. Answers will differ but students should point out that in both passages beauty is presented as universal and lasting.

To Autumn

John Keats

I

Season of mists and mellow fruitfulness,
    Close bosom-friend of the maturing sun;
Conspiring with him how to load and bless
    With fruit the vines that round the thatch-eves run;
5 To bend with apples the mossed cottage-trees,
    And fill all fruit with ripeness to the core;
      To swell the gourd, and plump the hazel shells
    With a sweet kernel; to set budding more,
And still more, later flowers for the bees,
10 Until they think warm days will never cease,
      For Summer has o'er-brimmed their clammy cells.

II

Who hath not seen thee oft amid thy store?
    Sometimes whoever seeks abroad may find
Thee sitting careless on a granary floor,
15   Thy hair soft-lifted by the winnowing[1] wind;
Or on a half-reaped furrow sound asleep,
    Drowsed with the fume of poppies, while thy hook[2]
      Spares the next swath and all its twined flowers:
And sometimes like a gleaner thou dost keep
20   Steady thy laden head across a brook;
    Or by a cider-press, with patient look,
      Thou watchest the last oozings hours by hours.

III

Where are the songs of Spring? Ay, where are they?
    Think not of them, thou hast thy music too—
25 While barred clouds bloom the soft-dying day,
    And touch the stubble-plains with rosy hue;
Then in a wailful choir the small gnats mourn
    Among the river sallows,[3] borne aloft
      Or sinking as the light wind lives or dies;

---

1. winnowing: Fanning; winnowing is a process in which the chaff is fanned from the grain.
2. hook: Scythe.
3. sallows: Willow trees.

30

And full-grown lambs loud bleat from hilly bourn;[4]
    Hedge-crickets sing; and now with treble soft
    The red-breast whistles from a garden croft;[5]
    And gathering swallows twitter in the skies.

---

4. bourn: Region.
5. croft: An enclosed plot of farm land.

Closure and Extension

THINKING ABOUT THE SELECTION
Recalling

1. (a) In stanza I of the poem, what is the season described as "doing"? (b) With whom is the season "conspiring"?
2. What are some of the songs of autumn?

Interpreting

3. In what way can Autumn be described as a "close bosom-friend of the maturing sun"?
4. (a) What activities frequently associated with the season are described in the second stanza? (b) What impression of Autumn is created by mentioning these activities?
5. Why do you think the speaker mentions the songs of Spring in stanza III?

Applying

6. What do you suppose was Keats's attitude toward winter? Explain your answer in terms of the three odes you have just read.

SPEAKING AND LISTENING
Selecting Music to Accompany a Poem

In "To Autumn," Keats mentions the songs of Spring and of Autumn. Many of the images he presents in the poem, in fact, suggest music. Find a piece of music that you feel would provide good background to Keats's poem about autumn. Try reading the poem aloud as the music plays. If possible, bring a recording of the music you select to class.

THINKING AND WRITING
Comparing and Contrasting Odes

Choose one of the odes by Shelley that you read. Reread it, noting such features as word choice, stanza structure, and overall message. In a one-page composition, discuss the ways in which the three odes by Keats are similar to and different from that of Shelley. Include mention of whose work you like better and state your reasons.

Grammar in Action

Use a **hyphen** to connect two or more words that are used as one word, unless the dictionary gives a contrary spelling. Compound expressions often convey abundance and suggest close relationships between the connected words. Because they are unusual, they draw attention to themselves and should be made and used with care. Notice John Keats's effective use of compound modifiers.

Prose

FISHERMAN UPON A LEE SHORE
J. M. W. Turner
The Iveagh Bequest, Kenwood,
Bridgeman/Art Resource

Humanities Note

Fine art, *Fisherman Upon a Lee Shore,* 1802, by J. M. W. Turner. John Mallord William Turner exhibited his first painting at the Royal Academy when he was fifteen. He became very successful, frequently exhibiting paintings there. Turner was stirred by wild and dramatically romantic scenes, like this. Many aspects of this piece are typical of Turner's work—filled with striking effects: an awe-inspiring storm, a battle with the raging seas, dazzling light and shadows. In Turner's work, nature reflects and expresses human emotions—the humans are small and overwhelmed in the face of powers beyond control.

Prose 731

Close *bosom-friend* of the maturing sun;

With fruit the vines that round the *thatch-eves* run;

For Summer has *o'er brimmed* their clammy cells

Or on a *half-reaped* furrow sound asleep,

Or by a *cider-press,* with patient look,

While barred clouds bloom the *soft-dying* day,
And touch the *stubble-plains* with rosy hue;

Hedge-crickets sing; and now with treble soft
The *red-breast* whistles from a garden croft;

The compound modifiers seem to capture some of the fullness of autumn's fruitfulness within the words themselves. Notice how much richness is lost by removing the hyphens: *Bosom friend, thatch eves, half reaped, cider press,* and *red breast* seem less tangible.

Student Activity. Choose a colorful time or place and write a small descriptive paragraph in which you use effective compound expressions joined by hyphens.

More About the Author Even had she not written *Frankenstein* and several other novels, Mary Wollstonecraft Shelley would probably still have become famous merely by association. Her father, William Godwin, was a brilliant political thinker; her mother, Mary Wollstonecraft, was a celebrated feminist, who wrote *A Vindication of the Rights of Women;* her husband, Percy Shelley, is now recognized as one of the finest Romantic poets; and she counted among her close friends another poetic genius, Lord Byron. In an age when a woman's role was often confined to the home, what influence do you think these people had on Mary Shelley's life?

Critical Evaluation Literary scholar Elizabeth MacAndrew wrote the following appraisal of Shelley's novel: "Mary Shelley's *Frankenstein* is the Gothic novel with the greatest claim to fame because it has become a modern myth. It . . . has a hero/villain, Victor Frankenstein, and makes use of the doubles figure to establish the relativity of moral values with great complexity. Victor is not simply good-gone-bad. Mary Shelley makes him a despairing human being by symbolically projecting the evil in him into the monstrous exterior of his creation. Mary Shelley's use of this device is in itself sufficient to have made *Frankenstein* a myth. . . . Throughout the terrible story he tells, Victor is an ordinary man in all but the extent of his suffering. His hold on us is inescapable, mythic, because the consequences of his deeds are horrible out of all proportion to his intent in performing them. It is just so that we look on the possibility of evil in ourselves, knowing as we do so many mitigating circumstances, convinced as we are that we are indeed compassionable beings. To the extent

MARY SHELLEY

1797–1851

Even the most serious and dedicated of writers have their lighter moments. It is interesting to note that had it not been for such a moment involving two of English literature's most gifted writers, one of the most celebrated Gothic novels of all time might never have seen the light of day. More interesting still, the novel in question, *Frankenstein,* was penned by neither of the aforementioned greats —the poets Percy Bysshe Shelley and Lord Byron—but by the wife of the former, Mary Shelley.

Born in London, Mary Wollstonecraft Godwin was the daughter of William Godwin, a political thinker and writer given to radical ideas. One of her father's books, *Political Justice,* managed to attract the attention of the young and equally radically minded Percy Shelley, who became one of Godwin's disciples. Mary Godwin in turn became a great admirer of the young poet, and the two of them eloped to Switzerland when she was seventeen.

Mary Shelley's first piece of writing, *Journal of a Six Weeks' Tour* (1817), was a collaborative effort with her husband. Her first solo work—the novel with which her name is most often associated today—grew, quite innocently, out of idle conversation between Byron and another friend during a visit to the Shelleys' home on Lake Geneva in 1816. As a result of the conversation, it was suggested as a means of passing the time that each of the four friends attempt to write a ghost story. Though the results of the contest were largely unremarkable, Mary Shelley's horrific tale of the creation of a monster so impressed the gathering that her husband later urged her to develop it into a full-length novel. Thus was born *Frankenstein* (1818), and the creature that has thrilled countless readers and fueled the imaginations of generations of film makers.

After *Frankenstein,* Mary Shelley produced five more novels: *Valperga* (1823) and *Perkin Warbeck* (1830), which are historical works; the autobiographical *Lodore* (1835); *Falkner* (1837), a complicated mystery tale; and *The Last Man* (1826).

If *Frankenstein* is, as scholars have noted, structurally weak, it is nevertheless a "good read." More important from a historical perspective, the novel was the first in a long line of works to explore the potential dangers of technology that falls into the wrong hands.

that our identification with Frankenstein is close, our fear of the evil that comes from him will be great."

Objectives

1 To recognize the Gothic tradition
2 To write in the Gothic tradition

Support Material

Teaching Portfolio
Teacher Backup, p. 877

Grammar in Action Worksheet, *Appreciating Repetition,* p. 881
Usage and Mechanics Worksheet, p. 883
Vocabulary Check, p. 884
Analyzing Literature Worksheet, *Recognizing the Gothic Tradition,* p. 885

Language Worksheet, *Understanding Greek and Latin Roots,* p. 886
Selection Test, p. 887

GUIDE FOR INTERPRETING

Introduction to *Frankenstein*

Gothic Tradition. The Gothic novel was a late eighteenth-century revival of the tale of terror, which has its roots in antiquity. Gothic fiction, or *Gothicism,* is formally defined by two elements—the historical and the "wonderful," or supernatural. One of the earliest and best-known Gothic novels was Horace Walpole's *The Castle of Otranto* (1765), a hair-raising account of a castle terrorized by a giant. Within the pages of Walpole's thriller, paintings and statues come to life for the first time in fiction. The next important contributor to the "renaissance of wonder" was Clara Reeve, a critic, whose *The Old English Baron* (1777) was, in her own humble opinion, an improvement on Walpole's haunted castle story. The Gothic tradition was refined considerably in the hands of Matthew Gregory Lewis, who, at the age of twenty, published *The Monk* (1796), a cleverly conceived and simply told tale of a Spanish friar who enters into a contract with the devil. The first novel to depict its horrors in graphic terms, *The Monk* paved the way for Mary Shelley's *Frankenstein* (1818), whose main character breathes life into one of the best-known and most terrifying monsters of all time.

Commentary

Mary Shelley's mother, Mary Wollstonecraft, was as radical a thinker as her father, William Godwin. Her 1792 book, *A Vindication of the Rights of Women,* was the first great work devoted to equality for women.

For centuries, she said, women had willingly served men. To escape from slavery, women must cultivate their minds, find new occupations, and refuse to accept an inferior role. Equality for women could help all people fulfill their potential, she wrote.

If her book had appeared earlier, it might merely have provoked amusement, but it fell upon a frightened world. Educators vetoed the freedom for which Wollstonecraft had pleaded. Female writers urged that women accept their subordinate position and use their "feminine wiles"—acting delicate and helpless, for example—to get their way with men.

Wollstonecraft died ten days after Mary's birth, but her ideas permeate her daughter's work. Where in the *Introduction to Frankenstein* do you see the influence of her writing and beliefs?

Writing

Give some thought to ideas that might be incorporated into a tale of terror. Well-used but always-dependable possibilities include graveyards at night, dark winding staircases, and ghosts. Sketch a rough outline to a story that contains some of these ideas.

Guide for Interpreting 733

Literary Focus The complete title of Mary Shelley's work is *Frankenstein; or, the Modern Prometheus*. The literary reference is to the mythological figure central to her husband's poem "Prometheus Unbound"—the Greek Titan who was chained and tortured by the god Zeus for stealing fire from heaven and giving it to humans. Prometheus was a popular figure in Romantic poetry, for he had the full range of Romantic moral sensibility and the full Romantic capacity for creation and destruction.

Have students make a list of Gothic novels they have read. Which ones are by modern writers? Which ones were written before the twentieth century? What aspects do these novels share?

Writing/Prior Knowledge Have your students brainstorm about other gothic-terror devices. The class might also attempt to suggest a skeletal plot outline.

Vocabulary

Preteach the following vocabulary words:
appendage (ə pen′dij) n.: Something added on (p. 734)
ungenial (un jēn′yəl) adj.: Unfriendly; characterized by bad weather (p. 234)
acceded (ak sēd′id) v.: (With to) Yielded to; agreed upon (p. 735)
platitude (plat′ ə tōōd′) n.: Statement lacking originality (p. 735)
phantasm (fan′ taz′m) n.: Supernatural form or shape (p. 736)
incitement (in sīt′ mənt) n.: Cause to perform; encouragement (p. 737)
progeny (präj′ ə nē) n.: Offspring; child (p. 737)

Teaching to Ability Levels For less advanced students, you may wish to read passages from the excerpt in class and use context clues to guide students toward an understanding of other difficult words.

Introduction to *Frankenstein*

Mary Wollstonecraft Shelley

In this introduction to the third edition of Frankenstein, *published in 1831, Mary Shelley recalls the circumstances that led her to write the novel during the summer of 1816.*

The Publishers of the Standard Novels, in selecting *Frankenstein* for one of their series, expressed a wish that I should furnish them with some account of the origin of the story. I am the more willing to comply, because I shall thus give a general answer to the question, so very frequently asked me: "How I, then a young girl, came to think of, and to dilate upon, so very hideous an idea?" It is true that I am very averse to bringing myself forward in print; but as my account will only appear as an appendage to a former production, and as it will be confined to such topics as have connection with my authorship alone, I can scarcely accuse myself of a personal intrusion. . . .

In the summer of 1816, we[1] visited Switzerland, and became the neighbors of Lord Byron. At first we spent our pleasant hours on the lake or wandering on its shores; and Lord Byron, who was writing the third canto of *Childe Harold,* was the only one among us who put his thoughts upon paper. These, as he brought them successively to us, clothed in all the light and harmony of poetry, seemed to stamp as divine the glories of heaven and earth, whose influences we partook with him.

But it proved a wet, ungenial summer, and incessant rain often confined us for days to the house. Some volumes of ghost stories, translated from the German into French,[2] fell into our hands. There was "The History of the Inconstant Lover,"[3] who, when he thought to clasp the bride to whom he had pledged his vows, found himself in the arms of the pale ghost of her whom he had deserted. There was the tale of the sinful founder of his race,[4] whose miserable doom it was to bestow the kiss of death on all the younger sons of his fated house, just when they reached the age of promise. His gigantic, shadowy form, clothed like the ghost in Hamlet, in complete armor but with the beaver[5] up, was seen at midnight, by the moon's fitful beams, to advance slowly along the gloomy avenue. The shape was lost beneath the shadow of the castle walls; but soon a gate swung back, a step was heard, the door of the chamber opened, and he advanced to the couch of the blooming youths, cradled in healthy sleep. Eternal sorrow sat upon his face as he bent down and kissed the foreheads of the boys, who from that hour withered like flowers snap-

---

1. we: Mary Shelley, her husband Percy Bysshe Shelley, and their two children.

2. volumes . . . French: *Fantasmagoriana,* or *Collected Stories of Apparitions of Specters, Ghosts, Phantoms, Etc.,* published anonymously in 1812.
3. "The History . . . Lover": The true name of the story is "The Dead Fiancée."
4. the tale . . . race: "Family Portraits."
5. beaver: The hinged piece of armor that covers the face.

A VIEW OF CHAMONIX AND MT. BLANC
Julius Schnon von Carolsfeld
Austrian Gallery, Vienna

Humanities Note

Fine art, *A View of Chamonix and Mt. Blanc,* 1824. Juius Schnon von Carolsfeld. Carolsfeld (1794–1872) was a German Nazarene painter. The Nazarenes were a group of Viennese artists who sought a return to the art of the Middle Ages. In their efforts to achieve the proper atmosphere, they occupied an abandoned monastery in Rome and worked as artist-monks. Their art was romantic, sentimental, and realistic.

The academically trained Julius von Carolsfeld often expressed this Nazarene form of Romanticism in landscape painting. *A View of Chamonix and Mt. Blanc* was painted in 1824. Beautifully detailed, it is a moonlit view of a famous glacier-covered mountain and a small village in the French Alps. As is common in German Romanticism, the painting has a weird or mysterious feeling to it, perhaps because of the extreme realism. This weirdness is the very quality that makes this an appropriate illustration for the environment in which Mary Shelley wrote the horror classic *Frankenstein:*

You might use the following questions for discussion.
1. How would you describe the setting of this painting?
2. Does this setting match the setting of the story?
3. What mood does this painting instill in you?

ped upon the stalk. I have not seen these stories since then, but their incidents are as fresh in my mind as if I had read them yesterday.

"We will each write a ghost story," said Lord Byron; and his proposition was acceded to. There were four of us.[6] The noble author began a tale, a fragment of which he printed at the end of his poem of Mazeppa. Shelley, more apt to embody ideas and sentiments in the radiance of brilliant imagery, and in the music of the most melodious verse that adorns our language, than to invent the machinery of a story, commenced one founded on the experiences of his early life. Poor Polidori had some terrible idea about a skull-headed lady, who was so punished for peeping through a keyhole —what to see I forget—something very shocking and wrong of course; but she

was reduced to a worse condition than the renowned Tom of Coventry,[7] he did not know what to do with her, and was obliged to despatch her to the tomb of the Capulets,[8] the only place for which she was fitted. The illustrious poets also, annoyed by the platitude of prose, speedily relinquished their uncongenial task.

I busied myself *to think of a story*— a story to rival those which had excited us to this task. One which would speak to the mysterious fears of our nature and awaken thrilling horror—one to make the reader dread to look round, to curdle the blood, and quicken the beatings of the heart. If I did not accomplish these things, my ghost story would be unworthy of its name. I thought and pondered—vainly. I felt that blank in-

---

7. Tom of Coventry: "Peeping Tom" who, according to legend, was struck blind for looking at Lady Godiva as she rode naked through Coventry.
8. tomb of the Capulets: Where Romeo and Juliet died.

---

6. four of us: Byron, the two Shelleys, and John William Polidori, Byron's physician.

Introduction to Frankenstein   735

4 **Discussion** What did Mary Shelley think of her husband's story-telling ability?

5 **Discussion** Why might Mary Shelley have had such a hard time thinking of a story?

Grammar in Action

Deliberate **repetition** of words or phrases can heighten effect and reinforce ideas. Emphasis achieved through repetition must be carefully planned, however, since the technique is dramatic and calls attention to itself. Notice how the repetition of *I saw* and *frightful* hammers home the fear Mary Shelley felt when she saw her vision.

I saw—with shut eyes but acute mental vision—I saw the pale student of unhallowed arts kneeling beside the thing he had put together. I saw the hideous phantasm of a man

stretched out, and then, on the working of some powerful engine, show signs of life and stir with an uneasy, half vital motion. Frightful must it be, for supremely frightful would be the effect of any human endeavor to mock the stupendous mechanism of the Creator of the world.

6 **Discussion** How is the Romantic concern about the nature of creativity reflected here?

7 **Discussion** What insight do these observations give into the personalities of Byron and Shelley?

8 **Discussion** Would the Romantics have admired or deplored Mary Shelley's imaginative reverie? Why?

9 **Enrichment** The twentieth-century writer W. Somerset Maugham wrote, ''Reverie is the groundwork of creative imagination; it is the privilege of the artist that with him it is not as with other men an escape from reality, but the means by which he accedes to it.'' Have students discuss the meaning of this quotation. How does it relate to Mary Shelley's reverie?

capability of invention which is the greatest misery of authorship, when dull Nothing replies to our anxious invocations. *Have you thought of a story?* I was asked each morning, and each morning I was forced to reply with a mortifying negative. . . .

Many and long were the conversations between Lord Byron and Shelley, to which I was a devout but nearly silent listener. During one of these, various philosophical doctrines were discussed, and among others the nature of the principle of life and whether there was any probability of its ever being discovered and communicated. They talked of the experiments of Dr. Darwin[9] (I speak not of what the Doctor really did or said that he did, but, as more to my purpose, of what was then spoken of as having been done by him), who preserved a piece of vermicelli in a glass case till by some extraordinary means it began to move with voluntary motion. Not thus, after all, would life be given. Perhaps a corpse would be reanimated: galvanism[10] had given token of such things. Perhaps the component parts of a creature might be manufactured, brought together, and endued with vital warmth.

Night waned upon this talk, and even the witching hour had gone by, before we retired to rest. When I placed my head on my pillow, I did not sleep, nor could I be said to think. My imagination, unbidden, possessed and guided me, gifting the successive images that arose in my mind with a vividness far beyond the usual bounds of reverie. I saw—with shut eyes but acute mental vision—I saw the pale student of unhallowed arts kneeling beside the thing he had put together. I saw the hideous phantasm of a man stretched out, and then, on the working of some powerful engine, show signs of life and stir with an uneasy, half vital motion. Frightful must it be, for supremely

6, 7

8

frightful would be the effect of any human endeavor to mock the stupendous mechanism of the Creator of the world. His success would terrify the artist; he would rush away from his odious handiwork, horror-stricken. He would hope that, left to itself, the slight spark of life which he had communicated would fade; that this thing, which had received such imperfect animation, would subside into dead matter; and he might sleep in the belief that the silence of the grave would quench forever the transient existence of the hideous corpse which he had looked upon as the cradle of life. He sleeps; but he is awakened; he opens his eyes; behold the horrid thing stands at his bedside, opening his curtains, and looking on him with yellow, watery, but speculative eyes.

I opened mine in terror. The idea so possessed my mind, that a thrill of fear ran through me, and I wished to exchange the ghastly image of my fancy for the realities around. I see them still: the very room, the dark parquet,[11] the closed shutters, with the moonlight struggling through, and the sense I had that the glassy lake and white high Alps were beyond. I could not so easily get rid of my hideous phantom: still it haunted me. I must try to think of something else. I recurred to my ghost story—my tiresome unlucky ghost story! O! if I could only contrive one which would frighten my reader as I myself had been frightened that night!

Swift as light and as cheering was the idea that broke in upon me. ''I have found it! What terrified me will terrify others, and I need only describe the specter which had haunted my midnight pillow.'' On the morrow I announced that I had *thought of a story.* I began that day with the words, *It was on a dreary night of November,* making only a transcript of the grim terrors of my waking dream.

At first I thought but of a few pages—of

9

---

9. Dr. Darwin: Erasmus Darwin (1731–1802), physician, natural scientist, and poet.
10. galvanism: The use of electric current to induce twitching in dead muscles.

11. parquet (pär kā'): Flooring made of wooden pieces arranged in a pattern.

Shelley's repeated *I saw* widens the readers' eyes and causes them to see the vision along with her. The third *I saw* adds horror. People in shock do not think of synonyms; they tend to repeat their first, vivid impressions. Her next sentence repeats *frightful* because, indeed, there is no better word to describe her reaction to a human playing God.

Student Activity. Recall a frightening experience from your childhood. Then write a paragraph in which you describe the experience using repetition to emphasize the fear you felt.

a short tale—but Shelley urged me to develop the idea at greater length. I certainly did not owe the suggestion of one incident, nor scarcely of one train of feeling, to my husband, and yet but for his incitement, it would never have taken the form in which it was presented to the world. From this declaration I must except the preface. As far as I can recollect, it was entirely written by him.

And now, once again, I bid my hideous progeny go forth and prosper. I have an affection for it, for it was the offspring of happy days, when death and grief were but words, which found no true echo in my heart. Its several pages speak of many a walk, many a drive, and many a conversation, when I was not alone; and my companion was one who, in this world, I shall never see more. But this is for myself: my readers have nothing to do with these associations.

10
11

10 **Discussion** Explain why the author says she has "an affection" for her horror story.

11 **Clarification** The name Frankenstein is commonly associated with the monster. It, in fact, refers to the creator.

Reader's Response Does this selection alter your thoughts and associations regarding "Frankenstein"? If so, how?

THINKING ABOUT THE SELECTION

Recalling

1. What question does the author say people frequently ask her?
2. (a) What forced the author, her husband, and their friends to stay indoors? (b) What did they do to pass the time?
3. What was Byron's proposition?
4. (a) What provided the author with inspiration for her story? (b) What "vision" came to the author after she retired for the night?

Interpreting

5. What do the goals the author sets for herself in writing her ghost story suggest about her as a person?
6. Based on her description of her "vision," what seems to be the author's attitude toward work of the sort carried out by Dr. Darwin?

Applying

7. Many areas of scientific investigation carry both potential benefits and potential dangers for humankind. (a) What such areas in our own age can you name? (b) Which areas do you believe human beings should never have become involved in? Give reasons for your answer.

ANALYZING LITERATURE

Recognizing Gothic Tradition

The Gothic tradition of the horror story, which began in the eighteenth century, traces back to ancient times. In *The Spirit of the Public Journals,* a 1797 pamphlet, a "recipe" for the Gothic novel is given. Among the "ingredients" listed are: an old castle, a long gallery with secret doors, three freshly murdered bodies, assorted skeletons, and "noises, whispers, and groans." In *Frankenstein,* Mary Shelley endeavored to improve slightly on that formula.

1. Based on your reading of her introduction, what most likely is the theme of *Frankenstein?*
2. Based on the French translations of ghost stories Shelley mentions, what other "ingredients" might be added to the above list?

THINKING AND WRITING

Writing in the Gothic Tradition

Review the ideas and outline you developed for the assignment under Writing on page 733. Then write an original story or episode that follows the Gothic tradition. You may add as many of the elements mentioned. If you can, build a theme into your horror story. When you revise make sure you have told your tale in chronological order.

settle for "second-best"—her ghost story had to be worthy of its name.
6. She saw any human attempt to create life as a mockery of the Creator.

Applying

7. (a) Answers will differ. Possible answers include the following: The attempt to create life in a test tube and experiments with nuclear energy are two examples of scientific investigation that carry both potential benefits and dangers. (b) Answers will differ; though nuclear weapons will be mentioned by many, because of their potential for destruction.

Challenge What other works of literature have been inspired by dreams?

ANSWERS TO ANALYZING LITERATURE

1. The theme of *Frankenstein* is that man should not try to interfere with the work of God.
2. She thought that a horror story should be terrifying, that death should be a prominent theme, and that the central character should atone for a sin by suffering a terrible fate.

THINKING AND WRITING

Publishing Student Writing Horror stories have always been popular with people of all ages. Suggest that students compile the best ghost stories into a book that might serve as a class fundraiser at Halloween.

Closure and Extension

ANSWERS TO THINKING ABOUT THE SELECTION
Recalling

1. She says that people ask her: How did a young girl conceive such a hideous idea?
2. (a) Rainy weather drove them indoors. (b) To pass the time they read ghost stories.

3. Byron proposed that each of them write a ghost story.
4. (a) Her inspiration was a discussion between Byron and Shelley about whether life could be manufactured. (b) She dreamed about a man who had created human life.

Interpreting

5. They suggest a somewhat insecure person. The presence of Shelley and Byron probably made her feel this way. She was not content to

Have students discuss stories about a person who sells his or her soul to the devil in exchange for knowledge or power. What do these stories have in common? How are they different? What makes this such a compelling idea?

More About the Author Johann Wolfgang von Goethe (gö tə) was not only a gifted writer, he was also a scientist, a painter, a statesman, a philosopher, and an educator.

Born in Frankfurt am Main, Goethe (1749–1832) was educated first by private tutors and later at the University of Leipzig. It was at the University that Goethe came under the influence of the *Sturm und Drang* literary movement.

Goethe's novel, *The Sorrows of Young Werther* (1774), brought him international fame. This autobiographical novel helped to form the conception of Romantic hero through the depiction of a restless, emotional, tormented, and individualist character.

Following the publication of the novel, Goethe was invited to the court of Charles Augustus, the reigning Duke of Weimar. Here he served for a time as the Duke's chief minister, conducted scientific studies, and directed the court theater. He also formed a fast friendship with Friedrich von Schiller, who provided Goethe with support, guidance, and advice for his writing. Schiller also assisted in revising a number of Goethe's most important works, including *Faust*.

Along with *Faust*, Goethe completed several other significant works during the late eighteenth and early nineteenth centuries. These works include the novels *Wilhelm Meister's Apprenticeship, Elective Affinities,* and *Wilhelm Meister's Travels,* the collection of poetry *Roman Elegies,* and his autobiographical work *Poetry and Truth.*

Thematic Idea An excerpt from Christopher Marlowe's *The Tragical History of the Life and Death of Doctor Faustus* appears on page 233. Unlike Goethe, Marlowe portrays Faust as a tragic character whose soul is condemned to eternal damnation at the end of the play.

CROSS CURRENTS

Goethe's *Faust*

The play opens in a narrow, high-vaulted Gothic room. Faust, a deeply learned scholar, speaks restlessly from his armchair by the desk:

> I have pursued, alas, philosophy,
> Jurisprudence, and medicine,
> And, help me God, theology,
> With fervent zeal through thick and thin.
> And here, poor fool, I stand once more,
> No wiser than before.

His life is dull, dusty, and empty; he has neither fame, fortune, nor contentment. In despair he tries a less legitimate road to knowledge and satisfaction:

> So I resorted to Magic's art,
> To see if by spirit mouth and might
> Many a secret might come to light;
> So I need toil no longer so,
> Propounding what I do not know.

Mephistopheles, the Devil, appears from the mist. Faust gladly signs a pact with him—in blood!—exchanging his soul for knowledge, "all treasures of the human mind." The Devil promises Faust that

> I shall be at your service by this bond
> Without relief or respite here on earth;

but makes the scholar swear

> And if or when we meet again beyond,
> You are to give me equal worth.

With this, a great change comes over the life of the learned doctor. He tastes experience through a great many wondrous adventures but does not find the happiness he is seeking until the very last act. And this is what Goethe is asking: What is happiness? Is it living within your abilities? Or is it daring to be more than human? Faust—and the audience—learn the answer as the curtain drops.

A LIFETIME OF WORK

The legend of Doctor Faustus, the famous magician who sells his soul to the devil in return for knowledge of mystical secrets, is a thrilling horror story with a moral. It was first published in 1587, and different versions were sold year after year at country fairs. In Christopher Marlowe's hands, the legend became a play for the Elizabethan stage. The theme was taken up by troupes of traveling puppeteers and soon became a favorite around the country.

Young Goethe, familiar with the Faust legend through the early books and puppet show, sensed that the wild tale could allow him to explore the exciting new aspirations of the human soul. In the early 1770's, he began to jot down the first scenes for a projected Faust play. When he moved to Weimar in the autumn of 1775—where he would settle for the rest of his life—he brought these sketches with him. He worked on the manuscript on and off for more than a decade. Fearing that he would never complete it, he issued an unfinished version in 1790. Encouraged by his friend Schiller, he finally published *Faust, Part One* in 1808. Meanwhile he had begun work on the second part, very different from the first in time, place, and style. Although he released portions of *Part Two* during his life, he worked on the manuscript right up until his death. The complete play was published in 1832, more than sixty years after he had first begun it. The lifetime of work yielded the masterpiece of Germany's finest poet.

FAUST AND ROMANTICISM

Although Romanticism didn't cause a political upheaval in Germany, it did spark the imagination of German writers. Like their English and French counterparts, young German writers began to rebel against the restraints of Neoclassicism.

The Romantic movement exploded on the German scene during the *Sturm und Drang* (storm and stress) movement of the 1770's. As the name suggests, the era saw the rise of highly emotional writing. Goethe, as with many writers of the time, was inspired by the movement to explore the new values of imagination and emotion.

To previous generations Faust was a symbol of humanity gone astray, and his story was taken as a warning. To the Romantics, in contrast, Faust represented human freedom from authority. Whether his decision would lead to salvation or not, his courage in venturing into the world of the forbidden makes him heroic. As he struggles between the real and the ideal, we see Goethe's deep love of humanity.

Goethe's *Faust* is the greatest and most famous version of the Faust legend, the one upon which all subsequent retellings are based. Fascinating, provocative, and compelling, *Faust* probes deeply into the human soul in its search for answers to the timeless quest for the meaning of human existence.

FAUST: HENRY IRVING AS MEPHISTOPHELES
Theatre Museum/E. T. Archive

→ Mr Henry Irving as Mephistopheles - Tw

Humanities Note

Fine Art, *Faust: Henry Irving as Mephistopheles*. Sir Henry Irving (1838–1905) was a major figure in the British theater. A descendant of the grand style of melodramatic performance, Irving was best known for his theatrically effective emotionalism. This style brought both praise and criticism from critics of his time. According to critic Max Beerbohm, "Irving may have sometimes overdone it; but he always overdid it beautifully." George Bernard Shaw attacked him for a lack of intellect, commenting that Irving "could not, even had the stage been as bare as a desert, have given us the true music and magic of Shakespeare's verse."

Despite this criticism, Irving had a tremendous impact on the style of nineteenth century theater. His melodramatic expression, as seen in this illustration of his role as Mephistopheles, became a standard by which other actors were measured. Today's restrained and naturalistic acting is far removed from Irving's histrionic, personal approach.

You might use the following questions for class discussion:
1. In what ways do you think the melodramatic style of acting favored by Irving would be appropriate for the Romantic age?
2. Why might critics have described this style of acting as "romantic"?

Questions

1. What evidence is there that the legend of Doctor Faustus was popular?
2. What does the name *Sturm und Drang* indicate about the focus of this literary movement?
3. Why did the Romantics consider Faust a heroic character?
4. Explain how Faust is an embodiment of Romantic ideals.

More About the Author Some
critics believe that Charles
Lamb's best essays were written
under the pen name "Elia." According to literary scholar Saxe
Commins, the "*nom de plume*
was derived from a fellow-clerk
in the South Sea House, an Italian. At the time, John Lamb
(Charles's brother) was working
there, and Charles, fearing that
John might not like certain allusions, merely appropriated the
name of the unwitting Italian.
When Charles Lamb went to confess to the original Elia his unsur-
pation of the name, he discovered that his fellow-clerk had
died the year before of consumption, totally unaware of the stir
created by the Essays written
over his name."

"Dream Children: A Reverie"
is one example of Elia's work.
A.C. Ward noted "As Elia, Lamb
was rarely dull . . . yet, as Lamb,
his pen at times drags wearily."
Do you think that by becoming
someone else in his imagination,
Lamb felt freer to express himself
and to deal with the unhappier
aspects of his life? Why?

CHARLES LAMB

1775–1834

A personal friend of most of the great English writers of his day,
Charles Lamb was considered one of the foremost prose writers of
the Romantic Era—a distinction he has retained through the present
time.

The son of a clerk and the grandson of a housekeeper, Lamb
was born in London. He was educated at Christ's Hospital, a school
for poor children, where he met and became lifelong friends with a
fellow student, Samuel Taylor Coleridge, who later became a
well-known poet and critic. At seventeen Lamb left school and took
a job with the South Sea House, a large London trading company.
He soon received a better position as an accountant at a rival firm,
the East India House, where he remained employed for thirty-three
years.

In 1796 an event occurred that shadowed the rest of Lamb's life.
His sister Mary, given to brief fits of insanity, killed their mother. After
this, Lamb, always a loving brother, devoted himself to Mary's care
and protection. Upon his retirement from East India House, he was
granted a comfortable pension and after his sister's confinement to
an asylum, took her to live in the country.

Throughout most of his life, Lamb wrote to supplement his
regular income. Although he composed a number of poems and
plays, it was with his essays and literary criticism that he made his
mark as a writer. In 1808 he published a book on Elizabethan
dramatic poets that established his reputation as a critic. Thereafter,
he began to contribute essays to periodicals such as the *Examiner,*
the *Quarterly Review*, the *London Magazine,* and the *Reflector,* a
magazine published by the poet Leigh Hunt.

It was in the *London Magazine* that Lamb's series of personal
essays written under the name Elia first appeared in printed form.
Later these essays were collected and published in the volumes
Essays of Elia (1832) and *Last Essays of Elia* (1833). Lamb also
collaborated with his sister Mary on a number of works, including
the ever-popular *Tales from Shakespeare* (1807), a collection designed to introduce young readers to Shakespeare's plays.

Many of Lamb's essays are autobiographical, with characters
modeled on his father, his grandmother, his brother John, and other
relatives. Though they are known for their gentle humor, the essays
often display an undercurrent of great sadness, the result of the
tragedies that Lamb experienced in his life.

Objectives

1 To understand the
   familiar essay
2 To infer a writer's tone
3 To recognize multiple
   meanings of words
4 To analyze a writer's
   attitudes

Support Material

Teaching Portfolio
Teacher Backup, p. 889
Usage and Mechanics Work-
   sheet, p. 892
Vocabulary Check, p. 893
Analyzing Literature Worksheet,
   *Understanding the Familiar Es-
   say,* p. 895
Language Worksheet, *Using the*

Multiple Meanings of Words,
p. 896
Selection Test, p. 897

GUIDE FOR INTERPRETING

Dream Children: A Reverie

Familiar Essay. An essay is a short prose composition that focuses on a single subject. A familiar or informal essay is a loosely constructed essay that uses conversational English to communicate a writer's thoughts in a manner that will interest or entertain the reader. Since familiar essays frequently include details from the author's own life, they are sometimes referred to as "personal" essays.

The familiar essay has its origins in the writings of Michel de Montaigne, a French author of the sixteenth century. It was Montaigne who first used the term *essai*—French for "attempt"—to describe the somewhat rambling, often amusing compositions in which he communicated highly personal thoughts to his readers.

Commentary

In their tone and style, Lamb's familiar essays no doubt drew on his frequent conversations with friends, a distinguished circle of great writers. Many anecdotes survive of their witty conversations. For example, the host of a party attended by Lamb, Wordsworth, and Keats, among others, remarked that Lamb's wit "so speeded the stream of conversation, that in my life I never passed a more delightful time." The following story describes an encounter between Lamb and Coleridge.

Coleridge had been especially talkative that evening. He had covered every topic imaginable, from Moses on downward. Finally his monologue came to his own concerns. He turned to Lamb and continued: "At this place, at Shrewsbury (which is not only remarkable for its celebrated cakes, and for having been the point of rendezvous for Falstaff's regiment of foot, but also, if I may presume to speak of it, for the first development of the imaginative faculty in myself, by which faculty I would be understood to mean, etc. etc.)—at Shrewsbury I was accustomed to preach. I believe, Charles Lamb, that you have heard me preach?" His exhausted friend quickly replied, "I—I—never heard you do anything else."

What characteristics of daily conversation do you see in the following familiar essay?

Writing

Choose a fairly light topic that allows some room for opinion, such as whether the school week should be shortened or lengthened. Freewrite, expressing your opinion on this topic, defending your position with abundant examples from your own life and experience.

Literary Focus Ask students to explain the meaning of the word *reverie* and to give examples of daydreams they have had. Point out that an informal essay, being loosely structured, is an especially appropriate form for the material of a reverie.

Writing/Prior Knowledge Allow your students a few minutes to offer their reasons for their opinion.

Vocabulary

Preteach the following vocabulary words:
reverie (rev′ər ē) n.: Daydream (p. 742)
upbraiding (up brād′iŋ) n.: Scolding (p. 742)
tawdry (tô′drē) adj.: Cheap; gaudy (p. 742)
desisted (di zist′əd) v.: Stopped (p. 742)
apparition (ap′ə rish′ən) n.: Ghost (p. 743)
impertinent (im pʉr′ t′n ənt) adj.: Rude; disrespectful (p. 743)
mettlesome (met″l səm) adj.: High-spirited (p. 743)

Dream Children: A Reverie

Charles Lamb

Children love to listen to stories about their elders when *they* were children; to stretch their imagination to the conception of a traditionary great-uncle, or grandame whom they never saw. It was in this spirit that my little ones crept about me the other evening to hear about their great-grandmother Field,[1] who lived in a great house in Norfolk (a hundred times bigger than that in which they and papa lived) which had been the scene—so at least it was generally believed in that part of the country—of the tragic incidents which they had lately become familiar with from the ballad of "The Children in the Wood."[2] Certain it is that the whole story of the children and their cruel uncle was to be seen fairly carved out in wood upon the chimney piece of the great hall, the whole story down to the Robin Redbreasts;[3] till a foolish rich person pulled it down to set up a marble one of modern invention in its stead, with no story upon it. Here Alice put out one of her dear mother's looks, too tender to be called upbraiding.

Then I went on to say, how religious and how good their great-grandmother Field was, how beloved and respected by everybody, though she was not indeed the mistress of this great house, but had only the charge of it (and yet in some respects she might be said to be the mistress of it too) committed to her by the owner, who preferred living in a newer and more fashionable mansion which he had purchased somewhere in the adjoining county; but still she lived in it in a manner as if it had been her own, and kept up the dignity of the great house in a sort while she lived, which afterwards came to decay, and was nearly pulled down, and all its old ornaments stripped and carried away to the owner's other house, where they were set up, and looked as awkward as if someone were to carry away the old tombs they had seen lately at the Abbey, and stick them up in Lady C.'s tawdry gilt drawing room. Here John smiled, as much as to say, "that would be foolish indeed."

And then I told how, when she came to die, her funeral was attended by a concourse of all the poor, and some of the gentry too, of the neighborhood for many miles round, to show their respect for her memory, because she had been such a good and religious woman; so good indeed that she knew all the Psaltery[4] by heart, ay, and a great part of the Testament besides. Here little Alice spread her hands.

Then I told what a tall, upright, graceful person their great-grandmother Field once was; and how in her youth she was esteemed the best dancer—here Alice's little right foot played an involuntary movement, till, upon my looking grave, it desisted—the

---

1. great-grandmother Field: Mary Field, Lamb's grandmother.
2. "The Children in the Wood": A popular ballad of the time about the mysterious disappearance of two children.
3. Robin Redbreasts: At the end of the story, the robin buries the bodies of the children with leaves.

4. Psaltery (sôl′ tə rē): The Psalms of David.

best dancer, I was saying, in the county, till a cruel disease, called a cancer, came, and bowed her down with pain; but it could never bend her good spirits, or make them stoop, but they were still upright, because she was so good and religious.

Then I told how she was used to sleep by herself in a lone chamber of the great lone house; and how she believed that an apparition of two infants was to be seen at midnight gliding up and down the great staircase near where she slept, but she said "those innocents would do her no harm"; and how frightened I used to be, though in those days I had my maid to sleep with me, because I was never half so good or religious as she—and yet I never saw the infants. Here John expanded all his eyebrows and tried to look courageous.

Then I told how good she was to all her grandchildren, having us to the great house in the holidays, where I in particular used to spend many hours by myself, in gazing upon the old busts of the Twelve Caesars that had been Emperors of Rome, till the old marble heads would seem to live again, or I to be turned into marble with them; how I never could be tired with roaming about that huge mansion, with its vast empty rooms, with their worn-out hangings, fluttering tapestry, and carved oaken panels, with the gilding almost rubbed out—sometimes in the spacious old-fashioned gardens, which I had almost to myself, unless when now and then a solitary gardening man would cross me—and how the nectarines and peaches hung upon the walls, without my ever offering to pluck them, because they were forbidden fruit, unless now and then—and because I had more pleasure in strolling about among the old melancholy-looking yew trees, or the firs, and picking up the red berries, and the fir apples,[5] which were good for nothing but to look at—or in lying about upon the fresh grass, with all the fine garden smells around me—or basking in the orangery, till I could almost fancy myself ripening too along with the oranges and the limes in that grateful warmth—or in watching the dace that darted to and fro in the fishpond, at the bottom of the garden, with here and there a great sulky pike hanging midway down the water in silent state, as if it mocked at their impertinent friskings—I had more pleasure in these busy-idle diversions than in all the sweet flavors of peaches, nectarines, oranges, and such like common baits of children. Here John slyly deposited back upon the plate a bunch of grapes, which, not unobserved by Alice, he had meditated dividing with her, and both seemed willing to relinquish them for the present as irrelevant.

Then in somewhat a more heightened tone, I told how, though their great-grandmother Field loved all her grandchildren, yet in an especial manner she might be said to love their uncle, John L—,[6] because he was so handsome and spirited a youth, and a king to the rest of us; and, instead of moping about in solitary corners, like some of us, he would mount the most mettlesome horse he could get, when but an imp no bigger than themselves, and make it carry him half over the county in a morning, and join the hunters when there were any out—and yet he loved the old great house and gardens too, but had too much spirit to be always pent up within their boundaries—and how their uncle grew up to man's estate as brave as he was handsome, to the admiration of everybody, but of their great-grandmother Field most especially; and how he used to carry me upon his back when I was a lame-footed boy—for he was a good bit older than me—many a mile when I could not walk for pain; and how in after life he became lame-footed too, and I did not always (I fear) make allowances enough for him when he was impatient, and in pain, nor remember sufficiently how considerate he had been to me when I was lame-footed;

---

5. fir apples: Fir cones.

6. John L—: John Lamb, Charles's brother.

4 **Discussion** How do these lines illustrate the chief purpose of a familiar essay?

5 **Discussion** What do these lines express about Lamb's attitude toward nature?

6 and how when he died, though he had not been dead an hour, it seemed as if he had died a great while ago, such a distance there is betwixt life and death; and how I bore his death as I thought pretty well at first, but afterwards it haunted and haunted me; and though I did not cry or take it to heart as some do, and as I think he would have done if I had died, yet I missed him all day long, and knew not till then how much I had loved him. I missed his kindness, and I missed his crossness, and wished him to be alive again, to be quarreling with him (for we quarreled sometimes) rather than not have him again, and was as uneasy without him, as he their poor uncle must have been when the doctor took off his limb. Here the children fell a-crying, and asked if their little mourning which they had on was not for uncle John, and they looked up, and prayed me not to go on about their uncle, but to tell them some stories about their pretty dead mother.

Then I told how for seven long years, in hope sometimes, sometimes in despair, yet persisting ever, I courted the fair Alice W—n;[7] and, as much as children could

---

7. Alice W—n: Alice Winterton, name given to Ann Simmons, whom Lamb loved in his earlier years.

understand, I explained to them what coyness, and difficulty, and denial meant in maidens—when suddenly, turning to Alice, the soul of the first Alice looked out at her eyes with such a reality of representment, that I became in doubt which of them stood there before me, or whose that bright hair was; and while I stood gazing, both the children gradually grew fainter to my view, receding, and still receding till nothing at last but two mournful features were seen in the uttermost distance, which, without speech, strangely impressed upon me the effects of speech: "We are not of Alice, nor of thee, nor are we children at all. The children of Alice called Bartrum father. We are nothing; less than nothing, and dreams. We are **7** only what might have been, and must wait upon the tedious shores of Lethe[8] millions of ages before we have existence, and a name"—and immediately awaking, I found myself quietly seated in my bachelor armchair, where I had fallen asleep, with the faithful Bridget[9] unchanged by my side—but John **8** L. (or James Elia) was gone forever.

---

8. Lethe (lē' thē): In classical mythology, the river of forgetfulness, flowing through Hades, the land of the dead.
9. Bridget: Name given to Lamb's sister, Mary.

THINKING ABOUT THE SELECTION
Recalling

1. (a) According to the opening paragraph, who is listening to the narrator's story? (b) Why are these listeners interested in hearing about great-grandmother Field?
2. (a) Besides his grandmother, which relative does the narrator speak of with deep affection? (b) What has happened to this relative?
3. (a) Who was Alice W—n? (b) According to the final paragraph, who closely resembles her?
4. (a) What is revealed about the narrator's audience in the final paragraph? (b) What is revealed about Alice W—n?

Interpreting

5. Why do you suppose the narrator's listeners are named John and Alice?
6. Identify three details in the essay that make the young John and Alice seem real.

Closure and Extension

ANSWERS TO THINKING ABOUT THE SELECTION

1. (a) The narrator's children are listening to the story. (b) Children like to listen to stories about their elders as children, to try to imagine what they were like when they were young.
2. (a) The narrator speaks of John L—, his brother and the grandchild of great-grandmother Field. (b) John L— has died.
3. (a) Alice was a woman whom the narrator courted. In reality, she was the woman (Ann Simmons) Charles Lamb loved but never married. (b) Alice, the child of the narrator, closely resembles Alice W—n.
4. (a) The narrator imagined the children in a daydream. (b) Alice W—n married a man named Bartrum and bore his children.

Interpreting

5. The narrator named his listeners after people he loved—his brother John and Alice Winterton.
6. Answers will differ. Possible answers include the following: The narrator describes Alice's reactions

7. In what ways does the apparition seen by great-grandmother Field foreshadow—that is, give the reader an advance glimpse of—the events at the end of the essay?
8. (a) What does this essay reveal about Charles Lamb's feelings toward his being unmarried and childless? (b) Why might such feelings be prompted by thoughts of his own childhood and especially of his brother John?

Applying

9. Do you think it is always important to know details of an author's life to fully appreciate the author's work? Explain.

ANALYZING LITERATURE
Understanding the Familiar Essay

A **familiar,** or informal, **essay** is a loosely constructed piece of prose that deals with a single topic and uses conversational English. Although a familiar essay may contain some short story elements, such as plot and character, it is nevertheless considered to be nonfiction, since its chief purpose is to communicate its author's thoughts and feelings, and not those of imaginary characters.
1. Which characters in Lamb's essay are real? Which are imaginary?
2. Which elements in the essay make it seem like a short story? Give several examples.
3. In what ways is the author's style characteristic of a familiar essay?

CRITICAL THINKING AND READING
Inferring Tone

The **tone** of a story, poem, or essay is the attitude the writer takes with respect to the audience, a character, or a situation. In much the way a person's tone of voice will affect how his or her words are understood, so the tone of a literary selection helps shape the reader's reaction toward it. Determine the tone Lamb takes

with respect to each of the following, and describe its effect on you.
1. Great-grandmother Field.
2. Young Alice and John.
3. The great house.
4. Alice W—n.

UNDERSTANDING LANGUAGE
Using Multiple Meaning of Words

While good authors as a rule use words precisely, they occasionally use words with second and even third meanings to enrich a thought or sentiment. A writer might, for instance, describe a character's state of mind as "cloudy," with the intention of conveying both the meanings "confused" and "bleak or unhappy." In "Dream Children: A Reverie," Charles Lamb uses several words in this fashion. For each sentence, give two meanings for the italicized word, and describe its impact.
1. "Then I told what a tall, *upright,* graceful person their great-grandmother . . . was." (page 742)
2. ". . . upon my looking *grave,* it desisted . . ." (page 742)
3. ". . . two mournful features . . . without speech, *strangely* impressed upon me the effects of speech. . . ." (page 744)

THINKING AND WRITING
Analyzing a Writer's Attitudes

Lamb's attitude toward his personal fantasy world and his attitude toward reality, as expressed in the essay, appear to be different. Discuss this difference in terms of his blend of factual and fictional details. Ask: What, exactly, is Lamb escaping from? What is he escaping to? What is his view of himself in the fantasy role of father? What relationship does this view bear to his real role as brother? Organize your thoughts and write the first draft of a brief essay. When you revise make sure you have included adequate details to support your main idea.

Dream Children: A Reverie   745

opening lines suggest that the piece will be a short story. The setting is established by the description of great-grandmother Field's house. Characters are introduced and brought to life. There is no firm plot, but the suggestion of a plot is there; for example, when the narrator talks about his brother John. There is a resolution to the story when the narrator wakes up.
3. The personal nature and rambling structure of the essay and the use of character, description, and colloquial language, including the frequent use of parentheses, are all characteristic of a familiar essay.

Challenge William Wordsworth claimed that poetry should have its origin in "emotion recollected in tranquillity." How do you think Wordsworth would react to this essay? Explain your answer.

ANSWERS TO CRITICAL THINKING AND READING

Answers will differ. Possible answers follow.
1. Great-grandmother Field is described with loving admiration and respect.
2. Young Alice and John are described with gentle amusement and affection.
3. The house is described with a tone that is a combination of wonder and nostalgia.
4. Alice W—n is described in a sad and regretful tone.

ANSWERS TO UNDERSTANDING LANGUAGE

1. *Upright* means "erect." *Upright* can also mean "honest" or "just," which adds an admirable dimension to great-grandmother's character.
2. *Grave* means "solemn." The word *grave* can also refer to a tomb, which carries greater impact due to the description of great-grandmother Field's funeral in the preceding sentences.
3. The word *strangely* means "oddly." It can also suggest "in an extraordinary way," which adds to the impact of the dream.

to his words, in such ways as "Alice put out one of her dear mother's looks" and "Alice spread her hands." He also describes John's reactions: "Here John smiled. . . ."
7. Great-grandmother Field saw the apparitions of two infants at midnight, which foreshadows the disclosure at the end of the essay that the children Alice and John are imaginary.
8. (a) The essay suggests that Lamb wished he had married Alice and

that they had had children. (b) His memories caused him to feel nostalgic about his family and rueful about his bachelorhood.

Applying

9. Answers will differ. Suggested response: Knowing details about an author's life and his or her attitudes can add to the appreciation of some works. However, in most cases the works can be appreciated on their own merit, without any special knowledge of the author.

ANSWERS TO ANALYZING LITERATURE

1. The characters of great-grandmother Field, John L—, and Alice W—n, and Bridget are real. The grandchildren Alice and John are imaginary.
2. Answers will differ. Possible answers include the following: The

More About the Author Hazlitt expressed his thoughts about writers in this excerpt from *On the Difference Between Writing and Speaking:* "They are never less alone than when alone. Mount them on a dinner-table, and they have nothing to say; shut them up in a room by themselves, and they are inspired. They are 'made fierce with dark keeping.' In revenge for being tongue-tied, a torrent of words flows from their pens, and the storm which was so long collecting comes down apace. It never rains but it pours. Is not this strange, unaccountable? Not at all so. . . . Till they can do justice to the feeling they have, they can do nothing. . . . What they would say (if they could) does not lie at the orifices of the mouth, ready for delivery, but is wrapped in the folds of the heart and registered in the chambers of the brain. . . . The whole of a man's thoughts and feelings cannot lie on the surface, made up for use; but the whole must be a greater quantity, a mightier power, if they could be got at, layer under layer, and brought into play by the levers of imagination and reflection. Such a person then sees farther and feels deeper than most others. He plucks up an argument at the roots, he tears out the very heart of his subject. He has more pride in conquering the difficulties of a question, than vanity in courting the favour of an audience. He wishes to satisfy himself before he pretends to enlighten the public."

Although he was greatly admired for his opinionated essays, Hazlitt was not nearly as successful in his personal life. He alienated many of his acquaintances, and both of his marriages ended in separation. Ask students what qualities that served Hazlitt well as a critic might have interfered with his personal relationships.

WILLIAM HAZLITT

1778–1830

Second only to Coleridge as a critic of the Romantic era, William Hazlitt was known in his day and is remembered in ours for his brisk and direct writing style. In addition Hazlitt was a true Romantic who lived life as he wrote about it—with gusto.

The son of a Unitarian minister who sympathized with the colonists during the American Revolution, Hazlitt sailed with his family to America when he was five and remained there for three years. He planned, like his father, to enter the clergy and was admitted to Hackney Theological Seminary in London. A difficulty in expressing himself both orally and on paper, however, forced him to abandon his goal and he returned to his family in Shropshire.

It was there in 1798 that Hazlitt met the poet Samuel Taylor Coleridge, who at the time was a house guest of Hazlitt's father. Recognizing Hazlitt's brilliance, Coleridge introduced the young man to his friends Wordsworth and Charles Lamb, who also found Hazlitt impressive.

Hazlitt, meanwhile, was still frustrated by his inability to communicate his ideas in writing, and at twenty-one he journeyed again to London, this time to study painting with his brother. Finding that his talents in this area were limited as well, he tried his hand once more at writing, and in 1805 published his first book, *An Essay on the Principles of Human Action.* In the six years that followed, he married, wrote two more books, and delivered a series of lectures on philosophy.

The year 1812 found Hazlitt penniless and his spirit broken. He took a paying job as a parliamentary reporter for a London newspaper and—much to his surprise and delight—he developed a following as a writer on a variety of subjects. In 1817 he published *Characters in Shakespeare's Plays,* which he followed up a year later with *A View of the English Stage,* a collection of drama criticism. At last, fame and respect had arrived!

Long an eccentric who judged everyone and everything according to his own rigid system of values, Hazlitt became more bitter and opinionated with age. He turned his talented pen to angry attacks on less liberal journalists than himself, as well as on poets and politicians, and in so doing made many enemies. Only the younger Romantic poets like Shelley and Keats admired Hazlitt's work of this period, and then only because of its intensity and dedication to the philosophy of Rousseau.

While to the modern mind Hazlitt's criticism tends to be overly subjective, scholars nevertheless respect him as one of the leading critics of Elizabethan and Romantic literature. Above all else Hazlitt is remembered for his ability to cut to the heart of an issue and to state his views firmly and honestly.

746   The Romantic Age

GUIDE FOR INTERPRETING

Macbeth

Literary Forms

Critical Essay. A critical essay is an essay that evaluates the merits of a given topic, usually artistic. While such an essay expresses the personal views and observations of its author, the essay will, if it is fair and honest, also appeal to some universal standard. Literary criticism, an area that gives rise to one of the best-known forms of critical essay, the literary essay, began with the Greek philosopher Plato and was later refined by Aristotle. From the fall of Rome through the Renaissance in the late fourteenth century, literary criticism was neglected in favor of church-related issues. With the Romantic movement came the first modern examples of the critical literary essay, as typified by the writings of Samuel Taylor Coleridge, Charles Lamb, and William Hazlitt.

Commentary

Drama criticism was a growing literary genre in the Romantic period because the theater had become an increasingly important feature of English life. By the 1820's, Romanticism dominated the plays presented throughout most of Europe. These plays were not characterized by one definite style, as in previous eras. Rather, they were generally strongly emotional, and their experimentation with form laid the groundwork for the later rejection of Neoclassicism.

The most important theaters in London were the Opera House, Drury Lane, and Covent Garden. Covent Garden, its wide rows packed with a stylish crowd, provided a strong contrast to the small, badly lit, makeshift theaters in which the finest plays of the Restoration period had been performed. Between acts, women walked around the theater selling apples and oranges, and it was possible to buy more filling food as well.

In the countryside, where any large building or barn had been considered appropriate for the staging of a play during the Restoration, a new group of theaters arose. Many were very well designed and built. Often, these rural theaters supported a permanent band of players.

What elements of Romanticism do you see in Hazlitt's criticism of *Macbeth*?

Writing

Imagine that you have been asked to review a play for your school newspaper. Make a list of the details of which you would need to take notice. Keep in mind that, in addition to such literary matters as character and theme, you would need to pay attention to how well the actors projected their voices, how effective the lighting was, and so on.

Guide for Interpreting 747

Writing/Prior Knowledge Hazlitt wrote this essay in reaction to seeing the play *Macbeth* performed in London. For extra credit, your **more advanced** students might enjoy writing a critical essay on a play, movie, or television show they have seen. Have them discuss the likenesses and differences between two major characters.

Vocabulary

Preteach the following vocabulary words:

preternatural (prēt′ər nach′ər əl) adj.: Outside the natural or normal order (p. 748)

tumultuous (too mul′ choo wəs) adj.: Disorderly; violent (p. 749)

vehemence (vē′ə məns) n.: Strength of feeling and emotion (p. 749)

obdurate (äb′ door ət, äb dyoor ət) adj.: Hardened against what is good or moral (p. 749)

ascendancy (ə send′ ən sē) n.: Major or dominating influence (p. 749)

inexorable (in ek′sər ə b′l) adj.: Ongoing, with no sign of stopping (p. 749)

baneful (bān′ fəl) adj.: Full of harm; destructive (p. 749)

compunctious (kəm punk shəs) adj.: Sorrowful; regretful (p. 750)

gratuitous (grə too′ə təs) adj.: Undeservedly or without reason (p. 750)

servile (sʉr′v′l) adj.: Slavelike (p. 750)

malignity (mə lig′ nə tē) n.: Deadliness (p. 750)

aggrandizement (ə gran′ diz mənt) n.: Increase in power (p. 750)

Literary Focus Explain that Hazlitt uses the present tense to write about his subject. As they read the essay, have students think about why Hazlitt chose the present tense and what effect this has on their reaction to his criticism.

Macbeth

William Hazlitt

"The poet's eye in a fine
*   frenzy rolling*
Doth glance from heaven to
*   earth, from earth to heaven;*
And as imagination bodies forth
The forms of things
*   unknown, the poet's pen*
Turns them to shape, and
*   gives to airy nothing*
A local habitation and a name."[1]

Macbeth and *Lear, Othello* and *Hamlet,* are usually reckoned Shakespeare's four principal tragedies. *Lear* stands first for the profound intensity of the passion; *Macbeth* for the wildness of the imagination and the rapidity of the action; *Othello* for the progressive interest and powerful alternations of feeling; *Hamlet* for the refined development of thought and sentiment. If the force of genius shown in each of these works is astonishing, their variety is not less so. They are like different creations of the same mind, not one of which has the slightest reference to the rest. This distinctness and originality is indeed the necessary consequence of truth and nature. Shakespeare's genius alone appeared to possess the resources of nature. He is "your only *tragedy maker*." His plays have the force of things upon the mind. What he represents is brought home to the bosom as a part of our experience, implanted in the memory as if we had known the places, persons, and things of which he treats. *Macbeth* is like a record of a preternatural and tragical event. It has the rugged severity of an old chronicle with all that the imagination of the poet can engraft upon traditional belief. The castle of Macbeth, round which "the air smells wooingly," and where "the temple-haunting martlet builds," has a real subsistence in the mind; the Weird Sisters meet us in person on "the blasted heath"; the "air-drawn dagger" moves slowly before our eyes; the "gracious Duncan," the "blood-boltered Banquo" stand before us; all that passed through the mind of Macbeth passes, without the loss of a tittle,[2] through ours. All that could actually take place, and all that is only possible to be conceived, what was said and what was done, the workings of passion, the spells of magic, are brought before us with the same absolute truth and vividness.

Shakespeare excelled in the openings of his plays: that of *Macbeth* is the most striking of any. The wildness of the scenery, the sudden shifting of the situations and characters, the bustle, the expectations excited, are equally extraordinary. From the first entrance of the Witches and the description of them when they meet Macbeth:

> *What are these*
> *So wither'd and so wild*
> *   in their attire,*
> *That look not like the*
> *   inhabitants of th' earth*
> *And yet are on't?*

the mind is prepared for all that follows.

This tragedy is alike distinguished for the lofty imagination it displays, and for the

---

1. "The poet's eye . . . name": From Shakespeare's *A Midsummer Night's Dream*, Act V, Scene i.

2. tittle *n.:* A very small particle.

Grammar in Action

Prefer **direct statement to understatement.** Positive statements can be written by negating a negative word, a technique called understatement. For example, *It was not an unappealing proposal* indicates that the proposal was appealing, but it is indirect, because of the double negative "not . . . unappealing." Normally, however, you would put statements in direct, positive form. Notice Hazlitt's positive statements.

tumultuous vehemence of the action; and the one is made the moving principle of the other. The overwhelming pressure of preternatural agency urges on the tide of human passion with redoubled force. Macbeth himself appears driven along by the violence of his fate like a vessel drifting before a storm: he reels to and fro like a drunken man; he staggers under the weight of his own purposes and the suggestions of others; he stands at bay with his situation; and from the superstitious awe and breathless suspense into which the communications of the Weird Sisters throw him is hurried on with daring impatience to verify their predictions, and with impious and bloody hand to tear aside the veil which hides the uncertainty of the future. He is not equal to the struggle with fate and conscience. He now "bends up each corporal instrument to the terrible feat"; at other times his heart misgives him, and he is cowed and abashed by his success. "The deed, no less than the attempt, confounds him." His mind is assailed by the stings of remorse, and full of "preternatural solicitings." His speeches and soliloquies are dark riddles on human life, baffling solution, and entangling him in their labyrinths. In thought he is absent and perplexed, sudden and desperate in act, from a distrust of his own resolution. His energy springs from the anxiety and agitation of his mind. His blindly rushing forward on the objects of his ambition and revenge, or his recoiling from them, equally betrays the harassed state of his feelings. This part of his character is admirably set off by being brought in connection with that of Lady Macbeth, whose obdurate strength of will and masculine firmness give her the ascendancy over her husband's faltering virtue. She at once seizes on the opportunity that offers for the accomplishment of all their wished-for greatness, and never flinches from her object till all is over. The magnitude of her resolution almost covers the magnitude of her guilt. She is a great bad woman, whom we hate, but whom we fear more than we hate. She does not excite our loathing and abhorrence like Regan and Goneril.[3] She is only wicked to gain a great end and is perhaps more distinguished by her commanding presence of mind and inexorable self-will, which do not suffer her to be diverted from a bad purpose, when once formed, by weak and womanly regrets, than by the hardness of her heart or want of natural affections. The impression which her lofty determination of character makes on the mind of Macbeth is well described where he exclaims:

> Bring forth men children only;
> For thy undaunted mettle should
>   compose
> Nothing but males!

Nor do the pains she is at to "screw his courage to the sticking-place," the reproach to him, not to be "lost so poorly in himself," the assurance that "a little water clears them of this deed," show anything but her greater consistency in depravity. Her strong-nerved ambition furnishes ribs of steel to "the sides of his intent"; and she is herself wound up to the execution of her baneful project with the same unshrinking fortitude in crime, that in other circumstances she would probably have shown patience in suffering. The deliberate sacrifice of all other considerations to the gaining "for their future days and nights sole sovereing sway and masterdom," by the murder of Duncan, is gorgeously expressed in her invocation on hearing of "his fatal entrance under her battlements":

> Come all you spirits
> That tend on mortal
>   thoughts, unsex me here:
> And fill me, from the
>   crown to th' toe, top-full
> Of direst cruelty; make
>   thick my blood,
> Stop up the access and
>   passage to remorse,

---

3. **Regan and Goneril:** King Lear's evil daughters in Shakespeare's *King Lear*.

4 **Discussion** Would this description of Macbeth be as effective if it were written in the past tense? Why or why not?

5 **Discussion** Contrast the personalities of Macbeth and Lady Macbeth, as described by Hazlitt. What does Hazlitt mean when he calls Lady Macbeth "a great bad woman"? Can you think of any other literary characters who might fit this description?

6 **Discussion** Do you agree with Hazlitt's assumption that Lady Macbeth would probably have been patient in suffering? Why or why not?

Macbeth himself appears driven along by the violence of his fate like a vessel drifting before a storm: he reels to and fro like a drunken man; . . . and from the superstitious awe and breathless suspense into which the communications of the Weird Sisters throw him is hurried on with daring impatience to verify their predictions . . .

Notice the confusing wordiness of the following:

Macbeth himself appers driven by the violence of his fate, not unlike a vessel drifting before a storm: he reels to and fro not unlike a drunken man; . . . and from the superstitious awe and breathless suspense into which the communications of the Weird Sisters throw him is hurried on with not undaring impatience to verify their predictions . . .

Student Activity. Change the following negative sentences into positive ones without changing their meanings.

1. George was not unhappy about his daughter's marriage.
2. Not unaware of the situation, Helena intervened on Ginny's behalf.
3. Satan, a not unworthy adversary, was cast into Hell.

7 **Discussion** What contrasts does Hazlitt see between the Witches and Lady Macbeth?

8 **Enrichment** According to the Gaelic tradition of tanistry, succession to the throne went to the most "worthy" kinsmen. Thus, in fact, Macbeth did have some claim to the throne. What might be some of the results of the custom of tanistry?

9 **Reading Strategy** Ask students to prepare a list of the contrasts Hazlitt sees in the play and challenge them to add contrasts of their own to the list.

Reader's Response If you are familiar with Shakespeare's *Macbeth,* how does this essay add to your understanding or opinion of the play? If you have not read or seen *Macbeth,* does this essay make you interested in reading or seeing it? Why or why not?

> That no compunctious
>   visitings of nature
> Shake my fell purpose,
>   nor keep peace between
> The effect and it. Come to
>   my woman's breasts,
> And take my milk for gall,
>   you murthering ministers,
> Wherever in your
>   sightless substances
> You wait on nature's
>   mischief. Come, thick
>   night!
> And pall thee in the
>   dunnest smoke of hell,
> That my keen knife see
>   not the wound it makes,
> Nor heav'n peep through
>   the blanket of the dark,
> To cry, hold, hold!

When she first hears that "Duncan comes there to sleep" she is so overcome by the news, which is beyond her utmost expectations, that she answers the messenger, "Thou 'rt mad to say it"; and on receiving her husband's account of the predictions of the Witches, conscious of his instability of purpose, and that her presence is necessary to goad him on to the consummation of his promised greatness, she exclaims:

> Hie thee hither,
> That I may pour my
>   spirits in thine ear,
> And chastise with the
>   valor of my tongue
> All that impedes thee
>   from the golden round,
> Which fate and
>   metaphysical aid doth seem
> To have thee crowned withal.

7 This swelling exultation and keen spirit of triumph, this uncontrollable eagerness of anticipation, which seems to dilate her form and take possession of all her faculties, this solid, substantial flesh and blood display of passion, exhibit a striking contrast to the cold, abstracted, gratuitous, servile malignity of the Witches, who are equally instrumental in urging Macbeth to his fate for the mere love of mischief, and from a disinterested delight in deformity and cruelty. They are hags of mischief, obscene panders to iniquity, malicious from their impotence of enjoyment, enamored of destruction, because they are themselves unreal, abortive, half-existences, who become sublime from their exemption from all human sympathies and contempt for all human affairs, as Lady Macbeth does by the force of passion! Her fault seems to have been an excess of that strong principle of self-interest and family aggrandizement, not amenable to the common feelings of compassion and justice, which is so marked a feature in barbarous nations and times. A passing reflection of this kind, on the resemblance of the sleeping king to her father, alone prevents her from slaying Duncan with her own hand. . . .

8

Macbeth (generally speaking) is done upon a stronger and more systematic principle of contrast than any other of Shakespeare's plays. It moves upon the verge of an abyss, and is a constant struggle between life and death. The action is desperate and the reaction is dreadful. It is a huddling together of fierce extremes, a war of opposite natures which of them shall destroy the other. There is nothing but what has a violent end or violent beginnings. The lights and shades are laid on with a determined hand; the transitions from triumph to despair, from the height of terror to the repose of death, are sudden and startling; every passion brings in its fellow-contrary, and the thoughts pitch and jostle against each other as in the dark. The whole play is an unruly chaos of strange and forbidden things, where the ground rocks under our feet. Shakespeare's genius here took its full swing, and trod upon the farthest bounds of nature and passion.

9

Closure and Extension

ANSWERS TO THINKING ABOUT THE SELECTION
Recalling

1. "*Lear* stands first for the profound intensity of passion; *Macbeth* for the wildness of the imagination and the rapidity of the action; *Othello*

THINKING ABOUT THE SELECTION

Recalling

1. According to Hazlitt, what does each of Shakespeare's "four principal tragedies" embody?
2. Which of these plays does Hazlitt say has the best dramatic opening? Why?
3. On pages 749–750, Hazlitt quotes a long passage spoken by Lady Macbeth that begins with the words, "Come all you spirits." What aspect of her character does he say this passage reveals?
4. In Hazlitt's opinion, what "systematic principle" sets *Macbeth* apart from Shakespeare's other plays?

Interpreting

5. On page 748, Hazlitt states that Shakespeare is "your only *tragedy maker*." (a) What do you think he means by this? (b) What do you think is the significance of the quotation marks around this phrase?
6. What two qualities does Hazlitt claim advance the action in the play, and what effect do they have on the characters of Macbeth and Lady Macbeth?
7. Hazlitt concludes his essay with the observation that in *Macbeth* Shakespeare's genius "took its full swing, and trod upon the farthest bounds of nature and passion." What evidence does he offer in support of this view?

Applying

8. How does Hazlitt's writing style compare with modern editorial style? Tell which you prefer and why you prefer it.

ANALYZING LITERATURE

Understanding a Critical Essay

A **critical essay** is a prose piece that reviews or critiques a work of art or literature. In the present day, standards for objective criticism have been established by experts. In the eighteenth century, by contrast, these standards varied pretty much from critic to critic. The essays of William Hazlitt, in particular, are marked by a tendency toward subjective, highly personal observations, although these observations are often supported with examples and quotations from the work. Reread Hazlitt's essay on *Macbeth*, and locate the following:

1. Three opinions that are supported by examples or quotes from the play.
2. Three opinions that are not supported.
3. Three phrases that demonstrate Hazlitt's enthusiasm for Shakespeare's writing in general and for *Macbeth* in particular.

CRITICAL THINKING AND READING

Finding Main Ideas

The **main idea** in a paragraph is the key point the author wishes to get across to the reader. Each main idea is backed up by one or more **supporting details.** Read the following quotations from Hazlitt's essay on *Macbeth*. Each is a supporting detail. Find the paragraph from which it was taken, and state the main idea of that paragraph.

1. "The wildness of the scenery, the sudden shifting of the situations and characters . . . are equally extraordinary." (page 748)
2. "The action is desperate and the reaction is dreadful." (page 750)
3. "The whole play is an unruly chaos of strange and forbidden things, where the ground rocks under our feet." (page 750)

THINKING AND WRITING

Evaluating Literary Criticism

In a magazine or newspaper, find a review of a book you have read or a play you have seen. As you read the review, ask yourself the following questions: What facts does the critic present? Which statements are opinions? What details does the critic offer in support of his or her opinions? Does the critic convey any strong feeling for the work? How interesting is the review?

After you have organized your thoughts regarding these and other questions that might occur to you, write an essay evaluating the review. When you revise make sure you have included adequate supporting details.

Macbeth 751

(Answers begin on p. 750.)

Applying

8. Answers will differ. Students should see that Hazlitt's style is more dramatic and emotional than that of most modern literary critics.

ANSWERS TO ANALYZING LITERATURE

1. Answers will differ. Suggested answers may include the following. Hazlitt quotes the description of the Witches to support his opinion that the first entrance of the Witches prepares the mind for what follows. That Lady Macbeth is steadfastly intent on the murder of Duncan is supported by quoting her words when she hears that Duncan had made his fatal entrance. That Lady Macbeth feels she is necessary to goad Macbeth to greatness is supported by a quotation.
2. Answers will differ. Suggested answers may include the following. Hazlitt does not support these three opinions: First, the plays *Macbeth, Lear, Othello,* and *Hamlet* are "like different creations of the same mind. . . ." Second, the Witches "are equally instrumental in urging Macbeth to his fate. . . ." Third, Lady Macbeth is "a woman . . . whom we fear more than we hate."
3. Answers will differ. Suggested answers may include the following. Hazlitt's enthusiasm for Shakespeare's writing is demonstrated by such phrases as "force of genius," "lofty imagination," and "absolute truth and vividness."

ANSWERS TO CRITICAL THINKING AND READING

1. Macbeth has the most striking opening of any of Shakespeare's plays.
2. In *Macbeth* Shakespeare pushes nature and passion to their limits by emphasizing extreme contrasts.
3. See number 2, Answers to Analyzing Literature, above.

THINKING AND WRITING

Publishing Student Writing

Using their essays as the basis, have students carry out a round-table discussion of the role of critics in today's society and the validity of contemporary criticism.

_____
751

---

for the progressive interest and powerful alternations of feeling; *Hamlet* for the refined development of thought and sentiment."
2. *Macbeth* has the best dramatic opening because of its wild scenery, the sudden shifts of situations and characters, the bustle, and the fact that it excites the reader's expectations.
3. The passage reveals Lady Macbeth's firmness of purpose and her "consistency in depravity."
4. *Macbeth* is set apart by its "sys-

tematic principle of contrast."

Interpreting

5. (a) Hazlitt calls Shakespeare the "only *tragedy maker*" because the characters and events in his plays seem to spring from real life, like a force of nature. (b) The quotation marks signify a kind of irony —through his plays Shakespeare "makes" tragedies happen; in life, however, tragedies result from seemingly unavoidable events.

6. Imagination and vehemence advance the action of the play. Although Macbeth is bothered by his conscience, he is too weak-willed to resist his wife's passionate ambition. Her determined wickedness undoes them both.
7. In the concluding paragraph Hazlitt offers no concrete evidence in the form of examples or quotes from the play to support this view. However, his view is very much in keeping with, and supported by, much of what precedes.

Motivation/Prior Knowledge
Have your female students imagine that they live in a world where the only road to security is a successful marriage. Have your male students imagine what it would be like to be a young man of wealth who may be judged more for his income than his personal qualities. Have students discuss how their expectations would be different from what they are today.

Master Teacher Note Discuss famous first lines of books, from "Call me Ishmael" to "It was a dark and stormy night." What makes some sentences so memorable and so resonant? Can students think of any examples of great first sentences from their own favorite books? Have a selection of popular and classic novels available, and compare their opening sentences. Is Austen's opening sentence an epigram or a hook? That is, does it seem to foreshadow following action or drag the reader into the story? Can students detect any change of pace between how books opened in Austen's time and today? If they do, what do they think accounts for the difference?

GREAT WORKS

PRIDE AND PREJUDICE
by Jane Austen

It is a truth universally acknowledged, that a single man in possession of a good fortune must be in want of a wife.

Illustration from PRIDE AND PREJUDICE
Hugh Thomson
The Granger Collection

"She is tolerable," Darcy said of Elizabeth.

So begins Jane Austen's *Pride and Prejudice,* a highly amusing examination of "the business of getting married" in early nineteenth-century England. Marriages are not based on the mutual pitter-patter of hearts in this society: It's money, social standing, and family connections that make the match. Marriage is like a shop where people people drive a hard bargain to conserve or improve their status in life.

As the novel opens, Mrs. Bennet, the mother of five marriageable daughters, is eagerly questioning her husband as to the identity of the "the young man of large fortune" who has just rented a mansion not far from the Bennet home. Since the girls have no inheritance and society affords almost no opportunity for employment, Mrs. Bennet has set as her life's work the successful marriage of her daughters. Frantic that Mrs. Lucas, who also has daughters to marry, may beat her to the punch, she insists that her husband visit the young man at once. Mr. Bennet refuses to take her seriously. Referring to his daughter, he says:

"They have none of them much to recommend them," replied he; "they are silly and ignorant, like other girls: but Lizzy has something more of quickness than her sisters."

752 *The Romantic Age*

"Mr. Bennet, how can you abuse your own children in such a way! You take delight in vexing me. You have no compassion for my poor nerves."

"You mistake me, my dear. I have a high respect for your nerves. They are my old friends. I have heard you mention them with consideration these twenty years at least."

It is clear from his comments that Mr. Bennet favors Lizzy—and with good reason. Her quick wit, common sense, and high moral standards reveal an intelligent person superior to the nonsense that swirls around her. To Austen herself, Elizabeth was "as delightful a creature as ever appeared in print, and how I shall be able to tolerate those who do not like her at least, I do not know."

The Plot Unfolds

Despite his protests, Mr. Bennet does call on Mr. Bingley, their new neighbor, who is pleasant and unpretentious despite his wealth. Bingley's friend Mr. Darcy, however, is as arrogant as Bingley is humble. Darcy's pride quickly becomes apparent when he refuses to dance with Elizabeth. "She is tolerable, but not handsome enough to tempt me," he huffs. Although offended, the slight appeals to her sense of humor, and Elizabeth takes great delight in relating the story to her friends. And so we have "pride" and "prejudice," as Darcy's pride—his sense of his own superior status—sparks Elizabeth's prejudice against him.

Pride and Prejudice

In many ways, the novel is the story of Elizabeth's education, as the twenty-year-old young woman learns about pride and prejudice in the world. Through her honesty, courage, and flexibility, we see action at last guided by reason.

In Chapter 19, for example, Elizabeth is cornered by a young man too proud to understand that she has no intention of accepting his astonishingly unromantic pro-

Great Works 753

Critical Evaluation Ian Watt described the esteem with which Austen was held by her contemporaries as follows: "Despite much public and private homage Jane Austen's position in the world of early nineteenth century letters was relatively obscure. The Romantic movement and its Victorian aftermath was in general unlikely to be favorable to Jane Austen's classical sense of order and control. All the Romantics were seeking in some way to transcend the limitations of actuality, to go beyond the bounds of society, reason, and individual experience, whether through political reform, through the imagination, or through spiritual self-exploration; and so it is not surprising that we find Keats, Shelley, and Byron silent about Jane Austen. Unlike these, Wordsworth read and commented upon Jane Austen's novels; but Sara Coleridge reports that, rather too predictably, 'Mr. Wordsworth used to say that though he admitted that her novels were an admirable copy of life, he could not be interested in productions of that kind; unless the truth of nature were presented to him clarified, as it were, by the pervading light of the imagination; it had scarce any attractions in his eyes.' Wordsworth's characteristic gravity also played a part in his lack of enthusiasm: as Sara Coleridge remarked, Wordsworth 'never in his life appreciated any genius in which (humour) is a large element. Hence his disregard for Jane Austen's novels.'"

She wanted to compose her own feelings and to make herself agreeable to all.

Illustration from PRIDE AND PREJUDICE
Hugh Thomson
The Granger Collection

posal of marriage. Here, Mr. Collins outlines his plan to Elizabeth:

> "Almost as soon as I entered the house, I singled you out as the companion of my future life. But before I run away with my feelings on this subject, perhaps it would be advisable for me to state my reasons for marrying . . .
>
> The idea of Mr. Collins, with all his solemn composure, being "run away with" by his feelings, made Elizabeth so near laughing that she could not use the short pause he allowed in any attempt to stop his going farther, and he continued:—
>
> "My reasons for marrying are, first, that I think it a right thing for every clergyman in easy circumstances (like myself) to set an example of matrimony in his parish; secondly, that I am convinced it will add very greatly to my happiness . . . "

The outcome? Her mother won't speak to her if she refuses; her father won't speak to her if she accepts! Elizabeth stands her ground, and the situation blows over . . . until Darcy's speech.

Soon, he is so taken with her that were it not for the "inferiority of her connections, he should be in some danger." She, however, feels no attraction to him at all. As the other characters begin to pair off in relationships, Elizabeth and Darcy are unable to judge each other accurately because of his pride and her prejudice.

Imagine, then, Elizabeth's shock when Darcy comes to visit her one day and says, "In vain have I struggled. It will not do. My feelings for you will not be repressed. You must allow me to tell you how ardently I admire and love you." What does she do?

After more than a century and a half, we return to *Pride and Prejudice* because it helps us retain our moral balance amid the temptation of pride, prejudice, and greed—and because it's highly entertaining!

Jane Austen

Who was the woman who wrote with such sensibility of pride and prejudice? If nothing else, the life and work of Jane Austen explode the myth that it is impossible to produce a great novel without having first sampled a broad range of life experiences. Her social comedies are considered by critics today to be masterpieces of character portrayal and dialogue.

Born at Steventon in southwestern England to loving parents of modest means, Jane Austen (1775–1817) was the seventh of eight children. From an early age she enjoyed writing, and entertained her family with parodies, or humorous sendups, of the syrupy, sentimental fiction and drama that were fashionable at the time. When she was in her late teens, she began her first novel, *Sense and Sensibility,* which is the story of two sisters. Prior to its completion, however, she put it aside to concentrate on another novel, *First Impressions*. Written as a series of letters, the work that would eventually be reshaped into her highly acclaimed *Pride and Prejudice* rapidly became the family favorite. So certain, in fact, was her father of its merits that he offered the work to a book publisher, who rejected it. Not easily discouraged, Austen plunged into a third novel, *Northanger Abbey*, a mock horror tale, which she finished in 1797.

In 1801 the family relocated to Bath, near the sea, where Austen for the first time in her life experienced unhappiness. In letters she described herself as an "exile" from the rural surroundings that she loved so much. When her father died in 1806, the family, or what remained of it—by now all the male children had married—left Bath for a cottage on an estate outside London. On the death of his wife, Austen's brother Edward and his eleven children came to live on the estate, and once again Austen found herself surrounded by relatives in a bustling household. The writer's block that had plagued her during her period of sadness vanished, and she eagerly returned to work, revising her early novels and completing three new ones.

Sense and Sensibility, the first to be published, appeared in 1811. It was followed two years later by *Pride and Prejudice*, and a year after that by *Mansfield Park*. In 1816 Austen became ill but continued to write, completing two more novels, *Persuasion* and *Northanger Abbey*, before her death. Her brother Henry saw to the publication of both works, including a biographical sketch of his sister, who during her life had insisted on anonymity.

Because in her writing Austen places intellect above emotion, she is seen by some as more neoclassical than Romantic. What all critics seem to be in agreement on, however, is that Jane Austen ranks as one of the greatest English novelists and *Pride and Prejudice* as one the greatest literary works of any period.

Illustration from PRIDE AND PREJUDICE
Hugh Thomson
The Granger Collection

Before she could reply to the entreaties of several that she would sing again, she was eagerly succeeded at the instrument by her sister Mary.

Writing Across the Curriculum
If students are interested, they might research and report on some aspect of life in England at the time *Pride and Prejudice* is set. Students might be especially interested in learning more about the social conventions of the middle and upper classes. You might inform the school or the local librarian, who can offer guidance and assistance with students' research. Have students report their findings to the rest of the class. Perhaps students with different topics can present their findings in the form of a panel discussion.

Cooperative Learning Students who choose to read *Pride and Prejudice* might want to work in a group on an oral presentation of a favorite scene from the novel. If so, have students form groups. Groups should choose a favorite scene, assign parts for each character and the narrator, and practice reading their scenes aloud. Encourage students to vary their tone of voice and use hand and facial gestures to enhance their performances. When groups have had sufficient time to practice their scenes, have them perform the scenes for the rest of the class.

The Romantic Age 1798–1832

BRITANNIA RULES THE WAVES

During the Romantic Age, Britannia ruled the waves and English ruled much of the land. Great Britain's smashing conquests in the course of the Napoleonic Wars in the beginning of the century—culminating in Nelson's famous victory at Trafalgar in 1805—had left her in a position of undisputed naval supremacy. This, in turn, gave her control over most of the world's commerce. As English ships traveled throughout the world, they left the language of the mother country in their wake.

New inventions and improvements affected the spread of English within the mother country as well. The establishment of the first affordable newspaper in 1816 and the creation of inexpensive postage in 1840 served to more closely unite the different parts of England and spread the influence of standard speech. Improved means of travel and communication brought about by the railroad, the steamboat, and the telegraph also served to unify the country and blanket the language across the land.

COLONIES ASSERT THEMSELVES

Not everyone accepted the dominance of British English quite so placidly, however. As England's larger colonies became increasingly independent, their citizens felt entitled to speak English in their fashion. Feisty Americans, for example, flushed with the acquisition of great tracts of land, asserted their right to speak American English, complete with such Native-American words as *caribou, hickory, moccasin, moose, opossum, raccoon, skunk, squaw, toboggan, tomahawk, totem,* and *wigwam.*

American English was also marked by borrowings from other peoples. From the Mexicans we took *chili, chocolate, tomato;* from Cuba and the West Indies came *barbecue, canoe,* and *hurricane.*

NEW PLACES, NEW VOCABULARY

The most obvious results of English expansion can be seen in growth of the vocabulary. The acquisition of new lands meant new experiences, new products, and new occupations to name. From India, English acquired such varied and important words as *bandanna, bangle, Bengal, Brahman, bungalow, calico, cashmere, china, chintz, coolie, cot, curry, dinghy, juggernaut, jungle, jute, loot, mandarin, nirvana, pariah, polo, punch* (beverage), *rajah, rupee, thug, toddy, tom-tom,* and *verandah.* From even farther East, the language welcomed terms that have today become commonplace: *gingham, indigo,* and *mango.* One of the most interesting new words was *seersucker,* an Indian corruption of a Persian expression meaning "milk and sugar" that came to be linked to a thin, striped cotton fabric. Many words entered English from Africa as well, either directly or from contact with Dutch and Portuguese traders. These include *banana, Boer, boorish, chimpanzee, gorilla, gumbo, voodoo,* and *zebra.* Although Australia has not given us many words, two have become extremely common: *boomerang* and *kangaroo.*

GRAMMAR REFORMS TAKE SHAPE

The language reforms begun in the Restoration and eighteenth century continued into the Romantic era. There was an especially strong movement to reorganize grammar, now that spelling improvements were well underway. Those seeking to mend grammar wanted to create rules, settle disputed points, and isolate errors to improve the language. As one writer commented in the preface to his grammar book:

> It is not the Language, but the Practice that is at fault. The Truth is, Grammar is very much neglected among us; and it is not the difficulty of the Language, but on the contrast the simplicity and the facility of it, that occasions this neglect. Were the Language less easy and simple, we should find ourselves under a necessity of studying it with more care and attention.

Many of the grammar rules we follow were first established during this period. The distinction between "lie" and "lay" was set out in the late eighteenth century; the preference for "different from" (rather than "different than") and the condemnation of "between you and I" and "it is me," in the early nineteenth. "Between" came to be used for groups of two; "among" came to be used for groups of three or more. It was decided that the comparative rather than the superlative should be used when only two things are involved ("the bigger," not "biggest," of two). Finally, we can note that the double negative was abolished in the late eighteenth century. One grammarian stated

the rule that now binds us: "Two Negatives in English destroy one another, or are equivalent to an Affirmative." Here, as elsewhere, grammar reformers were setting down what was apparently a frequent but not absolute tendency in the written language.

Although the rules many seem arbitrary and annoying, the results were noteworthy. English was no longer a language without rules. We now had guidelines to help us integrate the new words acquired through exploration and conquest.

Like people in the colonies, Scottish and Irish writers asserted their national identity. Sir Walter Scott is credited with reviving interest in the Scotts tongue.

SIR WALTER SCOTT
Sir Edwin Landseer
National Portrait Gallery, London,

YOU THE WRITER

Assignment

1. If there was one poetic form that permitted the Romantic poet to pour out his or her heart, it was the ode, a poem that pays tribute to an individual, quality, or place. Of course, the particular subject a poet chose for an ode was to an extent limited by circumstances of the times. Had Shelley and Keats lived in our present era of high technology, they might well have dedicated odes to the vastness of our universe.

Prewriting. Brainstorm to come up with an inspirational topic related to the current age, perhaps organ implants or high-speed electronic computers.

Writing. Write an original ode of at least three stanzas that expresses your awe for this modern wonder.

Revising. Review what you have written, making sure you have used vivid words. Check troublesome spellings.

Assignment

2. The Romantic movement grew out of an opposition to the tightly structured view of art and the reliance on scientific doctrine that typified writers of the previous age. The Romantic poet was concerned with emotions and concentrated on natural topics. Imagine you are the editor of a literary magazine and you have just received a poem by an unknown poet named Wordsworth or Coleridge (or any Romantic you have read).

Prewriting. List the tasks you think a magazine editor might be responsible for. Make notes for a response letter to this new poet.

Writing. Write a one-page letter explaining your feelings. State why you like or dislike this new submission.

Revising. Reread your letter for coherence and punctuation. Make sure you have maintained a single tone throughout.

Assignment

3. Essays, whether formal or personal, present the views of their authors in a well-organized and readable manner, sometimes using casual language to enhance a point. Imagine you are living during the Romantic Age. You are invited to write a guest column of approximately 500 words for a local newspaper.

Prewriting. Get your mind spinning to come up with a topic that is both timely and of general interest to the inhabitants of your city or community. Jot down notes to test your knowledge.

Writing. Do at least two drafts of your essay—one to develop the general structure and a second to iron out rough spots.

Revising. Check your essay for continuity. Be sure that any casual language you have used is general enough to be understood by your audience.

758   *The Romantic Age*

YOU THE CRITIC

Assignment

1. In the preface to the second edition of his *Lyrical Ballads,* William Wordsworth stated that his goal was "to choose incidents . . . from common life" and make them "interesting by tracing in them . . . the primary laws of our nature." It might be argued that this statement fairly summarized the goal of all Romantics. Write an essay demonstrating that the work of a Romantic poet of your choosing fits the above description.

    Prewriting. Before you begin to write, make sure you understand all parts of the Wordsworth statement. Decide in particular what you believe the phrase "primary laws of our nature" means.

    Writing. Write the first draft of your essay. Quote specific poems that illustrate your claim.

    Revising. Check to see that main subpoints of your essay support the thesis statement. Correct any run-on sentences or fragments.

Assignment

2. A writer's style is like a personal stamp that uniquely identifies his or her work. Style is determined by such features as word choice and sentence length. Evaluate the prose styles of two of the Romantic writers you have read and, in a comparative essay, tell which of the works you find more enjoyable.

    Prewriting. Plan your essay by comparing and contrasting the features mentioned above, along with such considerations as fit of style to subject matter. Organize your presentation of similarities and differences.

    Writing. Quote freely from the two writers' works. Devote one paragraph to a clear statement of preference, including reasons for your feelings.

    Revising. Reread your essay for internal consistency. Be sure you have anticipated and addressed any opposing views.

Assignment

3. Most of the major literary figures of the Romantic movement were supporters of the rebel cause in the French Revolution. Coleridge, for instance, while still in school, composed an ode celebrating the storming of the Bastille, the prison where "enemies" of the French state had been sent. In an expository paper, discuss what aspects of the Romantic temperament would logically lead to such a political stance.

    Prewriting. Divide a sheet of paper into two columns. In one, list traits of the liberal mind; in the other, list aspects of the Romantic world view. Draw lines connecting corresponding traits.

    Writing. Write your first draft. In the first paragraph include a definitive statement of your purpose in writing.

    Revising. Make sure you have adequately supported your main idea. Proofread your paper for possible errors and omissions.

You the Critic 759

Humanities Note

Fine art, *Queen Victoria's Visit to Cherbourg,* by Jules Achille Noel. Noel (1815–1881) was an English painter who worked during the Victorian Age. In his painting *Queen Victoria's Visit to Cherbourg,* he celebrates one of the events during her sixty-three year reign with the pomp and pageantry typical of the period.

Respect for the throne increased dramatically under Victoria's rule as Great Britain reached the height of its power. Although it was under her rule that the power of the British throne became largely symbolic, she aroused in the British people deep feelings of affection and admiration.

QUEEN VICTORIA'S VISIT TO CHERBOURG
Jules Achille Noel
Royal Academy, London

Objectives

1 To understand and appreciate life in the Victorian Age
2 To understand the British Empire and foreign policy
3 To understand Victorian thought
4 To have an overview of Victorian literature

THE VICTORIAN AGE
(1833–1901)

The year's at the spring
And the day's at the morn;
Morning's at seven;
The hillside's dew-pearled;
The lark's on the wing;
The snail's on the thorn;
God's in his heaven—
All's right with the world!
    From "Pippa Passes"
    Robert Browning

Historical Background During the nineteenth century, Great Britain was the leading industrial and commercial power in the world. Prosperous and content, the British took great pride in their achievements. Queen Victoria's reign of 63 years became the symbol of the nineteenth century. This prosperous time is called the Victorian Age.

Writing to Learn Encourage students to write, speculating about what changes might occur, especially in thinking and in literature, in the period following the Romantic Age.

Motivation/Prior Knowledge
Ask students if they have associations with the word *Victorian,* and if so, what they are. Point out that the word refers to and comes from the reign of Queen Victoria, who gave her name to this period.

Purpose-Setting Question How did the attitudes of society affect the literature of this period?

1 **Historical Context** This complacency somewhat resembles the attitude of eighteenth century Englishmen who felt that they were living in the best of all possible worlds; the main difference is in the breadth of social concern.

Humanities Note

London's Crystal Palace. Prosperity and growth marked the Victorian Age. This was clearly seen with the erection of London's Crystal Palace, which housed the Great Exhibition of 1851. Designed by Sir Joseph Paxton, the Crystal Palace was of iron-frame and glass-panel construction. Covering almost nineteen acres, the Crystal Palace was the first prefabricated structure with standardized sections constructed in the factory and assembled at the building site.

Queen Victoria reigned for sixty-four years, from 1837 to 1901—the longest reign of any British monarch. With occasional exceptions, those were years of prosperity for Britain. Robert Browning's lines on the preceding page echo the ringing optimism and self-assurance that marked the Victorian Age. The Victorians recognized that, in fact, all was not really "right with the world," and they worked hard to make improvements. Yet they firmly believed that theirs was the best nation in the best era history had yet produced.

LIVING IN THE VICTORIAN AGE

Britain's booming economy and rapid expansion encouraged great optimism. Profiting from its early industrial revolution, Britain became the world leader in manufacturing. Factories dotted the land. Factory towns grew into large cities. Banks, retail shops, and other businesses expanded. These changes in turn spurred the growth of two important classes—an industrial working class and a modern middle class, able to live a better life because of the low cost and large variety of mass-produced factory goods.

As its industry and commerce prospered, Britain expanded its merchant fleet and its powerful navy. Economic and military power helped Britain to acquire new colonies in far-flung parts of the globe. Victorians could quite literally boast that "the sun never sets on the British empire."

1 Yet, for all its self-satisfaction, the Victorian Age was also a time of social concern. Victorian writers exposed a dark underside of the industrial age—brutal factory conditions and stinking slums that bred poverty and disease. Goaded by reformers and radicals of many sorts, Victorian leaders took steps to expand democracy and better the lot of the poor. By the time Victoria died in 1901, Britain had shed some of its complacency and was grappling with the social and economic problems industrialization had caused.

LONDON'S CRYSTAL PALACE
The British Museum

762   *The Victorian Age*

Victoria and Albert

Victoria became queen at the age of eighteen. She impressed the members of Parliament with her grace and self-assurance, but she could also be very stubborn. In 1840 she insisted on marrying a first cousin, a minor German princeling named Albert of Saxe-Coburg-Gotha. Many Britons disliked the marriage: What if Prince Albert filled the queen's head with "European" notions of absolute rule? As it turned out, Albert understood the limited powers of British royalty. His wisdom and impartial advice did much to soften the personality of the queen. (It was she who reigned; Albert was not king but *prince consort*—the monarch's husband.)

Victoria and Albert produced a large family and restored to the monarchy a sense of decorum, sadly lacking since the madness of George III and the scandalous behavior of his sons. The twentieth century would tend to look back on Victoria as prim to the point of prudishness. However, we must remember that her restrained behavior came in reaction to those earlier royal excesses.

When Albert died of typhoid fever in 1861, Victoria went into deep mourning. For a time she was almost a recluse, leaving day-to-day government in the hands of her prime ministers. Victoria's limited involvement in political affairs helped to turn Britain into the modern constitutional monarchy it is today, in which the duties of the sovereign are largely ceremonial.

Victorian Politics

The prime ministers who govern Britain serve at the sufferance of Parliament, and can be dismissed at any time by a vote of no confidence. Such a system produces a more rapid turnover of leadership than does our own presidential system.

The years of Victoria's reign brought a change in the policies and even the names of the two parties that had dominated eighteenth-century politics. The Whig party formerly had championed Britain's commercial dominance and colonial empire. Gradually, the Whigs adopted new attitudes and became known as the Liberal party. Liberals often attacked colonial expansion and, under the leadership of William Gladstone, pressed for reforms at home and in Ireland. Meanwhile, the Tory party began to abandon its old stance of isolationism in foreign affairs and stubborn resistance to social change. The Tories (or Conservatives, as they came to be called) now supported imperialism—the expansion of empire. Under leaders like Benjamin Disraeli, the Conservatives also supported electoral reform. It was Disraeli who helped push through the Second Reform Bill of 1867, doubling the electorate by granting voting rights to tenant farmers and to better-paid male workers.

The Liberals and Conservatives alternated in power. Each party had its die-hard followers, but each had to compete for the same middle-of-the-road "swing" voters. As a result, Victorian politics emphasized compromise and slow reform.

Enrichment There were great differences between the early and late Victorians. During the early Victorian period, from 1832 to 1851, there was profound unrest and social change. The mid-Victorian period, 1851–1867, was the most optimistic, prosperous, and smug. During the late Victorian period, 1867–1901, advanced thinkers began to use the term *Victorian* contemptuously. The term connoted that attitude of comfortable smugness, an attitude becoming inappropriate for a period of growing democracy and socialism, even imperial expansion.

Enrichment Five years after the Reform Bill of 1867, Parliament passed a bill introducing the secret ballot. In 1884 and 1885, other reform bills gave the vote to rural working men. Thus, by 1885, most adult men in Britain had the right to vote. Women were still demanding the right to vote; however, their struggle did not succeed completely until 1928.

BRITISH EVENTS

1833   Slavery abolished in British empire.

1837   Victoria becomes queen.

Charles Dickens writes *The Pickwick Papers* and *Oliver Twist.*

Thomas Carlyle writes *The French Revolution.*

1840   Michael Faraday experiments with electric currents.

1843   **William Wordsworth** becomes poet laureate.

1844   George Williams founds YMCA.

1845   Irish Potato Famine begins.

1847   Factory Act passed.

Charlotte Brontë publishes *Jane Eyre.*

Emily Brontë publishes *Wuthering Heights.*

1848   First Public Health Act.

Women begin attending University of London.

1850   Public Libraries Act.

Elizabeth Barrett Browning publishes *Sonnets from the Portuguese.*

1854   Britain enters Crimean War.

Parliament abolishes religious restrictions for university attendance.

1856   Henry Bessemer introduces steelmaking process.

1859   Charles Darwin publishes *On the Origin of Species.*

1860   Florence Nightingale founds school for nurses.

Food and Drugs Act passed.

764   *The Victorian Age*

Queen Victoria

Charles Darwin

Battle from

Charlotte Brontë

Charles Dickens   Karl Marx

the Crimean War   Samuel Morse

Sepoy Mutiny   Richard Wagner

▮WORLD EVENTS▮

1836	United States: Ralph Waldo Emerson publishes *Nature*.
1841	South Pacific: New Zealand becomes a British colony.
	United States: Edgar Allan Poe publishes ''The Murders in the Rue Morgue.''
1842	Asia: Hong Kong becomes a British colony.
	France: Honoré de Balzac publishes *The Human Comedy*.
1844	America: Samuel F. B. Morse patents telegraph.
1846	America: Elias Howe patents sewing machine.
	France: Pierre Joseph Proudhon publishes *The Philosophy of Poverty*.
1848	France: Revolution establishes new republic under Louis Napoleon.
	Belgium: Marx and Engels publish *Communist Manifesto*.
1850	France: Life insurance introduced.
	Germany: Wagner's opera *Lohengrin* first performed.
1851	Australia: Gold discovered in New South Wales.
1853	Eastern Europe: Beginning of Crimean War.
1854	Japan: Trade with West reopened.
	United States: Henry David Thoreau publishes *Walden*.
1856	France: Gustave Flaubert publishes *Madame Bovary*.
1857	India: Sepoy Mutiny against British.
1858	India: Political power of East India Company abolished.

Introduction   765

Enrichment Thomas Hardy is viewed as a novelist who had the courage to portray life with the grimness that it possessed. *Tess of the D'Urbervilles*, one of Hardy's great tragic novels, embodies his ideas about a cruel universe indifferent to individual aspirations, while at the same time addressing modern attitudes and changes in attitudes. The role of fate is clear as Tess, a folk heroine, strives to make her life mean something. She becomes a genuinely tragic character when she sets out to make outward circumstances meet with her own vision of herself.

Literary Focus See the Great Works feature on *The Importance of Being Earnest,* p. 901.

BRITISH EVENTS

Illustration from *Treasure Island*

1863 Construction of London Underground begins.

1864 **Robert Browning** publishes *The Ring and the Book*.

1865 Joseph Lister initiates antiseptic surgery.

London Fire Department established.

Lewis Carroll publishes *Alice's Adventures in Wonderland*.

1867 **Matthew Arnold** publishes "Dover Beach."

1869 Debtors' prisons abolished.

1878 Salvation Army established.

1879 **George Meredith** publishes *The Egoist*.

1880 Joseph Swan installs first electric lighting.

1883 **Robert Louis Stevenson** publishes *Treasure Island*.

1884 First edition of *Oxford English Dictionary* published.

1886 English Lawn Tennis Association founded at Wimbledon.

1887 First Sherlock Holmes tale published.

1888 Jack the Ripper stalks London's East End.

1891 **Thomas Hardy** publishes *Tess of the d'Urbervilles*.

1892 **Rudyard Kipling** publishes *Barrack-room Ballads*.

1895 Oscar Wilde publishes *The Importance of Being Earnest*.

1896 **A. E. Housman** publishes *A Shropshire Lad*.

1901 Queen Victoria dies.

Robert Browning

Alice's Adventures

Suez Canal

Alexander Graham Bell

Civil War Begins

in Wonderland

Anton Chekhov

Boxer Rebellion

WORLD EVENTS

1861	United States: Civil War begins.
1865	Russia: Leo Tolstoy publishes *War and Peace*.
	Austria: Gregor Mendel proposes laws of heredity.
1866	Europe: Seven Weeks' War leads to unification of modern Germany.
1869	Egypt: Suez Canal completed.
1873	France: Jules Verne publishes *Around the World in Eighty Days*.
1876	United States: Alexander Graham Bell patents telephone.
1877	United States: Thomas Edison patents phonograph.
1878	Afghanistan: British troops fight Second Afghan War.
1879	South Africa: Zulu War against British.
1880	Russia: Feodor Dostoevsky publishes *The Brothers Karamazov*.
1882	Egypt: Britain invades and conquers nation.
1884	United States: Mark Twain publishes *The Adventures of Huckleberry Finn*.
1885	Belgium: van Gogh paints *The Potato Eaters*.
1894	Asia: Sino-Japanese War begins.
1896	Greece: First modern Olympics held.
1898	China: Boxer Rebellion against foreign influence.
	France: Marie and Pierre Curie discover radium.
1899	Russia: Anton Chekhov publishes *Uncle Vanya*.

Introduction 767

Enrichment During this time an aptitude for technological invention was becoming evident in the United States. Alexander Graham Bell and Thomas Edison were producing items that have since revolutionized our lives.

Enrichment Vincent van Gogh was producing a number of fine paintings at this time. However, he was unable to sell a single painting in his lifetime and lived largely on his brother Theo's goodwill. Ironically, in the 1980's and 1990's, several of van Gogh's paintings have sold for many millions of dollars, commanding the highest prices ever paid for works of art.

WARRINGTON HIGH STREET
T. Hesketh
Warrington Museum and Art Gallery

Domestic Problems and Reforms

Two key issues—trade policy and electoral reform—dominated domestic politics during the first half of the Victorian era. Trade debate centered on the Corn Laws, which had long slapped high tariffs on "corn" (grain). This discouraged food imports and helped British landlords and farmers. However, it also tended to keep food prices high, which angered consumers and the poorer classes. At stake was not just money but life itself, as became evident in 1845, when a failure of Ireland's potato crop caused a massive famine in which as many as one million Irish people died.

Seeking to increase the supply of food, Parliament repealed the Corn Laws in 1846. Over the following decade, Parliament changed other trade laws, putting an end to the policy of protectionism (restriction of imports to protect domestic producers). Instead, Britain now adopted a policy of free trade (allowing imports and exports with few or no restrictions). The new policy reflected the interests of rising British industries, which prospered by importing raw materials and exporting finished goods. Times had changed, and Britain was fast becoming an industrial rather than an agricultural nation.

Many Britons thought that the second issue—electoral reform—had been settled in 1832, when the Reform Law gave the vote to middle-class males. They were wrong; working-class people wanted further reform. In 1837, a group of radicals drew up a "People's Charter" demanding, among other things, universal suffrage for males. This so-called Chartist movement fizzled out after a decade or so, but new demands for electoral change led to the Second Reform Bill of 1867 and to almost complete male suffrage in 1885.

The urge for reform also affected many other areas. Women, although still not eligible to vote, began to attend universities. Parliament passed laws to reduce the working day for women and children, to establish a system of free grammar schools, and to legalize trade unions. It voted to improve public sanitation and to regulate factories and housing. Still, such measures did not go far enough to suit everyone, and agitation continued for further reform.

One of the most important issues left unresolved in the Victorian Age was the future of Ireland, where widespread poverty had bred bitter opposition to British control. In the 1880's and 1890's the Liberal leader William Gladstone supported Irish demands for home rule (self-government). However, a hard-line faction of Liberals joined Conservatives to block action on Gladstone's proposals.

EMPIRE AND FOREIGN POLICY

Britain was not alone in its drive to form a world empire in the Victorian Age. Other European powers were grabbing colonies too. British diplomats tried to protect and expand the British empire while promoting a balance of power within Europe.

768 *The Victorian Age*

The Imperialist Urge

Victorian Britons who supported a policy of imperialism could cite a long list of arguments: Colonies would provide raw materials and markets for British industry. They would offer a home for British settlers. Britain had no choice; if it didn't seize a territory, one of its European rivals would do so. Perhaps the clinching argument was the writer Rudyard Kipling's notion of "the white man's burden." Victorians tended to believe that Western civilization—commonly perceived as white, Christian, and progressive—was superior to all other cultures. This attitude led many Victorians to look condescendingly on non-Westerners as people in need of assistance. What could be more noble than to help those "natives" by offering them the protection of the British empire? While such an argument seems faintly ridiculous by today's lights, many Victorians sincerely believed it.

Britain's empire had two sorts of land—"settled" territories, where whites made up a large part of the population, and outright colonies, in which few whites lived. During the Victorian Age Britain granted considerable self-government to "settled" territories such as Canada, Australia, and New Zealand. On the other hand, it exercised strict rule over places such as Hong Kong (acquired from China in 1841). After a rebellion in 1856 by sepoys (Indian troops under British command), Britain shouldered aside the British East India Company and took direct control of India. Victoria would thus add "Empress of India" to her formal titles.

The Crimean War

The Victorian years were generally peaceful. Britain fought only one major European war—the Crimean War (1854–56), so called because it took place on the Crimean peninsula in southern Russia. Britain, France, and Turkey teamed up to thwart Russian expansion, but the battles were largely inconclusive. Today we remember the war mainly for the brave but disastrous charge of Britain's Light Brigade. This was commemorated in a famous poem by Alfred, Lord Tennyson, including these lines:

> Theirs not to make reply,
> Theirs not to reason why,
> Theirs but to do and die.

Britain as a World Power

In the last three decades of Victoria's rule, Britain reached new heights of wealth and power. It gained control of the new Suez Canal in Egypt. It acquired Cyprus, an island in the eastern Mediterranean. It joined other European powers in a scramble to carve up Africa, acquiring such territories as Kenya, Uganda, Nigeria, and Rhodesia (Zimbabwe). Also, Britain expanded its control over what is now South Africa, defeating Dutch settlers there in the Boer War of 1899–1902.

THE TRIUMPHS OF THE BRITISH ARMY AND NAVY, 1897
COMMEMORATING THE DIAMOND JUBILEE OF QUEEN VICTORIA
English Lithograph, 1897
The Granger Collection

Humanities Note

Fine art, *The Triumphs of the British Army and Navy,* 1897. This lithograph commemorates the Diamond Jubilee of Queen Victoria, or the sixtieth year of her reign. It shows the triumphs of the British Army and Navy at Balaclava in the Crimea and in the Sudan.

The armed forces of Great Britain, France, Turkey, and Sardinia fought the Russian forces for control of the Holy Lands. However, the underlying causes of the war were based on conflicting commercial interests, politics, and dynastic rivalries. This lithograph indicates the high level of patriotism felt by the British.

2 **Literary Movement** Tennyson's "Ulysses," page 779, affirms of this spirit of optimism. Tennyson creates an aging hero not content to rest on his laurels at home but eager to seek new worlds to conquer.

Even in those years of expansion, however, Britons could not help worrying about the future. Other nations, especially the United States and Germany, were rapidly building up industry and competing with Britain in world markets. How long could Britain maintain its economic superiority? How would economic changes affect the balance of power? For how long would Britain's navy "rule the waves"? By the end of Victoria's reign in 1901, British leaders had many disturbing questions to ponder.

VICTORIAN THOUGHT

2 Victorian thinkers often disagreed on the crucial issues of their times, but they shared a deep confidence in humanity's ability to better itself. "Man is not the creature of circumstances," said Benjamin Disraeli. "Circumstances are the creatures of man." This spirit of optimism prevailed up to the closing years of the Victorian era.

Responses to Industrialization

The changes brought about by the industrial revolution stirred conflicting feelings among Victorian thinkers. On the one hand, they admired the material benefits industrialization had brought. On the other, they deplored the brutality of factory life and of industrial slums.

We can divide into three groups the political and economic theories Victorians employed for dealing with the changed conditions of the industrial age:

Theories

- **Laissez-faire theory.** This theory holds that government should avoid meddling in the affairs of business—should "let it be" (the meaning of the French term). When allowed full freedom, the theory goes, industry will use the most efficient techniques and reach the highest possible level of prosperity.
- **Reformist liberalism.** Those who held this theory believed that rapid change brings problems that *laissez-faire* policies cannot solve. They argued that government intervention and regulation were sometimes necessary to protect the rights of the weak against the strong.
- **Socialism.** Some thinkers and activists favored a more far-reaching policy, ending private ownership of major industries and substituting public ownership. Supporters of socialism also called for sweeping government measures to promote equality and help the poor.

Religion and Science

At the same time they were debating the political problems posed by industrialization, the Victorians were grappling with the religious and philosophical implications of modern life. A religious movement called evangelicalism influenced many Victorians. The movement linked strict personal morality with a strong commitment to social reform, leading to the founding of such institutions as the Young Men's Christian Association (YMCA) and the Salvation Army. The Liberal leader William Gladstone was among those inspired by evangelicalism to devote his life to public service and social reform. The Oxford Movement expressed a second strain of religious thought, seeking a return to more traditional church ritual.

Other Victorians turned to science for answers. The theory of evolution proposed by Charles Darwin (1809–82) in *On the Origin of Species* (1859) stirred bitter controversy. Some Victorian thinkers saw Darwin's theory as a direct challenge to Biblical truth and traditional religious faith. Some accepted both Darwin's theory and religion, striving to reconcile scientific and religious insights.

Darwin believed that a process called natural selection guides evolution. By this process, some organisms survive (because they can adapt to changing conditions) and some die out (because they cannot adapt). A social scientist named Herbert Spencer (1820–1903) applied Darwin's idea—which Spencer called "the survival of the fittest"—to social life. In Spencer's harsh philosophy, called Social Darwinism, the "fittest" humans achieve social and economic success while the "unfit" fail. Neither government nor private charities should attempt to interfere with this "natural" process, said the Social Darwinists—applying *laissez-faire* theory to social as well as economic life.

VICTORIAN LITERATURE

The ideas of the Victorian Age—political and moral, scientific and religious—helped to shape the works you will read in this unit. Indeed, they helped to define the Victorians themselves. Education was spreading in the Victorian Age, and as literacy increased, so did the impact of the written word. Probably at no other time before or since did books enjoy such enormous popularity and influence.

Romanticism, Realism, and Naturalism

The Romantic movement continued to influence writers of the Victorian Age, but new styles of writing came into vogue. Romanticism had begun as a radical departure from literary practice; now it was part of mainstream culture, safe but slightly stale. A new generation of writers, coming of age in a time of rapid technological change, began to examine the social effects of that change. The heroes of the new generation's literature would be ordinary people

Enrichment The evangelical movement, which encouraged Puritan values, deeply affected the moral tone of England. In evangelicalism there was no place for the arts. The attitude was that art corrupts, because it distracts the mind from virtues.

Enrichment Matthew Arnold applied the term *Philistines* to people who, adopting the evangelical attitude, were hostile to any form of art. The term *Philistinism* has come to mean a smug indifference or antaganism to cultural or artistic values.

Humanities Note

Fine art, *Dudley Street, Seven Dials, London,* 1872, by Gustave Doré. Gustave Doré (1832–83) was an enormously popular illustrator of the mid-nineteenth century. Born in France, Doré illustrated some of the world's greatest classics, including the Bible, Dante's *Divine Comedy,* Tennyson's *Idylls of the King,* and Coleridge's "The Rime of the Ancient Mariner." As seen in this detail, his work is informed by his taste for romantic realism and reflects his taste for the dramatic.

Enrichment A group of artists shared a belief that art had become shallow, insincere, and even frivolous. They believed that they should return to the values of art before Raphael, and therefore called themselves the Pre-Raphaelite Brotherhood. They mounted an attack on academic art—everything that had descended from Raphael's painting. Wanting to reform the ills of modern civilization through their art, they strove for simplicity and sincerity, emulating the attitude of the medieval masters. Their subject matter was generally escapist, medieval, and sensuous. Their work included crowded canvases, flat figures, and often a return to nature. Dante Gabriel Rossetti was their leader and most gifted member. (See pages 773, 799, and 820 for examples of Pre-Raphaelite art.)

DUDLEY STREET, SEVEN DIALS, LONDON, 1872
Gustave Doré
The Granger Collection

facing the day-to-day problems of life. Life would be presented as it is, rather than as it might be. We call this new literary movement realism, because it sought to portray human life realistically, as it is actually lived, without sugar coating.

Romantic thinking had lent itself to poetic language, and we study the Romantic Age chiefly for its poetry. Realism, on the other hand, focused on more down-to-earth or prosaic events especially suited to prose. The shift in style helped to make the Victorian Age the great age of the British novel.

By focusing on ordinary people, realist literature reflected the nineteenth-century trend to democracy and appealed to a growing middle-class audience. Realist writing often dealt with family relationships, religion and morality, social change, and social reform—topics of special interest to middle-class readers.

New ideas in science also made their mark on Victorian literature. A movement known as naturalism—an outgrowth of realism—sought to apply the techniques of scientific observation to writing about life in the industrial age. Naturalists crammed their novels with details—the sour smells of poverty, the harsh sounds of factory life—often with the aim of promoting social reform. Naturalist writers directly contradicted the romantic view of nature as kindly and benevolent. To naturalists, the idea that nature mirrored human feelings was false—a "pathetic fallacy." Instead, naturalist writers portrayed nature as harsh and indifferent to the human suffering it often caused.

It would be a mistake to assume that Victorian writers abandoned romanticism altogether. Some writers blended romanticism with realism or naturalism; others sought to revive romanticism as the radical force it once had been. Two Victorian literary movements deserve special mention here. One is a group of painters and poets known as the Pre-Raphaelite Brotherhood. Formed about 1850, this short-lived group sought to ignore the ugliness of industrial life by portraying nature with the fidelity found in medieval Italian art before the Renaissance painter Raphael (1483–1520). The leading Pre-Raphaelite was Dante Gabriel Rossetti (1828–82), who excelled both as a painter and as a poet. The second group, known as the aesthetic movement, appeared toward the end of the Victorian Age. Aesthetes like the writer Oscar Wilde (1854–1900) turned away from the everyday world and sought to create "art for art's sake"—works whose sole reason for being was their perfection or beauty.

Victorian Poetry

The Victorian Age produced a large and diverse body of poetry. The Romantic style predominated at first, but realism and naturalism gained force as time went on.

The most popular poet of the era, however, was a romantic—Alfred, Lord Tennyson (1809–92). Influenced by earlier romantic poets, especially Walter Scott, Tennyson wrote many long narrative poems on ancient and medieval themes like the King Arthur legend. His verse displays a keen sense of the music of language, and some of his more sentimental lyrics reappeared in popular songs. Yet Tennyson also revealed a deeper, more thoughtful side in such powerful poems as "Ulysses" (1842) and *In Memoriam* (1850). Tennyson became poet laureate after Wordsworth died in 1850.

Robert Browning (1812–89) produced a body of poetry as diverse as Tennyson's, although in his lifetime he never achieved equal public acclaim. Many of Browning's poems display Romantic attitudes. Others, however, show the influence of realism in seeking to portray individuals with un-Romantic authenticity. Critics have especially admired Browning's use of the dramatic monologue—a long speech by an imaginary character—to expose pretense and

BEATA BEATRIX, c. 1863
Dante Gabriel Rossetti
The Granger Collection

Introduction 773

Humanities Note

Fine art, *Beata Beatrix,* c. 1863, by Dante Gabriel Rossetti. Dante Gabriel Rossetti (1828–82) was one of the founding members of the Pre-Raphaelite Brotherhood. This group of painters turned away from the materialism and ugliness they perceived in the industrialized world and toward the spirituality and idealism they associated with the past, especially the Middle Ages and the early Renaissance.

Rossetti, who was also a poet (see page 871), used literature as the subject matter of many of his paintings. He had a life-long fascination with his namesake, and created a series of paintings based on Dante's *Divine Comedy*, of which this painting of Beatrice is one.

5 **Enrichment** Robert Southey, a distinctly inferior Romantic poet, was chosen laureate in 1813; on his death in 1843 he was replaced by the aging Wordsworth. When Tennyson became poet laureate in 1850, the usual circumstance of back-to-back great poets in the laureateship occurred.

6 **Master Teacher Note** To analyze the differences between Tennyson's and Browning's attitudes toward death, you might have students compare and contrast "Crossing the Bar," page 808, and "Prospice," page 822.

7 **Literary Movement** Browning's "My Last Duchess," page 812, is his most famous example of this form. Because the critics had treated his early personal lyric poetry with contempt, Browning turned to the impersonal dramatic monologue in defense.

3 **Literary Movement** See Tennyson's "The Lady of Shalott," page 786, which combines a romantic fascination with the legendary past with the thoroughly modern concept of the artist experiencing life and love at second-hand.

4 **Literary Movement** See the excerpt from Tennyson's great elegy, "In Memoriam," page 797. In this poem, over a seventeen-year period, Tennyson works through his despair at the death of his beloved friend Arthur Hallam to a final acceptance of the wisdom of God.

Humanities Note

Alfred Lord Tennyson, Caricature, 1871, by Carlo Pellegrini. Caricature is a type of art that exaggerates the physical characteristics or mannerisms of its subject. Caricature is often used to poke fun at elevated subjects, such as the poet laureate.

This caricature of Tennyson gives great emphasis to certain characteristics. You might have students determine what the caricaturist is poking fun at.

8 Literary Movement See Elizabeth Browning's Sonnet 43, page 858, the most often-quoted of the forty-four poems in her sonnet sequence, *Sonnets from the Portuguese,* which she wrote to Browning during their courtship. He called them, somewhat extravagantly, "the finest sonnets in any language since Shakespeare." They have been judged with less hyperbole by more dispassionate critics as skillful, genuine, and sensitive.

9 Master Teacher Note Students might compare Elizabeth Barrett Browning's attitude toward love with Shakespeare's as voiced in his Sonnet 116, page 258.

10 Literary Movement See Christina Rossetti's "A Birthday," page 863, a lyric of great simplicity and charm.

11 Master Teacher Note Arnold's poem "To Marguerite—Continued," page 826, sees all men as islands. You might have students compare this attitude with John Donne's in Meditation 17, page 405.

12 Literary Movement Although Arnold's "Dover Beach," page 830, is "free" in the sense of an absence of a fixed pattern of meter and rhyme, its rhythm is mainly iambic pentameter; its rhyme is subtle, pervasive, and evocative; its staggered line lengths suggest the ebb and flow of the tide.

ALFRED, LORD TENNYSON, CARICATURE, 1871
Carlo Pellegrini
The Granger Collection

reveal a character's inner self. In 1846, Browning plunged into one of literature's most famous romances when he eloped with the poet Elizabeth Barrett, whose father had forbidden the marriage. At the time, Elizabeth was a more famous poet than Robert. History has since reversed that verdict, but Elizabeth Barrett Browning (1806 –61) is still remembered for the beautiful love poems she wrote her husband.

8, 9

A number of other Victorian poets also worked in the Romantic vein. You have already read of the Pre-Raphaelites, who include Dante Gabriel Rossetti; his sister, Christina Rossetti (1830–94); and George Meredith (1828–1909). Another poet with a Romantic style was Emily Brontë (1818–48), who often described characters and settings from the imaginative world of her own childhood.

10

Matthew Arnold (1822–88) was probably the first Victorian poet to focus on "the bewildering confusion" of the industrial age. Many of Arnold's poems deal with alienation: separation from nature, isolation from other human beings. In his most famous poem, "Dover Beach" (1867), he breaks with poetic tradition and employs free verse—poetry with no fixed rhythm—to portray the confusion and loss of faith of his times. Arnold was a forerunner of the more pessimistic naturalist writers.

11

12

Late Victorian naturalism found its strongest voice in Thomas Hardy (1840–1928), whose poetry, like his prose, focuses on workers and farmers overwhelmed by the forces of nature and society. Life's disappointments were also a frequent subject of A. E. Housman (1859–1936), whose quiet lyrics speak of personal loss and rural change.

13

14

Rudyard Kipling (1865–1936), who wrote fiction and children's stories as well as poetry, gained great popularity in the 1890's. Kipling created action-packed narrative poems such as "Gunga Din" (1892) and many short lyric poems that became popular songs. He employs the dialect of working-class soldiers in realist poems such as "Tommy" (1892):

15

> For it's Tommy this, an' Tommy that, an' "Chuck 'im out, the brute!"
> But it's "Savior of 'is Country" when the guns begin to shoot.

One final Victorian poet, Gerard Manley Hopkins (1844–89), remained unpublished during his own century but would later inspire twentieth-century poets. Hopkins, a Catholic priest, wrote deeply religious verse influenced by the earlier Romantic poets and the philosopher Duns Scotus. He was also an innovative craftsman, introducing a rhythmic pattern called sprung rhythm that abandoned traditional metric feet.

16, 17

Victorian Drama

Compared to poetry, drama in the Victorian Age seemed pale and uninspired. Playhouses were few in number and hemmed in by government restrictions. Only toward the end of the century did the

13 Literary Movement The pessimistic tone that pervades Hardy's poetry is particularly strong in "The Darkling Thrush," page 834.

14 Literary Movement More gentle and lyric than Hardy, Housman evokes the Shropshire countryside with poems like "Loveliest of Trees," page 852, and a poignant sense of loss with "To an Athlete Dying Young," page 850,

and "With Rue My Heart is Laden," page 854.

15 Literary Movement See Kipling's "Recessional," page 864, for an admonitory message from this spokesman for British imperialism.

16 Enrichment The Victorians weren't ready for Gerard Manley Hopkins; even when he was published in 1914, his poetry seemed

difficult and obscure. Time is making him more accessible.

17 Master Teacher Note Hopkins in "God's Grandeur," page 842, and Wordsworth in "The World Is Too Much With Us," page 657, voice attitudes toward Nature similar in some ways, vastly different in others. You might ask students to analyze both the similarities and the differences.

theater begin to show some sparkle, with serious dramas like Sir Arthur Wing Pinero's *The Second Mrs. Tanqueray* (1893) and satirical ones like Oscar Wilde's *The Importance of Being Earnest* (1895). **18**

Victorian Fiction

If one form of literature can be seen as quintessentially Victorian, it is the novel. Members of the new middle class were avid readers, and they loved novels—especially novels that reflected the main social issues of the day. Responding to the demand, weekly and monthly magazines published novels chapter by chapter, in serial form. Curious readers had to keep buying the magazine to learn what happened next. Most of the best novelists of the day wrote, at one time or another, for the magazines.

Romanticism heavily influenced early Victorian novels, especially those written by three sisters—Emily Brontë (1818–48), Charlotte Brontë (1816–55), and the lesser-known Anne Brontë (1820 –49). Emily's classic *Wuthering Heights* (1847) tells the poetic tale of the doomed passions of Catherine Earnshaw and of Heathcliff, one of English fiction's outstanding Byronic heroes. Charlotte's famous *Jane Eyre* (1847) recounts the adventures of a governess who falls in love with her mysterious employer, Mr. Rochester. Nevertheless, both works also contain elements of the new realism—as in *Jane Eyre*'s vivid portrait of the heroine's harsh childhood.

The realistic elements of *Jane Eyre* probably owe much to the influence of Charles Dickens (1812–70), who surpassed all other Victorian novelists in popularity. Dickens never forgot his impoverished childhood, filling his novels with poignant details that dramatized the problems of a grimy industrial England. Although Dickens treated social problems realistically and became an outspoken voice for social reform, he tempered his criticism with humor. Many of his characters are comic caricatures in which a particular human foible or vice is exaggerated. Dickens also showed a sentimental

BAYSWATER OMNIBUS
G. W. Joy
Museum of London

Humanities Note

Fine art, *Bayswater Omnibus*, by G. W. Joy. George William Joy (1844–1925) was a British painter who painted realistic scenes of everyday life. This scene in a public conveyance reflects the concerns of the social realists, showing the rapidly growing middle class.

18 Enrichment Like Oliver Goldsmith, Oscar Wilde has the distinction of having produced outstanding work in three distinct literary genres: in poetry, ''The Ballad of Reading Gaol;'' in Drama, *The Importance of Being Earnest*; in the novel, *The Picture of Dorian Gray*.

See the Great Works feature on *The Importance of Being Earnest,* p. 902.

Fine art, *Hyde Park near Grosvenor Gate,* 1842, by Thomas Shotter Boys. Thomas Shotter Boys (1803–72) was a British painter who sought to present everyday life in a realistic fashion. This painting captures the pageant of Victorian life in an age of opulence. The setting, Hyde Park, was an appropriate place to show Victorian people at leisure.

19 Literary Movement See Hardy's " 'Ah, Are You Digging on My Grave?' " page 850, for a poem that contains the same pessimistic and cynical tone that generally pervades his novels.

20 Master Teacher Note In both Hardy's "The Darkling Thrush," page 834, and Shelley's "To a Skylark," page 708, a bird seems to know something that man doesn't. You might ask students to analyze and compare this knowledge.

21 Enrichment It was Carlyle's *French Revolution* that inspired Dickens's writing of *A Tale of Two Cities.*

CHECK TEST

1. The prosperous economy and policy of expansionism in Britain produced a predominant feeling of _____ in Victorian life.
2. Victorian _____ emphasized compromise and slow reform.
3. The policy of _____ extended the British empire in the world.
4. The literary movements of _____ and _____ supplanted Romanticism during the Victorian period.
5. While poetry was important during the Victorian Age, the quintessential form of Victorian literature is considered to be _____ .

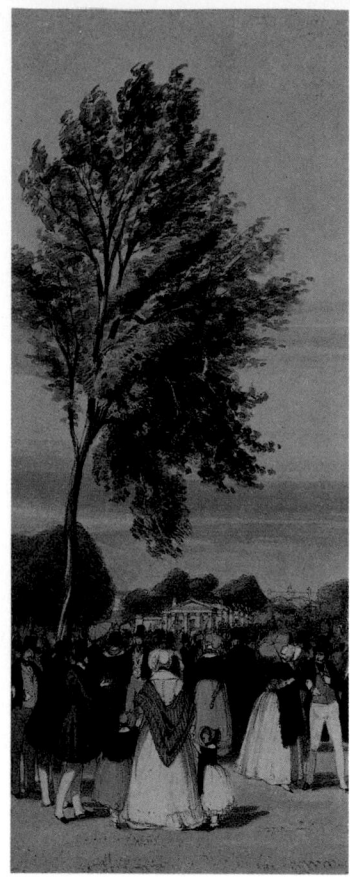

HYDE PARK NEAR GROSVENOR GATE, 1842
Thomas Shotter Boys
Guildhall Art Gallery

side, providing happy endings for many of his plucky heroes and heroines.

Other Victorian realists were less sentimental in their portraits of people and society. George Meredith, already mentioned as a romantic poet, produced careful psychological studies of characters and their motives in novels such as *The Egoist* (1879). Mary Ann Evans, writing under the pen name George Eliot (1819–80), examined moral issues and personal relationships in novels such as *Adam Bede* (1859). Also choosing realistic themes were William Makepeace Thackeray (1811–63), Anthony Trollope (1815–82), Elizabeth Gaskell (1810–65), and Samuel Butler (1835–1902).

As the century drew to a close, British novelists leaned more and more to naturalism. Thomas Hardy was the most highly regarded of late Victorian naturalists. Hardy set his fiction in western England, which he called by its old Saxon name, Wessex. His pessimistic novels often portray rural characters who have been disappointed in life and love.

19, 20

Such downbeat themes did not attract the enthusiastic reception for naturalist novels that earlier realist novels had won. Late Victorian readers tended to prefer the action-packed adventure stories of writers like Robert Louis Stevenson (1850–94) and Rudyard Kipling or the Sherlock Holmes mysteries of Sir Arthur Conan Doyle (1859–1930).

Nonfiction Prose

Novels, of course, were only one of the many types of prose available to Victorian readers. British writers poured out a steady stream of histories, biographies, essays, and criticism.

Greatest of the historians were Thomas Carlyle (1795–1881) and Thomas Babington Macaulay (1800–59). Carlyle also wrote historical biographies. Perhaps the outstanding literary biography of the era was Elizabeth Gaskell's *Life of Charlotte Brontë* (1857), still a primary source of information on the Brontë family.

21

All the great Victorian thinkers produced influential prose works. Matthew Arnold, for example, made a sharp attack on the British class system in *Culture and Anarchy* (1869), his most famous work of social criticism. Other influential works included *Modern Painters* (1843) by John Ruskin (1819–1900), *On Liberty* (1859) by John Stuart Mill (1806–73), *The Idea of a University Defined* (1873) by John Henry Newman (1801–90), and *Studies in the History of the Renaissance* (1873) by Walter Pater (1839–94).

All in all, the Victorian Age produced a diverse body of literature—entertaining, scholarly, humorous, profound. Because the era is so close to our own times—and because in it we see the beginnings of our own problems, many of them still unresolved —Victorian literature has a special relevance to readers in the twentieth century. In addition, the Victorian writers were brilliant storytellers, and we read their works not only for literary appreciation and historical understanding but for pure reading pleasure.

ANSWERS

1. optimism
2. politics
3. imperialism
4. realism, naturalism
5. the novel

ENGLISH VOICES
Quotations by Prominent Figures of the Period

Man is a tool-making animal.
Thomas Carlyle, *Sartor Resartus*

Youth is a blunder; manhood a struggle; old age a regret.
Benjamin Disraeli, *Coningsby*

If thou must love me, let it be for naught
Except for love's sake only.
Elizabeth Barrett Browning, *Sonnets from the Portuguese*

The only purpose for which power can be rightfully exercised over any member of a civilized community, against his will, is to prevent harm to others.
John Stuart Mill, *On Liberty*

You cannot fight against the future. Time is on our side.
William E. Gladstone, Speech on the Second Reform Bill

It's them as take advantage
that get advantage i'
this world.
George Eliot, *Adam Bede*

'Tis better to have loved and lost
Than never to have loved at all.
Alfred, Lord Tennyson, *In Memoriam, A.H.H.*

A man's reach should exceed his grasp,
Or what's a heaven for?
Robert Browning, "Andrea del Sarto"

He had used the word in its Pickwickian sense.
Charles Dickens, *The Pickwick Papers*

Additional Voices

The sole end for which mankind are warranted, individually or collectively, in interfering with the liberty of action of any of their number is self-protection.
John Stuart Mill, *Liberty*

The greatest happiness of the greatest number is the foundation of morals and legislation.
Jeremy Bentham, *The Commonplace Book*

I'm not denyin' the women are foolish; God Almighty made 'em to match the men.
George Eliot, *Adam Bede*

In order that people may be happy in their work, these three things are needed: They must be fit for it. They must not do too much of it. And they must have a sense of success in it.
John Ruskin, *Pre-Raphaelitism*

If any man has any poetry in him, he should paint it.
Dante Gabriel Rossetti

Reading Critically The information on this page is designed to help students read critically the literature of the Victorian Age. This information guides students to place a work of literature in its historical context, recognize the literary movements of the time, and appreciate the writers' techniques in conveying the ideas of the period.

As you discuss this information with your students, explain that the poem on the following pages, "Ulysses" by Alfred, Lord Tennyson, is a model for reading critically. The notes in the side column draw students' attention to the aspects of the poem that reflect the historical context, the literary movements, and Tennyson's techniques. Have students pay attention to the notes and make their own critical comments as they read the poem.
To give students further practice with the process of reading critically, use the selection in the Teaching Portfolio, "The Subjection of Women" by John Stuart Mill, page 936, which students can annotate themselves. Encourage students to use these strategies as they read the literature in this unit.

READING CRITICALLY

The Literature of 1832–1901

When you read literature it is important to place it in its historical context. Doing so will help you to see how the writer was influenced by the dominant ideas and attitudes of the time and how the work fits into a particular literary movement.

Historical Context

The Victorian Age was a period marked by industrial and scientific advances, social progress, political stability, and economic prosperity. When the period began, England was the world's wealthiest and most powerful nation, and the British Empire spanned the globe. As the age progressed, the nation continued to flourish, as industrial growth and development strengthened its economy and its empire reached its peak. With the expansion of industry, the middle class became a dominant force in British society, whose belief in hard work and strict morality came to represent the age. The middle class also possessed a sense of social responsibility that helped to bring about reforms that gradually improved the living and working conditions of the lower classes.

Literary Movements

The dominant attitudes and beliefs of the Victorian period are reflected in the literature of the time. While some writers embodied the Victorian ideals, others reacted against them. Many Victorian works conveyed the optimism and conservatism that characterized the age. Other works explored the problems that arose from industrialization and confronted the materialism, hypocrisy, and social pretense that accompanied the nation's prosperity. Because of the contrasting approaches of writers of the time, Victorian literature is extremely varied and diverse.

Writers' Techniques

The English novel came of age during the Victorian period. Often published in serial form, Victorian novels are generally characterized by their episodic plots and their realistic portrayal of nineteenth-century life. In poetry, writers displayed a wide array of voices and styles. However, Victorian poets were generally more detached and objective than their predecessors from the Romantic Age.

On the following pages is a poem by Alfred, Lord Tennyson, a major Victorian poet. The notes in the side column should help you to place the selection in its historical context.

Objectives

1 To understand a dramatic monologue
2 To understand a character's motivation
3 To write a continuation of the poem

Support Material

Teaching Portfolio
Teacher Backup, p. 933
Reading Critically, from "The Subjugation of Women," by John Stuart Mill
Grammar in Action Worksheet, *Verb Agreement in Inverted Sentences,* p. 939.
Usage and Mechanics Worksheet, p. 941

Analyzing Literature Worksheet, *Understanding the Speaker in Poetry,* p. 942
Language Worksheet, *Choosing the Meaning That Fits the Context,* p. 943
Selection Test, p. 945

Ulysses

Alfred, Lord Tennyson

In Homer's epic poem, the Odyssey, *Ulysses (yōō lĭs′ ēz), the hero of the poem, sets out for his home in Ithaca after ten years of fighting in the Trojan War. The journey is long and filled with adventure. Another decade passes before Ulysses finally reaches his destination. The story of Ulysses is continued in Tennyson's poem, as Ulysses finds himself growing restless years after his return to Ithaca, and he contemplates making a final voyage.*

It little profits that an idle king,
By this still hearth, among these barren crags,
Matched with an aged wife, I mete and dole[1]
Unequal[2] laws unto a savage race,
5 That hoard, and sleep, and feed, and know not me.
I cannot rest from travel; I will drink
Life to the lees.[3] All times I have enjoyed
Greatly, have suffered greatly, both with those
That loved me, and alone; on shore, and when
10 Through scudding drifts the rainy Hyades[4]
Vexed the dim sea. I am become a name;
For always roaming with a hungry heart
Much have I seen and known—cities of men
And manners, climates, councils, governments,
15 Myself not least, but honored of them all—
And drunk delight of battle with my peers,
Far on the ringing plains of windy Troy.
I am a part of all that I have met;
Yet all experience is an arch wherethrough
20 Gleams that untraveled world, whose margin fades
Forever and forever when I move.

Writer's Technique: Tennyson's poem is a dramatic monologue, a poem in which the speaker addresses one or more listeners whose replies are not given. The dramatic monologue was a popular poetic form during the Victorian age.

Writer's Technique: The poem is written in blank verse, or unrhymed lines of iambic pentameter.

Writer's Technique: Tennyson's imagery recalls Ulysses's adventures in Homer's *Iliad* and *Odyssey*.

---

1. mete and dole: Measure and give out.
2. unequal: Unfair.
3. lees: Sediment.
4. Hyades (hī′ ə dez): A group of stars whose rising was assumed to be followed by rain.

Ulysses   779

Presentation

Motivation/Prior Knowledge
Ask students to imagine that they have lived a life as a great adventurer. They have fame and respect around the world. What would it be like to grow old? How might aging change their lives? Relate this imagined situation to that of the great Greek hero Odysseus, also known as Ulysses.

Master Teacher Note Review with students the major episodes of the *Odyssey*, which they have probably read in an earlier grade. Elicit the heroic qualities of Odysseus, known as Ulysses to the Romans. Ask students to speculate on his life after the events of the *Odyssey*. Then tell them that in this poem Tennyson imagines the thoughts of Ulysses years after his return to Ithaca.

Purpose-Setting Question What force or need drives Ulysses?

Humanities Note

Fine art, *Ulysses*, by Jean Auguste Dominique Ingres. Ingres (1780–1867), a French painter of historical subjects and portraits, was exposed to art as a child by his father, a sculptor. He first studied music, but his interest in art proved stronger. He studied with various French artists, the foremost of whom was the classicist David. His travels to Italy exposed him to the works of Raphael, the Renaissance artist, by whom he was strongly influenced.

The painting *Ulysses* was completed in 1827. It demonstrates the commitment of Ingres to classicism (unemotional aesthetic principles in art imitating those of ancient Rome and Greece) in the beauty of line and restraint of color. Technically perfect, it is a formal, pure, graceful composition that shows Ingres's attraction to the monumental sculptures of ancient Rome and Greece.

You might use these questions for class discussion:

1. Does this seem to be a portrait of a man longing for adventure? Explain.
2. How does the formal, somewhat cold classicism of this painting compare to the language of Tennyson's poem?

ULYSSES
Jean-Auguste-Dominique Ingres
National Gallery of Art, Washington

How dull it is to pause, to make an end,
To rust unburnished, not to shine in use!
As though to breathe were life. Life piled on life
25 Were all too little, and of one to me
Little remains; but every hour is saved
From that eternal silence, something more,
A bringer of new things; and vile it were
For some three suns to store and hoard myself,
30 And this gray spirit yearning in desire
To follow knowledge like a sinking star,
Beyond the utmost bound of human thought.

Grammar in Action

When a sentence begins with the word *there* or *here,* the subject is always some other word. When you write such a sentence, be sure that the subject and verb agree in number. Do not let *there* or *here* incline you to use a singular verb merely because a plural subject does not appear until later in the sentence. Tennyson, in "Ulysses," demonstrates correct usage.

There lies the port; the vessel puffs her sail;
There gloom the dark broad seas.

In the first line, the singular verb "lies" is correct, because the subject is the singular noun "port." In the next line, the plural verb "gloom" agrees with the plural subject "seas." A less careful writer might have written incorrectly, *There glooms the dark broad seas.*

This is my son, mine own Telemachus,
To whom I leave the scepter and the isle⁵
35   Well-loved of me, discerning to fulfill
This labor, by slow prudence to make mild
A rugged people, and through soft degrees
Subdue them to the useful and the good.
Most blameless is he, centered in the sphere
40   Of common duties, decent not to fail
In offices of tenderness, and pay
Meet⁶ adoration to my household gods,
When I am gone. He works his work, I mine.
    There lies the port; the vessel puffs her sail;
45   There gloom the dark broad seas. My mariners,
Souls that have toiled and wrought, and thought with
        me—
That ever with a frolic welcome took
The thunder and the sunshine, and opposed
Free hearts, free foreheads—you and I are old;
50   Old age hath yet his honor and his toil;
Death closes all; but something ere the end,
Some work of noble note, may yet be done,
Not unbecoming men that strove with Gods.
The lights begin to twinkle from the rocks;
55   The long day wanes; the slow moon climbs; the deep
Moans round with many voices. Come, my friends,
'Tis not too late to seek a newer world.
Push off, and sitting well in order smite
The sounding furrows; for my purpose holds
60   To sail beyond the sunset, and the baths
Of all the western stars, until I die.
It may be that the gulfs will wash us down;
It may be we shall touch the Happy Isles,⁷
And see the great Achilles,⁸ whom we knew.
65   Though much is taken, much abides; and though
We are not now that strength which in old days
Moved earth and heaven, that which we are, we are—
One equal temper of heroic hearts,
Made weak by time and fate, but strong in will
70   To strive, to seek, to find, and not to yield.

Historical Context:
Ulysses's efforts to "subdue" the people of Ithaca parallels the efforts of the British Empire to "civilize" the natives of many of its colonies.

Literary Movement:
Ulysses's desires reflect the Victorian work ethic.

Writer's Technique: The sunset symbolizes Ulysses's advancing age and the approach of his death.

Literary Movement:
Ulysses's assertion reflects the sense of optimism and self-assurance that characterizes Victorian life.

---

5. isle: Ithaca, an island off the coast of Greece.
6. meet: Appropriate.
7. Happy Isles: Elysium, or the Islands of the Blessed; in classical mythology, the place where heroes went after death.
8. Achilles (ə' kil' ēz): The Greek hero of the Trojan War.

Ulysses   781

Enrichment This monologue occurs on the island of Ithaca, where Ulysses is now king. At the moment of the monologue, he is preparing to set sail for his legendary last voyage. It was predicted in the *Odyssey* that the hero would make a final voyage. During medieval times, Dante tells in the "Inferno," Canto XXVI, how Ulysses makes a fatal voyage into the unknown in his search for knowledge.

Reader's Response What do you think Ulysses' final voyage will hold for him?

For Further Study Biographical information on Tennyson appears on page 784, and additional poems by him are on pages 786–808.

Student Activity 1. Decide whether each of the following sentences shows agreement of number between subject and verb. If you find an error, correct it.

1. Here's your hat and coat.
2. There are still deer in these woods.
3. There is Tony, standing behind Jane and Mike.
4. Here are every penny that I owe you.
5. There was more cookies and cake than we could eat.

Student Activity 2. Write a brief paragraph in which one sentence contains the phrase *there is*, one contains *there are*, one contains *here is*, and one contains *here are*.

1. (a) Ulysses describes his situation as "barren," ruling an uncaring "savage race" who do not know him. (b) He describes his past experiences in the Trojan Wars and his travels among "cities of men" where he has encountered all sorts of people, governments, and scenes.
2. To Telemachus, he leaves the ruling of Ithaca and the paying of homage to the household gods.
3. His purpose, stated in lines 58-61, is to "sail beyond the sunset . . . until I die."
4. He comments that his physical strength has faded but his will "To strive, to seek, to find, and not to yield" is strong.

Interpreting

5. In his previous experiences, Ulysses was a strong, clever, heroic adventurer. In contrast, his life as ruler of Ithaca is uneventful; he is unknown and unappreciated there, and he longs for the old days of fame and adventure.
6. (a) Ulysses is proud of his past accomplishments. (b) Ulysses is feeling restless as he ages, yearning for one more chance to find knowledge and glory before he dies. (c) In general, Ulysses sees life as an opportunity for adventure.
7. Telemachus is attentive to his duties, content to live an ordered life.
8. Suggested Response: The theme might be that a hero continues to face life courageously even when aging and weary.

Applying

9. Answers will differ. Students might suggest that most people do not share the feelings of Ulysses about aging. Most people are content to reduce activities as they grow older.

ANSWERS TO ANALYZING LITERATURE

1. At this point in his life, Ulysses feels that he has little time left, that this

THINKING ABOUT THE SELECTION
Recalling

1. (a) How does Ulysses describe his current situation? (b) What past experiences does he describe?
2. What work is Ulysses leaving to Telemachus?
3. According to lines 58–61, what is Ulysses's purpose?
4. What comments does Ulysses make about his present condition in the final six lines?

Interpreting

5. How does Ulysses's current situation contrast with his previous experiences?
6. (a) What is Ulysses's attitude toward his experiences and accomplishments? (b) What are his feelings about aging? (c) What is his attitude toward life in general?
7. How is Telemachus different from his father?
8. What is the poem's theme?

Applying

9. Do you think that most people share Ulysses's feelings about aging? Why or why not?

ANALYZING LITERATURE
Understanding Dramatic Monologues

A dramatic monologue is a poem in which one character speaks to one or more silent listeners at a critical point in the speaker's life. The speaker's comments reveal the circumstances surrounding the conversation and offer insights into his or her personality. For example, in Tennyson's poem Ulysses reveals his attitudes concerning old age and death.

1. Why is the occasion of this poem a critical point in Ulysses's life?
2. What do Ulysses's comments reveal about his view concerning his purpose in life?
3. What are the dominant traits of Ulysses's personality?

CRITICAL THINKING AND READING
Understanding a Character's Motivation

In portraying any type of character, a writer must provide a motivation, or a stated or implied reason for the character's behavior, to make the character's actions believable. The motivation is the cause for the action. The ensuing action is the effect, or result. For example, in "Ulysses" Tennyson makes it clear that Ulysses's desire to make a final voyage is partly the result of his disenchantment with his current situation.

1. Name one other motivation for Ulysses's desire to make a final voyage.
2. How is this motivation conveyed in the poem?

THINKING AND WRITING
Writing a Continuation of the Poem

Write a dramatic monologue in which Ulysses describes the final voyage that he contemplates in Tennyson's poem. Brainstorm about the details and outcome of the journey. Arrange the details in chronological order. Then write your poem, using formal, dignified language similar to the language Tennyson uses in "Ulysses." When you revise, make sure you have used concrete details in describing the voyage. After you have finished revising, proofread your poem and share it with your classmates.

---

is his last chance for knowledge of the world.
2. He feels that his purpose in life is to seek knowledge, glory, and fame.
3. The major traits that Ulysses reveals in this poem are a strong will, determination, pride, and confidence in his abilities.

ANSWERS TO CRITICAL THINKING AND READING

1. Another motive for Ulysses' desire to make a final voyage is his great

yearning for knowledge of the world.
2. This belief is stated directly in lines 30-32, suggested in his memories of his past adventures, and evident in his urging to his companions "to seek a newer world" in line 57.

THINKING AND WRITING

Publishing Student Writing
After students have written their poems, you might have them read

their poems aloud in small groups. Each group can decide on the most effective poem and designate one person to read that poem to the class.

Major Victorian Poets

FAIR, QUIET AND SWEET REST
Luke Fildes
Warrington Museum and Art Gallery

More About the Author Alfred, Lord Tennyson's early education under the supervision of his father included a thorough immersion in classical literature. By the age of seven, Tennyson had not only read, but memorized, all of the odes written by the Latin poet Horace. How might Tennyson's classical education be related to his success as a poet?

Critical Evaluation The scholar Douglas Bush summarizes the merits of Tennyson as a writer of an earlier age: "First, he is of prime historical importance as the most fully representative mirror and interpreter of his great age, an age of bewildering progress and bewildering anxiety. . . . Secondly, when Tennyson's mediocre and bad writing has been stripped away, he still has, to quote Eliot, three qualities rarely found together except in the greatest poets: abundance, variety, and complete competence."

ALFRED, LORD TENNYSON

1809–1892

When Alfred Tennyson was named baron by Queen Victoria in 1883, he was doubly honored—first by the title *Lord,* second by being the first English writer so titled. The honor seemed fitting for one whom most Victorians regarded as the poetic voice of their age. His commitment to responsible action and his belief in the inherent goodness of people were just two of many traits that made Tennyson the object of his contemporaries' admiration and affection. Yet, beyond these qualities was the man himself, forever struggling to overcome shyness and self-doubt, his mind keenly attuned to the problems of his century. Tennyson's best poems reflect both the inner and outer being, expressing through a clear and richly haunting music those certainties that sustain the human spirit.

Tennyson was born in the rural town of Somersby in Lincolnshire, the fourth of twelve children. His father, a rector, had a large library and personally supervised his son's early education. In 1827 Tennyson entered Trinity College, Cambridge, where he became close friends with Arthur Henry Hallam, the son of a noted historian and a great fan of Tennyson's early efforts at poetry. In 1830, with Hallam's encouragement, Tennyson published *Poems, Chiefly Lyrical,* which he followed up two years later with the simply titled *Poems.* When Hallam died suddenly in Vienna in 1833, the loss left a void in Tennyson's life that nearly destroyed him.

Grief, however, was ultimately to prove to be the inspiration behind some of the poet's greatest work. Relatively soon after Hallam's death, Tennyson began work on a collection of memorial poems dedicated to his friend. When the lengthy tribute, titled *In Memoriam,* finally appeared in 1850, the Queen's husband, Prince Albert, was so impressed that he encouraged the Queen to appoint Tennyson next Poet Laureate of England. For the next forty years Tennyson continued to publish regularly. Among his most celebrated works was *Idylls of the King,* a series of poems based on the legend of King Arthur, which began appearing in 1859 and was completed in 1885.

Modern scholars are in general agreement that there is much of lasting value in Tennyson's works. Certainly, there is no denying what the twentieth-century poet and critic T. S. Eliot has called the "abundance, variety, and complete competence" in Tennyson's poetry. Nor can one ignore the number of quotable lines Tennyson has added to the language, among them "'Tis better to have loved and lost, than never to have loved at all." These aspects of his verse and others have earned Tennyson yet another honor—that of being one of the best-known poets of any age.

Objectives

1 To recognize meter and stanza structure
2 To understand the author's purpose
3 To find meanings that fit the context
4 To write a description of the poet's style

Support Material

Teaching Portfolio
Teacher Backup, p. 947
Grammar in Action Worksheet, *Using Details that Create Atmosphere,* p. 951
Usage and Mechanics Worksheet, p. 953
Vocabulary Check, p. 954
Analyzing Literature Worksheet, *Understanding Meter,* p. 955

Critical Thinking and Reading Worksheet, *Understanding the Author's Purpose,* p. 956
Selection Test, p. 947

GUIDE FOR INTERPRETING

The Lady of Shalott; Tears, Idle Tears; The Splendor Falls

Writer's Technique

Meter and Stanza Structure. Meter is the regular pattern of stressed and unstressed syllables in poetry. Stanza structure is a term that takes into account the meter, rhyme scheme, line length, and number of lines within each stanza of a poem. Through the structure of the stanza, the poet establishes unity, of both form and thought, within a poem.

For "The Lady of Shalott," a poem inspired by Arthurian legend, Tennyson appropriately chose a meter and stanza structure that recalled medieval romances—tales in verse that described the deeds of knights and ladies. The stanza of these romances, known as a "tail-rhyme stanza," was traditionally six lines long and composed of two pairs of rhyming lines, each followed by a short third line, or "tail." The rhyming lines, moreover, customarily contained four stressed syllables, or beats, while the tail contained three. Tennyson, as will be seen, altered this traditional pattern somewhat in "The Lady of Shalott," and in so doing, lent his poem a magical, almost dreamlike quality.

Commentary

"Modern fame is nothing," Tennyson remarked to a friend. "I'd rather have an acre of land. I shall go down, down! I'm up now. Action and reaction."

At the time of Tennyson's death, he was indeed immensely popular. But shortly thereafter, just as he had predicted, a reaction against his work set in, and as with a pebble thrown into a pond, rippled ever wider. It became fashionable in the 1920's and 1930's to belittle his work; critic Harold Nicholson, for example, called him "a morbid and unhappy mystic" who "should be read carelessly or not at all."

By the 1940's, however, the ripples had begun to die down, and critic Arthur J. Carr could write, "At some crucial points Tennyson is a modern poet, and there are compelling reasons why we should try to comprehend him."

Do you think such a swing in opinion is inevitable? Why do you think that Tennyson's poetry might appeal to us today?

Writing

Imagine that the only view of the world you had was a reflection of it, as through a mirror. Freewrite, describing what sensations you would miss in not experiencing life firsthand, and tell how this would make you feel.

Literary Focus Point out that Tennyson was a restless and inventive poet, with a keen ear for the music of poetry. Tell students that all of these factors may have influenced his adaptation of the tail-rhyme stanza.

Writing/Prior Knowledge Carry out the assignment literally by inviting student volunteers to sit facing a corner of the classroom in which a mirror has been set up. Ask them to record their impressions of the proceedings in the room over the space of five minutes. Discuss the results of the experiment.

Vocabulary

Preteach the following words:
casement (kās′ mənt) *n*.: Window that is hinged at the sides. (p. 786, l. 25)
burnished (bʉr′ nishd) *adj*.: Made shiny by daily use. (p. 789, l. 101)
waning (wān′ iŋ) *v*.: Gradually becoming dimmer. (p. 789, l. 119)
prow (prou) *n*.: Front of a boat. (p. 790, l. 125)
feigned (fānd) *v*.: Pretended. (p. 790, l. 17)
cataract (kat′ ə rakt′) *n*.: Waterfall. (p. 792, l. 4)
glens (glenz) *n*.: Valleys. (p. 792, l. 11)

Spelling Tip Have students notice the *ei* spelling of the long *a* sound and the silent *g* in *feigned*.

Motivation/Prior Knowledge
Have students discuss what they know about Arthurian legend and the Knights of the Round Table. Have them volunteer names and roles of such key characters as Sir Lancelot. What did King Arthur and his knights see as their purpose? What did they do to accomplish this purpose?

Master Teacher Note Tell students that the poem they are about to read involves a woman who has been placed under a curse. Elicit details of other stories, fables, and fairy tales they know of in which people are under spells or curses. Make a list of these details on the board. Generate a discussion about what happens in these tales when the spell is broken.

Thematic Idea Another selection that focuses on the legend of King Arthur is the excerpt from *Morte D'Arthur* by Thomas Malory, page 91.

Purpose-Setting Question What sorts of problems might confront a person whose life is devoted to creating art?

1 **Literary Focus** What is the rhyme scheme of the first stanza? How many accented syllables are there in each line?

2 **Discussion** What are the connotations of the word *gray*? What does the use of this word suggest about the Lady's existence?

The Lady of Shalott

Alfred, Lord Tennyson

Part I

On either side the river lie
Long fields of barley and of rye,
That clothe the wold[1] and meet the sky;
And through the field the road runs by
5   To many-towered Camelot,[2]
And up and down the people go,
Gazing where the lilies blow[3]
Round an island there below,
     The island of Shalott.

10 Willows whiten, aspens quiver,
Little breezes dusk and shiver
Through the wave that runs forever
By the island in the river
     Flowing down to Camelot.
15 Four gray walls, and four gray towers,
Overlook a space of flowers,
And the silent isle imbowers
     The Lady of Shalott.

By the margin, willow-veiled.
20 Slide the heavy barges trailed
By slow horses; and unhailed
The shallop[4] flitteth silken-sailed
     Skimming down to Camelot:
But who hath seen her wave her hand?
25 Or at the casement seen her stand?
Or is she known in all the land,
     The Lady of Shalott?

Only reapers, reaping early
In among the bearded barley,
30 Hear a song that echoes cheerly,

---

1. wold: Rolling plains.
2. Camelot: A legendary English town where King Arthur had his court and Round Table.
3. blow: Bloom.
4. shallop: A light open boat.

From the river winding clearly,
Down to towered Camelot:
And by the moon the reaper weary,
Piling sheaves in uplands airy,
35 Listening, whispers, "'Tis the fairy
Lady of Shalott."

Part II

There she weaves by night and day
A magic web with colors gay.
She has heard a whisper say,
40 A curse is on her if she stay
To look down to Camelot.
She knows not what the curse may be,
And so she weaveth steadily,
And little other care hath she,
45 The Lady of Shalott.

3

THE LADY OF SHALOTT
John Waterhouse
The Tate Gallery, London

3 Reading Strategy What impression do you have of the Lady so far? What details prompt this interpretation?

Humanities Note

Fine art, *The Lady of Shalott,* 1888, by John W. Waterhouse. John William Waterhouse (1849–1917) studied and exhibited at the Royal Academy in London. He is considered to be both a Classical and pre-Raphaelite painter of mainly romantic and poetic subjects. Much of his work was inspired by the poetry of Tennyson and Keats.

This painting, beautifully detailed and executed, was done in iridescent colors that lend a supernatural feel to it. The painting is rich in symbolism. The chain in the Lady's hand, for instance, represents her bondage to fate, and the guttering candle her soon-to-be-extinguished flame of life. Note, too, the Lady's grief-stricken expression, which registers her resignation to her fate.

Some additional points for class discussion include the following:
1. How true to the details of the poem do you feel the artist kept?
2. Do you feel that the mood of the painting effectively mirrors that of the poem?
3. What additional symbols can you locate in the painting? What do they represent?

788

4 Discussion How do the descriptions of these people differ from that of the Lady?

5 Reading Strategy What do you think the Lady might do about her plight?

6 Discussion How does the repetition of the *b* sound at the beginning of many of the stressed syllables enhance the description of Lancelot?

7 Discussion Compare the use of color in these lines with its use in line 15.

And moving through a mirror[5] clear
That hangs before her all the year,
Shadows of the world appear.
There she sees the highway near
     Winding down to Camelot:
50 There the river eddy whirls,
And there the surly village churls,
And the red cloaks of market girls,
     Pass onward from Shalott.

55 Sometimes a troop of damsels glad,
An abbot on an ambling pad,[6]
Sometimes a curly shepherd lad,
Or long-haired page in crimson clad,
     Goes by to towered Camelot;
60 And sometimes through the mirror blue
The knights come riding two and two:
She hath no loyal knight and true,
     The Lady of Shalott.

But in her web she still delights
65 To weave the mirror's magic sights,
For often through the silent nights
A funeral, with plumes and lights
     And music, went to Camelot:
Or when the moon was overhead,
70 Came two young lovers lately wed:
"I am half sick of shadows," said
     The Lady of Shalott.

Part III

A bow-shot from her bower eaves,
He rode between the barley sheaves,
75 The sun came dazzling through the leaves,
And flamed upon the brazen greaves[7]
     Of bold Sir Lancelot.
A red-cross knight[8] forever kneeled
To a lady in his shield,
80 That sparkled on the yellow field,
     Beside remote Shalott.

---

5. mirror: Weavers placed mirrors in front of their looms, so that they could view the progress of their work.
6. pad: An easy-paced horse.
7. greaves: Armor that protects the legs below the kneecaps.
8. red-cross knight: Refers to the Redcrosse Knight from *The Faerie Queene* by Edmund Spenser. In Spenser's work, the knight represents St. George, the patron saint of England, in addition to being a symbol of holiness.

Grammar in Action

The **atmosphere** is the mood or feeling conveyed by a literary work. Often writers use specific details—concrete nouns and precise adjectives, adverbs, and verbs—to evoke atmosphere. In "The Lady of Shalott," for example, Tennyson wants to evoke the atmosphere of medieval England. Notice the specific details he uses to accomplish this purpose:

The bridle bells rang merrily
     As he rode down to Camelot:
And from his blazoned baldric slung
A mighty silver bugle hung,
And as he rode his armor rung,
     Beside remote Shalott.

The gemmy[9] bridle glittered free,
Like to some branch of stars we see
Hung in the golden Galaxy.[10]
85　The bridle bells rang merrily
　　　As he rode down to Camelot:
And from his blazoned baldric[11] slung
A mighty silver bugle hung,
And as he rode his armor rung,
90　　　Beside remote Shalott.

All in the blue unclouded weather
Thick-jeweled shone the saddle leather,
The helmet and the helmet feather
Burned like one burning flame together,
95　　　As he rode down to Camelot.
As often through the purple night,
Below the starry clusters bright,
Some bearded meteor, trailing light,
　　　Moves over still Shalott.

100　His broad clear brow in sunlight glowed;
On burnish'd hooves his war horse trode;
From underneath his helmet flowed
His coal-black curls as on he rode,
　　　As he rode down to Camelot.
105　From the bank and from the river
He flashed into the crystal mirror,
"Tirra lirra," by the river
　　　Sang Sir Lancelot.

She left the web, she left the loom,
110　She made three paces through the room,
She saw the waterlily bloom,
She saw the helmet and the plume,
　　　She looked down to Camelot.
Out flew the web and floated wide;
115　The mirror cracked from side to side;
"The curse is come upon me," cried
　　　The Lady of Shalott.

8

Part IV

In the stormy east wind straining,
The pale yellow woods were waning,

---

9. gemmy: Jeweled.
10. Galaxy: The Milky Way.
11. blazoned baldric: A decorated sash worn diagonally across the chest.

The Lady of Shalott　789

8 Reading Strategy What do you think will happen to the Lady now?

Tennyson includes details such as the "blazoned baldric" and the "mighty silver bugle" to give his poem a medieval flavor. To portray this scene more fully, Tennyson even describes the sound of the knight's bridle bells and armor.

Student Activity 1. Identify other details in this poem that convey a medieval atmosphere and explain why they are effective. Specify the parts of speech that make up these details. For example, the phrase "blazoned baldric" consists of an adjective and a noun.

Student Activity 2. Write a brief description of a scene from a particular historical era. Use specific details to evoke the atmosphere of that time. Give your description to a classmate and see whether he or she can guess what era you meant to evoke.

9 **Discussion** Mischance is bad luck. Whose bad luck is referred to here, and what is the nature of that bad luck?

10 **Discussion** How does the Lady's song compare with that of Lancelot in line 107?

120   The broad stream in his banks complaining,
      Heavily the low sky raining
          Over towered Camelot;
      Down she came and found a boat
      Beneath a willow left afloat,
125   And round about the prow she wrote
          The Lady of Shalott.

      And down the river's dim expanse
      Like some bold seër in a trance,
      Seeing all his own mischance—
130   With a glassy countenance
          Did she look to Camelot.
      And at the closing of the day
      She loosed the chain, and down she lay;
      The broad stream bore her far away,
135   *The Lady of Shalott.*

      Lying, robed in snowy white
      That loosely flew to left and right—
      The leaves upon her falling light—
      Through the noises of the night
140   She floated down to Camelot:
      And as the boathead wound along
      The willowy hills and fields among,
      They heard her singing her last song,
          The Lady of Shalott.

145   Heard a carol, mournful, holy,
      Chanted loudly, chanted lowly,
      Till her blood was frozen slowly,
      And her eyes were darkened wholly,
          Turned to towered Camelot.
150   For ere she reached upon the tide
      The first house by the waterside,
      Singing in her song she died,
          The Lady of Shalott.

      Under tower and balcony,
155   By garden wall and gallery,
      A gleaming shape she floated by,
      Dead-pale between the houses high,
          Silent into Camelot.
      Out upon the wharfs they came,
160   Knight and burgher, lord and dame,
      And round the prow they read her name,
          The Lady of Shalott.

```
            Who is this? and what is here?
            And in the lighted palace near
      165   Died the sound of royal cheer;          11
            And they crossed themselves for fear,
            All the knights at Camelot:
            But Lancelot mused a little space;
            He said, "She has a lovely face;          12
      170   God in his mercy lend her grace,
            The Lady of Shalott."
```

THINKING ABOUT THE SELECTION
Recalling

1. (a) According to the poem, where does the Lady live? (b) How do the people of Camelot know of her existence?
2. What does the Lady spend all of her time doing, and why?
3. Where does she glimpse "shadows of the world"?
4. (a) What action does the Lady take when she sees Sir Lancelot in the mirror? (b) What happens to her as a result?

Interpreting

5. In line 42, the speaker says the Lady "knows not what the curse may be." Explain the curse in your own words?
6. Critics have seen this poem as a commentary on the plight of the artist. In the light of this interpretation, what is meant by the Lady's complaint in lines 71–72?
7. (a) Why do you think the author devotes so much space to his description of Sir Lancelot? (b) How does it relate to the Lady's action and to the overall meaning of the poem?

Applying

8. Why do you find the legend of King Arthur an especially effective—or especially poor —vehicle for the author's commentary on art and the artist in "The Lady of Shalott"?

ANALYZING LITERATURE
Recognizing Meter and Stanza Structure

Meter is a pattern of stressed and un-stressed syllables that creates a predictable rhythm in a poem. Meter is expressed in terms of units called *feet,* each consisting of one stressed syllable and one or more unstressed syllables. Meter is but one ingredient in a poem's **stanza structure,** which also takes into account such matters as variation in line length, overall number of lines, and rhyme scheme. In "The Lady of Shalott," Tennyson adapted—or altered to suit his needs—an ancient stanza form that had the following structure: 1. six lines per stanza; 2. four feet in lines 1, 2, 4, and 5; 3. three feet in lines 3 and 6; 4. the rhyme scheme *aabccb.*

Examine several stanzas of "The Lady of Shalott." Note the ways in which the stanza structure differs from the one above. Tell how the changes add to the poem's chantlike effect.

CRITICAL THINKING AND READING
Understanding the Author's Purpose

It has been suggested that Tennyson's purpose in writing "The Lady of Shalott" was to show how the past reflects the problems of the present day.
1. Which events or statements in the poem point to a possible problem?
2. What is the nature of that problem?
3. What specific instances of this problem are evident in modern society?

The Lady of Shalott   791

11 **Enrichment** King Arthur and the Knights of the Round Table are favorite subjects for students. Suggest further readings, such as T. H. White's *Once and Future King.*

12 **Reading Strategy** Ask students whether they suspect Lancelot was aware of his role in the death of the Lady.

Reader's Response What do you think the Lady of Shalott symbolizes? Explain.

Applying

8. Answers will differ. Students may find the setting effective because the artist's gift is elusive and mystical, like the legend.
   Challenge In what ways might the artist's life be considered richer than that of the non-artistic person?

ANSWERS TO ANALYZING LITERATURE

1. Each stanza contains nine lines.
2. Lines 1–8 each contain four beats.
3. Line 9 contains three beats.
4. The rhyme scheme is *aaaabcccb.* The additional rhyming lines, along with the invariable repetition of "Camelot" at the end of the fifth line and "Shalott" at the end of the ninth, conspire to lend the poem the character of a ritual chant.

ANSWERS TO CRITICAL THINKING AND READING

1. Suggested Response: The Lady's feelings of entrapment, artistic considerations aside, are indicative of a problem.
2. Suggested Response: The problem is that of alienation from society in an age of high technology. We must remember that the era in which Tennyson lived was marked by significant industrial advances that tended to minimize the self-worth of the individual.
3. Suggested Reponse: In the twentieth century this alienation is manifest in the devastating legions of the homeless found in inner cities.

Closure and Extension

ANSWERS TO THINKING ABOUT THE SELECTION
Recalling

1. (a) She lives in a tower on the island of Shalott. (b) Only reapers know of her existence and only through the song she sings.
2. She weaves a magic web to avoid invoking a curse that has been placed on her.
3. She sees them in a mirror.
4. (a) She boards a boat bound for Camelot. (b) She dies.

Interpreting

5. Suggested Response: The Lady is forbidden from glimpsing the real world.
6. Suggested Response: The complaint expresses dissatisfaction with the contrived world of art and a desire for human contact.
7. (a) The extensive description is intended perhaps to provide a glimpse of the dazzling colors of the real world. (b) It is precisely this world that the artist forsakes for the contrived world of art.

Motivation/Prior Knowledge
Ask students whether they have
ever had the experience of feeling especially happy or especially sad without knowing exactly
why. Ask them to attempt to recall what ran through their minds
on such an occasion. Were they
simply content to submit to the
feeling? Did they attempt to get
to the root of it? Did they try to
lose themselves in some mindless activity?

Master Teacher Note Have students look at the painting of
Tintern Abbey, page 645. What
feelings does the image of the
ruined church evoke? Explain that
a similar view of this church
prompted the poem students are
about to read.

Thematic Idea Another selection
that deals with the passage of
time and the impermanence of
human life is "Ozymandias" by
Percy Bysshe Shelley, page 702.

Purpose-Setting Question What
are the advantages and disadvantages of our ability to remember
the past?

1 **Discussion** What do autumn
fields represent to the speaker?

2 **Discussion** What is meant by
"friends up from the underworld"? What clues support your
interpretation?

3 **Enrichment** The reference to
"casement" here and "autumn
fields" in the first stanza are explained in a note from the poet as
harking directly to his view of the
woods "yellowing with autumn
seen through the ruined windows" of Tintern Abbey.

from # The Princess

Alfred, Lord Tennyson

*The Princess (1847) is a long narrative poem that con-
tains a number of songs. Some of these songs, including the
two that follow, are considered to be among the finest of
Tennyson's lyrics.*

Tears, Idle Tears

Tears, idle tears, I know not what they mean,
Tears from the depth of some divine despair
Rise in the heart, and gather to the eyes,
In looking on the happy autumn fields,
5 And thinking of the days that are no more.

Fresh as the first beam glittering on a sail,
That brings our friends up from the underworld,
Sad as the last which reddens over one
That sinks with all we love below the verge;
10 So sad, so fresh, the days that are no more.

Ah, sad and strange as in dark summer dawns
The earliest pipe of half-awakened birds
To dying ears, when unto dying eyes
The casement slowly grows a glimmering square;
15 So sad, so strange, the days that are no more.

Dear as remembered kisses after death,
And sweet as those by hopeless fancy feigned
On lips that are for others; deep as love,
Deep as first love, and wild with all regret;
20 O Death in Life, the days that are no more.

THINKING ABOUT THE SELECTION
Recalling

1. According to the first stanza, what causes the tears to rise?
2. In what three ways does the speaker describe "the days that are no more."

Interpreting

3. Why are the tears described as "idle"?
4. What do you think is meant in line 2 by "some divine despair"?
5. What comment is Tennyson making about our ability to remember things past?
6. A refrain is a repeated line or phrase in a poem or song. Identify the refrain in this poem, and explain how you think it was intended to make the reader feel.

Applying

7. (a) Why do you think people feel nostalgia for "days that are no more"? (b) In what way is nostalgia bittersweet?

UNDERSTANDING LANGUAGE
Fitting the Context

Words have great versatility. Often they can be used as more than one part of speech and have several different meanings. For example, consider the word *fancy* in line 17: "And sweet as those by hopeless fancy feigned." In this line,

fancy is a noun that means "imagination." However, one dictionary provides twenty different meanings for the word *fancy* and shows it used as four parts of speech.

For each sentence below, find the meaning of *fancy* that fits the context and tell as what part of speech the word is being used.
1. She refused to wear clothing with fancy trimming.
2. He didn't fancy the way the painting captured his likeness.
3. The young people took a fancy to each other.
4. "Well, fancy that!" exclaimed elderly Mrs. Kane.

THINKING AND WRITING
Describing the Poet's Style

A poet's **style** is the way he or she strings together words and ideas to communicate a particular image or message. In "Tears, Idle Tears," Tennyson's style includes the abundant use of repetition and the contrast between positive and negative impressions (such as "sad" and "fresh" in the second stanza). Write an essay explaining how Tennyson's style relates to his theme. Begin by stating the theme of the poem. Use quotations freely to illustrate the points you cover. When you revise, make sure you have quoted exactly and punctuated your quotations accurately.

Tears, Idle Tears 793

they are part of a lingering sadness.
4. Answers may differ. Students may interpret this phrase as meaning either a grievous loss or an inexplicable sadness of larger-than-human proportions.
5. Suggested Response: He is claiming that our ability to recall condemns us to recall happy bygone times wistfully—that this ability is, thus, a bittersweet phenomenon.
6. The refrain is "the days that are no more." The line was intended to evoke a melancholy feeling.

Applying

7. (a) Suggested Response: People feel nostalgia for "days that are no more" because they tend to romanticize the past. (b) It is bittersweet because it makes us feel happy to have experienced the times we are remembering but at the same time makes us feel sad that those times have passed.

Challenge Do you feel it would be an oversimplification, based on the message in this poem, to declare Tennyson a pessimist? Why or why not?

ANSWERS TO UNDERSTANDING LANGUAGE

1. fancy *adj.*: ornamental
2. fancy *v.*: Have a liking for
3. fancy *n.*: Liking
4. fancy *v.*: Can you imagine (that)

THINKING AND WRITING
Publishing Student Writing

After students have completed the assignment, go through the roll alphabetically asking each student as you call his or her name to provide one word describing the poet's style. Each time a new word is mentioned, write it on the board. When each student has spoken, determine, by a show of hands, which students have covered the most terms in their essays. Have three or four of them read their essays to the class.

Closure and Extension

ANSWERS TO THINKING ABOUT THE SELECTION
Recalling

1. Thoughts of "the days that are no more" cause the tears to rise.

2. He describes them as "so sad, so fresh," "so sad, so strange," and as "Death in life."

Interpreting

3. Suggested Response: The tears are described as "idle" because

793

Motivation/Prior Knowledge
Ask students to offer impressions
of exotic places to which they
have been or to imagine places
they would like to go. What qualities of these places were—or
would be—most memorable?
Apart from photographs, what
mementos help us remember
places we have been? What
kinds of sounds and sights tend
to come to mind when we think of
these places?

Master Teacher Note Ask a student who plays trumpet or bugle
to bring the instrument to class.
Have these students describe the
sorts of tones the instrument produces. If possible, arrange a demonstration. Then tell your students
that the poem they are about to
read was partly inspired by the
sounds of a bugle the poet heard
on a visit to Lake Killarney, in
Ireland.

Thematic Idea Another selection
that deals with the immortality of
beauty is Keat's "Ode on a Grecian Urn," page 726.

Purpose-Setting Question What
does the speaker hear, see, and
ask?

1 **Discussion** What feeling, or
mood, is established in the first
stanza? What words and images
create this mood?

2 **Reading Strategy** What is the
effect of the repetition of the word
dying?

3 **Clarification** Elfland is another
name for fairyland, which to the
Irish borders the "real" world.

4 **Discussion** What is meant by
"our echoes?"

The Splendor Falls

Alfred, Lord Tennyson

1   The splendor falls on castle walls
           And snowy summits old in story;
        The long light shakes across the lakes,
           And the wild cataract leaps in glory.
2 5 Blow, bugle, blow, set the wild echoes flying,
        Blow, bugle; answer, echoes, dying, dying, dying.

        O hark, O hear! how thin and clear,
           And thinner, clearer, farther going!
        O sweet and far from cliff and scar[1]
3 10   The horns of Elfland faintly blowing!
        Blow, let us hear the purple glens replying;
        Blow, bugle; answer, echoes, dying, dying, dying.

        O love, they die in yon rich sky,
           They faint on hill or field or river:
4 15   Our echoes roll from soul to soul,
           And grow forever and forever.
        Blow, bugle, blow, set the wild echoes flying,
        And answer, echoes, answer, dying, dying, dying.

---

1. scar: Mountainside.

THINKING ABOUT THE SELECTION
Recalling

1. Where exactly, according to the poem, does
the splendor fall?
2. What do the bugles "set flying"?

Interpreting

3. (a) What do you think is the meaning of the
phrase "horns of Elfland" in line 10? (b) Of

"wild echoes" in lines 5 and 17?

Applying

4. (a) This poem was published in 1847. What
"splendor" do you suppose Tennyson had in
mind that he felt was "dying" from the world
around him? (b) What "splendor" might a
contemporary poet have in mind in writing
about today's world?

Closure and Extension

ANSWERS TO THINKING ABOUT THE SELECTION
Recalling

1. The splendor falls on castle walls
and snowy summits.
2. They set the wild echoes flying.

Interpreting

3. (a) The suggestion is that the
speaker is so taken with the beauty
of the moment that the horns seem
almost to emanate from a mystical
region. (b) The suggestion is that
the echoes are part of a world
untainted by worldliness.

Applying

4. (a) Suggested Response: He might
have felt that the unspoiled beauty

of nature was disappearing. (b)
Suggested Response: A contemporary poet might also write about
the unspoiled beauty of nature.

Challenge This poem captures
the poet's response to beauty. To
what extent do you find the saying
"Beauty is in the eye of the beholder" to apply in this case?

THE BARD
John Martin
Yale Center for British Art

Humanities Note

Fine art, *The Bard,* 1817, by John Martin. John Martin (1789–1854) was a British painter of landscapes and historical scenes. He began his artistic endeavors painting heraldry on coaches and decorating china, activities that supported him while he studied painting in London. He eventually gained recognition for his paintings. He chose to paint historical scenes because it was the quickest and surest way to gain eminence and honors.

The painting *The Bard,* completed in 1817, exemplifies Martin's unique approach to the painting of historical events. He emphasized the landscape over the historical figures, an unheard-of choice in history painting at the time. This painting was inspired by a poem of the same name (written by Thomas Gray, 1757). It refers to an incident in the life of King Edward I. The figures are dwarfed by the vast, towering mountains and the magnificent, glowing castle. John Martin made this landscape into something astonishing and beautiful.

You may wish to use the following questions for discussion:

1. Although this painting was not specifically painted to illustrate this poem, which visual elements match Tennyson's descriptive phrases? There are at least four.
2. Tennyson refers to Elfland in his poem. Do you feel that this painting illustrates the magical allusions in the poem? Explain.

Presentation

Literary Focus Elegy is a fairly straightforward concept, and it might suffice here simply to point out to students that the form carries into music, where it is known also as requiem. The concept of symbolism can be reinforced by asking students to suggest some common symbols—the Statue of Liberty and Cupid are obvious choices—and to tell what each represents.

Writing As an alternative, divide the class into three groups, assigning one of the three emotions mentioned to each. After the groups have had a chance to brainstorm, a spokesperson can report the group's findings to the class.

Vocabulary

Preteach the following words:

divers (dī′ vərz) *adj.*: Varied; having many parts (archaic spelling) (p. 797, l. 2)

chrysalis (kris′ ′ləs) *n.*: Cocoon of a butterfly (p. 799, l. 36)

diffusive (di fyōō′ siv) *adj.*: Spread out (p. 799, l. 51)

languid (laŋ′ gwid) *adj.*: Slow, lacking energy (p. 801, l. 5)

slumbrous (slum′ brəs) *adj.*: Peaceful, suggesting sleep (p. 801, l. 13)

consumed (kən sōōm′d′) *adj.*: Overtaken, overwhelmed (p. 802, l. 57)

perpetual (pər pech′ oo wəl) *adj.*: Constant, unending (p. 803, l. 61)

waxing (waks′ iŋ) *v.*: Growing, ripening (p. 803, l. 77)

reconcile (rek′ ən sīl′) *v.*: Make up with (p. 804, l. 125)

doleful (dōl′ fəl) *adj.*: Filled with sadness (p. 806, l. 161)

GUIDE FOR INTERPRETING

Literary Forms	*from* **In Memoriam A. H. H.;** **The Lotos Eaters; Crossing the Bar**

from In Memoriam A. H. H.; The Lotos Eaters; Crossing the Bar

Literary Forms

Elegy. An *elegy* is any poem that mourns the passing of an individual. The writing of elegies traces back to ancient times and, since the Renaissance, has been an enduring tradition among English poets. Tennyson's *In Memoriam* is widely acknowledged as one of the finest elegies ever written. The poem not only laments the death of Tennyson's closest friend, Arthur Henry Hallam, but also provides a "chronicle" of the poet/speaker's emotions as he moves gradually away from sheer grief and doubt, and ultimately toward understanding, acceptance, and faith. In this sense *In Memoriam* is more about life, love, and hope than it is about death, anger, and despair.

Writer's Technique

Symbol. A *symbol* is a person, place, object, or action that represents an abstract idea. For example, a parent might be a symbol of authority and a spring flower might be a symbol of rebirth. Poets often use symbols to fill images with a deeper significance. In "The Lady of Shalott," for instance, Tennyson uses the web and mirror as symbols for, respectively, art and the artist's tendency to experience life secondhand.

Writing

The sudden death of a friend or relative, especially a young one, can stir up a wide range of emotions in the survivors, including despair, anger, and doubt. Describe what in particular might lead to these feelings about such a loss.

Primary Source

Critics have written enthusiastically about *In Memoriam*. Paul F. Baum, for instance, sees the *elegy* form as well matched to both its subject and to Tennyson's genius. "*In Memoriam*," he writes, "is not only a monument to Arthur Hallam and a record to Tennyson's personal suffering at Hallam's early death, it is also 'the way of the soul' . . . his representation of everyman's pain when confronted with death, the struggle with doubt, and the triumphant assertion of God's love."

Few scholars, however, have matched T. S. Eliot's impassioned response to the poem: "It is, in my opinion, in *In Memoriam* that Tennyson finds full expression. Its technical merit alone is enough to ensure its perpetuity. While Tennyson's technical competence is everywhere masterly and satisfying, *In Memoriam* is the most unapproachable of all his poems. Here are one hundred and thirty-two passages, each of several quatrains in the same form, and never monotony or repetition. . . . It is unique."

Spelling Tip Have students notice that, when the adjective *slumbrous* is formed from *slumber*, the *e* is dropped from the last syllable of slumber.

Objectives

1 To understand an elegy
2 To make inferences about the subject of an elegy
3 To recognize importance of allusions
4 To find antonyms
5 To recognize symbols
6 To compare attitudes
7 To write about symbols

Support Material

Teaching Portfolio
Teacher Backup, p. 959
Usage and Mechanics Worksheet, p. 962
Vocabulary Check, p. 954
Critical Thinking and Reading Worksheet, *Making Inferences About the Subject of an Elegy*, p. 965

from In Memoriam, A. H. H.

Alfred, Lord Tennyson

In Memoriam, A.H.H. is an elegiac poem that conveys Tennyson's feelings and reflections about the death of his close friend Arthur Hallam, a talented young man who died suddenly at the age of twenty-two. Though Milton's Lycidas and Shelley's Adonais also lamented the deaths of promising young men, the structure of Tennyson's poem is quite different from these earlier elegies. Unlike the earlier elegies, In Memoriam, A.H.H. is made up of 131 seemingly self-sustaining lyrics that were composed over a period of seventeen years, as the poet struggled to come to terms with the feelings of doubt and despair that stemmed from his friend's early death.

1

I held it truth, with him who sings
    To one clear harp in divers tones,
    That men may rise on stepping stones
Of their dead selves to higher things.

5 But who shall so forecast the years
    And find in loss a gain to match?
    Or reach a hand through time to catch
The far-off interest of tears?

Let Love clasp Grief lest both be drowned,
10   Let darkness keep her raven gloss.
    Ah, sweeter to be drunk with loss,
To dance with death, to beat the ground,

Than that the victor Hours should scorn
    The long result of love, and boast,
15   "Behold the man that loved and lost,
But all he was is overworn."

7

Dark house, by which once more I stand
    Here in the long unlovely street,
    Doors, where my heart was used to beat
20 So quickly, waiting for a hand,

from *In Memoriam A.H.H.*   797

Humanities Note

Fine art, *Nocturne: Grey and Gold —Chelsea Snow,* 1878, by James McNeill Whistler. Whistler (1834–1903) was an American painter who lived and worked in London. Both countries, England and the United States, claim him as their artist. His formal education as a painter consisted of a brief period of training in drawing and etching as a U.S. coastal surveyor and cartographer. It continued in Paris through close association with prominent French "modern" artists of his day. Whistler moved to London permanently in 1859 to paint.

The painting *Nocturne: Grey and Gold—Chelsea Snow* is one of a group of night scenes painted by Whistler. He used the musical term *nocturne* to suggest the poetic mood and subtle evening tones of the paintings. Whistler used the darkness of night to simplify and abstract shapes. The space in this painting is broken down into three simple shapes: the sky, the snow, and the dark mass of buildings and trees. The lone figure walking on the glowing snow seems to disappear into the darkness of the building.

You may wish to use the following questions for discussion:

1. What is the effect of the glowing lights in the window? Do they seem cheerful, or do they enhance the desolation of the scene?
2. Why might the person be walking alone in the dark?
3. What is the mood of the figure walking in the cold?

NOCTURNE: GREY AND GOLD—CHELSEA SNOW
James McNeill Whistler
The Fogg Art Museum, Cambridge, Mass.

Primary Source

The poet T. S. Eliot wrote the following about *In Memoriam.*

It is, in my opinion, in *In Memoriam* that Tennyson finds full expression. Its technical merit alone is enough to ensure its perpetuity. While Tennyson's technical competence is everywhere masterly and satisfying, *In Memoriam* is the less unapproachable of all his poems. Here are one hundred and thirty-two passages, each of several quatrains in the same form, and never monotony or repetition. And the poem has to be comprehended as a whole. We may not memorize a few passages, we cannot find a "fair sample"; we have to comprehend the whole of the poem which is essentially the length that it is. . . . *In Memoriam* . . . is unique: it is a long poem made by putting together lyrics, which have only the unity and continuity of a diary, the concentrated diary of a man confessing himself. It is a diary of which we have to read every word.

A hand that can be clasped no more—
    Behold me, for I cannot sleep,
    And like a guilty thing I creep   ⌐ 4
At earliest morning to the door.

25 He is not here; but far away
    The noise of life begins again,
    And ghastly through the drizzling rain   ⌐ 5
On the bald street breaks the blank day.

82

I wage not any feud with Death
30   For changes wrought on form and face;
    No lower life that earth's embrace
May breed with him, can fright my faith.

Eternal process moving on,
    From state to state the spirit walks;
35   And these are but the shattered stalks, ⌐ 6
Or ruined chrysalis of one.   ⌐ 7

Nor blame I Death, because he bare
    The use of virtue out of earth;
    I know transplanted human worth   ⌐ 8
40 Will bloom to profit, otherwhere.

For this alone on Death I wreak
    The wrath that garners in my heart;
    He put our lives so far apart
We cannot hear each other speak.

130

45 Thy voice is on the rolling air;
    I hear thee where the waters run;
    Thou standest in the rising sun,
And in the setting thou art fair.

What art thou then? I cannot guess;   9
50   But though I seem in star and flower
    To feel thee some diffusive power,
I do not therefore love thee less.

My love involves the love before;
    My love is vaster passion now;
55   Though mixed with God and Nature thou,
I seem to love thee more and more.

Far off thou art, but ever nigh;
    I have thee still, and I rejoice;
    I prosper, circled with thy voice;   ⌐ 10
60 I shall not lose thee though I die.

from *In Memoriam A.H.H.*   799

---

4 Discussion What might prompt feelings of guilt in the speaker?

5 Reading Strategy Have students describe the speaker's emotional state at this point.

6 Clarification The term *these* refers to the forms of lower life mentioned in line 30.

7 Critical Thinking and Reading Why is the use of the term *chrysalis* especially appropriate in light of Hallam's age when he died?

8 Discussion How might you state this sentiment in your own words?

9 Reading Strategy Have students compare the speaker's response to his loss here with those of the previous three stanzas.

10 Discussion What is the meaning of this line?

ANSWERS TO THINKING ABOUT THE SELECTION
Recalling

1. He now doubts that men may rise to higher things by treading on "their dead selves."
2. He is standing before the home of his late friend.
3. He is angry with death for making it impossible to speak with his friend.
4. It has increased.

Interpreting

5. (a) The corporeal, or bodily, manifestation is gone. (b) Hallam's spirit will live on in his friend's cherished memories.
6. Suggested Response: It means that although Hallam has disappeared from the physical world, his spirit remains embedded in the speaker's heart.
7. Students will note that in the first two excerpts, the speaker is still in deep pain. In the third and fourth, by contrast, he is respectively angry and resigned.

Applying

8. (a) Encourage students, in formulating answers, to avoid such clichés as "Time heals all wounds." (b) Answers will differ. Students may insist that their ideas would be close to those expressed in the poem.
9. (a) It means that people live on in the memories of others. (b) Hallam lives on in the speaker's memory.

ANSWERS TO ANALYZING LITERATURE

1. Answers will differ. Students may cite Tennyson's vigil before his late friend's home as something quite private and personal. His anger at death for making communication impossible with his friend is also a facet of his private loss.
2. Suggested Response: Tennyson's view of the world as a cold and bleak place (lines 26–28) is a typical manifestation of the human reaction to grief.

THINKING ABOUT THE SELECTION
Recalling

1. In Part 1, what truth does the speaker say he once held but now doubts?
2. Where is the speaker standing in Part 7?
3. For what one thing, in Part 82, does the speaker "wreak the wrath" in his heart on death?
4. In Part 130, what does the speaker say has happened to his love for his friend?

Interpreting

5. (a) According to the excerpts, what part of his friend does the poet finally accept is lost forever? (b) What part does he come to recognize will live forever?
6. Explain the paradox in line 57: "Far off thou art, but ever nigh."
7. Compare the first two excerpts with the last two. How have the poet's emotions changed?

Applying

8. (a) If you had to console someone who had lost a loved one, what advice might you give to help that person cope? (b) How close would your ideas be to those implied in the last excerpt of *In Memoriam*?
9. The English novelist Samuel Butler has written, "To die completely, a person must not only forget but be forgotten, and he who is not forgotten is not dead." (a) Discuss the meaning of this quotation. (b) How does it relate to *In Memoriam*?

ANALYZING LITERATURE
Understanding an Elegy

An **elegy** is a poem or song that laments a death, usually recent. *In Memoriam* is an especially strong elegy since, as Tennyson himself put it, the poem is "rather the cry of the whole human race than mine. In the poem altogether private grief swells out into thought of, and hope for, the whole world."
1. Which details in the four excerpts seem particularly "private"?
2. Which seem to apply to "the whole human race"?
3. What hope for future generations is implied in the final excerpt.

CRITICAL THINKING AND READING
Making Inferences About the Subject

In *In Memoriam* Tennyson never actually describes his friend directly but rather drops clues as to the man's personality. The reader must thus **infer,** or piece together from these clues, a picture of the man. What personality traits can you infer from the following?
1. Tennyson's reminiscence in Part 7 of his friend's hand clasp.
2. His comparing of his friend's remains to a "ruined crysalis."
3. His sensing in Part 130 of his friend's "diffusive power" in a star and flower.

---

3. Suggested Response: The speaker's rejoicing and prospering (lines 58–59) are indications that he has come a long way toward acceptance. As a poet he is able to concretize his thoughts so as to make them accessible to future generations who may, thus, benefit by his experience.

ANSWERS TO CRITICAL THINKING AND READING

1. The implication is that Hallam was a warm and sincere man, perhaps with a firm and friendly grasp.
2. The reference suggests that Hallam had great potential that was not fully realized.
3. One might infer that Hallam was a man who managed to make his presence felt.

The Lotos-Eaters

Alfred, Lord Tennyson

During their long voyage homeward in Homer's Odyssey, the Greek veterans of the Trojan War come to the land of the Lotos-Eaters, where, upon consuming the lotos's honeyed fruit, they are tempted by the desire to abandon their journey. Instead, the men wanted to forget about going home and stay in the land of the Lotos-Eaters forever.

In "The Lotos-Eaters," Tennyson expands upon Homer's brief account of the men's stay in the land of the Lotos-Eaters, delving into the men's desire for rest and the feelings of guilt that grew out of this desire.

"Courage!" he[1] said, and pointed toward the land,
"This mounting wave will roll us shoreward soon."
In the afternoon they came unto a land
In which it seemed always afternoon.
5   All round the coast the languid air did swoon,
Breathing like one that hath a weary dream.
Full-faced above the valley stood the moon;
And like a downward smoke, the slender stream
Along the cliff to fall and pause and fall did seem.

10   A land of streams! some, like a downward smoke,
Slow-dropping veils of thinnest lawn[2] did go;
And some through wavering lights and shadows broke,
Rolling a slumbrous sheet of foam below.
They saw the gleaming river seaward flow
15   From the inner land: far off, three mountaintops,
Three silent pinnacles of aged snow,
Stood sunset-flushed; and, dewed with showery drops,
Up clomb the shadowy pine above the woven copse.

The charmed sunset lingered low adown
20   In the red West: through mountain clefts the dale
Was seen far inland, and the yellow down[3]
Bordered with palm, and many a winding vale
And meadow, set with slender galingale;[4]
A land where all things always seemed the same!

---

1. he: Odysseus (ō dis′ ē əs) (or Ulysses), the hero of the *Odyssey*.
2. lawn *n.*: A fine, thin linen.
3. down *n.*: An expanse of open, high, grassy land.
4. galingale *n.*: A plant similar in appearance to tall grass.

Presentation

Motivation/Prior Knowledge Have students discuss the role of work in people's lives. How would it feel never to have to do work of any sort? How would it feel to be totally free of all responsibility? Would never-ending leisure eventually become tiresome?

Master Teacher Note Write the name *Odysseus* on the board. Ask students how much they know about this figure from Greek mythology. What modern English word is derived from the character's name? What is an odyssey? Inform students that they are about to read about one of Odysseus's adventures as seen through the eyes of a Victorian poet.

Thematic Idea Another selection that deals with the temptation of escape from the responsibilities of life is "Ode to a Nightingale" by John Keats, on page 721.

Purpose-Setting Question What qualities of modern life might make the prospect of escape tempting?

1 Discussion What qualities of the land strike you as particularly soothing and seductive?

2 **Discussion** What is the mental and physical state of the sailors? What circumstances do you suppose may have brought about these feelings?

3 **Critical Thinking and Reading** What island is the home of the sailors?

4 **Discussion** What is the effect of the repetition of the *s* sound in this passage?

5 **Reading Strategy** What does the speaker mean by his reference to "we" as "the first of things" (line 60) and as "the roof and crown of things" (line 68)?

25 And round about the keel with faces pale,
Dark faces pale against that rosy flame,
The mild-eyed melancholy Lotos-eaters came.

Branches they bore of that enchanted stem,
Laden with flower and fruit, whereof they gave
30 To each, but whoso did receive of them,
And taste, to him, the gushing of the wave
Far far away did seem to mourn and rave
On alien shores; and if his fellow spake,
His voice was thin, as voices from the grave;
35 And deep asleep he seemed, yet all awake,
And music in his ears his beating heart did make.

They sat them down upon the yellow sand,
Between the sun and moon upon the shore;
And sweet it was to dream of Fatherland,
40 Of child, and wife, and slave; but evermore
Most weary seemed the sea, weary the oar,
Weary the wandering fields of barren foam.
Then someone said, "We will return no more";
And all at once they sang, "Our island home[5]
45 Is far beyond the wave; we will no longer roam."

Choric Song[6]

I

There is sweet music here that softer falls
Than petals from blown roses on the grass,
Or night dews on still waters between walls
Of shadowy granite, in a gleaming pass;
50 Music that gentler on the spirit lies,
Than tired eyelids upon tired eyes;
Music that brings sweet sleep down from the blissful skies.
Here are cool mosses deep.
And through the moss the ivies creep,
And in the stream the long-leaved flowers weep,
55 And from the craggy ledge the poppy hangs in sleep.

II

Why are we weighed upon with heaviness
And utterly consumed with sharp distress,
While all things else have rest from weariness?
All things have rest: why should we toil alone,
60 We only toil, who are the first of things,

---

5. **home:** Ithaca, an island off the coast of Greece.
6. **Choric Song:** Sung by the Greek travelers in chorus.

802   *The Victorian Age*

And make perpetual moan,
Still from one sorrow to another thrown;
Nor ever fold our wings,
And cease from wanderings,
65   Nor steep our brows in slumber's holy balm;
Nor harken what the inner spirit sings,
"There is no joy but calm!"
Why should we only toil, the roof and crown of things?[7]

III

Lo! in the middle of the wood,
70   The folded leaf is wooed from out the bud
With winds upon the branch, and there
Grows green and broad, and takes no care,
Sun-steeped at noon, and in the moon
Nightly dew-fed; and turning yellow
75   Falls, and floats adown the air.
Lo! sweetened with the summer light,
The full-juiced apple, waxing over-mellow,
Drops in a silent autumn night.
All its allotted length of days,
80   The flower ripens in its place,
Ripens and fades, and falls, and hath no toil,
Fast-rooted in the fruitful soil.

IV

Hateful is the dark-blue sky,
Vaulted o'er the dark-blue sea.
85   Death is the end of life; ah, why
Should life all labor be?
Let us alone. Time driveth onward fast,
And in a little while our lips are dumb.
Let us alone. What is it that will last?
90   All things are taken from us, and become
Portions and parcels of the dreadful Past.
Let us alone. What pleasure can we have
To war with evil? Is there any peace
In ever climbing up the climbing wave?
95   All things have rest, and ripen toward the grave
In silence; ripen, fall and cease:
Give us long rest or death, dark death, or dreamful ease.[8]

---

7. Why . . . things?: This line echoes the following passage from
Edmund Spenser's *Faerie Queene*: "Why then dost thou, O man, that
of them all/Art Lord, and eke of nature Soveraine/willfully . . . waste
thy joyous hours in needless pain . . . ?"
8. All . . . ease: This passage echoes the following lines in Spenser's
Faerie Queene: "Sleep after toyle, port after stormie seas/Ease after
war, death after life does greatly please."

6 **Discussion** The phrase *Let us
alone* is repeated. With whom are
the sailors arguing?

7 **Critical Thinking and Reading**
What is the effect of the allusion to
Spenser's *Faerie Queen*?

8 **Reading Strategy** How does the speaker's mood here differ from that implied in lines 85–97? What does this mood swing tell you?

9 **Discussion** How would you state the speaker's thoughts here in your own words? What point is he driving at?

10 **Critical Thinking and Reading** Explain the allusion in this line.

11 **Clarification** The "pilot stars" were fixed celestial points used by sailors in ancient times for purposes of navigation.

V

How sweet it were, hearing the downward stream,
With half-shut eyes ever to seem
100 Falling asleep in a half dream!
To dream and dream, like yonder amber light,
Which will not leave the myrrh[9] bush on the height;
To hear each other's whispered speech;
Eating the Lotos day by day,
105 To watch the crisping[10] ripples on the beach,
And tender curving lines of creamy spray;
To lend our hearts and spirits wholly
To the influence of mild-minded melancholy;
To muse and brood and live again in memory,
110 With those old faces of our infancy
Heaped over with a mound of grass,
Two handfuls of white dust, shut in an urn of brass!

VI

Dear is the memory of our wedded lives,
And dear the last embraces of our wives
115 And their warm tears; but all hath suffered change;
For surely now our household hearths are cold,
Our sons inherit us, our looks are strange,
And we should come like ghosts to trouble joy.
Or else the island princes[11] over-bold
120 Have eat our substance, and the minstrel sings
Before them of the ten years' war in Troy,
And our great deeds, as half-forgotten things.
Is there confusion in the little isle?
Let what is broken so remain.
125 The Gods are hard to reconcile;
'Tis hard to settle order once again.
There *is* confusion worse than death,
Trouble on trouble, pain on pain,
Long labor unto aged breath,
130 Sore task to hearts worn out by many wars
And eyes grown dim with gazing on the pilot stars.

---

9. myrrh (mʉr) *n.*: A plant that produces a fragrant gum resin used in making incense and perfume.
10. crisping *adj.*: Curling.
11. princes: Suitors who were courting Ulysses' wife, Penelope.

Primary Source

In an essay entitled "Rites of Passage: 'The Lady of Shalott' and 'The Lotos-Eaters,'" David W. Shaw makes the following statements:

> Nowhere is the young Tennyson's ability to refine sensation, refracting it through thought, better demonstrated than in "The Lotos-Eaters." Whereas "The Lady of Shalott" presents the failure to carry alive the imagination of innocence into the stable forms of nature, "The Lotos-Eaters" illustrates the opposite problem: the failure to take the lessons of the wavering world outside, the world of quick decay and change, back into the timeless land of lotos. There are two rites of passage in the poem: one explicit, and the other merely proleptic, or ironically foreshadowed. The first rite occurs when Ulysses' men discover the essential anguish of being in time—the torment of "ever climbing up the climbing wave" (l. 94)—and they decide to escape into a changeless world. But lotos land is not

VII

But, propped on beds of amaranth[12] and moly,[13]
How sweet (while warm airs lull us, blowing lowly)
With half-dropped eyelid still,
135 Beneath a heaven dark and holy,
To watch the long bright river drawing slowly
His waters from the purple hill—
To hear the dewy echoes calling
From cave to cave through the thick-twined vine—
140 To watch the emerald-colored water falling
Through many a woven acanthus[14] wreath divine!
Only to hear and see the far-off sparkling brine,
Only to hear were sweet, stretched out beneath the pine.

---

12. amaranth (am′ ə ranth′) *n.*: An imaginary flower that never fades or dies.
13. moly (mō′ lē) *n.*: In classical mythology, an herb of magic powers. In the *Odyssey*, Ulysses uses moly to protect himself from the incantation of Circe (sər′ sē), an enchantress who turned men into swine.
14. acanthus (ə kan′ thəs) *n.*: A thistlelike plant.

ULYSSES MOURNING FOR HOME
Carved Gem of Light Brown Sardonyx
Roman 3rd to 2nd Century B.C.
Staatliche Museen zu Berlin

The Lotos Eaters 805

Humanities Note

Fine art, *Ulysses Mourning for Home*, Roman, (3rd–2nd Century, B.C). This gem, *Ulysses Mourning for Home*, is a cameo carved in sardonyx, a semi-precious gemstone prized for its varicolored bands of light and dark stone. Ornamental cameos, such as this, made their appearance in Roman jewelry craft about the third century B.C. They were used as personal ornaments, set in gold rings, brooches, and pendants, by both Roman men and women.

Emperors, gods, and heroes were the subjects for this cameo art. In this gem, Ulysses in a dejected pose, gazes at the empty sea. You might ask students these questions:

1. What feelings or mood are suggested by the face and attitude of Ulysses in this gem?
2. What might be on his mind?

paradise: . . . its satisfactions are enervating and narcotic. The mariners will have to undergo a second rite of passage by returning to their oars; there is no refuge from what Yeats calls "the murderous innocence of the sea" ("A Prayer for My Daughter, l. 16).

12 **Discussion** What facts is the speaker reporting in these lines?

13 **Enrichment** Have students read the episode of *The Odyssey* that tells of Odysseus's adventures in the land of the Lotos-Eaters. Ask them to compare and contrast the two writers' of the subject.

145 The Lotos blooms below the barren peak,
The Lotos blows by every winding creek;
All day the wind breathes low with mellower tone;
Through every hollow cave and alley lone
Round and round the spicy downs the yellow Lotos dust is
blown.
We have had enough of action, and of motion we,
150 Rolled to starboard, rolled to larboard, when the surge was
seething free,
Where the wallowing monster spouted his foam fountains
in the sea.
Let us swear an oath, and keep it with an equal mind,
In the hollow Lotos land to live and lie reclined
On the hills like Gods together, careless of mankind.
155 For they lie beside their nectar, and the bolts[15] are hurled
Far below them in the valleys, and the clouds are lightly
curled
Round their golden houses, girdled with the gleaming
world;
Where they smile in secret, looking over wasted lands,
Blight and famine, plague and earthquake, roaring deeps
and fiery sands,
160 Clanging fights, and flaming towns, and sinking ships, and
praying hands.
But they smile, they find a music centered in a doleful song.
Steaming up, a lamentation and an ancient tale of wrong,
Like a tale of little meaning though the words are strong;
Chanted from an ill-used race of men that cleave the soil,
165 Sow the seed, and reap the harvest with enduring toil,
Storing yearly little dues of wheat, and wine and oil;
Till they perish and they suffer—some, 'tis
whispered—down in hell
Suffer endless anguish, others in Elysian valleys[16] dwell,
Resting weary limbs at last on beds of asphodel.[17]
170 Surely, surely, slumber is more sweet than toil, the shore
Than labor in the deep mid-ocean, wind and wave and oar;
Oh rest ye, brother mariners, we will not wander more.

---

15. bolts: Thunderbolts.
16. Elysian (i lizh′ ən) **valleys:** In Greek mythology, heroes went to Elysia after death.
17. asphodel (as′ fə del′): A plant with yellow or white lilylike flowers.

THINKING ABOUT THE SELECTION
Recalling

1. What strange property of the land is mentioned in lines 4 and 24 of the poem?
2. (a) How do the men describe this new land in the poem's "choric song"? (b) How do they describe the lives they had led up till now? (c) What reasons do they give for wanting to remain?

Interpreting

3. (a) What do the men find so appealing about the land of the lotos-eaters? (b) What nagging concerns haunt them in spite of the effect of the lotos plants?
4. (a) What differences can you find between the odd-numbered and even-numbered stanzas of the poem's "choric song"? (b) What do these differences suggest about the decision the men have made?

Applying

5. To what extent do you think Tennyson is "prescribing" the sailors' decision in "The Lotos-Eaters" as a solution for problems of life in his time? Explain your answer.

CRITICAL THINKING AND READING
Recognizing Allusions

An **allusion** is a reference to a person, place, statement, or event in another work of art or cultural work. Writers use allusions to help the reader grasp a greater truth. Suppose that Tennyson had written "The Lotos-Eaters" without any of its allusions to classical mythology.

1. What general truth might have been missed?
2. What qualities of the poem would have been lost?
3. What other qualities might have been more evident?

UNDERSTANDING LANGUAGE
Finding Antonyms

Antonyms are words that have opposite or nearly opposite meanings. For example, in line 154 Tennyson writes, "On the hills like Gods together, careless of mankind." An antonym for the word *careless* is *concerned*.

Choose an antonym for each of the italicized words below.
1. "This *mounting* wave will roll us shoreward soon."
   a. swelling b. climbing c. falling d. dramatic
2. "And some through *wavering* lights and shadows broke . . ."
   a. uncertain b. trembling c. bright d. steady
3. "The charmed sunset *lingered* low adown . . ."
   a. faltered   b. departed
   c. operated   d. remained
4. "The mild-eyed *melancholy* Lotus-eaters came."
   a. sad   b. lonely   c. beautiful   d. joyful
5. "The folded leaf is *wooed* from out the bud . . ."
   a. coaxed   b. wed
   c. shunned   d. humored

Master Teacher Note Place Art Transparency 10, J. M. W. Turner's *Tours; Sunset,* on the overhead projector. Invite your students to express their impressions of the scene depicted and of Turner's artistry. You might then have them compare the subject and mood of this painting with the subject and mood of "Crossing the Bar." Is Turner's painting a good illustration for Tennyson's poem? Invite your students to discuss this question.

Thematic Idea Another poem that confronts the subject of death is "Prospice" by Robert Browning, page 822.

Purpose-Setting Question What are the speaker's feelings concerning death?

1 Discussion From whom do you think the speaker receives this "one clear call"?

2 Critical Thinking and Reading What thoughts do the words "evening bell" bring to mind?

3 Discussion How would you describe the speaker's outlook?

Humanities Note

Fine art, *The Angry Sea,* ca. 1880, by James Abbott McNeill Whistler (1834–1903). Whistler was an American artist who lived and worked in London. Although he had little formal training as a painter, his close association with leading Parisian "Modern" artists brought forth his talent. In 1859 he moved permanently to London and began to establish his reputation.

The Angry Sea reveals the strong influence of Japanese art on Whistler. In a few fluid strokes he captures the essence of the sea, sky, and sand with details such as the white waves and the ship.

Crossing the Bar

Alfred, Lord Tennyson

Tennyson requested that this poem, written three years before his death, be printed at the end of all editions of his poetry.

1

    Sunset and evening star,
        And one clear call for me!
And may there be no moaning of the bar,[1]
        When I put out to sea,

5   But such a tide as moving seems asleep,
        Too full for sound and foam,
When that[2] which drew from out the boundless deep
        Turns again home.

2

10   Twilight and evening bell,
    And after that the dark!
And may there be no sadness of farewell,
        When I embark;

3

    For though from out our bourne[3] of Time and Place
        The flood may bear me far,
15   I hope to see my Pilot face to face
        When I have crossed the bar.

---

1. bar: Sandbar.
2. that: The soul.
3. bourne: Boundary.

THE ANGRY SEA
James McNeill Whistler
Freer Gallery of Art, Smithsonian Institution

When discussing this painting with your students, point out that the subtle colors are in keeping with the reflective tone of the poem. Further points for class discussion include:

1. The artist used economy of line to express his visual message. Might the same be said of the poet and his use of words? Explain.

2. Although simple in form, this painting is quite dramatic. Is this in keeping with the mood of the poem? why or why not?

THINKING ABOUT THE SELECTION

Recalling

1. What does the speaker of the poem request in lines 3–4 and again in lines 11–12?

Interpreting

2. What do you think is actually meant by the phrase "crossing the bar"?
3. Who do you think the "Pilot" is?

Applying

4. Which excerpt from *In Memoriam* do you think is most in keeping with the attitude Tennyson expresses in "Crossing the Bar"? Explain why you feel as you do.

ANALYZING LITERATURE

Recognizing Symbols

A **symbol** is a thing, person, place, or idea whose meaning transcends, or goes beyond, its usual literal definition. When the reader of "Crossing the Bar" recognizes that the sea journey described in the poem is in actuality the passage into death, the symbolic meaning of many of the ideas and images becomes obvious. State the meaning symbolized by each of the following:

1. moaning of the bar.
2. putting out to sea.
3. twilight.
4. the dark.
5. the flood bearing one far.

CRITICAL THINKING AND READING

Comparing Attitudes

Writers may write about the same subject but take quite different positions. Read each statement below about death. Explain which one you feel comes closest to the attitude Tennyson expresses in "Crossing the Bar."

1. Oliver Wendell Holmes: "Death tugs at my ear and says: 'Live, I am coming.'"
2. John Dryden: "To die is landing on some distant shore."
3. Genesis 3:19: "Dust thou art, and unto dust shalt thou return."
4. Ralph Waldo Emerson: "Our fear of death is like our fear that summer will be short, but when we will have had our swing of pleasure, our fill of fruit, and our swelter of heat, we say we have had our day."
5. William Hazlitt: "Our repugnance to death increases in proportion to our consciousness of having lived in vain."

THINKING AND WRITING

Writing About Symbols

In "Crossing the Bar" Tennyson uses a series of interrelated symbols to deliver his thoughts on the issues of serenity at life's end and faith in an afterlife. He might, of course, have selected a different set of symbols to express these thoughts. Choose a symbolic vehicle other than a boat trip that could stand for the journey at life's end. Some possibilities are a walk up a hill, or the writing of the last chapter of a book. Make notes on the various details that might be used in such a symbolic representation. Then express Tennyson's ideas, in either a poem or brief story that uses this set of symbols.

ANSWERS TO THINKING ABOUT THE SELECTION
Recalling

1. He asks that there be no hesitation or sadness when he leaves.

Interpreting

2. The phrase refers to death.
3. The Pilot is God.

Applying

4. Answers will differ, but most students will probably agree that the last excerpt they read is most like this poem in its affirmation of the poet's faith.

ANSWERS TO ANALYZING LITERATURE

1. Suggested Response: The phrase symbolizes mourning.
2. This is another symbol for dying.
3. The phrase represents the end of life.
4. Suggested Response: The dark signifies the finality of death.
5. Suggested Response: The flood symbolizes the journey to the afterlife.

ANSWERS TO CRITICAL THINKING AND READING

Suggested Response: The attitude expressed by Dryden is most similar to Tennyson's attitude. Like Tennyson, Dryden views death as a journey to a distant, unknown world.

Writing Across the Curriculum
As an alternative, suggest that students choose an important event in history, possibly a war, and create a string of related symbols to represent facets of it. You might want to inform the history department about this assignment. History teachers might be able to aid the students in researching the event they choose.

More About the Author Robert Browning's relationship with the poet Elizabeth Barrett began with a series of letters, the first of which Browning wrote in 1844, before he himself had achieved any renown. The two maintained their correspondence for more than a decade before they finally met in person. What facet of Robert Browning's personality is revealed in this detail of his life? Why might such a character trait be important for a writer?

Critical Evaluation One of Browning's personal and poetic characteristics is a cheerful view of life. Much of his work celebrates love, heroism, and all that's "right with the world." Scholars Walter E. Houghton and G. Robert Stange, in *Victorian Poetry and Poetics,* feel that this "strain of complacent optimism that tinges Browning's work . . . seems to have prevented him from giving expression to the deepest levels of experience. Though his poetry is filled with potentially tragic situations, it never achieves the profound terror and the transcendent joy of genuine tragedy. He celebrated with incomparable vigor the life of aspiration, and in a great group of humane and subtle studies examined the effects of defeat and frustration. But he did not choose to look at man *in extremis,* and rarely do his poems provoke the shudder of pity and fear."

ROBERT BROWNING

1812–1889

In Victorian England, clubs to promote the works of the masters of English literature were fairly common. In 1881, a group of amateur scholars banded together to found another such club, the Browning Society. What made this literary club unique was that the poet it paid tribute to was *living.* Yet if honor in this form came unusually early to Robert Browning, then fame came unusually late, for it was not until nearly a half century after the publication of his first book that the public came to recognize his genius.

Robert Browning was born in London and spent the first twenty-eight years of his life there. Like Tennyson, he was educated mainly at home, spending much of his time during his early years in his father's large library. Here he immersed himself in art, history, literature, philosophy, religion, music, medicine, and zoology. At twenty-one, Browning published his first book, *Pauline,* a highly personal record of his religious skepticism, no doubt influenced by the writings of Shelley. Discouraged by the book's poor critical reception, Browning tried his hand next at something less personal, publishing *Paracelsus,* a long dramatic poem, in 1835. Failing again to please the critics, he turned to drama and two years later produced *Strafford,* which closed after five performances.

Despite his inability to establish himself in the public eye as a writer to be reckoned with, Browning was all the while shaping the distinctive dramatic voice that would ensure his eventual fame. In *Dramatic Lyrics* (1842), *Dramatic Romances and Lyrics* (1845), and *Men and Women* (1855) he reveals a rich and varied talent in both the short lyrical poem and the dramatic monologue.

In 1846 he married Elizabeth Barrett, a poet whose fame greatly exceeded his own. They established a home in Florence, Italy, a setting that figured in many of Browning's works. The marriage was an extremely happy one, and when his wife died in 1861, Browning, unable to face constant reminders of her in Florence, returned to London. Here, he soon became a popular figure, especially among university students, who were attracted to his next book, *Dramatis Personnae* (1864). This was followed by his masterpiece, *The Ring and the Book* (1868), which was hailed as the most "profound spiritual treasure that England had produced since the days of Shakespeare." Based on an actual seventeenth-century Italian murder trial, this long poem comprises ten dramatic monologues.

Browning's dramatic monologues have greatly influenced many twentieth-century poets. Today, he is admired not only for these complex psychological portraits, but also for his masterly blending of natural speech rhythms with strict poetic forms.

Objectives

1 To understand a dramatic monologue
2 To make inferences about the speaker
3 To appreciate diction
4 To write a dramatic monologue
5 To interpret tone
6 To write a comparison of two places
7 To make inferences about a poet's attitudes
8 To write a comparison of two poems

Support Material

Teaching Portfolio
Teacher Backup, p. 969
Grammar in Action Worksheets, *Using Parallelism,* p. 975; *Appreciating Contrasting Rhythms,* p. 977
Usage and Mechanics Worksheet, p. 979
Vocabulary Check, p. 980

GUIDE FOR INTERPRETING

My Last Duchess; Home-Thoughts, from Abroad; Love Among the Ruins; Prospice

Literary Forms

Dramatic Monologue. A dramatic monologue is a dramatic poem by a single speaker, much like a speech from a play. Unlike a play, however, where each speech is preceded by the name of its speaker, the dramatic monologue contains no such outward label. Rather, the identity of the speaker is revealed through his or her words. In "My Last Duchess," we learn, strictly through the speaker's conversation with an unnamed companion, the setting of the poem and—more importantly—the inner conflict that prompts the character's speech.

Writing

Write a brief fictional account of *your* life in the Oval Office titled "I, The President." Focus not on affairs of state but on the day-to-day routine in your household—your relationship with your family and friends, the stress that your job places on those relationships, and so on. Be sure to answer, somewhere in your account, the question "How has power changed me?"

Primary Source

In contemporary life, we often live by the dictum that less is more. Alfred, Lord Tennyson once told Robert Browning that "if he got rid of two-thirds, the remaining third would be much finer." After Browning had left the room, Tennyson expanded on his comments.

"It is necessary to respect the limits," he explained. "An artist is one who recognizes bounds to his work as a necessity, and does not overflow illimitably [boundlessly] to all extent about a matter. I soon found that if I meant to make any mark at all, it must be done by shortness, for all the men before me had been so diffuse, and all the big things had been done. To get workmanship as nearly perfect as possible is the best chance for going down the stream of time. A small vessel on fine lines is likely to float further than a great raft."

Do you agree with Tennyson's definition of an artist? What do you think he meant by the "big things," "a small vessel on fine lines," and "a great raft"? Would Browning's poems be better if he had followed Tennyson's advice?

Guide for Interpreting 811

Literary Focus To help the students understand the concept, refer them to one of the longer soliloquies in *Macbeth*. Point out that a dramatic monologue is essentially a soliloquy that is entirely self-contained.

Writing/Prior Knowledge As an alternative assignment, have students freewrite about their feelings concerning being away from home for an extended period of time.

Vocabulary

Preteach the following words:
countenance (koun′ tə nəns) *n.*: Face (p. 812, l. 7)
officious (ə fish′ əs) *adj.*: Overly eager to please (p. 812, l. 27)
munificence (myoo nif′ ə s′ns) *n.*: Great generosity (p. 814, l. 49)
avowed (ə voud′) *v.*: Swore (p. 814, l. 52)
sheaf (shēf) *n.*: Bundle of twigs or fibers (p. 817, l. 5)
bole (bōl) *n.*: Tree trunk (p. 817, l. 6)
dower (dou′ ər) *n.*: Gift (p. 817, l. 19)
rapture (rap′ chər) *n.*: Expression of great joy (p. 817, l. 16)
verdure (vʉr′ jər) *n.*: Green plants (p. 818, l. 15)
vestige (ves′ tij) *n.*: Trace; bit (p. 818, l. 29)
turret (tʉr′ it) *n.*: Small tower projecting from a building (p. 819, l. 37)
sublime (sə blīm′) *adj.*: Inspiring admiration through greatness or beauty (p. 819, l. 44)
minions (min′ yənz) *n.*: Attendants or agents (p. 819, l. 47)
brazen (brā′ z′n) *adj.*: Made of brass (p. 820, l. 75)
guerdon (gʉr′ d′n) *n.*: Reward (p. 822, l. 11)

Motivation/Prior Knowledge
Ask students what titles such as
Duke and *Count* conjure up in
their minds. What kinds of lives
do such individuals live? What
are their homes like? How does
one come to have such a title?

Thematic Idea Another selection
that focuses on a member of the
nobility is the excerpt from *Don
Juan* by Lord Byron, on page
697.

Purpose-Setting Question What
does the monologue reveal about
the speaker's personality?

1 Critical Thinking and Reading
What pattern of rhyme does
Browning establish in the first several lines?

2 Discussion What is the effect of
the speaker's hesitation in this
sentence?

3 Literary Focus What do these
lines reveal about the speaker's
personality?

My Last Duchess

Robert Browning

*This poem, set in the sixteenth century in a castle in
northern Italy, is based on events from the life of the Duke of
Ferrara, an Italian nobleman, whose first wife died after
only three years of marriage. Following his wife's death, the
Duke began making arrangements to remarry. In Browning's poem, the Duke is showing a painting of his first wife to
an agent who represents the father of the woman he hopes
to marry.*

That's my last Duchess painted on the wall,
Looking as if she were alive. I call
That piece a wonder, now: Frà Pandolf's[1] hands
Worked busily a day, and there she stands.
5 Will 't please you sit and look at her? I said
"Frà Pandolf" by design, for never read
Strangers like you that pictured countenance,
The depth and passion of its earnest glance,
But to myself they turned (since none puts by
10 The curtain I have drawn for you, but I)
And seemed as they would ask me, if they durst,[2]
How such a glance came there; so, not the first
Are you to turn and ask thus. Sir, 'twas not
Her husband's presence only, called that spot
Of joy into the Duchess' cheek: perhaps
15 Frà Pandolf chanced to say "Her mantle laps
Over my lady's wrist too much," or "Paint
Must never hope to reproduce the faint
Half-flush that dies along her throat"; such stuff
Was courtesy, she thought, and cause enough
20 For calling up that spot of joy. She had
A heart—how shall I say?—too soon made glad,
Too easily impressed; she liked whate'er
She looked on, and her looks went everywhere.
25 Sir, 'twas all one! My favor at her breast,
The dropping of the daylight in the West,
The bough of cherries some officious fool
Broke in the orchard for her, the white mule
She rode with round the terrace—all and each

---

1. Frà Pandolf's: The work of Brother Pandolf, an imaginary
painter.
2. durst: Dared.

Grammar in Action

Parallelism is the placement of equal ideas in words, phrases, or
clauses of similar types. To present a series of ideas of equal
importance, use similar grammatical constructions to guard
against jarring the reader and reducing clarity. Notice how Robert
Browning uses parallelism in the following sentence.

ANTEA PARMIGIANINO
Museo Nazionale di Capodimonte, Naples
Art Resource

My Last Duchess   813

Sir, 'twas all one! My favor at her breast,
The dropping of the daylight in the West,
The bough of cherries some officious fool
Broke in the orchard for her, the white mule
She rode with round the terrace— . . .

Browning introduces each item of the series with an article or possessive pronoun: "My fawn," "The dropping," "The bough," "the white mule." The Duke of Ferrara means to show his visitor that his wife cared equally for all of the things he mentions. The parallelism reinforces his meaning. Parallelism such as this also enhances readability. A good writer, therefore, will use this stylistic technique whenever it is appropriate.

Student Activity. Construct a long sentence containing a series of items written in parallel form. Suggestion: Begin with a clause similar to the following: *In the room I saw* . . . Then mention several persons or things, and modify, or describe, them with phrases or clauses of a similar grammatical structure.

30　Would draw from her alike the approving speech,
　　Or blush, at least. She thanked men—good! but thanked
　　Somehow—I know not how—as if she ranked
　　My gift of a nine-hundred-years-old name
　　With anybody's gift. Who'd stoop to blame
35　This sort of trifling? Even had you skill
　　In speech—(which I have not)—to make your will
　　Quite clear to such an one, and say, "Just this
　　Or that in you disgusts me; here you miss,
　　Or there exceed the mark"—and if she let
40　Herself be lessoned so, nor plainly set
　　Her wits to yours, forsooth,[3] and made excuse,
　　—E'en then would be some stooping; and I choose
　　Never to stoop. Oh sir, she smiled, no doubt,
　　Whene'er I passed her; but who passed without
45　Much the same smile? This grew; I gave commands;
　　Then all smiles stopped together. There she stands
　　As if alive. Will 't please you rise? We'll meet
　　The company below, then. I repeat,
　　The Count your master's known munificence
50　Is ample warrant that no one just pretense
　　Of mine for dowry will be disallowed;
　　Though his fair daughter's self, as I avowed
　　At starting, is my object. Nay, we'll go
　　Together down, sir! Notice Neptune,[4] though,
55　Taming a sea horse, thought a rarity,
　　Which Claus of Innsbruck[5] cast in bronze for me!

3. forsooth: In truth.
4. Neptune: In Roman mythology, the god of the sea.
5. Claus of Innsbruck: An imaginary Austrian sculptor.

THINKING ABOUT THE SELECTION
Recalling

1. (a) Where are the speaker and his companion? (b) What are they looking at?
2. What was the Duke's "gift" to his wife?

Interpreting

3. (a) What question are we to understand the speaker's companion to have asked. (b) What is the speaker's reply?

4. (a) What aspects of the Duke's personality are revealed in his keeping the painting behind a curtain? (b) What aspects are revealed in his being the only one allowed to draw the curtain?
5. (a) What has happened to the "last" Duchess? (b) Where in the poem is this revealed?
6. (a) How would you state the sentiment expressed in lines 21–22? (b) What examples does the speaker give as an illustration of this trait? (c) What feelings did it stir up in him?

814　*The Victorian Age*

Applying

7. The eighteenth century English statesman and writer Edmund Burke has written, "The greater the power, the more dangerous the abuse." What are your reactions to this statement?

ANALYZING LITERATURE

Dramatic Monologue

A **dramatic monologue** is a poem that reveals a character's personality through what he or she says in a dramatic situation. In most dramatic monologues, the character addresses another character who is merely a silent listener. By drawing conclusions based on the character's words, the reader can piece together the poem's setting, the situation that prompts the character to speak, and the character's motives and actions.

1. Imagine that this dramatic monologue is part of a play or movie that you are directing. Describe the setting and the situation that prompts the Duke's speech.
2. What tone of voice do you think the Duke uses? Explain your answer.
3. What motives do you suppose the Duke has for showing the Count's agent the portrait of his dead wife?
4. The Count's agent never speaks. How do you imagine he acts when he learns of the Duke's displeasure with his wife?
5. (a) What makes this kind of poem an especially strong vehicle for conveying information about a character? (b) How differently would you see the Duke if Browning had written "My Last Duchess" as a short story?

CRITICAL THINKING AND READING

Making Inferences About the Speaker

An **inference** is a conclusion arrived at through known facts or evidence. In "My Last Duchess," Browning never directly describes the Duke's personality. Rather, he relies upon the reader to make inferences, from selected information, about the sort of man the Duke is. Find evidence in the poem that the Duke is: (1) jealous, (2) overly proud, (3) determined to have things his way, (4) preoccupied with possessions, (5) a stern boss.

UNDERSTANDING LANGUAGE

Revealing Diction

The **diction,** or choice of words, in "My Last Duchess" is an important ingredient of the Duke's character. To show that the man is a member of the nobility and, therefore, schooled in the social graces, Browning has the Duke use such formal constructions as "Will't please you sit and look at her?" Yet, there are clues in his speech habits that suggest the Duke's good manners are only skin-deep. Locate examples of language in the poem that demonstrate:
1. that the Duke is rude and insulting to his staff
2. that he wants to appear humble
3. that he thinks of himself as reasonable

THINKING AND WRITING

Writing a Dramatic Monologue

Assume for the moment that the Duke has presented an accurate description of his last Duchess. List as many of her personality traits as you can. Then write an original dramatic monologue in which the Duchess reveals her impressions of her husband. In planning your monologue, consider the setting you want to convey and the occasion that prompts the speech. When you revise, make sure you have created a consistent picture of the Duchess.

My Last Duchess 815

through his or her comments. (b) Suggested Response: We would probably learn about the Duke's personality through his actions as well as his comments.

ANSWERS TO CRITICAL THINKING AND READING

1. The Duke's jealousy is manifest in his reaction to his wife and her "bad habit."
2. His feeling that it would be "stooping" to point out the Duchess's annoying habits is indicative of his pride.
3. This is shown in his high expectations from his wife and in his strict control.
4. His art collection and his treatment of his wife as a possession suggest this trait.
5. His reference to his gardener as an "officious fool" suggests that he is perhaps a stern boss.

ANSWERS TO UNDERSTANDING LANGUAGE

1. Suggested Response: He refers to his gardener as "some officious fool."
2. Suggested Response: Line 36 contains a self-effacing aside —"(which I have not)."
3. Suggested Response: His reference to the dowry in lines 48-51 conveys his belief that he is reasonable.

THINKING AND WRITING

For help with this assignment, students can refer to Lesson 18, "Writing a Poem," in the Handbook of Writing About Literature.

Publishing Student Writing After reading student compositions, choose two or three that best satisfy the terms of the assignment. Have the writer of each arrange an in-class presentation of the monologue complete with props.

Applying

7. Answers will differ. Students may comment that they agree with Burke's statement, because the actions of powerful people can have a tremendous impact on the lives of others.

Challenge How do you think Browning wants the reader to feel toward the Duke? Find evidence in support of your claim.

ANSWERS TO ANALYZING LITERATURE

1. Suggested Response: The setting is a gallery in the Duke's castle. The Duke and the agent are seated on a red velvet banquette. The Duke rises and draws a brocade curtain revealing a portrait.
2. Suggested Response: His tone of voice is arrogant and proud.

3. Suggested Response: He shows the portrait, because it provides him with an occasion to convey his expectations of a wife.
4. Suggested Response: He probably reports back to the Count that the Duke is an unfit suitor for the Count's daughter.
5. (a) Suggested Response: In a dramatic monologue we can learn about a character directly

Humanities Note

Fine art, *In Early Spring* by John William Inchbold. Inchbold (1830–1888) was a British landscape painter and etcher. John W. Inchbold received art training through his apprenticeship to a London lithography company and through a series of watercolor lessons. He was sympathetic to the precepts of the Pre-Raphaelite painters—a group of painters who emulated the primitive Italian artists who worked before Raphael. He was the first painter to bring the Pre-Raphaelite style to landscape painting.

This painting, *In Early Spring,* was completed in 1855. This depiction of tufts of grass breaking through the rich brown earth, early buds and flowers, and the new lambs of spring is realistically detailed. When first exhibited, it was highly praised for its strict attention to the minute details of nature. Inchbold saw the poetic possibilities of the English landscape and painted it with the truth, meticulous detail, and fresh colors of his Pre-Raphaelite beliefs.

You may wish to use the following questions for classroom discussion:

1. What feelings do both the artist and the poet share about England?
2. Could this be the English spring countryside that the poet longs for? Explain.

IN EARLY SPRING
John William Inchbold
Ashmolean Museum, Oxford

Home-Thoughts, from Abroad

Robert Browning

Oh, to be in England
Now that April's there,
And whoever wakes in England
Sees, some morning, unaware,

5 That the lowest boughs and the brushwood sheaf
Round the elm-tree bole are in tiny leaf,
While the chaffinch[1] sings on the orchard bough
In England—now!

And after April, when May follows,
10 And the whitethroat[2] builds, and all the swallows!
Hark, where my blossomed pear tree in the hedge
Leans to the field and scatters on the clover
Blossoms and dewdrops—at the bent spray's edge—
That's the wise thrush; he sings each song twice over,

15 Lest you should think he never could recapture
The first fine careless rapture!
And though the fields look rough with hoary dew,
All will be gay when noontide wakes anew
The buttercups, the little children's dower

20 —Far brighter than this gaudy melon flower![3]

---

1. chaffinch (chaf′ finch′) *n*.: A small European songbird.
2. whitethroat *n*.: Bird having white around the throat.
3. melon flower: The large, yellow flower of melon plants, native to a warm climate.

THINKING ABOUT THE SELECTION

Recalling

1. What time and place does the poem celebrate?
2. List four birds and six plants that the speaker says "whoever wakes in England" sees.

Interpreting

3. (a) Where do you suppose the speaker of the poem is? (b) What details of the poem provide clues?
4. How do you think the speaker is using the phrase "the little children's dower" in line 19?
5. Browning wrote this poem in England, following a trip to Italy. Why do you think he chose to write the poem as though he were far away at the time?

Applying

6. Think of a time when you were homesick, or try to imagine what it would be like. What details of home do you think would come to mind for you?

Home-Thoughts, from Abroad 817

817

Presentation

Motivation/Prior Knowledge
Ask students to volunteer what they know about empires that no longer exist. If there are students in your class who have visited the crumbling ancient forums of Rome or Greece, have them describe what they saw. What causes a civilization to vanish? Is it irreverent to walk on the ruins of a vanished civilization? Why or why not?

Master Teacher Note Obtain a photograph of the Parthenon. (A photo of the ruin appears in H. W. Janson's *History of Art,* Prentice-Hall/Abrams). Ask students what feelings the sight of the ancient Greek temple evokes in them. Ask them to explain these feelings.

Thematic Idea Another selection that deals with the ephemeral nature of greatness is "Ozymandias" by Percy Bysshe Shelley, on page 702.

Purpose-Setting Question What lessons can we learn from the mistakes of the past?

1 Discussion Where is the poem set? At what time of day?

2 Clarification The word *tinkle* adds an aural detail to this vividly described scene. The sound is made by bells around the necks of the sheep.

3 Discussion Contrast the image in these lines with that of the first sixteen lines.

4 Critical Thinking and Reading What do the words *plenty and perfection* suggest about the speaker's feelings toward the current state of the land? Toward its former state?

Love Among the Ruins

Robert Browning

This poem presents the contrast between past and present through the eyes of a shepherd, anxious to return to his waiting wife. The ruins that the shepherd and his wife live among may be the remains of ancient Babylon or Nineveh or one of the Etruscan cities of Italy.

Where the quiet-colored end of evening smiles,
    Miles and miles
On the solitary pastures where our sheep
    Halt asleep
5 Tinkle homeward through the twilight, stray or stop
    As they crop—
Was the site once of a city great and gay
    (So they say),
Of our country's very capital, its prince
10   Ages since
Held his court in, gathered councils, wielding far
    Peace or war.

Now—the country does not even boast a tree,
    As you see,
15 To distinguish slopes of verdure, certain rills
    From the hills
Intersect and give a name to (else they run
    Into one),
Where the domed and daring palace shot its spires
20   Up like fires
O'er the hundred-gated circuit of a wall
    Bounding all,
Made of marble, men might march on nor be pressed,
    Twelve abreast.

25 And such plenty and perfection, see, of grass
    Never was!
Such a carpet as, this summertime, o'erspreads
    And embeds
Every vestige of the city, guessed alone,[1]
30   Stock or stone—

---

1. guessed alone: Because the site of the city is now covered with grass, one can only guess where it was.

Grammar in Action

Skillful writers use **contrasting rhythms** to emphasize the themes of their work. The theme of Browning's "Love Among the Ruins" is the contrast between a glorious but empty past and a humble yet fulfilling present. Browning uses the contrast between a six-beat line and a two-beat line to suggest and reinforce that theme:

    Where a multitude of men breathed joy and woe
        Long ago

Where a multitude of men breathed joy and woe
    Long ago;
Lust of glory pricked their hearts up, dread of shame
    Struck them tame;
35 And that glory and that shame alike, the gold
    Bought and sold.

Now—the single little turret that remains
    On the plains,
By the caper[2] overrooted, by the gourd
40   Overscored,
While the patching houseleek's[3] head of blossom winks
    Through the chinks—
Marks the basement whence a tower in ancient time
    Sprang sublime,
45 And a burning ring, all round, the chariots traced
    As they raced,
And the monarch and his minions and his dames
    Viewed the games.

————————
2. caper *n.*: A prickly, trailing Mediterranean bush.
3. houseleek *n.*: A plant with yellow, pink, or red flowers and compact rosettes of thick, fleshy leaves.

ITALIAN RUINS
John Claude Nattes
Victoria & Albert Museum Trustees

In the couplet quoted above, the long line seems to swell out with the boisterous activity of an ancient kingdom. The short line, however, underscores the fact that past glory *is* past.

Student Activity 1. Show how the contrasting rhythms of the final couplet underscore the theme of the poem.

Student Activity 2. Write a prose description of two sharply contrasting activities. Vary the length and rhythm of your sentences to emphasize the contrast. For example, you might want to use long, flowing sentences to describe a dance movement and short, abrupt sentences to describe a carpenter hammering in a nail.

6 **Discussion** What is ironic about a shepherd and his wife living in one of the remnants of the castle?

7 **Reading Strategy** Have students summarize in their own words what they believe happened to the empire and why it happened.

8 **Discussion** What is the meaning of the final line?

50 And I know, while thus the quiet-colored eve
         Smiles to leave
    To their folding, all our many-tinkling fleece
         In such peace,
    And the slopes and rills, in undistinguished gray
         Melt away—
55 That a girl with eager eyes and yellow hair
         Waits me there
    In the turret whence the charioteers caught soul
         For the goal,
    When the king looked, where she looks now, breathless,
      dumb
60   Till I come.

    But he looked upon the city, every side,
         Far and wide,
    All the mountains topped with temples, all the glades'
         Colonnades,[4]
65 All the causeys,[5] bridges, aqueducts—and then,
         All the men!
    When I do come, she will speak not, she will stand,
         Either hand
    On my shoulder, give her eyes the first embrace
70   Of my face,
    Ere we rush, ere we extinguish sight and speech
         Each on each.

    In one year they sent a million fighters forth
         South and North,
75 And they built their gods a brazen pillar[6] high
         As the sky,
    Yet reserved a thousand chariots in full force—
         Gold, of course.
    Oh heart! oh blood that freezes, blood that burns!
80   Earth's returns
    For whole centuries of folly, noise and sin!
         Shut them in,
    With their triumphs and their glories and the rest!
         Love is best.

    ----

    4. Colonnades (käl' ə nādz') *n.*: Series of columns set at regular intervals; here, groups of trees surrounding an open area.
    5. causeys *n.*: Causeways or raised roads.
    6. brazen pillar: Built from the brass of captured chariots.

THINKING ABOUT THE SELECTION

Recalling

1. (a) What does the speaker say once stood where sheep pastures now stand? (b) What single trace remains?
2. What does the speaker say awaits him on the pastures at twilight?

Interpreting

3. What do you suppose is the identity of the speaker?
4. (a) How would you summarize the speaker's comments on the civilization mentioned in lines 33–36? (b) How would you describe his feelings toward this civilization?
5. (a) What do you think is the purpose of the speaker's noting in line 67 that his companion "will not speak" when he arrives? (b) What might he expect his companion to say?
6. (a) What do you think is the meaning of the speaker's lament in lines 81–82? (b) To what "folly" might he be referring?
7. Explain why "Love Among the Ruins" is or is not an appropriate title for the poem.

Applying

8. Reread "Ozymandias" by Shelley on page 702. (a) What similarities do you see between the messages in the two poems? (b) What differences do you see in the conclusions reached by the two poets?

CRITICAL THINKING AND READING

Interpreting Tone

Tone is the author's attitude toward his or her subject or audience. A work may have a tone that is lighthearted or serious, ironic or sincere, or any of numerous other possibilities. Just as a person's tone of voice can affect the way a remark is interpreted by others, so the tone of a literary work affects how the reader perceives the author's purpose.

1. (a) How would you describe the tone of the speaker of "Love Among the Ruins" with respect to the ruined splendor? (b) With respect to the civilzation? (c) With respect to his companion?
2. Consider what other tone Browning might have used to make the point he makes here. Would another tone strengthen or weaken the poem's impact? Explain your answer.

THINKING AND WRITING

Comparing and Contrasting Two Places

Think about how your town or city might have appeared 100 years ago. Write a description of the "two faces" of your city. Begin by listing ways in which the locale has undoubtedly changed, as well as ways in which it has probably remained the same, over the century. In writing your description, use vivid details so that your audience will be able to picture both the "old" city and the "new" one.

ment seems to be over the treacheries of the human heart. (b) The folly refers to the mistakes that brought about the destruction of the empire.

7. Suggested Response: It is an appropriate title, because the poem captures the ability of love to survive among the ruins that result from base desires.

Applying

8. (a) Answers will differ. Students should note that both poems deal with edifices of stone, now crumbled, that once demonstrated the power and invincibility of an individual or of a people. (b) Suggested Response: The difference is chiefly one of tone. Browning laments the folly that led to the fall of a civilization, while Shelley approaches his subject with a note of scorn, almost of triumph.

Challenge The metric pattern of the poem—a line of six feet followed by a line of two—seems almost playful. How well does this pattern relate to the poem's theme?

ANSWERS TO CRITICAL THINKING AND READING

1. (a) He seems to lament, though for the most part in a subdued fashion, the ruined splendor. (b) His tone toward the civilization is slightly more bitter—as though he feels the fate of the people was well-deserved. (c) His tone toward his wife is passionate—"a girl with eager eyes and yellow hair."
2. Suggested Response: Browning might have written the poem in an outwardly angry or outwardly mournful fashion. If this were the case, its subtle shadings and mild irony would have been lost.

Writing Across the Curriculum You might permit students to develop as an alternative topic the "two faces" of our planet—the earth today contrasted with the earth 1,000 years ago. Inform your science department about this assignment. Science teachers may be able to provide students with important details concerning the earth's appearance.

Closure and Extension

ANSWERS TO THINKING ABOUT THE SELECTION

Recalling

1. (a) He says a great city stood there. (b) All that remains are scattered ruins—a turret and a chariot track.
2. A "girl with eager eyes and yellow hair" awaits him.

Interpreting

3. The speaker is a shepherd.
4. (a) The suggestion is that these people succumbed to base desires and greed. (b) Suggested Response: The speaker feels contempt for this civilization.
5. (a) Suggested Response: He wants to convey the fact that they have a deep understanding of each other and do not need to speak. (b) He expects her to say nothing.
6. (a) Suggested Response: The la-

Prospice

Robert Browning

This poem, the title of which means "look forward," was written by Browning after the death of his wife. It is the classic expression of Browning's feelings about death.

Fear death?—to feel the fog in my throat,
 The mist in my face,
When the snow begins, and the blasts denote
 I am nearing the place,
5 The power of the night, the press of the storm,
 The post of the foe;
Where he stands, the Arch Fear in a visible form,
 Yet the strong man must go.
For the journey is done and the summit attained,
10 And the barriers fall,
Though a battle's to fight ere the guerdon be gained,
 The reward of it all.
I was ever a fighter, so—one fight more,
 The best and the last!
15 I would hate that death bandaged my eyes, and forbore,
 And bade me creep past.
No! let me taste the whole of it, fare like my peers,
 The heroes of old,
Bear the brunt, in a minute pay glad life's arrears
20 Of pain, darkness, and cold.
For sudden the worst turns the best to the brave,
 The black minute's at end,
And the elements' rage, the fiend-voices that rave,
 Shall dwindle, shall blend,
25 Shall change, shall become first a peace out of pain,
 Then a light, then thy breast,
Oh thou soul of my soul![1] I shall clasp thee again,
 And with God be the rest!

---

1. soul of my soul: Browning's wife.

THINKING ABOUT THE SELECTION
Recalling

1. (a) With what question does the speaker open the poem? (b) What is his answer in line 17?
2. (a) To what, in lines 1–14, does the speaker compare the process of dying? (b) Who, in lines 17–18, does the speaker say are his peers?

Interpreting

3. (a) What opposing forces does the speaker suggest are fighting at the moment of death? (b) What, according to line 21, is ironic about the nature of this battle?
4. (a) Whom do you think Browning is addressing in line 27 as "thou soul of my soul"? (b) What does this suggest about his belief in an afterlife?
5. In what way is this poem a look forward?

Applying

6. Browning has sometimes been criticized for being overly optimistic about situations in which others would be more skeptical. (a) Do you think this is true of his views in "Prospice?" Why or why not? (b) What other poets have you read who seem to share his attitudes?

CRITICAL THINKING AND READING
Making Inferences About Attitudes

Students of literature are warned repeatedly of the dangers of misidentifying the first-person narrator of a work with the work's author. Yet, in dealing with "Prospice," scholars generally assume that the attitudes reflected in the poem are precisely those of its author.

1. Based on what you have read about Robert Browning and his attitudes, how justified do you think scholars are in making this assumption?
2. What subjects besides death might an author choose to address without the use of a fictitious narrator?

THINKING AND WRITING
Comparing and Contrasting Two Poems

Both Tennyson's "Crossing the Bar" and Browning's "Prospice" express the poet's deepest feelings about dying. Reread the two poems, and think about the similarities and differences between them. Consider especially the following questions as you plan an essay comparing and contrasting the poems: What do Tennyson's image of the tide and Browning's image of the battle reveal about each poet's attitudes toward dying? How do the poets' notions of the afterlife differ? Which poem seems more effective to you? Begin your essay by summarizing your conclusions. Support your opinions by quoting freely from the poems. When you revise, make sure you have quoted precisely and have punctuated your sentences accurately.

ANSWERS TO THINKING ABOUT THE SELECTION
Recalling

1. (a) The question is "Fear death?" (b) His answer is a firm "No!"
2. (a) He compares it variously to struggling through a storm and to a battle. (b) He identifies himself with "the heroes of old."

Interpreting

3. (a) Suggested Response: The fear of death and the desire to continue living battles with the desire to surrender to death. (b) Suggested Response: The irony, in the speaker's view, is that something positive emerges out of this negative struggle.
4. (a) He is addressing his late wife. (b) The clear indication is that he believes in such a state.
5. It is a "look forward" to the poet's own death.

Applying

6. (a) Answers will differ. Many students may feel that Browning's view is overly optimistic. (b) Suggested Response: Tennyson expresses a similar view in "Crossing the Bar."

ANSWERS TO CRITICAL THINKING AND READING

1. Students should be in general agreement that this assumption is warranted. First, the poem fits the image presented in the biography of Browning as a perseverer—a man who refused to take "no" for an answer when his first publishing efforts failed. Second, the timeliness of the poem—its publication shortly after the death of the poet's wife—would indicate a personal stake in these sentiments.
2. Answers will differ. Students might suggest such subjects as war, nature, and industrialization.

THINKING AND WRITING

For help with this assignment, students can refer to Lesson 16, "Writing a Comparative Evaluation," in the Handbook of Writing About Literature.

More About the Author When Matthew Arnold's first volume of poems appeared in 1849 his sister commented that the book "almost like a new Introduction to him . . . I felt there was so much more of . . . practical questioning in Matt's book than I was prepared for. . . ." Is it surprising that Arnold's poetry revealed aspects of his personality of which those close to him had previously been unaware? Why or why not?

Critical Evaluation Lionel Trilling summarizes Arnold's work as follows: "Arnold's poetry in its most characteristic mood is elegiac—it mourns a loss, celebrates the lost thing, and tries to come to terms with the deprivation. What is this thing that is grieved for? The contemporary reader of English literature need not be long over this question. He will quite easily see that Arnold's loss is much the same as that which is at the center of the thought and feeling of such modern writers as T. S. Eliot, D. H. Lawrence, and W. B. Yeats. It is the loss of a certain culture—that is to say, of a certain body of assumptions, a certain way of looking at the world and of responding to it, a certain quality of temperament which seems no longer available.

"For Arnold, . . . the essential element of this sense of loss was the diminution of the intensity of religious faith."

MATTHEW ARNOLD

1822–1888

Of all the great Victorian poets, Matthew Arnold strikes twentieth-century readers as the most modern. The persistent theme of his poems—people's isolation and alienation from nature and from one another—has been echoed by many writers and thinkers of our own age. His pessimistic outlook too—that "there is everything to be endured, nothing to be done"—coincides with the view of many today that we are a generation of lost souls.

Matthew Arnold was born in Laleham, Middlesex, and educated at Rugby School, where his father, a believer in the good of social change, was headmaster. After entering Oxford in 1841, Arnold startled his contemporaries by dressing and behaving like an aristocratic dandy. Yet, behind this Byronic mask was developing the serious and sensitive social conscience that was to guide Arnold's career as a public servant, poet, and literary critic.

In 1851 Arnold accepted the post of Inspector of Schools, which he held until two years before his death. In this job he traveled through England and the Continent, and published reports that did much to improve public education in Great Britain. All the while, he remained a poet at heart, though his first two books, published in 1849 and 1851, met with little success.

His fortunes changed in 1853, with the publication of *Poems: A New Edition,* which included a long preface that established Arnold as a writer of clear critical prose as well as of quality poetry. With *New Poems* (1867), which contained his celebrated "Dover Beach," Arnold felt that he had expressed everything he had to say through poetry. From that point forward, he thus focused his creative energies on literary criticism.

The melancholy outlook of his poems, Arnold himself noted, was unrelieved by hope. Nevertheless, it was his belief that the role of literature was to "inspirit and rejoice the reader: that it shall convey a charm and infuse delight." In such critical works as *Culture and Anarchy* (1869), Arnold argued also that literature should train us to open our minds to what is true and valuable in life. For Arnold, then, literature's truth and cultural value lay in its ability to enlarge and develop humanity's "moral and social passion for doing good." Even his critical examinations of the classics and of Dante and Shakespeare were in part attempts to help readers of his day find permanent values in an industrialized society that Arnold viewed as increasingly materialistic and self-serving.

Despite his own opinions regarding the shortcomings of his poetic vision, Arnold's "dark" poems are a mirror of his critical beliefs: They charm and delight audiences, as well as point out enduring truths.

Objectives

1 To understand imagery and mood
2 To write about imagery and mood
3 To use figurative language
4 To write about a Victorian poet

Support Material

Teaching Portfolio
Teacher Backup, p. 987
Usage and Mechanics Worksheet, p. 991
Vocabulary Check, p. 992
Analyzing Literature Worksheet, *Appreciating Apostrophe,* p. 993
Language Worksheet, *Appreciating Vivid Words,* p. 994
Selection Test, p. 995

GUIDE FOR INTERPRETING

To Marguerite—Continued; Self-Dependence; Dover Beach

Writer's Technique

Imagery and Mood. Imagery is language that appeals to one or more of the senses. Poets rely on imagery to help establish *mood,* the overall feeling that a poem awakens in the reader. For example, if a poet wishes to create a mood of frustration, he or she may rely on imagery associated with a summer traffic jam—the sight of countless cars gleaming in the sunshine, the sound of motors humming, the feel of the heat rising from the pavement, the smell and perhaps even the taste of exhaust fumes. The same imagery, however, can be used to convey a mood of excitement and energy when the focus of the poem becomes a raceway, where roaring cars zoom past cheering spectators.

Figurative Language. Figurative language is the name applied to a group of literary devices that use words and phrases in an unorthodox way to create interesting effects. Figurative language is not to be taken literally. Among the many figures of speech used by poets are *apostrophe,* in which the poet directly addresses an absent person or some object or idea, and *personification,* the assigning of human qualities to nonhuman things. Both of these devices are used by Matthew Arnold in "Self-Dependence."

Commentary

Critics assume that Arnold wrote "Dover Beach" with his wife in mind. The lines ". . . the world, which seems/To lie before us like a land of dreams,/So various, so beautiful, so new," and the image of Dover Beach in the moonlight perhaps represent the stop that the poet and his wife made at Dover on their wedding journey in June of 1851. The wild beauty of the famed "white cliffs of Dover" continues to attract scores of people yearly.

The Straits of Dover, about twenty-one miles across, connect the English Channel and the Atlantic Ocean with the North Sea. It is a strikingly beautiful spot, for both the French and English shores are lined by high chalk cliffs. The outcropping of the stark white cliffs is the result of the swift erosion of the soft chalk. The lashing of the waves, wind, and rain and the seeping of groundwater combine to create striking shore-front sculpture.

Why do you think Arnold picked Dover Beach as the setting for his poem? How does the imagery help create the poem's mood?

Writing

Imagine yourself on a beach, watching the ebb and flow of the ocean. Freewrite, exploring the thoughts that spring to mind.

Guide for Interpreting 825

To Marguerite— Continued

Matthew Arnold

1   Yes! in the sea of life enisled,
With echoing straits between us thrown,
Dotting the shoreless watery wild,
2   We mortal millions live *alone*.
5   The islands feel the enclasping flow,
And then their endless bounds they know.

But when the moon their hollows lights,
And they are swept by balms of spring,
3   And in their glens, on starry nights,
10   The nightingales divinely sing;
And lovely notes, from shore to shore,
Across the sounds and channels pour—

Oh! then a longing like despair
Is to their farthest caverns sent;
15   For surely once, they feel, we were
Parts of a single continent!
Now round us spreads the watery plain—
4   Oh might our marges meet again!

Who ordered, that their longing's fire
20   Should be, as soon as kindled, cooled?
Who renders vain their deep desire?
5   A God, a God their severance ruled!
And bade betwixt their shores to be
The unplumbed, salt, estranging sea.

---

1. enisled (in īld') *adj.*: Isolated, as if placed on an island.

THINKING ABOUT THE SELECTION

Recalling

1. Where and how, according to lines 1–4, do "we mortal millions live"?
2. (a) According to lines 7–14, what sights and sounds seem to trigger "a longing like despair"? (b) What true cause for this longing is explained in lines 15–18?
3. According to the last stanza, who ordered that this longing's "fire" be "cooled"?

Interpreting

4. To what or whom do you think Arnold is comparing the islands?
5. What human condition is Arnold lamenting in this poem?
6. (a) Who do you suppose the "god" mentioned in line 22 might be? (b) What evidence do you have that this is not a "good" god?

Applying

7. John Donne wrote, "No man is an island entire of itself; every man is a piece of the continent, a part of the main." Arnold's "Yes!" at the beginning of this poem seems to be a flat contradiction of Donne's view. Which poet's view do you agree with more? Why?

ANALYZING LITERATURE

Creating Imagery and Mood

An **image** is a word or phrase that appeals to one or more of the five senses. Poets string together images to create a particular **mood,** or emotional response in the reader. In "To Marguerite—Continued," the dominant imagery is intended to help the reader form a mental picture of islands in a vast ocean. Arnold contrasts this imagery, however, with images of springtime in the second stanza.

1. What mood does Arnold establish with the island imagery in the first stanza? How do the sounds of the words themselves contribute to this mood?
2. What mood is suggested by the springtime images in the second stanza? How does the third stanza destroy this mood? How does this intentional undermining of a positive mood fit in with the theme of the poem?

THINKING AND WRITING

Writing About Imagery and Mood

The image of an island is an almost perfect vehicle for suggesting a mood of loneliness and, in the case of Arnold's poem, for a commentary on human isolation. Consider other images Arnold might have chosen that would have created a similar mood and been equally well suited to his theme. Make notes on one such image and on the senses to which it would appeal. Then write a brief poem or prose narrative that carries the message of "To Marguerite—Continued." When you revise, make sure you have used as many descriptive words as you can to enhance the vividness of your imagery and to sharpen the focus of the piece's mood.

To Marguerite—Continued 827

ANSWERS TO THINKING ABOUT THE SELECTION
Recalling

1. We live on islands, all alone.
2. (a) Moonlight, spring breezes, and the song of the nightingales trigger this longing. (b) The longing arises out of a desire that humanity might once again be single united race.
3. A God ordered the separation.

Interpreting

4. He is comparing the islands to human souls; each individual is an island.
5. He is alluding to the coldness and alienation that have developed among humans in these modern, technologically oriented times.
6. (a) Students will note that this is the "God of modern industry." (b) That the god is not a benevolent presence is indicated by his act of cooling the longing for togetherness with indifference.

Applying

7. Answers will differ. Those who agree with Donne will take the position that total independence is neither possible nor desirable, while those who side with Arnold will contend that solidarity is desirable but unattainable.

ANSWERS TO ANALYZING LITERATURE

1. He establishes a mood of cold isolation. The repetition of the $\bar{o}$ contributes to this mood.
2. The mood in the second stanza is one of quietude and tranquility. The third stanza destroys the mood by opening with a plaintive cry and the mention of a "longing like despair". The subverting of the positive mood is appropriate to the theme because it is precisely what the poet ascribes to the "God" of industry in line 22.

THINKING AND WRITING

For help with this assignment, students can refer to Lesson 4, "Writing About Imagery," in the Handbook of Writing About Literature.

Presentation

Motivation/Prior Knowledge Ask students to comment on what they experience when they look up at the stars at night. Do they merely see pretty twinkling lights, or do they entertain more profound thoughts? What associations might the stars and the vastness of the nighttime sky have had for thinkers of past generations?

Thematic Idea Another poem that deals with the concept of human self-sufficiency is "Not Waving, But Drowning," by Stevie Smith, on page 1307.

Purpose-Setting Question What credo does the speaker come to adopt through the experience he describes?

1 **Discussion** Have students discuss what "end" the poet might be referring to here and what this reveals about his intentions.

2 **Literary Focus** What are the objects of the apostrophe in these lines?

3 **Clarification** The word *unaffrighted* means "not frightened."

4 **Literary Focus** What human traits are ascribed to the stars and ocean in this passage?

5 **Enrichment** You might wish to have students read Arnold's short poem "The Last Word," which explores in more detail the "fever" that tends to erupt among "differing souls."

6 **Reading Strategy** Have students restate these thoughts in their own words.

Self-Dependence

Matthew Arnold

Weary of myself, and sick of asking
What I am, and what I ought to be,
At this vessel's prow I stand, which bears me
Forwards, forwards, o'er the starlit sea.

5 And a look of passionate desire
O'er the sea and to the stars I send:
"Ye who from my childhood up have calmed me,
Calm me, ah, compose me to the end!

"Ah, once more," I cried, "ye stars, ye waters,
10 On my heart your mighty charm renew;
Still, still let me, as I gaze upon you,
Feel my soul becoming vast like you!"

From the intense, clear, star-sown vault of heaven,
Over the lit sea's unquiet way,
15 In the rustling night air came the answer:
"Wouldst thou *be* as these are? *Live* as they.

"Unaffrighted by the silence round them,
Undistracted by the sights they see,
These demand not that the things without them
20 Yield them love, amusement, sympathy.

"And with joy the stars perform their shining,
And the sea its long moon-silvered roll;
For self-poised they live, nor pine with noting
All the fever of some differing soul.

25 "Bounded by themselves, and unregardful
In what state God's other works may be,
In their own tasks all their powers pouring,
These attain the mighty life you see."

O air-born voice! long since, severely clear,
30 A cry like thine in mine own heart I hear:
"Resolve to be thyself; and know that he,
Who finds himself, loses his misery!"

THINKING ABOUT THE SELECTION

Recalling

1. (a) What emotional state do we find the speaker in at the poem's beginning? (b) Where does the speaker say he is standing and going?
2. (a) What does the poet ask of the sea and the stars? (b) What answer does he receive in line 16?
3. What characteristics of the sea and stars enable them to "attain the mighty life" the speaker so admires?
4. What cry does the speaker finally hear in his own heart?
5. Why do you think the poet calls this poem "Self-Dependence," not "Independence"?

Interpreting

6. (a) In your own words, identify the problem that Arnold presents in the first two lines of the poem. (b) Identify the solution offered in the last two lines.
7. Lines 7–12 mention the speaker's childhood. What does the passage imply that the speaker has lost?
8. What do you suppose is the source of the "air-born voice" in the poem?
9. What is meant by "the fever of some differing soul" in line 24?

Applying

10. According to lines 19–20, nature is self-dependent because it does not require love, amusement, or sympathy. Do you think it is possible for human beings to attain such self-dependence? Explain your answer.

ANALYZING LITERATURE

Using Figurative Language

Figurative language is language not to be taken at face value. Many devices used by poets fall into the category of figurative language. In one such device, apostrophe, the poet directly addresses an absent human being or some object or idea. In personification, another device, human qualities are assigned to a nonhuman object. Both of these devices, or figures of speech, are used by Arnold in "Self-Dependence."

1. In which lines does Arnold use apostrophe? What or whom is he addressing?
2. What does Arnold personify in the poem? What human characteristics does he assign to these nonhuman things?
3. What reason might Arnold have had for using apostrophe and personification in this poem? How would the poem have been different had he not chosen to use these devices?

Self-Dependence 829

---

2. (a) He asks them to calm and compose him, as they did when he was younger. (b) He is told that if he would be like the sea and stars, he must live like them.
3. They are totally self-sufficient —needing neither love nor sympathy, nor concerned for the opinions of others.
4. He hears his own heart state that we are less miserable when we at least know our true selves.
5. The poem focuses on self-sufficiency rather than on independence.

Interpreting

6. (a) Students will note that the problem is one of discontent with the modern world and with what it has done to human relations. (b) The solution is to understand our own identities.
7. Suggested Response: He has lost his innocence.
8. Suggested Response: It is the voice of the heavens.
9. The phrase refers to the angry arguments of one whose opinion differs.

Applying

10. Answers will differ. Students may comment that they do believe that such self-dependence is possible.

Challenge Does the message in this poem conflict in any way with the message in "To Marguerite —Continued"? If so, how?

ANSWERS TO ANALYZING LITERATURE

1. Apostrophe is used in lines 7–12, and again in lines 29–30. In the first instance he is addressing the sea and stars, and in the second the air-born voice.
2. He personifies the sea and stars. The characteristics he assigns them include fear, distraction, sight, love, amusement, sympathy, joy, poise, pining, and arguing.
3. Answers will differ. Students might note that Arnold needed a nonhuman entity with which to compare what he saw as typical human behavior and that, in this regard, personification, at least, was virtually unavoidable.

Closure and Extension

ANSWERS TO THINKING ABOUT THE SELECTION
Recalling

1. (a) He is weary and full of self-doubt. (b) He is standing on the prow of a ship headed out to sea.

Dover Beach

Matthew Arnold

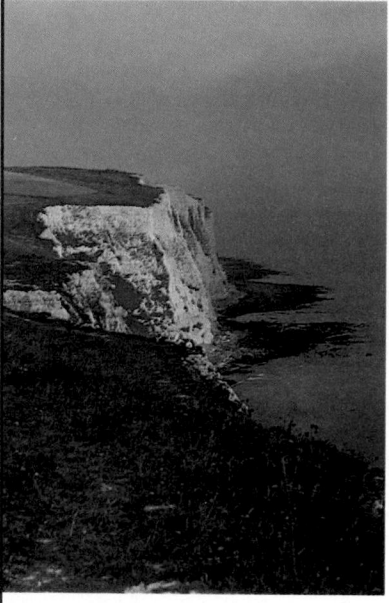

1
The sea is calm tonight.
The tide is full, the moon lies fair
Upon the straits:[1] on the French coast the light
Gleams and is gone; the cliffs of England stand,
5 Glimmering and vast, out in the tranquil bay.
Come to the window, sweet is the night air!
Only, from the long line of spray

2
Where the sea meets the moon-blanched land,
Listen! you hear the grating roar
10 Of pebbles which the waves draw back, and fling,
At their return, up the high strand,[2]
Begin, and cease, and then again begin,
With tremulous cadence slow, and bring
The eternal note of sadness in.

3
15 Sophocles[3] long ago
Heard it on the Aegaean,[4] and it brought
Into his mind the turbid ebb and flow
Of human misery; we
Find also in the sound a thought,
20 Hearing it by this distant northern sea.

4
The Sea of Faith
Was once, too, at the full, and round earth's shore
Lay like the folds of a bright girdle furled.
But now I only hear
25 Its melancholy, long, withdrawing roar,
Retreating, to the breath
Of the night wind, down the vast edges drear
And naked shingles[5] of the world.

---

1. straits: Strait of Dover, between England and France.
2. strand: Shore.
3. Sophocles (säf′ ə klēz′): A Greek tragic dramatist (496?–406 B.C.)
4. Aegaean (ē jē′ ən): The arm of the Mediterranean Sea between Greece and Turkey.
5. shingles *n.*: Beaches covered with large, coarse, waterworn gravel.

> Ah, love, let us be true
> 30   To one another! for the world, which seems
> To lie before us like a land of dreams,
> So various, so beautiful, so new,
> Hath really neither joy, nor love, nor light,
> Nor certitude, nor peace, nor help for pain;
> 35   And we are here as on a darkling[6] plain
> Swept with confused alarms of struggle and flight,
> Where ignorant armies clash by night.

---

6. darkling *adj.*: In the dark.

5 **Discussion** To whom do you think these lines are addressed? Explain your answer.

THINKING ABOUT THE SELECTION

Recalling

1. (a) According to the first stanza, what does the speaker see and hear from his window? (b) What does the "tremulous cadence" of the pebbles against the beach "bring in"? (c) Who else does the speaker say "long ago" heard this same sound?
2. What, according to lines 21–28, has happened to the "Sea of Faith?"
3. What sad reality does the speaker describe for his companion in lines 30–34?

Applying

4. A symbol is a thing, person, or place that stands for something beyond itself. (a) What might the "cliffs of England" symbolize in line 4? (b) The "naked shingles of the world" in line 28? (c) "Night" in line 37?
5. (a) What effect do you think Arnold aimed to achieve by varying the length of lines and using an irregular rhyme scheme? (b) How do these poetic devices relate to the theme?
6. (a) How is the battle image in the last three lines a fitting conclusion to this poem? (b) How would you state the message of these lines in your own words?

Applying

7. (a) To what extent does Arnold's plea to "be true to one another" in lines 29–30 provide a satisfactory solution to the "ebb and flow of human misery" he sees in the world? (b) Where does this solution break down?
8. (a) State the similarities in theme and imagery you find between this poem and "To Marguerite—Continued" on page 826. (b) State the differences.

THINKING AND WRITING

Writing About a Victorian Poet

From what you know of Victorian society and of Arnold's career, which attitudes of the Victorian Age do you think his poem's reflect? Consider, among other things, the effects that industrialization and science had on nineteenth-century England—both positive and negative. Comment on the effects of such forces in an essay that identifies Arnold's place as a poet of his time. When you revise, make sure you have mentioned mood and theme in your treatment of the topic.

Dover Beach   831

Applying

7. (a) Answers will differ. Students might note that this plea echoes the cry the speaker of "Self-Dependence" hears in his own heart at the end of that poem. (b) The solution breaks down inasmuch as honesty enables us to recognize, but not to deal with, the problems of the world delineated in the poem.
8. (a) Answers will differ. Students will note in particular the use of sea imagery and the conclusion that we are a race of lost and isolated souls. (b) The differences should include the views that "Dover Beach" is a more diffused and outwardly philosophical poem and that the metaphorical use of sea here (line 21) is much more direct.

Closure and Extension

ANSWERS TO THINKING ABOUT THE SELECTION

Recalling

1. (a) He sees and hears the ebb and flow of the tide. (b) It brings in "the eternal note of sadness." (c) He says that Sophocles heard the sound.
2. It has retreated.
3. He describes the world as a place without joy, love, light, certitude, peace, or help for pain.

Interpreting

4. (a) They might stand for England itself, or for mankind. (b) This is the world stripped of its illusion. (c) Night here represents the darkness of reality.
5. (a) The metric structure and rhyme scheme of the poem are uneven, like the ebb and flow of the tides. (b) Suggested Response: They reflect the opposing forces upon which the poem focuses.
6. (a) It sums up Arnold's view of the current state of the world and contrasts sharply with the opening lines. (b) Suggested Response: The message is that the human race is in hopeless turmoil.

Writing Across the Curriculum

As an alternative assignment, have students focus on the principles set down by Darwin and its effects on the artistic community in Victorian England at large. Science teachers may be able to aid students in conducting their research.

831

More About the Author At the age of sixteen Thomas Hardy was apprenticed to an architect. Following what for a time appeared to be his life's career path, he followed up this early training with formal study in London, ultimately winning a prize for his architectural work from the Royal Institute. What aspects of the study of architecture might prove useful to a writer and poet?

Critical Evaluation In *Victorian Poetry and Poetics,* Walter E. Houghton and G. Robert Stange make the following remarks about Hardy's poetry: "The poetry is, in some ways, difficult to approach. Hardy does not have the meilifluousness of Tennyson, the engaging vigor of Browning, or the surface wit and 'complexity' of some of his younger contemporaries. His style is rugged and idiosyncratic, and his sensibility does not lend itself to easy categorization. However, much of what is peculiar to his artistic nature can be understood in terms of his early life and his special reactions to the literary and intellectual environment of the end of the century. . . .

"Hardy's country environment . . . led him to focus on the bare essentials of existence. In the hamlets of Dorset, where the patterns of life were shaped by folk traditions, and the elemental round of birth and death, of love and suffering, was not concealed by the conventions of metropolitan society, Hardy, like Wordsworth or Robert Frost, could penetrate more readily to the central passions of life.

"It is this which gives his poems their symbolic richness. Though the diction is startlingly 'modern,' and the issues and incidents and characters obviously of a specific time and place, they are heightened to timelessness as are the particular names and events of a ballad."

THOMAS HARDY

1840–1928

Both a novelist and a poet, Thomas Hardy is sometimes called "the last of the great Victorians." Like Matthew Arnold, Hardy held a pessimistic view of the world. In his great novels he depicted people striving against overwhelming odds within a society and universe that were uncaring. Unlike Arnold, however, who sought to improve society, Hardy remained a passive observer of the ills of his century; if he offered comfort at all, it was in the uncertain hope that the future would be at least different, if not better.

Thomas Hardy was born in Dorset, a region in southwest England noted for its agriculture and, perhaps more importantly, for its ruins which date to Anglo–Saxon and Roman times. This "Wessex," as Hardy fictionalized the region in his poems and novels, is the setting for the works that established Hardy's reputation as a writer. In *Far from the Madding Crowd* (1874), *The Return of the Native* (1878), *The Mayor of Casterbridge* (1886), *Tess of the D'Urbervilles* (1891), and his masterpiece, *Jude the Obscure* (1895), Hardy's characters move against a haunting landscape that is at once ancient and modern, starkly beautiful yet indifferent to the tragic lives of its inhabitants.

Despite the undeniable greatness of Hardy's novels, the bleak view they presented was distressing to a public who much preferred the life-affirming optimism of Tennyson and Browning. So intense, in fact, was the angry response to *Jude the Obscure* upon its publication that Hardy thought it wise to abandon the novel in favor of his first literary love, poetry. An epic verse drama about the Napoleonic Wars, *The Dynasts* (1904–1908), earned Hardy immense public acclaim. With each book of verse that he produced over the next two decades, his reputation as a man of letters grew. When he died, the world honored him by burying his ashes in the Poet's Corner of Westminster Abbey, though, as a token to the region that he loved, his heart was buried in Dorset.

Hardy's poetry marks a bridge between the Victorian Age and the Modernist movement of the twentieth century. In his use of strict meters and stanza structure, Hardy was unmistakably Victorian. One contemporary critic called him "the most fertile inventor of stanza-forms in all English literature." Another critic, however, Leonard Woolf, viewed Hardy as one of the spiritual parents of the modern generation. Hardy's use of "nonpoetic" language and odd rhymes, coupled with his fatalistic outlook, were both source and inspiration to numerous twentieth-century writers, among them such important figures as Virginia Woolf, Siegfried Sassoon, and Robert Graves.

Objectives

1 To use similes and metaphors
2 To prepare an oral report on Wessex
3 To understand irony
4 To write a response to a poem

Support Material

Teaching Portfolio
Teacher Backup, p. 997-1000
Usage and Mechanics Worksheet, p. 1001
Vocabulary Check, p. 1002
Analyzing Literature Worksheet, *Understanding Simile and Metaphor,* p. 1003
Analyzing Literature Worksheet, *Understanding Irony,* p. 1004
Selection Test, p. 1005

GUIDE FOR INTERPRETING

The Darkling Thrush; The Man He Killed; "Ah, Are You Digging on My Grave?"

Writer's Technique

Simile and Metaphor. A simile is a figure of speech that compares two unlike things, using an explicit word such as *like* or *as*. In "Love Among the Ruins," Robert Browning uses a simile to compare the towers on a castle to flames: ". . . the doomed and daring palace shot its spires/Up *like* fires. . . ." A metaphor is a figure of speech that compares two unlike things directly, without the use of an intervening word. In "London, 1802," William Wordsworth laments the sorrowful state of affairs in the England of his day by comparing the country metaphorically to a swamp: "England hath need of thee: she is a fen/Of stagnant waters. . . ." Poets use similes and metaphors to broaden the meanings of their images by making surprising connections between generally unrelated things and ideas.

Writer's Technique

Irony. Irony is the intentional difference between expectation and reality in a poem or story. In *situational irony* the outcome of an event or situation is different from what the author has led the reader to predict. By using situational irony in "'Ah, Are You Digging on My Grave?'" Hardy communicates an especially strong message to the reader.

Writing

Write an account of an occasion when something relatively unimportant managed to change your mood entirely. Consider possibilities such as a beautiful flower growing through a crack in the pavement of a city sidewalk. Give details of how you felt before and after the mood-changing experience.

Primary Source

Although Hardy had written many poems in his late twenties, his first book of poetry was not published until he was fifty-eight years old. In the thirty years remaining to him, he published nearly one thousand poems. Why would a highly successful novelist abandon prose for poetry? We know that writing novels cause him great stress, and the uproar over *Jude the Obscure* sickened him. But there was more to it. Looking back in 1918, he wrote: "A sense of the truth of poetry, of its supreme place in literature, had awakened itself in me. At the risk of ruining all my wordly prospects I dabbled in it. . . . was forced out of it. . . . It came back upon me. . . . All was of the nature of being led by a mood, without foresight, or regard to whither it led."

Literary Focus To clarify the notion of situational irony, give students examples of the phenomenon as it occurs in everyday life. Then ask them to come up with their own examples of situational irony.

Writing If students are unable to come up with an actual example, ask them to invent an experience that fits the description of the assignment.

Vocabulary

Preteach the following words:
terrestrial (tə res′ trē əl) *adj.*: Of the earth; worldly (p. 834, l. 27)
gaunt (gônt) *adj.*: Thin (p. 834, l. 21)

The Darkling[1] Thrush

Thomas Hardy

I leant upon a coppice gate[2]
　　When Frost was specter-gray,
And Winter's dregs made desolate
　　The weakening eye of day.
5　The tangled bine-stems[3] scored the sky
　　Like strings of broken lyres,
And all mankind that haunted nigh
　　Had sought their household fires.

The land's sharp features seemed to be
10　　The Century's corpse[4] outleant,
His crypt the cloudy canopy,
　　The wind his death-lament.
The ancient pulse of germ[5] and birth
　　Was shrunken hard and dry,
15　And every spirit upon earth
　　Seemed fervorless as I.

At once a voice arose among
　　The bleak twigs overhead
In a full-hearted evensong
20　　Of joy illimited;
An aged thrush, frail, gaunt, and small,
　　In blast-beruffled plume,
Had chosen thus to fling his soul
　　Upon the growing gloom.

25　So little cause for carolings
　　Of such ecstatic sound
Was written on terrestrial things
　　Afar or nigh around,
That I could think there trembled through
30　　His happy good-night air
Some blessed Hope, whereof he knew
　　And I was unaware.

---

1. **darkling** *adj.*: In the dark.
2. **coppice** (kŏp′ ĭs) **gate:** Gate leading to a thicket, or small wood.
3. **bine-stems:** Twining stems.
4. **Century's corpse:** This poem was written on December 31, 1900, the last day of the nineteenth century.
5. **germ:** Seed or bud.

THINKING ABOUT THE SELECTION

Recalling

1. In what season of the year and at what time of day is the poem set?
2. What do the "land's sharp features" suggest to the speaker?
3. (a) What does the speaker suddenly hear in the third stanza? (b) What does the speaker think about as a result of this experience?

Interpreting

4. (a) What mood does the poet establish in the first two stanzas? (b) What images contribute to this mood? (c) With what does the poet contrast these images in the last two stanzas?
5. (a) Why do you think the poet characterizes the thrush as he does in lines 21–22? (b) What might the thrush symbolize?

Applying

6. Depressed people react in different ways to others who display "joys illimited." The poem describes one possible reaction. What are some other possibilities?
7. Reread "To a Skylark" by Shelley on page 708. (a) What similarities are evident in the speaker's response to the thrush in this poem? (b) What differences do you detect?

ANALYZING LITERATURE

Using Simile and Metaphor

A **simile** is a figure of speech that compares basically dissimilar things, using such connective words as *like* or *as*. Consider the following simile from Tennyson's "The Lotos-Eaters," which makes use of the connective word *than*: "There is sweet music here that softer falls/Than petals from blown roses on the grass. . . ." A **metaphor** compares basically dissimilar things as well, but without the use of a connective word.

When, again in "The Lotos-Eaters," Tennyson refers to the ocean as "fields of barren foam," he is speaking in metaphorical terms. Similes and metaphors are used by poets to heighten the meanings of their images.

1. Identify each of the following italicized images from "The Darkling Thrush" as either a simile or a metaphor. Tell what two objects are being compared in each case.
   a. Winter's *dregs* made desolate/The *weakening eye of day*. (Lines 3–4)
   b. The tangled bine-stems *scored* the sky/Like *strings of broken lyres*. . . . (Lines 5–6)
   c. An aged thrush . . . /Had chosen thus to *fling his soul*/Upon the *growing gloom*. (Lines 21–24)
2. To what are the land's sharp features compared in lines 9–11? Explain why this metaphor is especially appropriate for the time and place in which the poem is set.

SPEAKING AND LISTENING

Preparing an Oral Report on Wessex

Hardy's novels and many of his poems are set in "Wessex," his fictional name for the Dorset countryside that he loved. Using reference books, biographies of Hardy, histories of the Victorian Age, and Hardy's own works, prepare a five-to-ten-minute oral report on some aspect of Hardy's Wessex. You might consider one of the following topics:
   a. the geography of Wessex (Dorset)
   b. the history of the region (prehistoric, Roman, Anglo–Saxon)
   c. Wessex life in Victorian times
   d. Wessex as depicted in Hardy's works

The Darkling Thrush　835

Closure and Extension

ANSWERS TO THINKING ABOUT THE SELECTION
Recalling

1. It is wintertime and toward the close of day.
2. They suggest the corpse of the century laid out.
3. (a) He hears a thrush overhead. (b) He speculates on whether there is perhaps some hope in store.

Interpreting

4. (a) The mood is one of unrelieved gloom and pessimism. (b) Students might note such death-related images as "specter" and such decay-related images as "dregs," "weakening," and "tangled." (c) He contrasts them with slightly more upbeat images—"carolings" and "happy good-night air."
5. (a) Answers will differ. Students will perhaps note that this adds to the irony of the bird's song. (b) Suggested Response: The bird might symbolize the indomitability of the human spirit even in the most cheerless of times.

Applying

6. Answers will differ. Students may be acquainted with the tendency in some persons to bristle and lash out angrily at good cheer in others when their own spirits are low. Yet another possibility is that of a lapse still further into a depressed state.
7. (a) As in Shelley's poem, the speaker here is looking for a cause for at least guarded optimism. (b) The optimism in Shelley's poem is more direct and heartfelt, as though it were that of the poet himself.

ANSWERS TO ANALYZING LITERATURE

1. (a) The first is a metaphor comparing the end of a winter's day to dregs of wine; the second is a metaphor comparing the end of day to an eye losing its sight.
   (b) The first is a metaphor comparing the appearance of a network of twigs against the sky to the sky's having been crisscrossed or scored; the second is a simile comparing the above effect to the disconnected strings of a broken instrument.
   (c) The first is a metaphor comparing the act of singing to the flinging of a soul; the second is a metaphor comparing the oncoming darkness of day to increasing gloom.
2. They are compared respectively to a corpse, a crypt, and a dirge. The metaphors are apt insofar as the century is gloomily and unceremoniously winding down.

Motivation/Prior Knowledge
Write the expression "All's fair in love and war" on the board. Ask if students have ever heard this expression. Do students find the saying true? Are there some aspects of war that strike them as blatantly unfair? What other expressions do they know of that comment on war?

Master Teacher Note Distribute among your students a photograph of the *Marseillaise,* the sculpture by François Rude that crowns the Arc de Triomphe in Paris. (One appears on page 487 of H. W. Janson's *History of Art,* Prentice-Hall/Abrams.) Tell your students that this represents soldiers marching off to war, urged on by the Genius of Liberty, the figure at the top. Ask them whether this gives a realistic image of war. What problems arise out of the glorification of war?

Thematic Idea Another poem depicts the horrors of war is Stephen Spender's "What I Expected," page 1090.

Purpose-Setting Question What attitude toward war does the poem express?

1 **Discussion** What impression do you have of the age of the speaker? Of the other man? Why?

2 **Discussion** How would you describe the speaker's tone?

3 **Discussion** What was the speaker's reason for enlisting? How does this add to the poem's irony?

The Man He Killed

Thomas Hardy

1
"Had he and I but met
By some old ancient inn,
We should have sat us down to wet
Right many a nipperkin![1]

5 "But ranged as infantry,
And staring face to face,
I shot at him as he at me,
And killed him in his place.

2
"I shot him dead because—
10 Because he was my foe,
Just so: my foe of course he was;
That's clear enough; although

3
"He thought he'd 'list,[2] perhaps,
Off-hand like—just as I—
15 Was out of work—had sold his traps—
No other reason why.

"Yes; quaint and curious war is!
You shoot a fellow down
You'd treat if met where any bar is,
20 Or help to half-a-crown."[3]

---

1. **nipperkin** *n.*: A small glass for beer or wine.
2. **'list:** Enlist.
3. **half-a-crown:** A British coin.

THINKING ABOUT THE SELECTION

Recalling

1. (a) What does the speaker suggest might have happened had he and the other man met "by some old ancient inn"? (b) Where did they meet instead? (c) What happened?
2. What similarities between himself and the other man does the speaker note in lines 13–16?

Interpreting

3. (a) What do you think is the significance of the quotation marks in each stanza? (b) Who do you suppose the speaker is? (c) To whom do you think the poem is addressed?
4. Why do you think the speaker hesitates at the end of line 9?
5. (a) What point about the nature of war is Hardy making in this poem? (b) In what way is war "quaint and curious," as his speaker notes in line 17?
6. Do you think Hardy is writing about a specific war or about war in general? Explain your answer.

Applying

7. Why is it easier for an enemy to be faceless than to have a face?

AT THE WINDOW, 1960
Jacob Kainen

The Man He Killed 837

Closure and Extension

ANSWERS TO THINKING ABOUT THE SELECTION
Recalling

1. (a) They might have shared some refreshment together. (b) They met on the battlefield. (c) The speaker shot and killed the other man.
2. Both enlisted in an offhand manner; neither was a patriot.

Interpreting

3. (a) They indicate that the words are spoken by a character, not the poet. (b) The speaker is a soldier. (c) It is addressed to the world at large, to express the speaker's casual—and the poet's all-consuming—horror over this event.
4. Students will observe that the speaker needs to remind himself —or persuade himself—of the rationale behind his wanton act. The hesitation also adds a natural life-like quality to the narration.
5. (a) Suggested Response: He is pointing up the absurdity of a disagreement between major powers manifesting itself in the loss of innocent lives. (b) Suggested Response: War might be thought of as "quaint" because it often involves young, inexperienced people; it might be thought of as "curious" because these innocents are often the casualties.
6. Suggested Response: He is writing about war in general.

Applying

7. (a) Suggested Response: It is easier for the enemy to be faceless, because it makes it seem as if the deaths of enemy soldiers are in some way unreal.

Humanities Note

Fine art: *At The Window,* 1960, by Jacob Kainen. The American painter and graphic artist Jacob Kainen was born in 1909. Kainen felt his most valuable education came from association with other artists. As curator of the Department of Prints and Drawings of the National Collection of Fine Arts, he single-handedly built and expanded this collection during his twenty years in the position.

As a painter, Jacob Kainen has worked in many styles. *At the Window* is a figural abstraction. The painting is an amalgam of loose geometric shapes that represent a room, a window, and a man. The colors have no correspondence to reality but were used for their emotional impact on the viewer. The mood of the painting is one of depression, created in part by the prevalent low intensity blue. The unifying element in this and all of Kainen's work is the value uniformity of the colors.

Consider these questions for discussion:
1. What is the mood or effect of this painting?
2. In what ways does it illustrate "The Man He Killed"?

Motivation/Prior Knowledge
Ask students to describe, without naming names, the characteristics shared by most vain people. What makes people vain? Is vanity an easy flaw to correct? How do most people feel toward others who are vain?

Thematic Idea Another poem that explores the subject of human vanity is "To a Louse" by Robert Burns, page 599.

Purpose-Setting Question What is the unexpected answer to the title question of the poem?

1 Reading Strategy Caution students to pay strict attention to opening and closing quotation marks, signaling a change in speakers.

2 Reading Strategy Have students note that two key possibilities have now been eliminated. Are they able to identify the speaker?

3 Clarification The word *tendance,* an alternate form of *tending,* means "the acting of maintaining, as a garden."

4 Discussion Is it a natural state of affairs to have enemies? If not, what does this perhaps suggest about the deceased?

5 Discussion What other popular expression are you aware of that summarized this sentiment?

"Ah, Are You Digging on My Grave?"

Thomas Hardy

"Ah, are you digging on my grave
    My loved one?—planting rue?"
—"No: yesterday he went to wed
One of the brightest wealth has bred.
5 'It cannot hurt her now,' he said,
    'That I should not be true.'"

"Then who is digging on my grave?
    My nearest dearest kin?"
—"Ah, no: they sit and think, 'What use!
10 What good will planting flowers produce?
No tendance of her mound can loose
    Her spirit from Death's gin.'"[1]

"But some one digs upon my grave?
    My enemy?—prodding sly?"
15 —"Nay: when she heard you had passed the Gate
That shuts on all flesh soon or late,
She thought you no more worth her hate,
    And cares not where you lie."

"Then, who is digging on my grave?
20   Say—since I have not guessed!"
—"O it is I, my mistress dear,
Your little dog, who still lives near,
And much I hope my movements here
    Have not disturbed your rest?"

25   "Ah, yes! *You* dig upon my grave . . .
    Why flashed it not on me
That one true heart was left behind!
What feeling do we ever find
To equal among human kind
30   A dog's fidelity!"

---

1. gin *n.*: Trap.

"Mistress, I dug upon your grave
        To bury a bone, in case
I should be hungry near this spot
When passing on my daily trot.
35   I am sorry, but I quite forgot
        It was your resting-place."

THINKING ABOUT THE SELECTION

Recalling

1. (a) In the first stanza, who does the dead woman suspect is digging on her grave? (b) In the second stanza? (c) In the third stanza? (d) What response does she receive?
2. (a) Who in fact is doing the digging? (b) How does the woman react when she learns the answer to this question? (c) What reason does the digger give for disturbing the grave?

Interpreting

3. (a) At what point do you begin to suspect the identity of the voice responding to the woman's questions? (b) What effect does Hardy achieve by withholding this information?
4. (a) What mood does Hardy create by having a dead person speak? (b) How does this mood change once the digger is identified?
5. What point about human vanity and self-esteem is Hardy making in this poem?

Applying

6. (a) Of "The Darkling Thrush," "The Man He Killed," and this poem, which strikes you as the most pessimistic? (b) The least pessimistic? (c) Why?

ANALYZING LITERATURE

Understanding Irony

Irony is a purposeful contrast between expectation and reality. In "'Ah, Are You Digging on My Grave?'" Hardy uses situational irony. That is, he leads the reader to expect one kind of outcome but instead delivers another.

1. What is ironic about the voice in the last four lines of each of the first three stanzas?
2. What emotions does the dead woman express when she learns the identity of the digger? How do the digger's final words ironically alter the woman's emotional expectations?
3. Irony is often related to tone—the author's attitude toward the subject or audience. Explain how the irony in this poem is related to Hardy's pessimism and lack of sentimentality.

THINKING AND WRITING

Writing a Response to a Poem

In "'Ah, Are You Digging on My Grave?'" Hardy delivers pessimistic pronouncements on two different but related topics—human self-worth and human apathy. Consider your reaction to Hardy's views on these subjects by asking yourself questions such as the following. To what extent are Hardy's attitudes typical only of the era in which he lived? To what degree are tributes to the dead really tributes to the living? How thoroughly do we know the feelings others have toward us? How well do we understand our own feelings toward others? In an essay, sum up your response to the views Hardy presents. When you revise, make sure you have provided adequate support for your opinion.

2. (a) The digger is her dog. (b) She responds in essence that a dog is more loyal than any human. (c) The dog replies that it was burying a bone and quite forgot that this was his mistress's grave site.

Interpreting

3. (a) Answers will differ. Students may comment that they first begin to suspect the identity of the voice in the third stanza. (b) He builds suspense and creates humor.
4. (a) Suggested Response: He creates a mock-melancholic mood. (b) By the time the digger's identity is made known, any pretense of mourning has been cast aside.
5. Suggested Response: People are never as important as they think they are.

Applying

6. Answers will differ depending on particular tastes and emotional reactions. The majority of the students will probably name "The Darkling Thrust" as most pessimistic because of its somber air, and "'Ah, Are You Digging on My Grave?'" as least pessimistic because of its humor.

ANSWERS TO ANALYZING LITERATURE

1. The irony is that the voice is a dog—the very last soul, literally, that the dead woman might guess.
2. She seems consoled slightly that at least someone might mourn her. Her expectations are overturned when it is revealed that not even the dog has remembered her.
3. The irony is a function of Hardy's outlook. It thus stands to reason that the tone of a poem treating the subject of vanity will have a mocking, scornful tone.

THINKING AND WRITING

After students have completed their compositions, divide them into groups and have them read their rough drafts to one another and suggest ways in which they could be improved.

Closure and Extension

ANSWERS TO THINKING ABOUT THE SELECTION
Recalling

1. (a) She believes it is her widower. (b) She believes it is her relatives. (c) She believes it is her enemy. (d) The response each time is negative.

More About the Author As a student and, later, as a teacher, Gerard Manley Hopkins was a stickler for detail and organization. Intolerant of his own limitations, and even more so of those in others, he found it difficult to make and keep friends. How can such personality traits harm a writer? How can they help a writer?

Critical Evaluation Walter E. Houghton and G. Robert Stange, in *Victorian Poetry and Poetics,* discuss the strangeness of Hopkins's poetry. "Hopkins agreed: 'No doubt my poetry errs on the side of strangeness. I hope in time to have a more balanced and Miltonic style.' But, he added, 'it is the vice of distinctiveness to become queer.' The first impression Hopkins makes is often of a poet straining for originality and succeeding only in being eccentric. But further reflection suggests that seeming defects may be the function of his strengths. He was fired by the notion of 'inscape,' the special individualizing quality which distinguishes one person or object or emotion from every other, that pattern or form which is unique and inward. The response which the perception of inscape awakened in him he called 'instress' (or sometimes simply 'stress'). Many of his poems have as their aim the achieving of instress by a penetration of the inscape of an experience or object. Such an attempt requires novelty and boldness, an original style, and a fresh diction."

GERARD MANLEY HOPKINS

1844–1889

Though Gerard Manley Hopkins saw none of his work published during his lifetime, he was nevertheless the most innovative poet of the Victorian Age. Born in Essex, just outside London, Hopkins was the oldest of nine children in a well-educated and prosperous family. While still in grammar school, Hopkins began writing poetry, a practice that he maintained throughout his years at Oxford, where he also studied the classics.

It was during his third year at Oxford that Hopkins decided to become a Catholic, much to the dismay of his parents, who were devout Anglicans. Upon being accepted into the Society of Jesus in 1868, he symbolically burned his early poems, resolving "to write no more." Though he remained true to his word for the next seven years, Hopkins continued to keep detailed notebooks—as he had done ever since childhood—that recorded his fascination with words and his love of nature.

In 1874, as part of his preparation for the priesthood, Hopkins went to St. Bueno's College in Wales to study theology. There he learned to speak Welsh. He also began again to write poetry, though of a sort that was different not only from his earlier verse but from anything ever before done in English. Encouraged by a Jesuit superior, Hopkins wrote a long poem about a tragic shipwreck in which five nuns had drowned. "The Wreck of the Deutschland," apart from the great emotional power packed into it, was the first poem in which Hopkins used what he called "sprung rhythm." This is a system of versification in which accented syllables are grouped in emphatic patterns somewhat like those of Anglo-Saxon alliterative verse. The resulting meter is quite different from conventional English meter, in which accented and unaccented syllables alternate in regular patterns.

In 1877, the year he was ordained a priest, Hopkins wrote some of his best and best-known poems, including "God's Grandeur," "Pied Beauty," and "Hurrahing in Harvest." Like most of Hopkins's poems, the goal of these was to reveal and glorify the individual essence—or "inscape," as he called it—of everything in nature.

Hopkins served as a parish priest and missionary preacher among the poor in London, Liverpool, and Glasgow. Despite his total dedication to his calling, long hours and a tendency toward perfectionism left him depressed and in poor health. He died of typhoid fever one month before his forty-fifth birthday.

Objective

1 To write a reply by a character in a poem

Support Material

Teaching Portfolio
Teacher Backup, p. 1007
Usage and Mechanics Worksheet, p. 1011
Vocabulary Check, p. 1012
Analyzing Literature Worksheet, *Analyzing Rhythm and Rhyme,* p. 1013

Critical Thinking and Reading Worksheet, *Understanding the Effects of Imagery,* p. 1014
Selection Test, p. 1015

GUIDE FOR INTERPRETING

God's Grandeur; Hurrahing the Harvest; Pied Beauty; Spring and Fall

Writer's Technique

Rhythm and Rhyme. *Rhythm* is the pattern of stressed and unstressed syllables in a line of poetry. Every poem has rhythm, but not every poem has meter, a regular, predictable rhythmic pattern made up of units called "feet." Each foot consists of one stressed syllable and a fixed number of unstressed syllables. In the 1870's, Gerard Manley Hopkins created a new kind of rhythm that resembled natural speech. In *sprung rhythm,* as Hopkins termed his creation, the number of unstressed syllables varies from foot to foot. Precisely which syllables receive stress, moreover, is not accidental but carefully planned to help convey meaning and emotion. Finally, sprung rhythm calls for the innovative use of language, for the combining of existing words, the extending of word meanings, the invention of new words, and the elimination of words that do not add to the desired effect.

Rhyme is the repetition of the same or similar sounds in two or more words. When rhyme occurs at the ends of lines in a poem it is called *end rhyme.* When rhyme occurs within a single line it is called *internal rhyme.* Again breaking with tradition, Hopkins used both types of rhyme, as well as *approximate rhyme,* or rhyme that relates words similar in function or meaning.

Writing

Write the name of a prized possession, much-loved pastime, or favorite season at the top of a sheet of paper. Write whatever words and phrases come to mind. Read over what you have written. Note phrases and words whose *sounds* seem to relate to your topic.

Primary Source

In his work among the poor, Hopkins no doubt encountered scenes such as this one described by a fellow worker:

> I attended a family of thirteen—twelve of whom had typhus fever, without a bed in the *cellar,* without straw or timber shavings—frequent substitutes. They lay on the floor, and so crowded that I could scarcely pass between them . . . there is only one supply of water for all its inhabitants and it occupies a good deal of time to procure it and carry it back to the different rooms, where it soon becomes covered with black scum . . . One woman informed me that her husband lay dead, and that she could not obtain water without the greatest difficulty to wash his "rags" . . . there were for that year . . . 1 death to 14.6 persons.

Guide for Interpreting 841

Literary Focus Inform students that, in a number of his poems, Hopkins added accent marks to show which syllables receive stress.

Writing/Prior Knowledge After students have completed the assignment, have them compare results. Students whose lists seem less creative should be encouraged to make another attempt.

Vocabulary

Preteach the following words:
barbarous (bär′ bər əs) *adj.*: Primitive; uncivilized (p. 845, l. 1)
azurous (azh′ ər əs) *adj.*: Purple-blue (p. 845, l. 9)
dappled (dap′ 'ld) *adj.*: Speckled; having more than one color (p. 846, l. 1)
fickle (fik′ 'l) *adj.*: Unfaithful (p. 846, l. 8)
blight (blīt) *n.*: Condition of withering (p. 847, l. 15)

God's Grandeur

Gerard Manley Hopkins

1   The world is charged with the grandeur of God.
    It will flame out, like shining from shook foil;[1]
    It gathers to a greatness, like the ooze of oil
2   Crushed.[2] Why do men then now not reck his rod?[3]
    Generations have trod, have trod, have trod;
    And all is seared with trade; bleared, smeared with toil;
    And wears man's smudge and shares man's smell: the
        soil
    Is bare now, nor can foot feel, being shod.

3   And for all this, nature is never spent;
10   There lives the dearest freshness deep down things;
    And though the last lights off the black West went
        Oh, morning, at the brown brink eastward, springs—
    Because the Holy Ghost over the bent
4   World broods with warm breast and with ah! bright
        wings.

---

1. **foil** *n.*: Tinsel.
2. **crushed:** Squeezed from olives.
3. **reck his rod:** Heed God's authority.

THINKING ABOUT THE SELECTION
1. According to this poem, with what is the world charged?
Recalling
2. (a) According to lines 5–8, what has humankind done to God's grandeur? (b) According to line 9, what difference has man's behavior made? Explain.
3. (a) What is the Holy Ghost compared to in the last two lines? (b) What verb describes what it does? (c) What two adjectives describe it?

Interpreting
4. What kind of emotional response do you suppose Hopkins hoped to awaken in the reader of lines 1–4? Do you think he succeeds?
5. What do you think is the meaning of the question raised in line 4?
6. (a) What effect do you think the poet hoped to achieve by the repetition in line 5? (b) By the alliteration, or consonant repetition, of *sm* in lines 6–7?

842   The Victorian Age

BIRD'S NEST
Ros. W. Jenkins
Warrington Museum and Art Gallery

7. "God's Grandeur" is a sonnet, a poetic form with very specific rhyme requirements. Note, for instance, the number of words rhyming with *God* and *foil* in the first eight lines.
(a) Why do you suppose Hopkins chose so rigid a poetic form for this poem? In what way does the form reinforce his message? (b) What effect do you think Hopkins wanted to achieve by the sounds of the words *ooze, oil,* and *crushed* in lines 3 and 4? By the repetition of *d* sounds in line 10? Of *b* sounds in the last two lines?

Applying

8. (a) Although Hopkins notes many abuses in this poem, do you think his overall outlook is optimistic or pessimistic? Explain. (b) How would you define the difference between an optimist and a pessimist?

God's Grandeur 843

6. (a) Suggested Response: The repetition almost carries the sense of the soil being trampled underfoot. (b) Suggested Response: Again, the repetition of the *sm* sounds carries the suggestion of smudging or smearing.

7. (a) Suggested Response: The form reflects the dignity of the poem's message. (b) Suggested Response: In each case the repetition of sound echoes the image being created.

Applying

8. (a) Answers will differ. Students will perhaps feel for the most part that the poem is optimistic. (b) Suggested Response: An optimist is a person who looks for the positive side of a situation, while a pessimist looks for the negative side.

Challenge Do you find the image of God implied in the first several lines of the poem inconsistent with that presented in the last two lines? Why or why not?

Fine art, *Harvest Field with Gleaners, Haywood, Herefordshire,* by George Robert Lewis. Lewis (1782–1871) was an English portrait, genre, and landscape painter. He studied at the School of the Royal Academy, in London. He made his living painting portraits and illustrating travel books with descriptive landscape aquatints (an etching process that produces prints that look like watercolor paintings).

Harvest Field With Gleaners, Haywood, Herefordshire (1815), was painted in an area of England where Lewis completed many works. He shows the earth yielding its bounty to sturdy English peasants. A versatile artist, Lewis demonstrates in this work his narrative skill and his enthusiasm for nature.

You may wish to use the following questions for discussion:

1. What do you think are the artist's feelings about the bounty of nature?
2. How do the artist's feelings compare to those of Hopkins about the bounty of nature?

THINKING ABOUT THE SELECTION

Recalling

1. (a) In line 4, what does the speaker see on the ground? (b) In the sky? (c) How are these two things alike for the speaker?
2. (a) What does the speaker do in line 5? (b) What does he see?
3. According to the last stanza, what happens to someone who beholds nature's beauties?

Interpreting

4. How would you describe the speaker's emotional state in the poem? Support your answer

Closure and Extension

ANSWERS TO THINKING ABOUT THE SELECTION
Recalling

1. (a) He sees stacks of drying corn on the ground. (b) He sees fluffy clouds in the sky. (c) Both hold exquisite beauty for him.
2. (a) He walks and lifts up his heart and eyes. (b) He takes in the beauty that God has provided.
3. It knocks such a person off his or her feet.

Interpreting

4. Students will use such terms as *happy, ecstatic, delighted, rapturous.* Students might cite, among other possibilities, the exclamation in line 2, his rhetorical questions in lines 3–4, and lines 7–8.
5. The question here, like that in lines 3–4, is a rhetorical one. One possible paraphrase students might offer is: What greeting by a loved one could be more exhilarating to the senses than this one?
6. (a) The reference is to the observer of nature's bounty. (b) Students might paraphrase what is happening with the well-known expression: The person is being "knocked off his feet."

Applying

7. (a) Students should recall that the

Hurrahing in Harvest

Gerard Manley Hopkins

Summer ends now; now, barbarous in beauty, the stoks[1]
   arise
     Around; up above, what wind-walks! what lovely
      behavior
     Of silk-sack clouds! has wilder, wilful-wavier
Meal-drift molded ever and melted across skies?

5   I walk, I lift up, I lift up heart, eyes,
     Down all that glory in the heavens to glean our Savior;
     And, éyes, héart, what looks, what lips yet gave you a
Rapturous love's greeting of realer, of rounder replies?

And the azurous hung hills are his world-wielding shoulder
10   Majestic—as a stallion stalwart, very-violet-sweet!—
These things, these things were here and but the beholder
     Wanting; which two when they once meet,
The heart rears wings bold and bolder
     And hurls for him, O half hurls earth for him off under
     his feet.

---

1. stoks *n.*: Sheaves of corn stacked together on end to dry.

HARVEST FIELD WITH GLEANERS, HAYWOOD, HEREFORDSHIRE
George Robert Lewis
The Tate Gallery, London

with quotations.
5. In your own words, what question does the speaker ask in lines 7–8?
6. (a) Who is "him" in line 14? (b) What does the speaker say is happening to "him?"

Applying

7. (a) In what ways is this poem more typical of the Romantic than the Victorian period? (b) In what ways is it typical of neither?

Hurrahing in Harvest **845**

Romantics extolled the virtues of nature, unlike the Victorians who often wrote of doom and gloom. (b) The poem is typical of neither in its use of invented words and a highly personalized syntax.

Challenge How many examples of alliteration can the students come up with?

Presentation

Motivation/Prior Knowledge Ask students what the term *harvest* conjures up in their minds? At what time of year does harvesting take place? Where does it take place? What is harvested? What colors does the word summon up? Finally ask them what kind of mood they would expect in a poem that conveys the poet's impressions of the harvest.

Thematic Idea Another selection that pays homage to the fall is "To Autumn" by John Keats, on page 729.

Purpose-Setting Question What is the speaker celebrating?

1 Critical Thinking and Reading The title, like many of the lines of the poem, contains alliteration.

2 Discussion Where is the speaker located?

3 Critical Thinking and Reading What do you think the speaker means by "wind-walks"? Why is this an especially effective image?

4 Clarification The question here is a rhetorical one: The speaker is not expecting a reply.

5 Discussion Why is the word *glean* particularly appropriate here?

6 Clarification The syntax of these lines may be confusing to the students. Explain that "and but the beholder/Wanting" means "all that was missing was someone to behold these things."

Pied Beauty

Gerard Manley Hopkins

Glory be to God for dappled things—
    For skies of couple-color as a brinded[1] cow;
      For rose-moles all in stipple[2] upon trout that swim;
Fresh-firecoal chestnut-falls;[3] finches' wings;
5   Landscape plotted and pieced—fold, fallow, and plow;
      And áll trádes, their gear and tackle and trim.

All things counter,[4] original, spare, strange;
    Whatever is fickle, freckled (who knows how?)
      With swift, slow; sweet, sour; adazzle, dim;
10 He fathers-forth whose beauty is past change:
      Praise him.

----

1. brinded *adj.*: Having a gray or tawny coat streaked with a darker color.
2. stipple *n.*: Dots or small spots.
3. fresh-firecoal chestnut-falls: Roasted chestnuts.
4. counter: Contrary.

THINKING ABOUT THE SELECTION
Recalling

1. What five "dappled things" does the speaker name in the first five lines?
2. What does the speaker ask the reader to do in line 11?

Interpreting

3. (a) What do you think is the meaning of "couple-color" in line 2? (b) Why do you think Hopkins chose this, rather than a more conventional way, of expressing the thought?
4. What difference can you see between the "dappled things" of the first stanza and the sorts of things hinted at in the second?
5. What significance do you attach to the words in parentheses in line 8?
6. What do you think is meant by the phrase "whose beauty is past change" in line 10?

Applying

7. Compare "Pied Beauty" with "God's Grandeur." (a) In what ways are the two poems similar? (b) How are they different in their outlook on the world as altered by humans? (c) How might Hopkins have explained this apparent paradox, or self-contradiction.

Spring and Fall
To a Young Child

Gerard Manley Hopkins

A MOTHER AND CHILD ON THE ISLE OF WIGHT
James Collinson
Yale Center for British Art

Márgarét, are you grieving
Over Goldengrove unleaving?
Leáves, like the things of man, you
With your fresh thoughts care for, can you?
5 Ah! ás the heart grows older
It will come to such sights colder
By and by, nor spare a sigh
Though worlds of wanwood[1] leafmeal[2] lie;
And yet you will weep and know why.
1 10 Now no matter, child, the name:
Sórrow's spríngs áre the same.
Nor mouth had, no nor mind, expressed
What heart heard of, ghost[3] guessed:
2 15 It ís the blight man was born for,
It is Margaret you mourn for.

---

1. wanwood (wän′ wo͝od): Pale wood.
2. leafmeal: Ground-up decomposed leaves.
3. ghost: Spirit.

THINKING ABOUT THE SELECTION

Recalling

1. According to the speaker, in what way will Margaret change as she grows older?

Interpreting

2. What do you think is meant by "fresh thoughts" in line 4? By "worlds of wanwood leafmeal" in line 8?
3. What is the theme?

Applying

4. (a) What is the relevance of the title "Spring and Fall?" (b) What might "spring" stand for?

(c) What second meaning of "fall" might be relevant to the speaker's advice to the child?

THINKING AND WRITING

Writing Margaret's Reply

Imagine that you are Margaret. Try to put yourself in the position of a child who has just suffered a grave disappointment over something an adult would find trivial. Now write a response to the adult speaker of "Spring and Fall" that gives the child's view of the world and defends the child's right to his or her feelings, however inappropriate they might seem to an adult. Your response may take the form of either a poem or prose piece, but it should offer some insight on how children view the world of grownups.

Spring and Fall: To a Young Child **847**

More About the Author Although most of the poems in *A Shropshire Lad,* A. E. Housman's best-known volume, center on rural life in the village of Shropshire, all of them were composed in the Highgate section of London, where Housman lived between 1886 and 1905. What does this fact reveal about the capabilities of the artistic mind?

Critical Evaluation In *A Short History of English Literature,* Ifor Evans says of Housman "All his verse was composed in short lyrics, delusively simple in vocabulary, with quick dramatic themes, as in a ballad, and often with a tragic emphasis. The verses are full of cunningly contrived memories of other poets and the vocabulary, when seemingly it is the plainest English, has Latin recollections. . . . He was a poet who, like Gray, might have been with the greatest had he chosen to stretch his talent more fully."

A. E. HOUSMAN

1859–1936

A leading classical scholar of his age, Alfred Edward Housman devoted his life to teaching and translating the great Latin poets. Yet, most modern readers who know Housman know him as the author of three slender volumes of poetry that are as romantic and melancholy as any ever written.

Housman was born in Worcestershire, the oldest of seven children in a middle-class family. His childhood came to an end when his mother died, following a long illness, on his twelfth birthday. Money became a problem for the family, but Housman, a bright and resourceful young man, won a scholarship to Oxford, where he studied classical literature and philosophy. Though he was a brilliant student, his intolerance of any error by himself or others left him with few friends.

While at Oxford, Housman fell secretly in love with a person who was interested only in his friendship. His despair over this relationship combined with his unhappy teen years seems to have darkened the rest of Housman's life and to have given his poetry its bitter undertones.

Upon leaving Oxford, Housman went to work in the Patent Office. Determined to prove himself in the classics, he studied Greek and Latin at night and wrote scholarly articles for academic journals. In 1892, his hard-earned reputation as an expert in his field led to his appointment as professor of Latin at University College in London.

Though Housman spent the balance of his life engaged in scholarly pursuits, he found time to write poetry. His first and most famous collection of verse, *A Shropshire Lad* (1896), has as its fictitious narrator a homesick farmboy living in the city. In simple, precise language and brisk, regular rhythms, Housman focuses on the grim realities and fleeting joys of life. Housman paid for the first publication of *A Shropshire Lad* out of his own pocket, but it soon became highly popular. More than twenty-five years later, *Last Poems* (1922) was an instant best seller. After Housman's death, his brother Laurence edited and published *More Poems* (1936).

In a famous lecture that he delivered in 1933, Housman, who worked at projecting a public image as an emotionless intellectual, stated that the goal of poetry is to "transfuse emotion," not to transmit thought. A well-written poem, he maintained, makes a physical impact on the reader, like a shiver down the spine or a punch in the stomach. It is because of this impact in much of his own work that the best of A. E. Housman's poems have been marked for immortality.

Objectives

1 To recognize the theme of a poem
2 To write a response to literary criticism

Support Material

Teaching Portfolio
Teacher Backup, p. 1017
Usage and Mechanics Worksheet, p. 1021
Vocabulary Check, p. 1022
Analyzing Literature Worksheet, *Finding the Theme,* p. 1023
Language Worksheet, *Understanding the Multiple Meanings of Words,* p. 1024
Selection Test, p. 1025

GUIDE FOR INTERPRETING

To an Athlete Dying Young; Loveliest of Trees; When I Was One-and-Twenty; With Rue My Heart Is Laden

Writer's Technique

Theme. The theme in a literary work is the insight into life that it communicates to the reader. One of several recurring themes in Housman's verse is the bittersweet notion that youth is beautiful but that, like beauty itself, it passes too quickly. Even in those upbeat instances where Housman is describing happiness and glory, the reader senses an undercurrent of doom and a concern with the courage and endurance that will be required to face it. The charming, easy rhymes in his poems contrast sharply with his melancholy themes, which reflect both the pessimism of the late Victorian Age and the sadness in his own life.

Commentary

Housman led a life of harsh self-discipline and solitary habits: By the age of twenty-seven, he had fully embraced the monk-like seclusion that would characterize the rest of his life. Although a thorough teacher, he was distant and humorless. Much respected for his keen intelligence and devotion to his duties, neither his students nor colleagues were comfortable with him, and he had few close friends. By the time he was in his mid-forties, A *Shropshire Lad* had become a best seller. But despite his fame and affluence, he still spent his evenings working on his studies or reading detective stories, especially those of Conan Doyle, which were then very popular. His scholarly excellence was rewarded in 1911 when he was made Kennedy Professor of Latin at Cambridge University and a Fellow at Trinity College. He soon established the same reputation in his new positions as he had in his old: meticulous with his work, sour and surly with people. His rooms at Trinity were as grim as the man: The only decoration was a large tortoise shell; there was not even a comfortable chair. He refused the many honors and awards he was offered, including the royal Order of Merit; he would be condescended to by no one, not even the king. How do you see the man in his work?

Writing

Reflect on a topic to which you have a strong response—both positive and negative. Possibilities might include the promise of the future mixed with its uncertainties, or bittersweet memories of a favorite afterschool gathering spot that no longer exists. Freewrite, attempting to capture—using vivid details—the happy and sad sides of your topic.

Guide for Interpreting 849

Presentation

Motivation/Prior Knowledge
Discuss the effects of aging on professional athletes. How does the public's attitude toward athletes change as the athletes grow older? What psychological effects might this change in attitude have on the athletes? How does the public respond to the early death of certain athletes?

Thematic Idea Another poem that presents the poet's response to death is "Do Not Go Gentle into That Good Night" by Dylan Thomas, on page 1102.

Purpose-Setting Question What is the speaker's attitude toward death?

1 **Discussion** How does the meaning of "home" in this stanza differ from that implied in the first stanza?

2 **Discussion** What is the tone of this stanza?

3 **Clarification** *Betimes* is an archaic word meaning "early."

4 **Discussion** Lintels are not ordinarily low. What else might the speaker have in mind?

5 **Clarification** This is an inverted sentence; its subject is "the strengthless dead."

To an Athlete Dying Young

A. E. Housman

The time you won your town the race
We chaired you through the marketplace;
Man and boy stood cheering by,
And home we brought you shoulder-high.

5 Today, the road all runners come,
Shoulder-high we bring you home,
And set you at your threshold down,
Townsman of a stiller town.

Smart lad, to slip betimes away
10 From fields where glory does not stay
And early though the laurel[1] grows
It withers quicker than the rose.

Eyes the shady night has shut
Cannot see the record cut,
15 And silence sounds no worse than cheers
After earth has stopped the ears:

Now you will not swell the rout
Of lads that wore their honors out,
Runners whom renown outran
20 And the name died before the man.

So set, before its echoes fade,
The fleet foot on the sill of shade.
And hold to the low lintel up
The still-defended challenge cup.

25 And round that early-laureled head
Will flock to gaze the strengthless dead,
And find unwithered on its curls
The garland briefer than a girl's.

---

1. laurel: A symbol of victory.

THINKING ABOUT THE SELECTION

Recalling

1. (a) In what sport did the athlete excel? (b) What did the townspeople do to show their admiration for the athlete following the contest mentioned in the first stanza?
2. (a) Where is the athlete "today"? (b) What does the speaker say the athlete will not have to be concerned about "now"?

Interpreting

3. (a) What visual image presented in the first stanza is repeated in the second stanza? (b) How is the meaning of the image different in the second stanza. (c) How does this difference affect the mood, or reader's emotional reaction?
4. (a) How would you summarize the speaker's comments in lines 9–20? (b) What is meant by "the name died before the man"?
5. (a) In what way is the challenge cup mentioned in line 24 "still-defended"? (b) What double meaning might the poet have intended for the word "still"?

Applying

6. Tell whether you agree or disagree with the speaker in this poem. Give reasons for your answer.
7. What advice would you give an athlete who is concerned about growing old and losing his or her "glory"?

ANALYZING LITERATURE

Finding the Theme

The **theme** in a poem is its insight into life. A poem's theme should not be confused with its subject, which can usually be described in a single word, such as "love" or "war." Rather, the theme reflects the author's thoughts on that subject—for instance, "love is blind," "love is a battlefield." Since poets seldom state the theme directly, the reader must *infer*, or figure out, the theme from the events and descriptions in the poem. One effective way of doing this is by constructing a series of meaningful questions that take into account the facts of the poem, as well as such features as its setting, tone, and mood. Answer the following questions on "To an Athlete Dying Young." Then state the poem's theme.

1. (a) Who is the "main character" in the poem? (b) What is the character's main accomplishment?
2. (a) What has happened to this character that is the occasion for this poem? (b) What details in the second stanza alert you to this happening? (c) What is the speaker's tone—that is, what seems to be his true feelings toward this happening?
3. (a) What does the speaker assume in lines 9–20 might have happened to the main character in later years? (b) On what evidence does the speaker most likely base this assumption?
4. (a) What generalization might be made about the relationship between accomplishment and praise? (b) To what other areas of life might this generalization apply?
5. What is the speaker's attitude toward life and death?
6. What is the theme of the poem?

To an Athlete Dying Young 851

ANSWERS TO THINKING ABOUT THE SELECTION

Recalling

1. (a) He was a runner. (b) They carried him home on their shoulders.
2. (a) He is being carried to his grave. (b) He will not have to be concerned about his glory fading.

Interpreting

3. (a) The repeated image is that of the athlete being carried shoulder-high. (b) In the second stanza he is being carried by pall-bearers. (c) Students should express a feeling of being taken aback the second time.
4. (a) A possible summary might be the following: The athlete is wise to die before his reputation is worn out or his glory is diminished by the excellence of successive generations. (b) It means that the athletes were forgotten before their deaths.
5. (a) It is still-defended in the sense that the athlete has died before anyone had a chance to beat his record. (b) Students might note the use of *still* in the second stanza to designate the realm of the dead. The cup here is in the possession of the dead athlete.

Applying

6. Answers will differ. Many students may feel that the speaker's attitude is too pessimistic.
7. Answers will differ. Students might suggest that such an athlete could look forward to new "victories" off the playing field, rather than dwell on old ones on it.

ANSWERS TO ANALYZING LITERATURE

1. (a) The main character is a runner. (b) He has won a race for his town.
2. (a) The runner has died. (b) He is being carried to his grave. (c) Suggested Response: The tone is melancholy yet resolved.
3. (a) He assumes that the athlete's record would have been broken and his glory would have faded. (b) This often happens to athletes as they grow older.
4. (a) Suggested Response: The speaker suggests that praise does not come without accomplishment. (b) Suggested Response: The generalization can be applied to nearly all areas of life.
5. Suggested Response: The speaker seems to accept death as a natural part of the cycle of life.
6. Suggested Response: Glory does not last.

852

Loveliest of Trees

A. E. Housman

Loveliest of trees, the cherry now
Is hung with bloom along the bough,
And stands about the woodland ride
Wearing white for Eastertide.

5 Now, of my threescore years and ten,
Twenty will not come again,
And take from seventy springs a score,
It only leaves me fifty more.

And since to look at things in bloom
10 Fifty springs are little room,
About the woodlands I will go
To see the cherry hung with snow.

852   *The Victorian Age*

THINKING ABOUT THE SELECTION

Recalling

1. (a) During what season of the year is the poem set? (b) How can you tell?
2. What is the speaker of the poem doing?
3. (a) How old is the speaker? (b) To what age does he expect to live?

Interpreting

4. What realization does the speaker come to in the second stanza?
5. In the third stanza the speaker makes a resolution for himself. Do you think this resolution has to do only with trees? Explain.

Applying

6. (a) What is the theme of the poem? (b) Judging from this theme, what would you guess is the speaker/poet's attitude toward an afterlife?

When I Was One-and-Twenty

A. E. Housman

When I was one-and-twenty
    I heard a wise man say,
"Give crowns and pounds and guineas[1]
    But not your heart away;
5 Give pearls away and rubies
    But keep your fancy free."
But I was one-and-twenty,
    No use to talk to me.

When I was one-and-twenty
10   I heard him say again,
"The heart out of the bosom
    Was never given in vain;
'Tis paid with sighs a plenty
    And sold for endless rue."
15 And I am two-and-twenty,
    And oh, 'tis true, 'tis true.

---

1. crowns . . . guineas: Denominations of money.

THINKING ABOUT THE SELECTION

Recalling

1. (a) What does the speaker say he "heard a wise man say" when he was "one-and-twenty?" (b) What, according to lines 7–8, was the speaker's reaction to this advice?
2. What is the speaker's comment in the last line on the wise man's second piece of advice?

Interpreting

3. With what is the speaker/poet equating the age of one-and-twenty in this poem? Explain your answer.
4. (a) What is significant about the fact that the speaker has twice received advice? (b) How is this relevant in light of the poem's theme?
5. What do you suppose happened to the speaker that changed his mind?

Applying

6. What event in Housman's life may have prompted the writing of this poem?

Closure and Extension

Motivation/Prior Knowledge
Ask whether there are any students in the class who have moved from one city to another. Who among them were saddened by the experience? What was the saddest part of leaving? How long did the sadness last? How did these feelings change over time?

Thematic Idea Another selection that deals with the realities facing the aging is Sonnet 73 by Shakespeare, page 257.

Purpose-Setting Question What is the cause of the speaker's sadness?

1 **Enrichment** Housman wrote that Shakespeare's songs were a major influence on his poetry. Indeed the adjective "golden" here in conjunction with the references to "maiden" and "lad" echoes Shakespeare's song "Fear No More the Heat o' the Sun," on page 264.

2 **Discussion** What do you think is the age of the speaker? Why?

Closure and Extension

With Rue My Heart Is Laden

A. E. Housman

With rue my heart is laden
    For golden friends I had,
For many a rose-lipped maiden
    And many a lightfoot lad.

5 By brooks too broad for leaping
    The lightfoot boys are laid;
The rose-lipped girls are sleeping
    In fields where roses fade.

THINKING ABOUT THE SELECTION
Recalling

1. What has happened to the speaker's friends?

Interpreting

2. What is meant by "golden" in line 2?
3. What do the adjectives "rose-lipped" and "lightfoot" suggest about the speaker's memories of his friends?
4. (a) What do you suppose is the meaning of the phrase "too broad for leaping" in line 5? (b) By the phrase "where roses fade" in line 8?
5. The subjects of this poem are youth and beauty. What statement is the poet making about those subjects?

Applying

6. In what ways do you think young people and adults view the passage of time differently?

THINKING AND WRITING

Responding to Criticism

William Archer, a critic and contemporary of Housman, wrote in a review of *A Shropshire Lad* that "there is nothing whining about Mr. Housman's melancholy" in his verse. "Rather," the critic continued, "it is bracing, invigorating . . ." In an essay, state whether you agree or disagree with this assessment. Quote freely from the poems to support your view and to defend against the opposing view. In either case, respond to Archer's criticism as, itself, a product of the Victorian Age. Ask yourself what difference there might have been in his statements had they not been made at a time when the public was up in arms about the writings of such pessimists as Thomas Hardy. When you revise, make sure you have provided adequate support for your opinions.

ANSWERS TO THINKING ABOUT THE SELECTION
Recalling

1. They have died.

Interpreting

2. The word means "valuable" or "precious."
3. Both adjectives suggest that the speaker has retained images of his friends from the days when they were young and vital.
4. (a) Students might make the connection between the image and the boundaries between life and death. The brooks are too broad in the sense that the speaker's friends can never jump back from the Great Beyond. (b) The same inference may be made with respect to this image.
5. He appears to be saying that both youth and beauty inexorably end.

Applying

6. Suggested Response: Young people tend to be less aware of the passage of time, because they are not yet concerned with their advancing age.

THINKING AND WRITING
For help with this assignment, students can refer to Lesson 15, "Evaluating a Literary Work," in the Handbook of Writing About Literature.

Publishing Student Writing
After students have completed the assignment, divide the class into teams based on their position with respect to the subject, and stage a debate. Allow each side time to prepare and consolidate their information.

854

Other Victorian Poets

TEMPERANTIA, 1872
Sir Edward Burne-Jones
Christie's, London

Other Victorian Poets 855

Humanities Note

Fine art, *Temperantia*, 1872, Sir Edward Burne-Jones. Sir Edward Burne-Jones (1833–98) was a student of Dante Gabriel Rossetti. Like other members of the Pre-Raphaelite Brotherhood, he tried in his paintings to counter what he saw as the ugliness and soullessness of life in an industrialized society. Burne-Jones's paintings are characterized by a soft, almost languid style. Drawing his subject matter from myth and literature, Burne-Jones captures the world of trance and dream. In no sense do his paintings depict the real world.

Elizabeth Barrett Browning (1806–1861)

One of the best-known woman poets of her own or any time, Elizabeth Barrett was the oldest of twelve children in an upper middle class family. She received no formal education, but a zest for knowledge enabled her to learn eight languages on her own.

Barrett began writing poetry as a child and, by the time she reached adulthood, had published four immensely popular volumes of verse. Though she met many of the leading writers of the day, a longtime illness made her something of a recluse.

Then, in 1845, she began to receive letters from the poet Robert Browning, who, after five months of correspondence, paid her a visit. Her doctors suggested that she spend the winter of 1846 in Italy, which offered a warmer climate. When her stern father refused to allow her to leave, she and Browning eloped there.

In 1849 their son was born, whom they nicknamed "Pen." A year later, Mrs. Browning revised and published *Sonnets from the Portuguese,* a sequence of 44 love poems written to her husband. *Aurora Leigh* (1857), a love story in blank verse, was completed during the second of two trips she made back to London.

Dante Gabriel Rossetti (1828–1882)

A successful painter as well as a poet, Dante Gabriel Rossetti was the son of an Italian patriot who had been exiled from his homeland. Growing up in a bilingual household under the watchful eye of parents who, themselves, were devoted to literature and the arts, Rossetti began writing plays and poetry at the age of five.

In 1837 he was sent to King's College School, but when money became a problem for the family, the young Rossetti was encouraged to pursue a more lucrative career as a painter. He was admitted to the Royal Academy, a prestigious art school, but could not adjust to a structured education and left after two years to study privately.

At twenty Rossetti founded the Pre-Raphaelite Brotherhood, a group of painters and writers who favored a return to the styles of artists who had lived before the time of the Italian Renaissance artist Raphael. In 1860 he married Elizabeth Siddal, a model who had posed for him. She became the subject of many of the poems in *The House of Life* (1870), a sequence of sonnets reflecting different aspects of love. When his wife died, he buried his poems with her, but later had them retrieved.

Rossetti's poems, like his paintings, are filled—sometimes to the point of crowding—with color and pictorial detail. The despair in his later poems anticipated the pessimism of many modern writers.

856   *The Victorian Age*

Objective

1 To recognize sonnet form

GUIDE FOR INTERPRETING

Sonnet 43; Silent Noon

Literary Forms

The Sonnet. A sonnet is a lyric poem that has fourteen lines and a fixed rhyme scheme. Of the two most common forms of sonnet, the Italian and English, the Italian is the older, dating back to the thirteenth century. The form, also known as the Petrarchan sonnet, reached its height in the hands of Francesco Petrarch (1304–1374), who wrote over three hundred sonnets to a woman named Laura. The Italian sonnet has two parts—the *octave,* consisting of eight lines, which asks a question or raises a problem; and the *sestet,* consisting of six lines, which answers the question or resolves the problem. Though the rhyme scheme of the sestet varies, the octave always has the rhyme scheme *abbaabba.*

Despite occasional lapses in its popularity, the sonnet has surfaced again and again throughout the ages as the poetic form of choice among poets. In the nineteenth century, Elizabeth Barrett Browning and Dante Gabriel Rossetti, writing independently, revived the *sonnet cycle,* a series of sonnets loosely connected by subject or theme. Both of these cycles treat, in their own fashion, the subject of love.

Writing

Write the word *love* at the top of a sheet of paper. Then write ten complete sentences that explore your thoughts and feelings on the subject. Avoid mentioning specific names of individuals. When you have finished writing, read over your work and decide which of your impressions might be unique to you and could, therefore, be expanded into a poem or series of personal reflections.

Primary Source

Although the numerous reviews for Elizabeth Barrett Browning's 1844 *Poems* were complimentary, perhaps she would have been most pleased, had she been aware of it, by the praise of two teenage brothers, Dante Gabriel and William Michael Rossetti. Michael later recalled that "the poems of Miss Elizabeth Barrett Browning first caught the attention of my brother and myself. We revelled in them with profuse delight. Our perceptions of poetry were not then of the totally uncritical order, and we found some things which we thought faulty, both in excess and in defect; but in the main our pleasure was unalloyed. 'The Drama of Exile,' 'The Rhyme of the Duchess May,' 'The Lost Bower,' 'Lady Geraldine's Courtship,' 'A Vision of Poets,' and numerous other pieces, held us spellbound. In the course of two or three years we must have read some of these more than half-a-hundred times over; and either of us . . . could repeat them with great exactness."

Guide for Interpreting 857

Literary Focus Challenge your **more advanced** students to try their hand at this time-honored poetic form. Have them share their efforts with the class.

Teaching on Ability Levels Prepare your **less advanced** students for an analysis of the sestet rhyme scheme by alerting them to three commonly used formulas: *cdcdcd, cdeecd,* and *cdecde.*

Writing/Prior Knowledge Remind students that love has its good side and its bad side. You might suggest, in fact, that they divide their paper into two sections—one for each "side" of the emotion—before they begin taking notes.

Master Teacher Note Tell students that the poem they are about to read was part of a cycle presented by the poet to her husband shortly after breakfast one morning in 1847. Add that the poems held a meaning for Mrs. Browning so deep and private that it was only after much persuasion that she agreed to let her husband publish them, and then only under the title *Sonnets from the Portuguese,* which suggests that the poems were not originals but translations.

Purpose-Setting Question How well does the rigid form of the sonnet fit the poet's intentions?

1 Clarification Provide students with more details about the poet's health, explaining that she was plagued throughout her life with pain from a spine injury she sustained when she was fifteen.

Sonnet 43

Elizabeth Barrett Browning

How do I love thee? Let me count the ways.
I love thee to the depth and breadth and height
My soul can reach, when feeling out of sight
For the ends of Being and ideal Grace.
5 I love thee to the level of every day's
Most quiet need, by sun and candlelight.
I love thee freely, as men strive for Right;
I love thee purely, as they turn from Praise.
I love thee with the passion put to use
10 In my old griefs, and with my childhood's faith.
I love thee with a love I seemed to lose
With my lost saints—I love thee with the breath,
Smiles, tears, of all my life!—and, if God choose,
I shall but love thee better after death.

THINKING ABOUT THE SELECTION

Recalling

1. (a) What question does the speaker ask? (b) How many answers to this question does she give?
2. What does the speaker say she will do "if God choose"?

Interpreting

3. (a) What do you think the speaker means in lines 9–10 by "with the passion put to use/In my old griefs"? (b) By "with a love I seemed to lose/With my lost saints" in lines 11–12?
4. What effect is created by the repetition of the words "I love thee" throughout the poem?

Applying

5. Consult the list of ten sentences you wrote for the Writing assignment on page 857. What thoughts and feelings of your own might you add to those expressed by Elizabeth Barrett Browning in this poem?

ANALYZING LITERATURE

Understanding a Sonnet

A **sonnet** is a fourteen-line lyric poem with a fixed pattern of rhyme. The Italian sonnet has two parts. The first part, the octave, poses a question or presents a problem in eight lines. The second part, the sestet, answers that question or problem in six lines.

1. What line in the octet (first eight lines) ends with an irregular rhyming word? How might this irregularity be explained?
2. What is the rhyme scheme of the sestet?
3. Based on what you have learned about the Italian sonnet, tell in what critical way Sonnet 43 violates the rules. How does this violation help the poem to deliver its message?

Closure and Extension

ANSWERS TO THINKING ABOUT THE SELECTION
Recalling

1. (a) She asks herself in what ways she loves her husband. (b) She gives a total of seven answers.
2. She says that she will love her husband better after death.

Interpreting

3. (a) If students accept that this is a reference to the poet's infirmity, they may note the amount of energy a handicapped person must put into the simple routines of daily life. (b) Perhaps this again harks back to the poet's infirmity; in other words, her illness may have com-

858

promised religious convictions that she held till that time.
4. Students might view this either as a means of separating items in a catalogue or as the speaker's desire to repeat her feelings again and again for impact.

Applying

5. Answers will differ. One possibility is: I love you with every fiber of my body and soul.

ANSWERS TO ANALYZING LITERATURE

1. Alert students will note that the word "Grace" (line 4) ends in a different sibilant sound from the words ending lines 1, 5, and 8. Perhaps at the time the poem was written the pronunciation of the word was slightly different from that we give it today.

2. The rhyme scheme is *cdcdcd.*
3. The poem does not follow the formal division into octet and sestet. That is, the question raised in the octet is also answered, in part, in the octet—specifically in lines 2–8. Students may infer from this violation that the poet was intentionally emphasizing the complexity of the answer to her question by allowing it to occupy most of the space of the poem.

Silent Noon

Dante Gabriel Rossetti

Your hands lie open in the long fresh grass—
    The finger-points look through like rosy blooms:
    Your eyes smile peace. The pasture gleams and glooms ⎤ **1**
'Neath billowing skies that scatter and amass.
5 All round our nest, far as the eye can pass,
    Are golden kingcup fields with silver edge
    Where the cow-parsley skirts the hawthorn hedge.
'Tis visible silence, still as the hourglass.

Deep in the sun-searched growths the dragonfly ⎤
10 Hangs like a blue thread loosened from the sky— ⎬ **2**
    So this winged hour is dropped to us from above. ⎦
Oh! clasp we to our hearts, for deathless dower,
This close-companioned inarticulate hour
    When twofold silence was the song of love.

"WEY" CHINTZ
William Morris
The Granger Collection

THINKING ABOUT THE SELECTION
Recalling

1. (a) Where are the speaker and his companion? (b) What time of day is it? (c) What time of year? (d) How can you tell?

Interpreting

2. (a) What do you think the speaker means when he says the "pasture gleams and glooms"? (b) How might this detail be related to his training as an artist?
3. Is it possible for silence to be "visible," as the speaker states in line 8? Explain.
4. How do you explain the paradox in the last line?

Applying

5. Under what circumstances does silence have an effect opposite to the one described? What details might the poet have used to "paint" an impression of that kind of silence?

Silent Noon 859

Presentation

Thematic Idea Another poem that explores deeply felt emotions is "When I Have Fears that I May Cease to Be" by John Keats, page 719.

Purpose-Setting Question What is the relationship between the speaker and the person to whom the poem is addressed?

1 Discussion Can eyes smile? Can a person smile a message?

2 Discussion What do you suppose the speaker means in stating that this hour is "dropped to us from above"?

Humanities Note

Fabric design, "Wey" Chintz, by William Morris. Morris (1834–1896) was an English painter, designer, craftsman and poet. In 1861, William Morris set up a firm that produced decorative crafts such as furniture, wallpaper, and fabric. Inspired by the Pre-Raphaelite ideals, he sought to revive the "lost" medieval spirit of design, simplicity, good materials, sound workmanship, and rich decoration.

    The fabrics such as the "Wey Chintz" (of printed cotton, velveteen, and woven silk) designed by William Morris exploited the natural beauty of the fiber as part of the creation of the design. He looked to nature for his patterns, combining plant form with a strong structure.

    Consider these questions for discussion:
1. What do both the fabric design and the poem glorify?
2. Can you accept this fabric as an art form? Explain.

Closure and Extension

ANSWERS TO THINKING ABOUT THE SELECTION
Recalling

1. (a) They are lying in the grass. (b) It is noontime. (c) It is either spring or summer. (d) Flowers and plants are in bloom.

Interpreting

2. (a) Students should recognize this is a poetic way of describing the effects of the sunshine on the pasture, as it passes behind and emerges again from clouds. (b) Suggested Response: Artists have a deep awareness of the importance of light.
3. Suggested Response: Yes, silence is sometimes so pronounced that we feel as if we could almost see it.

4. Suggested Response: The paradox rests within the reference to silence as a "song" of love. While a song is defined in part by the presence of sound, the song in this instance is sounded out not in words, but in the message contained within the lovers' eyes and hearts.

Applying

5. Students should have no difficulty imagining circumstances under which silence communicates anger or hurt. As to what details might suggest this kind of silence, possibilities include mute staring, a frigid climate, and dagger-like eyes.

Between the years of 1862 and 1864, **George Meredith** shared a house in London with two prominent poets of his generation, A. C. Swinburne and Dante Gabriel Rossetti. How might this living arrangement both have helped and hindered Meredith's poetic career?

Despite the serious tone and religious themes that characterize much of her work, **Christina Rossetti** was so amused by a parody of her poem "A Birthday" that she pasted it into her copy of her *Poems* (1875). What does this action reveal about her personality?

Rudyard Kipling's two children, for whom he wrote his first *Jungle Book,* both died when they were young. How might these tragic events have shaped Kipling's vision as a writer?

One of **Robert Louis Stevenson's** more popular and well-known works is *A Child's Garden of Verses,* published in 1885. Written in a simple style, the poems in this volume present the world through a child's imagination. What qualities must a writer possess in order to appeal to both adults and children?

BIOGRAPHIES

George Meredith (1828–1909)

Meredith was born in the coastal city of Portsmouth. When his first volume of verse, *Poems* (1851), failed to sell, he turned to fiction but, again, enjoyed little success. It was not until the publication of *The Egoist* in 1879 that Meredith received the public recognition he had been seeking. Though Meredith is known primarily as a novelist, he always thought of himself first and foremost as a poet. Indeed, his best poems evoke the power of nature and the joy of humanity's relationship to it.

Christina Rossetti (1830–1894)

The younger sister of the poet Dante Gabriel Rossetti, Christina Rossetti is considered by some critics to be the greatest woman poet in all of English literature. In 1871 Rossetti fell victim to a disease that disfigured her and left her an invalid. In spite of this, she continued to write, turning out in the space of her lifetime five collections of verse, a book of poems for children, a book of prayers, and a book of religious meditations. Her simple lyrical poems exhibit a grace and precision that are rare.

Rudyard Kipling (1865–1936)

Rudyard Kipling was equally skillful as a poet and writer of prose. Born in Bombay, India, to English parents, Kipling was placed, when he was five, in a foster home in England. Kipling returned to India in 1882 to work as a journalist. During the next seven years, he published a number of witty poems and stories, and by the time he visited London in 1890, he was a celebrity. Kipling wrote several books that have since become children's classics: *The Jungle Books* (1895), *Captains Courageous* (1897), and *Kim* (1905).

Robert Louis Stevenson (1850–1894)

Robert Louis Stevenson was born in Edinburgh, Scotland. An essayist, poet, dramatist, and novelist, he is perhaps best remembered for such thrilling tales of suspense and adventure as *The Strange Case of Dr. Jekyll and Mr. Hyde, The Master of Ballantrae, Kidnapped,* and *Treasure Island.* Traveling constantly for his health, Stevenson died in Samoa, where he was buried "under the wide and starry sky."

Objectives

1 To understand how imagery is used in poetry
2 To write about a poem's historical context

Support Material

Teaching Portfolio
Teacher Backup, p. 1037
Grammar in Action Worksheet, *Appreciating Allusion,* p. 1044
Usage and Mechanics Worksheet, p. 1046
Vocabulary Check, p. 1047
Analyzing Literature Worksheet, *Understanding Imagery,* p. 1049

Language Worksheet, *Understanding Connotation and Denotation,* p. 1050
Selection Test, p. 1051

GUIDE FOR INTERPRETING

Lucifer in Starlight; A Birthday; Recessional; Requiem

Writer's Technique

Imagery. Imagery is language, often in the form of poetic details, that appeals to one or more of the five senses. Poets use imagery to communicate experience vividly, to make you see, feel, hear, smell, and taste the ideas they present to you in words. Since imagery is often visual, images are often thought of as "word pictures." The Pre-Raphaelite poets included images in their poems that would ordinarily go unnoticed, such as shadows on a wall or the scraping sound of chairs pushed across a floor. The poems of George Meredith and Christina Rossetti show influences of the Pre-Rapaelite movement. The sense-related details and elaborate word pictures in their verse provide a sharp contrast to the more stately images of Kipling's "Recessional."

Commentary

The Victorian tendency toward self-congratulation was especially evident at the Great Exhibition of 1851, the first international pubic display of commercial products. The Exhibition was hugely successful: Queen Victoria, for example, visited it forty-four times that summer. Addressing a dinner at the Exhibition, Albert, the Prince Consort, voiced the nation's optimism when he said:

> Nobody who has paid any attention to the peculiar features of our present era will doubt for a moment that we are living at a period of the most wonderful transition which tends rapidly to accomplish that Great End, to which, indeed, all history points—the realization of the unity of mankind . . .
>
> The distances which separated the different nations and parts of the globe are rapidly vanishing before the achievements of modern invention . . . thought is communicated with the rapidity, and even by the power of lightning. On the other hand, the great principle of the division of labor—which may be called the moving power of civilization, is being extended to all branches of science, industry and art.

How might the tone and content of Albert's speech move Kipling to write a poem such as "Recessional"?

Writing

Try to recall an experience you had that created vivid sense impressions, such as weathering a violent storm, or attempting to sleep on a blisteringly hot night without the aid of a fan or air conditioner. Freewrite about your experience.

Guide for Interpreting 861

Literary Focus Reinforce the notion of imagery by creating—and then having your students create—images related to several objects in the classroom.

Writing/Prior Knowledge Have students share their freewriting with the other members of the class.

Vocabulary

Preteach the following words:

dominion (də min′ yən) *n.*: Place of rule; home territory (p. 862, l. 2)

specter (spek′ tər) *n.*: Ghost or ghost-like appearance (p. 862, l. 4)

careened (kə rēnd) *v.*: Leaned to one side (p. 862, l. 7)

halcyon (hal′ sē ən) *adj.*: Calm (p. 863, l. 6)

dais (dā′ is) *n.*: Throne (p. 863, l. 9)

vair (ver) *n.*: Gray and white fur (p. 863, l. 10)

contrite (kən trīt′) *adj.*: Willing to repent or atone (p. 864, l. 10)

requiem (rek′ wē əm) *n.*: A dirge or mass for the dead (p. 876, title)

Motivation/Prior Knowledge
Ask students to name and describe their favorite terrifying creatures from film and fiction. Through a discussion, elicit what traits are common to these fantastic creations. If students were going to fashion a fiend of their own creation, what additional features would they incorporate to enhance its fright appeal?

Thematic Idea Another selection that deals with the fall of Satan is the excerpt from *Paradise Lost* by John Milton, page 449.

Purpose-Setting Question What does Satan encounter upon his rise?

1 Clarification The name *Lucifer* means "light-bearer."

2 Discussion What do these lines suggest about the size of the creature?

3 Discussion What do you suppose to be the meaning of "Awe"?

Closure and Extension

ANSWERS TO THINKING ABOUT THE SELECTION
Recalling

1. (a) He was tired of his dark dominion. (b) He rises up above the world.
2. (a) He looks at the stars that are the "brain of heaven." (b) He sinks once again.

Interpreting

3. It signifies earth.
4. Students might note that he has wings and that he is large enough to cast a shadow over much of a continent.
5. His scars were probably caused by his struggling against his descent from Paradise.
6. (a) The army is made up of the forces that represent the side of righteousness. (b) The inherent goodness of mankind is unalterable.

862

Lucifer in Starlight
George Meredith

On a starred night Prince Lucifer uprose.
Tired of his dark dominion swung the fiend
Above the rolling ball in cloud part screened,
Where sinners hugged their specter of repose.
5 Poor prey to his hot fit of pride were those.
And now upon his western wing he leaned,
Now his huge bulk o'er Afric's sands careened,
Now the black planet shadowed Arctic snows.
Soaring through wider zones that pricked his scars
10 With memory of the old revolt from Awe,
He reached a middle height, and at the stars,
Which are the brain of heaven, he looked, and sank.
Around the ancient track marched, rank on rank,
The army of unalterable law.

THINKING ABOUT THE SELECTIONS
Recalling

1. (a) Why does Prince Lucifer rise up? (b) Where does he go?
2. (a) What does he look at when he reaches "the middle height?" (b) What is his reaction to what he sees?

Interpreting

3. What do you understand "the rolling ball in cloud part screened" in line 3 to signify?
4. What are you able to gather about the appearance of "the fiend" from lines 6–9?
5. What do you think has caused Lucifer's scars, mentioned in line 9?
6. (a) Who or what makes up "the army of unalterable law"? (b) What situation is unalterable?
7. "Lucifer in Starlight" is a sonnet. (a) What question or problem is raised in the octet? (b) What answer or resolution is provided in the sestet?

8. In Milton's *Paradise Lost,* Satan (also known as Lucifer) is an angel who has fallen from grace and has, thus, been cast out of Heaven. How might this allusion explain Lucifer's feelings and "mission" in "Lucifer in Starlight?" What might be the meaning of "old revolt from Awe" in line 10?
9. In classical mythology, Lucifer (which means "lightbearer") was the morning star —that is, the planet Venus at dawn. The rising of Prince Lucifer, thus, also refers to the appearance of Venus on the horizon. How does knowing this enhance your appreciation of the poem?

Applying

10. Meredith may have come upon the idea for this poem while gazing up at a nighttime sky. What thoughts come to you when you gaze up at the stars? What themes might the vastness of the sky suggest?

862   *The Victorian Age*

7. (a) The problem raised in the octet is that of Lucifer attempting to reassert his supremacy. (b) The response in the sestet is that the forces of good will rally to forestall such a rise.
8. Suggested Response: The allusion makes it clear that Lucifer is seeking revenge. The "old revolt from Awe" refers to the actions that caused him to be cast out of heaven.
9. Answers will differ. Students may comment that this knowledge creates another possible interpretation of the poem.

Applying

10. Answers will differ. Some students may observe that the vastness of the sky suggests to them the infiniteness of the universe and of God's work—the very idea perhaps that came to Meredith's mind.

A Birthday

Christina Rossetti

My heart is like a singing bird
    Whose nest is in a watered shoot:
My heart is like an apple tree
    Whose boughs are bent with thickset fruit;
5 My heart is like a rainbow shell
    That paddles in a halcyon sea;
My heart is gladder than all these
    Because my love is come to me.

    Raise me a dais of silk and down;
10   Hang it with vair[1] and purple dyes;
Carve it in doves and pomegranates,
    And peacocks with a hundred eyes;
Work it in gold and silver grapes,
    In leaves and silver fleurs-de-lys;[2]
15 Because the birthday of my life
    Is come, my love is come to me.

---

1. vair *n.*: Squirrel fur.
2. fleurs-de-lys (flŭr′ də lēz′) *n*: Emblems resembling lilies or irises.

THINKING ABOUT THE SELECTION

Recalling

1. (a) To what three things does the speaker compare her heart in the first stanza? (b) Why does she feel as she does?
2. (a) What does the speaker ask for in the second stanza? (b) What does she say has come?

Interpreting

3. (a) What feeling does the poem convey? (b) Find three images that contribute to that feeling.

4. The poet makes abundant use of repetition, especially in the first stanza. How does this affect the mood of the poem?
5. What possible meanings might you attach to the phrase "the birthday of my life"?

Applying

6. The second stanza of "A Birthday" has been called a "fully Pre-Raphaelite word-picture." Using what you have learned about the Pre-Raphaelite movement along with evidence from the poem explain why you think this is so.

A Birthday 863

Motivation/Prior Knowledge
Ask students what they know of
the famous pleasure ship, the
Titanic. Ask what other phenomena they can think of that were
thought to be indestructible but
proved such thinking to be flawed. What do these phenomena
reveal about earthly ambition?

Thematic Idea Another poem
that deals with the vanity of a
fallen empire is "Love Among the
Ruins" by Robert Browning,
page 818.

Purpose-Setting Question What
is the speaker instructing his audience to remember?

1 **Clarification** As it is used here,
the word *awful* means "inspiring
awe."

2 **Reading Strategy** The phrase
"lest we forget" is repeated not
only within the line, but at the end
of the first two stanzas. Look
ahead to determine if it is repeated throughout. What effect does
repetition of this the phrase create?

Recessional[1]

Rudyard Kipling

*In 1897 a national celebration called the "Diamond
Jubilee" was held in honor of the sixtieth anniversary of
Queen Victoria's reign. The occasion prompted a great deal
of boasting about the strength and greatness of the empire.
Kipling responded to the celebration by writing this poem,
reminding the people of England that the British empire
might not last forever.*

God of our fathers, known of old—
    Lord of our far-flung battle-line—
Beneath whose awful Hand we hold
    Dominion over palm and pine—
5 Lord God of Hosts, be with us yet
Lest we forget—lest we forget!

The tumult and the shouting dies—
    The Captains and the Kings depart—
Still stands Thine ancient Sacrifice,
10   An humble and a contrite heart.[2]
Lord God of Hosts, be with us yet,
Lest we forget—lest we forget!

Far-called, our navies melt away—
    On dune and headland sinks the fire[3]—
15 Lo, all our pomp of yesterday
    Is one with Nineveh[4] and Tyre![5]
Judge of the Nations, spare us yet,
Lest we forget—lest we forget!

---

1. recessional *n.*: A hymn sung at the end of a religious service.
2. An . . . heart: An allusion to the Bible (Psalms 51:17): "The
sacrifices of God are a broken spirit: a broken and contrite heart, O
God, thou wilt not despise."
3. On . . . fire: Bonfires were lit on high ground all over Britain as
part of the opening ceremonies of the Jubilee celebration.
4. Nineveh (nin' ə və): The ancient capital of the Assyrian Empire,
the ruins of which were discovered buried in desert sands in the
1850's.
5. Tyre (tīr): Once a great port and the center of ancient Phoenician
culture, now a small town in Lebanon.

Grammar in Action

An **allusion** is a reference to a well-known person, place, event,
literary work, or work of art. Essayists, novelists, poets, and
speechmakers use allusions. In his "I Have a Dream" speech, for
example, Martin Luther King, Jr. alluded to the Bible: "I have a
dream that one day every valley shall be exalted, every hill and
mountain shall be made low. . . ." This reference to the writings
of the prophet Isaiah (40:4 and 5) gave King's words added
authority and suggested that he, too, was a prophet.

In "Recessional" Rudyard Kipling alludes to the ancient cities of Nineveh and Tyre:
    Lo, all our pomp of yesterday
      Is one with Nineveh and Tyre!
No longer glorious, these ancient cities were once the capitals of
mighty empires. Kipling's allusion, therefore, reminds Britons that
their own empire may decline as all previous empires have. The
mere mention of the names *Nineveh* and *Tyre* vividly conveys the
idea of faded glory.

If, drunk with sight of power, we loose
    Wild tongues that have not Thee in awe—
20 Such boasting as the Gentiles use
    Or lesser breeds without the Law[6]—
Lord God of Hosts, be with us yet,
Lest we forget—lest we forget!

25 For heathen heart that puts her trust
    In reeking tube[7] and iron shard[8]—
All valiant dust that builds on dust,
    And guarding calls not Thee to guard—
For frantic boast and foolish word,
30 Thy mercy on Thy People, Lord!

6. Such boasting . . . Law: An allusion to the Bible (Romans 2:14): "For when the Gentiles, which have not the law, do by nature things contained in the law, these, having not the law, are a law unto themselves."
7. tube: The barrel of a gun.
8. shard: Fragment of a bombshell.

THINKING ABOUT THE SELECTION

Recalling

1. (a) To whom is this poem addressed? (b) To whom is Kipling really speaking?
2. What does the speaker suggest, in lines 15–16, happens to "our pomp of yesterday?"
3. What does the speaker beg in the last line?

Interpreting

4. What qualities and actions does the poem condemn? Support your answer.
5. What is the poem's theme?

Applying

6. What differences do you detect in the images used by Kipling in "Recessional" and those used by George Meredith in "Lucifer in Starlight"? Which poet's imagery do you find more effective? Explain.

THINKING AND WRITING

Writing About Historical Context

Kipling's "Recessional" may be seen as a rejection of some of the values of the England in which he lived. Supplement what you have learned about Victorian England by consulting an encyclopedia or other historical reference. Note, in addition to the economic, political, and religious climates of the period, specific events that may have shaped the thoughts of the citizenry. Weigh all possible influences on Kipling at the time during which he composed this poem in 1897 and discard those that are irrelevant. Then write an explanatory paper in which you identify "Recessional" as a product of its period. Refer to specific lines of the poem to strengthen your thesis. When you revise, make sure your essay is organized in a logical order.

Motivation for Reading Have students discuss the purpose of epitaphs. What should an epitaph convey about a deceased individual?

Purpose-Setting Question How does the speaker wish to be remembered?

Closure and Extension

ANSWERS TO THINKING ABOUT THE SELECTION
Recalling

1. The speaker wishes to be buried "under the wide and starry sky."
2. The speaker approaches his death "gladly" and "with a will."

Interpreting

3. Suggested Response: The speaker's epitaph is appropriate because he has lived his life fully and happily and sees death and the grave as coming home to rest after his full and happy life.

Applying

4. Answers will differ. Suggested Response: People like to write their own epitaphs because they want others who come after them to know how they perceived their lives or perceived life in general.
5. Answers will differ. Students should highlight their most important qualities.

Requiem
Robert Louis Stevenson

Under the wide and starry sky
Dig the grave and let me lie.
Glad did I live and gladly die.
    And I laid me down with a will.

5 This be the verse you grave for me:
Here he lies where he longed to be;
Home is the sailor, home from sea,
    And the hunter home from the hill.

THINKING ABOUT THE SELECTION
Recalling

1. Where does the speaker wish to be buried?
2. How does the speaker approach his death?

Interpreting

3. Explain why the speaker's epitaph is appropriate.

Applying

4. Explain why you think people like to write their own epitaphs.
5. What epitaph would you create for yourself? Explain the reason for your choice.

Prose

A SUMMER DAY IN HYDE PARK
John Ritchie
Museum of London

Humanities Note

Fine Art, *A Summer Day in Hyde Park*, John Ritchie. John Ritchie was a genre painter who worked in London from 1858–1875. *A Summer Day in Hyde Park* is his best known painting. In it he shows a scene of leisure time in Victorian life.

More About the Author From his earliest years, when he went to work in a factory and took to wandering the streets of London, Charles Dickens absorbed not only the sights and sounds of urban life but also its bleak and oppressive spirit. He knew early-modern industrial civilization at first hand, and when he matured into a writer of fiction he expressed his poetic and prophetic sense of urban and industrial life with a degree of depth and insight few writers have ever equaled. Hence, though his dates of birth and death place him squarely in the Victorian age, as an artist he seems almost contemporary.

Critical Evaluation In an introduction to *Charles Dickens: Twentieth Century Views,* Wendell Stacy Johnson summarizes Dickens's work thus: "Dickens is the essential novelist, . . . ; he is himself a mixture, writing in a mixed form. He is both a reporter and a playwright of sorts. A journalist at the end of his career as at its beginning, he was always something of a dramatist (or maker of melodramas) and something of a player or speaker (a ham, a rhetorician)—with a need to communicate vocally. In stories he records the oddities along with the plain, hard facts of his times, and he reflects them to give these facts a mythic form, thus dramatizing himself as the teller, teacher, and the tale itself."

CHARLES DICKENS

(1812–1870)

No other writer since Shakespeare has occupied a more important place in popular culture than Charles Dickens. From his own time on, his works, with their unforgettable characters, have held special appeal for both scholars and the reading public at large, and have been transformed time and again into plays and films.

Dickens was born in Portsmouth on England's southern coast. Except for a few happy years at Chatham, east of London, his childhood was darkened by his father's wavering economic status. After years of eluding creditors, his father was finally sent to debtor's prison. Dickens in the meantime was sent to a "prison" of his own—to a factory where he worked long hours pasting labels. These experiences and other ills of the newly industrialized society figure prominently in his novels.

After becoming a law clerk at the age of fifteen, Dickens taught himself shorthand and became a court reporter. At twenty-one he began applying his keen powers of observation to humorous literary sketches of everyday life in London while reporting on the Parliamentary debates. A collection of these, *Sketches by Boz* (1835–36), earned him a small following, which he built up considerably with his first novel *The Pickwick Papers,* published in 1837.

Next came such favorites as *Oliver Twist* (1837), *Nicholas Nickleby* (1839), and, after a trip to America where his fame had already spread, *A Christmas Carol* (1843). In these early novels, which paint a sweeping satiric picture of Victorian England, Dickens displayed both a passion for social reform and a unique ability to combine humor with horror—themes and techniques that became the hallmark of all his fiction. He also developed his lifelong practice of writing for serial publications. Paid by the word, he wove elaborate plots with vast numbers of characters.

A turn toward more serious planning and characterization of greater psychological depth are evident in *Dombey and Son* (1848) and *David Copperfield* (1850), which also contain social criticism that is more direct and less optimistic. In the later novels Dickens blended these elements together most successfully, and the results were his masterpieces: *Bleak House* (1853), *Hard Times* (1854), and *Great Expectations* (1861). "The Signalman" was published in 1866 in a collection including several other railway stories.

Dickens never gave up journalism as a second outlet for his social conscience. In later life, the work load imposed by his many writing responsibilities coupled with his exhausting public reading tours took its toll on his health. In 1870, while at work on a novel, *The Mystery of Edwin Drood,* he died of a stroke.

Objectives

1 To appreciate plot in a ghost story
2 To be able to distinguish between realistic and supernatural detail
3 To select the correct meaning of a word for its context

Support Material

Teaching Portfolio
Teacher Backup, p. 1053
Grammar in Action Worksheet, *Using Single Quotation Marks,* p. 1057
Usage and Mechanics Worksheet, p. 1059
Vocabulary Check, p. 1060
Analyzing Literature Worksheet, *Understanding Plot: Foreshadowing,* p. 1061

Critical Thinking and Reading Worksheet, *Separating Realistic from Fantastic Details,* p. 1062
Selection Test, p. 1063
Art Transparency 12, *Going to Business,* by James Joseph Tissot

GUIDE FOR INTERPRETING

The Signalman

Plot in a Ghost Story. Plot is the ordered arrangement of happenings that make up a story or novel. Plot can be structured in a straight *chronological* progression, from the earliest event in time to the latest, or it can jump backwards and forward in time. In either case, plot generally builds on some *conflict,* or struggle between characters or forces, until it reaches a *climax,* or height of tension. The portion of the story from this point to the end, during which all remaining problems are solved, is called the *resolution*.

In a ghost story, the plot is built around *supernatural* elements —events beyond the normal order of things. The conflict is often between these supernatural forces and the human beings whose world they have invaded. At times, however, the conflict takes the form of a difference of opinion between two characters as to the explanation of certain mysterious events. In "The Signalman," for example, the first-person narrator attempts to explain away in rational terms the "ghost" that is plaguing a railroad employee.

Prepare the groundwork for an original ghost story. Consider the story's setting and characters by asking yourself questions such as the following: Is the story to take place in the here and now? What form will the "ghost" take? Who will be the person haunted by the ghost, and what will be the ghost's purpose? Jot down your answers to these and related questions.

Ghost stories are a special—and particularly enjoyable—type of fantastic literature. Alberto Manguel describes fantastic literature in the following manner:

> . . . fantastic literature deals with what can be best defined as the impossible seeping into the possible, what Wallace Stevens calls "black water breaking into reality." Fantastic literature never really explains everything. Like the ghost train at the fair, it takes us through the darkness of a real world, from terror to laughable terror, diving into walls that swing away at the very last minute, racing under eerie nothings that touch us with cobweb fingers, suddenly slowing down and lengthening that last encounter (with what? with what?), using our expectancy of horror more effectively than horror itself.

Literary Focus Dickens is considered to be a great portrayer of character as well as a masterly maker of plots. This short story highlights his psychological acumen as well. You might mention that in some of the best ghost stories, such as *The Turn of the Screw*, by Henry James, the psychological and the supernatural are often closely connected.

Writing/Prior Knowledge You might have your students discuss or speculate about how a psychological condition might lead to a person's seeing a ghost or some other supernatural phenomenon.

Vocabulary

Preteach the following words:

foreshortened (fôr shôr′ t'nd) *adj.*: Narrowed by observer's angle of vision (p. 870)

precipitate (pri sip′ ə tit) *adj.*: Steep (p. 870)

saturnine (sat′ ər nīn) *adj.*: Sluggish or gloomy (p. 871)

gesticulate (jes tik′ yə lāt′) *v.*: Communicate excitedly by gestures (p. 874)

ruminate (roo′ mə nāt′) *v.*: Think over; meditate (p. 876)

subordinate (sə bô′ də nit) *adj.*: Beneath another in rank (p. 876)

The Signalman

Charles Dickens

1 "Halloa! Below there!"

When he heard a voice thus calling to him, he was standing at the door of his box, with a flag in his hand, furled round its short pole. One would have thought, considering the nature of the ground, that he could not have doubted from what quarter the voice came; but instead of looking up to where I stood on the top of the steep cutting nearly over his head, he turned himself about, and looked down the Line. There was something remarkable in his manner of doing so, though I could not have said for my life what. But I know it was remarkable enough to attract my notice, even though his figure was foreshortened and shadowed, down in the deep trench, and mine was high above him, so steeped in the glow of an angry sunset, that I had shaded my eyes with my hand before I saw him at all.

"Halloa! Below!"

2 From looking down the Line, he turned himself about again, and, raising his eyes, saw my figure high above him.

"Is there any path by which I can come down and speak to you?"

He looked up at me without replying, and I looked down at him without pressing him too soon with a repetition of my idle question. Just then there came a vague vibration in the earth and air, quickly changing into a violent pulsation, and an oncoming rush that caused me to start back, as though it had force to draw me down. When such vapor as rose to my height from this rapid train had passed me and was skimming away over the landscape, I looked down again, and saw him refurling the flag he had shown while the train went by.

I repeated my inquiry. After a pause, during which he seemed to regard me with fixed attention, he motioned with his rolled-up flag towards a point on my level, some two or three hundred yards distant. I called down to him, "All right!" and made for that point. There, by dint of looking closely about me, I found a rough zigzag descending path notched out, which I followed.

3 The cutting was extremely deep, and unusually precipitate. It was made through a clammy stone, that became oozier and wetter as I went down. For these reasons, I found the way long enough to give me time to recall a singular air of reluctance or compulsion with which he had pointed out the path.

When I came down low enough upon the zigzag descent to see him again, I saw that he was standing between the rails on the way by which the train had lately passed, in an attitude as if he were waiting for me to appear. He had his left hand at his chin, and that left elbow rested on his right hand, crossed over his breast. His attitude was one of such expectation and watchfulness, that I stopped a moment, wondering at it.

4 I resumed my downward way, and stepping out upon the level of the railroad, and drawing nearer to him, saw that he was a dark sallow man, with a dark beard and rather heavy eyebrows. His post was in as solitary and dismal a place as ever I saw. On either side, a dripping-wet wall of jagged stone, excluding all view but a strip of sky; the perspective one way only a crooked prolongation of this great dungeon; the shorter perspective in the other direction terminating in a gloomy red light, and the gloomier

entrance to a black tunnel, in whose massive architecture there was a barbarous, depressing, and forbidding air. So little sunlight ever found its way to this spot, that it had an earthy, deadly smell; and so much cold wind rushed through it, that it struck chill to me, as if I had left the natural world.

Before he stirred, I was near enough to him to have touched him. Not even then removing his eyes from mine, he stepped back one step, and lifted his hand.

This was a lonesome post to occupy (I said), and it had riveted my attention when I looked down from up yonder. A visitor was a rarity, I should suppose; not an unwelcome rarity, I hoped? In me, he merely saw a man who had been shut up within narrow limits all his life, and who, being at last set free, had a newly awakened interest in these great works. To such purpose I spoke to him; but I am far from sure of the terms I used; for, besides that I am not happy in opening any conversation, there was something in the man that daunted me.

He directed a most curious look towards the red light near the tunnel's mouth, and looked all about it, as if something were missing from it, and then looked at me.

That light was part of his charge? Was it not?

He answered in a low voice, "Don't you know it is?"

The monstrous thought came into my mind, as I perused the fixed eyes and the saturnine face, that this was a spirit, not a man. I have speculated since, whether there may have been infection in his mind.

In my turn, I stepped back. But in making the action, I detected in his eyes some latent fear of me. This put the monstrous thought to flight.

"You look at me," I said, forcing a smile, "as if you had a dread of me."

"I was doubtful," he returned, "whether I had seen you before."

"Where?"

He pointed to the red light he had looked at.

"There?" I said.

Intently watchful of me, he replied (but without sound), "Yes."

"My good fellow, what should I do there? However, be that as it may, I never was there, you may swear."

"I think I may," he rejoined. "Yes, I am sure I may."

His manner cleared, like my own. He replied to my remarks with readiness, and in well-chosen words. Had he much to do there? Yes; that was to say, he had enough responsibility to bear; but exactness and watchfulness were what was required of him, and of actual work—manual labor—he had next to none. To change that signal, to trim those lights, and to turn this iron handle now and then, was all he had to do under that head. Regarding those many long and lonely hours of which I seemed to make so much, he could only say that the routine of his life had shaped itself into that form, and he had grown used to it. He had taught himself a language down here—if only to know it by sight, and to have formed his own crude ideas of its pronunciation, could be called learning it. He had also worked at fractions and decimals, and tried a little algebra; but he was, and had been as a boy, a poor hand at figures. Was it necessary for him when on duty always to remain in that channel of damp air, and could he never rise into the sunshine from between those high stone walls? Why, that depended upon times and circumstances. Under some conditions there would be less upon the Line than under others, and the same held good as to certain hours of the day and night. In bright weather, he did choose occasions for getting a little above these lower shadows; but, being at all times liable to be called by his electric bell, and at such times listening for it with redoubled anxiety, the relief was less than I would suppose.

He took me into his box, where there was a fire, a desk for an official book in which he had to make certain entries, a telegraphic instrument with its dial, face, and needles, and the little bell of which he had spoken. On my trusting that he would excuse the

The Signalman 871

5 **Discussion** What explanation does the narrator give for his interest in the tunnel and the signalman?

Fine art, *Two Tunnels,* 1975, by Guy Worsdell. The British wood engraver and painter Guy Worsdell was born in 1908. He studied at the Central School of Art and Design and with the wood engraver John Beedham. Worsdell is well known for his wood engraving prints. He did much to promote the creative aspects of the technique.

Wood engraving involves incising designs into a block of wood. This block is then inked and pressed onto paper, leaving a black and white image. It is an exacting art that requires strength and precision. The engraving *Two Tunnels* shows the degree of refinement in this technique attained by Guy Worsdell. In this sharp black-and-white image of a train, he has captured a sense of movement through his composition. The rich details of the landscape and train display a wide variety of textures and shading. Masterly wood engravings such as this helped to establish the technique as a fine art form.

You might use these questions for discussion:

1. Do you find the absence of color in this black and white image a benefit to this illustration? Explain.
2. What mood does this engraving evoke? Is it appropriate to "The Signalman"? Explain.
3. Does this sharp, direct image compare favorably with the language of the story?

TWO TUNNELS, 1975
Guy Worsdell

remark that he had been well educated, and (I hoped I might say without offense) perhaps educated above that station, he observed that instances of slight incongruity in such wise would rarely be found wanting among large bodies of men; that he had heard it was so in workhouses, in the police force, even in that last desperate resource, the army; and that he knew it was so, more or less, in any great railway staff. He had been, when young (if I could believe it, sitting in that hut—he scarcely could), a student of natural philosophy, and had attended lectures; but he had run wild, misused his opportunities, gone down, and never risen again. He had no complaint to offer about that. He had made his bed, and he lay upon it. It was far too late to make another.

All that I have here condensed, he said in a quiet manner, with his grave dark regards divided between me and the fire. He threw in the word, "Sir," from time to time, and especially when he referred to his youth, as though to request me to understand that he claimed to be nothing but what I found him. He was several times interrupted by the little bell, and had to read off messages, and send replies. Once he had to stand without the door, and display a flag as a train passed, and make some verbal communication to the driver. In the discharge of his duties, I observed him to be remarkably exact and vigilant, breaking off his discourse at a syllable, and remaining silent until what he had to do was done.

In a word, I should have set this man down as one of the safest of men to be employed in that capacity, but for the circumstance that while he was speaking to me he twice broke off with a fallen color, turned his face towards the little bell when it did NOT ring, opened the door of the hut (which was kept shut to exclude the unhealthy damp), and looked out towards the red light near the mouth of the tunnel. On both of those occasions, he came back to the fire with the inexplicable air upon him which I had remarked, without being able to define, when we were so far asunder.

Said I, when I rose to leave him, "You almost make me think that I have met with a contented man."

(I am afraid I must acknowledge that I said it to lead him on.)

"I believe I used to be so," he rejoined, in the low voice in which he had first spoken; "but I am troubled, sir, I am troubled."

He would have recalled the words if he could. He had said them, however, and I took them up quickly.

"With what? What is your trouble?"

"It is very difficult to impart, sir. It is very, very difficult to speak of. If ever you make me another visit, I will try to tell you."

"But I expressly intend to make you another visit. Say, when shall it be?"

"I go off early in the morning, and I shall be on again at ten tomorrow night, sir."

"I will come at eleven."

He thanked me, and went out at the door with me. "I'll show my white light, sir," he said, in his peculiar low voice, "till you have found the way up. When you have found it, don't call out! And when you are at the top, don't call out!"

His manner seemed to make the place strike colder to me, but I said no more than, "Very well."

"And when you come down tomorrow night, don't call out! Let me ask you a parting question. What made you cry, 'Halloa! Below there!' tonight?"

"Heaven knows," said I. "I cried something to that effect—"

"Not to that effect, sir. Those were the very words. I know them well."

"Admit those were the very words. I said them, no doubt, because I saw you below."

"For no other reason?"

"What other reason could I possibly have?"

"You had no feeling that they were conveyed to you in any supernatural way?"

"No."

He wished me good night, and held up his light. I walked by the side of the down Line of rails (with a very disagreeable sensation of a train coming behind me) until I found the path. It was easier to mount than to descend, and I got back to my inn without any adventure.

Punctual to my appointment, I placed my foot on the first notch of the zigzag next night, as the distant clocks were striking eleven. He was waiting for me at the bottom, with his white light on. "I have not called out," I said, when we came close together; "may I speak now?" "By all means, sir." "Good night, then, and here's my hand." "Good night, sir, and here's mine." With that we walked side by side to his box, entered it, closed the door, and sat down by the fire.

"I have made up my mind, sir," he began, bending forward as soon as we were seated, and speaking in a tone but a little above a whisper, "that you shall not have to ask me twice what troubles me. I took you for someone else yesterday evening. That troubles me."

"That mistake?"

"No. That someone else."

"Who is it?"

"I don't know."

"Like me?"

"I don't know. I never saw the face. The

6 **Reading Strategy** What does this curious action suggest about the signalman?

7 **Discussion** What one request does the signalman make of the narrator on his return visit?

left arm is across the face, and the right arm is waved—violently waved. This way."

I followed his action with my eyes, and it was the action of an arm gesticulating, with the utmost passion and vehemence, "For God's sake, clear the way!"

"One moonlight night," said the man, "I was sitting here, when I heard a voice cry, 'Halloa! Below there!' I started up, looked from that door, and saw this Someone else standing by the red light near the tunnel, waving as I just now showed you. The voice seemed hoarse with shouting, and it cried, 'Look out! Look out!' And then again, 'Halloa! Below there! Look out!' I caught up my lamp, turned it on red, and ran towards the figure, calling, 'What's wrong? What has happened? Where?' It stood just outside the blackness of the tunnel. I advanced so close upon it that I wondered at its keeping the sleeve across its eyes. I ran right up at it, and had my hand stretched out to pull the sleeve away, when it was gone."

"Into the tunnel," said I.

"No. I ran on into the tunnel, five hundred yards. I stopped, and held my lamp above my head, and saw the figures of the measured distance, and saw the wet stains stealing down the walls and trickling through the arch. I ran out again faster than I had run in (for I had a mortal abhorrence of the place upon me), and I looked all round the red light with my own red light, and I went up the iron ladder to the gallery top of it, and I came down again, and ran back here. I telegraphed both ways, 'An alarm has been given. Is anything wrong?' The answer came back, both ways, 'All well.'"

Resisting the slow touch of a frozen finger tracing out my spine, I showed him how that this figure must be a deception of his sense of sight; and how that figures, originating in disease of the delicate nerves that minister to the functions of the eye, were known to have often troubled patients, some of whom had become conscious of the nature of their affliction, and had even proved it by experiments upon themselves. "As to

an imaginary cry," said I, "do but listen for a moment to the wind in this unnatural valley while we speak so low, and to the wild harp it makes of the telegraph wires!"

That was all very well, he returned, after we had sat listening for a while, and he ought to know something of the wind and the wires—he who so often passed long winter nights there, alone and watching. But he would beg to remark that he had not finished.

I asked his pardon, and he slowly added these words, touching my arm:

"Within six hours after the Appearance, the memorable accident on this Line happened, and within ten hours the dead and wounded were brought along through the tunnel over the spot where the figure had stood."

A disagreeable shudder crept over me, but I did my best against it. It was not to be denied, I rejoined, that this was a remarkable coincidence, calculated deeply to impress his mind. But it was unquestionable that remarkable coincidences did continually occur, and they must be taken into account in dealing with such a subject. Though to be sure I must admit, I added (for I thought I saw that he was going to bring the objection to bear upon me), men of common sense did not allow much for coincidences in making the ordinary calculations of life.

He again begged to remark that he had not finished.

I again begged his pardon for being betrayed into interruptions.

"This," he said, again laying his hand upon my arm, and glancing over his shoulder with hollow eyes, "was just a year ago. Six or seven months passed, and I had recovered from the surprise and shock, when one morning, as the day was breaking, I, standing at the door, looked towards the red light, and saw the specter again." He stopped, with a fixed look at me.

"Did it cry out?"

"No. It was silent."

"Did it wave its arm?"

Grammar in Action

Use **single quotation marks** to indicate a quotation within a quotation. Any direct quotation or piece of dialogue must be enclosed within quotation marks. Sometimes, however, the person or character being quoted is also quoting someone else. To avoid confusion, single quotation marks appear around the inner quotations. Notice Charles Dickens's use of single quotation marks within dialogue.

"One moonlight night," said the man, "I was sitting here, when I heard a voice cry, 'Halloa! Below there!' I started up, looked from that door, and saw this Someone else standing by the red light near the tunnel, waving as I just now showed you. The voice seemed hoarse with shouting, and it cried, 'Look out! Look out!' And then again, 'Halloa! Below there! Look out!' I caught up my lamp, turned it on red, and ran towards the figure, calling, 'What's wrong? What has happened? Where?' It stood just outside the blackness of the tunnel. I advanced so close upon it that I wondered at its keeping the sleeve across its eyes. I ran right up at it, and

"No. It leaned against the shaft of the light, with both hands before the face. Like this."

Once more I followed his action with my eyes. It was an action of mourning. I have seen such an attitude in stone figures on tombs.

"Did you go up to it?"

"I came in and sat down, partly to collect my thoughts, partly because it had turned me faint. When I went to the door again, daylight was above me, and the ghost was gone."

"But nothing followed? Nothing came of this?"

He touched me on the arm with his forefinger twice or thrice, giving a ghastly nod each time:

"That very day, as a train came out of the tunnel, I noticed, at a carriage window on my side, what looked like a confusion of hands and heads, and something waved. I saw it just in time to signal the driver, Stop! He shut off, and put his brake on, but the train drifted past here a hundred and fifty yards or more. I ran after it, and, as I went along, heard terrible screams and cries. A beautiful young lady had died instantaneously in one of the compartments, and was brought in here, and laid on this floor between us."

Involuntarily I pushed my chair back, as I looked from the boards at which he pointed to himself.

"True, sir. True. Precisely as it happened, so I tell it you."

I could think of nothing to say, to any purpose, and my mouth was very dry. The wind and the wires took up the story with a long lamenting wail.

He resumed. "Now, sir, mark this, and judge how my mind is troubled. The specter came back a week ago. Ever since, it has been there, now and again, by fits and starts."

"At the light?"

"At the Danger light."

"What does it seem to do?"

He repeated, if possible with increased passion and vehemence, that former gesticulation of, "For God's sake, clear the way!"

Then he went on. "I have no peace or rest for it. It calls to me, for many minutes together, in an agonized manner, 'Below there! Look out! Look out!' It stands waving to me. It rings my little bell—"

I caught at that. "Did it ring your bell yesterday evening when I was here, and you went to the door?"

"Twice."

"Why, see," said I, "how your imagination misleads you. My eyes were on the bell, and my ears were open to the bell, and if I am a living man, it did NOT ring at those times. No, nor at any other time, except when it was rung in the natural course of physical things by the station communicating with you."

He shook his head. "I have never made a mistake as to that yet, sir. I have never confused the specter's ring with the man's. The ghost's ring is a strange vibration in the bell that it derives from nothing else, and I have not asserted that the bell stirs to the eye. I don't wonder that you failed to hear it. But I heard it."

"And did the specter seem to be there, when you looked out?"

"It WAS there."

"Both times?"

He repeated firmly: "Both times."

"Will you come to the door with me, and look for it now?"

He bit his under lip as though he were somewhat unwilling, but arose. I opened the door, and stood on the step, while he stood in the doorway. There was the Danger light. There was the dismal mouth of the tunnel. There were the high, wet stone walls of the cutting. There were the stars above them.

"Do you see it?" I asked him, taking particular note of his face. His eyes were prominent and strained, but not very much more so, perhaps, than my own had been when I had directed them earnestly towards the same spot.

8 **Discussion** What two events had followed the previous appearances of the apparition?

9 **Discussion** Why is the Signalman presently so troubled?

had my hand stretched out to pull the sleeve away, when it was gone."

During the signalman's speech to the narrator, he quotes what the voice had said and what he had said that moonlit night. To differentiate the speakers, single quotation marks are used.

Student Activity 1. Find another instance in Dickens's story in which he uses single quotation marks within dialogue to show a quotation within a quotation. Explain who is speaking in each instance.

Student Activity 2. Write a sentence of dialogue in which the speaker directly quotes another, and punctuate it correctly.

10 Discussion What is the signal-man's predicament?

"No," he answered. "It is not there."

"Agreed," said I.

We went in again, shut the door, and resumed our seats. I was thinking how best to improve this advantage, if it might be called one, when he took up the conversation in such a matter-of-course way, so assuming that there could be no serious question of fact between us, that I felt myself placed in the weakest of positions.

"By this time you will fully understand, sir," he said, "that what troubles me so dreadfully is the question, What does the specter mean?"

I was not sure, I told him, that I did fully understand.

"What is its warning against?" he said, ruminating, with his eyes on the fire, and only by times turning them on me. "What is the danger? Where is the danger? There is danger overhanging somewhere on the Line. Some dreadful calamity will happen. It is not to be doubted this third time, after what has gone before. But surely this is a cruel haunting of *me*. What can *I* do?"

He pulled out his handkerchief, and wiped the drops from his heated forehead.

10 "If I telegraph Danger, on either side of me, or on both, I can give no reason for it," he went on, wiping the palms of his hands. "I should get into trouble, and do no good. They would think I was mad. This is the way it would work: Message: "Danger! Take care!" Answer: "What Danger? Where?" Message: "Don't know. But for God's sake, take care!" They would displace me. What else could they do?"

His pain of mind was most pitiable to see. It was the mental torture of a conscientious man, oppressed beyond endurance by an unintelligible responsibility involving life.

"When it first stood under the Danger light," he went on, putting his dark hair back from his head, and drawing his hands outward across and across his temples in an extremity of feverish distress, "why not tell me where that accident was to happen—if it must happen? Why not tell me how it could be averted—if it could have been averted? When on its second coming it hid its face, why not tell me, instead, "She is going to die. Let them keep her at home"? If it came, on those two occasions, only to show me that its warnings were true, and so to prepare me for the third, why not warn me plainly now? And I, Lord help me! A mere poor signalman on this solitary station! Why not go to somebody with credit to be believed, and power to act?"

When I saw him in this state, I saw that for the poor man's sake, as well as for the public safety, what I had to do for the time was to compose his mind. Therefore, setting aside all question of reality or unreality between us, I represented to him that whoever thoroughly discharged his duty must do well, and that at least it was his comfort that he understood his duty, though he did not understand these confounding Appearances. In this effort I succeeded far better than in the attempt to reason him out of his conviction. He became calm; the occupations incidental to his post as the night advanced began to make larger demands on his attention: and I left him at two in the morning. I had offered to stay through the night, but he would not hear of it.

That I more than once looked back at the red light as I ascended the pathway, that I did not like the red light, and that I should have slept but poorly if my bed had been under it, I see no reason to conceal. Nor did I like the two sequences of the accident and the dead girl. I see no reason to conceal that either.

But what ran most in my thoughts was the consideration how ought I to act, having become the recipient of this disclosure? I had proved the man to be intelligent, vigilant, painstaking, and exact; but how long might he remain so, in his state of mind? Though in a subordinate position, still he held a most important trust, and would I (for

Commentary

Charles Dickens is one of the most popular writers who ever lived. In fact, his work colors our conceptions of nineteenth-century England. Part of our traditional view of English life is the view in his novels. His work divides itself chronologically. His early novels show his humor and his great ability as an entertainer. His later work was more serious, full of social criticism, and some consider it more important. However, all his work was well-received in his day and remains popular.

His popularity was high even during his lifetime. From 1858 to 1868 he had given readings of his novels in England and in the United States. The audiences loved Dickens, and he loved to please them. This was true not only of his readings but of the novels themselves. He created a world in which compassion and cheerfulness were elevated to supreme virtues. When Dickens died in 1870 something had gone out of English life that was irreplaceable, a bright voice amid the drab commercialism of the century, calling people to laughter and kindness.

RED VIRGINIA CREEPER
Edvard Munch
Three Lions

Humanities Note

Fine art, *Red Virginia Creeper* by Edvard Munch. Munch (1863–1944), a Norwegian painter and graphic artist, studied art at the School of Arts and Crafts in Oslo and in Paris. Munch's unique and complex psychological style is considered a forerunner of expressionism (nonobjective use of symbols and stereotypes, to give objective expression to inner experience).

The painting *Red Virginia Creeper* was painted in 1899–1900, during a period in Munch's life when he turned his focus outward to other people and the world around him. This, along with other paintings done at this time, was a motif he wished to use for a series of large decorative murals entitled "The Frieze of Life." The large house, covered with the red growth of the vine, has an air of mystery. The lonely figure in the foreground is surrounded by an aura of despair. The viewer is given no clue to the reasons behind his despair. Executed in a rhythmic, flowing style, this painting expresses isolation and spiritual unease.

You might use these questions for discussion:

1. How does the artist view the human condition?
2. How does this compare to Dickens's view of the human condition?

instance) like to stake my own life on the chances of his continuing to execute it with precision?

Unable to overcome a feeling that there would be something treacherous in my communicating what he had told me to his superiors in the Company, without first being plain with himself and proposing a middle course to him, I ultimately resolved to offer to accompany him (otherwise keeping his secret for the present) to the wisest medical practitioner we could hear of in those parts, and to take his opinion. A change in his time of duty would come round next night, he had apprised me, and he would be off an hour or two after sunrise, and on again soon after sunset. I had appointed to return accordingly.

The Signalman 877

11 Discussion What is the significance of the description of the signalman's face as "quite composed"?

12 Discussion How was the signalman killed?

13 Discussion Why was the engine driver seen in the same position as the ghost?

Next evening was a lovely evening, and I walked out early to enjoy it. The sun was not yet quite down when I traversed the field-path near the top of the deep cutting. I would extend my walk for an hour, I said to myself, half an hour on and half an hour back, and it would then be time to go to my signalman's box.

Before pursuing my stroll, I stepped to the brink, and mechanically looked down, from the point from which I had first seen him. I cannot describe the thrill that seized upon me, when, close at the mouth of the tunnel, I saw the appearance of a man, with his left sleeve across his eyes, passionately waving his right arm.

The nameless horror that oppressed me passed in a moment, for in a moment I saw that this appearance of a man was a man indeed, and that there was a little group of other men, standing at a short distance, to whom he seemed to be rehearsing the gesture he made. The Danger light was not yet lighted. Against its shaft, a little low hut, entirely new to me, had been made of some wooden supports and tarpaulin. It looked no bigger than a bed.

With an irresistible sense that something was wrong—with a flashing self-reproachful fear that fatal mischief had come of my leaving the man there, and causing no one to be sent to overlook or correct what he did—I descended the notched path with all the speed I could make.

"What is the matter?" I asked the men.

"Signalman killed this morning, sir."

"Not the man belonging to that box?"

"Yes, sir."

"Not the man I know?"

"You will recognize him, sir, if you knew him," said the man who spoke for the others, solemnly uncovering his own head, and raising an end of the tarpaulin, "for his face is quite composed."

"O, how did this happen, how did this happen?" I asked, turning from one to another as the hut closed in again.

"He was cut down by an engine, sir. No man in England knew his work better. But somehow he was not clear of the outer rail. It was just at broad day. He had struck the light, and had the lamp in his hand. As the engine came out of the tunnel, his back was towards her, and she cut him down. That man drove her, and was showing how it happened. Show the gentleman, Tom."

The man, who wore a rough dark dress, stepped back to his former place at the mouth of the tunnel.

"Coming round the curve in the tunnel, sir," he said, "I saw him at the end, like as if I saw him down a perspective-glass. There was no time to check speed, and I knew him to be very careful. As he didn't seem to take heed of the whistle, I shut it off when we were running down upon him, and called to him as loud as I could call."

"What did you say?"

"I said, 'Below there! Look out! Look out! For God's sake, clear the way!'"

I started.

"Ah! it was a dreadful time, sir. I never left off calling to him. I put this arm before my eyes not to see, and I waved this arm to the last; but it was no use."

Without prolonging the narrative to dwell on any one of its curious circumstances more than on any other, I may, in closing it, point out the coincidence that the warning of the Engine Driver included, not only the words which the unfortunate Signalman had repeated to me as haunting him, but also the words which I myself—not he—had attached and that only in my own mind, to the gesticulation he had imitated.

THINKING ABOUT THE SELECTION

Recalling

1. (a) How does the signalman behave during his first meeting with the narrator? (b) What explanation for this behavior is given in the second meeting?
2. (a) What tragedy followed the specter's first appearance? (b) Its second appearance? (c) How has it been warning the signalman lately?
3. What happens to the signalman?

Interpreting

4. Do you think the narrator is totally convinced of his own explanations of the events on the railroad line? Explain.
5. (a) What do you think is the narrator's view of the supernatural? (b) What evidence are you given that the events he narrates have changed his views?

Applying

6. In light of his description of the signalman's job, how does this story serve Dickens's goal of promoting social change in England?

ANALYZING LITERATURE

Following the Plot in a Ghost Story

The **plot** is the series of events in a story or novel that answers the question "What happens?" Plot usually involves a conflict, or clash between characters or opposing forces, that builds to a high point called the climax. In a ghost story, the plot revolves around supernatural—or "otherworldly"—elements.

1. What supernatural elements are featured in "The Signalman"? How do these elements tie in directly to the story's plot?
2. The story features several different conflicts. Identify:
   a. The conflict between the narrator and the signalman.
   b. The signalman's inner conflict.
   c. The narrator's inner conflict.

CRITICAL THINKING AND READING

Separating Details

Like any good ghost story, "The Signalman" is filled with details that lend themselves to both realistic and supernatural interpretation. What the signalman, for example, identifies as the specter's cry, the narrator "writes off" as the sound of the wind whistling through the telegraph wires. Yet not all details in the story can be explained away so simply. Identify the realistic and supernatural significance of each of the following details.

1. The ringing of the bell.
2. The words "For God's sake, clear the way!"
3. A figure with its left sleeve across its face and its right arm waving frantically.

UNDERSTANDING LANGUAGE

Fitting the Context

Occasionally writers use words that, in a given context, are *ambiguous,* or open to more than one interpretation. In each case below, give the intended meaning of the italicized word, and identify a second possible reading.

1. ". . . an oncoming rush . . . caused me to *start* back . . . " (page 870)
2. ". . . in [the tunnel's] architecture there was a . . . forbidding *air.* . . ." (page 871)
3. "That light was part of his *charge*?" (page 871)
4. "I have seen such an *attitude* in stone figures on tombs." (page 875)

THINKING AND WRITING

Writing a Ghost Story

Using the notes you developed earlier, write an original ghost story. Before you proceed, map out your story's plot. Ask: What will happen in the story, and in what order will you report the events? What is the conflict, and who does it involve? How will the conflict be resolved? When you have answered these questions, you may begin your first draft.

The Signalman 879

line. He concludes by speaking of "curious" circumstance and coincidence.

5. (a) At first, the narrator is doubtful of the supernatural. (b) The events he witnesses cause him to be uncertain of the meaning of the events.

Applying

6. Dickens's description of the signalman's job points up its hardships and dangers, thus contributing to his goal of promoting social change in England.

ANSWERS TO ANALYZING LITERATURE

1. "The Signalman" features a mysterious apparition, a series of warnings, and sudden tragedies.
2. (a) The narrator and the signalman are not certain whether or not to trust one another. (b) The signalman doesn't know if he should trust his feelings about the strange goings on at the train tunnel. (c) The narrator is in conflict over whether or not to believe the signalman.

ANSWERS TO CRITICAL THINKING AND READING

1. The narrator maintains the bell did not ring. The signalman points out that "the ghost's ring is a strange vibration in the bell that it derives from nothing else. . . ."
2. These are the words the narrator has mentally used. He hears them mysteriously repeated by a man who says they were uttered by the apparition.
3. The signalman as well as the apparition is said to assume this pose.

UNDERSTANDING LANGUAGE

1. to pull back—return
2. mood—smell
3. duty—obligation
4. appearance—facade

THINKING AND WRITING

For help with this assignment, students can refer to Lesson 19 "Writing a Short Story," in the Handbook of Writing About Literature.

Closure and Extension

ANSWERS TO THINKING ABOUT THE SELECTION

Recalling

1. (a) During his first meeting with the narrator, the signalman acts troubled. (b) In the second meeting, the signalman explains that he took the narrator for someone else.

2. (a) Within six hours after the specter's first appearance, there was a train crash. (b) After its second appearance, a young woman was killed. (c) Lately, it has been ringing a bell to warn the signalman.
3. The signalman is killed by a train.

Interpreting

4. The narrator does not seem to be totally convinced by his own explanations of the events on the railroad

THOMAS HARDY

1840–1928

In addition to being a highly regarded poet, Thomas Hardy was one of the most important fiction writers of the Victorian Age. Set in the imaginary region of Wessex, Hardy's novels and stories focused on the plight of the underdog in an unfeeling society.

Hardy was born in the Dorset countryside in southwestern England, the area upon which his fictional setting of Wessex is based. After leaving school at the age of fifteen, Hardy was trained to be an architect. He developed a strong interest in fiction and poetry, however, and eventually decided to focus his energy on writing. His first novel, *Desperate Remedies,* was published anonymously in 1871. The following year he achieved success as a novelist with the publication of *Under the Greenwood Tree.* Hardy went on to produce several more novels, but when his book *Jude the Obscure* (1896) prompted a hostile reaction, he turned to writing poetry.

In his novels and stories, Hardy often depicted characters whose destinies were shaped by forces beyond their control. Many of his works, including "The Three Strangers," also contain an element of mystery, resulting in part from the rough, unforgiving landscape that serves as their setting. (For additional information on Hardy, see page 832.)

GUIDE FOR INTERPRETING

Writer's Technique

Setting and Mood. Setting is the time when and place where the events in a story occur. This information is sometimes vital to a story's *mood,* or the feelings it stirs in the reader. If, for example, the story is set in a crowded, bustling city, the mood will be tense and hectic. If, on the other hand, the story is set on a lush tropical island, the mood will be calm and tranquil.

Writing

Imagine that a stranger appeared at the front door of your home one evening. Letting your imagination run free, describe this person's appearance, as well as yours and your family's initial reaction to him or her. Finally, state the reason for the stranger's visit.

Primary Source

One afternoon, Robert Graves, his wife, and T. E. Lawrence found themselves near Hardy's home in Dorchester. Since they had met Hardy not long before, when he had traveled to Oxford to receive an honorary degree from the university, they decided to stop in and visit him.

Graves, himself a well-known poet, novelist, and critic, wrote out a record of their conversation. It clearly shows the influence of setting and mood on Hardy's word choice and writing style.

> He said that he regarded professional critics as parasites no less noxious than autograph-hunters, and wished the world rid of them. He also wished that he had not listened to them when he was a young man; on their advice he had cut out dialect-words from his early poems, though they had no exact synonyms to fit the context. And still the critics were plaguing him. One of them recently complained of a poem of his where he had written "his shape *smalled* in the distance." Now what in the world else could he have written? Hardy then laughed a little and said that once or twice recently he had looked up a word in the dictionary for fear of being again acused of coining, and had found it there right enough—only to read on and find that the sole authority quoted was himself in a half-forgotten novel! He talked of early literary influences, and said that he had none at all, for he did not come of literary stock. Then he corrected himself and said that a friend, a fellow-apprentice in the architect's ofice where he had worked as a young man, used to lend him books.

How do you think the language of "The Three Strangers" might have differed if Hardy had used another setting and mood?

Guide for Interpreting 881

Literary Focus Point out that Hardy is sometimes considered a regional novelist because he consistently used the geographic area known as Wessex as the setting for his stories. His affection for this region and for those characters whose roots are there is in sharp contrast with his generally pessimistic view of life. Hardy's philosophical determinism as expressed in his novels is similar to the Greek view of fate as expressed in classical tragedy, which Hardy knew well.

Teaching to Ability Levels Have your less advanced students compile a list of the words and phrases that describe parts of the countryside. Have them separate their words and phrases into two columns—those that create a positive impression and those that create a negative one.

Writing/Prior Knowledge For an alternative exercise, have students discuss the similarities and differences between the reactions of rural Victorian society to strangers, as described in "The Three Strangers," and the reactions of modern urban society. Then have them complete the freewriting assignment, taking into consideration the points raised in the discussion.

Vocabulary

Preteach the following words:
inimical (in im′ i k′l) *adj.*: Unfriendly (p. 882)
salient (sāl′ yənt) *adj.*: Striking; easily noticeable (p. 885)
desultory (des′ 'l tôr′ ē) *adj.*: Jumping from point to point (p. 886)
alacrity (ə lak′ r tē) *n.*: Willingness (p. 890)
baleful (bāl′ fəl) *adj.*: Of or with evil intent (p. 893)

The Three Strangers

Thomas Hardy

Among the few features of agricultural England which retain an appearance but little modified by the lapse of centuries, may be reckoned the long, grassy and furzy downs, coombs,[1] or ewe-leases, as they are called according to their kind, that fill a large area of certain counties in the south and southwest. If any mark of human occupation is met with hereon, it usually takes the form of the solitary cottage of some shepherd.

Fifty years ago such a lonely cottage stood on such a down, and may possibly be standing there now. In spite of its loneliness, however, the spot, by actual measurement, was not three miles from a county town. Yet that affected it little. Three miles of irregular upland, during the long inimical seasons, with their sleets, snows, rains, and mists, afford withdrawing space enough to isolate a Timon[2] or a Nebuchadnezzar;[3] much less, in fair weather, to please that less repellent tribe, the poets, philosophers, artists, and others who "conceive and meditate of pleasant things."

Some old earthen camp or barrow,[4] some clump of trees, at least some starved fragment of ancient hedge is usually taken advantage of in the erection of these forlorn dwellings. But, in the present case, such a kind of shelter had been disregarded. Higher Crowstairs, as the house was called, stood quite detached and undefended. The only reason for its precise situation seemed to be the crossing of two footpaths at right angles hard by, which may have crossed there and thus for a good five hundred years. Hence the house was exposed to the elements on all sides. But, though the wind up here blew unmistakably when it did blow, and the rain hit hard whenever it fell, the various weathers of the winter season were not quite so formidable on the down as they were imagined to be by dwellers on low ground. The raw rimes[5] were not so pernicious as in the hollows, and the frosts were scarcely so severe. When the shepherd and his family who tenanted the house were pitied for their sufferings from the exposure, they said that upon the whole they were less inconvenienced by "wuzzes and flames" (hoarses and phlegms) than when they had lived by the stream of a snug neighboring valley.

The night of March 28, 182– was precisely one of the nights that were wont to call forth these expressions of commiseration. The level rainstorm smote walls, slopes, and hedges like the clothyard shafts of Senlac and Crecy.[6] Such sheep and outdoor animals as had no shelter stood with their buttocks to the winds; while the tails of little birds trying to roost on some scraggy thorn were blown inside out like umbrellas. The gable-end of the cottage was stained with wet, and the eavesdroppings flapped against the wall. Yet never was commiseration for the shepherd more misplaced. For that cheerful rustic was entertaining a large

1. **coombs** (ko͞oms) *n*: Deep, narrow valleys.
2. **Timon** (tī'mən): A fifth-century Greek hermit who lived in a cave.
3. **Nebuchadnezzar** (neb' yə kəd nez' ər): A Babylonian king who isolated himself in the fields after becoming insane.
4. **barrow** *n*.: A heap of earth or rocks marking a grave.

5. **rimes** (rīmz) *n*: White frost.
6. **clothyard . . . Crecy** (krā sē'): Yard-long arrows used in battles fought in England (at Senlac) and France (at Crecy).

party in glorification of the christening of his second girl.

The guests had arrived before the rain began to fall, and they were all now assembled in the chief or living room of the dwelling. A glance into the apartment at eight o'clock on this eventful evening would have resulted in the opinion that it was as cozy and comfortable a nook as could be wished for in boisterous weather. The calling of its inhabitant was proclaimed by a number of highly polished sheep crooks without stems that were hung ornamentally over the fireplace, the curl of each shining crook varying from the antiquated type engraved in the patriarchal pictures of old family Bibles to the most approved fashion of the last local sheep fair. The room was lighted by half a dozen candles, having wicks only a trifle smaller than the grease which enveloped them, in candlesticks that were never used but at high days, holy days, and family feasts. The lights were scattered about the room, two of them standing on the chimney piece. This position of candles was in itself significant. Candles on the chimney piece always meant a party.

On the hearth, in front of a backbrand to give substance, blazed a fire of thorns, that crackled "like the laughter of the fool."

Nineteen persons were gathered here. Of these, five women, wearing gowns of various bright hues, sat in chairs along the wall; girls shy and not shy filled the window bench; four men, including Charley Jake the hedge carpenter, Elijah New the parish clerk, and John Pitcher, a neighboring dairyman, the shepherd's father-in-law, lolled in the settle; a young man and maid, who were blushing over tentative *pourparlers*[7] on a life companionship, sat beneath the corner cupboard; and an elderly engaged man of fifty or upward moved restlessly about from spots where his betrothed was not to the spot where she was. Enjoyment was pretty general, and so much the more

prevailed in being unhampered by conventional restrictions. Absolute confidence in each other's good opinion begat perfect ease, while the finishing stroke of manner, amounting to a truly princely serenity, was lent to the majority by the absence of any expression or trait denoting that they wished to get on in the world, enlarge their minds, or do any eclipsing thing whatever —which nowadays so generally nips the bloom and *bonhomie*[8] of all except the two extremes of the social scale.

Shepherd Fennel had married well, his wife being a dairyman's daughter from a vale at a distance, who brought fifty guineas in her pocket—and kept them there, till they should be required for ministering to the needs of a coming family. This frugal woman had been somewhat exercised as to the character that should be given to the gathering. A sit-still party had its advantages; but an undisturbed position of ease in chairs and settles was apt to lead on the men to such an unconscionable deal of toping[9] that they would sometimes fairly drink the house dry. A dancing party was the alternative; but this, while avoiding the foregoing objection on the score of good drink, had a counterbalancing disadvantage in the matter of good victuals, the ravenous appetites engendered by the exercise causing immense havoc in the buttery. Shepherdess Fennel fell back upon the intermediate plan of mingling short dances with short periods of talk and singing, so as to hinder any ungovernable rage in either. But this scheme was entirely confined to her own gentle mind: the shepherd himself was in the mood to exhibit the most reckless phases of hospitality.

The fiddler was a boy of those parts, about twelve years of age, who had a wonderful dexterity in jigs and reels, though his fingers were so small and short as to necessitate a constant shifting for the high notes, from which he scrambled back to the first

---

7. *pourparlers* (po͞or′ pär lä′): Informal discussions (French).

8. *bonhomie* (bän′ ə mē′): Good nature (French).
9. *toping*: Drinking.

3 **Discussion** Compare and contrast the conditions inside and outside the cottage.

4 **Discussion** How do the people in the cottage feel about themselves and each other? Why?

5 **Discussion** You might mention that fennel is an herb of the parsley family. What is most appealing about Mrs. Fennel? What is least appealing?

Fine art, *Summer, Afternoon After a Shower* by John Constable. John Constable (1776–1837), a noteworthy British landscape painter was educated at the schools of the Royal Academy. He began his career in 1802 as a portrait and landscape painter. He is remembered today for his innovation of working out-of-doors and his resulting landscapes of vibrant color and light.

Summer, Afternoon After a Shower demonstrates Constable's constant interest in the effects of weather upon the landscape. Constable painted the skies in all atmospheric conditions. In this painting he attempts to describe truthfully the tempers of weather. The freshness and color of the wind-tossed landscape suffused with a vivid light were unknown qualities in his day, when formalized, studio versions of nature were the accepted mode.

You might use the following questions for discussion:

1. What features of this painting make it appropriate as an illustration for this story?
2. What is the mood of this painting?
3. Does it match the mood of the story?

SUMMER, AFTERNOON AFTER A SHOWER
John Constable
The Tate Gallery, London

position with sounds not of unmixed purity of tone. At seven the shrill tweedle-dee of this youngster had begun, accompanied by a booming ground bass from Elijah New, the parish clerk, who had thoughtfully brought with him his favorite musical instrument, the serpent.[10] Dancing was instantaneous, Mrs. Fennel privately enjoining the players on no account to let the dance exceed the length of a quarter of an hour.

But Elijah and the boy in the excitement of their position quite forgot the injunction. Moreover, Oliver Giles, a man of seventeen, one of the dancers, who was enamored of his partner, a fair girl of thirty-three rolling years, had recklessly handed a new crown-piece to the musicians, as a bribe to keep going as long as they had muscle and wind. Mrs. Fennel seeing the steam begin to generate on the countenances of her guests, crossed over and touched the fiddler's elbow and put her hand on the serpent's mouth. But they took no notice, and fearing she might lose her character of genial hostess if she were to interfere too markedly, she retired and sat down helpless. And so the dance whizzed on with cumulative fury, the performers moving in their planet-like courses, direct and retrograde,[11] from apogee to perigee,[12] till the hand of the well-kicked clock at the bottom of the room had traveled over the circumference of an hour.

While these cheerful events were in course of enactment within Fennel's pastoral dwelling an incident having considerable bearing on the party had occurred in the gloomy night without. Mrs. Fennel's concern about the growing fierceness of the dance corresponded in point of time with the ascent of a human figure to the solitary hill of Higher Crowstairs from the direction of the distant town. This personage strode on through the rain without a pause, following the little-worn path which, further on in its course, skirted the shepherd's cottage.

It was nearly the time of full moon, and on this account, though the sky was lined with a uniform sheet of dripping cloud, ordi-

---

10. serpent *n.*: An obsolete, coiled bass wind instrument.

11. direct and retrograde: Orbital directions.
12. from apogee to perigee: From the points in orbit farthest from and nearest to the earth.

nary objects out of doors were readily visible. The sad wan light revealed the lonely pedestrian to be a man of supple frame; his gait suggested that he had somewhat passed the period of perfect and instinctive agility, though not so far as to be otherwise than rapid of motion when occasion required. At a rough guess, he might have been about forty years of age. He appeared tall, but a recruiting sergeant, or other person accustomed to the judging of men's heights by the eye, would have discerned that this was chiefly owing to his gauntness, and that he was not more than five-feet-eight or nine.

Notwithstanding the regularity of his tread there was caution in it, as in that of one who mentally feels his way; and despite the fact that it was not a black coat nor a dark garment of any sort that he wore, there was something about him which suggested that he naturally belonged to the black-coated tribes[13] of men. His clothes were of fustian,[14] and his boots hobnailed, yet in his progress he showed not the mud-accustomed bearing of hobnailed and fustianed peasantry.

By the time that he had arrived abreast of the shepherd's premises the rain came down, or rather came along, with yet more determined violence. The outskirts of the little settlement partially broke the force of wind and rain, and this induced him to stand still. The most salient of the shepherd's domestic erections was an empty sty at the forward corner of his hedgeless garden, for in these latitudes the principle of masking the homelier features of your establishment by a conventional frontage was unknown. The traveler's eye was attracted to this small building by the pallid shine of the wet slates that covered it. He turned aside, and, finding it empty, stood under the pent roof for shelter.

While he stood the boom of the serpent within the adjacent house, and the lesser strains of the fiddler, reached the spot as an accompaniment to the surging hiss of the flying rain on the sod, its louder beating on the cabbage leaves of the garden, on the straw hackles of eight or ten beehives just discernible by the path, and its dripping from the eaves into a row of buckets and pans that had been placed under the walls of the cottage. For at Higher Crowstairs, as at all such elevated domiciles, the grand difficulty of housekeeping was an insufficiency of water; and a casual rainfall was utilized by turning out, as catchers, every utensil that the house contained. Some queer stories might be told of the contrivances for economy in suds and dishwaters that are absolutely necessitated in upland habitations during the droughts of summer. But at this season there were no such exigencies; a mere acceptance of what the skies bestowed was sufficient for an abundant store.

At last the notes of the serpent ceased and the house was silent. This cessation of activity aroused the solitary pedestrian from the reverie into which he had lapsed, and, emerging from the shed, with an apparently new intention, he walked up the path to the house door. Arrived here, his first act was to kneel down on a large stone beside the row of vessels, and to drink a copious draft from one of them. Having quenched his thirst he rose and lifted his hand to knock, but paused with his eye upon the panel. Since the dark surface of the wood revealed absolutely nothing, it was evident that he must be mentally looking through the door, as if he wished to measure thereby all the possibilities that a house of this sort might include, and how they might bear upon the question of his entry.

In his indecision he turned and surveyed the scene around. Not a soul was anywhere visible. The garden path stretched downward from his feet, gleaming like the track of a snail; the roof of the little well (mostly dry), the well cover, the top rail of the garden gate, were varnished with the same dull liquid glaze; while, far away in the vale, a faint whiteness of more than usual extent

---

13. **black-coated tribes:** Middle class.
14. **fustian** (fus'chən) *n.*: A coarse cotton cloth.

What part does fate play in this stranger's actions? What part did the man's own free will play?

7 Reading Strategy Based on what you have read so far, how would you react to the knock at the door if you were a guest at the party? What do you anticipate is going to happen because the shepherd has let a stranger into his house?

8 Discussion What is your first impression of the man? What do you think is the first impression of the party guests?

9 Discussion Why is it odd that the man has misplaced some objects? What are other reasons that he doesn't have his pipe and tobacco box with him?

showed that the rivers were high in the meads. Beyond all this winked a few bleared lamplights through the beating drops —lights that denoted the situation of the county town from which he had appeared to come. The absence of all notes of life in that direction seemed to clinch his intentions, and he knocked at the door.

Within, a desultory chat had taken the place of movement and musical sound. The hedge carpenter was suggesting a song to the company, which nobody just then was inclined to undertake, so that the knock afforded a not unwelcome diversion.

"Walk in!" said the shepherd promptly.

The latch clicked upward, and out of the night our pedestrian appeared upon the doormat. The shepherd arose, snuffed two of the nearest candles, and turned to look at him.

Their light disclosed that the stranger was dark in complexion and not unprepossessing as to feature. His hat, which for a moment he did not remove, hung low over his eyes, without concealing that they were large, open, and determined, moving with a flash rather than a glance around the room. He seemed pleased with his survey, and, baring his shaggy head, said, in a rich deep voice, "The rain is so heavy, friends, that I ask leave to come in and rest awhile."

"To be sure, stranger," said the shepherd. "And faith, you've been lucky in choosing your time, for we are having a bit of a fling for a glad cause—though, to be sure, a man could hardly wish that glad cause to happen more than once a year."

"Nor less," spoke up a woman. "For 'tis best to get your family over and done with, as soon as you can, so as to be all the earlier out of the fag o't."[15]

"And what may be this glad cause?" asked the stranger.

"A birth and christening," said the shepherd.

The stranger hoped his host might not be made unhappy either by too many or too

few of such episodes, and being invited by a gesture to a pull at the mug, he readily acquiesced. His manner, which, before entering, had been so dubious, was now altogether that of a careless and candid man.

"Late to be traipsing athwart this coomb —hey?" said the engaged man of fifty.

"Late it is, master, as you say.—I'll take a seat in the chimney corner, if you have nothing to urge against it, ma'am; for I am a little moist on the side that was next the rain."

Mrs. Shepherd Fennel assented, and made room for the self-invited comer, who, having got completely inside the chimney corner, stretched out his legs and his arms with the expansiveness of a person quite at home.

"Yes, I am rather cracked in the vamp,"[16] he said freely, seeing that the eyes of the shepherd's wife fell upon his boots, "and I am not well fitted either. I have had some rough times lately, and have been forced to pick up what I can get in the way of wearing, but I must find a suit better fit for working days when I reach home."

"One of hereabouts?" she inquired.

"Not quite that—farther up the country."

"I thought so. And so be I; and by your tongue you come from my neighborhood."

"But you would hardly have heard of me," he said quickly. "My time would be long before yours, ma'am, you see."

This testimony to the youthfulness of his hostess had the effect of stopping her cross-examination.

"There is only one thing more wanted to make me happy," continued the newcomer. "And that is a little baccy,[17] which I am sorry to say I am out of."

"I'll fill your pipe," said the shepherd.

"I must ask you to lend me a pipe likewise."

"A smoker, and no pipe about 'ee?"

---

15. fag o't: Fatigue of it.

16. vamp *n.*: The part of a shoe or boot covering the instep.
17. baccy: Tobacco.

COTTAGE AND POND, MOONLIGHT
Thomas Gainsborough

"I have dropped it somewhere on the road."

The shepherd filled and handed him a new clay pipe, saying, as he did so, "Hand me your baccy box—I'll fill that too, now I am about it."

The man went through the movement of searching his pockets.

"Lost that too?" said his entertainer, with some surprise.

"I am afraid so," said the man with some confusion. "Give it to me in a screw of paper." Lighting his pipe at the candle with a suction that drew the whole flame into the bowl, he resettled himself in the corner and bent his looks upon the faint steam from his damp legs, as if he wished to say no more.

Meanwhile the general body of guests had been taking little notice of this visitor by reason of an absorbing discussion in which they were engaged with the band about a tune for the next dance. The matter being settled, they were about to stand up when an interruption came in the shape of another knock at the door.

At sound of the same the man in the chimney corner took up the poker and began stirring the brands as if doing it thoroughly were the one aim of his existence; and a second time the shepherd said, "Walk in!" In a moment another man stood upon the straw-woven doormat. He too was a stranger.

This individual was one of a type radically different from the first. There was more of the commonplace in his manner, and a certain jovial cosmopolitanism sat upon his features. He was several years older than the first arrival, his hair being slightly frosted, his eyebrows bristly, and his whiskers cut back from his cheeks. His face was rather full and flabby, and yet it was not altogether a face without power. A few grog blossoms marked the neighborhood of his

The Three Strangers 887

Humanities Note

Fine art, *Cottage and Pond, Moonlight* by Thomas Gainsborough. Thomas Gainsborough (1727–1788), an important English painter of portraits and landscapes, was educated at St. Martins Lane Academy in London. Gainsborough slowly gained fame as a portrait painter. Although portraits were his main source of income, he preferred to paint landscapes. His progression in his art gained him considerable fame and the honor of being the favorite painter of King George III and Queen Charlotte. He is remembered today as the most accomplished and innovative painter of eighteenth-century England.

The painting *Cottage and Pond, Moonlight* is something of a curiosity. It is painted in transparent color on a foot-square pane of glass. It was intended for use in an invention of Gainsborough's, a candle-lit viewing box that he called "Gainsborough's Peep Show," which he used to amuse his family and friends. Gainsborough did a series of these paintings on glass of varying landscape subjects, ten of which are known to exist. Of the ten, this is perhaps the most effective. The cozy lit windows and the glowing moonlit sky lend a dramatic air to the scene. These slides are exhibited, backlit in a darkened hallway, in the Victoria and Albert Museum in London.

Below are questions you may use for discussion of this painting with your students:

1. In what ways does this painting visualize the setting of the story?
2. What is the effect of the lights pouring from the cottage windows? Is it one of invitation or hostility? Explain.

10 Clarification Hardy uses the name Casterbridge to refer to Dorchester, a town he knew very well, in the south of England. He uses Casterbridge again in his novel *The Mayor of Casterbridge*.

11 Discussion What is Mrs. Fennel's reaction to the two strangers?

nose. He flung back his long drab greatcoat, revealing that beneath it he wore a suit of cinder-gray shade throughout, large heavy seals, of some metal or other that would take a polish, dangling from his fob as his only personal ornament. Shaking the water drops from his low-crowned glazed hat, he said, "I must ask for a few minutes' shelter, comrades, or I shall be wetted to my skin before I get to Casterbridge."

"Make yourself at home, master," said the shepherd, perhaps a trifle less heartily than on the first occasion. Not that Fennel had the least tinge of niggardliness in his composition; but the room was far from large, spare chairs were not numerous, and damp companions were not altogether desirable at close quarters for the women and girls in their bright-colored gowns.

However, the second comer, after taking off his greatcoat, and hanging his hat on a nail in one of the ceiling beams as if he had been specially invited to put it there, advanced and sat down on the table. This had been pushed so closely into the chimney corner, to give all available room to the dancers, that its inner edge grazed the elbow of the man who had ensconced himself by the fire; and thus the two strangers were brought into close companionship. They nodded to each other by way of breaking the ice of unacquaintance, and the first stranger handed his neighbor the family mug—a huge vessel of brown ware, having its upper edge worn away like a threshold by the rub of whole generations of thirsty lips that had gone the way of all flesh, and bearing the following inscription burnt upon its rotund side in yellow letters:

THERE IS NO FUN

UNTiLL i CUM

The other man, nothing loth,[18] raised the mug to his lips, and drank on, and on, and on—till a curious blueness overspread the countenance of the shepherd's wife, who had regarded with no little surprise the first stranger's free offer to the second of what did not belong to him to dispense.

"I knew it!" said the toper to the shepherd with much satisfaction. "When I walked up your garden before coming in, and saw the hives all of a row, I said to myself, 'Where there's bees there's honey, and where there's honey there's mead.' But mead of such a truly comfortable sort as this I really didn't expect to meet in my older days." He took yet another pull at the mug, till it assumed an ominous elevation.

"Glad you enjoy it!" said the shepherd warmly.

"It is goodish mead," assented Mrs. Fennel, with an absence of enthusiasm which seemed to say that it was possible to buy praise for one's cellar at too heavy a price. "It is trouble enough to make—and really I hardly think we shall make any more. For honey sells well, and we ourselves can make shift with a drop o' small mead and metheglin[19] for common use from the comb-washings."

"O, but you'll never have the heart!" reproachfully cried the stranger in cinder gray, after taking up the mug a third time and setting it down empty. "I love mead, when 'tis old like this, as I love to go to church o' Sundays, or to relieve the needy any day of the week."

"Ha, ha, ha!" said the man in the chimney corner, who, in spite of the taciturnity induced by the pipe of tobacco, could not or would not refrain from this slight testimony to his comrade's humor.

Now the old mead of those days, brewed of the purest first-year or maiden honey, four pounds to the gallon—with its due complement of white of eggs, cinnamon, ginger, cloves, mace, rosemary, yeast, and processes of working, bottling, and cellaring—tasted remarkably strong; but it did not taste so strong as it actually was. Hence,

---

18. nothing loth: Not reluctant.

19. small mead and metheglin: Weaker types of mead.

Primary Source

Hardy's reputation rests largely on his novels. He wrote very little short fiction, but in it he employed the same techniques he employed in his novels. Ifor Evans, in *A Short History of English Literature* discusses Hardy's approach in fiction:

> An architect by profession, he gave to his novels a design that was architectural, employing each circumstance in the narrative to one accumulated effect. The final impression was one of a malign Fate functioning in men's lives, corrupting their possibilities of happiness, and beckoning them toward tragedy. While this intuition about life did not harden into a philosophy, it was so persistent that it had every aspect of a doctrine. His intellect contributed to it in revolting against the optimism of nineteenth-century materialism, and in refusing the consolations of the Christian faith. While he saw life thus as cruel and purposeless, he does not remain a detached spectator. He has pity for the puppets of Destiny, and it is a compassion that extends from man to the earthworms, and the diseased leaves of

presently, the stranger in cinder gray at the table, moved by its creeping influence, unbuttoned his waistcoat, threw himself back in his chair, spread his legs, and made his presence felt in various ways.

"Well, well, as I say," he resumed, "I am going to Casterbridge, and to Casterbridge I must go. I should have been almost there by this time; but the rain drove me into your dwelling, and I'm not sorry for it."

"You don't live in Casterbridge?" said the shepherd.

"Not as yet; though I shortly mean to move there."

"Going to set up in trade, perhaps?"

"No, no," said the shepherd's wife. "It is easy to see that the gentleman is rich, and don't want to work at anything."

The cinder-gray stranger paused, as if to consider whether he would accept that definition of himself. He presently rejected it by answering, "Rich is not quite the word for me, dame. I do work, and I must work. And even if I only get to Casterbridge by midnight I must begin work there at eight tomorrow morning. Yes, het or wet, blow or snow, famine or sword, my day's work tomorrow must be done."

"Poor man! Then, in spite o' seeming, you be worse off than we?" replied the shepherd's wife.

"'Tis the nature of my trade, men and maidens. 'Tis the nature of my trade more than my poverty. . . . But really and truly I must up and off, or I shan't get a lodging in the town." However, the speaker did not move, and directly added, "There's time for one more draft of friendship before I go; and I'd perform it at once if the mug were not dry."

"Here's a mug o' small," said Mrs. Fennel. "Small, we call it, though to be sure 'tis only the first wash o' the combs."

"No," said the stranger disdainfully. "I won't spoil your first kindness by partaking o' your second."

"Certainly not," broke in Fennel. "We don't increase and multiply every day, and I'll fill the mug again." He went away to the dark place under the stairs where the barrel stood. The shepherdess followed him.

"Why should you do this?" she said reproachfully, as soon as they were alone. "He's emptied it once, though it held enough for ten people; and now he's not contented wi' the small, but must needs call for more o' the strong! And a stranger unbeknown to any of us. For my part, I don't like the look o' the man at all."

"But he's in the house, my honey; and 'tis a wet night, and a christening. Daze it, what's a cup of mead more or less? There'll be plenty more next bee-burning."

"Very well—this time, then," she answered, looking wistfully at the barrel. "But what is the man's calling, and where is he one of, that he should come in and join us like this?"

"I don't know. I'll ask him again."

The catastrophe of having the mug drained dry at one pull by the stranger in cinder gray was effectually guarded against this time by Mrs. Fennel. She poured out his allowance in a small cup, keeping the large one at a discreet distance from him. When he had tossed off his portion, the shepherd renewed his inquiry about the stranger's occupation.

The latter did not immediately reply, and the man in the chimney corner, with sudden demonstrativeness, said, "Anybody may know my trade—I'm a wheelwright."

"A very good trade for these parts," said the shepherd.

"And anybody may know mine—if they've the sense to find it out," said the stranger in cinder gray.

"You may generally tell what a man is by his claws," observed the hedge carpenter, looking at his own hands. "My fingers be as full of thorns as an old pincushion is of pins."

The hands of the man in the chimney corner instinctively sought the shade, and he gazed into the fire as he resumed his pipe. The man at the table took up the hedge carpenter's remark, and added smartly, "True; but the oddity of my trade is that,

The Three Strangers   889

12 **Reading Strategy** Understanding irony will help students comprehend the author's message. How does Mrs. Fennel reveal how she feels about the second stranger in these ironic statements?

13 **Discussion** What does Hardy reveal about Mr. and Mrs. Fennel in this exchange under the stairs?

14 **Reading Strategy** What can you infer from this passage about the stranger's reluctance to discuss his trade?

15 **Discussion** What clue does the stranger provide in the last sentence of this bracketed section?

trees. Such a conception gave his novels a high seriousness which few of his contemporaries possessed. It was as if a scene of Greek tragedy were being played out among his Wessex rustics. An early criticism of his work lay in this very incongruity, that his rustic characters should have the high passions, the noble and tragic proportions, which he gave them.

16 **Enrichment** Although this musical riddle is certainly not the finest example of Hardy's poetry, he did consider himself a better poet than a novelist. In fact, he considered poetry to be far more important than fiction and hoped that he would be remembered as a poet.

17 **Discussion** How do the guests react to the second stranger's song and why?

18 **Discussion** What might make the first stranger ask for a second verse of the song?

19 **Discussion** What does the second stranger's song reveal about his profession?

instead of setting a mark upon me, it sets a mark upon my customers.''

No observation being offered by anybody in elucidation of this enigma the shepherd's wife once more called for a song. The same obstacles presented themselves as at the former time—one had no voice, another had forgotten the first verse. The stranger at the table, whose soul had now risen to a good working temperature, relieved the difficulty by exclaiming that, to start the company, he would sing himself. Thrusting one thumb into the armhole of his waistcoat, he waved the other hand in the air, and, with an extemporizing gaze at the shining sheep crooks above the mantelpiece, began:

> 16

> "O my trade it is the rarest one,
> Simple shepherds all—
> My trade is a sight to see;
> For my customers I tie, and
>   take them up on high,
> And waft 'em to a far countree!''

The room was silent when he had finished the verse—with one exception, that of the man in the chimney corner, who, at the singer's word, "Chorus!" joined him in a deep bass voice of musical relish—

> "And waft 'em to a far countree!''

> 17

Oliver Giles, John Pitcher the dairyman, the parish clerk, the engaged man of fifty, the row of young women against the wall, seemed lost in thought not of the gayest kind. The shepherd looked meditatively on the ground, the shepherdess gazed keenly at the singer, and with some suspicion; she was doubting whether this stranger were merely singing an old song from recollection, or was composing one there and then for the occasion. All were as perplexed at the obscure revelation as the guests at Belshazzar's Feast,[20] except the man in the chimney

***

20. as the . . . Belshazzar's (bel shaz′ərz) **Feast:** In the Old Testament, writing appeared on the wall during a feast held by the king of Babylon warning him of defeat (Ezekiel 5:1).

890   *The Victorian Age*

corner, who quietly said, ''Second verse, stranger,'' and smoked on.

> 18

The singer thoroughly moistened himself from his lips inwards, and went on with the next stanza as requested:

> 19

> "My tools are but common ones,
> Simple shepherds all—
> My tools are no sight to see:
> A little hempen string, and a post
>   whereon to swing,
> Are implements enough for me!''

Shepherd Fennel glanced round. There was no longer any doubt that the stranger was answering his question rhythmically. The guests one and all started back with suppressed exclamations. The young woman engaged to the man of fifty fainted halfway, and would have proceeded, but finding him wanting in alacrity for catching her she sat down trembling.

''Oh, he's the—!'' whispered the people in the background, mentioning the name of an ominous public officer. ''He's come to do it! 'Tis to be at Casterbridge jail tomorrow —the man for sheep-stealing—the poor clockmaker we heard of, who used to live away at Shottsford and had no work to do —Timothy Summers, whose family were a-starving, and so he went out of Shottsford by the high road, and took a sheep in open daylight, defying the farmer and the farmer's wife and the farmer's lad, and every man jack among 'em. He' (and they nodded towards the stranger of the deadly trade) 'is come from up the country to do it because there's not enough to do in his own county town, and he's got the place here now our own county man's dead; he's going to live in the same cottage under the prison wall.''

The stranger in cinder gray took no notice of this whispered string of observations, but again wetted his lips. Seeing that his friend in the chimney corner was the only one who reciprocated his joviality in any way, he held out his cup towards that appreciative comrade, who also held out his own. They clinked together, the eyes of the rest of the room hanging upon the singer's actions. He parted his lips for the third verse; but at that moment another knock was audible upon the door. This time the knock was faint and hesitating.

The company seemed scared; the shepherd looked with consternation towards the entrance, and it was with some effort that he resisted his alarmed wife's deprecatory glance, and uttered for the third time the welcoming words, "Walk in!"

The door was gently opened, and another man stood upon the mat. He, like those who had preceded him, was a stranger. This time it was a short, small personage, of fair complexion, and dressed in a decent suit of dark clothes.

"Can you tell me the way to—?" he began; when, gazing round the room to observe the nature of the company amongst whom he had fallen, his eyes lighted on the stranger in cinder gray. It was just at the instant when the latter, who had thrown his mind into his song with such a will that he scarcely heeded the interruption, silenced all whispers and inquiries by bursting into his third verse:

> *"Tomorrow is my working day,*
> *Simple shepherds all—*
> *Tomorrow is a working day for me:*
> *For the farmer's sheep is slain,*
> *and the lad who did it ta'en,*
> *And on his soul may God ha' merc-y!"*

The stranger in the chimney corner, waving cups with the singer so heartily that his mead splashed over on the hearth, repeated in his bass voice as before:—

21 *"And on his soul may God ha' merc-y!"*

22 All this time the third stranger had been standing in the doorway. Finding now that he did not come forward or go on speaking, the guests particularly regarded him. They noticed to their surprise that he stood before them the picture of abject terror—his knees trembling, his hand shaking so violently

that the door latch by which he supported himself rattled audibly; his white lips were parted, and his eyes fixed on the merry officer of justice in the middle of the room. A moment more and he had turned, closed the door, and fled.

"What a man can it be?" said the shepherd.

The rest, between the awfulness of their late discovery and the odd conduct of this third visitor, looked as if they knew not what to think, and said nothing. Instinctively they withdrew farther and farther from the grim gentleman in their midst, whom some of them seemed to take for the Prince of Darkness himself, till they formed a remote circle, an empty space of floor being left between them and him—. . . *circulus, cujus centrum diabolus.*[21] The room was so silent—though there were more than twenty people in it—that nothing could be heard but the patter of the rain against the window shutters, accompanied by the occasional hiss of a stray drop that fell down the chimney into the fire, and the steady puffing of the man in the corner, who had now resumed his pipe of long clay.

23

The stillness was unexpectedly broken. The distant sound of a gun reverberated through the air—apparently from the direction of the county town.

"Be jiggered!" cried the stranger who had sung the song, jumping up.

"What does that mean?" asked several.

"A prisoner escaped from the jail —that's what it means."

All listened. The sound was repeated, and none of them spoke but the man in the chimney corner, who said quietly, "I've often been told that in this county they fire a gun at such times; but I never heard it till now."

"I wonder if it is *my* man?" murmured the personage in cinder gray.

24

"Surely it is!" said the shepherd invol-

---

21. circulus . . . diabolus: A circle with the devil at its center.

20 Critical Reading and Thinking Fate is at work again in the arrival of the third stranger. What part does it play in the passage?

21 Reading Strategy Understanding irony increases reading comprehension. What is ironic about the first stranger's statement 'And on his soul may God ha' merc-y!'

22 Discussion What is the third stranger's reaction to the assembled group?

23 Critical Reading and Thinking Describe the part that fate plays in setting the tone of this passage.

24 Discussion What conclusions do the party guests reach about the third stranger? What has gone on before that contributes to their jumping to these conclusions?

untarily. "And surely we've zeed him! That little man who looked in at the door by now, and quivered like a leaf when he zeed ye and heard your song!"

"His teeth chattered, and the breath went out of his body," said the dairyman.

"And his heart seemed to sink within him like a stone," said Oliver Giles.

"And he bolted as if he'd been shot at," said the hedge carpenter.

"True—his teeth chattered, and his heart seemed to sink; and he bolted as if he'd been shot at," slowly summed up the man in the chimney corner.

"I didn't notice it," remarked the hangman.

"We were all a-wondering what made him run off in such a fright," faltered one of the women against the wall, "and now 'tis explained!"

The firing of the alarm gun went on at intervals, low and sullenly, and their suspicions became a certainty. The sinister gentleman in cinder gray roused himself. "Is there a constable here?" he asked, in thick tones. "If so, let him step forward."

The engaged man of fifty stepped quavering out from the wall, his betrothed beginning to sob on the back of the chair.

"You are a sworn constable?"

"I be, sir."

"Then pursue the criminal at once, with assistance, and bring him back here. He can't have gone far."

"I will, sir, I will—when I've got my staff. I'll go home and get it, and come sharp here, and start in a body."

"Staff!—never mind your staff; the man'll be gone!"

"But I can't do nothing without my staff—can I, William, and John, and Charles Jake? No; for there's the king's royal crown a painted on en in yaller and gold, and the lion and the unicorn, so as when I raise en up and hit my prisoner, 'tis made a lawful blow thereby. I wouldn't 'tempt to take up a man without my staff—no, not I. If I hadn't the law to gie me courage, why, instead o' my taking up him he might take up me!"

"Now, I'm a king's man myself, and can give you authority enough for this," said the formidable officer in gray. "Now then, all of ye, be ready. Have ye any lanterns?"

"Yes—have ye any lanterns?—I demand it!" said the constable.

"And the rest of you able-bodied—"

"Able-bodied men—yes—the rest of ye!" said the constable.

"Have you some good stout staves and pitchforks—"

"Staves and pitchforks—in the name o' the law! And take 'em in yer hands and go in quest, and do as we in authority tell ye!"

Thus aroused, the men prepared to give chase. The evidence was, indeed, though circumstantial, so convincing, that but little argument was needed to show the shepherd's guests that after what they had seen it would look very much like connivance if they did not instantly pursue the unhappy third stranger, who could not as yet have gone more than a few hundred yards over such uneven country.

A shepherd is always well provided with lanterns; and, lighting these hastily, and with hurdle staves in their hands, they poured out of the door, taking a direction along the crest of the hill, away from the town, the rain having fortunately a little abated.

Disturbed by the noise, or possibly by unpleasant dreams of her baptism, the child who had been christened began to cry heartbrokenly in the room overhead. These notes of grief came down through the chinks of the floor to the ears of the women below, who jumped up one by one, and seemed glad of the excuse to ascend and comfort the baby, for the incidents of the last half-hour greatly oppressed them. Thus in the space of two or three minutes the room on the ground floor was deserted quite.

But it was not for long. Hardly had the sound of footsteps died away when a man returned round the corner of the house from the direction the pursuers had taken. Peeping in at the door, and seeing nobody there, he entered leisurely. It was the stranger of the chimney corner, who had gone out with the rest. The motive of his return was shown by his helping himself to a cut piece of skimmer cake that lay on a ledge beside where he had sat, and which he had apparently forgotten to take with him. He also poured out half a cup more mead from the quantity that remained, ravenously eating and drinking these as he stood. He had not finished when another figure came in just as quietly—his friend in cinder gray.

"O—you here?" said the latter, smiling. "I thought you had gone to help in the capture." And this speaker also revealed the object of his return by looking solicitously round for the fascinating mug of old mead.

"And I thought you had gone," said the other, continuing his skimmer cake with some effort.

"Well, on second thoughts, I felt there were enough without me," said the first confidentially, "and such a night as it is, too. Besides, 'tis the business o' the government to take care of its criminals—not mine."

"True; so it is. And I felt as you did, that there were enough without me."

"I don't want to break my limbs running over the humps and hollows of this wild country."

"Nor I neither, between you and me."

"These shepherd people are used to it —simple-minded souls, you know, stirred up to anything in a moment. They'll have him ready for me before the morning, and no trouble to me at all."

"They'll have him, and we shall have saved ourselves all labor in the matter."

"True, true. Well, my way is to Caster-bridge; and 'tis as much as my legs will do to take me that far. Going the same way?"

"No, I am sorry to say! I have to get home over there" (he nodded indefinitely to the right), "and I feel as you do, that it is quite enough for my legs to do before bedtime."

The other had by this time finished the mead in the mug, after which, shaking hands heartily at the door, and wishing each other well, they went their several ways.

In the meantime the company of pursuers had reached the end of the hog's-back elevation which dominated this part of the down. They had decided on no particular plan of action; and, finding that the man of the baleful trade was no longer in their company, they seemed quite unable to form any such plan now. They descended in all directions down the hill, and straightway several of the party fell into the snare set by Nature for all misguided midnight ramblers over this part of the cretaceous formation. The 'lanchets,' or flint slopes, which belted the escarpment at intervals of a dozen yards, took the less cautious ones unawares, and losing their footing on the rubbly steep they slid sharply downwards, the lanterns rolling from their hands to the bottom, and there lying on their sides till the horn was scorched through.

When they had again gathered themselves together the shepherd, as the man who knew the country best, took the lead, and guided them round these treacherous inclines. The lanterns, which seemed rather to dazzle their eyes and warn the fugitive than to assist them in the exploration, were extinguished, due silence was observed; and in this more rational order they plunged into the vale. It was a grassy, briery, moist defile, affording some shelter to any person who had sought it; but the party perambulated it in vain, and ascended on the other side. Here they wandered apart, and after an interval closed together again to report progress. At the second time of closing in they found themselves near a lonely ash, the single tree on this part of the coomb, probably sown there by a passing bird some fifty years before. And here, standing a little to one side of the trunk, as motionless as the trunk itself, appeared the man they were in quest of, his outline being well defined against the sky beyond. The band noiselessly drew up and faced him.

The Three Strangers 893

26 **Discussion** What are the reactions of the first two strangers to the search for the third?

27 **Master Teacher Note** In regard to the second stranger's referring to the people as "simple-minded souls," you might want to point out that pride is a common fatal flaw in Greek tragedy. Pride is standing in the way of the second stranger's accomplishing his task. Because he is looking down his nose at the peasants, he fails to see what is in front of him.

28 **Literary Focus** Setting plays an important part in the development of Hardy's plots. Discuss how setting controls the action of this passage.

"Your money or your life!" said the constable sternly to the still figure.

"No, no," whispered John Pitcher. "'Tisn't our side ought to say that. That's the doctrine of vagabonds like him, and we be on the side of the law."

"Well, well," replied the constable impatiently; "I must say something, mustn't I? and if you had all the weight o' this undertaking upon your mind, perhaps you'd say the wrong thing too! Prisoner at the bar, surrender, in the name of the Father—the Crown, I mane!"

The man under the tree seemed now to notice them for the first time, and, giving them no opportunity whatever for exhibiting their courage, he strolled slowly towards them. He was, indeed, the little man, the third stranger; but his trepidation had in a great measure gone.

"Well, travelers," he said, "did I hear ye speak to me?"

"You did; you've got to come and be our prisoner at once!" said the constable. "We arrest 'ee on the charge of not biding in Casterbridge jail in a decent proper manner to be hung tomorrow morning. Neighbors, do your duty, and seize the culpet!"

On hearing the charge the man seemed enlightened, and, saying not another word, resigned himself with preternatural civility to the search party, who, with their staves in their hands, surrounded him on all sides, and marched him back towards the shepherd's cottage.

It was eleven o'clock by the time they arrived. The light shining from the open door, a sound of men's voices within, proclaimed to them as they approached the house that some new events had arisen in their absence. On entering they discovered the shepherd's living room to be invaded by two officers from Casterbridge jail, and a well-known magistrate who lived at the nearest county seat, intelligence of the escape having become generally circulated.

"Gentlemen," said the constable, "I have brought back your man—not without

risk and danger; but everyone must do his duty! He is inside this circle of able-bodied persons, who have lent me useful aid, considering their ignorance of Crown work. Men, bring forward your prisoner!" And the third stranger was led to the light.

"Who is this?" said one of the officials.

"The man," said the constable.

"Certainly not," said the turnkey; and the first corroborated his statement.

"But how can it be otherwise?" asked the constable. "Or why was he so terrified at sight o' the singing instrument of the law who sat there?" Here he related the strange behavior of the third stranger on entering the house during the hangman's song.

"Can't understand it," said the officer coolly. "All I know is that it is not the condemned man. He's quite a different character from this one; a gauntish fellow, with dark hair and eyes, rather good-looking, and with a musical bass voice that if you heard it once you'd never mistake as long as you lived."

"Why, souls—'twas the man in the chimney corner!"

"Hey—what?" said the magistrate, coming forward after inquiring particulars from the shepherd in the background. "Haven't you got the man after all?"

"Well, sir," said the constable, "he's the man we were in search of, that's true; and yet he's not the man we were in search of. For the man we were in search of was not the man we wanted, sir, if you understand my everyday way; for 'twas the man in the chimney corner!"

"A pretty kettle of fish altogether!" said the magistrate. "You had better start for the other man at once."

The prisoner now spoke for the first time. The mention of the man in the chimney corner seemed to have moved him as nothing else could do. "Sir," he said, stepping forward to the magistrate, "take no more trouble about me. The time is come when I may as well speak. I have done nothing; my crime is that the condemned

Grammar in Action

The **dash** is a strong, dramatic punctuation mark that should be used only infrequently. One of its valid uses is to indicate an abrupt change of thought, a dramatic interrupting idea, or a halt in speech such as is found in realistic dialogue. Hardy demonstrates correct use of the dash on page 894.

"Prisoner at the bar, surrender, in the name of the Father —the Crown, I mane!"

"Why, souls—'twas the man in the chimney corner!"
"Hey—what?" said the magistrate, coming forward after inquiring particulars from the shepherd in the background."

In all three of these examples, the dashes serve to reproduce the breaks that often occur in real speech, especially during moments of excitement.

One other common use of the dash is to set off a parenthetical expression, especially a long one, as in the following sentence.

man is my brother. Early this afternoon I left home at Shottsford to tramp it all the way to Casterbridge jail to bid him farewell. I was benighted, and called here to rest and ask the way. When I opened the door I saw before me the very man, my brother, that I thought to see in the condemned cell at Casterbridge. He was in this chimney corner; and jammed close to him, so that he could not have got out if he had tried, was the executioner who'd come to take his life, singing a song about it and not knowing that it was his victim who was close by, joining in to save appearances. My brother threw a glance of agony at me, and I knew he meant, 'Don't reveal what you see; my life depends on it.' I was so terror-struck that I could hardly stand, and, not knowing what I did, I turned and hurried away.''

The narrator's manner and tone had the stamp of truth, and his story made a great impression on all around. "And do you know where your brother is at the present time?'' asked the magistrate.

"I do not. I have never seen him since I closed this door.''

"I can testify to that, for we've been between ye ever since,'' said the constable.

"Where does he think to fly to? What is his occupation?''

"He's a watch-and-clock-maker, sir.''

"'A said 'a was a wheelwright—a wicked rogue,'' said the constable.

"The wheels of clocks and watches he meant, no doubt,'' said Shepherd Fennel. "I thought his hands were palish for's trade.''

"Well, it appears to me that nothing can be gained by retaining this poor man in custody,'' said the magistrate; "your business lies with the other, unquestionably.''

And so the little man was released off-hand; but he looked nothing the less sad on that account, it being beyond the power of magistrate or constable to raze out the written troubles in his brain, for they concerned another whom he regarded with more solicitude than himself. When this was done, and the man had gone his way, the night was found to be so far advanced that it was deemed useless to renew the search before the next morning.

Next day, accordingly, the quest for the clever sheep stealer became general and keen, to all appearance at least. But the intended punishment was cruelly disproportioned to the transgression, and the sympathy of a great many country folk in that district was strongly on the side of the fugitive. Moreover, his marvelous coolness and daring in hob-and-nobbing with the hangman, under the unprecedented circumstances of the shepherd's party, won their admiration. So that it may be questioned if all those who ostensibly made themselves so busy in exploring woods and fields and lanes were quite so thorough when it came to the private examination of their own lofts and outhouses. Stories were afloat of a mysterious figure being occasionally seen in some old overgrown trackway or other, remote from turnpike roads; but when a search was instituted in any of these suspected quarters nobody was found. Thus the days and weeks passed without tidings.

In brief, the bass-voiced man of the chimney corner was never recaptured. Some said that he went across the sea, others that he did not, but buried himself in the depths of a populous city. At any rate, the gentleman in cinder gray never did his morning's work at Casterbridge, nor met anywhere at all, for business purposes, the genial comrade with whom he had passed an hour of relaxation in the lonely house on the slope of the coomb.

The grass has long been green on the graves of Shepherd Fennel and his frugal wife; the guests who made up the christening party have mainly followed their entertainers to the tomb; the baby in whose honor they all had met is a matron in the sere and yellow leaf. But the arrival of the three strangers at the shepherd's that night, and the details connected therewith, is a story as well known as ever in the country about Higher Crowstairs.

30 Discussion What factors contribute to the sympathy toward the sheep thief? What can be inferred from his remaining free?

31 Reading Strategy What ironies have made this tale an interesting study of human nature? Have students compare this story to Thomas Hardy's poem "The Man He Killed."

On Thursday—I'll never forget that day—I went to work for the first time in my life.

Student Activity 1. Find six similar uses of the dash in "The Three Strangers."

Student Activity 2. Write a brief monologue such as a person would utter at an important moment in his or her life. Use dashes to indicate the speech pauses caused by strongly felt emotion.

Closure and Extension

ANSWERS TO THINKING ABOUT THE SELECTION
Recalling

1. (a) It takes place in and around a shepherd's cottage in Wessex on March 24, 182–. (b) a christening.
2. (a) The first stranger is about forty years old, gaunt, five-feet-eight or nine, dressed in a black coat. (b) The second stranger is several years older with slightly frosted hair, bristly eyebrows, and whiskers; his face is full and flabby with a nose marked by grog blossoms; he wears a cinder-grey suit and a greatcoat.
3. (a) The second stranger is a hangman. (b) He reveals his identity by singing a song about himself.
4. (a) Fennel assumes he is the sheepstealer (b) because of the terrified look on his face when he discovers who the hangman is.

Interpreting

5. They indicate that they are humble workers of the land.
6. Answers will differ.

Applying

7. Suggested response: Hardy's respect was limited.

Challenge How do you think Hardy wants you to feel toward the sheep stealer? Include evidence from the selection that supports your answer.

ANSWERS TO ANALYZING LITERATURE

Suggested response: Hardy's description of the outside of the cottage and the rain falling on the farm buildings and the surrounding downs creates a picture of bleak loneliness. This somber mood is alleviated and contrasted by his warm description of the convivial atmosphere inside the cottage.

THINKING ABOUT THE SELECTION
Recalling

1. (a) Where and when does the story take place? (b) What event is being celebrated?
2. (a) Describe the appearance of the first stranger. (b) Of the second stranger.
3. (a) What is the second stranger's occupation? (b) How is this revealed?
4. (a) Whom does Shepherd Fennel assume the third stranger to be? (b) Why?

Interpreting

5. What do the speech habits of the Fennels and their guests reveal about them?
6. (a) How early on did you guess the identity of the first stranger? (b) The second? (c) The third? (d) What clues did you use?

Applying

7. What does this story suggest about its author's respect for institutions such as the law in nineteenth-century England? Explain.

ANALYZING LITERATURE
Setting and Mood

The setting of a story is when and where the action occurs. In addition to such "factual" details as place names and historical references, setting also accounts for time of day, season, weather conditions, and the like. Aspects of setting, especially of the latter type help determine a story's mood—the emotional response it excites in its readers. Read the following details of setting from "The Three Strangers." Tell the mood suggested by each detail and by all of them taken together. Explain why each detail creates the mood it does.
1. Fifty years ago such a lonely cottage stood.
2. The level rainstorm smote walls, slopes, and hedges . . . ; the tails of little birds trying to roost on some scraggy thorn were blown inside out like umbrellas. The gable-end of the cottage was stained wet.
3. The room was lighted by half a dozen candles. . . . On the hearth . . . blazed a fire of thorns that crackled.

CRITICAL THINKING AND READING
Inferring the Author's Attitude

In "The Three Strangers" fate plays an important—and sometimes fickle—role. Had fate, for instance, not decreed a rainstorm, the sheep-stealer might never have come face-to-face with his executioner. And it is the same fateful rainstorm that enables the guilty man to escape capture by his pursuers. From these and other events in the story, attempt to **infer,** or arrive at an understanding of, Hardy's attitude toward the role of fate. Ask yourself: Does he seem to feel that fate governs our lives? To what extent does he believe that we can and should alter fate by exercising our own free will?

UNDERSTANDING LANGUAGE
Reading Dialect

Most of the characters in the story speak in a particular **dialect,** or manner of speech that typifies a particular region or group. The use of dialect in a story adds to both its realism and its local flavor. Restate each of the following quotations in standard English.
1. "Late to be traipsing athwart this coomb—hey?" (page 886)
2. "A smoker, and no pipe about 'ee?" (page 886)
3. ". . . That little man . . . quivered . . . when he zeed ye . . . !" (page 892)
4. "'A said 'a was a wheelwright . . ." (page 895)

THINKING AND WRITING
Describing a Place

Choose a place that you know well—perhaps the neighborhood you live in or a city that you have visited often. On a sheet of paper jot down as many details of the place as you can think of. Try to include in your list features that make the location unique, or at least easy to visualize. Then convert your notes into a description that would enable a stranger to picture it with little difficulty. Be prepared to share your description with your class.

ANSWERS TO CRITICAL THINKING AND READING

Suggested response: Hardy seems to demonstrate his belief in the supremacy of man's free will over fate when the criminal uses the hangman's pride against him and tricks him, thereby making escape possible.

ANSWERS TO UNDERSTANDING LANGUAGE

Suggested responses:

1. "It is rather late to be wandering around these barren hills, isn't it?"
2. "If you are a smoker, why don't you have a pipe?"
3. "That little man shook all over with fright when he saw you."
4. "He said that he was a wheelwright."

MASTERS OF THE VICTORIAN NOVEL

The Victorian Novel

From the sprawling canvas of Dickens's London to the compelling atmosphere of Emily Brontë's wild moors, the Victorian novel has made a lasting impression on literature and readers. Most of the novels written during this era are concerned with manners, morals, and money. Frequently the plot centers around the struggles of a main character to find self-knowledge with regard to others, in love or marriage, with family or neighbors, or within the working world. Sometimes the quest for self has spiritual overtones, as in the later novels of Thomas Hardy, although the major Victorian novelists in the main were more concerned with people's relationships to society than to religion.

The novels were frequently published in inexpensive monthly installments. To hold their readers' interest between parts, the writers built a minor climax into each installment. This led to a loose, episodic treatment with a vast, intricate plot, numerous characters, and much repetition to jog the reader's memory. Modern novelist Henry James called Victorian novels "large loose baggy monsters," but readers delighted in the suspenseful form.

Giants of the Victorian Novel

In such novels as *Ivanhoe* (1820), Sir Walter Scott, the first major historical novelist, created vivid portraits of Scotland, England, and the Continent from medieval times to the eighteenth century. William Makepeace Thackeray's foray into the historical novel, *Henry Esmond* (1852), was very successful, but *Vanity Fair* (1847) remains his masterpiece. Because of its narrative skill and vivid characterization, the satire immediately established his reputation as one of the major literary figures of the time. Many heroines were modeled on the main character, Becky Sharp. Charlotte Brontë's fictionalized autobiography of a young orphan, *Jane Eyre* (1847), sparked a series of novels on governesses, which became a popular genre through which to explore women's role in society. Her sister Emily's unique tale of love, revenge, and redemption, *Wuthering Heights,* comments on the tensions of nineteenth-century life in a different fashion. The most popular writer of the age, Charles Dickens, combined vivid storytelling, humor, pathos, and irony with sharp social criticism and acute observations of people and places, both real and imagined. His fame was based on an astonishing stream of novels, including *Nicholas Nickleby* (1837–1838), *Bleak House* (1852–1853), and *Great Expectations* (1860–1861).

"The art of novels," wrote Thackeray, "*is* to represent nature: to convey as strongly as possible the sentiment of reality." The continued appeal of Victorian novels comes in large part from their realistic portrayal of Victorian life.

Masters of the Victorian Novel 897

Presentation

Motivation/Prior Knowledge Have students define the novel, stating its characteristics and its elements. Let them discuss what types of novels they like to read. Point out that the novel has become the predominant form of literature, and it was in the nineteenth century that the novel as a form of literature reached its height.

Enrichment The novel as a literary form arose in the eighteenth century and flourished in the nineteenth century. With the rise of the middle class and the spread of minimal education in the nineteenth century, an audience arose for realistic fiction portraying middle-class society. Novelists became entertainers, suiting their writing to their audiences. They often wrote in installments, with the effect that many novels were episodic. Ask students how the novel changed in the twentieth century.

Activity Have each student read and report on a nineteenth-century novel. You might suggest novels by Walter Scott, Charles Dickens, the Brontë sisters, or any of the other writers mentioned on this page.

Tell students that *Wuthering Heights* presents a character at once repulsive and compelling. When *Wuthering Heights* first appeared, Heathcliff was seen as shocking and brutal. Heathcliff is Emily Brontë's version of a Byronic hero, that is, a character inspired by the poet Lord Byron. Typically the Byronic hero is dark, brooding, and unpredictable. Challenge students, as they read the novel, to outline their evolving reactions to Heathcliff.

Enrichment *Wuthering Heights* stands outside the tradition of the nineteenth-century novel. In many ways, it is more Elizabethan in its dramatic effects. Unlike most other nineteenth-century novels, which set up a social world, *Wuthering Heights* focuses on intense forces and passions—love, hate, and revenge—and the characters who embody these passions. These characters are almost devoid of the civilized habits, ways of thinking, and forms of social interaction that provide a familiar background in other fiction, particularly in the nineteenth century.

GREAT WORKS

WUTHERING HEIGHTS
by Emily Brontë

A Tale of Love

> If all else perished, and he remained I should continue to be; and if all else remained, and he were annihilated, the universe would turn to a mighty stranger: I should not seem a part of it. My love for Linton is like the foliage in the woods: time will change it, I'm well aware, as winter changes the trees. My love for Heathcliff resembles the eternal rocks beneath: a source of little visible delight, but necessary. Nelly, I am Heathcliff. He's always, always in my mind: not as a pleasure, any more than I am always a pleasure to myself, but as my own being.

Who could inspire such devotion in the heart of the willful, passionate Catherine Earnshaw? Only wild, fierce Heathcliff, more villain than hero, a man whose soul is torn between love and hate.

Heathcliff

Emily Brontë's *Wuthering Heights* opens in 1801 with the arrival of Mr. Lockwood at Thrushcross Grange, a house that he has rented on the windswept Yorkshire moor. He crosses the moor to meet his landlord, Heathcliff. His curiosity is sparked by gloomy, crumbling Wuthering Heights, Heathcliff's home. The savagely handsome Heathcliff is initially unfriendly but unbends enough to offer Lockwood some small social courtesy.

Lockwood's next visit goes far less smoothly. He is repulsed by the hatred among those gathered: Heathcliff, sullen young Hareton Earnshaw, and Heathcliff's beautiful, defiant daughter-in-law. Trapped by a raging snowstorm, he is reluctantly allowed to spend the night. During a violent nightmare, he imagines himself smashing the window, grabbing an icy cold hand, and hearing a voice sobbing, "I'm Catherine Linton, I'm home!" His scream awakens Heathcliff, who reacts violently to Lockwood's tale, wrenching open the window and crying, "Come in! come in! Cathy, do come. Oh do—*once* more! Oh! my heart's darling, hear me *this* time—Catherine, at last!" Lockwood makes his way home as soon as he can, soaked and chilled to the bone. What are we to make of all this?

Mrs. Dean's Tale

Lockwood questions his housekeeper, Nelly Dean, about the strange people he has met. We learn that Heathcliff was married to Isabella, sister of Mr. Linton, the previous owner of Wuthering Heights. Hareton Earn-

898 *The Victorian Age*

Literary Focus The point of view is extraordinarily complex in *Wuthering Heights*. It begins with an observing first-person narrator, Lockwood. Shortly, however, Lockwood ceases to report what he sees and begins to tell us what he hears from Nelly Dean, the housekeeper. The story of *Wuthering Heights* is retold through the double filter of one who saw first-hand what happened—Nelly—and an agent from the outside world—Lockwood.

shaw is Heathcliff's nephew. The rest of the wild story unfolds through Nelly's eyes.

Many years ago, Mr. Earnshaw, the former master, had returned from a trip with a "dirty, ragged, black-haired" waif he had picked up on the streets of Liverpool. Although both of Earnshaw's children—Hindley and Catherine—hated the boy on sight, Nelly named him "Heathcliff," and he remained. Catherine grew passionately attached to him, but with Mr. Earnshaw's death two years later, Hindley was freed to enact his resentment and mistreat Heathcliff fiercely. The outcast becomes even more brutal and morose. Catherine and Heathcliff, now closer than ever, seize any opportunity to escape, running wildly across the desolate moors. Hindley's wife gives birth to Hareton and dies; Hindley becomes a drunken brute.

One evening Catherine and Heathcliff end up at the Grange, and peer in the window at the spoiled Linton children, Edgar and Isabella. Catherine is injured and recuperates with the Lintons. A closeness grows between the families, and despite the love she feels for Heathcliff, she marries Edgar Linton. Tender, constant, and loving, he has all the qualities of the hero of conventional Victorial novels—and is no match for headstrong, selfish Catherine. Heathcliff bolts from Wuthering Heights.

When he returns six months later, he is rich and well-groomed. Torn between her love for Heathcliff and her husband's jealously, she weakens. After giving birth to Edgar's child, Cathy, she dies. For the next seventeen years, Heathcliff is bound on revenge. He marries Edgar's sister, Isabella, and turns Hindley into a drunken gambler,

Great Works 899

obtaining all his property. Isabella has a son, Linton, whom Heathcliff marries off to Cathy. His plans fall apart, however, when Linton dies and Cathy falls in love with and marries Hareton. Heathcliff's end is the most astonishing of all, however . . .

Emily Brontë

The daughter of an Irish clergyman, Emily Brontë (1818–1848) whose efforts gave the world *Wuthering Heights* in 1847, was one of three novel-writing sisters. Charlotte wrote *Jane Eyre* and Anne wrote *Agnes Grey.*

Born in the Yorkshire town of Hartshead-cum-Clifton, Brontë was raised, along with her brother and four sisters, by an aunt, following the early death of their mother. As children, the Brontës were often left to themselves. For recreation they walked the bleak moors near Haworth, where the family had moved from Hartshead, and invented imaginary "histories" for toy soldiers, a pastime they continued to pursue up through their teen years. In 1842 Emily went to Brussels with her sister Charlotte, to study at the Pensionnat Heger, in the hopes of starting their own school. The death of their aunt, however, brought the sisters prematurely back to Yorkshire.

In 1845 Charlotte accidentally discovered some poems that Emily had composed. The discovery led in turn to the revelation that Charlotte and Anne had secretly been writing poetry as well, and in 1846 the three talented Brontës published at their own expense a book of verses by "Currer, Ellis, and Acton Bell," the pen names that kept the sisters' initials but hid their real names. The book sold only two copies, but the venture had stoked the sisters' creative fires, and each began work on a novel.

For her project Emily chose to write about the Yorkshire countryside she knew so well. And she chose to write about it with the same poetic voice that typified the romantic tales she had produced as a child.

The result, *Wuthering Heights,* is a tale of love, revenge, and redemption that comments on the tensions of nineteenth-century society. Unlike Charlotte's *Jane Eyre,* which became an instant success, *Wuthering Heights* failed in its day to gain the recognition it deserved.

Emily, meanwhile, was in poor health, having long suffered from a respiratory condition. She died at the age of thirty.

That Emily Brontë may have intended her masterpiece as a visionary work is suggested by a study of her poetry, which expresses her impatience with social order and her yearning for a "dazzling sea" of infinity. As some contemporary critics have suggested, *Wuthering Heights* clouds rather than explains the mysteries of Brontë's brief life, yet there is no denying the enormous imaginative power behind the words.

An Unnoticed Masterpiece

Wuthering Heights went unnoticed when it was published in 1847. The handful of people who did read it were repulsed by the brutal violence of the characters and because it differed so much from the conventional romantic novels of the day. Critics today consider *Wuthering Heights* as the "one perfect work of art amid all the vast varied canvasses of Victorian fiction." Brontë died on December 19, 1848, knowing nothing at all of the overwhelming success that would finally be accorded to her book. "*Wuthering Heights* is a strange sort of book," said a critic the year after her death, "baffling all regular criticism; yet, it is impossible to begin and not finish it; and quite impossible to lay it aside afterwards and say nothing about it. . . . We strongly recommend all our readers who love novelty to get this story, for we can promise them that they will never have read anything like it before."

GREAT WORKS

THE IMPORTANCE OF BEING EARNEST
by Oscar Wilde

Presentation

Motivation/Prior Knowledge
Introduce the notion of farce: a dramatic piece that depends less on plot and character than on exaggerated, improbable situations for humorous effect. Students may have seen examples of farce on television. Although the nineteenth century is not noted for humor, Oscar Wilde, who was never one to stick to conventions, wrote a farce in *The Importance of Being Earnest*.

Humanities Note

Lithograph of Oscar Wilde, from *Vanity Fair,* May 24, 1884, issue. This lithograph is a caricature of Wilde. A caricature is a representation, pictorial or in words, in which a subject's distinctive features are deliberately exaggerated or distorted to produce a comic or ridiculous effect. Wilde became known as a "character," who affected outlandish manners and costume. In this caricature of him, the artist emphasizes Wilde's dandified attitude and appearance.

Caricature is more frequently associated with drawing than with writing, although Wilde himself in this play makes caricatures of his characters: through good, dull people, he mounts an assault on commonplace life and values.

Consider the following questions for discussion.
1. What details contribute to the caricature?
2. What attitude do you form of Wilde from this lithograph?

Oscar Wilde

Oscar Wilde (1854–1900) was born in Dublin, Ireland, the son of a famous surgeon and a Dublin poet. Educated at Trinity college, Dublin, and later at Magdalen College, Oxford, he took first class in Classical Moderations and Litterae Humaniores Newdigate prize for poetry. Wilde's full name was as extravagant as he was. The unconventional Oscar Fingall O'Flahertie Wills Wilde delighted in shocking his audiences. In plays like *Lady Windermere's Fan, A Woman of No Importance,* and *The Ideal Husband,* he turned the correct and proper on its head, poking fun at the conventions of Victorian behavior. As an advocate of the school of Aestheticism, Wilde championed the cause of "art for art's sake."

The Celebrated Mr. Wilde

The celebrated Oscar Wilde was known for his witty barbs and word play. On January 1882, he arrived in New York City by ocean liner to begin a lecture tour. The reporters who clustered around him were disappointed in the ordinary appearance of such a celebrated writer. He, too, was dissatisfied. Expecting inquiries about his planned lectures, he was instead bombarded with questions on how he liked his eggs fried, how he trimmed his fingernails, and what temperature he liked his bath to be. When his answers lacked the wit the reporters had come to expect, they buttonholed passengers for livelier responses. The passengers responded, recounting that they had heard him complain that the trip was dull and that the ocean did not roar.

The reporters gleefully printed that Wilde was "disappointed with the Atlantic Ocean," a phrase that got him far more publicity that any statement on his literary views could have done. Realizing that he had not done himself justice, Wilde made amends the moment he stepped ashore. "Have you anything to declare?" asked the customs official. "No, I have nothing to de-

LITHOGRAPH OF OSCAR WILDE FROM VANITY FAIR, MAY 24, 1984
Ape (also known as "Singe")
The Mansell Collection

Enrichment During the 1890's a literary and artistic movement arose, which brought together various theories and attitudes that had been brewing in the previous decades. This was the Aesthetic movement. In mid-century, the chief emphasis in art had been on the emotion and character of the artist. The new aesthetic attitudes centered on the qualities of the art itself. The rallying cry was "Art for Art's Sake." Art and artists were held to be free of any obligation or responsibility other than that of striving for beauty. Oscar Wilde embraced aestheticism. His critical writings, "The Decay of Lying" and "The Critic as Artist," express theories on such questions as the relation of art to nature and the function of art as a means of knowledge.

Some would say that Wilde lived the meaning of aestheticism with the brilliance of his conversation and the flamboyance of his dandyism. He perceived his life as art. "I have given my genius to my life," he said, "to my work only my talent."

clare," he replied. After a perfectly timed pause, he added "except my genius." Few remarks in history have circulated as widely and quickly as that one.

"The Importance of Being Earnest"

As the title proclaims, Wilde's 1895 farce is about earnestness, that is, Victorian solemnity. It's subtitle, *A Trivial Comedy for Serious People*, sets its tone, The play attacks the kind of false seriousness that means priggishness, hypocrisy, and lack of irony, all the qualities Wilde detested in nineteenth-century England. Now widely recognized as one of the finest comedies in English, *The Importance of Being Earnest* challenges almost everything we are likely to take seriously: death, money, marriage, status, economics, beauty and truth, morality, and the class system.

The play opens in the London apartment of Algernon Moncrieff, a young man about town. He is being visited by a friend whom he knows by the name of Ernest Worthing but whose real name is Jack. Jack lives in the country, where he is the guardian of Miss Cecily Cardew, a task he is anxious to escape. To do so, he invents a ne'er-do-well brother whom he must frequently visit in London to rescue from various scrapes. For no apparent reason, he uses the name "Ernest" in town and "Jack" in the country. As you can imagine, the confusion over names sets the plot spinning.

An Earnest by Any Other Name

Jack falls in love with Algernon's first cousin, Gwendolen Fairfax, and soon proposes:

JACK: [nervously] Miss Fairfax, ever since I met you I have admired you more than any

girl . . . I have ever met since . . . I met you.
GWENDOLYN: Yes, I am quite aware of the fact.
. . . For me you have always had an irresistible fascination. . . . my ideal has always
been to love someone of the name of Ernest.
There is something in that name that inspires absolute confidence. The moment
that Algernon first mentioned to me that he
had a friend called Ernest, I knew I was
destined to love you.

Jack anxiously inquires whether Gwendolyn could love him if his name were different; say, "Jack." "No," she protests, "The
only really safe name is Ernest."

In sails Gwendolyn's impossibly snob-
bish mother, Lady Bracknell, anxious to
make sure that Jack is an acceptable candidate for her daughter's hand. In the absurd
dialogue that follows, Wilde attacks all the
values most dear to Victorians:

LADY BRACKNELL: I have always been of the
opinion that a man who desires to get married should either know everything or nothing. Which do you know?
JACK: [after some hesitation] I know nothing,
Lady Bracknell.
LADY BRACKNELL: I am pleased to hear it. I do
not approve of anything that tampers with
natural ignorance. . . . The whole theory of
modern education is radically unsound. Fortunately in England, at any rate, education
produces no effect whatsoever. . . .

She next inquires after his assets:

JACK: Well, I own a house in Belgrave
Square. . . .
LADY BRACKNELL: What number in Belgrave
Square?
JACK: 149.
LADY BRACKNELL: [shaking her head] The un-
fashionable side. I thought there was some-
thing. However, that could easily be altered.
JACK: Do you mean the fashion, or the side?
LADY BRACKNELL: [sternly] Both, if necessary, I
presume. . . .

LADY BRACKNELL: Now to minor matters. Are
your parents living?
JACK: I have lost both my parents.
LADY BRACKNELL: Both? To lose one parent may
be regarded as a misfortune—to lose both
seems like carelessness. . . .

Weaving ridiculous characters and sparkling wit together in a delightfully unbelievable plot, Wilde challenges us to reexamine
the values we take most seriously. The result is an hilarious look at a totally absurd
world—ours! No wonder the play was an
immediate hit and has since become a theater classic.

A Tragic Ending

Unfortunately, Oscar Wilde's life ended
tragically with little time for him to enjoy his
success. His friendship with the son of the
Marquess of Queensberry led to his eventual
imprisonment for immoral conduct. During
the two years he spent in prison, his health
was ruined. He died, poor and alone—
having seen during his lifetime the peaks of
success and the abyss of failure.

More About the Author Oscar
Wilde developed his verbal talents as a youngster. His family
held frequent parties for the literary and social world of which
they were a part. At these gatherings the Wilde children were expected to be as witty as their
guests.

In school Oscar became
popular for his gift of storytelling
and his ability to create amusing
nicknames. Upon graduation
from Magdalene College, Oxford, Wilde was asked about his
plans. He replied, "Somehow or
other I'll be famous and if not
famous, I'll be notorious." How
would such an attitude affect a
career?

Presentation

Motivation/Prior Knowledge
Ask students about the role of women in society at different times as contrasted with today. Discuss function, responsibilities, rights, and so on. Then have them read this article.

Discussion Ask students how women have been portrayed in the literature they have read in each unit in this book?

CROSS CURRENTS

Changing Views of Women

SEVENTEETH-CENTURY VIEWS

Times were tough for women in seventeenth-century England. Although womanhood was idealized in the courtly love poetry of the day, the more common view held that women were conniving and inconstant. A popular writer expressed the general attitude against women in 1615:

> Eagles eat not men till they are
> dead but women devour them alive,
> for a woman will pick thy pocket
> and empty thy purse, laugh in thy
> face and cut thy throat, they are
> ungrateful, perjured, full of fraud,
> flouting and deceit, unconstant,
> waspish, toyish, light, sullen,
> proud, discourteous, and cruel.

Things were hardly better across the ocean. Although women in New England enjoyed relative equality battling side-by-side with their men to survive in a hostile land, there were limits to their rights. Mental, not physical, strength was at issue here, for women's minds were thought too frail to absorb excessive learning. Puritan culture reinforced the power of the father as the head of the family, and the penalty for trespassing the accepted order was dire indeed. Governor John Winthrop reported the following sad case in his diary entry for April 13, 1645:

> Mr. Hopkins, the governor of
> Hartford upon Connecticut, came to
> Boston, and brought his wife with
> him who was fallen into a sad
> infirmity, the loss of her
> understanding and reason, which
> had been growing upon her divers
> years, by occasion of her giving
> herself wholly to reading and

writing, and had written many books. Her husband, being very loving and tender with her, was loath to grieve her; but he saw his error, when it was too late. For if she had attended her household affairs, and such things as belong to women, and not gone out of her way and calling to meddle in such things as are proper for men, whose minds are stronger, etc., she had kept her wits, and might have improved them usefully and honorably in the place God had sent her.

RESTORATION VIEWS

Society's view of women had not changed drastically by the Restoration and early eighteenth century, although growing urbanization paved the way for the entrance of women into areas previously closed to them. After Charles II granted licenses to theaters, women dramatists such as Aphra Behn began publishing their own plays. With the end of the patronage system for the support of authors, women freely entered the ranks of novelists, wisely realizing that writing was one of the few careers open to them. Despite these inroads, women were still scorned. Many agreed with Alexander Pope's famous judgment—"Most women have no character at all." By the nineteenth century, satire gave way to sentiment, and views of women changed.

VICTORAN VIEWS

Women in Victorian England were considered incapable of governing themselves. A wife separated from her husband for whatever reason had no right to see her children. Married women could not own property; Charlotte Brontë was astonished to learn upon her marriage in 1854 that the copyrights of her novels and any royalties paid had passed from her hands to her husband's.

But the Victorian Age saw the start of women's emancipation. The first important step came in 1857, when the Divorce Act moved matrimonial cases from the religious to a nonreligious court. A woman could divorce her husband if he had been unfaithful and cruel, but divorce still carried a sizable social stigma. The greatest change came in 1881 with the Married Women's Property Act, granting women rights to their own possessions.

Despite these strides, many men—as well as women—still felt that women were best suited for hearth and home. A woman writing in 1837 stressed:

> "In everything that women attempt,
> they should show their
> consciousness of dependence.
> There is something so unpleasant
> in female self-sufficiency. . . . Their
> sex should ever teach them to be
> subordinate; and they should
> remember that, by them, influence
> is to be obtained, not by
> assumption, but by a delicate
> appeal to affection or principle.
> Women, in this respect, are
> something like children: the more
> they show their need of support,
> the more engaging they are."

Curiously, these rules held only for affluent women, who were thought too delicate for anything but the mildest pastimes. Their delicate nerves had to be cared for as carefully as their bodies. Although remarkably

SUFFRAGETTES EXPELLED AFTER DEMONSTRATING AT WESTMINSTER
A. Beltrame

productive, Elizabeth Barrett Browning, for example, spent six years in bed following her brother's death.

Someone had to pick up the slack—hence, a different view of working-class women. They were thought to be healthy and strong, although in truth they suffered far more from contagious diseases and complications from childbirth than their wealthy counterparts. A visitor to a cotton mill in 1897 reported on working conditions, "The place was full of women, young, all of them, some large with child, and obliged to stand twelve hours each day. . . . The heat was excessive in some of the rooms; the stink pestiferous, and in all an atmosphere of cotton flue. I nearly fainted."

By the twentieth century, the position of women and views toward them had changed dramatically, as men and women made strides toward equalizing all areas of life.

Cross Currents 905

Humanities Note

Lithograph, *Suffragettes expelled after demonstrating at Westminster,* 1906, by A. Beltrame. The desire of women for suffrage became very strong in England, as well as in other places, at the turn of the century. Women demonstrated in public places demanding the right to vote. Art like this print circulated widely, firing the cause. Students might enjoy noticing similarities between the action in this art with that in news photographs today of demonstrations for various causes.

Consider the following questions for discussion.
1. What do you think was the purpose of this piece of art?
2. Do you think it achieved its purpose?

Learning Across the Curriculum Have students do research on the achievements of women in various disciplines: science, technology, the arts, politics, medicine. Students may work on this individually or in groups. You might wish to have students share their findings with the class.

The Victorian Age 1833–1901

LANGUAGE CONTINUES TO GROW

The swift progress in every field of intellectual activity in the Victorian period was marked by a corresponding increase in new words. Great advances in industry, science, and modes of living all added new words to the vocabulary. In the field of electricity, for example, words like *dynamo, alternating current,* and *arc light* entered the language about 1870. The explosive number of words contributed by the field of science is especially dramatic.

Although some new words are technical terms used only by specialists, the vast numbers of new scientific words contributed to English during the Victorian age have since passed into general use. We now have names for medical conditions such as *anemia, appendicitis, bronchitis,* and *diphtheria,* to mention just a few.

Bacteriology and *immunology* were also coined during this age. Although the study of bacteria began with Dutch naturalist von Leeuwenhoek in 1683, the science of bacteriology was not firmly established until the nineteenth century. In 1860 Louis Pasteur established that bacteria come only from other similar organisms; in 1880 scientists began discovering immunity against specific bacteria. The bacteria for typhoid fever was isolated in 1880; tetanus, 1885; tuberculosis, 1890; and plague, 1894.

Thanks to Victorian scientists, we run *clinics* to help the ill, can *vaccinate* against many diseases, and use *anesthesia* to relieve pain. British chemist Sir Humphry Davis discovered nitrous oxide about 1800; it was first used by an American dentist, Horace Wells, in 1844. In 1847 British physician Sir James Simpson found chloroform to be an effective anesthesia.

We have efficient remedies such as *iodine* and *aspirin,* too. Although a crude aspirin compound found in the bark of the willow tree was used by the ancient Greeks and American Indians, it is bitter and irritates the stomach. German chemist Felix Hoffman first synthesized a purer form of aspirin in 1893 in response to the urging of his father, who suffered painfully from rheumatism.

And the movies! William Talbot in England and Louis Daguerre in France perfected the first practical photographic process in 1839; by 1861 American inventor Coleman Sellers had patented the Kinematoscope, the

DISRAELI AND QUEEN VICTORIA (cartoon)
John Tenniel
The Granger Collection

"NEW CROWNS FOR OLD ONES!"
(ALADDIN ADAPTED.)

first *moving picture.* Thomas Edison patented a refined version in 1891; by 1895 coin operated machines projecting fifty feet of film appeared in London, Berlin, and Paris. Edison's assistant produced a rudimentary talking picture in 1889, and the term *cinema* was coined.

ENGLISH BECOMES FORMAL

Despite the onslaught of new terms, the Victorians were extremely cautious about their language. Language was formal, polite—and a sure sign of social class. *Etiquette for the Ladies: Eighty Maxims on Dress, Manners and Accomplishments,* published in 1837, includes these guidelines on language:

> It is not only absurd, it is in bad taste, for people of inadequate means to ape the manners of the great. . . . Scarcely anything is so repulsive in a lady, so utterly plebeian, as speaking in a loud, harsh voice. . . . In speaking to her husband, a lady may address him by his Christian name. In speaking of him to others, it is more proper to style him Mr —. To degrade him to a mere initial, to call him *Mr. A.* or *Mr. B.,* is worse than vulgar, it is heathenish.

Not everyone was pleased by the stuffy formality English had acquired under Victoria's reign. Noted Victorian humorist Edward Lear, writing in 1844, remarked, "The uniform apathetic tone assumed by lofty society irks me *dreadfully*: nothing I long for half so much as to giggle heartily and to hop on one leg down the great gallery—but I dare not."

DIALECTS

Language was strictly conventional among the upper classes—and those who aspired to join their "betters"—but such was not the case among the common folk, as this excerpt from the Cockney Song "Wot Cher! O, Knocked 'em in the Old Kent Road" shows:

> Last week down our alley came a toff,
> Nice old geezer with a nasty cough,
> Sees my Missus, takes 'is topper off
>   In a very gentlemanly way!
>
> 'Ma'am,' says 'e, 'I'ave some news to tell,
> Your rich Uncle Tom of Camberwell
> Popped off recent, which it ain't a sell,
>   Leaving' you 'is little Donkey Shay.'
> 'Wot cher!' all the neighbors cried,
>   'Who're yer going' to meet, Bill?
>   Have yer bought the street, Bill?'
> Laugh! I thought I should 'ave died,
> Knocked 'em in the Old Kent Road!

A story is told that Tennyson stood looking at his grand home just after its completion, turned to his friend, and said, "You will live longer than I shall. That house will last five hundred years." His friend answered, "I think the English language will last longer."

By all indications, his friend was right.

The writing assignments on page 908 have students write creatively, while those on page 909 have them think about the selections and write critically.

YOU THE WRITER
Guidelines for Evaluating Assignment 1

1. Does the imaginary conversation between a Victorian poet and the student include the answers to three good questions about the poet's works or about life in Victorian England?
2. Does the dialogue include vivid details about the appearance of the poet and the setting of the conversation?
3. Are the poet's responses consistent with his or her writing style?
4. Is the dialogue lifelike and interesting with many vivid words?
5. Is the conversation free from grammar, usage, and mechanics errors?

Guidelines for Evaluating Assignment 2

1. Has the student written a new episode in the life of one of the characters?
2. Are any additions of character or setting reasonable in terms of the original story?
3. Is the addition consistent in the words and the actions of the main character?
4. Is the addition free from grammar, usage, and mechanics errors?

Guidelines for Evaluating Assignment 3

1. Has the student written an original poem in the style of a Victorian poet?
2. Has the student kept in mind the Victorian poets' tendency to be pessimistic?
3. Has the student been faithful to the line length, rhyme scheme, word choice, type of images used, and meter of the poet he or she imitated?
4. Is the poem free from grammar, usage, and mechanics errors?

YOU THE WRITER

Assignment

1. Suppose you had traveled back in time to Victorian England and met one of the poets whose works you have read. Record an imaginary conversation between you and that poet in which you asked and received answers to three good questions about his or her poetry or about life in the Victorian era.

Prewriting. Brainstorm to develop questions that will provide some insight into the art of the poet or into the social climate as reflected by the works and background material you have read.

Writing. Include in your composition details about the appearance of the poet and the setting of your conversation. Attempt to word the poet's responses in a manner consistent with his or her writing style.

Revising. Read your composition to see whether your description and dialogue are lifelike and interesting. Replace dull words with vivid ones.

Assignment

2. Choose one of the fiction selections you read and enjoyed in this unit, and write either a brief chapter that extends the action of the original or an entirely new episode in the life of one of the characters. Tell your story as you think the author of the original might have done.

Prewriting. Before you begin to write, make a study of the characters, paying particular attention to such details as physical appearance and speech habits. Familiarize yourself also with the author's style of narration.

Writing. Add new characters and settings, if you like, but make sure your additions are reasonable in terms of the original story. Strive for consistency in your characters' words and actions.

Revising. Compare the punctuation of your dialogue with that of the original, and correct any errors. Look for inconsistencies.

Assignment

3. Although every literary period has its outstanding poets, none rivals the Victorian era in the individuality of its poetic voices. This was the age when Browning was experimenting with his dramatic monologues, Hopkins with his sprung rhythm, Tennyson with his elaborate stanza forms. Write an original poem that imitates the style of one of the poets from this unit.

Prewriting. Get your creative juices flowing by considering possible subjects for a poem. Bear in mind that the majority of Victorian poets were quite pessimistic in their outlook on life.

Writing. As you write, be mindful of such details as line length, rhyme scheme, word choice, types of images used, and meter.

Revising. Adjust any weaknesses in structure and rhyme. Check the spellings of any words of which you are unsure.

YOU THE CRITIC

Assignment

1. Vivian de Sola Pinto, a scholar of Victorian literature, wrote that Thomas Hardy, unlike most other Victorian poets, was out "to produce a dramatic, rather than a pictorial or musical effect." Write an essay that either addresses this commentary on Hardy or explores the goals of another Victorian poet you have read.

Prewriting. Consider the possible meanings of the word *dramatic* as it is used in this sense. Scan the works by the poet you intend to focus on, and jot down words or phrases.

Writing. Open your essay with a clear thesis statement. Support each point you make with quotations from the poems or the background material on your poet.

Revising. Assess the first draft of your essay for clarity and coherence. Look out for any unwanted shifts in tense in the course of your discussion.

Assignment

2. A writer in the *Edinburgh Review* for July 1858 described the nineteenth century as an "age of transition—a period when changes, deeply and permanently affecting the whole condition of mankind, are occurring more rapidly . . . than at any prior time in human history." Extending the statement to include our own time, write a paper that agrees or disagrees.

Prewriting. On a sheet of paper note what you have learned about the history of the Victorian era, with specific regard to technological advances. On a second sheet make notes about similar advances in our own time.

Writing. Convert your notes into an essay. Back up each change with examples of the effects it has had on the human race, explaining in what way these effects are irreversible.

Revising. Examine your paper for evidence of faulty logic or grammar.

Assignment

3. The Victorian period is often regarded as one of pessimism. One need only recall the poetry of Arnold or Hardy to understand why. Yet at least two of the Victorians you read, Browning and Hopkins, were quite positive, or at least hopeful, most of the time. Select one pessimistic Victorian and one nonpessimistic one, and write an essay that compares and contrasts the two.

Prewriting. Begin by rereading the poetry of each of the poets you choose. As you read, jot down on separate sheets of paper thoughts and feelings the poem awakens in you.

Writing. State the purpose of your essay in your first paragraph. Quote specific lines and images from the poems to support the claims you make.

Revising. Proofread your paper to ensure that all your sentences make sense.

You the Critic 909

YOU THE CRITIC
Guidelines for Evaluating Assignment 1

1. Does the essay begin with a clear thesis statement about the goals of Hardy or another Victorian poet?
2. Is each point supported with quotes from the poems or background material on the poet?
3. Has the student commented on the dramatic aspects of the poet's works?
4. Is the essay free from grammar, usage, and mechanics errors?

Guidelines for Evaluating Assignment 2

1. Has the student agreed or disagreed with extending the statement to include our own time?
2. Has the student backed up each change mentioned with examples of the effects it has had on the human race, explaining in what ways those effects are irreversible?
3. Is the essay at least 250 words long?
4. Is the essay free from grammar, usage, and mechanics errors?

Guidelines for Evaluating Assignment 3

1. Does the student state the purpose of the essay, comparing a pessimistic and an optimistic poet, in the beginning of the paper?
2. Has the student quoted specific lines and images from the poems to support the claims made?
3. Has the student written a satisfying conclusion?
4. Is the essay free from grammar, usage, and mechanics errors?

Humanities Note

Fine art, *Big Ben,* 1905–06, by André Derain. French painter André Derain (1880–1954) traveled to England in the early 1900's and completed a series of very personal paintings of London. For Derain, that city had an undeniable charm, and he used dabs of paint in bright, almost playful colors to convey his sense of the liveliness of the scene. The massive architecture of England's Houses of Parliament and the familiar sight of the clock, "Big Ben," are made more human by Derain's light-hearted use of color, by the twirls of paint, by the deliberately decorative design of the sails of the boat passing by.

This painting is typical of Derain's early work. He went on to become one of the first Fauvists. The French word *fauve* means "wild beast" and the derisive name was hurled at Derain and other young artists, who cheerfully adopted it. The Fauvists painted in an expressionist style, characterized by bold distortion of forms and exhuberant color. The beginnings of that color can be seen in this early work.

Objectives

1 To understand the Edwardian Age
2 To understand World War I and its consequences
3 To understand the period between the wars
4 To understand the influence of World War II
5 To understand the role of modernism in the international artistic community
6 To appreciate the ideas of modernism
7 To appreciate the literature of the modern period

BIG BEN, 1905–1906
André Derain
Art Resource

THE MODERN PERIOD
1901–1945

Turning and turning in the widening gyre
The falcon cannot hear the falconer;
Things fall apart; the center cannot hold;
Mere anarchy is loosed upon the world,
The blood-dimmed tide is loosed, and everywhere
The ceremony of innocence is drowned.

from "The Second Coming,"
William Butler Yeats

Focus

Historical Background Tell students that although the modern period began on a note of complacency, the destruction caused by World War I caused widespread disillusionment. This mood led to the rejection of nineteenth century attitudes and techniques in many works of art. However, the arts also witnessed a surge of creativity just before the war: Picasso and Braque devised a new kind of painting called cubism, in which objects were viewed from different perspectives simultaneously; Stravinsky's music for the ballet *The Rite of Spring* used harsh sounds and primitive rhythms; and Ezra Pound founded a literary movement called Imagism, which rejected the wordiness and poetic diction of late nineteenth-century poetry.

Writing to Learn Have students write down what they know about the modern period. You might want to prompt them by writing the following on the chalkboard: World War I, World War II, Picasso, and Freud. After students have read the introduction, ask them to review what they have written and evaluate its accuracy.

Purpose-setting Question What were the main ways in which the modern period differed from the Victorian Age?

ESL Teaching Strategy Have ESL students tell the class how their country was affected by the two world wars. Pair up each ESL student with a native speaker who can help them read and understand the introduction.

Fine art, *An English Rose,* by Joseph Clark. Clark (1834–1926) was an English painter who worked in oils. Born in Dorset, he came to London at eighteen to study. He was a genre painter, using a realistic style to portray subjects from everyday life. The portrait called *An English Rose* captures a woman of the Edwardian Age. The light focused on the face and neck of this young woman gives her an almost luminous quality, and she appears relaxed, though expectant. There is a soft, almost affectionate treatment of the subject. This feeling is accomplished, in part, by the emphasis on rounded forms and proportions, ranging from the soft modeling of the features of the face, to the wave of the hair, to the shape and texture of the flowers. Harsh, angular lines are absent and there is a wispy, youthful quality to the rendering of her dress.

A complacent world floated into the twentieth century on a mood of hope and anticipation. Science and technology were off and soaring. *Progress* was the word on everyone's lips. What could possibly go wrong?

Plenty, as it turned out. While advances in communications and transportation drew the world closer together, modern warfare —William Butler Yeats's "blood-dimmed tide"—nearly destroyed it. World War I (1914–18) killed more than eight million people. World War II (1939–45) took an even higher toll. The wars, and the economic and moral upheaval they caused, shattered countless illusions.

British literature of the modern period (1901–1945) reflects these historical events, riding a swinging pendulum of hope and despair. First, the new century spurred a spirit of innovation in all the arts. Then World War I caused a backswing of disillusionment. Those two spirits, innovation and disillusionment, prompted modern writers to reject many of the traditions of nineteenth-century literature. It was time to experiment with fresh themes, fresh literary styles. "Make it new," exhorted American poet Ezra Pound, the London representative of Chicago's *Poetry* magazine. Pound's advice became the rallying cry of a generation of writers on both sides of the Atlantic.

THE EDWARDIAN AGE

When Queen Victoria died in 1901, her eldest son succeeded her as Edward VII. We call the years from 1901 to 1914 the Edwardian Age (although Edward died in 1910).

The rigid class distinctions and moral certainties of Victorian times lingered on into the Edwardian Age. We can read about the English country manors of this era in the novels of the American-born Henry James (1843–1916). James vividly portrays the opulence, the pampered gentry, the armies of servants. At the beginning of the century, one Briton in every six worked as a servant.

The rapid pace of change doomed this outdated way of life. Electricity became the "silent servant." It powered household appliances and made many of the jobs of servants obsolete. Telephones (and later radios) brought news from distant places. Automobiles (and later airplanes) opened new possibilities for travel.

As people gained new knowledge and greater sophistication, they began to question Victorian values and ideas. Women marched for the right to vote. A new Labor party, demanding greater rights for the working class, challenged the dominance of the existing Liberal and Conservative parties. In Ireland and in Britain's colonies, nationalists agitated for home rule or independence. By the time George V came to the throne in 1910, the nineteenth-century way of life was fading into memory.

AN ENGLISH ROSE
Joseph Clark
Gallerie George, London

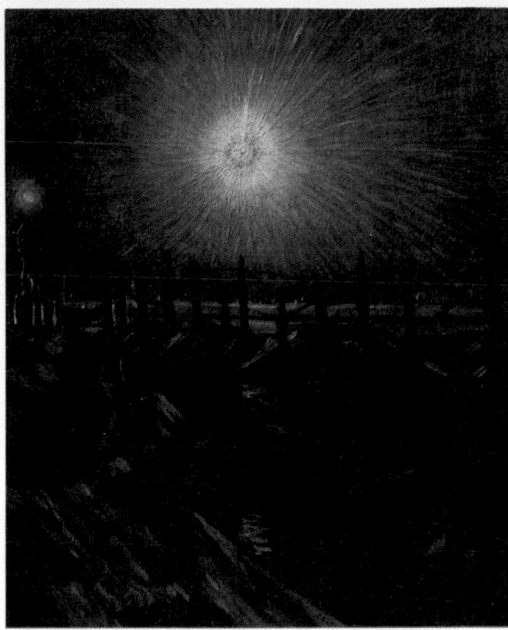

A STAR SHELL, c. 1916
Christopher Richard Wynne Nevinson
Tate Gallery

THE FIRST WORLD WAR AND ITS CONSEQUENCES

World War I erupted suddenly, but pressure had been building since the nineteenth century. Then, Britain and France had grabbed colonial empires, while Germany lagged behind. When the Germans later sought colonies of their own, their desires clashed with established British and French interests. The nations of Europe chose sides. Tensions grew. All it took was a spark to ignite the war—and the assassination in 1914 of Austria-Hungary's Archduke Ferdinand provided the spark.

Britain went to war in a light-hearted and confident spirit. Many had the romantic notion that the war would offer "good sport" and end in a few weeks. Sir Edward Grey, the foreign minister, saw more clearly. Gazing out on a London street at dusk, he said: "The lamps are going out all over Europe. We shall not see them lit again in our lifetime."

Poisonous gas, massive artillery barrages, and machine guns turned the fields of France and Belgium into a killing ground. Heroic cavalry charges and chivalrous hand-to-hand combat had little place in this first modern war. For four grim years of stalemate, the opposing armies slugged it out. The slaughter decimated a generation of young men and shredded the very fabric of British society. Poets perished by the scores. Many posthumously published poems tell the horrors of trench warfare and mourn the loss of heroic ideals.

BRITISH EVENTS

1901   Edward VII becomes king.

1902   **Joseph Conrad** publishes *Heart of Darkness*.

1903   Emmeline Pankhurst founds women's suffrage organization.

1904   **Saki** publishes his first stories.

1905   First London motor buses appear.

1908   Boy Scouts founded.

       London hosts Olympic games.

1910   George V becomes king.

1912   **George Bernard Shaw** publishes *Pygmalion*.

1913   **D.H. Lawrence** publishes *Sons and Lovers*.

1914   Britain enters World War I.

1916   Easter Rebellion in Ireland.

1917   **Siegfried Sassoon** publishes *Counter-Attack and Other Poems*.

1918   Women achieve right to vote.

       Rupert Brooke's *Collected Poems* published.

1919   Britain joins League of Nations.

       Lady Astor becomes first female member of Parliament.

1920   **Katherine Mansfield** publishes *Bliss and Other Stories*.

1921   Irish free state formed.

       BBC begins regular radio broadcasts.

914   *The Modern Period*

King Edward VII

Joseph Conrad

King George V and His Family

1908 Olympic Games

Battle Scene from World War I

Flight of the Wright Brothers at Kitty Hawk

Albert Einstein

Mohandas Gandhi

"STARS AND STRIPES NAILED TO THE NORTH POLE"

DR. FREDERICK A. COOK APRIL 21 1908   COMMANDER ROBERT E. PEARY APRIL 6 1909

TWO DAUNTLESS AMERICANS WHO REACHED THE GOAL OF A THOUSAND YEARS AND PLANTED THE STARS AND STRIPES UPON THE AXIS OF THE WORLD.

Postcard Commemorating Discovery of North Pole

WORLD EVENTS

1901	United States: Ragtime music develops.
	Germany: Thomas Mann publishes *Buddenbrooks*.
1903	United States: Orville and Wilbur Wright build first successful airplane.
1904	Asia: Russo-Japanese War begins.
1905	Germany: Albert Einstein proposes theory of relativity.
1909	Arctic: Explorers reach North Pole.
1911	China: Republic established under Sun Yat-sen.
	Antarctic: Explorers reach South Pole.
	Atlantic: *R.M.S. Titanic* sinks.
1913	Africa: Albert Schweitzer opens hospital in Congo.
	France: Marcel Proust publishes *Remembrance of Things Past*.
1914	Europe: Archduke Ferdinand assassinated; World War I begins.
	Central America: Panama Canal opens.
1917	Russia: Tsar overthrown; Bolsheviks seize power.
	Austria: Sigmund Freud publishes *Introduction to Psychoanalysis*.
1920	Switzerland: League of Nations holds first meeting.
	India: Gandhi leads nonviolent protests.
1921	Italy: Luigi Pirandello publishes *Six Characters in Search of an Author*.

Introduction 915

BRITISH EVENTS

London After Bombing by Germans

1922	**T.S. Eliot** publishes *The Waste Land*.
1924	First British airline begins regular operations.
	E.M. Forster publishes *A Passage to India*.
1925	John L. Baird transmits first television pictures.
1927	**Virginia Woolf** publishes *To the Lighthouse*.
1928	Shakespeare Theatre opens in Stratford-upon-Avon.
	W.B. Yeats writes "Sailing to Byzantium."
1930	**W.H. Auden** publishes *Poems*.
1934	**Dylan Thomas** writes "The Force That Through the Green Fuse...."
1935	Radar developed by British physicists.
1936	First BBC television broadcast.
1937	**Louis MacNeice** writes "The Sunlight on the Garden."
1938	**Graham Greene** publishes *Brighton Rock*.
1939	Britain enters World War II.
1940	Winston Churchill becomes prime minister.
	Bombing of Britain begins.
1945	**George Orwell** publishes *Animal Farm*.
	Elizabeth Bowen writes "The Demon Lover."

Winston Churchill

Charles Lindbergh

George VI and His Family

916 *The Modern Period*

Mandolin and Guitar

T.S. Eliot

Dylan Thomas

Persistence of Memory

Adolf Hitler

WORLD EVENTS

1922	Italy: Mussolini forms fascist government.
	France: James Joyce publishes *Ulysses*.
1923	France: Le Corbusier publishes *Towards a New Architecture*.
1924	Soviet Union: Lenin dies; Stalin comes to power.
1925	Germany: Adolf Hitler publishes *Mein Kampf*, part I.
	Austria: Franz Kafka's *The Trial* published.
1927	Charles Lindbergh crosses the Atlantic.
1928	France: Sixty-five nations sign Kellogg-Briand pact outlawing war.
1929	Beginning of worldwide depression.
1931	China: Japanese invade Manchuria.
	France: Salvador Dali paints *Persistence of Memory*.
1932	Soviet Union: Famine kills 5 million.
1933	Germany: Hitler comes to power.
	United States: Franklin D. Roosevelt becomes President.
1935	Africa: Mussolini invades Ethiopia.
1936	Spain: Civil War begins.
1937	France: Spanish artist Pablo Picasso creates *Guernica* mural.
1938	Europe: Hitler annexes Austria.
1939	Europe: Hitler invades Poland; World War II begins.
1941	Pacific: Pearl Harbor bombed; America enters war.
1945	Japan: Atomic bombs dropped on Hiroshima and Nagasaki.

Introduction 917

longing for his father's approval and resenting his strictness. Kafka lived with his family until he was thirty-two, and his relationship with his father, along with his feelings of familial obligation and guilt, is reflected in much of his writing.

Kafka began writing short stories and plays when he was very young. Despite his interest in writing, however, he chose to study law at the University of Prague. Eventually he took a position with the state Worker's Accident Insurance Institute, where he remained employed until 1922. Kafka's career in the insurance business never hindered his writing. In fact, his insurance career actually inspired him by revealing the bureaucratic chaos that often exists within government agencies.

As a German-speaking Jew in a country inhabited predominantly by Czech-speaking gentiles, Kafka had firsthand knowledge of what it was like to live outside the mainstream. His sense of alienation is apparent in nearly all his work. In his early works, including "The Metamorphosis" (1915), he explored the potentially disastrous results of ignoring one's true desires and aspirations and living according to the expectations of others.

In 1917 he was diagnosed as having tuberculosis. Shortly before his death in 1924, he instructed his friend Max Brod to destroy all his papers and personal documents, as well as his unfinished and unpublished works. Believing that Kafka never intended for him to follow the instructions, Brod ignored the request and arranged for the publication of Kafka's unfinished novels, *The Trial, The Castle,* and *America,* along with his personal diaries, *Letter to My Father,* and a number of his unpublished short stories. The publication of these works earned Kafka the critical acclaim that had eluded him during his lifetime.

Enrichment Tell students that Franz Kafka (1883–1924) grew up in Prague, Czechoslovakia, as the only son in a family of six. His father was a successful and domineering self-made businessman, and Kafka spent a good part of his life alternately

The Russian Revolution

Meanwhile, the war was toppling empires and convulsing whole societies. Russia's tottering monarchy collapsed in the spring of 1917. A democratic government took over and kept Russia in the war as an ally of Britain and France. Overwhelmed by the miserable conditions at the front, however, many Russian soldiers simply refused to fight on. Later in 1917, in a second spasm of revolution, Lenin's Bolsheviks ousted Russia's democratic leadership and set up the world's first Communist state. Russia's was the first of many European monarchies that the war would sweep away. Within a short time, the German and Austro-Hungarian monarchies vanished as well.

The Irish Rebellion

Meanwhile, unrest festered in Ireland. The Irish, predominantly Roman Catholic, had long resented British rule. At Easter of 1916 Irish nationalists in Dublin launched a rebellion that British troops quickly smashed. However, by executing the rebel leaders, Britain turned them into martyrs. Irish men and women who had previously held back—including major literary figures like William Butler Yeats (1865–1939)—now rallied to the cause of Irish independence.

The surge of Irish nationalism led to a hard-fought guerrilla war. In 1921 Britain capitulated. It granted independence to the Irish Free State. The new nation included all of Ireland except six mainly Protestant counties of the province of Ulster, in the north, which gained home rule but remained part of the United Kingdom. Violent disputes continue to this day over the future of the six counties of Northern Ireland.

OVER THE TOP (AT MARCOING, DECEMBER 1917)
John Nash

The Peace

In 1917 the United States entered the war on the side of Britain and France. World War I finally ground to a halt as Germany, starved and wracked by internal disputes, sued for peace. On armistice day—November 11, 1918—the guns fell silent. A year later, negotiators signed the Treaty of Versailles, calling for Germany to disarm and to pay huge reparations for war damages. ''This is not peace,'' prophesied France's Marshal Ferdinand Foch. ''This is an armistice for twenty years.'' The world would have to bear the legacy of bitterness spawned by the Great War and the Petty Peace, as writer H. G. Wells (1866–1946) called them.

BETWEEN THE WARS

European civilization struggled to recover from the war as hunger and hardship persisted into the 1920's. In Britain, strikes and unrest kept industry in turmoil. Although Britain's overseas empire remained intact, stirrings of discontent began to trouble the tranquility of colonies like India and Burma. More and more angry voices questioned the right of European powers to rule distant lands.

The Lost Generation

For years, "progress" had been undermining old traditions and values. World War I had added to the damage, exposing the sham of heroic myths and fostering an attitude of cynicism and despair. What modern values or rituals could fill the emptiness? In his poem *The Waste Land* (1922), T. S. Eliot expressed a widely felt disillusionment with twentieth-century life:

> You know only
> A heap of broken images, where the sun beats,
> And the dead tree gives no shelter, the cricket no relief,
> And the dry stone no sound of water. . . .
>   I think we are in rats' alley
> Where the dead men lost their bones.

People spoke of the disillusioned youth of postwar Europe as a "lost generation." Some drowned their cares in the pursuit of pleasure. They drove fast cars, danced to wild new jazz tunes, and experimented with many passing fads. Having won the right to vote in 1918, British women displayed a startling sense of independence. "Flappers" bobbed their hair short and wore low-waisted and daringly brief dresses. This postwar decade of extravagant behavior came to a shuddering halt when the New York Stock Market crash of 1929 began the worldwide Great Depression.

The Rise of Fascism

Hungry Europeans—people without jobs or future prospects —pinned their hopes on political extremes. Some embraced communism. Others, more numerous, leaned toward fascism—first in Italy under dictator Benito Mussolini, then in Germany under another dictator, Adolf Hitler.

As the 1930's wore on, the menace of fascism grew. Hitler built up Germany's military strength. Italy invaded Ethiopia. The two fascist dictators aided the rightist side in Spain's civil war, allied themselves with Japan, and threatened their neighbors.

A crucial moment came in 1938, when Hitler demanded territory from Czechoslovakia. Czechoslovakia's allies, Britain and France, agreed to the transfer of territory after Hitler promised he would make no more demands. "I believe it is peace for our time . . . peace with honor," British Prime Minister Neville Chamberlain proclaimed on returning from a meeting with Hitler in Munich, Germany, that September.

However, appeasement failed. In March 1939, Hitler seized what was left of Czechoslovakia. His invasion of Poland in September 1939 touched off World War II. Marshal Foch had been right: The armistice lasted barely twenty years.

3 Literary Movement This sense of disillusionment is evident in Eliot's "The Hollow Men," page 1081, in which he focuses on the spiritual emptiness of modern man.

THE SECOND WORLD WAR

The Second World War was, if anything, more destructive than the First. Hitler's "final solution" to "the Jewish problem" brought death to six million Jews. A German invasion of Russia killed soldiers and civilians by the millions. Battles raged all the way from Europe to North Africa, from the mountains of Burma and China to Hawaii. Massive bombing campaigns turned cities like London, Dresden, and Tokyo into raging infernos. Finally, in the waning days of the war in 1945, American atomic bombs blasted two Japanese cities, Hiroshima and Nagasaki, into cinder and ash. The war's death toll has been estimated at 35 million—not counting the millions who died in German concentration camps.

Somehow, Britain muddled through. The darkest days came in 1940, when France had fallen and Britain alone bore the brunt of German attacks. Inspired by Prime Minister Winston Churchill's ringing oratory, and joined in 1941 by two allies, the United States and Russia, Britain fought on to victory. However, it was a bitter, draining victory, ousting Britain from the ranks of first-rate powers and marking an end to Britain's long age of imperial glory.

MODERNISM AND THE INTERNATIONAL ARTISTIC COMMUNITY

Against this backdrop of chaos and violence, writers and other artists put forth a burst of creative energy. Often they left their own countries to work abroad—some as refugees from war, some by choice. Cultural centers like London, Paris, New York, and Berlin developed communities of painters, composers, architects, and writers—people who had come from many different lands. More than ever before, a truly international artistic community took shape.

This community of artistic people responded to the spirit of the times with a frenzy of innovation. How many ways were there to "make it new"? The ways seemed endless—and often puzzling. Controversy raged over radical new techniques in painting, music, architecture, and literature. What did the odd shapes and figures of cubist painters like Pablo Picasso of Spain and Georges Braque of France actually mean? Why did the Russian composer Igor Stravinsky put so much discordance into his *Rite of Spring* (1913)? Could people actually live and work in the modernistic buildings of architects such as France's Le Corbusier or Spain's Antonio Gaudí or in the glass-and-steel structures of Germany's Bauhaus school? Why did modern writers focus so much attention on human weakness and social decay?

In all fields of artistic life, innovators sought to create new art forms appropriate for the twentieth century. They all seemed to have one motto: "Out with the old, in with the new." Today we group the various schools and movements of this generation under the heading of modernism.

THE IDEAS OF MODERNISM

Although the specific movements that composed modernism were frequently short-lived, they shared a number of characteristics. First, all sought to be new and different, to experiment with new forms, to innovate, to startle, even to shock. In his poem "L'Art 1910," the American Ezra Pound (1885–1972) described a modernist painting:

Green arsenic smeared on an egg-white cloth,
Crushed strawberries! Come, let us feast our eyes.

Pound's poem illustrates some of the principles of a technique called imagism, which Pound helped introduce to British and American poetry. It uses *images*—details that can be perceived by the senses—to communicate its message. It employs *precise language*. It abandons nineteenth-century "poetic" diction for the vocabulary of *everyday speech*. It uses *free verse* instead of the fixed rhythm, or meter, of most nineteenth-century poetry. Finally, it *suggests* its message instead of stating it directly. Nowhere does Pound tell us that art in 1910 was startling. He merely implies it through words like "smeared" and through the juxtaposition of clashing images like "arsenic" and "strawberries."

One of the chief influences on modernism was the symbolist movement of the late nineteenth century. Symbolism originated with French poets like Charles Baudelaire (1821–67) and Stéphane Mallarmé (1842–98), whose methods then influenced such late Victorian writers as Oscar Wilde (1854–1900) and Algernon Swinburne (1837–1909). The symbolists rejected naturalism. Their poetry was deeply emotional and personal, like earlier romantic poetry, but it was at times far more subtle. It presented an array of imaginative symbols, seeking to evoke emotions in readers' minds.

EZRA POUND, 1938–39
Wyndham Lewis
The Granger Collection

Introduction 921

Humanities Note

Fine art, *Ezra Pound*, 1938–39 by Wyndham Lewis. Controversial American poet Ezra Pound (1885–1972) and British painter and author Wyndham Lewis (b. Maine 1886–d. England 1957) were good friends, brought together in England in the early part of the twentieth century as founders and champions of the short-lived radical art movement Vorticism. In painting, the vorticists used color as a means of expression of its own; the world of machines was as real to them as the world of nature, and they simplified forms into machine-like angularity. In writing, the Vorticists wanted to free post-Victorian verse from its confining structure. Pound was a major force in the shaping of twentieth-century poetry, and encouraged young writers such as James Joyce and T. S. Eliot.

By the time Lewis painted this arresting portrait, his own work had become more conventional, though forceful line and construction remained. There is great strength in the diagonal movement, set up by the lines of the figure. Pound himself seems entirely self-sufficient, indifferent to the viewer, and there is a definite sense of bones beneath the flesh of the face. The image of Pound at rest is a sharp contrast to the impending drama of his life. Pound broadcast Fascist propaganda for the Italians during World War II, and at the end of the war was brought to the United States to stand trial as a traitor. He was found mentally unfit to answer the charges and was hospitalized for more than a decade. Pound remains one of the most controversial literary figures of this century.

The use of images as subtle symbols would become characteristic of modernist poetry by Yeats and Eliot as well as the imagists.

A second characteristic of modernist art and literature was a tendency to present human experiences in fragments that viewers or readers had to piece together in their own minds. For example, Picasso's cubist paintings broke things into component parts. They showed the angles and planes that made up an object, an action, or a human form. The dadaists, who came after the cubists, saw the world as a meaningless jumble. One method of dadaist composition was simply to cut up words, dump them in a hat, and remove them in haphazard order to form a "poem." The message was not in the poem but in the method.

A third characteristic was the use of the techniques of realism and naturalism. Often this meant taking up subjects previously considered too trivial or too unpleasant for art and literature. Realism focused on the details of everyday life. Naturalism examined social and economic problems of the working class.

A fourth characteristic was attention to the new psychological insights of Austria's Sigmund Freud, Switzerland's Carl Jung, and other pioneer psychologists. Psychological realism—called expressionism in drama—sought to duplicate the inner workings of characters' minds, rather than merely to capture outer actions and experiences as earlier realism had done. Psychologist William James, brother of the American author Henry James, observed that the human mind works not in chronological order but in a series of associations. The mind leaps from thought to thought in what William James called the stream of consciousness.

LITERATURE OF THE MODERN PERIOD

British writing of the period 1900–45 does not fall into clear-cut categories or movements. However, we can divide the period into three broad stages: before 1910, from 1910 to 1930, and from 1930 to 1945. In the first, or Edwardian, stage, writers used the techniques of realism and naturalism to examine the social problems caused by rapid change. The most radical and characteristic works of modernism appeared during the second stage—especially in the years of disillusionment at the end of World War I. After 1930, writers tried to cope with the enormous problems posed by the Great Depression, the rise of fascism, and World War II. During this third stage a more direct, even somewhat didactic literature of conscience came into prominence.

Cutting across these three stages was an Irish Literary Revival, spurred by the explosion of nationalism in Ireland. The Revival—also called the Irish Literary Renaissance or Celtic Renaissance—began in late Victorian times. It sought to revive the dying Gaelic language, to explore early Celtic history and literature, and to express the Irish spirit.

THE ARTIST'S GARDEN AT DURBINS, c. 1915
Roger Fry
Yale Center for British Art, Paul Mellon Fund

Achievements in Poetry

The stages of the modern period appear clearly in poetry, and even within the evolving styles of individual poets. William Butler Yeats, a leading light of the Irish Literary Revival, provides an example. Yeats's early poetry (he was born in 1865) blends a Romantic love of nature with an interest in the myths and mysticism of Celtic antiquity. It uses traditional rhyme and verse patterns. In later years, Yeats abandoned Romanticism and relaxed the strictness of his form, often adopting the direct, more colloquial diction of the modernists. He employed symbolic images to delve into troubling questions of history and modern life. By the time of Yeats's death in 1939, many considered him the finest English-language poet of the twentieth century.

A Romantic strain also persisted in other British poetry of the early twentieth century. Even some of the brutally realistic poems that developed from World War I reflected romantic longings—to flee battle for the peace and beauty of the English countryside, for example. Among the best-known poets to die in the Great War was Rupert Brooke (1887–1915). The many other poets of World War I included Siegfried Sassoon (1886–1967), Ivor Gurney (1890–1937), Wilfred Owen (1893–1918), and Robert Graves (1895–1985).

Many of the poets who survived the war went on to express the attitudes of the "lost generation" in the modernist poetry of the 1920's. An important influence on these poets was the Victorian writer Gerard Manley Hopkins (1844–89), whose verse appeared posthumously in 1918. Hopkins used what he called sprung rhythm instead of more traditional metric patterns. Hopkins prepared the way for the modernists' experiments with new verse forms.

Preeminent among modernist poets of the 1920's was T. S. Eliot, whose verse reflects the influence of Freud and modern psychology. His "Love Song of J. Alfred Prufrock" (1917), for example, takes the form of a dramatic monologue. It offers the

Humanities Note

Fine art, *The Artist's Garden at Durbins,* c. 1915, by Roger Fry. Roger Fry (1866–1934) was an influential British art critic, still life and landscape painter. Born in London, he earned a degree in natural science at Cambridge. His scientist's curiosity was reflected in his art criticism and in his painting.

Fry drew as a child, and after attending Cambridge his interest in art was encouraged by several friends. He studied in London and Paris and introduced the French master Paul Cezanne and the post-impressionists to England. From 1905 to 1910 he was curator of paintings at New York's Metropolitan Museum of Art.

This painting depicts the view from the big windows in the country house Fry designed himself. A special feeling for simple, classic design structures the composition and guides the viewer, in an organized way, into the pleasant scene of the life in Surrey. The freedom in this painting is in the color and forms, which have movement and life independent of the objects they represent.

5 Literary Movement Typical of the images that Yeats employed in his mature poetry is the golden bird in "Sailing to Byzantium," page 1054, symbolic of unaging art.

6 Literary Movement See Rupert Brooke's "The Soldier," page 1068, and "The Great Lover," page 1069, for this romantic strain. Although Brooke was eventually a victim of World War I, he died before he ever reached the front, and his poetry contains none of the bitterness and disillusionment of other World War I poets like Siegfried Sassoon or Wilfred Owen.

7 Enrichment Eliot's verse play *Murder in the Cathedral* emerged from his belief that only a living faith could give meaning to life.

8 Literary Movement References to the disequilibrium of the political universe are also present in Auden's "In Memory of W. B. Yeats," page 1076; Yeats died in January, 1939, just a few months before the outbreak of World War II.

9 Literary Movement See Dylan Thomas's "Fern Hill," page 1098, for a celebration of the innocence and joy of life in childhood; see his "The Force That Through the Green Fuse Drives the Flower," page 1096, for an expression of the contention between the forces of life and death; see his "Do Not Go Gentle into That Good Night," page 1102, as an exhortation to his father to fight against encroaching annihilation.

10 Enrichment It is interesting to note that since Shakespeare, most of the great British writers of comedy have been Irish: William Congreve during the Restoration, Richard Brinsley Sheridan and Oliver Goldsmith in the eighteenth century, Oscar Wilde in the Victorian Age, and George Bernard Shaw in the twentieth century. Possibly their position as outsiders enabled them to see more clearly than insiders could the mockable faults of the society they depicted.

11 Enrichment Eliot's *Murder in the Cathedral* borrows from techniques of the past: a verse play combining the chorus of the Greek drama with the allegorical representations of the medieval morality play.

12 Enrichment The Abbey Theatre, along with the Moscow Art Theatre, was considered one of the two great theaters of the world in the early twentieth century. Although it still exists in Dublin, its stature has diminished.

fragmentary interior thoughts of a character's stream of consciousness. Eliot's long poem *The Waste Land* (1922) stands as a monument to the despair and bitterness of the "lost generation." Only later did Eliot shed some of his skepticism and find solace within the Anglican church.

In the 1930's and 1940's, poets showed greater interest in political and social topics. W. H. Auden (1907–73), Louis MacNeice (1907–63), Stephen Spender (born 1909), and Henry Reed (born 1914) continued to employ subtle symbolism and imagery. However, they also made direct statements of social protest. Consider these lines from Auden's famous "September 1, 1939," meditating on the eruption of World War II:

> I and the public know
> What all schoolchildren learn;
> Those to whom evil is done
> Do evil in return.

Romanticism did not die out completely, even in the latter years of the modern period. It flared into a wild brilliance in the verses of Dylan Thomas (1914–53), a Welsh poet who often focused on themes of life and death, as in "When, Like a Running Grave" (1934).

Achievements in Drama

The towering figure of late Victorian and modern drama is Irish-born George Bernard Shaw (1856–1960). Shaw was delving into the problems of a changing society even before the Edwardian Age. Blending realism with witty satire, he evoked laughter while prodding theatergoers to think about social issues such as class prejudice, the role of women, education, poverty, and war.

The Edwardian Age produced other important dramatists as well. James Matthew Barrie (1860–1937) wrote the classic children's fantasy *Peter Pan* (1904). John Galsworthy (1867–1933) wrote plays that each focus on a timely social problem. *Strife* (1909), for example, deals with labor-management relations. *Justice* (1910) looks at the prison system.

In the Depression years of the 1930's, Noel Coward (1899–1973) won attention for a series of smartly sophisticated dramas and musicals. The poet T. S. Eliot revived verse drama with works like *Murder in the Cathedral* (1935), a play about Thomas Becket, an archbishop of twelfth-century England.

The Irish Literary Revival led to the founding in 1904 of an Irish national theater (the Abbey Theater of Dublin) and produced some of the modern period's finest plays. John Millington Synge (1871–1909) vividly captures Irish rural life in plays like *Riders to the Sea* (1904). Sean O'Casey (1884–1964) turned to urban themes. He depicts the life of the poor in violence-torn Dublin in tragicomedies like *The Shadow of a Gunman* (1925).

Achievements in Fiction

We cannot fit the fiction of the modern period into neat, clear categories. The fiction swings between romanticism and realism, between misty fantasy and cynical disillusionment. Sometimes it probes the human mind, dwelling on the neuroses and longings of isolated individuals. Sometimes it sweeps across the vastness of history, pondering the mystery of human achievement and human suffering.

Arnold Bennett (1867–1931) was among several fiction writers of the Edwardian Age who produced brilliant works of realism and naturalism. In books such as *The Old Wives' Tale* (1901), Bennett depicted the working-class life of industrial England. He avoided authorial intrusion—the nineteenth-century practice of inserting the author's asides and opinions into a tale. Like Bennett, other modernist fiction writers want readers to draw their own conclusions about characters and events.

A second Edwardian novelist, Joseph Conrad (1857–1924), pioneered in the use of psychological realism. The Polish-born Conrad settled in London after learning English as a sailor on a British ship. He explored the individual's struggle with nature in tales of the sea such as *Lord Jim* (1900) and depicted colonialism in the brooding short novel *Heart of Darkness* (1902). Conrad's tales helped to popularize the short novel, or novella.

13

The British short story, earlier overshadowed by the Russian, the French, and the American short story, gained new attention in the modern period. Among the first masters of modern British short stories was the humorist H. H. Munro (1870–1916), who wrote under the pen name Saki. Another talented short-story writer was New Zealand-born Katherine Mansfield (1888–1923), who crafted sensitive tales of middle-class life.

The class system and the plight of the industrial worker emerged as key themes in the short stories and novels of D. H. Lawrence (1885–1930). Lawrence was a naturalist, but he had a Romantic abhorrence for the march of factories across the rural landscape. His savage hatred of conventional British manners and morals gives bite to novels like *Sons and Lovers* (1913) and the notorious *Lady Chatterley's Lover* (1928–29).

14

15

Perhaps the greatest pioneer of modernist fiction was the Irish writer James Joyce (1882–1941). Joyce revolutionized the form and structure of both the short story and the novel. In *The Dubliners* (1914), he presents a group of realistic short tales about working-class life in Dublin. Joyce tried to have each story achieve what he called an epiphany—a flash of awareness in which all the story elements come together to illuminate the story's meaning. Joyce's brilliant novel *Ulysses* (1922) was one of the first works of fiction to employ stream of consciousness. Joyce labored for years on this book, using an immense variety of techniques and symbols to pair an ancient Greek myth with a tale of twentieth-century Dublin.

STUDLAND BEACH (detail)
Vanessa Bell
The Tate Gallery

Introduction 925

15 Literary Movement See Lawrence's "The Rocking Horse Winner," page 974, for a bitter indictment of the destructive power of materialism in English society.

Humanities Note

Fine art, *Studland Beach,* 1911, by Vanessa Bell. Vanessa Bell (1879–1961) was a bold innovator in English art. She was the elder sister of writer Virginia Woolf who believed there was "something uncompromising" about her sister's art.

Bell painted figures and still lifes in oil. Her subjects are presented in broad masses —dramatically, directly, clearly and in an ordered fashion. In her work, there is bold division of the painted surface into simple, interrelated blocks of color. As in *Studland Beach* a strong diagonal divides the design, and all objects are integrated into it. She gives equal force to the blocks of color between the figures and to the figures themselves. Bell's interest in form and color led to a period of work that was completely abstract.

There is a strangeness to *Studland Beach* filled with faceless figures all intently focused on something the viewer cannot see. The painting is extreme and jarring: the figures are rooted, intensely, in a scene where, to the viewer, nothing seems to be happening.

13 Enrichment Eliot's poem "The Hollow Men" uses as one of its epigraphs a line from Conrad's *Heart of Darkness*: "Mistah Kurtz —he dead." Both works emphasize the tragic result of spiritual emptiness.

14 Master Teacher Note To demonstrate the way poets from totally different time periods and backgrounds can treat a similar theme, you might compare Lawrence's "Snake," page 1039, with Coleridge's "The Rime of the Ancient Mariner," page 660, particularly the section on the water-snakes.

Fine art, *The Mud Bath,* 1914, by David Bomberg. Bomberg (1890–1957) was a British painter of figures, landscapes, and still lifes in oil and water color. He studied in England and met Pablo Picasso in Paris. Bomberg wanted to translate the motion of life in urban times in an expressive, not a photographic, manner. He was influenced by the Cubists, but while many were painting machines, he preferred to use their techniques to paint figures and comment on modern life.

The starkly rigid, abstracted figures of *The Mud Bath* are animated by fierce energy, concretizing Bomberg's fascination with the harshness and vitality of urban existence. The clusters of figures are reduced to the most spare equations of brilliant color and form, symbols participating in a hectic drama born of twentieth-century existence.

16 **Literary Movement** Graham Greene, better known for his novels than for his short stories, is almost always concerned in his serious works (as opposed to his popular adventure stories or "entertainments") with the problems of good and evil. See his "Across the Bridge," page 1002, for a development of this theme.

Cooperative Learning Divide the class into small groups and have each group research a topic mentioned in the introduction. Possible topics include cubist painting, the development of radar, the Easter 1916 rising in Ireland, and the meeting of Chamberlain and Hitler at Munich. Then each group can report its findings to the class.

Check Test

1. One cause of World War I was the struggle among European nations for _____.
2. After World War I the disillusioned youth were called a "_____ generation."

THE MUD BATH
David Bomberg
The Tate Gallery

Another writer famous for capturing the stream of consciousness in fiction is Virginia Woolf (1882–1941). Woolf's major works include *Mrs. Dalloway* (1922) and *To the Lighthouse* (1927). She was the most distinguished member of a group of modernists known as the Bloomsbury set, named for the London neighborhood in which they congregated. E. M. Forster (1879–1970) also formed part of the Bloomsbury set. Forster portrayed the tragic clash of British and Indian cultures in his most famous novel, *A Passage to India* (1924).

As we have seen, social and political issues gained new attention in the 1930's and 1940's. In his futuristic novel *Brave New World* (1932), Aldous Huxley (1894–1963) used biting satire to criticize the misuse of science in totalitarian states. George Orwell (1903–50) ridiculed communism in his modern fable *Animal Farm* (1945) and in *1984* (1949). Like other dystopian novels, *1984* depicts a frightening future society, seeking to warn readers of the horror that may result from current trends. Other noteworthy British fiction writers of the era include Graham Greene (born 1904), Evelyn

16 Waugh (1903–66), Nancy Mitford (1904–73), C. P. Snow (1905–80), and the Irish writer Elizabeth Bowen (1899–1973).

It is probably too soon to evaluate fully the achievements of the modern period, but clearly the writers of the era had an enormous influence on those who would follow them. Writers such as Joyce and Woolf revolutionized the novel by developing new techniques suited to the chaotic confusions and groping skepticisms of modern times. Writers such as Yeats, Eliot, and Auden crafted new poetic tools and prepared a firm foundation for all subsequent twentieth-century verse. Moreover, the plays of Shaw and of the Irish Literary Revival became classics of the British theater, opening up new subject matter that would serve as a starting point for further innovation in later generations. The literature of the years 1900–1945 remains profoundly relevant in our contemporary period, in a world still chaotic, still torn by doubts, where people of talent are still eager to "make it new."

3. Economic depression in Germany provided a fertile ground for the rise of _____.
4. An artistic slogan of the modern period is Ezra Pound's imperative "Make it _____!"
5. An important characteristic of modernist art and literature was the tendency to present human experiences in _____.

Answers
1. colonies
2. lost
3. fascism
4. new
5. fragments

ENGLISH VOICES
Quotations by Prominent Figures of the Period

The greatest of evils and the worst of crimes is poverty.
George Bernard Shaw, *Major Barbara*

Vanity plays lurid tricks with our memory.
Joseph Conrad, *Lord Jim*

And what rough beast, its hour come round at last,
Slouches towards Bethlehem to be born?
William Butler Yeats, "The Second Coming"

Nothing could have been more obvious to the peoples of the early twentieth century than the rapidity with which war was becoming impossible. And as certainly they did not see it. They did not see it until the atomic bombs burst in their fumbling hands.
H. G. Wells, *The World Set Free*

Only two classes of books are of universal appeal: the very best and the very worst.
Joseph Conrad, *No More Parades*

I cannot forecast to you the actions of Russia. It is a riddle wrapped in a mystery inside an enigma.
Sir Winston Churchill, Radio broadcast

I have nothing to offer but blood, toil, tears, and sweat. . . .
Winston Churchill, First speech as Prime Minister

Impropriety is the soul of wit.
William Somerset Maugham, *The Moon and Sixpence*

Ireland is the old sow that eats her farrow.
James Joyce, *A Portrait of the Artist as a Young Man*

It is a symbol of Irish art. The cracked looking glass of a servant.
James Joyce, *Ulysses*

Women have served all these centuries as looking glasses possessing the magic and delicious power of reflecting the figure of man at twice its natural size.
Virginia Woolf, *A Room of One's Own*

Additional Voices

There is always one moment in childhood when the door opens and lets the future in.
Graham Greene, *The Power and the Glory*

There could be no honor in a sure success, but much might be wrested from a sure defeat.
T.E. Lawrence, *Revolt in the Desert*

April is the cruelest
 month, breeding
Lilacs out of the
 dead land, mixing
Memory and desire,
 stirring
Dull roots with
 spring rain.
T.S. Eliot, *The Waste Land*

Man is slightly nearer to the atom than to the star . . . From his central position man can survey the grandest works of Nature with the astronomer, or the minutest works with the physicist.
Sir Arthur Stanley Eddington, *Stars and Atoms*

Painting isn't an aesthetic operation; it's a form of magic designed as a mediator between this strange hostile world and us, a way of seizing the power by giving form to our terrors as well as our desires.
Pablo Picasso, from *Life with Picasso* by Francoise Gilot and Carlton Lake

READING CRITICALLY

The Literature of 1901–1945

When you read literature it is important to place it in its historical context. Doing so will help you to see how it was shaped by the events and attitudes of the time.

Historical Context

The Modern Age was one of the most turbulent and traumatic periods in British history. Numerous British colonies were granted their independence, and the British Empire was gradually transformed into the British Commonwealth, an association of self-governing countries. The country suffered through two tragic wars that caused the deaths of thousands of its citizens and experienced an economic depression that resulted in a startlingly high unemployment rate. At the same time, technological advances occurred that significantly changed the nature of people's lives. As a result of these events, there was a dramatic shift in the dominant attitudes and sentiments of the English people, as the sense of optimism and self-assurance that characterized the Victorian Age was replaced by a sense of uncertainty, disjointedness, and disillusionment.

Literary Movements

As the nation's attitude shifted, a new literary movement developed called Modernism. Rejecting previous literary traditions, the Modernists sought to capture the essence of modern life in both the form and content of their work. Delving into the minds of their characters, writers explored the sense of isolation, uncertainty, and disillusionment that had come to characterize modern life. The disjointedness of modern life was also reflected in the form of typical Modernist works, which often lack the expositions, resolutions, transitions, and explanations used in traditional works.

Writers' Techniques

During the Modern Age, writers explored a number of new literary techniques. Poets created works using free verse; fiction writers used shifting points of view; and both poets and fiction writers experimented with the stream-of-consciousness technique, attempting to recreate the natural flow of their characters' thoughts. At the same time, modern writers relied heavily on such traditional devices as symbols and allusions, often using these devices in conveying the themes of their works.

On the following pages is a short story by Katherine Mansfield, a prominent modern fiction writer. The notes in the side column should help you to place the selection in its historical context.

928 *The Modern Period*

A Dill Pickle

Katherine Mansfield

And then, after six years, she saw him again. He was seated at one of those little bamboo tables decorated with a Japanese vase of paper daffodils. There was a tall plate of fruit in front of him, and very carefully, in a way she recognized immediately as his "special" way, he was peeling an orange.

He must have felt that shock of recognition in her for he looked up and met her eyes. Incredible! He didn't know her! She smiled; he frowned. She came toward him. He closed his eyes an instant, but opening them his face lit up as though he had struck a match in a dark room. He laid down the orange and pushed back his chair, and she took her little warm hand out of her muff and gave it to him.

"Vera!" he exclaimed. "How strange. Really, for a moment I didn't know you. Won't you sit down? You've had lunch? Won't you have some coffee?"

She hesitated, but of course she meant to.

"Yes, I'd like some coffee." And she sat down opposite him.

"You've changed. You've changed very much," he said, staring at her with that eager, lighted look. "You look so well. I've never seen you look so well before."

"Really?" She raised her veil and unbuttoned her high fur collar. "I don't feel very well. I can't bear this weather, you know."

"Ah, no. You hate the cold. . . ."

"Loathe it." She shuddered. "And the worst of it is that the older one grows . . ."

He interrupted her. "Excuse me," and tapped on the table for the waitress. "Please bring some coffee and cream." To her: "You are sure you won't eat anything? Some fruit, perhaps. The fruit here is very good."

"No, thanks. Nothing."

"Then that's settled." And smiling just a hint too broadly he took up the orange again. "You were saying—the older one grows—"

Literary Movement: Like most modern short stories, this story begins without an exposition, and background information is revealed as the story progresses.

Writer's Technique: Vera's character is revealed through her actions and comments.

A Dill Pickle 929

Presentation

Motivation/Prior Knowledge Have students imagine running into someone they have not seen for a long time and this person does not recognize them. How would they react? Then tell them that this person is a former boyfriend or girlfriend. How would they react to this added information? Point out that this is the situation in "A Dill Pickle."

Purpose-Setting Question How does the dialogue in this story develop the characters, the theme, and the plot?

Critical Thinking and Reading You might point out that the male character in this story is referred to only as "him" or "he." What effect does this have on the story?

"The colder," she laughed. But she was thinking how well she remembered that trick of his—the trick of interrupting her—and of how it used to exasperate her six years ago. She used to feel then as though he, quite suddenly, in the middle of what she was saying, put his hand over her lips, turned from her, attended to something different, and then took his hand away, and with just the same slightly too broad smile, gave her his attention again. . . . Now we are ready. That is settled.

"The colder!" He echoed her words, laughing too. "Ah, ah. You still say the same things. And there is another thing about you that is not changed at all—your beautiful voice—your beautiful way of speaking." Now he was very grave; he leaned toward her, and she smelled the warm, stinging scent of the orange peel. "You have only to say one word and I would know your voice among all other voices. I don't know what it is—I've often wondered—that makes your voice such a—haunting memory. . . . Do you remember that first afternoon we spent together at Kew Gardens? You were so surprised because I did not know the names of any flowers. I am still just as ignorant for all your telling me. But whenever it is very fine and warm, and I see some bright colors—it's awfully strange—I hear your voice saying: 'Geranium, marigold and verbena.' And I feel those three words are all I recall of some forgotten, heavenly language. . . . You remember that afternoon?"

"Oh, yes, very well." She drew a long, soft breath, as though the paper daffodils between them were almost too sweet to bear. Yet, what had remained in her mind of that particular afternoon was an absurd scene over the tea table. A great many people taking tea in a Chinese pagoda, and he behaving like a maniac about the wasps—waving them away, flapping at them with his straw hat, serious and infuriated out of all proportion to the occasion. How delighted the sniggering tea drinkers had been. And how she had suffered.

But now, as he spoke, that memory faded. His was the truer. Yes, it had been a wonderful afternoon, full of geranium and marigold and verbena, and—warm sunshine. Her thoughts lingered over the last two words as though she sang them.

In the warmth, as it were, another memory unfolded. She saw herself sitting on a lawn. He lay beside her, and suddenly, after a long silence, he rolled over and put his head in her lap.

"I wish," he said, in a low, troubled voice, "I wish that I had taken poison and were about to die—here now!"

At that moment a little girl in a white dress, holding a long, dripping water lily, dodged from behind a bush, stared at them, and dodged back again. But he did not see. She leaned over him.

"Ah, why do you say that? I could not say that."

But he gave a kind of soft moan, and taking her hand he held it to his cheek.

"Because I know I am going to love you too much—far too much. And I shall suffer so terribly, Vera, because you never, never will love me."

He was certainly far better looking now than he had been then. He had lost all that dreamy vagueness and indecision. Now he had the air of a man who has found his place in life, and fills it with a confidence and an assurance which was, to say the least, impressive. He must have made money, too. His clothes were admirable, and at that moment he pulled a Russian cigarette case out of his pocket.

Writer's Technique: The man's personality is revealed through Vera's impressions of his appearance.

"Won't you smoke?"

"Yes, I will." She hovered over them. "They look very good."

"I think they are. I get them made for me by a little man in St. James's Street. I don't smoke very much. I'm not like you—but when I do, they must be delicious, very fresh cigarettes. Smoking isn't a habit with me; it's a luxury—like perfume. Are you still so fond of perfumes? Ah, when I was in Russia . . ."

She broke in: "You've really been to Russia?"

"Oh, yes. I was there for over a year. Have you forgotten how we used to talk of going there?"

"No, I've not forgotten."

He gave a strange half laugh and leaned back in his chair. "Isn't it curious. I have really carried out all those journeys that we planned. Yes, I have been to all those places that we talked of, and stayed in them long enough to—as you used to say, 'air oneself' in them. In fact, I have spent the last three years of my life traveling all the time. Spain, Corsica, Siberia, Russia, Egypt. The only country left is China, and I mean to go there, too, when the war is over."

As he spoke, so lightly, tapping the end of his cigarette against the ashtray, she felt the strange beast that had slumbered so long within her bosom stir, stretch itself, yawn, prick up its ears, and suddenly bound to its feet, and fix its longing, hungry stare upon those faraway places. But all she said was, smiling gently: "How I envy you."

He accepted that. "It has been," he said, "very wonderful

Writer's Technique: Mansfield uses a third-person limited point of view, focusing on Vera's thoughts and feelings. The use of a limited point of view reflects the Modernist belief that reality is shaped by people's perceptions.

A Dill Pickle 931

Master Teacher Note Mansfield's stories reflect the confusion and complexity of the modern age. She writes not about neat, controlled incidents but about common, fragmented incidents; her technique is to reveal the significance gradually of these incidents. "A Dill Pickle" is an example of such an incident.

—especially Russia. Russia was all that we had imagined, and far, far more. I even spent some days on a river boat on the Volga. Do you remember that boatman's song that you used to play?''

''Yes.'' It began to play in her mind as she spoke.

''Do you ever play it now?''

''No, I've no piano.''

He was amazed at that. ''But what has become of your beautiful piano?''

She made a little grimace. ''Sold. Ages ago.''

''But you were so fond of music,'' he wondered.

''I've no time for it now,'' said she.

He let it go at that. ''That river life,'' he went on, ''is something quite special. After a day or two you cannot realize that you have ever known another. And it is not necessary to know the language—the life of the boat creates a bond between you and the people that's more than sufficient. You eat with them, pass the day with them, and in the evening there is that endless singing.''

She shivered, hearing the boatman's song break out again loud and tragic, and seeing the boat floating on the darkening river with melancholy trees on either side. . . . ''Yes, I should like that,'' said she, stroking her muff.

''You'd like almost everything about Russian life,'' he said warmly. ''It's so informal, so impulsive, so free without question. And then the peasants are so splendid. They are such human beings—yes, that is it. Even the man who drives your carriage has—has some real part in what is happening. I remember the evening a party of us, two friends of mine and the wife of one of them, went for a picnic by the Black Sea. We took supper and champagne and ate and drank on the grass. And while we were eating the coachman came up. 'Have a dill pickle,' he said. He wanted to share with us. That seemed to me so right, so—you know what I mean?''

And she seemed at that moment to be sitting on the grass beside the mysteriously Black Sea, black as velvet and rippling against the banks in silent, velvet waves. She saw the carriage drawn up to one side of the road, and the little group on the grass, their faces and hands white in the moonlight. She saw the pale dress of the woman outspread and her folded parasol, lying on the grass like a huge pearl crochet hook. Apart from them, with his supper in a cloth on his knees, sat the coachman. ''Have a dill pickle,'' said he, and although she was not certain what a dill pickle was, she saw the greenish glass jar with a red chili like a parrot's beak glimmering through. She sucked in her cheeks; the dill pickle was terribly sour. . . .

"Yes, I know perfectly what you mean," she said.

In the pause that followed they looked at each other. In the past when they had looked at each other like that they had felt such a boundless understanding between them that their souls had, as it were, put their arms round each other and dropped into the same sea, content to be drowned, like mournful lovers. But now, the surprising thing was that it was he who held back. He who said:

"What a marvelous listener you are. When you look at me with those wild eyes I feel that I could tell you things that I would never breathe to another human being."

Was there just a hint of mockery in his voice or was it her fancy? She could not be sure.

"Before I met you," he said, "I had never spoken of myself to anybody. How well I remember one night, the night that I brought you the little Christmas tree, telling you all about my childhood. And of how I was so miserable that I ran away and lived under a cart in our yard for two days without being discovered. And you listened, and your eyes shone, and I felt that you had even made the little Christmas tree listen too, as in a fairy story."

But of that evening she had remembered a little pot of caviar. It had cost seven and sixpence. He could not get over it. Think of it—a tiny jar like that costing seven and sixpence. While she ate it he watched her, delighted and shocked.

"No, really, that is eating money. You could not get seven shillings into a little pot that size. Only think of the profit they must make. . . ." And he had begun some immensely complicated calculations. . . . But now good-bye to the caviar. The Christmas tree was on the table, and the little boy lay under the cart with his head pillowed on the yard dog.

"The dog was called Bosun," she cried delightedly.

But he did not follow. "Which dog? Had you a dog? I don't remember a dog at all."

"No, no. I mean the yard dog when you were a little boy." He laughed and snapped the cigarette case to.

"Was he? Do you know I had forgotten that. It seems such ages ago. I cannot believe that it is only six years. After I had recognized you today—I had to take such a leap—I had to take a leap over my whole life to get back to that time. I was such a kid then." He drummed on the table. "I've often thought how I must have bored you. And now I understand so

Writer's Technique What does the dill pickle suggest about the relationship between these two people?

Literary Movement: Modernist writers often explore the difficulty of establishing successful relationships in the modern world.

Literary Movement: The contrast in their recollections of the evening reflects the Modernist belief in the subjectivity of human experience.

Writer's Technique: The man's character is revealed through his comments.

A Dill Pickle   933

perfectly why you wrote to me as you did—although at the time that letter nearly finished my life. I found it again the other day, and I couldn't help laughing as I read it. It was so clever—such a true picture of me.'' He glanced up. ''You're not going?''

She had buttoned her collar again and drawn down her veil.

''Yes, I am afraid I must,'' she said, and managed a smile. Now she knew that he had been mocking.

''Ah, no, please,'' he pleaded. ''Don't go just for a moment,'' and he caught up one of her gloves from the table and clutched at it as if that would hold her. ''I see so few people to talk to nowadays, that I have turned into a sort of barbarian,'' he said. ''Have I said something to hurt you?''

> **Writer's Techniques:** Vera refuses to admit that his comments have hurt her, though it is clear from her actions that they have.

''Not a bit,'' she lied. But as she watched him draw her glove through his fingers, gently, gently, her anger really did die down, and besides, at the moment he looked more like himself of six years ago. . . .

''What I really wanted then,'' he said softly, ''was to be a sort of carpet—to make myself into a sort of carpet for you to walk on so that you need not be hurt by the sharp stones and the mud that you hated so. It was nothing more positive than that—nothing more selfish. Only I did desire, eventually, to turn into a magic carpet and carry you away to all those lands you longed to see.''

As he spoke she lifted her head as though she drank something; the strange beast in her bosom began to purr. . . .

> **Literary Movement:** The man's comment reflects the sense of pessimism that often characterizes modern life.

''I felt that you were more lonely than anybody else in the world,'' he went on, ''and yet, perhaps, that you were the only person in the world who was really, truly alive. Born out of your time,'' he murmured, stroking the glove, ''fated.''

What had she done! How had she dared to throw away her happiness like this. This was the only man who had ever understood her. Was it too late? Could it be too late? *She* was that glove that he held in his fingers. . . .

''And then the fact that you had no friends and never had made friends with people. How I understood that, for neither had I. Is it just the same now?''

''Yes,'' she breathed. ''Just the same. I am as alone as ever.''

''So am I,'' he laughed gently, ''just the same.''

Suddenly with a quick gesture he handed her back the glove and scraped his chair on the floor. ''But what seemed to me so mysterious then is perfectly plain to me now. And to you, too, of course. . . . It simply was that we were such egoists, so self-engrossed, so wrapped up in ourselves that we hadn't a corner in our hearts for anybody else. Do you know," he cried, naive and hearty, and dreadfully like another side of that old self again, "I began studying a Mind System when I was in Russia, and I found that we were not peculiar at all. It's quite a well known form of . . ."

She had gone. He sat there, thunderstruck, astounded beyond words. . . . And then he asked the waitress for his bill.

"But the cream has not been touched," he said. "Please do not charge me for it."

Historical Context: Psychology was a common interest in the Modernist period.

Literary Movement: Like most Modernist stories, the story ends abruptly, without a resolution.

Katherine Mansfield (1888-1923) was born Kathleen Mansfield Beauchamp in Wellington, New Zealand. At the age of fifteen she headed to London where she studied for three years at Queens College. In London she became acquainted with a number of literary figures, the most significant of whom were D. H. Lawrence and Virginia Woolf. It was the latter who, along with her husband, published Mansfield's first book of short stories, *Preludes,* in 1917. The overall bittersweet tone of the volume anticipated her second and more ambitious collection, *The Garden Party and Other Stories* (1922), in which she successfully combined her angry and sentimental impulses in portraits of impoverished single women.

Her writing brought her into contact with the literary critic J. Middleton Murray, whom she married. The two lived a nomadic and at times penniless life, moving back and forth between the Continent and London. Increasingly ill with tuberculosis, Mansfield spent the last few years of her life in and out of clinics and hospitals before the disease finally claimed her in 1923.

Critics credit Mansfield with having greatly refined the art of the short story. Her works have often been compared to those of Joyce and the Russian writer Chekhov, whom she greatly admired. When called upon to describe her motivation as a writer, Katherine Mansfield replied that she wrote out of both a sense of joy and a sense of doom. Indeed, her short stories—which alternately express cynicism toward the corruption of modern English society and recall fond memories of a blissful childhood—reflect this dual outlook.

THINKING ABOUT THE SELECTION

Recalling

1. (a) How does Vera's friend react when he first sees her? (b) How does this make Vera feel?

2. (a) What does the man remember about the first afternoon they spent together? (b) What does Vera remember?

3. Where has the man been for the past six years?

4. (a) What does Vera begin to feel toward the end of the story, as her friend explains their mutual loneliness? (b) What changes her mind?

A Dill Pickle 935

(Answers begin on p. 935.)

Interpreting

5. (a) He is very impressed with himself and is very caught up with impressing others. It is also clear that their love affair made a huge impression on her but not on him. (b) He sees none of his own faults and vanities. He tries to romanticize events after they happen, but she remembers the realities of what happened—in this instance, his obsession with the cost of the caviar.

6. Her decision that his memories are truer than hers shows that she *wants* it to have been that romantic —not that it was. It also indicates that she has a hard time not being taken in by his manipulation of her —now as in the days of their affair.

7. Suggested Response: Vera's action symbolizes her ambivalence towards him and her indecision whether to stay or go.

8. Suggested Response: The man truly seems to be an egoist: all of his conversation focuses on himself and his view of the world. Vera, however, seems to be able to think about and talk about people and events outside herself.

9. (a) Suggested Response: The title might be significant because of the man's reaction to the dill pickle, which reveals his condescension towards others, his egoism, his romanticizing of events for manipulative purposes. The dill pickle also symbolizes the man himself and what he offers to Vera—something sour rather than the sweetness and light that he thinks he offers. (b) Because of what it symbolizes, the title seems very appropriate for the story.

Applying

10. Answers will differ. Suggested Response: Unselfishness and a willingness to take risks are among the qualities necessary for people to be open to love.

ANSWERS TO ANALYZING LITERATURE

1. Suggested Response: This passage gives an impression of Vera through her feeling about cold, but, even more, the author indicates Vera's concern with aging.

Interpreting

5. (a) What difference between Vera and her friend is revealed in the first two paragraphs of the story? (b) What difference is revealed through their attitudes toward the pot of caviar?

6. Vera decides that her friend's recollections of the afternoon at Kew Gardens are "truer" than hers. What does this reveal about her?

7. What action do you think is symbolized by Vera's unbuttoning and buttoning her collar?

8. Do you think Vera's and the man's behavior reveal the truth of his statement about their being egoists? Support your answer with details from the story.

9. (a) What do you think is the significance of the story's title? (b) Do you think the title is an appropriate one? Explain.

Applying

10. The man claims that Vera and he were so wrapped up in themselves that they didn't have room in their hearts for anyone else. What qualities do you think are necessary for a person to be open to love?

ANALYZING LITERATURE

Understanding Dialogue

Dialogue is conversation that takes place between two or more characters in a literary work. One key purpose of dialogue is to present information about the characters in a direct and interesting manner. Knowing precisely when to let a character speak for himself or herself through dialogue and when to speak *for* that character requires great skill on the part of a writer.

Locate the following passages from the story, and read the paragraphs that precede and follow each. In each case explain what effect you feel the author achieves through dialogue that would be lost through direct narration.

1. "Loathe it." She shuddered. "And the worst of it is that the older one grows . . ." (page 929)

2. "The colder!" He echoed her words, laughing too. "Ah, ah. You still say the same things." (page 930)

3. "And while we were eating, the coachman came up. 'Have a dill pickle,' he said. He wanted to share with us. That seemed to me so right, so—you know what I mean?" (page 932)

4. "What a marvelous listener you are . . ." (page 933)

CRITICAL THINKING AND READING

Making Inferences Based on Dialogue

It has been said that language is "a window on the mind." If we accept this observation as true, then we can use dialogue to learn a great deal about the workings of a character's mind. Notice, for instance, Vera's tendency to speak in very short, almost clipped sentences—a habit that might lead us to infer that she is a guarded, cautious person, which, in fact, as the narrator assures us, she is. Her friend, too, reveals much about his thoughts, feelings, and ideas through his dialogue, though in this instance we receive no additional clues from the narrator.

What impression do you form of the narrator from what he says? Find lines of dialogue to back up your answer.

2. Suggested Response: The author shows in this one phrase that they had an intimate relationship and that he knew many things about her.

3. Suggested Response: The author shows that the young man is affected and in love with his perception of himself. The passage also shows condescension toward the peasants.

4. Suggested Response: The author shows the young man again as a flatterer and a manipulator. The words are also ironic because he does so much more talking than she that she can't help being a listener.

ANSWERS TO CRITICAL THINKING AND READING

Suggested Response: He thinks he is an expert on almost every subject, including what is good and what people ought to do: His statement "You are sure you won't eat anything? . . . The fruit here is very good" shows this.

He is overly dramatic and tries to manipulate people's emotions through this flattery and overdramatization. He is insincere; for example, he says "I wish that I had taken poison and were about to die—here now!"

He is tight with money. For example, he says "But the cream has not been touched . . . Please do not charge me for it." In context, this statement also shows how little real

Prose

GARDENS IN THE POUND, COOKHAM, 1936
Stanley Spencer
Leeds City Art Galleries

Prose 937

Fine art, *Gardens in the Pound, Cookham,* 1936, by Stanley Spencer. Stanley Spencer (1891–1959), trained in academic art at the prestigious Slade School in London. He lived his entire life in the small village of Cookham, near London. He considered it his "paradise on earth." Spencer is remembered for his landscapes of Cookham and paintings of mythical-religious fantasy set in Cookham.

Gardens in the Pound demonstrates Spencer's considerable skill as an artist. The natural detail is sensitively handled with a fresh point of view. The carefully rendered tones and textures of the vegetation and sunlight create interesting and random patterns. Spencer loved every aspect of Cookham, from alleyways to gardens and spent many hours recording them in paint.

feeling he has for Vera since she has just left and being charged for the cream is all he can think about.

More About the Author Joseph Conrad was the son of a Polish nobleman, who lived in exile in northern Russia. Growing up in the Ukraine, the young Conrad was isolated by language, culture, and customs from those around him. Both of his parents died when he was young, and this increased his isolation. How might Conrad's isolation have affected his writing?

Critical Evaluation The English novelist Christopher Isherwood made the following remarks about Conrad's feeling for the sea: "It is common to say of a man that he loves the sea. But Conrad was beyond loving or hating, he had dedicated himself to it absolutely. He writes about his sea-life with the unquestioning matter-of-factness of a monk speaking of his vocation. He did not marry until he had left it for good."

JOSEPH CONRAD

1857–1924

To become one of the most distinguished novelists of one's age would be accomplishment enough for most writers. To do so in a language other than one's own native tongue, as Joseph Conrad did, is an achievement almost without parallel.

Born in Poland to a scholarly father, Josef Teodor Konrad Nalecz Korzeniowski was orphaned at the age of ten. He fled his Russian-occupied homeland to France and England when he was sixteen, and spent the next dozen years as an apprentice seaman. The voyages that he made to exotic corners of the globe—Asia, Africa, and South America—were later put to use as the vivid settings for much of his fiction. In 1886, he became a ship's captain and an English citizen.

It was not until he was thirty-eight that Conrad published his first novel, *Almayer's Folly*. That year, 1895, also marked his marriage and his retirement from the sea. In the next few years, Conrad so far overcame the difficulties of writing in an adopted tongue (English was actually his third language; Polish and Russian were his first and second) that he became one of the masters of Modernist prose. In 1897 he published his first important novel, *The Nigger of The Narcissus*, and within the next seven years produced three master-pieces: *Lord Jim* (1900), *Youth*, a collection of shorter pieces that includes his well-known "Heart of Darkness" (1902), and the ambitious *Nostromo* (1904).

After a brief collaboration with novelist Ford Maddox Ford, Conrad came out with two novels about revolutionaries, *The Secret Agent* (1907) and *Under Western Eyes* (1911). Remaining active through the end of his life, he was at work on *Suspense*, an ambitious historical novel in the classic tradition, when he died in 1924.

Conrad often used the tradition of the sea yarn to create what, on the surface, were thrilling adventure tales. His serious thematic concerns, however, are readily apparent. Almost invariably the notion of "voyage" in a Conrad novel translates to a voyage of self-discovery. The menacing jungles and vast oceans that confront his characters become metaphors for the hidden depths of the self; the requirement for loyalty among crew members of a ship, often unmet, symbolizes the frailty of human relationships in a world filled with deception, corruption, and betrayal.

If Conrad's themes were Modernist, his technical treatments of those themes were even more so. Often, and memorably, as in "The Lagoon," he shifts the point of view from which the story is told.

GUIDE FOR INTERPRETING

The Lagoon

Writer's Technique

Shifting Point of View and Theme. Point of view is the vantage point from which an author elects to narrate a story. Traditionally, writers have narrated stories from either the first-person point of view, in which the speaker is also a character, or the third-person point of view, in which the speaker is not specifically identified by name. With the arrival of the Modernist movement in the early twentieth century, a third option was available—that of using both points of view within the space of a single narrative. By so doing, the writer was able to "move" the narrator from the foreground to the background as the action dictated. In "The Lagoon" Joseph Conrad shifts between a third- and first-person narrator with the additional purpose of emphasizing the story's theme, or central idea, that the line between reality and illusion is often blurred.

Commentary

"The Lagoon" is one of Conrad's most admired tales. Although it was only the fourth story he published, it nonetheless shows many elements that would become characteristic of his later work: exotic setting, intriguing ending, and unique narrative style. "The Lagoon" has the distinction of being the first tale in which Conrad borrowed from himself. When his editors requested a piece more characteristic of his exotic style, Conrad tried to reproduce the tangled landscape of his Malayan novels, complete with "forests rivers —stars—wind sunrise." Perhaps part of the story's enduring appeal stems from its eerie atmosphere, for "The Lagoon" is more of a mood piece than any of his other tales. Conrad was fond of the story himself: In 1897, thanking an acquaintance for a note of praise, he called it his favorite short story, written to please himself. Although the context of the letter and other information from his life suggest that his remark may have been voiced more out of politeness than genuine conviction, it nonetheless suggests that the mysterious tale exerted a story hold even over its author.

Writing

Try to recall, or invent, an occasion when a friend took you into his or her confidence and shared a problem with you. In a paragraph, describe the emotions you experienced as you listened to your friend. Note in particular whether you were sympathetic to your friend's dilemma, whether you were able to offer any useful advice, and whether there were implications of the problem that applied to yourself and others.

Literary Focus First-person point of view gives the reader access to the inner thoughts of the character, while third person narration allows other characters to speak their thoughts. Ask the students to keep in mind the central idea that even external realities can be illusions as they observe the point-of-view shift from first-person to third-person.

Writing/Prior Knowledge Ask the **less advanced** students to compare themselves to the white man as a friendly listener. Discuss sympathetic listening and compassion. Your **more advanced** students can analyze the way the white man serves as a bridge between the particular story of Arsat and the universal story of mankind, or the way he functions as a chorus.

Vocabulary

Preteach the following vocabulary words:
portals (pôr′t'lz) *n*.: Doors; gateways (p. 940)
invincible (in vin′səb'l) *adj*.: Unconquerable (p. 941)
propitiate (prə pish′ē āt) *v*.: Ease the burden of; appease (p. 942)
conflagration (kän′flə grā′ shən) *n*.: Great fire (p. 943)
august (ô gust′) *adj*.: Worthy of great respect (p. 944)

Objectives

1 To understand shifting points of view and theme
2 To make inferences about a moral code
3 To set up a reader's theater
4 To respond to theme

Support Material

Teaching Portfolio
Teacher Backup, p. 1115–1118
Grammar in Action Worksheet, *Appreciating Concrete Details*, p. 1119
Usage and Mechanics Worksheet, p. 1121
Vocabulary Check, p. 1122
Analyzing Literature Worksheet, *Understanding a Shifting Point of View*, p. 1123

Language Worksheet, *Using Context Clues*, p. 1124
Selection Test, p. 1125–1126
Art Transparency 13, *The Bridge, Etaples*, by Philip Wilson Steer

The Lagoon

Joseph Conrad

The white man, leaning with both arms over the roof of the little house in the stern of the boat, said to the steersman—

"We will pass the night in Arsat's clearing. It is late."

The Malay[1] only grunted, and went on looking fixedly at the river. The white man rested his chin on his crossed arms and gazed at the wake of the boat. At the end of the straight avenue of forests cut by the intense glitter of the river, the sun appeared unclouded and dazzling, poised low over the water that shone smoothly like a band of metal. The forests, somber and dull, stood motionless and silent on each side of the broad stream. At the foot of big, towering trees, trunkless nipa palms rose from the mud of the bank, in bunches of leaves enormous and heavy, that hung unstirring over the brown swirl of eddies. In the stillness of the air every tree, every leaf, every bough, every tendril of creeper and every petal of minute blossoms seemed to have been bewitched into an immobility perfect and final. Nothing moved on the river but the eight paddles that rose flashing regularly, dipped together with a single splash; while the steersman swept right and left with a periodic and sudden flourish of his blade describing a glinting semicircle above his head. The churned-up water frothed alongside with a confused murmur. And the

---

1. **Malay** (mã′ lã): A native of the Malay peninsula in Southeast Asia.

white man's canoe, advancing up stream in the short-lived disturbance of its own making, seemed to enter the portals of a land from which the very memory of motion had forever departed.

The white man, turning his back upon the setting sun, looked along the empty and broad expanse of the sea-reach. For the last three miles of its course the wandering, hesitating river, as if enticed irresistibly by the freedom of an open horizon, flows straight into the sea, flows straight to the east—to the east that harbors both light and darkness. Astern of the boat the repeated call of some bird, a cry discordant and feeble, skipped along over the smooth water and lost itself, before it could reach the other shore, in the breathless silence of the world.

The steersman dug his paddle into the stream, and held hard with stiffened arms, his body thrown forward. The water gurgled aloud; and suddenly the long straight reach seemed to pivot on its center, the forests swung in a semicircle, and the slanting beams of sunset touched the broadside of the canoe with a fiery glow, throwing the slender and distorted shadows of its crew upon the streaked glitter of the river. The white man turned to look ahead. The course of the boat had been altered at right-angles to the stream, and the carved dragonhead of its prow was pointing now at a gap in the fringing bushes of the bank. It glided through, brushing the overhanging twigs, and disappeared from the river like some

3 **Discussion** What mood does this description create?

4 **Discussion** What does the imagery suggest about the forest?

slim and amphibious creature leaving the water for its lair in the forests.

The narrow creek was like a ditch: tortuous, fabulously deep; filled with gloom under the thin strip of pure and shining blue of the heaven. Immense trees soared up, invisible behind the festooned draperies of creepers. Here and there, near the glistening blackness of the water, a twisted root of some tall tree showed amongst the tracery of small ferns, black and dull, writhing and motionless, like an arrested snake. The short words of the paddlers reverberated loudly between the thick and somber walls of vegetation. Darkness oozed out from between the trees, through the tangled maze of the creepers, from behind the great fantastic and unstirring leaves; the darkness, mysterious and invincible; the darkness scented and poisonous of impenetrable forests.

The men poled in the shoaling[2] water. The creek broadened, opening out into a wide sweep of a stagnant lagoon. The forests receded from the marshy bank, leaving a level strip of bright green, reedy grass to frame the reflected blueness of the sky. A fleecy pink cloud drifted high above, trailing the delicate coloring of its image under the floating leaves and the silvery blossoms of the lotus. A little house, perched on high piles, appeared black in the distance. Near it, two tall nibong palms, that seemed to have come out of the forests in the background, leaned slightly over the ragged roof, with a suggestion of sad tenderness and care in the droop of their leafy and soaring heads.

---

2. shoaling: Shallow.

The Lagoon   941

Grammar in Action

Concrete, accurate details create vivid pictures and convey an emotional impression. In describing the entry to Arsat's lagoon, notice how Joseph Conrad's precise details invest the place with character.

> The narrow creek was like a ditch: tortuous, fabulously deep; filled with gloom under the thin strip of pure and shining blue of the heaven. Immense trees soared up, invisible behind the festooned draperies of creepers. Here and there, near the glistening blackness of the water, a twisted root of some tall tree showed amongst the tracery of small ferns, black and dull, writhing and motionless, like an arrested snake.

Conrad infuses his description with a foreboding quality by heaping one disturbing detail upon another. The creek is "like a ditch," "fabulously deep," and therefore frighteningly perilous. "Immense trees soared up," threatening by their size. He adds to this "a twisted root" that appears snakelike, and he heaps yet

5 Discussion Why do the polers dislike stopping at Arsat's hut?

6 Reading Strategy Ask the students to summarize what the natives don't like, and to predict the role of "invisible dangers" or fate in this story.

7 Enrichment "Tuan" means lord and it is a malay term of respect which probably refers to Captain William Lingard, who was a local hero and father figure at the time Conrad sailed in the Malayan settlements. Lingard was the first European to establish a very isolated tracking post up the Berau river.

The steersman, pointing with his paddle, said, "Arsat is there. I see his canoe fast between the piles."

The polers ran along the sides of the boat glancing over their shoulders at the end of the day's journey. They would have preferred to spend the night somewhere else than on this lagoon of weird aspect and ghostly reputation. Moreover, they disliked Arsat, first as a stranger, and also because he who repairs a ruined house, and dwells in it, proclaims that he is not afraid to live amongst the spirits that haunt the places abandoned by mankind. Such a man can disturb the course of fate by glances or words; while his familiar ghosts are not easy to propitiate by casual wayfarers upon whom they long to wreak the malice of their human master. White men care not for such things, being unbelievers and in league with the Father of Evil, who leads them unharmed through the invisible dangers of this world. To the warnings of the righteous they oppose an offensive pretense of disbelief. What is there to be done?

So they thought, throwing their weight on the end of their long poles. The big canoe glided on swiftly, noiselessly, and smoothly, toward Arsat's clearing, till, in a great rattling of poles thrown down, and the loud murmurs of "Allah[3] be praised!" it came with a gentle knock against the crooked piles below the house.

The boatmen with uplifted faces shouted discordantly, "Arsat! O Arsat!" Nobody came. The white man began to climb the rude ladder giving access to the bamboo platform before the house. The juragan[4] of the boat said sulkily, "We will cook in the sampan,[5] and sleep on the water."

"Pass my blankets and the basket," said the white man curtly.

He knelt on the edge of the platform to

---

3. **Allah** (al′ ə): The Moslem name for God.
4. **juragan** (jōō rä′ gän): Captain or master.
5. **sampan:** A small flat-bottomed boat with a cabin formed by mats.

receive the bundle. Then the boat shoved off, and the white man, standing up, confronted Arsat, who had come out through the low door of his hut. He was a man young, powerful, with a broad chest and muscular arms. He had nothing on but his sarong.[6] His head was bare. His big, soft eyes stared eagerly at the white man, but his voice and demeanor were composed as he asked, without any words of greeting—

"Have you medicine, Tuan?"[7]

"No," said the visitor in a startled tone. "No. Why? Is there sickness in the house?"

"Enter and see," replied Arsat, in the same calm manner, and turning short round, passed again through the small doorway. The white man, dropping his bundles, followed.

In the dim light of the dwelling he made out on a couch of bamboos a woman stretched on her back under a broad sheet of red cotton cloth. She lay still, as if dead; but her big eyes, wide open, glittered in the gloom, staring upward at the slender rafters, motionless and unseeing. She was in a high fever, and evidently unconscious. Her cheeks were sunk slightly, her lips were partly open, and on the young face there was the ominous and fixed expression—the absorbed, contemplating expression of the unconscious who are going to die. The two men stood looking down at her in silence.

"Has she been long ill?" asked the traveler.

"I have not slept for five nights," answered the Malay, in a deliberate tone. "At first she heard voices calling her from the water and struggled against me who held her. But since the sun of today rose she hears nothing—she hears not me. She sees nothing. She sees not me—me!"

He remained silent for a minute, then asked softly—

---

6. **sarong:** A long, brightly colored strip of cloth worn like a skirt.
7. **Tuan** (twan): Malayan for "sir."

---

more discomfort on that detail by making the half-hidden snake "arrested" as if in wait.

Student Activity 1. Find the paragraph on page 963 quoted in the example, and cite the remaining concrete details, explaining their effects. Begin with "The short words of the paddlers . . .".

Student Activity 2. Write a descriptive paragraph, using concrete details to convey one dominant emotional impression.

"Tuan, will she die?"

"I fear so," said the white man sorrowfully. He had known Arsat years ago, in a far country in times of trouble and danger, when no friendship is to be despised. And since his Malay friend had come unexpectedly to dwell in the hut on the lagoon with a strange woman, he had slept many times there, in his journeys up and down the river. He liked the man who knew how to keep faith in council and how to fight without fear by the side of his white friend. He liked him—not so much perhaps as a man likes his favorite dog—but still he liked him well enough to help and ask no questions, to think sometimes vaguely and hazily in the midst of his own pursuits, about the lonely man and the long-haired woman with audacious face and triumphant eyes, who lived together hidden by the forests—alone and feared.

The white man came out of the hut in time to see the enormous conflagration of sunset put out by the swift and stealthy shadows that, rising like a black and impalpable vapor above the treetops, spread over the heaven, extinguishing the crimson glow of floating clouds and the red brilliance of departing daylight. In a few moments all the stars came out above the intense blackness of the earth, and the great lagoon gleaming suddenly with reflected lights resembled an oval patch of night sky flung down into the hopeless and abysmal night of the wilderness. The white man had some supper out of the basket, then collecting a few sticks that lay about the platform, made up a small fire, not for warmth, but for the sake of the smoke, which would keep off the mosquitos. He wrapped himself in his blankets and sat with his back against the reed wall of the house, smoking thoughtfully.

Arsat came through the doorway with noiseless steps and squatted down by the fire. The white man moved his outstretched legs a little.

"She breathes," said Arsat in a low voice, anticipating the expected question.

"She breathes and burns as if with a great fire. She speaks not; she hears not—and burns!"

He paused for a moment, then asked in a quiet, incurious tone—

"Tuan . . . will she die?"

The white man moved his shoulders uneasily, and muttered in a hesitating manner—

"If such is her fate."

"No, Tuan," said Arsat calmly. "If such is my fate. I hear, I see, I wait. I remember . . . Tuan, do you remember the old days? Do you remember my brother?"

"Yes," said the white man. The Malay rose suddenly and went in. The other, sitting still outside, could hear the voice in the hut. Arsat said: "Hear me! Speak!" His words were succeeded by a complete silence. "O Diamelen!" he cried suddenly. After that cry there was a deep sigh. Arsat came out and sank down again in his old place.

They sat in silence before the fire. There was no sound within the house, there was no sound near them; but far away on the lagoon they could hear the voices of the boatmen ringing fitful and distinct on the calm water. The fire in the bows of the sampan shone faintly in the distance with a hazy red glow. Then it died out. The voices ceased. The land and the water slept invisible, unstirring and mute. It was as though there had been nothing left in the world but the glitter of stars streaming, ceaseless and vain, through the black stillness of the night.

The white man gazed straight before him into the darkness with wide-open eyes. The fear and fascination, the inspiration and the wonder of death—of death near, unavoidable, and unseen, soothed the unrest of his race and stirred the most indistinct, the most intimate of his thoughts. The ever-ready suspicion of evil, the gnawing suspicion that lurks in our hearts, flowed out into the stillness round him—into the stillness profound and dumb, and made it appear untrustworthy and infamous, like

8

Critical Thinking and Reading Contrast Arsat and the white man in their attitudes toward friendship. What can you infer about Conrad from the narrator's ironical aside about the white man?

9 Enrichment The intense colors show the influence of the brilliant colors and heightened atmosphere of Conrad's tropical voyages.

10 Discussion What does the lagoon reflect?

11 Discussion Ask the students how the pairs of adjectives work.

12

12 Master Teacher Note Ask the students to observe the shift in person and atmosphere in this passage. The mysterious, ''phantom-filled'' struggle refers to the primitive feelings or the subconscious part of man. During the early decades of the twentieth century studies of Freud and others who studied the human unconscious made a deep impact on the art. Conrad's writing shows a fascination for the workings of the subconscious. Many of his primitive journeys and his primitive characters, like Arsat, can be viewed as symbols of our own primitive natures.

The exploration of the unconscious, along with the shifts in point of view, show why Conrad has been called the father of twentieth-century literature.

13 Clarification Conrad describes nature as indifferent to man at the lagoon. Conrad's theory of ''moral isolation'' claims man's weaknesses take over when a person is isolated. The lagoon also creates an atmosphere of isolation for the white man.

14 Enrichment Conrad said ''The artist, then, like the thinker or the scientist, seeks the truth and makes his appeal.'' How does Arsat make both the white man and the reader see the truth?

15 Reading Strategy Ask the students to predict the kind of love Arsat will describe.

16 Discussion What is the strength of brotherly love and what is its danger?

17 Clarification Conrad used facts about local people to enrich all of his Far East stories. Inche Maida was a local woman married to a chief of Perak. The princess of Perak was described as ''light, spare and a little witch like,'' and probably was the model for Inchi Midah.

the placid and impenetrable mask of an unjustifiable violence. In that fleeting and powerful disturbance of his being the earth enfolded in the starlight peace became a shadowy country of inhuman strife, a battlefield of phantoms terrible and charming, august or ignoble, struggling ardently for the possession of our helpless hearts. An unquiet and mysterious country of inextinguishable desires and fears.

A plaintive murmur rose in the night; a murmur saddening and startling, as if the great solitudes of surrounding woods had tried to whisper into his ear the wisdom of their immense and lofty indifference. Sounds hesitating and vague floated in the air round him, shaped themselves slowly into words; and at last flowed on gently in a murmuring stream of soft and monotonous sentences. He stirred like a man waking up and changed his position slightly. Arsat, motionless and shadowy, sitting with bowed head under the stars, was speaking in a low and dreamy tone—

''. . . for where can we lay down the heaviness of our trouble but in a friend's heart? A man must speak of war and of love. You, Tuan, know what war is, and you have seen me in time of danger seek death as other men seek life! A writing may be lost; a lie may be written; but what the eye has seen is truth and remains in the mind!''

''I remember,'' said the white man quietly. Arsat went on with mournful composure—

''Therefore I shall speak to you of love. Speak in the night. Speak before both night and love are gone—and the eye of day looks upon my sorrow and my shame; upon my blackened face; upon my burnt-up heart.''

A sigh, short and faint, marked an almost imperceptible pause, and then his words flowed on, without a stir, without a gesture.

''After the time of trouble and war was over and you went away from my country in the pursuit of your desires, which we, men of the islands, cannot understand, I and my

brother became again, as we had been before, the sword bearers of the Ruler. You know we were men of family, belonging to a ruling race, and more fit than any to carry on our right shoulder the emblem of power. And in the time of prosperity Si Dendring showed us favor, as we, in time of sorrow, had showed to him the faithfulness of our courage. It was a time of peace. A time of deer hunts and cock fights; of idle talks and foolish squabbles between men whose bellies are full and weapons are rusty. But the sower watched the young rice shoots grow up without fear, and the traders came and went, departed lean and returned fat into the river of peace. They brought news too. Brought lies and truth mixed together, so that no man knew when to rejoice and when to be sorry. We heard from them about you also. They had seen you here and had seen you there. And I was glad to hear, for I remembered the stirring times, and I always remembered you, Tuan, till the time came when my eyes could see nothing in the past, because they had looked upon the one who is dying there—in the house.''

He stopped to exclaim in an intense whisper, ''O Mara bahia! O Calamity!'' then went on speaking a little louder.

''There's no worse enemy and no better friend than a brother, Tuan, for one brother knows another, and in perfect knowledge is strength for good or evil. I loved my brother. I went to him and told him that I could see nothing but one face, hear nothing but one voice. He told me: 'Open your heart so that she can see what is in it—and wait. Patience is wisdom. Inchi Midah may die or our Ruler may throw off his fear of a woman!' . . . I waited! . . . You remember the lady with the veiled face, Tuan, and the fear of our Ruler before her cunning and temper. And if she wanted her servant, what could I do? But I fed the hunger of my heart on short glances and stealthy words. I loitered on the path to the bath houses in the daytime, and when the sun had fallen behind the forest I crept along the jasmine hedges of the wom-

Primary Source

Conrad's biographer Frederick Karl described William Lingard (see Enrichment Note #7) as follows:

William Lingard . . . was an energetic seaman, ship-owner, and trader, moving in and out of legal and illegal activities as befitting a man renowned as the 'Rajah Laut' [''King of the Sea'']. Although it is quite possible that Conrad never met him, Lingard caught the young seaman's imagination. . . . Lingard was as close as Conrad was ever to come to the Odysseus of his childhood dreams and reading. Very possibly, his mixture of shrewdness as a trader, daring as a contender with sea pirates for en's courtyard. Unseeing, we spoke to one another through the scent of flowers, through the veil of leaves, through the blades of long grass that stood still before our lips; so great was our prudence, so faint was the murmur of our great longing. The time passed swiftly . . . and there were whispers amongst women—and our enemies watched—my brother was gloomy, and I began to think of killing and of a fierce death. . . . We are of a people who take what they want—like you whites. There is a time when a man should forget loyalty and respect. Might and authority are given to rulers, but to all men is given love and strength and courage. My brother said, 'You shall take her from their midst. We are two who are like one.' And I answered, 'Let it be soon, for I find no warmth in sunlight that does not shine upon her.' Our time came when the Ruler and all the great people went to the mouth of the river to fish by torchlight. There were hundreds of boats, and on the white sand, between the water and the forests, dwellings of leaves were built for the households of the Rajahs.[8] The smoke of cooking fires was like a blue mist of the evening, and many voices rang in it joyfully. While they were making the boats ready to beat up the fish, my brother came to me and said, 'Tonight!' I looked to my weapons, and when the time came our canoe took its place in the circle of boats carrying the torches. The lights blazed on the water, but behind the boats there was darkness. When the shouting began and the excitement made them like mad we dropped out. The water swallowed our fire, and we floated back to the shore that was dark with only here and there the glimmer of embers. We could hear the talk of slave girls amongst the sheds. Then we found a place deserted and silent. We waited there. She came. She came running along the shore, rapid and leaving no trace, like a leaf driven by the wind into the sea. My brother said gloomily, 'Go and take

---

8. Rajahs (rä′ jəz): Malayan chiefs.

her; carry her into our boat.' I lifted her in my arms. She panted. Her heart was beating against my breast. I said, 'I take you from those people. You came to the cry of my heart, but my arms take you into my boat against the will of the great!' 'It is right,' said my brother. 'We are men who take what we want and can hold it against many. We should have taken her in daylight.' I said, 'Let us be off'; for since she was in my boat I began to think of our Ruler's many men. 'Yes. Let us be off,' said my brother. 'We are cast out and this boat is our country now —and the sea is our refuge.' He lingered with his foot on the shore, and I entreated him to hasten, for I remembered the strokes of her heart against my breast and thought that two men cannot withstand a hundred. We left, paddling downstream close to the bank; and as we passed by the creek where they were fishing, the great shouting had ceased, but the murmur of voices was loud like the humming of insects flying at noonday. The boats floated, clustered together, in the red light of torches, under a black roof of smoke; and men talked of their sport. Men that boasted, and praised, and jeered—men that would have been our friends in the morning, but on that night were already our enemies. We paddled swiftly past. We had no more friends in the country of our birth. She sat in the middle of the canoe with covered face; silent as she is now; unseeing as she is now—and I had no regret at what I was leaving because I could hear her breathing close to me—as I can hear her now.''

He paused, listened with his ear turned to the doorway, then shook his head and went on.

''My brother wanted to shout the cry of challenge—one cry only—to let the people know we were freeborn robbers who trusted our arms and the great sea. And again I begged him in the name of our love to be silent. Could I not hear her breathing close to me? I knew the pursuit would come quick enough. My brother loved me. He dipped his paddle without a splash. He only said,

---

18 **Discussion** What similarity to the whites is Arsat describing?

19 **Discussion** What is illusory here and what is real?

20 **Discussion** Why are they outcasts? How does isolation connect the brothers to the white man? In what way is Conrad an outcast also?

21 **Clarification** Conrad introduces pirates into ''The Lagoon'' since his Far East travels frequently brought him to a pirate haunt at that time.

---

routes and goods, and expertise as a handler of sailing vessels recalled to Conrad those daring adventurers, both real and fictitious, both Polish and Greek, with whom his own childhood was so closely connected. Further, Lingard, we know, was renowned as a storyteller, a spinner of tales, with his favorite resting place Emmerson's Tiffin Room in Singapore. As a teller of tales, there was in William Lingard many of the characteristics we also associate with Marlow, Conrad's own archetypal 'artist figure,' the narrator of four of his novels and tales.

22 **Discussion** In his brother's mind, what would Arsat have to do to become whole again?

23 **Reading Strategy** Predict what is going to happen to Arsat's brother.

24 **Clarification** The secret place Arsat's brother knows is probably a secret navigable channel up the Berau river which Captain Lingard found. Lingard was the only white man living in this very isolated place.

'There is half a man in you now—the other half is in that woman. I can wait. When you are a whole man again, you will come back with me here to shout defiance. We are sons of the same mother.' I made no answer. All my strength and all my spirit were in my hands that held the paddle—for I longed to be with her in a safe place beyond the reach of men's anger and of women's spite. My love was so great, that I thought it could guide me to a country where death was unknown, if I could only escape from Inchi Midah's fury and from our Ruler's sword. We paddled with haste, breathing through our teeth. The blades bit deep into the smooth water. We passed out of the river; we flew in clear channels amongst the shallows. We skirted the black coast; we skirted the sand beaches where the sea speaks in whispers to the land; and the gleam of white sand flashed back past our boat, so swiftly she ran upon the water. We spoke not. Only once I said, 'Sleep, Diamelen, for soon you may want all your strength.' I heard the sweetness of her voice, but I never turned my head. The sun rose and still we went on. Water fell from my face like rain from a cloud. We flew in the light and heat. I never looked back, but I knew that my brother's eyes, behind me, were looking steadily ahead, for the boat went as straight as a bushman's dart, when it leaves the end of the sumpitan.[9] There was no better paddler, no better steersman than my brother. Many times, together, we had won races in that canoe. But we never had put out our strength as we did then—then, when for the last time we paddled together! There was no braver or stronger man in our country than my brother. I could not spare the strength to turn my head and look at him, but every moment I heard the hiss of his breath getting louder behind me. Still he did not speak. The sun was high. The heat clung to my back like a flame of fire. My ribs were ready to burst, but I could no longer get enough air into my chest. And then I felt I must cry out with my last breath. 'Let us rest!' . . . 'Good!' he answered; and his voice was firm. He was strong. He was brave. He knew not fear and no fatigue . . . My brother!''

A murmur powerful and gentle, a murmur vast and faint; the murmur of trembling leaves, of stirring boughs, ran through the tangled depths of the forests, ran over the starry smoothness of the lagoon, and the water between the piles lapped the slimy timber once with a sudden splash. A breath of warm air touched the two men's faces and passed on with a mournful sound—a breath loud and short like an uneasy sigh of the dreaming earth.

Arsat went on in an even, low voice:

"We ran our canoe on the white beach of a little bay close to a long tongue of land that seemed to bar our road; a long wooded cape going far into the sea. My brother knew that place. Beyond the cape a river has its entrance, and through the jungle of that land there is a narrow path. We made a fire and cooked rice. Then we lay down to sleep on the soft sand in the shade of our canoe, while she watched. No sooner had I closed my eyes than I heard her cry of alarm. We leaped up. The sun was halfway down the sky already, and coming in sight in the opening of the bay we saw a prau[10] manned by many paddlers. We knew it at once; it was one of our Rajah's praus. They were watching the shore, and saw us. They beat the gong, and turned the head of the prau into the bay. I felt my heart become weak within my breast. Diamelen sat on the sand and covered her face. There was no escape by sea. My brother laughed. He had the gun you had given him, Tuan, before you went away, but there was only a handful of powder. He spoke to me quickly: 'Run with her along the path. I shall keep them back, for they have

---

9. **sumpitan** (sump' ə tăn): A Malayan blowgun which discharges poisonous darts.

10. **prau** (prou) *n.*: A swift Malayan boat with a large sail.

Primary Source

Conrad had to pass a difficult test to become the master of an English ship. His biographer, Frederick Karl, quotes from Conrad's own description of this oral examination:

"He [the examiner] began by trying to make me talk nonsense. But I had been warned of that fiendish trait, and contradicted him with great assurance. He kept inscrutably silent for a moment, and then, placing me in a ship of a certain size at sea, under certain conditions of weather, season, locality, etc., etc.—all very clear and precise—ordered me to execute a certain manoeuvre. Before I was half through with it he did some material damage to the ship. Directly I had grappled with the difficulty he caused another to present itself, and when that too was met he stuck another ship before me, creating a very dangerous situation. I felt slightly outraged by this ingenuity in piling up trouble upon a man."

Conrad argued that he would have seen the ship before that, but the examiner, imperturbable, says that the weather was thick. . . . At this point in the proceedings, the examiner has him so backed up with such little equipment no firearms, and landing in the face of a man with a gun is certain death for some. Run with her. On the other side of that wood there is a fisherman's house—and a canoe. When I have fired all the shots I will follow. I am a great runner, and before they can come up we shall be gone. I will hold out as long as I can, for she is but a woman—that can neither run nor fight, but she has your heart in her weak hands.' He dropped behind the canoe. The prau was coming. She and I ran, and as we rushed along the path I heard shots. My brother fired—once—twice—and the booming of the gong ceased. There was silence behind us. That neck of land is narrow. Before I heard my brother fire the third shot I saw the shelving shore, and I saw the water again: the mouth of a broad river. We crossed a grassy glade. We ran down to the water. I saw a low hut above the black mud, and a small canoe hauled up. I heard another shot behind me. I thought, 'That is his last charge.' We rushed down to the canoe; a man came running from the hut, but I leaped on him, and we rolled together in the mud. Then I got up, and he lay still at my feet. I don't know whether I had killed him or not. I and Diamelen pushed the canoe afloat. I heard yells behind me, and I saw my brother run across the glade. Many men were bounding after him. I took her in my arms and threw her into the boat, then leaped in myself. When I looked back I saw that my brother had fallen. He fell and was up again, but the men were closing round him. He shouted, 'I am coming!' The men were close to him. I looked. Many men. Then I looked at her. Tuan, I pushed the canoe! I pushed it into deep water. She was kneeling forward looking at me, and I said, 'Take your paddle,' while I struck the water with mine. Tuan, I heard him cry. I heard him cry my name twice; and I heard voices shouting, 'Kill! Strike!' I never turned back. I heard him calling my name again with a great shriek, as when life is going out together with the voice—and I never turned my head. My own name! . . . My brother! Three times he called—but I was not afraid of life. Was she not there in that canoe? And could I not with her find a country where death is forgotten—where death is unknown!''

The white man sat up. Arsat rose and stood, an indistinct and silent figure above the dying embers of the fire. Over the lagoon a mist drifting and low had crept, erasing slowly the glittering images of the stars. And now a great expanse of white vapor covered the land; it flowed cold and gray in the darkness, eddied in noiseless whirls round the tree-trunks and about the platform of the house, which seemed to float upon a restless and impalpable illusion of a sea. Only far away the tops of the trees stood outlined on the twinkle of heaven, like a somber and forbidding shore—a coast deceptive, pitiless and black.

Arsat's voice vibrated loudly in the profound peace.

"I had her there! I had her! To get her I would have faced all mankind. But I had her—and—"

His words went out ringing into the empty distances. He paused, and seemed to listen to them dying away very far—beyond help and beyond recall. Then he said quietly—

"Tuan, I loved my brother."

A breath of wind made him shiver. High above his head, high above the silent sea of mist the drooping leaves of the palms rattled together with a mournful and expiring sound. The white man stretched his legs. His chin rested on his chest, and he murmured sadly without lifting his head—

"We all love our brothers."

Arsat burst out with an intense whispering violence—

"What did I care who died? I wanted peace in my own heart."

He seemed to hear a stir in the house—listened—then stepped in noiselessly. The white man stood up. A breeze was coming in fitful puffs. The stars shone paler as if they had retreated into the frozen

The Lagoon 947

25 **Discussion** Why does Arsat's brother stay behind?

26 **Reading Strategy** Ask students to explain Arsat's illusion.

27 **Clarification** Sometimes Arsat breaks off, goes to check on Diamelen, and breaks the story. Thus, the reader experiences the story the same way the narrator does—with glimpses of the changes in Arsat's emotional reality.

28 **Literary Focus** What is Conrad telling us about choice? Look for proof that this statement is another illusion.

left that Conrad asks for time since "so many accidents have happened that I really can't remember what there's left for me to work with". . . . The examiner praises the young man's work thus far, draws him out a little more, and then tells him that if there is nothing more to do, he can always say his prayers. In forty minutes, Conrad "escaped from the room thankfully—passed!"

30 **Master Teacher Note** Conrad contrasts the lagoon's brilliance with Arsat's deep dark gloom when Diamelen dies. Diamelen has shone like a diamond or false light for Arsat. The realistic picture of the "merciless" sunshine contrasts with the earlier romantic landscape which seemed to sympathize with Arsat. Shifting from a romantic to a realistic point of view within the same story characterizes Conrad as modern, and it conveys Conrad's theme of the real world as illusion.

31 **Discussion** Relate the levels of meaning in this exchange to the theme of "The Lagoon."

32 **Critical Thinking and Reading** What does the white man's reaction show about Conrad's moral code?

33 **Reading Strategy** Ask students to summarize the cost of Arsat's obsession.

34 **Discussion** What does the darkness represent? What are Arsat's lost illusions?

Reader's Response In a way this story is about loyalty. Do you think loyalty is an important quality? Why or why not?

---

depths of immense space. After a chill gust of wind there were a few seconds of perfect calm and absolute silence. Then from behind the black and wavy line of the forests a column of golden light shot up into the heavens and spread over the semicircle of the eastern horizon. The sun had risen. The mist lifted, broke into drifting patches, vanished into thin flying wreaths; and the unveiled lagoon lay, polished and black, in the heavy shadows at the foot of the wall of trees. A white eagle rose over it with a slanting and ponderous flight, reached the clear sunshine and appeared dazzlingly brilliant for a moment, then soaring higher, became a dark and motionless speck before it vanished into the blue as if it had left the earth forever. The white man, standing gazing upward before the doorway, heard in the hut a confused and broken murmur of distracted words ending with a loud groan. Suddenly Arsat stumbled out with outstretched hands, shivered, and stood still for some time with fixed eyes. Then he said—

"She burns no more."

Before his face the sun showed its edge above the treetops, rising steadily. The breeze freshened; a great brilliance burst upon the lagoon, sparkled on the rippling water. The forests came out of the clear shadows of the morning, became distinct, as if they had rushed nearer—to stop short in a great stir of leaves, of nodding boughs, of swaying branches. In the merciless sunshine the whisper of unconscious life grew louder, speaking in an incomprehensible voice round the dumb darkness of that human sorrow. Arsat's eyes wandered slowly, then stared at the rising sun.

"I can see nothing," he said half aloud to himself.

"There is nothing," said the white man, moving to the edge of the platform and waving his hand to his boat. A shout came faintly over the lagoon and the sampan began to glide toward the abode of the friend of ghosts.

"If you want to come with me, I will wait all the morning," said the white man, looking away upon the water.

"No, Tuan," said Arsat softly. "I shall not eat or sleep in this house, but I must first see my road. Now I can see nothing—see nothing! There is no light and no peace in the world; but there is death—death for many. We were sons of the same mother—and I left him in the midst of enemies; but I am going back now."

He drew a long breath and went on in a dreamy tone:

"In a little while I shall see clear enough to strike—to strike. But she has died, and . . . now . . . darkness."

He flung his arms wide open, let them fall along his body, then stood still with unmoved face and stony eyes, staring at the sun. The white man got down into his canoe. The polers ran smartly along the sides of the boat, looking over their shoulders at the beginning of a weary journey. High in the stern, his head muffled up in white rags, the juragan sat moody, letting his paddle trail in the water. The white man, leaning with both arms over the grass roof of the little cabin, looked back at the shining ripple of the boat's wake. Before the sampan passed out of the lagoon into the creek he lifted his eyes. Arsat had not moved. He stood lonely in the searching sunshine; and he looked beyond the great light of a cloudless day into the darkness of a world of illusions.

Closure and Extension

ANSWERS TO THINKING ABOUT THE SELECTION
Recalling

1. The white man's crew want nothing to do with Arsat because they are afraid of him; he must be dangerously unafraid of the invisible spirits since he lives in a ruined house.
2. When he reaches Arsat's clearing the white man discovers that Diamelen is dying.
3. Arsat's brother was killed by the ruler's henchmen after Diamelen and Arsat desert him in the middle of the enemy.
4. Arsat says he will strike back at the enemies who killed his brother.

Interpreting

5. Arsat is more emotional and primitive than the white man, who is cold and objective. The white man and

THINKING ABOUT THE SELECTION
Recalling

1. Why do the members of the white man's crew want nothing to do with Arsat?
2. What does the white man discover when he reaches Arsat's clearing?
3. What happened to Arsat's brother?
4. At the end of the story, what does Arsat say he will do?

Interpreting

5. Compare and contrast the white man and Arsat?
6. Conrad devotes a good deal of space to descriptions of the sky and air. What events in the story are paralleled by the "conflagration of sunset" (page 943) and the rattling of the palm trees (page 947)?
7. When, following Diamelen's death, Arsat says "I can see nothing," the white man replies, "There is nothing" (page 948). (a) What do you think is meant by this remark? (b) How might it relate to the final line of the story?

Applying

8. (a) What might have been Conrad's purpose in not naming the white man in this story? (b) How does this decision reinforce the theme?

ANALYZING LITERATURE
Shifting Point of View and Theme

Point of view in a story is the vantage point from which the events are narrated. In a first-person narrative, the speaker is either a participant or observer in the story; whereas in a third-person narrative, the speaker is not directly identified. In "The Lagoon" Joseph Conrad narrates most of the story from the third-person point of view, though the "story within a story" —Arsat's tale—is narrated by Arsat himself.

1. What would have been lost if the entire story had been narrated by Arsat?
2. Why do you think Conrad chose to have Arsat narrate his own story?
3. How is the story's theme reinforced by the shift between points of view?

CRITICAL THINKING AND READING
Making Inferences About a Moral Code

When, for the second time in the story, Arsat says "I loved my brother" (page 947), the white man observes that "We all love our brothers." Though the remark might be taken at face value, the theme of the story suggests that its author is stating a larger truth about the "brotherhood" between all human beings and about the rules by which we should, but perhaps do not always, conduct our lives. Tell, based on Arsat's narrative, what you believe to be Conrad's views on the following moral issues:

1. The division of a society into classes.
2. The crossing of class lines in such a society.
3. The defiance of law in any society.
4. The degree to which we should feel free to pursue a goal at any cost.

SPEAKING AND LISTENING
Setting Up a Reader's Theater

Arrange a theatrical reading of "The Lagoon" in class. After assigning the parts of the narrator, the white man, and Arsat (you may wish to have several readers do the longer parts), consider what sound effects you will need and how they might be achieved. The sound of the natives in pursuit might be undertaken by the class as a whole. When you have finished planning and rehearsing, perform your reading.

THINKING AND WRITING
Responding to Theme

A lagoon is a pool of brackish water separated from the sea by sand bars and reefs. Knowing this, write an essay explaining the relevance of the story's title to its theme. Begin by stating the theme. Then develop your essay around the following questions. In Conrad's view of things, what does the lagoon represent? What is represented by the sea beyond? What does a voyage to and from the lagoon represent? Feel free to add and answer questions of your own that you feel clarify the relationship between theme and title.

The Lagoon 949

white man's esteem of him would have been lost if Arsat told the whole story.
2. Answers will differ. Conrad involves the reader's emotions and stirs up suspense and dramatic intensity by having Arsat narrate his own story.
3. The shift in person changes perspective and reinforces Conrad's theme of the uncertain distinction between reality and illusion.

ANSWERS TO CRITICAL THINKING AND READING

Suggested responses:
1. Conrad was an aristocrat but he associated class with inner worth.
2. Conrad probably saw the crossing of class lines as dangerous in a rigid society.
3. Conrad probably felt the defiance of law was dangerous since society needs the illusion of stability which laws give.
4. Conrad shows that it is extremely dangerous to pursue a goal to the point of obsession.

SPEAKING AND LISTENING

Discuss the possibility of using a mirror for the lagoon and a dark drapery for the sky. Analyze the dramatic strength of using doubles for Arsat and the white man, or identical-looking characters, one dressed in black, one in white. Ask the students to discuss Conrad's setting in terms of moral vulnerability in isolation.

THINKING AND WRITING

For help with this assignment, students can refer to Lesson 11, "Writing About Theme," in the Handbook of Writing About Literature.

Publishing Student Writing
Have students share their essays in groups. Each group can compile a composite image of the lagoon and share it with the class.

Arsat are both upper class, physically brave men who are used to taking what they want. Each one knows isolation since the captain is isolated from his crew and Arsat has become an outcast on the lagoon.
6. The "conflagration of sunset," is paralleled by the white man's answer to Arsat that Diamelen will probably die. The "rattling of the palm trees" parallels Arsat telling the white man that he loved his brother.

7. Suggested Responses: (a) The "nothing" refers to the world Arsat sees without Diamelen and without the illusions of honor and love. (b) The final line of the story refers to everything in this world as "illusion" or "nothing." It also refers to the godlessness Arsat experiences in his spirit.

Applying

8. (a) Conrad might have left the white man nameless so he could stand for every man. (b) By not naming the white man Conrad blurs the distinction between Arsat and the white man, softens his reality, and makes him seem almost like an illusion. The lack of a name allows him to enter into Arsat's story for everyone and to work as a bridge to the reader.

ANSWERS TO ANALYZING LITERATURE

1. The perspective on Arsat shed by the native's fear of him and the

SAKI (H. H. MUNRO)

1870–1916

The creation of an individualistic style and the adaptation of form to fit one's material are major challenges for every writer. Few can be said to have met these challenges as skillfully and elegantly as the satirist Saki (H. H. Munro).

Born in Burma, Hector Hugh Munro was raised by two aunts in the English county of Devon. He seems to have spent his childhood under a strict, authoritarian regime, if one is to judge by the satirical portraits of aunts in many of his later short stories. As a young adult, Munro returned to Burma to serve in that colony's military police force. After a couple of years, however, recurrent bouts of ill health forced his return to England where he remained for good. Determined to earn a living as a writer, he settled in London.

The turn of the century found Munro writing a regular column for the *Westminster Gazette*. After a year of writing political satire, he became a foreign news correspondent for the *Morning Post,* taking posts in Poland, Russia, and France. It was not until 1904 that Munro capitalized on his true calling, when he published a collection of short stories titled *Reginald,* writing under the pen name Saki (possibly borrowed from the name of the cupbearer in Edward Fitzgerald's popular poem *The Rubaiyat of Omar Khayyam*). The stories in *Reginald,* seldom over a few pages in length, were comically satirical glimpses of upper-class British society during the Edwardian period. With remarkable economy of language, Saki was able to re-create precisely the manners and costumes, not to mention the snobbery and boorishness, that typified the group.

The success of *Reginald* secured Saki's reputation as a master of the comedy of manners, and in his later collections—*Reginald in Russia* (1910) and *The Chronicles of Clovis* (1911)—he revived some of the zany characters from his original cast. The tone of many of these stories, which might be described as playful yet bitingly ironic, was similar to that used by Alexander Pope in *The Rape of the Lock*. Saki's refraining from serious treatments of his subject matter was probably rooted at least partly in the fact that he was a member of the very social class that he mocked.

With the outbreak of World War I in 1914, Saki enlisted for duty in the British army. Two years later he was killed in action in France. Among the collections of his stories published after his death are *The Toys of Peace* (1919) and *The Square Egg* (1924). Although some readers regard his stories as an acquired taste, Saki remains one of the present century's foremost "cupbearers" in the long tradition of English social satire.

The Schartz-Metterklume Method

Literary Forms

Satire. Satire is a mode of writing that exposes faults in human beings or institutions and holds those faults up to ridicule. Although virtually any literary form can be cast in the satiric mode, satire has its roots in the plays of ancient Greece and Rome. In the time between then and now, satire flourished especially in the eighteenth century and especially in such lengthy poems as Alexander Pope's mock-epic *The Rape of the Lock* and Samuel Johnson's intensely bitter "The Vanity of Human Wishes."

Despite the lack of any formal guidelines in the writing of satire, modern satirists make free use of irony, a discrepancy between what is said and what is actually intended or between appearances and reality. In his satirical "The Schartz-Metterklume Method," Saki uses irony, along with a companion device, understatement, to poke innocent fun at the pretentious manners of the English "upper crust" of the early twentieth century.

Commentary

What do critics think of Saki's work? While celebrated in his day chiefly for his short stories, critics now think that Saki's abilities were even more suited to drama and the novel. Playwright Noel Coward represents the critics of Saki's day when he isolates Saki's short stories for admiration. Believing that "high comedy was undoubtedly his greatest gift," he praises "The Schartz-Metterklume Method" as one of Saki's "masterpieces." But as Saki's career advanced, he turned to writing novels and plays as well. He was seeking a larger literary form in which to more fully develop characters and explore social issues, especially the question of Britain's survival on the eve of World War I. As with much of his drama, *The Watched Pot,* a comedy of manners completed just before he enlisted, shows his sparkling dialogue, complex plot, and brisk pace. Wherever his fullest talents lie, critics agree that Saki died before his writing attained its potential. "Let those who come after see to it that his name not be forgotten," concludes the scroll the king issued to honor Saki's memory. It seems certain that his work will continue to command a loyal following.

Writing

Imagine that on your way to school one day you were mistaken for someone famous. Suppose, moreover, that despite your assurances to the contrary, the person who mistook your identity refused to be dissuaded. Freewrite, telling whom you were mistaken for, and describing the funny sequence of events that followed this initial mistake.

Guide for Interpreting 951

Literary Focus Satire is a type of protest born of anger and indignation. A satirist is a self-appointed guardian of standards, ideals and truths. Saki uses satire to correct, censure, and ridicule the follies and vices of his society. Using contempt and laughter he reveals the cracks beneath society's false facade.

Writing/Prior Knowledge Have students discuss the tradition of mistaken identity in comedies such as Shakespeare's comedies or television comedies. Then have them complete the writing activity.

Vocabulary

Preteach the following Vocabulary words:
inventory (in'vən tôr'ē) *n.*: List of possessions (p. 952)
provoking (prə vōk'iŋ) *adj.*: Annoying, irritating (p. 952)
cowed (koud) *adj.*: Made to feel timid or fearful (p. 953)
condone (kən dōn') *v.*: Approve; authorize (p. 953)
castigation (kas'tə gā'shən) *n.*: Punishment (p. 954)
balustrade (bal'ə strād') *n.*: Railing supported by small pillars of stone or wood (p. 954)

Objectives

1 To understand satire
2 To make inferences about tone
3 To understand words with Latin roots
4 To compare and contrast approaches to satire

Support Material

Teaching Portfolio
Teacher Backup, pp. 1127–1130
Usage and Mechanics Worksheet, p. 1131
Vocabulary Check, p. 1132
Analyzing Literature Worksheet, *Understanding Satire,* p. 1133
Language Worksheet, *Understanding Words with Latin Roots,* p. 1134
Selection Test, pp. 1135–1136

The Schartz-Metterklume Method

Saki

Lady Carlotta stepped out onto the platform of the small wayside station and took a turn or two up and down its uninteresting length, to kill time till the train should be pleased to proceed on its way. Then, in the roadway beyond, she saw a horse struggling with a more than ample load, and a carter of the sort that seems to bear a sullen hatred against the animal that helps him to earn a living. Lady Carlotta promptly betook her to the roadway, and put rather a different complexion on the struggle. Certain of her acquaintances were wont to give her plentiful admonition as to the undesirability of interfering on behalf of a distressed animal, such interference being "none of her business." Only once had she put the doctrine of noninterference into practice, when one of its most eloquent exponents had been besieged for nearly three hours in a small and extremely uncomfortable may tree by an angry boar-pig, while Lady Carlotta, on the other side of the fence, had proceeded with the water-color sketch she was engaged on, and refused to interfere between the boar and his prisoner. It is to be feared that she lost the friendship of the ultimately rescued lady. On this occasion she merely lost the train, which gave way to the first sign of impatience it had shown throughout the journey, and steamed off without her. She bore the desertion with philosophical indifference; her friends and relations were thoroughly well used to the fact of her luggage arriving without her. She wired a vague noncommittal message to her destination to say that she was coming on "by another train." Before she had time to think what her next move might be she was confronted by an imposingly attired lady, who seemed to be taking a prolonged mental inventory of her clothes and looks.

"You must be Miss Hope, the governess I've come to meet," said the apparition, in a tone that admitted of very little argument.

"Very well, if I must I must," said Lady Carlotta to herself with dangerous meekness.

"I am Mrs. Quabarl," continued the lady; "and where, pray, is your luggage?"

"It's gone astray," said the alleged governess, falling in with the excellent rule of life that the absent are always to blame; the luggage had, in point of fact, behaved with perfect correctitude. "I've just telegraphed about it," she added, with a nearer approach to truth.

"How provoking," said Mrs. Quabarl; "these railway companies are so careless. However, my maid can lend you things for the night," and she led the way to her car.

During the drive to the Quabarl mansion Lady Carlotta was impressively introduced to the nature of the charge that had been thrust upon her; she learned that Claude and Wilfrid were delicate, sensitive young people, that Irene had the artistic temperament highly developed, and that Viola was something or other else of a mold equally commonplace among children of that class and type in the twentieth century.

"I wish them not only to be *taught,*" said

Mrs. Quabarl, "but *interested* in what they learn. In their history lessons, for instance, you must try to make them feel that they are being introduced to the life stories of men and women who really lived, not merely committing a mass of names and dates to memory. French, of course, I shall expect you to talk at mealtimes several days in the week."

"I shall talk French four days of the week and Russian in the remaining three."

"Russian? My dear Miss Hope, no one in the house speaks or understands Russian."

"That will not embarrass me in the least," said Lady Carlotta coldly.

Mrs. Quabarl, to use a colloquial expression, was knocked off her perch. She was one of those imperfectly self-assured individuals who are magnificent and autocratic as long as they are not seriously opposed. The least show of unexpected resistance goes a long way toward rendering them cowed and apologetic. When the new governess failed to express wondering admiration of the large newly purchased and expensive car, and lightly alluded to the superior advantages of one or two makes which had just been put on the market, the discomfiture of her patroness became almost abject. Her feelings were those which might have animated a general of ancient warfaring days, on beholding his heaviest battle-elephant ignominiously driven off the field by slingers and javelin throwers.

At dinner that evening, although reinforced by her husband, who usually duplicated her opinions and lent her moral support generally, Mrs. Quabarl regained none of her lost ground. The governess not only helped herself well and truly to wine, but held forth with considerable show of critical knowledge on various vintage matters, concerning which the Quabarls were in no wise able to pose as authorities. Previous governesses had limited their conversation on the wine topic to a respectful and doubtless sincere expression of a preference for water. When this one went as far as to recommend a wine firm in whose hands you could not go

very far wrong Mrs. Quabarl thought it time to turn the conversation into more usual channels.

"We got very satisfactory references about you from Canon Teep," she observed; "a very estimable man, I should think."

"Drinks like a fish and beats his wife, otherwise a very lovable character," said the governess imperturbably.

"My *dear* Miss Hope! I trust you are exaggerating," exclaimed the Quabarls in unison.

"One must in justice admit that there is some provocation," continued the romancer. "Mrs. Teep is quite the most irritating bridge player that I have ever sat down with; her leads and declarations would condone a certain amount of brutality in her partner, but to souse her with the contents of the only soda-water siphon in the house on a Sunday afternoon, when one couldn't get another, argues an indifference to the comfort of others which I cannot altogether overlook. You may think me hasty in my judgments, but it was practically on account of the siphon incident that I left."

"We will talk of this some other time," said Mrs. Quabarl hastily.

"I shall never allude to it again," said the governess with decision.

Mr. Quabarl made a welcome diversion by asking what studies the new instructress proposed to inaugurate on the morrow.

"History to begin with," she informed him.

"Ah, history," he observed sagely; "now in teaching them history you must take care to interest them in what they learn. You must make them feel that they are being introduced to the life stories of men and women who really lived—"

"I've told her all that," interposed Mrs. Quabarl.

"I teach history on the Schartz-Metterklume method," said the governess loftily.

"Ah, yes," said her listeners, thinking it expedient to assume an acquaintance at least with the name.

The Schartz-Metterklume Method 953

---

7 **Literary Focus** What is ironical about this discussion about languages?

8 **Literary Focus** What is the irony in Saki's comparison here? **Less advanced** students may wish to keep a list of "real" events in Saki's story so they don't get lost in Saki's ironical twists.

9 **Discussion** What does this discussion of wine reveal about Mrs. Quabarl?

10 **Clarification** Saki's names for his leading characters are typical Saki ironies. His fantastic imagination makes the Quabarls sound difficult, the Teeps sound like foolish little birds and Miss Hope sound like a mishap, which is indeed what Lady Carlotta engineers. The names are appropriate and improbable at the same time.

11 **Critical Thinking and Reading** What does the reader learn about Lady Carlotta as "a romancer?" **More advanced** students may wish to evaluate Saki as a romancer.

12 **Literary Focus** Ask the students to observe the irony and understatement in this delightful passage.

13 **Discussion** What characteristic does Mr. Quabarl reveal?

14 **Reading Strategy** Ask the students to take into consideration Lady Carlotta's behavior and to predict what "the Schartz-Metterklume method" will be like.

15 **Discussion** Why do the Quabarls pretend familiarity with Lady Carlotta's teaching method?

"What are you children doing out here?" demanded Mrs. Quabarl the next morning, on finding Irene sitting rather glumly at the head of the stairs, while her sister was perched in an attitude of depressed discomfort on the window seat behind her, with a wolfskin rug almost covering her.

"We are having a history lesson," came the unexpected reply. "I am supposed to be Rome, and Viola up there is the she-wolf; not a real wolf, but the figure of one that the Romans used to set store by—I forget why. Claude and Wilfrid have gone to fetch the shabby women."

"The shabby women?"

"Yes, they've got to carry them off. They didn't want to, but Miss Hope got one of father's fives bats[1] and said she'd give them a number nine spanking if they didn't, so they've gone to do it."

A loud, angry screaming from the direction of the lawn drew Mrs. Quabarl thither in hot haste, fearful lest the threatened castigation might even now be in process of infliction. The outcry, however, came principally from the two small daughters of the lodge-keeper, who were being hauled and pushed toward the house by the panting and disheveled Claude and Wilfrid, whose task was rendered even more arduous by the incessant, if not very effectual, attacks of the captured maidens' small brother. The governess, fives bat in hand, sat negligently on the stone balustrade, presiding over the scene with the cold impartiality of a goddess of battles. A furious and repeated chorus of "I'll tell muvver" rose from the lodge children, but the lodge mother, who was hard of hearing, was for the moment immersed in the preoccupation of her washtub. After an apprehensive glance in the direction of the lodge (the good woman was gifted with the highly militant temper which is sometimes the privilege of deafness) Mrs. Quabarl flew indignantly to the rescue of the struggling captives.

---

1. fives bats: Wooden bats used in playing a variation of *fives*, a kind of handball played in England.

"Wilfrid! Claude! Let those children go at once. Miss Hope, what on earth is the meaning of this scene?"

"Early Roman history; the Sabine women, don't you know? It's the Schartz-Metterklume method to make children understand history by acting it themselves; fixes it in their memory, you know. Of course, if, thanks to your interference, your boys go through life thinking that the Sabine women ultimately escaped, I really cannot be held responsible."

"You may be very clever and modern, Miss Hope," said Mrs. Quabarl firmly, "but I should like you to leave here by the next train. Your luggage will be sent after you as soon as it arrives."

"I'm not certain exactly where I shall be for the next few days," said the dismissed instructress of youth; "you might keep my luggage till I wire my address. There are only a couple of trunks and some golf clubs and a leopard cub."

"A leopard cub!" gasped Mrs. Quabarl. Even in her departure this extraordinary person seemed destined to leave a trail of embarrassment behind her.

"Well, it's rather left off being a cub; it's more than half grown, you know. A fowl every day and a rabbit on Sundays is what it usually gets. Raw beef makes it too excitable. Don't trouble about getting the car for me, I'm rather inclined for a walk."

And Lady Carlotta strode out of the Quabarl horizon.

The advent of the genuine Miss Hope, who had made a mistake as to the day on which she was due to arrive, caused a turmoil which that good lady was quite unused to inspiring. Obviously the Quabarl family had been woefully befooled, but a certain amount of relief came with the knowledge.

"How tiresome for you, dear Carlotta," said her hostess, when the overdue guest ultimately arrived; "how very tiresome losing your train and having to stop overnight in a strange place."

"Oh dear, no," said Lady Carlotta; "not at all tiresome—for me."

THINKING ABOUT THE SELECTION
Recalling

1. What causes Lady Carlotta to miss her train?
2. (a) What mistake does Mrs. Quabarl make when she sees Lady Carlotta on the platform? (b) How does Lady Carlotta react to this mistake?
3. What is the Schartz-Metterklume Method?
4. (a) Why do the Quabarls dismiss Lady Carlotta? (b) What is her reaction? (c) What request does she make as she is about to leave?
5. How do the Quabarls learn that they have been fooled?

Interpreting

6. (a) How would you describe the Quabarls? (b) How would you describe Lady Carlotta?
7. In your opinion do the characters' names enhance the story's humorous tone? Explain.

Applying

8. A contemporary of Saki, the critic Max Beerbohm remarked that laughter "rejoices in bonds [meaning chains]," if only to break them. Comment on whether you think Saki's humor in this story illustrates the remark.

ANALYZING LITERATURE
Understanding Satire

Satire is writing in which irony, humor, ridicule, or some combination of the three is used to make the reader aware of some evil or folly. In "The Schartz-Metterklume Method" Saki takes satiric aim at customs and attitudes of the English upper-class of his day.
1. Find at least two examples of irony in the story.
2. (a) How is the last sentence of the story an example of understatement? (b) How does the use of understatement bring home the satiric point of the story?
3. Do you think Saki's satire is characterized by biting wit or by more subtle methods? Support your answer.

CRITICAL THINKING AND READING
Making Inferences About Tone

Tone is the attitude taken by the author toward a particular character or subject. Although Saki never directly expresses his feelings about the Quabarls, and particularly Lady Quabarl, the reader has no trouble inferring his tone. Identify the character trait represented by each of the following details. Then, based on the sum of these traits, state Saki's tone.
1. Mrs. Quabarl's taking a "prolonged mental inventory" of Lady Carlotta on the platform
2. Mrs. Quabarl's assuming "in a tone that admitted of very little argument" that Lady Carlotta was the governess
3. Mr. Quabarl's duplicating his wife's opinions
4. The Quabarls' not admitting to never having heard of the Schartz-Metterklume Method

UNDERSTANDING LANGUAGE
Understanding Words with Latin Roots

The following words, which appear in "The Schartz-Metterklume Method," are each based on a Latin root. Look the words up in a good dictionary, noting the precise meaning of the root in each case. Find at least three words that share the root.
1. admonition   4. militant
2. eloquent   5. arduous
3. abject

THINKING AND WRITING
Comparing and Contrasting Approaches

Reread the introduction to and a portion of either *Gulliver's Travels* on page 520 or the excerpts from *The Rape of the Lock* on page 548. When you feel you have regained the flavor of the eighteenth-century work, write an essay in which you highlight the differences and similarities between this early satiric effort and the Saki story. Pay particular attention to language, tone, and theme. Conclude your essay by stating which satire you enjoyed more, giving your reasons. When you revise, make sure you have used details from the selections.

(Answers begin on p. 954.)

between the desired and actual results of the living history lesson or the "The Schartz-Metterklume Method."
2. (a) Lady Carlotta's response of "not tiresome" is certainly an understated description of the bizarre events she has precipitated. (b) The understatement emphasizes the advantage Carlotta has taken of the Quabarls.
3. Answers will differ. Students should use details from the story to support their answers.

ANSWERS TO CRITICAL READING AND THINKING

1. Shallowness, superficiality, materialism, and snobbishness.
2. Narrowness of vision; haste in making false assumptions.
3. Shallowness, powerlessness, and lack of imagination.
4. Superficiality and pretentiousness. Saki's tone is ironical and contemptuous.

Challenge Debate the premise and agree or disagree with the statement "Lady Carlotta escapes Saki's irony entirely because she speaks for the author." Use character traits and evidence of Saki's tone to defend your argument.

ANSWERS TO UNDERSTANDING LANGUAGE

1. *admonitio:* caution; advise against something; *admonish, admonitory, admonishment.*
2. *eloquens:* having the power of fluent and forceful speech; *loquacious, loquacity, eloquence.*
3. *abjectus:* utterly hopeless, or wretched; *abjectly, abjective, abjection.*
4. *militaris:* to have force as evidence; *militancy, militantly, militarism.*
5. *arduus:* requiring great exertion, difficult; *arduously, arduousness, ardor.*

THINKING AND WRITING

Publishing Student Writing Ask for volunteers to share the opinions stated in their essays.

dren unless they act out their history lesson. (b) Lady Carlotta asks Mrs. Quabarl to keep her trunks and to feed her leopard cub.
5. The Quabarls discover that they have been fooled when the real governess arrives the next day.

Interpreting

6. Suggested Responses: (a) The Quabarls are pretentious, shallow, snobs. (b) Lady Carlotta is eccen-

tric, sharp, and ironical.
7. Suggested Response: The characters' names enhance the story's humorous tone because they are ironical. The Quabarls are as ridiculous as their quarrelsome name, and "Miss Hope" is funny since she may bring them fresh hope or she may be a mistaken hope. Lady Carlotta does not act like a lady at all, and The Teeps sound like funny little birds.

Applying

8. Saki's humor breaks bonds since it cleanses away the social pretenses of the upper classes and the reader's belief in aristocrats' superiority.

ANSWERS TO ANALYZING LITERATURE

1. Mistaking Lady Carlotta for the governess and treating her highhandedly is situational irony; another example is the discrepancy

More About the Author Although travel to Italy and Greece contributed setting and characters for many of his works, E. M. Forster spent most of his life in England where he associated with the Bloomsbury group—a group that revolted against the artistic, social, and moral restrictions of Victorian society. These artists believed in the pleasure of communication and the enjoyment of beauty, and they profoundly affected the development of the avant-garde in literature in Britain. How might Forster's association with this group have affected his writing?

Critical Evaluation The English novelist Christopher Isherwood declared that Forster "is an author whose personality 'comes through' powerfully, even in a single paragraph. It is a personality that seems perennially boyish but not in the least naive, that is too sincerely warm–hearted to be capable of sentimentalism, that is defiantly and rashly frank but seldom aggressive, that is capable of the subtlest irony but never of spite."

Ask students if their reading of Forster's personality is the same as Isherwood's.

E. M. FORSTER

1879–1970

To understand who E. M. Forster was, it is perhaps best to start with what he was not. He was staunchly opposed to imperialism, to capitalism, to ecclesiasticism, and to just about any other *ism* except for humanism. Forster's ideal, in short, was a civilization in which the rights of the individual are held supreme over those of any collective or organization. It is precisely this message that serves as a theme in most of his novels.

Having lost his father at the age of one, Edward Morgan Forster was raised by his mother and a wealthy aunt. It was the latter's money that made it possible for him to attend the finest schools, beginning with Tonbridge School in Kent, which Forster later attacked as typifying what he called the "materialism of the English school system." In 1897 he entered King's College at Cambridge, which he considered his "spiritual home." After receiving his degree he traveled to Greece and then lived for some time in Italy.

While abroad he penned his first three novels. *Where Angels Fear to Tread* (1905) and *A Room with a View* (1908), set in Italy, examine the conflict between culture and falseness on the one hand, and passion and truth on the other. *The Longest Journey* (1907) recalls Forster's days at his beloved Cambridge, where he returned in 1910 to complete work on an advanced degree. It was in this same year that Forster published *Howard's End,* a carefully drawn portrait of pre-war society in England.

In 1912 Forster visited India. After serving in the International Red Cross during World War I, he returned there in 1921. His experiences and observations provided the inspiration for his most celebrated work, *A Passage to India* (1924). The novel, which treats the difficulties that arise in attempting to establish personal relationships, also delivered a prophetic glimpse of England's relations with India.

Dabbling in criticism and in shorter fiction as well, Forster turned out *Aspects of the Novel* in 1927 and *The External Moment,* a collection of short stories, the following year. He also produced several collections of essays, including *Abinger Harvest* (1936) and *Two Cheers for Democracy* (1951). In 1969 he was named to the Order of Merit.

Although some critics have suggested that Forster's novels deal ultimately with the age-old struggle between good and evil, the situation is more complicated than that. Invariably his villains value possessions over people and appearances over realities. And invariably, as in "The Helping Hand," those villains are made, in the end, to pay for their shallowness.

956   *The Modern Period*

Objectives

1 To understand characterization
2 To make inferences about character
3 To understand word origins
4 To write about character

Support Material

Teaching Portfolio
Teacher Backup, pp. 1137–1140
Grammar in Action Worksheet, *Understanding Complement–Subject–Verb Sentence Patterns,* p. 1141
Usage and Mechanics Worksheet, p. 1143
Vocabulary Check, p. 1144
Analyzing Literature Worksheet,

Analyzing Direct and Indirect Characterization, p. 1145
Language Worksheet, *Analyzing Changes in Definition,* p. 1146
Selection Test, pp. 1147–1148

GUIDE FOR INTERPRETING

The Helping Hand

Writer's Technique

Characterization. Characterization is the technique whereby a writer makes known the personality of the characters in a work of fiction. Characterization can be accomplished in one of two ways —directly or indirectly. In direct characterization the writer comments openly on the character's personality, using descriptive phrases and adjectives to telegraph impressions straight to the reader. In indirect characterization the writer permits the reader to make up his or her own mind as to what kind of person the character is. To equip the reader to do this, the writer provides information in the form of one or more of the following: (1) the character's words, including speech habits; (2) the character's actions; (3) the character's appearance; (4) the character's thoughts and feelings; and (5) the views of that character held by other characters in the story. Because it mimics the process we use in life to form impressions and opinions of the people we meet, indirect characterization has the effect of making the characters in a story seem real and lifelike.

Writing

Write a rough draft of a short poem or story titled "The Borrower." You may, if you wish, base it on a real-life occurrence, but avoid using the real names of individuals. The poem or story should tell about an individual who borrows habitually without ever returning the items borrowed. Include descriptions of the personalities of both the borrower and the lender.

Primary Source

Forster's work is unified by a concern with shared humanity and the importance of personal relationships, as the title of "The Helping Hand" suggests. The epigraph of his 1910 novel *Howards End* —"Only connect!"—introduces this theme, picked up later when one of the characters cries: "Only connect the prose and the passion, and both will be exalted, and human love will soon be at its height." But Forster's experience had taught him that this is far more easily said than done. *A Passage to India,* his last novel, represents the climax of this theme in his fiction. Some have seen the haunting image in the novel's end as representing the impossibility of forging true connections between people and cultures. The Englishman Fielding, debating the role of the British in India, asks the Indian Aziz, "Why can't we be friends now?" The novel ends with the narrator's answer: "But the horses didn't want it—they swerved apart; the earth didn't want it, sending up rocks through which riders must pass single file. . . ."

Do you think people can ever truly "connect" with each other?

Literary Focus In his *Aspects of the Novel* (1927) Forster divides characters into round and flat types. Flat characters derive from stock characters in early Italian comedy and they speak or act repetitively. Round characters are more detailed and diverse. Forster calls his round characters, "ready for extended life."

Writing/Prior Knowledge Students might prefer to present their characterizations in the form of a short script.

Vocabulary:

Preteach the following vocabulary words:

affected (ə fek′ tid) *adj.*: In a manner not true to the person (p. 958)

appropriated (ə prō′ prē āt′id) *v.*: Borrowed without giving credit (p. 958)

plagiarism (plā′ jə riz'm) *n.*: Passing off another's work as one's own (p. 958)

mortification (môr′ tə fi kā′ shən) *n.*: Feeling of great shock and upset (p. 960)

lucrative (lōō′ krə tiv) *adj.*: Profitable; rich (p. 960)

The Helping Hand

E. M. Forster

When Lady Anstey's book on Giovanni da Empoli[1] was published, Mr. Henderson found in it much that needed forgiveness. His friend did not write as charmingly as she talked: a horrid slime of culture oozed over her style, her criticisms were affected, her enthusiasms abominable. This he could have forgiven; but how could he forgive the subject matter? The dear lady had appropriated, without acknowledgement, facts and theories for which he, and he alone, was responsible. He had studied Giovanni da Empoli for years, and the premature fruit of his labors now lay upon the breakfast table —a little apple-green book, four shillings net, being one of Messrs. Angerstein's series of Pocket Painters.

Mrs. Henderson, a devoted wife, was turning over the leaves with a smile upon her face, for she was pleased that the words of Lady Anstey had been printed on such heavy paper. She knew nothing of the shameful plagiarism, her interest in art being sympathetic rather than intelligent: she was always glad when her friends and her husband got on in it, just as she was glad when her son got on at school.

"What a long list of books she has read to write it!" she observed. "Did you know she could read German? And when did she go to Italy? Wasn't Empoli[2] the place you made us go to—the dirty hotel where we had to hunt the chickens out of the bedroom window?"

"Yes," replied Mr. Henderson, remembering with anguish the nights at Empoli which he had spent and Lady Anstey had not.

"Why did we go there? I've forgotten."

"I had things to look up in the archives." He held up the newspaper as a screen.

"I think you look up too much. Here's Lady Anstey who a little time back knew no more about Italian art than I do, and yet look! I wish you'd write a little book like this. I'm sure you could do it."

"I haven't the knack of putting things brightly." He never said all he thought about the Pocket Painters and similar editions, believing that anything which induces people to look at pictures has its value.

"Yes: I dare say it's all superficial and wrong."

He answered with some animation, "What makes you think so?"

"Because I mistrust new theories—not that I should have known there was a theory. But she says there is one in the preface."

"Giovanni da Empoli," said Mr. Henderson eagerly, "is one of the great puzzles of the Quattrocento.[3] It is highly probable from internal and external evidence that many pictures attributed to other painters should be given to him."

---

1. Giovanni (jō van′ ē) **da Empoli** (em′ pō lē): A fictional painter.
2. Empoli: Town in central Italy.

3. Quattrocento (kwät′ trō chen′ tō): The fifteenth century.

"Cut your bread and butter, dear, do not bite it," said Mrs. Henderson to their son.

"If we take one of the Pieros[4] in the National Gallery, the portrait in the Poldi-Pezzoli at Milan, the so-called Baldovinetti[5] at Naples, and the *cassoni* attributed to Pesellino,[6] we notice in all a certain—"

"'Empoli is a quaint old town not untinged with the modern spirit,'" interrupted their son, who was reading out of Lady Anstey's book in the nasal twang that is considered humorous by the young. "'Here in 1409'—then a long note saying why not in 1429—"

---

4. **Pieros** (pyē′ rōz): Paintings by Italian painter Piero della Francesca (1410 or 1420–1492).
5. **Baldovinetti** (bäl′ dō vē net′ tē): Painting by Florentine painter Alessio Baldovinetti (1425–1499).
6. **Pesellino** (pes ə lē′ nō): Francesco Pesellino, an Italian Renaissance painter (1422–1457).

"Exactly," said his father.

"'—in 1409 young Giovanni was born, here, when not on his travels, he lived, and here he died in 1473. Our painter never married. Of his six children four—'"

"Don't read at meals, dear," said his mother, taking the book. "This is a great surprise to me and a great pleasure. I never thought Lady Anstey had it in her."

No more she had. The book was the work of Mr. Henderson. He had no one to blame but himself. Lady Anstey had said, "I want to write a book about Giovanni da Empoli: tell me everything you know," and he had told her, cautiously at first in barren statements, then, as he grew warm, infusing the facts with life, till at last the whole theory stood up before her delighted eyes. "Tell it me again," she said, for she was not quick at following, and he had told it her again and she had made notes of it, and he had placed his own notes at her disposal.

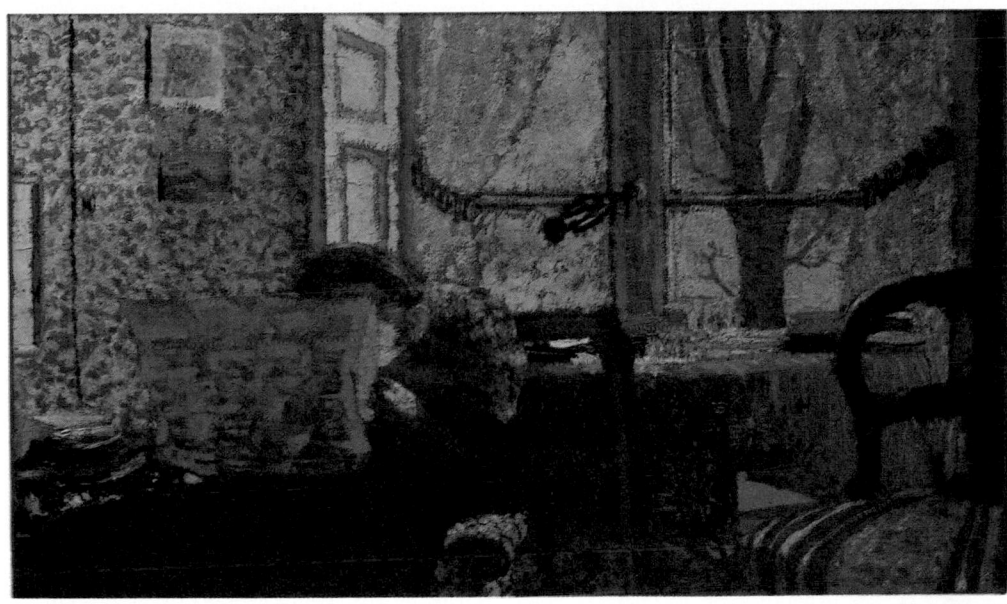

THE NEWSPAPER
Edouard Vuillard
The Phillips Collection

Humanities Note

Fine art, *The Newspaper,* Edouard Vuillard. Vuillard (1868-1940) was a pupil of artist Diogéne Maillart and studied at the Ecole des Beaux Arts and Academie Julien in Paris. He is considered to be a Post-Impressionist, a painter influenced but not guided by the vast changes in art brought about by the Impressionists, and a master Intimist painter, one who paints simple everyday scenes and objects. He was attracted to everyday life and all of its aspects and portrayed the comfortable French middle class in a most charming and decorative way in his paintings.

In this painting, *The Newspaper,* Vuillard shows his talent for finding beauty and poetry in the commonplace. The ordinary image of a man behind a newspaper is turned into a decorative pattern by the flat rhythm of the brush strokes and the pleasing subtle colors. You may point out the Impressionist influence on the painter evidenced in the way the dappling of light breaks up the picture plane. You may also ask the following questions:

1. What do you think the artist was trying to show in this painting?
2. Is the man behind the newspaper actually reading or might he be hiding from something? Explain.
3. Might this be considered a portrayal of the character Mr. Henderson? Explain.

7 Enrichment The artists working in Florence at the time in question all influenced one another.

One critic of Forster believes that the group of names in the story suggests that Giovanni da Empoli was Antonio Pollaiuolo rather than a fictional artist. Pollaiuolo, influenced by the revival of antiquity, worked on busts in the ancient manner in the area of Florence. If the artist is indeed Pollaiuolo, what is Forster saying about the need to view his characters in a fully rounded way?

8 Clarification Maria Cruttwell, who published the first criticism on Pollaiuolo in 1907, may be Lady Anstey. If so, she helped Forster announce the new information about da Empoli's (Pollaiuolo's) birth. Ask **more advanced** students to discuss the irony in the fact that Cruttwell's criticism of the model for da Empoli was published after Forster reputedly wrote "The Helping Hand," so that Forster was revealing new facts about the artist that he had "stolen" from the critics' notes.

9 Literary Focus How does Mrs. Henderson's reaction portray her character?

What do Mrs. Henderson's understatement and Mr. Henderson's silence reveal about the Hendersons?

Does internal and external evidence clarify the truth about Forster's characters in the same ironical way that Mr. Henderson's thesis clarifies the "truth" about da Empoli?

11 **Literary Focus** How do these characters contrast?

12 **Discussion** How does the miniature of the Italian contribute irony?

He reminded himself that facts are universal property, and it is no matter who gives them to the world. But ideas—should there not be some copyright in ideas? He had only meant to stimulate Lady Anstey, not to equip her. However, she had Virgil[7] on her side, and Molière[8] and Shakespeare, and all the ancient Greeks who had taken everything and said nothing to anybody, and splendid fellows they were.

She was perfectly open when they next met, greeting him with "And here is someone else to whom I owe more than I can say." For her book was a success, and Messrs. Angerstein had asked her to do one on Botticelli.[9]

"I'm so glad he's been of use," said Mrs. Henderson, imagining herself to be engaged in conventional civilities. "I never knew he had studied the man." For Mr. Henderson had decided to bear his burden in silence, and neither to his wife nor to anyone else did he give one hint of his mortification. He had in him something of the saint, and knew it would be wrong as well as undignified to repine.

"And now tell me all about Botticelli," said Lady Anstey. But Mr. Henderson told very little about Botticelli. He regarded Lady Anstey with frozen admiration, almost with terror, as a being devoid of conscience and consciousness. They continued great friends, but he saw her as seldom as possible.

Her book, in spite of its popular form, made a considerable impression in artistic circles, and she was soon drawn into the congenial and lucrative atmosphere of controversy. In a fortunate hour Sir William Magnus disagreed with her, and a duel ensued, conducted with courtesy on his side and spirit on hers. Wisely refraining from venturing into new fields, she contented herself with repeating the statements she

7. **Virgil:** Classical Roman poet (70–19 B.C.).
8. **Molière** (mōl yer′): French dramatist (1622–1673).
9. **Botticelli** (bät′ ə chel′ ē): Italian Renaissance painter (1445?–1510).

had made in her book. Mrs. Henderson, who always followed anything personal, was able to write her a hearty letter of congratulation on her victory.

Mr. Henderson did not write. The triumph of his theory gave him no pleasure, for it had triumphed in a mangled form. Lady Anstey had wielded it fairly well, but she had missed all the subtleties, she had spoiled the purity of its outline. Yet she had not spoiled it enough to justify his publishing it anew, under his own name.

He suffered a good deal, though he trained himself to laugh at the irony of the situation. He would like to have found someone to laugh with, but all his friends were embroiled on one side or the other, and he could not trust them to keep silent. As for his wife, she did not believe in irony. Meanwhile the book ran through several editions, and there was a rumor that the powers that be in the National Gallery were troubled, and meditated changing the label on the Piero della Francesca.

By the time Professor Rinaldi came to England, Mr. Henderson was tired of laughing and needed sympathy. Rinaldi, whom Mrs. Henderson called the Italian, was a man of great learning and artistic insight, who had become so disgusted with controversies over beauty that he had left Rome and retired to the curatorship of a small provincial gallery. There he lived, or as others said rotted, studying continually because he could not help it, but avowing his intention of never publishing again.

Here was a man to whom Mr. Henderson could speak freely. They were old friends, and he determined to pay him a visit in London.

"Do," said Mrs. Henderson, "and I will finish off the spring cleaning."

Mr. Henderson left on the Thursday, and Mrs. Henderson turned out the dining room. On Friday she did the drawing room. On Saturday she began at her husband's study, and came across a pasteboard box labeled Giovanni da Empoli.

Grammar in Action

Placing the **complement** before the subject and its verb produces an emphatic sentence, which adds variety and spice to a paragraph. Sentences cast in this pattern surprise the reader by expectations of ordinary sentence structure. Writers must use them sparingly, however, or risk artificial style. Notice E. M. Forster's well planned use of the complement-subject-verb pattern.

"What a long list of books she has read to write it!"

No more she had.

There he lived, or as others said rotted . . .

However, she had Virgil on her side, and Moliere and Shakespeare, and all the ancient Greeks who had taken everything and said nothing to anybody, and splendid fellows they were.

Forster's inverted patterns draw attention to the complements which are prominently placed. In these sentences, the complement

THE CONVERSATION
Hobson Pittman
The North Carolina Museum of Art, Raleigh, N.C.

Humanities Note

Fine art, *The Conversation,* by Hobson Pittman. Pittman (1898 –1972) was an American painter, engraver, and teacher. Born in Tarboro, North Carolina, Pittman studied at Pennsylvania State College, the Carnegie Institute, and Columbia University. He also expanded his artistic knowledge with extended travel abroad.

The painting *The Conversation* depicts a narrative subject rendered in a modern, realistic style. It shows the "artistic" interior of a studio, the large window of which shows a view of a spectacular landscape with an approaching storm. Seated before the window, impervious to nature's drama, two figures lean conspiratorially toward one another. It is painted with an interesting point of view, pleasant colors, and good humor.

You may wish to use the following questions for discussion:
1. Does the humorous and satiric nature of the painting suit the mood of the story? Explain.
2. How does the artist feel about the two women?

13 Discussion How does Mrs. Henderson discover the plagiarism?

14 Critical Thinking and Reading What can we infer from Mrs. Henderson's thinking time as opposed to her action time?

Recognizing the name, she opened it and read on the top sheet inside: "Reasons for believing G. to be born in 1409." A strange impulse moved her, and she went for Lady Anstey's book. It gave identical reasons.

Then in one moment the loving wife became a student of art. All Saturday she sat with the book and the papers before her, and discovered that they coincided, not here and there but everywhere. The last paper in the box was a letter from Lady Anstey saying "Many thanks for loan of notes, which have been most acceptable."

All Sunday she thought over the revelation, all Monday and all Tuesday she acted on it. Mr. Henderson returned on the Wednesday.

He was looking more cheerful than she had seen him for weeks. "The world is ruled by irony," he observed, and smiled, as if he found the rule easy to bear.

"And how is the Italian?" she asked, rather ill at ease.

"As fine as ever. 'A little less imagination in archaeology and a little more in art' was his advice to Sir William yesterday."

The word "art" gave her an opening, and she exclaimed, "Yes indeed! Yes indeed! Yes indeed!"

"Why this enthusiasm?"

"You dear thing!" she cried, embracing him; "you're too good to be alive!"

"What have I done?" he asked, looking grave.

The Helping Hand   961

placement suggests that the "long list of books" was indeed impressive; "No more" is emphatically negative; "There" suggests a close suburb of oblivion; and that the writers were "splendid fellows" was far beyond question.

Student Activity 1. Find two more sentences in which Forster uses the inverted complement-subject-verb pattern, and explain the effect created.

Student Activity 2. Write a sentence in the complement-subject-verb pattern.

15 Discussion Relate the Italian Professor's discovery to Mr. Henderson's statement, "the world is ruled by irony." What ironies exist in this story? What is the irony in the title?

Reader's Response Do you think plagiarism is destructive? Why or why not?

Closure and Extension

ANSWERS TO THINKING ABOUT THE SELECTION
Recalling

1. (a) Mr. Henderson feels angry and mortified when Lady Anstey's book first appears because she has plagiarized his research and his original theory about Giovanni da Empoli. (b) His wife is surprised and impressed that Lady Anstey could learn so much in so short a time.
2. (a) The publishers ask Lady Anstey to do another book using Botticelli as the subject this time. (b) Lady Anstey asks Mr. Henderson to tell her all about Botticelli.
3. (a) During her cleaning, Lady Anstey discovers her husband's box of original notes on da Empoli, and she realizes that Lady Anstey has stolen his research. (b) Mrs. Henderson tells the facts about the plagiarism to an editor. (c) Her husband is upset that she has exposed him as the originator of the theory because the Italian curator has discovered that Mr. Henderson's theory is wrong.

"I've found you out—that you wrote Lady Anstey's book—that she took all your facts and ideas and never said a word. And all these months you've let her talk and become famous and make money. I do admire and love you for it—but do be glad I'm different!"

"What have you been doing?" he said sternly.

"Nothing rude—don't be cross. I only let it out in the course of conversation, or put it in a letter if I was writing one."

"And to whom have you written?"

THINKING ABOUT THE SELECTION
Recalling

1. (a) How does Mr. Henderson feel when Lady Anstey's book appears? Why? (b) How does his wife feel? Why?
2. (a) What do Lady Anstey's publishers ask her to do following the success of her book? (b) What does she, in turn, ask of Mr. Henderson?
3. (a) What does Mr. Henderson come across during her cleaning? (b) What does she do as a result of this discovery? (c) What is her husband's response to her actions?

Interpreting

4. What is ironic about Lady Anstey's having the title "lady?"
5. Why do you suppose Mr. Henderson decides to "bear his burden in silence?"
6. (a) What does Mrs. Henderson's behavior at the breakfast table reveal about her? (b) What does Lady Anstey's request for information on Botticelli reveal about her?
7. Do you find the title of the story appropriate? Why or why not?

Interpreting

4. Lady Anstey's title is ironical because she does not act at all lady-like when she brashly steals Mr. Henderson's ideas and research.
5. Mr. Henderson is embarrassed and ashamed, and he feels that it would be undignified to expose Lady Anstey—who is one of his social peers—as a fraud.
6. (a) Mrs. Henderson acts foolish, flighty and superficial at the breakfast table. (b) Lady Anstey's request for information on Botticelli

reveals her audacity or nerve as well as her total lack of conscience.
7. The title is appropriate because of its irony on three levels. First, because Mr. Henderson gave Lady Anstey his help. Second, because Lady Anstey helped herself to all of Mr. Henderson's research and his original theory. Finally, because Mrs. Henderson wishes him success and she means to be helpful, but she ironically ends up harming Mr. Henderson more than Lady Anstey.

"Oh, not to Lady Anstey: to Lady Magnus about the vacuum cleaner, and one or two more. And yesterday I met the editor of the *Dudley* and he was horrified. Don't be angry—no, I don't mind if you are angry; it's simple justice I want; she shall *not* pick your brains and no one know; you *shall* have the credit for your own theory."

"Unfortunate," said Mr. Henderson. "Professor Rinaldi has just proved to me that the theory in question is wrong, that the facts are wrong, that the book is wrong, that I am wrong. Unfortunate."

Applying

8. (a) How did you feel at the end of the story? (b) How would you have behaved if you had been Mr. Henderson?

ANALYZING LITERATURE

Understanding Characterization

Characterization is the method a writer uses to reveal the personalities of characters in a story. In direct characterization, the writer tells us directly what sort of person the character is. In indirect characterization, the writer allows us to arrive at our own judgments based on what the character says, does, thinks, and looks like, as well as on how the character is regarded by other characters in the story. In "The Helping Hand," Forster uses a mixture of the two types of characterization. Identify the following characterizations as direct or indirect. For each example of indirect characterization, find the quoted words in the story. Then tell what trait each of the

Applying

8. (a) Suggested response: Many will feel amazed and amused by the irony at the end of the story. (b) Suggested response: Some will suggest that they would have exposed Lady Anstey as a plagiarist and a fraud.

Challenge Why doesn't Mr. Henderson get pleasure from the orig-indirect characterizations reveals and to which character each refers.

1. Mrs. Henderson, a devoted wife, was turning over the leaves with a smile . . . (page 958)
2. "I think you look up too much. . . ." (page 958)
3. He held up the newspaper as a screen. (page 958)
4. "I haven't the knack of putting things brightly." (page 958)
5. . . . he had told her, cautiously at first . . . , then, as he grew warm, infusing the facts with life. . . . (page 959)
6. Wisely refraining from venturing into new fields, she contented herself with repeating the statements she had made in her book. (page 960)
7. "Nothing rude—don't be cross. I only let it out in the course of a conversation, or put it in a letter if I was writing one." (page 962)
8. "Unfortunate," said Mr. Henderson. "Professor Rinaldi has just proved to me that the theory in question is wrong, that the facts are wrong, that the book is wrong, that I am wrong. Unfortunate." (page 962)

CRITICAL THINKING AND READING
Making Inferences About Character

When a writer uses indirect characterization, that writer is leaving it up to the reader to **infer,** or piece together from presented facts, a profile of the character. Read the following profiles of the three main characters in the story. State which of the traits you think are applicable and which are not, backing up your opinions with evidence from the story.
Mr. Henderson: defensive, overly cautious, meek, given to rationalization

Mrs. Henderson: simplistic, shallow, dishonest, a good friend
Lady Anstey: intelligent, poised, treacherous, self-centered

UNDERSTANDING LANGUAGE
Understanding Word Origins

As a rule, the meanings of words change over time. Some word meanings change so much, however, that they leave no trace of the word's original intent. One of the words in the story, *plagiarism*—the passing off of another's writing as one's own—has its roots in a Latin word meaning "kidnap." With the aid of a good dictionary, match up the ancient definitions in the second column with the words from the story.
1. abominable   a. fill with breath, soul
2. theory   b. beginning, first place
3. archives   c. shun as a bad omen
4. animation   d. observe, a viewing

THINKING AND WRITING
Writing About a Character

Choose one of the undeveloped characters in the story—the Hendersons' son, Sir William Magnus, or Professor Rinaldi—and, using the little information provided, create a personality for that character. You may describe the person's appearance and likes and dislikes, but focus the main part of your description on what the person is like. To begin, ask yourself in what ways this person is different from and similar to the other characters in the story. Strive for originality. Then write the first draft of your character sketch. When you revise make sure you have fleshed out your character with vivid details. Proofread your sketch and prepare a final draft.

The Helping Hand 963

inal success of his theory? How do you predict he will feel about being known as the creator of the theory after Professor Rinaldi's discovery?

ANSWERS TO ANALYZING LITERATURE

Suggested responses:

1. This direct characterization reveals Mrs. Henderson's devoted, sympathetic, generous nature.

2. This indirect characterization reveals that Mrs. Henderson is critical and shallow about her husband's field.
3. This indirect characterization shows that Mr. Henderson feels anguished about Mrs. Anstey's theft of his research.
4. This indirect characterization allows Mr. Henderson to protect his feelings while confirming that he is a scholar rather than a popular writer. It allows him to respond on

his wife's shallow level while apparently concealing his contempt for popular books.
5. This indirect characterization reveals Mr. Henderson's passion for his subject.
6. This indirect characterization reveals that although she is not a scholar, Lady Anstey is cunning enough to know how to protect herself.
7. This indirect characterization re-

(Answers begin on p. 962.)

veals Mrs. Henderson's naivete and concern.
8. This indirect characterization shows that Mr. Henderson is a man of great restraint with a sense of irony.

ANSWERS TO CRITICAL THINKING AND READING

Mr. Henderson shows that he is defensive and given to rationalization when he says that "he lacks the knack of putting things brightly." His final response shows that he can be seen as meek since he accepts his wife's meddling in his affairs, but his contact with Lady Anstey reveals that he is not overly cautious since he gave away his prized theory.

Mrs. Henderson shows that she is a good friend when she praises Lady Anstey's enterprise in writing the book. Her memories of their trip to Empoli, and her lack of understanding of her husband's work reveal that she is simplistic and shallow. She does not appear dishonest since she takes great pains to reveal the truth about Lady Anstey's fraud.

Lady Anstey has shown her treacherous side by stealing Mr. Henderson's hard work, and she reinforces this with her self-centered behavior when she asks him for new information. Her poise is shown in her ability to conceal her own ignorance in her debates with Sir William Magnus. She has a sly intelligence, like a thief, but she is not an original thinker.

ANSWERS TO UNDERSTANDING LANGUAGE

1. c   2. d   3. b   4. a

THINKING AND WRITING

For help with this assignment, students can refer to Lesson 9, "Writing About Character," in the Handbook of Writing About Literature.

More About the Author The famous intellectual discussions at Bloomsbury brought fresh ideas and attitudes to Virginia Woolf, helping to free her from the reserve of her family's Victorian upbringing. After she and her husband started Hogarth Press, writing, maintaining her delicate nerves, and keeping the comforting friends of Bloomsbury occupied the majority of her time. But Virginia Woolf did have a sensitivity to general social conditions, and particularly to the abuse of women's rights. Her intellectual and her privileged social background allowed her liberal beliefs to flourish. She resented the sexism and corruption of English universities and other aspects of male-dominated Victorian England, and she even refused the honorary degrees of several universities. Her extreme sensitivity and outbreaks of mental illness must have contributed to the feeling of isolation that readers can find in certain of her works.

Ask the students to look for Virginia Woolf's sensitivity to the isolated human condition as they read "The Lady in the Looking Glass: A Reflection." Ask them to also look for examples of Woolf's implied social criticism in this story.

Critical Evaluation The literary scholar David Daiches made the following evaluation of Woolf's fiction: "Woolf was a skilled exponent of the 'stream of consciousness' technique in her novels, exploring with great subtlety problems of personal identity and personal relationships as well as the significance of time, change, and memory for human personality. The delicate lyrical prose of her finest novels was a remarkable achievement."

VIRGINIA WOOLF

1882–1941

One can scarcely think of twentieth-century trends in fiction without thinking of "stream of consciousness," the technique whereby a character's innermost thoughts, emotions, and memories are woven together into a complex psychological fabric. And one can scarcely think of stream of consciousness without thinking of Virginia Woolf, the brilliant literary pioneer whose novels and short stories introduced this technique to the world.

Ironically for a writer who would become one of the leading lights of Modernism, Virginia Woolf was born into a family of prim and proper Victorians. Her father, Leslie Stephen, who served as the first editor of the renowned *Dictionary of National Biography,* saw to it that his daughter grew up surrounded by books, and at the age of twenty-three Virginia began contributing reviews to the Literary Supplement of *The Times of London.* In 1912 she married Leonard Woolf, an author and social reformer, with whom she founded the Hogarth Press. Their house in the Bloomsbury section of London became an informal meeting place for some of the more important thinkers of the era, attracting such figures as the writers E. M. Forster and Lytton Strachey, the art critic Roger Fry, and the economist John Maynard Keynes.

Woolf's first two novels, *The Voyage Out* (1915) and *Night and Day* (1919) were more or less conventional works. Her third was anything but. *Jacob's Room* (1922), which shattered the conventions of modern fiction-writing, tells the story of a young man's life entirely through an examination of his room and its cluttered contents. Although we never actually meet the title character, we come to know a great deal about him through an artful arrangement of photographs.

In the years between the wars, Woolf continued to refine her fluid, inward-looking style with three more stream-of-consciousness novels—*Mrs. Dalloway* (1925), *To the Lighthouse* (1927), and *The Waves* (1931)—and with four slightly less experimental ones. In her more revolutionary works, she virtually abolished the traditional concept of plot, preferring instead to concentrate on what she called "an ordinary mind on an ordinary day."

For much of her adult life Woolf suffered from painful bouts of depression brought on by poor health and a consuming hatred of war. In 1941, two years after the outbreak of World War II, she ended her life. Today Woolf is recognized, along with James Joyce, whose life span almost exactly paralleled her own, as one of the most influential shapers of contemporary modern fiction.

GUIDE FOR INTERPRETING

Writer's Technique

The Lady in the Looking Glass

Stream of Consciousness. Stream of consciousness is a narrative technique that relies on a character's feelings, memories, and thoughts, as well as associations between the three, to tell a story. Pioneered in the early 1920's by Virginia Woolf, James Joyce, and the American novelist William Faulkner, stream of consciousness marks an attempt to tune in directly to the workings of the character's mind—to capture the random flow of insights and thoughts much as they would naturally occur, moment by moment.

The stream-of-consciousness narrative dispenses with such conventions of traditional fiction as chronological ordering of events and the use of formal transitions. The responsibility for organizing the fragments into a meaningful whole often falls to the reader, who thus becomes more actively involved in the work than is the case with fiction of a more conventional design. The reader must piece together—from memories, unconnected thoughts, and glimpses of the subconscious mind—a meaningful whole. Though its demands on the reader are great, the result of the technique is often an intensely revealing, psychologically complete portrait of a human being.

Writing

Make a list of the contents of a person's room, using your own room at home, the room of someone you know, or one that you have invented for a fictional character. After each item on the list, jot down some notes as to its origin, its physical appearance, and its significance to the occupant.

Primary Source

Woolf's most famous explanation of her stream-of-consciousness technique appears in her essay "Modern Fiction." Focusing on an "ordinary mind on an ordinary day," Woolf notes: "The mind receives a myriad of impressions—trivial, fantastic, evanescent, or engraved with the sharpness of steel. From all sides they come, an incessant shower of innumerable atoms; and as they fall, as they shape themselves into the life of Monday or Tuesday, the accent falls differently from of old; the moment of importance came not here but there; so that, if a writer were a free man and not a slave, if he could write what he chose, not what he must, if he could base his work upon his own feeling and not upon convention, there would be no plot, no comedy, no tragedy, no love interest or catastrophe in the accepted style, and perhaps not a button sewn on as the Bond Street tailors would have it. . . . Life is a luminous halo, a semi-transparent envelope surrounding us from the beginning of consciousness to the end."

Guide for Interpreting 965

Literary Focus Stream-of-consciousness can be understood as an interior dialogue that describes the unspoken thoughts and feelings of characters without resorting to objective description or conventional dialogue. Thus, stream of consciousness concentrates on dreams, thoughts, and emotions of a character. Ask the students if they agree with this method of conveying reality.

Writing/Prior Knowledge Students might conclude by adding a person to the room they are describing.

Vocabulary

Preteach the following vocabulary words:
pirouetting (pir′ $\overline{oo}$ wet′ iŋ) *v*.: Dancing or whirling on foot (p. 966)
suffused (sə fyoōzd′) *v*.: Filled (p. 966)
transient (tran′ shənt) *adj*.: Temporary; passing through quickly (p. 966)
upbraidings (up brād′ iŋz) *n*.: Stern words of disapproval for an action (p. 968)
evanescence (ev′ ə nes′′ns) *n*.: Gradual disappearance, especially from sight (p. 969)
reticent (ret′ ə s′nt) *adj*.: Silent; reserved (p. 969)

Spelling Tip Point out that in *evanescence* the two s sounds are spelled *sc* and *c* respectively.

Objectives

1 To recognize stream of consciousness
2 To evaluate an author's purpose
3 To use stream of consciousness in writing

Support Material

Teaching Portfolio
Teacher Backup, pp. 1149–1152
Grammar in Action Worksheet, *Using Descriptive Details*, p. 1153
Usage and Mechanics Worksheet, p. 1155
Vocabulary Check, p. 1156
Analyzing Literature Worksheet, *Understanding · Stream-of-Consciousness Narration*, p. 1157
Critical Thinking and Reading Worksheet, p. 1158
Selection Test, pp. 1159–1160
Art Transparency 14, *The Artist and His Daemon*, by Cecil Collins

The Lady in the Looking Glass
A Reflection
Virginia Woolf

People should not leave looking glasses hanging in their rooms any more than they should leave open checkbooks or letters confessing some hideous crime. One could not help looking, that summer afternoon, in the long glass that hung outside in the hall. Chance had so arranged it. From the depths of the sofa in the drawing room one could see reflected in the Italian glass not only the marble-topped table opposite, but a stretch of the garden beyond. One could see a long grass path leading between banks of tall flowers until, slicing off an angle, the gold rim cut it off.

The house was empty, and one felt, since one was the only person in the drawing room, like one of those naturalists who, covered with grass and leaves, lie watching the shyest animals—badgers, otters, kingfishers—moving about freely, themselves unseen. The room that afternoon was full of such shy creatures, lights and shadows, curtains blowing, petals falling—things that never happen, so it seems, if someone is looking. The quiet old country room with its rugs and stone chimney pieces, its sunken bookcases and red and gold lacquer cabinets, was full of such nocturnal creatures. They came pirouetting across the floor, stepping delicately with high-lifted feet and spread tails and pecking allusive beaks as if they had been cranes or flocks of elegant flamingoes whose pink was faded, or peacocks whose trains were veiled with silver. And there were obscure flushes and darkening too, as if a cuttlefish had suddenly suffused the air with purple; and the room had its passions and rages and envies and sorrows coming over it and clouding it, like a human being. Nothing stayed the same for two seconds together.

But, outside, the looking glass reflected the hall table, the sunflowers, the garden path so accurately and so fixedly that they seemed held there in their reality unescapably. It was a strange contrast—all changing here, all stillness there. One could not help looking from one to the other. Meanwhile, since all the doors and windows were open in the heat, there was a perpetual sighing and ceasing sound, the voice of the transient and the perishing, it seemed, coming and going like human breath, while in the looking glass things had ceased to breathe and lay still in the trance of immortality.

Half an hour ago the mistress of the house, Isabella Tyson, had gone down the grass path in her thin summer dress, carrying a basket, and had vanished, sliced off by the gilt rim of the looking glass. She had gone presumably into the lower garden to pick flowers; or as it seemed more natural to

THE GARDEN OF LOVE
Walter Richard Sickert
The Fitzwilliam Museum, Cambridge

The Lady in the Looking-Glass: A Reflection 967

Humanities Note

Fine art, *The Garden of Love,* by Walter Richard Sickert. Sickert (1860-1942) was born in Munich, Germany, but became a British subject. His father, a painter, tried to discourage him from art in favor of a more financially rewarding career, to no avail. Sickert studied at the Slade School of Fine Art in London, but, discouraged by the strict academic atmosphere, he left to work and study at the studio of James McNeill Whistler. Later, in Paris, he studied with the French impressionist Edgar Degas. Sickert's greatest contribution to British art was his willingness to experiment with, defend, and teach new ideas in art.

The art of Walter Sickert can be described as impressionistic. *The Garden of Love* exemplifies his style. This study of sunlight on a garden in contrast to a cool interior shows an impressionist's interest in the effects of different types of light on colors.

You might ask the following questions:

1. How does this garden in the painting compare with the garden in the story?
2. Walter Sickert is notable for exploring new methods and subjects of painting. How does this reputation compare with Virginia Woolf's?

6 **Reading Strategy** Summarize what has occurred. Why is the observer alone in the room?

7 **Discussion** What does the imagery in this first impression of Isabella convey?

8 **Discussion** What does the narrator object to in the comparison of Isabella to the fantastic flower? Can this be seen as social concern about the treatment of women?

9 **Discussion** Does this pile of facts conflict with stream of consciousness? Is this pile up of facts meant as irony?

10 **Discussion** According to the observer, what types of things must be in the letters?

suppose, to pick something light and fantastic and leafy and trailing, traveler's-joy, or one of those elegant sprays of convolvulus that twine round ugly walls and burst here and there into white and violet blossoms. She suggested the fantastic and the tremulous convolvulus rather than the upright aster, the starched zinnia, or her own burning roses alight like lamps on the straight posts of their rose trees. The comparison showed how very little, after all these years, one knew about her; for it is impossible that any woman of flesh and blood of fifty-five or sixty should be really a wreath or a tendril. Such comparisons are worse than idle and superficial—they are cruel even, for they come like the convolvulus itself trembling between one's eyes and the truth. There must be truth; there must be a wall. Yet it was strange that after knowing her all these years one could not say what the truth about Isabella was; one still made up phrases like this about convolvulus and traveler's joy. As for facts, it was a fact that she was a spinster; that she was rich; that she had bought this house and collected with her own hands—often in the most obscure corners of the world and at great risk from poisonous stings and Oriental diseases—the rugs, the chairs, the cabinets which now lived their nocturnal life before one's eyes. Sometimes it seemed as if they knew more about her than we, who sat on them, wrote at them, and trod on them so carefully, were allowed to know. In each of these cabinets were many little drawers, and each almost certainly held letters, tied with bows of ribbon, sprinkled with sticks of lavender or rose leaves. For it was another fact—if facts were what one wanted—that Isabella had known many people, had had many friends; and thus if one had the audacity to open a drawer and read her letters, one would find the traces of many agitations, of appointments to meet, of upbraidings for not having met, long letters of intimacy and affection, violent letters of jealousy and reproach, terrible final words of parting—for all those inter-

views and assignations had led to nothing —that is, she had never married, and yet, judging from the masklike indifference of her face, she had gone through twenty times more of passion and experience than those whose loves are trumpeted forth for all the world to hear. Under the stress of thinking about Isabella, her room became more shadowy and symbolic; the corners seemed darker, the legs of chairs and tables more spindly and hieroglyphic.

Suddenly these reflections were ended violently and yet without a sound. A large black form loomed into the looking glass; blotted out everything, strewed the table with a packet of marble tablets veined with pink and gray, and was gone. But the picture was entirely altered. For the moment it was unrecognizable and irrational and entirely out of focus. One could not relate these tablets to any human purpose. And then by degrees some logical process set to work on them and began ordering and arranging them and bringing them into the fold of common experience. One realized at last that they were merely letters. The man had brought the post.

There they lay on the marble-topped table, all dripping with light and color at first and crude and unabsorbed. And then it was strange to see how they were drawn in and arranged and composed and made part of the picture and granted that stillness and immortality which the looking glass conferred. They lay there invested with a new reality and significance and with a greater heaviness, too, as if it would have needed a chisel to dislodge them from the table. And, whether it was fancy or not, they seemed to have become not merely a handful of casual letters but to be tablets graven with eternal truth—if one could read them, one would know everything there was to be known about Isabella, yes, and about life, too. The pages inside those marble-looking envelopes must be cut deep and scored thick with meaning. Isabella would come in, and take them, one by one, very slowly, and

Grammar in Action

When you write, re-create—rather than tell about—experience. Readers' imaginations are engaged by descriptive detail that allows them to experience a scene. Notice how Virginia Woolf shows what is in the glass.

Suddenly these reflections were ended violently and yet without a sound. A large black form loomed into the looking glass; blotted out everything, strewed the table with a packet of marble tablets veined with pink and gray, and was gone.

Woolf allows her reader to experience the disrupted picture within the glass along with the narrator, and thus the reader is drawn closer to the narrator. As the narrator assimilates the additions to the mirrored picture and pieces together what has happened—"The man had brought the post"—the reader shares the experience. If the narrator had simply declared "The reflections open them, and read them carefully word by word, and then with a profound sigh of comprehension, as if she had seen to the bottom of everything, she would tear the envelopes to little bits and tie the letters together and lock the cabinet drawer in her determination to conceal what she did not wish to be known.

The thought served as a challenge. Isabella did not wish to be known—but she should no longer escape. It was absurd, it was monstrous. If she concealed so much and knew so much one must prize her open with the first tool that came to hand—the imagination. One must fix one's mind upon her at that very moment. One must fasten her down there. One must refuse to be put off any longer with sayings and doings such as the moment brought forth—with dinners and visits and polite conversations. One must put oneself in her shoes. If one took the phrase literally, it was easy to see the shoes in which she stood, down in the lower garden, at this moment. They were very narrow and long and fashionable—they were made of the softest and most flexible leather. Like everything she wore, they were exquisite. And she would be standing under the high hedge in the lower part of the garden, raising the scissors that were tied to her waist to cut some dead flower, some overgrown branch. The sun would beat down on her face, into her eyes; but no, at the critical moment a veil of cloud covered the sun, making the expression of her eyes doubtful—was it mocking or tender, brilliant or dull? One could only see the indeterminate outline of her rather faded, fine face looking at the sky. She was thinking, perhaps, that she must order a new net for the strawberries; that she must send flowers to Johnson's widow; that it was time she drove over to see the Hippesleys in their new house. Those were the things she talked about at dinner certainly. But one was tired of the things that she talked about at dinner. It was her profounder state of being that one wanted to catch and turn to

words, the state that is to the mind what breathing is to the body, what one calls happiness or unhappiness. At the mention of those words it became obvious, surely, that she must be happy. She was rich; she was distinguished; she had many friends; she traveled—she bought rugs in Turkey and blue pots in Persia. Avenues of pleasure radiated this way and that from where she stood with her scissors raised to cut the trembling branches while the lacy clouds veiled her face.

Here with a quick movement of her scissors she snipped the spray of traveler's joy and it fell to the ground. As it fell, surely some light came in too, surely one could penetrate a little farther into her being. Her mind then was filled with tenderness and regret. . . . To cut an overgrown branch saddened her because it had once lived, and life was dear to her. Yes, and at the same time the fall of the branch would suggest to her how she must die herself and all the futility and evanescence of things. And then again quickly catching this thought up, with her instant good sense, she thought life had treated her well; even if fall she must, it was to lie on the earth and molder sweetly into the roots of violets. So she stood thinking. Without making any thought precise—for she was one of those reticent people whose minds hold their thoughts enmeshed in clouds of silence—she was filled with thoughts. Her mind was like her room, in which lights advanced and retreated, came pirouetting and stepping delicately, spread their tails, pecked their way; and then her whole being was suffused, like the room again, with a cloud of some profound knowledge, some unspoken regret, and then she was full of locked drawers, stuffed with letters, like her cabinets. To talk of "prizing her open" as if she were an oyster, to use any but the finest and subtlest and most pliable tools upon her was impious and absurd. One must imagine—here was she in the looking glass. It made one start.

11 **Literary Focus** Can you relate this passage to the technique of stream of consciousness?

12 **Clarification** *Interior monologue* has also been used to describe the inner movement of consciousness in a character's mind. What the narrator believes Isabella is thinking provides an indirect characterization of the narrator himself and an ironical comment on stream of consciousness.

13 **Discussion** Why does the narrator assume Isabella is happy?

14 **Literary Focus** What conflicting "thoughts" does Miss Tyson have about cutting the spray of traveler's joy? Are those her thoughts or the narrator's? In what way is this an example of stream of consciousness?

15 **Enrichment** In comparing Isabella's mind to the room, Woolf illustrates stream of consciousness. Virginia Woolf helped to create a revolution when she used stream of consciousness, or described changing thoughts, impressions, memories, and emotions without logical syntax or sequence. How much conventional dialogue takes place in this story? What does this say about the narrator?

16 **Critical Thinking and Reading** What does this passage imply about Woolf and the relationship of stream of consciousness to materialism or psychological realism?

ended violently and without a sound when the man brought the post and strewed letters across the table," the experience depicted would be less vivid.

Student Activity. Write a paragraph in which you use descriptive details to show one of the following:

1. My room was a mess.
2. The spring morning was beautiful.
3. My mother was very angry.
4. I was so embarrassed!

17 Discussion What is ironic in the imagery of Isabella within the still life in the mirror?

18 Discussion How does this passage tie in with the earlier reference to a naturalist? Does this picture seem overly judgmental or harshly realistic in contrast to the narrator's early romantic fantasies?

19 Discussion What is the irony in the letters? What is the greatest irony in the Isabella of the observer's imagination and her reality?

Reader's Response Have mirrors ever made you think about the differences between appearance and reality? Explain.

Closure and Extension

ANSWERS TO THINKING ABOUT THE SELECTION
Recalling

1. The story takes place in a quiet old country room.
2. (a) Isabella Tyson has gone out to the garden to cut flowers. (b) The mail arrives while she is out.
3. Cutting flowers makes Isabella feel sad because it reminds her of life's mortality.
4. The letters turn out to be bills.

Interpreting

5. Suggested response: The narrator sounds like a superficial friend or a

---

970

---

17 She was so far off at first that one could not see her clearly. She came lingering and pausing, here straightening a rose, there lifting a pink to smell it, but she never stopped; and all the time she became larger and larger in the looking glass, more and more completely the person into whose mind one had been trying to penetrate. One verified her by degrees—fitted the qualities one had discovered into this visible body. There were her gray-green dress, and her long shoes, her basket, and something sparkling at her throat. She came so gradually that she did not seem to derange the pattern in the glass, but only to bring in some new element which gently moved and altered the other objects as if asking them, courteously, to make room for her. And the letters and the table and the grass walk and the sunflowers which had been waiting in the looking glass separated and opened out so that she might be received among them. At last

there she was, in the hall. She stopped dead. She stood by the table. She stood perfectly still. At once the looking glass began to pour over her a light that seemed to fix her; that seemed like some acid to bite off the unessential and superficial and to leave only the truth. It was an enthralling spectacle. Everything dropped from her—clouds, dress, basket, diamond—all that one had called the creeper and convolvulus. Here was the hard wall beneath. Here was the woman herself. She stood naked in that pitiless light. And there was nothing. Isabella was perfectly empty. She had no thoughts. She had no friends. She cared for nobody. As for her letters, they were all bills. Look, as she stood there, old and angular, veined and lined, with her high nose and her wrinkled neck, she did not even trouble to open them.

People should not leave looking glasses hanging in their rooms.

18

19

THINKING ABOUT THE SELECTION
Recalling

1. Where does the story take place?
2. (a) What has Isabella Tyson gone to do? (b) What arrives while she is out?
3. How does Isabella feel about cutting the flower?
4. What do the letters turn out to be?

Interpreting

5. Who do you think is the narrator of the story? Explain your answer.
6. (a) Based on the information provided, how would you describe Isabella? (b) How would you summarize what the narrator wishes to "prize" from her?
7. The last sentence of the story repeats the first sentence. What is the effect of this repetition,

if you consider it together with the story's title and subtitle?
8. What, in your view, is the theme of the story?

Applying

9. Have you ever sought to know what made another person, perhaps a celebrity, "tick" and been disappointed by what you discovered? Give details of your experience and discuss the general truth it suggests.

ANALYZING LITERATURE
Recognizing Stream of Consciousness

Stream of consciousness is a literary technique that attempts to reproduce a character's thought processes as they might naturally occur

970   *The Modern Period*

---

writer who has researched many facts about Isabella. Certainly it is someone very well acquainted with the superficial aspects of Isabella's life since the narrator knows that she is a rich spinster who owns her own house with fabulous objects she has collected in travels all over the world. It is also obvious that the narrator is not a close family member or a friend, with a real understanding of Isabella's psyche or her life.

6. (a) Suggested response: Isabella is

an elderly, rich, spinster living in lonely unhappy isolation in a quiet old country house. (b) Suggested response: The narrator wishes to "prize" the inner truth or psychological reality of Isabella.

7. The last sentence reaffirms the dangers of mirrors, which are compared to "confessions" of crime in the first sentence and a "reflection" in the subtitle. Confession and reflection indicate personal revelation or the idea of the looking glass as a vehicle of exposure of

our private selves. The repetition emphasizes the irony because it simultaneously reflects Isabella, the narrator, and the reader. Thus, the mirror, like literature reflects the eye and imagination of the person looking into it.

8. Suggested response: The theme seems to be the discrepancy between inner reality and superficiality. The story also suggests the isolation of the individual and the need for personal relationships or human communion.

within the human mind. Often fragmented and seemingly unconnected, the thoughts, emotions, and memories that make up a stream-of-consciousness narrative paint a telling portrait of the character when seen from a larger perspective.

Reread carefully the paragraph of the story that begins, "Here with a quick movement of her scissors . . ." (page 969). Then answer the following questions.

1. If one traces her thought patterns from the cutting of the flower through the mention of the "locked drawers" of her mind, how many stages of thought can Isabella be seen to go through? What details of her personality are revealed in this paragraph?
2. What comment on her own technique of stream of consciousness does the author seem to be making in this paragraph?
3. What conclusion about Isabella does the narrator draw from this imaginative examination of Isabella's thoughts?

CRITICAL THINKING AND READING
Evaluating an Author's Purpose

Usually, behind a work of literature is a **purpose,** or intention, that was uppermost in the author's mind when he or she sat down to write. The purpose of some stories, for example, is to impart an understanding about people or life in general, while the purpose of others is merely to entertain. For Virginia Woolf, one ever-present purpose in her writing was to get beyond what she termed "the tyranny of plot"—that is, the requirement of "stylizing" a character's words and actions in accordance with the rules of traditional storytelling.

Give a short synopsis, or summary, of the "plot" implied in "The Lady in the Looking Glass." Then find evidence of the following aspects of Woolf's stream-of-consciousness technique in the story, and tell how they helped her achieve her purpose.

1. The use of random details to develop a character
2. The repetition of details of setting
3. The repetition of specific images, words, and phrases

THINKING AND WRITING
Using Stream of Consciousness

Use the list of possessions you developed earlier to tell a story about the occupant of the room. Use a stream-of-consciousness approach, modeling your story on Woolf's. Before you begin to write, map out what happens to the main character, using the time and manner in which the various objects were acquired as a guideline. When you revise make sure you capture the intermingling of conscious thought and memory. Be prepared to share your story with your class.

Commentary

In her fiction Virginia Woolf tried to find a way to convey the interplay of thought, emotion, and insight that lies below the surface of reality. In this attempt she boldly experimented with radical ways of telling her stories. Stream of consciousness, new structure, and innovative experiments with time were the result. Influential in her own day for her brilliant personality as well as for her literary criticism and fiction, her reputation has fallen somewhat in the postwar years. The violence of World War II made her subtleties of technique seem mild and old-fashioned. The revolution in technique she furthered is taken for granted where it has not been eclipsed by the political and social concerns of more recent works. Yet one critic believes that in the final analysis "she did supremely well what no one else has attempted to do. She mapped the world of the mind . . . under certain precise conditions of character and environment."

The Lady in the Looking-Glass: A Reflection 971

feelings, inner thoughts, hidden secrets, and imaginative memories.

ANSWERS TO CRITICAL THINKING AND READING

Suggested response. There is very little plot in the story since Virginia Woolf wished to move away from plot toward a stream-of-consciousness technique.

Isabella has disappeared into the garden; the observer's conception of her is suggested by her delightful home and her luxurious garden; her wealth implies happiness and success; her silence implies mystery and passion, and the bundle of letters flung on the marble table bear witness to this. But when Isabella reappears in the mirror, the light reveals a different truth of loneliness, indifference, emptiness, and age; the letters are only bills.

1. The random details helped Woolf develop her characters as lifelike. In real life only small illuminations occur and these cumulatively illuminate people to us.
2. The repetition and diffused quality of the images of the setting are lifelike and mirror real life's fragmentation.
3. Woolf repeats images, specific words and phrases into an artistic or musical repetition of impressions which form a collage of Isabella.

THINKING AND WRITING

Publishing Student Writing
Read aloud the students' stream-of-consciousness stories and discuss the degree of indirect characterization achieved.

Applying

9. Answers will differ. First appearances are deceptive. People are often quite otherwise than they first appear; when you follow a person's inner thoughts, dreams, beliefs, and fears you come closer to the "reality" of knowing that person.

Challenge What symbolizes the isolation of Isabella in contrast to her gregarious social appearance?

ANSWERS TO ANALYZING LITERATURE

1. Suggested Response: There seem to be approximately four stages here. Isabella feels regret for cutting away the life of the flower because she thinks of life's preciousness. Then she thinks about her own death and life's brevity and its futility. Next she accepts death because she reminds herself that life has treated her well. Isabella reveals that she is sensitive to flowers, and is philosophical or meditative at this point.

2. Woolf shows that the acts that we perform are only superficial outlines of ourselves as deep multidimensional thinking and feeling people. Thus she indicates that the natural thoughts, emotions, and memories which are reproduced in stream-of-consciousness narrative are the only approach to showing a real portrait of a person or character.

3. The narrator concludes that Isabella is reticent but filled with deep

1885–1930

More About the Author D. H. Lawrence was an influential leader in the movement of British literature into the world of modern interests, techniques, and honesty.

Because he was born into the working class, Lawrence was disconnected from the typical writers of the early twentieth century. His parents quarrelled continuously because they were ill-suited to each other. Lawrence's elopement with an older German woman reinforced his sense of isolation; their frequent travels separated him further from the British puritanism and snobbery which he bitterly disliked. Lawrence liked to consider himself a product of a "Mediterranean sensibility" because he looked back to more primitive societies for a wholeness and balance that he felt his contemporary industrial England had lost. As he traveled in search of a utopia, Lawrence studied psychoanalysis and wrote travel books as well as poetry. He had a stormy temperament and his life with his wife had many accusations and break-ups.

Critical Evaluation In *Aspects of the Novel,* E.M. Forster declared, "It is no wonder that D.H. Lawrence should have written two penetrating studies of Melville, for Lawrence himself is, as far as I know, the only prophetic novelist writing today—all the rest are fantasists or preachers: the only living novelist in whom the song predominates, who has the rapt bardic quality, and whom it is idle to criticize."

Review with students the role of prophets and prophecy in the Bible. Then ask them what they think Forster means by a prophetic novelist. Finally, have them determine whether or not this short story is in any way prophetic.

D. H. Lawrence occupies a unique position among the leading Modernist writers of the generation that came of age before the outbreak of the First World War. The originality of his literary achievements was partly clouded by the explosive controversy attached to his name during his lifetime and for some years after. As with Shelley and Byron before him, the controversy that swirled around Lawrence touched on several points, not the least of which were his unorthodox opinions on politics, society, and morality.

David Herbert Lawrence was born near Nottingham in the English Midlands, the son of a miner. His childhood was marked by poverty, illness, constant bickering between his parents, and his mother's driving ambition to make something of her son. After attending local schools, the young Lawrence spent several years as a teacher before turning to writing as a livelihood.

As a writer Lawrence was deeply influenced by the pioneering psychological theories of Sigmund Freud and by the philosophy of Friedrich Nietzsche. He restlessly searched and researched their writings, seeking confirmation of the underlying moral rightness of his strongest convictions—that the industrial social order was unjust, that open expression of sexuality was healthy, and that human beings could find true fulfillment only by living in harmony with nature.

In 1913, shortly before eloping to Germany with a woman several years older than himself, Lawrence published his first major novel, *Sons and Lovers*—a thinly disguised autobiographical account of his childhood and adolescent years. During World War I, he returned with his wife to England where he published his next major work, *The Rainbow* (1915). His frank treatment of sexuality in the book caused it to be declared obscene.

At the end of the war, the Lawrences left England for extended travels in Italy, Ceylon, Australia, Mexico, and the United States. Lawrence used many of these locales in his fiction: *Kangaroo* (1923), for example, is set in Australia; and *The Plumed Serpent* (1926) is steeped in the mythology of ancient Mexico. It was during his prolonged absence from England that Lawrence found a publisher for one of his greatest novels, *Women in Love* (1921). Ill from tuberculosis, Lawrence completed his last novel, *Lady Chatterley's Lover* (1928), while living in Italy.

In the half century since his death, society's views on Lawrence's writings have changed profoundly. Today, his fiction is almost universally admired for its vivid settings, fine craftsmanship, and psychological insight.

Objectives

1. To understand omniscient narration
2. To understand differences among synonyms
3. To tell the story from a different point of view

Support Material

Teaching Portfolio
Teacher Backup, pp. 1161–1164
Grammar in Action Worksheet, *Using Personification,* p. 1165
Usage and Mechanics Worksheet, p. 1167
Vocabulary Check, p. 1168
Critical Thinking and Reading Worksheet, *Understanding Cause–and–Effect Relationships,* p. 1169

Language Worksheet, *Understanding Differences Among Synonyms,* p. 1170
Selection Test, p. 1171–1172

GUIDE FOR INTERPRETING

Writer's Technique

The Rocking-Horse Winner

Omniscient Narration. Omniscient narration means an all-knowing third-person point of view. Unlike the first-person narrator, who doubles as a character, the third-person narrator is strictly an observer who reports the events of the story from a position beyond or outside them. Because of this remote vantage point, the third-person narrator is said to be omniscient, or all-knowing, privileged with the ability to see into the minds of the characters and to know what fate holds in store for them. While such a narrator is bound by literary convention to remain neutral—is prohibited, that is, from meddling in the affairs of the characters—the particular style of the narration often adds another, and sometimes colorful, dimension to the story. In "The Rocking-Horse Winner," for example, D. H. Lawrence adopts a third-person narrative style reminiscent of that used in fairy tales—a choice that is especially well-suited to the curious proceedings in the story.

Commentary

"The Rocking-Horse Winner," as with much of Lawrence's work, has sparked a staggering outpouring of critical commentary. There's even a film version! Nevertheless, the story's richness still leaves room for inquiry. In an article entitled "A Rocking-Horse: The Symbol, the Pattern, the Way to Live," critic W. D. Snodgrass scrutinizes the various meanings the rocking horse might have in the story. In one of his most intriguing points, Snodgrass examines the names of the horses upon which Paul, his uncle Oscar, and Bassett the gardener gamble. Snodgrass notes that Paul's first winner, Singhalese, and his last, Malabar, have names which refer to former British colonial regions in India. He sees in a third name, Mirza, the suggestion of still another colony, "Mirzapur." Did Lawrence deliberately select the names of former British colonies to make a point in his story? Snodgrass would have us think so. He notes that for years these colonies were winners for the British Empire. As with any colonial power or large corporation, the British tried to control peoples and materials with which they had little direct contact. He sees a clear parallel between the actions and fate of the British empire and Paul. Read the story and see what you think. Do you agree with Snodgrass's conclusion?

Writing

Think about people who believe in such things as superstitions, fortunetellers, and the like. List the qualities that these people have in common. Then attempt to develop a profile of the believer in what many others regard as coincidence or chance.

Literary Focus The omniscient narrator knows everything. He can enter at will into the mind of any character and tell the reader what the character is thinking. He can move physically and mentally at will. He can be in the present and the past. Using the third-person provides a comfortable form for modern writers because in a real sense the author does "know it all." The flexibility of omniscient narration eliminates limitations since the omniscient narrator can tell us just what the story demands. Although natural to the author, omniscience does not reflect life. We never know everything about other people.

Writing/Prior Knowledge Before students write, you might engage them in a discussion of the difference between superstition and fate.

Vocabulary

Preteach the following vocabulary words:
discreet (dis krēt′) *adj.*: Wise; prudent (p. 974)
brazening (brā′ z'n iŋ) *v.*: Daring boldly or shamelessly (p. 975)
careered (kə rird′) *v.*: Moved swiftly forward (p. 975)
uncanny (un kan′ ē) *adj.*: Mysterious; hard to explain (p. 980)
remonstrated (ri män′ strāt id) *v.*: Objected strongly (p. 981)

The Rocking-Horse Winner

D. H. Lawrence

1 There was a woman who was beautiful, who started with all the advantages, yet she had no luck. She married for love, and the love turned to dust. She had bonny children, yet she felt they had been thrust upon her, and she could not love them. They looked at her coldly, as if they were finding fault with her. And hurriedly she felt she must cover up some fault in herself. Yet what it was that she must cover up she never knew. Nevertheless, when her children were present, she always felt the center of her heart go 2 hard. This troubled her, and in her manner she was all the more gentle and anxious for her children, as if she loved them very much. Only she herself knew that at the center of her heart was a hard little place that could not feel love, no, not for anybody. Everybody else said of her: "She is such a good mother. She adores her children." Only she herself, and her children themselves, knew it was not so. They read it in each other's eyes.

There were a boy and two little girls. They lived in a pleasant house, with a garden, and they had discreet servants, and felt themselves superior to anyone in the neighborhood.

Although they lived in style, they felt always an anxiety in the house. There was never enough money. The mother had a small income, and the father had a small income, but not nearly enough for the social position which they had to keep up. The father went into town to some office. But though he had good prospects, these pros-

pects never materialized. There was always the grinding sense of the shortage of money, though the style was always kept up.

At last the mother said, "I will see if *I* can't make something." But she did not know where to begin. She racked her brains, and tried this thing and the other, but could not find anything successful. The failure made deep lines come into her face. Her children were growing up, they would have to go to school. There must be more money, there must be more money. The father, who was always very handsome and expensive in his tastes, seemed as if he never *would* be able to do anything worth doing. And the mother, who had a great belief in herself, did not succeed any better, and her tastes were just as expensive.

3 And so the house came to be haunted by the unspoken phrase: *There must be more money! There must be more money!* The children could hear it all the time, though nobody said it aloud. They heard it at Christmas, when the expensive and splendid toys filled the nursery. Behind the shining modern rocking horse, behind the smart doll's house, a voice would start whispering: "There *must* be more money! There *must* be more money!" And the children would stop playing, to listen for a moment. They would look into each other's eyes to see if they had all heard. And each one saw in the eyes of the other two that they too had heard. "There *must* be more money! There *must* be more money!"

It came whispering from the springs of

the still-swaying rocking horse, and even the horse, bending his wooden, champing head, heard it. The big doll, sitting so pink and smirking in her new pram,[1] could hear it quite plainly, and seemed to be smirking all the more self-consciously because of it. The foolish puppy, too, that took the place of the teddy bear, he was looking so extraordinarily foolish for no other reason but that he heard the secret whisper all over the house: "There *must* be more money."

Yet nobody ever said it aloud. The whisper was everywhere, and therefore no one spoke it. Just as no one ever says: "We are breathing!" in spite of the fact that breath is coming and going all the time.

"Mother!" said the boy Paul one day. "Why don't we keep a car of our own? Why do we always use uncle's, or else a taxi?"

"Because we're the poor members of the family," said the mother.

"But why *are* we, mother?"

"Well—I suppose," she said slowly and bitterly, "it's because your father has no luck."

The boy was silent for some time.

"Is luck money, mother?" he asked, rather timidly.

"No, Paul! Not quite. It's what causes you to have money."

"Oh!" said Paul vaguely. "I thought when Uncle Oscar said *filthy lucker,* it meant money."

"*Filthy lucre* does mean money," said the mother. "But it's lucre, not luck."

"Oh!" said the boy. "Then what *is* luck, mother?"

"It's what causes you to have money. If you're lucky you have money. That's why it's better to be born lucky than rich. If you're rich, you may lose your money. But if you're lucky, you will always get more money."

"Oh! Will you! And is father not lucky?"

"Very unlucky, I should say," she said bitterly.

---

1. pram: Baby carriage.

The boy watched her with unsure eyes.

"Why?" he asked.

"I don't know. Nobody ever knows why one person is lucky and another unlucky."

"Don't they? Nobody at all? Does *nobody* know?"

"Perhaps God! But He never tells."

"He ought to, then. And aren't you lucky either, mother?"

"I can't be, if I married an unlucky husband."

"But by yourself, aren't you?"

"I used to think I was, before I married. Now I think I am very unlucky indeed."

"Why?"

"Well—never mind! Perhaps I'm not really," she said.

The child looked at her, to see if she meant it. But he saw, by the lines of her mouth, that she was only trying to hide something from him.

"Well, anyhow," he said stoutly, "I'm a lucky person."

"Why?" said his mother, with a sudden laugh.

He stared at her. He didn't even know why he had said it.

"God told me," he asserted, brazening it out.

"I hope He did, dear!" she said, again with a laugh, but rather bitter.

"He did, mother!"

"Excellent!" said the mother, using one of her husband's exclamations.

The boy saw she did not believe him; or rather, that she paid no attention to his assertion. This angered him somewhere, and made him want to compel her attention.

He went off by himself, vaguely, in a childish way, seeking for the clue to "luck." Absorbed, taking no heed of other people, he went about with a sort of stealth, seeking inwardly for luck. He wanted luck, he wanted it, he wanted it. When the two girls were playing dolls, in the nursery, he would sit on his big rocking horse, charging madly into space, with a frenzy that made the little girls peer at him uneasily. Wildly the horse ca-

4 **Discussion** Where does the secret whisper originate?

5 **Discussion** How does Paul's mother define "luck?"

6 **Literary Focus** What aspect of third-person narration is conveyed by this encounter?

7 **Critical Reading and Thinking** What can we infer from Paul's frenzied riding? Why does Paul want luck?

The Rocking-Horse Winner 975

8 Enrichment Uncle Oscar is always joking, and he supplies the whip for the rocking horse and the incentive for Paul to keep wagering. Uncle Oscar implies a reference to Oscar Wilde, who published a volume of fairy tales written for his sons in 1888, called *The Happy Prince*. Wilde prefaced his Gothic novel *The Picture of Dorian Gray* with "there is no such thing as a moral or immoral book." The character of Uncle Oscar includes Wilde's individualism and his lack of morality. The "changeable" name of Paul's horse suggests a reference to Wilde's pen name, which was "Speranza." Wilde firmly believed that art must stand apart from life, and Uncle Oscar stays emotionally aloof like Lawrence's omniscient narrator in this story.

9 Critical Thinking and Reading What can you infer about Bassett?

reered, the waving dark hair of the boy tossed, his eyes had a strange glare in them. The little girls dared not speak to him.

When he had ridden to the end of his mad little journey, he climbed down and stood in front of his rocking horse, staring fixedly into its lowered face. Its red mouth was slightly open, its big eye was wide and glassy bright.

"Now!" he would silently command the snorting steed. "Now take me to where there is luck! Now take me!"

And he would slash the horse on the neck with the little whip he had asked Uncle Oscar for. He *knew* the horse could take him to where there was luck, if only he forced it. So he would mount again, and start on his furious ride, hoping at last to get there. He knew he could get there.

"You'll break your horse, Paul!" said the nurse.

"He's always riding like that! I wish he'd leave off!" said his elder sister Joan.

But he only glared down on them in silence. Nurse gave him up. She could make nothing of him. Anyhow he was growing beyond her.

One day his mother and his Uncle Oscar came in when he was on one of his furious rides. He did not speak to them.

"Hallo! you young jockey! Riding a winner?" said his uncle.

"Aren't you growing too big for a rocking horse? You're not a very little boy any longer, you know," said his mother.

But Paul only gave a blue glare from his big, rather close-set eyes. He would speak to nobody when he was in full tilt. His mother watched him with an anxious expression on her face.

At last he suddenly stopped forcing his horse into the mechanical gallop, and slid down.

"Well, I got there!" he announced fiercely, his blue eyes still flaring, and his sturdy long legs straddling apart.

"Where did you get to?" asked his mother.

"Where I wanted to go to," he flared back at her.

"That's right, son!" said Uncle Oscar. "Don't you stop till you get there. What's the horse's name?"

"He doesn't have a name," said the boy.

"Gets on without all right?" asked the uncle.

"Well, he has different names. He was called Sansovino last week."

"Sansovino, eh? Won the Ascot.[2] How did you know his name?"

"He always talks about horse races with Bassett," said Joan.

The uncle was delighted to find that his small nephew was posted with all the racing news. Bassett, the young gardener who had been wounded in the left foot in the war, and had got his present job through Oscar Cresswell, whose batman[3] he had been, was a perfect blade of the "turf."[4] He lived in the racing events, and the small boy lived with him.

Oscar Cresswell got it all from Bassett.

"Master Paul comes and asks me, so I can't do more than tell him, sir," said Bassett, his face terribly serious, as if he were speaking of religious matters.

"And does he ever put anything on a horse he fancies?"

"Well—I don't want to give him away—he's a young sport, a fine sport, sir. Would you mind asking him yourself? He sort of takes a pleasure in it, and perhaps he'd feel I was giving him away, sir, if you don't mind."

Bassett was serious as a church.

The uncle went back to his nephew, and took him off for a ride in the car.

"Say, Paul, old man, do you ever put anything on a horse?" the uncle asked.

The boy watched the handsome man closely.

"Why, do you think I oughtn't to?" he parried.

---

2. Ascot: A major English horse race.
3. batman: A British military officer's orderly.
4. blade . . . "turf": Horse-racing fan.

"Not a bit of it! I thought perhaps you might give me a tip for the Lincoln."[5]

The car sped on into the country, going down to Uncle Oscar's place in Hampshire.

"Honor bright?" said the nephew.

"Honor bright, son!" said the uncle.

"Well, then, Daffodil."

"Daffodil! I doubt it, sonny. What about Mirza?"

"I only know the winner," said the boy. "That's Daffodil!"

"Daffodil, eh?"

There was a pause. Daffodil was an obscure horse comparatively.

"Uncle!"

"Yes, son?"

"You won't let it go any further, will you? I promised Bassett."

"Bassett be hanged, old man! What's he got to do with it?"

"We're partners! We've been partners from the first! Uncle, he lent me my first five shillings, which I lost. I promised him, honor bright, it was only between me and him: only you gave me that ten-shilling note I started winning with, so I thought you were lucky. You won't let it go any further, will you?"

The boy gazed at his uncle from those big, hot, blue eyes, set rather close together. The uncle stirred and laughed uneasily.

"Right you are, son! I'll keep your tip private. Daffodil, eh! How much are you putting on him?"

"All except twenty pounds," said the boy. "I keep that in reserve."

The uncle thought it a good joke.

"You keep twenty pounds in reserve, do you, you young romancer? What are you betting, then?"

"I'm betting three hundred," said the boy gravely. "But it's between you and me, Uncle Oscar! Honor bright?"

The uncle burst into a roar of laughter.

"It's between you and me all right, you young Nat Gould,"[6] he said, laughing. "But where's your three hundred?"

"Bassett keeps it for me. We're partners."

"You are, are you! And what is Bassett putting on Daffodil?"

"He won't go quite as high as I do, I expect. Perhaps he'll go a hundred and fifty."

"What, pennies?" laughed the uncle.

"Pounds," said the child, with a surprised look at his uncle. "Bassett keeps a bigger reserve than I do."

Between wonder and amusement, Uncle Oscar was silent. He pursued the matter no further, but he determined to take his nephew with him to the Lincoln races.

"Now, son," he said, "I'm putting twenty on Mirza, and I'll put five for you on any horse you fancy. What's your pick?"

"Daffodil, uncle!"

"No, not the fiver on Daffodil!"

"I should if it was my own fiver," said the child.

"Good! Good! Right you are! A fiver for me and a fiver for you on Daffodil."

The child had never been to a race meeting before, and his eyes were blue fire. He pursed his mouth tight, and watched. A Frenchman just in front had put his money on Lancelot. Wild with excitement, he flayed his arms up and down, yelling *Lancelot! Lancelot!* in his French accent.

Daffodil came in first, Lancelot second, Mirza third. The child, flushed and with eyes blazing, was curiously serene. His uncle brought him five five-pound notes: four to one.

"What am I to do with these?" he cried, waving them before the boy's eyes.

"I suppose we'll talk to Bassett," said the boy. "I expect I have fifteen hundred now; and twenty in reserve; and this twenty."

---

5. Lincoln: A major English horse race.

6. Nat Gould: A famous English sportswriter and authority on horse racing.

10 Discussion Why makes Paul think that Uncle Oscar is lucky?

11 Discussion How does Uncle Oscar treat the whole affair?

12 Discussion What is Paul's connection with Uncle Oscar and Bassett?

13 Discussion How would you describe Bassett's attitude toward racing?

14 Discussion When are the bets successful?

His uncle studied him for some moments.

"Look here, son!" he said. "You're not serious about Bassett and that fifteen hundred, are you?"

"Yes, I am. But it's between you and me, uncle! Honor bright!"

"Honor bright all right, son! But I must talk to Bassett."

"If you'd like to be a partner, uncle, with Bassett and me, we could all be partners. Only you'd have to promise, honor bright, uncle, not to let it go beyond us three. Bassett and I are lucky, and you must be lucky, because it was your ten shillings I started winning with. . . ."

Uncle Oscar took both Bassett and Paul into Richmond Park for an afternoon, and there they talked.

"It's like this, you see, sir," Bassett said. "Master Paul would get me talking about racing events, spinning yarns, you know, sir. And he was always keen on knowing if I'd made or if I'd lost. It's about a year since, now, that I put five shillings on Blush of Dawn for him—and we lost. Then the luck turned, with that ten shillings he had from you, that we put on Singhalese. And since that time, it's been pretty steady, all things considering. What do you say, Master Paul?"

"We're all right when we're *sure*," said Paul. "It's when we're not quite sure that we go down."

"Oh, but we're careful then," said Bassett.

"But when are you *sure?*" smiled Uncle Oscar.

"It's Master Paul, sir," said Bassett, in a secret, religious voice. "It's as if he had it from heaven. Like Daffodil now, for the Lincoln. That was as sure as eggs."

"Did you put anything on Daffodil?" asked Oscar Cresswell.

"Yes, sir. I made my bit."

"And my nephew?"

Bassett was obstinately silent, looking at Paul.

"I made twelve hundred, didn't I, Bassett? I told uncle I was putting three hundred on Daffodil."

"That's right," said Bassett, nodding.

"But where's the money?" asked the uncle.

"I keep it safe locked up, sir. Master Paul, he can have it any minute he likes to ask for it."

"What, fifteen hundred pounds?"

"And twenty! And *forty*, that is, with the twenty he made on the course."

"It's amazing!" said the uncle.

"If Master Paul offers you to be partners, sir, I would, if I were you; if you'll excuse me," said Bassett.

Oscar Cresswell thought about it.

"I'll see the money," he said.

They drove home again, and sure enough, Bassett came round to the garden house with fifteen hundred pounds in notes. The twenty pounds reserve was left with Joe Glee, in the Turf Commission deposit.

"You see, it's all right, uncle, when I'm *sure!* Then we go strong, for all we're worth. Don't we, Bassett?"

"We do that, Master Paul."

"And when are you sure?" said the uncle, laughing.

"Oh, well, sometimes I'm *absolutely* sure, like about Daffodil," said the boy, "and sometimes I have an idea; and sometimes I haven't even an idea, have I, Bassett? Then we're careful, because we mostly go down."

"You do, do you! And when you're sure, like about Daffodil, what makes you sure, sonny?"

"Oh, well, I don't know," said the boy uneasily. "I'm sure, you know, uncle; that's all."

"It's as if he had it from heaven, sir," Bassett reiterated.

"I should say so!" said the uncle.

But he became a partner. And when the Leger was coming on, Paul was "sure" about Lively Spark, which was a quite inconsiderable horse. The boy insisted on putting a thousand on the horse, Bassett went for five hundred, and Oscar Cresswell two hundred. Lively Spark came in first, and the

Primary Source

Lawrence's remarks on Benjamin Franklin in his *Studies in Classic American Literature* relate to "The Rocking Horse Winner" as well:

> Why then did Benjamin set up this dummy of a perfect citizen as a pattern to America? Of course, he did it in perfect good faith, as far as he knew. He thought it simply was the true ideal. But what we *think* we do is not very important. We never really know what we are doing. Either we are materialistic instruments, like Benjamin, or we move in the gesture of creation, from our deepest self, usually unconscious. We are only the actors, we are never wholly the authors of our own deeds or works. IT is the author, the unknown inside us or outside us. The best we can do is to try to hold ourselves in unison with the deeps which are inside us. And the worse we can do is to try to have things our own way, when we run counter to IT, and in the long run get our knuckles rapped for our presumption.

Ask students how Lawrence's comment, "We never really know what we are doing," relates to Paul and his betting had been ten to one against him. Paul had made ten thousand.

"You see," he said. "I was absolutely sure of him."

Even Oscar Cresswell had cleared two thousand.

"Look here, son," he said, "this sort of thing makes me nervous."

"It needn't, uncle! Perhaps I shan't be sure again for a long time."

"But what are you going to do with your money?" asked the uncle.

"Of course," said the boy, "I started it for mother. She said she had no luck, because father is unlucky, so I thought if I was lucky, it might stop whispering."

"What might stop whispering?"

"Our house! I *hate* our house for whispering."

"What does it whisper?"

"Why—why"—the boy fidgeted— "why, I don't know! But it's always short of money, you know, uncle."

"I know it, son, I know it."

"You know people send mother writs, don't you, uncle?"

"I'm afraid I do," said the uncle.

"And then the house whispers like people laughing at you behind your back. It's awful, that is! I thought if I was lucky . . ."

"You might stop it," added the uncle.

The boy watched him with big blue eyes, that had an uncanny cold fire in them, and he said never a word.

"Well then!" said the uncle. "What are we doing?"

"I shouldn't like mother to know I was lucky," said the boy.

"Why not, son?"

"She'd stop me."

"I don't think she would."

"Oh!"—and the boy writhed in an odd way— "I *don't* want her to know, uncle."

"All right, son! We'll manage it without her knowing."

They managed it very easily. Paul, at the other's suggestion, handed over five thousand pounds to his uncle, who deposited it with the family lawyer, who was then to inform Paul's mother that a relative had put five thousand pounds into his hands, which sum was to be paid out a thousand pounds at a time, on the mother's birthday, for the next five years.

"So she'll have a birthday present of a thousand pounds for five successive years," said Uncle Oscar. "I hope it won't make it all the harder for her later."

Paul's mother had her birthday in November. The house had been "whispering" worse than ever lately, and even in spite of his luck, Paul could not bear up against it. He was very anxious to see the effect of the birthday letter, telling his mother about the thousand pounds.

When there were no visitors, Paul now took his meals with his parents, as he was beyond the nursery control. His mother went into town nearly every day. She had discovered that she had an odd knack of sketching furs and dress materials, so she worked secretly in the studio of a friend who was the chief "artist" for the leading drapers. She drew the figures of ladies in furs and ladies in silk and sequins for the newspaper advertisements. This young woman artist earned several thousand pounds a year, but Paul's mother only made several hundreds, and she was again dissatisfied. She so wanted to be first in something, and she did not succeed, even in making sketches for drapery advertisements.

She was down to breakfast on the morning of her birthday. Paul watched her face as she read her letters. He knew the lawyer's letter. As his mother read it, her face hardened and became more expressionless. Then a cold, determined look came on her mouth. She hid the letter under the pile of others, and said not a word about it.

"Didn't you have anything nice in the post for your birthday, mother?" said Paul.

"Quite moderately nice," she said, her voice cold and absent.

She went away to town without saying more.

But in the afternoon Uncle Oscar appeared. He said Paul's mother had had a

15 Critical Thinking and Reading Why does Paul need luck so desperately? What can we infer about Uncle Oscar from this exchange?

16 Critical Thinking and Reading What does Paul's birthday gift to his mother imply about him?

17 Discussion What frustrates Paul's mother? What do Paul and his mother have in common?

18 Discussion What does the reaction of Paul's mother show about her?

mother in this story. Are Paul and his mother "materialistic instruments?" Is either of them "in unison with the deeps . . . inside" them? Do they both "try to have things" their "own way?"

19 **Literary Focus** What can we infer about the inevitability of implying some attitude or point of view, even with an omniscient narrator, from this passage? What makes the voices go mad like "a chorus of frogs"?

20 **Discussion** What does Paul's mother infer from his refusal to leave for the seashore? What does this show about her?

21 **Master Teacher Note** "The Rocking-Horse Winner" revolves around the notion of fate, as in a Greek tragedy. Ask the students to relate "The Rocking-Horse Winner" to a Greek tragedy in terms of the working out of the tragic hero's fate, the use of Bassett as an evil spirit, and Uncle Oscar as a chorus.

22 **Literary Focus** How does Paul's "secret within a secret" show the neutrality of the omniscient narrator?

long interview with the lawyer, asking if the whole five thousand could not be advanced at once, as she was in debt.

"What do you think, uncle?" said the boy.

"I leave it to you, son."

"Oh, let her have it, then! We can get some more with the other," said the boy.

"A bird in the hand is worth two in the bush, laddie!" said Uncle Oscar.

"But I'm sure to *know* for the Grand National; or the Lincolnshire; or else the Derby.[7] I'm sure to know for *one* of them," said Paul.

So Uncle Oscar signed the agreement, and Paul's mother touched the whole five thousand. Then something very curious happened. The voices in the house suddenly went mad, like a chorus of frogs on a spring evening. There were certain new furnishings, and Paul had a tutor. He was *really* going to Eton,[8] his father's school, in the following autumn. There were flowers in the winter, and a blossoming of the luxury Paul's mother had been used to. And yet the voices in the house, behind the sprays of mimosa and almond blossom, and from under the piles of iridescent cushions, simply trilled and screamed in a sort of ecstasy: "There *must* be more money! Oh-h-h! There *must* be more money! Oh, now, now-w! now-w-w—there *must* be more money!—more than ever! More than ever!"

It frightened Paul terribly. He studied away at his Latin and Greek with his tutors. But his intense hours were spent with Bassett. The Grand National had gone by: he had not "known," and had lost a hundred pounds. Summer was at hand. He was in agony for the Lincoln. But even for the Lincoln he didn't "know," and he lost fifty pounds. He became wild-eyed and strange,

as if something were going to explode in him.

"Let it alone, son! Don't you bother about it!" urged Uncle Oscar. But it was as if the boy couldn't really hear what his uncle was saying.

"I've got to know for the Derby! I've *got* to know for the Derby!" the child reiterated, his big blue eyes blazing with a sort of madness.

His mother noticed how overwrought he was.

"You'd better go to the seaside. Wouldn't you like to go now to the seaside, instead of waiting? I think you'd better," she said, looking down at him anxiously, her heart curiously heavy because of him.

But the child lifted his uncanny blue eyes.

"I couldn't possibly go before the Derby, mother!" he said. "I couldn't possibly!"

"Why not?" she said, her voice becoming heavy when she was opposed. "Why not? You can still go from the seaside to see the Derby with your Uncle Oscar, if that's what you wish. No need for you to wait here. Besides, I think you care too much about these races. It's a bad sign. My family has been a gambling family, and you won't know till you grow up how much damage it has done. But it has done damage. I shall have to send Bassett away, and ask Uncle Oscar not to talk racing to you, unless you promise to be reasonable about it; go away to the seaside and forget it. You're all nerves!"

"I'll do what you like, mother, so long as you don't send me away till after the Derby," the boy said.

"Send you away from where? Just from this house?"

"Yes," he said, gazing at her.

"Why, you curious child, what makes you care about this house so much, suddenly? I never knew you loved it!"

He gazed at her without speaking. He had a secret within a secret, something he had not divulged, even to Bassett or to his Uncle Oscar.

---

7. Grand National . . . Derby: Major English horse races.
8. Eton: A prestigious private school in England.

Grammar in Action

Using **personification** to endow an inanimate object with human traits can be startlingly effective. Personification is a strong tool, and good writers use it only when they have a clear purpose in mind, since ill-planned personification can be pretentious and even ridiculous. Notice how D. H. Lawrence makes his house a character through personification.

And yet the voices in the house, behind the sprays of mimosa and almond blossom, and from under the piles of iridescent cushions, simply trilled and screamed in a sort of ecstasy: "There *must* be more money! Oh-h-h! There *must* be more money! Oh, now, now-w! now-w-w—there *must* be more money!—more than ever! More than ever!"

Lawrence gives the house a seething, greedy character by having it voice the material lust of Paul's family, and so he illuminates the family's true problem—love of things, not people—through the house itself, which seems to live and breathe and feed on money. If the house were not personified, the problem would never be voiced.

But his mother, after standing undecided and a little bit sullen for some moments, said:

"Very well, then! Don't go to the seaside till after the Derby, if you don't wish it. But promise me you won't let your nerves go to pieces! Promise you won't think so much about horse racing and *events,* as you call them!"

"Oh, no!" said the boy, casually. "I won't think much about them, mother. You needn't worry. I wouldn't worry, mother, if I were you."

"If you were me and I were you," said his mother, "I wonder what we *should* do!"

"But you know you needn't worry, mother, don't you?" the boy repeated.

"I should be awfully glad to know it," she said wearily.

"Oh, well, you *can,* you know. I mean you *ought* to know you needn't worry!" he insisted.

"Ought I? Then I'll see about it," she said.

Paul's secret of secrets was his wooden horse, that which had no name. Since he was emancipated from a nurse and a nursery governess, he had had his rocking horse removed to his own bedroom at the top of the house.

"Surely you're too big for a rocking horse!" his mother had remonstrated.

"Well, you see, mother, till I can have a *real* horse, I like to have *some* sort of animal about," had been his quaint answer.

"Do you feel he keeps you company?" she laughed.

"Oh, yes! He's very good, he always keeps me company, when I'm there," said Paul.

So the horse, rather shabby, stood in an arrested prance in the boy's bedroom.

The Derby was drawing near, and the boy grew more and more tense. He hardly heard what was spoken to him, he was very frail, and his eyes were really uncanny. His mother had sudden strange seizures of uneasiness about him. Sometimes, for half an hour, she would feel a sudden anxiety about him that was almost anguish. She wanted to rush to him at once, and know he was safe.

Two nights before the Derby, she was at a big party in town, when one of her rushes of anxiety about her boy, her firstborn, gripped her heart till she could hardly speak. She fought with the feeling, might and main, for she believed in common sense. But it was too strong. She had to leave the dance and go downstairs to telephone to the country. The children's nursery governess was terribly surprised and startled at being rung up in the night.

"Are the children all right, Miss Wilmot?"

"Oh yes, they are quite all right."

"Master Paul? Is he all right?"

"He went to bed as right as a trivet.[9] Shall I run up and look at him?"

"No!" said Paul's mother reluctantly. "No! Don't trouble. It's all right. Don't sit up. We shall be home fairly soon." She did not want her son's privacy intruded upon.

"Very good," said the governess.

It was about one o'clock when Paul's mother and father drove up to their house. All was still. Paul's mother went to her room and slipped off her white fur cloak. She had told her maid not to wait up for her. She heard her husband downstairs, mixing a whisky-and-soda.

And then, because of the strange anxiety at her heart, she stole upstairs to her son's room. Noiselessly she went along the upper corridor. Was there a faint noise? What was it?

She stood, with arrested muscles, outside his door, listening. There was a strange, heavy, and yet not loud noise. Her heart stood still. It was a soundless noise, yet rushing and powerful. Something huge, in violent, hushed motion. What was it? What in God's name was it? She ought to know. She felt that she *knew* the noise. She knew what it was.

---

9. right as a trivet: Perfectly right.

The Rocking-Horse Winner   981

Student Activity 1. Read the two paragraphs on pages 974 and 975 in which the voices first appear. Do you see any occurrences of personification apart from the house? Name what is personified and how.

Student Activity 2. Write a descriptive paragraph in which you personify one of the following inanimate objects: a toy train, an old car, a pair of sneakers, an armchair, a street. Be sure to choose a specific personality before you write, and assign the object characteristics that fit the personality.

25 Discussion What does Uncle Oscar's behavior demonstrate about his personality?

26 Discussion What simile does Lawrence use? Can a narrator be neutral?

27 Enrichment The word *fairy tale* comes from *Fata,* who was one of the Fates in ancient Roman mythology. *Fatum* means "fate," and Fata was a minor supernatural being who could assume diminutive human form and meddle in human affairs. Ask the students to discuss the description of Bassett in terms of his relation to fate or Puck or any imp-like spirit.

28 Discussion What is Paul's secret?

29 Clarification A bet is a thing staked or pledged between two parties upon the event of a contest. Historically a wager is the act of giving a pledge to abide the event of something. Thus historically one would pledge one's life on the outcome of a duel or battle. Ask the class to discuss these synonyms. How does Lawrence in "The Rocking-Horse Winner" play upon Paul as a "wager" in the ancient meaning of *wage* or "to stake down oneself as security"?

30 Discussion What was Paul searching for as he madly rode his rocking-horse? What could have made Paul a "winner"?

Reader's Response Why are children often especially sensitive to the emotions and unspoken wishes of a household?

Yet she could not place it. She couldn't say what it was. And on and on it went, like a madness.

Softly, frozen with anxiety and fear, she turned the door handle.

The room was dark. Yet in the space near the window, she heard and saw something plunging to and fro. She gazed in fear and amazement.

Then suddenly she switched on the light, and saw her son, in his green pajamas, madly surging on his rocking horse. The blaze of light suddenly lit him up, as he urged the wooden horse, and lit her up, as she stood, blond, in her dress of pale green and crystal, in the doorway.

"Paul!" she cried. "Whatever are you doing?"

"It's Malabar!" he screamed, in a powerful, strange voice. "It's Malabar!"

His eyes blazed at her for one strange and senseless second, as he ceased urging his wooden horse. Then he fell with a crash to the ground, and she, all her tormented motherhood flooding upon her, rushed to gather him up.

But he was unconscious, and unconscious he remained, with some brain fever. He talked and tossed, and his mother sat stonily by his side.

"Malabar! It's Malabar! Bassett, Bassett, I *know* it's Malabar!"

So the child cried, trying to get up and urge the rocking horse that gave him his inspiration.

"What does he mean by Malabar?" asked the heart-frozen mother.

"I don't know," said the father, stonily.

"What does he mean by Malabar?" she asked her brother Oscar.

"It's one of the horses running for the Derby," was the answer.

25 And, in spite of himself, Oscar Cresswell spoke to Bassett, and himself put a thousand on Malabar: at fourteen to one.

The third day of the illness was critical: they were watching for a change. The boy, with his rather long, curly hair, was tossing ceaselessly on the pillow. He neither slept nor regained consciousness, and his eyes were like blue stones. His mother sat, feeling her heart had gone, turned actually into a stone. **26**

In the evening, Oscar Cresswell did not come, but Bassett sent a message, saying could he come up for one moment, just one moment? Paul's mother was very angry at the intrusion, but on second thoughts she agreed. The boy was the same. Perhaps Bassett might bring him to consciousness.

The gardener, a shortish fellow with a little brown moustache and sharp little brown eyes, tiptoed into the room, touched his imaginary cap to Paul's mother, and stole to the bedside, staring with glittering, smallish eyes at the tossing, dying child. **27**

"Master Paul!" he whispered. "Master Paul! Malabar came in first all right, a clean win. I did as you told me. You've made over seventy thousand pounds, you have; you've got over eighty thousand. Malabar came in all right, Master Paul."

"Malabar! Malabar! Did I say Malabar, mother? Did I say Malabar? Do you think I'm lucky, mother? I knew Malabar, didn't I? Over eighty thousand pounds! I call that lucky, don't you, mother? Over eighty thousand pounds! I knew, didn't I know I knew? Malabar came in all right. If I ride my horse till I'm sure, then I tell you, Bassett, you can go as high as you like. Did you go for all you were worth, Bassett?" **28**

"I went a thousand on it, Master Paul."

"I never told you, mother, that if I can ride my horse, and *get there*, then I'm absolutely sure—oh, absolutely! Mother, did I ever tell you? I *am* lucky!" **29**

"No, you never did," said the mother.

But the boy died in the night.

And even as he lay dead, his mother heard her brother's voice saying to her: "My God, Hester, you're eighty-odd thousand to the good, and a poor devil of a son to the bad. But, poor devil, poor devil, he's best gone out of a life where he rides his rocking horse to find a winner." **30**

Closure and Extension

ANSWERS TO THINKING ABOUT THE SELECTION
Recalling

1. The mother blames the father's "bad luck" for the family's lack of money.

2. Paul tries to ride his rocking-horse to discover winners to bet on as a way of changing the family's luck.

3. (a) Paul gives his mother 1000 pounds a year for five years as a birthday present. (b) The mother reacts by wanting all of the money immediately.

4. On returning from the party, the mother finds Paul feverishly riding his rocking horse.

THINKING ABOUT THE SELECTION
Recalling

1. Why is the family in the story always short of money?
2. How does Paul try to change the family's luck?
3. (a) What birthday present does Paul give his mother? (b) What is her reaction to it?
4. What does Paul's mother discover upon returning from the big party?

Interpreting

5. What comment does Lawrence seem to be making about the concerns of Paul's parents?
6. On page 975 Paul's mother describes her husband as unlucky? (a) What do you think she means by this? (b) What does the remark reveal about her as a person?
7. What comment about life do you think the author is suggesting in Uncle Oscar's statement on Paul's death at the story's close?
8. Identify Lawrence's theme in this story.

Applying

9. Tell to what extent the problems he addresses are problems primarily of this century.

ANALYZING LITERATURE
Understanding Omniscient Narration

Omniscient narration is narration by a third-person speaker who, knowing all, is able to "read" the characters' minds and see into their futures. In "The Rocking-Horse Winner," D. H. Lawrence uses a narrative style of the sort ordinarily found in fairy tales. The opening line of the story, for example, has some of the ring of the familiar "Once upon a time" beginning.

1. Identify at least two other features of the story that give it the flavor of a fairy tale. Describe what you feel these features add to the impact of the ending.

2. (a) How different might your overall impression of the story be if Lawrence had used the mother as the narrator? (b) If he had used Uncle Oscar?

UNDERSTANDING LANGUAGE
Understanding Synonyms

Synonyms are words that share a common meaning. The word *luck,* for instance, which appears in one form or another throughout the story has synonyms in the words *fate, fortune,* and *chance,* to name a few. Yet, not all of these words mean the same thing, which suggests that *luck* has several related, but very different, meanings. Reread the section on page 975 where Paul's mother explains luck. Then turn to Paul's final words on page 982. Tell which synonyms apply to the mother's use of the word. Then tell which apply to Paul's use, and explain why that use is ironic.

THINKING AND WRITING
Telling the Story

Imagine that Paul, and not an omniscient narrator, were telling the story. Try to imagine, based on examples Lawrence provides of the child's language, what words Paul might use to express events. More important, try to envision what takes place inside Paul's mind when he is astride his horse and galloping toward another "victory." Then retell a portion of the story from Paul's point of view. You may wish to concentrate on the section that immediately precedes Paul's lapse into unconsciousness. When you revise make sure you have maintained a consistent point of view. Have you included information Paul would not know? Does your narrator sound like Paul? Proofread your story and prepare a final draft. Read it aloud to your classmates.

The Rocking-Horse Winner 983

ANSWERS TO ANALYZING LITERATURE

1. Suggested response: The supernatural powers of the rocking-horse, the anthropomorphic whispering house, plus the fairy tale setting of rich, beautiful, but miserable people with the intervention of the evil spirit Bassett, all give this story the flavor of a fairy tale. The fairy tale features contribute a mythic quality or greater dimension to the ironical end of the story.

2. Suggested Responses: (a) If Lawrence had used the mother as the narrator we would not have been able to see her superficiality or her shabby materialism. Also we could never have followed Paul's reasoning since his mother was oblivious to all but her own concerns. (b) Uncle Oscar would have changed our feeling of compassion for Paul's tragedy since he generally considered life a joke. We would have lost the morality and the social criticism if the narration changed from third-person to either the mother or Uncle Oscar.

ANSWERS TO UNDERSTANDING LANGUAGE

The mother's conversation about luck is based on fortune because she is concerned with money, and she attributes their lack of it to her husband's bad fortune or to chance. When Paul tells his mother that he is lucky, he means that he has wagered or taken a chance and won a fortune. Paul's usage reverses his mother's usage, and it is an ironic reversal. Actually, Paul has run into fate rather than chance and he has lost his life on his lucky wager. The final irony is that Paul and his mother are both entwined by fate and bad luck since the mother's good fortune costs her first-born's life.

THINKING AND WRITING

Divide students into groups, and have them read their rough drafts to one another and suggest ways in which they could be improved.

Interpreting

5. Lawrence seems to be criticizing the indifference and isolation as well as the materialism of Paul's parents.
6. (a) Paul's mother considers her husband unlucky because he has not made her rich. (b) This remark reveals that she is shallow, materialistic, and selfish.

7. Suggested response: Uncle Oscar seems to be saying that the boy was crazy or emotionally stunted so he's better off dead and that the mother is better off with the money.
8. Lawrence's theme might be the irony of greed or the distortion of people's understanding of one another due to their alienation.

Applying

9. Suggested Response: The problem of a desperate need for money and

the alienated fragmented family have a definite connection in this century. After industrialization, people left the family farm. Industrial work and the need for money in place of goods changed the nature of life for modern man. The loss of religion and its replacement with material obsession are primarily problems of this century.

Challenge Who are the winners in this story? Who are unlucky?

More About the Author James
Joyce's father drank a great deal,
which caused him to neglect his
affairs and sink first into debt and
then poverty. Joyce ended up
having to leave the Jesuit boarding school which he attended,
and he educated himself for two
years. As is the case with other
authors, Joyce's background is
apparent in much of his writing.
Tell students to be on the lookout
for references in "Araby" to influences from Joyce's life. Mention
that the story itself comes from
the collection of short stories
"Dubliners." Ask students to discuss what part is played by an
author's background in the works
of some of the other writers they
have read so far this year.

Critical Evaluation Richard Ellmann, Joyce's distinguished biographer, made the following
evaluation of Joyce's life and
work: "The surface of the life
Joyce lived seemed always erratic and provisional. But its central
meaning was directed as consciously as his work. The ingenuity with which he wrote his books
was the same with which he
forced the world to read them;
the smiling affection he extended
to Bloom and his other principal
characters was the same that he
gave to the members of his
family. . . . In whatever he did,
his two profound interests—his
family and his writings—kept
their place. . . . The intensity of
the first gave his work its sympathy and humanity; the intensity of
the second raised his life to dignity and high dedication."

JAMES JOYCE

1882–1941

Although James Joyce left Ireland early in his career and associated with the radical literary experimentalists on the Continent, he
never lost the respect for tradition that he had learned from his
Jesuit teachers. All of his works are set in his native Dublin, and all
have firm roots in the literature of the past. If Joyce's innovativeness
in the areas of plot, character, and language are undeniable, so
then is the notion that part of his greatness was his ability to
reinterpret and transform familiar literary forms.

James Joyce was born and educated in Dublin. Choosing,
much to the disappointment of his family and teachers, not to enter
the priesthood, he briefly considered careers in medicine and
singing. His true calling, however, was as a writer, and in 1907 he
published *Chamber Music,* a collection of poems. At the time of the
book's publication, Joyce was living in Trieste, Italy, where he
remained until the outbreak of the First World War.

The year he relocated to Zurich, 1914, also marks the appearance of his landmark volume of short stories *Dubliners.* This
collection of deceptively simple tales focuses on people who, on the
surface, are quite ordinary but whose minds are filled with raging
psychological and emotional conflicts. Each of the main characters
in *Dubliners* experiences in some way a growth of self-awareness
that leads to a climactic peak in the story.

This process is developed still more fully in *A Portrait of the
Artist as a Young Man,* a fictionalized account of Joyce's own life
from infancy through age twenty. Like Joyce, Stephen Dedalus, the
novel's main character, finds himself in conflict with his family, the
Roman Catholic Church, and the nationalistic fervor of his countrymen. The book also reveals a heightened awareness of the power of
language and a deeper immersion into the mind of the character.
Both these traits are carried forward into *Ulysses* (1922), whose
ultimate banning in England and the United States, made Joyce
famous, if not wealthy. This novel, which roughly parallels Homer's
Odyssey, presents a single day in the life of three Dubliners. The
world Joyce depicts, while as solidly three-dimensional as any
conjured up by nineteenth-century realists, is nevertheless one in
which language can be seen to provide keys to the exploration of
truth.

Joyce's last novel, *Finnegan's Wake* (1939), was in many ways
the most challenging. Written in what one scholar terms "a dream
language of Joyce's own invention," this highly experimental work
presents its author's view of human existence as moving through
various cycles.

Objectives

1 To recognize an
epiphany
2 To analyze Joyce's
attitude toward the
narrator
3 To appreciate
image-making words
4 To write an extended
conversation

Support Material

Teaching Portfolio
Teacher Backup, pp. 1173–1176
Grammar in Action Worksheet,
Using Semicolons, p. 1177
Usage and Mechanics Work-
sheet, p. 1179
Vocabulary Check, p. 1180
Analyzing Literature Worksheet,
Understanding Epiphany, p.
1181

Language Worksheet, *Appreciating Image–Making Words,* p.
1182
Selection Test, pp. 1183–1184

GUIDE FOR INTERPRETING

Araby

Writer's Technique

Epiphany. Epiphany (i pif′ ə nē) is a profound mental or spiritual revelation experienced by the hero of a literary work. The term is derived from Greek mythology, where it was used to describe the occasion when a god or goddess, wearing a disguise or concealed in a cloud, would suddenly reveal his or her true divine identity to a mortal. In modern fiction epiphany generally occurs in stories that operate on a mental, or "cerebral," level, rather than on a purely physical level. In such stories the major events are so constructed as to lead up to this dawning, or sudden awareness of an important truth, on the part of a character. What the character *thinks* under circumstances of this sort is more important than what he or she *does*. In his collection of stories *Dubliners,* James Joyce frequently depicts characters who experience epiphany.

Writing

Logan Pearsall Smith wrote, "All mirrors are magical mirrors; never can we see our faces in them." Freewrite, exploring the meaning of the quotation and your reactions to it.

Primary Source

The reactions people have to others may shed light on their own character. What was Joyce's reaction to William Butler Yeats, an older and more established writer? By 1905, when he was forty years old, Yeats was a famous man in Ireland: A greatly admired poet and playwright, he was also a leader in both the Irish Literary Revival and the Irish National Movement. In 1905 James Joyce was only twenty-three. In contrast to Yeats, he had yet to publish anything; his first work, a collection of poems called *Chamber Music,* was still two years off. One would think, then, that Joyce would be very much in awe of Yeats's accomplishments in light of his own youth and inexperience. Just the opposite was true, as revealed in the famous story his friend Oliver St. John Gogarty recounts: "We both lived on the north side of the city, and we were going up Rutland Square, I think it was a horse-drawn tram in those days. I happened to mention that thing that the newspapers were full of—that it was Yeats's fortieth birthday and that Lady Gregory had collected from his friends forty pounds with which she bought a Kelmscott edition of Chaucer by William Morris. Everybody knew that it was Yeats's birthday. But when I made an epiphany, so to speak, and told Joyce this, at the first tram stop he got out. Yeats was lodging in the Cavendish Hotel, in Rutland Square, and he solemnly walked in and knocked at Yeats's door. When Yeats opened the door of the sitting-room he said, 'What age are you, sir?' and Yeats said, 'I'm 40.'—'You are too old for me to help. I bid you goodbye.' And Yeats was greatly impressed at the impertinence of the thing."

Guide for Interpreting 985

Literary Focus Ask students if they know another context in which the word *epiphany* is used. Explain that the Epiphany, or Twelfth-night, is a Christian holiday celebrated twelve days after Christmas, on January 6. It is the day that the Magi were supposed to have visited the Christ child and the beasts in the stable were able to talk. Explain that religious symbols and references are common in literature, especially in the works of authors such as Joyce, who were heavily influenced by their religion.

Writing/Prior Knowledge Before they begin writing their paragraphs, have a student read the fifth paragraph of "Araby" beginning with "Her name sprang to my lips . . . " Have students notice the strong verbs and adjectives and concrete nouns Joyce uses to describe his emotions—*sprang, pour, strange prayers and praises, flood from my heart, my confused adoration.* Discuss in some detail the extended simile in the last line. Tell students to describe the emotions they experienced in their moments of epiphany with similar precision and clarity.

Vocabulary

Preteach the following vocabulary words:
imperturbable (im′ pər tʉr′ bə b'l) *adj.:* Calm; not easily ruffled (p. 987)
litanies (lit′'n ēz) *n.:* Form of prayer in which a congregation repeats a fixed response (p. 988)
garrulous (gar′ ə ləs) *adj.:* Tending to talk continuously (p. 989)
derided (di rīd′ id) *v.:* Made fun of; ridiculed (p. 990)

Humanities Note

Fine art, *St. Patrick's Close, Dublin*, by Walter Osborne. Walter Frederick Osborne (1859–1903) was an English landscape painter who lived in Ireland and received his art training there, at the Royal Hibernian Academy. He traveled through England and Europe and was briefly associated with a group of artists known as the Antwerp School in Belgium. His paintings are of urban scenes and the children that inhabited them. He painted the area around St. Patrick's Cathedral in Dublin many times.

The painting *St. Patrick's Close, Dublin*, portrays the poverty and squalor of the neighborhood around the cathedral. The placement of the children leads the eye into the picture plane, allowing it to go from one bleak scene to another. It is an effective portrayal of the indifference of children to the poverty around them.

Following are questions for class discussion:
1. Is this artist merely an observer of this scene or is he making a judgment about it?
2. Could this be a visualization of the street described in Joyce's story? Explain.

ST. PATRICK'S CLOSE
Walter Osborne
National Gallery of Ireland

Araby

James Joyce

North Richmond Street, being blind,[1] was a quiet street except at the hour when the Christian Brothers' School set the boys free. An uninhabited house of two stories stood at the blind end, detached from its neighbors in a square ground. The other houses of the street, conscious of decent lives within them, gazed at one another with brown imperturbable faces.

The former tenant of our house, a priest, had died in the back drawing room. Air, musty from having been long enclosed, hung in all the rooms, and the waste room behind the kitchen was littered with old useless papers. Among these I found a few paper-covered books, the pages of which were curled and damp: *The Abbot,* by Walter Scott, *The Devout Communicant* and *The Memoirs of Vidocq.*[2] I liked the last best because its leaves were yellow. The wild garden behind the house contained a central apple tree and a few straggling bushes under one of which I found the late tenant's rusty bicycle pump. He had been a very charitable priest; in his will he had left all his money to institutions and the furniture of his house to his sister.

When the short days of winter came dusk fell before we had well eaten our dinners. When we met in the street the houses had grown somber. The space of sky above us was the color of ever-changing violet and toward it the lamps of the street lifted their feeble lanterns. The cold air stung us and we played till our bodies glowed. Our shouts echoed in the silent street. The career of our play brought us through the dark muddy lanes behind the houses where we ran the gantlet of the rough tribes from the cottages, to the back doors of the dark dripping gardens where odors arose from the ashpits, to the dark odorous stables where a coachman smoothed and combed the horse or shook music from the buckled harness. When we returned to the street, light from the kitchen windows had filled the areas. If my uncle was seen turning the corner we hid in the shadow until we had seen him safely housed. Or if Mangan's sister came out on the doorstep to call her brother in to his tea we watched her from our shadow peer up and down the street. We waited to see whether she would remain or go in and, if she remained, we left our shadow and walked up to Mangan's steps resignedly. She was waiting for us, her figure defined by the light from the half-opened door. Her brother always teased her before he obeyed and I stood by the railings looking at her. Her dress swung as she moved her body and the soft rope of her hair tossed from side to side.

Every morning I lay on the floor in the front parlor watching her door. The blind was pulled down to within an inch of the sash so that I could not be seen. When she came out on the doorstep my heart leaped. I

---

1. **blind:** Dead end.
2. *The Abbot . . . Vidocq:* A historical tale, a religious manual, and the remembrances of a French adventurer, respectively.

Master Teacher Note Because Ireland and its internal struggles and conflicts with England are much in the news, have groups of students report briefly on various aspects of Irish history. Suggested topics might be the Battle of the Boyne, the effects of the potato famine of 1846–51, Fenianism, Orangemen, and home rule.

Enrichment In Great Britain, semi-detached houses are like duplexes in the United States and house middle-class people. Terraced houses are like row houses in certain parts of the United States and are the dwellings of working-class people. A detached house is a single house of the upper-middle classes. The neighborhood in ''Araby,'' except for the house on the end, is probably middle or lower-middle class.

Presentation

Motivation/Prior Knowledge Have students think of an event that they looked forward to for a long time. Tell them to think specifically of their feelings of anticipation. How did the imagined event and the real event differ?

Purpose-Setting Question What role does epiphany play in this story?

1 **Discussion** Ask students what figure of speech is used in this sentence. Briefly discuss personification.

2 **Critical Thinking and Reading** Ask students why they think Joyce chose a first-person narrator for his story. How would the story differ if it had been told in the third person?

3 **Discussion** Ask students what effect they think living in the same house as a priest might have on the narrator. Tell them to watch for indications of this influence as the story develops.

4 **Discussion** What kind of childhood did the narrator have? About how old are the boys in this story?

5 **Clarification** *Ran the gantlet* refers to an old method of determining someone's guilt or innocence by running between two rows of men with sticks, who would beat the accused. His or her reaction to this *ordeal* would indicate guilt or innocence. Joyce here refers to the boys' having to endure similar treatment from the local bullies.

6 **Discussion** What effect does Mangan's sister have on the boys? How is this effect related to their age?

ran to the hall, seized my books and followed her. I kept her brown figure always in my eye and, when we came near the point at which our ways diverged, I quickened my pace and passed her. This happened morning after morning. I had never spoken to her, except for a few casual words, and yet her name was like a summons to all my foolish blood.

Her image accompanied me even in places the most hostile to romance. On Saturday evenings when my aunt went marketing I had to go to carry some of the parcels. We walked through the flaring streets, jostled by drunken men and bargaining women, amid the curses of laborers, the shrill litanies of shopboys who stood on guard by the barrels of pigs' cheeks, the nasal chanting of street singers, who sang a *come-all-you* about O'Donovan Rossa,[3] or a ballad about the troubles in our native land. These noises converged in a single sensation of life for me: I imagined that I bore my chalice safely through a throng of foes. Her name sprang to my lips at moments in strange prayers and praises which I myself did not understand. My eyes were often full of tears (I could not tell why) and at times a flood from my heart seemed to pour itself out into my bosom. I thought little of the future. I did not know whether I would ever speak to her or not or, if I spoke to her, how I could tell her of my confused adoration. But my body was like a harp and her words and gestures were like fingers running upon the wires.

One evening I went into the back drawing room in which the priest had died. It was a dark rainy evening and there was no sound in the house. Through one of the broken panes I heard the rain impinge upon the earth, the fine incessant needles of water playing in the sodden beds. Some distant lamp or lighted window gleamed below me. I was thankful that I could see so little. All my senses seemed to desire to veil themselves and, feeling that I was about to

slip from them, I pressed the palms of my hands together until they trembled, murmuring: *"O love! O love!"* many times.

At last she spoke to me. When she addressed the first words to me I was so confused that I did not know what to answer. She asked me was I going to *Araby.* I forget whether I answered yes or no. It would be a splendid bazaar, she said; she would love to go.

"And why can't you?" I asked.

While she spoke she turned a silver bracelet round and round her wrist. She could not go, she said, because there would be a retreat[4] that week in her convent.[5] Her brother and two other boys were fighting for their caps and I was alone at the railings. She held one of the spikes, bowing her head towards me. The light from the lamp opposite our door caught the white curve of her neck, lit up her hair that rested there and, falling, lit up the hand upon the railing. It fell over one side of her dress and caught the white border of a petticoat, just visible as she stood at ease.

"It's well for you," she said.

"If I go," I said, "I will bring you something."

What innumerable follies laid waste my waking and sleeping thoughts after that evening! I wished to annihilate the tedious intervening days. I chafed against the work of school. At night in my bedroom and by day in the classroom her image came between me and the page I strove to read. The syllables of the word *Araby* were called to me through the silence in which my soul luxuriated and cast an Eastern enchantment over me. I asked for leave to go to the bazaar on Saturday night. My aunt was surprised and hoped it was not some Freemason[6] affair. I answered few questions in

---

3. come-all-you . . . Rossa: The opening of a ballad about an Irish hero.

4. retreat *n.*: A period of retirement or seclusion for prayer, religious study, and meditation.
5. convent *n.*: A school run by an order of nuns.
6. Freemason: The Free and Accepted Masons, an international secret society.

Grammar in Action

One of the uses of the **semicolon** is to join independent clauses that could be joined by a conjunction *(and, but, for, nor, or, so, or yet)*. Joyce uses the semicolon correctly in the following sentence.

> It would be a splendid bazaar, she said; she would love to go.

He might have written:

> It would be a splendid bazaar, she said, and she would love to go.

class. I watched my master's face pass from amiability to sternness; he hoped I was not beginning to idle. I could not call my wandering thoughts together. I had hardly any patience with the serious work of life which, now that it stood between me and my desire, seemed to me child's play, ugly monotonous child's play.

On Saturday morning I reminded my uncle that I wished to go to the bazaar in the evening. He was fussing at the hallstand, looking for the hat brush, and answered me curtly:

"Yes, boy, I know."

As he was in the hall I could not go into the front parlor and lie at the window. I left the house in bad humor and walked slowly toward the school. The air was pitilessly raw and already my heart misgave me.

When I came home to dinner my uncle had not yet been home. Still it was early. I sat staring at the clock for some time and, when its ticking began to irritate me, I left the room. I mounted the staircase and gained the upper part of the house. The high cold empty gloomy rooms liberated me and I went from room to room singing. From the front window I saw my companions playing below in the street. Their cries reached me weakened and indistinct and, leaning my forehead against the cool glass, I looked over at the dark house where she lived. I may have stood there for an hour, seeing nothing but the brown-clad figure cast by my imagination, touched discreetly by the lamplight at the curved neck, at the hand upon the railings and at the border below the dress.

When I came downstairs again I found Mrs. Mercer sitting at the fire. She was an old garrulous woman, a pawnbroker's widow, who collected used stamps for some pious purpose. I had to endure the gossip of the tea table. The meal was prolonged beyond an hour and still my uncle did not come. Mrs. Mercer stood up to go: she was sorry she couldn't wait any longer, but it was after eight o'clock and she did not like to be out late, as the night air was bad for her. When she had gone I began to walk up and down the room, clenching my fists. My aunt said:

"I'm afraid you may put off your bazaar for this night of Our Lord."

At nine o'clock I heard my uncle's latchkey in the hall door. I heard him talking to himself and heard the hallstand rocking when it had received the weight of his overcoat. I could interpret these signs. When he was midway through his dinner I asked him to give me the money to go to the bazaar. He had forgotten.

"The people are in bed and after their first sleep now," he said.

I did not smile. My aunt said to him energetically:

"Can't you give him the money and let him go? You've kept him late enough as it is."

My uncle said he was very sorry he had forgotten. He said he believed in the old saying: *All work and no play makes Jack a dull boy.* He asked me where I was going and, when I had told him a second time he asked me did I know *The Arab's Farewell to His Steed.*[7] When I left the kitchen he was about to recite the opening lines of the piece to my aunt.

I held a florin[8] tightly in my hand as I strode down Buckingham Street toward the station. The sight of the streets thronged with buyers and glaring with gas recalled to me the purpose of my journey. I took my seat in a third-class carriage of a deserted train. After an intolerable delay the train moved out of the station slowly. It crept onward among ruinous houses and over the twinkling river. At Westland Row Station a crowd of people pressed to the carriage doors; but the porters moved them back, saying that it was a special train for the bazaar. I remained alone in the bare car-

---

7. The Arab's . . . His Steed: A popular nineteenth-century poem.
8. florin *n.*: A former two-shilling coin.

He might even have written:

It would be a splendid bazaar, she said. She would love to go.

This last sentence implies a rule for using the semicolon to connect independent clauses: Use a semicolon where a period could be used. When trying to decide between a period and a semicolon, ask yourself, "Do these two clauses really amount to a single two-part statement?" If you answer yes, you can use a semicolon.

Student Activity. Look at each of the following pairs or groups of clauses, and decide whether a period or a semicolon is the more appropriate punctuation mark.

1. He swims well in fact, he is a state champion
2. He swims well I, however, have no interest in swimming
3. We gobbled down the cheese we gobbled down the Swedish meatballs we gobbled down the potato salad
4. We were so starved that we ate all the food we could find later, our stomachs didn't feel too well
5. I wish I were at the beach maybe next week I'll get there

15 Clarification The narrator was in such a hurry that he went in at a regular entrance, rather than paying a child's fare, which was much cheaper.

16 Discussion The narrator still uses religious imagery to express his romantic feelings, this time comparing the bazaar to a church. What is the irony of this comparison?

17 Discussion How did the bazaar differ from the narrator's expectations? What side of the bazaar —and life—did the boy confront that night? What does this confrontation make him realize?

18 Literary Focus How does the narrator's moment of epiphany make him feel at the time? How does it make him feel as he recalls it? What does this story tell you about the nature of literary epiphanies?

Reader's Response Do you agree with Joyce that people can experience sudden moments of insight into their motivation and nature? Explain.

---

riage. In a few minutes the train drew up beside an improvised wooden platform. I passed out onto the road and saw by the lighted dial of a clock that it was ten minutes to ten. In front of me was a large building which displayed the magical name.

15 I could not find any sixpenny entrance and, fearing that the bazaar would be closed, I passed in quickly through a turnstile, handing a shilling to a weary-looking man. I found myself in a big hall girdled at half its height by a gallery. Nearly all the stalls were closed and the greater part of the hall was in darkness. I recognized a silence like that which pervades a church after a service. I walked into the center of the bazaar timidly. A few people were gathered about the stalls which were still open. Before a curtain, over which the words *Café Chantant*[9] were written in colored lamps, **16**
17 two men were counting money on a salver.[10] I listened to the fall of the coins.

Remembering with difficulty why I had come I went over to one of the stalls and examined porcelain vases and flowered tea sets. At the door of the stall a young lady was talking and laughing with two young gentlemen. I remarked their English accents and listened vaguely to their conversation.

---

9. Café Chantant: A café with musical entertainment.
10. salver *n.*: A tray usually used for the presentation of letters or visiting cards.

"O, I never said such a thing!"
"O, but you did!"
"O, but I didn't!"
"Didn't she say that?"
"Yes. I heard her."
"O, there's a . . .fib!"

Observing me the young lady came over and asked me did I wish to buy anything. The tone of her voice was not encouraging; she seemed to have spoken to me out of a sense of duty. I looked humbly at the great jars that stood like Eastern guards at either side of the dark entrance to the stall and murmured:

"No, thank you."

The young lady changed the position of one of the vases and went back to the two young men. They began to talk of the same subject. Once or twice the young lady glanced at me over her shoulder.

I lingered before her stall, though I knew my stay was useless, to make my interest in her wares seem the more real. Then I turned away slowly and walked down the middle of the bazaar. I allowed the two pennies to fall against the sixpence in my pocket. I heard a voice call from one end of the gallery that the light was out. The upper part of the hall was now completely dark.

Gazing up into the darkness I saw myself as a creature driven and derided by vanity; and my eyes burned with anguish and anger. **18**

THINKING ABOUT THE SELECTION

Recalling

1. (a) What does the narrator feel toward Mangan's sister? (b) What are her first words to him?
2. (a) Why is going to the bazaar so important to the narrator? (b) Why is he late getting there?
(c) What does he buy?
3. How does the narrator feel at the end of the story?

Interpreting

4. How would you describe the mood, or feeling, established in the opening paragraphs?
5. What might have been the author's reason for

Closure and Extension

ANSWERS TO THINKING ABOUT THE SELECTION
Recalling

1. (a) She is his first love; his feelings towards her have a religious fervor to them. (b) She asks if he is going to the bazaar, Araby.

2. (a) He sees it as almost a religious pilgrimage from which he will bring his love a splendid gift. (b) He is late getting to the bazaar because his uncle, to whom the bazaar means nothing, forgets to give him the money for it. (c) The narrator buys nothing at the bazaar, because he suddenly realizes how foolish his romantic aspirations are.

3. (a) He feels silly, his pride is hurt, and he is angry for having put himself in a ridiculous position.

6. What makes the narrator feel as he does at the end of the story?
7. (a) Why do you think the author chose "Araby" as a name for the bazaar? (b) As a title for the story? (c) How does it relate to the narrator's experiences?

Applying

8. (a) Look up the meaning of the word *vanity*. Which meaning is intended in the last paragraph of this story? (b) Do you agree with the narrator that he is a "creature driven and derided by vanity"? Support your answer. (c) Do you think vanity is or is not necessary to some degree for survival in today's world? Explain your answer.

ANALYZING LITERATURE
Understanding Epiphany

Epiphany is the sudden recognition of an important truth by a character in a work of fiction. Tracing back to Greek mythology where it referred to the sudden disclosure to one character of a deity's identity, epiphany in contemporary fiction is the unmasking of a truth that was present all along in a character's mind. In the short stories of James Joyce, this truth usually relates to the essential nature of something commonplace—a person, situation, or object —that the character now sees in a new light.
1. Where in "Araby" does the epiphany occur?
2. What does the hero suddenly realize?
3. What suddenly causes him to feel this way?

CRITICAL THINKING AND READING
Analyzing Joyce's Attitude

It is important to keep in mind that, as with many stories told from the first-person point of view, the narrator of "Araby" is not the author. Yet as with any such story, the author expresses his attitude toward the character of the narrator through the character's words, thoughts, and actions. Read the following quotes from "Araby." Tell what they reveal, as a whole, about Joyce's attitude toward his narrator's romantic goals.
1. "Every morning I lay on the floor in the parlor watching her door." (page 987)
2. "Her image accompanied me even in places the most hostile to romance." (page 988)
3. "Her name sprang to my lips at moments in strange prayers. . . ." (page 988)
4. "'If I go,' I said, 'I will bring you something.'" (page 988)

UNDERSTANDING LANGUAGE
Appreciating Image-Making Words

An **image** is a word that appeals to the senses. Joyce is widely recognized as a master of imagery, and "Araby" amply demonstrates why. Identify which words help make each of the following images so vivid, and name the sense or senses to which the image appeals.
1. "The cold air stung us and we played till our bodies glowed." (page 987)
2. ". . . we ran . . . [to] the dark dripping gardens where odors rose from ashpits, to the dark odorous stables where a coachman smoothed and combed the horse or shook music from the buckled harness." (page 987)
3. "Her dress swung as she moved her body and the soft rope of her hair tossed from side to side." (page 987)
4. "The . . . streets thronged with buyers and glaring with gas recalled to me the purpose of my journey." (page 989)

THINKING AND WRITING
Writing an Extended Conversation

Choose an episode from the story involving the narrator and Mangan's sister—perhaps when he passes her going to school or when they talk about the bazaar. Imagine an extended conversation between them, giving particular emphasis to what they might say and the way in which they would most likely say it. Record this bit of dialogue, permitting yourself ample time to revise any sections that do not ring true.

Araby 991

(Answers begin on p. 990.)

Challenge Is Joyce sympathetic towards the narrator in "Araby"? How does he want the reader to feel both about the narrator and his experience?

ANSWERS TO ANALYZING LITERATURE

1. The epiphany in "Araby" occurs in the final paragraph.
2. The narrator suddenly realizes that his romantic notion of himself is vanity.
3. Imagining the bazaar as a romantic place, and seeing it in reality "ignites" the epiphany.

ANSWERS TO CRITICAL THINKING AND READING

1-4 The narrator sees and describes the girl in religious terms because they are probably the only ones, brought up Catholic as he was, that he would be familiar with to describe an emotion. He sees himself as her knight-protector. Joyce is spoofing the narrator's adolescent romanticism, but in a very gentle way.

ANSWERS TO UNDERSTANDING LANGUAGE

1. *stung:* touch; *glowed:* sight
2. *dripping:* sight, sound; *rose:* sight; *odorous:* smell; *smoothed:* touch; *combed:* touch
3. *swung:* sight; *moved:* sight; *tossed:* sight
4. *thronged: sight; glaring:* sight

THINKING AND WRITING

Writing Across the Curriculum
You may want some of the groups who reported on Irish history to write up their reports. You might want to inform the history department of the assignment so that they might provide guidance for research.

Interpreting

4. Joyce sets a mood of carefree youth on the verge of adolescence, but the serious and religious side of life—in the guise of the dead priest —is omnipresent.
5. By not naming Mangan's sister, Joyce makes her into a more mysterious, romantic figure—and more symbolic than real.
6. By comparing the reality of the bazaar with his preconceived notions about it, he sees that his devotion to Mangan's sister is silly. He is more in love with his idea of himself in love than he is actually in love with Mangan's sister.
7. (a) *Araby* is an exotic-sounding name that would have excited the imagination of both the boy and other people in the story. (b) The title was probably chosen by Joyce because it mirrors the narrator's concept of himself—that is, *Araby* itself is not as romantic a place as the local people thought it must be. (c) It is by going to the Araby bazaar that the narrator is able to see that his romantic vision of himself is just an illusion.

Applying

8. (a) The intended meaning is "anything or act that is vain, futile, idle, or worthless." (b) The narrator may be overstating the case, though answers to this question may differ. (c) A measure of vanity is probably unavoidable in all people. Whether it is needed for survival is open to debate.

ELIZABETH BOWEN

1899–1973

The fiction of Elizabeth Bowen is distinguished by the author's subtle observation of landscape, by her innovative and believable use of the supernatural, and by her haunting portrayal of England during one of the darkest eras of that country's history—the years between 1939 and 1945.

Bowen was born in Dublin and raised in County Cork, Ireland. She published her first novel, *The Hotel,* in 1927. During the 1930's she perfected her craft and in 1938, on the eve of the Second World War, completed one of her best-known works, *The Death of the Heart.* This novel traces the intertwining loves and fortunes of a group of sophisticated but vulnerable Londoners in the 1930's.

During the war Bowen observed England's hardships keenly and with compassion. The brutal realities of the conflict—air raids, blackouts, and espionage—were incorporated into some of her best short stories. Typically she played on the heightening of emotions and perceptions in wartime to probe the inner workings of her characters' minds. Shortly after the end of the war Bowen published another novel, *The Heat of the Day* (1949), which was received with much acclaim. Set in wartime London, the work movingly juxtaposes a tragic love affair with the larger national dilemma of a country's fight for its survival.

After the war, Bowen widened her literary activities to include literary criticism and book reviews for such journals as the *Tatler,* as well as scripts for the British Broadcasting Company. She was honored by her own country in 1948, when she received a prestigious award, the C.B.E. (Commander, Order of the British Empire). During the 1950's she spent a great deal of time in the United States, writing and lecturing.

After the death of her husband in 1952, Bowen returned to Ireland to live. Although her earlier work was influenced by the psychological realism of Henry James, her later novels—*A World of Love* (1955), *The Little Girls* (1964), and *Eva Trout* (1969)—exhibit a more symbolic, more poetic style. Bowen never fully adopted the stream-of-consciousness technique practiced by her contemporaries, Virginia Woolf and James Joyce. Yet readers may easily sense more than a trace of this technique in Bowen's novels and stories—such is her sensitivity to fine shades of emotion and her eye for small but important detail.

Bowen defined the novel as the "non-poetic statement of poetic truth," and in her straightforward, deceptively simple writing style and exploration of complex human relationships, she achieved this literary integrity and verisimilitude.

992   *The Modern Period*

GUIDE FOR INTERPRETING

The Demon Lover

Historical Context

War and the Ghost Story. Despite the number of times humans have waged warfare on one another throughout history, war has never, happily, become a natural state of affairs for the species. The unnaturalness of a civilization in wartime is especially evident off the battlefield, in the streets of a city. Here the horrors that attend war—loss of life, destruction of property, suffering, fear, and despair—seem ever so much like the work of a band of demonic spirits. The Second World War, in particular, struck individuals living in the war-ravaged cities of Europe as akin to a nightmare. Warning sirens and blackouts were a part of everyday life; whole communities were sometimes evacuated against the danger of an enemy attack, leaving street after street of deserted buildings. These "ghost towns" within metropolises like London impressed some writers as ideal backdrops for stories that deal in events of the supernatural, or ghost stories. One such writer was Elizabeth Bowen, who sought in "The Demon Lover" to pit the horrifying landscape of the battlefield against the still more horrifying landscape closer to home.

Commentary

"The Demon Lover" is, in part, a subtle reworking of an English ballad of the same name. In the ballad a faithless, fickle woman betrays her absent lover and marries another man. When the lover returns years later—now supposedly very wealthy—the woman is quick to abandon her husband and children to run off with him. Too late, she discovers that the lover is, in fact, not at all what she imagined. On a superficial level, Bowen's story resembles the ballad, and one critic, Douglas A. Hughes, has remarked that the author even relies on the poem to suggest how the story's main character, Mrs. Drover, views herself. But Bowen's genius in this story lies partly in the way she refashions the ballad's basic plot and terrifying atmosphere to suggest important things about the effect of war's devastation on the human psyche. In a recent study of Elizabeth Bowen, critic Allan E. Austin wrote that "'The Demon Lover' is a ghost story that builds up and then culminates like an Alfred Hitchcock movie."

Writing

Imagine that a mysterious letter or other piece of mail is delivered to your home. In a brief narrative, describe the specific contents of the letter, as well as your and your family's reaction to it. Conclude your account with an explanation of how the mystery was resolved.

Literary Focus Have students discuss works in which a war setting is used. Suggest *The Red Badge of Courage, All Quiet on the Western Front, War and Peace, The Guns of Navarone, Gunga Din, The Bridge on the River Kwai, The Bridges at Toko-Ri, Mother Courage,* or *A Tale of Two Cities* if they need ideas.

Writing/Prior Knowledge You may want the class to brainstorm ideas for the type of letter this might be and then let students come up with their own solutions to the mystery.

Vocabulary

Preteach the following vocabulary words:
parquet (pär kā′) *n.:* Wooden floors (p. 994)
escritoire (es′ krə twär′) *n.:* Ornamental writing desk (p. 994)
spectral (spek′ trəl) *adj.:* Ghostly (p. 996)
arboreal (är bôr′ ē əl) *adj.:* Situated near or among trees (p. 997)
circumscribed (sʉr′ kəm skrīb'd′) *adj.:* Limited; confined (p. 997)
weal (wēl) *n.:* Discolored ridge on the skin; blister (p. 998)
aperture (ap′ ər chr) *n.:* Opening (p. 999)

The Demon Lover

Elizabeth Bowen

Toward the end of her day in London Mrs. Drover went round to her shut-up house to look for several things she wanted to take away. Some belonged to herself, some to her family, who were by now used to their country life. It was late August; it had been a steamy, showery day: at the moment the trees down the pavement glittered in an escape of humid yellow afternoon sun. Against the next batch of clouds, already piling up ink-dark, broken chimneys and parapets stood out. In her once familiar street, as in any unused channel, an unfamiliar queerness had silted up; a cat wove itself in and out of railings, but no human eye watched Mrs. Drover's return. Shifting some parcels under her arm, she slowly forced round her latchkey in an unwilling lock, then gave the door, which had warped, a push with her knee. Dead air came out to meet her as she went in.

The staircase window having been boarded up, no light came down into the hall. But one door, she could just see, stood ajar, so she went quickly through into the room and unshuttered the big window in there. Now the prosaic woman, looking about her, was more perplexed than she knew by everything that she saw, by traces of her long former habit of life—the yellow smoke stain up the white marble mantelpiece, the ring left by a vase on the top of the escritoire;[1] the bruise in the wallpaper where, on the door being thrown open widely, the china handle had always hit the wall. The piano, having gone away to be stored, had left what looked like claw marks on its part of the parquet.[2] Though not much dust had seeped in, each object wore a film of another kind; and, the only ventilation being the chimney, the whole drawing room smelled of the cold hearth. Mrs. Drover put down her parcels on the escritoire and left the room to proceed upstairs; the things she wanted were in a bedroom chest.

She had been anxious to see how the house was—the part-time caretaker she shared with some neighbors was away this week on his holiday, known to be not yet back. At the best of times he did not look in often, and she was never sure that she trusted him. There were some cracks in the structure, left by the last bombing, on which she was anxious to keep an eye. Not that one could do anything—

A shaft of refracted daylight now lay across the hall. She stopped dead and stared at the hall table—on this lay a letter addressed to her.

She thought first—then the caretaker *must* be back. All the same, who, seeing the house shuttered, would have dropped a letter in at the box? It was not a circular, it was not a bill. And the post office redirected, to the address in the country, everything for her that came through the post. The care-

---

1. **escritoire** (es′ krə twär′) *n.*: A writing desk or table.

2. **parquet** (pär kā′) *n.*: A flooring of inlaid woodwork in geometric forms.

taker (even if he *were* back) did not know she was due in London today—her call here had been planned to be a surprise—so his negligence in the manner of this letter, leaving it to wait in the dusk and the dust, annoyed her. Annoyed, she picked up the letter, which bore no stamp. But it cannot be important, or they would know . . . She took the letter rapidly upstairs with her, without a stop to look at the writing till she reached what had been her bedroom, where she let in light. The room looked over the garden and other gardens: the sun had gone in; as the clouds sharpened and lowered, the trees and rank lawns seemed already to smoke with dark. Her reluctance to look again at the letter came from the fact that she felt intruded upon—and by someone contemptuous of her ways. However, in the tenseness preceding the fall of rain she read it: it was a few lines.

DEAR KATHLEEN,

You will not have forgotten that today is our anniversary, and the day we said. The years have gone by at once slowly and fast. In view of the fact that nothing has changed, I shall rely upon you to keep your promise. I was sorry to see you leave London, but was satisfied that you would be back in time. You may expect me, therefore, at the hour arranged.

Until then . . . K.

Mrs. Drover looked for the date: it was today's. She dropped the letter onto the bedsprings, then picked it up to see the writing again—her lips, beneath the remains of lipstick, beginning to go white. She felt so much the change in her own face that

HOLY BUSH HILL, HAMPSTEAD, 1921
Ethelbert White

9
10
11,
12
13
14
15

9 Clarification A *jumper* is a British word for "a pullover sweater." Be on the lookout for other unfamiliar British usages of commonly used English words.

10 Literary Focus Ask volunteers if they know what literary device is used in the next section. Discuss how flashbacks are used in movies as well as literature.

11 Literary Focus Note that this flashback takes place during World War I and that the rest of the story takes place in the middle of World War II. Ask students what they think the significance of these two time periods is in the story.

12 Discussion What are the sinister aspects of Mrs. Drover's final parting from her fiancé? What does this parting tell the reader about her lover? What do his words indicate about him?

13 Reading Strategy The reader is never told exactly what promise the fiancé extracts from Mrs. Drover? Why? What do you think that promise is?

14 Critical Thinking and Reading Discuss with students what "plight a troth" means. Ask when this archaic term is most commonly used. Ask how the use of the phrase is ironic in the story.

15 Discussion What was her reaction to her fiancé's death? Why do you think "she failed to attract men . . ." Why was marrying Mr. Drover such a relief to her?

she went to the mirror, polished a clear patch in it and looked at once urgently and stealthily in. She was confronted by a woman of forty-four, with eyes starting out under a hatbrim that had been rather carelessly pulled down. She had not put on any more powder since she left the shop where she ate her solitary tea. The pearls her husband had given her on their marriage hung loose round her now rather thinner throat, slipping into the V of the pink wool jumper her sister knitted last autumn as they sat round the fire. Mrs. Drover's most normal expression was one of controlled worry, but of assent. Since the birth of the third of her little boys, attended by a quite serious illness, she had had an intermittent muscular flicker to the left of her mouth, but in spite of this she could always sustain a manner that was at once energetic and calm.

Turning from her own face as precipitately as she had gone to meet it, she went to the chest where the things were, unlocked it, threw up the lid and knelt to search. But as rain began to come crashing down she could not keep from looking over her shoulder at the stripped bed on which the letter lay. Behind the blanket of rain the clock of the church that still stood struck six—with rapidly heightening apprehension she counted each of the slow strokes. "The hour arranged . . . My God," she said, "*What* hour? How should I . . . ? After twenty-five years. . . ."

The young girl talking to the soldier in the garden had not ever completely seen his face. It was dark; they were saying goodbye under a tree. Now and then—for it felt, from not seeing him at this intense moment, as though she had never seen him at all—she verified his presence for these few moments longer by putting out a hand, which he each time pressed, without very much kindness, and painfully, on to one of the breast buttons of his uniform. That cut of the button on the palm of her hand was, principally, what she was to carry away. This was so near the end of a leave from France that she could only wish him already gone. It was August 1916. Being not kissed, being drawn away from and looked at intimidated Kathleen till she imagined spectral glitters in the place of his eyes. Turning away and looking back up the lawn she saw, through branches of trees, the drawing-room window alight; she caught a breath for the moment when she could go running back there into the safe arms of her mother and sister, and cry: "What shall I do, what shall I do? He has gone."

Hearing her catch her breath, her fiancé said, without feeling: "Cold?"

"You're going away such a long way."

"Not so far as you think."

"I don't understand?"

"You don't have to," he said. "You will. You know what we said."

"But that was—suppose you—I mean, suppose."

"I shall be with you," he said, "sooner or later. You won't forget that. You need do nothing but wait."

Only a little more than a minute later she was free to run up the silent lawn. Looking in through the window at her mother and sister, who did not for the moment perceive her, she already felt that unnatural promise drive down between her and the rest of all humankind. No other way of having given herself could have made her feel so apart, lost and foresworn. She could not have plighted a more sinister troth.

Kathleen behaved well when, some months later, her fiancé was reported missing, presumed killed. Her family not only supported her but were able to praise her courage without stint because they could not regret, as a husband for her, the man they knew almost nothing about. They hoped she would, in a year or two, console herself—and had it been only a question of consolation things might have gone much straighter ahead. But her trouble, behind just a little grief, was a complete dislocation

Grammar in Action

When writing **dialogue,** use quotation marks around each speaker's words and begin a new paragraph with each change of speaker. Elizabeth Bowen demonstrates the correct style for dialogue.

Hearing her catch her breath, her fiance said, without feeling: "Cold?"

"You're going away such a long way."

"Not so far as you think."

"I don't understand?"

"You don't have to," he said. "You will. You know what we said."

Notice that by changing paragraphs as the speakers change, Bowen could leave out *he said* and *she said* without confusing the reader. Notice also that periods, commas, and question marks are from everything. She did not reject other lovers, for these failed to appear: for years she failed to attract men—and with the approach of her thirties she became natural enough to share her family's anxiousness on this score. She began to put herself out, to wonder; and at thirty-two she was very greatly relieved to find herself being courted by William Drover. She married him, and the two of them settled down in this quiet, arboreal part of Kensington; in this house the years piled up, her children were born and they all lived till they were driven out by the bombs of the next war. Her movements as Mrs. Drover were circumscribed, and she dismissed any idea that they were still watched.

As things were—dead or living the letter writer sent her only a threat. Unable, for some minutes, to go on kneeling with her back exposed to the empty room, Mrs. Drover rose from the chest to sit on an upright chair whose back was firmly against the wall. The desuetude of her former bedroom, her married London home's whole air of being a cracked cup from which memory, with its reassuring power, had either evaporated or leaked away, made a crisis—and at just this crisis the letter writer had, knowledgeably, struck. The hollowness of the house this evening canceled years on years of voices, habits and steps. Through the shut windows she only heard rain fall on the roofs around. To rally herself, she said she was in a mood—and, for two or three seconds shutting her eyes, told herself that she had imagined the letter. But she opened them—there it lay on the bed.

On the supernatural side of the letter's entrance she was not permitting her mind to dwell. Who, in London, knew she meant to call at the house today? Evidently, however, this had been known. The caretaker, *had* he come back, had had no cause to expect her: he would have taken the letter in his pocket, to forward it, at his own time, through the post. There was no other sign that the caretaker had been in—but, if not?

OX HOUSE, SHAFTESBURY, 1932
John R. Biggs

Letters dropped in at doors of deserted houses do not fly or walk to tables in halls. They do not sit on the dust of empty tables with the air of certainty that they will be found. There is needed some human hand—but nobody but the caretaker had a key. Under circumstances she did not care to consider, a house can be entered without a key. It was possible that she was not alone now. She might be being waited for, downstairs. Waited for—until when? Until "the hour arranged." At least that was not six o'clock; six has struck.

She rose from the chair and went over and locked the door.

The thing was, to get out. To fly? No, not that: she had to catch her train. As a woman whose utter dependability was the keystone of her family life she was not willing to

Humanities Notes

Wood engraving, *Ox House, Shaftesbury*, 1932, John R. Biggs. In this black-and-white wood block print, the artist John R. Biggs has used the medium effectively to create a scene of haunting quiet. The darkened room with an eerie light shining through the open door creates the feeling of a mysterious presence.

Consider these questions for discussion:
1. What is the mood of this scene?
2. How might this scene relate to the house in "The Demon Lover"?
3. Is this print an effective illustration for "The Demon Lover"? Explain.

16 Literary Focus How had the letter writer used the circumstances of the war and Mrs. Drover's psychological state against her?

17 Literary Focus What kind of figure of speech is this? What does it mean in the story and why is its use here so powerful?

18 Discussion How does Mrs. Drover's practicality—her "prosaicness"—work against her?

placed inside the quotation marks, and that the expression *he said* is placed outside them.

Student Activity. Write a passage of dialogue that reproduces a conversation such as you might have with an acquaintance. Follow the rules for writing dialogue as Bowen's passage illustrates them.

19 Discussion What do "the complete suspension of her existence" and the fact that she cannot remember his face tell about the fiancé? How does revealing only a little bit at a time about the fiancé affect the story?

20 Reading Strategy What figure of speech is used here and why is it so powerful? In the flashback, the author mentions that Mrs. Drover never clearly saw the fiancé's face. Watch for other references to his face to see how they tie together.

21 Discussion What was the draft that Mrs. Drover felt?

22 Literary Focus How does the atmosphere of war-torn London effect Mrs. Drover's state of mind?

23 Discussion Discuss how the events associated with the taxi heighten the tension to the story's climax when Mrs. Drover screams. Why does she scream?

Reader's Response Why do you think people enjoy reading ghost stories like this one?

return to the country, to her husband, her little boys and her sister, without the objects she had come up to fetch. Resuming work at the chest she set about making up a number of parcels in a rapid, fumbling-decisive way. These, with her shopping parcels, would be too much to carry; these meant a taxi—at the thought of the taxi her heart went up and her normal breathing resumed. I will ring up the taxi now; the taxi cannot come too soon; I shall hear the taxi out there running its engine, till I walk calmly down to it through the hall. I'll ring up—But no: the telephone is cut off . . . She tugged at a knot she had tied wrong.

The idea of flight . . . He was never kind to me, not really. I don't remember him kind at all. Mother said he never considered me. He was set on me, that was what it was —not love. Not love, not meaning a person well. What did he do, to make me promise like that? I can't remember—But she found that she could.

She remembered with such dreadful acuteness that the twenty-five years since then dissolved like smoke and she instinctively looked for the weal left by the button on the palm of her hand. She remembered not only all that he said and did but the complete suspension of *her* existence during that August week. I was not myself —they all told me so at the time. She remembered—but with one white burning blank as where acid has dropped on a photograph: *under no conditions* could she remember his face.

So wherever he may be waiting, I shall not know him. You have no time to run from a face you do not expect.

The thing was to get to the taxi before any clock struck what could be the hour. She would slip down the street and round the side of the square to where the square gave on the main road. She would return in the taxi, safe, to her own door, and bring the solid driver into the house with her to pick up the parcels from room to room. The idea

of the taxi driver made her decisive, bold; she unlocked her door, went to the top of the staircase and listened down.

She heard nothing—but while she was hearing nothing the *passé*[3] air of the staircase was disturbed by a draft that traveled up to her face. It emanated from the basement: down there a door or window was being opened by someone who chose this moment to leave the house.

The rain had stopped; the pavements steamily shone as Mrs. Drover let herself out by inches from her own front door into the empty street. The unoccupied houses opposite continued to meet her look with their damaged stare. Making toward the thoroughfare and the taxi, she tried not to keep looking behind. Indeed, the silence was so intense—one of those creeks of London silence exaggerated this summer by the damage of war—that no tread could have gained on hers unheard. Where her street debouched on the square where people went on living, she grew conscious of, and checked, her unnatural pace. Across the open end of the square two buses impassively passed each other; women, a perambulator,[4] cyclists, a man wheeling a barrow signalized, once again, the ordinary flow of life. At the square's most populous corner should be—and was—the short taxi rank. This evening, only one taxi—but this, although it presented its blank rump, appeared already to be alertly waiting for her. Indeed, without looking round the driver started his engine as she panted up from behind and put her hand on the door. As she did so, the clock struck seven. The taxi faced the main road. To make the trip back to her house it would have to turn—she had settled back on the seat and the taxi *had* turned before she, surprised by its knowing movement, recollected that she had not "said where." She leaned forward to scratch

---

3. **passé** (pa sä´) *adj.*: Stale.
4. **perambulator:** A baby carriage.

Closure and Extension

ANSWERS TO THINKING ABOUT THE SELECTION
Recalling

1. (a) The story takes place during World War II in London. (b) Mrs. Drover visits her house to pick up some things for her family, who are now living in the countryside to escape the bombing of London.

at the glass panel that divided the driver's head from her own.

The driver braked to what was almost a stop, turned round and slid the glass panel back. The jolt of this flung Mrs. Drover forward till her face was almost into the glass. Through the aperture driver and passenger, not six inches between them, remained for an eternity eye to eye. Mrs. Drover's mouth hung open for some seconds before she could issue her first scream. After that she continued to scream freely and to beat with her gloved hands on the glass all round as the taxi, accelerating without mercy, made off with her into the hinterland of deserted streets.

THINKING ABOUT THE SELECTION

Recalling

1. (a) Where and when does the story take place? (b) Why does Mrs. Drover visit her house in London?
2. (a) Who has written the letter Mrs. Drover discovers? (b) Why is she so upset by it?
3. (a) How does Mrs. Drover plan to escape from the house? (b) Does she succeed in her plan? Explain.

Interpreting

4. In the first paragraph the narrator remarks that "no human eye watched Mrs. Drover's return" to her house? In what way is this remark ironic?
5. (a) What words does the author use to describe Mrs. Drover's reaction to the letter? (b) What feelings do you think the author hoped this description would prompt in the reader?
6. One of the strengths of this short story is its ambiguity. Provide both a supernatural and a rational explanation for (a) the letter, and (b) the cab driver's knowing in which direction to take his passenger before she has spoken up.
7. Why do you think the author devotes so much space to Mrs. Drover's thought processes following the flashback?
8. What do you think is Mrs. Drover's ultimate fate? Explain the basis for your answer.

Applying

9. The story seems to be suggesting that one of the most damaging effects of war is the psychological vulnerability it produces in human beings? Do you agree? Defend your opinion.

ANALYZING LITERATURE

Considering War and the Ghost Story

The devastation that was war-torn London —shells of bombed-out dwellings facing empty streets, periods of blackout, the roar of airplane engines in the sky—provides a choice setting for a story involving the presence of a ghostlike figure. In fact, for the people who lived during that era, the specter was very real, lurking in every darkened doorway and known variously by the names of fear, desperation, and grief. Consider the following war-related details in "The Demon Lover," and explain how each in its own turn adds to the terror the reader feels on the part of Mrs. Drover.
1. The empty house in which the Drovers had lived
2. The break in the routine of mail delivery
3. The prospect of never knowing the fate of a loved one reported "missing in action"
4. The blocks of deserted streets in an evacuated neighborhood

The Demon Lover 999

edge is the presence of the ghostly lover. Rational explanations will differ, though students should support their opinions by reference to specific details of the story.
7. By devoting so much space to Mrs. Drover's thinking after the flashback, the reader sees her first rejecting the idea of who the letter writer could be and then coming to the slow realization of who it had to be. The reader also sees her plans to escape and how her own personality helps trap her (her unwillingness to run then and her insistence that she complete the task for which she came). It also increases the tension and suspense because the reader realizes that she doesn't know what he looks like.
8. One interpretation of Mrs. Drover's ultimate fate is that she goes to be the bride of her demon lover. However, if one prefers the psychological approach, it is that she has a nervous breakdown brought on by the war.

Applying

9. Suggested response: It is hard to say which is a worse consequence of war, psychological or physical suffering and damage. Death and destruction of property are terrible things, but the nightmares and psychological damage done to people are no less horrible than death.

ANSWERS TO ANALYZING LITERATURE

1. The empty house, deserted like many houses during the war by Londoners who feared the German bombing, seemed unnatural to Mrs. Drover. It is deserted in the way many "haunted" houses are.
2. The fact that her mail has been rerouted to the house in the country is one of the reasons that she has difficulty figuring out how the letter could have gotten there. The war has caused confusion in even this simple part of life.
3. Not knowing the fate of loved ones is a part of the uncertainty of war that sets the mood of the story.
4. The blocks of deserted streets give the impression of a ghost town —an unnatural setting for a residential neighborhood in London.

2. (a) The letter was written by Mrs. Drover's World War I fiancé. (b) Her fiancé died in the war—if indeed he was ever alive—and had gotten from her some sort of promise, complete with date and hour, to be reunited with him, no matter what happened to him.
3. (a) She plans to escape by leaving the house and returning with a taxi driver to carry her bundles, so she won't be vulnerable to the letter writer. (b) She does not succeed in her plan because the letter writer leaves the house before she does and poses as a taxi driver.

Interpreting

4. The phrase "no human eye watched Mrs. Drover's return" is ironic because an inhuman eye watches her. However, one only sees that this is the author's meaning as other clues about her fiancé mount up. In fact, the author has cleverly mentioned a cat to divert the reader's attention from what she meant by "inhuman."
5. (a) She "dropped the letter," her lips "[went] white," she "felt so much the change in her own face that she went to the mirror," "heightening apprehension" as she listened to the clock. (b) The author hopes this description will make the reader empathize with Mrs. Drover.
6. (a) and (b) The supernatural explanation for both the letter and the cab driver's apparent foreknowl-

GRAHAM GREENE

1904–

The search for a source of inner peace, launched earlier in the century by such poets as William Butler Yeats and T. S. Eliot, continues up through our own time in the novels and short stories of Graham Greene. A religious convert like Eliot, Greene writes—like Eliot—of pain, fear, despair, and alienation. His conclusion, which again mirrors the poet's, is that the ultimate key to salvation is a belief in God.

Greene was born in the town of Berkhamstead in Hertfordshire and educated at Berkhamstead School, where his father was headmaster. Though his grades were good enough to earn him admission to Oxford, he disliked school, describing it later as his "first impression of hell."

Much of Greene's early working life was spent as a journalist and travel writer. His training in these areas helped him develop the powers of keen observation, sensitivity to atmosphere, and simplicity of language that have become hallmarks of his fictional style. His journey to Mexico in 1938 provided the setting for his best-known novel, *The Power and the Glory* (1940). His trips to Africa resulted in travelogues as well as two novels, *The Heart of the Matter* (1944) and *A Burnt-Out Case* (1961).

Greene is also an author of books for children, an essayist, and an editor, and has enjoyed considerable success writing films and adapting his own stories for the screen. His cinematic work is tied to yet another outlet for his creativity, which Greene has called his "entertainments." These are adventure stories and spy thrillers, often dealing with the secret service and with pursuit. Among these are *Our Man in Havana* (1958) and *The Human Factor* (1978).

Greene's more serious work focuses more on the psychology of human character than on plot. Many of his protagonists are people without roots or beliefs—people in pain. They come across as real and believable individuals in whom good and evil, weakness and strength are intermingled. Though the characters in a Greene story often provide the reader with little reason for finding them likable, they almost always excite the reader's curiosity and pity—and, almost always, their author treats them with compassion.

The settings for Greene's fiction are usually hot, decaying, and poorly governed places, like the border town in "Across the Bridge." These parched, crumbling landscapes, presented to us in vivid detail, represent the distressed condition of a key character's troubled soul.

GUIDE FOR INTERPRETING

Across the Bridge

Writer's Technique

Theme and Point of View. Theme is the central idea of a work of literature. The theme of a work should not be confused with its subject, which can often be summed up in a single word or phrase, such as *love of money*. Rather, the theme is a commentary on the subject and is presented in the form of a statement: for example, *The love of money is the root of all evil*. Of the many fiction elements that bear on a work's theme, one of the most critical is point of view, or vantage point from which the events of the story are related. By choosing a first-person point of view—telling the story, that is, from the vantage point of "I" or "we"—an author creates an illusion of immediacy, which adds emphasis to certain themes. The theme suggested by the events described in "Across the Bridge," for example, comes home to the reader with special force, partly because those events are related by a firsthand observer of them.

Commentary

Graham Greene is among the most private of writers and has always discouraged speculation about his personality. His autobiographical writings discuss his publications, not his personal life, as if the man is created by his work and not the other way around. While he shares a number of characteristics with other writers of his generation—he comes from the English professional classes, his father was the headmaster of a private school, and he was aware of World War I but was too young to fight in it—his playful sense of humor sets him apart. He has been an active practical joker all of his life, a trait reflected in his writing. A surprising number of the characters in his works are named "Greene, as well as "Henry," the name he was christened. The tragic hero in *The Heart of the Matter* is named Henry Scobie; the narrator in *Travels with My Aunt* is Henry Pulling. *Yes and No* includes a character named Henry Privet, "privett" being an evergreen shrub. As with the illustrator Al Hirschfeld who often includes his daughter Nina's name in his cartoons, Greene frequently mentions the color green in his work. Can you find the reference to green in "Across the Bridge"?

Writing

After obtaining the person's permission, observe a friend or family member for an entire day, perhaps over the course of a weekend. Keep a detailed journal on where this person goes and what he or she does. Note any patterns of behavior in which the person engages, as well as any strange moves he or she might make.

Literary Focus Have students compare the point of view used in "Araby," "The Demon Lover," and other works of fiction recently read. How does the point of view affect each of these stories?

Writing/Prior Knowledge Before students begin this assignment, have them read a couple of appropriate newspaper articles for the type of journalistic style they ought to use in their writing. Or, if you have any access to diaries, having them look at a diary of a person's daily activities might also help them with this assignment.

Vocabulary

Preteach the following vocabulary words:
forlorn (fər lôrn′) *adj.:* Unhappy; in a pensive mood (p. 1002)
extradition (eks′ trə dish′ ən) *n.:* Release of an accused person into the custody of one state by another state (p. 1002)
awe (ô) *n.:* Fear mixed with great respect (p. 1004)
colossal (kə läs ′l) *adj.:* Enormous (p. 1005)
ordure (ôr′ jər) *n.:* Waste matter; excrement (p. 1006)

Motivation/Prior Knowledge
Tell students that the main figure in this story is a criminal. With that information, have students attempt to describe the main character of the story. They can draw on what they know about criminals from the movies, the newspapers, or any other source. After they have read the first three paragraphs of the story, have them compare Mr. Calloway with their descriptions of a criminal.

Master Teacher Note For students especially interested in Graham Greene or to whet interest for the story, suggest to students that they see one of the many movies that Greene wrote or that were based on his novels. Suggest *The Third Man, This Gun for Hire,* or the spoof of his spy novels, *Our Man in Havana.*

Purpose-Setting Question Why is it important to know the theme of a story?

1 Reading Strategy How does the first line of the story pique the reader's curiosity? Who is "he"? What do you know about him? How does this way of describing the character further pique the reader's curiosity in him?

2 Literary Focus What is the point of view of the story?

3 Discussion Why are the people of the town fascinated with Mr. Calloway? What did they think of him?

4 Discussion What purpose does the information about the shoeshine boys serve?

5 Literary Focus What is the effect of this simile?

6 Reading Strategy Ask students to describe the two towns in the story. How are they alike? How are they different?

Across the Bridge

Graham Greene

1 "They say he's worth a million," Lucia said. He sat there in the little hot damp Mexican square, a dog at his feet, with an air of immense and forlorn patience. The dog attracted your attention at once; for it was very nearly an English setter, only something had gone wrong with the tail and the feathering. Palms wilted over his head, it was all shade and stuffiness round the bandstand, radios talked loudly in Spanish from the little wooden sheds where they changed your pesos into dollars at a loss. I could tell he didn't understand a word from the way he read his newspaper—as I did **2** myself picking out the words which were like English ones. "He's been here a month," Lucia said. "They turned him out of Guatemala and Honduras."

You couldn't keep any secrets for five hours in this border town. Lucia had only been twenty-four hours in the place, but she knew all about Mr. Joseph Calloway. The only reason I didn't know about him (and I'd been in the place two weeks) was because I couldn't talk the language any more than Mr. Calloway could. There wasn't another soul in the place who didn't know the story—the whole story of the Halling Investment **3** Trust and the proceedings for extradition. Any man doing dusty business in any of the wooden booths in the town is better fitted by long observation to tell Mr. Calloway's tale than I am, except that I was in—literally—at the finish. They all watched the drama proceed with immense interest, sympathy and respect. For, after all, he had a million.

Every once in a while through the long **4** steamy day, a boy came and cleaned Mr. Calloway's shoes: he hadn't the right words to resist them—they pretended not to know his English. He must have had his shoes cleaned the day Lucia and I watched him at least half a dozen times. At midday he took a stroll across the square to the Antonio Bar and had a bottle of beer, the setter sticking to heel as if they were out for a country walk in England (he had, you may remember, one of the biggest estates in Norfolk). After his bottle of beer, he would walk down between the money changers' huts to the Rio Grande[1] and look across the bridge into the United States: people came and went constantly in cars. Then back to the square till lunchtime. He was staying in the best hotel, but you don't get good hotels in this border town: nobody stays in them more than a **5** night. The good hotels were on the other side of the bridge: you could see their electric signs twenty stories high from the little square at night, like lighthouses marking the United States.

You may ask what I'd been doing in so **6** drab a spot for a fortnight. There was no interest in the place for anyone; it was just damp and dust and poverty, a kind of shabby replica of the town across the river: both had squares in the same spots; both had the same number of cinemas. One was cleaner than the other, that was all, and more ex-

---

1. Rio Grande (rē′ ō grand′): River that flows between Mexico and Texas.

pensive, much more expensive. I'd stayed across there a couple of nights waiting for a man a tourist bureau said was driving down from Detroit to Yucatan and would sell a place in his car for some fantastically small figure—twenty dollars, I think it was. I don't know if he existed or was invented by the optimistic half-caste in the agency; anyway, he never turned up and so I waited, not much caring, on the cheap side of the river. It didn't much matter; I was living. One day I meant to give up the man from Detroit and go home or go south, but it was easier not to decide anything in a hurry. Lucia was just waiting for a car going the other way, but she didn't have to wait so long. We waited together and watched Mr. Calloway waiting —for God knows what.

I don't know how to treat this story—it was a tragedy for Mr. Calloway, it was poetic retribution, I suppose, in the eyes of the shareholders he'd ruined with his bogus transactions, and to Lucia and me, at this stage, it was pure comedy—except when he kicked the dog. I'm not a sentimentalist about dogs, I prefer people to be cruel to animals rather than to human beings, but I couldn't help being revolted at the way he'd kick that animal—with a hint of cold-blooded venom, not in anger but as if he were getting even for some trick it had played him a long while ago. That generally happened when he returned from the bridge: it was the only sign of anything resembling emotion he showed. Otherwise he looked a small, set, gentle creature with

7

7 **Discussion** Why does Mr. Calloway kick his dog every day when he returns from the bridge? What did it show about Mr. Calloway? What does the narrator think about his kicking the dog?

8 **Critical Thinking and Reading**
What does the narrator think the dog represents to Calloway? What else might the dog represent to Calloway?

9 **Discussion** This sentence elucidates the townspeople's reaction to Calloway. What did they think about him?

10 **Discussion** What does the policeman whom the narrator meets think about the town? Why is this ironic?

11 **Literary Focus** The narrator can't decide if the story is comedy or tragedy. Ask students why this particular scene is funny. What is the dramatic irony of the scene?

silver hair and a silver moustache, and gold-rimmed glasses, and one gold tooth like a flaw in character.

Lucia hadn't been accurate when she said he'd been turned out of Guatemala and Honduras; he'd left voluntarily when the extradition proceedings seemed likely to go through and moved north. Mexico is still not a very centralized state, and it is possible to get round governors as you can't get round cabinet ministers or judges. And so he waited there on the border for the next move. That earlier part of the story is, I suppose, dramatic, but I didn't watch it and I can't invent what I haven't seen—the long waiting in anterooms, the bribes taken and refused, the growing fear of arrest, and then the flight—in gold-rimmed glasses —covering his tracks as well as he could, but this wasn't finance and he was an amateur at escape. And so he'd washed up here, under my eyes and Lucia's eyes, sitting all day under the bandstand, nothing to read but a Mexican paper, nothing to do but look across the river at the United States, quite unaware, I suppose, that everyone knew everything about him, once a day kicking his dog. Perhaps in its semi-setter way it reminded him too much of the Norfolk estate —though that, too, I suppose, was the reason he kept it.

And the next act again was pure comedy. I hesitate to think what this man worth a million was costing his country as they edged him out from this land and that. Perhaps somebody was getting tired of the business, and careless; anyway, they sent across two detectives, with an old photograph. He'd grown his silvery moustache since that had been taken, and he'd aged a lot, and they couldn't catch sight of him. They hadn't been across the bridge two hours when everybody knew that there were two foreign detectives in town looking for Mr. Calloway—everybody knew, that is to say, except Mr. Calloway, who couldn't talk Spanish. There were plenty of people who could have told him in English, but they

didn't. It wasn't cruelty, it was a sort of awe and respect: like a bull, he was on show, sitting there mournfully in the plaza with his dog, a magnificent spectacle for which we all had ringside seats.

I ran into one of the policemen in the Bar Antonio. He was disgusted; he had had some idea that when he crossed the bridge life was going to be different, so much more color and sun, and—I suspect—love, and all he found were wide mud streets where the nocturnal rain lay in pools, and mangy dogs, smells and cockroaches in his bedroom, and the nearest to love, the open door of the Academia Comercial, where pretty mestizo[2] girls sat all the morning learning to typewrite. Tip-tap-tip-tap-tip—perhaps they had a dream, too—jobs on the other side of the bridge, where life was going to be so much more luxurious, refined and amusing.

We got into conversation; he seemed surprised that I knew who they both were and what they wanted. He said: "We've got information this man Calloway's in town."

"He's knocking around somewhere," I said.

"Could you point him out?"

"Oh, I don't know him by sight," I said.

He drank his beer and thought a while. "I'll go out and sit in the plaza. He's sure to pass sometime."

I finished my beer and went quickly off and found Lucia. I said, "Hurry, we're going to see an arrest." We didn't care a thing about Mr. Calloway, he was just an elderly man who kicked his dog and swindled the poor, and who deserved anything he got. So we made for the plaza; we knew Calloway would be there, but it had never occurred to either of us that the detectives wouldn't recognize him. There was quite a surge of people round the place; all the fruit-sellers and bootblacks in town seemed to have arrived together; we had to force our way through, and there in the little green stuffy

---

2. **mestizo** (mes tē′ zō) adj.: Of Spanish and Indian parentage.

Grammar in Action

Use a **dash** to set apart abrupt changes in thought. It is dramatic punctuation and must be used with purpose. Overusing the dash diminishes its effect and soon becomes a stylistic mannerism. Graham Greene uses the dash in several ways; notice how he sets off abrupt changes here:

We waited together and watched Mr. Calloway waiting—for God knows what.

I was in—literally—at the finish.

"I'd have expected over here there'd have been—you know what I mean—life.

Then they got up—they had a car outside.

Isolating words within dashes calls strong focus to the enclosed words. Notice how much more dramatic Greene's words are than the following:

center of the place, sitting on adjoining seats, were the two plainclothesmen and Mr. Calloway. I've never known the place so silent; everybody was on tiptoe, and the plainclothesmen were staring at the crowd looking for Mr. Calloway, and Mr. Calloway sat on his usual seat staring out over the money-changing booths at the United States.

"It can't go on. It just can't," Lucia said. But it did. It got more fantastic still. Somebody ought to write a play about it. We sat as close as we dared. We were afraid all the time we were going to laugh. The semi-setter scratched for fleas and Mr. Calloway watched the U.S.A. The two detectives watched the crowd, and the crowd watched the show with solemn satisfaction. Then one of the detectives got up and went over to Mr. Calloway. That's the end, I thought. But it wasn't, it was the beginning. For some reason they had eliminated him from their list of suspects. I shall never know why. The man said:

"You speak English?"

"I *am* English," Mr. Calloway said.

Even that didn't tear it, and the strangest thing of all was the way Mr. Calloway came alive. I don't think anybody had spoken to him like that for weeks. The Mexicans were too respectful—he was a man with a million—and it had never occurred to Lucia and me to treat him casually like a human being; even in our eyes he had been magnified by the colossal theft and the worldwide pursuit.

He said: "This is rather a dreadful place, don't you think?"

"It is," the policeman said.

"I can't think what brings anybody across the bridge."

"Duty," the policeman said gloomily. "I suppose you are passing through."

"Yes," Mr. Calloway said.

"I'd have expected over here there'd have been—you know what I mean—life. You read things about Mexico."

"Oh, life," Mr. Calloway said. He spoke firmly and precisely, as if to a committee of shareholders. "That begins on the other side."

"You don't appreciate your own country until you leave it."

"That's very true," Mr. Calloway said. "Very true."

At first it was difficult not to laugh, and then after a while there didn't seem to be much to laugh at; an old man imagining all the fine things going on beyond the international bridge. I think he thought of the town opposite as a combination of London and Norfolk—theaters and cocktail bars, a little shooting and a walk round the field at evening with the dog—that miserable imitation of a setter—poking the ditches. He'd never been across, he couldn't know that it was just the same thing over again—even the same layout; only the streets were paved and the hotels had ten more stories, and life was more expensive, and everything was a little bit cleaner. There wasn't anything Mr. Calloway would have called living—no galleries, no bookshops, just *Film Fun* and the local paper, and *Click* and *Focus* and the tabloids.

"Well," said Mr. Calloway, "I think I'll take a stroll before lunch. You need an appetite to swallow the food here. I generally go down and look at the bridge about now. Care to come, too?"

The detective shook his head. "No," he said, "I'm on duty. I'm looking for a fellow." And that, of course, gave *him* away. As far as Mr. Calloway could understand, there was only one "fellow" in the world anyone was looking for—his brain had eliminated friends who were seeking their friends, husbands who might be waiting for their wives, all objectives of any search but just the one. The power of elimination was what had made him a financier—he could forget the people behind the shares.

That was the last we saw of him for a while. We didn't see him going into the Botica Paris to get his aspirin, or walking back from the bridge with his dog. He simply

Across the Bridge 1005

12 **Critical Thinking and Reading** Why did the scene lose its humor for the narrator?

13 **Critical Thinking and Reading** What did the town across the bridge represent to Mr. Calloway?

14 **Thematic Idea** Compare Mr. Calloway's romanticized idea of the town across the bridge with the narrator's idea of the bazaar in "Araby."

We waited together and watched Mr. Calloway waiting for God knows what.

I was literally in at the finish.

"I'd have expected over here there'd have been (you know what I mean) life.

Then they all got up; they had a car outside.

Student Activity 1. Find three more places in Greene's story where dashes set off dramatic changes in thought.

Student Activity 2. Supply a dash for dramatic effect in the following sentences.

1. In fact, my mother always knows best sort of.
2. Would you I mean if you don't mind lend me your shoulder?
3. I'll be there for sure my mom's going to skin me you can count me in!

15 Discussion What does the author mean by this statement?

16 Discussion Why does the narrator suddenly see why Mr. Calloway longs for the town across the bridge? What does this revelation make him feel towards Mr. Calloway?

17 Discussion Why does the narrator feel sorry for Mr. Calloway in this paragraph?

18 Literary Focus What is ironic about the description of Mr. Calloway's "prize" for his efforts to avoid extradition?

19 Literary Focus What is ironic about this sentence? What is the narrator's attitude towards the policemen here?

20 Reading Strategy What is sadly ironic about the fact that everyone in the town speaks English? Why do you think the narrator is ambivalent about telling Mr. Calloway that everyone speaks English? What does this paragraph foreshadow?

21 Critical Thinking and Reading Mr. Calloway has very complex feelings for the dog. Have students discuss those feelings. Does he love or, as he claims, hate the dog?

disappeared, and when he disappeared, people began to talk, and the detectives heard the talk. They looked silly enough, and they got busy after the very man they'd been sitting next to in the garden. Then they, too, disappeared. They, as well as Mr. Calloway, had gone to the state capital to see the Governor and the Chief of Police, and it must have been an amusing sight there, too, as they bumped into Mr. Calloway and sat with him in the waiting rooms. I suspect Mr. Calloway was generally shown in first, for everyone knew he was worth a million. Only in Europe is it possible for a man to be a criminal as well as a rich man.

Anyway, after about a week the whole pack of them returned by the same train. Mr. Calloway traveled Pullman,[3] and the two policemen traveled in the day coach. It was evident that they hadn't got their extradition order.

Lucia had left by that time. The car came and went across the bridge. I stood in Mexico and watched her get out at the United States Customs. She wasn't anything in particular but she looked beautiful at a distance as she gave me a wave out of the United States and got back into the car. And I suddenly felt sympathy for Mr. Calloway, as if there were something over there which you couldn't find here, and turning round I saw him back on his old beat, with the dog at his heels.

I said "Good afternoon," as if it had been all along our habit to greet each other. He looked tired and ill and dusty, and I felt sorry for him—to think of the kind of victory he'd been winning, with so much expenditure of cash and care—the prize this dirty and dreary town, the booths of the money changers, the awful little beauty parlors with their wicker chairs and sofas looking like the reception rooms of brothels, that hot and stuffy garden by the bandstand.

He replied gloomily, "Good morning,"

---

3. Pullman: A railroad car with private compartments of seats that can be made into berths for sleeping.

and the dog started to sniff at some ordure and he turned and kicked it with fury, with depression, with despair.

And at that moment a taxi with the two policemen in it passed us on its way to the bridge. They must have seen that kick; perhaps they were cleverer than I had given them credit for, perhaps they were just sentimental about animals, and thought they'd do a good deed, and the rest happened by accident. But the fact remains—those two pillars of the law set about the stealing of Mr. Calloway's dog.

He watched them go by. Then he said, "Why don't you go across?"

"It's cheaper here," I said.

"I mean just for an evening. Have a meal at that place we can see at night in the sky. Go to the theater."

"There isn't a chance."

He said angrily, sucking his gold tooth, "Well, anyway, get away from here." He stared down the hill and up the other side. He couldn't see that that street climbing up from the bridge, contained only the same money-changers' booths as this one.

I said, "Why don't *you* go?"

He said evasively. "Oh—business."

I said, "It's only a question of money. You don't *have* to pass by the bridge."

He said with faint interest, "I don't talk Spanish."

"There isn't a soul here," I said, "who doesn't talk English."

He looked at me with surprise. "Is that so?" he said. "Is that so?"

It's as I have said; he'd never tried to talk to anyone, and they respected him too much to talk to him—he was worth a million. I don't know whether I'm glad or sorry that I told him that. If I hadn't he might be there now, sitting by the bandstand having his shoes cleaned—alive and suffering.

Three days later his dog disappeared. I found him looking for it, calling it softly and shamefacedly between the palms of the garden. He looked embarrassed. He said in a low angry voice, "I *hate* that dog. The beastly mongrel," and called "Rover, Rover" in a voice which didn't carry five yards. He said, "I bred setters once. I'd have shot a dog like that." It reminded him, I *was* right, of Norfolk, and he lived in the memory, and he hated it for its imperfection. He was a man without a family and without friends, and his only enemy was that dog. You couldn't call the law an enemy; you have to be intimate with an enemy.

Late that afternoon someone told him they'd seen the dog walking across the bridge. It wasn't true, of course, but we didn't know that then—they'd paid a Mexican five pesos to smuggle it across. So all that afternoon and the next Mr. Calloway sat in the garden having his shoes cleaned over and over again, and thinking how a dog could just walk across like that, and a human being, an immortal soul, was bound here in the awful routine of the little walk and the unspeakable meals and the aspirin at the botica. That dog was seeing things he couldn't see—that hateful dog. It made him mad—I think literally mad. You must remember the man had been going on for months. He had a million and he was living on two pounds a week, with nothing to spend his money on. He sat there and brooded on the hideous injustice of it. I think he'd have crossed over one day in any case, but the dog was the last straw.

Next day when he wasn't to be seen, I guessed he'd gone across and I went too. The American town is as small as the Mexican. I knew I couldn't miss him if he was there, and I was still curious. A little sorry for him, but not much.

I caught sight of him first in the only drugstore, having a Coca-Cola, and then once outside a cinema looking at the posters; he had dressed with extreme neatness, as if for a party, but there was no party. On my third time round, I came on the detectives—they were having Coca-Colas in the drugstore, and they must have missed Mr. Calloway by inches. I went in and sat down at the bar.

"Hello," I said, "you still about." I suddenly felt anxious for Mr. Calloway, I didn't want them to meet.

One of them said, "Where's Calloway?"

"Oh," I said, "he's hanging on."

"But not his dog," he said, and laughed. The other looked a little shocked, he didn't like anyone to *talk* cynically about a dog. Then they got up—they had a car outside.

"Have another?" I said.

"No thanks. We've got to keep moving."

The man bent close and confided to me: "Calloway's on this side."

"No!" I said.

"And his dog."

"He's looking for it," the other said.

"I'm damned if he is," I said, and again one of them looked a little shocked, as if I'd insulted the dog.

I don't think Mr. Calloway was looking for his dog, but his dog certainly found him. There was a sudden hilarious yapping from the car and out plunged the semi-setter and gamboled furiously down the street. One of the detectives—the sentimental one—was into the car before we got to the door and was off after the dog. Near the bottom of the long road to the bridge was Mr. Calloway—I do believe he'd come down to look at the Mexican side when he found there was nothing but the drugstore and the cinemas and the paper shops on the American. He saw the dog coming and yelled at it to go home—"home, home, home," as if they were in Norfolk—it took no notice at all, pelting towards him. Then he saw the police car coming, and ran. After that, everything happened too quickly, but I think the order of events was this—the dog started across the road right in front of the car, and Mr. Calloway yelled, at the dog or the car, I don't know which. Anyway, the detective swerved—he said later, weakly, at the inquiry, that he couldn't run over a dog, and down went Mr. Calloway, in a mess of broken glass and gold rims and silver hair, and blood. The dog was on to him before any of us could reach him, licking and whimpering and licking. I

22 **Discussion** Why did the two policemen steal Mr. Calloway's dog?

23 **Literary Focus** What is the irony Mr. Calloway sees in his situation that makes Mr. Calloway "mad—I think literally mad."

24 **Literary Focus** If you understand the narrator's foreshadowing of events, why is this description of Mr. Calloway ironic?

25 **Discussion** The narrator continues his ambivalent feelings towards Mr. Calloway. Why does he suddenly not want the policemen and Mr. Calloway to meet?

26 **Discussion** What does the dog feel about Mr. Calloway? What does Mr. Calloway think about the dog? Have students back their answers up with passages from the story.

27 **Critical Thinking and Reading** How does Greene set the stage for the sentimental policeman's accidental killing of Mr. Calloway? What is the irony in the policemen's statement at the inquiry?

Critical Thinking and Reading
What does the narrator mean in this sentence?

29 Discussion Why is the dog's reaction to Mr. Calloway's death a fitting one? Why was it both "comic and . . . pitiable?"

30 Critical Thinking and Reading
How might Mr. Calloway have deceived himself? Why does the narrator think that our "capacity for self-deception, our baseless optimism" is "so much more appalling than our despair"?

Reader's Response Do you think this story would make a good film? Why or why not?

Closure and Extension

ANSWERS TO THINKING ABOUT THE SELECTION
Recalling

1. (a) The story takes place in a dirty little Mexican border town on the Rio Grande River. (b) Mr. Calloway is hiding out there, having committed the crime of extortion of trust funds. (c) The narrator is waiting for a ride to the Yucatan peninsula from a man driving down from Detroit.
2. (a) Mr. Calloway's companion is his dog, a rather mangy-looking English setter. (b) He kicks the dog furiously once a day, usually after he looks across the bridge.
3. The two detectives do not recognize Mr. Calloway at first. When they do figure out who he is, they can't arrest him because he is not on American soil. They try to get extradition papers for him, but the governor refuses—the insinuation is that Mr. Calloway buys him off.
4. (a) The detectives steal his dog, and someone tells him that the dog went across the bridge. The narrator indicates that he really goes because he always wanted to see the town on the other side of the

saw Mr. Calloway put up his hand, and down it went across the dog's neck and the whimper rose to a stupid bark of triumph, but Mr. Calloway was dead—shock and a weak heart.

"Poor old geezer," the detective said, "I bet he really loved that dog," and it's true that the attitude in which he lay looked more like a caress than a blow. I thought it was meant to be a blow, but the detective may have been right. It all seemed to me a little too touching to be true as the old crook lay there with his arm over the dog's neck, dead with his million between the money-changers' huts, but it's as well to be humble in the face of human nature. He had come across the river for something, and it may, after all, have been the dog he was looking for. It sat there, baying its stupid and mongrel triumph across his body, like a piece of sentimental statuary. The nearest he could get to the fields, the ditches, the horizon of his home. It was comic and it was pitiable; but it wasn't less comic because the man was dead. Death doesn't change comedy to tragedy, and if that last gesture was one of affection, I suppose it was only one more indication of a human being's capacity for self-deception, our baseless optimism that is so much more appalling than our despair.

THINKING ABOUT THE SELECTION
Recalling

1. (a) Where does the story take place? (b) What is Mr. Calloway's reason for being there? (c) What is the narrator's reason?
2. (a) Who is Mr. Calloway's constant "companion"? (b) How does he treat this companion?
3. Why do the two detectives not arrest Mr. Calloway at first?
4. (a) What finally brings Mr. Calloway across the bridge? (b) What happens to him?

Interpreting

5. What effect does the repetition of the sentence "He was worth a million" have on you?
6. What trait of Mr. Calloway's personality is revealed by his not knowing that the inhabitants of the town speak English?

7. Both Mr. Calloway and the detectives are disappointed by what they find on the "other side" of the bridge. (a) What proverb does this call to mind? (b) How does this disappointment reflect the story's theme?
8. Consider the role of justice in the story. (a) In what ways is justice served by Mr. Calloway's death? (b) In what way is Mr. Calloway "saved"?

Applying

9. At the end of the story, the narrator says, " . . . I suppose it was only one more indication of a human being's capacity for self-deception, our baseless optimism that is so much more appalling than our despair." Explain your reactions to this statement.

bridge. (b) Mr. Calloway is hit by the car of the detectives, who swerve to avoid hitting the dog.

Interpreting

5. The repetition of "he was worth a million" reminds the reader that money and its influence is a central theme of the story, money is what gets Mr. Calloway into his present situation of exile and causes, eventually, his death.
6. Mr. Calloway does not know the

townspeople speak English because he feels too superior to them even to notice their bilingualism.
7. (a) The grass is always greener on the other side of the fence. (b) The story's theme centers on the debunking of great expectations—Mr. Calloway thought the town on the other side of the bridge would be wonderful because he was unable to leave the one he was in. Similarly, because of the money he stole, he thought his life would be wonderful; instead he was

trapped in a place where he didn't want to be.
8. (a) Because of the money he stole, it seems as if he got his "just deserts." (b) He is "saved" in his doing a noble thing—trying to save the dog and showing his affection for him.

Applying

9. Reactions will vary. You may wish to point out that Greene's Christianity is profoundly rooted in his sense of original sin—the fallen

ANALYZING LITERATURE

Understanding Theme and Point of View

Theme is the insight into life revealed through a literary work. Often misidentified with a story's subject, the theme is a statement about the subject. **Point of view**—the angle from which the story is told—can affect the reader's grasp of the theme. When a story is told, for instance, by a first-person narrator, the reader is made to feel almost a part of the events. This in turn brings the theme, or "moral," into sharp focus. Consider the theme of "Across the Bridge." Evaluate the impact that the following facts of narration have on the reader's awareness of the theme.

1. The narrator, in the fourth paragraph, gives us his firsthand impressions of the town on the American side.
2. The description of Mr. Calloway's relationship with the dog comes from one who is by his own admission not a lover of dogs.
3. The narrator begins to feel sympathy toward Mr. Calloway.

CRITICAL THINKING AND READING

Understanding Comedy and Tragedy

On page 1003 of the story, the narrator states, "I don't know how to treat this story—it was a tragedy for Mr. Calloway . . . [while to] me, at this stage, it was pure comedy. . . ." Again, at the end, after Mr. Calloway has died, he observes, "It was comic and it was pitiable; but it wasn't less comic because the man was dead. Death doesn't change comedy to tragedy. . . ."

1. In what sense might the death of Mr. Calloway have struck the narrator as comical?
2. Do you agree that death doesn't change comedy to tragedy? Why or why not?
3. The ancient Greeks defined comedy as a play in which the main character triumphs over opposing forces. According to this definition,

would you consider "Across the Bridge" more comedy than tragedy, or vice versa? Explain your answer.

UNDERSTANDING LANGUAGE

Learning About Word Completions

Suffixes, the meaning-bearing fragments added to the end of word roots to form new words, fall into two basic types. Derivational suffixes change the part of speech of the word root. The suffix -al, which converts the verb *arrive* to the noun *arrival,* is an example of a derivational suffix. Inflectional suffixes affect such matters as number and verb tense without changing the part of speech of the root. The suffix -es, which forms the plural noun *churches* from the singular noun *church,* is an example of an inflectional suffix. Identify the italicized part of each of the following words from the story as either a derivational or inflectional suffix. Use each in an original word.

1. pretend*ed*
2. stuff*iness*
3. invest*ment*
4. piti*able*
5. kick*ing*
6. expen*sive*

THINKING AND WRITING

Analyzing the Effects of Point of View

Choose another story that you read in this book, and identify its theme and its narrative point of view. In an essay explain how the point of view affects the theme. Structure your essay on the following questions: Would the impact of the theme have been different had the author used a first-person (or third-person) narrator? What details of narration helped make the theme apparent? What facets of the narrator's character were relevant to the theme? Make sure your essay opens with a clear thesis statement. When you revise make sure you have provided adequate support for your thesis. Proofread your essay and prepare a final draft.

Across the Bridge   1009

(Answers begin on p. 1008.)

elements—the two policemen missing him yet again in the drugstore, the dog running after him, the policemen chasing the dog, and the car swerving to miss the dog and yet killing Mr. Calloway, which seems ridiculous.

2. Suggested response: Greene thinks there are elements of comedy and tragedy in all parts of life. It is certain that one can be put in the uncomfortable position of laughing at the situation that just preceded Mr. Calloway's death and then feeling as if he or she were laughing at the death itself.

3. Suggested response: The Greeks also believed that the main character in a tragedy is a great person with a tragic flaw. Mr. Calloway is too little a person for his death to qualify as a tragedy—except in the sense that all human life is of value and therefore everyone's death is tragic. However, it does not appear that Mr. Calloway really triumphs over his own misplaced expectations; perhaps he reaches out and loves something—in this case, his dog—more than himself and his aspirations. The story has more comic elements in it than tragic, but it is not a comedy in the classical Greek sense.

ANSWERS TO UNDERSTANDING LANGUAGE

1. inflectional; retained
2. derivational; excessiveness
3. derivational; fulfillment
4. derivational; legible
5. inflectional; accepting
6. derivational; receptive

THINKING AND WRITING

For help with this assignment, students can refer to Lesson 12, "Writing About a Poem," in the Handbook of Writing About Literature.

You may wish to divide students into groups, and have them read their rough drafts to one another and suggest ways in which they could be improved.

state of the human race—and that this sense may account for his scorn of "baseless optimism."

ANSWERS TO ANALYZING LITERATURE

1. Through the narrator's eyes, we see the dusty, poverty-filled town as a sort of moral poverty against which the backdrop of Calloway's moral destitution plays. We see the narrator also focusing on money, just as everyone else in the town

does—and surely as Mr. Calloway does. So the narrator serves both to interpret the theme and also to represent it.

2. Perhaps the narrator cannot see or understand the relationship of Mr. Calloway and the dog. However, because we see the relationship through the narrator's eyes, he lets us try to figure out the relationship instead of our relying on him. In the same way, reading a piece of literature and figuring out the theme by oneself will have more impact than

if one is told exactly what to think. It also brings out one of the themes.

3. The narrator begins to move out of the general human condition of showing no concern for one's fellow man. He starts to see Mr. Calloway as a real person—not perfect, but certainly not all bad.

ANSWERS TO CRITICAL THINKING AND READING

1. The circumstances of Mr. Calloway's death have comic

George Orwell felt guilty for letting
the stereotypes of race and his
position as a police official interfere with his mingling with the
Burmese, he spent a period of his
life living with the indigent people
of Europe. He wore rags, shared
quarters with beggars and common laborers in East London and
Paris, and tramped around the
countryside as a vagrant, working
occasionally as a dishwasher, a
miner, or a field hand. His years in
Burma also changed him politically. His disgust with imperialism
and totalitarian governments led
him first to anarchism and then to
socialism and libertarianism systems that, respectively, claim to
help the downtrodden and es-
pouse freedom of will and freedom of action for all. Ask students
what other famous people they
might know—writers or others
—whose lives or, in the case of
authors, whose writing has been
altered by a profound experience
such as Orwell had in Burma.

Critical Evaluation The literary
scholar Jenni Calder said that "In
his writing Orwell covered almost
every aspect of modern life from
major political issues to tiny details of daily living. He was always swift and direct in his responses. His honesty sometimes
led to an impulsiveness which
marred the clarity of his style, but
generally his writing is taut, lucid,
detached and with a striking tendency for effective and sometimes shocking understatement.
. . . Few modern writers have
such a distinctive and exact
command of words."

Ask students whether or not
Orwell uses the device of understatement in this essay. Also,
have them find evidence of his
"distinctive and exact command
of words."

GEORGE ORWELL

1903–1950

Although George Orwell's popular fame is most directly linked to his
two novels of political satire, *Animal Farm* and *1984,* many discerning readers insist that his genius is most readily apparent in his
essays and nonfiction. Orwell's prose style, precise yet informal,
contributed to making his essays some of the most eloquent short
pieces in English writing of the twentieth century.

George Orwell was the pen name chosen by Eric Blair, born in
colonial Bengal, an eastern region of India. Schooled in England at
Eton, Orwell returned to the East—like H. H. Munro (Saki)—to serve
in the Imperial Police in Burma. His experiences in that post, which
span the years 1922 to 1927, form the basis of his first novel
Burmese Days (1934). Disillusioned by his country's policy in the
Orient, Orwell left military service to pursue jobs in journalism,
publishing, and bookselling in England and France. This period of
his life was marked by struggles with poverty, as he recalls in his
autobiographical *Down and Out in Paris and London* (1933).

During the 1930's Orwell became deeply involved in social and
international causes. *The Road to Wigan Pier* (1937) movingly
chronicles the miseries of the English working class during the later
phases of the Depression. The coming of the Spanish Civil War
(1936–1939) found Orwell firmly committed to the Republican
cause. Deploring what he saw as the totalitarianism of the National-
ist victors of the conflict, Orwell paid tribute to the victims in *Homage
to Catalonia* (1939).

During World War II Orwell served as literary editor of the
Tribune from 1943 to 1945 and also contributed political columns to
a number of newspapers and journals. In 1945 he published *Animal
Farm,* a savage fable that indirectly denounces the evils of both
Fascism and Communism. Suffering acutely from the tuberculosis
that would ultimately end his life, he completed *1984* (1948), a grim
vision of a future in which language and thought would be everywhere manipulated to serve totalitarian ends.

Orwell's passionate concern for the preservation of political
freedom was allied with his efforts to save the English language
from "double speak," jargon, and bureaucratic vagueness. In
"Politics and the English Language" he dramatically demonstrates
how language can be used subtly to conceal political corruption,
thereby blinding members of a society to the necessity of moral
choice. Although 1984 has come and gone without the fulfillment of
Orwell's grim prophecies, his lifelong commitment to political freedom and to the integrity of language remain as relevant today as
ever.

Objectives

1 To understand the use
  and importance of tone
  in a short story
2 To understand that
  stereotyping is a form of
  prejudice
3 To understand word
  origins
4 To support a written
  opinion

Support Material

Teaching Portfolio
Teacher Backup, pp. 1209–1212
Grammar in Action Worksheet,
Recognizing the Active Voice,
p. 1213
Usage and Mechanics Work-
sheet, p. 1215
Vocabulary Check, p. 1216
Analyzing Literature Worksheet,
Identifying Tone, p. 1217

Critical Thinking and Reading
Worksheet, *Understanding Ster-
eotypes,* p. 1218
Selection Test, pp. 1219–1220

GUIDE FOR INTERPRETING

Shooting an Elephant

Writer's Technique

Tone. Tone is the attitude the writer of a work of fiction takes toward his or her subject, his or her audience, or a character. Just as a speaker's tone of voice can affect the way in which a remark is taken, so the tone of a literary work will help shape the reader's response to it. Tone in a piece of literature is conveyed through the particular words the writer chooses as well as through details of description. For example, a writer who adopts a lighthearted and carefree tone toward the subject of sunshine might refer to the "kiss of warm rays," while the same writer, in approaching the subject with a bitter tone, might make reference to the sun's "cruel, harsh glare." In his essay, "Shooting an Elephant," George Orwell's diction, or word choice, reveals unambiguously his attitude toward the task that has fallen to him as a military police officer in Burma, as well as toward the people to whom he must account for his actions.

Commentary

Considerable family sacrifice and reduced tuition enabled Orwell's parents to send their only son to a fashionable preparatory school on the south coast of England while they remained in India. But the boy was intimidated by the wealth and position of the others at school: "I had no money, I was weak, I was ugly, I was unpopular, I had a chronic cough, I smelt," he later wrote. Despite his later academic success—at age thirteen he was awarded not one but two scholarships to England's most prestigious private high schools —he never lost his ability to identify with society's downtrodden. As he remarked: "The conviction that it was not possible for me to be a success went deep enough to influence my actions till far into adult life." Out of personal escape rather than any political conviction, therefore, he took a position with the Indian Imperial police in Burma rather than continuing his education at Cambridge University as expected. His ability to see life through the eyes of the underdog forms the basis of "Shooting an Elephant," and partly explains why the essay was ranked as a classic within his own lifetime. The essay relfects Orwell's own early humiliations and frustrations as a poor boy among wealthier classmates, recalled now in the difficult and hurtful official relationships between the British and Burmese.

Writing

What is power? Freewrite about the meaning of the word, exploring its effects on both the person who exerts power and the people on whom power is brought to bear.

Guide for Interpreting   1011

Literary Focus Remind students that the characters in a story can have many different feelings. For instance, in the first paragraphs of *Shooting an Elephant,* Orwell feels perplexed, upset, insulted, demeaned, and angry; the Burmese feel bitterness, superiority, anger. Tone refers to the *author's* feelings about the subject or characters of his or her story, not how his or her characters feel.

Writing/Prior Knowledge It would be useful to have your students discuss the meaning of power and its effects before writing about it.

Vocabulary

Preteach the following vocabulary words:

prostrate *(präs' trāt) adj.:* Defenseless; in a prone or lying position (p. 1012)

despotic (de spät' ik) *adj.:* Tyrannical (p. 1014)

squalid (skwäl' id) *adj.:* Miserably poor; wretched (p. 1014)

switch (swich) *n.:* Light whip (p. 1014)

orderly (ôr' dor lē) *n.:* Soldier assigned to carry out orders of a superior (p. 1014)

senility (si nil' ə tē) *n.:* Mental and physical decay due to old age (p. 1016)

Motivation/Prior Knowledge
Imagine that you go to a party where you know no one and you are dressed differently from any-one else. One of the people at the party knows someone from your school but doesn't think highly of that person and implies that everyone at your school must be the same way. You are mostly ignored; a few very rude people snicker at your outfit. What feelings do you have at the party? What do you think of the other people who are there? How do you describe the party to your friends?

Master Teacher Note You may wish to have students further their understanding of the essay by asking them to pick one of the following questions to research and answer. How and why did Britain become involved in Burma? What was the outcome of the three Anglo-Burmese Wars? Why did being made a province of India by the British infuriate the Burmese? How did religion fuel the fire of hatred towards the Brit-ish? What led to the peasant up-rising of 1931, which happened shortly after Orwell left Burma? How did Burma eventually be-come independent? Have them report on their findings in class.

Purpose-Setting Question What is the tone of the essay?

1 **Discussion** How would you feel if you had been treated as Orwell was by the Burmese? Why did the Burmese treat Orwell with con-tempt?

2 **Clarification** The Buddhist priests were probably "the worst of all" because, as a province of British-controlled India, the Bur-mese were subject to the Indian Hindus, whom they disdained.

3 **Literary Focus** What words ex-press Orwell's ambivalent feel-ings? How do they relate to the

Shooting an Elephant

George Orwell

In Moulmein, in lower Burma, I was hated by large numbers of people—the only time in my life that I have been important enough for this to happen to me. I was subdivisional police officer of the town, and in an aimless, petty kind of way anti-European feeling was very bitter. No one had the guts to raise a riot, but if a European woman went through the bazaars alone somebody would probably spit betel juice over her dress. As a police officer I was an obvious target and was baited whenever it seemed safe to do so. When a nimble Bur-man tripped me up on the football field and the referee (another Burman) looked the other way, the crowd yelled with hideous laughter. This happened more than once. In the end the sneering yellow faces of young men that met me everywhere, the insults hooted after me when I was at a safe dis-tance, got badly on my nerves. The young Buddhist priests were the worst of all. There were several thousands of them in the town and none of them seemed to have anything to do except stand on street corners and jeer at Europeans.

All this was perplexing and upsetting. For at that time I had already made up my mind that imperialism was an evil thing and the sooner I chucked up my job and got out of it the better. Theoretically—and secretly, of course—I was all for the Burmese and all against their oppressors, the British. As for the job I was doing, I hated it more bitterly than I can perhaps make clear. In a job like that you see the dirty work of Empire at close quarters. The wretched prisoners hud-dling in the stinking cages of the lockups, the gray, cowed faces of the long-term con-victs, the scarred buttocks of the men who had been flogged with bamboos—all these oppressed me with an intolerable sense of guilt. But I could get nothing into perspec-tive. I was young and ill educated and I had had to think out my problems in the utter silence that is imposed on every Englishman in the East. I did not even know that the British Empire is dying, still less did I know that it is a great deal better than the younger empires that are going to supplant it. All I knew was that I was stuck between my hatred of the empire I served and my rage against the evil-spirited little beasts who tried to make my job impossible. With one part of my mind I thought of the British Raj[1] as an unbreakable tyranny, as something clamped down, *in saecula saeculorum,*[2] upon the will of prostrate peoples; with an-other part I thought that the greatest joy in the world would be to drive a bayonet into a Buddhist priest's guts. Feelings like these are the normal byproducts of imperialism; ask any Anglo-Indian official, if you can catch him off duty.

One day something happened which in a roundabout way was enlightening. It was a tiny incident in itself, but it gave me a better glimpse than I had had before of the real

---

1. **Raj** (räj): Rule.
2. *in saecula saeculorum* (sē′ kōō lə sē′ kōō lôr′ əm): Forever and ever.

tone of the essay? What is the author's attitude towards his sub-ject? Why did he hate his job?

4 **Critical Thinking and Reading** What part did Orwell's age play in his ambivalent feelings towards the Burmese?

5 **Critical Thinking and Reading** Have students keep a list of phrases that Orwell uses to de-scribe the British. Discuss the conflict one would have from rep-resenting a government and yet not agreeing with its policies.

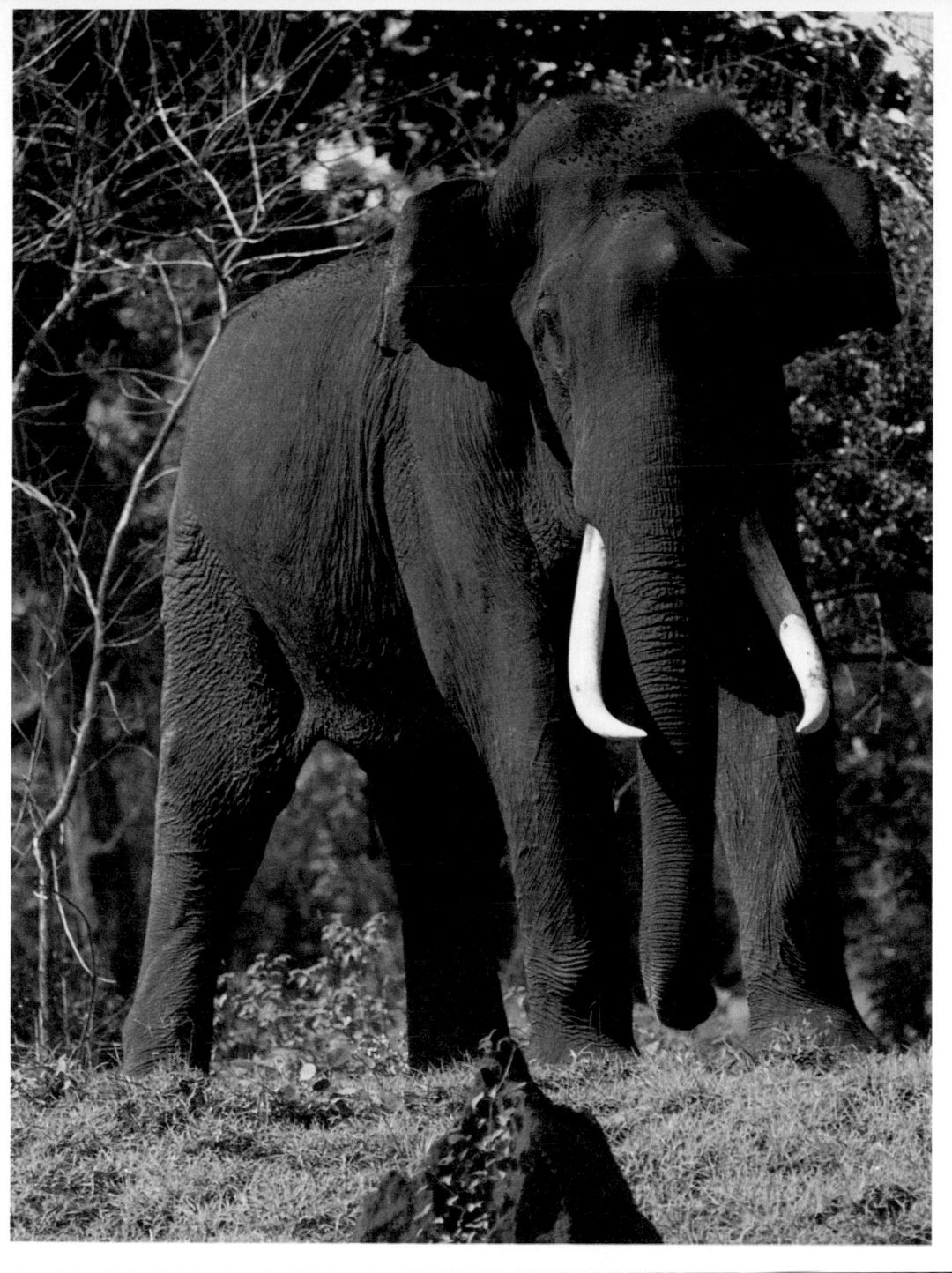

6 **Literary Focus** How is the atmosphere of the essay—the mood—affected by the comment on the weather?

7 **Discussion** Orwell sees, though confusedly, that two totally different cultures have great difficulty in understanding one another. What relationship does this comment have to Orwell's feelings of ambivalence about Burma and the inability for westerners to understand the Eastern way?

8 **Reading Strategy** What effect do you think borrowing the elephant gun will have on the story?

nature of imperialism—the real motives for which despotic governments act. Early one morning the subinspector at a police station the other end of the town rang me up on the phone and said that an elephant was ravaging the bazaar. Would I please come and do something about it? I did not know what I could do, but I wanted to see what was happening and I got onto a pony and started out. I took my rifle, an old .44 Winchester and much too small to kill an elephant, but I thought the noise might be useful *in terrorem.*[3] Various Burmans stopped me on the way and told me about the elephant's doings. It was not, of course, a wild elephant, but a tame one which had gone "must."[4] It had been chained up, as tame elephants always are when their attack of "must" is due, but on the previous night it had broken its chain and escaped. Its mahout,[5] the only person who could manage it when it was in that state, had set out in pursuit, but had taken the wrong direction and was now twelve hours' journey away, and in the morning the elephant had suddenly reappeared in the town. The Burmese population had no weapons and were quite helpless against it. It had already destroyed somebody's bamboo hut, killed a cow and raided some fruit stalls and devoured the stock; also it had met the municipal rubbish van and, when the driver jumped out and took to his heels, had turned the van over and inflicted violences upon it.

The Burmese subinspector and some Indian constables were waiting for me in the quarter where the elephant had been seen. It was a very poor quarter, a labyrinth of squalid bamboo huts, thatched with palm leaf, winding all over a steep hillside. I remember that it was a cloudy, stuffy morning at the beginning of the rains. We began questioning the people as to where the ele-

phant had gone and, as usual, failed to get any definite information. That is invariably the case in the East; a story always sounds clear enough at a distance, but the nearer you get to the scene of events the vaguer it becomes. Some of the people said that the elephant had gone in one direction, some said that he had gone in another, some professed not even to have heard of any elephant. I had almost made up my mind that the whole story was a pack of lies, when we heard yells a little distance away. There was a loud, scandalized cry of "Go away, child! Go away this instant!" and an old woman with a switch in her hand came round the corner of a hut, violently shooing away a crowd of naked children. Some more women followed, clicking their tongues and exclaiming; evidently there was something that the children ought not to have seen. I rounded the hut and saw a man's dead body sprawling in the mud. He was an Indian, a black Dravidian[6] coolie,[7] almost naked, and he could not have been dead many minutes. The people said that the elephant had come suddenly upon him round the corner of the hut, caught him with its trunk, put its foot on his back and ground him into the earth. This was the rainy season and the ground was soft, and his face had scored a trench a foot deep and a couple of yards long. He was lying on his belly with arms crucified and head sharply twisted to one side. His face was coated with mud, the eyes wide open, the teeth bared and grinning with an expression of unendurable agony. (Never tell me, by the way, that the dead look peaceful. Most of the corpses I have seen looked devilish.) The friction of the great beast's foot had stripped the skin from his back as neatly as one skins a rabbit. As soon as I saw the dead man I sent an orderly to a friend's house nearby to borrow an elephant rifle. I had already sent back the pony, not wanting it to

---

3. *in terrorem:* For terror.
4. **must:** Into a dangerous, frenzied state.
5. **mahout** (mə hōōt'): An elephant keeper and rider.

6. **Dravidian** (drə vid' ē ən): Belonging to the race of people inhabiting southern India.
7. **coolie:** Laborer.

Grammar in Action

When a verb's subject performs an action, that verb is in the **active voice.** Prefer the active to the passive voice when you write. The active voice is engaging, immediate, and direct. It enlivens writing that would be dull and distant in the passive voice. Notice how George Orwell's use of the active voice animates his essay.

> . . . his face had scored a trench a foot deep and a couple of yards long.

The friction of the great beast's foot had stripped the skin from his back as neatly as one skins a rabbit.

Notice how much vitality is lost in the following passive-voice equivalents:

> . . . a trench a foot deep and a couple of yards long was scored by his face.

The skin from his back was stripped by the friction of the great beast's foot as neatly as a rabbit is skinned.

go mad with fright and throw me if it smelled the elephant.

The orderly came back in a few minutes with a rifle and five cartridges, and meanwhile some Burmans had arrived and told us that the elephant was in the paddy fields[8] below, only a few hundred yards away. As I started forward practically the whole population of the quarter flocked out of the houses and followed me. They had seen the rifle and were all shouting excitedly that I was going to shoot the elephant. They had not shown much interest in the elephant when he was merely ravaging their homes, but it was different now that he was going to be shot. It was a bit of fun to them, as it would be to an English crowd; besides they wanted the meat. It made me vaguely uneasy. I had no intention of shooting the elephant—I had merely sent for the rifle to defend myself if necessary—and it is always unnerving to have a crowd following you. I marched down the hill, looking and feeling a fool, with the rifle over my shoulder and an ever-growing army of people jostling at my heels. At the bottom, when you got away from the huts, there was a metaled road[9] and beyond that a miry waste of paddy fields a thousand yards across, not yet plowed but soggy from the first rains and dotted with coarse grass. The elephant was standing eight yards from the road, his left side toward us. He took not the slightest notice of the crowd's approach. He was tearing up bunches of grass, beating them against his knees to clean them, and stuffing them into his mouth.

I had halted on the road. As soon as I saw the elephant I knew with perfect certainty that I ought not to shoot him. It is a serious matter to shoot a working elephant—it is comparable to destroying a huge and costly piece of machinery—and obviously one ought not to do it if it can possibly be avoided. And at that distance, peacefully eating, the elephant looked no more dangerous than a cow. I thought then and I think now that his attack of "must" was already passing off; in which case he would merely wander harmlessly about until the mahout came back and caught him. Moreover, I did not in the least want to shoot him. I decided that I would watch him for a little while to make sure that he did not turn savage again, and then go home.

But at that moment I glanced round at the crowd that had followed me. It was an immense crowd, two thousand at the least and growing every minute. It blocked the road for a long distance on either side. I looked at the sea of yellow faces above the garish clothes—faces all happy and excited over this bit of fun, all certain that the elephant was going to be shot. They were watching me as they would watch a conjurer about to perform a trick. They did not like me, but with the magical rifle in my hands I was momentarily worth watching. And suddenly I realized that I should have to shoot the elephant after all. The people expected it of me and I had got to do it; I could feel their two thousand wills pressing me forward, irresistibly. And it was at this moment, as I stood there with the rifle in my hands, that I first grasped the hollowness, the futility of the white man's dominion in the East. Here was I, the white man with his gun, standing in front of the unarmed native crowd—seemingly the leading actor of the piece; but in reality I was only an absurd puppet pushed to and fro by the will of those yellow faces behind. I perceived in this moment that when the white man turns tyrant it is his own freedom that he destroys. He becomes a sort of hollow, posing dummy, the conventionalized figure of a sahib.[10] For it is the condition of his rule that he shall spend his life in trying to impress the "natives," and so in every crisis he has got to do what

---

8. paddy fields: Rice fields.
9. metaled road: A road in which the pavement is reinforced with metal strips.

10. sahib (sä′ ib): Indian word for European gentleman.

Shooting an Elephant 1015

9 **Discussion** Why did a crowd form when Orwell set off with the gun? Why did the crowd make him "vaguely uneasy"? How else did it make him feel?

10 **Reading Strategy** Based on what you have read so far, do you think Orwell will shoot the elephant? Why or why not?

11 **Discussion** What does the simile "as they would watch a conjurer about to perform a trick" tell about Orwell's situation with the elephant?

12 **Critical Thinking and Reading** Why does Orwell think he has to kill the elephant? What is the realization he comes to about the real position of power of the British in Burma? What did Orwell fear more than the elephant? Orwell prefaced his essay with the remark that the real motives and nature of imperialism became clear to him in this incident. What are those motives? How did the incident illustrate them? What is the link between Burma and the elephant?

Student Activity 1. Rewrite the following sentences in the active voice. You will need to change words in some cases.

1. The road was blocked by the elephant for a long distance on either side.
2. When the trigger was pulled, I did not hear the bang or feel the kick.

Student Activity 2. Find three more active-voice sentences in Orwell's essay and explain what would be lost in each case if the voice were passive.

the "natives" expect of him. He wears a mask, and his face grows to fit it. I had got to shoot the elephant. I had committed myself to doing it when I sent for the rifle. A sahib has got to act like a sahib; he has got to appear resolute, to know his own mind and do definite things. To come all that way, rifle in hand, with two thousand people marching at my heels, and then to trail feebly away, having done nothing—no, that was impossible. The crowd would laugh at me. And my whole life, every white man's life in the East, was one long struggle not to be laughed at.

But I did not want to shoot the elephant. **13** I watched him beating his bunch of grass against his knees with that preoccupied grandmotherly air that elephants have. It seemed to me that it would be murder to shoot him. At that age I was not squeamish about killing animals, but I had never shot an elephant and never wanted to. (Somehow it always seems worse to kill a *large* animal.) Besides, there was the beast's owner to be considered. Alive, the elephant was worth at least a hundred pounds, dead, he would only be worth the value of his tusks, five pounds, possibly. But I had got to act quickly. I turned to some experienced-looking Burmans who had been there when we arrived, and asked them how the elephant had been behaving. They all said the same thing: he took no notice of you if you left him alone, but he might charge if you went too close to him.

It was perfectly clear to me what I ought to do. I ought to walk up to within, say, twenty-five yards of the elephant and test his behavior. If he charged, I could shoot; if he took no notice of me, it would be safe to leave him until the mahout came back. But also I knew that I was going to do no such thing. I was a poor shot with a rifle and the ground was soft mud into which one would sink at every step. If the elephant charged and I missed him. I should have about as much chance as a toad under a steam-roller. But even then I was not thinking particular-

ly of my own skin, only of the watchful yellow faces behind. For at that moment, with the crowd watching me, I was not afraid in the ordinary sense, as I would have been if I had been alone. A white man mustn't be frightened in front of "natives"; and so, in general, he isn't frightened. The sole thought in my mind was that if anything went wrong those two thousand Burmans would see me pursued, caught, trampled on, and reduced to a grinning corpse like that Indian up the hill. And if that happened it was quite probable that some of them would laugh. That would never do. There was only one alternative. I shoved the cartridges into the magazine and lay down on the road to get a better aim.

The crowd grew very still, and a deep, low, happy sigh, as of people who see the theater curtain go up at last, breathed from innumerable throats. They were going to have their bit of fun, after all. The rifle was a beautiful German thing with cross-hair sights. I did not then know that in shooting an elephant one would shoot to cut an imaginary bar running from ear hole to ear hole. I ought, therefore, as the elephant was sideways on, to have aimed straight at his ear-hole; actually I aimed several inches in front of this, thinking the brain would be further forward.

When I pulled the trigger I did not hear the bang or feel the kick—one never does when a shot goes home—but I heard the devilish roar of glee that went up from the crowd. In that instant, in too short a time, one would have thought, even for the bullet to get there, a mysterious, terrible change had come over the elephant. He neither stirred nor fell, but every line of his body had altered. He looked suddenly stricken, shrunken, immensely old, as though the frightful impact of the bullet had paralyzed him without knocking him down. At last, after what seemed a long time—it might have been five seconds, I dare say—he sagged flabbily to his knees. His mouth slobbered. An enormous senility seemed to have settled upon him. One could have imagined him thousands of years old. I fired again into the same spot. At the second shot he did not collapse but climbed with desperate slowness to his feet and stood weakly upright, with legs sagging and head drooping. I fired a third time. That was the shot that did for him. You could see the agony of it jolt his whole body and knock the last remnant of strength from his legs. But in falling he seemed for a moment to rise, for as his hind legs collapsed beneath him he seemed to tower upward like a huge rock toppling, his trunk reaching skyward like a tree. He trumpeted, for the first and only time. And then down he came, his belly toward me, with a crash that seemed to shake the ground even where I lay.

I got up. The Burmans were already racing past me across the mud. It was obvious that the elephant would never rise again, but he was not dead. He was breathing very rhythmically with long rattling gasps, his great mound of a side painfully rising and falling. His mouth was wide open—I could see far down into caverns of pale pink throat. I waited a long time for him to die, but his breathing did not weaken. Finally I fired my two remaining shots into the spot where I thought his heart must be. The thick blood welled out of him like red velvet, but still he did not die. His body did not even jerk when the shots hit him, the tortured breathing continued without a pause. He was dying, very slowly and in great agony, but in some world remote from me where not even a bullet could damage him further. I felt that I had got to put an end

14

to that dreadful noise. It seemed dreadful to see the great beast lying there, powerless to move and yet powerless to die, and not even to be able to finish him. I sent back for my small rifle and poured shot after shot into his heart and down his throat. They seemed to make no impression. The tortured gasps continued as steadily as the ticking of a clock.

In the end I could not stand it any longer and went away. I heard later that it took him half an hour to die. Burmans were bringing dahs[11] and baskets even before I left, and I was told they had stripped his body almost to the bones by the afternoon.

Afterward, of course, there were endless discussions about the shooting of the elephant. The owner was furious, but he was only an Indian and could do nothing. Besides, legally I had done the right thing, for a mad elephant has to be killed, like a mad dog, if its owner fails to control it. Among the Europeans opinion was divided. The older man said I was right, the younger men said it was a shame to shoot an elephant for killing a coolie, because an elephant was worth more than any Coringhee[12] coolie. And afterward I was very glad that the coolie had been killed; it put me legally in the right and it gave me a sufficient pretext for shooting the elephant. I often wondered whether any of the others grasped that I had done it solely to avoid looking a fool.

15

16

---

11. **dahs** (däz): Knives.
12. **Coringhee** (cor in' gē): Southern Indian.

14 **Discussion** What does the elephant symbolize to Orwell when he witnesses his painful, slow death "in some world remote from me . . ."? Why is he so upset when the elephant takes a long time to die?

15 **Critical Thinking and Reading** What do you infer from the phrases "only an Indian" and "it was a shame to shoot an elephant for killing a coolie, because an elephant was worth more . . ."?

16 **Critical Thinking and Reading** What is the irony in this statement? How does it further reveal Orwell's confusion and ambivalence about the Burmese?

mese; he agrees with their antipathy for imperialism, but their insulting treatment of him enrages him. The conflict between how he thinks he ought to feel towards the natives and how he actually feels "got badly on [his] nerves." He hates his job because it reveals the "dirty work of the Empire," particularly the wretchedness of prisoners. He therefore feels an overwhelming sense of guilt about his job.

7. The experience with the elephant is enlightening because through it he sees the position of England—and therefore himself—in Burma: that the "oppressors" are not really in charge, as they fancy; the Burmese are. The experience becomes symbolic of the British existence in Burma and through the experience he first understands the cause of his ambivalent feelings.

8. The author goes into great detail about the elephant's death so that the reader will experience the same revulsion as he does and will see the elephant as a symbol of Burma, whose spirit the British are killing just as needlessly and wastefully as he has killed the elephant.

9. (a) The direct language that Orwell uses does not hide the fact that he hates both the British tyranny and the "evil-spirited little beasts"—the Burmese." He also

---

Closure and Extension
(Questions begin on p. 1018.)

ANSWERS TO THINKING ABOUT THE SELECTION
Recalling

1. (a) Orwell was hated simply because he was British and therefore a symbol of British imperialism. (b) He agreed with the Burmese's hatred of imperialism, but their attitude towards him made him angry at them.

2. He sees the mangled and flayed body of the man that the elephant had trampled.

3. (a) He feels that killing the elephant would be murder, since it no longer seemed dangerous; the animal is worth a lot of money; its owner would be angry; although he does not feel squeamish about killing, he seems to have a respect for life that abhors needless slaughter. (b) He knows the crowd expects him to kill the elephant and realizes, as a British official,

that he can't "lose face" with the people.

4. The elephant sinks to its knees on the first shot but scrambles up with the second shot. The third shot makes it fall, but the fourth and fifth shots still cannot totally kill it.

5. After the animal is dead, the Burmese strip the meat off its bones.

Interpreting

6. Orwell is confused by his ambivalent feelings towards the Bur-

has a lot of sympathy for the elephant and yet the fact that he feels loyal to his country is evident when he decides, as his country's representative that he cannot appear foolish. (b) The theme of the essay is that man can commit heinous acts to appear "honorable" without looking foolish. Orwell's complex feelings lead him to do something he is morally against, but he has no recourse if he wants to save face. Until this incident, Orwell understands his motivations and actions as little as anyone.

Applying

10. Suggested responses: A student might say, No, because I am morally against killing animals under any circumstances. Or, yes; I agree with Orwell that it was the only thing he could do if he was to maintain the respect of the people.

ANSWERS TO ANALYZING LITERATURE

Suggested responses:

1. Orwell had ambivalent feelings about the Burmese. On the one hand, he agreed with their hatred of British imperialism and felt that he was a kindred spirit because of his anti-imperialism. ("Theoretically . . . I was all for the Burmese and all against their oppressors, the British.") However, their treatment of him made him so angry that his "greatest joy" would have been to "drive a bayonet into a Buddhist priest's guts." He hated their "sneering faces" and called them "evil-spirited little beasts."
2. He is "all against [the Burmese] oppressors, the British." Again, he probably means theoretically; he can have feelings of patriotism towards his country and still reject its policy decisions. He felt that although the British empire had problems, it was "a great deal better than the younger empires" that came after it.
3. Although Orwell does not feel "squeamish about killing animals," he does not like needless killing. He also feels sorry for the elephant, which is clear in his reference to it as having a "grandmotherly air,"

THINKING ABOUT THE SELECTION

Recalling

1. (a) Why was the narrator hated in Burma? (b) Why were his reactions to this hatred mixed?
2. What grisly sight does the narrator encounter when he arrives in the quarter where the elephant has been seen?
3. (a) What reasons does the narrator give for not wanting to shoot the elephant? (b) Why does he shoot it in spite of these reasons?
4. How many shots does it take to bring the elephant down?
5. What do the Burmans do once the elephant is dead?

Interpreting

6. How would you summarize the sentiments the narrator expresses in the first two paragraphs?
7. What do you think the narrator means when he states at the beginning of the third paragraph that this incident was "enlightening" in "a roundabout way"?
8. What do you think was the narrator's reason for providing his lengthy and detailed description of the elephant's death?
9. (a) What evidence is there in this essay that the narrator was divided in his sympathies? (b) How might the narrator's complex feelings be related to the essay's theme?

Applying

10. If you had been in the narrator's place do you think you would have shot the elephant? Why or why not?

ANALYZING LITERATURE

Identifying Tone

Tone is a writer's attitude toward his or her subject, audience, or a character. In a literary work, tone is communicated through details and the author's choice of words. As a recollection of an incident from a period of George Orwell's life that was "perplexing and upsetting," "Shooting an Elephant" sums up the author's attitude toward several separate but related subjects. In

your own words, identify the author's tone toward each of the following subjects, and locate specific words and passages that support your assumption.

1. The Burmans   3. Killing and death
2. The British Empire

CRITICAL THINKING AND READING

Understanding Stereotypes

A **stereotype** is a generalization about a whole group of people that does not apply to all individuals belonging to a certain group. The acceptance and use of stereotypes are forms of prejudice. In "Shooting an Elephant" Orwell explains that he was disliked by Burmans not because of any specific limitation of his own character but because he was European. The Burmans, thus, had a preconceived notion, or stereotype, of the European. What do you think is Orwell's reaction to stereotypes? Explain your answer.

UNDERSTANDING LANGUAGE

Understanding Word Origins

Several words used by Orwell in this selection are "Anglicizations," that is, words from another language which have been given English spellings and pronunciations that imitate the original. In a good dictionary, find each of the following Anglicized words, and trace their origins as far back as you can.

1. raj   4. sahib
2. mahout   5. dahs
3. coolie

THINKING AND WRITING

Supporting an Opinion

In an opinion paper, argue your belief that Orwell was justified, or not justified, in shooting the elephant. Your essay should not only support your own position but should pinpoint and refute arguments that might be raised by the opposition. Draw, if you can, from outside sources to drive home your point. When you revise make sure you have provided adequate support for your opinion.

---

and his detailed description of the elephant's death indicates what a impact it has on him.

ANSWERS TO CRITICAL THINKING AND READING

Suggested response: The Burmese stereotypically saw Europeans as despotic and bloodthirsty —as shown by their assumption that Orwell would shoot the elephant.

ANSWERS TO UNDERSTANDING LANGUAGE

1. raj: a Hindi word *raj* from the Sanskrit *rajati*, "he rules."
2. mahout: from Hindi *mahaut, mahawat,* from the Sanskrit *mahamatra* meaning "of great measure," which was originally an honorific title.
3. coolie: Hini *kuli* from *Kuli,* the name of an aboriginal tribe in India.

4. sahib: Hindi *sahib* from Arabic; "master."
5. dahs: from Burmese *dā,* "a large heavy knife."

GREAT WORKS

1984
by George Orwell

Presentation

Motivation/Prior Knowledge Ask students what it would be like to live in a society that denied them all the basic freedoms guaranteed by our Bill of Rights. Remind them that these freedoms include freedom of speech and freedom of assembly. After eliciting students' reactions to such a society, tell them that George Orwell portrayed the harmful effects of a police state in his novel *1984*.

Enrichment Tell students that slogans like "War is Peace" and "Freedom is Slavery" show how political abuses go hand in hand with abuses of language. Orwell wrote about this subject in his essay "Politics and the English Language." He argued that in defending the indefensible, "political language has to consist largely of euphemism, question–begging and sheer cloudy vagueness. Defenseless villages are bombarded from the air, the inhabitants driven out into the countryside, the cattle machine–gunned, the huts set on fire with incendiary bullets: this is called *pacification*. Millions of peasants are robbed of their farms and sent trudging along the roads with no more than they can carry: this is called *transfer of population* or *rectification of frontiers*. People are imprisoned for years without trial, or shot . . . this is called *elimination of unreliable elements*."

A Terrifying Warning

WAR IS PEACE
FREEDOM IS SLAVERY
IGNORANCE IS STRENGTH

Behind these seemingly contradictory phrases is the most terrifying warning that a writer has ever uttered—George Orwell's masterpiece, *1984*. Centering on the abuse of power, the novel portrays people in the not-so-distant future brutally crushed by the iron fist of repression. As the three slogans illustrate, in the world of *1984* language is manipulated to create a new—and utterly false—reality in which any lie can become a truth.

Orwell's horrifying vision of the future has become famous the world over. For instance, many terms Orwell coined to describe the perversion of language and personal freedom have entered daily speech. These include "Doublespeak," "Newspeak," and "Big Brother," to name just a few. Indeed, Orwell's very name has become synonymous with totalitarianism. The adjective "Orwellian" is used to describe the fear and horror of repressive governments. Just what did Orwell say in *1984* that has had such a lasting impression?

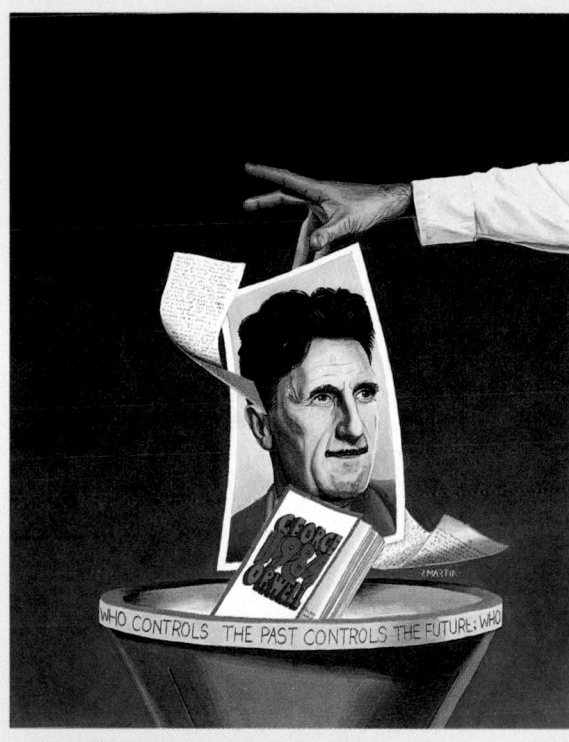

"WHO CONTROLS THE PAST CONTROLS THE FUTURE"
Quote from George Orwell
Illustration by Richard

Great Works   1019

The Near Future

The novel is set sometime in the near future—the date is never specified. As a matter of fact, Orwell decided on the title by simply transposing the last two digits of the book's intended publication date, 1948. Unfortunately, illness prevented him from completing the novel until 1949, and he lived less than a year after its publication before succumbing to the ravages of tuberculosis. Despite the title Orwell did not intend the reader to assume that the action was definitely set in 1984. Time, like truth, is fluid in the novel.

It is a world of new alliances. Countries as we presently know them have been reformed into three large nations: Oceania, Eurasia, and East Asia. Oceania is made up of the Americas, the Atlantic islands including the British Isles, Australia, and the southern portion of Africa. Eurasia includes the whole of the northern part of Europe and Asia from Portugal to the Bering Strait. Eastasia, smaller than the others and with a less definite western frontier, comprises China and the country to the south of it, the Japanese islands, and a large but fluctuating portion of Manchuria, Mongolia, and Tibet. The immediate action takes place in the part of Oceania called Air-Strip One (England), in a city still called London.

These three countries are constantly at war with one another, furiously shifting allegiances. When the novel opens, Oceania is at war with Eurasia, allied with Eastasia. Four years before, Oceania had been at war with Eastasia and allied with Eurasia; by the end of the book, the battlefield has shifted once again. It is against this background of never-ending war, uncertainty, and fear that the novel unfolds.

"A Bright Cold Day"

This is how the novel begins: "It was a bright cold day in April, and the clocks were striking thirteen. Winston Smith, his chin nuzzled into his breast in an effort to escape the vile wind, slipped quickly through the glass doors of Victory Mansions, though not quickly enough to prevent a swirl of gritty dust from entering along with him . . . On each landing, opposite the lift shaft, the poster with the enormous face gazed from the wall. It was one of those pictures which are so contrived that the eyes follow you about when you move. BIG BROTHER IS WATCHING YOU, the caption beneath it ran."

In most literary works, spring is a time of rebirth and love, happiness and promise. Instead, Orwell immediately plunges us here into a dirty, bitter world of "vile wind" and "gritty dust." It is very different from the shining future we often imagine. The clock tolls thirteen, a symbol of bad luck. The poster with Big Brother's ever-present eyes suggests that privacy, dignity, and peace have been swept away. Later in the opening chapter we see that bombs explode constantly; buildings are shabby and depressing. The name "Victory Mansions" is far more wish than reality, as the run-down state of Winston's small apartment shows. Because of the constant wars, all goods are in short supply, including necessities such as food, clothing, and housing. Since the kinds of consumer goods that we take for granted in our world—razor blades, tobacco, and chocolate—are nearly impossible to obtain, they are carefully hoarded. Telescreens, microphones, and networks of spies ("Thought Police") keep people under constant surveillance; children are taught to spy on their parents. The commanding face of the semi-mythical leader Big Brother gazes from every street corner. It is a world of pain, deprivation, and terror.

The Novel's Structure

The structure of the novel is somewhat unusual. The narrative is told in three sections, followed by a brief Appendix that is an important part of the story. Part One introduces us to Winston Smith and his bitterly lonely and fearful life in Oceania. Part Two describes his attempt to find hope by falling in love and rebelling against the ruling political party. Part Three shows what happens to his quest for a better life. The Appendix clarifies the structure and purpose of "Newspeak," the language Orwell created for *1984*.

In Part One we are introduced to the main character, Winston Smith. Although as a member of the Outer Party he is on the fringes of the ruling Inner Party, he nonetheless has no special privileges. As a result, he is frail and seems far older than his thirty-nine years. Decades of poor nourishment have taken their toll on his health and spirit.

Winston begins a diary, an act not strictly forbidden by law (for there are no written laws) but understood by the all-inclusive offense of "Thoughtcrime" to be punishable by death. Because of the unusual placement of the telescreen in his living room, he is able to scrape a crumb of privacy by huddling in an alcove, where he fearfully scribbles his thoughts. His thoughts drift to O'Brien, a member of the elite Inner Party. O'Brien is so important—and the Inner Party held in such fear—that a hush falls over the workers when he enters a room. We also learn that Winston works at the "Ministry of Truth," where he rewrites past documents —in effect forging history—to make the past conform to current Party doctrine. Winston wonders why a bold-looking dark-haired girl had caught his eye during the "Two Minutes Hate." Is she an agent of the Thought Police? Could she be spying on him? Will he mysteriously disappear as so many others have?

Part Two opens with the dark-haired girl's astonishing action: Risking death, she slips Winston a note declaring her love. After elaborate precautions they are able to meet and soon fall in love. Wanting a place in which to be alone, Winston and Julia risk everything by renting a room above an an-

tique store and setting up housekeeping. Amazingly, the room has no telescreen and the couple freely discuss rebellion against the Party and its symbol, Big Brother. Something almost as amazing happens one day at work: O'Brien, the Inner Party member, approaches Winston and invites him and Julia to his luxurious apartment. There he reveals that he is secretly involved in the resistance movement, The Brotherhood. Under his guidance Winston learns how the Party works—that its main goal is the exercise of power for its own sake. Part Two ends with a shattering climax.

In Part Three Winston learns the full truth about the Party—and himself. Under O'Brien's hand he sees what lies behind the resistance movement. This wrenching section lays bare the true effects of loss of freedom on the human soul. It contains some of the most unforgettable scenes you will ever read.

The Appendix explores how Newspeak, the official language of Oceania, provides a means of expression for the Party members while simultaneously making it impossible to express any unorthodox thought. In so doing it provides a detailed exploration of how language can be twisted to abolish free thinking.

Great Works 1021

Orwell (1903–1950) was the pseudonym used by an Englishman named Eric Blair. As a young man, he served with the Indian Imperial Police in Burma. When he returned to England, he became a writer. His firsthand experience with colonialism inspired his novel *Burmese Days* and the frequently anthologized essay "Shooting an Elephant." Orwell's hatred of totalitarianism led him to fight on the side of the Loyalists in the Spanish Civil War (1936–1939). He wrote about this experience in *Homage to Catalonia,* which the critic Lionel Trilling called "one of the important documents of our time."

Orwell died of a lung ailment at the age of 47.

Critical Evaluation The psychoanalyst Erich Fromm wrote that "Orwell . . . is not a prophet of disaster. He wants to warn and to awaken us. He still hopes—but in contrast to the writers of the utopias in the earlier phases of Western society, his hope is a desperate one. The hope can be realized only by recognizing, so *1984* teaches us, the danger with which all men are confronted today, the danger of a society of automatons who will have lost every trace of individuality, of love, of critical thought, and yet who will not be aware of it because of 'doublethink.' Books like Orwell's are powerful warnings, and it would be most unfortunate if the reader smugly interpreted *1984* as another description of Stalinist barbarism, and if he does not see that it means us, too."

Power Abused

The central question of life, Orwell once remarked, is "how to prevent power from being abused." O'Brien explains the Party's exercise of power to Winston's incredulous ears: "Power is inflicting pain and humiliation. Power is in tearing human minds to pieces and putting them together again in new shapes of your own choosing. Do you begin to see, then, what kind of world we are creating? It is the exact opposite of the stupid hedonistic Utopias that the old reformers imagined. A world of fear and treachery and torment, a world of trampling and being trampled upon, a world which will grow not less but more merciless as it refines itself. Progress in our world will be towards more pain . . . triumph after triumph: an endless pressing, pressing, pressing upon the nerve of power."

In part the novel's bleak despair emerged from the deep hopelessness of the 1930's and 1940's. It appeared for a time that most of the world would be ground under the heel of totalitarian dictatorships. Fascism, for example, required unquestioning loyalty to its leader. People were totally subordinated to the service of the state. As in *1984,* military supremacy was achieved at the expense of civilian standards of living. Orwell drew aspects of Big Brother, the Party, and the constant warfare from the Fascist oppression he saw burning through Europe. Fascism flowered in Italy, Spain, Japan, and Germany; even liberal democracies such as France and England had vocal Fascist movements. At the same time, terror and oppression were evident in Russia with the rise of Communism.

People have especially noted the similarities between "Big Brother" and the events of Orwell's day. Much has been written on the parallels between Big Brother and the Russian dictator Joseph Stalin, who consolidated his power in the mid-thirties through a major campaign of political terror. The purges, arrests, and deportations he ordered left few Russian families untouched. Much of his terror was exercised through a system of secret police, called the KGB. In their abuse of power, they greatly resemble the fictional "Thought Police" in *1984.* There are elements of the Nazi demagogue Adolph Hitler and the Spanish dictator Francisco Franco in Big Brother as well.

Orwell had raised his pen against dictatorships before. In his lucid essays and piercing satires, he had championed the cause of the downtrodden and oppressed. His 1945 fable *Animal Farm,* for example, grimly attacked the evils of both Fascism and Communism. Orwell felt so strongly about the threat of Fascism that he laid his life on the line to try to halt its encroachment. From 1936 to 1939, he fought on the front lines of the Spanish Civil War against the Fascist forces of General Francisco Franco. He regarded the actions of the Fascists in Spain as a betrayal of the popular revolution, which might otherwise have given the working classes real freedom and status. He was badly wounded in the throat.

But Orwell did not write *1984* to comment on life in the thirties and forties nor to predict the state of world leadership and society in the future. He exaggerates what life could be like in the future if totalitarian regimes seized control of governments to warn people to struggle to prevent the loss of decency and dignity in life. Recognizing that political freedom is solidly linked to linguistic freedom, he sought to warn readers that corrupting language corrupts life.

Poetry

HOUSES OF PARLIAMENT, 1903
Claude Monét
The Granger Collection

Humanities Note

Fine art, *Houses of Parliament,* 1903, by Claude Monet. The French painter Monet (1840–1926) was a founder of the impressionist school, and is one of the foremost landscape painters in the history of art. The impressionists used their broken-color technique to capture the transient variations of light and atmosphere brought on by changes of hour and season. They were interested in the subtle effects of light on form. Monet loosens the brushstrokes, allowing colors to fuse, not on canvas, but in the eye of the viewer. In impressionism, the actual act of painting becomes visible; every dab and touch is a record of the movement of the brush.

Houses of Parliament is one of 37 views of London's Thames River Monet exhibited in 1904. The painting is mysterious and visionary. Its theme is not the stone architecture, but silhouette and reflections, colored light suspended in air. The cool blue mass of the buildings is markedly contrasted to the fiery pastels of the sky and water, which seem to set the scene ablaze. Volume and depth in the painting are created by the variety of tones of color, which give the atmosphere as tangible a life and breath as that of the solid objects. The boatman in the foreground, moving through the fog, heightens the mysterious mood as do the narrow, tall Gothic towers and spires of the mass of buildings. The colors and technique themselves create a palpable drama.

WILLIAM BUTLER YEATS

1865–1939

Winner of the Nobel Prize for Literature in 1923, William Butler Yeats (yāts) is generally regarded as one of the finest poets of this century. Born near Dublin, Ireland, Yeats was educated there and in London, but his heart lay to the west, in County Sligo, Ireland, where he spent childhood vacations with his grandparents. In the shadow of Sligo's barren mountains, he became immersed in the mythology and legends of Ireland.

After three years of studying painting in Dublin, Yeats moved to London to pursue a literary career. He became friends with the poet Arthur Symons, who awakened his interest in the symbolic poetry of William Blake and the French Symbolists. Yeats's early poetry shows the Symbolist influence as well as that of the Pre-Raphaelites, a group who believed that art needs a moral center which they felt it had lost nearly three centuries earlier. Symbolism, Pre-Raphaelism, and Irish myth combined in Yeats's first important collection, *The Wanderings of Oisin,* published in 1889.

Yeats led the Irish Literary Revival, helping to establish the Irish Literary Society in London in 1892 and the Irish National Literary Society in Dublin. He was also active in the Irish National Movement, whose members sought Ireland's independence from England. In this, he was spurred by his unrequited love for the beautiful actress and revolutionary, Maud Gonne. To his sorrow—after many refusals of his proposals—she chose a soldier, and Yeats, years later, married another woman.

Near the end of the century, Yeats joined with his friend Lady Augusta Gregory in founding the Irish National Theatre Society. He turned his attention to writing plays, among them *The Shadowy Waters* (1900) and *Deirdre* (1907). When he returned to poetry, it was with a new voice, subtler but more powerful than the one he had used before that time. The poems in *The Tower,* published in 1928, show Yeats at the height of his abilities.

In 1922 Yeats was appointed a senator of the new Irish Free State, and on his seventieth birthday he was hailed by his nation as the greatest living Irishman. He continued to write poems until a day or two before his death at Roquebrune, France. One of his last poems contains his famous epitaph: Cast a cold eye / On life, on death. / Horseman, pass by!

GUIDE FOR INTERPRETING

When You Are Old; The Lake Isle of Innisfree; The Wild Swans at Coole; An Irish Airman Foresees His Death

Writer's Technique

Speaker and Lyric Voice. A lyric poem expresses personal thoughts and feelings on a specific subject. Among the most common subjects are love, death, nature, and war. Sometimes the speaker in a lyric poem—the one whose voice comes through—is, or appears to be, the poet. In Milton's "When I Consider How My Light Is Spent," for example, the speaker seems clearly to be the poet. In Christopher Marlowe's "The Passionate Shepherd to His Love," on the other hand, the speaker is almost certainly not the poet. In many lyric poems, such as William Blake's "The Tiger," you cannot tell for sure whether the speaker is or is not the poet.

Writing

Think of a subject about which you have strong feelings, either positive or negative, such as education, friendship, or marriage. Jot down some brief notes that express your feelings on the subject. Then think of a fictional character based either on your reading or your imagination. Write at least three sentences, or three lines of poetry, in which the fictional character expresses your feelings on the subject you have chosen.

Primary Source

Sean O'Faolain tried to explain the extraordinary influence William Butler Yeats exerted on all phases of Irish life. Elected a member of the Irish Academy of Letters founded the year before by Yeats and Shaw, O'Faolain worked with Yeats on several projects as Yeats's remarkable career drew to its close. "He had been our inspiration and our justification in the sense that all the rest of us younger men and women could not, between us, represent literature with anything like his achievement and authority in the eyes of the public. When he retired to Rapallo to die, and most of his generation had passed away or gone into exile one by one . . . there was nothing to do but wait until Time, if it ever did, created new reputations of equal authority. Time did not and could not. It was not a matter alone of literary achievement. Had, for example, Joyce returned to live in Dublin his presence would have made no difference. For the source of Yeats's authority, like the source of his poetry, was the extraordinary union in his nature of a powerful imagination, the will to enforce it, and a persistent dramatic self-image of himself as a seer and leader. . . . It was the blend that at once bestowed greatness on him and condemned him to loneliness. . . . It was his need of his nature, as poet and man, to live a foot off the ground, a foot or two, or more, away from common life."

Guide for Interpreting 1025

Motivation/Prior Knowledge
Encourage students to think about someone who disappointed them in rejecting their offer of friendship. What kind of polite response would be appropriate?

Master Teacher Note Elicit from students various meanings for *pilgrim*. Recall with them the pilgrims in Chaucer's *Canterbury Tales* and Pilgrim in Bunyan's *Pilgrim's Progress*. What do these pilgrims have in common? What religious connotations does *pilgrim* have?

Purpose-Setting Question How much self-pity is there in this poem?

Thematic Idea Another selection that you might want to use with this is Matthew Arnold's poem "To Marguerite-Continued," page 838.

1 Literary Focus Note that the speaker asks the woman to think about herself before he makes a transition to his own feelings. Why is this method effective?

2 Discussion What does Yeats mean by her "pilgrim soul"?

3 Discussion What does he mean by "the sorrows of your changing face"?

4 Literary Focus What does the imagery suggest about the outcome of this love?

Reader's Response How do you think the lady to whom this poem was addressed might have responded?

When You Are Old

William Butler Yeats

1
When you are old and gray and full of sleep,
And nodding by the fire, take down this book,
And slowly read, and dream of the soft look
Your eyes had once, and of their shadows deep;

2
5 How many loved your moments of glad grace,
And loved your beauty with love false or true,
But one man loved the pilgrim soul in you,
3
And loved the sorrows of your changing face;

4
And bending down beside the glowing bars,
10 Murmur, a little sadly, how Love fled
And paced upon the mountains overhead
And hid his face amid a crowd of stars.

THINKING ABOUT THE SELECTION

Recalling

1. What does the speaker ask the person being addressed to do?
2. What happened to Love?

Interpreting

3. Who do you think the "one man" in the second stanza is?
4. What does the phrase "pilgrim soul" suggest about the person being addressed?
5. Why is the word *Love* capitalized in line 10?

Applying

6. When love is not reciprocated, it may be withdrawn, as it apparently was in this poem. Under what circumstances do you think it is right to withdraw love that is not being returned?

ANALYZING LITERATURE
Understanding Speaker and Lyric Voice

The speaker in a lyric poem may or may not be the poet. Sometimes the identity of the speaker is obvious, but often it is hard to be sure. Knowing about the poet's life, while not essential to your enjoyment of a poem, may provide clues to the identity of the speaker.

1. Look back at the biography of Yeats. What event in his life might have prompted him to write this poem?
2. In line 2 the speaker advises the person being addressed to "take down this book." In what way might that advice furnish a clue to the identity of the speaker?

Closure and Extension

ANSWERS TO THINKING ABOUT THE SELECTION
Recalling

1. He asks her to read this book and dream about herself as a young woman.
2. Love fled, paced upon the mountains, and hid its face.

Interpreting

3. Suggested Response: The man is the speaker—Yeats himself.
4. Answers will differ. Students may respond that the phrase suggests the woman is a wanderer or seeker.
5. Suggested Response: The speaker is personifying love.

Applying

6. Answers will differ. Students may respond that a person always has the right to withdraw unreciprocated love.

ANSWERS TO ANALYZING LITERATURE

1. Suggested Response: Maud Gonne's choice of a different suitor could have prompted this poem.
2. Suggested Response: One would be reading this poem in a volume of verse, so one can infer that the speaker is a poet.

The Lake Isle of Innisfree

William Butler Yeats

I will arise and go now, and go to Innisfree,
And a small cabin build there, of clay and wattles[1] made:
Nine bean-rows will I have there, a hive for the honeybee,
And live alone in the bee-loud glade.

5 And I shall have some peace there, for peace comes
     dropping slow,
   Dropping from the veils of the morning to where the cricket
     sings;
   There midnight's all a glimmer, and noon a purple glow,
   And evening full of the linnet's wings.[2]

   I will arise and go now, for always night and day
10 I hear lake water lapping with low sounds by the shore;
   While I stand on the roadway, or on the pavements gray,
   I hear it in the deep heart's core.

_____

1. wattles *n*.: Stakes interwoven with twigs or branches.
2. linnet's wings: The wings of a European singing bird.

OLD HOUSE (IVY COTTAGE),
SHOREHAM, 1831–32
Samuel Palmer
Ashmolean Museum, Oxford

1 **Literary Focus** The metaphors here contrast with the first stanza's literal descriptions.

2 **Literary Focus** Note that stanza three returns to the directness of stanza one. How does this stanza, then, reinforce the message?

THINKING ABOUT THE SELECTION

Recalling

1. (a) What does the speaker want most to find at Innisfree? (b) How will each of the four times of day he mentions contribute to his goal?
2. According to line 11, where is the speaker when he hears the call of Innisfree?

Interpreting

3. Why do you think Innisfree, as the speaker describes it, has so much more appeal for him than where he is now?

4. (a) Do you think the speaker is expressing a wish or a genuine intent to go to Innisfree? (b) What evidence in the poem is there to support your answer?
5. What techniques or devices in the poem help to create a vivid picture of Innisfree?

Applying

6. Popular music sometimes deals with the theme of leaving one place and going to a more desirable place. What song or songs can you think of that have that theme?

The Lake Isle of Innisfree   1027

Presentation

Master Teacher Note You might tell students that Yeats had read Thoreau's *Walden* before writing this poem. Remind students that, in his book, Thoreau describes his experiment in living an isolated, self-sufficient life.

Purpose-Setting Question What is attractive about the way of life that Yeats imagines?

Humanities Note

Fine art; *Old House (Ivy Cottage), Shoreham* by Samuel Palmer. Samuel Palmer (1805–1881), was a British visionary painter of pastoral subjects. A precociously talented painter, Palmer exhibited watercolors at London's Royal Academy at the age of fourteen. The painting *Old House (Ivy Cottage), Shoreham* was completed in 1831–32. The contrast between the motionless shadowed figures and the bright cottage creates a mysterious tension. Even the foliage seems charged and still.

You may wish to discuss the following. This painting suggests a simple life, close to nature: How does this compare to the life Yeats writes of in his poem?

Closure and Extension

ANSWERS TO THINKING ABOUT THE SELECTION
Recalling

1. (a) The speaker desires peace. (b) Morning (mist and cricket song), noon ("a purple glow"), evening (flocks of linnets), and midnight ("all a glimmer") will contribute to the feeling of peace.
2. The speaker is on a city street.

Interpreting

3. Suggested Response: One may infer that the peaceful retreat is in direct contrast to the speaker's more frenetic city life.
4. (a) Suggested Response: The speaker seems to be expressing a deeply felt dream of an ideal type of existence rather than an intent to leave immediately. (b) Throughout the poem, he dwells more on visualizing the ideal than on a plan for departure.

5. Suggested Response: Students may note the repetition of the word "dropping;" the soothing *m, n,* and *l* sounds; the concrete, specific images; and the metaphors in the second stanza.

Applying

6. Answers will differ. Students will no doubt suggest currently popular songs.

Motivation/Prior Knowledge
Discuss why people think of swans as impressive birds, and note that the swan has become part of expressions such as *swansong*. What qualities do we associate with a swan?

Master Teacher Note You might want to tell students that Coole Park, where this poem is set, was the home of Lady Gregory. She was Yeats's patron and collaborator—they worked together in establishing a national theater. Yeats spent a great deal of time at Coole Park, a large estate with ponds for swans, forest paths, orchards, and so forth.

1 Discussion What scene does the poet set?

2 Discussion What is the effect of the poet's use of exact numbers?

3 Discussion The poet shifts the direction of his musings here; he turns from the outward scene to his inner feelings. How does he feel? Why is his heart sore? What in particular has changed in the past nineteen years?

4 Discussion What does he mean by "passion" and "conquest"? Are these qualities usually associated with the young? Explain.

5 Discussion Why does he call the swans "mysterious"?

6 Discussion What kind of wakening is he referring to?

Reader's Response Is there a type of bird that has a special, symbolic meaning for you? Explain.

The Wild Swans at Coole

William Butler Yeats

1
The trees are in their autumn beauty,
The woodland paths are dry,
Under the October twilight the water
Mirrors a still sky;
5 Upon the brimming water among
    the stones
Are nine-and-fifty swans.

2
The nineteenth autumn has come
    upon me
Since I first made my count;
I saw, before I had well finished,
10 All suddenly mount
And scatter wheeling in great broken
    rings
Upon their clamorous wings.

3
I have looked upon those brilliant
    creatures,
And now my heart is sore.
15 All's changed since I, hearing at twilight,
The first time on this shore,
The bell-beat of their wings above
    my head,
Trod with a lighter tread.

4
Unwearied still, lover by lover,
20 They paddle in the cold
Companionable streams or climb the air;
Their hearts have not grown old;
Passion or conquest, wander where
    they will,
Attend upon them still.

5
25 But now they drift on the still water,
Mysterious, beautiful;
Among what rushes will they build,
By what lake's edge or pool

6
Delight men's eyes when I awake
    some day
30 To find they have flown away?

THINKING ABOUT THE SELECTION

Recalling

1. (a) When did the speaker first begin counting the swans? (b) What did the swans do before he had finished counting?
2. (a) What was the speaker's reaction when he first heard "the bell-beat of their wings"? (b) Why is his reaction different now from what it was then?
3. What will the swans inevitably do?

Interpreting

4. For what thematic purpose does the speaker emphasize the setting in the first two stanzas?
5. In the fourth stanza, how does the speaker suggest that he and the swans are not alike?

Closure and Extension

ANSWERS TO THINKING ABOUT THE SELECTION
Recalling

1. (a) He began counting the swans nineteen years ago. (b) The swans flew away before he could finish counting.
2. (a) The speaker was younger then —"trod with a lighter tread"—and was perhaps happier. (b) He is older and tired now, envious of the swans' passion.
3. The swans will fly away.

Interpreting

4. Suggested Response: The speaker emphasizes autumn, generally symbolic of old age and of approaching death.
5. Suggested Response: The swans, in contrast to the speaker, are "unwearied still."

6. Suggested Response: The swans represent eternal youth and enduring love and passion.

Applying

7. Answers will differ but may center on the notion that beauty is fleeting; we know that a beautiful thing will not remain exactly as it is for long.

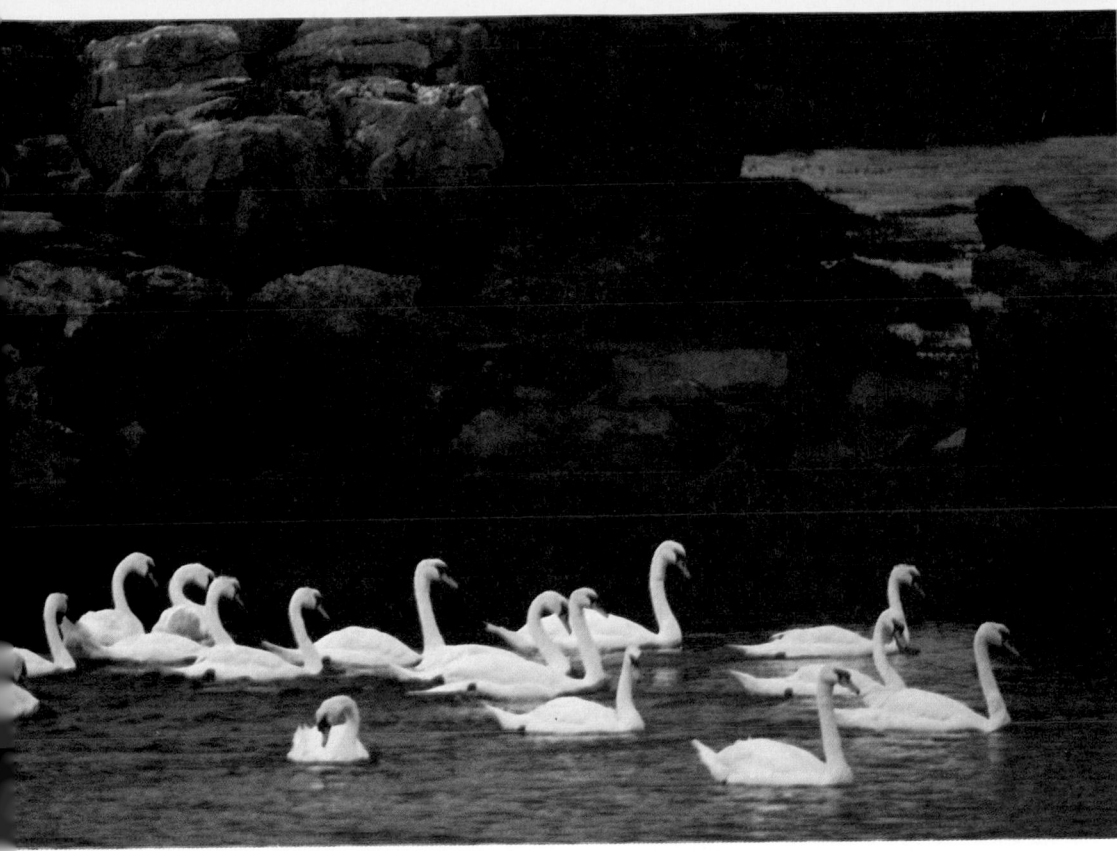

6. What do you think the swans symbolize to the speaker?

Applying

7. Although the wild swans in their natural setting are beautiful, the speaker feels a sense of sadness and loss. Why does great beauty sometimes arouse those feelings?

CRITICAL THINKING AND READING

Evaluating the Use of Imagery

Imagery in literature is created through the writer's use of words, singly or in combination, to produce a picture in the reader's mind. Images may appeal to any of the five senses. Sometimes they appeal to several senses at once. A writer who refers to "a crisp, shiny, sweet apple" is simultaneously appealing to hearing, sight, and taste. If imagery is to work effectively, readers must be familiar with the key words and their meanings. For example, a reader who has never heard the word *clamorous* will probably not appreciate the imagery of "clamorous wings." The following images are from "The Wild Swans of Coole." Locate each one in the poem and identify the sense or senses to which it appeals.

1. . . . the water/Mirrors a still sky
2. All suddenly mount/And scatter wheeling in great broken rings/Upon their clamorous wings
3. The bell-beat of their wings
4. They paddle in the cold/Companionable streams

The Wild Swans at Coole   1029

Motivation/Prior Knowledge
You may want to spur discussion by asking the following questions. Imagine that you are facing battle in a war. What do you think you would be thinking about?

Purpose-Setting Question Determine what is going through the airman's mind. Is there one central theme or just snatches of thought?

1 **Discussion** Why might the "I" of this poem say that his country is Kiltartan Cross rather than Ireland as a whole?

2 **Discussion** How does the speaker feel about the possible effects of the war?

3 **Discussion** What are the usual reasons that men go to war? Did any of these inspire the narrator? What did inspire him instead? What do you think he means by "A lonely impulse of delight"?

4 **Literary Focus** The final four lines explain why the narrator accepts the death that he foresaw in the two opening lines. Why do you think he values his lonely life and death as a pilot above all else?

An Irish Airman Foresees His Death

William Butler Yeats

Major Robert Gregory, a young Irish artist who was the son of Yeats's friend Lady Augusta Gregory, was killed during World War I while flying over Italy as a member of England's Royal Flying Corps. Gregory's death inspired Yeats to write this poem.

I know that I shall meet my fate
Somewhere among the clouds above;
Those that I fight I do not hate,
Those that I guard I do not love;[1]
My country is Kiltartan[2] Cross,   5
My countrymen Kiltartan's poor,
No likely end could bring them loss
Or leave them happier than before.
Nor law, nor duty bade me fight,
Nor public men, nor cheering crowds,   10
A lonely impulse of delight
Drove to this tumult in the clouds;
I balanced all, brought all to mind,
The years to come seemed waste of breath,
A waste of breath the years behind   15
In balance with this life, this death.

---

1. Those . . . love: Because Ireland was under English rule during World War I, many Irish fought as members of the English forces during the war. However, because of their desire for independence many of the Irish felt a great deal of resentment toward the English.
2. Kiltartan: A village near Lady Gregory's estate.

BURNING AIRPLANE
Photri

THINKING ABOUT THE SELECTION

Recalling

1. What does the Irish airman believe will happen to him?
2. (a) How does he feel about those he is fighting against? (b) Why is he fighting them?
3. How does he view (a) his past? (b) his future?

Interpreting

4. The airman does not love those he guards —the English. (a) Do you think his lack of love extends to those he calls his countrymen —Kiltartan's poor? (b) What lines in the poem support your answer?
5. (a) To what extent does the airman seem worried about his fate? (b) How would you describe the airman's character?

Applying

6. Suppose the airman were to survive the war. What do you think he might do with the rest of his life? Explain your answer.

THINKING AND WRITING

Writing About the Use of a Speaker

In writing "An Irish Airman Foresees His Death," Yeats had in mind Major Robert Gregory, the son of Yeats's close friend Lady Augusta Gregory. A volunteer in England's Royal Flying Corps, Major Gregory was killed during World War I while flying over Italy. Think about why Yeats may have chosen to write his poem with Major Gregory as the first-person speaker. Write a brief essay in which you explain why the poem, as written, allows Yeats to express his thoughts about the frailty of life, the futility of war, and the problems of Ireland more powerfully than a third-person point of view would have permitted. When you revise, make sure you have included details from the poem to support your opinion.

An Irish Airman Foresees His Death   1031

Closure and Extension

ANSWERS TO THINKING ABOUT THE SELECTION

Recalling

1. He foresees his death.
2. (a) He does not hate those that he fights. (b) He was motivated by "A lonely impulse of delight."
3. (a) and (b) He viewed his past and future as meaningless in comparison to his life and death as a pilot.

Interpreting

4. Suggested Responses: (a) He is sympathetic toward them, but does not believe that loss or victory in the war will change their lot. (b) Lines 7–9 support this response.
5. Suggested Responses: (a) He is not worried about his fate but accepts it. (b) He has a kind of tragic nobility and resignation.

Applying

6. Answers will differ. Some students might respond that he would not do anything constructive. Other students may feel that he would try to help his less fortunate countrymen.

THINKING AND WRITING

Publishing Student Writing You might want to have volunteers read their essays to the class.

Writing/Prior Knowledge To explore further the concept of symbols and to trigger their thinking before writing, ask students to think of objects in their own experience that are symbols. Then ask them to choose one symbol to represent themselves—it could be something that represents their interests, their personality, or a specific skill.

Vocabulary

Preteach the following vocabulary words:
anarchy (an′ ər kē) *n.:* Absence of government; confusion, disorder, and violence (p. 1033, l. 4)
conviction (kən vik′ shən) *n.:* Belief in something meaningful, such as a creed (p. 1033, l. 7)
descant (des kant′) *v.:* To talk at length (p. 1035, l. 5)
decrepitude (di krep′ ə tood) *n.:* State of being old and broken down (p. 1035, l. 7)

GUIDE FOR INTERPRETING

The Second Coming; After Long Silence; Sailing to Byzantium

Writer's Technique

Symbols. In its broadest, most basic sense, a symbol is something that stands for something else. The word *horse* is a symbol for an actual, recognizable animal. In our culture an olive branch is a symbol for peace. A symbol in literature is a word, person, object, or action that stands for something beyond itself. For example, the white whale in Herman Melville's *Moby-Dick* is often said to stand for evil. In the art and literature of the late nineteenth century, the word *symbolism* took on special significance. A group of French artists and poets, reacting against realism, promoted the use of symbols to achieve intensity and complexity in their work, a technique that sometimes approached mysticism. Yeats, an adherent of this type of symbolism in his early poetry, abandoned it later. However, in the last decade of his life, he created an elaborate symbolic system of his own, a system that is largely a curiosity for modern readers. His later poems abound in symbols, but Yeats remains first and foremost a poet, not a system-maker or a philosopher. In his best poems, the symbols do not require mastery of his system, but only the practiced eye of a careful reader.

As you read the poems by William Butler Yeats, look for his use of symbols and be alert to the possible meanings attached to them.

Writing

If you wished to picture Canada symbolically, you might draw a maple leaf; for Great Britain you might draw a lion and for New York City, an apple. Countries, states, cities, companies, high schools, professional athletic teams—all sometimes develop symbols for easy and perhaps emotional identification. Think about such symbols. Jot down a number of them, identifying what each one symbolizes.

Primary Source

It's tempting to think that famous writers are free from the doubts that the rest of us sometimes feel. That Eliot and Yeats both received great praise in their day does not mean that they were immune to a touch of professional jealousy. Writer Richard Ellmann noted their long incompatibility in this encounter:

"Among their various mild collisions none was more defined than the dinner at Wellesley College when Yeats, seated next to Eliot but oblivious of him, conversed with the guest on the other side until late in the meal. Then he turned and said, 'My friend here and I have been discussing the defects of T. S. Eliot's poetry. What do you think of that poetry?'

"Eliot held up his place card to excuse himself from the jury."

Objectives

1 To recognize and interpret symbols
2 To write a poem about silence

Support Material

Teaching Portfolio
Teacher Backup, p. 1231
Usage and Mechanics Worksheet, p. 1234
Vocabulary Check, p. 1235
Analyzing Literature Worksheet, *Understanding Symbols*, p. 1236
Language Worksheet, *Understanding Repetition*, p. 1237
Selection Test, p. 1238

The Second Coming

William Butler Yeats

"The Second Coming" was inspired by Yeats's belief that history occurs in two-thousand-year cycles, with one civilization passing through stages of development, growth, and decay, before crumbling and giving way to a new civilization that stands in direct opposition to the preceding civilization. The birth of Christ had brought about the end of one civilization and the birth of another, and Yeats believed that the society of the early twentieth century was in a state of decay that would lead to a similar sort of rebirth.

Turning and turning in the widening gyre
The falcon cannot hear the falconer;
Things fall apart; the center cannot hold;
Mere anarchy is loosed upon the world,
5   The blood-dimmed tide is loosed, and everywhere
The ceremony of innocence is drowned;
The best lack all conviction, while the worst
Are full of passionate intensity.[1]

Surely some revelation is at hand;
10   Surely the Second Coming is at hand.
The Second Coming! Hardly are those words out
When a vast image out of *Spiritus Mundi*[2]
Troubles my sight: somewhere in sands of the desert
A shape with lion body and the head of a man,[3]
15   A gaze blank and pitiless as the sun,
Is moving its slow thighs, while all about it
Reel shadows of the indignant desert birds.
The darkness drops again; but now I know
That twenty centuries[4] of stony sleep
20   Were vexed to nightmare by a rocking cradle,[5]
And what rough beast, its hour come round at last,
Slouches towards Bethlehem to be born?

---

1. Mere . . . intensity (lines 4-8): Refers to the Russian Revolution of 1917.
2. Spiritus Mundi (spir'i təs mōōn'dē): The Universal Spirit or soul, the Universal Subconscious in which the memories of the entire human race are forever preserved.
3. A . . . man: A sphinx.
4. twenty centuries: The historical cycle preceding the birth of Christ.
5. rocking cradle: The cradle of Jesus Christ.

The Second Coming   1033

Presentation

Motivation/Prior Knowledge Have students recall movies that they have seen about the fall of Rome or other civilizations, or newscasts about revolutions or anarchy in other countries. What usually followed the upheaval? What did the citizens hope for?

Master Teacher Note Present information about the role of a falconer. Point out the appropriateness of Yeats's choice of a falcon—a small hawk, a predatory bird—as opposed to some other bird in presenting his message.

Purpose-Setting Question What point is Yeats making in this poem?

1 Discussion The opening image, the circling flight of the bird, widening and widening until it loses contact with the center to which it should return, is a symbol for disunity. Why is this symbol effective?

2 Discussion Yeats speaks of anarchy and the blood-dimmed tide. What might these images represent in the modern world?

3 Literary Focus The monstrous threat, in the form of a rough, sphinx-like beast, slouches toward Bethlehem to be born, a frightening travesty of the birth of Christ almost two thousand years earlier.

Reader's Response If Yeats were alive today, would he feel that "Things fall apart"? Explain.

Enrichment This poem was written in 1919; Yeats felt that the anarchy in the world following World War I heralded the end of the Christian era.

Primary Source

The following passage from from Yeats's autobiography is particularly relevant to "The Second Coming":

A conviction that the world was now but a bundle of fragments possesed me without ceasing . . . . Doubtless because fragments broke into even smaller fragments we saw one another in a light of bitter comedy, and in the arts, where now one technical element reigned and now another, generation hated generation, and accomplished beauty was snatched away when it had most engaged our affections. One thing I did not foresee, not having the courage of my own thought: the growing murderousness of the world.

Closure and Extension

ANSWERS TO THINKING ABOUT THE SELECTION
Recalling

1. The falcon cannot hear its master.
2. Anarchy has been "loosed upon the world," drowning innocence.
3. The speaker believes that "some revelation is at hand."
4. A beast that has been dormant for twenty centuries has begun to stir in the desert.
5. A rough beast is about to be born.

Interpreting

6. Suggested Response: The unhearing falcon is symbolic of the disintegration of the natural order in the universe; it is symbolic of disunity and anarchy; it is a bird not obeying its master.
7. Suggested Response: Innocence is drowned in a bloody tide.
8. The twenty centuries are those following the birth of Christ.
9. (a) Answers will differ. (b) Students should point out differences between their expectations and Yeats's vision of a "shape with a lion body and the head of a man."

Applying

10. Answers will differ. Suggested Response: Predictions might be prompted by the awareness of the changes, especially cyclical changes, that run through human affairs.

ANSWERS TO ANALYZING LITERATURE

1. Suggested Responses: (a) He uses the stony, sleeping, sphinx-like creature to symbolize the twenty years of silence (b) Yeats concentrates on its features to emphasize its fearsomeness rather than letting the reader quickly name—and perhaps dismiss it—as a sphinx.
2. Suggested Responses: (a) This image symbolizes the loss of innocence in the modern world. (b) The indignant desert birds could represent those individuals aware of—and alarmed by—a change in the status quo.
3. Suggested Responses: (a) Yeats uses a sphinx-like beast to repre-

THINKING ABOUT THE SELECTION
Recalling

1. Why does the falcon not return to the falconer, as it ordinarily would in falconry (the hunting of game with falcons)?
2. In the first stanza, what is happening to government and innocence?
3. What does the speaker believe is at hand?
4. (a) What has begun to stir in the desert? (b) How long has it been dormant?
5. What does the speaker say is about to be born?

Interpreting

6. How does Yeats use the unhearing falcon as a symbol of what is happening in the world?
7. What is the imagery in lines 5-6?
8. When did the previous "twenty centuries of stony sleep" occur (that is, before the twentieth century)?
9. (a) What would you expect to appear at the Second Coming? (b) How does that differ from what the speaker suggests will appear?

Applying

10. What historical forces do you think prompt people, including poets, to predict vast upheavals, new civilizations, and even the end of the world?

ANALYZING LITERATURE
Understanding Symbols

A literary **symbol** is a word, person, object, or action that stands for something beyond itself. In "The Second Coming," for instance, the falcon flying in ever-widening circles is more than just a trained hunting bird that has lost its way. It represents something—it symbolizes something. A symbol always requires interpretation. With the falcon, it would help you to know Yeats's theories about "gyres," or cycles, which were a part of his symbolic system, although such knowledge is not really essential to an understanding of the poem.

1. Yeats does not merely talk about twenty centuries of silence. He symbolizes them. (a) What symbol does he use? (b) Why do you think he presents it through a description of its features rather than by naming it outright?
2. (a) What symbolism, if any, do you find in line 6: "The ceremony of innocence is drowned"? (b) What might the "indignant desert birds" in line 17 represent?
3. (a) What symbol does Yeats use to represent the coming era? (b) What characteristics do you associate with this symbol?

sent the coming era. (b) Possible characteristics are savagery, loathsomeness, and ugliness, among others.

After Long Silence

William Butler Yeats

1   Speech after long silence; it is right,
    All other lovers being estranged or dead,
2   Unfriendly lamplight hid under its shade,
    The curtains drawn upon unfriendly night,
3 5 That we descant and yet again descant
    Upon the supreme theme of Art and Song:
4   Bodily decrepitude is wisdom; young
5,6 We loved each other and were ignorant.

THINKING ABOUT THE SELECTION

Recalling

1. What does the speaker say should follow long silence?
2. The speaker describes two things as unfriendly. What are they?
3. What is the "supreme theme" that should be talked about after long silence?
4. Why does the speaker believe the old have more reason than the young to "descant and yet again descant"?

Interpreting

5. (a) What relationship exists between the people who are being urged to speak? (b) How can you tell?
6. What do you suppose was taking place during the period of long silence?
7. The speaker seems to have mixed feelings about old age. How would you describe his feelings?

Applying

8. How fully do you accept the idea that the young cannot talk meaningfully about "Art and Song"? Explain.

THINKING AND WRITING

Writing a Poem About Silence

"After Long Silence" treats the idea of silence symbolically. Silence, according to Yeats, is the time when human beings have little of intellectual importance to communicate to one another. That is one interpretation of silence, but only one. Choose another approach to the subject of silence. Think about it. Write some notes. Then write a poem that expresses your own view of silence. Remember that a poem requires revision just as much as an essay does —perhaps more.

Presentation

Motivation/Prior Knowledge Ask students to think about a person who had been a very close friend or relative whom they haven't seen in a long time. What might they talk about if they visited after many long years?

Purpose-Setting Question What is ironical about the speaker's situation?

1 **Discussion** What is the dramatic situation in this brief lyric?

2 **Literary Focus** Note the personifications in the phrases "unfriendly lamplight" and "unfriendly night." Why are lamplight and night unfriendly?

3 **Clarification** *Descant* here means "to talk at considerable length."

4 **Discussion** *Decrepitude* means "the state of being wasted by the infirmities of old age." How are lines 5 and 6 related to line 7?

5 **Discussion** Why, then, were these two ignorant when they were young? Do you think the poet is happier being old and wise?

6 **Discussion** What is the poem's tone?

Publishing Student Writing You may want to have students read their poems aloud in small groups and then discuss the various interpretations of silence that arise. Or you may want to encourage some students to give informal poetry readings to the full class.

Closure and Extension

ANSWERS TO THINKING ABOUT THE SELECTION
Recalling

1. Speech should follow long silence.
2. Lamplight and night are unfriendly.
3. The "supreme theme" is Art and Song.
4. The old are wiser in their "decrepitude."

Interpreting

5. Suggested Responses: (a) The two persons had been lovers. (b) In line 2, he says "All other lovers . . .," and in line 8, he says "We loved each other. . . ."
6. Suggested Response: Perhaps they had met and married others.
7. Suggested Response: The speaker deplores the physical infirmities but feels he has gained understanding.

Applying

8. Answers may differ. Students may respond that the young are more interested in action than talk.

THINKING AND WRITING

For help with this assignment, students can refer to Lesson 18, "Writing a Poem," in the Handbook of Writing About Literature.

Sailing to Byzantium[1]

W. B. Yeats

I

1 That is no country for old men. The young
In one another's arms, birds in the trees
—Those dying generations—at their song,
The salmon-falls, the mackerel-crowded seas,
2 5 Fish, flesh, or fowl, commend all summer long
Whatever is begotten, born, and dies.
3 Caught in that sensual music all neglect
Monuments of unaging intellect.

II

An aged man is but a paltry thing,
4 10 A tattered coat upon a stick, unless
Soul clap its hands and sing, and louder sing
For every tatter in its mortal dress,
Nor is there singing school but studying
Monuments of its own magnificence;
15 And therefore I have sailed the seas and come
5 To the holy city of Byzantium.

III

O sages standing in God's holy fire
As in the gold mosaic of a wall,[2]
Come from the holy fire, perne in a gyre,[3]
20 And be the singing-masters of my soul.
Consume my heart away; sick with desire
And fastened to a dying animal
It knows not what it is; and gather me
6 Into the artifice of eternity.

---

1. Byzantium (bi zan′ shē əm): The ancient capital of the Eastern Roman (or Byzantine) Empire and the seat of the Greek Orthodox Church; today, Istanbul, Turkey. For Yeats, it symbolized the sensual and artistic world as opposed to the natural and biological world.
2. sages . . . wall: Wise old men and saints portrayed in gold mosaic on the walls of Byzantine churches.
3. perne . . . gyre: Spin in a spiraling motion.

IV

25　Once out of nature I shall never take
　　My bodily form from any natural thing,
　　But such a form as Grecian goldsmiths make
　　Of hammered gold and gold enameling
　　To keep a drowsy Emperor awake;
30　Or set upon a golden bough to sing[4]
　　To lords and ladies of Byzantium
　　Of what is past, or passing, or to come.

_____

4. To . . . sing: Yeats wrote, "I have read somewhere that in the Emperor's palace at Byzantium was a tree made of gold and silver, and artificial birds that sang."

THINKING ABOUT THE SELECTION

Recalling

1. (a) What do the people of the country referred to in the first stanza "commend"? (b) What do they neglect?
2. How is "an aged man" described in lines 9-10?
3. What does the speaker do in lines 15-16?
4. What does the speaker ask of the sages in the third stanza?
5. What bodily form does the speaker wish to take when he is "out of nature"?

Interpreting

6. How does Byzantium contrast with the country described in the first two stanzas?
7. (a) What do the desires which the speaker expresses in stanzas 3 and 4 reveal about his attitude toward aging and death? (b) How does he hope to immortalize himself?
8. What does this poem suggest about the motives of artists and the purpose of art?

Applying

9. Do you think that most people hope to immortalize themselves in some way? Why or why not?

Sailing to Byzantium　1037

---

7 Discussion Compare and contrast this realm of artifice with the natural world in the first stanza.

8 Literary Focus The golden bird is a symbol of the artist who, through a work of art, has gone beyond the natural world. However, the artist sings about the very world he has transcended— the world of nature, time, and mortality!

You might want to remind students that a paradox is a statement or situation that has contradictory elements. Ask them how the golden bird is a paradoxical symbol.

Reader's Response Byzantium was Yeats's idea of a perfect city. What is yours?

Closure and Extension

ANSWERS TO THINKING ABOUT THE SELECTION
Recalling

1. (a) They commend "Whatever is begotten, born, and dies." (b) They "neglect/Monuments of unaging intellect."
2. "An aged man is . . ./A tattered coat upon a stick. . . ."
3. He sails the seas "To the holy city of Byzantium."
4. He asks them to move in a spiral, teach him to sing, consume his heart, and gather him "Into the artifice of eternity."
5. He wants to be a golden bird.

Interpreting

6. Suggested Response: Byzantium is an eternal, artificial city, not subject to the processes of mortality.
7. Suggested Response: (a) He wants to escape age and death. (b) He wants to immortalize himself by transcending nature. Paradoxically, however, as an artificial, golden bird, he will sing about mortality.
8. Suggested Response: The poem suggests that artists want to somehow escape age and death through their art.

Applying

9. Answers will differ. Students may respond that many people would like to immortalize themselves and that having children can even be viewed as a means to this end.

1037

More About the Author You might tell students that D. H. Lawrence believed a poem should reflect a momentary, spontaneous perception or feeling. Unlike Yeats, he did not view a poem as a carefully constructed, artificial work. Ask students to compare and contrast these two approaches to art. What are the advantages and disadvantages of each?

Literary Focus Consider explaining to students that many poets at the beginning of the century abandoned regular meters because they felt that every poetic expression required its own unique rhythm.

Writing/Prior Knowledge To open their thinking to a variety of possibilities, have students volunteer samples of "startling sights"—in nature, on a city street, or at a celebration of some kind, for example.

Critical Evaluation The literary scholars Richard Ellmann and Robert O'Clair asserted that Lawrence displays in his poems "a concentrated apprehension of the inner beings of animals and flowers."

Vocabulary

Preteach the following vocabulary words.
perversity (pər vur′ sə tē) *n.:* State of being wicked or wrong (l. 32)
convulsed (kən vulst′) *v.:* Shook; moved violently (l. 59)
accursed (ə kur′ sid) *adj.:* Hateful (l. 65)
expiate (ek′ spē āt′) *v.:* To make amends for; atone for (l. 74)

D.H. LAWRENCE

1885–1930

Although D. H. Lawrence is best known for his novels and short stories, he was also a fine poet. His poetry, like his prose, concentrates on the life-giving force of nature, exalting the physical and instinctual over the purely intellectual. Writing in free verse, Lawrence produced a number of powerful and original poems that evoke the "blood consciousness" and "dark gods" he sought. His "belief in the blood" was not merely his philosophy but was the dynamic force, the energy, that fueled his poetic imagination. For a fuller biography of D. H. Lawrence, see page 972.

Snake

Writer's Technique

Free Verse. Free verse is poetry that has no clearly defined rhyme scheme or rhythmic pattern. Lines are based on the natural phrasing of the language, and the rhythm follows normal voice cadences. Although no less a poet than Robert Frost has defined the writing of free verse as akin to "playing tennis with the net down," the issue is not that simple. Free verse poems are not merely works of prose laid out to resemble poetry. They *are* poetry, with a long and honored history going back to the Psalms in the bible. Free verse, never so "free" as prose, has its own rhythmic integrity and commonly makes use of the traditional devices of poetry, such as alliteration (repetition of consonant sounds), assonance (repetition of vowel sounds), and onomatopoeia (words or phrases that imitate the sound being described).

Writing

Try to recall the most startling sight you have ever come upon. Write a short account of this event. Describe in detail what you were doing when you first became aware of the sight. Explain your feelings at the time. Tell what happened after you began to watch. Describe how the event ended and what your thoughts and feelings were when it was over.

Primary Source

Imagine giving a book you have written to your folks. Lawrence describes his mother's reaction: "The very first copy of *The White Peacock* that was ever sent out, I put into my mother's hands when she was dying. She looked at the outside, and then at the title-page, and then at me, with darkening eyes. And though she loved me so much, I think she doubted whether it could be much of a book, since no one more important than I had written it. Somewhere, in the helpless privacies of her being, she had wistful respect for me. But for me in the face of the world, not much."

Objectives

1 To understand free verse
2 To make inferences about purpose

Support Material

Teaching Portfolio
Teacher Backup, p. 1241
Grammar in Action Worksheet, *Using the Colon,* p. 1244
Usage and Mechanics Worksheet, p. 1246
Vocabulary Check, p. 1247
Analyzing Literature Worksheet, *Understanding Free Verse,* p. 1248

Language Worksheet, *Classifying Compound Nouns,* p. 1249
Selection Test, p. 1250

Snake

D. H. Lawrence

A snake came to my water-trough
On a hot, hot day, and I in pajamas for the heat,
To drink there.

In the deep, strange-scented shade of the great dark
    carob tree
5 I came down the steps with my pitcher
And must wait, must stand and wait, for there he was at
    the trough before me.

He reached down from a fissure in the earth-wall in the
    gloom
And trailed his yellow-brown slackness soft-bellied down,
    over the edge of the stone trough
And rested his throat upon the stone bottom,
10 And where the water had dripped from the tap, in a small
    clearness,
He sipped with his straight mouth,
Softly drank through his straight gums, into his slack long
    body,
Silently.

Someone was before me at my water-trough,
15 And I, like a second comer, waiting.

He lifted his head from his drinking, as cattle do,
And looked at me vaguely, as drinking cattle do,
And flickered his two-forked tongue from his lips, and
    mused a moment,
And stooped and drank a little more,
20 Being earth-brown, earth-golden from the burning bowels
    of the earth
On the day of Sicilian July, with Etna[1] smoking.

The voice of my education said to me
He must be killed,
For in Sicily the black, black snakes are innocent, the gold
    are venomous.

---

1. Etna: A volcanic mountain in eastern Sicily.

Presentation

Motivation/Prior Knowledge
Ask students why so many people are both fascinated and repelled by snakes and other reptiles. Then tell them that this poem deals with such mixed feelings.

Purpose-Setting Question How do Lawrence's feelings about the snake change?

1 **Discussion** How do the first two stanzas set the scene?

2 **Discussion** Which words in Lawrence's description of the snake communicate his feelings of uneasiness and anxiety?

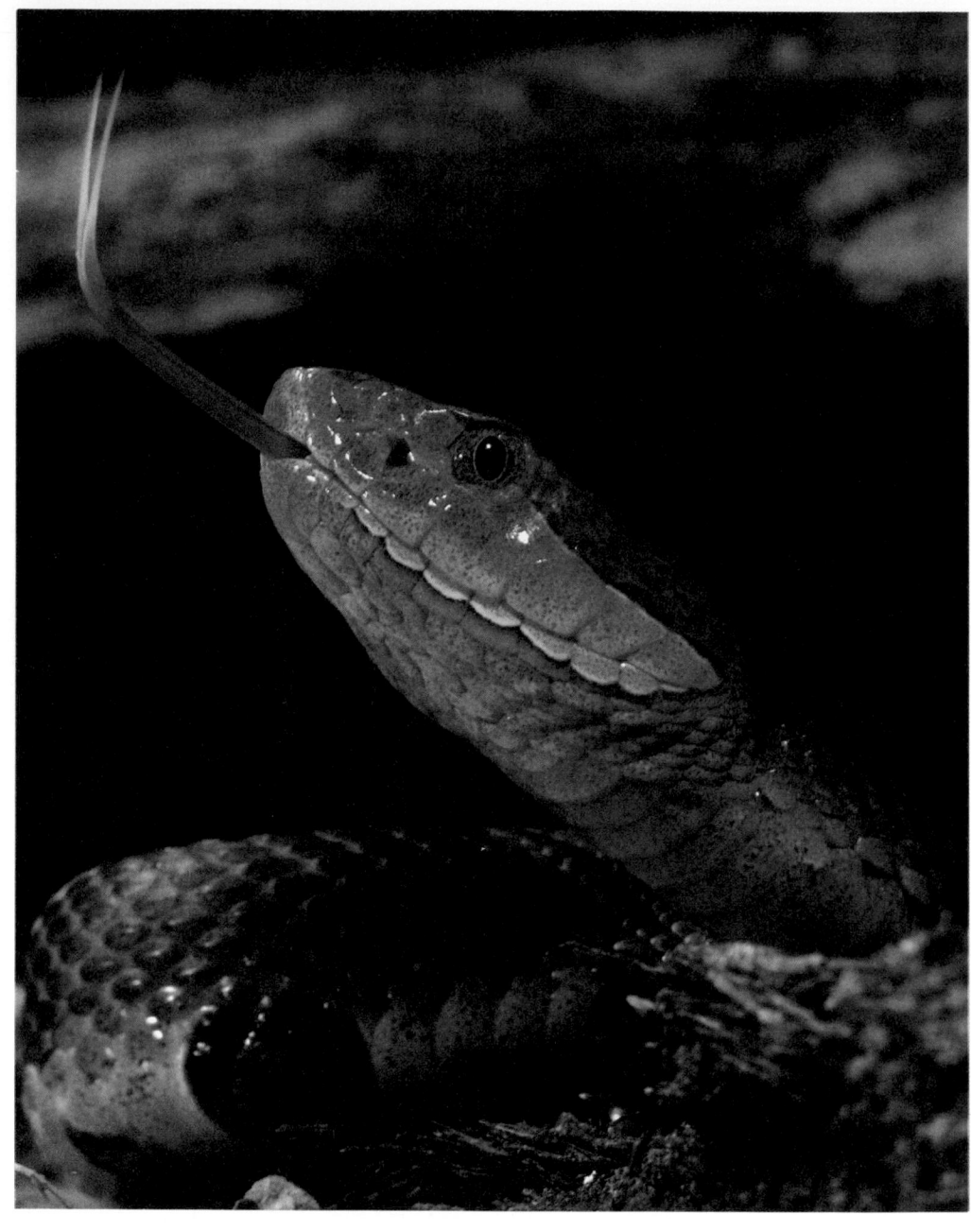

1040   *The Modern Period*

Grammar in Action

The **colon** has a number of uses. They include the following: to introduce a list of items following an independent clause, to introduce formal or lengthy quotations, to introduce a sentence that summarizes or explains the sentence before it, and to introduce an appositive following an independent clause. This last use is illustrated in "Snake."

And yet those voices:
If you were not afraid, you would kill him!

The second line above is an appositive because it refers to and explains "voices."

    Student Activity 1. "Snake" concludes with the following lines.

And I have something to expiate;
A pettiness.

25 And voices in me said, If you were a man
You would take a stick and break him now, and finish him
off.

But must I confess how I liked him,
How glad I was he had come like a guest in quiet, to drink
at my water-trough
And depart peaceful, pacified, and thankless,
30 Into the burning bowels of this earth?

Was it cowardice, that I dared not kill him?
Was it perversity, that I longed to talk to him?
Was it humility, to feel so honored?
I felt so honored.

35 And yet those voices:
If you were not afraid, you would kill him!

And truly I was afraid, I was most afraid,
But even so, honored still more
That he should seek my hospitality
40 From out the dark door of the secret earth.

He drank enough
And lifted his head, dreamily, as one who has drunken,
And flickered his tongue like a forked night on the air, so
black;
Seeming to lick his lips,
45 And looked around like a god, unseeing, into the air,
And slowly turned his head,
And slowly, very slowly, as if thrice adream,
Proceeded to draw his slow length curving round
And climb again the broken bank of my wall-face.

50 And as he put his head into that dreadful hole,
And as he slowly drew up, snake-easing his shoulders, and
entered farther,
A sort of horror, a sort of protest against his withdrawing
into that horrid black hole,
Deliberately going into the blackness, and slowly drawing
himself after,
Overcame me now his back was turned.

55 I looked round, I put down my pitcher,
I picked up a clumsy log
And threw it at the water-trough with a clatter.

Snake   1041

3 **Discussion** Explain the conflict that Lawrence experiences.

4 **Literary Focus** What effect does Lawrence create by shortening the fourth line of this stanza?

5 **Discussion** How does Lawrence seem to resolve his conflict?

6 **Discussion** Explain how Lawrence's inner conflict starts up again.

Could Lawrence have used a colon, instead of a semicolon, after
"expiate"? Explain your answer.

Student Activity 2. Write three sentences, each of which
illustrates a different use of the colon.

7 Discussion Why do you think he compares the snake to the albatross?

8 Literary Focus How do the varying line lengths in the final stanza reinforce the contrast between the greatness of the snake and Lawrence's pettiness?

9 Discussion How would you describe Lawrence's mood at the conclusion of the poem?

Reader's Response Have you known someone who had an experience similar to the speaker's? Explain.

I think it did not hit him,
But suddenly that part of him that was left behind
    convulsed in undignified haste,
60 Writhed like lightning, and was gone
Into the black hole, the earth-lipped fissure in the
    wall-front,
At which, in the intense still noon, I stared with
    fascination.

And immediately I regretted it.
I thought how paltry, how vulgar, what a mean act!
65 I despised myself and the voices of my accursed human
    education.

7 ⌈ And I thought of the albatross,[2]
  ⌊ And I wished he would come back, my snake.

For he seemed to me again like a king,
70 Like a king in exile, uncrowned in the underworld,
Now due to be crowned again.

8, ⌈ And so, I missed my chance with one of the lords
    Of life.
9 ⌊ And I have something to expiate;
75 A pettiness.

---

2. albatross: In Samuel Taylor Coleridge's "The Rime of the Ancient Mariner," the mariner shoots an albatross, a traditional symbol of good luck.

THINKING ABOUT THE SELECTION
Recalling

1. (a) What is the speaker on his way to do when he first becomes aware of the snake? (b) What is the snake doing?
2. (a) What does the "voice of [his] education" tell the speaker he should do? (b) How does he actually feel about the snake when the "voices" tell him he should kill it?
3. (a) What causes the speaker's horror toward the snake? (b) What does the speaker do? (c) How does he feel about having done it? (d) What three adjectives does he use to characterize his act?

Interpreting

4. In line 65 the speaker mentions "the voices of my accursed education." (a) What are these voices? (b) Why are they accursed?
5. Why does the speaker call the snake "a king in exile" and "one of the lords of life"?
6. The last two lines suggest that the speaker has committed a sin. (a) What is his sin? (b) Why does he call it a "pettiness"?

Closure and Extension

ANSWERS TO THINKING ABOUT THE SELECTION
Recalling

1. (a) The speaker is coming to the trough for a drink. (b) The snake is drinking from the trough.
2. (a) The voice says to kill the snake. (b) The speaker likes the snake and is glad it is a guest.
3. (a) The speaker is horrified by the snake disappearing into its hole. (b) He throws a log at the snake. (c) The speaker regrets his action. (d) The three are *paltry, vulgar,* and *mean.*

Interpreting

4. Suggested Responses: (a) The voices reflect what he has been taught to think about snakes. (b) They are accursed because they direct his thinking and his actions when he would rather respond to his true feelings.

5. Answers will differ. Students may respond that Lawrence views the snake as a symbol or embodiment of a ruler or god from beneath the earth.
6. Suggested Responses: (a) The speaker's sin is trying to kill the snake. (b) The action is petty or mean because the snake is a god-like, sacred animal.

Applying

7. Suggested Response: Yes, al-

Applying

7. Do you agree with the speaker that he has missed his chance? Explain your answer.

ANALYZING LITERATURE
Understanding Free Verse

Poetry with no clearly defined metric pattern or rhyme scheme is called **free verse.** Although inexperienced writers sometimes call their non-poetry "free verse," the truth is that free verse makes use of subtle, varying, but real rhythm as well as other traditional devices of poetry: repetition, alliteration, assonance, and onomatopoeia. It also has, in many cases, a high concentration of symbolism, figurative language, and imagery.

1. Notice how many lines of "Snake" begin with the word *And*. Notice also the repetition of words and phrases in the poem ("hot, hot" in line 2; "as cattle do" . . . "as drinking cattle do" in lines 16–17; and more). What effect do you think Lawrence intends to produce through this insistent repetition?
2. What devices—alliteration, assonance, onomatopoeia, repetition—do you find in each of the following excerpts. Some of them contain more than one device.

a. In the deep, strange-scented shade of the great dark carobtree
b. He sipped with his straight mouth,/Softly drank through his straight gums, into his slack long body,/Silently.
c. And flickered his two-forked tongue from his lips
d. Was it humility to feel so honored?/I felt so honored.

CRITICAL THINKING AND READING
Making Inferences About Purpose

On the surface "Snake" is a simple poem about Lawrence's (the speaker's/author's) unexpected encounter with a snake at a water-trough on a hot day in Sicily. If you look beneath the surface, however, you will see that his purpose in describing the incident transcends the basic narrative appeal of the poem. Lawrence makes his intent clear—although not his specific message—from his continuing, almost clinical analysis of his reactions to the snake. What underlying statement do you think he is making in "Snake" about human beings in general and himself in particular? Support your answer with quotations from the poem.

though his repentent attitude suggests he will not miss it again.

ANSWERS TO ANALYZING LITERATURE

1. Suggested Response: This insistent repetition emphasizes the strangeness, tension, and urgency of this encounter.
2. Suggested Responses: The poetic devices are (a) Assonance and alliteration (b) alliteration, onomatopoeia, repetition, and assonance (c) alliteration, assonance (d) repetition, alliteration.

ANSWERS TO CRITICAL THINKING AND READING

Answers will differ. Most students will realize that Lawrence is saying that we are educated away from our better, and deeper, impulses: "The voice of my education said to me/He must be killed. . . ."

More About the Author Siegfried Sassoon's poetry changed dramatically as a result of his experiences in the First World War—it became more satiric, realistic, and even shocking. Ask students to consider why his wartime experiences might have influenced his poetry in this way.

Critical Evaluation David Perkins wrote that Sassoon's book *Counter-Attack* (1918) "still impresses by its bitterness, anguish, and despair."

SIEGFRIED SASSOON

1886–1967

A decorated, twice-wounded soldier in World War I, Siegfried Sassoon witnessed first-hand the horrors of trench warfare in France. Like a number of other English writers and poets who saw action in the war, he resolved to portray for his own and future generations the grim reality of war, to show graphically its carnage and despair. No one did it better than he. Although Sassoon wrote for almost fifty years after the Armistice, he produced little to match his searing wartime verses that honor and mourn the "citizens of death's gray land."

Sassoon, born into a wealthy Jewish family in London, was something of a dilettante before the war. While attending Marlborough and Clare College, Cambridge, he found that he preferred hunting, cricket, golf, and ballet to more academic pursuits. Poetry aroused his interest also, and he published a number of pastoral poems and parodies while in his early twenties. In 1913, on the eve of World War I, his long poem, *The Daffodil Murderer,* gave evidence of his ability to combine parody with serious self-expression.

When war broke out in 1914, Sassoon joined the army the same day and showed such reckless courage in battle that he earned the nickname "Mad Jack" along with a medal for gallantry. But by the time he was wounded at Arras in April 1917, his attitude toward the supposed glory of war had changed. By then he was writing what he called "trench poems," the starkly realistic, agonized, sometimes horrifying verses on which his reputation rests. *The Old Huntsman* (1917) and *Counter-Attack* (1918) contain most of his memorable poems.

When Sassoon returned to the front in 1918, a British sentry shot him in the head by mistake, and Sassoon spent the rest of the war in a hospital.

After the Armistice, he continued to write, publishing his first prose work, *Memoirs of a Fox-Hunting Man,* in 1928. Billed as a novel, the book is essentially an autobiography, the first of several autobiographical works. Sassoon married at the age of forty-seven and settled down in rural Wiltshire. The literary innovations between the two World Wars passed him by. His niche in English literature had already been secured by a few dozen jarring, outraged, unforgettable poems from the trenches.

Support Material

Teaching Portfolio
Teacher Backup, p. 1253
Usage and Mechanics Worksheet, p. 1256
Vocabulary Check, p. 1257
Analyzing Literature Worksheet, *Understanding Historical Context,* p. 1258
Language Worksheet, *Understanding the Multiple Meanings of Words,* p. 1259
Selection Test, p. 1260

GUIDE FOR INTERPRETING

Wirers

Writer's Technique

Historical Context. Many poems deal with subjects unrelated to a particular time or place. A poem about love, for instance, deals with an emotion that is as old as the human race. But sometimes a historical event will create such an impact that poets feel impelled to comment on, and perhaps to explain, what happened. World War I was such an event. The war's devastation and slaughter, unprecedented at the time, gave rise to millions of words—patriotic, indignant, disillusioned, depending on the views of the writer. Those words were then, and are today, tied to their times. "Black Jack Pershing" was a household name in 1918. Soldiers were *doughboys,* and "Mademoiselle from Armentières" was a song familiar to everyone. Those names and facts are part of the history of World War I. A Siegfried Sassoon poem about World War I is likely to contain words and references unique to the war. As a reader, you must put such words and references into historical context—a perspective required by your distance in time from the events described. Ideally, you would be able to put all of World War I into historical context, but as a practical matter, you know enough about war in general to understand and appreciate a poem about World War I, even if you lack a thorough historical knowledge of the event.

Writing

Think of an abstract concept such as anger, betrayal, or loss and relate it to an experience that has affected you deeply. Freewrite about this experience, showing the feelings it caused.

Primary Source

By 1917 Sassoon was so strongly opposed to the war that he sent a formal protest to the House of Commons and threw his Military Cross into the River Mersey. In part his declaration read: "I believe that this war, on which I entered as a war of defense and liberation, has now become a war of aggression and conquest. . . . I can no longer be a party to prolong these sufferings for ends which I believe to be evil and unjust. I am not protesting against the conduct of the war, but against the political errors and insincerities for which the fighting men are being sacrificed." He was spared a formal court-martial through the intercession of fellow poet Robert Graves, who successfully pleaded that Sassoon was suffering from shellshock. As a result, in July 1917 Sassoon entered a war hospital in Edinburgh. There he befriended fellow patient and poet Wilfred Owen. When Owen was killed in battle during Armistice week, Sassoon collected and edited Owen's poems for publication.

Writing/Prior Knowledge You might want to divide the class into small groups and have them discuss their experiences before they begin to write.

Spelling Tip You might point out that the short *e* sound in *stealthy* is spelled *ea.*

Vocabulary

Preteach the following vocabulary words:
stealthy (stel' thē) *adj.:* In a quiet, secretive way (l. 4)
desolate (des'ə lit) *adj.:* Deserted; forlorn (l. 10)

Guide for Interpreting 1045

Motivation/Prior Knowledge
Bring in photographs or other pictures of action at the front lines in World War I, to help set the scene.

Purpose-Setting Question Identify the irony in this poem.

1 **Literary Focus** Note the sudden switch from the blackness of night to "ghastly dawn."

2 **Discussion** What irony is the poet pointing up in the last line?

Reader's Response What, if anything, did you learn from this poem about World War I? Explain.

Wirers[1]

Siegfried Sassoon

"Pass it along, the wiring party's going out"—
And yawning sentries mumble, "Wirers going out."
Unraveling; twisting; hammering stakes with muffled thud,
They toil with stealthy haste and anger in their blood.

5   The Boche[2] sends up a flare. Black forms stand rigid there,
Stock-still like posts; then darkness, and the clumsy ghosts
Stride hither and thither, whispering, tripped by clutching snare
Of snags and tangles.
        Ghastly dawn with vaporous coasts
10 Gleams desolate along the sky, night's misery ended.

Young Hughes was badly hit; I heard him carried away,
Moaning at every lurch; no doubt he'll die today.
But *we* can say the front-line wire's been safely mended.

---

1. wirers: Soldiers who were responsible for repairing the barbed-wire fences that protected the trenches in World War I.
2. Boche (bôsh): German soldier.

THINKING ABOUT THE SELECTION
Recalling

1. What are the wirers getting ready to do at the beginning of the poem?
2. What happens when an enemy flare lights the scene?
3. What does the speaker say will probably be the fate of the soldier named Hughes?

Interpreting

4. How do you think the wirers feel about the job they have to do?
5. (a) What is the speaker's attitude toward what has happened to young Hughes? (b) How do you explain that attitude?

Applying

6. (a) What kinds of nonmilitary jobs may lead to a routine acceptance of the daily presence of danger? (b) What is the difference between those jobs and a soldier's job?

ANALYZING LITERATURE
Historical Context

Actual events provide the historical context of "Wirers." If you knew no history at all, the

Closure and Extension

ANSWER TO THINKING ABOUT THE SELECTION
Recalling

1. The wirers are getting ready to lay barbed wire in no man's land.
2. The soldiers stand rigid.
3. Hughes will probably die before the end of the day.

Interpreting

4. Suggested Response: They probably hate their job and are afraid they will be killed.
5. Suggested Response: (a) The speaker is angered by Hughes's death. (b) His anger arises from the fact that a fence is given more importance than a human life.

Applying

6. (a) Answers will differ, but students may mention rescue teams, firemen, and policemen. (b) Answers will differ. One difference is that a soldier is expected to kill others, while civilian workers who take chances are engaged in more constructive activities.

ANSWERS TO ANALYZING LITERATURE

1. Suggested Responses: (a) The setting is not the Civil War because of the Boche. (b) It is probably not

DRAWING OF TANKS, WORLD WAR I
Photo Research Int.

Fine art, *Drawing of Tanks, World War I.* When a country goes to war, all members of society are affected. Artists and writers don soldiers' uniforms along with the professional warriors. Some artists, however, cannot forego expressing themselves through their art even on the battlefield.

This drawing is one unknown artist's comment on the war. Executed in easily portable materials, conté crayon (an oily earth-toned chalk) and paper, it is a quick sketch that gives an unglorified view of a field of battle. Troops advance across a field with trampled grass, blasted trees, and the fallen bodies of other soldiers. The faces of the troops are shocked and haggard as they follow the ominous shapes of the tanks. The sketchy immediacy of the drawing gives the impression that the artist will shortly rejoin the advancing troops. This brief and honest sketch is the work of someone who has experienced the horrors of war and paused to record its reality.

You might use these questions for discussion.
1. What do both the poet and the painter express in their works?
2. How does observation of this sketch affect you?

poem—without some kind of textual explanation—would be virtually meaningless to you. However, you know something about the trenches of World War I and about barbed-wire entanglements. You therefore have clues to the historical context of the poem.
1. How can you tell from the poem that its historical context is World War I (1914–18)

and not (a) the American Civil War (1861–65)? (b) World War II (1939–45)?
2. A historian has said that in World War I "cavalry was useless" and "artillery was absolutely indispensable." How does the content of the poem support the historian's statement?

World War II because barbed wire did not play as large a role in that war.

2. Suggested Response: Cavalry could not have charged across terrain obstructed by barbed wire.

More About the Author Tell students that "The Soldier" is a strongly patriotic poem. Review Rupert Brooke's background. Do you think his comfortable life increased his love of his country? What do you think contributes to a person's patriotism?

Critical Evaluation David Daiches wrote that "Brooke is often, and with considerable justice, taken as representative of the golden world of liberal culture immediately before World War I. His early death was symbolic of the death of a whole generation of dedicated English youth—brilliant and beautiful youth as they seemed in retrospect, for Brooke was noted for his physical beauty as well as for his talents. 'The Soldier,' traditional both in its sonnet form and its idealistic patriotic mood, represents the last significant expression of an attitude that could not survive the horrors of trench warfare."

RUPERT BROOKE

1887–1915

Although Rupert Brooke had established himself as a poet before World War I, it was the war and Brooke's early death that fostered his almost legendary fame. A handsome, privileged youth, an accomplished athlete and an intellectual, he attracted a host of influential friends who mourned his loss and celebrated his achievements. Brooke's best poems, filled with striking phrases, are exuberant with delight in the simple pleasures of living.

Brooke first wrote poetry as a child and by his teens was writing seriously. As an adolescent he remarked, "There are three good things in this world. One is to read poetry, another is to write poetry, and the best of all is to *live* poetry." His efforts to "live poetry" resulted in a man Churchill celebrated as "joyous, fearless, versatile . . . ruled by high, undoubting purpose . . . all that one could wish England's noblest sons to be."

Rupert Brooke was born in Rugby, Warwickshire, and educated at the famous public school there, where his father was an assistant master. He graduated from King's College, Cambridge, and studied for a time in Munich, Germany. A long love affair ended unhappily for Brooke, after which he traveled in the United States, Canada, and the South Pacific, making a pilgrimage to the home of Robert Louis Stevenson in Samoa. His poetry at the time echoes that of John Donne and occasionally A. E. Housman.

When war broke out in 1914, Brooke obtained a commission in the Hood Battalion of the Royal Naval Division. "Well, if Armageddon's *on*," he said at the time, "I suppose one should be there." After participating in the disastrous British expedition to Antwerp, he was ordered to the Dardanelles, where the British hoped to strike a blow against the Turks. He contracted blood poisoning on the way and entered a French military hospital on the Greek island of Skiros in the Aegean Sea. He died there on April 23, St. George's Day.

Brooke's war sonnets, which had appeared a few weeks before his death, gained extraordinary notice in the aftermath. Winston Churchill praised them in the London *Times*. The sonnets, traditional and idealistic, were among the last from the soldier-poets of World War I that expressed an unalloyed patriotism. Brooke had seen little of the trench warfare that so altered the vision of Siegfried Sassoon, Wilfred Owen, and other poets who served in the army.

Impressive as Brooke's poetry is, some of it lacks consistent vision. Contradictions abound. "Impulse was his god," wrote one critic, and it is impossible to speculate on the direction his work might have taken had he survived the war.

Objectives

1 To analyze the theme of patriotism in poetry
2 To understand and appreciate Georgian poetry
3 To appreciate specific words

Support Material

Teaching Portfolio
Teacher Backup, p. 1263
Usage and Mechanics Worksheet, p. 1266
Vocabulary Check, p. 1267
Analyzing Literature Worksheet, *Understanding Personifications,* p. 1268

Language Worksheet, *Appreciating Specific Words,* p. 1269
Selection Test, p. 1270
Art Transparency 15, *We Are Making a New World,* by Paul Nash

GUIDE FOR INTERPRETING

The Soldier; The Great Lover

Writer's Technique

The Theme of Patriotism. Patriotism, the love and loyal support of one's own country, has been a persistent theme in English literature. Shakespeare's lines in *King Richard II* are a stirring patriotic statement: "This royal throne of kings, this sceptered isle . . . This other Eden, demi-paradise . . . This precious stone set in the silver sea . . . This blessed plot, this earth, this realm, this England. . . ." Two centuries later, Sir Walter Scott sounded an equally patriotic note in *The Lay of the Last Minstrel:* "Breathes there the man with soul so dead,/Who never to himself hath said,/This is my own, my native land!" By the time of World War I, Great Britain had reached the height of its power, and Scott's proud boast, "The sun never sets on the immense empire," was the literal truth. At the outbreak of the war, the English were in a buoyantly patriotic mood, and Rupert Brooke's "The Soldier" catches that mood perfectly.

Writing

Freewrite about an occasion when you felt extreme pride in your country. The occasion might have been a flag-raising ceremony, the celebration of a national holiday, or a time of international crisis. Describe your feelings of patriotism, explaining what life in the United States meant to you at that moment.

Primary Source

In her diary young Vera Brittain recorded the enormous impact of Brooke's poems. One evening a friend "read us, at my request, five sonnets by Rupert Brooke, the most promising poet of the younger generation, who enlisted in the Navy when the war broke out & died at Lemnos a week or two ago—to the great loss & mourning of all modern writers & literature. The sonnets were all sad & moving, in spite of their spirit of courage & hope, & through them all ran a strangely prophetic note, a premonition of early death. I should not have asked her to read them if I had known, they were all so sad that I could scarcely keep back tears from my eyes." Mrs. Leighton, the mother of Vera's fiancé Roland, felt as strongly about Brooke's poems. Writing to her son in battle, Mrs. Leighton said, "I sent you a slip from a paper with a few quotations from the poems of Rupert Brooke. Will you let me have them back when you have read them? Because I cannot do without them, until I get the book. For they are Roland all over. . . . The last line in particular—they were from 'The Soldier,' If I should die, think only this of me'—cut through me with so many knife-stabs with their truth in the matter of likeness to him." Roland was later killed in battle.

Literary Focus Point out that "The Soldier" is a sonnet. Although the topic is quite different from those of Sidney, Spenser, Shakespeare, or Donne, why is the form appropriate for Brooke's message?

Writing/Prior Knowledge You might have students focus on the geographical features of the United States that inspire feelings of patriotism—powerful rivers, gorgeous canyons, fertile fields, and so forth.

Master Teacher Note After reading "The Soldier," place Art Transparency 15, *We Are Making a New World,* by Paul Nash, on the overhead projector. Ask your students to compare and contrast the poem and the painting for artistic intention, meaning, and overall effectiveness. You might pose this qustion: Which of the two works is more relevant to our situation today?

Vocabulary

Preteach the following vocabulary words:
illimitable (i lim′ it ə b'l) *adj.:* Without limit or bounds; immeasurable (p. 1051, l. 4)
inenarrable (in en′ ər ə b'l) *adj.:* Indescribable (p. 1051, l. 15)
benison (ben′ ə z'n) *n.:* Blessing; benediction (p. 1052, l. 39)
sacramented (sak′ rə ment id) *adj.:* Having the properties of religious rites or rituals (p. 1052, l. 62)
covenant (kuv′ ə nənt) *n.:* Solemn, binding agreement (p.1052, l. 62)

Motivation/Prior Knowledge
Have students consider the reasons that patriotism can be such a strong emotion. Then tell them that this feeling inspired Rupert Brooke's sonnet "The Soldier."

Purpose-Setting Question Why do you think this poem was praised by Winston Churchill —then a member of the government—during World War I?

1 Discussion Why will the "corner of a foreign field" be "forever England"?

2 Discussion What has England given the author?

3 Discussion How does the soldier plan to return the gifts of England, even in his death?

Reader's Response Is the sentiment expressed in this poem out of date? Why or why not?

Humanities Note

War poster. During both world wars, posters played an important part in communicating government instructions and propaganda to civilian and military communities. In graphic language, these posters urged people to support the war effort by enlisting, taking war jobs, buying bonds, conserving food and fuel, and above all, by being patriotic.
1. How does the sentiment expressed by this poster relate to that in the poem?
2. Do you feel that such posters would be as effective today? Explain.

BUY **VICTORY BONDS**

WAR POSTER
Photri

The Soldier

Rupert Brooke

If I should die, think only this of me:
    That there's some corner of a foreign field
That is forever England. There shall be
    In that rich earth a richer dust concealed;
5 A dust whom England bore, shaped, made aware,
    Gave, once, her flowers to love, her ways to roam,
A body of England's, breathing English air,
    Washed by the rivers, blest by suns of home.

And think, this heart, all evil shed away,
10   A pulse in the eternal mind, no less
      Gives somewhere back the thoughts by England
        given;
Her sights and sounds; dreams happy as her day;
    And laughter, learnt of friends; and gentleness,
      In hearts at peace, under an English heaven.

THINKING ABOUT THE SELECTION
Recalling

1. How does the speaker ask his readers to remember him if he should die?
2. What are three things that England gave to the speaker?
3. What will the speaker's heart give "somewhere back"?

Interpreting

4. (a) How does the speaker feel toward England? (b) How idealistic, or realistic, do you think his recollections are?
5. What is the "richer dust" that will be found in a foreign field?
6. The speaker says his heart will become a "pulse in the eternal mind." In your own words, what does he mean?

Applying

7. How would you define patriotism?

ANALYZING LITERATURE
Feeling Patriotism

    Patriotism is a deep and abiding love for one's country.
1. Why do you think Brooke's war poems, including "The Soldier," are strongly patriotic while many other poems from World War I, such as "Wirers," avoid patriotic sentiments?
2. A number of young English poets died in World War I. One of them, Charles Sorley, said of Rupert Brooke, "He has clothed his attitude in fine words; but he has taken the sentimental attitude." What is your opinion of this remark?

1050   *The Modern Period*

Closure and Extension

ANSWERS TO THINKING ABOUT THE SELECTION
Recalling

1. He asks the reader to think of him as being a part of England in foreign soil.
2. England gave flowers to appreciate, paths to roam, air, water, sun, and the laughter of friends.
3. The speaker's heart will give back thoughts of England.

Interpreting

4. Suggested Responses: (a) The speaker feels England is a kind of heaven. (b) The recollections seem generalized and idealized.
5. Suggested Response: The "richer dust" is the dust of the speaker's body.
6. Answers will differ, but students may interpret this statement to mean that the speaker's spirit has joined other heavenly spirits.

Applying

7. Students' answers will differ.

ANSWERS TO ANALYZING LITERATURE

1. Suggested Response: Other poems deal with the grim realities of front-line fighting, which Brooke did not experience.

The Great Lover

Rupert Brooke

I have been so great a lover: filled my days
So proudly with the splendor of Love's praise,
The pain, the calm, and the astonishment,
Desire illimitable, and still content,
5 And all dear names men use, to cheat despair,
For the perplexed and viewless streams that bear
Our hearts at random down the dark of life.
Now, ere the unthinking silence on that strife
Steals down, I would cheat drowsy Death so far,
10 My night shall be remembered for a star
That outshone all the suns of all men's days.
Shall I not crown them with immortal praise
Whom I have loved, who have given me, dared with me
High secrets, and in darkness knelt to see
15 The inenarrable godhead of delight?
Love is a flame:—we have beaconed the world's night.
A city:—and we have built it, these and I.
An emperor:—we have taught the world to die.
So, for their sakes I loved, ere I go hence,
20 And the high cause of Love's magnificence,
And to keep loyalties young, I'll write those names
Golden forever, eagles, crying flames,
And set them as a banner, that men may know,
To dare the generations, burn, and blow
25 Out on the wind of Time, shining and streaming. . . .
These I have loved:

    White plates and cups, clean-gleaming,
Ringed with blue lines; and feathery, fairy dust;
Wet roofs, beneath the lamp-light; the strong crust
Of friendly bread; and many-tasting food;

WHITE CUP AND SAUCER, NO 1016
Fantin-Latour
Fitzwilliam Museum, Cambridge

Presentation

Motivation/Prior Knowledge
Have students list the simple daily items and activities they enjoy. You might have them share some of these and make a class list. Then point out that Brooke's poem is a tribute to the things he has loved.

Master Teacher Note Review Brooke's life. Why is this poem especially poignant in light of that life?

Purpose-Setting Question How well does the title fit the poem?

1 **Discussion** How do the loves of the speaker enable him to "cheat despair"?

2 **Discussion** Explain what the poet means by the "star."

3 **Discussion** How has the speaker "taught the world to die"?

4 **Critical Thinking and Reading** Make some inferences about the speaker from his list of "loves."

5 **Reading Strategy** In one sentence, summarize what the poet is telling you that he loves in life.

2. Answers will differ. Some students may find the poem intensely sentimental, and others may see it as beautifully patriotic.

Humanities Note

Fine art, *White Cup and Saucer* by Henri Fantin Latour. Henri Fantin Latour (1836–1904) was a French painter. Although Latour enrolled at the Ecole des Beaux Arts in Paris, his studies there were unsuccessful. His self-training, which was more useful, consisted of his friendly association with the Impressionist Manet and the hours spent at the Louvre copying the works of the old masters.

White Cup and Saucer was painted in 1864. It shows the influence of the Impressionists in the simple, objective composition and the importance of the light on the object. A pleasing and direct painting, it shows the artist's awareness of innate beauty in everyday objects.

You might ask the following questions:
1. How do you think Rupert Brooke would feel about this painting?
2. Does this painting suit the thoughtful quality of the poem?

6 **Discussion** What will happen to the speaker's loves as he faces the "gate of Death"?

7 **Discussion** Are these last thoughts optimistic or pessimistic? Support your position with evidence from the poem.

30   Rainbows; and the blue bitter smoke of wood;
And radiant raindrops couching in cool flowers;
And flowers themselves, that sway through sunny hours,
Dreaming of moths that drink them under the moon;
Then, the cool kindliness of sheets, that soon
35   Smooth away trouble; and the rough male kiss
Of blankets; grainy wood; live hair that is
Shining and free; blue-massing clouds; the keen
Unpassioned beauty of a great machine;
The benison of hot water; furs to touch;
40   The good smell of old clothes; and others such—
The comfortable smell of friendly fingers,
Hair's fragrance, and the musty reek that lingers
About dead leaves and last year's ferns. . . .
                      Dear names,
And thousand others throng to me! Royal flames;
45   Sweet water's dimpling laugh from tap or spring;
Holes in the ground; and voices that do sing;
Voices in laughter, too; and body's pain,
Soon turned to peace; and the deep-panting train;
Firm sands; the little dulling edge of foam
50   That browns and dwindles as the wave goes home;
And washen stones, gay for an hour; the cold
Graveness of iron; moist black earthen mold;
Sleep; and high places; footprints in the dew;
And oaks; and brown horse-chestnuts, glossy-new;
55   And new-peeled sticks; and shining pools on grass;—

6
All these have been my loves. And these shall pass,
Whatever passes not, in the great hour,
Nor all my passion, all my prayers, have power
To hold them with me through the gate of Death.
60   They'll play deserter, turn with the traitor breath,
Break the high bond we made, and sell Love's trust
And sacramented covenant to the dust.

7
    —Oh, never a doubt but, somewhere, I shall wake,
And give what's left of love again, and make
New friends, now strangers. . . .
65   But the best I've known
Stays here, and changes, breaks, grows old, is blown
About the winds of the world, and fades from brains
Of living men, and dies.
                Nothing remains.

O dear my loves, O faithless, once again
70   This one last gift I give: that after men
Shall know, and later lovers, far-removed,
Praise you, "All these were lovely"; say, "He loved."

THINKING ABOUT THE SELECTION

Recalling

1. What does the speaker say he will "crown . . . with immortal praise"?
2. What are the first three items in the speaker's list of things he has loved?
3. What does the speaker say will happen to the things he loves after he is gone?
4. The speaker asks one last favor. What is it?

Interpreting

5. The title of this poem, "The Great Lover," might lead you to expect a different kind of poem. (a) In what sense is this not a traditional love poem? (b) In what sense is it a love poem?
6. In line 72 the speaker says, "O faithless." Whom or what is he addressing?
7. Who is being quoted in line 75, "All these were lovely"?
8. Walter de la Mare, the poet, said that Rupert Brooke delighted "in things for themselves." (a) How does this poem support that observation? (b) What properties are shared by (or missing from) all the items on Brooke's list?

Applying

9. If you were compiling a personal list of loves similar to those on Brooke's list, what five items might you add to the ones he includes? Suggest descriptive, image-making words to go with the items—not just "wood smoke," for example, but "the blue bitter smoke of wood."

CRITICAL THINKING AND READING

Identifying The Georgian Poets

Rupert Brooke, Siegfried Sassoon, and D. H. Lawrence, despite their artistic differences, are commonly identified with a group called the Georgian poets. The name stems from the fact that the poets were writing early in the reign of King George V of England. The group's anthology, *Georgian Poetry*, first appeared in 1912. Four more volumes, all featuring contemporary poets, were published biennially through 1922.

1. Georgian poetry has been accused of being "pleasant and almost nonpolitical." T. S. Eliot, a contemporary, said that the poets "insist upon the English countryside and are even positively patriotic." How closely do Brooke's two poems fit those two descriptions?
2. The Georgian poets appeared to be a vital new force in 1912. By 1922 they were clinging to "a tender and prettified Nature, to the false solace of dreams." Knowing something of Rupert Brooke's life and times, what do you think caused this rapid decline of Georgian poetry?

UNDERSTANDING LANGUAGE

Appreciating Specific Words

Rupert Brooke's choice of words in "The Great Lover" is extraordinarily effective. His words give the reader a vivid mental picture of what he is describing. Rather than merely writing "sheets," for instance (as on a scrawled shopping list), Brooke creates "the cool kindliness of sheets." Those two words—*cool* and *kindliness*—make all the difference. Find ten other specific words in "The Great Lover" that create striking images. (Include entire phrases in your answer, underlining the descriptive word or words. For example: *drowsy* Death.)

ANSWERS TO CRITICAL THINKING AND READING

1. Suggested Response: Both of Brooke's poems are positive about the English countryside and "The Soldier" is explicitly patriotic.
2. Suggested Response: The Georgians themselves may not have greatly changed. However, public attitudes may have been altered as a result of the horrors of World War I. Modernist poets like Pound and Eliot were more attuned to this shift than were the Georgians.

ANSWERS TO UNDERSTANDING LANGUAGE

Answers will differ. Students may include: "*feathery, fairy* dust"; "*many-tasting* food"; "*radiant* raindrops"; "*cool* flowers"; "*sunny* hours"; "*blue-massing* clouds"; and "the *comfortable smell* of *friendly* fingers."

Closure and Extension

ANSWERS TO THINKING ABOUT THE SELECTION

Recalling

1. The speaker will crown those he has loved.
2. He first lists white plates and cups trimmed in blue, dust, and wet roofs under lamplight.
3. They will remain but will eventually vanish.
4. The speaker asks to be remembered as having loved.

Interpreting

5. Suggested Responses: (a) This is not a poem of the love of one person for another. (b) It tells what Brooke has loved in his life.
6. Suggested Response: He calls the things he loves "faithless."
7. Suggested Response: Future reader and lovers are being quoted.
8. Suggested Responses: (a) His list indicates an interest in a variety of objects, which he seems to love just "for themselves." (b) All these items are passing sensations and impressions.

Applying

9. Answers will differ.

More About the Author You may want to tell students that T. S. Eliot was a pioneer in taking the urban environment as a subject. At the time he began writing, many poets still assumed that nature was the natural subject for poetry. Ask students what new types of subject matter poets might want to explore today.

Critical Evaluation Richard Ellmann and Robert O'Clair wrote that "Although Eliot deferred to Yeats as 'the greatest poet' of his time, he was himself the most famous. A man of keen intellect, capable of developing a philosophical position as well as a new rhythm and intonation, trained in classics, fluent in French and German, Eliot was better equipped than any other poet to bring verse fully into the twentieth century. As James Joyce remarked of him in a notebook, he abolished the idea of poetry for ladies."

T. S. ELIOT

1888–1965

Thomas Stearns Eliot is one of the dominant figures in twentieth-century English literature. A poet, playwright, critic, thinker, and cultural pioneer who changed the consciousness of an entire generation of writers, he emerged in the 1920's as the acknowledged leader of what is now called the Modernist movement. Eliot's work is often difficult to understand, drawing as it does upon a broad range of myth, history, religion, allusion, and symbol. His poems and plays raise fundamental questions about human aspirations and the nature of civilized society.

Eliot has ties to both the United States and Great Britain. Born in St. Louis, Missouri, he was educated at Smith and Milton Academies, Harvard University, the Sorbonne, and Oxford. The outbreak of World War I found Eliot in England, where he remained throughout most of his adult life, eventually acquiring British citizenship. In 1915 he married the sensitive, witty, but highly neurotic Vivienne Haigh-Wood. While writing poetry and critical reviews, Eliot taught school, worked for the banking firm of Lloyd's, and in 1925 took an editorial position with the publishing company that became Faber and Faber.

His earliest work, owing to its unconventional style, was greeted with less than universal acclaim, although the poet Ezra Pound was a vocal supporter from the beginning. Pound saw, as many did not, that Eliot spoke in an authentic new voice and offered an original, if bleak, vision. In *Prufrock and Other Observations* (1917) through *The Waste Land* (1922) and "The Hollow Men" (1925), Eliot pictured the disturbed, fragmented western world wrought by World War I and its aftermath. Then, gradually, came renewed hope through religion, his faith leading him to join the Church of England in 1927. "Journey of the Magi" (1927) and "Ash Wednesday" (1930) mark the new religious phase of his life and writing, capped by his poetic masterpiece, *Four Quartets,* published in 1943, during the dark days of World War II.

As he grew older, Eliot turned his attention increasingly to poetic drama and criticism. Although *Murder in the Cathedral* (1935) and *The Cocktail Party* (1950) are often performed, none of his plays have gained the widespread critical admiration accorded his poetry. As a literary critic, Eliot's influence on his contemporaries was profound. His *Notes Towards the Definition of Culture,* one of many noteworthy critical works, appeared in 1948, the same year in which he received the Nobel Prize for Literature. In 1967, on the second anniversary of Eliot's death, a memorial was unveiled in Poet's Corner, Westminster Abbey.

1054   *The Modern Period*

Objectives

1 To recognize and appreciate synecdoche
2 To select music that evokes the mood of a poem
3 To write a poem using synecdoche

Support Material

Teaching Portfolio
Teacher Backup, p. 1273
Usage and Mechanics Worksheet, p. 1277
Vocabulary Check, p. 1278
Analyzing Literature Worksheets, *Using Synecdoche,* p. 1279; *Conveying a Mood* p. 1281
Selection Test, p. 1282

GUIDE FOR INTERPRETING

Preludes; Journey of the Magi

Synecdoche. Synecdoche (si nĕk′ də kē) is a figure of speech in which a part stands for the whole, an individual for a class, a material for the thing—or the reverse of any of these. For example, in the sentence, "Give us this day our daily bread," the word *bread* (part) stands for *food* (whole). In the sentence "The thief knew that a loud noise would bring the law," the word *law* (whole) stands for *police officer* (part). As a poetic device, synecdoche can sometimes make thought-provoking connections that startle and enlighten the reader.

Mood. Mood is the dominant emotion created by a piece of writing. If the mood of a poem is serious and reflective, the reader, upon finishing it, will in all likelihood be somber and pensive. If, on the other hand, the mood of a poem is light and whimsical, the reader, upon completing it, should be in high spirits and perhaps smiling. Mood must not be confused with either theme or subject matter. For instance, "The Cremation of Sam McGee," a ballad by Robert Service, deals with the death and cremation of a man in the Yukon, but the mood of the ballad is anything but melancholy.

Look through a newspaper or magazine for examples of synecdoche. When you have collected ten or more examples, write a brief analysis of the device. In your analysis indicate (a) which kind of synecdoche occurs most often, and (b) why you think the device came into such common use in English.

Eliot's distinctive style and theme lend themselves very easily to parody; fortunately, he had a sense of humor where such imitations were concerned. "Most parodies of one's own work strike one as very poor," Mr. Eliot writes, "but there is one which deserves the success it has had, Henry Reed's 'Chard Whitlow.'" Judge for yourself from the following excerpt:

Chard Whitlow

(Mr. Eliot's Sunday Evening Postscript)
AS WE GET OLDER we do not get any younger.
Seasons return, and today I am fifty-five,
And this time last year I was fifty-four,
And this time next year I shall be sixty-two.
And I cannot say I should like (to speak for myself)
To see my time over again—if you can call it time:
Fidgeting uneasily under a draughty stair,
Or counting sleepless night in the crowded tube . . .

Focus

Literary Focus Help students to overcome some of their preconceptions about the negative connotations of the word *mood*, connotations that are associated, for instance, with the adjective *moody*. Emphasize that mood involves a state of mind as well as feeling. Have students think of places or events that put a person in a particular mood, for example, a sports event, a private party, a church service, or a graduation. List some of the moods that these places and occasions might inspire.

Writing/Prior Knowledge Help students to differentiate between a symbol and synecdoche. A police badge, for example, could be a symbol of an officer's authority, whereas the term "the law" stands for all policemen.

Vocabulary

Preteach the following vocabulary words:
galled (gôld) *adj.:* Injured or made sore by rubbing or chafing (p. 1059, l. 6)
refractory (ri frak′ tər ē) *adj.:* Hard to manage; stubborn (p. 1059, l. 6)
dispensation (dis′ pən sā′ shən) *n:* Religious system or belief (p. 1060, l. 41)

Motivation/Prior Knowledge
Ask students to recall an evening walk they took and the mood it inspired in them. Tell them that the first of Eliot's "Preludes" evokes a winter evening in a city.

Master Teacher Note You might tell students that at about the time Eliot was writing these poems in America, Ezra Pound was helping to create the imagist movement in England. That movement generally favored briefer poems, concrete descriptions, deletion of unnecessary words, and the use of free verse rather than traditional meters. Ask students to evaluate "The Preludes" using imagist criteria.

Purpose-Setting Question How are all these poems related?

1 Discussion Note the use of the adjectives in this stanza. What impression do they create?

2 Discussion What "masquerades" do you think the poet means?

Humanities Note

Fine art, *Bolton, 1938*, by Sir William Coldstream. The British artist and teacher Sir William Coldstream was born in 1908. He studied at the prestigious Slade School of Art in London. Coldstream dabbled in cinema for a few years and then returned to painting. Along with two other British modern artists, William Coldstream founded the Euston Road School of Drawing and Painting. The guiding principle of this school was that of his art: to speak directly to the viewing public with images that draw upon the simple beauty of the commonplace.

The painting *Bolton, 1938,* demonstrates this guiding principle. Painted in the industrialized North country of England, it is a somewhat romanticized view of a mill and worker's dwellings. The hazy atmosphere lends a mysterious and nostalgic mood to this landscape. Coldstream painted this scene realistically, in subdued colors.

You might use these questions for discussion:
1. In both works of art, the painting and the poem, the artist observes his surroundings. Which observations by the painter match observations by the poet?
2. Compare and contrast the moods evoked by the painting and the poem.

BOLTON, 1938 (detail)
William Coldstream
The National Gallery of Canada, Ottawa

Preludes
T. S. Eliot

I

The winter evening settles down
With smell of steaks[1] in passageways.
Six o'clock.
The burnt-out ends of smoky days.
5 And now a gusty shower wraps
The grimy scraps
Of withered leaves about your feet
And newspapers from vacant lots;
The showers beat
10 On broken blinds and chimney-pots,
And at the corner of the street
A lonely cab-horse steams and stamps.
And then the lighting of the lamps.

II

The morning comes to consciousness
15 Of faint stale smells of beer
From the sawdust-trampled street
With all its muddy feet that press
To early coffee-stands.
With the other masquerades
20 That time resumes,
One thinks of all the hands
That are raising dingy shades
In a thousand furnished rooms.

III

You tossed a blanket from the bed,
25 You lay upon your back, and waited;
You dozed, and watched the night revealing
The thousand sordid images
Of which your soul was constituted;
They flickered against the ceiling.

---

1. steaks: In 1910, when this poem was composed, steaks were inexpensive and were commonly eaten by members of the lower class.

30   And when all the world came back
     And the light crept up between the shutters
     And you heard the sparrows in the gutters,
     You had such a vision of the street
     As the street hardly understands;
35   Sitting along the bed's edge, where
     You curled the papers from your hair,
     Or clasped the yellow soles of feet
     In the palms of both soiled hands.

IV

     His soul stretched tight across the skies
40   That fade behind a city block,
     Or trampled by insistent feet
     At four and five and six o'clock;
     And short square fingers stuffing pipes,
     And evening newspapers, and eyes
45   Assured of certain certainties,
     The conscience of a blackened street
     Impatient to assume the world.

         I am moved by fancies that are curled
     Around these images, and cling:
50   The notion of some infinitely gentle
     Infinitely suffering thing.

     Wipe your hands across your mouth, and laugh;
     The worlds revolve like ancient women
     Gathering fuel in vacant lots.

Preludes   1057

3 **Discussion** What is the "vision of the street"?

4 **Discussion** What type of neighborhood is Eliot describing in I, II, and III? What words and phrases indicate this?

5 **Discussion** What do you think is the "infinitely gentle . . . suffering thing"?

6 **Discussion** What is the effect of this final image? How does it relate to the rest of "Preludes"?

Reader's Response What images would you use to describe a street you know very well?

Closure and Extension

ANSWERS TO THINKING ABOUT THE SELECTION
Recalling

1. The setting is a winter evening.
2. Dingy window shades are being raised.
3. The "you" of the poem "heard the sparrows in the gutters."
4. The ancient women are "Gathering fuel in vacant lots."

Interpreting

5. Suggested Response: The inhabitants of these city streets are laborers in the working class. Clues are broken blinds (line 10), stale smells of beer (15), and dingy shades (22).
6. Suggested Response: The cycle here is evening to day to evening again with little change or variety. The image in the final two lines also suggests a cycle.
7. Suggested Response: The mood is one of futility and dreariness, beneath which a great suffering is occurring.

Applying

8. Answers will differ. Students may respond that Eliot might have presented a more positive outlook and might have found more explicit religious meaning in these scenes.

ANSWERS TO ANALYZING LITERATURE

1. Suggested Response: The *morning* stands for everyone who is waking up. By suggesting a shared consciousness this synecdoche reinforces the impersonality of the poem.
2. Suggested Response: The *hands* represent people who are raising the shades; the image suggests a monotonous sameness.
3. Suggested Response: The *world* coming back refers to the visibility of people and objects in the morning light. This synecdoche implies a cyclic return rather than a renewal.
4. Suggested Response: The *street* refers to the people, objects, and whole life of the street. This synecdoche suggests a spiritual dimension behind the sordid appearances and tired cycles of life.

THINKING ABOUT THE SELECTION
Recalling

1. In Prelude I what is (a) the time of year? (b) The time of day?
2. In Prelude II what is taking place "in a thousand furnished rooms"?
3. What did "you" hear in Prelude III "when all the world came back"?
4. What are the "ancient women" in the simile doing in Prelude IV?

Interpreting

5. (a) To what social class do the people in "Preludes" belong? (b) How can you tell?
6. The symbol of cycles, or cyclic progression, says one critic, "is almost Mr. Eliot's trademark." What cycle do you find in "Preludes"?
7. A musical prelude can introduce a longer work or can stand alone. Each of Eliot's four preludes stands alone, but they all project a similar mood. How would you describe that mood?

Applying

8. "Preludes," written in 1910–11, reflects Eliot's views before the renewal of his religious faith. How might this poem be different if Eliot had written it twenty years later?

ANALYZING LITERATURE
Using Synecdoche

Synecdoche is a figure of speech in which a part stands for the whole ("Five thousand tongues applauded") or the whole for one of its parts ("Wall Street believes that . . ."). In literature, a synecdoche can enable readers to see an idea or an object in a new light. Sometimes, especially in Eliot's poetry, a synecdoche functions as a symbol. In Prelude II Eliot pictures the crowds of people that hurry to get their morning coffee before going to work. Rather than making such a prosaic statement, however, he uses the synecdoche "muddy feet" (line 17), providing the reader with a more visual and revealing image of the faceless morning bustle in a large city. For each of the following lines from "Preludes," (a) identify the synecdoche; (b) tell what the key word stands for; and (c) comment on how it adds to the mood of the poem.

1. The morning comes to consciousness (1. 14)
2. One thinks of all the hands (1. 21)
3. . . . all the world came back (1. 30)
4. You had such a vision of the street/As the street hardly understands (1. 33–34)
5. . . . and eyes/Assured of certain certainties (1. 44–45)

SPEAKING AND LISTENING
Selecting Music That Evokes the Poem

Like much of Eliot's early poetry, "Preludes" implies disenchantment with the twentieth century and reflects a bleak outlook on life. In this respect his poetry has much in common with the music composed in the early twentieth century. Do some library research on modern composers and their music, finding examples of music that expresses a similar disillusionment and seems to complement Eliot's poem. If possible, obtain a tape or tapes of this music to bring to class for listening and discussion.

THINKING AND WRITING
Writing a Poem Using Synecdoche

Choose a theme that interests you and write an original poem on it. You may choose any rhyme scheme and any metric pattern you like, and the poem may be of any reasonable length. Think carefully about how you can work two synecdoches into your poem—one using the part for the whole, the other using the whole for the part. Write the poem, using the synecdoches. Even with good planning, you will find that thoughtful revision is essential to a well-written poem.

5. Suggested Response: *Eyes* are the eyes of all these city people. This synecdoche reveals the closed state of mind of people in this environment. By referring to people only as "eyes" or, elsewhere, as feet or fingers, the poet hints at their lack of wholeness.

THINKING AND WRITING

For help with this assignment, students can refer to Lesson 18, "Writing a Poem," in the Handbook of Writing About Literature.

Publishing Student Writing Students may want to read their work to the class and then collect it in a class booklet.

Journey of the Magi

T. S. Eliot

In this poem, the speaker, one of the three wise men who traveled to Bethlehem to pay homage to the baby Jesus, reflects upon the meaning of his journey.

"A cold coming we had of it,
Just the worst time of the year
For a journey, and such a long journey:
The ways deep and the weather sharp,
5 The very dead of winter."[1]
And the camels galled, sore-footed, refractory,
Lying down in the melting snow.
There were times we regretted
The summer palaces on slopes, the terraces,
10 And the silken girls bringing sherbet.
Then the camel men cursing and grumbling
And running away, and wanting their liquor and women,
And the night-fires going out, and the lack of shelters,
And the cities hostile and the towns unfriendly
15 And the villages dirty and charging high prices:
A hard time we had of it.
At the end we preferred to travel all night,
Sleeping in snatches,
With the voices singing in our ears, saying
20 That this was all folly.

Then at dawn we came down to a temperate valley,
Wet, below the snow line, smelling of vegetation;
With a running stream and a water-mill beating the
    darkness,
And three trees on the low sky,
25 And an old white horse galloped away in the meadow.
Then we came to a tavern with vine-leaves over the lintel,
Six hands at an open door dicing for pieces of silver,
And feet kicking the empty wine-skins.

---

1. **"A . . . winter.":** Adapted from a part of a sermon delivered by 17th-century Bishop Lancelot Andrews: "A cold coming they had of it at this time of year, just the worst time of the year to take a journey, and specially a long journey in. The ways deep, the weather sharp, the days short, the sun farthest off . . . the very dead of winter."

Presentation

Motivation/Prior Knowledge
This journey is more than a physical one. Discuss with students the several connotations of journeys. What have they discovered about themselves and others on "personal" journeys?

Purpose-Setting Question How has the speaker changed as the result of his journey?

1 **Discussion** Describe the conditions of the journey of the Magi.

2 **Discussion** The author says that "this" is all folly. What is "this"?

3 **Discussion** Why do you think the speaker would make the journey again?

4 **Discussion** How is the birth of the savior both a birth and death for the men who witnessed it?

5 **Discussion** Why would the speaker welcome another death? Does his desire show faith or rejection of religion? Explain.

Reader's Response Why do you think a major change of belief, like the one the speaker experiences, can be so troubling?

30 But there was no information, and so we continued
And arrived at evening, not a moment too soon
Finding the place; it was (you may say) satisfactory.

3   All this was a long time ago, I remember,
And I would do it again, but set down
This set down
35 This: were we led all that way for
Birth or Death? There was a Birth, certainly,
4 We had evidence and no doubt. I had seen birth and death,
But had thought they were different; this Birth was
Hard and bitter agony for us, like Death, our death.
40 We returned to our places, these Kingdoms,
But no longer at ease here, in the old dispensation,
5 With an alien people clutching their gods.
I should be glad of another death.

THINKING ABOUT THE SELECTION

Recalling

1. What kind of weather did the speaker and his companions have on their journey?
2. What are three other problems they encountered?
3. (a) What did they find when they arrived at the tavern? (b) What did they not find?
4. How had circumstances changed for the speaker and his companions when they returned home?

Interpreting

5. Why did others, and perhaps the wise men themselves, think that "this was all folly"?
6. Why do you think the speaker uses understatement, including the parenthetical "you may say," in line 31?
7. In lines 33–35 the speaker says, and then repeats, the words "set down this." What do you think is the purpose of the repetition?
8. The last line of the poem is ambiguous; there is no single, agreed-upon meaning for it. What do you think it means?

Applying

9. In "Journey of the Magi" Eliot retells the story of the wise men traveling to Bethlehem to visit the newborn Jesus. He adds something of his own to the story. What other Biblical stories do you know that Eliot might have treated in a similar way?

ANALYZING LITERATURE

Conveying a Mood

The main feeling or atmosphere a piece of writing conveys is its **mood.** Mood is independent of content and theme, since the same story can be presented in various moods. Indeed, Eliot's "Journey of the Magi" has a different mood from the biblical story on which it is based. Read the original story (Matthew 2: 1–12).
1. How does the mood of Eliot's poem differ from the mood of the biblical story?
2. "Journey of the Magi" was published in 1927. How is the ending of the poem consistent with Eliot's views following his renewal of religious faith in the late 1920's?

Closure and Extension

ANSWERS TO THINKING ABOUT THE SELECTION
Recalling

1. The winter weather was cold and sharp.
2. They encountered the following problems: refractory, irritated camels; irresponsible camel drivers; lack of shelter and fires; hostile cities; unfriendly towns; dirty villages; and high prices.
3. At the tavern they found gamblers and drunkards but no information.
4. The speaker and his companion were uneasy at home, feeling alienated from the old forms of worship.

Interpreting

5. Suggested Response: They believed there was no point to this difficult journey.
6. Suggested Response: The understatement gives greater credibility to the speaker's words.
7. Suggested response: The repetition is to emphasize the importance of what follows. It also suggests that someone is taking down his words.
8. Answers will differ. Students might say that the speaker is anticipating his physical death or another spiritual rebirth like the one he experienced.

THINKING AND WRITING
Analyzing Eliot's Use of Ambiguity

Although Eliot's poetry was viewed by his contemporaries as a break from tradition, Eliot maintained, as do critics today, that it is steeped in tradition. The continuing challenge of his poems lies in their many layers of meaning and their seeming lack of connectedness. This intentional complexity grows out of Eliot's deep learning, his conscious use of the literature of the past, and a belief that serious themes demand the "logic of the imagination."

Ambiguity means having the potential for being understood in two or more ways. Once when a magazine editor wished to find out movie actor Cary Grant's age, he sent Grant's agent a telegram: "How old Cary Grant?" The telegraphic response came back: "Old Cary Grant fine." Poets often use ambiguity intentionally and quite seriously, as Eliot does in the last line of "Journey of the Magi." If your class has discussed question 8, you already have some idea of the different possible interpretations of that line. If not, think about them now. There are at least three reasonable and entirely different interpretations. Jot them down—and any others you can think of—before beginning to write. Then write a brief analytical essay in which you state these interpretations and comment on them. Indicate which one or more you think Eliot intended. Give your reasons. Before handing in the final draft of your paper, read it over carefully for logic. Refer to the poem, making sure that what you say is defensible in the context of what Eliot has written.

Primary Source

In Eliot's time as now, it was hard to make an adequate living as a writer, especially of poetry. Many influential poets toiled in unrelated jobs, writing in their free time. Eliot wrote what is likely the representative poem of the first half of the century, "The Waste-Land" (1921), while handling foreign exchanges for Lloyd's Bank. But then as now, society's expectations often clash with literature's calling, and many found it difficult to see why Eliot would prefer writing poetry to advancing in the bank. Critic I. A. Richards had this conversation with just such a man, one of Eliot's superiors in the bank:

Mr. W.: "You know him, I suppose, as a literary man, as a writer and . . . er . . . and . . . er . . . as a poet? Tell me, if you will—you won't mind my asking, will you? Tell me, is he, in your judgment, would you say, would you call him a good poet?"

Richards: "Well, in my judgment—not everyone would agree, of course, far from it—he *is* a good poet."

Mr. W: "Many of my colleagues . . . think a banker has no business whatever to be a poet. . . . But I believe that anything a man does, whatever his *hobby* may be, it's all the better if he is really keen on it and does it well. I think it helps him with his work. If you see our young friend, you might tell him that we think he's doing quite well at the bank. In fact, if he goes on as he has been doing, I don't see why—in time, of course, in time—he mightn't even become a bank manager."

Applying

9. Answers will differ. Students might refer to the story of Joseph and his brothers.

ANSWERS TO ANALYZING LITERATURE

1. Suggested Response: The mood of Eliot's poem is one of complaint or difficulty rather than joy.
2. Suggested Response: The ending reflects the "death" of one way of thinking and believing and the birth of a new religious consciousness. It also suggests the difficulty of such a change.

THINKING AND WRITING

For help with this assignment students can consult Lesson 13, "Writing About a Poem" in the Handbook of Writing About Literature.

Publishing Student Writing

Place students in groups of three or four and assign a recorder for each group. Have students share their interpretations and compile a list of these. Have the recorder report for the group to the class. Students can then note varying interpretations and defenses.

Literary Focus You might want to tell students that reading a poem aloud can often provide a clue to its tone.

Writing/Prior Knowledge You might want to divide the class into small groups so that students can read the original and revised letters to fellow group members.

Vocabulary

Preteach the following vocabulary words:

supplication (sup′ lə ka′ shən) *n.*: Act of praying (l. 43)

tumid (too′ mid) *adj.*: Swollen (l. 60)

The Hollow Men

Writer's Technique

Tone. A speaker uses a certain tone in communicating a message to his or her audience. A writer does much the same thing, but a writer—lacking pitch, stress, and other features of spoken language —must rely on the choice of details, words, and syntax to convey tone. In poetry, tone reveals a great deal about the writer's attitude toward the subject. In fact, identifying the tone of a poem is vital to a full understanding of the poem's meaning.

Writing

Find a short letter to the editor in your local newspaper that is written in a tone that is easy to recognize and describe. Ordinarily you can describe tone with a single word—*outraged,* perhaps, or *reasonable,* or *amused.* Then rewrite the letter in an entirely different tone. If the tone is outraged, make it sweet and pleasant. If the tone is amused, make it bitter and angry.

Primary Source

The tone of a poem such as "The Hollow Men" makes T. S. Eliot seem very stern and removed from the concerns and cares of daily life. His wide learning and brilliant publications—combined with his deep religious faith—made him seem even more unapproachable and intimidating. But Dylan Thomas's friend Roy Campbell recalls an encounter with Eliot (whom they had nicknamed the "Archbishop") that shows a very different side to his character:

> Dylan Thomas had failed his medical test for the army, and he and Caitlin [Thomas's wife] were broke. My three pounds a week did not carry far: so one day Dylan and I decided to go on a borrowing raid. "But you must stay outside, Roy," he said. "We'll never raise a penny if they see you with me, except in the case of so-and-so and so-and-so." Dylan proposed to make a vast tour . . . of all the newly rich poets in their new offices in the Central Office of Information and the Ministry of Information. . . . But we raised no cash. Dylan said that it had been the same in every office where he had been without me. We stood outside the M.O.I. scratching our heads. "What about His Grace?" I asked, "He lives around there." "You mean the Archbishop?" gasped Dylan, "I wouldn't dare."—"Come on, you'll see. He's not only a saint in his poems, he's a bloody saint in his life too." We went to see Eliot, and the great man helped us so lavishly that it lasted till by some curious coincidence we both got our first considerable radio jobs, almost simultaneously, and were able to pay Elliot back. (Dylan never forgot his kindness. Neither do I.)

Objectives

1 To analyze a poem's tone
2 To interpret allusions
3 To write about tone

Support Material

Teaching Portfolio
Teacher Backup, p. 1285
Grammar in Action Worksheet, *Omitting Punctuation for Effect,* p. 1288
Usage and Mechanics Worksheet, p. 1290
Vocabulary Check, p. 1291
Analyzing Literature Worksheet, *Conveying Tone,* p. 1292

Critical Thinking and Reading Worksheet, *Interpreting Allusions,* p. 1293
Selection Test, p. 1294

The Hollow Men

'T. S. Eliot

Mistah Kurtz[1]—*he dead.*

A penny for the Old Guy[2]

I

We are the hollow men
We are the stuffed men
Leaning together
Headpiece filled with straw. Alas!
5 Our dried voices, when
We whisper together
Are quiet and meaningless
As wind in dry grass
Or rats' feet over broken glass
10 In our dry cellar

Shape without form, shade without color,
Paralyzed force, gesture without motion;

Those who have crossed
With direct eyes, to death's other Kingdom[3]
15 Remember us—if at all—not as lost
Violent souls, but only
As the hollow men
The stuffed men.

1, 2

---

1. Mistah Kurtz: A character in Joseph Conrad's *Heart of Darkness* who travels to Africa hoping to improve the lives of the natives, but finds that, instead, he is corrupted by the worst elements of native life. Horrified by what he had become, Kurtz dies in the jungle.
2. A . . . Guy: A traditional cry used by children on Guy Fawkes Day. Guy Fawkes (1570–1606) was executed for participating in a plot to blow up the king and both Houses of Parliament in 1605. Each year on November 5, children beg for pennies to buy firecrackers which they use to destroy stuffed dummies representing Fawkes.
3. Those . . . Kingdom: An allusion to Dante's *Paradiso*, in which those "with direct eyes" are blessed by God in Heaven.

3 **Discussion** Whose "eyes" is the speaker afraid of meeting? Why is the speaker afraid?

4 **Discussion** Why do you think this speaker would want to wear "disguises"?

5 **Discussion** What is "death's other kingdom"?

II

3
20 Eyes I dare not meet in dreams
In death's dream kingdom
These do not appear:
There, the eyes are
Sunlight on a broken column
There, is a tree swinging
25 And voices are
In the wind's singing
More distant and more solemn
Than a fading star.

Let me be no nearer
30 In death's dream kingdom
Let me also wear
Such deliberate disguises
4 Rat's coat, crowskin, crossed staves
In a field[4]
35 Behaving as the wind behaves
No nearer—

Not that final meeting
In the twilight kingdom

III

This is the dead land
40 This is cactus land
Here the stone images
Are raised, here they receive
The supplication of a dead man's hand
Under the twinkle of a fading star.

45 Is it like this
5 In death's other kingdom
Waking alone
At the hour when we are
Trembling with tenderness
50 Lips that would kiss
Form prayers to broken stone.

---

4. crossed . . . field: Scarecrows.

Grammar in Action

Skillful writers occasionally **omit punctuation for effect.** They know how a passage or poem would normally be punctuated, but they leave punctuation marks out in order to achieve a carefully calculated result. T.S. Eliot, for example, omits many commas and end marks from "The Hollow Men":

This is the dead land
This is cactus land

Here the stone images
Are raised, here they receive
The supplication of a dead man's hand
Under the twinkle of a fading star.

Ordinarily, the first and second lines would end with periods, and the comma in line three should be a period. However, in this passage, as in other sections of the poem, no sentence ever really ends or begins. Like "the hollow men" themselves, the sentences are suspended in a kind of limbo.

Student Activity 1. Find another passage in the poem that is missing punctuation. Add the missing punctuation marks. Then

IV

The eyes are not here
There are no eyes here
In this valley of dying stars
55 In this hollow valley
This broken jaw of our lost kingdoms

In this last of meeting places
We grope together
And avoid speech
60 Gathered on this beach of the tumid river[5]

Sightless, unless
The eyes reappear
As the perpetual star[6]
Multifoliate rose[7]
65 Of death's twilight kingdom
The hope only
Of empty men.

V

Here we go round the prickly pear
Prickly pear prickly pear
70 *Here we go round the prickly pear*
At five o'clock in the morning.[8]

Between the idea
And the reality
Between the motion
75 And the act[9]
Falls the Shadow

For Thine is the Kingdom[10]

---

5. river: From Dante's *Inferno*, the river Archeron, the river which the dead cross over as they pass into Hell.
6. star: A traditional symbol for Christ.
7. Multifoliate rose: In Dante's *Paradiso*, Paradise was described as a "multifoliate rose," or a rose with many leaves. Also, the rose is a traditional symbol for the Virgin Mary.
8. Here . . . morning: Adaptation of a common nursery rhyme. A prickly pear is a cactus.
9. Between . . . act: A reference to *Julius Caesar*, Act II, Scene i, 63–65: "Between the acting of a dreadful thing/And the first motion, all the interim is/Like a phantasma or hideous dream."
10. For . . . Kingdom: From the ending of the Lord's Prayer.

The Hollow Men   1065

6 **Literary Focus** Is the tone of these lines hopeful? Explain.

7 **Discussion** Explain the significance of the children's song. What do its words and rhythm suggest? How is it appropriate?

8 **Discussion** What do you think Eliot means by "the Shadow"?

9 **Discussion** What is the effect of including the last line of "The Lord's Prayer"?

compare the correctly punctuated passage with the one from the poem and determine which is more effective.

Student Activity 2. Describe a person who is very talkative. Deliberately omit punctuation to convey the speed and quantity of this person's speech.

10 **Discussion** Explain the effect of
the repetition in lines 95–97. How
does the repetition add to the
meaning of the last line?

Reader's Response Why do you
think the last four lines of this
poem are among the best-known
lines Eliot wrote?

Between the conception
And the creation
80 Between the emotion
And the response
Falls the Shadow

                       Life is very long[11]

Between the desire
85 And the spasm
Between the potency
And the existence
Between the essence
And the descent
90 Falls the Shadow

             For Thine is the Kingdom

For Thine is
Life is
For Thine is the

95 *This is the way the world ends*
    This is the way the world ends
    This is the way the world ends
    Not with a bang but a whimper.

10

11. Life . . . long: Quotation from Joseph Conrad's *An Outcast of the
Islands.*

THINKING ABOUT THE SELECTION

Recalling

1. How does the speaker say that he and others like him are remembered by those "with direct eyes"?
2. In "death's dream kingdom" what disguise will the speaker wear?
3. What do the hollow men do in the "hollow valley . . . this last of meeting places"?
4. What is it that forever falls between idea and achievement, preventing the hollow men from accomplishing anything?
5. According to the speaker, how does the world end?

Interpreting

6. Although Kurtz was a "hollow sham" and Guy Fawkes was a traitor, the speaker suggests that they were superior to the hollow men. Why were they superior?
7. What aspects of modern life might the "stone images" in part III represent?
8. Both part III and part V suggest a particular kind of landscape in which the hollow men exist. What kind of landscape is it?
9. What do you think "the Shadow" is in part V?

Applying

10. In "The Hollow Men," published in 1925, Eliot presents a bleak picture of his generation. To what extent, if at all, do you think his implied criticism applies to the people of today?

ANALYZING LITERATURE

Conveying Tone

The **tone** of a poem reveals the writer's attitude toward the subject or theme. Tone is conveyed through details and images—hollow men stuffed with straw, a cactus land, a twilight kingdom. It is also carried by words and their connotations—*hollow, meaningless, fading, death, Shadow, whimper.* Syntax, the way in which words are put together, plays a part, too—"Shape without form, shade without color"

(parallelism); "The hope only/Of empty men" (ambiguity). How would you describe the tone of "The Hollow Men"? (One adjective can usually describe tone, but since Eliot's poem is more complex than most, you may find it necessary to go into greater detail.)

CRITICAL THINKING AND READING

Interpreting Allusions

An **allusion** in literature is a brief, often indirect reference to a person, a place, an event, or another literary work. "The Hollow Men" is a poem rich in allusions. Choose any three of the following allusions from "The Hollow Men." Explain each one. Tell how the allusion adds meaning to the poem by introducing, as a kind of literary shorthand, a number of associations through the use of only a few words. Try to go somewhat beyond the footnote text.

1. *Mistah Kurtz—he dead.*
2. Those who have crossed/With direct eyes, to death's other Kingdom
3. As the perpetual star/Multifoliate rose
4. Between the motion/And the act
5. *For Thine is the Kingdom*

THINKING AND WRITING

Writing About Tone

Write an essay in which you analyze the tone of T. S. Eliot's poetry. Describe the tone of each of the three Eliot poems in this unit and explain how the tone adds to the meaning of each one. Use quotations from the poems to illustrate and support your points. Follow the three basic steps in the writing process. In prewriting, take notes and make a rough outline. Then write your first draft, using appropriate quotations. In revising, make any major changes that are needed —structural, logical, organizational—as well as checking your grammar and usage. Finally, make any needed proofreading corrections.

ages could represent skyscrapers or any falsely worshiped material objects.
8. Suggested Response: The landscape is desolate, arid, and unproductive.
9. Answers may differ. Some students may say the Shadow is the fear of taking any action.

Applying

10. Answers will differ. Some students may find this picture too negative; others may feel it is applicable today.

ANSWERS TO ANALYZING LITERATURE

Suggested Response: The tone may be described as bleak, hopeless, enervated, and anxious.

ANSWERS TO CRITICAL THINKING AND READING

1. Suggested Response: The allusion may suggest that even the energetic evil of Kurtz is beyond the capabilities of the hollow men.
2. Suggested Response: These are the eyes of the blessed who see the figures in the poem as hollow.
3. Suggested Response: The only hope of hollow men is some sort of heavenly mercy, perhaps from a compassionate figure like the Virgin Mary.
4. Suggested Response: This phrase from Shakespeare's *Julius Caesar* suggests that all positive action seems dreadful to the hollow men, who are living in a kind of nightmare.
5. Suggested Response: This cut-off phrase from the Lord's Prayer suggests that the hollow men cannot fully pray and therefore cannot get beyond their situation.

THINKING AND WRITING

For help with this assignment, students can refer to Lesson 13, "Writing about a Poem," in the Handbook of Writing About Literature.

Publishing Student Writing Ask student volunteers to read their essays aloud so that students can learn from the variety of points raised.

Closure and Extension

ANSWERS TO THINKING ABOUT THE SELECTION

Recalling

1. He and others are remembered as hollow men and stuffed men.
2. The speaker will be disguised as a scarecrow.
3. The hollow men, sightless, grope together and avoid speech.
4. A shadow falls between the idea and the achievement.
5. The world ends *"Not with a bang but with a whimper."*

Interpreting

6. Suggested Response: These individuals had a direction to their lives and were not afraid of dying.
7. Suggested Response: Stone im-

1068

More About the Author You might want to tell students that Graves preferred a simple life on the island of Majorca to life in England. Ask students what might have motivated Graves to make this choice.

Critical Evaluation David Daiches wrote that Graves "has published over 15 volumes of poetry, of which *Collected Poems 1959* represents most of what he wants to preserve. He has continued to publish slim volumes of new poetry. . . , but the 1959 volume well represents the range and quality of his genius. Its publication was the sign for clear critical affirmation, on both sides of the Atlantic, that Graves is a major English poet of our time."

ROBERT GRAVES

1895–1985

Robert Graves has written successfully in almost every literary form, but he is perhaps best known as the author of the best-selling novel *I, Claudius* (1934), which was made into an outstanding BBC television series a few years ago. Graves achieved his first fame in 1929 with a classic memoir of World War I, *Good-bye to All That.* Despite his prose efforts, however, Graves's true calling is poetry, as he has said. Ever since his first two volumes appeared in 1916, he has been recognized as a major British poet.

The son of a prominent poet, Robert Graves grew up in a London household with an extensive private library, which provided much of his early education. World War I began while he was attending the Charterhouse School and producing his earliest poems. Graves enlisted in the Royal Welsh Fusiliers, the same outfit to which Siegfried Sassoon belonged. Fighting in the trenches, he was severely wounded and reported dead. He later suffered shell shock and received a medical discharge. Graves, like Sassoon, lost all illusions about the glory of war, as shown by his two wartime poetry collections, *Over the Brazier* (1916) and *Fairies and Fusiliers* (1917).

Graves studied at Oxford, received his degree, and in 1927 took a teaching position at the Royal Egyptian University in Cairo. For a number of years he collaborated with the American poet Laura Riding on many writing and publishing projects. In 1929 he and Riding settled in Majorca, an island off the coast of Spain, where he remained except for intervals during the Spanish Civil War, World War II, and a teaching stint at Oxford in the 1960's.

A respected scholar and critic, Graves aroused controversy in 1948 with the publication of *The White Goddess,* a critical study of the origin, value, and history of poetry, whose main thesis—the dominance of a mythic female Muse—is impressively argued but widely questioned. Its influence on Graves's poetry, however, has been substantial and beneficial. His poems, a blend of traditional and modern, sometimes exhibit a deceptive simplicity. According to the American poet Richard Wilbur, they "have the air of being spontaneous answers to actual experience."

Graves refused to seek praise, for fame would make him hostage to public opinion. A poet who writes for others has forsaken his honor, which "consists in his not forming ties that can impair critical independence, or prevent him from telling the whole truth about anything, or force him to do anything out of character." Yet in his independence Graves achieved immortality.

Objectives

1 To understand the Modernist Movement
2 To write about the Modernist Movement

Support Material

Teaching Portfolio
Teacher Backup, p. 1297
Usage and Mechanics Worksheet, p. 1300
Vocabulary Check, p. 1301
Critical Thinking and Reading Worksheet, *Recognizing Traditional Symbolism,* p. 1302

Language Worksheet, *Understanding Coined Words,* p. 1303
Selection Test, p. 1304

GUIDE FOR INTERPRETING

Interruption; One Hard Look;
She Tells Her Love While Half Asleep

Period Trends

The Modernist Movement. The Modernist movement, or Modernism, followed World War I. Art, architecture, dance, and literature —all were in revolt against the rigid traditional forms of earlier periods. Disillusioned by the war and unhappy with the postwar world, artists sought new forms, new techniques, new subjects. It was a time of ferment. The Modernist writers, like the Georgian poets, demanded a break with the past, but the Modernists were much more radical than the Georgians. The aftermath of war, which doomed the pastoral-minded Georgians, spurred the Modernists to action. Many poets who began as Georgians—D. H. Lawrence, Siegfried Sassoon, Robert Graves—changed and grew. In the 1920's T. S. Eliot in England, James Joyce in Ireland, and E. E. Cummings in the United States experimented in ways that earlier generations would have found incomprehensible.

Commentary

What is the difference between "major" and "minor" achievements —especially in a field as personal as literature? George Stade judges Graves to be "a minor poet of major proportions." Stade claims that Graves has deliberately chosen to be a minor poet, citing as support Graves's remark: "Minor poetry, so called to differentiate it from major, is the real stuff." Graves thinks of himself as a traditional poet, but not himself a tradition, as is the case with Chaucer and Shakespeare. But a great many others claim that he is indeed a major poet, "the most important poet writing in English and the best model for young poets seeking to establish a new tradition or recover the native one." To Stade, Graves's steadfast refusal to be "major" establishes much of what is unique and valuable about his career. In contrast to the Modernist trend of impersonality, for example, Graves stresses sincerity, emotion, and suggestiveness. As Daniel Hoffman has remarked, "In prose as well as poetry, Graves was an original."

Writing

Choose an everyday object to write about. Set an alarm to go off at the end of five minutes. Then, on a sheet of paper, begin writing nonstop, putting down any thoughts or associations that come to mind in regard to your subject. You need not write full sentences, but try to keep your pen or pencil in motion until the alarm sounds. When your time is up, read over your random jottings. Select the most interesting of them and share them with your classmates.

Literary Focus You may point out that the American poet Ezra Pound was instrumental in creating the modernist movement in poetry. Influenced by the British novelist Ford Maddox Ford and the Philosopher T. E. Hulme, Pound started writing brief poems in free verse that focused on a single image. The group of writers who adopted this approach called themselves imagists and were active in London before World War I.

Writing/Prior Knowledge Have students practice thinking by association. Name an item and have a student volunteer an immediate association. Have students continue to associate, for two or three minutes. See where the association leads them. Then assign the writing.

Interruption

Robert Graves

If ever against this easy blue and silver
Hazed-over countryside of thoughtfulness,
Far behind in the mind and above,
Boots from before and below approach trampling,
5 Watch how their premonition will display
A forward countryside, low in the distance—
A picture-postcard square of June grass;
Will warm a summer season, trim the hedges,
Cast the river about on either flank,
10 Start the late cuckoo emptily calling,
Invent a rambling tale of moles and voles,
Furnish a path with stiles.
Watch how the field will broaden, the feet nearing,
Sprout with great dandelions and buttercups,
15 Widen and heighten. The blue and silver
Fogs at the border of this all-grass.
Interruption looms gigantified,
Lurches against, treads thundering through,
Blots the landscape, scatters all,
20 Roars and rumbles like a dark tunnel,
Is gone.
      The picture-postcard grass and trees
Swim back to central: it is a large patch,
It is a modest, failing patch of green,
25 The postage stamp of its departure,
Clouded with blue and silver, closing in now
To a plain countryside of less and less,
Unpeopled and unfeatured blue and silver,
Before, behind, above.

SUN, WIND, AND RAIN
David Cox
The City Museum and Art Gallery, Birmingham

Humanities Note

Fine art, *Sun, Wind, and Rain* by David Cox. David Cox (1783 –1859), an English landscape painter, learned his craft through various jobs held early in his life —as miniaturist, paint maker, and scene painter. He took a few watercolor lessons from the famous English watercolorist John Varley, after which he taught drawing and sold watercolor sketches for a living. He eventually gained a small reputation as a painter and continued to teach for the rest of his life.

The painting *Sun, Wind, and Rain* was completed in 1845. It was painted in North Wales in oil, a medium that Cox only began to use in 1839. Painted with simple vigor, it is a striking celebration of the caprices of nature.

You might ask the following questions:
1. What do both the poem and the painting describe?
2. Which verbal images in the poem match visual images in the painting?

THINKING ABOUT THE SELECTION

Recalling

1. (a) Where does the interruption occur? (b) What time of year is it?
2. With what does the field sprout when the feet near it?
3. What is the sound of the interruption at its height?
4. When the interruption is over, how is the "blue and silver" countryside described?

Interpreting

5. (a) What is the interruption? (b) What is the first indication of the nature of the interruption?

6. Why do you think the interruption is described as being "all-grass"?
7. Why do you think the poet chose to break line 21 abruptly?
8. The meaning of "Interruption" is not expressed in a series of logically ordered sentences. How is it expressed?

Applying

9. Short stories sometimes have an interruption as their main plot device. (a) What short story do you know that uses this device? (b) What is the nature of the interruption? (c) What precedes and follows the interruption?

Closure and Extension

ANSWERS TO THINKING ABOUT THE SELECTION
Recalling

1. (a) and (b) The interruption occurs while the speaker is in a "blue and silver" countryside in June. It occurs in the person's thoughts.
2. The field sprouts with dandelions and buttercups.
3. At its height, the sound "Roars . . . like a dark tunnel."
4. The blue and silver countryside is plain, unpeopled, and unfeatured.

Interpreting

5. Suggested Responses: (a) The interruption is the sound of footsteps approaching. (b) The first indication is line 4.
6. Suggested Response: The grass covers the whole landscape.
7. Suggested Response: The break is to emphasize the contrast—the interruption has left, and the summer countryside returns.
8. Suggested Response: It is expressed as a series of associated images.

Applying

9. Answers will differ.

One Hard Look

Robert Graves

Small gnats that fly
In hot July
And lodge in sleeping ears,
Can rouse therein
5 A trumpet's din
With Day of Judgment fears.

Small mice at night
Can wake more fright
Than lions at midday;
10 A straw will crack
The camel's back—
There is no easier way.

One smile relieves
A heart that grieves
15 Though deadly sad it be,
And one hard look
Can close the book
That lovers love to see.

THINKING ABOUT THE SELECTION

Recalling

1. What does the buzz of a gnat sound like in the ear of a sleeper?
2. What can one hard look do?

Interpreting

3. What is the common characteristic of gnats, mice, and straw that contribute to the meaning of the poem?
4. What main observation does the poem make?

Applying

5. (a) Do you agree with Graves's observation? (b) What experience have you had that supports or casts doubt on what he says?

She Tells Her Love While Half Asleep

Robert Graves

She tells her love while half asleep,
   In the dark hours,
      With half-words whispered low: **1**
As Earth stirs in her winter sleep
5   And puts out grass and flowers
      Despite the snow,
      Despite the falling snow.   **2**

THINKING ABOUT THE SELECTION

Recalling

1. What is the time of day in the poem?
2. "Despite the falling snow," what does the earth do?

Interpreting

3. To what in nature are the "half-words whispered low" compared?
4. What might falling snow represent metaphorically in the relationship between the speaker and the one who "tells her love"?

Applying

5. The flowers of spring are probably the most widely used symbol of rebirth. Why do you think this is so?

THINKING AND WRITING

Writing About the Modernist Movement

The modernist movement began and peaked in the 1920's. To understand the movement, you need a general understanding of that tumultuous decade. You also should know the works of a few of the major writers—T. S. Eliot, Robert Graves, James Joyce, and Virginia Woolf. Do some library research on the modernism of the Twenties. Take notes, particularly on the changes in style that modernism introduced.

Write an essay in which you explain why writers and other artists in that decade felt compelled to strike out in new directions. Include quotations from the sources you have used. When you revise your first draft, check to make sure you have introduced and punctuated the quotations properly.

Presentation

Motivation/Prior Knowledge Have students describe a winter field. What is happening to the seeds under the earth? Then tell them that the poet uses the growth of plants as a figure of speech.

Purpose-Setting Question How does the poet feel toward his subject?

1 Discussion How are "dark hours" and "winter sleep" similar images?

2 Discussion How does the word "falling" add to the snow image? Would the omission of the last line make a difference in the intent of the poem?

Closure and Extension

ANSWERS TO THINKING ABOUT THE SELECTION
Recalling

1. The setting is nighttime.
2. The earth begins to grow grass and flowers.

Interpreting

3. Suggested Response: The words are compared to the Earth's stirring.
4. Suggested Response: It may represent a period of waiting or quiescence during which the love is preparing for growth.

Applying

5. Answers will differ. Students may respond that flowers, though dormant in winter, sprout vigorously, beautifully, and trustingly after the winter season.

THINKING AND WRITING
Publishing Student Writing You might want to collect students' essays in a book.

Writing Across the Curriculum You may want to work with the members of the history department to assist students in learning more about the 1920's. Perhaps members of that department could give lectures and suggest movies or other resources to help students place the Modernists in a social context.

W. H. AUDEN

1907–1977

Much as T. S. Eliot became established as the poetic voice of the 1920's, so W. H. Auden emerged as the poetic voice of the 1930's. Born in York, England, Auden moved to the United States at the age of thirty-two and took out citizenship papers, reversing the odyssey of Eliot, who was born in St. Louis, Missouri, and became a British subject. The youthful Auden was greatly influenced by Eliot's *The Waste Land,* but in later life both men replaced their anger and despair with a staunch Christian faith. Versatility, wit, and dazzling technique characterize Auden's poetry.

Wystan Hugh Auden, the son of a doctor, was interested in science as a child and planned to become an engineer. He received his education at St. Edmund's School and Gresham's School, and later attended Oxford University. His first appearance in print was in *Oxford Poetry,* a series of annual collections of verse by the university's undergraduates. The volumes in which his poems appear—1926, 1927, and 1928—also contain poems by Stephen Spender, C. Day Lewis, and Louis MacNeice, all of whom became important poets.

Auden's first published collection, entitled simply *Poems,* appeared in 1930. These poems, innovative and eloquent, struck many readers of the day as strange, even impenetrable. His second volume, *On This Island,* published in 1937, is more down-to-earth and generated greater enthusiasm. He was awarded the King's Poetry Medal that year. In 1939 Auden left England for the United States, where he taught in a number of universities while continuing to write. He became an American citizen in 1946, and his poetry collection, *The Age of Anxiety,* won a Pulitzer Prize in 1948. In 1956, having been elected Professor of Poetry at Oxford University, he returned to England where he remained through 1961.

Auden was a more prolific poet than Eliot, and his output is remarkable for its variety, originality, and craftsmanship. He writes equally well in the current idiom of the street or in the archaic measures of *Beowulf,* in the sing-song manner of a traditional ballad or in the formal cadences of an elegy. He has been called "the most provocative as well as the most unpredictable poet of his generation." With Yeats and Eliot, he shares honors as the most significant British poet of the first half of the twentieth century.

GUIDE FOR INTERPRETING

In Memory of W. B. Yeats;
Musée des Beaux Arts

Writer's Technique

Elegy and Figurative Language. An elegy is a poem of mourning for the dead. The great Greek and Latin elegies, forerunners of elegies in English, were written in distichs. A *distich* is a pair of rhyming lines considered as a unit. The third part of W. H. Auden's "In Memory of W. B. Yeats" is composed of distichs, or couplets, similar to those in a classical elegy. Elegies sum up, often in heroic terms, the lifetime accomplishments of an individual, or, as in Gray's "Elegy Written in a Country Churchyard," a group of people. Elegies frequently make use of figurative language; that is, language rich in figures of speech such as simile, metaphor, and personification. An elegy may also contain literary devices such as paradox and allusion.

Commentary

One of Auden's friends has remarked that Auden thinks of himself as "a giant personal enterprise—Auden, Auden, Auden, and Company." The remark is fitting, for it suggests that the poet is made up of many different sides, bounded by contrast and intricacy. Early poems such as "Musée des Beaus Arts" (1938) and "In Memory of W. B. Yeats" (1939) are deeply serious explorations of the nature and function of poetry and the artist's special role in society. Later poems, in contrast, are lighter in tone. They often use surprising, comic touches to probe the place of art in the world and eternity. Auden's discussion of the role of art and the artist in *Secondary Worlds*, a series of lectures he delivered in 1967, serves to reaffirm what he created thirty years earlier in "Musée des Beaux Arts," and "In Memory of W. B. Yeats," as well as in much of his later work. "To believe in the value of art," he wrote, "is to believe that it is possible to make an object, be it an epic or a two-line epigram, which will remain permanently on hand in the world." This function of art, Auden emphasizes, is the opposite of much of the work of the world, which is to make things designed to be obsolete. To Auden, then, a work of art can give us the moral and intellectual nourishment we need to survive. What role do you think art serves in today's world?

Writing

Think of a person, living or dead, whom you greatly admire. This person can be either someone you know (or knew) firsthand or someone famous. Write a few memorial lines for the person, using a figure of speech in each of the lines. Try to use at least one simile, one metaphor, and one personification.

Literary Focus You may want to point out to students that each section of this elegy has a different form. The first is in free verse, the second uses iambic pentameter, and the third—the most formal section—is cast in quatrains. The meter of the last section is trochaic tetrameter (a trochee foot is the reverse of an iamb).

Writing/Prior Knowledge Ask students why they might admire a person. Is it for what the person does? Is it for what the person stands? Is it for the personal qualities of wit, or gentleness, or honesty? Encourage a variety of responses. Then assign the writing.

Vocabulary

Preteach the following vocabulary word:
sequestered (si kwes′ tərd) *v.*: Kept apart from others (l. 61)

1 Discussion Explain how the death of the poet is kept from his poems.

2 Discussion What is the general reaction to this death?

In Memory of W. B. Yeats

W. H. Auden

1

He disappeared in the dead of winter:
The brooks were frozen, the airports almost deserted,
And snow disfigured the public statues;
The mercury sank in the mouth of the dying day.
5 O all the instruments agree
The day of his death was a dark cold day.

Far from his illness
The wolves ran on through the evergreen forests,
The peasant river was untempted by fashionable quays;[1]
10 By mourning tongues
The death of the poet was kept from his poems.

But for him it was his last afternoon as himself,
An afternoon of nurses and rumors;
The provinces of his body revolted,
15 The squares of his mind were empty,
Silence invaded the suburbs,
The current of his feeling failed: he became his admirers.

Now he is scattered among a hundred cities
And wholly given over to unfamiliar affections;
20 To find his happiness in another kind of wood
And be punished by another code of conscience.
The words of a dead man
Are modified in the guts of the living.

But in the importance and noise of tomorrow
25 When the brokers are roaring like beasts on the floor of the
    Bourse,[2]
And the poor have the sufferings to which they are fairly
    accustomed,

---

1. **quays** (kēz): Wharfs with facilities for loading or unloading ships.
2. **Bourse** (boŏrs): The Paris Stock Exchange.

Grammar in Action

Tone, which is an author's attitude toward his or her subject, is directly related to the **form** of a work. For example, sonnets and other elaborately structured forms tend to promote the use of a more serious tone.

Auden makes use of this connection between form and tone in his poem about Yeats. The first part of his poem, which is conversational and informal, is written in free verse. In the second part of the poem, Auden's tone becomes more serious and elegiac (*elegiac* means "expressing lament and praise for someone who has died"). To accommodate this new tone, Auden tightens his form by using rhyme (for the most part, slant rhyme) and making his lines approximately the same length. The third section of the poem is still more formal; it has a regular rhyme scheme (aabb) and meter (trochaic tetrameter). As a result of this tightening of form, the third section has an even more exalted and serious tone.

And each in the cell of himself is almost convinced of his
    freedom;
A few thousand will think of this day
As one thinks of a day when one did something slightly
    unusual.

30   O all the instruments agree
The day of his death was a dark cold day.

2

You were silly like us: your gift survived it all;
The parish of rich women, physical decay,
Yourself; mad Ireland hurt you into poetry.
35   Now Ireland has her madness and her weather still,
For poetry makes nothing happen: it survives
In the valley of its saying where executives
Would never want to tamper; it flows south
From ranches of isolation and the busy griefs,
40   Raw towns that we believe and die in; it survives,
A way of happening, a mouth.

3

Earth, receive an honored guest;
William Yeats is laid to rest:
Let the Irish vessel lie
45   Emptied of its poetry.

Time that is intolerant
Of the brave and innocent,
And indifferent in a week
To a beautiful physique,

50   Worships language and forgives
Everyone by whom it lives;
Pardons cowardice, conceit
Lays its honors at their feet.

Time with this strange excuse
55   Pardoned Kipling and his views,[3]

---

3. Kipling . . . views: English writer Rudyard Kipling (1865–1936)
was a supporter of imperialism.

In Memory of W.B. Yeats   1077

3 **Literary Focus** Note that the poet is now addressing Yeats directly. What is the effect of this shift?

4 **Literary Focus** Note that Part 3 focuses on the enduring qualities of Yeats's poetry. Why do you think this part of the poem is the most formal?

5 **Literary Focus** How do the shorter stanzas and the use of rhyming couplets—distichs—change the tone?

6 **Discussion** According to the speaker, time worships language and pardons the cowardice of good writers. Do you think either of these concepts is true?

Student Activity 1. Could the poem have been equally effective if Auden had begun with a tighter form and more serious tone and then proceeded to a looser form and less serious tone? Explain.

Student Activity 2. Write an elegy for a person you knew or a figure from history. Follow Auden's pattern by dividing your poem into two or more sections and changing the form and tone of your poem as you move from section to section.

7 **Discussion** How do these stanzas contrast? What is the role of
poetry in the times the poet describes?

8 **Discussion** Explain the paradox.
How can there be a ''rapture of
distress''?

Reader's Response Is there a
person whose death you would
like to commemorate in some
way? Explain.

And will pardon Paul Claudel,[4]
Pardons him for writing well.

In the nightmare of the dark
All the dogs of Europe bark,
60 And the living nations wait,
Each sequestered in its hate;

7

Intellectual disgrace
Stares from every human face,
And the seas of pity lie
65 Locked and frozen in each eye.

Follow, poet, follow right
To the bottom of the night,
With your unconstraining voice
Still persuade us to rejoice;

8

70 With the farming of a verse
Make a vineyard of the curse,
Sing of human unsuccess
In a rapture of distress;

In the deserts of the heart
75 Let the healing fountain start,
In the prison of his days
Teach the free man how to praise.

---

4. pardon Paul Claudel (klō del'): French poet, dramatist, and
diplomat. Paul Claudel (1868–1955) had antidemocratic political
views, which Yeats at times shared.

THINKING ABOUT THE SELECTION
Recalling

1. What two things were present on Yeats's last
afternoon ''as himself''?
2. How many people are likely to remember
Yeats's death the next day?
3. What was it that ''hurt'' Yeats into writing
poetry?

4. According to the third section of the poem,
to whom is time (a) intolerant? (b) indifferent?
5. What does the speaker ask the poet to teach
free men?

Interpreting

6. Twice in the first section, the speaker uses
the words ''all the instruments agree.'' What
instruments might he mean (a) in a literal

Closure and Extension

ANSWERS TO THINKING
ABOUT THE SELECTION
Recalling

1. Nurses and rumors were present.
2. The speaker says a few thousand
may remember Yeats's death.
3. ''Mad Ireland'' hurt Yeats into writing poetry.
4. (a and b) Time is intolerant of the

brave and innocent and indifferent
to a beautiful physique.
5. The speaker asks the poet to
teach free men how to praise.

Interpreting

6. Suggested Responses: (a) The literal instruments are thermome-
ters and barometers. (b) Metaphorically the instruments might
be the minds and hearts of those
who loved the poet's work.
7. Suggested Response: Yeats is in

the minds of people in hundreds
of cities.
8. Suggested Response: (a) Auden
is addressing Yeats in the second
section and (b) the Earth and a
generic poet in the third section.
9. Suggested Response: (a) The
speaker says that Europe is full of
hatred. (b) He feels the poet
should ''persuade us to rejoice''
and teach us how to praise.

sense? (b) in a metaphorical sense?

7. What do you think the poet means by stating in line 18 that Yeats is now "scattered among a hundred cities"?

8. Whom is the speaker addressing in (a) the second section? (b) the third section?

9. (a) How favorably or unfavorably does the speaker view the situation in Europe? (b) How does he think the poet should react to it? Find evidence to support your answer.

Applying

10. This poem is an elegy to William Butler Yeats. Yet, in a sense, it could be addressed to any poet, for Auden sets down the responsibilities and rewards he thinks belong to the poet. What are these responsibilities and rewards?

ANALYZING LITERATURE
Understanding Elegy

An **elegy** is a poem that pays tribute to a person (or, less commonly, more than one person) who has died. Throughout history elegies have been written to immortalize people who, at least in the eyes of the poet, have achieved greatness. Most elegies contain imaginative comparisons—figures of speech such as simile, metaphor, and personification. W. H. Auden uses all three of these kinds of figurative language in "In Memory of W. B. Yeats." Write the line or lines of the poem in which each of the following occurs.

1. Personification in which a day coming to an end is said to display a facial feature,
2. Personification of a body of water as being susceptible to temptation,
3. Metaphor that compares body and mind to geographic areas,
4. Simile in which certain professional people are compared to wild animals,
5. Simile that compares thinking about the death of a great man with thinking about doing something unusual,

6. Personification where something inanimate and abstract has the power to worship and pardon,
7. Metaphor that relates something bad to a place where grapes are grown.

CRITICAL THINKING AND READING
Understanding the Legacy of an Artist

"In Memory of W. B. Yeats" is a poet's tribute not to a lost friend but to a fellow poet. Auden never knew Yeats personally, but he knew of him by reading his poetry. Most poets, as you might suppose, read poetry as well as write it. They are aware of the classics and trends. Poetry —indeed, all literature—is part of an ever-expanding archive, one in which, as in the National Archives, "the past is prologue." Auden, in his elegy, is responding to the loss he believes the world should feel at the loss of a great artist. Yet he is also aware, as the poem makes clear, that while Yeats himself is gone, the poetry of Yeats lives on.

1. What does Auden mean in line 11, "The death of the poet was kept from his poems"?
2. In the third section of the poem, what evidence is there that Auden is mourning the passing of an artist more than the passing of Yeats the man?

THINKING AND WRITING
Writing About a Paradox

In line 36 Auden observes that "poetry makes nothing happen." But in the next section of the poem he beseeches the poet (any poet) to use his or her gift to lead the human race out of the darkness of hatred. How, you may ask, is it possible for a poet to accomplish this monumental task if "poetry makes nothing happen"? In an essay explain how you might get around this apparent contradiction—this paradox—by drawing upon other insights from the poem. When you revise make sure your essay is well organized and that you have provided adequate support for your thesis.

In Memory of W.B. Yeats 1079

Musée des Beaux Arts[1]

W. H. Auden

About suffering they were never wrong,
The Old Masters: how well they understood
Its human position; how it takes place
While someone else is eating or opening a window or just
    walking dully along;
5 How, when the aged are reverently, passionately waiting
For the miraculous birth, there always must be
Children who did not specially want it to happen, skating
On a pond at the edge of the wood:
They never forgot
10 That even the dreadful martyrdom must run its course
Anyhow in a corner, some untidy spot
Where the dogs go on with their doggy life and the
    torturer's horse
Scratches its innocent behind on a tree.

In Brueghel's *Icarus*,[2] for instance: how everything turns
    away
15 Quite leisurely from the disaster; the ploughman may
Have heard the splash, the forsaken cry,
But for him it was not an important failure; the sun shone
As it had to on the white legs disappearing into the green
Water; and the expensive delicate ship that must have seen
20 Something amazing, a boy falling out of the sky,
Had somewhere to get to and sailed calmly on.

---

1. Musée des Beaux Arts: The Museum of Fine Arts in Brussels, Belgium.
2. Brueghel's (br$\overline{oo}$′ gəlz) *Icarus* (ik′ ə rəs): *The Fall of Icarus,* a painting by Flemish painter Pieter Brueghel (1522?–1599).

THE FALL OF ICARUS
Pieter Bruegel
Musées Royaux des Beaux-Arts de Belgique

Humanities Note

Fine art, *Landscape With the Fall of Icarus*, by Pieter Bruegel. Pieter Bruegel the Elder (1530–1569) was a Flemish painter. He roamed the countryside, often in disguise, to make candid drawings of peasants at work and play that he would later use for his paintings.

The painting *Landscape With the Fall of Icarus* was influenced by Ovid's tale of Icarus, in which a fisherman, a shepherd, and a peasant go about their daily work oblivious to the drama of the flight and fall of Icarus. Bruegel's painting is composed of little scenes of the events described in Ovid's story. The colors are jewellike; the detail is exquisite.

You might use the following questions for discussion:

1. In his poem, Auden comments on the indifference of humans to each other's disasters. How does Bruegel show this indifference in this painting?
2. What is the poet's attitude toward this indifference? What is the artist's attitude toward this indifference?

THINKING ABOUT THE SELECTION

Recalling

1. (a) What do the Old Masters show "someone else" doing while suffering occurs? (b) According to the speaker, what do the Old Masters understand about martyrdom?
2. (a) How does the ploughman react to the disaster in the Brueghel painting, *Icarus*? (b) How does the ship respond?

Interpreting

3. What do you think Auden intends the activities in line 4 to represent?
4. What is your understanding of the "miraculous birth" the aged are awaiting?
5. Icarus is a figure in Greek mythology who flies with artificial wings. Coming too close to the sun, the wax of his wings melts, and he falls into the sea and drowns. (a) What does Brueghel mean to imply by calling his painting *Icarus* but showing only Icarus's disappearing legs in the corner of the picture? (b) How closely does Auden's poem adhere to the same theme?

Applying

6. The poem describes an age-old irony. (a) In your own words, what is this irony? (b) What are some examples of it that exist today?

Musée des Beaux Arts 1081

Closure and Extension

ANSWERS TO THINKING ABOUT THE SELECTION
Recalling

1. (a) Observers to suffering are doing commonplace things such as eating, walking, or opening a window. (b) Martyrdom occurs, unremarked, in some "untidy spot."
2. (a) The ploughman ignores Icarus's fall, (b) and the ship sails on.

Interpreting

3. Suggested Response: The activities represent daily, ordinary, somewhat mindless tasks.
4. Suggested Response: The miraculous birth is life after death.
5. Suggested Responses: (a) Bruegel implies that people are indifferent to suffering. (b) Auden's poem adheres closely to that theme.

Applying

6. Answers will differ, but students may respond as follows: (a) The irony is that even the most spectacular sufferings occur in a context of indifference. (b) Students should cite examples from literature or experience.

LOUIS MACNEICE

1907–1963

Four members of the "Auden group" at Oxford went on to achieve an honored place in English literature: Auden himself, C. Day Lewis, Stephen Spender, and Louis MacNeice. Of these, MacNeice was generally regarded as the junior member, not because of age but rather because he lacked the artistic certainty and political commitments of the others. A lyric and reflective poet of distinction, he was always modest about the aims of poetry, doubting that poetry could truly change the world. MacNeice's reputation has risen steadily over the years, and today many consider him second only to Auden among the poets of his generation.

MacNeice, the son of a Protestant clergyman, was born in Belfast, Northern Ireland. Surrounded by books as a child, he began to write poetry at the age of seven. By the time he went to Merton College, Oxford, he was familiar with the works of T. S. Eliot and other modern poets. MacNeice's first collection of poems, *Blind Fireworks,* appeared in 1929, while he was still an undergraduate. *Poems,* the collection that established his reputation, came out six years later.

A teacher during the 1930's, MacNeice lectured in Classics at the University of Birmingham from 1930 to 1936 and in Greek at Bedford College for Women from 1936 to 1940. As a writer, he tried his hand at various genres, including drama, but his lasting achievements are in poetry. One of his notable books from the late 1930's, *Letters from Iceland* (1937), co-authored by W. H. Auden, is an unusual travel book in which the poetry outweighs the prose.

In 1941 MacNeice joined the British Broadcasting Company as a feature writer and producer. Among his radio credits are two powerful BBC plays, *Christopher Columbus* (1944) and *The Dark Tower* (1947). He wrote *The Poetry of W. B. Yeats* (1941), a critical summary of that author's work, and produced a number of excellent translations, including Aeschylus' *Agamemnon* and Goethe's *Faust.* MacNeice died in London in 1963 while he was working on his autobiography.

MacNeice's poetry, usually dealing with contemporary life, is restrained and precise, with overtones of melancholy. It is the poetry of a man who, as the poet Edwin Muir put it, "is never swept off his feet."

GUIDE FOR INTERPRETING

The Sunlight on the Garden; Sunday Morning

Writer's Technique

Scansion. Scansion is the analysis of lines of poetry according to their patterns of rhythm. The key to scansion is meter. Meter is a recurring pattern of stressed and unstressed syllables in poetry. Meter is to poetry approximately what beat is to music. In scansion, stressed syllables are marked with a /; unstressed syllables are marked with a ∪. Each group of syllables makes up a foot. Feet are marked off with a |. In scansion, do not expect to find perfectly regular patterns repeated over and over. After you have identified a metrical foot, look for and expect to find irregularities or breaks from the pattern.

Writing

Choose four lines from any poem that appears earlier in this book. First, mark all the syllables in the lines as either stressed or unstressed. To do this, say the lines aloud. Next, find the pattern of stress that predominates. There are four common patterns:

1. Unstressed/stressed (iambic)
2. Stressed/unstressed (trochaic)
3. Stressed/unstressed/unstressed (dactylic)
4. Unstressed/unstressed/stressed (anapaestic)

Finally, put in the vertical bars that show the end of one foot and the beginning of another. Notice that a vertical bar may divide a word rather than going between two words, as in the line below from a poem by William Wordsworth.

```
 ∪   /  ∪ /  ∪  /  ∪  / ∪   /
With sac|rifice|before|the ris|ing morn
```

Primary Source

MacNeice's 1938 book *Modern Poetry* is primarily a defense of modern verse, especially the work of Auden, Spender, Day-Lewis, and MacNeice himself. It also offers an intriguing glimpse into MacNeice's own poetic theories. Mainly, he tried to bridge the gap between the poet and the ordinary person. He felt that the poet should communicate and, to best accomplish this goal, be "a blend of the entertainer and the critic or informer." In fact, the poet is a great deal like MacNeice himself: "I would have a poet able-bodied, fond of talking, a reader of newspapers, capable of pity and laughter, informed in economics, appreciative of women, involved in personal relationships, actively interested in politics, susceptible to physical impressions."

Guide for Interpreting 1083

Literary Focus Have students determine the rhythms of their favorite songs. This exercise should give them a greater appreciation of rhythm in poetry.

Writing/Prior Knowledge To reinforce the *sounds* of stress patterns, place single words on the board that exemplify a stress pattern, for example, *about*=iambic; *maybe*=trochaic; *finishing*=dactylic; *introduce*=anapestic. Have students volunteer more words and identify stress patterns until students are comfortable with the identifications.

You may want to have students construct their own examples of these various types of metrical feet.

Presentation

Motivation/Prior Knowledge
Have students think about time passing quickly from year to year. What concerns them most? What do they like to recall from the past?

Purpose-Setting Question What is the tone of this poem?

Master Teacher Note Consider telling students that the fifth line of each stanza is shorter than the others. Have them determine how its meter differs. Also have them consider why the poet chose to insert a shorter line at this point.

1 Reading Strategy Offer a one-sentence summary of what this stanza says.

2 Discussion What rhyme scheme does MacNeice use?

3 Discussion What does the allusion contribute to the meaning of the poem?

4 Discussion How do the repetitions contribute to the meaning?

The Sunlight on the Garden

Louis MacNeice

1
The sunlight on the garden
Hardens and grows cold,
We cannot cage the minute
Within its nets of gold,
5 When all is told
We cannot beg for pardon.

2
Our freedom as free lances
Advances towards its end;
The earth compels, upon it
10 Sonnets and birds descend;
And soon, my friend,
We shall have no time for dances.

The sky was good for flying
Defying the church bells
15 And every evil iron
Siren and what it tells:
The earth compels,
3 We are dying, Egypt, dying[1]

4
And not expecting pardon,
20 Hardened in heart anew,
But glad to have sat under
Thunder and rain with you,
And grateful too
For sunlight on the garden.

---

1. We . . . dying: An allusion to a line spoken by Antony to Cleopatra after he has been mortally wounded in Shakespeare's *Antony and Cleopatra*: "I am dying, Egypt, dying."

OLD THATCHED SUMMER HOUSE
Lillian Stannard
Christopher Wood Gallery, London

Humanities Note

Fine art, *Old Thatched Summer House* by Lillian Stannard. Lillian Stannard (1884–1944) was a British watercolorist. Born into a family of painters, Lillian learned from her mother, Emily, and her father, Henry. Her brother and sister also painted. She specialized in the painting of landscapes, flowers, and gardens.

Old Thatched Summer House was painted at Blackheath. It is a charming rendering of an English garden in full flower. The bright blossoms, flooding sunlight, and thatched hut are painted with sensitivity and dedication to detail. This little-known artist skillfully evokes the true essence of a summer garden through the medium of watercolor.

You might use the following questions for discussion:

1. What do both the poem and this painting celebrate?
2. The purpose of this painting is to provide a pleasant subject to view. How does this purpose compare with that of the poem?

THINKING ABOUT THE SELECTION
Recalling

1. What does the speaker say we shall soon have no time for?
2. What two things does the speaker say he is happy to have experienced?

Interpreting

3. In line 6 and again in line 19 the speaker uses the word *pardon*. From what do you think he is implying there is no pardon?
4. There is an apparent reference to wartime in this poem. What is it?
5. What or whom do you think is dying in this poem—the speaker, a generation, a nation, or something or someone else? Explain your answer.

Applying

6. Death is a familiar theme in poetry. (a) What other poem have you read that conveys an attitude similar to the one expressed here? (b) How does that poem differ from MacNeice's?

ANALYZING LITERATURE
Understanding Scansion

Most poems contain regular rhythmic patterns of stressed and unstressed syllables. The identification of these patterns is called **scansion,** and the act of reading a poem to identify its patterns is called **scanning.**

1. On a sheet of paper, copy "The Sunlight on the Garden." Scan the poem, analyzing it for unstressed and stressed syllables and for feet. Your analysis will show both the recurring patterns and any deviations from them.
2. The poem has an unusual rhyme scheme. Look carefully at the rhyming words MacNeice uses. What makes his rhyme scheme different from that in most poems?

The Sunlight on the Garden   1085

Primary Source

In *A History of Modern Poetry,* David Perkins made the following comments about "The Sunlight on the Garden":

Though the wish is to hold or prolong the moment, the recognition is that we cannot. But the form of the poem enacts the impossible wish: with echoing rhymes (garden/Hardens; minute/Within its); with the rhyming of the first and last lines in each stanza; with the repetition of the opening line of the poem in the final one. . . . 'Anew' [in line 20] suggests that we have been 'hardened in heart' before, and hence that the nostalgia and regret of the poem express a moment of backsliding self-indulgence. If so, the poem ends in anything but renewed readiness for the future, for the final lines turn fondly again toward the past and the present.

Presentation

Motivation/Prior Knowledge
Have students think about what they like to do on a summer Sunday morning. What do their friends like to do? What sorts of activities are different on Sundays from those during the week?

Purpose-Setting Question What feelings does the poet have about Sunday?

Master Teacher Note You may want to have students determine the meter and rhyme scheme of this poem. Then have them consider how the regular form of the poem contributes to its meaning.

1 Literary Focus Point out the simile. Note the humor in the comparison.

2 Discussion What do the images in these lines suggest about Sunday mornings? Is the metaphor of a "great bazaar" appropriate? Why or why not?

3 Discussion Why are the church bells described as "skulls' mouths"? What does their music remind us of?

Reader's Response Does this poem reflect your feelings about Sunday? Why or why not?

Sunday Morning

Louis MacNeice

Down the road someone is practicing scales,
The notes like little fishes vanish with a wink of tails,
Man's heart expands to tinker with his car
For this is Sunday morning, Fate's great bazaar;
5   Regard these means as ends, concentrate on this Now,
And you may grow to music or drive beyond Hindhead[1]
    anyhow,
Take corners on two wheels until you go so fast
That you can clutch a fringe or two of the windy past,
That you can abstract this day and make it to the week of
    time
10 A small eternity, a sonnet self-contained in rhyme.

But listen, up the road, something gulps, the church spire
Opens its eight bells out, skulls' mouths which will not tire
To tell how there is no music or movement which secures
Escape from the weekday time. Which deadens and
    endures.

---

1. Hindhead: A district in the county of Surrey, England.

THINKING ABOUT THE SELECTION

Recalling

1. What are two Sunday-morning activities the speaker mentions?
2. What will "skulls' mouths" never tire of telling?

Interpreting

3. Why do you think the speaker refers to Sunday morning as "Fate's great bazaar"?
4. What does the speaker suggest is required to make the most of a Sunday?
5. The last four lines contrast rather sadly with the first ten. What is the point of the contrast?

Applying

6. "The Sunlight on the Garden" and "Sunday Morning" express a similar futile wish. In your own words, what is that wish?

THINKING AND WRITING

Writing About Rhyme and Rhythm

Modern poets differ in their use of rhyme and rhythm. In "Sunday Morning," MacNeice uses a basic *aabb* rhyme scheme. Scan the poem to determine its metric pattern. Then, in a brief essay, explain what effects the rhyme and rhythm of the poem have on your appreciation of it. Also, try to answer these broader questions: (a) Do you generally prefer rhyming poems to free verse? (b) What effect, if any, does rhyme have on meaning? (c) Do you think subject matter helps to determine the appropriate rhyme and rhythm for a poem?)

Before you start to write, make at least a sketchy outline of the main points you will cover. Your first draft may follow this outline closely or may deviate from it as necessary. When you revise the paper for your final draft, pay special attention to organization. See that your points appear in logical and persuasive order.

Primary Source

As with T. S. Eliot and W. H. Auden, Louis MacNeice believed that one function of poetry should be to convey important, difficult ideas about the modern experience. But everyday language proved insufficient to express the complexity of today's dilemmas. Instead, he and others explored the poetic use of wit and symbols to make their ideas known. Thus, the old ways of looking at a poem no longer work. Critics Wright Thomas and Stuart Gerry Brown explain how MacNeice used wit in "The Sunlight on the Garden" to convey his theme. While we can see "the sunlight on the garden" clearly enough, we cannot see it "hardening," they begin. Similarly, we can see "nets of gold" but we cannot visualize a "minute" being "caged." When we look

more closely, we see that in spite of what we feel about being unable to understand, we have in fact made the comparisons and been able to imagine the experience that he describes. As Thomas and Brown conclude: "We do in fact know what he means by the sunlight hardening and by caging a minute within golden nets. But we have not understood him by means of impossible sensory reactions; we have got beyond or beside or perhaps through sensory experience into intellectual experience. We have understood what we could not imagine. . . . It is the impossibility of the thing which makes the poem, paradoxical as that may be. . . . The trick by which this is managed is called 'wit.'"

In this way MacNeice uses language to explore the dilemmas of modern life.

Sunday Morning 1087

More About the Authors Ask students why they might suppose Stephen Spender became interested in political activism? You might ask students to look for any resemblance between the irony of Reed's "Naming of Parts" and the poems of Thomas Hardy, whom Reed admired.

Critical Evaluation Richard Ellmann and Robert O'Clair made the following evaluation of Stephen Spender's work: "The poems which Spender writes are incursions into the tenous and unresolved, repeated efforts—rather heroic in their kind—to make firm the infirm, to grip, without idealization, the possible. . . . The center of his verse is his aroused, suffering consciousness, but he is not self-flattering, and with relentless severity exposes what may be 'corrupt, insubstantial' in himself."

BIOGRAPHIES

Stephen Spender (1909–   )

No poet of the 1930's has provided posterity with a more detailed and honest picture of the era between the wars than has Stephen Spender. Much of his early poetry deals with the world of the Thirties, that "low dishonest decade" that saw the world lurch from depression to fascism to war. Yet Spender, never a pessimist in the manner of T. S. Eliot, celebrates technology at the same time he confronts the problems of industrial civilization.

The son of a political journalist, Spender was born in London and educated at University College, Oxford, where he met and fell under the spell of W. H. Auden. In 1928, while at Oxford, he hand-printed a limited edition of Auden's *Poems*. Spender contributed his own early poems to *Oxford Poetry*. He lived in Germany in the early 1930's and published his first important book, *Poems*, in 1933, the year Hitler became chancellor of the Third Reich.

Spender, a political activist, traveled to Spain to promote antifascist propaganda during the Spanish Civil War. From 1939 to 1941, he coedited the literary magazine *Horizon* and later coedited the political, cultural, and literary review *Encounter*. In his autobiography *World Within World* (1951), Spender is candid and perceptive about people, politics, and himself, as he explores and attempts to integrate his lyrical and idealistic vision with the realities of society.

Henry Reed (1914–   )

Although Henry Reed is well-known in England for his many radio plays, his reputation as a poet rests mainly on one slim volume, *A Map of Verona*, published in 1946. In fact, it rests principally on thirty lines in that collection—"Naming of Parts," which is a satirical section of a longer poem, "Lessons of War." Reed's few poems, always precise and assured, vary widely in subject matter, mood, and theme. So do his highly regarded radio plays, among which are an adaptation of *Moby-Dick*, the partly autobiographical *Return to Naples*, and a dramatic prose poem, *The Streets of Pompeii*.

Henry Reed was born in Birmingham, England, and educated at King Edward VI School and the University of Birmingham. After graduation he worked for several years on a biography of Thomas Hardy, then taught school for a year before being drafted into the army in 1941. He received a transfer to the Foreign Office, where he worked in Naval Intelligence. Most of Reed's career since the end of World War II has involved radio drama for the British Broadcasting Corporation (BBC), with some time out for translating and for teaching at the University of Washington in Seattle. His poetic output, though limited, is of high quality.

Support Material

Teaching Portfolio
Teacher Backup, p. 1327
Usage and Mechanics Worksheet, p. 1331
Vocabulary Check, p. 1332
Analyzing Literature Worksheet, *Determining the Speaker*, p. 1333

Language Worksheet, *Using Word Roots*, p. 1334
Selection Test, p. 1335

GUIDE FOR INTERPRETING

Writer's Technique

What I Expected; Naming of Parts

Speaker. The speaker in a poem is the poem's narrator. Narration can occur either in the first person *(I, we)* or in the third person *(he, she, it, they)*. Often a first-person speaker is a persona created by the poet. Consider, for instance, the first-person speakers who are already dead, as, for example, in Edgar Lee Masters's *Spoon River Anthology*. But even if the speaker is represented as being alive, he or she may not be the poet. In Robert Browning's "My Last Duchess," for example, no one would mistake the speaker (the cruel Duke of Ferrara) for the likable Browning. Sometimes a poet uses a first-person speaker to lend immediacy to the poem's content.

Satire. Satire is writing that uses wit and humor to attack human follies, stupidities, and abuses. It can be directed at a single person or at an entire society. Satire can be written in any genre—novels, short stories, poems, or plays. Always a mixture of humor and criticism, it is intended to persuade the reader, without the use of formal argument, to accept the author's viewpoint. Among the most famous satires in English are Jonathan Swift's *Gulliver's Travels* and George Orwell's *Animal Farm*.

Commentary

Henry Reed and Louis MacNeice led an astonishing array of brilliant talent onto the airwaves during the twenty years after the war. With such poets as Dylan Thomas, Sylvia Plath, Ted Hughes, and Stevie Smith, Reed and MacNeice created a series of masterpieces for the British Broadcasting System. Office hours were largely ignored, and a generation of talent was nurtured in the BBC studios and two adjacent pubs. Reed was closely involved with the exceptional groups of writers, composers, actors, and technical staff that essentially constituted a permanent company. Consequently he wrote many of his radio scripts with particular players in mind, and their individual ability often sparked his imagination. *The Complete Lessons of War*, broadcast in 1960, for example, was written with actor Frank Duncan in the role of the drill sergeant; Reed spoke the descriptive passages himself.

Writing

Choose an event in history that happened long before you were born. Possibilities include the signing of the Declaration of Independence, the defense of the Alamo, and the assassination of Abraham Lincoln. Put yourself in the place of a participant in the event. Jot down notes in the first person, just as if you had observed what happened. Include as many details as you can that, prior to your account, were unknown to the general public.

Guide for Interpreting 1089

What I Expected

Stephen Spender

What I expected, was
Thunder, fighting,
Long struggles with men
And climbing.
5   After continual straining
I should grow strong;
Then the rocks would shake
And I rest long.

What I had not foreseen
10 Was the gradual day
Weakening the will
Leaking the brightness away,
The lack of good to touch,
The fading of body and soul
15 Smoke before wind,
Corrupt, unsubstantial.

The wearing of Time,
And the watching of cripples pass
With limbs shaped like questions
20 In their odd twist,
The pulverous grief
Melting the bones with pity,
The sick falling from earth—
These, I could not foresee.

25 Expecting always
Some brightness to hold in trust
Some final innocence
Exempt from dust,
That, hanging solid,
30 Would dangle through all
Like the created poem,
Or the faceted crystal.

THINKING ABOUT THE SELECTION
Recalling

1. What are four things the speaker says he expected?
2. What are six things he had not foreseen?
3. Besides "Some brightness to hold in trust," what was the speaker always expecting?

Interpreting

4. (a) What do you think is the setting of this poem? (b) What lines in the poem support your answer?
5. In line 12 and again in line 26 the speaker uses the word *brightness*. What do you think this brightness represents?
6. In line 22 the speaker mentions the melting of bones. To whose bones is he referring?

Applying

7. The speaker seems to have been deeply disappointed when reality did not match his expectations. In the eighteenth century, the poet Alexander Pope wrote, "Blessed is he who expects nothing, for he shall never be disappointed." How do you think the speaker would react to this statement? Support your answer.

ANALYZING LITERATURE
Determining the Speaker

The speaker in a poem is the individual who does the telling, the narrator. Speakers fall into two main categories, (1) first person *(I, we)*, in which the speaker is in essence a character in the poem; (2) third-person *(he, she, it, they)*, in which the speaker is an outsider. Sometimes a first-person speaker is the poet, but more often he or she is not. Rather, the speaker is assuming a particular role to create a desired effect. In determining whether a first-person speaker is probably the poet, it may help you to know something of the poet's life. For instance, you know that Rupert Brooke and the soldier-speaker in "The Soldier" might be one and the same. On the other hand, if you know that Stephen Spender was not a front-line soldier in World War II, you would know he could not have written a first-person battlefield scene except through an assumed identity.

1. Identify the kind of speaker in Stephen Spender's "What I Expected."
2. In view of the subject matter of the poem, why is this kind of speaker a logical one?
3. The speaker and the poet are not one and the same in "What I Expected." How do you know?

THINKING AND WRITING
Comparing and Contrasting Two Poems

Reread Louis MacNeice's "The Sunlight on the Garden," noting in particular the references to flying and to sirens in the third stanza. Some critics have called this a war poem, pointing to "flying" as a reference to fighter planes and to the "evil iron siren" as an air-raid siren. Assuming that this interpretation is correct, write an essay in which you compare and contrast MacNeice's "The Sunlight on the Garden" with Spender's "What I Expected." Concentrate not only on the subject matter of the two poems, but also on their structure—speakers, metric patterns, line lengths, and rhyme schemes. Begin by making notes on both poems. When you write your first draft, quote lines from the poems where appropriate. In revising, be sure you have made your comparisons and contrast clear.

What I Expected 1091

Closure and Extension

ANSWERS TO THINKING ABOUT THE SELECTION
Recalling

1. The author lists his expectations in lines 2–8.
2. What he had not foreseen is listed in lines 10–24.
3. The speaker was also always expecting "Some final innocence."

Interpreting

4. Suggested Response: (a) There is no specific locale for the poem, but it is set during the speaker's declining years. (b) Lines 10-13 suggest this.
5. Suggested Response: The brightness represents ideals or goals to be reached.
6. Suggested Resonse: The speaker refers to his own bones.

Applying

7. Answers will differ. Students may respond that the speaker would not be able to follow Pope's advice.

ANSWERS TO ANALYZING LITERATURE

1. Suggested Response: The speaker is an elderly person, probably a man.
2. Suggested Response: The images of struggles with men and climbing suggest this type of speaker.
3. Suggested Response: The poet *has* created a poem, though the speaker could not.

THINKING AND WRITING

For help with this assignment, students can consult Lesson 16, "Writing a Comparative Evaluation," in the Handbook of Writing About Literature.

Publishing Student Writing Select five or six of the student essays that are representative, and offer them to the school newspaper as poetry reviews.

Naming of Parts

Henry Reed

1, 2

Today we have naming of parts. Yesterday,
We had daily cleaning. And tomorrow morning,
We shall have what to do after firing. But today,
Today we have naming of parts. Japonica[1]
5 Glistens like coral in all of the neighboring gardens,
    And today we have naming of parts.

3

This is the lower sling swivel. And this
Is the upper sling swivel, whose use you will see,
When you are given your slings. And this is the piling swivel,
10 Which in your case you have not got. The branches
Hold in the gardens their silent, eloquent gestures,
    Which in our case we have not got.

This is the safety-catch, which is always released
With an easy flick of the thumb. And please do not let me
15 See anyone using his finger. You can do it quite easy
If you have any strength in your thumb. The blossoms
Are fragile and motionless, never letting anyone see
    Any of them using their finger.

4

And this you can see is the bolt. The purpose of this
20 Is to open the breech, as you see. We can slide it
Rapidly backwards and forwards: we call this
Easing the spring. And rapidly backwards and forwards
The early bees are assaulting and fumbling the flowers:
    They call it easing the Spring.

25 They call it easing the Spring: it is perfectly easy
If you have any strength in your thumb; like the bolt,
And the breech, and the cocking-piece, and the point of balance,

5

Which in our case we have not got; and the almond-blossom
Silent in all of the gardens and the bees going backwards and forwards,
30   For today we have naming of parts.

---

1. japonica (jə pän′ i kə): A spiny plant with pink or red flowers.

THINKING ABOUT THE SELECTION

Recalling

1. (a) What does the speaker say the members of his group ("we") had yesterday? (b) What will they have tomorrow?
2. What part of the rifle does the speaker not have?
3. What is the purpose of the bolt?
4. What is silent in the gardens?

Interpreting

5. (a) Who are the members of the group identified as "we" in the poem? (b) Why are they having "naming of parts"?
6. (a) In the fourth stanza, what are the two meanings of "easing the Spring"? (b) In the fifth stanza, what are two possible meanings of "the point of balance"?

Applying

7. Suppose you were the instructor giving the "naming of parts" lesson, and you became aware of what is on the mind of the speaker (or second voice). (a) How would you react? (b) How would you rate the chances of the recruit becoming a good soldier?

ANALYZING LITERATURE

Using Satire

Satire is writing that shows the folly or evil of something through the use of wit and humor. In "Naming of Parts," the poet is not directly attacking war or the military, despite the sharp contrast he draws between instruction in rifle parts and the wonders of spring.

1. What specifically is Reed satirizing in the poem?
2. How does he use the repetition of words and phrases to make his point? Give at least two examples.

CRITICAL THINKING AND READING

Comparing and Contrasting Speakers

There may be two speakers in this poem, one the instructor-speaker, the other the trainee-speaker. Or there may be only one speaker who first parrots the dull, mechanical words of the instructor, then gives his own personal thoughts on the attractions of nature in springtime. Whichever way you interpret Reed's method (two different speakers or two opposing voices within the same speaker), the satiric message is the same.

1. (a) Which lines, or parts of lines, in each stanza are the instructor's words or mechanical repetitions of them? (b) Which express the personal feelings of the trainee?
2. Which stanza deviates from this pattern?
3. Describe the similarities and differences between the language of the two voices (or speakers).

THINKING AND WRITING

Writing About Satire

A number of newspaper and magazine columnists write satire. Erma Bombeck's satiric columns on domestic life and Art Buchwald's on politics, among others, have been reprinted in many books. Find a modern satirical column, either original or reprinted, and write an essay analyzing it. Before you start to write, read the column carefully, making a list of devices the writer uses—exaggeration, understatement, analogy, figurative language, and so on. Jot down an example of each device. When you begin to write, first identify the author, topic, and source of the column you are analyzing. Then write the first draft of your essay. Stick to the point; avoid clever but irrelevant comments. When you revise, pay special attention to unity. Every sentence in your essay should relate to the main point you want to make.

3. The purpose of the bolt is to open the breech.
4. The almond blossom is silent in the garden.

Interpreting

5. Suggested Response: (a) The "we" is a group of young recruits. (b) They are being trained in riflery.
6. Suggested Response: (a) Two meanings of "Easing the spring" are the literal, careful movement of the spring of the rifle and the slow beginning of the season of spring. (b) The meanings are the balanced weight of a rifle and mental or moral balance.

Applying

7. Answers will differ. (a) Responses will probably note that the instructor would be annoyed or angered at the recruit. (b) The chances of the recruit becoming a good soldier are slim.

ANSWERS TO ANALYZING LITERATURE

1. Suggested Response: Reed is satirizing the mechanistic and unproductive instruction.
2. Suggested Response: He uses repetition to point up ironic similarities between the instruction and the emerging spring. See lines 24 and 28.

ANSWERS TO CRITICAL THINKING

1. The instructor's words are lines 7–10, 13–16, 19–22, 25–28; lines of the trainee are 4–6, 10–12, 16–18, 22–24.
2. The final stanza deviates.
3. Suggested Response: The young recruit uses the instructor's words in an ironic context.

THINKING AND WRITING
Publishing Student Writing
Have students share their analyses in small groups. They can test their own observations with each other and expand their thinking as well.

Closure and Extension

ANSWERS TO THINKING ABOUT THE SELECTION
Recalling

1. (a) The speaker says they had "daily cleaning" and (b) tomorrow they will have "what to do after firing."
2. The piling swivel is not available.

1914–1953

When Dylan Thomas burst upon the literary scene in 1933, he was barely twenty years old. His poems, romantic, effusive, and melodic, spoke to readers then, as now, in a voice that could be mistaken for no one else's. Despite some critical bewilderment at first, Thomas gained remarkable popularity in his lifetime, probably greater than that of any poet since Byron. The rich, glowing magic of his language propels the reader onward in spite of its often complex imagery, visionary landscapes, and puzzling ambiguities. Stephen Spender called Thomas "a linguistic genius." The critic Louis Untermeyer says that his lines "leap and shout and all but leave the printed page. . . ."

Dylan Thomas was born in Swansea, an industrial city on the southern coast of Wales. His father was a school teacher, and young Dylan, surrounded by his father's books, seems to have spent his childhood in training to be a poet. He attended Swansea Grammar School until 1931, after which he worked intermittently as a newspaper reporter, radio broadcaster, and film scriptwriter. In 1941 he published a collection of stories about his childhood and youth, *Portrait of the Artist as a Young Dog.* He recorded a number of his poems, as well as his "play for voices," *Under Milk Wood,* which premiered in May 1953 at the Fogg Theater of Harvard University, with Thomas reading all the parts.

Thomas did his best work while living in Wales, far from the temptations of London and New York. At work, he was a meticulous craftsman, shy when sober, exercising strict formal control over what on paper seems so spontaneous. But in London, and on his four speaking tours to the United States, he was a different man, flamboyant, childish, hard-drinking, dissolute, an "outlaw defiant." His marriage to the Irish beauty Caitlin Macnamara was stormy but enduring. She was at his side when he died of the effects of alcoholism at St. Vincent's Hospital in New York City.

Poetry, to Thomas, was "the rhythmic, inevitably narrative, movement from an overclothed blindness to a naked vision." That vision is almost always free of the political themes and overtones found in the works of such contemporaries as Auden and Spender. On Thomas's place in literary history, the verdict is mixed. The poet Conrad Aiken sums him up as a "language-lover and language-juggler." The critic David Daiches says that "he was growing in poetic stature to the last" but, more important, "he wrote some poems that the world will not willingly let die."

GUIDE FOR INTERPRETING

The Force That Through the Green Fuse Drives the Flower; Fern Hill; Do Not Go Gentle into That Good Night

Writer's Technique

Parallelism. Parallelism is the matching or contrasting of two or more ideas through the use of similar phrasing. Sometimes parallelism can produce almost a list or catalog, as in *Ecclesiastes* 3:4: "A time to weep, and a time to laugh; a time to mourn, and a time to dance." Another well-known example of this kind of parallelism, also featuring contrasts, is the beginning of Charles Dickens's *A Tale of Two Cities:* "It was the best of times; it was the worst of times. . . ." In poetry, parallelism can appear within a single line, as in Coleridge's "Without a breeze, without a tide." Or it can be within a stanza, as in Shelley's "The seed ye sow, another reaps/The wealth ye find, another keeps." Or it can be from stanza to stanza, as in Byron's "And there lay the steed with his nostril all wide" [stanza four]; "And there lay the rider distorted and pale" [stanza five].

Villanelle. A villanelle is a nineteen-line poem with specific and rather complicated requirements. The first fifteen lines are arranged in three-line stanzas. The first and third lines of the opening stanza are repeated alternately as the closing line of each of the remaining three-line stanzas. They then appear together as a concluding couplet. Only two rhymes are permitted throughout the poem, the rhyme scheme being this: *aba aba aba aba aba abaa.* The villanelle originated in fifteenth-century France, where its aim was to lend a surface simplicity to pastoral poems. Following its revival in the nineteenth century, the villanelle has been used for a broad range of subjects.

Commentary

What image do you get when you think of a "poet"? According to critic David Daiches, Dylan Thomas was "the most poetical poet of our time. He talked and dressed and behaved like a poet; he was reckless, flamboyant, irreverent, innocent. . . . His verse, too, had a romantic wildness about it that even a reader who could make nothing of it recognized as 'poetic.'"

Writing

Describe a chain of events in your life, beginning each link of the chain with the words, "If it were not for . . ." You might write, for example, "If it were not for my family moving to this city two years ago, I would not have attended this school. If it were not for my attending this school, I would not have met my best friend. If it were not for having met my best friend . . ." and so on. See how far you can take your chain by the end of one page.

Literary Focus Students may find that the form of the villanelle will become clearer when they work through an actual poem. It may be helpful to have students consider why poets are interested in such intricate forms. What, for instance, does repetition and regularity contribute to a poem?

Writing/Prior Knowledge You might want to divide the class into small groups so they can discuss key events in their lives before they begin to write.

The Force That Through the Green Fuse Drives the Flower

Dylan Thomas

The force that through the green fuse drives the flower
Drives my green age; that blasts the roots of trees
Is my destroyer.
And I am dumb to tell[1] the crooked rose
5   My youth is bent by the same wintry fever.

The force that drives the water through the rocks
Drives my red blood; that dries the mouthing streams
Turns mine to wax.
And I am dumb to mouth unto my veins
10   How at the mountain spring the same mouth sucks.

The hand that whirls the water in the pool
Stirs the quicksand; that ropes the blowing wind
Hauls my shroud sail.
And I am dumb to tell the hanging man
15   How of my clay is made the hangman's lime.[2]

The lips of time leech to the fountain head;
Love drips and gathers, but the fallen blood
Shall calm her sores.
And I am dumb to tell a weather's wind
20   How time has ticked a heaven round the stars.

And I am dumb to tell the lover's tomb
How at my sheet goes the same crooked worm.

---

1. dumb to tell: Unable to tell.
2. hangman's lime: Quicklime used to bury those who had been hanged.

Grammar in Action

Students sometimes do not know whether to use *that* or *which* to introduce a clause. Normally, you should use *which* to introduce a nonessential clause and either *that* or *which* (preferably *that*) to introduce an essential clause. (An essential clause is one that is necessary to the meaning of a sentence.) In Thomas's poem, the first line of each of the first three stanzas contains an essential clause. Notice that Thomas uses *that* to introduce each clause and

THINKING ABOUT THE SELECTION

Recalling

1. (a) What does the speaker say he is unable to tell the hangman? (b) What is he unable to tell the lover's tomb?

Interpreting

2. What do you think the speaker means by the phrase (a) "green fuse"? (b) "green age"?
3. (a) What force do you think the speaker has in mind in the first two stanzas? (b) What word does he use in the third stanza to refer to this force?
4. The force in the poem brings about two very different outcomes. In general terms what are they?

Applying

5. To what extent would you describe this poem as one about faith? Explain.

ANALYZING LITERATURE

Using Parallelism

Parallelism, which is a form of repetition, matches or contrasts ideas through the use of similar phrasing or grammatical structures. In "The Force That Through the Green Fuse Drives the Flower," Dylan Thomas uses a complex, interlocking parallelism within stanzas:

    The force   that   drives the green fuse
                   drives the flower
                   Drives my green age
           that   blasts the roots of trees

He also uses parallelism from stanza to stanza.

1. In what way are the second lines of the first three stanzas parallel?
2. In what way are the fourth lines of the first four stanzas parallel?
3. What parallel element exists in the last lines of the last four stanzas?

Primary Source

Like Joyce, Yeats, and Hopkins, Thomas was in love with words. "The world is too much with us," says the hero of "The Orchards," "creating a world of words." According to critic William York Tindall, "words were Thomas's matter, his tool, and his refuge; but so great his delight in them and in what Rimbaud [a French symbolist poet] called their 'alchemy' that, as Thomas complains, they sometimes got between him and the object. Sometimes they became the object." People are often bothered by the ambiguity of language, but Thomas celebrated the different meanings that words held and the ways in which they could be manipulated to suggest layers of meaning. He fiddled with the sound and shape of words to create his poetic images. In an often-quoted letter, he remarks, "A poem by myself needs a host of images, because its center is a host of images. I make one image . . . let it breed another, let that image contradict the first, make of the third image bred out of the two together, a fourth contradictory image, and let them all, within my formal imposed limits, conflict." Once in New York, not long before he died, he was talking to a friend about writing. "When I experience anything," he said, "I experience it as a thing and a word at the same time, both equally amazing." Writing the "Ballad of the Long Legged Bait," he said, had been like carrying a huge armful of words to a table he thought was upstairs, and wondering if he could reach it in time, or if it would still be there.

The Force That Through the Green Fuse Drives the Flower 1097

ANSWERS TO THINKING ABOUT THE SELECTION
Recalling

1. (a) He cannot tell the hanging man that he, the poet, is made of "the hangman's lime." (b) The same crooked worm goes at his sheet.

Interpreting

2. Suggested Response: (a) The phrase "green fuse" may refer to the stem of a plant. (b) The phrase "green age" means a youthful, energetic age.
3. Suggested Response: (a) In these stanzas the speaker means vigorous life forces. (b) He uses the word "hand" to refer to this force.
4. Suggested Response: The two outcomes are life and death.

Applying

5. Answers will differ.

ANSWERS TO ANALYZING LITERATURE

1. Suggested Response: Each second line of those stanzas begins with a strong verb-object construction: "Drives my green age"; "Drives my red blood"; and "Stirs the quicksand."
2. The fourth lines of these stanzas all repeat the phrase, "And I am dumb to tell [mouth, in one case] . . ."
3. Suggested Response: Each of these statements begins with the word "How" and explains an interconnection between the poet—except in line 20—and nature or other humans.

the clause is not separated by commas from the rest of the sentence.

The force that through the green fuse drives the flower . . .

The force that drives the water . . .

The hand that whirls the water . . .

It would also have been grammatically correct for Thomas to use *which* to introduce these clauses.
    Now consider this sentence.

The man's hand, which whirled the water in the pool, stirred up the sand.

Since *hand* is identified by *The man's,* the modifying phrase is nonessential. Therefore, it begins with *which* and is separated by commas from the rest of the sentence.

    Student Activity. Write five sentences containing essential clauses and five containing nonessential clauses.

Motivation/Prior Knowledge
Ask students: What are some of your best recollections of your childhood? If you could choose one or two adjectives to describe that whole time, what would those adjectives be? Tell them that Thomas writes about his childhood in this poem.

Master Teacher Note You might want to point out to students that the words *green* and *golden* appear often in this poem. Have students consider the connotations of these words. How do these connotations contribute to the theme of the poem.

1 Discussion What impression of the speaker's childhood do you get from these lines? Which words and phrases contribute to this impression?

2 Discussion What is the meaning of this statement?

3 Discussion What is the effect of the repeated use of the word *And*?

4 Discussion Where else in the poem does Thomas use personification? How do these personifications contribute to the poem's mood or meaning?

Fern Hill

Dylan Thomas

1

Now as I was young and easy under the apple boughs
About the lilting house and happy as the grass was green,
  The night above the dingle starry,
   Time let me hail and climb
5 Golden in the heydays of his eyes,
And honored among wagons I was prince of the apple
 towns
And once below a time I lordly had the trees and leaves
   Trail with daisies and barley
  Down the rivers of the windfall light.

2

10 And as I was green and carefree, famous among the barns
About the happy yard and singing as the farm was home,
  In the sun that is young once only,
   Time let me play and be
  Golden in the mercy of his means,
15 And green and golden I was huntsman and herdsman, the
 calves
Sang to my horn, the foxes on the hills barked clear and
 cold,
   And the sabbath rang slowly
  In the pebbles of the holy streams.

3

All the sun long it was running, it was lovely, the hay
20 Fields high as the house, the tunes from the chimneys, it
 was air
   And playing, lovely and watery
    And fire green as grass.
  And nightly under the simple stars
As I rode to sleep the owls were bearing the farm away,
25 All the moon long I heard, blessed among stables, the
 nightjars[1]
   Flying with the ricks,[2] and the horses
    Flashing into the dark.

4

And then to awake, and the farm, like a wanderer white
With the dew, come back, the cock on his shoulder; it was
 all

---

1. nightjars *n.*: Common nocturnal birds, named for the whirring sound which the male makes.
2. ricks *n.*: Haystacks.

Grammar in Action

Use specific words in unique ways to make your meaning vivid. Unique uses excite the reader's imagination and engage the emotions. Good writers use specific words and look for new ways to apply language. Notice Dylan Thomas's unique use of specific language.

About the *lilting house* and *happy as the grass was green* . . .

And *honored among wagons* I was prince of the apple towns . . .

And *once below a time* . . .

And as I was green and carefree, *famous among the barns* . . .

About the *happy yard* and *singing as the farm was home* . . .

Humanities Note

Fine art, *The Magic Apple Tree* by Samuel Palmer. The British painter Samuel Palmer (1805–1881) was influenced by the art and literature of the mystic poet and artist William Blake. Classified by history as a Romantic painter, Palmer took Romanticism one step further toward mysticism. As a member of a group called "the Ancients," who turned to artists of the past for inspiration for their art, Palmer settled in the village of Shoreham, Kent. Here he produced his most memorable works, landscapes full of magic, dreams, and vision.

Samuel Palmer painted *The Magic Apple Tree* while at Shoreham. This is a pastoral in which everything—the hillside, the animals, and the trees—seems to vibrate with a secret life. The sheep seem to be mesmerized by the music played by the boy. The apple tree, bowed with ripe fruit, seems to be leaning toward the pipe-playing boy. Palmer's interpretation of this scene is atmospheric and timeless. It is a worshipful and intense homage to the beauty and goodness of nature.

You might use the following questions for discussion:
1. How does this painting convey a sense of timelessness?
2. How does this timeless quality enhance the painting's suitability as an illustration of Dylan Thomas's childhood reminiscence?
3. What visual elements of this painting match things mentioned in the poem?

Thomas shows an almost religious reverence for the simple wonder and happiness of his childhood. His specific and unique word usage awakens that reverence in the reader. A house does not normally "lilt" nor is a yard "happy," and yet in this poem the words suggest that the child's happiness affects even the inanimate objects. "Happy as the grass was green" and "singing as the farm was home" show the inexpressible extent of the happiness and the singing, since we can assume the grass was exceptionally green, and the farm was absolutely home. Neither of those clauses makes literal sense, but both make imaginative and emotional sense. "Honored among wagons" and "famous among the barns" are similar unique uses that kindle almost mythical reverence.

Student Activity. Find three more unique uses of words in the poem, and analyze their effectiveness.

5 Discussion To which legend or story is this an allusion? How does this allusion add to the poem's meaning?

6 Discussion How is the passage of time suggested?

7 Discussion Explain the paradox in the phrase "green and dying." How does this paradox relate to the theme of the poem?

Reader's Response Does this poem reflect some of your feelings about childhood? Explain.

5 **30** Shining, it was Adam and maiden,
          The sky gathered again
        And the sun grew round that very day.
      So it must have been after the birth of the simple light
      In the first, spinning place, the spellbound horses walking
        warm
35   Out of the whinnying green stable
          On to the fields of praise.

      And honored among foxes and pheasants by the gay house
      Under the new made clouds and happy as the heart was
        long,
          In the sun born over and over,
40   I ran my heedless ways,
          My wishes raced through the house-high hay
      And nothing I cared, at my sky blue trades, that time allows
      In all his tuneful turning so few and such morning songs
          Before the children green and golden
45   Follow him out of grace,

6   Nothing I cared, in the lamb white days, that time would
        take me
      Up to the swallow thronged loft by the shadow of my hand,
          In the moon that is always rising,
            Nor that riding to sleep
50   I should hear him fly with the high fields
      And wake to the farm forever fled from the childless land.
      Oh as I was young and easy in the mercy of his means,
7   Time held me green and dying
      Though I sang in my chains like the sea.

THINKING ABOUT THE SELECTION
Recalling

1. What two colors does the speaker use repeatedly to describe himself as a youth?
2. What descriptive words about the hayfields suggest that the speaker was a youngster when observing them?
3. What does the speaker say happened each night as he "rode to sleep"?
4. In the last stanza, where does the speaker suggest that time has taken him?

Interpreting

5. (a) How would you describe the speaker's feelings about his childhood? (b) What are some of the words and phrases that convey this feeling?
6. What do you think is meant in lines 33–34 by "the birth of the simple light/In the first, spinning place"?
7. The mood in the last stanza changes from that in the preceding stanzas. (a) What is the change? (b) What are two lines or phrases earlier in the poem that foreshadow this change?
8. Line 53, "Time held me green and dying," expresses the basic idea of the poem. In your own words, what does the line mean?

Applying

9. Passing from the innocence of childhood to the reality and responsibility of adulthood is the subject of many rituals, proverbs, and literary works. What are a few of these?

CRITICAL READING AND THINKING
Interpreting Connotative Meaning

The **connotation** of a word is the meaning the word has beyond its dictionary definition. For example, *lilting,* in line 2, means "metrical, rhythmic," but, beyond that meaning—or *denotation* —the word has favorable connotations of melodic singing and cheerfulness. By contrast, the word *eurhythmic* has a denotation similar to that of *lilting,* but its connotations, if not actually unfavorable, are rather stuffy and academic.

Poets take great care with the connotations of the words they use. (Dylan Thomas is said to have been unhappy with the word *heedless* in line 40, but could not find a word he considered more appropriate for his meaning.)

Find the following words and phrases in "Fern Hill." Explain what connotations you believe the poet intends:
(1) apple towns (l. 6); (2) sun (l. 18); (3) moon (l. 25); (4) sky blue trades (l. 42); (5) lamb white (l. 46); (6) swallow thronged loft (l. 47); (7) in my chains (l. 54); (8) like the sea (l. 54).

UNDERSTANDING LANGUAGE
Using Words from Middle English

Middle English, the English language as it existed from about 1150 to 1500, included many words that are in widespread use today. It also included some that are less familiar—for example, *dingle* (l. 3) and *ricks* (l. 26). "Fern Hill" contains a high percentage of words from Middle English.

1. Using a good dictionary, check the etymologies of *young, easy, green, sabbath, sun, house.*
2. Explain why many of the etymologies show ME (Middle English) being directly preceded by OF (Old French) rather than by OE (Old English) or something else.

THINKING AND WRITING
Writing a Poem About Childhood

The farm in "Fern Hill" belonged to Ann Jones, Dylan Thomas's aunt. As a child, Thomas spent many vacations and holidays there. As an adult, he remembered it as a happy world, an innocent Eden, forever lost. Write a poem about the place where you spent some or all of your childhood. You may have pleasant recollections, like Thomas, or ones that are less pleasant. Write in whatever poetic form you wish. Include as many images as you can to help a reader visualize both the setting and your experiences. Remember that a poem requires prewriting and revision, just as other forms of composition do.

Fern Hill   1101

8. Suggested Response: Even as I was young and growing, I was dying—though I did not know it.

Applying

9. Answers will differ. A confirmation and a Bar Mitzvah are two applicable religious rituals.

ANSWERS TO CRITICAL THINKING AND READING

1. Suggested Response: Small country towns, or places the poet imagined among the apple boughs.
2. Suggested Response: This word seems to mean all the days of his youth.
3. Suggested Response: This word means all the nights of his youth.
4. Suggested Response: This phrase means the innocent, carefree activities of youth.
5. Suggested Response: Innocent days of childhood are suggested.
6. Suggested Response: This phrase may connote aproaching adulthood or an adult's perspective.
7. Suggested Response: This phrase implies that we are all enchained in our dying bodies.
8. Suggested Response: The sea seems wild and free and powerful, yet it is bounded by the land.

ANSWERS TO UNDERSTANDING LANGUAGE

1. young—Middle English; Old English
   easy—Middle English; Old French
   green—Middle English; Old English
   sabbath—Middle English; Old French and Old English
   sun—Middle English; Old English
   house—Middle English; Old English
2. Suggested Response: Many words came into English from French.

THINKING AND WRITING

For help with this assignment, students can consult Lesson 18, "Writing a Poem," in the Handbook of Writing About Literature.

Publishing Student Writing Arrange for students to share their poems in small groups. Encourage them to submit their work to the school literary magazine.

Closure and Extension

ANSWERS TO THINKING ABOUT THE SELECTION
Recalling

1. The speaker was green and golden.

2. The hayfields were "high as a house," indicating he was small.
3. He says, figuratively, that owls carried the house away.
4. The speaker suggests that time has taken him to adulthood.

Interpreting

5. Suggested Response: (a) The speaker has joyful memories of childhood. (b) Numerous words and phrases indicate that joy.

Some are "young and easy," "lilting house," "green and carefree," "happy yard," "singing," "playing," "it was all and Shining," "nothing I cared."

6. Suggested Response: That description refers to the creation of the world.
7. (a) The change is that the poet begins to express regret for the passing of time. (b) Lines 4–5 and 12–14 foreshadow that change.

Do Not Go Gentle into That Good Night

Dylan Thomas

1

Do not go gentle into that good night,
Old age should burn and rave at close of day;
Rage, rage against the dying of the light.

Though wise men at their end know dark is right,
5 Because their words had forked no lightning they
Do not go gentle into that good night.

Good men, the last wave by, crying how bright
Their frail deeds might have danced in a green bay,
Rage, rage against the dying of the light.

2

10 Wild men who caught and sang the sun in flight,
And learn, too late, they grieved it on its way,
Do not go gentle into that good night.

Grave men, near death, who see with blinding sight
Blind eyes could blaze like meteors and be gay,
15 Rage, rage against the dying of the light.

3

And you, my father, there on the sad height,
Curse, bless, me now with your fierce tears, I pray.
Do not go gentle into that good night.

4

Rage, rage against the dying of the light.

THINKING ABOUT THE SELECTION
Recalling

1. Starting with the second stanza of this villa-nelle, what four kinds of men does the speak-er describe as they go "into that good night"?

Interpreting

2. (a) In this poem, what does *night* seem to represent? (b) What does *light* represent?
3. Considering the speaker's advice to "rage" against the "dying of the light," why do you think he regards night as "good"?
4. What double meaning does the word *grave* have in line 13?
5. How would you paraphrase the speaker's advice in the final couplet?

Applying

6. Do you think "Do Not Go Gentle into That Good Night" might have been a better poem if Thomas had chosen to work with a less restrictive poetic form than the villanelle? Explain your reasoning.

Drama

SET DESIGN OF COVENT GARDEN FOR PYGMALION
Donald Oenslager
Harvard Theater Collection

Humanities Note

Fine art, *Set Design of Covent Garden for Pygmalion*, 1945, by Donald Oenslager. Oenslager (1902–1975) designed scenic productions for many first-run plays and operas in the United States and abroad and made a major contribution to the American theater. He believed a set was more than a background; to Oenslager the stage setting was like a still life, a silent character who spoke to the audience as the curtain was raised, conveying the designer's feeling about the nature of the play.

This set, which is both realistic and fanciful, was designed for a 1945 British production of the George Bernard Shaw masterpiece, *Pygmalion*. The set is architectural in its strong use of perspective to create depth, dimension, and separation between the dominant pillars in the foreground and the receding street beyond. The dramatic perspective engages the imagination and invites the viewer to enter and see what is to come.

More About the Author Music was an integral part of Shaw's household as he was growing up. He began his career as a music critic. Discuss what you think Shaw's reactions might have been to his "didactic drama about phonetics," *Pygmalion*, being turned into a highly successful musical, *My Fair Lady*.

Critical Evaluation The literary scholar Reuben A. Brower made the following comments about *Pygmalion*: "The closing dialogue of the play, in which Eliza and Higgins tell each other off and attain their pure if precarious freedom from sentiment and class, is perhaps the finest that Shaw ever wrote. Anyone who has watched a good actress play this scene—or who has the imagination to see and hear Eliza as she dances about the stage delivering the twists and turns of her attack with perfect balance between new cultivation and old coarseness—will know what is meant by the poetic art of Shaw. Borrowing Johnson's query to the critics of Pope, we may ask, 'If this be not poetry, where is poetry to be found?'"

GEORGE BERNARD SHAW

1856–1950

During his ninety-four years, George Bernard Shaw was a novelist, a critic on many subjects, a champion of all sorts of reform, and, finally, a playwright. Original, witty, and opinionated, he often managed to offend people when he was not busy charming them.

Born in Ireland to a family with musical talent but little money, Shaw saw to his own education. At the age of twenty he arrived in London, where he remained for the rest of his life. After trying, and essentially failing, as a writer of fiction, he turned to reviewing—first books, then paintings, and finally music.

Shaw was a restless man, however, with boundless tastes and interests. In 1884 he joined the Fabian Society, an organization whose aim was the peaceful reform of social, economic, and political systems. His personal ambition, as he put it, was "to force the public to reconsider its morals," and toward this end he invested every ounce of his energies. In the process he established himself as a debater and public speaker of some stature.

The enjoyment he derived from crafting lines for his public addresses coupled with his earlier enthusiasm for writing criticism naturally led him in the direction of drama criticism. From there it was a short jump to playwriting itself. Shaw's first play, *Widower's House* (1892), was a rather heavy-handed and ironical exposure of the slum landlord practices and municipal graft that were common ills of the day. His next effort, *Mrs. Warren's Profession* (1894), ran into trouble with official censorship due to its serious treatment of prostitution and the inequities of industrialism. In the same year, *Arms and the Man* enjoyed a limited success.

If people would not attend productions of his plays, Shaw reasoned, they might at least read them. In 1898 he published his first collection, *Plays Pleasant and Unpleasant,* adding the prefaces and epilogues that came to be his trademark.

Shaw's plays, forty-seven in all, continued to challenge the "spiritual sleep" of England's "middle-class morality." When *Pygmalion* was completed in 1913, it was produced in German in Vienna, as a means of avoiding the usual bad press. Its success there led it to London, where, in April of 1914, it opened to immediate acclaim. Like his professor of phonetics, Henry Higgins, Shaw believed in the power of language to break down class barriers. In his will he left a sizable bequest to furthering a system of phonetic spelling. In the interests of spelling simplification, he left out the apostrophe in some contractions, as in this text.

Objectives

1 To understand historical context in drama
2 To use generalizations properly
3 To understand dialect
4 To write about historical context

Support Material

Teaching Portfolio
Teacher Backup, p. 1351
Grammar in Action Worksheet, p. 1355
Usage and Mechanics Worksheet, p. 1357
Vocabulary Check, p. 1358
Critical Thinking and Reading Worksheet, *Generalizing,* p. 1360

Language Worksheet, *Understanding Dialect,* p. 1361
Selection Test, p. 1362
Art Transparency 16, *Picadilly Circus,* by Charles Ginner
Library of Video Classics, Pygmalion

GUIDE FOR INTERPRETING

Preface to Pygmalion and Pygmalion, Act I

Historical Context

The Play. Historical context refers both to the backdrop of historical events against which a work is set and to attitudes and events of the time during which the author lived. The first of these two aspects relates to such matters as when and where the work takes place, to whether the author has used real places and people, and to the degree to which the events have been fictionalized. The second aspect of historical context—the relevance of "current events" and attitudes of the author's day—takes into account any social conditions and values that may have impacted on the subject matter of the work or its execution.

Writing

To demonstrate the irregularities of English spelling, George Bernard Shaw once suggested that the word *fish* be written *ghoti.* (The *gh,* he explained, was to be pronounced as it is in *rough,* the *o* as in *women,* and the *ti* as in *station.)* Play with English spellings until you have devised three or four "outrageous" words of your own. Show these to your classmates on paper, and see if anyone can read them correctly.

Primary Source

More than any of Shaw's other plays, *Pygmalion* shows how seemingly minor events simmered in his mind, emerging years later transformed in his work. According to Shaw, the play's opening scene was suggested by the following incident:

> Some time ago, happening to be caught in a pelting shower in St. Martin's Lane on a gloomy evening, I took refuge in the entry to a narrow court, where I was presently joined by three men of prosaic appearance, apparently respectable artisans. To my surprise, instead of beginning to talk about horses, they began to talk about music— . . . illustrating their conversation by singing passages in which certain pet singers of theirs had come out wonderfully. This led to a discussion as to whether they could remember some work which had been an old favorite of theirs. Finally, one of them pulled out a pitch pipe; the three sang a chord; and away they went, *sotto voce,* but very prettily, into a three-part song, raising their voices a little when they found that the passers-by were too preoccupied by the deluge to notice them. They were wholly untroubled by a consciousness of the distinguished critic lurking in the shadow a few feet off, greatly pleased with the performance but withal sufficiently master of his business not to be surprised at this survival.

Guide for Interpreting   1105

Literary Focus Shaw's portrayal of the place of women in society was accurate for the time period in which *Pygmalion* takes place; however, the climate seems to have changed. In the early 1980's, Rex Harrison again played Henry Higgins in a revival of *My Fair Lady;* his speeches that indicated Higgins's ideas of the roles of women were greeted with exclamations of disagreement from the audience.

Writing/Prior Knowledge Remind students that at the bottom of the page in most dictionaries is a guide to the diacritical marks that designate the sounds that words have.

Vocabulary

Preteach the following vocabulary words:
conciliatory (ken sil′ ē ə tôr′ ē) *adj.:* Agreeable (p. 1006)
derisive (di rī′ siv) *adj.:* Mocking (p. 1006)
repudiation (ri pyo͞o′ dē ā′ shən) *n.:* Rejection; denial (p. 1007)
cyrptograms (krip′ tə gramz) *n.:* Coded messages (p. 1007)
prodigious (prə dij′ əs) *adj.:* Large; impressive (p. 1008)
didactic (dī dak′ tik) *adj.:* Instructive (p. 1008)
plutocracy (plo͞o tök′ rə sē) *n.:* Wealthy governing class (p. 1008)
impertinent (im pʉr′ t'n ənt) *adj.:* Bold; impudent (p. 1014
mendacity (men das′ ə tē) *n.:* Lying (p. 1015)
prodigal (präd′ i gəl) *adj.:* Wasteful (p. 1018)

Preface to *Pygmalion*

George Bernard Shaw

A Professor of Phonetics

The English have no respect for their language, and will not teach their children to speak it. They cannot spell it because they have nothing to spell it with but an old foreign alphabet of which only the consonants—and not all of them—have any agreed speech value. Consequently no man can teach himself what it should sound like from reading it; and it is impossible for an Englishman to open his mouth without making some other Englishman despise him. Most European languages are now accessible in black and white to foreigners: English and French are not thus accessible even to Englishmen and Frenchmen. The reformer we need most today is an energetic phonetic enthusiast: that is why I have made such a one the hero of a popular play.

There have been heroes of that kind crying in the wilderness for many years past. When I became interested in the subject towards the end of the eighteen-seventies, the illustrious Alexander Melville Bell, the inventor of Visible Speech, had emigrated to Canada, where his son invented the telephone; but Alexander J. Ellis[1] was still a London Patriarch, with an impressive head always covered by a velvet skull cap, for which he would apologize to public meetings in a very courtly manner. He and Tito Pagliardini, another phonetic veteran, were men whom it was impossible to dislike.

Henry Sweet,[2] then a young man, lacked their sweetness of character: he was about as conciliatory to conventional mortals as Ibsen[3] or Samuel Butler.[4] His great ability as a phonetician (he was, I think the best of them all at his job) would have entitled him to high official recognition, and perhaps enabled him to popularize his subject, but for his Satanic contempt for all academic dignitaries and persons in general who thought more of Greek than of phonetics. Once, in the days when the Imperial Institute rose in South Kensington, and Joseph Chamberlain[5] was booming the Empire, I induced the editor of a leading monthly review to commission an article from Sweet on the imperial importance of his subject. When it arrived, it contained nothing but a savagely derisive attack on a professor of language and literature whose chair Sweet regarded as proper to a phonetic expert only. The article, being libellous, had to be returned as impossible; and I had to renounce my dream of dragging its author into the limelight. When I met him afterwards, for the first time for many years, I found to my astonishment that he, who had been a quite tolerably presentable young man, had actually managed by sheer scorn to alter his personal appearance until he had become a sort of

---

1. Alexander J. Ellis: English phonetician and mathematician (1814–1890).

2. Henry Sweet: English phonetician (1845–1912).
3. Ibsen: Norwegian playwright Henrik Ibsen (1828–1906).
4. Samuel Butler: English novelist (1835–1902).
5. Joseph Chamberlain: British statesman (1836–1914).

Grammar in Action

The main features of **persuasive writing** are a persuasive purpose and an appropriate, convincing tone. In the "Preface to *Pygmalion*," Shaw wants to convince readers that phonetics is an important study, that English spelling is in need of reform, and that the ideal person to reform it would be "an energetic phonetic enthusiast."

Shaw uses a number of devices to make these points. For example, he uses an authoritative tone, with hints of humor, to impress readers with the appalling state of English spelling: "The English have no respect for their language, and will not teach their children to speak it." Although he does not give examples to support this point, his tone is sure to gain a reader's attention.

The amusing and vivid portraits of phoneticians that Shaw provides are calculated to arouse a reader's interest in the subject and to establish Shaw's credentials as a knowledgeable layman: "When I met him afterwards, for the first time for many years, I found to my astonishment that he, who had been a quite tolerably presentable young man, had actually managed by sheer scorn to alter his personal appearance until he had walking repudiation of Oxford and all its traditions. It must have been largely in his own despite that he was squeezed into something called a Readership[6] of phonetics there. The future of phonetics rests probably with his pupils, who all swore by him; but nothing could bring the man himself into any sort of compliance with the university to which he nevertheless clung by divine right in an intensely Oxonian[7] way. I daresay his papers, if he has left any, include some satires that may be published without too destructive results fifty years hence. He was, I believe, not in the least an ill-natured man: very much the opposite, I should say; but he would not suffer fools gladly; and to him all scholars who were not rabid phoneticians were fools.

Those who knew him will recognize in my third act the allusion to the Current Shorthand in which he used to write postcards. It may be acquired from a four and sixpenny manual published by the Clarendon Press. The postcards which Mrs Higgins describes are such as I have received from Sweet. I would decipher a sound which a cockney would represent by *zerr*, and a Frenchman by *seu*, and then write demanding with some heat what on earth it meant. Sweet, with boundless contempt for my stupidity, would reply that it not only meant but obviously was the word Result, as no other word containing that sound, and capable of making sense with the context, existed in any language spoken on earth. That less expert mortals should require fuller indications was beyond Sweet's patience. Therefore, though the whole point of his Current Shorthand is that it can express every sound in the language perfectly, vowels as well as consonants, and that your hand has to make no stroke except the easy and current ones with which you write m, n, and u, l, p, and q, scribbling them at whatev-

er angle comes easiest to you, his unfortunate determination to make this remarkable and quite legible script serve also as a shorthand reduced it in his own practice to the most inscrutable of cryptograms. His true objective was the provision of a full, accurate, legible script for our language; but he was led past that by his contempt for the popular Pitman system of shorthand, which he called the Pitfall system. The triumph of Pitman was a triumph of business organization: there was a weekly paper to persuade you to learn Pitman: there were cheap textbooks and exercise books and transcripts of speeches for you to copy, and schools where experienced teachers coached you up to the necessary proficiency. Sweet could not organize his market in that fashion. He might as well have been the Sybil[8] who tore up the leaves of prophecy that nobody would attend to. The four and sixpenny manual, mostly in his lithographed handwriting, that was never vulgarly advertized, may perhaps some day be taken up by a syndicate and pushed upon the public as The Times[9] pushed the Encyclopoedia Britannica; but until then it will certainly not prevail against Pitman. I have bought three copies of it during my lifetime; and I am informed by the publishers that its cloistered existence is still a steady and healthy one. I actually learned the system two several times; and yet the shorthand in which I am writing these lines is Pitman's. And the reason is, that my secretary cannot transcribe Sweet, having been perforce taught in the schools of Pitman. In America I could use the commercially organized Gregg shorthand, which has taken a hint from Sweet by making its letters writable (current, Sweet would have called them) instead of having to be geometrically drawn like Pitman's; but all these systems, including

---

6. Readership *n.*: A position as a lecturer or instructor.
7. Oxonian *adj.*: Pertaining to Oxford University.

8. Sybil: One of the women consulted as prophetesses by the ancient Greeks or Romans.
9. The Times: The *London Times*, a British newspaper.

become a sort of walking repudiation of Oxford and all its traditions."

Student Activity 1. Does Shaw convince you of the points he is making? Explain.

Student Activity 2. Imitate Shaw and write a brief essay explaining why a subject that has been previously ignored is worthy of public attention. If possible, use humor to make your essay even more persuasive.

Sweet's, are spoilt by making them available for verbatim reporting, in which complete and exact spelling and word division are impossible. A complete and exact phonetic script is neither practicable nor necessary for ordinary use; but if we enlarge our alphabet to the Russian size, and make our spelling as phonetic as Spanish, the advance will be prodigious.

Pygmalion Higgins is not a portrait of Sweet, to whom the adventure of Eliza Doolittle would have been impossible; still, as will be seen, there are touches of Sweet in the play. With Higgins's physique and temperament Sweet might have set the Thames on fire. As it was, he impressed himself professionally on Europe to an extent that made his comparative personal obscurity, and the failure of Oxford to do justice to his eminence, a puzzle to foreign specialists in his subject. I do not blame Oxford, because I think Oxford is quite right in demanding a certain social amenity from its nurslings (heavens knows it is not exorbitant in its requirement!); for although I well know how hard it is for a man of genius with a seriously underrated subject to maintain serene and kindly relations with the men who underrate it, and who keep all the best places for less important subjects which they profess without originality and sometimes without much capacity for them, still, if he overwhelms them with wrath and disdain, he cannot expect them to heap honors on him.

Of the later generations of phoneticians I know little. Among them towered Robert Bridges, to whom perhaps Higgins may owe his Miltonic sympathies, though here again I must disclaim all portraiture. But if the play makes the public aware that there are such people as phoneticians, and that they are among the most important people in England at present, it will serve its turn.

I wish to boast that Pygmalion has been an extremely successful play, both on stage and screen, all over Europe and North America as well as at home. It is so intensely and deliberately didactic, and its subject is esteemed so dry, that I delight in throwing it at the heads of the wiseacres who repeat the parrot cry that art should never be didactic. It goes to prove my contention that great art can never be anything else.

Finally, and for the encouragement of people troubled with accents that cut them off from all high employment, I may add that the change wrought by Professor Higgins in the flower-girl is neither impossible nor uncommon. The modern concierge's daughter who fulfills her ambition by playing the Queen of Spain in Ruy Blas[10] at the Théâtre Français is only one of many thousands of men and women who have sloughed off their native dialects and acquired a new tongue. Our West End shop assistants and domestic servants are bilingual. But the thing has to be done scientifically, or the last state of the aspirant may be worse than the first. An honest slum dialect is more tolerable than the attempts of phonetically untaught persons to imitate the plutocracy. Ambitious flower-girls who read this play must not imagine that they can pass themselves off as fine ladies by untutored imitation. They must learn their alphabet over again, and different, from a phonetic expert. Imitation will only make them ridiculous.

---

10. Ruy Blas (rōō ē′ blas′): A play by French writer Victor Hugo (1802–1885).

NOTE FOR TECHNICIANS. A complete representation of the play as printed in this edition is technically possible only on the cinema screen or on stages furnished with exceptionally elaborate machinery. For ordinary theatrical use the scenes separated by rows of asterisks are to be omitted.

In the dialogue an e upside down indicates the indefinite vowel, sometimes called obscure or neutral, for which, though it is one of the commonest sounds in English speech, our wretched alphabet has no letter.

Pygmalion

CHARACTERS

Henry Higgins	Eliza Doolittle	Taximen
Colonel Pickering	Mrs Eynsford Hill	Count Nepommuck
Freddy Eynsford Hill	Miss Eynsford Hill	Host
Alfred Doolittle	Mrs Higgins	Hostess
Bystanders	Mrs Pearce	Footmen
	Parlormaid	Constables

1 **Reading Strategy** Have those students who will benefit from a graphic presentation of information prepare an enlarged map of the part of London in which the play takes place. Being able to locate the centers of activity will help them remember the events that took place in each location. Have them find each place on the map as it is introduced in the play.

2 **Discussion** What classes in London society are brought together in the shelter? How do they reveal their classes? What does the author think of the class presented by the mother? How do you know?

ACT I

1 *London at* 11.15 P.M. *Torrents of heavy summer rain. Cab whistles blowing frantically in all directions. Pedestrians running for shelter into the portico of St Paul's church (not Wren's cathedral but Inigo Jones's church in Covent Garden vegetable market), among them a lady and her daughter in evening dress. All are peering out gloomily at the rain, except one man with his back turned to the rest, wholly preoccupied with a notebook in which he is writing.*

The church clock strikes the first quarter.[1]

THE **DAUGHTER** [*in the space between the central pillars, close to the one on her left*] I'm getting chilled to the bone. What can Freddy be doing all this time? He's been gone twenty minutes.

THE **MOTHER** [*on her daughter's right*] Not so long. But he ought to have got us a cab by this.

A **BYSTANDER** [*on the lady's right*] He wont get no cab not until half-past eleven, missus, when they come back after dropping their theatre fares.

THE **MOTHER.** But we must have a cab. We cant stand here until half-past eleven. It's too bad.

2 THE **BYSTANDER.** Well, it ain't my fault, missus.

THE **DAUGHTER.** If Freddy had a bit of gumption, he would have got one at the theatre door.

THE **MOTHER.** What could he have done, poor boy?

THE **DAUGHTER.** Other people got cabs. Why couldn't he?

FREDDY *rushes in out of the rain from the Southampton Street side, and comes between them closing a dripping umbrella.*

He is a young man of twenty, in evening dress, very wet round the ankles.

THE **DAUGHTER.** Well, havnt you got a cab?

FREDDY. Theres not one to be had for love or money.

THE **MOTHER.** Oh, Freddy, there must be one. You cant have tried.

THE **DAUGHTER.** It's too tiresome. Do you expect us to go and get one ourselves?

FREDDY. I tell you theyre all engaged. The rain was so sudden: nobody was prepared; and everybody had to take a cab. Ive been to Charing Cross one way and nearly to Ludgate Circus the other; and they were all engaged.

THE **MOTHER.** Did you try Trafalgar Square?

FREDDY. There wasn't one at Trafalgar Square.

THE **DAUGHTER.** Did you try?

FREDDY. I tried as far as Charing Cross Station. Did you expect me to walk to Hammersmith?

THE **DAUGHTER.** You havnt tried at all.

THE **MOTHER.** You really are very helpless, Freddy. Go again; and dont come back until you have found a cab.

FREDDY. I shall simply get soaked for nothing.

THE **DAUGHTER.** And what about us? Are we to stay here all night in this draught,[2] with next to nothing on? You selfish pig—

FREDDY. Oh, very well: I'll go, I'll go. [*He opens his umbrella and dashes off Strandwards, but comes into collision with a flower girl who is hurrying in for shelter, knocking her basket out of her hands. A blinding flash of lightning, followed instantly by a rattling peal of thunder, orchestrates the incident*].

THE **FLOWER GIRL.** Nah then, Freddy: look wh' y' gowin, deah.

---

1. **first quarter:** Fifteen minutes past the hour.

2. **draught** (draft): Draft.

Primary Source

Stella Campbell, the 48-year-old actress who played the teenage Eliza Doolittle, had broken off her relationship with Shaw a year before *Pygmalion* opened. The following is an excerpt from a letter that Shaw wrote in response to this rejection:

Very well, go: the loss of a woman is not the end of the world. The sun shines: it is pleasant to swim: it is good to work: my soul can stand alone. But I am deeply, deeply, deeply wounded. You have tried me; and you are not comfortable with me: I cannot bring you peace, or rest, or even fun: there is nothing really frank in our comradeship after all. It is I who have been happy, carelessly happy, comfortable, able to walk for miles after dinner at top speed in search of you, singing all the way (I had walked eight miles in the morning, by the way, and written a scene of my play). . . . Bah! You have no nerve: you have no brain. . . . Go then: the Shavian oxygen burns up your little lungs: seek some stuffiness that suits you. You will not marry George! [George Cornwallis West, a much younger man whom she did marry in 1914, while she was rehears-

FREDDY. Sorry [*he rushes off*].

THE FLOWER GIRL [*picking up her scattered flowers and replacing them in the basket*] Theres menners f' yer! Tə-oo banches o voylets trod into the mad. [*She sits down on the plinth³ of the column sorting her flowers, on the lady's right. She is not at all a romantic figure. She is perhaps eighteen, perhaps twenty, hardly older. She wears a little sailor hat of black straw that has long been exposed to the dust and soot of London and has seldom if ever been brushed. Her hair needs washing rather badly: its mousy color can hardly be natural. She wears a shoddy black coat that reaches nearly to her knees and is shaped to her waist. She has a brown skirt with a coarse apron. Her boots are much the worse for wear. She is no doubt as clean as she can afford to be; but compared to the ladies she is very dirty. Her features are no worse than theirs; but their condition leaves something to be desired; and she needs the services of a dentist*].

THE MOTHER. How do you know that my son's name is Freddy, pray?

THE FLOWER GIRL. Ow, eez yə-ooa, san, is e? Wal, fewd dan y' də-ooty bawmz a mather should, eed now bettern to spawl a pore gel's flahrzn than ran away athaht pyin. Will ye-oo py me f'them? [*Here, with apologies, this desperate attempt to represent her dialect without a phonetic alphabet must be abandoned as unintelligible outside London*].

THE DAUGHTER. Do nothing of the sort, mother. The idea!

THE MOTHER. Please allow me, Clara. Have you any pennies?

THE DAUGHTER. No. Ive nothing smaller than sixpence.

THE FLOWER GIRL [*hopefully*] I can give you change for a tanner,⁴ kind lady.

---

3. plinth: The block at the base of a column.
4. tanner: Slang for a sixpence.

THE MOTHER [*to* CLARA] Give it to me. [CLARA *parts reluctantly*]. Now [*to the* GIRL] This is for your flowers.

THE FLOWER GIRL. Thank you kindly, lady.

THE DAUGHTER. Make her give you the change. These things are only a penny a bunch.

THE MOTHER. Do hold your tongue, Clara. [*To the* GIRL] You can keep the change.

THE FLOWER GIRL. Oh, thank you, lady.

THE MOTHER. Now tell me how you know that young gentleman's name.

THE FLOWER GIRL. I didnt.

THE MOTHER. I heard you call him by it. Dont try to deceive me.

THE FLOWER GIRL [*protesting*] Who's trying to deceive you? I called him Freddy or Charlie same as you might yourself if you was talking to a stranger and wished to be pleasant.

THE DAUGHTER. Sixpence thrown away! Really, mamma, you might have spared Freddy that. [*She retreats in disgust behind the pillar*].

An elderly gentleman of the amiable military type rushes into the shelter, and closes a dripping umbrella. He is in the same plight as FREDDY, *very wet above the ankles. He is in evening dress, with a light overcoat. He takes the place left vacant by* THE DAUGHTER.

THE GENTLEMAN. Phew!

THE MOTHER. [*to the* GENTLEMAN] Oh, sir, is there any sign of its stopping?

THE GENTLEMAN. I'm afraid not. It started worse than ever about two minutes ago [*he goes to the plinth beside the* FLOWER GIRL: *puts up his foot on it; and stoops to turn down his trouser ends*].

THE MOTHER. Oh dear! [*She retires sadly and joins her daughter*].

Pygmalion, Act I   1111

3 Speaking and Listening Have several volunteers give this speech. As a comparison to their work, you might play a recording of this speech from either the play or *My Fair Lady*.

4 Clarification A penny, the plural is *pence,* is a coin—originally silver, then copper, and from 1860 bronze. At the time of the play, it was worth ½ of a shilling or 1/240 of a pound sterling. A sixpence was equal to six pennies. Now a penny is worth 1/100 of a pound sterling.

ing the role of Eliza for *Pygmalion*] At the last moment you will funk him or be ousted by a bolder soul. You have wounded my vanity: an inconceivable audacity, an unpardonable crime.

Farewell, wretch that I loved.
G.B.S.

THE FLOWER GIRL [*taking advantage of the military gentleman's proximity to establish friendly relations with him*] If it's worse, it's a sign it's nearly over. So cheer up, Captain; and buy a flower off a poor girl.

THE GENTLEMAN. I'm sorry. I havnt any change.

THE FLOWER GIRL. I can give you change, Captain.

THE GENTLEMAN. For a sovereign? Ive nothing less.

THE FLOWER GIRL. Garn! Oh do buy a flower off me, Captain. I can change half-a-crown. Take this for tuppence.

THE GENTLEMAN. Now dont be troublesome: theres a good girl. [*Trying his pockets*] I really havnt any change—Stop: heres three hapence, if thats any use to you [*he retreats to the other pillar*].

THE FLOWER GIRL [*disappointed, but thinking three half-pence better than nothing*] Thank you, sir.

THE BYSTANDER [*to the* GIRL] You be careful: give him a flower for it. Theres a bloke here behind taking down every blessed word youre saying. [*All turn to the man who is taking notes*].

THE FLOWER GIRL [*springing up terrified*] I aint done nothing wrong by speaking to the gentleman. Ive a right to sell flowers if I keep off the kerb. [*Hysterically*] I'm a respectable girl: so help me, I never spoke to him except to ask him to buy a flower off me.

General hubbub, mostly sympathetic to the FLOWER GIRL, *but deprecating her excessive sensibility. Cries of* Dont start hollerin. Who's hurting you? Nobody's going to touch you. Whats the good of fussing? Steady on. Easy, easy, etc., *come from the elderly staid spectators, who pat her comfortingly. Less patient ones bid her shut her head, or ask her roughly what is wrong with her. A remoter group, not knowing what the matter is, crowd in and increase the noise with* question and answer: What's the row? What-she do? Where is he? A tec[5] taking her down. What! him? Yes: him over there: Took money off the gentleman, etc.

THE FLOWER GIRL [*breaking through them to the* GENTLEMAN, *crying wildly*] Oh, sir, dont let him charge me. You dunno what it means to me. Theyll take away my character and drive me on the streets for speaking to gentlemen. They—

THE NOTE TAKER [*coming forward on her right, the rest crowding after him*] There! there! there! there! who's hurting you, you silly girl? What do you take me for?

THE BYSTANDER. It's aw rawt: e's a genleman: look at his bə-oots. [*Explaining to the* NOTE TAKER] She thought you was a copper's nark, sir.

THE NOTE TAKER [*with quick interest*] Whats a copper's nark?

THE BYSTANDER [*inapt at definition*] It's a—well, it's a copper's nark, as you might say. What else would you call it? A sort of informer.

THE FLOWER GIRL [*still hysterical*] I take my Bible oath I never said a word—

THE NOTE TAKER [*overbearing but good-humored*] Oh, shut up, shut up. Do I look like a policeman?

THE FLOWER GIRL [*far from reassured*] Then what did you take down my words for? How do I know whether you took me down right? You just shew me what youve wrote about me. [*The* NOTE TAKER *opens his book and holds it steadily under her nose, though the pressure of the mob trying to read it over his shoulders would upset a weaker man*]. Whats that? That aint proper writing. I cant read that.

THE NOTE TAKER. I can. [*Reads, reproducing her pronunciation exactly*] "Cheer ap, Keptin; n' baw ya flahr orf a pore gel."

---

5. tec: A slang abbreviation for detective.

THE FLOWER GIRL [*much distressed*] It's because I called him Captain. I meant no harm. [*To the* GENTLEMAN] Oh, sir, dont let him lay a charge agen me for a word like that. You—

THE GENTLEMAN. Charge! I make no charge. [*To the* NOTE TAKER] Really, sir, if you are a detective, you need not begin protecting me against molestation by young women until I ask you. Anybody could see that the girl meant no harm.

THE BYSTANDERS GENERALLY [*demonstrating against police espionage*] Course they could. What business is it of yours? You mind your own affairs. He wants promotion, he does. Taking down people's words! Girl never said a word to him. What harm if she did? Nice thing a girl cant shelter from the rain without being insulted, etc., etc., etc. [*She is conducted by the more sympathetic demonstrators back to her plinth, where she resumes her seat and struggles with her emotion*].

THE BYSTANDER. He aint a tec. He's a blooming busybody: thats what he is. I tell you, look at his bə-oots.

THE NOTE TAKER [*turning on him genially*] And how are all your people down at Selsey?

THE BYSTANDER [*suspiciously*] Who told you my people come from Selsey?

THE NOTE TAKER. Never you mind. They did. [*To the* GIRL] How do you come to be up so far east? You were born in Lisson Grove.

THE FLOWER GIRL [*appalled*] Oh, what harm is there in my leaving Lisson Grove? It wasnt fit for a pig to live in; and I had to pay four-and-six a week. [*In tears*] Oh, boo —hoo—oo—

THE NOTE TAKER. Live where you like; but stop that noise.

THE GENTLEMAN [*to the* GIRL] Come, come! he cant touch you: you have a right to live where you please.

A SARCASTIC BYSTANDER [*thrusting himself between the* NOTE TAKER *and the* GENTLEMAN] Park Lane, for instance. I'd like to go into the Housing Question with you, I would.

THE FLOWER GIRL [*subsiding into a brooding melancholy over her basket, and talking very low-spiritedly to herself*] I'm a good girl, I am.

THE SARCASTIC BYSTANDER [*not attending to her*] Do you know where I come from?

THE NOTE TAKER [*promptly*] Hoxton.

Titterings. Popular interest in the NOTE TAK-ER's *performance increases.*

THE SARCASTIC ONE [*amazed*] Well, who said I didnt? Bly me! you know everything, you do.

THE FLOWER GIRL [*still nursing her sense of injury*] Aint no call to meddle with me, he aint.

THE BYSTANDER [*to her*] Of course he aint. Dont you stand it from him. [*To the* NOTE TAKER] See here: what call have you to know about people what never offered to meddle with you?

THE FLOWER GIRL. Let him say what he likes. I dont want to have no truck with him.

THE BYSTANDER. You take us for dirt under your feet, dont you? Catch you taking liberties with a gentleman!

THE SARCASTIC BYSTANDER. Yes: tell him where he come from if you want to go fortune-telling.

THE NOTE TAKER. Cheltenham, Harrow, Cambridge, and India.

THE GENTLEMAN. Quite right.

Great laughter. Reaction in the NOTE TAKER's *favor. Exclamations of* He knows all about it. Told him proper. Hear him tell the toff[6] where he come from? etc.

---

6. **toff:** English slang for a fashionable person.

Pygmalion, Act I 1113

---

8 **Discussion** How does the Note Taker know where the bystander and the girl originated?

9 **Clarification** The Flower Girl paid four shillings and six pence a week in rent.

10 **Critical Thinking and Reading** What generalizations can you make about the Bystander's attitudes and background?

11 **Clarification** The gentleman was brought up in Cheltenham, west of London, in Gloucestershire; went to Harrow, a public (controlled enrollment, privately funded) school for boys; went to university at Cambridge; and served in the military in India.

12 **Discussion** Discuss the difference between the Note Taker's response to the Flower Girl and the Daughter and their responses to him.

13 **Critical Thinking and Reading** How does the exchange support the generalization that the English judge each other as soon as they open their mouths?

14 **Discussion** Why is the Note Taker interested in the girl?

THE GENTLEMAN. May I ask, sir, do you do this for your living at a music hall?

THE NOTE TAKER. I've thought of that. Perhaps I shall some day.

The rain has stopped; and the persons on the outside of the crowd begin to drop off.

THE FLOWER GIRL [*resenting the reaction*] He's no gentleman, he aint, to interfere with a poor girl.

THE DAUGHTER [*out of patience, pushing her way rudely to the front and displacing the* GENTLEMAN, *who politely retires to the other side of the pillar*] What on earth is Freddy doing? I shall get pneumownia if I stay in this draught any longer.

THE NOTE TAKER [*to himself, hastily making a note of her pronunciation of "monia"*] Earlscourt.

THE DAUGHTER [*violently*] Will you please keep your impertinent remarks to yourself.

THE NOTE TAKER. Did I say that out loud? I didn't mean to. I beg your pardon. Your mother's Epsom, unmistakeably.

THE MOTHER [*advancing between the* DAUGHTER *and the* NOTE TAKER] How very curious! I was brought up in Largelady Park, near Epsom.

THE NOTE TAKER [*uproariously amused*] Ha! ha! What a devil of a name! Excuse me. [*To the* DAUGHTER] You want a cab, do you?

12 THE DAUGHTER. Dont dare speak to me.

THE MOTHER. Oh please, please, Clara. [*Her daughter repudiates her with an angry shrug and retires haughtily*] We should be so grateful to you, sir, if you found us a cab. [*The* NOTE TAKER *produces a whistle*] Oh, thank you. [*She joins her daughter*].
The NOTE TAKER *blows a piercing blast.*

THE SARCASTIC BYSTANDER. There! I knowed he was a plainclothes copper.

THE BYSTANDER. That aint a police whistle: thats a sporting whistle.

1114   The Modern Period

THE FLOWER GIRL [*still preoccupied with her wounded feelings*] He's no right to take away my character. My character is the same to me as any lady's.

THE NOTE TAKER. I dont know whether youve noticed it; but the rain stopped about two minutes ago.

THE BYSTANDER. So it has. Why didn't you say so before? and us losing our time listening to your silliness! [*He walks off towards the Strand*].

THE SARCASTIC BYSTANDER. I can tell where you come from. You come from Anwell. Go back there.

13

THE NOTE TAKER [*helpfully*] Hanwell.

THE SARCASTIC BYSTANDER [*affecting great distinction of speech*] Thenk you, teacher. Haw haw! So long [*he touches his hat with mock respect and strolls off*].

THE FLOWER GIRL. Frightening people like that! How would he like it himself?

THE MOTHER. It's quite fine now, Clara. We can walk to a motor bus. Come. [*She gathers her skirts above her ankles and hurries off towards the Strand*].

THE DAUGHTER. But the cab—[*her mother is out of hearing*]. Oh, how tiresome! [*She follows angrily*].

All the rest have gone except the NOTE TAKER, *the* GENTLEMAN, *and the* FLOWER GIRL, *who sits arranging her basket, and still pitying herself in murmurs.*

THE FLOWER GIRL. Poor girl! Hard enough for her to live without being worried and chivied.[7]

THE GENTLEMAN [*returning to his former place on the* NOTE TAKER*'s left*] How do you do it, if I may ask?

THE NOTE TAKER. Simple phonetics. The science of speech. Thats my profession: also

_____

7. worrited and chivied: Worried and tormented.

my hobby. Happy is the man who can make a living by his hobby! You can spot an Irishman or a Yorkshireman by his brogue. *I* can place any man within six miles. I can place him within two miles in London. Sometimes within two streets.

THE FLOWER GIRL. Ought to be ashamed of himself, unmanly coward.

THE GENTLEMAN. But is there a living in that?

THE NOTE TAKER. Oh yes. Quite a fat one. This is an age of upstarts. Men begin in Kentish Town with £80 a year, and end in Park Lane with a hundred thousand. They want to drop Kentish Town; but they give themselves away every time they open their mouths. Now I can teach them—

THE FLOWER GIRL. Let him mind his own business and leave a poor girl—

THE NOTE TAKER [*explosively*] Woman: cease this detestable boohooing instantly; or else seek the shelter of some other place of worship.

THE FLOWER GIRL [*with feeble defiance*] Ive a right to be here if I like, same as you.

THE NOTE TAKER. A woman who utters such depressing and disgusting sounds has no right to be anywhere—no right to live. Remember that you are a human being with a soul and the divine gift of articulate speech: that your native language is the language of Shakespear and Milton and The Bible; and dont sit there crooning like a bilious pigeon.

THE FLOWER GIRL [*quite overwhelmed, looking up at him in mingled wonder and deprecation without daring to raise her head*] Ah-ah-ah-ow-ow-ow-oo!

THE NOTE TAKER [*whipping out his book*] Heavens! what a sound! [*He writes; then holds out the book and reads, reproducing her vowels exactly*] Ah-ah-ah-ow-ow-ow-oo!

THE FLOWER GIRL [*tickled by the performance, and laughing in spite of herself*] Garn!

THE NOTE TAKER. You see this creature with her kerbstone English: the English that will keep her in the gutter to the end of her days. Well, sir, in three months I could pass that girl off as a duchess at an ambassador's garden party. I could even get her a place as lady's maid or shop assistant, which requires better English.

THE FLOWER GIRL. What's that you say?

THE NOTE TAKER. Yes, you squashed cabbage leaf, you disgrace to the noble architecture of these columns, you incarnate insult to the English language: I could pass you off as the Queen of Sheba. [*To the* GENTLEMAN] Can you believe that?

THE GENTLEMAN. Of course I can. I am myself a student of Indian dialects; and—

THE NOTE TAKER [*eagerly*] Are you? Do you know Colonel Pickering, the author of Spoken Sanscrit?

THE GENTLEMAN. I am Colonel Pickering. Who are you?

THE NOTE TAKER. Henry Higgins, author of Higgins's Universal Alphabet.

PICKERING [*with enthusiasm*] I came from India to meet you.

HIGGINS. I was going to India to meet you.

PICKERING. Where do you live?

HIGGINS. 27A Wimpole Street. Come and see me tomorrow.

PICKERING. I'm at the Carlton. Come with me now and lets have a jaw over some supper.

HIGGINS. Right you are.

THE FLOWER GIRL [*to* PICKERING, *as he passes her*] Buy a flower, kind gentleman. I'm short for my lodging.

PICKERING. I really havnt any change. I'm sorry [*he goes away*].

HIGGINS [*shocked at the* GIRL'*s mendacity*] Liar. You said you could change half-a-crown.

Pygmalion, Act I 1115

15 **Enrichment** London was once a small village surrounded by other small villages. Even though these villages eventually grew together into the large city we call London today, the individual villages and their individual inhabitants have maintained distinct identities, including their own dialects.

16 **Literary Focus** What is there about the Note Taker and the society in which he lives that causes and permits him to be so verbally abusive to this young girl?

17 **Discussion** Compare what you learn about the Note Taker in this speech with what you know about Henry Sweet from reading the Preface.

18 **Discussion** What are the economic side effects of the way the girl speaks?

19 **Enrichment** People of the gentleman's class normally ate a rather extensive breakfast, had a hot, complete meal called *dinner* near noon, had a meal called *tea*—consisting of rather delicate sandwiches and cakes and tea—at 4:00 P.M., and ate a lavish meal called *supper* late in the evening.

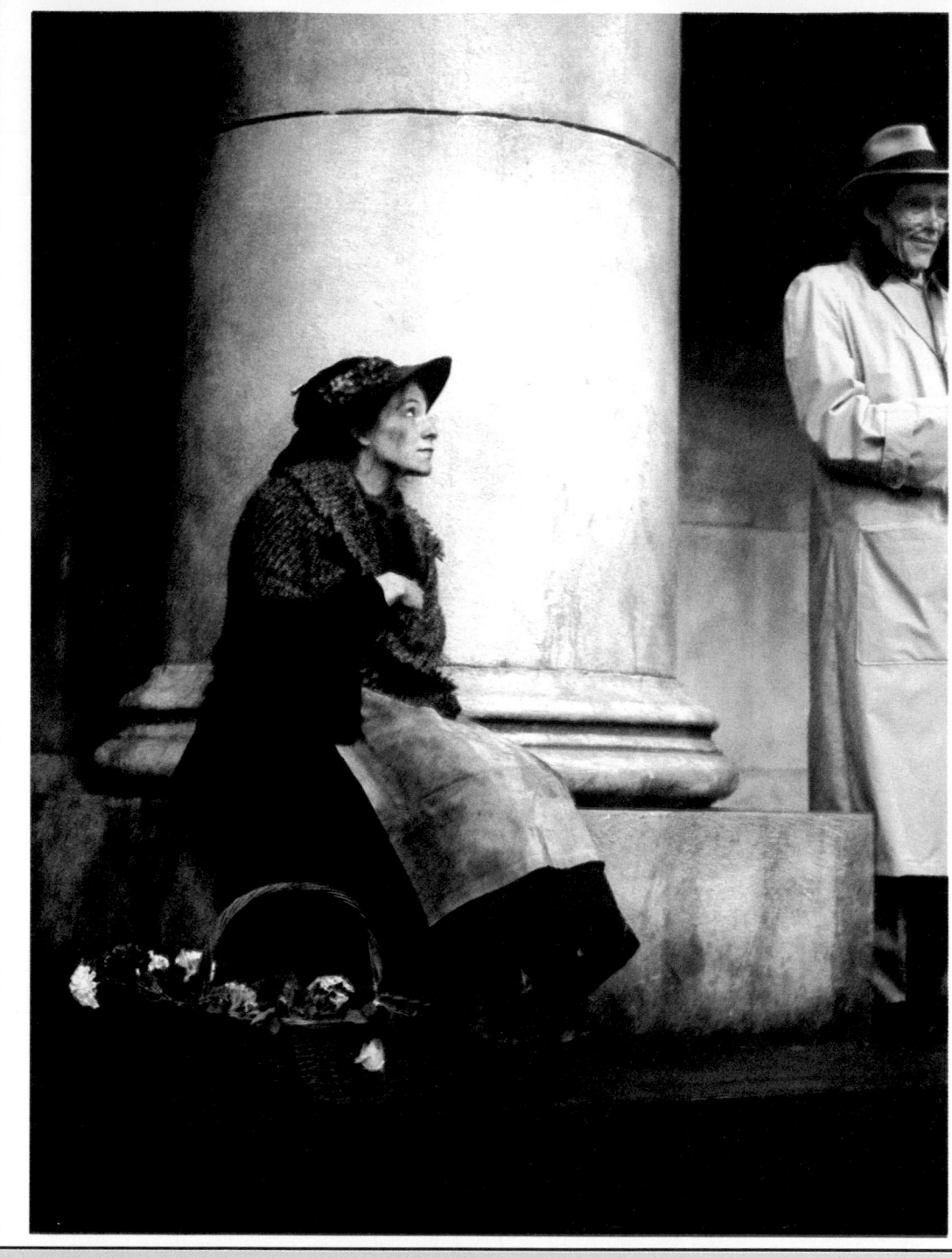

Primary Source

The drama critic Eric Bentley made the following comments on Shavian comedy:

It is the dialogue of Shavian comedy that has attracted most attention. It was praised by Max Beerbohm and G.K. Chesterton forty years ago, and it is praised by Edmund Wilson and Jacques Barzun today. But Shaw's talent is not merely for conversation, it is also for dramaturgy. In all

justice it should be said that Max Beerbohm pointed this out in a retraction of his earlier view that Shaw was a writer of conversations, not plays. This view, says Beerbohm, collapses when you actually see Shaw in the theater: 'To deny that he is a dramatist merely because he chooses, for the most part, to get drama out of contrasted types of character and thought, without action, and without appeal to the emotions, seems to be both unjust and absurd.'

But these words of Beerbohm's, written in 1905, have not always been heeded. There are histories of the drama in which Bernard Shaw has been relegated to a humble role beside now forgotten mediocrities. Most of those who

THE FLOWER GIRL [*rising in desperation*] You ought to be stuffed with nails, you ought. [*Flinging the basket at his feet*] Take the whole blooming basket for sixpence.

The church clock strikes the second quarter.

HIGGINS [*hearing in it the voice of God, rebuking him for his Pharisaic[8] want of charity to the poor girl*] A reminder. [*He raises his hat solemnly; then throws a handful of money into the basket and follows* PICKERING].

20

THE FLOWER GIRL [*picking up a half-crown*] Ah-ow-ooh! [*Picking up a couple of florins*] Aaah-ow-ooh! [*Picking up several coins*] Aaaaah-ow-ooh! [*Picking up a half-sovereign*] Aaaaaaaaaaaah-ow-ooh!!!

FREDDY [*springing out of a taxicab*] Got one at last. Hello! [*To the* GIRL] Where are the two ladies that were here?

THE FLOWER GIRL. They walked to the bus when the rain stopped.

FREDDY. And left me with a cab on my hands! Damnation!

THE FLOWER GIRL [*with grandeur*] Never mind, young man. *I'm* going home in a taxi. [*She sails off to the cab. The driver puts his hand behind him and holds the door firmly shut against her. Quite understanding his mistrust, she shews him her handful of money*]. A taxi fare aint no object to me, Charlie. [*He grins and opens the door*]. Here. What about the basket?

THE TAXIMAN. Give it here. Tuppence extra.

LIZA. No: I dont want nobody to see it. [*She crushes it into the cab and gets in, continuing the conversation through the window*] Good-bye, Freddy.

FREDDY [*dazedly raising his hat*] Goodbye.

TAXIMAN. Where to?

---

8. Pharisaic (far′ ə sā′ ik) *adj.*: Referring to the Pharisees, an ancient Jewish party or fellowship that carefully observed the written law; hypocritically self-righteous.

LIZA. Bucknam Pellis [Buckingham Palace].

TAXIMAN. What d'ye mean—Bucknam Pellis?

LIZA. Dont you know where it is? In the Green Park, where the King lives. Goodbye, Freddy. Dont let me keep you standing there. Goodbye.

21

FREDDY. Goodbye [*He goes*].

TAXIMAN. Here? Whats this about Bucknam Pellis? What business have you at Bucknam Pellis?

LIZA. Of course I havnt none. But I wasn't going to let him know that. You drive me home.

TAXIMAN. And wheres home?

LIZA. Angel Court, Drury Lane, next Meiklejohn's oil shop.

TAXIMAN. That sounds more like it, Judy. [*He drives off*].

* * * * * *

Let us follow the taxi to the entrance to Angel Court, a narrow little archway between two shops, one of them Meiklejohn's oil shop. When it stops there, Eliza gets out, dragging her basket with her.

LIZA. How much?

TAXIMAN [*indicating the taximeter*] Cant you read? A shilling.

LIZA. A shilling for two minutes!!

TAXIMAN. Two minutes or ten: it's all the same.

LIZA. Well, I dont call it right.

22

TAXIMAN. Ever been in a taxi before?

LIZA [*with dignity*] Hundreds and thousands of times, young man.

TAXIMAN [*laughing at her*] Good for you, Judy. Keep the shilling, darling, with best love from all at home. Good luck! [*He drives off*].

20 **Discussion** Why does Higgins throw the girl a handful of money?

21 **Enrichment** Buckingham Palace, the home of the reigning monarch in London, sits next to Green Park, between Hyde Park and St. James Park—three of the many green spaces maintained as public gardens and parks in London.

22 **Discussion** What do we learn about the Flower Girl and the Taximan in this exchange between them?

discover the artistry of Shaw discover the prose style much more than the dramaturgy. Even Beerbohm's praise is left-handed in its assertion that Shavian drama is 'without action and without appeal to the emotions.' . . . It is curious, because it shows how a man can revert to the cliche conception of Shaw—'a giant brain and no heart,' to cite one of the critics in *Fanny's First Play*—after a momentary escape from it.

23 Enrichment It is still a rather common practice in some homes and boarding houses in Great Britain to have coin-operated gas heaters, water heaters, and lights. The meters allow people to budget carefully the amount of gas, hot water, and electricity that they use.

Reader's Response Do you think Liza and Higgins will meet again? Why or why not?

LIZA [*humiliated*] Impidence!

She picks up the basket and trudges up the alley with it to her lodging: a small room with very old wall paper hanging loose in the damp places. A broken pane in the window is mended with paper. A portrait of a popular actor and a fashion plate of ladies' dresses, all wildly beyond poor ELIZA's *means, both torn from newspapers, are pinned up on the wall. A birdcage hangs in the window; but its tenant died long ago: it remains as a memorial only.*

These are the only visible luxuries: the rest is the irreducible minimum of poverty's needs: a wretched bed heaped with all sorts of coverings that have any warmth in them, a draped packing case with a basin and jug on it and a little looking glass over it, a chair and table, the refuse of some suburban kitchen, and an American alar-um clock on the shelf above the unused fireplace: the whole lighted with a gas lamp with a penny in the slot meter. Rent: four shillings a week.

Here Eliza, chronically weary, but too excited to go to bed, sits, counting her new riches and dreaming and planning what to do with them, until the gas goes out, when she enjoys for the first time the sensation of being able to put in another penny without grudging it. This prodigal mood does not extinguish her gnawing sense of the need for economy sufficiently to prevent her from calculating that she can dream and plan in bed more cheaply and warmly than sitting up without a fire. So she takes off her shawl and skirt and adds them to the miscellaneous bedclothes. Then she kicks off her shoes and gets into bed without any further change.

THINKING ABOUT THE SELECTION
Recalling

1. What kind of reformer does Shaw claim, in the Preface, that "we need most today"?
2. (a) What is the point of Current Shorthand? (b) Why does Shaw find it superior to previous systems?
3. (a) Where and when does the play open? (b) What are the mother and daughter doing?
4. How does The Note Taker amaze the crowd?
5. What feat does The Note Taker say he could accomplish in three months?

Interpreting

6. Based on Shaw's description of Henry Sweet in the Preface, what traits might you say the two men shared?
7. (a) What effect does Shaw achieve by spelling out words according to the speaker's pronunciation? (b) by identifying characters by labels at first?

Applying

8. In the seventh century, Ali ibn-abi-Talib, who was fourth caliph of the Moslems, wrote, "A man is hid under his tongue." (a) Explain the meaning of this quotation. (b) Under what circumstances do you feel that a person's speech habits are important?

ANALYZING LITERATURE
Understanding Historical Context

Historical context refers both to a play's historical validity (if it depicts events at a time other than that at which it was written) and to events and attitudes of the author's day that may have been influential. *Pygmalion* provides us

---

Closure and Extension

ANSWERS TO THINKING ABOUT THE SELECTION
Recalling

1. We need an "energetic phonetic enthusiast"; that was why he made such a man the hero of his play.
2. (a) Current Shorthand made it possible to express every sound —every vowel and consonant—in the English language perfectly. (b) It used "no stroke except the easy and current ones with which you write m, n, and u, l, p, and q."
3. (a) The play opens in the portico of St. Paul's church near the Covent Garden vegetable market in London. It is 11:15 P.M., and it is raining heavily. (b) They are standing in the portico to avoid getting wet, while Freddy, the son, tries to find a taxi to take them home.
4. The Note Taker guesses where several people are from, just by hearing them speak.
5. The Note Taker says that within three months he could pass the Flower Girl off as a duchess at an ambassador's garden party.

Interpreting

6. Shaw says that Higgins is not a portrait of Sweet but that there are touches of Sweet in the play, such as the irascible arrogance with which they both dealt with those they thought to be fools. Shaw also

with a glimpse of English city life shortly after the turn of the century. Tell what the following details from Act I reveal about that lifestyle, and describe any differences you might expect today in your own city.

1. Freddy's searching for a cab while his mother and sister remain sheltered.
2. The crowd's suspicions about The Note Taker.
3. (a) The verbal exchanges between The Note Taker and The Flower Girl. (b) between The Flower Girl and the Taximan.

CRITICAL THINKING AND READING
Generalizing About People

The Note Taker in Act I bases his assumptions about the speech habits of Eliza and the others on well-founded **generalizations,** or observations that apply to classes of people. While such observations, when based on scientific principles as they are here, can be valid, generalizing as a rule is a dangerous practice. Tell what generalizations underlie the following acts, and judge their validity.

1. Shaw's remarking in the Preface that "it is impossible for an Englishman to open his mouth without making some other Englishman despise him."
2. Eliza's assuming that Higgins is a "tec."
3. The crowd's sizing up Pickering as a "toff."
4. The Taximan's holding the door shut against Eliza when she first approaches.

SPEAKING AND LISTENING
Understanding Dialect

A **dialect** is a collection of speech habits that typifies a particular social class or region. A dialect may vary from the standard form of a language in pronunciation, in grammar, and in the use of certain expressions. Whatever its defining features may be, every dialect is *systematic*—or governed by rules. The Cockney accent used by Eliza is used to this day by lower-class inhabitants of London's East End. Arrange for members of the class to read aloud Eliza's speeches on pages 1130 and 1135. After "translating" them into standard English, develop as many rules of pronunciation and grammar as you can for the Cockney dialect.

THINKING AND WRITING
Writing About Historical Context

Reread Shaw's Preface to the play. Then write a short essay evaluating the Preface's contribution to the play's historical context. Begin by asking yourself the following questions. How relevant are Shaw's attitudes about language to the events of Act I? How important is the background information on Henry Sweet? On systems of shorthand? When you revise, make sure you have provided details from the Preface and from Act I to support your thesis. Proofread your essay and prepare a final draft.

(Answers begin on p. 1118.)

confront such a person as openly and directly as these people did.
3. Suggested Responses: (a) It appears that those of the upper class could speak to everyone else in any way that they might choose; even though, the Flower Girl and some bystanders objected, no one could make the Note Taker stop. Today, there is a real possibility that this confrontation would have gotten violent very quickly and that no one in the crowd would have stepped into help. (b) The Taximan and the Flower Girl are both from the working class and value money in the same way. Only when she showed him that she could pay, did he allow her to get in the taxi. However, when he got to her street, he let her out without paying. Today, it is unlikely that someone would be challenged by Taximan about whether he or she could pay the fare, and it is equally unlikely that the ride would end up being free.

ANSWERS TO CRITICAL THINKING AND READING

1. The generalization that the English judge each other on how they speak is an accurate statement; that they despise each other upon hearing each other speak is an assumption that cannot be made.
2. Eliza became distraught when she assumed that Higgins was a detective; her generalization that anyone taking down notes about his surroundings must be on a case proved to be wrong.
3. That Pickering is a "toff" is an accurate observation; because a toff is a fashionable person whose quality could be easily assessed by anyone who saw him. He dress was that of a gentlemen with class.
4. The Taximan assumed by her manner and by the clothes she wore that Eliza had no money; it turns out that this time his generalization was wrong. She had a fistful of money with which to pay him.

SPEAKING AND LISTENING

Have volunteers put together a list of expressions from the rhyming slang of the Cockneys. Have them present the list orally to the rest of the class, with translations, and have them teach the usage and pronunciation of the expressions.

says that if Sweet had had Higgins's physique and temperament Sweet might have been more successful in his attempts to change the way that the English looked at their language.
7. (a) Shaw's spelling allows the reader to see and to sound out the differences in the dialects that Higgins is studying. (b) His identification of characters by labels enables the reader to connect the character's speech with his or her profession or role.

Applying
8. (a) Answers will differ, though the general idea of the quotation seems to be that people conceal themselves by what they say. (b) Speech habits are important whenever we are likely to be known or judged primarily by them—as, for instance, during a job interview.

ANSWERS TO ANALYZING LITERATURE

1. Suggested Response: Men, seen as the stronger sex, were more capable of withstanding rain and were expected to "take care of" women. Today, many women take the initiative in their lives and feel they can take care of themselves.
2. Suggested Response: The crowd thought that if the Note Taker was watching them carefully he must be a policeman; it seems that policeman were seen as intrusive by this society. This attitude still exists in today's society, although most people would not feel as free to

Literary Focus Remind students what they have learned about round and flat characters and the importance of character development—external and internal—to the development of the story.

Writing/Prior Knowledge When they have completed their writing, have them exchange their paragraphs with a partner and offer comments that will improve them. Have them return the paragraphs and make whatever changes they feel are necessary.

Vocabulary

Preteach the following vocabulary words:

impetuous (im pech′ o͞o wəs) *adj.:* Given to doing things on the spur of the moment (p. 1121)

petulance (pech′ o͞o ləns) *n.:* Peevishness; moodiness (p. 1121)

peremptorily (pə remp′ tə ri lē) *adv.:* Decisively (p. 1123)

zephyr (zef′ ər) *n.:* Gentle wind (p. 1125)

elocution (el′ə kyo͞o′ shən) *n.:* Art of public speaking (p. 1125)

remonstrance (ri män′ strəns) *n.:* Protest (p. 1126)

presumptuous (pri zump′ cho͞o wəs) *adj.:* Unduly confident or bold (p. 1128)

GUIDE FOR INTERPRETING

Pygmalion, Act II

Writer's Technique

Character Development. Character development is the fleshing out of a character in a work of fiction through confrontations with other characters or forces. Depending upon the extent to which a character changes as a result of these confrontations, he or she is said to be either static or dynamic. A *static character* is one who remains relatively unchanged by events. A *dynamic character,* by contrast, is one who changes considerably, sometimes shedding altogether character traits which he or she possessed earlier in the work. In Shakespeare's *The Taming of the Shrew,* for example, the character Kate begins as a feisty, hot-tempered individual who, through the course of the play, is transformed into a mellow, even-tempered person.

Commentary

Shaw's own character, as with the ones he created, was developed through encounters with different forces. These forces must have been powerful, for at twenty-four Shaw did not seem destined for greatness. He was considered a total failure, ignored by his mother, despised by his sister, passed over by relatives and family friends. St. John Ervine describes him as "tall, over six feet in height, and pale with the pallor of people with red hair, although his was not notably red. . . . It was worn flat on his head, divided in the middle, and was matched on his chin by a thin, scrubby beard which was slow in its growth. . . . His eyes were his most notable feature, far more notable than the long, slightly twisted nose which seemed at first sight to prevail over the whole face, or the tightly-drawn lips or the large projecting ears. The eyebrows . . . revealed already the strange dissimilarity between the two sides of his face. . . . One side was genial, almost benign and full of fun and laughter; the other side had a brooding look that was to become almost tormented in his old age. . . . He wears the features of a sober young man, over-earnest, perhaps about the state of the world and eager to deliver messages, though unable yet to find an audience which will listen for more than a minute or two; but he shows in his laughing eye as well as in the eye that is somber, and in the resolute lips, that he will one day make the casual and disinterested passers-by stand and look and listen."

Writing

What motivates people to change? Why do people decide to alter the way they look, behave, or even speak? Freewrite, exploring your thoughts on these questions.

Objectives

1 To understand character development
2 To make inferences about characters
3 To read dialogue aloud
4 To write comparing and contrasting characters

Support Material

Teaching Portfolio
Teacher Backup, p. 1365
Grammar in Action Worksheet, *Appreciating Dialect,* p. 1369
Usage and Mechanics Worksheet, p. 1371
Vocabulary Check, p. 1372
Analyzing Literature Worksheet, *Understanding Character Development,* p. 1373

Critical Thinking and Reading Worksheet, *Making Inferences About Characters,* p. 1374
Selection Test, p. 1375

ACT II

Next day at 11 A.M. HIGGINS'S *laboratory in Wimpole Street. It is a room on the first floor, looking on the street, and was meant for the drawing room. The double doors are in the middle of the back wall; and persons entering find in the corner to their right two tall file cabinets at right angles to one another against the walls. In this corner stands a flat writing-table, on which are a phonograph, a laryngoscope,[1] a row of tiny organ pipes with a bellows, a set of lamp chimneys for singing flames with burners attached to a gas plug in the wall by an indiarubber tube, several tuning-forks of different sizes, a life-size image of half a human head, shewing in section the vocal organs, and a box containing a supply of wax cylinders for the phonograph.*

Further down the room, on the same side, is a fireplace, with a comfortable leather-covered easy-chair at the side of the hearth nearest the door, and a coal-scuttle. There is a clock on the mantlepiece. Between the fireplace and the phonograph table is a stand for newspapers.

On the other side of the central door, to the left of the visitor, is a cabinet of shallow drawers. On it is a telephone and the telephone directory. The corner beyond, and most of the side wall, is occupied by a grand piano, with the keyboard at the end furthest from the door, and a bench for the players extending the full length of the keyboard. On the piano is a dessert dish heaped with fruit and sweets, mostly chocolates.

The middle of the room is clear. Besides the easy-chair, the piano bench, and two chairs at the phonograph table, there is one stray chair. It stands near the fireplace. On the walls, engravings: mostly Piranesis[2] and mezzotint[3] portraits. No paintings.

---

1. laryngoscope (lə riŋ′ gō skōp′) *n.*: An instrument for examining the throat.
2. Piranesis (pēr′ ə nā′ zēz): Works of Italian artist Giambattista Piranesi (1720–1778).
3. mezzotint: An engraving made from a copper or steel plate.

PICKERING *is seated at the table, putting down some cards and a tuning-fork which he has been using.* HIGGINS *is standing up near him, closing two or three file drawers which are hanging out. He appears in the morning light as a robust, vital, appetizing sort of man of forty or thereabouts, dressed in a professional-looking black frock-coat with a white linen collar and black silk tie. He is of energetic, scientific type, heartily, even violently interested in everything that can be studied as a scientific subject, and careless about himself and other people, including their feelings. He is, in fact, but for his years and size, rather like a very impetuous baby "taking notice" eagerly and loudly, and requiring almost as much watching to keep him out of unintended mischief. His manner varies from genial bullying when he is in a good humor to stormy petulance when anything goes wrong; but he is so entirely frank and void of malice that he remains likeable even in his least reasonable moments.*

HIGGINS [*as he shuts the last drawer*] Well, I think thats the whole show.

PICKERING. It's really amazing. I havnt taken half of it in, you know.

HIGGINS. Would you like to go over any of it again?

PICKERING [*rising and coming to the fireplace, where he plants himself with his back to the fire*] No, thank you: not now. I'm quite done up for this morning.

HIGGINS [*following him, and standing beside him on his left*] Tired of listening to sounds?

PICKERING. Yes. It's a fearful strain. I rather fancied myself because I can pronounce twenty-four distinct vowel sounds; but your hundred and thirty beat me. I cant hear a bit of difference between most of them.

HIGGINS [*chuckling, and going over to the piano to eat sweets*] Oh, that comes with practice. You hear no difference at first; but you keep on listening, and presently you

---

3 Critical Thinking and Reading
What inferences can you make about the part that Mrs. Pearce plays in the Higgins household?

4 Discussion How does Eliza feel about herself?

5 Literary Focus Which of these characters are more likely to be static characters and which are more likely to be dynamic characters as the play progresses?

find theyre all as different as A from B. [MRS PEARCE *looks in; she is* HIGGINS's *housekeeper*]. Whats the matter?

MRS PEARCE [*hesitating, evidently perplexed*] A young woman asks to see you, sir.

HIGGINS. A young woman! What does she want?

MRS PEARCE. Well, sir, she says youll be glad to see her when you know what she's come about. She's quite a common girl, sir. Very common indeed. I should have sent her away, only I thought perhaps you wanted her to talk into your machines. I hope Ive not done wrong; but really you see such queer people sometimes—youll excuse me, I'm sure, sir—

HIGGINS. Oh, thats all right, Mrs Pearce. Has she an interesting accent?

MRS PEARCE. Oh, something dreadful, sir, really. I dont know how you can take an interest in it.

HIGGINS [*to* PICKERING] Lets have her up. Shew her up, Mrs Pearce [*he rushes across to his working table and picks out a cylinder to use on the phonograph*].

MRS PEARCE [*only half resigned to it*] Very well, sir. It's for you to say. [*She goes downstairs*].

HIGGINS. This is rather a bit of luck. I'll shew you how I make records. We'll set her talking; and I'll take it down first in Bell's Visible Speech; then in broad Romic; and then we'll get her on the phonograph so that you can turn her on as often as you like with the written transcript before you.

MRS PEARCE [*returning*] This is the young woman, sir.

The FLOWER GIRL *enters in state. She has a hat with three ostrich feathers, orange, sky-blue, and red. She has a nearly clean apron, and the shoddy coat has been tidied a little. The pathos of this deplorable figure, with its innocent vanity and consequential*

air, touches PICKERING, *who has already straightened himself in the presence of* MRS PEARCE. *But as to* HIGGINS, *the only distinction he makes between men and women is that when he is neither bullying nor exclaiming to the heavens against some featherweight cross,[4] he coaxes women as a child coaxes its nurse when it wants to get anything out of her.*

HIGGINS [*brusquely, recognizing her with unconcealed disappointment, and at once, babylike, making an intolerable grievance of it*] Why, this is the girl I jotted down last night. She's no use: I've got all the records I want of the Lisson Grove lingo; and I'm not going to waste another cylinder on it. [*To the* GIRL] Be off with you: I dont want you.

THE FLOWER GIRL. Dont you be so saucy. You aint heard what I come for yet. [*To* MRS PEARCE, *who is waiting at the door for further instructions*] Did you tell him I come in a taxi?

MRS PEARCE. Nonsense, girl! What do you think a gentleman like Mr Higgins cares what you came in?

THE FLOWER GIRL. Oh, we are proud! He aint above giving lessons, not him: I heard him say so. Well, I aint come here to ask for any compliment; and if my money's not good enough I can go elsewhere.

HIGGINS. Good enough for what?

THE FLOWER GIRL. Good enough for yə-oo. Now you know, dont you? I've come to have lessons, I am. And to pay for em tə-oo: make no mistake.

HIGGINS [*stupent[5]*] Well!!! [*Recovering his breath with a gasp*] What do you expect me to say to you?

THE FLOWER GIRL. Well, if you was a gentleman, you might ask me to sit down, I think. Dont I tell you I'm bringing you business?

---

4. **feather-weight cross:** A very minor inconvenience.
5. **stupent:** Astonished.

Primary Source

The literary scholar Reuben A. Brower made the following comment about Shaw's ability to create character through dialogue:

> The basis of Shaw's comedy, as we might expect, is talk, but essentially *dramatic* talk, speech that exactly defines and projects character. The talk is not simply the conversation of the man George Bernard Shaw, transferred to the stage and headed by different names—a common criticism of Shaw's work, though certainly not applicable to his better plays. Like Shakespeare or any dramatist of the first rank, he possessed a fine talent for writing dialogue of character, a talent that puzzled late nineteenth-century actors who had grown accustomed to half-written plays and who took it for granted that they must 'build up' a part by introducing their own variations of speech and manner. (Oddly enough, they thought that Shakespeare too needed a good deal of 'filling out' of the same sort.) Beerbohm Tree [a prominent British actor-theater manager (1853–1917)]

HIGGINS. Pickering: shall we ask this baggage to sit down, or shall we throw her out of the window?

THE FLOWER GIRL [*running away in terror to the piano, where she turns at bay*] Ah-ah-oh-ow-ow-ow-oo! [*Wounded and whimpering*] I wont be called a baggage when Ive offered to pay like any lady.

Motionless, the two men stare at her from the other side of the room, amazed.

PICKERING [*gently*] But what is it you want?

THE FLOWER GIRL. I want to be a lady in a flower shop stead of sellin at the corner of Tottenham Court Road. But they wont take me unless I can talk more genteel. He said he could teach me. Well, here I am ready to pay him—not asking any favor—and he treats me zif I was dirt.

MRS PEARCE. How can you be such a foolish ignorant girl as to think you could afford to pay Mr Higgins?

THE FLOWER GIRL. Why shouldnt I? I know what lessons cost as well as you do; and I'm ready to pay.

HIGGINS. How much?

THE FLOWER GIRL [*coming back to him, triumphant*] Now youre talking! I thought youd come off it when you saw a chance of getting back a bit of what you chucked at me last night. [*Confidentially*] Youd had a drop in,[6] hadn't you?

HIGGINS [*peremptorily*] Sit down.

THE FLOWER GIRL. Oh, if youre going to make a compliment of it—

HIGGINS [*thundering at her*] Sit down.

MRS PEARCE [*severely*] Sit down, girl. Do as youre told.

THE FLOWER GIRL. Ah-ah-ah-ow-ow-oo! [*She stands, half rebellious, half bewildered*].

———
6. had a drop in: Been drinking.

PICKERING [*very courteous*] Wont you sit down? [*He places the stray chair near the hearthrug between himself and* HIGGINS].

LIZA [*coyly*] Dont mind if I do. [*She sits down.* PICKERING *returns to the hearthrug*].

HIGGINS. Whats your name?

THE FLOWER GIRL. Liza Doolittle.

HIGGINS [*declaiming gravely*]
Eliza, Elizabeth, Betsy and Bess,
They went to the woods to get a bird's nes':

PICKERING. They found a nest with four eggs in it:

HIGGINS. They took one apiece, and left three in it.
They laugh heartily at their own fun.
LIZA. Oh, dont be silly.

MRS PEARCE [*placing herself behind* ELIZA's *chair*] You mustnt speak to the gentleman like that.

LIZA. Well, why wont he speak sensible to me?

HIGGINS. Come back to business. How much do you propose to pay me for the lessons?

LIZA. Oh, I know whats right. A lady friend of mine gets French lessons for eighteenpence an hour from a real French gentleman. Well, you wouldnt have the face to ask me the same for teaching me my own language as you would for French; so I wont give more than a shilling. Take it or leave it.

HIGGINS [*walking up and down the room, rattling his keys and his cash in his pockets*] You know, Pickering, if you consider a shilling, not as a simple shilling, but as a percentage of this girl's income, it works out as fully equivalent to sixty or seventy guineas from a millionaire.

PICKERING. How so?

HIGGINS. Figure it out. A millionaire has about £150 a day. She earns about half-a-crown.

Pygmalion, Act II 1123

6 Critical Thinking and Reading
What inferences can be made about the relative status and class of these three characters?

7 Reading Strategy What is the meaning of this riddle?

found to his surprise that "Shaw, with his platform technique, could build up speeches by tricks that were beyond the compass of his [Tree's] voice."

1123

LIZA [*haughtily*] Who told you I only—

HIGGINS [*continuing*] She offers me two-fifths of her day's income for a lesson. Two-fifths of a millionaire's income for a day would be somewhere about £60. It's handsome. By George, it's enormous! it's the biggest offer I ever had.

LIZA [*rising, terrified*] Sixty pounds! What are you talking? I never offered you sixty pounds. Where would I get—

HIGGINS. Hold your tongue.

LIZA [*weeping*] But I aint got sixty pounds. Oh—

MRS PEARCE. Dont cry, you silly girl. Sit down. Nobody is going to touch your money.

HIGGINS. Somebody is going to touch you, with a broomstick, if you dont stop snivelling. Sit down.

LIZA [*obeying slowly*] Ah-ah-ah-ow-oo-o! One would think you was my father.

HIGGINS. If I decide to teach you, I'll be worse than two fathers to you. Here [*he offers her his silk handkerchief*]!

LIZA. Whats this for?

HIGGINS. To wipe your eyes. To wipe any part of your face that feels moist. Remember: thats your handkerchief; and thats your sleeve. Dont mistake the one for the other if you wish to become a lady in a shop. LIZA, *utterly bewildered, stares helplessly at him.*

MRS PEARCE. It's no use talking to her like that, Mr Higgins: she doesnt understand you. Besides, youre quite wrong: she doesnt do it that way at all [*she takes the handkerchief*].

LIZA [*snatching it*] Here! You give me that handkerchief. He gev it to me, not to you.

PICKERING [*laughing*] He did. I think it must be regarded as her property, Mrs Pearce.

MRS PEARCE [*resigning herself*] Serve you right, Mr Higgins.

PICKERING. Higgins: I'm interested. What about the ambassador's garden party? I'll say youre the greatest teacher alive if you make that good. I'll bet you all the expenses of the experiment you cant do it. And I'll pay for the lessons.

LIZA. Oh, you are real good. Thank you, Captain.

HIGGINS [*tempted, looking at her*] It's almost irresistible. She's so deliciously low—so horribly dirty—

LIZA [*protesting extremely*] Ah-ah-ah-ah-ow-ow-oo-oo!!! I aint dirty: I washed my face and hands afore I come, I did.

PICKERING. Youre certainly not going to turn her head with flattery, Higgins.

MRS PEARCE [*uneasy*] Oh, dont say that, sir: theres more ways than one of turning a girl's head; and nobody can do it better than Mr Higgins, though he may not always mean it. I do hope, sir, you wont encourage him to do anything foolish.

HIGGINS [*becoming excited as the idea grows on him*] What is life but a series of inspired follies? The difficulty is to find them to do. Never lose a chance: it doesnt come every day. I shall make a duchess of this draggle-tailed guttersnipe.

LIZA [*strongly deprecating this view of her*] Ah-ah-ah-ow-ow-oo!

HIGGINS [*carried away*] Yes: in six months —in three if she has a good ear and a quick tongue—I'll take her anywhere and pass her off as anything. We'll start today: now! this moment! Take her away and clean her, Mrs Pearce. Monkey Brand,[7] if it wont come off any other way. Is there a good fire in the kitchen?

MRS PEARCE [*protesting*] Yes; but—

HIGGINS [*storming on*] Take all her clothes off and burn them. Ring up Whitely or some-

---

7. Monkey Brand: A strong cleaning agent.

body for new ones. Wrap her up in brown paper til they come.

LIZA. Youre no gentleman, youre not, to talk of such things. I'm a good girl, I am; and I know what the like of you are, I do.

HIGGINS. We want none of your Lisson Grove prudery here, young woman. Youve got to learn to behave like a duchess. Take her away, Mrs Pearce. If she gives you any trouble, wallop her.

LIZA [*springing up and running between* PICKERING *and* MRS PEARCE *for protection*] No! I'll call the police, I will.

MRS PEARCE. But Ive no place to put her.

HIGGINS. Put her in the dustbin.

LIZA. Ah-ah-ah-ow-ow-oo!

PICKERING. O come, Higgins! be reasonable.

MRS PEARCE [*resolutely*] You must be reasonable, Mr Higgins: really you must. You cant walk over everybody like this.

HIGGINS, *thus scolded, subsides. The hurricane is succeeded by a zephyr of amiable surprise.*

HIGGINS [*with professional exquisiteness of modulation*] I walk over everybody! My dear Mrs Pearce, my dear Pickering, I never had the slightest intention of walking over anyone. All I propose is that we should be kind to this poor girl. We must help her to prepare and fit herself for her new station in life. If I did not express myself clearly it was because I did not wish to hurt her delicacy, or yours.

LIZA, *reassured, steals back to her chair.*

MRS PEARCE [*to* PICKERING] Well, did you ever hear anything like that, sir?

PICKERING [*laughing heartily*] Never, Mrs Pearce: never.

HIGGINS [*patiently*] Whats the matter?

MRS PEARCE. Well, the matter is, sir, that you cant take a girl up like that as if you were picking up a pebble on the beach.

HIGGINS. Why not?

MRS PEARCE. Why not! But you dont know anything about her. What about her parents? She may be married.

LIZA. Garn!

HIGGINS. There! As the girl very properly says, Garn! Married indeed! Dont you know that a woman of that class looks a worn out drudge of fifty a year after she's married?

LIZA. Whood marry me?

HIGGINS [*suddenly resorting to the most thrillingly beautiful low tones in his best elocutionary style*] By George, Eliza, the streets will be strewn with the bodies of men shooting themselves for your sake before Ive donc with you.

MRS PEARCE. Nonsense, sir. You mustnt talk like that to her.

LIZA [*rising and squaring herself determinedly*] I'm going away. He's off his chump, he is. I dont want no balmies teaching me.

HIGGINS [*wounded in his tenderest point by her insensibility to his elocution*] Oh, indeed! I'm mad, am I? Very well, Mrs Pearce: you neednt order the new clothes for her. Throw her out.

LIZA [*whimpering*] Nah-ow. You got no right to touch me.

MRS PEARCE. You see now what comes of being saucy. [*Indicating the door*] This way, please.

LIZA [*almost in tears*] I didnt want no clothes. I wouldnt have taken them [*she throws away the handkerchief*]. I can buy my own clothes.

HIGGINS [*deftly retrieving the handkerchief and intercepting her on her reluctant way to the door*] Youre an ungrateful wicked girl. This is my return for offering to take you out of the gutter and dress you beautifully and make a lady of you.

Pygmalion, Act II 1125

13 Reading Strategy Discuss the irony in walloping a woman to turn her into a duchess.

14 Clarification A dustbin is the equivalent of a garbage can or trash barrel in the United States.

15 Critical Thinking and Reading What can you infer about Higgins and his own understanding of himself from this passage?

16 Discussion What do we learn about Eliza from this remark?

17 Discussion What admirable qualities has Eliza demonstrated thus far?

18 Discussion Why won't Higgins admit that Eliza has feelings? Do you think that he really does not perceive her as a human being?

19 Discussion Has Eliza made an accurate assessment of Higgins's character?

MRS PEARCE. Stop, Mr Higgins. I wont allow it. It's you that are wicked. Go home to your parents, girl; and tell them to take better care of you.

LIZA. I aint got no parents. They told me I was big enough to earn my own living and turned me out.

MRS PEARCE. Wheres your mother?

LIZA. I aint got no mother. Her that turned me out was my sixth stepmother. But I done without them. And I'm a good girl, I am.

HIGGINS. Very well, then, what on earth is all this fuss about? The girl doesnt belong to anybody—is no use to anybody but me. [*He goes to* MRS PEARCE *and begins coaxing*]. You can adopt her, Mrs Pearce: I'm sure a daughter would be a great amusement to you. Now don't make any more fuss. Take her downstairs; and—

MRS PEARCE. But whats to become of her? Is she to be paid anything? Do be sensible, sir.

HIGGINS. Oh, pay her whatever is necessary: put it down in the housekeeping book. [*Impatiently*] What on earth will she want with money? She'll have her food and her clothes. She'll only drink if you give her money.

LIZA [*turning on him*] Oh you are a brute. It's a lie: nobody ever saw the sign of liquor on me. [*To* PICKERING] Oh, sir: youre a gentleman: dont let him speak to me like that.

PICKERING [*in good-humored remonstrance*] Does it occur to you, Higgins, that the girl has some feelings?

HIGGINS [*looking critically at her*] Oh no, I dont think so. Not any feelings that we need bother about. [*Cheerily*] Have you, Eliza?

LIZA. I got my feelings same as anyone else.

HIGGINS [*to* PICKERING, *reflectively*] You see the difficulty?

PICKERING. Eh? What difficulty?

HIGGINS. To get her to talk grammar. The mere pronunciation is easy enough.

LIZA. I dont want to talk grammar. I want to talk like a lady in a flower-shop.

MRS PEARCE. Will you please keep to the point, Mr Higgins. I want to know on what terms the girl is to be here. Is she to have any wages? And what is to become of her when youve finished your teaching? You must look ahead a little.

HIGGINS [*impatiently*] Whats to become of her if I leave her in the gutter? Tell me that, Mrs Pearce.

MRS PEARCE. Thats her own business, not yours, Mr Higgins.

HIGGINS. Well, when Ive done with her, we can throw her back into the gutter; and then it will be her own business again; so thats all right.

LIZA. Oh, youve no feeling heart in you: you dont care for nothing but yourself. [*She rises and takes the floor resolutely*]. Here! Ive had enough of this. I'm going [*making for the door*]. You ought to be ashamed of yourself, you ought.

HIGGINS [*snatching a chocolate cream from the piano, his eyes suddenly beginning to twinkle with mischief*] Have some chocolates, Eliza.

LIZA [*halting, tempted*] How do I know what might be in them? Ive heard of girls being drugged by the like of you.

HIGGINS *whips out his penknife; cuts a chocolate in two; puts one half into his mouth and bolts it; and offers her the other half.*

HIGGINS. Pledge of good faith, Eliza. I eat one half: you eat the other. [LIZA *opens her mouth to retort: he pops the half chocolate into it*]. You shall have boxes of them, barrels of them, every day. You shall live on them. Eh?

LIZA [*who has disposed of the chocolate after being nearly choked by it*] I wouldnt have ate it, only I'm too ladylike to take it out of my mouth.

HIGGINS. Listen, Eliza. I think you said you came in a taxi.

LIZA. Well, what if I did? Ive as good a right to take a taxi as anyone else.

HIGGINS. You have, Eliza; and in future you shall have as many taxis as you want. You shall go up and down and round the town in a taxi every day. Think of that, Eliza.

20 **MRS PEARCE.** Mr Higgins: youre tempting the girl. It's not right. She should think of the future.

HIGGINS. At her age! Nonsense! Time enough to think of the future when you havnt any future to think of. No, Eliza: do as this lady does: think of other people's futures; but never think of your own. Think of chocolates, and taxis, and gold, and diamonds.

LIZA. No: I dont want no gold and no diamonds. I'm a good girl, I am. [*She sits down again, with an attempt at dignity*].

21

HIGGINS. You shall remain so, Eliza, under the care of Mrs Pearce. And you shall marry an officer in the Guards, with a beautiful moustache: the son of a marquis, who will disinherit him for marrying you, but will relent when he sees your beauty and goodness—

PICKERING. Excuse me, Higgins; but I really must interfere. Mrs Pearce is quite right. If this girl is to put herself in your hands for six months for an experiment in teaching, she must understand thoroughly what she's doing.

HIGGINS. How can she? She's incapable of understanding anything. Besides, do any of

20 Discussion On whose side is Mrs. Pearce and why?

21 Discussion What does Eliza mean when she repeats, ''I'm a good girl, I am''?

us understand what we are doing? If we did, would we ever do it?

PICKERING. Very clever, Higgins; but not to the present point. [*To* ELIZA] Miss Doolittle—

LIZA [*overwhelmed*] Ah-ah-ow-oo!

HIGGINS. There! Thats all youll get out of Eliza. Ah-ah-ow-oo! No use explaining. As a military man you ought to know that. Give her her orders: thats enough for her. Eliza: you are to live here for the next six months, learning how to speak beautifully, like a lady in a florist's shop. If youre good and do whatever youre told, you shall sleep in a proper bedroom, and have lots to eat, and money to buy chocolates and take rides in taxis. If youre naughty and idle you will sleep in the back kitchen among the black beetles, and be walloped by Mrs Pearce with a broomstick. At the end of six months you shall go to Buckingham Palace in a carriage, beautifully dressed. If the King finds out youre not a lady, you will be taken by the police to the Tower of London, where your head will be cut off as a warning to other presumptuous flower girls. If you are not found out, you shall have a present of seven-and-sixpence to start life with as a lady in a shop. If you refuse this offer you will be a most ungrateful wicked girl; and the angels will weep for you. [*To* PICKERING] Now are you satisfied, Pickering? [*To* MRS PEARCE] Can I put it more plainly and fairly, Mrs Pearce?

MRS PEARCE [*patiently*] I think youd better let me speak to the girl properly in private. I dont know that I can take charge of her or consent to the arrangement at all. Of course I know you dont mean her any harm; but when you get what you call interested in people's accents, you never think or care what may happen to them or you. Come with me, Eliza.

HIGGINS. Thats all right. Thank you, Mrs Pearce. Bundle her off to the bath-room.

LIZA [*rising reluctantly and suspiciously*] Youre a great bully, you are. I wont stay here

if I dont like. I wont let nobody wallop me. I never asked to go to Bucknam Palace, I didnt. I was never in trouble with the police, not me. I'm a good girl—

MRS PEARCE. Dont answer back, girl. You dont understand the gentleman. Come with me. [*She leads the way to the door, and holds it open for* ELIZA].

LIZA [*as she goes out*] Well, what I say is right. I wont go near the King, not if I'm going to have my head cut off. If I'd known what I was letting myself in for, I wouldnt have come here. I always been a good girl; and I never offered to say a word to him; and I dont owe him nothing; and I dont care; and I wont be put upon; and I have my feelings the same as anyone else—

MRS PEARCE *shuts the door; and* ELIZA*'s plaints are no longer audible.*

*   *   *   *   *   *

Eliza is taken upstairs to the third floor greatly to her surprise; for she expected to be taken down to the scullery.[8] There Mrs Pearce opens a door and takes her into a spare bedroom.

MRS PEARCE. I will have to put you here. This will be your bedroom.

LIZA. O-h, I couldn't sleep here, missus. It's too good for the likes of me. I should be afraid to touch anything. I aint a duchess yet, you know.

MRS PEARCE. You have got to make yourself as clean as the room: then you wont be afraid of it. And you must call me Mrs Pearce, not missus. [*She throws open the door of the dressingroom, now modernized as a bathroom*].

LIZA. Gawd! whats this? Is this where you wash clothes? Funny sort of copper[9] I call it.

---

8. scullery *n.*: A room adjoining the kitchen, where pots and pans are cleaned and stored.
9. copper *n.*: A large metal container or boiler used for washing clothes.

Grammar in Action

A nonstandard **dialect** is a form of English that makes use of words, pronunciations, and sentence structures not used in standard English. In *Pygmalion* Eliza Doolittle speaks the cockney dialect associated with natives of the East End of London. Cockney is characterized by a loss of the letter *h* at the start of words and an extensive use of complex vowel sounds called diphthongs (a diphthong is said to be complex because it

combines two different vowel sounds: the diphthong in *down,* for example, combines the sounds of *o* and *u*).

Shaw uses a technique employed by many writers who introduce dialect into their work: He exaggerates the dialect at first to call the audience's attention to it, and then he allows it to sound more like standard speech. Compare, for instance, these two examples of Eliza's speech from Act I and Act II:

"Ow, eez y -ooa, san, is e? Wal, fewd dan y' d -ooty bawmz a mather should, eed now bettern to spawl a pore gel's flahrzn than ran awy athaht pyin." (Act I)

"I always been a good girl; and I never offered to say a word to him; and I dont owe him nothing. . . ." (Act II)

MRS PEARCE. It is not a copper. This is where we wash ourselves, Eliza, and where I am going to wash you.

LIZA. You expect me to get into that and wet myself all over! Not me. I should catch my death. I knew a woman did it every Saturday night; and she died of it.

MRS PEARCE. Mr Higgins has the gentlemen's bathroom downstairs; and he has a bath every morning, in cold water.

LIZA. Ugh! He's made of iron, that man.

MRS PEARCE. If you are to sit with him and the Colonel and be taught you will have to do the same. They wont like the smell of you if you don't. But you can have the water as hot as you like. There are two taps: hot and cold.

LIZA [*weeping*] I couldnt. I dursnt. Its not natural: it would kill me. I've never had a bath in my life: not what youd call a proper one.

MRS PEARCE. Well, dont you want to be clean and sweet and decent, like a lady? You know you cant be a nice girl inside if youre a dirty slut outside.

LIZA. Boohoo!!!!

MRS PEARCE. Now stop crying and go back into your room and take off all your clothes. Then wrap yourself in this [*Taking down a gown from its peg and handing it to her*] and come back to me. I will get the bath ready.

LIZA [*all tears*] I cant. I wont. I'm not used to it. Ive never took off all my clothes before. It's not right: it's not decent.

MRS PEARCE. Nonsense, child. Dont you take off all your clothes every night when you go to bed?

LIZA [*amazed*] No. Why should I? I should catch my death. Of course I take off my skirt.

MRS PEARCE. Do you mean that you sleep in the underclothes you wear in the daytime?

LIZA. What else have I to sleep in?

MRS PEARCE. You will never do that again as long as you live here. I will get you a proper nightdress.

LIZA. Do you mean change into cold things and lie awake shivering half the night? You want to kill me, you do.

MRS PEARCE. I want to change you from a frowzy slut to a clean respectable girl fit to sit with the gentlemen in the study. Are you going to trust me and do what I tell you or be thrown out and sent back to your flower basket?

LIZA. But you dont know what the cold is to me. You dont know how I dread it.

MRS PEARCE. Your bed won't be cold here: I will put a hot water bottle in it. [*Pushing her into the bedroom*] Off with you and undress.

LIZA. Oh, if only I'd known what a dreadful thing it is to be clean I'd never have come. I didnt know when I was well off. I—[MRS PEARCE *pushes her through the door, but leaves it partly open lest her prisoner should take to flight*].

MRS PEARCE *puts on a pair of white rubber sleeves, and fills the bath, mixing hot and cold, and testing the result with the bath thermometer. She perfumes it with a handful of bath salts and adds a palmful of mustard. She then takes a formidable looking long handled scrubbing brush and soaps it profusely with a ball of scented soap.*

ELIZA *comes back with nothing on but the bath gown huddled tightly round her, a piteous spectacle of abject terror.*

MRS PEARCE. Now come along. Take that thing off.

LIZA. Oh I couldnt, Mrs Pearce: I reely couldnt. I never done such a thing.

MRS PEARCE. Nonsense. Here: step in and tell me whether its hot enough for you.

LIZA. Ah-oo! Ah-oo! It's too hot.

Pygmalion, Act II 1129

23 Discussion Why would this statement be valid to Eliza?

24 Discussion What surprising information does Eliza reveal about herself as she prepares for her bath? What does this information reveal about the living conditions of the people whom she represents?

Notice that in the first speech, Eliza drops the *h* in front of *he* (*eez* is her way of saying, "he is") and complicates the vowel sounds in words like *your* (y-ooa) and *duty* (d-ooty). Her second speech sounds more like standard English (and this is before Higgins has given her any lessons!). She begins *him* with an *h*, although she omits the helping verb *have* in her first sentence.

Student Activity Give an example of a dialect with which you are familiar. How does it differ from standard English?

25 Discussion Why does Higgins say he is a confirmed bachelor? What reason or reasons would you infer from his behavior?

MRS PEARCE [*deftly snatching the gown away and throwing* ELIZA *down on her back*]. It wont hurt you. [*She sets to work with the scrubbing brush*].

ELIZA*'s screams are heartrending.*

*   *   *   *   *   *

Meanwhile the Colonel has been having it out with Higgins about Eliza. Pickering has come from the hearth to the chair and seated himself astride of it with his arms on the back to cross-examine him.

PICKERING. Excuse the straight question, Higgins. Are you a man of good character where women are concerned?

HIGGINS [*moodily*] Have you ever met a man of good character where women are concerned?

PICKERING. Yes: very frequently.

HIGGINS [*dogmatically, lifting himself on his hands to the level of the piano, and sitting on it with a bounce*] Well, I havnt. I find that the moment I let a woman make friends with me, she becomes jealous, exacting, suspicious, and a damned nuisance. I find that the moment I let myself make friends with a woman, I become selfish and tyrannical. Women upset everything. When you let them into your life, you find that the woman is driving at one thing and youre driving at another.

PICKERING. At what, for example?

HIGGINS [*coming off the piano restlessly*] Oh, Lord knows! I suppose the woman wants to live her own life; and the man wants to live his; and each tries to drag the other on to the wrong track. One wants to go north and the other south; and the result is that both have to go east, though they both hate the east wind. [*He sits down on the bench at the keyboard*]. So here I am, a confirmed old bachelor, and likely to remain so.

PICKERING [*rising and standing over him gravely*] Come, Higgins! You know what I mean. If I'm to be in this business I shall feel responsible for that girl. I hope it's understood that no advantage is to be taken of her position.

HIGGINS. What! That thing! Sacred, I assure you. [*Rising to explain*] You see, she'll be a pupil; and teaching would be impossible unless pupils were sacred. Ive taught scores of American millionairesses how to speak English: the best looking women in the world. I'm seasoned. They might as well be blocks of wood. *I* might as well be a block of wood. It's—

MRS PEARCE *opens the door. She has* ELIZA*'s hat in her hand.* PICKERING *retires to the easy-chair at the hearth and sits down.*

HIGGINS [*eagerly*] Well, Mrs Pearce is it all right?

MRS PEARCE [*at the door*] I just wish to trouble you with a word, if I may, Mr. Higgins.

HIGGINS. Yes, certainly. Come in. [*She comes forward*]. Dont burn that, Mrs Pearce. I'll keep it as a curiosity. [*He takes the hat*].

MRS PEARCE. Handle it carefully, sir, please. I had to promise her not to burn it; but I had better put it in the oven for a while.

HIGGINS [*putting it down hastily on the piano*] Oh! thank you. Well, what have you to say to me?

PICKERING. Am I in the way?

MRS PEARCE. Not in the least, sir. Mr Higgins: will you please be very particular what you say before the girl?

HIGGINS [*sternly*] Of course. I'm always particular about what I say. Why do you say this to me?

MRS PEARCE [*unmoved*] No, sir: youre not at all particular when youve mislaid anything or when you get a little impatient. Now it doesnt matter before me: I'm used to it. But you really must not swear before the girl.

HIGGINS [*indignantly*] I swear! [*Most emphatically*] I never swear. I detest the habit. What the devil do you mean?

MRS PEARCE [*stolidly*] Thats what I mean, sir. You swear a great deal too much. I dont mind your damning and blasting, and what the devil and where the devil and who the devil—

HIGGINS. Mrs Pearce: this language from your lips! Really!

MRS PEARCE [*not to be put off*]—but there is a certain word I must ask you not to use. The girl used it herself when she began to enjoy the bath. It begins with the same letter as bath. She knows no better: she learnt it at her mother's knee. But she must not hear it from your lips.

HIGGINS [*loftily*] I cannot charge myself with having ever uttered it, Mrs Pearce. [*She looks at him steadfastly. He adds, hiding an uneasy conscience with a judicial air*] Except perhaps in a moment of extreme and justifiable excitement.

26 **MRS PEARCE.** Only this morning, sir, you applied it to your boots, to the butter, and to the brown bread.

27 **HIGGINS.** Oh, that! Mere alliteration, Mrs Pearce, natural to a poet.

MRS PEARCE. Well, sir, whatever you choose to call it, I beg you not to let the girl hear you repeat it.

HIGGINS. Oh, very well, very well. Is that all?

MRS PEARCE. No, sir. We shall have to be very particular with this girl as to personal cleanliness.

HIGGINS. Certainly. Quite right. Most important.

MRS PEARCE. I mean not to be slovenly about her dress or untidy in leaving things about.

HIGGINS [*going to her solemnly*] Just so. I intended to call your attention to that. [*He passes on to* PICKERING, *who is enjoying the conversation immensely*]. It is these little things that matter, Pickering. Take care of the pence and the pounds will take care of themselves is as true of personal habits as of money. [*He comes to anchor on the hearthrug, with the air of a man in an unassailable position*].

28 **MRS PEARCE.** Yes, sir. Then might I ask you not to come down to breakfast in your dressing-gown, or at any rate not to use it as a napkin to the extent you do, sir. And if you would be so good as not to eat everything off the same plate, and to remember not to put the porridge saucepan out of your hand on the clean tablecloth, it would be a better example to the girl. You know you nearly choked yourself with a fishbone in a jam only last week.

29 **HIGGINS** [*routed from the hearthrug and drifting back to the piano*] I may do these things sometimes in absence of mind; but surely I dont do them habitually. [*Angrily*] By the way: my dressing-gown smells most damnably of benzine.

MRS PEARCE. No doubt it does, Mr Higgins. But if you will wipe your fingers—

30 **HIGGINS** [*yelling*] Oh very well, very well: I'll wipe them in my hair in future.

MRS PEARCE. I hope youre not offended, Mr Higgins.

HIGGINS [*shocked at finding himself thought capable of an unamiable sentiment*] Not at all, not at all. Youre quite right, Mrs Pearce: I shall be particularly careful before the girl. Is that all?

MRS PEARCE. No, sir. Might she use some of those Japanese dresses you brought from abroad? I really cant put her back into her old things.

HIGGINS. Certainly. Anything you like. Is that all?

MRS PEARCE. Thank you, sir. Thats all. [*She goes out*].

31 **HIGGINS.** You know, Pickering, that woman has the most extraordinary ideas about me. Here I am, a shy, diffident sort of man. I've never been able to feel really grown-up and

---

26 Reading Strategy What message does Mrs. Pearce wish to convey by using irony?

27 Discussion What is Higgins's rationalization for swearing when he finally admits that he does swear?

28 Critical Thinking and Reading What can you infer in this passage about how Mrs. Pearce feels about Higgins and about how he feels about her?

29 Clarification Benzine is a coal-tar based liquid that is used as a solvent and, in this case, as a cleaning fluid.

30 Discussion Is this practice in character for Higgins? If so, why? If not, why not?

31 Discussion Do you think Higgins believes what he is saying? Why or why not?

32 Discussion How does the saying "The best defense is a good offense" apply here?

33 Discussion How does Higgins catch Mr. Doolittle off guard?

tremendous, like other chaps. And yet she's firmly persuaded that I'm an arbitrary overbearing bossing kind of person. I cant account for it.

MRS PEARCE *returns.*

MRS PEARCE. If you please, sir, the trouble's beginning already. Theres a dustman[10] downstairs, Alfred Doolittle, wants to see you. He says you have his daughter here.

PICKERING [*rising*] Phew! I say!

HIGGINS [*promptly*] Send the blackguard[11] up.

MRS PEARCE. Oh, very well, sir. [*She goes out*].

PICKERING. He may not be a blackguard, Higgins.

HIGGINS. Nonsense. Of course he's a blackguard.

PICKERING. Whether he is or not, I'm afraid we shall have some trouble with him.

HIGGINS [*confidently*] Oh no: I think not. If theres any trouble he shall have it with me, not I with him. And we are sure to get something interesting out of him.

PICKERING. About the girl?

HIGGINS. No. I mean his dialect.

PICKERING. Oh!

MRS PEARCE [*at the door*] Doolittle, sir. [*She admits* DOOLITTLE *and retires*].

ALFRED *is an elderly but vigorous dustman, clad in the costume of his profession, including a hat with a back brim covering his neck and shoulders. He has well marked and rather interesting features, and seems equally free from fear and conscience. He has a remarkably expressive voice, the result of a habit of giving vent to his feelings without reserve. His present pose is that of wounded honor and stern resolution.*

---

10. dustman *n.*: A garbage collector.
11. blackguard (blag' ərd) *n.*: Scoundrel.

DOOLITTLE [*at the door, uncertain which of the two gentlemen is his man*] Professor Iggins?

HIGGINS. Here. Good morning. Sit down.

DOOLITTLE. Morning, Governor. [*He sits down magisterially*]. I come about a very serious matter, Governor.

HIGGINS [*to* PICKERING] Brought up in Hounslow. Mother Welsh, I should think. [DOOLITTLE *opens his mouth, amazed.* HIGGINS *continues*] What do you want, Doolittle?

DOOLITTLE [*menacingly*] I want my daughter: thats what I want. See?

HIGGINS. Of course you do. Youre her father, arnt you? You dont suppose anyone else wants her, do you? I'm glad to see you have some spark of family feeling left. She's upstairs. Take her away at once.

DOOLITTLE [*rising, fearfully taken aback*] What!

HIGGINS. Take her away. Do you suppose I'm going to keep your daughter for you?

DOOLITTLE [*remonstrating*] Now, now, look here, Governor. Is it reasonable? Is it fairity to take advantage of a man like this? The girl belongs to me. You got her. Where do I come in? [*He sits down again*].

HIGGINS. Your daughter had the audacity to come to my house and ask me to teach her how to speak properly so that she could get a place in a flower-shop. This gentleman and my housekeeper have been here all the time. [*Bullying him*] How dare you come here and attempt to blackmail me? You sent her here on purpose.

DOOLITTLE [*protesting*] No, Governor.

HIGGINS. You must have. How else could you possibly know that she is here?

DOOLITTLE. Don't take a man up like that, Governor.

HIGGINS. The police shall take you up. This is a plant—a plot to extort money by threats. I

Primary Source

The literary scholar Maurice Valency made the following comment on Shaw's belief in the importance of correct speech:

> In *Pygmalion* there is nothing to suggest that Higgins is a socialist, and he has apparently no idea of leveling the classes under a common phonetic system. But the implication is that what could be done with Eliza Doolittle can be done, more or less successfully, with anyone who shows the necessary aptitude. Shaw himself had learned upper-class English ways in somewhat the same manner as Eliza, and he evidently liked the idea that in order to transform a clever garbageman into a prime minister all that is necessary is a course in speech. Such ideas were certainly current in the early decades of this century, and the vast proliferation of speech courses in those years attests to the influence of the theory.

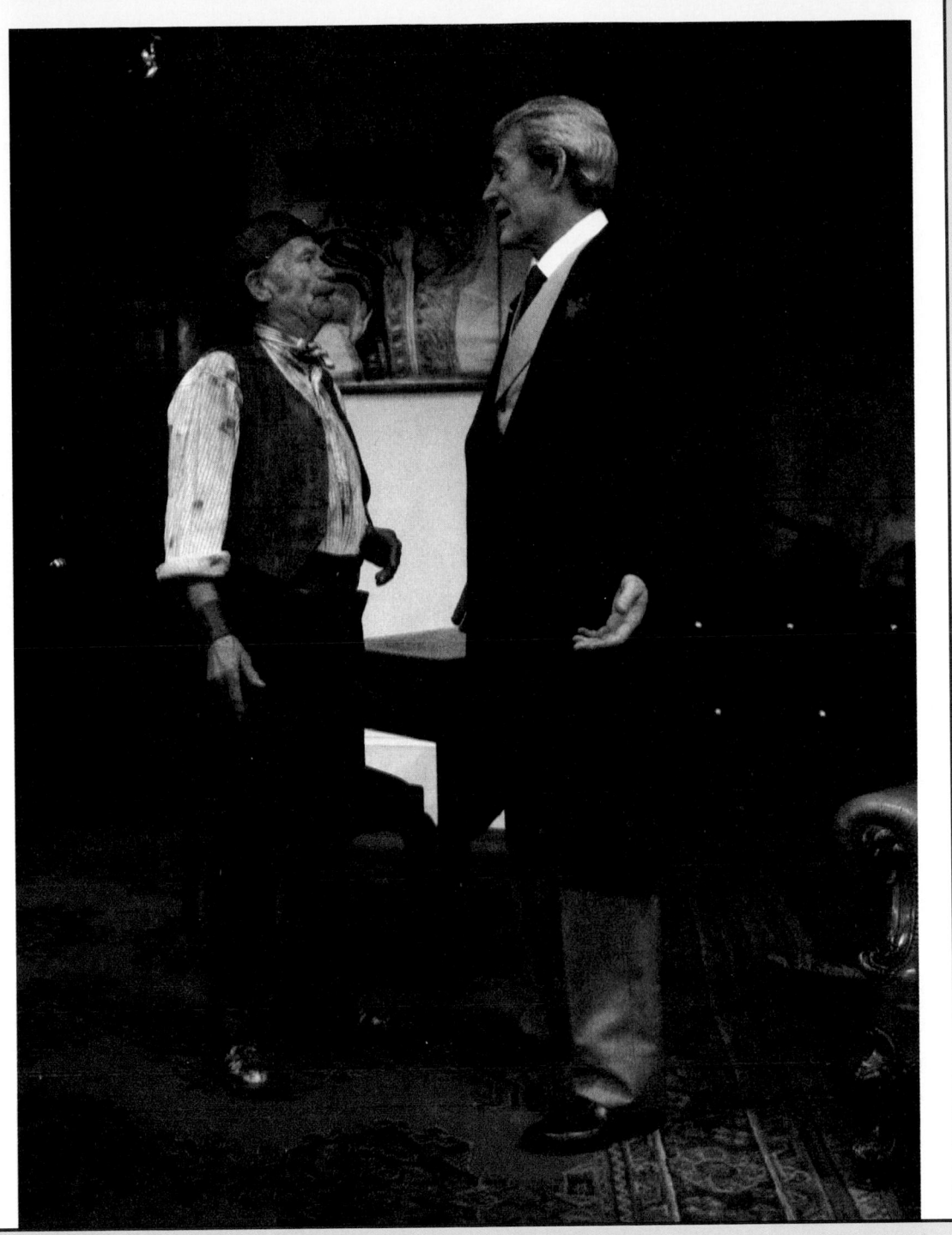

shall telephone for the police [*he goes resolutely to the telephone and opens the directory*]

DOOLITTLE. Have I asked you for a brass farthing? I leave it to the gentleman here: have I said a word about money?

HIGGINS [*throwing the book aside and marching down on* DOOLITTLE *with a poser*] What else did you come for?

DOOLITTLE [*sweetly*] Well, what would a man come for? Be human, Governor.

HIGGINS [*disarmed*] Alfred: did you put her up to it?

DOOLITTLE. So help me, Governor. I never did. I take my Bible oath I aint seen the girl these two months past.

HIGGINS. Then how did you know she was here?

DOOLITTLE [*"most musical, most melancholy"*] I'll tell you, Governor, if youll only let me get a word in. I'm willing to tell you. I'm wanting to tell you. I'm waiting to tell you.

HIGGINS. Pickering: this chap has a certain natural gift of rhetoric. Observe the rhythm of his native woodnotes wild. "I'm willing to tell you: I'm wanting to tell you: I'm waiting to tell you." Sentimental rhetoric! thats the Welsh strain in him. It also accounts for his mendacity and dishonesty.

PICKERING. Oh, please, Higgins: I'm west country myself. [*To* DOOLITTLE] How did you know the girl was here if you didnt send her?

DOOLITTLE. It was like this, Governor. The girl took a boy in the taxi to give him a jaunt. Son of her landlady, he is. He hung about on the chance of her giving him another ride home. Well, she sent him back for her luggage when she heard you was willing for her to stop here. I met the boy at the corner of Long Acre and Endell Street.

HIGGINS. Public house. Yes?

DOOLITTLE. The poor man's club, Governor: why shouldnt I?

PICKERING. Do let him tell his story, Higgins.

DOOLITTLE. He told me what was up. And I ask you, what was my feelings and my duty as a father? I says to the boy, "You bring me the luggage," I says—

PICKERING. Why didnt you go for it yourself?

DOOLITTLE. Landlady wouldnt have trusted me with it, Governor. She's that kind of woman: you know. I had to give the boy a penny afore he trusted me with it, the little swine. I brought it to her just to oblige you like, and make myself agreeable. Thats all.

HIGGINS. How much luggage?

DOOLITTLE. Musical instrument, Governor. A few pictures, a trifle of jewelry, and a birdcage. She said she didn't want no clothes. What was I to think from that, Governor? I ask you as a parent what was I to think?

HIGGINS. So you came to rescue her from worse than death, eh?

DOOLITTLE [*appreciatively: relieved at being so well understood*] Just so, Governor. That's right.

PICKERING. But why did you bring her luggage if you intended to take her away?

DOOLITTLE. Have I said a word about taking her away? Have I now?

HIGGINS [*determinedly*] Youre going to take her away, double quick. [*He crosses to the hearth and rings the bell*].

DOOLITTLE [*rising*] No, Governor. Dont say that. I'm not the man to stand in my girl's light. Heres a career opening for her, as you might say; and—

MRS PEARCE *opens the door and awaits orders.*

HIGGINS. Mrs Pearce: this is Eliza's father. He has come to take her away. Give her to him. [*He goes back to the piano, with an air of* *washing his hands of the whole affair*].

DOOLITTLE. No. This is a misunderstanding. Listen here—

MRS PEARCE. He cant take her away. Mr Higgins: how can he? You told me to burn her clothes.

DOOLITTLE. Thats right. I cant carry the girl through the streets like a blooming monkey, can I? I put it to you.

HIGGINS. You have put it to me that you want your daughter. Take your daughter. If she has no clothes go out and buy her some.

DOOLITTLE [*desperate*] Wheres the clothes she come in? Did I burn them or did your missus here?

MRS PEARCE. I am the housekeeper, if you please. I have sent for some clothes for your girl. When they come you can take her away. You can wait in the kitchen. This way, please.

DOOLITTLE, *much troubled, accompanies her to the door; then hesitates; finally turns confidentially to* HIGGINS.

DOOLITTLE. Listen here, Governor. You and me is men of the world, aint we?

HIGGINS. Oh! Men of the world, are we? Youd better go, Mrs Pearce.

MRS PEARCE. I think so, indeed, sir. [*She goes, with dignity*].

PICKERING. The floor is yours, Mr Doolittle.

DOOLITTLE [*to* PICKERING] I thank you, Governor. [*To* HIGGINS, *who takes refuge on the piano bench, a little overwhelmed by the proximity of his visitor; for* DOOLITTLE *has a professional flavour of dust about him*]. Well, the truth is, I've taken a sort of fancy to you, Governor; and if you want the girl, I'm not so set on having her back home again but what I might be open to an arrangement. Regarded in the light of a young woman, she's a fine handsome girl. As a daughter she's not worth her keep; and so I tell you straight. All I ask is my rights as a father; and youre the last man alive to expect me to let her go for nothing; for I can see youre one of the straight sort, Governor. Well, whats a five-pound note to you? and whats Eliza to me? [*He turns to his chair and sits down judicially*].

PICKERING. I think you ought to know, Doolittle, that Mr Higgins's intentions are entirely honorable.

DOOLITTLE. Course they are, Governor. If I thought they wasnt, I'd ask fifty.

HIGGINS [*revolted*] Do you mean to say that you would sell your daughter for £50?

DOOLITTLE. Not in a general way I would; but to oblige a gentleman like you I'd do a good deal, I do assure you.

PICKERING. Have you no morals, man?

DOOLITTLE [*unabashed*] Cant afford them, Governor. Neither could you if you was as poor as me. Not that I mean any harm, you know. But if Liza is going to have a bit out of this, why not me too?

HIGGINS [*troubled*] I dont know what to do, Pickering. There can be no question that as a matter of morals it's a positive crime to give this chap a farthing. And yet I feel a sort of rough justice in his claim.

DOOLITTLE. Thats it, Governor. Thats all I say. A father's heart, as it were.

PICKERING. Well, I know the feeling; but really it seems hardly right—

DOOLITTLE. Dont say that, Governor. Dont look at it that way. What am I, Governors both? I ask you, what am I? I'm one of the undeserving poor: thats what I am. Think of what that means to a man. It means that he's up agen middle class morality all the time. If theres anything going, and I put in for a bit of it, it's always the same story: "Youre undeserving; so you cant have it." But my needs is as great as the most deserv-

---

35 **Discussion** What is Mr. Doolittle's real motivation for seeking his daughter?

36 **Critical Thinking and Reading** What can you infer about the lower class from this statement?

37 **Literary Focus** What is it about Mr. Doolittle that gives him the potential to be a dynamic character?

38 **Discussion** In your own words, what did ''middle class morality'' mean during the Victorian period?

39 **Discussion** How has your view of Mr. Doolittle changed since he was first introduced?

40 **Discussion** What advice does Mr. Doolittle give Pickering concerning Eliza?

41 **Critical Thinking and Reading** What can you infer about the place of women in Victorian society from this statement?

38 ing widows' that ever got money out of six different charities in one week for the death of the same husband. I dont need less than a deserving man: I need more. I dont eat less hearty than him; and I drink a lot more. I want a bit of amusement, cause I'm a thinking man. I want cheerfulness and a song and a band when I feel low. Well, they charge me just the same for everything as they charge the deserving. What is middle class morality? Just an excuse for never giving me anything. Therefore, I ask you, as two gentlemen, not to play that game on me. I'm playing straight with you. I aint pretending to be deserving. I'm undeserving; and I mean to go on being undeserving. I like it; and thats the truth. Will you take advantage of a man's nature to do him out of the price of his own daughter what he's brought up and fed and clothed by the sweat of his brow until she's growed big enough to be interesting to you two gentlemen? Is five pounds unreasonable? I put it to you; and I leave it to you.

HIGGINS [*rising, and going over to* PICKERING] Pickering: if we were to take this man in hand for three months, he could choose between a seat in the Cabinet and a popular pulpit in Wales.

PICKERING. What do you say to that, Doolittle?

DOOLITTLE. Not me, Governor, thank you kindly. Ive heard all the preachers and all the prime ministers—for I'm a thinking man and game for politics or religion or social reform same as all the other amusements—and I tell you it's a dog's life any way you look at it. Undeserving poverty is my line. Taking one station in society with another, it's—it's—well, it's the only one that has any ginger in it, to my taste.

HIGGINS. I suppose we must give him a fiver.

PICKERING. He'll make a bad use of it, I'm afraid.

DOOLITTLE. Not me, Governor, so help me I wont. Dont you be afraid that I'll save it and

spare it and live idle on it. There wont be a penny of it left by Monday: I'll have to go to work same as if I'd never had it. It wont pauperize me, you bet. Just one good spree for myself and the missus, giving pleasure to ourselves and employment to others, and satisfaction to you to think it's not been throwed away. You couldn't spend it better.

39 **HIGGINS** [*taking out his pocket book and coming between* DOOLITTLE *and the piano*] This is irresistible. Lets give him ten. [*He offers two notes to the* DUSTMAN]

DOOLITTLE. No, Governor. She wouldnt have the heart to spend ten; and perhaps I shouldnt neither. Ten pounds is a lot of money: it makes a man feel prudent like; and then good-bye to happiness. You give me what I ask you, Governor: not a penny more, and not a penny less.

PICKERING. Why dont you marry that missus of yours? I rather draw the line at encouraging that sort of immorality.

41 **DOOLITTLE.** Tell her so, Governor: tell her so. I'm willing. It's me that suffers by it. Ive no hold on her. I got to be agreeable to her. I got to give her presents. I got to buy her clothes something sinful. I'm a slave to that woman, Governor, just because I'm not her lawful husband. And she knows it too. Catch her marrying me! Take my advice, Governor: marry Eliza while she's young and dont know no better. If you dont youll be sorry for it after. If you do, she'll be sorry for it after; but better her than you, because youre a man, and she's only a woman and dont know how to be happy anyhow.

HIGGINS. Pickering: if we listen to this man another minute, we shall have no convictions left. [*To* DOOLITTLE] Five pounds I think you said.

DOOLITTLE. Thank you kindly, Governor.

HIGGINS. Youre sure you wont take ten?

DOOLITTLE. Not now. Another time, Governor.

HIGGINS [*handing him a five-pound note*] Here you are.

DOOLITTLE. Thank you, Governor. Good morning. [*He hurries to the door, anxious to get away with his booty. When he opens it he is confronted with a dainty and exquisitely clean young Japanese lady in a simple blue cotton kimono printed cunningly with small white jasmine blossoms.* MRS PEARCE *is with her. He gets out of her way deferentially and apologizes*]. Beg pardon, miss.

THE JAPANESE LADY. Garn! Dont you know your own daughter?

DOOLITTLE	[*exclaiming*	Bly me! it's Eliza!
HIGGINS	*simul-*	Whats that? This!
PICKERING	*taneously*	By Jove!

LIZA. Dont I look silly?

HIGGINS. Silly?

MRS PEARCE [*at the door*] Now, Mr Higgins, please dont say anything to make the girl conceited about herself.

HIGGINS [*conscientiously*] Oh! Quite right, Mrs Pearce. [*To* ELIZA] Yes: damned silly.

MRS PEARCE. Please, sir.

HIGGINS [*correcting himself*] I mean extremely silly.

LIZA. I should look all right with my hat on. [*She takes up her hat; puts it on; and walks across the room to the fireplace with a fashionable air*].

HIGGINS. A new fashion, by George! And it ought to look horrible!

DOOLITTLE [*with fatherly pride*] Well, I never thought she'd clean up as good looking as that, Governor. She's a credit to me, aint she?

LIZA. I tell you, it's easy to clean up here. Hot and cold water on tap, just as much as you like, there is. Woolly towels, there is; and a towel horse[12] so hot, it burns your fingers. Soft brushes to scrub yourself, and a wooden bowl of soap smelling like primroses. Now I know why ladies is so clean. Washing's a treat for them. Wish they could see what it is for the like of me!

HIGGINS. I'm glad the bathroom met with your approval.

LIZA. It didnt: not all of it; and I dont care who hears me say it. Mrs Pearce knows.

HIGGINS. What was wrong, Mrs Pearce?

MRS PEARCE [*blandly*] Oh, nothing, sir. It doesnt matter.

LIZA. I had a good mind to break it. I didnt know which way to look. But I hung a towel over it, I did.

HIGGINS. Over what?

MRS PEARCE. Over the looking-glass, sir.

HIGGINS. Doolittle: you have brought your daughter up too strictly.

DOOLITTLE. Me! I never brought her up at all, except to give her a lick of a strap now and again. Dont put it on me, Governor. She aint accustomed to it, you see: thats all. But she'll soon pick up your free-and-easy ways.

LIZA. I'm a good girl, I am; and I wont pick up no free-and-easy ways.

HIGGINS. Eliza: if you say again that youre a good girl, your father shall take you home.

LIZA. Not him. You dont know my father. All he come here for was to touch you for some money to get drunk on.

DOOLITTLE. Well, what else would I want money for? To put into the plate in church, I suppose. [*She puts out her tongue at him. He is so incensed by this that* PICKERING *presently finds it necessary to step between*

---

12. **towel horse:** Towel rack; in this case the rack is heated to dry the towels.

42 Discussion How has Eliza's attitude toward bathing changed now that she has taken a bath?

42

them]. Dont you give me none of your lip; and dont let me hear you giving this gentleman any of it neither, or youll hear from me about it. See?

HIGGINS. Have you any further advice to give her before you go, Doolittle? Your blessing, for instance.

DOOLITTLE. No, Governor: I aint such a mug as to put up my children to all I know myself. Hard enough to hold them in without that. If you want Eliza's mind improved, Governor, you do it yourself with a strap. So long, gentlemen. [*He turns to go*].

HIGGINS [*impressively*] Stop. Youll come regularly to see your daughter. It's your duty, you know. My brother is a clergyman; and he could help you in your talks with her.

DOOLITTLE [*evasively*] Certainly, I'll come, Governor. Not just this week, because I have a job at a distance. But later on you may depend on me. Afternoon, gentlemen. Afternoon, maam. [*He touches his hat to* MRS PEARCE, *who disdains the salutation and goes out. He winks at* HIGGINS, *thinking him probably a fellow-sufferer from* MRS PEARCE's *difficult disposition, and follows her*].

1138　　The Modern Period

LIZA. Dont you believe the old liar. He'd as soon you set a bulldog on him as a clergyman. You wont see him again in a hurry.

HIGGINS. I dont want to, Eliza. Do you?

LIZA. Not me. I dont want never to see him again, I dont. He's a disgrace to me, he is, collecting dust,[13] instead of working at his trade.

PICKERING. What is his trade, Eliza?

LIZA. Talking money out of other people's pockets into his own. His proper trade's a navvy;[14] and he works at it sometimes too —for exercise—and earns good money at it. Aint you going to call me Miss Doolittle any more?

PICKERING. I beg your pardon, Miss Doolittle. It was a slip of the tongue.

LIZA. Oh, I dont mind; only it sounded so genteel. I should just like to take a taxi to the corner of Tottenham Court Road and get out there and tell it to wait for me, just to put the girls in their place a bit. I wouldnt speak to them, you know.

PICKERING. Better wait til we get you something really fashionable.

HIGGINS. Besides, you shouldnt cut your old friends now that you have risen in the world. Thats what we call snobbery.

LIZA. You dont call the like of them my friends now, I should hope. Theyve took it out of me often enough with their ridicule when they had the chance; and now I mean to get a bit of my own back. But if I'm to have fashionable clothes, I'll wait. I should like to have some. Mrs Pearce says youre going to give me some to wear in bed at night different to what I wear in the daytime; but it do seem a waste of money when you could get something to shew. Besides, I never could fancy changing into cold things on a winter night.

---

13. **collecting dust:** Picking up garbage.
14. **navvy** (nav′ ē) *n.*: An unskilled laborer.

MRS PEARCE [*coming back*] Now, Eliza. The new things have come for you to try on.

LIZA. Ah-ow-oo-ooh! [*She rushes out*].

MRS PEARCE [*following her*] Oh, dont rush about like that, girl. [*She shuts the door behind her*].

HIGGINS. Pickering: we have taken on a stiff job.

PICKERING [*with conviction*] Higgins: we have.

★　　★　　★　　★　　★　　★

There seems to be some curiosity as to what Higgins's lessons to Eliza were like. Well, here is a sample: the first one.

Picture Eliza, in her new clothes, and feeling her inside put out of step by a lunch, dinner, and breakfast of a kind to which it is unaccustomed, seated with Higgins and the Colonel in the study, feeling like a hospital out-patient at a first encounter with the doctors.

Higgins, constitutionally unable to sit still, discomposes her still more by striding restlessly about. But for the reassuring presence and quietude of her friend the Colonel she would run for her life, even back to Drury Lane.

HIGGINS. Say your alphabet.

LIZA. I know my alphabet. Do you think I know nothing? I dont need to be taught like a child.

HIGGINS [*thundering*] Say your alphabet.

PICKERING. Say it, Miss Doolittle. You will understand presently. Do what he tells you; and let him teach you in his own way.

LIZA. Oh well, if you put it like that—Ahyee, bəyee, cəyee, dəyee—

HIGGINS [*with the roar of a wounded lion*] Stop. Listen to this, Pickering. This is what we pay for as elementary education. This unfortunate animal has been locked up for nine years in school at our expense to teach her to speak and read the language of

43 Discussion What keeps Eliza from giving up and leaving Higgins's house?

Reader's Response Would you advise Liza to study with Higgins? Explain.

Shakespear and Milton. And the result is Ahyee, Bə-yee, Cə-yee, Dəyee. [*To* ELIZA] Say A, B, C, D.

LIZA [*almost in tears*] But I'm sayin it. Ahyee, Bəyee, Cəyee—

HIGGINS. Stop. Say a cup of tea.

LIZA. A cappətə-ee.

HIGGINS. Put your tongue forward until it squeezes against the top of your lower teeth. Now say cup.

LIZA. C-c-c—I cant. C-Cup.

PICKERING. Good. Splendid, Miss Doolittle.

HIGGINS. By Jupiter, she's done it the first shot. Pickering: we shall make a duchess of her. [*To* ELIZA] Now do you think you could possibly say tea? Not tə-yee, mind: if you ever say bə-yee cə-yee də-yee again you shall be dragged round the room three times by the hair of your head. [*Fortissimo*] T, T, T, T.

LIZA [*weeping*] I cant hear no difference cep that it sounds more genteel-like when you say it.

HIGGINS. Well, if you can hear the difference, what the devil are you crying for? Pickering: give her a chocolate.

PICKERING. No, no. Never mind crying a little, Miss Doolittle: you are doing very well; and the lessons wont hurt. I promise you I wont let him drag you round the room by your hair.

HIGGINS. Be off with you to Mrs Pearce and tell her about it. Think about it. Try to do it by yourself: and keep your tongue well forward in your mouth instead of trying to roll it up and swallow it. Another lesson at half-past four this afternoon. Away with you.

ELIZA. *still sobbing, rushes from the room.*

And that is the sort of ordeal Eliza has to go through for months before we meet her again on her first appearance in London society of the professional class.

THINKING ABOUT THE SELECTION

Recalling

1. (a) Why has Eliza come to see Higgins? (b) With what does she offer to pay him?
2. What are the terms of the bet Pickering proposes?
3. (a) What are Mrs. Pearce's concerns with regard to the arrangement? (b) What are Pickering's?
4. (a) What is the purpose of Alfred Doolittle's visit? (b) How does Higgins respond to his demands?

Interpreting

5. What differences between Higgins and Pickering are pointed out in Act II?

6. (a) What is revealed about the role of women of this era? (b) About middle-class and lower-class ideals?

Applying

7. (a) How does Higgins's treatment of Eliza strike you? (b) Do you think this was Shaw's intention? Explain.

ANALYZING LITERATURE

Understanding Character Development

Character development is the technique of adding depth to characters by causing them to grow by reacting to other characters and events. A static character is essentially unaltered by

Closure and Extension

ANSWERS TO THINKING ABOUT THE SELECTION
Recalling

1. (a) Eliza has come to ask Higgins to give her lessons in speaking so that she can speak like a lady and get a proper job in a flower shop. (b) She offers to pay daily with what is approximately half of what she

makes in a day.
2. Pickering says that he will pay for all the expenses of having Eliza live at Higgins home and of teaching her if Eliza can pass as a fine lady at an ambassador's garden party.
3. (a) Mrs. Pearce is concerned about how the girl will fit into the household, what the girl's family will think, and then what will happen to the girl after she has finished her lessons. (b) Pickering is concerned about the girl's feelings and the fact that she must thoroughly un-

derstand what she is getting herself into.
4. (a) Mr. Doolittle, who says that he has come to get his daughter, has really come to see what monetary benefit he can receive for "allowing" his daughter to live in the Higgins household. (b) Higgins calls his bluff and tells him that he can take his daughter with him immediately.

involvements of plot, whereas a dynamic character is affected, sometimes radically. In order to observe changes in a character, we must have a clear idea of what qualities that character possesses in the first place.

Using at least five adjectives or descriptive phrases, profile each of the five characters appearing in Act II. Then tell which of the characters is static and which is dynamic, giving your reasons for your classifications.

CRITICAL THINKING AND READING
Making Inferences About Characters

Occasionally, in a literary work, we receive conflicting reports on a character's ambitions, motives, and thoughts. This is because, as in real life, a character's self-image often differs drastically from the image other characters hold of her or him. It is the responsibility of the alert reader to consider all information and then to *infer*, or assemble, from it an accurate picture of the character in question. Tell what impression the speaker of each of the following lines hopes to convey, and what impression he or she succeeds in conveying.

1. THE FLOWER GIRL. Did you tell him I come in a taxi? (page 1122)
2. HIGGINS. *I* walk over everybody! My dear Mrs Pearce, my dear Pickering, I never had the slightest intention of walking over anyone. (page 1125)
3. DOOLITTLE. I come about a very serious matter, Governor. (page 1132)

SPEAKING AND LISTENING
Reading Dialogue Aloud

Dialogue consists of lines that represent the actual speech utterances or conversations of the characters in a literary work. In a play, dialogue is everything. Ideally, dialogue should give the impression of actual conversation, not separate speeches. Shaw orchestrated his dialogue like music, varying tempo and intonation to emphasize the ideas and attitudes being expressed. Choose sections of Act II, assign roles, and stage an in-class reading. To make the dialogue as natural and lifelike as possible, readers should consider what they know about each character, including his or her speech habits.

THINKING AND WRITING
Comparing and Contrasting Characters

Using information you have accumulated about the characters thus far, write an essay that explores similarities and differences between any two of the characters in Act II. First select the characters and jot down notes about them. Then write your first draft, remembering to pay attention to underlying motives and stage directions in arriving at an understanding of each character. When you revise, make sure your essay is ordered logically and that you have supported your thesis with details from the play. Proofread your essay and prepare a final draft.

(Answers begin on p. 1140.)

cite specific aspects of the play to support their interpretations.

ANSWERS TO ANALYZING LITERATURE

Answers will differ. Encourage your students to tell which actions or speeches of characters they had in mind when they formed their views.

ANSWERS TO ANALYZING CRITICAL THINKING AND READING

Suggested responses:
1. Because Eliza equates riding in a taxi with being important, she wants to be certain that Higgins knows that she arrived at his door in a taxi. Higgins, to whom riding in a taxi is commonplace, doesn't care and, therefore, doesn't think any the better of her because she did.
2. Higgins is aghast to find out that anyone thinks that he "walks over anyone." To everyone else it is quite apparent that he does; to Higgins, that is the last thing that he would do.
3. Doolittle is trying to sound serious so that he will be taken seriously; he is not. Higgins will not be blackmailed, so Doolittle must tell him his true intent—to get some money for his own good times from his daughter's good fortune.

Challenge What inferences can you make from about the relationship between Higgins and Eliza in Act II that will help you predict how they will feel about each other by the end of the play?

SPEAKING AND LISTENING

Have students practice in groups before they present their readings to the class.

Writing Across the Curriculum In conjunction with the music department, you might have the students write a critique of the music from *My Fair Lady*, including an analysis of how well the music supported the story.

Interpreting

5. Even though Pickering is as single-minded about accomplishing the goal of getting Eliza to speak properly as Higgins is, he appears to be much more aware of the social graces—more genteel—and cares more about others and their feelings.
6. Suggested responses: (a) Women were expected to rely on their men to take care of them, and in turn, men looked on women as more or less their property. Because women were possessions, they could be treated in any way that men chose to treat them, including being beaten if they "needed it." (b) The lower class did what they had to in order to survive and to get some pleasure out of their lives. The middle class tried to maintain a sense of dignity and morality, in some ways emulating the upper class that they aspired to join.

(b) The lower class did what they had to in order to survive and to get some pleasure out of their lives. The middle class tried to maintain a sense of dignity and morality, in some ways emulating the upper class that they aspired to join.

Applying

7. (a) Answers will differ, though students should support their responses with reasons. (b) Answers will again differ. Students should

Pygmalion, Act III

Writer's Technique

Satire. Satire is a technique that combines humor with criticism to expose flaws and shortcomings in institutions or human beings. Shaw, as an advocate of reform, saw in this brand of "serious comedy" an effective tool. "After all," he wrote, "the salvation of the world depends on the men who will not take evil good-humoredly, and whose laughter destroys the fool instead of encouraging him." The targets, methods, and styles of satire are many and varied. Unfair or outdated laws, pointless rules and regulations, prejudices and mindless conventions, illogical political policies, fads and styles—all have been held up to ridicule in poems, novels, essays, and plays. Today satire flourishes in such diverse media as film, television, cartoons, comic strips, and comedy acts, not to mention, of course, literature. Novels such as George Orwell's *Nineteen Eighty-four,* Evelyn Waugh's *The Loved One,* and Joseph Heller's *Catch-22* satirize many aspects of twentieth-century life.

Writing/Prior Knowledge When students have completed this activity, have them read their work aloud to their groups, eliminating all direct references to the subject that they are satirizing. Have the rest of the group discuss the possibilities and guess the subject.

Writing

Brainstorm in small groups in an effort to come up with a list of styles and habits that you find especially laughable. Attempt to pinpoint the features of your subject that seem silly, unreasonable, or unfair.

Spelling Tip You might point out that the ending of *incorrigible* is spelled *ible,* the less common spelling of this adjective ending.

Primary Source

One of the literary weapons that Shaw used in *Pygmalion* to right society's wrongs was satire. In his criticism as well he pointed out society's faults through whatever means might be effective—and he never hesitated to voice his opinion. Answering complaints that his criticism was full of personal feeling, he said,

> It is the capacity for making good or bad art a personal matter that makes a man a critic. When people do less than their best, and do that less at once badly and self-complacently, I hate them, loathe them, detest them, long to tear them limb from limb. . . . In the same way, really fine artists inspire me with the warmest personal regard, which I gratify in writing my notices without the smallest reference to . . . justice, impartiality, and the rest of the ideals. When my critical mood is at its height, personal feeling is not the word: it is passion: the passion for artistic perfection—for the noblest beauty of sound, sight, and action—that rages in me. Let all young artists look to it, and pay no heed to the idiots who declare that criticism should be free from personal feeling. The true critic, I repeat, is the man who becomes your personal enemy on the sole provocation of a bad performance and will only be appeased by a good performance.

Vocabulary

Preteach the following vocabulary words:
pretension (pri ten′ shən) *n.:* Rank or class (p. 1143)
cynical (sin′ i k'l) *adj.:* Distrustful; sneering (p. 1148)
imprecations (im′ prə kā′ shənz) *n.:* Curses (p. 1149)
somnambulist (säm nam′ byo͞o list) *n.:* Sleepwalker (p. 1155)
morosely (mə rōs′ lē) *adv.:* Sullenly; in bad humor (p. 1155)
incorrigible (in kôr′ i jə b'l) *adj.:* Not capable of being corrected or of behaving better (p. 1156)

Objectives

1 To recognize satire
2 To compare and contrast attitudes
3 To understand slang
4 To evaluate the effectiveness of satire

Support Material

Teaching Portfolio
Teacher Backup, p. 1377
Grammar in Action Worksheet, *Understanding a Comedy of Manners,* p. 1380
Usage and Mechanics Worksheet, p. 1382
Vocabulary Check, p. 1383
Critical Thinking and Reading Worksheet, *Comparing and Contrasting Characters' Attitudes,* p. 1384
Language Worksheet, *Understanding Slang,* p. 1385
Selection Test, p. 1386

ACT III

It is MRS HIGGINS's *at-home day.*[1] *Nobody has yet arrived. Her drawing room, in a flat on Chelsea Embankment, has three windows looking on the river; and the ceiling is not so lofty as it would be in an older house of the same pretension. The windows are open, giving access to a balcony with flowers in pots. If you stand with your face to the windows, you have the fireplace on your left and the door in the right-hand wall close to the corner nearest the windows.*

MRS HIGGINS *was brought up on Morris*[2] *and Burne Jones;*[3] *and her room, which is very unlike her son's room in Wimpole Street, is not crowded with furniture and little tables and nicknacks. In the middle of the room there is a big ottoman; and this, with the carpet, the Morris wall-papers, and the Morris chintz window curtains and brocade covers of the ottoman and its cushions, supply all the ornament, and are much too handsome to be hidden by odds and ends of useless things. A few good oil-paintings from the exhibitions in the Grosvenor Gallery thirty years ago (the Burne Jones, not the Whistler*[4] *side of them) are on the walls. The only landscape is a Cecil Lawson*[5] *on the scale of a Rubens.*[6] *There is a portrait of* MRS HIGGINS *as she was when she defied the fashion in her youth in one of the beautiful Rossettian*[7] *costumes which, when caricatured by people who did not understand, led to the absurdities of popular estheticism in the eighteen-seventies.*

In the corner diagonally opposite the door MRS HIGGINS, *now over sixty and long past taking the trouble to dress out of the fashion, sits writing at an elegantly simple writing-table with a bell button within reach of her hand. There is a Chippendale chair further back in the room between her and the window nearest her side. At the other side of the room, further forward, is an Elizabethan chair roughly carved in the taste of Inigo Jones.*[8] *On the same side a piano in a decorated case. The corner between the fireplace and the window is occupied by a divan cushioned in Morris chintz.*

It is between four and five in the afternoon.

The door is opened violently; and HIGGINS *enters with his hat on.*

MRS HIGGINS [*dismayed*] Henry! [*Scolding him*] What are you doing here today? It is my at-home day: you promised not to come. [*As he bends to kiss her, she takes his hat off, and presents it to him*].

HIGGINS. Oh bother! [*He throws the hat down on the table*].

MRS HIGGINS. Go home at once.

HIGGINS [*kissing her*] I know, mother. I came on purpose.

MRS HIGGINS. But you mustnt. I'm serious, Henry. You offend all my friends: they stop coming whenever they meet you.

HIGGINS. Nonsense! I know I have no small talk; but people dont mind. [*He sits on the settee*].

MRS HIGGINS. Oh! dont they? Small talk indeed! What about your large talk? Really, dear, you mustnt stay.

---

1. **at-home day:** The day of the week when a lady regularly receives visitors.
2. **Morris:** William Morris (1834–1896), English poet, artist, and craftsman.
3. **Burne Jones:** Sir Edward Corley Burne-Jones (1833–1898), English painter and designer.
4. **Whistler:** James Abbott McNeill Whistler (1834–1903), an American painter who lived in England.
5. **Cecil Lawson:** Cecil Gordon Lawson (1851–1882), English landscape painter.
6. **Rubens:** Peter Paul Rubens (1577–1640), a Flemish painter famous for his large paintings.
7. **Rossettian:** Referring to Dante Gabriel Rossetti (1828–1882), English poet and painter.
8. **Inigo Jones:** English architect and stage designer (1573–1652).

HIGGINS. I must. Ive a job for you. A phonetic job.

MRS HIGGINS. No use, dear. I'm sorry; but I cant get round your vowels; and though I like to get pretty postcards in your patent shorthand, I always have to read the copies in ordinary writing you so thoughtfully send me.

HIGGINS. Well, this isn't a phonetic job.

MRS HIGGINS. You said it was.

HIGGINS. Not your part of it. Ive picked up a girl.

MRS HIGGINS. Does that mean that some girl has picked you up?

HIGGINS. Not at all. I dont mean a love affair.

MRS HIGGINS. What a pity!

HIGGINS. Why?

MRS HIGGINS. Well, you never fall in love with anyone under forty-five. When will you discover that there are some rather nice-looking young women about?

HIGGINS. Oh, I cant be bothered with young women. My idea of a lovable woman is somebody as like you as possible. I shall never get into the way of seriously liking young women: some habits lie too deep to be changed. [*Rising abruptly and walking about, jingling his money and his keys in his trouser pockets*] Besides, theyre all idiots.

MRS HIGGINS. Do you know what you would do if you really loved me, Henry?

HIGGINS. Oh bother! What? Marry, I suppose.

MRS HIGGINS. No. Stop fidgeting and take your hands out of your pockets. [*With a gesture of despair, he obeys and sits down again*]. Thats a good boy. Now tell me about the girl.

HIGGINS. She's coming to see you.

MRS HIGGINS. I dont remember asking her.

HIGGINS. You didn't. *I* asked her. If youd known her you wouldnt have asked her.

MRS HIGGINS. Indeed! Why?

HIGGINS. Well, it's like this. She's a common flower girl. I picked her off the kerbstone.

MRS HIGGINS. And invited her to my at-home!

HIGGINS [*rising and coming to her to coax her*] Oh, thatll be all right. Ive taught her to speak properly; and she has strict orders as to her behavior. She's to keep to two subjects: the weather and everybody's health —Fine day and How do you do, you know —and not to let herself go on things in general. That will be safe.

MRS HIGGINS. Safe! To talk about our health! about our insides! perhaps about our outsides! How could you be so silly, Henry?

HIGGINS [*impatiently*] Well, she must talk about something. [*He controls himself and sits down again*]. Oh, she'll be all right: dont you fuss. Pickering is in it with me. Ive a sort of bet on that I'll pass her off as a duchess in six months. I started on her some months ago; and she's getting on like a house on fire. I shall win my bet. She has a quick ear; and she's easier to teach than my middle-class pupils because she's had to learn a complete new language. She talks English almost as you talk French.

MRS HIGGINS. Thats satisfactory, at all events.

HIGGINS. Well, it is and it isnt.

MRS HIGGINS. What does that mean?

HIGGINS. You see, Ive got her pronunciation all right; but you have to consider not only how a girl pronounces, but what she pronounces; and that's where—

They are interrupted by the PARLORMAID, *announcing guests.*

THE PARLORMAID. Mrs and Miss Eynsford Hill. [*She withdraws*].

HIGGINS. Oh Lord! [*He rises; snatches his hat from the table; and makes for the door; but before he reaches it his mother introduces him*].

Grammar in Action

In a **comedy of manners,** a writer satirically challenges the manners of a society or particular group of people within it. Shaw satirizes both upper class and lower class manners in *Pygmalion.* When Higgins tries to pass off Eliza as a respectable upper class girl, Shaw mocks the pretensions of "good" society as well as Eliza's social ineptitude. Before Eliza even appears at the tea party in Act III, however, Higgins's disregard of manners makes the overbred Mrs. Eynsford Hill seem ridiculous:

Mrs. Eynsford Hill [*half rising*] Are we in the way?

Mrs. Higgins [*rising and making her sit down again*] No, no. You couldn't have come more fortunately: we want you to meet a friend of ours.

Higgins [*turning hopefully*] Yes, by George! We want two or three people. You'll do as well as anybody else.

Higgins is saying, in effect, that in upper class society, good manners make everyone interchangeable: One polite person is as dull and proper as any other!

Mrs and Miss Eynsford Hill are the mother and daughter who sheltered from the rain in Covent Garden. The mother is well bred, quiet, and has the habitual anxiety of straitened means. The daughter has acquired a gay air of being very much at home in society: the bravado of genteel poverty.

MRS EYNSFORD HILL [*to* MRS HIGGINS] How do you do? [*They shake hands*].

MISS EYNSFORD HILL. How d'you do? [*She shakes*].

MRS HIGGINS [*introducing*] My son Henry.

MRS EYNSFORD HILL. Your celebrated son! I have so longed to meet you, Professor Higgins.

HIGGINS [*glumly, making no movement in her direction*] Delighted. [*He backs against the piano and bows brusquely*].

MISS EYNSFORD HILL [*going to him with confident familiarity*] How do you do?

HIGGINS [*staring at her*] Ive seen you before somewhere. I havnt the ghost of a notion where; but Ive heard your voice. [*Drearily*] It doesnt matter. Youd better sit down.

MRS HIGGINS. I'm sorry to say that my celebrated son has no manners. You mustnt mind him.

MISS EYNSFORD HILL [*gaily*] I dont. [*She sits in the Elizabethan chair*].

MRS EYNSFORD HILL [*a little bewildered*] Not at all. [*She sits on the ottoman between her daughter and* MRS HIGGINS, *who has turned her chair away from the writing-table*].

HIGGINS. Oh, have I been rude? I didnt mean to be.

He goes to the central window, through which, with his back to the company, he contemplates the river and the flowers in Battersea Park on the opposite bank as if they were a frozen desert.

The PARLORMAID *returns, ushering in* PICKERING.

THE PARLORMAID. Colonel Pickering. [*She withdraws*].

PICKERING. How do you do, Mrs Higgins?

MRS HIGGINS. So glad youve come. Do you know Mrs Eynsford Hill—Miss Eynsford Hill? [*Exchange of bows. The* COLONEL *brings the Chippendale chair a little forward between* MRS HILL *and* MRS HIGGINS, *and sits down*].

PICKERING. Has Henry told you what weve come for?

HIGGINS. [*over his shoulder*] We were interrupted: damn it!

MRS HIGGINS. Oh, Henry, Henry, really!

MRS EYNSFORD HILL [*half rising*] Are we in the way?

MRS HIGGINS [*rising and making her sit down again*] No, no. You couldnt have come more fortunately: we want you to meet a friend of ours.

HIGGINS [*turning hopefully*] Yes, by George! We want two or three people. You'll do as well as anybody else.
The PARLORMAID *returns, ushering* FREDDY.
THE PARLORMAID. Mr Eynsford Hill.

HIGGINS [*almost audibly, past endurance*] God of Heaven! another of them.

FREDDY [*shaking hands with* MRS HIGGINS] Ahdedo?

MRS HIGGINS. Very good of you to come. [*Introducing*] Colonel Pickering.

FREDDY [*bowing*] Ahdedo?

MRS HIGGINS. I don't think you know my son, Professor Higgins.

FREDDY [*going to* HIGGINS] Ahdedo?

HIGGINS [*looking at him much as if he were a pickpocket*] I'll take my oath Ive met you before somewhere. Where was it?

Pygmalion, Act III 1145

6 Literary Focus What about Higgins's manner lets you know that Shaw is going to treat this scene satirically?

7 Discussion How does Henry feel about the Eynsford Hills, individually and collectively?

Student Activity 1. Find a passage in the tea party scene where Eliza's incomplete mastery of upper class manners produces a humorous effect. Then explain what aspect of upper class manners Shaw is satirizing in the scene.

Student Activity 2. Write a comedy-of-manners scene in which you satirize the manners of a particular group. You may want to use mimickry and exaggeration to generate comedy; however, make your satire affectionate rather than savage.

1146   *The Modern Period*

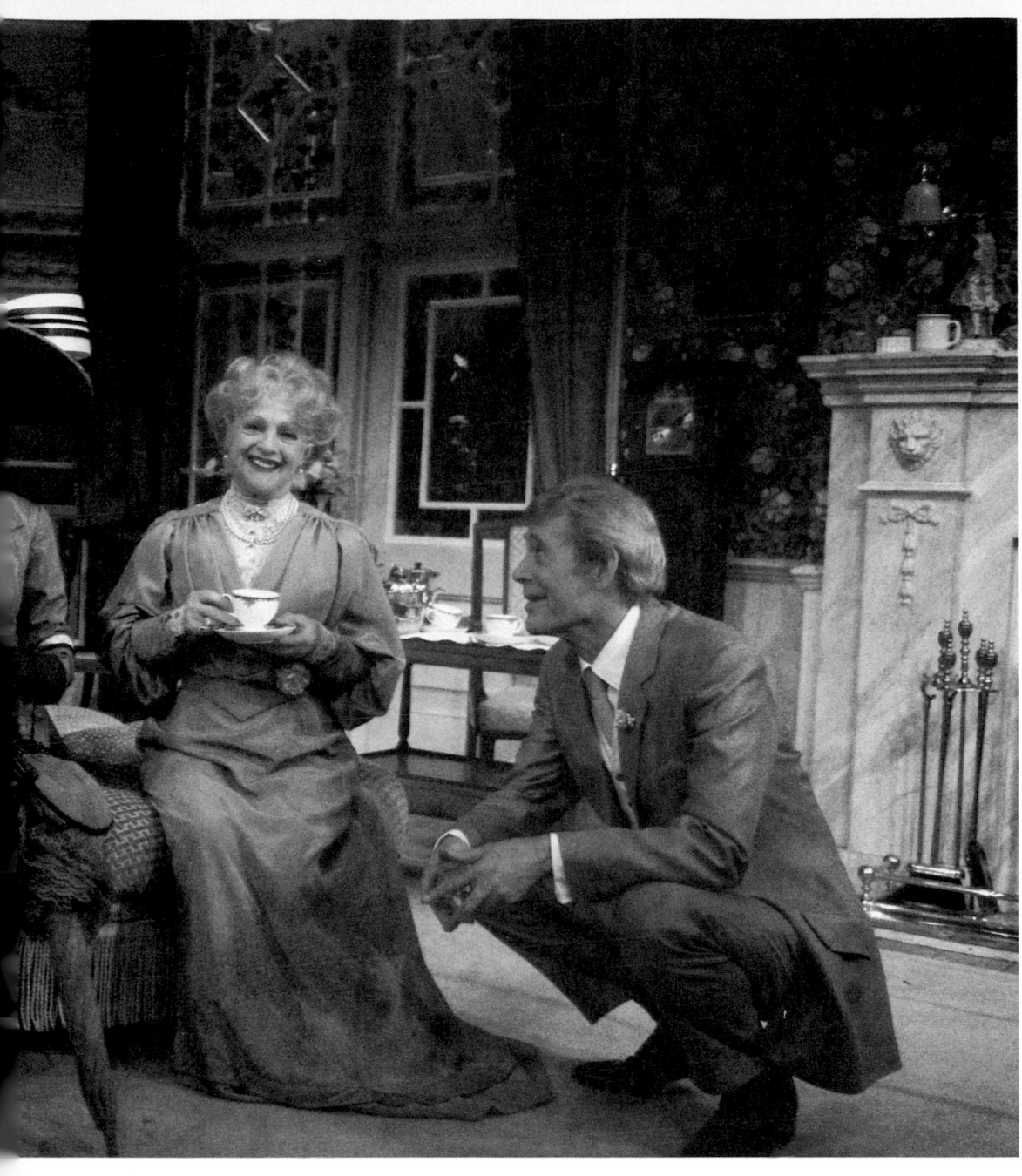

Pygmalion, Act III 1147

8 Discussion Ask students whether Higgins is exaggerating and overstating his case. What does his manner reveal about his personality?

FREDDY. I dont think so.

HIGGINS [*resignedly*] It dont matter, anyhow. Sit down.

He shakes FREDDY's *hand, and almost slings him on to the ottoman with his face to the window; then comes round to the other side of it.*

HIGGINS. Well, here we are, anyhow! [*He sits down on the ottoman next* MRS EYNSFORD HILL, *on her left*] And now, what the devil are we going to talk about until Eliza comes?

MRS HIGGINS. Henry: you are the life and soul of the Royal Society's soirées;[9] but really youre rather trying on more commonplace occasions.

HIGGINS. Am I? Very sorry. [*Beaming suddenly*] I suppose I am, you know. [*Uproariously*] Ha, ha!

MISS EYNSFORD HILL [*who considers* HIGGINS *quite eligible matrimonially*] I sympathize. I havnt any small talk. If people would only be frank and say what they really think!

HIGGINS [*relapsing into gloom*] Lord forbid!

MRS EYNSFORD HILL [*taking up her daughter's cue*] But why?

HIGGINS. What they think they ought to think is bad enough, Lord knows; but what they really think would break up the whole show. Do you suppose it would be really agreeable if I were to come out now with what *I* really think?

MISS EYNSFORD HILL [*gaily*] Is it so very cynical?

HIGGINS. Cynical! Who the dickens said it was cynical? I mean it wouldnt be decent.

MRS EYNSFORD HILL [*seriously*] Oh! I'm sure you dont mean that, Mr Higgins.

HIGGINS. You see, we're all savages, more or less. We're supposed to be civilized and

---

9. **soirées** (swä räz') *n.*: Parties held in the evening.

cultured—to know all about poetry and philosophy and art and science, and so on; but how many of us know even the meanings of these names? [*To* MISS HILL] What do you know of poetry? [*To* MRS HILL] What do you know of science? [*Indicating* FREDDY] What does he know of art or science or anything else? What the devil do you imagine I know of philosophy?

MRS HIGGINS [*warningly*] Or of manners, Henry?

THE PARLORMAID [*opening the door*] Miss Doolittle. [*She withdraws*].

HIGGINS [*rising hastily and running to* MRS HIGGINS] Here she is, mother. [*He stands on tiptoe and makes signs over his mother's head to* ELIZA *to indicate to her which lady is her hostess*].

ELIZA, *who is exquisitely dressed, produces an impression of such remarkable distinction and beauty as she enters that they all rise, quite fluttered. Guided by* HIGGINS's *signals, she comes to* MRS HIGGINS *with studied grace.*

LIZA [*speaking with pedantic correctness of pronunciation and great beauty of tone*] How do you do, Mrs Higgins? [*She gasps slightly in making sure of the H in Higgins, but is quite successful*]. Mr Higgins told me I might come.

MRS HIGGINS [*cordially*] Quite right: I'm very glad indeed to see you.

PICKERING. How do you do, Miss Doolittle?

LIZA [*shaking hands with him*] Colonel Pickering, is it not?

MRS EYNSFORD HILL. I feel sure we have met before, Miss Doolittle. I remember your eyes.

LIZA. How do you do? [*She sits down on the ottoman gracefully in the place just left vacant by* HIGGINS].

MRS EYNSFORD HILL [*introducing*] My daughter Clara.

LIZA. How do you do?

9 **CLARA** [*impulsively*] How do you do? [*She sits down on the ottoman beside* ELIZA, *devouring her with her eyes*].

FREDDY [*coming to their side of the ottoman*] Ive certainly had the pleasure.

MRS EYNSFORD HILL [*introducing*] My son Freddy.

LIZA. How do you do?

FREDDY *bows and sits down in the Elizabethan chair, infatuated.*

HIGGINS [*suddenly*] By George, yes: it all comes back to me! [*They stare at him*]. Covent Garden! [*Lamentably*] What a damned thing!

MRS HIGGINS. Henry, please! [*He is about to sit on the edge of the table*] Dont sit on my writing-table: youll break it.

HIGGINS [*sulkily*] Sorry.

10 *He goes to the divan, stumbling into the fender and over the fire-irons on his way; extricating himself with muttered imprecations; and finishing his disastrous journey by throwing himself so impatiently on the divan that he almost breaks it.* MRS HIGGINS *looks at him, but controls herself and says nothing.*

A long and painful pause ensues.

MRS HIGGINS [*at last, conversationally*] Will it rain, do you think?

LIZA. The shallow depression in the west of these islands is likely to move slowly in an easterly direction. There are no indications of any great change in the barometrical situation.

FREDDY. Ha! ha! how awfully funny!

LIZA. What is wrong with that, young man? I bet I got it right.

FREDDY. Killing!

MRS EYNSFORD HILL. I'm sure I hope it wont turn cold. Theres so much influenza about. It runs right through our whole family regularly every spring.

LIZA [*darkly*] My aunt died of influenza: so they said.

MRS EYNSFORD HILL [*clicks her tongue sympathetically*]!!!

LIZA [*in the same tragic tone*] But it's my belief they done the old woman in.

MRS HIGGINS [*puzzled*] Done her in?

LIZA. Y-e-e-e-es, Lord love you! Why should she die of influenza? She come through diphtheria right enough the year before. I saw her with my own eyes. Fairly blue with it, she was. They all thought she was dead; but my father he kept ladling gin down her throat til she came to so sudden that she bit the bowl off the spoon.

MRS EYNSFORD HILL [*startled*] Dear me!

LIZA [*piling up the indictment*] What call would a woman with that strength in her have to die of influenza? What become of her new straw hat that should have come to me? Somebody pinched it; and what I say is, them as pinched it done her in.

MRS EYNSFORD HILL. What does doing her in mean?

HIGGINS [*hastily*] Oh, thats the new small talk. To do a person in means to kill them.

MRS EYNSFORD HILL [*to* ELIZA, *horrified*] You surely dont believe that your aunt was killed?

LIZA. Do I not! Them she lived with would have killed her for a hat-pin, let alone a hat.

MRS EYNSFORD HILL. But it cant have been right for your father to pour spirits down her throat like that. It might have killed her.

11 **LIZA.** Not her. Gin was mother's milk to her. Besides, he'd poured so much down his own throat that he knew the good of it.

MRS EYNSFORD HILL. Do you mean that he drank?

9 Discussion What do you learn about Clara's character in this speech?

10 Reading Strategy What is the irony between Higgins's image of himself and the display that he puts on here?

11 Discussion Although Eliza's pronunciation might be perfect, what does she lack in her conversation with the Eynsford Hills?

12 Discussion What does it show about the Eynsford Hills when they are so cordially responsive to Eliza's "small talk"? What is the author making fun of here?

LIZA. Drank! My word! Something chronic.

MRS EYNSFORD HILL. How dreadful for you!

LIZA. Not a bit. It never did him no harm what I could see. But then he did not keep it up regular. [*Cheerfully*] On the burst, as you might say, from time to time. And always more agreeable when he had a drop in. When he was out of work, my mother used to give him fourpence and tell him to go out and not come back until he'd drunk himself cheerful and loving-like. Theres lots of women has to make their husbands drunk to make them fit to live with. [*Now quite at her ease*] You see, it's like this. If a man has a bit of conscience, it always takes him when he's sober; and then it makes him low-spirited. A drop of booze just takes that off and makes him happy. [*To* FREDDY, *who is in convulsions of suppressed laughter*] Here! what are you sniggering at?

FREDDY. The new small talk. You do it so awfully well.

LIZA. If I was doing it proper, what was you laughing at? [*To* HIGGINS] Have I said anything I oughtnt?

MRS HIGGINS [*interposing*] Not at all, Miss Doolittle.

LIZA. Well, thats a mercy, anyhow. [*Expansively*] What I always say is—

HIGGINS [*rising and looking at his watch*] Ahem!

LIZA [*looking round at him; taking the hint; and rising*] Well: I must go. [*They all rise.* FREDDY *goes to the door*]. So pleased to have met you. Goodbye. [*She shakes hands with* MRS HIGGINS].

MRS HIGGINS. Goodbye.

LIZA. Goodbye, Colonel Pickering.

PICKERING. Goodbye, Miss Doolittle. [*They shake hands*].

LIZA [*nodding to the others*] Goodbye, all.

FREDDY [*opening the door for her*] Are you walking across the Park, Miss Doolittle? If so—

LIZA [*with perfectly elegant diction*] Walk! Not bloody likely. [*Sensation*]. I am going in a taxi. [*She goes out*].

PICKERING *gasps and sits down.* FREDDY *goes out on the balcony to catch another glimpse of* ELIZA.

MRS EYNSFORD HILL [*suffering from shock*] Well, I really cant get used to the new ways.

CLARA [*throwing herself discontentedly into the Elizabethan chair*] Oh, it's all right, mamma, quite right. People will think we never go anywhere or see anybody if you are so old-fashioned.

MRS EYNSFORD HILL. I daresay I am very old-fashioned; but I do hope you wont begin using that expression, Clara. I have got accustomed to hear you talking about men as rotters, and calling everything filthy and beastly; though I do think it horrible and unladylike. But this last is really too much. Dont you think so, Colonel Pickering?

PICKERING. Dont ask me. Ive been away in India for several years; and manners have changed so much that I sometimes dont know whether I'm at a respectable dinnertable or in a ship's forecastle.

CLARA. It's all a matter of habit. Theres no right or wrong in it. Nobody means anything by it. And it's so quaint, and gives such a smart emphasis to things that are not in themselves very witty. I find the new small talk delightful and quite innocent.

MRS EYNSFORD HILL [*rising*] Well, after that, I think it's time for us to go.

PICKERING *and* HIGGINS *rise*.

CLARA [*rising*] Oh yes: we have three at-homes to go to still. Goodbye, Mrs Higgins. Goodbye, Colonel Pickering. Goodbye, Professor Higgins.

HIGGINS [*coming grimly at her from the divan, and accompanying her to the door*] Goodbye. Be sure you try on that small talk at the three at-homes. Dont be nervous about it. Pitch it in strong.

CLARA [*all smiles*] I will. Goodbye. Such nonsense, all this early Victorian prudery!

HIGGINS [*tempting her*] Such damned nonsense!

CLARA. Such bloody nonsense!

MRS EYNSFORD HILL [*convulsively*] Clara!

CLARA. Ha! Ha! [*She goes out radiant, conscious of being thoroughly up to date, and is heard descending the stairs in a stream of silvery laughter*].

FREDDY [*to the heavens at large*] Well, I ask you— [*He gives it up, and comes to* MRS HIGGINS]. Goodbye.

MRS HIGGINS [*shaking hands*] Goodbye. Would you like to meet Miss Doolittle again?

FREDDY [*eagerly*] Yes, I should, most awfully.

MRS HIGGINS. Well, you know my days.

FREDDY. Yes. Thanks awfully. Goodbye. [*He goes out*].

MRS EYNSFORD HILL. Goodbye, Mr Higgins.

HIGGINS. Goodbye. Goodbye.

MRS EYNSFORD HILL [*to* PICKERING] It's no use. I shall never be able to bring myself to use that word.

PICKERING. Dont. It's not compulsory, you know. Youll get on quite well without it.

MRS EYNSFORD HILL. Only, Clara is so down on me if I am not positively reeking with the latest slang. Goodbye.

PICKERING. Goodbye [*They shake hands*].

MRS EYNSFORD HILL. [*to* MRS HIGGINS] You mustnt mind Clara. [PICKERING, *catching from her lowered tone that this is not meant for him to hear, discreetly joins* HIGGINS *at the window*]. We're so poor! and she gets so few parties, poor child! She doesn't quite know. [MRS HIGGINS, *seeing that her eyes are moist, takes her hand sympathetically and goes with her to the door*]. But the boy is nice. Dont you think so?

MRS HIGGINS. Oh, quite nice. I shall always be delighted to see him.

MRS EYNSFORD HILL. Thank you, dear. Goodbye. [*She goes out*].

HIGGINS [*eagerly*] Well? Is Eliza presentable [*he swoops on his mother and drags her to the ottoman, where she sits down in* ELIZA's *place with her son on her left*]?

PICKERING *returns to his chair on her right*.

MRS HIGGINS. You silly boy, of course she's not presentable. She's a triumph of your art and of her dressmaker's; but if you suppose for a moment that she doesn't give herself away in every sentence she utters, you must be perfectly cracked about her.

PICKERING. But dont you think something might be done? I mean something to eliminate the sanguinary[10] element from her conversation.

MRS HIGGINS. Not as long as she is in Henry's hands.

HIGGINS [*aggrieved*] Do you mean that my language is improper?

MRS HIGGINS. No, dearest: it would be quite proper—say on a canal barge; but it would not be proper for her at a garden party.

HIGGINS [*deeply injured*] Well I must say—

PICKERING [*interrupting him*] Come, Higgins: you must learn to know yourself. I havnt heard such language as yours since we used to review the volunteers in Hyde Park twenty years ago.

HIGGINS [*sulkily*] Oh, well, if you say so, I suppose I dont always talk like a bishop.

---

10. sanguinary (saŋ′ gwi ner′ ē) *adj.*: Bloody.

13

14

13 Discussion What is Higgins's motive in encouraging Clara to use the new small talk during her other three visits?

14 Reading Strategy What is the intended play on words in this speech? To what is it referring?

15 Discussion What does Higgins reveal about his feelings for Eliza?

16 Discussion Why does Mrs. Pearce end all conversations about Eliza with "You don't think, sir"?

17 Discussion What is Higgins overlooking in this metamorphosis of Eliza?

MRS HIGGINS [*quieting* HENRY *with a touch*] Colonel Pickering: will you tell me what is the exact state of things in Wimpole Street?

PICKERING [*cheerfully: as if this completely changed the subject*] Well, I have come to live there with Henry. We work together at my Indian Dialects; and we think it more convenient—

MRS HIGGINS. Quite so. I know all about that: it's an excellent arrangement. But where does this girl live?

HIGGINS. With us, of course. Where should she live?

MRS HIGGINS. But on what terms? Is she a servant? If not, what is she?

PICKERING [*slowly*] I think I know what you mean, Mrs Higgins.

15 HIGGINS. Well, dash me if *I* do! Ive had to work at the girl every day for months to get her to her present pitch. Besides, she's useful. She knows where my things are, and remembers my appointments and so forth.

MRS HIGGINS. How does your housekeeper get on with her?

HIGGINS. Mrs Pearce? Oh, she's jolly glad to get so much taken off her hands; for before Eliza came, she used to have to find things and remind me of my appointments. But she's got some silly bee in her bonnet about Eliza. She keeps saying "You dont think, sir": doesn't she, Pick?

16 PICKERING. Yes: thats the formula. "You dont think, sir." Thats the end of every conversation about Eliza.

HIGGINS. As if I ever stop thinking about the girl and her confounded vowels and consonants. I'm worn out, thinking about her, and watching her lips and her teeth and her tongue, not to mention her soul, which is the quaintest of the lot.

MRS HIGGINS. You certainly are a pretty pair of babies, playing with your live doll.

HIGGINS. Playing! The hardest job I ever tackled: make no mistake about that, mother. But you have no idea how frightfully interesting it is to take a human being and change her into a quite different human being by creating a new speech for her. It's filling up the deepest gulf that separates class from class and soul from soul. **17**

PICKERING [*drawing his chair closer to* MRS HIGGINS *and bending over to her eagerly*] Yes: it's enormously interesting. I assure you, Mrs Higgins, we take Eliza very seriously. Every week—every day almost—there is some new change. [*Closer again*] We keep records of every stage—dozens of gramophone disks and photographs—

HIGGINS [*assailing her at the other ear*] Yes, by George: it's the most absorbing experiment I ever tackled. She regularly fills our lives up: doesn't she, Pick?

PICKERING. We're always talking Eliza.

HIGGINS. Teaching Eliza.

PICKERING. Dressing Eliza.

MRS HIGGINS. What!

HIGGINS. Inventing new Elizas.

HIGGINS.	(*speaking together*)	You know, she has the most extraordinary quickness of ear: I assure you, my dear Mrs Higgins, that girl
PICKERING.		
HIGGINS.		just like a parrot. Ive tried her with every
PICKERING.		is a genius. She can play the piano quite beautifully.
HIGGINS.		possible sort of sound that a human being can make—
PICKERING.		We have taken her to classical concerts and to music
HIGGINS.		Continental dialects, African dialects, Hottentot

PICKERING. {(speaking together)} halls; and it's all the same to her: she plays everything

HIGGINS. clicks, things it took me years to get hold of; and

PICKERING. she hears right off when she comes home, whether it's

HIGGINS. she picks them up like a shot, right away, as if she had Beethoven and Brahms or Lehar, and Lionel Monckton;

PICKERING.

HIGGINS. been at it all her life. though six months ago, she'd never as much as touched a piano—

PICKERING.

MRS HIGGINS [putting her fingers in her ears, as they are by this time shouting one another down with an intolerable noise] Sh-sh-sh—sh! [They stop].

PICKERING. I beg your pardon. [He draws his chair back apologetically].

HIGGINS. Sorry. When Pickering starts shouting nobody can get a word in edgeways.

MRS HIGGINS. Be quiet, Henry. Colonel Pickering: dont you realize that when Eliza walked in Wimpole Street, something walked in with her?

PICKERING. Her father did. But Henry soon got rid of him.

MRS HIGGINS. It would have been more to the point if her mother had. But as her mother didnt something else did.

PICKERING. But what?

MRS HIGGINS. (unconsciously dating herself by the word) A problem.

PICKERING. Oh, I see. The problem of how to pass her off as a lady.

HIGGINS. I'll solve that problem. Ive half solved it already.

MRS HIGGINS. No, you two infinitely stupid male creatures: the problem of what is to be done with her afterwards.

HIGGINS. I dont see anything in that. She can go her own way, with all the advantages I have given her.

MRS HIGGINS. The advantages of that poor woman who was here just now! The manners and habits that disqualify a fine lady from earning her own living without giving her a fine lady's income! Is that what you mean?

PICKERING. [Indulgently, being rather bored] Oh, that will be all right, Mrs Higgins. [He rises to go].

HIGGINS. [Rising also] We'll find her some light employment.

PICKERING. She's happy enough. Dont you worry about her. Goodbye. [He shakes hands as if he were consoling a frightened child, and makes for the door].

HIGGINS. Anyhow, theres no good bothering now. The thing's done. Goodbye, mother. [He kisses her, and follows PICKERING].

PICKERING [turning for a final consolation] There are plenty of openings. We'll do whats right. Goodbye.

HIGGINS [to Pickering as they go out together] Lets take her to the Shakespear exhibition at Earls Court.

PICKERING. Yes: lets. Her remarks will be delicious.

HIGGINS. She'll mimic all the people for us when we get home.

PICKERING. Ripping. [Both are heard laughing as they go downstairs].

MRS HIGGINS [rises with an impatient bounce, and returns to her work at the writing-table. She sweeps a litter of disarranged papers out of the way; snatches a

18 **Discussion** What dawns on Higgins and Pickering during this exchange?

19 **Discussion** What future problem regarding Eliza does Mrs. Higgins warn her son about?

20 **Discussion** Besides an experiment in phonetics, what has Eliza become to both men?

18

19

20

21 **Reading Strategy** Predict what this speech may foreshadow.

22 **Enrichment** *Cockney* can refer to the London working-class dialect or to anyone from London's working class, but it is more specifically anyone in the working class born within the sound of Bow Bells, which are in a church tower in the heart of London.

sheet of paper from her stationery case; and tries resolutely to write. At the third time she gives it up; flings down her pen; grips the table angrily and exclaims] Oh, men! men!! men!!!

*   *   *   *   *   *

Clearly Eliza will not pass as a duchess yet; and Higgins's bet remains unwon. But the six months are not yet exhausted and just in time Eliza does actually pass as a princess. For a glimpse of how she did it imagine an Embassy in London one summer evening after dark. The hall door has an awning and a carpet across the sidewalk to the kerb, because a grand reception is in progress. A small crowd is lined up to see the guests arrive.

A Rolls-Royce car drives up. Pickering in evening dress, with medals and orders, alights, and hands out Eliza, in opera cloak, evening dress, diamonds, fan, flowers and all accessories. Higgins follows. The car drives off; and the three go up the steps and into the house, the door opening for them as they approach.

Inside the house they find themselves in a spacious hall from which the grand staircase rises. On the left are the arrangements for the gentlemen's cloaks. The male guests are depositing their hats and wraps there.

On the right is a door leading to the ladies' cloakroom. Ladies are going in cloaked and coming out in splendor. Pickering whispers to Eliza and points out the ladies' room. She goes into it. Higgins and Pickering take off their overcoats and take tickets for them from the attendant.

One of the guests, occupied in the same way, has his back turned. Having taken his ticket, he turns round and reveals himself as an important looking young man with an astonishingly hairy face. He has an enormous moustache, flowing out into luxuriant whiskers. Waves of hair cluster on his brow. His hair is cropped closely at the back, and glows with oil. Otherwise he is very smart. He wears several worthless orders. He is evidently a foreigner, guessable as a whis-

kered Pandour[11] from Hungary; but in spite of the ferocity of his moustache he is amiable and genially voluble.

Recognizing Higgins, he flings his arms wide apart and approaches him enthusiastically.

WHISKERS. Maestro, maestro. [*He embraces* HIGGINS *and kisses him on both cheeks*]. You remember me?

HIGGINS. No I dont. Who the devil are you?

WHISKERS. I am your pupil: your first pupil, your best and greatest pupil. I am little Nepommuck, the marvellous boy. I have made your name famous throughout Europe. You teach me phonetic. You cannot forget ME.

HIGGINS. Why dont you shave?

NEPOMMUCK. I have not your imposing appearance, your chin, your brow. Nobody notice me when I shave. Now I am famous: they call me Hairy Faced Dick.

HIGGINS. And what are you doing here among all these swells?

NEPOMMUCK. I am interpreter. I speak 32 languages. I am indispensable at these international parties. You are great cockney specialist: you place a man anywhere in London the moment he open his mouth. I place any man in Europe.

A FOOTMAN *hurries down the grand staircase and comes to* NEPOMMUCK.

FOOTMAN. You are wanted upstairs. Her Excellency cannot understand the Greek gentleman.

NEPOMMUCK. Thank you, yes, immediately.

The FOOTMAN *goes and is lost in the crowd.*

NEPOMMUCK [*to* HIGGINS] This Greek diplomatist pretends he cannot speak nor understand English. He cannot deceive me. He is the son of a Clerkenwell watchmaker. He

21, 22

---

11. Pandour: A bodyguard or servant of Hungarian nobles.

Primary Source

The literary scholar Maurice Valency pointed out the fairy-tale basis of *Pygmalion:*

> By the time *Pygmalion* was written there were in existence innumerable stage versions of Cinderella. . . . In all likelihood the direct ancestor of *Pygmalion* was Boucicault's melodrama, *Grimaldi, or the Life of an Actress* (1862), in which a Covent Garden flower-girl is educated, brought to fame, and finally adopted by a broken-down

actor, who turns out to be a duke in disguise. Many other analogies have been collected. It seems clear that Shaw intended to follow in *Pygmalion* the traditional formula of such plays—the discovery, the education, the preliminary test, the crucial scene, and so on—up to the point at which the prince and the beggar maid are finally united. Shaw said of the traditional scene of the ball, which *Pygmalion* omits:

> "The obligatory scene, the scene in which Eliza makes her successful debut at the Ambassador's party, was at the root of the play at its inception. But when I got to work I left it to the imagination of the audience, as the theatre

speaks English so villainously that he dare not utter a word of it without betraying his origin. I help him to pretend; but I make him pay through the nose. I make them all pay. Ha ha! [*He hurries upstairs*].

PICKERING. Is this fellow really an expert? Can he find out Eliza and blackmail her?

HIGGINS. We shall see. If he finds her out I lose my bet.

ELIZA *comes from the cloakroom and joins them.*

PICKERING. Well, Eliza, now for it. Are you ready?

LIZA. Are you nervous, Colonel?

PICKERING. Frightfully. I feel exactly as I felt before my first battle. It's the first time that frightens.

LIZA. It is not the first time for me, Colonel. I have done this fifty times—hundreds of times—in my little piggery in Angel Court in my day-dreams. I am in a dream now. Promise me not to let Professor Higgins wake me; for if he does I shall forget everything and talk as I used to in Drury Lane.

PICKERING. Not a word, Higgins. [*To* ELIZA] Now, ready?

LIZA. Ready.

PICKERING. Go.

They mount the stairs, HIGGINS *last.* PICKERING *whispers to the* FOOTMAN *on the first landing.*

FIRST LANDING FOOTMAN. Miss Doolittle, Colonel Pickering, Professor Higgins.

SECOND LANDING FOOTMAN. Miss Doolittle, Colonel Pickering, Professor Higgins.

At the top of the staircase the AMBASSADOR *and his* WIFE, *with* NEPOMMUCK *at her elbow, are receiving.*

HOSTESS [*taking* ELIZA*'s hand*] How d'ye do?

HOST [*same play*] How d'ye do? How d'ye do, Pickering?

LIZA [*with a beautiful gravity that awes her hostess*] How do you do? [*She passes on to the drawingroom*].

HOSTESS. Is that your adopted daughter, Colonel Pickering? She will make a sensation.

PICKERING. Most kind of you to invite her for me. [*He passes on*].

HOSTESS [*to* NEPOMMUCK] Find out all about her.

NEPOMMUCK [*bowing*] Excellency—[*he goes into the crowd*].

HOST. How d'ye do, Higgins? You have a rival here tonight. He introduced himself as your pupil. Is he any good?

HIGGINS. He can learn a language in a fortnight—knows dozens of them. A sure mark of a fool. As a phonetician, no good whatever.

HOSTESS. How d'ye do, Professor?

HIGGINS. How do you do? Fearful bore for you this sort of thing. Forgive my part in it. [*He passes on*].

23

In the drawing room and its suite of salons the reception is in full swing. Eliza passes through. She is so intent on her ordeal that she walks like a somnambulist in a desert instead of a débutante in a fashionable crowd. They stop talking to look at her, admiring her dress, her jewels, and her strangely attractive self. Some of the younger ones at the back stand on their chairs to see.

The Host and Hostess come in from the staircase and mingle with their guests. Higgins, gloomy and contemptuous of the whole business, comes into the group where they are chatting.

HOSTESS. Ah, here is Professor Higgins: he will tell us. Tell us all about the wonderful young lady, Professor.

HIGGINS [*almost morosely*] What wonderful young lady?

HOSTESS. You know very well. They tell me there has been nothing like her in London since people stood on their chairs to look at

23 Discussion How do you think the hostess would react to this comment, when Higgins was out of the range of her voice?

could not afford the expense, and it made the play too long. Sir James Barrie spotted this at once and remonstrated. So when the play was screened, I added the omitted scene." [Shaw included this scene in subsequent texts of the play.]

The scene of the ball which Shaw added to the screen version of the play was not, however, obligatory. It was merely decorative. A love scene at the end of the play was really obligatory. It was therefore regularly supplied by the actors from the time of Beerbohm Tree [a well-known actor-manager], in the teeth of the author's peremptory instructions to the contrary.

Reader's Response Does Liza's success at the ball have a fairy-tale dimension? Explain.

Closure and Extension

ANSWERS TO THINKING ABOUT THE SELECTION

1. Mrs. Higgins is upset because she is "at home" that day, and Higgins always offended her friends by refusing to engage in small talk.
2. Eliza is told to talk about the weather and everybody's health.
3. Higgins tells them that Eliza is using the "new small talk," which makes them feel very much behind the times.
4. Nepommuck declares that Eliza is Hungarian of royal, albeit, illegitimate birth.
5. Higgins wins the bet: Eliza passes as a duchess.

Interpreting

6. (a) Eliza goes on at great length about the ill health and eventual death of her gin-guzzling aunt. (b)

Mrs Langtry.[12]

NEPOMMUCK *joins the group, full of news.*

HOSTESS. Ah, here you are at last, Nepommuck. Have you found out all about the Doolittle lady?

NEPOMMUCK. I have found out all about her. She is a fraud.

HOSTESS. A fraud! Oh no.

NEPOMMUCK. YES, yes. She cannot deceive me. Her name cannot be Doolittle.

HIGGINS. Why?

NEPOMMUCK. Because Doolittle is an English name. And she is not English.

HOSTESS. Oh, nonsense! She speaks English perfectly.

NEPOMMUCK. Too perfectly. Can you shew me any English woman who speaks English as it should be spoken? Only foreigners who have been taught to speak it speak it well.

HOSTESS. Certainly she terrified me by the way she said How d'ye do. I had a schoolmistress who talked like that; and I was mortally afraid of her. But if she is not English what is she?

NEPOMMUCK. Hungarian.

ALL THE REST. Hungarian!

NEPOMMUCK. Hungarian. And of royal blood. I am Hungarian. My blood is royal.

HIGGINS. Did you speak to her in Hungarian?

NEPOMMUCK. I did. She was very clever. She said "Please speak to me in English: I do not understand French." French! She pretend not to know the difference between Hungarian and French. Impossible: she knows both.

HIGGINS. And the blood royal? How did you find that out?

NEPOMMUCK. Instinct, maestro, instinct. Only the Magyar races can produce that air of the

---

12. Mrs. Langtry: Lily Langtry (1852–1929), a beautiful English actress.

---

divine right, those resolute eyes. She is a princess.

HOST. What do you say, Professor?

HIGGINS. I say an ordinary London girl out of the gutter and taught to speak by an expert. I place her in Drury Lane.

NEPOMMUCK. Ha ha ha! Oh, maestro, maestro, you are mad on the subject of cockney dialects. The London gutter is the whole world for you.

HIGGINS [*to the* HOSTESS] What does your Excellency say?

HOSTESS. Oh, of course I agree with Nepommuck. She must be a princess at least.

HOST. Not necessarily legitimate, of course. Morganatic[13] perhaps. But that is undoubtedly her class.

HIGGINS. I stick to my opinion.

HOSTESS. Oh, you are incorrigible.
The group breaks up, leaving HIGGINS *isolated.* PICKERING *joins him.*

PICKERING. Where is Eliza? We must keep an eye on her.

ELIZA *joins them.*

LIZA. I don't think I can bear much more. The people all stare so at me. An old lady has just told me that I speak exactly like Queen Victoria. I am sorry if I have lost your bet. I have done my best; but nothing can make me the same as these people.

PICKERING. You have not lost it, my dear. You have won it ten times over.

HIGGINS. Let us get out of this. I have had enough of chattering to these fools.

PICKERING. Eliza is tired; and I am hungry. Let us clear out and have supper somewhere.

---

13. Morganatic (môr′ gə nat′ ik) *adj.*: Referring to a form of marriage in which a person of royalty or nobility marries a spouse of inferior social status. While such a marriage is considered valid, children produced by it do not inherit titles.

Nepommuck considers himself an authority on phonetics, Higgins's star pupil. The fact that he is so loud in his pronouncements and so far wrong about Eliza makes Higgins's victory even sweeter.

7. (a) Even though Eliza has been able to fool everyone at the ball, she knows that she is not one of them, and she is well aware that if they knew the truth about her she would not be accepted on any level. (b) He may be suggesting her humble self-knowledge as well as

her acute awareness of class differences.

Applying

8. Answers will differ. Such a custom is not generally found in our society.

ANSWERS TO ANALYZING LITERATURE

1. Shaw satirizes the need to make small talk when Eliza discusses the

weather and her aunt's influenza in shocking terms, and Higgins tells everyone that she is just being fashionable by using the "new small talk."
2. Shaw satirizes the "at home" custom by having Higgins barge in, unannounced, and tell his mother that he has invited a flower girl of questionable origin to be his mother's guest.
3. Eliza's visit to Mrs. Higgins and her

THINKING ABOUT THE SELECTION
Recalling

1. Why is Mrs. Higgins upset when her son arrives at her house?
2. To what two "safe" topics is Eliza limited?
3. How does Higgins explain Eliza's language to the Eynsford Hills?
4. Who does Nepommuck declare Eliza to be?
5. Explain the outcome of Pickering's bet with Higgins.

Interpreting

6. (a) What humor arises out of Higgins's telling Eliza to limit her conversation to two topics? (b) Out of Nepommuck's "investigation" of Eliza?
7. At the end of the embassy ball Eliza comments that "nothing can make me the same as these people." (a) What do you suppose to be her state of mind as she utters this comment? Why? (b) What is Shaw suggesting about Eliza through this comment?

Applying

8. What parallels to an "at-home day," if any, can you find in modern American social customs? Explain the similarities and point out any differences.

ANALYZING LITERATURE
Using Satire

Satire is a technique that unites comedy and criticism to ridicule an offensive behavior or institution. The targets of satire, since its origins in ancient Greek and Roman drama, have included unjust or overly harsh laws, mindless social customs, and shallow trends. In Act III of *Pygmalion,* Shaw aims his satiric arrows at several customs and foibles of his day that continue to exist in our own. These include
1. the need (of some) to make small talk,
2. proper social etiquette,
3. the effort to pass oneself off as someone one is not.
Locate and describe the places in the act where Shaw pokes fun at each of these human failings.

CRITICAL THINKING AND READING
Comparing and Contrasting Attitudes

In Act III of *Pygmalion,* the characters express a variety of attitudes on a number of topics. Compare and contrast the following characters' views on the topics mentioned, and tell how you believe each of the characters came by those views.
1. Good manners: Higgins, Mrs. Higgins.
2. Love: Higgins, Mrs. Higgins, Freddy.
3. Slang: Mrs. Eynsford Hill, her daughter.
4. The fate of Eliza: Mrs. Higgins, Higgins, Pickering.
5. Formal dress affairs: Eliza, Higgins, Pickering.

UNDERSTANDING LANGUAGE
Understanding Slang

Slang is language used and understood by members of a particular group or culture. Unlike words from the standard language, which change very slowly over long periods of time, slang terms are literally "in" one year, "out" the next. Give the meaning of the following slang terms from Act III. Note any slang used by your own culture—modern-day high school students —to convey the same idea.
1. *Done her in?* (page 1149)
2. Somebody *pinched* it. (page 1149)
3. *On the burst,* as you might say. (page 1150)
4. [And always more agreeable] when he *had a drop in.* (page 1150)

THINKING AND WRITING
Evaluating the Effectiveness of Satire

Satire is a difficult form of comedy to write. A well-conceived satire will neither be so light as to lack punch nor so biting as to lack humor. In a short essay, explain whether or not you find the humor and criticism of Shaw's satire in Act III well-balanced. To get yourself started, answer questions such as the following. What is funny and why? What is being criticized? How clear are Shaw's intentions? When you revise, make sure you have included examples from Act III to back up your theses.

Pygmalion, Act III   1157

(*Answers begin on p. 1156.*)

thought was the new slang very difficult to listen to; her daughter thought that using it made her sound chic and used what she thought were slang expressions without understanding what they were or what they meant.

4. Probably because she was a woman and Henry's mother, Mrs. Higgins was worried about Henry mistreating Eliza, using her to his advantage, and forgetting about her. Higgins saw Eliza as an experiment, and because his work was the most important thing in his life he saw nothing wrong with dropping her when he was finished and going on to the next project. Pickering was equally interested in Eliza as a project, but he was also concerned about her feelings; Pickering has a history of helping people in need.

5. Eliza, because she has only dreamed about such events, is enchanted and does not want the evening to end. Higgins hates such formal affairs, probably because he had spent his younger years going to them, and is there only because he wants to win the bet. Pickering is a gentleman and enjoys the evening without making a fuss either way; as a military man, he is trained to do his duty.

ANSWERS TO UNDERSTANDING LANGUAGE

Suggested responses:

1. killed, destroyed
2. lifted it; stole it
3. when he felt like; every so often
4. when he was tipsy

Challenge Rewrite Eliza's account of her aunt's influenza in modern slang.

THINKING AND WRITING

Publishing Student Writing Have students write what they think Eliza was thinking as she left the ball with Higgins and Pickering. Have them read their selections to each other aloud, using a British accent and mimicking Eliza's personality as much as possible.

appearance at the ball are both examples of people attempting to be what they are not. The Eynsford Hills are a more subtle example of the same; they are hanging on desperately to the appearance that they belong in the upper class.

ANSWERS TO CRITICAL THINKING AND READING

1. Mrs. Higgins would have been a young woman during the most intensely Victorian years in England, and she was of the class that practiced all the polite customs with precision. Possibly because of her very strict adherence to the rules of etiquette, her son Henry would have nothing to do with them as an adult. He could not be bothered to perform as society would want him to and enjoyed making those who did follow the rules look foolish.

2. Higgins saw love as something that would stand in the way of his doing what he wanted to do, probably because he had grown up not having to do anything for anyone but himself. Mrs. Higgins desperately wanted Henry to find love, probably because she had felt loved by Henry's father and because society demanded that men of Henry's age be married. Freddy sought love because he needed someone to lean on; his mother always let him know how incompetent he was, and he had not learned to rely on himself.

3. Mrs. Eynsford Hill found what she

1157

Literary Focus Remind students that a play can have subplots that run parallel to the major plot. Each subplot has its own crisis, or climax.

Writing/Prior Knowledge Have students brainstorm as a group about what is likely to happen in Act IV.

Vocabulary

Preteach the following vocabulary words:
cant (kant) *n*.: Insincere talk (p. 1164)
dudgeon (duj′ ən) *n*.: Angry resentment; rage (p. 1164)
perfunctorily (pər fuŋk′ tə ri lē) *adv*.: Carelessly (p. 1164)

GUIDE FOR INTERPRETING

Writer's Technique

Writing

Primary Source

Pygmalion, Act IV

Crisis. Crisis is a highpoint of emotion or action that occurs near the end of a work of fiction. Also known as *climax,* the crisis is one key point in the carefully arranged sequence of elements in a story known as *plot.* Historically the plot contains five such elements, the first of which, the *exposition,* is a playbill of sorts. The exposition tells us who the characters are and what sort of *conflict,* or struggle, they face. Often this conflict is between the characters themselves, although at times an outside force like nature or society is involved. In any event *complications* arise in one form or another, causing the action or emotional intensity to build. Once the crisis has been reached, the work begins to wind down. In this final stage, known as the *resolution* or *denouement,* all problems are solved and any loose ends are tied up. This pattern of elements has been abandoned in whole or in part by a number of modern writers. Shaw, in an effort to create a more lifelike drama, deviated somewhat from this formula, especially in his comedies.

Imagine you are sitting in a theater watching this play. The curtain has come down on Act III. During intermission, you turn to the person sitting next to you and discuss the play. Create a conversation in which both of you provide ideas on what will happen next.

Shaw broke away from the traditional arrangement of plot elements, such as crisis, in a drama. He explained his reasoning this way:

> You will understand that my plays are not constructed plays: they grow naturally. If you "construct" a play: that is, if you plan your play beforehand, and then carry out your plan, you will find yourself in the position of a person putting together a jig-saw puzzle . . . which, to a spectator, is unbearably dull. The scenes must be born alive. If they are not new to you as you write, and sometimes quite contrary to the expectations with which you have begun them, they are dead wood. A live play constructs itself with a subtlety, and often with a mechanical ingenuity, that often deludes critics into holding the author up as the most crafty of artificers when he has never, in writing his play, known what one of his characters would say until another gave the clue. . . . Now what the drama can do, and what it actually does, is to take this unmeaning, haphazard show of life . . . and arrange it in such a way as to make you think very much more deeply about it than you ever dreamed of thinking about actual incidents that came to your knowledge.

Objectives

1 To explain crisis in a dramatic work
2 To understand cause and effect
3 To understand synonyms and antonyms
4 To write a letter of advice

Support Material

Teaching Portfolio
Teacher Backup, p. 1389
Usage and Mechanics Worksheet, p. 1392
Vocabulary Check, p. 1393
Critical Thinking and Reading Worksheet, *Understanding Cause and Effect,* p. 1394
Language Worksheet, *Understanding Synonyms and Antonyms,* p. 1395
Selection Test, p. 1396

ACT IV

The Wimpole Street laboratory. Midnight. Nobody in the room. The clock on the man-telpiece strikes twelve. The fire is not alight: it is a summer night.

Presently HIGGINS *and* PICKERING *are heard on the stairs.*

HIGGINS [*calling down to* PICKERING] I say, Pick: lock up, will you? I shant be going out again.

PICKERING. Right. Can Mrs Pearce go to bed? We dont want anything more, do we?

HIGGINS. Lord, no!

ELIZA *opens the door and is seen on the lighted landing in all the finery in which she has just won* HIGGINS*'s bet for him. She comes to the hearth, and switches on the electric lights there. She is tired: her pallor contrasts strongly with her dark eyes and hair; and her expression is almost tragic. She takes off her cloak; puts her fan and gloves on the piano; and sits down on the bench, brooding and silent.* HIGGINS, *in eve-ning dress, with overcoat and hat, comes in, carrying a smoking jacket which he has picked up downstairs. He takes off the hat and overcoat; throws them carelessly on the newspaper stand; disposes of his coat in the same way; puts on the smoking jacket; and throws himself wearily into the easy-chair at the hearth.* PICKERING, *similar-ly attired, comes in. He also takes off his hat and overcoat, and is about to throw them on* HIGGINS*'s when he hesitates.*

PICKERING. I say: Mrs Pearce will row if we leave these things lying about in the drawing room.

HIGGINS. Oh, chuck them over the bannisters into the hall. She'll find them there in the morning and put them away all right. She'll think we were drunk.

PICKERING. We are, slightly. Are there any letters?

HIGGINS. I didnt look. [PICKERING *takes the overcoats and hats and goes downstairs.* HIGGINS *begins half singing half yawning an air from* La Fanciulla Del Golden West.[1] *Suddenly he stops and exclaims*] I wonder where the devil my slippers are!

ELIZA *looks at him darkly; then rises sud-denly and leaves the room.*

HIGGINS *yawns again, and resumes his song.*

PICKERING *returns, with the contents of the letter-box in his hand.*

---

1. La Fanciulla (fan cho͞o′ la) **del Golden West:** *The Girl of the Golden West,* an opera by Italian composer Giacomo Puccini (1858–1924).

Pygmalion, Act IV 1159

2 **Clarification** A fender is a screen-like guard against live coals in front of a fireplace.

3 **Literary Focus** How does this exchange contribute to the crisis between Higgins and Eliza?

4 **Reading Strategy** Explain the irony in this speech.

5 **Discussion** How does Pickering's military career affect his attitude?

6 **Discussion** What one thing do Pickering and Higgins seem to have forgotten in their joy over their success?

7 **Critical Thinking and Reading** What do you think finally causes Eliza to break down and to show her true feelings?

PICKERING. Only circulars, and this coroneted billet-doux[2] for you. [*He throws the circulars into the fender, and posts himself on the hearthrug, with his back to the grate*].

HIGGINS [*glancing at the billet-doux*] Money-lender. [*He throws the letter after the circulars*].

ELIZA *returns with a pair of large down-at-heel slippers. She places them on the carpet before* HIGGINS, *and sits as before without a word.*

HIGGINS [*yawning again*] Oh Lord! What an evening! What a crew! What a silly tomfoolery! [*He raises his shoe to unlace it, and catches sight of the slippers. He stops unlacing and looks at them as if they had appeared there of their own accord*]. Oh! theyre there, are they?

PICKERING [*stretching himself*]. Well, I feel a bit tired. It's been a long day. The garden party, a dinner party, and the reception! Rather too much of a good thing. But youve won your bet, Higgins. Eliza did the trick, and something to spare, eh?

HIGGINS [*fervently*] Thank God it's over!

ELIZA *flinches violently; but they take no notice of her; and she recovers herself and sits stonily as before.*

PICKERING. Were you nervous at the garden party? *I* was. Eliza didnt seem a bit nervous.

HIGGINS. Oh, she wasnt nervous. I knew she'd be all right. No: it's the strain of putting the job through all these months that has told on me. It was interesting enough at first, while we were at the phonetics; but after that I got deadly sick of it. If I hadnt backed myself to do it I should have chucked the whole thing up two months ago. It was a silly notion: the whole thing has been a bore.

PICKERING. Oh come! the garden party was

---

2. **billet-doux** (bĭl′ ä dōō′): Love letter.

frightfully exciting. My heart began beating like anything.

HIGGINS. Yes, for the first three minutes. But when I saw we were going to win hands down, I felt like a bear in a cage, hanging about doing nothing. The dinner was worse: sitting gorging there for over an hour, with nobody but a damned fool of a fashionable woman to talk to! I tell you, Pickering, never again for me. No more artificial duchesses. The whole thing has been simple purgatory.

PICKERING. Youve never been broken in properly to the social routine. [*Strolling over to the piano*] I rather enjoy dipping into it occasionally myself: it makes me feel young again. Anyhow, it was a great success: an immense success. I was quite frightened once or twice because Eliza was doing it so well. You see, lots of the real people cant do it at all: theyre such fools that they think style comes by nature to people in their position; and so they never learn. Theres always something professional about doing a thing superlatively well.

HIGGINS. Yes: thats what drives me mad: the silly people dont know their own silly business. [*Rising*] However, it's over and done with; and now I can go to bed at last without dreading tomorrow.

ELIZA*'s beauty becomes murderous.*

PICKERING. I think I shall turn in too. Still, it's been a great occasion: a triumph for you. Goodnight. [*He goes*].

HIGGINS [*following him*] Goodnight. [*Over his shoulder, at the door*] Put out the lights, Eliza; and tell Mrs Pearce not to make coffee for me in the morning: I'll take tea. [*He goes out*].

ELIZA *tries to control herself and feel indifferent as she rises and walks across to the hearth to switch off the lights. By the time she gets there she is on the point of screaming. She sits down in* HIGGINS*'s chair and holds on hard to the arms. Finally she gives way and flings herself furiously on the floor, raging.*

8 **Reading Strategy** What do Higgins's slippers symbolize to Eliza?

9 **Critical Thinking and Reading** What causes Higgins to lose a bit of his confidence and to become uneasy?

10 **Discussion** What does Higgins mean when he says that this "irritation is purely subjective"?

8 **Reading Strategy** What do Higgins's slippers symbolize to Eliza?

9 **Critical Thinking and Reading** What causes Higgins to lose a bit of his confidence and to become uneasy?

10 **Discussion** What does Higgins mean when he says that this "irritation is purely subjective"?

HIGGINS [*in despairing wrath outside*] What the devil have I done with my slippers? [*He appears at the door*].

8 LIZA [*snatching up the slippers, and hurling them at him one after the other with all her force*] There are your slippers. And there. Take your slippers; and may you never have a day's luck with them!

HIGGINS [*astounded*] What on earth—! [*He comes to her*]. Whats the matter? Get up. [*He pulls her up*] Anything wrong?

LIZA [(*breathless*] Nothing wrong—with you. Ive won your bet for you, havnt I? Thats enough for you. *I* dont matter, I suppose.

HIGGINS. You won my bet! You! Presumptuous insect! *I* won it. What did you throw those slippers at me for?

LIZA. Because I wanted to smash your face. I'd like to kill you, you selfish brute. Why didnt you leave me where you picked me out of—in the gutter? You thank God it's all over, and that now you can throw me back again there, do you? [*She crisps her fingers³ frantically*].

HIGGINS [*looking at her in cool wonder*] The creature is nervous, after all.

LIZA [*gives a suffocated scream of fury, and instinctively darts her nails at his face*]!!

HIGGINS [*catching her wrists*] Ah! would you? Claws in, you cat. How dare you shew your temper to me? Sit down and be quiet. [*He throws her roughly into the easy-chair*].

LIZA [*crushed by superior strength and weight*] Whats to become of me? Whats to become of me?

HIGGINS. How the devil do I know whats to become of you? What does it matter what becomes of you?

LIZA. You dont care. I know you dont care. You wouldnt care if I was dead. I'm nothing

---

3. **crisps her fingers:** Clenches her fingers into fists.

to you—not so much as them slippers.

HIGGINS [*thundering*] Those slippers.

LIZA [*with bitter submission*]. Those slippers. I didnt think it made any difference now.

A pause. ELIZA *hopeless and crushed.* HIGGINS *a little uneasy.* **9**

HIGGINS [*in his loftiest manner*] Why have you begun going on like this? May I ask whether you complain of your treatment here?

LIZA. No.

HIGGINS. Has anybody behaved badly to you? Colonel Pickering? Mrs Pearce? Any of the servants?

LIZA. No.

HIGGINS. I presume you dont pretend that *I* have treated you badly?

LIZA. No.

HIGGINS. I am glad to hear it. [*He moderates his tone*]. Perhaps youre tired after the strain of the day. Will you have a glass of champagne? [*He moves towards the door*].

LIZA. No. [*Recollecting her manners*] Thank you.

HIGGINS [*good-humored again*] This has been coming on you for some days. I suppose it was natural for you to be anxious about the garden party. But thats all over now. [*He pats her kindly on the shoulder. She writhes*]. Theres nothing more to worry about.

LIZA. No. Nothing more for you to worry about. [*She suddenly rises and gets away from him by going to the piano bench, where she sits and hides her face*]. Oh God! I wish I was dead.

HIGGINS [*staring after her in sincere surprise*] Why? In heaven's name, why? [*Reasonably, going to her*] Listen to me, Eliza. All this irritation is purely subjective. **10**

Primary Source

Shaw had written as a music critic and knew a great deal about music in general and opera in particular. Reuben A. Brower commented on the link between Shaw's plays and opera:

> But Shaw was a joker and a musician. He could "never resist a joke," and had been pleasantly corrupted by a taste for opera, the most absurd and least realistic of dramatic forms. Via opera he leaped easily back to eighteenth-century drama, with its simplified type-characters who exercise the art of witty conversation. But Shaw's more immediate inspiration was drawn from Mozart. (It should be noted, too, that the traditions of comedy and comic opera were very closely connected in the eighteenth century.) In Shaw, as in music drama, we have the constant sense that the stage is a stage and the actors quite free to step forward and sound off at length on any emotion or idea suggested by the situation. In opera, too, we expect the most preposterous and unlikely action. . . . Finally there is in Shaw as in opera the extreme emphasis on a role as "a voice," rather than a person. Note, as evidence, Shaw's very exact directions as to the kind of voice required for

LIZA. I dont understand. I'm too ignorant.

HIGGINS. It's only imagination. Low spirits and nothing else. Nobody's hurting you. Nothing's wrong. You go to bed like a good girl and sleep it off. Have a little cry and say your prayers: that will make you comfortable.

LIZA. I heard your prayers. "Thank God it's all over!"

HIGGINS [*impatiently*] Well, dont you thank God it's all over? Now you are free and can do what you like.

LIZA [*pulling herself together in desperation*] What am I fit for? What have you left me fit for? Where am I to go? What am I to do? Whats to become of me?

HIGGINS [*enlightened, but not at all impressed*] Oh, thats whats worrying you, is it? [*He thrusts his hands into his pockets, and walks about in his usual manner, rattling the contents of his pockets, as if condescending to a trivial subject out of pure kindness*]. I shouldnt bother about it if I were you. I should imagine you wont have much difficulty in settling yourself somewhere or other, though I hadnt quite realized that you were going away. [*She looks quickly at him: he does not look at her, but examines the dessert stand on the piano and decides that he will eat an apple*]. You might marry, you know. [*He bites a large piece out of the apple and munches it noisily*]. You see, Eliza, all men are not confirmed old bachelors like me and the Colonel. Most men are the marrying sort [poor devils!]; and youre not bad-looking: it's quite a pleasure to look at you sometimes—not now, of course, because youre crying and looking as ugly as the very devil; but when youre all right and quite yourself, youre what I should call attractive. That is, to the people in the marrying line, you understand. You go to bed and have a good nice rest; and then get up and look at yourself in the glass; and you wont feel so cheap.

ELIZA *again looks at him, speechless, and does not stir.*

The look is quite lost on him: he eats his apple with a dreamy expression of happiness, as it is quite a good one.

HIGGINS [*a genial afterthought occurring to him*] I daresay my mother could find some chap or other who would do very well.

LIZA. We were above that at the corner of Tottenham Court Road.

HIGGINS [*waking up*] What do you mean?

LIZA. I sold flowers. I didnt sell myself. Now youve made a lady of me I'm not fit to sell anything else. I wish youd left me where you found me.

Pygmalion, Act IV 1163

11 Reading Strategy Predict whether Eliza will leave or stay.

12 Reading Strategy Discuss the irony in Eliza's statement about her old life.

each part. He maintains this operatic quality by his wonderful skill in molding the tones and rhythms of his speakers, in building up a strong sense of rhythm in whole speeches and in whole passages of the dialogue.

13 **Discussion** What do you think Eliza would really like Higgins to say at this point?

14 **Discussion** Why is Higgins becoming more and more abusive?

HIGGINS [*slinging the core of the apple decisively into the grate*] Tosh, Eliza. Dont you insult human relations by dragging all this cant about buying and selling into it. You neednt marry the fellow if you dont like him.

LIZA. What else am I to do?

HIGGINS. Oh, lots of things. What about your old idea of a florist's shop? Pickering could set you up in one: he has lots of money. [*Chuckling*] He'll have to pay for all those togs you have been wearing today; and that, with the hire of the jewellery, will make a big hole in two hundred pounds. Why, six months ago you would have thought it the millennium to have a flower shop of your own. Come! youll be all right. I must clear off to bed: I'm devilish sleepy. By the way, I came down for something: I forgot what it was.

LIZA. Your slippers.

HIGGINS. Oh yes, of course. You shied them at me. [*He picks them up, and is going out when she rises and speaks to him*].

LIZA. Before you go, sir—

HIGGINS [*dropping the slippers in his surprise at her calling him Sir*] Eh?

LIZA. Do my clothes belong to me or to Colonel Pickering?

HIGGINS [*coming back into the room as if her question were the very climax of unreason*] What the devil use would they be to Pickering?

LIZA. He might want them for the next girl you pick up to experiment on.

HIGGINS [*shocked and hurt*] Is that the way you feel towards us?

LIZA. I dont want to hear anything more about that. All I want to know is whether anything belongs to me. My own clothes were burnt.

HIGGINS. But what does it matter? Why need you start bothering about that in the middle of the night?

LIZA. I want to know what I may take away with me. I dont want to be accused of stealing.

HIGGINS [*now deeply wounded*] Stealing! You shouldnt have said that, Eliza. That shews a want of feeling.

LIZA. I'm sorry. I'm only a common ignorant girl; and in my station I have to be careful. There cant be any feelings between the like of you and the like of me. Please will you tell me what belongs to me and what doesnt?

HIGGINS [*very sulky*] You may take the whole damned houseful if you like. Except the jewels. Theyre hired. Will that satisfy you? [*He turns on his heel and is about to go in extreme dudgeon*].

LIZA [*drinking in his emotion like nectar, and nagging him to provoke a further supply*] Stop, please. [*She takes off her jewels*]. Will you take these to your room and keep them safe? I don't want to run the risk of their being missing.   **13**

HIGGINS [*furious*] Hand them over. [*She puts them into his hands*]. If these belonged to me instead of to the jeweller, I'd ram them down your ungrateful throat. [*He perfunctorily thrusts them into his pockets, unconsciously decorating himself with the protruding ends of the chains*].   **14**

LIZA [*taking a ring off*]. This ring isnt the jeweller's: it's the one you bought me in Brighton. I dont want it now. [HIGGINS *dashes the ring violently into the fireplace, and turns on her so threateningly that she crouches over the piano with her hands over her face, and exclaims*] Dont you hit me.

HIGGINS. Hit you! You infamous creature, how dare you accuse me of such a thing? It is you who have hit me. You have wounded me to the heart.

LIZA [*thrilling with hidden joy*] I'm glad. Ive got a little of my own back, anyhow.

HIGGINS [*with dignity, in his finest professional style*] You have caused me to lose my temper: a thing that has hardly ever happened to me before. I prefer to say nothing more tonight. I am going to bed.

LIZA [*pertly*] Youd better leave a note for Mrs Pearce about the coffee; for she wont be told by me.

HIGGINS [*formally*] Damn Mrs Pearce; and damn the coffee; and damn you; and [*wildly*] damn my own folly in having lavished my hard-earned knowledge and the treasure of my regard and intimacy on a heartless guttersnipe. [*He goes out with impressive decorum, and spoils it by slamming the door savagely*].

ELIZA *goes down on her knees on the hearth-rug to look for the ring. When she finds it she considers for a moment what to do with it. Finally she flings it down on the dessert stand and goes upstairs in a tearing rage.*

 * * * * * *

The furniture of Eliza's room has been increased by a big wardrobe and a sumptuous dressing-table. She comes in and switches on the electric light. She goes to the wardrobe; opens it; and pulls out a walking dress, a hat, and a pair of shoes, which she throws on the bed. She takes off her evening dress and shoes; then takes a padded hanger from the wardrobe; adjusts it carefully in the evening dress; and hangs it in the wardrobe, which she shuts with a slam. She puts on her walking shoes, her walking dress, and hat. She takes her wrist watch from the dressing-table and fastens it on. She pulls on her gloves; takes her vanity bag; and looks into it to see that her purse is there before hanging it on her wrist. She makes for the door. Every movement expresses her furious resolution.

She takes a last look at herself in the glass.

She suddenly puts out her tongue at herself; then leaves the room, switching off the electric light at the door.

Meanwhile, in the street outside, Freddy Eynsford Hill, lovelorn, is gazing up at the second floor, in which one of the windows is still lighted.

The light goes out.

FREDDY. Goodnight, darling, darling, darling.

ELIZA *comes out, giving the door a considerable bang behind her.*

LIZA. Whatever are you doing here?

FREDDY. Nothing. I spend most of my nights here. It's the only place where I'm happy. Dont laugh at me, Miss Doolittle.

LIZA. Dont you call me Miss Doolittle, do you hear? Liza's good enough for me. [*She breaks down and grabs him by the shoulders*] Freddy: you dont think I'm a heartless guttersnipe, do you?

FREDDY. Oh no, no, darling: how can you imagine such a thing? You are the loveliest, dearest—

He loses all self-control and smothers her with kisses. She, hungry for comfort, responds. They stand there in one another's arms.

 An elderly police constable arrives.

CONSTABLE [*scandalized*] Now then! Now then!! Now then!!!

They release one another hastily.

FREDDY. Sorry, constable. Weve only just become engaged.

They run away.

The constable shakes his head, reflecting on his own courtship and on the vanity of human hopes. He moves off in the opposite direction with slow professional steps.

The flight of the lovers takes them to Cavendish Square. There they halt to consider their next move.

LIZA [*out of breath*] He didnt half give me a fright, that copper. But you answered him proper.

FREDDY. I hope I havnt taken you out of your way. Where were you going?

15 Critical Thinking and Reading What causes Higgins to change his behavior so abruptly?

16 Discussion Why do Higgins and Eliza shift so quickly throughout this exchange from being furious at each other to trying to be kind and back to being furious?

17 Critical Thinking and Reading What causes Eliza to stick her tongue out at herself as she leaves?

18 Discussion Do you think that Eliza really planned to go to the river? Why or why not?

19 **Discussion** Would you have felt safe walking about London at night during Victorian times? Why or why not?

20 **Enrichment** Wimbledon Common is about a forty-five minute ride south and west of London and not a ride usually taken in a taxi.

Reader's Response Do you think Liza and Higgins will marry? Why or why not?

LIZA. To the river.

FREDDY. What for?

LIZA. To make a hole in it.

FREDDY [*horrified*] Eliza, darling. What do you mean? What's the matter?

LIZA. Never mind. It doesnt matter now. There's nobody in the world now but you and me, is there?

FREDDY. Not a soul.

They indulge in another embrace, and are again surprised by a much younger constable.

SECOND CONSTABLE. Now then, you two! What's this? Where do you think you are? Move along here, double quick.

FREDDY. As you say, sir, double quick.

They run away again, and are in Hanover Square before they stop for another conference.

FREDDY. I had no idea the police were so devilishly prudish.

LIZA. It's their business to hunt girls off the street.

FREDDY. We must go somewhere. We cant wander about the streets all night.

LIZA. Cant we? I think it'd be lovely to wander about for ever.

FREDDY. Oh, darling.

They embrace again, oblivious of the arrival of a crawling taxi. It stops.

TAXIMAN. Can I drive you and the lady anywhere, sir? | 19

They start asunder.

LIZA. Oh, Freddy, a taxi. The very thing.

FREDDY. But, damn it, I've no money.

LIZA. I have plenty. The Colonel thinks you should never go out without ten pounds in your pocket. Listen. We'll drive about all night; and in the morning I'll call on old Mrs Higgins and ask her what I ought to do. I'll tell you all about it in the cab. And the police wont touch us there.

FREDDY. Righto! Ripping. [*To the* TAXIMAN] Wimbledon Common. [*They drive off*]. | 20

THINKING ABOUT THE SELECTION

Recalling

1. (a) How are Higgins and Pickering feeling as the act opens? (b) How does Eliza feel?
2. What does Higgins suggest when Eliza asks what will become of her?
3. (a) What does Eliza do after Higgins goes to bed? (b) Whom does she run into?

Interpreting

4. (a) What two characters earlier in the play anticipated the concern Eliza expresses here? (b) What was Higgins's response to them?

5. (a) In what ways does Higgins act differently from how he behaved earlier in the play? (b) In what ways is his behavior predictable? (c) What does his behavior reveal about him?

Applying

6. What aspects of being a woman of this era compound Eliza's problems?

ANALYZING LITERATURE

Explaining Crisis

The **crisis** in a work of fiction is the turning point—that moment when the conflict presented

Closure and Extension

ANSWERS TO THINKING ABOUT THE SELECTION
Recalling

1. (a) Higgins and Pickering are very proud of themselves and of what they have accomplished by passing Eliza off as royalty. (b) Eliza had a wonderful evening but is very frustrated when the two men give her no credit for the evening's success, when they—in fact—ignore her presence.
2. Higgins says that he doesn't know and he doesn't care what will happen to her.
3. (a) Eliza packs her things and leaves the house. (b) She runs straight into the arms of Freddy, who happens to be watching the house as he does every evening —hoping to catch a glimpse of her.

Interpreting

4. (a) Both Pickering and Mrs. Pearce were concerned from the beginning about what would happen to Eliza after she had learned to be a lady. (b) Higgins alternately said that Eliza could go back where she came from, raged at them for even worrying about the problem, or goodheartedly assured everyone that things would work out fine.
5. (a) Higgins is still as insensitive and abusive as always, but he genuine-

earlier in the work comes to a head. Also referred to as the *climax,* this highpoint, which occurs close to the end of the work, is followed by a resolution of all problems. The crisis in Act IV of *Pygmalion* is quite obviously the outgrowth of a conflict between Higgins and Eliza.

1. What is the nature of that conflict; that is, what has each of the two characters been trying to achieve from the start?
2. What problems mentioned (or raised) in Act IV remain to be resolved? How do you think they will be resolved? Explain why you feel as you do.

CRITICAL THINKING AND READING
Understanding Cause and Effect

Events, both in real life and in fiction, seldom happen in a vacuum. More commonly put, one thing "usually leads to another." Your ride to school does not show up and, therefore, you are late to your first-period class. Because of your lateness, you miss getting down an important assignment due the following day. And so on. An event that leads to a particular result is called a **cause.** The result of the cause is called an **effect.** Most works of fiction are chains of causes and effects.

For each of the following events, supply one cause and one effect.
1. Eliza pays Professor Higgins a visit.
2. Pickering proposes a bet with Higgins.

3. Higgins appears at his mother's "at-home."
4. Eliza throws Higgins's slippers at him.

UNDERSTANDING LANGUAGE
Finding Synonyms and Antonyms

Two words with the same or similar meanings are **synonyms.** *Boy* and *lad* are examples of synonyms. Two words opposite in meaning are **antonyms.** *Light* and *dark* are examples of antonyms. The word in italics to the left of each list appears in Act IV. From each list, select the one synonym and the one antonym. Consult a dictionary if necessary.
1. *resumes:* desists, incites, continues, inures
2. *genial:* reclusive, mystical, cordial, glacial
3. *infamous:* disgraceful, attractive, adorable, obscure
4. *intimacy:* estrangement, confidence, befuddlement, familiarity
5. *oblivious:* apparent, unmindful, self-effacing, self-conscious

THINKING AND WRITING
Writing a Letter of Advice

What do you think about the engagement of Eliza and Freddy? Is she making the right choice? Does she have other options? List any suggestions you would offer Eliza. Then write a letter to her offering advice. When you revise your letter, make sure your advice is practical. Have you presented it in a persuasive manner? Proofread your letter and prepare a final draft.

(Answers begin on p. 1166.)

Challenge How do you predict each conflict will be resolved? Support your answers with details from the play.

ANSWERS TO CRITICAL THINKING AND READING

1. *Cause:* Eliza wants to learn to speak properly.
   Effect: Higgins takes her on as a pupil.
2. *Cause:* Pickering wants to see the girl taken care of.
   Effect: Higgins takes Eliza's life over and makes her into a lady.
3. *Cause:* Higgins wants to see if Eliza can fool a few select people in polite society.
   Effect: Eliza seems to be accepted as upper class, if a little odd.
4. *Cause:* Higgins has been totally insensitive to Eliza's feelings.
   Effect: Eliza makes up her mind to leave Higgins and his lessons.

ANSWERS TO UNDERSTANDING LANGUAGE

1. synonym: continues; antonym: desists
2. synonym: cordial; antonym: reclusive
3. synonym: disgraceful; antonym: adorable
4. synonym: confidence; antonym: estrangement
5. synonym: unmindful; antonym: self-conscious

THINKING AND WRITING

In groups have students read one another's drafts and make suggestions for improvements. The writers can then include suggestions for improvement in their revisions.

Challenge Have students write what they think Eliza was thinking as she listened to Higgins and Pickering congratulate each other after the ball. Have them read their selections to each other aloud, using a British accent and mimicking Eliza's personality as much as possible.

---

ly seems to be trying to find a solution to the problem that he has created for Eliza. (b) It is predictable that he is going to be angry, that he will not really understand someone else's needs because he has so few on the personal level, and that he will take all the credit for Eliza's success. (c) It reveals him to be a consistent personality —he is essentially unchanged from what he was at the outset, though he has developed an unacknowledged affection for Eliza.

Applying

6. Most women of the upper class were considered to be little more than decoration on the arms of their men. Because she doesn't have a man to take care of her or an occupation, she is left with nothing to live on.

ANSWERS TO ANALYZING LITERATURE

1. Higgins has devoted all of his energies to seeing that Eliza is mistaken

for a lady in polite society so that he will gain recognition as a teacher and so that he can say that he fooled the upper class at their own game. Eliza has been trying to reach the same goal but primarily to better herself and to please Higgins.
2. We don't know whether Eliza will marry Higgins or Freddy, whether Eliza will be found out, or whether Eliza will return to the Higgins's house. Resolutions and reasons for those resolutions will differ.

Literary Focus Playwrights must make their work universally true enough to allow the audience to identify with some part of their plays—the characters, the conflicts, the resolutions. Playwrights accomplish this by convincing their audiences that they should trust them to portray life so that it can be understood; they encourage their audiences to "willingly suspend their disbelief" so that their plays can deliver their messages.

Writing/Prior Knowledge Have students include the resolution of each of the character's conflicts. Then have them choose the combination of resolutions that they prefer and formulate their own endings to the play from those.

Pygmalion, Act V

Writer's Technique

The Complete Play. A play consists of many elements. The first of these is plot, the sequence of events. Will the plot be structured *chronologically*, moving ever forward in time? Or will it contain flashbacks? Next comes setting, the *when* and *where* of the play. How will time and location be conveyed to the audience? Through speakers' words? Through stage sets? Another element is characters, the people in the action. How many characters will be *round*, that is, complex and true-to-life? How many will be *flat*, one-dimensional figures included purely to advance the plot? Then comes tone, the playwright's attitude toward his or her subject or audience. Will the tone be lighthearted? Serious? A mixture? There is the issue of symbols—people, places, and events that stand for something beyond themselves. Last but not least is theme, the central idea of the play. What central idea or insight into life does the play communicate to the audience?

Writing

How will the play end? Based on the first four acts, draft your own ending. What will become of Eliza? Of Higgins? Of Freddy? Compare your hunches with those of your classmates.

Primary Source

Much of *Pygmalion* was radically different from what theatergoers were accustomed to seeing. In "An Aside" in *To Myself and My Friends*, Shaw explained the radical changes he introduced into modern English theater. He began:

> In a generation which knew nothing of any sort of acting but drawing-room acting, and which considered a speech of more than twenty words impossibly long, I went back to the classical style and write long rhetorical speeches like operatic solos, regarding my plays as musical perfomances precisely as Shakespeare did. As a producer I went back to the forgotten heroic stage business and the exciting or impressive declamation I had learnt from oldtimers like Risotori, Salvini, and Barry Sullivan. Yet so novel was my post-Marx post-Ibsen outlook on life that nobody suspected that my methods were as old as the stage itself. They would have seemed the merest routine to Kemble or Mrs. Siddons; but to the Victorian leading ladies they seemed to be unleadingladylike barnstorming. . . . I was continually struggling with the conscientious efforts of our players to underdo their parts lest they should be considered stagey. . . . It took a European war to cure them of wanting to be ladies and gentlemen first and actresses and actors later.

Vocabulary

Preteach the following vocabulary words:

resplendently (ri splen′ dənt lē) *adj.*: Splendidly; gorgeously (p. 1170)

vehement (vē′ ə mənt) *adj.*: Energetic; forceful (p. 1170)

magnanimous (mag nan′ ə məs) *adj.*: Generously forgiving (p. 1178)

transfiguration (trans fig′ yoo ra′ shən) *n.*: Change in outward appearance (p. 1184)

coquetting (kō ket′ iŋ) *v.*: Flirting (p. 1184)

impetuous (im pech′ oo wəs) *adj.*: Given to rash or hasty action (p. 1185)

transcendence (tran sen′ dəns) *n.*: Rising above (p. 1187)

odious (ō′ dē əs) *adj.*: Hateful; offensive (p. 1189)

pretentious (pri ten′ shes) *adj.*: Making false claims (p. 1189)

Objectives

1 To understand a complete play
2 To summarize a play
3 To write about the title of a play

Support Material

Teaching Portfolio
Teacher Backup, p. 1399
Grammar in Action Worksheets, *Using Transitions*, p. 1403; *Understanding Narrative Writing*, 1405
Usage and Mechanics Worksheet, p. 1407
Vocabulary Check, p. 1408

Critical Thinking and Reading Worksheet, *Summarizing*, p. 1410
Language Worksheet, *Using Prefixes*, p. 1411
Selection Test, p. 1412

ACT V

MRS HIGGINS's *drawing room. She is at her writing-table as before. The* PARLORMAID *comes in.*

THE PARLORMAID [*at the door*] Mr Henry, maam, is downstairs with Colonel Pickering.

MRS HIGGINS. Well, shew them up.

THE PARLORMAID. Theyre using the telephone, maam. Telephoning to the police, I think.

MRS HIGGINS. What!

THE PARLORMAID [*coming further in and lowering her voice*] Mr Henry is in a state, maam. I thought I'd better tell you.

MRS HIGGINS. If you had told me that Mr Henry was not in a state it would have been more surprising. Tell them to come up when theyve finished with the police. I suppose he's lost something.

THE PARLORMAID. Yes, maam [*going*].

MRS HIGGINS. Go upstairs and tell Miss Doolittle that Mr Henry and the Colonel are here. Ask her not to come down til I send for her.

THE PARLORMAID. Yes, maam.

HIGGINS *bursts in. He is, as the* PARLORMAID *has said, in a state.*

HIGGINS. Look here, mother: heres a confounded thing!

MRS HIGGINS. Yes, dear. Good morning. [*He checks his impatience and kisses her, whilst the* PARLORMAID *goes out*]. What is it?

HIGGINS. Eliza's bolted.

MRS HIGGINS [*calmly continuing her writing*] You must have frightened her.

HIGGINS. Frightened her! nonsense! She was left last night, as usual, to turn out the lights and all that; and instead of going to bed she changed her clothes and went right off: her bed wasnt slept in. She came in a cab for her things before seven this morning; and that fool Mrs Pearce let her have them without telling me a word about it. What am I to do?

MRS HIGGINS. Do without, I'm afraid, Henry. The girl has a perfect right to leave if she chooses.

HIGGINS [*wandering distractedly across the room*] But I cant find anything. I dont know what appointments Ive got. I'm—[PICKERING *comes in.* MRS HIGGINS *puts down her pen and turns away from the writing-table*].

PICKERING [*shaking hands*] Good morning, Mrs Higgins. Has Henry told you? [*He sits down on the ottoman*].

HIGGINS. What does that ass of an inspector say? Have you offered a reward?

MRS HIGGINS [*rising in indignant amazement*] You dont mean to say you have set the police after Eliza.

HIGGINS. Of course. What are the police for? What else could we do? [*He sits in the Elizabethan chair*].

PICKERING. The inspector made a lot of difficulties. I really think he suspected us of some improper purpose.

MRS HIGGINS. Well, of course, he did. What right have you to go to the police and give the girl's name as if she were a thief, or a lost umbrella, or something? Really! [*She sits down again, deeply vexed*].

HIGGINS. But we want to find her.

PICKERING. We cant let her go like this, you know, Mrs Higgins. What were we to do?

MRS HIGGINS. You have no more sense, either of you, than two children. Why—

The PARLORMAID *comes in and breaks off the conversation.*

THE PARLORMAID. Mr Henry: a gentleman wants to see you very particular. He's been sent on from Wimpole Street.

HIGGINS. Oh, bother! I cant see anyone now. Who is it?

Presentation

Motivation/Prior Knowledge
Have students put themselves in Eliza's place and discuss the following questions. Should I stay with Higgins and Pickering? Should I marry Freddy? Should I go back to being a flower girl? Have them predict what Eliza will do, based on their answers to these questions.

Master Teacher Note When students have finished reading *Pygmalion,* you might show the movie *My Fair Lady,* asking students to compare and contrast the two plays and the effectiveness of each while they watch. Have students write a review explaining which of the two they prefer and why.

Purpose-Setting Question Does Shaw make use of all the elements of a play?

1 **Discussion** Why is Higgins looking for Eliza? Do you think that he's worried about her? Justify your answer based on his past behavior.

2 **Discussion** Discuss the alternative possibilities of why Higgins might be so distracted by Eliza's disappearance.

3 Reading Strategy Have students predict what has caused Mr. Doolittle to be dressed so finely and what part Higgins had to play in Doolittle's situation. Have them evaluate their predictions when they discover what has happened.

4 Discussion Is Mr. Doolittle's discomfort at not noticing Mrs. Higgins part of his former self or his present self?

THE PARLORMAID. A Mr Doolittle, sir.

PICKERING. Doolittle! Do you mean the dustman?

THE PARLORMAID. Dustman! Oh no, sir: a gentleman.

HIGGINS [*springing up excitedly*] By George, Pick, it's some relative of hers that she's gone to. Somebody we know nothing about. [*To the* PARLORMAID] Send him up, quick.

THE PARLORMAID. Yes, sir. [*She goes*].

HIGGINS [*eagerly, going to his mother*] Genteel relatives! now we shall hear something. [*He sits down in the Chippendale chair*].

MRS HIGGINS. Do you know any of her people?

PICKERING. Only her father: the fellow we told you about.

THE PARLORMAID [*announcing*] Mr Doolittle. [*She withdraws*].

> DOOLITTLE *enters. He is resplendently dressed as for a fashionable wedding, and might, in fact, be the bridegroom. A flower in his buttonhole, a dazzling silk hat, and patent leather shoes complete the effect. He is too concerned with the business he has come on to notice* MRS HIGGINS. *He walks straight to* HIGGINS, *and accosts him with vehement reproach.*

DOOLITTLE [*indicating his own person*] See here! Do you see this? You done this.

HIGGINS. Done what, man?

DOOLITTLE. This, I tell you. Look at it. Look at this hat. Look at this coat.

PICKERING. Has Eliza been buying you clothes?

DOOLITTLE. Eliza! not she. Why would she buy me clothes?

MRS HIGGINS. Good morning, Mr Doolittle. Wont you sit down?

DOOLITTLE [*taken aback as he becomes conscious that he has forgotten his hostess*] Asking your pardon, maam. [*He approaches her and shakes her proffered hand*]. Thank you. [*He sits down on the ottoman, on* PICKERING*'s right*]. I am that full of what has happened to me that I cant think of anything else.

HIGGINS. What the dickens has happened to you?

DOOLITTLE. I shouldn't mind if it had only happened to me: anything might happen to anybody and nobody to blame but Providence, as you might say. But this is something that you done to me: yes, you, Enry Iggins.

HIGGINS. Have you found Eliza?

DOOLITTLE. Have you lost her?

HIGGINS. Yes.

DOOLITTLE. You have all the luck, you have. I aint found her; but she'll find me quick enough now after what you done to me.

MRS HIGGINS. But what has my son done to you, Mr Doolittle?

DOOLITTLE. Done to me! Ruined me. Destroyed my happiness. Tied me up and delivered me into the hands of middle class morality.

HIGGINS [*rising intolerantly and standing over* DOOLITTLE] Youre raving. Youre drunk. Youre mad. I gave you five pounds. After that I had two conversations with you, at half-a-crown an hour. Ive never seen you since.

DOOLITTLE. Oh! Drunk am I? Mad am I? Tell me this. Did you or did you not write a letter to an old blighter in America that was giving five millions to found Moral Reform Societies all over the world, and that wanted you to invent a universal language for him?

HIGGINS. What! Ezra D. Wannafeller! He's dead. [*He sits down again carelessly*].

DOOLITTLE. Yes: he's dead; and I'm done for. Now did you or did you not write a letter to him to say that the most original moralist at

1170 *The Modern Period*

5 **Discussion** What unexpected inheritance did Mr. Doolittle receive? What are its conditions? What role did Higgins play in the inheritance? Compare your predictions to these answers.

present in England, to the best of your knowledge, was Alfred Doolittle, a common dustman?

HIGGINS. Oh, after your first visit I remember making some silly joke of the kind.

DOOLITTLE. Ah! You may well call it a silly joke. It put the lid on me right enough. Just give him the chance he wanted to shew that Americans is not like us: that they reckonize and respect merit in every class of life, however humble. Them words is in his blooming will, in which, Henry Higgins, thanks to your silly joking, he leaves me a share in his Predigested Cheese Trust worth [three] thousand a year on condition that I lecture for his Wannafeller Moral Reform World League as often as they ask me up to six times a year.

HIGGINS. The devil he does! Whew! [*Brightening suddenly*] What a lark!

PICKERING. A safe thing for you, Doolittle. They wont ask you twice.

DOOLITTLE. It aint the lecturing I mind. I'll lecture them blue in the face, I will, and not turn a hair. It's making a gentleman of me that I object to. Who asked him to make a gentleman of me? I was happy. I was free. I touched pretty nigh everybody for money when I wanted it, same as I touched you, Enry Iggins. Now I am worrited; tied neck and heels; and everybody touches me for money. It's a fine thing for you, says my solicitor.[1] Is it? says I. You mean it's a good

---

1. solicitor *n.*: A member of the legal profession who is not allowed to plead cases in superior court.

Pygmalion, Act V   1171

6 Discussion What does Mr. Doolittle see as advantages and disadvantages of his new status?

7 Reading Strategy Discuss the meaning of this allusion and list some of the modern versions, such as "between a rock and a hard place."

8 Literary Focus What does the speech say about Higgins as a representative of his class?

6

thing for you, I says. When I was a poor man and had a solicitor once when they found a pram[2] in the dust cart, he got me off, and got shut of me and got me shut of him as quick as he could. Same with the doctors: used to shove me out of the hospital before I could hardly stand on my legs, and nothing to pay. Now they finds out that I'm not a healthy man and cant live unless they looks after me twice a day. In the house I'm not let do a hand's turn for myself: somebody else must do it and touch me for it. A year ago I hadnt a relative in the world except two or three that wouldn't speak to me. Now Ive fifty, and not a decent week's wages among the lot of them. I have to live for others and not for myself: that middle class morality. You talk of losing Eliza. Dont you be anxious: I bet she's on my doorstep by this: she that could support herself easy by selling flowers if I wasnt respectable. And the next one to touch me will be you, Enry Iggins. I'll have to learn to speak middle class language from you, instead of speaking proper English. Thats where youll come in; and I daresay thats what you done it for.

MRS HIGGINS. But, my dear Mr Doolittle, you need not suffer all this if you are really in earnest. Nobody can force you to accept this bequest. You can repudiate it. Isnt that so, Colonel Pickering?

PICKERING. I believe so.

DOOLITTLE [*softening his manner in deference to her sex*] Thats the tragedy of it, maam. It's easy to say chuck it; but I havnt the nerve. Which of us has? We're all intimidated. Intimidated, maam: thats what we are. What is there for me if I chuck it but the workhouse in my old age? I have to dye my hair already to keep my job as a dustman. If I was one of the deserving poor, and had put by a bit, I could chuck it; but then why should I, acause the deserving poor might as well be millionaires for all the happiness they ever has. They dont know what happi-

ness is. But I, as one of the undeserving poor, have nothing between me and the pauper's uniform but this here blasted three thousand a year that shoves me into the middle class. (Excuse the expression, maam; youd use it yourself if you had my provocation). Theyve got you every way you turn: it's a choice between the Skilly of the workhouse and the Char Bydis[3] of the middle class; and I havnt the nerve for the workhouse. Intimidated: thats what I am. Broke. Bought up. Happier men than me will call for my dust, and touch me for their tip; and I'll look on helpless, and envy them. And thats what your son has brought me to. [*He is overcome by emotion*].

7

MRS HIGGINS. Well, I'm very glad youre not going to do anything foolish, Mr Doolittle. For this solves the problem of Eliza's future. You can provide for her now.

DOOLITTLE [*with melancholy resignation*] Yes, maam: I'm expected to provide for everyone now, out of [three] thousand a year.

HIGGINS [*jumping up*] Nonsense! he cant provide for her. He shant provide for her. She doesnt belong to him. I paid him five pounds for her. Doolittle: either youre an honest man or a rogue.

8

DOOLITTLE [*tolerantly*] A little of both, Henry, like the rest of us: a little of both.

HIGGINS. Well, you took that money for the girl; and you have no right to take her as well.

MRS HIGGINS. Henry: dont be absurd. If you want to know where Eliza is, she is upstairs.

HIGGINS [*amazed*] Upstairs!!! Then I shall

---

2. pram *n*.: Baby carriage.

---

3. Skilly . . . Char Bydis: Doolittle means Scylla (sil′ ə) and Charybdis (kə rib′ dis), a dangerous rock and whirlpool on either side of the narrow passage between Italy and Sicily. Scylla and Charybdis, personified by the ancient Greeks as two monsters, have come to stand for any two dangers neither of which can be evaded without risking the other.

jolly soon fetch her downstairs. [*He makes resolutely for the door*].

MRS HIGGINS [*rising and following him*] Be quiet, Henry. Sit down.

HIGGINS. I—

MRS HIGGINS. Sit down, dear; and listen to me.

HIGGINS. Oh very well, very well, very well. [*He throws himself ungraciously on the ottoman, with his face towards the windows*]. But I think you might have told us this half an hour ago.

MRS HIGGINS. Eliza came to me this morning. She told me of the brutal way you two treated her.

HIGGINS [*bounding up again*] What!

PICKERING [*rising also*] My dear Mrs Higgins, she's been telling you stories. We didnt treat her brutally. We hardly said a word to her; and we parted on particularly good terms. [*Turning on* Higgins] Higgins: did you bully her after I went to bed?

HIGGINS. Just the other way about. She threw my slippers in my face. She behaved in the most outrageous way. I never gave her the slightest provocation. The slippers came bang into my face the moment I entered the room—before I had uttered a word. And used perfectly awful language.

PICKERING [*astonished*] But why? What did we do to her?

MRS HIGGINS. I think I know pretty well what you did. The girl is naturally rather affectionate, I think. Isnt she, Mr Doolittle?

DOOLITTLE. Very tender-hearted, maam. Takes after me.

MRS HIGGINS. Just so. She had become attached to you both. She worked very hard for you, Henry. I don't think you quite realize what anything in the nature of brain work means to a girl of her class. Well, it seems that when the great day of trial came, and she did this wonderful thing for you without making a single mistake, you two sat there and never said a word to her, but talked together of how glad you were that it was all over and how you had been bored with the whole thing. And then you were surprised because she threw your slippers at you! *I* should have thrown the fire-irons at you.

HIGGINS. We said nothing except that we were tired and wanted to go to bed. Did we, Pick?

PICKERING [*shrugging his shoulders*] That was all.

MRS HIGGINS [*ironically*] Quite sure?

PICKERING. Absolutely. Really, that was all.

MRS HIGGINS. You didnt thank her, or pet her, or admire her, or tell her how splendid she'd been.

HIGGINS [*impatiently*] But she knew all about that. We didnt make speeches to her, if thats what you mean.

PICKERING [*conscience stricken*] Perhaps we were a little inconsiderate. Is she very angry?

MRS HIGGINS [*returning to her place at the writing-table*] Well, I'm afraid she wont go back to Wimpole Street, especially now that Mr Doolittle is able to keep up the position you have thrust on her; but she says she is quite willing to meet you on friendly terms and to let bygones be bygones.

HIGGINS [*furious*] Is she, by George? Ho!

MRS HIGGINS. If you promise to behave yourself, Henry, I'll ask her to come down. If not, go home; for you have taken up quite enough of my time.

HIGGINS. Oh, all right. Very well. Pick: you behave yourself. Let us put on our best Sunday manners for this creature that we picked out of the mud. [*He flings himself sulkily into the Elizabethan chair*].

DOOLITTLE [*remonstrating*] Now, now, Enry Iggins! Have some consideration for my feelings as a middle class man.

---

9 **Discussion** Decide if Higgins is fooling himself or if he really believes what he is saying and explain your choice.

10 **Discussion** On whose side is Mrs. Higgins and why?

11 **Reading Strategy** What is the irony in this statement?

12 Discussion Why is it important for Eliza not to know what has happened to her father until after she has made her decision?

13 Discussion What causes Higgins to choke?

14 Literary Focus If you knew nothing else about Higgins but what you can learn in this speech, how would you describe his character?

12

MRS HIGGINS. Remember your promise, Henry. [*She presses the bell-button on the writing-table*]. Mr Doolittle: will you be so good as to step out on the balcony for a moment. I dont want Eliza to have the shock of your news until she has made it up with these two gentlemen. Would you mind?

DOOLITTLE. As you wish, lady. Anything to help Henry to keep her off my hands. [*He disappears through the window*].

The PARLORMAID *answers the bell.* PICKERING *sits down in* DOOLITTLE'S *place.*

MRS HIGGINS. Ask Miss Doolittle to come down, please.

THE PARLORMAID. Yes, maam. [*She goes out*].

MRS HIGGINS. Now, Henry: be good.

HIGGINS. I am behaving myself perfectly.

PICKERING. He is doing his best, Mrs Higgins.

A pause. HIGGINS *throws back his head; stretches out his legs; and begins to whistle.*

MRS HIGGINS. Henry, dearest, you dont look at all nice in that attitude.

HIGGINS [*pulling himself together*] I was not trying to look nice, mother.

MRS HIGGINS. It doesnt matter, dear. I only wanted to make you speak.

HIGGINS. Why?

MRS HIGGINS. Because you cant speak and whistle at the same time.

HIGGINS *groans. Another very trying pause.*

HIGGINS [*springing up, out of patience*] Where the devil is that girl? Are we to wait here all day?

ELIZA *enters, sunny, self-possessed, and giving a staggeringly convincing exhibition of ease of manner. She carries a little work-basket, and is very much at home.* PICKERING *is too much taken aback to rise.*

LIZA. How do you do, Professor Higgins? Are you quite well?

HIGGINS [*choking*] Am I— [*He can say no more*].

13

LIZA. But of course you are: you are never ill. So glad to see you again, Colonel Pickering. [*He rises hastily; and they shake hands*]. Quite chilly this morning, isn't it? [*She sits down on his left. He sits beside her*].

HIGGINS. Dont you dare try this game on me. I taught it to you; and it doesnt take me in. Get up and come home; and dont be a fool.

ELIZA *takes a piece of needlework from her basket, and begins to stitch at it, without taking the least notice of this outburst.*

MRS HIGGINS. Very nicely put, indeed, Henry. No woman could resist such an invitation.

HIGGINS. You let her alone, mother. Let her speak for herself. You will jolly soon see whether she has an idea that I havnt put into her head or a word that I havnt put into her mouth. I tell you I have created this thing out of the squashed cabbage leaves of Covent Garden; and now she pretends to play the fine lady with me.

14

MRS HIGGINS [*placidly*] Yes, dear; but youll sit down, wont you?

HIGGINS *sits down again, savagely.*

LIZA [*to* PICKERING, *taking no apparent notice of* HIGGINS, *and working away deftly*] Will you drop me altogether now that the experiment is over, Colonel Pickering?

PICKERING. Oh dont. You mustnt think of it as an experiment. It shocks me, somehow.

LIZA. Oh, I'm only a squashed cabbage leaf—

PICKERING [*impulsively*] No.

LIZA [*continuing quietly*]—but I owe so much to you that I should be very unhappy if you forgot me.

PICKERING. It's very kind of you to say so, Miss Doolittle.

15 Reading Strategy What irony is involved in Eliza's explanation to Pickering?

16 Literary Focus What effect has having self-respect had on the development of Eliza's character?

17 Discussion Of what significance is the fact that Higgins took off his boots in front of Eliza?

18 Literary Focus Have students cite examples from the play that support Eliza's observation that the difference between a flower girl and a lady is not in the way that she behaves but in the way that she is treated.

19 Discussion What has caused the final separation between Eliza's past and present?

15

LIZA. It's not because you paid for my dresses. I know you are generous to everybody with money. But it was from you that I learnt really nice manners; and that is what makes one a lady, isnt it? You see it was so very difficult for me with the example of Professor Higgins always before me. I was brought up to be just like him, unable to control myself, and using bad language on the slightest provocation. And I should never have known that ladies and gentlemen didnt behave like that if you hadnt been there.

HIGGINS. Well!!

PICKERING. Oh, thats only his way, you know. He doesnt mean it.

LIZA. Oh, *I* didnt mean it either, when I was a flower girl. It was only my way. But you see I did it; and thats what makes the difference after all.

PICKERING. No doubt. Still, he taught you to speak; and I couldn't have done that, you know.

LIZA [*trivially*] Of course: that is his profession.

HIGGINS. Damnation!

LIZA [*continuing*] It was just like learning to dance in the fashionable way: there was nothing more than that in it. But do you know what began my real education?

PICKERING. What?

16

LIZA [*stopping her work for a moment*] Your calling me Miss Doolittle that day when I first came to Wimpole Street. That was the beginning of self-respect for me. [*She resumes her stitching*] And there were a hundred little things you never noticed, because they came naturally to you. Things about standing up and taking off your hat and opening doors—

PICKERING. Oh, that was nothing.

LIZA. Yes: things that shewed you thought and felt about me as if I were something better than a scullery-maid; though of course I know you would have been just the same to a scullery-maid if she had been let into the drawing room. You never took off your boots in the dining room when I was there.

17

PICKERING. You mustnt mind that. Higgins takes off his boots all over the place.

LIZA. I know. I am not blaming him. It is his way, isn't it? But it made such a difference to me that you didnt do it. You see, really and truly, apart from the things anyone can pick up (the dressing and the proper way of speaking, and so on), the difference between a lady and a flower girl is not how she behaves, but how she's treated. I shall always be a flower girl to Professor Higgins, because he always treats me as a flower girl, and always will; but I know I can be a lady to you, because you always treat me as a lady, and always will.

18

MRS HIGGINS. Please dont grind your teeth, Henry.

PICKERING. Well, this is really very nice of you, Miss Doolittle.

LIZA. I should like you to call me Eliza, now, if you would.

PICKERING. Thank you. Eliza, of course.

LIZA. And I should like Professor Higgins to call me Miss Doolittle.

HIGGINS. I'll see you damned first.

MRS HIGGINS. Henry! Henry!

PICKERING [*laughing*] Why dont you slang back at him? Dont stand it. It would do him a lot of good.

19

LIZA. I cant. I could have done it once; but now I cant go back to it. You told me, you know, that when a child is brought to a foreign country, it picks up the language in a few weeks, and forgets its own. Well, I am a child in your country. I have forgotten my own language, and can speak nothing but yours. Thats the real break-off with the corner of Tottenham Court Road. Leaving Wimpole Street finishes it.

PICKERING [*much alarmed*] Oh! but youre coming back to Wimpole Street, arnt you? Youll forgive Higgins?

HIGGINS [*rising*] Forgive! Will she, by George! Let her go. Let her find out how she can get on without us. She will relapse into the gutter in three weeks without me at her elbow.

DOOLITTLE *appears at the centre window. With a look of dignified reproach at* HIGGINS, *he comes slowly and silently to his daughter, who, with her back to the window, is unconscious of his approach.*

PICKERING. He's incorrigible, Eliza. You wont relapse, will you?

20

LIZA. No: not now. Never again. I have learnt my lesson. I dont believe I could utter one of the old sounds if I tried. [DOOLITTLE *touches her on the left shoulder. She drops her work, losing her self-possession utterly at the spectacle of her father's splendor*] A-a-a-a-ah-ow-ooh!

HIGGINS [*With a crow of triumph*] Aha! Just so. A-a-a-a-ahowooh! A-a-a-a-ahowooh! A-a-a-a-ahowooh! Victory! Victory! [*He throws himself on the divan, folding his arms, and spraddling arrogantly*].

DOOLITTLE. Can you blame the girl? Dont look at me like that, Eliza. It aint my fault. Ive come into some money.

LIZA. You must have touched a millionaire this time, dad.

DOOLITTLE. I have. But I'm dressed something special today. I'm going to St George's, Hanover Square. Your stepmother is going to marry me.

LIZA [*angrily*] Youre going to let yourself down to marry that low common woman!

PICKERING [*quietly*] He ought to, Eliza. [*To* DOOLITTLE] Why has she changed her mind?

DOOLITTLE [*sadly*] Intimidated, Governor. Intimidated. Middle class morality claims its victim. Wont you put on your hat, Liza, and come and see me turned off?

LIZA. If the Colonel says I must, I—I'll [*almost sobbing*] I'll demean myself. And get insulted for my pains, like enough.

DOOLITTLE. Dont be afraid: she never comes to words with anyone now, poor woman! respectability has broke all the spirit out of her.

21

PICKERING [*squeezing* ELIZA'S *elbow gently*] Be kind to them, Eliza. Make the best of it.

LIZA [*forcing a little smile for him through her vexation*] Oh well, just to shew theres no ill feeling. I'll be back in a moment. [*She goes out*].

DOOLITTLE [*sitting down beside* PICKERING] I feel uncommon nervous about the ceremony, Colonel. I wish youd come and see me through it.

PICKERING. But youve been through it before, man. You were married to Eliza's mother.

DOOLITTLE. Who told you that, Colonel?

PICKERING. Well, nobody told me. But I concluded—naturally——

DOOLITTLE. No: that aint the natural way, Colonel: it's only the middle class way. My way was always the undeserving way. But dont say nothing to Eliza. She dont know: I always had a delicacy about telling her.

PICKERING. Quite right. We'll leave it so, if you dont mind.

DOOLITTLE. And youll come to the church, Colonel, and put me through straight?

PICKERING. With pleasure. As far as a bachelor can.

MRS HIGGINS. May I come, Mr Doolittle? I should be very sorry to miss your wedding.

22

DOOLITTLE. I should indeed be honored by your condescension, maam; and my poor old

20 Reading Strategy Explore the irony and humor in Eliza's reaction.

21 Literary Focus What changes has middle-class morality brought to the character of Mr. Doolittle's future wife? Explain how this change shows Shaw poking fun at this morality.

22 Discussion Why might someone in Mrs. Higgins's social position go to Mr. Doolittle's wedding? What is her motivation?

23 **Discussion** What is Mr. Doolittle saying to Eliza and Pickering about the relationship between the three of them?

24 **Discussion** What is the relationship between Higgins's statement and Shaw's feelings about the class structure of England?

25 **Literary Focus** What is Shaw saying about manners and class in this paragraph that support the theme of the play?

woman would take it as a tremenjous compliment. She's been very low, thinking of the happy days that are no more.

MRS HIGGINS [*rising*] I'll order the carriage and get ready. [*The men rise, except* HIGGINS]. I shant be more than fifteen minutes. [*As she goes to the door* ELIZA *comes in, hatted and buttoning her gloves*]. I'm going to the church to see your father married, Eliza. You had better come in the brougham[4] with me. Colonel Pickering can go on with the bridegroom.

MRS HIGGINS *goes out.* ELIZA *comes to the middle of the room between the centre window and the ottoman.* PICKERING *joins her.*

DOOLITTLE. Bridegroom. What a word! It makes a man realize his position, somehow. [*He takes up his hat and goes towards the door*].

PICKERING. Before I go, Eliza, do forgive Higgins and come back to us.

LIZA. I dont think dad would allow me. Would you, dad?

DOOLITTLE [*sad but magnanimous*] They played you off very cunning, Eliza, them two sportsmen. If it had been only one of them, you could have nailed him. But you see, there was two; and one of them chaperoned the other, as you might say. [*To* PICKERING] It was artful of you, Colonel; but I bear no malice: I should have done the same myself. I been the victim of one woman after another all my life, and I dont grudge you two getting the better of Liza. I shant interfere. It's time for us to go, Colonel. So long, Henry. See you in St George's, Eliza. [*He goes out*].

PICKERING. [*coaxing*] Do stay with us, Eliza. [*He follows Doolittle*].

ELIZA *goes out on the balcony to avoid being alone with* HIGGINS. *He rises and joins her there. She immediately comes back into the room and makes for the door; but he*

---

4. **brougham** (broom) *n.*: A type of carriage.

goes along the balcony and gets his back to the door before she reaches it.

HIGGINS. Well, Eliza, you've had a bit of your own back, as you call it. Have you had enough? and are you going to be reasonable? Or do you want any more?

LIZA. You want me back only to pick up your slippers and put up with your tempers and fetch and carry for you.

HIGGINS. I havnt said I wanted you back at all.

LIZA. Oh, indeed. Then what are we talking about?

HIGGINS. About you, not about me. If you come back I shall treat you just as I have always treated you. I cant change my nature; and I dont intend to change my manners. My manners are exactly the same as Colonel Pickering's.

LIZA. That's not true. He treats a flower girl as if she was a duchess.

HIGGINS. And I treat a duchess as if she was a flower girl.

LIZA. I see [*She turns away composedly, and sits on the ottoman, facing the window*]. The same to everybody.

HIGGINS. Just so.

LIZA. Like father.

HIGGINS [*grinning, a little taken down*] Without accepting the comparison at all points, Eliza, it's quite true that your father is not a snob, and that he will be quite at home in any station of life to which his eccentric destiny may call him. [*Seriously*] The great secret, Eliza, is not having bad manners or good manners or any other particular sort of manners, but having the same manner for all human souls: in short, behaving as if you were in Heaven, where there are no third-class carriages, and one soul is as good as another.

LIZA. Amen. You are a born preacher.

Primary Source

Following is an excerpt from a letter that Shaw wrote to Edmund Gurney, who was rehearsing the part of Alfred Doolittle:

In the first act your whole scene is played on the point of your being one of the undeserving poor. You get the very last inch out of it, and the slightest attempt to come back to it in the last act would be quite fatal. When it is alluded to there, there must be no emphasis whatever on it: you must play the last act altogether on your melancholy downfall as a captive of middle-class morality. When you come on the stage, Higgins will be somewhere—God knows where. . . . The point for you is that no matter where he is . . . go straight to him and have it out with him about the clothes close up nose to nose with him, and make it clear that you are quite oblivious of the presence of Mrs. Higgins. . . . From the moment she speaks to you, you must adapt your manner to her presence, and throw yourself with instinctive good manners, and the gallantry that has made you a slave to women all your life, on her sympathy. I want it to be clear that the dustman has much more social talent than anybody present.

HIGGINS [irritated] The question is not whether I treat you rudely, but whether you ever heard me treat anyone else better.

LIZA [with sudden sincerity] I dont care how you treat me. I dont mind you swearing at me. I shouldnt mind a black eye: Ive had one before this. But [standing up and facing him] I wont be passed over.

HIGGINS. Then get out of my way; for I wont stop for you. You talk about me as if I were a motor bus.

LIZA. So you are a motor bus: all bounce and go, and no consideration for anyone. But I can do without you: dont think I cant.

HIGGINS. I know you can. I told you you could.

LIZA [wounded, getting away from him to the other side of the ottoman with her face to the hearth] I know you did, you brute. You wanted to get rid of me.

HIGGINS. Liar.

LIZA. Thank you. [She sits down with dignity]

HIGGINS. You never asked yourself, I suppose, whether I could do without you.

LIZA. [earnestly] Don't you try to get round me. You'll have to do without me.

26

HIGGINS [arrogant] I can do without anybody. I have my own soul: my own spark of divine fire. But [with sudden humility] I shall miss you, Eliza. [He sits down near her on the ottoman] I have learnt something from your idiotic notions: I confess that humbly and gratefully. And I have grown accustomed to your voice and appearance. I like them, rather.

LIZA. Well, you have both of them on your gramophone and in your book of photographs. When you feel lonely without me, you can turn the machine on. It's got no feelings to hurt.

HIGGINS. I cant turn your soul on. Leave me those feelings; and you can take away the voice and the face. They are not you.

LIZA. Oh, you are a devil. You can twist the heart in a girl as easy as some could twist her arms to hurt her. Mrs Pearce warned me. Time and again she has wanted to leave you; and you always got round her at the last minute. And you dont care a bit for her. And you dont care a bit for me.

HIGGINS. I care for life, for humanity; and you are a part of it that has come my way and been built into my house. What more can you or anyone ask?

LIZA. I wont care for anybody that doesnt care for me.

HIGGINS. Commercial principles, Eliza. Like [reproducing her Covent Garden pronunciation with professional exactness] s'yollin voylets [selling violets], isnt it?

LIZA. Dont sneer at me. It's mean to sneer at me.

HIGGINS. I have never sneered in my life. Sneering doesnt become either the human face or the human soul. I am expressing my righteous contempt for Commercialism. I dont and wont trade in affection. You call me a brute because you couldnt buy a claim on me by fetching my slippers and finding my spectacles. You were a fool: I think a woman fetching a man's slippers is a disgusting sight: did I ever fetch your slippers? I think a good deal more of you for throwing them in my face. No use slaving for me and then saying you want to be cared for: who cares for a slave? If you come back, come back for the sake of good fellowship; for youll get nothing else. Youve had a thousand times as much out of me as I have out of you; and if you dare to set up your little dog's tricks of fetching and carrying slippers against my creation of a Duchess Eliza, I'll slam the door in your silly face.

27

LIZA. What did you do it for if you didnt care for me?

HIGGINS [heartily] Why, because it was my job.

Pygmalion, Act V   1179

26 **Literary Focus** Is this speech consistent with Higgins's character? If so, why? If not, why not?

27 **Discussion** What universal truth does Higgins—speaking for Shaw—present here for anyone interested in relationships between men and women? What new light does Higgins's explanation shed on him?

28 **Discussion** According to Higgins, what is the cause of violence in life?

29 **Discussion** Why does Eliza consider herself a slave?

30 **Discussion** Why—when he doesn't appear to be asking her —does Eliza tell Higgins that she won't marry him?

31 **Discussion** What *are* Eliza and Higgins really quarreling about?

LIZA. You never thought of the trouble it would make for me.

28 HIGGINS. Would the world ever have been made if its maker had been afraid of making trouble? Making life means making trouble. Theres only one way of escaping trouble; and thats killing things. Cowards, you notice, are always shrieking to have troublesome people killed.

LIZA. I'm no preacher: I dont notice things like that. I notice that you dont notice me.

HIGGINS [*jumping up and walking about intolerantly*] Eliza: youre an idiot. I waste the treasures of my Miltonic mind by spreading them before you. Once for all, understand that I go my way and do my work without caring twopence what happens to either of us. I am not intimidated, like your father and your stepmother. So you can come back or go to the devil: which you please.

LIZA. What am I to come back for?

HIGGINS [*bouncing up on his knees on the ottoman and leaning over it to her*] For the fun of it. Thats why I took you on.

LIZA [*with averted face*] And you may throw me out tomorrow if I dont do everything you want me to?

HIGGINS. Yes; and you may walk out tomorrow if I dont do everything you want me to.

LIZA. And live with my stepmother?

HIGGINS. Yes, or sell flowers.

29 LIZA. Oh, if I only could go back to my flower basket! I should be independent of both you and father and all the world! Why did you take my independence from me? Why did I give it up? I'm a slave now, for all my fine clothes.

30 HIGGINS. Not a bit. I'll adopt you as my daughter and settle money on you if you like. Or would you rather marry Pickering?

LIZA [*looking fiercely round at him*] I wouldnt marry you if you asked me; and youre nearer my age than what he is.

HIGGINS [*gently*] Than he is: not "than what he is."

LIZA [*losing her temper and rising*] I'll talk as I like. Youre not my teacher now.

HIGGINS [*reflectively*] I dont suppose Pickering would, though. He's as confirmed an old bachelor as I am.

LIZA. Thats not what I want; and dont you think it. I've always had chaps enough wanting me that way. Freddy Hill writes to me twice and three times a day, sheets and sheets.

HIGGINS [*disagreeably surprised*] Damn his impudence! [*He recoils and finds himself sitting on his heels*].

LIZA. He has a right to if he likes, poor lad. And he does love me.

HIGGINS [*getting off the ottoman*] You have no right to encourage him.

LIZA. Every girl has a right to be loved.

HIGGINS. What! By fools like that?

31 LIZA. Freddy's not a fool. And if he's weak and poor and wants me, may be he'd make me happier than my betters that bully me and dont want me.

HIGGINS. Can he make anything of you? Thats the point.

LIZA. Perhaps I could make something of him. But I never thought of us making anything of one another; and you never think of anything else. I only want to be natural.

HIGGINS. In short, you want me to be as infatuated about you as Freddy? Is that it?

LIZA. No I dont. Thats not the sort of feeling I want from you. And dont you be too sure of yourself or of me. I could have been a bad girl if I'd liked. Ive seen more of some things than you, for all your learning. Girls like me can drag gentlemen down to make love to them easy enough. And they wish each other dead the next minute.

HIGGINS. Of course they do. Then what in thunder are we quarrelling about?

LIZA [*much troubled*] I want a little kindness. I know I'm a common ignorant girl, and you a book-learned gentleman; but I'm not dirt under your feet. What I done [*correcting herself*] what I did was not for the dresses and the taxis: I did it because we were pleasant together and I come—came—to care for you; not to want you to make love to me, and not forgetting the difference between us, but more friendly like.

HIGGINS. Well, of course. Thats just how I feel. And how Pickering feels. Eliza: youre a fool.

LIZA. Thats not a proper answer to give me [*she sinks on the chair at the writing-table in tears*].

HIGGINS. It's all youll get until you stop being a common idiot. If youre going to be a lady, youll have to give up feeling neglected if the men you know dont spend half their time snivelling over you and the other half giving you black eyes. If you cant stand the coldness of my sort of life, and the strain of it, go back to the gutter. Work til youre more a brute than a human being; and then cuddle and squabble and drink til you fall asleep. Oh, it's a fine life, the life of the gutter. It's real: it's warm: it's violent: you can feel it through the thickest skin: you can taste it and smell it without any training or any work. Not like Science and Literature and Classical Music and Philosophy and Art. You find me cold, unfeeling, selfish, dont you? Very well: be off with you to the sort of people you like. Marry some sentimental hog or other with lots of money, and a thick pair of lips to kiss you with and a thick pair of boots to kick you with. If you cant appreciate what youve got, youd better get what you can appreciate.

LIZA. [*Desperate*] Oh, you are a cruel tyrant. I cant talk to you: you turn everything against me: I'm always in the wrong. But you know very well all the time that youre nothing but a bully. You know I cant go back to the gutter, as you call it, and that I have no real friends in the world but you and the Colonel. You know well I couldnt bear to live with a low common man after you two; and it's wicked and cruel of you to insult me by pretending I could. You think I must go back to Wimpole Street because I have nowhere else to go but father's. But dont you be too sure that you have me under your feet to be trampled on and talked down. I'll marry Freddy, I will, as soon as I'm able to support him.

HIGGINS [*thunderstruck*] Freddy!!! that young fool! That poor devil who couldnt get a job as an errand boy even if he had the guts to try for it! Woman: do you not understand that I have made you a consort for a king?

LIZA. Freddy loves me: that makes him king enough for me. I dont want him to work: he wasnt brought up to it as I was. I'll go and be a teacher.

HIGGINS. Whatll you teach, in heaven's name?

LIZA. What you taught me. I'll teach phonetics.

HIGGINS. Ha! ha! ha!

LIZA. I'll offer myself as an assistant to that hairyfaced Hungarian.

HIGGINS [*rising in a fury*] What! That imposter! that humbug! that toadying ingoramus! Teach him my methods! my discoveries! You take one step in his direction and I'll wring your neck. [*He lays hands on her*]. Do you hear?

LIZA [*defiantly non-resistant*] Wring away. What do I care? I knew youd strike me some day. [*He lets her go, stamping with rage at having forgotten himself, and recoils so hastily that he stumbles back into his seat on the ottoman*]. Aha! Now I know how to deal with you. What a fool I was not to think of it before! You cant take away the knowledge you gave me. You said I had a finer ear than you. And I can be civil and kind to people, which is more than you can. Aha!

32 Discussion Why is Higgins so shocked this time when Eliza tells him that she's going to marry Freddy?

33 Discussion What does Eliza say and do that earns her new respect from Higgins?

Reader's Response Were you satisfied by the way the play ended? Why or why not?

[*Purposely dropping her aitches to annoy him*] Thats done you, Enry Iggins, it az. Now I dont care that [*snapping her fingers*] for your bullying and your big talk. I'll advertize it in the papers that your duchess is only a flower girl that you taught, and that she'll teach anybody to be a duchess just the same in six months for a thousand guineas. Oh, when I think of myself crawling under your feet and being trampled on and called names, when all the time I had only to lift up my finger to be as good as you, I could just kick myself.

HIGGINS [*wondering at her*] You damned impudent slut, you! But it's better than snivelling; better than fetching slippers and finding spectacles, isnt it? [*Rising*] By George, Eliza. I said I'd make a woman of you; and I have. I like you like this.

LIZA. Yes: you turn round and make up to me now that I'm not afraid of you, and can do without you.

34

HIGGINS. Of course I do, you little fool. Five minutes ago you were like a millstone round my neck. Now youre a tower of strength: a consort battleship. You and I and Pickering will be three old bachelors instead of only two men and a silly girl.

MRS HIGGINS *returns, dressed for the wedding.* ELIZA *instantly becomes cool and elegant.*

MRS HIGGINS. The carriage is waiting, Eliza. Are you ready?

LIZA. Quite. Is the Professor coming?

MRS HIGGINS. Certainly not. He cant behave himself in church. He makes remarks out loud all the time on the clergyman's pronunciation.

LIZA. Then I shall not see you again, Professor. Goodbye. [*She goes to the door*].

MRS HIGGINS [*coming to* HIGGINS] Goodbye, dear.

HIGGINS. Goodbye, mother. [*He is about to kiss her, when he recollects something*]. Oh, by the way, Eliza, order a ham and a Stilton cheese, will you? And buy me a pair of reindeer gloves, number eights, and a tie to match that new suit of mine. You can choose the color. [*His cheerful, careless, vigorous voice shews that he is incorrigible*].

LIZA [*disdainfully*] Number eights are too small for you if you want them lined with lamb's wool. You have three new ties that you have forgotten in the drawer of your washstand. Colonel Pickering prefers double Gloucester to Stilton; and you dont notice the difference. I telephoned Mrs Pearce this morning not to forget the ham. What you are to do without me I cannot imagine. [*She sweeps out*].

MRS HIGGINS. I'm afraid youve spoilt that girl, Henry. I should be uneasy about you and her if she were less fond of Colonel Pickering.

HIGGINS. Pickering! Nonsense: she's going to marry Freddy. Ha ha! Freddy! Freddy!! Ha ha ha ha ha!!!!! [*He roars with laughter as the play ends*].

Primary Source

The literary scholar Stanley Weintraub explained how Shaw came to write the epilogue to *Pygmalion:*

> The play's London success in 1914 outraged as well as delighted Shaw. Sir Herbert Beerbohm Tree, the Henry Higgins of the production, having played a lifetime of romantic endings, had devised a way to distort Shaw's ironic and ambiguous conclusion without altering a word; in the interval between the last lines of the play and the last lowering of the curtain he would provide by demonstrative affection for Eliza a broad hint that matrimony was in store for the professor and his pupil. Shaw was furious at the Cinderella suggestion and wrote to Tree telling him what he thought of the performance. "My ending makes money; you ought to be grateful," Tree answered smugly. Shaw fired back, "Your ending is damnable: you ought to be shot." And to prevent future fairy-tale endings Shaw wrote an unsentimental short-story epilogue for the published play which "proved" that Eliza would marry the weak Freddy Eynsford Hill and open a successful flower shop with money proferred from Colonel Pickering. "It does not

follow in the least," Shaw defended himself to his Edinburgh printer, William Maxwell, nearly twenty years later, "that Liza and Higgins were sexually insensible to each other, or that their sensibility took the form of repugnance . . . ; but the fact stands that their marriage would have been a revolting tragedy and that the marriage with Freddy is the natural and happy ending to the story." But no one acts an undramatized prose epilogue, and Shaw's bittersweet ending to the actual play leaves the Higgins-Eliza relationship more dramatically at its appropriate—and unsettled—point.

Epilogue

The rest of the story need not be shewn in action, and indeed, would hardly need telling if our imaginations were not so enfeebled by their lazy dependence on the ready-mades and reach-me-downs of the ragshop in which Romance keeps its stock of "happy endings" to misfit all stories. Now, the history of Eliza Doolittle, though called a romance because the transfiguration it records seems exceedingly improbable, is common enough. Such transfigurations have been achieved by hundreds of resolutely ambitious young women since Nell Gwynne[1] set them the example by playing queens and fascinating kings in the theatre in which she began by selling oranges. Nevertheless, people in all directions have assumed, for no other reason than that she became the heroine of a romance, that she must have married the hero of it. This is unbearable, not only because her little drama, if acted on such a thoughtless assumption, must be spoiled, but because the true sequel is patent to anyone with a sense of human nature in general, and of feminine instinct in particular.

Eliza, in telling Higgins she would not marry him if he asked her, was not coquetting: she was announcing a well-considered decision. When a bachelor interests, and dominates, and teaches, and becomes important to a spinster, as Higgins with Eliza, she always, if she has character enough to be capable of it, considers very seriously indeed whether she will play for becoming that bachelor's wife, especially if he is so little interested in marriage that a determined and devoted woman might capture him if she set herself resolutely to do it. Her decision will depend a good deal on whether she is really free to choose; and that, again, will depend on her age and income. If she is at the end of her youth, and has no security for her livelihood, she will marry him because she must marry anybody who will provide for her. But at Eliza's age a good-looking girl does not feel that pressure: she feels free to pick and choose. She is therefore guided by her instinct in the matter. Eliza's instinct tells her not to marry Higgins. It does not tell her to give him up. It is not in the slightest doubt as to his remaining one of the strongest personal interests in her life. It would be very sorely strained if there was another woman likely to supplant her with him. But as she feels sure of him on that last point, she has no doubt at all as to her course, and would not have any, even if the difference of twenty years in age, which seems so great to youth, did not exist between them.

As our own instincts are not appealed to by her conclusion, let us see whether we

---

1. **Nell Gwynne:** Eleanor Gwynne (1650–1687), an English actress and favorite of Charles II.

Grammar in Action

Transitions aid connection and coherence in writing. A reader must follow the flow of ideas throughout a passage; transitions point the way toward the next thought. Write with transitions to guide your reader smoothly through your thoughts. Notice George Bernard Shaw's transitions.

Now, though Eliza was incapable of *thus* explaining to herself Higgins's formidable powers of resistance to the charm that prostrated Freddy at the first glance, she was instinctively aware that she could never obtain a complete grip of him, or come between him and his mother (the first necessity of the married woman). *To put it shortly,* she knew that for some mysterious reason he had not the makings of a married man in him . . .

Now and *thus* relate the sentence in which they occur back to the preceding paragraph. "Now" establishes a smooth bridge between the two, and "thus" identifies the kind of explanation for which Eliza has no capacity. *To put it shortly* paves the way for the cannot discover some reason in it. When Higgins excused his indifference to young women on the ground that they had an irresistible rival in his mother, he gave the clue to his inveterate old-bachelordom. The case is uncommon only to the extent that remarkable mothers are uncommon. If an imaginative boy has a sufficiently rich mother who has intelligence, personal grace, dignity of character without harshness, and a cultivated sense of the best art of her time to enable her to make her house beautiful, she sets a standard for him against which very few women can struggle, besides effecting for him a disengagement of his affections, his sense of beauty, and his idealism from his specifically sexual impulses. This makes him a standing puzzle to the huge number of uncultivated people who have been brought up in tasteless homes by commonplace or disagreeable parents, and to whom, consequently, literature, painting, sculpture, music, and affectionate personal relations come as modes of sex if they come at all. The word passion means nothing else to them; and that Higgins could have a passion for phonetics and idealize his mother instead of Eliza, would seem to them absurd and unnatural. Nevertheless, when we look round and see that hardly anyone is too ugly or disagreeable to find a wife or a husband if he or she wants one, whilst many old maids and bachelors are above the average in quality and culture, we cannot help suspecting that the disentanglement of sex from the associations with which it is so commonly confused, a disentanglement which persons of genius achieve by sheer intellectual analysis, is sometimes produced or aided by parental fascination.

Now, though Eliza was incapable of thus explaining to herself Higgins's formidable powers of resistance to the charm that prostrated Freddy at the first glance, she was instinctively aware that she could never obtain a complete grip of him, or come between him and his mother (the first necessity of

the married woman). To put it shortly, she knew that for some mysterious reason he had not the makings of a married man in him, according to her conception of a husband as one to whom she would be his nearest and fondest and warmest interest. Even had there been no mother-rival, she would still have refused to accept an interest in herself that was secondary to philosophic interests. Had Mrs Higgins died, there would still have been Milton and the Universal Alphabet. Landor's[2] remark that to those who have the greatest power of loving, love is a secondary affair, would not have recommended Landor to Eliza. Put that along with her resentment of Higgins's domineering superiority, and her mistrust of his coaxing cleverness in getting round her and evading her wrath when he had gone too far with his impetuous bullying, and you will see that Eliza's instinct had good grounds for warning her not to marry her Pygmalion.

And now, whom did Eliza marry? For if Higgins was a predestinate old bachelor, she was most certainly not a predestinate old maid. Well, that can be told very shortly to those who have not guessed it from the indications she has herself given them.

Almost immediately after Eliza is stung into proclaiming her considered determination not to marry Higgins, she mentions the fact that young Mr Frederick Eynsford Hill is pouring out his love for her daily through the post. Now Freddy is young, practically twenty years younger than Higgins: he is a gentleman [or, as Eliza would qualify him, a toff], and speaks like one. He is nicely dressed, is treated by the Colonel as an equal, loves her unaffectedly, and is not her master, nor ever likely to dominate her in spite of his advantage of social standing. Eliza has no use for the foolish romantic tradition that all women love to be mastered, if not actually bullied and beaten. "When

35

---

2. **Landor's:** Referring to Walter Savage Landor (1775–1864), an English writer.

Pygmalion, Epilogue 1185

35 **Discussion** What does this passage say about the basis for the dominance and abuse of women during this period? How does Eliza feel about the status of women?

next thought, making its connection to the previous one smoother and more readily acceptable.

Student Activity 1. Identify the transitions in the following passage.

Jenny returned to class. Meanwhile, her mother arrived in Mr. Peterson's office. She had, indeed, ignored Jenny's plea that she stay away. Moreover, she was determined to speak her mind. As a result, Mr. Peterson summoned Jenny back to his office once again, and, accordingly, she came.

Student Activity 2. Write a paragraph in which you use transitional words or phrases to establish smoothness and clarity of thought.

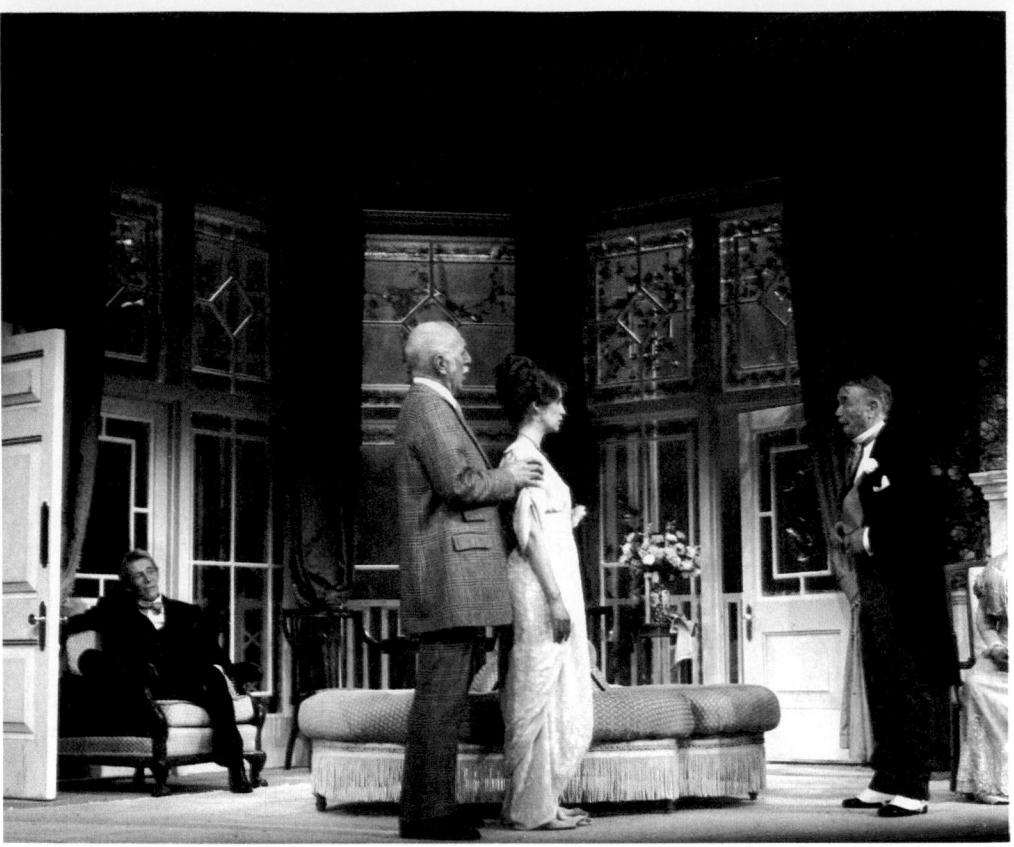

you go to women" says Nietzsche[3] "take your whip with you." Sensible despots have never confined that precaution to women: they have taken their whips with them when they have dealt with men, and been slavishly idealized by the men over whom they have flourished the whip much more than by women. No doubt there are slavish women as well as slavish men; and women, like men, admire those that are stronger than themselves. But to admire a strong person and to live under that strong person's thumb are two different things. The weak may not be admired and hero-worshipped; but they are by no means disliked or shunned; and they never seem to have the least difficulty in marrying people who are too good for them. They may fail in emergencies; but life is not one long emergency: it is mostly a string of situations for which no exceptional strength is needed, and with which even rather weak people can cope if they have a stronger partner to help them out. Accordingly, it is a truth everywhere in evidence that strong people, masculine or feminine, not only do not marry stronger people, but do not shew any preference for them in selecting their

---

3. Nietzsche (nē′ chə): German philosopher Friedrich Wilhelm Nietzsche (1844–1900).

friends. When a lion meets another with a louder roar "the first lion thinks the last a bore." The man or woman who feels strong enough for two, seeks for every other quality in a partner than strength.

The converse is also true. Weak people want to marry strong people who do not frighten them too much; and this often leads them to make the mistake we describe metaphorically as "biting off more than they can chew." They want too much for too little; and when the bargain is unreasonable beyond all bearing, the union becomes impossible: it ends in the weaker party being either discarded or borne as a cross, which is worse. People who are not only weak, but silly or obtuse as well, are often in these difficulties.

This being the state of human affairs, what is Eliza fairly sure to do when she is placed between Freddy and Higgins? Will she look forward to a lifetime of fetching Higgins's slippers or to a lifetime of Freddy fetching hers? There can be no doubt about the answer. Unless Freddy is biologically repulsive to her, and Higgins biologically attractive to a degree that overwhelms all her other instincts, she will, if she marries either of them, marry Freddy.

And that is just what Eliza did.

Complications ensued; but they were economic, not romantic. Freddy had no money and no occupation. His mother's jointure,[4] a last relic of the opulence of Largelady Park, had enabled her to struggle along in Earlscourt with an air of gentility, but not to procure any serious secondary education for her children, much less give the boy a profession. A clerkship at thirty shillings a week was beneath Freddy's dignity, and extremely distasteful to him besides. His prospects consisted of a hope that if he kept up appearances somebody would do something for him. The something appeared vaguely to his imagination as a pri-

vate secretaryship or a sinecure[5] of some sort. To his mother it perhaps appeared as a marriage to some lady of means who could not resist her boy's niceness. Fancy her feelings when he married a flower girl who had become disclassed under extraordinary circumstances which were now notorious!

It is true that Eliza's situation did not seem wholly ineligible. Her father, though formerly a dustman, and now fantastically disclassed, had become extremely popular in the smartest society by a social talent which triumphed over every prejudice and every disadvantage. Rejected by the middle class, which he loathed, he had shot up at once into the highest circles by his wit, his dustmanship (which he carried like a banner), and his Nietzschean transcendence of good and evil. At intimate ducal dinners he sat on the right hand of the Duchess; and in country houses he smoked in the pantry and was made much of by the butler when he was not feeding in the dining room and being consulted by cabinet ministers. But he found it almost as hard to do all this on [three] thousand a year as Mrs Eynsford Hill to live in Earlscourt on an income so pitiably smaller that I have not the heart to disclose its exact figure. He absolutely refused to add the last straw to his burden by contributing to Eliza's support.

Thus Freddy and Eliza, now Mr and Mrs Eynsford Hill, would have spent a penniless honeymoon but for a wedding present of £500 from the Colonel to Eliza. It lasted a long time because Freddy did not know how to spend money, never having had any to spend, and Eliza, socially trained by a pair of old bachelors, wore her clothes as long as they held together and looked pretty, without the least regard to their being many months out of fashion. Still, £500 will not last two young people for ever; and they both knew, and Eliza felt as well, that they must

---

4. jointure n.: Widow's inheritance.

5. sinecure (sī′ nə kyōōr′) n.: Any office or position that brings advantage but involves little or no work.

shift for themselves in the end. She could quarter herself on Wimpole Street because it had come to be her home; but she was quite aware that she ought not to quarter Freddy there, and that it would not be good for his character if she did.

Not that the Wimpole Street bachelors objected. When she consulted them, Higgins declined to be bothered about her housing problem when that solution was so simple. Eliza's desire to have Freddy in the house with her seemed of no more importance than if she had wanted an extra piece of bedroom furniture. Pleas as to Freddy's character, and the moral obligation on him to earn his own living, were lost on Higgins. He denied that Freddy had any character, and declared that if he tried to do any useful work some competent person would have the trouble of undoing it: a procedure involving a net loss to the community, and great unhappiness to Freddy himself, who was obviously intended by Nature for such light work as amusing Eliza, which, Higgins declared, was a much more useful and honorable occupation than working in the city. When Eliza referred again to her project of teaching phonetics, Higgins abated not a jot of his violent opposition to it. He said she was not within ten years of being qualified to meddle with his pet subject; and as it was evident that the Colonel agreed with him, she felt she could not go against them in this grave matter, and that she had no right, without Higgins's consent, to exploit the knowledge he had given her; for his knowledge seemed to her as much his private property as his watch: Eliza was no communist. Besides, she was superstitiously devoted to them both, more entirely and frankly after her marriage than before it.

It was the Colonel who finally solved the problem, which had cost him much perplexed cogitation. He one day asked Eliza, rather shyly, whether she had quite given up her notion of keeping a flower shop. She replied that she had thought of it, but had put it out of her head, because the Colonel had said, that day at Mrs Higgins's, that it would never do. The Colonel confessed that when he said that, he had not quite recovered from the dazzling impression of the day before. They broke the matter to Higgins that evening. The sole comment vouchsafed by him very nearly led to a serious quarrel with Eliza. It was to the effect that she would have in Freddy an ideal errand boy.

Freddy himself was next sounded on the subject. He said he had been thinking of a shop himself; though it had presented itself to his pennilessness as a small place in which Eliza should sell tobacco at one counter whilst he sold newspapers at the opposite one. But he agreed that it would be extraordinarily jolly to go early every morning with Eliza to Covent Garden and buy flowers on the scene of their first meeting: a sentiment which earned him many kisses from his wife. He added that he had always been afraid to propose anything of the sort, because Clara would make an awful row about a step that must damage her matrimonial chances, and his mother could not be expected to like it after clinging for so many years to that step of the social ladder on which retail trade is impossible.

This difficulty was removed by an event highly unexpected by Freddy's mother. Clara, in the course of her incursions into those artistic circles which were the highest within her reach, discovered that her conversational qualifications were expected to include a grounding in the novels of Mr H. G. Wells.[6] She borrowed them in various directions so energetically that she swallowed them all within two months. The result was a conversion of a kind quite common today. A modern Acts of the Apostles would fill fifty whole Bibles if anyone were capable of writing it.

Poor Clara, who appeared to Higgins and

---

6. **H. G. Wells:** Herbert George Wells (1866–1946), English novelist and historian.

his mother as a disagreeable and ridiculous person, and to her own mother as in some inexplicable way a social failure, had never seen herself in either light; for, though to some extent ridiculed and mimicked in West Kensington like everybody else there, she was accepted as a rational and normal—or shall we say inevitable?—sort of human being. At worst they called her The Pusher; but to them no more than to herself had it ever occurred that she was pushing the air, and pushing it in a wrong direction. Still, she was not happy. She was growing desperate. Her one asset, the fact that her mother was what the Epsom greengrocer called a carriage lady, had no exchange value, apparently. It had prevented her from getting educated, because the only education she could have afforded was education with the Earlscourt greengrocer's daughter. It had led her to seek the society of her mother's class; and that class simply would not have her, because she was much poorer than the greengrocer, and, far from being able to afford a maid, could not afford even a housemaid, and had to scrape along at home with an illiberally treated general servant. Under such circumstances nothing could give her an air of being a genuine product of Largelady Park. And yet its tradition made her regard a marriage with anyone within her reach as an unbearable humiliation. Commercial people and professional people in a small way were odious to her. She ran after painters and novelists; but she did not charm them; and her bold attempts to pick up and practise artistic and literary talk irritated them. She was, in short, an utter failure, an ignorant, incompetent, pretentious, unwelcome, penniless, useless little snob; and though she did not admit these disqualifications (for nobody ever faces unpleasant truths of this kind until the possibility of a way out dawns on them) she felt their effects too keenly to be satisfied with her position.

Clara had a startling eyeopener when,
on being suddenly wakened to enthusiasm by a girl of her own age who dazzled her and produced in her a gushing desire to take her for a model, and gain her friendship, she discovered that this exquisite apparition had graduated from the gutter in a few months time. It shook her so violently, that when Mr H. G. Wells lifted her on the point of his puissant[7] pen, and placed her at the angle of view from which the life she was leading and the society to which she clung appeared in its true relation to real human needs and worthy social structure, he effected a conversion and a conviction of sin comparable to the most sensational feats of General Booth[8] or Gypsy Smith.[9] Clara's snobbery went bang. Life suddenly began to move with her. Without knowing how or why, she began to make friends and enemies. Some of the acquaintances to whom she had been a tedious or indifferent or ridiculous affliction, dropped her: others became cordial. To her amazement she found that some "quite nice" people were saturated with Wells, and that this accessibility to ideas was the secret of their niceness. People she had thought deeply religious, and had tried to conciliate on that tack with disastrous results, suddenly took an interest in her, and revealed a hostility to conventional religion which she had never conceived possible except among the most desperate characters. They made her read Galsworthy; and Galsworthy exposed the vanity of Largelady Park and finished her. It exasperated her to think that the dungeon in which she had languished for so many unhappy years had been unlocked all the time, and that the impulses she had so carefully struggled with and stifled for the sake of keeping well with society, were pre-

---

7. puissant (pyo͞o′ i sənt) *adj.*: Powerful.
8. General Booth: William Booth (1829–1912), the founder of the Salvation Army.
9. Gypsy Smith: Gipsy Rodney Smith (1860–1947), an English evangelist.

cisely those by which alone she could have come into any sort of sincere human contact. In the radiance of these discoveries, and the tumult of their reaction, she made a fool of herself as freely and conspicuously as when she so rashly adopted Eliza's expletive in Mrs Higgins's drawing room; for the new-born Wellsian had to find her bearings almost as ridiculously as a baby; but nobody hates a baby for its ineptitudes, or thinks the worse of it for trying to eat the matches; and Clara lost no friends by her follies. They laughed at her to her face this time; and she had to defend herself and fight it out as best she could.

When Freddy paid a visit to Earlscourt (which he never did when he could possibly help it) to make the desolating announcement that he and his Eliza were thinking of blackening the Largelady scutcheon[10] by opening a shop, he found the little household already convulsed by a prior announcement from Clara that she also was going to work in an old furniture shop in Dover Street, which had been started by a fellow Wellsian. This appointment Clara owed, after all, to her old social accomplishment of Push. She had made up her mind that, cost what it might, she would see Mr Wells in the flesh; and she had achieved her end at a garden party. She had better luck than so rash an enterprise deserved. Mr Wells came up to her expectations. Age had not withered him, nor could custom stale his infinite variety in half an hour. His pleasant neatness and compactness, his small hands and feet, his teeming ready brain, his unaffected accessibility, and a certain fine apprehensiveness which stamped him as susceptible from his topmost hair to his tipmost toe, proved irresistible. Clara talked of nothing else for weeks and weeks afterwards. And as she happened to talk to the lady of the furniture shop, and that lady also desir-

ed above all things to know Mr Wells and sell pretty things to him, she offered Clara a job on the chance of achieving that end through her.

And so it came about that Eliza's luck held, and the expected opposition to the flower shop melted away. The shop is in the arcade of a railway station not very far from the Victoria and Albert Museum; and if you live in that neighbourhood you may go there any day and buy a buttonhole from Eliza.

Now here is a last opportunity for romance. Would you not like to be assured that the shop was an immense success, thanks to Eliza's charms and her early business experience in Covent Garden? Alas! the truth is the truth: the shop did not pay for a long time, simply because Eliza and her Freddy did not know how to keep it. True, Eliza had not to begin at the very beginning: she knew the names and prices of the cheaper flowers; and her elation was unbounded when she found that Freddy, like all youths educated at cheap, pretentious, and thoroughly inefficient schools, knew a little Latin. It was very little, but enough to make him appear to her a Porson or Bentley,[11] and to put him at his ease with botanical nomenclature. Unfortunately he knew nothing else; and Eliza, though she could count money up to eighteen shillings or so, and had acquired a certain familiarity with the language of Milton from her struggles to qualify herself for winning Higgins's bet, could not write out a bill without utterly disgracing the establishment. Freddy's power of stating in Latin that Balbus built a wall and that Gaul was divided into three parts[12] did not carry with it the slightest knowledge of accounts or business: Colonel

10. **scutcheon** (skuch′ ən) n.: Coat of arms.

11. **Porson, Bentley:** Richard Porson (1759–1808) and Richard Bentley (1662–1742), English classical scholars.
12. **Balbus . . . parts:** Referring to elementary Latin exercises.

Grammar in Action

Narrative writing tells a series of related events in story form and graphic language. Usually there is no narrative writing in plays, but Shaw has added an epilogue to *Pygmalion* that narrates what occurred after the play ended. One of Shaw's purposes was to prevent readers from imagining the typical happy ending; as the epilogue makes clear, Higgins and Eliza do not end up as a cozy couple.

In writing the epilogue, Shaw had to tell what happened swiftly and yet with enough plausible and amusing details to keep the attention of his readers. He solved this problem admirably. Notice, for example, how a single image quickly summarizes a whole chapter in Eliza and Freddy's life:

"On the piteous spectacle of the pair spending their evenings in shorthand schools and polytechnic classes, learning bookkeeping and typewriting with incipient junior clerks, male and female, from the elementary schools, let me not dwell."

Student Activity 1. Find another passage in which Shaw combines a rapid narrative pace with specific and amusing details. Then justify your choice.

Pickering had to explain to him what a cheque book and a bank account meant. And the pair were by no means easily teachable. Freddy backed up Eliza in her obstinate refusal to believe that they could save money by engaging a bookkeeper with some knowledge of the business. How, they argued, could you possible save money by going to extra expense when you already could not make both ends meet? But the Colonel, after making the ends meet over and over again, at last gently insisted; and Eliza, humbled to the dust by having to beg from him so often, and stung by the uproarious derision of Higgins, to whom the notion of Freddy succeeding at anything was a joke that never palled, grasped the fact that business, like phonetics, has to be learned.

On the piteous spectacle of the pair spending their evenings in shorthand schools and polytechnic classes, learning bookkeeping and typewriting with incipient junior clerks, male and female, from the elementary schools, let me not dwell. There were even classes at the London School of Economics, and a humble personal appeal to the director of that institution to recommend a course bearing on the flower business. He, being a humorist, explained to them the method of the celebrated Dickensian essay on Chinese Metaphysics by the gentleman who read an article on China and an article on Metaphysics and combined the information. He suggested that they should combine the London School with Kew Gardens. Eliza, to whom the procedure of the Dickensian gentleman seemed perfectly correct (as in fact it was) and not in the least funny (which was only her ignorance), took the advice with entire gravity. But the effort that cost her the deepest humiliation was a request to Higgins, whose pet artistic fancy, next to Milton's verse, was calligraphy, and who himself wrote a most beautiful Italian hand, that he would teach her to write. He declared that she was congenitally incapable of forming a single letter worthy of the least of Milton's words; but she persisted; and again he suddenly threw himself into the task of teaching her with a combination of stormy intensity, concentrated patience, and occasional bursts of interesting disquisition on the beauty and nobility, the august mission and destiny, of human handwriting. Eliza ended by acquiring an extremely uncommercial script which was a positive extension of her personal beauty, and spending three times as much on stationery as anyone else because certain qualities and shapes on paper became indispensable to her. She could not even address an envelope in the usual way because it made the margins all wrong.

Their commercial schooldays were a period of disgrace and despair for the young couple. They seemed to be learning nothing about flower shops. At last they gave it up as hopeless, and shook the dust of the shorthand schools, and the polytechnics, and the London School of Economics from their feet for ever. Besides, the business was in some mysterious way beginning to take care of itself. They had somehow forgotten their objections to employing other people. They came to the conclusion that their own way was the best, and that they had really a remarkable talent for business. The Colonel, who had been compelled for some years to keep a sufficient sum on current account at his bankers to make up their deficits, found that the provision was unnecessary: the young people were prospering. It is true that there was not quite fair play between them and their competitors in trade. Their week-ends in the country cost them nothing, and saved them the price of their Sunday dinners; for the motor car was the Colonel's; and he and Higgins paid the hotel bills. Mr F. Hill, florist and greengrocer (they soon discovered that there was money in asparagus; and asparagus led to other vegetables), had an air which stamped the business as classy; and in private life he was still Frederick Eynsford Hill, Esquire. Not that

Student Activity 2. Write an epilogue to one of your favorite stories. Briefly tell what happened to the main characters after the story ended and include enough graphic details to keep your audience interested. Remember to narrate events in the order they occurred and to indicate how one event flowed from another.

38 Discussion How does the author explain Eliza's continuing interest in and attachment to Higgins? Explain the allusion to the story of Pygmalion, including whether the play is appropriately titled.

38

there was any swank[13] about him: nobody but Eliza knew that he had been christened Frederick Chaloner. Eliza herself swanked like anything.

That is all. That is how it has turned out. It is astonishing how much Eliza still manages to meddle in the housekeeping at Wimpole Street in spite of the shop and her own family. And it is notable that though she never nags her husband, and frankly loves the Colonel as if she were his favorite daughter, she has never got out of the habit of nagging Higgins that was established on the fatal night when she won his bet for him. She snaps his head off on the faintest provocation, or on none. He no longer dares to tease her by assuming an abysmal inferiority of Freddy's mind to his own. He storms and bullies and derides; but she stands up to him so ruthlessly that the Colonel has to ask her from time to time to be kinder to Higgins; and it is the only request of his that brings a mulish expression into her face. Nothing but some emergency or calamity great enough to break down all likes and dislikes, and throw them both back on their common humanity—and may they be spared any such trial!—will ever alter this. She knows that Higgins does not need her, just as her father did not need her. The very

scrupulousness with which he told her that day that he had become used to having her there, and dependent on her for all sorts of little services, and that he should miss her if she went away (it would never have occurred to Freddy or the Colonel to say anything of the sort) deepens her inner certainty that she is "no more to him than them slippers"; yet she has a sense, too, that his indifference is deeper than the infatuation of commoner souls. She is immensely interested in him. She has even secret mischievous moments in which she wishes she could get him alone, on a desert island, away from all ties and with nobody else in the world to consider, and just drag him off his pedestal and see him making love like any common man. We all have private imaginations of that sort. But when it comes to business, to the life that she really leads as distinguished from the life of dreams and fancies, she likes Freddy and she likes the Colonel; and she does not like Higgins and Mr Doolittle. Galatea never does quite like Pygmalion:[14] his relation to her is too godlike to be altogether agreeable.

---

13. swank *n.*: Ostentatious behavior.

14. Galatea (gal'ə tē'ə) **. . . Pygmalion:** Pygmalion was a mythological king of Cyprus who carved a statue of a woman so beautiful that he fell in love with her. The king prayed to the gods to bring the statue, Galatea, to life, and his prayers were answered by Aphrodite, the goddess of love.

Closure and Extension

ANSWERS TO THINKING ABOUT THE SELECTION
Recalling

1. Pickering has been talking to the police to see if they can help find Eliza.
2. (a) On the recommendation of Higgins, Mr. Doolittle has become a lecturer for the Wannafeller Moral Reform World League. Because of

1192

that association, he will inherit stock worth three thousand pounds a year by the founder of the league, Mr. Wannafeller. (b) He has been made a gentlemen, with gentlemen's responsibilities; he is no longer a free man. Eliza's latest stepmother and he are getting married that very day.
3. It was from Pickering that Eliza learned really nice manners; he showed her how real ladies and gentlemen behave, something Higgins could not do.

4. (a) Eliza wants Higgins to care for her. (b) Higgins wants Eliza to come back to his house for the fun of it.
5. (a) She marries Freddy, is set up by Pickering as the operator of a flower shop, spends a great deal of time learning how to make the shop successful, lives with Freddy at Higgins's house, and makes a success of the business. (b) Clara becomes a follower of H. G. Wells and ends up working in a furniture shop.

Interpreting

6. Suggested Response: Because Mr. Doolittle has been able to put middle-class morality on like his new suit, remaining very much his own man, but passing as middle class, Shaw suggests that such morality is superficial and not to be taken seriously.
7. Suggested Response: By this time, Higgins and Eliza are too attached to each other to break their relationship off completely. Higgins is so difficult to deal with that it was

THINKING ABOUT THE SELECTION

Recalling

1. Who has Pickering been talking with on the phone at the beginning of Act V? Why?
2. (a) What has happened to Alfred Doolittle? (b) How has this change affected his life?
3. Why is Eliza grateful to Pickering?
4. (a) In their conversation together what does Eliza tell Higgins she wants from him? (b) What does he want from her?
5. (a) What, according to the Epilogue, becomes of Eliza? (b) Of Clara Eynsford Hill?

Interpreting

6. Explain what the changes in Alfred Doolittle suggest is Shaw's attitude toward "middle-class morality."
7. Do you think the outcome of Higgins's last discussion with Eliza was inevitable? Why or why not?

Applying

8. The Epilogue describes developments in Eliza's life after the action of the play. Would you have preferred to see these developments played out? Explain your reasons.

ANALYZING LITERATURE

Understanding the Complete Play

The paradoxical saying that "the whole is greater than the sum of its parts" is true of works of art. A play is a weaving-together of many elements, among them: the plot (or story line), the setting (time and place of the action), the characters (roles), the tone (playwright's attitude toward the subject or audience), the symbols (representative values attached to events, people, or things), and the theme (main idea). When these separate elements come together, a "chemical reaction" results. Create a checklist similar to the following for *Pygmalion*.

plot	setting	character	tone	symbol	theme

Write a brief description for each of the play's elements, entering "NA" when the element is not applicable. Then discuss how the various elements interact in Shaw's play. (Consider, for example, how setting affects theme.)

CRITICAL THINKING AND READING

Summarizing a Play

When a newspaper or magazine critic writes a review of a play, he or she includes a **summary,** or brief description of the action. A good summary captures a sense of the play as a whole, focusing not only on what is said and done but on such details as setting. The amount of information that a summary provides depends, of course, on its overall length. List the details you find important to include in a one-page summary of *Pygmalion*. Decide how you would handle such matters as Shaw's Preface and Epilogue.

THINKING AND WRITING

Writing About the Title

At the end of the Epilogue, Shaw mentions Pygmalion and Galatea, who are figures from Greek mythology. The sculptor Pygmalion created a statue of a beautiful woman. After he fell in love with his creation, the goddess Aphrodite brought her to life. Write an essay and discuss the effectiveness of the title Shaw chose for his play. Proceed by addressing the following questions: How godlike do you think Eliza finds Higgins? To what extent has Higgins "created" a new person? Might Higgins's feelings toward Eliza at any point in the play be fairly described as "love?" How much impact will the title have on a person who views, rather than reads, the play and who is, therefore, unfamiliar with the Epilogue? When you revise, make sure you have included adequate support for your theses.

Pygmalion, Epilogue 1193

inevitable that they would not marry, but it is also inevitable that their relationship would continue for the rest of their lives.

Applying

8. Suggested Response: No. The play ends just after Eliza indicates that she will remain associated with Higgins but will marry Freddy; yet, there is still some question. Because the play ends before everything is definitely resolved, the audience is left wondering what really

will happen to both of them. If Shaw had written the Epilogue as another act, he would have left the audience with nothing to ponder, nothing to work through for themselves.

ANSWERS TO ANALYZING LITERATURE

Suggested response:

Plot: The plot concerns the transformation of a lower-class flower girl into a woman accepted as a

duchess by upper-class society.

Setting: The play is set in Victorian England, where what one sees in a situation or understands about a person isn't always an accurate indication of what the actual situation is or what the person is really like.

Character: The characters are representatives of the different classes in Victorian society; each

(Answers begin on p. 1192.)

plays out his or her role to determine where each really fits in that class structure.

Tone: The tone is satirical; Shaw is poking fun at all the classes, indicating that all of them are less than honest about who they are and that the boundaries between them are less rigid than is assumed.

Symbol: As representatives of their classes and the moral ethic of that class, each character becomes a symbol and their changes represent the changes possible for all members of their class; Higgins is an independent, one who refuses to seek acceptance in any class.

Theme: The theme concerns the idea that the barriers between the classes in England are artificial at best; scratch the surface and there is a dustman and a duchess in everyone.

Each of these elements is focused on the roles and characteristics of the various classes in England. Because of this focus, the elements support each other to produce a cohesive whole, a play that works through the plot to deliver the playwright's message in a clear and entertaining manner.

Challenge Keeping in mind the same elements of a play that Shaw uses, students might be challenged to write their own ending to *Pygmalion*.

ANSWERS TO CRITICAL THINKING AND READING

Answers will differ. You might list on the board key details that different students have chosen.

Challenge Have students write their one-page summaries of the play and read them aloud to a partner. Have them discuss and recommend changes that should be made in both papers and then prepare their final drafts.

1193

Pygmalion Becomes My Fair Lady

Presentation

Motivation/Prior Knowledge
Ask students if they have ever heard of the songs "I Could Have Danced All Night," "The Rain in Spain," and "Get Me to the Church on Time." If some students know these songs, have them sing the lyrics. Then tell students that they will be reading about the show for which these famous songs were written.

Enrichment Tell students that years before the musical was written, Shaw himself wrote a screenplay for the movie version of *Pygmalion* (1938). [This movie and an accompanying guide are available from the Prentice Hall Library of Video Classics.] The movie starred Leslie Howard as Higgins and introduced Wendy Hiller as Eliza Doolittle.

In adapting his play for the screen, Shaw added a scene at the ball where Eliza is taken for a great lady. He then incorporated this scene into the play, along with narrative material and other short scenes that were prepared for the film.

It was the undisputed smash musical of 1956. From the moment the first hints drifted north from Philadelphia—where the musical was having its tryout run—tickets were eagerly snatched up. By March 15, when the show officially opened in New York City, only a few tickets were still available. By March 16 tickets were sold out for months ahead. Critics raved: "One of the best musicals of the century!" Writer James Thurber proclaimed it to be "the finest union of comedy and music" in his experience. Its male lead made the cover of the July 23 issue of *Time* magazine. Although it was one of those rare musicals that did not have a title song—it took its name from an old poem about London Bridge falling down—within weeks an astonishing number of its songs were famous. People were humming "The Rain in Spain," "I Could Have Danced

All Night," and "Get Me to the Church on Time." By 1962, when it completed its run of 2,717 performances, its 1912 period costumes had even influenced American fashion. What play had taken America by such storm? Why, *My Fair Lady*, of course!

LERNER AND LOEWE

What could account for the play's outrageous success and impact on American culture? Obviously much of its success was due to Lerner and Loewe, the brilliant duo responsible for such classic hits as *Brigadoon* (1947) and *Camelot* (1960). Except for the play's girl-gets-boy ending that Shaw would not have tolerated, Lerner had the sense not to tamper with a good thing—almost all of *My Fair Lady* comes directly from Shaw's *Pygmalion*.

Recall that Shaw declared in the Epilogue to *Pygmalion* that to assume that the heroine of a romance "must have married the hero of it" is "unbearable." But perhaps in his adaptation Lerner was only doing what so many had wanted to do before him. Take, for instance, the case of the first actor to play Henry Higgins, Beerbohm Tree. Handpicked by Shaw for the role, the actor nonetheless chose to ignore Shaw's directions and play the role his own way. Accounts have it that Shaw was absolutely livid with Tree who, when the curtain fell in the last act, threw a flower to Eliza—indicating his affections for her and holding out the hope that they would indeed be united. Aside from the ending, Lerner was much more respectful of Shaw's writing and made almost no changes in the original.

In at least one spot, Lerner changed a scene's location, though the plot remains the same. In *Pygmalion* Henry Higgins first presents Eliza to society at his mother's house. In *My Fair Lady* her presentation is at the Ascot races, where there are many more chances for Eliza to slip back into her Tottenham Court Road lingo. He has also eliminated or added minor characters to point up situations. In the main, however, he has faithfully followed Shaw's lead. Stage directions are, for the most part, word for word from Shaw. As the critic for *Time* magazine remarked, "At bottom, *My Fair Lady* is nothing more than George Bernard Shaw's play *Pygmalion* with music added."

A GLITTERING CAST

Credit is also due to the glittering cast. Theatergoers and fellow actors alike were stunned by Harrison's brilliant performance as Henry Higgins. Famed actor Charles Laughton rushed backstage to offer his congratulations to his friend Harrison: "In all my theater experience," he raved, "I've only seen a handful of performances to match Rex's. He makes every man in the audience laugh at himself, and every woman laugh at the man beside her." Interestingly, Harrison had met Shaw in person in the course of performing in Shaw's play *Major Barbara* in 1934. *My Fair Lady* marked the debut of twenty-year-old English actress Julie Andrews, who was described as playing the role of the flower-girl Eliza with "heart-lifting simplicity."

THE MOVIE VERSION

If possible, the 1964 movie version was as splendid as the stage play. Studio head Jack Warner originally wanted Cary Grant or Rock Hudson to play Higgins and James

Cagney to be Doolittle. Cary Grant refused Warner's offer by saying that if the studio mogul chose anyone but Rex Harrison for the role of Higgins he would not even bother to see the film. Without a bankable leading man, Warner was worried: After all, he had put up more than five million for the rights to the musical, set aside nearly twenty million for production costs, and promised the authors and producers of the stage show almost fifty percent of the net. As it turned out, his fears were groundless. The screen version proved a stunning hit, earning Oscars for Best Picture, Best Actor, Best Director, Best Color Cinematography, Best Costume Design, Best Musical Score, Best Sound, and Best Art Direction. The only major award it did not win was Best Actress. In one of life's little twists of fate, Julie Andrews won Best Actress that year for her role in Mary Poppins—and Audrey Hepburn did not even receive a nomination as Eliza Doolittle.

In the long run, however, we must go back to Shaw and present our laurels to him, for without him there would be no *Pygmalion;* and without *Pygmalion* there would be no *My Fair Lady.*

Cross Currents 1195

YOU THE WRITER
Guidelines for Evaluating Assignment 1

1. Does the 250-word character sketch begin with a description of the relevance of the character to the story in which he or she appears?
2. Has the student used the author's terms, along with vivid original terms, to describe the character's physical appearance, habits, behaviors, and beliefs?
3. Has the student noted details that seem to have symbolic significance?
4. Is the character sketch logically organized and free from grammar, usage, and mechanics errors?

Guidelines for Evaluating Assignment 2

1. Has the student written an original poem in free verse?
2. Has the student modeled the poem on the work of one of the poets in this unit?
3. Has the student used vivid images, figures of speech, and other appropriate poetic devices?
4. Is the poem free from grammar, usage, and mechanics errors?

Guidelines for Evaluating Assignment 3

1. Has the student used stream-of-consciousness technique to write his or her short fictional piece?
2. Does an object seen by the character trigger a string of mental associations?
3. Is it apparent that the character is whole?
4. Is the fictional piece free from grammar, usage, and mechanics errors?

YOU THE WRITER

Assignment

1. A character sketch is like a painting in words. Unlike a visual portrait, however, a character sketch delves into the mind of the subject, revealing his or her innermost thoughts and attitudes. Choose one of the characters you read about in this unit and write a character sketch.

Prewriting. In selecting a character, make sure there is ample material to develop. Divide a sheet of paper into several sections, labeling one "Physical Details," another "Habits and Behaviors," and a third "Beliefs."

Writing. Begin your sketch by describing the relevance of your character to the story in which he or she appears. Use the author's terms, along with vivid terms of your own, to describe the character's appearance and mental makeup.

Revising. Make sure you have arranged your information in an orderly way.

Assignment

2. Robert Frost, the prominent twentieth-century poet, described the writing of free verse as "like playing tennis with the net down." As the careful reader of this unit will have observed, free verse is more structured than Frost's glib dismissal suggests. Write an original poem in free verse. Model your effort on the work of one of the poets you read and admired.

Prewriting. Get your wheels spinning to come up with a topic. When you have selected one, write it at the center of a sheet of paper and cluster ideas around it.

Writing. Write your first draft. Attempt to use vivid images and figures of speech.

Revising. Put your poem aside for several hours. Then reread it. Look for areas that are weak or in need of clarification.

Assignment

3. The stream-of-consciousness technique perfected by Virginia Woolf and others was one of the significant literary breakthroughs of the Modernist period. Write a short fictional account in which a character enters a room and sees an object—either familiar or new—that triggers a string of mental associations.

Prewriting. Brainstorm for details about your character, including his or her appearance, habits, attitudes, and so on. Create in outline form a past for your character.

Writing. In your first draft, mention the object the character sees and then let your mind lead you. Freewrite without regard to correctness of form, spelling, or sentence structure.

Revising. Check doubtful spellings and polish any rough edges.

YOU THE CRITIC

Assignment

1. Several of the writers in this unit—Shaw, Saki, and the poet Henry Reed among them—use satire or irony to put across their ideas to the reader. Select a satirical work and a work that expresses its theme in a totally straightforward manner. In an essay, compare and contrast the two approaches. Tell which you believe to be more effective, and give reasons.

    Prewriting. Review the concept of satire and the manner in which the author of your satirical selection uses it. In a single sentence, identify the theme of each of the selections.

    Writing. In an opening paragraph, discuss the relationship between theme and satire. Devote some space to speculation on how the impact of the two works would have been altered had the authors opted for a different approach.

    Revising. Check your essay for coherence and economy of language.

Assignment

2. T. S. Eliot wrote that William Butler Yeats "was one of those few [poets] whose history is the history of their own times, who are part of the consciousness of an age which cannot be understood without them." In an essay, evaluate this statement as it applies to Yeats, to Eliot himself, or to some other poet of the Modernist period.

    Prewriting. Prepare for your composition by reviewing the background material on your poet and on the history of the period. Jot down notes on this interrelation.

    Writing. Write your first draft. Spend at least a paragraph describing the uniqueness of your poet's contribution to his or her age. Quote the poems where relevant.

    Revising. Examine your essay for unity and logic. Substitute strong, specific words for any that strike you as vague or weak.

Assignment

3. Perhaps the two events that most profoundly shaped the literature of the Modernist period were World Wars I and II. Select any three writers of the period and describe the differences and similarities the impact of the wars had on their lives and works.

    Prewriting. After you have selected your three writers, develop a profile for each in which you identify the relevance of the wars. Note whether the individual saw action on the battlefield, whether he or she used the notion of war literally or figuratively in stories or poems, and so on.

    Writing. Begin your composition with a brief biographical sketch of each writer. Quote liberally from the literary works in your discussion.

    Revising. Review your composition to be sure you have covered all points raised in your outline.

You the Critic 1197

YOU THE CRITIC
Guidelines for Evaluating Assignment 1

1. Does the opening paragraph of the comparison discuss the relationship between theme and satire?
2. Does the student speculate on how the impact of the two works would have been altered had the authors chosen a different approach?
3. Is the essay coherent and does it demonstrate economy of language?
4. Is the essay free from grammar, usage, and mechanics errors?

Guidelines for Evaluating Assignment 2

1. Has the student evaluated Eliot's statement as it applies to Yeats, Eliot himself, or another poet?
2. Does the student describe the uniqueness of the poet's contribution to his or her age in a paragraph or more?
3. Does the student quote from the author's works to support main points?
4. Does the student use strong, specific words?
5. Is the essay free from grammar, usage, and mechanics errors?

Guidelines for Evaluating Assignment 3

1. Has the student selected three authors of the Modern period and described the differences and similarities the impact of the two world wars had on their lives and works?
2. Has the student begun the essay with a brief biographical sketch of each writer including their wartime experiences?
3. Has the student quoted from the literary works of the writers to support all points?
4. Is the essay free from grammar, usage, and mechanics errors?

Humanities Note

Fine art, *Papagena*, 1983, by Gillian Ayres. *Papagena* was painted by the contemporary British artist Gillian Ayres (b. 1930). Ayres studied at the Camberwell School of Art and has taught at the Bath Academy, St. Martins. She is presently head of painting at the Winchester School of Art. In her painting Gillian Ayres tries to create spatial scale and balance, vision and humor, through the expressive use of color. *Papagena* shows those characteristics. Her paintings are in the collections of leading museums, including London's Tate Gallery and New York's Museum of Modern Art.

PAPAGENA
Gillian Ayres
Photograph Courtesy of The South Bank Center

Objectives

1 To understand the aftermath of World War II in Britain
2 To understand Britain's recovery from World War II and the problems it faced
3 To appreciate the variety and richness of contemporary British literature

CONTEMPORARY WRITERS
1945–present

We are living at one of the great turning points
of history. . . . Yesterday, we split the atom.
We assaulted that colossal citadel of power, the
tiny unit of the substance of the universe. And
because of this, the great dream and the great
nightmare of centuries of human thought have taken
flesh and walk beside us all, day and night.*

from "The Small Personal Voice,"
Doris Lessing

1199

A new world dawned in 1945—a world of great promise and yet of great danger. First the United States, then the Soviet Union, then Britain, France, and a number of other nations gained the ability to build massively destructive atomic weapons. Henceforth all humanity would dwell in the shadow of the bomb. That fact made a deep impression on writers like Doris Lessing, whose words are quoted on the preceding page.

The postwar period has not been kind to Britain. Its Empire has crumbled, its military rank has declined, and its traditional industries have rusted away. However, Britain has struggled gamely to resolve its problems while taking pride in a still-vibrant literary and artistic life.

THE AFTERMATH OF WAR

World War II shook British society to its very core. The months after the fighting stopped were a time of privation and misery, as people made do with meager food rations and walked through streets lined with bombed-out ruins. Faced with the urgent need for reconstruction, Britons sought to shape a new social and political climate. Out went the wartime coalition government of Winston Churchill. In came a peacetime Labor government, bubbling with optimism. The Labor party's goals were sweeping: nationalize major industries, improve social services, attack the system of class privileges. Parliament set to work to transform class-bound Britain into a twentieth-century welfare state. The Age of the Common Man had dawned.

An End to Empire

Meanwhile, shadows descended on the British Empire. Nationalists in Asia and Africa were demanding their freedom—by force if necessary, by negotiation if possible. British leaders hesitated. They sent troops to put down rebellions, but they also sent diplomats to negotiate an orderly transfer of power.

The dismantling of empire did not always go smoothly. In South Asia, seeking to avert conflict between Hindus and Moslems, Britain split the Indian subcontinent into two nations, India and Pakistan. Partition and independence came in 1947. Almost immediately, bloody communal fighting swept the subcontinent. In the Middle East, unable to mediate the bitter Arab-Jewish feud over Palestine, Britain withdrew from its Palestine mandate. Israel's birth in 1948 touched off the first of many Arab-Israeli wars. In Malaya, Kenya, Rhodesia, and other territories too, bloodshed accompanied the process of withdrawal.

Slowly, the British Empire passed into history. In its place emerged a new Commonwealth of Nations, its members bound together not by force and the myth of empire but by common loyalties and common needs.

Evolving Europe

On the Continent, too, British power declined sharply after the war. By 1947 disputes and quarrels had ended the wartime alliance that linked Britain, the United States, and the Soviet Union. An Iron Curtain (Churchill's term) divided Europe. East of the Iron Curtain, the Soviet Union dominated a string of dependent or "satellite" nations with Socialist governments. West of the Iron Curtain, Britain and many other nations huddled under the umbrella of United States power. In 1949 they joined together in a military alliance called the North Atlantic Treaty Organization (NATO). Later Britain would join the European Economic Community, or Common Market, a group of nations (now numbering twelve) that are trying to merge their economic systems into a "united Europe."

RECOVERY AND CONTEMPORARY PROBLEMS

War memories faded, Britons cleared away the rubble, and life got better. By the 1960's Britain was once again a center of cultural excitement. The dazzling popularity of the Beatles carried British rock music to the far corners of the world. Trendy young people on

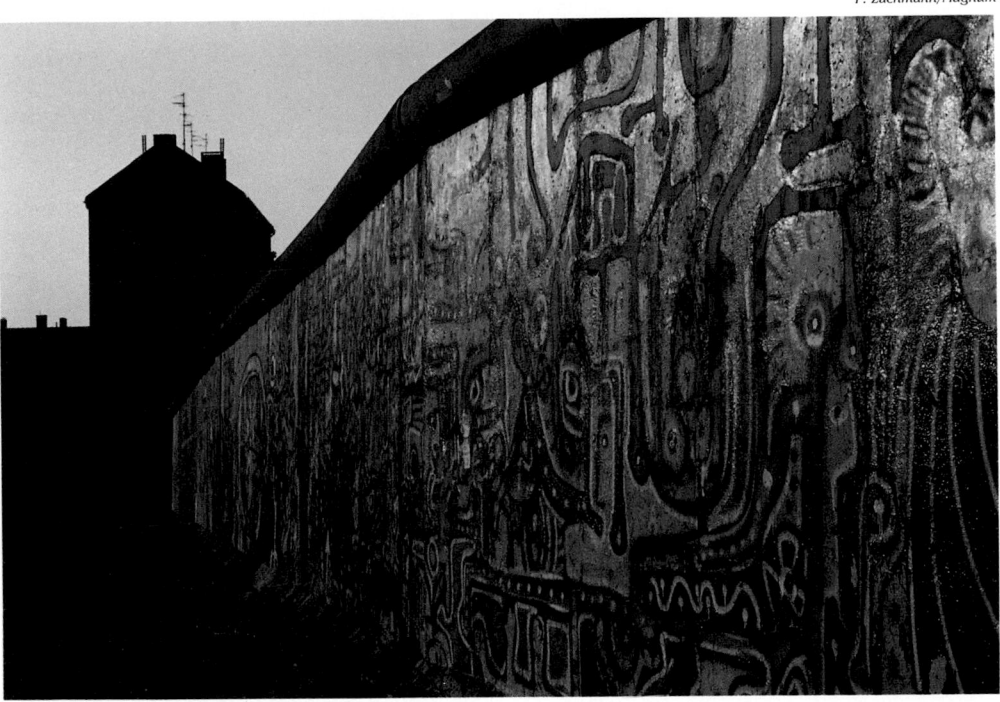

BERLIN WALL
P. Zachmann/Magnum

BRITISH EVENTS

1945   Churchill resigns.

1946   United Nations meets in London.

1947   Coal mines nationalized.

1949   Britain joins NATO.

         Irish Free State becomes Republic of Ireland.

1950   London dock strike.

1952   Elizabeth II becomes queen.

1953   Winston Churchill knighted, wins Nobel Prize for Literature.

1954   Track star Roger Bannister breaks four-minute mile.

         William Golding publishes *Lord of the Flies*.

         Philip Larkin publishes *The Less Deceived*.

1956   British troops sent to Egypt in Suez Crisis.

1957   P.G. Wodehouse publishes *The World of Jeeves*.

1959   First televised election coverage.

1960   Alan Sillitoe publishes *The Loneliness of the Long Distance Runner*.

1962   Doris Lessing publishes *The Golden Notebook*.

1964   Stevie Smith publishes *Selected Poems*.

1966   Seamus Heaney publishes *Death of a Naturalist*.

1967   New Scotland Yard opens.

Albert Camus

Sir Winston Churchill

Hungarian Uprising

World War II Ends

WORLD EVENTS

1945	World War II ends.
1947	India and Pakistan gain independence from Britain.
	France: Albert Camus publishes *The Plague*.
1948	Mideast: Palestine partitioned; nation of Israel established.
	South Africa: Alan Paton publishes *Cry, the Beloved Country*.
1949	China: Mao Tse-tung establishes People's Republic.
1950	Asia: Korean War begins.
	South Africa: Riots against apartheid crushed.
1952	United States: Ernest Hemingway publishes *The Old Man and the Sea*.
1953	Tibet: Edmund Hillary climbs Mount Everest.
1954	United States: Jonas Salk begins inoculations against polio.
	Algeria: War of independence from France begins.
1955	Eastern Europe: Communist nations sign Warsaw Pact.
	United States: Martin Luther King, Jr. leads black boycott of Montgomery buses.
	Australia: Patrick White publishes *The Tree of Life*.
1956	Hungary: Revolt against Russian influence crushed.
1957	Russia: Sputnik I, first spaceship, launched.
1959	Cuba: Fidel Castro seizes power.
	Canada: St. Lawrence Seaway opens.

Mao Tse-tung

Martin Luther King, Jr.

Fidel Castro

Doris Lessing

Introduction   1203

1204

Enrichment Give students the following background information on the Common Market. After World War II, the European nations of France, West Germany, Italy, Belgium, the Netherlands, and Luxembourg agreed to the Schuman Plan (1951). This plan provided for the pooling of coal and steel resources and the elimination of tariffs on these materials. The success of the Schuman Plan led to the development of the European Economic Community (1957), often called the Common Market. Member nations integrated their economies by reducing tariffs and making it easier for people to travel from one country to another.

Throughout the 1960's, Great Britain tried repeatedly to enter the Common Market. Its entry, however, was opposed by France, partly because of Britain's special economic relationship with nations of the British Commonwealth. In 1973 Britain finally succeeded in joining the Common Market, along with the Republic of Ireland and Denmark.

BRITISH EVENTS

1972   Britain imposes direct rule on Northern Ireland.

1973   Britain and Ireland join Common Market.

1975   North Sea oil production begins.

1976   First supersonic passenger flight leaves London.

1977   John Fowles publishes *Daniel Martin*.

1979   Margaret Thatcher becomes first female prime minister.

1980   V.S. Naipaul publishes *A Bend in the River*.

        Britain suffers worst recession since 1930s.

        Strikes in government-run steel and mining industries.

1981   Unemployment and racial tensions lead to Brixton riots.

        Royal wedding of Prince Charles and Princess Diana.

1982   Britain defeats Argentina in Falklands war.

1983   William Golding wins Nobel Prize for Literature.

1984   Ted Hughes named poet laureate.

1985   Hillsborough Agreement gives Republic of Ireland voice in governing Northern Ireland.

1986   First American football game played in England.

1987   Poetry recitations given in London's Waterloo Station.

1990   Violent protests arise in response to proposed poll tax.

Direct Rule Imposed on Northern Ireland

Margaret Thatcher   Labor Strike

Famine in Ethiopia

V. S. Naipaul

Jean Anouilh   Gabriel Garcia Marquez

North Sea Oil Platforms

Corazon Aquino   Ayatollah Khomeini

WORLD EVENTS

1960	Russia: Yuri Gagarin becomes first person in space.
	Germany: Berlin Wall built.
1961	France: Jean Anouilh publishes *Becket*.
1962	Caribbean: Cuban Missile Crisis.
1963	United States: President John F. Kennedy assassinated.
	Germany: Günther Grass publishes *Dog Years*.
1964	Vietnam: American troops begin fighting.
1966	India: Indira Gandhi becomes prime minister.
1967	South Africa: Christiaan Bernard performs first heart transplant.
1968	Colombia: Gabriel García Márquez publishes *A Hundred Years of Solitude*.
1969	America's *Apollo 11* lands on moon.
1971	Switzerland: Women gain right to vote.
1973	Worldwide energy crisis.
1974	France: Russia's Alexander Solzhenitsyn publishes *The Gulag Archipelago*.
1977	Africa: Djibouti, last remaining European colony, granted independence.
1979	Iran: Ayatollah Khomeini overthrows Shah.
	Nicaragua: Sandinistas oust Somoza government.
1980	Poland: Lech Walesa leads Solidarity movement.
1985	Ethiopia: Warfare and drought result in great famine.
1986	Russia: Accident at Chernobyl nuclear plant.
	Philippines: Democratic government established under Corazon Aquino.
1989	Germany: Closed border, symbolized by Berlin Wall, opens between East and West Germany.

Introduction   1205

Fine art, *Industrial Landscape,* by L. S. Lowry. Laurence Stephen Lowry(1887-1976), a British painter, was educated at the Muncipal College of Art. Lowry developed a highly individualistic style of painting industrial scenes. These seemingly naive views of factories, workers, and dreary mill towns are Lowry's satiric observation of England's deteriorating industrialized society.

Industrial Landscape is a panoramic view of factories and workers' barracks populated by characteristic scurrying stick figures. His palette is restricted to a few basic colors applied to a stark white background. The impersonality of the scene is Lowry's comment on the dehumanization loneliness imposed by industrialization. Despite this bleak message the landscape has a poetry that is peculiar to his work.

the Continent and in America looked to London for inspiration. They wore their hair long like the Beatles, and they bought "mod" fashions from London's Carnaby Street.

A Series of Shocks

Unfortunately, rock bands and boutiques did not suffice to restore Britain's economic vitality. The industries that had hauled Britain and the world into the industrial revolution of the eighteenth century—textiles, steelmaking, shipbuilding—had lost their old magic. Now British industries were lagging behind. First in America, then in Japan and other Asian countries, new factories sprang up that could turn out goods more cheaply than could Britain's aging factories. By the score, British factories closed their gates. By the thousands, laid-off British workers "went on the dole" (signed up for welfare benefits).

For Britons, economic troubles were not the only shocks of the postwar period. British society was changing rapidly. The many changes included the following:

- *Large-scale immigration.* Indians, Africans, West Indians, and others poured in from Britain's former colonies and Britain was transformed into a multiracial, "melting-pot" society.
- *Greater equality.* The barriers that had long divided Britons by social class began to break down, as changes in the system of education opened new opportunities to working-class people.
- *New roles for women.* Despite Britain's long history of ruling queens, women had held few other prominent positions. In 1979

INDUSTRIAL LANDSCAPE
L. S. Lowry
Tate Gallery, London

the nation elected its first female prime minister, Margaret Thatcher. At the same time, more and more women began rising to prominence in politics, science, business, education, and the arts.

The Thatcher Era

Thatcher was a woman with a mission. She prescribed a stiff dose of free enterprise as the cure for Britain's troubles. Her Conservative-party government set about selling off state-owned industries and imposing cost-cutting measures on Britain's welfare agencies. Her government also encouraged the growth of new-style industries based on computer technology.

Thatcher's task would not be an easy one. Britain's economy remained shaky, despite the discovery and exploitation of oil deposits in the North Sea. The country also faced a number of challenges. In 1982 it fought a war with Argentina over Britain's tiny South Atlantic possession, the Falkland Islands. Britain won the war, but paid a high price in blood and money. Meanwhile, the violence in Ulster (Northern Ireland) dragged on. A 1985 agreement gave the Republic of Ireland a consultative role in Ulster's affairs. But hard-line Ulster Catholics continued to fight for union with Ireland, and hard-line Ulster Protestants rejected any cooperation with that Catholic country.

Today, Britain seeks to adapt to a much-changed postwar world. In some ways the most modern of nations, Britain is in other ways among the most traditional. The ancient institutions of monarchy still play a central role in British life, inspiring awe and reverence in many

MARGARET THATCHER, 1983
Stuart Franklin-Sygma

ARCHBISHOP OF CANTERBURY LEADING PRINCE AND PRINCESS TO HIGH ALTAR OF ST. PAUL'S, JULY 29, 1981
The Granger Collection

Humanities Note

Fine art, *Great Black-Backed Gull,* by Douglas Anderson. England's Douglas Anderson (b. 1934) is best known for his portraits in oil. His studies, however, with Italy's Pieter Annigoni prepared him to paint other subjects as well. The atmospheric painting *Great Black-Backed Gull* is a modern view of an old subject. The flat, simplified treatment of the water and sky contrasts with the detailed rocks and pebbles in the foreground. The bird perched there lends a touch of loneliness to the scene.

Enrichment Tell students that in recent years, Britain has achieved success in a field that was previously dominated by Americans: the musical theater. The key to Britain's success has been the young composer Andrew Lloyd Webber. (See the remarks on Andrew Lloyd Webber in the Cross Currents Feature, p. 1325.) His hit shows include *Cats* and *Phantom of the Opera.*

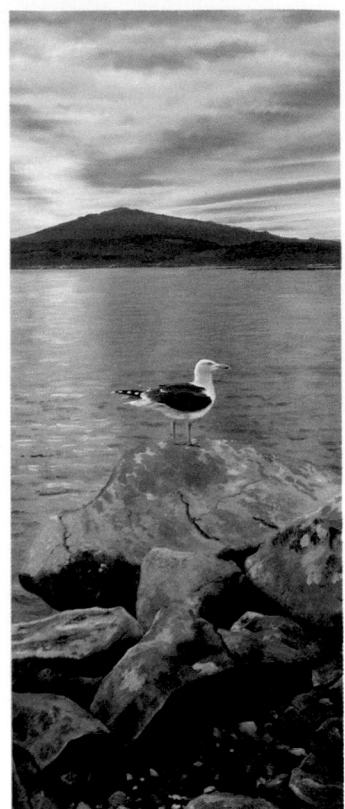

GREAT BLACK-BACKED GULL
Douglas Anderson
Oscar and Peter Johnson Ltd., London

Britons. Huge, happy crowds celebrated the marriages of the heir to the throne—Charles, Prince of Wales—in 1981 and of his brother Andrew in 1986. For each occasion, the pomp and splendor of honored traditions blended with the glitz and glamor of the media age. Like the poet T. S. Eliot, Britons seem to have turned to the past as a source of comfort while moving ahead into the swirl and bustle of contemporary life.

CONTEMPORARY BRITISH LITERATURE

Both in subject matter and in style, British literature since World War II has displayed enormous diversity. Faced with an ever-shrinking world, many British writers have turned outward. They have addressed such global concerns as the destruction of the environment and the threat of nuclear war. Other writers have turned inward, exploring personal relationships and the individual's attempts to cope with modern urban and suburban life. Many recent works have examined Britain's past or its new role as a secondary power. Other works have addressed the specific problems and concerns of the British working class, whose problems and attitudes they address in their writings. Finally, with the decline of empire has come a blossoming of "post-colonial" literature. Writers in Ireland and in many former British colonies often use the English language to explore the legacy of empire.

Achievements in Drama

Britain has continued to enjoy preeminence in the world of drama. In New York City, America's theater capital, for example, Broadway's most successful new dramas are often British imports. Many British plays go on to become films seen the world over. British television, too, has produced a string of noteworthy original dramas and a number of fine adaptations of classic novels and plays.

Many contemporary British dramatists use the techniques of realism. For example, Shelagh Delaney (born 1939) specializes in slice-of-life dramas like *A Taste of Honey* (1958). Her works are acutely realistic in depicting the lives of ordinary people. A group of dramatists known as Britain's "angry young men" also used realistic techniques in plays of the 1950's and 1960's attacking the injustices of Britain's class system. Typical of their work is John Osborne's *Look Back in Anger,* which focuses on a working-class youth rebelling against the establishment.

A second strain of contemporary British drama is represented by the so-called theater of the absurd. Plays of this school often feature dialogue and actions that seem disconnected and senseless—as if to say that life itself is an absurd series of tribulations. The Irish-born Samuel Beckett (born 1906), author of *Waiting for Godot* (1952), is foremost among the playwrights who use such techniques. The early plays of Harold Pinter (born 1930) also show the influence of the theater of the absurd.

A third type of contemporary British play is the historical drama that explores figures, events, and attitudes from times gone by. One such play is *A Man for All Seasons* (1960) by Robert Bolt (born 1924), which tells the story of Thomas More, the sixteenth-century scholar and Catholic martyr. Employing powerful, almost Shakespearean language, the play captures the grandeur of times past. Yet Bolt also creates a narrator called the Common Man, through whose eyes More's life unfolds—a strikingly contemporary touch. Tom Stoppard employs a similar device in *Rosencrantz and Guildenstern Are Dead* (1967).

Achievements in Poetry

Contemporary British poets are less widely known than British playwrights. Still, many poets have come to teach at American universities and have won international reputations. During the 1950's and 1960's, a number of outstanding British poets associated themselves with what is called simply the Movement—the poetic equivalent of drama's angry young men. These poets rejected the style of Romantic poets such as Dylan Thomas, aiming to capture everyday experiences in the language of "the common man." Philip Larkin (1922–85), among the finest poets in the Movement, brought

KING'S COOKHAM RISE, 1947
Stanley Spencer
The Metropolitan Museum of Art

4 Enrichment Another poet who taught and wrote in America was Ted Hughes who in 1956 married an American poet, the late Sylvia Plath.

5 Literary Movement See "Hawk Roosting," page 1302, in which the poet emphasizes the bird's predatory nature.

6 Master Teacher Note To develop an understanding of the classical view of man as fallible rather than perfectible, you might have students compare Golding's view in *Lord of the Flies* with Conrad's in *Heart of Darkness.*

4 to his well-crafted verse a background as a music critic. Also part of the Movement were Thom Gunn (born 1929) and Donald Davie (born 1922), both of whom went on to teach and write in America.

The British have plucked poets out of musty libraries and thrust them before live audiences. Colorful festivals keep alive the Anglo-Saxon and Celtic traditions of oral poetry recitation. Poets have even recited their verse for rush-hour commuters at London's Waterloo Station. One of the first contemporary poets to stress oral performance was Stevie Smith, born Florence Margaret Smith (1902–71). Influenced by traditional English lyrics and early church music, Smith often recited her verse aloud in the singsong manner of traditional British bards.

5 British poets of recent years have exhibited a great deal of diversity in the form and content of their work. Ted Hughes (born 1930), named Britain's poet laureate in 1984, writes frequently of the beauty and violence of nature. His best-known volumes include *Hawk in the Rain* (1957) and *Crow* (1971). Nature is also a common subject in the work of Irish poet Seamus Heaney (born 1939). In his poetry Heaney also frequently explores the terror and hope of Ireland's stormy history. Another well-known contemporary poet, Elaine Feinstein (born 1930) writes a lyric poetry that balances an awareness of human limitations against a deep faith in human endurance. Other significant contemporary poets include William Empson (1906–84), Molly Holden (1927–81), Geoffrey Hill (born 1932), and the Irish poets Patrick Kavanagh (1905–67) and Thomas Kinsella (born 1928).

Achievements in Prose

The English novel has continued to flourish in the contemporary period. With the introduction of the inexpensive paperback, books have become more accessible to the general public, and people have been able to to build larger personal libraries than ever before.

Several writers who began their careers in the modern period continued to prosper in contemporary times. On such writer was Graham Greene who produced a string of best sellers which often dealt with Cold War politics. Another was P. G. Wodehouse (1881–1975), who began his series of charming novels about dimwitted Bertie Wooster and his clever butler, Jeeves, in 1939. As late as the 1960's, Wodehouse was delighting readers with new Jeeves books.

Many new novelists also came on the scene. Four of the most successful have been William Golding (born 1911 and winner of the 1983 Nobel Prize for Literature), Anthony Burgess (born 1917), Kingsley Amis (born 1922), and John Fowles (born 1926). Golding's 6 *Lord of the Flies* (1954) tells of a group of British schoolboys who revert to savage behavior after being stranded on a tropical island. Burgess has carried on in the tradition of George Orwell's *1984,* imagining a brutal future in the dystopian novel *A Clockwork Orange* (1962). Amis gives a comic touch to novels like *Lucky Jim* (1953)

P. G. WODEHOUSE, 1958
The Granger Collection

and *Stanley and the Women* (1984). Fowles often experiments with novel forms, as in *The Collector* (1963), which tells the same story twice—from two characters' different points of view.

In literature as in other realms of British life, women have risen to 7 the forefront since 1945. Margaret Drabble (born 1939) has produced such well-received novels as *The Summer Birdcage* (1963) and *The Needle's Eye* (1972). The Irish-born Iris Murdoch (born 1919) has written many intricate novels exploring human relationships. Doris Lessing (born 1919), who grew up in Rhodesia (Zimbabwe), gained fame for a series of novels set in Africa about a 8 character named Martha Guest. Later she wrote *The Golden Notebook* (1962) and a string of novels with futuristic settings. Another important female author is Nadine Gordimer (born 1923), who writes well-crafted novels and short stories that examine the moral and political dilemmas of racially divided South Africa, where she lives.

Many British fiction writers in addition to Gordimer have excelled at writing short stories. Sean O'Faolain (born 1900) creates stories that capture the flavor of rural life in his native Ireland. Michael McLaverty (born 1907), another Irishman, usually deals with plots and themes relating to nature. Among the finest of England's native short-story writers is Alan Sillitoe (born 1928), whose lyrical tales often focus on the painful predicaments of working-class people.

Meanwhile, a number of talented writers from what used to be called "the colonies" have added to the richness of contemporary British literature. These authors include Mordecai Richler (born 1931) of Canada, Wilson Harris (born 1921) of Guyana, V. S. Naipaul (born 1932) of Trinidad, Frank Sargeson (1903–82) of New Zealand, and Patrick White (born 1912) of Australia.

Nonfiction has also prospered in contemporary times. The Irish writer Lawrence Durrell (born 1912), who is also a skilled novelist and poet, has earned praise for his travel writing and humorous sketches. Antonia Fraser (born 1932), wife of the playwright Harold Pinter, is a widely read popular historian. Bertrand Russell (1872–1970), the controversial philosopher, mathematician, and political activist, produced one of the best British autobiographies of recent decades. Several writers have also earned widespread recognition as literary critics. These writers include V. S. Pritchett (born 1900) and David Daiches (born 1912), as well as the poets Donald Davie and Thom Gunn, and the novelists Anthony Burgess and Margaret Drabble.

ENGLISH VOICES
Quotations by Prominent Figures of the Period

So always look for the silver lining
And try to find the sunny side of life.
P. G. Wodehouse, *Sally*

Why does my Muse only speak when she is unhappy?
She does not, I only listen when I am unhappy.
Stevie (Florence Margaret) Smith, "My Muse"

So winter closed its fist
And got it stuck in the pump.
Seamus Heaney, "Rite of Spring" (from *Door Into the Dark*)

The point is, . . . the point is, that as far as I can see, everything's cracking up.
Doris Lessing, Anne in *The Golden Notebook*

Columbus' huckstering breath
Blew inland through North America

Killing the last of the mammoths.
Ted Hughes, "Fourth of July" (from *Lupercal*)

Duty largely consists of pretending that the trivial is critical.
John Fowles, *The Magus*

Life should be a humane
undertaking. I know. I
undertook it. Yet have found
that in every move
I prevent someone
from stepping where I step.
Thom Gunn, "Positives"

While we can, for as long as we can, oh let us believe.
Isabel Colegate, *The Shooting Party*

Eternity is a terrible thought. I mean, where's it going to end?
Tom Stoppard, *Rosencrantz and Guildenstern Are Dead*

Source: Doris Lessing, *A Small Personal Voice: Essays, Reviews, Interviews* (New York: Vintage Books, 1975) p. 7. Essay "The Small Personal Voice" first appeared 1957.

Introduction 1213

Reading Critically The purpose of this page is to guide students in critical reading of contemporary English literature. The information offered here will enable students to place a work of literature in its historical context, identify literary movements of the time, and appreciate the writers' techniques used to convey the ideas of the period.

Reading Critically The purpose of this page is to guide students in critical reading of contemporary English literature. The information offered here will enable students to place a work of literature in its historical context, identify literary movements of the time, and appreciate the writers' techniques used to convey the ideas of the period.

As you discuss the information on this page with your class, explain that the short story on the following pages, "The Distant Past" by William Trevor, is a model for reading critically. The side columns contain notes that draw attention to elements that reflect the historical context, the influence of the literary movements, and the writer's technique.

To give students further practice with the process of reading critically, use the selection in the Teaching Portfolio, "The Lost Symbols" By Elizabeth Jennings, page 1441, following the Teacher Backup, which students can annotate themselves. Encourage students to use these strategies as they read the literature in this unit.

Teaching to Ability Levels For **less advanced** students, you might want to discuss some of the words and phrases that are particularly Irish before they read the story: *mince, custom, BBC, public house, bogs, cutlery.* For **more advanced** students, you might offer more background about the Irish struggle. Ask the history department for primary sources about the time. Perhaps you might present speeches by Eamon De Balera, Bernadatte Devlin, or other leaders to the class.

The Literature of 1945–Present

Because writers tend to be influenced by literary movements and historical trends, placing a literary work in its historical context can help you to fully understand and appreciate it.

Historical Context

The period from 1945 to the present has been a time of transition for the English nation and people. During World War II London and other English towns and cities were severely damaged by German air raids, and in the aftermath of the war the British people struggled to rebuild their nation. At the same time, as the transformation of the British Empire into the British Commonwealth was completed, the nation was forced to accept a sharp decline in its economic and political status. Despite the decline in its status, however, the government has taken strong measures to insure adequate health care, housing, education, and pensions for the entire British population.

Literary Movements

Contemporary British literature is extremely diverse in content. Like their predecessors from the modern period, many contemporary writers have delved into the human mind, focusing on people's inner thoughts and feelings. Responding to the changing complexion of British life, some writers have explored the effects of change on the British traditions, institutions, and people. Others have confronted additional problems and issues facing today's British society, and still others have presented shocking visions of futuristic societies in which personal freedoms are denied.

Writer's Techniques

Although contemporary British writers have used a wide variety of literary forms and devices, few new techniques have been developed. While many contemporary poets have relied on traditional poetic forms, others have used the unconventional forms that became popular during the Modern Age. In fiction, writers have generally modeled their stories and novels after typical modern works, omitting expositions, transitions, and resolutions, and using the stream-of-consciousness technique.

On the following pages is a story by William Trevor, a highly regarded contemporary fiction writer. The notes in the side column should help you to place the selection in its historical context.

1214   *Contemporary Writers*

Objectives

1 To recognize types of characters
2 To understand characters' motivations
3 To write a dialogue

Support Materials

Teaching Portfolio
Teacher Backup, p. 1437
Reading Critically, "The Lost Symbols," by Elizabeth Jennings, p. 1441
Grammar in Action Worksheet, *Appreciating Dialect,* p. 1442
Usage and Mechanics Worksheet, p. 1444

Analyzing Literature Worksheet, *Recognizing Character*, p. 1445
Critical Thinking and Reading Worksheet, *Understanding a Character's Motivation,* p. 1446
Selection Test, p. 1447

The Distant Past

William Trevor

In the town and beyond it they were regarded as harmlessly peculiar. Odd, people said, and in time this reference took on a burnish of affection.

They had always been thin, silent with one another, and similar in appearance: a brother and sister who shared a family face. It was a bony countenance, with pale blue eyes and a sharp, well-shaped nose and high cheekbones. Their father had had it too, but unlike them their father had been an irresponsible and careless man, with red flecks in his cheeks that they didn't have at all. The Middletons of Carraveagh the family had once been known as, but now the brother and sister were just the Middletons, for Carraveagh didn't count any more, except to them.

They owned four Herefords,[1] a number of hens, and the house itself, three miles outside the town. It was a large house, built in the reign of George II,[2] a monument that reflected in its glory and later decay the fortunes of a family. As the brother and sister aged, its roof increasingly ceased to afford protection, rust ate at its gutters, grass thrived in two thick channels all along its avenue. Their father had mortgaged his inherited estate, so local rumor claimed, in order to keep a Catholic Dublin woman in brandy and jewels. When he died, in 1924, his two children discovered that they possessed only a dozen acres. It was locally said also that this adversity hardened their will and that because of it they came to love the remains of Carraveagh more than they could ever have loved a husband or a wife. They blamed for their ill-fortune the Catholic Dublin woman whom they'd never met and they blamed as well the new national regime, contriving in their eccentric way to relate the two. In the days of the union jack[3] such women would have known their place—wasn't it all part and parcel?

Writer's Technique: Unlike most contemporary stories, the story begins with an exposition, in which background information is provided.

Literary Movements: The decay of the Middleton estate parallels the decline of the British Empire.

Historical Context: The story is set in southern Ireland. After being ruled by the English for hundreds of years, the Irish people rebelled against British rule in 1920. Following a period of bloody conflict, the British granted southern Ireland its independence in 1921, and the Irish Free State was established.

---

1. **Herefords** *n.*: A breed of cattle.
2. **reign of George II:** 1727-1760.
3. **union jack:** The British flag; the symbol of British rule.

The Distant Past 1215

Literary Movement: Like Trevor's characters, many British people have had difficulty accepting the dramatic changes that have occurred during the twentieth century and have tried to cling to the institutions and traditions of the past.

Twice a week, on Fridays and Sundays, the Middletons journeyed into the town, first of all in a trap[4] and later in a Ford Anglia car. In the shops and elsewhere they made, quite gently, no secret of their continuing loyalty to the past. They attended on Sundays St. Patrick's Protestant Church, a place that matched their mood, for prayers were still said there for the King whose sovereignty their country had denied. The revolutionary regime would not last, they quietly informed the Reverend Packham—what sense was there in green-painted pillar boxes[5] and a language that nobody understood?

4. **trap** *n.*: A two-wheeled horse-drawn carriage.
5. **pillar boxes:** Mail collection boxes.

Primary Source

The following quotation comes from Neil Hepburn's review of William Trevor's *Angels at the Ritz,* the book of short stories that contains "The Distant Past":

[If William Trevor's] novels have excited respectful admiration, it is perhaps because enthusiasm does not come easily to reviewers—and perhaps because the area within which Mr. Trevor works with something like obsession is an extremely uncomfortable one, quite rapidly giving rise to ill-defined feelings of guilt and despair in his readers. For Mr. Trevor worries about the separation of human beings, from one another, from feeling, from the past, particularly from love and from childhoods retrospectively illuminated (whether in fact or illusion) by golden and perfect companionship. So meticulously articulated is this worry in the 12 stories of *Angels at the Ritz,* so expertly judged the writing, that you cannot help yourself from feeling strong compassion (amounting to heartbreak in the beautiful 'Mrs. Actland's Ghosts') for the poor creatures of

On Fridays, when they took seven or eight dozen eggs to the town, they dressed in pressed tweeds and were accompanied over the years by a series of red setters, the breed there had always been at Carraveagh. They sold the eggs in Keogh's grocery and then had a drink with Mrs. Keogh in the part of her shop that was devoted to the consumption of refreshment. They enjoyed the occasion, for they liked Mrs. Keogh and were liked by her in return. Afterwards they shopped, chatting to the shopkeepers about whatever news there was, and then they went to Healy's Hotel for a few more drinks before driving home.

In spite of their loyalty to the past, they built up convivial relationships with the people of the town. Fat Driscoll, who kept the butcher's shop, used even to joke about the past when he stood with them in Healy's Hotel or stood behind his own counter cutting their slender chops or thinly slicing their liver. "Will you ever forget it, Mr. Middleton? I'd ha' run like a rabbit if you'd lifted a finger at me." Fat Driscoll would laugh then, rocking back on his heels with a glass of stout in his hand or banging their meat on to his weighing-scales. Mr. Middleton would smile. "There was alarm in your eyes, Mr. Driscoll,' Miss Middleton would murmur, smiling also at the memory of the distant occasion.

Fat Driscoll, with a farmer called Maguire and another called Breen, had stood in the hall of Carraveagh, each of them in charge of a shotgun. The Middletons, children then, had been locked with their mother and father and an aunt into an upstairs room. Nothing else had happened: the expected British soldiers had not, after all, arrived and the men in the hall had eventually relaxed their vigil. "A massacre they wanted," the Middletons' father said after they'd gone. "Bloody ruffians."

The Second World War took place. Two Germans, a man and his wife called Winkelmann who ran a glove factory in the town, were suspected by the Middletons of being spies for the Third Reich.[6] People laughed, for they knew the Winkelmanns well and could lend no credence to the Middletons' latest fantasy—typical of them, they explained to the Winkelmanns, who had been worried. Soon after the War the Reverend Packham died and was replaced by the Reverend Bradshaw, a younger man who laughed also and regarded the Middletons as an anachronism. They protested when prayers

---

6. Third Reich (rīk): The German government under the Nazis (1933–1945).

his fancy, cast thoughtlessly adrift on the silent-roaring sea of their aloneness. Nor, a moment later—and here is the discomfort—can you help the breaking in of a bitter self-knowledge: your compassion is, after all, for clever artifacts, and your own, real, companionable virtues are neither golden nor perfect. Too much of this can make you resentful, even blind you to Mr. Trevor's excellence. This is why collections are inimical to the proper love of short stories and why, marvelously well as these 12 are done, it is better to resist the temptation to gulp them all down at a sitting.

were no longer said for the Royal Family in St. Patrick's, but the Reverend Bradshaw considered that their protests were as absurd as the prayers themselves had been. Why pray for the monarchy of a neighboring island when their own island had its chosen President now? The Middletons didn't reply to that argument. In the Reverend Bradshaw's presence they rose to their feet when the BBC played "God Save the King," and on the day of the coronation of Queen Elizabeth II they drove into the town with a small union jack propped up in the back window of their Ford Anglia. "Bedad, you're a holy terror, Mr. Middleton!" Fat Driscoll laughingly exclaimed, noticing the flag as he lifted a tray of pork steaks from his display shelf. The Middletons smiled. It was a great day for the Commonwealth of Nations, they replied, a remark which further amused Fat Driscoll and which he later repeated in Phelan's public house. "Her Britannic Majesty," guffawed his friend Mr. Breen.

Situated in a valley that was noted for its beauty and with convenient access to rich rivers and bogs over which game-birds flew, the town benefited from post-war tourism. Healy's Hotel changed its title and became, overnight, the New Ormonde. Shopkeepers had their shopfronts painted and Mr. Healy organized an annual Salmon Festival. Even Canon Kelly, who had at first commented severely on the habits of the tourists, and in particular on the summertime dress of the women, was in the end obliged to confess that the morals of his flock remained unaffected. "God and good sense," he proclaimed, meaning God and his own teaching. In time he even derived pride from the fact that people with other values came briefly to the town and that the values esteemed by his parishioners were in no way diminished.

From the windows of their convent the Loretto nuns observed the long, sleek cars with G.B. plates; English and American accents drifted on the breeze to them. Mothers cleaned up their children and sent them to the Golf Club to seek employment as caddies. Sweet shops sold holiday mementoes. The brown, soda and currant breads of Murphy-Flood's bakery were declared to be delicious. Mr. Healy doubled the number of local girls who served as waitresses in his dining room, and in the winter of 1961 he had the builders in again, working on an extension for which the Munster and Leinster Bank had lent him twenty-two thousand pounds.

But as the town increased its prosperity Carraveagh continued its decline. The Middletons were in their middle sixties now and were reconciled to a life that became more uncomfortable with every passing year. Together they roved the vast lofts of their house, placing old paint tins and flowerpot saucers beneath the drips from the roof. At night they sat over their thin chops in a dining room that had once been gracious and which in a way was gracious still, except for the faded appearance of furniture that was dry from lack of polish and of a wallpaper that time had rendered colorless. In the hall their father gazed down at them, framed in ebony and gilt, in the uniform of the Irish Guards. He had conversed with Queen Victoria, and even in their middle sixties they could still hear him saying that God and Empire and Queen formed a trinity unique in any worthy soldier's heart. In the hall hung the family crest, and on ancient Irish linen the Cross of St. George.[7]

The dog that accompanied the Middletons now was called Turloch, an animal whose death they dreaded for they felt they couldn't manage the antics of another pup. Turloch, being thirteen, moved slowly and was blind and a little deaf. He was a reminder to them of their own advancing years and of the effort it had become to tend the Herefords and collect the weekly eggs. More and more they looked forward to Fridays, to the warm companionship of Mrs. Keogh and Mr. Healy's chatter in the hotel. They stayed longer now with Mrs. Keogh and in the hotel, and idled longer in the shops, and drove home more slowly. Dimly, but with no less loyalty, they still recalled the distant past and were listened to without ill-feeling when they spoke of it and of Carraveagh as it had been, and of the Queen whose company their careless father had known.

The visitors who came to the town heard about the Middletons and were impressed. It was a pleasant wonder, more than one of them remarked, that old wounds could heal so completely, that the Middletons continued in their loyalty to the past and that, in spite of it, they were respected in the town. When Miss Middleton had been ill with a form of pneumonia in 1958 Canon Kelly had driven out to Carraveagh twice a week with pullets and young ducks that his housekeeper had dressed. "An upright couple," was the Canon's public opinion of the Middletons, and he had been known to add that eccentric views would hurt you less than malice. "We can disagree without guns in this town," Mr. Healy pronounced in his cocktail room, and his visitors usually replied that as far as they could see that was the

---

7. St. George: The patron saint of England.

Historical Context: Their father's portrait reminds them of the Victorian age, an era in which British life was characterized by a sense of optimism and patriotism.

The Distant Past 1219

Writer's Technique: The Middletons' personalities are revealed through the descriptions of their thoughts and actions.

Historical Context: The bombing was carried out by Catholics in Northern Ireland who believed that the Protestant majority in that country was discriminating against them. This was the beginning of a violent conflict between Catholics and Protestants in Northern Ireland.

result of living in a Christian country. That the Middletons bought their meat from a man who had once locked them into an upstairs room and had then waited to shoot soldiers in their hall was a fact that amazed the seasonal visitors. You lived and learned, they remarked to Mr. Healy.

The Middletons, privately, often considered that they led a strange life. Alone in their two beds at night they now and again wondered why they hadn't just sold Carraveagh forty-eight years ago when their father had died—why had the tie been so strong and why had they in perversity encouraged it? They didn't fully know, nor did they attempt to discuss the matter in any way. Instinctively they had remained at Carraveagh, instinctively feeling that it would have been cowardly to go. Yet often it seemed to them now to be no more than a game they played, this worship of the distant past. And at other times it seemed as real and as important as the remaining acres of land, and the house itself.

"Isn't that shocking?" Mr. Healy said one day in 1967. "Did you hear about that, Mr. Middleton, blowing up them post offices in Belfast?"

Mr. Healy, red-faced and short-haired, spoke casually in his Cocktail Room, making midday conversation. He had commented in much the same way at breakfast-time, looking up from the *Irish Independent*. Everyone in the town had said it too: that the blowing up of sub-post offices in Belfast was a shocking matter.

"A bad business," Fat Driscoll remarked, wrapping the Middletons' meat. "We don't want that old stuff all over again."

"We didn't want it in the first place," Miss Middleton reminded him. He laughed, and she laughed, and so did her brother. Yes, it was a game, she thought—how could any of it be as real or as important as the afflictions and problems of the old butcher himself, his rheumatism and his reluctance to retire? Did her brother, she wondered, privately think so too?

"Come on, old Turloch," he said, stroking the flank of the red setter with the point of his shoe, and she reflected that you could never tell what he was thinking. Certainly it wasn't the kind of thing you wanted to talk about.

"I've put him in a bit of mince," Fat Driscoll said, which was something he often did these days, pretending the mince would otherwise be thrown away. There'd been a red setter about the place that night when he waited in the hall for the soldiers; Breen and Maguire had pushed it down into a cellar, frightened of it.

Grammar in Action

A **nonstandard dialect** is a form of English that uses words, pronunciations, and sentence structures not used in standard English. Writers use nonstandard dialect to add local color to their stories and present a more realistic picture of a setting. Language can indicate a certain setting just as effectively as a detailed physical description. The phrase "toidy-toid street," for example, evokes Brooklyn, New York, just as surely as the first line of Robert Burns's poem "To a Mouse" calls up pictures of a Scottish landscape: "Wee, sleekit, cow'rin, tim'rous beastie."

In "The Distant Past," William Trevor effectively suggests a setting in the North of Ireland with a bit of Irish dialect:

"We're hit, Mr. Middleton," Mr. Healy said one Friday morning. "If there's a dozen visitors this summer *it'll be God's own stroke of luck for us.*"

"Luck?"

"*Sure,* who wants to come to a country with all that malarkey in it?"

The italicized word and clause are characteristic of Irish

"There's a heart of gold in you, Mr. Driscoll," Miss Middleton murmured, nodding and smiling at him. He was the same age as she was, sixty-six—he should have shut up shop years ago. He would have, he'd once told them, if there'd been a son to leave the business to. As it was, he'd have to sell it and when it came to the point he found it hard to make the necessary arrangements. "Like us and Carraveagh," she'd said, even though on the face of it it didn't seem the same at all.

Every evening they sat in the big old kitchen, hearing the news. It was only in Belfast and Derry, the wireless said; outside Belfast and Derry you wouldn't know anything was happening at all. On Fridays they listened to the talk in Mrs. Keogh's bar and in the hotel. "Well, thank God it has nothing to do with the South," Mr. Healy said often, usually repeating the statement.

The first British soldiers landed in the North of Ireland, and soon people didn't so often say that outside Belfast and Derry you wouldn't know anything was happening. There were incidents in Fermanagh and Armagh, in border villages and towns. One Prime Minister resigned and then another one. The troops were unpopular, the newspapers said; internment became part of the machinery of government. In the town, in St. Patrick's Protestant Church and in the Church of the Holy Assumption, prayers for peace were offered, but no peace came.

Historical Context: In 1969, following bloody riots in the cities of Belfast and Londonderry, British troops were sent into Northern Ireland. In 1972, as the violence continued, the British government took over direct control of the country.

"We're hit, Mr. Middleton," Mr. Healy said one Friday morning. "If there's a dozen visitors this summer it'll be God's own stroke of luck for us."

"Luck?"

"Sure, who wants to come to a country with all that malarkey in it?"

"But it's only in the North."

"Tell that to your tourists, Mr. Middleton."

The town's prosperity ebbed. The border was more than sixty miles away, but over that distance had spread some wisps of the fog of war. As anger rose in the town at the loss of fortune so there rose also the kind of talk there had been in the distant past. There was talk of atrocities and counteratrocities, and of guns and gelignite[8] and the rights of people. There was bitterness suddenly in Mrs. Keogh's bar because of the lack of trade, and in the empty hotel there was bitterness also.

Writer's Techniques: Trevor implies that the townspeople's resentment of the British has resurfaced as a result of the violence in Northern Ireland and the implications of the violence.

---

8. gelegnite *n.*: An explosive.

The Distant Past 1221

speech. By using dialect, Trevor conveys the Irish setting in a particularly economical manner. He does not need to add very much in the way of physical description.

Student Activity 1. Find another example in this story where Trevor uses dialect to convey a setting.

Student Activity 2. Write a brief dialogue in which you communicate the setting to a reader purely by means of an immediately recognizable dialect. Assume that the reader will be one of your classmates, and remember that a dialect uses nonstandard words, pronunciations, and sentence structures.

Clarification Belfast is the capital of Ulster, or Northern Ireland. Derry, also known as Londonderry, is a seaport there.

Master Teacher Note William Trevor taught history at a school in Armagh, Northern Ireland from 1950 to 1952.

On Fridays, only sometimes at first, there was a silence when the Middletons appeared. It was as though, going back nearly twenty years, people remembered the union jack in the window of their car and saw it now in a different light. It wasn't something to laugh at any more, nor were certain words that the Middletons had gently spoken, nor were they themselves just an old, peculiar couple. Slowly the change crept about, all around them in the town, until Fat Driscoll didn't wish it to be remembered that he had ever given them mince for their dog. He had stood with a gun in the enemy's house, waiting for soldiers so that soldiers might be killed—it was better that people should remember that.

One day Canon Kelly looked the other way when he saw the Middletons' car coming and they noticed this movement of his head, although he hadn't wished them to. And on another day Mrs. O'Brien, who had always been keen to talk to them in the hotel, didn't reply when they addressed her.

The Middletons naturally didn't discuss these rebuffs but they each of them privately knew that there was no conversation they could have at this time with the people of the town. The stand they had taken and kept to for so many years no longer seemed ridiculous in the town. Had they driven with a union jack now they would, astoundingly, have been shot.

"It will never cease." He spoke disconsolately one night, standing by the dresser where the wireless was.

She washed the dishes they'd eaten from, and the cutlery. "Not in our time," she said.

"It is worse than before."

"Yes, it is worse than before."

They took from the walls of the hall the portrait of their father in the uniform of the Irish Guards because it seemed wrong to them that at this time it should hang there. They took down also the crest of their family and the Cross of St. George, and from a vase on the drawing-room mantelpiece they removed the small union jack that had been there since the coronation of Queen Elizabeth II. They did not remove these articles in fear but in mourning for the *modus vivendi*[9] that had existed for so long between them and the people of the town. They had given their custom to a butcher who had planned to shoot down soldiers in their hall and he, in turn, had given them mince for their dog. For fifty years they had experienced, after suspicion had seeped away, a tolerance

---

9. *modus vivendi* (vi ven' di): Manner of getting along.

that never again in the years that were left to them would they know.

One November night their dog died and he said to her after he had buried it that they must not be depressed by all that was happening. They would die themselves and the house would become a ruin because there was no one to inherit it, and the distant past would be set to rest. But she disagreed: the *modus vivendi* had been easy for them, she pointed out, because they hadn't really minded the dwindling of their fortunes while the town prospered. It had given them a life, and a kind of dignity: you could take a pride out of living in peace.

He did not say anything and then, because of the emotion that both of them felt over the death of their dog, he said in a rushing way that they could no longer at their age hope to make a living out of the remains of Carraveagh. They must sell the hens and the four Herefords. As he spoke, he watched her nodding, agreeing with the sense of it. Now and again, he thought, he would drive slowly into the town, to buy groceries and meat with the money they had saved, and to face the silence that would sourly thicken as their own two deaths came closer and death increased in another part of their island. She felt him thinking that and she knew that he was right. Because of the distant past they would die friendless. It was worse than being murdered in their beds.

Literary Movement: The fate of the Middleton family and estate reflects the disappearance of a glorious age in British history

William Trevor (1928–   ) was born and educated in Ireland, but he moved to England after beginning his writing career. Set in both Ireland and England, his stories explore a wide variety of subjects and themes. Displaying a deep understanding of human nature, Trevor often portrays the seemingly pointless misunderstandings that develop between people and groups of people. Perhaps Trevor's deep understanding of people comes from his unusual education. The son of a bank manager, he was enrolled in thirteen different schools. For long periods, however, he simply roamed the countryside, occasionally tutored by neighboring farmers or failed clergymen. Interestingly, he completed his education formally, graduating from Trinity College in 1950. Initially a history teacher and sculptor, he turned to writing, he said, to express a humanity he could not find in his art. Trevor has published numerous collections of short stories, including *The Collected Stories of William Trevor*.

The Distant Past   1223

(Answers begin on p. 1223.)

3. (a) The Middletons drive into town with a union jack propped up in the back window. (b) The townspeople laugh at them.
4. The town prospers because tourists found it a charming, pleasant place to visit.
5. (a) The relationship of the townspeople and the Middletons is friendly at first. Although they are considered eccentric, they are respected and welcome. (b) Bitter, the townspeople turn away from the Middletons by ignoring them. They are no longer welcome.

Interpreting

6. Just as the British Empire was diminished after World War I as colonies demanded and received independence, the Middletons lost property and their home deteriorated. They both were relics of the past.
7. As long as the town was prosperous, the Middletons were respected even though they were avid Anglophiles. When British soldiers came to Northern Ireland and trouble started there, the townspeople began to ignore and reject them.
8. Suggested Response: The change in the townspeople's attitude reveals that terrorism can affect people far away, old wounds never completely heal, and economic adversity can create bitterness and cruelty.

Applying

9. Answers will differ. One possible response would include the fact that since the Irish had been oppressed by the English for hundreds of years, denied their civil rights, and considered second-class citizens in their own country, they are bound to harbor ill feelings toward the English.

Challenge Imagine that you were a tourist who had visited the town during the tranquil years of the early '60's. You have decided to return and, much to your surprise, you notice a change in the town's atmosphere. Write a postcard home, telling what you think of the difference.

1224

THINKING ABOUT THE SELECTION
Recalling

1. Whom do the Middletons blame for the decay of their estate?
2. What event do Fat Driscoll and the Middletons recall when they visit Driscoll's butcher shop?
3. (a) What do the Middletons do on the day of Queen Elizabeth II's coronation? (b) How do the townspeople respond to this action?
4. Why does the town prosper in the years after World War II?
5. (a) What type of relationship do the Middletons have with the townspeople? (b) How does the relationship change after the town's prosperity fades?

Interpreting

6. How does the decline of the Middletons' fortunes parallel the decline of the British Empire?
7. What is ironic, or surprising, about the fact that throughout most of the story the townspeople respected the Middletons?
8. What does the change in the townspeople's attitude toward the Middletons reveal about human nature?

Applying

9. Why do you think that many Irish people feel a sense of resentment toward the British?

ANALYZING LITERATURE
Recognizing Character

A variety of different types of characters are used in literary works. When a character is well-developed and posseses a variety of traits, he or she is referred to as a round character. A character who embodies a single trait, ideal, or quality is referred to as a flat character. Static characters are characters who do not change during the course of a literary work. Dynamic characters are characters who do change.

1. Are the Middletons flat characters or round characters? Support your answer.
2. Are the Middletons static characters or dynamic characters? Support your answer.
3. Are the townspeople static characters or dynamic characters? Support your answer.

CRITICAL THINKING AND READING
Understanding a Character's Motivation

In portraying any type of character, a writer must provide a motivation, or a stated or implied reason for the character's behavior, to make the character's actions believable. For example, in "The Distant Past" it is clear that the Middletons' actions on the day of Queen Elizabeth II's coronation are motivated by their loyalty to Great Britain.

1. What motivates the townspeople to change their behavior toward the Middletons?
2. How does Trevor reveal this motivation?

THINKING AND WRITING
Writing a Dialogue

Write a dialogue in which the Middletons discuss the decline in their fortunes and the change in the townspeoples' attitude toward them. Reread the story, trying to put yourself in the Middletons' place. Then write your dialogue, having the Middletons discuss the reasons for and feelings about their present situation. When you finish writing, revise your dialogue and share it with your classmates.

ANSWERS TO ANALYZING LITERATURE

1. The Middletons are round characters because the reader knows what they are thinking and feeling.
2. The Middletons are dynamic characters, for they change when they, mourning for the way they had related to the townspeople, remove the symbols of England.
3. The townspeople are also dynamic characters because their attitude towards the Middletons changes from friendly respect to cold bitterness.

ANSWERS TO CRITICAL THINKING AND READING

1. The townspeople's change in behavior is motivated by loss of income because of terrorism in the North. They associate the Middletons' loyalty to Britain with the trouble caused by British soldiers.
2. Trevor reveals this by the actions of the townspeople—pointedly ignoring the Middletons, becoming silent when they appear, and no longer accepting their eccentricity.

THINKING AND WRITING

Publishing Student Writing Have students work with a partner to tape their dialogues, adding any sound effects that would be appropriate. Play the tapes for the class.

Prose

THE IDENTI-KIT MAN, 1974
Derek Boshier
Tate Gallery Publications Department

Fine art, *The Identi-kit Man*, 1974, Derek Boshier. *The Identi-kit Man* was done by the British artist Derek Boshier (1937-   ). Boshier studied at the Yeovil School of Art and the Royal College of Art in London. His radical Pop Art statements first gained notice in the sixties. He has since worked in many styles and media, including photography, video, and film. His statements are never bland or common. They explore political issues and archetypes, morality, and modern life situations. *The Identi-kit Man* starkly presents items as symbols. The work of Derek Boshier brashly forces viewers to re-evaluate their heroes and re-examine their values.

More About the Author One of the sources for Sean O'Faolain's rich fictional characterizations might be his biographical writing. In addition to novels and short stories, O'Faolain wrote biographies of Eamon De Valera, Daniel O'Connell, Hugh O'Neill, and others. These factual portrayals of men who had a role in Irish history demanded O'Faolain's probing into the *whys* and *hows* of their lives. While his fiction derives from imagination, the engaging and well-rounded characters in O'Faolain's stories correlate to the types of men in his biographies—they question values, challenge their environment, and attempt to find meaning in their lives. As O'Faolain said, "There is only one admirable form of the imagination—the imagination that is so intense that it creates a new reality, that it makes things happen, whether it be a political thing, or a social thing, or a work of art." His own intense imagination, fueled by factual research, has yielded sympathetic and complex characters. Discuss how factual research can influence or enhance a writers' imaginative creation.

Critical Evaluation Literary scholar Gordon Henderson wrote that "O'Faolain's reputation rests most firmly on his short stories, which critics have tended to rank with those of James Joyce and Frank O'Connor. His later stories won a wide popular audience in such mass-circulation magazines as *Colliers, McCall's, Redbook, Saturday Evening Post, Ladies' Home Journal,* and *Playboy.* Their popular appeal, however, does not reduce his stature as a writer of serious fiction. Like Joyce and O'Connor, he took the short story as he received it from Maupassant and Chekhov and transformed it into something uniquely his own and uniquely Irish."

SEAN O'FAOLAIN

1900–

Although the Irish writer Sean O'Faolain is best known for his short stories, he has written widely in many genres—novels, plays, biographies, travel books, literary criticism. His works, which draw upon a powerful sense of tradition, deal with Ireland and its people with a universality that transcends their locale. Over the past fifty years, his writings have promoted liberal, humane values in a state that he, as a revolutionary, helped to bring into existence.

Sean O'Faolain, originally named John Whelan, was born in the city of Cork in southern Ireland, the son of a policeman and a theatrical landlady. Schooled by priests and later at University College, Cork, he "became one with the emotion of Ireland" in the aftermath of the Easter Rebellion of 1916. He joined the Irish volunteers, learned Gaelic, and changed his name to its Gaelic variant. During the Irish revolution, 1918–1921, he served as director of publicity for the Irish Republican Army. An idealist, he found himself disillusioned by the struggle and its consequences and drifted away from war and politics.

After a year of graduate study at Harvard, O'Faolain sent for Eileen Gould, whom he had met during the revolution. He married her, and for their honeymoon they took a camping trip across the United States. Although both he and Eileen loved America, they returned to Ireland "where every field, every path, every ruin had its memories, where every last corner had its story."

The war, which made O'Faolain a bitter young man, furnished the material for his first short stories, collected in *Midsummer Night Madness* (1932). His later collections, such as *A Purse of Coppers* (1937) and *The Man Who Invented Sin* (1948), show increasing maturity. They depict everyday Irish life in a lyrical yet unsentimental manner.

O'Faolain wrote that "the longing . . . not merely to describe chaos but to bring it, before God, to imaginative form" led him to become a writer. He concludes: "Being a writer I had to—as the spider must spin, and the clouds must drift and fall, and the trees grow and shed and grow again—go on writing, waiting and watching for the appearance, within me, of the theme . . . to say: 'This is what you dreamed as a boy. There is no break, no chasm, just a larger shape, a more human, a more complex form.'"

O'Faolain, who says his aim in writing is a "blend of reason and sensibility," founded *The Bell,* an Irish literary journal, in 1940, and edited it for a number of years. A reformer, deeply concerned with Irish culture, he has not always been popular with conservatives in Ireland. Nevertheless, his compassion and humor have never left him, and his portraits of Irish life are sympathetic and compelling.

Objectives

1 To understand first-person narration
2 To identify subjective information
3 To understand the meaning of caricature
4 To write about a thematic statement

Support Material

Teaching Portfolio
Teacher Backup, p. 1449
Grammar in Action Worksheet, *Using Sentence Fragments,* p. 1453
Usage and Mechanics Worksheet, p. 1455
Vocabulary Check, p. 1456
Analyzing Literature Worksheet, *Understanding First-Person Narration,* p. 1458

GUIDE FOR INTERPRETING

A Touch of Autumn in the Air

First-person Narration. The purpose of narration is to tell a story. Narration may be either factual (as is history and biography) or fictional (as in novels and short stories). In fictional narration, the story may be told from various perspectives, depending on the narrator's point of view. The narrator—the person who tells the story—may be someone within the story or someone outside it. A first-person narrator is a character within the story. He or she uses the word *I* in telling it. A third-person narrator stands outside the story and uses *he, she, they,* or *it.*

First-person narration, or point of view, falls into two main types. A first-person narrator, using the pronoun *I,* may be a main character in a story—a first-person participant—like the narrator in Mary Wollstonecraft Shelley's *Frankenstein.* Or the narrator, using *I,* may be a first-person observer, like Dr. Watson in the Sherlock Holmes stories.

In either kind of role, the narrator serves as a persona, or mask, through which the writer tells the story. He or she relates events in accordance with the writer's artistic purpose. The narrator, being a fictional creation, does *not* necessarily reflect the writer's own attitudes or beliefs.

Commentary

Writers whose careers span a long period of time face a particular problem: Should they go back and revise earlier works to reflect their changed style? For example, if like O'Faolain they wrote their early works in a romantic style that is not characteristic of their current work, should they rewrite these early works to make the style consistent with their later writing?

Critics have noted that the realistic style of "A Touch of Autumn" is characteristic of much of O'Faolain's work from the fifties to the present. However, it contrasts with that of his earlier short stories, which were far more heavily poetical, "full of romantic words, such as *dawn, dew, onwards, youth, world, adamant,* and *dusk,*" as O'Faolain himself remarks. However, this romantic mood has passed out of fashion now, replaced by the harder edge found in his later stories.

O'Faolain resisted the impulse to rewrite his stories once they were published. Explaining his decision not to rewrite, O'Faolain said, "You can rewrite while you are the same man. To rewrite years after is a form of forgery."

Writing

What is memory? Why do we remember some things and not others? Why do some events spring to mind after lying dormant in memory for many years? Freewrite, exploring your answers.

Guide for Interpreting 1227

Literary Focus Point out that narration is the way that a writer tells a story. Explain to students that writers must choose different types of narration for different purposes. Ask students to discuss the advantages and disadvantages of first-person narration. Elicit that an advantage of first-person narration is that the reader learns the thoughts and feelings of one character. The reader becomes involved in the story because the narrator is directly involved in the events. A possible disadvantage of first-person narration is that the reader is limited to learning only what the narrator knows, experiences, or finds out from other characters or from direct observation. Have students think about other stories that they have read. Ask your **less advanced** students to identify the point of view in each story. Ask your **more advanced** students to analyze the writer's use of first-person narration or third-person narration.

Writing/Prior Knowledge Have students discuss a vivid childhood memory, an incident that they wish might happen to them, or a historical event that they will never forget. Then have them complete the freewriting assignment, using their discussion as a basis for the writing topic. Ask students to consider the advantages and disadvantages of first-person narration to a writer. Your **more advanced** students might try using first-person narration and third-person narration in their writing.

Vocabulary

Preteach the following vocabulary words:

obstinacy (äb′ stə nə sē) *n.*: Stubbornness (p. 1228)

mesmerism (mez′ mər iz′m) *n.*: Hypnotism (p. 1229)

advert (ad vʉrt′) *v.*: To call attention to (p. 1229)

demesne (di mān′) *n.*: Lands of an estate (p. 1229)

sinuous (sin′ yo͞o wəs) *adj.*: Bending; curving in and out (p. 1229)

premonitory (pri män′ ə tôr′ ē) *adj.*: Giving warning beforehand (p. 1232)

phosphorescence (fäs′ fə res′ 'ns) *n.*: The property of shining in the dark (p. 1234)

imperiously (im pir′ ē əs lē) *adv.*: Arrogantly (p. 1234)

A Touch of Autumn
in the Air

Sean O'Faolain

It was, of all people, Daniel Cashen of
Roscommon who first made me realize that
the fragments of any experience that remain
in a man's memory, like bits and scraps of a
ruined temple, are preserved from time not
at random but by the inmost desires of his
personality.

Cashen was neither sensitive nor intelligent. He was a caricature of the self-made,
self-educated, nineteenth-century businessman. Some seventy years ago he had set
up a small woollen factory in County Roscommon which, by hard work from early
morning to late at night, and by making
everybody around him work at the same
pace, he developed into a thriving industry
which he personally owned. His Swansdown
Blankets, for example, were the only kind of
blankets my mother ever bought. Though
old when I made his acquaintance, he was
still a powerful horse of a man, always
dressed in well-pressed Irish tweeds, heavy
countryman's boots, and a fawn, flat-topped
bowler hat set squat above a big, red, square
face, heavy handlebar moustaches and pale
blue, staring eyes of which one always saw
the complete circle of the iris, challenging,
concentrated, slightly mad.

One would not expect such a man to say
anything very profound about the workings
of the memory, and he did not. All he did
was to indulge in a brief burst of reminiscence in a hotel foyer, induced by my casual
remark that it was a lovely, sunny day outside but that there was a touch of autumn in
the air. The illuminating thing was the bewildered look that came into those pale,
staring eyes as he talked. It revealed that he
was much more touched and troubled by the
Why of memory than by the Fact of memory.
He was saying, in effect: Why do I remember
that? Why do I not remember the other
thing? For the first time in his life something
within him had gone out of control.

What he started to talk about was a
holiday he spent when just under fifteen, in
what was at that time called the Queen's
County. It had lasted two months, September and October. "Lovely, sunny weather,
just like today." What had begun to bother
him was not so much that the days had
merged and melted together in his memory
—after so many years that was only natural
—but that here and there, from a few days
of no more evident importance than any
other days, a few trivial things stuck up
above the tides of forgetfulness. And as he
mentioned them I could see that he was
fumbling, a little fearfully, towards the notion that there might be some meaning in
the pattern of those indestructible bits of
the jigsaw of his youth, perhaps even some
sort of revelation in their obstinacy after so
much else had dropped down the crevices of
time.

He did not come directly to the major
memory that had set his mind working in
this way. He mentioned a few lesser memo-

ries first, staring out through the revolving glass doors at the sunny street. There was the afternoon when, by idle chance, he leaned over a small stone bridge near his Uncle Bartle's farm and became held for an hour by the mesmerism of the stream flickering through the chickweed. As could happen likewise to a great number of busy men, who normally never think at all about the subjective side of themselves, and are overwhelmed by the mystery of it if once they do advert to it, he attached an almost magical import to the discovery that he had never forgotten the bright pleasure of that casual hour.

"No, John! Although it must be near sixty years ago. And I don't believe I ever will forget it. Why is that?"

Of course, he admitted modestly, he had a phenomenal memory, and to prove it he invited me to ask him the telephone numbers of any half-dozen shops in town. But, yet, there was that red hay barn where he and his cousin, Kitty Bergin, played and tumbled a score of times—it was a blur.

"I can't even remember whether the thing was made of timber or corrugated iron!"

Or there was the sunken river, away back on the level leas, a stream rather than a river, where one warm September Sunday after Mass he saw, with distasteful pleasure, the men splashing around naked, roughly ducking a boy who had joined them, laughing at his screams. But, whereas he also still possessed the soft, surrounding fields, the imperceptibly moving clouds, the crunch of a jolting cart far away, the silence so deep that you could have heard an apple falling, he had lost every detail of the walk to and from the river, and every hour before and after it. A less arrogant man might have accepted the simple explanation that the mind wavers in and out of alertness, is bright at one moment, dim at the next. Those mad, round irises glared at the suggestion that his mind could at any time be dim.

He pointed out that he knew the country for miles around, intimately, walking it and cycling it day after day: what clung to him of it all, like burrs, were mere spots—a rusty iron gate falling apart, a crossroads tree with a black patch burnt at its base, an uneventful turn off the main road, a few undistinguished yards of the three miles of wall around the local demesne. He laughed scornfully at my idea that his mind became bright only for those few yards of wall.

"Well, perhaps it became dim then? You were thinking hard about other things up to that point in your walk?"

Here he allowed his real trouble to expose itself. He had not only remembered pointless scraps, but, I found, those scraps had been coming back to him repeatedly during the last few days with a tormenting joy, so that here he was, an old man, fondling nothings as lovingly as if he were fondling a lock of a dead woman's hair. It was plain, at last, that he was thinking of all those fragments of his boyhood as the fish scales of some wonderful fish, never-to-be-seen, sinuous and shining, that had escaped from his net into the ocean.

What had started him off was simple. (I reconstruct it as well as I can, intuiting and enlarging from his own brief, blunt words.) A few mornings before our meeting, fine and sunny also, he had happened to go into a toyshop where they also sold sweets. He was suddenly transfixed by the smell peculiar to these shops—scented soaps, the paint on the tin toys and the sprayed wooden trucks, the smell of the children's gift books, the sweetness of the sweets. At once he was back in that holiday, with his cousin Kitty Bergin, on the leas behind her father's farmhouse (his Uncle Bartle's), one sunny, mistified October morning, driving in a donkey cart down to where his uncle and his cousin Jack were ditching a small meadow that they had retrieved from the rushes and the bog water.

As Kitty and he slowly jolted along the rutted track deeper and deeper into this

A Touch of Autumn in the Air   1229

5 **Clarification** Who is speaking? What effect does the dialogue have?

6 **Discussion** Discuss the sensory details of Cashen's memory. List as many different senses that the writer appeals to as you can.

7 **Reading Strategy** Why is Cashen's memory like a fish? Do you think that Cashen would compare his recollection of boyhood to a fish?

8 **Clarification** A lea is a pasture that is used temporarily for haying or grazing. Uncle Bartle and cousin Jack are making a ditch so that excess water will run off from the pasture.

9 **Reading Strategy** When does the action described take place? Explain the shift in time in this sentence.

10 **Literary Focus** Describe the point of view used in this passage. Who is the narrator?

Humanities Note

Fine art, *The Soothsayer from the Green Island,* 1946, by John Petts. The contemporary British artist John Petts was born in 1914 in London. He was educated at the Hornsley College of Art and the Central School, Royal Academy of Art. Not content to express himself in one medium, Petts works in sculpture, mosaic, engraving, and stained-glass design. He is internationally known for the large window he designed for the people of Wales to present as a goodwill gift to the Afro-American Church in Birmingham, Alabama, which was bombed in a notorious racial incident.

John Petts did wood-engraving illustrations for England's Golden Cockerel Press. This engraving, *The Soothsayer,* was executed in 1946. This example shows Petts's engraving skills in the interesting variety of textures, masterly composition, and combination of unconventional point of view with rhythmic curving lines.

You might ask the following questions:

1. What kind of person would you guess the man in this print to be?
2. What is the mood or atmosphere of this print?

THE SOOTHSAYER FROM THE GREEN ISLAND, 1946
John Petts

1230   *Contemporary Writers*

wide, flat river basin of the Barrow, whose hundreds of streams and dikes feed into what, by a gradual addition, becomes a river some twenty miles away, the two men whom they were approaching looked so minute on the level bog, under the vast sky, that Dan got a queer feeling of his own smallness in observing theirs. As he looked back, the white, thatched farmhouse nestling into the earth had never seemed so homely, cozy and comforting.

Ferns crackled at the hub. When he clutched one its fronds were warm but wet. It was the season when webs are flung with a wild energy across chasms. He wiped his face several times. He saw dew drops in a row in midair, invisibly supported between frond and frond. A lean swath of mist, or was it low cloud, floated beneath far hills. Presently they saw behind the two men a pond with a fringe of reeds. Against an outcrop of delicately decayed limestone was a bent hawthorn in a cloud of ruby berries. Or could it have been a rowan tree? The sky was a pale green. The little shaven meadow was as lemon-bright as fallen ash leaves before the dew dries on their drifts, so that it would have been hard to say whether the liquid lemon of the meadow was evaporating into the sky or the sky melting down into the field.

They were on a happy mission. Mulvaney the postman had brought two letters to the farmhouse from two other sons: Owen, who was a pit manager in the mines at Castlecomer, and Christopher (who, out of respect, was never referred to as Christy), then studying for the priesthood in a Dublin seminary. Aunt Molly had sent them off with the letters, a jug of hot tea and thick rounds of fresh, homemade bread and homemade apple jam smelling of cloves, a great favorite of Uncle Bartle's. They duly reached the two men, relieved the donkey of bridle, bit and winkers so that he could graze in the meadow, spread sacks to sit on, and while Kitty poured the tea into mugs Bartle reverently wiped his clayey hands on the sides of his trousers and took the letters. As he read them aloud in a slow, singsong voice, like a man intoning his prayers, it was clear that those two sons had gone so far outside his own experience of the big world that he stood a little in awe of them both. It was a picture to be remembered for years: the meadow, the old man, the smoke of the distant farmhouse, partriarchal, sheltered, simple.

When he laid down the letter from the priest-to-be he said:

"He's doing well. A steady lad."

When he had read the letter from the mines he said:

"He's doing fine. If he escapes the danger he will go far."

While Jack was reading the letters Kitty whispered to Danny, thumbing the moon's faint crescent:

"Look! It says D for Danny."

"Or," he murmured to her boldly, 'it could be D for Dear?"

Her warning glare towards her father was an admission.

"I see here," Jack commented, while his father sucked at the tea, "that Christopher is after visiting Fanny Emphie. Her name in religion is Sister Fidelia."

Dan had seen this girl at the Curragh Races during the first week of his holidays, a neighbor's daughter who, a few weeks later, entered the convent. He had heard them joking one night about how she and Christopher had at one time been "great" with one another. He remembered a slight, skinny girl with a cocked nose, laughing moist lips and shining white teeth.

"Read me out that bit," Bartle ordered. "I didn't note that."

"'I got special leave from the President to visit Sister Fidelia, last week, at Saint Joachim's. She is well and happy but looked pale. She asked after you all. Saint Joachim's has nice grounds, but the trams pass outside the wall and she said that for the first couple of weeks she could hardly sleep at all.'"

A Touch of Autumn in the Air   1231

11 Reading Strategy What do you think is being described in this passage?

12 Master Teacher Note This selection is rich in sensory detail. Provide students with books of photographs or paintings that graphically represent the pastoral beauty of Ireland. Emphasize the rural photographs or paintings. If students have been to Ireland, ask them to describe the landscape.

13 Clarification A bridle is the restraint by which a rider controls a horse or donkey. A bit is the steel part of the bridle that fits into animal's mouth. Winkers are the blinkers or blinders worn by the donkey so that it is not distracted or suddenly frightened as it walks or works.

14 Reading Strategy How do Dan and Kitty feel about one another?

15 Clarification In the Catholic religion, women who become nuns are addressed as "Sister." Because a woman who enters the convent for religious service is giving up her old life and making a pledge for a new life, she changes her name to signify this new commitment. Fanny Emphie took the name "Sister Fidelia" when she became a nun. *Fidelia* is related to *fidelity,* which means "loyalty."

16 Clarification A curragh, or coracle, is a small boat made of broad hoops that are covered with animal hide or tarpaulin. The curragh is traditionally used in Ireland and the British Isles.

17 Discussion Describe in your own words what Kitty looks like. What do her actions reveal about Kitty's personality?

18 Master Teacher Note The Conversation Lozenges made a lasting impression on Cashen. Try to find "conversation lozenges" in the stores to help students understand the flavor of his recollection. These candies are often sold for Valentine's Day. Have students compare and contrast the messages written on those that Cashen buys and those that you supply.

19 Reading Strategy What series of coincidences happen to Cashen? Why does Cashen notice the nun in the sweets-and-toys shop?

The two men went on drinking their tea. It occurred to Dan that they did not care much for Fanny Emphie. He saw her now in her black robes walking along a graveled path under the high walls of the convent, outside which the trams at night drew their glow in the air overhead. It also occurred to him, for no reason, that Kitty Bergin might one day think of becoming a nun, and he looked at her with a pang of premonitory loss. Why should any of them leave this quiet place?

"Ha!" said old Bartle suddenly, and winked at Danny, and rubbed his dusty hands and drew out his pipe. This meant that they must all get back to work.

Kitty gathered up the utensils, Danny tackled the donkey, the others went back to their ditching and she and Danny drove back to where the fern was plentiful for bedding. Taking two sickles, they began to rasp through the stalks. After a while she straightened up, so did he, and they regarded one another, waist-deep in the fern.

"Do you think," she asked him pertly, "would I make a nice nun?"

"You!" he said, startled that the same thought had entered their heads at the same time.

She came across to him, slipped from his pocket the big blue handkerchief in which the bread had been wrapped, cast it in an arc about her fair head, drew it tightly under her chin with her left hand, and then with a deft peck of her right finger and thumb cowled it forward over her forehead and her up-looking blue eyes.

"Sister Fidelia, sir," she curtsied, provokingly.

He grappled with her as awkwardly as any country boy, paying the sort of homage he expected was expected of him, and she, laughing, wrestled strongly with him. They swayed in one another's arms, aware of each other's bodies, until she cried, "Here's Daddy," and when he let her go mocked him from a safe distance for his innocence. But

as they cut the fern again her sidelong glances made him happy.

They piled the cut fern into the cart, climbed on top of it, and lay face down on it, feeling the wind so cold that they instinctively pressed closer together. They jolted out to the main road, and as they ambled along they talked, and it seemed to him that it was very serious talk, but he forgot every word of it. When they came near the crossroads with its little sweetshop, they decided to buy a half-penny-worth of their favorite sweets, those flat, odd-shaped sweets —diamonds, hearts, hexagonals—called Conversation Lozenges because each sweet bore on its coarse surface a ring posy[1] in colored ink, such as Mizpah, Truth Tries Troth, Do You Care? or All for Love. Some bore girls' names, such as Gladys or Alice. His first sweet said, Yours in Heart. He handed it to her with a smile; she at once popped it into her mouth, laughing at his folly. As they ambled along so, slowly, chatting and chewing, the donkey's hooves whispering through the fallen beech leaves, they heard high above the bare arches of the trees the faint honking of the wild geese called down from the north by the October moon.

It was to those two or three hours of that October morning many years ago that he was whirled back as he stood transfixed by the smells of the sweets-and-toys shop. Forgetting what he had come there to buy, he asked them if they sold Conversation Lozenges. They had never heard of them. As he turned to go he saw a nun leafing through the children's gift books. He went near her and, pretending to look at a book, peered under her cowl. To his surprise she was a very old nun. On the pavement he glanced up at the sky and was startled to see there the faint crescent moon. He was startled because he remembered that he had seen it earlier in the morning, and had quite forgotten the fact.

---

1. **ring posy:** A verse or motto inscribed in a circle.

Grammar in Action

Use short **elliptical sentences,** or **sentence fragments,** to add emphasis or to mimic speech. For special purposes, a sentence with missing elements may occasionally be used to advantage, but only if the reader may be expected to understand what has been left out. If the reader cannot supply the omissions without confusion, the fragment should not be used. Notice Sean O'Faolain's use of fragments on page 1234.

He said he hadn't thought of it for sixty years. Perhaps not? But he was thinking of it now, when the adventure was pretty well over. As it was. "Aha!" he cried triumphantly. "Better than ever."

O'Faolain uses the easily understood fragment "Perhaps not?" rather than *And perhaps he had not* to suggest doubt about Daniel Cashen's statement and to engage the reader with his thoughts. The fragment "As it was" strongly emphasizes that the "adventure was pretty well over" while reminding the reader that Cashen's life was over as well. The fragment makes a full and abrupt stop, befitting this life perhaps not fully lived. The second example shows how nicely a fragment mimics speech.

He at once distrusted the message of his memory. Perhaps it was not that the smells had reminded him of little Kitty Bergin eating Yours in Heart, or pretending to be a nun, or wrestling with him in the fern? Perhaps what had called him back was the indifference of those two men to the fate of the nun? Or was there some special meaning for him in those arrowing geese? Or in the cozy, sheltered farmhouse? Maybe the important thing that day had been the old man humbly reading the letters? Why had the two men looked so small under the open sky of the bogland? D, she had said, for Danny . . .

As he stared at me there in the hotel foyer, my heart softened towards him. The pain in his eyes was the pain of a man who has begun to lose one of the great pleasures of life in the discovery that we can never truly remember anything at all, that we are for a great part of our lives at the mercy of uncharted currents of the heart. It would have been futile to try to comfort him by

20

21

22

20 **Literary Focus** Discuss the point of view used in this passage. What are the disadvantages of third-person narration? What are the advantages?

21 **Literary Focus** Who is the narrator? What signifies a shift in narration?

22 **Critical Thinking and Reading** What is the main idea of this passage? Is the information given by the narrator objective or subjective? How do you know?

Humanities Note

Fine art, *Knockalla Hills, Donegal,* by Dan O'Neill. Irish artist Dan O'Neill was born in Belfast in 1920. His splendid landscape paintings have never given in to the modern trends in art. He has maintained a consistent palette and style throughout his painting career.

Knockalla Hills, Donegal is an example of O'Neill's original style of landscape painting, in which a simple view is made interesting through his choice of harmonious colors and pleasing shapes. He captures the essence of a cool fall day in Ireland.

You might use these questions for discussion:

1. Is there anything in this painting to indicate that the scene is in Ireland? Elaborate.
2. How has the artist shown the viewer the season?

KNOCKALLA HILLS, DONEGAL
Dan O'Neill
Ulster Museum, Belfast

A Touch of Autumn in the Air 1233

Student Activity 1. State which of the following contain useful fragments. Tell why each either works or does not.

1. He looked out the window. Rain soon.
2. Billy stole quietly from the kitchen. Cookie in hand.
3. "Tomorrow, then." He rose and left quickly.

Student Activity 2. Write a short paragraph in which, with a firm purpose in mind, you use one effective sentence fragment. Remember to use quotation marks if you mimic speech.

23 Literary Focus What effect does the use of dialogue have on the tone of the story? Why does the narrator's question comfort Daniel Cashen?

24 Critical Thinking and Reading Identify the part of this sentence that is objective and the part that is subjective.

25 Critical Thinking and Reading How does the narrator feel about Cashen? Do you agree or disagree with the narrator's opinion? Why?

26 Enrichment O'Faolain compares Cashen's search for the meaning of his boyhood with archaeology. An archaeologist finds and studies delicate shards of pottery, scraps of clothing, and so on in an attempt to piece together the history and customs of a particular civilization. Often these scraps and shards offer nothing more than puzzling clues. O'Faolain's reference to archaeology is interesting for two reasons: he "digs" through factual material to write his biographies and explain his subjects; and his native country possesses a rich archaeological past buried in layers of peat found in Ireland's many bogs.

Reader's Response Why do you think people sometimes remember apparently insignificant things?

Closure and Extension

ANSWERS TO THINKING ABOUT THE SELECTION
Recalling

1. (a) The narrator's casual remark about the day being sunny but with a touch of autumn in the air prompts Daniel Cashen to talk about the holiday he spent long ago. (b) He engages in this reminiscence in a hotel foyer.
2. (a) Kitty Bergin is Daniel Cashen's cousin. (b) Aunt Molly sends Kitty and Dan to the meadow to bring

saying that those currents may be charted elsewhere, that even when those revolving glass doors in front of us flashed in the October sun the whole movement of the universe since time began was involved in that coincidence of light. Daniel Cashen of Roscommon would get small comfort out of thinking of himself as a little blob of phosphorescence running along the curl of a wave at night.

And then, by chance, I did say something that comforted him, because as he shook hands with me and said he must be off, I said, without thinking:

"I hope the blankets are doing well?"

"Aha!" he cried triumphantly. "Better than ever."

And tapped his flat-topped hat more firmly on his head and whirled the doors before him out into the sunny street as imperiously as any man accustomed to ordering everything that comes his way.

Through the slowing doors I watched him halt on the pavement. He looked slowly to the right, and then he looked towards his left, and then, slowly, he looked up around the sky until he found what he was looking for. After a few moments he shivered up his shoulders around his neck, looked at the ground at his feet, put his two hands into his pockets, and moved very slowly away, still down-looking, out of sight.

Poor man, I thought when he was gone; rash, blunt, undevious; yet, in his own crude way, more true to life than his famous French contemporary[2] who recaptured lost time only by dilating, inventing, suppressing, merging such of its realities as he could recall, and inventing whatever he could not. Cashen was playing archaeology with his boyhood, trying to deduce a whole self out of a few dusty shards.[3] It was, of course, far too late. My guess was that of the few scraps that he now held in his hands the clue lay not so much in the offer of love and the images of retirement, the girl's courtship, the white farmhouse snuggling down cozily into the earth under the vast dome of the sky, and the old man left behind by his sons, as in the challenging sight of his own littleness on that aqueous plain whose streams barely trickled to the open sea. He said he hadn't thought of it for sixty years. Perhaps not? But he was thinking of it now, when the adventure was pretty well over. As it was. A week later a friend rang me up and said, "Did you hear who's died?" I knew at once, but I asked the question.

He left nearly a hundred and fifty thousand pounds—a lot of money in our country—and, since he never married, he divided it all up among his relatives by birth, most of them comparatively poor people and most of them living in what used to be called, in his boyhood, the Queen's County.

---

2. famous French contemporary: French novelist Marcel Proust (1871-1922).
3. shards *n.*: Fragments or broken pieces.

THINKING ABOUT THE SELECTION

Recalling

1. (a) What prompts Daniel Cashen to start talking about the holiday he spent long ago? (b) Where does he engage in this "brief burst of reminiscence"?
2. (a) Who is Kitty Bergin? (b) Why did Aunt Molly send her and Dan to the meadow?
3. (a) Whom did Kitty pretend to be? (b) How did Dan respond to her play-acting? (c) Why?
4. What does the narrator ask that brings Cashen back from his reminiscence?
5. What does the narrator think affected Cashen most about his boyhood recollection?

hot tea, homemade bread and apple jam, and letters from Owen and Christopher to Jack and Uncle Bartle.
3. (a) Kitty pretended to be Sister Fidelia, a nun. (b) Dan wrestled with Kitty. (c) He grappled with her because he thought she wanted him to.
4. The narrator asks about the blankets Cashen's company manufactures; the question brings him back from his remembrance.

5. The narrator thinks that Cashen's recollection made him feel small and insignificant.

Interpreting

6. The narrator thinks that Cashen is troubled by his memories because of the look in Cashen's eye when he remembers the holiday; he appears bewildered by the remembrance and by why he remembers certain things and not others.

7. Answers will differ. Cashen most likely asks for Conversation Lozenges in the candy shop as a sentimental gesture; he bought such sweets more than fifty years ago with Kitty Bergin. The lozenges remind him of this blissful time in his life.
8. The narrator's heart softens toward Cashen near the end of the story because he recognizes the pain Cashen feels upon realizing that his memory is incomplete and

Interpreting

6. Why does the narrator think Cashen is troubled by his memories?
7. Why do you think Cashen, as an old man, asks for Conversation Lozenges in the candy shop?
8. Near the end of the story, why does the narrator's heart soften toward Cashen?
9. What is the significance of the story's title?
10. What is your own interpretation of Daniel Cashen's story and his motives for telling it?

Applying

11. Do you agree with the narrator that we can never truly remember anything at all? Explain your answer.

ANALYZING LITERATURE
First-person Narration

A first-person observer may be a fully developed character, with a name, a life history, and a personality, as is Dr. Watson in the Sherlock Holmes stories. On the other hand, a first-person observer, as in Sean O'Faolain's "A Touch of Autumn in the Air," may exist mostly in the background of the story.

1. In "A Touch of Autumn in the Air," the narrator introduces the story of Daniel Cashen and then lets the story take over. (a) What does the narrator say the story made him realize? (b) If this is true, what does the story reveal about the "inmost desires" of Cashen's personality?
2. What inferences do you make about the narrator, based on the story he tells?

CRITICAL THINKING AND READING
Identifying Subjective Information

A narrator will often provide you with subjective information—that is, information based on the narrator's own personal thoughts, feelings, and judgments. The reader has to judge the reliability of information about characters, taking into consideration not only the source of the information but also its nature. Purely factual information—for instance, that Cashen was just under fifteen at the time of the incident—seems objective enough. But that Cashen "looked at her [Kitty] with a pang of premonitory loss" is subjective regardless of who is doing the narrating.

Reread "A Touch of Autumn in the Air," identifying at least *five* apparently objective statements about Daniel Cashen and at least *five* subjective statements about him.

UNDERSTANDING LANGUAGE
Learning What a Caricature Is

When the narrator says that Daniel Cashen is "a caricature of the self-made, self-educated, nineteenth-century businessman," he means that Cashen is an exaggerated or distorted example of that type of person. In using the word *caricature,* he is ridiculing Cashen. The word *caricature* comes from the Italian noun *caricatura,* meaning "an overloading," which in turn comes from the verb *caricare,* "to load, exaggerate." One type of caricature is a picture or cartoon in which a person's features are exaggerated or distorted to produce an absurd effect. Political cartoonists produce caricatures.

Taking the whole story into account, how accurate do you think the narrator's statement about Cashen being a caricature of the self-made businessman is? Support your answer.

THINKING AND WRITING
Responding to a Thematic Statement

Very few short stories begin with an explicit statement of the story's theme. This story does. Write a brief composition in which you explain how "A Touch of Autumn in the Air" develops the theme stated in the opening sentence. First, restate the opening sentence in your own words. Then reread the story, making notes for your composition. Write your first draft, telling how the events in the story demonstrate the truth of the opening sentence. Revise your paper before handing it in. Proofread carefully to eliminate misspellings and mistakes in grammar, usage, and punctuation.

A Touch of Autumn in the Air **1235**

---

title also refers to the time of year when Cashen had this experience sixty years ago; the gentle "touch" of autumn is what helps him recall the experience.
10. Answers will differ. Students should give support for their interpretations.

Applying

11. Answers will differ. Suggested response: We can remember things. Daniel Cashen remembers a

happy time in his childhood that made a deep impression.

Challenge What do you think Cashen learns about choice in the story? What irony does his name reveal about his values? Find evidence in the selection to support your answer.

ANSWERS TO ANALYZING LITERATURE

1. (a) The story makes the narrator realize that people's memories are shaped by their inmost desires. (b) It would seem that Cushen's inmost desire was to love Kitty Bergin.
2. Suggested response: Cashen is a successful but lonely old man, who has not attained his inmost desire in life.

ANSWERS TO CRITICAL THINKING AND READING

Answers will differ. The examples students give of apparently objective statements about Cashen should include factual information that is based on objective truth or statements that can be proven. The examples students give of subjective statements about Cashen should state an opinion or make a judgment.

ANSWERS TO UNDERSTANDING LANGUAGE

Suggested response: In appearance, Cashen is a caricature of the self-made businessman. However, by the end of the story, it is apparent that Cashen has the capacity for deep emotion and sensitivity, which he has revealed by telling his story. The narrator's statement that Cashen is a caricature is only partly true; as his personality is revealed, he seems more complex and profound than a mere caricature.

THINKING AND WRITING
Publishing Student Writing Ask for student volunteers to read their compositions aloud. Have students compile a list of events that demonstrate the truth of the theme, based on each composition.

More About the Author P.G. Wodehouse obviously loved to write. As he told an interviewer, "I was writing stories when I was five. I don't remember what I did before that. Just loafed, I suppose." In the course of his long career, Wodehouse demonstrated not only a polished, well-crafted writing style but diversity as well. In addition to writing novels, short stories, and plays. Wodehouse achieved some fame for his witty Tin Pan Alley songs. He wrote the lyrics for dozens of songs for musicals of the early 1900s. This unexpected application of his writing talent flourished while Wodehouse was living in the United States, where he met Jerome Kern and Guy Bolton. The three men, who shared tastes in musical comedy, collaborated on many popular Broadway productions. While Wodehouse incorporated his talent for writing and his deft use of humor and word play in his song lyrics, his interest in musical comedy often fed into his humorous novels and stories. He made numerous direct and indirect references to his "other" passion in much of his fiction. You might ask students how writers weave personal interests or sidelights into their work.

Critical Evaluation Hilaire Belloc said of Wodehouse, "Everything this author has seen he has observed; everything he has observed he has engraved; but, what is more remarkable than observation (which is common to many), or even than the record of observation (which is, though rare in any excellent degree, yet fairly well known) is the presentation of the thing observed so that it rises almost violently before the eye to which it is presented."

P. G. WODEHOUSE

1881–1975

P(elham) G(renville) Wodehouse (pronounced wood-house) wrote for eighty years, indifferent to fame, fortune, and age. He did so, he once said, for the "pleasure of turning out the stuff." A prolific writer of humorous short stories, plays, novels, and essays, P. G. Wodehouse, known to his friends as "Plum," insisted that he had no message for humanity in his delightfully zany works. Nevertheless, his spoofs of the British gentry of a bygone era, often involving the befuddled Bertie Wooster and his unflappable valet Jeeves, are a unique contribution to modern English literature.

Wodehouse, born to a well-to-do family in Surrey, England, was educated in English boarding schools and at Dulwich College, near London. Even at an early age, Wodehouse seemed early destined for greatness: In *A Portrait of a Master,* David A. Jasen quotes one of his classmates: "Plum's talk was exhilarating. I had never known such talk. Even at . . . seventeen he could discuss lucidly writers of whom I had never heard . . . But it was impossible to say who were his favorite authors. He liked so many and all kinds. And from the first time I met him, he had decided to write. He never swerved." As a trainee in banking, he began writing humorous fiction, articles, and verse for publication. He joined the staff of the London *Globe* in 1901 as a humor columnist, and in 1908 published his first adult novel, *Love Among the Chickens.*

He first visited the United States, "the land of romance," in 1904, and within a few years became a transatlantic commuter. After a two-month courtship, he married Ethel Rowley, a young English widow whom he had met in New York. His popularity and his income rose rapidly when his stories began appearing in *The Saturday Evening Post,* which at that time was the leading publisher of short fiction in the United States.

Wodehouse had a long and distinguished career in the theater, writing parts of more than forty plays and screenplays. His theatrical experience affected his books, for he began to think of episodes as scenes and characters as actors, and he wrote a number of stories set in Hollywood. His reputation, however, rests primarily on his novels, of which he wrote nearly a hundred, and on his more than three hundred short stories. Among his many notable books are *Carry On, Jeeves* (1934), *The Code of the Woosters* (1938), *Spring Fever* (1948), and *Plum Pie* (1966).

An international commuter for much of his life, Wodehouse lived in Paris after World War II, then moved to Long Island in 1952. Four Wodehouse novels appeared at about the time he was celebrating his ninetieth birthday. He was knighted in 1975, shortly before his death.

GUIDE FOR INTERPRETING

The Truth About George

Writer's Techniques

Humor. Humor is the quality that makes something seem amusing, funny, or comic. It emphasizes the ludicrous aspects of life. Yet the elements that make up humor—those characteristics that can be listed as making something humorous—are not easy to identify. What one person finds funny, another may not. The word *humor* (the British spell it *humour)* was originally a physiological term describing the fluids, or humors, in the human body, especially the four "cardinal humors" that were thought to be responsible for one's health and disposition. As time went on, the word came to mean "a mood or state of mind," then "a whim or fancy," and finally "the quality that makes something seem amusing, funny, or comic." Humor, in the modern sense, often relies upon exaggeration, misunderstandings, odd juxtapositions, repetition, wordplay, stock characters, and so on. But such explanations of humor, like similar explanations of music or art, add very little to one's understanding or enjoyment. It is the experience that counts.

Writing

Think about something that has made you laugh recently. Jot down a few notes about the incident, including your opinion of the source of the humor. What was it that made you laugh?

Primary Source

Interviewed on his eightieth birthday, Wodehouse said:

> From my earliest years I had always wanted to be a writer. It was not that I had any particular message for humanity. I am still plugging away and not the ghost of one so far, so it begins to look as though, unless I suddenly hit mid-season form in my eighties, humanity will remain a message short. The curious thing about those early days is that, in spite of the blizzard of rejection slips, I had the most complete confidence in myself. . . . It was only later that doubts on this point began to creep in. . . . Today I am a mass of diffidence and I-wonder-if-this-is-going-to-be-all-right-ness, and I envy those tough authors, square-jawed and spitting out of the side of their mouths, who are perfectly sure, every time they start a new book, that it will be a masterpiece. But with each new book of mine I have always the feeling that this time I have picked a lemon in the garden of literature. A good thing . . . keeps one up on one's toes and makes one write every sentence ten times. . . . When in due course Charon ferries me across the Styx and everyone is telling eveyone else what a rotten writer I was, I hope at least one voice will be heard piping up: "But he did take trouble."

Guide for Interpreting 1237

---

incident or character, relate a funny remark, or depict a comical act, a writer might use parody, anecdotes, irony, caricature, or other forms of humor. Humor in cartoons, for instance, is conveyed graphically through pictures and associations. Emphasize the idea that humor evokes laughter because it appeals to the reader's sense of what is absurd or incongruous. Preview for students how P.G. Wodehouse uses several distinct forms of humor in "The Truth about George."

Writing/Prior Knowledge Discuss the expression "laugh, and the whole world laughs with you." Then have students note a humorous incident, explaining why the incident made them laugh. If students have difficulty recalling something humorous, guide them to think about a joke that they have recently heard, a comical incident that they have observed, or a situation that they found humorous. Guide students to identify the reasons that they laughed.

Vocabulary

Preteach the following vocabulary words:
maligned (mə līnd′) *v.*: Spoke evil of; defamed (p. 1238)
sibilant (sib′ ′l ənt) *adj.*: Hissing (p. 1239)
deleterious (del′ ə tir′ ē əs) *adj.*: Harmful to health; injurious (p. 1240)
choleric (käl′ ər ik) *adj.*: Easily provoked to anger (p. 1240)
irascibly (i ras′ ə b'lē) *adv.*: Irritably (p. 1240)
largess (lär jes′) *n.*: Generous gift (p. 1242)
ostentation (äs′ tən tā′ shən) *n.*: Showy display (p. 1243)
contretemps (kōn trə tän′) *n.*: Awkward mishap (p. 1246)

Objectives

1 To understand humor in a short story
2 To recognize caricature
3 To use synonyms
4 To write about humor

Support Material

Teaching Portfolio
Teacher Backup, p. 1463
Grammar in Action Worksheet, *Recognizing Participial Phrases,* p. 1467
Usage and Mechanics Worksheet, p. 1469
Vocabulary Check, p. 1470
Analyzing Literature Worksheet, *Understanding Humor,* p. 1472

Language Worksheet, *Using Synonyms,* p. 1473
Selection Test, p. 1474

Literary Focus Point out that a writer may use different forms of humor for different purposes. For example, to describe an amusing

Motivation/Prior Knowledge
Tell students that "The Truth about George" contains some made-up song lyrics that are based on real songs. As they read, have them try to guess the real lyrics of each song that George sings. After they have finished reading, you might wish to have students find the actual lyrics to each song and explain why P.G. Wodehouse might have used each one in the story.

Master Teacher Note The song lyrics that P.G. Wodehouse adapts so that George can communicate are playful and humorous. Find recordings of "Tea for Two," "If You Knew Susie," and so on. Have students listen to the songs to get an idea of the light-hearted tone of this story. You might also wish to find recordings of P.G. Wodehouse's Tin Pan Alley songs to give them an insight into his type of humor. Explain that Wodehouse himself wrote the lyrics to the songs.

Purpose-Setting Question What *is* the truth about George?

1 **Enrichment** Point out that an angler is someone who fishes with a hook. The assumption that the narrator makes in this paragraph is that he is hearing two fishermen tell a "fish story," in which the men exaggerate their success in fishing. A fish story is a tall tale in which the teller keeps exaggerating the details of the story.

2 **Literary Focus** Point out that the narrator has misunderstood the conversation that he heard. The two men are actually talking about an illness and not a fish. Explain that the humor comes from the narrator's mistaken impressions.

3 **Discussion** What are the difficulties and challenges that someone with a stammer might encounter?

The Truth About George

P. G. Wodehouse

Two men were sitting in the bar parlor of the Anglers' Rest as I entered it; and one of them, I gathered from his low, excited voice and wide gestures, was telling the other a story. I could hear nothing but an occasional "Biggest I ever saw in my life!" and "Fully as large as that!" but in such a place it was not difficult to imagine the rest; and when the second man, catching my eye, winked at me with a sort of humorous misery, I smiled sympathetically back at him.

The action had the effect of establishing a bond between us; and when the storyteller finished his tale and left, he came over to my table as if answering a formal invitation.

"Dreadful liars some men are," he said genially.

"Fishermen," I suggested, "are traditionally careless of the truth."

"He wasn't a fisherman," said my companion. "That was our local doctor. He was telling me about his latest case of dropsy. Besides"—he tapped me earnestly on the knee—"you must not fall into the popular error about fishermen. Tradition has maligned them. I am a fisherman myself, and I have never told a lie in my life."

I could well believe it. He was a short, stout, comfortable man of middle age, and the thing that struck me first about him was the extraordinary childlike candor of his eyes. They were large and round and honest. I would have bought oil stock from him without a tremor.

The door leading into the white dusty road opened, and a small man with rimless pince-nez[1] and an anxious expression shot in like a rabbit. He stood looking at us, seemingly ill at ease.

"N-n-n-n-n-n—" he said.

We looked at him inquiringly.

"N-n-n-n-n-n-ice d-d-d-d—"

His nerve appeared to fail him, and he vanished as abruptly as he had come.

"I think he was leading up to telling us that it was a nice day," hazarded my companion.

"It must be very embarrassing," I said, "for a man with such a painful impediment in his speech to open conversation with strangers."

"Probably trying to cure himself. Like my nephew George. Have I ever told you about my nephew George?"

I reminded him that we had only just met, and that this was the first time I had learned that he had a nephew George.

"Young George Mulliner. My name is Mulliner. I will tell you about George's case—in many ways a rather remarkable one."

My nephew George (said Mr. Mulliner) was as nice a young fellow as you would ever wish to meet, but from childhood up he had been cursed with a terrible stammer. If he had had to earn his living, he would undoubtedly have found this affliction a great handicap, but fortunately his father had left

---

1. **pince-nez** (pans′ nā′): Eyeglasses without sidepieces, held in place by springs gripping the bridge of the nose.

him a comfortable income; and George spent a not unhappy life, residing in the village where he had been born and passing his days in the usual country sports and his evenings in doing crossword puzzles. By the time he was thirty he knew more about Eli,[2] the prophet, Ra,[3] the sun god, and the bird Emu than anybody else in the county except Susan Blake, the vicar's daughter, who had also taken up the solving of crossword puzzles and was the first girl in Worcestershire to find out the meaning of "stearine" and "crepuscular."

It was his association with Miss Blake that first turned George's thoughts to a serious endeavor to cure himself of his stammer. Naturally, with this hobby in common, the young people saw a great deal of one another; for George was always looking in at the vicarage to ask her if she knew a word of seven letters meaning "appertaining to the profession of plumbing," and Susan was just as constant a caller at George's cozy little cottage—being frequently stumped, as girls will be, by words of eight letters signifying "largely used in the manufacture of poppet valves." The consequence was that one evening, just after she had helped him out of a tight place with the word "disestablishmentarianism," the boy suddenly awoke to the truth and realized that she was all the world to him—or, as he put it to himself from force of habit, precious, beloved, darling, much-loved, highly esteemed or valued.

And yet, every time he tried to tell her so, he could get no farther than a sibilant gurgle which was no more practical use than a hiccup.

Something obviously had to be done, and George went to London to see a specialist.

"I-I-I-I-I-I—" said George.

"You were saying—?"

"Woo-woo-woo-woo-woo-woo—"

---

2. **Eli:** From the Bible, a high priest of Israel.
3. **Ra:** The sun god and principal deity of the ancient Egyptians.

"Sing it," said the specialist.

"S-s-s-s-s-s-s-s—?" said George, puzzled.

The specialist explained. He was a kindly man with moth-eaten whiskers and an eye like a meditative codfish.

"Many people," he said, "who are unable to articulate clearly in ordinary speech find themselves lucid and bell-like when they burst into song."

It seemed a good idea to George. He thought for a moment; then threw his head back, shut his eyes, and let it go in a musical baritone.

"I love a lassie, a bonny, bonny lassie," sang George. "She's as pure as the lily in the dell."

"No doubt," said the specialist, wincing a little.

"She's as sweet as the heather, the bonny purple heather—Susan, my Worcestershire bluebell."

"Ah!" said the specialist. "Sounds a nice girl. Is this she?" he asked, adjusting his glasses and peering at the photograph which George had extracted from the interior of the left side of his undervest.

George nodded and drew in breath.

"Yes, sir," he caroled, "that's my baby. No, sir, don't mean maybe. Yes, sir, that's my baby now. And, by the way, by the way, when I meet that preacher I shall say: 'Yes, sir, that's my . . .'"

"Quite," said the specialist hurriedly. He had a sensitive ear. "Quite, quite."

"If you knew Susie like I know Susie," George was beginning, but the other stopped him.

"Quite. Exactly. I shouldn't wonder. And now," said the specialist, "what precisely is the trouble? No" he added hastily, as George inflated his lungs, "don't sing it. Write the particulars on this piece of paper."

George did so.

"H'm!" said the specialist, examining the screed. "You wish to woo, court, and become betrothed, engaged, affianced to this girl, but you find yourself unable, incapable,

3 Reading Strategy Why do you think that George knows so much about Eli, Ra, and Emu?

4 Literary Focus How does George feel about Susan? Why is the way George expresses his realization humorous?

5 Enrichment Each time that George tries to explain his problem and how he feels about Susan Blake, he sings. In order to communicate his thoughts, George changes the lyrics of some popular songs. "Yes Sir, That's My Baby" (1925), written by Gus Kahn, and "If You Knew Susie" (1925), written by Buddy De Sylva, are famous Tin Pan Alley standards. These popular songs were published by music publishers located on 28th Street in New York City, which was dubbed Tin Pan Alley because of the lively sound of piano playing. Although the music produced here may have sounded to some like tin pans banging in an alley, these songs were extremely popular from the early 1900's through the 1940's. P.G. Wodehouse undoubtedly refers to Tin Pan Alley lyrics in "The Truth about George" because he knew them well.

6 Critical Thinking and Reading
Do you think that this description of the specialist is a caricature? Why or why not?

7 Enrichment Some scientists believe that stammering is caused by a biological process in which the brain's signals for speech are delayed by fractions of a second. Others believe that stammering is a learned behavior related to stress about talking or to pressure to speak precisely. Another theory states that stammering may represent a psychological block in which a person cannot express his or her feelings.

8 Discussion What advice does the specialist give to George? Do you think the advice will work? How realistic is the advice?

9 Clarification A guinea is an English monetary unit that equals one pound and one shilling.

10 Literary Focus Explain why George's interaction with the stranger on the train is humorous. Point out that Wodehouse uses irony, one form of humor, to describe this encounter.

11 Clarification The stranger attempts to say "I asked you a civil question. Are you deaf?"

incompetent, impotent, and powerless. Every time you attempt it, your vocal cords fail, fall short, are insufficient, wanting, deficient, and go blooey.''

George nodded.

''A not unusual case. I have had to deal with this sort of thing before. The effect of love on the vocal cords of even a normally eloquent subject is frequently deleterious. As regards the habitual stammerer, tests have shown that in ninety-seven point five six nine recurring of cases the divine passion reduces him to a condition where he sounds like a soda-water siphon trying to recite 'Gunga Din.' There is only one cure.''

''W-w-w-w-w—?'' asked George.

''I will tell you. Stammering,'' proceeded the specialist, putting the tips of his fingers together and eyeing George benevolently, ''is mainly mental and is caused by shyness, which is caused by the inferiority complex, which in its turn is caused by suppressed desires or introverted inhibitions or something. The advice I give to all young men who come in here behaving like soda-water siphons is to go out and make a point of speaking to at least three perfect strangers every day. Engage these strangers in conversation, persevering no matter how priceless a chump you may feel, and before many weeks are out you will find that the little daily dose has had its effect. Shyness will wear off, and with it the stammer.''

And, having requested the young man—in a voice of the clearest timbre, free from all trace of impediment—to hand over a fee of five guineas, the specialist sent George out into the world.

The more George thought about the advice he had been given, the less he liked it. He shivered in the cab that took him to the station to catch the train back to East Wobsley. Like all shy young men, he had never hitherto looked upon himself as shy—preferring to attribute his distaste for the society of his fellows to some subtle rareness of soul. But now that the thing had been put squarely up to him, he was compelled to realize that in all essentials he was a perfect rabbit. The thought of accosting perfect strangers and forcing his conversation upon them sickened him.

But no Mulliner has ever shirked an unpleasant duty. As he reached the platform and strode along it to the train, his teeth were set, his eyes shone with an almost fanatical light of determination, and he intended before his journey was over to conduct three heart-to-heart chats if he had to sing every bar of them.

The compartment into which he had made his way was empty at the moment, but just before the train started a very large, fierce-looking man got in. George would have preferred somebody a little less formidable for his first subject, but he braced himself and bent forward, And, as he did so, the man spoke.

''The wur-wur-wur-wur-weather,'' he said, ''sus-sus-seems to be ter-ter-taking a tur-tur-turn for the ber-ber-better, der-doesn't it?''

George sank back as if he had been hit between the eyes. The train had moved out of the dimness of the station by now, and the sun was shining brightly on the speaker, illuminating his knobbly shoulders, his craggy jaw, and, above all, the shockingly choleric look in his eyes. To reply ''Y-y-y-y-y-y-y-yes'' to such a man would obviously be madness.

But to abstain from speech did not seem to be much better as a policy. George's silence appeared to arouse this man's worst passions. His face had turned purple and he glared painfully.

''I uk-uk-asked you a sus-sus-civil quk-quk-quk,'' he said irascibly. ''Are you d-d-d-d-deaf?''

All we Mulliners have been noted for our presence of mind. To open his mouth, point to his tonsils, and utter a strangled gurgle was with George the work of a moment.

The tension relaxed. The man's annoyance abated.

"D-d-d-dumb?" he said commiseratingly. "I beg your p-p-p-p-pup. I t-t-trust I have not caused you p-p-p-p-pup. It m must be tut-tut-tut-tut-tut not to be able to to sus-sus-speak fuf-fuf-fuf-fuf-fluently."

He then buried himself in his paper, and George sank back in his corner, quivering in every limb.

To get to East Wobsley, as you doubtless know, you have to change at Ippleton and take the branch line. By the time the train reached this junction, George's composure was somewhat restored. He deposited his belongings in a compartment of the East Wobsley train, which was waiting in a glued manner on the other side of the platform, and, finding that it would not start for some ten minutes, decided to pass the time by strolling up and down in the pleasant air.

It was a lovely afternoon. The sun was gilding the platform with its rays, and a gentle breeze blew from the west. A little brook ran tinkling at the side of the road; birds were singing in the hedgerows; and through the trees could be discerned dimly the noble façade of the County Lunatic Asylum. Soothed by his surroundings, George began to feel so refreshed that he regretted that in this wayside station there was no one present whom he could engage in talk.

It was at this moment that the distinguished-looking stranger entered the platform.

The newcomer was a man of imposing physique, simply dressed in pajamas, brown boots, and a mackintosh. In his hand he carried a top hat, and into this he was dipping his fingers, taking them out, and then waving them in a curious manner to right and left. He nodded so affably to George that the latter, though a little surprised at the other's costume, decided to speak. After all, he reflected, clothes do not make the man, and, judging from the other's smile, a warm heart appeared to beat beneath that orange-and-mauve striped pajama jacket.

14 Enrichment The actual quotation that Wodehouse paraphrases here is, "Be thou familiar, but by no means vulgar;/Those friends thou hast, and their adoption tried,/Grapple them to thy soul with hoops of steel." The lines appear in Shakespeare's *Hamlet*, Act 1, scene iii.

15 Clarification The stranger uses *lark* in the sense of harmless fun, mischief, or an escapade. George is startled by the remark, mistakenly thinking of birds, another meaning of lark.

"N-n-n-n-nice weather," he said.

"Glad you like it," said the stranger. "I ordered it specially."

George was a little puzzled by this remark, but he persevered.

"M-might I ask wur-wur-what you are dud-doing?"

"Doing?"

"With that her-her-her-her-hat?"

"Oh, with this hat? I see what you mean. Just scattering largess to the multitude," replied the stranger, dipping his fingers once more and waving them with a generous gesture. "Devil of a bore, but it's expected of a man in my position. The fact is," he said, linking his arm in George's and speaking in a confidential undertone, "I'm the Emperor of Abyssinia. That's my palace over there," he said, pointing through the trees. "Don't let it go any farther. It's not supposed to be generally known."

It was with a rather sickly smile that George now endeavored to withdraw his arm from that of his companion, but the other would have none of this aloofness. He seemed to be in complete agreement with Shakespeare's dictum that a friend, when found, should be grappled to you with hoops of steel. He held George in a viselike grip and drew him into a recess of the platform. He looked about him and seemed satisfied.

"We are alone at last," he said.

This fact had already impressed itself with sickening clearness on the young man. There are few spots in the civilized world more deserted than the platform of a small country station. The sun shone on the smooth asphalt, on the gleaming rails, and on the machine which, in exchange for a penny placed in the slot marked "Matches," would supply a package of wholesome butterscotch—but on nothing else.

What George could have done with at the moment was a posse of police armed with stout clubs, and there was not even a dog in sight.

"I've been wanting to talk to you for a long time," said the stranger genially.

"Huh-huh-have you?" said George.

"Yes. I want your opinion of human sacrifices."

George said he didn't like them.

"Why not?" asked the other, surprised.

George said it was hard to explain. He just didn't.

"Well, I think you're wrong," said the Emperor. "I know there's a school of thought growing up that holds your views, but I disapprove of it. I hate all this modern advanced thought. Human sacrifices have always been good enough for the Emperors of Abyssinia, and they're good enough for me. Kindly step in here, if you please."

He indicated the lamp-and-mop room, at which they had now arrived. It was a dark and sinister apartment, smelling strongly of oil and porters, and was probably the last place on earth in which George would have wished to be closeted with a man of such peculiar views. He shrank back.

"You go in first," he said.

"No larks," said the other suspiciously. | 15

"L-l-l-l-larks?"

"Yes. No pushing a fellow in and locking the door and squirting water at him through the window. I've had that happen to me before."

"Sus-certainly not."

"Right!" said the Emperor. "You're a gentleman and I'm a gentleman. Both gentlemen. Have you a knife, by the way? We shall need a knife."

"No. No knife."

"Ah, well," said the Emperor, "then we'll have to look about for something else. No doubt we shall manage somehow."

And with the debonair manner which so became him, he scattered another handful of largess and walked into the lamp room.

It was not the fact that he had given his word as a gentleman that kept George from locking the door. There is probably no family on earth more nicely scrupulous as regards keeping its promises than the Mulliners, but I am compelled to admit that, had George been able to find the key, he would

Grammar in Action

A **participial phrase** acts as an adjective and modifies a noun or pronoun. It can be used to combine closely related ideas. A participial phrase embedded within a sentence is set off by commas if it is nonessential. Notice P. G. Wodehouse's use of embedded participial phrases.

Then, glancing along the floor, he perceived feminine ankles.

It was a dark and sinister apartment, smelling strongly of oil and porters, and was probably the last place on earth George would have wished . . .

The first example combines the ideas that George was glancing along the floor and that he saw feminine ankles. His glancing is the reason he saw, so the two are closely related. Seeing ankles is the essential idea, so the lesser idea is subordinated in the participial phrase modifying "he." In the second have locked the door without hesitation. Not being able to find the key, he had to be satisfied with banging it. This done, he leaped back and raced away down the platform. A confused noise within seemed to indicate that the Emperor had become involved with some lamps.

George made the best of the respite. Covering the ground at a high rate of speed, he flung himself into the train and took refuge under the seat.

There he remained, quaking. At one time he thought that his uncongenial acquaintance had got upon his track, for the door of the compartment opened and a cool wind blew in upon him. Then, glancing along the floor, he perceived feminine ankles. The relief was enormous, but even in his relief George, who was the soul of modesty, did not forget his manners. He closed his eyes.

A voice spoke.

"Porter!"

"Yes, ma'am?"

"What was all that disturbance as I came into the station?"

"Patient escaped from the asylum, ma'am."

"Good gracious!"

The voice would undoubtedly have spoken further, but at this moment the train began to move. There came the sound of a body descending upon a cushioned seat, and some little time later the rustling of a paper.

George had never before traveled under the seat of a railway carriage; and, though he belonged to the younger generation, which is supposed to be so avid of new experiences, he had no desire to do so now. He decided to emerge, and, if possible, to emerge with the minimum of ostentation. Little as he knew of women, he was aware that as a sex they are apt to be startled by the sight of men crawling out from under the seats of compartments. He began his maneuvers by poking out his head and surveying the terrain.

All was well. The woman, in her seat across the way, was engrossed in her paper. Moving in a series of noiseless wriggles, George extricated himself from his hiding place and, with a twist which would have been impossible to a man not in the habit of doing Swedish exercises daily before breakfast, heaved himself into the corner seat. The woman continued reading her paper.

The events of the past quarter of an hour had tended rather to drive from George's mind the mission which he had undertaken on leaving the specialist's office. But now, having leisure for reflection, he realized that, if he meant to complete his first day of the cure, he was allowing himself to run sadly behind schedule. Speak to three strangers, the specialist had told him, and up to the present he had spoken to only one. True, this one had been a pretty considerable stranger, and a less conscientious young man than George Mulliner might have considered himself justified in chalking him up on the scoreboard as one and a half or even two. But George had the dogged, honest Mulliner streak in him, and he refused to quibble.

He nerved himself for action and cleared his throat.

"Ah-h'rm!" said George.

And, having opened the ball, he smiled a winning smile and waited for his companion to make the next move.

The move which his companion made was in an upwards direction, and measured from six to eight inches. She dropped her paper and regarded George with a pale-eyed horror. One pictures her a little in the position of Robinson Crusoe[4] when he saw the footprint in the sand. She had been convinced that she was completely alone, and lo! out of space a voice had spoken to her. Her face worked, but she made no remark.

George, on his side, was also feeling a little ill at ease. Women always increased his

---

4. **Robinson Crusoe:** The hero of Daniel Defoe's novel *Robinson Crusoe* (1719), a sailor who is shipwrecked on a tropical island.

The Truth About George 1243

16 **Literary Focus** Why is this sentence humorous? What type of humor does Wodehouse use here?

17 **Reading Strategy** Explain in your own words how the woman on the train reacts. Why do you think she reacts this way? What assumption do you think the woman makes?

16

17

example, "smelling strongly of oil and porters" describes the apartment. Neither phrase is essential, so both are set off by commas.

Student Activity 1. Find three more participial phrases in the story. Identify the noun or pronoun each modifies.

Student Activity 2. Combine each of the following pairs of clauses into one sentence by making the subordinate idea a participial phrase.

1. Peter loves his new car. He drives it carefully.
2. My mother was amazed. I gave the speech without fear.
3. I heard the news this morning. I suppressed my horror.

natural shyness. He never knew what to say to them.

Then a happy thought struck him. He had just glanced at his watch and found the hour to be nearly four-thirty. Women, he knew, loved a drop of tea at about this time, and fortunately there was in his suitcase a full thermos flask.

"Pardon me, but I wonder if you would care for a cup of tea?" was what he wanted to say, but, as so often happened with him when in the presence of the opposite sex, he could get no farther than a sort of sizzling sound like a cockroach calling to its young.

The woman continued to stare at him. Her eyes were now about the size of regulation standard golf balls, and her breathing suggested the last stages of asthma. And it was at this point that George, struggling for speech, had one of those inspirations which frequently came to Mulliners. There flashed into his mind what the specialist had told him about singing. Say it with music—that was the thing to do.

He delayed no longer.

"Tea for two and two for tea and me for you and you for me—"

He was shocked to observe his companion turning Nile green. He decided to make his meaning clearer.

"I have a nice thermos. I have a full thermos. Won't you share my thermos, too? When skies are gray and you feel you are blue, tea sends the sun smiling through. I have a nice thermos. I have a full thermos. May I pour out some for you?"

You will agree with me, I think, that no invitation could have been more happily put, but his companion was not responsive. With one last agonized look at him, she closed her eyes and sank back in her seat. Her lips had now turned a curious gray-blue color, and they were moving feebly. She reminded George, who, like myself, was a keen fisherman, of a newly gaffed salmon.

George sat back in his corner, brooding. Rack his brain as he might, he could think of no topic which could be guaranteed to interest, elevate, and amuse. He looked out of the window with a sigh.

The train was now approaching the dear old familiar East Wobsley country. He began to recognize landmarks. A wave of sentiment poured over George as he thought of Susan, and he reached for the bag of buns which he had bought at the refreshment room at Ippleton. Sentiment always made him hungry.

He took his thermos out of the suitcase, and, unscrewing the top, poured himself out a cup of tea. Then, placing the thermos on the seat, he drank.

He looked across at his companion. Her eyes were still closed, and she uttered little sighing noises. George was half inclined to renew his offer of tea, but the only tune he could remember was "Hard-Hearted Hannah, the Vamp from Savannah," and it was difficult to fit suitable words to it. He ate his bun and gazed out at the familiar scenery.

Now, as you approach East Wobsley, the train, I must mention, has to pass over some points; and so violent is the sudden jerking that strong men have been known to spill their beer. George, forgetting this in his preoccupation, had placed the thermos only a few inches from the edge of the seat. The result was that, as the train reached the points, the flask leaped like a live thing, dived to the floor, and exploded.

Even George was distinctly upset by the sudden sharpness of the report. His bun sprang from his hand and was dashed to fragments. He blinked thrice in rapid succession. His heart tried to jump out of his mouth and loosened a front tooth.

But on the woman opposite the effect of the untoward occurrence was still more marked. With a single piercing shriek, she rose from her seat straight into the air like a rocketing pheasant; and, having clutched the communication cord, fell back again. Impressive as her previous leap had been, she excelled it now by several inches. I do not know what the existing record for the

18 **Critical Thinking and Reading** What makes this description of the woman a caricature?

19 **Enrichment** Wodehouse uses more lyrics from Tin Pan Alley standards. The first lyrics come from "Tea for Two" (1924) by Irving Caesar and Vincent Youmans.

20 **Literary Focus** Discuss the type of humor that Wodehouse employs in this passage.

sitting high jump is, but she undoubtedly lowered it; and if George had been a member of the Olympic Games Selection Committee, he would have signed this woman up immediately.

It is a curious thing that, in spite of the railway companies' sporting willingness to let their patrons have a tug at the extremely moderate price of five pounds a go, very few people have ever either pulled a communication cord or seen one pulled. There is, thus, a widespread ignorance as to what precisely happens on such occasions.

The procedure, George tells me, is as follows: First there comes a grinding noise, as the brakes are applied. Then the train stops. And finally, from every point of the compass, a seething mob of interested onlookers begins to appear.

It was about a mile and a half from East Wobsley that the affair had taken place, and as far as the eye could reach the countryside was totally devoid of humanity. A moment before nothing had been visible but smiling cornfields and broad pasturelands; but now from east, west, north, and south running figures began to appear. We must remember that George at the time was in a somewhat overwrought frame of mind, and his statements should therefore be accepted with caution; but he tells me that out of the middle of a single empty meadow, entirely devoid of cover, no fewer than twenty-seven distinct rustics suddenly appeared, having undoubtedly shot up through the ground.

The rails, which had been completely unoccupied, were now thronged with so dense a crowd of navvies[5] that it seemed to George absurd to pretend that there was any unemployment in England. Every member of the laboring classes throughout the country was so palpably present. Moreover, the train, which at Ippleton had seemed sparsely occupied, was disgorging passengers from every door. It was the sort of mob scene which would have made David W. Griffith[6] scream with delight; and it looked, George says, like Guest Night at the Royal Automobile Club. But, as I say, we must remember that he was overwrought.

It is difficult to say what precisely would have been the correct behavior of your polished man of the world in such a situation. I think myself that a great deal of sang-froid[7] and address would be required even by the most self-possessed in order to pass off such a contretemps. To George, I may say at once, the crisis revealed itself immediately as one which he was totally incapable of handling. The one clear thought that stood out from the welter of his emotions was the reflection that it was advisable to remove himself, and to do so without delay. Drawing a deep breath, he shot swiftly off the mark.

All we Mulliners have been athletes; and George, when at the University, had been noted for his speed of foot. He ran now as he had never run before. His statement, however, that as he sprinted across the first field he distinctly saw a rabbit shoot an envious glance at him as he passed and shrug its shoulders hopelessly, I am inclined to discount. George, as I have said before, was a little overexcited.

Nevertheless, it is not to be questioned that he made good going. And he had need to, for after the first instant of surprise, which had enabled him to secure a lead, the whole mob was pouring across country after him; and dimly, as he ran, he could hear voices in the throng informally discussing the advisability of lynching him. Moreover, the field through which he was running, a moment before a bare expanse of green, was now black with figures, headed by a man with a beard who carried a pitchfork. George swerved sharply to the right,

---

5. **navvies** (năv′ ēz): Laborers.

6. **David W. Griffith:** American motion-picture director and producer (1875–1948).
7. **sang-froid** (sän′ frwä′): Composure.

Primary Source

In 1940, after Wodehouse had been captured by the Germans, George Orwell wrote the following evaluation of his work:

By their subject-matter ye shall know them, and the subject-matter of Mr. Wodehouse's books is almost invariably the Edwardian house party, the comic man-servant and the idle young man with private means. Behind the farcical incidents there is manifest a vision of life in which the dividends flow in for ever and ever . . . After reading him steadily for a quarter of a century I cannot remember a single one of his books in which the *jeune premier* [French for "leading man"] really works for his living. His heroes either have private incomes, like Bertie Wooster, or they end up with some kind of sinecure job in the retinue of a millionaire. And that, however lightly he may choose to treat it, is obviously the way in which he considers it desirable for a young man to live. . . .

When Mr. Wodehouse was led off into captivity by the Germans, he is said to have remarked to a friend, "Perhaps after this I shall write a serious book." I wonder. It might be casting a swift glance over his shoulder at his pursuers. He disliked them all, but especially the man with the pitchfork.

It is impossible for one who was not an eyewitness to say how long the chase continued and how much ground was covered by the interested parties. I know the East Wobsley country well, and I have checked George's statements; and, if it is true that he traveled east as far as Little-Wigmarsh-in-the-Dell and as far west as Higgleford-cum-Wortlebury-beneath-the-Hill, he must undoubtedly have done a lot of running.

23 But a point which must not be forgotten is that, to a man not in a condition to observe closely, the village of Higgleford-cum-Wortlebury-beneath-the-Hill might easily not have been Higgleford-cum-Wortlebury-beneath-the-Hill at all, but another hamlet which in many respects closely resembles it. I need scarcely say that I allude to Lesser-Snodsbury-in-the-Vale.

Let us assume, therefore, that George, having touched Little-Wigmarsh-in-the-Dell, shot off at a tangent and reached Lesser-Snodsbury-in-the-Vale. This would be a considerable run. And, as he remembers flitting past Farmer Higgins's pigsty and the Dog and Duck at Pondlebury Parva and splashing through the brook Wipple at the point where it joins the River Wopple, we can safely assume that, wherever else he went, he got plenty of exercise.

But the pleasantest of functions must end, and, just as the setting sun was gilding the spire of the ivy-covered church of St. Barnabas the Resilient, where George as a child had sat so often, enlivening the tedium of the sermon by making faces at the choirboys, a damp and bedraggled figure might have been observed crawling painfully along the High Street of East Wobsley in the direction of the cozy little cottage known to its builder as Chatsworth and to the village tradesmen as "Mulliner's."

It was George, home from the hunting field.

Slowly George Mulliner made his way to the familiar door, and, passing through it, flung himself into his favorite chair. But a moment later a more imperious need than the desire to rest forced itself upon his attention. Rising stiffly, he tottered to the kitchen and mixed himself a revivifying drink. Then, refilling his glass, he returned to the sitting room, to find that it was no longer empty. A slim, fair girl, tastefully attired in tailor-made tweeds, was leaning over the desk on which he kept his Dictionary of English Synonyms.

She looked up as he entered, startled.

"Why, Mr. Mulliner!" she exclaimed. "What has been happening? Your clothes are torn, rent, ragged, tattered, and your hair is all disheveled, untrimmed, hanging loose or negligently, at loose ends!"

George smiled a wan smile.

"You are right," he said. "And, what is more, I am suffering from extreme fatigue, weariness, lassitude, exhaustion, prostration, and languor." 24

The girl gazed at him, a divine pity in her soft eyes.

"I'm so sorry," she murmured. "So very sorry, grieved, distressed, afflicted, pained, mortified, dejected, and upset."

George took her hand. Her sweet sympathy had effected the cure for which he had been seeking so long. Coming on top of the violent emotions through which he had been passing all day, it seemed to work on him like some healing spell, charm, or incantation. Suddenly, in a flash, he realized that he was no longer a stammerer. Had he wished at that moment to say, "Peter Piper picked a peck of pickled peppers," he could have done it without a second thought.

But he had better things to say than that.

"Miss Blake—Susan—Susie." He took her other hand in his. His voice rang out clear and unimpeded. It seemed to him incredible that he had ever yammered at this girl like an overheated steam radiator. "It cannot have escaped your notice that I have 25

very interesting if he did. But what I think is certain is that he cannot continue in the Psmith and Jeeves tradition very much longer. It is already decades out of date. . . . now the whole of that way of life is being destroyed too completely to survive even in fantasy. . . . I hope the Germans are treating Mr. Wodehouse decently, and I hope that later on he will write that serious book. Few writers of our time have used words more skillfully, or squandered better talents.

23 **Enrichment** Explain to students that Wodehouse is satirizing characteristically English place names. His fictional place names mock those in England that consist of long hyphenated strings of descriptive words.

24 **Discussion** Note the synonyms in this passage. Discuss the shades of meaning of each word.

25 **Literary Focus** Why is George's speech humorous? What type of humor does Wodehouse use in writing the speech this way?

Master Teacher Note Give students the following aphorisms: *love conquers all* and *all's well that ends well*. Have them respond to these expressions in terms of the last sentence of "The Truth About George." Guide students in analyzing the meaning of the last sentence in relation to the story as a whole and in relation to the aphorisms.

Reader's Response Do you think that being in love can change someone's personality? Explain.

Closure and Extension

ANSWERS TO THINKING ABOUT THE SELECTION
Recalling

1. A man who stutters comes into the Anglers' Rest, where the narrator and two men are sitting. Mulliner then tells the story of how his nephew George tried to cure himself of a stammer.

2. (a) George decides to seek a cure for his stutter because he realizes that he loves Susan Blake and wishes to tell her so. (b) George travels to London to see a specialist who can treat his stammer. (c) The specialist tells George to sing when he wants to express something and to talk to at least three perfect strangers every day.

3. (a) When George tries to talk to the first stranger, he attempts to talk to someone who also stammers. George is embarrassed and pretends that he is dumb. (b) When George tries to talk to the second stranger, he finds out that the man has just escaped from the County Lunatic Asylum. George runs to board a train to get away from the stranger.

long entertained toward you sentiments warmer and deeper than those of ordinary friendship. It is love, Susan, that has been animating my bosom. Love, first a tiny seed, has burgeoned in my heart till, blazing into flame, it has swept away on the crest of its wave my diffidence, my doubt, my fears, and my foreboding, and now, like the topmost topaz of some ancient tower, it cries to all the world in a voice of thunder: 'You are mine!· My mate! Predestined to me since Time first began!' As the star guides the mariner when, battered by boiling billows, he hies him home to the haven of hope and happiness, so do you gleam upon me along life's rough road and seem to say, 'Have courage, George! I am here!' Susan, I am not an eloquent man—I cannot speak fluently as I could wish—but these simple words which you have just heard come from the heart, from the unspotted heart of an English gentleman. Susan, I love you. Will you be my wife, married woman, matron, spouse, helpmeet, consort, partner or better half?"

"Oh, George!" said Susan. "Yes, yea, ay, aye! Decidedly, unquestionably, indubitably, incontrovertibly, and past all dispute!"

He folded her in his arms. And, as he did so, there came from the street outside —faintly, as from a distance—the sound of feet and voices. George leaped to the window. Rounding the corner, just by the Cow and Wheelbarrow public house, licensed to sell ales, wines, and spirits, was the man with the pitchfork, and behind him followed a vast crowd.

"My darling," said George. "For purely personal and private reasons, into which I need not enter, I must now leave you. Will you join me later?"

"I will follow you to the ends of the earth," replied Susan passionately.

"It will not be necessary," said George. "I am only going down to the coal cellar. I shall spend the next half hour or so there. If anybody calls and asks for me, perhaps you would not mind telling them that I am out."

"I will, I will," said Susan. "And, George, by the way. What I really came here for was to ask you if you knew a word of nine letters, ending in k and signifying an implement employed in the pursuit of agriculture."

"Pitchfork, sweetheart," said George. "But you may take it from me, as one who knows, that agriculture isn't the only thing it is used in pursuit of."

And since that day (concluded Mr. Mulliner) George, believe me or believe me not, has not had the slightest trace of an impediment in his speech. He is now the chosen orator at all political rallies for miles around; and so offensively self-confident has his manner become that only last Friday he had his eye blacked by a hay-corn-and-feed merchant of the name of Stubbs. It just shows you, doesn't it?

THINKING ABOUT THE SELECTION
Recalling

1. What incident prompts Mulliner to tell the story of his nephew George?
2. (a) Why does George decide to seek a cure? (b) What action does he take? (c) What two pieces of advice does he receive?
3. What happens when George tries to speak to (a) the first stranger? (b) the second stranger?
4. How does the woman on the train react when George begins singing "Tea for Two"?
5. (a) What cures George's stammering? (b) To what does he credit the cure?

Interpreting

6. (a) Why does George think it would be

4. The woman on the train turns green when George begins to sing "Tea for Two." His attempt to convey the idea that he would like to share his thermos of tea with her terrifies her. The woman does not speak and merely stares at George. Wodehouse suggests that the woman has a heart attack.

5. (a) George's stammering is cured when he indirectly gains confidence through his adventures that day. In a sense, George has

cured himself. (b) After a day of adventures and a harrowing escape home, George is soothed by Susan's concern. George credits his cure to Susan's sympathy.

Interpreting

6. (a) George thinks it would be madness to reply to the stutterer because it would appear that he was mocking him. (b) George's response placates the stutterer, who realizes that George was not

being rude.

7. (a) The woman in the train compartment thinks that George is the escapee from County Lunatic Asylum. (b) Suggested response: George's attempt to speak to the woman only frightens her more. His behavior only confirms her worst suspicions.

8. Suggested response: The explanation of George's chase is humorous because of the quaint names of the hamlets he suppos-

madness to reply to the stutterer on the train? (b) Why does his response placate the stutterer?

7. (a) Who does the woman in the train compartment think George is? (b) What effect do you think George's "sizzling . . . like a cockroach" has on the woman?

8. What is humorous about the explanation of the amount of ground George must have covered while being chased?

9. Why do George and Susan both use long strings of synonyms in their speech?

Applying

10. George is a timid soul who becomes "offensively self-confident." (a) What conditions make a person timid? (b) What conditions can make the same person self-confident?

ANALYZING LITERATURE

Understanding Humor

Humor, the quality that makes something seem amusing, funny, or comic, is easier to recognize than it is to explain. Exaggeration is often a part of humor, as when the doctor in "The Truth About George" says of the habitual stammerer that "tests have shown that in ninety-seven point five six nine" percent of cases, love "reduces him to a condition where he sounds like a soda-water siphon trying to recite 'Gunga Din.'" Misunderstandings often figure in humor, as when George tries to communicate with the woman in the train compartment by singing, and she takes it as proof of his being a lunatic. Look through "The Truth About George" and find what you consider to be the five most amusing incidents, situations, or statements. Try to explain what it is about each one that makes it humorous.

CRITICAL THINKING AND READING

Recognizing Caricature

When P. G. Wodehouse describes the antics of George and other characters in this story, you know that real people do not behave or talk that way. Yet there is a core of truth, greatly exaggerated and distorted, in what the characters do and say. Wodehouse is creating caricatures, just as a cartoonist creates caricatures by drawing people with recognizable but grotesque features. George is a caricature of a person who stutters. Point out three other caricatures in this story and explain why each fits that category.

UNDERSTANDING LANGUAGE

Using Synonyms

A **synonym** is a word that means almost the same thing as another word. Since one word seldom has exactly the same meaning as another, you cannot arbitrarily substitute synonyms for each other in speaking and writing. In "The Truth About George," both George and Susan use a series of synonyms for comic effect. George says, "Will you be my wife, married woman, matron, spouse, helpmeet, consort, partner or better half?" Those words are all synonyms, but they do not all have precisely the same meaning. A *spouse,* for instance, may be either a husband or a wife; a *matron* is usually an older woman; a *consort* is often a royal partner.

The following groups of synonyms appear in the story. Using a good dictionary, define each word, distinguishing it from the synonyms included with it.

1. incapable, incompetent, powerless
2. torn, rent, ragged
3. fatigue, lassitude, prostration
4. pained, mortified, dejected

THINKING AND WRITING

Writing About Humor

Does "The Truth About George" make you laugh, chuckle, snicker, giggle, guffaw? What do you find funny in it? Why do you find it funny? Look back at your answers in Analyzing Literature. Use the five examples of humor that you chose in that assignment as the basis for a composition on the topic, "What Is Humor?" Make further notes, if necessary. In your first draft, be as precise and specific as you can. When you revise the material for your final draft, check to make sure that your sentences are clear and to the point, not simply abstract thoughts or unsupported generalizations.

The Truth About George 1249

---

edly runs between: from Little-Wig-marsh-in-the-Dell to Higgleford-cum-Wortlebury-beneath-the-Hill.

9. George and Susan use synonyms when they speak because they are both avid crossword puzzle fans. They're always looking for words to help them solve their puzzles.

Applying

10. Answers will differ. Suggested Responses: (a) A person might be timid in whatever circumstances he or she is not comfortable. (b) The same person might be self-confident in circumstances in which he or she is comfortable and in control.

Challenge Think about the title of this story. What do you think the "truth" is about George? Find evidence in the story to support your answer.

across the countryside; George finally professing his love for Susan Blake. Each incident or situation is humorous because it is exaggerated, absurd, unexpected, or unbelievable.

ANSWERS TO CRITICAL THINKING AND READING

Answers will differ. Three examples of caricatures include the description of the specialist, who seems overly concerned with statistical data and scientific proof and who gives George some absurdly theoretical advice for curing his stammer; the description of the escapee from the lunatic asylum, who believes himself to be the Emperor of Abyssinia; the description of the mob that pursues George, which includes train passengers and laborers and a leader carrying a pitchfork. Each caricature includes physical descriptions that exaggerate or emphasize what that person or group of people might look like as well as an exaggeration of personality

ANSWERS TO UNDERSTANDING LANGUAGE

Suggested responses:

1. incapable: lacking in ability
   incompetent: not qualified
   powerless: unable to change something.
2. torn: ripped apart by force
   rent: violently severed
   ragged: having an irregular edge
3. fatigue: tiredness
   lassitude: weariness
   prostration: physical and mental exhaustion
4. pained: hurt
   mortified: shamed or embarrassed
   dejected: depressed

ANSWERS TO ANALYZING LITERATURE

Answers will differ. Five examples of humorous incidents or situations include the following: George singing to explain his problem to the specialist; George meeting the "Emperor of Abyssinia"; George's attempt at being polite to the woman on the train and singing his offer of tea to her; George being pursued by a mob

THINKING AND WRITING

Publishing Student Writing You might wish to have your students form debate teams to discuss the topic "What is humor?" Have them choose specific aspects of humor to consider.

Focus

More About the Author Like many twentieth-century artists and writers, Doris Lessing is concerned with the related topics of consciousness, sanity, and psychology. She argues, somewhat surprisingly, that there are some circumstances in which the only healthy thing to do is to become sick. Since so much of modern civilization is mad, madness may be a necessary stage in becoming whole. She frequently portrays breaking down as a means of breaking through. In *The Four-Gated City,* the final novel in her *Children of Violence* series, Lessing's protagonist, Martha Quest, is severely depressed and unwell. Lessing cleverly recalls *Jane Eyre* by creating a many-leveled house in which two women, one "mad" and one "sane," cooperate in creating a new level of consciousness. Discuss other stories, poems, plays, and movies that present eccentric characters who possess a wisdom so-called normal society needs.

Critical Evaluation David Daiches and Jon Stallworthy made the following evaluation of Lessing's work: "The novels convey the scope of human suffering in the twentieth century with an imaginative power that surmounts their sometimes proselytizing tone. Some of her short stories, which deal with racial and social dilemmas as well as with loneliness, the claims of politics, the problems of aging (especially for women), the conflict between the generations, and a whole spectrum of problems of alienation and isolation, have a pungency and force lacking in her more discursive novels."

1919–

Doris Lessing is one of the most powerful of contemporary authors. Her novels and short stories explore the evils of racism, the role of women in modern life, the importance of intuition, and the limits of idealism in solving the problems facing society. Her books, profound and highly personal, confront a host of post-World War II issues, supplying almost a history of the times, with special emphasis on Africa and feminism.

The focus on Africa in Doris Lessing's work is not surprising. Born in Persia of British parents, she grew up on a three-thousand-acre farm in Southern Rhodesia (now Zimbabwe), where her parents raised maize with the help of native labor. She remained in Africa through two unsuccessful marriages, living principally in the Rhodesian capital of Salisbury, until she was thirty.

Explaining how her career began, Lessing said: "I've always been a writer . . . but not until I was quite old—twenty-six or -seven—did I realize that I'd better . . . get down to business. I was working in a lawyer's office at the time, and I remember walking in and saying to my boss, 'I'm giving up my job because I'm going to write a novel.' He very properly laughed, and I indignantly walked home and wrote *The Grass Is Singing.*"

She moved to London in 1949 and published her first novel, *The Grass Is Singing,* the next year, having brought the manuscript with her from Rhodesia. Her African experiences provided the material for this deeply moving, highly acclaimed work. In an interview in 1962, Lessing commented, "I feel the best thing that ever happened to me was that I was brought up out of England. I took for granted kinds of experiences that would be impossible to a middle-class girl here."

The Golden Notebook, published in 1962, is her most renowned and technically sophisticated work. It represents a junction between the two main paths her fiction has taken—her realistic, sometimes reportorial early style, and her visionary, at times apocalyptic, "inner space fiction" that came later. The dominant theme in *The Golden Notebook* is that of the free woman who struggles for individuality and equality despite her social and psychological conditioning.

A self-described "architect of the soul," Lessing is one of the most serious and intelligent of today's writers. Hers is a uniquely twentieth-century odyssey. Writing in what she calls a "straight, broad, direct" manner, she has produced a remarkable body of novels and short stories, works that are distinguished not only for their breadth of subject matter but also for their breadth of vision.

GUIDE FOR INTERPRETING

A Mild Attack of Locusts

Conflict. One of the ingredients of an effective story or play is conflict, the struggle between a main character and another person or force. Often the conflict involves two main characters—protagonist and antagonist—as in many of Shakespeare's tragedies. Sometimes the conflict is between a main character and society as a whole, or between a main character and nature. These conflicts are external. An external conflict is one between a main character and another person or between a character and an outside force. There may also be internal conflict, or psychological conflict. Internal conflict occurs within the mind of a main character. Many plots contain both external and internal conflicts. Fictional conflicts, like real-life conflicts, are often complex, and you may occasionally find them puzzling to sort out.

Writing

Human beings are often pitted against nature in both real life and in fiction. For example, a family may struggle against a fast-flowing river, or fire fighters may battle a forest fire. Make a list of natural forces against which human beings must battle—and win—to survive.

Primary Source

Lessing describes life on an isolated South African farm.

> Our neighbors were four, five, seven miles off. . . . The seasons were bad, prices bad, crops failed. This was the sort of thing that made it impossible for him [her father] ever to "get off the farm," which, he agreed with my mother, was what he most wanted to do. . . . But it was my mother who suffered. After a period of neurotic illness, which was a protest against her situation, she became brave and resourceful. But she never saw that her husband was not living in a real world, that he had made a captive of her common sense. We were always about to "get off the farm." A miracle would do it—a sweepstake, a goldmine, a legacy. And then? What a question! We would go to England where life would be normal with people coming in for musical evenings and nice supper parties at the Trocadero after a show. Poor woman, for the twenty years we were on the farm, she waited for when life would begin for her and for her children, for she never understood that what was a calamity for her was for them a blessing.

As you read "A Mild Attack of Locusts," see how Margaret's conflicts parallel those Lessing's mother faced.

Guide for Interpreting   1251

Literary Focus In literature as in life, it is a great deal easier to recognize external than internal conflict. Indeed, the most difficult aspect of internal conflict is acknowledging that it exists. The locust attack in Lessing's story serves as a sort of mirror in which Margaret is first able to see her own inner turmoil. Curiously, the attack serves as an agent of healing.

Writing/Prior Knowledge Encourage your students to describe these conflicts before the class. Have them specify the forces in conflict and tell how the conflicts were resolved or likely to be. Have students discuss the meaning of the story's title, "A Mild Attack of Locusts." Encourage students to incorporate the insights gained during discussion in their compositions on paradox.

Vocabulary

Preteach the following vocabulary words:
acrid (ak′ rid) *adj.:* Sharp; bitter (p. 1253).
myriads (mir′ē ədz) *n.:* Great numbers of things (p. 1253)
veldt (velt) *n.:* Open, grassy country (p. 1253)
serrated (ser′āt əd) *adj.:* Toothed or notched like a saw (p. 1253).
perverted (pər vʉr′tid) *adj.:* Distorted; corrupted (p. 1254)
irremediable (ir i mē′dē ə b′l) *adj.:* Incurable; incapable of being remedied (p. 1255)
haggard (hag′ərd) *adj.:* Having a worn, gaunt, or wild look (p. 1255)
imminent (im′ə nənt) *adj.:* Likely to happen soon (p. 1256)

Objectives

1 To recognize conflict
2 To appreciate the role of style
3 To write about paradox

Support Material

Teaching Portfolio
Teacher Backup, p. 1477
Grammar in Action Worksheet, *Using Varied Sentence Structures,* p. 1481
Usage and Mechanics Worksheet, p. 1483
Vocabulary Check, p. 1484
Analyzing Literature Worksheet, *Recognizing Conflict,* p. 1486

Critical Thinking and Reading Worksheet, *Understanding Style,* p. 1487
Selection Test, p. 1488

Motivation/Prior Knowledge
Ask students to think of this story
by Lessing as a sort of mystery.
Tell them to read carefully so that
they will be able to state clearly
the problem the protagonist
solves.

Master Teacher Note Lessing
often writes of people, particularly
women, who find themselves
trapped in situations they do not
recall creating. Suggest that
more advanced students read
Lessing's "Room 19," a somewhat longer story, about a desperate woman. Compare this protagonist with Margaret.

Thematic Idea Death-and-
resurrection is a paradox at the
heart of life. Lessing's Margaret
is initiated into this mystery, a
theme recurrent in fiction and
particularly in poetry. This paradox often appears in the poems
of John Donne.

Purpose-Setting Question How
does Margaret change over the
course of the story?

1 **Critical Thinking and Reading**
What might you infer about Margaret from this passage?

2 **Discussion** What three things did
the farmers discuss that Margaret
knew nothing about? What does
the word *language* mean in this
context?

A Mild Attack of Locusts

Doris Lessing

1 The rains that year were good; they were coming nicely just as the crops needed them —or so Margaret gathered when the men said they were not too bad. She never had an opinion of her own on matters like the weather, because even to know about what seems a simple thing like the weather needs experience. Which Margaret had not got. The men were Richard her husband, and old Stephen, Richard's father, a farmer from way back; and these two might argue for hours whether the rains were ruinous or just ordinarily exasperating. Margaret had

2 been on the farm three years. She still did not understand how they did not go bank-rupt altogether, when the men never had a good word for the weather, or the soil, or the Government. But she was getting to learn the language. Farmers' language. And they neither went bankrupt nor got very rich. They jogged along doing comfortably.

Their crop was maize.[1] Their farm was three thousand acres on the ridges that rise up toward the Zambesi escarpment[2]—high, dry windswept country, cold and dusty in winter, but now, in the wet season, steamy with the heat rising in wet soft waves off miles of green foliage. Beautiful it was, with the sky blue and brilliant halls of air, and the bright green folds and hollows of coun-try beneath, and the mountains lying sharp and bare twenty miles off across the rivers.

The sky made her eyes ache; she was not used to it. One does not look so much at the sky in the city she came from. So that evening when Richard said: "The Govern-ment is sending out warnings that locusts are expected, coming down from the breed-ing grounds up North," her instinct was to look about her at the trees. Insects —swarms of them—horrible! But Richard and the old man had raised their eyes and were looking up over the mountain. "We haven't had locusts in seven years," they said. "They go in cycles, locusts do." And then: "There goes our crop for this season!"

But they went on with the work of the farm just as usual until one day they were coming up the road to the homestead for the midday break, when old Stephen stopped, raised his finger and pointed: "Look, look, there they are!"

Out ran Margaret to join them, looking at the hills. Out came the servants from the kitchen. They all stood and gazed. Over the rocky levels of the mountain was a streak of rust-colored air. Locusts. There they came.

At once Richard shouted at the cookboy. Old Stephen yelled at the houseboy. The cookboy ran to beat the old plowshare[3] hanging from a tree branch, which was used to summon the laborers at moments of cri-sis. The houseboy ran off to the store to collect tin cans, any old bit of metal. The farm was ringing with the clamor of the gong; and they could see the laborers come

---

1. **maize** (māz) *n*.: Corn.
2. **Zambesi** (zam bē′ zē) **escarpment:** Steep cliffs along the Zambesi River in southern Africa.

3. **plowshare** *n*.: The cutting blade of a plow.

Primary Source

In an essay on her father, Doris Lessing described the house she lived in as a girl in Southern Rhodesia:

> Soon, there was my father in a cigar-shaped house of thatch and mud on the top of a kopje [a small hill] that overlooked in all directions a great system of mountains, rivers, valleys, while overhead the sky arched from horizon to empty horizon. This was a couple of hundred miles south from the Zambesi [a river in southern Africa], a hundred or so west from Mozambique, in the district of Banket, so called because certain of its reefs were of the same formation as those called *banket* on the Rand [short for Witwatersrand, a region in South Africa consisting of ranges of hills which contain rich gold fields]. Lomagundi —gold country, tobacco country, maize country—wild,

pouring out of the compound, pointing at the hills and shouting excitedly. Soon they had all come up to the house, and Richard and old Stephen were giving them orders —Hurry, hurry, hurry.

And off they ran again, the two white men with them, and in a few minutes Margaret could see the smoke of fires rising from all around the farmlands. Piles of wood and grass had been prepared there. There were seven patches of bared soil, yellow and ox-blood color and pink, where the new meal-ies[4] were just showing, making a film of bright green; and around each drifted up thick clouds of smoke. They were throwing wet leaves on to the fires now, to make it acrid and black. Margaret was watching the hills. Now there was a long, low cloud advancing, rust-color still, swelling forward and out as she looked. The telephone was ringing. Neighbors—quick, quick, there come the locusts. Old Smith had had his crop eaten to the ground. Quick, get your fires started. For of course, while every farmer hoped the locusts would overlook his farm and go on to the next, it was only fair to warn each other; one must play fair. Everywhere, fifty miles over the countryside, the smoke was rising from myriads of fires. Margaret answered the telephone calls, and between calls she stood watching the locusts. The air was darkening. A strange darkness, for the sun was blazing—it was like the darkness of a veldt fire, when the air gets thick with smoke. The sunlight comes down distorted, a thick, hot orange. Oppressive it was, too, with the heaviness of a storm. The locusts were coming fast. Now half the sky was darkened. Behind the reddish veils in front, which were the advance guards of the swarm, the main swarm showed in dense black cloud, reaching almost to the sun itself.

Margaret was wondering what she could do to help. She did not know. Then up came

---

4. **mealies** *n.*: Ears of corn.

old Stephen from the lands. ''We're finished, Margaret, finished! Those beggars can eat every leaf and blade off the farm in half an hour! And it is only early afternoon—if we can make enough smoke, make enough noise till the sun goes down, they'll settle somewhere else perhaps. . . .'' And then: ''Get the kettle going. It's thirsty work, this.''

So Margaret went to the kitchen, and stoked up the fire, and boiled the water. Now, on the tin roof of the kitchen she could hear the thuds and bangs of falling locusts, or a scratching slither as one skidded down. Here were the first of them. From down on the lands came the beating and banging and clanging of a hundred gasoline cans and bits of metal. Stephen impatiently waited while one gasoline can was filled with tea, hot, sweet and orange-colored, and the other with water. In the meantime, he told Margaret about how twenty years back he was eaten out, made bankrupt, by the locust armies. And then, still talking, he hoisted up the gasoline cans, one in each hand, by the wood pieces set cornerwise across each, and jogged off down to the road to the thirsty laborers. By now the locusts were falling like hail on to the roof of the kitchen. It sounded like a heavy storm. Margaret looked out and saw the air dark with a criss-cross of the insects, and she set her teeth and ran out into it—what the men could do, she could. Overhead the air was thick, locusts everywhere. The locusts were flopping against her, and she brushed them off, heavy red-brown creatures, looking at her with their beady old-men's eyes while they clung with hard, serrated legs. She held her breath with disgust and ran through into the house. There it was even more like being in a heavy storm. The iron roof was reverberating, and the clamor of iron from the lands was like thunder. Looking out, all the trees were queer and still, clotted with insects, their boughs weighed to the ground. The earth seemed to be moving, locusts crawling everywhere, she could not see the lands at

almost empty. (The Africans had been turned off it into reserves.) Our neighbors were four, five, seven miles off. In front of the house . . . no neighbors, nothing; no farms, just wild bush with two rivers but no fences to the mountains seven miles away. And beyond these mountains and bush again to the Portuguese border, over which ''our boys'' used to escape when wanted by the police for pass or other offenses.

3 Discussion Why do you suppose Lessing has chosen so carefully to include colors in this passage? What is the effect of their juxtaposition?

4 Literary Focus How does this paradox reinforce the conflict portrayed in the story?

5 Reading Strategy What previous passage(s) does this question recall? Watch for its repetition, in somewhat altered form, later in the story.

6 Literary Focus Why does Lessing repeat the verb, *clotted*? Is it stylistically purposeful and, if so, how? Why, do you suppose, does she use this particular verb? What are its connotations? Do they support the story's theme?

7 Discussion Contrast Margaret's reaction to the locust attack with Stephen's. Why do they differ so?

all, so thick was the swarm. Towards the mountains it was like looking into driving rain—even as she watched, the sun was blotted out with a fresh onrush of them. It was a half-night, a perverted blackness. Then came a sharp crack from the bush—a branch had snapped off. Then another. A tree down the slope leaned over and settled heavily to the ground. Through the hail of insects a man came running. More tea, more water was needed. She supplied them. She kept the fires stoked and filled cans with liquid, and then it was four in the afternoon, and the locusts had been pouring across overhead for a couple of hours. Up came old Stephen again, crunching locusts underfoot with every step, locusts clinging all over him; he was cursing and swearing, banging with his old hat at the air. At the doorway he stopped briefly, hastily pulling at the clinging insects and throwing them off, then he plunged into the locust-free living-room.

"All the crops finished. Nothing left," he said.

But the gongs were still beating, the men still shouting, and Margaret asked: "Why do you go on with it, then?"

"The main swarm isn't settling. They are heavy with eggs. They are looking for a place to settle and lay. If we can stop the main body settling on our farm, that's everything. If they get a chance to lay their eggs, we are going to have everything eaten flat with hoppers[5] later on." He picked a stray locust off his shirt and split it down with his thumbnail—it was clotted inside with eggs. "Imagine that multiplied by millions. You ever seen a hopper swarm on the march? Well, you're lucky."

Margaret thought an adult swarm was bad enough. Outside now the light on the earth was a pale, thin yellow, clotted with moving shadows; the clouds of moving insects thickened and lightened like driving rain. Old Stephen said, "They've got the wind behind them, that's something."

"Is it very bad?" asked Margaret fearfully, and the old man said emphatically: "We're finished. This swarm may pass over, but once they've started, they'll be coming down from the North now one after another. And then there are the hoppers—it might go on for two or three years."

Margaret sat down helplessly, and thought: Well, if it's the end, it's the end. What now? We'll all three have to go back to town. . . . But at this, she took a quick look at Stephen, the old man who had farmed forty years in this country, been bankrupt twice, and she knew nothing would make him go and become a clerk in the city. Yet her heart ached for him, he looked so tired, the worry lines deep from nose to mouth. Poor old man. . . . He had lifted up a locust that had got itself somehow into his pocket, holding it in the air by one leg. "You've got the strength of a steel-spring in those legs of yours," he was telling the locust, good-humoredly. Then, although he had been fighting locusts, squashing locusts, yelling at locusts, sweeping them in great mounds into the fires to burn for the last three hours, nevertheless he took this one to the door and carefully threw it out to join its fellows, as if

_____

5. hoppers *n.:* Baby locusts.

Grammar in Action

Varied sentence structures make lively writing. Good writers combine sentence styles within a passage to add interest and enhance meaning. Notice Doris Lessing's varied structures.

> Then came a sharp crack from the bush—a branch had snapped off. Then another. A tree down the slope leaned over and settled heavily to the ground. Through the hail of insects a man came running. More tea, more water was

needed. She supplied them. She kept the fires stoked and filled cans with liquid, and then it was four in the afternoon, and the locusts had been pouring across overhead for a couple of hours.

Lessing keeps the reader's interest as much by the way she expresses each idea as she does by the ideas themselves. In each case, the sentence style heightens the meaning it bears. The first sentence uses an inverted independent clause followed by an interrupting idea set off by a dash. She accentuates the idea of the snapped branch by following it with an abrupt fragment, "Then another." That she follows with a simple declarative statement he would rather not harm a hair of its head. This comforted Margaret; all at once she felt irrationally cheered. She remembered it was not the first time in the last three years the man had announced their final and irremediable ruin.

"Get me a drink, lass," he then said, and she set the bottle of whisky by him.

In the meantime, out in the pelting storm of insects, her husband was banging the gong, feeding the fires with leaves, the insects clinging to him all over—she shuddered. "How can you bear to let them touch you?" she asked. He looked at her, disapproving. She felt suitably humble—just as she had when he had first taken a good look at her city self, hair waved and golden, nails red and pointed. Now she was a proper farmer's wife, in sensible shoes and a solid skirt. She might even get to letting locusts settle on her—in time.

Having tossed back a whisky or two, old Stephen went back into the battle, wading now through glistening brown waves of locusts.

Five o'clock. The sun would set in an hour. Then the swarm would settle. It was as thick overhead as ever. The trees were ragged mounds of glistening brown.

Margaret began to cry. It was all so hopeless—if it wasn't a bad season, it was locusts; if it wasn't locusts, it was army worm[6] or veldt fires. Always something. The rustling of the locust armies was like a big forest in the storm; their settling on the roof was like the beating of the rain; the ground was invisible in a sleek, brown, surging tide—it was like being drowned in locusts, submerged by the loathsome brown flood. It seemed as if the roof might sink in under the weight of them, as if the door might give in under their pressure and these rooms fill with them—and it was getting so dark . . . she looked up. The air was thinner; gaps of blue showed in the dark, moving clouds. The

---

6. **army worm:** Larva of certain moths that travel in large groups, ruining crops.

blue spaces were cold and thin—the sun must be setting. Through the fog of insects she saw figures approaching. First old Stephen, marching bravely along, then her husband, drawn and haggard with weariness. Behind them the servants. All were crawling all over with insects. The sound of the gongs had stopped. She could hear nothing but the ceaseless rustle of a myriad wings.

The two men slapped off the insects and came in.

"Well," said Richard, kissing her on the cheek, "the main swarm has gone over."

"For the Lord's sake," said Margaret angrily, still half-crying, "what's here is bad enough, isn't it?" For although the evening air was no longer black and thick, but a clear blue, with a pattern of insects whizzing this way and that across it, everything else—trees, buildings, bushes, earth, was gone under the moving brown masses.

"If it doesn't rain in the night and keep them here—if it doesn't rain and weight them down with water, they'll be off in the morning at sunrise."

"We're bound to have some hoppers. But not the main swarm—that's something."

Margaret roused herself, wiped her eyes, pretended she had not been crying, and fetched them some supper, for the servants were too exhausted to move. She sent them down to the compound to rest.

She served the supper and sat listening. There is not one maize plant left, she heard. Not one. The men would get the planters out the moment the locusts had gone. They must start all over again.

But what's the use of that, Margaret wondered, if the whole farm was going to be crawling with hoppers? But she listened while they discussed the new government pamphlet that said how to defeat the hoppers. You must have men out all the time, moving over the farm to watch for movement in the grass. When you find a patch of hoppers, small lively black things, like crickets, then you dig trenches around the

---

8 **Literary Focus** List as many of the conflicts presented by this passage as you can.

9 **Discussion** How does this passage embody Margaret's conflict?

---

whose style suggests the way a distant tree might gradually fall to the ground. The introductory phrase, "Through the hail of insects," has the man appear from behind the hail, just as the sentence says he does. By using passive voice and ellipsis in "More tea, more water was needed," Lessing allows us to hear the man talk to Margaret and to note his urgency. Margaret complies quickly in a short declarative sentence, but her response to his request continues to fill her day, and Lessing frames that in a compound, coordinated sentence that subtly shows the nonstop quality of her work.

Student Activity. Write a descriptive paragraph in which you consciously vary the sentence structures to heighten meaning.

10 Literary Focus What is the significance of the word *shadow* here? Where else has Lessing used it? What parallel does she make?

11 Discussion Why is it significant that Margaret shares the moment of seeing the beauty of the locusts fanning their wings? What has she gained that she lacked before?

12 Discussion Why is the comment of the men ironic, yet totally revealing of character, in view of their constant predictions of doom?

Reader's Response What are some problems that face farmers in our country?

patch or spray them with poison from pumps supplied by the Government. The Government wanted them to cooperate in a world plan for eliminating this plague forever. You should attack locusts at the source. Hoppers, in short. The men were talking as if they were planning a war, and Margaret listened, amazed.

In the night it was quiet; no sign of the settled armies outside, except sometimes a branch snapped, or a tree could be heard crashing down.

Margaret slept badly in the bed beside Richard, who was sleeping like the dead, exhausted with the afternoon's fight. In the morning she woke to yellow sunshine lying across the bed—clear sunshine, with an occasional blotch of shadow moving over it. She went to the window. Old Stephen was ahead of her. There he stood outside, gazing down over the bush. And she gazed, astounded—and entranced, much against her will. For it looked as if every tree, every bush, all the earth, were lit with pale flames. The locusts were fanning their wings to free them of the night dews. There was a shimmer of red-tinged gold light everywhere.

She went out to join the old man, stepping carefully among the insects. They stood and watched. Overhead the sky was blue, blue and clear.

"Pretty," said old Stephen, with satisfaction.

Well, thought Margaret, we may be ruined, we may be bankrupt, but not everyone has seen an army of locusts fanning their wings at dawn.

Over the slopes, in the distance, a faint red smear showed in the sky, thickened and spread. "There they go," said old Stephen. "There goes the main army, off south."

And now from the trees, from the earth all round them, the locusts were taking wing. They were like small aircraft, maneuvering for the take-off, trying their wings to see if they were dry enough. Off they went. A reddish-brown steam was rising off the miles of bush, off the lands, the earth. Again the sunlight darkened.

And as the clotted branches lifted, the weight on them lightening, there was nothing but the black spines of branches, trees. No green left, nothing. All morning they watched, the three of them, as the brown crust thinned and broke and dissolved, flying up to mass with the main army, now a brownish-red smear in the southern sky. The lands which had been filmed with green, the new tender mealie plants, were stark and bare. All the trees stripped. A devastated landscape. No green, no green anywhere.

By midday the reddish cloud had gone. Only an occasional locust flopped down. On the ground were the corpses and the wounded. The African laborers were sweeping these up with branches and collecting them in tins.

"Ever eaten sun-dried locust?" asked old Stephen. "That time twenty years ago, when I went broke, I lived on mealie meal and dried locusts for three months. They aren't bad at all—rather like smoked fish, if you come to think of it."

But Margaret preferred not even to think of it.

After the midday meal the men went off to the lands. Everything was to be replanted. With a bit of luck another swarm would not come traveling down just this way. But they hoped it would rain very soon, to spring some new grass, because the cattle would die otherwise—there was not a blade of grass left on the farm. As for Margaret, she was trying to get used to the idea of three or four years of locusts. Locusts were going to be like bad weather, from now on, always imminent. She felt like a survivor after war—if this devastated and mangled countryside was not ruin, well, what then was ruin?

But the men ate their supper with good appetites.

"It could have been worse," was what they said. "It could be much worse."

THINKING ABOUT THE SELECTION

Recalling

1. (a) How long has Margaret lived on the farm? (b) Where did she come from? (c) How has her appearance changed since coming to the farm?
2. What are the farmers' two main defenses against the locusts?
3. Why do the farmers want to prevent the main swarm of locusts from settling?
4. What three problems besides locusts do the farmers sometimes have to face?
5. (a) How much damage do the locusts do to the farm? (b) When morning comes, what do the locusts do?

Interpreting

6. What is Margaret's attitude toward the locust attack?
7. Why does old Stephen fight on even after saying they are finished?
8. Why do you think Margaret is comforted when Stephen releases the locust that was in his pocket?
9. In what sense is the locust attack ''mild,'' as the title of the story calls it?

Applying

10. People react differently when faced with what seems to be a hopeless situation. (a) How does this story make that point? (b) What have you seen in your own experience that proves it?

ANALYZING LITERATURE

Recognizing Conflict

In a work of fiction, the opposition between a character and another force is the story's conflict. This conflict may be external, as between the farmers and the invading locusts in ''A Mild Attack of Locusts.'' Or it may be internal, as in Margaret's love for her husband opposed to her despair for his future as a farmer on the veldt.

1. There are a number of conflicts in ''A Mild Attack of Locusts.'' One of them concerns Margaret's struggle to define herself as a farmer's wife. What evidence is there in the story that she does not regard herself as entirely satisfied with her role in life?
2. The immediate external conflict in the story is the locust attack. But there is a long-term conflict as well, one that is unresolved by the farmers' minor victory in keeping the main swarm from settling. (a) What is the long-term, unresolved external conflict? (b) How successful do you think Richard, Stephen, and Margaret will be in resolving it?

CRITICAL THINKING AND READING

Understanding the Role of Style

A writer's **style** is his or her distinctive way of using language to express thoughts. Style is a broad term. It includes word choice, sentence structure, point of view, and all aspects of organization. A writer's style is influenced by the literary fashion of the times and by his or her own personality and preferences. Some writers pay close attention to their style; others do not. The style of some writers stands out in sharp relief; that of others is hardly noticeable. Doris Lessing's style in ''A Mild Attack of Locusts'' is plain and precise. Her use of inverted sentence structure is perhaps its most noticeable feature —''Beautiful it was, with the sky blue.''

What makes Lessing's ''straight, broad, direct'' style effective in this story?

THINKING AND WRITING

Writing About a Paradox

A **paradox** is a statement or circumstance that at first seems untrue or self-contradictory but upon reflection proves to be true in some sense. In ''A Mild Attack of Locusts,'' Margaret, after a day of feeling revulsion for the locusts, is entranced the next morning as they fan their wings, making ''a shimmer of red-tinged gold light everywhere.'' Her feelings are paradoxical. Write a composition in which you explain the paradox of how something so destructive and even loathsome can also be beautiful. When revising your first draft, make sure you have supported your ideas with specific details.

A Mild Attack of Locusts   1257

Closure and Extension

ANSWERS TO THINKING ABOUT THE SELECTION
Recalling

1. (a) ''Margaret has been on the farm three years.'' (b) Margaret came from the city. (c) Margaret has traded in ''her city self, hair waved and golden, nails red and pointed'' for the image of ''a proper farmer's wife, in sensible shoes and a solid skirt.''
2. The farmers' two main defenses against the locusts are noise and fire.

3. The farmers want to prevent the main swarm of locusts from settling so they can keep them from laying their eggs.
4. Besides locusts, farmers must contend with ''a bad season,'' ''army worm,'' and ''veldt fires.''
5. (a) The locusts strip the farm of everything green and growing. (b) In the morning, they leave for the south.

Interpreting

6. Margaret prefers to not think about the locust attack.
7. Old Stephen fights on because he is a survivor.
8. Margaret is comforted by Stephen's releasing the locust in his pocket because it shows his humaneness.
9. It is mild because it could have been worse.

Applying

10. (a) Margaret reacts differently from the farmers. (b) Answers will differ. Students should mention the different reactions of people in the same set of circumstances.

ANSWERS TO ANALYZING LITERATURE

1. Margaret's constant feeling of not understanding her surroundings suggests that she doesn't regard herself as entirely satisfied with her role in life. Her memory of her city self suggests nostalgia and preference for an earlier time.
2. (a) The long-term, unresolved conflict concerns the advisability of continuing the farm at all. (b) Answers will differ. Students should give reasons for their answers.

ANSWERS TO CRITICAL THINKING AND READING

The story is a modern parable. ''Straight, broad, direct'' suits its lesson.

THINKING AND WRITING

Publishing Student Writing Have students read their compositions in small groups. Each group can then select one or two compositions to share with the class.

More About the Author Nadine Gordimer is often compared, artistically, with her fellow South African and fellow author, Doris Lessing. Both characteristically deal with the twin themes of freedom and estrangement on a personal as well as a political level. While Lessing has become famous for the ways in which she employs structure to support and reinforce theme, Gordimer is more well-known for her careful crafting of language.

Critical Evaluation A reviewer in the *Times Literary Supplement* wrote that "Nadine Gordimer . . . makes a point well by not stating it directly. South Africa is her home, and is the setting for many of her stories, but even when she is making use of politics in a story she is never guilty of pushing her characters to the sideline in order to make an overt political point—a fact which, paradoxically, enables her to demonstrate South Africa's political oddities more exactly: the country lives through the characters' experience of it. . . ."

1923–

The fiction of Nadine Gordimer has been shaped by her life in South Africa and by her firm opposition to the government's policy of apartheid. Initially honored for her short fiction, she says that in time she found the short story "too delicate for what I have to say." In recent years her novels, some of them banned in South Africa, have gained an international reputation.

Nadine Gordimer was born in Springs, South Africa, a small town near Johannesburg. Her mother took her out of a local private school when she was eleven, and from then until she was sixteen she "read tremendously," wrote much fiction, and published her first adult short story, "Come Again Tomorrow," when she was fifteen. She studied for a year at the University of Witwatersrand, continuing to write short stories. *The Soft Voice of the Serpent* (1952) was the first collection of her stories to be published in the United States.

Following the critical success of that book, Gordimer's stories began appearing in *The New Yorker,* the *Atlantic, Harper's,* and other well-known periodicals. In her stories she often describes the enforced entrapment of whites who have inherited political and economic power in South Africa's closed society. Frequently she builds a personal tale around a fleeting but sharply focused moment of insight.

In her short stories, and later in her novels—including the critically acclaimed *A Guest of Honor* (1970), *The Conservationist* (1974), and *Burger's Daughter* (1979)—she displays an ability to write from the perspectives of Anglo, black, and Afrikaner and to delineate a variety of economic and social settings. She writes as a compassionate observer of the human condition. In lyric tones yet without sentimentality, she pictures the South African scene with awareness and humanity, stressing the themes of understanding, adjustment, and forgiveness.

Until she was thirty, Nadine Gordimer had never been outside South Africa. Since then she has traveled widely and lectured in a number of universities, including Princeton, Columbia, and the University of Michigan. In recent years she has won many literary awards.

Since 1954, Gordimer has been married to Reinhold Cassier, the director of the Johannesburg branch of Sotheby Parke Bernet. She has two children, one by a previous marriage. Called "a luminous symbol of at least one white person's understanding of the black man's burden," there can be little doubt that she is the leading African novelist writing in English.

GUIDE FOR INTERPRETING

The Train from Rhodesia

Theme. Theme is the insight into life revealed by a work of literature. In fiction the writer's central idea becomes the theme of the work. Often the theme can be stated in a single sentence, such as "A small mistake in judgment can have serious consequences." Sometimes it demands a more detailed description. A work of fiction may have one theme or several. In developing a theme, the writer introduces conflict, typically a problem or problems that must be solved by the protagonist, or main character.

When the protagonist has to choose between two or more undesirable alternatives, he or she faces a dilemma. In familiar terms a dilemma is a choice between the frying pan and the fire; in mythological terms, between Scylla and Charybdis. A dilemma involves a difficult choice between actions or values, and any choice that the character makes may have unfortunate results.

An author's entire literary output is frequently characterized by one overriding theme that ties together all the individual works. Each work rarely states the same theme in the same way. Rather, readers can see one general concern expressed differently in each poem, story, novel, or essay. These themes can be drawn from the writer's personal situation, or combined with some political, social, or moral concern of the day. On the surface, it would not seem possible that Nadine Gordimer's work would show one dominant theme, since she writes about such a wide range of people and places. Indeed, one critic has remarked that "the image of the bazaar comes to mind when one thinks of Miss Gordimer's variety and resourcefulness." For example, many of her stories concern wealthy, sophisticated, and frequently bored urban and suburban people in Johannesburg, South Africa. Other tales deal with people on the lowest economic rung eking out a bare living among the wretched thatched roofs and mud floors of native locations. Many of her best tales, such as "The Train from Rhodesia," intermingle these two worlds to more fully illuminate the situation in contemporary South Africa. But critic Robert F. Haugh has identified a tension between "what might be" and "what is " in a majority of her work. How do you see this theme in "The Train form Rhodesia"?

According to an African proverb, "The earth is a beehive; we all enter by the same door but live in different cells." Freewrite, exploring the meaning of this proverb.

Guide for Interpreting 1259

Literary Focus Fiction requires conflict to make it move. Dilemma, a special type of inner conflict, requires a character, usually the protagonist, to decide between difficult alternatives.

Writing/Prior Knowledge Have the students discuss the relationship between the story's opening sentence and its central theme. Encourage them to bear this discussion in mind as they complete the freewriting assignment.

Vocabulary

Preteach the following vocabulary words:
heraldic (hə ral′dik) *adj.:* Resembling an English coat of arms (p. 1260)
impressionistic (im presh′ ə nis′ tik) *adj.:* Conveying a quick, overall picture (p. 1260)
elongated (i lôŋ′gāt id) *adj.:* Lengthened; stretched (p. 1262)
valance (val′əns) *n.:* Decorative facing (p. 1262)
segmented (seg′ment id) *adj.:* Separated into parts (p. 1263)
splaying (splā′iŋ) *v.:* Spreading (p. 1263)
atrophy (a′trə fē) *v.:* Waste away (p. 1264)

Objectives

1 To understand theme
2 To understand cultural attitudes and customs
3 To distinguish between concrete and abstract words
4. To write about theme in fiction

Support Material

Teaching Portfolio
Teacher Backup, p. 1491
Grammar in Action Worksheet, *Recognizing Prepositional Phrases,* p. 1495
Usage and Mechanics Worksheet, p. 1497
Vocabulary Check, p. 1498

Critical Thinking and Reading Worksheet, *Understanding Cultural Attitudes,* p. 1500
Language Worksheet, *Recognizing Concrete and Abstract Words,* p. 1501
Selection Test, p. 1502

The Train from Rhodesia[1]

Nadine Gordimer

The train came out of the red horizon and bore down toward them over the single straight track.

The stationmaster came out of his little brick station with its pointed chalet roof, feeling the creases in his serge uniform in his legs as well. A stir of preparedness rippled through the squatting native vendors waiting in the dust; the face of a carved wooden animal, eternally surprised, stuck out of a sack. The stationmaster's barefoot children wandered over. From the gray mud huts with the untidy heads that stood within a decorated mud wall, chickens, and dogs with their skin stretched like parchment over their bones, followed the piccanins[2] down to the track. The flushed and perspiring west cast a reflection, faint, without heat, upon the station, upon the tin shed marked "Goods," upon the walled kraal,[3] upon the gray tin house of the stationmaster and upon the sand, that lapped all around, from sky to sky, cast little rhythmical cups of shadow, so that the sand became the sea, and closed over the children's black feet softly and without imprint.

The stationmaster's wife sat behind the mesh of her veranda. Above her head the hunk of a sheep's carcass moved slightly, dangling in a current of air.

They waited.

The train called out, along the sky; but there was no answer; and the cry hung on: I'm coming . . . I'm coming . . .

The engine flared out now, big, whisking a dwindling body behind it; the track flared out to let it in.

Creaking, jerking, jostling, gasping, the train filled the station.

Here, let me see that one—the young woman curved her body further out of the corridor window. Missus? smiled the old boy, looking at the creatures he held in his hand. From a piece of string on his gray finger hung a tiny woven basket; he lifted it, questioning. No, no, she urged, leaning down toward him, across the height of the train, toward the man in the piece of old rug; that one, that one, her hand commanded. It was a lion, carved out of soft dry wood that looked like spongecake; heraldic, black and white, with impressionistic detail burnt in. The old man held it up to her still smiling, not from the heart, but at the customer. Between its Vandyke[4] teeth, in the mouth opened in an endless roar too terrible to be heard, it had a black tongue. Look, said the young husband, if you don't mind! And round the neck of the thing, a piece of fur (rat? rabbit? meerkat?); a real mane, majestic, telling you somehow that the artist had delight in the lion.

---

1. Rhodesia (rō de′ zhə): Former name of Zimbabwe (zim bä′ bwe), a country in southern Africa.
2. piccanins *n.*: Native children.
3. kraal (kräl) *n.*: A fenced-in enclosure for cattle or sheep.

4. Vandyke (van dīk′) *adj.*: In the style of the subjects of the portraits of Flemish painter Anthony Vandyke (1599–1641).

Discussion What is the significance of the artists being described as animals who "sprang, walking bent"?

5 **Discussion** Explain why the faces of the passengers suddenly look different after their contact with those outside the train.

6 **Reading Strategy** What can be inferred about the relationship between the young man and woman and about the reason for their trip. In other words, why are they on this train together?

4 All up and down the length of the train in the dust the artists sprang, walking bent, like performing animals, the better to exhibit the fantasy held toward the faces on the train. Buck, startled and stiff, staring with round black and white eyes. More lions, standing erect, grappling with strange, thin, elongated warriors who clutched spears and showed no fear in their slits of eyes. How much, they asked from the train, how much?

Give me penny, said the little ones with nothing to sell. The dogs went and sat, quite still, under the dining car, where the train breathed out the smell of meat cooking with onion.

A man passed beneath the arch of reaching arms meeting gray-black and white in the exchange of money for the staring wooden eyes, the stiff wooden legs sticking up in the air; went along under the voices and the bargaining, interrogating the wheels. Past the dogs; glancing up at the dining car where he could stare at the faces, behind glass, drinking beer, two by two, on either side of a uniform railway vase with its pale dead flower. Right to the end, to the guard's van, where the stationmaster's children had just collected their mother's two loaves of bread; to the engine itself, where the stationmaster and the driver stood talking against the steaming complaint of the resting beast.

The man called out to them, something loud and joking. They turned to laugh, in a twirl of steam. The two children careered over the sand, clutching the bread, and burst through the iron gate and up the path through the garden in which nothing grew.

5 Passengers drew themselves in at the corridor windows and turned into compartments to fetch money, to call someone to look. Those sitting inside looked up: suddenly different, caged faces, boxed in, cut off, after the contact of outside. There was an orange a piccanin would like. . . . What about that chocolate? It wasn't very nice. . . .

A young girl had collected a handful of the hard kind, that no one liked, out of the chocolate box, and was throwing them to the dogs, over at the dining car. But the hens darted in, and swallowed the chocolates, incredibly quick and accurate, before they had even dropped in the dust, and the dogs, a little bewildered, looked up with their brown eyes, not expecting anything.

—No, leave it, said the girl, don't take it. . . .

Too expensive, too much, she shook her head and raised her voice to the old boy, giving up the lion. He held it up where she had handed it to him. No, she said, shaking her head. Three-and-six?[5] insisted her husband, loudly. Yes baas! laughed the boy. *Three-and-six?*—the young man was incredulous. Oh leave it—she said. The young man stopped. Don't you want it? he said, keeping his face closed to the boy. No, never mind, she said, leave it. The old native kept his head on one side, looking at them sideways, holding the lion. Three-and-six, he murmured, as old people repeat things to themselves.

6 The young woman drew her head in. She went into the coupé[6] and sat down. Out of the window, on the other side, there was nothing; sand and bush; a thorn tree. Back through the open doorway, past the figure of her husband in the corridor, there was the station, the voices, wooden animals waving, running feet. Her eye followed the funny little valance of scrolled wood that outlined the chalet roof of the station; she thought of the lion and smiled. That bit of fur round the neck. But the wooden buck, the hippos, the elephants, the baskets that already bulked out of their brown paper under the seat and on the luggage rack! How will they look at home? Where will you put them? What will they mean away from the places you found

---

5. **three-and-six:** Three shillings and sixpence.
6. **coupé** (kōō pā′) *n.:* A half-compartment at the end, with seats on only one side.

Grammar in Action

Prepositional phrases contain a preposition and a noun or pronoun called the object of the preposition. Such phrases can modify a noun or a verb.

EXAMPLE: He collided with the table *beside the door*. (The prepositional phrase is an adjective phrase modifying the noun "table.")
In Prospect Park, you can ride thoroughbred horses. (The prepositional phrase is an adverb phrase modifying the verb "ride.")

Writers use prepositional phrases to make their descriptions more precise and colorful. Notice the way in which Nadine Gordimer employs such phrases in the following passage from "The Train from Rhodesia."

Out of the window, on the other side, there was nothing; sand and bush; a thorn tree. *Back through the open doorway, past the figure of her husband in the corridor,* there was the station, the voices, wooden animals waving, running feet.

The four adverbial phrases and the one adjective phrase are essential to this description. With them, Gordimer leads the them? Away from the unreality of the last few weeks? The man outside. But he is not part of the unreality; he is for good now. Odd . . . somewhere there was an idea that he, that living with him, was part of the holiday, the strange places.

Outside, a bell rang. The stationmaster was leaning against the end of the train, green flag rolled in readiness. A few men who had got down to stretch their legs sprang on to the train, clinging to the observation platforms, or perhaps merely standing on the iron step, holding the rail; but on the train, safe from the one dusty platform, the one tin house, the empty sand.

There was a grunt. The train jerked. Through the glass the beer drinkers looked out, as if they could not see beyond it. Behind the flyscreen, the stationmaster's wife sat facing back at them beneath the darkening hunk of meat.

There was a shout. The flag drooped out. Joints not yet coordinated, the segmented body of the train heaved and bumped back against itself. It began to move; slowly the scrolled chalet moved past it, the yells of the natives, running alongside, jetted up into the air, fell back at different levels. Staring wooden faces waved drunkenly, there, then gone, questioning for the last time at the windows. Here, one-and-six baas!—As one automatically opens a hand to catch a thrown ball, a man fumbled wildly down his pocket, brought up the shilling and sixpence and threw them out; the old native, gasping, his skinny toes splaying the sand, flung the lion.

The piccanins were waving, the dogs stood, tails uncertain, watching the train go: past the mud huts, where a woman turned to look, up from the smoke of the fire, her hand pausing on her hip.

The stationmaster went slowly in under the chalet.

The old native stood, breath blowing out the skin between his ribs, feet tense, balanced in the sand, smiling and shaking his head. In his opened palm, held in the attitude of receiving, was the retrieved shilling and sixpence.

The blind end of the train was being pulled helplessly out of the station. **7**

The young man swung in from the corridor, breathless. He was shaking his head with laughter and triumph. Here! he said. And waggled the lion at her. One-and-six!

What? she said.

He laughed. I was arguing with him for fun, bargaining—when the train had pulled out already, he came tearing after. . . . One-and-six baas! So there's your lion.

She was holding it away from her, the head with the open jaws, the pointed teeth, the black tongue, the wonderful ruff of fur facing her. She was looking at it with an expression of not seeing, of seeing something different. Her face was drawn up, wryly, like the face of a discomforted child. Her mouth lifted nervously at the corner. Very slowly, cautious, she lifted her finger and touched the mane, where it was joined to the wood.

But how could you, she said. He was shocked by the dismay of her face.

Good heavens, he said, what's the matter?

If you wanted the thing, she said, her voice rising and breaking with the shrill impotence of anger, why didn't you buy it in the first place? If you wanted it, why didn't you pay for it? Why didn't you take it decently, when he offered it? Why did you have to wait for him to run after the train with it, and give him one-and-six? One-and-six!

She was pushing it at him, trying to force him to take it. He stood astonished, his hands hanging at his sides.

But you wanted it! You liked it so much?

—It's a beautiful piece of work, she said fiercely, as if to protect it from him.

You liked it so much! You said yourself it was too expensive—

Oh *you*—she said, hopeless and furious. *You*. . . . She threw the lion onto the seat.

reader's eye through the scene, almost the way a movie camera would. This movement also gives the scene depth, a foreground and background; for example, we are taken past the husband in the foreground to the flurry of activity behind him.

Student Activity 1. Identify two other passages where Gordimer uses prepositional phrases and explain how they contribute to her description.

Student Activity 2. Find a descriptive passage written by your favorite author. Identify all the prepositional phrases he or she has used, then copy over the description eliminating these phrases. Finally, compare and contrast the original passage with the new one you have created.

8

8 Reading Strategy What is the "void" that the young woman discovers? What clues are there to suggest it?

9 Discussion Why does the story end as it does?

10 Reading Strategy Ask students to review the descriptions of the train throughout the short story. How is it personified? What similarity to the young woman could the train represent?

Reader's Response Have you ever witnessed a small incident that revealed important truths? Explain.

He stood looking at her.

She sat down again in the corner and, her face slumped in her hand, stared out of the window. Everything was turning around inside her. One-and-six. One-and-six. One-and-six for the wood and the carving and the sinews of the legs and the switch of the tail. The mouth open like that and the teeth. The black tongue, rolling, like a wave. The mane round the neck. To give one-and-six for that. The heat of shame mounted through her legs and body and sounded in her ears like the sound of sand pouring. Pouring, pouring. She sat there, sick. A weariness, a tastelessness, the discovery of a void made her hands slacken their grip, atrophy emptily, as if the hour was not worth their grasp. She was feeling like this

again. She had thought it was something to do with singleness, with being alone and belonging too much to oneself.

She sat there not wanting to move or speak, or to look at anything, even; so that the mood should be associated with nothing, no object, word or sight that might recur and so recall the feeling again. . . . Smuts blew in grittily, settled on her hands. Her back remained at exactly the same angle, turned against the young man sitting with his hands drooping between his sprawled legs, and the lion, fallen on its side in the corner.

The train had cast the station like a skin. It called out to the sky, I'm coming, I'm coming; and again, there was no answer.

8

9, 10

THINKING ABOUT THE SELECTION
Recalling

1. At the beginning of the story, what are three details that show the isolation of the small-town railway station?
2. (a) How much money does the vendor want for the carved lion? (b) How much does he finally accept?
3. (a) What have the young couple already bought on their holiday? (b) After the "unreality" of the vacation, what does the wife realize "is for good now"?
4. (a) At the end of the story, how is the young woman sitting in her seat? (b) Where is the lion?

Interpreting

5. Why is the arrival of the train important to the people in the town?
6. Why do you think the young woman wants the carved lion?
7. (a) Why is the young woman angry when her

husband bargains for and obtains the lion at a low price? (b) What does she mean to imply when she says, "If you wanted the thing . . . why didn't you pay for it"?
8. This story is highly symbolic. (a) What may the train symbolize? (b) The station?

Applying

9. At the end of the story, the young wife feels isolated and alone. Her husband is confused by her unexpected reactions. (a) What has happened in this apparently trivial incident to make her feel shame, sickness, weariness, and emptiness? (b) How would you advise her husband to try to reassure her?

ANALYZING LITERATURE
Understanding Theme

Theme is the central idea in a literary work. Conflict, which occurs as the theme is developed, may present one or more dilemmas. A

1264   *Contemporary Writers*

dilemma is a situation in which the main character, or protagonist, has to choose between undesirable alternatives. A short-story writer will not necessarily resolve all dilemmas, but may leave them for the reader to ponder. With a partner or in a small group, discuss two of the dilemmas —apart from isolation in marriage—that the young woman in "The Train from Rhodesia" appears to be facing. For example:

1. The dilemma of belonging to the well-to-do white minority in an impoverished black nation
2. The dilemma of trying to make connections with other people in a setting that makes it hard to do so

CRITICAL THINKING AND READING
Understanding Cultural Attitudes

The scene at the railway station that is described in "The Train from Rhodesia" is probably unfamiliar to you. The custom of white train passengers bargaining with native craftsmen for the purchase of their hand-carved wares reflects circumstances in southern Africa at the time the fictional incident occurs. Both the passengers on the train and the natives at the station accept the custom as normal. They see nothing to object to, although to an outside observer it might suggest inequality, racism, and exploitation.

Describe the scene at a subway, bus station, train station, or airport in your community or nearby. Your viewpoint should be that of total stranger to your community—a visitor from another country, perhaps. Point out any behavior, habits, or activities that appear unusual to you as an outsider.

UNDERSTANDING LANGUAGE
Using Concrete and Abstract Words

A **concrete word** is one that names a person or an object that can be directly observed through the senses. For example, you can see a pencil, hear a dog bark, taste salt. The words *pencil, bark,* and *salt* are concrete words. An **abstract word** is one that names qualities, conditions, or ideas that cannot be directly observed. Some interpretation is required. For example, while you can define *heroism, joy,* and *freedom,* you cannot point to them as objects. You must base your definition, instead, on specific examples of them.

Since a good short-story writer like Nadine Gordimer seldom moralizes, she favors concrete words in telling the story, although she may use abstract words in dialogue or to show the feelings of the main characters.

1. List and define five concrete words that contribute to the atmosphere of the story.
2. List and define five abstract words that show the thoughts or emotions of the characters.
3. The woman complains that her husband did not take the lion "decently." How do you think she would define the word decency? Explain your answer.

THINKING AND WRITING
Writing About Theme

The events in "The Train from Rhodesia" work together to reveal an insight into life. Identify the major theme in "The Train from Rhodesia." Write it in one carefully considered sentence. Then choose another short story in this book that has a similar theme. Write this theme, too, in a single sentence. Then write an essay in which you explain the similarities and differences between the two stories. Be specific. Give examples to support your main points. In revising the first draft, pay close attention to word choice. Have you chosen the right word in each place where an exact word is important—not merely a word that comes close? Careful word choice is one distinguishing mark of a good writer. Proofread your essay and share it with your classmates.

her husband, and their class routinely exploit natives.

8. (a) Suggested Response: The train represents a powerful force. It embodies authority, government, and the dominant civilization. (b) Suggested Response: The station seems to be a receptive, oppressed sufferer. It represents the people, popular culture, and the way life is actually lived.

Applying

9. (a) The ugliness in which she has been involved, that is, buying native artifacts for pennies, has suddenly been revealed to her. (b) Answers may differ. Suggested Response: Move away from Rhodesia would be one possibility.

ANSWERS TO ANALYZING LITERATURE

Have a member of each group report on the group's conclusions. Suggested Responses:
1. This dilemma may engender guilt.
2. This dilemma probably gives rise to frustration.

ANSWERS TO CRITICAL READING AND THINKING

Answers may differ. Emphasize that students should point out specific details.

ANSWERS TO UNDERSTANDING LANGUAGE

1. Answers will differ. Five concrete words that contribute to the mood of the story are *perspiring, carcass, creaking, jerking,* and *jostling.*
2. Answers will differ. Five abstract words that show the thoughts or emotions of the characters are *fear, unreality, laughter, triumph,* and *dismay.*
3. Answers will differ. The woman might define *decency* as "applying fair and considerate standards." She thought her husband should not take advantage of the natives.

THINKING AND WRITING

For help with this assignment, students can refer to Lesson 11, "Writing About Theme," in the Handbook of Writing About Literature.

Closure and Extension

ANSWERS TO THINKING ABOUT THE SELECTION
Recalling

1. Three details are the fact that the train "came out of the red horizon," the mention of the "single straight track," and the mention of the "sand, that lapped all around, from sky to sky. . . ."

2. (a) The vendor wants three-and-six. (b) He finally accepts one-and-six.
3. (a) The young couple have already bought "the wooden buck, the hippos, the elephants, the baskets." (b) After the "unreality" of their vacation, the wife realizes that her relationship with "the man outside . . . is for good now."
4. (a) At the end of the story, the young woman sits with her back to the young man. (b) The lion, "fallen on its side in the corner" is, likewise, behind her.

Interpreting

5. The train means trade and the possibility of boosting the economy.
6. The young woman seems to want the lion because it is so beautifully made.
7. (a) She is suddenly disgusted by the way in which her husband has taken advantage of the native artist. (b) Answers may differ. Suggested Response: Perhaps she is disgusted by the way in which she,

ALAN SILLITOE

More About the Author Alan Sillitoe himself worked in factories from the age of fourteen until he entered the air force during World War II. After the war, he lived in Majorca and became acquainted with Robert Graves, a successful writer, who encouraged Sillitoe to begin writing. His stories often deal with the ways in which young laborers like himself escape from the despair of their lives. How do you think Sillitoe felt about his life when he was young? How might he feel about his background now that he is successful?

Critical Evaluation The reviewer Clancy Sigal wrote that "Of all living English writers none can match Alan Sillitoe's sharp instinct for the grinding pain and convulsive joys of working-class life. *Saturday Night and Sunday Morning* and *The Loneliness of the Long Distance Runner* probably are this generation's most vivid documents of how the majority of English people live and think."

1928–

When Alan Sillitoe's first novel, *Saturday Night and Sunday Morning,* was published in 1958, one critic commented, "For the first time, English working-class life is treated . . . as a normal aspect of the human condition and as normal subject matter for a writer." Most of Sillitoe's heroes are rebellious members of the laboring class, "simple men caught in the cog-wheels of society."

Alan Sillitoe, the son of a tannery worker, was born and raised in Nottingham, an industrial city northwest of London. He left school at fourteen and worked in a bicycle plant and a plywood mill. From 1946 to 1949 he served in the Royal Air Force as a radio operator in Malaya.

He began to write while in Malaya, scrapping the manuscripts of nine complete novels before publishing and achieving immediate success with *Saturday Night and Sunday Morning.*

Sillitoe has been called one of the last of Britain's "angry young men," a group of writers in the 1950's and 1960's whose protagonists defy what they regard as outmoded political traditions and social norms. Like the other authors in this group, Sillitoe explores the theme of rebellion. Unlike them, he keeps his heroes firmly rooted in the working class, seeking self-discovery through a shared opposition to much of organized society.

His first collection of short stories, *The Loneliness of the Long-Distance Runner,* appeared in 1959. This collection, like his first novel, won immediate acclaim. The title story tells of a young juvenile delinquent who refuses to repent of the crimes that have landed him in an English reform school.

Sillitoe has also written poems and plays. Although his later work extends the range of his protagonists' rebellion, he remains primarily a chronicler of the English working classes. His restless energy has produced a body of work that is sometimes compared with that of D. H. Lawrence, another writer from Nottingham.

As with Lawrence, being poor left a permanent impression on Sillitoe's writing. Most of his work revolves around those scratching out a living on the lowest rungs of society's ladder. His understanding of poverty's effects is shown in this excerpt from his essay on the subject: "The very poor are too busy surviving to want to get on. To get on is something often dinned into them, handed down by the culture beneath which they exist. They are unable to take advantage of it, for to reach next week with clothes on your back, food still on the table, and enough life in your brain to face another week is the most they can do."

Support Material

Teaching Portfolio
Teacher Backup, p. 1505
Grammar in Action Worksheet, *Recognizing The Passive Voice,* p. 1509
Usage and Mechanics Worksheet, p. 1511
Vocabulary Check, p. 1512
Analyzing Literature Worksheet,

Understanding Setting, p. 1513
Language Worksheet, *Understanding Slang,* p. 1514
Selection Test, p. 1515
Art Transparency 17, *Beulah Road,* by Eric Holt

GUIDE FOR INTERPRETING

The Fiddle

Literary Focus Remind students that several authors use setting as if it were a character in their works—the Brontës, Dickens, and Hardy. The areas in which these authors lived and wrote had such an impact on them that they saw setting as a determining factor in their stories as well. The settings used by these authors have something else in common. Whether it's the urban blight of London and Radford or the wind-swept bleakness of the Yorkshire moors and the southwest downs, these settings set a controlling tone of despair.

Writing/Prior Knowledge Have students complete the writing activity by organizing the sentences into a paragraph that describes the setting that they have chosen. Remind them to organize their sentences in a logical sequence and to include transitions between sentences.

Writer's Techniques

Setting. The setting in a work of fiction is the place and time in which the action occurs. In some stories the setting is of great importance; in others it is not. A writer presents setting in various ways. A playwright can use costumes and stage scenery to help establish the place and time of the events. A novelist or short-story writer, on the other hand, has to do it all with words. The most direct way is through extended description, although this tends to slow down the action. Many contemporary writers prefer to establish the setting by interspersing description with ongoing narration. If the setting is vital to the theme and action of the story, the writer is likely to give it prominence, often through detailed and memorable description.

Writing

Every time and every place provides a setting. As you read this assignment, you are in a setting of your own. You may be in a classroom. You may be in a living room, or a bedroom, or a kitchen. Think of some words and ideas that you associate with your present setting. Jot them down. Then write ten descriptive sentences that show the main features of your immediate environment.

Primary Source

From 1953 to 1958, Sillitoe and his wife lived as inexpensively as possible in Majorca while he tried to get his work published. He supplemented his small service pension by translating and teaching; his wife worked for a travel agency. Sillitoe sent several of his poems to Robert Graves, already famous. Graves, too, was living in Majorca, in a home he had built from the royalties from *I Claudius.* At Graves's invitation, Sillitoe visited him one Sunday, riding a borrowed bicycle. Graves autographed a copy of his book while they talked of England and the problems which writers face. Sillitoe recorded this exchange:

> "Some of your poems are good," he said, still looking at me as if waiting for some sort of recognition. "At least you end them well. So many people get off to a good start, then fizzle out half way through" . . . I said I found his remarks about my poetry encouraging, but that so far none had been published. "That doesn't matter," he replied. "As long as you keep on writing them." This wasn't the sort of truth I wanted to hear: "I'd like to see them in print." "That's no problem if you keep writing."

Graves was right; soon after, Sillitoe published his first book and has published steadily ever since.

Guide for Interpreting 1267

Vocabulary

Preteach the following vocabulary words:

sinewy (sin′yo͞o wē) *adj.:* Tough; vigorous; powerful (p. 1268)

persistent (pər sis′tənt) *adj.:* Continuing (p. 1268)

obliterate (ə blit′ə rāt) *v.:* To destroy utterly (p. 1269)

sublimity (sə blim′ə tē) *n.:* The quality of being majestic or noble (p. 1271)

harried (har′ēd) *v.:* Harassed (p. 1271)

brazen (brā′z'n) *adj.:* Bold; shameless (p. 1272)

The Fiddle

Alan Sillitoe

On the banks of the sinewy River Leen, where it flowed through Radford, stood a group of cottages called Harrison's Row. There must have been six to eight of them, all in a ruinous condition, but lived in nevertheless.

They had been put up for stockingers[1] during the Industrial Revolution a hundred years before, so that by now the usual small red English housebricks had become weatherstained and, in some places, almost black.

Harrison's Row had a character all of its own, both because of its situation, and the people who lived there. Each house had a space of pebbly soil rising in front, and a strip of richer garden sloping away from the kitchen door down to the diminutive River Leen at the back. The front gardens had almost merged into one piece of common ground, while those behind had in most cases retained their separate plots.

As for the name of the isolated row of cottages, nobody knew who Harrison had been, and no one was ever curious about it. Neither did they know where the Leen came from, though some had a general idea as to where it finished up.

A rent man walked down cobblestoned Leen Place every week to collect what money he could. This wasn't much, even at the best of times which, in the "thirties," were not too good—though no one in their conversation was able to hark back to times when they had been any better.

From the slight rise on which the houses stood, the back doors and windows looked across the stream into green fields, out towards the towers and pinnacles of Wollaton Hall in one direction, and the woods of Aspley Manor in the other.

After a warm summer without much rain the children were able to wade to the fields on the other side. Sometimes they could almost paddle. But after a three-day downpour when the air was still heavy with undropped water, and colored a menacing gun-metal blue, it was best not to go anywhere near the river, for one false slip and you would get sucked in, and be dragged by the powerful current along to the Trent some miles away. In that case there was no telling where you'd end up. The water seemed to flow into the River Amazon[2] itself, indicated by the fact that Frankie Buller swore blind how one day he had seen a crocodile snapping left and right downstream with a newborn baby in its mouth. You had to be careful—and that was a fact. During the persistent rain of one autumn water came up over the gardens and almost in at the back doors.

Harrison's Row was a cut-off place in that not many people knew about it unless they were familiar with the district. You went to it along St. Peter's Street, and down

---

1. stockingers *n.*: Stocking weavers.

2. River Amazon: The largest, most powerful river in South America.

HILLSIDE IN WALES (detail)
L.S. Lowry
The Tate Gallery, London

Leen Place. But it was delightful for the kids who lived there because out of the back gardens they could go straight into the stream of the Leen. In summer an old tin hip bath would come from one of the houses. Using it for a boat, and stripped to their white skins, the children were happy while sun and weather lasted.

The youths and older kids would eschew this fun and set out in a gang, going far beyond, to a bend of the canal near Wollaton Pit where the water was warm—almost hot —due to some outlet from the mine itself. This place was known as "'otties," and they'd stay all day with a bottle of lemonade and a piece of bread, coming back late in the evening looking pink and tired as if out of a prolonged dipping in the ritual bath. But a swim in 'otties was only for the older ones, because a boy of four had once been drowned there.

Harrison's Row was the last of Nottingham where it met the countryside. Its houses were at the very edge of the city, in the days before those numerous housing estates had been built beyond. The line of dwellings called Harrison's Row made a sort of outpost bastion before the country began.

Yet the houses in the city didn't immediately start behind, due to gardens and a piece of wasteground, which gave to Harrison's Row a feeling of isolation. It stood somewhat on its own, as if the city intended one day to leapfrog over it and obliterate the country beyond.

On the other hand, any foreign army attacking from the west, over the green fields that glistened in front, would first have to flatten Harrison's Row before getting into the innumerable streets of houses behind.

Across the Leen, horses were sometimes to be seen in the fields and, in other fields beyond, the noise of combine harvesters could be heard at work in the summer. Children living there, and adults as well, had the advantage of both town and country. On a fine evening late in August one of the unemployed husbands might be seen looking across at the noise of some machinery working in a field, his cap on but wearing no shirt, as if wondering why he was here and not over there, and why in fact he had ever left those same fields in times gone by to be forced into this bit of a suburb where he now had neither work nor purpose in life. He was not bitter, and not much puzzled perhaps, yet he couldn't help being envious of those still out there in the sunshine.

The Fiddle   1269

Humanities Note

Fine art: Detail, *Hillside in Wales,* by L.S. Lowry. The British artist Laurence Stephen Lowry (1887–1976) is best remembered for his simple and highly personal industrial landscapes populated with antlike figures. He was educated at the Municipal College of Art in Manchester and the Salford School of Art. His work was nationally famous in his lifetime and is now in the collections of leading museums.

The painting *Hillside in Wales* is one of his panoramic, detached views of the countryside. The canvas is packed with visual information presented in a deliberately naive way. The dots of people scurrying about, the rows of houses, the rushing river, and the hillside beyond all work together to form this patchwork commentary on modern life.

You might use the following questions for discussion:

1. What statement is the artist attempting to make with this landscape?
2. What is the effect of the seemingly naive technique of this painting?

5 Discussion What does the dropping of the *h* tells us about the people of Harrison Row?

6 Clarification Wasteground is land that may have once had a building on it or was used for another purpose but because of misuse can no longer be used at all.

7 Reading Strategy What does this image tell us about the future of Nottingham?

8 Critical Thinking and Reading Of what is the stark contrast between the green countryside and Harrison Row a symbol?

9 Discussion Why do you think that this man wasn't bitter?

10

10 Discussion What effect does the revelation that the narrator is the author have on the story?

11 Reading Strategy What is ironic about Ted's arrest?

12 Enrichment Part of the reason that the Industrial Revolution took place in this area was that rich coal veins supplied the fuel for the new machinery.

13 Clarification *Brilliantine* is "a dressing that makes hair look glossy, almost like patent leather."

14 Literary Focus What effect does this parenthetical anecdote have on your understanding of the setting?

15 Discussion Why did deaf Mrs. Deaffy enjoy Jeff's music so much?

16 Clarification An escarpment is a very steep side of a hill or rock.

17 Discussion What might you infer about Jeff from this passage?

---

10 In my visions of leaving Nottingham for good—and they were frequent in those days—I never reckoned on doing so by the high road or railway. Instead I saw myself wading or swimming the Leen from Harrison's Row, and setting off west once I was on the other side.

A tale remembered with a laugh at that time told about how young Ted Griffin, who had just started work, saw two policemen one day walking down Leen Place towards Harrison's Row. Convinced they had come to arrest him for meter-breaking, he ran through the house and garden, went over the fence, jumped into the Leen—happily not much swollen—waded across to the field, then four-legged it over the railway, and made his way to Robins Wood a mile or so beyond. A perfect escape route. He stayed two days in hiding, and then crept home at night, famished and soaked, only to find that the police had not come for him, but to question Blonk next door, who was suspected of poaching. When they did get Ted Griffin **11** he was pulled out of bed one morning even before he'd had time to open his eyes and think about a spectacular escape across the Leen.

12 Jeff Bignal was a young unmarried man of twenty-four. His father had been killed in the Great War,[3] and he lived with his mother at Number Six Harrison's Row, and worked down nearby Radford Pit. He was short in height, and plump, his white skin scarred back and front with livid blue patches where he had been knocked with coal at the mine **13** face. When he went out on Saturday night he brilliantined his hair.

After tea in summer while it was still light and warm he would sit in his back garden playing the fiddle, and when he did everybody else came out to listen. Or they opened the doors and windows so that the sound of his music drifted in, while the woman stayed at the sink or wash-copper,

---

3. Great War: World War I.

or the man at his odd jobs. Anyone with a wireless would turn it down or off.

Even tall dark sallow-faced elderly Mrs. Deaffy (a kid sneaked into her kitchen one day and thieved her last penny-packet of cocoa and she went crying to tell Mrs. Atkin who, when her youngest came in, hit him so hard with her elbow that one of his teeth shot out and the blood washed away most of the cocoa-stains around his mouth)—old **14** Mrs. Deaffy stood by her back door as if she weren't stone deaf any more and could follow each note of Jeffrey Bignal's exquisite violin. She smiled at seeing everyone occupied, fixed or entranced, and therefore no **15** torment to herself, which was music enough to her whether she could hear it or not.

And Blonk, in the secretive dimness of the kitchen, went on mending his poaching nets before setting out with Arthur Bede next door on that night's expedition to Gunthorpe by the banks of the Trent, where the green escarpment between there and Knee- **16** ton was riddled with warrens and where, so it was said, if you stood sufficiently still the rabbits ran over your feet, and it was only necessary to make a quick grab to get one.

Jeff sat on a chair, oblivious to everybody, fed up with his day's work at the pit and only wanting to lose himself in his own music. The kids stopped splashing and shouting in the water, because if they didn't they might get hauled in and clouted with just the right amount of viciousness to suit the crime and the occasion. It had happened before, though Jeff had always been too far off to notice.

His face was long, yet generally cheerful—contrary to what one would expect—a smile settling on it whenever he met and passed anybody on the street, or on his way to the group of shared lavatories at the end of the Row. But his face was almost down and lost to the world as he sat on his chair and brought forth his first sweet notes of a summer's evening.

It was said that a neighbor in the last place they had lived had taught him to play **17**

Grammar in Action

Although it must be used sparingly, the **passive voice** is acceptable when the doer of an action is of little importance and the emphasis is naturally on the recipient of the action. The passive voice is acceptable, and probably desirable, in all three of the following excerpts.

Across the Leen, horses were sometimes to be seen in the fields and, in other fields beyond, the noise of combine harvesters could be heard at work in the summer. (page 1269)

The reception was held at the chapel on St. Peter's Street, which seemed to be a sort of halfway house . . .(page 1272)

. . . and not long afterwards meat as well as nearly everything else was put on the ration. (page 1272) like that. Others maintained it was an uncle who had shown him how. But nobody knew for sure because when someone asked directly he said that if he had any gift at all it must have come from God above. It was known that on some Sundays of the year, if the sun was out, he went to the Methodist chapel on St. Peter's Street.

He could play anything from "Greensleeves" to "Mademoiselle from Armentières'." He could do a beautiful heart-pulling version of Handel's *Largo,* and throw in bits from *The Messiah* as well. He would go from one piece to another with no rhyme or reason, from ridiculousness to sublimity, with almost shocking abruptness, but as the hour or so went by it all appeared easy and natural, part of a long piece coming from Jeff Bignal's fiddle while the ball of the sun went down behind his back.

To a child it seemed as if the songs lived in the hard collier's muscle at the top of his energetic arm, and that they queued one by one to get out. Once free, they rushed along his flesh from which the shirtsleeves had been rolled up, and split into his fingertips, where they were played out with ease into the warm evening air.

The grass in the fields across the stream was livid and lush, almost blue, and a piebald horse stood with bent head, eating oats out of a large old pram whose wheels had long since gone. The breeze wafted across from places farther out, from Robins Wood and the Cherry Orchard, Wollaton Roughs and Bramcote Hills and even, on a day that was not too hot, from the tops of the Pennines in Derbyshire.

Jeff played for himself, for the breeze against his arm, for the soft hiss of the flowing Leen at the end of the garden, and maybe also for the horse in the field, which took no notice of anything and which, having grown tired of its oats in the pram, bent its head over the actual grass and began to roam in search of succulent pastures.

In the middle of the winter Jeff's fiddling was forgotten. He went into the coal mine before it was light, and came up only after it had got dark. Walking down Leen Place, he complained to Blonk that it was hard on a man not to see daylight for weeks at a time.

"That's why I wain't go anywhere near the bleddy pit," Blonk said vehemently, though he had worked there from time to time, and would do so again when harried by his wife and children. "You'd do better to come out on a bit o' poaching with me and Arthur," he suggested.

It was virtually true that Jeff saw no daylight, because even on Sunday he stayed in bed most of the day, and if it happened to be dull there was little enough sky to be seen through his front bedroom window, which looked away from the Leen and up the hill.

The upshot of his complaint was that he would do anything to change such a situation. A man was less than an animal for putting up with it.

"I'd do anything," he repeated to his mother over his tea in the single room downstairs.

"But what, though?" she asked. "What can you do, Jeff?"

"Well, how do I know?" he almost snapped at her. "But I'll do summat,[4] you can be sure of that."

He didn't do anything till the weather got better and life turned a bit sweeter. Maybe this improvement finally got him going, because it's hard to help yourself towards better things when you're too far down in the dumps.

On a fine blowy day with both sun and cloud in the sky Jeff went out in the morning, walking up Leen Place with his fiddle under his arm. The case had been wiped and polished.

In the afternoon he came back without it.

"Where's your fiddle?" Ma Jones asked.

He put an awkward smile on to his pale face, and told her: "I sold it."

---

4. summat: Something.

The Fiddle 1271

---

18 Discussion Why is this image of how Jeff's music is produced appropriate for a child of this district?

19 Clarification A piebald horse has black-and-white patches.

20 Reading Strategy What "anything" do you predict he will do to change his life?

Who sees the horses, holds the reception, or puts meat on the ration does not matter at all. Therefore, it is reasonable to use the passive voice to focus on what is seen, what is held, and what is rationed.

Student Activity 1. Find another sentence Sillitoe framed in the passive voice and rewrite it actively. What is the difference between your active-voice sentence and his passive one? Which is better?

Student Activity 2. Write a sentence in the active voice recalling a personal memory that seems to be passing into legend. Now rewrite it using the passive voice. What changes in effect can you find between the two sentences?

21 Reading Strategy Predict how he will change his life with four quid.

22 Discussion Comment on the use of *rattled* here. Would the verb *traveled* be as effective?

23 Discussion Why would a look on his face make people question whether he would be able to play the violin again?

24 Discussion Why were the people amazed at how easy Jeff's transition had been?

25 Enrichment Chitterlings are the smaller intestines of a pig or other edible animal, and black pudding is a dessert made with blood. Both are considered delicacies or special treats by some segments of the British population.

26 Discussion What was an advantage to the loss of Jeff's music?

27 Reading Strategy What do you think happened to Jeff?

Reader's Response Why do you think people sometimes surrender their dreams and hopes?

Master Teacher Note Place Art Transparency 17, *Beulah Road* by Eric Holt, on the overhead projector. You might mention that Holt is a contemporary British artist who has won praise and fame for his representations of British life today. When students have had a chance to look at this painting, ask them to offer their opinions on what the artist was trying to express. How does the painting compare with Sillitoe's story? When the story and painting are considered together, what impression of contemporary British society do the students get?

"Well I never! How much for?"

He was too shocked at her brazen question not to tell the truth: "Four quid."

"That ain't much."

"It'll be enough," he said roughly.

21 | "Enough for what, Jeff?"

22 | He didn't say, but the fact that he had sold his fiddle for four quid rattled up and down the line of cottages till everybody knew of it. Others swore he'd got ten pounds for it, because something that made such music must be worth more than a paltry four, and in any case Jeff would never say how much he'd really got for it, for fear that someone would go in and rob him.

They wondered why he'd done it, but had to wait for the answer, as one usually does. But there was nothing secretive about Jeff Bignal, and if he'd sold his music for a mess of pottage he saw no point in not letting them know why. They'd find out sooner or later, anyway.

All he'd had to do was make up his mind, and he'd done that lying on his side at the pit face while ripping coal out with his pick and shovel. Decisions made like that can't be undone, he knew. He'd brooded on it all winter, till the fact of having settled it seemed to have altered the permanent expression of his face, and given it a new look **23** which caused people to wonder whether he would ever be able to play the fiddle again anyway—at least with his old spirit and dash.

With the four quid he paid the first week's rent on a butcher's shop on Denman Street, and bought a knife, a chopper, and a bit of sharpening stone, as well as a wooden block. Maybe he had a quid or two more knocking around, though if he had it couldn't have been much, but with four quid and a slice of bluff he got enough credit from a wholesaler at the meat market downtown to stock his shop with mutton and beef, and in a couple of days he was in trade. The **24** people of Harrison's Row were amazed at how easy it was, though nobody had ever thought of doing it themselves.

Like a serious young man of business Mr. Bignal—as he was now known—parted his hair down the middle, so that he didn't look so young any more, but everyone agreed that it was better than being at Radford Pit. They'd seen how he had got fed up with selling the sweat of his brow.

No one could say that he prospered, but they couldn't deny that he made a living. And he didn't have to suffer the fact of not seeing daylight for almost the whole of the winter.

Six months after opening the shop he got married. The reception was held at the chapel on St. Peter's Street, which seemed to be a sort of halfway house between Harrison's Row on the banks of the Leen and the butcher's shop on Denman Street farther up.

Everybody from Harrison's Row was invited for a drink and something to eat; but he knew them too well to let any have either chops or chitterlings (or even black puddings) on tick[5] when they came into his **25** shop.

The people of Harrison's Row missed the sound of his fiddle on long summer evenings, though the children could splash and shout with their tin bathtub undisturbed, **26** floundering through shallows and scrambling up to grass on the other bank, and wondering what place they'd reach if they walked without stopping till it got dark.

Two years later the Second World War began, and not long afterwards meat as well as nearly everything else was put on the ration. Apart from which, Jeff was only twenty-six, so got called up into the army. **27** He never had much chance to make a proper start in life, though people said that he came out all right in the end.

The houses of Harrison's Row were condemned as unfit to live in, and a bus depot stands on the site.

---

5. tick: Credit.

Closure and Extension

ANSWERS TO THINKING ABOUT THE SELECTION
Recalling

1. (a) The story takes place during the depression, one hundred years after the Industrial Revolution. (b) Harrison's Row is in Radford, a suburb of Nottingham. (c) The Rad-

ford mine is very near where he lives.

2. (a) The younger children swim in an old tin hip bath or the River Leen when the water ebbs a bit in the summer. (b) The water in the river rises and turns it into a dangerous torrent. (c) The older swimmers go to a bend in the canal near the Wollaton Pit; the water is warm because of some outlet from the mine itself.

3. (a) Jeff says that his ability is a gift

The packed mass of houses on the hill behind—forty years after Jeff Dignal sold his violin—is also vanishing, and high-rise hencoops (as the people call them) are put in their place. The demolition crew knock down ten houses a day—though the foreman told me there was still work for another two years.

28

Some of the houses would easily have lasted a few more decades, for the bricks were perfect, but as the foreman went on:

"You can't let them stand in the way of progress"—whatever that means.

The people have known each other for generations but, when they are moved to their new estates and blocks of flats,[6] they will know each other for generations more, because as I listen to them talking, they speak a language which, in spite of everything and everyone, never alters.

29

___

6. flats: Apartments.

28 Discussion How is the demolition of the houses on Harrison Row "in the way of progress" related to Jeff Bignal's act of selling his fiddle?

29 Discussion What is the relationship between Jeff Bignal's music and the "language" of the people of Harrison's Row?

___

(Answers begin on p. 1272.)

THINKING ABOUT THE SELECTION

Recalling

1. (a) What is the time, or era, of the events in this story? (b) In what city is Harrison's Row? (c) In what section of the city is the mine in which Jeff Bignal works?
2. (a) Where do the younger children swim? (b) Why do they not swim there after a heavy rain? (c) Where do the older children swim?
3. (a) Whom does Jeff Bignal credit for his ability to play the violin? (b) Whom do his neighbors credit?
4. (a) What does Jeff finally do with his fiddle? (b) Why does he do this?

Interpreting

5. Why is the River Leen important to the people of Harrison's Row?
6. Why is the fiddle important to Jeff Bignal?
7. (a) How does Jeff rebel against his situation in life? (b) How does Blonk rebel?
8. Why will Jeff not extend credit to the people from Harrison's Row?
9. (a) What do you think the fiddle symbolizes? (b) How does this symbol help reveal the story's theme?

Applying

10. (a) What do you think of Jeff's decision to sell his fiddle? (b) How happy do you think Jeff's butcher shop made him? Explain.

ANALYZING LITERATURE

Understanding Setting

Setting is the time and place in which the events in a literary work occur. In "The Fiddle" Alan Sillitoe describes the physical setting of Harrison's Row and the activities that formerly went on there. The entire first section of the story establishes the setting. You learn a great deal about Harrison's Row before you learn anything at all about the protagonist, Jeff Bignal. The setting helps to define the people in the story.

1. The narrator is deeply interested in the history and geography of Harrison's Row. Nevertheless, he says that "no one knew who Harrison had been, and no one was ever curious about it. Neither did they know where the Leen came from, though some had a general idea as to where it finished up." How do those details about the setting help to characterize the people who live in Harrison's Row?
2. The brief last section of the story returns to the setting. How do you think the narrator feels about a bus depot standing on the site of Harrison's Row and the construction of "high rise hencoops"? Explain.
3. Slang is highly informal language that is appropriate among friends or in casual situations. (a) Find three examples of slang in "The Fiddle." (b) How does the use of slang add local color to the story?

The Fiddle 1273

More About the Author In terms of her fiction, Margaret Drabble's involvement in the theater and with acting is more than a mere biographical footnote. Drabble, who acted with the Royal Shakespeare Company, learned important strategies for creating convincing characterization on the stage. This ability to draw upon experience and theatrical artifice to create characters has undoubtedly enriched her fictional portraits. In writing the play *Bird of Paradise* (1969) and several screenplays for film and for television, Drabble directly calls upon theatrical training in order to bring believable, dynamic characters to life. In writing fiction, Drabble indirectly employs theatrical technique in her attentiveness to details of dress, gesture, speech, mood, atmosphere, and setting. Her work contains direct references to theater as well. For example, the main character in her novel *The Garrick Year* (1964) marries an actor in a theater company. Drabble's images and rich adjective-filled descriptions bring forth characters that, for a moment, live on the page. Discuss how an understanding of theater and acting might affect a writer's work.

Critical Evaluation The literary scholar Virginia K. Beards wrote that "Margaret Drabble's bleak pessimism regarding love, marriage, and the casual disasters besetting the female locked into heterosexuality and a less radical life style is the focus of her first five novels, written since 1964. Published and praised in England, she seems little read in the United States, a transatlantic reader's loss, since the currency of her vision is remarkable."

MARGARET DRABBLE

1939–

If Margaret Drabble had not become a novelist, she might have become a famous actress. While at Cambridge University she concentrated on the theater and at one point played opposite the noted actor Derek Jacobi. Upon graduation, she joined the Royal Shakespeare Company, understudying Vanessa Redgrave as Imogen in *Cymbeline*. She then left the theater, began writing fiction, and succeeded so well in her new career that a critic in 1980 observed, "She is becoming the novelist people will turn to a hundred years from now to find out how things were. . . ."

Born in Sheffield, Drabble came from a cultured and well-educated family. Her father was a circuit judge and her mother an English teacher. "A fiery child with a hyperactive mind," according to her mother, Margaret attended a Quaker boarding school prior to Cambridge. After college, she abandoned the theater for motherhood. While she was pregnant with the first of her three children, she began to write fiction. Her first novel, *A Summer Bird-Cage,* was published in 1962. Over the years she has continued to write novels that have gained both critical and popular success. Among her best-known works are *The Millstone* (1965), *The Waterfall* (1969), *The Realms of Gold* (1975), and *The Middle Ground* (1980). Most of Drabble's protagonists are, like their creator, well-educated professional women: scholars, poets, journalists.

Sociable, composed, and levelheaded, Drabble is in great demand for interviews and personal appearances. In the fall of 1980, she received a great honor when the Queen Mother dubbed her a Commander of the British Empire. Although she possesses enormous creative energy, Drabble does not regard herself as remarkable, but—in keeping with her themes—"ordinary" and fortunate. She is a clear and perceptive writer whose dry humor, and penetrating technical skill have become the hallmarks of her style. Her work has steadily flowered; many critics and readers believe that in its maturity it will achieve greatness.

Drabble, in commenting on her own work, declares that she is firmly committed to the realistic tradition of the nineteenth century. Although sometimes called a "women's novelist," she disavows feminism as a theme, believing that equal rights and opportunity for women are part of a larger whole. She maintains that her fundamental concerns are "privilege, justice, and salvation." Working in the literary tradition of Jane Austen, Charlotte Brontë, and George Eliot, she creates brilliantly realized characters who reflect the dilemmas of women in the modern world, women who are trying to integrate the demands of family life and a career.

1274   Contemporary Writers

GUIDE FOR INTERPRETING

A Voyage to Cythera

Writer's Techniques

Flat and Round Characters. A flat character, sometimes called a stereotype or stock character, is a one-dimensional human being in literature. For example, in "The Schartz-Metterklume Method," Saki does not portray the Quabarls family in depth. It is their very shallowness, in fact, that he wishes to satirize. He has therefore made them flat characters, or stereotypes. They do not change in the course of the story, and they contribute to the plot in a predictable way.

The fictional opposite of a flat character is a round character. A round character is a three-dimensional portrait that readers can accept as resembling an actual person. The writer may provide a detailed description of the character. More important, the writer will reveal the character's motivations, emotions, and inner conflicts. Round characters may be complex, unpredictable, and inconsistent, just like real people. In narrative fiction they are generally *dynamic*—that is, they change or grow in some way during the story. (Flat characters are *static*—they do not change or grow.) An example of a round character in a short story is Margaret in Doris Lessing's "A Mild Attack of Locusts."

Writing

An epigraph is a quotation at the beginning of a book, chapter, or story. Read the epigraph to Margaret Drabble's story carefully. Then brainstorm for several minutes on the associations and emotions suggested by this fragment of Rilke's poetry. Jot down your impressions of what the epigraph (and the story's title) may suggest about the narrative to follow.

Primary Source

Margaret Drabble's comments in *A Woman Writer* relate closely to the dilemma that Helen, the main character in "A Voyage to Cythera," faces. Drabble thinks that the large amount of fiction written by women recently shows that "a lot of women worry about the same things at the same time, and turned to fiction to express their anxieties—not only because . . . they still had nowhere else to turn, but also because fiction is ideally suited to such themes. . . . Many people read novels in order to find patterns or images for a possible future—to know how to behave, what to hope to be like. We do not want to resemble the women of the past, but where is our future. . . . We live in an uncharted world, as far as manners and morals are concerned, we are having to make up our own morality as we go. Our subject matter is enormous, there are whole new patterns to create."

Guide for Interpreting 1275

Literary Focus Point out that characterization is the way a writer chooses to reveal characters. A writer may reveal what a character is like through dialogue, description, and narration. Explain to students that they may learn what characters are like by carefully reading details in a story. For example, what does a character look like? How does he or she dress? What does a character say? How does he or she speak? What does a character think and feel? What actions does a character take? To create a round character, a writer provides details. When a writer provides few details, then the character is more likely a flat character. Point out that both flat and round characters appear in "A Voyage to Cythera."

Vocabulary

Preteach the following vocabulary words:
piazzas (pē az′əs) *n.:* Open public squares (p. 1276)
irrepressible (ir′i pres′ə b′l) *adj.:* Not able to be restrained (p. 1277)
solace (säl′is) *n.:* Comfort in grief or trouble (p. 1280)
divination (div′ə nā′shən) *n.:* Clever guess (p. 1280)
intimation (in′tə mā′shən) *n.:* Hint (p. 1281)
anterior (an tir′ē ər) *adj.:* At or toward the front (p. 1285)

1

A Voyage to Cythera[1]
Margaret Drabble

Beloved, lost to begin with, never greeted,
I do not know what tones most please you.
No more when the future's wave
hangs poised is it you I try to discern there.
All the greatest images in me,
far-off experienced landscape,
towers and towns and bridges and
unsuspected turns of the way,
and the power of those lands
once intertwined with the life of the gods:
mount up within me to mean you,
who forever elude.

Oh, you are the garden. . . .
—_Rainer Maria Rilke_[2]

2

3,4

There are some people who cannot get onto a train without imagining that they are about to voyage into the significant unknown; as though the notion of movement were inseparably connected with the notion of discovery, as though each displacement of the body were a displacement of the soul. Helen was so much this way, and with so little lasting justification, that she was continually surprising herself by the intensity of her expectation; she could get excited by the prospect of any journey longer than 30 miles, and the thought of travel to the Conti-

nent was enough to reduce her to a state of feverish anticipation. The mere mention of the names of certain places would make her tremble, and she was addicted to railway stations, air terminals, ports, motorways, travel brochures, and all other points and emblems of departure. A phrase in a novel could make her feel weak with desire, and when once at the Gare de l'Est[3] in Paris she saw a train with Budapest written on it, she felt her skin tighten and her hair stand on end. Her most erotic dreams were not of men but of places; she would dream of piazzas and marble fountains, of mountains and terraces with great lumps of baroque statuary, of great buildings abandoned in green fields, and she would wake from these dreams cold with the sweat of fading passion. There was a certain angle of road that never failed to affect her, whenever she approached it: a rising angle, with a bare empty curve breasting infinity, the blue-sky space of infinity. She always felt that the sea might lie beyond such rising nothingness, and sometimes it was the sea, but more often it was the Caledonian[4] Market or a row of Hampstead houses; though whatever it was was somehow irrelevant, for it was that tense moment of expectation before revelation that she so much cherished.

Once she talked of this preoccupation of hers to a much-traveled old man, and he said that she felt this way because whenever

5

6

7

---

1. **Cythera** (si thir′ ə): A Greek island, near which the Greek goddess of love, Aphrodite, was supposed to have arisen full-grown from the sea.
2. **Rainer Maria Rilke:** A German poet (1875–1926). The lines are from an untitled poem by Rilke.

3. **Gare de l'Est** (gär də lest): A Paris train station.
4. **Caledonian:** Scottish.

she went to a new place she hoped to fall in love. He had been the same, he said; restless, expectant; and she knew that he was telling the truth, for his life illustrated his explanation. "When I was young," he said, "I thought there was a woman waiting for me in every railway compartment, on every airplane, in every hotel. How can one not think this? One thinks the plane will crash, and that one will die, and that one must die in the arms of the woman in the next seat. Isn't that so?"

And she had, in a way, thought that it was so, though the truth was that she herself would never fall in love in any of these temporary places, for she could not speak to strangers. Though that in itself proved nothing, for she supposed that nevertheless she might one day do so, and that it might be for this one moment of sudden communication that she so persistently sought. People spoke to her, from time to time, but always the wrong people, always the motherly and the fatherly men and the dull irrepressible youths. Her own kind did not speak to her, nor she to them. She traveled once overnight from Milan, alone in a compartment with a girl who was reading the same book she herself was reading; a book both of them might have been proud to acknowledge and not a word did they exchange. Another time, in a crowded train from Edinburgh, she sat opposite a woman who started to weep as the train left the station; she wept silently and effortlessly for hours, great tears rolling down her white cheeks into the neck of her emerald-green sweater, and at York Helen offered her a cigarette, and she declined it, and ceased weeping. On another occasion a man kissed her in a corridor as they drew into Oxford; she liked him, he was a lovely man, but he was drunk and she turned away her face and turned up the collar of her coat.

And yet despite these wasted opportunities she continued to expect. Truly, she thought to herself, as she got into the London train at Reading Station late one cold night, truly, it is a proof of madness that the prospect of this journey should not appall. It is cold, the train is half an hour late, I am hungry; this is the kind of situation about which I hear my friends most tirelessly and tiresomely complain. And yet I am looking forward to it. I shall sit here in the dark and the cold, with nothing to watch but the reflection of my own face in the cold pane, and I shall not care. As soon as the train moves, I shall sit back, and feel it move with me, and feel that I am moving, although I know quite well that all I am doing is going back home again to an empty flat.[5] There will be rain and steam on the glass of this window by my face, and I shall look at it, and that will be all. What a hardened case I am, that such dull mileage should recall those other landscapes, those snowy precipices, those sunny plains, those fields of corn, those gritty swaying breakfasts in the pale light of transient Switzerland or angel-watched Marseilles. I am a child, I like to rock and dream, I dream as if I were in a cradle.

And she shut her eyes, waiting for the whistle and the metallic connections of machinery; so with her eyes shut she did not see the man come into the compartment, and could never know for certain whether he had seen her, whether he had joined her because he had wanted to join her. All she knew was that when she opened her eyes, aware of the intrusion, aware of the draft from the opened door, he was already there, putting his overcoat up on the rack, arranging his books and papers on the seat next to him, settling himself in the empty compartment as far away from her as he could, on the corridor side, diagonally opposite, where she could not fail to watch him. She turned her fur collar up defensively against her face, and arranged her legs more tidily together, and opened her book upon her knee, disclaiming all threat of human contact, coldly repelling any acknowledgment of her

---

5. flat *n.*: Apartment.

8 Critical Thinking and Reading What sort of person is Helen? How do you know? Is the evidence given direct or indirect?

9 Critical Thinking and Reading Discuss Helen's travel experiences. Explain how this passage reveals her attitude toward travel either directly or indirectly.

10 Literary Focus How does Helen describe herself? What do you think she is like? Is Helen a flat or a round character? Explain your answer.

Humanities Note

Fine art, *Shunters,* 1965, by James Dolby. Dolby (1909–1975) was a British wood engraver and teacher. Educated at the Keighly School of Art and the Royal Academy of Art, Dolby taught art at many of England's prestigious schools. He is best known for his pioneering efforts to revive the ancient art of wood engraving. Wood engraving was one of the earliest means of reproducing words and images. Designs are incised in a block of soft wood with a sharp tool. The blocks are then inked and pressed onto paper, leaving a black-and-white image. With the advent of photography this method of reproduction fell into disuse. Its revival in the twentieth century is strictly as a fine art form.

Works such as *Shunters* show us how modern images and style can effectively use the technique of wood engraving. The forms of the train and station are executed in a sharp, simplified style, which pares the shapes into geometric components. The striking black-and-white image produced by the engraving complements the streamlined spareness of the work. A benefit of this technique is that it allows the artist to produce multiple copies of the work. The result is an original art form that is more affordable to the public than a painting.

Consider using this question for discussion: How does this engraving convey a sense of urgency and motion?

SHUNTERS 1965
James Dolby

1278   *Contemporary Writers*

Primary Source Note

Nancy S. Hardin, who interviewed Margaret Drabble, said that she "is a warm and friendly person with an intense quality that finds expression both in her demeanor and her works. It seems appropriate that her concern is frequently, among other things, with 'the holiness of the heart's affections,' for there is a kinship between her and the early nineteenth-century romantic writers who tended to give primacy to emotion over reason and who honestly trusted their inner perceptions. She is equally in tune with those later nineteenth-century novelists whose world involves predestined paths and fate. Yet, she is also very much of her own time, and her characters and their self-confrontations are burdened with choices relevant to the 1960s and 1970s. . . ."

presence, and all the time she watched him discreetly through her half-shut eyes. Because the truth was that not since she was 17, more years ago than she cared to think, had she sat on a train so near to such a man. When she was 17 she had sat in a compartment with an actor, on the late night train to Brighton, and he had talked to her all the way, and amused her by imitating Laurence Olivier[6] for her and other famous men whom she did not recognize and when they had parted on the station he had kissed her soft and girlish and impressionable cheek, and murmured, "Bless you, bless you," as though he had a right to bless. She had subsequently followed his unremarkable career, catching sight of his name in the *Radio Times*, admiring him once on the television, glimpsing him as he passed on the cinema screen; she felt quietly possessive about him, quietly amused by her sense of intimacy with one who must so long ago have forgotten her, and who would hardly now recognize her from what she then had been. Sometimes she wondered idly whether her preoccupation with journeys might not date from this experience; but chronologically this was not so, for her preoccupation had long preceded it. She had been this way since childhood, when she had shrunk and trembled at the sight of the huge pistons, when she had stopped her ears in delighted terror as she heard the roar of the approaching seaside train.

This man, this night, did not look as though he wished to amuse her with imitations of Laurence Olivier. He looked preoccupied. In fact, the more she watched him, the more she realized that he was almost grotesquely preoccupied. He was restless; he could not sit still: he kept picking up one book from his pile, then another, then turning over the pages of his *New Statesman*, then staring out into the corridor and onto the dark platform. At first she thought that he might be waiting for someone to come, half-expecting somebody to join him, but she decided that this was not so, for she could perceive no augmenting of his anxiety as the time drew on, no sudden start when the loudspeaker apologized for the delay and said that the train would leave in two minutes; nor did his nervousness seem to be directed toward the door and the platform, as it would have been had he been waiting. She recalled that she herself had once developed a dreadful pain in the neck from sitting with her neck to the window through which she knew that she might glimpse the first sign of a long-awaited arrival. But this man's nervousness was as it were diffused, rather than directed; it attached itself to nothing and to everything. She could not take her eyes off him, and not only because of the nakedness of his condition, which in another might have appeared merely ludicrous; indeed, embarrassment would have turned away her eyes, had it not been for the extreme elegance of his gestures, and the lovely angles into which each struggle against immobility brought him. There was the way he had of clutching his eyebrows with one wide-spanned long nicotine-fingered hand that filled her with an intense delight; the hand covered the eyes, bringing to him no doubt an illusion of concealment, but she could see beneath it the anxious movement of the lips, trembling with some expression that she could not catch, with speech or smiling or perhaps with a sigh. And as he made this gesture, each time, he tossed his head slightly backward, and then again forward, so that his long hair fell tenderly over his fingers. It was the color that she had always liked, but she had never before seen it adorning such vexed, haggard, and experienced features: for it was a dark gold, the color of health and innocence. It was a dark golden yellow, and it was streaked with gray. It was soft hair, and it fell gently.

---

6. Laurence Olivier: A famous British actor (1907–1989).

11 **Reading Strategy** How old do you think Helen is?

12 **Enrichment** Margaret Drabble's own involvement in theater is evoked in this passage. The man that Helen met on a train long ago was an actor who entertained her with impressions; she followed his career on radio, television, and in films.

13 **Literary Focus** Describe the man on the train in your own words. Is he a flat or a round character? How do you know?

14 **Clarification** The *New Statesman* is a British journal that began publication in 1913. It is a review that frequently expresses political views of the left.

15 **Critical Thinking and Reading** How does Helen feel about the man on the train? How do you know? Is the evidence given direct or indirect?

16 **Discussion** What is Helen's interpretation of the man's emotions? Why does Helen find washing cups and emptying bins comforting?

17 Critical Thinking and Reading What significance do the letters hold for Helen? Is Helen's assumption based on direct or indirect evidence?

18 Discussion Why does Helen weep? Whom do you think Helen is actually describing?

19 Critical Thinking and Reading What do you infer that the man is doing? What kind of evidence is given to help you make this inference?

When the train moved off, he flung himself back into his corner, and shut his eyes, with an appearance of resolution, as though his own restlessness had finally begun to irritate him: as though he had decided to sit still. Helen looked out of the window by her face, into the lights and darkness of the disappearing town. In one piece of glass she could see the reflection of his face, and she watched it, quite confidently aware that he would not be able to keep his eyes shut, and after a few minutes he was leaning forward in his seat once more, his elbows on his knees, staring at the ground. Then, even as she watched, she saw a thought strike him: she saw the conception of the idea, she saw him reach into his pocket and take out a pack of cigarettes and a box of matches, and abstract a cigarette, and light it, all with the dreamy movements of a habitual smoker, and yet with a kind of surprise, for the truth was, as she could so clearly see, that he had even in his abstraction forgotten the possibility of such a trivial solace. As he drew on the cigarette she could see his relief, his gratitude toward his own recollection. The smoke consoled him, and she could feel in her the nature of the consolation: for she herself, when tormented by love, had found comfort in the repetition of small and necessary acts, in washing cups and emptying bins and fastening her stockings and remembering that it was time to have a meal. It seemed clear to her that it was love that was tormenting him: she knew those painful symptoms of disease.

And indeed, ten minutes later, when the ash of his last activity lay scattered all over the floor and all over his trousers, he stood up and got a packet of letters out of his overcoat pocket, and began to read them. He could not more clearly have indicated his malady if he had turned to her and told her what was in his mind. She watched the reflection of his face as he read, ashamed now to watch him directly, though she knew that he could not know that she so keenly watched him, that she was so expert in the intimate language of his state. She felt that she could tell everything from the way he handled those letters: he was still rapt in the first five minutes of love, that brief and indefinite breathless pause before familiarity, affection, disillusion, rot, decay. The number of letters in his hands supported her divination, as well as the quality of his attention; there were five of them, only five, and the paper of them was new, although they were crumbling wearily at the folds from overuse. She felt such pangs, in his presence, of she knew not what: of envy, of regret, of desire. At his age, with those graying strands and those profound wrinkles, he must surely know the folly of his obsession, and the inevitable tragic close before him; and she found such a willful confrontation of pain almost unbearably moving. She herself, enduring daily the painful death of such an attitude, the chilly destination of such deliberately romantic embarkations, could hardly prevent the tears from rising to her eyes; and in fact, they rose, warm in the cold skin of her lids, making her nose prick and her eyes ache, yet warm, coming from within her, and chilling only at the touch of the outside air. Absurd, she said to herself, absurd: absurd to weep. His image turned into a blur, and it was like the image of time itself, human, lovely, perishing, intent.

When he had read and reread his letters, he stood up again, and got a pen out of his coat pocket, and tore a piece of paper off a block of typing paper, and started to write. He wrote slowly, after the first three words, hesitantly, as though what he was saying was of no interest, as though all the interest lay in the way of saying it. She wondered what he was, who he was, what his woman was, and jealously whether she were worth such care. He took a quarter of an hour to write his letter, and when he had finished it he had covered only half a page. She wondered whether he would have an envelope,

Grammar in Action

Express a series of equally weighted items in similar form. Such use of **parallel structure** indicates the equality between the items of the series. Notice how Margaret Drabble uses parallel structure.

. . . he was still rapt in the first five minutes of love, that brief and indefinite breathless pause before familiarity, affection, disillusion, rot, decay.

She felt such pangs, in his presence, of she knew not what: of envy, of regret, of desire.

She wondered what he was, who he was, what his woman was, and jealously whether she were worth such care.

Drabble uses parallel structure here for series of words, phrases, and clauses. The first example consists of abstract nouns, the second of prepositional phrases, and the third of clauses.

Student Activity 1. Locate another sentence in which Drabble uses parallelism in a series. What change in effect would occur if one item in the series were not parallel to the others?

and saw that he had; it was a brown business envelope. He folded his letter up and put it in the envelope, and then sealed it up. She waited for him to write the address, but he did not write the address: he sat there looking down at the small brown oblong, and as he looked at it she became in some indefinable way aware that he had become aware of her own presence, that he was at last considering her, in some significant way. Later, she wondered how this shadowy and delicate intimation could ever have reached her—for reach her it did, and she was one of those who believe that no intimations are too delicate to exist—and she concluded that it could only have been a sudden stillness on his part, a sudden fading of restlessness, as he returned from whatever other place he had been in to contemplate her in her proximity. She felt his attention: she endured it, for five minutes at least, before he spoke.

She was pretending to read when he spoke to her. He said to her, "I wonder, I wonder if you would do something for me?" and she looked up and met his eyes, and found that he was smiling at her with a most peculiar mixture of diffidence and vanity: he was truly nervous at the prospect of speaking to her, and those five silent minutes were a measure of his nervousness, and yet at the same time he had taken the measure of her curiosity and helpless attraction: she knew that he knew that she would like to be addressed. And his tone enchanted her, for it was her own tone: a tone of cool, anxious, irresistible appeal. She knew that he too did not speak often to strangers.

"It depends what it is," she said, smiling back at him with his own smile.

"It's a very simple thing," he said, "not at all incriminating. Or at least, not for you."

"It would be, then, for you?" she said.

"Of course it would," he said. "That's why I'm making the effort of asking you to do it."

"What is it?" she said.

"I wondered if you would address this envelope for me," he said.

"Well, yes," she said. "I don't see any harm in that. I'd do that for you."

"I thought you would do it," he said. "If I hadn't thought that you would, I wouldn't have asked you. I wouldn't have liked it if you had said no."

"I might ask you what it was about me that made you think I would say yes," she said, "but such a question might embarrass you."

"Oh," he said, "oh, no," rising to his feet and crossing to her with the envelope, "oh, no, I don't mind answering, it was because of that book you're reading, and the kind of shoes you're wearing, and the way your hair is. I liked that book when I read it."

And then he sat down by her, and handed her the envelope, and said, "Look, I'll write it down for you and you can copy it. It's hard to hear when people dictate things, isn't it?"

And he wrote the name and address on another piece of his block of paper. He wrote:

> Mrs. H. Smithson,
> 24 Victoria Place,
> London N.W.1.

And Helen dutifully copied it out, on the brown envelope, then handed it back to him.

"I hope," she said, "that my handwriting is sufficiently unlike yours."

"I was thinking," he said, "that after all it's rather similar. But dissimilar enough."

Then he said no more, but he remained sitting by her. She would in a way have preferred him to move, because where he now was she could not really see him, either overtly or covertly. And she had nothing to say to him: for she could hardly have said, I was right about you, I guessed right. He said

20 Reading Strategy Describe in your own words how the man looks at Helen.

21 Discussion Discuss why the man on the train might make this request.

22 Critical Thinking and Reading How did the man know that Helen would carry out his request? Is the evidence given direct or indirect?

23 Discussion Discuss the significance of this address. To whom is the man writing?

24 Clarification A fourpenny stamp is one that costs four pennies. A fourpenny is an old silver coin worth fourpence.

Student Activity 2. Correct these sentences by setting the series in parallel form.

1. The photographer shot several deer, a buck that was young, three fawns, and an old bear.
2. The article will cover the birth of the company, the progress of its development, and how its future outlook seems.
3. The vacationers hiked, sunbathed, went swimming, and talked.

25 Enrichment London is divided into postal units that designate areas by compass direction and by number. For example, *S.W.* refers to southwestern London. Other designations include N.W., N.E., and S.E., for northwest, northeast, and southeast. The numbers in London addresses pinpoint a smaller region within each compass region. Point out that the corollary to these postal divisions in the United States might be the zip code, which indicates state and city locations.

26 Literary Focus What does the dialogue reveal? How do you learn more about each character through their words? Analyze how dialogue helps create round characters.

27 Discussion Compare and contrast Helen's encounter with the man on the train with those "wasted opportunities" for contact on page 1277.

28 Enrichment The Sirens were mythical sea nymphs who lived on a Greek island. The Sirens, part bird and part woman, sang such tempting songs that they lured sailors to their destruction. When the Greek hero Odysseus, the king of Ithaca, was returning home from the Trojan War, he put wax in the sailors' ears so that they would not be tempted by the Sirens' songs. Today the meaning of the word *siren,* a tempting or seductive woman, reflects this tale. Helen alludes to this myth, told by Homer in the *Odyssey,* because she, too, is lured by a beautiful illusion that could potentially harm her. In pursuing the illusion of love, Helen may become as detached from the real world as do the sailors who allow themselves to be lured by the Sirens.

29 Literary Focus Discuss Helen's attempt to give form to Mrs. Smithson. Is Mrs. Smithson a flat or a round character? How do you know?

nothing to her, for a while: he got a wallet from his pocket, and took out a sheet of fourpenny stamps, and tore one off, licked it, and stuck it on. She liked watching his hands, and the way they moved. Then, still holding the letter, he said to her, "Where do you live?"

She must have recoiled slightly from the question, because immediately he followed it up with, "Only, I was meaning, from the point of view of postmarks."

"Oh," she said. "I see. Yes. I live in S.W.7. You want me to post it, do you?"

"Would you mind posting it?" he asked.

"No. I would post it for you," she said.

"You take my point very quickly," he said, then, with some difficulty, looking downward and away from her, hardly able to bring himself to thank her more formally.

"I've had to make such points before myself," she said.

"I thought, somehow, that you would not mind about such things," he said.

"You wouldn't have asked me if you'd thought I minded. Tell me, do you really trust me to remember to post it?"

"Of course I do," he said. "One wouldn't not post a stranger's letter."

And this was so exactly the truth that it silenced her, and they said no more to each other until the train drew into Paddington: and as they walked together off the platform, he said, "Thank you, and good-bye."

And she said, "Good-bye," and she carried the letter in her hand all the way home, and dropped it into the letterbox on her block. Then she went down the basement steps to her dark flat, and she knew that the name and the address, written there in her own writing, so strangely, were imprinted upon her memory forever.

And indeed, over the next month, she sometimes fancied that she thought of little else. She knew that this was not the truth, that it was merely a fancy, because of course she did think of other things; of her job, of her friends, of her mother, of what to buy for supper, of whether she wanted to go to the cinema on Wednesday night. But she did not think of these other things in the mad, romantic, obsessive way that she thought of Mrs. H. Smithson, and the nameless man, and the whole curious, affecting incident: in a sense she resented the incident, because it did so much to vindicate her own crazy expectancy, her foolish faith in revelation. She knew, in her better, saner self, that such faith was foolish, and she suspected that such partial hints of its validity were a delusion, a temptation, and that if she heeded them she would be disabled forever, and disqualified from real life, as Odysseus would have been by the Sirens.[7] And yet at the same time she knew, in her other self, that it was that man she was thinking about, however unreasonably. She looked for him as she walked along the streets of London, and she could not convince herself that it was not for him that she was looking. She speculated about the identity and appearance of Mrs. Smithson, and supplied her endlessly with Christian names, until she remembered that the H. might well have stood for her husband's name, not hers. She speculated about the deceived husband. Although most of her own friends were married and had children, she still found it hard to acknowledge that Mrs. Smithson might well be a woman of her own generation, for the prefix *Mrs.* invariably supplied her with a material image, the image of her own mother: and she would realize from time to time, with a start, that the women that she thought of as mothers were in fact grandmothers, and that the young girls she saw pushing prams on Saturday mornings and quarreling with vigorous toddlers on buses were not in fact elder sisters but mothers,

---

7. **Odysseus . . . Sirens:** In Homer's *Odyssey,* Odysseus, the hero, plugs his ears so that he will not be tempted by the singing of the sirens, sea nymphs whose enchanting songs lured sailors to their deaths on rocky coastlines.

Mrs. Smithson, Mrs. Smithson. She could not give form to Mrs. Smithson.

It was in the week before Christmas that she decided to go and have a look at Mrs. Smithson. The idea occurred to her at lunchtime one day, in the middle of a lunchtime business Christmas party. She stood there, drinking too much and not getting enough to eat, defeated as ever by the problems of buffet technique, and as she listened to a very nice man whom she had known and liked for several years describe to her the felicities of his new central heating, she suddenly decided to go and look at Mrs. Smithson. After all, she said to herself, what could be more harmless, what more undetectable? All I need to do is to knock on her door and ask, say, for Alice. And then I would know. I don't know what I would know, but I would know it. And she smiled at the man, and allowed her glass to be once more filled, and then told him politely all about some other friends of hers whose central heating had entirely ruined all their antique furniture, and split all the antique paneling of their rather priceless house. And as she talked, she was already in her heart on her way to Mrs. Smithson's, already surrendering to the lure of that fraught, romantic, painful world, which seemed to call her, to call her continually from the endurable sorrows of daily existence to some possible other country of the passions, a country where she felt she would recognize, though strange to it, the scenery and landmarks. She thought often of this place, as of some place perpetually existing, and yet concealed: and she could describe it to herself only in terms of myth or allegory, unsatisfactory terms, she felt, and perniciously implanted in her by her classical education. It was a place other than the real world, or what she felt to be the real world, and it was both more beautiful and more valid, though valid in itself only: and it could be entered not at will, but intermittently, by accident, and yet always with some sense of temptation and surrender. Some people, she could see, passed most of their lives in its confines, and governed by its laws only, like that old man, himself a poet, who had first defined for her the nature of her expectations. There were enough of such people in the world to keep alive before her the possibility of a permanent, irreversible entry through those mysteriously inscribed and classic gates: a poet, a drunken Frenchman, a girl she had known who said one day: "I will go to Baghdad," and went. They crossed her path, these people, or their names came to her, garlanded with wreaths of that unfamiliar foliage: Yves was seen in Marseilles carrying a lobster, Esther was seen in a bookshop in New York wearing a fur coat and with diamonds in her hair, Esther was in Marrakesh, living in one room with an Arab. Yves had gone to Ireland and started a lobster farm. Oh, messages from a foreign country, oh, disquieting glimpses of brightness. Helen gulped down the remains of her fourth glass of wine, and looked at her watch, which said that it was five past three; and said to the central-heating man that she must go.

She walked to Victoria Place, pausing dazed at traffic lights, stumbling at each irregularity of the pavement, running her hand idly along grimy railings. It was cold, but she could not feel the cold: her face was burning. She knew her way because she had looked Victoria Place up a month ago, the day after she had posted the letter, in her *A to Z Guide to London:* she remembered the moment when she had done so, because she had pretended to herself that she was doing no such thing, and her mind had not known what her hands and eyes were doing. But her mind now remembered what it had then refused to acknowledge, and she took herself there as though entranced, the trance persisting long after the effects of walking had dispelled the effects of so much drink on so empty a stomach. I must be mad, she said

30 Literary Focus Is the man at the Christmas party a flat or a round character? How do you know?

31 Reading Strategy Summarize the meaning of this passage. Why is Helen fascinated with Mrs. Smithson? What characteristics of "the country of the passions" does Helen describe? What does Helen admire about the people who live there?

32 Discussion Why does Helen feel dazed?

to herself more than once: I must be mad. And at the very end of the journey she began, very slightly, to lose her nerve: she thought that she would not dare to knock upon the door, she thought that perhaps after all only insignificant disaffection could await her, that she could do no more than dispel what had already in its own way been perfection.

But there was no need to knock at the door. Victoria Place, when she reached it, was a short main street of tall terraced houses, either newly recovered or so smart that they had never lapsed: the number 24 was brightly illuminated, shining brightly forth into the gathering darkness. She walked slowly toward it, realizing that she would be able to see whatever there was to see without knocking: realizing that fate had connived with her curiosity by providing a bus stop directly outside the house, so that she could stand there and wait without fear of detection. She took her place at the bus stop, and stood there for a moment before she gathered her courage to turn around, and then she turned. The lights were on in the two lower floors, and she could see straight into the basement, a room which most closely resembled in shape the one where she herself lived. The room seemed at first sight to be full of people, and there was so much activity that it took some time to sort them out. There were two women, and four children; no, five children, for there was a baby sitting in a corner on a blue rug. The larger children were putting up a Christmas tree, and one of the women was laying the table for tea, while the other, her back to the window, one elbow on the mantelpiece, appeared to be reading aloud a passage from a book. It was a large, bright room, with a green carpet, and white walls, and red painted wooden furniture; even the table was painted red. A children's room. It shone, it glittered. A mobile of golden fishes hung from the ceiling, and the carpet was strewn with colored glass and tinsel decorations for the tree. The plates on the table

were blue and white, and the silver knives caught the light; on the mantelpiece stood two many-faceted cut glasses and an open bottle of wine. Two of the children had fair hair, and the other three were dark: and the woman laying the table had red hair, a huge coil of dark red hair from which whole heavy locks escaped, dragging down the back of her neck, falling against her face at each movement, and she moved endlessly, restlessly, vigorously, taking buns out of a bag, slicing bread, pouring black currant juice into beakers, turning to listen to the other woman, and suddenly laughing, throwing back her head with a kind of violence and laughing: and the other woman at the mantelpiece laughed too, her thin shoulders shaking, and the children, irritated by their mother's laughter, flung themselves at her, clinging angrily onto her knees, shouting, until the red-haired woman tried to silence them with slices of bread and butter, which were rejected and flung around the floor: so she followed them up with the iced buns, tossing them round and yet talking, all the time talking, to the other woman and not to the children, intent upon some point, some anecdote too precious to lose, and the children chewed at the buns while she scooped up the torn pieces of bread and bestowed them all, with a smile of such lovely passing affection, upon the baby, a smile so tender and amused and solicitous that Helen, overseeing it, felt her heart stand still.

And as she stood there, out there in the cold, and watched, she felt herself stiffen slowly into the breathlessness of attention: because it seemed to her that she had been given, freely, a vision of something so beautiful that its relevance could not be measured. The hints and arrows that had led her here took on the mysterious significance of fate itself: she felt that everything was joined and drawn together, that all things were part of some pattern of which she caught by sheer chance a sudden hopeful sense: and that those two women, and their children, and the man on the train, and the bright and radiant uncurtained room, an island in the surrounding darkness, were symbols to her of things too vague to name, of happiness, of hope, of brightness, warmth, and celebration. She gazed into that room, where emotion lay, like water unimaginably profound. The red-haired woman was kneeling now, on the green carpet, rubbing with a corner of the tea towel at a buttery mark on the carpet, and at the same time looking up and listening, with an expression upon her face in which vexation with the children, carelessness of her own vexation, and a kind of soft rapt delight in the other woman's company were inextricably confused; and the other woman had turned slightly, so that Helen from the window could see her face, and she was twisting in her hands a length of red-and-silver tinsel, idly pulling shreds from it as she spoke. And Helen thought of all the other dark cold rooms of London and the world, of loneliness, of the blue chilly flickerings of television sets, of sad children, silenced mothers, and unmarried girls and she wondered if so much delight were truly gathered up and concentrated into one place, or whether these windows were not windows through which she viewed the real huge spacious anterior lovely world. And it seemed possible to see them so, because she did not know that house, nor those women, nor their names, nor the name of the man who had led her there: the poetry of inspiration being to a certain extent, as she knew, the poetry of ignorance, and the connections between symbols a destructive folly to draw. She did not even know which of these women was Mrs. Smithson, whom she had come to see, for if one woman had laid the table, the other cleared it, equally at home. She knew nothing, and could therefore believe everything, drawing faith from such a vision, as she had drawn faith from unfamiliar cities: drawing faith from the passionate vision of intimacy, where intimacy itself failed her; as Wordsworth turned from his life to his keener recollec-

tions,[8] and Yeats to lions and towers and hawks.[9]

By the time that one of the children was sent to draw the curtains, she was stiff and white with cold. She turned away, as the child, a small girl with straight dark hair and a face suddenly grave with the weight of her task, began to struggle with the heavy floor-length hangings, shutting inch by inch away from her the colored angles of refracted light, the Christmas tree, the airy fishes, the verdant green, the small angelic innocent faces, the shining spheres of glass, and those two young worn women: and as she turned she felt the first snowflakes of the year settle softly on her skin, and looking up, she saw the dim blue sky full of snow. She glanced back, to see if the child had seen it, but the curtains were already drawn, and she saw nothing but her own image, pale in the glass. So she started to walk down the street, away from the house, away from the bus stop, but before she had taken ten steps a car drew up, just by her side, a slow yard from her, and there was the man from the train, sitting there and looking at her. She paused, and he opened the door, and sitting there still he said to her, "I don't know what to say to you, you look so fragile that a word might hurt you." And she smiled at him, a slow dazed smile, knowing that as he for her, so she for him was some mysterious apparition, some faintly gleaming memorable image: and she turned away, and walked down the street away from him into the snowy darkness, and he got out of his car and went into the house.

She walked carefully, because her ankles were so brittle from the cold that she feared that if she stumbled, they would snap.

---

8. Wordsworth . . . recollections: British poet William Wordsworth (1770–1850) delved into memories of his youth in his poetry, recollecting the emotion of childhood in the tranquility of adulthood.
9. Yeats . . . hawks: British poet William Butler Yeats (1865–1939) developed his own mythology.

A Voyage to Cythera 1285

---

37 Discussion Compare and contrast the scene that Helen observes in the room with the world that Helen describes sympathetically and that she herself experiences.

38 Enrichment William Wordsworth, an English Romantic poet, wrote the first analytical autobiography in the form of a poem. *The Prelude,* consisting of fourteen "books," was written between 1798 and 1839.

Twentieth-century Irish poet W. B. Yeats frequently used towers, lions, and hawks in his poems, such as "The Second Coming." Yeats's tower with its winding stair symbolized for him both intellectual pursuit and the necessary abandonment of the world. His identification with the tower, also a symbol of Irish history, of isolation, and of security, was so strong that at one time he actually purchased a tower and lived in it.

39 Reading Strategy Why does Helen think that the man at the end of this story is an apparition?

Reader's Response Who was the most memorable stranger you ever saw on the street or talked with for a few minutes?

Closure and Extension

ANSWERS TO THINKING ABOUT THE SELECTION
Recalling

1. (a) Helen is obsessed with travel and with the idea of discovery and the changes that travel affords. She believes that each trip leads to revelation. (b) Helen hopes to fall in love whenever she journeys to a new place.
2. Helen concludes that the man on the train is the victim of a tragic love affair. She bases her conclusion on the fact that the man appears to be restless and troubled. (b) The man on the train asks Helen to address a letter that he has just written; he then asks her to mail it.
3. (a) The man discusses the virtues of central heating with Helen. (b) Helen points out that central heat-

ing ruined some friends' antique furniture and paneling. (c) Helen leaves after she finishes her fourth glass of wine; she departs at five minutes to three.
4. (a) Helen plans to knock on the door of 24 Victoria Place and inquire for "Alice," in order to meet Mrs. Smithson. (b) Helen actually stands at the bus stop directly in front of the house and pretends to be waiting for a bus. (c) Helen observes a large, bright room.

There are two women there, one reading aloud from a book and the other setting tea. Helen sees five children in the room; the oldest children are decorating a Christmas tree. (d) The man from the train arrives.

Interpreting

5. Answers will differ. Helen wishes to solve the mystery that the man on the train involves her in. She is also irrationally jealous of Mrs. Smithson and the fact that the man has some sort of relationship with her.

6. (a) Suggested Response: Helen's vision of the room at 24 Victoria Place is one of harmony, happiness, and love. The vision is both beautiful and frightening to her. (b) Suggested Response: Helen thinks that it is dangerous to draw connections between symbols because in so doing one can lose sight of reality and be tempted by delusion or one's own desires.

7. Suggested Response: The implications of the story's title are that the story is about a journey and the story will have a happy ending. Indeed, the story is about a journey, not to a particular place but to a level of understanding. Yet instead of finding love, Helen finds that it does not exist for her.

8. Suggested Response: Helen has learned about her needs and expectations. She better comprehends her own complex motivations and her reasons for travel. She seems to understand that she stands apart from the world unveiled to her in the room.

Applying

9. Answers will differ. It is doubtful that Helen will ever fall in love with a specific man, because she seems to be more in love with the idea of love than with a particular person. When she looks into the room, she is stunned and moved; she has no hope of ever having the kind of life she observes. As Helen points out at the end of the story, the man on the train seems to be a ghostly image. To her, he is not real.

ANSWERS TO CRITICAL THINKING AND READING

1. (a) direct; (b) direct; (c) indirect; (d) indirect

2. (a) Helen almost entirely uses indirect evidence to make her assumptions. She observes his actions and interprets his gestures and expres-

THINKING ABOUT THE SELECTION
Recalling

1. (a) At the beginning of the story, what is Helen's attitude toward journeys? (b) According to "a much-traveled old man," why does she feel this way?

2. (a) What conclusion does Helen reach about the man on the train from Reading to London? (b) What does the man ask her to do?

3. (a) What does the man at the office Christmas party talk about? (b) How does Helen respond? (c) At what point does she leave?

4. (a) When Helen visits Victoria Place, what does she plan to do there? (b) What does she actually do? (c) What does she observe? (d) Who arrives as she starts to walk away?

Interpreting

5. Why do you think Helen is so obsessed with catching a glimpse of Mrs. Smithson?

6. (a) In the last scene of the story, what meaning does the "vision" that Helen sees have for her? (b) Why does Helen think that connections between symbols are "a destructive folly to draw"?

7. (a) The title of this story is an allusion. The reader is expected to know that Cythera is a Greek island where Aphrodite, the goddess of love, arose full-grown from the sea. How are the implications of the story's title fulfilled in an unexpected way at the end? (b) How does the title relate to the theme?

8. In what way or ways has Helen changed or grown as a consequence of her experiences?

Applying

9. What do you think the chances are that Helen will ever fall in love with a specific man?

CRITICAL THINKING AND READING
Identifying Kinds of Evidence

Direct evidence is straightforward factual information that leads to an obvious conclusion. When the narrator says that the man on the train "took out a sheet of fourpenny stamps, and tore one off, licked it, and stuck it on" the envelope, you have direct evidence of an intent to mail the letter or to have it mailed. **Indirect evidence** requires much more interpretation. For example, when the narrator says that "there was no need to knock at the door" of the house on Victoria Place, you can infer that Helen is relieved to avoid a face-to-face meeting with Mrs. Smithson. But the evidence is indirect; you have to use other information about Helen's personality to reach that conclusion.

1. Identify the kind of evidence—direct or indirect—in each of the following inferences: (a) that Helen had been to France; (b) that Helen liked the man who kissed her on a train as it drew into Oxford; (c) that Helen had received an excellent education; (d) that Helen was bored by the man's talk about central heating at the Christmas party.

2. (a) What kind of evidence does Helen use on the train to support her conclusion about the unnamed man? (b) How accurately does she seem to have interpreted the evidence?

THINKING AND WRITING
Writing About Characterization

Fictional characters, whether flat or round, must be believable. They may sometimes act in unexpected ways, but they should not act out of character. A flat, stock-character clown should not suddenly and for no apparent reason become a dashing hero. A round, carefully developed character like Helen in "A Voyage to Cythera" may change and grow, but she must do so within the personality given her by the writer. Helen is a complex but consistent character. Write an essay in which you discuss three of Helen's encounters with other people, explaining how in each one she acts true to the personality that the author has given her. Begin by choosing the three encounters. Make notes about them. Then write your first draft, showing Helen's consistency from one encounter to the next. In revising your first draft, make sure you have supplied clear connections.

sions but does not actually speak to him. When he does speak to Helen, she uses direct evidence to infer that his letter is somehow important. (b) Helen seems to have interpreted some of the indirect evidence correctly; the man is alone on the train, he is preoccupied, and his request does seem mysterious. She correctly interprets the evidence that he wishes to speak to her.

THINKING AND WRITING

For help with this assignment, students can refer to Lesson 9, "Writing About Character," in the Handbook of Writing About Literature.

Publishing Student Writing Ask student volunteers to read their compositions aloud. Have students choose one of the best compositions about Helen's en-

counters. You might wish to ask them to write a class play based on one of the encounters from this composition. Have students work in small groups to write dialogue, design a set, describe costumes, and decide on details about lighting and sound effects.

Challenge How do you feel about Helen's "voyage to Cythera"? What is the point of the voyage? Is it successful? Why or why not?

GREAT WORKS

LORD OF THE FLIES
by William Golding

Picture yourself on an unspoiled, isolated tropical island. Lush green palm trees wave in the soft breeze and the sun glitters like a coin pasted on the clear blue sky. The waves gently roll over the warm golden sand. Maybe you would pass endless afternoons catching the rays, watching the sparkling ocean, and listening to the monkeys chattering as they swing among the vines. How about gathering fragrant blood-red blossoms? If you were hungry, you need only reach up to the nearest tree to pluck luscious fruit still warm from the sun or drink sweet coconut milk. Now add a group of classmates your own age—no adults, please!—and paradise would certainly be complete. This is the setting for William Golding's 1954 classic story of good and evil, *Lord of the Flies.* But on Golding's fictional tropical island, things turn out very differently from what we would expect . . .

A Futuristic Tale

The novel opens sometime in the future, in the modern age of hostile superpowers, murderous weapons, and vicious battles. The world has been plunged into a deadly atomic war. A group of English schoolboys, aged six to twelve, has been ejected from a flaming airplane onto a South Sea island in

a last-ditch effort to save their lives. Fortunately, none of the boys has been injured. The first boy we encounter is tall, blond-haired, and good-looking. Soon we learn that his name is Ralph, that he is about twelve years old, and that he is cheerful and decent. His father was a commander in the Navy, and his well-to-do home in England was a pleasant place, with "treats" before bed, books to read, and a walled garden visited by wild ponies. As he picks his way toward the lagoon, he hears a voice.

The voice belongs to a stout, nearsighted, and asthmatic boy of about the same age as Ralph. He is identified only by the unflattering nickname "Piggy." With his thin hair, soft body, and eyeglasses, it is plain to see that he would be the butt of schoolboy jokes. As they play by the lagoon, Piggy speaks of a background very different from

Motivation/Prior Knowledge
Have students imagine what would happen if the class were marooned on an island without teachers or other adults. After students have outlined various scenarios, tell them that *Lord of the Flies* describes what happens to a group of English schoolboys isolated on a tropical island.

Discussion Have students discuss how young people with different backgrounds might react differently to the situation described in the novel. What experiences, for example, would best prepare one to be self-reliant? What kinds of skills would be most helpful in this new and strange environment?

Ralph's. His father dead, his mother run off, Piggy was raised by his aunt, who ran a sweet shop, a decidedly working-class occupation. Although neither handsome nor charming, Piggy seems far more intelligent than Ralph: He tells Ralph what he overheard the pilot saying about the atomic attack, stresses how slim is the possibility of rescue, and questions how to determine whether they are on an island or peninsula.

Suddenly the boys spot something large and creamy-colored in the lagoon. Ralph pulls a sapling from the bank, enabling Piggy to pull the object from the water. It is a huge conch shell, fully eighteen inches across. At Piggy's direction, Ralph blows into the shell, which emits a deep, booming cry. The blast acts like a siren, summoning the other boys.

First, a number of small boys wander over to Ralph and Piggy. Ragged and dirty, their faces smeared with sticky masses of fruit, the little boys arrange themselves on the fallen palm trunks at Ralph's feet. They are joined by a pair of identical towheaded twins, who give their names as Sam and Eric. Like an outstretched black snake, a line of boys dressed incongruously in long black cloaks with silver crosses on their chests appears on the horizon. As the line of boys approaches the others, their leader vaults to the platform and confronts Ralph. This is Jack Merridew. Tall, red-haired, and ugly, he leads his black-cloaked church choir with an iron fist. Only when Simon—a small, thin boy with a pointed chin and bright eyes—faints, does he allow the others to rest in the shade. From the way the choir obeys him, it is plain that he has leadership abilities. Yet despite the choir's allegiance, Ralph is elected chief on the basis of his appearance and his possession of the already-powerful symbol of the conch. Ralph selects Jack and Simon to accompany him on an expedition to discover whether they are indeed on an island. If you were in Ralph's place, what action would you have undertaken first—exploring, building shelter, or gathering food?

Scrambling up the cliffs and through the underbrush, the three boys learn that they are indeed stranded on an island. They also see the place where they crashed and encounter wild pigs. Upon their return, Ralph and Jack ignore Piggy's advice and order a signal fire built before they erect shelter. The chilling fear lurking just below the surface emerges that evening, when the little ones wail about a monster they call the "beastie." Things turn decidedly nasty when a little one disappears in the fire . . .

Not a Paradise After All

Slowly, we begin to see that the tropical island may not be the paradise it first appeared—and the boys' subsequent adventure will be very different from what we expect. First, take the matter of food. Although the boys have only to pluck the fruit off the trees to eat, the fruit is often green and frequently makes them ill. At times, the island is torn by fierce tropical storms that uproot whole trees. Annoying insects, sharp thorns, rot, and decay are everywhere visible. The boys are plagued by hunger, stomach upsets, insect bites, deep scratches, and sunburn. Then there is the boys' terror of isolation and their desperate attempts to signal a passing ship which can return them to the world they have lost. Will a passing ship spot their signal fire and rescue them? But by far the most important element is the struggle for power, and with it, survival. Who will be in charge? How will he rule? And how will the others react?

Other Tales of Castaways

Now, stories about people castaway on idyllic tropical islands are nothing new. Ever since 1719, when Daniel Defoe landed Robinson Crusoe on a desert island, literature has abounded with tales of castaways. Probably the most well-known among these are Jonathan Swift's *Gulliver's Travels*, Jules Verne's *The Mysterious Island*, and J. D. Wyss's *The Swiss Family Robinson*.

Themes in *Lord of the Flies*

We know, then, that romantic adventure tales of castaways are not unique, and that Golding even modeled *Lord of the Flies* on one of the most well-known of these novels, *The Coral Island* by R. M. Ballantyne. But Golding is using the time-honored castaway story to a very different end. His purpose is to address the main concern we have today: the nature of the human personality and the reflection of that personality on society. The message that underlies Golding's tale, however, is so startling and controversial that *Lord of the Flies* has become the most influential novel among American high school and college students since J. D. Salinger's *Catcher in the Rye*, published in 1945. Speaking of the success of *Lord of the Flies*, noted critic Lionel Trilling remarked, "First, apparently, in the colleges, then in secondary schools, it seems to have captured the imagination of a whole generation." This first novel—from the unlikely hand of a forty-three-year-old teacher and wartime commander in the British Royal Navy—established its author as one of the most "dynamic, exciting, and controversial figures in contemporary British literature."

For *Lord of the Flies* is a bloody, tragic tale about how human behavior changes when the ordinary social controls are absent. In a completely convincing and often very frightening way, the novel shows what happens when all the trappings of everyday society are slowly stripped away.

Great Works 1289

Enrichment Tell students that Daniel Defoe (1660–1731) published nine novels, including *Robinson Crusoe,* during the years 1719 to 1724. In writing *Robinson Crusoe,* Defoe relied on narratives of shipwrecks written by sailors. One such narrative was written by Alexander Selkirk, who had been stranded on a desert island for four years. Selkirk was so influenced by these years of solitude that after his rescue and return to England, he built himself a cave. Defoe attempted to interview Selkirk in order to gather material for his novel, but there is no evidence that he actually met the man.

Defoe's narrative is, in one sense, an homage to the rising middle classes. Robinson Crusoe is the perfect middle-class entrepreneur, bustling with energy and filled with ideas to better his lot. Defoe's optimism stands in sharp contrast to Golding's pessimistic view of human nature. This contrast demonstrates how a single genre, the shipwreck story, can be used for vastly different purposes.

What do you think would happen in a world without social controls? Obviously your answer depends on whether you believe that people are basically good or basically evil. Do you think people are fundamentally decent and kind but have had the misfortune of being born into a very bad world? If so, you would agree with French philosopher Jean Jacques Rousseau. He wrote that people are born noble and moral, but they are systematically corrupted by an evil society. Do you think, as Rousseau did, that if society were to change, all our troubles would lessen? Steinbeck's *The Grapes of Wrath,* Salinger's *The Catcher in the Rye,* and Shakespeare's *Hamlet* all provide examples of good people whose troubles are forced on them from the society in which they live.

Or do you think that people are basically evil? In this case, society acts as a brake to hold their vicious impulses under control. If so, you would agree with Golding's point in *Lord of the Flies.* Vividly, with a brilliantly conveyed sense of mounting terror, *Lord of the Flies* exposes Golding's view of the desperate wickedness of the human heart. As the boys attempt to impose order on chaos,

they reveal the irrationality at the heart of existence. With gruesome detail, the story unfolds the end of innocence and the realization of universal evil. It is easy to see how the view Golding takes in *Lord of the Flies* has sparked a heated controversy that continues to ignite millions of readers.

The title hints of the novel's main point. The "Lord of the Flies" is the name Simon gives to the head of a wild pig that the others have slaughtered. After the kill, the pig's skull is impaled on a stick, where it is promptly infested by flies. The term "Lord of the Flies" is a translation of the Hebrew word "Baalzebub" or "Beelzebub"–the "chief of the devils." In referring to the devil, Simon is commenting on what he sees happening around him.

In its message and method, *Lord of the Flies* seems at first glance to resemble Orwell's equally grim view of the future, *1984;* however, the novels are fundamentally very different. First, Orwell is writing as a satirist in *1984.* As such, he does not want to symbolize humanity's condition or even the plight of modern man. His object is simply to record as forcefully as he can the fearful symptoms which he had observed developing in Russia, America, and England in the thirties and forties. To do this, he exaggerates what he has seen of the abuses of power. *1984* is not about eternal values or about the future of the world; it is about the present. *Lord of the Flies,* in contrast, offers no such specific portrait of the modern world. Rather, it is an attempt to trace the defects of society back to the defects of the human race. In so doing, it offers a crushing commentary on humanity's doomed attempt to build a rational society.

According to critics Ian Gregor and Mark Kinkead-Weekes, "Mr. Golding's book is valuable to us, not because it 'tells us about' the darkness of man's heart, but because it shows us, because it is a work of art which enables us to enter into the world it creates and live at the level of a deeply perceptive and intelligent man."

Poetry

MOUNT FUJI AND FLOWERS, 1972
David Hockney
Metropolitan Museum of Art

Humanities Note

Fine art, *Mount Fuji and Flowers*, 1972, David Hockney. David Hockney, born in 1937, is Britain's best known contemporary painter and graphic artist. Educated at Bradford College and the Royal College of Art in London, Hockney first attracted public notice with his radical "Pop" statements. Today he is known as a painter of difficult effects, such as sunlight on pool water, and for his stunning graphic designs.

Mount Fuji and Flowers is a striking combination of reality and fantasy. A delicate spray of spring flowers leans gracefully in a vase fashioned from a section of bamboo. The vase rests on a narrow rose-colored ledge, beyond which the balance of the canvas is filled with an abstract vision of Mt. Fuji painted in dreamy layers of celestial blue. This is the artist's homage to things Japanese, which have inspired his conception of art.

More About the Author Philip
Larkin had a seemingly uneventful
childhood. He was a mediocre
student, finding school at times a
"tiresome interruption" to things
he liked to do better. Among
those things was reading. A voracious reader, he read everything
from detective stories to contemporary fiction to the classics. As a
very young child he played highly
creative and imaginative games,
building a private childhood world.
In his early teens he began a
lifelong interest in jazz, something
he came to love "even more than
poetry." Have your students discuss the importance of childhood
experiences on the development
of an author. What types of experiences might most shape an author's development?

Critical Evaluation David
Daiches and Jon Stallworthy
made the following statement
about Larkin's work: "No other
poet presents the welfare-state
world of post-Imperial Britain so
vividly, so unsparingly, and in the
last analysis so tenderly. Much
has been written of Larkin's
Hardyesque pessimism, his depiction of loneliness, age, and
death, but the many negatives in
his poems imply positives, out of
reach of the ironic and self-
depreciating speaker, but available perhaps to others more fortunate, elsewhere."

PHILIP LARKIN

1922–1985

Should a poem be heavily symbolic and filled with images or should
it be simple and straightforward? Few poets made better use of the
ordinary in both content and style than did Philip Larkin. Once
connected with "the Movement," a group of poets whose work first
appeared in Robert Conquest's 1956 anthology *New Lines,* Larkin
then established his own unique place in contemporary literature.
Writing in a poetic form that approximates conversation, he raised
familiar experiences to the level of art. His poems were often wry,
self-critical, and understated, "part sigh, part affirmation," as one
critic stated. Poetry for Larkin was a part-time job; his full-time job
was that of librarian at the University of Hull, a major seaport on the
east coast of England.

Philip Larkin was born in Coventry, England. A graduate of St.
John's College, Oxford, Larkin began his writing career as a
novelist. He later served as jazz correspondent of the *Daily Telegraph.* His poetry, which was the source of his international fame,
displays a clear-eyed honesty that captures moments of startling
truth. Often it contains a narrator who observes the world around
him with detachment. Larkin's poetry has frequently been compared with that of Thomas Hardy, whom he admired.

The detachment central to much of Larkin's verse was apparent
during his childhood as well. He wrote that "I was not happy in
school. Admittedly it was an affair of being more frightened than
hurt, but it was being hurt sometimes, and being frightened was not
very pleasant." Regardless, he distinguished himself early, and won
numerous academic prizes. No doubt part of his achievement was
due to the strong influence of his father, Sydney Larkin. The brilliant
administrator of the City Treasury of Coventry, the senior Larkin
could be merciless with those who fell short of his rigid standards.
Noel Hughes, Philip's childhood friend, recalled Mr. Larkin's forceful
personality and the cool feeling in the household. "In spite of the
unfailing graciousness of Mrs. Larkin's welcome," Huges commented, "the atmosphere of Philip's home, with its intimidating tidiness,
its highly waxed furniture and practice of hushed conversation,
impressed me as solemn." Hughes believes that "there is in Philip
much that is reminiscent of his father."

From his father Larkin absorbed his love for the writings of D. H.
Lawrence, his superb mastery of languages, and his attention to
appearance. He was cultured and polite in manner—almost courtly.
To the poets of ensuing generations he has left a legacy of high
standards, learning, and attention to detail.

Objectives

1 To understand and
identify the tone of a
poem
2 To recognize how the
tone can differ be-
tween poems and how
tone affects the poem's
meaning
3 To compare and con-
trast the tone of sever-
al poems

Support Material

Teaching Portfolio
Teacher Backup, p. 1529
Usage and Mechanics Work-
sheet, p. 1533
Vocabulary Check, p. 1534
Analyzing Literature Worksheet,
Understanding Tone, p. 1535

Language Worksheet, *Under-
standing Multiple Meanings of
Words,* p. 1536
Selection Test, p. 1537
Art Transparency 19, *Shipbuild-
ing on the Clyde,* by Stanley
Spencer

GUIDE FOR INTERPRETING

Days; The Explosion; Coming

Writer's Techniques

Tone. In casual conversation, the words people use and the way they say them suggest an attitude and create a mood. In poetry, the writer's attitude toward his or her subject and the mood created by the language are called **tone**. Tone can be solemn, playful, cynical, angry; or it can have any of dozens of other attributes. In general, tone reflects the writer's attitude and puts the reader in the same kind of mood. Tone is created by the ideas in the poem as well as by verbal elements such as meter, sentence structure, diction, and imagery.

Writing

Write a short imperative sentence. (*Do the dishes,* for example; or *Mow the lawn.*) Then rewrite it, putting the same thought into *five* different sentences, each with a different tone. Your rewritten sentences will probably be longer than the original. Choose your five different tones from the following list.

| angry | bored | eager | friendly | timid |
| blunt | desperate | formal | pompous | vague |

Be prepared to read your sentences in class to see if your classmates can identify the tone of each sentence.

Primary Source

One day fellow writer Kingsley Amis spoke with longtime friend Philip Larkin about two of the greatest prizes writers can receive: the Nobel Prize for Literature and the Poet Laureateship of Great Britain. Amis was astonished at his friend's reaction. Anthony Thwaite records his reaction in *Larkin At Sixty.*

> In 1976 or so he and I were in a taxi on our way to a drink in London. I said into a silence, without premeditation,
> "What chance of the Nobel?"
> "Oh, that's gone," he said decisively. "I thought they might be keeping it warm for a chap like me—you know, a chap who never *writes* anything or *does* anything or *says* anything. But now I find they've just given it to a . . . [fellow] who never *writes* anything or *does* anything or *says* anything. No, that's *gone.*"
> After a pause, I asked, "What about the Laureateship?"
> "I dream about that sometimes," he said in the same tone, "*and wake up screaming.* Nah, with any luck they'll pass me over."

Guide for Interpreting 1293

Motivation/Prior Knowledge
Have the students try to recall what they did yesterday, or a week ago. Do they take tomorrow for granted? Do we often reflect on the days in our lives? Is it important or valuable to do this? What factors in a person's life might affect how they interpret and look at days?

Purpose-Setting Question Does this poem provide a satisfying answer to the question "What are days for?"

1 Discussion What is the tone of the poem in these lines? Do lines 2–5 answer the question the way you might answer it?

2 Discussion Are there other places than days in which to live? Why does the author ask this question here?

3 Critical Thinking and Reading Which of the questions in stanza one interests Larkin most? What is the meaning of the priest and doctor? How are they involved in "solving" the question?

4 Discussion Why are the priest and doctor "running over the fields"? Does this ending seem strange in light of the poem's questions?

Days

Philip Larkin

1
What are days for?
Days are where we live.
They come, they wake us
Time and time over.
5   They are to be happy in;
2   Where can we live but days?

3   Ah, solving that question
Brings the priest and the doctor
In their long coats
4 10 Running over the fields.

THINKING ABOUT THE SELECTION

Recalling

1. In your own words, what is the speaker's answer to the first question in the poem?

Interpreting

2. Why does the answer to the second question bring the priest and the doctor running?

Applying

3. What would be different about the thought in this poem if Larkin had substituted the word *life* for the word *days*?

ANALYZING LITERATURE

Understanding Tone

Tone is the attitude that a writer takes toward his or her subject, characters, or audience. In a poem, tone is conveyed to a great extent by word choice.

1. How would you describe the tone of "Days"?
2. How does the interjection *Ah* at the beginning of line 7 affect the tone of the poem?
3. How would the tone of the poem be different if lines 6–10 did not exist?

Closure and Extension

ANSWERS TO THINKING ABOUT THE SELECTION
Recalling

1. The author suggests that days form a place or space for living and to "be happy in."

1294

Interpreting

2. Suggested Response: The need to know "where can we live but days" comes most urgently at the time of death. One often calls in a priest or minister and a doctor at that time.

Applying

3. Suggested Response: Using the word *life* would certainly change the poem's meaning, since Larkin refers to days as a place for living, questioning where else we might live but days.

ANSWERS TO ANALYZING LITERATURE

1. Suggested Response: The tone is bland, almost matter-of-fact in the first stanza, but more actively reflective in the second stanza.
2. The word injects more emotion than the poem has previously expressed.
3. The tone would be unvaried.

Challenge Do you agree with the attitude Larkin expresses in this poem? How might you rephrase the poem to express your attitude? Try writing your response in a brief composition.

The Explosion

Philip Larkin

On the day of the explosion
Shadows pointed towards the pithead:
In the sun the slagheap slept.

Down the lane came men in pitboots
5 Coughing oath-edged talk and pipe-smoke,
Shouldering off the freshened silence.

One chased after rabbits; lost them;
Came back with a nest of lark's eggs;
Showed them; lodged them in the grasses.

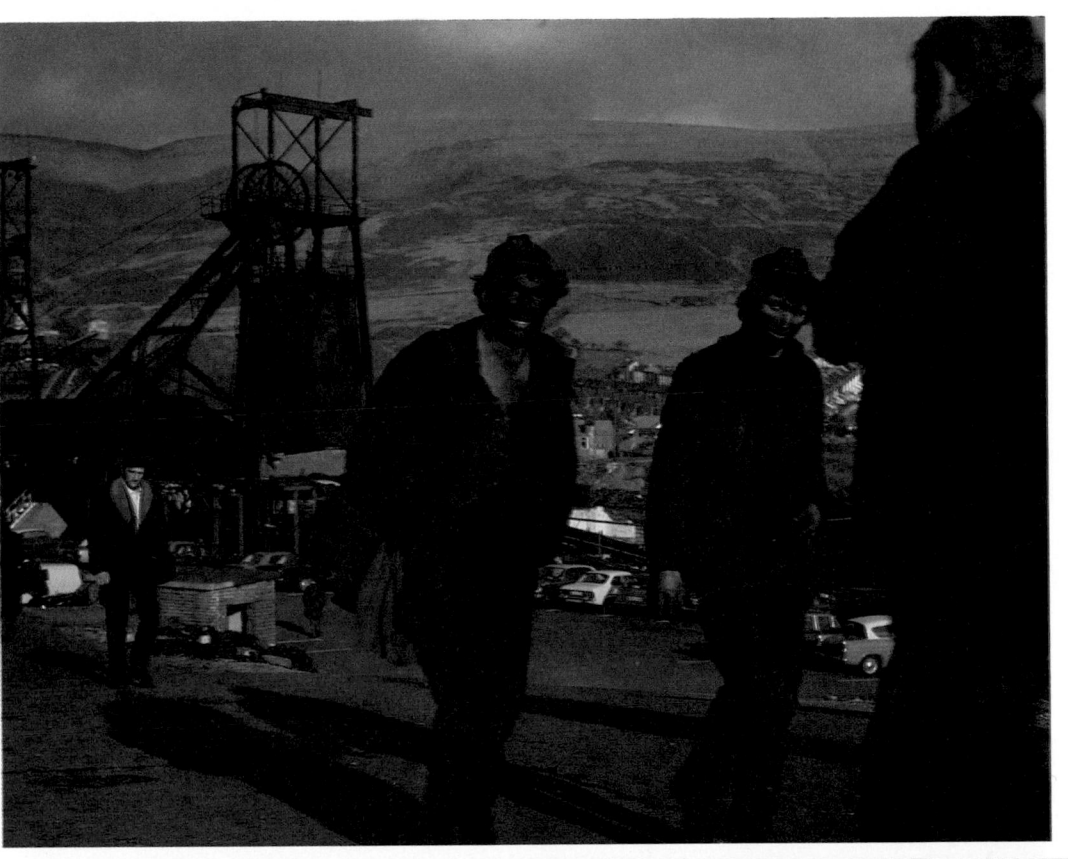

Presentation

Motivation/Prior Knowledge
Have the students imagine they are with a group of people going off to work in the morning. The workers are mostly friends. The talk and actions are ordinary and everyday. Later in the day a tragedy happens. Some of the workers die. How significant would their morning's actions now become? How would you, as an onlooker, feel? How would the survivors of the tragedy feel?

Master Teacher Note This poem records an incident familiar to Larkin, who grew up in an industrial town. To set the background discuss facts about coal mining. If possible read an account of a mining accident from a newspaper or magazine.

Purpose-Setting Question How has the author used carefully selected incidents and details to create a touching and poignant effect?

1 **Discussion** What is the effect of knowing about the explosion from the beginning of the poem?

2 **Discussion** What do the details about the miners contribute to the poem's impact? What is ironic and chilling about the image of "tall gates standing open"?

Master Teacher Note After reading Larkin's "The Explosion," display Art Transparency 19, Stanley Spencer's *Shipbuilding on the Clyde*, on the overhead projector. Point out that both the poem and the painting deal with modern British industrial life. Ask: Do the two works have anything else in common? What point might each be trying to make? Which work, Larkin's or Spencer's, do you admire more, and why?

3 **Discussion** What is contrasted in these two stanzas? Is the contrast effective? What meaning does it add to the poem?

4 **Critical Thinking and Reading** The sudden shift in time and place between stanzas four and five and between stanzas five and six helps to set the tone of the poem. Notice that the shifts are dramatic but done so that the careful reader can still catch the meaning.

5 **Discussion** What is especially poignant about introducing the wives here? How does the image of the sun contrast with that in line 2?

Challenge What is the author's reaction to the incident of the explosion? What feelings has it touched in him? Support your response with specific images and incidents from the poem.

Reader's Response Which details in this poem affected you the most? Explain.

Closure and Extension

ANSWERS TO THINKING ABOUT THE SELECTION
Recalling

1. The events in the poem occur near a coal mine shaft and at funeral services.
2. The earth tremor resulting from the explosion causes the cows to stop chewing and creates a hazy effect around the sun.
3. (a) For a second the widows see their men walking towards them. (b) The earth tremor causes the cows to stop chewing for a second.

Interpreting

4. Line 1 speaks about the explosion, while in line 2 there are shadows pointing towards the mine.
5. Suggested Response: Some of the men going into the mine are pipe smokers. They are coughing, perhaps from smoking or from

10 So they passed in beards and moleskins,
    Fathers, brothers, nicknames, laughter,
    Through the tall gates standing open.

    At noon, there came a tremor; cows
15 Stopped chewing for a second; sun,
    Scarfed as in a heat-haze, dimmed.

    The dead go on before us, they
    Are sitting in God's house in comfort,
    We shall see them face to face—

    Plain as lettering in the chapels
20 It was said, and for a second
    Wives saw men of the explosion

    Larger than in life they managed—
    Gold as on a coin, or walking
    Somehow from the sun towards them,

25 One showing the eggs unbroken.

THINKING ABOUT THE SELECTION
Recalling

1. Where do the events in the poem occur?
2. What immediate effect does the explosion have on life above ground?
3. (a) What do the widows of the miners see "for a second" at the funeral services? (b) What else in the poem lasts "for a second"?

Interpreting

4. How does the first stanza foreshadow events in the poem?

5. In your own words, explain line 5.
6. (a) What is the mood of the men going to work? (b) What details show this mood?
7. Why are lines 16–18 printed in italics?
8. What is the symbolic meaning of the eggs?
9. How would you describe the tone of "The Explosion"?

Applying

10. What relationship is there between the theme of "Days" and the theme of "The Explosion"?

working the mines. Their speech is punctuated by oaths.
6. (a) The men going to work are in a normal, everyday, somewhat cheerful mood. (b) They are talking, smoking, and coughing. One stops to chase a rabbit and pick up a nest of lark's eggs. They are relatives and friends, calling each other nicknames and laughing together.
7. Lines 16–18 are in italics because they are words of a funeral service.

8. Answers will differ. Suggested Response: The lark's eggs are a sign of spring, rebirth, and renewal of nature. The unbroken eggs symbolize that nature will survive.
9. Answers will differ. Suggested Response: The tone of the poem is poignant and tragic. Good, kind working men suddenly die in a mining accident.

Applying

10. Answers will differ. Suggested Re-

sponse: Both poems explore the meaning of life and death. People seek to live and be happy, yet death is a reality to be confronted, something not under our control.

Coming

Philip Larkin

On longer evenings,
Light, chill and yellow,
Bathes the serene
Foreheads of houses.
5   A thrush sings,
Laurel-surrounded
In the deep bare garden,
Its fresh-peeled voice
Astonishing the brickwork.
10 It will be spring soon,
It will be spring soon—
And I, whose childhood
Is a forgotten boredom,
Feel like a child
15 Who comes on a scene
Of adult reconciling,
And can understand nothing
But the unusual laughter,
And starts to be happy.

1

2

3

4

THINKING ABOUT THE SELECTION
Recalling

1. In "Coming" what are two signs of spring that the speaker notices?
2. With what kind of attitude does the speaker look back on childhood?

Interpreting

3. The speaker draws a comparison between the coming of spring and a child witnessing the end of an adult argument. What similarities are there between the two occasions?

Applying

4. In writing about the seasons, the nature writer Hal Borland observed, "April is a promise that May is bound to keep." Explain this statement.

THINKING AND WRITING
Writing About Tone

Write an essay in which you compare and contrast the tone of the three Larkin poems. Find and jot down words, phrases, or lines that support your assessment of the tone of each poem. In your first draft, be sure that the quoted lines actually make the points you say they do. When revising, eliminate vague or meaningless statements. You will find that in writing about literature, you can easily fall into the trap of writing sentences that, upon analysis, convey very little information.

Coming   1297

More About the Author Thom Gunn tends to praise strength, insensitivity, and action over thought. Violent action is seen as "a valid means of self-expression." Led by his personal quest for self-identity and life's meaning, in the early 1960's Gunn changed his poetic stance. He moved towards writing free verse dealing with more positive themes. Discuss with your students the problems faced by an author who is growing and changing. Is it valid to compare works from one period with another?

Critical Evaluation In the second volume of his book *A History of Modern Poetry,* David Perkins makes the following statement about the work of Thom Gunn: "The poetry of Thom Gunn (b. 1929) shares, on the one hand, moral attitudes and stylistic modes that are typical of poets in the United States today and especially of poets in California. On the other hand, it bears the stamp of Gunn's early training in a different school, so that amid the hot tubs, LSD, sunny flesh, sleeping bags under the stars, and general quest for Adamic innocence and spontaneous wholeness of being Gunn preserves the strong discipline of such masters as William Empson, F.R. Leavis, and Yvor Winters."

Literary Focus T.S. Eliot once noticed that each age has its own poetic diction. Note that poets choose words with great care and that their choices are integral to their unique style. To highlight that diction is part of everyday language, have the students read over several recent compositions. Have they repeated certain words and phrases? Are they developing a certain diction in their writing?

Taylor Street

Thom William Gunn (1929-   ) was born in Gravesend, England and educated at Cambridge. He became, to his own surprise, one of "the Movement" poets of the 1950's. In the mid-1950's he moved to California, studied at Stanford University, and taught at the University of California, Berkeley. In 1960 Gunn decided to settle permanently in San Francisco, give up teaching, and devote himself full-time to writing. In his verse as well as in his life, he straddles the English and American traditions. Some critics say that his celebration of men of action (such as soldiers, motorcyclists, and tough boys), his fascination with violence, and his glorification of popular heroes such as Elvis Presley come from the American culture; his low-keyed, cool, informal manner, the British. This synthesis of the two cultures partly accounts for the intense critical controversy that swirls around him. An American reviewer labeled him "a fashionable, rote versifier of some skill and intelligence . . . [whose work] has not the slightest power to touch you." Yet he is very highly regarded in England, and his first book, *Fighting Terms,* was praised by noted critic A. Alvarez as "the most impressive first book of poems since Robert Lowell's." Gunn, who has published steadily since the 1950's, is well represented in anthologies and has won many literary awards.

Writer's Techniques

Diction. Diction is word choice. Choosing the best and most appropriate words is essential to effective writing. A writer—especially a poet—must select his or her words carefully to express the exact nuances intended. Diction can be as simple as that in a primer's "See Spot run" or as ornate as that in John Milton's *Paradise Lost:*

> Nor was his name unheard or unadored
> In ancient Greece, and in Ausonian land
> Men called him Mulciber; and how he fell
> From Heaven, they fabled, thrown by angry Jove
> Over the crystal battlements.

Diction can be as formal as a speech to Parliament or as informal as current Cockney slang. In choosing their words, writers take into account the subject, the theme, and the audience. Intent determines diction.

As you read Thom Gunn's "Taylor Street," pay close attention to the words he uses. Try to determine the effect of the words.

Objective

To recognize an author's diction

Support Material

Teaching Portfolio
Teacher Backup, p. 1539
Usage and Mechanics Worksheet, p. 1542
Analyzing Literature Worksheet, *Recognizing the Importance of Diction,* p. 1543
Language Worksheet, *Choosing Synonyms,* p. 1544
Selection Test, p. 1545

Closure and Extension

ANSWERS TO THINKING ABOUT THE SELECTION
Recalling

1. (a) He is sitting on the porch facing the street. (b) His face is yellowish and he wears a floppy brown hat. His eyes are small.
2. (a) He is watching people pass by the house. (b) Lines 18–19 make it

Taylor Street

Thom Gunn

1
The small porch of imitation
marble is never sunny, but
outside the front door he
sits on his kitchen chair facing
5 the street. In the bent yellowish
face, from under the brim
of a floppy brown hat,
his small eyes watch what
he is not living. But he
10 lives what he can:

2
watches without a smile, with
a certain strain, the warmth
of his big crumpled
body anxiously cupped
15 by himself in himself, as
he leans over himself not
over the cold railing, unmoving but carefully getting
a little strength from the sight of the

3
20 passers-by. He has it
all planned: he will live
here morning by morning.

THINKING ABOUT THE SELECTION

Recalling

1. (a) Where is the man in the poem sitting? (b) What are three details of his appearance?
2. (a) According to lines 8 and 9, what is the man watching? (b) How is this activity made more definite in lines 19 and 20?

Interpreting

3. What two lines suggest that the man is not leading an inactive life by choice?
4. How do you think the man "is getting a little strength from the sight of the passers-by"?
5. How would you describe the tone of this poem?
6. The poem focuses on a single man, yet its title is "Taylor Street." Why?

Applying

7. The poet provides enough information for an imaginative reader to speculate about the life of the man on the porch. What do you think the man's background is?

ANALYZING LITERATURE

Recognizing the Importance of Diction

The importance of **diction,** or word choice, in a brief poem cannot be overemphasized. The poet must make every word count, and Thom Gunn does.

1. Why is it significant that the porch is (a) *small?* (b) *imitation marble?* (c) *never sunny?*
2. The man is not just sitting in a chair. He is sitting in a *kitchen* chair. Why?
3. The man's body is *crumpled.* The word *crumpled,* while specific and powerful, is open to interpretation. How do you interpret it?
4. What is symbolic about the *cold railing?*
5. (a) Why does the word *planned* seem somehow inappropriate? (b) How does it add an encouraging note?

Taylor Street 1299

Hughes once commented that his poems are "not about violence but vitality." Poetry became his whole life when he married Sylvia Plath. Prior to that he had worked as a gardener, a groundskeeper for the Royal Canadian Air Force, and a script reader. Hughes was born in 1930, eight years after Donald Davie and Philip Larkin. Therefore, he missed some of their direct experiences with World War II. He noted that he was far more willing than they to deal directly with issues of violence and savagery in his writing. Ask the students to discuss the effect of an author's birthday on his or her writing. What might be different about the writings of an author born in 1940, 1950, or 1960 simply because of their differences in age?

Critical Evaluation The literary scholar David Perkins said that "in Hughes's better poems the vision of a brutally harsh world is complicated (though not mitigated) by the strangeness and originality of the imaginative experience and by the humor of tough survival. And his later volumes admit somewhat hopeful possibilities in existence that were absent from his earlier ones. He still portrays a mindless, ruthless nature, but he seems to sympathize or identify with it less."

TED HUGHES

1930–

A major contemporary poet, Ted Hughes has been widely praised for his portrayal of nature in all its fierceness and primitive cruelty. Hughes differs from "the Movement" poets, who, he says, "wanted it cozy." There is nothing cozy about Hughes's starkly defined animal world. His diction, in the words of one critic, is "a solid phalanx of buffeting verbs and steel-heeled nouns." Yet Hughes, despite his verbal violence, shows a masterful ability to describe nature, seeking links between its universal force and the human condition.

Nature is a dominant theme in Hughes's poetry. His first book of poems, *The Hawk in the Rain,* appeared in 1957 and brought him immediate success. *Crow* (1970), *Crow Wakes* (1971), and *Eat Crow* (1972) reveal his characteristic style. In them, an animal observes and comments upon the human condition. Because of his use of animal characters, Hughes has been compared to both Aesop and George Orwell. The British critic A. Alvarez calls Hughes "the most powerful and original poet now writing in this country."

Hughes's fascination with nature and animals can be traced back to his childhood in the Calder Valley in western Yorkshire. The valley was full of animals of all kinds, and Hughes often went hunting with his brother, a gamekeeper. This interest in nature led to his university studies in archaeology and anthropology. After graduation in 1954, he spent the next two years in a variety of jobs: He was a rose gardener, a night watchman, a zoo attendant, a schoolteacher, and a reader at a film studio.

In 1956 Hughes and his friends published a poetry magazine called *St. Botolph's Review.* Although the magazine was a failure —it lasted only one issue—at the party held to celebrate its beginning Hughes met Sylvia Plath. They married in June of that year. After teaching briefly at universities in Massachusetts, the couple returned to England in 1959 to devote their full attention to writing. Initially, both were highly productive—Hughes writing most of the poems that later appeared in a volume called *Wodwo,* Plath completing her autobiographical novel *The Bell Jar* and beginning her famous *Ariel* poems. But despite the birth of two children, the union was not happy. The couple separated in August of 1962; the marriage ended the following February with Plath's death. Hughes was unable to write again until 1966, but since then he has produced a number of major collections of poetry. He has been called the most important figure to emerge on the British poetic scene since World War II.

1 To understand the meaning of personification in poetry
2 To use personification in original writing
3 To write a poem in which personification is used

Support Material

Teaching Portfolio
Teacher Backup, p. 1547
Usage and Mechanics Worksheet, p. 1551
Vocabulary Check, p. 1552
Analyzing Literature Worksheet, *Using Personification,* p. 1553

Language Worksheet, *Choosing Antonyms,* p. 1554
Selection Test, p. 1555

GUIDE FOR INTERPRETING

Hawk Roosting; The Horses

Writer's Techniques

Personification. Personification is a figure of speech in which a thing, a quality, or an idea is given human attributes. For example, when Edmund Spenser writes that envy "rode upon a ravenous wolf," he is using personification. Sometimes personification is extended well beyond a phrase or sentence and involves point of view. Events are observed through the eyes or mind of a nonhuman narrator. A familiar example of such extended personification is Jack London's *The Call of the Wild,* in which the story is told from the viewpoint of Buck, a dog. Like simile, metaphor, and other figures of speech, personification presents ideas and details in fresh, original ways.

Commentary

Ted Hughes believes that he acquired a sense of violence very early in life. In fact, he has traced this awareness back to his earliest childhood. As the son of one of only seventeen men from a regiment of several hundred to return form Gallipoli during World War I, he learned about life's tragedy from his father's experiences. As the poems "Out" and "TV Off" recount, Hughes's father was wounded and left piled with the dead for two days; although his visible wounds healed, he never recovered from the terrifying experience. It may be true, as Hughes says, that "the shrapnel that shattered my father's paybook/Gripped me," and that his poetry replays his own visions of the horror and misery of trench warfare. Regardless of its source, his work is shot through with a sense of violence. This is apparent in his style as well as in his subjects. Notice the violent phrases and explosive verbs in these two poems, for example. Critic Calvin Bedine believes that "Hughes's great talent is for a dramatic grip of language, dead cold but bleakly pungent . . . His style is emotionally dry, yet burns." Critics have often remarked that Hughes's violent nature imagery represents a descent into the unconscious, noting parallels between the poetry of Hughes and D. H. Lawrence. What parallels do you see between the contemporary world and the world of nature in Hughes's poems?

Writing

Choose at least five inanimate objects—a pencil, a painting, a computer, for instance—and write a sentence about each one, giving the object human attributes. ("My pencil stopped short at the word *goodbye,* refusing to finish the sentence.") Although animals and plants can be the subjects of personification, try to limit your examples to purely inanimate (lifeless) objects, qualities, or ideas.

Guide for Interpreting 1301

Literary Focus An author's use of personification may grow out of his or her basic recognition of "self" as related to nature. Artists often try to personify complex ideas, for example, using an eagle to personify freedom or even creating a sculpture such as the Statue of Liberty.

Writing/Prior Knowledge We speak of raging storms, stars looking down, giggling dogs, and crafty cats. Have the students listen carefully to conversations and to television and radio dialogue. How many examples of personification do they find? Add examples from their freewriting. Do any especially interesting examples or patterns emerge?

Motivation/Prior Knowledge
Have students imagine a favorite animal-cartoon character. Notice how the character is humanized—a person in animal clothing. Now imagine the animal could speak from its own viewpoint. How would it describe its life? What might it say about itself and its surroundings? Would the animal's outlook be the same as our outlook towards it?

Master Teacher Note ''Hawk Roosting'' explores the inner being of a hawk. To vivify his portrait, Hughes isolates the bird from everything and everybody. The effect is surrealistic and frightening. Imagine the effect if you were to clip away objects in a black-and-white photo one by one, leaving the remaining objects on a black or gray background. How does the effect of the photograph change as objects are removed? What happens when only one object or detail remains?

Purpose-Setting Question What is the total effect created by having the hawk speak?

1 Discussion Why does the author place the hawk ''in the top of the wood''? What is the effect of this on the reader?

2 Critical Thinking and Reading Hughes immediately clarifies that it is a hawk speaking, not a person. Note the hawk's thoughts while sleeping. Why does the author repeat the word *hooked* to describe hawk's head and feet?

3 Literary Focus How do these lines show with the hawk's feelings? Is the use of personification here more or less effective than the author's just describing how the hawk felt?

4 Literary Focus Notice how the author has expressed a complex idea in a few words. In what way

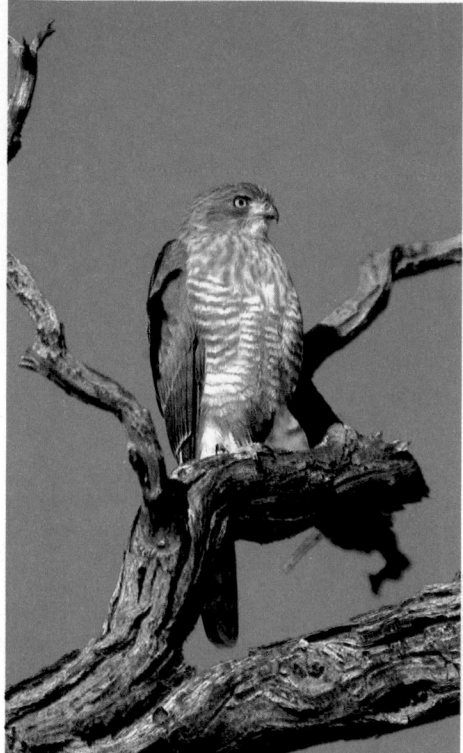

Hawk Roosting

Ted Hughes

I sit in the top of the wood, my eyes closed.   1
Inaction, no falsifying dream
Between my hooked head and hooked feet: 2
Or in sleep rehearse perfect kills and eat.

5 The convenience of the high trees!
The air's buoyancy and the sun's ray
Are of advantage to me;   3
And the earth's face upward for my inspection.

My feet are locked upon the rough bark.
10 It took the whole of Creation
To produce my foot, my each feather:
Now I hold Creation in my foot   4

Or fly up, and revolve it all slowly—
I kill where I please because it is all mine.
15 There is no sophistry in my body:
My manners are tearing off heads—

The allotment of death.
For the one path of my flight is direct   5
Through the bones of the living.
20 No arguments assert my right:

The sun is behind me.
Nothing has changed since I began.
My eye has permitted no change.   6
I am going to keep things like this.

can the hawk ''hold Creation'' in its foot?

5 Discussion How has the tone of the hawk's conversation changed? Does what is said here follow logically from what was said in stanzas one and two?

6 Discussion Is it good that ''Nothing has changed''? Why is the sun behind the hawk's head?

Reader's Response If you could be any animal in the world, which would you choose? Why?

THINKING ABOUT THE SELECTION

Recalling

1. (a) Who is the speaker in the poem? (b) Where is the speaker sitting?
2. What does the speaker do while sleeping?
3. What are three advantages that allow the speaker to "kill where I please"?

Interpreting

4. What does stanza 3 suggest about the physical makeup and abilities of the speaker?
5. In lines 14–16, how does the speaker refute the "falsifying dream" that nature is invariably pleasant and nonviolent?
6. (a) What do you think the speaker means by "Nothing has changed since I began"? (b) How might you interpret the line in another way?
7. (a) What does the poet's (not the speaker's) view of nature seem to be? (b) How do you feel about that view?

Applying

8. Nature can be violent. What have you seen in your own experience that shows this to be true? What other moods can you identify in nature? Provide examples that reveal these moods.

ANALYZING LITERATURE

Using Personification

Giving human attributes to a thing, a quality, or an idea is called **personification.** In "Hawk Roosting," Ted Hughes uses the technique to present his ideas about nature in an unusual and striking way.

1. Personification requires giving human attributes to something nonhuman. How is the hawk personified in Hughes's poem?
2. Why do you think Hughes has the hawk speak for itself in the poem rather than having a human speaker interpret what the hawk might be thinking?

THINKING AND WRITING

Using Personification in a Poem

Choose a bird very unlike the hawk. For example, you might choose a sparrow or a lark. Freewrite, exploring what this animal might see as it looks at the world. Then write a poem in which you personify this creature. Your poem can be short or long, rhymed or unrhymed. Have the bird speak, telling what it sees. When you revise make sure you have given your bird human characteristics.

Commentary

In view of the striking personifications of nature's creatures and often merciless view of the world in Hughes's poetry, it is especially surprising that he is a prolific and important writer of children's books. His books for children include six books of poetry, two of fiction, and one of plays, though several of his children's plays for radio have never been collected. In addition, he has written an introduction to poetry for young readers. Originally published in England under the title *Poetry in the Making,* the American edition is called *Poetry Is.*

In part, his dedication to children's literature arises from his belief that "every new child is nature's chance to correct culture's error." To Hughes, children have the ability to reclaim the world's goodness. Their innocence and wonder can defeat evil and darkness. How does he express this idea in the following stanza?

In the little girl's angel gaze
Crow lost every feather
In the little boy's wondering eyes
Crow's bones splintered

---

claws and fly away with it. It can kill and feed where it pleases.

Interpreting

4. Answers will differ. Suggested Response: Stanza three suggests that the hawk is an extraordinary physical creature. His feet are perfectly designed both for living in his environment and for holding onto live prey.
5. In lines 14–16 the hawk describes his merciless, mechanical way of killing. In nature animals kill prey without feeling or remorse.
6. Answers will differ. Suggested Responses: (a) The hawk is suggesting the even plan of its existence. Complex thoughts and interactions have no part in its life. (b) Perhaps the speaker is referring to nature's seemingly unchanging life-cycle that carries on from generation to generation.
7. Answers will differ. Suggested Responses: (a) Some ideas might be that nature is cruel, violent, and mechanistic. Creatures do not act feelingly toward one another. (b) Some students might want to soften Hughes's view by describing their feelings toward nature. Others may point to the truth of the idea that animals are not human.

Applying

8. Answers will differ. Suggested Response: Students may have observed such things as a blue jay cracking open and eating a stolen robin's egg. Students will probably mention a number of human moods that nature seems to display—for example, a violent storm, which can suggest anger.

ANSWERS TO ANALYZING LITERATURE

1. The hawk is endowed with the capacity of uttering humanlike thoughts.
2. Hughes's method leads to a direct, more vivid presentation of the hawk.

THINKING AND WRITING

For help with this assignment, students can refer to Lesson 18, "Writing a Poem," in the Handbook of Writing About Literature.

Closure and Extension

ANSWERS TO THINKING ABOUT THE SELECTION
Recalling

1. (a) The hawk is the speaker in the poem. (b) The hawk is sitting high in the top of the tree.
2. While sleeping the hawk rehearses ways to kill prey and the feeling of eating it.
3. Suggested Response: The hawk can spot prey from high in the air. It can hold live prey in its hooked

Motivation/Prior Knowledge
Ask the students to imagine or recall a special experience that somehow won't go away—a picture of the sun rising over the lake, or the view from a mountaintop on a perfect winter day. The event crops up in memory, and we search for new meanings for it. Are such experiences common for people? Are they important for living? Can they in any way help determine the direction of someone's life?

Master Teacher Note Ted Hughes's poem tells about a person's experience of seeing horses in a woods and the effect of the experience on the person at a much later time. Discuss the effect of a simple incident on some artists—Dante's seeing Beatrice, for example. Bring in examples of the work of artists who paint the same or similar things—over and over—Van Gogh's sunflowers, Georgia O'Keeffe's Arizona mountain.

Purpose-Setting Question What does this poem suggest about the effect of a memory on a person's life?

1 **Literary Focus** Describe the scene, using the author's own words. What was the speaker's mood then? How might someone else have described the same scene?

2 **Discussion** What is the only action of the horses? What do the details in these lines contribute to the poem's meaning?

3 **Discussion** What characteristic of the horses made the most lasting impression on the speaker? How do you know this?

The Horses

Ted Hughes

1

I climbed through woods in the hour-before-dawn dark.
Evil air, a frost-making stillness,

Not a leaf, not a bird—
A world cast in frost. I came out above the wood

5 Where my breath left tortuous statues in the iron light.
But the valleys were draining the darkness

Till the moorline—blackening dregs of the brightening
  gray—
Halved the sky ahead. And I saw the horses:

2

Huge in the dense gray—ten together—
10 Megalith-still. They breathed, making no move,

With draped manes and tilted hind-hooves,
Making no sound.

3

I passed: not one snorted or jerked its head.
Gray silent fragments

15 Of a gray silent world.

I listened in emptiness on the moor-ridge.
The curlew's[1] tear turned its edge on the silence.

Slowly detail leafed from the darkness. Then the sun
Orange, red, red erupted

20 Silently, and splitting to its core tore and flung cloud,
Shook the gulf open, showed blue,

And the big planets hanging—
I turned

Stumbling in the fever of a dream, down towards
25 The dark woods, from the kindling tops.

---

1. curlew (kʉr′ lo͞o) *n.*: A large, brownish wading bird with long legs.

And came to the horses.
                                        There, still they stood,
But now steaming and glistening under the flow of light,

Their draped stone manes, their tilted hind-hooves
30 Stirring under a thaw while all around them

The frost showed its fires. But still they made no sound.
Not one snorted or stamped,

Their hung heads patient as the horizons,
High over valleys, in the red leveling rays—

35 In din of the crowded streets, going among the years, the
    faces,
May I still meet my memory in so lonely a place

Between the streams and the red clouds, hearing curlews,
Hearing the horizons endure.

4

THINKING ABOUT THE SELECTION
Recalling

1. What are four words in lines 1–15 that depict the atmosphere of the morning?
2. How are the horses different in the second sighting than in the first?
3. What wish does the speaker make in the last four lines of the poem?

Interpreting

4. (a) In your own words, what does "detail leafed from the darkness" in line 18 mean? (b) What does "the sun/Orange, red, red erupted" in lines 19 and 20 mean?
5. (a) What is the figure of speech in line 33? (b) How do you explain the comparison?
6. The view of nature is different in "The Horses" from that in "Hawk Roosting." What is the basic difference?

Applying

7. Think of a place you would like to remember later, in "the crowded streets, going among the years." (a) What kind of place is it? (b) Why would you like to remember it?

THINKING AND WRITING
Comparing Poems

Reread William Wordsworth's "Lines Composed a Few Miles Above Tintern Abbey." Then write an essay in which you compare Wordsworth's view of nature with that of Ted Hughes in "The Horses." Make notes before you begin to write. Jot down a few specific lines from each poem to support your comparison. In writing your first draft, be willing to speculate on the reasons for the differences between the poems. When you revise your first draft, check to be sure that your statements are supported by evidence from the poems.

The Horses   1305

4 **Discussion** Looking back over the whole poem, why is this memory so important for the speaker? What do the horses represent to him?

---

ing of dawn, the shapes of individual objects become clearer, as upon closer inspection one can see individual leaves on a tree. (b) Sometimes, especially on a stormy day, the sun at sunrise will look like a bright red ball. Hughes's description is eerie and suggests something ominous is about to happen.
5. (a) The simile in line 33 compares the patient horses to the patient horizon high over the valley, awaiting the sunrise. (b) Answers will differ. Suggested Response: The comparison is tied to the speaker's reaction. He judges both the horses and the horizon to be patient. Nature's patient waiting is important as it implies confidence that the sun will indeed rise.
6. Answers will differ. Suggested Response: In "Hawk Roosting" the message comes entirely through the hawk, who views nature as mechanistic, isolating, and without compassion. In "The Horses," nature is seen through human eyes. The speaker finds in his experience with nataure an important message to help him endure his life.

Applying

7. Answers will differ. Encourage students to think of experiences in places and to note that the place, as in the poem, might be an ordinary and even familiar spot.

Challenge Does the author clearly define what the experience with the horses meant to the speaker? How important is this information to understanding the meaning of the poem?

THINKING AND WRITING

Publishing Student Writing Have students help design a classroom or library bulletin board on Personification. Include student artwork and writing as well as examples from cartoons and artworks by major artists and writers.

Closure and Extension

ANSWERS TO THINKING ABOUT THE SELECTION
Recalling

1. Some words depicting the morning atmosphere are *dark, evil, frost,* and *grey.*

2. In the second sighting the horses are "steaming and glistening." They have started to move their hind hooves.
3. The speaker wishes he might still meet the memory of his experience in the midst of his ongoing busy life.

Interpreting

4. Answers will differ. Suggested Responses: (a) With the gradual com-

1305

GUIDE FOR INTERPRETING

Not Waving but Drowning; Pretty

Stevie Smith (1902-1971) shows intelligence, honesty, and wit in her poetry. Her poems are hard to categorize because of their variations in tone, form, and perspective. One critic calls her work "a forest of themes and attitudes." She is, the critic continues, "as surprising as she is skillful, her finesse equal to her boldness."

This independent-minded poet was born Florence Margaret Smith in Hull, Yorkshire. Small as a child, she was nicknamed "Stevie" after a famous jockey. When she was three, Smith moved with her mother and sister from the rural Yorkshire of her birth to an unfashionable London suburb. Because her mother's health was poor and her father had deserted the family to go to sea, Smith and her sister Molly were raised mainly by an aunt. The bond between "Auntie Lion" and Smith was warm and close, and the two were to live together for Smith's entire life.

Smith worked for many years in a magazine publisher's office in London, and often gave poetry readings on English radio and television. She first published her poetry and fiction when she was in her early thirties, ultimately publishing three novels and more than ten collections of poetry. Her first novel, *Novel on Yellow Paper,* appeared in 1936, and her first collection of poems, *A Good Time Was Had by All,* in 1937. "Not Waving but Drowning" was published in 1957.

Writer's Techniques

Voice. When a poet writes, the poet has a voice—a speaker's voice that can use idiom, rhythm, intonation, and other devices to achieve its effects. When you, the reader, scan a poem (even though silently), you "hear" a voice expressing the words in the poem. You notice, often without conscious thought, the pauses, the pitch, the stresses on certain words and syllables. If you are alert, you will also perceive the feelings behind the voice, such as excitement, panic, despair, or indifference. Voice, then, is an aspect of tone and can be described by an adjective or adjectives, just as tone can.

Writing

Freewrite for a few minutes, using your own natural voice. Make no effort to put your words into complete, grammatically correct sentences. Simply write as you think, quickly and even disjointedly. When you have finished, look back on what you have written. How would you describe your written voice? Serious? Amusing? Casual? Try to decide on the adjective that best describes it.

1306   *Contemporary Writers*

Not Waving but Drowning

Stevie Smith

Nobody heard him, the dead man,
But still he lay moaning:
I was much further out than you thought
And not waving but drowning.

5   Poor chap, he always loved larking
And now he's dead
It must have been too cold for him his heart gave way,
They said.

Oh, no no no, it was too cold always
10   (Still the dead one lay moaning)
I was much too far out all my life
And not waving but drowning.

(margin brackets labeled 1, 2, 3, 4)

THINKING ABOUT THE SELECTION

Recalling

1. Five lines in the poem are spoken by the dead man. Which lines are they?
2. (a) How did the spectators interpret the dead man's waving? (b) What led them to make this interpretation?
3. What caused the man's death?

Interpreting

4. What does the *it* represent in line 9, "Oh, no no no, it was too cold always"?
5. In what sense was the dead man "too far out" all his life?
6. In line 4, the phrase "not waving but drowning" seems to be the literal truth. In line 12, the same phrase has a metaphorical meaning. What is its metaphorical meaning?

Applying

7. What kinds of distress signals in ordinary life might be interpreted as "waving"?

ANALYZING LITERATURE

Understanding Voice

"Not Waving but Drowning" appears to be simple, but the appearance is deceptive. Three speakers can be identified in it: a narrator, a spectator (or spectators), and the dead man. The narrator's voice (lines 1, 2 and 10) is matter-of-fact and neutral, if a bit puzzled. The narrator's double use of the word *moaning* adds to your understanding of the dead man's distress.

1. Study lines 5–7. (a) What adjective or adjectives do you think accurately describe the voice of the spectators? (b) Explain.
2. (a) What adjective or adjectives describe the voice of the dead man? (b) Explain.

Not Waving But Drowning   1307

Master Teacher Note This poem clearly reflects the author's love for the rhythm and intonation of language. Behind a genial appearance lies a frightening reality; behind an optimistic front lies powerful, sometimes terrible truth. To help students appreciate the use of connotation, have them list several common adjectives and change their meanings by using them in different situations. Include both positive and negative adjectives in the list. Students should understand that word meanings can change with circumstances and a person's mood.

Purpose-Setting Question In what way is this poem about much more than the author's concern for the word *pretty* or her desire to describe a scene in nature?

1 **Reading Strategy** Have the students list the images in lines 1–16 in order. What pattern emerges from the list?

2 **Discussion** How can an eye "not see enough"? Why might the author introduce the person viewing the scene in this way?

3 **Discussion** Why does the author use "thief" to describe a person here? From whose viewpoint is the person a thief?

4 **Discussion** How does the author answer the question posed in line 1 here? Is the answer unusual?

Reader's Response Do you think "Nature is always careless and indifferent"? Why or why not?

Pretty

Stevie Smith

Why is the word pretty so underrated?
In November the leaf is pretty when it falls
The stream grows deep in the woods after rain
And in the pretty pool the pike stalks

5 He stalks his prey, and this is pretty too,
The prey escapes with an underwater flash
But not for long, the great fish has him now
The pike is a fish who always has his prey

And this is pretty. The water rat is pretty
10 His paws are not webbed, he cannot shut his nostrils
As the otter can and the beaver, he is torn between
The land and water. Not "torn," he does not mind.

The owl hunts in the evening and it is pretty
The lake water below him rustles with ice
15 There is frost coming from the ground, in the air mist
All this is pretty, it could not be prettier.

Yes, it could always be prettier, the eye abashes
It is becoming an eye that cannot see enough,
Out of the wood the eye climbs. This is prettier
20 A field in the evening, tilting up.

The field tilts to the sky. Though it is late
The sky is lighter than the hill field
All this looks easy but really it is extraordinary
Well, it is extraordinary to be so pretty.

25 And it is careless, and that is always pretty
This field, this owl, this pike, this pool are careless,
As Nature is always careless and indifferent
Who sees, who steps, means nothing, and this is pretty.

So a person can come along like a thief—pretty!—
30 Stealing a look, pinching the sound and feel,
Lick the icicle broken from the bank
And still say nothing at all, only cry pretty.

Cry pretty, pretty, pretty and you'll be able
Very soon not even to cry pretty
35 And so be delivered entirely from humanity
This is prettiest of all, it is very pretty.

THINKING ABOUT THE SELECTION
Recalling

1. In the first four stanzas, what are seven things that the speaker says are pretty?
2. Why does the speaker feel the need to see beyond the wood?
3. What is "prettiest of all"?

Interpreting

4. The speaker does not define *pretty* directly but only through examples. What is the speaker's implied definition of *pretty*?
5. How does the speaker feel about the fact that nature is "careless and indifferent"?
6. (a) What do you think the speaker means by "being delivered entirely from humanity"? (b) Why might the speaker regard that as pretty?

Applying

7. What aspect of nature—other than its prettiness—can serve as a useful example for human beings? Explain.

CRITICAL THINKING AND READING
Comparing and Contrasting Attitudes

Both Ted Hughes in "Hawk Roosting" and Stevie Smith in "Pretty" accept the everyday violence in nature. To Hughes, the hawk's "manners are tearing off heads." To Smith, the pike's stalking and capture of its prey are "pretty." Yet Hughes and Smith express themselves very differently about nature's unconcern.

1. Both the Hughes poem and the Smith poem have been described as "chilling." Which poet—or neither or both of them—do you think views nature as being essentially benign? Explain.
2. A poet's attitudes are expressed in words. List ten key words from each poem that support your answer to the preceding question.

THINKING AND WRITING
Evaluating a Poem

Write an essay evaluating either of Stevie Smith's poems. Begin by deciding which poem you prefer, or which poem you believe will allow you to express the most convincing opinion. Write a thesis sentence that states your opinion clearly. Use lines from the poem in writing your first draft. When you revise, make a special effort to see that the quoted lines fit smoothly and effectively into what you have written. Your final draft should be as error-free as you can make it. Prepare this draft and share it with your classmates. Compare your reaction to the poems with theirs.

Pretty 1309

Interpreting

4. The speaker implies that pretty is the quality of being striking to the eye, vivid, or vital, because it includes even things not thought of as "pretty." Pretty describes a kind of cosmic truth about nature and reality.
5. The speaker feels it is somehow nature's right and privilege to be careless and indifferent.
6. (a) Answers will differ. Suggested Response: The phrase might refer to death, but more clearly means deliverance from association with ordinary, insensitive humanity. (b) Answers will differ. Suggested Response: The speaker feels disassociated from most people, viewing nature and life in a different way.

Applying

7. Answers will differ. Suggested Response: Some aspects of nature that can serve as useful examples are breeding cycles, living habits, and so on.

ANSWERS TO CRITICAL THINKING AND READING

1. Answers will differ. Suggested Response: The word *benign* is defined as "good natured or kindly" or "not malignant." The hawk is portrayed as totally isolated, not relating to anyone or anything. It is clearly not good natured, nor is it not malignant, since it accepts "tearing off heads" as a way of life. In Smith's poem, nature is portrayed as "indifferent" and "careless." The word *benign* might be used for this poem, in the sense of not malignant.
2. The word choices will differ but may include for "Hawk Roosting"—*hooked, head, hooked feet, perfect kills, feet locked, tearing off heads, allotment of death,* and *through bones of the living;* and for "Pretty"—*pike stalks, beaver is torn, field tilling up, it is careless,* and *indifferent.*

THINKING AND WRITING

For help with this assignment, students can refer to Lesson 15, "Evaluating a Literary Work," in the Handbook of Writing About Literature.

Closure and Extension

ANSWERS TO THINKING ABOUT THE SELECTION
Recalling

1. Seven things the speaker says are pretty are a falling leaf, a pool, a pike stalking prey, a pike getting prey, a water rat, an owl hunting, and frost forming.
2. A view beyond the woods is "extraordinary" and more cosmic, including sky and hills.
3. Being "delivered entirely from humanity" is prettiest.

Writer's Techniques

Writing

Anniversary; Out

Elaine Feinstein (1930-   ) is an inventive poet. Her first collection of poems, *In a Green Eye*, appeared in 1966, and her first novel, *The Circle,* four years later. In both prose and poetry, Feinstein displays a sly sense of humor coupled with a discerning fidelity to her own experience. Born in Bootle, Lancashire, Feinstein received her B.A. and M.A. from Cambridge University, then worked as an editor, teacher, translator, and journalist.

Feinstein was raised in the English Midlands, the daughter of a cabinet maker who ran his own factory until economic problems forced him to start anew. As such, her background was typical of the generation who profited from the 1944 Education Act, which made it possible for many to obtain a higher education. For ten years beginning in 1956, when she married biochemist Arnold Feinstein, she spent much of her time raising their three children. After the pulication of her first book, she came into contact with fellow poet Donald Davie, who urged her to apply for a lectureship at Essex University, where he taught. Her application was successful, and she spent 1967–1969 collaborating with a number of fellow poets to publish their poems in a weekly mineographed pamphlet. Through the group, she came to feel that her roots were not truly English. Many see her subsequent writing as a quest for those roots in European history and culture.

Style. Feinstein says: "I began to write poetry in the '60s very consciously influenced by American poets (Emily Dickinson and William Carlos Williams, in particular), at a time when line, and spacing, to indicate the movement of poetry was much less fashionable than it is now among young British poets."

Word associations are the uniquely personal images, experiences, or thoughts that particular words bring to mind. For example, the word *diesel* denotes a particular kind of internal-combustion engine, but its associations are not easy to predict. It might remind one person of her first close-up view of a huge locomotive in a train station. It might remind another of the distinctive smell of diesel exhaust fumes on a busy highway. Think of a common word that has unique associations for you. Jot down the random thoughts that occur to you in connection with the word.

Anniversary

Elaine Feinstein

Suppose I took out a slender ketch from
under the pokes of Palace pier tonight to
catch a sea going fish for you   **1**

or dressed in antique goggles and wings and
5   flew down through sycamore leaves into the park   **2**

or luminescent through some planetary strike
put one delicate flamingo leg over the sill of your lab

Could I surprise you? or would you insist on   **3**
keeping a pattern to link every transfiguration?   **4**

10   Listen, I shall have to whisper it
into your heart directly: we are all
supernatural / every day
we rise new creatures / cannot be predicted   **5**

THINKING ABOUT THE SELECTION

Recalling

1. What is the second "transfiguration" the speaker might make to surprise the *you*?
2. Where does the speaker suggest that the *you*—the person spoken to—might be found?
3. What descriptive word does the speaker say applies to all people?

Interpreting

4. (a) What kind of person is the *you* who is being addressed? (b) How can you tell?
5. (a) What kind of person is the speaker? (b) How can you tell?
6. In what way is the speaker's meaning for *supernatural* different from the meaning that moviegoers or readers of science fiction might be inclined to give the word?
7. Why do you think the poet calls this poem "Anniversary"?
8. What makes it clear that each of the first three stanzas is complete even though none has end punctuation?
9. Why does the poet not put the second question in stanza 4 into a separate stanza?
10. What purpose do the slashes (/) serve in the last two lines of the poem?

Applying

11. In the poem the speaker and the person spoken to seem to have quite different temperaments. How valid a perception on the poet's part do you think that is? Explain.

Motivation/Prior Knowledge
Have the students imagine they are asked to help someone write a factual report. Then have them imagine they are asked to help the person write a poem. Which helping job is harder? Do professional poets ever need help with writing? What kind of help? Who or what might provide that help?

Master Teacher Note This poem uses a scene to reflect a person's mood. Show the students several photos and paintings of people with things in the background. How does the background detail contribute to their understanding more about the person? If you can clip away the background detail, let them notice the effect created by looking at the people or person alone.

Purpose-Setting Question What kind of mentor would most help a creative person such as a poet?

1 **Critical Thinking and Reading** The poem begins with two three-word simple sentences. The next two sentences contain personification, similes, and imagery. Examine the imagery carefully. How does the poet use all these elements to illustrate something about the speaker's state of mind?

2 **Clarification** *Camel-thorn* is "a plant or tree in the mimosa family, which bears yellow flowers."

3 **Discussion** Why has the author placed this line here, rather than at the opening of the next stanza?

4 **Discussion** Why is the person referred to as a "spirit of invention"? Is there is a contradiction in asking for someone who is "holy" and "innocent" and using the word "unnaturally"?

5 **Discussion** What is the relationship between the builder's cranes "like birds" and the "white gulls"?

Out

Elaine Feinstein

1, 2
The diesel stops. It is morning. Gray sky
is falling into the mud. At the waterside
two builders' cranes are sitting like birds

3
and the yellow gorse[1] pushes up
5 like camel-thorn between oil-drums and old cars.
Who shall I take for my holy poet

4
to lead me out of this plain? I want an
innocent spirit of invention: a Buster Keaton[2]
to sail unnaturally overhead by simple leverage and

10 fire the machinery. Then we should all spring out of our
heads, dazzled with hope, even the white-faced ticket
collector dozing over his fag,[3] at such an intervention

5
suddenly in this stopped engine, we should
see the white gulls rising out of the rain over
15 the fen: and know our own freedom.

---

1. gorse *n.*: A prickly green shrub with yellow flowers.
2. Buster Keaton: An American motion-picture actor (1895–1966), who was among the most popular silent film comedians, having created a character who, though he never smiled, was able to overcome all obstacles.
3. fag: Cigarette.

THINKING ABOUT THE SELECTION
Recalling

1. What is the setting of this poem?
2. How does the speaker describe the kind of holy poet she is seeking?
3. What would happen if someone were to appear and "fire the machinery"?

Interpreting

4. To what extent would the effect of the scene be different if the cranes were busily at work rather than standing idle?
5. The speaker wants to be led "out of this plain." In your own words, define *plain* as the poet is using the word.
6. Why do you think a "Buster Keaton" is needed to shake things up?
7. Explain the analogy suggested in the last stanza.

Applying

8. Besides poetry, what is a healthful and effective way to lift oneself out of a bleak mood?

THINKING AND WRITING
Writing About Style

Write an essay about Elaine Feinstein's style. Consider her remarks about her own poetry (see Writer's Techniques, page 1310). Then review "Anniversary" and "Out" carefully. Think about Feinstein's subject matter and her ideas as well as about her word choice, imagery, sentence structure, usage, and punctuation. Style is a very broad concept. Make a chart comparing and contrasting the style in both. When you write your first draft, include lines from the poem to illustrate and clarify your statements. When you revise the first draft, pay close attention to your own style. A good essay should be enjoyable and thought-provoking—and your writing style largely determines if it is. Make sure you have supported your main idea with details from the poems. Have you quoted precisely and accurately? Have you punctuated quotations accurately? Proofread your essay and prepare a final draft.

Commentary

In addition to writing poetry, Elaine Feinstein also writes novels, short stories, and television scripts. Talent in more than one literary genre is unusual. As a result, reviewers have encountered some difficulty characterizing her style and achievements in her nonpoetic writing. For example, she has been labeled a "poetic novelist" by one reviewer. This inability to pin a label on her writing is not limited to critics; Feinstein herself has described her first novel as a "prose poem," thereby acknowledging her interweaving of poetic techniques into prose writing. Indeed, she once remarked that she first wrote prose as "an extension of the poetic impulse."

Her first novel, *The Circle* (1970), clearly shows how she created a different style by adapting some traditional poetic devices to the form of the novel. This is especially seen in her use of spacing and pauses for emphasis and the way she fragments syntax to mirror rhythm and pacing. As with all her novels, in *The Circle* Feinstein pares down her language—as a poet would—to say what she wants in the most economical and effective manner.

Her stylistic innovations are designed, in the words of one reviewer, to enable her "to write novels which move her readers, as the great novels of the past have done, and to involve them in the fate of her characters so that they will care about what happens to them."

Out   1313

ANSWERS TO THINKING ABOUT THE SELECTION
Recalling

1. The setting is a bleak railroad siding where an engine is pulled in for refueling.
2. The speaker describes the holy poet as an "innocent spirit of invention."
3. If someone were to "fire the machinery," the speaker and others would know their own freedom.

Interpreting

4. Answers will differ. Suggested Response: If the cranes were busy it would indicate that something was being built today, a suggestion of growth and aliveness.
5. Answers will differ. Suggested Response: *Plain* here has the meaning of a personal dry place, where originality and creativity have seemingly fled.
6. Answers will differ. Suggested Response: The presence of such a character would add interest, humor, the unusual, and the alive to a drab scene.
7. Answers will differ. Suggested Response: The last line suggests an analogy between knowledge of our freedom and seeing white gulls rise out of a fen.

Applying

8. Answers will differ. Suggested Response: There are many ways to lift oneself out of a bleak mood, such as walking, listening to music, or calling a friend.

Challenge What kinds of things could be spirits of invention? Discuss those things mentioned in the poem and add your own ideas.

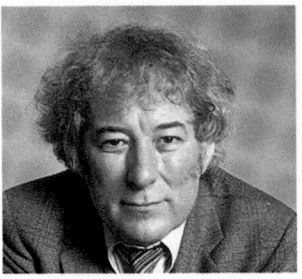

Follower; Shore Woman

Seamus Heaney (1939-   ), born in county Derry, Northern Ireland, has devoted much of his poetry to the life, history, and conflict of his homeland. He is a gifted tradionalist whom the American poet Robert Lowell has called "the most important Irish poet since Yeats." The eldest of nine children, Heaney spent a happy childhood on the farm that had been in his family for generations. He has said that his deep regard for tradition and the past grew from his early experiences in the rich boggy land of his ancestors. After graduating from the local primary school in 1951, he left home to board in St. Columba's College in Londonderry. He first published as an undergraduate at Queen's University. Long having struggled with the role of the artist in political situations, Heaney left Northern Ireland in 1972, when a cottage on the Synge estate in County Wicklow became available. His departure was termed by some an artistic necessity; by others, a betrayal.

Despite his fame, Heaney is known to be modest and natural. A friend recalls when he met Heaney "fresh from reading at Harvard and dressed for dinner at the Princeton Club, he still managed to convey the easy intimacy of a gathering around a peat fire."

Writer's Techniques

Figurative Language. A poet, like every other writer and speaker, uses two kinds of language: literal and figurative. *Literal language* is that which means exactly what it says. "The audience applauded the candidate's speech loudly" is a literal statement. "The candidate's speech brought down the house," by contrast, is not literal. It is figurative. *Figurative language* (language containing one or more *figures of speech*) has meaning beyond its literal meaning, or apart from it.

Writing

The English language contains a great deal of onomatopoeia —words whose natural sound matches their meaning. Three examples are *buzz, tinkle,* and *twang.* Think about the sounds you hear every day. What words describe them? Write down at least ten examples of onomatopoeia, not including the words already given.

Follower

Seamus Heaney

My father worked with a horse plow,
His shoulders globed like a full sail strung
Between the shafts and the furrow.
The horses strained at his clicking tongue.

5 An expert. He would set the wing
And fit the bright steel-pointed sock.
The sod rolled over without breaking.
At the headrig, with a single pluck

Of reins, the sweating team turned round
10 And back into the land. His eye
Narrowed and angled at the ground,
Mapping the furrow exactly.

I stumbled in his hobnailed wake,
Fell sometimes on the polished sod;
15 Sometimes he rode me on his back
Dipping and rising to his plod.

I wanted to grow up and plow,
To close one eye, stiffen my arm.
All I ever did was follow
20 In his broad shadow round the farm.

I was a nuisance, tripping, falling,
Yapping always. But today
It is my father who keeps stumbling
Behind me, and will not go away.

Closure and Extension

ANSWERS TO THINKING ABOUT THE SELECTION
Recalling

1. The speaker describes how his father would expertly put together the plow and break ground.
2. The boy wanted to grow up to imitate his father and become a farmer.
3. (a) The speaker says he stumbled, fell, and rode behind the plow. (b) He uses the verb *stumbling* to describe his father today.

Interpreting

4. (a) Suggested response: The child was probably about three or four years old. (b) He describes how the father picked him up and rode him piggyback after he stumbled. He was always talking.
5. Answers will differ. Suggested response: The boy wants to close his eye and stiffen his arm in imitation of his father as he mapped out furrows.
6. Answers will differ. Suggested responses: The lines suggest the speaker always tried to follow after his father and was never able to equal him. The speaker remained obscured, behind his father's shadow.
7. The tone is reflective, admiring, and affectionate. Students may cite different lines and phrases in support of their descriptions of the poem's tone.

Applying

8. (a) Time and age radically change the roles. (b) Suggested response: Most young people have to adjust and get used to such changing roles.

ANSWERS TO ANALYZING LITERATURE

1. Answers will differ. (a) "Mapping the furrow" is figurative because the father is not drawing a map showing how the furrows will go. (b) As he plowed, my father carefully planned where each furrow would go. (c) The figurative language adds to the impression of the father's expertise. He is mental-ly planning perfect rows, even as he plows his field.
2. Answers will differ. (a) "My father . . . stumbling" is figurative because the father is not physically tripping and falling. (b) The father may be older now and may need the speaker's care and attention, or the father may be an internal stumbling block for the speaker, who is trying to be a free and independent adult.

THINKING ABOUT THE SELECTION
Recalling

1. How does the speaker show that his father was an expert at plowing?
2. As the boy accompanied his father, what did he want to do?
3. (a) What three verbs does the speaker use to describe the father's actions behind the plow? (b) What parallel verb does he use in speaking of his father today?

Interpreting

4. (a) What do you think is the approximate age of the speaker in the plowing scene he describes? (b) How can you tell?
5. Why do you think the boy wanted to close one eye and stiffen his arm?
6. The speaker says: "All I ever did was follow/In his broad shadow. . . ." What double meaning do those words suggest?
7. What is the tone of this poem? Find evidence to support your answer.

Applying

8. (a) What does this poem suggest about the changing roles of parents and children? (b)

Do you think most young people are prepared for these changing roles? Explain your answer.

ANALYZING LITERATURE
Understanding Figurative Language

Figurative language is language that is not meant to be interpreted literally. When Heaney writes that his father's shoulders "globed like a full sail," he does not mean that they became an actual sphere or that they were as large as a ship's wind-filled sail. Yet the points of resemblance give you a clear, striking picture of his father walking behind the plow.

1. "Mapping the furrow" (line 12) is an example of figurative language. (a) Why? (b) How would you express the idea literally? (c) What does the figurative language add to the thought?
2. The line about "my father . . . stumbling" (line 23) is figurative. (a) Why? (b) How would you express the idea literally?

Commentary

Ireland's distinctive basin-like shape—a low-lying plain ringed by mountains—results in an unusual geographic phenomenon. Since drainage is blocked by the mountains, the deep central plain retains moisture, slowing down the decay of organic matter. The ground remains wet and spongy. As a result, thick layers of dark, rich vegetation develop. Since until very recently the area was relatively untouched, astonishingly well-preserved bodies, clothing, food, tools, and artifacts have been unearthed. For centuries the peat from these bogs was cut, dried, and used as fuel; today it is also exported as peat moss after all its moisture is extracted. But the peat bogs are more than a commodity: They spark the creative imagination as well.

Heaney found in the bogs echoes of ancient Ireland. In his famous "bog" poems, Heaney sought to define and explain the present by relating it to the past. Thus, he connects the history and strife of Northern Ireland to the northern European experience. Aided by *The Bog People,* a study with fascinating photographs of the preserved bodies of Iron Age people unearthed from peat bogs, he links in *Wintering Out* and *North* the battles of long-gone Vikings to the struggles of the present-day Irish.

Shore Woman

Seamus Heaney

Man to the hills, woman to the shore.
                    Gaelic proverb

I have crossed the dunes with their whistling bent
Where dry loose sand was riddling round the air
And I'm walking the firm margin. White pocks
Of cockle, blanched roofs of clam and oyster
5   Hoard the moonlight, woven and unwoven
Off the bay. At the far rocks
A pale sud comes and goes.

Under boards the mackerel slapped to death
Yet still we took them in at every cast,
10 Stiff flails of cold convulsed with their first breath.
My line plumbed certainly the undertow,
Loaded against me once I went to draw
And flashed and fattened up towards the light.
He was all business in the stern. I called
15 "This is so easy that it's hardly right,"
But he unhooked and coped with frantic fish
Without speaking. Then suddenly it lulled,
We'd crossed where they were running, the line rose
Like a let-down and I was conscious
20 How far we'd drifted out beyond the head.
"Count them up at your end," was all he said
Before I saw the porpoises' thick backs
Cartwheeling like the flywheels[1] of the tide,
Soapy and shining. To have seen a hill
25 Splitting the water could not have numbed me more
Than the close irruption of that school,
Tight viscous muscle, hooped from tail to snout,
Each one revealed complete as it bowled out
And under.
30   They will attack a boat.

---

1. **flywheels** *n.*: Heavy wheels for regulating the speed and uniformity of motion of a machine.

Presentation

Motivation/Prior Knowledge
Ask the students to imagine they are a child out fishing with their father. The fishing is going well, when suddenly there is a crisis. The child fears the boat will sink, while the father, who is an experienced sailor, remains calm and unmoved. How might it feel to recall this scene years later? Do we sometimes use scenes in our lives to stand for many different experiences?

Master Teacher Note Particularly with **less advanced** students, you may wish to paraphrase those passages that are unclear upon first reading.

Purpose-Setting Question What is this poem saying about the process of forming identity?

1 **Discussion** What is the feel and rhythm of lines 1–2? How is that changed in line 3? What is the contrast between the actions of nature and the speaker?

2 **Discussion** Why does the author place the sea far off in line 7 and then abruptly move both back in time and out to sea in line 8? What is the effect of this?

3 **Critical Thinking and Reading** Heaney's precise choice of words and use of rhythm create multiple levels of meaning. Note the way the father is introduced and the use of the word *stern*. What is the effect of the "But" coming directly after the boy's comment?

Discussion Why has the author used the words "a boat" rather than "this boat"? On what do the father and son disagree?

Thematic Idea Another poem dealing with a relationship between father and son is Dylan Thomas's "Do Not Go Gentle into That Good Night" on page 1102. You might have students compare the father-son relationship in Thomas's poem with that suggested in the two poems by Seamus Heaney.

ANSWERS TO THINKING ABOUT THE SELECTION
Recalling

1. In the first stanza the speaker is walking along a strand at the edge of the dunes.
2. (a) The father and speaker were out in a boat fishing. (b) The fishing was very successful. (c) The speaker became aware of how far out they were when there was a lull and the fish stopped biting.
3. (a) The speaker was frightened about the number, size, and power of the porpoises. (b) The father felt the boy was reacting to a myth about porpoises being dangerous. (c) The father was right, in that they survived being near the porpoises.
4. In the last stanza the speaker is back walking along the strand.

Interpreting

5. Answers will differ. The father takes the coming of the porpoises as a challenge to prove an old yarn is false. The speaker reacts in fear, wanting to simply go back to shore.
6. Answers will differ. (a) The father and speaker seem somewhat distant, the father businesslike and silent and the speaker talkative and enthusiastic. (b) On land their relationship seems remote, with the father contradicting the son and still not communicating with him.
7. Answers will differ. Among things to note are where the speaker was and where he is now, the details of relationship between father and son, and the speaker's words and attitudes then and now.

THINKING ABOUT THE SELECTION
Recalling

1. Where is the speaker in the first stanza?
2. (a) What were the father and the speaker doing in the open boat? (b) How successful were they? (c) When did the speaker become aware of how far the boat had drifted?
3. (a) Why was the speaker frightened at the sight of the porpoises? (b) What was the father's reaction? (c) Who was right about the porpoises—father or speaker?
4. Where is the speaker in the last stanza?

Interpreting

5. What basic difference is there between the father and speaker in the encounter with the porpoises? Explain your answer.
6. (a) How close does the relationship between father and speaker appear to be when the two are at sea? (b) How close is it on land? Explain.
7. What relationship is there between the Gaelic proverb and the title and theme of the poem?

Applying

8. To what extent do you think the speaker's fear suggests weakness? Provide support for your answer.
9. What, if anything, do you think the father said to the speaker after the porpoises had left? What makes you think he said this?

Primary Source Note

In his book *A History of Modern Poetry,* David Perkins made the following comments about Seamus Heaney's collection of poems *Station Island* (1984):

> The second part of *Station Island,* the title sequence, is the most ambitious and also the most directly personal work Heaney has published thus far. Station Island is a place of religious pilgrimage on Lough Derg in Ireland. Making this pilgrimage, Heaney encounters ghosts of dead persons from his own past or from Irish literary history. The encounters are partly modeled on the one with the ghost in Eliot's 'Little Gidding' III and even more on Dante (the verse of some sections is a modified *terza rima*), and from Dante the concrete, direct phrasing acquires a weight that is new in Heaney:
>
> > And then as if a shower were blackening
> > already blackened stubble, the dark weather
> > of his unspoken pain came over him.
>
> Yet other passages are pleasantly swift, simple, and colloquial: "I met a young priest, glossy as a blackbird." Most

I knew it and I asked him to put in
But he would not, declared it was a yarn
My people had been fooled by far too long
And he would prove it now and settle it.
35 Maybe he shrank when those sloped oily backs
Propelled towards us: I lay and screamed
Under splashed brine in an open rocking boat
Feeling each dunt and slither through the timber,
Sick at their huge pleasures in the water.

40 I sometimes walk this strand for thanksgiving
Or maybe it's to get away from him
Skittering his spit across the stove. Here
Is the taste of safety, the shelving sand
Harbors no worse than razorshell[2] or crab—
45 Though my father recalls carcasses of whales
Collapsed and gasping, right up to the dunes.
But tonight such moving sinewed dreams lie out
In darker fathoms, far beyond the head.
Astray upon a debris of scrubbed shells
50 Between parched dunes and salivating wave,
I have rights on this fallow avenue,
A membrane between moonlight and my shadow.

5

---

2. razorshell *n.*: The shell of razor clams, burrowing clams with
elongated, narrow shells that resemble a straight razor.

CRITICAL THINKING AND READING
Recognizing Sound and Meaning

Poets use a number of devices to create the
kinds of sounds that complement the meaning of
their words. Rhyme, rhythm, repetition, harsh-or-
soft consonants and vowels, and onomatopoeia
all help to produce the desired effects.
1. What is one example of onomatopoeia in the
first stanza?
2. What are three examples of repetition of
sound in the second stanza?
3. Sound is used very effectively in line 42. What
devices that make this line work so well?

THINKING AND WRITING
Analyzing the Use of Sound in a Poem

Write an essay in which you analyze the
devices for creating sound in "Shore Woman." To
appreciate the sound effects in the poem, read it
aloud at least once before you begin. Jot down
notes about the sound devices. What impression
do they create? Then write your first draft. Remember that when you write an analysis of this
kind, you have to do more than just point out the
devices. You also have to explain how they work.
When you revise, make sure you have provided
details from the poem to support your analysis.

Shore Woman 1319

Focus

More About the Authors
Donald Davie has stated his belief that the poet "is responsible to the community in which he writes for purifying and correcting the spoken language." Recognized as much for his scholarly work and criticism as for his poetry, Davie's poems are often restrained, carefully wrought statements. Though his roots are clearly English, he has lived and worked in America for many years. His feelings towards his homeland have often tended to be negative and bitter. How might a move as an adult away from one's homeland affect an author's writings? How related is an author's homeland to his work? Can a writer ever get completely away from his or her basic roots?

Molly Holden was in her mid-thirties when she was disabled by multiple sclerosis, a degenerative disease which affects muscle control. In addition to writing adult poetry, she was an award-winning author of children's poetry and fiction. She also developed plays and programs for the British Broadcasting Company. Some have suggested that Holden's progressive illness increased her identity with the earth and affected her themes and the content of her poetry. Discuss the effects of ill health or handicaps on an author's work. Might a serious illness or disability change the direction of an author's work? How?

Critical Evaluation In the second volume of his book *A History of Modern Poetry,* David Perkins notes the paradoxical quality of Davie's allegiances: ". . . though Davie opposed the Modernist-Symbolist premises in poetry, he admired many Modernist poets, especially Pound. And with similar paradox he repeatedly conceded that Augustan poetry [poetry from the era of Pope and Addison], despite or even because of its responsible virtue, was generally minor. He hoped his criticism might help contemporaries to write a poetry of 'urbane and momentous statement,' but the emphasis he attached to this was to some extent a relative and historical one. The moral attitude implied in Augustan style . . . was now especially necessary as a corrective of the present."

Donald Davie
1922–

Donald Davie, one of "the Movement" poets of the 1950's, is noted today for the quiet elegance and urbane perception of his work. He is often compared to the eighteenth-century Augustan poets, whose tone, diction, and verse forms he admires and sometimes emulates. Davie, born in Yorkshire, England, has taught in England, Ireland, and the United States. A traditionalist, he believes that formal discipline in writing can free rather than restrict the poetic imagination. One of his best-known collections, *The Shires* (1974), consists of one poem for each of the forty counties of England.

Davie developed an early interest in poetry from his mother, Alice Sugden Davie, who was so fond of verse that her son was later able to remark that she knew "the greater part, perhaps the whole" of Palgrave's massive *The Golden Treasury of the Best Songs and Lyrical Poems in the English Language* (1861, 1897) by heart. Another influence in the creation of his style was what he calls the "industrially ravaged landscape" of his youth, which contributed to his favoring literature that is "spare and lean."

Molly Holden
1927–1981

Born in London, Molly Holden was twelve when her family moved to the heart of Wiltshire, an area which became the geographical center of her writing. She earned her B.A. and M.A. in English at King's College, London, married, and began a family. Although her poetry was late in coming—her first creative success, *The Bright Cloud,* was published when she was thirty-seven—her verse gained in power and creativity in the 1960's and 1970's. Her work subsequently won many prizes and much critical praise.

Molly Holden wrote poetry that is subtle and sparkling. It is based on close attention to precise, telling details. Although Holden was disabled with multiple sclerosis in 1964, she did not let this progressive illness impede her writing. Her keen observation became, if anything, more acute, and her three finest collections—*To Make Me Grieve* (1968), *Air and Chill Earth* (1972), *The Country Over* (1975)—are testaments to her creative power and indomitable spirit. As she wrote, "Doubly urgent longing fills my days/to put down surely what is my obsession."

> **Objective**
>
> To write a poem using imagery

Support Material

Teaching Portfolio
Teacher Backup, p. 1589
Usage and Mechanics Worksheet, p. 1593
Vocabulary Check, p. 1594
Analyzing Literature Worksheet, *Understanding Imagery,* p. 1596
Language Worksheet, *Understanding Concrete Language,* p. 1597
Selection Test, p. 1598

GUIDE FOR INTERPRETING

For Doreen: A Voice from the Garden; Some Men Create

Writer's Techniques

Imagery. When a writer's words or phrases create a picture in the reader's mind, the writer is using imagery. The mental pictures of imagery do not always involve sight; the images can also come from touch, taste, smell, or hearing. Verbal images based on the five senses are called sensory images. Imagery is important in poetry because it adds color to descriptions and helps to give concrete reality to abstract ideas.

Writing

Imagery is not restricted to poetry. It occurs in all forms of writing and may come up in everyday conversation. A good storyteller uses imagery to create pictures in his or her listeners' minds. For one day, keep a list of the images you hear in conversation or read in newspapers or magazines.

Primary Source

Do writers—especially poets—think differently from the rest of us? Is there such a thing as a "poetic mind"? If so, do poets think in mental pictures of imagery? If not, can nonpoets write poetry? Donald Davie attempted to answer these questions in a recent interview. He began with the assertion that although he wanted above all else to be a "natural poet," he has come to realize that he is not a poet by nature, only by inclination. He continued:

> Most of the poems I have written are not natural poems, in one sense not truly poems, simply because the thought in them could have been expressed—at whatever cost to terseness and point—in a nonpoetic way. This does not mean however that they are worthless, or that they are shams; for as much can be said of much of the poetry of the past that by common consent is worth reading and remembering. Nevertheless I have taken a decision to write no more poems of this kind, only poems which are, if not *naturally*, in all events *truly* poems throughout. For a true poem can be written by a mind not naturally poetic —though by the inhuman labor of thwarting at every point the natural grain and bent. This working against the grain does not damage the mind, nor is it foolish; on the contrary, only by doing this does each true poem as it is written become an authentic widening of experience—a truth won from life against all odds . . .

Guide for Interpreting   1321

Literary Focus Imagery is an essential part of poetry because our first experience of anything comes through our senses. We feel a cool breeze, hear wind rustle through trees, and touch a smooth stone. Point out that we have internal senses such as hunger and thirst, and even a sense of motion.

Writing/Prior Knowledge Ask the students what images they see when they hear a word such as *successful*. When they have completed their writing assignment, they might categorize the images according to the various senses. An analysis of the pattern of images used in a particular newspaper or magazine article could be used as an extra credit assignment.

Vocabulary

Preteach the following vocabulary words:

trellis (trel′ is) *n*.: Frame of crossed strips, usually of wood; used as a screen or support for climbing plants (p. 1322, l. 4)

trefoil (trē′ foil) *n*.: Clover (p. 1322, l. 5)

envisage (en viz′ ij) *v*.: To form a mental picture of; imagine (p. 1322, l. 11)

anglophobia (aŋ glə fo′ bē ə) *n*.: Hatred or fear of England or things English (p. 1322, l. 19)

sough (sou) *n*.: A groan or sighing sound (p. 1322, l. 25)

parapet (par′ ə pit) *n*.: A low wall or railing (p. 1323, l. 7)

husbandry (huz′ bən drē) *n*.: Farming (p. 1323, l. 13)

For Doreen: A Voice from the Garden

Donald Davie

1

We have a lawn of moss.
The next house is called The Beeches.
A towering squirrel-haunted
Trellis of trees, across
5 Our matt and trefoil, reaches
Shade where our guests have sauntered.

2

Cars snap by in the road.
In a famous photographed village
The High Street is our address.
10 Our guests write from abroad
Delighted to envisage
Rose arbor and wilderness.

They get them, and the lilacs.
Some frenzy in us discards
15 Lilacs and all. It will harden,
However England stacks
Her dear discolored cards
Against us, us to her garden.

3

Anglophobia rises
20 In Brooklyn to hysteria
At some British verses.
British, one sympathizes.
Diesel fumes cling to wistaria.[1]
One conceives of worse reverses.

25 The sough of the power brake
Makes every man an island;
But we are the island race.
We must be mad to take
Offense at our poisoned land
And the gardens that pock her face.

---

1. wistaria (wis tir′ ē ə) *n.*: Vines of shrubs with clusters of bluish, white, pink, or purplish flowers.

THINKING ABOUT THE SELECTION
Recalling

1. What are three of the natural features near the speaker's house?
2. (a) Where are the guests from? (b) What delights them about the grounds near the speaker's house?
3. How does the "frenzy in us" cause the speaker (or the English perhaps) to regard garden-like settings such as this one?
4. What does the speaker say the English "must be mad" to dislike?

Interpreting

5. Why do you think the English ignore, or discard, the beauties that foreign guests see there?
6. How does the speaker react to Brooklyn's dislike of certain British verses?
7. If the gardens of England are in fact beautiful, why does the speaker say they "pock her face"?
8. One interpretation of this poem is that its basic theme is English literature, not the English landscape. What evidence do you find in the poem to support this interpretation?

Applying

9. Critics have remarked on Davie's relationship with England—a somewhat antagonistic one —and on his stylistic tendency to "shut the reader out." To what extent do you think these two comments apply to this poem?

Some Men Create

Molly Holden

Some men create an unintended
    beauty by default,
never cut back the creeping ivy
    so its stragglers vault

  5 from crumbling wall to neighboring bridge
    beside the arched lane,
to swing like hair from the parapet,
    shining with spring rain;

never gravel out the timber pile
10   nor lop the dead oak
so that the seeding traveler's joy
    smothers them like smoke.

So among orderly husbandry
    leave some plots alone
15 that the eye may reap with pleasure what
    the hand has not sown.

THINKING ABOUT THE SELECTION

Recalling

1. What does the uncut ivy do?
2. What advice does the speaker give to gardeners?

Interpreting

3. How is the beauty described in this poem created "by default"?
4. What causes the "traveler's joy" in stanza 3?

Applying

5. What are some examples you can point to of "beauty by default"?

6. How do you think a professional gardener or landscaper would respond to this poem?

THINKING AND WRITING

Writing a Poem Using Imagery

    Write an original poem using imagery. The writing assignment on page 1321 should have uncovered many examples of imagery used to brighten up everyday conversation. Perhaps you can use some of these examples in your poem. Remember that your object is to choose words and phrases that will create pictures in the minds of your readers. Once you have a topic for your poem, write your first draft. When you revise, make sure your language is fresh and vivid.

London Moves to Broadway

THE BRITISH INVASION

Although it's commonly supposed that the British have invaded the American stage only recently, they've actually been trodding our boards from the very beginning. Take musicals, for example—those entertaining productions in which a story is told by a combination of spoken dialogue and musical numbers. America claims the first musical —*The Black Crook* (1866)—but England says hers were better. Perhaps we can't settle that dispute, but no one can argue that British plays were imported to America from the time the first curtain was raised. For example, only five years after England's first musical comedy—Osmond Carr's 1892 *In Town*—debuted in London, it was staged in New York.

The balance of trade leveled out somewhat in the next few years, as musical comedy became more firmly established. *The Belle of New York* premiered in New York in 1897, but achieved its major success a year later in London, where it became the first American musical to run for over a year. On the other hand, *Florodora* was a hit in London in 1899 but ran even longer in New York after opening there in 1900. The balance was still tipped in England's favor, however. Although the American stage prospered during the next few years, musicals imported from England (and Vienna!) continued to hold sway here in the early years of the twentieth century.

A SUDDEN SHIFT

Things shifted suddenly with the outbreak of World War I. Swollen with anti-German feeling, Americans no longer wanted European musicals. At the same time, English playwrights suffered a dry spell, and American playwrights and composers flowered as never before. Jerome Kern, Cole Porter, and Irving Berlin set Broadway ablaze with a series of magnificent productions. Oscar Hammerstein II set toes tapping on both sides of the Atlantic with his catchy lyrics. Al Jolson crooned the smash hits from George Gershwin's musicals. Many of these productions found their way to British shores.

After a slow start in the early twenties, American musicals stormed American and British footlights. Fred Astaire and his sister Adele hoofed their way through the first musical collaboration of brothers George and Ira Gershwin; the team of Richard Rodgers and Lorenzo Hart debuted in 1925. In 1927 to 1928 more than fifty musicals opened on Broadway. Paul Robeson sang the haunting "Old Man River" from the smash *Show Boat* in the 1928 London production. The heyday of the American musical continued into the thirties, with the first Pulitzer Prize awarded to a musical (*Of Thee I Sing*, 1931). The American musical continued to grow in the forties and fifties with such hits as Rodgers and Hammerstein's *South Pacific* (1949) and *The King and I* (1951), and Lerner and Loewe's *My Fair Lady* (1956).

SIGNS OF REVIVAL

Meanwhile, the English musical had been showing signs of revival, most notably with the 1960 hit *Oliver!*, seen in New York in 1963. The heyday of the American musical was over; the stage was set for London's invasion of Broadway. Critics—and audiences—agree that England produced the only major theatrical talent of the seventies and eighties.

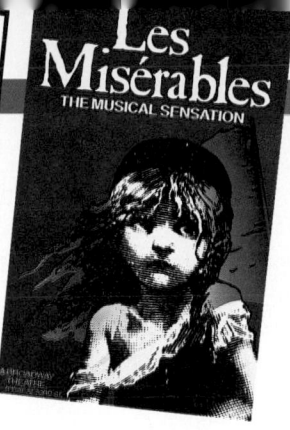

In an interesting reversal, a number of British musical hits debuted in America and then traveled back home. The most famous of these is the remarkable *Jesus Christ Superstar*, a musical based on the life of Christ. The smash team of lyricist Tim Rice and composer Andrew Lloyd Webber opened the play first in New York in 1971, then journeyed back with it to London a year later. But for their next success, *Evita*, the duo returned to the old pattern: This musical opened first in London in 1978, a year later in New York. In the same decade, the American stage also imported England's *Billy*, a musical based on the play *Billy Liar; The Good Companions; Joseph and the Amazing Technicolor Dreamcoat;* and *The Moony Shapiro Songbook* as well as a number of excellent dramas. Lloyd Webber scored big again in 1981 when he brought *Cats* to the New York stage. Based on T. S. Eliot's *Old Possum's Book of Practical Cats*, this dazzling production is marked by extravagant makeup, costumes, and creative staging.

THE 1980's

By the eighties, England had become seemingly the only source of successful musicals; of the twenty-one shows on Broadway at the beginning of 1983, more than a third came from England's theatre district, the West End. And these shows were good, too: In 1987, for example, twelve of Broadway's nineteen Tony Awards went to musicals that originated on the London stage. The musical *Me and My Girl*, for example, capitulated English actor Robert Lindsay to stardom. But the brightest light on Broadway belongs to Andrew Lloyd Webber.

Webber added to his string of commercial successes when he imported his musical wonderland *Starlight Express;* more noted for its roller skating and clever set than plot, it nonetheless delighted packed audiences. His astonishingly successful *Les Misérables* set the stage for the megahit *Phantom of the Opera*. Tickets are virtually unavailable for this quasi-operatic retelling of the monster-meets-girl melodrama.

Perhaps the most striking example of the way London has moved to Broadway is *Follies*, not so much an import from the West End as a complete restaging of American Stephen Sondheim's 1971 musical. Although the original version won five Tony Awards during its Broadway run, it lost nearly its entire investment. British producer Cameron Mackintosh's invitation to Sondheim to "have a wee think" about the play resulted in an entirely revamped show. The three million dollar London production opened to huge advance sales, and Mackintosh hopes to bring *Follies* back to Broadway, a rare reverse transfer that would be both welcome yet humbling.

As one British paper put it, "The Great White Way seems to have become an overseas colony of the West End."

Cross Currents   1325

Questions

1. What factors explained the diminishing of British influence on Broadway around the time of World War I?
2. What musical signaled the revival of the English musical stage?
3. (a) Which English composer revived the English musical stage almost singlehandedly? (b) Name two of his biggest hits.
4. How does the revamping of Stephen Sondheim's 1971 musical *Follies* illustrate the new strength of the English musical stage?

Activities

1. Bring in recordings, tapes, or compact disks of some of Andrew Lloyd Webber's musicals and play them for the class.
2. Have students research the way in which Eliot's *Old Possum's Book of Practical Cats* was adapted for the musical stage. Ask them to report their findings to the class.

The writing assignments on page 1326 have students write creatively, while those on page 1327 have them think about the selections and write critically.

YOU THE WRITER
Guidelines for Evaluating Assignment 1

1. Does the new ending begin at the turning point of the story?
2. Does the story move in a different direction to achieve surprise?
3. Is the new ending logically linked to something presented earlier?
4. Does the new ending seem as if it had been written by the author of the story?
5. Is the ending free from grammar, usage, and mechanics errors?

Guidelines for Evaluating Assignment 2

1. Has the student written an interesting, dramatic, or startling letter to a friend that discusses a character from a story in this unit?
2. Does the letter include what the character is like, how he or she relates to the events of the story, the student's feelings about the character, and an interesting and memorable ending?
3. Is the letter written in conventional letter form?
4. Is the letter free from grammar, usage, and mechanics errors?

Guidelines for Evaluating Assignment 3

1. Has the student written a poem with a strong central image or idea, using a poem from this unit as a model?
2. Has the student followed the model for rhythm, rhyme, and structure but modified it where appropriate to the central ideas he or she is expressing?
3. Is the poem expressive and clear?
4. Is the poem free from grammar, usage, and mechanics errors?

Assignment

1. Write an alternate ending for one of the stories in this unit. Make the ending follow logically from preceding events and from the nature of the characters.

Prewriting. Reread the story to see how its earlier parts prepare for the present ending. Then ask, "How might these parts lead up to a different ending?"

Writing. Now write your alternate ending. Start at the turning point, and, to achieve surprise, have the story move in a different direction. To make the new ending logical, link it to something presented earlier.

Revising. Revise with the aim of making your new ending seem as if it had been written by the author of the story.

Assignment

2. Write a letter to a friend in which you discuss a character in a story from this unit. Write as if the character were real and you had been present at the events recounted in the story.

Prewriting. Ask, "What is the character like? What are his or her key traits? How are they seen in the events of the story? What is the main idea I should express about the character? How can I develop and conclude my letter in an interesting and memorable way?" Freewrite exploring your answer to these questions.

Writing. When you have arrived at clear and definite answers to these questions, write a personal letter in conventional form.

Revising. Can you make your letter more interesting, more dramatic, or more startling? Have you captured the characters personality accurately? Make changes with these possibilities in view.

Assignment

3. Sometimes a poem has a central image or idea that spreads itself throughout the poem like the branches and roots of a tree. Write a poem with a central image or idea, using a poem in this unit as a model.

Prewriting. Find a subject you would like to write about. Then think of a central image or idea that can tie together and express your thoughts and feelings about the subject. Ask, "How might the author of my model have treated this subject?"

Writing. Write the first draft of your poem. Follow your model poem for rhythm, rhyme, and structure. However, make whatever modifications you feel are appropriate to what you are trying to express.

Revising. Make changes to improve the expressiveness of your poem. Be sure to read your verses aloud to see if their rhythm and sound can be improved.

YOU THE CRITIC

Assignment

1. Choose two characters from two different stories in this section and write an essay discussing (1) the important actions they took, and (2) the consequences of these actions.

Prewriting. For each character, divide a sheet of paper into two columns. In the first column, list the major actions the characters took. In the second column, list the consequences of these actions.

Writing. In your opening paragraph, describe in general the actions of each character and the consequences of the actions. In the body paragraphs, treat each story separately. For both stories, discuss the characters' actions first and the consequences second.

Revising. Carefully review the organization of your essay to see if you can establish connections by comparison and contrast between the two characters you have discussed.

Assignment

2. Much contemporary fiction is quite different from earlier, more traditional fiction. Write an essay in which you explain why you prefer contemporary or earlier stories.

Prewriting. First decide on the chief differences between earlier and more recent stories. Which of these differences explain your likes and dislikes? Which specific stories would you cite to illustrate these differences?

Writing. Write your first draft. Begin by stating your preference. Give your reasons by discussing the qualities you like or dislike in older or contemporary fiction.

Revising. Revise your essay by attempting to clarify or support more strongly your reasons for your preference. See if you can use comparison and contrast to reveal more vividly the chief differences between the two periods of fiction.

Assignment

3. Some lines in a poem are memorable either because of what they say or how they say it, or both. Choose at least three poems from this unit and write an essay identifying the lines you consider most memorable, explaining why you think they are memorable.

Prewriting. Scan the poems in this unit for the ones you think contain the most memorable lines. Copy these lines and note why you liked them. Were you impressed by the content? Was the imagery sharp? Was the phrasing beautiful?

Writing. Write an introductory paragraph in which you announce your subject and indicate how you will approach it. Then discuss each of the memorable lines, quoting the line first and then explaining why you think it is memorable.

Revising. See if you can use transitional words and phrases to improve the unity and coherence of your essay.

You the Critic   1327

1. Does the comparison begin with a general description of the action of two characters from different stories?
2. Do the body paragraphs treat the stories separately and discuss the characters' actions first and the consequences second?
3. Has the student established connections by comparing and contrasting the characters?
4. Is the essay free from grammar, usage, and mechanics errors?

Guidelines for Evaluating Assignment 2

1. Does the student begin the essay by stating a preference for contemporary or traditional fiction?
2. Does the student give reasons by discussing the qualities he or she likes or dislikes in traditional or contemporary literature?
3. Does the student use evidence from the literature to support his or her reasons?
4. Is the essay free from grammar, usage, and mechanics errors?

Guidelines for Evaluating Assignment 3

1. Is there an introductory paragraph that announces the three poems and indicates that they are memorable?
2. Has the student discussed each of the memorable lines, quoting the lines first and then explaining why they are memorable?
3. Has the student used transitional words and phrases to improve the unity and coherence of the essay?
4. Is the essay free from grammar, usage, and mechanics errors?

Literary Map of Great Britain

N

King Duncan's palace (Macbeth)
●Macbeth's castle
Dunsinane
(Macbeth slain)

Johnson and
Boswell tour
Hebrides, 1773

Outer Hebrides
Isle of Skye
Inner Hebrides
SCOTTISH HIGHLANDS

Loch Ness

SCOTLAND

NORTH SEA

Sir Patrick Spens
and Scottish lords drown:
"The Seafarer"

Loch Lomond

Dumferling *"Sir Patrick Spens"*

ATLANTIC OCEAN

Ayshire
Burn's "Sweet Afton,"
"To a Mouse"

English-Scottish border.
Setting of many early ballads

NORTHERN IRELAND

Kelloe
E.B. Browning born

Sligo
Yeat's
"Lake Isle
of Innisfree"

Lake District
Wordsworth's poetry

Whitby
Caedmon's hymns

IRISH SEA

Haworth Moor
Setting of *Jane Eyre*

Wakefield
Medieval mystery
and morality plays

Humberside
Marvell lives, writes

Dublin ✵
Birthplace of Steele,
Swift, Shaw, Wilde,
Yeats, Joyce

Gawain vs.
Green Knight

A Shropshire Lad,
Housman

Lichfield
Samuel Johnson
born

IRELAND

Stratford-on-Avon
Shakespeare

ENGLAND

Kilcolman ●
Spenser composes
Fairie Queene

WALES

Cambridge*

Swansea
Dylan Thomas's poetry

●**Oxford***

London

Wordsworth's Tintern Abbey

Stonehenge

Thames River

Canterbury
Destination of
Chaucer's pilgrims;
Marlowe born

Salisbury
Geo. Herbert's
Temple

Route of
Chaucer's pilgrims

Dover
Arnold's
"Dover Beach"

Dorset
Hardy's Wessex
("Three Strangers")

Portsmouth
Dickens born

Tintagel
Legendary birthplace
of King Arthur

Dean Prior
Herrick a
country parson
here

ENGLISH CHANNEL

FRANCE

***Oxford**
Authors who studied here include
Addison, Arnold, Donne,
T.S. Eliot, Hopkins, Housman,
Johnson, Lovelace, MacNeice,
Raleigh, Shelley, Sidney,
and Steele.

***Cambridge**
Authors who studied here include
Bacon, Brooke, Byron, Coleridge,
Dryden, Forster, Gray, Herbert,
Herrick, Marlowe, Marvell,
Pepys, Sassoon, Spenser,
Tennyson, Wordsworth,
and Wyatt.

Rulers of England and Great Britain (including dates of reign)

This chart presents the rulers of England and Great Britain from Anglo-Saxon times to the present. The earliest English kings were rulers not of England in its entirety but of kingdoms within England. The first of an unbroken succession of kings or queens of England was William I (1066-87). In 1707, upon the passage of the Act of Union, which united England and Scotland, Queen Anne became the first monarch of Great Britain.

[Kingdom of Kent]
Ethelbert, 560-616

[Kingdom of Northumbria]
Ethelfrith, 593-617
Edwin, 617-633
Oswald, 635-642
Oswy, 642-670
Ecgfrith, 670-685

[Kingdom of Mercia]
Penda, 626-655
Ethelbald, 716-757
Offa II, 757-796
Cenulf, 796-821

[Kingdom of Wessex]
Ine, 688-726

Saxons and Danes
Egbert, 802-39
Æthelwulf, 839-58
Æthelbald, 858-60
Æthelbert, 860-65
Æthelred, 865-71
Alfred, 871-99
Edward 899-924
Athelstan, 924-39
Edmund, 946-55
Edred, 946-55
Edway, 955-59
Edgar, 959-78
Edward (the Martyr), 978-1016
Æthelred (the Unready), 978-1016
Edmund (Ironside), son of Æthelred 1016
Canute, by conquest, 1016-35
Harold I (Harefoot), 1037-40
Harthacunute, 1040-42
Edward (the Confessor), 1042-66
Harold II, 1066

House of Normandy
William I The Conquerer, 1066-87
William II, 1087-1100
Henry I, 1100-1135

House of Blois
Stephen, 1135-54

House of Plantagenet
Henry II, 1154-89
Richard I, (Coeur de Lion) 1189-99
John, 1199-1216
Henry III, 1216-72
Edward I, 1272-1307
Edward II, 1302-27
Edward III, 1327-77
Richard II, 1327-99

House of Lancaster
Henry IV, 1399-1413
Henry V, 1413-22
Henry VI, 1422-61, 1470-99

House of York
Edward IV, 1461-70, 1471-83
Edward V, 1483
Richard III, 1483-85

House of Tudor
Henry VII, 1485-1509
Henry VIII, 1509-47
Edward VI, 1547-53
Mary I, 1553-58
Elizabeth I, 1558-1603

House of Stuart
James I (James VI of Scotland), 1603-25
Charles I, 1625-49

Commonwealth and Protectorate
Council of State, 1649-53
Cromwell, Oliver, lord protector, 1653-58
Cromwell, Richard, lord protector, 1658-59

House of Stuart (restored)
Charles II, 1660-85
James II, 1685-88
William III, ruled jointly with Mary II, 1689-94; ruled alone, 1694-1702
Mary II, ruled jointly with William III, 1689-94
Anne, 1702-14

House of Hanover
George I, 1714-27
George II, 1727-60
George III, 1760-1820
George IV, 1820-30
William IV, 1830-37
Victoria, 1837-1901

House of Saxe-Cobury
Edward VII, 1901-10

House of Windsor
(family name changed during World War I)
George V, 1910-36
Edward VIII, 1936
George VI, 1936-1952
Elizabeth II, 1952

The lessons in the Handbook of Thinking and Writing About Literature may be used for direct instruction in the writing process, specifically the process of writing about literature. In addition, students may use these lessons for reference and support when they are doing the Thinking and Writing assignments with the selections. References to appropriate lessons are suggested on the Annotated Teacher's Edition page with the assignment.

HANDBOOK OF WRITING ABOUT LITERATURE

SECTION 1: UNDERSTANDING THE WRITING PROCESS

Lesson 1: Prewriting

You may wish that you could just sit down, spend a few minutes, and magically write out a polished paragraph or essay. Unfortunately, most writing is not so easy. It takes time and hard work. Nevertheless, you can write more confidently if you understand that writing is a process, not a single step. Most writers go through these stages.

1. *Prewriting:* getting and organizing ideas for writing
2. *Drafting:* writing down ideas in a rough first draft
3. *Revising:* reworking and improving the written draft
4. *Proofreading:* finding and correcting errors in spelling, punctuation, capitalization, grammar, usage, and manuscript form
5. *Publishing:* sharing the writing with other people

STEP 1: ANALYZE THE SITUATION

Instead of just starting to write your paper, begin by thinking through what you need and want to accomplish. Ask yourself the following questions.

1. *Assignment:* To what extent does the assignment define what you should do? Does it specify a topic? Does it require a paragraph or an essay? Does the assignment contain any key words such as *explain, compare, identify, retell, discuss, contrast, describe, cite, analyze, define, develop,* or *show*?
2. *Topic:* What will you write about? How can you state your subject precisely? Is your topic exact and narrow enough? Can you sum it up

in a topic sentence or thesis statement that suggests your position or viewpoint?
3. *Purpose:* What is your goal? Will you explain, describe, tell, or argue? Do you want your reader to react by understanding, imagining, being entertained, or being persuaded?
4. *Audience:* Who will read your writing? What should you assume about the reader's background and knowledge?
5. *Voice:* How should your writing sound to a reader? Should it sound informal, formal, calm, emotional, logical, ironic, or straightforward?
6. *Content:* What information will you need to provide about the topic? Can you gather all the information you need by analyzing your reading or by thinking about the topic? Do you need to do research? If so, what resources should you draw on?
7. *Form:* How will you shape your writing? Is it to be creative—a play, a poem, or a story? Is it to be an essay, a paragraph, a report, or a term paper? What parts will the writing include? What plan will you use to arrange the parts? What will come first, second, third, and so on?

STEP 2: MAKE A PLAN

After analyzing your writing situation, you can plan what to do next. Often you will need to find a topic or to narrow the one assigned. Then you can return to any unresolved questions that remain. For example, suppose that you are assigned an informal essay explaining to your classmates three techniques used in a poem you select. Your assignment defines your purpose (to explain), audience (classmates), and voice (informal). Your essay's topic (the poem and your point about it), content (your explanation and examples of three techniques), and form (the order of the paragraphs) will be clearer after you select and analyze a specific poem.

STEP 3: GATHER INFORMATION

Your assignment may or may not tell you exactly what topic to work on. Either way, instead of just hoping for a brilliant idea, try one of these prewriting methods to get ideas for or about a topic.

1. *Freewriting:* Write about the topic for several minutes. Don't worry about spelling, punctuation, or logical connections between ideas. Simply get down on paper everything that comes to mind about the topic. Later you can rephrase your best ideas.
2. *Clustering:* On a blank piece of paper, write and circle your topic. Add other ideas, circling them and using lines to connect them to the topic.
3. *Questioning:* Act like a reporter and ask questions about your topic. Begin your questions with *who, what, where, when, why,* and *how.*
4. *Listing:* Make a list of events in sequence, pro and con arguments, differences, similarities, subtypes, examples, or causes.
5. *Analyzing:* Identify the parts of your topic. That is, look for subtopics and for relationships among the parts and the whole.
6. *Researching:* Look up terms, details, or whatever background you need to know.

STEP 4: ORGANIZE YOUR NOTES

After gathering ideas, you are ready to organize your material and to work out a rough outline. Whatever order you choose should suit your topic, be logical, build from idea to idea,

and interest a reader. Try one of these patterns or the reverse of one of these patterns.

1. *Chronological order:* first to last
2. *Spatial order:* nearest to farthest, topmost to bottommost, and so on
3. *Order of complexity:* simplest to most elaborate
4. *Order of familiarity:* best to least understood
5. *Order of frequency:* most to least numerous
6. *Order of importance:* least to most significant
7. *Order of effectiveness:* least to most convincing

CASE STUDY: PREWRITING

Brian's English teacher assigned an informal paragraph. Brian was to pick a reading that he found especially interesting and then explain briefly how and why he reacted to it as he did.

Brian decided to write about Mary Shelley's Introduction to *Frankenstein.* First he analyzed the writing situation.

- Assignment: paragraph—explain reaction
- Topic: Shelley's Introduction to *Frankenstein*—but what about it?
- Purpose: explain so reader understands
- Audience: Ms. Burton—maybe class? all have read Shelley's essay
- Voice: informal, personal reactions
- Content: why like it? why interesting?
- Form: paragraph—needs topic sentence and examples—which ones? what order?

Brian decided to try freewriting to figure out what to say about his topic.

Shelley wrote this famous story. It is also famous in movies. I thought she must of been a natural writer. Didn't expect her to have trouble writing. Byron and Shelley wrote OK stories even tho they are famous poets. But she can't get an idea. After hearing about these experiments she gets this vision. She still doesn't think she can write a story, then she sees its her story.

ANSWERS TO ACTIVITIES AND ASSIGNMENTS,
Section A

1. He focused on a topic—Mary Shelley's trouble with writing. He could now include this in his original chart.
2. He misspells words and writes ungrammatical sentences. He rightly ignores these errors during his freewriting.
3. He uses chronological order.

Brian saw two main ideas in his freewriting: Mary Shelley had written a famous story, and she had trouble writing, just as he did. He did not know how to develp the first idea but he thought he could figure out a topic sentence about the second. He made this rough outline, using details from the essay.

- Topic: I did not expect Shelley to have trouble writing.
    She can't get an idea—others can
    She gets a vision
    Finally she sees that it's her story
    conclusion?

ACTIVITIES AND ASSIGNMENTS

A. Answer these questions about the case study:
1. Review Brian's freewriting and rough outline. Did he finally resolve all the questions about his writing situation? Revise his first chart to include his later decisions.
2. Review Brian's freewriting. What mistakes in grammar or phrasing did Brian make? Why didn't he take the time to correct these at this stage?
3. What order did Brian use to arrange the three details in his rough outline?
    B. Choose a selection that interests you. Follow these prewriting steps to prepare for writing an informal paragraph about it:
1. Make notes to analyze your writing situation.
2. Decide what your next step should be. Use one of the prewriting techniques explained above to gather ideas.
3. Work out a rough outline, using your prewriting notes. Make sure that you have a specific topic and an idea about how to organize your ideas. Save all of your notes.

Lesson 2: Drafting and Revising

DRAFTING YOUR PAPER

Drafting is the process of putting ideas down on paper. The following guidelines will help you with the drafting stage of the writing process:

1. Choose a drafting method that is right for you. Some people like to make a detailed outline or prewriting plan and then to write a slow, meticulous draft based on this outline or plan. Other people like to write a very quick and very rough draft and then to revise this draft several times.

2. Whichever drafting method you choose, it is a good idea to do at least some planning before writing. In other words, you should have some idea about what you are going to say and in what order. You may wish to make a rough outline before you begin drafting.

3. Concentrate on getting your ideas down on paper. You can revise and proofread your work later.

4. Be open to new ideas that occur to you as you write. If necessary, change your writing plan to accommodate these new ideas.

REVISING YOUR DRAFT

Revising is the process of reworking and refining your draft. To revise a paper, read it over carefully and ask yourself the questions in the Checklist for Revision.

If your answer to any of the questions is "no," rework your draft until you can answer "yes." You may find that you need to revise your draft several times.

CASE STUDY: DRAFTING AND REVISING

Brian used his prewriting notes to begin writing his informal paragraph on Mary Shelley's Introduction to *Frankenstein.* After reviewing the assignment, his freewriting, and his rough out-

---

CHECKLIST FOR REVISION

Topic and Purpose
- ☐ Is my topic clear?
- ☐ Does the writing have a specific purpose?
- ☐ Does the writing achieve its purpose?

Audience
- ☐ Will everything I have written be clear to my audience?
- ☐ Will my audience find the writing interesting?
- ☐ Will my audience respond in the way I would like?

Voice and Word Choice
- ☐ Is the impression my writing conveys the one I intended it to convey?
- ☐ Is my language appropriately formal or informal?
- ☐ Have I avoided vague, undefined terms?
- ☐ Have I used vivid, specific nouns, verbs, and adjectives?
- ☐ Have I avoided jargon that my audience will not understand?
- ☐ Have I avoided clichés?
- ☐ Have I avoided slang, odd connotations, euphemisms, and gobbledygook (except for novelty or humor)?

Content/Development
- ☐ Have I avoided including unnecessary or unrelated ideas?
- ☐ Have I developed my topic completely?
- ☐ Have I supplied examples or details that support the statements that I have made?
- ☐ Are my sources of information unbiased, up-to-date, and authoritative?
- ☐ Are my quotations verbatim, or word for word?

Form
- ☐ Have I followed a logical method of organization?
- ☐ Have I used transitions, or connecting words, to make the organization clear?
- ☐ Does the writing have a clear introduction, body, and conclusion?

Drafting and Revising 1335

Motivation for Writing Explain to your students that if they have done their prewriting and have taken the time to plan or outline their first drafts they will find the actual writing far easier than if they attempt to begin with a draft. The preliminary work will give them material to work on and a sense of direction. Moreover, they will be less likely to lose control of their subject when they need to pause and search for words and phrases.

Tell students that if they use a checklist like the one in their textbooks, revision can be done far more easily and effectively than if they merely look over their writing with no specific objectives and standards in mind. With more advanced students discuss the idea that to revise one's writing is to revise—and improve—one's mind.

1. He added *Instead* and *Finally*.
2. The sentence is irrelevant.
3. He changes it to make it more exact.
4. They sum up his main point.
5. He changed the phrasing to express his ideas more clearly and coherently.

line, Brian decided that he needed to work on a topic sentence. Here's how he drafted and revised that topic sentence:

- Topic idea: I did not expect Shelley to have trouble writing.

- Topic sentence: I enjoyed reading it because I found out about her trouble writing which was not what I expected.

- Revised version: I enjoyed reading Mary Shelley's Introduction to *Frankenstein* because I found out about something I didn't expect—that she had trouble coming up with ideas for writing.

Next Brian used this topic sentence to get started drafting his paragraph, shown at right.

ACTIVITIES AND ASSIGNMENTS

A. Answer the following questions about Brian's revisions of his rough draft:
1. What transitions did Brian add to his paragraph?
2. Why did Brian delete the sentence, "She is just real terrified"?
3. Why did Brian change some of the wording in his sentence about Mary Shelley's vision?
4. Why did he add the last sentences?
5. What other changes did Brian make? Why did he make these changes?

B. Using your notes from the preceding lesson, draft and revise your own paragraph. Follow these steps:
1. Review your notes and your rough outline.
2. Work on your topic sentence, refining it so that your specific topic and your approach to or attitude toward the topic is clear.
3. If necessary, revise your rough outline. Note your subtopics (the parts of your main topic),

and add any new significant details that occur to you.
4. Use your revised topic sentence to start your paragraph.
5. Write the body of your paragraph, presenting the subtopics and details from your outline.
6. Write a conclusion.
7. Revise your draft using the Checklist for Revision on page 1335. Keep all of your notes and drafts.

I enjoyed reading Mary Shelley's Introduction to Frankenstein because I found out about something I didn't expect—that she had trouble coming up with ideas for writing *Since* Her story has become so famous, I thought Shelley was just a natural writer. *Instead, I found out, that* she had trouble getting an idea for a story. *Even though her husband,* ~~Shelley,~~ Byron, and Polidori had wrote theres, *She could not think of an idea.* Finally she has this ~~weird~~ *imaginative* vision about ~~an~~ ex- *a terrifying creating life.* periment ~~in science. She is just real terrified.~~ *At first, recognize* She ~~just does not see~~ this as her story she just wishes she did write something ~~just~~ as *frightening this is* ~~creepy.~~ Then she realizes that ~~she has~~ her idea for a story. *Her problem surprised me but they also reassured me. I hadn't expected to find out that a writer like her had the same writing problem I usually do.*

Lesson 3: Proofreading and Publishing

USING EDITORIAL SYMBOLS

The last lesson discussed reorganizing, adding, cutting, and otherwise revising your writing. Once you have made these major revisions, you are ready to make more detailed changes such as adding punctuation, correcting capitalization, and refining word order. The editorial symbols on the right are especially helpful for marking such changes on your final draft.

PROOFREADING YOUR FINAL DRAFT

Proofreading is your last careful review of your paper. As you proofread, look for minor errors and for rough passages that you missed earlier. If possible, let your revised draft sit for a few hours or a day before going over it. Taking a break from your manuscript should make it easier for you to see flaws. Ask yourself the questions listed on the next page as you proofread.

Use a dictionary, a style manual, or a writing textbook to check spellings and rules for punctuation, capitalization, and manuscript form. Once your paper has been proofread, make a clean final copy, if necessary. Check your final version carefully to catch any errors in copying.

PUBLISHING, OR SHARING YOUR WORK WITH OTHERS

After proofreading your paper, you are ready to share it with readers. When you write papers for school, your teachers will be your primary readers. Nevertheless, you or your class can expand your audience in the following ways:
1. Exchange papers with a small group of students from your class.
2. Read your paper aloud to your class or to another class.
3. Share your writing with your friends and relatives.
4. Make a booklet of your writing at the end of the semester or year.
5. Make a class booklet with a paper by every student.
6. Contribute some of your writing to the school literary magazine.

EDITORIAL SYMBOLS		
Symbol	Meaning	Example
⟲	move text	She never again published because of this
ℓ or —	delete	in this ~~this~~ book
∧	insert	the poem's ∧scheme *rhyme*
⌒	no space	mono logue
⊙	add period	a line ends it⊙
∧	add comma	sonnets, odes∧and other lyric poems
∨	add apostrophe	writers style
∨ ∨	add quotation marks	The Train from Rhodesia
∿	transpose	to wildly run
¶	begin paragraph	the stanza. The next image
/	lower case	The Poet writes
≡	capitalize	in "Shore woman"

Proofreading and Publishing   1337

Motivation for Writing Encourage your students to let time pass before they proofread their revised drafts. Tell them that if they do so they will find it easy to pretend that they are proofreading someone else's work—a practice that will enable them to look at their writing objectively and with a greater alertness to errors.

You might have a class discussion on the publishing opportunities that are, or can be made, available to your students.

7. If your school does not have a literary magazine, start one.
8. Contribute your writing to your school or community newspaper.
9. Enter writing contests for student writers sponsored by community groups or by magazines.

10. Send your writing to magazines that publish student writing.

CASE STUDY: PROOFREADING AND PUBLISHING

Brian revised his draft paragraph and made a new copy, including all his additions and changes. Then he used the Checklist for Proofreading on the left to locate any remaining problems. This is Brian's proofread draft:

CHECKLIST FOR PROOFREADING

Grammar and Usage
☐ Are all of my sentences complete? That is, have I avoided sentence fragments?
☐ Do all of my sentences express only one complete thought? That is, have I avoided run-on sentences?
☐ Do the verbs I have used agree with their subjects?
☐ Have all the words in my paper been used correctly? Am I sure about the meanings of all these words?
☐ Is the thing being referred to by each pronoun (*I, me, this, each,* etc.) clear?
☐ Have I used adjectives and adverbs correctly?

Spelling
☐ Am I absolutely sure that each word has been spelled correctly?

Punctuation
☐ Does every sentence end with a punctuation mark?
☐ Have I used commas, semicolons, colons, hyphens, dashes, parentheses, quotation marks, and apostrophes correctly?

Capitalization
☐ Have I capitalized any words that should not be capitalized?
☐ Should I capitalize any words that I have not capitalized?

Manuscript Form
☐ Have I indented the first line(s) of my paragraph(s)?
☐ Have I written my name and the page number in the top right-hand corner of each page?
☐ Have I double-spaced the manuscript?
☐ Is my manuscript neat and legible?

I enjoyed reading Mary Shelley's Introduction to <u>Frankenstein</u> because I found out about ~~something I didn't expect~~ that she had trouble coming up with ideas for writing. Since her story ₍about Frankenstein₎ has become so famous, I thought Shelly was just a natural writer. Instead, I found out that she had trouble getting an idea for ₍her₎ ~~a~~ story. Even though her husband, Byron, and Polidori had ₍written₎ ~~wrote theres~~ ₍their stories₎ she could not think of an idea. Finally she ₍had an₎ ~~has this~~ imaginative vision about a terrifying experiment in creating life. At first, she ₍did₎ ~~does~~ not recognize this as her story, she just ~~wish-~~ ₍wished₎ ~~es~~ she ~~old~~ ₍could₎ write something as frightening. Then she ~~realizes~~ ₍realized₎ that this ~~is~~ ₍was₎ her idea for a story. Her problems surprised me, but they also reassured me. I hadn't expected to find out that a writer like her had the same writing problem I usually do.

Brian recopied his paper, read it through for careless errors, and then exchanged papers with a small group in class.

ACTIVITIES AND ASSIGNMENTS

A. Answer the following questions about Brian's proofreading in the case study.

1. Explain why Brian made each change that he did.
2. What other changes do you think Brian might have made? Explain why you would have made those changes.

B. Proofread and publish your draft from the preceding lesson on Drafting and Revising. Follow these steps:

1. Use the Checklist for Proofreading on page 1338 to review your draft. Correct any problems that the checklist helps you to identify.
2. Recopy your corrected paper. Read through this final version to make sure that you copied everything correctly.
3. Share your draft with your teacher and with the other students in class.

ANSWERS TO ACTIVITIES AND ASSIGNMENTS, *Section A*

1. Students should see that, in general, Brian's changes remove the mechanical, stylistic, and grammatical flaws that tend to persist in written work until careful, systematic proofreading is done.
2. His phrasing could still be improved—made less loose and juvenile. The word *about* should be removed from the first sentence. Students may find other weak spots.

SECTION 2: UNDERSTANDING THE PARTS OF A LITERARY WORK: ANALYSIS AND INTERPRETATION

Lesson 4: Writing About Images

WHAT IS AN IMAGE?

An *image* is a word or a phrase that presents an experience that can be sensed—a sight, sound, touch, taste, smell, or other physical sensation. For example, Stevie Smith begins "In the Park" this way:

Walking one day in the park in winter
I heard two silvered gentlemen talking,
Two old friends, elderly, walking, talking
There by the silver lake mid-pooled
    black in winter.

These images of sight, sound, and movement create a picture, in words, of the scene in the park.

WHY WRITERS USE IMAGES

Writers use images for several purposes:
1. To create vivid descriptions of the things they write about
2. To suggest emotions or feelings about these things
3. To create figures of speech such as metaphors, similes, and personifications

Sir Philip Sidney begins "Sonnet 31" with these lines:

With how sad steps, O Moon, thou
    climb'st the skies!
How silently, and with how wan a face!

The images in these lines:
1. Describe the sight and sound of the moon moving across the sky,
2. Suggest a sad feeling, and
3. Personify the moon as a person with a wan face who can climb the sky despondently.

CASE STUDY: WRITING ABOUT IMAGES

Jason's teacher asked each student to write a short essay about the imagery used in a favorite poem. Jason chose to write about William Butler Yeats's "The Lake Isle of Innisfree," on page 1027.

Prewriting

Jason first read the poem several times. Then he made the following list of the images in the poem:

- Images of sight:
    "a small cabin . . . of clay and wattles made"
    "nine bean rows"
    "a hive for the honeybee"
    "glade"
    "the veils of the morning"
    "midnight's all a glimmer"
    "noon a purple glow"
    "roadway . . . pavements gray"

- Images of sound:
    "the bee-loud glade"
    "the cricket sings"
    "the linnet's wings"
    "lake water lapping with low sounds by the shore"
    "I hear it in the deep heart's core"

Jason looked up *Innisfree, wattles, glade,* and *linnet* in a dictionary. Then he added these definitions to his notes:

- Innisfree: an island on a lake in County Sligo, Ireland

- wattles: sticks interwined with twigs and branches to make crude fences or walls

- glade: an open space in a forest

- linnet: a small songbird found in Europe, Asia, and Africa

As Jason thought about the images in the poem, he noticed that the speaker describes two scenes. The first two stanzas describe a rural setting—the island of Innisfree. The last stanza describes a city scene. Jason added these observations to his notes:

- Stanzas 1 and 2: images used to create a picture of the natural beauty on the island of Innisfree. The mood created by these images is one of peacefulness.

- Stanza 3: images used to create a picture of a street scene in a city. The mood created by these images is one of unpleasantness.

Next Jason wrote this topic sentence:

In "The Lake Isle of Innisfree," by William Butler Yeats, the speaker uses images to contrast living in an ugly city with living in a beautiful natural setting.

Finally, Jason made the following rough outline for an essay:

- Introductory paragraph: Begin by pointing out how city-dwellers often long to escape to a simpler existence in the country. End paragraph with thesis statement.

- Body paragraph 1: Discuss images used in poem to create a beautiful country scene.

- Body paragraph 2: Discuss contrast between beautiful country scene and the city in which the speaker lives.

- Conclusion: Make point that modern urban life creates many pressures and that escape often seems desirable. Point out that Yeats's beautiful imagery makes living in the country seem very desirable indeed.

Drafting and Revising

Jason used his notes to write a rough draft of a four-paragraph essay. Then he revised his essay, using the Checklist for Revision on page 1335.

Proofreading and Publishing

After revising his draft, Jason made a clean copy and proofread it carefully. Then he shared this proofread copy with his parents and with his teacher.

ACTIVITIES AND ASSIGNMENTS

A. Use Jason's prewriting notes to write an essay about imagery in "The Lake Isle of Innisfree," on page 1027. Revise and proofread your essay. Then share it with your classmates and with your teacher.

B. Choose a poem from your textbook and write a short essay about its imagery. Follow these steps:
1. Read the poem carefully, noting as many of the images as you can.
2. Prepare a chart of the images, arranged by type (sight, sound, taste, touch, and smell).
3. Make notes about why the writer may have used these images—what pictures they create and how they affect the reader.
4. Review your prewriting notes to decide which ideas seem most likely to produce a thoughtful and persuasive paper. Draft a thesis sentence that sums up your topic and your point about it.
5. Make a rough outline, grouping the ideas that belong together in each paragraph.
6. Write a draft of your paper, including an introductory paragraph, one or more body paragraphs, and a conclusion.
7. Revise your paper and then proofread it, using the checklists on pages 1335 and 1338.
8. Share your final copy with your family, with a friend, or with a classmate.

Motivation for Writing After reviewing the most important sound
devices and the most common
metrical patterns, you might have
a contest in the form of a test that
will not be submitted for a grade.
The test can consist of examples
of the sound devices and metrical
patterns, which the students are
asked to identify. You might then
select an appropriate passage
from a poem or Shakespeare play
and have the class discuss the
use of sound devices.

Lesson 5: Writing About Sound

DEVICES OF SOUND IN LITERATURE

Literary works, especially poems, often contain special devices of sound that are used to suggest or to reinforce meaning. Consider, for example, the use of words to imitate the sounds of musical instruments in these lines from John Dryden's "A Song for Saint Cecilia's Day":

The soft complaining flute
In dying notes discovers
The woes of hopeless lovers,
Whose dirge is whispered by the
    warbling lute.

The list on the right describes some of the most commonly used devices of sound.

CASE STUDY: WRITING ABOUT SOUND

Janine's English teacher asked the class to choose a passage from *The Tragedy of Macbeth* and to write about the use of devices of sound in the passage. Janine chose to write about the opening scene of the play.

Prewriting

Janine began by reading the passage aloud several times and listening to its sounds. Then she copied the passage into her notebook and marked its devices of sound, as shown on page 1343.

Then Janine took the following notes about the devices of sound used in the passage:

- Opening sounds like a chant, very rhythmical; four-beat lines (tetrameter)

- Rhyming lines: again/rain, done/won/sun, fair/air

- Onomatopoeia: hurlyburly

- Alliteration: *f* sounds in last two lines

- Parallelism: "Fair is foul, and foul is fair"

- Break in pattern: four-beat lines continue until the Third Witch's line "There to meet with Macbeth." This change in the rhythm

SOUND DEVICES
Alliteration: the repetition of initial consonant sounds, as in "O, my *l*uve is *l*ike a *r*ed, *r*ed *r*ose"
Assonance: a partial rhyme involving repetition of a stressed vowel sound but not of the surrounding consonant sounds, as in "about the ho*u*se"
Consonance: a partial rhyme involving repetition of similar consonant sounds but not of the intervening vowel sounds, as in "a mon*k*ey's un*cl*e" or "dan*c*ing zebras."
Rhyme: the repetition of sounds at the ends of words, as in "Then look ar*ound*, and choose thy gr*ound*"
Cacophony: the use of harsh, unpleasant sounds, as in "hectic red,/Pestilence-stricken multitudes"
Euphony: the use of beautiful, pleasant sounds, as in "Much have I traveled in the realms of gold"
Onomatopoeia: the use of words that sound like what they refer to, as in "And full-grown lambs loud *bleat* from hilly bourn"
Meter: the use of a regular, recurring rhythmical pattern, as in "In Xanadu did Kubla Khan/A stately pleasure-dome decree"
Parallelism: the repetition of a grammatical pattern, as in "the night was dark, no father was there;/The child was wet with dew"
Repetition: the use, again, of a sound, word, phrase, sentence, grammatical pattern, or rhythmical pattern. Note that alliteration, assonance, consonance, rhyme, meter, and parallelism are all varieties of repetition.

1342   *Handbook of Writing About Literature*

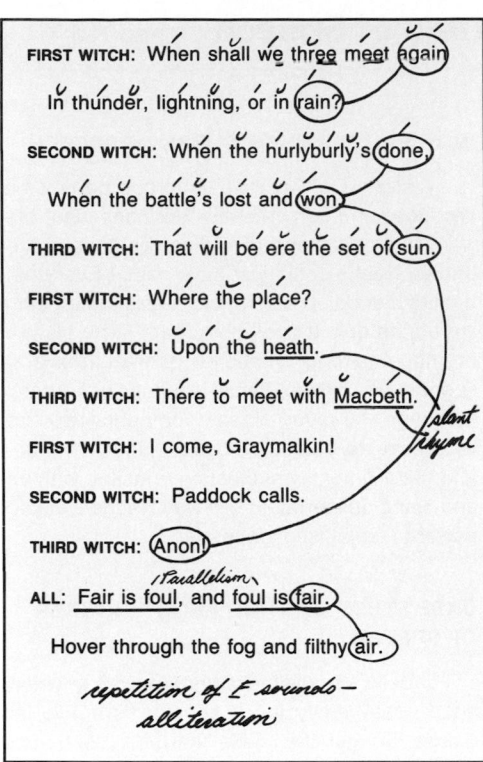

FIRST WITCH: When shall we three meet again

In thunder, lightning, or in rain?

SECOND WITCH: When the hurlyburly's done,

When the battle's lost and won.

THIRD WITCH: That will be ere the set of sun.

FIRST WITCH: Where the place?

SECOND WITCH: Upon the heath.

THIRD WITCH: There to meet with Macbeth.

FIRST WITCH: I come, Graymalkin!

SECOND WITCH: Paddock calls.

THIRD WITCH: Anon!

Parallelism

ALL: Fair is foul, and foul is fair.

Hover through the fog and filthy air.

slant rhyme

repetition of F sounds — alliteration

emphasizes the name "Macbeth" and is a little disconcerting.

- The parallelism of "Fair is foul and foul is fair" emphasizes the witches' desire to confuse fair things with foul things.

Drafting and Revising

Based on these notes, Janine wrote the following rough draft:

Shakespeare's MacBeth begins with a dramatic chant. As if the withces were casting some evil spell. The chant is written in four-beat, tetrameter lines. These opening lines rhyme. As in a chant or spell. The rhyming, four beat lines continue until line 8. Which introduces Macbeth. Line 8 is peculiar because it contains only three lines and because the word *Macbeth* does not rhyme, precisely, with the word *heath,* in the preceeding line. Thus the

introduction of the name of Macbeth upsets the rhythmical pattern, just as Macbeth will upset the ordered pattern of life in the kingdom of scotland. The opening scene ends with a rhyming, chantlike couplet. The parallelism of "Fair is foul, and foul is fair" emphasizes the witches desire to confuse foulness with fairness. The repeition, or alliteration, of *f* sounds in these last lines ties together and emphasizes the words fair, foul, fog, and filthey. Thus creating a mood, or atmosphere, of ugliness and impending horror.

After finishing her rough draft, Janine revised it carefully.

Proofreading and Publishing

Janine proofread her revised rough draft, made a clean final copy, and handed in her paper to her English teacher.

ACTIVITIES AND ASSIGNMENTS

A. Revise Janine's rough draft from the preceding case study. Follow these steps:
1. Correct all the sentence fragments in the draft.
2. Correct the misspellings and the improper punctuation. Italicize or underline the title of the play.
3. Make any other corrections you feel are necessary.
4. Proofread the revised draft, and then share the proofread copy with your classmates.

B. Choose a poem or a passage from a play or short story and write an analysis of the devices of sound used in it. Follow the procedure outlined in the case study. Begin by copying the passage or poem into your notebook. Then mark its devices of sound and make notes about them. Finally, write a paragraph presenting your analysis of the devices of sound, organized in order of their appearance in the poem or passage. Revise and proofread your paragraph. Then share it with your teacher and with your classmates.

Lesson 6: Writing About Figures of Speech

WHAT ARE FIGURES OF SPEECH?

When expressions or words are used imaginatively, rather than literally, they are called *figures of speech.* The following lines from "A Litany in Time of Plague," by Thomas Nashe, illustrate *metaphor,* a figure of speech in which one thing is described as though it were something else:

> Beauty is but a flower
> Which wrinkles will devour.

Besides identifying beauty with a flower that will soon wilt, Nashe implies a comparison between the flower and youthful human skin. The skin's beauty, like the flower's, soon will be gone, eaten by wrinkles as if they were hungry animals.

The following lines from "A Birthday," by Christina Rossetti, contain *similes.* A simile is a figure of speech that compares two subjects using *like* or *as:*

> My heart is like a singing bird . . .
> My heart is like an apple tree . . .
> My heart is like a rainbow shell . . .

Other figures of speech are listed in the chart later in this lesson and in the Handbook of Literary Terms and Techniques.

Such figures of speech can be analyzed to figure out how they work. The literal subject in a metaphor or simile is sometimes called the *tenor.* This subject shares a certain characteristic with the *vehicle,* the figurative term to which it is compared. For example, in Rossetti's third line above, the heart is the tenor. It is compared with the vehicle, a rainbow shell. Different as a heart and a shell are, the comparison makes sense because both share the characteristic of being in a happy situation.

WHY WRITERS USE FIGURES OF SPEECH

Writers use figurative language because its vividness and concreteness enriches what they want to say. Instead of writing the lines quoted earlier, Nashe could just have said, "Everything beautiful ends up getting old." This statement is literal and dull. It does not create lively pictures or trigger strong emotional or imaginative responses in a reader. In just two lines of figurative language, however, Nashe compares two fragile, desirable subjects—beauty and a flower—and two frightening subjects—wrinkling with age and being devoured. In this way Nashe awakens powerful feelings in his reader.

CASE STUDY: WRITING ABOUT FIGURES OF SPEECH

Ladelle's English assignment was to write a short essay analyzing a poem's figurative language. To get the class started, the teacher listed figures of speech on the chalkboard.

Prewriting

Ladelle started her prewriting by reviewing these terms and making a list of how each works. As she analyzed her chosen poem, "Ode to the West Wind," by Percy Bysshe Shelley, she noted figures of speech:

- Antithesis: Use of parallelism to present contrasting ideas
  Maybe "Destroyer and preserver" (first stanza)

- Apostrophe: Direct address of an object, idea, or absent person
  "O wild West Wind . . . Thou breath of Autumn's being Thou" (first stanza)

- Hyperbole: Exaggeration/overstatement

"azure moss and flowers/So sweet, the sense faints picturing them" (third stanza)

- Irony: Contrast between what is and what seems
  Double nature of west wind (first and fourth stanzas)—both destroyer and preserver

- Metaphor: Comparison through identification
  "I fall upon the thorns of life! I bleed!" (fourth stanza)
  "Ashes and sparks, my words among mankind!" (fifth stanza)

- Metonymy: Substitution of closely related thing
  "A heavy weight of hours" for time (fourth stanza)

- Paradox: Contradiction which is true
  "Destroyer and preserver" (first stanza)

- Personification: Use of human qualities for animal, thing, or idea
  Mediterranean Sea sleeps and dreams (third stanza)

- Simile: Comparison with *like* or *as*
  Leaves "driven, like ghosts" fleeing (first stanza)
  Seeds "Each like a corpse" in a grave (first stanza)
  Clouds shed like "decaying leaves" (second stanza)
  Clouds spread like "bright hair" (second stanza)
  "Make me thy lyre" as forest is (fifth stanza)
  "dead thought" driven like leaves (fifth stanza)

- Synecdoche: Substitution of part for the whole
  "Be through my lips," meaning through his voice and words as a poet (fifth stanza)

- Understatement: Statement of less than is meant
  can't find example in poem

Next Ladelle tried to sum up Shelley's point, or theme, so that she could see the purpose of the poem's figurative language. She turned this idea into her thesis statement and jotted it down:

- Thesis: Shelley uses figurative language to describe the west wind and to explain his ambition as a poet.

Since she had found many figures of speech but was writing only a short essay, Ladelle knew that she had to decide which figures and examples were most important. These choices resulted in her rough outline for a four-paragraph essay:

- Paragraph 1: Thesis and introduction

- Paragraph 2: Description of west wind apostrophe, paradox, and simile (transition to next paragraph)

- Paragraph 3: Explanation of Shelley's ambition as poet simile, metaphor, and synecdoche

- Paragraph 4: Conclusion and summary

Drafting and Revising

After drafting her first paragraph, Ladelle started on her second. Here is the rough draft of her second paragraph:

Shelley uses apostrophe, paradox, and simile to discribe the wind. The paradox, "Destroyer and preserver," tells how the wind both blows away the autum leaves and saving the seeds for next spring. The poem opens with apostrophe, as Shelly talks directly to the wind. He hails it, saying, "O wild West Wind, thou breath of Autumn's being" (line 1). Finally, the similes in the first two sections. They discribe how the wind effects the things around it. The west wind blows dead leaves "like ghosts from an enchanter fleeing." It drops the seeds on the gound where they wait "like a corpse within its grave" (line 8) for spring. It carries along clouds

1. She has sensibly decided to write about only the most important ones.
2. She should treat the three figures of speech in the order in which she mentions them in the first sentence. Spelling errors ("discribe," "Shelly") and a sentence fragment (after the fourth sentence) need to be corrected. The syntax of the second sentence needs improvement.

like leaves, like "bright hair." All these figures of speech discribe the wind.

Ladelle completed her essay and revised it.

Proofreading and Publishing

After proofreading her final copy, Ladelle shared her paper with her best friend and then handed it in.

ACTIVITIES AND ASSIGNMENTS

A. Answer the following questions about Ladelle's writing in the case study:
1. Why doesn't Ladelle's rough outline list every figure of speech in her chart?
2. How might Ladelle reorganize the rough draft of her second paragraph? What grammatical errors and other problems need to be corrected? Based on your answers to this question, revise and proofread Ladelle's paragraph.

B. Write a short essay about the figures of speech in a poem by Blake, Wordsworth, Byron, Keats, Hardy, Meredith, Auden, or Heaney. Follow these steps:
1. Read the poem aloud and make a handwritten copy.
2. On your copy, mark the figures of speech that you find. List them by type in a chart.
3. Decide how you want to organize your essay. Each paragraph might make a single point about the poem, using figures of speech as subtopics or examples; or each paragraph might focus on a different figure of speech, explaining how it works and what it adds to the poem. Make a rough outline and draft a thesis statement.
4. Draft your essay, following your outline. Include an introduction, several body paragraphs, and a conclusion.
5. Revise and proofread your draft using the checklists on pages 1335 and 1338.
6. Share your final copy with your teacher and with a friend.

Lesson 7: Writing About Setting

WHAT IS SETTING?

The *setting* of a literary work is the environment within which the action occurs. Using images and details, the writer may describe the geographical location, the historical period, the season of the year, the weather, a building or room, the furniture, the characters' clothes, their jobs or social circumstances, the local customs —whatever elements will create the sense of a particular time and place.

Often a description of the setting opens a narrative, as in Katherine Mansfield's "A Dill Pickle," on page 929.

> And then, after six years, she saw him again. He was seated at one of those little bamboo tables decorated with a Japanese vase of paper daffodils. There was a tall plate of fruit in front of him, and ... he was peeling an orange.

This description immediately sets the scene in the restaurant, thus helping the reader imagine the two characters meeting there.

Although Mansfield uses images of sight to introduce this setting, details of sound, taste, touch, or smell may also help create a setting, as in this description of a carpenter's workshop from George Eliot's *Adam Bede:*

> The afternoon sun was warm on the five workmen there, busy upon doors and window-frames and wainscoting. A scent of pine-wood from a tent-like pile of planks outside the open door mingled itself with the scent of the elder-bushes which were spreading their summer snow close to the open window opposite....

In the rest of the passage, Eliot describes the appearance of the dog lying in the workshop, the texture of its bed, and the sound of a worker singing.

HOW WRITERS USE SETTINGS

Writers use settings for various purposes. Here are some of the ways in which setting may be used.

USES OF SETTING
To make a work more believable through vivid, precise descriptions
To create a mood, or atmosphere
To create a conflict, as when a character struggles against something in his or her environment
To symbolize a key concept that the writer wants to express

A setting may also reflect a character's situation, complicate the plot, highlight the theme, or otherwise add to the overall effect of the work.

CASE STUDY: WRITING ABOUT SETTING

Anthony's class was studying Victorian prose and novels. Each student was to write a paragraph or two about the significance of the setting in one of the Victorian selections in this book.

Prewriting

After deciding to work on the Victorian novel *Jane Eyre,* Anthony started his prewriting by listing answers to key questions about the setting:

- What is the setting?
  Place—the Reed family's house
  Time—an afternoon long ago, probably about when Brontë lived
  Season—wintry November
  Weather—cold, windy, rainy

Writing About Setting   1347

Janes and *Reeds* need apostrophes. *Wintrish* should be *wintry*. *Penny-less* should be *penniless*. *Made* should be *makes*. "and her inferior" is a fragment. Similar errors of usage occur in the remainder of the paragraph. Have students look at each sentence and find the errors.

• What details are used to create the setting?
Description of day (paragraphs 1–2)—wind, clouds, and rain
Drawing room—Mrs. Reed lying on sofa by fireplace with children around
Window seat in breakfast room—enclosed by curtains; bookcases; outside view of wintry day
Social background—John Reed says Jane is a poor dependent (fight scene)

• What is significance of the setting?
Description of day (paragraphs 1–2)—dreary cold; sad and "humbled" feelings from walks (mood: shows and reflects Jane's situation); cold outside like cold people inside
Drawing room—Mrs. Reed has "her darlings about her" but not Jane (shows Jane's conflict with Reeds)
Window seat—curtains and glass "protecting, but not separating" from the wintry day, followed by John's attack and throwing book (mood: shows Jane's feelings)

Anthony reviewed his notes. He decided that he wanted to focus on the way the setting added to the mood and symbolized Jane's situation at the beginning of the novel. He worked next on a rough outline and on a topic sentence.

Drafting and Revising

As Anthony worked on his draft, he discovered that he was explaining Jane Eyre's situation more than the mood of the story. He then revised his topic sentence so that it more accurately reflected the content of his paragraph. On the right is Anthony's revised draft.

Proofreading and Publishing

After Anthony finished revising his draft, he let it sit overnight. Then he proofread his paragraph, made a final copy, and read it to his discussion group during class.

The setting ~~adds to the mood of the novel~~ *at the beginning of Jane Eyre* ~~and~~ symbolizes Janes situation. Her story *begins* ~~starts~~ (on this wintrish afternoon) at the Reeds home where she is *a penny-less* dependent. *The* cold wind, the 'clouds so somber,' and the 'rain so penetrating' prevent ~~an afternoon walk~~ *on a* *her* ~~that afternoon.~~ The walks always made ~~Jane~~ *and* feel sad. ~~They also made~~ her feel inferior.

This opening setting immediately helps to point out ~~that Jane is very isolated and very unhappy in this situation.~~ *Jane's isolated and unhappy situation.* The indoor setting also contrasts the *comfortable* life of the Reeds *up* ~~against~~ *cruel treatment and* Jane's isolation. The window *in the breakfast room* seat hides and protects Jane ~~Jane~~ temporarily but even their the ~~the~~ window is "protecting, but not separating me from the drear Nov. day." *Indoors or out, isolated cold and dreary* Jane is ~~separated~~ from others, facing a setting *with the Reed* that symbolizes her life.

ACTIVITIES AND ASSIGNMENTS

A. Proofread Anthony's paragraph. What additional changes or corrections are needed in his final copy?

B. Choose from this book a short story or an excerpt from a novel. Write a paper of one or two paragraphs analyzing the significance of the setting. Follow these steps.

1. Read your selection several times. First concentrate on the action of the story. Then read

the selection again, paying close attention to details of the setting.

2. Write out answers to these key questions about setting:

    a. What is the setting? the time? the place?

    b. What details are used to create the setting?

    c. What is the significance of the setting?

As you do this prewriting, make notes of your answers to each question.

3. Draft a topic sentence that presents your main point. Then use your notes to prepare a rough outline.

4. Draft your paper, following your rough outline. If you want to develop two main points, you may need to write two paragraphs rather than just one.

5. Revise your paper, following the Checklist for Revision on page 1335. Make sure that your topic sentence accurately reflects the content of your paper and that it focuses on the significance of the setting.

6. Proofread your paper, using the Checklist for Proofreading on page 1338. Share your final copy with other students who have written about or are interested in the same selection.

Lesson 8: Writing About Plot

WHAT IS PLOT?

A *plot* is a series of events, or occurrences, each of which is causally related to those that have preceded it. One event in a plot causes the next, which causes the next, and so on to the end of the story. Most plots involve a *central conflict,* or struggle, that is introduced, developed, and then resolved. Typically, the plot of a story, drama, or narrative poem is divided into the following parts:

1. Introduction, or exposition: presents the setting, the major characters, and the basic situation
2. Inciting incident: introduces the central conflict
3. Development: events that occur because of the central conflict
4. Climax: high point of interest or suspense that culminates the development
5. Resolution: event that ends the central conflict
6. Denouement: any events that occur after the resolution

Some critics refer to the introduction, inciting incident, development, and climax as the *rising action,* and to the resolution and denouement as the *falling action.*

Some stories do not contain all these parts in exactly this order. An author may choose, for example, to begin a story *in medias res* (literally, "in the middle part"), after the inciting incident has occurred. The inciting incident of Milton's *Paradise Lost,* for instance, is the expulsion of Satan from heaven. However, Milton begins the poem in the middle of the action, after this expulsion has taken place. In some stories the climax and the resolution are the same event. In some there is no denouement, or tying up of loose ends after the resolution.

SPECIAL DEVICES OF PLOT

Most plots are presented in chronological order. That is, the events follow one another in time as they would in real life. However, an author may choose to vary this pattern by using flashbacks. A *flashback* is a section of a literary work that interrupts the normal sequence of events to present an event from an earlier time. The following special devices of plot are also commonly used by authors:

1. Foreshadowing: hinting about events yet to occur
2. Subplot: a series of events outside but related to the main plot; common in long works such as novels and full-length dramas
3. Suspense: the creation of a feeling of anxious uncertainty about the outcome of events
4. Surprise ending: an unexpected event occurring at the end of the story

CASE STUDY: WRITING ABOUT PLOT

Nikki's teacher asked each student to select a short story from the text and to write a paragraph about some aspect of its plot. Nikki decided to write about Elizabeth Bowen's "The Demon Lover," on page 994.

Prewriting

Nikki began by analyzing the plot so that she could pick one aspect to focus on in her paragraph. She worked out a list like this:

- Exposition: Mrs. Drover visits house
- Inciting incident: Mrs. Drover finds letter and feels afraid
- Development: Mrs. Drover recalls her fiancé in a flashback, remembers the promise that she made, feels afraid, wants to escape, leaves for safety of taxi
- False climax and resolution: Mrs. Drover arrives at taxi stand and thinks that she is safe

- Real climax and resolution (surprise ending): sees driver eye to eye, screams

- Denouement: taxi carries Mrs. Drover off

Nikki also noted some of Bowen's special techniques:

- Foreshadowing:
  Beginning—"dead air" in house
  Mysterious unstamped letter from K.
  "spectral glitters" in fiancé's eyes
  "suspension of her existence" during week with fiancé in August of 1916
  No memory of her fiancé's face
  Someone leaves house before she does

- Flashbacks (Mrs. Drover's memories):
  Last evening with fiancé—August, 1916
  Her life after fiancé is declared missing in action
  Why she made promise to her fiancé

- Suspense:
  Wondering who (or what) is after her
  Wondering if she will get away

- Surprise ending:
  Thinks she is safe in taxi but taxi driver carries her off screaming

Nikki wrote several possible topic sentences, as follows:

In "The Demon Lover" Elizabeth Bowen makes use of several special plot devices, including flashbacks, foreshadowing, and a surprise ending.

Elizabeth Bowen's "The Demon Lover" has a traditional plot structure consisting of an exposition, an inciting incident, a development, a climax, and a brief denouement.

In "The Demon Lover" Elizabeth Bowen builds suspense and then tricks the reader with a false resolution.

Drafting and Revising

Nikki liked all of her topic sentences. However, she couldn't write about all of them, so she chose the third one. She wrote a quick draft of her paper, pouring all her ideas onto the page and not stopping to worry about proper spelling, grammar, and punctuation. Then she revised her paragraph several times. As she revised, she cut a lot of nonessential details, and she added direct quotations from the story to support her claims.

Proofreading and Publishing

After her revisions were done, Nikki proofread her paper carefully to get it ready for a reader. Then she shared her final proofread paper with classmates in a small group discussion.

ACTIVITIES AND ASSIGNMENTS

A. Read or reread "The Demon Lover," on page 994. Use Nikki's prewriting notes, plus your own ideas, to write a paragraph about an unusual or striking feature of the story's plot. Follow these steps:

1. Combine your own ideas and examples from the story with Nikki's prewriting notes. Work out a rough outline of main points and examples, using one of her narrowed topics or your own topic.
2. Begin your paragraph with a topic sentence that makes a specific point about the plot. Refine one of Nikki's topic sentences or write your own.
3. Write the body of your paragraph, following your outline. Explain the main points needed to defend your topic sentence. Quote and summarize as needed, but do not simply retell the story.
4. Write a concluding sentence.
5. Revise and proofread, using the checklists on pages 1335 and 1339.
6. Hand in your paper after sharing it with other students in your class.

B. Choose one of the following works: "The Rocking-Horse Winner," on page 974; "Araby," on page 987; "A Mild Attack of Locusts," on page 1252; *Macbeth,* on page 271; or "The Rime of the Ancient Mariner," on page 660. Then write a paragraph about some aspect of its plot. Follow these steps:

1. After reading the story twice, list the events in the story. Organize them as Nikki did in the case study. Note the parts of the plot and any special techniques used by the writer.

2. Use your prewriting notes to choose a specific focus for your paragraph. Prepare a rough outline and a statement of your topic.

3. Write a rough draft. Follow your outline, develop your topic sentence, and add a conclusion.

4. Revise and proofread your draft, using the checklists on pages 1335 and 1338.

5. Share your final paragraph with a friend in your class.

Lesson 9: Writing About Character

WHAT IS CHARACTERIZATION?

In a literary work, each person, or each animal or object treated like a person, is called a *character.* The *protagonist,* or *main character,* plays the central role in the work and often wins the reader's admiration or sympathy. In some works the main character is in direct conflict with another character, known as the *antagonist.* Many works contain other major and minor characters as well, each with his or her contribution to make to the work as a whole.

Characterization is the act of introducing and developing characters in such a way as to make them real or believable. Here is the way Jane Austen introduces the protagonist in *Emma:*

> Emma Woodhouse, handsome, clever, and rich, with a comfortable home and happy disposition, seemed to unite some of the best blessings of existence; and had lived nearly twenty-one years in the world with very little to distress or vex her.

HOW WRITERS CREATE CHARACTERS

A writer may reveal the personality of a character directly or indirectly. When a writer uses *direct characterization,* he or she simply tells the reader what the character is like. When a writer uses *indirect characterization,* he or she presents the actions, words, and thoughts of a character as clues to the personality of that character or of another character.

A writer may decide to create a *round character*—one who is complex, just like a real person—or a *flat character*—one who has only a few distinguishing characteristics. The main character in a work is usually round, or complex. Minor characters are often flat.

In developing a character, a writer provides information about the following:
1. *Physical Appearance:* What does the charac-ter look like? What does the character wear?
2. *Background:* Where does the character come from? Who are the character's friends? Who are the character's relatives? What has the character experienced before the time of the story?
3. *Personality:* What are the character's special qualities and habits? How does the character tend to react to events or relate to others? How does the character think or feel?
4. *Actions:* How does the character behave? How does the character act toward others or cause others to act?
5. *Words:* What does the character say? What do others say about the character?
6. *Motivation:* Why does the character act or react in certain ways? What does the character want or need?
7. *Conflict:* Does the character have an external or internal conflict? How is the conflict resolved?
8. *Change:* Does the character change in the course of the story? If so, why, and in what ways?

CASE STUDY: WRITING ABOUT CHARACTERS

Each student in Sarah's class was asked to write a paragraph about a character in a short story. Sarah decided to analyze the woman on the train in "The Train from Rhodesia," on page 1260.

Prewriting

After rereading the story, Sarah spent five minutes writing down everything that came to mind as she thought about the character. She worked as quickly as possible, without worrying

Writing About Character 1353

about her wording or her grammar. Here is Sarah's freewriting:

> The woman ends up feeling very sad—sort of empty and tired. She thought getting married would make her less lonesome. But her husband seems strange and unreal. Like everything else on their vacation. They have a fight because of the carved lion. He got it for her because she liked it and he liked bargaining for it. She loves the lion—it's artistic and beautiful. But she is angry and ashamed—something beautiful should not be bargained for. It should just be paid for—have its dignity. The lion and the fight make her realize how alone she still is because her husband doesn't understand. Maybe she's like the train—calling to the sky but getting no answer.

Next Sarah turned to the questions listed earlier in the lesson. She skipped those that the story did not answer and then concentrated on answering those that seemed most important.

- Motivation:
  The woman sees the lion's beauty.
  She seems afraid to take it home in case it doesn't mean anything there.
  She feels ashamed at bargaining for something beautiful.
  She wanted her husband to share her feelings—but she still feels alone.

- Conflict:
  The lion causes conflict with her husband—not resolved at the end.

- Change:
  She doesn't exactly change—she just realizes that things are the same inside her—still empty.

Now Sarah felt prepared to plan her character study. She decided that the key to the character was her loneliness at the end. Sarah worked next on listing her main ideas:

- My main points:
  woman ends up feeling very sad—empty

lion causes conflict—not resolved
she loved lion but he loved bargaining
she is ashamed at bargaining for beauty
because of this conflict she realizes that the same feelings are still inside her—empty, tired, lonely

Drafting and Revising

Once Sarah had an outline and a topic sentence, she was ready to write her rough draft. She wrote a paragraph, let it sit several hours, and then revised it.

Proofreading and Publishing

Sarah proofread her paper and then took it to class. She read it aloud during the class discussion of character motivation.

ACTIVITIES AND ASSIGNMENTS

A. Use information from the case study to complete these steps:
1. Read or reread "The Train from Rhodesia," on page 1260. Review Sarah's prewriting notes and add other notes of your own.
2. Turn Sarah's list of main points into an outline for a one-paragraph character study. Revise Sarah's notes as necessary. Then write a topic sentence for your paragraph.
3. Draft a paragraph based on your topic sentence and outline. Make sure that you include evidence from the story to support your conclusions about the character.
4. Revise and proofread your paragraph, using the checklists on pages 1335 and 1338.
5. Exchange papers with one or two other students in your class to see how your final paragraphs differ.

B. Select a short story from this book. Write a paragraph about one of the characters. Follow these steps:
1. Read the story several times, first to select a character and then to note how the character

looks, acts, speaks, thinks, and feels.

2. Freewrite for five minutes about the character as if you're trying to figure out a real person. Concentrate on getting your ideas on paper; do not worry about phrasing, spelling, punctuation, or grammar.

3. Add other notes to your freewriting, using the list of questions about character. Make sure that all your conclusions are supported by the story.

4. Decide on your main point about the charac-ter. Write a topic sentence stating this point. Then make a rough outline that presents your main ideas and your supporting examples.

5. Begin your paragraph with a topic sentence.

6. Following your outline, draft the body of your paragraph.

7. Write a concluding sentence that sums up and re-emphasizes your point.

8. Revise and proofread your draft, using the checklists on pages 1335 and 1338. Share your final copy in class.

Lesson 10: Writing About Point of View

WHAT IS POINT OF VIEW?

Point of view is the vantage point, or perspective, from which a story is told. If the *narrator,* or storyteller, is one of the characters in the story, then the story is written from the *first-person point of view*. If the narrator is *not* one of the characters but stands outside the action and tells about it, then the story is written from the *third-person point of view*.

In most stories written from the first-person point of view, the actions or events are reported from one person's perspective. Everything is seen through the eyes of the character/narrator. Such a point of view is said to be *limited.*

In some stories written from the third-person point of view, the narrator tells the tale from one character's limited perspective. However, in other third-person stories the narrator is all-knowing, or *omniscient,* and can present the perspectives of all or several of the characters.

To summarize, most stories are written from one of the following points of view:

1. *Limited first-person point of view:* The narrator is a character in the story and presents the action from his or her own perspective.
2. *Limited third-person point of view:* The narrator is *not* a character in the story and presents the action from the perspective of one of the characters.
3. *Omniscient third-person point of view:* The narrator is *not* a character in the story. He or she is all-knowing and can present the internal states or viewpoints of all the characters.

DIFFERENCES BETWEEN POINTS OF VIEW

Stories told from a limited point of view tend to be highly personal and immediate in their impact. The reader usually identifies with the one character from whose perspective the story is told. However, the narrator in such a story is unable to reveal, directly, the private thoughts and feelings of all the characters.

Stories told from an omniscient point of view tend not to be as focused on a single individual. In such stories the narrator has a godlike ability to see all things and know all things. Often the narrator in such a story is able to point out or to reveal interesting or amusing contradictions between the thoughts, feelings, and perceptions of the various characters.

OTHER QUALITIES OF NARRATORS

You have learned about two important respects in which narrators differ. Some narrators participate in the action, and some do not. Some narrators view the events from a limited perspective, and some from an omniscient perspective. Narrators also differ in the following ways:

1. *Reliability:* Some narrators can be counted on to tell the truth. Such narrators are *reliable.* Other narrators grossly distort the truth. Such narrators are *unreliable* or *ironic.*
2. *Objectivity:* Some narrators are cool, calm, and reserved. They simply report events as they occur. Such narrators are *objective.* Other narrators are highly emotional or make their attitudes toward characters and events quite clear. Such narrators are *subjective.*

CASE STUDY: WRITING ABOUT NARRATION AND POINT OF VIEW

Travis was assigned a brief paper on point of view in a fictional narrative. He decided to analyze Emily Brontë's *Wuthering Heights,* which is introduced on page 898.

Prewriting

Travis's class had already read the selection from *Wuthering Heights,* so Travis knew that the first-person narrator is Mr. Lockwood. Travis began his prewriting by rereading the selection and taking these notes:

- Point of view: first-person

- Narrator: Mr. Lockwood
  Tries to be reliable and give good account (even if embarrassing to him), but makes too many assumptions
  Starts out assuming that Heathcliff is like him (subjective, not objective)
  Lockwood and Healthcliff very different:
  L.'s fussy and pompous chattering vs. H.'s yelling and growling
  L. expects regular social set-up (servants, tea) and plans visits whereas H. is unsociable (dogs, barred doors, refuses guide in snowstorm).

- Effect of point of view:
  Suggests there's a hidden story since L. doesn't know what's going on
  L. guesses everybody's position in household and is totally wrong.
  Makes us curious about H. and his past because he's so different from L.
  L. seems ordinary, especially in contrast to H.; this suggests that H.'s story will be unusual.

Next Travis worked on organizing all of his material.

Drafting and Revising

Travis planned two paragraphs: one analyzing Mr. Lockwood as the narrator, and the other discussing how Mr. Lockwood's point of view affects the reader. Here is the beginning of Travis's rough draft:

> I am writing about *Wuthering Heights.* Brontë has Mr. Lockwood tell the story. He is the narrator. He has a first-person point of view. (He is a character in the story and speaks in the first person as "I"). He tries to give an accurate account of Heathcliff. Heathcliff is his landlord. He starts out assuming that Heathcliff is like him. This is a subjective viewpoint. In fact, they are very different.

Travis finished drafting his two paragaphs.

Then he revised them several times.

Proofreading and Publishing

Travis proofread his paragraphs and shared his final paper with his discussion group in class.

ACTIVITIES AND ASSIGNMENTS

A. If you haven't already done so, read the selection from *Wuthering Heights,* on page 898. Revise and complete Travis's draft from the case study. Combine his short sentences to make the draft read more smoothly. Add details to the paragraph, especially at the end, to support the claims made. Rewrite and strengthen Travis's topic sentence. Then add a conclusion to the paragraph. Finally, write a paragraph about the effect of Lockwood's limited point of view on a reader.

B. Select a short story from this text. Analyze the narrator and the point of view. Then write two paragraphs discussing the narrator's point of view and its effect on the reader. Follow these steps:

1. After you have read the story once, identify the narrator and the point of view.
2. Analyze the point of view. Determine whether it is limited or omniscient, first person or third. Also determine whether the narrator is reliable or unreliable, subjective or objective.
3. Reread the story and take notes on the narrator and the point of view. Make sure that your notes address the question of the effect of the point of view on the reader.
4. Organize your ideas. First plan a rough outline. Then work on a topic sentence that states your main idea about the point of view.
5. Draft your two paragraphs. Analyze the narrator and the point of view in the first paragraph. Then discuss how the point of view influences the reader's reaction to the story.
6. Revise your paragraphs, using the Checklist for Revision on page 1335.
7. Proofread your paragraphs, using the Checklist for Proofreading on page 1338.
8. Share your writing with your classmates.

Lesson 11: Writing About Theme

WHAT IS A THEME?

The central idea of a literary work is its *theme.* The theme is an insight about life or the human experience that is revealed through the details of the literary work. For example, the problems characters face and the way they resolve them may provide insight into the human condition. This insight is the theme of the work.

HOW WRITERS EXPRESS THEMES

Occasionally, the theme of a work is stated directly. Usually, however, the theme is not stated directly. Instead, it is implied by the work as a whole. The many separate aspects of the work combine to suggest its central idea.

For instance, in the morality play *Everyman,* on page 188, the Messenger in the first scene says that the play "of our lives and ending shows/How transitory we be all day." Later in the play, the Doctor sums up the implication of Everyman's death for the playgoers:

> Ye hearers, take it of worth, old and
>   young.
> And forsake Pride, for he deceiveth you
>   in the end.
> And remember Beauty, Five-Wits,
>   Strength, and Discretion,
> They all at the last do Everyman
>   forsake.
> Save his Good Deeds there doth he
>   take

This passage expresses quite directly the theme of the play: Live a good life, full of good deeds, so that you will find salvation when you die.

Many works, however, are less didactic and thus more difficult to interpret. Raleigh's "The Nymph's Reply to the Shepherd" shows how a work of literature may suggest a theme:

> If all the world and love were young,
> And truth in every shepherd's tongue,
> These pretty pleasures might me move
> To live with thee, and be thy love.

Here the nymph tells the shepherd that she would be willing to be his love under certain conditions. The last stanza echoes the same idea:

> But could youth last and love still
>   breed,
> Had joys no date nor age no need,
> Then those delights my mind might move,
> To live with thee and be thy love.

These first and last stanzas set up conditions for the nymph's agreement. She says that an idyllic love might flourish—*if* everything could stay young and *if* men always spoke the truth. Of course, she and the reader both know that the conditions in the first and last stanzas cannot be met in real life. All is not permanently young and true, and love does not always increase. Raleigh does not directly say that everything, including youth and love, changes over time. Nevertheless, careful readers will conclude that this is, in fact, the poem's theme.

CASE STUDY: WRITING ABOUT THEME

Liz was asked to write a paragraph about the theme of a short story. She selected Doris Lessing's "A Mild Attack of Locusts," on page 1252.

Prewriting

Liz read the story several times because she knew that finding the theme meant understanding the whole work. Then she worked on writing out a statement of the theme. When she had trouble getting started, she tried freewriting just to get something on paper.

> I am stuck. So why am I? I really do like this story. The best parts are the descriptions and the characters. Margaret keeps being amazed and feeling discouraged. Her husband and Stephen especially just keep on going. They even end up saying that it could have been worse—though everything green is eaten up. I guess Lessing is saying how amazing it is that people just keep going even when disaster strikes.

When Liz stopped freewriting, she knew that she had begun to work out the theme. After she rephrased her idea, she went back to the story to examine how Lessing actually revealed the theme.

- Theme:
  Despite disasters, human beings can show great strength and resilience.

- Expressions of theme in story:
  Opening of story—Margaret is learning "farmer's language."
  Always problems but they still manage & get along OK
  While waiting for the locusts to come and eat their crops, they keep on working as usual.
  Locusts arrive and they fight them.
  Stephen says they are finished, tells about locusts bankrupting him 20 yrs ago, and goes back out with tea.
  When crops are all eaten, they keep on fighting to prevent locusts from laying eggs (hoppers hatch later).
  Stephen tosses out locust after admiring its strength; Margaret remembers he's said they were ruined before and they've survived.
  Men are cheered because main swarm has gone by—they begin planning to fight hoppers.

  Margaret admires beauty of locusts at dawn despite the damage they've done.

- Conclusion:
  Margaret feels like "a survivor after war" & men say, "It could have been worse."

Drafting and Revising

Liz used her prewriting notes to draft her paragraph. She started with a clear topic sentence about the theme, developed the body of the paragraph, using details from the story, and then wrote a concluding sentence that summarized her analysis. Next Liz revised her paragraph, making sure that her points were clearly stated and organized.

Proofreading and Publishing

After proofreading, Liz exchanged papers with the student sitting next to her before they both handed in their paragraphs.

ACTIVITIES AND ASSIGNMENTS

A. Refer to the case study as you write a paragraph, following these directions:

1. Read or reread "A Mild Attack of Locusts," on page 1252. Review Liz's prewriting notes, and add other notes of your own about the theme. Use the notes to work out a rough outline of points about how the theme is revealed to the reader.
2. Write a topic sentence, identifying the story and its theme.
3. Draft the body of your paragraph, discussing how the theme is revealed or expressed in the story. Use your rough outline and Liz's and your prewriting notes to supply detailed supporting evidence from the story.
4. Write a concluding sentence that sums up your analysis of the story's theme.
5. Revise and proofread your paragraph, using the checklists on pages 1335 and 1338.

6. Share your final copy with a classmate before handing it in.

   B. Write a paragraph about a literary work in this book. In your paragraph, identify the work's theme, and explain how this theme is expressed or revealed in the work. You may select any literary work or write about one of these: Shakespeare's *Macbeth*, on page 271; Orwell's "Shooting an Elephant," on page 1012; Lawrence's "The Rocking-Horse Winner," on page 974; or Blake's "A Poison Tree," on page 614. Follow these steps:

1. Read the work once or twice. Write a single sentence stating its theme. (Use freewriting if you get stuck.)
2. Refine your statement of theme. Then go through the work, taking notes on points in the work that express, reveal, or illustrate the theme.
3. Work out a rough outline of your ideas.
4. Begin your rough draft with a topic sentence identifying the work and its theme.
5. Follow your rough outline and your prewriting notes as you draft the body of your paragraph. Do not just generalize about the idea of the theme. Be sure to include details from the work to show how the writer conveys the theme.
6. Write a concluding sentence that sums up your main point.
7. Revise your paragraph, using the Checklist for Revision on page 1335.
8. Use the Checklist for Proofreading, on page 1338, to check your final version.
9. Share your paper with your classmates and with your teacher.

SECTION 3: UNDERSTANDING THE WORK AS A WHOLE: INTERPRETATION AND SYNTHESIS

Lesson 12: Writing About a Short Story

When you write about a short story, your task begins not with writing but with reading and understanding the story. Follow these guidelines when studying a story:

1. Read the story through to find out what happens in the plot.
2. Look up any unfamiliar words in the Glossary or in a dictionary.
3. Read the story again, this time concentrating on how the writer has created its key features.
4. Refer to the story as you analyze its main elements.

HOW TO ANALYZE A SHORT STORY

The following list outlines the main elements of short stories (and of longer fictional works as well). Once you have made prewriting notes about these aspects of a story, you are prepared to think about how each contributes to the story's meaning.

1. *Author and title:* Who wrote the story? What is the title of the story? Does the title suggest the subject or theme of the story?
2. *Plot:* What are the story's main events? What happens during each part of the plot: the exposition, the inciting incident, the development, the climax, the resolution, and the denouement? Does the story use special plot techniques such as foreshadowing, flashbacks, suspense, or a surprise ending?
3. *Central conflict:* What is the cental conflict? Is the conflict external? Is the protagonist pitted against another character, society, or nature? Is the conflict internal? Is there a struggle between different emotions and feelings within the protagonist?
4. *Setting:* What is the place, time, and social situation of the setting? What details create the setting? What is the setting's significance? Does it contribute to the conflict or mood?
5. *Characterization:* Who is the protagonist? Is there an antagonist? If so, who is the antagonist? Who are the other major and minor characters? What roles do they play? What do readers learn about each character's appearance, background, personality, actions, words, relationships, motivations, conflicts, and changes?
6. *Point of view:* Who is the storyteller, or narrator? Is the narrator omniscient or limited, first person or third? Is the narrator subjective or objective, reliable or unreliable?
7. *Language:* Does the story contain figures of speech such as hyperbole, irony, metaphor, or simile? Does the story contain special devices of sound such as onomatopoeia or parallelism?
8. *Theme:* What is the theme—the story's insight or central idea? How is the theme expressed?
9. *Other elements:* Is the story addressed to a specific audience? if so, who? Is the story an example of a specific genre such as fantasy, science fiction, psychological fiction, mystery fiction, detective fiction, or regional fiction?

CASE STUDY: WRITING ABOUT A SHORT STORY

Javier's English teacher assigned an essay

1. Students should be able to spot the spelling and usage errors easily. Aside from them, many of the changes raise the level of the diction from substandard to standard; e.g., *crazy about* becomes *infatuated*; *real foolish* becomes *very foolish*.

2. A full paragraph devoted to such a summary would have been a needless and tedious digression.

about the significance of a short story. Javier decided to analyze and write about James Joyce's "Araby," on page 987.

Prewriting

Javier read the story twice and got this idea for his thesis:

> "Araby" shows how we all get ideas about how things will be and then feel disappointed with ourselves when things don't work out as expected.

Next Javier began taking prewriting notes on the story's key features, using the list found earlier in the lesson. Here are his notes about the story's setting:

- Place: boy's home with aunt and uncle, town (Ireland), train ride, and bazaar

- Details: blind street and houses
  Priest's former room with blinds where he watches Mangan's sister
  Town market full of people and shops
  Empty train going to bazaar
  Bazaar dark with stalls closed, money counting, girl flirting. Significant because reality contrasts with what he wants and imagines.
  Real market vs. knight with chalice
  Lonely train ride foreshadows bazaar
  His idea of Araby vs. real bazaar. Significant because setting suggests his state (symbolic?).
  Lives in "blind" street and watches Mangan's sister from behind blinds
  Lights are out at bazaar, leaving him in the dark but able to "see"

Javier finished his analysis, concentrating on point of view and characterization. Then he planned how to organize his essay and made a list of his main points.

Drafting and Revising

Based on his thesis idea and on his other prewriting notes, Javier drafted a thesis state-ment and an introductory paragraph. For the body of his essay, he wrote one paragraph apiece about setting, characterization, and point of view, relating each to his thesis about the significance of the story. Then he drafted a concluding paragraph that summed up his main point about the story's theme. Finally, he revised his story, reorganizing, adding examples, and rephrasing as needed.

Proofreading and Publishing

Next Javier proofread his paper, looking for minor errors and making a few more changes in wording. Here is his first paragraph with his proofreading changes:

> The experiences of the boy in James
> Joyce's *Araby* illustrates how people often
> expects more than ordinary reality can provide
> and then feel disillusioned and disappointed
> with themselves. The boy is infatuated with Man-
> gan's sister, imagines that he will heroically
> brings her something from the
> bazaar, and then feels very foolish when Araby is not
> what he expects. The story expresses its
> idea through the setting
> and the characterization of the boy and his
> point of view as the narrator.

Javier recopied his paper, read it through for copying errors, and shared it with his class discussion group.

ACTIVITIES AND ASSIGNMENTS

A. Use the draft in the case study to answer these questions:

1. Explain why Javier made each of his proofreading changes.
2. Why didn't Javier explain the plot in a full paragraph instead of summing it up in his second sentence?
3. Javier's first paragraph previews the next three paragraphs—one each on setting, characterization of the boy, and point of view. Read "Araby" carefully, take prewriting notes on these elements of the story, and then write the body paragraphs. Your paragraphs should support Javier's thesis and should each focus on a single element of the story. Revise and proofread your draft carefully, using the checklists on pages 1335 and 1338.

   B. Write an essay interpreting a short story in this book. Follow these steps:

1. Read the story, and use the lists found earlier in this lesson to analyze it.
2. Draft a thesis statement about the significance of the story, concentrating on its theme, purpose, or overall effect.
3. Use your prewriting notes to decide which elements of the story will best support your thesis. Prepare an outline that notes the element each paragraph will discuss plus the evidence from the story that will illustrate each feature and relate it to your thesis.
4. Draft your paper, following your outline.
5. Revise and proofread your paper, using the checklists on pages 1335 and 1338.
6. Share your paper with your class.

Lesson 13: Writing About a Poem

Writing about a poem requires that you understand it well. Follow these general steps as you begin the process of analysis:

1. Read the poem to yourself. Look up any unfamiliar words. Identify the poem's speaker, subject, and genre (narrative, dramatic, or lyric).
2. Read the poem again, and note any images, figurative language, or allusions. Think about the functions served by these.
3. Read the poem aloud. Listen for special devices of sound such as rhythm, rhyme, alliteration, or onomatopoeia.
4. Read the poem again carefully and paraphrase it, sentence by sentence or line by line. Your paraphrase should reflect both what the poem states directly and what it implies.
5. Make notes on the genre, form, imagery, figurative language, devices of sound, theme, and other elements of the poem.

HOW TO ANALYZE A POEM

When you take prewriting notes about a poem as a whole, look at the elements frequently used in poetry to see what features set apart this particular poem—to see what makes it different or especially meaningful. Then you will have a basis for deciding what to emphasize in your paper about the poem. The following list of elements in poetry will help you look for the key features of a poem. Once you have identified these features, you can begin to ask questions about them and to analyze how they create the poem's meaning.

1. *Author and title:* Who wrote the poem? What is the title of the poem? Does the title suggest the topic or theme of the poem?
2. *Genre:* Is the poem a lyric, such as an ode, an elegy, or a sonnet? That is, does it use musical language to express the emotions of a single speaker? If so, who is the speaker? What audience is being addressed? What is the occasion or situation? Is the poem a narrative, such as a ballad, an epic, or a metrical romance? That is, does it tell a story? If so, what plot, characters, settings, and point of view does this story have? Is it a dramatic poem, one that uses monologue, dialogue, or other dramatic techniques? What point of view, characters, setting, and situation does the poem present?
3. *Form:* Does the poem have a traditional form or pattern? If the poem is divided into stanzas, what form does each stanza take? Describe the number of lines, rhyme scheme, and metrical pattern of each stanza. Does the poem make use of couplets, quatrains, or some other standard stanza form? Does each stanza function, like a paragraph, as an independent unit of meaning? Does the poem have a unique shape or structure that adds to its meaning?
4. *Imagery:* What images of sight, sound, taste, touch, smell, and movement are used? What emotions do the images suggest?
5. *Figurative language:* What figures of speech are used in the poem? Does the poem contain examples of antithesis, apostrophe, irony, hyperbole, metaphor, metonymy, oxymoron, paradox, personification, simile, synecdoche, or understatement? Does the poem contain symbols or allusions? Is it allegorical?
6. *Devices of sound:* Does the poem contain rhyming words? Does it have a regular rhyme scheme? Does the poem contain alliteration, assonance, or consonance? Does it contain euphony, cacophony, parallel structure, or repetition? What is the poem's meter? What type and number of metrical feet does it have

1364   *Handbook of Writing About Literature*

in each line? If the poem is in free verse, how does it use rhythm?

7. *Other elements:* Has the poet taken liberties with spelling, mechanics, or grammar? Has the poet used words in unusual ways? If so, why has he or she done so? What tone does the speaker use? What is the mood of the poem? Does this mood change during the poem? What is the poem's theme? What overall effects do the separate parts of the poem combine to create?

CASE STUDY: WRITING ABOUT A POEM

Jeremy's English assignment was to write an essay about a poem. He decided to write about Molly Holden's "Some Men Create," on page 1323.

Prewriting

Jeremy began his prewriting by reading through the poem several times, studying it in detail, and making notes about its key features. here are a few of his notes:

- Author: Molly Holden

- Title: "Some Men Create"

- Form: 4 quatrains—show the situation (1), consequences (2–3), and point (4)

- Genre: lyric poem

- Imagery: sight (so that "eye may reap")
  ivy vaulting, swinging, and shining

- Figurative language: two similes
  Ivy will "swing like hair" (sounds like Rapunzel?)
  "seeding traveler's joy smothers" timber and oak "like smoke"

- Devices of sound:
  Rhyme scheme (*abcb*)
  Alliteration: *sm*others/*sm*oke
  Assonance: suggests "Oh" of wonder?

o in so, oak/smoke, alone/sown
  Repetition: word *so* used three times
  Meter: variations match meaning example: 4th lines of stanzas are all the same (´ ˘ ´ ˘ ´) except in last stanza, where variation emphasizes "not sown"
  Examples: line "vaults" between first two stanzas (just like ivy); line 10 (about cutting dead tree) has 5 one-syllable words—snap off like branches from dead tree

- Theme (last stanza especially):
  Even in an orderly life, people should allow some spontaneous and unanticipated things to develop.

After Jeremy read through his prewriting notes, he felt that the poem not only explains but also illustrates its theme. He outlined his paper, selecting as examples the features he thought would best support his thesis.

- Paragraph 1 Introduce poem: Name author and title; state thesis that the poem both explains & illustrates its theme

- Paragraph 2 Form is orderly (rhyme, meter): 4 quatrains follow logical pattern—show the situation, illustrate the consequences, and explain point

- Paragraph 3 Form has surprises ("not sown"):
  Meter in line 4 of last stanza
  Line that "vaults " between stanzas
  Line 10 with short words

- Paragraph 4 Language also helps reader see the point that eye likes to "reap":
  Images of sight (ivy)
  Similes (also visual)
  Assonance (suggests awe or wonder)

- Paragraph 5 Conclusion: Poem states and illustrates its point, showing us that we like order but we also like unexpected pleasures.

1. He left them out because they are irrelevant to his point about eyes liking to leap. He might have worked them into paragraph 5.
2. The poem both explains and illustrates its theme that people should allow for the spontaneous and unanticipated.

Drafting and Revising

Jeremy used his outline and notes to write a rough draft. Then he revised his draft, making sure that both his interpretation and his examples were clear.

Proofreading and Publishing

Jeremy carefully proofread his paper and then exchanged papers with a classmate.

ACTIVITIES AND ASSIGNMENTS

A. Read or reread Molly Holden's poem, on page 1323. Then use the case study for these activities:

1. Jeremy's outline does not include alliteration and repetition. Why do you think he left them out? Could he have added them? If so, where?
2. Jeremy's outline notes the idea for his thesis. Write this out in a sentence.
3. Add your own ideas to Jeremy's prewriting notes. Use your notes and the notes from the case study to draft, revise, and proofread your own analysis.

B. Write an interpretive essay on any poem in this text. Follow these steps:

1. Read the poem and analyze it, using the steps and key elements outlined at the beginning of this lesson.
2. Use your prewriting notes to develop a working outline and a thesis statement about the poem's overall effect, purpose, or theme.
3. Follow your outline as you write an introductory paragraph, body paragraphs, and a conclusion. Be sure to use supporting examples and quotations.
4. Revise and proofread your essay, using the checklists on pages 1335 and 1338.
5. Share the poem and your paper with your classmates.

Lesson 14: Writing About Drama

When you analyze a play, you will find that it contains many of the literary elements found in short stories and in poetry. Like a short story, a play has a plot, a central conflict, characters, a setting, and a theme. Like poetry, a play may use poetic forms, imagery, figurative language, and devices of sound. Refer to the previous two lessons for information on analyzing and writing about these literary elements.

No matter how much a play resembles a story or a poem, it necessarily differs in one major respect. A play is written to be performed before an audience. Its action is physical and takes place on stage. Its lines are written to be spoken by actors and to be accompanied by their expressions and movements. Unlike most stories and poems, a play has dialogue for actors to speak and stage directions to explain the actors' movements, the appearance of the set, the props needed, the lighting and sound effects, and other aspects of performance and production. In addition, a play may use such *dramatic conventions* as the *aside* (a speech or comment made directly to the audience as though other characters on stage could not hear it) and the *soliloquy* (a speech delivered by a lone character on the stage, one that reveals the character's inner thoughts).

HOW TO ANALYZE DRAMA

A play can be analyzed as a written work of literature or as a performance, as the following questions suggest.

The drama as literature:
1. What happens during the exposition, inciting incident, development, climax, resolution, and denouement of the plot? What happens during each act and scene?
2. What is the central conflict?

4. Who are the characters? What does each add to the play?
5. What does the audience learn about each character's background, personality, relationships, motivations, conflicts, and changes?
6. How is the theme revealed?
7. What imagery does the writer use?
8. What figurative language does the writer use?
9. What symbols does the play present?
10. What devices of sound does the language of the play include?

The drama as performance:
1. How is the stage set, and how does that setting affect the audience?
2. How effectively and accurately is each character portrayed in the performance?
3. How effective is the delivery of the dialogue? (Consider such factors as pacing, volume, pitch, stress, tone, and vocal quality.)
4. What is the overall effect of the performance?
5. How would you review the performance as a whole? (Consider such factors as the acting, the set, the costumes, the sound, the lighting, the direction, the properties, the makeup, and any other facts in the production.)

CASE STUDY: WRITING ABOUT DRAMA

Michael's English teacher assigned an essay about one scene in *Macbeth*. The focus of the essay was to be how the scene contributes to the significance of the play as a whole.

Prewriting

Michael decided to analyze Act I, Scene iii, when Macbeth first meets the three witches. He wanted to figure out how the scene moves the play forward and what significant information it

Motivation for Writing Make available to your class drama reviews and criticism from newspapers and magazines. Reading them will give students some idea of how entertaining and useful such writing can be. You might ask the class to point out what they can learn from such reviews about how to write about drama. You might then have them apply their developing sense of drama criticism to writing about a television play or movie. At that point, they should be well prepared to study this lesson.

1. They are *As Banquo points out,*
Still, Finally, and *In contrast.* These
transitions knit his observations
into a coherent whole.

gives the audience. Here is a chart Michael made to examine the play's plot, setting, characters, and themes.

Michael worked on organizing his notes into a logical outline for his essay.

ELEMENT	SIGNIFICANCE
Plot: three witches on heath meet Macbeth and Banquo	nature of witches
hail Macbeth with three titles	Macbeth is absorbed, wants to hear more from them
hail Banquo as father of kings	Banquo may become a threat to Macbeth's ambitions
Ross and Angus arrive to greet Macbeth as Thane of Cawdor	confirm witches about Cawdor raise question about crown
Setting: thunderstorm on heath "foul and fair" day	threatening, evil weather foreshadows events to come
Character: Macbeth is shaken by prophecy but wants to know more	ready to think of murdering Duncan decides not to act but leave it to chance
Banquo suspects betrayal from witches	contrast with Macbeth: Banquo is not ambitious and senses evil, does not react as Macbeth does warns of evil
Themes: ambition control of future—choice or destiny?	Macbeth considers how far he'll go to make prophecy true

Drafting and Revising

Michael began his introduction with this thesis statement:

> Through its plot, setting, and characterization, Act I, Scene iii, of *Macbeth* alerts the audience to the problem of knowing one's destiny and wanting to control the future.

Michael drafted and revised his essay, including an introductory paragraph, a concluding paragraph, and separate paragraphs on plot, setting, and character. Here is his revised version of paragraph four, on character:

> Both Macbeth and Banquo hear the prophecies and their first confirmation out on the heath. From the beginning, the two characters react differently. As Banquo points out, Macbeth acts distracted and shaken. He wants to hear more and does not want to judge the prophecy as evil or good. Still, his first thought is not of some accident to the king but of murder—of how his own action could secure the future. Finally he decides that chance may bring him the crown without any action on his part. In contrast, Banquo sees the witches as evil and warns Macbeth. Though he wants to hear their prediction he does not want anything from them. Unlike Macbeth, he has no thought of trying to control the future.

Proofreading and Publishing

Michael proofread his paper for spelling and mechanical errors. Then he shared the paper with his older brother, who is an actor.

ACTIVITIES AND ASSIGNMENTS

A. Use the case study to answer these questions:

1. Point out the transitional words and phrases in Michael's paragraph. Explain how Michael uses transitions to help organize his discussion of the two characters.

2. Michael does not use any quotations from the play to support his arguments. Revise his

paragraph, adding appropriate quotations. Be sure to punctuate properly and to quote the exact words of the play.

B. Choose one of these topics for an essay about a play: (1) analyze the main elements of one scene in a play from this text, and explain their contributions to the significance of the play as a whole; or (2) evaluate the ways in which Higgins and Liza change in *Pygmalion,* on page 1109. For either topic, follow these steps.

1. Read the section of the play carefully several times. Try to imagine how the scene would be presented on stage.
2. Take prewriting notes as you analyze the play.

Use the first list in this lesson for guidelines; return to the last two lessons if you need more suggestions.

3. Work out a thesis statement and an outline. Note the main point of each paragraph and the supporting evidence or details from the play. Decide whether you should organize element by element or chronologically as presented in the play.
4. Follow your outline and support your thesis statement as you draft your essay.
5. Revise and proofread your draft, using the checklists on pages 1335 and 1338.
6. Share your essay with your classmates.

SECTION 4: JUDGING A LITERARY WORK: EVALUATION

Lesson 15: Evaluating a Literary Work

WHAT IS EVALUATION?

When you *evaluate* something, you judge its value. In everyday life you regularly perform this mental task—evaluating a new album, clothes that you want to buy, or the food at a new restaurant. Each evaluation states your opinion and is based on *evidence,* the facts you discover when you listen to the album, try on the clothes, or eat at the restaurant. In other words, your evaluation is based on appropriate standards or criteria—the sound and style of the music, the appearance and cost of the clothes, and the taste and price of the food.

Evaluating a literary work is just like making other judgments: You state an opinion based on certain standards or criteria. Then you support your opinion with specific evidence and details. Your opinion is your own, but it will not be accepted by anyone else unless you can marshal the facts to support it.

For example, if you argued that *The Tempest* is a juvenile play because two of the characters are a sprite and a monster, your opinion could not be supported by evidence. Since it was common for supernatural beings to appear in plays on the Elizabethan stage, their presence does not make the play juvenile. Therefore, your opinion is not sound since it cannot be supported by evidence. If, on the other hand, you argued that the overall mood of the *The Tempest* is more tragic than cheerful, some people would disagree with you, but you could provide evidence from the play to support your evaluation so that readers would understand your position.

CRITERIA FOR EVALUATING A LITERARY WORK

Your judgment of the quality of a story, poem, play, or other work may be based on many different criteria. Here are some standards often applied to literature:

1. To what extent does the work accomplish its purpose or achieve its effect? Do you think that it succeeds in doing what it sets out to do—entertaining, amusing, scaring, surprising, persuading, teaching, or emotionally moving its reader?

2. Is its purpose or effect worth accomplishing? Do you consider its purpose more important or significant than other purposes?

3. Does the work have an ethical or moral message? Do you feel that its message is important? Do you agree with the message?

4. How original or inventive is the work? Do you find the topic or its treatment new?

5. How clear and understandable is the work? If the work is difficult, does it nonetheless reward the reader's efforts to understand it? Does the work seem indefensibly unclear or confused?

6. To what extent does the work meet other criteria important to you as a reader? Do you have personal views about its genre, subject, or style?

CASE STUDY: EVALUATING A LITERARY WORK

Ben's teacher asked the class to suggest poems that might provoke different opinions from different people. Then each student was to write an essay stating and supporting an evaluation of the poem.

Prewriting

Ben decided to write about Rupert Brooke's "The Soldier," on page 1050. Ben himself had mixed feelings about the poem that depended on whether he based his judgment on realistic criteria or on the poem's success in accomplishing its purpose. He used clustering to test both ideas:

Ben decided to write about the opinion that he could most persuasively defend with evidence from the poem. He added to and reorganized his prewriting notes until he had outlined a four-paragraph essay.

Drafting and Revising

Ben refined his thesis statement and drafted his essay. The next day he revised his paper, carefully checking the clarity of his arguments and evidence.

Proofreading and Publishing

After Ben proofread his paper, he shared the poem and his paper with a friend.

ACTIVITIES AND ASSIGNMENTS

A. Read or reread Brooke's poem, on page 1050. Then review Ben's clustering notes in the case study and follow these steps:

1. Select one of Ben's criteria, and add your own notes to his; start with your own criteria for judging the poem, and use clustering or another prewriting technique to develop your ideas. Whatever your view, the prewriting notes should specify your standards or criteria for judging, your opinion about how well the poem meets those standards or criteria, and your supporting evidence (quotations, paraphrases, and analyses of the poem).

2. Write a thesis statement that states your opinion. Then outline your main points and your evidence.

3. Draft your essay, including an introduction, several body paragraphs that develop your main points, and a conclusion.

4. Revise and proofread your paper, using the checklists on pages 1335 and 1338. Check especially carefully to see that your opinions and reasons are clearly stated and that your evidence is pertinent and clear.

5. Exchange your work with someone in class who wrote a paper using a different standard for judgment. Compare your papers.

B. Select a poem, story, or other literary work about which you have a definite opinion. Write a four- or five-paragraph essay evaluating that work. Follow these steps:

1. Use freewriting, clustering, or another prewriting technique to figure out the criterion or standard for judgment, your precise opinion, and the supporting evidence on which you will base your judgment. If you have a strong view but cannot find evidence to support it, your opinion will not be persuasive. In that case, start over with another work, or do more prewriting to develop your ideas.

2. Work out a thesis statement that presents your opinion about the work. Organize your prewriting ideas in a paragraph-by-paragraph outline. Make sure that your paper is clearly organized. You might choose to concentrate, in each paragraph, on a specific element of the work, showing how it supports your opinion. On the other hand, you might devote a paragraph to each reason for your opinion, drawing supporting examples of different kinds from the work.

3. Draft your essay, starting with an introduction to the literary work, your criterion for judging it, and your evaluation or opinion, based on the criterion. Next write your body paragraphs and a conclusion.

4. If possible, wait a few hours or a day so that you have more perspective about your own writing. Then revise your essay, using the checklist on page 1335. Make sure that your ideas are stated clearly and that your opinions are supported by evidence.

5. Proofread your paper, using the checklist on page 1338.

6. If possible, exchange papers with a classmate who has a different opinion about the same work.

Lesson 16: Writing a Comparative Evaluation

WHAT IS A COMPARATIVE EVALUATION?

A *comparative evaluation* follows the same pattern explained in the last lesson. First state your opinion about which of two works is better or worse, based on specific criteria or standards for judgment. Your basis for comparison may include one or more specific points of comparison (similarities) or contrast (differences). Then use specific evidence from both works to support your views.

CHOOSING WORKS FOR COMPARATIVE EVALUATION

When you select two works for comparative evaluation, they should have something in common—perhaps the same theme, topic, or literary form. If the two works are totally unlike, comparison serves little purpose. You could only conclude that they are very different—that one, for example, is an Anglo-Saxon epic poem and the other, a modern short story about a fiddle.

To compare or contrast the two works effectively, you need to find comparable points in each. These points might be the elements characteristic of the type of writing. For example, you could compare and contrast the form, imagery, figurative language, and sound devices in two lyric poems with the same subject and theme. Similarly, you might look at characterization, setting, and symbolism in a short story and a play with similar plots and themes. (See the lessons in Sections 2 and 3 of this handbook for advice about how to analyze specific elements and types of literary works.)

ORGANIZING A COMPARATIVE EVALUATION

Begin by selecting the points of comparison and contrast that seem most pertinent. Then make a chart listing each point of comparison or contrast. Allow room for an entry about each work in its own column. For each work and each point of comparison, note comments and evidence.

Next plan an outline based on the points that fit your essay. Use the organizational method that is best for the complexity and balance of your material:

METHOD 1	METHOD 2
Introduction	Introduction
Work #1 —Point A —Point B —Point C	Point A —Work #1 —Work #2
Work #2 —Point A —Point B —Point C	Point B —Work #1 —Work #2
Conclusion	Point C —Work #1 —Work #2
	Conclusion

CASE STUDY: WRITING A COMPARATIVE EVALUATION

Melissa's English teacher assigned a comparative evaluation of two poems. Melissa picked two sonnets, Shakespeare's Sonnet 29, on page 255, and Rossetti's "Silent Noon," on page 859.

Prewriting

Melissa began the assignment by carefully rereading the two poems. She knew that she

1. She will use Method 1: she will first discuss Sonnet 29, and then "Silent Noon."
2. She might discuss both poems together for each of several points.
3. Answers will vary. Students should be asked to explain how they would use whichever outline form they prefer.

liked Shakespeare's better, but she needed to analyze why. Using elements from the lesson on writing about a poem, she worked out this chart:

ELEMENT	SONNET 29	"SILENT NOON"
Form	Shakespearean	Petrarchan
Imagery	sound—cries and curses, then little until thinks of beloved and lark sings	sight—lush imagery is almost too much
Figures of Speech	simile—he feels like a lark singing when he thinks of beloved idea of joy bursting up fits well	simile—the dragonfly hangs like a blue thread; so this hour is dropped to lovers thread, hour, and dragonfly are less attractive silence like hourglass is OK but no special fit overdone!
Sound Devices	repetition "like him" parallelism and trouble/ look/curse this man's/ that man's structure of lines emphasizes rut he's in	alliteration: *gl*eams/*gl*ooms *s*kies/*sc*atter *s*un/*s*earched *d*eathless/*d*ower lines 8 and 14 hiss instead of hush
Language Choices	older words "beweep" "bootless" but actually direct clear language	showy l. 13 is too dense "This close-companioned inarticulate hour"
Theme	love poem: remembers love when downcast and wouldn't change with a king it's a bigger compliment	love poem: treasures beautiful hour together more ordinary idea than in Shakespeare sonnet

After Melissa had enough evidence to support her opinion, she worked out an outline for her paper.

Drafting and Revising

Melissa began her draft with this thesis statement:

> Shakespeare's Sonnet 29 is a deeper and more moving love poem than Rosetti's "Silent Noon." Although some of Shakespeare's older vocabulary is harder to understand, his sonnet's form and meaning are better matched to each other through his use of sound devices, imagery, and figurative language.

Melissa continued drafting her paper, following her outline. She then revised carefully, checking to make sure that she had included all her main points of comparison and contrast for each poem.

Proofreading and Publishing

After proofreading, Melissa shared her paper with Ms. Thomas, her English teacher from the preceding year, who had given her extra help with comparisons and contrasts.

ACTIVITIES AND ASSIGNMENTS

A. Use the case study to answer the following questions.
1. Which organizational plan does Melissa's thesis statement suggest that she will use? Use her prewriting notes to write out the outline that you think she has planned.
2. How else might Melissa organize her paper?

Work out a second possible outline for her paper. Write a revised thesis statement that suits this new outline.

3. Which outline better suits her material? Explain the advantages and disadvantages of each.

B. For your own comparative evaluation, select two literary works such as any of the following pairs: Marlowe's "The Passionate Shepherd to His Love," on page 230, and Raleigh's "The Nymph's Reply to the Shepherd," on page 238; Nashe's "A Litany in Time of Plague," on page 250, and the selection from Defoe's *A Journal of the Plague Year,* on page 514; Marvell's "To His Coy Mistress," on page 418, and Herrick's "To the Virgins, to Make Much of Time," on page 432; or Tennyson's "Crossing the Bar," on page 808, and Thomas's "Do Not Go Gentle into That Good Night," on page 1102. Follow these steps in writing your essay:

1. Read both works carefully.
2. Tentatively decide which you like better and for what reasons.
3. Set up a chart like the one in the case study, listing the points of comparison and contrast for both works. Begin working on the points that seem most important, but stay flexible in case other ideas occur to you.
4. Work out a rough outline and a thesis statement. Try one of the two methods of organizing outlined earlier.
5. Begin drafting your paper's introduction, including the titles and authors of the two works and your thesis statement with your evaluation. Draft the body paragraphs, following your outline and including clear supporting evidence from the works. Then write a concluding paragraph summarizing your argument.
6. Check for clear and consistent organization. Try outlining your draft itself to identify any problems or omissions.
7. Revise and proofread your essay, using the checklists on pages 1335 and 1338.
8. Share your essay with a classmate.

Motivation for Writing To galva-
nize student interest in this lesson, you might present your class
with speeches, editorials, or
propaganda-like writing that
forcefully expresses a point of
view with which students are likely to disagree. Let them first voice
their reactions, and then challenge them to disprove logically
the writer's assertions. If you can
make your students see the need
for logical, intelligent criticism of
persuasive writing, they should be
receptive to the principles explained in this lesson.

Lesson 17: Evaluating Persuasion

A nonfiction work is *persuasive* if its purpose
is to move readers or listeners to take some
action or to adopt some view. Examples of persuasive nonfiction include editorials, advertisements, campaign speeches, and public relations
materials. Often people write essays and even
whole books specifically to persuade others to
think or act in certain ways.

SOUND REASONING ABOUT PERSUASION

Persuasive writing and speech present
opinions—statements about which people may
disagree. When evaluating persuasive language, a reader or listener must determine
whether the opinions presented are sound. The
following are some criteria for evaluating the
soundness of opinions:

The Consistency Principle

Is the opinion consistent with known facts?
For example, the opinion that one should not
take illegal drugs is consistent with the fact that
illegal drugs can cause great physical and psychological harm.

The Utility Principle

Does accepting the opinion led to consequences that are themselves acceptable? For
example, the opinion that one should not drive
beyond the speed limit is sound because acting
on this opinion has desirable consequences.
When people drive within the speed limit, there
are fewer traffic accidents.

The Principle of Appeal to Authority

Is the opinion consistent with the views of
knowledgeable and reliable authorities? For example, the opinion that one should eat high-
fiber, low-fat foods is consistent with the views of
medical scientists and researchers. These people have found that eating such foods decreases
one's risk of developing heart disease or cancer.

Each of these principles is related to the
more general principle that an opinion must be
supported by reasoned, logical arguments.

UNSOUND REASONING ABOUT OPINIONS

When people write or speak persuasively,
they sometimes present arguments that are unreasonable or illogical. Such arguments make
use of propaganda and logical fallacies. *Propaganda* is language that is emotionally charged
and intentionally misleading. A *logical fallacy* is
an error in reasoning. The following propaganda
devices and logical fallacies are often found in
persuasive writing and speech:

Propaganda Techniques:
1. *Bandwagon:* urging support for an opinion
   simply because many other people support
   the opinion
2. *Loaded language:* using emotionally charged
   words that have little meaning beyond arous-
   ing positive or negative feelings
3. *Argument ad hominem:* (literally, "argument
   to the person") criticizing or attacking the
   opponent instead of the oponent's argument
4. *Snob appeal:* urging support for an opinion
   solely because an admired person or group
   supports it
5. *Straw man:* exaggerating or misrepresenting
   the opposing position so that it sounds more
   ridiculous than it actually it
6. *Stereotyping:* assuming, without sufficient evidence, that everyone in a particular group has
   certain characteristics

Logical Fallacies:
1. *Begging the question:* stating an opinion with-

out giving evidence to support it; simply assuming the truth of the opinion to be proved

2. *Either/or fallacy:* treating a complicated issue as if there were only two sides or two alternatives when there are actually more

3. *Post hoc, ergo propter hoc:* (literally, "after this, therefore because of this") assuming that one action or event caused another simply because it came earlier in time

4. *False analogy:* falsely treating two subjects as similar in one respect simply because they are similar in some other respect

5. *Non sequitur:* (literally, "it does not follow") stating a conclusion that is not a necessary consequence of the reasons given

6. *Overgeneralization:* making a statement that is broader in its application than the facts would warrant

When evaluating written or spoken persuasion, make sure that the opinions presented are well supported. Also make sure that the speaker or writer has avoided propaganda devices and logical fallacies.

CASE STUDY: EVALUATING PROPAGANDA AND ARGUMENT

Carrie's English class was working on the logical evaluation of arguments. Each student brought to class an example of propaganda or faulty logic. Examples were found in editorials, in political speeches, in a letter to the editor of a newspaper, and in similar material. After the class discussion each student was asked to write a paragraph evaluating his or her example.

Prewriting

Carrie found this letter to the editor in her local newspaper:

Dear Editor:

The recent car accident on Tunley Lane shows how irresponsible pet owners are. If that dog had not been walking along the side of the road, the car would not have run into the mailbox. People should not have pets unless they are willing to care for them. All good citizens agree that the public should not have to risk car crashes, highway mayhem, and wanton violence just because these people are nincompoops!

Sincerely,
Roger Loxley

Carrie began analyzing this letter, first noting its highly emotional vocabulary and tone as well as the lack of evidence for its assertions. She then listed some of the letter's flaws:

• Argument ad hominem and loaded language—calling people "nincompoops"

• Bandwagon appeal or snob appeal—calling on "all good citizens"

• Non sequitur—assuming that the dog by the road was not cared for and assuming that pet owners are responsible for "car crashes, highway mayhem, and wanton violence"

• Post hoc, ergo propter hoc—assuming that the dog caused the accident

• Stereotyping—characterizing all pet owners as irresponsible people

Carrie decided that the letter contained two basic flaws—lack of respect for other people, both pet owners and readers, and an illogical analysis of causes and effects.

Drafting and Revising

Carrie used her prewriting notes to supply details for her paragraph. After drafting her paragraph, she carefully revised it, making sure that her own points were presented reasonably.

Proofreading and Publishing

Carrie proofread her paragraph and then read it aloud to the class.

ANSWERS TO ACTIVITIES AND ASSIGNMENTS,
Section A

1. The list provides her with a good outline for a paragraph. Students could use her list as it stands for an outline, but with the addition of a thesis statement, such as *This letter shows lack of respect for people and illogical analysis.*
2. Other logical flaws include snob appeal, stereotyping, and overgeneralization.
3. It lacks emotional restraint, sufficiency of information, utility.

ACTIVITIES AND ASSIGNMENTS

A. Use the case study to answer the following questions:
1. How could Carrie use her list of logical flaws to illustrate that the letter lacked respect for people and presented a faulty analysis of causes? Work out an outline for her paragraph. Feel free to add or to leave out points.
2. Do you see other logical flaws in the letter? If so, what are they?
3. What general characteristics of sound argument does the letter lack?

B. Analyze an example of faulty argument or of propaganda. Write a paragraph about it, following these steps:
1. Find an example such as a letter to the editor, an editorial, a political brochure, some campaign material, or an advertisement.
2. Analyze why your example is not a sound argument. Examine its general characteristics, its specific logical fallacies, and its propaganda techniques. List these problems. Then use the materials on your list to make an outline.
3. Begin your paragraph with a topic sentence. Then explain and illustrate your main points. Add a conclusion.
4. Revise and proofread your draft, using the checklists on pages 1335 and 1338.
5. Share your paragraph with a class discussion group.

SECTION 5: WRITING CREATIVELY
Lesson 18: Writing a Short Story

Writing a short story means arranging and telling about incidents, describing scenes, and developing characters in ways that will interest and entertain a reader. A short story may begin with an idea about any of the standard features of the short story—character, setting, plot, mood, or theme.

FINDING A STORY IDEA

Here are some suggestions about how to find an idea for a short story:

1. *What happens? (plot):* Think of an incident or a conflict that could make a good story. Consider internal conflicts (choices, decisions, or other pressures) or external conflicts (struggles between people, battles with social or physical forces, contests, or other oppositions).
2. *Where does it happen? (setting):* Think of an interesting time (past, present, or future) and place (real or imaginary), perhaps someplace where you have lived or that you have visited.
3. *Who is involved? (characters):* Think of someone you know who is interesting, admirable, or unusual. Create a character based on this person.
4. *What does it mean? (theme):* Think of an insight that you would like to pass along to others.
5. *Who tells the story? (point of view):* Imagine a narrator who has a complete overview, the more limited view of an observer, or the even more limited view of a participating character.

DEVELOPING YOUR STORY

To develop your story idea more fully, ask yourself these questions:

1. *Character:* Who will be the main character? What will be the character's name? How will he or she look and talk? What will be the character's background, personality, education, job, or status? What will be the character's motivations? Why will the character act as he or she does? What will he or she want or believe? Will the character change? If so, how and why? What will the character learn? What relationships with others will the character have? What internal or external conflicts will the character need to resolve? Who will be the minor characters? What will be their roles? What will they be like? How will they relate to the protagonist?
2. *Setting:* When will the story take place? Where will it take place? What sensory images will help you create this place for a reader?
3. *Plot:* What will happen in the story? In what order will you tell the story? Will you use flashbacks, foreshadowing, or a surprise ending? How will you build suspense? What background information will you supply at the beginning of the story? What will happen to begin the conflict? How will the conflict develop? What will be its consequences? What will be the most suspenseful moment? How will the conflict end? Will anything happen after the conflict ends? If so, what?
4. *Point of View:* Who will tell the story—an observer or a character? How much will the storyteller know—everything or what one character knows? Will the narrator speak in the first person or in the third person?
5. *Theme:* What will be your short story's central idea or insight into life? How will you express this point in the short story?

Motivation for Writing You might begin with the five suggestions for finding a story idea. Let the class use them to come up with at least several possible ideas. Tell your students that they are free to use any of these ideas, or one of their own devising, to write a story. If students have a concrete idea in mind, the suggestions for developing a story are more likely to prove useful.

CASE STUDY: WRITING A SHORT STORY

Erica wanted to enter a short story contest, but she did not want to write a typical romance or adventure story. She wanted to write about the future, but she needed an idea.

Prewriting

Since the school district computers were down most of that day, Erica began to wonder what life would be like without computers. She wrote down a few notes about this idea to test whether it would make a good short story.

- Title ideas: maybe "Computers on Strike" or "The Great Computer Scam"

- What happens? (plot):
  Something damages one computer
  It breaks down; spreads to others
  All overload and stop working
  Now what? Consequences? Solution?
  Get them fixed? Live without them?

- Where does it happen? (setting):
  Future, maybe 50 years from now
  Society even more dependent on computers; people need them to work, run houses, make decisions
  Should place look cold and mechanical? or should it have deceptive surface, looking natural but depending on the computers to keep it all going?

- Who is involved? (characters):
  Probably need good person, but does he or she want to fix the computers? Would character rather help people become independent of them again? also need source of conflict: computers themselves? or evil character? (not mad scientist!) maybe the electric power company?

- What does it mean? (theme):
  What is my central idea?
  Should story show human ability to solve problems? or the need to stay human in an over-controlled society? or the need for people to find solutions using their intelligence?

- Who tells the story? (point of view):
  Maybe all-knowing narrator?
  —maybe the main character who feels the conflict or even the computer that causes the mess?

Erica finally had an idea. She used the list of questions in this lesson to develop her idea further.

Drafting and Revising

Erica drafted her story in one sitting. Then she waited a day, read it through once, and began to revise section by section.

Proofreading and Publishing

After proofreading her paper and handing it in for her teacher's reactions, Erica made a few more changes. Then she entered her work in the short story contest.

ACTIVITIES AND ASSIGNMENTS

A. Review Erica's prewriting notes and complete them yourself, using the list of questions for developing a short story. Work out your own story outline and draft your story. After revising and proofreading your story, exchange papers with other students in your class to see how differently they developed the story.

B. Write an original story. Follow these suggestions:
1. Use the first list (the one with the *who, when, where,* and *what* questions) to come up with an idea for a story.
2. Develop your ideas by answering the questions in the second list in this lesson.
3. Make a list of the events in your story.
4. Draft your story.
5. Review your draft, checking the development

of all the elements in the second chart. Make any necessary additions, cuts, or changes so that the sequence of events, the characters' motivations, and the conflict are clear.

6. Revise your draft as you would any other paper, using the checklist on page 1335.

7. Proofread your paper using the checklist on page 1338.

8. Share your story with a reader whom you think would especially enjoy it—your parents, your English teacher, a past English teacher, a teacher in another class, or a friend.

Lesson 19: Writing a Poem

Writing poetry can be a wonderful, rewarding experience. In this lesson you will review some common poetic forms and then try writing some poetry yourself.

SOME COMMON VERSE FORMS

A *couplet* is a pair of rhyming lines, each with the same number of strong stresses, or beats. Long poems are often made of strings of couplets that may or may not be separated by spaces. For examples of poems written in couplets, see Marvell's "To His Coy Mistress," on page 418; the selections by Pope, on pages 548 and 561; and Hopkins's "Spring and Fall: To a Young Child," on page 847.

A *ballad* is a poem that tells a story in short, rhyming stanzas. The traditional ballad, often set to music, has four- or six-line rhyming stanzas. Most ballads have a recurring rhythmical pattern. Examples of traditional ballads appear on pages 104–112. Many traditional English and American songs are ballads, as are many popular songs.

Free verse is poetry that does not follow a recurring rhythmical or metrical pattern. A writer of free verse is free in the sense that he or she can ignore tha standard conventions of language and can divide up his or her lines in any way that seems appropriate to what is being said. Examples of free verse in your text include Lawrence's "Snake," on page 1039, and Smith's "Not Waving But Drowning," on page 1307.

CASE STUDY: WRITING A POEM

Greg's class was writing poetry. He decided to write a ballad, hoping to publish it in the school newspaper.

Prewriting

Although Greg knew roughly what a ballad was, he first read the examples of traditional ballads in the text and reviewed the definition of *ballad* in the Handbook of Literary Terms and Techniques.

Next Greg started to work on an idea. He wanted to write a ballad that would interest everybody who read the newspaper. He also thought, given his personality, that he could write a better humorous ballad than a serious or tragic one. During the next few days, he listed events at school or involving students that might be topics:

- College applications—not a story, but could be one student's trauma

- SAT scores—maybe about valiant survivors on test days

- Accident at Bell and River Road—too serious to be funny; could be done like "Sir Partick Spens," but probably not a good idea

- Cafeteria—food is always a complaint for students; maybe I could tell the story of one student braving the lunch lines, especially on a day with "mystery stew"

Greg liked his second idea and thought other students would too.

Drafting and Revising

Greg started work on his first stanza with these lines:

> Young Bobby was a valiant lad,
> He had faced the SAT,
> He had filed his college forms
> And he . . .

Greg did not like this beginning. He decided not to specify Bobby's grade level because he wanted the poem to appeal to an audience broader than just one class. He also felt stuck after the ending with *forms.* Then Greg decided to start over with another topic. He wrote until he finished the first draft, alternating between adding new lines and rephrasing completed lines as he got new ideas. Here is the beginning of his revised ballad:

Young Bobby was a valiant lad,
A soccer man was he.
~~He had faced the SAT.~~

He never flinched from pain or grief,
'Til
~~Until~~ after period three.

Then came the line that scared the brave,

The line that scared the bold,

The line that led ~~our~~ *brave* Bobby on

~~To a meal ... told.~~
~~To a lunch never told.~~
To a lunch never told.

Proofreading and Publishing

After proofreading his ballad, Greg submitted his final copy to the school newspaper, where it was published two weeks later.

ACTIVITIES AND ASSIGNMENTS

A. Answer the following questions about the case study:

1. Identify these features of traditional ballads in Greg's poem:
   a. division into four-line stanzas
   b. use of a regular rhyme scheme
   c. use of repetition
   d. use of a regular rhythmical pattern
2. Write the rest of Greg's ballad, using your imagination or adding details about your schools's cafeteria. Stick to the traditional ballad form that Greg used.

B. Try writing your own poem, following the directions below.

Couplet (one or more)

1. Read some of the poems written in couplets that appear in this book.
2. Choose an idea that suits the compact style of the couplet.
3. Once you have an idea, write it out. Experiment with rhymes to end the lines.
4. Rework each line until the metrical pattern is regular and the end rhyme fits.
5. Revise and proofread your poem.
6. share your poem with your class.

Ballad

1. Begin by thinking of an event or situation for a ballad story. Brainstorm a list of ideas until you have one you like.
2. Read the ballads in this book to review the pattern of the ballad stanza.
3. Begin writing stanza by stanza, using the traditional ballad form.
4. Add other ballad characteristics as you work. Use simple language, direct dialogue, dramatic action without extra detail, repetition, and perhaps a refrain.
5. Revise and proofread your ballad.
6. Submit it to your school newspaper or to some other student publication.

Free verse

1. Read a number of free-verse poems to see how they work.
2. Jot down your ideas for a subject. Use prewriting techniques such as brainstorming, clustering, freewriting, and charting.
3. Write out your poem in a prose paragraph.
4. Divide your prose into lines. Each line should be a complete grammatical unit—a phrase, a clause, or a sentence.
5. Revise and proofread your poem, paying particular attention to word choice, imagery, and special devices of sound.

Once your poem is finished, share it with friends and submit it to your school's literary magazine or to another student publication.

ANSWERS TO ACTIVITIES AND ASSIGNMENTS,
Section A

1. The division occurs after line 4. The rhymes are *he/three* and *bold/told.* The phrase *the line* is repeated. The pattern is alternating lines of iambic tetrameter and iambic trimeter.

Lesson 20: Writing a Short Dramatic Sketch

A full-length drama or play may last several hours and have many scenes and acts. A *dramatic sketch,* however, lasts only a few minutes and is a single short scene. A sketch uses the same form as a longer play and can be either comic or tragic, but it makes only a single point. Because of its restricted length and focus, the dramatic sketch adapts well to the pace of television and is a popular feature of comedy and variety shows.

UNDERSTANDING THE CONVENTIONS USED IN A DRAMATIC SKETCH

Like longer dramatic works, the dramatic sketch has these features:

1. *Title*
2. *List of characters*
3. *Stage directions:* underlined or italicized in square brackets or parentheses
4. *Dialogue:* with character names in all capitals (sometimes in boldface or italic type), followed by the exact words the actors are to say

The beginning of Shaw's *Pygmalion,* on page 1109, illustrates these conventions:

Act I

London at 11:15 P.M. Torrents of heavy summer rain. Cab whistles blowing frantically in all directions. Pedestrians running for shelter. . . .
The church clock strikes the first quarter.

THE DAUGHTER *(in the space between the central pillars, close to the one on her left)* I'm getting chilled to the bone. What can Freddy be doing all this time? he's been gone twenty minutes.

THE MOTHER *(on her daughter's right)* Not so long. But he ought to have got us a cab by this.

Stage directions can explain what the set should look like and what lighting, sound, or special effects are required in production. They can explain which characters are on stage and what they are doing as a scene opens. When a character speaks, the stage directions can clarify how the actor should be positioned, how he or she should move, and what expression or tone he or she should use. The dialogue, on the other hand, supplies only the exact words the actor should speak.

PLANNING A DRAMATIC SKETCH

Like any other creative projects, a dramatic sketch requires many decisions. As you make each decision, consider whether what you imagine can happen on stage. Ask yourself these questions as you begin your planning:

1. Will the sketch be comic or serious? How do I want the audience to react? What should be the overall effect?
2. What will be the time and place of the action? How will the set represent the setting?
3. Who will the characters be? How will they speak, move, and act? How should they look and sound to the audience? What costumes will they wear?
4. What events will occur as part of the plot? What conflict will complicate the plot? What will happen in the beginning, the middle, and the end?
5. What props, special effects, or other extras will be needed?

CASE STUDY: WRITING A DRAMATIC SKETCH

Tamara's school service club was in charge of planning a show for the spring orientation for students who would be entering the school next fall. The show was to encourage their school spirit and to make them feel welcome.

Prewriting

Tamara and two of her friends were in charge of drafting a script for the show. Since their English class had read *Everyman* earlier in the year, they decided to model their dramatic sketch on a morality play. Tamara wrote out their plans:

- Title: Every[fresh]man
- Characters:

Every[fresh]man	School Spirit
Apathy	Energy
Rowdy	Loyalty
Foggy	Pride
Lazy	Hard Work
Wacky	

- Plot summary: Every[fresh]man arrives on campus to start next year. Apathy, Rowdy, Foggy, Lazy, and Wacky try to lead Every[fresh]man astray. School Spirit, assisted by Energy, Loyalty, Pride, and Hard Work, come to the rescue. They send away the others, except Wacky, and help Every[fresh]man start the year right.

- Setting: The school—probably just a door and a walk to suggest the edge of the school building

Drafting and Revising

Next Tamara drafted the script, and her friends helped her to revise it. Here's how their dramatic sketch began:

Every[fresh]man

[The scene opens near Building A on the first day of school in the fall. The building door is at the back left and the front walk leads off to the right. New students are arriving, hunting for their lockers, turning their schedules and maps around, looking lost. Every[fresh]man enters from the left, drops a map, picks it up, and looks around. Every[fresh]man is printed on the character's T-shirt.]

EVERY[FRESH]MAN. *[sounding confused and turning map upside down]* This looks like Building B, except that this walk is in the wrong place. Maybe I should try this way. . . .

ROWDY. *[runs in from right and playfully shadow boxes with Every[fresh]man]* Hiya, kiddo. What's new? Har, har.

EVERY[FRESH]MAN. Well, I'm new here, and I don't know how to find Building B.

ROWDY. *[grabbing map]* Gimme that. Har, har. Looks like an upside-down map!

APATHY. *[drifts in from right]* Oh, who cares, Rowdy?

ROWDY. *[sarcastically]* Oh, my! *[shadow boxing with Apathy, who just yawns]* You sure don't, do you, Apathy?

FOGGY. *[wandering in from right]* Now was today Wednesday or Thursday? I can't remember if I have chemistry this year. Maybe it's Algebra instead.

ROWDY. Get your station tuned in, Foggy. We've got a problem here. Definitely looks like a lost one. *[tosses map aside]*

FOGGY. *[ignores Rowdy and talks to Every[fresh]man]* Well, if you want Building B, it's here somewhere, unless it's over there now. Nope, that's definitely the gym. *[picks up map while talking and puzzling over buildings in distance]*

Proofreading and Publishing

After proofreading, Tamara made copies of her final version for the club members in the cast and for their club advisor.

ACTIVITIES AND ASSIGNMENTS

A. Refer to the case study as you answer these questions.

1. How does Tamara tell the audience her characters' names? Why does she describe how they act as well as what they say?

2. Add another section to Tamara's sketch. Introduce the rest of the characters, who try to lead Every[fresh]man astray. Show how they confront School Spirit, or show School Spirit and friends rescuing Every[fresh]man from the others. Follow Tamara's format for dialogue and stage directions.

B. Write your own short dramatic sketch,

following these steps:

1. Select a topic, an occasion, and an audience for your sketch.
2. Use the planning chart to work out your ideas. Write notes on your title, characters, setting, and plot.
3. Draft your sketch. Begin with the title, character list, and stage directions for the set. Then write the dialogue and the stage directions for the actors. Give only essential directions.
4. Read your draft aloud to test whether the dialogue sounds natural.
5. Revise carefully. Cut unneeded description or conversations that do not advance the plot. Add information needed for clarity, and revise your dialogue so it sounds natural.
6. Proofread your script. Share it with your classmates.

Lesson 21: Writing an Essay

WHAT IS AN ESSAY?

An essay allows you, the writer, to communicate directly with a reader about something that matters to you. It communicates your experiences, ideas, and feelings. This lesson explains how to adapt the steps outlined in the first section of this handbook to the personal essay.

PLANNING AN ESSAY

In your essay, you are likely to want to sound like one thoughtful person talking with another about something that concerns or interests you. Make sure that you have some personal experience or knowledge about your topic. Even if your topic is assigned, your own viewpoint makes your essay personal.

Essays have many purposes, depending on what you write about and how you want to affect a reader. Suppose you work as a volunteer at a local nature center and care very much about its future. You might write about that topic in many ways as this list suggests:

1. *Narrative essay:* telling a story to entertain and interest a reader:

   My first trip up Waterfall Trail, at the Davis Valley Nature Center, began peacefully, giving no clue of the danger to come.

2. *Descriptive essay:* describing something so that a reader can imagine it:

   Even though the Davis Valley Nature Center is only five minutes from homes and businesses, I feel hundreds of miles from civilization when I see the sun rise there on a crisp autumn morning.

3. *Expository essay:* Explaining something so that a reader can understand it:

   The three trails at the Davis Valley Nature Center seem confusing, but they actually form a pretzel shape, all meeting at the Education Center.

4. *Argumentative or persuasive essay:* convincing people to act or think in a certain way:

   Proposition 4 must be passed if we are to protect the plants and animals in preserves like the Davis Valley Nature Center.

For your essay, freewriting and clustering are especially helpful. They can help you to relax and to think freely about your topic. Questioning, listing, and analyzing are useful if you need to figure out how to approach or develop your idea.

Your prewriting activities also may vary with your purpose. For a narrative essay, a time line of events may help organize the key incidents in the story. A list of images, arranged by sense (sight, sound, taste, touch, and smell), can enrich a descriptive essay. For an expository essay, you may want to list examples, subtypes, or steps in a process. You may need a chart that lists causes and effects or that identifies points of comparison or contrast. Should your purpose be argumentative, you may want to list your arguments, your opponent's arguments, and reasons that support or contradict them.

CASE STUDY: WRITING AN ESSAY

Patrick's English teacher assigned an essay. Students could select their own topics, but each essay had to have a clear thesis statement and an orderly, logical development.

Prewriting

Patrick began prewriting by thinking about his college applications. He used clustering to pinpoint a topic, as shown on the next page.

Patrick looked over his clustering chart and decided that he wanted to explain his college

Motivation for Writing This lesson represents a good occasion to inform your students that the word *essay* originally meant "an attempt, or trying out." If they understand that an essay need not be the last word on a particular subject, they are more likely to write with ease. To demonstrate just how relaxed and personal a good essay can be, you might read aloud some passages from Montaigne's essays or some of the "Notes and Comments" pieces in *The New Yorker*. If presented properly, such writings may inspire students with the idea "I can write like that, too."

choice. He reorganized his ideas in a list, identifying subtopics and details for the body of his essay:

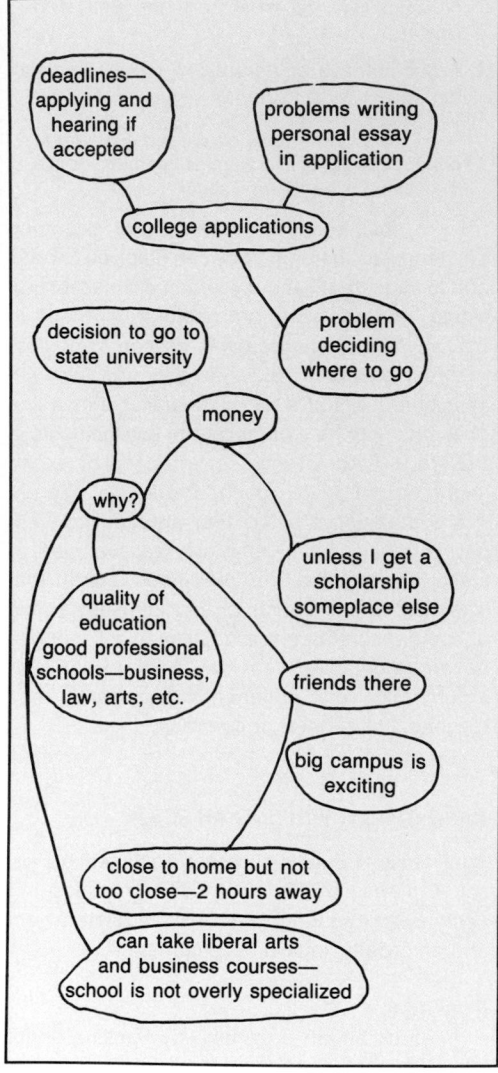

- Topic: state university is my first choice for college

- Paragraph 1   Introduction and thesis statement:
    Why state university is my first choice (add reasons to thesis)
    Qualify: unless I get a scholarship elsewhere and must take money to be fair to family

- Paragraph 2   Money:
    Most people assume money is my reason (add tuition example?)
    College is so expensive that money has to be a factor
    But it is not my main reason

- Paragraph 3   Other supposed reasons:
    Friends there
    Exciting, big campus
    Close to home but not too close (2 hours by car)
    All are factors, but all could be supplied by other schools

- Paragraph 4   Real reason is the quality of school:
    Not overly specialized, so I can take both liberal arts and business
    Good professional schools, so degree will be well regarded and faculty will be top level
    Most important is recent national honors for architecture school; architecture will be my major field

- Paragraph 5   Conclusion about reasons for choice:
    Not for economic or social reasons but for academic reasons
    Lucky to get the other benefits while getting the one that matters most about any college

Drafting and Revising

Because his outline was so detailed, Patrick quickly drafted a thesis statement and wrote the rest of his paper. Next he revised his essay, concentrating mainly on sentence structure and style because he felt that his organization was already clear.

Proofreading and Publishing

After Patrick proofread his paper, he left a copy with his guidance counselor.

ACTIVITIES AND ASSIGNMENTS

A. Use the case study to answer the following questions:

1. Carefully review Patrick's outline. Do all of his points follow logically and support his thesis statement? What important explanation, not in his clustering, has he added to his outline?
2. Use Patrick's outline to draft a possible thesis statement for his essay. Be sure that your statement specifies the topic, states the approach or viewpoint, and prepares a reader for the content and order of the body paragraphs.
3. Given Patrick's outline, what transition would you expect to find in his essay? Point to places in his outline that suggest how he planned to link his paragraphs and sentences.

B. Write your own essay, following these steps:

1. Think of a topic that interests or concerns you. Decide whether your essay will be narrative, descriptive, expository, persuasive, or entertaining. If you have trouble thinking of a topic, try freewriting or clustering.
2. Use one of the prewriting techniques to develop ideas. Then arrange your ideas in an outline.
3. Write a thesis statement that specifies your topic and your viewpoint. If possible, also prepare a reader for the content and organization of your essay.
4. Use your thesis statement as the basis of your introductory paragraph.
5. Write body paragraphs, each developing a main point. Each should have a topic sentence that follows from your thesis plus transitions, clear explanations, and details or examples.
6. Write a concluding paragraph that sums up your essay in an interesting way.
7. Revise and proofread your essay, using the checklists on pages 1335 and 1338.
8. Share your essay with a friend.

ACT See *Drama.*

ALEXANDRINE An *alexandrine* is a line of poetry written in iambic hexameter. The line is made up of six feet, each containing one weakly stressed syllable followed by one strongly stressed syllable. The following lines from Michael Drayton's *Polyolbion,* which was written in 1613, are alexandrines:

Mŭse, fírst | ŏf Ar|dĕn téll, | whŏse
    fóot|stĕps yet | ăre found
Ĭn hér | roŭgh wóod|lănds, móre |thăn ań|ў
  óth|ĕr ground

The alexandrine takes its name from the fact that the meter was often used in Old French poems about Alexander the Great. Alexandrines never became popular in England. However, Edmund Spenser did use them at the ends of stanzas in *The Faerie Queene.*
See *Meter* and *Spenserian Stanza.*

ALLEGORY An *allegory* is a literary work with two or more levels of meaning—one literal level and one or more symbolic levels. The events, settings, objects, or characters in an allegory stand for ideas or qualities beyond themselves. Allegorical writing was common in the Middle Ages. Thereafter, the popularity of allegory declined, but Spenser revived the form in *The Faerie Queene,* and John Bunyan revived it yet again in *The Pilgrim's Progress.* Some modern novels, such as Joseph Conrad's *Heart of Darkness,* can be read allegorically. When reading a work allegorically, one tries to match every element at the literal level with a corresponding element at the symbolic level.

ALLITERATION *Alliteration* is the repetition of initial consonant sounds. Emily Brontë used alliteration of *l* sounds in the first stanza of her poem "The Old Stoic":

Riches I hold in *l*ight esteem,
  And *L*ove I *l*augh to scorn;
And *l*ust of fame was but a dream
  That vanished with the morn

Alliteration is often used, especially in poetry, to emphasize and to link words as well as to create pleasing, musical sounds. Alliteration of stressed syllables was one of the characteristic features of Anglo-Saxon poetry.
See *Anglo-Saxon Poetry.*

ALLUSION An *allusion* is a reference to a well-known person, place, event, literary work, or work of art. Writers often make allusions to tales from the Bible, classical Greek and Roman myths, plays by Shakespeare, historical or political events, and other materials with which they expect their readers to be familiar. An allusion appears in Shakespeare's *A Midsummer Night's Dream,* when Hermia swears "by Cupid's strongest bow," thus referring to the god of love in Roman mythology. Writers sometimes use allusions as a sort of shorthand to suggest ideas in a simple and concise manner.

ANAPEST See *Meter.*

ANECDOTE An *anecdote* is a brief story about an interesting, amusing, or strange event. In *The Life of Samuel Johnson,* an excerpt from which appears on page 576, James Boswell tells both serious and humorous anecdotes about Johnson. These anecdotes illustrate features of Johnson's temperament and character and explain why Boswell regarded Johnson as one of the most extraordinary figures in all literary history.

ANGLO-SAXON POETRY *Anglo-Saxon poetry* is the rhythmic poetry composed in Old English before A.D. 1100. It generally has four accented syllables and an indefinite number of unaccented syllables in each line. Each line is divided in half by a caesura, or pause, and the halves are linked by the alliteration of two or three of the accented syllables. The following lines, translated from "Wulf and Eadwacer," show the alliteration and caesuras used in Anglo-Saxon poetry:

I *w*aited for my *W*ulf//with far-*W*andering
   yearnings,
*W*hen it was rainy *w*eather//and I sat
   *w*eeping.

Anglo-Saxon poetry was originally composed orally and then sung or chanted to the accompaniment of a primitive harp.
See *Alliteration, Caesura,* and *Kenning.*

ANTAGONIST An *antagonist* is a character or force in conflict with the main character, or protagonist, in a literary work. In many stories the plot is based on a conflict between the antagonist and the protagonist. In *Beowulf,* on page 24, the protagonist faces two antagonists—Grendel and Grendel's mother.
See *Character* and *Protagonist.*

ANTITHESIS *Antithesis* is a figure of speech in which contrasting or paradoxical ideas are presented in parallel form. The following examples of antithesis come from Alexander Pope's *An Essay on Criticism:*
1. Some praise at morning what they blame at night
2. To err is human, to forgive, divine.

Antithesis was popular among the Neoclassical English poets of the eighteenth century, who often used it to make witty or satirical comments.

APHORISM An *aphorism* is a general truth or observation about life, usually stated concisely and pointedly. Often witty or wise, memorable aphorisms appear in the works of Chaucer, Shakespeare, Pope, Johnson, and many other writers. An essay writer may have an *aphoristic style*—a style characterized by use of such statements—as does Francis Bacon. The following aphorisms come from Bacon's "Of Studies":
1. Crafty men condemn studies, simple men admire them, and wise men use them.
2. Reading maketh a full man, conference a ready man, and writing an exact man.

Used in an essay, an aphorism can be a memorable way to sum up or to reinforce a point or argument.

APOSTROPHE An *apostrophe* is a figure of speech in which a speaker directly addresses an absent person or a personified quality, object, or idea. Shelley opens his poem "Ode to the West Wind" with an apostrophe that addresses the wind. Apostrophe is often used in poetry and in speeches to add emotional intensity.
See *Figurative Language.*

ARGUMENTATION *Argumentation* is the type of writing that presents and logically supports the writer's views about an issue. Argumentation is one of the forms, or modes, of discourse. The term *argumentation* is sometimes used as though it were synonymous with *persuasion.* However, some critics and scholars distinguish between the two terms, using argumentation for works that support opinions with logical reasoning and persuasion for works that support opinions with appeals to emotion.
See *Forms of Discourse* and *Persuasion.*

ASIDE An *aside* is a statement delivered by an actor to an audience in such a way that other characters on stage are presumed not to hear what is said. In an aside the character reveals his or her private thoughts, reactions, or motivations. Act III, Scene iv of *Macbeth* contains the following aside:

MURDERER. Most royal sir, Fleance is scaped.
MACBETH. [*Aside*] Then comes my fit again. I
   had else been perfect;
Whole as the marble, founded as the rock,
As broad and general as the casing air.
But now I am cabined, cribbed,

confined, bound in
To saucy doubts and fears.—but
Banquo's safe?

In this aside, Macbeth reveals his fearful reaction to the news that Fleance is still alive.

ASSONANCE   *Assonance* is the repetition of vowel sounds in stressed syllables containing dissimilar consonant sounds. Robert Browning used assonance in the following famous line from his poem "Andrea del Sarto":

Ah, but a man's reach should exceed his
    grasp

The long *e* sound is repeated in the words *reach* and *exceed* in stressed syllables containing these consonants: *r–ch* and *c–d*.
See *Consonance.*

ATMOSPHERE   See *Mood.*

AUTOBIOGRAPHY   An *autobiography* is a form of nonfiction in which a person tells his or her own life story. Unlike a diary or a letter, an autobiography is written for a public audience. George Orwell's "Shooting an Elephant," on page 1014, is a fine example of the autobiographical essay.
See *Biography.*

BALLAD   A *ballad* is a songlike poem that tells a story, often one dealing with adventure or romance. Most ballads have the following characteristics:
1. four- or six-line stanzas
2. rhyme
3. simple language
4. dramatic action

Many ballads employ repetition of a refrain. Some make use of incremental repetition, in which a refrain is varied slightly each time it appears.

The British Isles have a rich tradition of *folk ballads*—songs that originated among illiterate peoples and were passed from singer to singer by word of mouth. Examples in your text include "Sir Patrick Spens," "The Two Corbies," and "Barbara Allan." Many English, Scottish, Welsh, and Irish writers have also created *literary ballads*—sophisticated poems in the style of folk ballads. One such literary ballad in your text is Samuel Taylor Coleridge's *The Rime of the Ancient Mariner,* on page 660.
See *Ballad Stanza, Incremental Repetition,* and *Refrain.*

BALLAD STANZA   A *ballad stanza* is a four- or six-line stanza form used in folk ballads and in literary imitations of folk ballads. In a typical four-line ballad stanza, the first and third lines each have four stresses; the second and fourth lines each have three stresses and also rhyme. Thus the usual rhyme scheme is *abcb,* although some ballads follow the scheme *abab.* This typical four-line ballad stanza comes from Dudley Randall's "Ballad of Birmingham":

Mother dear, may I go downtown,
Instead of out to play,
And march the streets of Birmingham
In a Freedom March today?

See *Ballad.*

BIOGRAPHY   A *biography* is a form of nonfiction in which a writer tells the life story of another person. A good biographer uses many sources of information, including, perhaps, the subject's letters and journals, interviews with the subject or with people who know the subject, personal knowledge about the subject, and books and other works about the subject. James Boswell's *The Life of Samuel Johnson,* an excerpt from which appears on page 576, is one of the most famous of all biographies. Boswell's work has been widely praised for its accuracy of reporting and its liveliness of style.
See *Autobiography.*

BLANK VERSE   *Blank verse* is poetry written in unrhymed iambic pentameter lines. Each iambic foot has one weakly stressed syllable followed by one strongly stressed syllable. A pentameter line has five of these feet. Blank verse usually contains occasional variations in rhythm—variations that are introduced to create emphasis, variety, and naturalness of sound. Because blank verse sounds much like ordinary spoken English, it is often used in drama and in poetry. Great English writers of blank verse have included Shakespeare, Wordsworth, Browning, and Auden. The following lines come from Wordsworth's blank-verse poem "Lines Composed a Few Miles Above Tintern Abbey," on page 644:

> Fŏr thóu | art with | mĕ hére |ŭpón | thĕ bánks
> Ŏf thís | faír ŕív|er̆; thóu |my̆ déar|ĕst
>   friĕnd

See *Meter*.

CAESURA A *caesura* is a natural pause, or break, in the middle of a line of poetry. The symbol // has been used to mark the caesuras in the following lines from Kathleen Raine's "In the Beck":

> There is a fish,//that quivers in the
>   pool,
> itself a shadow,//but its shadow, clear.
> Catch it again and again,//it still is
>   there.

A poet can draw attention to a word by placing it just before or just after a caesura. In Anglo-Saxon poetry a caesura divides each four-stress line in half and thus is essential to the rhythm.
See *Anglo-Saxon Poetry*.

CANTO A *canto* is a section of a long poem. Both Alexander Pope's *The Rape of the Lock* and Edmund Spenser's *The Faerie Queene* were written in cantos.

CARICATURE A *caricature* is a distorted or exaggerated portrayal of a person. The portrayal of Lady Bracknell, in Oscar Wilde's *The Importance of Being Earnest,* is an example. Caricature is used to ridicule personal flaws and general social failings.

CARPE DIEM *Carpe diem* is a Latin phrase meaning "seize the day." Many great literary works have been written with the *carpe diem* theme. All have in common the fact that they urge people to enjoy life in the present, while such enjoyment is still possible. One of the best-known poems on this theme is Robert Herrick's "To the Virgins, to Make Much of Time," on page 432, which begins with the line, "Gather ye rosebuds while ye may." Another famous work that deals with the *carpe diem* theme is Marvell's "To His Coy Mistress," on page 418.

CATALOG A *catalog* is a list included in a literary work. Taking his cue from classical epics, which list warriors, ships, weapons, and other items, John Milton uses this convention in *Paradise Lost* to list the fallen angels. Alexander Pope uses the catalog in *The Rape of the Lock* to list the duties of the sylphs. Writers use catalogs to instruct readers and to convey a great deal of information concisely. The effect of a catalog is usually to overwhelm the reader with the numbers of items mentioned.
See *Epic Convention*.

CHARACTER A *character* is a person or animal who takes part in the action of a literary work. Characters can be described in many different ways, as follows:
1. In terms of the importance of their roles: A character who plays an important role in a story is called a *major character.* A character who does not play an important role is called a *minor character.*
2. In terms of their roles: A character who plays the central role in a story is called the *protagonist.* A character who opposes the protagonist is called the *antagonist.*
3. In terms of their complexity: A complex character is called *round,* while a simple character is called *flat.*

4. In terms of the degree to which they change: A character who changes is called *dynamic;* a character who does not change is called *static.*

Character types that readers recognize easily, such as the hard-boiled detective or the wicked stepmother, are called *stereotypes,* or *stock charcters.*
See *Characterization* and *Motivation.*

CHARACTERIZATION   *Characterization* is the act of creating and developing a character. A writer uses *direct characterization* when he or she states a character's traits explicitly. *Indirect characterization* occurs when the writer reveals a character's traits by some other means. A character's traits can be revealed indirectly by means of what he or she says, thinks, or does; by means of a description of his or her appearance; or by means of the statements, thoughts, or actions of other characters. When using indirect characterization, the writer depends on the reader to infer a character's traits from the clues provided.
See *Character.*

CLASSICISM   *Classicism* is an approach to literature and to the other arts that stresses reason, harmony, balance, proportion, clarity, and idealism in imitation of the philosophers and artists of ancient Greece and Rome. The European Neoclassicists of the eighteenth century revived the Greek and Roman classical tradition and aspired to produce works worthy of this tradition. Classicism is often contrasted with Romanticism, which places a premium on imagination and emotion, sometimes at the expense of reason and proportion. Classicism also differs from Realism, which concentrates on the actual rather than on the ideal.
See *Neoclassicism, Realism,* and *Romanticism.*

CLIMAX   The *climax* is the high point of interest or suspense in a literary work. Often the climax is also the *crisis* in the plot, the point at which the protagonist changes his or her understanding or situation. Sometimes the climax coincides with the *resolution,* the point at which the central conflict is ended. In a story the climax generally occurs near the end. For example, Charles Dickens's "The Signalman," on page 870, reaches its climax with the death of the signalman. In a play the climax often falls more toward the middle and marks the end of the rising action and the beginning of the falling action. For example, in William Shakespeare's *Macbeth,* the climax is the banquet scene, in Act III. This scene begins the inevitable movement toward Macbeth's downfall.
See *Plot.*

CLOSED COUPLET   See *Couplet.*

COMEDY   A *comedy* is a work of literature, especially a play, that has a happy ending. Comedies often show ordinary characters in conflict with their societies. Their problems are resolved through laughter, reconciliation, and the correction of moral faults or social wrongs. Types of comedy include the *romantic comedy,* which involves problems among lovers, and the *comedy of manners,* which satirically challenges the social customs of a sophisticated society. George Bernard Shaw's *Pygmalion,* on page 1109, is a modern comedy of manners. Many comedies feature humorous physical action and witty dialogue. Comedy is often contrasted with tragedy, in which the central character, or protagonist, meets an unfortunate end.
See *Drama* and *Tragedy.*

COMEDY OF MANNERS   See *Comedy.*

COMIC RELIEF   *Comic relief* is the feeling created by a humorous action or speech that appears within a serious work of literature. For example, the so-called "Porter Scene" in *Macbeth,* at the beginning of Act II, Scene iii, provides comic relief after the murder of Duncan. As this scene illustrates, comic relief is often used to emphasize, by contrast, the seriousness of the main action.

CONCEIT A *conceit* is an unusual and surprising comparison between two very different things. This special kind of metaphor or complicated analogy is often the basis for a whole poem. During the Elizabethan period, sonnets commonly included *Petrarchan conceits,* ones that extravagantly compared the beloved's beauty or the speaker's suffering to something else. For example, the sonnets of Sir Thomas Wyatt compare the lover's state to a storm-tossed ship, to the Alps, and to a soldier's camp. Shakespeare satirizes such overblown conceits in his Sonnet 130:

> I love to hear her speak; yet well I know
> That music hath a far more pleasing sound:
> I grant I never saw a goddess go;
> My mistress, when she walks, treads on the
>   ground.
> And yet, by heaven, I think my love as rare
> As any she belied with false compare.

The seventeenth-century metaphysical poets were especially fond of elaborate, unusual, highly intellectual conceits. For example, in "Love's Alchemy," John Donne compares the unreliability of love to the unreliability of alchemy for making gold.
See *Metaphor.*

CONCRETE POEM A *concrete poem* is one with a shape that suggests its subject. An example in this text is George Herbert's "Easter Wings," on page 412.
See *Emblematic Image.*

CONFLICT A *conflict* is a struggle between opposing forces. Sometimes this struggle is *internal,* or within a character. At other times the struggle is *external,* or between the character and some outside force. The outside force may be another character, nature, or some element

of society such as a custom or a political institution. Often the conflict in a work is complicated and combines several of these possibilities. For example, Macbeth struggles against the better parts of his own nature, against Banquo and Fleance, against fate, and against the forces led by Malcolm, Macduff, and Siward.
See *Antagonist, Plot,* and *Protagonist.*

CONNOTATION A *connotation* is an association that a word calls to mind in addition to its dictionary meaning. For example, the words *home* and *domicile* have the same dictionary meanings. However, the first has positive connotations of warmth and security while the second does not. Therefore, a writer who wants to convey a sense of warmth and security will be more likely to use the word *home* than the word *domicile,* even though the two words refer to the same thing. Because the connotations of words are so powerful, writers carefully choose words with connotations that suggest the shades of meaning they intend.
See *Denotation.*

CONSONANCE *Consonance* is the repetition of consonant sounds in stressed syllables containing dissimilar vowel sounds. D.H. Lawrence uses consonance in the opening lines of "Snake":

> A snake came to my water-trough
> On a *hot, hot,* day, and I in pajamas for the
>   *heat,*
> To drink there.

The words *hot* and *heat* have the same consonants but different vowels. (Note also the assonance in the words *snake* and *came* and in the words *water* and *pajamas.*) When used at the ends of lines, consonance can create *approximate* or *slant rhyme.*
See *Assonance.*

COUPLET A *couplet* is a pair of rhyming lines written in the same meter. The following iambic tetrameter couplets come from John Milton's "L'Allegro":

> And if I give thee honor due,
> Mirth, admit me of the crew
> To live with her, and live with thee,
> In unreproved pleasures free.

A *heroic couplet* is a rhymed pair of iambic pentameter lines. During the Neoclassical Period, the popular heroic couplet was often also a *closed couplet,* with its meaning and grammar complete within two lines. These lines from Alexander Pope's *An Essay on Criticism* illustrate the closed heroic couplet:

> True ease in writing comes from art, not
>   chance,
> As those move easiest who have learned to
>   dance.

Sonnets written in the English, or Shakespearean, style usually end with heroic couplets.
See *Sonnet.*

CRISIS   The *crisis* in the plot of a story or play is the turning point for the protagonist—the point at which his or her situation or understanding is changed. This point often coincides with the *climax,* or emotional high point, of the story.
See *Climax* and *Plot.*

DACTYL   See *Meter.*

DEAD METAPHOR   See *Metaphor.*

DENOTATION   The *denotation* of a word is its objective meaning, that to which the word refers, independent of other associations the word calls to mind. Dictionaries list the denotative meanings of words. Another term for denotative meaning is *referential meaning.*
See *Connotation.*

DENOUEMENT   The *denouement* in a literary work is anything that happens after the resolution of the plot. At this point the central conflict is resolved, and the consequences for the protago-

nist are already decided. Essentially, a denouement is a tying up of loose ends. In some works no denouement is needed.
See *Plot.*

DESCRIPTION   A *description* is a portrait, in words, of a person, place, or object. Its purpose is to provide the concrete details and lively images that make people, places, and things become clear to readers.

Descriptions use *imagery*—words and phrases that appeal to the senses of sight, sound, touch, taste, and smell. Description is one of the major forms, or modes, of discourse and is often found in conjunction with other types of writing such as narration, exposition, or persuasion.
See *Forms of Discourse* and *Imagery.*

DEVELOPMENT   See *Plot.*

DIALECT   A *dialect* is the form of a language spoken by people in a particular region or group. Dialects differ from one another in grammar, vocabulary, and pronunciation. Authors often write in regional dialects, as did Robert Burns, who used a Scots dialect in such poems as "Auld Lang Syne":

> Should auld acquaintance be forgot,
> And never brought to mind?
> Should auld acquaintance be forgot,
> And auld lang syne?

Dialect is sometimes used by writers as a part of characterization. For example, the social status of each character in George Bernard Shaw's *Pygmalion,* on page 1109, is revealed by the dialect the character speaks. In the course of Shaw's play, the central character, Eliza Doolittle, is trained to speak Received Standard English—a dialect with high social prestige—rather than her native Cockney dialect.
See *Vernacular.*

DIALOGUE   A *dialogue* is a conversation between characters. Writers use dialogue to reveal character, to present events, to add variety to narratives, and to interest readers. The dialogue in a story or play is usually set off by quotation marks and paragraphing. The dialogue in a play script generally follows the characters' names.

DIARY   A *diary* is a personal record of daily events, usually written in prose. Most diaries are not written for publication; sometimes, however, interesting diaries or diaries by influential people do find their way into print. One example of a published diary is that of Samuel Pepys, a selection from which appears on page 506. In his diary Pepys recorded anecdotes and details about his life in the 1660's.
See *Journal.*

DICTION   *Diction* is word choice. A writer's diction can be a major determinant of his or her style. Diction can be described as formal or informal, abstract or concrete, plain or ornate, ordinary or technical.
See *Style.*

DIMETER   See *Meter.*

DIRECT CHARACTERIZATION   See *Characterization.*

DRAMA   A *drama* is a story written to be performed by actors. It may consist of one or more large sections called *acts,* which are made up of any number of smaller sections called *scenes.*

Drama originated in the religious rituals and symbolic re-enactments of primitive peoples. The ancient Greeks developed drama into a sophisticated art and created such dramatic forms as tragedy and comedy.

The first dramas in England were the miracle plays and morality plays of the Middle Ages. *Miracle plays* told Biblical stories. *Morality plays,* such as *Everyman,* on page 188, dealt with personified virtues and vices. The English Re-

naissance saw a great flowering of drama in England, culminating in the works of William Shakespeare, who wrote many of the world's greatest comedies, tragedies, histories, and romances. During the Neoclassical Age, English drama turned to witty, satirical comedies of manners that probed the virtues of upper-class society. Superb examples of Neoclassical comedy include Goldsmith's *She Stoops to Conquer* and Congreve's *The Way of the World.* The Romantic and Victorian ages were not great periods for drama in England. However, a few good verse plays were written, including Percy Bysshe Shelley's *The Cenci* and *Prometheus Unbound* and Robert Browning's *Pippa Passes.* The end of the nineteenth and beginning of the twentieth centuries saw a resurgence of the drama in England and throughout the English-speaking world. Great plays of the Modern Period include George Bernard Shaw's *Pygmalion,* on page 1109, and the many plays by William Butler Yeats, John Millington Synge, Christopher Fry, T. S. Eliot, Harold Pinter, and Samuel Beckett.

DRAMATIC IRONY   See *Irony.*

DRAMATIC MONOLOGUE   A *dramatic monologue* is a poem in which an imaginary character speaks to a silent listener. During the monologue, the speaker reveals his or her personality, usually at a moment of crisis. Examples of dramatic monologues in this text are Robert Browning's "My Last Duchess," on page 812 and Alfred, Lord Tennyson's "Ulysses," on page 779.

DRAMATIC POETRY   See *Poetry.*

DYNAMIC CHARACTER   See *Character.*

ELEGY   An *elegy* is a solemn and formal lyric poem about death. It may mourn a particular person or reflect on a serious or tragic theme, such as the passing of youth, beauty, or a way of

life. See Thomas Gray's "Elegy Written in a Country Churchyard," on page 586.
See *Lyric Poem.*

EMBLEMATIC IMAGE   An *emblematic image* is a symbolic figure or shape presented through the arrangement of the lines of a poem. For example, George Herbert's "Easter Wings," on page 412, is shaped like a pair of wings.
See *Concrete Poem.*

END RHYME   See *Rhyme.*

END-STOPPED LINE   An *end-stopped line* of poetry concludes with a break in the meter and in the meaning. This pause at the end of a line often is punctuated by a period, comma, dash, or semicolon. These lines from "Away, Melancholy," by Stevie Smith, are end-stopped:

> Are not the trees green,
> The earth as green?
> Does not the wind blow,
> Fire leap and the rivers flow?
> Away melancholy.

See *Run-on Line.*

EPIC   An *epic* is a long narrative poem about the adventures of gods or of a hero. *Beowulf,* on page 24, is a *folk epic,* one that was composed orally and then passed from storyteller to storyteller by word of mouth. The ancient Greek epics attributed to Homer—the *Iliad* and the *Odyssey* —are also folk epics. The *Aeneid,* by the Roman poet Virgil, and *The Divine Comedy,* by the Italian poet Dante Alighieri, are examples of literary epics from the Classical and Medieval periods, respectively. John Milton's *Paradise Lost,* a selection from which appears on page 449, is also a literary epic. Milton's goal in creating *Paradise Lost* was to write a Christian epic similar in form and equal in value to the great epics of antiquity. Because of an epic's length and seriousness of theme, it presents an encyclopedic portrait of the culture in which it was produced. One can learn a great deal about ancient Greece by reading Homer and a great deal about thirteenth- and fourteenth-century Italy by reading Dante.
See *Epic Convention.*

EPIC CONVENTION   An *epic convention* is a traditional characteristic of epic poems. These characteristics include an opening statement of the theme; an appeal for supernatural help in telling the story; a beginning *in medias res* (Latin: "in the middle of things"), long lists, or catalogs, of people and things; accounts of past events; and descriptive phrases such as kennings, Homeric similes, and Homeric epithets.
See *Catalog, Epic, Epithet,* In Medias Res, *Invocation,* and *Kenning.*

EPIGRAM   An *epigram* is a brief, pointed statement in prose or in verse. The concluding couplet in an English sonnet may be epigrammatic. An essay may be written in an *epigrammatic style,* one that is characterized by frequent use of epigrams.

EPIGRAPH   An *epigraph* is a quotation that appears at the beginning of a literary work, as is illustrated by Rainer Maria Rilke's lines at the beginning of Margaret Drabble's "A Voyage to Cythera," on page 1276. An epigraph generally introduces a motif or a theme that is developed in the work itself.

EPIPHANY   *Epiphany* is a term introduced by James Joyce to describe a moment of revelation or insight in which a character recognizes some truth. In Joyce's "Araby," the boy's epiphany comes at the end of the story, on page 987, when he recognizes the falsity of his dream.

EPITAPH   An *epitaph* is an inscription written on a tomb or burial place. In literature, epitaphs also include serious or humorous lines written as if they were intended for such use. Examples are the epitaph at the end of Thomas Gray's "Elegy

Written in a Country Churchyard," which appears on page 586, and this epitaph for Sir Isaac Newton, written by Alexander Pope:

Nature and Nature's laws lay hid in night:
God said, Let Newton be! and all was light.

EPITHET An *epithet* is a word or phrase that states a characteristic quality of some person or thing. A.E. Housman uses epithets such as "golden friends" and "lightfoot lad" in "With Rue My Heart Is Laden," on page 854. Homeric epithets, such as "wide-wayed city," "clear-voiced heralds," and "high-hearted princes" in the *Iliad,* were common in classical epics and in later imitations of classical epics.
See *Epic Convention.*

ESSAY An *essay* is a short, nonfiction work about a particular subject. Essays are of many types but may be classified by tone or style as formal or informal.

An essay may also be classed by its main purpose as descriptive, narrative, expository, argumentative, or persuasive.

EXACT RHYME See *Rhyme.*

EXEMPLUM An *exemplum* is a short tale or anecdote with a moral, especially one used in a medieval sermon. Geoffrey Chaucer's "The Pardoner's Tale," on page 159, illustrates the moral that "love of wealth is the root of all evil."

EXPOSITION *Exposition* is writing or speech that explains, informs, or presents information. Types of exposition include analysis, classification, comparison and contrast, definition, and exemplification.

In the plot of a story or drama, the *exposition* is the part of the work that introduces the characters, the setting, and the basic situation. For example, in William Shakespeare's *A Midsummer Night's Dream,* the first scene introduces the lovers and their problems, locates the action in the palace at Athens near a wood, and establishes the light mood of a romantic comedy.
See *Forms of Discourse* and *Plot.*

EXPRESSIONISM *Expressionism* was an artistic movement early in the twentieth century. The Expressionists emphasized the inner experiences of individuals rather than objective external realities. This movement influenced many dramatists and poets, including T.S. Eliot, whose poem "The Hollow Men," appears on page 1063.

EXTENDED METAPHOR See *Metaphor.*

FABLE A *fable* is a brief story, usually with animal characters, that teaches a lesson, or moral. The earliest extant fables are those attributed to Aesop, a Greek writer of the sixth century B.C. In modern times fables are popular both as nursery tales and as vehicles for satire. In his novella *Animal Farm,* George Orwell adapted the fable form for use in a satirical allegory about the Russian Revolution and its aftermath.

FALLING ACTION The *falling action* is all of the action that takes place after the climax in a literary work. During this time, the conflict is resolved and the suspense decreases.
See *Plot* and *Rising Action.*

FANTASY *Fantasy* is highly imaginative writing that contains elements not found in real life. Elizabeth Bowen's "The Demon Lover," on page 994, is a fantasy. Writers use fantasies to entertain readers and sometimes to make serious points about reality.

FARCE *Farce* is a kind of comedy that features physical horseplay, stereotypical characters, and absurd plots, often ones involving mistaken identities and recognition scenes. The writer of a farce uses exaggeration, irony, and witty dialogue to move his or her audience to laughter. A farce may be a complete play or a scene used for contrast or comic relief within a serious work.

FICTION *Fiction* is a prose writing that tells about imaginary characters and events. Some writers of fiction base their stories on real people and events, while others rely solely on their imaginations.
See *Narration, Nonfiction,* and *Prose.*

FIGURATIVE LANGUAGE *Figurative language* is writing or speech not meant to be interpreted literally. Poets and other writers use figurative language to create vivid word pictures, to make their writing emotionally intense and concentrated, and to state their ideas in new and unusual ways that satisfy readers' imaginations.
See *Figure of Speech.*

FIGURE OF SPEECH A *figure of speech* is an expression or a word used imaginatively rather than literally. Among the types of figurative language are antithesis, apostrophe, hyperbole, irony, metaphor, metonymy, oxymoron, paradox, personification, simile, synecdoche, and understatement.
See *Figurative Language.* See also the entries for individual figures of speech.

FIRST-PERSON POINT OF VIEW See *Point of View.*

FLASHBACK A *flashback* is a section of a literary work that interrupts the sequence of events to relate an event from an earlier time. The writer may present the flashback as a character's memory or recollection, as part of an account or story told by a character, or as a dream or daydream. For example, in Elizabeth Bowen's "The Demon Lover," on page 994, Mrs. Drover remembers saying farewell to her fiancé twenty-five years earlier. Writers use flashbacks to show what motivates a character and to supply background information in a dramatic way.
See *Foreshadowing.*

FLAT CHARACTER See *Character.*

FOIL A *foil* is a character who provides a contrast to another character, thus intensifying the impact of that other character. For example, Banquo and Duncan act as foils for the ambitious and tyrannical Macbeth.

FOLK BALLAD See *Ballad.*

FOLKLORE *Folklore* includes the stories, legends, myths, ballads, riddles, sayings, and other traditional works produced orally by illiterate or semi-literate peoples. Folklore influences written literature in many ways, as is suggested by the beheading contest in *Sir Gawain and the Green Knight,* on page 170, and the fiancé in Elizabeth Bowen's "The Demon Lover," on page 994.

FOLK TALE A *folk tale* is a story composed orally and then passed from person to person by word of mouth. Many of Chaucer's stories were based on folk tales.
See *Folklore.*

FOOT See *Meter.*

FORESHADOWING *Foreshadowing* is the use, in a literary work, of clues that suggest events that have yet to occur. Writers use foreshadowing to create suspense or to prepare the audience for the eventual outcome of events.
See *Flashback.*

FORM The *form* of a literary work is its structure, shape, pattern, organization, or style—the way it is made. A work's form is often distinguished from its *content*—what it is about.

FORMS OF DISCOURSE The *forms of discourse* are the main types of writing—description, narration, exposition, and persuasion or argumentation. Each has a different purpose and may be a writer's main emphasis. Often, however, the forms of discourse are used together to support each other. For instance, a narrative may include description, or an argument may begin with exposition.

See *Argumentation, Description, Exposition, Narration,* and *Persuasion.*

FREE VERSE   *Free verse* is poetry not written in a regular rhythmical pattern, or meter. Instead of having metrical feet and lines, free verse has a rhythm that suits its meaning and that uses the sounds of spoken language in lines of different lengths. Free verse has been widely used in twentieth-century poetry. An example is "The Galloping Cat," by Stevie Smith:

> All the same I
> Intend to go on being
> A cat that likes to
> Gallop about doing good
> So
> Now with my bald head I go,
> Chopping the untidy flowers down, to and fro.

GOTHIC   *Gothic* is a term used to describe literary works that make extensive use of primitive, Medieval, wild, mysterious, or natural elements. Gothic elements offended eighteenth-century Neoclassical writers but appealed to the Romantic writers who followed them. *Gothic novels,* such as Mary Wollstonecraft Shelley's *Frankenstein,* a selection from which appears on page 734, are often set in gloomy castles where horrifying, supernatural events take place.

HEPTAMETER   See *Meter.*

HEPTASTICH   See *Stanza.*

HERO/HEROINE   A *hero* or *heroine* is a character whose actions are inspiring or noble. Often heroes struggle to overcome foes or to escape from difficulties. The most obvious examples of heroes and heroines are the larger-than-life characters in myths and legends, ones like Beowulf or Odysseus. However, more ordinary characters can, and often do, perform heroic deeds.

HEROIC COUPLET   See *Couplet.*

HEXAMETER   See *Meter.*

HOMERIC EPITHET   See *Epithet.*

HYPERBOLE   A *hyperbole* is a deliberate exaggeration or overstatement. In "On Monsieur's Departure," Queen Elizabeth I used this figure of speech:

> I grieve and dare not show my discontent,
> I love and yet am forced to seem to hate,
> I do, yet dare not say I ever meant,
> I seem stark mute but inwardly to prate.
> I am and not, I freeze and yet am burned,
> Since from myself another self I turned.

Of course, Queen Elizabeth was not turned by love into another person, she was not mute or burned, and she did not act in total opposition to her true feelings. Such excessive claims are examples of hyperbole. In Oscar Wilde's *The Importance of Being Earnest,* Algernon's claims likewise illustrate hyperbole:

> ALGERNON: I really don't see anything romantic in proposing. It is very romantic to be in love. But there is nothing romantic about a definite proposal. Why, one may be accepted. One usually is, I believe. Then the excitement is all over. The very essence of romance is uncertainty. If ever I get married, I'll certainly try to forget the fact.

As these examples suggest, hyperbole may be used for heightened seriousness or for comic effect.

See *Figurative Language.*

IAMB   See *Meter.*

IAMBIC PENTAMETER   See *Meter.*

IMAGE   An *image* is a word or a phrase that

appeals to one or more of the five senses—sight, hearing, touch, taste, or smell. In a famous essay on Hamlet, T.S. Eliot explained how a group of images can be used as an "objective correlative." By this phrase Eliot meant to suggest that a complex emotional state can be suggested by images that are carefully chosen to evoke this state.
See *Imagery.*

IMAGERY   *Imagery* is the descriptive language used in literature to re-create sensory experiences. The following lines from William Collins's "Ode to Evening," show how a poet can use imagery to appeal to several senses:

> Now air is hushed, save where the weak-eyed
>   bat,
> With short shrill shrieks flits by on leathern
>   wing,
> Or where the beetle winds
> His small but sullen horn,
> As oft he rises 'midst the twilight path,
> Against the pilgrim borne in heedless hum.

These lines describe the sounds, sights, and movements of evening, just as if a reader were out walking with the poem's speaker. Imagery can enrich writing by making it more vivid, setting a tone, suggesting emotions, and guiding a reader's reactions.

INCITING INCIDENT   See *Plot.*

INCONGRUITY   An *incongruity* is a juxtaposition of incompatible or opposite elements. For example, sometimes a writer's style and subject may be incongruous, as in Alexander Pope's *The Rape of the Lock,* on page 548. Pope uses the formal language and conventions of epic poetry, but his subject is only the social battle surrounding a lock of hair. When a writer talks about something trivial in formal language, the exaggeration and surprise of the incongruity may create a comic or humorous effect.

INCREMENTAL REPETITION   *Incremental repetition,* used in ballads and in other oral poetry, is the technique of repeating a line or a stanza with slight but significant changes. Incremental repetition is used in the ballad "Lord Randal":

> "O where have you been, Lord Randal, my son?
> O where have you been, my handsome young
>   man?—
> "I have been to the greenwood; O make my
>   bed soon,
> For I'm weary with hunting, and fain would lie
>   down."

Each stanza uses this question-and-answer pattern, supplying and repeating details that add to the story and increase suspense.
See *Ballad.*

INDIRECT CHARACTERIZATION   See *Characterization.*

IN MEDIAS RES   The phrase *in medias res,* Latin for "in the middle of things," is a storytelling method used in epic poems and in other narratives. When a writer begins *in medias res,* the story starts in the middle, jumping right into the action. The background and the initial events are introduced later by means of one or more flashbacks. John Milton's *Paradise Lost,* like the great epics of classical antiquity, follows this pattern. Milton's epic begins with Satan and the fallen angels on the burning lake in Chaos. Not until Books V and VI does Raphael tell Adam about the great battle that occurred just before those angels fell from heaven.
See *Epic Convention.*

INTERNAL RHYME   See *Rhyme.*

INVERSION   An *inversion* is a reversal or change in the regular word order of a sentence. For instance, Anne Killigrew begins the poem

"Upon the Saying That My Verses Were Made by Another" in this way:

> Next Heaven, my vows to thee, O sacred Muse!
> I offered up, nor didst thou them refuse.

These lines reverse the usual subject-verb-object order, "I offered up my vows to thee," and the usual negative construction, "nor didst thou refuse them." Poets, in particular, use inversion to emphasize words and sometimes to fit them to the meter of a poem.

INVOCATION An *invocation* is an appeal to a Muse or to another divine being for help in writing the poem. In ancient Greece and Rome, writers often began their works by calling for the aid of the Muses, who were the nine daughters of Apollo responsible for the various arts. In *Paradise Lost,* on page 449, John Milton appeals to his "Heavenly Muse," the Holy Spirit of the Christian trinity.
See *Epic Convention.*

IRONY *Irony* is the general name given to literary techniques that involve surprising, interesting, or amusing contradictions. In *verbal irony,* words are used to suggest the opposite of their usual meaning. In *dramatic irony,* there is a contradiction between what a character thinks and what the reader or audience knows to be true. In *irony of situation,* an event occurs that directly contradicts the expectations of the characters, the reader, or the audience.

IRONY OF SITUATION See *Irony.*

JOURNAL A *journal* is a daily autobiographical account of events and personal reactions. Daniel Defoe adapted this form to fictional use in his *A Journal of the Plague Year,* an excerpt from which appears on page 514.
See *Diary.*

KENNING A *kenning* is a metaphorical phrase, used in Anglo-Saxon poetry to replace a concrete noun. In "The Seafarer," on page 17, the cuckoo is called "summer's sentinel" and the sea "the whale's home."
See *Anglo-Saxon Poetry* and *Epic Convention.*

LEGEND A *legend* is a widely told story about the past, one that may or may not have a foundation in fact. A legend often reflects a people's identity or cultural values, generally with more historical truth and less emphasis on the supernatural than in a myth. English legends include the stories of King Arthur, of Robin Hood, and of other folk heroes.
See *Myth.*

LIMITED POINT OF VIEW See *Point of View.*

LITERARY BALLAD See *Ballad.*

LITERARY CRITICISM *Literary criticism* is the art of analyzing, interpreting, and evaluating literary works. There are many different types, or schools, of literary criticism, as follows:
1. *Impressionistic* or *Reader-Response Criticism* deals with the subjective responses of individual readers.
2. *Biographical* or *Historical Criticism* deals with details of literary history as these relate to particular works.
3. *Archetypal Criticism* deals with universal patterns of meaning or symbolism believed to be part of the biological or cultural heritage of humankind as a whole.
4. *Psychological Criticism* interprets texts based on concepts derived from any of a number of psychological models, such as the Gestalt Model of perception or the Freudian model of personality.
5. *Linguistic Criticism* applies to literary criticism borrowed from the scientific study of language.
6. *Moral* or *Ethical Criticism* evaluates literary works based on the moral or ethical mes-

sages that they convey. *Political Criticism* is a type of moral or ethical criticism.

7. The so-called *New Criticism* concentrates on the characteristics or qualities of literary works themselves, apart from any extra-textual material such as information about authors' lives or literary movements.

8. *Reconstructionist Criticism* views the literary text as an occasion for a creative act in which the reader in effect makes a new text by virtue of what he or she brings to it.

LYRIC POEM   A *lyric poem* is a poem that expresses the observations and feelings of a single speaker. Unlike a narrative poem, it presents an experience or a single effect, but it does not tell a full story. Types of lyrics include the elegy, the ode, and the sonnet. The lyric flourished in the songs and sonnets of the Renaissance, was revived by the Romantic poets, and has remained the most common poetic form during the nineteenth and twentieth centuries. Alfred, Lord Tennyson; Robert Browning; Elizabeth Barrett Browning; Matthew Arnold; William Butler Yeats; T.S. Eliot; W.H. Auden; Dylan Thomas, and Stevie Smith—all were great writers of lyric poems.

MAJOR CHARACTER   See *Character.*

MEMENTO MORI   *Memento mori* is a Latin phrase meaning "remember that you must die." Many great literary works have been written on the *memento mori* theme, including Marvell's "To His Coy Mistress," on page 418, and Gray's "Elegy Written in a Country Churchyard," on page 586.

METAPHOR   A *metaphor* is a figure of speech in which one thing is spoken of as though it were something else, as in "death, that long sleep." Through this identification of dissimilar things, a comparison is suggested or implied. Emily Brontë uses the following metaphor in the sec-

ond stanza of her poem "Remembrance": "my thoughts no longer hover . . . resting their wings." The metaphor suggests similarities between the speaker's thoughts and the wings of a bird.

An *extended metaphor* is one that is developed at length and that involves several points of comparison. Elizabeth Daryush uses extended metaphor in "November Sun":

His face is pale and shrunk, his shining hair
    Is prison-shorn;
Trailing his grey cloak, up the short dark
    stair
    He creeps each morn,

Looks out to his lost throne, to the
    noon-height
    Once his, then turns
Back to the alien dungeon, where all night
    Unseen he burns.

This poem metaphorically describes the November sun as a royal prisoner.

A *mixed metaphor* occurs when two metaphors are jumbled together. For example, thorns and rain are illogically mixed in "The thorns of life rained down on him."

A *dead metaphor* is one that has been so overused that its original metaphorical impact has been lost. Examples of dead metaphors include "the foot of the bed" and "toe the line." See *Figurative Language.*

METAPHYSICAL POETRY   *Metaphysical poetry* is the term used to describe the works of such seventeenth-century English poets as Richard Crashaw, John Donne, George Herbert, Andrew Marvell, Thomas Traherne, and Henry Vaughan. The term was first used by Samuel Johnson in an attack on writers who fill their works with far-fetched conceits and who make poetry a vehicle for displays of learning. Characteristic features of metaphysical poetry include intellectual playfulness, argument, paradoxes, irony, elaborate and unusual conceits, incongruity, and the rhythms of ordinary speech. Examples of metaphysical poems in this text include

Donne's "Song," on page 398, and Marvell's "To His Coy Mistress," on page 418.

METER The *meter* of a poem is its rhythmical pattern. This pattern is determined by the number and types of stresses, or beats, in each line. To describe the meter of a poem, you must *scan* its lines. *Scanning* involves marking the strongly stressed and weakly stressed syllables, as follows:

Twéen | thăt, whĕn |thĕ gráve's | dărk wáll
Dĭd fírst | hĕr fórm | rĕtáin,
Thĕy thought thĕir héarts coŭld ne'er rĕcáll
Thĕ líght | ŏf jóy | ăgáin.
　　—Emily Brontë, "Song"

As you can see, each strong stress is marked with a slanted line (´) and each weak stress with a horseshoe symbol (˘). The weak and strong stresses are then divided by vertical lines into groups called *feet*. The following types of feet are common in English poetry:

1. *Iamb:* a foot with one weak stress followed by one strong stress, as in the word "ăfráid"

2. *Trochee:* a foot with one strong stress followed by one weak stress, as in the word "héathĕr"

3. *Anapest:* a foot with two weak stresses followed by one strong stress, as in the word "dĭsĕmbárk"

4. *Dactyl:* a foot with one strong stress followed by two weak stresses, as in the word "sólĭtŭde"

5. *Spondee:* a foot with two strong stresses, as in the word "wórkdáy"

6. *Pyrrhic:* a foot with two weak stresses, as in the last foot of the word "ŭnspéak|ăblў"

7. *Amphibrach:* a foot with a weak syllable, one strong syllable, and another weak syllable, as in the word "ănóthĕr"

8. *Amphimacer:* a foot with a strong syllable, one weak syllable, and another strong syllable, as in "úp ănd dówn"

A line of poetry is described as *iambic, trochaic, anapestic,* or *dactylic* according to what kind of foot appears most often in the line.

Lines are also described in terms of the number of feet that occur in them, as follows:

1. *Monometer:* verse written in one-foot lines:

Soúnd thĕ Flúte!
Nŏw ít's mŭte.
Bírds dĕlíght
Dáy ănd Níght.
　　—William Blake, "Spring"

2. *Dimeter:* verse written in two-foot lines:

Ŏ Róse | thŏu ărt síck.
Thĕ ínvís | ĭblĕ wórm,
Thăt flíes | ĭn thĕ níght
Ĭn thĕ hów | lĭng storm:
Hăs found | ŏut thў bĕd
Ŏf crím | sŏn jóy:
Ănd hís dárk | sécrĕt lóve
Dŏes thў lífe | dĕstróy.
　　—William Blake, "The Sick Rose"

3. *Trimeter:* verse written in three-foot lines:

Ĭ wént | tŏ thĕ Gárd | ĕn ŏf Lóve
Ănd sáw | whăt Ĭ név | ĕr hăd séen:
Ă Cháp | ĕl wăs buílt ĭn thĕ mídst,
Whĕre Ĭ úsed | tŏ pláy | ŏn thĕ gréen.
　　—William Blake, "The Garden of Love"

4. *Tetrameter:* verse written in four-foot lines:

Ĭ wánd | ĕr thró' | eăch chart | er'd stréet,
Neăr whére | thĕ chart | er'd Thámes | dŏes flów
Ănd márk | ĭn ev | ĕrў face | Ĭ méet
Márks ŏf | wéaknĕss, | márks ŏf | wóe.
　　—William Blake, "London"

5. *Pentameter:* verse written in five-foot lines:

Ănd wé | ăre pút | ŏn earth | ă lítt | lĕ spáce,
Thăt wé | măy léarn | tŏ béar | thĕ béams | ŏf lóve
　　—William Blake, "The Little Black Boy"

A six-foot line is called a *hexameter*. A line with seven feet is a *heptameter*.

A complete description of the meter of a line tells both how many feet there are in the line and what kind of foot is most common. Thus the stanza from Emily Brontë's poem, quoted at the beginning of this entry, would be described as being made up of alternating iambic tetrameter and iambic trimeter lines. Poetry that does not have a regular meter is called *free verse*.

METONYMY   *Metonymy* is a figure of speech that substitutes something closely related for the thing actually meant. In the opening line of "The Lost Leader," Robert Browning says, "Just for a handful of silver he left us," using silver to refer to money in the form of a government grant. Browning's reference to silver is also an allusion to the handful of silver that Judas earned for betraying Christ in the Bible.
See *Figurative Language*.

MINOR CHARACTER   See *Character*.

MIRACLE PLAY   See *Drama*.

MIXED METAPHOR   See *Metaphor*.

MOCK EPIC   A *mock epic* is a poem about a trivial matter written in the style of a serious epic. The incongruity of the style and the subject matter produces comic effects. Alexander Pope's *The Rape of the Lock,* on page 548, is a mock epic.
See *Epic* and *Epic Convention*.

MONOLOGUE   A *monologue* is a speech or performance given entirely by one person or by one character.
See *Dramatic Monologue* and *Soliloquy*.

MOOD   *Mood,* or atmosphere, is the feeling created in the reader by a literary work or passage. The mood may be suggested by the writer's choice of words, by events in the work, or by the physical setting. Nadine Gordimer begins "The Train from Rhodesia," on page 1260, with a mood-evoking description of the brick, mud, and tin buildings at the hot, sandy train station. Everyone there—the stationmaster, his wife, the native vendors, and the children—awaits the train, the only relief expected in this inactive and restricted environment.

See *Setting* and *Tone*.

MONOMETER   See *Meter*.

MORALITY PLAY   See *Drama*.

MOTIF   A *motif* is a recurring literary convention or an element that is repeated within a literary work. For example, Titania and Bottom in William Shakespeare's *A Midsummer Night's Dream* exemplify a motif from folklore—the mortal enchanted by a fairy lover. D.H. Lawrence, in "The Rocking-Horse Winner," on page 974, repeats the motif of luck throughout his story. Whether a motif is part of the literary tradition or is an author's own invention, it generally unifies a work and adds to its theme.

MOTIVATION   A *motivation* is a reason that explains or partially explains a character's thoughts, feelings, actions, or speech. Characters may be motivated by their physical needs; by their wants, wishes, desires, or dreams; or by their beliefs, values, and ideals. Effective characterization involves creating motivations that make characters seem believable.
See *Character*.

MYTH   A *myth* is a fictional tale, originally with religious significance, that explains the actions of gods or heroes, the causes of natural phenomena, or both. Allusions to characters and motifs from Greek, Roman, Norse, and Celtic myths are common in English literature. In addition, mythological stories are often retold or adapted, as George Bernard Shaw's *Pygmalion,* on page 1109, illustrates. Pygmalion was a character from Greek mythology who created a beautiful sculpture of a woman and then fell in love with his own creation.
See *Legend*.

NARRATION   *Narration* is writing that tells a story. The act of telling a story is also called

narration. The *narrative,* or story, is told by a storyteller called the *narrator.* Narration is one of the major forms of discourse and appears in many guises. Biographies, autobiographies, journals, reports, novels, short stories, plays, narrative poems, anecdotes, fables, parables, myths, legends, folktales, ballads, and epic poems are all narratives, or types of narration.
See *Forms of Discourse.*

NARRATIVE   See *Narration.*

NARRATIVE POEM   A *narrative poem* tells a story in verse. Three traditional types of narrative poems include ballads, such as "Sir Patrick Spens" and "Barbara Allan"; epics, such as *Beowulf;* and metrical romances, such as *Sir Gawain and the Green Knight.* Other narrative poems in this text include the selection from Spenser's *The Faerie Queene,* on page 244; the selection from Milton's *Paradise Lost,* on page 449; Coleridge's "The Rime of the Ancient Mariner," on page 660; and Tennyson's "The Lady of Shalott," on page 786.

NARRATOR   See *Narration.*

NATURALISM   *Naturalism* was a literary movement among writers at the end of the nineteenth century and during the early decades of the twentieth century. The Naturalists, influenced by the theories of Social Darwinists like Sir Herbert Spencer, tended to view people as hopeless victims of immutable natural laws. Important Naturalist writers included the Norwegian playwright Henrik Ibsen and the French novelist Emile Zola.
See *Realism.*

NEOCLASSICISM   *Neoclassicism* was a literary movement during the Restoration and the eighteenth century in which writers turned to classical Greek and Roman literary models and standards. Like the ancient Greeks, the Neo-classicists stressed reason, order, harmony, restraint, correctness, and decorum. The way these qualities took literary form is illustrated by the balanced and controlled heroic couplet, perfected by John Dryden and Alexander Pope. Much Neoclassical literature dealt with themes related to proper and tasteful human conduct. The most popular literary forms of the day—essays, letters, early novels, epigrams, parodies, and satires—reflected this emphasis on society as subject matter. Just as the Neoclassicists rejected the individualism and extravagance of the Renaissance in favor of classical restraint, so the nineteenth-century Romantics rejected Neoclassicism in favor of imagination, emotion, and the individual.
See *Classicism* and *Romanticism.*

NONFICTION   *Nonfiction* is prose writing that presents and explains ideas or that tells about real people, places, objects, or events.
See *Fiction.*

NOVEL   A *novel* is a long work of fiction. A novel often has a complicated plot, many major and minor characters, a significant theme, and several settings. Novels can be grouped in many ways based on the historical periods in which they are written (such as Romantic or Victorian), on the subjects and themes that they treat (such as Gothic or regional), on the techniques used in them (such as stream of consciousness), or on their debts to literary movements (such as Naturalism or Realism). Among early novels were Samuel Richardson's works *Pamela* and *Clarissa Harlowe,* and Henry Fielding's *Tom Jones.* Other classic English novels include Jane Austen's *Pride and Prejudice,* Sir Walter Scott's *Waverley,* Charles Dickens's *David Copperfield,* and George Eliot's *The Mill on the Floss.* Major twentieth-century novelists include James Joyce, Virginia Woolf, D.H. Lawrence, Henry James, Graham Greene, and Patrick White. A *novella* is not as long as a novel but is longer than a short story. See, for example, Joseph Conrad's novella *Heart of Darkness.*

OBJECTIVE CORRELATIVE   See *Image.*

OCTAVE   See *Stanza.*

ODE   An *ode* is a long, formal lyric poem with a serious theme. It may or may not have a traditional structure with three alternating stanza patterns called the *strophe,* the *antistrophe,* and the *epode.* An ode may be written for a private occasion, as was John Keats's "Ode to a Nightingale," on page 721, which was written about a bird nesting near a friend's home. On the other hand, an ode may be prepared for a public ceremony, as was John Dryden's "A Song for St. Cecilia's Day," on page 499, which was performed in 1687 at an annual festival. Odes often honor people, commemorate events, respond to natural scenes, or consider serious human problems.
See *Lyric.*

OMNISCIENT POINT OF VIEW   See *Point of View.*

ONOMATOPOEIA   *Onomatopoeia* is the use of words that imitate sounds. Examples of such words are *buzz, hiss, murmur,* and *rustle.* Seamus Heaney uses onomatopoeia in "Churning Day" to suggest the sounds of making butter:

> My mother took first turn, set up rhythms
> that slugged and thumped for hours. Arms
>   ached.
> Hands blistered. Cheeks and clothes were
>   splattered
> with flabbymilk.

Onomatopoeia is used to create musical effects and to reinforce meaning, especially in poetry.

ORAL TRADITION   *Oral tradition* is the passing of songs, stories, and poems from genera-

tion to generation by word of mouth. Among the many materials composed or preserved through oral tradition in Great Britain are *Beowulf,* on page 24, and the folk ballads on pages 104–114. In his *Morte d'Arthur,* Sir Thomas Malory drew on written French sources and on Arthurian legends from the oral tradition. Edmund Spenser drew on the same sources when composing *The Faerie Queene.* Shakespeare drew on materials from the oral tradition to create the *sprites* and *fairies* of *A Midsummer Night's Dream.* Folk epics, ballads, myths, legends, folktales, folk songs, proverbs, nursery rhymes—all such products of the oral tradition were originally spoken or sung rather than written down.
See *Ballad, Folklore, Legend,* and *Myth.*

OTTAVA RIMA   *Ottava rima* is a stanza with eight iambic pentameter lines that rhyme *abababcc.* Lord Byron used this stanza for his *Don Juan,* a selection from which appears on page 697. William Butler Yeats was fond of this stanza form and used it in a number of his finest poems, including "Sailing to Byzantium," on page 1036.

OVERSTATEMENT   See *Hyperbole.*

OXYMORON   *Oxymoron* is a figure of speech that fuses two contradictory or opposing ideas. An oxymoron, such as "freezing fire" or "happy grief," thus suggests a paradox in just a few words. In Book I of *Paradise Lost,* Milton uses the oxymoron "darkness visible" to describe the pit into which Satan and the other rebellious angels have been thrown.
See *Figurative Language* and *Paradox.*

PARADOX   A *paradox* is a statement that seems to be contradictory but that actually presents a truth. In "Love's Growth," John Donne presents the following paradox:

> Methinks I lied all winter, when I swore
> My love was infinite, if spring make it more.

Because a paradox is surprising or even shocking, it draws the reader's attention to what is being said.

See *Figurative Language* and *Oxymoron.*

PARALLELISM *Parallelism* is the repetition of a grammatical pattern. Stevie Smith uses parallel infinitive verbs in the first stanza of her poem "Is It Wise?":

> Is it wise
> To hug misery
> To make a song of Melancholy
> To weave a garland of sighs
> To abandon hope wholly?
> No, it is not wise.

Parallelism is used in poetry and in other writing to emphasize and to link related ideas.

PARODY A *parody* is a humorous, mocking imitation of a literary work. The play-within-the-play in William Shakespeare's *A Midsummer Night's Dream* parodies the poor performances and versions of classical tales that were current in Shakespeare's day.

PASTORAL A literary work is *pastoral* if it deals with the pleasures of a simple, rural life or with escape to a simpler place and time. The tradition of pastoral literature began in ancient Greece with the poetic idylls of Theocritus. Theocritus wrote about the simple lives of shepherds and goatherds. The Roman poet Virgil also wrote a famous collection of pastoral poems, the *Eclogues,* in imitation of Theocritus. Virgil's characters were, like Theocritus's, idealized rustics.

During the European Renaissance, pastoral writing became quite popular. One famous example of the genre is *The Countess of Pembroke's Arcadia,* by Sir Phillip Sidney. Another example is Christopher Marlowe's "The Passionate Shepherd to His Love," on page 230.

Today the term *pastoral* is commonly applied to any work in which a speaker longs to escape to a simpler, rural life. By this definition both William Wordsworth's "The World Is Too Much with Us," on page 657, and William Butler Yeats's "The Lake Isle of Innisfree," on page 1027, are pastoral poems.

PATHOS *Pathos* is the quality in a literary work that arouses feelings of pity, sorrow, or compassion in readers or in an audience. In *Macbeth,* the murdering of Macduff's family is a source of pathos, causing the audience to feel great sympathy for Macduff.

PENTAMETER See *Meter.*

PERSONIFICATION *Personification* is a type of figurative language in which a nonhuman subject is given human characteristics. Percy Bysshe Shelley used personification in these lines from "To Night":

> Swiftly walk o'er the western wave,
>   Spirit of the Night!
> Out of the misty eastern cave
> Where, all the long and lone daylight
> Thou wovest dreams of joy and fear,
> Which make thee terrible and dear,
>   Swift be thy flight!

Effective personification of things or ideas makes them seem vital and alive, as if they were human.

See *Figurative Language* and *Metaphor.*

PERSUASION *Persuasion* is writing or speech that attempts to convince the audience to take some action or to adopt some opinion. Persuasion is one of the major forms of discourse and is used in advertising, in editorials, in sermons, in political speeches, and in other such writings. Some people use the terms *persuasion* and *argument* synonymously. Others use *persuasion* to refer to works that appeal to the emotions and *argument* to refer to works that appeal to reason.

See *Forms of Discourse.*

PETRARCHAN CONCEIT   See *Conceit.*

PETRARCHAN SONNET   See *Sonnet.*

PLOT   *Plot* is the sequence of events in a literary work. The two primary elements of any plot are characters and a conflict. Most plots can be analyzed into most or all of the following parts:

1. The *exposition* introduces the setting, the characters, and the basic situation.
2. The *inciting incident* introduces the central conflict.
3. During the *development,* the conflict runs its course and usually intensifies.
4. At the *climax,* the conflict reaches a high point of interest or suspense.
5. At the *resolution,* the conflict is ended.
6. The *denouement* ties up loose ends that remain after the resolution of the conflict.

There are many variations on the standard plot structure. Some stories begin *in medias res* ("in the middle of things"), after the inciting incident has already occurred. In some stories the expository material appears toward the middle, in flashbacks. In many stories there is no denouement. Occasionally, though not often, the conflict is left unresolved.

POETRY   *Poetry* is one of the three major types, or genres, of literature, the others being prose and drama. Poetry defies simple definition because there is no single characteristic that is found in all poems and not found in all non-poems. In other words, poems are what philosophers of language call an "ill-defined set."

Often poems are divided into lines and stanzas. Many poems employ regular rhythmical patterns, or meters. However, some poems are written out just like prose, and some are written in free verse. Most poems make use of highly concise, musical, and emotionally charged language. Many also make use of imagery, figurative language, and special devices of sound such as rhyme.

Types of poetry include narrative poetry (ballads, epics, and metrical romances), dramatic poetry (dramatic monologues and dramatic dialogues), lyrics (sonnets, odes, elegies, and love poems), and concrete poetry.

POINT OF VIEW   *Point of view* is the perspective, or vantage point, from which a story is told. If a character within the story tells the story, then it is told from the *first-person* point of view. If a voice from outside the story tells it, then the story is told from the *third-person* point of view. If the knowledge of the storyteller is limited to the internal states of one character, then the storyteller has a *limited* point of view. If the storyteller's knowledge extends to the internal states of all of the characters, then the storyteller has an *omniscient* point of view. The point of view from which a story is told determines what view of events will be presented.

PROSE   *Prose* is the ordinary form of written language and one of the three major types of literature. Most writing that is not poetry, drama, or song is considered prose. Prose occurs in two major forms: fiction and nonfiction.

PROTAGONIST   The *protagonist* is the main character in a literary work. In D. H. Lawrence's "The Rocking-Horse Winner," on page 974, the protagonist is Paul.
See *Antagonist* and *Character.*

PSALM   A *psalm* is a song or hymn of praise, especially one included in the Book of Psalms in the Bible.

PUN   A *pun* is a play on words. A pun may involve using a word or a phrase that has two different meanings or it may involve using two different words or phrases with the same sound, as in *sun* and *son.* The title of George Herbert's poem "The Collar" is a pun that suggests both the clerical collar of an Anglican minister and "choler," or anger, the emotion expressed at the beginning of the poem but calmed by God's call to the poem's speaker. Puns are often humorous but may serve serious purposes as well, as the example from Herbert shows.

PYRRHIC See *Meter.*

QUATRAIN See *Stanza.*

REALISM *Realism* is the presentation in art of the details of actual life. Another term for Realism, one that derives from Aristotle's *Poetics,* is *mimesis,* the Greek word for "imitation." During the last part of the nineteenth century and the first part of the twentieth, Realism enjoyed considerable popularity among writers in the English-speaking world. Nowhere, perhaps, was Realism more evident than in the novel. Novels often dealt with grim social realities and often presented realistic portrayals of the psychological states of characters. Realism also had considerable influence on theater in the early Modern Era. During the first part of this century, for example, the most common sort of stage setting was that in which a room was presented as though one wall had been removed and the audience were peering inside.

REFERENTIAL MEANING See *Denotation.*

REFRAIN A *refrain* is a regularly repeated line or group of lines in a poem or song. See, for example, the refrain "Lord, have mercy on us!" in Thomas Nashe's "A Litany in Time of Plague," on page 250.

REGIONALISM *Regionalism* is the tendency to confine one's writing to the presentation of materials drawn from a particular geographical area. George Eliot, for example, tended to set her tales in the English Midlands. The Brontës wrote about Yorkshire. Thomas Hardy wrote about Dorset and Wessex. D. H. Lawrence wrote about Nottinghamshire. A Regionalist writer presents the distinct culture of an area, including its speech, customs, landscape, and history.

REPETITION *Repetition* is the use, more than once, of any element of language—a sound, a word, a phrase, a clause, a sentence, a grammatical pattern, or a rhythmical pattern. Alliteration, assonance, consonance, meter, parallelism, refrains, and rhyme are all types of repetition.

RESOLUTION See *Plot.*

RHYME *Rhyme* is the repetition of sounds at the ends of words. *End rhyme* occurs when the rhyming words are repeated at the ends of lines. *Internal rhyme* occurs when the rhyming words fall within a line. *Exact rhyme* is the use of identical rhyming sounds, as in *love* and *dove. Approximate,* or *slant rhyme,* is the use of sounds that are similar but not identical, as in *prove* and *glove.*

RHYME SCHEME A *rhyme scheme* is a regular pattern of rhyming words in a poem or stanza. To indicate a rhyme scheme, one assigns each final sound in the poem or stanza a different letter. Consider, for example, how the following lines from Charlotte Brontë's "On the Death of Anne Brontë" have been marked:

There's little joy in life for *me,*	a
And little terror in the *grave;*	b
I've lived the parting hour to *see*	a
Of one I would have died to *save.*	b

The rhyme scheme of this stanza is *abab.*

RHYTHM See *Meter.*

RISING ACTION The *rising action* is that part of a plot that leads up to the climax. During the rising action, suspense increases as the complications of the conflict develop.
See *Falling Action* and *Plot.*

ROMANCE   A *romance* is a story that presents remote or imaginative incidents rather than ordinary, realistic experience. The term *romance* was originally used to refer to medieval tales of the deeds and loves of noble knights and ladies. These early romances, or tales of chivalry and courtly love, are exemplified by *Sir Gawain and the Green Knight,* on page 170, and by Malory's *Morte d'Arthur,* on page 91. During the Renaissance in England, many writers drew heavily on the romance tradition. One such writer was Edmund Spenser, whose *The Faerie Queene* combines elements of romance and elements of the epic. From the eighteenth century on, the term *romance* has been commonly used to describe sentimental novels about love.

ROMANTIC COMEDY   See *Comedy.*

ROMANTICISM   *Romanticism* was a literary and artistic movement of the eighteenth and nineteenth centuries. In reaction against Neoclassicism, the Romantics emphasized imagination, fancy, freedom, emotion, wildness, the beauty of the untamed natural world, the rights of the individual, the nobility of the common man, and the attractiveness of pastoral life. Important figures in the Romantic movement included William Wordsworth; Samuel Taylor Coleridge; Percy Bysshe Shelley; John Keats; and George Gordon, Lord Byron.

ROUND CHARACTER   See *Character.*

RUN-ON LINE   A *run-on line* is one that does not contain a pause or a stop at the end. A run-on line ends in the middle of a statement and of a grammatical unit, and the reader must therefore read the next line to find the end of the statement and the completion of the grammatical unit. The beginning of Molly Holden's "The

Double Nature of White" illustrates the run-on line:

> White orchards are the earliest, stunning
> the spirit resigned to winter's black, white thorn
> sprays first the bare wet branches of the
>   hedge.

See *End-Stopped Line.*

SATIRE   *Satire* is writing that ridicules or holds up to contempt the faults of individuals or of groups. A satirist may use a sympathetic tone or an angry, bitter tone. Some satire, like Jonathan Swift's *Gulliver's Travels,* an excerpt from which appears on page 520, is written in prose. Other satire, such as Henry Reed's "The Naming of Parts," on page 1094, is written in poetry. Although a satire is often humorous, its purpose is not simply to make readers laugh but also to correct, through laughter, the flaws and shortcomings that it points out.

SCANSION   *Scansion* is the process of analyzing the metrical pattern of a poem.
See *Meter.*

SCENE   See *Drama.*

SESTET   See *Stanza.*

SETTING   The *setting* of a literary work is the time and place of the action. A setting can serve many different purposes. It can provide a backdrop for the action. It can be the force that the protagonist struggles against and thus the source of the central conflict. It can also be used to create a mood, or atmosphere. In many works the setting symbolizes some point that the author wishes to emphasize. Much of Emily Brontë's novel *Wuthering Heights,* which is discussed on pages 898–901, is set in the house named in the novel's title. When Lockwood visits this house at the beginning of the story, he finds it standing on a cold hilltop on the moors, built to

withstand the north wind and inhabited by fierce dogs and unsociable people. This setting creates a specific mood and suggests, symbolically, the wild emotional history of the past inhabitants of the house.
See *Mood* and *Symbol.*

SHAKESPEAREAN SONNET See *Sonnet.*

SHORT STORY A *short story* is a brief work of fiction. The short story resembles the longer novel but generally has a simpler plot and setting. In addition, a short story tends to reveal character at a crucial moment rather than to develop it through many incidents.

SIMILE A *simile* is a figure of speech that compares two dissimilar things by using a key word such as *like* or *as.* Christina Rossetti uses similes in her poem "Goblin Market" to describe two sisters:

> Like two blossoms on one stem,
> Like two flakes of new-fallen snow,
> Like two wands of ivory
> Tipped with gold for awful kings.

By comparing dissimilar things, the writer of a simile shocks the reader into appreciation of the qualities of the things being compared. Thus a simile makes a description more vivid and memorable.
See *Figurative Language.*

SLANT RHYME See *Rhyme.*

SOLILOQUY A *soliloquy* in a play or prose work is a long speech made by a character who is alone and who thus reveals his or her private thoughts and feelings to the audience or reader. William Shakespeare's Act III of *Macbeth* opens with a soliloquy in which Banquo speculates on what Macbeth has done to fulfill the prophecy of the witches.
See *Monologue.*

SONNET A *sonnet* is a fourteen-line lyric poem focused on a single theme. Sonnets have many variations but are usually written in iambic pentameter, following one of two traditional patterns.

The *Petrarchan* or *Italian sonnet* is divided into two parts, the eight-line octave and the six-line sestet. The octave rhymes *abba abba,* while the sestet generally rhymes *cde cde* or uses some combination of *cd* rhymes. The two parts of the Petrarchan sonnet work together. The octave raises a question, states a problem, or presents a brief narrative, and the sestet answers the question, solves the problem, or comments on the narrative.

The *Shakespearean* or *English sonnet* has three four-line quatrains plus a concluding two-line couplet. The rhyme scheme of such a sonnet is usually *abab cdcd efef gg.* Each of the three quatrains usually explores a different variation of the main theme. Then the couplet presents a summarizing or concluding statement.
See *Lyric* and *Sonnet Sequence.*

SONNET SEQUENCE A *sonnet sequence* is a series or group of sonnets written to one person or on one theme. Although each sonnet can stand alone as a separate poem, the sequence lets the poet trace the development of a relationship or examine different aspects of a single subject. Examples of sonnet sequences are Sir Philip Sidney's *Astrophel and Stella,* Edmund Spenser's *Amoretti,* and Elizabeth Barrett Browning's *Sonnets from the Portuguese.*
See *Sonnet.*

SPEAKER The *speaker* is the imaginary voice assumed by the writer of a poem. In other words, the speaker is the character who tells the poem.

This character often is not identified by name. The title of William Blake's poem "The Chimney Sweeper" identifies the speaker, a child who gives this account of his life:

When my mother died I was very young,
And my father sold me while yet my tongue
Could scarcely cry " 'weep! 'weep! 'weep!
  'weep!"
So your chimneys I sweep and in soot I sleep.

Although this speaker matter-of-factly accepts his life, the poem is ironic because the poet expects readers to have a different view of the child's situation. Recognizing the speaker and thinking about his or her characteristics is often central to interpreting a lyric poem.
See *Point of View*.

SPENSERIAN STANZA   The *Spenserian stanza*, invented by Edmund Spenser for use in *The Faerie Queene*, has nine iambic lines rhymed *ababbcbcc*. All the lines are pentameters except the last, which is a hexameter or alexandrine. This close-knit rhyme scheme unifies the stanza, and the final line provides a dignified summary. This stanza form is used in George Gordon, Lord Byron's *Childe Harold's Pilgrimage*, on page 692, and in poems by William Wordsworth, John Keats, Percy Bysshe Shelley, and Alfred, Lord Tennyson.
See *Alexandrine*.

SPONDEE   See *Meter*.

SPRUNG RHYTHM   *Sprung rhythm* is the term used by Gerard Manley Hopkins to describe the idiosyncratic meters of his poems. Discovering the underlying metrical pattern of a poem written in sprung rhythm is difficult if not impossible. The rhythm is quite varied and contains such violations of traditional metrical rules as several strong stresses in a row or feet containing more than two weak stresses. The following lines from Gerard Manley Hopkins's "Spring" illustrate sprung rhythm:

What is all this juice and all this joy?
A strain of the earth's sweet being in
  the beginning
In Eden garden.—Have, get, before it
  cloy,
Before it cloud, Christ, lord, and sour
  with sinning,
Innocent mind and Mayday in girl and boy

STAGE DIRECTIONS   *Stage directions* are notes included in a drama to describe how the work is to be performed or staged. Stage directions are usually printed in italics and enclosed within parentheses or brackets. They may mention how the characters should speak or move, what the costumes or scenery should look like, how the set should be arranged, what lighting should be used, and so on.

STANZA   A *stanza* is a group of lines in a poem, considered as a unit. Many poems are divided into stanzas that are separated by spaces. Stanzas often function just like paragraphs in prose. Each stanza states and develops a single main idea.

Stanzas are commonly named according to the number of lines found in them, as follows:
1. *Couplet:* a two-line stanza
2. *Tercet:* a three-line stanza
3. *Quatrain:* a four-line stanza
4. *Cinquain:* a five-line stanza
5. *Sestet:* a six-line stanza
6. *Heptastich:* a seven-line stanza
7. *Octave:* an eight-line stanza
See *Sonnet* and *Spenserian Stanza*.

STATIC CHARACTER   See *Character*.

STEREOTYPE   See *Character*.

STOCK CHARACTER   See *Character*.

STREAM OF CONSCIOUSNESS *Stream of consciousness* is a narrative technique that presents thoughts as if they were coming directly from a character's mind. Instead of being arranged in chronological order, the events in a stream-of-consciousness narrative are presented from the character's point of view, mixed in with the character's ongoing feelings and memories. Developed by writers such as James Joyce and Virginia Woolf, stream-of-consciousness writing is used to reveal a character's complex psychology and to present it in realistic detail.
See *Point of View.*

STYLE A writer's *style* is his or her typical way of writing. Determinants of a writer's style include his or her formality, use of figurative language, use of rhythm, typical grammatical patterns, typical sentence lengths, and typical methods of organization. John Milton is noted for a grand, heroic style that contrasts with John Keats's rich, sensory style and with T.S. Eliot's allusive, ironic style.
See *Diction.*

SUBPLOT A *subplot* is a second, less important plot within a story or play. One subplot in William Shakespeare's *A Midsummer Night's Dream* deals with the presentation of a play by Bottom and his fellows. Another deals with the quarrel between Titania and Oberon. A subplot may add to, reflect, vary, or contrast with the main plot.
See *Plot.*

SUSPENSE *Suspense* is a feeling of growing curiosity or anxious uncertainty about the outcome of events in a literary work. Writers create suspense by raising questions in the minds of their readers.

SYMBOL A *symbol* is anything that stands for or represents something else. Thus a flag is a symbol of a country, a group of letters can symbolize a spoken word, a spoken word can symbolize an object, a fine car can symbolize wealth, and so on. In literary criticism a distinction is often made between *traditional* or *conventional symbols*—ones that are part of our general cultural inheritance—and *personal symbols*—ones that are created by particular authors for use in particular works. For example, the lamb in William Blake's poem "The Lamb" is a conventional symbol for peace, gentleness, and innocence, one that Blake inherited from the Bible and from the pastoral tradition. However, the tiger in Blake's poem "The Tiger" is not a conventional or inherited symbol. Blake created this symbol of evil specifically for this poem.

Conventional symbolism is often based on elements of the natural world. For example, youth is often symbolized by greenery or springtime, middle age by summer, and old age by autumn or winter. Death is often symbolized by darkness or cold. The sun is often used as a symbol of power or authority. Roses are symbols of love and beauty. Doves are symbols of peace. Foxes are symbols of craftiness, and owls of wisdom.

Conventional symbols are also sometimes borrowed from the spheres of religion and politics. For example, a cross may be a symbol of Christianity or the color red a symbol of Marxist ideology.

SYMBOLISM *Symbolism* was a literary movement of nineteenth-century France. The Symbolist writers reacted against Realism and stressed, instead, the importance of suggestion and evocation of emotional states, especially by means of symbols corresponding to these states. The Symbolists were also quite concerned with using sound to achieve emotional effects. Important Symbolist writers included Stéphane Mallarmé, Paul Verlaine, and Arthur Rimbaud. English writers who were influenced by the Symbolist movement included William Butler Yeats and T. S. Eliot.

SYNECDOCHE *Synecdoche* is a figure of speech in which a part of something is used to stand for the whole. In the preface to his long poem entitled *Milton,* William Blake includes these lines: "And did those feet in ancient time/ Walk upon England's mountains green?" The feet, of course, stand for the whole body, and "England's mountains green" stand for England generally.
See *Figurative Language.*

TERCET　See *Stanza.*

TERZA RIMA　*Terza rima* is a three-line stanza pattern with interlocking rhymes that connect stanza to stanza. The middle line of one tercet rhymes with the first and last lines of the next so that *aba* is followed by *bcb, cdc, ded,* and so on. "The Triumph of Life," by Percy Bysshe Shelley, illustrates this pattern:

As in that trance of wondrous thought I lay	*a*
This was the tenour of my waking dream,	*b*
Methought I sat beside a public way	*a*
Thick strewn with summer dust, and a great 　stream	*b*
Of people there was hurrying to and fro	*c*
Numerous as gnats upon the evening 　gleam	*b*

As the name suggests, *terza rima* is an Italian verse form. The form was made famous by Dante Alighieri, who used it in his *The Divine Comedy.* Terza rima is a difficult form because of the rhymes required, but it has been used successfully by Sir Thomas Wyatt, Lord Byron, Robert Browning, and William Butler Yeats.

TETRAMETER　See *Meter.*

THEME　The *theme* is a central idea, concern, or purpose in a literary work. In an essay the theme might be directly stated in what is known as a thesis statement. In a serious literary work, the theme is usually expressed indirectly rather than directly. A light work, one written strictly for entertainment, may not have a theme.

THIRD-PERSON POINT OF VIEW　See *Point of View.*

TONE　The *tone* of a literary work is the writer's attitude toward the readers and toward the subject. A writer's tone may be formal or informal, friendly or distant, personal or pompous. For example, William Hazlitt's tone in his essay on Macbeth, on page 748, is earnest and respectful, while James Boswell's tone in *The Life of Samuel Johnson,* which begins on page 576, is familiar and engaging.
See *Mood.*

TRAGEDY　*Tragedy* is a type of drama or literature that shows the downfall or destruction of a noble or outstanding person, traditionally one who possesses a character weakness called a *tragic flaw.* Macbeth, for example, is a brave and noble figure led astray by ambition. The *tragic hero,* through choice or circumstance, is caught up in a sequence of events that inevitably results in disaster. Because the protagonist is neither a wicked villain nor an innocent victim, the audience reacts with mixed emotions—both pity and fear, according to the Greek philosopher Aristotle, who defined tragedy in his famous work, the *Poetics.* The outcome of a tragedy, in which the protagonist is isolated from society, contrasts with the happy resolution of a comedy, in which the protagonist makes peace with society.
See *Comedy* and *Drama.*

TRIMETER　See *Meter.*

TROCHEE　See *Meter.*

UNDERSTATEMENT　*Understatement* is the literary technique of saying less than is actually

meant, generally in an ironic way. An example of understatement is the description of a flooded area as "slightly soggy."
See *Figurative Language*.

VERBAL IRONY   See *Irony*.

VERNACULAR   *Vernacular* is the ordinary language of the people living in a particular region. Instead of using more formal literary language, writers may use vernacular to create realistic characters or to approach readers informally. See *Dialect*.

VILLANELLE   A *villanelle* is a nineteen-line French verse form. It has two refrains formed by repeating line 1 in lines 6, 12, and 18 and by repeating line 3 in lines 9, 15, and 19. The three lines in each of the first five stanzas rhyme *aba*. The final quatrain rhymes *abaa*. An example of a villanelle in this text is Dylan Thomas's "Do Not Go Gentle into That Good Night," on page 1102.

HANDBOOK OF CRITICAL THINKING AND READING TERMS

ABSTRACT *adj.* Anything that is not concrete or definite is *abstract.* A building is concrete because its details can be perceived by the senses. A set of blueprints is abstract because most of these details are left out. Words and the ideas that they represent can also be abstract. Examples of abstract words include *love, truth, history, realism, courage, nature,* and *society.*

People can make abstract ideas clear by using specific examples and illustrations. Suppose, for instance, that a novelist wants to communicate the abstract idea of a society. To do so, he or she might create characters representing a cross section of ethnic, economic, and political backgrounds: a coal miner, an immigrant, a pop star, a farmer, an aristocrat, and a labor leader. The novelist might make this depiction seem realistic by including many specific details and allusions to actual places, styles of clothing, customs, and historical events.

Another way to express abstract ideas clearly is to use symbols and figures of speech. For example, in the poem "Do Not Go Gentle into That Good Night," on page 1102, Dylan Thomas uses a concrete image—light—as a symbol for an abstraction—life.

ANALOGY *n.* An *analogy* is a comparison that explains one subject by pointing out its similarities to another subject. Writers often use analogies to explain the unfamiliar in familiar terms. For example, a writer might explain the organization of a theatrical troupe by comparing it to the organization of a baseball team. An analogy is possible only when the two items being compared have elements or characteristics in common. Writers use a number of techniques to state or to suggest analogies, including metaphor, simile, and extended metaphor.

Whenever you read or hear an analogy, ask yourself what characteristics the two things being compared have in common. Whenever you create an analogy, make sure that the two things being compared do in fact share common elements or characteristics. Avoid false analogy—the fallacy of assuming that two things are similar in one respect simply because they are similar in another respect.

ANALYSIS *n.* *Analysis* is the process of studying a whole by examining its parts. When you analyze something, follow these steps: First, break the thing down into its parts. Next, study the properties and functions of the parts. Then, look for relationships among the parts and between each part and the whole. For example, you might analyze the plot of a short story into the exposition, the inciting incident, the development, the climax, the resolution, and the denouement. After breaking the events of the story down into these parts, you would then study each part and think about how each part advances the action and contributes to the whole.

There are many different types of analysis. A *functional analysis* is one in which a thing is broken down into parts and then the functions of each part are studied. A *cause-and-effect analysis* is one in which a series of events is broken down into separate events that are then identified as causes or effects.

ARGUMENT *n.* An *argument* is a set of logically-related statements consisting of a conclusion and one or more premises. The premises are the reasons for accepting the conclusion. For example, you might argue in a paper that Macbeth, the protagonist in Shakespeare's tragedy, is essentially a good man who is tempted by ambition to commit acts that he knows to be wrong. To support this argument, you might present the following evidence from the play:

1. Before committing the murder, Macbeth thinks aloud about the duty that he owes to Duncan and about the great evil involved in killing one's king, one's kinsman, and one's guest.
2. Macbeth has such a guilty conscience that he is driven to have hallucinations, seeing first a bloody dagger in the air and then the ghost of Banquo.
3. At the end of the play, in the "Tomorrow" soliloquy, Macbeth reveals that life has become completely meaningless for him.

Whenever you state an interpretation or an evaluation of a literary work, you should support your statement with reasons drawn from the work itself.

The term *argument* is also used to refer to a brief summary, or synopsis, of a literary work. Thus a summary of the plot of *Paradise Lost* might be described as presenting "the argument of the poem."
See *Conclusion, Deduction, Evidence, Induction,* and *Inference.*

BANDWAGON   See *Propaganda Technique.*

BEGGING THE QUESTION   See *Logical Fallacy.*

CATEGORIZATION *n.   Categorization* is the process of placing objects or ideas into groups. These groups may be called classes or categories. Categorization is always done according to some shared property or characteristic. For example, one might place Coleridge's "The Rime of the Ancient Mariner," on page 660, and Tennyson's "The Lady of Shallot," on page 786, into the same category because these poems share two important characteristics: Both tell stories, and both deal with extraordinary or supernatural events.

To categorize something, follow these steps:
1. Observe the characteristics of the thing to be categorized.
2. Think of other things that have the same characteristics.
3. Find or create a name for the group of things with the shared characteristic.

Categorization is a useful tool for organizing information. Information about literary works is organized by categorizing works into groups called *genres.* The major genres of literature are prose, poetry, and drama. Prose can be divided into the subcategories of fiction and nonfiction; poetry into the subcategories of lyric, narrative, dramatic, and epic poetry; and drama into the subcategories of comedy, serious drama, tragedy, melodrama, and farce.

CAUSE AND EFFECT *n. phrase*   When one event precedes and brings about another event, the first is said to be a *cause* and the second an *effect.* A *sufficient cause* is one that, by itself, is enough to bring about the effect. A *necessary cause* is one that is required in order to bring about an effect but that may or may not be sufficient to bring about the effect.

Cause-and-effect relationships are extremely important in literary study. The plot of a story, for example, is a series of events related by cause and effect. One event causes the next, which causes the next, and so on to the end of the story. Literary history often involves tracing the forces that caused the writer to produce particular works. Such forces might include the author's personal experiences and reading or the social, political, and cultural circumstances in which the author wrote.

The act of reading also involves cause and effect. Particular aspects of the text—the imagery or tone, for example—cause certain reactions in the reader. To understand the work, the reader must account for these reactions by determining what aspects of the text caused them.

CIRCULAR REASONING   See *Logical Fallacy.*

COMPARISON *n.   Comparison* is the process

of observing and pointing out similarities. For example, a comparison of Samuel Pepys and James Boswell might note that each author possessed an excellent eye for detail, that each was a skillful storyteller, and that each displayed a love for social life.

See *Contrast*.

CONCLUSION *n.* A *conclusion* is anything that follows reasonably from something else. In an argument, the conclusion is a statement that follows from supporting facts and reasons. In a literary work, the conclusion is the final part, or ending, of the work.

CONTRAST *n.* *Contrast* is the process of observing and pointing out differences. If, for example, you were to contrast writers of the Neoclassical and Romantic eras, you might point out the following differences:

1. Politics: The Neoclassicists were conservatives; the Romantics were liberals or radicals.
2. Style: The Neoclassicists used harmonious, ordered, stylized language; the Romanticists used language modeled on ordinary speech or language that was grand, heroic, and exuberant.
3. Social or ethical stance: The Neoclassicists stressed acceptable social norms; the Romanticists stressed the freedom of the individual.
4. Attitude toward nature: The Neoclassicists loved nature when it was controlled and ordered, as in a garden; the Romanticists loved nature in its uncontrolled, wild state.

See *Comparison*.

DEDUCTION *n.* *Deduction* is a form of argument in which the conclusion has to be true if the premises are true. Consider the following arguments:

Major premise: People living in the eighteenth century had no experience of electric lights, automobiles, computers, or airplanes.

Minor premise: Dr. Johnson lived in the eighteenth century.
Conclusion: Dr. Johnson had no experience of electric lights, automobiles, computers, or airplanes.

Major premise: All sonnets have fourteen lines.
Minor premise: Andrew Marvell's "To His Coy Mistress" has forty-six lines.
Conclusion: Andrew Marvell's "To His Coy Mistress" is not a sonnet.

If you accept the premises of these arguments, then you must also accept their conclusions. Therefore, these arguments are deductions.

See *Generalization, Induction,* and *Inference*.

DEFINITION *n.* *Definition* is the process of explaining the meaning of a word or a phrase. Definition is essential to communication because it establishes agreed-upon meanings for words.

The simplest type of definition, *ostensive definition,* involves pointing to something and saying its name. If, for example, you point to an object and say, "typewriter," you are giving an ostensive definition of the word *typewriter.* The word is defined by the observable characteristics of the object that is referred to.

Another common type of definition is the kind found in dictionaries, *lexical definition.* Lexical definition uses words to explain the meanings of other words. Some common types of lexical definition are definitions by synonym, by antonym, by example, and by genus and differentia.

In a *definition by synonym,* one uses a word or a phrase that has the same meaning as the word being defined: A *drama* is "a play."

In a *definition by antonym,* one uses a word or a phrase with an opposite meaning along with a negation such as *no* or *not: Free verse* is "poetry that does not have a regular meter."

In a definition by example, one lists things to which the term being defined applies: *Epic poems* include Homer's *Iliad* and *Odyssey,* Virgil's

Aeneid, Dante's *The Divine Comedy,* and Milton's *Paradise Lost.*

In a *genus and differentia* definition, one places the thing to be defined into a general category, or *genus,* and then one shows how the thing being defined differs from other things in the general category:

> To be defined: Epic
> Genus, or category: narrative poem
> Differentia: long
>   about the adventures of heroes or gods
> Definition: An *epic* is "a long narrative poem about the adventures of heroes or gods."

Whenever you use words that your audience may not understand, define these words. Use the methods of lexical definition explained here.

EITHER/OR FALLACY See *Logical Fallacy.*

EVALUATION *n.* *Evaluation* is the process of making a judgment about the quality or value of something. When you make an evaluation of a work of literature, bear in mind these guidelines:

1. Make your evaluation specific. An evaluation such as "I hated it" or "It's a wonderful book" is too vague.
2. Base your evaluation on a clear standard, or criterion, of judgment.
3. Support your evaluation with evidence drawn from the work.

For more information on criteria for evaluation, see the lesson on Evaluating a Literary Work, on page 1376.
See *Opinion* and *Judgment.*

EVIDENCE *n.* *Evidence* is factual information presented to support an argument. When you write or speak about literature, the evidence that you use to support your statements will be details drawn from literary works. For example, consider the statement "The Old Man in Chaucer's 'The Pardoner's Tale' is Death personified." To support this interpretation you might provide the following evidence: The Old Man is described as being extremely aged, the Old Man possesses a ghostlike appearance, and the three young revellers are killed shortly after meeting the Old Man.

FACT *n.* A *fact* is a statement that can be proved true or false by evidence. For example, the following facts are true by definition:

> A *dollar* is equal to one hundred cents.
> A *conceit* is an extravagant or farfetched metaphor.

The following facts are true by observation:

> "Barbara Allan" and "Sir Patrick Spens" are both ballads.
> Some lyric poems are very short, and some are quite long.

When you write or speak about a literary work, use facts from the work to support the assertions that you make.
See *Opinion.*

FALSE ANALOGY See *Logical Fallacy.*

GENERALIZATION *n.* A *generalization* is a statement that applies to more than one thing. The following statements are generalizations:

> Elizabethan poetry often praised Queen Elizabeth I.
> Samuel Johnson's works contain many examples of the technique known as parallelism.

The first statement applies to more than one Elizabethan poem and the second to more than one of Samuel Johnson's works.

Deductive arguments often begin with generalizations. Consider the following deductive argument:

> Premise: (generalization) Novels are written in prose.
> Conclusion: Mary Shelley's novel *Frankenstein* is written in prose.

Inductive arguments often end with generalizations. Consider the following inductive argument:

> Premise: Tennyson's "The Splendor Falls" rhymes.
> Premise: Tennyson's "Crossing the Bar" rhymes.
> Premise: Tennyson's "The Lotos-Eaters" rhymes.
> Conclusion: (generalization) Many of Tennyson's poems rhyme.

When making generalizations, be careful to avoid overgeneralization, or making statements that are too broad. For example, the statement "All of Tennyson's poems rhyme" is too broad because some of his poems, such as "Ulysses," do not rhyme. To avoid overgeneralization, use qualifiers, or words that limit statements. Some common qualifiers include a *few, some, many,* and *most.*
See *Deduction, Induction,* and *Stereotype.*

INDUCTION *n.* *Induction* is a form of argument in which the conclusion is probably but not necessarily true. For example, if you read several comic plays and notice that each ends with a marriage, you might conclude that "All comedies end with marriages." However, you could not be certain of the truth of this statement unless you had read all the comedies ever written.

Most of what people know about the world is learned by induction. Each individual generalizes, based on his or her limited experience. Thus a small child sees several objects with wheels, each of which is called a car, and the child thus generalizes that all wheeled objects are cars. Eventually, the child will learn to limit this inductive generalization based on additional information.

Literary study often involves using induction. After you have read several works by one author or several works written in a particular period, you might, for example, make generalizations about the author or about the period. Remember, however, that such generalizations are subject to error and should be qualified by words and phrases such as *probably* or *most likely.*
See *Deduction, Generalization,* and *Inference.*

INFERENCE *n.* An *inference* is any logical or reasonable conclusion based on known facts or accepted premises. The conclusions of both deductive and inductive arguments are inferences. Reading actively involves continually making inferences based on details presented in the work being read.
See *Conclusion, Deduction,* and *Induction.*

INTERPRETATION *n.* *Interpretation* is the process of determining the meaning or significance of speech, writing, art, music, or actions. The interpretation of a literary work involves many different processes. These include the following:
1. Reading carefully and actively and responding to each new detail
2. Examining one's own responses to the work and identifying the details that create these responses
3. Being alert to patterns and relations that emerge during the reading of the work
4. Analyzing the work into its parts, studying these parts, and determining how the parts relate to one another and to the whole
5. Pulling together one's observations about the work to make generalizations about the significance, or meaning, of the work as a whole.

Interpretation usually aims at making clear the central theme of a work. For example, an interpretation of Percy Bysshe Shelley's "Ozymandias," on page 702 might read as follows: "'Ozymandias' is a poem about the vanity of worldly pretension." Of course, any such interpretation must be supported by evidence from the work. A sound interpretation is one that accounts for all the important parts of a work and that is not contradicted by any part of the work.
See *Analysis.*

JUDGMENT *n.* A *judgment* is a statement about the quality or value of something. A sound

judgment of a literary work is one that is based on evidence derived from careful reading and thoughtful analysis.
See *Evaluation* and *Opinion*.

LOADED WORDS See *Propaganda Technique*.

LOGICAL FALLACY *n. phrase* A *logical fallacy* is an error in reasoning. In the attempt to make persuasive arguments, people often fall into such errors. The following logical fallacies are quite common:

1. *Begging the question:* This fallacy occurs when someone assumes the truth of the statement to be proved without providing any evidence to support the statement. For example: "Of course, everyone knows that contemporary poetry is obscure." (No evidence is given to support the claim.)
2. *Circular reasoning:* This fallacy occurs when the evidence given to support a claim is simply a restatement of the claim in other words. For example: "Wordsworth should be considered a nature poet because he wrote poems about nature." (The second part of the sentence simply restates the claim made in the first part.)
3. *Either/or fallacy:* This fallacy occurs when someone claims that there are only two alternatives when there are actually more. For example: "William Blake was either a madman or a confused mystic." (The statement ignores a third possibility—that Blake was a sane but highly idiosyncratic writer who invented his own elaborate code, or symbol system, in which to express his ideas.)
4. *False analogy:* This fallacy occurs when someone falsely assumes that two subjects are similar in one respect just because they are similar in some other respect. For example: "The English people and the American people speak the same language. Therefore, their cultures must be alike." (The false assumption is made that because these peoples are similar in one respect they are similar in all respects.)
5. *Overgeneralization:* This fallacy occurs when someone makes a statement that is too broad or too inclusive. For example: "The Victorians were imperialists." (This statement is only partially true, for some British citizens of the Victorian Age opposed the government's imperialistic colonial policies.)
6. *Post hoc, ergo propter hoc:* (a Latin phrase meaning "After this, therefore because of this") This fallacy occurs when someone falsely assumes that an event is caused by another event simply because of the order of the events in time. For example: "After adopting the Christian religion, the Anglo-Saxons were defeated by the Normans. Therefore, the adoption of Christianity must have led to the Anglo-Saxon defeat." (This argument is, of course, completely fallacious. The adoption of Christianity took place long before the Norman invasion, and the Normans themselves were Christians. The defeat was actually due to other factors such as the divisiveness among the Anglo-Saxons, the surprise nature of the invasion, and the superiority of the Norman soldiers.)

When you do persuasive writing or speaking, try to avoid these logical fallacies. Also be on guard against these fallacies in other people's writing and speech.

MAIN IDEA *n. phrase* The *main idea* is the central point that a speaker or writer wants to communicate. Sometimes, as in the thesis statement of an essay, the main idea is stated directly. However, often the main idea of a literary work is implied. The reader must identify the main idea based on clues provided by other elements of the work.
See *Purpose*.

OBJECTIVE *adj.* Something is *objective* if it has to do with a reality that is independent of any

particular person's mind or personal, internal experiences. Statements of fact are objective because anyone can, at least in principle, verify them. Statements of opinion, on the other hand, are not objective because they express an individual's personal feelings and impressions. However, statements of opinion can be supported by objective facts. When you write about a literary work, you should strive to be objective. That is, you should support your statements with factual evidence that other people can verify by reading the work themselves.
See *Subjective.*

OPINION *n.* An *opinion* is a statement that can be supported by facts but that is not itself a fact. Opinions may be judgments, predictions, or statements of policy or obligation. The following are opinions:

Judgment: William Butler Yeats is the greatest poet of the twentieth century.
Prediction: Third World writers will play an increasingly prominent role in the literature of the late twentieth and early twenty-first centuries.
Obligation: We must continually affirm the value of a literary education.

Whenever you express an opinion, you should support it with facts and with reasoned arguments.
See *Fact, Judgment,* and *Prediction.*

OVERGENERALIZATION See *Logical Fallacy.*

PARAPHRASE *n.* A *paraphrase* is a restatement in different words. When writing about literature, paraphrase can be used to support an interpretation or an analysis when the exact words of the original are not essential to the argument. However, when paraphrasing, be careful not to alter the meaning of the original. Simply translate what the writer said into equivalent words of your own.

POST HOC, ERGO PROPTER HOC See *Logical Fallacy.*

PREDICTION *n.* *Prediction* is the act of making statements about the future. An active reader continually makes and tests predictions on the basis of details presented in the work being read. For example, while reading about the Lilliputians' adoption of Lemuel Gulliver, on page 520, you might predict that these tiny people will put the giant Gulliver to military use. Gulliver's size in comparison to his hosts' makes this an obvious possibility, one that the story confirms.

Authors often supply hints or clues as to what will happen later in their works. This technique of providing clues to later events is called *foreshadowing,* and foreshadowing is one of the reasons why prediction of events in a literary work is possible. Often, of course, readers simply base their predictions on expectations related to the genre of the work being read or on general knowledge about how people, and thus characters, react in certain situations.

Sometimes an author will intentionally mislead readers into making predictions that later prove false. This technique, often used in mystery and detective fiction, makes possible the occurrence of surprise endings.
See *Opinion.*

PROBLEM SOLVING *n. phrase* *Problem solving* is the process by which a person comes up with a solution to some difficulty. The following are some general guidelines for solving any sort of problem:
1. State the problem as precisely as possible.
2. Identify your goal.
3. Identify the differences between the goal state (the situation that will exist when the problem is solved) and the initial state (the situation that exists at the beginning of your work on the problem).
4. Take steps to reduce the differences between the goal state and the initial state.

The following rules of thumb, or *heuristics,* are useful for solving many types of problems.

1. Break the problem down into parts and solve the parts separately.
2. Think of similar problems that you have solved before and see whether the same solutions can be used.
3. Draw a diagram or sketch to clarify the problem.
4. Make a pros-and-cons chart.
5. Use brainstorming, freewriting, clustering, and other general thinking strategies to generate possible solutions.
6. Restate the problem in various ways or from several points of view.
7. Define any key terms or concepts related to the problem.
8. Examine your ideas about the problem to see whether they are too rigid. See if there aren't new ways of conceiving the problem and its solution.
9. Ask yourself "What if" questions to generate possible solutions.
10. Ask someone to help you with parts of the problem that are especially difficult.
11. Use means/ends analysis. That is, at each point in your work toward solving the problem, pause to determine whether you are advancing toward a solution.

Use these techniques or strategies to solve the many types of problems that you encounter in everyday life, including problems related to writing and to interpreting works of literature.

PROPAGANDA TECHNIQUE *n. phrase* A *propaganda technique* is an improper appeal to emotion used for the purpose of swaying the opinions of an audience. The following propaganda techniques often appear in persuasive writing and speech.

1. *Bandwagon:* This technique involves encouraging people to think or act in some way simply because other people are doing so. For example: "Everyone's reading this new thriller. You should, too."
2. *Loaded words:* This technique involves using words with strong positive or negative connotations. Name-calling is an example of the use of loaded words. So is any use of words that are charged with emotional associations. For example: "I detest Kipling because his writings are *undemocratic.*"
3. *Snob appeal:* This technique involves making a direct or implied claim that one should act or think in a certain way because of the high social status associated with the action or thought. For example: "All really sophisticated readers appreciate Alexander Pope."
4. *Vague, undefined terms:* This technique involves promoting or challenging an opinion by using words that are so vague or so poorly defined as to be almost meaningless. For example: "Librarians shouldn't be allowed to purchase *awful* books like these."

Try to avoid propaganda techniques in your own speech and writing, and be on guard against these techniques in the speech and writing of others.

PURPOSE *n.* The *purpose* is the goal, or aim, of a literary work. Works are often classified as narrative, descriptive, expository, or persuasive, based on their purposes. A narrative work tells a story. A descriptive work portrays a person, place, or thing. An expository work explains something or provides information. A persuasive work attempts to move an audience to adopt some opinion or to take some action. Many works combine these purposes. For example, a narrative work may also be, in places, descriptive, or a persuasive work may be, in places, expository.

Of course, most works also have more specific purposes. For example, Milton claimed that the purpose of *Paradise Lost,* an excerpt from which appears on page 449, was "to justify

God's ways to man.'' When used in this specific sense, the word *purpose* is equivalent to *theme*.

REASON *n.* A *reason* is a statement made in support of some conclusion. The term *reason* is also used as a verb to signify the human ability to think logically and rationally.

SNOB APPEAL See *Propaganda Technique.*

SOURCE *n.* A *source* is anything from which ideas and information are taken. Some books, such as dictionaries, encyclopedias, atlases, almanacs, and biographies are specifically designed to be used as sources. Other types of sources include interviews with people, magazine articles, computerized information services, booklets, television programs, films, and recordings. Of course, every writer draws on at least one other very important source—his or her own experiences.

There are two basic types of sources, primary and seconary. A *primary source* is a first-hand account. Conversations, speeches, legal documents, and letters are examples of primary sources. *Secondary sources* are accounts or compilations written or prepared by people who are not eyewitnesses. A recent biography of Samuel Johnson would be a secondary source about Johnson's life. A collection of Johnson's letters would be a primary source. Boswell's *Life of Samuel Johnson,* an excerpt from which appears on page 576, is a primary source for some facts and a secondary source for others.

Whenever you gather information for use in a speech or in a paper, make sure that your sources are unbiased, up-to-date, authoritative, and reliable. Also make sure that you credit your sources properly by means of footnotes, endnotes, or in-text references.

STEREOTYPE *n.* A *stereotype* is a fixed or conventional notion or characterization. Examples of stereotypical characters include the absent-minded professor, the suffering artist, the backroom politician, and the mad scientist. Although writers occasionally use stereotypes when they haven't the space to develop complete, rounded characters, good writers generally avoid stereotyping. Of course, in everyday life stereotyping leads people to make false assumptions about other people and groups of people. Stereotyping occurs because of the unfortunate human tendency to overgeneralize. See *Generalization.*

SUBJECTIVE *adj.* Something is *subjective* if it is based on personal reactions or emotions rather than on some objective reality. A reader's reaction to a work of literature is, therefore, subjective. However, this subjective reaction can be supported by means of objective evidence drawn from the work. See *Objective.*

SUMMARIZE *v.* To *summarize* something is to restate it briefly in other words. Generally, one summarizes long works and paraphrases short passages. When writing about literary works, you may sometimes find it useful to summarize events from literary history, positions taken by critics, or events in the works themselves. Always make sure that your summary is an accurate reflection of the original. In particular, make sure not to give more or less weight to particular parts than was given in the material that you are summarizing.

VAGUE, UNDEFINED TERMS See *Propaganda Technique.*

GLOSSARY

READING THE GLOSSARY ENTRIES

The words in this glossary are from selections appearing in your textbook. Each entry in the glossary contains the following parts:

1. Entry Word. This word appears at the beginning of the entry, in boldface type.

2. Pronunciation. The symbols in parentheses tell how the entry word is pronounced. If a word has more than one possible pronunciation, the most common of these pronunciations is given first.

3. Part of Speech. Appearing after the pronunciation, in italics, is an abbreviation that tells the part of speech of the entry word. The following abbreviations have been used:

n. noun   **p.** pronoun   **v.** verb
adj. adjective   **adv.** adverb   **conj.** conjunction

4. Definition. This part of the entry follows the part-of-speech abbreviation and gives the meaning of the entry word as used in the selection in which it appears.

KEY TO PRONUNCIATION SYMBOLS USED IN THE GLOSSARY

The following symbols are used in the pronunciations that follow the entry words:

Symbol	Key Words	Symbol	Key Words
a	asp, fat, parrot	b	bed, fable, dub
ā	ape, date, play	d	dip, beadle, had
ä	ah, car, father	f	fall, after, off
		g	get, haggle, dog
e	elf, ten, berry	h	he, ahead, hotel
ē	even, meet, money	j	joy, agile, badge
		k	kill, tackle, bake
I	is, hit, mirror	l	let, yellow, ball
ī	ice, bite, high	m	met, camel, trim
		n	not, flannel, ton
ō	open, tone, go	p	put, apple, tap
ô	all, horn, law	r	red, port, dear
o͞o	ooze, tool, crew	s	sell, castle, pass
o͝o	look, pull, moor	t	top, cattle, hat
yo͞o	use, cute, few	v	vat, hovel, have
yo͝o	united, cure, globule	w	will, always, swear
oi	oil, point, toy	y	yet, onion, yard
ou	out, crowd, plow	z	zebra, dazzle, haze
u	up, cut, color	ch	chin, catcher, arch
ʉr	urn, fur, deter	sh	she, cushion, dash
		t/h	thin, nothing, truth
ə	a in ago	t͟h	then, father, lathe
	e in agent	zh	azure, leisure
	i in sanity	ŋ	ring, anger, drink
	o in comply	′	[indicates that a
	u in focus		following l or n is a
ər	perhaps, murder		syllabic consonant, as in
			able (ā′ b'l)]

This pronunciation key is from *Webster's New World Dictionary,* Second College Edition. Copyright © 1986 by Simon & Schuster. Used by permission.

A

abasement (ə bās′ mənt)   *n.* Condition of being put down or humbled

abash (ə bash′)   *v.* To make ashamed or ill at ease

abate (ə bāt′)   *v.* To lessen; to put an end to

abhorred (əb hôrd′)   *adj.* Something that is regarded with horror or loathing

abjure (əb jo͝or′)   *v.* To vow to give up; repudiate

ablution (ab lo͞o′ shən)   *n.* Washing or cleansing of the body

abstract (ab′ strakt)   *n.* Brief summary stating main points

acanthus (ə kan′ t/həs)   *n.* Thistlelike plant

accede (ak sēd′)   *v.* (With to) To yield to; agree upon

accursed (ə kʉr′ sid)   *adj.* Hateful

acrid (ak′ rid)   *adj.* Sharp; bitter

adamantine (ad′ ə man′ tēn)   *adj.* Unbreakable

adjure (ə jo͝or′)   *v.* To appeal to earnestly

advert (ad vʉrt′)   *v.* To call attention

affectation (af′ ek tā′ shən)   *n.* Pretense

affected (ə fek′ tid)   *adj.* In a manner not true to the person

affliction (ə flik′ shən)   *n.* State of pain or misery, pain; suffering

aggrandizement (ə gran′ diz mənt)   *n.* Increase in power

alacrity (ə lak′ rə tē)   *n.* Willingness

allure (ə lo͞or′)   *v.* To entice; charm; induce

amaranth (am′ ə rant/h′)   *n.* Imaginary flower that never fades or dies

amass (ə mas′)   *v.* To gather together

amity (am′ ə tē)   *n.* Peaceful relations

anarchy (an′ ər kē)   *n.* Absence of government; confusion, disorder, and violence

anglophobia (aŋ glə fō′ bē ə)   *n.* Hatred or fear of England or things English

animadversion (an′ ə mad vʉr′ zhən)   *n.* Unfavorable comment

anointed (ə noint′ id)   *adj.* Declared sacred

anterior (an tir′ ē ər)   *adj.* At or toward the front

antiquity (an tik′ wə tē)   *n.* Ancient times

apace (ə pās′)   *adv.* Swiftly: with speed

aperture (ap′ ər chər)   *n.* An opening

apostate (ə päs′ tāt′)   *adj.* Denying former religious conviction

apothecary (ə pät/h′ ə ker ē)   *n.* A pharmacist or druggist; person who formerly prepared drugs

apparition (ap′ ə rish′ ən)   *n.* A ghost

appendage (ə pen′ dij)   *n.* Something added on

application (ap′ lə kā′ shən)   *n.* A specific act or case

apprehension (ap rə hen′ shən)   *n.* Fear, concern

appropriate (ə prō′ prē āt′)   *v.* To borrow without giving credit

arbiter (är′ bə tər)   *n.* Judge, umpire

arboreal (är bôr′ ē əl)   *adj.* Situated near or among trees

ardor (är′ dər)   *n.* Great warmth or intensity of passion, emotion, desire and so forth

armament (är′ mə mənt)   *n.* Arms, weapon

ascendancy (ə send′ ən sē)   *n.* A major or dominating influence

aspire (ə spīr′)   v. To be ambitious

asperity (as per′ ə tē)   n. Ill temper; irritability

asphodel (as′ fə del′)   n. Plant with yellow or white lilylike flowers

assay (a sā′)   v. To try, attempt; prove or test

assiduity (as ə dyōō′ ə tē)   n. Diligence

assignation (as′ ig nā′ shən)   n. An appointment to meet

asunder (ə sun′ dər)   adv. Apart; in separate directions

atrophy (a′ trə fē)   v. To waste away

augment (ôg ment′)   v. To make greater; enlarge

august (ô gust′)   adj. Inspiring awe and reverence

austere (ô stir′)   adj. Having a stern personality or appearance; somber

avarice (av′ ər is)   n. Greed

aver (ə vur′)   v. To state to be true

avocation (av′ ə kā′ shən)   n. Something that calls one away or distracts from something

avouch (ə vouch′)   v. To assert positively; affirm

avow (ə vou′)   v. To swear

awe (ô)   n. Fear mixed with great respect

azurous (az′ ər əs)   adj. Purple-blue

B

baleful (bāl′ fəl)   adj. Of or with evil intent

balm (bäm)   n. Anything healing or soothing

balustrade (bal′ ə strād′)   n. A railing supported by small pillars of stone or wood

baneful (bān′ fəl)   adj. Full of harm; destructive

barbarous (bär′ bər əs)   adj. Primitive; uncivilized

barrow (bar′ ō)   n. Heap of earth or rocks marking a grave

Beelzebub (bē el′ zə bub′)   n. Traditionally, the chief devil, or Satan

beget (bi get′)   v. To bring into being

belie (bi lī′)   v. To prove false; contradict

benison (ben′ ə z′n)   n. Blessing; benediction

bent (bent)   adj. Determined; resolved

beseech (bi sēch′)   v. To ask earnestly; entreat; implore

betokeneth (bi tō′ k'n et/h)   v. To be a sign of; to indicate

blasphemous (blas′ fə məs)   adj. Disrespectful of God; impious

blight (blīt)   n. Condtion of withering

blithe (blīt/h)   adj. Cheerful

boatswain (bō′ s'n)   n. Warrant officer or petty officer in charge of a ship's deck crew, rigging, and anchors

bole (bōl)   n. Tree trunk

boon (bōōn)   n. Something good or pleasant that is given, as a blessing

brazen (brā′ z'n)   adj. 1. Made of brass; 2. bold; shameless

burnished (bur′ nisht)   adj. Made shiny by daily use

C

caitiff (kāt′ if)   n. Evil person

canker (kaŋ′ kər)   n. Ulcer-like sore on the lips or in the mouth

cant (kant)   n. Insincere talk

caprice (kə prēs′)   n. A tendency to act on whim

careen (kə rēn′)   v. To lean to one side

career (kə rir′)   v. To move swiftly forward

carriage (kar′ ij)   n. A way of bearing oneself; deportment

casement (kās′ mənt)   n. A window that is hinged at the sides

castigation (kas′ tə gā shən)   n. A punishment

cataract (kat′ ə rakt′)   n. A waterfall

cavil (kav′ 'l)   v. To raise trivial objections

certitude (sur′ tə tōod)   n. A certainty

chaffinch (chaf′ finch′)   n. Small European songbird

chary (cher′ ē)   adj. Not giving freely

chaste (chāst)   adj. Pure; untainted; unblemished

chastise (chas tīz′)   v. To condemn sharply; scold

chide (chīd)   v. To scold; rebuke

chimerical (ki mir′ i k'l)   adj. Imaginary; unreal

choleric (käl′ ər ik)   adj. Easily provoked to anger

chrysalis (kris′ əl əs)   n. A cocoon of a butterfly

churl (churl)   n. 1. same as ceorl; farm laborer; peasant: 2. Surly, ill-bred person; boor

circumscribe (sur′ kəm skrīb′)   v. To limit; confine

circumspection (sur′ kəm spek′ shən)   n. Caution

clamorous (klam′ ər əs)   adj. Noisy

cleave (klēv)   v. Split apart

cloyed (kloid)   adj. Made sick by an overdose

cluster (klus′ tər)   n. A group, gathering; bunch, as of grapes for wine

cockle (käk′ 'l)   n. An edible shellfish with two heart-shaped shells

colonnade (käl′ ə nād′)   n. A series of columns set at regular intervals

colossal (kə läs′ 'l)   adj. Enormous

compact (kəm pakt′)   v. To put together

complaisance (kəm plā′ z'ns)   n. A desire to be agreeable

compose (kəm pōz′)   v. To get oneself together emotionally; calm

compound (käm′ pound)   v. To join; combine

compunctious (kəm punk′ shəs)   adj. Sorrowful; regretful

conciliatory (kən sil′ ē ə tôr′ ē)   adj. Agreeable

condone (kən dōn′)   v. To approve; authorize

conflagration (kän′ flə grā′ shən)   n. A great fire

conjecture (kən jek′ chər)   v. To guess

constant (kän′ stənt)   adj. Faithful; unchanging; unceasing

constitution (kän′ stə tōō′ shən)   n. Makeup (of a person)

consummation (kän′ sə mā′ shən)   n. State of fulfillment or completion

consumed (kən sōōm'd′)   adj. Overtaken, overwhelmed

contention (kən ten′ shən)   n. A controversy; dispute

contentious (kən ten′ shəs)   adj. Of questionable validity

contretemps (kōn trə tän′)   n. An awkward mishap

contrite (kən trīt′)   adj. Willing to repent or atone

conviction (kən vik′ shən)   n. A belief in something meaningful, such as a creed

convulse (kən vuls′)   v. To shake; move violently

coomb (kōōm)   n. A deep, narrow valley

copious (kō′ pē əs)   adj. Abundant, plentiful

coquet (kō ket′)   v. To flirt

corporeal (kôr pôr′ ē əl)   adj. Of the body

countenance (koun' tə nəns)   *n.* A face

coupe (kōō pā')   *n.* A closed carriage with seats on one side

courtier (kôr' tē ər)   *n.* An attendant at a royal court

covenant (kuv' ə nənt)   *n.* A solemn, binding agreement

coveted (kuv' it əd)   *v.* Wanted eagerly

covetousness (kuv' it əs nəs)   *n.* Greediness

cowed (koud)   *adj.* Made to feel timid or fearful

coy (koi)   *adj.* Unwilling to make a commitment, *not* the modern sense of "pretending to be shy."

credulity (krə dōō' lə tē)   *n.* Tendency to believe too readily

crimp (krimp)   *v.* To shape; crease

cryptogram (krip' tə gram)   *n.* A coded message

cur (kʉr)   *n.* A dog of mixed breeds

curb (kʉrb)   *n.* Chain or strap around a horse's lower jaw attached to the bit to check the horse

curlew (kʉr' lōō)   *n.* Large, brownish wading bird with long legs

cynical (sin' i k'l)   *adj.* Distrustful; sneering

D

dah (dä)   *n.* A knife

dais (dā' is)   *n.* A platform

dale (dāl)   *n.* A hollow; valley

dappled (dap' 'ld)   *adj.* Speckled; having more than one color

dauntless (dônt' lis)   *adj.* Fearless

decamp (di kamp')   *v.* To leave suddenly

decrepitude (di krep' ə tōōd)   *n.* State of being old and broken down

deference (def' ər əns)   *n.* Courtesy

degree (di grē')   *n.* Social class

deign (dān)   *v.* To condescend; lower oneself

deleterious (del' ə tir' ē əs)   *adj.* Harmful to health; injurious

demesne (di mān')   *n.* The lands of an estate

deride (di rīd')   *v.* To make fun of; ridicule

derisive (di rī' siv)   *adj.* Mocking

descant (des kant')   *v.* To talk at length

desist (di zist')   *v.* To stop

desolate (des' ə lit)   *adj.* Deserted; forlorn

despoil (di spoil')   *v.* To take away one's possessions

despotic (de spät' ik)   *adj.* Tyrannical

destitute (des' tə tōōt)   *adj.* Lacking

desultory (des' 'l tôr ē)   *adj.* Passing from point to point aimlessly

didactic (dī dak' tik)   *adj.* Instructive

diffidence (dif' ə dəns)   *n.* Shyness; hesitation

diffusive (di fyōō' siv)   *adj.* Spread out

dirge (dʉrj)   *n.* A song of mourning

disabused (dis' ə byōōzd')   *adj.* Freed from false ideas

discourse (dis kôrs')   *v.* To talk about; discussing

discreet (dis krēt')   *adj.* Wise; prudent

discursive (dis kʉr' siv)   *adj.* Reaching conclusions by a series of logical steps, as opposed to intuition

dispensation (dis pən sā' s/hən)   *n.* Religious system or belief

distemper (dis tem' pər)   *n.* Infectious disease, in this case the plague

divers (dī' vərz)   *adj.* Varied; having many parts (archaic spelling)

diversion (də vər' z/hən)   *n.* A pastime; amusement

divination (dlv' ə nā' s/hən)   *n.* A clever guess

divining (də vīn' iŋ)   *adj.* Guessing; intuitive

doleful (dōl' fəl)   *adj.* Filled with sadness

dominion (də min' yən)   *n.* A place of rule; home territory

dotage (dōt' ij)   *n.* Second childhood, state of senility

doughty (dout' ē)   *adj.* Brave

dower (dou' ər)   *n.* A gift

dowry (dou' rē)   *n.* The property that a woman brings to her husband at marriage

drear (drir)   *adj.* Dreary; melancholy

dregs (dregz)   *n.* Sediment of liquids

dryad (drī əd)   *n.* In classical mythology, a wood nymph

dudgeon (duj' ən)   *n.* Angry resentment; rage

dulcimer (dul' sə mər)   *n.* Musical instrument with metal strings which produce sounds when struck by two small hammers

dun (dun)   *adj.* Dull grayish brown

dunt (dunt)   *n.* Heavy, dull-sounding blow

E

eglantine (eg' lən tīn)   *n.* Sweetbrier or honeysuckle

elocution (el' ə kyōō' s/hən)   *n.* The art of public speaking

elongated (i lôŋ' gāt id)   *adj.* Lengthened; stretched

eloquent (el' ə kwənt)   *adj.* Very expressive

empyreal (em pir' ē əl)   *adj.* Referring to the indestructible substance of which Heaven, or the empyrean, is composed

encomium (en kō' mē əm)   *n.* The formal expression of praise or tribute

encumber (in kum' bər)   *v.* To weigh down with a load

engender (in jen' dər)   *v.* To bring into being; cause to exist

enisled (in īld')   *adj.* Isolated, as if placed on an island

entreat (in trēt')   *v.* To beg; plead

envisage (en viz' ij)   *v.* To form a mental picture of; imagine

equipage (ek' wə pij)   *n.* Horses and carriages

equivocate (i kwiv' ə kāt')   *v.* To tell falsehoods

escritoire (es' krə twär')   *n.* An ornamental writing desk or table

eternize (i tʉr' nīz)   *v.* To make everlasting

evanescence (ev' ə nes' 'ns)   *n.* Gradual disappearance, especially from sight

even (ē' vən)   *adj.* Parallel; on the same level with; conforming to

exact (ig zakt')   *v.* To demand; compel

exorciser (ek' sôr sīz' ər)   *n.* A sorcerer; magician

expanse (ik spans')   *n.* A wide, continuous stretch, as of land

expedient (ik spē' dē ənt)   *n.* Device used in an emergency

expiate (ek' spē āt')   *v.* To make amends for; atone for; forgive; absolve

expostulate (ik späs' o/hə lāt)   *v.* To reason earnestly with

extradition (eks′ trə di∫′ ən)   *n.* The release of an accused person into the custody of one state by another state

F

faceted (fas′ ə tid)   *adj.* Having many sides
fathom (fa∫′ əm)   *n.* A unit of measure for the depth of water; a fathom is six feet
fastidious (fas tid′ ē əs)   *adj.* Hard to please
feign (fān)   *v.* To pretend
felicity (fə lis′ ə tē)   *n.* An apt expression or thought
fen (fen)   *n.* Marsh or bog
fettered (fet′ ər'd)   *adj.* Chained; confined
fickle (fik′ ′l)   *adj.* Unfaithful
firmament (fʉr′ mə mənt)   *n.* Sky, viewed poetically as a solid arch or vault
firth (furth)   *n.* The narrow arm of a sea
fleur-de-lys (flʉr′ də lēz′)   *n.* An emblem resembling a lily or iris
fluency (floo′ ən sē)   *n.* Easy flow; smoothness
fold (fōld)   *n.* Pen in which to keep sheep
folly (fäl′ e)   *n.* A foolish action or belief
foment (fō ment′)   *v.* To stir up; incite
fond (fänd)   *adj.* Archaic: Foolish, not the modern sense of having affection for someone or something
foreshortened (fôr ∫hor′ t'nd)   *adj.* Narrowed by observer's angle of vision
forethink (fôr think′)   *v.* To foretell; predict
forlorn (fər lôrn′)   *adj.* Unhappy; in a pensive mood
former (fôr′ mər)   *adj.* Earlier; coming before
fret (fret)   *v.* To eat away
frolic (fräl′ ik)   *adj.* Merry
furbished (fʉr′ bi∫hd)   *adj.* Brightened; polished
furlong (fʉr′ lôŋ)   *n.* A unit for measuring distance; a furlong is equal to one eighth of a mile
fustian (fus′ ∫hən)   *n.* A coarse cotton cloth

G

gaiters (gāt′ ərz)   *n.* Cloth coverings for the instep and lower leg
gall (gôl)   *n.* Something bitter or distasteful
galled (gôld)   *adj.* Injured or made sore by rubbing or chafing
gang (gaŋ)   *v.* To go or walk (Scot.)
garnished (gär′ ni∫ht)   *adj.* Decorated; trimmed
garrulous (gar′ ə ləs)   *adj.* Tending to talk continuously
gaudy (gôd′ ē)   *adj.* Showy in a tasteless way
gaunt (gônt)   *adj.* Thin
genial (jēn′ yəl)   *adj.* Kindly, cordial
gesticulate (jes tik′ yə lāt′)   *v.* To communicate excitedly by gestures
gigantified (jī gan′ tə fīd)   *adj.* Made to seem much larger
gisarme (gi zärm′)   *n.* A battle-ax
glean (glēn)   *v.* To pick from, as crops
glen (glen)   *n.* A valley
gowden (gou′ d'n)   *adj.* Golden
grace (grās)   *n.* God's favor or approval
grate (grāt)   *n.* Frame of metal bars used as a partition
gratuitous (grə too′ ə təs)   *adj.* Undeservedly or without reason
guerdon (gʉr′ d'n)   *n.* A reward
guile (gīl)   *n.* Artful trickery; cunning

H

habitation (hab′ ə tā′ ∫hən)   *n.* A home; dwelling
habituate (hə bi∫h′ oo wāt′)   *v.* To accustom to; to make used to
haft (haft)   *n.* Handle of a weapon or tool
haggard (hag′ ərd)   *adj.* Having a worn, gaunt, or wild look
halcyon (hal′ sē ən)   *adj.* Calm
halter (hôl′ tər)   *n.* Rope for hanging; hangman's noose
haply (hap′ lē)   *adv.* By chance
harbinger (här′ bin jər)   *n.* A forerunner
harmonious (här mō′ nē əs)   *adj.* In a manner that is in accordance
harry (har′ ē)   *v.* To harass
hauberk (hô′ bərk)   *n.* A coat of armor
haughty (hôt′ ē)   *adj.* Lofty
headrig (hed′ rig)   *n.* The part of a plow that turns over the soil; moldboard
health (helt∫h)   *n.* A wish for happiness, as in drinking a series of toasts
heraldic (hə ral′ dik)   *adj.* Resembling an English coat of arms
hermitage (hʉr′ mit ij)   *n.* A retreat suitable for meditation; originally, a hermit's dwelling
hew (hyoo)   *n.* Color; hue
hoary (hôr′ ē)   *adj.* White or gray with age
hobnailed (häb′ nāld)   *adj.* Studded with nails to prevent wear or slipping
husbandry (huz′ bən drē)   *n.* Farming

I

ignominy (ig′ nə min′ ē)   *n.* Humiliation; dishonor; disgrace
illimitable (i lim′ it ə b'l)   *adj.* Without limit or bounds; immeasurable
illumine (i loo′ min)   *v.* To light up
imminent (im′ ə nənt)   *adj.* Likely to happen soon
impaired (im perd′)   *v.* Diminished
imperiously (im pir′ ē əs lē)   *adv.* Arrogantly
impertinence (im pʉr′ t'n əns)   *n.* Rudeness
imperturbable (im′ pər tʉr′ bə b'l)   *adj.* Calm; not easily ruffled
impetuous (im pe∫h′ oo wəs)   *adj.* Given to rash or hasty action; doing things on the spur of the moment; tending to act impulsively, without thinking
impious (im′ pē əs)   *adj.* Disrespectful; irreverent, ungodly
importune (im′ pôr toon′)   *v.* To press with frequent requests; ask insistently
importuning (im pôr toon′ iŋ)   *v.* Begging, urging
imprecation (im′ prə kā′ ∫hən)   *n.* A curse
impressionistic (im pre∫h′ ə nis′ tik)   *adj.* Conveying a quick, overall picture
impudence (im′ pyoo dəns)   *n.* The quality of being rash or contrary
inarticulate (in′ är tik′ yə lit)   *adj.* Not able to speak
incessant (in ses′ 'nt)   *adj.* Never ceasing
incitement (in sīt′ mənt)   *n.* A cause to perform; encouragement
inconstancy (in kän′ stən sē)   *n.* A contradiction; fickleness; changeableness

incorrigible   (in kôr′ i jə b′l)   *adj.* Not capable of being corrected or of behaving better

inculcate   (in kul′ kāt)   *v.* To impress upon the mind by frequent repetition

indissoluble   (in′ di säl′ yoo b′l)   *adj.* Not able to be dissolved or undone

inexorable   (in ek′ sər ə b′l)   *adj.* Ongoing, with no sign of stopping

infirmity   (in fur′ mə tē)   *n.* Physical or mental defect; illness

ingenuous   (in jen′ yoo wəs)   *adj.* Naive; simple

inglorious   (in glôr′ ē əs)   *adj.* Little-known

inimical   (in im′ i k′l)   *adj.* Hostile; unfriendly

iniquity   (in ik′ wə tē)   *n.* Wickedness

innumerable   (in noo′ mər ə b′l)   *adj.* Too many to count

inordinate   (in ôr′ d′n it)   *adj.* Beyond reasonable limits

inquisition   (in′ kwə zish′ ən)   *n.* Any investigation that violates the privacy or rights of individuals

insipid   (in sip′ id)   *adj.* Not exciting or interesting; dull, lifeless

intemperance   (in tem′ pər əns)   *n.* Lack of restraint

intermit   (in tər mit′)   *v.* To stop for a time

intimation   (in′ tə mā′ s/hən)   *n.* A hint

inventory   (in′ vən tôr′ ē)   *n.* A list of possessions

invincible   (in vin′ sə b′l)   *adj.* Unconquerable

irascibly   (i ras′ ə b′lē)   *adv.* Irritably

irremediable   (ir i mē′ dē ə b′l)   *adj.* Incurable; incapable of being remedied

irrepressible   (ir′ i pres′ ə b′l)   *adj.* Not able to be restrained

isthmus   (is′ məs)   *n.* A narrow strip of land, with water on each side, connecting two larger land masses

J

Japonica   (jə pän′ i kə)   *n.* A spiny plant with pink or red flowers

jocund   (jäk′ ənd)   *adj.* Cheerful; pleasant; jovial

judicious   (joo dish′ əs)   *adj.* having or showing good judgment

K

keen   (kēn)   *adj.* Having a sharp edge or point

ken   (ken)   *n.* The range of sight or knowledge

ketch   (kech)   *n.* A two-masted sailing vessel

kindred   (kin′ drid)   *n.* Relatives; relations

knave   (nāv)   *n.* A scoundrel; cheater

knell   (nel)   *n.* The sound of a bell, especially one rung slowly, as at a funeral

kraal   (kräl)   *n.* A fenced-in enclosure for cattle or sheep

L

laboriously   (lə bôr′ ē əs lē)   *adv.* In a manner involving much hard work

laden   (lād′ ′n)   *adj.* Burdened; weighed down

lament   (lə ment′)   *v.* To mourn; wail; bemoan

lamentable   (lam′ ən tə b′l)   *adj.* Distressing

languid   (laŋ′ gwid)   *adj.* Slow, lacking energy

languish   (laŋ′ gwish)   *v.* To become weak or sickly looking

languor   (laŋ′ gər)   *n.* Weakness, fatigue

largess   (lär jes′)   *n.* Generous gift

largesse   (lär′ jes)   *n.* A nobility of spirit

lark   (lärk′)   *v.* To play around

laryngoscope   (lə riŋ′ gō skōp′)   *n.* An instrument for examining the throat

lay   (lā)   *n.* A short poem to be sung

leviathan   (lə vī′ ə thən)   *n.* A great sea monster

lexicographer   (lek′ sə käg′ rə fər)   *n.* One who compiles a dictionary

liege   (lēj)   *n.* A lord or king

lintel   (lin′ t′l)   *n.* A beam over a door

litany   (lit′ ′n ē)   *n.* A form of prayer in which a congregation repeats a fixed response

loath   (lōt/h)   *adj.* Reluctant; unwilling

lucrative   (loo′ krə tiv)   *adj.* Profitable

luminescent   (loo mə nes′ ′nt)   *adj.* Giving out light without much heat

lyric   (lir′ ik)   *n.* A poem, one of the major categories of poetry; in classical literature, a song accompanied by a lyre

M

madrigal   (mad′ ri gəl)   *n.* A song with parts for several voices with no musical accompaniment

magnanimous   (mag nan′ ə məs)   *adj.* Generously forgiving

mahout   (mə hoot′)   *n.* An elephant keeper and rider

mail   (māl)   *n.* A flexible body armor made of metal

maize   (māz)   *n.* Corn

malevolence   (mə lev′ ə ləns)   *n.* Ill will; spitefulness

malign   (mə līn′)   *v.* To speak evil of; defame

malignity   (mə lig′ nə tē)   *n.* A strong desire to harm others; deadliness

manifold   (man′ ə fōld)   *adj.* Of many kinds; varied

mead-hall   (mēd′ hôl)   *n.* A banquet hall; mead is a beverage made from fermented honey and water

measure   (mezh′ ər)   *n.* A quantity, dimension, size

megalith   (meg′ ə lit/h′)   *n.* A huge stone, especially one used in prehistoric monuments

melancholy   (mel′ ən käl′ ē)   *n.* Sadness; lowness of spirit

mendacity   (men das′ ə tē)   *n.* Lying

mesmerism   (mez′ mər iz′m)   *n.* Hypnotism

mestizo   (mes tē′ zō)   *adj.* Of Spanish and Indian parentage

metaphysical   (met ə fiz′ i k′l)   *adj.* Very abstract

mettlesome   (met′ ′l səm)   *adj.* High-spirited

minion   (min′ yən)   *n.* Attendant or agent

miscreant   (mis′ crē ənt)   *n.* A villain

misanthropist   (mis an′ t/hrə pist)   *n.* One who hates or mistrusts others

modish   (mōd′ ish)   *adj.* Fashionable

moleskin   (mōl′ skin)   *n.* Work clothes made from strong, twilled cotton fabric

molt   (mōlt)   *v.* Cast off; shed, as skin or feathers

moly   (mō′ lē)   *n.* In classical mythology, an herb of magic powers; European wild garlic

moorline   (moor′ līn)   *n.* The horizon where open, rolling wasteland meets the sky

morosely   (mə rōs′ lē)   *adv.* Sullenly; in bad humor

mortification   (môr′ tə fi kā′ s/hən)   *n.* A feeling of great shock and upset

multitudinous   (mul′ tə tood′ ′n əs)   *adj.* Existing in great numbers

munificence   (myoo nif′ ə s′ns)   *n.* Great generosity

myriad (mir′ ē əd)   *n.* Ten thousand; a great number of things

myrrh (mur)   *n.* A plant that produces a fragrant gum resin used in making incense and perfume

N

nativity (nə tiv′ ə tē′)   *n.* A birth, especially in regard to place and time

nunnery (nun′ ər ē)   *n.* A convent, a dwelling place for nuns

nymph (nimf)   *n.* In classical mythology, a minor nature goddess usually shown as a lovely young girl

O

obdurate (äb′ door ət, äb′ dyoor ət)   *adj.* Hardened against what is good or moral; stubborn, unyielding

obliquely (ə blēk′ lē)   *adv.* At a slant; indirectly

obliterate (ə blit′ ə rāt)   *v.* to destroy utterly

obstinacy (äb′ stə nə sē)   *n.* Stubbornness

ode (ōd)   *n.* A poem of varying line lengths and usually several stanzas, often addressed to someone; in classical literature, a poem to be sung, usually in praise of someone

odious (ō′ dē əs)   *adj.* Exciting repugnance or aversion; abhorrent; hateful; offensive; disgusting

officious (ə fish′ əs)   *adj.* Overly eager to please (obsolete meaning); offering unnecessary advice or services

ope (ōp)   *v.* To open

opiate (ō′ pē it)   *n.* Something that brings on relaxation or sleep

oppress (ə pres′)   *v.* To burden

oracle (ôr′ ə k'l)   *n.* In classical antiquity, the shrine in which a god spoke through a priest or priestess

orderly (ôr′ dər lē)   *n.* A soldier assigned to carry out orders of a superior

ordure (ôr′ jər)   *n.* Waste matter; excrement

ostentation (äs′ tən tā′ shən)   *n.* A showy display

overplus (ō′ vər plus′)   *n.* A surplus, abundance; enough over for others

overscrupulous (ō′ vər skroo′ pyə ləs)   *adj.* Overly concerned about details

P

pallor (pal′ ər)   *n.* An unnatural lack of color; paleness

palpable (pal′ pə b'l)   *adj.* Capable of being touched or felt

panegyric (pan′ ə jir′ ik)   *n.* A speech giving praise

parapet (par′ ə pit)   *n.* A low wall or railing

parley (pär′ lē)   *n.* A discussion

parquet (pär kā′)   *n.* A flooring of inlaid woodwork in geometric forms; wooden floors

passé (pa sā′)   *adj.* Stale

pastoral (pas′ tər al)   *adj.* Pertaining to country life

patron (pā′ trən)   *n.* One who gives financial aid to an artist or writer

penetrailia (pen′ ə trā′ lē ə)   *n.* The innermost parts

penitent (pen′ ə tənt)   *adj.* Feeling or showing sorrow for one's misdeeds or sins

penury (pen′ yə rē)   *n.* Poverty

perchance (pər chans′)   *adv.* Perhaps, possibly

peremptorily (pə remp′ tə ri lē)   *adv.* Decisively; without showing cause

perfidious (pər fid′ ē əs)   *adj.* Disloyal; treacherous

perfidiousness (pə fid′ ē əs nis)   *n.* The betrayal of trust

perfunctorily (pər funk′ tə ri lē)   *adv.* Carelessly

periwig (per′ ə wig′)   *n.* A type of wig often worn by men during the seventeenth and eighteenth centuries

pernicious (pər nish′ əs)   *adj.* Causing serious injury; deadly; evil; wicked

perpetual (pər pech′ oo wəl)   *adj.* Constant, unending

persistent (pər sis′ tənt)   *adj.* Continuing

perturbation (pur′ tər bā′ shən)   *n.* A disorder

peruke (pə rook′)   *n.* A wig

perversity (pər vur′ sə tē)   *n.* State of being wicked or wrong

perverted (pər vur′ tid)   *adj.* Distorted; corrupted

pestilence (pes′ t'l əns)   *n.* A highly contagious disease, such as plague

petulance (pech′ oo ləns)   *n.* Insolent behavior; peevishness; moodiness

phantasm (fan′ taz'm)   *n.* A supernatural form or shape

phlegm (flem)   *n.* Sluggishness

phoenix (fē′ niks)   *n.* A fabled bird of Arabia said to consume itself by fire every five hundred years and to rise renewed from its own ashes

phosphorescence (fäs′ fə res′ 'ns)   *n.* The property of shining in the dark

physiognomy (fiz′ ē äg′ nə mē)   *n.* Facial features thought to reveal character or disposition

piazza (pē az′ ə)   *n.* An open public square

piety (pī′ ə tē)   *n.* Devotion

pike (pīk)   *n.* A voracious freshwater fish

pince-nez (pans′ nā′)   *n.* Eyeglasses without sidepieces, held in place by springs gripping the bridge of the nose

pirouette (pir′ oo wet′)   *v.* To dance or whirl on one foot

pithead (pit′ hed)   *n.* The top of a mining pit or coal shaft

plagiarism (plā′ jə riz'm)   *n.* The passing off of another's work as one's own

platitude (plat′ ə tood′)   *n.* A statement lacking originality

plebian (pli bē′ ən)   *adj.* Common; ordinary

plutocracy (ploo täk′ rə sē)   *n.* The wealthy governing class

poke (pōk)   *n.* An overhanging projection, such as the brim on a woman's poke bonnet

portal (pôr′ t'l)   *n.* A door; gateway

posy (pō′ zē)   *n.* A bouquet

prate (prāt′)   *n.* To talk much and foolishly

prau (prau)   *n.* A swift Malayan boat with a large sail

prebendary (preb′ ən der′ ē)   *n.* In the Church of England, honorary clergyman

precedency (pres′ ə dən sē)   *n.* Priority because of rank

precipitate (pri sip′ ə tit)   *adj.* Steep

predominance (pri däm′ ə nans)   *n.* Superiority

preferment (pri fur′ mənt)   *n.* An advancement in rank

pregnant (preg′ nənt)   *adj.* Full of ideas; inventive

premonition (prē mə nish′ ən)   *n.* A warning in advance

premonitory (pri män′ ə tôr′ ē)   *adj.* Giving warning beforehand

presume (pri zōōm′)   v. To suppose

presumptuous (pri zump′ choo wǝs)   adj. Unduly confident or bold

pretence (pri tens′)   n. A claim (British spelling)

pretension (pri ten′ shǝn)   n. A claim to a rank or class

pretentious (pri ten′ shǝs)   adj. Making false claims

preternatural (prēt′ ǝr nach′ ǝr ǝl)   adj. Outside the natural or normal order

prevarication (pri var ǝ kā′ shǝn)   n. An evasion of truth

prime (prīm)   n. The best stage or time; most mature period

pristine (pris′ tēn)   adj. Pure; untouched; unspoiled

prodigal (präd′ i gǝl)   adj. Addicted to wasteful expenditure

prodigious (prǝ dij′ ǝs)   adj. Enormous; huge; impressive

profuse (prǝ fyōōs′)   adj. Abundant, pouring out

progeny (präj′ ǝ nē)   n. Offspring; a child

promiscuously (prǝ mis′ kyoo wǝs lē)   adv. Without care or thought

promontory (präm′ ǝn tôr′ ē)   n. The land that juts out into a body of water; high point of land extending into the sea

propagator (präp′ ǝ gāt′ ǝr)   n. One who causes something to happen or to spread

prophesy (präf′ ǝ sī)   v. Predict

prophetic (prǝ fet′ ik)   adj. Having the power to predict or foreshadow

propitiate (prǝ pish′ ē āt′)   v. Ease the burden of; appease

prostrate (präs′ trāt)   adj. Defenseless; in a prone or lying position

protracted (prō trak′ tid)   v. Drawn out; prolonged

providence (präv′ ǝ dens)   n. Divine forethought, guidance, and care; also, God

provoking (prǝ vōk′ iŋ)   adj. Annoying, irritating

prow (prou)   n. The front of a boat

prudence (prōōd′ 'ns)   n. Care in avoiding errors; discretion

puissant (pyōō′ i sǝnt)   adj. Powerful

pulverous (pul′ vǝ rǝs)   adj. Crumbling

pumice (pum′ is)   n. A volcanic rock

Q

quay (kē)   n. A wharf with facilities for loading or unloading ships

R

raiment (rā′ mǝnt)   n. Clothing

Raj (raj)   n. Rule

rapture (rap′ chǝr)   n. An expression of great joy

ravish (rav′ ish)   v. To violate

recompense (rek′ ǝm pens′)   n. A payment in return; reward

reconcile (rek′ ǝn sīl′)   v. To make up with

recreant (rek′ rē ǝnt)   adj. Cowardly

rectify (rek′ tǝ fī)   v. To set right; correct

refractory (ri frak′ tǝr ē)   adj. Hard to manage; stubborn

refulgent (ri ful′ jǝnt)   adj. Shining; radiant

remonstrance (ri män′ strǝns)   n. A protest

remonstrate (ri män′ strāt)   v. To object strongly

repose (ri pōz′)   v. Lie back

repository (ri päz′ ǝ tôr ē)   n. A center for accumulation and storage

repudiation (ri pyōō′ dē ā′ shǝn)   n. A rejection; denial

requiem (rek′ wē ǝm)   n. Dirge or mass for the dead; Musical composition or service honoring the dead

respite (res′ pit)   n. A postponement; delay

resplendently (ri splen′ dǝnt lē)   adj. Splendidly, gorgeously

reticent (ret′ ǝ s'nt)   adj. Laid back; uncommunicative

retort (ri tôrt′)   n. A comeback with a smart answer or wisecrack

retreat (ri trēt′)   n. A period of retirement or seclusion for prayer, religious study, and meditation

reverence (rev′ ǝr ǝns)   n. A great respect; deep respect or awe

reverie (rev′ ǝr ē)   n. A daydream

righteousness (rī′ chǝs nis)   n. Doing what is fair and just

rill (ril)   n. A little brook

rime (rīm)   n. A white frost

rioter (rī′ ǝt ǝr)   n. A loud, dissolute bully

rostral (räs′ trǝl)   adj. Having a beaklike projection, or rostrum, as at the prow of a ship

rout (rout)   n. An overwhelming defeat

rue (rōō)   n. Sorrow

ruminate (rōō′ mǝ nāt)   v. To think over; meditate

rummage (rum′ ij)   v. To search by thoroughly examining

S

sacramented (sak′ rǝ ment id)   adj. Having the properties of religious rites or rituals

sagacity (sǝ gas′ ǝ tē)   n. Wisdom: judgment

salient (sāl′ yǝnt)   adj. Striking; easily noticeable

salver (sal′ vǝr)   n. A tray usually used for the presentation of letters or visiting cards

sampan (sam′ pan)   n. A small flat-bottomed boat with a cabin formed by mats

sanguinary (saŋ′ gwi ner′ ē)   adj. Bloody

sanguine (san′ gwin)   adj. Of cheerful temperament

sarong (sǝ rôŋ′)   n. A long, brightly colored strip of cloth worn like a skirt

satiety (sǝ tī′ ǝ tē)   n. State of being filled to excess

saturnine (sat′ ǝr nin)   adj. Sluggish or gloomy

schism (siz′ 'm)   n. A division into groups or factions

screed (skrēd)   n. A long, tiresome piece of writing

scutcheon (skuch′ ǝn)   n. A coat of arms

segmented (seg′ ment id)   adj. Separated into parts

semblance (sem′ blǝns)   n. Appearance; image

senility (si nil′ ǝ tē)   n. Mental and physical decay due to old age

sepulcher (sep′ 'l kǝr)   n. A tomb

sequacious (si kwā′ shǝs)   adj. (Archaic.) Tending to follow dutifully, in service of

sequester (si kwes′ tǝr)   v. To keep apart from others

Seraphim (ser′ ǝ fim)   n. The highest order of angels

serrated (ser′ āt ǝd)   adj. Toothed or notched like a saw

servile (sur′ v'l)   adj. Slavelike

severance (sev′ ǝr ǝns)   n. State of being kept separate

shard (shärd)   n. A fragment or broken pieces

sheaf   (s/hēf)   *n.* A bundle of twigs or fibers

sibilant   (sib′ 'l ənt)   *adj.* Hissing

signet   (sig′ nit)   *n.* A seal

sinecure   (sī′ nə kyoor′)   *n.* Any office or position that brings advantage but involves little or no work

sinew   (sin′ yōō)   *n.* Muscular power; force

sinewy   (sin′ yoo wē)   *adj.* Tough; vigorous; powerful

sinuous   (sin′ yōō əs)   *adj.* Winding, twisting; bending; curving in and out

slagheap   (slag′ hēp)   *n.* A pile of waste material from mining

slumbrous   (slum′ brəs)   *adj.* Peaceful, suggesting sleep

sock   (säk)   *n.* The blade of a plow

sojourn   (sō′ jurn)   *v.* To stay for a while

solace   (säl′ is)   *n.* A comfort in grief or trouble; relief

solicit   (sə lis′ it)   *v.* Ask for, plead for

solicitous   (sə lis′ ə təs)   *adj.* Showing care or concern

soliloquize   (sə lil′ ə kwīz′)   *v.* To talk to oneself

somnambulist   (säm nam′ byoo list)   *n.* A sleepwalker

sophist   (säf′ ist)   *n.* One who makes misleading arguments

sordid   (sor′ did)   *adj.* Unclean, dirty

soiree   (swä rä′)   *n.* Party held in the evening

sophistry   (säf′ is trē)   *n.* Clever but unsound reasoning

sough   (sou)   *n.* A groan or sighing sound

sovereign   (säv′ rən)   *adj.* Supreme in power, rank, or authority

specter   (spek′ tər)   *n.* A ghost or ghost-like appearance

spectral   (spek′ trəl)   *adj.* Ghostly

spendthrift   (spend′ thrift′)   *n.* A person who spends money wastefully or foolishly

spent   (spent)   *adj.* Used up; gone

splaying   (splā′ iŋ)   *v.* Spreading

sprightly   (sprīt′ lē)   *adj.* Lively

squalid   (skwäl′ id)   *adj.* Miserably poor; wretched

squire   (skwīr)   *n.* A country gentleman or landed proprietor

stagnant   (stag′ nənt)   *adj.* Standing still, as water

stealthy   (stel′ thē)   *adj.* In a quiet, secretive way; sly; furtive

steep   (stēp)   *v.* To become saturated with

stem   (stem)   *v.* To stop; dam up

stile   (stīl)   *n.* A step or set of steps used in climbing over a fence or wall

stoic   (stō′ ik)   *n.* A person indifferent to pleasure or pain

sublimity   (sə blim′ ə tē)   *n.* The quality of being majestic or noble

subordinate   (sə bôr′ də nit)   *adj.* Beneath another in rank

subtle   (sut′ 'l)   *adj.* Cunning; ingenious

succeed   (sək sēd)   *v.* To follow; come after

succinct   (sək siŋkt′)   *adj.* Belted (Archaic); terse

suffuse   (sə fyōōz′)   *v.* To fill

sullen   (sul′ ən)   *adj.* Gloomy; dismal

sumpitan   (sump′ ə tan)   *n.* A Malayan blowgun which discharges poisonous darts

sundry   (sun′ drē)   *adj.* Various; miscellaneous

superfluity   (sōō′ pər flōō′ ə tē)   *n.* An excess

supplant   (sə plant′)   *v.* To take the place of; supersede

suppliant   (sup′ lē ənt)   *adj.* Beseeching prayerfully; imploring

supplication   (sup′ lə kā′ s/hən)   *n.* The act of praying

surfeit   (sur′ fit)   *n.* Too much of something; an excess

surmise   (sər mīz′)   *v.* To guess, assume; to form an opinion from inconclusive evidence

swaddling   (swäd′ liŋ)   *adj.* Long, narrow bands of cloth wrapped around newborn babies

swain   (swān)   *n.* A country youth

switch   (swich)   *n.* A light whip

sylvan   (sil′ vən)   *adj.* Wooded

symmetry   (sim′ ə trē)   *n.* Beauty resulting from balance of form

T

taffeta   (taf′ i tə)   *n.* A fine silk fabric

talent   (tal′ ənt)   *n.* A Biblical unit of money; native ability

tarry   (tar′ ē)   *v.* To delay, linger, be tardy, abide; continue in the same condition

tawdry   (tô′ drē)   *adj.* Cheap; gaudy

teeming   (tēm′ iŋ)   *adj.* Filled to overflowing

temperate   (tem′ pər it)   *adj.* Exercising moderation and self-restraint

tempest   (tem′ pist)   *n.* A violent storm accompanied by rain; any violent commotion or tumult, an uproar

tempestuous   (tem pes′ choo wəs)   *adj.* Turbulent; violently stormy

tenor   (ten′ ər)   *n.* A general tendency or course

terrestrial   (tə res′ trē əl)   *adj.* Of this world; earthly

thane   (thān)   *n.* In early England, a member of a class of freemen who held land of the king or a lord in return for military services

thrall   (thrôl)   *n.* A slave; serf

timorous   (tim′ ər əs)   *adj.* Fearful; timid

tincture   (tiŋk′ chər)   *n.* A tint

tithe   (tīth)   *n.* One tenth of a person's income, paid as a tax to support the church

tor   (tôr)   *n.* A high, rocky hill; crag

torrid   (tôr′ id)   *adj.* Hot, scorching

traffic   (traf′ ik)   *n.* Business

transcendence   (tran sen′ dəns)   *n.* A rising above

transfiguration   (trans fig yoo rā′ s/hən)   *n.* A change in outward form or appearance

transgress   (trans′ gres)   *v.* To violate a law or command; overstep or break

transient   (tran′ s/hənt)   *adj.* A person who passes quickly through a place

transitory   (tran′ sə tôr′ ē)   *adj.* Temporary; fleeting

trefoil   (trē′ foil)   *n.* Clover

trellis   (trel′ is)   *n.* A frame or crossed strips, usually of wood, used as a screen or support for climbing plants

tremulous   (trem′ yoo ləs)   *adj.* Trembling; timid

tress   (tres)   *n.* A lock of human hair

tryst   (trist)   *n.* A meeting

tuft   (tuft)   *n.* A grouping of fibers such as hair or grass

tumid   (tōō′ mid)   *adj.* Swollen

tumult   (tōō′ mult)   *n.* Commotion, disturbance; uproar; noisy confusion

tumultuous   (tōō mul′ choo wəs)   *adj.* Disorderly; violent

turbid   (tur′ bid)   *adj.* Muddy or cloudy; confused

turret   (tur′ it)   *n.* A small tower projecting from a building

twa   (twä)   *n.* Two (Scot.)

U

uncanny (un kan′ ē) *adj.* Mysterious; hard to explain
unctuous (uŋk′ choo wəs) *adj.* Oily
ungenial (un jēn′ yəl) *adj.* Unfriendly; characterized by bad weather
unmitigable (un mit′ i gə b′l) *adj.* Not able to be diminished in intensity
unravished (un rav′ ishd) *adj.* Undisturbed, unspoiled
unbraiding (up brād′ iŋ) *n.* Stern words of disapproval for an action; scolding
usurious (yoo zhoor′ ē əs) *adj.* Lending money at a high rate of interest
unsurped (yoo surp′d′) *adj.* Wrongfully seized

V

vain (vān) *adj.* Foolish; worthless
vair (ver) *n.* A gray and white fur
valance (val′ əns) *n.* A decorative facing
vale (vāl) *n.* A valley
vanity (van′ ə tē) *n.* A trifle, knicknack, or other insignificant thing
vaunt (vônt) *v.* To speak boastfully
vehemence (vē′ ə məns) *n.* Strength of feeling and emotion
vehement (vē′ ə mənt) *adj.* Energetic, forceful
veldt (velt) *n.* Open, grassy country
verdure (vur′ jər) *n.* Green plants
verge (vurj) *n.* An edge, rim
vestige (ves′ tij) *n.* A trace; bit
vestry (ves′ trē) *n.* A church meeting room
vexation (vek sā′ shən) *n.* An annoyance
vignettes (vin yets′) *n.* Decorative designs or borderless pictures in a book
vintage (vin′ tij) *n.* A wine or nectar of high quality
virago (və rā′ gō) *n.* A scolding woman
virtuous (vur′ choo wəs) *adj.* Pure, righteous

virulency (vir′ yoo lən sē) *n.* Harmfulness
visage (viz′ ij) *n.* A person's face or facial expression
vis-à-vis (vē′ zə vē′) Face to face with
viscous (vis′ kəs) *adj.* Semifluid; sticky
vizard (viz′ ərd) *n.* A mask

W

wan (wän) *adj.* Sickly pale; (Archaic) gloomy, not the modern sense of sickly pale
wane (wān′) *v.* To gradually become dimmer
wanton (wän′ t′n) *adj.* Luxuriant: said of vegetation; frisky; playful
wantonness (wän′ t′n nis) *n.* State of being reckless or undisciplined
wanwood (wän′ wood) *n.* A pale wood
wax (waks) *v.* To grow, ripen
weal (wēl) *n.* A discolored ridge on the skin; blister
whelk (hwelk) *n.* A pimple
wisteria (wis tir′ ē ə) *n.* Vines of shrubs with clusters of bluish, white, pink, or purplish flowers
wit (wit) *n.* Intelligence, wisdom
wrangle (raŋ′ g′l) *v.* To argue noisily and angrily; bicker

Y

yare (yer) *adj.* Ready; prepared
yoke (yōk) *n.* A wooden contrivance joining the heads of two draft animals, such as oxen, to make them capable of pulling heavier loads
ycladd (i klad′) *pp.* Clothed, dressed
yclept (i klept′) *pp.* Called; named

Z

zephyr (zef′ ər) *n.* A gentle wind

INDEX OF FINE ART

Index of Fine Art   1437

1438   *Index of Fine Art*

INDEX OF SKILLS

ANALYZING LITERATURE

CRITICAL THINKING AND READING

UNDERSTANDING LANGUAGE

INDEX OF TITLES BY THEMES

INDEX OF AUTHORS AND TITLES

ACKNOWLEDGMENTS (continued)

Jonathan Clowes Ltd., London, on behalf of Doris Lessing (continued)
sonal Voice: Essays, Reviews, Interviews by Doris Lessing. Copyright © 1957 by Doris Lessing. Reprinted by permission of Jonathan Clowes Ltd., London, on behalf of Doris Lessing.

Jonathan Clowes Ltd., London, on behalf of Doris Lessing and Harper & Row, Publishers, Inc.
"A Mild Attack of Locusts" from *The Habit of Loving* by Doris Lessing. Copyright © 1957 by Doris Lessing. Reprinted by permission.

Doubleday, a division of Bantam, Doubleday, Dell Publishing Group, Inc.
"The Lagoon" from *Tales of Unrest* by Joseph Conrad, Doubleday, Page & Company.

Faber and Faber Ltd.
"Days" from *The Whitsun Weddings* by Phillip Larkin. Copyright © 1960, 1961, 1962, 1964 by Phillip Larkin. "Sunday Morning" and "The Sunlight on the Garden" from *The Collected Poems of Louis MacNeice* by Louis MacNeice. Copyright © the Estate of Louis MacNeice 1966. Reprinted by permission of Faber and Faber Ltd.

Farrar, Straus and Giroux, Inc. and Faber and Faber Ltd.
"Taylor Street" from *Selected Poems 1950–1975* by Thom Gunn. Copyright © 1957, 1958, 1961, 1967, 1971, 1973, 1974, 1975, 1976, 1979 by Thom Gunn. Published in London in *Touch* by Thom Gunn. "Follower," "Shore Woman," and excerpt from "Rite of Spring" from *Poems 1965–1975* by Seamus Heaney. Copyright © 1966, 1969, 1972, 1975, 1980 by Seamus Heaney. "Follower" published in London in *Death of a Naturalist* by Seamus Heaney and "Shore Woman" published in London in *Wintering Out* by Seamus Heaney. "The Explosion" from *High Windows* by Philip Larkin. Copyright © 1974 by Philip Larkin. Reprinted by permission of the publishers.

Harcourt Brace Jovanovich, Inc.
From *Shakespeare: The Complete Works,* edited by G. B. Harrison, copyright 1948, 1952, 1968 by Harcourt Brace Jovanovich, Inc. Reprinted by permission of the publisher.

Harcourt Brace Jovanovich, Inc. and Faber and Faber Ltd.
"The Hollow Men," "Journey of the Magi," and "Preludes" from *Collected Poems 1909–1962* by T. S. Eliot, copyright 1935, 1936 by Harcourt Brace Jovanovich, Inc.; copyright © 1964 by T. S. Eliot. Reprinted by permission of the publishers.

Harcourt Brace Jovanovich, Inc., A. M. Heath & Company Ltd., the Estate of the Late Sonia Brownell Orwell, and Secker & Warburg Ltd.
"Shooting an Elephant" from *Shooting an Elephant and Other Essays* by George Orwell, copyright 1950 by Sonia Brownell Orwell; renewed 1978 by Sonia Pitt-Rivers. Reprinted by permission.

Harcourt Brace Jovanovich, Inc., The Hogarth Press Ltd., and the author's Estate
"The Lady in the Looking Glass: A Reflection" from *The Complete Shorter Fiction of Virginia Woolf* edited by Susan Dick, copyright © 1985 by Quentin Bell and Angelica Garnett. Reprinted by permission.

Harper & Row, Publishers, Inc.
"Woman" from *The Works of Oliver Goldsmith* edited by Peter Cunningham, Harper & Brothers. "The Horses" from *New Selected Poems* by Ted Hughes. Copyright © 1957, 1982 by Ted Hughes. Reprinted by permission of Harper & Row, Publishers, Inc.

Harper & Row, Publishers, Inc. and Faber and Faber Ltd.
"Hawk Roosting" from *New Selected Poems* by Ted Hughes. Copyright © 1959, 1982 by Ted Hughes. Published in London in *Lupercal* by Ted Hughes. Excerpt from "Fourth of July" from *Lupercal* by Ted Hughes. Copyright © 1960 by Ted Hughes. Copyright renewal © 1988 by Ted Hughes. Reprinted by permission of the publishers.

Alan W. Holden
"Some Men Create" from *To Make Me Grieve* by Molly Holden, Chatto and Windus Ltd. Exclusive copyright Alan Holden.

Henry Holt and Company, Inc.
"Loveliest of trees, the cherry now," "To an athlete dying young," "When I was one-and-twenty," and "With rue my heart is laden" from *The Collected Poems of A. E. Housman.* Copyright © 1939, 1940, 1965 by Holt, Rinehart and Winston, Inc. Copyright © 1967, 1968 by Robert E. Symons. Reprinted by permission of Henry Holt and Company, Inc.

Houghton Mifflin Company
Lines from "Childe Harold's Pilgrimage" ("Apostrophe to the Ocean"), lines from "Don Juan," "She Walks in Beauty," and "So We'll Go No More A-Roving" reprinted from *The Complete Poetical Works of Lord Byron.* From "A Voyage to Brobdingnag" and from "A Voyage to Lilliput" reprinted from *Gulliver's Travels and Other Writings* by Jonathan Swift, edited by Louis A. Landa. Riverside Edition. Copyright © 1960 by Houghton Mifflin Company. Used by permission.

Olwyn Hughes
"Anniversary" and "Out" from *The Magic Apple Tree* by Elaine Feinstein. Copyright © 1971 by Elaine Feinstein. Reprinted by permission of Olwyn Hughes.

Alfred A. Knopf, Inc.
"The Demon Lover" copyright 1946 and renewed 1974 by Elizabeth Bowen. Reprinted from *The Demon Lover and Other Stories* by Elizabeth Bowen. "A Dill Pickle" copyright 1920 by Alfred A. Knopf, Inc. and renewed 1948 by John Middleton Murry. Reprinted from *The Short Stories of Katherine Mansfield* by Katherine Mansfield. Reprinted by permission of Alfred A. Knopf, Inc.

Little, Brown and Company, in association with The Atlantic Monthly Press
"A Touch of Autumn in the Air" from *The Collected Stories of*

Sean O'Faolain by Sean O'Faolain. Copyright © 1962 by Sean O'Faolain. Reprinted by permission.

Louisiana State University Press
"A Birthday" reprinted from *The Complete Poems of Christina Rossetti*, Volume I, edited by R. W. Crump. Copyright © 1979 by Louisiana State University Press.

Macmillan London Ltd.
"A Song for St. Cecilia's Day" from *The Poetical Works of John Dryden* edited by W. D. Christie. "The Three Strangers" from *Wessex Tales* by Thomas Hardy.

Macmillan Publishing Company
"Ah, Are You Digging on My Grave?," "The Darkling Thrush," and "The Man He Killed" from *The Complete Poems of Thomas Hardy* edited by James Gibson (New York: Macmillan, 1978). This collection was published outside the U.S. by Macmillan (London) Ltd. in 1976. "The Lake Isle of Innisfree" and "When You Are Old" from *The Poems of W. B. Yeats: A New Edition,* edited by Richard J. Finneran (New York: Macmillan, 1983).

Macmillan Publishing Company and A. P. Watt Ltd. on behalf of Michael B. Yeats and Macmillan London Ltd.
"An Irish Airman Foresees His Death" and "The Wild Swans at Coole" copyright 1919 by Macmillan Publishing Company, renewed 1947 by Bertha Georgie Yeats; "The Second Coming" copyright 1924 by Macmillan Publishing Company, renewed 1952 by Bertha Georgie Yeats; "Sailing to Byzantium" copyright 1928 by Macmillan Publishing Company, renewed 1956 by Bertha Georgie Yeats; and "After Long Silence" copyright 1933 by Macmillan Publishing Company, renewed 1961 by Bertha Georgie Yeats. All poems reprinted with permission.

The Marvell Press
"Coming" by Philip Larkin is reprinted from *The Less Deceived* by Philip Larkin, by permission of The Marvell Press, England.

Methuen & Company Ltd.
"The Passionate Shepherd to His Love" and lines from *The Tragical History of the Life and Death of Dr. Faustus* from *Marlowe's Poems* edited by L. C. Martin. Lines from "An Essay on Man," "Canto III," and lines from "Canto V" reprinted from *The Poems of Alexander Pope* edited by John Butt. Published by Methuen & Co. Ltd., London.

New American Library, a division of Penguin Books U.S.A. Inc.
From *Beowulf* translated by Burton Raffel. Copyright © 1963 by Burton Raffel. From *The Tragedy of Macbeth* by William Shakespeare, edited by Sylvan Barnet. Copyright © 1963 by Sylvan Barnet. *The Tempest* by William Shakespeare, edited by Robert Langaum and Sylvan Barnet. Copyright © 1987 by Robert Langaum and Sylvan Barnet. Reprinted by arrangement with New American Library, a division of Penguin Books U.S.A. Inc., New York, New York.

New Directions Publishing Corporation
Lines from "In the Park," lines from "The Galloping Cat," and lines from "My Muse" from Stevie Smith, *The Collected Poems of Stevie Smith.* Copyright © 1972 by Stevie Smith.

"Not Waving but Drowning" and "Pretty" from Stevie Smith, *The Collected Poems of Stevie Smith.* Copyright © 1972 by Stevie Smith. Reprinted by permission of New Directions Publishing Corporation.

New Directions Publishing Corporation and David Higham Associates Ltd.
"Do Not Go Gentle into That Good Night," "Fern Hill," and "The Force That Through the Green Fuse Drives the Flower" from Dylan Thomas, *The Poems of Dylan Thomas.* Copyright 1939 by New Directions Publishing Corporation. Copyright 1945 by the Trustees for the Copyrights of Dylan Thomas. Copyright 1952 by Dylan Thomas. Published in London by J. M. Dent & Sons Ltd. Reprinted by permission.

W. W. Norton & Company, Inc.
Reprinted from *Sir Gawain and the Green Knight, A New Verse Translation* by Marie Borroff, by permission of W. W. Norton & Company, Inc. Copyright © 1967 by W. W. Norton & Company, Inc.

Oxford University Press
"The Wanderer" from *An Anthology of Old English Poetry,* translated by Charles W. Kennedy. Copyright 1960. Reprinted by permission.

Oxford University Press, Inc. and A. P. Watt Ltd. on behalf of the Executors of the Estate of Robert Graves
"Interruption," "One Hard Look," and "She Tells Her Love ..." from *Collected Poems* by Robert Graves. Copyright © 1975 in this edition by Robert Graves. Reprinted by permission.

Oxford University Press, England
"A Poison Tree," "Holy Thursday," "Infant Sorrow," "The Human Abstract," "The Lamb," and "The Tiger" from *The Poetical Works of William Blake* edited by John Sampson. From "The Life of Samuel Johnson" in *Boswell's Life of Johnson* by James Boswell, edited by C. B. Tinker. From *Wuthering Heights* by Emily Brontë, edited by H. W. Garrod. "Sonnet 43" from *The Poetical Works of Elizabeth Barrett Browning,* Oxford Edition. "Kubla Khan" and "The Rime of the Ancient Mariner" from *The Poems of Samuel Taylor Coleridge.* "Easter Wings," "Man," and "Virtue" from *The Poems of George Herbert,* edited by Helen Gardner. "An Ode for Him" and "To the Virgins, to Make Much of Time" from *The Poems of Robert Herrick* edited by L. C. Martin. "God's Grandeur," "Hurrahing in Harvest," "Pied Beauty," and "Spring and Fall" from *Poems of Gerard Manley Hopkins,* 4th edition, edited by W. H. Gardner and N. H. MacKenzie. "Letter to Lord Chesterfield" from *The Letters of Samuel Johnson,* Volume I: 1719–1774, collected and edited by R. W. Chapman. "Dream Children: A Reverie" from *The Works of Charles Lamb* edited by Thomas Hutchinson. "To Althea" and "To Lucasta, On Going to the Wars" from *The Poems of Richard Lovelace* edited by C. H. Wilkinson. "Sonnet 31" and "Sonnet 39" from *The Poems of Sir Philip Sidney* edited by William A. Ringler, Jr. Lines from "The Faerie Queen," "Sonnet 1," "Sonnet 26," and "Sonnet 75" from *The Poetical Works of Edmund Spenser* edited by J. C. Smith and E. de Selincourt. From "Thoughts on Various Subjects" in *Satires and Personal Writings* by Jonathan Swift, edited by William Alfred Eddy. "Crossing the Bar," lines from "In

Memoriam A.H.H.," "Tears, Idle Tears," "The Lady of Shalott," "The Lotos-Eaters," lines from "The Princess' ("The
Splendor Falls"), and "Ulysses" from *Alfred Tennyson: Poetical Works*.

Pantheon Books, a division of Random House, Inc.
From "The Preface" and from "A Dictionary of the English
Language" by Samuel Johnson in *Johnson's Dictionary: A
Modern Selection* edited by E. L. McAdam, Jr. and George
Milne.

Penguin Books Ltd.
"The Nun's Priest's Tale" from *The Canterbury Tales* by
Geoffrey Chaucer, translated by Nevill Coghill (Penguin
Classics, Revised Edition, 1977), copyright © Nevill Coghill,
1951, 1958, 1960, 1975, 1977. Reprinted by permission of
Penguin Books Ltd. From *A History of the English Church and
People* by Venerable Bede, translated with an introduction by
Leo Sherley-Price, revised by R. E. Latham (Penguin Clas-
sics, 1955, 1965, 1968), copyright © Leo Sherley-Price,
1955, 1965, 1968, copyright © R. E. Latham, 1968, pp. 37–
40. "The Prologue" and 238 lines from "The Pardoner's
Tale" from *The Canterbury Tales* by Geoffrey Chaucer, translated into modern English by Nevill Coghill (Penguin Classics, 1951, 1958, 1960), copyright © Nevill Coghill, 1951,
1958, 1960, pp. 19–41, 268–274. Reprinted by permission of
Penguin Books Ltd.

Peters Fraser & Dunlop Group Ltd.
"A Voyage to Cythera" by Margaret Drabble, published in
Mademoiselle Magazine, December 1967. Reprinted by per-
mission of the Peters Fraser & Dunlop Group Ltd.

Random House, Inc.
from *Jane Eyre* by Charlotte Brontë. "Holy Sonnet 10," "Holy
Sonnet 14," "Meditation 17," and "Song" from *Complete
Poetry and Selected Prose of John Donne* by John Donne,
edited by John Hayward.

Random House, Inc. and Faber and Faber Ltd.
"In Memory of W.B. Yeats" and "Musée des Beaux Arts"
copyright 1940 and renewed 1968 by W. H. Auden. Reprinted from *W. H. Auden: Collected Poems* by W. H. Auden,
edited by Edward Mendelson. "What I Expected" copyright
1934 and renewed 1962 by Stephen Spender. Reprinted
from *Collected Poems 1928–1985* by Stephen Spender. Reprinted by permission of the publishers.

Routledge & Kegan Paul
"For Doreen: A Voice from the Garden" from *Collected
Poems 1950–1970* by Donald Davie. Copyright © Donald
Davie 1972.

**Routledge & Kegan Paul and Associated Book Publishers
(U.K.) Ltd.**
"The Picture of Little T.C. in a Prospect of Flowers" and "To
His Coy Mistress" from *The Poems of Andrew Marvell* edited
by Hugh MacDonald.

Simon & Schuster, Inc.
"The Truth about George" from *The Most of P. G. Wode-
house* by P. G. Wodehouse. Copyright © 1960 by Pelham
Grenville Wodehouse. Reprinted by permission of Simon &
Schuster, Inc. Pronunciation key from *Webster's New World
Dictionary*—Second College Edition. Copyright © 1984 by
Simon & Schuster, Inc. Reprinted by permission.

**The Society of Authors on behalf of the Estate of Bernard
Shaw**
Pygmalion by Bernard Shaw. Copyright 1913, 1914, 1916,
1930, 1941, 1944 George Bernard Shaw. Copyright 1957
The Public Trustee as Executor of the Estate of George
Bernard Shaw. Reprinted by permission.

**The University of Chicago Press and Faber and
Faber Ltd.**
Lines from "Positives" in *Positives: Verses* by Thom Gunn.
Copyright © 1967 by Tom Gunn. Reprinted by permission of
the publishers.

University of Nebraska Press
"The Seafarer" reprinted from *Poems From the Old English*,
translated, with an introduction by Burton Raffel, by permission of University of Nebraska Press. Copyright © 1960,
1964, by the University of Nebraska Press.

Unwin Hyman Ltd.
Lines from "In the Beck" from *The Collected Poems of
Kathleen Raine* by Kathleen Raine. © Copyright 1956 by
Kathleen Raine. Reprinted by permission of Unwin Hyman
Ltd.

Viking Penguin Inc.
"The Train from Rhodesia" from *Selected Stories* by Nadine
Gordimer. Copyright 1952 by Nadine Gordimer. "Snake"
from *The Complete Poems of D. H. Lawrence* edited by Vivian
de Sola Pinto and F. Warren Roberts. Copyright © 1964,
1971 by Angelo Ravagli and C. M. Weekley, Executors of the
Estate of Frieda Lawrence Ravagli. "The Rocking-Horse
Winner" from *The Complete Short Stories of D. H. Lawrence*,
Vol. III. Copyright 1933 by the Estate of D. H. Lawrence;
copyright renewed © 1961 by Angelo Ravagli and C. M.
Weekley, Executors of the Estate of Frieda Lawrence
Ravagli. "The Schartz-Metterklume Method" from *The Complete Short Stories of Saki* by Saki (H. H. Munro). Copyright
1930, renewed © 1958 by The Viking Press, Inc. "Sonnet
29," "Sonnet 73," "Sonnet 116," and "Sonnet 130" from
William Shakespeare: The Complete Works edited by Alfred
Harbage. Copyright © 1969 by Penguin Books, Inc. Reprinted by permission of Viking Penguin Inc.

**Viking Penguin Inc., Jonathan Cape Ltd., and the
Executors of the James Joyce Estate**
"Araby" from *Dubliners* by James Joyce. Copyright 1916 by
B. W. Huebsch. Definitive text copyright © 1967 by the
Estate of James Joyce. Reprinted by permission.

Viking Penguin Inc. and John Johnson Ltd.
"The Distant Past" from *Angels at the Ritz and Other Stories*
by William Trevor. Copyright © 1973 by William Trevor.
Reprinted by permission.

Viking Penguin Inc. and Laurence Pollinger Ltd.
"Across the Bridge" from *Nineteen Stories* by Graham
Greene. Copyright 1947, renewed © 1975 by Graham
Greene. Published in London in *Collected Stories* by Graham

Greene by William Heinemann, Ltd. and The Bodley Head Ltd. Reprinted by permission.

Viking Penguin Inc. and George Sassoon
"Wirers" from *The Colleted Poems of Siegfried Sassoon* by Siegfried Sassoon. Copyright 1918 by E. P. Dutton Co. Copyright renewed 1946 by Siegfried Sassoon. Reprinted by permission.

Wallace & Sheil Agency, Inc. and Tessa Sayle Agency, London
"The Fiddle" from *The Second Chance and Other Stories* by Alan Sillitoe. Copyright © 1981 by Alan Sillitoe. Reprinted by permission.

Note: Every effort has been made to locate the copyright owner of material reprinted in this book. Omissions brought to our attention will be corrected in subsequent editions.

ART CREDITS

Cover and Title Page: *The Sisters,* 1900, Ralph Peacock, The Tate Gallery, London, Art Resource (N1772); **p. 1:** Bayeux Tapestry: Norman Cavalry Charge at the Shieldwall at the Battle of Hastings, The Granger Collection; **p. 3:** Religious Ceremony of the Druids, Forrest C. Crooks, Three Lions; **pp. 4, 5:** Stonehenge, D. E. Szymanski/D.P.I.; St. Augustine, Giuseppe Ribera/Three Lions; A Viking Sword, Viking, X Century, Sword, Iron, copper and silver, the Metropolitan Museum of Art, Rogers Fund, 1955, Copyright © 1980/87 by The Metropolitan Museum of Art; Danes Attacking a British Town, English ms., illumination c. 1130, The Granger Collection; Buddha Addressing a Disciple, The Granger Collection; The Coronation of William the Conqueror, ms. illumination c. 1470, The Granger Collection; A Roman Town After the Fall of the Empire, Roman Town at the Foot of the Alps After the Conquest by the Gauls, Octave Penguilly-L'Haridon, Three Lions; Charles Martel Battling the Moors, The Granger Collection; King Charlemagne, jeweled gold reliquary bust, c. 1350, Domschatz, Aachen, The Granger Collection; **p. 6:** Insignia of the Roman Civil Governor in Charge of the Five British Provinces, early 15th-century copy of a page from the now-lost Notitia Dignitatum Utriusque Imperii, a 4th-century list of the symbols of their provinces, The Granger Collection; **p. 8:** Saxons, Jutes, and Angles Arriving in Britain by Sea, English manuscript illumination, The Granger Collection; **p. 9:** An English Monk Exactly Contemporary with Bede, illumination from an early 8th-century Northumbrian codex, The Granger Collection; **p. 10:** The 9th-Century Oseberg Viking Ship, The Granger Collection; **p. 11:** Alfred the Great Acknowledged as King by All Men of England, 871 A.D., Three Lions; Page from an Early 12th-Century Manuscript of the *Anglo-Saxon Chronicle* Describing the Norman Conquest, The Granger Collection; **p. 12:** The Bayeux Tapestry: Edward the Confessor Speaks to Harold of Wessex, The Granger Collection; **p. 14:** A Page from the Caedmon Manuscript, c. 1000, The Granger Collection; **p. 18:** Ships with Three Men, Fish, ms. Ashmole 1511, folio 86 verso, Bodleian Library, Oxford; **p. 20:** (detail), see credit for p. 18; **p. 22:** Statens Historiska Museet, Stockholm, Werner Forman Archive; **p. 25:** The Dragon for "The High Kings," George Sharp; **p. 28:** Arthur Going to Avalon for "The High Kings"

(detail), George Sharp; **p. 34:** The So-Called "Sigurd's Helmet," Statens Historiska Museet, Stockholm, Werner Forman Archive; Coins Depicting Viking Longships, Statens Historiska Museet, Stockholm, Werner Forman Archive; The Gokstad Ship, Viking Ships, Museum, Bygdøy, Oslo, Werner Forman Archive; **p. 35:** Head of Carved Post from the Ship Burial at Oseberg, Werner Forman Archive; Helmet, Statens Historiska Museet, Stockholm, Werner Forman Archive; Golden Horns, National Museet Copenhagen, photo by Lennard Larsen; **p. 41:** *Slaying of a Bull on the base of a Cauldron, 100 B.C.,* Werner Forman Archive/National Museum, Copenhagen; **p. 42:** *Handle fixture of a bucket,* Celtic/Viking, Werner Forman Archive; **p. 43:** *Detail of a dragon head on the Mammen horse collar,* Viking, 10th century, Werner Forman Archive; **p. 44:** *Gilt-bronze winged dragon—bridal mounting,* 8th century, Werner Forman Archive/Statens Historiska Museet, Stockholm; **p. 47:** *Gilt silver brooch,* Viking migration period, Werner Forman Archive/Statens Historiska Museet, Stockholm; **p. 48:** *Silver pendant showing the helmet of the Vendel,* Viking 10th century, Werner Forman Archive/Statens Historiska Museet, Stockholm; **p. 49:** *The Oseberg Ship,* Viking, c. A.D. 850, Werner Forman Archive/Viking Ship Museum, Bygdøy, Oslo; **p. 53:** *Beowulf,* ms. page, The British Museum/The Bettmann Archive (p. 3955) (7779); **p. 55:** "Grendel" Frontispiece from *Beowulf,* 1908, Pattern Wilson, The British Library; **p. 57:** *Serra flying over a boat,* illumination from an English bestiary, c. 1185, The Granger Collection; **p. 59:** *Sutton Hoo Ship Burial,* A.D. 7th century, The Granger Collection; **p. 62:** (detail) and **p. 65:** Cotton ms. Tiberius C. II Folio 5 Verso, Page of Bede's History, The British Library; **p. 66:** Monks, ms. University College, 165 piii, Bodleian Library, Oxford; **p. 69:** *The Anglo Saxon Chronicle* (Ms. Cott TIB B1. Fol 132), The British Museum; **p. 72:** Pilgrims to Canterbury: Detail of an English illuminated manuscript, c. 1400, The Granger Collection; **p. 74:** Bayeux Tapestry: Duke William Encourages His Men at Hastings by Raising His Helmet, The Granger Collection; **p. 75:** A bailiff supervising the harvest (the month of August): Manuscript illumination, English, early 14th century, The Granger Collection; **pp. 76, 77:** The Murder of Thomas Becket, illumination from an English psalter, c. 1200, The Granger Collection; King John Signs the Magna Carta, The Granger Collection; Pope Gregory IX, mosaic head from the Old Basilica of St. Peter, The Granger Collection; The Siege of Jerusalem During the First Crusade, late 13th-century French ms. illumination, The Granger Collection; Roger Bacon, mid-15th-century Italian ms. illumination, The Granger Collection; Genghis Khan, Chinese silk album leaf, Yuan Dynasty; Manuscript of the Song of Roland, Anglo-Norman text from a 12th-century English ms., The Granger Collection; Twelfth-century Chess Piece, The Granger Collection; **pp. 78, 79:** François Villon (1431–after 1463), colored woodcut from the Grand Testament de Maitre François Villon, Paris, 1489, The Granger Collection; Printer's Device Used by Caxton, The Granger Collection; Marco Polo Entering Peking, 14th-century miniature from the Livre de Merveilles, The Granger Collection; Joan of Arc at the Coronation of Charles VII, canvas, 1854, by J. A. D. Ingres, The Granger Collection; Johann Gutenberg Printing First Bible, The Granger Collection; Black Death Sweeps Through England, Fear of plague in house of Fitzeisulf (detail) Trinity Chapel window, Canterbury Cathedral, 14th century, The Granger Collection; Canterbury Tales, The beginning of the prologue to Chaucer's Canterbury Tales, a 15th-century ms. page, The Granger Collection; *Battle During the Hundred Years' War, Battle of Poitiers,* Eugene Delacroix, Three Lions; **p. 81:** King John signing Magna Carter at Runnymede, 15th June 1215, colored engraving, 18th century, The Granger Collection; Four Kings of England depicted on a page of a 13th-century manuscript, The Granger Collection; **p. 82:** Funeral of plague victim in House of Fitzeisulf Trinity Chapel Window, Canterbury Cathedral, 14th century, The Granger Collection; **p. 83:** King Henry VII of England, panel, 1505, by Michiel Sittow, The Granger Collection; **p. 84:** *Sir Galahad,* 1864 (watercolor), Dante Gabriel Rossetti, The Granger Collection; **p. 85:** Johann Gutenberg examining the first proof his printed Bible from his press at Mainz, after the painting by J. L. G. Ferris (detail), The Granger Collection; **p. 86:** A page from the Lansdowne ms of Geoffrey Chaucer's *Canterbury Tales,* The Granger Collection; **p. 87:** *Robin Hood,* 1852, Richard Dadd, Yale Center for British Art, Paul Mellon Collection; **p. 94:** The Nine Heroes Tapestries, Christian Heroes: Arthur with Three Cardinals, Detail: Arthur, upper half, probably Nicolas Bataille, Paris, The Metropolitan Museum of Art, The Cloisters Collection, Munsey Fund, 1932, © Copyright 1985 by the Metropolitan Museum of Art, **p. 104:** Medieval Baron Dining, from *Breviarium Grimari,* 15th century, The Bettmann Archive; **p. 112:** *Veronica Veronese,* Dante Gabriel Rossetti, Delaware Art Museum, Samuel and Mary Bancroft Memorial Collection; **p. 114:** Geoffrey Chaucer, unknown artist, The Granger Collection; **p. 118:** The Tabard Inn, Arthur Szyk for *The Canterbury Tales,* The George Macy Companies; **p. 121:** The Yeoman, Arthur Szyk for *The Canterbury Tales,* The George Macy Companies; **p. 123:** The Monk, Arthur Szyk for *The Canterbury Tales,* The George Macy Companies; **p. 126:** The Student, Arthur Szyk for *The Canterbury Tales,* The George Macy Companies; **p. 130:** The Wife of Bath, Arthur Szyk for *The Canterbury Tales,* The George Macy Companies; **p. 143:** *English Travelers Setting Forth from Chaucer's Canterbury Tales,* Trustees of the British Library, (Roy 18.0.11 f.148 detail); **p. 146:** *Woman Feeding Chicken,* (Cod. ser. nov. 2644, fol. 65) Italian manuscript, Osterreichische National Bibliothek, Bild-archiv und Portrat-sammlung; **p. 151:** *The Nun's Priest* from *The Canterbury Tales* by Chaucer, The Huntington Library, San Marino, California; **p. 153:** *Chaucer reciting Troilus and Cressida before a court gathering (frontpiece),* Corpus Christi College; **p. 154:** *Chaucer's Canterbury Pilgrims,* 1810, William Blake, The Huntington Library, San Marino, California; **p. 162:** The Pardoner, Arthur Szyk for *The Canterbury Tales,* The George Macy Companies; **p. 166:** *World Map: Cathay and the Empire of the Great Khan,* 1459, Mauro, Biblioteca Nazionale Marciana, Venice/E. T. Archive; **p. 167:** *A Medieval View of the Universe,* © Ronald Sheridan, Ancient Art and Architecture Collection; **p. 171:** From *The Romance of King Arthur and His Knights of the Round Table,* Arthur Rackham, Weathervane Books; **p. 177:** Sir Gawain and the Green Knight, ms Douce 199, folio 157 verso, The Bodleian Library, Oxford; **p. 183:** Gawain Receiving the Green Girdle, woodcut by Fritz Kredel from Gardner, *The Complete Works of the Gawain Poet* © 1965, The University of Chicago; **p. 194:** *The Old Man and Death,* c. 1774, Joseph Wright of Derby, Wadsworth Atheneum, Hartford, Ella Gallup Sumner and Mary Catlin Sumner Collection, © Wadsworth Atheneum; **p. 196:** *Bayeux Tapestry/The Normans Attack the English,* Michael Holford; **p. 197:** Begining of the prologue to *Canterbury Tales,* 15th century ms. page, The Granger Collection; **p. 200–01:** *Queen Elizabeth and Sir Walter Raleigh,* Charles Edouard Boutibonne, Three Lions; **p. 203:** *Mona Lisa,* Leonardo da Vinci, Three Lions; **pp. 204–05:** *Sir Thomas More with His Family,* The Granger Collection; *Queen Elizabeth I,* The Granger Collection; *Copernicus's Treatise of Astronomy,* The Granger Collection; *The Last Supper,* Leonardo Da Vinci, Three Lions; *Columbus Sets Sail from Spain,* The Granger Collection; *English Navy Attacking Spanish Armada,* The Granger Collection; London, c. 1558, The Granger Collection; *Francisco Pizarro,* The Granger Collection; **pp. 206–07:** Globe Theatre, The Granger Collection; *Galileo,* The Granger Collection; *The Pilgrims Land at Plymouth Rock,* The Granger Collection; *Cervantes,* The Granger Collection; Engraving of William Shakespeare by Martin Droeshout on title page of the First Folio, 1623, The Granger Collection; Pieter Bruegel the Elder, *Wedding Dance in the Open Air,* Panel, 1566, The Granger Collection; *Akbar the Great,* Indian Mughal miniature by Manohar, c. 1600, The Granger Collection; **p. 208:** *Portrait of Erasmus,* Hans Holbein, National Gallery, Parma, Scala/Art Resource; **p. 209:** Martin Luther Fastening His 95 Theses on the Door of All Saints Church, Wittenburg, Germany, on 31 October, 1517, 19th-century engraving, The Granger Collection; **p. 210:** *King Henry VII of England,* Hans Holbein, The Granger Collection; **p. 211:** *Queen Elizabeth I of England,* c. 1588, by or after George Gower, The Granger Collection; **p. 212:** Queen Elizabeth I Knighting Francis Drake on Board the *Golden Hind* at Deptford, 4 April 1581, 19th-century engraving, The Granger Collection; The Launching of Fire ships Against the Spanish Armada, National Maritime Museum, Greenwich, England; **p. 214:** *Sir Walter Raleigh,* N. Hilliard, Three Lions; **p. 215:** *William Shakespeare,* artist unknown, Three Lions; **p. 216:** Title Page of the First Edition of the King James Bible, London, 1611, The Granger Collection; **p. 219:** *View of a Park, with Huntsmen and Deer,* Peter Tillemans, Victoria & Albert Museum Trustees; **p. 220:** The Granger Collection; **p. 222:** Sir Philip Sidney (detail), c. 1576, unknown artist, by courtesy of the National Portrait Gallery, London; **p. 225:** *Shepherds Under a Full Moon,* Samuel Palmer, c. 1830, © Ashmolean Museum, Oxford; **p. 228:** The Granger Collection; **p. 230:** The Hireling Shepherd, William Holman Hunt, The Manchester City Art Galleries; **p. 236:** *Sir Walter Raleigh* (detail), unknown artist, The Granger Collection; **p. 241:** *Portrait of an Unknown Man,* Nicholas Hilliard, Victoria & Albert Museum Trustees; **p. 242:** The Granger Collection; **p. 248:** New York Public Library, Picture Collection; **p. 252:** *William Shakespeare,* unknown artist, by courtesy of the National Portrait Gallery, London; **p. 256:** *The Sonnet,* William Mulready, Victoria & Albert Museum Trustees; **p. 263:** *The Woodcutter Courting the Milkmaid,* Thomas Gainsborough, Woburn Abbey, by kind permission of the Marquess of Tavistock, and the Trustees of the Bedford Estates; **p. 267:** The Granger Collection; **p. 272:** *The Three Witches,* Henry Fuseli, Courtauld Institute Galleries, London (Witt Collection No. 4533); **p. 277:** *Macbeth and the Witches,* Clarkson Stanfield, Leicestershire Museums, Art Galleries and Records Service; **p. 287:** *Scene from Macbeth,* Cattermole, from the art collection of the Folger Shakespeare Library; **p. 293:** *Ellen Terry as Lady Macbeth,* 1889, John Singer Sargent, The Tate Gallery, on loan to the National Portrait Gallery, London; **p. 298:** *Lady Macbeth Seizing the Daggers,* Henry Fuseli, The Tate Gallery, London; **p. 310:**

Wood engraving after Sir John Gilbert, The Granger Collection; **p. 325:** Macbeth and the Witches, engraved by Thew after Reynolds, Royal Academy of Arts, London; **p. 328:** Wood engraving after Sir John Gilbert, The Granger Collection; **p. 340:** *Mrs. Siddons as Lady Macbeth,* Garrick Club/G. H. Harlow; **p. 352:** *Delacroix as Hamlet,* Delacroix, Paris, Louvre/Giraudon/Art Resource (CFL 2050) (617P6); **p. 353:** *Ophelia,* 1852, Sir John Everett Millais, The Tate Gallery, London/Bridgeman/Art Resource (2078) (617P7); **p. 354:** *Hamlet and Horacio,* Delacroix, Paris, Louvre/Giraudon/Art Resource (LAC46564) (617P5) **p. 355:** *The Play Scene in Hamlet,* Exh1842, Daniel Maclise, The Tate Gallery, London/ Art Resource (N422) (617P10); **p. 356:** *Francis Bacon* (detail), John Vanderbank, 1731 copy of painting c. 1618, by courtesy of the National Portrait Gallery, London; **p. 360:** "The Cosmographical Glasse," London, 1559 (p. 50), from William Cuningham, The Huntington Library at San Marino, California; **p. 365:** King James Bible, 1611, title page of the New Testament, by permission of the Folger Shakespeare Library; **p. 369:** Letters Patent from Elizabeth I to Francis Drake, 1687, E. T. Archive; **pp. 372–73:** *The Thames at Westminster Stairs,* 1631 or 1637, Claude de Jongh, c. 1631 or 1637, Yale Center for British Art, Paul Mellon Collection; **pp. 376–77:** *Francis Bacon,* John Vanderbank, 1731 copy of painting, c. 1618, by courtesy of the National Portrait Gallery, London; *Execution of King Charles I of England, 30 January 1649,* contemporary painting by "Weeson," The Granger Collection; John Milton, engraved from an original by William Faithorne, The Bettmann Archive; *The Night Watch,* Rembrandt van Rijn, Three Lions; *Covent Garden Market,* Three Lions; *New Amsterdam,* The Granger Collection; *Molière at Extreme Left with French and Italian Comedians,* oil attributed to Verio, 1670, The Granger Collection; *King Louis XIV,* canvas by Hyacinthe Rigaud, The Granger Collection; *Andrew Marvell,* oil on canvas, c. 1655–60 by an unknown artist, The Granger Collection; **p. 378:** *Portrait of Charles I,* Anthony Van Dyck, The Louvre, Paris, Art Resource; **p. 380:** *The Execution of King Charles I of England at Whitehall, London, January 30, 1649,* colored woodcut from contemporary balladsheet, The Granger Collection; **p. 382:** *Oliver Cromwell,* Sir Peter Lely (Peter Van der Faes), Firenze, Galleria Palatina, Art Resource; **p. 383:** *Ben Jonson,* The Granger Collection; **p. 385:** *John Donne,* The Granger Collection; **p. 387:** *George Herbert,* The Granger Collection; **p. 392:** *Shakespeare and Ben Jonson at Chess,* Karel van Mander, photo courtesy of William M. deHeyman, Philadelphia, Pennsylvania; **p. 395:** *Greenwich Palace from the Northeast with a Man-of-War at Anchor* (detail), c. 1630, National Maritime Museum; **p. 396:** *John Donne,* oil on canvas after Isaac Oliver, The Granger Collection; **p. 401:** *Sir Thomas Aston at the Deathbed of His Wife,* John Souch, Manchester City Art Galleries; **p. 408:** *George Herbert,* The Granger Collection; **p. 411:** *The Milkmaid,* Myles Birket Foster, Victoria & Albert Museum Trustees, Bridgeman/Art Resource; **p. 416:** *Andrew Marvell,* oil on canvas, c. 1655–60, unknown artist, The Granger Collection; **p. 422:** *Ben Jonson,* oil on canvas (detail), after Abraham van Blyenberch, The Granger Collection; **p. 427:** *Marriage à la Mode IV: The Countess's Morning Levée* (detail), William Hogarth, National Gallery, London; **p. 428:** New York Public Library Picture Collection; **p. 433:** *Three Ladies Adorning a Term of Hymen,* 1773, Sir Joshua Reynolds, The Tate Gallery, London; **p. 434:** (top) *Sir John Suckling,* Anthony Van Dyck, The Granger Collection; (bottom) *Richard Lovelace,* The Granger Collection; **p. 436:** Boucher, François, *The Interrupted Sleep,* The Metropolitan Museum of Art, The Jules Bach Collection 1949, © Copyright 1984 by The Metropolitan Museum of Art; **p. 437:** *Fair Is My Love* (detail), Edwin A. Abbey, The Harris Museum and Art Gallery, Preston; **p. 438:** Edward Burne-Jones, *Going to the Battle,* 1858, Fitzwilliam Museum, Cambridge; **p. 441:** *The Farrier's Shop,* c. 1620–87, Gael Barend, Guildhall Art Gallery, London, Bridgeman/Art Resource; **p. 442:** *John Milton,* c. 1629, detail of painting by an unknown artist, The Granger Collection; **p. 454:** *Paradise Lost,* 1688, angels/devil/death figures, John Milton, from the British Library; **p. 459:** *The Garden of Eden,* Erastus S. Field, Superstock; **p. 460:** John Bunyan, The Granger Collection; **p. 463:** Pilgrim's Progress (angels, pilgrim, knight figures), John Bunyan, The British Library; **p. 466:** *Captain John Smith (1580–1631): detail from Smith's Map of Virginia, 1616,* The Granger Collection; **pp. 470–71:** Morville Hall, Shropshire, John Inigo Richards, Roy Miles Fine Paintings, London, Bridgeman/Art Resource; **p. 474–75:** Palace at Versailles, Painting by Pierre Patel, The Granger Collection; The Syndics, Rembrandt, Three Lions; Samuel Pepys, painting by John Hayls, 1666, The Granger Collection; The Great Fire of London, 1666 Contemporary painting, Dutch School, The Granger Collection; John Locke (1632–1704), detail of oil on canvas, 1704, after Sir G. Kneller, The Granger Collection; La Salle Received in the Village of the Caddo Indians, May 1686, oil on canvas by George Catlin, The Granger Collection; Major Port for Trade with China, Portuguese colony of Macao, colored engraving, 1598, The Granger Collection; Johann Sebastian Bach, Gustav Zerner, Three Lions; **pp. 476–77:** Illustration from Gulliver's Travels, The Granger Collection; The American Revolution Begins, The Granger Collection; *Robert Burns (1759–96),* oil on panel by Alexander Nasmyth, The Granger Collection; James Boswell talking to Samuel Johnson 'till near two in the morning', satirical caricature etching by Thomas Rowlandson, 1786, The Granger Collection; *Captain Cook Explores the South Pacific,* painting by William Hodges, The Granger Collection; The Storming of the Bastille, Gouache by Claude Cholat, an eyewitness, The Granger Collection; Benjamin Franklin, with his lightning detector, English mezzotint, 1763, by Edward Fisher, The Granger Collection; The Boston Tea Party, The Granger Collection; *W. A. Mozart (1756–91),* posthumous portrait by Johann Peter Krafft, The Granger Collection; **p. 474:** *Queen Anne and the Knights of the Garter, 1713,* Peter Angelis, The Granger Collection; **p. 479:** *King George III of England, c. 1760,* Allan Ramsay, The Granger Collection; **p. 488:** *A Philosopher Lecturing on the Orrery,* Joseph Wright of Derby, Derby Art Gallery; **p. 483:** *The Rake's Progress: No. 5, The Marriage,* William Hogarth, The Granger Collection; **p. 486:** *Sir Isaac Newton, c. 1726,* Attributed to John Vanderbank, The Granger Collection; **p. 491:** *The Election—The Polling,* William Hogarth, Sir John Soane's Museum, London, Bridgeman/Art Resource; **p. 492:** *John Dryden* (detail), J. Maubert, by courtesy of the National Portrait Gallery, London; **p. 495:** *Shakespeare and his Contemporaries,* John Faed, From the Collection of Mr. and Mrs. Sandor Korein; **p. 500:** *The Music of a Bygone Age,* John Melhuish Strudwick, The Pre-Raphaelite Trust, Bridgeman/Art Resource; **p. 504:** *Samuel Pepys (detail) c. 1695,* John Closterman, The Granger Collection; **p. 508:** *The Great Fire of London, 1666,* The Museum of London; **p. 511:** *Conversa-*

tion in a Park, Thomas Gainsborough, The Louvre, Paris, Giraudon/Art Resources; **p. 512:** The Bettmann Archive; **p. 514:** Journal of the Plague Year: The Dead Cart, The British Library; **p. 518:** *Jonathan Swift,* Charles Jervas, The Granger Collection; **p. 522:** Illustration by Willy Pogany, The Donnell Library Children's Room, The Research Libraries, New York Public Library, Astor, Lenox and Tilden Foundations; **p. 526:** Illustration by Willy Pogany, The Donnell Library Children's Room, The Research Libraries, New York Public Library, Astor, Lenox and Tilden Foundations; **pp. 532, 533, 534, 535:** Illustrations from *Robinson Crusoe,* 1920, N. C. Wyeth, The Granger Collection; **p. 536:** *Joseph Addison* (detail), Sir Geoffrey Kneller, The Granger Collection; *Sir Richard Steele (detail), 1712,* Jonathan Richardson, The Granger Collection; **p. 542:** St. Edmund's Chapel, Westminster Abbey, John Fulleylove; **p. 546:** *Alexander Pope (detail) c. 1738–43,* William Hoare, The Granger Collection; **p. 549:** *The Barge,* 1895–6, From *The Rape of the Lock,* Smithers, 1896, from *The Best of Beardsley,* collected and edited by R. A. Walker, copyright © 1948 by The Bodley Head, published in the USA by Excalibur Books, plate 63; **p. 552:** The Rape of the Lock, 1895–6, from The Rape of the Lock, Smithers, 1986, from The Best of Beardsley, collected and edited by R. A. Walker, copyright © 1948 by The Bodley Head, published in the USA by Excalibur Books, plate 64; **p. 557:** The Battle of the Beaux and Belles, Aubrey Beardsley, The Barber Institute of Fine Arts, The University of Birmingham; **p. 563:** Oliver Goldsmith, James Boswell, and Samuel Johnson At The Mitre Tavern, Nineteenth-century colored engraving, The Granger Collection; **p. 564:** *Samuel Johnson (detail) 1756,* Sir Joshua Reynolds, The Granger Collection; **p. 574:** *James Boswell (detail) 1785,* Sir Joshua Reynolds, The Granger Collection; **p. 577:** Johnson and Boswell, © The Trustees of the British Museum; **p. 583:** *Haymakers, 1785,* George Stubbs, The Granger Collection; **p. 584:** *Thomas Gray (detail) 1748,* J. G. Eccardt, The Granger Collection; **p. 592:** *Oliver Goldsmith (detail) c. 1770* Studio of J. Reynolds, The Granger Collection; **p. 594:** *Robert Burns,* A. Nasmyth, National Portrait Gallery, London; **p. 602:** *The River Dee Near Eton Hall,* Richard Wilson, The Barber Institute, The University of Birmingham; **p. 606:** *William Blake (detail) 1807,* Thomas Phillips, The Granger Collection; **p. 609:** From a manuscript of "The Lamb" by William Blake, Lessing J. Rosenwald Collection, Library of Congress, Washington, D.C.; **p. 610:** Blake, William, The Tyger, A page from Songs of Innocence and Experience, The Metropolitan Museum of Art, Rogers Fund, 1917, © 1984 by The Metropolitan Museum of Art; **p. 614:** From a manuscript of "A Poison Tree" by William Blake, Lessing J. Rosenwald Collection, Library of Congress, Washington, D.C.; **p. 617:** An Allegory of the Royal Society, Hollar, The Mansell Collection; **pp. 620–21:** *View in Hampshire,* Patrick Nasmyth Guild Hall Art Gallery, City of London, Bridgeman/Art Resource; **p. 622:** *Capture of the Bastille, July 14, 1789,* Claude Cholat, The Granger Collection; **pp. 624–25:** *William Wordsworth, (1770–1850),* oil on canvas 1842, by Benjamin Haydon, The Granger Collection; *Jane Austen,* The Granger Collection; *'The Meeting of Sir Walter Scott and Robert Burns',* painting by C. M. Hardie, The Granger Collection; George Stephenson's Locomotive, The Granger Collection; Union Jack, The Granger Collection; Rosetta Stone, The Granger Collection; *Napoleon Bonaparte as First Consul,* J. A. Ingres, Three Lions; *Beethoven composing in his studio,* a late nineteenth-century painting by Carl Schlosser, The Granger Collection; Robert Fulton's Steamboat, The Granger Collection; **pp. 626–27:** *John Keats Listening to the Nightingale on Hampstead Heath,* oil, c. 1845, by Joseph Severn, The Granger Collection; London in the 1820's, The Granger Collection; Charles Lamb, The Granger Collection; *The Grove, or Admiral's House, Hampstead,* oil on canvas, 1820 by John Constable, The Granger Collection; Liverpool-Manchester Railway, The Granger Collection; The Peterloo Massacre; The Last of the Mohicans, The Granger Collection; Savannah, the First Steamer to Cross the Atlantic, The Granger Collection; *Edgar Allan Poe,* Thomas C. Corner, Three Lions; **p. 628:** *The Battle of Trafalgar,* J. M. W. Turner, The Granger Collection; **p. 629:** (top) *Napoleon (The Campaign in France, 1814),* J. L. E. Meissonier, The Granger Collection; (bottom) *King William of England,* Sir Martin Archer Shee, The Granger Collection; **p. 630:** *Sketch for Hadleigh Castle, c. 1828–29,* John Constable, The Granger Collection; **p. 631:** *Rain, Steam and Speed—The Great Western Railway, Before 1844,* J. M. W. Turner, The Granger Collection; **p. 632:** *Portrait of Goethe,* Joseph Karl Steiler, Three Lions; **p. 633:** (top) *Calais Pier: An English Packet Arriving,* J. M. W. Turner, The Granger Collection; (bottom) *Samuel Taylor Coleridge,* Peter Vandyke, The Granger Collection; **p. 635:** *John Keats,* Joseph Severn, The Granger Collection; **p. 636:** *Sir Walter Scott/Abbotsford Family, 1804,* Sir David Wilkie, The Granger Collection; **p. 641:** *Salisbury Cathedral,* John Constable, Musea de Arte, São Paolo, Giraudon/Art Resource; **p. 642:** *William Wordsworth (detail) 1842),* Benjamin Haydon, The Granger Collection; **p. 645:** *Tintern Abbey,* J. M. W. Turner, Reproduced by Courtesy of the Trustees of the British Museum; **p. 650:** *Landscape With Rainbow,* Joseph Wright of Derby, Derby Art Collection; **p. 655:** *Cornfield by Moonlight,* Samuel Palmer, Reproduced by Courtesy of the Trustees of the British Museum; **p. 658:** *Samuel Taylor Coleridge* (detail), by Courtesy of the National Portrait Gallery, London; **pp. 663–73:** Engravings by Gustav Doré for The Rime of the Ancient Mariner, by Samuel Taylor Coleridge; **p. 687:** *Chinese Silk Album Leaf, Yuan Dynasty, Kublai Khan,* The Granger Collection; **p. 688:** *Lord Byron (detail),* William West, The Granger Collection; **p. 693:** *Shipwreck,* J. C. C. Dahl, Munich Neue Pinakothek/Kavaler, Kavaler/Art Resource; **p. 700:** *Percy Bysshe Shelley* (detail), A. Curran, The Granger Collection; **p. 705:** *Cirrus Cloud Study,* John Constable, Victoria & Albert Museum, Trustees; **p. 709:** *Cloud Study, 1821,* John Constable, Yale Center for British Art, Paul Mellon Collection; **p. 714:** *John Keats* (detail), Joseph Severn, The Granger Collection; **p. 717:** Frontispiece, Homer's Iliad and Odyssey, 1612, G. Chapman, The British Library; **p. 719:** *John Keats, 1821,* J. Severn, By Courtesy of the National Portrait Gallery, London; **p. 722:** *Small Bird on a Flowering Plum Branch,* The Goto Museum; **p. 727:** Greek Vase, terracotta c. 460 B.C., attributed to the Orchard Painter, Column Crater (called the "Orchard Vase"), Side A: Women Gathering Apples,The Metropolitan Museum of Art, Rogers Fund, 1907 © copyright 1984 by The Metropolitan Museum of Art; **p. 731:** *Fishermen Upon a Lee Shore,* J. M. W. Turner, The Iveagh Bequest, Kenwood, Bridgeman/Art Resource; **p. 732:** *Mary Shelley,* (detail) c. 1840, Richard Rothwell, By Courtesy of the National Portrait Gallery, London; **p. 735:** *A View of Chamonix and Mt. Blanc,* Julius Schnon von Caròlsfeld, Austrian Gallery, Vienna; **p. 739:** *Faust: Henry Irving as Mephistopheles,* c. 1885,

Theatre Museum/E. T. Archive; **p. 740:** *Charles Lamb* (detail), After Henry Hopper Meyer, By Courtesy of the National Portrait Gallery, London; **p. 746:** *William Hazlitt,* 1825, William Bewick, By Courtesy of the National Portrait Gallery, London; **pp. 752, 754, 755:** Illustrations from *Pride and Prejudice,* 19th century engraving, Hugh Thomson, The Granger Collection; **p. 757:** *Sir Walter Scott,* 1824, Sir Edwin Landseer, National Portrait Gallery, London/Jean-Loup Charmet; **pp. 760–61:** *Queen Victoria's Visit to Cherbourg,* Jules Achille Noel, Royal Academy, London, Bridgeman/Art Resource; **p. 762:** Painting of London's Crystal Palace, Done for the Great Exhibition of 1851, Reproduced by the courtesy of the Trustees of the British Museum; **pp. 764–65:** *Queen Victoria of England,* oil on canvas, 1838, by Sir George Hayter, The Granger Collection; *Charles Darwin in his greenhouse at Down House,* posthumous Russian painting, The Granger Collection; *Charlotte Brontë,* The Granger Collection; *Charles Dickens,* The Granger Collection; *Battle from the Crimean War,* The Granger Collection; *Sepoy Mutiny,* The Granger Collection; *Karl Marx,* The Granger Collection; *Samuel F. B. Morse with his telegraph:* mezzotint by John Sartain, The Granger Collection; *Richard Wagner (1813–1883),* oil by Franz von Lenback, The Granger Collection; **pp. 766–67:** Illustration, 1911, by N. C. Wyeth for Robert Louis Stevenson's *Treasure Island,* The Granger Collection; *Robert Browning,* Rudolph Lehman, Three Lions; *Suez Canal,* The Granger Collection; *Alexander Graham Bell,* The Granger Collection; *The Mad Tea Party,* colored engraving after the design by Sir John Tenniel for the first edition of Lewis Carroll's *Alice's Adventures in Wonderland,* 1865, The Granger Collection; *The (First) Battle of Bull Run, 21 July 1861,* lithograph, 1889, by Kurz & Allison, The Granger Collection; *Anton Chekhov,* The Granger Collection; *Marines Fight in the Boxer Rebellion Outside Peking Legation,* John Clymer, Three Lions; **p. 768:** *Warrington High Street,* T. Hesketh, Warrington Museum and Art Gallery, Bridgeman/Art Resource; **p. 769:** The Triumphs of the British Army and Navy, 1897, Commemorating the Diamond Jubilee of Queen Victoria, English lithograph, 1897, The Granger Collection; **p. 772:** *Dudley Street, Seven Dials, London,* 1872, Gustav Doré, The Granger Collection; **p. 773:** *Beata Beatrix, c. 1863,* Dante Gabriel Rossetti, The Granger Collection; **p. 774:** *Alfred, Lord Tennyson,* Caricature, 1871, Carlo Pellegrini, The Granger Collection; **p. 775:** *Bayswater Omnibus,* G. W. Joy, Museum of London; **p. 776:** *Hyde Park Near Grosvenor Gate,* 1842 (detail), Thomas Shotter Boys, Guildhall Art Gallery, Bridgeman/Art Resource; **p. 780:** *Ulysses c. 1827,* Jean-Auguste-Dominique Ingres, National Gallery of Art, Washington; Chester Dale Collection; **p. 783:** *Fair, Quiet, and Sweet Rest* (detail), Luke Fildes, Warrington Museum and Art Gallery, Bridgeman/Art Resource; **p. 784:** *Baron Alfred Tennyson c. 1840,* S. Laurence, By Courtesy of the National Portrait Gallery, London; **p. 787:** *The Lady of Shalott,* John Waterhouse, The Tate Gallery, London; **p. 795:** *The Bard,* John Martin, Yale Center for British Art, Paul Mellon Collection; **pp. 810–11:** *Nocturne: Grey and Gold—Chelsea Snow, 1876,* James McNeill Whistler, The Fogg Art Museum, Cambridge, Mass. Bequest—Grenville L. Winthrop; **p. 805:** Carved Gem of Light Brown Sardonyx, Roman 3rd to 2nd Century B.C., Ulysses Mourning for Home, Staatliche Museen zu Berlin; **p. 808:** *The Angry Sea* (detail), James McNeill Whistler, Courtesy of the Freer Gallery of Art, Smithsonian Institution, Washington, D.C.; **p. 810:** *Robert Browning,* M. Gordigiani, The Granger Collection; **p. 813:** *Portrait of a Lady (or Antea),* Parmagianino, Museo Nationale di Capodimonte, Naples; **p. 816:** *In Early Spring,* Inchbold, Ashmolean Museum, Oxford; **p. 819:** *Italian Ruins,* John Claude Nattes, Victoria & Albert Museum Trustees; **p. 824:** *Matthew Arnold* (detail) 1888, G. J. Watts, By Courtesy of the National Portrait Gallery, London; **pp. 832:** *Thomas Hardy,* By Courtesy of the National Portrait Gallery, London; **p. 837:** *At the Window, 1960,* Jacob Kainen, 1979.83, oil on canvas 47⅞ × 59⅞ ", National Museum of American Art, Smithsonian Institution, Gift of Mr. and Mrs. Wallace F. Holladay; **p. 840:** *Gerard Manley Hopkins,* A. E. Hopkins, By Courtesy of the National Portrait Gallery, London; **p. 843:** *Bird's Nest,* Ros W. Jenkins, Warrington Museum and Art Gallery, Bridgeman/Art Resource; **p. 844–45:** *Harvest Field with Gleaners, Haywood, Herefordshire, 1815,* George Robert Lewis, The Tate Gallery, London; **p. 847:** *A Mother and Child of the Isle of Wight c. 1849–51,* James Collinson, Yale Center for British Art, Paul Mellon Collection; **p. 848:** Alfred Edward Housman, F. Dodd, The Granger Collection; **p. 855:** *Temperantia* (detail) *1872,* Sir Edward Burne-Jones, Christie's, London, Bridgeman/Art Resource; **p. 856:** (top) *Elizabeth Barrett Browning, 1859,* Field Talfourd, The Granger Collection; (bottom) *Dante Gabriel Rossetti, 1847,* Self Portrait, The Granger Collection; **p. 859:** "Wey" Chintz, 1884, William Morris, The Granger Collection; **p. 860:** George Meredith, The Granger Collection; *Christina Rossetti,* D. G. Rossetti, By Courtesy of the National Portrait Gallery, London; *Rudyard Kipling,* (detail) *1899,* P. Burne-Jones, By Courtesy of the National Portrait Gallery, London; *Robert Louis Stevenson (Detail),* John Singer Sargent, The Taft Museum, Gift of Mr. and Mrs. Charles Phelps Taft; **p. 867:** *A Summer Day in Hyde Park,* John Ritchie, Museum of London; **p. 868:** Charles Dickens, The Granger Collection; **p. 872:** *Two Tunnels,* 1975, Guy Worsdell; **p. 877:** *Red Virginia Creeper,* Edvard Munch, Three Lions; **p. 880:** *Thomas Hardy,* By Courtesy of the National Portrait Gallery, London; **p. 884:** *Summer, Afternoon After a Shower,* (detail), John Constable, The Tate Gallery, London; **p. 887:** *Cottage and Pond, Moonlight,* Thomas Gainsborough, Victoria & Albert Museum Trustees; **p. 901:** Lithograph of Oscar Wilde from *Vanity Fair,* May 24, 1884, Ape (also known as "Singe"), The Mansell Collection; **p. 905:** *Suffragettes Expelled After Demonstrating at Westminster,* 1906, A. Beltrame, E. T. Archive (SOH/111/A); **p. 906:** *Disraeli and Queen Victoria* (cartoon), 1878, John Tenniel, The Granger Collection (4E524.14); **pp. 910–12:** *Big Ben, 1905–1906,* André Derain, Art Resource; *An English Rose,* Joseph Clark, Gallerie George, London, Bridgeman/Art Resource; **p. 913:** *A Star Shell, c. 1916,* Christopher Richard Wynne Nevinson, Tate Gallery London; **pp. 914–15:** *King Edward VII of England, Canvas by Sir Luke Fildes,* The Granger Collection; *King George V and Royal Family of England,* Canvas, 1913, by J. Lavery, The Granger Collection; 1908 Olympic Games, The Granger Collection; *Joseph Conrad (1857–1924),* oil on canvas 1923–24, by Walter Tittle, The Granger Collection; *Albert Einstein,* Frank Einzheimer, Three Lions; *Bombardment of Trenches,* watercolor, 1918, by Raoul Lespagne; *Flight of the Wright Brothers at Kitty Hawk,* The Granger Collection; Postcard Commemorating Discovery of North Pole, The Granger Collection; **pp. 916–17:** *Devastation, 1941: An East End Street, London,* Graham Sutherland, watercolor, 1941, The Granger Collection; *Winston Churchill (1874–1965),* oil on canvas, 1946, by Douglas

Chandor, The Granger Collection; *Conversation Piece (George VI of England with Family)*, Herbert James Gunn, Three Lions; *The Persistence of Memory, 1931*, Salvador Dali, The Granger Collection; *Mandolin and Guitar, 1924*, Pablo Picasso, The Granger Collection; *Dylan Thomas (1914–1953)*, oil on canvas, 1940, Rupert Shephard; Adolf Hitler, The Granger Collection; **p. 918:** *Over the Top (at Marcoing, December 1917)*, The Granger Collection; **p. 921:** *Ezra Pound, 1938–39*, Wyndham Lewis, The Granger Collection; **p. 923:** *The Artist's Garden at Durbins, c. 1915*, Roger Fry, Yale Center for British Art, Paul Mellon fund; **p. 925:** *Studland Beach (Detail)*, Vanessa Bell, The Tate Gallery, London; **p. 926:** *The Mud Bath*, David Bromberg, The Tate Gallery, London; **p. 937:** *Gardens in the Pound, Cookham, 1936*, Stanley Spencer, Collection, Leeds City Art Galleries; **p. 938:** *Joseph Conrad* (detail) *1923–24*, Walter Tittle, By courtesy of the National Portrait Gallery, London; **p. 956:** *Edward Morgan Forster, 1920*, Dora Carrington, By Courtesy of the National Portrait Gallery, London; **p. 959:** *The Newspaper*, Edouard Vuillard, The Phillips Collection, Washington, D.C.; **p. 961:** *The Conversation*, Hobson Pittman, The North Carolina Museum of Art, Raleight, N.C. Gift of the Artist; **p. 967:** *The Garden of Love*, Walter Richard Sickert, The Fitzwilliam Museum, Cambridge; **p. 972:** *D. H. Lawrence (detail) 1920*, Jan Juta, By Courtesy of the National Portrait Gallery, London; **p. 984:** *James Joyce (detail) 1935*, Jacques-Emile Blanche, The Granger Collection; **p. 986:** *St. Patrick's Close*, Walter Osborne, National Gallery of Ireland; **p. 995:** *Holy Bush Hill, Hampstead, 1921*, Ethelbert White; **p. 997:** *Ox House, Shaftesbury, 1932*, John R. Biggs; **p. 1019:** "Who controls the Past controls the Future," George Orwell, illustration by Richard Martin; **p. 1023:** *Houses of Parliament, Sunset, 1903*, Claude Monét, The Granger Collection; **p. 1024:** *William Butler Yeats*, Augustus Johns, The Granger Collection; **p. 1027:** *Old House (Ivy Cottage), Shoreham, 1831–32*, Samuel Palmer, Ashmolean Museum, Oxford; **p. 1031:** *Burning Airplane*, Photri; **p. 1038:** *D. H. Lawrence (detail) 1920*, Jan Juta, By courtesy of the National Portrait Gallery, London; **p. 1045:** Drawing of Tanks, World War I, Photri, Inc.; **p. 1048:** *Rupert Brooke 1911*, Clara Ewald, The Granger Collection; **p. 1050:** War Poster, Photri; **p. 1051:** *White Cup and Saucer, No. 1016*, Fantin-Latour, Fitzwilliam Museum, Cambridge; **p. 1054:** *T. S. Eliot (detail) 1888–1965*, Sir Gerald Kelly, National Portrait Gallery, Smithsonian Institution; **p. 1056:** *Bolton, 1938* (detail), William Coldstream, The National Gallery of Canada, Ottawa, Gift of the Massey Foundation, 1946; **p. 1068:** *Robert Graves, 1968*, J. Aldridge, The Granger Collection; **p. 1071:** *Sun, Wind, and Rain, 1845*, David Cox, The City Museum and Art Gallery, Birmingham; **p. 1081:** *The Fall of Icarus*, P. I. Bruegel, Musées Royeaux des Beaux-Arts de Belgique, Bruxelles; **pp. 1084–85:** *Old Thatched Summer House*, Lillian Stannard, Christopher Wood Gallery, London; Bridgeman/Art Resource; **p. 1099:** *The Magic Apple Tree, c. 1830*, Samuel Palmer, Fitzwilliam Museum, Cambridge; **p. 1103:** *Set design of Covent Garden for Pygmalion*, Donald Oenslager, Harvard Theater Collection; **p. 1104:** *George Bernard Shaw*, The Bettmann Archive; **pp. 1198–99:** *Papagena 1983*, Gillian Ayres, Private Collection, Photograph courtesy of The South Bank Center; **Time Line, 2nd spread** (between pp. 1201 and 1206): *Mao Tse-tung*, The Granger Collection; Martin Luther King, Jr., Gruerio/Three Lions; **p. 1206:** *Industrial Landscape*, L. S. Lowry, The Tate Gallery,

London; **p. 1208:** *Great Black-Backed Gull*, Douglas Anderson, Oscar and Peter Johnson Ltd., London, Bridgeman/Art Resource; **p. 1209:** *King's Cookham Rise, 1947*, Stanley Spencer, The Metropolitan Museum of Art, Purchase Lila Acheson Wallace Gift, 1981, © copyright 1986 by the Metropolitan Museum of Art; **p. 1225:** *The Identi-Kit Man*, Derek Boshier, The Tate Gallery, London; **p. 1242:** The Soothsayer from the Green Island, 1946, John Petts; **p. 1233:** *Knockalla Hills, Donegal*, Dan O'Neill, Ulster Museum, Belfast; **p. 1269:** *Hillside in Wales* (detail), L. S. Lowry, The Tate Gallery, London; **p. 1278:** *Shunters, 1965*, James Dolby; **p. 1291:** *Mount Fuji and Flowers, 1972*, David Hockney, The Metropolitan Museum of Art, Purchase Mr. and Mrs. Arthur Hays Sulzberger Gift, 1972, © copyright 1987 by The Metropolitan Museum of Art; **p. 1292:** *Philip Larkin (detail) 1984*, Humphrey Ocean, By courtesy of the National Portrait Gallery, London.

PHOTOGRAPH CREDITS

p. 247: Bodego Bay, California, Pacific Ocean, © Peter Arnold; **p. 404:** Messerschmidt/Leo deWys, Inc.; **p. 545:** Photo by Rex Joseph; **p. 587:** Ian Berry/Magnum; **p. 596:** Alvin E. Staffan; Photo Researchers; **p. 703:** Diane Rawson, Photo Researchers; **p. 753:** Masterpiece Theater © BBC; **p. 830:** Thomas Hollyman/Photo Researchers; **p. 834:** Marshall Sklar/Photo Researchers; **p. 852:** Kees Van Den Berg/Photo Researchers; **p. 899:** Still from "Wuthering Heights," Laurence Olivier and Merle Oberon, Movie Still Archives; **pp. 902, 903:** Production stills from "The Importance of Being Earnest," 1977, Martha Swope; **p. 915:** Mohandas Gandhi, The Granger Collection; **p. 916:** Charles Lindbergh, The Granger Collection; **p. 917:** T. S. Eliot, The Granger Collection; **p. 941:** Dieter and Mary Plage; Bruce Coleman; **p. 950:** The Granger Collection; **p. 964:** The Granger Collection; **p. 992:** Alfred A. Knopf; **p. 1000:** The Granger Collection; **p. 1003:** ABBAS/Magnum; **p. 1010:** The Granger Collection; **p. 1013:** R. Dev/Photo Researchers; **pp. 1021, 1022:** Film stills from "1984," with Richard Burton and John Hurt, Photofest; **pp. 1028–29:** Dennis Stock/Magnum; **p. 1040:** Joe McDonald/Animals Animals; **p. 1044:** Siegfried Sassoon (detail) 1920, Bassano, By courtesy of the National Portrait Gallery, London; **p. 1074:** The Bettmann Archive/BBC Hulton; **p. 1082:** Louis MacNeice (detail) c. 1936, N. Coster, By courtesy of the National Portrait Gallery, London; **p. 1088:** (top) The Granger Collection; (bottom) Rollie McKenna; **pp. 1109, 1116, 1127, 1133, 1138, 1146–47, 1159, 1161, 1163, 1171, 1175, 1183, 1186:** Martha Swope; **pp. 1194, 1195:** Audrey Hepburn in "My Fair Lady," Warner Brothers, Movie Still Archives; **p. 1201:** Berlin Wall, P. Zachmann/Magnum; **Time Line 1st spread** (between pp. 1201 and 1206): Bruno Barbey/Magnum; Peter Marlow/Sygma; F. Scianna/Magnum; Peter Marlow/Sygma; Henri Cartier-Bresson/Magnum; Sygma; Ian Berry/Magnum Photos; Susan Meiselas/Magnum; Stuart Franklin/Sygma; Abbas/Magnum; **Time Line 2nd spread:** The Granger Collection; The Granger Collection; Erich Lessing/Magnum; Three Lions; Henri Cartier-Bresson/Magnum; Morath/Magnum; **p. 1207:** (top) Stuart Franklin/Sygma; (bottom) The Granger Collection; **p. 1211:** The Granger Collection; **p. 1216:** Nicholas Devore/Bruce Coleman; **p. 1223:** Mark

Gerson; **p. 1226:** Godfrey Graham; **p. 1232:** UPI/Bettmann Archive; **p. 1250:** Thomas Victor; **p. 1254:** Brian Brake/Photo Researchers; **p. 1258:** Thomas Victor; **p. 1266:** The Bettmann Archive/BBC Hulton; **p. 1274:** Thomas Victor; **p. 1287:** Photo by Rex Joseph; **pp. 1288, 1290:** Stills from Peter Brook's, "Lord of the Flies," Photofest; **p. 1295:** David Hurn/Magnum; **p. 1298:** Thomas Victor; **p. 1300:** Thomas Victor; **p. 1302:** Clem Haagner/Bruce Coleman; **p. 1306:** Stevie Smith (detail) 1970, Godfrey Argent, By Courtesy of the National Portrait Gallery, London; **p. 1310:** Layle Silbert; **p. 1314:** Thomas Victor; **p. 1318:** J. G. Ross/Photo Researchers; **p. 1320:** (top) Doreen Davie; (bottom) Alan Holden; **p. 1325:** Photos by Rex Joseph.

ILLUSTRATION CREDITS

pp. 7, 22, 1241, 1244, 1260: The Art Source.